ShopIngenix.com is now **OptumCoding.com**

NEW ADDRESS. SAME GREAT WEBSITE.

- Find the products you need quickly and easily with our powerful search engine
- View all available formats and edition years on the same page with consolidated product pages

- Browse our eCatalog online
- Chat live with a customer service representative; ask questions about the site or the checkout process

- Visit Coding Central for expert resources including articles, *Inside Track to ICD-10,* and coding scenarios to test your knowledge

Register on OptumCoding.com for a customized website experience:

- **View special website promotions/ discounts**
- **Get product recommendations based on your order history**
- **Research your order history**
- **Check on shipment status and tracking**
- **View invoices and payment history**
- **Pay outstanding invoices online**
- **Manage your address book**

- **Ship orders to multiple locations**
- **Renew your order with a single click**
- **Compile a wish list of the products you want and purchase when you're ready**
- **Receive a $50 coupon for every $500 you spend on OptumCoding.com (for customers who are not a part of our Medallion or Reseller programs). When logged in, the eRewards meter keeps track of purchases toward your next reward**

Don't have an OptumCoding.com account yet?

It's easy to create one:

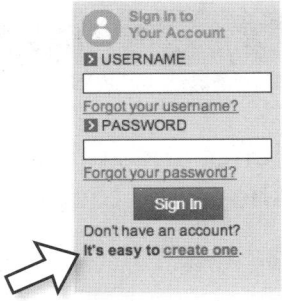

>> **REGISTER TO SAVE 15% ON YOUR NEXT ONLINE ORDER.**

Call toll-free 1.800.464.3649, option 1

FOBA13D

INGENIX.

Ingenix is now Optum
—a leading health services business.

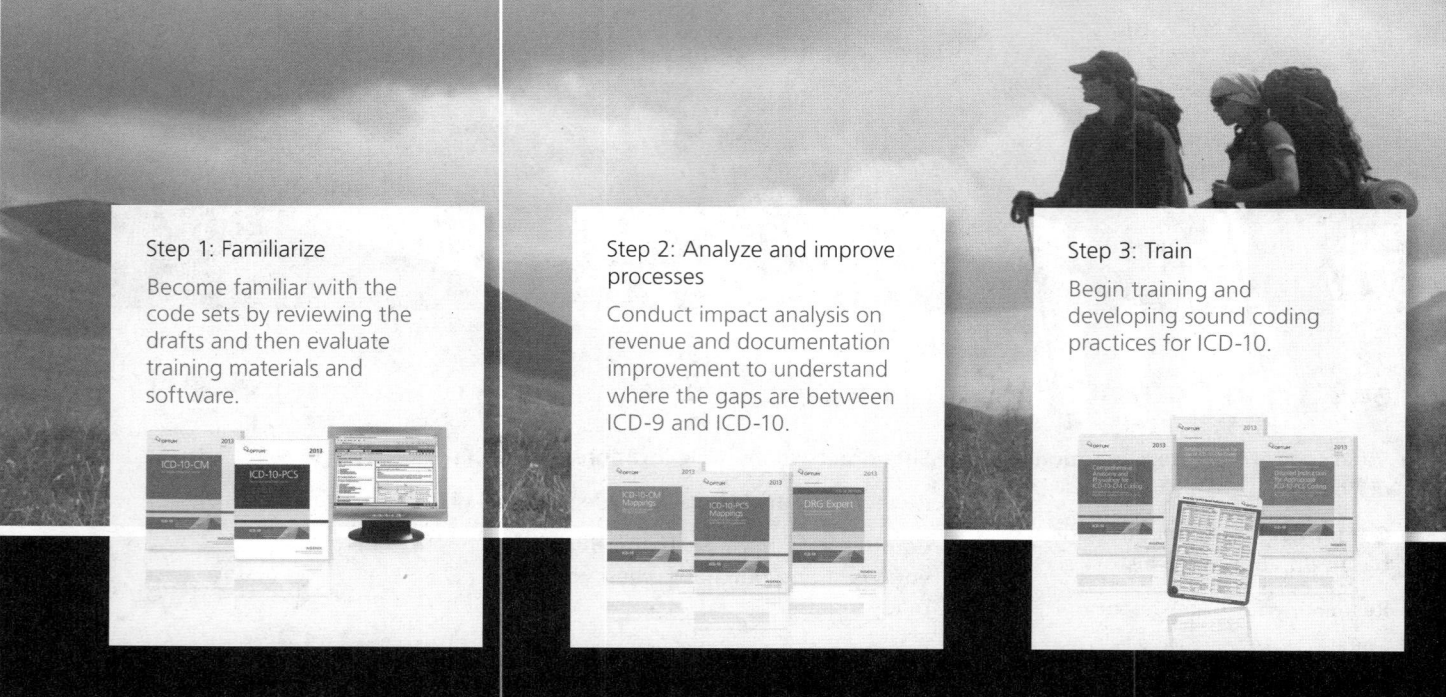

Tackle the transition one step at a time. **Optum can help.**

Take steps to prepare for ICD-10. No matter where you are in the process, we have solutions that can help ease the transition.

Step 1: Familiarize

Become familiar with the code sets by reviewing the drafts and then evaluate training materials and software.

Step 2: Analyze and improve processes

Conduct impact analysis on revenue and documentation improvement to understand where the gaps are between ICD-9 and ICD-10.

Step 3: Train

Begin training and developing sound coding practices for ICD-10.

Experience the full power of Optum ICD-10 resources.
Start shopping today and save up to 30%.*

 Save 30%. Visit www.optumcoding.com to order online.

 Save 20%. Call 800.464.3649, option 1.

Use promo code **FOBA13B** to receive your discounts.

INGENIX®

Ingenix is now Optum
—a leading health services business.

DRG Expert

A comprehensive guidebook to the MS-DRG classification system

Changes effective with discharges on or after October 1, 2012

2013

29th Edition

OptumInsight Notice

The *DRG Expert* has been prepared based upon subjective medical judgment and upon the information available as of the date of publication. This publication is designed to provide accurate and authoritative information in regard to the subject covered, and every reasonable effort has been made to ensure the accuracy of the information contained within these pages. However, the book does not replace an ICD-9-CM code book; it serves only as a guide. OptumInsight, its employees, agents, and staff make no representation or guarantee that this book is error-free or that the use of this book will prevent differences of opinion or disputes with Medicare as to the amounts that will be paid to providers of services, and will bear no responsibility for the results or consequences of its use.

Our Commitment to Accuracy

OptumInsight is committed to producing accurate and reliable materials. To report corrections, please visit www.optumcoding.com/accuracy or email accuracy@optum.com. You can also reach customer service by calling 1.800.464.3649, option 1.

Copyright

Acknowledgments

Ken Kracker, *Product Manager*
Lynn Speirs, *Senior Director, Editorial/Desktop Publishing*
Karen Schmidt, BSN, *Senior Director, Clinical Technical Editors*
Stacy Perry, *Manager, Desktop Publishing*
Lisa Singley, *Project Manager*
Kelly Canter, BA, RHIT, CCS, *Technical Editor*
Brigid T. Caffrey, BA, BS, CCS, *Technical Editor*
Tracy Betzler, *Desktop Publishing Specialist*
Kate Holden, *Editor*
Jan Welsh, *Sales Executive,* OptumInsight Data Analytics

About the Technical Editors

Kelly V. Canter, BA, RHIT, CCS

Ms. Canter has expertise in hospital inpatient and outpatient coding and compliance, utilization review, and ICD-9-CM and CPT/HCPCS coding. Her experience includes conducting coding and medical necessity audits, providing staff education, revenue cycle management, and hospital quality incentive programs. Most recently she was responsible for coding audits and compliance of a health information management services company. She is an active member of the American Health Information Management Association (AHIMA).

Brigid T. Caffrey, BA, BS, CCS

Ms. Caffrey has expertise in hospital inpatient and outpatient coding and compliance and ICD-9-CM and CPT/HCPCS coding. Her experience includes conducting coding audits, providing staff education inclusive of physician education, and creating internal coding guidelines. She has a background in professional component coding, with expertise in radiology procedure coding. Most recently Ms. Caffrey was responsible for coding audits and compliance of a health information management services company. She is an active member of the American Health Information Management Association (AHIMA).

Summary of Changes

DRG Expert Website

Ingenix now maintains a website to accompany *DRG Expert*. Ingenix will post special reports, Centers for Medicare and Medicaid Services (CMS) information, and updated data files on this website so that the information is available before the next book update. This website address is:

> http://www.optumcoding.com/Product/Updates/DRG

This website is available only to customers who purchase the *DRG Expert*. The following password is needed to access this site:

DRG2013pub

The password will change annually and Ingenix will supply customers with the new password when it changes.

Available on eBook

The *DRG Expert* is now available as an eBook for your convenience. The eBook version of *DRG Expert* contains a complete copy of this book, including appendixes, and may be purchased separately.

Summary of Changes for FY 2013

The Centers for Medicare and Medicaid Services has issued its final rule on changes to the hospital inpatient prospective payment system (IPPS) and fiscal 2013 rates (*Federal Register,* August, 2012). The MS-DRGs are now considered Version 30.0 Medicare DRGs, and are effective for discharges occurring on or after October 1, 2012.

DRG and Code Changes

- Add one new procedure code, 00.95 Injection or infusion of glucarpidase.
- Reassign cases with a principal diagnosis of 487.0 (Influenza with pneumonia) and one pneumonia code from a newly created list of secondary diagnosis codes to MS-DRGs 177-179 Respiratory Infections and Inflammations with MCC, with CC, or without CC/MCC from MS-DRGs 193-195 Simple Pneumonia and Pleurisy with MCC, with CC, or without CC/MCC.
- Reassign cases with procedure code 39.78 (Endovascular implantation of branching or fenestrated graft[s] in aorta) to MS-DRGs 237-238 Major Cardiovascular Procedures with MCC and without MCC from MS-DRGs 252-254 Other Vascular Procedures with MCC, with CC, and without CC/MCC.
- Delete 584.8 (Acute kidney failure with other specified pathological lesion in kidney) from the MS-DRG MCC list and add it to the MS-DRG CC list.
- Add three new CCs to the MS-DRG CC list 263.0 (Malnutrition of moderate degree), 263.1 (Malnutrition of mild degree), and 440.4 (Chronic total occlusion of artery of the extremities).
- Create a new MCE edit to identify claims that report procedure code 96.72 (Continuous invasive mechanical ventilation for 96 consecutive hours or more) with a length of stay less than four days.
- Remove sleeve gastrectomy from the MCE Noncovered Procedure edit.
- Add Surgical Site Infection (SSI) Following Cardiac Implantable Electronic Device (CIED) Procedures as a subcategory within the SSI HAC category.
- Add a new hospital-acquired condition (HAC), Iatrogenic Pneumothorax with Venous Catheterization.
- Add diagnosis codes 999.32 (Bloodstream infection due to central venous catheter) and 999.33 (Local infection due to central venous catheter) to the existing Vascular Catheter-Associated Infection HAC category.
- Recalibrate the DRG relative weights as required by the Social Security Act.

Contents

Numeric Listing of DRGs

Numeric Listing of DRGs

Numeric Listing of DRGs

Numeric Listing of DRGs

Numeric Listing of DRGs

Numeric Listing of DRGs

Numeric Listing of DRGs

DRG Listing by Major Diagnostic Category

MDC 8   Diseases And Disorders Of The Musculoskeletal System And Connective Tissue

SURGICAL

MEDICAL

MDC 9 Diseases And Disorders Of The Skin, Subcutaneous Tissue And Breast

SURGICAL

MEDICAL

MDC 10 Endocrine, Nutritional And Metabolic Diseases And Disorders

SURGICAL

MEDICAL

MDC 11   Diseases And Disorders Of The Kidney And Urinary Tract

SURGICAL

MEDICAL

MDC 12   Diseases And Disorders Of The Male Reproductive System

SURGICAL

MEDICAL

MDC 13   Diseases And Disorders Of The Female Reproductive System

SURGICAL

DRG Listing by Major Diagnostic Category

Introduction

The Medicare Severity Diagnosis-Related Group (MS-DRG) system organizes ICD-9-CM diagnosis and procedure codes into a complex, comprehensive system based on a few simple principles.

Understanding how the DRG system works enables providers to recover the appropriate payment for inpatient services rendered in an acute care hospital facility, which is consistent with the intent of the federal government when the DRG system was devised. The *DRG Expert* helps providers understand DRGs, thus ensuring appropriate payment.

Note: For information concerning the DRG classification system for long-term acute care hospitals (LTCHs), refer to the section titled "Long Term Acute Care Hospital Prospective Payment System (LTCH PPS)" on page xxvii.

Source of Information

Information in the book is taken from the official data published by the Centers for Medicare and Medicaid Services (CMS) in the *Federal Register*, Volume 77, No. 170 August 31, 2012 ("Hospital Inpatient Prospective Payment Systems for Acute Care Hospitals and the Long Term Care Hospital Prospective Payment System Changes and FY2013 Rates; Final Rule"). The information presented is consistent with the fiscal 2013 Grouper, version 30.0.

Basic Characteristics of DRG Classification

A DRG is one of 751 groups that classify patients into clinically cohesive groups that demonstrate similar consumption of hospital resources and length-of-stay patterns. In 1983, Congress mandated a national inpatient prospective payment system (IPPS) for all Medicare inpatients. The following types of hospitals are excluded from the IPPS:

- Psychiatric hospitals and units
- Rehabilitation hospitals and units
- Children's hospitals
- Long-term care hospitals
- Cancer hospitals
- Critical access hospitals

This IPPS uses DRGs to determine hospital reimbursement. CMS administers the IPPS and issues all rules and changes with regard to DRGs.

In addition to calculating reimbursement, DRGs have two major functions. The first is to help evaluate the quality of care. Not only are critical pathways designed around DRGs, but benchmarking and outcomes analysis can be launched using the DRG clinical framework, and quality reviews can be performed to assess coding practices and physician documentation. Ongoing education of physicians, coders, nurses, and utilization review personnel can be guided by the results of DRG analysis.

Second, DRGs assist in evaluating utilization of services. Each DRG represents the average resources needed to treat patients grouped to that DRG relative to the national average of resources used to treat all Medicare patients. The DRG assigned to each hospital inpatient stay also relates to the hospital case mix (i.e., the types of patients the hospital treats). A hospital's Medicare population case complexity is measured by calculation of the case mix index, which is an average of all MS-DRG relative weights for the facility during a given period of time. The higher the case mix index, the more complex the patient population and the higher the required level of resources utilized. Since severity is such an essential component of MS-DRG assignment and case mix index calculation, documentation and code assignment to the highest degree of accuracy and specificity is of utmost importance.

Medicare computes the case-mix adjustment for each fiscal year for all hospitals based upon the case-mix data received. This CMI is then used to adjust the hospital base rate, which is a factor in computing the total hospital payment under IPPS.

The formula for computing the hospital payment for each DRG is as follows:

DRG Relative Weight x Hospital Base Rate = Hospital Payment

The hospital case mix complexity includes the following patient attributes:

- Severity of illness — the level of loss of function or mortality associated with disease
- Prognosis — defined as probable outcome of illness
- Treatment difficulty — patient management problems
- Need for intervention — severity of illness that would result due to lack of immediate or continuing care
- Resource intensity — volume and types of services required for patient management

The DRG system was developed to relate case mix to resource utilization. Reimbursement is adjusted to reflect the resource utilization and does not take into consideration severity of illness, prognosis, treatment difficulty, or need for intervention.

Case mix and complexity can be analyzed and monitored in relation to cost and utilization of services. In addition, high-volume conditions and services can be identified and monitored, and DRG trend analysis can aid in forecasting future staff and facility requirements. One important operating parameter is the CMI, which measures the cost of a hospital's Medicare patient mix in relation to the cost of all Medicare patients. A low case mix may indicate unnecessary revenue loss.

DRG Assignment Process

DRGs are assigned using the principal diagnosis; secondary diagnoses, which include complication/comorbidities; surgical or other invasive procedures; sex of the patient and discharge status. One DRG is assigned to each inpatient stay. Diagnoses and procedures are designated by ICD-9-CM codes. The following describes the typical decision process used to assign a DRG to a case.

A case is assigned to one of 25 major diagnostic categories (MDC), which are mutually exclusive groups based on principal diagnosis. DRG assignment is based upon the following considerations:

- Principal and secondary diagnosis and procedure codes
- Sex of the patient

- Discharge status
- Presence or absence of major complications and comorbidities (MCCs) and/or presence or absence of complications and comorbidities (CCs)
- Birth weight for neonates

Each MDC is organized into one of two sections — surgical or medical. The surgical section classifies all surgical conditions based upon operating room procedures. The medical section classifies all diagnostic conditions based upon diagnosis codes. The majority of MDCs are organized by major body system and/or are associated with a particular medical specialty.

There are two groups of DRGs that are not assigned to MDCs. First, there is the group that may be associated with all MDCs. This group includes DRGs created specifically to report admissions into a facility that have been assigned invalid principal diagnoses (DRG 998), have O.R. procedures unrelated to a principal diagnosis (DRGs 981–983, 984–986, and 987–989), or are ungroupable principal diagnoses (DRG 999). Although the scope is too broad for clinical analysis, the DRGs encompass clinically coherent cases.

Another group not assigned to MDCs is called Pre-MDC DRGs, which consist of cases that are grouped by surgical procedure rather than principal diagnosis. The Pre-MDC DRG group includes bone marrow and organ transplant cases as well as tracheostomy cases.

Further sorting of medical classifications is performed by principal diagnosis type and/or surgical classifications by type of surgery. Finally, the case is analyzed for the presence of MCCs and/or CCs as indicated by ICD-9-CM diagnosis codes, and a DRG is assigned.

Each year, effective October 1 through September 30, DRG assignments are adjusted based on relative weight (RW), arithmetic mean length of stay (AMLOS), and geometric mean length of stay (GMLOS). Annually, new ICD-9-CM codes are also incorporated into the existing DRGs or new DRGs are added for the next fiscal year.

The information contained in this manual reflects the DRG classification system for fiscal 2013, Grouper Version 30.0.

Grouper Version	Effective Time Period
MS 30.0	10/01/2012 – 09/30/2013
MS 29.0	10/01/2011 – 09/30/2012
MS 28.0	10/01/2010 – 09/30/2011
MS 27.0	10/01/2009 – 09/30/2010
MS 26.0	10/01/2008 – 09/30/2009
MS 25.0	10/01/2007 – 09/30/2008
CMS 24.0	10/01/2006 – 09/30/2007
CMS 23.0	10/01/2005 – 09/30/2006
CMS 22.0	10/01/2004 – 09/30/2005
CMS 21.0	10/01/2003 – 09/30/2004
CMS 20.0	10/01/2002 – 09/30/2003
CMS 19.0	10/01/2001 – 09/30/2002
CMS 18.0	10/01/2000 – 09/30/2001
CMS 17.0	10/01/1999 – 09/30/2000
CMS 16.0	10/01/1998 – 09/30/1999
CMS 15.0	10/01/1997 – 09/30/1998
CMS 14.0	10/01/1996 – 09/30/1997
CMS 13.0	10/01/1995 – 09/30/1996
CMS 12.0	10/01/1994 – 09/30/1995
CMS 11.0	10/01/1993 – 09/30/1994
CMS 10.0	10/01/1992 – 09/30/1993
CMS 9.0	10/01/1991 – 09/30/1992
CMS 8.0	10/01/1990 – 09/30/1991
CMS 7.0	10/01/1989 – 09/30/1990
CMS 6.0	10/01/1988 – 09/30/1989
CMS 5.0	10/01/1987 – 09/30/1988
CMS 4.0	10/01/1986 – 09/30/1987
CMS 3.0	05/01/1986 – 09/30/1986
CMS 2.0	10/01/1983 – 04/30/1986

Complications and Comorbidities

CMS developed lists of MCC and CC conditions for assignment of hospital cases to appropriate MS-DRGs. When a CC or MCC is present as a secondary diagnosis, it may affect DRG assignment.

The MCC/CC lists are updated annually and can be found at http://www.cms.hhs.gov/AcuteInpatientPPS in Tables 6A, 6C, and 6E. However due to the ICD-9-CM code freeze, there were no new, revised, or deleted diagnosis codes for 2013 and hence there are no Tables 6A, 6C, or 6E available for MS-DRG Grouper version 30.0. These lists instead are compiled within the *Federal Register* in Tables 6I.1., I.2., 6J.1., and 6J.2.

For certain principal diagnoses, conditions generally considered CCs are not seen as such because a closely related condition deemed a CC would result in duplicative or inconsistent coding. The following parameters determine those secondary diagnoses that are excluded from the CC list:

- Chronic and acute manifestations of the same condition should not be considered CCs for one another.
- Specific and nonspecific diagnosis codes for the same condition should not be considered CCs for one another.
- Conditions that may not coexist such as partial/total, unilateral/bilateral, obstructed/unobstructed, and benign/malignant should not be considered CCs for one another.
- The same condition in anatomically proximal sites should not be considered CCs for one another.
- Closely related conditions should not be considered CCs for one another.

Some conditions are an MCC only if the patient is discharged alive.

Certain MCC/CCs that are considered preventable conditions acquired during the hospital stay, identified as Hospital Acquired Conditions (HAC), with a Present on Admission indicator of "N" and "U" will effect MS-DRG payment. Medicare will not assign the higher paying MS-DRG if the HAC was not present on admission (NPOA) and will be paid as though it was not present. The HAC list may be revised in consultation with CDC, as long as the list contains at least two conditions, and can be found at: http://www.cms.gov/Medicare/Medicare-Fee-for-Service-Payment/HospitalAcqCond/Hospital-Acquired_Conditions.html.

Long Term Acute Care Hospital Prospective Payment System (LTCH PPS)

Use of postacute care services has grown rapidly since the implementation of the acute care hospital inpatient prospective payment system. The average length of stay in acute care hospitals has decreased, and patients are increasingly being discharged to postacute care settings such as long term care hospitals (LTCH), skilled nursing facilities (SNF), home health agencies (HHA), and inpatient rehabilitation facilities (IRF) to complete their course of treatment. The increased use of postacute care providers, including hospitals excluded from the acute care hospital inpatient PPS, has resulted in the rapid growth in Medicare payments to these hospitals in recent years.

Under the provisions of the Balanced Budget Refinement Act of 1999 and the Medicare, Medicaid, and SCHIP Benefits Improvement and Protection Act of 2000, over a five-year period LTCHs were transitioned from a blend of reasonable cost-based reimbursement to prospective payment rates beginning October 1, 2002. LTCHs are defined as facilities that have an average length of stay greater than 25 days.

The LTC-DRG system is based on the current DRG system under the acute care hospital inpatient PPS (MS-DRG). The LTC-DRGs model uses the existing hospital inpatient DRG classification system with weights calibrated to account for the difference in resource use by patients exhibiting the case complexity and multiple medical problems characteristic of LTCHs. The existing MS-DRGs were regrouped into classification groups based on patient data called case-mix groups (CMG).

After screening through the Medicare Code Editor, each claim is classified into the appropriate LTC-DRG by the Medicare LTCH Grouper. The LTCH Grouper is specialized computer software based on the Grouper used by the acute care hospital inpatient PPS, which was developed as a means of classifying each case into a DRG on the basis of diagnosis and procedure codes and other demographic information (age and discharge status). Following the LTC-DRG assignment, the Medicare fiscal intermediary determines the prospective payment by using the Medicare Pricer program, which accounts for hospital-specific adjustments.

CMS modified the DRGs for the LTCH PPS by developing LTCH-specific relative weights to account for the fact that LTCHs generally treat patients with multiple medical problems. Therefore, CMS developed a crosswalk of IPPS MS-DRGs to LTC-DRG data, including relative weight (RW), GMLOS, and 5/6 GMLOS for short stay outlier case payment adjustment.

The LTC-DRG is linked to the recalibration and reclassification of the MS-DRGs under the IPPS to be effective with discharges occurring on or after October 1 through September 30 each year.

Appendix C of this manual is the LTC-DRG crosswalk based upon the Grouper Version 30.0.

Keys to a Financially Successful DRG Program

CMS assigns each DRG a relative weight based upon charge data for all Medicare inpatient hospital discharges. Each hospital has a customized base rate that adjusts payment commensurate with the hospital's cost of providing services. The type of hospital and the wage index for the geographic area determines the hospital base rate. DRG relative weights and hospital base rates are adjusted yearly (effective October 1 through September 30) to reflect changes in health care resource consumption as well as economic factors. Payment is determined by multiplying the DRG relative weight by the hospital base rate. The DRG with the highest relative weight is the highest-paying DRG. Regardless of actual costs incurred, the hospital receives only the calculated payment.

The DRG payment system is based on averages. Payment is determined by the resource needs of the average Medicare patient for a given set of diseases or disorders. These resources include the length of stay and the number and intensity of services provided. Therefore, the more efficiently a provider delivers care, the greater the operating margin will be.

The keys to a financially successful DRG program are:

- Decreased length of stay
- Decreased resource utilization (tests and procedures)
- Increased intensity of case-management services resulting in optimal length of stay for the patient and facility
- Increased preadmission testing
- Improved medical record documentation

The Physician's Role

Proper DRG assignment requires a complete and thorough accounting of the following:

- Principal diagnosis
- Procedures
- Complications
- Comorbidities (all relevant pre-existing conditions)
- Signs and symptoms when diagnoses are not established
- Discharge status

Because DRG assignment is based on documentation in the medical record, the record should:

- Be comprehensive and complete
- Include all diagnoses, procedures, complications, and comorbidities, as well as abnormal test results documented by the physician. It should also include any suspected conditions and what was done to investigate or evaluate them.
- Be timely

All dictation, signatures, etc., should be completed in the medical record as patient care is provided and must be:

- Legible
- Well documented

The information should be documented properly. With complete information in the medical record, coders can effectively analyze, code, and report the required information. This ensures that proper payment is received. For example, if the physician documents that a patient with a skull fracture was in a coma for less than one hour, DRGs 085–087 may be assigned. If the physician documents that the coma lasted for more than one hour, DRGs 082–084 may be assigned, with a resulting payment difference.

Physicians must be actively involved in the query process. They should respond to a query in a timely fashion and document their response, as established by the process, to ensure it meets regulatory requirements and is maintained in some form on the permanent medical record.

DRG Expert Organization

Summary of Changes
As a special feature, a summary of all the important changes in the DRG system for the current year is presented in this section.

Numeric DRG Listing
This section is a numeric listing of all DRGs with MDC, and page reference.

DRG Listing by Major Diagnostic Category
The "MDC List" section is a numerical listing of the MDCs with the category title. Each MDC then is separated into a surgical DRG list and medical DRG list for the MDC. Also, the page reference for each DRG is noted.

Introduction
The introduction addresses the basic characteristics of DRG classification, a brief overview of the DRG assignment process inclusive of complications and comorbidities, Long Term Acute Care Hospital Prospective Payment System, keys to a financially successful DRG program, and the physician's role in proper DRG assignment.

Glossary of DRG Terms
This section of the introduction contains definitions of terms associated with the DRG classification system.

Definitions of the DRGs
The book contains a list of the 25 MDCs. Preceding each MDC is a list of all ICD-9-CM diagnosis codes that are assigned to each MDC. They are listed in numeric order, beginning with MDC 1. Please note that there are no diagnosis codes for the Pre-MDC DRGs, since they are grouped according to procedure code. Each MDC is divided into surgical and medical sections (when appropriate). Listed in each section are the applicable DRGs and their associated diagnosis and/or procedure codes. Beside each DRG title is its GMLOS, AMLOS, and RW. Under each DRG is a list of diagnosis and/or procedure codes that determine assignment of the case to that DRG.

Indexes
Your *DRG Expert* allows you to locate a DRG by searching alphabetically (code narrative) or numerically (ICD-9-CM codes) by either disease or procedure.

The indexes are arranged in the following order at the back of the book:

- Alphabetic Index to Diseases
- Numeric Index to Diseases
- Alphabetic Index to Procedures
- Numeric Index to Procedures

Appendix A, Lists of CCs and MCCs
CMS conducted a review of over 13,500 diagnosis codes to determine which codes should be classified as CCs as part of their process to develop MS-DRGs. CMS then did an additional analysis to further refine secondary diagnoses into what will now be known as Major CCs (MCCs). The lists in this section represent diagnosis codes designated as CCs and MCCs under the MS-DRGs.

Appendix B, MS-DRG Surgical Hierarchy Table
Since patients may be assigned to only one DRG per admission, a tool was necessary to enable the evaluation of the relative resource consumption for cases involving multiple surgeries that individually group to different surgical DRGs within an MDC. The surgical hierarchy table in this section reflects the relative resource requirements of the various surgical procedures of each MDC. Arranging the surgical DRGs in this manner helps you assign the DRG that accurately reflects the resource utilization for multiple surgery cases and, thereby, assign the case to the highest surgical DRG.

Appendix C, MS-LTC-DRG Crosswalk
CMS modified the DRGs for the LTCH PPS by developing LTCH-specific relative weights to account for the fact that LTCHs generally treat patients with multiple medical problems. Therefore, CMS developed a crosswalk of IPPS MS-DRG to LTC-DRG data, including RW, GMLOS, and short stay outlier thresholds. Appendix C of this manual is the LTC-DRG based upon the Grouper Version 30.0.

Appendix D, National Average Payment Table
This section lists all DRGs in numerical order. Each DRG is listed with the DRG title, the symbol Ⓣ indicating that the DRG was selected as a qualified discharge that may be paid as a transfer case, the symbol ⓢ indicating that the DRG is subject to the special payment methodology, the GMLOS, the ALMOS, the relative weight, and the average national payment.

CMS established a postacute care transfer policy effective October 1, 1998. The purpose of the IPPS postacute care transfer payment policy is to avoid providing an incentive for a hospital to transfer patients to another hospital early in the patients' stay in order to minimize costs while still receiving the full DRG payment. The transfer policy adjusts the payments to approximate the reduced costs of transfer cases. CMS adopted new criteria to expand the postacute care transfer policy beginning with the FY 2006 IPPS. The new criteria to determine which DRGs should be included are as follows:

- The DRG has at least 2,050 postacute care transfer cases;
- At least 5.5 percent of the cases in the DRG are discharged to postacute care prior to the geometric mean length of stay for the DRG;
- The DRG has a geometric mean length of stay of at least 3.0 days; and,
- If the DRG is one of a paired set of DRGs based on the presence or absence of a comorbidity or complication, both paired DRGs are included if either one meets the first three criteria.

If a DRG is included on the list of Post-Acute Transfer or Special Payment DRGs and has one of the following discharge disposition (patient status) codes assigned, it is subject to the reimbursement policy:

02   Discharged/Transferred to a Short-Term General Hospital for Inpatient Care (both participating and non-participating hospitals are included in the transfer policy)

03   Discharged/Transferred to SNF with Medicare Certification in Anticipation of Covered Skilled Care

05   Discharged/Transferred to a Designated Cancer Center or Children's Hospital

06   Discharged/Transferred to Home Under Care of Organized Home Health Service Organization in Anticipation of Covered Skilled Care

07   Left against medical advice
62   Discharged/Transferred to an Inpatient Rehabilitation Facility (IRF) Including Rehabilitation Distinct Part Units of a Hospital
63   Discharged/Transferred to a Medicare Certified Long-term Care Hospital
65   Discharged/Transferred to a Psychiatric Hospital or Psychiatric Distinct Part Unit of a Hospital
66   Discharged/Transferred to a Critical Access Hospital

CMS conformed the previous postacute care transfer policy to the new MS-DRGs. Consistent with policy under which both DRGs in a CC/non CC pair are qualifying DRGs if one of the pair qualifies, each MS-DRG that shares a base MS-DRG will be a qualifying DRG if one of the MS-DRGs in the subgroup qualifies.

The same rationale will apply to MS-DRGs subject to special payment methodology. An MS-DRG will be subject to the special payment methodology if it shares a base MS-DRG with an MS-DRG that meets criteria for receiving the special payment methodology.

This section provides comprehensive lists of the MS-DRGs that meet the postacute care transfer criteria and the MS-DRGs that meet the special payment criteria. All DRGs subject to the special payment provisions are also included under the post-acute transfer policies, so those DRGs appear in the special payment list only.

The national average payment for each DRG is calculated by multiplying the current RW of the DRG and national average hospital Medicare base rate. The national average hospital Medicare base rate is the sum of the full update labor-related and nonlabor-related amounts published in the *Federal Register*, FY 2013 Final Rule, Table 1A. National Adjusted Operating Standardized Amounts; Labor/Nonlabor (if wage index greater than 1) or Table 1B. National Adjusted Operating Standardized Amounts; Labor/Nonlabor (if wage index less than or equal to 1).

Appendix E, 2011 MedPAR National Data Table

The MedPAR Benchmarking Data represents Inpatient Medicare 2011 MedPAR benchmarking data designed to provide a high-level benchmark of discharges, length of stay, age, total charges, and total reimbursement on a DRG basis at a national level for hospitals. In order to provide data in the format presented, the data from the MedPAR dataset requires manipulation. Listed below is a definition of each data element as well as other terms used in the section. Any required calculations used to derive calculated amounts are also described below.

Weighted Average - Aggregated results for the selected peer group are reported as weighted averages. To calculate a weighted average for the peer group amounts, we multiply the volume by the individual item to get the hospital's total. For example, if a hospital had 100 cases of DRG 127 with an average charge of $10,000, we'd multiply 100 times $10,000 to get $1,000,000. We then sum these amounts (charge, cost, length of stay etc) for all of the hospitals in the peer group. Next, we divide those sums by the total number of admissions for that DRG. This produces a weighted average result for the group.

Average Length of Stay - The sum of all days reported by a hospital or peer group for a DRG divided by the number of times the DRG was reported. Peer groups are weighted averages.

Charge Per Admit - The average charge for all times the service was supplied by the facility. Average charge is the sum of all charges for the reported DRG divided by the number of discharges for that DRG.

Discharges - The total number of times this DRG was reported by the provider. Because of privacy rules, no information is shown where a provider or peer group's volume is less than 11 cases. When this happens, all corresponding fields will be blank and the case mix index will be shown as a 0. Note: Some reports use the term "admissions" to identify the number of patients receiving care under a specific DRG. This report uses the term discharges, which can be used interchangeably with the term admissions.

Average Allowed - The average amount allowed for the claim from all sources. The average allowed is the sum of the outlier payments, disproportionate share, indirect medical education, capital total, copayments and deductibles and bill total per diem.

Average Age - The average age is calculated using the Census Bureau's Middle Population Projection Series to assign specific ages to claims based on the age range reported and the weighted distribution within the range for that population group. In total, the age ranges will match the distribution reported by the Census Bureau. These assigned ages are then averaged by DRG and by severity to produce the average age in the report.

For questions or additional information specific to Appendixes E and F contact,

Jan Welsh, Data Analytics
Ingenix OptumInsight
1.800.859.2447, option 2, or
614.410.7637.

Appendix F, Medicare Case Mix Index Table

The Medicare Case Mix Index (CMI) is a ratio calculated from publicly available data from the 2013 Medicare IPPS Impact File using acute care hospitals where CMI > 0.0. The formula to calculate this ratio is as follows, add all the Medicare relative weights and then divide that number by the total number of Medicare discharges. The CMI data is important benchmark information that allows organizations to set goals based on best practices in the industry. It is an indicator that shows the increase or decrease in severity to Medicare patients at a facility. It can also reflect issues with documentation and proper code assignment. If the documentation is not as comprehensive as it should be it is difficult to assign a code at the greatest level of specificity, determine the principal diagnosis or primary procedure, and identify secondary conditions that may have impact on the proper DRG assignment therefore impacting reimbursement. Also included is average daily census and average daily beds.

Instructions for Using *DRG Expert*

If the DRG is known, use the "Numeric DRG Listing." The DRGs are numerically ordered in this section. Locate the designated DRG and check the DRG title, the MDC into which the DRG falls, and the reference page number. Turn to the referenced page for a complete list of codes that group to the DRG, as well as the reimbursement data for the DRG. Scan the list for codes with an asterisk (*). The asterisk indicates a sequence or range of codes, and all codes within that code category or subcategory are represented. See an ICD-9-CM code book for specific codes.

If the MDC to which the case groups is known but the specific DRG is not, use the "DRG Listed by Major Diagnostic Category" to locate potential DRG selections. Find the MDC, determine whether the case is surgical or medical, scan the DRG and title list, and then turn to the referenced page for further information.

If the DRG is not known, follow the steps below to determine DRG assignment:

1. Determine whether the case had an operating room procedure (certain operating room procedures do not qualify and do not appear in this book). If so, refer to either the alphabetic or numeric procedure index to locate all potential DRG assignments.

   Look for the specific code or search by main term with qualifier, then body site and qualifier. Main terms are listed as specific operative procedures.

   Example:

   57.85 Cystourethroplasty and plastic repair of bladder neck

   Use the main term "Operation" when the procedure is unspecified.

   Example:

   07.5* Operations on pineal gland

   To locate a diagnostic procedure, look for the specific code under "Diagnostic procedure," and the body site, in that order.

   Example:

   67.1* Diagnostic procedures on cervix

   Note: An asterisk denotes an incomplete code that represents a sequence or range of codes. Refer to the ICD-9-CM code book for the specific codes.

2. If the case lacks an operating room procedure, look up the diagnosis by using either the alphabetic or numeric diagnosis index.

   To locate a diagnosis, look for the specific code or the condition, qualifier, then body site and qualifier, in that order.

   Example:

   805* Fracture of vertebral column without mention of spinal cord injury

3. In some cases it is necessary to scan the list of codes in the index for both the category code (three-digit code) and the subcategory (four-digit code) level of the code, listed in the index with an asterisk. Note the pages referenced for the DRG to which the category code and the subcategory code ranges are assigned. Turn to the page or pages and review the DRG descriptions to determine the correct DRG to assign to the case.

   Example:

   In the index, code 263.0 Malnutrition, degree, moderate, directs the coder to DRG 791 Prematurity with Major Problems. Code 263.0 is listed as a secondary diagnosis of major problem. However, this DRG assignment is appropriate only for newborns and other neonates. The category level, 263*, refers the coder to DRGs 640 Miscellaneous Disorders of Nutrition, Metabolism, and Fluids and Electrolytes with MCC, and to DRG 977 HIV With or Without Other Related Condition. The coder must make the final determination of the correct DRG assignment using these DRG choices.

4. Turn to the page(s) and review the DRG descriptions. Determine which is the correct DRG.

   Often a diagnosis or procedure code is assigned to more than one DRG. Not every DRG entry has a full list of the codes that group to the particular DRG, but refers to a DRG entry that does contain the full list. As in the example above for 263* Other and unspecified protein-calorie malnutrition, the index refers the coder to DRG 640 Miscellaneous Disorders of Nutrition, Metabolism, and Fluids and Electrolytes with MCC. However, DRG 640 and 641 are considered DRGs in a subgroup. The only difference in the assignment of either of the DRGs is the presence or absence of an MCC. In the guidebook a note appears under DRG 641 that says "Select principal diagnosis listed under DRG 640." That means that code 263* groups to

DRGs 640 & 641 depending on the presence or absence of an MCC. Be careful to examine all possible potential DRG assignments when the DRG title includes qualifiers such as "with MCC" versus "without MCC," "with CC" versus "without CC," and "with CC/MCC" versus "without CC/MCC." These qualifiers are highlighted in the title as an alert to the coder.

Also note those codes listed with an asterisk (*). The asterisk indicates a sequence or range of codes, and all codes within that code category or subcategory are represented. See an ICD-9-CM code book for specific codes.

5. Examine the medical record closely for the following considerations: the patient's principal diagnosis, secondary diagnoses, which include complication/comorbidities; surgical or other invasive procedures; sex of the patient and discharge status; and birth weight for neonates. Documentation must support selection of the final DRG.

6. Know and follow the Official Coding Guidelines for Coding and Reporting. The rules for selection of principal diagnosis are essential in DRG assignment, especially those related to admission to inpatient status from outpatient observation and outpatient ambulatory surgery

Important Protocols of *DRG Expert*

More than one DRG: Many diagnosis and procedure codes group to more than one DRG. Be sure to check every DRG referenced.

Asterisks: Some codes are followed by an asterisk, which indicates that the ICD-9-CM code is incomplete and represents a sequence or range of codes. Refer to the ICD-9-CM code book for the specific codes included in the code range.

A complete DRG title is necessary to understand the nature of the cases the DRG comprises.

Example:

DRG 698   **Other Kidney and Urinary Tract Diagnoses with MCC**

DRG 699   **Other Kidney and Urinary Tract Diagnoses with CC**

DRG 700   **Other Kidney and Urinary Tract Diagnoses without CC/MCC**

A complete review of the DRG title is necessary to understand that correct DRG assignment depends on two factors — the presence/absence of a MCC and/or CC and patient disposition. Review DRGs that precede or follow the target DRG, and determine how their narrative descriptions differ. It is possible another DRG with a higher relative weight may be assigned appropriately.

The symbol Ⓣ indicates a DRG selected as a qualified discharge that may be paid as a transfer case.

The symbol ⓢ indicates a DRG that is subject to the special payment methodology.

The symbol ▽ indicates that the DRG is one of the targeted subgroups of DRGs identified as a DRG having the potential for "upcoding" or "DRG creep." These DRGs should be considered as probable targets of an audit. The symbol reminds the coder to carefully consider the documentation that supports the DRG assignment.

The symbol ☑ indicates that there is the potential for assigning a more appropriate, higher-paying DRG. The coder should review the medical documentation to identify all the major factors that might justify assigning the case to a higher-paying DRG.

A red color bar indicates a surgical DRG.

A blue color bar indicates a medical DRG.

A pink color bar indicates an MCC.

A gray color bar indicates a CC.

A yellow color bar indicates a procedure proxy, whereby the inclusion of a specific procedure code acts as a proxy for the MCC or CC for the case. If the procedure code is assigned, the MCC or CC code typically required would not be necessary for DRG grouping.

The terms principal or secondary diagnosis indicates DRGs that are based on specific principal or secondary diagnosis requirements.

Bold text OR, AND, WITH, and WITHOUT alerts the user to those complex DRGs that have additional diagnosis or procedure qualifications.

Glossary of DRG Terms

against medical advice: The discharge status of patients who leave the hospital after signing a form that releases the hospital from responsibility, or who leave the hospital premises without notifying hospital personnel.

arithmetic mean length of stay (AMLOS): The average number of days patients within a given DRG stay in the hospital, also referred to as the average length of stay. The AMLOS is used to determine payment for outlier cases.

base rate: A number assigned to a hospital that is used to calculate DRG reimbursement. Base rates vary from hospital to hospital. The base rate adjusts reimbursement to allow for such individual characteristics of the hospital as geographic location, status (urban/rural, teaching), and local labor costs.

case-mix index (CMI): The sum of all DRG relative weights, divided by the number of Medicare cases. A low CMI may denote DRG assignments that do not adequately reflect the resources used to treat Medicare patients.

charges: The dollar amount of hospital bills.

complication/comorbidity (CC): A condition that when present leads to substantially increased hospital resource use such as intensive monitoring, expensive and technically complex services, and extensive care requiring a greater number of caregivers. Significant acute disease, acute exacerbations of significant chronic diseases, advanced or end stage chronic diseases, and chronic diseases associated with extensive debility are representative of CC conditions.

diagnosis-related group (DRG): One of the 751 valid classifications of diagnoses in which patients demonstrate similar resource consumption and length-of-stay patterns.

discharge: A situation in which the patient leaves an acute care (prospective payment) hospital after receiving complete acute care treatment.

discharge status: Disposition of the patient at discharge (for example: left against medical advice, discharged home, transferred to an acute care hospital, expired).

geometric mean length of stay (GMLOS): Used to compute reimbursement, the GMLOS is a statistically adjusted value for all cases for a given DRG, allowing for the outliers, transfer cases, and negative outlier cases that would normally skew the data. The GMLOS is used to determine payment only for transfer cases — i.e., the per diem rate.

Grouper: The software program that assigns DRGs.

homogeneous: Adjective describing patients who consume similar types and amounts of hospital resources.

major complication/comorbidity (MCC): Diagnosis codes that reflect the highest level of severity (see also complication/comorbidity).

major diagnostic category (MDC): Broad classification of diagnoses typically grouped by body system.

nonoperating room procedure: A procedure that does not normally require the use of the operating room and that can affect DRG assignment.

operating room (OR) procedure: A procedure that falls into a defined group of procedures that normally require the use of an operating room.

other diagnoses (*see also* complication/comorbidity): All conditions (secondary) that exist at the time of admission or that develop subsequently that affect the treatment received and/or the length of stay. Diagnoses that relate to an earlier episode and that have no bearing on the current hospital stay are not to be reported.

outliers: There are two types of outliers: day and cost outliers. Payment for day outliers was eliminated with discharges occurring on or after October 1, 1997. A cost outlier is a case in which the costs for treating the patient are extraordinarily high in relation to the costs for other patients in the DRG. An increase in cost outlier payments compensates for the elimination of day outlier payments. Hospital-specific cost-to-charge ratios are applied to the covered charges (operating and capital costs computed separately) for the case to determine whether the costs of the case exceed the fixed loss outlier threshold.

per diem rate: Payment made to the hospital from which a patient is transferred for each day of stay. Per diem rate is determined by dividing the full DRG payment by the GMLOS for the DRG. The payment rate for the first day of stay is twice the per diem rate, and subsequent days are paid at the per diem rate up to the full DRG amount.

PMDC (Pre-MDC): There are 15 DRGs to which cases are directly assigned based upon procedure codes. Cases are assigned to these DRGs before classification to an MDC. The PMDC includes DRGs for heart transplant or implant of a heart assist system, liver and/or intestinal, three DRGs for bone marrow, simultaneous pancreas/kidney transplant, pancreas transplant, lung transplant, and five DRGs for tracheostomies. These DRGs are listed in the section of this manual entitled "Pre-MDC."

principal diagnosis: The condition established after study to be chiefly responsible for occasioning the admission of the patient to the hospital for care.

principal procedure: A procedure performed for definitive treatment rather than diagnostic or exploratory purposes, or that was necessary to treat a complication. The principal procedure usually is related to the principal diagnosis.

relative weight (RW): An assigned weight that is intended to reflect the relative resource consumption associated with each DRG. The higher the relative weight, the greater the payment to the hospital.

The relative weights are calculated by CMS and published in the final PPS rule.

surgical hierarchy: Surgical hierarchy is defined as an ordering of surgical cases from most to least resource intensive. Application of this decision rule is necessary when patient stays involve multiple surgical procedures, each one of which, occurring by itself, could result in assignment to a different DRG. All patients must be assigned to only one DRG per admission.

transfer: A situation in which the patient is transferred to another acute care hospital for related care.

volume: The number of patients in each DRG.

Pre MDC

SURGICAL

DRG 001 **Heart Transplant or Implant of Heart Assist System with MCC**
| GMLOS 29.4 | AMLOS 38.5 | RW 26.0295 |

Operating Room Procedures
33.6   Combined heart-lung transplantation
37.51   Heart transplantation
37.52   Implantation of total internal biventricular heart replacement system
37.66   Insertion of implantable heart assist system
OR
37.60   Implantation or insertion of biventricular external heart assist system
OR
37.63   Repair of heart assist system
OR
37.65   Implant of single ventricular (extracorporeal) external heart assist system
AND
37.64   Removal of external heart assist system(s) or device(s)

DRG 002 **Heart Transplant or Implant of Heart Assist System without MCC**
| GMLOS 15.5 | AMLOS 19.7 | RW 13.9131 | ☑ |

Select operating room procedure OR any procedure combinations listed under DRG 001

DRG 003 **ECMO or Tracheostomy with Mechanical Ventilation 96+ Hours or Principal Diagnosis Except Face, Mouth and Neck with Major O.R.**
| GMLOS 28.2 | AMLOS 34.5 | RW 17.7369 | T |

Operating Room Procedure
39.65   Extracorporeal membrane oxygenation (ECMO)
OR
Nonoperating Room Procedure
31.1   Temporary tracheostomy
OR
Operating Room Procedures
31.21   Mediastinal tracheostomy
31.29   Other permanent tracheostomy
AND EITHER
Principal Diagnosis
Any diagnosis EXCEPT mouth, larynx and pharynx disorders listed under DRG 011
OR
Nonoperating Room Procedure
96.72   Continuous invasive mechanical ventilation for 96 consecutive hours or more

WITH
Operating Room Procedures
Any O.R. procedure not listed in DRGs 984-989

DRG 004 **Tracheostomy with Mechanical Ventilation 96+ Hours or Principal Diagnosis Except Face, Mouth and Neck without Major O.R.**
| GMLOS 20.9 | AMLOS 25.5 | RW 10.8833 | T ☑ |

Nonoperating Room Procedure
31.1   Temporary tracheostomy
OR
Operating Room Procedures
31.21   Mediastinal tracheostomy
31.29   Other permanent tracheostomy
AND EITHER
Principal Diagnosis
Any diagnosis EXCEPT mouth, larynx and pharynx disorders listed under DRG 011
OR
Nonoperating Room Procedure
96.72   Continuous invasive mechanical ventilation for 96 consecutive hours or more

DRG 005 **Liver Transplant with MCC or Intestinal Transplant**
| GMLOS 16.0 | AMLOS 21.7 | RW 10.9894 |

Operating Room Procedures
46.97   Transplant of intestine
50.51   Auxiliary liver transplant
50.59   Other transplant of liver

DRG 006 **Liver Transplant without MCC**
| GMLOS 8.0 | AMLOS 8.9 | RW 4.7178 | ☑ |

Operating Room Procedures
50.51   Auxiliary liver transplant
50.59   Other transplant of liver

DRG 007 **Lung Transplant**
| GMLOS 14.7 | AMLOS 18.2 | RW 9.6127 | ☑ |

Operating Room Procedures
33.5*   Lung transplant

DRG 008 **Simultaneous Pancreas/Kidney Transplant**
| GMLOS 9.8 | AMLOS 11.4 | RW 5.1110 |

Principal or Secondary Diagnosis
249*   Secondary diabetes mellitus
250.0*   Diabetes mellitus without mention of complication
250.1*   Diabetes with ketoacidosis
250.2*   Diabetes with hyperosmolarity
250.3*   Diabetes with other coma
250.4*   Diabetes with renal manifestations
250.5*   Diabetes with ophthalmic manifestations
250.6*   Diabetes with neurological manifestations
250.7*   Diabetes with peripheral circulatory disorders

Pre MDC—SURGICAL

Surgical   *Medical*   *CC Indicator*   *MCC Indicator*   *Procedure Proxy*

© 2012 OptumInsight, Inc.   Valid 10/01/2012-09/30/2013   1

Pre MDC—SURGICAL

250.8*	Diabetes with other specified manifestations
250.9*	Diabetes with unspecified complication
251.3	Postsurgical hypoinsulinemia

AND

Principal or Secondary Diagnosis

403.01	Hypertensive chronic kidney disease, malignant, with chronic kidney disease stage V or end stage renal disease
403.11	Hypertensive chronic kidney disease, benign, with chronic kidney disease stage V or end stage renal disease
403.91	Hypertensive chronic kidney disease, unspecified, with chronic kidney disease stage V or end stage renal disease
404.02	Hypertensive heart and chronic kidney disease, malignant, without heart failure and with chronic kidney disease stage V or end stage renal disease
404.03	Hypertensive heart and chronic kidney disease, malignant, with heart failure and with chronic kidney disease stage V or end stage renal disease
404.12	Hypertensive heart and chronic kidney disease, benign, without heart failure and with chronic kidney disease stage V or end stage renal disease
404.13	Hypertensive heart and chronic kidney disease, benign, with heart failure and chronic kidney disease stage V or end stage renal disease
404.92	Hypertensive heart and chronic kidney disease, unspecified, without heart failure and with chronic kidney disease stage V or end stage renal disease
404.93	Hypertensive heart and chronic kidney disease, unspecified, with heart failure and chronic kidney disease stage V or end stage renal disease
585*	Chronic kidney disease (CKD)
V42.0	Kidney replaced by transplant
V43.89	Other organ or tissue replaced by other means

AND

Any of the following procedure combinations

52.80	Pancreatic transplant, not otherwise specified
	AND
55.69	Other kidney transplantation
OR	
52.82	Homotransplant of pancreas
	AND
55.69	Other kidney transplantation

DRG 009   Bone Marrow Transplant

GMLOS 0.0	AMLOS 0.0	RW 0.0000

Omitted in October 2011 grouper version

DRG 010   Pancreas Transplant

GMLOS 8.0	AMLOS 8.6	RW 3.8954	☑

Principal or Secondary Diagnosis

249*	Secondary diabetes mellitus
250.0*	Diabetes mellitus without mention of complication
250.1*	Diabetes with ketoacidosis
250.2*	Diabetes with hyperosmolarity
250.3*	Diabetes with other coma
250.4*	Diabetes with renal manifestations
250.5*	Diabetes with ophthalmic manifestations
250.6*	Diabetes with neurological manifestations
250.7*	Diabetes with peripheral circulatory disorders
250.8*	Diabetes with other specified manifestations
250.9*	Diabetes with unspecified complication
251.3	Postsurgical hypoinsulinemia

AND

Operating Room Procedures

52.80	Pancreatic transplant, not otherwise specified
52.82	Homotransplant of pancreas

DRG 011   Tracheostomy for Face, Mouth, and Neck Diagnoses with MCC

GMLOS 11.9	AMLOS 14.9	RW 4.8434	☑

Operating Room Procedures

30.3	Complete laryngectomy
30.4	Radical laryngectomy

OR

Principal Diagnosis

012.3*	Tuberculous laryngitis
032.0	Faucial diphtheria
032.1	Nasopharyngeal diphtheria
032.2	Anterior nasal diphtheria
032.3	Laryngeal diphtheria
034.0	Streptococcal sore throat
054.2	Herpetic gingivostomatitis
074.0	Herpangina
098.6	Gonococcal infection of pharynx
099.51	Chlamydia trachomatis infection of pharynx
101	Vincent's angina
102.5	Gangosa due to yaws
112.0	Candidiasis of mouth
140*	Malignant neoplasm of lip
141*	Malignant neoplasm of tongue
142*	Malignant neoplasm of major salivary glands
143*	Malignant neoplasm of gum
144*	Malignant neoplasm of floor of mouth
145*	Malignant neoplasm of other and unspecified parts of mouth
146*	Malignant neoplasm of oropharynx
147*	Malignant neoplasm of nasopharynx
148*	Malignant neoplasm of hypopharynx
149*	Malignant neoplasm of other and ill-defined sites within the lip, oral cavity, and pharynx
160*	Malignant neoplasm of nasal cavities, middle ear, and accessory sinuses
161*	Malignant neoplasm of larynx
165.0	Malignant neoplasm of upper respiratory tract, part unspecified
170.1	Malignant neoplasm of mandible
173.0*	Other and unspecified malignant neoplasm of skin of lip
176.2	Kaposi's sarcoma of palate
193	Malignant neoplasm of thyroid gland
195.0	Malignant neoplasm of head, face, and neck
196.0	Secondary and unspecified malignant neoplasm of lymph nodes of head, face, and neck
200.01	Reticulosarcoma of lymph nodes of head, face, and neck
200.11	Lymphosarcoma of lymph nodes of head, face, and neck
200.21	Burkitt's tumor or lymphoma of lymph nodes of head, face, and neck
200.81	Other named variants of lymphosarcoma and reticulosarcoma of lymph nodes of head, face, and neck
201.01	Hodgkin's paragranuloma of lymph nodes of head, face, and neck
201.11	Hodgkin's granuloma of lymph nodes of head, face, and neck
201.21	Hodgkin's sarcoma of lymph nodes of head, face, and neck
201.41	Hodgkin's disease, lymphocytic-histiocytic predominance of lymph nodes of head, face, and neck
201.51	Hodgkin's disease, nodular sclerosis, of lymph nodes of head, face, and neck
201.61	Hodgkin's disease, mixed cellularity, involving lymph nodes of head, face, and neck
201.71	Hodgkin's disease, lymphocytic depletion, of lymph nodes of head, face, and neck
201.91	Hodgkin's disease, unspecified type, of lymph nodes of head, face, and neck
202.01	Nodular lymphoma of lymph nodes of head, face, and neck
202.11	Mycosis fungoides of lymph nodes of head, face, and neck

T Transfer DRG   SP Special Payment   ☑ Optimization Potential   ﹀ Targeted Potential   * Code Range   ● New DRG   ▲ Revised DRG Title

2

Valid 10/01/2012–09/30/2013   © 2012 OptumInsight, Inc.

202.21	Sezary's disease of lymph nodes of head, face, and neck
202.31	Malignant histiocytosis of lymph nodes of head, face, and neck
202.41	Leukemic reticuloendotheliosis of lymph nodes of head, face, and neck
202.51	Letterer-Siwe disease of lymph nodes of head, face, and neck
202.61	Malignant mast cell tumors of lymph nodes of head, face, and neck
202.81	Other malignant lymphomas of lymph nodes of head, face, and neck
202.91	Other and unspecified malignant neoplasms of lymphoid and histiocytic tissue of lymph nodes of head, face, and neck
210*	Benign neoplasm of lip, oral cavity, and pharynx
212.0	Benign neoplasm of nasal cavities, middle ear, and accessory sinuses
212.1	Benign neoplasm of larynx
213.0	Benign neoplasm of bones of skull and face
213.1	Benign neoplasm of lower jaw bone
226	Benign neoplasm of thyroid glands
228.00	Hemangioma of unspecified site
228.01	Hemangioma of skin and subcutaneous tissue
228.09	Hemangioma of other sites
230.0	Carcinoma in situ of lip, oral cavity, and pharynx
231.0	Carcinoma in situ of larynx
235.0	Neoplasm of uncertain behavior of major salivary glands
235.1	Neoplasm of uncertain behavior of lip, oral cavity, and pharynx
235.6	Neoplasm of uncertain behavior of larynx
242*	Thyrotoxicosis with or without goiter
245*	Thyroiditis
246.2	Cyst of thyroid
246.3	Hemorrhage and infarction of thyroid
246.8	Other specified disorders of thyroid
246.9	Unspecified disorder of thyroid
327.2*	Organic sleep apnea
327.3*	Circadian rhythm sleep disorder
327.4*	Organic parasomnia
327.5*	Organic sleep related movement disorders
327.8	Other organic sleep disorders
460	Acute nasopharyngitis (common cold)
462	Acute pharyngitis
463	Acute tonsillitis
464.00	Acute laryngitis, without mention of obstruction
464.01	Acute laryngitis, with obstruction
464.2*	Acute laryngotracheitis
464.3*	Acute epiglottitis
464.4	Croup
464.50	Unspecified supraglottis, without mention of obstruction
464.51	Unspecified supraglottis, with obstruction
465*	Acute upper respiratory infections of multiple or unspecified sites
470	Deviated nasal septum
472.1	Chronic pharyngitis
472.2	Chronic nasopharyngitis
474*	Chronic disease of tonsils and adenoids
475	Peritonsillar abscess
476.0	Chronic laryngitis
476.1	Chronic laryngotracheitis
478.2*	Other diseases of pharynx, not elsewhere classified
478.3*	Paralysis of vocal cords or larynx
478.4	Polyp of vocal cord or larynx
478.5	Other diseases of vocal cords
478.6	Edema of larynx
478.7*	Other diseases of larynx, not elsewhere classified
478.8	Upper respiratory tract hypersensitivity reaction, site unspecified
478.9	Other and unspecified diseases of upper respiratory tract
519.0*	Tracheostomy complications
519.11	Acute bronchospasm
519.19	Other diseases of trachea and bronchus
520*	Disorders of tooth development and eruption
521*	Diseases of hard tissues of teeth
522*	Diseases of pulp and periapical tissues
523*	Gingival and periodontal diseases
524*	Dentofacial anomalies, including malocclusion
525*	Other diseases and conditions of the teeth and supporting structures
526*	Diseases of the jaws
527*	Diseases of the salivary glands
528*	Diseases of the oral soft tissues, excluding lesions specific for gingiva and tongue
529*	Diseases and other conditions of the tongue
682.0	Cellulitis and abscess of face
682.1	Cellulitis and abscess of neck
748.2	Congenital web of larynx
748.3	Other congenital anomaly of larynx, trachea, and bronchus
749.0*	Cleft palate
749.1*	Cleft lip
749.2*	Cleft palate with cleft lip
750.0	Tongue tie
750.1*	Other congenital anomalies of tongue
750.21	Congenital absence of salivary gland
750.22	Congenital accessory salivary gland
750.23	Congenital atresia, salivary duct
750.24	Congenital fistula of salivary gland
750.25	Congenital fistula of lip
750.26	Other specified congenital anomalies of mouth
750.27	Congenital diverticulum of pharynx
750.29	Other specified congenital anomaly of pharynx
780.51	Insomnia with sleep apnea, unspecified
780.53	Hypersomnia with sleep apnea, unspecified
780.57	Unspecified sleep apnea
784.8	Hemorrhage from throat
784.92	Jaw pain
802.0	Mandible, closed fracture
802.3*	Mandible, open fracture
802.4	Malar and maxillary bones, closed fracture
802.5	Malar and maxillary bones, open fracture
802.6	Orbital floor (blow-out), closed fracture
802.7	Orbital floor (blow-out), open fracture
802.8	Other facial bones, closed fracture
802.9	Other facial bones, open fracture
807.5	Closed fracture of larynx and trachea
807.6	Open fracture of larynx and trachea
830*	Dislocation of jaw
873.2*	Open wound of nose, without mention of complication
873.3*	Open wound of nose, complicated
873.40	Open wound of face, unspecified site, without mention of complication
873.41	Open wound of cheek, without mention of complication
873.43	Open wound of lip, without mention of complication
873.44	Open wound of jaw, without mention of complication
873.50	Open wound of face, unspecified site, complicated
873.51	Open wound of cheek, complicated
873.53	Open wound of lip, complicated
873.54	Open wound of jaw, complicated
873.60	Open wound of mouth, unspecified site, without mention of complication
873.61	Open wound of buccal mucosa, without mention of complication
873.62	Open wound of gum (alveolar process), without mention of complication
873.64	Open wound of tongue and floor of mouth, without mention of complication
873.65	Open wound of palate, without mention of complication
873.69	Open wound of mouth, other and multiple sites, without mention of complication
873.70	Open wound of mouth, unspecified site, complicated
873.71	Open wound of buccal mucosa, complicated

873.72	Open wound of gum (alveolar process), complicated
873.74	Open wound of tongue and floor of mouth, complicated
873.75	Open wound of palate, complicated
873.79	Open wound of mouth, other and multiple sites, complicated
874.00	Open wound of larynx with trachea, without mention of complication
874.01	Open wound of larynx, without mention of complication
874.02	Open wound of trachea, without mention of complication
874.10	Open wound of larynx with trachea, complicated
874.11	Open wound of larynx, complicated
874.12	Open wound of trachea, complicated
874.2	Open wound of thyroid gland, without mention of complication
874.3	Open wound of thyroid gland, complicated
874.4	Open wound of pharynx, without mention of complication
874.5	Open wound of pharynx, complicated
874.8	Open wound of other and unspecified parts of neck, without mention of complication
874.9	Open wound of other and unspecified parts of neck, complicated
900.82	Injury to multiple blood vessels of head and neck
900.89	Injury to other specified blood vessels of head and neck
900.9	Injury to unspecified blood vessel of head and neck
925*	Crushing injury of face, scalp, and neck
933*	Foreign body in pharynx and larynx
935.0	Foreign body in mouth
947.0	Burn of mouth and pharynx
959.0*	Injury, other and unspecified, head face, and neck
V10.01	Personal history of malignant neoplasm of tongue
V10.02	Personal history of malignant neoplasm of other and unspecified parts of oral cavity and pharynx
V10.21	Personal history of malignant neoplasm of larynx

AND EITHER

Nonoperating Room Procedure

31.1	Temporary tracheostomy

OR

Operating Room Procedures

31.21	Mediastinal tracheostomy
31.29	Other permanent tracheostomy

DRG 012   Tracheostomy for Face, Mouth, and Neck Diagnoses with CC

GMLOS 8.5   AMLOS 10.0   RW 3.1576   ☑

Select principal diagnosis and operating and nonoperating room procedures listed under DRG 011

DRG 013   Tracheostomy for Face, Mouth, and Neck Diagnoses without CC/MCC

GMLOS 5.6   AMLOS 6.5   RW 1.9566   ☑

Select principal diagnosis and operating and nonoperating room procedures listed under DRG 011

DRG 014   Allogeneic Bone Marrow Transplant

GMLOS 18.6   AMLOS 25.8   RW 10.5255

Operating Room Procedures

41.02	Allogeneic bone marrow transplant with purging
41.03	Allogeneic bone marrow transplant without purging
41.05	Allogeneic hematopoietic stem cell transplant without purging
41.06	Cord blood stem cell transplant
41.08	Allogeneic hematopoietic stem cell transplant with purging

DRG 015   Autologous Bone Marrow Transplant

GMLOS 0.0   AMLOS 0.0   RW 0.0000

Omitted in October 2012 grouper version

DRG 016   Autologous Bone Marrow Transplant with CC/MCC

GMLOS 17.9   AMLOS 19.9   RW 6.0932   ☑

Operating Room Procedures

41.00	Bone marrow transplant, not otherwise specified
41.01	Autologous bone marrow transplant without purging
41.04	Autologous hematopoietic stem cell transplant without purging
41.07	Autologous hematopoietic stem cell transplant with purging
41.09	Autologous bone marrow transplant with purging

DRG 017   Autologous Bone Marrow Transplant without CC/MCC

GMLOS 11.0   AMLOS 14.2   RW 4.5817   ☑

Operating Room Procedures

41.00	Bone marrow transplant, not otherwise specified
41.01	Autologous bone marrow transplant without purging
41.04	Autologous hematopoietic stem cell transplant without purging
41.07	Autologous hematopoietic stem cell transplant with purging
41.09	Autologous bone marrow transplant with purging

Pre MDC—SURGICAL

Ⓣ Transfer DRG   ⑤⑨ Special Payment   ☑ Optimization Potential   ▽ Targeted Potential   * Code Range   ● New DRG   ▲ Revised DRG Title

4   Valid 10/01/2012-09/30/2013   © 2012 OptumInsight, Inc.

003.21	045.00	072.72	237.72	327.34	335.24	342.90	346.50	353.9
006.5	045.01	078.81	237.73	327.35	335.29	342.91	346.51	354.0
013.00	045.02	090.40	237.79	327.36	335.8	342.92	346.52	354.1
013.01	045.03	090.41	237.9	327.37	335.9	343.0	346.53	354.2
013.02	045.10	090.42	239.6	327.39	336.0	343.1	346.60	354.3
013.03	045.11	090.49	249.60	327.41	336.1	343.2	346.61	354.4
013.04	045.12	091.81	249.61	327.43	336.2	343.3	346.62	354.5
013.05	045.13	094.0	250.60	327.51	336.3	343.4	346.63	354.8
013.06	045.90	094.1	250.61	327.52	336.8	343.8	346.70	354.9
013.10	045.91	094.2	250.62	330.0	336.9	343.9	346.71	355.0
013.11	045.92	094.3	250.63	330.1	337.00	344.00	346.72	355.1
013.12	045.93	094.81	307.20	330.2	337.01	344.01	346.73	355.2
013.13	046.0	094.82	307.21	330.3	337.09	344.02	346.80	355.3
013.14	046.11	094.85	307.22	330.8	337.1	344.03	346.81	355.4
013.15	046.19	094.87	307.23	330.9	337.20	344.04	346.82	355.5
013.16	046.2	094.89	307.81	331.0	337.21	344.09	346.83	355.6
013.20	046.3	094.9	310.2	331.11	337.22	344.1	346.90	355.71
013.21	046.71	098.82	310.81	331.19	337.29	344.2	346.91	355.79
013.22	046.72	100.81	310.89	331.2	337.3	344.30	346.92	355.8
013.23	046.79	100.89	315.35	331.3	337.9	344.31	346.93	355.9
013.24	046.8	112.83	320.0	331.4	338.0	344.32	347.00	356.0
013.25	046.9	114.2	320.1	331.5	338.21	344.40	347.01	356.1
013.26	047.0	115.01	320.2	331.6	338.22	344.41	347.10	356.2
013.30	047.1	115.11	320.3	331.7	338.28	344.42	347.11	356.3
013.31	047.8	115.91	320.7	331.81	338.29	344.5	348.0	356.4
013.32	047.9	130.0	320.81	331.82	338.4	344.60	348.1	356.8
013.33	048	137.1	320.82	331.83	339.00	344.81	348.2	356.9
013.34	049.0	138	320.89	331.89	339.01	344.89	348.30	357.0
013.35	049.1	139.0	320.9	331.9	339.02	344.9	348.31	357.1
013.36	049.8	191.0	321.0	332.0	339.03	345.00	348.39	357.2
013.40	049.9	191.1	321.1	332.1	339.04	345.01	348.4	357.3
013.41	052.0	191.2	321.2	333.0	339.05	345.10	348.5	357.4
013.42	052.2	191.3	321.3	333.1	339.09	345.11	348.81	357.5
013.43	053.0	191.4	321.4	333.2	339.10	345.2	348.82	357.6
013.44	053.10	191.5	321.8	333.3	339.11	345.3	348.89	357.7
013.45	053.11	191.6	322.0	333.4	339.12	345.40	348.9	357.81
013.46	053.12	191.7	322.1	333.5	339.20	345.41	349.0	357.82
013.50	053.13	191.8	322.2	333.6	339.21	345.50	349.1	357.89
013.51	053.14	191.9	322.9	333.71	339.22	345.51	349.2	357.9
013.52	053.19	192.0	323.01	333.72	339.3	345.60	349.81	358.00
013.53	054.3	192.1	323.02	333.79	339.41	345.61	349.82	358.01
013.54	054.72	192.2	323.1	333.82	339.42	345.70	349.89	358.1
013.55	054.74	192.3	323.2	333.83	339.43	345.71	349.9	358.2
013.56	055.0	192.8	323.41	333.84	339.44	345.80	350.1	358.30
013.60	056.00	192.9	323.42	333.85	339.81	345.81	350.2	358.31
013.61	056.01	194.4	323.51	333.89	339.82	345.90	350.8	358.39
013.62	056.09	194.5	323.52	333.90	339.83	345.91	350.9	358.8
013.63	058.21	194.6	323.61	333.91	339.84	346.00	351.0	358.9
013.64	058.29	198.3	323.62	333.92	339.85	346.01	351.1	359.0
013.65	062.0	198.4	323.63	333.93	339.89	346.02	351.8	359.1
013.66	062.1	225.0	323.71	333.94	340	346.03	351.9	359.21
013.80	062.2	225.1	323.72	333.99	341.0	346.10	352.0	359.22
013.81	062.3	225.2	323.81	334.0	341.1	346.11	352.1	359.23
013.82	062.4	225.3	323.82	334.1	341.20	346.12	352.2	359.24
013.83	062.5	225.4	323.9	334.2	341.21	346.13	352.3	359.29
013.84	062.8	225.8	324.0	334.3	341.22	346.20	352.4	359.3
013.85	062.9	225.9	324.1	334.4	341.8	346.21	352.5	359.4
013.86	063.0	227.4	324.9	334.8	341.9	346.22	352.6	359.5
013.90	063.1	227.5	325	334.9	342.00	346.23	352.9	359.6
013.91	063.2	227.6	326	335.0	342.01	346.30	353.0	359.81
013.92	063.8	228.02	327.21	335.10	342.02	346.31	353.1	359.89
013.93	063.9	237.1	327.25	335.11	342.10	346.32	353.2	359.9
013.94	064	237.3	327.27	335.19	342.11	346.33	353.3	377.00
013.95	066.2	237.5	327.30	335.20	342.12	346.40	353.4	377.01
013.96	071	237.6	327.31	335.21	342.80	346.41	353.5	377.04
036.0	072.1	237.70	327.32	335.22	342.81	346.42	353.6	377.51
036.1	072.2	237.71	327.33	335.23	342.82	346.43	353.8	377.52

377.53	438.7	794.19	800.86	801.80	803.72	804.64	806.70	851.74
377.54	438.81	796.1	800.89	801.81	803.73	804.65	806.71	851.75
377.61	438.82	798.0	800.90	801.82	803.74	804.66	806.72	851.76
377.62	438.83	799.53	800.91	801.83	803.75	804.69	806.79	851.79
377.63	438.84	800.00	800.92	801.84	803.76	804.70	806.8	851.80
377.71	438.85	800.01	800.93	801.85	803.79	804.71	806.9	851.81
377.72	438.89	800.02	800.94	801.86	803.80	804.72	850.0	851.82
377.73	438.9	800.03	800.95	801.89	803.81	804.73	850.11	851.83
377.75	723.2	800.04	800.96	801.90	803.82	804.74	850.12	851.84
377.9	723.3	800.05	800.99	801.91	803.83	804.75	850.2	851.85
378.86	723.4	800.06	801.00	801.92	803.84	804.76	850.3	851.86
379.45	729.2	800.09	801.01	801.93	803.85	804.79	850.4	851.89
388.61	736.05	800.10	801.02	801.94	803.86	804.80	850.5	851.90
430	736.06	800.11	801.03	801.95	803.89	804.81	850.9	851.91
431	736.07	800.12	801.04	801.96	803.90	804.82	851.00	851.92
432.0	736.74	800.13	801.05	801.99	803.91	804.83	851.01	851.93
432.1	740.0	800.14	801.06	803.00	803.92	804.84	851.02	851.94
432.9	740.1	800.15	801.09	803.01	803.93	804.85	851.03	851.95
433.00	740.2	800.16	801.10	803.02	803.94	804.86	851.04	851.96
433.01	741.00	800.19	801.11	803.03	803.95	804.89	851.05	851.99
433.10	741.01	800.20	801.12	803.04	803.96	804.90	851.06	852.00
433.11	741.02	800.21	801.13	803.05	803.99	804.91	851.09	852.01
433.20	741.03	800.22	801.14	803.06	804.00	804.92	851.10	852.02
433.21	741.90	800.23	801.15	803.09	804.01	804.93	851.11	852.03
433.30	741.91	800.24	801.16	803.10	804.02	804.94	851.12	852.04
433.31	741.92	800.25	801.19	803.11	804.03	804.95	851.13	852.05
433.80	741.93	800.26	801.20	803.12	804.04	804.96	851.14	852.06
433.81	742.0	800.29	801.21	803.13	804.05	804.99	851.15	852.09
433.90	742.1	800.30	801.22	803.14	804.06	806.00	851.16	852.10
433.91	742.2	800.31	801.23	803.15	804.09	806.01	851.19	852.11
434.00	742.3	800.32	801.24	803.16	804.10	806.02	851.20	852.12
434.01	742.4	800.33	801.25	803.19	804.11	806.03	851.21	852.13
434.10	742.51	800.34	801.26	803.20	804.12	806.04	851.22	852.14
434.11	742.53	800.35	801.29	803.21	804.13	806.05	851.23	852.15
434.90	742.59	800.36	801.30	803.22	804.14	806.06	851.24	852.16
434.91	742.8	800.39	801.31	803.23	804.15	806.07	851.25	852.19
435.0	742.9	800.40	801.32	803.24	804.16	806.08	851.26	852.20
435.1	747.81	800.41	801.33	803.25	804.19	806.09	851.29	852.21
435.2	747.82	800.42	801.34	803.26	804.20	806.10	851.30	852.22
435.3	756.17	800.43	801.35	803.29	804.21	806.11	851.31	852.23
435.8	759.5	800.44	801.36	803.30	804.22	806.12	851.32	852.24
435.9	779.7	800.45	801.39	803.31	804.23	806.13	851.33	852.25
436	780.01	800.46	801.40	803.32	804.24	806.14	851.34	852.26
437.0	780.03	800.49	801.41	803.33	804.25	806.15	851.35	852.29
437.1	780.09	800.50	801.42	803.34	804.26	806.16	851.36	852.30
437.2	780.31	800.51	801.43	803.35	804.29	806.17	851.39	852.31
437.3	780.32	800.52	801.44	803.36	804.30	806.18	851.40	852.32
437.4	780.33	800.53	801.45	803.39	804.31	806.19	851.41	852.33
437.5	780.39	800.54	801.46	803.40	804.32	806.20	851.42	852.34
437.6	780.72	800.55	801.49	803.41	804.33	806.21	851.43	852.35
437.7	781.0	800.56	801.50	803.42	804.34	806.22	851.44	852.36
437.8	781.1	800.59	801.51	803.43	804.35	806.23	851.45	852.39
437.9	781.2	800.60	801.52	803.44	804.36	806.24	851.46	852.40
438.0	781.3	800.61	801.53	803.45	804.39	806.25	851.49	852.41
438.10	781.4	800.62	801.54	803.46	804.40	806.26	851.50	852.42
438.11	781.6	800.63	801.55	803.49	804.41	806.27	851.51	852.43
438.12	781.8	800.64	801.56	803.50	804.42	806.28	851.52	852.44
438.13	781.91	800.65	801.59	803.51	804.43	806.29	851.53	852.45
438.14	781.92	800.66	801.60	803.52	804.44	806.30	851.54	852.46
438.19	781.94	800.69	801.61	803.53	804.45	806.31	851.55	852.49
438.20	781.99	800.70	801.62	803.54	804.46	806.32	851.56	852.50
438.21	782.0	800.71	801.63	803.55	804.49	806.33	851.59	852.51
438.22	784.0	800.72	801.64	803.56	804.50	806.34	851.60	852.52
438.30	784.3	800.73	801.65	803.59	804.51	806.35	851.61	852.53
438.31	784.51	800.74	801.66	803.60	804.52	806.36	851.62	852.54
438.32	784.52	800.75	801.69	803.61	804.53	806.37	851.63	852.55
438.40	784.59	800.76	801.70	803.62	804.54	806.38	851.64	852.56
438.41	792.0	800.79	801.71	803.63	804.55	806.39	851.65	852.59
438.42	793.0	800.80	801.72	803.64	804.56	806.4	851.66	853.00
438.50	794.00	800.81	801.73	803.65	804.59	806.5	851.69	853.01
438.51	794.01	800.82	801.74	803.66	804.60	806.60	851.70	853.02
438.52	794.02	800.83	801.75	803.69	804.61	806.61	851.71	853.03
438.53	794.09	800.84	801.76	803.70	804.62	806.62	851.72	853.04
438.6	794.10	800.85	801.79	803.71	804.63	806.69	851.73	853.05

853.06	854.03	905.0	951.1	952.05	952.18	953.8	955.7	957.8
853.09	854.04	907.0	951.2	952.06	952.19	953.9	955.8	957.9
853.10	854.05	907.1	951.3	952.07	952.2	954.0	955.9	996.2
853.11	854.06	907.2	951.4	952.08	952.3	954.1	956.0	996.63
853.12	854.09	907.3	951.6	952.09	952.4	954.8	956.1	996.75
853.13	854.10	907.4	951.7	952.10	952.8	954.9	956.2	997.00
853.14	854.11	907.5	951.8	952.11	952.9	955.0	956.3	997.01
853.15	854.12	907.9	951.9	952.12	953.0	955.1	956.4	997.02
853.16	854.13	950.1	952.00	952.13	953.1	955.2	956.5	997.09
853.19	854.14	950.2	952.01	952.14	953.2	955.3	956.8	V53.01
854.00	854.15	950.3	952.02	952.15	953.3	955.4	956.9	V53.02
854.01	854.16	950.9	952.03	952.16	953.4	955.5	957.0	V53.09
854.02	854.19	951.0	952.04	952.17	953.5	955.6	957.1	

MDC 1: Diseases And Disorders Of The Nervous System

SURGICAL

MDC 1: Diseases And Disorders Of The Nervous System—SURGICAL

DRG 020 Intracranial Vascular Procedures with Principal Diagnosis of Hemorrhage with MCC

GMLOS 14.5   **AMLOS 17.6**   **RW 9.1016**

Principal Diagnosis
094.87	Syphilitic ruptured cerebral aneurysm
430	Subarachnoid hemorrhage
431	Intracerebral hemorrhage
432*	Other and unspecified intracranial hemorrhage

Operating Room Procedures
02.13	Ligation of meningeal vessel
38.01	Incision of intracranial vessels
38.11	Endarterectomy of intracranial vessels
38.31	Resection of intracranial vessels with anastomosis
38.41	Resection of intracranial vessels with replacement
38.51	Ligation and stripping of varicose veins of intracranial vessels
38.61	Other excision of intracranial vessels
38.81	Other surgical occlusion of intracranial vessels
39.28	Extracranial-intracranial (EC-IC) vascular bypass
39.51	Clipping of aneurysm
39.52	Other repair of aneurysm
39.53	Repair of arteriovenous fistula
39.72	Endovascular (total) embolization or occlusion of head and neck vessels
39.75	Endovascular embolization or occlusion of vessel(s) of head or neck using bare coils
39.76	Endovascular embolization or occlusion of vessel(s) of head or neck using bioactive coils
39.79	Other endovascular procedures on other vessels

DRG 021 Intracranial Vascular Procedures with Principal Diagnosis of Hemorrhage with CC

GMLOS 11.8   **AMLOS 13.5**   **RW 6.6400**   ☑

Select principal diagnosis and operating room procedures listed under DRG 020

DRG 022 Intracranial Vascular Procedures with Principal Diagnosis of Hemorrhage without CC/MCC

GMLOS 6.5   **AMLOS 8.0**   **RW 4.5056**   ☑

Select principal diagnosis and operating room procedures listed under DRG 020

DRG 023 Craniotomy with Major Device Implant/Acute Complex Central Nervous System Principal Diagnosis with MCC or Chemo Implant

GMLOS 7.9   **AMLOS 11.1**   **RW 5.2378**   ⊤

Operating Room Procedures
00.62	Percutaneous angioplasty of intracranial vessel(s)
01.12	Open biopsy of cerebral meninges
01.14	Open biopsy of brain
01.15	Biopsy of skull
01.18	Other diagnostic procedures on brain and cerebral meninges
01.19	Other diagnostic procedures on skull
01.21	Incision and drainage of cranial sinus
01.22	Removal of intracranial neurostimulator lead(s)
01.23	Reopening of craniotomy site
01.24	Other craniotomy
01.25	Other craniectomy
01.28	Placement of intracerebral catheter(s) via burr hole(s)
01.31	Incision of cerebral meninges
01.32	Lobotomy and tractotomy
01.39	Other incision of brain
01.41	Operations on thalamus
01.42	Operations on globus pallidus
01.51	Excision of lesion or tissue of cerebral meninges
01.52	Hemispherectomy
01.53	Lobectomy of brain
01.59	Other excision or destruction of lesion or tissue of brain
01.6	Excision of lesion of skull
02.0*	Cranioplasty
02.1*	Repair of cerebral meninges
02.2*	Ventriculostomy
02.91	Lysis of cortical adhesions
02.92	Repair of brain
02.93	Implantation or replacement of intracranial neurostimulator lead(s)
02.94	Insertion or replacement of skull tongs or halo traction device
02.99	Other operations on skull, brain, and cerebral meninges
04.01	Excision of acoustic neuroma
04.41	Decompression of trigeminal nerve root
07.13	Biopsy of pituitary gland, transfrontal approach
07.14	Biopsy of pituitary gland, transsphenoidal approach
07.15	Biopsy of pituitary gland, unspecified approach
07.17	Biopsy of pineal gland
07.5*	Operations on pineal gland
07.6*	Hypophysectomy
07.7*	Other operations on hypophysis
17.54	Percutaneous atherectomy of intracranial vessel(s)
17.61	Laser interstitial thermal therapy [LITT] of lesion or tissue of brain under guidance
29.92	Division of glossopharyngeal nerve
38.01	Incision of intracranial vessels
38.11	Endarterectomy of intracranial vessels
38.31	Resection of intracranial vessels with anastomosis
38.41	Resection of intracranial vessels with replacement
38.51	Ligation and stripping of varicose veins of intracranial vessels
38.61	Other excision of intracranial vessels
38.81	Other surgical occlusion of intracranial vessels
39.28	Extracranial-intracranial (EC-IC) vascular bypass
39.51	Clipping of aneurysm
39.52	Other repair of aneurysm
39.53	Repair of arteriovenous fistula
39.72	Endovascular (total) embolization or occlusion of head and neck vessels
39.74	Endovascular removal of obstruction from head and neck vessel(s)
39.75	Endovascular embolization or occlusion of vessel(s) of head or neck using bare coils
39.76	Endovascular embolization or occlusion of vessel(s) of head or neck using bioactive coils
39.79	Other endovascular procedures on other vessels

AND

Any of the following

Acute Complex CNS Principal Diagnosis
003.21	Salmonella meningitis
006.5	Amebic brain abscess
013*	Tuberculosis of meninges and central nervous system
036.0	Meningococcal meningitis
036.1	Meningococcal encephalitis
045.0*	Acute paralytic poliomyelitis specified as bulbar
045.1*	Acute poliomyelitis with other paralysis
045.9*	Acute unspecified poliomyelitis
052.2	Postvaricella myelitis
053.14	Herpes zoster myelitis
054.3	Herpetic meningoencephalitis
054.72	Herpes simplex meningitis
054.74	Herpes simplex myelitis

⊤ *Transfer DRG*   SP *Special Payment*   ☑ *Optimization Potential*   ▽ *Targeted Potential*   * *Code Range*   ● *New DRG*   ▲ *Revised DRG Title*

055.0	Postmeasles encephalitis
058.21	Human herpesvirus 6 encephalitis
058.29	Other human herpesvirus encephalitis
062*	Mosquito-borne viral encephalitis
063*	Tick-borne viral encephalitis
064	Viral encephalitis transmitted by other and unspecified arthropods
066.2	Venezuelan equine fever
071	Rabies
072.1	Mumps meningitis
072.2	Mumps encephalitis
091.81	Early syphilis, acute syphilitic meningitis (secondary)
094.2	Syphilitic meningitis
094.81	Syphilitic encephalitis
098.82	Gonococcal meningitis
100.8*	Other specified leptospiral infections
112.83	Candidal meningitis
114.2	Coccidioidal meningitis
115.01	Histoplasma capsulatum meningitis
115.11	Histoplasma duboisii meningitis
115.91	Unspecified Histoplasmosis meningitis
130.0	Meningoencephalitis due to toxoplasmosis
320*	Bacterial meningitis
321.0	Cryptococcal meningitis
321.1	Meningitis in other fungal diseases
321.2	Meningitis due to viruses not elsewhere classified
321.3	Meningitis due to trypanosomiasis
323.0*	Encephalitis, myelitis, and encephalomyelitis in viral diseases classified elsewhere
323.1	Encephalitis, myelitis, and encephalomyelitis in rickettsial diseases classified elsewhere
323.2	Encephalitis, myelitis, and encephalomyelitis in protozoal diseases classified elsewhere
323.4*	Other encephalitis, myelitis, and encephalomyelitis due to other infections classified elsewhere
323.5*	Encephalitis, myelitis, and encephalomyelitis following immunization procedures
323.6*	Postinfectious encephalitis, myelitis, and encephalomyelitis
323.7*	Toxic encephalitis, myelitis, and encephalomyelitis
323.8*	Other causes of encephalitis, myelitis, and encephalomyelitis
323.9	Unspecified causes of encephalitis, myelitis, and encephalomyelitis
324*	Intracranial and intraspinal abscess
325	Phlebitis and thrombophlebitis of intracranial venous sinuses
341.2*	Acute (transverse) myelitis
430	Subarachnoid hemorrhage
431	Intracerebral hemorrhage
432.9	Unspecified intracranial hemorrhage
433.01	Occlusion and stenosis of basilar artery with cerebral infarction
433.11	Occlusion and stenosis of carotid artery with cerebral infarction
433.21	Occlusion and stenosis of vertebral artery with cerebral infarction
433.31	Occlusion and stenosis of multiple and bilateral precerebral arteries with cerebral infarction
433.81	Occlusion and stenosis of other specified precerebral artery with cerebral infarction
433.91	Occlusion and stenosis of unspecified precerebral artery with cerebral infarction
434.01	Cerebral thrombosis with cerebral infarction
434.11	Cerebral embolism with cerebral infarction
434.91	Unspecified cerebral artery occlusion with cerebral infarction
851.1*	Cortex (cerebral) contusion with open intracranial wound
851.2*	Cortex (cerebral) laceration without mention of open intracranial wound
851.3*	Cortex (cerebral) laceration with open intracranial wound

851.5*	Cerebellar or brain stem contusion with open intracranial wound
851.6*	Cerebellar or brain stem laceration without mention of open intracranial wound
851.7*	Cerebellar or brain stem laceration with open intracranial wound
851.8*	Other and unspecified cerebral laceration and contusion, without mention of open intracranial wound
851.9*	Other and unspecified cerebral laceration and contusion, with open intracranial wound
852.0*	Subarachnoid hemorrhage following injury without mention of open intracranial wound
852.1*	Subarachnoid hemorrhage following injury, with open intracranial wound
852.3*	Subdural hemorrhage following injury, with open intracranial wound
853.0*	Other and unspecified intracranial hemorrhage following injury, without mention of open intracranial wound
853.1*	Other and unspecified intracranial hemorrhage following injury with open intracranial wound
854.1*	Intracranial injury of other and unspecified nature with open intracranial wound

OR

The following procedure combination

02.93	Implantation or replacement of intracranial neurostimulator lead(s)
	AND
01.20	Cranial implantation or replacement of neurostimulator pulse generator

OR

02.93	Implantation or replacement of intracranial neurostimulator lead(s)
	AND
86.95	Insertion or replacement of multiple array neurostimulator pulse generator, not specified as rechargeable

OR

02.93	Implantation or replacement of intracranial neurostimulator lead(s)
	AND
86.98	Insertion or replacement of multiple array (two or more) rechargeable neurostimulator pulse generator

OR

Nonoperating Room Procedure

00.10	Implantation of chemotherapeutic agent

DRG 024　Craniotomy with Major Device Implant/Acute Complex Central Nervous System Principal Diagnosis without MCC

　　　　　GMLOS 4.3　　　AMLOS 6.5　　　RW 3.5279　　　Ⓣ ☑

Operating Room Procedures

00.62	Percutaneous angioplasty of intracranial vessel(s)
01.12	Open biopsy of cerebral meninges
01.14	Open biopsy of brain
01.15	Biopsy of skull
01.18	Other diagnostic procedures on brain and cerebral meninges
01.19	Other diagnostic procedures on skull
01.21	Incision and drainage of cranial sinus
01.22	Removal of intracranial neurostimulator lead(s)
01.23	Reopening of craniotomy site
01.24	Other craniotomy
01.25	Other craniectomy
01.28	Placement of intracerebral catheter(s) via burr hole(s)
01.31	Incision of cerebral meninges
01.32	Lobotomy and tractotomy
01.39	Other incision of brain
01.41	Operations on thalamus

MDC 1: Diseases And Disorders Of The Nervous System—SURGICAL

01.42	Operations on globus pallidus
01.51	Excision of lesion or tissue of cerebral meninges
01.52	Hemispherectomy
01.53	Lobectomy of brain
01.59	Other excision or destruction of lesion or tissue of brain
01.6	Excision of lesion of skull
02.0*	Cranioplasty
02.1*	Repair of cerebral meninges
02.2*	Ventriculostomy
02.91	Lysis of cortical adhesions
02.92	Repair of brain
02.93	Implantation or replacement of intracranial neurostimulator lead(s)
02.94	Insertion or replacement of skull tongs or halo traction device
02.99	Other operations on skull, brain, and cerebral meninges
04.01	Excision of acoustic neuroma
04.41	Decompression of trigeminal nerve root
07.13	Biopsy of pituitary gland, transfrontal approach
07.14	Biopsy of pituitary gland, transsphenoidal approach
07.15	Biopsy of pituitary gland, unspecified approach
07.17	Biopsy of pineal gland
07.5*	Operations on pineal gland
07.6*	Hypophysectomy
07.7*	Other operations on hypophysis
17.54	Percutaneous atherectomy of intracranial vessel(s)
17.61	Laser interstitial thermal therapy [LITT] of lesion or tissue of brain under guidance
29.92	Division of glossopharyngeal nerve
38.01	Incision of intracranial vessels
38.11	Endarterectomy of intracranial vessels
38.31	Resection of intracranial vessels with anastomosis
38.41	Resection of intracranial vessels with replacement
38.51	Ligation and stripping of varicose veins of intracranial vessels
38.61	Other excision of intracranial vessels
38.81	Other surgical occlusion of intracranial vessels
39.28	Extracranial-intracranial (EC-IC) vascular bypass
39.51	Clipping of aneurysm
39.52	Other repair of aneurysm
39.53	Repair of arteriovenous fistula
39.72	Endovascular (total) embolization or occlusion of head and neck vessels
39.74	Endovascular removal of obstruction from head and neck vessel(s)
39.75	Endovascular embolization or occlusion of vessel(s) of head or neck using bare coils
39.76	Endovascular embolization or occlusion of vessel(s) of head or neck using bioactive coils
39.79	Other endovascular procedures on other vessels

AND

Any of the following

Acute Complex CNS Principal Diagnosis

003.21	Salmonella meningitis
006.5	Amebic brain abscess
013*	Tuberculosis of meninges and central nervous system
036.0	Meningococcal meningitis
036.1	Meningococcal encephalitis
045.0*	Acute paralytic poliomyelitis specified as bulbar
045.1*	Acute poliomyelitis with other paralysis
045.9*	Acute unspecified poliomyelitis
052.2	Postvaricella myelitis
053.14	Herpes zoster myelitis
054.3	Herpetic meningoencephalitis
054.72	Herpes simplex meningitis
054.74	Herpes simplex myelitis
055.0	Postmeasles encephalitis
058.21	Human herpesvirus 6 encephalitis
058.29	Other human herpesvirus encephalitis
062*	Mosquito-borne viral encephalitis
063*	Tick-borne viral encephalitis
064	Viral encephalitis transmitted by other and unspecified arthropods
066.2	Venezuelan equine fever
071	Rabies
072.1	Mumps meningitis
072.2	Mumps encephalitis
091.81	Early syphilis, acute syphilitic meningitis (secondary)
094.2	Syphilitic meningitis
094.81	Syphilitic encephalitis
098.82	Gonococcal meningitis
100.8*	Other specified leptospiral infections
112.83	Candidal meningitis
114.2	Coccidioidal meningitis
115.01	Histoplasma capsulatum meningitis
115.11	Histoplasma duboisii meningitis
115.91	Unspecified Histoplasmosis meningitis
130.0	Meningoencephalitis due to toxoplasmosis
320*	Bacterial meningitis
321.0	Cryptococcal meningitis
321.1	Meningitis in other fungal diseases
321.2	Meningitis due to viruses not elsewhere classified
321.3	Meningitis due to trypanosomiasis
323.01	Encephalitis and encephalomyelitis in viral diseases classified elsewhere
323.02	Myelitis in viral diseases classified elsewhere
323.1	Encephalitis, myelitis, and encephalomyelitis in rickettsial diseases classified elsewhere
323.2	Encephalitis, myelitis, and encephalomyelitis in protozoal diseases classified elsewhere
323.41	Other encephalitis and encephalomyelitis due to other infections classified elsewhere
323.42	Other myelitis due to other infections classified elsewhere
323.51	Encephalitis and encephalomyelitis following immunization procedures
323.52	Myelitis following immunization procedures
323.61	Infectious acute disseminated encephalomyelitis [ADEM]
323.62	Other postinfectious encephalitis and encephalomyelitis
323.63	Postinfectious myelitis
323.71	Toxic encephalitis and encephalomyelitis
323.72	Toxic myelitis
323.81	Other causes of encephalitis and encephalomyelitis
323.82	Other causes of myelitis
323.9	Unspecified causes of encephalitis, myelitis, and encephalomyelitis
324*	Intracranial and intraspinal abscess
325	Phlebitis and thrombophlebitis of intracranial venous sinuses
341.20	Acute (transverse) myelitis NOS
341.21	Acute (transverse) myelitis in conditions classified elsewhere
341.22	Idiopathic transverse myelitis
430	Subarachnoid hemorrhage
431	Intracerebral hemorrhage
432.9	Unspecified intracranial hemorrhage
433.01	Occlusion and stenosis of basilar artery with cerebral infarction
433.11	Occlusion and stenosis of carotid artery with cerebral infarction
433.21	Occlusion and stenosis of vertebral artery with cerebral infarction
433.31	Occlusion and stenosis of multiple and bilateral precerebral arteries with cerebral infarction
433.81	Occlusion and stenosis of other specified precerebral artery with cerebral infarction
433.91	Occlusion and stenosis of unspecified precerebral artery with cerebral infarction
434.01	Cerebral thrombosis with cerebral infarction
434.11	Cerebral embolism with cerebral infarction

T Transfer DRG   SP Special Payment   ☑ Optimization Potential   ▽ Targeted Potential   * Code Range   ● New DRG   ▲ Revised DRG Title

10

Valid 10/01/2012-09/30/2013

© 2012 OptumInsight, Inc.

434.91	Unspecified cerebral artery occlusion with cerebral infarction
851.1*	Cortex (cerebral) contusion with open intracranial wound
851.2*	Cortex (cerebral) laceration without mention of open intracranial wound
851.3*	Cortex (cerebral) laceration with open intracranial wound
851.5*	Cerebellar or brain stem contusion with open intracranial wound
851.6*	Cerebellar or brain stem laceration without mention of open intracranial wound
851.7*	Cerebellar or brain stem laceration with open intracranial wound
851.8*	Other and unspecified cerebral laceration and contusion, without mention of open intracranial wound
851.9*	Other and unspecified cerebral laceration and contusion, with open intracranial wound
852.0*	Subarachnoid hemorrhage following injury without mention of open intracranial wound
852.1*	Subarachnoid hemorrhage following injury, with open intracranial wound
852.3*	Subdural hemorrhage following injury, with open intracranial wound
853.0*	Other and unspecified intracranial hemorrhage following injury, without mention of open intracranial wound
853.1*	Other and unspecified intracranial hemorrhage following injury with open intracranial wound
854.1*	Intracranial injury of other and unspecified nature with open intracranial wound

OR

The following procedure combination

02.93	Implantation or replacement of intracranial neurostimulator lead(s)
	AND
01.20	Cranial implantation or replacement of neurostimulator pulse generator

OR

02.93	Implantation or replacement of intracranial neurostimulator lead(s)
	AND
86.95	Insertion or replacement of multiple array neurostimulator pulse generator, not specified as rechargeable

OR

02.93	Implantation or replacement of intracranial neurostimulator lead(s)
	AND
86.98	Insertion or replacement of multiple array (two or more) rechargeable neurostimulator pulse generator

DRG 025 Craniotomy and Endovascular Intracranial Procedures with MCC
GMLOS 8.1   AMLOS 10.5   RW 4.5958   T ☑

Operating Room Procedures

00.62	Percutaneous angioplasty of intracranial vessel(s)
01.12	Open biopsy of cerebral meninges
01.14	Open biopsy of brain
01.15	Biopsy of skull
01.18	Other diagnostic procedures on brain and cerebral meninges
01.19	Other diagnostic procedures on skull
01.21	Incision and drainage of cranial sinus
01.22	Removal of intracranial neurostimulator lead(s)
01.23	Reopening of craniotomy site
01.24	Other craniotomy
01.25	Other craniectomy
01.28	Placement of intracerebral catheter(s) via burr hole(s)
01.31	Incision of cerebral meninges
01.32	Lobotomy and tractotomy
01.39	Other incision of brain
01.41	Operations on thalamus
01.42	Operations on globus pallidus
01.51	Excision of lesion or tissue of cerebral meninges
01.52	Hemispherectomy
01.53	Lobectomy of brain
01.59	Other excision or destruction of lesion or tissue of brain
01.6	Excision of lesion of skull
02.01	Opening of cranial suture
02.02	Elevation of skull fracture fragments
02.03	Formation of cranial bone flap
02.04	Bone graft to skull
02.05	Insertion of skull plate
02.06	Other cranial osteoplasty
02.07	Removal of skull plate
02.1*	Repair of cerebral meninges
02.2*	Ventriculostomy
02.91	Lysis of cortical adhesions
02.92	Repair of brain
02.93	Implantation or replacement of intracranial neurostimulator lead(s)
02.94	Insertion or replacement of skull tongs or halo traction device
02.99	Other operations on skull, brain, and cerebral meninges
04.01	Excision of acoustic neuroma
04.41	Decompression of trigeminal nerve root
07.13	Biopsy of pituitary gland, transfrontal approach
07.14	Biopsy of pituitary gland, transsphenoidal approach
07.15	Biopsy of pituitary gland, unspecified approach
07.17	Biopsy of pineal gland
07.5*	Operations on pineal gland
07.6*	Hypophysectomy
07.7*	Other operations on hypophysis
17.54	Percutaneous atherectomy of intracranial vessel(s)
17.61	Laser interstitial thermal therapy [LITT] of lesion or tissue of brain under guidance
29.92	Division of glossopharyngeal nerve
38.01	Incision of intracranial vessels
38.11	Endarterectomy of intracranial vessels
38.31	Resection of intracranial vessels with anastomosis
38.41	Resection of intracranial vessels with replacement
38.51	Ligation and stripping of varicose veins of intracranial vessels
38.61	Other excision of intracranial vessels
38.81	Other surgical occlusion of intracranial vessels
39.28	Extracranial-intracranial (EC-IC) vascular bypass
39.51	Clipping of aneurysm
39.52	Other repair of aneurysm
39.53	Repair of arteriovenous fistula
39.72	Endovascular (total) embolization or occlusion of head and neck vessels
39.74	Endovascular removal of obstruction from head and neck vessel(s)
39.75	Endovascular embolization or occlusion of vessel(s) of head or neck using bare coils
39.76	Endovascular embolization or occlusion of vessel(s) of head or neck using bioactive coils
39.79	Other endovascular procedures on other vessels

DRG 026 Craniotomy and Endovascular Intracranial Procedures with CC
GMLOS 5.3   AMLOS 6.8   RW 2.9555   T ☑

Select operating room procedures listed under DRG 025

DRG 027 Craniotomy and Endovascular Intracranial Procedures without CC/MCC
GMLOS 2.8 AMLOS 3.6 RW 2.1631 T ☑

Select operating room procedures listed under DRG 025

DRG 028 Spinal Procedures with MCC
GMLOS 9.9 AMLOS 12.9 RW 5.6028 SP ☑

Operating Room Procedures
03.0* Exploration and decompression of spinal canal structures
03.1 Division of intraspinal nerve root
03.2* Chordotomy
03.32 Biopsy of spinal cord or spinal meninges
03.39 Other diagnostic procedures on spinal cord and spinal canal structures
03.4 Excision or destruction of lesion of spinal cord or spinal meninges
03.5* Plastic operations on spinal cord structures
03.6 Lysis of adhesions of spinal cord and nerve roots
03.7* Shunt of spinal theca
03.93 Implantation or replacement of spinal neurostimulator lead(s)
03.94 Removal of spinal neurostimulator lead(s)
03.97 Revision of spinal thecal shunt
03.98 Removal of spinal thecal shunt
03.99 Other operations on spinal cord and spinal canal structures
77.81 Other partial ostectomy of scapula, clavicle, and thorax (ribs and sternum)
77.91 Total ostectomy of scapula, clavicle, and thorax (ribs and sternum)
80.50 Excision or destruction of intervertebral disc, unspecified
80.51 Excision of intervertebral disc
80.53 Repair of the anulus fibrosus with graft or prosthesis
80.54 Other and unspecified repair of the anulus fibrosus
80.59 Other destruction of intervertebral disc
81.00 Spinal fusion, not otherwise specified
81.01 Atlas-axis spinal fusion
81.02 Other cervical fusion of the anterior column, anterior technique
81.03 Other cervical fusion of the posterior column, posterior technique
81.04 Dorsal and dorsolumbar fusion of the anterior column, anterior technique
81.05 Dorsal and dorsolumbar fusion of the posterior column, posterior technique
81.06 Lumbar and lumbosacral fusion of the anterior column, anterior technique
81.07 Lumbar and lumbosacral fusion of the posterior column, posterior technique
81.08 Lumbar and lumbosacral fusion of the anterior column, posterior technique
81.3* Refusion of spine
84.59 Insertion of other spinal devices
84.6* Replacement of spinal disc
84.80 Insertion or replacement of interspinous process device(s)
84.82 Insertion or replacement of pedicle-based dynamic stabilization device(s)
84.84 Insertion or replacement of facet replacement device(s)

DRG 029 Spinal Procedures with CC or Spinal Neurostimulator
GMLOS 4.7 AMLOS 6.4 RW 2.9277 SP ☑

Operating Room Procedures
03.0* Exploration and decompression of spinal canal structures
03.1 Division of intraspinal nerve root
03.2* Chordotomy
03.32 Biopsy of spinal cord or spinal meninges
03.39 Other diagnostic procedures on spinal cord and spinal canal structures

03.4 Excision or destruction of lesion of spinal cord or spinal meninges
03.5* Plastic operations on spinal cord structures
03.6 Lysis of adhesions of spinal cord and nerve roots
03.7* Shunt of spinal theca
03.93 Implantation or replacement of spinal neurostimulator lead(s)
03.94 Removal of spinal neurostimulator lead(s)
03.97 Revision of spinal thecal shunt
03.98 Removal of spinal thecal shunt
03.99 Other operations on spinal cord and spinal canal structures
77.81 Other partial ostectomy of scapula, clavicle, and thorax (ribs and sternum)
77.91 Total ostectomy of scapula, clavicle, and thorax (ribs and sternum)
80.50 Excision or destruction of intervertebral disc, unspecified
80.51 Excision of intervertebral disc
80.53 Repair of the anulus fibrosus with graft or prosthesis
80.54 Other and unspecified repair of the anulus fibrosus
80.59 Other destruction of intervertebral disc
81.00 Spinal fusion, not otherwise specified
81.01 Atlas-axis spinal fusion
81.02 Other cervical fusion of the anterior column, anterior technique
81.03 Other cervical fusion of the posterior column, posterior technique
81.04 Dorsal and dorsolumbar fusion of the anterior column, anterior technique
81.05 Dorsal and dorsolumbar fusion of the posterior column, posterior technique
81.06 Lumbar and lumbosacral fusion of the anterior column, anterior technique
81.07 Lumbar and lumbosacral fusion of the posterior column, posterior technique
81.08 Lumbar and lumbosacral fusion of the anterior column, posterior technique
81.3* Refusion of spine
84.59 Insertion of other spinal devices
84.6* Replacement of spinal disc
84.80 Insertion or replacement of interspinous process device(s)
84.82 Insertion or replacement of pedicle-based dynamic stabilization device(s)
84.84 Insertion or replacement of facet replacement device(s)
OR

Any of the following procedure combinations
03.93 Implantation or replacement of spinal neurostimulator lead(s)
AND
86.94 Insertion or replacement of single array neurostimulator pulse generator, not specified as rechargeable
OR
03.93 Implantation or replacement of spinal neurostimulator lead(s)
AND
86.95 Insertion or replacement of multiple array neurostimulator pulse generator, not specified as rechargeable
OR
03.93 Implantation or replacement of spinal neurostimulator lead(s)
AND
86.97 Insertion or replacement of single array rechargeable neurostimulator pulse generator
OR
03.93 Implantation or replacement of spinal neurostimulator lead(s)
AND
86.98 Insertion or replacement of multiple array (two or more) rechargeable neurostimulator pulse generator

MDC 1: Diseases And Disorders Of The Nervous System—SURGICAL

DRG 030 Spinal Procedures without CC/MCC
GMLOS 2.4   AMLOS 3.2   RW 1.7854   SP ☑

Operating Room Procedures

03.0*	Exploration and decompression of spinal canal structures
03.1	Division of intraspinal nerve root
03.2*	Chordotomy
03.32	Biopsy of spinal cord or spinal meninges
03.39	Other diagnostic procedures on spinal cord and spinal canal structures
03.4	Excision or destruction of lesion of spinal cord or spinal meninges
03.5*	Plastic operations on spinal cord structures
03.6	Lysis of adhesions of spinal cord and nerve roots
03.7*	Shunt of spinal theca
03.93	Implantation or replacement of spinal neurostimulator lead(s)
03.94	Removal of spinal neurostimulator lead(s)
03.97	Revision of spinal thecal shunt
03.98	Removal of spinal thecal shunt
03.99	Other operations on spinal cord and spinal canal structures
77.81	Other partial ostectomy of scapula, clavicle, and thorax (ribs and sternum)
77.91	Total ostectomy of scapula, clavicle, and thorax (ribs and sternum)
80.50	Excision or destruction of intervertebral disc, unspecified
80.51	Excision of intervertebral disc
80.53	Repair of the anulus fibrosus with graft or prosthesis
80.54	Other and unspecified repair of the anulus fibrosus
80.59	Other destruction of intervertebral disc
81.00	Spinal fusion, not otherwise specified
81.01	Atlas-axis spinal fusion
81.02	Other cervical fusion of the anterior column, anterior technique
81.03	Other cervical fusion of the posterior column, posterior technique
81.04	Dorsal and dorsolumbar fusion of the anterior column, anterior technique
81.05	Dorsal and dorsolumbar fusion of the posterior column, posterior technique
81.06	Lumbar and lumbosacral fusion of the anterior column, anterior technique
81.07	Lumbar and lumbosacral fusion of the posterior column, posterior technique
81.08	Lumbar and lumbosacral fusion of the anterior column, posterior technique
81.3*	Refusion of spine
84.59	Insertion of other spinal devices
84.6*	Replacement of spinal disc
84.80	Insertion or replacement of interspinous process device(s)
84.82	Insertion or replacement of pedicle-based dynamic stabilization device(s)
84.84	Insertion or replacement of facet replacement device(s)

DRG 031 Ventricular Shunt Procedures with MCC
GMLOS 8.5   AMLOS 12.0   RW 4.2645   T ☑

Operating Room Procedures

02.3*	Extracranial ventricular shunt
02.42	Replacement of ventricular shunt
02.43	Removal of ventricular shunt

DRG 032 Ventricular Shunt Procedures with CC
GMLOS 3.6   AMLOS 5.3   RW 2.0348   T ☑

Select operating room procedures listed under DRG 031

DRG 033 Ventricular Shunt Procedures without CC/MCC
GMLOS 2.0   AMLOS 2.6   RW 1.4381   T ☑

Select operating room procedures listed under DRG 031

DRG 034 Carotid Artery Stent Procedure with MCC
GMLOS 4.7   AMLOS 7.0   RW 3.6918

Operating Room Procedures

00.61	Percutaneous angioplasty of extracranial vessel(s)
17.53	Percutaneous atherectomy of extracranial vessel(s)

AND

Nonoperating Room Procedure

00.63	Percutaneous insertion of carotid artery stent(s)

DRG 035 Carotid Artery Stent Procedure with CC
GMLOS 2.1   AMLOS 3.2   RW 2.1965   ☑

Select operating and nonoperating room procedures listed under DRG 034

DRG 036 Carotid Artery Stent Procedure without CC/MCC
GMLOS 1.3   AMLOS 1.5   RW 1.6610   ☑

Select operating and nonoperating room procedures listed under DRG 034

DRG 037 Extracranial Procedures with MCC
GMLOS 5.6   AMLOS 8.3   RW 3.1870   ☑

Operating Room Procedures

00.61	Percutaneous angioplasty of extracranial vessel(s)
17.53	Percutaneous atherectomy of extracranial vessel(s)
17.56	Atherectomy of other non-coronary vessel(s)
38.10	Endarterectomy, unspecified site
38.12	Endarterectomy of other vessels of head and neck
38.32	Resection of other vessels of head and neck with anastomosis
38.62	Other excision of other vessels of head and neck
39.22	Aorta-subclavian-carotid bypass
39.29	Other (peripheral) vascular shunt or bypass
39.3*	Suture of vessel
39.50	Angioplasty of other non-coronary vessel(s)
39.56	Repair of blood vessel with tissue patch graft
39.57	Repair of blood vessel with synthetic patch graft
39.58	Repair of blood vessel with unspecified type of patch graft
39.59	Other repair of vessel
39.77	Temporary (partial) therapeutic endovascular occlusion of vessel
39.92	Injection of sclerosing agent into vein

DRG 038 Extracranial Procedures with CC
GMLOS 2.4   AMLOS 3.5   RW 1.5741   ☑

Select operating room procedures listed under DRG 037

DRG 039 Extracranial Procedures without CC/MCC
GMLOS 1.4   AMLOS 1.6   RW 1.0285   ☑

Select operating room procedures listed under DRG 037

DRG 040 Peripheral/Cranial Nerve and Other Nervous System Procedures with MCC
GMLOS 8.9   AMLOS 11.7   RW 3.8680   SP ☑

Operating Room Procedures

01.20	Cranial implantation or replacement of neurostimulator pulse generator
01.29	Removal of cranial neurostimulator pulse generator

MDC 1: Diseases And Disorders Of The Nervous System—SURGICAL

Surgical	*Medical*	CC Indicator	MCC Indicator	*Procedure Proxy*

MDC 1: Diseases And Disorders Of The Nervous System—SURGICAL

04.02	Division of trigeminal nerve
04.03	Division or crushing of other cranial and peripheral nerves
04.04	Other incision of cranial and peripheral nerves
04.05	Gasserian ganglionectomy
04.06	Other cranial or peripheral ganglionectomy
04.07	Other excision or avulsion of cranial and peripheral nerves
04.12	Open biopsy of cranial or peripheral nerve or ganglion
04.19	Other diagnostic procedures on cranial and peripheral nerves and ganglia
04.3	Suture of cranial and peripheral nerves
04.42	Other cranial nerve decompression
04.43	Release of carpal tunnel
04.44	Release of tarsal tunnel
04.49	Other peripheral nerve or ganglion decompression or lysis of adhesions
04.5	Cranial or peripheral nerve graft
04.6	Transposition of cranial and peripheral nerves
04.7*	Other cranial or peripheral neuroplasty
04.91	Neurectasis
04.92	Implantation or replacement of peripheral neurostimulator lead(s)
04.93	Removal of peripheral neurostimulator lead(s)
04.99	Other operations on cranial and peripheral nerves
05.0	Division of sympathetic nerve or ganglion
05.1*	Diagnostic procedures on sympathetic nerves or ganglia
05.2*	Sympathectomy
05.8*	Other operations on sympathetic nerves or ganglia
05.9	Other operations on nervous system
07.19	Other diagnostic procedures on adrenal glands, pituitary gland, pineal gland, and thymus
07.8*	Thymectomy
07.95	Thoracoscopic incision of thymus
07.98	Other and unspecified thoracoscopic operations on thymus
08.5*	Other adjustment of lid position
27.62	Correction of cleft palate
27.69	Other plastic repair of palate
29.4	Plastic operation on pharynx
29.59	Other repair of pharynx
37.74	Insertion or replacement of epicardial lead (electrode) into epicardium
37.75	Revision of lead (electrode)
37.76	Replacement of transvenous atrial and/or ventricular lead(s) (electrode(s))
37.77	Removal of lead(s) (electrodes) without replacement
37.79	Revision or relocation of cardiac device pocket
37.80	Insertion of permanent pacemaker, initial or replacement, type of device not specified
37.85	Replacement of any type of pacemaker device with single-chamber device, not specified as rate responsive
37.86	Replacement of any type of pacemaker device with single-chamber device, rate responsive
37.87	Replacement of any type of pacemaker device with dual-chamber device
37.89	Revision or removal of pacemaker device
38.02	Incision of other vessels of head and neck
38.21	Biopsy of blood vessel
38.42	Resection of other vessels of head and neck with replacement
38.7	Interruption of the vena cava
38.82	Other surgical occlusion of other vessels of head and neck
40.11	Biopsy of lymphatic structure
44.00	Vagotomy, not otherwise specified
54.95	Incision of peritoneum
81.71	Arthroplasty of metacarpophalangeal and interphalangeal joint with implant
81.72	Arthroplasty of metacarpophalangeal and interphalangeal joint without implant
81.74	Arthroplasty of carpocarpal or carpometacarpal joint with implant

81.75	Arthroplasty of carpocarpal or carpometacarpal joint without implant
81.79	Other repair of hand, fingers, and wrist
82.5*	Transplantation of muscle and tendon of hand
82.6*	Reconstruction of thumb
82.7*	Plastic operation on hand with graft or implant
82.8*	Other plastic operations on hand
83.13	Other tenotomy
83.14	Fasciotomy
83.19	Other division of soft tissue
83.21	Open biopsy of soft tissue
83.41	Excision of tendon for graft
83.43	Excision of muscle or fascia for graft
83.45	Other myectomy
83.49	Other excision of soft tissue
83.7*	Reconstruction of muscle and tendon
83.81	Tendon graft
83.82	Graft of muscle or fascia
83.83	Tendon pulley reconstruction on muscle, tendon, and fascia
83.85	Other change in muscle or tendon length
83.87	Other plastic operations on muscle
83.88	Other plastic operations on tendon
83.89	Other plastic operations on fascia
83.92	Insertion or replacement of skeletal muscle stimulator
83.93	Removal of skeletal muscle stimulator
84.11	Amputation of toe
84.12	Amputation through foot
84.13	Disarticulation of ankle
84.14	Amputation of ankle through malleoli of tibia and fibula
84.15	Other amputation below knee
84.16	Disarticulation of knee
84.17	Amputation above knee
86.06	Insertion of totally implantable infusion pump
86.22	Excisional debridement of wound, infection, or burn
86.4	Radical excision of skin lesion
86.60	Free skin graft, not otherwise specified
86.61	Full-thickness skin graft to hand
86.62	Other skin graft to hand
86.63	Full-thickness skin graft to other sites
86.65	Heterograft to skin
86.66	Homograft to skin
86.67	Dermal regenerative graft
86.69	Other skin graft to other sites
86.70	Pedicle or flap graft, not otherwise specified
86.71	Cutting and preparation of pedicle grafts or flaps
86.72	Advancement of pedicle graft
86.74	Attachment of pedicle or flap graft to other sites
86.75	Revision of pedicle or flap graft
86.81	Repair for facial weakness
86.91	Excision of skin for graft
86.93	Insertion of tissue expander
86.94	Insertion or replacement of single array neurostimulator pulse generator, not specified as rechargeable
86.95	Insertion or replacement of multiple array neurostimulator pulse generator, not specified as rechargeable
86.96	Insertion or replacement of other neurostimulator pulse generator
86.97	Insertion or replacement of single array rechargeable neurostimulator pulse generator
86.98	Insertion or replacement of multiple array (two or more) rechargeable neurostimulator pulse generator
92.27	Implantation or insertion of radioactive elements

OR

Any of the following procedure combinations

37.70	Initial insertion of lead (electrode), not otherwise specified
	AND
37.80	Insertion of permanent pacemaker, initial or replacement, type of device not specified

---

T *Transfer DRG*   SP *Special Payment*   ☑ *Optimization Potential*   ▽ *Targeted Potential*   * *Code Range*   ● *New DRG*   ▲ *Revised DRG Title*

OR

37.70	Initial insertion of lead (electrode), not otherwise specified
AND	
37.81	Initial insertion of single-chamber device, not specified as rate responsive

OR

37.70	Initial insertion of lead (electrode), not otherwise specified
AND	
37.82	Initial insertion of single-chamber device, rate responsive

OR

37.70	Initial insertion of lead (electrode), not otherwise specified
AND	
37.85	Replacement of any type of pacemaker device with single-chamber device, not specified as rate responsive

OR

37.70	Initial insertion of lead (electrode), not otherwise specified
AND	
37.86	Replacement of any type of pacemaker device with single-chamber device, rate responsive

OR

37.70	Initial insertion of lead (electrode), not otherwise specified
AND	
37.87	Replacement of any type of pacemaker device with dual-chamber device

OR

37.71	Initial insertion of transvenous lead (electrode) into ventricle
AND	
37.80	Insertion of permanent pacemaker, initial or replacement, type of device not specified

OR

37.71	Initial insertion of transvenous lead (electrode) into ventricle
AND	
37.81	Initial insertion of single-chamber device, not specified as rate responsive

OR

37.71	Initial insertion of transvenous lead (electrode) into ventricle
AND	
37.82	Initial insertion of single-chamber device, rate responsive

OR

37.71	Initial insertion of transvenous lead (electrode) into ventricle
AND	
37.85	Replacement of any type of pacemaker device with single-chamber device, not specified as rate responsive

OR

37.71	Initial insertion of transvenous lead (electrode) into ventricle
AND	
37.86	Replacement of any type of pacemaker device with single-chamber device, rate responsive

OR

37.71	Initial insertion of transvenous lead (electrode) into ventricle
AND	
37.87	Replacement of any type of pacemaker device with dual-chamber device

OR

37.72	Initial insertion of transvenous leads (electrodes) into atrium and ventricle
AND	
37.80	Insertion of permanent pacemaker, initial or replacement, type of device not specified

OR

37.72	Initial insertion of transvenous leads (electrodes) into atrium and ventricle
AND	
37.83	Initial insertion of dual-chamber device

OR

37.73	Initial insertion of transvenous lead (electrode) into atrium
AND	
37.80	Insertion of permanent pacemaker, initial or replacement, type of device not specified

OR

37.73	Initial insertion of transvenous lead (electrode) into atrium
AND	
37.81	Initial insertion of single-chamber device, not specified as rate responsive

OR

37.73	Initial insertion of transvenous lead (electrode) into atrium
AND	
37.82	Initial insertion of single-chamber device, rate responsive

OR

37.73	Initial insertion of transvenous lead (electrode) into atrium
AND	
37.85	Replacement of any type of pacemaker device with single-chamber device, not specified as rate responsive

OR

37.73	Initial insertion of transvenous lead (electrode) into atrium
AND	
37.86	Replacement of any type of pacemaker device with single-chamber device, rate responsive

OR

37.73	Initial insertion of transvenous lead (electrode) into atrium
AND	
37.87	Replacement of any type of pacemaker device with dual-chamber device

OR

37.74	Insertion or replacement of epicardial lead (electrode) into epicardium
AND	
37.80	Insertion of permanent pacemaker, initial or replacement, type of device not specified

OR

37.74	Insertion or replacement of epicardial lead (electrode) into epicardium
AND	
37.81	Initial insertion of single-chamber device, not specified as rate responsive

OR

37.74	Insertion or replacement of epicardial lead (electrode) into epicardium
AND	
37.82	Initial insertion of single-chamber device, rate responsive

OR

37.74	Insertion or replacement of epicardial lead (electrode) into epicardium
AND	
37.83	Initial insertion of dual-chamber device

OR

37.74	Insertion or replacement of epicardial lead (electrode) into epicardium
AND	
37.85	Replacement of any type of pacemaker device with single-chamber device, not specified as rate responsive

OR

37.74	Insertion or replacement of epicardial lead (electrode) into epicardium
AND	
37.86	Replacement of any type of pacemaker device with single-chamber device, rate responsive

MDC 1: Diseases And Disorders Of The Nervous System—SURGICAL

OR

| 37.74 | Insertion or replacement of epicardial lead (electrode) into epicardium |

AND

| 37.87 | Replacement of any type of pacemaker device with dual-chamber device |

OR

| 37.76 | Replacement of transvenous atrial and/or ventricular lead(s) (electrode(s)) |

AND

| 37.80 | Insertion of permanent pacemaker, initial or replacement, type of device not specified |

OR

| 37.76 | Replacement of transvenous atrial and/or ventricular lead(s) (electrode(s)) |

AND

| 37.85 | Replacement of any type of pacemaker device with single-chamber device, not specified as rate responsive |

OR

| 37.76 | Replacement of transvenous atrial and/or ventricular lead(s) (electrode(s)) |

AND

| 37.86 | Replacement of any type of pacemaker device with single-chamber device, rate responsive |

OR

| 37.76 | Replacement of transvenous atrial and/or ventricular lead(s) (electrode(s)) |

AND

| 37.87 | Replacement of any type of pacemaker device with dual-chamber device |

OR

Nonoperating Room Procedures

| 92.3* | Stereotactic radiosurgery |

DRG 041 **Peripheral/Cranial Nerve and Other Nervous System Procedures with CC or Peripheral Neurostimulator**
     GMLOS 5.0   AMLOS 6.4   RW 2.1330   SP ☑

Operating Room Procedures

01.20	Cranial implantation or replacement of neurostimulator pulse generator
01.29	Removal of cranial neurostimulator pulse generator
04.02	Division of trigeminal nerve
04.03	Division or crushing of other cranial and peripheral nerves
04.04	Other incision of cranial and peripheral nerves
04.05	Gasserian ganglionectomy
04.06	Other cranial or peripheral ganglionectomy
04.07	Other excision or avulsion of cranial and peripheral nerves
04.12	Open biopsy of cranial or peripheral nerve or ganglion
04.19	Other diagnostic procedures on cranial and peripheral nerves and ganglia
04.3	Suture of cranial and peripheral nerves
04.42	Other cranial nerve decompression
04.43	Release of carpal tunnel
04.44	Release of tarsal tunnel
04.49	Other peripheral nerve or ganglion decompression or lysis of adhesions
04.5	Cranial or peripheral nerve graft
04.6	Transposition of cranial and peripheral nerves
04.7*	Other cranial or peripheral neuroplasty
04.91	Neurectasis
04.92	Implantation or replacement of peripheral neurostimulator lead(s)
04.93	Removal of peripheral neurostimulator lead(s)
04.99	Other operations on cranial and peripheral nerves
05.0	Division of sympathetic nerve or ganglion
05.1*	Diagnostic procedures on sympathetic nerves or ganglia
05.2*	Sympathectomy
05.8*	Other operations on sympathetic nerves or ganglia
05.9	Other operations on nervous system
07.19	Other diagnostic procedures on adrenal glands, pituitary gland, pineal gland, and thymus
07.8*	Thymectomy
07.95	Thoracoscopic incision of thymus
07.98	Other and unspecified thoracoscopic operations on thymus
08.5*	Other adjustment of lid position
27.62	Correction of cleft palate
27.69	Other plastic repair of palate
29.4	Plastic operation on pharynx
29.59	Other repair of pharynx
37.74	Insertion or replacement of epicardial lead (electrode) into epicardium
37.75	Revision of lead (electrode)
37.76	Replacement of transvenous atrial and/or ventricular lead(s) (electrode(s))
37.77	Removal of lead(s) (electrodes) without replacement
37.79	Revision or relocation of cardiac device pocket
37.80	Insertion of permanent pacemaker, initial or replacement, type of device not specified
37.85	Replacement of any type of pacemaker device with single-chamber device, not specified as rate responsive
37.86	Replacement of any type of pacemaker device with single-chamber device, rate responsive
37.87	Replacement of any type of pacemaker device with dual-chamber device
37.89	Revision or removal of pacemaker device
38.02	Incision of other vessels of head and neck
38.21	Biopsy of blood vessel
38.42	Resection of other vessels of head and neck with replacement
38.7	Interruption of the vena cava
38.82	Other surgical occlusion of other vessels of head and neck
40.11	Biopsy of lymphatic structure
44.00	Vagotomy, not otherwise specified
54.95	Incision of peritoneum
81.71	Arthroplasty of metacarpophalangeal and interphalangeal joint with implant
81.72	Arthroplasty of metacarpophalangeal and interphalangeal joint without implant
81.74	Arthroplasty of carpocarpal or carpometacarpal joint with implant
81.75	Arthroplasty of carpocarpal or carpometacarpal joint without implant
81.79	Other repair of hand, fingers, and wrist
82.5*	Transplantation of muscle and tendon of hand
82.6*	Reconstruction of thumb
82.7*	Plastic operation on hand with graft or implant
82.8*	Other plastic operations on hand
83.13	Other tenotomy
83.14	Fasciotomy
83.19	Other division of soft tissue
83.21	Open biopsy of soft tissue
83.41	Excision of tendon for graft
83.43	Excision of muscle or fascia for graft
83.45	Other myectomy
83.49	Other excision of soft tissue
83.7*	Reconstruction of muscle and tendon
83.81	Tendon graft
83.82	Graft of muscle or fascia
83.83	Tendon pulley reconstruction on muscle, tendon, and fascia
83.85	Other change in muscle or tendon length
83.87	Other plastic operations on muscle
83.88	Other plastic operations on tendon
83.89	Other plastic operations on fascia
83.92	Insertion or replacement of skeletal muscle stimulator
83.93	Removal of skeletal muscle stimulator
84.11	Amputation of toe

T Transfer DRG   SP Special Payment   ☑ Optimization Potential   ▽ Targeted Potential   * Code Range   ● New DRG   ▲ Revised DRG Title

84.12	Amputation through foot
84.13	Disarticulation of ankle
84.14	Amputation of ankle through malleoli of tibia and fibula
84.15	Other amputation below knee
84.16	Disarticulation of knee
84.17	Amputation above knee
86.06	Insertion of totally implantable infusion pump
86.22	Excisional debridement of wound, infection, or burn
86.4	Radical excision of skin lesion
86.60	Free skin graft, not otherwise specified
86.61	Full-thickness skin graft to hand
86.62	Other skin graft to hand
86.63	Full-thickness skin graft to other sites
86.65	Heterograft to skin
86.66	Homograft to skin
86.67	Dermal regenerative graft
86.69	Other skin graft to other sites
86.70	Pedicle or flap graft, not otherwise specified
86.71	Cutting and preparation of pedicle grafts or flaps
86.72	Advancement of pedicle graft
86.74	Attachment of pedicle or flap graft to other sites
86.75	Revision of pedicle or flap graft
86.81	Repair for facial weakness
86.91	Excision of skin for graft
86.93	Insertion of tissue expander
86.94	Insertion or replacement of single array neurostimulator pulse generator, not specified as rechargeable
86.95	Insertion or replacement of multiple array neurostimulator pulse generator, not specified as rechargeable
86.96	Insertion or replacement of other neurostimulator pulse generator
86.97	Insertion or replacement of single array rechargeable neurostimulator pulse generator
86.98	Insertion or replacement of multiple array (two or more) rechargeable neurostimulator pulse generator
92.27	Implantation or insertion of radioactive elements

OR

Any of the following procedure combinations

37.70	Initial insertion of lead (electrode), not otherwise specified
AND	
37.80	Insertion of permanent pacemaker, initial or replacement, type of device not specified

OR

37.70	Initial insertion of lead (electrode), not otherwise specified
AND	
37.81	Initial insertion of single-chamber device, not specified as rate responsive

OR

37.70	Initial insertion of lead (electrode), not otherwise specified
AND	
37.82	Initial insertion of single-chamber device, rate responsive

OR

37.70	Initial insertion of lead (electrode), not otherwise specified
AND	
37.85	Replacement of any type of pacemaker device with single-chamber device, not specified as rate responsive

OR

37.70	Initial insertion of lead (electrode), not otherwise specified
AND	
37.86	Replacement of any type of pacemaker device with single-chamber device, rate responsive

OR

37.70	Initial insertion of lead (electrode), not otherwise specified
AND	
37.87	Replacement of any type of pacemaker device with dual-chamber device

OR

37.71	Initial insertion of transvenous lead (electrode) into ventricle
AND	
37.80	Insertion of permanent pacemaker, initial or replacement, type of device not specified

OR

37.71	Initial insertion of transvenous lead (electrode) into ventricle
AND	
37.81	Initial insertion of single-chamber device, not specified as rate responsive

OR

37.71	Initial insertion of transvenous lead (electrode) into ventricle
AND	
37.82	Initial insertion of single-chamber device, rate responsive

OR

37.71	Initial insertion of transvenous lead (electrode) into ventricle
AND	
37.85	Replacement of any type of pacemaker device with single-chamber device, not specified as rate responsive

OR

37.71	Initial insertion of transvenous lead (electrode) into ventricle
AND	
37.86	Replacement of any type of pacemaker device with single-chamber device, rate responsive

OR

37.71	Initial insertion of transvenous lead (electrode) into ventricle
AND	
37.87	Replacement of any type of pacemaker device with dual-chamber device

OR

37.72	Initial insertion of transvenous leads (electrodes) into atrium and ventricle
AND	
37.80	Insertion of permanent pacemaker, initial or replacement, type of device not specified

OR

37.72	Initial insertion of transvenous leads (electrodes) into atrium and ventricle
AND	
37.83	Initial insertion of dual-chamber device

OR

37.73	Initial insertion of transvenous lead (electrode) into atrium
AND	
37.80	Insertion of permanent pacemaker, initial or replacement, type of device not specified

OR

37.73	Initial insertion of transvenous lead (electrode) into atrium
AND	
37.81	Initial insertion of single-chamber device, not specified as rate responsive

OR

37.73	Initial insertion of transvenous lead (electrode) into atrium
AND	
37.82	Initial insertion of single-chamber device, rate responsive

OR

37.73	Initial insertion of transvenous lead (electrode) into atrium
AND	
37.85	Replacement of any type of pacemaker device with single-chamber device, not specified as rate responsive

OR

37.73	Initial insertion of transvenous lead (electrode) into atrium
AND	
37.86	Replacement of any type of pacemaker device with single-chamber device, rate responsive

MDC 1: Diseases And Disorders Of The Nervous System—MEDICAL

OR

37.73	Initial insertion of transvenous lead (electrode) into atrium
	AND
37.87	Replacement of any type of pacemaker device with dual-chamber device

OR

37.74	Insertion or replacement of epicardial lead (electrode) into epicardium
	AND
37.80	Insertion of permanent pacemaker, initial or replacement, type of device not specified

OR

37.74	Insertion or replacement of epicardial lead (electrode) into epicardium
	AND
37.81	Initial insertion of single-chamber device, not specified as rate responsive

OR

37.74	Insertion or replacement of epicardial lead (electrode) into epicardium
	AND
37.82	Initial insertion of single-chamber device, rate responsive

OR

37.74	Insertion or replacement of epicardial lead (electrode) into epicardium
	AND
37.83	Initial insertion of dual-chamber device

OR

37.74	Insertion or replacement of epicardial lead (electrode) into epicardium
	AND
37.85	Replacement of any type of pacemaker device with single-chamber device, not specified as rate responsive

OR

37.74	Insertion or replacement of epicardial lead (electrode) into epicardium
	AND
37.86	Replacement of any type of pacemaker device with single-chamber device, rate responsive

OR

37.74	Insertion or replacement of epicardial lead (electrode) into epicardium
	AND
37.87	Replacement of any type of pacemaker device with dual-chamber device

OR

37.76	Replacement of transvenous atrial and/or ventricular lead(s) (electrode(s))
	AND
37.80	Insertion of permanent pacemaker, initial or replacement, type of device not specified

OR

37.76	Replacement of transvenous atrial and/or ventricular lead(s) (electrode(s))
	AND
37.85	Replacement of any type of pacemaker device with single-chamber device, not specified as rate responsive

OR

37.76	Replacement of transvenous atrial and/or ventricular lead(s) (electrode(s))
	AND
37.86	Replacement of any type of pacemaker device with single-chamber device, rate responsive

OR

37.76	Replacement of transvenous atrial and/or ventricular lead(s) (electrode(s))
	AND
37.87	Replacement of any type of pacemaker device with dual-chamber device

OR

Nonoperating Room Procedures

92.3*	Stereotactic radiosurgery

OR

Any of the following procedure combinations

04.92	Implantation or replacement of peripheral neurostimulator lead(s)
	AND
86.94	Insertion or replacement of single array neurostimulator pulse generator, not specified as rechargeable

OR

04.92	Implantation or replacement of peripheral neurostimulator lead(s)
	AND
86.95	Insertion or replacement of multiple array neurostimulator pulse generator, not specified as rechargeable

OR

04.92	Implantation or replacement of peripheral neurostimulator lead(s)
	AND
86.97	Insertion or replacement of single array rechargeable neurostimulator pulse generator

OR

04.92	Implantation or replacement of peripheral neurostimulator lead(s)
	AND
86.98	Insertion or replacement of multiple array (two or more) rechargeable neurostimulator pulse generator

DRG 042	**Peripheral/Cranial Nerve and Other Nervous System Procedures without CC/MCC**
	GMLOS 2.6 **AMLOS 3.4** **RW 1.7744** SP ☑

Select operating room procedures or procedure combinations listed under DRG 040

MEDICAL

DRG 052	**Spinal Disorders and Injuries with CC/MCC**
	GMLOS 4.3 **AMLOS 5.8** **RW 1.4903** ☑

Principal Diagnosis

343.0	Diplegic infantile cerebral palsy
343.1	Hemiplegic infantile cerebral palsy
343.2	Quadriplegic infantile cerebral palsy
343.4	Infantile hemiplegia
344.0*	Quadriplegia and quadriparesis
344.1	Paraplegia
344.2	Diplegia of upper limbs
780.72	Functional quadriplegia
806*	Fracture of vertebral column with spinal cord injury
907.2	Late effect of spinal cord injury
952*	Spinal cord injury without evidence of spinal bone injury

---

Ⓣ Transfer DRG   SP Special Payment   ☑ Optimization Potential   ▽ Targeted Potential   * Code Range   ● New DRG   ▲ Revised DRG Title

18   Valid 10/01/2012-09/30/2013

© 2012 OptumInsight, Inc.

DRG 053 Spinal Disorders and Injuries without CC/MCC
GMLOS 2.9   AMLOS 3.5   RW 0.9046   ☑

Select principal diagnosis listed under DRG 052

DRG 054 Nervous System Neoplasms with MCC
GMLOS 4.2   AMLOS 5.7   RW 1.3962   T☑

Principal Diagnosis
191*   Malignant neoplasm of brain
192*   Malignant neoplasm of other and unspecified parts of nervous system
194.4   Malignant neoplasm of pineal gland
194.5   Malignant neoplasm of carotid body
194.6   Malignant neoplasm of aortic body and other paraganglia
198.3   Secondary malignant neoplasm of brain and spinal cord
198.4   Secondary malignant neoplasm of other parts of nervous system
225*   Benign neoplasm of brain and other parts of nervous system
227.4   Benign neoplasm of pineal gland
227.5   Benign neoplasm of carotid body
227.6   Benign neoplasm of aortic body and other paraganglia
237.1   Neoplasm of uncertain behavior of pineal gland
237.3   Neoplasm of uncertain behavior of paraganglia
237.5   Neoplasm of uncertain behavior of brain and spinal cord
237.6   Neoplasm of uncertain behavior of meninges
237.9   Neoplasm of uncertain behavior of other and unspecified parts of nervous system
239.6   Neoplasm of unspecified nature of brain

DRG 055 Nervous System Neoplasms without MCC
GMLOS 3.2   AMLOS 4.3   RW 1.0486   T☑

Select principal diagnosis listed under DRG 054

DRG 056 Degenerative Nervous System Disorders with MCC
GMLOS 5.4   AMLOS 7.1   RW 1.7194   T☑

Principal Diagnosis
046*   Slow virus infections and prion diseases of central nervous system
094.0   Tabes dorsalis
094.1   General paresis
094.82 Syphilitic Parkinsonism
094.85 Syphilitic retrobulbar neuritis
094.89 Other specified neurosyphilis
094.9   Unspecified neurosyphilis
310.8* Other specified nonpsychotic mental disorder following organic brain damage
330*   Cerebral degenerations usually manifest in childhood
331.0   Alzheimer's disease
331.1* Frontotemporal dementia
331.2   Senile degeneration of brain
331.3   Communicating hydrocephalus
331.4   Obstructive hydrocephalus
331.5   Idiopathic normal pressure hydrocephalus [INPH]
331.6   Corticobasal degeneration
331.7   Cerebral degeneration in diseases classified elsewhere
331.82 Dementia with Lewy bodies
331.83 Mild cognitive impairment, so stated
331.89 Other cerebral degeneration
331.9   Unspecified cerebral degeneration
332*   Parkinson's disease
333.0   Other degenerative diseases of the basal ganglia
333.4   Huntington's chorea
333.5   Other choreas
333.6   Genetic torsion dystonia
333.71 Athetoid cerebral palsy
333.90 Unspecified extrapyramidal disease and abnormal movement disorder
333.94 Restless legs syndrome [RLS]
333.99 Other extrapyramidal disease and abnormal movement disorder
335*   Anterior horn cell disease
336.0   Syringomyelia and syringobulbia
342*   Hemiplegia and hemiparesis
358.0* Myasthenia gravis
358.1   Myasthenic syndromes in diseases classified elsewhere
358.3* Lambert-Eaton syndrome
379.45 Argyll Robertson pupil, atypical
438*   Late effects of cerebrovascular disease

DRG 057 Degenerative Nervous System Disorders without MCC
GMLOS 3.6   AMLOS 4.7   RW 0.9680   T☑

Select principal diagnosis listed under DRG 056

DRG 058 Multiple Sclerosis and Cerebellar Ataxia with MCC
GMLOS 5.4   AMLOS 7.0   RW 1.6472   ☑

Principal Diagnosis
334*   Spinocerebellar disease
340   Multiple sclerosis
341.0   Neuromyelitis optica
341.1   Schilder's disease
341.8   Other demyelinating diseases of central nervous system
341.9   Unspecified demyelinating disease of central nervous system

DRG 059 Multiple Sclerosis and Cerebellar Ataxia with CC
GMLOS 3.9   AMLOS 4.7   RW 1.0088   ☑

Select principal diagnosis listed under DRG 058

DRG 060 Multiple Sclerosis and Cerebellar Ataxia without CC/MCC
GMLOS 3.1   AMLOS 3.6   RW 0.7807   ☑

Select principal diagnosis listed under DRG 058

DRG 061 Acute Ischemic Stroke with Use of Thrombolytic Agent with MCC
GMLOS 6.0   AMLOS 7.8   RW 2.8668

Principal Diagnosis
433.01 Occlusion and stenosis of basilar artery with cerebral infarction
433.11 Occlusion and stenosis of carotid artery with cerebral infarction
433.21 Occlusion and stenosis of vertebral artery with cerebral infarction
433.31 Occlusion and stenosis of multiple and bilateral precerebral arteries with cerebral infarction
433.81 Occlusion and stenosis of other specified precerebral artery with cerebral infarction
433.91 Occlusion and stenosis of unspecified precerebral artery with cerebral infarction
434.01 Cerebral thrombosis with cerebral infarction
434.11 Cerebral embolism with cerebral infarction
434.91 Unspecified cerebral artery occlusion with cerebral infarction

AND

Nonoperating Room Procedure
99.10   Injection or infusion of thrombolytic agent

Surgical   Medical   CC Indicator   MCC Indicator   Procedure Proxy

DRG 062 Acute Ischemic Stroke with Use of Thrombolytic Agent with CC

GMLOS 4.5   AMLOS 5.2   RW 1.9551   ☑

Select principal diagnosis AND nonoperating room procedure listed under DRG 061

DRG 063 Acute Ischemic Stroke with Use of Thrombolytic Agent without CC/MCC

GMLOS 3.2   AMLOS 3.7   RW 1.5366   ☑

Select principal diagnosis AND nonoperating room procedure listed under DRG 061

DRG 064 Intracranial Hemorrhage or Cerebral Infarction with MCC

GMLOS 4.8   AMLOS 6.6   RW 1.8424   Ⓣ ☑ ▽

Principal Diagnosis

430	Subarachnoid hemorrhage
431	Intracerebral hemorrhage
432*	Other and unspecified intracranial hemorrhage
433.01	Occlusion and stenosis of basilar artery with cerebral infarction
433.11	Occlusion and stenosis of carotid artery with cerebral infarction
433.21	Occlusion and stenosis of vertebral artery with cerebral infarction
433.31	Occlusion and stenosis of multiple and bilateral precerebral arteries with cerebral infarction
433.81	Occlusion and stenosis of other specified precerebral artery with cerebral infarction
433.91	Occlusion and stenosis of unspecified precerebral artery with cerebral infarction
434.01	Cerebral thrombosis with cerebral infarction
434.11	Cerebral embolism with cerebral infarction
434.91	Unspecified cerebral artery occlusion with cerebral infarction

DRG 065 Intracranial Hemorrhage or Cerebral Infarction with CC

GMLOS 3.7   AMLOS 4.5   RW 1.1345   Ⓣ ☑ ▽

Select principal diagnosis listed under DRG 064

DRG 066 Intracranial Hemorrhage or Cerebral Infarction without CC/MCC

GMLOS 2.6   AMLOS 3.1   RW 0.8135   Ⓣ ☑ ▽

Select principal diagnosis listed under DRG 064

DRG 067 Nonspecific Cerebrovascular Accident and Precerebral Occlusion without Infarction with MCC

GMLOS 4.1   AMLOS 5.4   RW 1.5074   ☑ ▽

Principal Diagnosis

433.00	Occlusion and stenosis of basilar artery without mention of cerebral infarction
433.10	Occlusion and stenosis of carotid artery without mention of cerebral infarction
433.20	Occlusion and stenosis of vertebral artery without mention of cerebral infarction
433.30	Occlusion and stenosis of multiple and bilateral precerebral arteries without mention of cerebral infarction
433.80	Occlusion and stenosis of other specified precerebral artery without mention of cerebral infarction
433.90	Occlusion and stenosis of unspecified precerebral artery without mention of cerebral infarction
434.00	Cerebral thrombosis without mention of cerebral infarction
434.10	Cerebral embolism without mention of cerebral infarction
434.90	Unspecified cerebral artery occlusion without mention of cerebral infarction
436	Acute, but ill-defined, cerebrovascular disease

DRG 068 Nonspecific Cerebrovascular Accident and Precerebral Occlusion without Infarction without MCC

GMLOS 2.6   AMLOS 3.2   RW 0.8899   ☑ ▽

Select principal diagnosis listed under DRG 067

DRG 069 Transient Ischemia

GMLOS 2.2   AMLOS 2.7   RW 0.7449   ☑ ▽

Principal Diagnosis

435*	Transient cerebral ischemia
437.1	Other generalized ischemic cerebrovascular disease

DRG 070 Nonspecific Cerebrovascular Disorders with MCC

GMLOS 5.1   AMLOS 6.8   RW 1.7056   Ⓣ ☑

Principal Diagnosis

348.3*	Encephalopathy, not elsewhere classified
348.81	Temporal sclerosis
348.89	Other conditions of brain
348.9	Unspecified condition of brain
349.89	Other specified disorder of nervous system
349.9	Unspecified disorders of nervous system
437.0	Cerebral atherosclerosis
437.7	Transient global amnesia
437.8	Other ill-defined cerebrovascular disease
437.9	Unspecified cerebrovascular disease

DRG 071 Nonspecific Cerebrovascular Disorders with CC

GMLOS 3.7   AMLOS 4.7   RW 1.0174   Ⓣ ☑

Select principal diagnosis listed under DRG 070

DRG 072 Nonspecific Cerebrovascular Disorders without CC/MCC

GMLOS 2.5   AMLOS 3.0   RW 0.7506   Ⓣ ☑

Select principal diagnosis listed under DRG 070

DRG 073 Cranial and Peripheral Nerve Disorders with MCC

GMLOS 4.1   AMLOS 5.4   RW 1.2820   ☑

Principal Diagnosis

053.10	Herpes zoster with unspecified nervous system complication
053.11	Geniculate herpes zoster
053.12	Postherpetic trigeminal neuralgia
053.13	Postherpetic polyneuropathy
053.19	Other herpes zoster with nervous system complications
056.00	Unspecified rubella neurological complication
072.72	Mumps polyneuropathy
249.6*	Secondary diabetes mellitus with neurological manifestations
250.6*	Diabetes with neurological manifestations
337*	Disorders of the autonomic nervous system
344.60	Cauda equina syndrome without mention of neurogenic bladder
350*	Trigeminal nerve disorders
351*	Facial nerve disorders
352*	Disorders of other cranial nerves
353*	Nerve root and plexus disorders
354*	Mononeuritis of upper limb and mononeuritis multiplex
355*	Mononeuritis of lower limb and unspecified site
356.0	Hereditary peripheral neuropathy
356.1	Peroneal muscular atrophy
356.2	Hereditary sensory neuropathy

Ⓣ Transfer DRG   ⓈⓅ Special Payment   ☑ Optimization Potential   ▽ Targeted Potential   * Code Range   ● New DRG   ▲ Revised DRG Title

20   Valid 10/01/2012-09/30/2013   © 2012 OptumInsight, Inc.

356.4	Idiopathic progressive polyneuropathy
356.8	Other specified idiopathic peripheral neuropathy
356.9	Unspecified hereditary and idiopathic peripheral neuropathy
357.1	Polyneuropathy in collagen vascular disease
357.2	Polyneuropathy in diabetes
357.3	Polyneuropathy in malignant disease
357.4	Polyneuropathy in other diseases classified elsewhere
357.5	Alcoholic polyneuropathy
357.6	Polyneuropathy due to drugs
357.7	Polyneuropathy due to other toxic agents
357.8*	Other inflammatory and toxic neuropathy
357.9	Unspecified inflammatory and toxic neuropathy
358.2	Toxic myoneural disorders
358.8	Other specified myoneural disorders
358.9	Unspecified myoneural disorders
723.2	Cervicocranial syndrome
723.3	Cervicobrachial syndrome (diffuse)
723.4	Brachial neuritis or radiculitis NOS
729.2	Unspecified neuralgia, neuritis, and radiculitis
736.05	Wrist drop (acquired)
736.06	Claw hand (acquired)
736.07	Club hand, acquired
736.74	Claw foot, acquired
951.0	Injury to oculomotor nerve
951.1	Injury to trochlear nerve
951.2	Injury to trigeminal nerve
951.3	Injury to abducens nerve
951.4	Injury to facial nerve
951.6	Injury to accessory nerve
951.7	Injury to hypoglossal nerve
951.8	Injury to other specified cranial nerves
951.9	Injury to unspecified cranial nerve
953*	Injury to nerve roots and spinal plexus
954*	Injury to other nerve(s) of trunk, excluding shoulder and pelvic girdles
955*	Injury to peripheral nerve(s) of shoulder girdle and upper limb
956*	Injury to peripheral nerve(s) of pelvic girdle and lower limb
957*	Injury to other and unspecified nerves

DRG 074   Cranial and Peripheral Nerve Disorders without MCC
GMLOS 3.1   AMLOS 4.0   RW 0.8837   ☑

Select principal diagnosis listed under DRG 073

DRG 075   Viral Meningitis with CC/MCC
GMLOS 5.5   AMLOS 7.0   RW 1.7611   ☑

Principal Diagnosis
047*	Meningitis due to enterovirus
048	Other enterovirus diseases of central nervous system
049.0	Lymphocytic choriomeningitis
049.1	Meningitis due to adenovirus
053.0	Herpes zoster with meningitis
054.72	Herpes simplex meningitis
072.1	Mumps meningitis

DRG 076   Viral Meningitis without CC/MCC
GMLOS 3.2   AMLOS 3.9   RW 0.8947   ☑

Select principal diagnosis listed under DRG 075

DRG 077   Hypertensive Encephalopathy with MCC
GMLOS 4.8   AMLOS 6.0   RW 1.6426   ☑

Principal Diagnosis
437.2	Hypertensive encephalopathy

DRG 078   Hypertensive Encephalopathy with CC
GMLOS 3.2   AMLOS 4.0   RW 0.9790   ☑

Select principal diagnosis listed under DRG 077

DRG 079   Hypertensive Encephalopathy without CC/MCC
GMLOS 2.4   AMLOS 2.9   RW 0.7297   ☑

Select principal diagnosis listed under DRG 077

DRG 080   Nontraumatic Stupor and Coma with MCC
GMLOS 3.7   AMLOS 5.2   RW 1.2616   ☑

Principal Diagnosis
348.4	Compression of brain
348.5	Cerebral edema
348.82	Brain death
780.01	Coma
780.03	Persistent vegetative state
780.09	Other alteration of consciousness

DRG 081   Nontraumatic Stupor and Coma without MCC
GMLOS 2.7   AMLOS 3.4   RW 0.7416   ☑

Select principal diagnosis listed under DRG 080

DRG 082   Traumatic Stupor and Coma, Coma Greater Than One Hour with MCC
GMLOS 3.3   AMLOS 5.6   RW 1.9249   ☑

Principal Diagnosis of Traumatic Stupor and Coma > 1 Hour
800.03	Closed fracture of vault of skull without mention of intracranial injury, moderate (1-24 hours) loss of consciousness
800.04	Closed fracture of vault of skull without mention of intracranial injury, prolonged (more than 24 hours) loss of consciousness and return to pre-existing conscious level
800.05	Closed fracture of vault of skull without mention of intracranial injury, prolonged (more than 24 hours) loss of consciousness, without return to pre-existing conscious level
800.06	Closed fracture of vault of skull without mention of intracranial injury, loss of consciousness of unspecified duration
800.13	Closed fracture of vault of skull with cerebral laceration and contusion, moderate (1-24 hours) loss of consciousness
800.14	Closed fracture of vault of skull with cerebral laceration and contusion, prolonged (more than 24 hours) loss of consciousness and return to pre-existing conscious level
800.15	Closed fracture of vault of skull with cerebral laceration and contusion, prolonged (more than 24 hours) loss of consciousness, without return to pre-existing conscious level
800.16	Closed fracture of vault of skull with cerebral laceration and contusion, loss of consciousness of unspecified duration
800.23	Closed fracture of vault of skull with subarachnoid, subdural, and extradural hemorrhage, moderate (1-24 hours) loss of consciousness
800.24	Closed fracture of vault of skull with subarachnoid, subdural, and extradural hemorrhage, prolonged (more than 24 hours) loss of consciousness and return to pre-existing conscious level
800.25	Closed fracture of vault of skull with subarachnoid, subdural, and extradural hemorrhage, prolonged (more than 24 hours) loss of consciousness, without return to pre-existing conscious level
800.26	Closed fracture of vault of skull with subarachnoid, subdural, and extradural hemorrhage, loss of consciousness of unspecified duration

800.33 Closed fracture of vault of skull with other and unspecified intracranial hemorrhage, moderate (1-24 hours) loss of consciousness

800.34 Closed fracture of vault of skull with other and unspecified intracranial hemorrhage, prolonged (more than 24 hours) loss of consciousness and return to pre-existing conscious level

800.35 Closed fracture of vault of skull with other and unspecified intracranial hemorrhage, prolonged (more than 24 hours) loss of consciousness, without return to pre-existing conscious level

800.36 Closed fracture of vault of skull with other and unspecified intracranial hemorrhage, loss of consciousness of unspecified duration

800.43 Closed fracture of vault of skull with intracranial injury of other and unspecified nature, moderate (1-24 hours) loss of consciousness

800.44 Closed fracture of vault of skull with intracranial injury of other and unspecified nature, prolonged (more than 24 hours) loss of consciousness and return to pre-existing conscious level

800.45 Closed fracture of vault of skull with intracranial injury of other and unspecified nature, prolonged (more than 24 hours) loss of consciousness, without return to pre-existing conscious level

800.46 Closed fracture of vault of skull with intracranial injury of other and unspecified nature, loss of consciousness of unspecified duration

800.53 Open fracture of vault of skull without mention of intracranial injury, moderate (1-24 hours) loss of consciousness

800.54 Open fracture of vault of skull without mention of intracranial injury, prolonged (more than 24 hours) loss of consciousness and return to pre-existing conscious level

800.55 Open fracture of vault of skull without mention of intracranial injury, prolonged (more than 24 hours) loss of consciousness, without return to pre-existing conscious level

800.56 Open fracture of vault of skull without mention of intracranial injury, loss of consciousness of unspecified duration

800.63 Open fracture of vault of skull with cerebral laceration and contusion, moderate (1-24 hours) loss of consciousness

800.64 Open fracture of vault of skull with cerebral laceration and contusion, prolonged (more than 24 hours) loss of consciousness and return to pre-existing conscious level

800.65 Open fracture of vault of skull with cerebral laceration and contusion, prolonged (more than 24 hours) loss of consciousness, without return to pre-existing conscious level

800.66 Open fracture of vault of skull with cerebral laceration and contusion, loss of consciousness of unspecified duration

800.73 Open fracture of vault of skull with subarachnoid, subdural, and extradural hemorrhage, moderate (1-24 hours) loss of consciousness

800.74 Open fracture of vault of skull with subarachnoid, subdural, and extradural hemorrhage, prolonged (more than 24 hours) loss of consciousness and return to pre-existing conscious level

800.75 Open fracture of vault of skull with subarachnoid, subdural, and extradural hemorrhage, prolonged (more than 24 hours) loss of consciousness, without return to pre-existing conscious level

800.76 Open fracture of vault of skull with subarachnoid, subdural, and extradural hemorrhage, loss of consciousness of unspecified duration

800.83 Open fracture of vault of skull with other and unspecified intracranial hemorrhage, moderate (1-24 hours) loss of consciousness

800.84 Open fracture of vault of skull with other and unspecified intracranial hemorrhage, prolonged (more than 24 hours) loss of consciousness and return to pre-existing conscious level

800.85 Open fracture of vault of skull with other and unspecified intracranial hemorrhage, prolonged (more than 24 hours) loss of consciousness, without return to pre-existing conscious level

800.86 Open fracture of vault of skull with other and unspecified intracranial hemorrhage, loss of consciousness of unspecified duration

800.93 Open fracture of vault of skull with intracranial injury of other and unspecified nature, moderate (1-24 hours) loss of consciousness

800.94 Open fracture of vault of skull with intracranial injury of other and unspecified nature, prolonged (more than 24 hours) loss of consciousness and return to pre-existing conscious level

800.95 Open fracture of vault of skull with intracranial injury of other and unspecified nature, prolonged (more than 24 hours) loss of consciousness, without return to pre-existing conscious level

800.96 Open fracture of vault of skull with intracranial injury of other and unspecified nature, loss of consciousness of unspecified duration

801.03 Closed fracture of base of skull without mention of intracranial injury, moderate (1-24 hours) loss of consciousness

801.04 Closed fracture of base of skull without mention of intracranial injury, prolonged (more than 24 hours) loss of consciousness and return to pre-existing conscious level

801.05 Closed fracture of base of skull without mention of intracranial injury, prolonged (more than 24 hours) loss of consciousness, without return to pre-existing conscious level

801.06 Closed fracture of base of skull without mention of intracranial injury, loss of consciousness of unspecified duration

801.13 Closed fracture of base of skull with cerebral laceration and contusion, moderate (1-24 hours) loss of consciousness

801.14 Closed fracture of base of skull with cerebral laceration and contusion, prolonged (more than 24 hours) loss of consciousness and return to pre-existing conscious level

801.15 Closed fracture of base of skull with cerebral laceration and contusion, prolonged (more than 24 hours) loss of consciousness, without return to pre-existing conscious level

801.16 Closed fracture of base of skull with cerebral laceration and contusion, loss of consciousness of unspecified duration

801.23 Closed fracture of base of skull with subarachnoid, subdural, and extradural hemorrhage, moderate (1-24 hours) loss of consciousness

801.24 Closed fracture of base of skull with subarachnoid, subdural, and extradural hemorrhage, prolonged (more than 24 hours) loss of consciousness and return to pre-existing conscious level

801.25 Closed fracture of base of skull with subarachnoid, subdural, and extradural hemorrhage, prolonged (more than 24 hours) loss of consciousness, without return to pre-existing conscious level

801.26 Closed fracture of base of skull with subarachnoid, subdural, and extradural hemorrhage, loss of consciousness of unspecified duration

801.33 Closed fracture of base of skull with other and unspecified intracranial hemorrhage, moderate (1-24 hours) loss of consciousness

801.34 Closed fracture of base of skull with other and unspecified intracranial hemorrhage, prolonged (more than 24 hours) loss of consciousness and return to pre-existing conscious level

801.35   Closed fracture of base of skull with other and unspecified intracranial hemorrhage, prolonged (more than 24 hours) loss of consciousness, without return to pre-existing conscious level

801.36   Closed fracture of base of skull with other and unspecified intracranial hemorrhage, loss of consciousness of unspecified duration

801.43   Closed fracture of base of skull with intracranial injury of other and unspecified nature, moderate (1-24 hours) loss of consciousness

801.44   Closed fracture of base of skull with intracranial injury of other and unspecified nature, prolonged (more than 24 hours) loss of consciousness and return to pre-existing conscious level

801.45   Closed fracture of base of skull with intracranial injury of other and unspecified nature, prolonged (more than 24 hours) loss of consciousness, without return to pre-existing conscious level

801.46   Closed fracture of base of skull with intracranial injury of other and unspecified nature, loss of consciousness of unspecified duration

801.53   Open fracture of base of skull without mention of intracranial injury, moderate (1-24 hours) loss of consciousness

801.54   Open fracture of base of skull without mention of intracranial injury, prolonged (more than 24 hours) loss of consciousness and return to pre-existing conscious level

801.55   Open fracture of base of skull without mention of intracranial injury, prolonged (more than 24 hours) loss of consciousness, without return to pre-existing conscious level

801.56   Open fracture of base of skull without mention of intracranial injury, loss of consciousness of unspecified duration

801.63   Open fracture of base of skull with cerebral laceration and contusion, moderate (1-24 hours) loss of consciousness

801.64   Open fracture of base of skull with cerebral laceration and contusion, prolonged (more than 24 hours) loss of consciousness and return to pre-existing conscious level

801.65   Open fracture of base of skull with cerebral laceration and contusion, prolonged (more than 24 hours) loss of consciousness, without return to pre-existing conscious level

801.66   Open fracture of base of skull with cerebral laceration and contusion, loss of consciousness of unspecified duration

801.73   Open fracture of base of skull with subarachnoid, subdural, and extradural hemorrhage, moderate (1-24 hours) loss of consciousness

801.74   Open fracture of base of skull with subarachnoid, subdural, and extradural hemorrhage, prolonged (more than 24 hours) loss of consciousness and return to pre-existing conscious level

801.75   Open fracture of base of skull with subarachnoid, subdural, and extradural hemorrhage, prolonged (more than 24 hours) loss of consciousness, without return to pre-existing conscious level

801.76   Open fracture of base of skull with subarachnoid, subdural, and extradural hemorrhage, loss of consciousness of unspecified duration

801.83   Open fracture of base of skull with other and unspecified intracranial hemorrhage, moderate (1-24 hours) loss of consciousness

801.84   Open fracture of base of skull with other and unspecified intracranial hemorrhage, prolonged (more than 24 hours) loss of consciousness and return to pre-existing conscious level

801.85   Open fracture of base of skull with other and unspecified intracranial hemorrhage, prolonged (more than 24 hours) loss of consciousness, without return to pre-existing conscious level

801.86   Open fracture of base of skull with other and unspecified intracranial hemorrhage, loss of consciousness of unspecified duration

801.93   Open fracture of base of skull with intracranial injury of other and unspecified nature, moderate (1-24 hours) loss of consciousness

801.94   Open fracture of base of skull with intracranial injury of other and unspecified nature, prolonged (more than 24 hours) loss of consciousness and return to pre-existing conscious level

801.95   Open fracture of base of skull with intracranial injury of other and unspecified nature, prolonged (more than 24 hours) loss of consciousness, without return to pre-existing conscious level

801.96   Open fracture of base of skull with intracranial injury of other and unspecified nature, loss of consciousness of unspecified duration

803.03   Other closed skull fracture without mention of intracranial injury, moderate (1-24 hours) loss of consciousness

803.04   Other closed skull fracture without mention of intracranial injury, prolonged (more than 24 hours) loss of consciousness and return to pre-existing conscious level

803.05   Other closed skull fracture without mention of intracranial injury, prolonged (more than 24 hours) loss of consciousness, without return to pre-existing conscious level

803.06   Other closed skull fracture without mention of intracranial injury, loss of consciousness of unspecified duration

803.13   Other closed skull fracture with cerebral laceration and contusion, moderate (1-24 hours) loss of consciousness

803.14   Other closed skull fracture with cerebral laceration and contusion, prolonged (more than 24 hours) loss of consciousness and return to pre-existing conscious level

803.15   Other closed skull fracture with cerebral laceration and contusion, prolonged (more than 24 hours) loss of consciousness, without return to pre-existing conscious level

803.16   Other closed skull fracture with cerebral laceration and contusion, loss of consciousness of unspecified duration

803.23   Other closed skull fracture with subarachnoid, subdural, and extradural hemorrhage, moderate (1-24 hours) loss of consciousness

803.24   Other closed skull fracture with subarachnoid, subdural, and extradural hemorrhage, prolonged (more than 24 hours) loss of consciousness and return to pre-existing conscious level

803.25   Other closed skull fracture with subarachnoid, subdural, and extradural hemorrhage, prolonged (more than 24 hours) loss of consciousness, without return to pre-existing conscious level

803.26   Other closed skull fracture with subarachnoid, subdural, and extradural hemorrhage, loss of consciousness of unspecified duration

803.33   Other closed skull fracture with other and unspecified intracranial hemorrhage, moderate (1-24 hours) loss of consciousness

803.34   Other closed skull fracture with other and unspecified intracranial hemorrhage, prolonged (more than 24 hours) loss of consciousness and return to pre-existing conscious level

803.35   Other closed skull fracture with other and unspecified intracranial hemorrhage, prolonged (more than 24 hours) loss of consciousness, without return to pre-existing conscious level

803.36   Other closed skull fracture with other and unspecified intracranial hemorrhage, loss of consciousness of unspecified duration

803.43   Other closed skull fracture with intracranial injury of other and unspecified nature, moderate (1-24 hours) loss of consciousness

803.44   Other closed skull fracture with intracranial injury of other and unspecified nature, prolonged (more than 24 hours) loss of consciousness and return to pre-existing conscious level

803.45   Other closed skull fracture with intracranial injury of other and unspecified nature, prolonged (more than 24 hours) loss of consciousness, without return to pre-existing conscious level

803.46   Other closed skull fracture with intracranial injury of other and unspecified nature, loss of consciousness of unspecified duration

803.53   Other open skull fracture without mention of intracranial injury, moderate (1-24 hours) loss of consciousness

803.54   Other open skull fracture without mention of intracranial injury, prolonged (more than 24 hours) loss of consciousness and return to pre-existing conscious level

803.55   Other open skull fracture without mention of intracranial injury, prolonged (more than 24 hours) loss of consciousness, without return to pre-existing conscious level

803.56   Other open skull fracture without mention of intracranial injury, loss of consciousness of unspecified duration

803.63   Other open skull fracture with cerebral laceration and contusion, moderate (1-24 hours) loss of consciousness

803.64   Other open skull fracture with cerebral laceration and contusion, prolonged (more than 24 hours) loss of consciousness and return to pre-existing conscious level

803.65   Other open skull fracture with cerebral laceration and contusion, prolonged (more than 24 hours) loss of consciousness, without return to pre-existing conscious level

803.66   Other open skull fracture with cerebral laceration and contusion, loss of consciousness of unspecified duration

803.73   Other open skull fracture with subarachnoid, subdural, and extradural hemorrhage, moderate (1-24 hours) loss of consciousness

803.74   Other open skull fracture with subarachnoid, subdural, and extradural hemorrhage, prolonged (more than 24 hours) loss of consciousness and return to pre-existing conscious level

803.75   Other open skull fracture with subarachnoid, subdural, and extradural hemorrhage, prolonged (more than 24 hours) loss of consciousness, without return to pre-existing conscious level

803.76   Other open skull fracture with subarachnoid, subdural, and extradural hemorrhage, loss of consciousness of unspecified duration

803.83   Other open skull fracture with other and unspecified intracranial hemorrhage, moderate (1-24 hours) loss of consciousness

803.84   Other open skull fracture with other and unspecified intracranial hemorrhage, prolonged (more than 24 hours) loss of consciousness and return to pre-existing conscious level

803.85   Other open skull fracture with other and unspecified intracranial hemorrhage, prolonged (more than 24 hours) loss of consciousness, without return to pre-existing conscious level

803.86   Other open skull fracture with other and unspecified intracranial hemorrhage, loss of consciousness of unspecified duration

803.93   Other open skull fracture with intracranial injury of other and unspecified nature, moderate (1-24 hours) loss of consciousness

803.94   Other open skull fracture with intracranial injury of other and unspecified nature, prolonged (more than 24 hours) loss of consciousness and return to pre-existing conscious level

803.95   Other open skull fracture with intracranial injury of other and unspecified nature, prolonged (more than 24 hours) loss of consciousness, without return to pre-existing conscious level

803.96   Other open skull fracture with intracranial injury of other and unspecified nature, loss of consciousness of unspecified duration

804.03   Closed fractures involving skull or face with other bones, without mention of intracranial injury, moderate (1-24 hours) loss of consciousness

804.04   Closed fractures involving skull or face with other bones, without mention or intracranial injury, prolonged (more than 24 hours) loss of consciousness and return to pre-existing conscious level

804.05   Closed fractures involving skull of face with other bones, without mention of intracranial injury, prolonged (more than 24 hours) loss of consciousness, without return to pre-existing conscious level

804.06   Closed fractures involving skull of face with other bones, without mention of intracranial injury, loss of consciousness of unspecified duration

804.13   Closed fractures involving skull or face with other bones, with cerebral laceration and contusion, moderate (1-24 hours) loss of consciousness

804.14   Closed fractures involving skull or face with other bones, with cerebral laceration and contusion, prolonged (more than 24 hours) loss of consciousness and return to pre-existing conscious level

804.15   Closed fractures involving skull of face with other bones, with cerebral laceration and contusion, prolonged (more than 24 hours) loss of consciousness, without return to pre-existing conscious level

804.16   Closed fractures involving skull or face with other bones, with cerebral laceration and contusion, loss of consciousness of unspecified duration

804.23   Closed fractures involving skull or face with other bones with subarachnoid, subdural, and extradural hemorrhage, moderate (1-24 hours) loss of consciousness

804.24   Closed fractures involving skull or face with other bones with subarachnoid, subdural, and extradural hemorrhage, prolonged (more than 24 hours) loss of consciousness and return to pre-existing conscious level

804.25   Closed fractures involving skull or face with other bones with subarachnoid, subdural, and extradural hemorrhage, prolonged (more than 24 hours) loss of consciousness, without return to pre-existing conscious level

804.26   Closed fractures involving skull or face with other bones with subarachnoid, subdural, and extradural hemorrhage, loss of consciousness of unspecified duration

804.33   Closed fractures involving skull or face with other bones, with other and unspecified intracranial hemorrhage, moderate (1-24 hours) loss of consciousness

804.34   Closed fractures involving skull or face with other bones, with other and unspecified intracranial hemorrhage, prolonged (more than 24 hours) loss of consciousness and return to preexisting conscious level

804.35   Closed fractures involving skull or face with other bones, with other and unspecified intracranial hemorrhage, prolonged (more than 24 hours) loss of consciousness, without return to pre-existing conscious level

804.36   Closed fractures involving skull or face with other bones, with other and unspecified intracranial hemorrhage, loss of consciousness of unspecified duration

804.43   Closed fractures involving skull or face with other bones, with intracranial injury of other and unspecified nature, moderate (1-24 hours) loss of consciousness

804.44   Closed fractures involving skull or face with other bones, with intracranial injury of other and unspecified nature, prolonged (more than 24 hours) loss of consciousness and return to pre-existing conscious level

804.45   Closed fractures involving skull or face with other bones, with intracranial injury of other and unspecified nature, prolonged (more than 24 hours) loss of consciousness, without return to pre-existing conscious level

Ⓣ *Transfer DRG*   ⓢ *Special Payment*   ☑ *Optimization Potential*   ⱽ *Targeted Potential*   * *Code Range*   ● *New DRG*   ▲ *Revised DRG Title*

24   Valid 10/01/2012-09/30/2013   © 2012 OptumInsight, Inc.

804.46   Closed fractures involving skull or face with other bones, with intracranial injury of other and unspecified nature, loss of consciousness of unspecified duration

804.53   Open fractures involving skull or face with other bones, without mention of intracranial injury, moderate (1-24 hours) loss of consciousness

804.54   Open fractures involving skull or face with other bones, without mention of intracranial injury, prolonged (more than 24 hours) loss of consciousness and return to pre-existing conscious level

804.55   Open fractures involving skull or face with other bones, without mention of intracranial injury, prolonged (more than 24 hours) loss of consciousness, without return to pre-existing conscious level

804.56   Open fractures involving skull or face with other bones, without mention of intracranial injury, loss of consciousness of unspecified duration

804.63   Open fractures involving skull or face with other bones, with cerebral laceration and contusion, moderate (1-24 hours) loss of consciousness

804.64   Open fractures involving skull or face with other bones, with cerebral laceration and contusion, prolonged (more than 24 hours) loss of consciousness and return to pre-existing conscious level

804.65   Open fractures involving skull or face with other bones, with cerebral laceration and contusion, prolonged (more than 24 hours) loss of consciousness, without return to pre-existing conscious level

804.66   Open fractures involving skull or face with other bones, with cerebral laceration and contusion, loss of consciousness of unspecified duration

804.73   Open fractures involving skull or face with other bones with subarachnoid, subdural, and extradural hemorrhage, moderate (1-24 hours) loss of consciousness

804.74   Open fractures involving skull or face with other bones with subarachnoid, subdural, and extradural hemorrhage, prolonged (more than 24 hours) loss of consciousness and return to pre-existing conscious level

804.75   Open fractures involving skull or face with other bones with subarachnoid, subdural, and extradural hemorrhage, prolonged (more than 24 hours) loss of consciousness, without return to pre-existing conscious level

804.76   Open fractures involving skull or face with other bones with subarachnoid, subdural, and extradural hemorrhage, loss of consciousness of unspecified duration

804.83   Open fractures involving skull or face with other bones, with other and unspecified intracranial hemorrhage, moderate (1-24 hours) loss of consciousness

804.84   Open fractures involving skull or face with other bones, with other and unspecified intracranial hemorrhage, prolonged (more than 24 hours) loss of consciousness and return to pre-existing conscious level

804.85   Open fractures involving skull or face with other bones, with other and unspecified intracranial hemorrhage, prolonged (more than 24 hours) loss of consciousness, without return to pre-existing conscious level

804.86   Open fractures involving skull or face with other bones, with other and unspecified intracranial hemorrhage, loss of consciousness of unspecified duration

804.93   Open fractures involving skull or face with other bones, with intracranial injury of other and unspecified nature, moderate (1-24 hours) loss of consciousness

804.94   Open fractures involving skull or face with other bones, with intracranial injury of other and unspecified nature, prolonged (more than 24 hours) loss of consciousness and return to pre-existing conscious level

804.95   Open fractures involving skull or face with other bones, with intracranial injury of other and unspecified nature, prolonged (more than 24 hours) loss of consciousness, without return to pre-existing level

804.96   Open fractures involving skull or face with other bones, with intracranial injury of other and unspecified nature, loss of consciousness of unspecified duration

851.03   Cortex (cerebral) contusion without mention of open intracranial wound, moderate (1-24 hours) loss of consciousness

851.04   Cortex (cerebral) contusion without mention of open intracranial wound, prolonged (more than 24 hours) loss of consciousness and return to pre-existing conscious level

851.05   Cortex (cerebral) contusion without mention of open intracranial wound, prolonged (more than 24 hours) loss of consciousness, without return to pre-existing conscious level

851.06   Cortex (cerebral) contusion without mention of open intracranial wound, loss of consciousness of unspecified duration

851.13   Cortex (cerebral) contusion with open intracranial wound, moderate (1-24 hours) loss of consciousness

851.14   Cortex (cerebral) contusion with open intracranial wound, prolonged (more than 24 hours) loss of consciousness and return to pre-existing conscious level

851.15   Cortex (cerebral) contusion with open intracranial wound, prolonged (more than 24 hours) loss of consciousness, without return to pre-existing conscious level

851.16   Cortex (cerebral) contusion with open intracranial wound, loss of consciousness of unspecified duration

851.23   Cortex (cerebral) laceration without mention of open intracranial wound, moderate (1-24 hours) loss of consciousness

851.24   Cortex (cerebral) laceration without mention of open intracranial wound, prolonged (more than 24 hours) loss of consciousness and return to pre-existing conscious level

851.25   Cortex (cerebral) laceration without mention of open intracranial wound, prolonged (more than 24 hours) loss of consciousness, without return to pre-existing conscious level

851.26   Cortex (cerebral) laceration without mention of open intracranial wound, loss of consciousness of unspecified duration

851.33   Cortex (cerebral) laceration with open intracranial wound, moderate (1-24 hours) loss of consciousness

851.34   Cortex (cerebral) laceration with open intracranial wound, prolonged (more than 24 hours) loss of consciousness and return to pre-existing conscious level

851.35   Cortex (cerebral) laceration with open intracranial wound, prolonged (more than 24 hours) loss of consciousness, without return to pre-existing conscious level

851.36   Cortex (cerebral) laceration with open intracranial wound, loss of consciousness of unspecified duration

851.43   Cerebellar or brain stem contusion without mention of open intracranial wound, moderate (1-24 hours) loss of consciousness

851.44   Cerebellar or brain stem contusion without mention of open intracranial wound, prolonged (more than 24 hours) loss consciousness and return to pre-existing conscious level

851.45   Cerebellar or brain stem contusion without mention of open intracranial wound, prolonged (more than 24 hours) loss of consciousness, without return to pre-existing conscious level

851.46   Cerebellar or brain stem contusion without mention of open intracranial wound, loss of consciousness of unspecified duration

851.53   Cerebellar or brain stem contusion with open intracranial wound, moderate (1-24 hours) loss of consciousness

851.54   Cerebellar or brain stem contusion with open intracranial wound, prolonged (more than 24 hours) loss of consciousness and return to pre-existing conscious level

MDC 1: Diseases And Disorders Of The Nervous System—MEDICAL

851.55 Cerebellar or brain stem contusion with open intracranial wound, prolonged (more than 24 hours) loss of consciousness, without return to pre-existing conscious level

851.56 Cerebellar or brain stem contusion with open intracranial wound, loss of consciousness of unspecified duration

851.63 Cerebellar or brain stem laceration without mention of open intracranial wound, moderate (1-24 hours) loss of consciousness

851.64 Cerebellar or brain stem laceration without mention of open intracranial wound, prolonged (more than 24 hours) loss of consciousness and return to pre-existing conscious level

851.65 Cerebellar or brain stem laceration without mention of open intracranial wound, prolonged (more than 24 hours) loss of consciousness, without return to pre-existing conscious level

851.66 Cerebellar or brain stem laceration without mention of open intracranial wound, loss of consciousness of unspecified duration

851.73 Cerebellar or brain stem laceration with open intracranial wound, moderate (1-24 hours) loss of consciousness

851.74 Cerebellar or brain stem laceration with open intracranial wound, prolonged (more than 24 hours) loss of consciousness and return to pre-existing conscious level

851.75 Cerebellar or brain stem laceration with open intracranial wound, prolonged (more than 24 hours) loss of consciousness, without return to pre-existing conscious level

851.76 Cerebellar or brain stem laceration with open intracranial wound, loss of consciousness of unspecified duration

851.83 Other and unspecified cerebral laceration and contusion, without mention of open intracranial wound, moderate (1-24 hours) loss of consciousness

851.84 Other and unspecified cerebral laceration and contusion, without mention of open intracranial wound, prolonged (more than 24 hours) loss of consciousness and return to preexisting conscious level

851.85 Other and unspecified cerebral laceration and contusion, without mention of open intracranial wound, prolonged (more than 24 hours) loss of consciousness, without return to pre-existing conscious level

851.86 Other and unspecified cerebral laceration and contusion, without mention of open intracranial wound, loss of consciousness of unspecified duration

851.93 Other and unspecified cerebral laceration and contusion, with open intracranial wound, moderate (1-24 hours) loss of consciousness

851.94 Other and unspecified cerebral laceration and contusion, with open intracranial wound, prolonged (more than 24 hours) loss of consciousness and return to pre-existing conscious level

851.95 Other and unspecified cerebral laceration and contusion, with open intracranial wound, prolonged (more than 24 hours) loss of consciousness, without return to pre-existing conscious level

851.96 Other and unspecified cerebral laceration and contusion, with open intracranial wound, loss of consciousness of unspecified duration

852.03 Subarachnoid hemorrhage following injury, without mention of open intracranial wound, moderate (1-24 hours) loss of consciousness

852.04 Subarachnoid hemorrhage following injury, without mention of open intracranial wound, prolonged (more than 24 hours) loss of consciousness and return to pre-existing conscious level

852.05 Subarachnoid hemorrhage following injury, without mention of open intracranial wound, prolonged (more than 24 hours) loss of consciousness, without return to pre-existing conscious level

852.06 Subarachnoid hemorrhage following injury, without mention of open intracranial wound, loss of consciousness of unspecified duration

852.13 Subarachnoid hemorrhage following injury, with open intracranial wound, moderate (1-24 hours) loss of consciousness

852.14 Subarachnoid hemorrhage following injury, with open intracranial wound, prolonged (more than 24 hours) loss of consciousness and return to pre-existing conscious level

852.15 Subarachnoid hemorrhage following injury, with open intracranial wound, prolonged (more than 24 hours) loss of consciousness, without return to pre-existing conscious level

852.16 Subarachnoid hemorrhage following injury, with open intracranial wound, loss of consciousness of unspecified duration

852.23 Subdural hemorrhage following injury, without mention of open intracranial wound, moderate (1-24 hours) loss of consciousness

852.24 Subdural hemorrhage following injury, without mention of open intracranial wound, prolonged (more than 24 hours) loss of consciousness and return to pre-existing conscious level

852.25 Subdural hemorrhage following injury, without mention of open intracranial wound, prolonged (more than 24 hours) loss of consciousness, without return to pre-existing conscious level

852.26 Subdural hemorrhage following injury, without mention of open intracranial wound, loss of consciousness of unspecified duration

852.33 Subdural hemorrhage following injury, with open intracranial wound, moderate (1-24 hours) loss of consciousness

852.34 Subdural hemorrhage following injury, with open intracranial wound, prolonged (more than 24 hours) loss of consciousness and return to pre-existing conscious level

852.35 Subdural hemorrhage following injury, with open intracranial wound, prolonged (more than 24 hours) loss of consciousness, without return to pre-existing conscious level

852.36 Subdural hemorrhage following injury, with open intracranial wound, loss of consciousness of unspecified duration

852.43 Extradural hemorrhage following injury, without mention of open intracranial wound, moderate (1-24 hours) loss of consciousness

852.44 Extradural hemorrhage following injury, without mention of open intracranial wound, prolonged (more than 24 hours) loss of consciousness and return to pre-existing conscious level

852.45 Extradural hemorrhage following injury, without mention of open intracranial wound, prolonged (more than 24 hours) loss of consciousness, without return to pre-existing conscious level

852.46 Extradural hemorrhage following injury, without mention of open intracranial wound, loss of consciousness of unspecified duration

852.53 Extradural hemorrhage following injury, with open intracranial wound, moderate (1-24 hours) loss of consciousness

852.54 Extradural hemorrhage following injury, with open intracranial wound, prolonged (more than 24 hours) loss of consciousness and return to pre-existing conscious level

852.55 Extradural hemorrhage following injury, with open intracranial wound, prolonged (more than 24 hours) loss of consciousness, without return to pre-existing conscious level

852.56 Extradural hemorrhage following injury, with open intracranial wound, loss of consciousness of unspecified duration

Ⓣ *Transfer DRG*   ⓈⓅ *Special Payment*   ☑ *Optimization Potential*   ▽ *Targeted Potential*   * *Code Range*   ● *New DRG*   ▲ *Revised DRG Title*

26   Valid 10/01/2012-09/30/2013   © 2012 OptumInsight, Inc.

853.03 Other and unspecified intracranial hemorrhage following injury, without mention of open intracranial wound, moderate (1-24 hours) loss of consciousness

853.04 Other and unspecified intracranial hemorrhage following injury, without mention of open intracranial wound, prolonged (more than 24 hours) loss of consciousness and return to preexisting conscious level

853.05 Other and unspecified intracranial hemorrhage following injury. Without mention of open intracranial wound, prolonged (more than 24 hours) loss of consciousness, without return to pre-existing conscious level

853.06 Other and unspecified intracranial hemorrhage following injury, without mention of open intracranial wound, loss of consciousness of unspecified duration

853.13 Other and unspecified intracranial hemorrhage following injury, with open intracranial wound, moderate (1-24 hours) loss of consciousness

853.14 Other and unspecified intracranial hemorrhage following injury, with open intracranial wound, prolonged (more than 24 hours) loss of consciousness and return to pre-existing conscious level

853.15 Other and unspecified intracranial hemorrhage following injury, with open intracranial wound, prolonged (more than 24 hours) loss of consciousness, without return to pre-existing conscious level

853.16 Other and unspecified intracranial hemorrhage following injury, with open intracranial wound, loss of consciousness of unspecified duration

854.03 Intracranial injury of other and unspecified nature, without mention of open intracranial wound, moderate (1-24 hours) loss of consciousness

854.04 Intracranial injury of other and unspecified nature, without mention of open intracranial wound, prolonged (more than 24 hours) loss of consciousness and return to pre-existing conscious level

854.05 Intracranial injury of other and unspecified nature, without mention of open intracranial wound, prolonged (more than 24 hours) loss of consciousness, without return to pre-existing conscious level

854.06 Intracranial injury of other and unspecified nature, without mention of open intracranial wound, loss of consciousness of unspecified duration

854.13 Intracranial injury of other and unspecified nature, with open intracranial wound, moderate (1-24 hours) loss of consciousness

854.14 Intracranial injury of other and unspecified nature, with open intracranial wound, prolonged (more than 24 hours) loss of consciousness and return to pre-existing conscious level

854.15 Intracranial injury of other and unspecified nature, with open intracranial wound, prolonged (more than 24 hours) loss of consciousness, without return to pre-existing conscious level

854.16 Intracranial injury of other and unspecified nature, with open intracranial wound, loss of consciousness of unspecified duration

OR

Principal Diagnosis of Traumatic Stupor and Coma

800.00 Closed fracture of vault of skull without mention of intracranial injury, unspecified state of consciousness

800.01 Closed fracture of vault of skull without mention of intracranial injury, no loss of consciousness

800.02 Closed fracture of vault of skull without mention of intracranial injury, brief (less than one hour) loss of consciousness

800.09 Closed fracture of vault of skull without mention of intracranial injury, unspecified concussion

800.10 Closed fracture of vault of skull with cerebral laceration and contusion, unspecified state of consciousness

800.11 Closed fracture of vault of skull with cerebral laceration and contusion, no loss of consciousness

800.12 Closed fracture of vault of skull with cerebral laceration and contusion, brief (less than one hour) loss of consciousness

800.19 Closed fracture of vault of skull with cerebral laceration and contusion, unspecified concussion

800.20 Closed fracture of vault of skull with subarachnoid, subdural, and extradural hemorrhage, unspecified state of consciousness

800.21 Closed fracture of vault of skull with subarachnoid, subdural, and extradural hemorrhage, no loss of consciousness

800.22 Closed fracture of vault of skull with subarachnoid, subdural, and extradural hemorrhage, brief (less than one hour) loss of consciousness

800.29 Closed fracture of vault of skull with subarachnoid, subdural, and extradural hemorrhage, unspecified concussion

800.30 Closed fracture of vault of skull with other and unspecified intracranial hemorrhage, unspecified state of consciousness

800.31 Closed fracture of vault of skull with other and unspecified intracranial hemorrhage, no loss of consciousness

800.32 Closed fracture of vault of skull with other and unspecified intracranial hemorrhage, brief (less than one hour) loss of consciousness

800.39 Closed fracture of vault of skull with other and unspecified intracranial hemorrhage, unspecified concussion

800.40 Closed fracture of vault of skull with intracranial injury of other and unspecified nature, unspecified state of consciousness

800.41 Closed fracture of vault of skull with intracranial injury of other and unspecified nature, no loss of consciousness

800.42 Closed fracture of vault of skull with intracranial injury of other and unspecified nature, brief (less than one hour) loss of consciousness

800.49 Closed fracture of vault of skull with intracranial injury of other and unspecified nature, unspecified concussion

800.50 Open fracture of vault of skull without mention of intracranial injury, unspecified state of consciousness

800.51 Open fracture of vault of skull without mention of intracranial injury, no loss of consciousness

800.52 Open fracture of vault of skull without mention of intracranial injury, brief (less than one hour) loss of consciousness

800.59 Open fracture of vault of skull without mention of intracranial injury, unspecified concussion

800.60 Open fracture of vault of skull with cerebral laceration and contusion, unspecified state of consciousness

800.61 Open fracture of vault of skull with cerebral laceration and contusion, no loss of consciousness

800.62 Open fracture of vault of skull with cerebral laceration and contusion, brief (less than one hour) loss of consciousness

800.69 Open fracture of vault of skull with cerebral laceration and contusion, unspecified concussion

800.70 Open fracture of vault of skull with subarachnoid, subdural, and extradural hemorrhage, unspecified state of consciousness

800.71 Open fracture of vault of skull with subarachnoid, subdural, and extradural hemorrhage, no loss of consciousness

800.72 Open fracture of vault of skull with subarachnoid, subdural, and extradural hemorrhage, brief (less than one hour) loss of consciousness

800.79 Open fracture of vault of skull with subarachnoid, subdural, and extradural hemorrhage, unspecified concussion

800.80 Open fracture of vault of skull with other and unspecified intracranial hemorrhage, unspecified state of consciousness

800.81 Open fracture of vault of skull with other and unspecified intracranial hemorrhage, no loss of consciousness

800.82 Open fracture of vault of skull with other and unspecified intracranial hemorrhage, brief (less than one hour) loss of consciousness

MDC 1: Diseases And Disorders Of The Nervous System—MEDICAL

Surgical | Medical | CC Indicator | MCC Indicator | Procedure Proxy

800.89	Open fracture of vault of skull with other and unspecified intracranial hemorrhage, unspecified concussion
800.90	Open fracture of vault of skull with intracranial injury of other and unspecified nature, unspecified state of consciousness
800.91	Open fracture of vault of skull with intracranial injury of other and unspecified nature, no loss of consciousness
800.92	Open fracture of vault of skull with intracranial injury of other and unspecified nature, brief (less than one hour) loss of consciousness
800.99	Open fracture of vault of skull with intracranial injury of other and unspecified nature, unspecified concussion
801.00	Closed fracture of base of skull without mention of intracranial injury, unspecified state of consciousness
801.01	Closed fracture of base of skull without mention of intracranial injury, no loss of consciousness
801.02	Closed fracture of base of skull without mention of intracranial injury, brief (less than one hour) loss of consciousness
801.09	Closed fracture of base of skull without mention of intracranial injury, unspecified concussion
801.10	Closed fracture of base of skull with cerebral laceration and contusion, unspecified state of consciousness
801.11	Closed fracture of base of skull with cerebral laceration and contusion, no loss of consciousness
801.12	Closed fracture of base of skull with cerebral laceration and contusion, brief (less than one hour) loss of consciousness
801.19	Closed fracture of base of skull with cerebral laceration and contusion, unspecified concussion
801.20	Closed fracture of base of skull with subarachnoid, subdural, and extradural hemorrhage, unspecified state of consciousness
801.21	Closed fracture of base of skull with subarachnoid, subdural, and extradural hemorrhage, no loss of consciousness
801.22	Closed fracture of base of skull with subarachnoid, subdural, and extradural hemorrhage, brief (less than one hour) loss of consciousness
801.29	Closed fracture of base of skull with subarachnoid, subdural, and extradural hemorrhage, unspecified concussion
801.30	Closed fracture of base of skull with other and unspecified intracranial hemorrhage, unspecified state of consciousness
801.31	Closed fracture of base of skull with other and unspecified intracranial hemorrhage, no loss of consciousness
801.32	Closed fracture of base of skull with other and unspecified intracranial hemorrhage, brief (less than one hour) loss of consciousness
801.39	Closed fracture of base of skull with other and unspecified intracranial hemorrhage, unspecified concussion
801.40	Closed fracture of base of skull with intracranial injury of other and unspecified nature, unspecified state of consciousness
801.41	Closed fracture of base of skull with intracranial injury of other and unspecified nature, no loss of consciousness
801.42	Closed fracture of base of skull with intracranial injury of other and unspecified nature, brief (less than one hour) loss of consciousness
801.49	Closed fracture of base of skull with intracranial injury of other and unspecified nature, unspecified concussion
801.50	Open fracture of base of skull without mention of intracranial injury, unspecified state of consciousness
801.51	Open fracture of base of skull without mention of intracranial injury, no loss of consciousness
801.52	Open fracture of base of skull without mention of intracranial injury, brief (less than one hour) loss of consciousness
801.59	Open fracture of base of skull without mention of intracranial injury, unspecified concussion
801.60	Open fracture of base of skull with cerebral laceration and contusion, unspecified state of consciousness
801.61	Open fracture of base of skull with cerebral laceration and contusion, no loss of consciousness
801.62	Open fracture of base of skull with cerebral laceration and contusion, brief (less than one hour) loss of consciousness
801.69	Open fracture of base of skull with cerebral laceration and contusion, unspecified concussion
801.70	Open fracture of base of skull with subarachnoid, subdural, and extradural hemorrhage, unspecified state of consciousness
801.71	Open fracture of base of skull with subarachnoid, subdural, and extradural hemorrhage, no loss of consciousness
801.72	Open fracture of base of skull with subarachnoid, subdural, and extradural hemorrhage, brief (less than one hour) loss of consciousness
801.79	Open fracture of base of skull with subarachnoid, subdural, and extradural hemorrhage, unspecified concussion
801.80	Open fracture of base of skull with other and unspecified intracranial hemorrhage, unspecified state of consciousness
801.81	Open fracture of base of skull with other and unspecified intracranial hemorrhage, no loss of consciousness
801.82	Open fracture of base of skull with other and unspecified intracranial hemorrhage, brief (less than one hour) loss of consciousness
801.89	Open fracture of base of skull with other and unspecified intracranial hemorrhage, unspecified concussion
801.90	Open fracture of base of skull with intracranial injury of other and unspecified nature, unspecified state of consciousness
801.91	Open fracture of base of skull with intracranial injury of other and unspecified nature, no loss of consciousness
801.92	Open fracture of base of skull with intracranial injury of other and unspecified nature, brief (less than one hour) loss of consciousness
801.99	Open fracture of base of skull with intracranial injury of other and unspecified nature, unspecified concussion
803.00	Other closed skull fracture without mention of intracranial injury, unspecified state of consciousness
803.01	Other closed skull fracture without mention of intracranial injury, no loss of consciousness
803.02	Other closed skull fracture without mention of intracranial injury, brief (less than one hour) loss of consciousness
803.09	Other closed skull fracture without mention of intracranial injury, unspecified concussion
803.10	Other closed skull fracture with cerebral laceration and contusion, unspecified state of consciousness
803.11	Other closed skull fracture with cerebral laceration and contusion, no loss of consciousness
803.12	Other closed skull fracture with cerebral laceration and contusion, brief (less than one hour) loss of consciousness
803.19	Other closed skull fracture with cerebral laceration and contusion, unspecified concussion
803.20	Other closed skull fracture with subarachnoid, subdural, and extradural hemorrhage, unspecified state of consciousness
803.21	Other closed skull fracture with subarachnoid, subdural, and extradural hemorrhage, no loss of consciousness
803.22	Other closed skull fracture with subarachnoid, subdural, and extradural hemorrhage, brief (less than one hour) loss of consciousness
803.29	Other closed skull fracture with subarachnoid, subdural, and extradural hemorrhage, unspecified concussion
803.30	Other closed skull fracture with other and unspecified intracranial hemorrhage, unspecified state of unconsciousness
803.31	Other closed skull fracture with other and unspecified intracranial hemorrhage, no loss of consciousness
803.32	Other closed skull fracture with other and unspecified intracranial hemorrhage, brief (less than one hour) loss of consciousness
803.39	Other closed skull fracture with other and unspecified intracranial hemorrhage, unspecified concussion

---

803.40 Other closed skull fracture with intracranial injury of other and unspecified nature, unspecified state of consciousness

803.41 Other closed skull fracture with intracranial injury of other and unspecified nature, no loss of consciousness

803.42 Other closed skull fracture with intracranial injury of other and unspecified nature, brief (less than one hour) loss of consciousness

803.49 Other closed skull fracture with intracranial injury of other and unspecified nature, unspecified concussion

803.50 Other open skull fracture without mention of injury, state of consciousness unspecified

803.51 Other open skull fracture without mention of intracranial injury, no loss of consciousness

803.52 Other open skull fracture without mention of intracranial injury, brief (less than one hour) loss of consciousness

803.59 Other open skull fracture without mention of intracranial injury, unspecified concussion

803.60 Other open skull fracture with cerebral laceration and contusion, unspecified state of consciousness

803.61 Other open skull fracture with cerebral laceration and contusion, no loss of consciousness

803.62 Other open skull fracture with cerebral laceration and contusion, brief (less than one hour) loss of consciousness

803.69 Other open skull fracture with cerebral laceration and contusion, unspecified concussion

803.70 Other open skull fracture with subarachnoid, subdural, and extradural hemorrhage, unspecified state of consciousness

803.71 Other open skull fracture with subarachnoid, subdural, and extradural hemorrhage, no loss of consciousness

803.72 Other open skull fracture with subarachnoid, subdural, and extradural hemorrhage, brief (less than one hour) loss of consciousness

803.79 Other open skull fracture with subarachnoid, subdural, and extradural hemorrhage, unspecified concussion

803.80 Other open skull fracture with other and unspecified intracranial hemorrhage, unspecified state of consciousness

803.81 Other open skull fracture with other and unspecified intracranial hemorrhage, no loss of consciousness

803.82 Other open skull fracture with other and unspecified intracranial hemorrhage, brief (less than one hour) loss of consciousness

803.89 Other open skull fracture with other and unspecified intracranial hemorrhage, unspecified concussion

803.90 Other open skull fracture with intracranial injury of other and unspecified nature, unspecified state of consciousness

803.91 Other open skull fracture with intracranial injury of other and unspecified nature, no loss of consciousness

803.92 Other open skull fracture with intracranial injury of other and unspecified nature, brief (less than one hour) loss of consciousness

803.99 Other open skull fracture with intracranial injury of other and unspecified nature, unspecified concussion

804.00 Closed fractures involving skull or face with other bones, without mention of intracranial injury, unspecified state of consciousness

804.01 Closed fractures involving skull or face with other bones, without mention of intracranial injury, no loss of consciousness

804.02 Closed fractures involving skull or face with other bones, without mention of intracranial injury, brief (less than one hour) loss of consciousness

804.09 Closed fractures involving skull of face with other bones, without mention of intracranial injury, unspecified concussion

804.10 Closed fractures involving skull or face with other bones, with cerebral laceration and contusion, unspecified state of consciousness

804.11 Closed fractures involving skull or face with other bones, with cerebral laceration and contusion, no loss of consciousness

804.12 Closed fractures involving skull or face with other bones, with cerebral laceration and contusion, brief (less than one hour) loss of consciousness

804.19 Closed fractures involving skull or face with other bones, with cerebral laceration and contusion, unspecified concussion

804.20 Closed fractures involving skull or face with other bones with subarachnoid, subdural, and extradural hemorrhage, unspecified state of consciousness

804.21 Closed fractures involving skull or face with other bones with subarachnoid, subdural, and extradural hemorrhage, no loss of consciousness

804.22 Closed fractures involving skull or face with other bones with subarachnoid, subdural, and extradural hemorrhage, brief (less than one hour) loss of consciousness

804.29 Closed fractures involving skull or face with other bones with subarachnoid, subdural, and extradural hemorrhage, unspecified concussion

804.30 Closed fractures involving skull or face with other bones, with other and unspecified intracranial hemorrhage, unspecified state of consciousness

804.31 Closed fractures involving skull or face with other bones, with other and unspecified intracranial hemorrhage, no loss of consciousness

804.32 Closed fractures involving skull or face with other bones, with other and unspecified intracranial hemorrhage, brief (less than one hour) loss of consciousness

804.39 Closed fractures involving skull or face with other bones, with other and unspecified intracranial hemorrhage, unspecified concussion

804.40 Closed fractures involving skull or face with other bones, with intracranial injury of other and unspecified nature, unspecified state of consciousness

804.41 Closed fractures involving skull or face with other bones, with intracranial injury of other and unspecified nature, no loss of consciousness

804.42 Closed fractures involving skull or face with other bones, with intracranial injury of other and unspecified nature, brief (less than one hour) loss of consciousness

804.49 Closed fractures involving skull or face with other bones, with intracranial injury of other and unspecified nature, unspecified concussion

804.50 Open fractures involving skull or face with other bones, without mention of intracranial injury, unspecified state of consciousness

804.51 Open fractures involving skull or face with other bones, without mention of intracranial injury, no loss of consciousness

804.52 Open fractures involving skull or face with other bones, without mention of intracranial injury, brief (less than one hour) loss of consciousness

804.59 Open fractures involving skull or face with other bones, without mention of intracranial injury, unspecified concussion

804.60 Open fractures involving skull or face with other bones, with cerebral laceration and contusion, unspecified state of consciousness

804.61 Open fractures involving skull or face with other bones, with cerebral laceration and contusion, no loss of consciousness

804.62 Open fractures involving skull or face with other bones, with cerebral laceration and contusion, brief (less than one hour) loss of consciousness

804.69 Open fractures involving skull or face with other bones, with cerebral laceration and contusion, unspecified concussion

804.70 Open fractures involving skull or face with other bones with subarachnoid, subdural, and extradural hemorrhage, unspecified state of consciousness

804.71 Open fractures involving skull or face with other bones with subarachnoid, subdural, and extradural hemorrhage, no loss of consciousness

Surgical   Medical   CC Indicator   MCC Indicator   Procedure Proxy

MDC 1: Diseases And Disorders Of The Nervous System—MEDICAL

804.72	Open fractures involving skull or face with other bones with subarachnoid, subdural, and extradural hemorrhage, brief (less than one hour) loss of consciousness
804.79	Open fractures involving skull or face with other bones with subarachnoid, subdural, and extradural hemorrhage, unspecified concussion
804.80	Open fractures involving skull or face with other bones, with other and unspecified intracranial hemorrhage, unspecified state of consciousness
804.81	Open fractures involving skull or face with other bones, with other and unspecified intracranial hemorrhage, no loss of consciousness
804.82	Open fractures involving skull or face with other bones, with other and unspecified intracranial hemorrhage, brief (less than one hour) loss of consciousness
804.89	Open fractures involving skull or face with other bones, with other and unspecified intracranial hemorrhage, unspecified concussion
804.90	Open fractures involving skull or face with other bones, with intracranial injury of other and unspecified nature, unspecified state of consciousness
804.91	Open fractures involving skull or face with other bones, with intracranial injury of other and unspecified nature, no loss of consciousness
804.92	Open fractures involving skull or face with other bones, with intracranial injury of other and unspecified nature, brief (less than one hour) loss of consciousness
804.99	Open fractures involving skull or face with other bones, with intracranial injury of other and unspecified nature, unspecified concussion
851.00	Cortex (cerebral) contusion without mention of open intracranial wound, state of consciousness unspecified
851.01	Cortex (cerebral) contusion without mention of open intracranial wound, no loss of consciousness
851.02	Cortex (cerebral) contusion without mention of open intracranial wound, brief (less than 1 hour) loss of consciousness
851.09	Cortex (cerebral) contusion without mention of open intracranial wound, unspecified concussion
851.10	Cortex (cerebral) contusion with open intracranial wound, unspecified state of consciousness
851.11	Cortex (cerebral) contusion with open intracranial wound, no loss of consciousness
851.12	Cortex (cerebral) contusion with open intracranial wound, brief (less than 1 hour) loss of consciousness
851.19	Cortex (cerebral) contusion with open intracranial wound, unspecified concussion
851.20	Cortex (cerebral) laceration without mention of open intracranial wound, unspecified state of consciousness
851.21	Cortex (cerebral) laceration without mention of open intracranial wound, no loss of consciousness
851.22	Cortex (cerebral) laceration without mention of open intracranial wound, brief (less than 1 hour) loss of consciousness
851.29	Cortex (cerebral) laceration without mention of open intracranial wound, unspecified concussion
851.30	Cortex (cerebral) laceration with open intracranial wound, unspecified state of consciousness
851.31	Cortex (cerebral) laceration with open intracranial wound, no loss of consciousness
851.32	Cortex (cerebral) laceration with open intracranial wound, brief (less than 1 hour) loss of consciousness
851.39	Cortex (cerebral) laceration with open intracranial wound, unspecified concussion
851.40	Cerebellar or brain stem contusion without mention of open intracranial wound, unspecified state of consciousness
851.41	Cerebellar or brain stem contusion without mention of open intracranial wound, no loss of consciousness
851.42	Cerebellar or brain stem contusion without mention of open intracranial wound, brief (less than 1 hour) loss of consciousness
851.49	Cerebellar or brain stem contusion without mention of open intracranial wound, unspecified concussion
851.50	Cerebellar or brain stem contusion with open intracranial wound, unspecified state of consciousness
851.51	Cerebellar or brain stem contusion with open intracranial wound, no loss of consciousness
851.52	Cerebellar or brain stem contusion with open intracranial wound, brief (less than 1 hour) loss of consciousness
851.59	Cerebellar or brain stem contusion with open intracranial wound, unspecified concussion
851.60	Cerebellar or brain stem laceration without mention of open intracranial wound, unspecified state of consciousness
851.61	Cerebellar or brain stem laceration without mention of open intracranial wound, no loss of consciousness
851.62	Cerebellar or brain stem laceration without mention of open intracranial wound, brief (less than 1 hour) loss of consciousness
851.69	Cerebellar or brain stem laceration without mention of open intracranial wound, unspecified concussion
851.70	Cerebellar or brain stem laceration with open intracranial wound, state of consciousness unspecified
851.71	Cerebellar or brain stem laceration with open intracranial wound, no loss of consciousness
851.72	Cerebellar or brain stem laceration with open intracranial wound, brief (less than one hour) loss of consciousness
851.79	Cerebellar or brain stem laceration with open intracranial wound, unspecified concussion
851.80	Other and unspecified cerebral laceration and contusion, without mention of open intracranial wound, unspecified state of consciousness
851.81	Other and unspecified cerebral laceration and contusion, without mention of open intracranial wound, no loss of consciousness
851.82	Other and unspecified cerebral laceration and contusion, without mention of open intracranial wound, brief (less than 1 hour) loss of consciousness
851.89	Other and unspecified cerebral laceration and contusion, without mention of open intracranial wound, unspecified concussion
851.90	Other and unspecified cerebral laceration and contusion, with open intracranial wound, unspecified state of consciousness
851.91	Other and unspecified cerebral laceration and contusion, with open intracranial wound, no loss of consciousness
851.92	Other and unspecified cerebral laceration and contusion, with open intracranial wound, brief (less than 1 hour) loss of consciousness
851.99	Other and unspecified cerebral laceration and contusion, with open intracranial wound, unspecified concussion
852.00	Subarachnoid hemorrhage following injury, without mention of open intracranial wound, unspecified state of consciousness
852.01	Subarachnoid hemorrhage following injury, without mention of open intracranial wound, no loss of consciousness
852.02	Subarachnoid hemorrhage following injury, without mention of open intracranial wound, brief (less than 1 hour) loss of consciousness
852.09	Subarachnoid hemorrhage following injury, without mention of open intracranial wound, unspecified concussion
852.10	Subarachnoid hemorrhage following injury, with open intracranial wound, unspecified state of consciousness
852.11	Subarachnoid hemorrhage following injury, with open intracranial wound, no loss of consciousness

Ⓣ *Transfer DRG*   Ⓢᴾ *Special Payment*   ☑ *Optimization Potential*   ▽ *Targeted Potential*   * *Code Range*   ● *New DRG*   ▲ *Revised DRG Title*

30   Valid 10/01/2012–09/30/2013   © 2012 OptumInsight, Inc.

852.12 Subarachnoid hemorrhage following injury, with open intracranial wound, brief (less than 1 hour) loss of consciousness
852.19 Subarachnoid hemorrhage following injury, with open intracranial wound, unspecified concussion
852.20 Subdural hemorrhage following injury, without mention of open intracranial wound, unspecified state of consciousness
852.21 Subdural hemorrhage following injury, without mention of open intracranial wound, no loss of consciousness
852.22 Subdural hemorrhage following injury, without mention of open intracranial wound, brief (less than one hour) loss of consciousness
852.29 Subdural hemorrhage following injury, without mention of open intracranial wound, unspecified concussion
852.30 Subdural hemorrhage following injury, with open intracranial wound, state of consciousness unspecified
852.31 Subdural hemorrhage following injury, with open intracranial wound, no loss of consciousness
852.32 Subdural hemorrhage following injury, with open intracranial wound, brief (less than 1 hour) loss of consciousness
852.39 Subdural hemorrhage following injury, with open intracranial wound, unspecified concussion
852.40 Extradural hemorrhage following injury, without mention of open intracranial wound, unspecified state of consciousness
852.41 Extradural hemorrhage following injury, without mention of open intracranial wound, no loss of consciousness
852.42 Extradural hemorrhage following injury, without mention of open intracranial wound, brief (less than 1 hour) loss of consciousness
852.49 Extradural hemorrhage following injury, without mention of open intracranial wound, unspecified concussion
852.50 Extradural hemorrhage following injury, with open intracranial wound, state of consciousness unspecified
852.51 Extradural hemorrhage following injury, with open intracranial wound, no loss of consciousness
852.52 Extradural hemorrhage following injury, with open intracranial wound, brief (less than 1 hour) loss of consciousness
852.59 Extradural hemorrhage following injury, with open intracranial wound, unspecified concussion
853.00 Other and unspecified intracranial hemorrhage following injury, without mention of open intracranial wound, unspecified state of consciousness
853.01 Other and unspecified intracranial hemorrhage following injury, without mention of open intracranial wound, no loss of consciousness
853.02 Other and unspecified intracranial hemorrhage following injury, without mention of open intracranial wound, brief (less than 1 hour) loss of consciousness
853.09 Other and unspecified intracranial hemorrhage following injury, without mention of open intracranial wound, unspecified concussion
853.10 Other and unspecified intracranial hemorrhage following injury, with open intracranial wound, unspecified state of consciousness
853.11 Other and unspecified intracranial hemorrhage following injury, with open intracranial wound, no loss of consciousness
853.12 Other and unspecified intracranial hemorrhage following injury, with open intracranial wound, brief (less than 1 hour) loss of consciousness
853.19 Other and unspecified intracranial hemorrhage following injury, with open intracranial wound, unspecified concussion
854.00 Intracranial injury of other and unspecified nature, without mention of open intracranial wound, unspecified state of consciousness
854.01 Intracranial injury of other and unspecified nature, without mention of open intracranial wound, no loss of consciousness
854.02 Intracranial injury of other and unspecified nature, without mention of open intracranial wound, brief (less than 1 hour) loss of consciousness
854.09 Intracranial injury of other and unspecified nature, without mention of open intracranial wound, unspecified concussion
854.10 Intracranial injury of other and unspecified nature, with open intracranial wound, unspecified state of consciousness
854.11 Intracranial injury of other and unspecified nature, with open intracranial wound, no loss of consciousness
854.12 Intracranial injury of other and unspecified nature, with open intracranial wound, brief (less than 1 hour) loss of consciousness
854.19 Intracranial injury of other and unspecified nature, with open intracranial wound, with unspecified concussion

AND

Secondary Diagnosis of Traumatic Stupor and Coma > 1 Hour

Above listed diagnoses with description of loss of consciousness greater than one hour or of unspecified duration

DRG 083 Traumatic Stupor and Coma, Coma Greater Than One Hour with CC
GMLOS 3.4   AMLOS 4.5   RW 1.3458   ☑

Select principal diagnosis of coma greater than one hour OR principal diagnosis of traumatic stupor AND a secondary diagnosis of coma greater than one hour listed under DRG 082

DRG 084 Traumatic Stupor and Coma, Coma Greater Than One Hour without CC/MCC
GMLOS 2.2   AMLOS 2.7   RW 0.8696   ☑

Select principal diagnosis of coma greater than one hour OR principal diagnosis of traumatic stupor AND a secondary diagnosis of coma greater than one hour listed under DRG 082

DRG 085 Traumatic Stupor and Coma, Coma Less Than One Hour with MCC
GMLOS 5.0   AMLOS 6.8   RW 2.0387   T ☑

Select principal diagnosis listed under DRG 082 excluding those with loss of consciousness of greater than one hour or of unspecified duration

DRG 086 Traumatic Stupor and Coma, Coma Less Than One Hour with CC
GMLOS 3.4   AMLOS 4.3   RW 1.1874   T ☑

Select principal diagnosis listed under DRG 082 excluding those with loss of consciousness of greater than one hour or of unspecified duration

DRG 087 Traumatic Stupor and Coma, Coma Less Than One Hour without CC/MCC
GMLOS 2.2   AMLOS 2.7   RW 0.7605   T ☑

Select principal diagnosis listed under DRG 082 excluding those with loss of consciousness of greater than one hour or of unspecified duration

DRG 088 Concussion with MCC
GMLOS 4.1   AMLOS 5.3   RW 1.5687   ☑

Principal Diagnosis
850*   Concussion

MDC 1: Diseases And Disorders Of The Nervous System—MEDICAL

DRG 089   **Concussion with CC**
GMLOS 2.7   AMLOS 3.4   RW 0.9791   ☑

Select principal diagnosis listed under DRG 088

DRG 090   **Concussion without CC/MCC**
GMLOS 1.8   AMLOS 2.2   RW 0.7218   ☑

Select principal diagnosis under DRG 088

DRG 091   **Other Disorders of Nervous System with MCC**
GMLOS 4.3   AMLOS 6.0   RW 1.6583   T ☑

Principal Diagnosis

078.81	Epidemic vertigo
094.87	Syphilitic ruptured cerebral aneurysm
137.1	Late effects of central nervous system tuberculosis
138	Late effects of acute poliomyelitis
139.0	Late effects of viral encephalitis
228.02	Hemangioma of intracranial structures
237.7*	Neurofibromatosis
307.2*	Tics
315.35	Childhood onset fluency disorder
323.71	Toxic encephalitis and encephalomyelitis
323.72	Toxic myelitis
325	Phlebitis and thrombophlebitis of intracranial venous sinuses
326	Late effects of intracranial abscess or pyogenic infection
327.21	Primary central sleep apnea
327.25	Congenital central alveolar hypoventilation syndrome
327.27	Central sleep apnea in conditions classified elsewhere
327.3*	Circadian rhythm sleep disorder
327.41	Confusional arousals
327.43	Recurrent isolated sleep paralysis
327.51	Periodic limb movement disorder
327.52	Sleep related leg cramps
331.81	Reye's syndrome
333.1	Essential and other specified forms of tremor
333.2	Myoclonus
333.3	Tics of organic origin
333.72	Acute dystonia due to drugs
333.79	Other acquired torsion dystonia
333.82	Orofacial dyskinesia
333.83	Spasmodic torticollis
333.84	Organic writers' cramp
333.85	Subacute dyskinesia due to drugs
333.89	Other fragments of torsion dystonia
333.91	Stiff-man syndrome
333.92	Neuroleptic malignant syndrome
333.93	Benign shuddering attacks
336.1	Vascular myelopathies
336.2	Subacute combined degeneration of spinal cord in diseases classified elsewhere
336.3	Myelopathy in other diseases classified elsewhere
336.8	Other myelopathy
336.9	Unspecified disease of spinal cord
338.0	Central pain syndrome
338.2*	Chronic pain
338.4	Chronic pain syndrome
343.3	Monoplegic infantile cerebral palsy
343.8	Other specified infantile cerebral palsy
343.9	Unspecified infantile cerebral palsy
344.3*	Monoplegia of lower limb
344.4*	Monoplegia of upper limb
344.5	Unspecified monoplegia
344.8*	Other specified paralytic syndromes
344.9	Unspecified paralysis
347*	Cataplexy and narcolepsy
348.0	Cerebral cysts
348.1	Anoxic brain damage
349.1	Nervous system complications from surgically implanted device
349.2	Disorders of meninges, not elsewhere classified
349.81	Cerebrospinal fluid rhinorrhea
349.82	Toxic encephalopathy
356.3	Refsum's disease
359.0	Congenital hereditary muscular dystrophy
359.1	Hereditary progressive muscular dystrophy
359.21	Myotonic muscular dystrophy
359.22	Myotonia congenita
359.23	Myotonic chondrodystrophy
359.24	Drug-induced myotonia
359.29	Other specified myotonic disorder
359.3	Periodic paralysis
359.4	Toxic myopathy
359.5	Myopathy in endocrine diseases classified elsewhere
359.6	Symptomatic inflammatory myopathy in diseases classified elsewhere
359.81	Critical illness myopathy
359.89	Other myopathies
359.9	Unspecified myopathy
377.00	Unspecified papilledema
377.01	Papilledema associated with increased intracranial pressure
377.04	Foster-Kennedy syndrome
377.5*	Disorders of optic chiasm
377.6*	Disorders of other visual pathways
377.7*	Disorders of visual cortex
377.9	Unspecified disorder of optic nerve and visual pathways
378.86	Internuclear ophthalmoplegia
388.61	Cerebrospinal fluid otorrhea
437.3	Cerebral aneurysm, nonruptured
437.5	Moyamoya disease
437.6	Nonpyogenic thrombosis of intracranial venous sinus
740*	Anencephalus and similar anomalies
741*	Spina bifida
742*	Other congenital anomalies of nervous system
747.81	Congenital anomaly of cerebrovascular system
747.82	Congenital spinal vessel anomaly
756.17	Spina bifida occulta
759.5	Tuberous sclerosis
779.7	Periventricular leukomalacia
781.0	Abnormal involuntary movements
781.1	Disturbances of sensation of smell and taste
781.2	Abnormality of gait
781.3	Lack of coordination
781.4	Transient paralysis of limb
781.6	Meningismus
781.8	Neurological neglect syndrome
781.91	Loss of height
781.92	Abnormal posture
781.94	Facial weakness
781.99	Other symptoms involving nervous and musculoskeletal systems
782.0	Disturbance of skin sensation
784.3	Aphasia
784.5*	Other speech disturbance
792.0	Nonspecific abnormal finding in cerebrospinal fluid
793.0	Nonspecific (abnormal) findings on radiological and other examination of skull and head
794.0*	Nonspecific abnormal results of function study of brain and central nervous system
794.10	Nonspecific abnormal response to unspecified nerve stimulation
794.19	Other nonspecific abnormal result of function study of peripheral nervous system and special senses
796.1	Abnormal reflex
798.0	Sudden infant death syndrome
799.53	Visuospatial deficit
905.0	Late effect of fracture of skull and face bones

☐T☐ Transfer DRG   ☐SP☐ Special Payment   ☑ Optimization Potential   ▽ Targeted Potential   * Code Range   ● New DRG   ▲ Revised DRG Title

907.0	Late effect of intracranial injury without mention of skull fracture
907.1	Late effect of injury to cranial nerve
907.3	Late effect of injury to nerve root(s), spinal plexus(es), and other nerves of trunk
907.4	Late effect of injury to peripheral nerve of shoulder girdle and upper limb
907.5	Late effect of injury to peripheral nerve of pelvic girdle and lower limb
907.9	Late effect of injury to other and unspecified nerve
950.1	Injury to optic chiasm
950.2	Injury to optic pathways
950.3	Injury to visual cortex
950.9	Injury to unspecified optic nerve and pathways
996.2	Mechanical complication of nervous system device, implant, and graft
996.63	Infection and inflammatory reaction due to nervous system device, implant, and graft
996.75	Other complications due to nervous system device, implant, and graft
997.0*	Nervous system complications
V53.0*	Fitting and adjustment of devices related to nervous system and special senses

DRG 092 Other Disorders of Nervous System with CC
GMLOS 3.1   AMLOS 4.0   RW 0.9214   T ☑

Select principal diagnosis listed under DRG 091

DRG 093 Other Disorders of Nervous System without CC/MCC
GMLOS 2.3   AMLOS 2.8   RW 0.6938   T ☑

Select principal diagnosis listed under DRG 091

DRG 094 Bacterial and Tuberculous Infections of Nervous System with MCC
GMLOS 8.9   AMLOS 11.5   RW 3.5656

Principal Diagnosis

003.21	Salmonella meningitis
013*	Tuberculosis of meninges and central nervous system
036.0	Meningococcal meningitis
036.1	Meningococcal encephalitis
098.82	Gonococcal meningitis
320*	Bacterial meningitis
324*	Intracranial and intraspinal abscess
357.0	Acute infective polyneuritis

DRG 095 Bacterial and Tuberculous Infections of Nervous System with CC
GMLOS 6.3   AMLOS 7.9   RW 2.4627   ☑

Select principal diagnosis listed under DRG 094

DRG 096 Bacterial and Tuberculous Infections of Nervous System without CC/MCC
GMLOS 4.4   AMLOS 5.5   RW 2.0158   ☑

Select principal diagnosis listed under DRG 094

DRG 097 Nonbacterial Infections of Nervous System Except Viral Meningitis with MCC
GMLOS 8.9   AMLOS 11.5   RW 3.3714   ☑

Principal Diagnosis

006.5	Amebic brain abscess
045.0*	Acute paralytic poliomyelitis specified as bulbar
045.1*	Acute poliomyelitis with other paralysis
045.9*	Acute unspecified poliomyelitis

049.8	Other specified non-arthropod-borne viral diseases of central nervous system
049.9	Unspecified non-arthropod-borne viral disease of central nervous system
052.0	Postvaricella encephalitis
052.2	Postvaricella myelitis
053.14	Herpes zoster myelitis
054.3	Herpetic meningoencephalitis
054.74	Herpes simplex myelitis
055.0	Postmeasles encephalitis
056.01	Encephalomyelitis due to rubella
056.09	Other neurological rubella complications
058.21	Human herpesvirus 6 encephalitis
058.29	Other human herpesvirus encephalitis
062*	Mosquito-borne viral encephalitis
063*	Tick-borne viral encephalitis
064	Viral encephalitis transmitted by other and unspecified arthropods
066.2	Venezuelan equine fever
071	Rabies
072.2	Mumps encephalitis
090.4*	Juvenile neurosyphilis
091.81	Early syphilis, acute syphilitic meningitis (secondary)
094.2	Syphilitic meningitis
094.3	Asymptomatic neurosyphilis
094.81	Syphilitic encephalitis
100.8*	Other specified leptospiral infections
112.83	Candidal meningitis
114.2	Coccidioidal meningitis
115.01	Histoplasma capsulatum meningitis
115.11	Histoplasma duboisii meningitis
115.91	Unspecified Histoplasmosis meningitis
130.0	Meningoencephalitis due to toxoplasmosis
321*	Meningitis due to other organisms
322*	Meningitis of unspecified cause
323.0*	Encephalitis, myelitis, and encephalomyelitis in viral diseases classified elsewhere
323.1	Encephalitis, myelitis, and encephalomyelitis in rickettsial diseases classified elsewhere
323.2	Encephalitis, myelitis, and encephalomyelitis in protozoal diseases classified elsewhere
323.4*	Other encephalitis, myelitis, and encephalomyelitis due to other infections classified elsewhere
323.5*	Encephalitis, myelitis, and encephalomyelitis following immunization procedures
323.6*	Postinfectious encephalitis, myelitis, and encephalomyelitis
323.8*	Other causes of encephalitis, myelitis, and encephalomyelitis
323.9	Unspecified causes of encephalitis, myelitis, and encephalomyelitis
341.2*	Acute (transverse) myelitis

DRG 098 Nonbacterial Infections of Nervous System Except Viral Meningitis with CC
GMLOS 6.1   AMLOS 7.7   RW 1.8418   ☑

Select principal diagnosis listed under DRG 097

DRG 099 Nonbacterial Infections of Nervous System Except Viral Meningitis without CC/MCC
GMLOS 4.1   AMLOS 4.9   RW 1.2427   ☑

Select principal diagnosis listed under DRG 097

DRG 100 Seizures with MCC
GMLOS 4.3   AMLOS 5.8   RW 1.5570   T ☑

Principal Diagnosis

345*	Epilepsy and recurrent seizures
780.3*	Convulsions

MDC 1: Diseases And Disorders Of The Nervous System—MEDICAL

DRG 101 **Seizures without MCC**
       GMLOS 2.6   AMLOS 3.3   RW 0.7643   T ☑

Select principal diagnosis listed under DRG 100

DRG 102 **Headaches with MCC**
       GMLOS 3.0   AMLOS 4.1   RW 1.0209   ☑

Principal Diagnosis
307.81	Tension headache
310.2	Postconcussion syndrome
339*	Other headache syndromes
346*	Migraine
348.2	Benign intracranial hypertension
349.0	Reaction to spinal or lumbar puncture
437.4	Cerebral arteritis
784.0	Headache

DRG 103 **Headaches without MCC**
       GMLOS 2.3   AMLOS 2.9   RW 0.6893   ☑

Select principal diagnosis listed under DRG 102

MDC 1: Diseases And Disorders Of The Nervous System—MEDICAL

T Transfer DRG   SP Special Payment   ☑ Optimization Potential   TGT Targeted Potential   * Code Range   ● New DRG   ▲ Revised DRG Title

34   Valid 10/01/2012-09/30/2013   © 2012 OptumInsight, Inc.

MDC 2
Diseases And Disorders Of The Eye

017.30	224.1	360.89	362.56	364.00	365.60	368.00	369.63	371.30
017.31	224.2	360.9	362.57	364.01	365.61	368.01	369.64	371.31
017.32	224.3	361.00	362.60	364.02	365.62	368.02	369.65	371.32
017.33	224.4	361.01	362.61	364.03	365.63	368.03	369.66	371.33
017.34	224.5	361.02	362.62	364.04	365.64	368.10	369.67	371.40
017.35	224.6	361.03	362.63	364.05	365.65	368.11	369.68	371.41
017.36	224.7	361.04	362.64	364.10	365.70	368.12	369.69	371.42
032.81	224.8	361.05	362.65	364.11	365.71	368.13	369.70	371.43
036.81	224.9	361.06	362.66	364.21	365.72	368.14	369.71	371.44
053.20	228.03	361.07	362.70	364.22	365.73	368.15	369.72	371.45
053.21	232.1	361.10	362.71	364.23	365.74	368.16	369.73	371.46
053.22	234.0	361.11	362.72	364.24	365.81	368.2	369.74	371.48
053.29	249.50	361.12	362.73	364.3	365.82	368.30	369.75	371.49
054.40	249.51	361.13	362.74	364.41	365.83	368.31	369.76	371.50
054.41	250.50	361.14	362.75	364.42	365.89	368.32	369.8	371.51
054.42	250.51	361.19	362.76	364.51	365.9	368.33	369.9	371.52
054.43	250.52	361.2	362.77	364.52	366.00	368.34	370.00	371.53
054.44	250.53	361.30	362.81	364.53	366.01	368.40	370.01	371.54
054.49	264.0	361.31	362.82	364.54	366.02	368.41	370.02	371.55
055.71	264.1	361.32	362.83	364.55	366.03	368.42	370.03	371.56
076.0	264.2	361.33	362.84	364.56	366.04	368.43	370.04	371.57
076.1	264.3	361.81	362.85	364.57	366.09	368.44	370.05	371.58
076.9	264.4	361.89	362.89	364.59	366.10	368.45	370.06	371.60
077.0	264.5	361.9	362.9	364.60	366.11	368.46	370.07	371.61
077.1	264.6	362.01	363.00	364.61	366.12	368.47	370.20	371.62
077.2	264.7	362.02	363.01	364.62	366.13	368.51	370.21	371.70
077.3	333.81	362.03	363.03	364.63	366.14	368.52	370.22	371.71
077.4	360.00	362.04	363.04	364.64	366.15	368.53	370.23	371.72
077.8	360.01	362.05	363.05	364.70	366.16	368.54	370.24	371.73
077.98	360.02	362.06	363.06	364.71	366.17	368.55	370.31	371.81
077.99	360.03	362.07	363.07	364.72	366.18	368.59	370.32	371.82
090.3	360.04	362.10	363.08	364.73	366.19	368.60	370.33	371.89
091.50	360.11	362.11	363.10	364.74	366.20	368.61	370.34	371.9
091.51	360.12	362.12	363.11	364.75	366.21	368.62	370.35	372.00
091.52	360.13	362.13	363.12	364.76	366.22	368.63	370.40	372.01
094.83	360.14	362.14	363.13	364.77	366.23	368.69	370.44	372.02
094.84	360.19	362.15	363.14	364.81	366.30	368.8	370.49	372.03
095.0	360.20	362.16	363.15	364.82	366.31	368.9	370.50	372.04
098.40	360.21	362.17	363.20	364.89	366.32	369.00	370.52	372.05
098.41	360.23	362.18	363.21	364.9	366.33	369.01	370.54	372.06
098.42	360.24	362.20	363.22	365.00	366.34	369.02	370.55	372.10
098.43	360.29	362.21	363.30	365.01	366.41	369.03	370.59	372.11
098.49	360.30	362.22	363.31	365.02	366.42	369.04	370.60	372.12
098.81	360.31	362.23	363.32	365.03	366.43	369.05	370.61	372.13
115.02	360.32	362.24	363.33	365.04	366.44	369.06	370.62	372.14
115.12	360.33	362.25	363.34	365.05	366.45	369.07	370.63	372.15
115.92	360.34	362.26	363.35	365.06	366.46	369.08	370.64	372.20
130.1	360.40	362.27	363.40	365.10	366.50	369.10	370.8	372.21
130.2	360.41	362.29	363.41	365.11	366.51	369.11	370.9	372.22
139.1	360.42	362.30	363.42	365.12	366.52	369.12	371.00	372.30
172.1	360.43	362.31	363.43	365.13	366.53	369.13	371.01	372.31
173.10	360.44	362.32	363.50	365.14	366.8	369.14	371.02	372.33
173.11	360.50	362.33	363.51	365.15	366.9	369.15	371.03	372.34
173.12	360.51	362.34	363.52	365.20	367.0	369.16	371.04	372.39
173.19	360.52	362.35	363.53	365.21	367.1	369.17	371.05	372.40
190.0	360.53	362.36	363.54	365.22	367.20	369.18	371.10	372.41
190.1	360.54	362.37	363.55	365.23	367.21	369.20	371.11	372.42
190.2	360.55	362.40	363.56	365.24	367.22	369.21	371.12	372.43
190.3	360.59	362.41	363.57	365.31	367.31	369.22	371.13	372.44
190.4	360.60	362.42	363.61	365.32	367.32	369.23	371.14	372.45
190.5	360.61	362.43	363.62	365.41	367.4	369.24	371.15	372.50
190.6	360.62	362.50	363.63	365.42	367.51	369.25	371.16	372.51
190.7	360.63	362.51	363.70	365.43	367.52	369.3	371.20	372.52
190.8	360.64	362.52	363.71	365.44	367.53	369.4	371.21	372.53
190.9	360.65	362.53	363.72	365.51	367.81	369.60	371.22	372.54
216.1	360.69	362.54	363.8	365.52	367.89	369.61	371.23	372.55
224.0	360.81	362.55	363.9	365.59	367.9	369.62	371.24	372.56

MDC 2: Diseases And Disorders Of The Eye

372.61	374.23	375.33	376.50	378.12	378.85	379.54	743.48	918.0
372.62	374.30	375.41	376.51	378.13	378.87	379.55	743.49	918.1
372.63	374.31	375.42	376.52	378.14	378.9	379.56	743.51	918.2
372.64	374.32	375.43	376.6	378.15	379.00	379.57	743.52	918.9
372.71	374.33	375.51	376.81	378.16	379.01	379.58	743.53	921.0
372.72	374.34	375.52	376.82	378.17	379.02	379.59	743.54	921.1
372.73	374.41	375.53	376.89	378.18	379.03	379.60	743.55	921.2
372.74	374.43	375.54	376.9	378.20	379.04	379.61	743.56	921.3
372.75	374.44	375.55	377.02	378.21	379.05	379.62	743.57	921.9
372.81	374.45	375.56	377.03	378.22	379.06	379.63	743.58	930.0
372.89	374.46	375.57	377.10	378.23	379.07	379.8	743.59	930.1
372.9	374.50	375.61	377.11	378.24	379.09	379.90	743.61	930.2
373.00	374.52	375.69	377.12	378.30	379.11	379.91	743.62	930.8
373.01	374.53	375.81	377.13	378.31	379.12	379.92	743.63	930.9
373.02	374.54	375.89	377.14	378.32	379.13	379.93	743.64	940.0
373.11	374.55	375.9	377.15	378.33	379.14	379.99	743.65	940.1
373.12	374.56	376.00	377.16	378.34	379.15	694.61	743.66	940.2
373.13	374.81	376.01	377.21	378.35	379.16	743.00	743.69	940.3
373.2	374.82	376.02	377.22	378.40	379.19	743.03	743.8	940.4
373.31	374.83	376.03	377.23	378.41	379.21	743.06	743.9	940.5
373.32	374.84	376.04	377.24	378.42	379.22	743.10	794.11	940.9
373.33	374.85	376.10	377.30	378.43	379.23	743.11	794.12	941.02
373.34	374.86	376.11	377.31	378.44	379.24	743.12	794.13	941.12
373.4	374.87	376.12	377.32	378.45	379.25	743.20	794.14	941.22
373.5	374.89	376.13	377.33	378.50	379.26	743.21	802.6	941.32
373.6	374.9	376.21	377.34	378.51	379.27	743.22	802.7	941.42
373.8	375.00	376.22	377.39	378.52	379.29	743.30	870.0	941.52
373.9	375.01	376.30	377.41	378.53	379.31	743.31	870.1	950.0
374.00	375.02	376.31	377.42	378.54	379.32	743.32	870.2	976.5
374.01	375.03	376.32	377.43	378.55	379.33	743.33	870.3	996.51
374.02	375.11	376.33	377.49	378.56	379.34	743.34	870.4	996.53
374.03	375.12	376.34	378.00	378.60	379.39	743.35	870.8	998.82
374.04	375.13	376.35	378.01	378.61	379.40	743.36	870.9	V42.5
374.05	375.14	376.36	378.02	378.62	379.41	743.37	871.0	V43.0
374.10	375.15	376.40	378.03	378.63	379.42	743.39	871.1	V43.1
374.11	375.16	376.41	378.04	378.71	379.43	743.41	871.2	V45.78
374.12	375.20	376.42	378.05	378.72	379.46	743.42	871.3	
374.13	375.21	376.43	378.06	378.73	379.49	743.43	871.4	
374.14	375.22	376.44	378.07	378.81	379.50	743.44	871.5	
374.20	375.30	376.45	378.08	378.82	379.51	743.45	871.6	
374.21	375.31	376.46	378.10	378.83	379.52	743.46	871.7	
374.22	375.32	376.47	378.11	378.84	379.53	743.47	871.9	

SURGICAL

DRG 113   Orbital Procedures with CC/MCC
GMLOS 4.1   AMLOS 5.6   RW 1.8587

Operating Room Procedures
16.0*   Orbitotomy
16.22   Diagnostic aspiration of orbit
16.23   Biopsy of eyeball and orbit
16.29   Other diagnostic procedures on orbit and eyeball
16.3*   Evisceration of eyeball
16.4*   Enucleation of eyeball
16.5*   Exenteration of orbital contents
16.6*   Secondary procedures after removal of eyeball
16.7*   Removal of ocular or orbital implant
16.8*   Repair of injury of eyeball and orbit
16.92   Excision of lesion of orbit
16.98   Other operations on orbit
76.46   Other reconstruction of other facial bone
76.79   Other open reduction of facial fracture
76.91   Bone graft to facial bone
76.92   Insertion of synthetic implant in facial bone

DRG 114   Orbital Procedures without CC/MCC
GMLOS 2.2   AMLOS 2.9   RW 0.9589   ☑

Select operating room procedures listed under DRG 113

DRG 115   Extraocular Procedures Except Orbit
GMLOS 3.4   AMLOS 4.5   RW 1.2407   ☑

Operating Room Procedures
08.11   Biopsy of eyelid
08.2*   Excision or destruction of lesion or tissue of eyelid
08.3*   Repair of blepharoptosis and lid retraction
08.4*   Repair of entropion or ectropion
08.5*   Other adjustment of lid position
08.6*   Reconstruction of eyelid with flaps or grafts
08.7*   Other reconstruction of eyelid
08.9*   Other operations on eyelids
09*   Operations on lacrimal system
10*   Operations on conjunctiva
11.0   Magnetic removal of embedded foreign body from cornea
11.2*   Diagnostic procedures on cornea
11.3*   Excision of pterygium
11.4*   Excision or destruction of tissue or other lesion of cornea
11.61   Lamellar keratoplasty with autograft
11.62   Other lamellar keratoplasty
11.71   Keratomileusis
11.72   Keratophakia
11.74   Thermokeratoplasty
11.76   Epikeratophakia
11.91   Tattooing of cornea
12.84   Excision or destruction of lesion of sclera
12.87   Scleral reinforcement with graft
12.88   Other scleral reinforcement
12.89   Other operations on sclera
14.6   Removal of surgically implanted material from posterior segment of eye
15*   Operations on extraocular muscles
16.93   Excision of lesion of eye, unspecified structure
16.99   Other operations on eyeball
38.21   Biopsy of blood vessel
86.22   Excisional debridement of wound, infection, or burn
86.4   Radical excision of skin lesion
95.04   Eye examination under anesthesia

DRG 116   Intraocular Procedures with CC/MCC
GMLOS 3.5   AMLOS 5.1   RW 1.5022

Operating Room Procedures
11.1   Incision of cornea
11.5*   Repair of cornea
11.60   Corneal transplant, not otherwise specified
11.63   Penetrating keratoplasty with autograft
11.64   Other penetrating keratoplasty
11.69   Other corneal transplant
11.73   Keratoprosthesis
11.75   Radial keratotomy
11.79   Other reconstructive surgery on cornea
11.92   Removal of artificial implant from cornea
11.99   Other operations on cornea
12.0*   Removal of intraocular foreign body from anterior segment of eye
12.1*   Iridotomy and simple iridectomy
12.21   Diagnostic aspiration of anterior chamber of eye
12.22   Biopsy of iris
12.29   Other diagnostic procedures on iris, ciliary body, sclera, and anterior chamber
12.31   Lysis of goniosynechiae
12.32   Lysis of other anterior synechiae
12.33   Lysis of posterior synechiae
12.34   Lysis of corneovitreal adhesions
12.35   Coreoplasty
12.39   Other iridoplasty
12.40   Removal of lesion of anterior segment of eye, not otherwise specified
12.41   Destruction of lesion of iris, nonexcisional
12.42   Excision of lesion of iris
12.43   Destruction of lesion of ciliary body, nonexcisional
12.44   Excision of lesion of ciliary body
12.51   Goniopuncture without goniotomy
12.52   Goniotomy without goniopuncture
12.53   Goniotomy with goniopuncture
12.54   Trabeculotomy ab externo
12.55   Cyclodialysis
12.59   Other facilitation of intraocular circulation
12.6*   Scleral fistulization
12.7*   Other procedures for relief of elevated intraocular pressure
12.81   Suture of laceration of sclera
12.82   Repair of scleral fistula
12.83   Revision of operative wound of anterior segment, not elsewhere classified
12.85   Repair of scleral staphyloma with graft
12.86   Other repair of scleral staphyloma
12.91   Therapeutic evacuation of anterior chamber
12.92   Injection into anterior chamber
12.93   Removal or destruction of epithelial downgrowth from anterior chamber
12.97   Other operations on iris
12.98   Other operations on ciliary body
12.99   Other operations on anterior chamber
13*   Operations on lens
14.0*   Removal of foreign body from posterior segment of eye
14.1*   Diagnostic procedures on retina, choroid, vitreous, and posterior chamber
14.21   Destruction of chorioretinal lesion by diathermy
14.22   Destruction of chorioretinal lesion by cryotherapy
14.26   Destruction of chorioretinal lesion by radiation therapy
14.27   Destruction of chorioretinal lesion by implantation of radiation source
14.29   Other destruction of chorioretinal lesion
14.31   Repair of retinal tear by diathermy
14.32   Repair of retinal tear by cryotherapy
14.39   Other repair of retinal tear
14.4*   Repair of retinal detachment with scleral buckling and implant

MDC 2: Diseases And Disorders Of The Eye—SURGICAL

14.5*	Other repair of retinal detachment
14.7*	Operations on vitreous
14.9	Other operations on retina, choroid, and posterior chamber
16.1	Removal of penetrating foreign body from eye, not otherwise specified

DRG 117 Intraocular Procedures without CC/MCC
GMLOS 1.7   AMLOS 2.3   RW 0.7234   ☑

Select operating room procedures listed under DRG 116

MEDICAL

DRG 121 Acute Major Eye Infections with CC/MCC
GMLOS 3.9   AMLOS 4.9   RW 0.9589   ☑

Principal Diagnosis

360.00	Unspecified purulent endophthalmitis
360.01	Acute endophthalmitis
360.02	Panophthalmitis
360.04	Vitreous abscess
360.13	Parasitic endophthalmitis NOS
360.19	Other endophthalmitis
370.00	Unspecified corneal ulcer
370.03	Central corneal ulcer
370.04	Hypopyon ulcer
370.05	Mycotic corneal ulcer
370.06	Perforated corneal ulcer
370.55	Corneal abscess
375.01	Acute dacryoadenitis
375.31	Acute canaliculitis, lacrimal
375.32	Acute dacryocystitis
376.01	Orbital cellulitis
376.02	Orbital periostitis
376.03	Orbital osteomyelitis
376.04	Orbital tenonitis

DRG 122 Acute Major Eye Infections without CC/MCC
GMLOS 3.2   AMLOS 3.9   RW 0.6533   ☑

Select principal diagnosis listed under DRG 121

DRG 123 Neurological Eye Disorders
GMLOS 2.2   AMLOS 2.7   RW 0.7542   ☑

Principal Diagnosis

036.81	Meningococcal optic neuritis
362.3*	Retinal vascular occlusion
365.12	Low tension open-angle glaucoma
367.52	Total or complete internal ophthalmoplegia
368.11	Sudden visual loss
368.12	Transient visual loss
368.2	Diplopia
368.40	Unspecified visual field defect
368.41	Scotoma involving central area in visual field
368.43	Sector or arcuate defects in visual field
368.44	Other localized visual field defect
368.45	Generalized contraction or constriction in visual field
368.46	Homonymous bilateral field defects in visual field
368.47	Heteronymous bilateral field defects in visual field
368.55	Acquired color vision deficiencies
374.30	Unspecified ptosis of eyelid
374.31	Paralytic ptosis
374.32	Myogenic ptosis
374.45	Other sensorimotor disorders of eyelid
376.34	Intermittent exophthalmos
376.35	Pulsating exophthalmos

376.36	Lateral displacement of globe of eye
376.82	Myopathy of extraocular muscles
377.10	Unspecified optic atrophy
377.11	Primary optic atrophy
377.12	Postinflammatory optic atrophy
377.15	Partial optic atrophy
377.16	Hereditary optic atrophy
377.21	Drusen of optic disc
377.24	Pseudopapilledema
377.3*	Optic neuritis
377.4*	Other disorders of optic nerve
378.5*	Paralytic strabismus
378.72	Progressive external ophthalmoplegia
378.73	Strabismus in other neuromuscular disorders
378.87	Other dissociated deviation of eye movements
379.40	Unspecified abnormal pupillary function
379.41	Anisocoria
379.42	Miosis (persistent), not due to miotics
379.43	Mydriasis (persistent), not due to mydriatics
379.46	Tonic pupillary reaction
379.49	Other anomaly of pupillary function
379.50	Unspecified nystagmus
379.52	Latent nystagmus
379.54	Nystagmus associated with disorders of the vestibular system
379.55	Dissociated nystagmus
379.57	Nystagmus with deficiencies of saccadic eye movements
379.58	Nystagmus with deficiencies of smooth pursuit movements

DRG 124 Other Disorders of the Eye with MCC
GMLOS 3.6   AMLOS 4.9   RW 1.1885

Principal Diagnosis

017.3*	Tuberculosis of eye
032.81	Conjunctival diphtheria
053.2*	Herpes zoster with ophthalmic complications
054.4*	Herpes simplex with ophthalmic complications
055.71	Measles keratoconjunctivitis
076*	Trachoma
077*	Other diseases of conjunctiva due to viruses and Chlamydiae
090.3	Syphilitic interstitial keratitis
091.5*	Early syphilis, uveitis due to secondary syphilis
094.83	Syphilitic disseminated retinochoroiditis
094.84	Syphilitic optic atrophy
095.0	Syphilitic episcleritis
098.4*	Gonococcal infection of eye
098.81	Gonococcal keratosis (blennorrhagica)
115.02	Histoplasma capsulatum retinitis
115.12	Histoplasma duboisii retinitis
115.92	Unspecified Histoplasmosis retinitis
130.1	Conjunctivitis due to toxoplasmosis
130.2	Chorioretinitis due to toxoplasmosis
139.1	Late effects of trachoma
172.1	Malignant melanoma of skin of eyelid, including canthus
173.1*	Other and unspecified malignant neoplasm of eyelid, including canthus
190*	Malignant neoplasm of eye
216.1	Benign neoplasm of eyelid, including canthus
224*	Benign neoplasm of eye
228.03	Hemangioma of retina
232.1	Carcinoma in situ of eyelid, including canthus
234.0	Carcinoma in situ of eye
249.5*	Secondary diabetes mellitus with ophthalmic manifestations
250.5*	Diabetes with ophthalmic manifestations
264.0	Vitamin A deficiency with conjunctival xerosis
264.1	Vitamin A deficiency with conjunctival xerosis and Bitot's spot
264.2	Vitamin A deficiency with corneal xerosis
264.3	Vitamin A deficiency with corneal ulceration and xerosis

MDC 2: Diseases And Disorders Of The Eye—MEDICAL

Ⓣ *Transfer DRG*   ⓢ *Special Payment*   ☑ *Optimization Potential*   ▽ *Targeted Potential*   * *Code Range*   ● *New DRG*   ▲ *Revised DRG Title*

38   Valid 10/01/2012-09/30/2013   © 2012 OptumInsight, Inc.

264.4	Vitamin A deficiency with keratomalacia
264.5	Vitamin A deficiency with night blindness
264.6	Vitamin A deficiency with xerophthalmic scars of cornea
264.7	Other ocular manifestations of vitamin A deficiency
333.81	Blepharospasm
360.03	Chronic endophthalmitis
360.11	Sympathetic uveitis
360.12	Panuveitis
360.14	Ophthalmia nodosa
360.2*	Degenerative disorders of globe
360.3*	Hypotony of eye
360.4*	Degenerated conditions of globe
360.5*	Retained (old) intraocular foreign body, magnetic
360.6*	Retained (old) intraocular foreign body, nonmagnetic
360.8*	Other disorders of globe
360.9	Unspecified disorder of globe
361.0*	Retinal detachment with retinal defect
361.1*	Retinoschisis and retinal cysts
361.2	Serous retinal detachment
361.3*	Retinal defects without detachment
361.8*	Other forms of retinal detachment
361.9	Unspecified retinal detachment
362.0*	Diabetic retinopathy
362.1*	Other background retinopathy and retinal vascular changes
362.2*	Other proliferative retinopathy
362.4*	Separation of retinal layers
362.5*	Degeneration of macula and posterior pole of retina
362.6*	Peripheral retinal degenerations
362.7*	Hereditary retinal dystrophies
362.8*	Other retinal disorders
362.9	Unspecified retinal disorder
363*	Chorioretinal inflammations, scars, and other disorders of choroid
364.0*	Acute and subacute iridocyclitis
364.1*	Chronic iridocyclitis
364.2*	Certain types of iridocyclitis
364.3	Unspecified iridocyclitis
364.41	Hyphema
364.42	Rubeosis iridis
364.5*	Degenerations of iris and ciliary body
364.6*	Cysts of iris, ciliary body, and anterior chamber
364.7*	Adhesions and disruptions of iris and ciliary body
364.8*	Other disorders of iris and ciliary body
364.9	Unspecified disorder of iris and ciliary body
365.0*	Borderline glaucoma (glaucoma suspect)
365.10	Unspecified open-angle glaucoma
365.11	Primary open-angle glaucoma
365.13	Pigmentary open-angle glaucoma
365.14	Open-angle glaucoma of childhood
365.15	Residual stage of open angle glaucoma
365.2*	Primary angle-closure glaucoma
365.3*	Corticosteroid-induced glaucoma
365.4*	Glaucoma associated with congenital anomalies, dystrophies, and systemic syndromes
365.5*	Glaucoma associated with disorders of the lens
365.6*	Glaucoma associated with other ocular disorders
365.7*	Glaucoma stage
365.8*	Other specified forms of glaucoma
365.9	Unspecified glaucoma
366*	Cataract
367.0	Hypermetropia
367.1	Myopia
367.2*	Astigmatism
367.3*	Anisometropia and aniseikonia
367.4	Presbyopia
367.51	Paresis of accommodation
367.53	Spasm of accommodation
367.8*	Other disorders of refraction and accommodation
367.9	Unspecified disorder of refraction and accommodation
368.0*	Amblyopia ex anopsia
368.10	Unspecified subjective visual disturbance
368.13	Visual discomfort
368.14	Visual distortions of shape and size
368.15	Other visual distortions and entoptic phenomena
368.16	Psychophysical visual disturbances
368.3*	Other disorders of binocular vision
368.42	Scotoma of blind spot area in visual field
368.51	Protan defect in color vision
368.52	Deutan defect in color vision
368.53	Tritan defect in color vision
368.54	Achromatopsia
368.59	Other color vision deficiencies
368.6*	Night blindness
368.8	Other specified visual disturbances
368.9	Unspecified visual disturbance
369*	Blindness and low vision
370.01	Marginal corneal ulcer
370.02	Ring corneal ulcer
370.07	Mooren's ulcer
370.2*	Superficial keratitis without conjunctivitis
370.3*	Certain types of keratoconjunctivitis
370.4*	Other and unspecified keratoconjunctivitis
370.50	Unspecified interstitial keratitis
370.52	Diffuse interstitial keratitis
370.54	Sclerosing keratitis
370.59	Other interstitial and deep keratitis
370.6*	Corneal neovascularization
370.8	Other forms of keratitis
370.9	Unspecified keratitis
371*	Corneal opacity and other disorders of cornea
372*	Disorders of conjunctiva
373*	Inflammation of eyelids
374.0*	Entropion and trichiasis of eyelid
374.1*	Ectropion
374.2*	Lagophthalmos
374.33	Mechanical ptosis
374.34	Blepharochalasis
374.41	Eyelid retraction or lag
374.43	Abnormal innervation syndrome of eyelid
374.44	Sensory disorders of eyelid
374.46	Blepharophimosis
374.50	Unspecified degenerative disorder of eyelid
374.52	Hyperpigmentation of eyelid
374.53	Hypopigmentation of eyelid
374.54	Hypertrichosis of eyelid
374.55	Hypotrichosis of eyelid
374.56	Other degenerative disorders of skin affecting eyelid
374.8*	Other disorders of eyelid
374.9	Unspecified disorder of eyelid
375.00	Unspecified dacryoadenitis
375.02	Chronic dacryoadenitis
375.03	Chronic enlargement of lacrimal gland
375.1*	Other disorders of lacrimal gland
375.2*	Epiphora
375.30	Unspecified dacryocystitis
375.33	Phlegmonous dacryocystitis
375.4*	Chronic inflammation of lacrimal passages
375.5*	Stenosis and insufficiency of lacrimal passages
375.6*	Other changes of lacrimal passages
375.8*	Other disorders of lacrimal system
375.9	Unspecified disorder of lacrimal system
376.00	Unspecified acute inflammation of orbit
376.1*	Chronic inflammatory disorders of orbit
376.2*	Endocrine exophthalmos
376.30	Unspecified exophthalmos
376.31	Constant exophthalmos
376.32	Orbital hemorrhage
376.33	Orbital edema or congestion
376.4*	Deformity of orbit
376.5*	Enophthalmos

Surgical	Medical	CC Indicator	MCC Indicator	Procedure Proxy

MDC 2: Diseases And Disorders Of The Eye—MEDICAL

376.6	Retained (old) foreign body following penetrating wound of orbit
376.81	Orbital cysts
376.89	Other orbital disorder
376.9	Unspecified disorder of orbit
377.02	Papilledema associated with decreased ocular pressure
377.03	Papilledema associated with retinal disorder
377.13	Optic atrophy associated with retinal dystrophies
377.14	Glaucomatous atrophy (cupping) of optic disc
377.22	Crater-like holes of optic disc
377.23	Coloboma of optic disc
378.0*	Esotropia
378.1*	Exotropia
378.2*	Intermittent heterotropia
378.3*	Other and unspecified heterotropia
378.4*	Heterophoria
378.6*	Mechanical strabismus
378.71	Duane's syndrome
378.81	Palsy of conjugate gaze
378.82	Spasm of conjugate gaze
378.83	Convergence insufficiency or palsy in binocular eye movement
378.84	Convergence excess or spasm in binocular eye movement
378.85	Anomalies of divergence in binocular eye movement
378.9	Unspecified disorder of eye movements
379.0*	Scleritis and episcleritis
379.1*	Other disorders of sclera
379.2*	Disorders of vitreous body
379.3*	Aphakia and other disorders of lens
379.51	Congenital nystagmus
379.53	Visual deprivation nystagmus
379.56	Other forms of nystagmus
379.59	Other irregularities of eye movements
379.6*	Inflammation (infection) of postprocedural bleb
379.8	Other specified disorders of eye and adnexa
379.9*	Unspecified disorder of eye and adnexa
694.61	Benign mucous membrane pemphigoid with ocular involvement
743*	Congenital anomalies of eye
794.11	Nonspecific abnormal retinal function studies
794.12	Nonspecific abnormal electro-oculogram (EOG)
794.13	Nonspecific abnormal visually evoked potential
794.14	Nonspecific abnormal oculomotor studies
802.6	Orbital floor (blow-out), closed fracture
802.7	Orbital floor (blow-out), open fracture
870*	Open wound of ocular adnexa
871*	Open wound of eyeball
918*	Superficial injury of eye and adnexa
921.0	Black eye, not otherwise specified
921.1	Contusion of eyelids and periocular area
921.2	Contusion of orbital tissues
921.3	Contusion of eyeball
921.9	Unspecified contusion of eye
930*	Foreign body on external eye
940*	Burn confined to eye and adnexa
941.02	Burn of unspecified degree of eye (with other parts of face, head, and neck)
941.12	Erythema due to burn (first degree) of eye (with other parts face, head, and neck)
941.22	Blisters, with epidermal loss due to burn (second degree) of eye (with other parts of face, head, and neck)
941.32	Full-thickness skin loss due to burn (third degree NOS) of eye (with other parts of face, head, and neck)
941.42	Deep necrosis of underlying tissues due to burn (deep third degree) of eye (with other parts of face, head, and neck), without mention of loss of a body part
941.52	Deep necrosis of underlying tissues due to burn (deep third degree) of eye (with other parts of face, head, and neck), with loss of a body part
950.0	Optic nerve injury

976.5	Poisoning by eye anti-infectives and other eye drugs
996.51	Mechanical complication due to corneal graft
996.53	Mechanical complication due to ocular lens prosthesis
998.82	Cataract fragments in eye following surgery
V42.5	Cornea replaced by transplant
V43.0	Eye globe replaced by other means
V43.1	Lens replaced by other means
V45.78	Acquired absence of organ, eye

DRG 125   Other Disorders of the Eye without MCC

GMLOS 2.5	AMLOS 3.2	RW 0.6850	☑

Select principal diagnosis listed under DRG 124

Ⓣ *Transfer DRG*   ⓢ*Special Payment*   ☑ *Optimization Potential*   ▽ *Targeted Potential*   * *Code Range*   ● *New DRG*   ▲ *Revised DRG Title*

40   Valid 10/01/2012-09/30/2013   © 2012 OptumInsight, Inc.

MDC 3
Diseases And Disorders Of The Ear, Nose, Mouth And Throat

012.30	144.9	231.0	382.2	386.33	389.8	478.33	522.6	524.60
012.31	145.0	235.0	382.3	386.34	389.9	478.34	522.7	524.61
012.32	145.1	235.1	382.4	386.35	460	478.4	522.8	524.62
012.33	145.2	235.6	382.9	386.40	461.0	478.5	522.9	524.63
012.34	145.3	327.20	383.00	386.41	461.1	478.6	523.00	524.64
012.35	145.4	327.23	383.01	386.42	461.2	478.70	523.01	524.69
012.36	145.5	327.24	383.02	386.43	461.3	478.71	523.10	524.70
015.60	145.6	327.26	383.1	386.48	461.8	478.74	523.11	524.71
015.61	145.8	327.29	383.20	386.50	461.9	478.75	523.20	524.72
015.62	145.9	327.40	383.21	386.51	462	478.79	523.21	524.73
015.63	146.0	327.42	383.22	386.52	463	478.8	523.22	524.74
015.64	146.1	327.44	383.30	386.53	464.00	478.9	523.23	524.75
015.65	146.2	327.49	383.31	386.54	464.01	487.1	523.24	524.76
015.66	146.3	327.53	383.32	386.55	464.20	520.0	523.25	524.79
017.40	146.4	327.59	383.33	386.56	464.21	520.1	523.30	524.81
017.41	146.5	327.8	383.81	386.58	464.30	520.2	523.31	524.82
017.42	146.6	380.00	383.89	386.8	464.31	520.3	523.32	524.89
017.43	146.7	380.10	383.9	386.9	464.4	520.4	523.33	524.9
017.44	146.8	380.11	384.00	387.0	464.50	520.5	523.40	525.0
017.45	146.9	380.12	384.01	387.1	464.51	520.6	523.41	525.10
017.46	147.0	380.13	384.09	387.2	465.0	520.7	523.42	525.11
032.0	147.1	380.14	384.1	387.8	465.8	520.8	523.5	525.12
032.1	147.2	380.15	384.20	387.9	465.9	520.9	523.6	525.13
032.2	147.3	380.16	384.21	388.00	470	521.00	523.8	525.19
032.3	147.8	380.21	384.22	388.01	471.0	521.01	523.9	525.20
034.0	147.9	380.22	384.23	388.02	471.1	521.02	524.00	525.21
053.71	148.0	380.23	384.24	388.10	471.8	521.03	524.01	525.22
054.2	148.1	380.30	384.25	388.11	471.9	521.04	524.02	525.23
054.73	148.2	380.31	384.81	388.12	472.0	521.05	524.03	525.24
055.2	148.3	380.32	384.82	388.2	472.1	521.06	524.04	525.25
074.0	148.8	380.39	384.9	388.30	472.2	521.07	524.05	525.26
094.86	148.9	380.4	385.00	388.31	473.0	521.08	524.06	525.3
098.6	149.0	380.50	385.01	388.32	473.1	521.09	524.07	525.40
099.51	149.1	380.51	385.02	388.40	473.2	521.10	524.09	525.41
101	149.8	380.52	385.03	388.41	473.3	521.11	524.10	525.42
102.5	149.9	380.53	385.09	388.42	473.8	521.12	524.11	525.43
112.0	160.0	380.81	385.10	388.43	473.9	521.13	524.12	525.44
112.82	160.1	380.89	385.11	388.44	474.00	521.14	524.19	525.50
140.0	160.2	380.9	385.12	388.5	474.01	521.15	524.20	525.51
140.1	160.3	381.00	385.13	388.60	474.02	521.20	524.21	525.52
140.3	160.4	381.01	385.19	388.69	474.10	521.21	524.22	525.53
140.4	160.5	381.02	385.21	388.70	474.11	521.22	524.23	525.54
140.5	160.8	381.03	385.22	388.71	474.12	521.23	524.24	525.60
140.6	160.9	381.04	385.23	388.72	474.2	521.24	524.25	525.61
140.8	161.0	381.05	385.24	388.8	474.8	521.25	524.26	525.62
140.9	161.1	381.06	385.30	388.9	474.9	521.30	524.27	525.63
141.0	161.2	381.10	385.31	389.00	475	521.31	524.28	525.64
141.1	161.3	381.19	385.32	389.01	476.0	521.32	524.29	525.65
141.2	161.8	381.20	385.33	389.02	476.1	521.33	524.30	525.66
141.3	161.9	381.29	385.35	389.03	477.0	521.34	524.31	525.67
141.4	165.0	381.3	385.82	389.04	477.1	521.35	524.32	525.69
141.5	176.2	381.4	385.83	389.05	477.2	521.40	524.33	525.71
141.6	195.0	381.50	385.89	389.06	477.8	521.41	524.34	525.72
141.8	210.0	381.51	385.9	389.08	477.9	521.42	524.35	525.73
141.9	210.1	381.52	386.00	389.10	478.0	521.49	524.36	525.79
142.0	210.2	381.60	386.01	389.11	478.11	521.5	524.37	525.8
142.1	210.3	381.61	386.02	389.12	478.19	521.6	524.39	525.9
142.2	210.4	381.62	386.03	389.13	478.20	521.7	524.4	526.0
142.8	210.5	381.63	386.04	389.14	478.21	521.81	524.50	526.1
142.9	210.6	381.7	386.10	389.15	478.22	521.89	524.51	526.2
143.0	210.7	381.81	386.11	389.16	478.24	521.9	524.52	526.3
143.1	210.8	381.89	386.12	389.17	478.25	522.0	524.53	526.4
143.8	210.9	381.9	386.19	389.18	478.26	522.1	524.54	526.5
143.9	212.0	382.00	386.2	389.20	478.29	522.2	524.55	526.61
144.0	212.1	382.01	386.30	389.21	478.30	522.3	524.56	526.62
144.1	213.1	382.02	386.31	389.22	478.31	522.4	524.57	526.63
144.8	230.0	382.1	386.32	389.7	478.32	522.5	524.59	526.69

MDC 3: Diseases And Disorders Of The Ear, Nose, Mouth And Throat

526.81	528.72	744.22	749.04	750.25	802.1	807.6	873.22	873.75
526.89	528.79	744.23	749.10	750.26	802.20	830.0	873.23	873.79
526.9	528.8	744.24	749.11	750.27	802.21	830.1	873.29	874.00
527.0	528.9	744.29	749.12	750.29	802.22	848.1	873.30	874.01
527.1	529.0	744.3	749.13	780.4	802.23	872.00	873.31	874.10
527.2	529.1	744.41	749.14	780.51	802.24	872.01	873.32	874.11
527.3	529.2	744.42	749.20	780.53	802.25	872.02	873.33	874.4
527.4	529.3	744.43	749.21	780.57	802.26	872.10	873.39	874.5
527.5	529.4	744.46	749.22	784.1	802.27	872.11	873.43	931
527.6	529.5	744.47	749.23	784.40	802.28	872.12	873.44	932
527.7	529.6	744.49	749.24	784.41	802.29	872.61	873.53	933.0
527.8	529.8	744.81	749.25	784.42	802.30	872.62	873.54	933.1
527.9	529.9	744.82	750.0	784.43	802.31	872.63	873.60	935.0
528.00	738.0	744.83	750.10	784.44	802.32	872.64	873.61	947.0
528.01	738.7	744.84	750.11	784.49	802.33	872.69	873.62	951.5
528.02	744.00	744.89	750.12	784.7	802.34	872.71	873.63	993.0
528.09	744.01	748.0	750.13	784.8	802.35	872.72	873.64	993.1
528.1	744.02	748.1	750.15	784.91	802.36	872.73	873.65	994.6
528.2	744.03	748.2	750.16	784.92	802.37	872.74	873.69	
528.3	744.04	748.3	750.19	784.99	802.38	872.79	873.70	
528.4	744.05	749.00	750.21	792.4	802.39	872.8	873.71	
528.5	744.09	749.01	750.22	794.15	802.4	872.9	873.72	
528.6	744.1	749.02	750.23	794.16	802.5	873.20	873.73	
528.71	744.21	749.03	750.24	802.0	807.5	873.21	873.74	

SURGICAL

DRG 129 Major Head and Neck Procedures with CC/MCC or Major Device
GMLOS 3.7   AMLOS 5.4   RW 2.1500   ☑

Operating Room Procedures
20.96	Implantation or replacement of cochlear prosthetic device, not otherwise specified
20.97	Implantation or replacement of cochlear prosthetic device, single channel
20.98	Implantation or replacement of cochlear prosthetic device, multiple channel
25.3	Complete glossectomy
25.4	Radical glossectomy
27.32	Wide excision or destruction of lesion or tissue of bony palate
30.1	Hemilaryngectomy
30.29	Other partial laryngectomy
40.40	Radical neck dissection, not otherwise specified
40.41	Radical neck dissection, unilateral
40.42	Radical neck dissection, bilateral
40.50	Radical excision of lymph nodes, not otherwise specified
40.59	Radical excision of other lymph nodes
76.31	Partial mandibulectomy
76.41	Total mandibulectomy with synchronous reconstruction
76.42	Other total mandibulectomy

DRG 130 Major Head and Neck Procedures without CC/MCC
GMLOS 2.3   AMLOS 2.9   RW 1.2065   ☑

Operating Room Procedures
25.3	Complete glossectomy
25.4	Radical glossectomy
27.32	Wide excision or destruction of lesion or tissue of bony palate
30.1	Hemilaryngectomy
30.29	Other partial laryngectomy
40.40	Radical neck dissection, not otherwise specified
40.41	Radical neck dissection, unilateral
40.42	Radical neck dissection, bilateral
40.50	Radical excision of lymph nodes, not otherwise specified
40.59	Radical excision of other lymph nodes
76.31	Partial mandibulectomy
76.41	Total mandibulectomy with synchronous reconstruction
76.42	Other total mandibulectomy

DRG 131 Cranial/Facial Procedures with CC/MCC
GMLOS 4.2   AMLOS 6.1   RW 2.3443   ☑

Operating Room Procedures
01.23	Reopening of craniotomy site
01.24	Other craniotomy
01.25	Other craniectomy
01.6	Excision of lesion of skull
02.01	Opening of cranial suture
02.02	Elevation of skull fracture fragments
02.03	Formation of cranial bone flap
02.04	Bone graft to skull
02.05	Insertion of skull plate
02.06	Other cranial osteoplasty
02.07	Removal of skull plate
02.99	Other operations on skull, brain, and cerebral meninges
16.01	Orbitotomy with bone flap
16.02	Orbitotomy with insertion of orbital implant
16.09	Other orbitotomy
16.51	Exenteration of orbit with removal of adjacent structures
16.52	Exenteration of orbit with therapeutic removal of orbital bone
16.59	Other exenteration of orbit
16.63	Revision of enucleation socket with graft
16.64	Other revision of enucleation socket
16.89	Other repair of injury of eyeball or orbit
16.92	Excision of lesion of orbit
16.98	Other operations on orbit
21.4	Resection of nose
21.72	Open reduction of nasal fracture
76.01	Sequestrectomy of facial bone
76.19	Other diagnostic procedures on facial bones and joints
76.2	Local excision or destruction of lesion of facial bone
76.39	Partial ostectomy of other facial bone
76.43	Other reconstruction of mandible
76.44	Total ostectomy of other facial bone with synchronous reconstruction
76.45	Other total ostectomy of other facial bone
76.46	Other reconstruction of other facial bone
76.6*	Other facial bone repair and orthognathic surgery
76.70	Reduction of facial fracture, not otherwise specified
76.72	Open reduction of malar and zygomatic fracture
76.74	Open reduction of maxillary fracture
76.76	Open reduction of mandibular fracture
76.77	Open reduction of alveolar fracture
76.79	Other open reduction of facial fracture
76.91	Bone graft to facial bone
76.92	Insertion of synthetic implant in facial bone
76.94	Open reduction of temporomandibular dislocation
76.97	Removal of internal fixation device from facial bone
76.99	Other operations on facial bones and joints

DRG 132 Cranial/Facial Procedures without CC/MCC
GMLOS 2.1   AMLOS 2.7   RW 1.2362   ☑

Select operating room procedures listed under DRG 131

DRG 133 Other Ear, Nose, Mouth and Throat O.R. Procedures with CC/MCC
GMLOS 3.6   AMLOS 5.4   RW 1.7818   ☑

Operating Room Procedures
04.01	Excision of acoustic neuroma
04.02	Division of trigeminal nerve
04.03	Division or crushing of other cranial and peripheral nerves
04.04	Other incision of cranial and peripheral nerves
04.05	Gasserian ganglionectomy
04.06	Other cranial or peripheral ganglionectomy
04.07	Other excision or avulsion of cranial and peripheral nerves
04.12	Open biopsy of cranial or peripheral nerve or ganglion
04.19	Other diagnostic procedures on cranial and peripheral nerves and ganglia
04.41	Decompression of trigeminal nerve root
04.42	Other cranial nerve decompression
04.49	Other peripheral nerve or ganglion decompression or lysis of adhesions
04.71	Hypoglossal-facial anastomosis
04.72	Accessory-facial anastomosis
04.73	Accessory-hypoglossal anastomosis
04.74	Other anastomosis of cranial or peripheral nerve
04.75	Revision of previous repair of cranial and peripheral nerves
04.76	Repair of old traumatic injury of cranial and peripheral nerves
04.92	Implantation or replacement of peripheral neurostimulator lead(s)
04.93	Removal of peripheral neurostimulator lead(s)
04.99	Other operations on cranial and peripheral nerves
05.21	Sphenopalatine ganglionectomy
05.22	Cervical sympathectomy
06.09	Other incision of thyroid field

MDC 3: Diseases And Disorders Of The Ear, Nose, Mouth And Throat—SURGICAL

06.6	Excision of lingual thyroid
06.7	Excision of thyroglossal duct or tract
09.12	Biopsy of lacrimal sac
09.19	Other diagnostic procedures on lacrimal system
09.43	Probing of nasolacrimal duct
09.44	Intubation of nasolacrimal duct
09.81	Dacryocystorhinostomy (DCR)
09.99	Other operations on lacrimal system
16.65	Secondary graft to exenteration cavity
16.66	Other revision of exenteration cavity
18.21	Excision of preauricular sinus
18.3*	Other excision of external ear
18.5	Surgical correction of prominent ear
18.6	Reconstruction of external auditory canal
18.7*	Other plastic repair of external ear
18.9	Other operations on external ear
19*	Reconstructive operations on middle ear
20.01	Myringotomy with insertion of tube
20.23	Incision of middle ear
20.32	Biopsy of middle and inner ear
20.39	Other diagnostic procedures on middle and inner ear
20.5*	Other excision of middle ear
20.6*	Fenestration of inner ear
20.7*	Incision, excision, and destruction of inner ear
20.91	Tympanosympathectomy
20.93	Repair of oval and round windows
20.95	Implantation of electromagnetic hearing device
20.99	Other operations on middle and inner ear
21.04	Control of epistaxis by ligation of ethmoidal arteries
21.05	Control of epistaxis by (transantral) ligation of the maxillary artery
21.06	Control of epistaxis by ligation of the external carotid artery
21.07	Control of epistaxis by excision of nasal mucosa and skin grafting of septum and lateral nasal wall
21.09	Control of epistaxis by other means
21.5	Submucous resection of nasal septum
21.6*	Turbinectomy
21.82	Closure of nasal fistula
21.83	Total nasal reconstruction
21.84	Revision rhinoplasty
21.85	Augmentation rhinoplasty
21.86	Limited rhinoplasty
21.87	Other rhinoplasty
21.88	Other septoplasty
21.89	Other repair and plastic operations on nose
21.99	Other operations on nose
27.54	Repair of cleft lip
27.62	Correction of cleft palate
27.63	Revision of cleft palate repair
27.69	Other plastic repair of palate
28.0	Incision and drainage of tonsil and peritonsillar structures
28.11	Biopsy of tonsils and adenoids
28.19	Other diagnostic procedures on tonsils and adenoids
28.2	Tonsillectomy without adenoidectomy
28.3	Tonsillectomy with adenoidectomy
28.4	Excision of tonsil tag
28.5	Excision of lingual tonsil
28.6	Adenoidectomy without tonsillectomy
28.7	Control of hemorrhage after tonsillectomy and adenoidectomy
28.91	Removal of foreign body from tonsil and adenoid by incision
28.92	Excision of lesion of tonsil and adenoid
28.99	Other operations on tonsils and adenoids
29.0	Pharyngotomy
29.2	Excision of branchial cleft cyst or vestige
29.31	Cricopharyngeal myotomy
29.32	Pharyngeal diverticulectomy
29.33	Pharyngectomy (partial)
29.39	Other excision or destruction of lesion or tissue of pharynx
29.4	Plastic operation on pharynx
29.51	Suture of laceration of pharynx
29.52	Closure of branchial cleft fistula
29.53	Closure of other fistula of pharynx
29.54	Lysis of pharyngeal adhesions
29.59	Other repair of pharynx
29.92	Division of glossopharyngeal nerve
29.99	Other operations on pharynx
30.0*	Excision or destruction of lesion or tissue of larynx
30.21	Epiglottidectomy
30.22	Vocal cordectomy
31.3	Other incision of larynx or trachea
31.45	Open biopsy of larynx or trachea
31.5	Local excision or destruction of lesion or tissue of trachea
31.6*	Repair of larynx
31.71	Suture of laceration of trachea
31.72	Closure of external fistula of trachea
31.73	Closure of other fistula of trachea
31.74	Revision of tracheostomy
31.75	Reconstruction of trachea and construction of artificial larynx
31.79	Other repair and plastic operations on trachea
31.91	Division of laryngeal nerve
31.92	Lysis of adhesions of trachea or larynx
31.98	Other operations on larynx
31.99	Other operations on trachea
34.22	Mediastinoscopy
38.00	Incision of vessel, unspecified site
38.02	Incision of other vessels of head and neck
38.12	Endarterectomy of other vessels of head and neck
38.21	Biopsy of blood vessel
38.32	Resection of other vessels of head and neck with anastomosis
38.42	Resection of other vessels of head and neck with replacement
38.62	Other excision of other vessels of head and neck
38.82	Other surgical occlusion of other vessels of head and neck
39.98	Control of hemorrhage, not otherwise specified
39.99	Other operations on vessels
40.11	Biopsy of lymphatic structure
40.19	Other diagnostic procedures on lymphatic structures
40.21	Excision of deep cervical lymph node
40.23	Excision of axillary lymph node
40.29	Simple excision of other lymphatic structure
40.3	Regional lymph node excision
40.9	Other operations on lymphatic structures
42.01	Incision of esophageal web
42.09	Other incision of esophagus
42.10	Esophagostomy, not otherwise specified
42.11	Cervical esophagostomy
42.12	Exteriorization of esophageal pouch
42.19	Other external fistulization of esophagus
42.21	Operative esophagoscopy by incision
42.25	Open biopsy of esophagus
42.31	Local excision of esophageal diverticulum
42.32	Local excision of other lesion or tissue of esophagus
42.39	Other destruction of lesion or tissue of esophagus
42.40	Esophagectomy, not otherwise specified
42.41	Partial esophagectomy
42.42	Total esophagectomy
42.51	Intrathoracic esophagoesophagostomy
42.52	Intrathoracic esophagogastrostomy
42.53	Intrathoracic esophageal anastomosis with interposition of small bowel
42.54	Other intrathoracic esophagoenterostomy
42.55	Intrathoracic esophageal anastomosis with interposition of colon
42.56	Other intrathoracic esophagocolostomy
42.58	Intrathoracic esophageal anastomosis with other interposition
42.59	Other intrathoracic anastomosis of esophagus

42.61	Antesternal esophagoesophagostomy
42.62	Antesternal esophagogastrostomy
42.63	Antesternal esophageal anastomosis with interposition of small bowel
42.64	Other antesternal esophagoenterostomy
42.65	Antesternal esophageal anastomosis with interposition of colon
42.66	Other antesternal esophagocolostomy
42.68	Other antesternal esophageal anastomosis with interposition
42.69	Other antesternal anastomosis of esophagus
42.7	Esophagomyotomy
42.82	Suture of laceration of esophagus
42.83	Closure of esophagostomy
42.84	Repair of esophageal fistula, not elsewhere classified
42.86	Production of subcutaneous tunnel without esophageal anastomosis
42.87	Other graft of esophagus
42.89	Other repair of esophagus
50.12	Open biopsy of liver
76.09	Other incision of facial bone
76.11	Biopsy of facial bone
76.5	Temporomandibular arthroplasty
77.19	Other incision of other bone, except facial bones, without division
77.30	Other division of bone, unspecified site
77.40	Biopsy of bone, unspecified site
77.49	Biopsy of other bone, except facial bones
77.69	Local excision of lesion or tissue of other bone, except facial bones
77.79	Excision of other bone for graft, except facial bones
77.89	Other partial ostectomy of other bone, except facial bones
77.99	Total ostectomy of other bone, except facial bones
79.29	Open reduction of fracture of other specified bone, except facial bones, without internal fixation
79.39	Open reduction of fracture of other specified bone, except facial bones, with internal fixation
79.69	Debridement of open fracture of other specified bone, except facial bones
83.02	Myotomy
83.39	Excision of lesion of other soft tissue
83.49	Other excision of soft tissue
86.22	Excisional debridement of wound, infection, or burn
86.4	Radical excision of skin lesion
86.63	Full-thickness skin graft to other sites
86.66	Homograft to skin
86.67	Dermal regenerative graft
86.69	Other skin graft to other sites
86.70	Pedicle or flap graft, not otherwise specified
86.71	Cutting and preparation of pedicle grafts or flaps
86.72	Advancement of pedicle graft
86.74	Attachment of pedicle or flap graft to other sites
86.75	Revision of pedicle or flap graft
86.81	Repair for facial weakness
86.82	Facial rhytidectomy
86.84	Relaxation of scar or web contracture of skin
86.87	Fat graft of skin and subcutaneous tissue
86.89	Other repair and reconstruction of skin and subcutaneous tissue
86.91	Excision of skin for graft
86.93	Insertion of tissue expander
92.27	Implantation or insertion of radioactive elements

DRG 134 Other Ear, Nose, Mouth and Throat O.R. Procedures without CC/MCC

GMLOS 1.8   AMLOS 2.2   RW 0.9177   ☑

Select operating room procedures listed under DRG 133

DRG 135 Sinus and Mastoid Procedures with CC/MCC

GMLOS 4.0   AMLOS 5.9   RW 2.0002

Operating Room Procedures

20.21	Incision of mastoid
20.22	Incision of petrous pyramid air cells
20.4*	Mastoidectomy
20.92	Revision of mastoidectomy
22.12	Open biopsy of nasal sinus
22.3*	External maxillary antrotomy
22.4*	Frontal sinusotomy and sinusectomy
22.5*	Other nasal sinusotomy
22.6*	Other nasal sinusectomy
22.7*	Repair of nasal sinus
22.9	Other operations on nasal sinuses

DRG 136 Sinus and Mastoid Procedures without CC/MCC

GMLOS 1.8   AMLOS 2.3   RW 1.0697   ☑

Select operating room procedures listed under DRG 135

DRG 137 Mouth Procedures with CC/MCC

GMLOS 3.8   AMLOS 5.0   RW 1.3192   ☑

Operating Room Procedures

24.2	Gingivoplasty
24.4	Excision of dental lesion of jaw
24.5	Alveoloplasty
25.02	Open biopsy of tongue
25.1	Excision or destruction of lesion or tissue of tongue
25.2	Partial glossectomy
25.59	Other repair and plastic operations on tongue
25.94	Other glossotomy
25.99	Other operations on tongue
27.0	Drainage of face and floor of mouth
27.1	Incision of palate
27.21	Biopsy of bony palate
27.22	Biopsy of uvula and soft palate
27.31	Local excision or destruction of lesion or tissue of bony palate
27.42	Wide excision of lesion of lip
27.43	Other excision of lesion or tissue of lip
27.49	Other excision of mouth
27.53	Closure of fistula of mouth
27.55	Full-thickness skin graft to lip and mouth
27.56	Other skin graft to lip and mouth
27.57	Attachment of pedicle or flap graft to lip and mouth
27.59	Other plastic repair of mouth
27.61	Suture of laceration of palate
27.7*	Operations on uvula
27.92	Incision of mouth, unspecified structure
27.99	Other operations on oral cavity

DRG 138 Mouth Procedures without CC/MCC

GMLOS 1.9   AMLOS 2.3   RW 0.7388   ☑

Select operating room procedures listed under DRG 137

DRG 139 Salivary Gland Procedures

GMLOS 1.4   AMLOS 1.8   RW 0.8922   ☑

Operating Room Procedures

26.12	Open biopsy of salivary gland or duct
26.2*	Excision of lesion of salivary gland
26.3*	Sialoadenectomy
26.4*	Repair of salivary gland or duct
26.99	Other operations on salivary gland or duct

| *Surgical* | *Medical* | *CC Indicator* | *MCC Indicator* | *Procedure Proxy* |

MEDICAL

DRG 146　Ear, Nose, Mouth and Throat Malignancy with MCC
GMLOS 6.3　　　AMLOS 9.1　　　RW 2.2347　　☑

Principal Diagnosis
140*	Malignant neoplasm of lip
141*	Malignant neoplasm of tongue
142*	Malignant neoplasm of major salivary glands
143*	Malignant neoplasm of gum
144*	Malignant neoplasm of floor of mouth
145*	Malignant neoplasm of other and unspecified parts of mouth
146*	Malignant neoplasm of oropharynx
147*	Malignant neoplasm of nasopharynx
148*	Malignant neoplasm of hypopharynx
149*	Malignant neoplasm of other and ill-defined sites within the lip, oral cavity, and pharynx
160*	Malignant neoplasm of nasal cavities, middle ear, and accessory sinuses
161*	Malignant neoplasm of larynx
165.0	Malignant neoplasm of upper respiratory tract, part unspecified
176.2	Kaposi's sarcoma of palate
195.0	Malignant neoplasm of head, face, and neck
230.0	Carcinoma in situ of lip, oral cavity, and pharynx
231.0	Carcinoma in situ of larynx
235.0	Neoplasm of uncertain behavior of major salivary glands
235.1	Neoplasm of uncertain behavior of lip, oral cavity, and pharynx
235.6	Neoplasm of uncertain behavior of larynx

DRG 147　Ear, Nose, Mouth and Throat Malignancy with CC
GMLOS 3.9　　　AMLOS 5.4　　　RW 1.2486　　☑

Select principal diagnosis listed under DRG 146

DRG 148　Ear, Nose, Mouth and Throat Malignancy without CC/MCC
GMLOS 2.4　　　AMLOS 3.2　　　RW 0.7488　　☑

Select principal diagnosis listed under DRG 146

DRG 149　Dysequilibrium
GMLOS 2.1　　　AMLOS 2.5　　　RW 0.6462　　☑

Principal Diagnosis
386.0*	Meniere's disease
386.1*	Other and unspecified peripheral vertigo
386.2	Vertigo of central origin
386.3*	Labyrinthitis
386.5*	Labyrinthine dysfunction
386.8	Other disorders of labyrinth
386.9	Unspecified vertiginous syndromes and labyrinthine disorders
780.4	Dizziness and giddiness
994.6	Motion sickness

DRG 150　Epistaxis with MCC
GMLOS 3.8　　　AMLOS 5.2　　　RW 1.3890　　☑

Principal Diagnosis
784.7	Epistaxis

DRG 151　Epistaxis without MCC
GMLOS 2.2　　　AMLOS 2.8　　　RW 0.6458　　☑

Select principal diagnosis listed under DRG 150

DRG 152　Otitis Media and Upper Respiratory Infection with MCC
GMLOS 3.4　　　AMLOS 4.4　　　RW 1.0166　　☑

Principal Diagnosis
034.0	Streptococcal sore throat
055.2	Postmeasles otitis media
074.0	Herpangina
098.6	Gonococcal infection of pharynx
099.51	Chlamydia trachomatis infection of pharynx
101	Vincent's angina
380.00	Unspecified perichondritis of pinna
381.0*	Acute nonsuppurative otitis media
381.1*	Chronic serous otitis media
381.2*	Chronic mucoid otitis media
381.3	Other and unspecified chronic nonsuppurative otitis media
381.4	Nonsuppurative otitis media, not specified as acute or chronic
381.5*	Eustachian salpingitis
382*	Suppurative and unspecified otitis media
383.0*	Acute mastoiditis
383.1	Chronic mastoiditis
383.2*	Petrositis
383.9	Unspecified mastoiditis
384.0*	Acute myringitis without mention of otitis media
384.1	Chronic myringitis without mention of otitis media
460	Acute nasopharyngitis (common cold)
461*	Acute sinusitis
462	Acute pharyngitis
463	Acute tonsillitis
464.00	Acute laryngitis, without mention of obstruction
464.01	Acute laryngitis, with obstruction
464.2*	Acute laryngotracheitis
464.3*	Acute epiglottitis
464.4	Croup
464.50	Unspecified supraglottis, without mention of obstruction
464.51	Unspecified supraglottis, with obstruction
465*	Acute upper respiratory infections of multiple or unspecified sites
472*	Chronic pharyngitis and nasopharyngitis
473*	Chronic sinusitis
474.00	Chronic tonsillitis
474.01	Chronic adenoiditis
474.02	Chronic tonsillitis and adenoiditis
475	Peritonsillar abscess
476*	Chronic laryngitis and laryngotracheitis
477*	Allergic rhinitis
478.21	Cellulitis of pharynx or nasopharynx
478.22	Parapharyngeal abscess
478.24	Retropharyngeal abscess
478.71	Cellulitis and perichondritis of larynx
478.8	Upper respiratory tract hypersensitivity reaction, site unspecified
478.9	Other and unspecified diseases of upper respiratory tract
487.1	Influenza with other respiratory manifestations
993.0	Barotrauma, otitic
993.1	Barotrauma, sinus

DRG 153　Otitis Media and Upper Respiratory Infection without MCC
GMLOS 2.5　　　AMLOS 3.1　　　RW 0.6605　　☑

Select principal diagnosis listed under DRG 152

DRG 154　Other Ear, Nose, Mouth and Throat Diagnoses with MCC
GMLOS 4.3　　　AMLOS 5.7　　　RW 1.4138　　☑

Principal Diagnosis
012.3*	Tuberculous laryngitis
015.6*	Tuberculosis of mastoid
017.4*	Tuberculosis of ear
032.0	Faucial diphtheria

Ⓣ *Transfer DRG*　　ⓈⓅ *Special Payment*　　☑ *Optimization Potential*　　▽ *Targeted Potential*　　* *Code Range*　　● *New DRG*　　▲ *Revised DRG Title*

032.1	Nasopharyngeal diphtheria
032.2	Anterior nasal diphtheria
032.3	Laryngeal diphtheria
053.71	Otitis externa due to herpes zoster
054.73	Herpes simplex otitis externa
094.86	Syphilitic acoustic neuritis
102.5	Gangosa due to yaws
112.82	Candidal otitis externa
210.2	Benign neoplasm of major salivary glands
210.5	Benign neoplasm of tonsil
210.6	Benign neoplasm of other parts of oropharynx
210.7	Benign neoplasm of nasopharynx
210.8	Benign neoplasm of hypopharynx
210.9	Benign neoplasm of pharynx, unspecified
212.0	Benign neoplasm of nasal cavities, middle ear, and accessory sinuses
212.1	Benign neoplasm of larynx
327.20	Organic sleep apnea, unspecified
327.23	Obstructive sleep apnea (adult) (pediatric)
327.24	Idiopathic sleep related nonobstructive alveolar hypoventilation
327.26	Sleep related hypoventilation/hypoxemia in conditions classifiable elsewhere
327.29	Other organic sleep apnea
327.40	Organic parasomnia, unspecified
327.42	REM sleep behavior disorder
327.44	Parasomnia in conditions classified elsewhere
327.49	Other organic parasomnia
327.53	Sleep related bruxism
327.59	Other organic sleep related movement disorders
327.8	Other organic sleep disorders
380.1*	Infective otitis externa
380.2*	Other otitis externa
380.3*	Noninfectious disorders of pinna
380.4	Impacted cerumen
380.5*	Acquired stenosis of external ear canal
380.8*	Other disorders of external ear
380.9	Unspecified disorder of external ear
381.6*	Obstruction of Eustachian tube
381.7	Patulous Eustachian tube
381.8*	Other disorders of Eustachian tube
381.9	Unspecified Eustachian tube disorder
383.3*	Complications following mastoidectomy
383.8*	Other disorders of mastoid
384.2*	Perforation of tympanic membrane
384.8*	Other specified disorders of tympanic membrane
384.9	Unspecified disorder of tympanic membrane
385*	Other disorders of middle ear and mastoid
386.4*	Labyrinthine fistula
387*	Otosclerosis
388.0*	Degenerative and vascular disorders of ear
388.1*	Noise effects on inner ear
388.2	Unspecified sudden hearing loss
388.3*	Tinnitus
388.40	Unspecified abnormal auditory perception
388.41	Diplacusis
388.42	Hyperacusis
388.43	Impairment of auditory discrimination
388.44	Other abnormal auditory perception, recruitment
388.5	Disorders of acoustic nerve
388.60	Unspecified otorrhea
388.69	Other otorrhea
388.7*	Otalgia
388.8	Other disorders of ear
388.9	Unspecified disorder of ear
389*	Hearing loss
470	Deviated nasal septum
471*	Nasal polyps
474.1*	Hypertrophy of tonsils and adenoids
474.2	Adenoid vegetations
474.8	Other chronic disease of tonsils and adenoids
474.9	Unspecified chronic disease of tonsils and adenoids
478.0	Hypertrophy of nasal turbinates
478.1*	Other diseases of nasal cavity and sinuses
478.20	Unspecified disease of pharynx
478.25	Edema of pharynx or nasopharynx
478.26	Cyst of pharynx or nasopharynx
478.29	Other disease of pharynx or nasopharynx
478.3*	Paralysis of vocal cords or larynx
478.4	Polyp of vocal cord or larynx
478.5	Other diseases of vocal cords
478.6	Edema of larynx
478.70	Unspecified disease of larynx
478.74	Stenosis of larynx
478.75	Laryngeal spasm
478.79	Other diseases of larynx
527*	Diseases of the salivary glands
738.0	Acquired deformity of nose
738.7	Cauliflower ear
744.0*	Congenital anomalies of ear causing impairment of hearing
744.1	Congenital anomalies of accessory auricle
744.2*	Other specified congenital anomalies of ear
744.3	Unspecified congenital anomaly of ear
744.4*	Congenital branchial cleft cyst or fistula; preauricular sinus
744.89	Other specified congenital anomaly of face and neck
748.0	Congenital choanal atresia
748.1	Other congenital anomaly of nose
748.2	Congenital web of larynx
748.3	Other congenital anomaly of larynx, trachea, and bronchus
750.21	Congenital absence of salivary gland
750.22	Congenital accessory salivary gland
750.23	Congenital atresia, salivary duct
750.24	Congenital fistula of salivary gland
750.27	Congenital diverticulum of pharynx
750.29	Other specified congenital anomaly of pharynx
780.51	Insomnia with sleep apnea, unspecified
780.53	Hypersomnia with sleep apnea, unspecified
780.57	Unspecified sleep apnea
784.1	Throat pain
784.4*	Voice and resonance disorders
784.8	Hemorrhage from throat
784.91	Postnasal drip
784.99	Other symptoms involving head and neck
792.4	Nonspecific abnormal finding in saliva
794.15	Nonspecific abnormal auditory function studies
794.16	Nonspecific abnormal vestibular function studies
802.0	Nasal bones, closed fracture
802.1	Nasal bones, open fracture
807.5	Closed fracture of larynx and trachea
807.6	Open fracture of larynx and trachea
872*	Open wound of ear
873.20	Open wound of nose, unspecified site, without mention of complication
873.21	Open wound of nasal septum, without mention of complication
873.22	Open wound of nasal cavity, without mention of complication
873.23	Open wound of nasal sinus, without mention of complication
873.29	Open wound of nose, multiple sites, without mention of complication
873.3*	Open wound of nose, complicated
874.00	Open wound of larynx with trachea, without mention of complication
874.01	Open wound of larynx, without mention of complication
874.10	Open wound of larynx with trachea, complicated
874.11	Open wound of larynx, complicated
874.4	Open wound of pharynx, without mention of complication
874.5	Open wound of pharynx, complicated
931	Foreign body in ear

Surgical   **Medical**   CC Indicator   MCC Indicator   Procedure Proxy

932	Foreign body in nose
933*	Foreign body in pharynx and larynx
947.0	Burn of mouth and pharynx
951.5	Injury to acoustic nerve

DRG 155   Other Ear, Nose, Mouth and Throat Diagnoses with CC
GMLOS 3.2   AMLOS 4.1   RW 0.9137   ☑

Select principal diagnosis listed under DRG 154

DRG 156   Other Ear, Nose, Mouth and Throat Diagnoses without CC/MCC
GMLOS 2.3   AMLOS 2.8   RW 0.6349   ☑

Select principal diagnosis listed under DRG 154

DRG 157   Dental and Oral Diseases with MCC
GMLOS 4.7   AMLOS 6.6   RW 1.6010   ☑

Principal Diagnosis

054.2	Herpetic gingivostomatitis
112.0	Candidiasis of mouth
210.0	Benign neoplasm of lip
210.1	Benign neoplasm of tongue
210.3	Benign neoplasm of floor of mouth
210.4	Benign neoplasm of other and unspecified parts of mouth
213.1	Benign neoplasm of lower jaw bone
520*	Disorders of tooth development and eruption
521*	Diseases of hard tissues of teeth
522*	Diseases of pulp and periapical tissues
523*	Gingival and periodontal diseases
524*	Dentofacial anomalies, including malocclusion
525*	Other diseases and conditions of the teeth and supporting structures
526*	Diseases of the jaws
528*	Diseases of the oral soft tissues, excluding lesions specific for gingiva and tongue
529*	Diseases and other conditions of the tongue
744.81	Macrocheilia
744.82	Microcheilia
744.83	Macrostomia
744.84	Microstomia
749*	Cleft palate and cleft lip
750.0	Tongue tie
750.1*	Other congenital anomalies of tongue
750.25	Congenital fistula of lip
750.26	Other specified congenital anomalies of mouth
784.92	Jaw pain
802.2*	Mandible, closed fracture
802.3*	Mandible, open fracture
802.4	Malar and maxillary bones, closed fracture
802.5	Malar and maxillary bones, open fracture
830*	Dislocation of jaw
848.1	Sprain and strain of jaw
873.43	Open wound of lip, without mention of complication
873.44	Open wound of jaw, without mention of complication
873.53	Open wound of lip, complicated
873.54	Open wound of jaw, complicated
873.6*	Open wound of internal structures of mouth, without mention of complication
873.7*	Open wound of internal structure of mouth, complicated
935.0	Foreign body in mouth

DRG 158   Dental and Oral Diseases with CC
GMLOS 3.2   AMLOS 4.1   RW 0.8988   ☑

Select principal diagnosis listed under DRG 157

DRG 159   Dental and Oral Diseases without CC/MCC
GMLOS 2.1   AMLOS 2.6   RW 0.5969   ☑

Select principal diagnosis listed under DRG 157

Ⓣ Transfer DRG   ⓢⓟ Special Payment   ☑ Optimization Potential   ▽ Targeted Potential   * Code Range   ● New DRG   ▲ Revised DRG Title

48   Valid 10/01/2012-09/30/2013   © 2012 OptumInsight, Inc.

MDC 4
Diseases And Disorders Of The Respiratory System

003.22	011.34	012.13	163.1	482.1	493.90	516.0	748.60	807.16
006.4	011.35	012.14	163.8	482.2	493.91	516.1	748.61	807.17
010.00	011.36	012.15	163.9	482.30	493.92	516.2	748.69	807.18
010.01	011.40	012.16	164.2	482.31	494.0	516.30	748.8	807.19
010.02	011.41	012.20	164.3	482.32	494.1	516.31	748.9	807.2
010.03	011.42	012.21	164.8	482.39	495.0	516.32	754.81	807.3
010.04	011.43	012.22	164.9	482.40	495.1	516.33	754.82	807.4
010.05	011.44	012.23	165.8	482.41	495.2	516.34	756.3	839.61
010.06	011.45	012.24	165.9	482.42	495.3	516.35	756.6	839.71
010.10	011.46	012.25	176.4	482.49	495.4	516.36	770.7	848.3
010.11	011.50	012.26	195.1	482.81	495.5	516.37	781.5	848.40
010.12	011.51	012.80	197.0	482.82	495.6	516.4	786.00	848.41
010.13	011.52	012.81	197.1	482.83	495.7	516.5	786.01	848.42
010.14	011.53	012.82	197.2	482.84	495.8	516.61	786.02	848.49
010.15	011.54	012.83	197.3	482.89	495.9	516.62	786.03	860.0
010.16	011.55	012.84	209.21	482.9	496	516.63	786.04	860.1
010.80	011.56	012.85	209.61	483.0	500	516.64	786.05	860.2
010.81	011.60	012.86	212.2	483.1	501	516.69	786.06	860.3
010.82	011.61	020.3	212.3	483.8	502	516.8	786.07	860.4
010.83	011.62	020.4	212.4	484.1	503	516.9	786.09	860.5
010.84	011.63	020.5	212.5	484.3	504	517.1	786.1	861.20
010.85	011.64	021.2	212.8	484.5	505	517.2	786.2	861.21
010.86	011.65	022.1	212.9	484.6	506.0	517.3	786.30	861.22
010.90	011.66	031.0	213.3	484.7	506.1	517.8	786.31	861.30
010.91	011.70	033.0	214.2	484.8	506.2	518.0	786.39	861.31
010.92	011.71	033.1	231.1	485	506.3	518.1	786.4	861.32
010.93	011.72	033.8	231.2	486	506.4	518.2	786.52	862.0
010.94	011.73	033.9	231.8	487.0	506.9	518.3	786.6	862.1
010.95	011.74	039.1	231.9	488.01	507.0	518.4	786.7	862.21
010.96	011.75	052.1	235.7	488.02	507.1	518.51	786.8	862.29
011.00	011.76	055.1	235.8	488.11	507.8	518.52	786.9	862.31
011.01	011.80	073.0	235.9	488.12	508.0	518.53	793.11	862.39
011.02	011.81	074.1	239.1	488.81	508.1	518.6	793.19	874.02
011.03	011.82	095.1	277.02	488.82	508.2	518.7	794.2	874.12
011.04	011.83	112.4	278.03	490	508.8	518.81	795.51	908.0
011.05	011.84	114.0	306.1	491.0	508.9	518.82	795.52	934.0
011.06	011.85	114.4	327.22	491.1	510.0	518.83	799.01	934.1
011.10	011.86	114.5	415.11	491.20	510.9	518.84	799.02	934.8
011.11	011.90	115.05	415.12	491.21	511.0	518.89	799.1	934.9
011.12	011.91	115.15	415.13	491.22	511.1	519.00	807.00	947.1
011.13	011.92	115.95	415.19	491.8	511.81	519.01	807.01	958.0
011.14	011.93	121.2	416.2	491.9	511.89	519.02	807.02	958.1
011.15	011.94	122.1	464.10	492.0	511.9	519.09	807.03	958.7
011.16	011.95	130.4	464.11	492.8	512.0	519.11	807.04	996.84
011.20	011.96	135	466.0	493.00	512.1	519.19	807.05	997.31
011.21	012.00	136.3	466.11	493.01	512.2	519.2	807.06	997.32
011.22	012.01	137.0	466.19	493.02	512.81	519.3	807.07	997.39
011.23	012.02	162.0	480.0	493.10	512.82	519.4	807.08	999.1
011.24	012.03	162.2	480.1	493.11	512.83	519.8	807.09	V42.6
011.25	012.04	162.3	480.2	493.12	512.84	519.9	807.10	V45.76
011.26	012.05	162.4	480.3	493.20	512.89	573.5	807.11	V55.0
011.30	012.06	162.5	480.8	493.21	513.0	714.81	807.12	V71.2
011.31	012.10	162.8	480.9	493.22	513.1	733.6	807.13	
011.32	012.11	162.9	481	493.81	514	748.4	807.14	
011.33	012.12	163.0	482.0	493.82	515	748.5	807.15	

SURGICAL

53.7*	Repair of diaphragmatic hernia, abdominal approach
53.8*	Repair of diaphragmatic hernia, thoracic approach

DRG 163   Major Chest Procedures with MCC
GMLOS 11.3   AMLOS 13.7   RW 5.1193   T ☑

Operating Room Procedures

07.16	Biopsy of thymus
07.8*	Thymectomy
07.9*	Other operations on thymus
17.69	Laser interstitial thermal therapy [LITT] of lesion or tissue of other and unspecified site under guidance
31.73	Closure of other fistula of trachea
31.75	Reconstruction of trachea and construction of artificial larynx
31.79	Other repair and plastic operations on trachea
32.09	Other local excision or destruction of lesion or tissue of bronchus
32.1	Other excision of bronchus
32.20	Thoracoscopic excision of lesion or tissue of lung
32.21	Plication of emphysematous bleb
32.22	Lung volume reduction surgery
32.23	Open ablation of lung lesion or tissue
32.25	Thoracoscopic ablation of lung lesion or tissue
32.26	Other and unspecified ablation of lung lesion or tissue
32.27	Bronchoscopic bronchial thermoplasty, ablation of airway smooth muscle
32.29	Other local excision or destruction of lesion or tissue of lung
32.3*	Segmental resection of lung
32.4*	Lobectomy of lung
32.5*	Pneumonectomy
32.6	Radical dissection of thoracic structures
32.9	Other excision of lung
33.0	Incision of bronchus
33.1	Incision of lung
33.25	Open biopsy of bronchus
33.28	Open biopsy of lung
33.34	Thoracoplasty
33.39	Other surgical collapse of lung
33.4*	Repair and plastic operation on lung and bronchus
33.92	Ligation of bronchus
33.98	Other operations on bronchus
33.99	Other operations on lung
34.02	Exploratory thoracotomy
34.03	Reopening of recent thoracotomy site
34.27	Biopsy of diaphragm
34.3	Excision or destruction of lesion or tissue of mediastinum
34.5*	Pleurectomy
34.6	Scarification of pleura
34.73	Closure of other fistula of thorax
34.74	Repair of pectus deformity
34.8*	Operations on diaphragm
34.93	Repair of pleura
37.12	Pericardiotomy
37.24	Biopsy of pericardium
37.31	Pericardiectomy
37.91	Open chest cardiac massage
38.05	Incision of other thoracic vessels
38.15	Endarterectomy of other thoracic vessels
38.35	Resection of other thoracic vessels with anastomosis
38.45	Resection of other thoracic vessels with replacement
38.55	Ligation and stripping of varicose veins of other thoracic vessel
38.65	Other excision of other thoracic vessel
38.85	Other surgical occlusion of other thoracic vessel
39.54	Re-entry operation (aorta)
39.98	Control of hemorrhage, not otherwise specified
40.22	Excision of internal mammary lymph node
40.52	Radical excision of periaortic lymph nodes
40.6*	Operations on thoracic duct

DRG 164   Major Chest Procedures with CC
GMLOS 5.8   AMLOS 7.0   RW 2.6191   T ☑

Select operating room procedures listed under DRG 163

DRG 165   Major Chest Procedures without CC/MCC
GMLOS 3.5   AMLOS 4.1   RW 1.7922   T ☑

Select operating room procedures listed under DRG 163

DRG 166   Other Respiratory System O.R. Procedures with MCC
GMLOS 9.1   AMLOS 11.5   RW 3.7513   T ☑

Operating Room Procedures

17.56	Atherectomy of other non-coronary vessel(s)
30.01	Marsupialization of laryngeal cyst
30.09	Other excision or destruction of lesion or tissue of larynx
30.1	Hemilaryngectomy
30.2*	Other partial laryngectomy
31.3	Other incision of larynx or trachea
31.45	Open biopsy of larynx or trachea
31.5	Local excision or destruction of lesion or tissue of trachea
31.6*	Repair of larynx
31.71	Suture of laceration of trachea
31.72	Closure of external fistula of trachea
31.74	Revision of tracheostomy
31.91	Division of laryngeal nerve
31.92	Lysis of adhesions of trachea or larynx
31.98	Other operations on larynx
31.99	Other operations on trachea
32.24	Percutaneous ablation of lung lesion or tissue
33.20	Thoracoscopic lung biopsy
33.27	Closed endoscopic biopsy of lung
33.29	Other diagnostic procedures on lung or bronchus
33.93	Puncture of lung
34.06	Thoracoscopic drainage of pleural cavity
34.1	Incision of mediastinum
34.20	Thoracoscopic pleural biopsy
34.21	Transpleural thoracoscopy
34.22	Mediastinoscopy
34.26	Open biopsy of mediastinum
34.28	Other diagnostic procedures on chest wall, pleura, and diaphragm
34.29	Other diagnostic procedures on mediastinum
34.4	Excision or destruction of lesion of chest wall
34.79	Other repair of chest wall
34.99	Other operations on thorax
38.21	Biopsy of blood vessel
38.7	Interruption of the vena cava
39.29	Other (peripheral) vascular shunt or bypass
39.31	Suture of artery
39.50	Angioplasty of other non-coronary vessel(s)
39.99	Other operations on vessels
40.11	Biopsy of lymphatic structure
40.19	Other diagnostic procedures on lymphatic structures
40.21	Excision of deep cervical lymph node
40.23	Excision of axillary lymph node
40.24	Excision of inguinal lymph node
40.29	Simple excision of other lymphatic structure
40.3	Regional lymph node excision
40.4*	Radical excision of cervical lymph nodes
40.50	Radical excision of lymph nodes, not otherwise specified
40.59	Radical excision of other lymph nodes
50.12	Open biopsy of liver
54.11	Exploratory laparotomy
77.01	Sequestrectomy of scapula, clavicle, and thorax (ribs and sternum)

T Transfer DRG   SP Special Payment   ☑ Optimization Potential   Targeted Potential   * Code Range   ● New DRG   ▲ Revised DRG Title

50   Valid 10/01/2012-09/30/2013   © 2012 OptumInsight, Inc.

MDC 4: Diseases And Disorders Of The Respiratory System—SURGICAL

77.11   Other incision of scapula, clavicle, and thorax (ribs and sternum) without division

77.21   Wedge osteotomy of scapula, clavicle, and thorax (ribs and sternum)

77.31   Other division of scapula, clavicle, and thorax (ribs and sternum)

77.41   Biopsy of scapula, clavicle, and thorax (ribs and sternum)

77.49   Biopsy of other bone, except facial bones

77.61   Local excision of lesion or tissue of scapula, clavicle, and thorax (ribs and sternum)

77.71   Excision of scapula, clavicle, and thorax (ribs and sternum) for graft

77.81   Other partial ostectomy of scapula, clavicle, and thorax (ribs and sternum)

77.91   Total ostectomy of scapula, clavicle, and thorax (ribs and sternum)

78.01   Bone graft of scapula, clavicle, and thorax (ribs and sternum)

78.11   Application of external fixator device, scapula, clavicle, and thorax [ribs and sternum]

78.41   Other repair or plastic operations on scapula, clavicle, and thorax (ribs and sternum)

78.51   Internal fixation of scapula, clavicle, and thorax (ribs and sternum) without fracture reduction

78.61   Removal of implanted device from scapula, clavicle, and thorax (ribs and sternum)

78.71   Osteoclasis of scapula, clavicle, and thorax (ribs and sternum)

78.81   Diagnostic procedures on scapula, clavicle, and thorax (ribs and sternum) not elsewhere classified

78.91   Insertion of bone growth stimulator into scapula, clavicle and thorax (ribs and sternum)

83.21   Open biopsy of soft tissue

84.94   Insertion of sternal fixation device with rigid plates

86.06   Insertion of totally implantable infusion pump

86.22   Excisional debridement of wound, infection, or burn

86.69   Other skin graft to other sites

92.27   Implantation or insertion of radioactive elements

DRG 167   Other Respiratory System O.R. Procedures with CC
GMLOS 5.4   AMLOS 6.8   RW 2.0043   T ☑

Select operating room procedures listed under DRG 166

DRG 168   Other Respiratory System O.R. Procedures without CC/MCC
GMLOS 3.1   AMLOS 4.1   RW 1.3153   T ☑

Select operating room procedures listed under DRG 166

MEDICAL

DRG 175   Pulmonary Embolism with MCC
GMLOS 5.5   AMLOS 6.6   RW 1.5870   T ☑

Principal Diagnosis

415.1*   Pulmonary embolism and infarction

416.2   Chronic pulmonary embolism

958.0   Air embolism as an early complication of trauma

958.1   Fat embolism as an early complication of trauma

999.1   Air embolism as complication of medical care, not elsewhere classified

DRG 176   Pulmonary Embolism without MCC
GMLOS 3.9   AMLOS 4.6   RW 1.0379   T ☑

Select principal diagnosis listed under DRG 175

DRG 177   Respiratory Infections and Inflammations with MCC
GMLOS 6.6   AMLOS 8.2   RW 2.0549   T ☑ ᵀᴿᴬ

Principal Diagnosis

003.22   Salmonella pneumonia

006.4   Amebic lung abscess

010*   Primary tuberculous infection

011*   Pulmonary tuberculosis

012.0*   Tuberculous pleurisy

012.1*   Tuberculosis of intrathoracic lymph nodes

012.2*   Isolated tracheal or bronchial tuberculosis

012.8*   Other specified respiratory tuberculosis

020.3   Primary pneumonic plague

020.4   Secondary pneumonic plague

020.5   Pneumonic plague, unspecified

021.2   Pulmonary tularemia

022.1   Pulmonary anthrax

031.0   Pulmonary diseases due to other mycobacteria

039.1   Pulmonary actinomycotic infection

052.1   Varicella (hemorrhagic) pneumonitis

055.1   Postmeasles pneumonia

073.0   Ornithosis with pneumonia

095.1   Syphilis of lung

112.4   Candidiasis of lung

114.0   Primary coccidioidomycosis (pulmonary)

114.4   Chronic pulmonary coccidioidomycosis

114.5   Unspecified pulmonary coccidioidomycosis

115.05   Histoplasma capsulatum pneumonia

115.15   Histoplasma duboisii pneumonia

115.95   Unspecified Histoplasmosis pneumonia

121.2   Paragonimiasis

122.1   Echinococcus granulosus infection of lung

130.4   Pneumonitis due to toxoplasmosis

136.3   Pneumocystosis

277.02   Cystic fibrosis with pulmonary manifestations

482.0   Pneumonia due to Klebsiella pneumoniae

482.1   Pneumonia due to Pseudomonas

482.4*   Pneumonia due to Staphylococcus

482.8*   Pneumonia due to other specified bacteria

484*   Pneumonia in infectious diseases classified elsewhere

507*   Pneumonitis due to solids and liquids

510*   Empyema

511.1   Pleurisy with effusion, with mention of bacterial cause other than tuberculosis

513*   Abscess of lung and mediastinum

519.2   Mediastinitis

795.5*   Nonspecific reaction to test for tuberculosis

V71.2   Observation for suspected tuberculosis

OR

Principal Diagnosis

487.0   Influenza with pneumonia

AND

Secondary Diagnosis

482.0   Pneumonia due to Klebsiella pneumoniae

482.1   Pneumonia due to Pseudomonas

482.40   Pneumonia due to Staphylococcus, unspecified

482.41   Methicillin susceptible pneumonia due to Staphylococcus aureus

482.42   Methicillin resistant pneumonia due to Staphylococcus aureus

482.49   Other Staphylococcus pneumonia

482.81   Pneumonia due to anaerobes

482.82   Pneumonia due to Escherichia coli (E. coli)

482.83   Pneumonia due to other gram-negative bacteria

482.84   Legionnaires' disease

482.89   Pneumonia due to other specified bacteria

DRG 178 Respiratory Infections and Inflammations with CC

GMLOS 5.3 AMLOS 6.4 RW 1.4403 T ☑ ▽

Select principal diagnosis listed under DRG 177

DRG 179 Respiratory Infections and Inflammations without CC/MCC

GMLOS 3.8 AMLOS 4.6 RW 0.9799 T ☑ ▽

Select principal diagnosis listed under DRG 177

DRG 180 Respiratory Neoplasms with MCC

GMLOS 5.6 AMLOS 7.3 RW 1.7567 ☑

Principal Diagnosis

162*	Malignant neoplasm of trachea, bronchus, and lung
163*	Malignant neoplasm of pleura
164.2	Malignant neoplasm of anterior mediastinum
164.3	Malignant neoplasm of posterior mediastinum
164.8	Malignant neoplasm of other parts of mediastinum
164.9	Malignant neoplasm of mediastinum, part unspecified
165.8	Malignant neoplasm of other sites within the respiratory system and intrathoracic organs
165.9	Malignant neoplasm of ill-defined sites within the respiratory system
176.4	Kaposi's sarcoma of lung
195.1	Malignant neoplasm of thorax
197.0	Secondary malignant neoplasm of lung
197.1	Secondary malignant neoplasm of mediastinum
197.2	Secondary malignant neoplasm of pleura
197.3	Secondary malignant neoplasm of other respiratory organs
209.21	Malignant carcinoid tumor of the bronchus and lung
209.61	Benign carcinoid tumor of the bronchus and lung
212.2	Benign neoplasm of trachea
212.3	Benign neoplasm of bronchus and lung
212.4	Benign neoplasm of pleura
212.5	Benign neoplasm of mediastinum
212.8	Benign neoplasm of other specified sites of respiratory and intrathoracic organs
212.9	Benign neoplasm of respiratory and intrathoracic organs, site unspecified
213.3	Benign neoplasm of ribs, sternum, and clavicle
214.2	Lipoma of intrathoracic organs
231.1	Carcinoma in situ of trachea
231.2	Carcinoma in situ of bronchus and lung
231.8	Carcinoma in situ of other specified parts of respiratory system
231.9	Carcinoma in situ of respiratory system, part unspecified
235.7	Neoplasm of uncertain behavior of trachea, bronchus, and lung
235.8	Neoplasm of uncertain behavior of pleura, thymus, and mediastinum
235.9	Neoplasm of uncertain behavior of other and unspecified respiratory organs
239.1	Neoplasm of unspecified nature of respiratory system
511.81	Malignant pleural effusion

DRG 181 Respiratory Neoplasms with CC

GMLOS 3.9 AMLOS 5.1 RW 1.2108 ☑

Select principal diagnosis listed under DRG 180

DRG 182 Respiratory Neoplasms without CC/MCC

GMLOS 2.7 AMLOS 3.4 RW 0.8275 ☑

Select principal diagnosis listed under DRG 180

DRG 183 Major Chest Trauma with MCC

GMLOS 5.0 AMLOS 6.2 RW 1.4804 ☑

Principal Diagnosis

807.03	Closed fracture of three ribs
807.04	Closed fracture of four ribs
807.05	Closed fracture of five ribs
807.06	Closed fracture of six ribs
807.07	Closed fracture of seven ribs
807.08	Closed fracture of eight or more ribs
807.09	Closed fracture of multiple ribs, unspecified
807.1*	Open fracture of rib(s)
807.2	Closed fracture of sternum
807.3	Open fracture of sternum
807.4	Flail chest
839.61	Closed dislocation, sternum
839.71	Open dislocation, sternum
861.22	Lung laceration without mention of open wound into thorax
861.32	Lung laceration with open wound into thorax
862.0	Diaphragm injury without mention of open wound into cavity
862.1	Diaphragm injury with open wound into cavity
862.21	Bronchus injury without mention of open wound into cavity
862.31	Bronchus injury with open wound into cavity
874.02	Open wound of trachea, without mention of complication
874.12	Open wound of trachea, complicated

DRG 184 Major Chest Trauma with CC

GMLOS 3.5 AMLOS 4.2 RW 1.0171 ☑

Select principal diagnosis listed under DRG 183

DRG 185 Major Chest Trauma without CC/MCC

GMLOS 2.4 AMLOS 2.9 RW 0.6961 ☑

Select principal diagnosis listed under DRG 183

DRG 186 Pleural Effusion with MCC

GMLOS 4.9 AMLOS 6.4 RW 1.5746 T ☑

Principal Diagnosis

511.89	Other specified forms of effusion, except tuberculous
511.9	Unspecified pleural effusion

DRG 187 Pleural Effusion with CC

GMLOS 3.7 AMLOS 4.7 RW 1.1169 T ☑

Select principal diagnosis listed under DRG 186

DRG 188 Pleural Effusion without CC/MCC

GMLOS 2.6 AMLOS 3.3 RW 0.7544 T ☑

Select principal diagnosis listed under DRG 186

DRG 189 Pulmonary Edema and Respiratory Failure

GMLOS 4.1 AMLOS 5.2 RW 1.2461 ☑ ▽

Principal Diagnosis

506.1	Acute pulmonary edema due to fumes and vapors
514	Pulmonary congestion and hypostasis
518.4	Unspecified acute edema of lung
518.5*	Pulmonary insufficiency following trauma and surgery
518.81	Acute respiratory failure
518.83	Chronic respiratory failure
518.84	Acute and chronic respiratory failure

T Transfer DRG *SP Special Payment* *☑ Optimization Potential* *▽ Targeted Potential* ** Code Range* *● New DRG* *▲ Revised DRG Title*

© 2012 OptumInsight, Inc.

DRG 190   Chronic Obstructive Pulmonary Disease with MCC

GMLOS 4.3   AMLOS 5.3   RW 1.1860   T ☑ ▽

Principal Diagnosis

491.1	Mucopurulent chronic bronchitis
491.2*	Obstructive chronic bronchitis
491.8	Other chronic bronchitis
491.9	Unspecified chronic bronchitis
492.0	Emphysematous bleb
492.8	Other emphysema
493.20	Chronic obstructive asthma, unspecified
493.21	Chronic obstructive asthma with status asthmaticus
493.22	Chronic obstructive asthma, with (acute) exacerbation
494*	Bronchiectasis
496	Chronic airway obstruction, not elsewhere classified
506.4	Chronic respiratory conditions due to fumes and vapors
506.9	Unspecified respiratory conditions due to fumes and vapors
748.61	Congenital bronchiectasis

DRG 191   Chronic Obstructive Pulmonary Disease with CC

GMLOS 3.6   AMLOS 4.4   RW 0.9521   T ☑ ▽

Select principal diagnosis listed under DRG 190

DRG 192   Chronic Obstructive Pulmonary Disease without CC/MCC

GMLOS 2.9   AMLOS 3.4   RW 0.7072   T ☑ ▽

Select principal diagnosis listed under DRG 190

DRG 193   Simple Pneumonia and Pleurisy with MCC

GMLOS 5.1   AMLOS 6.3   RW 1.4893   T ☑ ▽

Principal Diagnosis

074.1	Epidemic pleurodynia
480*	Viral pneumonia
481	Pneumococcal pneumonia (streptococcus pneumoniae pneumonia)
482.2	Pneumonia due to Hemophilus influenzae (H. influenzae)
482.3*	Pneumonia due to Streptococcus
482.9	Unspecified bacterial pneumonia
483*	Pneumonia due to other specified organism
485	Bronchopneumonia, organism unspecified
486	Pneumonia, organism unspecified
487.0	Influenza with pneumonia
488.01	Influenza due to identified avian influenza virus with pneumonia
488.02	Influenza due to identified avian influenza virus with other respiratory manifestations
488.11	Influenza due to identified 2009 H1N1 influenza virus with pneumonia
488.12	Influenza due to identified 2009 H1N1 influenza virus with other respiratory manifestations
488.81	Influenza due to identified novel influenza A virus with pneumonia
488.82	Influenza due to identified novel influenza A virus with other respiratory manifestations
511.0	Pleurisy without mention of effusion or current tuberculosis

DRG 194   Simple Pneumonia and Pleurisy with CC

GMLOS 3.9   AMLOS 4.7   RW 0.9996   T ☑ ▽

Select principal diagnosis listed under DRG 193

DRG 195   Simple Pneumonia and Pleurisy without CC/MCC

GMLOS 3.0   AMLOS 3.5   RW 0.7078   T ☑

Select principal diagnosis listed under DRG 193

DRG 196   Interstitial Lung Disease with MCC

GMLOS 5.5   AMLOS 6.9   RW 1.6820   T ☑

Principal Diagnosis

135	Sarcoidosis
137.0	Late effects of respiratory or unspecified tuberculosis
495*	Extrinsic allergic alveolitis
500	Coal workers' pneumoconiosis
501	Asbestosis
502	Pneumoconiosis due to other silica or silicates
503	Pneumoconiosis due to other inorganic dust
504	Pneumonopathy due to inhalation of other dust
505	Unspecified pneumoconiosis
508.1	Chronic and other pulmonary manifestations due to radiation
515	Postinflammatory pulmonary fibrosis
516*	Other alveolar and parietoalveolar pneumonopathy
517.1	Rheumatic pneumonia
517.2	Lung involvement in systemic sclerosis
517.3	Acute chest syndrome
517.8	Lung involvement in other diseases classified elsewhere
518.3	Pulmonary eosinophilia
518.6	Allergic bronchopulmonary aspergillosis
714.81	Rheumatoid lung
770.7	Chronic respiratory disease arising in the perinatal period

DRG 197   Interstitial Lung Disease with CC

GMLOS 3.9   AMLOS 4.8   RW 1.1209   T ☑

Select principal diagnosis listed under DRG 196

DRG 198   Interstitial Lung Disease without CC/MCC

GMLOS 2.9   AMLOS 3.6   RW 0.7879   T ☑

Select principal diagnosis listed under DRG 196

DRG 199   Pneumothorax with MCC

GMLOS 6.1   AMLOS 7.8   RW 1.8915   ☑

Principal Diagnosis

512.0	Spontaneous tension pneumothorax
512.1	Iatrogenic pneumothorax
512.2	Postoperative air leak
512.8*	Other pneumothorax and air leak
518.1	Interstitial emphysema
860*	Traumatic pneumothorax and hemothorax
958.7	Traumatic subcutaneous emphysema

DRG 200   Pneumothorax with CC

GMLOS 3.5   AMLOS 4.5   RW 1.0242   ☑ ▽

Select principal diagnosis listed under DRG 199

DRG 201   Pneumothorax without CC/MCC

GMLOS 2.6   AMLOS 3.3   RW 0.6792   ☑

Select principal diagnosis listed under DRG 199

DRG 202   Bronchitis and Asthma with CC/MCC

GMLOS 3.3   AMLOS 4.0   RW 0.8704   ☑ ▽

Principal Diagnosis

033*	Whooping cough
464.1*	Acute tracheitis
466*	Acute bronchitis and bronchiolitis
490	Bronchitis, not specified as acute or chronic
491.0	Simple chronic bronchitis
493.0*	Extrinsic asthma
493.1*	Intrinsic asthma
493.8*	Other forms of asthma

MDC 4: Diseases And Disorders Of The Respiratory System—MEDICAL

MDC 4: Diseases And Disorders Of The Respiratory System—MEDICAL

493.9*	Unspecified asthma
519.1*	Other diseases of trachea and bronchus, not elsewhere classified

DRG 203   Bronchitis and Asthma without CC/MCC

GMLOS 2.5   AMLOS 3.0   RW 0.6228   ☑ ▽

Select principal diagnosis listed under DRG 202

DRG 204   Respiratory Signs and Symptoms

GMLOS 2.1   AMLOS 2.7   RW 0.6822   ☑

Principal Diagnosis

327.22	High altitude periodic breathing
518.82	Other pulmonary insufficiency, not elsewhere classified
786.0*	Dyspnea and respiratory abnormalities
786.1	Stridor
786.2	Cough
786.3*	Hemoptysis
786.4	Abnormal sputum
786.52	Painful respiration
786.6	Swelling, mass, or lump in chest
786.7	Abnormal chest sounds
786.8	Hiccough
786.9	Other symptoms involving respiratory system and chest
793.19	Other nonspecific abnormal finding of lung field

DRG 205   Other Respiratory System Diagnoses with MCC

GMLOS 4.0   AMLOS 5.3   RW 1.3809   Ⓣ ☑

Principal Diagnosis

278.03	Obesity hypoventilation syndrome
306.1	Respiratory malfunction arising from mental factors
506.0	Bronchitis and pneumonitis due to fumes and vapors
506.2	Upper respiratory inflammation due to fumes and vapors
506.3	Other acute and subacute respiratory conditions due to fumes and vapors
508.0	Acute pulmonary manifestations due to radiation
508.2	Respiratory conditions due to smoke inhalation
508.8	Respiratory conditions due to other specified external agents
508.9	Respiratory conditions due to unspecified external agent
518.0	Pulmonary collapse
518.2	Compensatory emphysema
518.7	Transfusion related acute lung injury [TRALI]
518.89	Other diseases of lung, not elsewhere classified
519.0*	Tracheostomy complications
519.3	Other diseases of mediastinum, not elsewhere classified
519.4	Disorders of diaphragm
519.8	Other diseases of respiratory system, not elsewhere classified
519.9	Unspecified disease of respiratory system
573.5	Hepatopulmonary syndrome
733.6	Tietze's disease
748.4	Congenital cystic lung
748.5	Congenital agenesis, hypoplasia, and dysplasia of lung
748.60	Unspecified congenital anomaly of lung
748.69	Other congenital anomaly of lung
748.8	Other specified congenital anomaly of respiratory system
748.9	Unspecified congenital anomaly of respiratory system
754.81	Pectus excavatum
754.82	Pectus carinatum
756.3	Other congenital anomaly of ribs and sternum
756.6	Congenital anomaly of diaphragm
781.5	Clubbing of fingers
793.11	Solitary pulmonary nodule
794.2	Nonspecific abnormal results of pulmonary system function study
799.0*	Asphyxia and hypoxemia
799.1	Respiratory arrest

807.00	Closed fracture of rib(s), unspecified
807.01	Closed fracture of one rib
807.02	Closed fracture of two ribs
848.3	Sprain and strain of ribs
848.4*	Sprain and strain of sternum
861.20	Unspecified lung injury without mention of open wound into thorax
861.21	Lung contusion without mention of open wound into thorax
861.30	Unspecified lung injury with open wound into thorax
861.31	Lung contusion with open wound into thorax
862.29	Injury to other specified intrathoracic organs without mention of open wound into cavity
862.39	Injury to other specified intrathoracic organs with open wound into cavity
908.0	Late effect of internal injury to chest
934.0	Foreign body in trachea
934.1	Foreign body in main bronchus
934.8	Foreign body in other specified parts of trachea, bronchus, and lung
934.9	Foreign body in respiratory tree, unspecified
947.1	Burn of larynx, trachea, and lung
996.84	Complications of transplanted lung
997.3*	Respiratory complications
V42.6	Lung replaced by transplant
V45.76	Acquired absence of organ, lung
V55.0	Attention to tracheostomy

DRG 206   Other Respiratory System Diagnoses without MCC

GMLOS 2.5   AMLOS 3.2   RW 0.7763   Ⓣ ☑

Select principal diagnosis listed under DRG 205

DRG 207   Respiratory System Diagnosis with Ventilator Support 96+ Hours

GMLOS 12.5   AMLOS 14.6   RW 5.3619   Ⓣ ☑ ▽

Select principal diagnosis from MDC 4
AND

Nonoperating Room Procedure

96.72	Continuous invasive mechanical ventilation for 96 consecutive hours or more

DRG 208   Respiratory System Diagnosis with Ventilator Support <96 Hours

GMLOS 5.1   AMLOS 7.0   RW 2.2899   ☑ ▽

Select principal diagnosis from MDC 4
AND

Nonoperating Room Procedures

96.70	Continuous invasive mechanical ventilation of unspecified duration
96.71	Continuous invasive mechanical ventilation for less than 96 consecutive hours

---

Ⓣ *Transfer DRG*   ⓈⓅ *Special Payment*   ☑ *Optimization Potential*   ▽ *Targeted Potential*   * *Code Range*   ● *New DRG*   ▲ *Revised DRG Title*

MDC 5
Diseases And Disorders Of The Circulatory System

032.82	395.2	410.60	422.93	427.9	442.3	453.52	745.61	785.9
036.40	395.9	410.61	422.99	428.0	442.81	453.6	745.69	786.50
036.41	396.0	410.62	423.0	428.1	442.82	453.71	745.7	786.51
036.42	396.1	410.70	423.1	428.20	442.83	453.72	745.8	786.59
036.43	396.2	410.71	423.2	428.21	442.84	453.73	745.9	793.2
074.20	396.3	410.72	423.3	428.22	442.89	453.74	746.00	794.30
074.21	396.8	410.80	423.8	428.23	442.9	453.75	746.01	794.31
074.22	396.9	410.81	423.9	428.30	443.1	453.76	746.02	794.39
074.23	397.0	410.82	424.0	428.31	443.21	453.77	746.09	796.2
086.0	397.1	410.90	424.1	428.32	443.22	453.79	746.1	796.3
093.0	397.9	410.91	424.2	428.33	443.24	453.81	746.2	798.1
093.1	398.0	410.92	424.3	428.40	443.29	453.82	746.3	798.2
093.20	398.90	411.0	424.90	428.41	443.81	453.83	746.4	861.00
093.21	398.91	411.1	424.91	428.42	443.82	453.84	746.5	861.01
093.22	398.99	411.81	424.99	428.43	443.89	453.85	746.6	861.02
093.23	401.0	411.89	425.0	428.9	443.9	453.86	746.7	861.03
093.24	401.1	412	425.11	429.0	444.01	453.87	746.81	861.10
093.81	401.9	413.0	425.18	429.1	444.09	453.89	746.82	861.11
093.82	402.00	413.1	425.2	429.2	444.1	453.9	746.83	861.12
093.89	402.01	413.9	425.3	429.3	444.21	454.0	746.84	861.13
093.9	402.10	414.00	425.4	429.4	444.22	454.1	746.85	908.3
098.83	402.11	414.01	425.5	429.5	444.81	454.2	746.86	908.4
098.84	402.90	414.02	425.7	429.6	444.89	454.8	746.87	996.00
098.85	402.91	414.03	425.8	429.71	444.9	454.9	746.89	996.01
112.81	404.00	414.04	425.9	429.79	445.01	456.3	746.9	996.02
115.03	404.01	414.05	426.0	429.81	445.02	456.8	747.0	996.03
115.04	404.03	414.06	426.10	429.82	445.89	458.0	747.10	996.04
115.13	404.10	414.07	426.11	429.83	447.0	458.1	747.11	996.09
115.14	404.11	414.10	426.12	429.89	447.1	458.21	747.20	996.1
115.93	404.13	414.11	426.13	429.9	447.2	458.29	747.21	996.61
115.94	404.90	414.12	426.2	440.0	447.5	458.8	747.22	996.62
130.3	404.91	414.19	426.3	440.20	447.70	458.9	747.29	996.71
164.1	404.93	414.2	426.4	440.21	447.71	459.0	747.31	996.72
212.7	405.01	414.3	426.50	440.22	447.72	459.10	747.32	996.73
228.00	405.09	414.4	426.51	440.23	447.73	459.11	747.39	996.74
228.09	405.11	414.8	426.52	440.24	447.8	459.12	747.40	996.83
249.70	405.19	414.9	426.53	440.29	447.9	459.13	747.41	997.1
249.71	405.91	415.0	426.54	440.30	448.0	459.19	747.42	997.2
250.70	405.99	416.0	426.6	440.31	448.9	459.2	747.49	997.79
250.71	410.00	416.1	426.7	440.32	449	459.30	747.5	999.2
250.72	410.01	416.8	426.81	440.4	451.0	459.31	747.60	999.31
250.73	410.02	416.9	426.82	440.8	451.11	459.32	747.61	999.32
306.2	410.10	417.0	426.89	440.9	451.19	459.33	747.62	999.33
391.0	410.11	417.1	426.9	441.00	451.2	459.39	747.63	999.81
391.1	410.12	417.8	427.0	441.01	451.81	459.81	747.64	999.82
391.2	410.20	417.9	427.1	441.02	451.82	459.89	747.69	999.88
391.8	410.21	420.0	427.2	441.03	451.83	459.9	747.89	V42.1
391.9	410.22	420.90	427.31	441.1	451.84	745	747.9	V42.2
392.0	410.30	420.91	427.32	441.2	451.89	745.10	759.82	V43.21
392.9	410.31	420.99	427.41	441.3	451.9	745.11	780.2	V43.22
393	410.32	421.0	427.42	441.4	453.1	745.12	785.0	V43.3
394.0	410.40	421.1	427.5	441.5	453.2	745.19	785.1	V43.4
394.1	410.41	421.9	427.60	441.6	453.40	745.2	785.2	V53.31
394.2	410.42	422.0	427.61	441.7	453.41	745.3	785.3	V53.32
394.9	410.50	422.90	427.69	441.9	453.42	745.4	785.4	V53.39
395.0	410.51	422.91	427.81	442.0	453.50	745.5	785.50	V71.7
395.1	410.52	422.92	427.89	442.2	453.51	745.60	785.51	

MDC 5: Diseases And Disorders Of The Circulatory System—SURGICAL

SURGICAL

DRG 215   Other Heart Assist System Implant
GMLOS 8.5   AMLOS 15.0   RW 14.1036   ☑

Operating Room Procedures
37.53	Replacement or repair of thoracic unit of (total) replacement heart system
37.54	Replacement or repair of other implantable component of (total) replacement heart system
37.60	Implantation or insertion of biventricular external heart assist system
37.62	Insertion of temporary non-implantable extracorporeal circulatory assist device
37.63	Repair of heart assist system
37.65	Implant of single ventricular (extracorporeal) external heart assist system

DRG 216   Cardiac Valve and Other Major Cardiothoracic Procedures with Cardiac Catheterization with MCC
GMLOS 13.8   AMLOS 16.4   RW 9.5190   SP

Operating Room Procedures
35.05	Endovascular replacement of aortic valve
35.06	Transapical replacement of aortic valve
35.07	Endovascular replacement of pulmonary valve
35.08	Transapical replacement of pulmonary valve
35.09	Endovascular replacement of unspecified heart valve
35.1*	Open heart valvuloplasty without replacement
35.2*	Open and other replacement of heart valve
35.33	Annuloplasty
37.68	Insertion of percutaneous external heart assist device
38.45	Resection of other thoracic vessels with replacement
39.73	Endovascular implantation of graft in thoracic aorta

AND

Nonoperating Room Procedures
37.21	Right heart cardiac catheterization
37.22	Left heart cardiac catheterization
37.23	Combined right and left heart cardiac catheterization
37.26	Catheter based invasive electrophysiologic testing
88.52	Angiocardiography of right heart structures
88.53	Angiocardiography of left heart structures
88.54	Combined right and left heart angiocardiography
88.55	Coronary arteriography using single catheter
88.56	Coronary arteriography using two catheters
88.57	Other and unspecified coronary arteriography
88.58	Negative-contrast cardiac roentgenography

DRG 217   Cardiac Valve and Other Major Cardiothoracic Procedures with Cardiac Catheterization with CC
GMLOS 9.0   AMLOS 10.2   RW 6.3495   SP ☑

Select operating room procedure AND nonoperating room procedure listed under DRG 216

DRG 218   Cardiac Valve and Other Major Cardiothoracic Procedures with Cardiac Catheterization without CC/MCC
GMLOS 6.5   AMLOS 7.4   RW 5.3429   SP ☑

Select operating room procedure AND nonoperating room procedure listed under DRG 216

DRG 219   Cardiac Valve and Other Major Cardiothoracic Procedures without Cardiac Catheterization with MCC
GMLOS 10.3   AMLOS 12.5   RW 7.8390   SP ☑

Operating Room Procedures
35.05	Endovascular replacement of aortic valve
35.06	Transapical replacement of aortic valve
35.07	Endovascular replacement of pulmonary valve
35.08	Transapical replacement of pulmonary valve
35.09	Endovascular replacement of unspecified heart valve
35.1*	Open heart valvuloplasty without replacement
35.2*	Open and other replacement of heart valve
35.33	Annuloplasty
37.68	Insertion of percutaneous external heart assist device
38.45	Resection of other thoracic vessels with replacement
39.73	Endovascular implantation of graft in thoracic aorta

DRG 220   Cardiac Valve and Other Major Cardiothoracic Procedures without Cardiac Catheterization with CC
GMLOS 6.8   AMLOS 7.5   RW 5.2438   SP ☑

Select operating room procedures listed under DRG 219

DRG 221   Cardiac Valve and Other Major Cardiothoracic Procedures without Cardiac Catheterization without CC/MCC
GMLOS 5.1   AMLOS 5.6   RW 4.4232   SP ☑

Select operating room procedures listed under DRG 219

DRG 222   Cardiac Defibrillator Implant with Cardiac Catheterization with Acute Myocardial Infarction/Heart Failure/Shock with MCC
GMLOS 9.9   AMLOS 12.0   RW 8.5506   ☑

Principal Diagnosis
398.91	Rheumatic heart failure (congestive)
402.01	Malignant hypertensive heart disease with heart failure
402.11	Benign hypertensive heart disease with heart failure
402.91	Hypertensive heart disease, unspecified, with heart failure
404.01	Hypertensive heart and chronic kidney disease, malignant, with heart failure and with chronic kidney disease stage I through stage IV, or unspecified
404.03	Hypertensive heart and chronic kidney disease, malignant, with heart failure and with chronic kidney disease stage V or end stage renal disease
404.11	Hypertensive heart and chronic kidney disease, benign, with heart failure and with chronic kidney disease stage I through stage IV, or unspecified
404.13	Hypertensive heart and chronic kidney disease, benign, with heart failure and chronic kidney disease stage V or end stage renal disease
404.91	Hypertensive heart and chronic kidney disease, unspecified, with heart failure and with chronic kidney disease stage I through stage IV, or unspecified
404.93	Hypertensive heart and chronic kidney disease, unspecified, with heart failure and chronic kidney disease stage V or end stage renal disease
410.01	Acute myocardial infarction of anterolateral wall, initial episode of care
410.11	Acute myocardial infarction of other anterior wall, initial episode of care
410.21	Acute myocardial infarction of inferolateral wall, initial episode of care
410.31	Acute myocardial infarction of inferoposterior wall, initial episode of care
410.41	Acute myocardial infarction of other inferior wall, initial episode of care
410.51	Acute myocardial infarction of other lateral wall, initial episode of care

Ⓣ *Transfer DRG*   SP *Special Payment*   ☑ *Optimization Potential*   ▽ *Targeted Potential*   * *Code Range*   ● *New DRG*   ▲ *Revised DRG Title*

56   Valid 10/01/2012-09/30/2013   © 2012 OptumInsight, Inc.

410.61	Acute myocardial infarction, true posterior wall infarction, initial episode of care
410.71	Acute myocardial infarction, subendocardial infarction, initial episode of care
410.81	Acute myocardial infarction of other specified sites, initial episode of care
410.91	Acute myocardial infarction, unspecified site, initial episode of care
428.0	Congestive heart failure, unspecified
428.1	Left heart failure
428.2*	Systolic heart failure
428.3*	Diastolic heart failure
428.4*	Combined systolic and diastolic heart failure
428.9	Unspecified heart failure
785.50	Unspecified shock
785.51	Cardiogenic shock

AND

Operating Room Procedures

00.51	Implantation of cardiac resynchronization defibrillator, total system (CRT-D)
17.51	Implantation of rechargeable cardiac contractility modulation [CCM], total system
37.94	Implantation or replacement of automatic cardioverter/defibrillator, total system (AICD)

OR

Any of the following procedure combinations

00.52	Implantation or replacement of transvenous lead (electrode) into left ventricular coronary venous system
	AND
00.54	Implantation or replacement of cardiac resynchronization defibrillator pulse generator device only (CRT-D)

OR

37.74	Insertion or replacement of epicardial lead (electrode) into epicardium
	AND
00.54	Implantation or replacement of cardiac resynchronization defibrillator pulse generator device only (CRT-D)

OR

37.74	Insertion or replacement of epicardial lead (electrode) into epicardium
	AND
37.96	Implantation of automatic cardioverter/defibrillator pulse generator only

OR

37.74	Insertion or replacement of epicardial lead (electrode) into epicardium
	AND
37.98	Replacement of automatic cardioverter/defibrillator pulse generator only

OR

37.95	Implantation of automatic cardioverter/defibrillator leads(s) only
	AND
00.54	Implantation or replacement of cardiac resynchronization defibrillator pulse generator device only (CRT-D)

OR

37.95	Implantation of automatic cardioverter/defibrillator leads(s) only
	AND
37.96	Implantation of automatic cardioverter/defibrillator pulse generator only

OR

| 37.97 | Replacement of automatic cardioverter/defibrillator leads(s) only |

| | **AND** |
| 00.54 | Implantation or replacement of cardiac resynchronization defibrillator pulse generator device only (CRT-D) |

OR

37.97	Replacement of automatic cardioverter/defibrillator leads(s) only
	AND
37.98	Replacement of automatic cardioverter/defibrillator pulse generator only

AND

Nonoperating Room Procedures

37.21	Right heart cardiac catheterization
37.22	Left heart cardiac catheterization
37.23	Combined right and left heart cardiac catheterization
88.52	Angiocardiography of right heart structures
88.53	Angiocardiography of left heart structures
88.54	Combined right and left heart angiocardiography
88.55	Coronary arteriography using single catheter
88.56	Coronary arteriography using two catheters
88.57	Other and unspecified coronary arteriography
88.58	Negative-contrast cardiac roentgenography

DRG 223 Cardiac Defibrillator Implant with Cardiac Catheterization with Acute Myocardial Infarction/Heart Failure/Shock without MCC

GMLOS 4.4   AMLOS 5.9   RW 6.1065 ☑

Select principal diagnosis AND operating room procedure OR procedure combinations AND nonoperating room procedure listed under DRG 222

DRG 224 Cardiac Defibrillator Implant with Cardiac Catheterization without Acute Myocardial Infarction/Heart Failure/Shock with MCC

GMLOS 8.1   AMLOS 10.0   RW 7.6758 ☑

Select any principal diagnosis listed under MDC 5 excluding acute myocardial infarction, heart failure and shock

Select any operating room procedure OR procedure combination AND nonoperating room procedure listed under DRG 222

DRG 225 Cardiac Defibrillator Implant with Cardiac Catheterization without Acute Myocardial Infarction/Heart Failure/Shock without MCC

GMLOS 4.0   AMLOS 5.0   RW 5.7605 ☑

Select any principal diagnosis listed under MDC 5 excluding acute myocardial infarction, heart failure and shock

Select any operating room procedure OR procedure combination AND nonoperating room procedure listed under DRG 222

DRG 226 Cardiac Defibrillator Implant without Cardiac Catheterization with MCC

GMLOS 6.1   AMLOS 8.7   RW 6.7354 ☑

Operating Room Procedures

00.51	Implantation of cardiac resynchronization defibrillator, total system (CRT-D)
17.51	Implantation of rechargeable cardiac contractility modulation [CCM], total system
37.94	Implantation or replacement of automatic cardioverter/defibrillator, total system (AICD)

OR

Any of the following procedure combinations

| 00.52 | Implantation or replacement of transvenous lead (electrode) into left ventricular coronary venous system |

AND

00.54 Implantation or replacement of cardiac resynchronization defibrillator pulse generator device only (CRT-D)

OR

37.74 Insertion or replacement of epicardial lead (electrode) into epicardium

AND

00.54 Implantation or replacement of cardiac resynchronization defibrillator pulse generator device only (CRT-D)

OR

37.74 Insertion or replacement of epicardial lead (electrode) into epicardium

AND

37.96 Implantation of automatic cardioverter/defibrillator pulse generator only

OR

37.74 Insertion or replacement of epicardial lead (electrode) into epicardium

AND

37.98 Replacement of automatic cardioverter/defibrillator pulse generator only

OR

37.95 Implantation of automatic cardioverter/defibrillator leads(s) only

AND

00.54 Implantation or replacement of cardiac resynchronization defibrillator pulse generator device only (CRT-D)

OR

37.95 Implantation of automatic cardioverter/defibrillator leads(s) only

AND

37.96 Implantation of automatic cardioverter/defibrillator pulse generator only

OR

37.97 Replacement of automatic cardioverter/defibrillator leads(s) only

AND

00.54 Implantation or replacement of cardiac resynchronization defibrillator pulse generator device only (CRT-D)

OR

37.97 Replacement of automatic cardioverter/defibrillator leads(s) only

AND

37.98 Replacement of automatic cardioverter/defibrillator pulse generator only

DRG 227 Cardiac Defibrillator Implant without Cardiac Catheterization without MCC

GMLOS 2.1   AMLOS 3.1   RW 5.1886   ☑

Select operating room procedure OR procedure combination listed under DRG 226

DRG 228 Other Cardiothoracic Procedures with MCC

GMLOS 11.2   AMLOS 13.4   RW 7.0815   ☑

Operating Room Procedures

35.31 Operations on papillary muscle
35.32 Operations on chordae tendineae
35.34 Infundibulectomy
35.35 Operations on trabeculae carneae cordis
35.39 Operations on other structures adjacent to valves of heart
35.42 Creation of septal defect in heart
35.50 Repair of unspecified septal defect of heart with prosthesis
35.51 Repair of atrial septal defect with prosthesis, open technique

35.53 Repair of ventricular septal defect with prosthesis, open technique
35.54 Repair of endocardial cushion defect with prosthesis
35.55 Repair of ventricular septal defect with prosthesis, closed technique
35.6* Repair of atrial and ventricular septa with tissue graft
35.7* Other and unspecified repair of atrial and ventricular septa
35.8* Total repair of certain congenital cardiac anomalies
35.91 Interatrial transposition of venous return
35.92 Creation of conduit between right ventricle and pulmonary artery
35.93 Creation of conduit between left ventricle and aorta
35.94 Creation of conduit between atrium and pulmonary artery
35.95 Revision of corrective procedure on heart
35.98 Other operations on septa of heart
35.99 Other operations on valves of heart
36.03 Open chest coronary artery angioplasty
36.2 Heart revascularization by arterial implant
36.3* Other heart revascularization
36.9* Other operations on vessels of heart
37.10 Incision of heart, not otherwise specified
37.11 Cardiotomy
37.32 Excision of aneurysm of heart
37.33 Excision or destruction of other lesion or tissue of heart, open approach
37.35 Partial ventriculectomy
37.37 Excision or destruction of other lesion or tissue of heart, thoracoscopic approach

DRG 229 Other Cardiothoracic Procedures with CC

GMLOS 7.1   AMLOS 8.0   RW 4.6279   ☑

Select operating room procedure OR procedure combination listed under DRG 228

DRG 230 Other Cardiothoracic Procedures without CC/MCC

GMLOS 4.8   AMLOS 5.6   RW 3.8111   ☑

Select operating room procedure OR procedure combination listed under DRG 228

DRG 231 Coronary Bypass with PTCA with MCC

GMLOS 10.3   AMLOS 12.1   RW 7.5297

Operating Room Procedures

36.1* Bypass anastomosis for heart revascularization

AND

Operating Room Procedures

00.66 Percutaneous transluminal coronary angioplasty [PTCA]
17.55 Transluminal coronary atherectomy
35.96 Percutaneous balloon valvuloplasty
35.97 Percutaneous mitral valve repair with implant

DRG 232 Coronary Bypass with PTCA without MCC

GMLOS 8.3   AMLOS 9.1   RW 5.7151   ☑

Select operating room procedures listed under DRG 231

DRG 233 Coronary Bypass with Cardiac Catheterization with MCC

GMLOS 11.9   AMLOS 13.4   RW 7.2292   ☐☑

Operating Room Procedures

36.1* Bypass anastomosis for heart revascularization

AND

Nonoperating Room Procedures

37.21 Right heart cardiac catheterization
37.22 Left heart cardiac catheterization
37.23 Combined right and left heart cardiac catheterization

Ⓣ Transfer DRG   ⓢⓅ Special Payment   ☑ Optimization Potential   ▽ Targeted Potential   * Code Range   ● New DRG   ▲ Revised DRG Title

58   Valid 10/01/2012-09/30/2013   © 2012 OptumInsight, Inc.

88.52	Angiocardiography of right heart structures
88.53	Angiocardiography of left heart structures
88.54	Combined right and left heart angiocardiography
88.55	Coronary arteriography using single catheter
88.56	Coronary arteriography using two catheters
88.57	Other and unspecified coronary arteriography
88.58	Negative-contrast cardiac roentgenography

DRG 234 Coronary Bypass with Cardiac Catheterization without MCC

GMLOS 8.1   AMLOS 8.7   RW 4.8413   T ☑

Select operating room procedure AND nonoperating room procedure listed under DRG 233

DRG 235 Coronary Bypass without Cardiac Catheterization with MCC

GMLOS 9.2   AMLOS 10.7   RW 5.8014   T ☑

Operating Room Procedures
| 36.1* | Bypass anastomosis for heart revascularization |

DRG 236 Coronary Bypass without Cardiac Catheterization without MCC

GMLOS 6.0   AMLOS 6.5   RW 3.7777   T ☑

Select operating room procedure listed under DRG 235

DRG 237 Major Cardiovascular Procedures with MCC

GMLOS 7.1   AMLOS 10.0   RW 5.1170   ☑

Operating Room Procedures
35.0*	Closed heart valvotomy or transcatheter replacement of heart valve
37.12	Pericardiotomy
37.24	Biopsy of pericardium
37.31	Pericardiectomy
37.4*	Repair of heart and pericardium
37.55	Removal of internal biventricular heart replacement system
37.61	Implant of pulsation balloon
37.64	Removal of external heart assist system(s) or device(s)
37.67	Implantation of cardiomyostimulation system
37.91	Open chest cardiac massage
37.99	Other operations on heart and pericardium
38.04	Incision of aorta
38.05	Incision of other thoracic vessels
38.06	Incision of abdominal arteries
38.07	Incision of abdominal veins
38.14	Endarterectomy of aorta
38.15	Endarterectomy of other thoracic vessels
38.16	Endarterectomy of abdominal arteries
38.34	Resection of aorta with anastomosis
38.35	Resection of other thoracic vessels with anastomosis
38.36	Resection of abdominal arteries with anastomosis
38.37	Resection of abdominal veins with anastomosis
38.44	Resection of abdominal aorta with replacement
38.46	Resection of abdominal arteries with replacement
38.47	Resection of abdominal veins with replacement
38.55	Ligation and stripping of varicose veins of other thoracic vessel
38.64	Other excision of abdominal aorta
38.65	Other excision of other thoracic vessel
38.66	Other excision of abdominal arteries
38.67	Other excision of abdominal veins
38.84	Other surgical occlusion of abdominal aorta
38.85	Other surgical occlusion of other thoracic vessel
38.86	Other surgical occlusion of abdominal arteries
38.87	Other surgical occlusion of abdominal veins
39.0	Systemic to pulmonary artery shunt

39.1	Intra-abdominal venous shunt
39.21	Caval-pulmonary artery anastomosis
39.22	Aorta-subclavian-carotid bypass
39.23	Other intrathoracic vascular shunt or bypass
39.24	Aorta-renal bypass
39.25	Aorta-iliac-femoral bypass
39.26	Other intra-abdominal vascular shunt or bypass
39.52	Other repair of aneurysm
39.54	Re-entry operation (aorta)
39.71	Endovascular implantation of other graft in abdominal aorta
39.72	Endovascular (total) embolization or occlusion of head and neck vessels
39.75	Endovascular embolization or occlusion of vessel(s) of head or neck using bare coils
39.76	Endovascular embolization or occlusion of vessel(s) of head or neck using bioactive coils
39.78	Endovascular implantation of branching or fenestrated graft(s) in aorta
39.79	Other endovascular procedures on other vessels

DRG 238 Major Cardiovascular Procedures without MCC

GMLOS 2.7   AMLOS 3.9   RW 3.1863   ☑

Operating Room Procedures
35.0*	Closed heart valvotomy or transcatheter replacement of heart valve
37.12	Pericardiotomy
37.24	Biopsy of pericardium
37.31	Pericardiectomy
37.4*	Repair of heart and pericardium
37.55	Removal of internal biventricular heart replacement system
37.61	Implant of pulsation balloon
37.64	Removal of external heart assist system(s) or device(s)
37.67	Implantation of cardiomyostimulation system
37.91	Open chest cardiac massage
37.99	Other operations on heart and pericardium
38.04	Incision of aorta
38.05	Incision of other thoracic vessels
38.06	Incision of abdominal arteries
38.07	Incision of abdominal veins
38.14	Endarterectomy of aorta
38.15	Endarterectomy of other thoracic vessels
38.16	Endarterectomy of abdominal arteries
38.34	Resection of aorta with anastomosis
38.35	Resection of other thoracic vessels with anastomosis
38.36	Resection of abdominal arteries with anastomosis
38.37	Resection of abdominal veins with anastomosis
38.44	Resection of abdominal aorta with replacement
38.46	Resection of abdominal arteries with replacement
38.47	Resection of abdominal veins with replacement
38.55	Ligation and stripping of varicose veins of other thoracic vessel
38.64	Other excision of abdominal aorta
38.65	Other excision of other thoracic vessel
38.66	Other excision of abdominal arteries
38.67	Other excision of abdominal veins
38.84	Other surgical occlusion of abdominal aorta
38.85	Other surgical occlusion of other thoracic vessel
38.86	Other surgical occlusion of abdominal arteries
38.87	Other surgical occlusion of abdominal veins
39.0	Systemic to pulmonary artery shunt
39.1	Intra-abdominal venous shunt
39.21	Caval-pulmonary artery anastomosis
39.22	Aorta-subclavian-carotid bypass
39.23	Other intrathoracic vascular shunt or bypass
39.24	Aorta-renal bypass
39.25	Aorta-iliac-femoral bypass
39.26	Other intra-abdominal vascular shunt or bypass
39.52	Other repair of aneurysm
39.54	Re-entry operation (aorta)

MDC 5: Diseases And Disorders Of The Circulatory System—SURGICAL

| Surgical | Medical | CC Indicator | MCC Indicator | Procedure Proxy |

MDC 5: Diseases And Disorders Of The Circulatory System—SURGICAL

39.71 Endovascular implantation of other graft in abdominal aorta
39.72 Endovascular (total) embolization or occlusion of head and neck vessels
39.75 Endovascular embolization or occlusion of vessel(s) of head or neck using bare coils
39.76 Endovascular embolization or occlusion of vessel(s) of head or neck using bioactive coils
39.78 Endovascular implantation of branching or fenestrated graft(s) in aorta
39.79 Other endovascular procedures on other vessels

DRG 239 Amputation for Circulatory System Disorders Except Upper Limb and Toe with MCC
GMLOS 11.1   AMLOS 14.1   RW 4.6194   T

Operating Room Procedures
84.10 Lower limb amputation, not otherwise specified
84.12 Amputation through foot
84.13 Disarticulation of ankle
84.14 Amputation of ankle through malleoli of tibia and fibula
84.15 Other amputation below knee
84.16 Disarticulation of knee
84.17 Amputation above knee
84.18 Disarticulation of hip
84.19 Abdominopelvic amputation
84.91 Amputation, not otherwise specified

DRG 240 Amputation for Circulatory System Disorders Except Upper Limb and Toe with CC
GMLOS 7.4   AMLOS 9.1   RW 2.6531   T ☑

Select operating room procedures listed under DRG 239

DRG 241 Amputation for Circulatory System Disorders Except Upper Limb and Toe without CC/MCC
GMLOS 4.7   AMLOS 5.7   RW 1.4825   T ☑

Select operating room procedures listed under DRG 239

DRG 242 Permanent Cardiac Pacemaker Implant with MCC
GMLOS 6.1   AMLOS 7.8   RW 3.7314   T ☑

Operating Room Procedure
00.50 Implantation of cardiac resynchronization pacemaker without mention of defibrillation, total system (CRT-P)

OR

Any of the following procedure combinations
00.52 Implantation or replacement of transvenous lead (electrode) into left ventricular coronary venous system
AND
00.53 Implantation or replacement of cardiac resynchronization pacemaker pulse generator only (CRT-P)

OR
37.70 Initial insertion of lead (electrode), not otherwise specified
AND
00.53 Implantation or replacement of cardiac resynchronization pacemaker pulse generator only (CRT-P)

OR
37.70 Initial insertion of lead (electrode), not otherwise specified
AND
37.80 Insertion of permanent pacemaker, initial or replacement, type of device not specified

OR
37.70 Initial insertion of lead (electrode), not otherwise specified
AND
37.81 Initial insertion of single-chamber device, not specified as rate responsive

OR
37.70 Initial insertion of lead (electrode), not otherwise specified
AND
37.82 Initial insertion of single-chamber device, rate responsive

OR
37.70 Initial insertion of lead (electrode), not otherwise specified
AND
37.85 Replacement of any type of pacemaker device with single-chamber device, not specified as rate responsive

OR
37.70 Initial insertion of lead (electrode), not otherwise specified
AND
37.86 Replacement of any type of pacemaker device with single-chamber device, rate responsive

OR
37.70 Initial insertion of lead (electrode), not otherwise specified
AND
37.87 Replacement of any type of pacemaker device with dual-chamber device

OR
37.71 Initial insertion of transvenous lead (electrode) into ventricle
AND
00.53 Implantation or replacement of cardiac resynchronization pacemaker pulse generator only (CRT-P)

OR
37.71 Initial insertion of transvenous lead (electrode) into ventricle
AND
37.80 Insertion of permanent pacemaker, initial or replacement, type of device not specified

OR
37.71 Initial insertion of transvenous lead (electrode) into ventricle
AND
37.81 Initial insertion of single-chamber device, not specified as rate responsive

OR
37.71 Initial insertion of transvenous lead (electrode) into ventricle
AND
37.82 Initial insertion of single-chamber device, rate responsive

OR
37.71 Initial insertion of transvenous lead (electrode) into ventricle
AND
37.85 Replacement of any type of pacemaker device with single-chamber device, not specified as rate responsive

OR
37.71 Initial insertion of transvenous lead (electrode) into ventricle
AND
37.86 Replacement of any type of pacemaker device with single-chamber device, rate responsive

OR
37.71 Initial insertion of transvenous lead (electrode) into ventricle
AND
37.87 Replacement of any type of pacemaker device with dual-chamber device

OR
37.72 Initial insertion of transvenous leads (electrodes) into atrium and ventricle
AND
00.53 Implantation or replacement of cardiac resynchronization pacemaker pulse generator only (CRT-P)

OR
37.72 Initial insertion of transvenous leads (electrodes) into atrium and ventricle

AND

37.80   Insertion of permanent pacemaker, initial or replacement, type of device not specified

OR

37.72   Initial insertion of transvenous leads (electrodes) into atrium and ventricle

     AND

37.83   Initial insertion of dual-chamber device

OR

37.73   Initial insertion of transvenous lead (electrode) into atrium

     AND

00.53   Implantation or replacement of cardiac resynchronization pacemaker pulse generator only (CRT-P)

OR

37.73   Initial insertion of transvenous lead (electrode) into atrium

     AND

37.80   Insertion of permanent pacemaker, initial or replacement, type of device not specified

OR

37.73   Initial insertion of transvenous lead (electrode) into atrium

     AND

37.81   Initial insertion of single-chamber device, not specified as rate responsive

OR

37.73   Initial insertion of transvenous lead (electrode) into atrium

     AND

37.82   Initial insertion of single-chamber device, rate responsive

OR

37.73   Initial insertion of transvenous lead (electrode) into atrium

     AND

37.85   Replacement of any type of pacemaker device with single-chamber device, not specified as rate responsive

OR

37.73   Initial insertion of transvenous lead (electrode) into atrium

     AND

37.86   Replacement of any type of pacemaker device with single-chamber device, rate responsive

OR

37.73   Initial insertion of transvenous lead (electrode) into atrium

     AND

37.87   Replacement of any type of pacemaker device with dual-chamber device

OR

37.74   Insertion or replacement of epicardial lead (electrode) into epicardium

     AND

00.53   Implantation or replacement of cardiac resynchronization pacemaker pulse generator only (CRT-P)

OR

37.74   Insertion or replacement of epicardial lead (electrode) into epicardium

     AND

37.80   Insertion of permanent pacemaker, initial or replacement, type of device not specified

OR

37.74   Insertion or replacement of epicardial lead (electrode) into epicardium

     AND

37.81   Initial insertion of single-chamber device, not specified as rate responsive

OR

37.74   Insertion or replacement of epicardial lead (electrode) into epicardium

     AND

37.82   Initial insertion of single-chamber device, rate responsive

OR

37.74   Insertion or replacement of epicardial lead (electrode) into epicardium

     AND

37.83   Initial insertion of dual-chamber device

OR

37.74   Insertion or replacement of epicardial lead (electrode) into epicardium

     AND

37.85   Replacement of any type of pacemaker device with single-chamber device, not specified as rate responsive

OR

37.74   Insertion or replacement of epicardial lead (electrode) into epicardium

     AND

37.86   Replacement of any type of pacemaker device with single-chamber device, rate responsive

OR

37.74   Insertion or replacement of epicardial lead (electrode) into epicardium

     AND

37.87   Replacement of any type of pacemaker device with dual-chamber device

OR

37.76   Replacement of transvenous atrial and/or ventricular lead(s) (electrode(s))

     AND

00.53   Implantation or replacement of cardiac resynchronization pacemaker pulse generator only (CRT-P)

OR

37.76   Replacement of transvenous atrial and/or ventricular lead(s) (electrode(s))

     AND

37.80   Insertion of permanent pacemaker, initial or replacement, type of device not specified

OR

37.76   Replacement of transvenous atrial and/or ventricular lead(s) (electrode(s))

     AND

37.85   Replacement of any type of pacemaker device with single-chamber device, not specified as rate responsive

OR

37.76   Replacement of transvenous atrial and/or ventricular lead(s) (electrode(s))

     AND

37.86   Replacement of any type of pacemaker device with single-chamber device, rate responsive

OR

37.76   Replacement of transvenous atrial and/or ventricular lead(s) (electrode(s))

     AND

37.87   Replacement of any type of pacemaker device with dual-chamber device

---

DRG 243   **Permanent Cardiac Pacemaker Implant with CC**
     GMLOS 3.7   AMLOS 4.7   RW 2.6204   T ☑

Select operating room procedure or combinations listed under DRG 242

DRG 244   **Permanent Cardiac Pacemaker Implant without CC/MCC**
     GMLOS 2.3   AMLOS 2.8   RW 2.0624   T ☑

Select operating room procedure or combinations listed under DRG 242

DRG 245   AICD Generator Procedures
GMLOS 2.9   AMLOS 4.3   RW 4.2540   ☑

Operating Room Procedures
00.54   Implantation or replacement of cardiac resynchronization defibrillator pulse generator device only (CRT-D)
17.52   Implantation or replacement of cardiac contractility modulation [CCM] rechargeable pulse generator only
37.96   Implantation of automatic cardioverter/defibrillator pulse generator only
37.98   Replacement of automatic cardioverter/defibrillator pulse generator only

DRG 246   Percutaneous Cardiovascular Procedure with Drug-Eluting Stent with MCC or 4+ Vessels/Stents
GMLOS 3.8   AMLOS 5.2   RW 3.1566   ☑

Operating Room Procedures
00.66   Percutaneous transluminal coronary angioplasty [PTCA]
17.55   Transluminal coronary atherectomy
35.96   Percutaneous balloon valvuloplasty
35.97   Percutaneous mitral valve repair with implant
36.09   Other removal of coronary artery obstruction
37.34   Excision or destruction of other lesion or tissue of heart, endovascular approach

OR

Nonoperating Room Procedures
37.26   Catheter based invasive electrophysiologic testing
37.27   Cardiac mapping

AND

Nonoperating Room Procedure
36.07   Insertion of drug-eluting coronary artery stent(s)

OR

Any of the following procedure combinations:
00.43   Procedure on four or more vessels
      AND
00.66   Percutaneous transluminal coronary angioplasty [PTCA]
OR
00.48   Insertion of four or more vascular stents
      AND
00.66   Percutaneous transluminal coronary angioplasty [PTCA]

DRG 247   Percutaneous Cardiovascular Procedure with Drug-Eluting Stent without MCC
GMLOS 2.0   AMLOS 2.5   RW 1.9911   ☑

Operating Room Procedures
00.66   Percutaneous transluminal coronary angioplasty [PTCA]
17.55   Transluminal coronary atherectomy
35.96   Percutaneous balloon valvuloplasty
35.97   Percutaneous mitral valve repair with implant
36.09   Other removal of coronary artery obstruction
37.34   Excision or destruction of other lesion or tissue of heart, endovascular approach

OR

Nonoperating Room Procedures
37.26   Catheter based invasive electrophysiologic testing
37.27   Cardiac mapping

AND

Nonoperating Room Procedure
36.07   Insertion of drug-eluting coronary artery stent(s)

DRG 248   Percutaneous Cardiovascular Procedure with Non Drug-Eluting Stent with MCC or 4+ Vessels/Stents
GMLOS 4.7   AMLOS 6.4   RW 3.0003   ☑

Operating Room Procedures
00.66   Percutaneous transluminal coronary angioplasty [PTCA]
17.55   Transluminal coronary atherectomy
35.96   Percutaneous balloon valvuloplasty
35.97   Percutaneous mitral valve repair with implant
36.09   Other removal of coronary artery obstruction
37.34   Excision or destruction of other lesion or tissue of heart, endovascular approach

OR

Nonoperating Room Procedures
37.26   Catheter based invasive electrophysiologic testing
37.27   Cardiac mapping

AND

Nonoperating Room Procedure
36.06   Insertion of non-drug-eluting coronary artery stent(s)

OR

Operating Room Procedure
92.27   Implantation or insertion of radioactive elements

OR

Any of the following procedure combinations:
00.43   Procedure on four or more vessels
      AND
00.66   Percutaneous transluminal coronary angioplasty [PTCA]
OR
00.48   Insertion of four or more vascular stents
      AND
00.66   Percutaneous transluminal coronary angioplasty [PTCA]

DRG 249   Percutaneous Cardiovascular Procedure with Non Drug-Eluting Stent without MCC
GMLOS 2.3   AMLOS 2.9   RW 1.7961   ☑

Operating Room Procedures
00.66   Percutaneous transluminal coronary angioplasty [PTCA]
17.55   Transluminal coronary atherectomy
35.96   Percutaneous balloon valvuloplasty
35.97   Percutaneous mitral valve repair with implant
36.09   Other removal of coronary artery obstruction
37.34   Excision or destruction of other lesion or tissue of heart, endovascular approach

OR

Nonoperating Room Procedures
37.26   Catheter based invasive electrophysiologic testing
37.27   Cardiac mapping

AND

Operating Room Procedure
92.27   Implantation or insertion of radioactive elements

OR

Nonoperating Room Procedure
36.06   Insertion of non-drug-eluting coronary artery stent(s)

DRG 250   Percutaneous Cardiovascular Procedure without Coronary Artery Stent with MCC
GMLOS 5.2   AMLOS 7.1   RW 2.9988   ☑

Operating Room Procedures
00.66   Percutaneous transluminal coronary angioplasty [PTCA]
17.55   Transluminal coronary atherectomy

MDC 5: Diseases And Disorders Of The Circulatory System—SURGICAL

Ⓣ *Transfer DRG*   SP *Special Payment*   ☑ *Optimization Potential*   *Targeted Potential*   * *Code Range*   ● *New DRG*   ▲ *Revised DRG Title*

62   Valid 10/01/2012–09/30/2013   © 2012 OptumInsight, Inc.

35.52	Repair of atrial septal defect with prosthesis, closed technique
35.96	Percutaneous balloon valvuloplasty
35.97	Percutaneous mitral valve repair with implant
36.09	Other removal of coronary artery obstruction
37.34	Excision or destruction of other lesion or tissue of heart, endovascular approach

OR

Nonoperating Room Procedures

37.26	Catheter based invasive electrophysiologic testing
37.27	Cardiac mapping
37.90	Insertion of left atrial appendage device

DRG 251 Percutaneous Cardiovascular Procedure without Coronary Artery Stent without MCC
GMLOS 2.2   AMLOS 3.0   RW 1.9237   ☑

Select operating procedures OR nonoperating room procedures listed under DRG 250

DRG 252 Other Vascular Procedures with MCC
GMLOS 5.3   AMLOS 7.8   RW 3.0224   ☑

Operating Room Procedures

00.61	Percutaneous angioplasty of extracranial vessel(s)
00.62	Percutaneous angioplasty of intracranial vessel(s)
04.92	Implantation or replacement of peripheral neurostimulator lead(s)
17.53	Percutaneous atherectomy of extracranial vessel(s)
17.54	Percutaneous atherectomy of intracranial vessel(s)
17.56	Atherectomy of other non-coronary vessel(s)
38.00	Incision of vessel, unspecified site
38.02	Incision of other vessels of head and neck
38.03	Incision of upper limb vessels
38.08	Incision of lower limb arteries
38.10	Endarterectomy, unspecified site
38.12	Endarterectomy of other vessels of head and neck
38.13	Endarterectomy of upper limb vessels
38.18	Endarterectomy of lower limb arteries
38.21	Biopsy of blood vessel
38.29	Other diagnostic procedures on blood vessels
38.30	Resection of vessel with anastomosis, unspecified site
38.32	Resection of other vessels of head and neck with anastomosis
38.33	Resection of upper limb vessels with anastomosis
38.38	Resection of lower limb arteries with anastomosis
38.40	Resection of vessel with replacement, unspecified site
38.42	Resection of other vessels of head and neck with replacement
38.43	Resection of upper limb vessels with replacement
38.48	Resection of lower limb arteries with replacement
38.52	Ligation and stripping of varicose veins of other vessels of head and neck
38.57	Ligation and stripping of abdominal varicose veins
38.60	Other excision of vessels, unspecified site
38.62	Other excision of other vessels of head and neck
38.63	Other excision of upper limb vessels
38.68	Other excision of lower limb arteries
38.7	Interruption of the vena cava
38.80	Other surgical occlusion of vessels, unspecified site
38.82	Other surgical occlusion of other vessels of head and neck
38.83	Other surgical occlusion of upper limb vessels
38.88	Other surgical occlusion of lower limb arteries
39.29	Other (peripheral) vascular shunt or bypass
39.30	Suture of unspecified blood vessel
39.31	Suture of artery
39.41	Control of hemorrhage following vascular surgery
39.49	Other revision of vascular procedure
39.50	Angioplasty of other non-coronary vessel(s)

39.51	Clipping of aneurysm
39.53	Repair of arteriovenous fistula
39.55	Reimplantation of aberrant renal vessel
39.56	Repair of blood vessel with tissue patch graft
39.57	Repair of blood vessel with synthetic patch graft
39.58	Repair of blood vessel with unspecified type of patch graft
39.59	Other repair of vessel
39.77	Temporary (partial) therapeutic endovascular occlusion of vessel
39.8*	Operations on carotid body, carotid sinus and other vascular bodies
39.91	Freeing of vessel
39.94	Replacement of vessel-to-vessel cannula
39.99	Other operations on vessels
86.96	Insertion or replacement of other neurostimulator pulse generator

DRG 253 Other Vascular Procedures with CC
GMLOS 4.4   AMLOS 5.9   RW 2.4739   ☑

Select operating room procedures listed under DRG 252

DRG 254 Other Vascular Procedures without CC/MCC
GMLOS 2.1   AMLOS 2.7   RW 1.6609   ☑

Select operating room procedures listed under DRG 252

DRG 255 Upper Limb and Toe Amputation for Circulatory System Disorders with MCC
GMLOS 6.7   AMLOS 8.8   RW 2.4381   T ☑

Operating Room Procedures

84.0*	Amputation of upper limb
84.11	Amputation of toe
84.3	Revision of amputation stump

DRG 256 Upper Limb and Toe Amputation for Circulatory System Disorders with CC
GMLOS 5.5   AMLOS 6.8   RW 1.5934   T ☑

Select operating room procedures listed under DRG 255

DRG 257 Upper Limb and Toe Amputation for Circulatory System Disorders without CC/MCC
GMLOS 3.2   AMLOS 4.2   RW 0.9535   T ☑

Select operating room procedures listed under DRG 255

DRG 258 Cardiac Pacemaker Device Replacement with MCC
GMLOS 5.0   AMLOS 6.5   RW 2.6945   ☑

Operating Room Procedures

00.53	Implantation or replacement of cardiac resynchronization pacemaker pulse generator only (CRT-P)
00.57	Implantation or replacement of subcutaneous device for intracardiac or great vessel hemodynamic monitoring
37.80	Insertion of permanent pacemaker, initial or replacement, type of device not specified
37.85	Replacement of any type of pacemaker device with single-chamber device, not specified as rate responsive
37.86	Replacement of any type of pacemaker device with single-chamber device, rate responsive
37.87	Replacement of any type of pacemaker device with dual-chamber device

DRG 259 Cardiac Pacemaker Device Replacement without MCC
GMLOS 2.5   AMLOS 3.3   RW 1.8590   ☑

Select operating room procedures listed under DRG 258

| *Surgical* | *Medical* | *CC Indicator* | *MCC Indicator* | *Procedure Proxy* |

MDC 5: Diseases And Disorders Of The Circulatory System—SURGICAL

DRG 260 Cardiac Pacemaker Revision Except Device Replacement with MCC
GMLOS 7.7   AMLOS 10.5   RW 3.6624   ☑

Operating Room Procedures
00.56 Insertion or replacement of implantable pressure sensor with lead for intracardiac or great vessel hemodynamic monitoring
37.74 Insertion or replacement of epicardial lead (electrode) into epicardium
37.75 Revision of lead (electrode)
37.76 Replacement of transvenous atrial and/or ventricular lead(s) (electrode(s))
37.77 Removal of lead(s) (electrodes) without replacement
37.79 Revision or relocation of cardiac device pocket
37.89 Revision or removal of pacemaker device

DRG 261 Cardiac Pacemaker Revision Except Device Replacement with CC
GMLOS 3.4   AMLOS 4.4   RW 1.6769   ☑

Select operating room procedures listed under DRG 260

DRG 262 Cardiac Pacemaker Revision Except Device Replacement without CC/MCC
GMLOS 2.1   AMLOS 2.7   RW 1.2343   ☑

Select operating room procedures listed under DRG 260

DRG 263 Vein Ligation and Stripping
GMLOS 3.8   AMLOS 5.9   RW 1.9091   ☑

Operating Room Procedures
38.09 Incision of lower limb veins
38.39 Resection of lower limb veins with anastomosis
38.49 Resection of lower limb veins with replacement
38.50 Ligation and stripping of varicose veins, unspecified site
38.53 Ligation and stripping of varicose veins of upper limb vessels
38.59 Ligation and stripping of lower limb varicose veins
38.69 Other excision of lower limb veins
38.89 Other surgical occlusion of lower limb veins
39.32 Suture of vein
39.92 Injection of sclerosing agent into vein

DRG 264 Other Circulatory System O.R. Procedures
GMLOS 5.6   AMLOS 8.3   RW 2.6674   T☑

Operating Room Procedures
05.0 Division of sympathetic nerve or ganglion
05.2* Sympathectomy
05.89 Other operations on sympathetic nerves or ganglia
17.32 Laparoscopic cecectomy
17.33 Laparoscopic right hemicolectomy
17.34 Laparoscopic resection of transverse colon
17.35 Laparoscopic left hemicolectomy
17.39 Other laparoscopic partial excision of large intestine
21.04 Control of epistaxis by ligation of ethmoidal arteries
21.05 Control of epistaxis by (transantral) ligation of the maxillary artery
21.06 Control of epistaxis by ligation of the external carotid artery
21.07 Control of epistaxis by excision of nasal mucosa and skin grafting of septum and lateral nasal wall
21.09 Control of epistaxis by other means
25.1 Excision or destruction of lesion or tissue of tongue
31.72 Closure of external fistula of trachea
31.74 Revision of tracheostomy
33.20 Thoracoscopic lung biopsy
33.27 Closed endoscopic biopsy of lung

33.28 Open biopsy of lung
34.02 Exploratory thoracotomy
34.03 Reopening of recent thoracotomy site
34.1 Incision of mediastinum
34.21 Transpleural thoracoscopy
34.22 Mediastinoscopy
34.26 Open biopsy of mediastinum
34.29 Other diagnostic procedures on mediastinum
38.26 Insertion of implantable pressure sensor without lead for intracardiac or great vessel hemodynamic monitoring
39.27 Arteriovenostomy for renal dialysis
39.42 Revision of arteriovenous shunt for renal dialysis
39.43 Removal of arteriovenous shunt for renal dialysis
39.93 Insertion of vessel-to-vessel cannula
39.98 Control of hemorrhage, not otherwise specified
40.1* Diagnostic procedures on lymphatic structures
40.21 Excision of deep cervical lymph node
40.23 Excision of axillary lymph node
40.24 Excision of inguinal lymph node
40.29 Simple excision of other lymphatic structure
40.3 Regional lymph node excision
41.5 Total splenectomy
43.6 Partial gastrectomy with anastomosis to duodenum
43.7 Partial gastrectomy with anastomosis to jejunum
43.82 Laparoscopic vertical (sleeve) gastrectomy
43.89 Open and other partial gastrectomy
43.99 Other total gastrectomy
44.38 Laparoscopic gastroenterostomy
44.39 Other gastroenterostomy without gastrectomy
45.61 Multiple segmental resection of small intestine
45.62 Other partial resection of small intestine
45.72 Open and other cecectomy
45.73 Open and other right hemicolectomy
45.74 Open and other resection of transverse colon
45.75 Open and other left hemicolectomy
45.79 Other and unspecified partial excision of large intestine
45.8* Total intra-abdominal colectomy
45.93 Other small-to-large intestinal anastomosis
46.03 Exteriorization of large intestine
46.13 Permanent colostomy
47.09 Other appendectomy
48.25 Open biopsy of rectum
48.35 Local excision of rectal lesion or tissue
48.62 Anterior resection of rectum with synchronous colostomy
48.63 Other anterior resection of rectum
48.69 Other resection of rectum
50.12 Open biopsy of liver
54.0 Incision of abdominal wall
54.11 Exploratory laparotomy
54.19 Other laparotomy
54.93 Creation of cutaneoperitoneal fistula
54.95 Incision of peritoneum
55.91 Decapsulation of kidney
84.94 Insertion of sternal fixation device with rigid plates
86.06 Insertion of totally implantable infusion pump
86.22 Excisional debridement of wound, infection, or burn
86.4 Radical excision of skin lesion
86.60 Free skin graft, not otherwise specified
86.61 Full-thickness skin graft to hand
86.62 Other skin graft to hand
86.63 Full-thickness skin graft to other sites
86.65 Heterograft to skin
86.66 Homograft to skin
86.67 Dermal regenerative graft
86.69 Other skin graft to other sites
86.70 Pedicle or flap graft, not otherwise specified
86.71 Cutting and preparation of pedicle grafts or flaps
86.72 Advancement of pedicle graft
86.74 Attachment of pedicle or flap graft to other sites
86.75 Revision of pedicle or flap graft

86.91	Excision of skin for graft
86.93	Insertion of tissue expander
92.27	Implantation or insertion of radioactive elements

OR

The following procedure combination

00.56	Insertion or replacement of implantable pressure sensor with lead for intracardiac or great vessel hemodynamic monitoring

AND

00.57	Implantation or replacement of subcutaneous device for intracardiac or great vessel hemodynamic monitoring

DRG 265 AICD Lead Procedures
GMLOS 2.5   AMLOS 3.8   RW 2.4394   ☑

Operating Room Procedures

00.52	Implantation or replacement of transvenous lead (electrode) into left ventricular coronary venous system
37.95	Implantation of automatic cardioverter/defibrillator leads(s) only
37.97	Replacement of automatic cardioverter/defibrillator leads(s) only

MEDICAL

DRG 280 Acute Myocardial Infarction, Discharged Alive with MCC
GMLOS 4.9   AMLOS 6.3   RW 1.7999   T ☑ ▽

Principal or Secondary Diagnosis

410.01	Acute myocardial infarction of anterolateral wall, initial episode of care
410.11	Acute myocardial infarction of other anterior wall, initial episode of care
410.21	Acute myocardial infarction of inferolateral wall, initial episode of care
410.31	Acute myocardial infarction of inferoposterior wall, initial episode of care
410.41	Acute myocardial infarction of other inferior wall, initial episode of care
410.51	Acute myocardial infarction of other lateral wall, initial episode of care
410.61	Acute myocardial infarction, true posterior wall infarction, initial episode of care
410.71	Acute myocardial infarction, subendocardial infarction, initial episode of care
410.81	Acute myocardial infarction of other specified sites, initial episode of care
410.91	Acute myocardial infarction, unspecified site, initial episode of care

DRG 281 Acute Myocardial Infarction, Discharged Alive with CC
GMLOS 3.2   AMLOS 4.0   RW 1.0961   T ☑ ▽

Select principal or secondary diagnoses listed under DRG 280

DRG 282 Acute Myocardial Infarction, Discharged Alive without CC/MCC
GMLOS 2.1   AMLOS 2.6   RW 0.7736   T ☑ ▽

Select principal or secondary diagnoses listed under DRG 280

DRG 283 Acute Myocardial Infarction, Expired with MCC
GMLOS 3.2   AMLOS 5.1   RW 1.7539   ☑

Select principal or secondary diagnoses listed under DRG 280

DRG 284 Acute Myocardial Infarction, Expired with CC
GMLOS 1.9   AMLOS 2.6   RW 0.8042   ☑

Select principal or secondary diagnosis listed under DRG 280

DRG 285 Acute Myocardial Infarction, Expired without CC/MCC
GMLOS 1.4   AMLOS 1.7   RW 0.5353   ☑

Select principal or secondary diagnosis listed under DRG 280

DRG 286 Circulatory Disorders Except Acute Myocardial Infarction, with Cardiac Catheterization with MCC
GMLOS 4.9   AMLOS 6.6   RW 2.0617   ☑ ▽

Select any principal diagnosis listed under MDC 5 excluding AMI

Nonoperating Room Procedures

37.21	Right heart cardiac catheterization
37.22	Left heart cardiac catheterization
37.23	Combined right and left heart cardiac catheterization
88.52	Angiocardiography of right heart structures
88.53	Angiocardiography of left heart structures
88.54	Combined right and left heart angiocardiography
88.55	Coronary arteriography using single catheter
88.56	Coronary arteriography using two catheters
88.57	Other and unspecified coronary arteriography
88.58	Negative-contrast cardiac roentgenography

DRG 287 Circulatory Disorders Except Acute Myocardial Infarction, with Cardiac Catheterization without MCC
GMLOS 2.4   AMLOS 3.1   RW 1.0709   ☑ ▽

Select any principal diagnosis listed under MDC 5 excluding AMI

Select nonoperating room procedure listed under DRG 286

DRG 288 Acute and Subacute Endocarditis with MCC
GMLOS 7.9   AMLOS 9.9   RW 2.8229   T

Principal Diagnosis

036.42	Meningococcal endocarditis
093.20	Unspecified syphilitic endocarditis of valve
098.84	Gonococcal endocarditis
112.81	Candidal endocarditis
115.04	Histoplasma capsulatum endocarditis
115.14	Histoplasma duboisii endocarditis
115.94	Unspecified Histoplasmosis endocarditis
421.0	Acute and subacute bacterial endocarditis
421.1	Acute and subacute infective endocarditis in diseases classified elsewhere
421.9	Unspecified acute endocarditis

DRG 289 Acute and Subacute Endocarditis with CC
GMLOS 5.9   AMLOS 7.2   RW 1.8145   T ☑

Select principal diagnosis listed under DRG 288

DRG 290 Acute and Subacute Endocarditis without CC/MCC
GMLOS 4.1   AMLOS 5.0   RW 1.2092   T ☑

Select principal diagnosis listed under DRG 288

DRG 291 Heart Failure and Shock with MCC
GMLOS 4.7   AMLOS 6.0   RW 1.5174   T ☑ ▽

Principal Diagnosis

398.91	Rheumatic heart failure (congestive)
402.01	Malignant hypertensive heart disease with heart failure
402.11	Benign hypertensive heart disease with heart failure
402.91	Hypertensive heart disease, unspecified, with heart failure

---

Surgical   *Medical*   *CC Indicator*   *MCC Indicator*   *Procedure Proxy*

MDC 5: Diseases And Disorders Of The Circulatory System—MEDICAL

404.01	Hypertensive heart and chronic kidney disease, malignant, with heart failure and with chronic kidney disease stage I through stage IV, or unspecified
404.03	Hypertensive heart and chronic kidney disease, malignant, with heart failure and with chronic kidney disease stage V or end stage renal disease
404.11	Hypertensive heart and chronic kidney disease, benign, with heart failure and with chronic kidney disease stage I through stage IV, or unspecified
404.13	Hypertensive heart and chronic kidney disease, benign, with heart failure and chronic kidney disease stage V or end stage renal disease
404.91	Hypertensive heart and chronic kidney disease, unspecified, with heart failure and with chronic kidney disease stage I through stage IV, or unspecified
404.93	Hypertensive heart and chronic kidney disease, unspecified, with heart failure and chronic kidney disease stage V or end stage renal disease
428*	Heart failure
785.50	Unspecified shock
785.51	Cardiogenic shock

DRG 292 Heart Failure and Shock with CC
GMLOS 3.8   AMLOS 4.6   RW 1.0034   T ☑ ▽

Select principal diagnosis listed under DRG 291

DRG 293 Heart Failure and Shock without CC/MCC
GMLOS 2.7   AMLOS 3.2   RW 0.6751   T ☑ ▽

Select principal diagnosis listed under DRG 291

DRG 294 Deep Vein Thrombophlebitis with CC/MCC
GMLOS 4.2   AMLOS 5.1   RW 1.0229   ☑ ▽

Principal Diagnosis

451.1*	Phlebitis and thrombophlebitis of deep veins of lower extremities
451.2	Phlebitis and thrombophlebitis of lower extremities, unspecified
451.81	Phlebitis and thrombophlebitis of iliac vein
453.2	Other venous embolism and thrombosis, of inferior vena cava

DRG 295 Deep Vein Thrombophlebitis without CC/MCC
GMLOS 3.5   AMLOS 4.0   RW 0.6476   ☑ ▽

Select principal diagnosis listed under DRG 294

DRG 296 Cardiac Arrest, Unexplained with MCC
GMLOS 1.9   AMLOS 2.8   RW 1.2878   ☑

Principal Diagnosis

427.5	Cardiac arrest
798.1	Instantaneous death
798.2	Death occurring in less than 24 hours from onset of symptoms, not otherwise explained

DRG 297 Cardiac Arrest, Unexplained with CC
GMLOS 1.3   AMLOS 1.5   RW 0.6455   ☑

Select principal diagnosis listed under DRG 296

DRG 298 Cardiac Arrest, Unexplained without CC/MCC
GMLOS 1.1   AMLOS 1.2   RW 0.4571   ☑

Select principal diagnosis listed under DRG 296

DRG 299 Peripheral Vascular Disorders with MCC
GMLOS 4.5   AMLOS 5.8   RW 1.4186   T ☑ ▽

Principal Diagnosis

249.7*	Secondary diabetes mellitus with peripheral circulatory disorders
250.7*	Diabetes with peripheral circulatory disorders
440.0	Atherosclerosis of aorta
440.2*	Atherosclerosis of native arteries of the extremities
440.3*	Atherosclerosis of bypass graft of extremities
440.4	Chronic total occlusion of artery of the extremities
440.8	Atherosclerosis of other specified arteries
440.9	Generalized and unspecified atherosclerosis
441.0*	Dissection of aorta
441.1	Thoracic aneurysm, ruptured
441.2	Thoracic aneurysm without mention of rupture
441.3	Abdominal aneurysm, ruptured
441.4	Abdominal aneurysm without mention of rupture
441.5	Aortic aneurysm of unspecified site, ruptured
441.6	Thoracoabdominal aneurysm, ruptured
441.7	Thoracoabdominal aneurysm without mention of rupture
441.9	Aortic aneurysm of unspecified site without mention of rupture
442.0	Aneurysm of artery of upper extremity
442.2	Aneurysm of iliac artery
442.3	Aneurysm of artery of lower extremity
442.8*	Aneurysm of other specified artery
442.9	Other aneurysm of unspecified site
443.1	Thromboangiitis obliterans (Buerger's disease)
443.21	Dissection of carotid artery
443.22	Dissection of iliac artery
443.24	Dissection of vertebral artery
443.29	Dissection of other artery
443.8*	Other specified peripheral vascular diseases
443.9	Unspecified peripheral vascular disease
444.0*	Arterial embolism and thrombosis of abdominal aorta
444.1	Embolism and thrombosis of thoracic aorta
444.2*	Embolism and thrombosis of arteries of the extremities
444.8*	Embolism and thrombosis of other specified artery
444.9	Embolism and thrombosis of unspecified artery
445.0*	Atheroembolism of extremities
445.89	Atheroembolism of other site
447.0	Arteriovenous fistula, acquired
447.1	Stricture of artery
447.2	Rupture of artery
447.5	Necrosis of artery
447.7*	Aortic ectasia
447.8	Other specified disorders of arteries and arterioles
447.9	Unspecified disorders of arteries and arterioles
448.0	Hereditary hemorrhagic telangiectasia
448.9	Other and unspecified capillary diseases
449	Septic arterial embolism
451.0	Phlebitis and thrombophlebitis of superficial vessels of lower extremities
451.82	Phlebitis and thrombophlebitis of superficial veins of upper extremities
451.83	Phlebitis and thrombophlebitis of deep veins of upper extremities
451.84	Phlebitis and thrombophlebitis of upper extremities, unspecified
451.89	Phlebitis and thrombophlebitis of other site
451.9	Phlebitis and thrombophlebitis of unspecified site
453.1	Thrombophlebitis migrans
453.4*	Acute venous embolism and thrombosis of deep vessels of lower extremity
453.5*	Chronic venous embolism and thrombosis of deep vessels of lower extremity
453.6	Venous embolism and thrombosis of superficial vessels of lower extremity

---

T *Transfer DRG*   SP *Special Payment*   ☑ *Optimization Potential*   ▽ *Targeted Potential*   * *Code Range*   ● *New DRG*   ▲ *Revised DRG Title*

66   Valid 10/01/2012-09/30/2013   © 2012 OptumInsight, Inc.

453.7*	Chronic venous embolism and thrombosis of other specified vessels
453.8*	Acute venous embolism and thrombosis of other specified veins
453.9	Embolism and thrombosis of unspecified site
454.0	Varicose veins of lower extremities with ulcer
454.1	Varicose veins of lower extremities with inflammation
454.2	Varicose veins of lower extremities with ulcer and inflammation
454.8	Varicose veins of the lower extremities with other complications
454.9	Asymptomatic varicose veins
456.3	Sublingual varices
456.8	Varices of other sites
459.1*	Postphlebitic syndrome
459.2	Compression of vein
459.3*	Chronic venous hypertension
459.81	Unspecified venous (peripheral) insufficiency
747.5	Congenital absence or hypoplasia of umbilical artery
747.6*	Other congenital anomaly of peripheral vascular system
747.89	Other specified congenital anomaly of circulatory system
747.9	Unspecified congenital anomaly of circulatory system
785.4	Gangrene
908.3	Late effect of injury to blood vessel of head, neck, and extremities
908.4	Late effect of injury to blood vessel of thorax, abdomen, and pelvis
997.2	Peripheral vascular complications
997.79	Vascular complications of other vessels

DRG 300　Peripheral Vascular Disorders with CC
GMLOS 3.7　　　AMLOS 4.6　　　RW 0.9679　　☑ T ☑ ▽

Select principal diagnosis listed under DRG 299

DRG 301　Peripheral Vascular Disorders without CC/MCC
GMLOS 2.7　　　AMLOS 3.4　　　RW 0.6679　　☑ T ☑ ▽

Select principal diagnosis listed under DRG 299

DRG 302　Atherosclerosis with MCC
GMLOS 2.9　　　AMLOS 3.9　　　RW 1.0142　　☑ ▽

Principal Diagnosis

412	Old myocardial infarction
414.0*	Coronary atherosclerosis
414.2	Chronic total occlusion of coronary artery
414.3	Coronary atherosclerosis due to lipid rich plaque
414.4	Coronary atherosclerosis due to calcified coronary lesion
414.8	Other specified forms of chronic ischemic heart disease
414.9	Unspecified chronic ischemic heart disease
429.2	Unspecified cardiovascular disease
429.3	Cardiomegaly
429.89	Other ill-defined heart disease
429.9	Unspecified heart disease
459.89	Other specified circulatory system disorders
459.9	Unspecified circulatory system disorder
793.2	Nonspecific (abnormal) findings on radiological and other examination of other intrathoracic organs

DRG 303　Atherosclerosis without MCC
GMLOS 1.9　　　AMLOS 2.3　　　RW 0.5773　　☑ ▽

Select principal diagnosis listed under DRG 302

DRG 304　Hypertension with MCC
GMLOS 3.4　　　AMLOS 4.4　　　RW 1.0503　　☑

Principal Diagnosis

401.0	Essential hypertension, malignant

401.1	Essential hypertension, benign
401.9	Unspecified essential hypertension
402.00	Malignant hypertensive heart disease without heart failure
402.10	Benign hypertensive heart disease without heart failure
402.90	Unspecified hypertensive heart disease without heart failure
404.00	Hypertensive heart and chronic kidney disease, malignant, without heart failure and with chronic kidney disease stage I through stage IV, or unspecified
404.10	Hypertensive heart and chronic kidney disease, benign, without heart failure and with chronic kidney disease stage I through stage IV, or unspecified
404.90	Hypertensive heart and chronic kidney disease, unspecified, without heart failure and with chronic kidney disease stage I through stage IV, or unspecified
405*	Secondary hypertension

DRG 305　Hypertension without MCC
GMLOS 2.1　　　AMLOS 2.6　　　RW 0.6187　　☑

Select principal diagnosis listed under DRG 304

DRG 306　Cardiac Congenital and Valvular Disorders with MCC
GMLOS 4.0　　　AMLOS 5.2　　　RW 1.3122　　☑

Principal Diagnosis

074.22	Coxsackie endocarditis
093.0	Aneurysm of aorta, specified as syphilitic
093.1	Syphilitic aortitis
093.21	Syphilitic endocarditis, mitral valve
093.22	Syphilitic endocarditis, aortic valve
093.23	Syphilitic endocarditis, tricuspid valve
093.24	Syphilitic endocarditis, pulmonary valve
391.1	Acute rheumatic endocarditis
394*	Diseases of mitral valve
395*	Diseases of aortic valve
396*	Diseases of mitral and aortic valves
397*	Diseases of other endocardial structures
424*	Other diseases of endocardium
429.5	Rupture of chordae tendineae
429.6	Rupture of papillary muscle
429.81	Other disorders of papillary muscle
745.0	Bulbus cordis anomalies and anomalies of cardiac septal closure, common truncus
745.1*	Transposition of great vessels
745.2	Tetralogy of Fallot
745.3	Bulbus cordis anomalies and anomalies of cardiac septal closure, common ventricle
745.4	Ventricular septal defect
745.5	Ostium secundum type atrial septal defect
745.60	Unspecified type congenital endocardial cushion defect
745.61	Ostium primum defect
745.69	Other congenital endocardial cushion defect
745.7	Cor biloculare
745.8	Other bulbus cordis anomalies and anomalies of cardiac septal closure
745.9	Unspecified congenital defect of septal closure
746.0*	Congenital anomalies of pulmonary valve
746.1	Congenital tricuspid atresia and stenosis
746.2	Ebstein's anomaly
746.3	Congenital stenosis of aortic valve
746.4	Congenital insufficiency of aortic valve
746.5	Congenital mitral stenosis
746.6	Congenital mitral insufficiency
746.7	Hypoplastic left heart syndrome
746.81	Congenital subaortic stenosis
746.82	Cor triatriatum
746.83	Congenital infundibular pulmonic stenosis
746.84	Congenital obstructive anomalies of heart, not elsewhere classified
746.85	Congenital coronary artery anomaly

Surgical	_Medical_	CC Indicator	MCC Indicator	Procedure Proxy

746.87	Congenital malposition of heart and cardiac apex
746.89	Other specified congenital anomaly of heart
746.9	Unspecified congenital anomaly of heart
747.0	Patent ductus arteriosus
747.1*	Coarctation of aorta
747.2*	Other congenital anomaly of aorta
747.3*	Anomalies of pulmonary artery
747.4*	Congenital anomalies of great veins
759.82	Marfan's syndrome
785.2	Undiagnosed cardiac murmurs
996.02	Mechanical complication due to heart valve prosthesis

DRG 307 Cardiac Congenital and Valvular Disorders without MCC
GMLOS 2.6   AMLOS 3.3   RW 0.7840   ☑

Select principal diagnosis listed under DRG 306

DRG 308 Cardiac Arrhythmia and Conduction Disorders with MCC
GMLOS 3.9   AMLOS 5.0   RW 1.2285   ☑ ▽

Principal Diagnosis

426*	Conduction disorders
427.0	Paroxysmal supraventricular tachycardia
427.1	Paroxysmal ventricular tachycardia
427.2	Unspecified paroxysmal tachycardia
427.3*	Atrial fibrillation and flutter
427.4*	Ventricular fibrillation and flutter
427.6*	Premature beats
427.8*	Other specified cardiac dysrhythmias
427.9	Unspecified cardiac dysrhythmia
746.86	Congenital heart block
785.0	Unspecified tachycardia
785.1	Palpitations
996.01	Mechanical complication due to cardiac pacemaker (electrode)
996.04	Mechanical complication due to automatic implantable cardiac defibrillator

DRG 309 Cardiac Arrhythmia and Conduction Disorders with CC
GMLOS 2.8   AMLOS 3.5   RW 0.8098   ☑ ▽

Select principal diagnosis listed under DRG 308

DRG 310 Cardiac Arrhythmia and Conduction Disorders without CC/MCC
GMLOS 2.0   AMLOS 2.3   RW 0.5541   ☑ ▽

Select principal diagnosis listed under DRG 308

DRG 311 Angina Pectoris
GMLOS 1.8   AMLOS 2.2   RW 0.5207   ☑ ▽

Principal Diagnosis

411.1	Intermediate coronary syndrome
411.81	Acute coronary occlusion without myocardial infarction
411.89	Other acute and subacute form of ischemic heart disease
413.0	Angina decubitus
413.1	Prinzmetal angina
413.9	Other and unspecified angina pectoris

DRG 312 Syncope and Collapse
GMLOS 2.4   AMLOS 2.9   RW 0.7339   ☑

Principal Diagnosis

458.0	Orthostatic hypotension
458.2*	Iatrogenic hypotension
780.2	Syncope and collapse

DRG 313 Chest Pain
GMLOS 1.7   AMLOS 2.1   RW 0.5617   ☑ ▽

Principal Diagnosis

786.50	Chest pain, unspecified
786.51	Precordial pain
786.59	Chest pain, other
V71.7	Observation for suspected cardiovascular disease

DRG 314 Other Circulatory System Diagnoses with MCC
GMLOS 4.9   AMLOS 6.7   RW 1.8508   Ⓣ ☑

Principal Diagnosis

032.82	Diphtheritic myocarditis
036.40	Meningococcal carditis, unspecified
036.41	Meningococcal pericarditis
036.43	Meningococcal myocarditis
074.20	Coxsackie carditis, unspecified
074.21	Coxsackie pericarditis
074.23	Coxsackie myocarditis
086.0	Chagas' disease with heart involvement
093.8*	Other specified cardiovascular syphilis
093.9	Unspecified cardiovascular syphilis
098.83	Gonococcal pericarditis
098.85	Other gonococcal heart disease
115.03	Histoplasma capsulatum pericarditis
115.13	Histoplasma duboisii pericarditis
115.93	Unspecified Histoplasmosis pericarditis
130.3	Myocarditis due to toxoplasmosis
164.1	Malignant neoplasm of heart
212.7	Benign neoplasm of heart
228.00	Hemangioma of unspecified site
228.09	Hemangioma of other sites
306.2	Cardiovascular malfunction arising from mental factors
391.0	Acute rheumatic pericarditis
391.2	Acute rheumatic myocarditis
391.8	Other acute rheumatic heart disease
391.9	Unspecified acute rheumatic heart disease
392*	Rheumatic chorea
393	Chronic rheumatic pericarditis
398.0	Rheumatic myocarditis
398.90	Unspecified rheumatic heart disease
398.99	Other and unspecified rheumatic heart diseases
410.00	Acute myocardial infarction of anterolateral wall, episode of care unspecified
410.02	Acute myocardial infarction of anterolateral wall, subsequent episode of care
410.10	Acute myocardial infarction of other anterior wall, episode of care unspecified
410.12	Acute myocardial infarction of other anterior wall, subsequent episode of care
410.20	Acute myocardial infarction of inferolateral wall, episode of care unspecified
410.22	Acute myocardial infarction of inferolateral wall, subsequent episode of care
410.30	Acute myocardial infarction of inferoposterior wall, episode of care unspecified
410.32	Acute myocardial infarction of inferoposterior wall, subsequent episode of care
410.40	Acute myocardial infarction of other inferior wall, episode of care unspecified
410.42	Acute myocardial infarction of other inferior wall, subsequent episode of care
410.50	Acute myocardial infarction of other lateral wall, episode of care unspecified
410.52	Acute myocardial infarction of other lateral wall, subsequent episode of care
410.60	Acute myocardial infarction, true posterior wall infarction, episode of care unspecified

---

Ⓣ *Transfer DRG*   ⓈⓅ *Special Payment*   ☑ *Optimization Potential*   ▽ *Targeted Potential*   * *Code Range*   ● *New DRG*   ▲ *Revised DRG Title*

410.62	Acute myocardial infarction, true posterior wall infarction, subsequent episode of care	
410.70	Acute myocardial infarction, subendocardial infarction, episode of care unspecified	
410.72	Acute myocardial infarction, subendocardial infarction, subsequent episode of care	
410.80	Acute myocardial infarction of other specified sites, episode of care unspecified	
410.82	Acute myocardial infarction of other specified sites, subsequent episode of care	
410.90	Acute myocardial infarction, unspecified site, episode of care unspecified	
410.92	Acute myocardial infarction, unspecified site, subsequent episode of care	
411.0	Postmyocardial infarction syndrome	
414.1*	Aneurysm and dissection of heart	
415.0	Acute cor pulmonale	
416.0	Primary pulmonary hypertension	
416.1	Kyphoscoliotic heart disease	
416.8	Other chronic pulmonary heart diseases	
416.9	Unspecified chronic pulmonary heart disease	
417*	Other diseases of pulmonary circulation	
420*	Acute pericarditis	
422*	Acute myocarditis	
423*	Other diseases of pericardium	
425*	Cardiomyopathy	
429.0	Unspecified myocarditis	
429.1	Myocardial degeneration	
429.4	Functional disturbances following cardiac surgery	
429.71	Acquired cardiac septal defect	
429.79	Other certain sequelae of myocardial infarction, not elsewhere classified	
429.82	Hyperkinetic heart disease	
429.83	Takotsubo syndrome	
458.1	Chronic hypotension	
458.8	Other specified hypotension	
458.9	Unspecified hypotension	
459.0	Unspecified hemorrhage	
785.3	Other abnormal heart sounds	
785.9	Other symptoms involving cardiovascular system	
794.30	Nonspecific abnormal unspecified cardiovascular function study	
794.31	Nonspecific abnormal electrocardiogram (ECG) (EKG)	
794.39	Other nonspecific abnormal cardiovascular system function study	
796.2	Elevated blood pressure reading without diagnosis of hypertension	
796.3	Nonspecific low blood pressure reading	
861.0*	Heart injury, without mention of open wound into thorax	
861.1*	Heart injury, with open wound into thorax	
996.00	Mechanical complication of unspecified cardiac device, implant, and graft	
996.03	Mechanical complication due to coronary bypass graft	
996.09	Mechanical complication of cardiac device, implant, and graft, other	
996.1	Mechanical complication of other vascular device, implant, and graft	
996.61	Infection and inflammatory reaction due to cardiac device, implant, and graft	
996.62	Infection and inflammatory reaction due to other vascular device, implant, and graft	
996.71	Other complications due to heart valve prosthesis	
996.72	Other complications due to other cardiac device, implant, and graft	
996.73	Other complications due to renal dialysis device, implant, and graft	
996.74	Other complications due to other vascular device, implant, and graft	
996.83	Complications of transplanted heart	
997.1	Cardiac complications	

999.2	Other vascular complications of medical care, not elsewhere classified
999.31	Other and unspecified infection due to central venous catheter
999.32	Bloodstream infection due to central venous catheter
999.33	Local infection due to central venous catheter
999.81	Extravasation of vesicant chemotherapy
999.82	Extravasation of other vesicant agent
999.88	Other infusion reaction
V42.1	Heart replaced by transplant
V42.2	Heart valve replaced by transplant
V43.2*	Heart replaced by other means
V43.3	Heart valve replaced by other means
V43.4	Blood vessel replaced by other means
V53.3*	Fitting and adjustment of cardiac device

DRG 315   Other Circulatory System Diagnoses with CC

GMLOS 3.1	AMLOS 4.0	RW 0.9527	T ☑

Select principal diagnosis listed under DRG 314

DRG 316   Other Circulatory System Diagnoses without CC/MCC

GMLOS 2.0	AMLOS 2.5	RW 0.6224	T ☑

Select principal diagnosis listed under DRG 314

001.0	014.81	151.5	209.67	531.01	534.70	551.00	562.02	578.1
001.1	014.82	151.6	209.74	531.10	534.71	551.01	562.03	578.9
001.9	014.83	151.8	211.0	531.11	534.90	551.02	562.10	579.0
003.0	014.84	151.9	211.1	531.20	534.91	551.03	562.11	579.1
004.0	014.85	152.0	211.2	531.21	535.00	551.1	562.12	579.2
004.1	014.86	152.1	211.3	531.30	535.01	551.20	562.13	579.3
004.2	017.80	152.2	211.4	531.31	535.10	551.21	564.00	579.4
004.3	017.81	152.3	211.8	531.40	535.11	551.29	564.01	579.8
004.8	017.82	152.8	211.9	531.41	535.20	551.3	564.02	579.9
004.9	017.83	152.9	214.3	531.50	535.21	551.8	564.09	617.5
005.0	017.84	153.0	228.04	531.51	535.30	551.9	564.1	619.1
005.2	017.85	153.1	230.1	531.60	535.31	552.00	564.2	750.3
005.3	017.86	153.2	230.2	531.61	535.40	552.01	564.3	750.4
005.4	021.1	153.3	230.3	531.70	535.41	552.02	564.4	750.5
005.81	022.2	153.4	230.4	531.71	535.50	552.03	564.5	750.6
005.89	032.83	153.5	230.5	531.90	535.51	552.1	564.6	750.7
005.9	039.2	153.6	230.6	531.91	535.60	552.20	564.7	750.8
006.0	040.2	153.7	230.7	532.00	535.61	552.21	564.81	750.9
006.1	054.71	153.8	230.9	532.01	535.70	552.29	564.89	751.0
006.2	078.82	153.9	235.2	532.10	535.71	552.3	564.9	751.1
007.0	091.1	154.0	235.4	532.11	536.0	552.8	565.0	751.2
007.1	091.69	154.1	235.5	532.20	536.1	552.9	565.1	751.3
007.2	095.2	154.2	239.0	532.21	536.2	553.00	566	751.4
007.3	098.7	154.3	251.5	532.30	536.3	553.01	567.0	751.5
007.4	098.86	154.8	271.2	532.31	536.40	553.02	567.1	751.8
007.5	099.52	158.8	271.3	532.40	536.41	553.03	567.21	751.9
007.8	099.56	158.9	277.03	532.41	536.42	553.1	567.22	756.70
007.9	112.84	159.0	289.2	532.50	536.49	553.20	567.23	756.71
008.00	112.85	159.8	306.4	532.51	536.8	553.21	567.29	756.72
008.01	123.0	159.9	447.4	532.60	536.9	553.29	567.31	756.73
008.02	123.1	176.3	455.0	532.61	537.0	553.3	567.38	756.79
008.03	123.2	195.2	455.1	532.70	537.1	553.8	567.39	759.3
008.04	123.3	197.4	455.2	532.71	537.2	553.9	567.81	759.4
008.09	123.4	197.5	455.3	532.90	537.3	555.0	567.82	787.01
008.1	123.5	197.6	455.4	532.91	537.4	555.1	567.89	787.02
008.2	123.6	197.8	455.5	533.00	537.5	555.2	567.9	787.03
008.3	123.8	209.00	455.6	533.01	537.6	555.9	568.0	787.04
008.41	123.9	209.01	455.7	533.10	537.81	556.0	568.81	787.1
008.42	126.0	209.02	455.8	533.11	537.82	556.1	568.82	787.20
008.43	126.1	209.03	455.9	533.20	537.83	556.2	568.89	787.21
008.44	126.2	209.10	456.0	533.21	537.84	556.3	568.9	787.22
008.45	126.3	209.11	456.1	533.30	537.89	556.4	569.0	787.23
008.46	126.8	209.12	456.20	533.31	537.9	556.5	569.1	787.24
008.47	126.9	209.13	456.21	533.40	538	556.6	569.2	787.29
008.49	127.0	209.14	530.0	533.41	539.01	556.8	569.3	787.3
008.5	127.1	209.15	530.10	533.50	539.09	556.9	569.41	787.4
008.61	127.2	209.16	530.11	533.51	539.81	557.0	569.42	787.5
008.62	127.3	209.17	530.12	533.60	539.89	557.1	569.43	787.60
008.63	127.4	209.23	530.13	533.61	540.0	557.9	569.44	787.61
008.64	127.5	209.25	530.19	533.70	540.1	558.1	569.49	787.62
008.65	127.6	209.26	530.20	533.71	540.9	558.2	569.5	787.63
008.66	127.7	209.27	530.21	533.90	541	558.3	569.60	787.7
008.67	127.9	209.40	530.3	533.91	542	558.41	569.61	787.91
008.69	129	209.41	530.4	534.00	543.0	558.42	569.62	787.99
008.8	150.0	209.42	530.5	534.01	543.9	558.9	569.69	789.0
009.0	150.1	209.43	530.6	534.10	550.00	560.0	569.71	789.01
009.1	150.2	209.50	530.7	534.11	550.01	560.1	569.79	789.02
009.2	150.3	209.51	530.81	534.20	550.02	560.2	569.81	789.03
009.3	150.4	209.52	530.82	534.21	550.03	560.30	569.82	789.04
014.00	150.5	209.53	530.83	534.30	550.10	560.31	569.83	789.05
014.01	150.8	209.54	530.84	534.31	550.11	560.32	569.84	789.06
014.02	150.9	209.55	530.85	534.40	550.12	560.39	569.85	789.07
014.03	151.0	209.56	530.86	534.41	550.13	560.81	569.86	789.09
014.04	151.1	209.57	530.87	534.50	550.90	560.89	569.87	789.30
014.05	151.2	209.63	530.89	534.51	550.91	560.9	569.89	789.31
014.06	151.3	209.65	530.9	534.60	550.92	562.00	569.9	789.32
014.80	151.4	209.66	531.00	534.61	550.93	562.01	578.0	789.33

789.34	789.46	789.69	796.75	863.29	863.49	863.89	936	V55.1
789.35	789.47	789.7	796.76	863.30	863.50	863.90	937	V55.2
789.36	789.49	789.9	796.77	863.31	863.51	863.95	938	V55.3
789.37	789.60	792.1	796.78	863.39	863.52	863.99	947.2	V55.4
789.39	789.61	793.4	796.79	863.40	863.53	868.00	947.3	
789.40	789.62	793.6	862.22	863.41	863.54	868.03	997.41	
789.41	789.63	796.70	862.32	863.42	863.55	868.10	997.49	
789.42	789.64	796.71	863.0	863.43	863.56	868.13	997.71	
789.43	789.65	796.72	863.1	863.44	863.59	908.1	V53.50	
789.44	789.66	796.73	863.20	863.45	863.80	935.1	V53.51	
789.45	789.67	796.74	863.21	863.46	863.85	935.2	V53.59	

MDC 6: Diseases And Disorders Of The Digestive System—SURGICAL

SURGICAL

DRG 326   Stomach, Esophageal and Duodenal Procedures with MCC
GMLOS 12.0   AMLOS 15.4   RW 5.6118   T

Operating Room Procedures

29.3*	Excision or destruction of lesion or tissue of pharynx
31.73	Closure of other fistula of trachea
38.05	Incision of other thoracic vessels
38.35	Resection of other thoracic vessels with anastomosis
38.45	Resection of other thoracic vessels with replacement
38.65	Other excision of other thoracic vessel
38.85	Other surgical occlusion of other thoracic vessel
39.1	Intra-abdominal venous shunt
42.01	Incision of esophageal web
42.09	Other incision of esophagus
42.1*	Esophagostomy
42.21	Operative esophagoscopy by incision
42.25	Open biopsy of esophagus
42.31	Local excision of esophageal diverticulum
42.32	Local excision of other lesion or tissue of esophagus
42.39	Other destruction of lesion or tissue of esophagus
42.4*	Excision of esophagus
42.5*	Intrathoracic anastomosis of esophagus
42.6*	Antesternal anastomosis of esophagus
42.7	Esophagomyotomy
42.82	Suture of laceration of esophagus
42.83	Closure of esophagostomy
42.84	Repair of esophageal fistula, not elsewhere classified
42.85	Repair of esophageal stricture
42.86	Production of subcutaneous tunnel without esophageal anastomosis
42.87	Other graft of esophagus
42.89	Other repair of esophagus
42.91	Ligation of esophageal varices
43.0	Gastrotomy
43.3	Pyloromyotomy
43.42	Local excision of other lesion or tissue of stomach
43.49	Other destruction of lesion or tissue of stomach
43.5	Partial gastrectomy with anastomosis to esophagus
43.6	Partial gastrectomy with anastomosis to duodenum
43.7	Partial gastrectomy with anastomosis to jejunum
43.8*	Other partial gastrectomy
43.9*	Total gastrectomy
44.0*	Vagotomy
44.11	Transabdominal gastroscopy
44.15	Open biopsy of stomach
44.21	Dilation of pylorus by incision
44.29	Other pyloroplasty
44.3*	Gastroenterostomy without gastrectomy
44.40	Suture of peptic ulcer, not otherwise specified
44.41	Suture of gastric ulcer site
44.42	Suture of duodenal ulcer site
44.5	Revision of gastric anastomosis
44.61	Suture of laceration of stomach
44.63	Closure of other gastric fistula
44.64	Gastropexy
44.65	Esophagogastroplasty
44.66	Other procedures for creation of esophagogastric sphincteric competence
44.67	Laparoscopic procedures for creation of esophagogastric sphincteric competence
44.68	Laparoscopic gastroplasty
44.69	Other repair of stomach
44.91	Ligation of gastric varices
44.92	Intraoperative manipulation of stomach
44.99	Other operations on stomach
45.01	Incision of duodenum
45.31	Other local excision of lesion of duodenum

45.32	Other destruction of lesion of duodenum
46.71	Suture of laceration of duodenum
46.72	Closure of fistula of duodenum
51.82	Pancreatic sphincterotomy
51.83	Pancreatic sphincteroplasty
52.7	Radical pancreaticoduodenectomy
53.7*	Repair of diaphragmatic hernia, abdominal approach
53.8*	Repair of diaphragmatic hernia, thoracic approach

DRG 327   Stomach, Esophageal and Duodenal Procedures with CC
GMLOS 6.3   AMLOS 8.2   RW 2.6811   T ☑

Select operating room procedures listed under DRG 326

DRG 328   Stomach, Esophageal and Duodenal Procedures without CC/MCC
GMLOS 2.5   AMLOS 3.3   RW 1.4413   T ☑

Select operating room procedures listed under DRG 326

DRG 329   Major Small and Large Bowel Procedures with MCC
GMLOS 12.1   AMLOS 14.9   RW 5.2599   T ☑

Operating Room Procedures

17.3*	Laparoscopic partial excision of large intestine
45.5*	Isolation of intestinal segment
45.6*	Other excision of small intestine
45.7*	Open and other partial excision of large intestine
45.8*	Total intra-abdominal colectomy
45.9*	Intestinal anastomosis
46.0*	Exteriorization of intestine
46.10	Colostomy, not otherwise specified
46.11	Temporary colostomy
46.13	Permanent colostomy
46.20	Ileostomy, not otherwise specified
46.21	Temporary ileostomy
46.22	Continent ileostomy
46.23	Other permanent ileostomy
46.73	Suture of laceration of small intestine, except duodenum
46.74	Closure of fistula of small intestine, except duodenum
46.75	Suture of laceration of large intestine
46.76	Closure of fistula of large intestine
46.79	Other repair of intestine
46.80	Intra-abdominal manipulation of intestine, not otherwise specified
46.81	Intra-abdominal manipulation of small intestine
46.82	Intra-abdominal manipulation of large intestine
46.91	Myotomy of sigmoid colon
46.92	Myotomy of other parts of colon
46.93	Revision of anastomosis of small intestine
46.94	Revision of anastomosis of large intestine
46.99	Other operations on intestines
47.92	Closure of appendiceal fistula
48.1	Proctostomy
48.71	Suture of laceration of rectum
48.72	Closure of proctostomy
48.74	Rectorectostomy
48.75	Abdominal proctopexy
48.76	Other proctopexy
70.52	Repair of rectocele
70.53	Repair of cystocele and rectocele with graft or prosthesis
70.55	Repair of rectocele with graft or prosthesis
70.72	Repair of colovaginal fistula
70.73	Repair of rectovaginal fistula
70.74	Repair of other vaginoenteric fistula

T *Transfer DRG*   SP *Special Payment*   ☑ *Optimization Potential*   ▽ *Targeted Potential*   * *Code Range*   ● *New DRG*   ▲ *Revised DRG Title*

DRG 330   Major Small and Large Bowel Procedures with CC
GMLOS 7.4   AMLOS 8.6   RW 2.5731   T ☑

Select operating room procedures listed under DRG 329

DRG 331   Major Small and Large Bowel Procedures without CC/MCC
GMLOS 4.5   AMLOS 5.0   RW 1.6361   T ☑

Select operating room procedures listed under DRG 329

DRG 332   Rectal Resection with MCC
GMLOS 11.2   AMLOS 13.4   RW 4.6143   T ☑

Operating Room Procedures
48.4*   Pull-through resection of rectum
48.5*   Abdominoperineal resection of rectum
48.6*   Other resection of rectum
49.75   Implantation or revision of artificial anal sphincter
49.76   Removal of artificial anal sphincter
68.8   Pelvic evisceration

DRG 333   Rectal Resection with CC
GMLOS 6.7   AMLOS 7.8   RW 2.4814   T ☑

Select operating room procedures listed under DRG 332

DRG 334   Rectal Resection without CC/MCC
GMLOS 4.0   AMLOS 4.6   RW 1.6181   T ☑

Select operating room procedures listed under DRG 332

DRG 335   Peritoneal Adhesiolysis with MCC
GMLOS 11.2   AMLOS 13.4   RW 4.3146   T

Operating Room Procedures
54.5*   Lysis of peritoneal adhesions

DRG 336   Peritoneal Adhesiolysis with CC
GMLOS 7.0   AMLOS 8.4   RW 2.3529   T ☑

Select operating room procedures listed under DRG 335

DRG 337   Peritoneal Adhesiolysis without CC/MCC
GMLOS 4.0   AMLOS 5.0   RW 1.5538   T ☑

Select operating room procedures listed under DRG 335

DRG 338   Appendectomy with Complicated Principal Diagnosis with MCC
GMLOS 8.3   AMLOS 10.0   RW 3.2008   ☑

Principal Diagnosis
153.5   Malignant neoplasm of appendix
209.11   Malignant carcinoid tumor of the appendix
540.0   Acute appendicitis with generalized peritonitis
540.1   Acute appendicitis with peritoneal abscess

Operating Room Procedures
47.0*   Appendectomy
47.2   Drainage of appendiceal abscess
47.99   Other operations on appendix

DRG 339   Appendectomy with Complicated Principal Diagnosis with CC
GMLOS 5.4   AMLOS 6.4   RW 1.8675   ☑

Select principal diagnosis and operating room procedure listed under DRG 338

DRG 340   Appendectomy with Complicated Principal Diagnosis without CC/MCC
GMLOS 3.0   AMLOS 3.6   RW 1.2024   ☑

Select principal diagnosis and operating room procedure listed under DRG 338

DRG 341   Appendectomy without Complicated Principal Diagnosis with MCC
GMLOS 4.8   AMLOS 6.6   RW 2.3116   ☑

Operating Room Procedures
47.0*   Appendectomy
47.2   Drainage of appendiceal abscess
47.99   Other operations on appendix

DRG 342   Appendectomy without Complicated Principal Diagnosis with CC
GMLOS 2.9   AMLOS 3.7   RW 1.3516   ☑

Select operating room procedures listed under DRG 341

DRG 343   Appendectomy without Complicated Principal Diagnosis without CC/MCC
GMLOS 1.6   AMLOS 1.9   RW 0.9547   ☑

Select operating room procedures listed under DRG 341

DRG 344   Minor Small and Large Bowel Procedures with MCC
GMLOS 9.0   AMLOS 11.5   RW 3.4094   ☑

Operating Room Procedures
45.00   Incision of intestine, not otherwise specified
45.02   Other incision of small intestine
45.03   Incision of large intestine
45.11   Transabdominal endoscopy of small intestine
45.15   Open biopsy of small intestine
45.21   Transabdominal endoscopy of large intestine
45.26   Open biopsy of large intestine
45.34   Other destruction of lesion of small intestine, except duodenum
45.49   Other destruction of lesion of large intestine
46.5*   Closure of intestinal stoma
46.6*   Fixation of intestine
47.91   Appendicostomy
48.0   Proctotomy
48.21   Transabdominal proctosigmoidoscopy
48.25   Open biopsy of rectum
56.84   Closure of other fistula of ureter
57.83   Repair of fistula involving bladder and intestine
69.42   Closure of fistula of uterus
70.75   Repair of other fistula of vagina
71.72   Repair of fistula of vulva or perineum

DRG 345   Minor Small and Large Bowel Procedures with CC
GMLOS 5.6   AMLOS 6.6   RW 1.7123   ☑

Select operating room procedures listed under DRG 344

DRG 346   Minor Small and Large Bowel Procedures without CC/MCC
GMLOS 3.9   AMLOS 4.4   RW 1.1608   ☑

Select operating room procedures listed under DRG 344

MDC 6: Diseases And Disorders Of The Digestive System—SURGICAL

DRG 347   Anal and Stomal Procedures with MCC
GMLOS 6.4   AMLOS 8.6   RW 2.5169   ☑

Operating Room Procedures
45.33	Local excision of lesion or tissue of small intestine, except duodenum
45.41	Excision of lesion or tissue of large intestine
46.4*	Revision of intestinal stoma
48.35	Local excision of rectal lesion or tissue
48.73	Closure of other rectal fistula
48.79	Other repair of rectum
48.8*	Incision or excision of perirectal tissue or lesion
48.9*	Other operations on rectum and perirectal tissue
49.01	Incision of perianal abscess
49.02	Other incision of perianal tissue
49.04	Other excision of perianal tissue
49.1*	Incision or excision of anal fistula
49.39	Other local excision or destruction of lesion or tissue of anus
49.44	Destruction of hemorrhoids by cryotherapy
49.45	Ligation of hemorrhoids
49.46	Excision of hemorrhoids
49.49	Other procedures on hemorrhoids
49.5*	Division of anal sphincter
49.6	Excision of anus
49.71	Suture of laceration of anus
49.72	Anal cerclage
49.73	Closure of anal fistula
49.79	Other repair of anal sphincter
49.9*	Other operations on anus

DRG 348   Anal and Stomal Procedures with CC
GMLOS 4.2   AMLOS 5.4   RW 1.3900   ☑

Select operating room procedures listed under DRG 347

DRG 349   Anal and Stomal Procedures without CC/MCC
GMLOS 2.3   AMLOS 2.8   RW 0.8343   ☑

Select operating room procedures listed under DRG 347

DRG 350   Inguinal and Femoral Hernia Procedures with MCC
GMLOS 5.9   AMLOS 7.8   RW 2.5082   ☑

Operating Room Procedures
17.1*	Laparoscopic unilateral repair of inguinal hernia
17.2*	Laparoscopic bilateral repair of inguinal hernia
53.0*	Other unilateral repair of inguinal hernia
53.1*	Other bilateral repair of inguinal hernia
53.2*	Unilateral repair of femoral hernia
53.3*	Bilateral repair of femoral hernia

DRG 351   Inguinal and Femoral Hernia Procedures with CC
GMLOS 3.4   AMLOS 4.4   RW 1.3755   ☑

Select operating room procedures listed under DRG 350

DRG 352   Inguinal and Femoral Hernia Procedures without CC/MCC
GMLOS 2.0   AMLOS 2.4   RW 0.9043   ☑

Select operating room procedures listed under DRG 350

DRG 353   Hernia Procedures Except Inguinal and Femoral with MCC
GMLOS 6.3   AMLOS 8.2   RW 2.8192   ☑

Operating Room Procedures
53.4*	Repair of umbilical hernia
53.5*	Repair of other hernia of anterior abdominal wall (without graft or prosthesis)
53.6*	Repair of other hernia of anterior abdominal wall with graft or prosthesis

53.9	Other hernia repair
54.71	Repair of gastroschisis
54.72	Other repair of abdominal wall

DRG 354   Hernia Procedures Except Inguinal and Femoral with CC
GMLOS 4.0   AMLOS 5.0   RW 1.5976   ☑

Select operating room procedures listed under DRG 353

DRG 355   Hernia Procedures Except Inguinal and Femoral without CC/MCC
GMLOS 2.4   AMLOS 2.9   RW 1.1172   ☑

Select operating room procedures listed under DRG 353

DRG 356   Other Digestive System O.R. Procedures with MCC
GMLOS 8.9   AMLOS 12.0   RW 3.9463   T ☑

Operating Room Procedures
17.56	Atherectomy of other non-coronary vessel(s)
17.63	Laser interstitial thermal therapy [LITT] of lesion or tissue of liver under guidance
38.04	Incision of aorta
38.06	Incision of abdominal arteries
38.07	Incision of abdominal veins
38.14	Endarterectomy of aorta
38.16	Endarterectomy of abdominal arteries
38.34	Resection of aorta with anastomosis
38.36	Resection of abdominal arteries with anastomosis
38.37	Resection of abdominal veins with anastomosis
38.46	Resection of abdominal arteries with replacement
38.47	Resection of abdominal veins with replacement
38.57	Ligation and stripping of abdominal varicose veins
38.64	Other excision of abdominal aorta
38.66	Other excision of abdominal arteries
38.67	Other excision of abdominal veins
38.7	Interruption of the vena cava
38.84	Other surgical occlusion of abdominal aorta
38.86	Other surgical occlusion of abdominal arteries
38.87	Other surgical occlusion of abdominal veins
39.26	Other intra-abdominal vascular shunt or bypass
39.27	Arteriovenostomy for renal dialysis
39.49	Other revision of vascular procedure
39.50	Angioplasty of other non-coronary vessel(s)
39.91	Freeing of vessel
39.98	Control of hemorrhage, not otherwise specified
39.99	Other operations on vessels
40.1*	Diagnostic procedures on lymphatic structures
40.21	Excision of deep cervical lymph node
40.23	Excision of axillary lymph node
40.24	Excision of inguinal lymph node
40.29	Simple excision of other lymphatic structure
40.3	Regional lymph node excision
40.5*	Radical excision of other lymph nodes
40.9	Other operations on lymphatic structures
41.5	Total splenectomy
49.74	Gracilis muscle transplant for anal incontinence
50.12	Open biopsy of liver
50.14	Laparoscopic liver biopsy
50.19	Other diagnostic procedures on liver
50.23	Open ablation of liver lesion or tissue
50.24	Percutaneous ablation of liver lesion or tissue
50.25	Laparoscopic ablation of liver lesion or tissue
50.26	Other and unspecified ablation of liver lesion or tissue
50.29	Other destruction of lesion of liver
51.03	Other cholecystostomy
51.13	Open biopsy of gallbladder or bile ducts
51.19	Other diagnostic procedures on biliary tract
51.22	Cholecystectomy
51.23	Laparoscopic cholecystectomy

MDC 6: Diseases And Disorders Of The Digestive System—SURGICAL

51.32	Anastomosis of gallbladder to intestine
51.36	Choledochoenterostomy
51.37	Anastomosis of hepatic duct to gastrointestinal tract
51.59	Incision of other bile duct
51.62	Excision of ampulla of Vater (with reimplantation of common duct)
51.63	Other excision of common duct
51.69	Excision of other bile duct
51.81	Dilation of sphincter of Oddi
52.12	Open biopsy of pancreas
52.19	Other diagnostic procedures on pancreas
52.92	Cannulation of pancreatic duct
52.99	Other operations on pancreas
54.0	Incision of abdominal wall
54.1*	Laparotomy
54.21	Laparoscopy
54.22	Biopsy of abdominal wall or umbilicus
54.23	Biopsy of peritoneum
54.29	Other diagnostic procedures on abdominal region
54.3	Excision or destruction of lesion or tissue of abdominal wall or umbilicus
54.4	Excision or destruction of peritoneal tissue
54.6*	Suture of abdominal wall and peritoneum
54.73	Other repair of peritoneum
54.74	Other repair of omentum
54.75	Other repair of mesentery
54.92	Removal of foreign body from peritoneal cavity
54.93	Creation of cutaneoperitoneal fistula
54.94	Creation of peritoneovascular shunt
54.95	Incision of peritoneum
70.50	Repair of cystocele and rectocele
86.06	Insertion of totally implantable infusion pump
86.22	Excisional debridement of wound, infection, or burn
86.60	Free skin graft, not otherwise specified
86.63	Full-thickness skin graft to other sites
86.65	Heterograft to skin
86.66	Homograft to skin
86.67	Dermal regenerative graft
86.69	Other skin graft to other sites
86.70	Pedicle or flap graft, not otherwise specified
86.71	Cutting and preparation of pedicle grafts or flaps
86.72	Advancement of pedicle graft
86.74	Attachment of pedicle or flap graft to other sites
86.75	Revision of pedicle or flap graft
86.93	Insertion of tissue expander
92.27	Implantation or insertion of radioactive elements

DRG 357 Other Digestive System O.R. Procedures with CC
GMLOS 5.5   AMLOS 7.1   RW 2.1747   ☑☑

Select operating room procedures listed under DRG 356

DRG 358 Other Digestive System O.R. Procedures without CC/MCC
GMLOS 3.1   AMLOS 4.0   RW 1.3629   ☑☑

Select operating room procedures listed under DRG 356

MEDICAL

DRG 368 Major Esophageal Disorders with MCC
GMLOS 5.1   AMLOS 6.6   RW 1.8327   ☑

Principal Diagnosis
017.8*	Tuberculosis of esophagus
112.84	Candidiasis of the esophagus
456.0	Esophageal varices with bleeding
456.1	Esophageal varices without mention of bleeding
456.20	Esophageal varices with bleeding in diseases classified elsewhere
530.4	Perforation of esophagus
530.7	Gastroesophageal laceration-hemorrhage syndrome
530.82	Esophageal hemorrhage
530.84	Tracheoesophageal fistula
750.3	Congenital tracheoesophageal fistula, esophageal atresia and stenosis
750.4	Other specified congenital anomaly of esophagus
862.22	Esophagus injury without mention of open wound into cavity
947.2	Burn of esophagus

DRG 369 Major Esophageal Disorders with CC
GMLOS 3.5   AMLOS 4.2   RW 1.0664   ☑

Select principal diagnosis listed under DRG 368

DRG 370 Major Esophageal Disorders without CC/MCC
GMLOS 2.5   AMLOS 3.0   RW 0.7593   ☑

Select principal diagnosis listed under DRG 368

DRG 371 Major Gastrointestinal Disorders and Peritoneal Infections with MCC
GMLOS 6.5   AMLOS 8.4   RW 2.0200   ☑☑

Principal Diagnosis
001*	Cholera
003.0	Salmonella gastroenteritis
004*	Shigellosis
005.0	Staphylococcal food poisoning
005.2	Food poisoning due to Clostridium perfringens (C. welchii)
005.3	Food poisoning due to other Clostridia
005.4	Food poisoning due to Vibrio parahaemolyticus
005.8*	Other bacterial food poisoning
006.0	Acute amebic dysentery without mention of abscess
006.1	Chronic intestinal amebiasis without mention of abscess
006.2	Amebic nondysenteric colitis
007*	Other protozoal intestinal diseases
008.00	Intestinal infection due to unspecified E. coli
008.01	Intestinal infection due to enteropathogenic E. coli
008.02	Intestinal infection due to enterotoxigenic E. coli
008.03	Intestinal infection due to enteroinvasive E. coli
008.04	Intestinal infection due to enterohemorrhagic E. coli
008.09	Intestinal infection due to other intestinal E. coli infections
008.1	Intestinal infection due to Arizona group of paracolon bacilli
008.2	Intestinal infection due to aerobacter aerogenes
008.3	Intestinal infections due to proteus (mirabilis) (morganii)
008.41	Intestinal infections due to staphylococcus
008.42	Intestinal infections due to pseudomonas
008.43	Intestinal infections due to campylobacter
008.44	Intestinal infections due to yersinia enterocolitica
008.45	Intestinal infections due to clostridium difficile
008.46	Intestinal infections due to other anaerobes
008.47	Intestinal infections due to other gram-negative bacteria
008.49	Intestinal infection due to other organisms
008.5	Intestinal infection due to unspecified bacterial enteritis
014*	Tuberculosis of intestines, peritoneum, and mesenteric glands
021.1	Enteric tularemia
022.2	Gastrointestinal anthrax
032.83	Diphtheritic peritonitis
039.2	Abdominal actinomycotic infection
095.2	Syphilitic peritonitis
098.86	Gonococcal peritonitis
123.1	Cysticercosis
123.5	Sparganosis (larval diphyllobothriasis)
123.6	Hymenolepiasis
123.8	Other specified cestode infection

123.9	Unspecified cestode infection
126*	Ancylostomiasis and necatoriasis
540.0	Acute appendicitis with generalized peritonitis
540.1	Acute appendicitis with peritoneal abscess
567.0	Peritonitis in infectious diseases classified elsewhere
567.1	Pneumococcal peritonitis
567.2*	Other suppurative peritonitis
567.3*	Retroperitoneal infections
567.89	Other specified peritonitis
567.9	Unspecified peritonitis
569.5	Abscess of intestine

DRG 372   Major Gastrointestinal Disorders and Peritoneal Infections with CC

GMLOS 4.9   AMLOS 5.9   RW 1.2275   T ☑

Select principal diagnosis listed under DRG 371

DRG 373   Major Gastrointestinal Disorders and Peritoneal Infections without CC/MCC

GMLOS 3.6   AMLOS 4.3   RW 0.8401   T ☑

Select principal diagnosis listed under DRG 371

DRG 374   Digestive Malignancy with MCC

GMLOS 6.3   AMLOS 8.5   RW 2.1284   T ☑

Principal Diagnosis

150*	Malignant neoplasm of esophagus
151*	Malignant neoplasm of stomach
152*	Malignant neoplasm of small intestine, including duodenum
153*	Malignant neoplasm of colon
154*	Malignant neoplasm of rectum, rectosigmoid junction, and anus
158.8	Malignant neoplasm of specified parts of peritoneum
158.9	Malignant neoplasm of peritoneum, unspecified
159.0	Malignant neoplasm of intestinal tract, part unspecified
159.8	Malignant neoplasm of other sites of digestive system and intra-abdominal organs
159.9	Malignant neoplasm of ill-defined sites of digestive organs and peritoneum
176.3	Kaposi's sarcoma of gastrointestinal sites
195.2	Malignant neoplasm of abdomen
197.4	Secondary malignant neoplasm of small intestine including duodenum
197.5	Secondary malignant neoplasm of large intestine and rectum
197.6	Secondary malignant neoplasm of retroperitoneum and peritoneum
197.8	Secondary malignant neoplasm of other digestive organs and spleen
209.0*	Malignant carcinoid tumors of the small intestine
209.1*	Malignant carcinoid tumors of the appendix, large intestine, and rectum
209.23	Malignant carcinoid tumor of the stomach
209.25	Malignant carcinoid tumor of foregut, not otherwise specified
209.26	Malignant carcinoid tumor of midgut, not otherwise specified
209.27	Malignant carcinoid tumor of hindgut, not otherwise specified
209.74	Secondary neuroendocrine tumor of peritoneum
230.1	Carcinoma in situ of esophagus
230.2	Carcinoma in situ of stomach
230.3	Carcinoma in situ of colon
230.4	Carcinoma in situ of rectum
230.5	Carcinoma in situ of anal canal
230.6	Carcinoma in situ of anus, unspecified
230.7	Carcinoma in situ of other and unspecified parts of intestine
230.9	Carcinoma in situ of other and unspecified digestive organs
235.2	Neoplasm of uncertain behavior of stomach, intestines, and rectum
235.4	Neoplasm of uncertain behavior of retroperitoneum and peritoneum
235.5	Neoplasm of uncertain behavior of other and unspecified digestive organs
239.0	Neoplasm of unspecified nature of digestive system

DRG 375   Digestive Malignancy with CC

GMLOS 4.3   AMLOS 5.5   RW 1.2738   T ☑

Select principal diagnosis listed under DRG 374

DRG 376   Digestive Malignancy without CC/MCC

GMLOS 2.8   AMLOS 3.5   RW 0.8809   T ☑

Select principal diagnosis listed under DRG 374

DRG 377   GI Hemorrhage with MCC

GMLOS 4.9   AMLOS 6.3   RW 1.7817   T ☑ ▽

Principal Diagnosis

531.0*	Acute gastric ulcer with hemorrhage
531.2*	Acute gastric ulcer with hemorrhage and perforation
531.4*	Chronic or unspecified gastric ulcer with hemorrhage
531.6*	Chronic or unspecified gastric ulcer with hemorrhage and perforation
532.0*	Acute duodenal ulcer with hemorrhage
532.2*	Acute duodenal ulcer with hemorrhage and perforation
532.4*	Chronic or unspecified duodenal ulcer with hemorrhage
532.6*	Chronic or unspecified duodenal ulcer with hemorrhage and perforation
533.0*	Acute peptic ulcer, unspecified site, with hemorrhage
533.2*	Acute peptic ulcer, unspecified site, with hemorrhage and perforation
533.4*	Chronic or unspecified peptic ulcer, unspecified site, with hemorrhage
533.6*	Chronic or unspecified peptic ulcer, unspecified site, with hemorrhage and perforation
534.0*	Acute gastrojejunal ulcer with hemorrhage
534.2*	Acute gastrojejunal ulcer with hemorrhage and perforation
534.4*	Chronic or unspecified gastrojejunal ulcer with hemorrhage
534.6*	Chronic or unspecified gastrojejunal ulcer with hemorrhage and perforation
535.01	Acute gastritis with hemorrhage
535.11	Atrophic gastritis with hemorrhage
535.21	Gastric mucosal hypertrophy with hemorrhage
535.31	Alcoholic gastritis with hemorrhage
535.41	Other specified gastritis with hemorrhage
535.51	Unspecified gastritis and gastroduodenitis with hemorrhage
535.61	Duodenitis with hemorrhage
535.71	Eosinophilic gastritis with hemorrhage
537.83	Angiodysplasia of stomach and duodenum with hemorrhage
537.84	Dieulafoy lesion (hemorrhagic) of stomach and duodenum
562.02	Diverticulosis of small intestine with hemorrhage
562.03	Diverticulitis of small intestine with hemorrhage
562.12	Diverticulosis of colon with hemorrhage
562.13	Diverticulitis of colon with hemorrhage
569.3	Hemorrhage of rectum and anus
569.85	Angiodysplasia of intestine with hemorrhage
578*	Gastrointestinal hemorrhage

DRG 378   GI Hemorrhage with CC

GMLOS 3.4   AMLOS 4.0   RW 1.0168   T ☑ ▽

Select principal diagnosis listed under DRG 377

Ⓣ *Transfer DRG*   ⓈⓅ *Special Payment*   ☑ *Optimization Potential*   ▽ *Targeted Potential*   * *Code Range*   ● *New DRG*   ▲ *Revised DRG Title*

76   Valid 10/01/2012-09/30/2013   © 2012 OptumInsight, Inc.

DRG 379   GI Hemorrhage without CC/MCC

GMLOS 2.4   AMLOS 2.9   RW 0.7015   T ☑ ▽

Select principal diagnosis listed under DRG 377

DRG 380   Complicated Peptic Ulcer with MCC

GMLOS 5.6   AMLOS 7.2   RW 1.9311   T ☑

Principal Diagnosis

251.5	Abnormality of secretion of gastrin
530.2*	Ulcer of esophagus
530.85	Barrett's esophagus
531.1*	Acute gastric ulcer with perforation
531.31	Acute gastric ulcer without mention of hemorrhage or perforation, with obstruction
531.5*	Chronic or unspecified gastric ulcer with perforation
531.71	Chronic gastric ulcer without mention of hemorrhage or perforation, with obstruction
531.91	Gastric ulcer, unspecified as acute or chronic, without mention of hemorrhage or perforation, with obstruction
532.1*	Acute duodenal ulcer with perforation
532.31	Acute duodenal ulcer without mention of hemorrhage or perforation, with obstruction
532.5*	Chronic or unspecified duodenal ulcer with perforation
532.71	Chronic duodenal ulcer without mention of hemorrhage or perforation, with obstruction
532.91	Duodenal ulcer, unspecified as acute or chronic, without mention of hemorrhage or perforation, with obstruction
533.1*	Acute peptic ulcer, unspecified site, with perforation
533.31	Acute peptic ulcer, unspecified site, without mention of hemorrhage and perforation, with obstruction
533.5*	Chronic or unspecified peptic ulcer, unspecified site, with perforation
533.71	Chronic peptic ulcer of unspecified site without mention of hemorrhage or perforation, with obstruction
533.91	Peptic ulcer, unspecified site, unspecified as acute or chronic, without mention of hemorrhage or perforation, with obstruction
534.1*	Acute gastrojejunal ulcer with perforation
534.3*	Acute gastrojejunal ulcer without mention of hemorrhage or perforation
534.5*	Chronic or unspecified gastrojejunal ulcer with perforation
534.7*	Chronic gastrojejunal ulcer without mention of hemorrhage or perforation
534.9*	Gastrojejunal ulcer, unspecified as acute or chronic, without mention of hemorrhage or perforation
537.0	Acquired hypertrophic pyloric stenosis
537.3	Other obstruction of duodenum
751.0	Meckel's diverticulum

DRG 381   Complicated Peptic Ulcer with CC

GMLOS 3.7   AMLOS 4.6   RW 1.1130   T ☑

Select principal diagnosis listed under DRG 380

DRG 382   Complicated Peptic Ulcer without CC/MCC

GMLOS 2.8   AMLOS 3.4   RW 0.7917   T ☑

Select principal diagnosis listed under DRG 380

DRG 383   Uncomplicated Peptic Ulcer with MCC

GMLOS 4.4   AMLOS 5.6   RW 1.3384   ☑

Principal Diagnosis

531.30	Acute gastric ulcer without mention of hemorrhage, perforation, or obstruction
531.70	Chronic gastric ulcer without mention of hemorrhage, perforation, without mention of obstruction
531.90	Gastric ulcer, unspecified as acute or chronic, without mention of hemorrhage, perforation, or obstruction
532.30	Acute duodenal ulcer without mention of hemorrhage, perforation, or obstruction
532.70	Chronic duodenal ulcer without mention of hemorrhage, perforation, or obstruction
532.90	Duodenal ulcer, unspecified as acute or chronic, without hemorrhage, perforation, or obstruction
533.30	Acute peptic ulcer, unspecified site, without mention of hemorrhage, perforation, or obstruction
533.70	Chronic peptic ulcer, unspecified site, without mention of hemorrhage, perforation, or obstruction
533.90	Peptic ulcer, unspecified site, unspecified as acute or chronic, without mention of hemorrhage, perforation, or obstruction

DRG 384   Uncomplicated Peptic Ulcer without MCC

GMLOS 2.9   AMLOS 3.5   RW 0.8365   ☑

Select principal diagnosis listed under DRG 383

DRG 385   Inflammatory Bowel Disease with MCC

GMLOS 6.3   AMLOS 8.3   RW 1.9078   ☑

Principal Diagnosis

555*	Regional enteritis
556*	Ulcerative colitis

DRG 386   Inflammatory Bowel Disease with CC

GMLOS 4.1   AMLOS 5.1   RW 1.0505   ☑

Select principal diagnosis listed under DRG 385

DRG 387   Inflammatory Bowel Disease without CC/MCC

GMLOS 3.1   AMLOS 3.8   RW 0.7878   ☑

Select principal diagnosis listed under DRG 385

DRG 388   GI Obstruction with MCC

GMLOS 5.4   AMLOS 7.1   RW 1.6564   T ☑ ▽

Principal Diagnosis

560*	Intestinal obstruction without mention of hernia

DRG 389   GI Obstruction with CC

GMLOS 3.7   AMLOS 4.6   RW 0.9217   T ☑ ▽

Select principal diagnosis listed under DRG 388

DRG 390   GI Obstruction without CC/MCC

GMLOS 2.7   AMLOS 3.2   RW 0.6372   T ☑ ▽

Select principal diagnosis listed under DRG 388

DRG 391   Esophagitis, Gastroenteritis and Miscellaneous Digestive Disorders with MCC

GMLOS 3.9   AMLOS 5.1   RW 1.1897   ☑ ▽

Principal Diagnosis

005.9	Unspecified food poisoning
008.6*	Intestinal infection, enteritis due to specified virus
008.8	Intestinal infection due to other organism, NEC
009*	Ill-defined intestinal infections
078.82	Epidemic vomiting syndrome
112.85	Candidiasis of the intestine
123.0	Taenia solium infection, intestinal form
123.2	Taenia saginata infection
123.3	Taeniasis, unspecified
123.4	Diphyllobothriasis, intestinal
127.0	Ascariasis
127.1	Anisakiasis

MDC 6: Diseases And Disorders Of The Digestive System—MEDICAL

127.2	Strongyloidiasis
127.3	Trichuriasis
127.4	Enterobiasis
127.5	Capillariasis
127.6	Trichostrongyliasis
127.7	Other specified intestinal helminthiasis
127.9	Unspecified intestinal helminthiasis
129	Unspecified intestinal parasitism
228.04	Hemangioma of intra-abdominal structures
271.2	Hereditary fructose intolerance
271.3	Intestinal disaccharidase deficiencies and disaccharide malabsorption
306.4	Gastrointestinal malfunction arising from mental factors
447.4	Celiac artery compression syndrome
530.0	Achalasia and cardiospasm
530.1*	Esophagitis
530.3	Stricture and stenosis of esophagus
530.5	Dyskinesia of esophagus
530.6	Diverticulum of esophagus, acquired
530.81	Esophageal reflux
530.83	Esophageal leukoplakia
530.89	Other specified disorder of the esophagus
530.9	Unspecified disorder of esophagus
535.00	Acute gastritis without mention of hemorrhage
535.10	Atrophic gastritis without mention of hemorrhage
535.20	Gastric mucosal hypertrophy without mention of hemorrhage
535.30	Alcoholic gastritis without mention of hemorrhage
535.40	Other specified gastritis without mention of hemorrhage
535.50	Unspecified gastritis and gastroduodenitis without mention of hemorrhage
535.60	Duodenitis without mention of hemorrhage
535.70	Eosinophilic gastritis without mention of hemorrhage
536.0	Achlorhydria
536.1	Acute dilatation of stomach
536.2	Persistent vomiting
536.3	Gastroparesis
536.8	Dyspepsia and other specified disorders of function of stomach
536.9	Unspecified functional disorder of stomach
537.1	Gastric diverticulum
537.2	Chronic duodenal ileus
537.4	Fistula of stomach or duodenum
537.5	Gastroptosis
537.6	Hourglass stricture or stenosis of stomach
537.81	Pylorospasm
537.82	Angiodysplasia of stomach and duodenum (without mention of hemorrhage)
537.89	Other specified disorder of stomach and duodenum
537.9	Unspecified disorder of stomach and duodenum
538	Gastrointestinal mucositis (ulcerative)
552.3	Diaphragmatic hernia with obstruction
553.3	Diaphragmatic hernia without mention of obstruction or gangrene
558.3	Gastroenteritis and colitis, allergic
558.4*	Eosinophilic gastroenteritis and colitis
558.9	Other and unspecified noninfectious gastroenteritis and colitis
562.00	Diverticulosis of small intestine (without mention of hemorrhage)
562.01	Diverticulitis of small intestine (without mention of hemorrhage)
562.10	Diverticulosis of colon (without mention of hemorrhage)
562.11	Diverticulitis of colon (without mention of hemorrhage)
564.0*	Constipation
564.1	Irritable bowel syndrome
564.2	Postgastric surgery syndromes
564.3	Vomiting following gastrointestinal surgery
564.4	Other postoperative functional disorders
564.5	Functional diarrhea

564.6	Anal spasm
564.8*	Other specified functional disorders of intestine
564.9	Unspecified functional disorder of intestine
579*	Intestinal malabsorption
617.5	Endometriosis of intestine
787*	Symptoms involving digestive system
789.0*	Abdominal pain
789.3*	Abdominal or pelvic swelling, mass, or lump
789.6*	Abdominal tenderness
789.7	Colic
789.9	Other symptoms involving abdomen and pelvis
792.1	Nonspecific abnormal finding in stool contents
793.4	Nonspecific (abnormal) findings on radiological and other examination of gastrointestinal tract
793.6	Nonspecific (abnormal) findings on radiological and other examination of abdominal area, including retroperitoneum

DRG 392   **Esophagitis, Gastroenteritis and Miscellaneous Digestive Disorders without MCC**

GMLOS 2.8	AMLOS 3.4	RW 0.7375	☑ ▽

Select principal diagnosis listed under DRG 391

DRG 393   **Other Digestive System Diagnoses with MCC**

GMLOS 4.8	AMLOS 6.6	RW 1.6666	☑ ▽

Principal Diagnosis

040.2	Whipple's disease
054.71	Visceral herpes simplex
091.1	Primary anal syphilis
091.69	Early syphilis, secondary syphilis of other viscera
098.7	Gonococcal infection of anus and rectum
099.52	Chlamydia trachomatis infection of anus and rectum
099.56	Chlamydia trachomatis infection of peritoneum
209.4*	Benign carcinoid tumors of the small intestine
209.5*	Benign carcinoid tumors of the appendix, large intestine, and rectum
209.63	Benign carcinoid tumor of the stomach
209.65	Benign carcinoid tumor of foregut, not otherwise specified
209.66	Benign carcinoid tumor of midgut, not otherwise specified
209.67	Benign carcinoid tumor of hindgut, not otherwise specified
211.0	Benign neoplasm of esophagus
211.1	Benign neoplasm of stomach
211.2	Benign neoplasm of duodenum, jejunum, and ileum
211.3	Benign neoplasm of colon
211.4	Benign neoplasm of rectum and anal canal
211.8	Benign neoplasm of retroperitoneum and peritoneum
211.9	Benign neoplasm of other and unspecified site of the digestive system
214.3	Lipoma of intra-abdominal organs
277.03	Cystic fibrosis with gastrointestinal manifestations
289.2	Nonspecific mesenteric lymphadenitis
455*	Hemorrhoids
456.21	Esophageal varices without mention of bleeding in diseases classified elsewhere
530.86	Infection of esophagostomy
530.87	Mechanical complication of esophagostomy
536.4*	Gastrostomy complications
539*	Complications of bariatric procedures
540.9	Acute appendicitis without mention of peritonitis
541	Appendicitis, unqualified
542	Other appendicitis
543*	Other diseases of appendix
550*	Inguinal hernia
551*	Other hernia of abdominal cavity, with gangrene
552.0*	Femoral hernia with obstruction
552.1	Umbilical hernia with obstruction
552.2*	Ventral hernia with obstruction
552.8	Hernia of other specified site, with obstruction
552.9	Hernia of unspecified site, with obstruction

Ⓣ *Transfer DRG*   ⓢⓟ *Special Payment*   ☑ *Optimization Potential*   ▽ *Targeted Potential*   * *Code Range*   ● *New DRG*   ▲ *Revised DRG Title*

553.0*	Femoral hernia without mention of obstruction or gangrene
553.1	Umbilical hernia without mention of obstruction or gangrene
553.2*	Ventral hernia without mention of obstruction or gangrene
553.8	Hernia of other specified sites of abdominal cavity without mention of obstruction or gangrene
553.9	Hernia of unspecified site of abdominal cavity without mention of obstruction or gangrene
557*	Vascular insufficiency of intestine
558.1	Gastroenteritis and colitis due to radiation
558.2	Toxic gastroenteritis and colitis
564.7	Megacolon, other than Hirschsprung's
565*	Anal fissure and fistula
566	Abscess of anal and rectal regions
567.81	Choleperitonitis
567.82	Sclerosing mesenteritis
568*	Other disorders of peritoneum
569.0	Anal and rectal polyp
569.1	Rectal prolapse
569.2	Stenosis of rectum and anus
569.4*	Other specified disorders of rectum and anus
569.6*	Colostomy and enterostomy complications
569.7*	Complications of intestinal pouch
569.81	Fistula of intestine, excluding rectum and anus
569.82	Ulceration of intestine
569.83	Perforation of intestine
569.84	Angiodysplasia of intestine (without mention of hemorrhage)
569.86	Dieulafoy lesion (hemorrhagic) of intestine
569.87	Vomiting of fecal matter
569.89	Other specified disorder of intestines
569.9	Unspecified disorder of intestine
619.1	Digestive-genital tract fistula, female
750.5	Congenital hypertrophic pyloric stenosis
750.6	Congenital hiatus hernia
750.7	Other specified congenital anomalies of stomach
750.8	Other specified congenital anomalies of upper alimentary tract
750.9	Unspecified congenital anomaly of upper alimentary tract
751.1	Congenital atresia and stenosis of small intestine
751.2	Congenital atresia and stenosis of large intestine, rectum, and anal canal
751.3	Hirschsprung's disease and other congenital functional disorders of colon
751.4	Congenital anomalies of intestinal fixation
751.5	Other congenital anomalies of intestine
751.8	Other specified congenital anomalies of digestive system
751.9	Unspecified congenital anomaly of digestive system
756.7*	Congenital anomaly of abdominal wall
759.3	Situs inversus
759.4	Conjoined twins
789.4*	Abdominal rigidity
796.7*	Abnormal cytologic smear of anus and anal HPV
862.32	Esophagus injury with open wound into cavity
863.0	Stomach injury without mention of open wound into cavity
863.1	Stomach injury with open wound into cavity
863.2*	Small intestine injury without mention of open wound into cavity
863.3*	Small intestine injury with open wound into cavity
863.4*	Colon or rectal injury without mention of open wound into cavity
863.5*	Injury to colon or rectum with open wound into cavity
863.80	Gastrointestinal tract injury, unspecified site, without mention of open wound into cavity
863.85	Appendix injury without mention of open wound into cavity
863.89	Injury to other and unspecified gastrointestinal sites without mention of open wound into cavity
863.90	Gastrointestinal tract injury, unspecified site, with open wound into cavity
863.95	Appendix injury with open wound into cavity

863.99	Injury to other and unspecified gastrointestinal sites with open wound into cavity
868.00	Injury to unspecified intra-abdominal organ without mention of open wound into cavity
868.03	Peritoneum injury without mention of open wound into cavity
868.10	Injury to unspecified intra-abdominal organ, with open wound into cavity
868.13	Peritoneum injury with open wound into cavity
908.1	Late effect of internal injury to intra-abdominal organs
935.1	Foreign body in esophagus
935.2	Foreign body in stomach
936	Foreign body in intestine and colon
937	Foreign body in anus and rectum
938	Foreign body in digestive system, unspecified
947.3	Burn of gastrointestinal tract
997.4*	Digestive system complications, not elsewhere classified
997.71	Vascular complications of mesenteric artery
V53.5*	Fitting and adjustment of other gastrointestinal appliance and device
V55.1	Attention to gastrostomy
V55.2	Attention to ileostomy
V55.3	Attention to colostomy
V55.4	Attention to other artificial opening of digestive tract

DRG 394 **Other Digestive System Diagnoses with CC**

GMLOS 3.5	AMLOS 4.4	RW 0.9837	☑ ▽

Select principal diagnosis listed under DRG 393

DRG 395 **Other Digestive System Diagnoses without CC/MCC**

GMLOS 2.4	AMLOS 3.0	RW 0.6791	☑ ▽

Select principal diagnosis listed under DRG 393

MDC 6: Diseases And Disorders Of The Digestive System—MEDICAL

Surgical		_Medical_		_CC Indicator_		_MCC Indicator_		_Procedure Proxy_

006.3	070.59	155.2	452	572.8	574.60	576.1	793.3	864.13
070.0	070.6	156.0	453.0	573.0	574.61	576.2	794.8	864.14
070.1	070.70	156.1	570	573.1	574.70	576.3	863.81	864.15
070.20	070.71	156.2	571.0	573.2	574.71	576.4	863.82	864.19
070.21	070.9	156.8	571.1	573.3	574.80	576.5	863.83	868.02
070.22	072.3	156.9	571.2	573.4	574.81	576.8	863.84	868.12
070.23	072.71	157.0	571.3	573.8	574.90	576.9	863.91	996.82
070.30	091.62	157.1	571.40	573.9	574.91	577.0	863.92	996.86
070.31	095.3	157.2	571.41	574.00	575.0	577.1	863.93	V02.60
070.32	120.1	157.3	571.42	574.01	575.10	577.2	863.94	V02.61
070.33	121.0	157.4	571.49	574.10	575.11	577.8	864.00	V02.62
070.41	121.1	157.8	571.5	574.11	575.12	577.9	864.01	V02.69
070.42	121.3	157.9	571.6	574.20	575.2	751.60	864.02	V42.7
070.43	121.4	197.7	571.8	574.21	575.3	751.61	864.03	V42.83
070.44	122.0	209.72	571.9	574.30	575.4	751.62	864.04	V59.6
070.49	122.5	211.5	572.0	574.31	575.5	751.69	864.05	
070.51	122.8	211.6	572.1	574.40	575.6	751.7	864.09	
070.52	130.5	230.8	572.2	574.41	575.8	782.4	864.10	
070.53	155.0	235.3	572.3	574.50	575.9	789.1	864.11	
070.54	155.1	277.4	572.4	574.51	576.0	791.4	864.12	

SURGICAL

DRG 405　**Pancreas, Liver and Shunt Procedures with MCC**
　　　　　GMLOS 11.3　　　AMLOS 15.2　　　RW 5.5575　　[T]

Operating Room Procedures
17.63　Laser interstitial thermal therapy [LITT] of lesion or tissue of liver under guidance
39.1　Intra-abdominal venous shunt
50.0　Hepatotomy
50.21　Marsupialization of lesion of liver
50.22　Partial hepatectomy
50.23　Open ablation of liver lesion or tissue
50.24　Percutaneous ablation of liver lesion or tissue
50.25　Laparoscopic ablation of liver lesion or tissue
50.26　Other and unspecified ablation of liver lesion or tissue
50.29　Other destruction of lesion of liver
50.3　Lobectomy of liver
50.4　Total hepatectomy
50.61　Closure of laceration of liver
50.69　Other repair of liver
51.43　Insertion of choledochohepatic tube for decompression
51.82　Pancreatic sphincterotomy
51.83　Pancreatic sphincteroplasty
52.0*　Pancreatotomy
52.22　Other excision or destruction of lesion or tissue of pancreas or pancreatic duct
52.3　Marsupialization of pancreatic cyst
52.4　Internal drainage of pancreatic cyst
52.5*　Partial pancreatectomy
52.6　Total pancreatectomy
52.7　Radical pancreaticoduodenectomy
52.80　Pancreatic transplant, not otherwise specified
52.81　Reimplantation of pancreatic tissue
52.82　Homotransplant of pancreas
52.83　Heterotransplant of pancreas
52.92　Cannulation of pancreatic duct
52.95　Other repair of pancreas
52.96　Anastomosis of pancreas
52.99　Other operations on pancreas
54.94　Creation of peritoneovascular shunt

DRG 406　**Pancreas, Liver and Shunt Procedures with CC**
　　　　　GMLOS 6.2　　　AMLOS 7.9　　　RW 2.7303　　[T][✓]

Select operating room procedures listed under DRG 405

DRG 407　**Pancreas, Liver and Shunt Procedures without CC/MCC**
　　　　　GMLOS 4.1　　　AMLOS 5.0　　　RW 1.8280　　[T][✓]

Select operating room procedures listed under DRG 405

DRG 408　**Biliary Tract Procedures Except Only Cholecystectomy with or without C.D.E. with MCC**
　　　　　GMLOS 10.3　　　AMLOS 12.8　　　RW 3.8375

Operating Room Procedures
51.02　Trocar cholecystostomy
51.03　Other cholecystostomy
51.04　Other cholecystotomy
51.3*　Anastomosis of gallbladder or bile duct
51.49　Incision of other bile ducts for relief of obstruction
51.59　Incision of other bile duct
51.61　Excision of cystic duct remnant
51.62　Excision of ampulla of Vater (with reimplantation of common duct)
51.63　Other excision of common duct
51.69　Excision of other bile duct

51.7*　Repair of bile ducts
51.81　Dilation of sphincter of Oddi
51.89　Other operations on sphincter of Oddi
51.91　Repair of laceration of gallbladder
51.92　Closure of cholecystostomy
51.93　Closure of other biliary fistula
51.94　Revision of anastomosis of biliary tract
51.95　Removal of prosthetic device from bile duct
51.99　Other operations on biliary tract

WITH OR WITHOUT

Operating Room Procedures
51.41　Common duct exploration for removal of calculus
51.42　Common duct exploration for relief of other obstruction
51.51　Exploration of common bile duct

DRG 409　**Biliary Tract Procedures Except Only Cholecystectomy with or without C.D.E. with CC**
　　　　　GMLOS 6.9　　　AMLOS 8.3　　　RW 2.2680　　[✓]

Select operating room procedures listed under DRG 408

DRG 410　**Biliary Tract Procedures Except Only Cholecystectomy with or without C.D.E. without CC/MCC**
　　　　　GMLOS 4.8　　　AMLOS 5.7　　　RW 1.6875　　[✓]

Select operating room procedures listed under DRG 408

DRG 411　**Cholecystectomy with C.D.E. with MCC**
　　　　　GMLOS 9.7　　　AMLOS 11.7　　　RW 3.8040　　[✓]

Operating Room Procedures
51.41　Common duct exploration for removal of calculus
51.42　Common duct exploration for relief of other obstruction
51.51　Exploration of common bile duct
AND

Operating Room Procedures
51.2*　Cholecystectomy

DRG 412　**Cholecystectomy with C.D.E. with CC**
　　　　　GMLOS 7.0　　　AMLOS 8.2　　　RW 2.5989　　[✓]

Select operating room procedures listed under DRG 411

DRG 413　**Cholecystectomy with C.D.E. without CC/MCC**
　　　　　GMLOS 4.6　　　AMLOS 5.3　　　RW 1.8582　　[✓]

Select operating room procedures listed under DRG 411

DRG 414　**Cholecystectomy Except by Laparoscope without C.D.E. with MCC**
　　　　　GMLOS 9.0　　　AMLOS 10.9　　　RW 3.5643　　[T][✓]

Operating Room Procedures
51.21　Other partial cholecystectomy
51.22　Cholecystectomy

DRG 415　**Cholecystectomy Except by Laparoscope without C.D.E. with CC**
　　　　　GMLOS 6.0　　　AMLOS 6.9　　　RW 2.0728　　[T][✓]

Select operating room procedures listed under DRG 414

DRG 416　**Cholecystectomy Except by Laparoscope without C.D.E. without CC/MCC**
　　　　　GMLOS 3.7　　　AMLOS 4.4　　　RW 1.3354　　[T][✓]

Select operating room procedures listed under DRG 414

Surgical	Medical	CC Indicator	MCC Indicator	Procedure Proxy

MDC 7: Diseases And Disorders Of The Hepatobiliary System And Pancreas—MEDICAL

DRG 417   Laparoscopic Cholecystectomy without C.D.E. with MCC
GMLOS 6.1   AMLOS 7.7   RW 2.5189   ☑

Operating room procedures
51.23   Laparoscopic cholecystectomy
51.24   Laparoscopic partial cholecystectomy

DRG 418   Laparoscopic Cholecystectomy without C.D.E. with CC
GMLOS 4.2   AMLOS 5.1   RW 1.7007   ☑

Select operating room procedures listed under DRG 417

DRG 419   Laparoscopic Cholecystectomy without C.D.E. without CC/MCC
GMLOS 2.5   AMLOS 3.0   RW 1.2050   ☑

Select operating room procedures listed under DRG 417

DRG 420   Hepatobiliary Diagnostic Procedures with MCC
GMLOS 8.7   AMLOS 12.3   RW 3.8509   ☑

Operating Room Procedures
44.11   Transabdominal gastroscopy
50.12   Open biopsy of liver
50.14   Laparoscopic liver biopsy
50.19   Other diagnostic procedures on liver
51.13   Open biopsy of gallbladder or bile ducts
51.19   Other diagnostic procedures on biliary tract
52.12   Open biopsy of pancreas
52.19   Other diagnostic procedures on pancreas
54.11   Exploratory laparotomy
54.19   Other laparotomy
54.21   Laparoscopy
54.23   Biopsy of peritoneum
54.29   Other diagnostic procedures on abdominal region
87.53   Intraoperative cholangiogram

DRG 421   Hepatobiliary Diagnostic Procedures with CC
GMLOS 4.6   AMLOS 6.2   RW 1.7381   ☑

Select operating room procedures listed under DRG 420

DRG 422   Hepatobiliary Diagnostic Procedures without CC/MCC
GMLOS 3.2   AMLOS 4.0   RW 1.3006   ☑

Select operating room procedures listed under DRG 420

DRG 423   Other Hepatobiliary or Pancreas O.R. Procedures with MCC
GMLOS 10.2   AMLOS 13.6   RW 4.3308   ☑

Operating Room Procedures
03.2*   Chordotomy
17.56   Atherectomy of other non-coronary vessel(s)
38.7   Interruption of the vena cava
39.26   Other intra-abdominal vascular shunt or bypass
39.29   Other (peripheral) vascular shunt or bypass
39.49   Other revision of vascular procedure
39.50   Angioplasty of other non-coronary vessel(s)
39.98   Control of hemorrhage, not otherwise specified
40.11   Biopsy of lymphatic structure
42.91   Ligation of esophageal varices
43.0   Gastrotomy
43.42   Local excision of other lesion or tissue of stomach
44.32   Percutaneous [endoscopic] gastrojejunostomy
44.38   Laparoscopic gastroenterostomy
44.39   Other gastroenterostomy without gastrectomy
44.63   Closure of other gastric fistula
44.91   Ligation of gastric varices
44.92   Intraoperative manipulation of stomach
45.01   Incision of duodenum

45.31   Other local excision of lesion of duodenum
45.32   Other destruction of lesion of duodenum
46.80   Intra-abdominal manipulation of intestine, not otherwise specified
46.81   Intra-abdominal manipulation of small intestine
46.82   Intra-abdominal manipulation of large intestine
46.99   Other operations on intestines
54.0   Incision of abdominal wall
54.12   Reopening of recent laparotomy site
54.4   Excision or destruction of peritoneal tissue
54.5*   Lysis of peritoneal adhesions
54.61   Reclosure of postoperative disruption of abdominal wall
54.62   Delayed closure of granulating abdominal wound
54.64   Suture of peritoneum
54.72   Other repair of abdominal wall
54.73   Other repair of peritoneum
54.74   Other repair of omentum
54.75   Other repair of mesentery
54.93   Creation of cutaneoperitoneal fistula
54.95   Incision of peritoneum
86.06   Insertion of totally implantable infusion pump
86.22   Excisional debridement of wound, infection, or burn

DRG 424   Other Hepatobiliary or Pancreas O.R. Procedures with CC
GMLOS 6.3   AMLOS 8.3   RW 2.4081   ☑

Select operating room procedures listed under DRG 423

DRG 425   Other Hepatobiliary or Pancreas O.R. Procedures without CC/MCC
GMLOS 3.8   AMLOS 4.9   RW 1.5756   ☑

Select operating room procedures listed under DRG 423

MEDICAL

DRG 432   Cirrhosis and Alcoholic Hepatitis with MCC
GMLOS 4.8   AMLOS 6.3   RW 1.6792   ☑

Principal Diagnosis
571.1   Acute alcoholic hepatitis
571.2   Alcoholic cirrhosis of liver
571.3   Unspecified alcoholic liver damage
571.5   Cirrhosis of liver without mention of alcohol
571.6   Biliary cirrhosis

DRG 433   Cirrhosis and Alcoholic Hepatitis with CC
GMLOS 3.4   AMLOS 4.2   RW 0.9316   ☑

Select principal diagnosis listed under DRG 432

DRG 434   Cirrhosis and Alcoholic Hepatitis without CC/MCC
GMLOS 2.6   AMLOS 3.2   RW 0.6343   ☑

Select principal diagnosis listed under DRG 432

DRG 435   Malignancy of Hepatobiliary System or Pancreas with MCC
GMLOS 5.4   AMLOS 7.1   RW 1.7816   ☑

Principal Diagnosis
155*   Malignant neoplasm of liver and intrahepatic bile ducts
156*   Malignant neoplasm of gallbladder and extrahepatic bile ducts
157*   Malignant neoplasm of pancreas
197.7   Secondary malignant neoplasm of liver
209.72   Secondary neuroendocrine tumor of liver
230.8   Carcinoma in situ of liver and biliary system

Ⓣ Transfer DRG   ⑤ᴾ Special Payment   ☑ Optimization Potential   ᵀᴳᵈ Targeted Potential   * Code Range   ● New DRG   ▲ Revised DRG Title

235.3	Neoplasm of uncertain behavior of liver and biliary passages

DRG 436   Malignancy of Hepatobiliary System or Pancreas with CC
GMLOS 4.0   AMLOS 5.2   RW 1.1934   ☑

Select principal diagnosis listed under DRG 435

DRG 437   Malignancy of Hepatobiliary System or Pancreas without CC/MCC
GMLOS 2.8   AMLOS 3.6   RW 0.9537   ☑

Select principal diagnosis listed under DRG 435

DRG 438   Disorders of Pancreas Except Malignancy with MCC
GMLOS 5.3   AMLOS 7.2   RW 1.7844   ☑

Principal Diagnosis

072.3	Mumps pancreatitis
211.6	Benign neoplasm of pancreas, except islets of Langerhans
577*	Diseases of pancreas
751.7	Congenital anomalies of pancreas
863.81	Pancreas head injury without mention of open wound into cavity
863.82	Pancreas body injury without mention of open wound into cavity
863.83	Pancreas tail injury without mention of open wound into cavity
863.84	Pancreas injury, multiple and unspecified sites, without mention of open wound into cavity
863.91	Pancreas head injury with open wound into cavity
863.92	Pancreas body injury with open wound into cavity
863.93	Pancreas tail injury with open wound into cavity
863.94	Pancreas injury, multiple and unspecified sites, with open wound into cavity
996.86	Complications of transplanted pancreas
V42.83	Pancreas replaced by transplant

DRG 439   Disorders of Pancreas Except Malignancy with CC
GMLOS 3.7   AMLOS 4.6   RW 0.9603   ☑

Select principal diagnosis listed under DRG 438

DRG 440   Disorders of Pancreas Except Malignancy without CC/MCC
GMLOS 2.8   AMLOS 3.3   RW 0.6790   ☑

Select principal diagnosis listed under DRG 438

DRG 441   Disorders of Liver Except Malignancy, Cirrhosis, Alcoholic Hepatitis with MCC
GMLOS 5.1   AMLOS 7.0   RW 1.8767   T☑

Principal Diagnosis

006.3	Amebic liver abscess
070*	Viral hepatitis
072.71	Mumps hepatitis
091.62	Early syphilis, secondary syphilitic hepatitis
095.3	Syphilis of liver
120.1	Schistosomiasis due to schistosoma mansoni
121.0	Opisthorchiasis
121.1	Clonorchiasis
121.3	Fascioliasis
121.4	Fasciolopsiasis
122.0	Echinococcus granulosus infection of liver
122.5	Echinococcus multilocularis infection of liver
122.8	Unspecified echinococcus of liver
130.5	Hepatitis due to toxoplasmosis
211.5	Benign neoplasm of liver and biliary passages
277.4	Disorders of bilirubin excretion
452	Portal vein thrombosis

453.0	Budd-Chiari syndrome
570	Acute and subacute necrosis of liver
571.0	Alcoholic fatty liver
571.4*	Chronic hepatitis
571.8	Other chronic nonalcoholic liver disease
571.9	Unspecified chronic liver disease without mention of alcohol
572*	Liver abscess and sequelae of chronic liver disease
573.0	Chronic passive congestion of liver
573.1	Hepatitis in viral diseases classified elsewhere
573.2	Hepatitis in other infectious diseases classified elsewhere
573.3	Unspecified hepatitis
573.4	Hepatic infarction
573.8	Other specified disorders of liver
573.9	Unspecified disorder of liver
751.62	Congenital cystic disease of liver
751.69	Other congenital anomaly of gallbladder, bile ducts, and liver
782.4	Jaundice, unspecified, not of newborn
789.1	Hepatomegaly
791.4	Biliuria
794.8	Nonspecific abnormal results of liver function study
864*	Injury to liver
996.82	Complications of transplanted liver
V02.6*	Carrier or suspected carrier of viral hepatitis
V42.7	Liver replaced by transplant
V59.6	Liver donor

DRG 442   Disorders of Liver Except Malignancy, Cirrhosis, Alcoholic Hepatitis with CC
GMLOS 3.5   AMLOS 4.4   RW 0.9545   T☑

Select principal diagnosis listed under DRG 441

DRG 443   Disorders of Liver Except Malignancy, Cirrhosis, Alcoholic Hepatitis without CC/MCC
GMLOS 2.6   AMLOS 3.2   RW 0.6473   T☑

Select principal diagnosis listed under DRG 441

DRG 444   Disorders of the Biliary Tract with MCC
GMLOS 4.7   AMLOS 6.2   RW 1.6039   ☑

Principal Diagnosis

574*	Cholelithiasis
575*	Other disorders of gallbladder
576*	Other disorders of biliary tract
751.60	Unspecified congenital anomaly of gallbladder, bile ducts, and liver
751.61	Congenital biliary atresia
793.3	Nonspecific (abnormal) findings on radiological and other examination of biliary tract
868.02	Bile duct and gallbladder injury without mention of open wound into cavity
868.12	Bile duct and gallbladder injury, with open wound into cavity

DRG 445   Disorders of the Biliary Tract with CC
GMLOS 3.5   AMLOS 4.3   RW 1.0720   ☑

Select principal diagnosis listed under DRG 444

DRG 446   Disorders of the Biliary Tract without CC/MCC
GMLOS 2.4   AMLOS 3.0   RW 0.7583   ☑

Select principal diagnosis listed under DRG 444

MDC 7: Diseases And Disorders Of The Hepatobiliary System And Pancreas—MEDICAL

Surgical   **Medical**   **CC Indicator**   **MCC Indicator**   **Procedure Proxy**

MDC 8

Diseases And Disorders Of The Musculoskeletal System And Connective Tissue

003.23	136.1	390	711.43	712.18	715.11	716.28	717.40	718.52
003.24	137.3	443.0	711.44	712.19	715.12	716.29	717.41	718.53
015.00	170.0	446.0	711.45	712.20	715.13	716.30	717.42	718.54
015.01	170.1	446.1	711.46	712.21	715.14	716.31	717.43	718.55
015.02	170.2	446.20	711.47	712.22	715.15	716.32	717.49	718.56
015.03	170.3	446.21	711.48	712.23	715.16	716.33	717.5	718.57
015.04	170.4	446.29	711.49	712.24	715.17	716.34	717.6	718.58
015.05	170.5	446.3	711.50	712.25	715.18	716.35	717.7	718.59
015.06	170.6	446.4	711.51	712.26	715.20	716.36	717.81	718.65
015.10	170.7	446.5	711.52	712.27	715.21	716.37	717.82	718.70
015.11	170.8	446.6	711.53	712.28	715.22	716.38	717.83	718.71
015.12	170.9	446.7	711.54	712.29	715.23	716.39	717.84	718.72
015.13	171.0	447.6	711.55	712.30	715.24	716.40	717.85	718.73
015.14	171.2	696.0	711.56	712.31	715.25	716.41	717.89	718.74
015.15	171.3	710.0	711.57	712.32	715.26	716.42	717.9	718.75
015.16	171.4	710.1	711.58	712.33	715.27	716.43	718.00	718.76
015.20	171.5	710.2	711.59	712.34	715.28	716.44	718.01	718.77
015.21	171.6	710.3	711.60	712.35	715.30	716.45	718.02	718.78
015.22	171.7	710.4	711.61	712.36	715.31	716.46	718.03	718.79
015.23	171.8	710.5	711.62	712.37	715.32	716.47	718.04	718.80
015.24	171.9	710.8	711.63	712.38	715.33	716.48	718.05	718.81
015.25	198.5	710.9	711.64	712.39	715.34	716.49	718.07	718.82
015.26	209.73	711.00	711.65	712.80	715.35	716.50	718.08	718.83
015.50	213.0	711.01	711.66	712.81	715.36	716.51	718.09	718.84
015.51	213.2	711.02	711.67	712.82	715.37	716.52	718.10	718.85
015.52	213.4	711.03	711.68	712.83	715.38	716.53	718.11	718.86
015.53	213.5	711.04	711.69	712.84	715.80	716.54	718.12	718.87
015.54	213.6	711.05	711.70	712.85	715.89	716.55	718.13	718.88
015.55	213.7	711.06	711.71	712.86	715.90	716.56	718.14	718.89
015.56	213.8	711.07	711.72	712.87	715.91	716.57	718.15	718.90
015.70	213.9	711.08	711.73	712.88	715.92	716.58	718.17	718.91
015.71	215.0	711.09	711.74	712.89	715.93	716.59	718.18	718.92
015.72	215.2	711.10	711.75	712.90	715.94	716.60	718.19	718.93
015.73	215.3	711.11	711.76	712.91	715.95	716.61	718.20	718.94
015.74	215.4	711.12	711.77	712.92	715.96	716.62	718.21	718.95
015.75	215.5	711.13	711.78	712.93	715.97	716.63	718.22	718.97
015.76	215.6	711.14	711.79	712.94	715.98	716.64	718.23	718.98
015.80	215.7	711.15	711.80	712.95	716.00	716.65	718.24	718.99
015.81	215.8	711.16	711.81	712.96	716.01	716.66	718.25	719.00
015.82	215.9	711.17	711.82	712.97	716.02	716.67	718.26	719.01
015.83	238.0	711.18	711.83	712.98	716.03	716.68	718.27	719.02
015.84	238.1	711.19	711.84	712.99	716.04	716.80	718.28	719.03
015.85	239.2	711.20	711.85	713.0	716.05	716.81	718.29	719.04
015.86	268.0	711.21	711.86	713.1	716.06	716.82	718.30	719.05
015.90	268.1	711.22	711.87	713.2	716.07	716.83	718.31	719.06
015.91	268.2	711.23	711.88	713.3	716.08	716.84	718.32	719.07
015.92	274.00	711.24	711.89	713.4	716.09	716.85	718.33	719.08
015.93	274.01	711.25	711.90	713.5	716.10	716.86	718.34	719.09
015.94	274.02	711.26	711.91	713.6	716.11	716.87	718.35	719.10
015.95	274.03	711.27	711.92	713.7	716.12	716.88	718.36	719.11
015.96	274.81	711.28	711.93	713.8	716.13	716.89	718.37	719.12
036.82	274.82	711.29	711.94	714.0	716.14	716.90	718.38	719.13
040.81	274.89	711.30	711.95	714.1	716.15	716.91	718.39	719.14
056.71	274.9	711.31	711.96	714.2	716.16	716.92	718.40	719.15
091.61	277.30	711.32	711.97	714.30	716.17	716.93	718.41	719.16
095.5	277.31	711.33	711.98	714.31	716.18	716.94	718.42	719.17
095.6	277.39	711.34	711.99	714.32	716.19	716.95	718.43	719.18
095.7	279.41	711.35	712.10	714.33	716.20	716.96	718.44	719.19
098.50	279.49	711.36	712.11	714.4	716.21	716.97	718.45	719.20
098.51	306.0	711.37	712.12	714.89	716.22	716.98	718.46	719.21
098.52	359.71	711.38	712.13	714.9	716.23	716.99	718.47	719.22
098.53	359.79	711.39	712.14	715.00	716.24	717.0	718.48	719.23
098.59	380.01	711.40	712.15	715.04	716.25	717.1	718.49	719.24
099.3	380.02	711.41	712.16	715.09	716.26	717.2	718.50	719.25
102.6	380.03	711.42	712.17	715.10	716.27	717.3	718.51	719.26

719.27	721.41	726.65	729.73	730.95	736.1	754.41	756.16	810.10
719.28	721.42	726.69	729.79	730.96	736.20	754.42	756.19	810.11
719.29	721.5	726.70	729.81	730.97	736.21	754.43	756.2	810.12
719.30	721.6	726.71	729.82	730.98	736.22	754.44	756.4	810.13
719.31	721.7	726.72	729.89	730.99	736.29	754.50	756.50	811.00
719.32	721.8	726.73	729.90	731.0	736.30	754.51	756.51	811.01
719.33	721.90	726.79	729.91	731.1	736.31	754.52	756.52	811.02
719.34	721.91	726.8	729.92	731.2	736.32	754.53	756.53	811.03
719.35	722.0	726.90	729.99	731.3	736.39	754.59	756.54	811.09
719.36	722.10	726.91	730.00	731.8	736.41	754.60	756.55	811.10
719.37	722.11	727.00	730.01	732.0	736.42	754.61	756.56	811.11
719.38	722.2	727.01	730.02	732.1	736.5	754.62	756.59	811.12
719.39	722.30	727.02	730.03	732.2	736.6	754.69	756.81	811.13
719.40	722.31	727.03	730.04	732.3	736.70	754.70	756.82	811.19
719.41	722.32	727.04	730.05	732.4	736.71	754.71	756.83	812.00
719.42	722.39	727.05	730.06	732.5	736.72	754.79	756.89	812.01
719.43	722.4	727.06	730.07	732.6	736.73	754.89	756.9	812.02
719.44	722.51	727.09	730.08	732.7	736.75	755.00	759.7	812.03
719.45	722.52	727.1	730.09	732.8	736.76	755.01	759.81	812.09
719.46	722.6	727.2	730.10	732.9	736.79	755.02	759.89	812.10
719.47	722.70	727.3	730.11	733.00	736.81	755.10	781.93	812.11
719.48	722.71	727.40	730.12	733.01	736.89	755.11	793.7	812.12
719.49	722.72	727.41	730.13	733.02	736.9	755.12	794.17	812.13
719.50	722.73	727.42	730.14	733.03	737.0	755.13	795.6	812.19
719.51	722.80	727.43	730.15	733.09	737.10	755.14	802.8	812.20
719.52	722.81	727.49	730.16	733.10	737.11	755.20	802.9	812.21
719.53	722.82	727.50	730.17	733.11	737.12	755.21	805.00	812.30
719.54	722.83	727.51	730.18	733.12	737.19	755.22	805.01	812.31
719.55	722.90	727.59	730.19	733.13	737.20	755.23	805.02	812.40
719.56	722.91	727.60	730.20	733.14	737.21	755.24	805.03	812.41
719.57	722.92	727.61	730.21	733.15	737.22	755.25	805.04	812.42
719.58	722.93	727.62	730.22	733.16	737.29	755.26	805.05	812.43
719.59	723.0	727.63	730.23	733.19	737.30	755.27	805.06	812.44
719.60	723.1	727.64	730.24	733.20	737.31	755.28	805.07	812.49
719.61	723.5	727.65	730.25	733.21	737.32	755.29	805.08	812.50
719.62	723.7	727.66	730.26	733.22	737.33	755.30	805.10	812.51
719.63	723.8	727.67	730.27	733.29	737.34	755.31	805.11	812.52
719.64	723.9	727.68	730.28	733.3	737.39	755.32	805.12	812.53
719.65	724.00	727.69	730.29	733.40	737.40	755.33	805.13	812.54
719.66	724.01	727.81	730.30	733.41	737.41	755.34	805.14	812.59
719.67	724.02	727.82	730.31	733.42	737.42	755.35	805.15	813.00
719.68	724.03	727.83	730.32	733.43	737.43	755.36	805.16	813.01
719.69	724.09	727.89	730.33	733.44	737.8	755.37	805.17	813.02
719.7	724.1	727.9	730.34	733.45	737.9	755.38	805.18	813.03
719.80	724.2	728.0	730.35	733.49	738.10	755.39	805.2	813.04
719.81	724.3	728.10	730.36	733.5	738.11	755.4	805.3	813.05
719.82	724.4	728.11	730.37	733.7	738.12	755.50	805.4	813.06
719.83	724.5	728.12	730.38	733.81	738.19	755.51	805.5	813.07
719.84	724.6	728.13	730.39	733.82	738.2	755.52	805.6	813.08
719.85	724.70	728.19	730.70	733.90	738.3	755.53	805.7	813.10
719.86	724.71	728.2	730.71	733.91	738.4	755.54	805.8	813.11
719.87	724.79	728.3	730.72	733.92	738.5	755.55	805.9	813.12
719.88	724.8	728.4	730.73	733.93	738.6	755.56	808.0	813.13
719.89	724.9	728.5	730.74	733.94	738.8	755.57	808.1	813.14
719.90	725	728.6	730.75	733.95	738.9	755.58	808.2	813.15
719.91	726.0	728.71	730.76	733.96	739.0	755.59	808.3	813.16
719.92	726.10	728.79	730.77	733.97	739.1	755.60	808.41	813.17
719.93	726.11	728.81	730.78	733.98	739.2	755.61	808.42	813.18
719.94	726.12	728.82	730.79	733.99	739.3	755.62	808.43	813.20
719.95	726.13	728.83	730.80	734	739.4	755.63	808.44	813.21
719.96	726.19	728.84	730.81	735.0	739.5	755.64	808.49	813.22
719.97	726.2	728.85	730.82	735.1	739.6	755.65	808.51	813.23
719.98	726.30	728.86	730.83	735.2	739.7	755.66	808.52	813.30
719.99	726.31	728.87	730.84	735.3	739.8	755.67	808.53	813.31
720.0	726.32	728.88	730.85	735.4	739.9	755.69	808.54	813.32
720.1	726.33	728.89	730.86	735.5	754.0	755.8	808.59	813.33
720.2	726.39	728.9	730.87	735.8	754.1	755.9	808.8	813.40
720.81	726.4	729.0	730.88	735.9	754.2	756.0	808.9	813.41
720.89	726.5	729.1	730.89	736.00	754.30	756.10	809.0	813.42
720.9	726.60	729.4	730.90	736.01	754.31	756.11	809.1	813.43
721.0	726.61	729.5	730.91	736.02	754.32	756.12	810.00	813.44
721.1	726.62	729.6	730.92	736.03	754.33	756.13	810.01	813.45
721.2	726.63	729.71	730.93	736.04	754.35	756.14	810.02	813.46
721.3	726.64	729.72	730.94	736.09	754.40	756.15	810.03	813.47

813.50	816.02	823.10	827.1	834.12	839.03	842.00	880.21	997.61
813.51	816.03	823.11	829.0	835.00	839.04	842.01	880.22	997.62
813.52	816.10	823.12	829.1	835.01	839.05	842.02	880.23	997.69
813.53	816.11	823.20	831.00	835.02	839.06	842.09	880.29	V42.4
813.54	816.12	823.21	831.01	835.03	839.07	842.10	881.20	V43.60
813.80	816.13	823.22	831.02	835.10	839.08	842.11	881.21	V43.61
813.81	817.0	823.30	831.03	835.11	839.10	842.12	881.22	V43.62
813.82	817.1	823.31	831.04	835.12	839.11	842.13	882.2	V43.63
813.83	818.0	823.32	831.09	835.13	839.12	842.19	883.2	V43.64
813.90	818.1	823.40	831.10	836.0	839.13	843.0	884.2	V43.65
813.91	820.00	823.41	831.11	836.1	839.14	843.1	890.2	V43.66
813.92	820.01	823.42	831.12	836.2	839.15	843.8	891.2	V43.69
813.93	820.02	823.80	831.13	836.3	839.16	843.9	892.2	V43.7
814.00	820.03	823.81	831.14	836.4	839.17	844.0	893.2	V52.0
814.01	820.09	823.82	831.19	836.50	839.18	844.1	894.2	V52.1
814.02	820.10	823.90	832.00	836.51	839.20	844.2	905.1	V53.7
814.03	820.11	823.91	832.01	836.52	839.21	844.3	905.2	V54.01
814.04	820.12	823.92	832.02	836.53	839.30	844.8	905.3	V54.02
814.05	820.13	824.0	832.03	836.54	839.31	844.9	905.4	V54.09
814.06	820.19	824.1	832.04	836.59	839.40	845.00	905.5	V54.10
814.07	820.20	824.2	832.09	836.60	839.41	845.01	905.6	V54.11
814.08	820.21	824.3	832.10	836.61	839.42	845.02	905.7	V54.12
814.09	820.22	824.4	832.11	836.62	839.49	845.03	905.8	V54.13
814.10	820.30	824.5	832.12	836.63	839.50	845.09	905.9	V54.14
814.11	820.31	824.6	832.13	836.64	839.51	845.10	958.6	V54.15
814.12	820.32	824.7	832.14	836.69	839.52	845.11	996.40	V54.16
814.13	820.8	824.8	832.19	837.0	839.59	845.12	996.41	V54.17
814.14	820.9	824.9	832.2	837.1	839.69	845.13	996.42	V54.19
814.15	821.00	825.0	833.00	838.00	839.79	845.19	996.43	V54.20
814.16	821.01	825.1	833.01	838.01	839.8	846.0	996.44	V54.21
814.17	821.10	825.20	833.02	838.02	839.9	846.1	996.45	V54.22
814.18	821.11	825.21	833.03	838.03	840.0	846.2	996.46	V54.23
814.19	821.20	825.22	833.04	838.04	840.1	846.3	996.47	V54.24
815.00	821.21	825.23	833.05	838.05	840.2	846.8	996.49	V54.25
815.01	821.22	825.24	833.09	838.06	840.3	846.9	996.66	V54.26
815.02	821.23	825.25	833.10	838.09	840.4	847.0	996.67	V54.27
815.03	821.29	825.29	833.11	838.10	840.5	847.1	996.77	V54.29
815.04	821.30	825.30	833.12	838.11	840.6	847.2	996.78	V54.81
815.09	821.31	825.31	833.13	838.12	840.7	847.3	996.90	V54.82
815.10	821.32	825.32	833.14	838.13	840.8	847.4	996.91	V54.89
815.11	821.33	825.33	833.15	838.14	840.9	847.9	996.92	V54.9
815.12	821.39	825.34	833.19	838.15	841.0	848.0	996.93	V59.2
815.13	822.0	825.35	834.00	838.16	841.1	848.2	996.94	
815.14	822.1	825.39	834.01	838.19	841.2	848.5	996.95	
815.19	823.00	826.0	834.02	839.00	841.3	848.8	996.96	
816.00	823.01	826.1	834.10	839.01	841.8	848.9	996.99	
816.01	823.02	827.0	834.11	839.02	841.9	880.20	997.60	

SURGICAL

DRG 453   Combined Anterior/Posterior Spinal Fusion with MCC
GMLOS 10.1   AMLOS 12.6   RW 10.5952

Operating Room Procedures

81.02	Other cervical fusion of the anterior column, anterior technique
81.04	Dorsal and dorsolumbar fusion of the anterior column, anterior technique
81.06	Lumbar and lumbosacral fusion of the anterior column, anterior technique
81.32	Refusion of other cervical spine, anterior column, anterior technique
81.34	Refusion of dorsal and dorsolumbar spine, anterior column, anterior technique
81.36	Refusion of lumbar and lumbosacral spine, anterior column, anterior technique

AND

Operating Room Procedures

81.03	Other cervical fusion of the posterior column, posterior technique
81.05	Dorsal and dorsolumbar fusion of the posterior column, posterior technique
81.07	Lumbar and lumbosacral fusion of the posterior column, posterior technique
81.08	Lumbar and lumbosacral fusion of the anterior column, posterior technique
81.33	Refusion of other cervical spine, posterior column, posterior technique
81.35	Refusion of dorsal and dorsolumbar spine, posterior column, posterior technique
81.37	Refusion of lumbar and lumbosacral spine, posterior column, posterior technique
81.38	Refusion of lumbar and lumbosacral spine, anterior column, posterior technique

DRG 454   Combined Anterior/Posterior Spinal Fusion with CC
GMLOS 5.3   AMLOS 6.3   RW 7.7979   ☑

Select operating room procedures listed under DRG 453

DRG 455   Combined Anterior/Posterior Spinal Fusion without CC/MCC
GMLOS 3.1   AMLOS 3.6   RW 5.8705   ☑

Select operating room procedures listed under DRG 453

DRG 456   Spinal Fusion Except Cervical with Spinal Curvature/Malignancy/Infection or 9+ Fusions with MCC
GMLOS 10.6   AMLOS 13.1   RW 9.5204   ☑

Principal Diagnosis

015.02	Tuberculosis of vertebral column, bacteriological or histological examination unknown (at present)
015.04	Tuberculosis of vertebral column, tubercle bacilli not found (in sputum) by microscopy, but found by bacterial culture
015.05	Tuberculosis of vertebral column, tubercle bacilli not found by bacteriological examination, but tuberculosis confirmed histologically
170.2	Malignant neoplasm of vertebral column, excluding sacrum and coccyx
198.5	Secondary malignant neoplasm of bone and bone marrow
209.73	Secondary neuroendocrine tumor of bone
213.2	Benign neoplasm of vertebral column, excluding sacrum and coccyx
238.0	Neoplasm of uncertain behavior of bone and articular cartilage
239.2	Neoplasms of unspecified nature of bone, soft tissue, and skin
730.08	Acute osteomyelitis, other specified site
730.18	Chronic osteomyelitis, other specified sites
730.28	Unspecified osteomyelitis, other specified sites
732.0	Juvenile osteochondrosis of spine
733.13	Pathologic fracture of vertebrae
737.0	Adolescent postural kyphosis
737.1*	Kyphosis (acquired)
737.2*	Lordosis (acquired)
737.3*	Kyphoscoliosis and scoliosis
737.8	Other curvatures of spine associated with other conditions
737.9	Unspecified curvature of spine associated with other condition
754.2	Congenital musculoskeletal deformity of spine
756.51	Osteogenesis imperfecta

OR

Secondary Diagnosis

737.4*	Curvature of spine associated with other conditions

AND

Operating Room Procedures

81.00	Spinal fusion, not otherwise specified
81.04	Dorsal and dorsolumbar fusion of the anterior column, anterior technique
81.05	Dorsal and dorsolumbar fusion of the posterior column, posterior technique
81.06	Lumbar and lumbosacral fusion of the anterior column, anterior technique
81.07	Lumbar and lumbosacral fusion of the posterior column, posterior technique
81.08	Lumbar and lumbosacral fusion of the anterior column, posterior technique
81.30	Refusion of spine, not otherwise specified
81.34	Refusion of dorsal and dorsolumbar spine, anterior column, anterior technique
81.35	Refusion of dorsal and dorsolumbar spine, posterior column, posterior technique
81.36	Refusion of lumbar and lumbosacral spine, anterior column, anterior technique
81.37	Refusion of lumbar and lumbosacral spine, posterior column, posterior technique
81.38	Refusion of lumbar and lumbosacral spine, anterior column, posterior technique
81.39	Refusion of spine, not elsewhere classified

OR

Nonoperating Room Procedure

81.64	Fusion or refusion of 9 or more vertebrae

DRG 457   Spinal Fusion Except Cervical with Spinal Curvature/Malignancy/Infection or 9+ Fusions with CC
GMLOS 5.6   AMLOS 6.5   RW 6.4171   ☑

Select principal or secondary diagnosis and operating room procedures listed under DRG 456

OR

Nonoperating room procedure

81.64	Fusion or refusion of 9 or more vertebrae

MDC 8: Diseases And Disorders Of The Musculoskeletal System And Connective Tissue—SURGICAL

MDC 8: Diseases And Disorders Of The Musculoskeletal System And Connective Tissue—SURGICAL

DRG 458 **Spinal Fusion Except Cervical with Spinal Curvature/Malignancy/Infection or 9+ Fusions without CC/MCC**
GMLOS 3.3   AMLOS 3.7   RW 4.9491

Select principal or secondary diagnosis and operating room procedures listed under DRG 456
OR

Nonoperating room procedure
81.64   Fusion or refusion of 9 or more vertebrae

DRG 459 **Spinal Fusion Except Cervical with MCC**
GMLOS 7.3   AMLOS 9.1   RW 6.5390   T ☑

Includes any of the following procedure codes, as long as any combination of procedure codes would not otherwise result in assignment to DRG 453
81.00   Spinal fusion, not otherwise specified
81.04   Dorsal and dorsolumbar fusion of the anterior column, anterior technique
81.05   Dorsal and dorsolumbar fusion of the posterior column, posterior technique
81.06   Lumbar and lumbosacral fusion of the anterior column, anterior technique
81.07   Lumbar and lumbosacral fusion of the posterior column, posterior technique
81.08   Lumbar and lumbosacral fusion of the anterior column, posterior technique
81.30   Refusion of spine, not otherwise specified
81.34   Refusion of dorsal and dorsolumbar spine, anterior column, anterior technique
81.35   Refusion of dorsal and dorsolumbar spine, posterior column, posterior technique
81.36   Refusion of lumbar and lumbosacral spine, anterior column, anterior technique
81.37   Refusion of lumbar and lumbosacral spine, posterior column, posterior technique
81.38   Refusion of lumbar and lumbosacral spine, anterior column, posterior technique
81.39   Refusion of spine, not elsewhere classified

DRG 460 **Spinal Fusion Except Cervical without MCC**
GMLOS 3.1   AMLOS 3.6   RW 3.8783   T ☑

Select operating room procedures listed under DRG 459

DRG 461 **Bilateral or Multiple Major Joint Procedures of Lower Extremity with MCC**
GMLOS 6.4   AMLOS 7.7   RW 4.9062

Any combination of two or more of the following procedures
00.70   Revision of hip replacement, both acetabular and femoral components
00.80   Revision of knee replacement, total (all components)
00.85   Resurfacing hip, total, acetabulum and femoral head
00.86   Resurfacing hip, partial, femoral head
00.87   Resurfacing hip, partial, acetabulum
81.51   Total hip replacement
81.52   Partial hip replacement
81.54   Total knee replacement
81.56   Total ankle replacement

DRG 462 **Bilateral or Multiple Major Joint Procedures of Lower Extremity without MCC**
GMLOS 3.5   AMLOS 3.8   RW 3.3745   ☑

Select any combination of two or more procedures listed under DRG 461

DRG 463 **Wound Debridement and Skin Graft Except Hand, for Musculo-Connective Tissue Disorders with MCC**
GMLOS 10.9   AMLOS 15.1   RW 5.4443   T

Operating Room Procedures
80.05   Arthrotomy for removal of prosthesis without replacement, hip
80.06   Arthrotomy for removal of prosthesis without replacement, knee
86.22   Excisional debridement of wound, infection, or burn
86.60   Free skin graft, not otherwise specified
86.63   Full-thickness skin graft to other sites
86.65   Heterograft to skin
86.66   Homograft to skin
86.67   Dermal regenerative graft
86.69   Other skin graft to other sites
86.70   Pedicle or flap graft, not otherwise specified
86.71   Cutting and preparation of pedicle grafts or flaps
86.72   Advancement of pedicle graft
86.74   Attachment of pedicle or flap graft to other sites
86.75   Revision of pedicle or flap graft
86.93   Insertion of tissue expander

DRG 464 **Wound Debridement and Skin Graft Except Hand, for Musculo-Connective Tissue Disorders with CC**
GMLOS 6.5   AMLOS 8.2   RW 2.9406   T ☑

Select operating room procedures listed under DRG 463

DRG 465 **Wound Debridement and Skin Graft Except Hand, for Musculo-Connective Tissue Disorders without CC/MCC**
GMLOS 3.9   AMLOS 5.0   RW 1.8802   T ☑

Select operating room procedures listed under DRG 463

DRG 466 **Revision of Hip or Knee Replacement with MCC**
GMLOS 7.0   AMLOS 8.7   RW 5.0078   T

Operating Room Procedures
00.70   Revision of hip replacement, both acetabular and femoral components
00.71   Revision of hip replacement, acetabular component
00.72   Revision of hip replacement, femoral component
00.73   Revision of hip replacement, acetabular liner and/or femoral head only
00.80   Revision of knee replacement, total (all components)
00.81   Revision of knee replacement, tibial component
00.82   Revision of knee replacement, femoral component
81.53   Revision of hip replacement, not otherwise specified
81.55   Revision of knee replacement, not otherwise specified

DRG 467 **Revision of Hip or Knee Replacement with CC**
GMLOS 4.1   AMLOS 4.6   RW 3.2516   T ☑

Select operating room procedures listed under DRG 466

DRG 468 **Revision of Hip or Knee Replacement without CC/MCC**
GMLOS 3.1   AMLOS 3.3   RW 2.6070   T ☑

Select operating room procedures listed under DRG 466

DRG 469 **Major Joint Replacement or Reattachment of Lower Extremity with MCC**
GMLOS 6.4   AMLOS 7.6   RW 3.4196   T ☑

Operating Room Procedures
00.85   Resurfacing hip, total, acetabulum and femoral head
00.86   Resurfacing hip, partial, femoral head
00.87   Resurfacing hip, partial, acetabulum

81.51	Total hip replacement
81.52	Partial hip replacement
81.54	Total knee replacement
81.56	Total ankle replacement
84.26	Foot reattachment
84.27	Lower leg or ankle reattachment
84.28	Thigh reattachment

DRG 470   Major Joint Replacement or Reattachment of Lower Extremity without MCC

     GMLOS 3.2   AMLOS 3.5   RW 2.0953   T ☑

Select operating room procedures listed under DRG 469

DRG 471   Cervical Spinal Fusion with MCC

     GMLOS 6.5   AMLOS 9.0   RW 4.7075   ☑

Operating Room Procedures

81.01	Atlas-axis spinal fusion
81.02	Other cervical fusion of the anterior column, anterior technique
81.03	Other cervical fusion of the posterior column, posterior technique
81.31	Refusion of Atlas-axis spine
81.32	Refusion of other cervical spine, anterior column, anterior technique
81.33	Refusion of other cervical spine, posterior column, posterior technique

DRG 472   Cervical Spinal Fusion with CC

     GMLOS 2.5   AMLOS 3.6   RW 2.8041   ☑

Select operating room procedures listed under DRG 471

DRG 473   Cervical Spinal Fusion without CC/MCC

     GMLOS 1.5   AMLOS 1.8   RW 2.1254   ☑

Select operating room procedures listed under DRG 471

DRG 474   Amputation for Musculoskeletal System and Connective Tissue Disorders with MCC

     GMLOS 8.9   AMLOS 11.6   RW 3.5676   T ☑

Operating Room Procedures

84.00	Upper limb amputation, not otherwise specified
84.03	Amputation through hand
84.04	Disarticulation of wrist
84.05	Amputation through forearm
84.06	Disarticulation of elbow
84.07	Amputation through humerus
84.08	Disarticulation of shoulder
84.09	Interthoracoscapular amputation
84.10	Lower limb amputation, not otherwise specified
84.12	Amputation through foot
84.13	Disarticulation of ankle
84.14	Amputation of ankle through malleoli of tibia and fibula
84.15	Other amputation below knee
84.16	Disarticulation of knee
84.17	Amputation above knee
84.18	Disarticulation of hip
84.19	Abdominopelvic amputation
84.3	Revision of amputation stump
84.91	Amputation, not otherwise specified

DRG 475   Amputation for Musculoskeletal System and Connective Tissue Disorders with CC

     GMLOS 5.9   AMLOS 7.4   RW 2.0071   T ☑

Select operating room procedures listed under DRG 474

DRG 476   Amputation for Musculoskeletal System and Connective Tissue Disorders without CC/MCC

     GMLOS 3.0   AMLOS 3.9   RW 1.0171   T ☑

Select operating room procedures listed under DRG 474

DRG 477   Biopsies of Musculoskeletal System and Connective Tissue with MCC

     GMLOS 8.9   AMLOS 11.0   RW 3.2681   SP

Operating Room Procedures

01.15	Biopsy of skull
01.19	Other diagnostic procedures on skull
76.1*	Diagnostic procedures on facial bones and joints
77.40	Biopsy of bone, unspecified site
77.41	Biopsy of scapula, clavicle, and thorax (ribs and sternum)
77.42	Biopsy of humerus
77.43	Biopsy of radius and ulna
77.45	Biopsy of femur
77.46	Biopsy of patella
77.47	Biopsy of tibia and fibula
77.48	Biopsy of tarsals and metatarsals
77.49	Biopsy of other bone, except facial bones
78.80	Diagnostic procedures on bone, not elsewhere classified, unspecified site
78.81	Diagnostic procedures on scapula, clavicle, and thorax (ribs and sternum) not elsewhere classified
78.82	Diagnostic procedures on humerus, not elsewhere classified
78.83	Diagnostic procedures on radius and ulna, not elsewhere classified
78.85	Diagnostic procedures on femur, not elsewhere classified
78.86	Diagnostic procedures on patella, not elsewhere classified
78.87	Diagnostic procedures on tibia and fibula, not elsewhere classified
78.89	Diagnostic procedures on other bone, except facial bones, not elsewhere classified
81.98	Other diagnostic procedures on joint structures

DRG 478   Biopsies of Musculoskeletal System and Connective Tissue with CC

     GMLOS 5.5   AMLOS 6.8   RW 2.2663   SP ☑

Select operating room procedures listed under DRG 477

DRG 479   Biopsies of Musculoskeletal System and Connective Tissue without CC/MCC

     GMLOS 3.2   AMLOS 4.1   RW 1.6922   SP ☑

Select operating room procedures listed under DRG 477

DRG 480   Hip and Femur Procedures Except Major Joint with MCC

     GMLOS 7.2   AMLOS 8.5   RW 3.0367   SP ☑

Operating Room Procedures

77.05	Sequestrectomy of femur
77.25	Wedge osteotomy of femur
77.35	Other division of femur
77.85	Other partial ostectomy of femur
77.95	Total ostectomy of femur
78.05	Bone graft of femur
78.15	Application of external fixator device, femur
78.25	Limb shortening procedures, femur
78.35	Limb lengthening procedures, femur
78.45	Other repair or plastic operations on femur
78.55	Internal fixation of femur without fracture reduction
78.75	Osteoclasis of femur
78.95	Insertion of bone growth stimulator into femur
79.15	Closed reduction of fracture of femur with internal fixation
79.25	Open reduction of fracture of femur without internal fixation

Surgical	Medical	CC Indicator	MCC Indicator	Procedure Proxy

MDC 8: Diseases And Disorders Of The Musculoskeletal System And Connective Tissue—SURGICAL

79.35	Open reduction of fracture of femur with internal fixation
79.45	Closed reduction of separated epiphysis of femur
79.55	Open reduction of separated epiphysis of femur
79.65	Debridement of open fracture of femur
79.85	Open reduction of dislocation of hip
79.95	Unspecified operation on bone injury of femur
80.15	Other arthrotomy of hip
80.45	Division of joint capsule, ligament, or cartilage of hip
80.75	Synovectomy of hip
80.95	Other excision of hip joint
81.21	Arthrodesis of hip
81.40	Repair of hip, not elsewhere classified
83.12	Adductor tenotomy of hip

DRG 481   Hip and Femur Procedures Except Major Joint with CC
GMLOS 4.9   AMLOS 5.3   RW 1.9345   SP ☑

Select operating room procedures listed under DRG 480

DRG 482   Hip and Femur Procedures Except Major Joint without CC/MCC
GMLOS 4.0   AMLOS 4.3   RW 1.5660   SP ☑

Select operating room procedures listed under DRG 480

DRG 483   Major Joint and Limb Reattachment Procedures of Upper Extremity with CC/MCC
GMLOS 2.9   AMLOS 3.5   RW 2.5314   T ☑

Operating Room Procedures
81.73	Total wrist replacement
81.80	Other total shoulder replacement
81.81	Partial shoulder replacement
81.84	Total elbow replacement
81.88	Reverse total shoulder replacement
84.23	Forearm, wrist, or hand reattachment
84.24	Upper arm reattachment

DRG 484   Major Joint and Limb Reattachment Procedures of Upper Extremity without CC/MCC
GMLOS 1.9   AMLOS 2.1   RW 2.0950   T ☑

Select operating room procedures listed under DRG 483

DRG 485   Knee Procedures with Principal Diagnosis of Infection with MCC
GMLOS 8.6   AMLOS 10.3   RW 3.0583   ☑

Principal Diagnosis
711.06	Pyogenic arthritis, lower leg
730.06	Acute osteomyelitis, lower leg
730.16	Chronic osteomyelitis, lower leg
730.26	Unspecified osteomyelitis, lower leg
996.66	Infection and inflammatory reaction due to internal joint prosthesis
996.67	Infection and inflammatory reaction due to other internal orthopedic device, implant, and graft

Operating Room Procedures
00.83	Revision of knee replacement, patellar component
00.84	Revision of total knee replacement, tibial insert (liner)
77.06	Sequestrectomy of patella
77.26	Wedge osteotomy of patella
77.36	Other division of patella
77.86	Other partial ostectomy of patella
77.96	Total ostectomy of patella
78.06	Bone graft of patella
78.16	Application of external fixator device, patella
78.46	Other repair or plastic operations on patella

78.56	Internal fixation of patella without fracture reduction
78.76	Osteoclasis of patella
78.96	Insertion of bone growth stimulator into patella
79.86	Open reduction of dislocation of knee
80.16	Other arthrotomy of knee
80.46	Division of joint capsule, ligament, or cartilage of knee
80.6	Excision of semilunar cartilage of knee
80.76	Synovectomy of knee
80.96	Other excision of knee joint
81.22	Arthrodesis of knee
81.42	Five-in-one repair of knee
81.43	Triad knee repair
81.44	Patellar stabilization
81.45	Other repair of the cruciate ligaments
81.46	Other repair of the collateral ligaments
81.47	Other repair of knee

DRG 486   Knee Procedures with Principal Diagnosis of Infection with CC
GMLOS 5.8   AMLOS 6.8   RW 2.0808   ☑

Select principal diagnosis and operating room procedures listed under DRG 485

DRG 487   Knee Procedures with Principal Diagnosis of Infection without CC/MCC
GMLOS 4.2   AMLOS 4.9   RW 1.4863   ☑

Select principal diagnosis and operating room procedures listed under DRG 485

DRG 488   Knee Procedures without Principal Diagnosis of Infection with CC/MCC
GMLOS 3.5   AMLOS 4.3   RW 1.6865   T ☑

Select only operating room procedures listed under DRG 485

DRG 489   Knee Procedures without Principal Diagnosis of Infection without CC/MCC
GMLOS 2.4   AMLOS 2.8   RW 1.2486   T ☑

Select only operating room procedures listed under DRG 485

DRG 490   Back and Neck Procedures Except Spinal Fusion with CC/MCC or Disc Device/Neurostimulator
GMLOS 3.2   AMLOS 4.5   RW 1.8154   ☑

Operating Room Procedures
03.02	Reopening of laminectomy site
03.09	Other exploration and decompression of spinal canal
03.1	Division of intraspinal nerve root
03.32	Biopsy of spinal cord or spinal meninges
03.39	Other diagnostic procedures on spinal cord and spinal canal structures
03.4	Excision or destruction of lesion of spinal cord or spinal meninges
03.53	Repair of vertebral fracture
03.59	Other repair and plastic operations on spinal cord structures
03.6	Lysis of adhesions of spinal cord and nerve roots
03.93	Implantation or replacement of spinal neurostimulator lead(s)
03.94	Removal of spinal neurostimulator lead(s)
03.97	Revision of spinal thecal shunt
03.98	Removal of spinal thecal shunt
03.99	Other operations on spinal cord and spinal canal structures
80.50	Excision or destruction of intervertebral disc, unspecified
80.51	Excision of intervertebral disc
80.53	Repair of the anulus fibrosus with graft or prosthesis
80.54	Other and unspecified repair of the anulus fibrosus

T Transfer DRG   SP Special Payment   ☑ Optimization Potential   Targeted Potential   * Code Range   ● New DRG   ▲ Revised DRG Title

80.59	Other destruction of intervertebral disc
84.59	Insertion of other spinal devices
84.6*	Replacement of spinal disc
84.80	Insertion or replacement of interspinous process device(s)
84.82	Insertion or replacement of pedicle-based dynamic stabilization device(s)
84.84	Insertion or replacement of facet replacement device(s)

OR

Any of the following procedure code combinations

03.93	Implantation or replacement of spinal neurostimulator lead(s)

AND

86.94	Insertion or replacement of single array neurostimulator pulse generator, not specified as rechargeable

OR

03.93	Implantation or replacement of spinal neurostimulator lead(s)

AND

86.95	Insertion or replacement of multiple array neurostimulator pulse generator, not specified as rechargeable

OR

03.93	Implantation or replacement of spinal neurostimulator lead(s)

AND

86.97	Insertion or replacement of single array rechargeable neurostimulator pulse generator

OR

03.93	Implantation or replacement of spinal neurostimulator lead(s)

AND

86.98	Insertion or replacement of multiple array (two or more) rechargeable neurostimulator pulse generator

DRG 491   Back and Neck Procedures Except Spinal Fusion without CC/MCC

GMLOS 1.7   AMLOS 2.1   RW 1.0354   ☑

Operating Room Procedures

03.02	Reopening of laminectomy site
03.09	Other exploration and decompression of spinal canal
03.1	Division of intraspinal nerve root
03.32	Biopsy of spinal cord or spinal meninges
03.39	Other diagnostic procedures on spinal cord and spinal canal structures
03.4	Excision or destruction of lesion of spinal cord or spinal meninges
03.53	Repair of vertebral fracture
03.59	Other repair and plastic operations on spinal cord structures
03.6	Lysis of adhesions of spinal cord and nerve roots
03.93	Implantation or replacement of spinal neurostimulator lead(s)
03.94	Removal of spinal neurostimulator lead(s)
03.97	Revision of spinal thecal shunt
03.98	Removal of spinal thecal shunt
03.99	Other operations on spinal cord and spinal canal structures
80.50	Excision or destruction of intervertebral disc, unspecified
80.51	Excision of intervertebral disc
80.53	Repair of the anulus fibrosus with graft or prosthesis
80.54	Other and unspecified repair of the anulus fibrosus
80.59	Other destruction of intervertebral disc
84.60	Insertion of spinal disc prosthesis, not otherwise specified
84.61	Insertion of partial spinal disc prosthesis, cervical
84.63	Insertion of spinal disc prosthesis, thoracic
84.64	Insertion of partial spinal disc prosthesis, lumbosacral
84.66	Revision or replacement of artificial spinal disc prosthesis, cervical

84.67	Revision or replacement of artificial spinal disc prosthesis, thoracic
84.68	Revision or replacement of artificial spinal disc prosthesis, lumbosacral
84.69	Revision or replacement of artificial spinal disc prosthesis, not otherwise specified

DRG 492   Lower Extremity and Humerus Procedures Except Hip, Foot, Femur with MCC

GMLOS 6.7   AMLOS 8.3   RW 3.1039   SP ☑

Operating Room Procedures

77.02	Sequestrectomy of humerus
77.07	Sequestrectomy of tibia and fibula
77.22	Wedge osteotomy of humerus
77.27	Wedge osteotomy of tibia and fibula
77.32	Other division of humerus
77.37	Other division of tibia and fibula
77.82	Other partial ostectomy of humerus
77.87	Other partial ostectomy of tibia and fibula
77.92	Total ostectomy of humerus
77.97	Total ostectomy of tibia and fibula
78.02	Bone graft of humerus
78.07	Bone graft of tibia and fibula
78.12	Application of external fixator device, humerus
78.17	Application of external fixator device, tibia and fibula
78.22	Limb shortening procedures, humerus
78.27	Limb shortening procedures, tibia and fibula
78.32	Limb lengthening procedures, humerus
78.37	Limb lengthening procedures, tibia and fibula
78.42	Other repair or plastic operation on humerus
78.47	Other repair or plastic operations on tibia and fibula
78.52	Internal fixation of humerus without fracture reduction
78.57	Internal fixation of tibia and fibula without fracture reduction
78.72	Osteoclasis of humerus
78.77	Osteoclasis of tibia and fibula
78.92	Insertion of bone growth stimulator into humerus
78.97	Insertion of bone growth stimulator into tibia and fibula
79.11	Closed reduction of fracture of humerus with internal fixation
79.16	Closed reduction of fracture of tibia and fibula with internal fixation
79.21	Open reduction of fracture of humerus without internal fixation
79.26	Open reduction of fracture of tibia and fibula without internal fixation
79.31	Open reduction of fracture of humerus with internal fixation
79.36	Open reduction of fracture of tibia and fibula with internal fixation
79.41	Closed reduction of separated epiphysis of humerus
79.46	Closed reduction of separated epiphysis of tibia and fibula
79.51	Open reduction of separated epiphysis of humerus
79.56	Open reduction of separated epiphysis of tibia and fibula
79.61	Debridement of open fracture of humerus
79.66	Debridement of open fracture of tibia and fibula
79.87	Open reduction of dislocation of ankle
79.91	Unspecified operation on bone injury of humerus
79.96	Unspecified operation on bone injury of tibia and fibula
79.97	Unspecified operation on bone injury of tarsals and metatarsals
80.17	Other arthrotomy of ankle
80.47	Division of joint capsule, ligament, or cartilage of ankle
80.77	Synovectomy of ankle
80.87	Other local excision or destruction of lesion of ankle joint
80.97	Other excision of ankle joint
80.99	Other excision of joint of other specified site
81.11	Ankle fusion
81.12	Triple arthrodesis
81.49	Other repair of ankle

84.48   Implantation of prosthetic device of leg

DRG 493   Lower Extremity and Humerus Procedures Except Hip, Foot, Femur with CC
GMLOS 4.0   AMLOS 4.8   RW 1.9310   SP ☑

Select operating room procedures listed under DRG 492

DRG 494   Lower Extremity and Humerus Procedures Except Hip, Foot, Femur without CC/MCC
GMLOS 2.6   AMLOS 3.1   RW 1.3938   SP ☑

Select operating room procedures listed under DRG 492

DRG 495   Local Excision and Removal Internal Fixation Devices Except Hip and Femur with MCC
GMLOS 7.5   AMLOS 9.8   RW 2.9977   SP ☑

Operating Room Procedures
01.6   Excision of lesion of skull
34.4   Excision or destruction of lesion of chest wall
76.09   Other incision of facial bone
76.2   Local excision or destruction of lesion of facial bone
76.97   Removal of internal fixation device from facial bone
77.10   Other incision of bone without division, unspecified site
77.11   Other incision of scapula, clavicle, and thorax (ribs and sternum) without division
77.12   Other incision of humerus without division
77.13   Other incision of radius and ulna without division
77.16   Other incision of patella without division
77.17   Other incision of tibia and fibula without division
77.19   Other incision of other bone, except facial bones, without division
77.60   Local excision of lesion or tissue of bone, unspecified site
77.61   Local excision of lesion or tissue of scapula, clavicle, and thorax (ribs and sternum)
77.62   Local excision of lesion or tissue of humerus
77.63   Local excision of lesion or tissue of radius and ulna
77.66   Local excision of lesion or tissue of patella
77.67   Local excision of lesion or tissue of tibia and fibula
77.69   Local excision of lesion or tissue of other bone, except facial bones
77.70   Excision of bone for graft, unspecified site
77.71   Excision of scapula, clavicle, and thorax (ribs and sternum) for graft
77.72   Excision of humerus for graft
77.73   Excision of radius and ulna for graft
77.76   Excision of patella for graft
77.77   Excision of tibia and fibula for graft
77.79   Excision of other bone for graft, except facial bones
78.60   Removal of implanted device, unspecified site
78.61   Removal of implanted device from scapula, clavicle, and thorax (ribs and sternum)
78.62   Removal of implanted device from humerus
78.63   Removal of implanted device from radius and ulna
78.64   Removal of implanted device from carpals and metacarpals
78.66   Removal of implanted device from patella
78.67   Removal of implanted device from tibia and fibula
78.68   Removal of implanted device from tarsal and metatarsals
78.69   Removal of implanted device from other bone
80.00   Arthrotomy for removal of prosthesis without replacement, unspecified site
80.01   Arthrotomy for removal of prosthesis without replacement, shoulder
80.02   Arthrotomy for removal of prosthesis without replacement, elbow
80.03   Arthrotomy for removal of prosthesis without replacement, wrist

80.04   Arthrotomy for removal of prosthesis without replacement, hand and finger
80.07   Arthrotomy for removal of prosthesis without replacement, ankle
80.08   Arthrotomy for removal of prosthesis without replacement, foot and toe
80.09   Arthrotomy for removal of prosthesis without replacement, other specified site
80.80   Other local excision or destruction of lesion of joint, unspecified site
80.81   Other local excision or destruction of lesion of shoulder joint
80.82   Other local excision or destruction of lesion of elbow joint
80.86   Other local excision or destruction of lesion of knee joint
80.89   Other local excision or destruction of lesion of joint of other specified site

DRG 496   Local Excision and Removal Internal Fixation Devices Except Hip and Femur with CC
GMLOS 4.0   AMLOS 5.2   RW 1.6306   SP ☑

Select operating room procedures listed under DRG 495

DRG 497   Local Excision and Removal Internal Fixation Devices Except Hip and Femur without CC/MCC
GMLOS 2.0   AMLOS 2.5   RW 1.1202   SP ☑

Select operating room procedures listed under DRG 495

DRG 498   Local Excision and Removal Internal Fixation Devices of Hip and Femur with CC/MCC
GMLOS 5.3   AMLOS 7.2   RW 2.1304   ☑

Operating Room Procedures
77.15   Other incision of femur without division
77.65   Local excision of lesion or tissue of femur
77.75   Excision of femur for graft
78.65   Removal of implanted device from femur
80.85   Other local excision or destruction of lesion of hip joint

DRG 499   Local Excision and Removal Internal Fixation Devices of Hip and Femur without CC/MCC
GMLOS 2.1   AMLOS 2.6   RW 1.0106   ☑

Select operating room procedures listed under DRG 498

DRG 500   Soft Tissue Procedures with MCC
GMLOS 7.8   AMLOS 10.2   RW 3.1368   SP ☑

Operating Room Procedures
54.3   Excision or destruction of lesion or tissue of abdominal wall or umbilicus
80.70   Synovectomy, unspecified site
80.79   Synovectomy of other specified site
81.95   Suture of capsule or ligament of other lower extremity
83.0*   Incision of muscle, tendon, fascia, and bursa
83.13   Other tenotomy
83.14   Fasciotomy
83.19   Other division of soft tissue
83.2*   Diagnostic procedures on muscle, tendon, fascia, and bursa, including that of hand
83.3*   Excision of lesion of muscle, tendon, fascia, and bursa
83.4*   Other excision of muscle, tendon, and fascia
83.5   Bursectomy
83.61   Suture of tendon sheath
83.62   Delayed suture of tendon
83.64   Other suture of tendon
83.65   Other suture of muscle or fascia
83.7*   Reconstruction of muscle and tendon
83.81   Tendon graft

MDC 8: Diseases And Disorders Of The Musculoskeletal System And Connective Tissue—SURGICAL

83.82	Graft of muscle or fascia
83.83	Tendon pulley reconstruction on muscle, tendon, and fascia
83.85	Other change in muscle or tendon length
83.86	Quadricepsplasty
83.87	Other plastic operations on muscle
83.88	Other plastic operations on tendon
83.89	Other plastic operations on fascia
83.91	Lysis of adhesions of muscle, tendon, fascia, and bursa
83.92	Insertion or replacement of skeletal muscle stimulator
83.93	Removal of skeletal muscle stimulator
83.99	Other operations on muscle, tendon, fascia, and bursa
86.4	Radical excision of skin lesion
86.81	Repair for facial weakness

DRG 501   Soft Tissue Procedures with CC

GMLOS 4.5   AMLOS 5.7   RW 1.5940   SP ☑

Select operating room procedures listed under DRG 500

DRG 502   Soft Tissue Procedures without CC/MCC

GMLOS 2.4   AMLOS 2.9   RW 1.0670   SP ☑

Select operating room procedures listed under DRG 500

DRG 503   Foot Procedures with MCC

GMLOS 6.8   AMLOS 8.7   RW 2.3006   ☑

Operating Room Procedures

04.44	Release of tarsal tunnel
77.08	Sequestrectomy of tarsals and metatarsals
77.18	Other incision of tarsals and metatarsals without division
77.28	Wedge osteotomy of tarsals and metatarsals
77.38	Other division of tarsals and metatarsals
77.5*	Excision and repair of bunion and other toe deformities
77.68	Local excision of lesion or tissue of tarsals and metatarsals
77.78	Excision of tarsals and metatarsals for graft
77.88	Other partial ostectomy of tarsals and metatarsals
77.98	Total ostectomy of tarsals and metatarsals
78.08	Bone graft of tarsals and metatarsals
78.18	Application of external fixator device, tarsals and metatarsals
78.28	Limb shortening procedures, tarsals and metatarsals
78.38	Limb lengthening procedures, tarsals and metatarsals
78.48	Other repair or plastic operations on tarsals and metatarsals
78.58	Internal fixation of tarsals and metatarsals without fracture reduction
78.78	Osteoclasis of tarsals and metatarsals
78.88	Diagnostic procedures on tarsals and metatarsals, not elsewhere classified
78.98	Insertion of bone growth stimulator into tarsals and metatarsals
79.17	Closed reduction of fracture of tarsals and metatarsals with internal fixation
79.18	Closed reduction of fracture of phalanges of foot with internal fixation
79.27	Open reduction of fracture of tarsals and metatarsals without internal fixation
79.28	Open reduction of fracture of phalanges of foot without internal fixation
79.37	Open reduction of fracture of tarsals and metatarsals with internal fixation
79.38	Open reduction of fracture of phalanges of foot with internal fixation
79.67	Debridement of open fracture of tarsals and metatarsals
79.68	Debridement of open fracture of phalanges of foot
79.88	Open reduction of dislocation of foot and toe
79.98	Unspecified operation on bone injury of phalanges of foot
80.18	Other arthrotomy of foot and toe
80.48	Division of joint capsule, ligament, or cartilage of foot and toe

80.78	Synovectomy of foot and toe
80.88	Other local excision or destruction of lesion of joint of foot and toe
80.98	Other excision of joint of foot and toe
81.13	Subtalar fusion
81.14	Midtarsal fusion
81.15	Tarsometatarsal fusion
81.16	Metatarsophalangeal fusion
81.17	Other fusion of foot
81.57	Replacement of joint of foot and toe
81.94	Suture of capsule or ligament of ankle and foot
83.11	Achillotenotomy
83.84	Release of clubfoot, not elsewhere classified
84.11	Amputation of toe
84.25	Toe reattachment

DRG 504   Foot Procedures with CC

GMLOS 4.8   AMLOS 5.9   RW 1.5641   ☑

Select operating room procedures listed under DRG 503

DRG 505   Foot Procedures without CC/MCC

GMLOS 2.6   AMLOS 3.2   RW 1.1478   ☑

Select operating room procedures listed under DRG 503

DRG 506   Major Thumb or Joint Procedures

GMLOS 3.0   AMLOS 4.0   RW 1.3003   ☑

Operating Room Procedures

80.13	Other arthrotomy of wrist
80.14	Other arthrotomy of hand and finger
81.71	Arthroplasty of metacarpophalangeal and interphalangeal joint with implant
81.72	Arthroplasty of metacarpophalangeal and interphalangeal joint without implant
81.74	Arthroplasty of carpocarpal or carpometacarpal joint with implant
81.75	Arthroplasty of carpocarpal or carpometacarpal joint without implant
81.79	Other repair of hand, fingers, and wrist
82.6*	Reconstruction of thumb

DRG 507   Major Shoulder or Elbow Joint Procedures with CC/MCC

GMLOS 4.0   AMLOS 5.6   RW 1.8689   ☑

Operating Room Procedures

80.11	Other arthrotomy of shoulder
80.12	Other arthrotomy of elbow
81.23	Arthrodesis of shoulder
81.24	Arthrodesis of elbow
81.83	Other repair of shoulder
81.85	Other repair of elbow

DRG 508   Major Shoulder or Elbow Joint Procedures without CC/MCC

GMLOS 1.8   AMLOS 2.2   RW 1.2071   ☑

Select operating room procedures listed under DRG 507

DRG 509   Arthroscopy

GMLOS 2.6   AMLOS 3.7   RW 1.3494   ☑

Operating Room Procedures

80.2*	Arthroscopy

Surgical	Medical	CC Indicator	MCC Indicator	Procedure Proxy

MDC 8: Diseases And Disorders Of The Musculoskeletal System And Connective Tissue—SURGICAL

DRG 510 Shoulder, Elbow or Forearm Procedure, Except Major Joint Procedure with MCC

GMLOS 5.0   AMLOS 6.3   RW 2.2963   T ☑

Operating room procedures

77.03	Sequestrectomy of radius and ulna
77.23	Wedge osteotomy of radius and ulna
77.33	Other division of radius and ulna
77.83	Other partial ostectomy of radius and ulna
77.93	Total ostectomy of radius and ulna
78.03	Bone graft of radius and ulna
78.13	Application of external fixator device, radius and ulna
78.23	Limb shortening procedures, radius and ulna
78.33	Limb lengthening procedures, radius and ulna
78.43	Other repair or plastic operations on radius and ulna
78.53	Internal fixation of radius and ulna without fracture reduction
78.73	Osteoclasis of radius and ulna
78.93	Insertion of bone growth stimulator into radius and ulna
79.12	Closed reduction of fracture of radius and ulna with internal fixation
79.22	Open reduction of fracture of radius and ulna without internal fixation
79.32	Open reduction of fracture of radius and ulna with internal fixation
79.42	Closed reduction of separated epiphysis of radius and ulna
79.52	Open reduction of separated epiphysis of radius and ulna
79.62	Debridement of open fracture of radius and ulna
79.81	Open reduction of dislocation of shoulder
79.82	Open reduction of dislocation of elbow
79.92	Unspecified operation on bone injury of radius and ulna
80.41	Division of joint capsule, ligament, or cartilage of shoulder
80.42	Division of joint capsule, ligament, or cartilage of elbow
80.71	Synovectomy of shoulder
80.72	Synovectomy of elbow
80.91	Other excision of shoulder joint
80.92	Other excision of elbow joint
81.82	Repair of recurrent dislocation of shoulder
81.93	Suture of capsule or ligament of upper extremity
83.63	Rotator cuff repair
84.44	Implantation of prosthetic device of arm

DRG 511 Shoulder, Elbow or Forearm Procedure, Except Major Joint Procedure with CC

GMLOS 3.2   AMLOS 3.8   RW 1.5222   T ☑

Select operating room procedures listed under DRG 510

DRG 512 Shoulder, Elbow or Forearm Procedure, Except Major Joint Procedure without CC/MCC

GMLOS 1.9   AMLOS 2.2   RW 1.1201   T ☑

Select operating room procedures listed under DRG 510

DRG 513 Hand or Wrist Procedures, Except Major Thumb or Joint Procedures with CC/MCC

GMLOS 3.6   AMLOS 4.8   RW 1.3409   ☑

Operating Room Procedures

04.43	Release of carpal tunnel
77.04	Sequestrectomy of carpals and metacarpals
77.14	Other incision of carpals and metacarpals without division
77.24	Wedge osteotomy of carpals and metacarpals
77.34	Other division of carpals and metacarpals
77.44	Biopsy of carpals and metacarpals
77.64	Local excision of lesion or tissue of carpals and metacarpals
77.74	Excision of carpals and metacarpals for graft
77.84	Other partial ostectomy of carpals and metacarpals
77.94	Total ostectomy of carpals and metacarpals

78.04	Bone graft of carpals and metacarpals
78.14	Application of external fixator device, carpals and metacarpals
78.24	Limb shortening procedures, carpals and metacarpals
78.34	Limb lengthening procedures, carpals and metacarpals
78.44	Other repair or plastic operations on carpals and metacarpals
78.54	Internal fixation of carpals and metacarpals without fracture reduction
78.74	Osteoclasis of carpals and metacarpals
78.84	Diagnostic procedures on carpals and metacarpals, not elsewhere classified
78.94	Insertion of bone growth stimulator into carpals and metacarpals
79.13	Closed reduction of fracture of carpals and metacarpals with internal fixation
79.14	Closed reduction of fracture of phalanges of hand with internal fixation
79.23	Open reduction of fracture of carpals and metacarpals without internal fixation
79.24	Open reduction of fracture of phalanges of hand without internal fixation
79.33	Open reduction of fracture of carpals and metacarpals with internal fixation
79.34	Open reduction of fracture of phalanges of hand with internal fixation
79.63	Debridement of open fracture of carpals and metacarpals
79.64	Debridement of open fracture of phalanges of hand
79.83	Open reduction of dislocation of wrist
79.84	Open reduction of dislocation of hand and finger
79.93	Unspecified operation on bone injury of carpals and metacarpals
79.94	Unspecified operation on bone injury of phalanges of hand
80.43	Division of joint capsule, ligament, or cartilage of wrist
80.44	Division of joint capsule, ligament, or cartilage of hand and finger
80.73	Synovectomy of wrist
80.74	Synovectomy of hand and finger
80.83	Other local excision or destruction of lesion of wrist joint
80.84	Other local excision or destruction of lesion of joint of hand and finger
80.93	Other excision of wrist joint
80.94	Other excision of joint of hand and finger
81.25	Carporadial fusion
81.26	Metacarpocarpal fusion
81.27	Metacarpophalangeal fusion
81.28	Interphalangeal fusion
82.01	Exploration of tendon sheath of hand
82.02	Myotomy of hand
82.03	Bursotomy of hand
82.09	Other incision of soft tissue of hand
82.1*	Division of muscle, tendon, and fascia of hand
82.2*	Excision of lesion of muscle, tendon, and fascia of hand
82.3*	Other excision of soft tissue of hand
82.4*	Suture of muscle, tendon, and fascia of hand
82.5*	Transplantation of muscle and tendon of hand
82.7*	Plastic operation on hand with graft or implant
82.8*	Other plastic operations on hand
82.91	Lysis of adhesions of hand
82.99	Other operations on muscle, tendon, and fascia of hand
84.01	Amputation and disarticulation of finger
84.02	Amputation and disarticulation of thumb
84.21	Thumb reattachment
84.22	Finger reattachment
86.61	Full-thickness skin graft to hand
86.62	Other skin graft to hand
86.73	Attachment of pedicle or flap graft to hand
86.85	Correction of syndactyly

T Transfer DRG   SP Special Payment   ☑ Optimization Potential   ▽ Targeted Potential   * Code Range   ● New DRG   ▲ Revised DRG Title

DRG 514   Hand or Wrist Procedures, Except Major Thumb or Joint Procedures without CC/MCC

      GMLOS 2.1   AMLOS 2.6   RW 0.8655   ☑

Select operating room procedures listed under DRG 513

DRG 515   Other Musculoskeletal System and Connective Tissue O.R. Procedure with MCC

      GMLOS 7.7   AMLOS 9.7   RW 3.2831   SP

Operating Room Procedures

01.25	Other craniectomy
02.0*	Cranioplasty
02.94	Insertion or replacement of skull tongs or halo traction device
02.99	Other operations on skull, brain, and cerebral meninges
04.03	Division or crushing of other cranial and peripheral nerves
04.04	Other incision of cranial and peripheral nerves
04.06	Other cranial or peripheral ganglionectomy
04.07	Other excision or avulsion of cranial and peripheral nerves
04.12	Open biopsy of cranial or peripheral nerve or ganglion
04.19	Other diagnostic procedures on cranial and peripheral nerves and ganglia
04.49	Other peripheral nerve or ganglion decompression or lysis of adhesions
04.92	Implantation or replacement of peripheral neurostimulator lead(s)
04.93	Removal of peripheral neurostimulator lead(s)
04.99	Other operations on cranial and peripheral nerves
06.13	Biopsy of parathyroid gland
06.19	Other diagnostic procedures on thyroid and parathyroid glands
16.51	Exenteration of orbit with removal of adjacent structures
16.59	Other exenteration of orbit
17.56	Atherectomy of other non-coronary vessel(s)
21.72	Open reduction of nasal fracture
21.83	Total nasal reconstruction
21.84	Revision rhinoplasty
21.85	Augmentation rhinoplasty
21.86	Limited rhinoplasty
21.87	Other rhinoplasty
21.88	Other septoplasty
21.89	Other repair and plastic operations on nose
22.62	Excision of lesion of maxillary sinus with other approach
33.20	Thoracoscopic lung biopsy
33.28	Open biopsy of lung
34.74	Repair of pectus deformity
34.79	Other repair of chest wall
34.81	Excision of lesion or tissue of diaphragm
38.21	Biopsy of blood vessel
38.7	Interruption of the vena cava
39.50	Angioplasty of other non-coronary vessel(s)
39.98	Control of hemorrhage, not otherwise specified
40.1*	Diagnostic procedures on lymphatic structures
40.21	Excision of deep cervical lymph node
40.23	Excision of axillary lymph node
40.24	Excision of inguinal lymph node
40.29	Simple excision of other lymphatic structure
40.3	Regional lymph node excision
40.51	Radical excision of axillary lymph nodes
40.52	Radical excision of periaortic lymph nodes
40.53	Radical excision of iliac lymph nodes
40.54	Radical groin dissection
40.59	Radical excision of other lymph nodes
41.43	Partial splenectomy
41.5	Total splenectomy
50.12	Open biopsy of liver
55.24	Open biopsy of kidney
59.00	Retroperitoneal dissection, not otherwise specified
62.41	Removal of both testes at same operative episode

76.01	Sequestrectomy of facial bone
76.31	Partial mandibulectomy
76.39	Partial ostectomy of other facial bone
76.4*	Excision and reconstruction of facial bones
76.5	Temporomandibular arthroplasty
76.6*	Other facial bone repair and orthognathic surgery
76.70	Reduction of facial fracture, not otherwise specified
76.72	Open reduction of malar and zygomatic fracture
76.74	Open reduction of maxillary fracture
76.76	Open reduction of mandibular fracture
76.77	Open reduction of alveolar fracture
76.79	Other open reduction of facial fracture
76.91	Bone graft to facial bone
76.92	Insertion of synthetic implant in facial bone
76.94	Open reduction of temporomandibular dislocation
76.99	Other operations on facial bones and joints
77.00	Sequestrectomy, unspecified site
77.01	Sequestrectomy of scapula, clavicle, and thorax (ribs and sternum)
77.09	Sequestrectomy of other bone, except facial bones
77.20	Wedge osteotomy, unspecified site
77.21	Wedge osteotomy of scapula, clavicle, and thorax (ribs and sternum)
77.29	Wedge osteotomy of other bone, except facial bones
77.30	Other division of bone, unspecified site
77.31	Other division of scapula, clavicle, and thorax (ribs and sternum)
77.39	Other division of other bone, except facial bones
77.80	Other partial ostectomy, unspecified site
77.81	Other partial ostectomy of scapula, clavicle, and thorax (ribs and sternum)
77.89	Other partial ostectomy of other bone, except facial bones
77.90	Total ostectomy, unspecified site
77.91	Total ostectomy of scapula, clavicle, and thorax (ribs and sternum)
77.99	Total ostectomy of other bone, except facial bones
78.00	Bone graft, unspecified site
78.01	Bone graft of scapula, clavicle, and thorax (ribs and sternum)
78.09	Bone graft of other bone, except facial bones
78.10	Application of external fixator device, unspecified site
78.11	Application of external fixator device, scapula, clavicle, and thorax [ribs and sternum]
78.19	Application of external fixator device, other
78.20	Limb shortening procedures, unspecified site
78.29	Limb shortening procedures, other
78.30	Limb lengthening procedures, unspecified site
78.39	Other limb lengthening procedures
78.40	Other repair or plastic operations on bone, unspecified site
78.41	Other repair or plastic operations on scapula, clavicle, and thorax (ribs and sternum)
78.49	Other repair or plastic operations on other bone, except facial bones
78.50	Internal fixation of bone without fracture reduction, unspecified site
78.51	Internal fixation of scapula, clavicle, and thorax (ribs and sternum) without fracture reduction
78.59	Internal fixation of other bone, except facial bones, without fracture reduction
78.70	Osteoclasis, unspecified site
78.71	Osteoclasis of scapula, clavicle, and thorax (ribs and sternum)
78.79	Osteoclasis of other bone, except facial bones
78.90	Insertion of bone growth stimulator, unspecified site
78.91	Insertion of bone growth stimulator into scapula, clavicle and thorax (ribs and sternum)
78.99	Insertion of bone growth stimulator into other bone
79.10	Closed reduction of fracture with internal fixation, unspecified site
79.19	Closed reduction of fracture of other specified bone, except facial bones, with internal fixation

Surgical	Medical	CC Indicator	MCC Indicator	Procedure Proxy

MDC 8: Diseases And Disorders Of The Musculoskeletal System And Connective Tissue—MEDICAL

79.20	Open reduction of fracture without internal fixation, unspecified site
79.29	Open reduction of fracture of other specified bone, except facial bones, without internal fixation
79.30	Open reduction of fracture with internal fixation, unspecified site
79.39	Open reduction of fracture of other specified bone, except facial bones, with internal fixation
79.40	Closed reduction of separated epiphysis, unspecified site
79.49	Closed reduction of separated epiphysis of other specified bone
79.50	Open reduction of separated epiphysis, unspecified site
79.59	Open reduction of separated epiphysis of other specified bone
79.60	Debridement of open fracture, unspecified site
79.69	Debridement of open fracture of other specified bone, except facial bones
79.80	Open reduction of dislocation of unspecified site
79.89	Open reduction of dislocation of other specified site, except temporomandibular
79.90	Unspecified operation on bone injury, unspecified site
79.99	Unspecified operation on bone injury of other specified bone
80.10	Other arthrotomy, unspecified site
80.19	Other arthrotomy of other specified site
80.40	Division of joint capsule, ligament, or cartilage, unspecified site
80.49	Division of joint capsule, ligament, or cartilage of other specified site
80.90	Other excision of joint, unspecified site
81.18	Subtalar joint arthroereisis
81.20	Arthrodesis of unspecified joint
81.29	Arthrodesis of other specified joint
81.59	Revision of joint replacement of lower extremity, not elsewhere classified
81.65	Percutaneous vertebroplasty
81.66	Percutaneous vertebral augmentation
81.96	Other repair of joint
81.97	Revision of joint replacement of upper extremity
81.99	Other operations on joint structures
84.29	Other reattachment of extremity
84.40	Implantation or fitting of prosthetic limb device, not otherwise specified
84.81	Revision of interspinous process device(s)
84.83	Revision of pedicle-based dynamic stabilization device(s)
84.85	Revision of facet replacement device(s)
84.92	Separation of equal conjoined twins
84.93	Separation of unequal conjoined twins
84.94	Insertion of sternal fixation device with rigid plates
84.99	Other operations on musculoskeletal system
86.06	Insertion of totally implantable infusion pump

DRG 516   Other Musculoskeletal System and Connective Tissue O.R. Procedure with CC
GMLOS 4.6   AMLOS 5.6   RW 1.9744   SP ☑

Select operating room procedures listed under DRG 515

DRG 517   Other Musculoskeletal System and Connective Tissue O.R. Procedure without CC/MCC
GMLOS 2.8   AMLOS 3.5   RW 1.5767   SP ☑

Select operating room procedures listed under DRG 515

MEDICAL

DRG 533   Fractures of Femur with MCC
GMLOS 4.5   AMLOS 6.1   RW 1.4725   T ☑

Principal Diagnosis
821*   Fracture of other and unspecified parts of femur

DRG 534   Fractures of Femur without MCC
GMLOS 3.0   AMLOS 3.7   RW 0.7366   T ☑

Select principal diagnosis listed under DRG 533

DRG 535   Fractures of Hip and Pelvis with MCC
GMLOS 4.2   AMLOS 5.4   RW 1.2790   T ☑

Principal Diagnosis
808*   Fracture of pelvis
820*   Fracture of neck of femur

DRG 536   Fractures of Hip and Pelvis without MCC
GMLOS 3.1   AMLOS 3.5   RW 0.7146   T ☑

Select principal diagnosis listed under DRG 535

DRG 537   Sprains, Strains, and Dislocations of Hip, Pelvis and Thigh with CC/MCC
GMLOS 3.4   AMLOS 4.0   RW 0.8638   ☑

Principal Diagnosis
835*   Dislocation of hip
843*   Sprains and strains of hip and thigh
848.5   Pelvic sprain and strains

DRG 538   Sprains, Strains, and Dislocations of Hip, Pelvis and Thigh without CC/MCC
GMLOS 2.4   AMLOS 2.8   RW 0.6405   ☑

Select principal diagnosis listed under DRG 537

DRG 539   Osteomyelitis with MCC
GMLOS 6.6   AMLOS 8.7   RW 1.9982   T ☑

Principal Diagnosis
003.24   Salmonella osteomyelitis
015.0*   Tuberculosis of vertebral column
015.5*   Tuberculosis of limb bones
015.7*   Tuberculosis of other specified bone
091.61   Early syphilis, secondary syphilitic periostitis
095.5   Syphilis of bone
098.53   Gonococcal spondylitis
730.0*   Acute osteomyelitis
730.1*   Chronic osteomyelitis
730.2*   Unspecified osteomyelitis
730.8*   Other infections involving bone in diseases classified elsewhere
730.9*   Unspecified infection of bone

DRG 540   Osteomyelitis with CC
GMLOS 5.0   AMLOS 6.1   RW 1.2692   T ☑

Select principal diagnosis listed under DRG 539

DRG 541   Osteomyelitis without CC/MCC
GMLOS 3.8   AMLOS 4.8   RW 0.9770   T ☑

Select principal diagnosis listed under DRG 539

DRG 542   Pathological Fractures and Musculoskeletal and Connective Tissue Malignancy with MCC
GMLOS 6.3   AMLOS 8.2   RW 2.0293   T ☑ 🔻

Principal Diagnosis
170*   Malignant neoplasm of bone and articular cartilage
171*   Malignant neoplasm of connective and other soft tissue
198.5   Secondary malignant neoplasm of bone and bone marrow
209.73 Secondary neuroendocrine tumor of bone
238.0   Neoplasm of uncertain behavior of bone and articular cartilage
446.3   Lethal midline granuloma
446.4   Wegener's granulomatosis
733.1* Pathologic fracture
733.93 Stress fracture of tibia or fibula
733.94 Stress fracture of the metatarsals
733.95 Stress fracture of other bone
733.96 Stress fracture of femoral neck
733.97 Stress fracture of shaft of femur
733.98 Stress fracture of pelvis

DRG 543   Pathological Fractures and Musculoskeletal and Connective Tissue Malignancy with CC
GMLOS 4.3   AMLOS 5.4   RW 1.1749   T ☑ 🔻

Select principal diagnosis listed under DRG 542

DRG 544   Pathological Fractures and Musculoskeletal and Connective Tissue Malignancy without CC/MCC
GMLOS 3.3   AMLOS 3.9   RW 0.8012   T ☑ 🔻

Select principal diagnosis listed under DRG 542

DRG 545   Connective Tissue Disorders with MCC
GMLOS 6.1   AMLOS 8.7   RW 2.4785   T

Principal Diagnosis
099.3   Reiter's disease
136.1   Behcet's syndrome
277.3* Amyloidosis
279.4* Autoimmune disease, not elsewhere classified
359.7* Inflammatory and immune myopathies, NEC
390   Rheumatic fever without mention of heart involvement
443.0   Raynaud's syndrome
446.0   Polyarteritis nodosa
446.1   Acute febrile mucocutaneous lymph node syndrome (MCLS)
446.2* Hypersensitivity angiitis
446.5   Giant cell arteritis
446.6   Thrombotic microangiopathy
446.7   Takayasu's disease
447.6   Unspecified arteritis
696.0   Psoriatic arthropathy
710*   Diffuse diseases of connective tissue
711.1* Arthropathy associated with Reiter's disease and nonspecific urethritis
711.2* Arthropathy in Behcet's syndrome
714.0   Rheumatoid arthritis
714.1   Felty's syndrome
714.2   Other rheumatoid arthritis with visceral or systemic involvement
714.3* Juvenile chronic polyarthritis
714.89 Other specified inflammatory polyarthropathies
720.0   Ankylosing spondylitis
725   Polymyalgia rheumatica
795.6   False positive serological test for syphilis

DRG 546   Connective Tissue Disorders with CC
GMLOS 4.1   AMLOS 5.2   RW 1.1767   T ☑

Select principal diagnosis listed under DRG 545

DRG 547   Connective Tissue Disorders without CC/MCC
GMLOS 2.9   AMLOS 3.5   RW 0.7581   T ☑

Select principal diagnosis listed under DRG 545

DRG 548   Septic Arthritis with MCC
GMLOS 5.8   AMLOS 7.6   RW 1.7465   ☑

Principal Diagnosis
003.23 Salmonella arthritis
015.1* Tuberculosis of hip
015.2* Tuberculosis of knee
015.8* Tuberculosis of other specified joint
015.9* Tuberculosis of unspecified bones and joints
036.82 Meningococcal arthropathy
098.50 Gonococcal arthritis
098.51 Gonococcal synovitis and tenosynovitis
098.52 Gonococcal bursitis
098.59 Other gonococcal infection of joint
102.6   Bone and joint lesions due to yaws
711.0* Pyogenic arthritis
711.4* Arthropathy associated with other bacterial diseases
711.6* Arthropathy associated with mycoses
711.7* Arthropathy associated with helminthiasis
711.8* Arthropathy associated with other infectious and parasitic diseases
711.9* Unspecified infective arthritis

DRG 549   Septic Arthritis with CC
GMLOS 4.6   AMLOS 5.6   RW 1.1683   ☑

Select principal diagnosis listed under DRG 548

DRG 550   Septic Arthritis without CC/MCC
GMLOS 3.1   AMLOS 3.8   RW 0.7723   ☑

Select principal diagnosis listed under DRG 548

DRG 551   Medical Back Problems with MCC
GMLOS 5.0   AMLOS 6.4   RW 1.6345   T ☑ 🔻

Principal Diagnosis
720.1   Spinal enthesopathy
720.2   Sacroiliitis, not elsewhere classified
720.8* Other inflammatory spondylopathies
720.9   Unspecified inflammatory spondylopathy
721*   Spondylosis and allied disorders
722*   Intervertebral disc disorders
723.0   Spinal stenosis in cervical region
723.1   Cervicalgia
723.5   Torticollis, unspecified
723.7   Ossification of posterior longitudinal ligament in cervical region
723.8   Other syndromes affecting cervical region
723.9   Unspecified musculoskeletal disorders and symptoms referable to neck
724*   Other and unspecified disorders of back
737*   Curvature of spine
738.4   Acquired spondylolisthesis
738.5   Other acquired deformity of back or spine
739.1   Nonallopathic lesion of cervical region, not elsewhere classified
739.2   Nonallopathic lesion of thoracic region, not elsewhere classified

MDC 8: Diseases And Disorders Of The Musculoskeletal System And Connective Tissue—MEDICAL

MDC 8: Diseases And Disorders Of The Musculoskeletal System And Connective Tissue—MEDICAL

739.3	Nonallopathic lesion of lumbar region, not elsewhere classified
739.4	Nonallopathic lesion of sacral region, not elsewhere classified
756.10	Congenital anomaly of spine, unspecified
756.11	Congenital spondylolysis, lumbosacral region
756.12	Congenital spondylolisthesis
756.13	Congenital absence of vertebra
756.14	Hemivertebra
756.15	Congenital fusion of spine (vertebra)
756.19	Other congenital anomaly of spine
781.93	Ocular torticollis
805*	Fracture of vertebral column without mention of spinal cord injury
839.0*	Closed dislocation, cervical vertebra
839.1*	Open dislocation, cervical vertebra
839.2*	Closed dislocation, thoracic and lumbar vertebra
839.3*	Open dislocation, thoracic and lumbar vertebra
839.4*	Closed dislocation, other vertebra
839.5*	Open dislocation, other vertebra
846*	Sprains and strains of sacroiliac region
847*	Sprains and strains of other and unspecified parts of back
905.1	Late effect of fracture of spine and trunk without mention of spinal cord lesion

DRG 552   Medical Back Problems without MCC
GMLOS 3.2   AMLOS 3.9   RW 0.8533   T ☑ ▽

Select principal diagnosis listed under DRG 551

DRG 553   Bone Diseases and Arthropathies with MCC
GMLOS 4.3   AMLOS 5.6   RW 1.2087   ☑

Principal Diagnosis

056.71	Arthritis due to rubella
268.0	Rickets, active
268.1	Rickets, late effect
268.2	Osteomalacia, unspecified
274.0*	Gouty arthropathy
274.8*	Gout with other specified manifestations
274.9	Gout, unspecified
711.3*	Postdysenteric arthropathy
711.5*	Arthropathy associated with other viral diseases
712*	Crystal arthropathies
713*	Arthropathy associated with other disorders classified elsewhere
714.4	Chronic postrheumatic arthropathy
714.9	Unspecified inflammatory polyarthropathy
715*	Osteoarthrosis and allied disorders
716*	Other and unspecified arthropathies
718.5*	Ankylosis of joint
719.1*	Hemarthrosis
719.2*	Villonodular synovitis
719.3*	Palindromic rheumatism
730.30	Periostitis, without mention of osteomyelitis, unspecified site
730.31	Periostitis, without mention of osteomyelitis, shoulder region
730.32	Periostitis, without mention of osteomyelitis, upper arm
730.33	Periostitis, without mention of osteomyelitis, forearm
730.34	Periostitis, without mention of osteomyelitis, hand
730.35	Periostitis, without mention of osteomyelitis, pelvic region and thigh
730.36	Periostitis, without mention of osteomyelitis, lower leg
731*	Osteitis deformans and osteopathies associated with other disorders classified elsewhere
732*	Osteochondropathies
733.0*	Osteoporosis
733.2*	Cyst of bone
733.4*	Aseptic necrosis of bone

733.5	Osteitis condensans
733.92	Chondromalacia

DRG 554   Bone Diseases and Arthropathies without MCC
GMLOS 2.9   AMLOS 3.6   RW 0.6916   ☑

Select principal diagnosis listed under DRG 553

DRG 555   Signs and Symptoms of Musculoskeletal System and Connective Tissue with MCC
GMLOS 3.8   AMLOS 5.1   RW 1.2348   ☑

Principal Diagnosis

719.4*	Pain in joint
719.5*	Stiffness of joint, not elsewhere classified
719.6*	Other symptoms referable to joint
719.7	Difficulty in walking
719.8*	Other specified disorders of joint
719.9*	Unspecified disorder of joint
728.85	Spasm of muscle
728.87	Muscle weakness (generalized)
729.0	Rheumatism, unspecified and fibrositis
729.1	Unspecified myalgia and myositis
729.5	Pain in soft tissues of limb
729.81	Swelling of limb
729.82	Cramp of limb
729.89	Other musculoskeletal symptoms referable to limbs
729.9*	Other and unspecified disorders of soft tissue
739.0	Nonallopathic lesion of head region, not elsewhere classified
739.5	Nonallopathic lesion of pelvic region, not elsewhere classified
739.6	Nonallopathic lesion of lower extremities, not elsewhere classified
739.7	Nonallopathic lesion of upper extremities, not elsewhere classified
739.8	Nonallopathic lesion of rib cage, not elsewhere classified
739.9	Nonallopathic lesion of abdomen and other sites, not elsewhere classified

DRG 556   Signs and Symptoms of Musculoskeletal System and Connective Tissue without MCC
GMLOS 2.6   AMLOS 3.2   RW 0.7039   ☑

Select principal diagnosis listed under DRG 555

DRG 557   Tendonitis, Myositis and Bursitis with MCC
GMLOS 5.2   AMLOS 6.5   RW 1.5613   T ☑

Principal Diagnosis

040.81	Tropical pyomyositis
095.6	Syphilis of muscle
095.7	Syphilis of synovium, tendon, and bursa
306.0	Musculoskeletal malfunction arising from mental factors
726.0	Adhesive capsulitis of shoulder
726.1*	Rotator cuff syndrome of shoulder and allied disorders
726.2	Other affections of shoulder region, not elsewhere classified
726.3*	Enthesopathy of elbow region
726.4	Enthesopathy of wrist and carpus
726.5	Enthesopathy of hip region
726.6*	Enthesopathy of knee
726.70	Unspecified enthesopathy of ankle and tarsus
726.71	Achilles bursitis or tendinitis
726.72	Tibialis tendinitis
726.79	Other enthesopathy of ankle and tarsus
726.8	Other peripheral enthesopathies
726.9*	Unspecified enthesopathy
727.00	Unspecified synovitis and tenosynovitis
727.01	Synovitis and tenosynovitis in diseases classified elsewhere

T Transfer DRG   SP Special Payment   ☑ Optimization Potential   ▽ Targeted Potential   * Code Range   ● New DRG   ▲ Revised DRG Title

98   Valid 10/01/2012-09/30/2013   © 2012 OptumInsight, Inc.

727.03	Trigger finger (acquired)
727.04	Radial styloid tenosynovitis
727.05	Other tenosynovitis of hand and wrist
727.06	Tenosynovitis of foot and ankle
727.09	Other synovitis and tenosynovitis
727.2	Specific bursitides often of occupational origin
727.3	Other bursitis disorders
727.4*	Ganglion and cyst of synovium, tendon, and bursa
727.5*	Rupture of synovium
727.6*	Rupture of tendon, nontraumatic
727.8*	Other disorders of synovium, tendon, and bursa
727.9	Unspecified disorder of synovium, tendon, and bursa
728.0	Infective myositis
728.1*	Muscular calcification and ossification
728.2	Muscular wasting and disuse atrophy, not elsewhere classified
728.3	Other specific muscle disorders
728.4	Laxity of ligament
728.5	Hypermobility syndrome
728.6	Contracture of palmar fascia
728.7*	Other fibromatoses of muscle, ligament, and fascia
728.81	Interstitial myositis
728.82	Foreign body granuloma of muscle
728.83	Rupture of muscle, nontraumatic
728.84	Diastasis of muscle
728.86	Necrotizing fasciitis
728.88	Rhabdomyolysis
728.89	Other disorder of muscle, ligament, and fascia
728.9	Unspecified disorder of muscle, ligament, and fascia
729.4	Unspecified fasciitis
729.7*	Nontraumatic compartment syndrome

DRG 558   Tendonitis, Myositis and Bursitis without MCC
GMLOS 3.5   AMLOS 4.1   RW 0.8594   T ☑

Select principal diagnosis listed under DRG 557

DRG 559   Aftercare, Musculoskeletal System and Connective Tissue with MCC
GMLOS 5.2   AMLOS 7.0   RW 1.8741   T ☑

Principal Diagnosis

905.2	Late effect of fracture of upper extremities
905.3	Late effect of fracture of neck of femur
905.4	Late effect of fracture of lower extremities
905.5	Late effect of fracture of multiple and unspecified bones
905.8	Late effect of tendon injury
905.9	Late effect of traumatic amputation
996.4*	Mechanical complication of internal orthopedic device, implant, and graft
996.66	Infection and inflammatory reaction due to internal joint prosthesis
996.67	Infection and inflammatory reaction due to other internal orthopedic device, implant, and graft
996.77	Other complications due to internal joint prosthesis
996.78	Other complications due to other internal orthopedic device, implant, and graft
996.9*	Complications of reattached extremity or body part
V52.0	Fitting and adjustment of artificial arm (complete) (partial)
V52.1	Fitting and adjustment of artificial leg (complete) (partial)
V53.7	Fitting and adjustment of orthopedic device
V54.0*	Aftercare involving internal fixation device
V54.1*	Aftercare for healing traumatic fracture
V54.2*	Aftercare for healing pathologic fracture
V54.8*	Other orthopedic aftercare
V54.9	Unspecified orthopedic aftercare

DRG 560   Aftercare, Musculoskeletal System and Connective Tissue with CC
GMLOS 3.5   AMLOS 4.4   RW 1.0300   T ☑

Select principal diagnosis listed under DRG 559

DRG 561   Aftercare, Musculoskeletal System and Connective Tissue without CC/MCC
GMLOS 2.0   AMLOS 2.5   RW 0.6115   T ☑

Select principal diagnosis listed under DRG 559

DRG 562   Fractures, Sprains, Strains and Dislocations Except Femur, Hip, Pelvis and Thigh with MCC
GMLOS 4.4   AMLOS 5.6   RW 1.3989   T ☑

Principal Diagnosis

717.0	Old bucket handle tear of medial meniscus
717.1	Derangement of anterior horn of medial meniscus
717.2	Derangement of posterior horn of medial meniscus
717.3	Other and unspecified derangement of medial meniscus
717.4*	Derangement of lateral meniscus
717.5	Derangement of meniscus, not elsewhere classified
717.7	Chondromalacia of patella
717.8*	Other internal derangement of knee
717.9	Unspecified internal derangement of knee
718.01	Articular cartilage disorder, shoulder region
718.02	Articular cartilage disorder, upper arm
718.03	Articular cartilage disorder, forearm
718.04	Articular cartilage disorder, hand
718.07	Articular cartilage disorder, ankle and foot
718.20	Pathological dislocation of joint, site unspecified
718.21	Pathological dislocation of shoulder joint
718.22	Pathological dislocation of upper arm joint
718.23	Pathological dislocation of forearm joint
718.24	Pathological dislocation of hand joint
718.26	Pathological dislocation of lower leg joint
718.27	Pathological dislocation of ankle and foot joint
718.31	Recurrent dislocation of shoulder joint
718.32	Recurrent dislocation of upper arm joint
718.33	Recurrent dislocation of forearm joint
718.34	Recurrent dislocation of hand joint
718.36	Recurrent dislocation of lower leg joint
718.37	Recurrent dislocation of ankle and foot joint
754.41	Congenital dislocation of knee (with genu recurvatum)
810*	Fracture of clavicle
811.00	Closed fracture of unspecified part of scapula
811.01	Closed fracture of acromial process of scapula
811.02	Closed fracture of coracoid process of scapula
811.03	Closed fracture of glenoid cavity and neck of scapula
811.10	Open fracture of unspecified part of scapula
811.11	Open fracture of acromial process of scapula
811.12	Open fracture of coracoid process
811.13	Open fracture of glenoid cavity and neck of scapula
812*	Fracture of humerus
813*	Fracture of radius and ulna
814*	Fracture of carpal bone(s)
815*	Fracture of metacarpal bone(s)
816*	Fracture of one or more phalanges of hand
817*	Multiple fractures of hand bones
818*	Ill-defined fractures of upper limb
822*	Fracture of patella
823*	Fracture of tibia and fibula
824*	Fracture of ankle
825.0	Closed fracture of calcaneus
825.1	Open fracture of calcaneus
825.2*	Closed fracture of other tarsal and metatarsal bones
825.3*	Open fracture of other tarsal and metatarsal bones
826*	Fracture of one or more phalanges of foot
827*	Other, multiple, and ill-defined fractures of lower limb

Surgical	Medical	CC Indicator	MCC Indicator	Procedure Proxy

MDC 8: Diseases And Disorders Of The Musculoskeletal System And Connective Tissue—MEDICAL

829*	Fracture of unspecified bones
831*	Dislocation of shoulder
832*	Dislocation of elbow
833*	Dislocation of wrist
834*	Dislocation of finger
836*	Dislocation of knee
837*	Dislocation of ankle
838*	Dislocation of foot
839.69	Closed dislocation, other location
839.79	Open dislocation, other location
839.8	Closed dislocation, multiple and ill-defined sites
839.9	Open dislocation, multiple and ill-defined sites
840*	Sprains and strains of shoulder and upper arm
841*	Sprains and strains of elbow and forearm
842*	Sprains and strains of wrist and hand
844*	Sprains and strains of knee and leg
845.0*	Ankle sprain and strain
845.1*	Foot sprain and strain
848.8	Other specified sites of sprains and strains
848.9	Unspecified site of sprain and strain
905.6	Late effect of dislocation
905.7	Late effect of sprain and strain without mention of tendon injury

DRG 563   Fractures, Sprains, Strains and Dislocations Except Femur, Hip, Pelvis and Thigh without MCC

GMLOS 3.0	AMLOS 3.5	RW 0.7463	T ☑

Select principal diagnosis listed under DRG 562

DRG 564   Other Musculoskeletal System and Connective Tissue Diagnoses with MCC

GMLOS 4.7	AMLOS 6.2	RW 1.4459	☑

Principal Diagnosis

137.3	Late effects of tuberculosis of bones and joints
213.0	Benign neoplasm of bones of skull and face
213.2	Benign neoplasm of vertebral column, excluding sacrum and coccyx
213.4	Benign neoplasm of scapula and long bones of upper limb
213.5	Benign neoplasm of short bones of upper limb
213.6	Benign neoplasm of pelvic bones, sacrum, and coccyx
213.7	Benign neoplasm of long bones of lower limb
213.8	Benign neoplasm of short bones of lower limb
213.9	Benign neoplasm of bone and articular cartilage, site unspecified
215*	Other benign neoplasm of connective and other soft tissue
238.1	Neoplasm of uncertain behavior of connective and other soft tissue
239.2	Neoplasms of unspecified nature of bone, soft tissue, and skin
380.01	Acute perichondritis of pinna
380.02	Chronic perichondritis of pinna
380.03	Chondritis of pinna
717.6	Loose body in knee
718.00	Articular cartilage disorder, site unspecified
718.05	Articular cartilage disorder, pelvic region and thigh
718.08	Articular cartilage disorder, other specified site
718.09	Articular cartilage disorder, multiple sites
718.1*	Loose body in joint
718.25	Pathological dislocation of pelvic region and thigh joint
718.28	Pathological dislocation of joint of other specified site
718.29	Pathological dislocation of joint of multiple sites
718.30	Recurrent dislocation of joint, site unspecified
718.35	Recurrent dislocation of pelvic region and thigh joint
718.38	Recurrent dislocation of joint of other specified site
718.39	Recurrent dislocation of joint of multiple sites
718.4*	Contracture of joint
718.65	Unspecified intrapelvic protrusion acetabulum, pelvic region and thigh

718.7*	Developmental dislocation of joint
718.8*	Other joint derangement, not elsewhere classified
718.9*	Unspecified derangement of joint
719.0*	Effusion of joint
726.73	Calcaneal spur
727.02	Giant cell tumor of tendon sheath
727.1	Bunion
729.6	Residual foreign body in soft tissue
730.37	Periostitis, without mention of osteomyelitis, ankle and foot
730.38	Periostitis, without mention of osteomyelitis, other specified sites
730.39	Periostitis, without mention of osteomyelitis, multiple sites
730.7*	Osteopathy resulting from poliomyelitis
733.3	Hyperostosis of skull
733.7	Algoneurodystrophy
733.8*	Malunion and nonunion of fracture
733.90	Disorder of bone and cartilage, unspecified
733.91	Arrest of bone development or growth
733.99	Other disorders of bone and cartilage
734	Flat foot
735*	Acquired deformities of toe
736.00	Unspecified deformity of forearm, excluding fingers
736.01	Cubitus valgus (acquired)
736.02	Cubitus varus (acquired)
736.03	Valgus deformity of wrist (acquired)
736.04	Varus deformity of wrist (acquired)
736.09	Other acquired deformities of forearm, excluding fingers
736.1	Mallet finger
736.2*	Other acquired deformities of finger
736.3*	Acquired deformities of hip
736.4*	Genu valgum or varum (acquired)
736.5	Genu recurvatum (acquired)
736.6	Other acquired deformities of knee
736.70	Unspecified deformity of ankle and foot, acquired
736.71	Acquired equinovarus deformity
736.72	Equinus deformity of foot, acquired
736.73	Cavus deformity of foot, acquired
736.75	Cavovarus deformity of foot, acquired
736.76	Other acquired calcaneus deformity
736.79	Other acquired deformity of ankle and foot
736.8*	Acquired deformities of other parts of limbs
736.9	Acquired deformity of limb, site unspecified
738.1*	Other acquired deformity of head
738.2	Acquired deformity of neck
738.3	Acquired deformity of chest and rib
738.6	Acquired deformity of pelvis
738.8	Acquired musculoskeletal deformity of other specified site
738.9	Acquired musculoskeletal deformity of unspecified site
754.0	Congenital musculoskeletal deformities of skull, face, and jaw
754.1	Congenital musculoskeletal deformity of sternocleidomastoid muscle
754.2	Congenital musculoskeletal deformity of spine
754.3*	Congenital dislocation of hip
754.40	Congenital genu recurvatum
754.42	Congenital bowing of femur
754.43	Congenital bowing of tibia and fibula
754.44	Congenital bowing of unspecified long bones of leg
754.5*	Congenital varus deformities of feet
754.6*	Congenital valgus deformities of feet
754.7*	Other congenital deformity of feet
754.89	Other specified nonteratogenic anomalies
755*	Other congenital anomalies of limbs
756.0	Congenital anomalies of skull and face bones
756.16	Klippel-Feil syndrome
756.2	Cervical rib
756.4	Chondrodystrophy
756.5*	Congenital osteodystrophies
756.8*	Other specified congenital anomalies of muscle, tendon, fascia, and connective tissue

T *Transfer DRG*   SP *Special Payment*   ☑ *Optimization Potential*   ▽ *Targeted Potential*   * *Code Range*   ● *New DRG*   ▲ *Revised DRG Title*

100   Valid 10/01/2012-09/30/2013   © 2012 OptumInsight, Inc.

756.9	Other and unspecified congenital anomaly of musculoskeletal system
759.7	Multiple congenital anomalies, so described
759.81	Prader-Willi syndrome
759.89	Other specified multiple congenital anomalies, so described
793.7	Nonspecific (abnormal) findings on radiological and other examination of musculoskeletal system
794.17	Nonspecific abnormal electromyogram (EMG)
802.8	Other facial bones, closed fracture
802.9	Other facial bones, open fracture
809.0	Fracture of bones of trunk, closed
809.1	Fracture of bones of trunk, open
811.09	Closed fracture of other part of scapula
811.19	Open fracture of other part of scapula
848.0	Sprain and strain of septal cartilage of nose
848.2	Sprain and strain of thyroid region
880.2*	Open wound of shoulder and upper arm, with tendon involvement
881.2*	Open wound of elbow, forearm, and wrist, with tendon involvement
882.2	Open wound of hand except finger(s) alone, with tendon involvement
883.2	Open wound of finger(s), with tendon involvement
884.2	Multiple and unspecified open wound of upper limb, with tendon involvement
890.2	Open wound of hip and thigh, with tendon involvement
891.2	Open wound of knee, leg (except thigh), and ankle, with tendon involvement
892.2	Open wound of foot except toe(s) alone, with tendon involvement
893.2	Open wound of toe(s), with tendon involvement
894.2	Multiple and unspecified open wound of lower limb, with tendon involvement
958.6	Volkmann's ischemic contracture
997.6*	Amputation stump complication
V42.4	Bone replaced by transplant
V43.6*	Joint replaced by other means
V43.7	Limb replaced by other means
V59.2	Bone donor

DRG 565 **Other Musculoskeletal System and Connective Tissue Diagnoses with CC**

GMLOS 3.6   AMLOS 4.5   RW 0.9386   ☑

Select principal diagnosis listed under DRG 564

DRG 566 **Other Musculoskeletal System and Connective Tissue Diagnoses without CC/MCC**

GMLOS 2.6   AMLOS 3.2   RW 0.6786   ☑

Select principal diagnosis listed under DRG 564

Surgical	Medical	CC Indicator	MCC Indicator	Procedure Proxy

Diseases And Disorders Of The Skin, Subcutaneous Tissue And Breast

006.6	114.1	174.8	611.81	692.82	702.0	709.09	881.02	914.8
017.00	120.3	174.9	611.82	692.83	702.11	709.1	882.0	914.9
017.01	132.0	175.0	611.83	692.84	702.19	709.2	883.0	915.0
017.02	132.1	175.9	611.89	692.89	702.8	709.3	884.0	915.1
017.03	132.2	176.0	611.9	692.9	703.0	709.4	890.0	915.2
017.04	132.3	176.1	612.0	693.0	703.8	709.8	891.0	915.3
017.05	132.9	176.8	612.1	693.1	703.9	709.9	892.0	915.4
017.06	133.0	176.9	617.6	693.8	704.00	723.6	893.0	915.5
017.10	133.8	198.2	680.0	693.9	704.01	729.30	894.0	915.6
017.11	133.9	198.81	680.1	694.0	704.02	729.31	906.0	915.7
017.12	134.0	209.31	680.2	694.1	704.09	729.39	906.2	915.8
017.13	134.1	209.32	680.3	694.2	704.1	744.5	906.3	915.9
017.14	134.2	209.33	680.4	694.3	704.2	744.9	906.4	916.0
017.15	134.8	209.34	680.5	694.4	704.3	757.0	906.5	916.1
017.16	134.9	209.35	680.6	694.5	704.41	757.1	906.6	916.2
022.0	172.0	209.36	680.7	694.60	704.42	757.2	906.7	916.3
031.1	172.2	214.0	680.8	694.8	704.8	757.31	906.8	916.4
032.85	172.3	214.1	680.9	694.9	704.9	757.32	906.9	916.5
035	172.4	214.8	681.00	695.0	705.0	757.33	910.0	916.6
039.0	172.5	214.9	681.01	695.10	705.1	757.39	910.1	916.7
039.3	172.6	216.0	681.02	695.11	705.21	757.4	910.2	916.8
039.4	172.7	216.2	681.10	695.12	705.22	757.5	910.3	916.9
051.1	172.8	216.3	681.11	695.13	705.81	757.6	910.4	917.0
051.2	172.9	216.4	681.9	695.14	705.82	757.8	910.5	917.1
053.9	173.00	216.5	682.0	695.15	705.83	757.9	910.6	917.2
054.0	173.01	216.6	682.1	695.19	705.89	780.8	910.7	917.3
054.6	173.02	216.7	682.2	695.2	705.9	782.1	910.8	917.4
054.9	173.09	216.8	682.3	695.3	706.0	782.2	910.9	917.5
058.81	173.20	216.9	682.4	695.4	706.1	782.8	911.0	917.6
058.82	173.21	217	682.5	695.50	706.2	782.9	911.1	917.7
058.89	173.22	228.01	682.6	695.51	706.3	784.2	911.2	917.8
078.0	173.29	232.0	682.7	695.52	706.8	793.80	911.3	917.9
078.10	173.30	232.2	682.8	695.53	706.9	793.81	911.4	919.0
078.11	173.31	232.3	682.9	695.54	707.00	793.82	911.5	919.1
078.12	173.32	232.4	684	695.55	707.01	793.89	911.6	919.2
078.19	173.39	232.5	685.0	695.56	707.02	873.0	911.7	919.3
085.1	173.40	232.6	685.1	695.57	707.03	873.1	911.8	919.4
085.2	173.41	232.7	686.00	695.58	707.05	873.40	911.9	919.5
085.3	173.42	232.8	686.01	695.59	707.06	873.41	912.0	919.6
085.4	173.49	232.9	686.09	695.81	707.07	873.42	912.1	919.7
085.5	173.50	233.0	686.1	695.89	707.09	873.49	912.2	919.8
091.3	173.51	238.2	686.8	695.9	707.10	873.50	912.3	919.9
091.82	173.52	238.3	686.9	696.1	707.11	873.51	912.4	920
102.0	173.59	239.3	690.10	696.2	707.12	873.52	912.5	922.0
102.1	173.60	306.3	690.11	696.3	707.13	873.59	912.6	922.1
102.2	173.61	374.51	690.12	696.4	707.14	873.8	912.7	922.2
102.3	173.62	448.1	690.18	696.5	707.15	873.9	912.8	922.31
102.4	173.69	457.0	690.8	696.8	707.19	874.8	912.9	922.32
103.0	173.70	457.1	691.0	697.0	707.20	874.9	913.0	922.33
103.1	173.71	457.2	691.8	697.1	707.21	875.0	913.1	922.8
103.3	173.72	610.0	692.0	697.8	707.22	876.0	913.2	922.9
110.0	173.79	610.1	692.1	697.9	707.23	876.1	913.3	923.00
110.1	173.80	610.2	692.2	698.0	707.24	877.0	913.4	923.01
110.2	173.81	610.3	692.3	698.2	707.25	877.1	913.5	923.02
110.3	173.82	610.4	692.4	698.3	707.8	879.0	913.6	923.03
110.4	173.89	610.8	692.5	698.4	707.9	879.1	913.7	923.09
110.5	173.90	610.9	692.6	698.8	708.0	879.2	913.8	923.10
110.6	173.91	611.0	692.70	698.9	708.1	879.4	913.9	923.11
110.8	173.92	611.1	692.71	700	708.2	879.6	914.0	923.20
110.9	173.99	611.2	692.72	701.0	708.3	879.8	914.1	923.21
111.0	174.0	611.3	692.73	701.1	708.4	880.00	914.2	923.3
111.1	174.1	611.4	692.74	701.2	708.5	880.01	914.3	923.8
111.2	174.2	611.5	692.75	701.3	708.8	880.02	914.4	923.9
111.3	174.3	611.6	692.76	701.4	708.9	880.03	914.5	924.00
111.8	174.4	611.71	692.77	701.5	709.00	880.09	914.6	924.01
111.9	174.5	611.72	692.79	701.8	709.01	881.00	914.7	924.10
112.3	174.6	611.79	692.81	701.9		881.01		924.11

| 924.20 | 924.3 | 924.5 | 924.9 | V42.3 | V50.1 | V51.0 | V59.1 | |
| 924.21 | 924.4 | 924.8 | 996.54 | V50.0 | V50.41 | V51.8 | | |

SURGICAL

DRG 570   Skin Debridement with MCC
GMLOS 7.5   AMLOS 9.9   RW 2.4688   ☑☑

Operating Room Procedure
86.22   Excisional debridement of wound, infection, or burn

DRG 571   Skin Debridement with CC
GMLOS 5.5   AMLOS 6.7   RW 1.4969   ☑☑

Select operating room procedure listed under DRG 570

DRG 572   Skin Debridement without CC/MCC
GMLOS 3.9   AMLOS 4.7   RW 1.0036   ☑☑

Select operating room procedure listed under DRG 570

DRG 573   Skin Graft for Skin Ulcer or Cellulitis with MCC
GMLOS 8.6   AMLOS 13.0   RW 3.5637   ☑☑

Principal Diagnosis
681*   Cellulitis and abscess of finger and toe
682*   Other cellulitis and abscess
707*   Chronic ulcer of skin

Operating Room Procedures
85.82   Split-thickness graft to breast
85.83   Full-thickness graft to breast
85.84   Pedicle graft to breast
85.85   Muscle flap graft to breast
86.4   Radical excision of skin lesion
86.60   Free skin graft, not otherwise specified
86.61   Full-thickness skin graft to hand
86.62   Other skin graft to hand
86.63   Full-thickness skin graft to other sites
86.65   Heterograft to skin
86.66   Homograft to skin
86.67   Dermal regenerative graft
86.69   Other skin graft to other sites
86.7*   Pedicle grafts or flaps
86.91   Excision of skin for graft
86.93   Insertion of tissue expander

DRG 574   Skin Graft for Skin Ulcer or Cellulitis with CC
GMLOS 7.2   AMLOS 9.5   RW 2.4469   ☑☑

Select principal diagnosis and operating room procedures listed under DRG 573

DRG 575   Skin Graft for Skin Ulcer or Cellulitis without CC/MCC
GMLOS 4.0   AMLOS 5.3   RW 1.3266   ☑☑

Select principal diagnosis and operating room procedures listed under DRG 573

DRG 576   Skin Graft Except for Skin Ulcer or Cellulitis with MCC
GMLOS 8.5   AMLOS 12.9   RW 4.2457   ☑

Select only operating room procedures listed under DRG 573

DRG 577   Skin Graft Except for Skin Ulcer or Cellulitis with CC
GMLOS 3.9   AMLOS 5.8   RW 1.8963   ☑

Select only operating room procedures listed under DRG 573

DRG 578   Skin Graft Except for Skin Ulcer or Cellulitis without CC/MCC
GMLOS 2.3   AMLOS 3.2   RW 1.1312   ☑

Select only operating room procedures listed under DRG 573

DRG 579   Other Skin, Subcutaneous Tissue and Breast Procedures with MCC
GMLOS 7.3   AMLOS 9.6   RW 2.7186   ☑☑

Operating Room Procedures
06.09   Other incision of thyroid field
07.22   Unilateral adrenalectomy
07.3   Bilateral adrenalectomy
07.63   Partial excision of pituitary gland, unspecified approach
07.64   Total excision of pituitary gland, transfrontal approach
07.65   Total excision of pituitary gland, transsphenoidal approach
07.68   Total excision of pituitary gland, other specified approach
07.69   Total excision of pituitary gland, unspecified approach
07.72   Incision of pituitary gland
07.79   Other operations on hypophysis
08.20   Removal of lesion of eyelid, not otherwise specified
08.22   Excision of other minor lesion of eyelid
08.23   Excision of major lesion of eyelid, partial-thickness
08.24   Excision of major lesion of eyelid, full-thickness
08.25   Destruction of lesion of eyelid
08.38   Correction of lid retraction
08.44   Repair of entropion or ectropion with lid reconstruction
08.5*   Other adjustment of lid position
08.6*   Reconstruction of eyelid with flaps or grafts
08.7*   Other reconstruction of eyelid
08.99   Other operations on eyelids
09.73   Repair of canaliculus
16.93   Excision of lesion of eye, unspecified structure
17.56   Atherectomy of other non-coronary vessel(s)
18.21   Excision of preauricular sinus
18.3*   Other excision of external ear
18.5   Surgical correction of prominent ear
18.6   Reconstruction of external auditory canal
18.71   Construction of auricle of ear
18.79   Other plastic repair of external ear
18.9   Other operations on external ear
21.4   Resection of nose
21.72   Open reduction of nasal fracture
21.83   Total nasal reconstruction
21.84   Revision rhinoplasty
21.85   Augmentation rhinoplasty
21.86   Limited rhinoplasty
21.87   Other rhinoplasty
21.88   Other septoplasty
21.89   Other repair and plastic operations on nose
21.99   Other operations on nose
27.0   Drainage of face and floor of mouth
27.42   Wide excision of lesion of lip
27.43   Other excision of lesion or tissue of lip
27.54   Repair of cleft lip
27.55   Full-thickness skin graft to lip and mouth
27.56   Other skin graft to lip and mouth
27.57   Attachment of pedicle or flap graft to lip and mouth
27.59   Other plastic repair of mouth
27.63   Revision of cleft palate repair
27.69   Other plastic repair of palate
27.92   Incision of mouth, unspecified structure
29.2   Excision of branchial cleft cyst or vestige
29.52   Closure of branchial cleft fistula
31.72   Closure of external fistula of trachea
31.74   Revision of tracheostomy
34.4   Excision or destruction of lesion of chest wall
34.79   Other repair of chest wall
37.79   Revision or relocation of cardiac device pocket

☐ Transfer DRG   ☐ Special Payment   ☑ Optimization Potential   ▽ Targeted Potential   * Code Range   ● New DRG   ▲ Revised DRG Title

39.25	Aorta-iliac-femoral bypass
39.29	Other (peripheral) vascular shunt or bypass
39.31	Suture of artery
39.50	Angioplasty of other non-coronary vessel(s)
39.59	Other repair of vessel
39.98	Control of hemorrhage, not otherwise specified
40.0	Incision of lymphatic structures
40.1*	Diagnostic procedures on lymphatic structures
40.2*	Simple excision of lymphatic structure
40.3	Regional lymph node excision
40.4*	Radical excision of cervical lymph nodes
40.5*	Radical excision of other lymph nodes
40.9	Other operations on lymphatic structures
48.35	Local excision of rectal lesion or tissue
48.73	Closure of other rectal fistula
48.8*	Incision or excision of perirectal tissue or lesion
49.01	Incision of perianal abscess
49.02	Other incision of perianal tissue
49.04	Other excision of perianal tissue
49.11	Anal fistulotomy
49.12	Anal fistulectomy
49.39	Other local excision or destruction of lesion or tissue of anus
49.71	Suture of laceration of anus
49.72	Anal cerclage
49.73	Closure of anal fistula
49.75	Implantation or revision of artificial anal sphincter
49.76	Removal of artificial anal sphincter
49.79	Other repair of anal sphincter
50.12	Open biopsy of liver
50.14	Laparoscopic liver biopsy
50.19	Other diagnostic procedures on liver
54.0	Incision of abdominal wall
54.11	Exploratory laparotomy
54.21	Laparoscopy
54.22	Biopsy of abdominal wall or umbilicus
54.3	Excision or destruction of lesion or tissue of abdominal wall or umbilicus
54.63	Other suture of abdominal wall
54.72	Other repair of abdominal wall
59.00	Retroperitoneal dissection, not otherwise specified
64.11	Biopsy of penis
64.2	Local excision or destruction of lesion of penis
64.49	Other repair of penis
65.5*	Bilateral oophorectomy
65.61	Other removal of both ovaries and tubes at same operative episode
65.63	Laparoscopic removal of both ovaries and tubes at same operative episode
67.1*	Diagnostic procedures on cervix
67.39	Other excision or destruction of lesion or tissue of cervix
70.24	Vaginal biopsy
70.33	Excision or destruction of lesion of vagina
70.71	Suture of laceration of vagina
71.09	Other incision of vulva and perineum
71.1*	Diagnostic procedures on vulva
71.24	Excision or other destruction of Bartholin's gland (cyst)
71.3	Other local excision or destruction of vulva and perineum
71.62	Bilateral vulvectomy
71.71	Suture of laceration of vulva or perineum
76.43	Other reconstruction of mandible
77.28	Wedge osteotomy of tarsals and metatarsals
77.4*	Biopsy of bone
80.83	Other local excision or destruction of lesion of wrist joint
82.09	Other incision of soft tissue of hand
82.21	Excision of lesion of tendon sheath of hand
82.29	Excision of other lesion of soft tissue of hand
82.39	Other excision of soft tissue of hand
82.45	Other suture of other tendon of hand
82.72	Plastic operation on hand with graft of muscle or fascia
82.79	Plastic operation on hand with other graft or implant

82.89	Other plastic operations on hand
82.91	Lysis of adhesions of hand
83.02	Myotomy
83.09	Other incision of soft tissue
83.14	Fasciotomy
83.21	Open biopsy of soft tissue
83.32	Excision of lesion of muscle
83.39	Excision of lesion of other soft tissue
83.44	Other fasciectomy
83.45	Other myectomy
83.49	Other excision of soft tissue
83.65	Other suture of muscle or fascia
83.71	Advancement of tendon
83.82	Graft of muscle or fascia
83.87	Other plastic operations on muscle
83.88	Other plastic operations on tendon
83.89	Other plastic operations on fascia
84.0*	Amputation of upper limb
84.1*	Amputation of lower limb
84.3	Revision of amputation stump
84.91	Amputation, not otherwise specified
86.06	Insertion of totally implantable infusion pump
86.21	Excision of pilonidal cyst or sinus
86.25	Dermabrasion
86.8*	Other repair and reconstruction of skin and subcutaneous tissue
86.90	Extraction of fat for graft or banking
92.27	Implantation or insertion of radioactive elements

OR

Nonoperating Room Procedures

86.07	Insertion of totally implantable vascular access device (VAD)
86.09	Other incision of skin and subcutaneous tissue
86.3	Other local excision or destruction of lesion or tissue of skin and subcutaneous tissue

DRG 580 Other Skin, Subcutaneous Tissue and Breast Procedures with CC

GMLOS 3.7	AMLOS 5.1	RW 1.4875	T ☑

Select operating room procedures or nonoperating room procedures listed under DRG 579

DRG 581 Other Skin, Subcutaneous Tissue and Breast Procedures without CC/MCC

GMLOS 2.0	AMLOS 2.5	RW 0.9916	T ☑

Select operating room procedures or nonoperating room procedures listed under DRG 579

DRG 582 Mastectomy for Malignancy with CC/MCC

GMLOS 2.0	AMLOS 2.7	RW 1.1283	☑

Principal or Secondary Diagnosis

174*	Malignant neoplasm of female breast
175*	Malignant neoplasm of male breast
198.2	Secondary malignant neoplasm of skin
198.81	Secondary malignant neoplasm of breast
233.0	Carcinoma in situ of breast
238.3	Neoplasm of uncertain behavior of breast

Operating Room Procedures

85.22	Resection of quadrant of breast
85.23	Subtotal mastectomy
85.3*	Reduction mammoplasty and subcutaneous mammectomy
85.4*	Mastectomy
85.7*	Total reconstruction of breast

Surgical	Medical	CC Indicator	MCC Indicator	Procedure Proxy

MDC 9: Diseases And Disorders Of The Skin, Subcutaneous Tissue And Breast—MEDICAL

DRG 583   Mastectomy for Malignancy without CC/MCC
GMLOS 1.5   AMLOS 1.7   RW 0.8992   ☑

Select principal or secondary diagnosis and operating room procedures listed under DRG 582

DRG 584   Breast Biopsy, Local Excision and Other Breast Procedures with CC/MCC
GMLOS 3.7   AMLOS 5.3   RW 1.6550   ☑

Operating Room Procedures
17.69   Laser interstitial thermal therapy [LITT] of lesion or tissue of other and unspecified site under guidance
85.12   Open biopsy of breast
85.20   Excision or destruction of breast tissue, not otherwise specified
85.21   Local excision of lesion of breast
85.22   Resection of quadrant of breast
85.23   Subtotal mastectomy
85.24   Excision of ectopic breast tissue
85.25   Excision of nipple
85.3*   Reduction mammoplasty and subcutaneous mammectomy
85.4*   Mastectomy
85.50   Augmentation mammaplasty, not otherwise specified
85.53   Unilateral breast implant
85.54   Bilateral breast implant
85.55   Fat graft to breast
85.6   Mastopexy
85.7*   Total reconstruction of breast
85.86   Transposition of nipple
85.87   Other repair or reconstruction of nipple
85.89   Other mammoplasty
85.93   Revision of implant of breast
85.94   Removal of implant of breast
85.95   Insertion of breast tissue expander
85.96   Removal of breast tissue expander (s)
85.99   Other operations on the breast

DRG 585   Breast Biopsy, Local Excision and Other Breast Procedures without CC/MCC
GMLOS 1.8   AMLOS 2.2   RW 1.1381   ☑

Select operating room procedures listed under DRG 584

MEDICAL

DRG 592   Skin Ulcers with MCC
GMLOS 5.3   AMLOS 6.9   RW 1.4632   T☑

Principal Diagnosis
707*   Chronic ulcer of skin

DRG 593   Skin Ulcers with CC
GMLOS 4.4   AMLOS 5.3   RW 0.9912   T☑

Select principal diagnosis listed under DRG 592

DRG 594   Skin Ulcers without CC/MCC
GMLOS 3.2   AMLOS 3.9   RW 0.6782   T☑

Select principal diagnosis listed under DRG 592

DRG 595   Major Skin Disorders with MCC
GMLOS 5.9   AMLOS 7.7   RW 1.8803   ☑

Principal Diagnosis
017.1*   Erythema nodosum with hypersensitivity reaction in tuberculosis
053.9   Herpes zoster without mention of complication
172.0   Malignant melanoma of skin of lip
172.2   Malignant melanoma of skin of ear and external auditory canal
172.3   Malignant melanoma of skin of other and unspecified parts of face
172.4   Malignant melanoma of skin of scalp and neck
172.5   Malignant melanoma of skin of trunk, except scrotum
172.6   Malignant melanoma of skin of upper limb, including shoulder
172.7   Malignant melanoma of skin of lower limb, including hip
172.8   Malignant melanoma of other specified sites of skin
172.9   Melanoma of skin, site unspecified
209.31   Merkel cell carcinoma of the face
209.32   Merkel cell carcinoma of the scalp and neck
209.33   Merkel cell carcinoma of the upper limb
209.34   Merkel cell carcinoma of the lower limb
209.35   Merkel cell carcinoma of the trunk
209.36   Merkel cell carcinoma of other sites
694.4   Pemphigus
694.5   Pemphigoid
694.60   Benign mucous membrane pemphigoid without mention of ocular involvement
694.8   Other specified bullous dermatosis
694.9   Unspecified bullous dermatosis
695.0   Toxic erythema
695.1*   Erythema multiforme
695.2   Erythema nodosum
695.4   Lupus erythematosus
695.81   Ritter's disease
696.1   Other psoriasis
696.2   Parapsoriasis

DRG 596   Major Skin Disorders without MCC
GMLOS 3.6   AMLOS 4.5   RW 0.8880   ☑

Select principal diagnosis listed under DRG 595

DRG 597   Malignant Breast Disorders with MCC
GMLOS 5.4   AMLOS 7.2   RW 1.6026   ☑

Principal Diagnosis
174*   Malignant neoplasm of female breast
175*   Malignant neoplasm of male breast
198.2   Secondary malignant neoplasm of skin
198.81   Secondary malignant neoplasm of breast
233.0   Carcinoma in situ of breast
238.3   Neoplasm of uncertain behavior of breast

DRG 598   Malignant Breast Disorders with CC
GMLOS 4.1   AMLOS 5.5   RW 1.2280   ☑

Select principal diagnosis listed under DRG 597

DRG 599   Malignant Breast Disorders without CC/MCC
GMLOS 2.3   AMLOS 3.1   RW 0.6650   ☑

Select principal diagnosis listed under DRG 597

DRG 600   Nonmalignant Breast Disorders with CC/MCC
GMLOS 4.0   AMLOS 5.0   RW 0.9968   ☑

Principal Diagnosis
239.3   Neoplasm of unspecified nature of breast

457.0	Postmastectomy lymphedema syndrome
610*	Benign mammary dysplasias
611*	Other disorders of breast
612*	Deformity and disproportion of reconstructed breast
757.6	Specified congenital anomalies of breast
793.8*	Nonspecific abnormal findings on radiological and other examinations of body structure, breast
996.54	Mechanical complication due to breast prosthesis
V50.41	Prophylactic breast removal

DRG 601   Nonmalignant Breast Disorders without CC/MCC
GMLOS 3.0   AMLOS 3.6   RW 0.6247   ☑

Select principal diagnosis listed under DRG 600

DRG 602   Cellulitis with MCC
GMLOS 5.2   AMLOS 6.5   RW 1.4883   ☐☑

Principal Diagnosis

035	Erysipelas
457.2	Lymphangitis
680*	Carbuncle and furuncle
681*	Cellulitis and abscess of finger and toe
682*	Other cellulitis and abscess
684	Impetigo
685*	Pilonidal cyst
686*	Other local infection of skin and subcutaneous tissue
910.1	Face, neck, and scalp except eye, abrasion or friction burn, infected
910.5	Face, neck, and scalp except eye, insect bite, nonvenomous, infected
910.7	Face, neck, and scalp except eye, superficial foreign body (splinter), without major open wound, infected
910.9	Other and unspecified superficial injury of face, neck, and scalp, infected
911.1	Trunk abrasion or friction burn, infected
911.3	Trunk blister, infected
911.5	Trunk, insect bite, nonvenomous, infected
911.7	Trunk, superficial foreign body (splinter), without major open wound, infected
911.9	Other and unspecified superficial injury of trunk, infected
912.1	Shoulder and upper arm, abrasion or friction burn, infected
912.3	Shoulder and upper arm, blister, infected
912.5	Shoulder and upper arm, insect bite, nonvenomous, infected
912.7	Shoulder and upper arm, superficial foreign body (splinter), without major open wound, infected
912.9	Other and unspecified superficial injury of shoulder and upper arm, infected
913.1	Elbow, forearm, and wrist, abrasion or friction burn, infected
913.3	Elbow, forearm, and wrist, blister infected
913.5	Elbow, forearm, and wrist, insect bite, nonvenomous, infected
913.7	Elbow, forearm, and wrist, superficial foreign body (splinter), without major open wound, infected
913.9	Other and unspecified superficial injury of elbow, forearm, and wrist, infected
914.1	Hand(s) except finger(s) alone, abrasion or friction burn, infected
914.3	Hand(s) except finger(s) alone, blister, infected
914.5	Hand(s) except finger(s) alone, insect bite, nonvenomous, infected
914.7	Hand(s) except finger(s) alone, superficial foreign body (splinter) without major open wound, infected
914.9	Other and unspecified superficial injury of hand(s) except finger(s) alone, infected
915.1	Finger, abrasion or friction burn, infected
915.3	Finger, blister, infected
915.5	Finger, insect bite, nonvenomous, infected
915.7	Finger, superficial foreign body (splinter), without major open wound, infected
915.9	Other and unspecified superficial injury of finger, infected
916.1	Hip, thigh, leg, and ankle, abrasion or friction burn, infected
916.3	Hip, thigh, leg, and ankle, blister, infected
916.5	Hip, thigh, leg, and ankle, insect bite, nonvenomous, infected
916.7	Hip, thigh, leg, and ankle, superficial foreign body (splinter), without major open wound, infected
916.9	Other and unspecified superficial injury of hip, thigh, leg, and ankle, infected
917.1	Foot and toe(s), abrasion or friction burn, infected
917.3	Foot and toe(s), blister, infected
917.5	Foot and toe(s), insect bite, nonvenomous, infected
917.7	Foot and toe(s), superficial foreign body (splinter), without major open wound, infected
917.9	Other and unspecified superficial injury of foot and toes, infected
919.1	Other, multiple, and unspecified sites, abrasion or friction burn, infected
919.3	Other, multiple, and unspecified sites, blister, infected
919.5	Other, multiple, and unspecified sites, insect bite, nonvenomous, infected
919.7	Other, multiple, and unspecified sites, superficial foreign body (splinter), without major open wound, infected
919.9	Other and unspecified superficial injury of other, multiple, and unspecified sites, infected

DRG 603   Cellulitis without MCC
GMLOS 3.6   AMLOS 4.3   RW 0.8392   ☐☑

Select principal diagnosis listed under DRG 602

DRG 604   Trauma to the Skin, Subcutaneous Tissue and Breast with MCC
GMLOS 3.9   AMLOS 5.3   RW 1.3297   ☑

Principal Diagnosis

873.0	Open wound of scalp, without mention of complication
873.1	Open wound of scalp, complicated
873.40	Open wound of face, unspecified site, without mention of complication
873.41	Open wound of cheek, without mention of complication
873.42	Open wound of forehead, without mention of complication
873.49	Open wound of face, other and multiple sites, without mention of complication
873.50	Open wound of face, unspecified site, complicated
873.51	Open wound of cheek, complicated
873.52	Open wound of forehead, complicated
873.59	Open wound of face, other and multiple sites, complicated
873.8	Other and unspecified open wound of head without mention of complication
873.9	Other and unspecified open wound of head, complicated
874.8	Open wound of other and unspecified parts of neck, without mention of complication
874.9	Open wound of other and unspecified parts of neck, complicated
875.0	Open wound of chest (wall), without mention of complication
876*	Open wound of back
877*	Open wound of buttock
879.0	Open wound of breast, without mention of complication
879.1	Open wound of breast, complicated
879.2	Open wound of abdominal wall, anterior, without mention of complication
879.4	Open wound of abdominal wall, lateral, without mention of complication
879.6	Open wound of other and unspecified parts of trunk, without mention of complication

MDC 9: Diseases And Disorders Of The Skin, Subcutaneous Tissue And Breast—MEDICAL

879.8	Open wound(s) (multiple) of unspecified site(s), without mention of complication
880.0*	Open wound of shoulder and upper arm, without mention of complication
881.0*	Open wound of elbow, forearm, and wrist, without mention of complication
882.0	Open wound of hand except finger(s) alone, without mention of complication
883.0	Open wound of finger(s), without mention of complication
884.0	Multiple and unspecified open wound of upper limb, without mention of complication
890.0	Open wound of hip and thigh, without mention of complication
891.0	Open wound of knee, leg (except thigh), and ankle, without mention of complication
892.0	Open wound of foot except toe(s) alone, without mention of complication
893.0	Open wound of toe(s), without mention of complication
894.0	Multiple and unspecified open wound of lower limb, without mention of complication
906*	Late effects of injuries to skin and subcutaneous tissues
910.0	Face, neck, and scalp, except eye, abrasion or friction burn, without mention of infection
910.6	Face, neck, and scalp, except eye, superficial foreign body (splinter), without major open wound or mention of infection
910.8	Other and unspecified superficial injury of face, neck, and scalp, without mention of infection
911.0	Trunk abrasion or friction burn, without mention of infection
911.6	Trunk, superficial foreign body (splinter), without major open wound and without mention of infection
911.8	Other and unspecified superficial injury of trunk, without mention of infection
912.0	Shoulder and upper arm, abrasion or friction burn, without mention of infection
912.2	Shoulder and upper arm, blister, without mention of infection
912.6	Shoulder and upper arm, superficial foreign body (splinter), without major open wound and without mention of infection
912.8	Other and unspecified superficial injury of shoulder and upper arm, without mention of infection
913.0	Elbow, forearm, and wrist, abrasion or friction burn, without mention of infection
913.6	Elbow, forearm, and wrist, superficial foreign body (splinter), without major open wound and without mention of infection
913.8	Other and unspecified superficial injury of elbow, forearm, and wrist, without mention of infection
914.0	Hand(s) except finger(s) alone, abrasion or friction burn, without mention of infection
914.6	Hand(s) except finger(s) alone, superficial foreign body (splinter), without major open wound and without mention of infection
914.8	Other and unspecified superficial injury of hand(s) except finger(s) alone, without mention of infection
915.0	Abrasion or friction burn of finger, without mention of infection
915.6	Finger, superficial foreign body (splinter), without major open wound and without mention of infection
915.8	Other and unspecified superficial injury of finger without mention of infection
916.0	Hip, thigh, leg, and ankle, abrasion or friction burn, without mention of infection
916.6	Hip, thigh, leg, and ankle, superficial foreign body (splinter), without major open wound and without mention of infection
916.8	Other and unspecified superficial injury of hip, thigh, leg, and ankle, without mention of infection

917.0	Abrasion or friction burn of foot and toe(s), without mention of infection
917.6	Foot and toe(s), superficial foreign body (splinter), without major open wound and without mention of infection
917.8	Other and unspecified superficial injury of foot and toes, without mention of infection
919.0	Abrasion or friction burn of other, multiple, and unspecified sites, without mention of infection
919.6	Other, multiple, and unspecified sites, superficial foreign body (splinter), without major open wound and without mention of infection
919.8	Other and unspecified superficial injury of other, multiple, and unspecified sites, without mention of infection
920	Contusion of face, scalp, and neck except eye(s)
922.0	Contusion of breast
922.1	Contusion of chest wall
922.2	Contusion of abdominal wall
922.3*	Contusion of trunk
922.8	Contusion of multiple sites of trunk
922.9	Contusion of unspecified part of trunk
923*	Contusion of upper limb
924*	Contusion of lower limb and of other and unspecified sites

DRG 605 **Trauma to the Skin, Subcutaneous Tissue & Breast without MCC**

GMLOS 2.6	AMLOS 3.2	RW 0.7552	☑

Select principal diagnosis listed under DRG 604

DRG 606 **Minor Skin Disorders with MCC**

GMLOS 4.2	AMLOS 6.0	RW 1.3936	☑

Principal Diagnosis

006.6	Amebic skin ulceration
017.0*	Tuberculosis of skin and subcutaneous cellular tissue
022.0	Cutaneous anthrax
031.1	Cutaneous diseases due to other mycobacteria
032.85	Cutaneous diphtheria
039.0	Cutaneous actinomycotic infection
039.3	Cervicofacial actinomycotic infection
039.4	Madura foot
051.1	Pseudocowpox
051.2	Contagious pustular dermatitis
054.0	Eczema herpeticum
054.6	Herpetic whitlow
054.9	Herpes simplex without mention of complication
058.8*	Other human herpesvirus infections
078.0	Molluscum contagiosum
078.1*	Viral warts
085.1	Cutaneous leishmaniasis, urban
085.2	Cutaneous leishmaniasis, Asian desert
085.3	Cutaneous leishmaniasis, Ethiopian
085.4	Cutaneous leishmaniasis, American
085.5	Mucocutaneous leishmaniasis, (American)
091.3	Secondary syphilis of skin or mucous membranes
091.82	Early syphilis, syphilitic alopecia
102.0	Initial lesions of yaws
102.1	Multiple papillomata and wet crab yaws due to yaws
102.2	Other early skin lesions due to yaws
102.3	Hyperkeratosis due to yaws
102.4	Gummata and ulcers due to yaws
103.0	Primary lesions of pinta
103.1	Intermediate lesions of pinta
103.3	Mixed lesions of pinta
110*	Dermatophytosis
111*	Dermatomycosis, other and unspecified
112.3	Candidiasis of skin and nails
114.1	Primary extrapulmonary coccidioidomycosis
120.3	Cutaneous schistosomiasis
132*	Pediculosis and phthirus infestation

Ⓣ *Transfer DRG*   SP *Special Payment*   ☑ *Optimization Potential*   ▽ *Targeted Potential*   * *Code Range*   ● *New DRG*   ▲ *Revised DRG Title*

108   Valid 10/01/2012-09/30/2013   © 2012 OptumInsight, Inc.

133*	Acariasis
134*	Other infestation
173.0*	Other and unspecified malignant neoplasm of skin of lip
173.2*	Other and unspecified malignant neoplasm of skin of ear and external auditory canal
173.3*	Other and unspecified malignant neoplasm of skin of other and unspecified parts of face
173.4*	Other and unspecified malignant neoplasm of scalp and skin of neck
173.5*	Other and unspecified malignant neoplasm of skin of trunk, except scrotum
173.6*	Other and unspecified malignant neoplasm of skin of upper limb, including shoulder
173.7*	Other and unspecified malignant neoplasm of skin of lower limb, including hip
173.8*	Other and unspecified malignant neoplasm of other specified sites of skin
173.9*	Other and unspecified malignant neoplasm of skin, site unspecified
176.0	Kaposi's sarcoma of skin
176.1	Kaposi's sarcoma of soft tissue
176.8	Kaposi's sarcoma of other specified sites
176.9	Kaposi's sarcoma of unspecified site
214.0	Lipoma of skin and subcutaneous tissue of face
214.1	Lipoma of other skin and subcutaneous tissue
214.8	Lipoma of other specified sites
214.9	Lipoma of unspecified site
216.0	Benign neoplasm of skin of lip
216.2	Benign neoplasm of ear and external auditory canal
216.3	Benign neoplasm of skin of other and unspecified parts of face
216.4	Benign neoplasm of scalp and skin of neck
216.5	Benign neoplasm of skin of trunk, except scrotum
216.6	Benign neoplasm of skin of upper limb, including shoulder
216.7	Benign neoplasm of skin of lower limb, including hip
216.8	Benign neoplasm of other specified sites of skin
216.9	Benign neoplasm of skin, site unspecified
217	Benign neoplasm of breast
228.01	Hemangioma of skin and subcutaneous tissue
232.0	Carcinoma in situ of skin of lip
232.2	Carcinoma in situ of skin of ear and external auditory canal
232.3	Carcinoma in situ of skin of other and unspecified parts of face
232.4	Carcinoma in situ of scalp and skin of neck
232.5	Carcinoma in situ of skin of trunk, except scrotum
232.6	Carcinoma in situ of skin of upper limb, including shoulder
232.7	Carcinoma in situ of skin of lower limb, including hip
232.8	Carcinoma in situ of other specified sites of skin
232.9	Carcinoma in situ of skin, site unspecified
238.2	Neoplasm of uncertain behavior of skin
306.3	Skin malfunction arising from mental factors
374.51	Xanthelasma of eyelid
448.1	Nevus, non-neoplastic
457.1	Other noninfectious lymphedema
617.6	Endometriosis in scar of skin
690*	Erythematosquamous dermatosis
691*	Atopic dermatitis and related conditions
692*	Contact dermatitis and other eczema
693*	Dermatitis due to substances taken internally
694.0	Dermatitis herpetiformis
694.1	Subcorneal pustular dermatosis
694.2	Juvenile dermatitis herpetiformis
694.3	Impetigo herpetiformis
695.3	Rosacea
695.5*	Exfoliation due to erythematous conditions according to extent of body surface involved
695.89	Other specified erythematous condition
695.9	Unspecified erythematous condition
696.3	Pityriasis rosea
696.4	Pityriasis rubra pilaris
696.5	Other and unspecified pityriasis
696.8	Psoriasis related disease NEC
697*	Lichen
698.0	Pruritus ani
698.2	Prurigo
698.3	Lichenification and lichen simplex chronicus
698.4	Dermatitis factitia (artefacta)
698.8	Other specified pruritic conditions
698.9	Unspecified pruritic disorder
700	Corns and callosities
701*	Other hypertrophic and atrophic conditions of skin
702*	Other dermatoses
703*	Diseases of nail
704*	Diseases of hair and hair follicles
705*	Disorders of sweat glands
706*	Diseases of sebaceous glands
708*	Urticaria
709*	Other disorders of skin and subcutaneous tissue
723.6	Panniculitis specified as affecting neck
729.3*	Unspecified panniculitis
744.5	Congenital webbing of neck
744.9	Unspecified congenital anomaly of face and neck
757.0	Hereditary edema of legs
757.1	Ichthyosis congenita
757.2	Dermatoglyphic anomalies
757.31	Congenital ectodermal dysplasia
757.32	Congenital vascular hamartomas
757.33	Congenital pigmentary anomaly of skin
757.39	Other specified congenital anomaly of skin
757.4	Specified congenital anomalies of hair
757.5	Specified congenital anomalies of nails
757.8	Other specified congenital anomalies of the integument
757.9	Unspecified congenital anomaly of the integument
780.8	Generalized hyperhidrosis
782.1	Rash and other nonspecific skin eruption
782.2	Localized superficial swelling, mass, or lump
782.8	Changes in skin texture
782.9	Other symptoms involving skin and integumentary tissues
784.2	Swelling, mass, or lump in head and neck
910.2	Face, neck, and scalp except eye, blister, without mention of infection
910.3	Face, neck, and scalp except eye, blister, infected
910.4	Face, neck, and scalp except eye, insect bite, nonvenomous, without mention of infection
911.2	Trunk blister, without mention of infection
911.4	Trunk, insect bite, nonvenomous, without mention of infection
912.4	Shoulder and upper arm, insect bite, nonvenomous, without mention of infection
913.2	Elbow, forearm, and wrist, blister, without mention of infection
913.4	Elbow, forearm, and wrist, insect bite, nonvenomous, without mention of infection
914.2	Hand(s) except finger(s) alone, blister, without mention of infection
914.4	Hand(s) except finger(s) alone, insect bite, nonvenomous, without mention of infection
915.2	Finger, blister, without mention of infection
915.4	Finger, insect bite, nonvenomous, without mention of infection
916.2	Hip, thigh, leg, and ankle, blister, without mention of infection
916.4	Hip, thigh, leg, and ankle, insect bite, nonvenomous, without mention of infection
917.2	Foot and toe(s), blister, without mention of infection
917.4	Foot and toe(s), insect bite, nonvenomous, without mention of infection
919.2	Other, multiple, and unspecified sites, blister, without mention of infection

Surgical	Medical	CC Indicator	MCC Indicator	Procedure Proxy

919.4	Other, multiple, and unspecified sites, insect bite, nonvenomous, without mention of infection
V42.3	Skin replaced by transplant
V50.0	Elective hair transplant for purposes other than remedying health states
V50.1	Other plastic surgery for unacceptable cosmetic appearance
V51*	Aftercare involving the use of plastic surgery
V59.1	Skin donor

DRG 607   Minor Skin Disorders without MCC

GMLOS 2.8   AMLOS 3.6   RW 0.6892   ☑

Select principal diagnosis listed under DRG 606

Ⓣ *Transfer DRG*   ⓈⓅ *Special Payment*   ☑ *Optimization Potential*   ▽ *Targeted Potential*   * *Code Range*   ● *New DRG*   ▲ *Revised DRG Title*

110   Valid 10/01/2012-09/30/2013   © 2012 OptumInsight, Inc.

MDC 10
Endocrine, Nutritional And Metabolic Diseases And Disorders

017.50	240.9	246.2	250.82	255.13	263.0	271.4	276.51	779.34
017.51	241.0	246.3	250.83	255.14	263.1	271.8	276.52	781.7
017.52	241.1	246.8	250.90	255.2	263.2	271.9	276.61	783.0
017.53	241.9	246.9	250.91	255.3	263.8	272.0	276.69	783.1
017.54	242.00	249.00	250.92	255.41	263.9	272.1	276.7	783.21
017.55	242.01	249.01	250.93	255.42	264.8	272.2	276.8	783.22
017.56	242.10	249.10	251.0	255.5	264.9	272.3	276.9	783.3
017.60	242.11	249.11	251.1	255.6	265.0	272.4	277.00	783.40
017.61	242.20	249.20	251.2	255.8	265.1	272.5	277.09	783.41
017.62	242.21	249.21	251.3	255.9	265.2	272.6	277.1	783.42
017.63	242.30	249.30	251.4	257.0	266.0	272.7	277.2	783.43
017.64	242.31	249.31	251.8	257.1	266.1	272.8	277.5	783.5
017.65	242.40	249.80	251.9	257.2	266.2	272.9	277.6	783.6
017.66	242.41	249.81	252.00	257.8	266.9	273.4	277.7	783.7
122.2	242.80	249.90	252.01	257.9	267	275.01	277.81	783.9
193	242.81	249.91	252.02	258.01	268.9	275.02	277.82	790.21
194.0	242.90	250.00	252.08	258.02	269.0	275.03	277.83	790.22
194.1	242.91	250.01	252.1	258.03	269.1	275.09	277.84	790.29
194.3	243	250.02	252.8	258.1	269.2	275.1	277.85	791.5
194.8	244.0	250.03	252.9	258.8	269.3	275.2	277.86	791.6
194.9	244.1	250.10	253.0	258.9	269.8	275.3	277.87	794.5
198.7	244.2	250.11	253.1	259.0	269.9	275.40	277.89	794.6
211.7	244.3	250.12	253.2	259.1	270.0	275.41	277.9	794.7
226	244.8	250.13	253.3	259.2	270.1	275.42	278.00	868.01
227.0	244.9	250.20	253.4	259.3	270.2	275.49	278.01	868.11
227.1	245.0	250.21	253.5	259.4	270.3	275.5	278.02	874.2
227.3	245.1	250.22	253.6	259.50	270.4	275.8	278.1	874.3
227.8	245.2	250.23	253.7	259.51	270.5	275.9	278.2	V85.41
227.9	245.3	250.30	253.8	259.52	270.6	276.0	278.3	V85.42
237.0	245.4	250.31	253.9	259.8	270.7	276.1	278.4	V85.43
237.2	245.8	250.32	255.0	259.9	270.8	276.2	278.8	V85.44
237.4	245.9	250.33	255.10	260	270.9	276.3	306.6	V85.45
239.7	246.0	250.80	255.11	261	271.0	276.4	759.1	
240.0	246.1	250.81	255.12	262	271.1	276.50	759.2	

SURGICAL

DRG 614 **Adrenal and Pituitary Procedures with CC/MCC**
GMLOS 4.2   AMLOS 5.7   RW 2.3998

Operating Room Procedures
07.0*   Exploration of adrenal field
07.12   Open biopsy of adrenal gland
07.13   Biopsy of pituitary gland, transfrontal approach
07.14   Biopsy of pituitary gland, transsphenoidal approach
07.15   Biopsy of pituitary gland, unspecified approach
07.17   Biopsy of pineal gland
07.19   Other diagnostic procedures on adrenal glands, pituitary gland, pineal gland, and thymus
07.2*   Partial adrenalectomy
07.3   Bilateral adrenalectomy
07.4*   Other operations on adrenal glands, nerves, and vessels
07.5*   Operations on pineal gland
07.6*   Hypophysectomy
07.7*   Other operations on hypophysis

DRG 615 **Adrenal and Pituitary Procedures without CC/MCC**
GMLOS 2.3   AMLOS 2.7   RW 1.4036   ☑

Select operating room procedures listed under DRG 614

DRG 616 **Amputation of Lower Limb for Endocrine, Nutritional, and Metabolic Disorders with MCC**
GMLOS 11.5   AMLOS 14.1   RW 4.3525   ☐☑

Operating Room Procedures
84.10   Lower limb amputation, not otherwise specified
84.11   Amputation of toe
84.12   Amputation through foot
84.13   Disarticulation of ankle
84.14   Amputation of ankle through malleoli of tibia and fibula
84.15   Other amputation below knee
84.16   Disarticulation of knee
84.17   Amputation above knee

DRG 617 **Amputation of Lower Limb for Endocrine, Nutritional, and Metabolic Disorders with CC**
GMLOS 6.2   AMLOS 7.5   RW 1.9716   ☐☑

Select operating room procedures listed under DRG 616

DRG 618 **Amputation of Lower Limb for Endocrine, Nutritional, and Metabolic Disorders without CC/MCC**
GMLOS 4.0   AMLOS 5.0   RW 1.1287   ☐☑

Select operating room procedures listed under DRG 616

DRG 619 **O.R. Procedures for Obesity with MCC**
GMLOS 4.6   AMLOS 7.3   RW 3.4876

Operating Room Procedures
43.82   Laparoscopic vertical (sleeve) gastrectomy
43.89   Open and other partial gastrectomy
44.3*   Gastroenterostomy without gastrectomy
44.5   Revision of gastric anastomosis
44.68   Laparoscopic gastroplasty
44.69   Other repair of stomach
44.95   Laparoscopic gastric restrictive procedure
44.96   Laparoscopic revision of gastric restrictive procedure
44.97   Laparoscopic removal of gastric restrictive device(s)
44.98   (Laparoscopic) adjustment of size of adjustable gastric restrictive device
44.99   Other operations on stomach

45.90   Intestinal anastomosis, not otherwise specified
45.91   Small-to-small intestinal anastomosis
85.31   Unilateral reduction mammoplasty
85.32   Bilateral reduction mammoplasty
86.83   Size reduction plastic operation
86.87   Fat graft of skin and subcutaneous tissue
86.89   Other repair and reconstruction of skin and subcutaneous tissue

DRG 620 **O.R. Procedures for Obesity with CC**
GMLOS 2.5   AMLOS 3.1   RW 1.8601   ☑

Select operating room procedures listed under DRG 619

DRG 621 **O.R. Procedures for Obesity without CC/MCC**
GMLOS 1.6   AMLOS 1.9   RW 1.5026   ☑

Select operating room procedures listed under DRG 619

DRG 622 **Skin Grafts and Wound Debridement for Endocrine, Nutritional and Metabolic Disorders with MCC**
GMLOS 9.7   AMLOS 12.8   RW 3.5668   ☐☑

Operating Room Procedures
84.3   Revision of amputation stump
86.22   Excisional debridement of wound, infection, or burn
86.60   Free skin graft, not otherwise specified
86.63   Full-thickness skin graft to other sites
86.67   Dermal regenerative graft
86.69   Other skin graft to other sites
86.70   Pedicle or flap graft, not otherwise specified
86.71   Cutting and preparation of pedicle grafts or flaps
86.72   Advancement of pedicle graft
86.74   Attachment of pedicle or flap graft to other sites
86.75   Revision of pedicle or flap graft
86.91   Excision of skin for graft
86.93   Insertion of tissue expander

DRG 623 **Skin Grafts and Wound Debridement for Endocrine, Nutritional and Metabolic Disorders with CC**
GMLOS 5.9   AMLOS 7.3   RW 1.8221   ☐☑

Select operating room procedures listed under DRG 622

DRG 624 **Skin Grafts and Wound Debridement for Endocrine, Nutritional and Metabolic Disorders without CC/MCC**
GMLOS 3.6   AMLOS 4.4   RW 0.9662   ☐☑

Select operating room procedures listed under DRG 622

DRG 625 **Thyroid, Parathyroid and Thyroglossal Procedures with MCC**
GMLOS 4.4   AMLOS 6.8   RW 2.3606

Operating Room Procedures
06.02   Reopening of wound of thyroid field
06.09   Other incision of thyroid field
06.12   Open biopsy of thyroid gland
06.13   Biopsy of parathyroid gland
06.19   Other diagnostic procedures on thyroid and parathyroid glands
06.2   Unilateral thyroid lobectomy
06.3*   Other partial thyroidectomy
06.4   Complete thyroidectomy
06.5*   Substernal thyroidectomy
06.6   Excision of lingual thyroid
06.7   Excision of thyroglossal duct or tract
06.8*   Parathyroidectomy
06.91   Division of thyroid isthmus

☐ *Transfer DRG*   ⑤ⓟ *Special Payment*   ☑ *Optimization Potential*   ▽ *Targeted Potential*   * *Code Range*   ● *New DRG*   ▲ *Revised DRG Title*

112   Valid 10/01/2012-09/30/2013   © 2012 OptumInsight, Inc.

06.92	Ligation of thyroid vessels	
06.93	Suture of thyroid gland	
06.94	Thyroid tissue reimplantation	
06.95	Parathyroid tissue reimplantation	
06.98	Other operations on thyroid glands	
06.99	Other operations on parathyroid glands	
17.62	Laser interstitial thermal therapy [LITT] of lesion or tissue of head and neck under guidance	

DRG 626   Thyroid, Parathyroid and Thyroglossal Procedures with CC
GMLOS 2.0   AMLOS 2.9   RW 1.2163   ☑

Select operating room procedures listed under DRG 625

DRG 627   Thyroid, Parathyroid and Thyroglossal Procedures without CC/MCC
GMLOS 1.2   AMLOS 1.4   RW 0.8217   ☑

Select operating room procedures listed under DRG 625

DRG 628   Other Endocrine, Nutritional and Metabolic O.R. Procedures with MCC
GMLOS 6.8   AMLOS 10.0   RW 3.2936   ☐T

Operating Room Procedures

00.70	Revision of hip replacement, both acetabular and femoral components
00.71	Revision of hip replacement, acetabular component
00.72	Revision of hip replacement, femoral component
00.73	Revision of hip replacement, acetabular liner and/or femoral head only
00.86	Resurfacing hip, partial, femoral head
00.87	Resurfacing hip, partial, acetabulum
01.15	Biopsy of skull
07.16	Biopsy of thymus
07.8*	Thymectomy
07.9*	Other operations on thymus
08.20	Removal of lesion of eyelid, not otherwise specified
08.38	Correction of lid retraction
08.70	Reconstruction of eyelid, not otherwise specified
12.64	Trabeculectomy ab externo
12.72	Cyclocryotherapy
12.79	Other glaucoma procedures
13.1*	Intracapsular extraction of lens
13.59	Other extracapsular extraction of lens
14.49	Other scleral buckling
14.54	Repair of retinal detachment with laser photocoagulation
14.6	Removal of surgically implanted material from posterior segment of eye
14.72	Other removal of vitreous
14.74	Other mechanical vitrectomy
16.99	Other operations on eyeball
17.35	Laparoscopic left hemicolectomy
17.56	Atherectomy of other non-coronary vessel(s)
34.26	Open biopsy of mediastinum
34.3	Excision or destruction of lesion or tissue of mediastinum
34.4	Excision or destruction of lesion of chest wall
38.00	Incision of vessel, unspecified site
38.02	Incision of other vessels of head and neck
38.03	Incision of upper limb vessels
38.08	Incision of lower limb arteries
38.12	Endarterectomy of other vessels of head and neck
38.13	Endarterectomy of upper limb vessels
38.18	Endarterectomy of lower limb arteries
38.21	Biopsy of blood vessel
38.29	Other diagnostic procedures on blood vessels
38.30	Resection of vessel with anastomosis, unspecified site
38.33	Resection of upper limb vessels with anastomosis
38.38	Resection of lower limb arteries with anastomosis
38.43	Resection of upper limb vessels with replacement

38.48	Resection of lower limb arteries with replacement
38.55	Ligation and stripping of varicose veins of other thoracic vessel
38.60	Other excision of vessels, unspecified site
38.63	Other excision of upper limb vessels
38.68	Other excision of lower limb arteries
38.7	Interruption of the vena cava
38.83	Other surgical occlusion of upper limb vessels
38.88	Other surgical occlusion of lower limb arteries
39.25	Aorta-iliac-femoral bypass
39.27	Arteriovenostomy for renal dialysis
39.29	Other (peripheral) vascular shunt or bypass
39.31	Suture of artery
39.41	Control of hemorrhage following vascular surgery
39.42	Revision of arteriovenous shunt for renal dialysis
39.49	Other revision of vascular procedure
39.50	Angioplasty of other non-coronary vessel(s)
39.56	Repair of blood vessel with tissue patch graft
39.57	Repair of blood vessel with synthetic patch graft
39.58	Repair of blood vessel with unspecified type of patch graft
39.59	Other repair of vessel
39.91	Freeing of vessel
39.93	Insertion of vessel-to-vessel cannula
39.98	Control of hemorrhage, not otherwise specified
40.1*	Diagnostic procedures on lymphatic structures
40.21	Excision of deep cervical lymph node
40.29	Simple excision of other lymphatic structure
40.3	Regional lymph node excision
40.4*	Radical excision of cervical lymph nodes
40.52	Radical excision of periaortic lymph nodes
40.53	Radical excision of iliac lymph nodes
43.0	Gastrotomy
43.42	Local excision of other lesion or tissue of stomach
43.7	Partial gastrectomy with anastomosis to jejunum
44.92	Intraoperative manipulation of stomach
45.41	Excision of lesion or tissue of large intestine
45.62	Other partial resection of small intestine
45.75	Open and other left hemicolectomy
45.93	Other small-to-large intestinal anastomosis
45.94	Large-to-large intestinal anastomosis
50.12	Open biopsy of liver
52.12	Open biopsy of pancreas
52.19	Other diagnostic procedures on pancreas
52.22	Other excision or destruction of lesion or tissue of pancreas or pancreatic duct
52.5*	Partial pancreatectomy
52.80	Pancreatic transplant, not otherwise specified
52.82	Homotransplant of pancreas
52.83	Heterotransplant of pancreas
54.11	Exploratory laparotomy
54.3	Excision or destruction of lesion or tissue of abdominal wall or umbilicus
54.4	Excision or destruction of peritoneal tissue
54.59	Other lysis of peritoneal adhesions
62.7	Insertion of testicular prosthesis
65.22	Wedge resection of ovary
65.24	Laparoscopic wedge resection of ovary
77.27	Wedge osteotomy of tibia and fibula
77.38	Other division of tarsals and metatarsals
77.4*	Biopsy of bone
77.61	Local excision of lesion or tissue of scapula, clavicle, and thorax (ribs and sternum)
77.68	Local excision of lesion or tissue of tarsals and metatarsals
77.69	Local excision of lesion or tissue of other bone, except facial bones
77.88	Other partial ostectomy of tarsals and metatarsals
77.89	Other partial ostectomy of other bone, except facial bones
78.65	Removal of implanted device from femur
79.35	Open reduction of fracture of femur with internal fixation
80.10	Other arthrotomy, unspecified site

Surgical   *Medical*   CC Indicator   MCC Indicator   Procedure Proxy

80.12	Other arthrotomy of elbow
80.16	Other arthrotomy of knee
80.26	Arthroscopy of knee
80.6	Excision of semilunar cartilage of knee
80.82	Other local excision or destruction of lesion of elbow joint
80.88	Other local excision or destruction of lesion of joint of foot and toe
80.98	Other excision of joint of foot and toe
81.11	Ankle fusion
81.23	Arthrodesis of shoulder
81.52	Partial hip replacement
81.53	Revision of hip replacement, not otherwise specified
82.21	Excision of lesion of tendon sheath of hand
82.33	Other tenonectomy of hand
83.13	Other tenotomy
83.31	Excision of lesion of tendon sheath
83.39	Excision of lesion of other soft tissue
83.65	Other suture of muscle or fascia
83.75	Tendon transfer or transplantation
83.79	Other muscle transposition
85.12	Open biopsy of breast
85.21	Local excision of lesion of breast
86.06	Insertion of totally implantable infusion pump
92.27	Implantation or insertion of radioactive elements

OR

Nonoperating Room Procedures

92.3*	Stereotactic radiosurgery

DRG 629 **Other Endocrine, Nutritional and Metabolic O.R. Procedures with CC**
GMLOS 6.1   AMLOS 7.4   RW 2.1440   T ☑

Select operating or nonoperating room procedures listed under DRG 628

DRG 630 **Other Endocrine, Nutritional and Metabolic O.R. Procedures without CC/MCC**
GMLOS 3.1   AMLOS 4.1   RW 1.2266   T ☑

Select operating or nonoperating room procedures listed under DRG 628

MEDICAL

DRG 637 **Diabetes with MCC**
GMLOS 4.3   AMLOS 5.7   RW 1.4070   T ☑

Principal Diagnosis

249.0*	Secondary diabetes mellitus without mention of complication
249.1*	Secondary diabetes mellitus with ketoacidosis
249.2*	Secondary diabetes mellitus with hyperosmolarity
249.3*	Secondary diabetes mellitus with other coma
249.8*	Secondary diabetes mellitus with other specified manifestations
249.9*	Secondary diabetes mellitus with unspecified complication
250.0*	Diabetes mellitus without mention of complication
250.1*	Diabetes with ketoacidosis
250.2*	Diabetes with hyperosmolarity
250.3*	Diabetes with other coma
250.8*	Diabetes with other specified manifestations
250.9*	Diabetes with unspecified complication
791.5	Glycosuria

DRG 638 **Diabetes with CC**
GMLOS 3.1   AMLOS 3.8   RW 0.8218   T ☑

Select principal diagnosis listed under DRG 637

DRG 639 **Diabetes without CC/MCC**
GMLOS 2.2   AMLOS 2.7   RW 0.5558   T ☑

Select principal diagnosis listed under DRG 637

DRG 640 **Miscellaneous Disorders of Nutrition, Metabolism, and Fluids and Electrolytes with MCC**
GMLOS 3.4   AMLOS 4.7   RW 1.1076   T ☑ ▽

Principal Diagnosis

251.0	Hypoglycemic coma
251.2	Hypoglycemia, unspecified
251.3	Postsurgical hypoinsulinemia
260	Kwashiorkor
261	Nutritional marasmus
262	Other severe protein-calorie malnutrition
263*	Other and unspecified protein-calorie malnutrition
264.8	Other manifestations of vitamin A deficiency
264.9	Unspecified vitamin A deficiency
265*	Thiamine and niacin deficiency states
266*	Deficiency of B-complex components
267	Ascorbic acid deficiency
268.9	Unspecified vitamin D deficiency
269*	Other nutritional deficiencies
275.2	Disorders of magnesium metabolism
275.4*	Disorders of calcium metabolism
275.5	Hungry bone syndrome
276*	Disorders of fluid, electrolyte, and acid-base balance
277.00	Cystic fibrosis without mention of meconium ileus
277.09	Cystic fibrosis with other manifestations
278.00	Obesity, unspecified
278.01	Morbid obesity
278.02	Overweight
278.1	Localized adiposity
278.2	Hypervitaminosis A
278.3	Hypercarotinemia
278.4	Hypervitaminosis D
278.8	Other hyperalimentation
779.34	Failure to thrive in newborn
781.7	Tetany
783*	Symptoms concerning nutrition, metabolism, and development
790.2*	Abnormal glucose
791.6	Acetonuria
V85.4*	Body Mass Index 40 and over, adult

DRG 641 **Miscellaneous Disorders of Nutrition, Metabolism, and Fluids and Electrolytes without MCC**
GMLOS 2.7   AMLOS 3.4   RW 0.6920   T ☑ ▽

Select principal diagnosis listed under DRG 640

DRG 642 **Inborn and Other Disorders of Metabolism**
GMLOS 3.3   AMLOS 4.6   RW 1.1233

Principal Diagnosis

270*	Disorders of amino-acid transport and metabolism
271.0	Glycogenosis
271.1	Galactosemia
271.4	Renal glycosuria
271.8	Other specified disorders of carbohydrate transport and metabolism
271.9	Unspecified disorder of carbohydrate transport and metabolism
272*	Disorders of lipoid metabolism

T Transfer DRG   SP Special Payment   ☑ Optimization Potential   ▽ Targeted Potential   * Code Range   ● New DRG   ▲ Revised DRG Title

114   Valid 10/01/2012-09/30/2013   © 2012 OptumInsight, Inc.

273.4	Alpha-1-antitrypsin deficiency
275.0*	Disorders of iron metabolism
275.1	Disorders of copper metabolism
275.3	Disorders of phosphorus metabolism
275.8	Other specified disorders of mineral metabolism
275.9	Unspecified disorder of mineral metabolism
277.1	Disorders of porphyrin metabolism
277.2	Other disorders of purine and pyrimidine metabolism
277.5	Mucopolysaccharidosis
277.6	Other deficiencies of circulating enzymes
277.7	Dysmetabolic Syndrome X
277.81	Primary carnitine deficiency
277.82	Carnitine deficiency due to inborn errors of metabolism
277.83	Iatrogenic carnitine deficiency
277.84	Other secondary carnitine deficiency
277.85	Disorders of fatty acid oxidation
277.86	Peroxisomal disorders
277.87	Disorders of mitochondrial metabolism
277.89	Other specified disorders of metabolism
277.9	Unspecified disorder of metabolism

DRG 643 Endocrine Disorders with MCC
GMLOS 5.7   AMLOS 7.1   RW 1.7094   T ☑

Principal Diagnosis

017.5*	Tuberculosis of thyroid gland
017.6*	Tuberculosis of adrenal glands
122.2	Echinococcus granulosus infection of thyroid
193	Malignant neoplasm of thyroid gland
194.0	Malignant neoplasm of adrenal gland
194.1	Malignant neoplasm of parathyroid gland
194.3	Malignant neoplasm of pituitary gland and craniopharyngeal duct
194.8	Malignant neoplasm of other endocrine glands and related structures
194.9	Malignant neoplasm of endocrine gland, site unspecified
198.7	Secondary malignant neoplasm of adrenal gland
211.7	Benign neoplasm of islets of Langerhans
226	Benign neoplasm of thyroid glands
227.0	Benign neoplasm of adrenal gland
227.1	Benign neoplasm of parathyroid gland
227.3	Benign neoplasm of pituitary gland and craniopharyngeal duct (pouch)
227.8	Benign neoplasm of other endocrine glands and related structures
227.9	Benign neoplasm of endocrine gland, site unspecified
237.0	Neoplasm of uncertain behavior of pituitary gland and craniopharyngeal duct
237.2	Neoplasm of uncertain behavior of adrenal gland
237.4	Neoplasm of uncertain behavior of other and unspecified endocrine glands
239.7	Neoplasm of unspecified nature of endocrine glands and other parts of nervous system
240*	Simple and unspecified goiter
241*	Nontoxic nodular goiter
242*	Thyrotoxicosis with or without goiter
243	Congenital hypothyroidism
244*	Acquired hypothyroidism
245*	Thyroiditis
246*	Other disorders of thyroid
251.1	Other specified hypoglycemia
251.4	Abnormality of secretion of glucagon
251.8	Other specified disorders of pancreatic internal secretion
251.9	Unspecified disorder of pancreatic internal secretion
252*	Disorders of parathyroid gland
253*	Disorders of the pituitary gland and its hypothalamic control
255*	Disorders of adrenal glands
257*	Testicular dysfunction
258*	Polyglandular dysfunction and related disorders
259*	Other endocrine disorders

306.6	Endocrine malfunction arising from mental factors
759.1	Congenital anomalies of adrenal gland
759.2	Congenital anomalies of other endocrine glands
794.5	Nonspecific abnormal results of thyroid function study
794.6	Nonspecific abnormal results of other endocrine function study
794.7	Nonspecific abnormal results of basal metabolism function study
868.01	Adrenal gland injury without mention of open wound into cavity
868.11	Adrenal gland injury, with open wound into cavity
874.2	Open wound of thyroid gland, without mention of complication
874.3	Open wound of thyroid gland, complicated

DRG 644 Endocrine Disorders with CC
GMLOS 4.0   AMLOS 4.9   RW 1.0508   T ☑

Select principal diagnosis listed under DRG 643

DRG 645 Endocrine Disorders without CC/MCC
GMLOS 2.8   AMLOS 3.4   RW 0.7233   T ☑

Select principal diagnosis listed under DRG 643

MDC 11
Diseases And Disorders Of The Kidney And Urinary Tract

016.00	098.30	239.4	581.3	589.0	595.3	599.5	788.30	866.13
016.01	098.31	239.5	581.81	589.1	595.4	599.60	788.31	867.0
016.02	099.54	249.40	581.89	589.9	595.81	599.69	788.32	867.1
016.03	120.0	249.41	581.9	590.00	595.82	599.70	788.33	867.2
016.04	137.2	250.40	582.0	590.01	595.89	599.71	788.34	867.3
016.05	188.0	250.41	582.1	590.10	595.9	599.72	788.35	868.04
016.06	188.1	250.42	582.2	590.11	596.0	599.81	788.36	868.14
016.10	188.2	250.43	582.4	590.2	596.1	599.82	788.37	939.0
016.11	188.3	274.10	582.81	590.3	596.2	599.83	788.38	939.9
016.12	188.4	274.11	582.89	590.80	596.3	599.84	788.39	958.5
016.13	188.5	274.19	582.9	590.81	596.4	599.89	788.41	996.30
016.14	188.6	277.88	583.0	590.9	596.51	599.9	788.42	996.31
016.15	188.7	306.50	583.1	591	596.52	753.0	788.43	996.39
016.16	188.8	306.53	583.2	592	596.53	753.10	788.5	996.64
016.20	188.9	306.59	583.4	592.1	596.54	753.11	788.61	996.65
016.21	189.0	344.61	583.6	592.9	596.55	753.12	788.62	996.76
016.22	189.1	403.00	583.7	593.0	596.59	753.13	788.63	996.81
016.23	189.2	403.01	583.81	593.1	596.6	753.14	788.64	997.5
016.24	189.3	403.10	583.89	593.2	596.7	753.15	788.65	997.72
016.25	189.4	403.11	583.9	593.3	596.81	753.16	788.69	V42.0
016.26	189.8	403.90	584.5	593.4	596.82	753.17	788.7	V43.5
016.30	189.9	403.91	584.6	593.5	596.83	753.19	788.8	V45.74
016.31	198.0	404.02	584.7	593.6	596.89	753.20	788.91	V53.6
016.32	198.1	404.12	584.8	593.70	596.9	753.21	788.99	V55.5
016.33	209.24	404.92	584.9	593.71	597.0	753.22	791.0	V55.6
016.34	209.64	440.1	585.1	593.72	597.80	753.23	791.1	V56.0
016.35	223.0	442.1	585.2	593.73	597.81	753.29	791.2	V56.1
016.36	223.1	443.23	585.3	593.81	597.89	753.3	791.7	V56.2
016.90	223.2	445.81	585.4	593.82	598.00	753.4	791.9	V56.31
016.91	223.3	447.3	585.5	593.89	598.01	753.5	793.5	V56.32
016.92	223.81	453.3	585.6	593.9	598.1	753.6	794.4	V56.8
016.93	223.89	580.0	585.9	594.0	598.2	753.7	794.9	V59.4
016.94	223.9	580.4	586	594.1	598.8	753.8	866.00	
016.95	233.7	580.81	587	594.2	598.9	753.9	866.01	
016.96	233.9	580.89	588.0	594.8	599.0	788.0	866.02	
032.84	236.7	580.9	588.1	594.9	599.1	788.1	866.03	
078.6	236.90	581.0	588.81	595	599.2	788.20	866.10	
095.4	236.91	581.1	588.89	595.1	599.3	788.21	866.11	
098.11	236.99	581.2	588.9	595.2	599.4	788.29	866.12	

SURGICAL

DRG 652 Kidney Transplant
GMLOS 6.0   AMLOS 7.0   RW 3.0825   ☑

Operating Room Procedure
55.69   Other kidney transplantation

DRG 653 Major Bladder Procedures with MCC
GMLOS 13.1   AMLOS 16.0   RW 6.1649   ⊤

Operating Room Procedures
57.6   Partial cystectomy
57.7*   Total cystectomy
57.83   Repair of fistula involving bladder and intestine
57.84   Repair of other fistula of bladder
57.85   Cystourethroplasty and plastic repair of bladder neck
57.86   Repair of bladder exstrophy
57.87   Reconstruction of urinary bladder
57.88   Other anastomosis of bladder
57.89   Other repair of bladder
70.53   Repair of cystocele and rectocele with graft or prosthesis

DRG 654 Major Bladder Procedures with CC
GMLOS 7.9   AMLOS 9.0   RW 3.1279   ⊤ ☑

Select operating room procedures listed under DRG 653

DRG 655 Major Bladder Procedures without CC/MCC
GMLOS 4.7   AMLOS 5.6   RW 2.0913   ⊤ ☑

Select operating room procedures listed under DRG 653

DRG 656 Kidney and Ureter Procedures for Neoplasm with MCC
GMLOS 7.3   AMLOS 9.5   RW 3.5136   ☑

Principal Diagnosis
188*   Malignant neoplasm of bladder
189*   Malignant neoplasm of kidney and other and unspecified urinary organs
198.0   Secondary malignant neoplasm of kidney
198.1   Secondary malignant neoplasm of other urinary organs
209.24   Malignant carcinoid tumor of the kidney
209.64   Benign carcinoid tumor of the kidney
223*   Benign neoplasm of kidney and other urinary organs
233.7   Carcinoma in situ of bladder
233.9   Carcinoma in situ of other and unspecified urinary organs
236.7   Neoplasm of uncertain behavior of bladder
236.9*   Neoplasm of uncertain behavior of other and unspecified urinary organs
239.4   Neoplasm of unspecified nature of bladder
239.5   Neoplasm of unspecified nature of other genitourinary organs

Operating Room Procedures
39.24   Aorta-renal bypass
39.26   Other intra-abdominal vascular shunt or bypass
39.55   Reimplantation of aberrant renal vessel
40.52   Radical excision of periaortic lymph nodes
40.53   Radical excision of iliac lymph nodes
40.54   Radical groin dissection
40.59   Radical excision of other lymph nodes
55.0*   Nephrotomy and nephrostomy
55.1*   Pyelotomy and pyelostomy
55.24   Open biopsy of kidney
55.29   Other diagnostic procedures on kidney
55.3*   Local excision or destruction of lesion or tissue of kidney
55.4   Partial nephrectomy
55.5*   Complete nephrectomy

55.61   Renal autotransplantation
55.7   Nephropexy
55.8*   Other repair of kidney
55.91   Decapsulation of kidney
55.97   Implantation or replacement of mechanical kidney
55.98   Removal of mechanical kidney
55.99   Other operations on kidney
56.1   Ureteral meatotomy
56.2   Ureterotomy
56.34   Open biopsy of ureter
56.39   Other diagnostic procedures on ureter
56.4*   Ureterectomy
56.5*   Cutaneous uretero-ileostomy
56.6*   Other external urinary diversion
56.7*   Other anastomosis or bypass of ureter
56.8*   Repair of ureter
56.92   Implantation of electronic ureteral stimulator
56.93   Replacement of electronic ureteral stimulator
56.94   Removal of electronic ureteral stimulator
56.95   Ligation of ureter
56.99   Other operations on ureter
59.00   Retroperitoneal dissection, not otherwise specified
59.02   Other lysis of perirenal or periureteral adhesions
59.03   Laparoscopic lysis of perirenal or periureteral adhesions
59.09   Other incision of perirenal or periureteral tissue

DRG 657 Kidney and Ureter Procedures for Neoplasm with CC
GMLOS 4.6   AMLOS 5.4   RW 1.9904   ☑

Select principal diagnosis and operating room procedures listed under DRG 656

DRG 658 Kidney and Ureter Procedures for Neoplasm without CC/MCC
GMLOS 2.9   AMLOS 3.2   RW 1.4836   ☑

Select principal diagnosis and operating room procedures listed under DRG 656

DRG 659 Kidney and Ureter Procedures for Non-neoplasm with MCC
GMLOS 7.9   AMLOS 10.8   RW 3.5192   ⊤ ☑

Select only operating room procedures listed under DRG 656

DRG 660 Kidney and Ureter Procedures for Non-neoplasm with CC
GMLOS 4.4   AMLOS 5.8   RW 1.8829   ⊤ ☑

Select only operating room procedures listed under DRG 656

DRG 661 Kidney and Ureter Procedures for Non-neoplasm without CC/MCC
GMLOS 2.3   AMLOS 2.9   RW 1.3335   ⊤ ☑

Select only operating room procedures listed under DRG 656

DRG 662 Minor Bladder Procedures with MCC
GMLOS 7.5   AMLOS 10.3   RW 2.9941   ☑

Operating Room Procedures
57.12   Lysis of intraluminal adhesions with incision into bladder
57.18   Other suprapubic cystostomy
57.19   Other cystotomy
57.2*   Vesicostomy
57.34   Open biopsy of bladder
57.39   Other diagnostic procedures on bladder
57.5*   Other excision or destruction of bladder tissue
57.81   Suture of laceration of bladder
57.82   Closure of cystostomy
57.91   Sphincterotomy of bladder
57.93   Control of (postoperative) hemorrhage of bladder

MDC 11: Diseases And Disorders Of The Kidney And Urinary Tract—SURGICAL

57.96	Implantation of electronic bladder stimulator
57.97	Replacement of electronic bladder stimulator
57.98	Removal of electronic bladder stimulator
57.99	Other operations on bladder
58.93	Implantation of artificial urinary sphincter (AUS)
59.1*	Incision of perivesical tissue
59.2*	Diagnostic procedures on perirenal and perivesical tissue
59.3	Plication of urethrovesical junction
59.4	Suprapubic sling operation
59.5	Retropubic urethral suspension
59.6	Paraurethral suspension
59.71	Levator muscle operation for urethrovesical suspension
59.79	Other repair of urinary stress incontinence
59.91	Excision of perirenal or perivesical tissue
59.92	Other operations on perirenal or perivesical tissue
70.50	Repair of cystocele and rectocele
70.51	Repair of cystocele
70.54	Repair of cystocele with graft or prosthesis
70.77	Vaginal suspension and fixation
70.78	Vaginal suspension and fixation with graft or prosthesis

DRG 663 Minor Bladder Procedures with CC
GMLOS 3.8 AMLOS 5.2 RW 1.5295 ☑

Select operating room procedures listed under DRG 662

DRG 664 Minor Bladder Procedures without CC/MCC
GMLOS 1.6 AMLOS 2.0 RW 1.1260 ☑

Select operating room procedures listed under DRG 662

DRG 665 Prostatectomy with MCC
GMLOS 9.5 AMLOS 11.9 RW 3.0737 ☑

Operating Room Procedures
60.2*	Transurethral prostatectomy
60.3	Suprapubic prostatectomy
60.4	Retropubic prostatectomy
60.5	Radical prostatectomy
60.62	Perineal prostatectomy
60.69	Other prostatectomy
60.96	Transurethral destruction of prostate tissue by microwave thermotherapy
60.97	Other transurethral destruction of prostate tissue by other thermotherapy

DRG 666 Prostatectomy with CC
GMLOS 4.5 AMLOS 6.2 RW 1.6602 ☑

Select operating room procedures listed under DRG 665

DRG 667 Prostatectomy without CC/MCC
GMLOS 2.0 AMLOS 2.6 RW 0.8760 ☑

Select operating room procedures listed under DRG 665

DRG 668 Transurethral Procedures with MCC
GMLOS 6.7 AMLOS 8.8 RW 2.4731 ☑

Operating Room Procedures
56.0	Transurethral removal of obstruction from ureter and renal pelvis
57.33	Closed (transurethral) biopsy of bladder
57.4*	Transurethral excision or destruction of bladder tissue
60.12	Open biopsy of prostate
60.95	Transurethral balloon dilation of the prostatic urethra

DRG 669 Transurethral Procedures with CC
GMLOS 3.1 AMLOS 4.2 RW 1.3015 ☑

Select operating room procedures listed under DRG 668

DRG 670 Transurethral Procedures without CC/MCC
GMLOS 1.9 AMLOS 2.4 RW 0.8326 ☑

Select operating room procedures listed under DRG 668

DRG 671 Urethral Procedures with CC/MCC
GMLOS 3.7 AMLOS 5.2 RW 1.4513 ☑

Operating Room Procedures
58.0	Urethrotomy
58.1	Urethral meatotomy
58.4*	Repair of urethra
58.5	Release of urethral stricture
58.91	Incision of periurethral tissue
58.92	Excision of periurethral tissue
58.99	Other operations on urethra and periurethral tissue

DRG 672 Urethral Procedures without CC/MCC
GMLOS 1.8 AMLOS 2.3 RW 0.8383 ☑

Select operating room procedures listed under DRG 671

DRG 673 Other Kidney and Urinary Tract Procedures with MCC
GMLOS 6.4 AMLOS 9.8 RW 3.0591

Operating Room Procedures
03.93	Implantation or replacement of spinal neurostimulator lead(s)
03.94	Removal of spinal neurostimulator lead(s)
04.92	Implantation or replacement of peripheral neurostimulator lead(s)
06.8*	Parathyroidectomy
17.56	Atherectomy of other non-coronary vessel(s)
33.20	Thoracoscopic lung biopsy
33.28	Open biopsy of lung
34.02	Exploratory thoracotomy
38.06	Incision of abdominal arteries
38.07	Incision of abdominal veins
38.16	Endarterectomy of abdominal arteries
38.21	Biopsy of blood vessel
38.36	Resection of abdominal arteries with anastomosis
38.37	Resection of abdominal veins with anastomosis
38.46	Resection of abdominal arteries with replacement
38.47	Resection of abdominal veins with replacement
38.66	Other excision of abdominal arteries
38.67	Other excision of abdominal veins
38.7	Interruption of the vena cava
38.86	Other surgical occlusion of abdominal arteries
38.87	Other surgical occlusion of abdominal veins
39.27	Arteriovenostomy for renal dialysis
39.42	Revision of arteriovenous shunt for renal dialysis
39.43	Removal of arteriovenous shunt for renal dialysis
39.49	Other revision of vascular procedure
39.50	Angioplasty of other non-coronary vessel(s)
39.52	Other repair of aneurysm
39.56	Repair of blood vessel with tissue patch graft
39.57	Repair of blood vessel with synthetic patch graft
39.58	Repair of blood vessel with unspecified type of patch graft
39.59	Other repair of vessel
39.71	Endovascular implantation of other graft in abdominal aorta
39.72	Endovascular (total) embolization or occlusion of head and neck vessels
39.73	Endovascular implantation of graft in thoracic aorta
39.75	Endovascular embolization or occlusion of vessel(s) of head or neck using bare coils

39.76	Endovascular embolization or occlusion of vessel(s) of head or neck using bioactive coils
39.79	Other endovascular procedures on other vessels
39.93	Insertion of vessel-to-vessel cannula
39.94	Replacement of vessel-to-vessel cannula
39.98	Control of hemorrhage, not otherwise specified
40.11	Biopsy of lymphatic structure
40.19	Other diagnostic procedures on lymphatic structures
40.24	Excision of inguinal lymph node
40.29	Simple excision of other lymphatic structure
40.3	Regional lymph node excision
40.50	Radical excision of lymph nodes, not otherwise specified
40.9	Other operations on lymphatic structures
50.12	Open biopsy of liver
50.14	Laparoscopic liver biopsy
50.19	Other diagnostic procedures on liver
54.0	Incision of abdominal wall
54.1*	Laparotomy
54.21	Laparoscopy
54.5*	Lysis of peritoneal adhesions
54.92	Removal of foreign body from peritoneal cavity
54.93	Creation of cutaneoperitoneal fistula
54.95	Incision of peritoneum
64.95	Insertion or replacement of non-inflatable penile prosthesis
64.96	Removal of internal prosthesis of penis
64.97	Insertion or replacement of inflatable penile prosthesis
77.4*	Biopsy of bone
86.06	Insertion of totally implantable infusion pump
86.22	Excisional debridement of wound, infection, or burn
92.27	Implantation or insertion of radioactive elements

OR

Principal Diagnosis

277.88	Tumor lysis syndrome
403.00	Hypertensive chronic kidney disease, malignant, with chronic kidney disease stage I through stage IV, or unspecified
403.01	Hypertensive chronic kidney disease, malignant, with chronic kidney disease stage V or end stage renal disease
403.10	Hypertensive chronic kidney disease, benign, with chronic kidney disease stage I through stage IV, or unspecified
403.11	Hypertensive chronic kidney disease, benign, with chronic kidney disease stage V or end stage renal disease
403.90	Hypertensive chronic kidney disease, unspecified, with chronic kidney disease stage I through stage IV, or unspecified
403.91	Hypertensive chronic kidney disease, unspecified, with chronic kidney disease stage V or end stage renal disease
404.02	Hypertensive heart and chronic kidney disease, malignant, without heart failure and with chronic kidney disease stage V or end stage renal disease
404.12	Hypertensive heart and chronic kidney disease, benign, without heart failure and with chronic kidney disease stage V or end stage renal disease
404.92	Hypertensive heart and chronic kidney disease, unspecified, without heart failure and with chronic kidney disease stage V or end stage renal disease
584.5	Acute kidney failure with lesion of tubular necrosis
584.6	Acute kidney failure with lesion of renal cortical necrosis
584.7	Acute kidney failure with lesion of medullary [papillary] necrosis
584.8	Acute kidney failure with other specified pathological lesion in kidney
584.9	Acute kidney failure, unspecified
585*	Chronic kidney disease (CKD)
586	Unspecified renal failure
788.5	Oliguria and anuria
958.5	Traumatic anuria

AND

Nonoperating Room Procedure

86.07	Insertion of totally implantable vascular access device (VAD)

OR

Principal Diagnosis

250.41	Diabetes with renal manifestations, type I [juvenile type], not stated as uncontrolled
250.43	Diabetes with renal manifestations, type I [juvenile type], uncontrolled

AND

Nonoperating Room Procedures

52.84	Autotransplantation of cells of islets of Langerhans
52.85	Allotransplantation of cells of islets of Langerhans

DRG 674   **Other Kidney and Urinary Tract Procedures with CC**

GMLOS 5.1	AMLOS 7.0	RW 2.1887	☑

Select principal diagnosis and operating and nonoperating room procedures listed under DRG 673

DRG 675   **Other Kidney and Urinary Tract Procedures without CC/MCC**

GMLOS 1.8	AMLOS 2.5	RW 1.3558	☑

Select principal diagnosis and operating and nonoperating room procedures listed under DRG 673

MEDICAL

DRG 682   **Renal Failure with MCC**

GMLOS 4.9	AMLOS 6.5	RW 1.5862	T ☑

Principal Diagnosis

277.88	Tumor lysis syndrome
403.00	Hypertensive chronic kidney disease, malignant, with chronic kidney disease stage I through stage IV, or unspecified
403.01	Hypertensive chronic kidney disease, malignant, with chronic kidney disease stage V or end stage renal disease
403.10	Hypertensive chronic kidney disease, benign, with chronic kidney disease stage I through stage IV, or unspecified
403.11	Hypertensive chronic kidney disease, benign, with chronic kidney disease stage V or end stage renal disease
403.90	Hypertensive chronic kidney disease, unspecified, with chronic kidney disease stage I through stage IV, or unspecified
403.91	Hypertensive chronic kidney disease, unspecified, with chronic kidney disease stage V or end stage renal disease
404.02	Hypertensive heart and chronic kidney disease, malignant, without heart failure and with chronic kidney disease stage V or end stage renal disease
404.12	Hypertensive heart and chronic kidney disease, benign, without heart failure and with chronic kidney disease stage V or end stage renal disease
404.92	Hypertensive heart and chronic kidney disease, unspecified, without heart failure and with chronic kidney disease stage V or end stage renal disease
584.5	Acute kidney failure with lesion of tubular necrosis
584.6	Acute kidney failure with lesion of renal cortical necrosis
584.7	Acute kidney failure with lesion of medullary [papillary] necrosis
584.8	Acute kidney failure with other specified pathological lesion in kidney
584.9	Acute kidney failure, unspecified
585*	Chronic kidney disease (CKD)

586	Unspecified renal failure
788.5	Oliguria and anuria
958.5	Traumatic anuria

DRG 683   Renal Failure with CC
GMLOS 3.8   AMLOS 4.7   RW 0.9958   T ☑ ▽

Select principal diagnosis listed under DRG 682

DRG 684   Renal Failure without CC/MCC
GMLOS 2.6   AMLOS 3.1   RW 0.6432   T ☑ ▽

Select principal diagnosis listed under DRG 682

DRG 685   Admit for Renal Dialysis
GMLOS 2.5   AMLOS 3.5   RW 0.8899   ☑

Principal Diagnosis
| V56* | Encounter for dialysis and dialysis catheter care |

DRG 686   Kidney and Urinary Tract Neoplasms with MCC
GMLOS 5.4   AMLOS 7.2   RW 1.6823   ☑

Principal Diagnosis
188*	Malignant neoplasm of bladder
189*	Malignant neoplasm of kidney and other and unspecified urinary organs
198.0	Secondary malignant neoplasm of kidney
198.1	Secondary malignant neoplasm of other urinary organs
209.24	Malignant carcinoid tumor of the kidney
209.64	Benign carcinoid tumor of the kidney
223*	Benign neoplasm of kidney and other urinary organs
233.7	Carcinoma in situ of bladder
233.9	Carcinoma in situ of other and unspecified urinary organs
236.7	Neoplasm of uncertain behavior of bladder
236.9*	Neoplasm of uncertain behavior of other and unspecified urinary organs
239.4	Neoplasm of unspecified nature of bladder
239.5	Neoplasm of unspecified nature of other genitourinary organs

DRG 687   Kidney and Urinary Tract Neoplasms with CC
GMLOS 3.6   AMLOS 4.7   RW 1.0499   ☑

Select principal diagnosis listed under DRG 686

DRG 688   Kidney and Urinary Tract Neoplasms without CC/MCC
GMLOS 2.2   AMLOS 2.9   RW 0.6805   ☑

Select principal diagnosis listed under DRG 686

DRG 689   Kidney and Urinary Tract Infections with MCC
GMLOS 4.5   AMLOS 5.5   RW 1.1784   T ☑ ▽

Principal Diagnosis
016.0*	Tuberculosis of kidney
016.1*	Tuberculosis of bladder
016.2*	Tuberculosis of ureter
016.3*	Tuberculosis of other urinary organs
016.9*	Genitourinary tuberculosis, unspecified
032.84	Diphtheritic cystitis
078.6	Hemorrhagic nephrosonephritis
095.4	Syphilis of kidney
098.11	Gonococcal cystitis (acute)
098.30	Chronic gonococcal infection of upper genitourinary tract, site unspecified
098.31	Gonococcal cystitis, chronic
099.54	Chlamydia trachomatis infection of other genitourinary sites
120.0	Schistosomiasis due to schistosoma haematobium
137.2	Late effects of genitourinary tuberculosis

590*	Infections of kidney
593.3	Stricture or kinking of ureter
595.0	Acute cystitis
595.1	Chronic interstitial cystitis
595.2	Other chronic cystitis
595.3	Trigonitis
595.4	Cystitis in diseases classified elsewhere
595.81	Cystitis cystica
595.89	Other specified types of cystitis
595.9	Unspecified cystitis
597*	Urethritis, not sexually transmitted, and urethral syndrome
599.0	Urinary tract infection, site not specified

DRG 690   Kidney and Urinary Tract Infections without MCC
GMLOS 3.2   AMLOS 3.9   RW 0.7810   T ☑ ▽

Select principal diagnosis listed under DRG 689

DRG 691   Urinary Stones with ESW Lithotripsy with CC/MCC
GMLOS 3.0   AMLOS 4.0   RW 1.5632   ☑

Principal Diagnosis
274.11	Uric acid nephrolithiasis
591	Hydronephrosis
592*	Calculus of kidney and ureter
593.4	Other ureteric obstruction
593.5	Hydroureter
594.1	Other calculus in bladder
594.2	Calculus in urethra
594.8	Other lower urinary tract calculus
594.9	Unspecified calculus of lower urinary tract
788.0	Renal colic

WITH

Nonoperating Room Procedure
| 98.51 | Extracorporeal shockwave lithotripsy (ESWL) of the kidney, ureter and/or bladder |

DRG 692   Urinary Stones with ESW Lithotripsy without CC/MCC
GMLOS 1.7   AMLOS 2.1   RW 1.0563   ☑

Select principal diagnosis and nonoperating room procedure listed under DRG 691

DRG 693   Urinary Stones without ESW Lithotripsy with MCC
GMLOS 4.0   AMLOS 5.2   RW 1.4169   ☑

Select only principal diagnosis listed under DRG 691

DRG 694   Urinary Stones without ESW Lithotripsy without MCC
GMLOS 2.0   AMLOS 2.4   RW 0.7017   ☑

Select only principal diagnosis listed under DRG 691

DRG 695   Kidney and Urinary Tract Signs and Symptoms with MCC
GMLOS 4.2   AMLOS 5.5   RW 1.2944   ☑

Principal Diagnosis
599.7*	Hematuria
788.1	Dysuria
788.2*	Retention of urine
788.3*	Urinary incontinence
788.4*	Frequency of urination and polyuria
788.6*	Other abnormality of urination
788.7	Urethral discharge
788.8	Extravasation of urine
788.9*	Other symptoms involving urinary system
791.0	Proteinuria
791.1	Chyluria
791.2	Hemoglobinuria

T Transfer DRG   SP Special Payment   ☑ Optimization Potential   ▽ Targeted Potential   * Code Range   ● New DRG   ▲ Revised DRG Title

Valid 10/01/2012-09/30/2013

791.7	Other cells and casts in urine
791.9	Other nonspecific finding on examination of urine
793.5	Nonspecific (abnormal) findings on radiological and other examination of genitourinary organs
794.4	Nonspecific abnormal results of kidney function study
794.9	Nonspecific abnormal results of other specified function study

DRG 696 Kidney and Urinary Tract Signs and Symptoms without MCC

GMLOS 2.5   **AMLOS 3.1**   **RW 0.6639**   ☑

Select principal diagnosis listed under DRG 695

DRG 697 Urethral Stricture

GMLOS 2.5   **AMLOS 3.2**   **RW 0.8246**   ☑

Principal Diagnosis

598*	Urethral stricture

DRG 698 Other Kidney and Urinary Tract Diagnoses with MCC

GMLOS 5.2   **AMLOS 6.6**   **RW 1.5995**   T ☑ ▽

Principal Diagnosis

249.4*	Secondary diabetes mellitus with renal manifestations
250.4*	Diabetes with renal manifestations
274.10	Gouty nephropathy, unspecified
274.19	Other gouty nephropathy
306.50	Psychogenic genitourinary malfunction, unspecified
306.53	Psychogenic dysuria
306.59	Other genitourinary malfunction arising from mental factors
344.61	Cauda equina syndrome with neurogenic bladder
440.1	Atherosclerosis of renal artery
442.1	Aneurysm of renal artery
443.23	Dissection of renal artery
445.81	Atheroembolism of kidney
447.3	Hyperplasia of renal artery
453.3	Embolism and thrombosis of renal vein
580*	Acute glomerulonephritis
581*	Nephrotic syndrome
582*	Chronic glomerulonephritis
583*	Nephritis and nephropathy, not specified as acute or chronic
587	Unspecified renal sclerosis
588*	Disorders resulting from impaired renal function
589*	Small kidney of unknown cause
593.0	Nephroptosis
593.1	Hypertrophy of kidney
593.2	Acquired cyst of kidney
593.6	Postural proteinuria
593.7*	Vesicoureteral reflux
593.8*	Other specified disorders of kidney and ureter
593.9	Unspecified disorder of kidney and ureter
594.0	Calculus in diverticulum of bladder
595.82	Irradiation cystitis
596*	Other disorders of bladder
599.1	Urethral fistula
599.2	Urethral diverticulum
599.3	Urethral caruncle
599.4	Urethral false passage
599.5	Prolapsed urethral mucosa
599.6*	Urinary obstruction
599.8*	Other specified disorder of urethra and urinary tract
599.9	Unspecified disorder of urethra and urinary tract
753*	Congenital anomalies of urinary system
866*	Injury to kidney
867.0	Bladder and urethra injury without mention of open wound into cavity
867.1	Bladder and urethra injury with open wound into cavity
867.2	Ureter injury without mention of open wound into cavity
867.3	Ureter injury with open wound into cavity

868.04	Retroperitoneum injury without mention of open wound into cavity
868.14	Retroperitoneum injury with open wound into cavity
939.0	Foreign body in bladder and urethra
939.9	Foreign body in unspecified site in genitourinary tract
996.30	Mechanical complication of unspecified genitourinary device, implant, and graft
996.31	Mechanical complication due to urethral (indwelling) catheter
996.39	Mechanical complication of genitourinary device, implant, and graft, other
996.64	Infection and inflammatory reaction due to indwelling urinary catheter
996.65	Infection and inflammatory reaction due to other genitourinary device, implant, and graft
996.76	Other complications due to genitourinary device, implant, and graft
996.81	Complications of transplanted kidney
997.5	Urinary complications
997.72	Vascular complications of renal artery
V42.0	Kidney replaced by transplant
V43.5	Bladder replaced by other means
V45.74	Acquired absence of organ, other parts of urinary tract
V53.6	Fitting and adjustment of urinary device
V55.5	Attention to cystostomy
V55.6	Attention to other artificial opening of urinary tract
V59.4	Kidney donor

DRG 699 Other Kidney and Urinary Tract Diagnoses with CC

GMLOS 3.6   **AMLOS 4.5**   **RW 0.9998**   T ☑ ▽

Select principal diagnosis listed under DRG 698

DRG 700 Other Kidney and Urinary Tract Diagnoses without CC/MCC

GMLOS 2.6   **AMLOS 3.3**   **RW 0.6854**   T ☑ ▽

Select principal diagnosis listed under DRG 698

Surgical   *Medical*   *CC Indicator*   *MCC Indicator*   *Procedure Proxy*

MDC 12
Diseases And Disorders Of The Male Reproductive System

016.40	098.10	099.8	198.82	600.11	603.1	607.85	608.9	867.7
016.41	098.12	099.9	214.4	600.20	603.8	607.89	698.1	867.8
016.42	098.13	112.2	222.0	600.21	603.9	607.9	752.51	867.9
016.43	098.14	131.00	222.1	600.3	604.0	608.0	752.52	878.0
016.44	098.19	131.02	222.2	600.90	604.90	608.1	752.61	878.1
016.45	098.2	131.03	222.3	600.91	604.91	608.20	752.62	878.2
016.46	098.32	131.09	222.4	601.0	604.99	608.21	752.63	878.3
016.50	098.33	185	222.8	601.1	605	608.22	752.64	878.8
016.51	098.34	186.0	222.9	601.2	606.0	608.23	752.65	878.9
016.52	098.39	186.9	233.4	601.3	606.1	608.24	752.69	908.2
016.53	099.0	187.1	233.5	601.4	606.8	608.3	752.7	922.4
016.54	099.1	187.2	233.6	601.8	606.9	608.4	752.81	926.0
016.55	099.2	187.3	236.4	601.9	607.0	608.81	752.89	939.3
016.56	099.40	187.4	236.5	602.0	607.1	608.82	752.9	V25.2
054.10	099.41	187.5	236.6	602.1	607.2	608.83	758.6	V26.0
054.13	099.49	187.6	456.4	602.2	607.3	608.84	758.7	V45.77
054.19	099.50	187.7	456.5	602.3	607.81	608.85	758.81	V50.2
072.0	099.53	187.8	600.00	602.8	607.82	608.86	758.89	
091.0	099.55	187.9	600.01	602.9	607.83	608.87	792.2	
098.0	099.59	195.3	600.10	603.0	607.84	608.89	867.6	

SURGICAL

DRG 707 **Major Male Pelvic Procedures with CC/MCC**
GMLOS 3.0   AMLOS 4.1   RW 1.8134   ☑

Operating Room Procedures
40.52	Radical excision of periaortic lymph nodes
40.53	Radical excision of iliac lymph nodes
40.54	Radical groin dissection
40.59	Radical excision of other lymph nodes
48.69	Other resection of rectum
54.11	Exploratory laparotomy
57.6	Partial cystectomy
57.7*	Total cystectomy
59.00	Retroperitoneal dissection, not otherwise specified
60.3	Suprapubic prostatectomy
60.4	Retropubic prostatectomy
60.5	Radical prostatectomy
60.62	Perineal prostatectomy
60.69	Other prostatectomy

DRG 708 **Major Male Pelvic Procedures without CC/MCC**
GMLOS 1.5   AMLOS 1.7   RW 1.2936   ☑

Select operating room procedures listed under DRG 707

DRG 709 **Penis Procedures with CC/MCC**
GMLOS 4.0   AMLOS 6.4   RW 2.0087   ☑

Operating Room Procedures
58.43	Closure of other fistula of urethra
58.45	Repair of hypospadias or epispadias
58.46	Other reconstruction of urethra
58.49	Other repair of urethra
58.5	Release of urethral stricture
64.11	Biopsy of penis
64.2	Local excision or destruction of lesion of penis
64.3	Amputation of penis
64.4*	Repair and plastic operation on penis
64.5	Operations for sex transformation, not elsewhere classified
64.92	Incision of penis
64.93	Division of penile adhesions
64.95	Insertion or replacement of non-inflatable penile prosthesis
64.96	Removal of internal prosthesis of penis
64.97	Insertion or replacement of inflatable penile prosthesis
64.98	Other operations on penis
64.99	Other operations on male genital organs

DRG 710 **Penis Procedures without CC/MCC**
GMLOS 1.5   AMLOS 1.8   RW 1.2991   ☑

Select operating room procedures listed under DRG 709

DRG 711 **Testes Procedures with CC/MCC**
GMLOS 5.5   AMLOS 7.8   RW 1.9631   ☑

Operating Room Procedures
61.2	Excision of hydrocele (of tunica vaginalis)
61.42	Repair of scrotal fistula
61.49	Other repair of scrotum and tunica vaginalis
61.92	Excision of lesion of tunica vaginalis other than hydrocele
61.99	Other operations on scrotum and tunica vaginalis
62.0	Incision of testis
62.12	Open biopsy of testis
62.19	Other diagnostic procedures on testes
62.2	Excision or destruction of testicular lesion
62.3	Unilateral orchiectomy
62.4*	Bilateral orchiectomy
62.5	Orchiopexy
62.6*	Repair of testes
62.7	Insertion of testicular prosthesis
62.99	Other operations on testes
63.09	Other diagnostic procedures on spermatic cord, epididymis, and vas deferens
63.1	Excision of varicocele and hydrocele of spermatic cord
63.2	Excision of cyst of epididymis
63.3	Excision of other lesion or tissue of spermatic cord and epididymis
63.4	Epididymectomy
63.51	Suture of laceration of spermatic cord and epididymis
63.53	Transplantation of spermatic cord
63.59	Other repair of spermatic cord and epididymis
63.81	Suture of laceration of vas deferens and epididymis
63.82	Reconstruction of surgically divided vas deferens
63.83	Epididymovasostomy
63.85	Removal of valve from vas deferens
63.89	Other repair of vas deferens and epididymis
63.92	Epididymotomy
63.93	Incision of spermatic cord
63.94	Lysis of adhesions of spermatic cord
63.95	Insertion of valve in vas deferens
63.99	Other operations on spermatic card, epididymis, and vas deferens

DRG 712 **Testes Procedures without CC/MCC**
GMLOS 2.3   AMLOS 3.2   RW 0.8418   ☑

Select operating room procedures listed under DRG 711

DRG 713 **Transurethral Prostatectomy with CC/MCC**
GMLOS 3.1   AMLOS 4.4   RW 1.3234   ☑

Operating Room Procedures
60.2*	Transurethral prostatectomy
60.96	Transurethral destruction of prostate tissue by microwave thermotherapy
60.97	Other transurethral destruction of prostate tissue by other thermotherapy

DRG 714 **Transurethral Prostatectomy without CC/MCC**
GMLOS 1.6   AMLOS 1.8   RW 0.6983   ☑

Select operating room procedures listed under DRG 713

DRG 715 **Other Male Reproductive System O.R. Procedures for Malignancy with CC/MCC**
GMLOS 4.4   AMLOS 6.6   RW 1.9149   ☑

Principal Diagnosis
185	Malignant neoplasm of prostate
186*	Malignant neoplasm of testis
187*	Malignant neoplasm of penis and other male genital organs
195.3	Malignant neoplasm of pelvis
198.82	Secondary malignant neoplasm of genital organs
233.4	Carcinoma in situ of prostate
233.5	Carcinoma in situ of penis
233.6	Carcinoma in situ of other and unspecified male genital organs
236.4	Neoplasm of uncertain behavior of testis
236.5	Neoplasm of uncertain behavior of prostate
236.6	Neoplasm of uncertain behavior of other and unspecified male genital organs

Operating Room Procedures
03.93	Implantation or replacement of spinal neurostimulator lead(s)
03.94	Removal of spinal neurostimulator lead(s)

Surgical   *Medical*   CC Indicator   *MCC Indicator*   *Procedure Proxy*

MDC 12: Diseases And Disorders Of The Male Reproductive System—MEDICAL

04.92	Implantation or replacement of peripheral neurostimulator lead(s)
04.93	Removal of peripheral neurostimulator lead(s)
17.69	Laser interstitial thermal therapy [LITT] of lesion or tissue of other and unspecified site under guidance
38.7	Interruption of the vena cava
39.98	Control of hemorrhage, not otherwise specified
40.1*	Diagnostic procedures on lymphatic structures
40.24	Excision of inguinal lymph node
40.29	Simple excision of other lymphatic structure
40.3	Regional lymph node excision
40.50	Radical excision of lymph nodes, not otherwise specified
40.9	Other operations on lymphatic structures
50.12	Open biopsy of liver
56.41	Partial ureterectomy
56.5*	Cutaneous uretero-ileostomy
56.6*	Other external urinary diversion
56.71	Urinary diversion to intestine
56.72	Revision of ureterointestinal anastomosis
56.73	Nephrocystanastomosis, not otherwise specified
56.75	Transureteroureterostomy
56.83	Closure of ureterostomy
56.84	Closure of other fistula of ureter
57.18	Other suprapubic cystostomy
57.2*	Vesicostomy
57.33	Closed (transurethral) biopsy of bladder
57.34	Open biopsy of bladder
57.39	Other diagnostic procedures on bladder
57.49	Other transurethral excision or destruction of lesion or tissue of bladder
57.5*	Other excision or destruction of bladder tissue
57.82	Closure of cystostomy
57.83	Repair of fistula involving bladder and intestine
57.84	Repair of other fistula of bladder
57.88	Other anastomosis of bladder
58.1	Urethral meatotomy
58.47	Urethral meatoplasty
58.99	Other operations on urethra and periurethral tissue
59.02	Other lysis of perirenal or periureteral adhesions
59.03	Laparoscopic lysis of perirenal or periureteral adhesions
59.09	Other incision of perirenal or periureteral tissue
59.1*	Incision of perivesical tissue
59.2*	Diagnostic procedures on perirenal and perivesical tissue
59.91	Excision of perirenal or perivesical tissue
59.92	Other operations on perirenal or perivesical tissue
60.0	Incision of prostate
60.12	Open biopsy of prostate
60.14	Open biopsy of seminal vesicles
60.15	Biopsy of periprostatic tissue
60.18	Other diagnostic procedures on prostate and periprostatic tissue
60.19	Other diagnostic procedures on seminal vesicles
60.61	Local excision of lesion of prostate
60.72	Incision of seminal vesicle
60.73	Excision of seminal vesicle
60.79	Other operations on seminal vesicles
60.8*	Incision or excision of periprostatic tissue
60.93	Repair of prostate
60.94	Control of (postoperative) hemorrhage of prostate
60.95	Transurethral balloon dilation of the prostatic urethra
60.99	Other operations on prostate
77.4*	Biopsy of bone
86.06	Insertion of totally implantable infusion pump
86.22	Excisional debridement of wound, infection, or burn
92.27	Implantation or insertion of radioactive elements

DRG 716 Other Male Reproductive System O.R. Procedures for Malignancy without CC/MCC
GMLOS 1.3   AMLOS 1.5   RW 0.9656   ☑

Select principal diagnosis and operating room procedures listed under DRG 715

DRG 717 Other Male Reproductive System O.R. Procedures Except Malignancy with CC/MCC
GMLOS 4.5   AMLOS 6.2   RW 1.7261   ☑

Select only operating room procedures listed under DRG 715

DRG 718 Other Male Reproductive System O.R. Procedures Except Malignancy without CC/MCC
GMLOS 2.2   AMLOS 3.0   RW 0.8657   ☑

Select only operating room procedures listed under DRG 715

MEDICAL

DRG 722 Malignancy, Male Reproductive System with MCC
GMLOS 5.4   AMLOS 7.2   RW 1.6690   ☑

Principal Diagnosis
185	Malignant neoplasm of prostate
186*	Malignant neoplasm of testis
187*	Malignant neoplasm of penis and other male genital organs
195.3	Malignant neoplasm of pelvis
198.82	Secondary malignant neoplasm of genital organs
233.4	Carcinoma in situ of prostate
233.5	Carcinoma in situ of penis
233.6	Carcinoma in situ of other and unspecified male genital organs
236.4	Neoplasm of uncertain behavior of testis
236.5	Neoplasm of uncertain behavior of prostate
236.6	Neoplasm of uncertain behavior of other and unspecified male genital organs

DRG 723 Malignancy, Male Reproductive System with CC
GMLOS 4.0   AMLOS 5.1   RW 1.1066   ☑

Select principal diagnosis listed under DRG 722

DRG 724 Malignancy, Male Reproductive System without CC/MCC
GMLOS 2.0   AMLOS 2.6   RW 0.6509   ☑

Select principal diagnosis listed under DRG 722

DRG 725 Benign Prostatic Hypertrophy with MCC
GMLOS 4.6   AMLOS 5.9   RW 1.2976   ☑

Principal Diagnosis
600*	Hyperplasia of prostate

DRG 726 Benign Prostatic Hypertrophy without MCC
GMLOS 2.7   AMLOS 3.4   RW 0.7085   ☑

Select principal diagnosis listed under DRG 725

DRG 727 Inflammation of the Male Reproductive System with MCC
GMLOS 5.0   AMLOS 6.3   RW 1.4014

Principal Diagnosis
016.4*	Tuberculosis of epididymis
016.5*	Tuberculosis of other male genital organs
054.10	Unspecified genital herpes

054.13	Herpetic infection of penis
054.19	Other genital herpes
072.0	Mumps orchitis
091.0	Genital syphilis (primary)
098.0	Gonococcal infection (acute) of lower genitourinary tract
098.10	Gonococcal infection (acute) of upper genitourinary tract, site unspecified
098.12	Gonococcal prostatitis (acute)
098.13	Gonococcal epididymo-orchitis (acute)
098.14	Gonococcal seminal vesiculitis (acute)
098.19	Other gonococcal infections (acute) of upper genitourinary tract
098.2	Gonococcal infections, chronic, of lower genitourinary tract
098.32	Gonococcal prostatitis, chronic
098.33	Gonococcal epididymo-orchitis, chronic
098.34	Gonococcal seminal vesiculitis, chronic
098.39	Other chronic gonococcal infections of upper genitourinary tract
099.0	Chancroid
099.1	Lymphogranuloma venereum
099.2	Granuloma inguinale
099.4*	Other nongonococcal urethritis (NGU)
099.50	Chlamydia trachomatis infection of unspecified site
099.53	Chlamydia trachomatis infection of lower genitourinary sites
099.55	Chlamydia trachomatis infection of unspecified genitourinary site
099.59	Chlamydia trachomatis infection of other specified site
099.8	Other specified venereal diseases
099.9	Unspecified venereal disease
112.2	Candidiasis of other urogenital sites
131.00	Unspecified urogenital trichomoniasis
131.02	Trichomonal urethritis
131.03	Trichomonal prostatitis
131.09	Other urogenital trichomoniasis
601*	Inflammatory diseases of prostate
603.1	Infected hydrocele
604*	Orchitis and epididymitis
605	Redundant prepuce and phimosis
607.1	Balanoposthitis
607.2	Other inflammatory disorders of penis
607.81	Balanitis xerotica obliterans
608.0	Seminal vesiculitis
608.4	Other inflammatory disorder of male genital organs
V50.2	Routine or ritual circumcision

DRG 728　Inflammation of the Male Reproductive System without MCC
　　　　　GMLOS 3.3　　　　AMLOS 3.9　　　　RW 0.7721　　☑

Select principal diagnosis listed under DRG 727

DRG 729　Other Male Reproductive System Diagnoses with CC/MCC
　　　　　GMLOS 3.4　　　　AMLOS 4.4　　　　RW 1.0357　　☑

Principal Diagnosis

214.4	Lipoma of spermatic cord
222*	Benign neoplasm of male genital organs
456.4	Scrotal varices
456.5	Pelvic varices
602*	Other disorders of prostate
603.0	Encysted hydrocele
603.8	Other specified type of hydrocele
603.9	Unspecified hydrocele
606*	Male infertility
607.0	Leukoplakia of penis
607.3	Priapism
607.82	Vascular disorders of penis
607.83	Edema of penis
607.84	Impotence of organic origin
607.85	Peyronie's disease

607.89	Other specified disorder of penis
607.9	Unspecified disorder of penis
608.1	Spermatocele
608.2*	Torsion of testis
608.3	Atrophy of testis
608.8*	Other specified disorder of male genital organs
608.9	Unspecified disorder of male genital organs
698.1	Pruritus of genital organs
752.5*	Undescended and retractile testicle
752.6*	Hypospadias and epispadias and other penile anomalies
752.7	Indeterminate sex and pseudohermaphroditism
752.8*	Other specified congenital anomalies of genital organs
752.9	Unspecified congenital anomaly of genital organs
758.6	Gonadal dysgenesis
758.7	Klinefelter's syndrome
758.8*	Other conditions due to chromosome anomalies
792.2	Nonspecific abnormal finding in semen
867.6	Injury to other specified pelvic organs without mention of open wound into cavity
867.7	Injury to other specified pelvic organs with open wound into cavity
867.8	Injury to unspecified pelvic organ without mention of open wound into cavity
867.9	Injury to unspecified pelvic organ with open wound into cavity
878.0	Open wound of penis, without mention of complication
878.1	Open wound of penis, complicated
878.2	Open wound of scrotum and testes, without mention of complication
878.3	Open wound of scrotum and testes, complicated
878.8	Open wound of other and unspecified parts of genital organs, without mention of complication
878.9	Open wound of other and unspecified parts of genital organs, complicated
908.2	Late effect of internal injury to other internal organs
922.4	Contusion of genital organs
926.0	Crushing injury of external genitalia
939.1	Foreign body in penis
V25.2	Sterilization
V26.0	Tuboplasty or vasoplasty after previous sterilization
V45.77	Acquired absence of organ, genital organs

DRG 730　Other Male Reproductive System Diagnoses without CC/MCC
　　　　　GMLOS 2.0　　　　AMLOS 2.5　　　　RW 0.6113　　☑

Select principal diagnosis listed under DRG 729

Surgical　　　　　　*Medical*　　　　　　*CC Indicator*　　　　　　*MCC Indicator*　　　　　　*Procedure Proxy*

016.60	099.59	219.0	614.7	618.82	622.3	625.9	752.10	795.13
016.61	099.8	219.1	614.8	618.83	622.4	626.0	752.11	795.14
016.62	099.9	219.8	614.9	618.84	622.5	626.1	752.19	795.15
016.63	112.1	219.9	615.0	618.89	622.6	626.2	752.2	795.16
016.64	112.2	220	615.1	618.9	622.7	626.3	752.31	795.18
016.65	131.00	221.0	615.9	619.0	622.8	626.4	752.32	795.19
016.66	131.01	221.1	616.0	619.2	622.9	626.5	752.33	867.4
016.70	131.02	221.2	616.10	619.8	623.0	626.6	752.34	867.5
016.71	131.09	221.8	616.11	619.9	623.1	626.7	752.35	867.6
016.72	179	221.9	616.2	620.0	623.2	626.8	752.36	867.7
016.73	180.0	233.1	616.3	620.1	623.3	626.9	752.39	867.8
016.74	180.1	233.2	616.4	620.2	623.4	627.0	752.40	867.9
016.75	180.8	233.30	616.50	620.3	623.5	627.1	752.41	878.4
016.76	180.9	233.31	616.51	620.4	623.6	627.2	752.42	878.5
054.10	181	233.32	616.81	620.5	623.7	627.3	752.43	878.6
054.11	182.0	233.39	616.89	620.6	623.8	627.4	752.44	878.7
054.12	182.1	236.0	616.9	620.7	623.9	627.8	752.45	878.8
054.19	182.8	236.1	617.0	620.8	624.01	627.9	752.46	878.9
091.0	183.0	236.2	617.1	620.9	624.02	628.0	752.47	908.2
098.0	183.2	236.3	617.2	621.0	624.09	628.1	752.49	922.4
098.10	183.3	256.0	617.3	621.1	624.1	628.2	752.7	926.0
098.15	183.4	256.1	617.4	621.2	624.2	628.3	752.89	939.1
098.16	183.5	256.2	617.8	621.30	624.3	628.4	752.9	939.2
098.17	183.8	256.31	617.9	621.31	624.4	628.8	758.6	947.4
098.19	183.9	256.39	618.00	621.32	624.5	628.9	758.81	996.32
098.2	184.0	256.4	618.01	621.33	624.6	629.0	758.89	V25.2
098.35	184.1	256.8	618.02	621.34	624.8	629.1	795.00	V25.3
098.36	184.2	256.9	618.03	621.35	624.9	629.20	795.01	V26.0
098.37	184.3	306.51	618.04	621.4	625.0	629.21	795.02	V45.77
098.39	184.4	306.52	618.05	621.5	625.1	629.22	795.03	V50.42
099.0	184.8	456.5	618.09	621.6	625.2	629.23	795.04	V55.7
099.1	184.9	456.6	618.1	621.7	625.3	629.29	795.05	V61.5
099.2	195.3	614.0	618.2	621.8	625.4	629.31	795.06	V88.01
099.40	198.6	614.1	618.3	621.9	625.5	629.32	795.07	V88.02
099.41	198.82	614.2	618.4	622.0	625.6	629.81	795.08	V88.03
099.49	218.0	614.3	618.5	622.10	625.70	629.89	795.09	
099.50	218.1	614.4	618.6	622.11	625.71	629.9	795.10	
099.53	218.2	614.5	618.7	622.12	625.79	698.1	795.11	
099.55	218.9	614.6	618.81	622.2	625.8	752.0	795.12	

SURGICAL

DRG 734   Pelvic Evisceration, Radical Hysterectomy and Radical Vulvectomy with CC/MCC
GMLOS 5.0   AMLOS 7.1   RW 2.6652   ☑

Operating Room Procedures
40.50   Radical excision of lymph nodes, not otherwise specified
40.52   Radical excision of periaortic lymph nodes
40.53   Radical excision of iliac lymph nodes
40.54   Radical groin dissection
40.59   Radical excision of other lymph nodes
68.61   Laparoscopic radical abdominal hysterectomy
68.69   Other and unspecified radical abdominal hysterectomy
68.71   Laparoscopic radical vaginal hysterectomy [LRVH]
68.79   Other and unspecified radical vaginal hysterectomy
68.8   Pelvic evisceration
71.5   Radical vulvectomy

DRG 735   Pelvic Evisceration, Radical Hysterectomy and Radical Vulvectomy without CC/MCC
GMLOS 1.9   AMLOS 2.3   RW 1.1682   ☑

Select operating room procedures listed under DRG 734

DRG 736   Uterine and Adnexa Procedures for Ovarian or Adnexal Malignancy with MCC
GMLOS 10.7   AMLOS 13.0   RW 4.4140

Principal Diagnosis
183*   Malignant neoplasm of ovary and other uterine adnexa
198.6   Secondary malignant neoplasm of ovary
236.2   Neoplasm of uncertain behavior of ovary

Operating Room Procedures
65*   Operations on ovary
66.0*   Salpingotomy
66.1*   Diagnostic procedures on fallopian tubes
66.4   Total unilateral salpingectomy
66.5*   Total bilateral salpingectomy
66.61   Excision or destruction of lesion of fallopian tube
66.62   Salpingectomy with removal of tubal pregnancy
66.69   Other partial salpingectomy
66.7*   Repair of fallopian tube
66.92   Unilateral destruction or occlusion of fallopian tube
66.93   Implantation or replacement of prosthesis of fallopian tube
66.94   Removal of prosthesis of fallopian tube
66.96   Dilation of fallopian tube
66.97   Burying of fimbriae in uterine wall
66.99   Other operations on fallopian tubes
68.0   Hysterotomy
68.13   Open biopsy of uterus
68.14   Open biopsy of uterine ligaments
68.19   Other diagnostic procedures on uterus and supporting structures
68.23   Endometrial ablation
68.29   Other excision or destruction of lesion of uterus
68.3*   Subtotal abdominal hysterectomy
68.41   Laparoscopic total abdominal hysterectomy
68.49   Other and unspecified total abdominal hysterectomy
68.5*   Vaginal hysterectomy
68.9   Other and unspecified hysterectomy
69.19   Other excision or destruction of uterus and supporting structures
69.3   Paracervical uterine denervation
69.4*   Uterine repair

DRG 737   Uterine and Adnexa Procedures for Ovarian or Adnexal Malignancy with CC
GMLOS 5.4   AMLOS 6.4   RW 2.0049   ☑

Select principal diagnosis and operating room procedures listed under DRG 736

DRG 738   Uterine and Adnexa Procedures for Ovarian or Adnexal Malignancy without CC/MCC
GMLOS 3.0   AMLOS 3.4   RW 1.2853   ☑

Select principal diagnosis and operating room procedures listed under DRG 736

DRG 739   Uterine, Adnexa Procedures for Nonovarian/Adnexal Malignancy with MCC
GMLOS 6.8   AMLOS 9.2   RW 3.3219   ☑

Principal Diagnosis
179   Malignant neoplasm of uterus, part unspecified
180*   Malignant neoplasm of cervix uteri
181   Malignant neoplasm of placenta
182*   Malignant neoplasm of body of uterus
184*   Malignant neoplasm of other and unspecified female genital organs
195.3   Malignant neoplasm of pelvis
198.82   Secondary malignant neoplasm of genital organs
233.1   Carcinoma in situ of cervix uteri
233.2   Carcinoma in situ of other and unspecified parts of uterus
233.3*   Carcinoma in situ, other and unspecified female genital organs
236.0   Neoplasm of uncertain behavior of uterus
236.1   Neoplasm of uncertain behavior of placenta
236.3   Neoplasm of uncertain behavior of other and unspecified female genital organs

Operating Room Procedures
65*   Operations on ovary
66.0*   Salpingotomy
66.1*   Diagnostic procedures on fallopian tubes
66.4   Total unilateral salpingectomy
66.5*   Total bilateral salpingectomy
66.61   Excision or destruction of lesion of fallopian tube
66.62   Salpingectomy with removal of tubal pregnancy
66.69   Other partial salpingectomy
66.7*   Repair of fallopian tube
66.92   Unilateral destruction or occlusion of fallopian tube
66.93   Implantation or replacement of prosthesis of fallopian tube
66.94   Removal of prosthesis of fallopian tube
66.96   Dilation of fallopian tube
66.97   Burying of fimbriae in uterine wall
66.99   Other operations on fallopian tubes
68.0   Hysterotomy
68.13   Open biopsy of uterus
68.14   Open biopsy of uterine ligaments
68.19   Other diagnostic procedures on uterus and supporting structures
68.23   Endometrial ablation
68.29   Other excision or destruction of lesion of uterus
68.3*   Subtotal abdominal hysterectomy
68.41   Laparoscopic total abdominal hysterectomy
68.49   Other and unspecified total abdominal hysterectomy
68.5*   Vaginal hysterectomy
68.9   Other and unspecified hysterectomy
69.19   Other excision or destruction of uterus and supporting structures
69.3   Paracervical uterine denervation
69.4*   Uterine repair

MDC 13: Diseases And Disorders Of The Female Reproductive System—SURGICAL

Surgical	Medical	CC Indicator	MCC Indicator	Procedure Proxy

DRG 740 Uterine, Adnexa Procedures for Nonovarian/Adnexal Malignancy with CC

GMLOS 3.3   AMLOS 4.2   RW 1.5688   ☑

Select principal diagnosis and operating room procedures listed under DRG 739

DRG 741 Uterine, Adnexa Procedures for Nonovarian/Adnexal Malignancy without CC/MCC

GMLOS 1.8   AMLOS 2.2   RW 1.1499   ☑

Select principal diagnosis and operating room procedures listed under DRG 739

DRG 742 Uterine and Adnexa Procedures for Nonmalignancy with CC/MCC

GMLOS 2.9   AMLOS 3.9   RW 1.4157   ☑

Principal Diagnosis

016.6*	Tuberculous oophoritis and salpingitis
016.7*	Tuberculosis of other female genital organs
054.10	Unspecified genital herpes
054.11	Herpetic vulvovaginitis
054.12	Herpetic ulceration of vulva
054.19	Other genital herpes
091.0	Genital syphilis (primary)
098.0	Gonococcal infection (acute) of lower genitourinary tract
098.10	Gonococcal infection (acute) of upper genitourinary tract, site unspecified
098.15	Gonococcal cervicitis (acute)
098.16	Gonococcal endometritis (acute)
098.17	Gonococcal salpingitis, specified as acute
098.19	Other gonococcal infections (acute) of upper genitourinary tract
098.2	Gonococcal infections, chronic, of lower genitourinary tract
098.35	Gonococcal cervicitis, chronic
098.36	Gonococcal endometritis, chronic
098.37	Gonococcal salpingitis (chronic)
098.39	Other chronic gonococcal infections of upper genitourinary tract
099.0	Chancroid
099.1	Lymphogranuloma venereum
099.2	Granuloma inguinale
099.4*	Other nongonococcal urethritis (NGU)
099.50	Chlamydia trachomatis infection of unspecified site
099.53	Chlamydia trachomatis infection of lower genitourinary sites
099.55	Chlamydia trachomatis infection of unspecified genitourinary site
099.59	Chlamydia trachomatis infection of other specified site
099.8	Other specified venereal diseases
099.9	Unspecified venereal disease
112.1	Candidiasis of vulva and vagina
112.2	Candidiasis of other urogenital sites
131.00	Unspecified urogenital trichomoniasis
131.01	Trichomonal vulvovaginitis
131.02	Trichomonal urethritis
131.09	Other urogenital trichomoniasis
218*	Uterine leiomyoma
219*	Other benign neoplasm of uterus
220	Benign neoplasm of ovary
221*	Benign neoplasm of other female genital organs
256*	Ovarian dysfunction
306.51	Psychogenic vaginismus
306.52	Psychogenic dysmenorrhea
456.5	Pelvic varices
456.6	Vulval varices
614*	Inflammatory disease of ovary, fallopian tube, pelvic cellular tissue, and peritoneum
615*	Inflammatory diseases of uterus, except cervix
616.0	Cervicitis and endocervicitis
616.1*	Vaginitis and vulvovaginitis
616.2	Cyst of Bartholin's gland
616.3	Abscess of Bartholin's gland
616.4	Other abscess of vulva
616.5*	Ulceration of vulva
616.8*	Other specified inflammatory diseases of cervix, vagina, and vulva
616.9	Unspecified inflammatory disease of cervix, vagina, and vulva
617.0	Endometriosis of uterus
617.1	Endometriosis of ovary
617.2	Endometriosis of fallopian tube
617.3	Endometriosis of pelvic peritoneum
617.4	Endometriosis of rectovaginal septum and vagina
617.8	Endometriosis of other specified sites
617.9	Endometriosis, site unspecified
618*	Genital prolapse
619.0	Urinary-genital tract fistula, female
619.2	Genital tract-skin fistula, female
619.8	Other specified fistula involving female genital tract
619.9	Unspecified fistula involving female genital tract
620*	Noninflammatory disorders of ovary, fallopian tube, and broad ligament
621*	Disorders of uterus, not elsewhere classified
622*	Noninflammatory disorders of cervix
623*	Noninflammatory disorders of vagina
624*	Noninflammatory disorders of vulva and perineum
625*	Pain and other symptoms associated with female genital organs
626*	Disorders of menstruation and other abnormal bleeding from female genital tract
627*	Menopausal and postmenopausal disorders
628*	Female infertility
629*	Other disorders of female genital organs
698.1	Pruritus of genital organs
752.0	Congenital anomalies of ovaries
752.1*	Congenital anomalies of fallopian tubes and broad ligaments
752.2	Congenital doubling of uterus
752.3*	Other congenital anomaly of uterus
752.4*	Congenital anomalies of cervix, vagina, and external female genitalia
752.7	Indeterminate sex and pseudohermaphroditism
752.89	Other specified anomalies of genital organs
752.9	Unspecified congenital anomaly of genital organs
758.6	Gonadal dysgenesis
758.8*	Other conditions due to chromosome anomalies
795.0*	Abnormal Papanicolaou smear of cervix and cervical HPV
795.1*	Abnormal Papanicolaou smear of vagina and vaginal HPV
867.4	Uterus injury without mention of open wound into cavity
867.5	Uterus injury with open wound into cavity
867.6	Injury to other specified pelvic organs without mention of open wound into cavity
867.7	Injury to other specified pelvic organs with open wound into cavity
867.8	Injury to unspecified pelvic organ without mention of open wound into cavity
867.9	Injury to unspecified pelvic organ with open wound into cavity
878.4	Open wound of vulva, without mention of complication
878.5	Open wound of vulva, complicated
878.6	Open wound of vagina, without mention of complication
878.7	Open wound of vagina, complicated
878.8	Open wound of other and unspecified parts of genital organs, without mention of complication
878.9	Open wound of other and unspecified parts of genital organs, complicated
908.2	Late effect of internal injury to other internal organs
922.4	Contusion of genital organs
926.0	Crushing injury of external genitalia

☐ Transfer DRG   ⑤ᴾ Special Payment   ☑ Optimization Potential   ⱽᵉˢ Targeted Potential   * Code Range   ● New DRG   ▲ Revised DRG Title

939.1	Foreign body in uterus, any part
939.2	Foreign body in vulva and vagina
947.4	Burn of vagina and uterus
996.32	Mechanical complication due to intrauterine contraceptive device
V25.2	Sterilization
V25.3	Menstrual extraction
V26.0	Tuboplasty or vasoplasty after previous sterilization
V45.77	Acquired absence of organ, genital organs
V50.42	Prophylactic ovary removal
V55.7	Attention to artificial vagina
V61.5	Multiparity
V88.0*	Acquired absence of cervix and uterus

Operating Room Procedures

65*	Operations on ovary
66.0*	Salpingotomy
66.1*	Diagnostic procedures on fallopian tubes
66.4	Total unilateral salpingectomy
66.5*	Total bilateral salpingectomy
66.61	Excision or destruction of lesion of fallopian tube
66.62	Salpingectomy with removal of tubal pregnancy
66.69	Other partial salpingectomy
66.7*	Repair of fallopian tube
66.92	Unilateral destruction or occlusion of fallopian tube
66.93	Implantation or replacement of prosthesis of fallopian tube
66.94	Removal of prosthesis of fallopian tube
66.96	Dilation of fallopian tube
66.97	Burying of fimbriae in uterine wall
66.99	Other operations on fallopian tubes
68.0	Hysterotomy
68.13	Open biopsy of uterus
68.14	Open biopsy of uterine ligaments
68.19	Other diagnostic procedures on uterus and supporting structures
68.23	Endometrial ablation
68.29	Other excision or destruction of lesion of uterus
68.3*	Subtotal abdominal hysterectomy
68.41	Laparoscopic total abdominal hysterectomy
68.49	Other and unspecified total abdominal hysterectomy
68.5*	Vaginal hysterectomy
68.9	Other and unspecified hysterectomy
69.19	Other excision or destruction of uterus and supporting structures
69.3	Paracervical uterine denervation
69.4*	Uterine repair

DRG 743 **Uterine and Adnexa Procedures for Nonmalignancy without CC/MCC**
GMLOS 1.7   AMLOS 1.9   RW 0.9653   ☑

Select principal diagnosis and operating room procedures listed under DRG 742

DRG 744 **D&C, Conization, Laparoscopy and Tubal Interruption with CC/MCC**
GMLOS 4.1   AMLOS 5.9   RW 1.5573   ☑

Operating Room Procedures

54.21	Laparoscopy
66.2*	Bilateral endoscopic destruction or occlusion of fallopian tubes
66.3*	Other bilateral destruction or occlusion of fallopian tubes
66.63	Bilateral partial salpingectomy, not otherwise specified
67.1*	Diagnostic procedures on cervix
67.2	Conization of cervix
68.15	Closed biopsy of uterine ligaments
68.16	Closed biopsy of uterus
68.21	Division of endometrial synechiae
68.22	Incision or excision of congenital septum of uterus

69.09	Other dilation and curettage of uterus
92.27	Implantation or insertion of radioactive elements

DRG 745 **D&C, Conization, Laparoscopy and Tubal Interruption without CC/MCC**
GMLOS 1.8   AMLOS 2.2   RW 0.8109   ☑

Select operating room procedures listed under DRG 744

DRG 746 **Vagina, Cervix and Vulva Procedures with CC/MCC**
GMLOS 3.0   AMLOS 4.4   RW 1.3850   ☑

Operating Room Procedures

48.73	Closure of other rectal fistula
57.18	Other suprapubic cystostomy
57.21	Vesicostomy
67.3*	Other excision or destruction of lesion or tissue of cervix
67.4	Amputation of cervix
67.51	Transabdominal cerclage of cervix
67.59	Other repair of cervical os
67.6*	Other repair of cervix
69.95	Incision of cervix
69.97	Removal of other penetrating foreign body from cervix
70.13	Lysis of intraluminal adhesions of vagina
70.14	Other vaginotomy
70.23	Biopsy of cul-de-sac
70.24	Vaginal biopsy
70.29	Other diagnostic procedures on vagina and cul-de-sac
70.3*	Local excision or destruction of vagina and cul-de-sac
70.71	Suture of laceration of vagina
70.72	Repair of colovaginal fistula
70.73	Repair of rectovaginal fistula
70.74	Repair of other vaginoenteric fistula
70.75	Repair of other fistula of vagina
70.76	Hymenorrhaphy
70.79	Other repair of vagina
70.91	Other operations on vagina
70.92	Other operations on cul-de-sac
70.93	Other operations on cul-de-sac with graft or prosthesis
71.0*	Incision of vulva and perineum
71.1*	Diagnostic procedures on vulva
71.22	Incision of Bartholin's gland (cyst)
71.23	Marsupialization of Bartholin's gland (cyst)
71.24	Excision or other destruction of Bartholin's gland (cyst)
71.29	Other operations on Bartholin's gland
71.3	Other local excision or destruction of vulva and perineum
71.4	Operations on clitoris
71.6*	Other vulvectomy
71.7*	Repair of vulva and perineum
71.8	Other operations on vulva

DRG 747 **Vagina, Cervix and Vulva Procedures without CC/MCC**
GMLOS 1.5   AMLOS 1.8   RW 0.8818   ☑

Select operating room procedures listed under DRG 746

DRG 748 **Female Reproductive System Reconstructive Procedures**
GMLOS 1.4   AMLOS 1.7   RW 0.9773   ☑

Operating Room Procedures

57.85	Cystourethroplasty and plastic repair of bladder neck
59.4	Suprapubic sling operation
59.5	Retropubic urethral suspension
59.6	Paraurethral suspension
59.71	Levator muscle operation for urethrovesical suspension
59.79	Other repair of urinary stress incontinence
64.5	Operations for sex transformation, not elsewhere classified
69.2*	Repair of uterine supporting structures
69.98	Other operations on supporting structures of uterus
70.4	Obliteration and total excision of vagina

Surgical   Medical   CC Indicator   MCC Indicator   Procedure Proxy

MDC 13: Diseases And Disorders Of The Female Reproductive System—SURGICAL

MDC 13: Diseases And Disorders Of The Female Reproductive System—MEDICAL

70.5*	Repair of cystocele and rectocele
70.6*	Vaginal construction and reconstruction
70.77	Vaginal suspension and fixation
70.78	Vaginal suspension and fixation with graft or prosthesis
70.8	Obliteration of vaginal vault

DRG 749   Other Female Reproductive System O.R. Procedures with CC/MCC
GMLOS 6.1   AMLOS 8.6   RW 2.5755

Operating Room Procedures

03.93	Implantation or replacement of spinal neurostimulator lead(s)
03.94	Removal of spinal neurostimulator lead(s)
04.92	Implantation or replacement of peripheral neurostimulator lead(s)
04.93	Removal of peripheral neurostimulator lead(s)
05.24	Presacral sympathectomy
38.7	Interruption of the vena cava
39.98	Control of hemorrhage, not otherwise specified
40.11	Biopsy of lymphatic structure
40.24	Excision of inguinal lymph node
40.29	Simple excision of other lymphatic structure
40.3	Regional lymph node excision
47.1*	Incidental appendectomy
50.12	Open biopsy of liver
54.1*	Laparotomy
54.23	Biopsy of peritoneum
54.29	Other diagnostic procedures on abdominal region
54.4	Excision or destruction of peritoneal tissue
54.5*	Lysis of peritoneal adhesions
54.61	Reclosure of postoperative disruption of abdominal wall
54.62	Delayed closure of granulating abdominal wound
56.41	Partial ureterectomy
56.5*	Cutaneous uretero-ileostomy
56.6*	Other external urinary diversion
56.71	Urinary diversion to intestine
56.72	Revision of ureterointestinal anastomosis
56.73	Nephrocystanastomosis, not otherwise specified
56.75	Transureteroureterostomy
56.83	Closure of ureterostomy
56.84	Closure of other fistula of ureter
57.22	Revision or closure of vesicostomy
57.33	Closed (transurethral) biopsy of bladder
57.34	Open biopsy of bladder
57.5*	Other excision or destruction of bladder tissue
57.6	Partial cystectomy
57.7*	Total cystectomy
57.82	Closure of cystostomy
57.83	Repair of fistula involving bladder and intestine
57.84	Repair of other fistula of bladder
57.89	Other repair of bladder
58.0	Urethrotomy
58.43	Closure of other fistula of urethra
58.49	Other repair of urethra
58.5	Release of urethral stricture
58.99	Other operations on urethra and periurethral tissue
59.00	Retroperitoneal dissection, not otherwise specified
59.02	Other lysis of perirenal or periureteral adhesions
59.03	Laparoscopic lysis of perirenal or periureteral adhesions
59.09	Other incision of perirenal or periureteral tissue
59.1*	Incision of perivesical tissue
66.95	Insufflation of therapeutic agent into fallopian tubes
68.24	Uterine artery embolization [UAE] with coils
68.25	Uterine artery embolization [UAE] without coils
69.99	Other operations on cervix and uterus
70.12	Culdotomy
71.9	Other operations on female genital organs
86.06	Insertion of totally implantable infusion pump
86.22	Excisional debridement of wound, infection, or burn

DRG 750   Other Female Reproductive System O.R. Procedures without CC/MCC
GMLOS 2.4   AMLOS 3.0   RW 1.0675   ☑

Select operating room procedures listed under DRG 749

MEDICAL

DRG 754   Malignancy, Female Reproductive System with MCC
GMLOS 5.9   AMLOS 8.1   RW 1.9833   ☑

Principal Diagnosis

179	Malignant neoplasm of uterus, part unspecified
180*	Malignant neoplasm of cervix uteri
181	Malignant neoplasm of placenta
182*	Malignant neoplasm of body of uterus
183*	Malignant neoplasm of ovary and other uterine adnexa
184*	Malignant neoplasm of other and unspecified female genital organs
195.3	Malignant neoplasm of pelvis
198.6	Secondary malignant neoplasm of ovary
198.82	Secondary malignant neoplasm of genital organs
233.1	Carcinoma in situ of cervix uteri
233.2	Carcinoma in situ of other and unspecified parts of uterus
233.3*	Carcinoma in situ, other and unspecified female genital organs
236.0	Neoplasm of uncertain behavior of uterus
236.1	Neoplasm of uncertain behavior of placenta
236.2	Neoplasm of uncertain behavior of ovary
236.3	Neoplasm of uncertain behavior of other and unspecified female genital organs

DRG 755   Malignancy, Female Reproductive System with CC
GMLOS 3.8   AMLOS 5.0   RW 1.0990   ☑

Select principal diagnosis listed under DRG 754

DRG 756   Malignancy, Female Reproductive System without CC/MCC
GMLOS 2.1   AMLOS 2.7   RW 0.5777   ☑

Select principal diagnosis listed under DRG 754

DRG 757   Infections, Female Reproductive System with MCC
GMLOS 6.0   AMLOS 7.8   RW 1.6945   ☑

Principal Diagnosis

016.6*	Tuberculous oophoritis and salpingitis
016.7*	Tuberculosis of other female genital organs
054.10	Unspecified genital herpes
054.11	Herpetic vulvovaginitis
054.12	Herpetic ulceration of vulva
054.19	Other genital herpes
091.0	Genital syphilis (primary)
098.0	Gonococcal infection (acute) of lower genitourinary tract
098.10	Gonococcal infection (acute) of upper genitourinary tract, site unspecified
098.15	Gonococcal cervicitis (acute)
098.16	Gonococcal endometritis (acute)
098.17	Gonococcal salpingitis, specified as acute
098.19	Other gonococcal infections (acute) of upper genitourinary tract
098.2	Gonococcal infections, chronic, of lower genitourinary tract
098.35	Gonococcal cervicitis, chronic
098.36	Gonococcal endometritis, chronic
098.37	Gonococcal salpingitis (chronic)
098.39	Other chronic gonococcal infections of upper genitourinary tract

---

Ⓣ *Transfer DRG*   ⓢⓟ *Special Payment*   ☑ *Optimization Potential*   ▽ *Targeted Potential*   * *Code Range*   ● *New DRG*   ▲ *Revised DRG Title*

099.0	Chancroid
099.1	Lymphogranuloma venereum
099.2	Granuloma inguinale
099.4*	Other nongonococcal urethritis (NGU)
099.50	Chlamydia trachomatis infection of unspecified site
099.53	Chlamydia trachomatis infection of lower genitourinary sites
099.55	Chlamydia trachomatis infection of unspecified genitourinary site
099.59	Chlamydia trachomatis infection of other specified site
099.8	Other specified venereal diseases
099.9	Unspecified venereal disease
112.1	Candidiasis of vulva and vagina
112.2	Candidiasis of other urogenital sites
131.00	Unspecified urogenital trichomoniasis
131.01	Trichomonal vulvovaginitis
131.02	Trichomonal urethritis
131.09	Other urogenital trichomoniasis
614.0	Acute salpingitis and oophoritis
614.1	Chronic salpingitis and oophoritis
614.2	Salpingitis and oophoritis not specified as acute, subacute, or chronic
614.3	Acute parametritis and pelvic cellulitis
614.4	Chronic or unspecified parametritis and pelvic cellulitis
614.5	Acute or unspecified pelvic peritonitis, female
614.7	Other chronic pelvic peritonitis, female
614.8	Other specified inflammatory disease of female pelvic organs and tissues
614.9	Unspecified inflammatory disease of female pelvic organs and tissues
615*	Inflammatory diseases of uterus, except cervix
616.0	Cervicitis and endocervicitis
616.1*	Vaginitis and vulvovaginitis
616.3	Abscess of Bartholin's gland
616.4	Other abscess of vulva
616.8*	Other specified inflammatory diseases of cervix, vagina, and vulva
616.9	Unspecified inflammatory disease of cervix, vagina, and vulva
625.71	Vulvar vestibulitis
698.1	Pruritus of genital organs

DRG 758 Infections, Female Reproductive System with CC

GMLOS 4.4   AMLOS 5.4   RW 1.0790   ☑

Select principal diagnosis listed under DRG 757

DRG 759 Infections, Female Reproductive System without CC/MCC

GMLOS 3.1   AMLOS 3.7   RW 0.7173   ☑

Select principal diagnosis listed under DRG 757

DRG 760 Menstrual and Other Female Reproductive System Disorders with CC/MCC

GMLOS 2.8   AMLOS 3.6   RW 0.8062   ☑

Principal Diagnosis

218*	Uterine leiomyoma
219*	Other benign neoplasm of uterus
220	Benign neoplasm of ovary
221*	Benign neoplasm of other female genital organs
256*	Ovarian dysfunction
306.51	Psychogenic vaginismus
306.52	Psychogenic dysmenorrhea
456.5	Pelvic varices
456.6	Vulval varices
614.6	Pelvic peritoneal adhesions, female (postoperative) (postinfection)
616.2	Cyst of Bartholin's gland
616.5*	Ulceration of vulva
617.0	Endometriosis of uterus

617.1	Endometriosis of ovary
617.2	Endometriosis of fallopian tube
617.3	Endometriosis of pelvic peritoneum
617.4	Endometriosis of rectovaginal septum and vagina
617.8	Endometriosis of other specified sites
617.9	Endometriosis, site unspecified
618*	Genital prolapse
619.0	Urinary-genital tract fistula, female
619.2	Genital tract-skin fistula, female
619.8	Other specified fistula involving female genital tract
619.9	Unspecified fistula involving female genital tract
620*	Noninflammatory disorders of ovary, fallopian tube, and broad ligament
621*	Disorders of uterus, not elsewhere classified
622*	Noninflammatory disorders of cervix
623*	Noninflammatory disorders of vagina
624*	Noninflammatory disorders of vulva and perineum
625.0	Dyspareunia
625.1	Vaginismus
625.2	Mittelschmerz
625.3	Dysmenorrhea
625.4	Premenstrual tension syndromes
625.5	Pelvic congestion syndrome
625.6	Female stress incontinence
625.70	Vulvodynia, unspecified
625.79	Other vulvodynia
625.8	Other specified symptom associated with female genital organs
625.9	Unspecified symptom associated with female genital organs
626*	Disorders of menstruation and other abnormal bleeding from female genital tract
627*	Menopausal and postmenopausal disorders
628*	Female infertility
629.0	Hematocele, female, not elsewhere classified
629.1	Hydrocele, canal of Nuck
629.2*	Female genital mutilation status
629.3*	Complication of implanted vaginal mesh and other prosthetic materials
629.8*	Other specified disorders of female genital organs
629.9	Unspecified disorder of female genital organs
752.0	Congenital anomalies of ovaries
752.1*	Congenital anomalies of fallopian tubes and broad ligaments
752.2	Congenital doubling of uterus
752.3*	Other congenital anomaly of uterus
752.4*	Congenital anomalies of cervix, vagina, and external female genitalia
752.7	Indeterminate sex and pseudohermaphroditism
752.89	Other specified anomalies of genital organs
752.9	Unspecified congenital anomaly of genital organs
758.6	Gonadal dysgenesis
758.8*	Other conditions due to chromosome anomalies
795.0*	Abnormal Papanicolaou smear of cervix and cervical HPV
795.1*	Abnormal Papanicolaou smear of vagina and vaginal HPV
867.4	Uterus injury without mention of open wound into cavity
867.5	Uterus injury with open wound into cavity
867.6	Injury to other specified pelvic organs without mention of open wound into cavity
867.7	Injury to other specified pelvic organs with open wound into cavity
867.8	Injury to unspecified pelvic organ without mention of open wound into cavity
867.9	Injury to unspecified pelvic organ with open wound into cavity
878.4	Open wound of vulva, without mention of complication
878.5	Open wound of vulva, complicated
878.6	Open wound of vagina, without mention of complication
878.7	Open wound of vagina, complicated
878.8	Open wound of other and unspecified parts of genital organs, without mention of complication

MDC 13: Diseases And Disorders Of The Female Reproductive System—MEDICAL

878.9	Open wound of other and unspecified parts of genital organs, complicated
908.2	Late effect of internal injury to other internal organs
922.4	Contusion of genital organs
926.0	Crushing injury of external genitalia
939.1	Foreign body in uterus, any part
939.2	Foreign body in vulva and vagina
947.4	Burn of vagina and uterus
996.32	Mechanical complication due to intrauterine contraceptive device
V25.2	Sterilization
V25.3	Menstrual extraction
V26.0	Tuboplasty or vasoplasty after previous sterilization
V45.77	Acquired absence of organ, genital organs
V50.42	Prophylactic ovary removal
V55.7	Attention to artificial vagina
V61.5	Multiparity
V88.0*	Acquired absence of cervix and uterus

DRG 761   **Menstrual and Other Female Reproductive System Disorders without CC/MCC**

   GMLOS 1.8   AMLOS 2.2   RW 0.4951   ☑

Select principal diagnosis listed under DRG 760

⊤ *Transfer DRG*   ⓢⓟ *Special Payment*   ☑ *Optimization Potential*   ▽ *Targeted Potential*   * *Code Range*   ● *New DRG*   ▲ *Revised DRG Title*

132   Valid 10/01/2012-09/30/2013   © 2012 OptumInsight, Inc.

MDC 14
Pregnancy, Childbirth And The Puerperium

630	635.72	638.0	642.41	646.40	647.91	649.23	652.33	654.40
631.0	635.80	638.1	642.42	646.41	647.92	649.24	652.40	654.41
631.8	635.81	638.2	642.43	646.42	647.93	649.30	652.41	654.42
632	635.82	638.3	642.44	646.43	647.94	649.31	652.43	654.43
633.00	635.90	638.4	642.50	646.44	648.00	649.32	652.50	654.44
633.01	635.91	638.5	642.51	646.50	648.01	649.33	652.51	654.50
633.10	635.92	638.6	642.52	646.51	648.02	649.34	652.53	654.51
633.11	636.00	638.7	642.53	646.52	648.03	649.40	652.60	654.52
633.20	636.01	638.8	642.54	646.53	648.04	649.41	652.61	654.53
633.21	636.02	638.9	642.60	646.54	648.10	649.42	652.63	654.54
633.80	636.10	639.0	642.61	646.60	648.11	649.43	652.70	654.60
633.81	636.11	639.1	642.62	646.61	648.12	649.44	652.71	654.61
633.90	636.12	639.2	642.63	646.62	648.13	649.50	652.73	654.62
633.91	636.20	639.3	642.64	646.63	648.14	649.51	652.80	654.63
634.00	636.21	639.4	642.70	646.64	648.20	649.53	652.81	654.64
634.01	636.22	639.5	642.71	646.70	648.21	649.60	652.83	654.70
634.02	636.30	639.6	642.72	646.71	648.22	649.61	652.90	654.71
634.10	636.31	639.8	642.73	646.73	648.23	649.62	652.91	654.72
634.11	636.32	639.9	642.74	646.80	648.24	649.63	652.93	654.73
634.12	636.40	640.00	642.90	646.81	648.30	649.64	653.00	654.74
634.20	636.41	640.01	642.91	646.82	648.31	649.70	653.01	654.80
634.21	636.42	640.03	642.92	646.83	648.32	649.71	653.03	654.81
634.22	636.50	640.80	642.93	646.84	648.33	649.73	653.10	654.82
634.30	636.51	640.81	642.94	646.90	648.34	649.81	653.11	654.83
634.31	636.52	640.83	643.00	646.91	648.40	649.82	653.13	654.84
634.32	636.60	640.90	643.01	646.93	648.41	650	653.20	654.90
634.40	636.61	640.91	643.03	647.00	648.42	651.00	653.21	654.91
634.41	636.62	640.93	643.10	647.01	648.43	651.01	653.23	654.92
634.42	636.70	641.00	643.11	647.02	648.44	651.03	653.30	654.93
634.50	636.71	641.01	643.13	647.03	648.50	651.10	653.31	654.94
634.51	636.72	641.03	643.20	647.04	648.51	651.11	653.33	655.00
634.52	636.80	641.10	643.21	647.10	648.52	651.13	653.40	655.01
634.60	636.81	641.11	643.23	647.11	648.53	651.20	653.41	655.03
634.61	636.82	641.13	643.80	647.12	648.54	651.21	653.43	655.10
634.62	636.90	641.20	643.81	647.13	648.60	651.23	653.50	655.11
634.70	636.91	641.21	643.83	647.14	648.61	651.30	653.51	655.13
634.71	636.92	641.23	643.90	647.20	648.62	651.31	653.53	655.20
634.72	637.00	641.30	643.91	647.21	648.63	651.33	653.60	655.21
634.80	637.01	641.31	643.93	647.22	648.64	651.40	653.61	655.23
634.81	637.02	641.33	644.00	647.23	648.70	651.41	653.63	655.30
634.82	637.10	641.80	644.03	647.24	648.71	651.43	653.70	655.31
634.90	637.11	641.81	644.10	647.30	648.72	651.50	653.71	655.33
634.91	637.12	641.83	644.13	647.31	648.73	651.51	653.73	655.40
634.92	637.20	641.90	644.20	647.32	648.74	651.53	653.80	655.41
635.00	637.21	641.91	644.21	647.33	648.80	651.60	653.81	655.43
635.01	637.22	641.93	645.10	647.34	648.81	651.61	653.83	655.50
635.02	637.30	642.00	645.11	647.40	648.82	651.63	653.90	655.51
635.10	637.31	642.01	645.13	647.41	648.83	651.70	653.91	655.53
635.11	637.32	642.02	645.20	647.42	648.84	651.71	653.93	655.60
635.12	637.40	642.03	645.21	647.43	648.90	651.73	654.00	655.61
635.20	637.41	642.04	645.23	647.44	648.91	651.80	654.01	655.63
635.21	637.42	642.10	646.00	647.50	648.92	651.81	654.02	655.70
635.22	637.50	642.11	646.01	647.51	648.93	651.83	654.03	655.71
635.30	637.51	642.12	646.03	647.52	648.94	651.90	654.04	655.73
635.31	637.52	642.13	646.10	647.53	649.00	651.91	654.10	655.80
635.32	637.60	642.14	646.11	647.54	649.01	651.93	654.11	655.81
635.40	637.61	642.20	646.12	647.60	649.02	652.00	654.12	655.83
635.41	637.62	642.21	646.13	647.61	649.03	652.01	654.13	655.90
635.42	637.70	642.22	646.14	647.62	649.04	652.03	654.14	655.91
635.50	637.71	642.23	646.20	647.63	649.10	652.10	654.20	655.93
635.51	637.72	642.24	646.21	647.64	649.11	652.11	654.21	656.00
635.52	637.80	642.30	646.22	647.80	649.12	652.13	654.23	656.01
635.60	637.81	642.31	646.23	647.81	649.13	652.20	654.30	656.03
635.61	637.82	642.32	646.24	647.82	649.14	652.21	654.31	656.10
635.62	637.90	642.33	646.30	647.83	649.20	652.23	654.32	656.11
635.70	637.91	642.34	646.31	647.84	649.21	652.30	654.33	656.13
635.71	637.92	642.40	646.33	647.90	649.22	652.31	654.34	656.20

656.21	659.40	661.33	664.41	666.34	669.70	671.91	674.94	676.63
656.23	659.41	661.40	664.44	667.00	669.71	671.92	675.00	676.64
656.30	659.43	661.41	664.50	667.02	669.80	671.93	675.01	676.80
656.31	659.50	661.43	664.51	667.04	669.81	671.94	675.02	676.81
656.33	659.51	661.90	664.54	667.10	669.82	672.00	675.03	676.82
656.40	659.53	661.91	664.60	667.12	669.83	672.02	675.04	676.83
656.41	659.60	661.93	664.61	667.14	669.84	672.04	675.10	676.84
656.43	659.61	662.00	664.64	668.00	669.90	673.00	675.11	676.90
656.50	659.63	662.01	664.80	668.01	669.91	673.01	675.12	676.91
656.51	659.70	662.03	664.81	668.02	669.92	673.02	675.13	676.92
656.53	659.71	662.10	664.84	668.03	669.93	673.03	675.14	676.93
656.60	659.73	662.11	664.90	668.04	669.94	673.04	675.20	676.94
656.61	659.80	662.13	664.91	668.10	670.00	673.10	675.21	677
656.63	659.81	662.20	664.94	668.11	670.02	673.11	675.22	678.00
656.70	659.83	662.21	665.00	668.12	670.04	673.12	675.23	678.01
656.71	659.90	662.23	665.01	668.13	670.10	673.13	675.24	678.03
656.73	659.91	662.30	665.03	668.14	670.12	673.14	675.80	678.10
656.80	659.93	662.31	665.10	668.20	670.14	673.20	675.81	678.11
656.81	660.00	662.33	665.11	668.21	670.20	673.21	675.82	678.13
656.83	660.01	663.00	665.20	668.22	670.22	673.22	675.83	679.00
656.90	660.03	663.01	665.22	668.23	670.24	673.23	675.84	679.01
656.91	660.10	663.03	665.24	668.24	670.30	673.24	675.90	679.02
656.93	660.11	663.10	665.30	668.80	670.32	673.30	675.91	679.03
657.00	660.13	663.11	665.31	668.81	670.34	673.31	675.92	679.04
657.01	660.20	663.13	665.34	668.82	670.80	673.32	675.93	679.10
657.03	660.21	663.20	665.40	668.83	670.82	673.33	675.94	679.11
658.00	660.23	663.21	665.41	668.84	670.84	673.34	676.00	679.12
658.01	660.30	663.23	665.44	668.90	671.00	673.80	676.01	679.13
658.03	660.31	663.30	665.50	668.91	671.01	673.81	676.02	679.14
658.10	660.33	663.31	665.51	668.92	671.02	673.82	676.03	792.3
658.11	660.40	663.33	665.54	668.93	671.03	673.83	676.04	796.5
658.13	660.41	663.40	665.60	668.94	671.04	673.84	676.10	V23.0
658.20	660.43	663.41	665.61	669.00	671.10	674.00	676.11	V23.1
658.21	660.50	663.43	665.64	669.01	671.11	674.01	676.12	V23.2
658.23	660.51	663.50	665.70	669.02	671.12	674.02	676.13	V23.3
658.30	660.53	663.51	665.71	669.03	671.13	674.03	676.14	V23.41
658.31	660.60	663.53	665.72	669.04	671.14	674.04	676.20	V23.42
658.33	660.61	663.60	665.74	669.10	671.20	674.10	676.21	V23.49
658.40	660.63	663.61	665.80	669.11	671.21	674.12	676.22	V23.5
658.41	660.70	663.63	665.81	669.12	671.22	674.14	676.23	V23.7
658.43	660.71	663.80	665.82	669.13	671.23	674.20	676.24	V23.81
658.80	660.73	663.81	665.83	669.14	671.24	674.22	676.30	V23.82
658.81	660.80	663.83	665.84	669.20	671.30	674.24	676.31	V23.83
658.83	660.81	663.90	665.90	669.21	671.31	674.30	676.32	V23.84
658.90	660.83	663.91	665.91	669.22	671.33	674.32	676.33	V23.85
658.91	660.90	663.93	665.92	669.23	671.40	674.34	676.34	V23.86
658.93	660.91	664.00	665.93	669.24	671.42	674.40	676.40	V23.87
659.00	660.93	664.01	665.94	669.30	671.44	674.42	676.41	V23.89
659.01	661.00	664.04	666.00	669.32	671.50	674.44	676.42	V23.9
659.03	661.01	664.10	666.02	669.34	671.51	674.50	676.43	V24.0
659.10	661.03	664.11	666.04	669.40	671.52	674.51	676.44	V28.0
659.11	661.10	664.14	666.10	669.41	671.53	674.52	676.50	V28.1
659.13	661.11	664.20	666.12	669.42	671.54	674.53	676.51	V28.2
659.20	661.13	664.21	666.14	669.43	671.80	674.54	676.52	V61.6
659.21	661.20	664.24	666.20	669.44	671.81	674.80	676.53	V61.7
659.23	661.21	664.30	666.22	669.50	671.82	674.82	676.54	
659.30	661.23	664.31	666.24	669.51	671.83	674.84	676.60	
659.31	661.30	664.34	666.30	669.60	671.84	674.90	676.61	
659.33	661.31	664.40	666.32	669.61	671.90	674.92	676.62	

SURGICAL

DRG 765   **Cesarean Section with CC/MCC**

GMLOS 3.8   AMLOS 4.8   RW 1.2194

Principal Diagnosis

640.01	Threatened abortion, delivered
640.81	Other specified hemorrhage in early pregnancy, delivered
640.91	Unspecified hemorrhage in early pregnancy, delivered
641.01	Placenta previa without hemorrhage, with delivery
641.11	Hemorrhage from placenta previa, with delivery
641.21	Premature separation of placenta, with delivery
641.31	Antepartum hemorrhage associated with coagulation defects, with delivery
641.81	Other antepartum hemorrhage, with delivery
641.91	Unspecified antepartum hemorrhage, with delivery
642.01	Benign essential hypertension with delivery
642.02	Benign essential hypertension, with delivery, with current postpartum complication
642.11	Hypertension secondary to renal disease, with delivery
642.12	Hypertension secondary to renal disease, with delivery, with current postpartum complication
642.21	Other pre-existing hypertension, with delivery
642.22	Other pre-existing hypertension, with delivery, with current postpartum complication
642.31	Transient hypertension of pregnancy, with delivery
642.32	Transient hypertension of pregnancy, with delivery, with current postpartum complication
642.41	Mild or unspecified pre-eclampsia, with delivery
642.42	Mild or unspecified pre-eclampsia, with delivery, with current postpartum complication
642.51	Severe pre-eclampsia, with delivery
642.52	Severe pre-eclampsia, with delivery, with current postpartum complication
642.61	Eclampsia, with delivery
642.62	Eclampsia, with delivery, with current postpartum complication
642.71	Pre-eclampsia or eclampsia superimposed on pre-existing hypertension, with delivery
642.72	Pre-eclampsia or eclampsia superimposed on pre-existing hypertension, with delivery, with current postpartum complication
642.91	Unspecified hypertension, with delivery
642.92	Unspecified hypertension, with delivery, with current postpartum complication
643.01	Mild hyperemesis gravidarum, delivered
643.11	Hyperemesis gravidarum with metabolic disturbance, delivered
643.21	Late vomiting of pregnancy, delivered
643.81	Other vomiting complicating pregnancy, delivered
643.91	Unspecified vomiting of pregnancy, delivered
644.21	Early onset of delivery, delivered, with or without mention of antepartum condition
645.11	Post term pregnancy, delivered, with or without mention of antepartum condition
645.21	Prolonged pregnancy, delivered, with or without mention of antepartum condition
646.00	Papyraceous fetus, unspecified as to episode of care
646.01	Papyraceous fetus, delivered, with or without mention of antepartum condition
646.11	Edema or excessive weight gain in pregnancy, with delivery, with or without mention of antepartum complication
646.12	Edema or excessive weight gain in pregnancy, with delivery, with current postpartum complication
646.21	Unspecified renal disease in pregnancy, with delivery
646.22	Unspecified renal disease in pregnancy, with delivery, with current postpartum complication
646.31	Pregnancy complication, recurrent pregnancy loss, with or without mention of antepartum condition
646.41	Peripheral neuritis in pregnancy, with delivery
646.42	Peripheral neuritis in pregnancy, with delivery, with current postpartum complication
646.51	Asymptomatic bacteriuria in pregnancy, with delivery
646.52	Asymptomatic bacteriuria in pregnancy, with delivery, with current postpartum complication
646.61	Infections of genitourinary tract in pregnancy, with delivery
646.62	Infections of genitourinary tract in pregnancy, with delivery, with current postpartum complication
646.71	Liver and biliary tract disorders in pregnancy, delivered, with or without mention of antepartum condition
646.81	Other specified complication of pregnancy, with delivery
646.82	Other specified complications of pregnancy, with delivery, with current postpartum complication
646.91	Unspecified complication of pregnancy, with delivery
647.01	Maternal syphilis, complicating pregnancy, with delivery
647.02	Maternal syphilis, complicating pregnancy, with delivery, with current postpartum complication
647.11	Maternal gonorrhea with delivery
647.12	Maternal gonorrhea, with delivery, with current postpartum complication
647.21	Other maternal venereal diseases with delivery
647.22	Other maternal venereal diseases with delivery, with current postpartum complication
647.31	Maternal tuberculosis with delivery
647.32	Maternal tuberculosis with delivery, with current postpartum complication
647.41	Maternal malaria with delivery
647.42	Maternal malaria with delivery, with current postpartum complication
647.51	Maternal rubella with delivery
647.52	Maternal rubella with delivery, with current postpartum complication
647.61	Other maternal viral disease with delivery
647.62	Other maternal viral disease with delivery, with current postpartum complication
647.81	Other specified maternal infectious and parasitic disease with delivery
647.82	Other specified maternal infectious and parasitic disease with delivery, with current postpartum complication
647.91	Unspecified maternal infection or infestation with delivery
647.92	Unspecified maternal infection or infestation with delivery, with current postpartum complication
648.01	Maternal diabetes mellitus with delivery
648.02	Maternal diabetes mellitus with delivery, with current postpartum complication
648.11	Maternal thyroid dysfunction with delivery, with or without mention of antepartum condition
648.12	Maternal thyroid dysfunction with delivery, with current postpartum complication
648.21	Maternal anemia, with delivery
648.22	Maternal anemia with delivery, with current postpartum complication
648.31	Maternal drug dependence, with delivery
648.32	Maternal drug dependence, with delivery, with current postpartum complication
648.41	Maternal mental disorders, with delivery
648.42	Maternal mental disorders, with delivery, with current postpartum complication
648.51	Maternal congenital cardiovascular disorders, with delivery
648.52	Maternal congenital cardiovascular disorders, with delivery, with current postpartum complication
648.61	Other maternal cardiovascular diseases, with delivery
648.62	Other maternal cardiovascular diseases, with delivery, with current postpartum complication
648.71	Bone and joint disorders of maternal back, pelvis, and lower limbs, with delivery
648.72	Bone and joint disorders of maternal back, pelvis, and lower limbs, with delivery, with current postpartum complication
648.81	Abnormal maternal glucose tolerance, with delivery

648.82	Abnormal maternal glucose tolerance, with delivery, with current postpartum complication
648.91	Other current maternal conditions classifiable elsewhere, with delivery
648.92	Other current maternal conditions classifiable elsewhere, with delivery, with current postpartum complication
649.01	Tobacco use disorder complicating pregnancy, childbirth, or the puerperium, delivered, with or without mention of antepartum condition
649.02	Tobacco use disorder complicating pregnancy, childbirth, or the puerperium, delivered, with mention of postpartum complication
649.11	Obesity complicating pregnancy, childbirth, or the puerperium, delivered, with or without mention of antepartum condition
649.12	Obesity complicating pregnancy, childbirth, or the puerperium, delivered, with mention of postpartum complication
649.21	Bariatric surgery status complicating pregnancy, childbirth, or the puerperium, delivered, with or without mention of antepartum condition
649.22	Bariatric surgery status complicating pregnancy, childbirth, or the puerperium, delivered, with mention of postpartum complication
649.31	Coagulation defects complicating pregnancy, childbirth, or the puerperium, delivered, with or without mention of antepartum condition
649.32	Coagulation defects complicating pregnancy, childbirth, or the puerperium, delivered, with mention of postpartum complication
649.41	Epilepsy complicating pregnancy, childbirth, or the puerperium, delivered, with or without mention of antepartum condition
649.42	Epilepsy complicating pregnancy, childbirth, or the puerperium, delivered, with mention of postpartum complication
649.51	Spotting complicating pregnancy, delivered, with or without mention of antepartum condition
649.61	Uterine size date discrepancy, delivered, with or without mention of antepartum condition
649.62	Uterine size date discrepancy, delivered, with mention of postpartum complication
649.71	Cervical shortening, delivered, with or without mention of antepartum condition
649.8*	Onset (spontaneous) of labor after 37 completed weeks of gestation but before 39 completed weeks gestation, with delivery by (planned) cesarean section
650	Normal delivery
651.01	Twin pregnancy, delivered
651.11	Triplet pregnancy, delivered
651.21	Quadruplet pregnancy, delivered
651.31	Twin pregnancy with fetal loss and retention of one fetus, delivered
651.41	Triplet pregnancy with fetal loss and retention of one or more, delivered
651.51	Quadruplet pregnancy with fetal loss and retention of one or more, delivered
651.61	Other multiple pregnancy with fetal loss and retention of one or more fetus(es), delivered
651.71	Multiple gestation following (elective) fetal reduction, delivered, with or without mention of antepartum condition
651.81	Other specified multiple gestation, delivered
651.91	Unspecified multiple gestation, delivered
652.01	Unstable lie of fetus, delivered
652.11	Breech or other malpresentation successfully converted to cephalic presentation, delivered
652.21	Breech presentation without mention of version, delivered
652.31	Transverse or oblique fetal presentation, delivered
652.41	Fetal face or brow presentation, delivered
652.51	High fetal head at term, delivered
652.61	Multiple gestation with malpresentation of one fetus or more, delivered
652.71	Prolapsed arm of fetus, delivered
652.81	Other specified malposition or malpresentation of fetus, delivered
652.91	Unspecified malposition or malpresentation of fetus, delivered
653.01	Major abnormality of bony pelvis, not further specified, delivered
653.11	Generally contracted pelvis in pregnancy, delivered
653.21	Inlet contraction of pelvis in pregnancy, delivered
653.31	Outlet contraction of pelvis in pregnancy, delivered
653.41	Fetopelvic disproportion, delivered
653.51	Unusually large fetus causing disproportion, delivered
653.61	Hydrocephalic fetus causing disproportion, delivered
653.71	Other fetal abnormality causing disproportion, delivered
653.81	Fetal disproportion of other origin, delivered
653.91	Unspecified fetal disproportion, delivered
654.01	Congenital abnormalities of pregnant uterus, delivered
654.02	Congenital abnormalities of pregnant uterus, delivered, with mention of postpartum complication
654.11	Tumors of body of uterus, delivered
654.12	Tumors of body of uterus, delivered, with mention of postpartum complication
654.21	Previous cesarean delivery, delivered, with or without mention of antepartum condition
654.31	Retroverted and incarcerated gravid uterus, delivered
654.32	Retroverted and incarcerated gravid uterus, delivered, with mention of postpartum complication
654.41	Other abnormalities in shape or position of gravid uterus and of neighboring structures, delivered
654.42	Other abnormalities in shape or position of gravid uterus and of neighboring structures, delivered, with mention of postpartum complication
654.51	Cervical incompetence, delivered
654.52	Cervical incompetence, delivered, with mention of postpartum complication
654.61	Other congenital or acquired abnormality of cervix, with delivery
654.62	Other congenital or acquired abnormality of cervix, delivered, with mention of postpartum complication
654.71	Congenital or acquired abnormality of vagina, with delivery
654.72	Congenital or acquired abnormality of vagina, delivered, with mention of postpartum complication
654.81	Congenital or acquired abnormality of vulva, with delivery
654.82	Congenital or acquired abnormality of vulva, delivered, with mention of postpartum complication
654.91	Other and unspecified abnormality of organs and soft tissues of pelvis, with delivery
654.92	Other and unspecified abnormality of organs and soft tissues of pelvis, delivered, with mention of postpartum complication
655.01	Central nervous system malformation in fetus, with delivery
655.11	Chromosomal abnormality in fetus, affecting management of mother, with delivery
655.21	Hereditary disease in family possibly affecting fetus, affecting management of mother, with delivery
655.31	Suspected damage to fetus from viral disease in mother, affecting management of mother, with delivery
655.41	Suspected damage to fetus from other disease in mother, affecting management of mother, with delivery
655.51	Suspected damage to fetus from drugs, affecting management of mother, delivered
655.61	Suspected damage to fetus from radiation, affecting management of mother, delivered
655.71	Decreased fetal movements, affecting management of mother, delivered
655.81	Other known or suspected fetal abnormality, not elsewhere classified, affecting management of mother, delivery

T Transfer DRG   SP Special Payment   ☑ Optimization Potential   ᵀᴬᴿ Targeted Potential   * Code Range   ● New DRG   ▲ Revised DRG Title

136   Valid 10/01/2012-09/30/2013   © 2012 OptumInsight, Inc.

655.91	Unspecified fetal abnormality affecting management of mother, delivery
656.01	Fetal-maternal hemorrhage, with delivery
656.11	Rhesus isoimmunization affecting management of mother, delivered
656.21	Isoimmunization from other and unspecified blood-group incompatibility, affecting management of mother, delivered
656.30	Fetal distress affecting management of mother, unspecified as to episode of care
656.31	Fetal distress affecting management of mother, delivered
656.40	Intrauterine death affecting management of mother, unspecified as to episode of care
656.41	Intrauterine death affecting management of mother, delivered
656.51	Poor fetal growth, affecting management of mother, delivered
656.61	Excessive fetal growth affecting management of mother, delivered
656.71	Other placental conditions affecting management of mother, delivered
656.81	Other specified fetal and placental problems affecting management of mother, delivered
656.91	Unspecified fetal and placental problem affecting management of mother, delivered
657.01	Polyhydramnios, with delivery
658.01	Oligohydramnios, delivered
658.10	Premature rupture of membranes in pregnancy, unspecified as to episode of care
658.11	Premature rupture of membranes in pregnancy, delivered
658.20	Delayed delivery after spontaneous or unspecified rupture of membranes, unspecified as to episode of care
658.21	Delayed delivery after spontaneous or unspecified rupture of membranes, delivered
658.30	Delayed delivery after artificial rupture of membranes, unspecified as to episode of care
658.31	Delayed delivery after artificial rupture of membranes, delivered
658.40	Infection of amniotic cavity, unspecified as to episode of care
658.41	Infection of amniotic cavity, delivered
658.81	Other problem associated with amniotic cavity and membranes, delivered
658.91	Unspecified problem associated with amniotic cavity and membranes, delivered
659.00	Failed mechanical induction of labor, unspecified as to episode of care
659.01	Failed mechanical induction of labor, delivered
659.10	Failed medical or unspecified induction of labor, unspecified as to episode of care
659.11	Failed medical or unspecified induction of labor, delivered
659.20	Unspecified maternal pyrexia during labor, unspecified as to episode of care
659.21	Unspecified maternal pyrexia during labor, delivered
659.30	Generalized infection during labor, unspecified as to episode of care
659.31	Generalized infection during labor, delivered
659.41	Grand multiparity, delivered, with or without mention of antepartum condition
659.50	Elderly primigravida, unspecified as to episode of care
659.51	Elderly primigravida, delivered
659.60	Elderly multigravida, unspecified as to episode of care or not applicable
659.61	Elderly multigravida, delivered, with mention of antepartum condition
659.70	Abnormality in fetal heart rate or rhythm, unspecified as to episode of care or not applicable
659.71	Abnormality in fetal heart rate or rhythm, delivered, with or without mention of antepartum condition
659.80	Other specified indication for care or intervention related to labor and delivery, unspecified as to episode of care
659.81	Other specified indication for care or intervention related to labor and delivery, delivered
659.90	Unspecified indication for care or intervention related to labor and delivery, unspecified as to episode of care
659.91	Unspecified indication for care or intervention related to labor and delivery, delivered
660.00	Obstruction caused by malposition of fetus at onset of labor, unspecified as to episode of care
660.01	Obstruction caused by malposition of fetus at onset of labor, delivered
660.10	Obstruction by bony pelvis during labor and delivery, unspecified as to episode of care
660.11	Obstruction by bony pelvis during labor and delivery, delivered
660.20	Obstruction by abnormal pelvic soft tissues during labor and delivery, unspecified as to episode of care
660.21	Obstruction by abnormal pelvic soft tissues during labor and delivery, delivered
660.30	Deep transverse arrest and persistent occipitoposterior position during labor and delivery, unspecified as to episode of care
660.31	Deep transverse arrest and persistent occipitoposterior position during labor and deliver, delivered
660.40	Shoulder (girdle) dystocia during labor and delivery, unspecified as to episode of care
660.41	Shoulder (girdle) dystocia during labor and deliver, delivered
660.50	Locked twins during labor and delivery, unspecified as to episode of care in pregnancy
660.51	Locked twins, delivered
660.60	Unspecified failed trial of labor, unspecified as to episode
660.61	Unspecified failed trial of labor, delivered
660.70	Unspecified failed forceps or vacuum extractor, unspecified as to episode of care
660.71	Unspecified failed forceps or vacuum extractor, delivered
660.80	Other causes of obstructed labor, unspecified as to episode of care
660.81	Other causes of obstructed labor, delivered
660.90	Unspecified obstructed labor, unspecified as to episode of care
660.91	Unspecified obstructed labor, with delivery
661.00	Primary uterine inertia, unspecified as to episode of care
661.01	Primary uterine inertia, with delivery
661.10	Secondary uterine inertia, unspecified as to episode of care
661.11	Secondary uterine inertia, with delivery
661.20	Other and unspecified uterine inertia, unspecified as to episode of care
661.21	Other and unspecified uterine inertia, with delivery
661.30	Precipitate labor, unspecified as to episode of care
661.31	Precipitate labor, with delivery
661.40	Hypertonic, incoordinate, or prolonged uterine contractions, unspecified as to episode of care
661.41	Hypertonic, incoordinate, or prolonged uterine contractions, with delivery
661.90	Unspecified abnormality of labor, unspecified as to episode of care
661.91	Unspecified abnormality of labor, with delivery
662.00	Prolonged first stage of labor, unspecified as to episode of care
662.01	Prolonged first stage of labor, delivered
662.10	Unspecified prolonged labor, unspecified as to episode of care
662.11	Unspecified prolonged labor, delivered
662.20	Prolonged second stage of labor, unspecified as to episode of care
662.21	Prolonged second stage of labor, delivered
662.30	Delayed delivery of second twin, triplet, etc., unspecified as to episode of care
662.31	Delayed delivery of second twin, triplet, etc., delivered
663.00	Prolapse of cord, complicating labor and delivery, unspecified as to episode of care

Surgical *Medical* *CC Indicator* *MCC Indicator* *Procedure Proxy*

MDC 14: Pregnancy, Childbirth And The Puerperium—SURGICAL

663.01	Prolapse of cord, complicating labor and delivery, delivered
663.10	Cord around neck, with compression, complicating labor and delivery, unspecified as to episode of care
663.11	Cord around neck, with compression, complicating labor and delivery, delivered
663.20	Other and unspecified cord entanglement, with compression, complicating labor and delivery, unspecified as to episode of care
663.21	Other and unspecified cord entanglement, with compression, complicating labor and delivery, delivered
663.30	Other and unspecified cord entanglement, without mention of compression, complicating labor and delivery, unspecified as to episode of care
663.31	Other and unspecified cord entanglement, without mention of compression, complicating labor and delivery, delivered
663.40	Short cord complicating labor and delivery, unspecified as to episode of care
663.41	Short cord complicating labor and delivery, delivered
663.50	Vasa previa complicating labor and delivery, unspecified as to episode of care
663.51	Vasa previa complicating labor and delivery, delivered
663.60	Vascular lesions of cord complicating labor and delivery, unspecified as to episode of care
663.61	Vascular lesions of cord complicating labor and delivery, delivered
663.80	Other umbilical cord complications during labor and delivery, unspecified as to episode of care
663.81	Other umbilical cord complications during labor and delivery, delivered
663.90	Unspecified umbilical cord complication during labor and delivery, unspecified as to episode of care
663.91	Unspecified umbilical cord complication during labor and delivery, delivered
664.00	First-degree perineal laceration, unspecified as to episode of care in pregnancy
664.01	First-degree perineal laceration, with delivery
664.10	Second-degree perineal laceration, unspecified as to episode of care in pregnancy
664.11	Second-degree perineal laceration, with delivery
664.20	Third-degree perineal laceration, unspecified as to episode of care in pregnancy
664.21	Third-degree perineal laceration, with delivery
664.30	Fourth-degree perineal laceration, unspecified as to episode of care in pregnancy
664.31	Fourth-degree perineal laceration, with delivery
664.40	Unspecified perineal laceration, unspecified as to episode of care in pregnancy
664.41	Unspecified perineal laceration, with delivery
664.50	Vulvar and perineal hematoma, unspecified as to episode of care in pregnancy
664.51	Vulvar and perineal hematoma, with delivery
664.60	Anal sphincter tear complicating delivery, not associated with third-degree perineal laceration, unspecified as to episode of care or not applicable
664.61	Anal sphincter tear complicating delivery, not associated with third-degree perineal laceration, delivered, with or without mention of antepartum condition
664.80	Other specified trauma to perineum and vulva, unspecified as to episode of care in pregnancy
664.81	Other specified trauma to perineum and vulva, with delivery
664.90	Unspecified trauma to perineum and vulva, unspecified as to episode of care in pregnancy
664.91	Unspecified trauma to perineum and vulva, with delivery
665.00	Rupture of uterus before onset of labor, unspecified as to episode of care
665.01	Rupture of uterus before onset of labor, with delivery
665.10	Rupture of uterus during labor, unspecified as to episode
665.11	Rupture of uterus during labor, with delivery
665.20	Inversion of uterus, unspecified as to episode of care in pregnancy
665.22	Inversion of uterus, delivered with postpartum complication
665.30	Laceration of cervix, unspecified as to episode of care in pregnancy
665.31	Laceration of cervix, with delivery
665.40	High vaginal laceration, unspecified as to episode of care in pregnancy
665.41	High vaginal laceration, with delivery
665.50	Other injury to pelvic organs, unspecified as to episode of care in pregnancy
665.51	Other injury to pelvic organs, with delivery
665.60	Damage to pelvic joints and ligaments, unspecified as to episode of care in pregnancy
665.61	Damage to pelvic joints and ligaments, with delivery
665.70	Pelvic hematoma, unspecified as to episode of care
665.71	Pelvic hematoma, with delivery
665.72	Pelvic hematoma, delivered with postpartum complication
665.80	Other specified obstetrical trauma, unspecified as to episode of care
665.81	Other specified obstetrical trauma, with delivery
665.82	Other specified obstetrical trauma, delivered, with postpartum
665.90	Unspecified obstetrical trauma, unspecified as to episode of care
665.91	Unspecified obstetrical trauma, with delivery
665.92	Unspecified obstetrical trauma, delivered, with postpartum complication
666.02	Third-stage postpartum hemorrhage, with delivery
666.12	Other immediate postpartum hemorrhage, with delivery
666.22	Delayed and secondary postpartum hemorrhage, with delivery
666.32	Postpartum coagulation defects, with delivery
667.02	Retained placenta without hemorrhage, with delivery, with mention of postpartum complication
667.12	Retained portions of placenta or membranes, without hemorrhage, delivered, with mention of postpartum complication
668.00	Pulmonary complications of the administration of anesthesia or other sedation in labor and delivery, unspecified as to episode of care
668.01	Pulmonary complications of the administration of anesthesia or other sedation in labor and delivery, delivered
668.02	Pulmonary complications of the administration of anesthesia or other sedation in labor and delivery, delivered, with mention of postpartum complication
668.10	Cardiac complications of the administration of anesthesia or other sedation in labor and delivery, unspecified as to episode of care
668.11	Cardiac complications of the administration of anesthesia or other sedation in labor and delivery, delivered
668.12	Cardiac complications of the administration of anesthesia or other sedation in labor and delivery, delivered, with mention of postpartum complication
668.20	Central nervous system complications of the administration of anesthesia or other sedation in labor and delivery, unspecified as to episode of care
668.21	Central nervous system complications of the administration of anesthesia or other sedation in labor and delivery, delivered
668.22	Central nervous system complications of the administration of anesthesia or other sedation in labor and delivery, delivered, with mention of postpartum complication
668.80	Other complications of the administration of anesthesia or other sedation in labor and delivery, unspecified as to episode of care
668.81	Other complications of the administration of anesthesia or other sedation in labor and delivery, delivered
668.82	Other complications of the administration of anesthesia or other sedation in labor and delivery, delivered, with mention of postpartum complication

MDC 14: Pregnancy, Childbirth And The Puerperium—SURGICAL

T Transfer DRG   SP Special Payment   ☑ Optimization Potential   ▽ Targeted Potential   * Code Range   ● New DRG   ▲ Revised DRG Title

138   Valid 10/01/2012–09/30/2013   © 2012 OptumInsight, Inc.

668.90	Unspecified complication of the administration of anesthesia or other sedation in labor and delivery, unspecified as to episode of care
668.91	Unspecified complication of the administration of anesthesia or other sedation in labor and delivery, delivered
668.92	Unspecified complication of the administration of anesthesia or other sedation in labor and delivery, delivered, with mention of postpartum complication
669.00	Maternal distress complicating labor and delivery, unspecified as to episode of care
669.01	Maternal distress, with delivery, with or without mention of antepartum condition
669.02	Maternal distress, with delivery, with mention of postpartum complication
669.10	Shock during or following labor and delivery, unspecified as to episode of care
669.11	Shock during or following labor and delivery, with delivery, with or without mention of antepartum condition
669.12	Shock during or following labor and delivery, with delivery, with mention of postpartum complication
669.20	Maternal hypotension syndrome complicating labor and delivery, unspecified as to episode of care
669.21	Maternal hypotension syndrome, with delivery, with or without mention of antepartum condition
669.22	Maternal hypotension syndrome, with delivery, with mention of postpartum complication
669.30	Acute kidney failure following labor and delivery, unspecified as to episode of care or not applicable
669.32	Acute kidney failure following labor and delivery, delivered, with mention of postpartum complication
669.40	Other complications of obstetrical surgery and procedures, unspecified as to episode of care
669.41	Other complications of obstetrical surgery and procedures, with delivery, with or without mention of antepartum condition
669.42	Other complications of obstetrical surgery and procedures, with delivery, with mention of postpartum complication
669.50	Forceps or vacuum extractor delivery without mention of indication, unspecified as to episode of care
669.51	Forceps or vacuum extractor delivery without mention of indication, delivered, with or without mention of antepartum condition
669.60	Breech extraction, without mention of indication, unspecified as to episode of care
669.61	Breech extraction, without mention of indication, delivered, with or without mention of antepartum condition
669.70	Cesarean delivery, without mention of indication, unspecified as to episode of care
669.71	Cesarean delivery, without mention of indication, delivered, with or without mention of antepartum condition
669.80	Other complication of labor and delivery, unspecified as to episode of care
669.81	Other complication of labor and delivery, delivered, with or without mention of antepartum condition
669.82	Other complication of labor and delivery, delivered, with mention of postpartum complication
669.90	Unspecified complication of labor and delivery, unspecified as to episode of care
669.91	Unspecified complication of labor and delivery, with delivery, with or without mention of antepartum condition
669.92	Unspecified complication of labor and delivery, with delivery, with mention of postpartum complication
670.02	Major puerperal infection, unspecified, delivered, with mention of postpartum complication
670.12	Puerperal endometritis, delivered, with mention of postpartum complication
670.22	Puerperal sepsis, delivered, with mention of postpartum complication
670.32	Puerperal septic thrombophlebitis, delivered, with mention of postpartum complication
670.82	Other major puerperal infection, delivered, with mention of postpartum complication
671.01	Varicose veins of legs, with delivery, with or without mention of antepartum condition
671.02	Varicose veins of legs, with delivery, with mention of postpartum complication
671.11	Varicose veins of vulva and perineum, with delivery, with or without mention of antepartum condition
671.12	Varicose veins of vulva and perineum, with delivery, with mention of postpartum complication
671.21	Superficial thrombophlebitis with delivery, with or without mention of antepartum condition
671.22	Superficial thrombophlebitis with delivery, with mention of postpartum complication
671.31	Deep phlebothrombosis, antepartum, with delivery
671.42	Deep phlebothrombosis, postpartum, with delivery
671.51	Other phlebitis and thrombosis with delivery, with or without mention of antepartum condition
671.52	Other phlebitis and thrombosis with delivery, with mention of postpartum complication
671.81	Other venous complication, with delivery, with or without mention of antepartum condition
671.82	Other venous complication, with delivery, with mention of postpartum complication
671.91	Unspecified venous complication, with delivery, with or without mention of antepartum condition
671.92	Unspecified venous complication, with delivery, with mention of postpartum complication
672.02	Puerperal pyrexia of unknown origin, delivered, with mention of postpartum complication
673.01	Obstetrical air embolism, with delivery, with or without mention of antepartum condition
673.02	Obstetrical air embolism, with delivery, with mention of postpartum complication
673.11	Amniotic fluid embolism, with delivery, with or without mention of antepartum condition
673.12	Amniotic fluid embolism, with delivery, with mention of postpartum complication
673.21	Obstetrical blood-clot embolism, with delivery, with or without mention of antepartum condition
673.22	Obstetrical blood-clot embolism, with mention of postpartum complication
673.31	Obstetrical pyemic and septic embolism, with delivery, with or without mention of antepartum condition
673.32	Obstetrical pyemic and septic embolism, with delivery, with mention of postpartum complication
673.81	Other obstetrical pulmonary embolism, with delivery, with or without mention of antepartum condition
673.82	Other obstetrical pulmonary embolism, with delivery, with mention of postpartum complication
674.01	Cerebrovascular disorder, with delivery, with or without mention of antepartum condition
674.02	Cerebrovascular disorder, with delivery, with mention of postpartum complication
674.12	Disruption of cesarean wound, with delivery, with mention of postpartum complication
674.22	Disruption of perineal wound, with delivery, with mention of postpartum complication
674.32	Other complication of obstetrical surgical wounds, with delivery, with mention of postpartum complication
674.42	Placental polyp, with delivery, with mention of postpartum complication
674.51	Peripartum cardiomyopathy, delivered, with or without mention of antepartum condition
674.52	Peripartum cardiomyopathy, delivered, with mention of postpartum condition
674.82	Other complication of puerperium, with delivery, with mention of postpartum complication
674.92	Unspecified complications of puerperium, with delivery, with mention of postpartum complication

Surgical   Medical   CC Indicator   MCC Indicator   Procedure Proxy

MDC 14: Pregnancy, Childbirth And The Puerperium—SURGICAL

675.01	Infection of nipple associated with childbirth, delivered, with or without mention of antepartum condition
675.02	Infection of nipple associated with childbirth, delivered with mention of postpartum complication
675.11	Abscess of breast associated with childbirth, delivered, with or without mention of antepartum condition
675.12	Abscess of breast associated with childbirth, delivered, with mention of postpartum complication
675.21	Nonpurulent mastitis, delivered, with or without mention of antepartum condition
675.22	Nonpurulent mastitis, delivered, with mention of postpartum complication
675.81	Other specified infection of the breast and nipple associated with childbirth, delivered, with or without mention of antepartum condition
675.82	Other specified infection of the breast and nipple associated with childbirth, delivered, with mention of postpartum complication
675.91	Unspecified infection of the breast and nipple, delivered, with or without mention of antepartum condition
675.92	Unspecified infection of the breast and nipple, delivered, with mention of postpartum complication
676.01	Retracted nipple, delivered, with or without mention of antepartum condition
676.02	Retracted nipple, delivered, with mention of postpartum complication
676.11	Cracked nipple, delivered, with or without mention of antepartum condition
676.12	Cracked nipple, delivered, with mention of postpartum complication
676.21	Engorgement of breasts, delivered, with or without mention of antepartum condition
676.22	Engorgement of breasts, delivered, with mention of postpartum complication
676.31	Other and unspecified disorder of breast associated with childbirth, delivered, with or without mention of antepartum condition
676.32	Other and unspecified disorder of breast associated with childbirth, delivered, with mention of postpartum complication
676.41	Failure of lactation, with delivery, with or without mention of antepartum condition
676.42	Failure of lactation, with delivery, with mention of postpartum complication
676.51	Suppressed lactation, with delivery, with or without mention of antepartum condition
676.52	Suppressed lactation, with delivery, with mention of postpartum complication
676.61	Galactorrhea, with delivery, with or without mention of antepartum condition
676.62	Galactorrhea, with delivery, with mention of postpartum complication
676.81	Other disorder of lactation, with delivery, with or without mention of antepartum condition
676.82	Other disorder of lactation, with delivery, with mention of postpartum complication
676.91	Unspecified disorder of lactation, with delivery, with or without mention of antepartum condition
676.92	Unspecified disorder of lactation, with delivery, with mention of postpartum complication
678.01	Fetal hematologic conditions, delivered, with or without mention of antepartum condition
678.11	Fetal conjoined twins, delivered, with or without mention of antepartum condition
679.00	Maternal complications from in utero procedure, unspecified as to episode of care or not applicable
679.01	Maternal complications from in utero procedure, delivered, with or without mention of antepartum condition
679.02	Maternal complications from in utero procedure, delivered, with mention of postpartum complication

| 679.11 | Fetal complications from in utero procedure, delivered, with or without mention of antepartum condition |
| 679.12 | Fetal complications from in utero procedure, delivered, with mention of postpartum complication |

Operating Room Procedures
74.0	Classical cesarean section
74.1	Low cervical cesarean section
74.2	Extraperitoneal cesarean section
74.4	Cesarean section of other specified type
74.99	Other cesarean section of unspecified type

DRG 766   Cesarean Section without CC/MCC
GMLOS 2.9   AMLOS 3.1   RW 0.8586   ☑

Select principal diagnosis and operating room procedure listed under DRG 765

DRG 767   Vaginal Delivery with Sterilization and/or D&C
GMLOS 2.5   AMLOS 3.2   RW 0.9225   ☑

Select principal diagnosis listed under DRG 765

Operating Room Procedures
66.2*	Bilateral endoscopic destruction or occlusion of fallopian tubes
66.3*	Other bilateral destruction or occlusion of fallopian tubes
66.4	Total unilateral salpingectomy
66.5*	Total bilateral salpingectomy
66.63	Bilateral partial salpingectomy, not otherwise specified
66.69	Other partial salpingectomy
66.92	Unilateral destruction or occlusion of fallopian tube
66.97	Burying of fimbriae in uterine wall
69.02	Dilation and curettage following delivery or abortion
69.09	Other dilation and curettage of uterus
69.52	Aspiration curettage following delivery or abortion

DRG 768   Vaginal Delivery with O.R. Procedure Except Sterilization and/or D&C
GMLOS 4.7   AMLOS 5.8   RW 1.8304

Select principal diagnosis listed under DRG 765

Operating Room Procedures
38.7	Interruption of the vena cava
39.98	Control of hemorrhage, not otherwise specified
39.99	Other operations on vessels
40.24	Excision of inguinal lymph node
40.3	Regional lymph node excision
48.79	Other repair of rectum
49.46	Excision of hemorrhoids
54.11	Exploratory laparotomy
54.21	Laparoscopy
66.62	Salpingectomy with removal of tubal pregnancy
67.1*	Diagnostic procedures on cervix
67.2	Conization of cervix
67.3*	Other excision or destruction of lesion or tissue of cervix
67.62	Repair of fistula of cervix
68.0	Hysterotomy
68.3*	Subtotal abdominal hysterectomy
68.41	Laparoscopic total abdominal hysterectomy
68.49	Other and unspecified total abdominal hysterectomy
68.5*	Vaginal hysterectomy
68.61	Laparoscopic radical abdominal hysterectomy
68.69	Other and unspecified radical abdominal hysterectomy
68.71	Laparoscopic radical vaginal hysterectomy [LRVH]
68.79	Other and unspecified radical vaginal hysterectomy
68.9	Other and unspecified hysterectomy
69.41	Suture of laceration of uterus
69.49	Other repair of uterus
69.95	Incision of cervix

70.12	Culdotomy
70.23	Biopsy of cul-de-sac
70.29	Other diagnostic procedures on vagina and cul-de-sac
70.32	Excision or destruction of lesion of cul-de-sac
71.22	Incision of Bartholin's gland (cyst)
71.23	Marsupialization of Bartholin's gland (cyst)
71.24	Excision or other destruction of Bartholin's gland (cyst)
71.29	Other operations on Bartholin's gland
73.94	Pubiotomy to assist delivery
74.3	Removal of extratubal ectopic pregnancy
75.36	Correction of fetal defect
75.52	Repair of current obstetric laceration of corpus uteri
75.93	Surgical correction of inverted uterus
75.99	Other obstetric operations

DRG 769 Postpartum and Postabortion Diagnoses with O.R. Procedure
GMLOS 3.3 AMLOS 5.0 RW 1.4668

Select principal diagnosis listed under DRG 776 with any operating room procedure

DRG 770 Abortion with D&C, Aspiration Curettage or Hysterotomy
GMLOS 1.6 AMLOS 2.0 RW 0.6489 ☑

Select principal diagnosis listed under DRG 779

Operating Room Procedures

69.0*	Dilation and curettage of uterus
69.51	Aspiration curettage of uterus for termination of pregnancy
69.52	Aspiration curettage following delivery or abortion
74.91	Hysterotomy to terminate pregnancy

MEDICAL

DRG 774 Vaginal Delivery with Complicating Diagnoses
GMLOS 2.6 AMLOS 3.3 RW 0.7217 ☑

Principal Diagnosis

641.01	Placenta previa without hemorrhage, with delivery
641.11	Hemorrhage from placenta previa, with delivery
641.21	Premature separation of placenta, with delivery
641.31	Antepartum hemorrhage associated with coagulation defects, with delivery
641.81	Other antepartum hemorrhage, with delivery
641.91	Unspecified antepartum hemorrhage, with delivery
642.01	Benign essential hypertension with delivery
642.02	Benign essential hypertension, with delivery, with current postpartum complication
642.11	Hypertension secondary to renal disease, with delivery
642.12	Hypertension secondary to renal disease, with delivery, with current postpartum complication
642.21	Other pre-existing hypertension, with delivery
642.22	Other pre-existing hypertension, with delivery, with current postpartum complication
642.41	Mild or unspecified pre-eclampsia, with delivery
642.42	Mild or unspecified pre-eclampsia, with delivery, with current postpartum complication
642.51	Severe pre-eclampsia, with delivery
642.52	Severe pre-eclampsia, with delivery, with current postpartum complication
642.61	Eclampsia, with delivery
642.62	Eclampsia, with delivery, with current postpartum complication
642.71	Pre-eclampsia or eclampsia superimposed on pre-existing hypertension, with delivery
642.72	Pre-eclampsia or eclampsia superimposed on pre-existing hypertension, with delivery, with current postpartum complication
642.91	Unspecified hypertension, with delivery
642.92	Unspecified hypertension, with delivery, with current postpartum complication
647.01	Maternal syphilis, complicating pregnancy, with delivery
647.02	Maternal syphilis, complicating pregnancy, with delivery, with current postpartum complication
647.11	Maternal gonorrhea with delivery
647.12	Maternal gonorrhea, with delivery, with current postpartum complication
647.21	Other maternal venereal diseases with delivery
647.22	Other maternal venereal diseases with delivery, with current postpartum complication
647.31	Maternal tuberculosis with delivery
647.32	Maternal tuberculosis with delivery, with current postpartum complication
647.41	Maternal malaria with delivery
647.42	Maternal malaria with delivery, with current postpartum complication
647.51	Maternal rubella with delivery
647.52	Maternal rubella with delivery, with current postpartum complication
647.61	Other maternal viral disease with delivery
647.62	Other maternal viral disease with delivery, with current postpartum complication
647.81	Other specified maternal infectious and parasitic disease with delivery
647.82	Other specified maternal infectious and parasitic disease with delivery, with current postpartum complication
647.91	Unspecified maternal infection or infestation with delivery
647.92	Unspecified maternal infection or infestation with delivery, with current postpartum complication
648.01	Maternal diabetes mellitus with delivery
648.02	Maternal diabetes mellitus with delivery, with current postpartum complication
648.51	Maternal congenital cardiovascular disorders, with delivery
648.52	Maternal congenital cardiovascular disorders, with delivery, with current postpartum complication
648.61	Other maternal cardiovascular diseases, with delivery
648.62	Other maternal cardiovascular diseases, with delivery, with current postpartum complication
649.8*	Onset (spontaneous) of labor after 37 completed weeks of gestation but before 39 completed weeks gestation, with delivery by (planned) cesarean section
659.21	Unspecified maternal pyrexia during labor, delivered
659.31	Generalized infection during labor, delivered
666.02	Third-stage postpartum hemorrhage, with delivery
666.12	Other immediate postpartum hemorrhage, with delivery
666.22	Delayed and secondary postpartum hemorrhage, with delivery
666.32	Postpartum coagulation defects, with delivery
667.02	Retained placenta without hemorrhage, with delivery, with mention of postpartum complication
667.12	Retained portions of placenta or membranes, without hemorrhage, delivered, with mention of postpartum complication
668.01	Pulmonary complications of the administration of anesthesia or other sedation in labor and delivery, delivered
668.02	Pulmonary complications of the administration of anesthesia or other sedation in labor and delivery, delivered, with mention of postpartum complication
668.11	Cardiac complications of the administration of anesthesia or other sedation in labor and delivery, delivered
668.12	Cardiac complications of the administration of anesthesia or other sedation in labor and delivery, delivered, with mention of postpartum complication

MDC 14: Pregnancy, Childbirth And The Puerperium—MEDICAL

668.21	Central nervous system complications of the administration of anesthesia or other sedation in labor and delivery, delivered
668.22	Central nervous system complications of the administration of anesthesia or other sedation in labor and delivery, delivered, with mention of postpartum complication
668.81	Other complications of the administration of anesthesia or other sedation in labor and delivery, delivered
668.82	Other complications of the administration of anesthesia or other sedation in labor and delivery, delivered, with mention of postpartum complication
668.91	Unspecified complication of the administration of anesthesia or other sedation in labor and delivery, delivered
668.92	Unspecified complication of the administration of anesthesia or other sedation in labor and delivery, delivered, with mention of postpartum complication
669.11	Shock during or following labor and delivery, with delivery, with or without mention of antepartum condition
669.12	Shock during or following labor and delivery, with delivery, with mention of postpartum complication
669.32	Acute kidney failure following labor and delivery, delivered, with mention of postpartum complication
669.41	Other complications of obstetrical surgery and procedures, with delivery, with or without mention of antepartum condition
669.42	Other complications of obstetrical surgery and procedures, with delivery, with mention of postpartum complication
670.02	Major puerperal infection, unspecified, delivered, with mention of postpartum complication
670.12	Puerperal endometritis, delivered, with mention of postpartum complication
670.22	Puerperal sepsis, delivered, with mention of postpartum complication
670.32	Puerperal septic thrombophlebitis, delivered, with mention of postpartum complication
670.82	Other major puerperal infection, delivered, with mention of postpartum complication
671.31	Deep phlebothrombosis, antepartum, with delivery
671.42	Deep phlebothrombosis, postpartum, with delivery
671.51	Other phlebitis and thrombosis with delivery, with or without mention of antepartum condition
671.52	Other phlebitis and thrombosis with delivery, with mention of postpartum complication
672.02	Puerperal pyrexia of unknown origin, delivered, with mention of postpartum complication
673.01	Obstetrical air embolism, with delivery, with or without mention of antepartum condition
673.02	Obstetrical air embolism, with delivery, with mention of postpartum complication
673.11	Amniotic fluid embolism, with delivery, with or without mention of antepartum condition
673.12	Amniotic fluid embolism, with delivery, with mention of postpartum complication
673.21	Obstetrical blood-clot embolism, with delivery, with or without mention of antepartum condition
673.22	Obstetrical blood-clot embolism, with mention of postpartum complication
673.31	Obstetrical pyemic and septic embolism, with delivery, with or without mention of antepartum condition
673.32	Obstetrical pyemic and septic embolism, with delivery, with mention of postpartum complication
673.81	Other obstetrical pulmonary embolism, with delivery, with or without mention of antepartum condition
673.82	Other obstetrical pulmonary embolism, with delivery, with mention of postpartum complication
674.01	Cerebrovascular disorder, with delivery, with or without mention of antepartum condition
674.02	Cerebrovascular disorder, with delivery, with mention of postpartum complication
674.12	Disruption of cesarean wound, with delivery, with mention of postpartum complication
674.22	Disruption of perineal wound, with delivery, with mention of postpartum complication
674.32	Other complication of obstetrical surgical wounds, with delivery, with mention of postpartum complication
674.51	Peripartum cardiomyopathy, delivered, with or without mention of antepartum condition
674.52	Peripartum cardiomyopathy, delivered, with mention of postpartum condition
674.82	Other complication of puerperium, with delivery, with mention of postpartum complication
675.01	Infection of nipple associated with childbirth, delivered, with or without mention of antepartum condition
675.02	Infection of nipple associated with childbirth, delivered with mention of postpartum complication
675.11	Abscess of breast associated with childbirth, delivered, with or without mention of antepartum condition
675.12	Abscess of breast associated with childbirth, delivered, with mention of postpartum complication
675.21	Nonpurulent mastitis, delivered, with or without mention of antepartum condition
675.22	Nonpurulent mastitis, delivered, with mention of postpartum complication
679.01	Maternal complications from in utero procedure, delivered, with or without mention of antepartum condition
679.02	Maternal complications from in utero procedure, delivered, with mention of postpartum complication

OR

Principal Diagnosis

640.01	Threatened abortion, delivered
640.81	Other specified hemorrhage in early pregnancy, delivered
640.91	Unspecified hemorrhage in early pregnancy, delivered
642.31	Transient hypertension of pregnancy, with delivery
642.32	Transient hypertension of pregnancy, with delivery, with current postpartum complication
643.01	Mild hyperemesis gravidarum, delivered
643.11	Hyperemesis gravidarum with metabolic disturbance, delivered
643.21	Late vomiting of pregnancy, delivered
643.81	Other vomiting complicating pregnancy, delivered
643.91	Unspecified vomiting of pregnancy, delivered
644.21	Early onset of delivery, delivered, with or without mention of antepartum condition
645.11	Post term pregnancy, delivered, with or without mention of antepartum condition
645.21	Prolonged pregnancy, delivered, with or without mention of antepartum condition
646.00	Papyraceous fetus, unspecified as to episode of care
646.01	Papyraceous fetus, delivered, with or without mention of antepartum condition
646.11	Edema or excessive weight gain in pregnancy, with delivery, with or without mention of antepartum complication
646.12	Edema or excessive weight gain in pregnancy, with delivery, with current postpartum complication
646.21	Unspecified renal disease in pregnancy, with delivery
646.22	Unspecified renal disease in pregnancy, with delivery, with current postpartum complication
646.31	Pregnancy complication, recurrent pregnancy loss, with or without mention of antepartum condition
646.41	Peripheral neuritis in pregnancy, with delivery
646.42	Peripheral neuritis in pregnancy, with delivery, with current postpartum complication
646.51	Asymptomatic bacteriuria in pregnancy, with delivery
646.52	Asymptomatic bacteriuria in pregnancy, with delivery, with current postpartum complication
646.61	Infections of genitourinary tract in pregnancy, with delivery
646.62	Infections of genitourinary tract in pregnancy, with delivery, with current postpartum complication

T *Transfer DRG*   SP *Special Payment*   ☑ *Optimization Potential*   ▽ *Targeted Potential*   * *Code Range*   ● *New DRG*   ▲ *Revised DRG Title*

142   Valid 10/01/2012-09/30/2013   © 2012 OptumInsight, Inc.

646.71	Liver and biliary tract disorders in pregnancy, delivered, with or without mention of antepartum condition
646.81	Other specified complication of pregnancy, with delivery
646.82	Other specified complications of pregnancy, with delivery, with current postpartum complication
646.91	Unspecified complication of pregnancy, with delivery
648.11	Maternal thyroid dysfunction with delivery, with or without mention of antepartum condition
648.12	Maternal thyroid dysfunction with delivery, with current postpartum complication
648.21	Maternal anemia, with delivery
648.22	Maternal anemia with delivery, with current postpartum complication
648.31	Maternal drug dependence, with delivery
648.32	Maternal drug dependence, with delivery, with current postpartum complication
648.41	Maternal mental disorders, with delivery
648.42	Maternal mental disorders, with delivery, with current postpartum complication
648.71	Bone and joint disorders of maternal back, pelvis, and lower limbs, with delivery
648.72	Bone and joint disorders of maternal back, pelvis, and lower limbs, with delivery, with current postpartum complication
648.81	Abnormal maternal glucose tolerance, with delivery
648.82	Abnormal maternal glucose tolerance, with delivery, with current postpartum complication
648.91	Other current maternal conditions classifiable elsewhere, with delivery
648.92	Other current maternal conditions classifiable elsewhere, with delivery, with current postpartum complication
649.01	Tobacco use disorder complicating pregnancy, childbirth, or the puerperium, delivered, with or without mention of antepartum condition
649.02	Tobacco use disorder complicating pregnancy, childbirth, or the puerperium, delivered, with mention of postpartum complication
649.11	Obesity complicating pregnancy, childbirth, or the puerperium, delivered, with or without mention of antepartum condition
649.12	Obesity complicating pregnancy, childbirth, or the puerperium, delivered, with mention of postpartum complication
649.21	Bariatric surgery status complicating pregnancy, childbirth, or the puerperium, delivered, with or without mention of antepartum condition
649.22	Bariatric surgery status complicating pregnancy, childbirth, or the puerperium, delivered, with mention of postpartum complication
649.31	Coagulation defects complicating pregnancy, childbirth, or the puerperium, delivered, with or without mention of antepartum condition
649.32	Coagulation defects complicating pregnancy, childbirth, or the puerperium, delivered, with mention of postpartum complication
649.41	Epilepsy complicating pregnancy, childbirth, or the puerperium, delivered, with or without mention of antepartum condition
649.42	Epilepsy complicating pregnancy, childbirth, or the puerperium, delivered, with mention of postpartum complication
649.51	Spotting complicating pregnancy, delivered, with or without mention of antepartum condition
649.61	Uterine size date discrepancy, delivered, with or without mention of antepartum condition
649.62	Uterine size date discrepancy, delivered, with mention of postpartum complication
649.71	Cervical shortening, delivered, with or without mention of antepartum condition
649.81	Onset (spontaneous) of labor after 37 completed weeks of gestation but before 39 completed weeks gestation, with delivery by (planned) cesarean section, delivered, with or without mention of antepartum condition
649.82	Onset (spontaneous) of labor after 37 completed weeks of gestation but before 39 completed weeks gestation, with delivery by (planned) cesarean section, delivered, with mention of postpartum complication
650	Normal delivery
651.01	Twin pregnancy, delivered
651.11	Triplet pregnancy, delivered
651.21	Quadruplet pregnancy, delivered
651.31	Twin pregnancy with fetal loss and retention of one fetus, delivered
651.41	Triplet pregnancy with fetal loss and retention of one or more, delivered
651.51	Quadruplet pregnancy with fetal loss and retention of one or more, delivered
651.61	Other multiple pregnancy with fetal loss and retention of one or more fetus(es), delivered
651.71	Multiple gestation following (elective) fetal reduction, delivered, with or without mention of antepartum condition
651.81	Other specified multiple gestation, delivered
651.91	Unspecified multiple gestation, delivered
652.01	Unstable lie of fetus, delivered
652.11	Breech or other malpresentation successfully converted to cephalic presentation, delivered
652.21	Breech presentation without mention of version, delivered
652.31	Transverse or oblique fetal presentation, delivered
652.41	Fetal face or brow presentation, delivered
652.51	High fetal head at term, delivered
652.61	Multiple gestation with malpresentation of one fetus or more, delivered
652.71	Prolapsed arm of fetus, delivered
652.81	Other specified malposition or malpresentation of fetus, delivered
652.91	Unspecified malposition or malpresentation of fetus, delivered
653.01	Major abnormality of bony pelvis, not further specified, delivered
653.11	Generally contracted pelvis in pregnancy, delivered
653.21	Inlet contraction of pelvis in pregnancy, delivered
653.31	Outlet contraction of pelvis in pregnancy, delivered
653.41	Fetopelvic disproportion, delivered
653.51	Unusually large fetus causing disproportion, delivered
653.61	Hydrocephalic fetus causing disproportion, delivered
653.71	Other fetal abnormality causing disproportion, delivered
653.81	Fetal disproportion of other origin, delivered
653.91	Unspecified fetal disproportion, delivered
654.01	Congenital abnormalities of pregnant uterus, delivered
654.02	Congenital abnormalities of pregnant uterus, delivered, with mention of postpartum complication
654.11	Tumors of body of uterus, delivered
654.12	Tumors of body of uterus, delivered, with mention of postpartum complication
654.21	Previous cesarean delivery, delivered, with or without mention of antepartum condition
654.31	Retroverted and incarcerated gravid uterus, delivered
654.32	Retroverted and incarcerated gravid uterus, delivered, with mention of postpartum complication
654.41	Other abnormalities in shape or position of gravid uterus and of neighboring structures, delivered
654.42	Other abnormalities in shape or position of gravid uterus and of neighboring structures, delivered, with mention of postpartum complication
654.51	Cervical incompetence, delivered
654.52	Cervical incompetence, delivered, with mention of postpartum complication
654.61	Other congenital or acquired abnormality of cervix, with delivery

Surgical   Medical   CC Indicator   MCC Indicator   Procedure Proxy

654.62	Other congenital or acquired abnormality of cervix, delivered, with mention of postpartum complication
654.71	Congenital or acquired abnormality of vagina, with delivery
654.72	Congenital or acquired abnormality of vagina, delivered, with mention of postpartum complication
654.81	Congenital or acquired abnormality of vulva, with delivery
654.82	Congenital or acquired abnormality of vulva, delivered, with mention of postpartum complication
654.91	Other and unspecified abnormality of organs and soft tissues of pelvis, with delivery
654.92	Other and unspecified abnormality of organs and soft tissues of pelvis, delivered, with mention of postpartum complication
655.01	Central nervous system malformation in fetus, with delivery
655.11	Chromosomal abnormality in fetus affecting management of mother, with delivery
655.21	Hereditary disease in family possibly affecting fetus, affecting management of mother, with delivery
655.31	Suspected damage to fetus from viral disease in mother, affecting management of mother, with delivery
655.41	Suspected damage to fetus from other disease in mother, affecting management of mother, with delivery
655.51	Suspected damage to fetus from drugs, affecting management of mother, delivered
655.61	Suspected damage to fetus from radiation, affecting management of mother, delivered
655.71	Decreased fetal movements, affecting management of mother, delivered
655.81	Other known or suspected fetal abnormality, not elsewhere classified, affecting management of mother, delivery
655.91	Unspecified fetal abnormality affecting management of mother, delivery
656.01	Fetal-maternal hemorrhage, with delivery
656.11	Rhesus isoimmunization affecting management of mother, delivered
656.21	Isoimmunization from other and unspecified blood-group incompatibility, affecting management of mother, delivered
656.30	Fetal distress affecting management of mother, unspecified as to episode of care
656.31	Fetal distress affecting management of mother, delivered
656.40	Intrauterine death affecting management of mother, unspecified as to episode of care
656.41	Intrauterine death affecting management of mother, delivered
656.51	Poor fetal growth, affecting management of mother, delivered
656.61	Excessive fetal growth affecting management of mother, delivered
656.71	Other placental conditions affecting management of mother, delivered
656.81	Other specified fetal and placental problems affecting management of mother, delivered
656.91	Unspecified fetal and placental problem affecting management of mother, delivered
657.01	Polyhydramnios, with delivery
658.01	Oligohydramnios, delivered
658.10	Premature rupture of membranes in pregnancy, unspecified as to episode of care
658.11	Premature rupture of membranes in pregnancy, delivered
658.20	Delayed delivery after spontaneous or unspecified rupture of membranes, unspecified as to episode of care
658.21	Delayed delivery after spontaneous or unspecified rupture of membranes, delivered
658.30	Delayed delivery after artificial rupture of membranes, unspecified as to episode of care
658.31	Delayed delivery after artificial rupture of membranes, delivered
658.40	Infection of amniotic cavity, unspecified as to episode of care
658.41	Infection of amniotic cavity, delivered
658.81	Other problem associated with amniotic cavity and membranes, delivered
658.91	Unspecified problem associated with amniotic cavity and membranes, delivered
659.00	Failed mechanical induction of labor, unspecified as to episode of care
659.01	Failed mechanical induction of labor, delivered
659.10	Failed medical or unspecified induction of labor, unspecified as to episode of care
659.11	Failed medical or unspecified induction of labor, delivered
659.20	Unspecified maternal pyrexia during labor, unspecified as to episode of care
659.30	Generalized infection during labor, unspecified as to episode of care
659.41	Grand multiparity, delivered, with or without mention of antepartum condition
659.50	Elderly primigravida, unspecified as to episode of care
659.51	Elderly primigravida, delivered
659.60	Elderly multigravida, unspecified as to episode of care or not applicable
659.61	Elderly multigravida, delivered, with mention of antepartum condition
659.70	Abnormality in fetal heart rate or rhythm, unspecified as to episode of care or not applicable
659.71	Abnormality in fetal heart rate or rhythm, delivered, with or without mention of antepartum condition
659.80	Other specified indication for care or intervention related to labor and delivery, unspecified as to episode of care
659.81	Other specified indication for care or intervention related to labor and delivery, delivered
659.90	Unspecified indication for care or intervention related to labor and delivery, unspecified as to episode of care
659.91	Unspecified indication for care or intervention related to labor and delivery, delivered
660.00	Obstruction caused by malposition of fetus at onset of labor, unspecified as to episode of care
660.01	Obstruction caused by malposition of fetus at onset of labor, delivered
660.10	Obstruction by bony pelvis during labor and delivery, unspecified as to episode of care
660.11	Obstruction by bony pelvis during labor and delivery, delivered
660.20	Obstruction by abnormal pelvic soft tissues during labor and delivery, unspecified as to episode of care
660.21	Obstruction by abnormal pelvic soft tissues during labor and delivery, delivered
660.30	Deep transverse arrest and persistent occipitoposterior position during labor and delivery, unspecified as to episode of care
660.31	Deep transverse arrest and persistent occipitoposterior position during labor and deliver, delivered
660.40	Shoulder (girdle) dystocia during labor and delivery, unspecified as to episode of care
660.41	Shoulder (girdle) dystocia during labor and deliver, delivered
660.50	Locked twins during labor and delivery, unspecified as to episode of care in pregnancy
660.51	Locked twins, delivered
660.60	Unspecified failed trial of labor, unspecified as to episode
660.61	Unspecified failed trial of labor, delivered
660.70	Unspecified failed forceps or vacuum extractor, unspecified as to episode of care
660.71	Unspecified failed forceps or vacuum extractor, delivered
660.80	Other causes of obstructed labor, unspecified as to episode of care
660.81	Other causes of obstructed labor, delivered
660.90	Unspecified obstructed labor, unspecified as to episode of care
660.91	Unspecified obstructed labor, with delivery
661.00	Primary uterine inertia, unspecified as to episode of care
661.01	Primary uterine inertia, with delivery

661.10	Secondary uterine inertia, unspecified as to episode of care
661.11	Secondary uterine inertia, with delivery
661.20	Other and unspecified uterine inertia, unspecified as to episode of care
661.21	Other and unspecified uterine inertia, with delivery
661.30	Precipitate labor, unspecified as to episode of care
661.31	Precipitate labor, with delivery
661.40	Hypertonic, incoordinate, or prolonged uterine contractions, unspecified as to episode of care
661.41	Hypertonic, incoordinate, or prolonged uterine contractions, with delivery
661.90	Unspecified abnormality of labor, unspecified as to episode of care
661.91	Unspecified abnormality of labor, with delivery
662.00	Prolonged first stage of labor, unspecified as to episode of care
662.01	Prolonged first stage of labor, delivered
662.10	Unspecified prolonged labor, unspecified as to episode of care
662.11	Unspecified prolonged labor, delivered
662.20	Prolonged second stage of labor, unspecified as to episode of care
662.21	Prolonged second stage of labor, delivered
662.30	Delayed delivery of second twin, triplet, etc., unspecified as to episode of care
662.31	Delayed delivery of second twin, triplet, etc., delivered
663.00	Prolapse of cord, complicating labor and delivery, unspecified as to episode of care
663.01	Prolapse of cord, complicating labor and delivery, delivered
663.10	Cord around neck, with compression, complicating labor and delivery, unspecified as to episode of care
663.11	Cord around neck, with compression, complicating labor and delivery, delivered
663.20	Other and unspecified cord entanglement, with compression, complicating labor and delivery, unspecified as to episode of care
663.21	Other and unspecified cord entanglement, with compression, complicating labor and delivery, delivered
663.30	Other and unspecified cord entanglement, without mention of compression, complicating labor and delivery, unspecified as to episode of care
663.31	Other and unspecified cord entanglement, without mention of compression, complicating labor and delivery, delivered
663.40	Short cord complicating labor and delivery, unspecified as to episode of care
663.41	Short cord complicating labor and delivery, delivered
663.50	Vasa previa complicating labor and delivery, unspecified as to episode of care
663.51	Vasa previa complicating labor and delivery, delivered
663.60	Vascular lesions of cord complicating labor and delivery, unspecified as to episode of care
663.61	Vascular lesions of cord complicating labor and delivery, delivered
663.80	Other umbilical cord complications during labor and delivery, unspecified as to episode of care
663.81	Other umbilical cord complications during labor and delivery, delivered
663.90	Unspecified umbilical cord complication during labor and delivery, unspecified as to episode of care
663.91	Unspecified umbilical cord complication during labor and delivery, delivered
664.00	First-degree perineal laceration, unspecified as to episode of care in pregnancy
664.01	First-degree perineal laceration, with delivery
664.10	Second-degree perineal laceration, unspecified as to episode of care in pregnancy
664.11	Second-degree perineal laceration, with delivery
664.20	Third-degree perineal laceration, unspecified as to episode of care in pregnancy
664.21	Third-degree perineal laceration, with delivery

664.30	Fourth-degree perineal laceration, unspecified as to episode of care in pregnancy
664.31	Fourth-degree perineal laceration, with delivery
664.40	Unspecified perineal laceration, unspecified as to episode of care in pregnancy
664.41	Unspecified perineal laceration, with delivery
664.50	Vulvar and perineal hematoma, unspecified as to episode of care in pregnancy
664.51	Vulvar and perineal hematoma, with delivery
664.60	Anal sphincter tear complicating delivery, not associated with third-degree perineal laceration, unspecified as to episode of care or not applicable
664.61	Anal sphincter tear complicating delivery, not associated with third-degree perineal laceration, delivered, with or without mention of antepartum condition
664.80	Other specified trauma to perineum and vulva, unspecified as to episode of care in pregnancy
664.81	Other specified trauma to perineum and vulva, with delivery
664.90	Unspecified trauma to perineum and vulva, unspecified as to episode of care in pregnancy
664.91	Unspecified trauma to perineum and vulva, with delivery
665.00	Rupture of uterus before onset of labor, unspecified as to episode of care
665.01	Rupture of uterus before onset of labor, with delivery
665.10	Rupture of uterus during labor, unspecified as to episode
665.11	Rupture of uterus during labor, with delivery
665.20	Inversion of uterus, unspecified as to episode of care in pregnancy
665.22	Inversion of uterus, delivered with postpartum complication
665.30	Laceration of cervix, unspecified as to episode of care in pregnancy
665.31	Laceration of cervix, with delivery
665.40	High vaginal laceration, unspecified as to episode of care in pregnancy
665.41	High vaginal laceration, with delivery
665.50	Other injury to pelvic organs, unspecified as to episode of care in pregnancy
665.51	Other injury to pelvic organs, with delivery
665.60	Damage to pelvic joints and ligaments, unspecified as to episode of care in pregnancy
665.61	Damage to pelvic joints and ligaments, with delivery
665.70	Pelvic hematoma, unspecified as to episode of care
665.71	Pelvic hematoma, with delivery
665.72	Pelvic hematoma, delivered with postpartum complication
665.80	Other specified obstetrical trauma, unspecified as to episode of care
665.81	Other specified obstetrical trauma, with delivery
665.82	Other specified obstetrical trauma, delivered, with postpartum
665.90	Unspecified obstetrical trauma, unspecified as to episode of care
665.91	Unspecified obstetrical trauma, with delivery
665.92	Unspecified obstetrical trauma, delivered, with postpartum complication
668.00	Pulmonary complications of the administration of anesthesia or other sedation in labor and delivery, unspecified as to episode of care
668.10	Cardiac complications of the administration of anesthesia or other sedation in labor and delivery, unspecified as to episode of care
668.20	Central nervous system complications of the administration of anesthesia or other sedation in labor and delivery, unspecified as to episode of care
668.80	Other complications of the administration of anesthesia or other sedation in labor and delivery, unspecified as to episode of care
668.90	Unspecified complication of the administration of anesthesia or other sedation in labor and delivery, unspecified as to episode of care

MDC 14: Pregnancy, Childbirth And The Puerperium—MEDICAL

Surgical   *Medical*   CC Indicator   MCC Indicator   Procedure Proxy

MDC 14: Pregnancy, Childbirth And The Puerperium—MEDICAL

669.00 Maternal distress complicating labor and delivery, unspecified as to episode of care
669.01 Maternal distress, with delivery, with or without mention of antepartum condition
669.02 Maternal distress, with delivery, with mention of postpartum complication
669.10 Shock during or following labor and delivery, unspecified as to episode of care
669.20 Maternal hypotension syndrome complicating labor and delivery, unspecified as to episode of care
669.21 Maternal hypotension syndrome, with delivery, with or without mention of antepartum condition
669.22 Maternal hypotension syndrome, with delivery, with mention of postpartum complication
669.30 Acute kidney failure following labor and delivery, unspecified as to episode of care or not applicable
669.40 Other complications of obstetrical surgery and procedures, unspecified as to episode of care
669.50 Forceps or vacuum extractor delivery without mention of indication, unspecified as to episode of care
669.51 Forceps or vacuum extractor delivery without mention of indication, delivered, with or without mention of antepartum condition
669.60 Breech extraction, without mention of indication, unspecified as to episode of care
669.61 Breech extraction, without mention of indication, delivered, with or without mention of antepartum condition
669.70 Cesarean delivery, without mention of indication, unspecified as to episode of care
669.71 Cesarean delivery, without mention of indication, delivered, with or without mention of antepartum condition
669.80 Other complication of labor and delivery, unspecified as to episode of care
669.81 Other complication of labor and delivery, delivered, with or without mention of antepartum condition
669.82 Other complication of labor and delivery, delivered, with mention of postpartum complication
669.90 Unspecified complication of labor and delivery, unspecified as to episode of care
669.91 Unspecified complication of labor and delivery, with delivery, with or without mention of antepartum condition
669.92 Unspecified complication of labor and delivery, with delivery, with mention of postpartum complication
671.01 Varicose veins of legs, with delivery, with or without mention of antepartum condition
671.02 Varicose veins of legs, with delivery, with mention of postpartum complication
671.11 Varicose veins of vulva and perineum, with delivery, with or without mention of antepartum condition
671.12 Varicose veins of vulva and perineum, with delivery, with mention of postpartum complication
671.21 Superficial thrombophlebitis with delivery, with or without mention of antepartum condition
671.22 Superficial thrombophlebitis with delivery, with mention of postpartum complication
671.81 Other venous complication, with delivery, with or without mention of antepartum condition
671.82 Other venous complication, with delivery, with mention of postpartum complication
671.91 Unspecified venous complication, with delivery, with or without mention of antepartum condition
671.92 Unspecified venous complication, with delivery, with mention of postpartum complication
674.42 Placental polyp, with delivery, with mention of postpartum complication
674.92 Unspecified complications of puerperium, with delivery, with mention of postpartum complication
675.81 Other specified infection of the breast and nipple associated with childbirth, delivered, with or without mention of antepartum condition

675.82 Other specified infection of the breast and nipple associated with childbirth, delivered, with mention of postpartum complication
675.91 Unspecified infection of the breast and nipple, delivered, with or without mention of antepartum condition
675.92 Unspecified infection of the breast and nipple, delivered, with mention of postpartum complication
676.01 Retracted nipple, delivered, with or without mention of antepartum condition
676.02 Retracted nipple, delivered, with mention of postpartum complication
676.11 Cracked nipple, delivered, with or without mention of antepartum condition
676.12 Cracked nipple, delivered, with mention of postpartum complication
676.21 Engorgement of breasts, delivered, with or without mention of antepartum condition
676.22 Engorgement of breasts, delivered, with mention of postpartum complication
676.31 Other and unspecified disorder of breast associated with childbirth, delivered, with or without mention of antepartum condition
676.32 Other and unspecified disorder of breast associated with childbirth, delivered, with mention of postpartum complication
676.41 Failure of lactation, with delivery, with or without mention of antepartum condition
676.42 Failure of lactation, with delivery, with mention of postpartum complication
676.51 Suppressed lactation, with delivery, with or without mention of antepartum condition
676.52 Suppressed lactation, with delivery, with mention of postpartum complication
676.61 Galactorrhea, with delivery, with or without mention of antepartum condition
676.62 Galactorrhea, with delivery, with mention of postpartum complication
676.81 Other disorder of lactation, with delivery, with or without mention of antepartum condition
676.82 Other disorder of lactation, with delivery, with mention of postpartum complication
676.91 Unspecified disorder of lactation, with delivery, with or without mention of antepartum condition
676.92 Unspecified disorder of lactation, with delivery, with mention of postpartum complication
678.01 Fetal hematologic conditions, delivered, with or without mention of antepartum condition
678.11 Fetal conjoined twins, delivered, with or without mention of antepartum condition
679.00 Maternal complications from in utero procedure, unspecified as to episode of care or not applicable
679.11 Fetal complications from in utero procedure, delivered, with or without mention of antepartum condition
679.12 Fetal complications from in utero procedure, delivered, with mention of postpartum complication

AND

Secondary Diagnosis
641.01 Placenta previa without hemorrhage, with delivery
641.11 Hemorrhage from placenta previa, with delivery
641.21 Premature separation of placenta, with delivery
641.31 Antepartum hemorrhage associated with coagulation defects, with delivery
641.81 Other antepartum hemorrhage, with delivery
641.91 Unspecified antepartum hemorrhage, with delivery
642.01 Benign essential hypertension with delivery
642.02 Benign essential hypertension, with delivery, with current postpartum complication
642.11 Hypertension secondary to renal disease, with delivery

Ⓣ *Transfer DRG*   🆂🅿 *Special Payment*   ☑ *Optimization Potential*   🆅 *Targeted Potential*   * *Code Range*   ● *New DRG*   ▲ *Revised DRG Title*

146   Valid 10/01/2012–09/30/2013   © 2012 OptumInsight, Inc.

642.12 Hypertension secondary to renal disease, with delivery, with current postpartum complication
642.21 Other pre-existing hypertension, with delivery
642.22 Other pre-existing hypertension, with delivery, with current postpartum complication
642.41 Mild or unspecified pre-eclampsia, with delivery
642.42 Mild or unspecified pre-eclampsia, with delivery, with current postpartum complication
642.51 Severe pre-eclampsia, with delivery
642.52 Severe pre-eclampsia, with delivery, with current postpartum complication
642.61 Eclampsia, with delivery
642.62 Eclampsia, with delivery, with current postpartum complication
642.71 Pre-eclampsia or eclampsia superimposed on pre-existing hypertension, with delivery
642.72 Pre-eclampsia or eclampsia superimposed on pre-existing hypertension, with delivery, with current postpartum complication
642.91 Unspecified hypertension, with delivery
642.92 Unspecified hypertension, with delivery, with current postpartum complication
647.01 Maternal syphilis, complicating pregnancy, with delivery
647.02 Maternal syphilis, complicating pregnancy, with delivery, with current postpartum complication
647.11 Maternal gonorrhea with delivery
647.12 Maternal gonorrhea, with delivery, with current postpartum complication
647.21 Other maternal venereal diseases with delivery
647.22 Other maternal venereal diseases with delivery, with current postpartum complication
647.31 Maternal tuberculosis with delivery
647.32 Maternal tuberculosis with delivery, with current postpartum complication
647.41 Maternal malaria with delivery
647.42 Maternal malaria with delivery, with current postpartum complication
647.51 Maternal rubella with delivery
647.52 Maternal rubella with delivery, with current postpartum complication
647.61 Other maternal viral disease with delivery
647.62 Other maternal viral disease with delivery, with current postpartum complication
647.81 Other specified maternal infectious and parasitic disease with delivery
647.82 Other specified maternal infectious and parasitic disease with delivery, with current postpartum complication
647.91 Unspecified maternal infection or infestation with delivery
647.92 Unspecified maternal infection or infestation with delivery, with current postpartum complication
648.01 Maternal diabetes mellitus with delivery
648.02 Maternal diabetes mellitus with delivery, with current postpartum complication
648.51 Maternal congenital cardiovascular disorders, with delivery
648.52 Maternal congenital cardiovascular disorders, with delivery, with current postpartum complication
648.61 Other maternal cardiovascular diseases, with delivery
648.62 Other maternal cardiovascular diseases, with delivery, with current postpartum complication
659.21 Unspecified maternal pyrexia during labor, delivered
659.31 Generalized infection during labor, delivered
666.02 Third-stage postpartum hemorrhage, with delivery
666.12 Other immediate postpartum hemorrhage, with delivery
666.22 Delayed and secondary postpartum hemorrhage, with delivery
666.32 Postpartum coagulation defects, with delivery
667.02 Retained placenta without hemorrhage, with delivery, with mention of postpartum complication
667.12 Retained portions of placenta or membranes, without hemorrhage, delivered, with mention of postpartum complication
668.01 Pulmonary complications of the administration of anesthesia or other sedation in labor and delivery, delivered
668.02 Pulmonary complications of the administration of anesthesia or other sedation in labor and delivery, delivered, with mention of postpartum complication
668.11 Cardiac complications of the administration of anesthesia or other sedation in labor and delivery, delivered
668.12 Cardiac complications of the administration of anesthesia or other sedation in labor and delivery, delivered, with mention of postpartum complication
668.21 Central nervous system complications of the administration of anesthesia or other sedation in labor and delivery, delivered
668.22 Central nervous system complications of the administration of anesthesia or other sedation in labor and delivery, delivered, with mention of postpartum complication
668.81 Other complications of the administration of anesthesia or other sedation in labor and delivery, delivered
668.82 Other complications of the administration of anesthesia or other sedation in labor and delivery, delivered, with mention of postpartum complication
668.91 Unspecified complication of the administration of anesthesia or other sedation in labor and delivery, delivered
668.92 Unspecified complication of the administration of anesthesia or other sedation in labor and delivery, delivered, with mention of postpartum complication
669.11 Shock during or following labor and delivery, with delivery, with or without mention of antepartum condition
669.12 Shock during or following labor and delivery, with delivery, with mention of postpartum complication
669.32 Acute kidney failure following labor and delivery, delivered, with mention of postpartum complication
669.41 Other complications of obstetrical surgery and procedures, with delivery, with or without mention of antepartum condition
669.42 Other complications of obstetrical surgery and procedures, with delivery, with mention of postpartum complication
670.02 Major puerperal infection, unspecified, delivered, with mention of postpartum complication
670.12 Puerperal endometritis, delivered, with mention of postpartum complication
670.22 Puerperal sepsis, delivered, with mention of postpartum complication
670.32 Puerperal septic thrombophlebitis, delivered, with mention of postpartum complication
670.82 Other major puerperal infection, delivered, with mention of postpartum complication
671.31 Deep phlebothrombosis, antepartum, with delivery
671.42 Deep phlebothrombosis, postpartum, with delivery
671.51 Other phlebitis and thrombosis with delivery, with or without mention of antepartum condition
671.52 Other phlebitis and thrombosis with delivery, with mention of postpartum complication
672.02 Puerperal pyrexia of unknown origin, delivered, with mention of postpartum complication
673.01 Obstetrical air embolism, with delivery, with or without mention of antepartum condition
673.02 Obstetrical air embolism, with delivery, with mention of postpartum complication
673.11 Amniotic fluid embolism, with delivery, with or without mention of antepartum condition
673.12 Amniotic fluid embolism, with delivery, with mention of postpartum complication
673.21 Obstetrical blood-clot embolism, with delivery, with or without mention of antepartum condition
673.22 Obstetrical blood-clot embolism, with mention of postpartum complication

673.31 Obstetrical pyemic and septic embolism, with delivery, with or without mention of antepartum condition
673.32 Obstetrical pyemic and septic embolism, with delivery, with mention of postpartum complication
673.81 Other obstetrical pulmonary embolism, with delivery, with or without mention of antepartum condition
673.82 Other obstetrical pulmonary embolism, with delivery, with mention of postpartum complication
674.01 Cerebrovascular disorder, with delivery, with or without mention of antepartum condition
674.02 Cerebrovascular disorder, with delivery, with mention of postpartum complication
674.12 Disruption of cesarean wound, with delivery, with mention of postpartum complication
674.22 Disruption of perineal wound, with delivery, with mention of postpartum complication
674.32 Other complication of obstetrical surgical wounds, with delivery, with mention of postpartum complication
674.51 Peripartum cardiomyopathy, delivered, with or without mention of antepartum condition
674.52 Peripartum cardiomyopathy, delivered, with mention of postpartum condition
674.82 Other complication of puerperium, with delivery, with mention of postpartum complication
675.01 Infection of nipple associated with childbirth, delivered, with or without mention of antepartum condition
675.02 Infection of nipple associated with childbirth, delivered with mention of postpartum complication
675.11 Abscess of breast associated with childbirth, delivered, with or without mention of antepartum condition
675.12 Abscess of breast associated with childbirth, delivered, with mention of postpartum complication
675.21 Nonpurulent mastitis, delivered, with or without mention of antepartum condition
675.22 Nonpurulent mastitis, delivered, with mention of postpartum complication
679.01 Maternal complications from in utero procedure, delivered, with or without mention of antepartum condition
679.02 Maternal complications from in utero procedure, delivered, with mention of postpartum complication

AND

Only Operating Room Procedures
48.71 Suture of laceration of rectum
49.59 Other anal sphincterotomy
67.51 Transabdominal cerclage of cervix
67.59 Other repair of cervical os
67.61 Suture of laceration of cervix
67.69 Other repair of cervix
70.13 Lysis of intraluminal adhesions of vagina
70.14 Other vaginotomy
70.24 Vaginal biopsy
70.31 Hymenectomy
70.33 Excision or destruction of lesion of vagina
70.71 Suture of laceration of vagina
70.79 Other repair of vagina
71.0* Incision of vulva and perineum
71.1* Diagnostic procedures on vulva
71.3 Other local excision or destruction of vulva and perineum
71.71 Suture of laceration of vulva or perineum
71.79 Other repair of vulva and perineum
73.99 Other operations to assist delivery
75.50 Repair of current obstetric laceration of uterus, not otherwise specified
75.51 Repair of current obstetric laceration of cervix
75.61 Repair of current obstetric laceration of bladder and urethra

OR

No Operating Room Procedures

DRG 775 Vaginal Delivery without Complicating Diagnoses
GMLOS 2.1   AMLOS 2.4   RW 0.5755   ☑

Principal Diagnosis
640.01 Threatened abortion, delivered
640.81 Other specified hemorrhage in early pregnancy, delivered
640.91 Unspecified hemorrhage in early pregnancy, delivered
642.31 Transient hypertension of pregnancy, with delivery
642.32 Transient hypertension of pregnancy, with delivery, with current postpartum complication
643.01 Mild hyperemesis gravidarum, delivered
643.11 Hyperemesis gravidarum with metabolic disturbance, delivered
643.21 Late vomiting of pregnancy, delivered
643.81 Other vomiting complicating pregnancy, delivered
643.91 Unspecified vomiting of pregnancy, delivered
644.21 Early onset of delivery, delivered, with or without mention of antepartum condition
645.11 Post term pregnancy, delivered, with or without mention of antepartum condition
645.21 Prolonged pregnancy, delivered, with or without mention of antepartum condition
646.00 Papyraceous fetus, unspecified as to episode of care
646.01 Papyraceous fetus, delivered, with or without mention of antepartum condition
646.11 Edema or excessive weight gain in pregnancy, with delivery, with or without mention of antepartum complication
646.12 Edema or excessive weight gain in pregnancy, with delivery, with current postpartum complication
646.21 Unspecified renal disease in pregnancy, with delivery
646.22 Unspecified renal disease in pregnancy, with delivery, with current postpartum complication
646.31 Pregnancy complication, recurrent pregnancy loss, with or without mention of antepartum condition
646.41 Peripheral neuritis in pregnancy, with delivery
646.42 Peripheral neuritis in pregnancy, with delivery, with current postpartum complication
646.51 Asymptomatic bacteriuria in pregnancy, with delivery
646.52 Asymptomatic bacteriuria in pregnancy, with delivery, with current postpartum complication
646.61 Infections of genitourinary tract in pregnancy, with delivery
646.62 Infections of genitourinary tract in pregnancy, with delivery, with current postpartum complication
646.71 Liver and biliary tract disorders in pregnancy, delivered, with or without mention of antepartum condition
646.81 Other specified complication of pregnancy, with delivery
646.82 Other specified complications of pregnancy, with delivery, with current postpartum complication
646.91 Unspecified complication of pregnancy, with delivery
648.11 Maternal thyroid dysfunction with delivery, with or without mention of antepartum condition
648.12 Maternal thyroid dysfunction with delivery, with current postpartum complication
648.21 Maternal anemia, with delivery
648.22 Maternal anemia with delivery, with current postpartum complication
648.31 Maternal drug dependence, with delivery
648.32 Maternal drug dependence, with delivery, with current postpartum complication
648.41 Maternal mental disorders, with delivery
648.42 Maternal mental disorders, with delivery, with current postpartum complication
648.71 Bone and joint disorders of maternal back, pelvis, and lower limbs, with delivery
648.72 Bone and joint disorders of maternal back, pelvis, and lower limbs, with delivery, with current postpartum complication
648.81 Abnormal maternal glucose tolerance, with delivery

648.82	Abnormal maternal glucose tolerance, with delivery, with current postpartum complication
648.91	Other current maternal conditions classifiable elsewhere, with delivery
648.92	Other current maternal conditions classifiable elsewhere, with delivery, with current postpartum complication
649.01	Tobacco use disorder complicating pregnancy, childbirth, or the puerperium, delivered, with or without mention of antepartum condition
649.02	Tobacco use disorder complicating pregnancy, childbirth, or the puerperium, delivered, with mention of postpartum complication
649.11	Obesity complicating pregnancy, childbirth, or the puerperium, delivered, with or without mention of antepartum condition
649.12	Obesity complicating pregnancy, childbirth, or the puerperium, delivered, with mention of postpartum complication
649.21	Bariatric surgery status complicating pregnancy, childbirth, or the puerperium, delivered, with or without mention of antepartum condition
649.22	Bariatric surgery status complicating pregnancy, childbirth, or the puerperium, delivered, with mention of postpartum complication
649.31	Coagulation defects complicating pregnancy, childbirth, or the puerperium, delivered, with or without mention of antepartum condition
649.32	Coagulation defects complicating pregnancy, childbirth, or the puerperium, delivered, with mention of postpartum complication
649.41	Epilepsy complicating pregnancy, childbirth, or the puerperium, delivered, with or without mention of antepartum condition
649.42	Epilepsy complicating pregnancy, childbirth, or the puerperium, delivered, with mention of postpartum complication
649.51	Spotting complicating pregnancy, delivered, with or without mention of antepartum condition
649.61	Uterine size date discrepancy, delivered, with or without mention of antepartum condition
649.62	Uterine size date discrepancy, delivered, with mention of postpartum complication
649.71	Cervical shortening, delivered, with or without mention of antepartum condition
649.8*	Onset (spontaneous) of labor after 37 completed weeks of gestation but before 39 completed weeks gestation, with delivery by (planned) cesarean section
650	Normal delivery
651.01	Twin pregnancy, delivered
651.11	Triplet pregnancy, delivered
651.21	Quadruplet pregnancy, delivered
651.31	Twin pregnancy with fetal loss and retention of one fetus, delivered
651.41	Triplet pregnancy with fetal loss and retention of one or more, delivered
651.51	Quadruplet pregnancy with fetal loss and retention of one or more, delivered
651.61	Other multiple pregnancy with fetal loss and retention of one or more fetus(es), delivered
651.71	Multiple gestation following (elective) fetal reduction, delivered, with or without mention of antepartum condition
651.81	Other specified multiple gestation, delivered
651.91	Unspecified multiple gestation, delivered
652.01	Unstable lie of fetus, delivered
652.11	Breech or other malpresentation successfully converted to cephalic presentation, delivered
652.21	Breech presentation without mention of version, delivered
652.31	Transverse or oblique fetal presentation, delivered
652.41	Fetal face or brow presentation, delivered
652.51	High fetal head at term, delivered
652.61	Multiple gestation with malpresentation of one fetus or more, delivered
652.71	Prolapsed arm of fetus, delivered
652.81	Other specified malposition or malpresentation of fetus, delivered
652.91	Unspecified malposition or malpresentation of fetus, delivered
653.01	Major abnormality of bony pelvis, not further specified, delivered
653.11	Generally contracted pelvis in pregnancy, delivered
653.21	Inlet contraction of pelvis in pregnancy, delivered
653.31	Outlet contraction of pelvis in pregnancy, delivered
653.41	Fetopelvic disproportion, delivered
653.51	Unusually large fetus causing disproportion, delivered
653.61	Hydrocephalic fetus causing disproportion, delivered
653.71	Other fetal abnormality causing disproportion, delivered
653.81	Fetal disproportion of other origin, delivered
653.91	Unspecified fetal disproportion, delivered
654.01	Congenital abnormalities of pregnant uterus, delivered
654.02	Congenital abnormalities of pregnant uterus, delivered, with mention of postpartum complication
654.11	Tumors of body of uterus, delivered
654.12	Tumors of body of uterus, delivered, with mention of postpartum complication
654.21	Previous cesarean delivery, delivered, with or without mention of antepartum condition
654.31	Retroverted and incarcerated gravid uterus, delivered
654.32	Retroverted and incarcerated gravid uterus, delivered, with mention of postpartum complication
654.41	Other abnormalities in shape or position of gravid uterus and of neighboring structures, delivered
654.42	Other abnormalities in shape or position of gravid uterus and of neighboring structures, delivered, with mention of postpartum complication
654.51	Cervical incompetence, delivered
654.52	Cervical incompetence, delivered, with mention of postpartum complication
654.61	Other congenital or acquired abnormality of cervix, with delivery
654.62	Other congenital or acquired abnormality of cervix, delivered, with mention of postpartum complication
654.71	Congenital or acquired abnormality of vagina, with delivery
654.72	Congenital or acquired abnormality of vagina, delivered, with mention of postpartum complication
654.81	Congenital or acquired abnormality of vulva, with delivery
654.82	Congenital or acquired abnormality of vulva, delivered, with mention of postpartum complication
654.91	Other and unspecified abnormality of organs and soft tissues of pelvis, with delivery
654.92	Other and unspecified abnormality of organs and soft tissues of pelvis, delivered, with mention of postpartum complication
655.01	Central nervous system malformation in fetus, with delivery
655.11	Chromosomal abnormality in fetus, affecting management of mother, with delivery
655.21	Hereditary disease in family possibly affecting fetus, affecting management of mother, with delivery
655.31	Suspected damage to fetus from viral disease in mother, affecting management of mother, with delivery
655.41	Suspected damage to fetus from other disease in mother, affecting management of mother, with delivery
655.51	Suspected damage to fetus from drugs, affecting management of mother, delivered
655.61	Suspected damage to fetus from radiation, affecting management of mother, delivered
655.71	Decreased fetal movements, affecting management of mother, delivered
655.81	Other known or suspected fetal abnormality, not elsewhere classified, affecting management of mother, delivery

Surgical	*Medical*	CC Indicator	MCC Indicator	*Procedure Proxy*

655.91	Unspecified fetal abnormality affecting management of mother, delivery
656.01	Fetal-maternal hemorrhage, with delivery
656.11	Rhesus isoimmunization affecting management of mother, delivered
656.21	Isoimmunization from other and unspecified blood-group incompatibility, affecting management of mother, delivered
656.30	Fetal distress affecting management of mother, unspecified as to episode of care
656.31	Fetal distress affecting management of mother, delivered
656.40	Intrauterine death affecting management of mother, unspecified as to episode of care
656.41	Intrauterine death affecting management of mother, delivered
656.51	Poor fetal growth, affecting management of mother, delivered
656.61	Excessive fetal growth affecting management of mother, delivered
656.71	Other placental conditions affecting management of mother, delivered
656.81	Other specified fetal and placental problems affecting management of mother, delivered
656.91	Unspecified fetal and placental problem affecting management of mother, delivered
657.01	Polyhydramnios, with delivery
658.01	Oligohydramnios, delivered
658.10	Premature rupture of membranes in pregnancy, unspecified as to episode of care
658.11	Premature rupture of membranes in pregnancy, delivered
658.20	Delayed delivery after spontaneous or unspecified rupture of membranes, unspecified as to episode of care
658.21	Delayed delivery after spontaneous or unspecified rupture of membranes, delivered
658.30	Delayed delivery after artificial rupture of membranes, unspecified as to episode of care
658.31	Delayed delivery after artificial rupture of membranes, delivered
658.40	Infection of amniotic cavity, unspecified as to episode of care
658.41	Infection of amniotic cavity, delivered
658.81	Other problem associated with amniotic cavity and membranes, delivered
658.91	Unspecified problem associated with amniotic cavity and membranes, delivered
659.00	Failed mechanical induction of labor, unspecified as to episode of care
659.01	Failed mechanical induction of labor, delivered
659.10	Failed medical or unspecified induction of labor, unspecified as to episode of care
659.11	Failed medical or unspecified induction of labor, delivered
659.20	Unspecified maternal pyrexia during labor, unspecified as to episode of care
659.30	Generalized infection during labor, unspecified as to episode of care
659.41	Grand multiparity, delivered, with or without mention of antepartum condition
659.50	Elderly primigravida, unspecified as to episode of care
659.51	Elderly primigravida, delivered
659.60	Elderly multigravida, unspecified as to episode of care or not applicable
659.61	Elderly multigravida, delivered, with mention of antepartum condition
659.70	Abnormality in fetal heart rate or rhythm, unspecified as to episode of care or not applicable
659.71	Abnormality in fetal heart rate or rhythm, delivered, with or without mention of antepartum condition
659.80	Other specified indication for care or intervention related to labor and delivery, unspecified as to episode of care
659.81	Other specified indication for care or intervention related to labor and delivery, delivered
659.90	Unspecified indication for care or intervention related to labor and delivery, unspecified as to episode of care
659.91	Unspecified indication for care or intervention related to labor and delivery, delivered
660.00	Obstruction caused by malposition of fetus at onset of labor, unspecified as to episode of care
660.01	Obstruction caused by malposition of fetus at onset of labor, delivered
660.10	Obstruction by bony pelvis during labor and delivery, unspecified as to episode of care
660.11	Obstruction by bony pelvis during labor and delivery, delivered
660.20	Obstruction by abnormal pelvic soft tissues during labor and delivery, unspecified as to episode of care
660.21	Obstruction by abnormal pelvic soft tissues during labor and delivery, delivered
660.30	Deep transverse arrest and persistent occipitoposterior position during labor and delivery, unspecified as to episode of care
660.31	Deep transverse arrest and persistent occipitoposterior position during labor and deliver, delivered
660.40	Shoulder (girdle) dystocia during labor and delivery, unspecified as to episode of care
660.41	Shoulder (girdle) dystocia during labor and deliver, delivered
660.50	Locked twins during labor and delivery, unspecified as to episode of care in pregnancy
660.51	Locked twins, delivered
660.60	Unspecified failed trial of labor, unspecified as to episode
660.61	Unspecified failed trial of labor, delivered
660.70	Unspecified failed forceps or vacuum extractor, unspecified as to episode of care
660.71	Unspecified failed forceps or vacuum extractor, delivered
660.80	Other causes of obstructed labor, unspecified as to episode of care
660.81	Other causes of obstructed labor, delivered
660.90	Unspecified obstructed labor, unspecified as to episode of care
660.91	Unspecified obstructed labor, with delivery
661.00	Primary uterine inertia, unspecified as to episode of care
661.01	Primary uterine inertia, with delivery
661.10	Secondary uterine inertia, unspecified as to episode of care
661.11	Secondary uterine inertia, with delivery
661.20	Other and unspecified uterine inertia, unspecified as to episode of care
661.21	Other and unspecified uterine inertia, with delivery
661.30	Precipitate labor, unspecified as to episode of care
661.31	Precipitate labor, with delivery
661.40	Hypertonic, incoordinate, or prolonged uterine contractions, unspecified as to episode of care
661.41	Hypertonic, incoordinate, or prolonged uterine contractions, with delivery
661.90	Unspecified abnormality of labor, unspecified as to episode of care
661.91	Unspecified abnormality of labor, with delivery
662.00	Prolonged first stage of labor, unspecified as to episode of care
662.01	Prolonged first stage of labor, delivered
662.10	Unspecified prolonged labor, unspecified as to episode of care
662.11	Unspecified prolonged labor, delivered
662.20	Prolonged second stage of labor, unspecified as to episode of care
662.21	Prolonged second stage of labor, delivered
662.30	Delayed delivery of second twin, triplet, etc., unspecified as to episode of care
662.31	Delayed delivery of second twin, triplet, etc., delivered
663.00	Prolapse of cord, complicating labor and delivery, unspecified as to episode of care
663.01	Prolapse of cord, complicating labor and delivery, delivered

T Transfer DRG   SP Special Payment   ☑ Optimization Potential   TRG Targeted Potential   * Code Range   ● New DRG   ▲ Revised DRG Title

150   Valid 10/01/2012-09/30/2013   © 2012 OptumInsight, Inc.

663.10	Cord around neck, with compression, complicating labor and delivery, unspecified as to episode of care
663.11	Cord around neck, with compression, complicating labor and delivery, delivered
663.20	Other and unspecified cord entanglement, with compression, complicating labor and delivery, unspecified as to episode of care
663.21	Other and unspecified cord entanglement, with compression, complicating labor and delivery, delivered
663.30	Other and unspecified cord entanglement, without mention of compression, complicating labor and delivery, unspecified as to episode of care
663.31	Other and unspecified cord entanglement, without mention of compression, complicating labor and delivery, delivered
663.40	Short cord complicating labor and delivery, unspecified as to episode of care
663.41	Short cord complicating labor and delivery, delivered
663.50	Vasa previa complicating labor and delivery, unspecified as to episode of care
663.51	Vasa previa complicating labor and delivery, delivered
663.60	Vascular lesions of cord complicating labor and delivery, unspecified as to episode of care
663.61	Vascular lesions of cord complicating labor and delivery, delivered
663.80	Other umbilical cord complications during labor and delivery, unspecified as to episode of care
663.81	Other umbilical cord complications during labor and delivery, delivered
663.90	Unspecified umbilical cord complication during labor and delivery, unspecified as to episode of care
663.91	Unspecified umbilical cord complication during labor and delivery, delivered
664.00	First-degree perineal laceration, unspecified as to episode of care in pregnancy
664.01	First-degree perineal laceration, with delivery
664.10	Second-degree perineal laceration, unspecified as to episode of care in pregnancy
664.11	Second-degree perineal laceration, with delivery
664.20	Third-degree perineal laceration, unspecified as to episode of care in pregnancy
664.21	Third-degree perineal laceration, with delivery
664.30	Fourth-degree perineal laceration, unspecified as to episode of care in pregnancy
664.31	Fourth-degree perineal laceration, with delivery
664.40	Unspecified perineal laceration, unspecified as to episode of care in pregnancy
664.41	Unspecified perineal laceration, with delivery
664.50	Vulvar and perineal hematoma, unspecified as to episode of care in pregnancy
664.51	Vulvar and perineal hematoma, with delivery
664.60	Anal sphincter tear complicating delivery, not associated with third-degree perineal laceration, unspecified as to episode of care or not applicable
664.61	Anal sphincter tear complicating delivery, not associated with third-degree perineal laceration, delivered, with or without mention of antepartum condition
664.80	Other specified trauma to perineum and vulva, unspecified as to episode of care in pregnancy
664.81	Other specified trauma to perineum and vulva, with delivery
664.90	Unspecified trauma to perineum and vulva, unspecified as to episode of care in pregnancy
664.91	Unspecified trauma to perineum and vulva, with delivery
665.00	Rupture of uterus before onset of labor, unspecified as to episode of care
665.01	Rupture of uterus before onset of labor, with delivery
665.10	Rupture of uterus during labor, unspecified as to episode
665.11	Rupture of uterus during labor, with delivery
665.20	Inversion of uterus, unspecified as to episode of care in pregnancy
665.22	Inversion of uterus, delivered with postpartum complication
665.30	Laceration of cervix, unspecified as to episode of care in pregnancy
665.31	Laceration of cervix, with delivery
665.40	High vaginal laceration, unspecified as to episode of care in pregnancy
665.41	High vaginal laceration, with delivery
665.50	Other injury to pelvic organs, unspecified as to episode of care in pregnancy
665.51	Other injury to pelvic organs, with delivery
665.60	Damage to pelvic joints and ligaments, unspecified as to episode of care in pregnancy
665.61	Damage to pelvic joints and ligaments, with delivery
665.70	Pelvic hematoma, unspecified as to episode of care
665.71	Pelvic hematoma, with delivery
665.72	Pelvic hematoma, delivered with postpartum complication
665.80	Other specified obstetrical trauma, unspecified as to episode of care
665.81	Other specified obstetrical trauma, with delivery
665.82	Other specified obstetrical trauma, delivered, with postpartum
665.90	Unspecified obstetrical trauma, unspecified as to episode of care
665.91	Unspecified obstetrical trauma, with delivery
665.92	Unspecified obstetrical trauma, delivered, with postpartum complication
668.00	Pulmonary complications of the administration of anesthesia or other sedation in labor and delivery, unspecified as to episode of care
668.10	Cardiac complications of the administration of anesthesia or other sedation in labor and delivery, unspecified as to episode of care
668.20	Central nervous system complications of the administration of anesthesia or other sedation in labor and delivery, unspecified as to episode of care
668.80	Other complications of the administration of anesthesia or other sedation in labor and delivery, unspecified as to episode of care
668.90	Unspecified complication of the administration of anesthesia or other sedation in labor and delivery, unspecified as to episode of care
669.00	Maternal distress complicating labor and delivery, unspecified as to episode of care
669.01	Maternal distress, with delivery, with or without mention of antepartum condition
669.02	Maternal distress, with delivery, with mention of postpartum complication
669.10	Shock during or following labor and delivery, unspecified as to episode of care
669.20	Maternal hypotension syndrome complicating labor and delivery, unspecified as to episode of care
669.21	Maternal hypotension syndrome, with delivery, with or without mention of antepartum condition
669.22	Maternal hypotension syndrome, with delivery, with mention of postpartum complication
669.30	Acute kidney failure following labor and delivery, unspecified as to episode of care or not applicable
669.40	Other complications of obstetrical surgery and procedures, unspecified as to episode of care
669.50	Forceps or vacuum extractor delivery without mention of indication, unspecified as to episode of care
669.51	Forceps or vacuum extractor delivery without mention of indication, delivered, with or without mention of antepartum condition
669.60	Breech extraction, without mention of indication, unspecified as to episode of care
669.61	Breech extraction, without mention of indication, delivered, with or without mention of antepartum condition
669.70	Cesarean delivery, without mention of indication, unspecified as to episode of care

669.71 Cesarean delivery, without mention of indication, delivered, with or without mention of antepartum condition

669.80 Other complication of labor and delivery, unspecified as to episode of care

669.81 Other complication of labor and delivery, delivered, with or without mention of antepartum condition

669.82 Other complication of labor and delivery, delivered, with mention of postpartum complication

669.90 Unspecified complication of labor and delivery, unspecified as to episode of care

669.91 Unspecified complication of labor and delivery, with delivery, with or without mention of antepartum condition

669.92 Unspecified complication of labor and delivery, with delivery, with mention of postpartum complication

671.01 Varicose veins of legs, with delivery, with or without mention of antepartum condition

671.02 Varicose veins of legs, with delivery, with mention of postpartum complication

671.11 Varicose veins of vulva and perineum, with delivery, with or without mention of antepartum condition

671.12 Varicose veins of vulva and perineum, with delivery, with mention of postpartum complication

671.21 Superficial thrombophlebitis with delivery, with or without mention of antepartum condition

671.22 Superficial thrombophlebitis with delivery, with mention of postpartum complication

671.81 Other venous complication, with delivery, with or without mention of antepartum condition

671.82 Other venous complication, with delivery, with mention of postpartum complication

671.91 Unspecified venous complication, with delivery, with or without mention of antepartum condition

671.92 Unspecified venous complication, with delivery, with mention of postpartum complication

674.42 Placental polyp, with delivery, with mention of postpartum complication

674.92 Unspecified complications of puerperium, with delivery, with mention of postpartum complication

675.81 Other specified infection of the breast and nipple associated with childbirth, delivered, with or without mention of antepartum condition

675.82 Other specified infection of the breast and nipple associated with childbirth, delivered, with mention of postpartum complication

675.91 Unspecified infection of the breast and nipple, delivered, with or without mention of antepartum condition

675.92 Unspecified infection of the breast and nipple, delivered, with mention of postpartum complication

676.01 Retracted nipple, delivered, with or without mention of antepartum condition

676.02 Retracted nipple, delivered, with mention of postpartum complication

676.11 Cracked nipple, delivered, with or without mention of antepartum condition

676.12 Cracked nipple, delivered, with mention of postpartum complication

676.21 Engorgement of breasts, delivered, with or without mention of antepartum condition

676.22 Engorgement of breasts, delivered, with mention of postpartum complication

676.31 Other and unspecified disorder of breast associated with childbirth, delivered, with or without mention of antepartum condition

676.32 Other and unspecified disorder of breast associated with childbirth, delivered, with mention of postpartum complication

676.41 Failure of lactation, with delivery, with or without mention of antepartum condition

676.42 Failure of lactation, with delivery, with mention of postpartum complication

676.51 Suppressed lactation, with delivery, with or without mention of antepartum condition

676.52 Suppressed lactation, with delivery, with mention of postpartum complication

676.61 Galactorrhea, with delivery, with or without mention of antepartum condition

676.62 Galactorrhea, with delivery, with mention of postpartum complication

676.81 Other disorder of lactation, with delivery, with or without mention of antepartum condition

676.82 Other disorder of lactation, with delivery, with mention of postpartum complication

676.91 Unspecified disorder of lactation, with delivery, with or without mention of antepartum condition

676.92 Unspecified disorder of lactation, with delivery, with mention of postpartum complication

678.01 Fetal hematologic conditions, delivered, with or without mention of antepartum condition

678.11 Fetal conjoined twins, delivered, with or without mention of antepartum condition

679.00 Maternal complications from in utero procedure, unspecified as to episode of care or not applicable

679.11 Fetal complications from in utero procedure, delivered, with or without mention of antepartum condition

679.12 Fetal complications from in utero procedure, delivered, with mention of postpartum complication

AND

Only operating room procedures listed under DRG 774
OR

No operating room procedures

DRG 776   Postpartum and Postabortion Diagnoses without O.R. Procedure

GMLOS 2.5   AMLOS 3.2   RW 0.6565   ☑

Principal Diagnosis

639* Complications following abortion or ectopic and molar pregnancies

642.04 Benign essential hypertension, complicating pregnancy, childbirth, and the puerperium, postpartum condition or complication

642.14 Hypertension secondary to renal disease, complicating pregnancy, childbirth, and the puerperium, postpartum condition or complication

642.24 Other pre-existing hypertension complicating pregnancy, childbirth, and the puerperium, postpartum condition or complication

642.34 Transient hypertension of pregnancy, postpartum condition or complication

642.44 Mild or unspecified pre-eclampsia, postpartum condition or complication

642.54 Severe pre-eclampsia, postpartum condition or complication

642.64 Eclampsia, postpartum condition or complication

642.74 Pre-eclampsia or eclampsia superimposed on pre-existing hypertension, postpartum condition or complication

642.94 Unspecified hypertension complicating pregnancy, childbirth, or the puerperium, postpartum condition or complication

646.14 Edema or excessive weight gain in pregnancy, without mention of hypertension, postpartum condition or complication

646.24 Unspecified renal disease in pregnancy, without mention of hypertension, postpartum condition or complication

646.44 Peripheral neuritis in pregnancy, postpartum condition or complication

646.54 Asymptomatic bacteriuria in pregnancy, postpartum condition or complication

Ⓣ Transfer DRG   🆂🅿 Special Payment   ☑ Optimization Potential   🆈🅻🅳 Targeted Potential   * Code Range   ● New DRG   ▲ Revised DRG Title

152   Valid 10/01/2012–09/30/2013   © 2012 OptumInsight, Inc.

646.64	Infections of genitourinary tract in pregnancy, postpartum condition or complication
646.84	Other specified complications of pregnancy, postpartum condition or complication
647.04	Maternal syphilis complicating pregnancy, childbrith, or the puerperium, postpartum condition or complication
647.14	Maternal gonorrhea complicating pregnancy, childbrith, or the puerperium, postpartum condition or complication
647.24	Other venereal diseases complicating pregnancy, childbrith, or the puerperium, postpartum condition or complication
647.34	Maternal tuberculosis complicating pregnancy, childbirth, or the puerperium, postpartum condition or complication
647.44	Maternal malaria, complicating pregnancy, childbirth, or the puerperium, postpartum condition or complication
647.54	Maternal rubella complicating pregnancy, childbirth, or the puerperium, postpartum condition or complication
647.64	Other maternal viral diseases complicating pregnancy, childbirth, or the puerperium, postpartum condition or complication
647.84	Other specified maternal infectious and parasitic diseases complicating pregnancy, childbirth, or the puerperium, postpartum condition or complication
647.94	Unspecified maternal infection or infestation complicating pregnancy, childbirth, or the puerperium, postpartum condition or complication
648.04	Maternal diabetes mellitus, complicating pregnancy, childbirth, or the puerperium, postpartum condition or complication
648.14	Maternal thyroid dysfunction complicating pregnancy, childbirth, or the puerperium, postpartum condition or complication
648.24	Maternal anemia complicating pregnancy, childbirth, or the puerperium, postpartum condition or complication
648.34	Maternal drug dependence complicating pregnancy, childbirth, or the puerperium, postpartum condition or complication
648.44	Maternal mental disorders complicating pregnancy, childbirth, or the puerperium, postpartum condition or complication
648.54	Maternal congenital cardiovascular disorders complicating pregnancy, childbirth, or the puerperium, postpartum condition or complication
648.64	Other maternal cardiovascular diseases complicating pregnancy, childbirth, or the puerperium, postpartum condition or complication
648.74	Bone and joint disorders of maternal back, pelvis, and lower limbs complicating pregnancy, childbirth, or the puerperium, postpartum condition or complication
648.84	Abnormal maternal glucose tolerance complicating pregnancy, childbirth, or the puerperium, postpartum condition or complication
648.94	Other current maternal conditions classifiable elsewhere complicating pregnancy, childbirth, or the puerperium, postpartum condition or complication
649.04	Tobacco use disorder complicating pregnancy, childbirth, or the puerperium, postpartum condition or complication
649.14	Obesity complicating pregnancy, childbirth, or the puerperium, postpartum condition or complication
649.24	Bariatric surgery status complicating pregnancy, childbirth, or the puerperium, postpartum condition or complication
649.34	Coagulation defects complicating pregnancy, childbirth, or the puerperium, postpartum condition or complication
649.44	Epilepsy complicating pregnancy, childbirth, or the puerperium, postpartum condition or complication
649.64	Uterine size date discrepancy, postpartum condition or complication
654.04	Congenital abnormalities of uterus, postpartum condition or complication
654.14	Tumors of body of uterus, postpartum condition or complication
654.34	Retroverted and incarcerated gravid uterus, postpartum condition or complication
654.44	Other abnormalities in shape or position of gravid uterus and of neighboring structures, postpartum condition or complication
654.54	Cervical incompetence, postpartum condition or complication
654.64	Other congenital or acquired abnormality of cervix, postpartum condition or complication
654.74	Congenital or acquired abnormality of vagina, postpartum condition or complication
654.84	Congenital or acquired abnormality of vulva, postpartum condition or complication
654.94	Other and unspecified abnormality of organs and soft tissues of pelvis, postpartum condition or complication
664.04	First-degree perineal laceration, postpartum condition or complication
664.14	Second-degree perineal laceration, postpartum condition or complication
664.24	Third-degree perineal laceration, postpartum condition or complication
664.34	Fourth-degree perineal laceration, postpartum condition or complication
664.44	Unspecified perineal laceration, postpartum condition or complication
664.54	Vulvar and perineal hematoma, postpartum condition or complication
664.64	Anal sphincter tear complicating delivery, not associated with third-degree perineal laceration, postpartum condition or complication
664.84	Other specified trauma to perineum and vulva, postpartum condition or complication
664.94	Unspecified trauma to perineum and vulva, postpartum condition or complication
665.24	Inversion of uterus, postpartum condition or complication
665.34	Laceration of cervix, postpartum condition or complication
665.44	High vaginal laceration, postpartum condition or complication
665.54	Other injury to pelvic organs, postpartum condition or complication
665.64	Damage to pelvic joints and ligaments, postpartum condition or complication
665.74	Pelvic hematoma, postpartum condition or complication
665.84	Other specified obstetrical trauma, postpartum condition or complication
665.94	Unspecified obstetrical trauma, postpartum condition or complication
666.04	Third-stage postpartum hemorrhage, postpartum condition or complication
666.14	Other immediate postpartum hemorrhage, postpartum condition or complication
666.24	Delayed and secondary postpartum hemorrhage, postpartum condition or complication
666.34	Postpartum coagulation defects, postpartum condition or complication
667.04	Retained placenta without hemorrhage, postpartum condition or complication
667.14	Retained portions of placenta or membranes, without hemorrhage, postpartum condition or complication
668.04	Pulmonary complications of the administration of anesthesia or other sedation in labor and delivery, postpartum condition or complication
668.14	Cardiac complications of the administration of anesthesia or other sedation in labor and delivery, postpartum condition or complication
668.24	Central nervous system complications of the administration of anesthesia or other sedation in labor and delivery, postpartum condition or complication

MDC 14: Pregnancy, Childbirth And The Puerperium—MEDICAL

Surgical	*Medical*	CC Indicator	MCC Indicator	*Procedure Proxy*

668.84   Other complications of the administration of anesthesia or other sedation in labor and delivery, postpartum condition or complication

668.94   Unspecified complication of the administration of anesthesia or other sedation in labor and delivery, postpartum condition or complication

669.04   Maternal distress complicating labor and delivery, postpartum condition or complication

669.14   Shock during or following labor and delivery, postpartum condition or complication

669.24   Maternal hypotension syndrome, postpartum condition or complication

669.34   Acute kidney failure following labor and delivery, postpartum condition or complication

669.44   Other complications of obstetrical surgery and procedures, postpartum condition or complication

669.84   Other complication of labor and delivery, postpartum condition or complication

669.94   Unspecified complication of labor and delivery, postpartum condition or complication

670.04   Major puerperal infection, unspecified, postpartum condition or complication

670.14   Puerperal endometritis, postpartum condition or complication

670.24   Puerperal sepsis, postpartum condition or complication

670.34   Puerperal septic thrombophlebitis, postpartum condition or complication

670.84   Other major puerperal infection, postpartum condition or complication

671.04   Varicose veins of legs, postpartum condition or complication

671.14   Varicose veins of vulva and perineum, postpartum condition or complication

671.24   Superficial thrombophlebitis, postpartum condition or complication

671.44   Deep phlebothrombosis, postpartum condition or complication

671.54   Other phlebitis and thrombosis, postpartum condition or complication

671.84   Other venous complications, postpartum condition or complication

671.94   Unspecified venous complication, postpartum condition or complication

672.04   Puerperal pyrexia of unknown origin, postpartum condition or complication

673.04   Obstetrical air embolism, postpartum condition or complication

673.14   Amniotic fluid embolism, postpartum condition or complication

673.24   Obstetrical blood-clot embolism, postpartum condition or complication

673.34   Obstetrical pyemic and septic embolism, postpartum condition or complication

673.84   Other obstetrical pulmonary embolism, postpartum condition or complication

674.04   Cerebrovascular disorders in the puerperium, postpartum condition or complication

674.14   Disruption of cesarean wound, postpartum condition or complication

674.24   Disruption of perineal wound, postpartum condition or complication

674.34   Other complications of obstetrical surgical wounds, postpartum condition or complication

674.44   Placental polyp, postpartum condition or complication

674.54   Peripartum cardiomyopathy, postpartum condition or complication

674.84   Other complications of puerperium, postpartum condition or complication

674.94   Unspecified complications of puerperium, postpartum condition or complication

675.04   Infection of nipple, postpartum condition or complication

675.14   Abscess of breast, postpartum condition or complication

675.24   Nonpurulent mastitis, postpartum condition or complication

675.84   Other specified infections of the breast and nipple, postpartum condition or complication

675.94   Unspecified infection of the breast and nipple, postpartum condition or complication

676.04   Retracted nipple, postpartum condition or complication

676.14   Cracked nipple, postpartum condition or complication

676.24   Engorgement of breasts, postpartum condition or complication

676.34   Other and unspecified disorder of breast associated with childbirth, postpartum condition or complication

676.44   Failure of lactation, postpartum condition or complication

676.54   Suppressed lactation, postpartum condition or complication

676.64   Galactorrhea, postpartum condition or complication

676.84   Other disorders of lactation, postpartum condition or complication

676.94   Unspecified disorder of lactation, postpartum condition or complication

679.04   Maternal complications from in utero procedure, postpartum condition or complication

679.14   Fetal complications from in utero procedure, postpartum condition or complication

V24.0   Postpartum care and examination immediately after delivery

DRG 777   Ectopic Pregnancy
        GMLOS 1.9   AMLOS 2.3   RW 0.8777   ☑

Principal Diagnosis
633*   Ectopic pregnancy

DRG 778   Threatened Abortion
        GMLOS 2.1   AMLOS 3.1   RW 0.5049   ☑

Principal Diagnosis
640.00   Threatened abortion, unspecified as to episode of care
640.03   Threatened abortion, antepartum
640.80   Other specified hemorrhage in early pregnancy, unspecified as to episode of care
640.83   Other specified hemorrhage in early pregnancy, antepartum
640.90   Unspecified hemorrhage in early pregnancy, unspecified as to episode of care
640.93   Unspecified hemorrhage in early pregnancy, antepartum
644.00   Threatened premature labor, unspecified as to episode of care
644.03   Threatened premature labor, antepartum

DRG 779   Abortion without D&C
        GMLOS 1.6   AMLOS 1.9   RW 0.4962   ☑

Principal Diagnosis
632   Missed abortion
634*   Spontaneous abortion
635*   Legally induced abortion
636*   Illegally induced abortion
637*   Abortion, unspecified as to legality
638*   Failed attempted abortion
V61.7   Other unwanted pregnancy

DRG 780   False Labor
        GMLOS 1.1   AMLOS 1.2   RW 0.1896   ☑

Principal Diagnosis
644.10   Other threatened labor, unspecified as to episode of care
644.13   Other threatened labor, antepartum

Ⓣ Transfer DRG   SP Special Payment   ☑ Optimization Potential   Targeted Potential   * Code Range   ● New DRG   ▲ Revised DRG Title

154   Valid 10/01/2012-09/30/2013   © 2012 OptumInsight, Inc.

DRG 781   Other Antepartum Diagnoses with Medical Complications

GMLOS 2.6   **AMLOS 3.8**   **RW 0.6687**   ☑

Principal Diagnosis

630	Hydatidiform mole
631*	Other abnormal product of conception
641.03	Placenta previa without hemorrhage, antepartum
641.13	Hemorrhage from placenta previa, antepartum
641.23	Premature separation of placenta, antepartum
641.33	Antepartum hemorrhage associated with coagulation defect, antepartum
641.83	Other antepartum hemorrhage, antepartum
641.93	Unspecified antepartum hemorrhage, antepartum
642.03	Benign essential hypertension antepartum
642.13	Hypertension secondary to renal disease, antepartum
642.23	Other pre-existing hypertension, antepartum
642.33	Transient hypertension of pregnancy, antepartum
642.43	Mild or unspecified pre-eclampsia, antepartum
642.53	Severe pre-eclampsia, antepartum
642.63	Eclampsia, antepartum
642.73	Pre-eclampsia or eclampsia superimposed on pre-existing hypertension, antepartum
642.93	Unspecified hypertension antepartum
643.03	Mild hyperemesis gravidarum, antepartum
643.13	Hyperemesis gravidarum with metabolic disturbance, antepartum
643.23	Late vomiting of pregnancy, antepartum
643.83	Other vomiting complicating pregnancy, antepartum
643.93	Unspecified vomiting of pregnancy, antepartum
644.20	Early onset of delivery, unspecified as to episode of care
645.13	Post term pregnancy, antepartum condition or complication
645.23	Prolonged pregnancy, antepartum condition or complication
646.03	Papyraceous fetus, antepartum
646.13	Edema or excessive weight gain, antepartum
646.23	Unspecified antepartum renal disease
646.33	Pregnancy complication, recurrent pregnancy loss, antepartum condition or complication
646.43	Peripheral neuritis antepartum
646.53	Asymptomatic bacteriuria antepartum
646.63	Infections of genitourinary tract antepartum
646.73	Liver and biliary tract disorders in pregnancy, antepartum condition or complication
646.83	Other specified complication, antepartum
646.93	Unspecified complication of pregnancy, antepartum
647.03	Maternal syphilis, antepartum
647.13	Maternal gonorrhea, antepartum
647.23	Other maternal venereal diseases, antepartum condition or complication
647.33	Maternal tuberculosis, antepartum
647.43	Maternal malaria, antepartum
647.53	Maternal rubella, antepartum
647.63	Other maternal viral disease, antepartum
647.83	Other specified maternal infectious and parasitic disease, antepartum
647.93	Unspecified maternal infection or infestation, antepartum
648.03	Maternal diabetes mellitus, antepartum
648.13	Maternal thyroid dysfunction, antepartum condition or complication
648.23	Maternal anemia, antepartum
648.33	Maternal drug dependence, antepartum
648.43	Maternal mental disorders, antepartum
648.53	Maternal congenital cardiovascular disorders, antepartum
648.63	Other maternal cardiovascular diseases, antepartum
648.73	Bone and joint disorders of maternal back, pelvis, and lower limbs, antepartum
648.83	Abnormal maternal glucose tolerance, antepartum
648.93	Other current maternal conditions classifiable elsewhere, antepartum
649.03	Tobacco use disorder complicating pregnancy, childbirth, or the puerperium, antepartum condition or complication
649.13	Obesity complicating pregnancy, childbirth, or the puerperium, antepartum condition or complication
649.23	Bariatric surgery status complicating pregnancy, childbirth, or the puerperium, antepartum condition or complication
649.33	Coagulation defects complicating pregnancy, childbirth, or the puerperium, antepartum condition or complication
649.43	Epilepsy complicating pregnancy, childbirth, or the puerperium, antepartum condition or complication
649.53	Spotting complicating pregnancy, antepartum condition or complication
649.63	Uterine size date discrepancy, antepartum condition or complication
649.73	Cervical shortening, antepartum condition or complication
651.03	Twin pregnancy, antepartum
651.13	Triplet pregnancy, antepartum
651.23	Quadruplet pregnancy, antepartum
651.33	Twin pregnancy with fetal loss and retention of one fetus, antepartum
651.43	Triplet pregnancy with fetal loss and retention of one or more, antepartum
651.53	Quadruplet pregnancy with fetal loss and retention of one or more, antepartum
651.63	Other multiple pregnancy with fetal loss and retention of one or more fetus(es), antepartum
651.73	Multiple gestation following (elective) fetal reduction, antepartum condition or complication
651.83	Other specified multiple gestation, antepartum
651.93	Unspecified multiple gestation, antepartum
652.03	Unstable lie of fetus, antepartum
652.13	Breech or other malpresentation successfully converted to cephalic presentation, antepartum
652.23	Breech presentation without mention of version, antepartum
652.33	Transverse or oblique fetal presentation, antepartum
652.43	Fetal face or brow presentation, antepartum
652.53	High fetal head at term, antepartum
652.63	Multiple gestation with malpresentation of one fetus or more, antepartum
652.73	Prolapsed arm of fetus, antepartum condition or complication
652.83	Other specified malposition or malpresentation of fetus, antepartum
652.93	Unspecified malposition or malpresentation of fetus, antepartum
653.03	Major abnormality of bony pelvis, not further specified, antepartum
653.13	Generally contracted pelvis in pregnancy, antepartum
653.23	Inlet contraction of pelvis in pregnancy, antepartum
653.33	Outlet contraction of pelvis in pregnancy, antepartum
653.43	Fetopelvic disproportion, antepartum
653.53	Unusually large fetus causing disproportion, antepartum
653.63	Hydrocephalic fetus causing disproportion, antepartum
653.73	Other fetal abnormality causing disproportion, antepartum
653.83	Fetal disproportion of other origin, antepartum
653.93	Unspecified fetal disproportion, antepartum
654.03	Congenital abnormalities of pregnant uterus, antepartum
654.13	Tumors of body of uterus, antepartum condition or complication
654.23	Previous cesarean delivery, antepartum condition or complication
654.33	Retroverted and incarcerated gravid uterus, antepartum
654.43	Other abnormalities in shape or position of gravid uterus and of neighboring structures, antepartum
654.53	Cervical incompetence, antepartum condition or complication
654.63	Other congenital or acquired abnormality of cervix, antepartum condition or complication

654.73	Congenital or acquired abnormality of vagina, antepartum condition or complication
654.83	Congenital or acquired abnormality of vulva, antepartum condition or complication
654.93	Other and unspecified abnormality of organs and soft tissues of pelvis, antepartum condition or complication
655.03	Central nervous system malformation in fetus, antepartum
655.13	Chromosomal abnormality in fetus, affecting management of mother, antepartum
655.23	Hereditary disease in family possibly affecting fetus, affecting management of mother, antepartum condition or complication
655.33	Suspected damage to fetus from viral disease in mother, affecting management of mother, antepartum condition or complication
655.43	Suspected damage to fetus from other disease in mother, affecting management of mother, antepartum condition or complication
655.53	Suspected damage to fetus from drugs, affecting management of mother, antepartum
655.63	Suspected damage to fetus from radiation, affecting management of mother, antepartum condition or complication
655.73	Decreased fetal movements, affecting management of mother, antepartum condition or complication
655.83	Other known or suspected fetal abnormality, not elsewhere classified, affecting management of mother, antepartum condition or complication
655.93	Unspecified fetal abnormality affecting management of mother, antepartum condition or complication
656.03	Fetal-maternal hemorrhage, antepartum condition or complication
656.13	Rhesus isoimmunization affecting management of mother, antepartum condition
656.23	Isoimmunization from other and unspecified blood-group incompatibility, affecting management of mother, antepartum
656.33	Fetal distress affecting management of mother, antepartum
656.43	Intrauterine death affecting management of mother, antepartum
656.53	Poor fetal growth, affecting management of mother, antepartum condition or complication
656.63	Excessive fetal growth affecting management of mother, antepartum
656.73	Other placental conditions affecting management of mother, antepartum
656.83	Other specified fetal and placental problems affecting management of mother, antepartum
656.93	Unspecified fetal and placental problem affecting management of mother, antepartum
657.03	Polyhydramnios, antepartum complication
658.03	Oligohydramnios, antepartum
658.13	Premature rupture of membranes in pregnancy, antepartum
658.23	Delayed delivery after spontaneous or unspecified rupture of membranes, antepartum
658.33	Delayed delivery after artificial rupture of membranes, antepartum
658.43	Infection of amniotic cavity, antepartum
658.83	Other problem associated with amniotic cavity and membranes, antepartum
658.93	Unspecified problem associated with amniotic cavity and membranes, antepartum
659.03	Failed mechanical induction of labor, antepartum
659.13	Failed medical or unspecified induction of labor, antepartum
659.23	Unspecified maternal pyrexia, antepartum
659.33	Generalized infection during labor, antepartum
659.43	Grand multiparity with current pregnancy, antepartum
659.53	Elderly primigravida, antepartum
659.63	Elderly multigravida, with antepartum condition or complication
659.73	Abnormality in fetal heart rate or rhythm, antepartum condition or complication
659.83	Other specified indication for care or intervention related to labor and delivery, antepartum
659.93	Unspecified indication for care or intervention related to labor and delivery, antepartum
660.03	Obstruction caused by malposition of fetus at onset of labor, antepartum
660.13	Obstruction by bony pelvis during labor and delivery, antepartum
660.23	Obstruction by abnormal pelvic soft tissues during labor and delivery, antepartum
660.33	Deep transverse arrest and persistent occipitoposterior position during labor and delivery, antepartum
660.43	Shoulder (girdle) dystocia during labor and delivery, antepartum
660.53	Locked twins, antepartum
660.63	Unspecified failed trial of labor, antepartum
660.73	Failed forceps or vacuum extractor, unspecified, antepartum
660.83	Other causes of obstructed labor, antepartum
660.93	Unspecified obstructed labor, antepartum
661.03	Primary uterine inertia, antepartum
661.13	Secondary uterine inertia, antepartum
661.23	Other and unspecified uterine inertia, antepartum
661.33	Precipitate labor, antepartum
661.43	Hypertonic, incoordinate, or prolonged uterine contractions, antepartum
661.93	Unspecified abnormality of labor, antepartum
662.03	Prolonged first stage of labor, antepartum
662.13	Unspecified prolonged labor, antepartum
662.23	Prolonged second stage of labor, antepartum
662.33	Delayed delivery of second twin, triplet, etc., antepartum
663.03	Prolapse of cord, complicating labor and delivery, antepartum
663.13	Cord around neck, with compression, complicating labor and delivery, antepartum
663.23	Other and unspecified cord entanglement, with compression, complicating labor and delivery, antepartum
663.33	Other and unspecified cord entanglement, without mention of compression, complicating labor and delivery, antepartum
663.43	Short cord complicating labor and delivery, antepartum
663.53	Vasa previa complicating labor and delivery, antepartum
663.63	Vascular lesions of cord complicating labor and delivery, antepartum
663.83	Other umbilical cord complications during labor and delivery, antepartum
663.93	Unspecified umbilical cord complication during labor and delivery, antepartum
665.03	Rupture of uterus before onset of labor, antepartum
665.83	Other specified obstetrical trauma, antepartum
665.93	Unspecified obstetrical trauma, antepartum
668.03	Pulmonary complications of the administration of anesthesia or other sedation in labor and delivery, antepartum
668.13	Cardiac complications of the administration of anesthesia or other sedation in labor and delivery, antepartum
668.23	Central nervous system complications of the administration of anesthesia or other sedation in labor and delivery, antepartum
668.83	Other complications of the administration of anesthesia or other sedation in labor and delivery, antepartum
668.93	Unspecified complication of the administration of anesthesia or other sedation in labor and delivery, antepartum
669.03	Maternal distress complicating labor and delivery, antepartum condition or complication
669.13	Shock during or following labor and delivery, antepartum shock
669.23	Maternal hypotension syndrome, antepartum

MDC 14: Pregnancy, Childbirth And The Puerperium—MEDICAL

Ⓣ *Transfer DRG*   ⓈⓅ *Special Payment*   ☑ *Optimization Potential*   ᵗᵍᵈ *Targeted Potential*   * *Code Range*   ● *New DRG*   ▲ *Revised DRG Title*

669.43	Other complications of obstetrical surgery and procedures, antepartum condition or complication
669.83	Other complication of labor and delivery, antepartum condition or complication
669.93	Unspecified complication of labor and delivery, antepartum condition or complication
671.03	Varicose veins of legs, antepartum
671.13	Varicose veins of vulva and perineum, antepartum
671.23	Superficial thrombophlebitis, antepartum
671.33	Deep phlebothrombosis, antepartum
671.53	Other antepartum phlebitis and thrombosis
671.83	Other venous complication, antepartum
671.93	Unspecified venous complication, antepartum
673.03	Obstetrical air embolism, antepartum condition or complication
673.13	Amniotic fluid embolism, antepartum condition or complication
673.23	Obstetrical blood-clot embolism, antepartum
673.33	Obstetrical pyemic and septic embolism, antepartum
673.83	Other obstetrical pulmonary embolism, antepartum
674.03	Cerebrovascular disorder, antepartum
674.53	Peripartum cardiomyopathy, antepartum condition or complication
675.03	Infection of nipple, antepartum
675.13	Abscess of breast, antepartum
675.23	Nonpurulent mastitis, antepartum
675.83	Other specified infection of the breast and nipple, antepartum
675.93	Unspecified infection of the breast and nipple, antepartum
676.03	Retracted nipple, antepartum condition or complication
676.13	Cracked nipple, antepartum condition or complication
676.23	Engorgement of breast, antepartum
676.33	Other and unspecified disorder of breast associated with childbirth, antepartum condition or complication
676.43	Failure of lactation, antepartum condition or complication
676.53	Suppressed lactation, antepartum condition or complication
676.63	Galactorrhea, antepartum condition or complication
676.83	Other disorder of lactation, antepartum condition or complication
676.93	Unspecified disorder of lactation, antepartum condition or complication
678.03	Fetal hematologic conditions, antepartum condition or complication
678.13	Fetal conjoined twins, antepartum condition or complication
679.03	Maternal complications from in utero procedure, antepartum condition or complication
679.13	Fetal complications from in utero procedure, antepartum condition or complication
792.3	Nonspecific abnormal finding in amniotic fluid
796.5	Abnormal finding on antenatal screening
V28.0	Screening for chromosomal anomalies by amniocentesis
V28.1	Screening for raised alpha-fetoprotein levels in amniotic fluid
V28.2	Other antenatal screening based on amniocentesis
V61.6	Illegitimacy or illegitimate pregnancy

AND

Secondary Diagnosis

641.30	Antepartum hemorrhage associated with coagulation defects, unspecified as to episode of care
641.33	Antepartum hemorrhage associated with coagulation defect, antepartum
642.03	Benign essential hypertension antepartum
642.13	Hypertension secondary to renal disease, antepartum
642.23	Other pre-existing hypertension, antepartum
642.43	Mild or unspecified pre-eclampsia, antepartum
642.50	Severe pre-eclampsia, unspecified as to episode of care
642.53	Severe pre-eclampsia, antepartum

642.60	Eclampsia complicating pregnancy, childbirth or the puerperium, unspecified as to episode of care
642.63	Eclampsia, antepartum
642.70	Pre-eclampsia or eclampsia superimposed on pre-existing hypertension, complicating pregnancy, childbirth, or the puerperium, unspecified as to episode of care
642.73	Pre-eclampsia or eclampsia superimposed on pre-existing hypertension, antepartum
642.93	Unspecified hypertension antepartum
643.00	Mild hyperemesis gravidarum, unspecified as to episode of care
643.03	Mild hyperemesis gravidarum, antepartum
643.10	Hyperemesis gravidarum with metabolic disturbance, unspecified as to episode of care
643.13	Hyperemesis gravidarum with metabolic disturbance, antepartum
643.20	Late vomiting of pregnancy, unspecified as to episode of care
643.23	Late vomiting of pregnancy, antepartum
643.80	Other vomiting complicating pregnancy, unspecified as to episode of care
643.83	Other vomiting complicating pregnancy, antepartum
643.90	Unspecified vomiting of pregnancy, unspecified as to episode of care
643.93	Unspecified vomiting of pregnancy, antepartum
646.10	Edema or excessive weight gain in pregnancy, unspecified as to episode of care
646.13	Edema or excessive weight gain, antepartum
646.20	Unspecified renal disease in pregnancy, unspecified as to episode of care
646.23	Unspecified antepartum renal disease
646.43	Peripheral neuritis antepartum
646.60	Infections of genitourinary tract in pregnancy, unspecified as to episode of care
646.63	Infections of genitourinary tract antepartum
646.70	Liver and biliary tract disorders in pregnancy, unspecified as to episode of care or not applicable
646.73	Liver and biliary tract disorders in pregnancy, antepartum condition or complication
646.80	Other specified complication of pregnancy, unspecified as to episode of care
646.83	Other specified complication, antepartum
647.03	Maternal syphilis, antepartum
647.13	Maternal gonorrhea, antepartum
647.23	Other maternal venereal diseases, antepartum condition or complication
647.33	Maternal tuberculosis, antepartum
647.43	Maternal malaria, antepartum
647.53	Maternal rubella, antepartum
647.63	Other maternal viral disease, antepartum
647.83	Other specified maternal infectious and parasitic disease, antepartum
647.93	Unspecified maternal infection or infestation, antepartum
648.03	Maternal diabetes mellitus, antepartum
648.13	Maternal thyroid dysfunction, antepartum condition or complication
648.23	Maternal anemia, antepartum
648.33	Maternal drug dependence, antepartum
648.43	Maternal mental disorders, antepartum
648.53	Maternal congenital cardiovascular disorders, antepartum
648.63	Other maternal cardiovascular diseases, antepartum
648.73	Bone and joint disorders of maternal back, pelvis, and lower limbs, antepartum
648.83	Abnormal maternal glucose tolerance, antepartum
648.93	Other current maternal conditions classifiable elsewhere, antepartum

Surgical	Medical	CC Indicator	MCC Indicator	Procedure Proxy

DRG 782 Other Antepartum Diagnoses without Medical Complications

GMLOS 1.8	AMLOS 2.6	RW 0.4050	☑

Principal Diagnosis

630 Hydatidiform mole
631* Other abnormal product of conception
641.03 Placenta previa without hemorrhage, antepartum
641.13 Hemorrhage from placenta previa, antepartum
641.23 Premature separation of placenta, antepartum
641.83 Other antepartum hemorrhage, antepartum
641.93 Unspecified antepartum hemorrhage, antepartum
642.33 Transient hypertension of pregnancy, antepartum
644.20 Early onset of delivery, unspecified as to episode of care
645.13 Post term pregnancy, antepartum condition or complication
645.23 Prolonged pregnancy, antepartum condition or complication
646.03 Papyraceous fetus, antepartum
646.33 Pregnancy complication, recurrent pregnancy loss, antepartum condition or complication
646.53 Asymptomatic bacteriuria antepartum
646.93 Unspecified complication of pregnancy, antepartum
649.03 Tobacco use disorder complicating pregnancy, childbirth, or the puerperium, antepartum condition or complication
649.13 Obesity complicating pregnancy, childbirth, or the puerperium, antepartum condition or complication
649.23 Bariatric surgery status complicating pregnancy, childbirth, or the puerperium, antepartum condition or complication
649.33 Coagulation defects complicating pregnancy, childbirth, or the puerperium, antepartum condition or complication
649.43 Epilepsy complicating pregnancy, childbirth, or the puerperium, antepartum condition or complication
649.53 Spotting complicating pregnancy, antepartum condition or complication
649.63 Uterine size date discrepancy, antepartum condition or complication
649.73 Cervical shortening, antepartum condition or complication
651.03 Twin pregnancy, antepartum
651.13 Triplet pregnancy, antepartum
651.23 Quadruplet pregnancy, antepartum
651.33 Twin pregnancy with fetal loss and retention of one fetus, antepartum
651.43 Triplet pregnancy with fetal loss and retention of one or more, antepartum
651.53 Quadruplet pregnancy with fetal loss and retention of one or more, antepartum
651.63 Other multiple pregnancy with fetal loss and retention of one or more fetus(es), antepartum
651.73 Multiple gestation following (elective) fetal reduction, antepartum condition or complication
651.83 Other specified multiple gestation, antepartum
651.93 Unspecified multiple gestation, antepartum
652.03 Unstable lie of fetus, antepartum
652.13 Breech or other malpresentation successfully converted to cephalic presentation, antepartum
652.23 Breech presentation without mention of version, antepartum
652.33 Transverse or oblique fetal presentation, antepartum
652.43 Fetal face or brow presentation, antepartum
652.53 High fetal head at term, antepartum
652.63 Multiple gestation with malpresentation of one fetus or more, antepartum
652.73 Prolapsed arm of fetus, antepartum condition or complication
652.83 Other specified malposition or malpresentation of fetus, antepartum
652.93 Unspecified malposition or malpresentation of fetus, antepartum
653.03 Major abnormality of bony pelvis, not further specified, antepartum
653.13 Generally contracted pelvis in pregnancy, antepartum
653.23 Inlet contraction of pelvis in pregnancy, antepartum
653.33 Outlet contraction of pelvis in pregnancy, antepartum
653.43 Fetopelvic disproportion, antepartum
653.53 Unusually large fetus causing disproportion, antepartum
653.63 Hydrocephalic fetus causing disproportion, antepartum
653.73 Other fetal abnormality causing disproportion, antepartum
653.83 Fetal disproportion of other origin, antepartum
653.93 Unspecified fetal disproportion, antepartum
654.03 Congenital abnormalities of pregnant uterus, antepartum
654.13 Tumors of body of uterus, antepartum condition or complication
654.23 Previous cesarean delivery, antepartum condition or complication
654.33 Retroverted and incarcerated gravid uterus, antepartum
654.43 Other abnormalities in shape or position of gravid uterus and of neighboring structures, antepartum
654.53 Cervical incompetence, antepartum condition or complication
654.63 Other congenital or acquired abnormality of cervix, antepartum condition or complication
654.73 Congenital or acquired abnormality of vagina, antepartum condition or complication
654.83 Congenital or acquired abnormality of vulva, antepartum condition or complication
654.93 Other and unspecified abnormality of organs and soft tissues of pelvis, antepartum condition or complication
655.03 Central nervous system malformation in fetus, antepartum
655.13 Chromosomal abnormality in fetus, affecting management of mother, antepartum
655.23 Hereditary disease in family possibly affecting fetus, affecting management of mother, antepartum condition or complication
655.33 Suspected damage to fetus from viral disease in mother, affecting management of mother, antepartum condition or complication
655.43 Suspected damage to fetus from other disease in mother, affecting management of mother, antepartum condition or complication
655.53 Suspected damage to fetus from drugs, affecting management of mother, antepartum
655.63 Suspected damage to fetus from radiation, affecting management of mother, antepartum condition or complication
655.73 Decreased fetal movements, affecting management of mother, antepartum condition or complication
655.83 Other known or suspected fetal abnormality, not elsewhere classified, affecting management of mother, antepartum condition or complication
655.93 Unspecified fetal abnormality affecting management of mother, antepartum condition or complication
656.03 Fetal-maternal hemorrhage, antepartum condition or complication
656.13 Rhesus isoimmunization affecting management of mother, antepartum condition
656.23 Isoimmunization from other and unspecified blood-group incompatibility, affecting management of mother, antepartum
656.33 Fetal distress affecting management of mother, antepartum
656.43 Intrauterine death affecting management of mother, antepartum
656.53 Poor fetal growth, affecting management of mother, antepartum condition or complication
656.63 Excessive fetal growth affecting management of mother, antepartum
656.73 Other placental conditions affecting management of mother, antepartum
656.83 Other specified fetal and placental problems affecting management of mother, antepartum

---

Ⓣ *Transfer DRG*   ⓢ *Special Payment*   ☑ *Optimization Potential*   ▽ *Targeted Potential*   * *Code Range*   ● *New DRG*   ▲ *Revised DRG Title*

158   Valid 10/01/2012–09/30/2013   © 2012 OptumInsight, Inc.

656.93 Unspecified fetal and placental problem affecting management of mother, antepartum
657.03 Polyhydramnios, antepartum complication
658.03 Oligohydramnios, antepartum
658.13 Premature rupture of membranes in pregnancy, antepartum
658.23 Delayed delivery after spontaneous or unspecified rupture of membranes, antepartum
658.33 Delayed delivery after artificial rupture of membranes, antepartum
658.43 Infection of amniotic cavity, antepartum
658.83 Other problem associated with amniotic cavity and membranes, antepartum
658.93 Unspecified problem associated with amniotic cavity and membranes, antepartum
659.03 Failed mechanical induction of labor, antepartum
659.13 Failed medical or unspecified induction of labor, antepartum
659.23 Unspecified maternal pyrexia, antepartum
659.33 Generalized infection during labor, antepartum
659.43 Grand multiparity with current pregnancy, antepartum
659.53 Elderly primigravida, antepartum
659.63 Elderly multigravida, with antepartum condition or complication
659.73 Abnormality in fetal heart rate or rhythm, antepartum condition or complication
659.83 Other specified indication for care or intervention related to labor and delivery, antepartum
659.93 Unspecified indication for care or intervention related to labor and delivery, antepartum
660.03 Obstruction caused by malposition of fetus at onset of labor, antepartum
660.13 Obstruction by bony pelvis during labor and delivery, antepartum
660.23 Obstruction by abnormal pelvic soft tissues during labor and delivery, antepartum
660.33 Deep transverse arrest and persistent occipitoposterior position during labor and delivery, antepartum
660.43 Shoulder (girdle) dystocia during labor and delivery, antepartum
660.53 Locked twins, antepartum
660.63 Unspecified failed trial of labor, antepartum
660.73 Failed forceps or vacuum extractor, unspecified, antepartum
660.83 Other causes of obstructed labor, antepartum
660.93 Unspecified obstructed labor, antepartum
661.03 Primary uterine inertia, antepartum
661.13 Secondary uterine inertia, antepartum
661.23 Other and unspecified uterine inertia, antepartum
661.33 Precipitate labor, antepartum
661.43 Hypertonic, incoordinate, or prolonged uterine contractions, antepartum
661.93 Unspecified abnormality of labor, antepartum
662.03 Prolonged first stage of labor, antepartum
662.13 Unspecified prolonged labor, antepartum
662.23 Prolonged second stage of labor, antepartum
662.33 Delayed delivery of second twin, triplet, etc., antepartum
663.03 Prolapse of cord, complicating labor and delivery, antepartum
663.13 Cord around neck, with compression, complicating labor and delivery, antepartum
663.23 Other and unspecified cord entanglement, with compression, complicating labor and delivery, antepartum
663.33 Other and unspecified cord entanglement, without mention of compression, complicating labor and delivery, antepartum
663.43 Short cord complicating labor and delivery, antepartum
663.53 Vasa previa complicating labor and delivery, antepartum
663.63 Vascular lesions of cord complicating labor and delivery, antepartum
663.83 Other umbilical cord complications during labor and delivery, antepartum

663.93 Unspecified umbilical cord complication during labor and delivery, antepartum
665.03 Rupture of uterus before onset of labor, antepartum
665.83 Other specified obstetrical trauma, antepartum
665.93 Unspecified obstetrical trauma, antepartum
668.03 Pulmonary complications of the administration of anesthesia or other sedation in labor and delivery, antepartum
668.13 Cardiac complications of the administration of anesthesia or other sedation in labor and delivery, antepartum
668.23 Central nervous system complications of the administration of anesthesia or other sedation in labor and delivery, antepartum
668.83 Other complications of the administration of anesthesia or other sedation in labor and delivery, antepartum
668.93 Unspecified complication of the administration of anesthesia or other sedation in labor and delivery, antepartum
669.03 Maternal distress complicating labor and delivery, antepartum condition or complication
669.13 Shock during or following labor and delivery, antepartum shock
669.23 Maternal hypotension syndrome, antepartum
669.43 Other complications of obstetrical surgery and procedures, antepartum condition or complication
669.83 Other complication of labor and delivery, antepartum condition or complication
669.93 Unspecified complication of labor and delivery, antepartum condition or complication
671.03 Varicose veins of legs, antepartum
671.13 Varicose veins of vulva and perineum, antepartum
671.23 Superficial thrombophlebitis, antepartum
671.33 Deep phlebothrombosis, antepartum
671.53 Other antepartum phlebitis and thrombosis
671.83 Other venous complication, antepartum
671.93 Unspecified venous complication, antepartum
673.03 Obstetrical air embolism, antepartum condition or complication
673.13 Amniotic fluid embolism, antepartum condition or complication
673.23 Obstetrical blood-clot embolism, antepartum
673.33 Obstetrical pyemic and septic embolism, antepartum
673.83 Other obstetrical pulmonary embolism, antepartum
674.03 Cerebrovascular disorder, antepartum
674.53 Peripartum cardiomyopathy, antepartum condition or complication
675.03 Infection of nipple, antepartum
675.13 Abscess of breast, antepartum
675.23 Nonpurulent mastitis, antepartum
675.83 Other specified infection of the breast and nipple, antepartum
675.93 Unspecified infection of the breast and nipple, antepartum
676.03 Retracted nipple, antepartum condition or complication
676.13 Cracked nipple, antepartum condition or complication
676.23 Engorgement of breast, antepartum
676.33 Other and unspecified disorder of breast associated with childbirth, antepartum condition or complication
676.43 Failure of lactation, antepartum condition or complication
676.53 Suppressed lactation, antepartum condition or complication
676.63 Galactorrhea, antepartum condition or complication
676.83 Other disorder of lactation, antepartum condition or complication
676.93 Unspecified disorder of lactation, antepartum condition or complication
678.03 Fetal hematologic conditions, antepartum condition or complication
678.13 Fetal conjoined twins, antepartum condition or complication
679.03 Maternal complications from in utero procedure, antepartum condition or complication

| Surgical | Medical | CC Indicator | MCC Indicator | Procedure Proxy |

679.13	Fetal complications from in utero procedure, antepartum condition or complication
792.3	Nonspecific abnormal finding in amniotic fluid
796.5	Abnormal finding on antenatal screening
V28.0	Screening for chromosomal anomalies by amniocentesis
V28.1	Screening for raised alpha-fetoprotein levels in amniotic fluid
V28.2	Other antenatal screening based on amniocentesis
V61.6	Illegitimacy or illegitimate pregnancy

DRG 998   Principal Diagnosis Invalid as Discharge Diagnosis
    GMLOS 0.0   AMLOS 0.0   RW 0.0000

Note: If there is no value in either the GMLOS or the AMLOS, the volume of cases for this DRG is insufficient to determine a meaningful computation of these statistics.

Principal diagnoses listed for MDC 14 considered invalid as discharge diagnosis

641.00	Placenta previa without hemorrhage, unspecified as to episode of care
641.10	Hemorrhage from placenta previa, unspecified as to episode of care
641.20	Premature separation of placenta, unspecified as to episode of care
641.30	Antepartum hemorrhage associated with coagulation defects, unspecified as to episode of care
641.80	Other antepartum hemorrhage, unspecified as to episode of care
641.90	Unspecified antepartum hemorrhage, unspecified as to episode of care
642.00	Benign essential hypertension complicating pregnancy, childbirth, and the puerperium, unspecified as to episode of care
642.10	Hypertension secondary to renal disease, complicating pregnancy, childbirth, and the puerperium, unspecified as to episode of care
642.20	Other pre-existing hypertension complicating pregnancy, childbirth, and the puerperium, unspecified as to episode of care
642.30	Transient hypertension of pregnancy, unspecified as to episode of care
642.40	Mild or unspecified pre-eclampsia, unspecified as to episode of care
642.50	Severe pre-eclampsia, unspecified as to episode of care
642.60	Eclampsia complicating pregnancy, childbirth or the puerperium, unspecified as to episode of care
642.70	Pre-eclampsia or eclampsia superimposed on pre-existing hypertension, complicating pregnancy, childbirth, or the puerperium, unspecified as to episode of care
642.90	Unspecified hypertension complicating pregnancy, childbirth, or the puerperium, unspecified as to episode of care
643.00	Mild hyperemesis gravidarum, unspecified as to episode of care
643.10	Hyperemesis gravidarum with metabolic disturbance, unspecified as to episode of care
643.20	Late vomiting of pregnancy, unspecified as to episode of care
643.80	Other vomiting complicating pregnancy, unspecified as to episode of care
643.90	Unspecified vomiting of pregnancy, unspecified as to episode of care
645.10	Post term pregnancy, unspecified as to episode of care or not applicable
645.20	Prolonged pregnancy, unspecified as to episode of care or not applicable
646.10	Edema or excessive weight gain in pregnancy, unspecified as to episode of care
646.20	Unspecified renal disease in pregnancy, unspecified as to episode of care
646.30	Pregnancy complication, recurrent pregnancy loss, unspecified as to episode of care
646.40	Peripheral neuritis in pregnancy, unspecified as to episode of care
646.50	Asymptomatic bacteriuria in pregnancy, unspecified as to episode of care
646.60	Infections of genitourinary tract in pregnancy, unspecified as to episode of care
646.70	Liver and biliary tract disorders in pregnancy, unspecified as to episode of care or not applicable
646.80	Other specified complication of pregnancy, unspecified as to episode of care
646.90	Unspecified complication of pregnancy, unspecified as to episode of care
647.00	Maternal syphilis, complicating pregnancy, childbirth, or the puerperium, unspecified as to episode of care
647.10	Maternal gonorrhea complicating pregnancy, childbirth, or the puerperium, unspecified as to episode of care
647.20	Other maternal venereal diseases, complicating pregnancy, childbirth, or the puerperium, unspecified as to episode of care
647.30	Maternal tuberculosis complicating pregnancy, childbirth, or the puerperium, unspecified as to episode of care
647.40	Maternal malaria complicating pregnancy, childbirth or the puerperium, unspecified as to episode of care
647.50	Maternal rubella complicating pregnancy, childbirth, or the puerperium, unspecified as to episode of care
647.60	Other maternal viral disease complicating pregnancy, childbirth, or the puerperium, unspecified as to episode of care
647.80	Other specified maternal infectious and parasitic disease complicating pregnancy, childbirth, or the puerperium, unspecified as to episode of care
647.90	Unspecified maternal infection or infestation complicating pregnancy, childbirth, or the puerperium, unspecified as to episode of care
648.00	Maternal diabetes mellitus, complicating pregnancy, childbirth, or the puerperium, unspecified as to episode of care
648.10	Maternal thyroid dysfunction complicating pregnancy, childbirth, or the puerperium, unspecified as to episode of care or not applicable
648.20	Maternal anemia of mother, complicating pregnancy, childbirth, or the puerperium, unspecified as to episode of care
648.30	Maternal drug dependence complicating pregnancy, childbirth, or the puerperium, unspecified as to episode of care
648.40	Maternal mental disorders, complicating pregnancy, childbirth, or the puerperium, unspecified as to episode of care
648.50	Maternal congenital cardiovascular disorders, complicating pregnancy, childbirth, or the puerperium, unspecified as to episode of care
648.60	Other maternal cardiovascular diseases complicating pregnancy, childbirth, or the puerperium, unspecified as to episode of care
648.70	Bone and joint disorders of maternal back, pelvis, and lower limbs, complicating pregnancy, childbirth, or the puerperium, unspecified as to episode of care
648.80	Abnormal maternal glucose tolerance, complicating pregnancy, childbirth, or the puerperium, unspecified as to episode of care
648.90	Other current maternal conditions classifiable elsewhere, complicating pregnancy, childbirth, or the puerperium, unspecified as to episode of care
649.00	Tobacco use disorder complicating pregnancy, childbirth, or the puerperium, unspecified as to episode of care or not applicable

649.10 Obesity complicating pregnancy, childbirth, or the puerperium, unspecified as to episode of care or not applicable

649.20 Bariatric surgery status complicating pregnancy, childbirth, or the puerperium, unspecified as to episode of care or not applicable

649.30 Coagulation defects complicating pregnancy, childbirth, or the puerperium, unspecified as to episode of care or not applicable

649.40 Epilepsy complicating pregnancy, childbirth, or the puerperium, unspecified as to episode of care or not applicable

649.50 Spotting complicating pregnancy, unspecified as to episode of care or not applicable

649.60 Uterine size date discrepancy, unspecified as to episode of care or not applicable

649.70 Cervical shortening, unspecified as to episode of care or not applicable

651.00 Twin pregnancy, unspecified as to episode of care

651.10 Triplet pregnancy, unspecified as to episode of care

651.20 Quadruplet pregnancy, unspecified as to episode of care

651.30 Twin pregnancy with fetal loss and retention of one fetus, unspecified as to episode of care or not applicable

651.40 Triplet pregnancy with fetal loss and retention of one or more, unspecified as to episode of care or not applicable

651.50 Quadruplet pregnancy with fetal loss and retention of one or more, unspecified as to episode of care or not applicable

651.60 Other multiple pregnancy with fetal loss and retention of one or more fetus(es), unspecified as to episode of care or not applicable

651.70 Multiple gestation following (elective) fetal reduction, unspecified as to episode of care or not applicable

651.80 Other specified multiple gestation, unspecified as to episode of care

651.90 Unspecified multiple gestation, unspecified as to episode of care

652.00 Unstable lie of fetus, unspecified as to episode of care

652.10 Breech or other malpresentation successfully converted to cephalic presentation, unspecified as to episode of care

652.20 Breech presentation without mention of version, unspecified as to episode of care

652.30 Transverse or oblique fetal presentation, unspecified as to episode of care

652.40 Fetal face or brow presentation, unspecified as to episode of care

652.50 High fetal head at term, unspecified as to episode of care

652.60 Multiple gestation with malpresentation of one fetus or more, unspecified as to episode of care

652.70 Prolapsed arm of fetus, unspecified as to episode of care

652.80 Other specified malposition or malpresentation of fetus, unspecified as to episode of care

652.90 Unspecified malposition or malpresentation of fetus, unspecified as to episode of care

653.00 Major abnormality of bony pelvis, not further specified in pregnancy, unspecified as to episode of care

653.10 Generally contracted pelvis in pregnancy, unspecified as to episode of care in pregnancy

653.20 Inlet contraction of pelvis in pregnancy, unspecified as to episode of care in pregnancy

653.30 Outlet contraction of pelvis in pregnancy, unspecified as to episode of care in pregnancy

653.40 Fetopelvic disproportion, unspecified as to episode of care

653.50 Unusually large fetus causing disproportion, unspecified as to episode of care

653.60 Hydrocephalic fetus causing disproportion, unspecified as to episode of care

653.70 Other fetal abnormality causing disproportion, unspecified as to episode of care

653.80 Fetal disproportion of other origin, unspecified as to episode of care

653.90 Unspecified fetal disproportion, unspecified as to episode of care

654.00 Congenital abnormalities of pregnant uterus, unspecified as to episode of care

654.10 Tumors of body of pregnant uterus, unspecified as to episode of care in pregnancy

654.20 Previous cesarean delivery, unspecified as to episode of care or not applicable

654.30 Retroverted and incarcerated gravid uterus, unspecified as to episode of care

654.40 Other abnormalities in shape or position of gravid uterus and of neighboring structures, unspecified as to episode of care

654.50 Cervical incompetence, unspecified as to episode of care in pregnancy

654.60 Other congenital or acquired abnormality of cervix, unspecified as to episode of care in pregnancy

654.70 Congenital or acquired abnormality of vagina, unspecified as to episode of care in pregnancy

654.80 Congenital or acquired abnormality of vulva, unspecified as to episode of care in pregnancy

654.90 Other and unspecified abnormality of organs and soft tissues of pelvis, unspecified as to episode of care in pregnancy

655.00 Central nervous system malformation in fetus, unspecified as to episode of care in pregnancy

655.10 Chromosomal abnormality in fetus, affecting management of mother, unspecified as to episode of care in pregnancy

655.20 Hereditary disease in family possibly affecting fetus, affecting management of mother, unspecified as to episode of care in pregnancy

655.30 Suspected damage to fetus from viral disease in mother, affecting management of mother, unspecified as to episode of care in pregnancy

655.40 Suspected damage to fetus from other disease in mother, affecting management of mother, unspecified as to episode of care in pregnancy

655.50 Suspected damage to fetus from drugs, affecting management of mother, unspecified as to episode of care

655.60 Suspected damage to fetus from radiation, affecting management of mother, unspecified as to episode of care

655.70 Decreased fetal movements, unspecified as to episode of care

655.80 Other known or suspected fetal abnormality, not elsewhere classified, affecting management of mother, unspecified as to episode of care

655.90 Unspecified fetal abnormality affecting management of mother, unspecified as to episode of care

656.00 Fetal-maternal hemorrhage, unspecified as to episode of care in pregnancy

656.10 Rhesus isoimmunization unspecified as to episode of care in pregnancy

656.20 Isoimmunization from other and unspecified blood-group incompatibility, unspecified as to episode of care in pregnancy

656.50 Poor fetal growth, affecting management of mother, unspecified as to episode of care

656.60 Excessive fetal growth affecting management of mother, unspecified as to episode of care

656.70 Other placental conditions affecting management of mother, unspecified as to episode of care

656.80 Other specified fetal and placental problems affecting management of mother, unspecified as to episode of care

656.90 Unspecified fetal and placental problem affecting management of mother, unspecified as to episode of care

657.00 Polyhydramnios, unspecified as to episode of care

658.00 Oligohydramnios, unspecified as to episode of care

658.80 Other problem associated with amniotic cavity and membranes, unspecified as to episode of care

| Surgical | Medical | CC Indicator | MCC Indicator | Procedure Proxy |

658.90	Unspecified problem associated with amniotic cavity and membranes, unspecified as to episode of care
659.40	Grand multiparity with current pregnancy, unspecified as to episode of care
666.00	Third-stage postpartum hemorrhage, unspecified as to episode of care
666.10	Other immediate postpartum hemorrhage, unspecified as to episode of care
666.20	Delayed and secondary postpartum hemorrhage, unspecified as to episode of care
666.30	Postpartum coagulation defects, unspecified as to episode of care
667.00	Retained placenta without hemorrhage, unspecified as to episode of care
667.10	Retained portions of placenta or membranes, without hemorrhage, unspecified as to episode of care
670.00	Major puerperal infection, unspecified, unspecified as to episode of care or not applicable
670.10	Puerperal endometritis, unspecified as to episode of care or not applicable
670.20	Puerperal sepsis, unspecified as to episode of care or not applicable
670.30	Puerperal septic thrombophlebitis, unspecified as to episode of care or not applicable
670.80	Other major puerperal infection, unspecified as to episode of care or not applicable
671.00	Varicose veins of legs complicating pregnancy and the puerperium, unspecified as to episode of care
671.10	Varicose veins of vulva and perineum complicating pregnancy and the puerperium, unspecified as to episode of care
671.20	Superficial thrombophlebitis complicating pregnancy and the puerperium, unspecified as to episode of care
671.30	Deep phlebothrombosis, antepartum, unspecified as to episode of care
671.40	Deep phlebothrombosis, postpartum, unspecified as to episode of care
671.50	Other phlebitis and thrombosis complicating pregnancy and the puerperium, unspecified as to episode of care
671.80	Other venous complication of pregnancy and the puerperium, unspecified as to episode of care
671.90	Unspecified venous complication of pregnancy and the puerperium, unspecified as to episode of care
672.00	Puerperal pyrexia of unknown origin, unspecified as to episode of care
673.00	Obstetrical air embolism, unspecified as to episode of care
673.10	Amniotic fluid embolism, unspecified as to episode of care
673.20	Obstetrical blood-clot embolism, unspecified as to episode of care
673.30	Obstetrical pyemic and septic embolism, unspecified as to episode of care
673.80	Other obstetrical pulmonary embolism, unspecified as to episode of care
674.00	Cerebrovascular disorder occurring in pregnancy, childbirth, or the puerperium, unspecified as to episode of care
674.10	Disruption of cesarean wound, unspecified as to episode of care
674.20	Disruption of perineal wound, unspecified as to episode of care in pregnancy
674.30	Other complication of obstetrical surgical wounds, unspecified as to episode of care
674.40	Placental polyp, unspecified as to episode of care
674.50	Peripartum cardiomyopathy, unspecified as to episode of care or not applicable
674.80	Other complication of puerperium, unspecified as to episode of care
674.90	Unspecified complications of puerperium, unspecified as to episode of care
675.00	Infection of nipple associated with childbirth, unspecified as to episode of care
675.10	Abscess of breast associated with childbirth, unspecified as to episode of care
675.20	Nonpurulent mastitis, unspecified as to episode of prenatal or postnatal care
675.80	Other specified infection of the breast and nipple associated with childbirth, unspecified as to episode of care
675.90	Unspecified infection of the breast and nipple, unspecified as to prenatal or postnatal episode of care
676.00	Retracted nipple, unspecified as to prenatal or postnatal episode of care
676.10	Cracked nipple, unspecified as to prenatal or postnatal episode of care
676.20	Engorgement of breasts, unspecified as to prenatal or postnatal episode of care
676.30	Other and unspecified disorder of breast associated with childbirth, unspecified as to episode of care
676.40	Failure of lactation, unspecified as to episode of care
676.50	Suppressed lactation, unspecified as to episode of care
676.60	Galactorrhea associated with childbirth, unspecified as to episode of care
676.80	Other disorder of lactation, unspecified as to episode of care
676.90	Unspecified disorder of lactation, unspecified as to episode of care
677	Late effect of complication of pregnancy, childbirth, and the puerperium
678.00	Fetal hematologic conditions, unspecified as to episode of care or not applicable
678.10	Fetal conjoined twins, unspecified as to episode of care or not applicable
679.10	Fetal complications from in utero procedure, unspecified as to episode of care or not applicable
V23.0	Pregnancy with history of infertility
V23.1	Pregnancy with history of trophoblastic disease
V23.2	Pregnancy with history of abortion
V23.3	Pregnancy with grand multiparity
V23.4*	Pregnancy with other poor obstetric history
V23.5	Pregnancy with other poor reproductive history
V23.7	Insufficient prenatal care
V23.8*	Supervision of other high-risk pregnancy
V23.9	Unspecified high-risk pregnancy

MDC 15

Newborns And Other Neonates With Conditions Originating In The Perinatal Period

277.01	762.2	764.14	765.10	768.1	770.9	774.31	777.8	V32.00
747.83	762.3	764.15	765.11	768.2	771.0	774.39	777.9	V32.01
760.0	762.4	764.16	765.12	768.3	771.1	774.4	778.0	V32.1
760.1	762.5	764.17	765.13	768.4	771.2	774.5	778.1	V32.2
760.2	762.6	764.18	765.14	768.5	771.3	774.6	778.2	V33.00
760.3	762.7	764.19	765.15	768.6	771.4	774.7	778.3	V33.01
760.4	762.8	764.20	765.16	768.70	771.5	775.0	778.4	V33.1
760.5	762.9	764.21	765.17	768.71	771.6	775.1	778.5	V33.2
760.61	763.0	764.22	765.18	768.72	771.7	775.2	778.6	V34.00
760.62	763.1	764.23	765.19	768.73	771.81	775.3	778.7	V34.01
760.63	763.2	764.24	765.20	768.9	771.82	775.4	778.8	V34.1
760.64	763.3	764.25	765.21	769	771.83	775.5	778.9	V34.2
760.70	763.4	764.26	765.22	770.0	771.89	775.6	779.0	V35.00
760.71	763.5	764.27	765.23	770.10	772.0	775.7	779.1	V35.01
760.72	763.6	764.28	765.24	770.11	772.10	775.81	779.2	V35.1
760.73	763.7	764.29	765.25	770.12	772.11	775.89	779.31	V35.2
760.74	763.81	764.90	765.26	770.13	772.12	775.9	779.32	V36.00
760.75	763.82	764.91	765.27	770.14	772.13	776.0	779.33	V36.01
760.76	763.83	764.92	765.28	770.15	772.14	776.1	779.4	V36.1
760.77	763.84	764.93	765.29	770.16	772.2	776.2	779.5	V36.2
760.78	763.89	764.94	766.0	770.17	772.3	776.3	779.6	V37.00
760.79	763.9	764.95	766.1	770.18	772.4	776.4	779.81	V37.01
760.8	764.00	764.96	766.21	770.2	772.5	776.5	779.82	V37.1
760.9	764.01	764.97	766.22	770.3	772.6	776.6	779.83	V37.2
761.0	764.02	764.98	767.0	770.4	772.8	776.7	779.84	V39.00
761.1	764.03	764.99	767.11	770.5	772.9	776.8	779.85	V39.01
761.2	764.04	765.00	767.19	770.6	773.0	776.9	779.89	V39.1
761.3	764.05	765.01	767.2	770.81	773.1	777.1	779.9	V39.2
761.4	764.06	765.02	767.3	770.82	773.2	777.2	V30.00	
761.5	764.07	765.03	767.4	770.83	773.3	777.3	V30.01	
761.6	764.08	765.04	767.5	770.84	773.4	777.4	V30.1	
761.7	764.09	765.05	767.6	770.85	773.5	777.50	V30.2	
761.8	764.10	765.06	767.7	770.86	774.0	777.51	V31.00	
761.9	764.11	765.07	767.8	770.87	774.1	777.52	V31.01	
762.0	764.12	765.08	767.9	770.88	774.2	777.53	V31.1	
762.1	764.13	765.09	768.0	770.89	774.30	777.6	V31.2	

MEDICAL

DRG 789   Neonates, Died or Transferred to Another Acute Care Facility

GMLOS 1.8   AMLOS 1.8   RW 1.5035

Discharge status of transfer to an acute care facility or expired

DRG 790   Extreme Immaturity or Respiratory Distress Syndrome, Neonate

GMLOS 17.9   AMLOS 17.9   RW 4.9579

Principal or Secondary Diagnosis

765.01	Extreme fetal immaturity, less than 500 grams
765.02	Extreme fetal immaturity, 500-749 grams
765.03	Extreme fetal immaturity, 750-999 grams
765.04	Extreme fetal immaturity, 1,000-1,249 grams
765.05	Extreme fetal immaturity, 1,250-1,499 grams
765.21	Less than 24 completed weeks of gestation
765.22	24 completed weeks of gestation
765.23	25-26 completed weeks of gestation
769	Respiratory distress syndrome in newborn

DRG 791   Prematurity with Major Problems

GMLOS 13.3   AMLOS 13.3   RW 3.3861   ☑

Principal or Secondary Diagnosis of Prematurity

765.00	Extreme fetal immaturity, unspecified (weight)
765.06	Extreme fetal immaturity, 1,500-1,749 grams
765.07	Extreme fetal immaturity, 1,750-1,999 grams
765.08	Extreme fetal immaturity, 2,000-2,499 grams
765.1*	Other preterm infants
765.24	27-28 completed weeks of gestation
765.25	29-30 completed weeks of gestation
765.26	31-32 completed weeks of gestation
765.27	33-34 completed weeks of gestation
765.28	35-36 completed weeks of gestation

AND

Principal or Secondary Diagnosis of Major Problem

277.01	Cystic fibrosis with meconium ileus
747.83	Persistent fetal circulation
763.4	Fetus or newborn affected by cesarean delivery
764.11	Light-for-dates with signs of fetal malnutrition, less than 500 grams
764.12	Light-for-dates with signs of fetal malnutrition, 500-749 grams
764.13	Light-for-dates with signs of fetal malnutrition, 750-999 grams
764.14	Light-for-dates with signs of fetal malnutrition, 1,000-1,249 grams
764.15	Light-for-dates with signs of fetal malnutrition, 1,250-1,499 grams
764.16	Light-for-dates with signs of fetal malnutrition, 1,500-1,749 grams
764.17	Light-for-dates with signs of fetal malnutrition, 1,750-1,999 grams
764.18	Light-for-dates with signs of fetal malnutrition, 2,000-2,499 grams
764.21	Fetal malnutrition without mention of "light-for-dates", less than 500 grams
764.22	Fetal malnutrition without mention of "light-for-dates", 500-749 grams
764.23	Fetal malnutrition without mention of "light-for-dates", 750-999 grams
764.24	Fetal malnutrition without mention of "light-for-dates", 1,000-1,249 grams
764.25	Fetal malnutrition without mention of "light-for-dates", 1,250-1,499 grams
764.26	Fetal malnutrition without mention of "light-for-dates", 1,500-1,749 grams
764.27	Fetal malnutrition without mention of "light-for-dates", 1,750-1,999 grams
764.28	Fetal malnutrition without mention of "light-for-dates", 2,000-2,499 grams
767.0	Subdural and cerebral hemorrhage, birth trauma
767.11	Birth trauma, epicranial subaponeurotic hemorrhage (massive)
767.4	Injury to spine and spinal cord, birth trauma
767.7	Other cranial and peripheral nerve injuries, birth trauma
768.5	Severe birth asphyxia
768.72	Moderate hypoxic-ischemic encephalopathy
768.73	Severe hypoxic-ischemic encephalopathy
770.0	Congenital pneumonia
770.1*	Fetal and newborn aspiration
770.2	Interstitial emphysema and related conditions of newborn
770.3	Pulmonary hemorrhage of fetus or newborn
770.4	Primary atelectasis of newborn
770.84	Respiratory failure of newborn
770.85	Aspiration of postnatal stomach contents without respiratory symptoms
770.86	Aspiration of postnatal stomach contents with respiratory symptoms
771.0	Congenital rubella
771.1	Congenital cytomegalovirus infection
771.2	Other congenital infection specific to the perinatal period
771.4	Omphalitis of the newborn
771.5	Neonatal infective mastitis
771.8*	Other infection specific to the perinatal period
772.0	Fetal blood loss affecting newborn
772.1*	Intraventricular hemorrhage
772.2	Fetal and neonatal subarachnoid hemorrhage of newborn
772.4	Fetal and neonatal gastrointestinal hemorrhage
772.5	Fetal and neonatal adrenal hemorrhage
773.2	Hemolytic disease due to other and unspecified isoimmunization of fetus or newborn
773.3	Hydrops fetalis due to isoimmunization
773.4	Kernicterus due to isoimmunization of fetus or newborn
773.5	Late anemia due to isoimmunization of fetus or newborn
774.4	Perinatal jaundice due to hepatocellular damage
774.7	Kernicterus of fetus or newborn not due to isoimmunization
775.1	Neonatal diabetes mellitus
775.2	Neonatal myasthenia gravis
775.3	Neonatal thyrotoxicosis
775.4	Hypocalcemia and hypomagnesemia of newborn
775.5	Other transitory neonatal electrolyte disturbances
775.6	Neonatal hypoglycemia
775.7	Late metabolic acidosis of newborn
776.0	Hemorrhagic disease of newborn
776.1	Transient neonatal thrombocytopenia
776.2	Disseminated intravascular coagulation in newborn
776.3	Other transient neonatal disorders of coagulation
776.6	Anemia of neonatal prematurity
777.1	Fetal and newborn meconium obstruction
777.2	Neonatal intestinal obstruction due to inspissated milk
777.5*	Necrotizing enterocolitis in newborn
777.6	Perinatal intestinal perforation
778.0	Hydrops fetalis not due to isoimmunization
779.0	Convulsions in newborn
779.1	Other and unspecified cerebral irritability in newborn
779.2	Cerebral depression, coma, and other abnormal cerebral signs in fetus or newborn
779.32	Bilious vomiting in newborn
779.4	Drug reactions and intoxications specific to newborn
779.5	Drug withdrawal syndrome in newborn
779.85	Cardiac arrest of newborn

Ⓣ Transfer DRG   SP Special Payment   ☑ Optimization Potential   ᵀᴱᴸ Targeted Potential   * Code Range   ● New DRG   ▲ Revised DRG Title

164   Valid 10/01/2012-09/30/2013   © 2012 OptumInsight, Inc.

OR

Secondary Diagnosis of Major Problem

036.3	Waterhouse-Friderichsen syndrome, meningococcal
036.4*	Meningococcal carditis
036.81	Meningococcal optic neuritis
036.82	Meningococcal arthropathy
037	Tetanus
038*	Septicemia
040.0	Gas gangrene
040.41	Infant botulism
046.2	Subacute sclerosing panencephalitis
052.0	Postvaricella encephalitis
052.1	Varicella (hemorrhagic) pneumonitis
052.7	Chickenpox with other specified complications
052.8	Chickenpox with unspecified complication
052.9	Varicella without mention of complication
053.0	Herpes zoster with meningitis
053.10	Herpes zoster with unspecified nervous system complication
053.11	Geniculate herpes zoster
053.12	Postherpetic trigeminal neuralgia
053.13	Postherpetic polyneuropathy
053.19	Other herpes zoster with nervous system complications
053.20	Herpes zoster dermatitis of eyelid
053.21	Herpes zoster keratoconjunctivitis
053.22	Herpes zoster iridocyclitis
053.29	Other ophthalmic herpes zoster complications
053.71	Otitis externa due to herpes zoster
053.79	Other specified herpes zoster complications
053.8	Unspecified herpes zoster complication
053.9	Herpes zoster without mention of complication
054.0	Eczema herpeticum
054.2	Herpetic gingivostomatitis
054.3	Herpetic meningoencephalitis
054.4*	Herpes simplex with ophthalmic complications
054.5	Herpetic septicemia
054.71	Visceral herpes simplex
054.72	Herpes simplex meningitis
054.73	Herpes simplex otitis externa
054.79	Other specified herpes simplex complications
054.8	Unspecified herpes simplex complication
055.0	Postmeasles encephalitis
055.1	Postmeasles pneumonia
055.2	Postmeasles otitis media
055.7*	Measles, with other specified complications
055.8	Unspecified measles complication
056.0*	Rubella with neurological complications
056.7*	Rubella with other specified complications
056.8	Unspecified rubella complications
058.10	Roseola infantum, unspecified
058.11	Roseola infantum due to human herpesvirus 6
058.12	Roseola infantum due to human herpesvirus 7
058.21	Human herpesvirus 6 encephalitis
058.29	Other human herpesvirus encephalitis
070.2*	Viral hepatitis B with hepatic coma
070.3*	Viral hepatitis B without mention of hepatic coma
070.4*	Other specified viral hepatitis with hepatic coma
070.5*	Other specified viral hepatitis without mention of hepatic coma
070.6	Unspecified viral hepatitis with hepatic coma
070.9	Unspecified viral hepatitis without mention of hepatic coma
072.0	Mumps orchitis
072.1	Mumps meningitis
072.2	Mumps encephalitis
072.3	Mumps pancreatitis
072.7*	Mumps with other specified complications
072.8	Unspecified mumps complication
079.6	Respiratory syncytial virus (RSV)
112.4	Candidiasis of lung
112.5	Disseminated candidiasis
112.81	Candidal endocarditis
112.82	Candidal otitis externa
112.83	Candidal meningitis
112.84	Candidiasis of the esophagus
112.85	Candidiasis of the intestine
114.2	Coccidioidal meningitis
114.3	Other forms of progressive coccidioidomycosis
115.01	Histoplasma capsulatum meningitis
115.02	Histoplasma capsulatum retinitis
115.03	Histoplasma capsulatum pericarditis
115.04	Histoplasma capsulatum endocarditis
115.05	Histoplasma capsulatum pneumonia
115.11	Histoplasma duboisii meningitis
115.12	Histoplasma duboisii retinitis
115.13	Histoplasma duboisii pericarditis
115.14	Histoplasma duboisii endocarditis
115.15	Histoplasma duboisii pneumonia
115.91	Unspecified Histoplasmosis meningitis
115.92	Unspecified Histoplasmosis retinitis
115.93	Unspecified Histoplasmosis pericarditis
115.94	Unspecified Histoplasmosis endocarditis
115.95	Unspecified Histoplasmosis pneumonia
116.0	Blastomycosis
116.1	Paracoccidioidomycosis
117.3	Aspergillosis
117.4	Mycotic mycetomas
117.5	Cryptococcosis
117.6	Allescheriosis (Petriellidiosis)
117.7	Zygomycosis (Phycomycosis or Mucormycosis)
118	Opportunistic mycoses
130.0	Meningoencephalitis due to toxoplasmosis
130.1	Conjunctivitis due to toxoplasmosis
130.2	Chorioretinitis due to toxoplasmosis
130.3	Myocarditis due to toxoplasmosis
130.4	Pneumonitis due to toxoplasmosis
130.5	Hepatitis due to toxoplasmosis
130.7	Toxoplasmosis of other specified sites
130.8	Multisystemic disseminated toxoplasmosis
136.3	Pneumocystosis
251.0	Hypoglycemic coma
252.1	Hypoparathyroidism
253.5	Diabetes insipidus
254.1	Abscess of thymus
261	Nutritional marasmus
262	Other severe protein-calorie malnutrition
263.0	Malnutrition of moderate degree
263.1	Malnutrition of mild degree
263.8	Other protein-calorie malnutrition
263.9	Unspecified protein-calorie malnutrition
276*	Disorders of fluid, electrolyte, and acid-base balance
277.88	Tumor lysis syndrome
282.40	Thalassemia, unspecified
282.41	Sickle-cell thalassemia without crisis
282.42	Sickle-cell thalassemia with crisis
282.43	Alpha thalassemia
282.44	Beta thalassemia
282.45	Delta-beta thalassemia
282.47	Hemoglobin E-beta thalassemia
282.49	Other thalassemia
283.1*	Non-autoimmune hemolytic anemias
283.2	Hemoglobinuria due to hemolysis from external causes
283.9	Acquired hemolytic anemia, unspecified
285.1	Acute posthemorrhagic anemia
286.6	Defibrination syndrome
287.4*	Secondary thrombocytopenia
289.84	Heparin-induced thrombocytopenia [HIT]
292.0	Drug withdrawal
320*	Bacterial meningitis
321*	Meningitis due to other organisms
322.0	Nonpyogenic meningitis

322.1	Eosinophilic meningitis
322.9	Unspecified meningitis
324*	Intracranial and intraspinal abscess
348.1	Anoxic brain damage
349.0	Reaction to spinal or lumbar puncture
349.1	Nervous system complications from surgically implanted device
349.3*	Dural tear
349.81	Cerebrospinal fluid rhinorrhea
349.82	Toxic encephalopathy
377.00	Unspecified papilledema
377.01	Papilledema associated with increased intracranial pressure
377.02	Papilledema associated with decreased ocular pressure
383.01	Subperiosteal abscess of mastoid
383.81	Postauricular fistula
398.91	Rheumatic heart failure (congestive)
402.01	Malignant hypertensive heart disease with heart failure
402.11	Benign hypertensive heart disease with heart failure
402.91	Hypertensive heart disease, unspecified, with heart failure
404.01	Hypertensive heart and chronic kidney disease, malignant, with heart failure and with chronic kidney disease stage I through stage IV, or unspecified
404.03	Hypertensive heart and chronic kidney disease, malignant, with heart failure and with chronic kidney disease stage V or end stage renal disease
404.11	Hypertensive heart and chronic kidney disease, benign, with heart failure and with chronic kidney disease stage I through stage IV, or unspecified
404.13	Hypertensive heart and chronic kidney disease, benign, with heart failure and chronic kidney disease stage V or end stage renal disease
404.91	Hypertensive heart and chronic kidney disease, unspecified, with heart failure and with chronic kidney disease stage I through stage IV, or unspecified
404.93	Hypertensive heart and chronic kidney disease, unspecified, with heart failure and chronic kidney disease stage V or end stage renal disease
414.10	Aneurysm of heart
415*	Acute pulmonary heart disease
416.2	Chronic pulmonary embolism
420.0	Acute pericarditis in diseases classified elsewhere
421*	Acute and subacute endocarditis
422.0	Acute myocarditis in diseases classified elsewhere
422.92	Septic myocarditis
423.0	Hemopericardium
424.9*	Endocarditis, valve unspecified
425.8	Cardiomyopathy in other diseases classified elsewhere
426.0	Atrioventricular block, complete
426.53	Other bilateral bundle branch block
426.54	Trifascicular block
426.7	Anomalous atrioventricular excitation
426.89	Other specified conduction disorder
427.1	Paroxysmal ventricular tachycardia
427.3*	Atrial fibrillation and flutter
427.4*	Ventricular fibrillation and flutter
427.5	Cardiac arrest
428.0	Congestive heart failure, unspecified
428.1	Left heart failure
428.2*	Systolic heart failure
428.3*	Diastolic heart failure
428.4*	Combined systolic and diastolic heart failure
428.9	Unspecified heart failure
429.4	Functional disturbances following cardiac surgery
429.81	Other disorders of papillary muscle
429.82	Hyperkinetic heart disease
430	Subarachnoid hemorrhage
431	Intracerebral hemorrhage
432*	Other and unspecified intracranial hemorrhage
433.01	Occlusion and stenosis of basilar artery with cerebral infarction
433.11	Occlusion and stenosis of carotid artery with cerebral infarction
433.21	Occlusion and stenosis of vertebral artery with cerebral infarction
433.31	Occlusion and stenosis of multiple and bilateral precerebral arteries with cerebral infarction
433.81	Occlusion and stenosis of other specified precerebral artery with cerebral infarction
433.91	Occlusion and stenosis of unspecified precerebral artery with cerebral infarction
434*	Occlusion of cerebral arteries
436	Acute, but ill-defined, cerebrovascular disease
440.24	Atherosclerosis of native arteries of the extremities with gangrene
444*	Arterial embolism and thrombosis
449	Septic arterial embolism
451.1*	Phlebitis and thrombophlebitis of deep veins of lower extremities
451.2	Phlebitis and thrombophlebitis of lower extremities, unspecified
451.81	Phlebitis and thrombophlebitis of iliac vein
453.2	Other venous embolism and thrombosis, of inferior vena cava
457.2	Lymphangitis
459.0	Unspecified hemorrhage
478.22	Parapharyngeal abscess
478.24	Retropharyngeal abscess
478.3*	Paralysis of vocal cords or larynx
478.75	Laryngeal spasm
481	Pneumococcal pneumonia (streptococcus pneumoniae pneumonia)
482*	Other bacterial pneumonia
483*	Pneumonia due to other specified organism
485	Bronchopneumonia, organism unspecified
486	Pneumonia, organism unspecified
488.01	Influenza due to identified avian influenza virus with pneumonia
488.02	Influenza due to identified avian influenza virus with other respiratory manifestations
488.11	Influenza due to identified 2009 H1N1 influenza virus with pneumonia
488.12	Influenza due to identified 2009 H1N1 influenza virus with other respiratory manifestations
488.81	Influenza due to identified novel influenza A virus with pneumonia
488.82	Influenza due to identified novel influenza A virus with other respiratory manifestations
493.01	Extrinsic asthma with status asthmaticus
493.11	Intrinsic asthma with status asthmaticus
493.91	Asthma, unspecified with status asthmaticus
507.0	Pneumonitis due to inhalation of food or vomitus
507.8	Pneumonitis due to other solids and liquids
508.0	Acute pulmonary manifestations due to radiation
510*	Empyema
511.1	Pleurisy with effusion, with mention of bacterial cause other than tuberculosis
511.89	Other specified forms of effusion, except tuberculous
511.9	Unspecified pleural effusion
513*	Abscess of lung and mediastinum
516.6*	Interstitial lung diseases of childhood
518.0	Pulmonary collapse
518.1	Interstitial emphysema
518.4	Unspecified acute edema of lung
518.52	Other pulmonary insufficiency, not elsewhere classified, following trauma and surgery
519.2	Mediastinitis
530.4	Perforation of esophagus
530.84	Tracheoesophageal fistula
536.1	Acute dilatation of stomach

T *Transfer DRG*   SP *Special Payment*   ☑ *Optimization Potential*   ▽ *Targeted Potential*   * *Code Range*   ● *New DRG*   ▲ *Revised DRG Title*

550.00	Inguinal hernia with gangrene, unilateral or unspecified, (not specified as recurrent)
550.02	Inguinal hernia with gangrene, bilateral
550.10	Inguinal hernia with obstruction, without mention of gangrene, unilateral or unspecified, (not specified as recurrent)
550.12	Inguinal hernia with obstruction, without mention gangrene, bilateral, (not specified as recurrent)
551.00	Femoral hernia with gangrene, unilateral or unspecified (not specified as recurrent)
551.02	Femoral hernia with gangrene, bilateral, (not specified as recurrent)
551.1	Umbilical hernia with gangrene
551.2*	Ventral hernia with gangrene
551.3	Diaphragmatic hernia with gangrene
551.8	Hernia of other specified sites, with gangrene
551.9	Hernia of unspecified site, with gangrene
552.00	Unilateral or unspecified femoral hernia with obstruction
552.02	Bilateral femoral hernia with obstruction
552.1	Umbilical hernia with obstruction
552.2*	Ventral hernia with obstruction
552.3	Diaphragmatic hernia with obstruction
552.8	Hernia of other specified site, with obstruction
552.9	Hernia of unspecified site, with obstruction
557.0	Acute vascular insufficiency of intestine
558.2	Toxic gastroenteritis and colitis
560.0	Intussusception
560.1	Paralytic ileus
560.2	Volvulus
560.30	Unspecified impaction of intestine
560.32	Fecal impaction
560.39	Impaction of intestine, other
560.89	Other specified intestinal obstruction
560.9	Unspecified intestinal obstruction
566	Abscess of anal and rectal regions
567*	Peritonitis and retroperitoneal infections
568.81	Hemoperitoneum (nontraumatic)
569.3	Hemorrhage of rectum and anus
569.7*	Complications of intestinal pouch
569.83	Perforation of intestine
570	Acute and subacute necrosis of liver
572.0	Abscess of liver
572.1	Portal pyemia
572.2	Hepatic encephalopathy
572.4	Hepatorenal syndrome
573.3	Unspecified hepatitis
573.4	Hepatic infarction
576.1	Cholangitis
577.0	Acute pancreatitis
577.2	Cyst and pseudocyst of pancreas
578*	Gastrointestinal hemorrhage
579.3	Other and unspecified postsurgical nonabsorption
580*	Acute glomerulonephritis
584*	Acute kidney failure
590.1*	Acute pyelonephritis
590.2	Renal and perinephric abscess
590.3	Pyeloureteritis cystica
590.8*	Other pyelonephritis or pyonephrosis, not specified as acute or chronic
590.9	Unspecified infection of kidney
591	Hydronephrosis
593.5	Hydroureter
595.0	Acute cystitis
595.4	Cystitis in diseases classified elsewhere
595.81	Cystitis cystica
595.89	Other specified types of cystitis
595.9	Unspecified cystitis
596.0	Bladder neck obstruction
596.1	Intestinovesical fistula
596.2	Vesical fistula, not elsewhere classified

596.4	Atony of bladder
596.6	Nontraumatic rupture of bladder
596.7	Hemorrhage into bladder wall
597.0	Urethral abscess
599.0	Urinary tract infection, site not specified
599.6*	Urinary obstruction
599.7*	Hematuria
619.1	Digestive-genital tract fistula, female
619.8	Other specified fistula involving female genital tract
620.7	Hematoma of broad ligament
682*	Other cellulitis and abscess
683	Acute lymphadenitis
693.0	Dermatitis due to drugs and medicines taken internally
695.0	Toxic erythema
708.0	Allergic urticaria
733.1*	Pathologic fracture
740*	Anencephalus and similar anomalies
741*	Spina bifida
742*	Other congenital anomalies of nervous system
745.4	Ventricular septal defect
756.72	Omphalocele
756.73	Gastroschisis
759.4	Conjoined twins
779.7	Periventricular leukomalacia
780.01	Coma
780.03	Persistent vegetative state
780.31	Febrile convulsions (simple), unspecified
780.39	Other convulsions
781.7	Tetany
785.0	Unspecified tachycardia
785.4	Gangrene
785.50	Unspecified shock
788.2*	Retention of urine
790.7	Bacteremia
791.1	Chyluria
799.1	Respiratory arrest
820*	Fracture of neck of femur
821.0*	Closed fracture of shaft or unspecified part of femur
821.1*	Open fracture of shaft or unspecified part of femur
860*	Traumatic pneumothorax and hemothorax
865*	Injury to spleen
900.0*	Injury to carotid artery
900.1	Internal jugular vein injury
900.81	External jugular vein injury
901.0	Thoracic aorta injury
901.1	Innominate and subclavian artery injury
901.2	Superior vena cava injury
901.3	Innominate and subclavian vein injury
901.41	Pulmonary artery injury
901.42	Pulmonary vein injury
902.0	Abdominal aorta injury
902.10	Unspecified inferior vena cava injury
953.4	Injury to brachial plexus
958.0	Air embolism as an early complication of trauma
958.1	Fat embolism as an early complication of trauma
958.2	Secondary and recurrent hemorrhage as an early complication of trauma
958.3	Posttraumatic wound infection not elsewhere classified
958.4	Traumatic shock
958.5	Traumatic anuria
958.7	Traumatic subcutaneous emphysema
995.20	Unspecified adverse effect of unspecified drug, medicinal and biological substance
995.21	Arthus phenomenon
995.22	Unspecified adverse effect of anesthesia
995.23	Unspecified adverse effect of insulin
995.27	Other drug allergy
995.29	Unspecified adverse effect of other drug, medicinal and biological substance
995.4	Shock due to anesthesia not elsewhere classified

MDC 15: Newborns And Other Neonates With Conditions Originating In The Perinatal Period—MEDICAL

MDC 15: Newborns And Other Neonates With Conditions Originating In The Perinatal Period—MEDICAL

997.0*	Nervous system complications
997.1	Cardiac complications
997.2	Peripheral vascular complications
997.3*	Respiratory complications
997.4*	Digestive system complications, not elsewhere classified
997.5	Urinary complications
997.71	Vascular complications of mesenteric artery
997.72	Vascular complications of renal artery
997.79	Vascular complications of other vessels
998.0*	Postoperative shock
998.11	Hemorrhage complicating a procedure
998.12	Hematoma complicating a procedure
998.13	Seroma complicating a procedure
998.2	Accidental puncture or laceration during procedure
998.4	Foreign body accidentally left during procedure, not elsewhere classified
998.51	Infected postoperative seroma
998.59	Other postoperative infection
998.6	Persistent postoperative fistula, not elsewhere classified
998.7	Acute reaction to foreign substance accidentally left during procedure, not elsewhere classified
998.9	Unspecified complication of procedure, not elsewhere classified
999.1	Air embolism as complication of medical care, not elsewhere classified
999.2	Other vascular complications of medical care, not elsewhere classified
999.34	Acute infection following transfusion, infusion, or injection of blood and blood products
999.39	Complications of medical care, NEC, infection following other infusion, injection, transfusion, or vaccination
999.4*	Anaphylactic reaction due to serum
999.5*	Other serum reaction, not elsewhere classified
999.6*	ABO incompatibility reaction due to transfusion of blood or blood products
999.7*	Rh and other non-ABO incompatibility reaction due to transfusion of blood or blood products
999.8*	Other and unspecified infusion and transfusion reaction

DRG 792   Prematurity without Major Problems

GMLOS 8.6	AMLOS 8.6	RW 2.0431	☑

Principal or Secondary Diagnosis of Prematurity

765.00	Extreme fetal immaturity, unspecified (weight)
765.06	Extreme fetal immaturity, 1,500-1,749 grams
765.07	Extreme fetal immaturity, 1,750-1,999 grams
765.08	Extreme fetal immaturity, 2,000-2,499 grams
765.1*	Other preterm infants
765.24	27-28 completed weeks of gestation
765.25	29-30 completed weeks of gestation
765.26	31-32 completed weeks of gestation
765.27	33-34 completed weeks of gestation
765.28	35-36 completed weeks of gestation

DRG 793   Full Term Neonate with Major Problems

GMLOS 4.7	AMLOS 4.7	RW 3.4783	☑

Principal or Secondary Diagnosis of Major Problem

277.01	Cystic fibrosis with meconium ileus
747.83	Persistent fetal circulation
763.4	Fetus or newborn affected by cesarean delivery
764.11	Light-for-dates with signs of fetal malnutrition, less than 500 grams
764.12	Light-for-dates with signs of fetal malnutrition, 500-749 grams
764.13	Light-for-dates with signs of fetal malnutrition, 750-999 grams
764.14	Light-for-dates with signs of fetal malnutrition, 1,000-1,249 grams

764.15	Light-for-dates with signs of fetal malnutrition, 1,250-1,499 grams
764.16	Light-for-dates with signs of fetal malnutrition, 1,500-1,749 grams
764.17	Light-for-dates with signs of fetal malnutrition, 1,750-1,999 grams
764.18	Light-for-dates with signs of fetal malnutrition, 2,000-2,499 grams
764.21	Fetal malnutrition without mention of "light-for-dates", less than 500 grams
764.22	Fetal malnutrition without mention of "light-for-dates", 500-749 grams
764.23	Fetal malnutrition without mention of "light-for-dates", 750-999 grams
764.24	Fetal malnutrition without mention of "light-for-dates", 1,000-1,249 grams
764.25	Fetal malnutrition without mention of "light-for-dates", 1,250-1,499 grams
764.26	Fetal malnutrition without mention of "light-for-dates", 1,500-1,749 grams
764.27	Fetal malnutrition without mention of "light-for-dates", 1,750-1,999 grams
764.28	Fetal malnutrition without mention of "light-for-dates", 2,000-2,499 grams
767.0	Subdural and cerebral hemorrhage, birth trauma
767.11	Birth trauma, epicranial subaponeurotic hemorrhage (massive)
767.4	Injury to spine and spinal cord, birth trauma
767.7	Other cranial and peripheral nerve injuries, birth trauma
768.5	Severe birth asphyxia
768.72	Moderate hypoxic-ischemic encephalopathy
768.73	Severe hypoxic-ischemic encephalopathy
770.0	Congenital pneumonia
770.1*	Fetal and newborn aspiration
770.2	Interstitial emphysema and related conditions of newborn
770.3	Pulmonary hemorrhage of fetus or newborn
770.4	Primary atelectasis of newborn
770.84	Respiratory failure of newborn
770.85	Aspiration of postnatal stomach contents without respiratory symptoms
770.86	Aspiration of postnatal stomach contents with respiratory symptoms
771.0	Congenital rubella
771.1	Congenital cytomegalovirus infection
771.2	Other congenital infection specific to the perinatal period
771.4	Omphalitis of the newborn
771.5	Neonatal infective mastitis
771.8*	Other infection specific to the perinatal period
772.0	Fetal blood loss affecting newborn
772.1*	Intraventricular hemorrhage
772.2	Fetal and neonatal subarachnoid hemorrhage of newborn
772.4	Fetal and neonatal gastrointestinal hemorrhage
772.5	Fetal and neonatal adrenal hemorrhage
773.2	Hemolytic disease due to other and unspecified isoimmunization of fetus or newborn
773.3	Hydrops fetalis due to isoimmunization
773.4	Kernicterus due to isoimmunization of fetus or newborn
773.5	Late anemia due to isoimmunization of fetus or newborn
774.4	Perinatal jaundice due to hepatocellular damage
774.7	Kernicterus of fetus or newborn not due to isoimmunization
775.1	Neonatal diabetes mellitus
775.2	Neonatal myasthenia gravis
775.3	Neonatal thyrotoxicosis
775.4	Hypocalcemia and hypomagnesemia of newborn
775.5	Other transitory neonatal electrolyte disturbances
775.6	Neonatal hypoglycemia
775.7	Late metabolic acidosis of newborn
776.0	Hemorrhagic disease of newborn
776.1	Transient neonatal thrombocytopenia
776.2	Disseminated intravascular coagulation in newborn

Ⓣ Transfer DRG   ⓈⓅ Special Payment   ☑ Optimization Potential   ⃝ᵀᵍᵗ Targeted Potential   * Code Range   ● New DRG   ▲ Revised DRG Title

168   Valid 10/01/2012-09/30/2013   © 2012 OptumInsight, Inc.

776.3	Other transient neonatal disorders of coagulation
776.6	Anemia of neonatal prematurity
777.1	Fetal and newborn meconium obstruction
777.2	Neonatal intestinal obstruction due to inspissated milk
777.5*	Necrotizing enterocolitis in newborn
777.6	Perinatal intestinal perforation
778.0	Hydrops fetalis not due to isoimmunization
779.0	Convulsions in newborn
779.1	Other and unspecified cerebral irritability in newborn
779.2	Cerebral depression, coma, and other abnormal cerebral signs in fetus or newborn
779.32	Bilious vomiting in newborn
779.4	Drug reactions and intoxications specific to newborn
779.5	Drug withdrawal syndrome in newborn
779.85	Cardiac arrest of newborn

OR

Secondary Diagnosis of Major Problem

036.3	Waterhouse-Friderichsen syndrome, meningococcal
036.4*	Meningococcal carditis
036.81	Meningococcal optic neuritis
036.82	Meningococcal arthropathy
037	Tetanus
038*	Septicemia
040.0	Gas gangrene
040.41	Infant botulism
046.2	Subacute sclerosing panencephalitis
052.0	Postvaricella encephalitis
052.1	Varicella (hemorrhagic) pneumonitis
052.7	Chickenpox with other specified complications
052.8	Chickenpox with unspecified complication
052.9	Varicella without mention of complication
053.0	Herpes zoster with meningitis
053.10	Herpes zoster with unspecified nervous system complication
053.11	Geniculate herpes zoster
053.12	Postherpetic trigeminal neuralgia
053.13	Postherpetic polyneuropathy
053.19	Other herpes zoster with nervous system complications
053.20	Herpes zoster dermatitis of eyelid
053.21	Herpes zoster keratoconjunctivitis
053.22	Herpes zoster iridocyclitis
053.29	Other ophthalmic herpes zoster complications
053.71	Otitis externa due to herpes zoster
053.79	Other specified herpes zoster complications
053.8	Unspecified herpes zoster complication
053.9	Herpes zoster without mention of complication
054.0	Eczema herpeticum
054.2	Herpetic gingivostomatitis
054.3	Herpetic meningoencephalitis
054.4*	Herpes simplex with ophthalmic complications
054.5	Herpetic septicemia
054.71	Visceral herpes simplex
054.72	Herpes simplex meningitis
054.73	Herpes simplex otitis externa
054.79	Other specified herpes simplex complications
054.8	Unspecified herpes simplex complication
055.0	Postmeasles encephalitis
055.1	Postmeasles pneumonia
055.2	Postmeasles otitis media
055.7*	Measles, with other specified complications
055.8	Unspecified measles complication
056.0*	Rubella with neurological complications
056.7*	Rubella with other specified complications
056.8	Unspecified rubella complications
058.10	Roseola infantum, unspecified
058.11	Roseola infantum due to human herpesvirus 6
058.12	Roseola infantum due to human herpesvirus 7
058.21	Human herpesvirus 6 encephalitis
058.29	Other human herpesvirus encephalitis

070.2*	Viral hepatitis B with hepatic coma
070.3*	Viral hepatitis B without mention of hepatic coma
070.4*	Other specified viral hepatitis with hepatic coma
070.5*	Other specified viral hepatitis without mention of hepatic coma
070.6	Unspecified viral hepatitis with hepatic coma
070.9	Unspecified viral hepatitis without mention of hepatic coma
072.0	Mumps orchitis
072.1	Mumps meningitis
072.2	Mumps encephalitis
072.3	Mumps pancreatitis
072.7*	Mumps with other specified complications
072.8	Unspecified mumps complication
079.6	Respiratory syncytial virus (RSV)
112.4	Candidiasis of lung
112.5	Disseminated candidiasis
112.81	Candidal endocarditis
112.82	Candidal otitis externa
112.83	Candidal meningitis
112.84	Candidiasis of the esophagus
112.85	Candidiasis of the intestine
114.2	Coccidioidal meningitis
114.3	Other forms of progressive coccidioidomycosis
115.01	Histoplasma capsulatum meningitis
115.02	Histoplasma capsulatum retinitis
115.03	Histoplasma capsulatum pericarditis
115.04	Histoplasma capsulatum endocarditis
115.05	Histoplasma capsulatum pneumonia
115.11	Histoplasma duboisii meningitis
115.12	Histoplasma duboisii retinitis
115.13	Histoplasma duboisii pericarditis
115.14	Histoplasma duboisii endocarditis
115.15	Histoplasma duboisii pneumonia
115.91	Unspecified Histoplasmosis meningitis
115.92	Unspecified Histoplasmosis retinitis
115.93	Unspecified Histoplasmosis pericarditis
115.94	Unspecified Histoplasmosis endocarditis
115.95	Unspecified Histoplasmosis pneumonia
116.0	Blastomycosis
116.1	Paracoccidioidomycosis
117.3	Aspergillosis
117.4	Mycotic mycetomas
117.5	Cryptococcosis
117.6	Allescheriosis (Petriellidiosis)
117.7	Zygomycosis (Phycomycosis or Mucormycosis)
118	Opportunistic mycoses
130.0	Meningoencephalitis due to toxoplasmosis
130.1	Conjunctivitis due to toxoplasmosis
130.2	Chorioretinitis due to toxoplasmosis
130.3	Myocarditis due to toxoplasmosis
130.4	Pneumonitis due to toxoplasmosis
130.5	Hepatitis due to toxoplasmosis
130.7	Toxoplasmosis of other specified sites
130.8	Multisystemic disseminated toxoplasmosis
136.3	Pneumocystosis
251.0	Hypoglycemic coma
252.1	Hypoparathyroidism
253.5	Diabetes insipidus
254.1	Abscess of thymus
261	Nutritional marasmus
262	Other severe protein-calorie malnutrition
263.0	Malnutrition of moderate degree
263.1	Malnutrition of mild degree
263.8	Other protein-calorie malnutrition
263.9	Unspecified protein-calorie malnutrition
276*	Disorders of fluid, electrolyte, and acid-base balance
277.88	Tumor lysis syndrome
282.40	Thalassemia, unspecified
282.41	Sickle-cell thalassemia without crisis
282.42	Sickle-cell thalassemia with crisis

Surgical   *Medical*   *CC Indicator*   *MCC Indicator*   *Procedure Proxy*

MDC 15: Newborns And Other Neonates With Conditions Originating In The Perinatal Period—MEDICAL

282.43	Alpha thalassemia
282.44	Beta thalassemia
282.45	Delta-beta thalassemia
282.47	Hemoglobin E-beta thalassemia
282.49	Other thalassemia
283.1*	Non-autoimmune hemolytic anemas
283.2	Hemoglobinuria due to hemolysis from external causes
283.9	Acquired hemolytic anemia, unspecified
285.1	Acute posthemorrhagic anemia
286.6	Defibrination syndrome
287.4*	Secondary thrombocytopenia
289.84	Heparin-induced thrombocytopenia [HIT]
292.0	Drug withdrawal
320*	Bacterial meningitis
321*	Meningitis due to other organisms
322.0	Nonpyogenic meningitis
322.1	Eosinophilic meningitis
322.9	Unspecified meningitis
324*	Intracranial and intraspinal abscess
348.1	Anoxic brain damage
349.0	Reaction to spinal or lumbar puncture
349.1	Nervous system complications from surgically implanted device
349.3*	Dural tear
349.81	Cerebrospinal fluid rhinorrhea
349.82	Toxic encephalopathy
377.00	Unspecified papilledema
377.01	Papilledema associated with increased intracranial pressure
377.02	Papilledema associated with decreased ocular pressure
383.01	Subperiosteal abscess of mastoid
383.81	Postauricular fistula
398.91	Rheumatic heart failure (congestive)
402.01	Malignant hypertensive heart disease with heart failure
402.11	Benign hypertensive heart disease with heart failure
402.91	Hypertensive heart disease, unspecified, with heart failure
404.01	Hypertensive heart and chronic kidney disease, malignant, with heart failure and with chronic kidney disease stage I through stage IV, or unspecified
404.03	Hypertensive heart and chronic kidney disease, malignant, with heart failure and with chronic kidney disease stage V or end stage renal disease
404.11	Hypertensive heart and chronic kidney disease, benign, with heart failure and with chronic kidney disease stage I through stage IV, or unspecified
404.13	Hypertensive heart and chronic kidney disease, benign, with heart failure and chronic kidney disease stage V or end stage renal disease
404.91	Hypertensive heart and chronic kidney disease, unspecified, with heart failure and with chronic kidney disease stage I through stage IV, or unspecified
404.93	Hypertensive heart and chronic kidney disease, unspecified, with heart failure and chronic kidney disease stage V or end stage renal disease
414.10	Aneurysm of heart
415*	Acute pulmonary heart disease
416.2	Chronic pulmonary embolism
420.0	Acute pericarditis in diseases classified elsewhere
421*	Acute and subacute endocarditis
422.0	Acute myocarditis in diseases classified elsewhere
422.92	Septic myocarditis
423.0	Hemopericardium
424.9*	Endocarditis, valve unspecified
425.8	Cardiomyopathy in other diseases classified elsewhere
426.0	Atrioventricular block, complete
426.53	Other bilateral bundle branch block
426.54	Trifascicular block
426.7	Anomalous atrioventricular excitation
426.89	Other specified conduction disorder
427.1	Paroxysmal ventricular tachycardia
427.3*	Atrial fibrillation and flutter

427.4*	Ventricular fibrillation and flutter
427.5	Cardiac arrest
428.0	Congestive heart failure, unspecified
428.1	Left heart failure
428.2*	Systolic heart failure
428.3*	Diastolic heart failure
428.4*	Combined systolic and diastolic heart failure
428.9	Unspecified heart failure
429.4	Functional disturbances following cardiac surgery
429.81	Other disorders of papillary muscle
429.82	Hyperkinetic heart disease
430	Subarachnoid hemorrhage
431	Intracerebral hemorrhage
432*	Other and unspecified intracranial hemorrhage
433.01	Occlusion and stenosis of basilar artery with cerebral infarction
433.11	Occlusion and stenosis of carotid artery with cerebral infarction
433.21	Occlusion and stenosis of vertebral artery with cerebral infarction
433.31	Occlusion and stenosis of multiple and bilateral precerebral arteries with cerebral infarction
433.81	Occlusion and stenosis of other specified precerebral artery with cerebral infarction
433.91	Occlusion and stenosis of unspecified precerebral artery with cerebral infarction
434*	Occlusion of cerebral arteries
436	Acute, but ill-defined, cerebrovascular disease
440.24	Atherosclerosis of native arteries of the extremities with gangrene
444*	Arterial embolism and thrombosis
449	Septic arterial embolism
451.1*	Phlebitis and thrombophlebitis of deep veins of lower extremities
451.2	Phlebitis and thrombophlebitis of lower extremities, unspecified
451.81	Phlebitis and thrombophlebitis of iliac vein
453.2	Other venous embolism and thrombosis, of inferior vena cava
457.2	Lymphangitis
459.0	Unspecified hemorrhage
478.22	Parapharyngeal abscess
478.24	Retropharyngeal abscess
478.3*	Paralysis of vocal cords or larynx
478.75	Laryngeal spasm
481	Pneumococcal pneumonia (streptococcus pneumoniae pneumonia)
482*	Other bacterial pneumonia
483*	Pneumonia due to other specified organism
485	Bronchopneumonia, organism unspecified
486	Pneumonia, organism unspecified
488.01	Influenza due to identified avian influenza virus with pneumonia
488.02	Influenza due to identified avian influenza virus with other respiratory manifestations
488.11	Influenza due to identified 2009 H1N1 influenza virus with pneumonia
488.12	Influenza due to identified 2009 H1N1 influenza virus with other respiratory manifestations
488.81	Influenza due to identified novel influenza A virus with pneumonia
488.82	Influenza due to identified novel influenza A virus with other respiratory manifestations
493.01	Extrinsic asthma with status asthmaticus
493.11	Intrinsic asthma with status asthmaticus
493.91	Asthma, unspecified with status asthmaticus
507.0	Pneumonitis due to inhalation of food or vomitus
507.8	Pneumonitis due to other solids and liquids
508.0	Acute pulmonary manifestations due to radiation
510*	Empyema

T *Transfer DRG*   SP *Special Payment*   ☑ *Optimization Potential*   ▽ *Targeted Potential*   * *Code Range*   ● *New DRG*   ▲ *Revised DRG Title*

511.1	Pleurisy with effusion, with mention of bacterial cause other than tuberculosis
511.89	Other specified forms of effusion, except tuberculous
511.9	Unspecified pleural effusion
513*	Abscess of lung and mediastinum
516.6*	Interstitial lung diseases of childhood
518.0	Pulmonary collapse
518.1	Interstitial emphysema
518.4	Unspecified acute edema of lung
518.52	Other pulmonary insufficiency, not elsewhere classified, following trauma and surgery
519.2	Mediastinitis
530.4	Perforation of esophagus
530.84	Tracheoesophageal fistula
536.1	Acute dilatation of stomach
550.00	Inguinal hernia with gangrene, unilateral or unspecified, (not specified as recurrent)
550.02	Inguinal hernia with gangrene, bilateral
550.10	Inguinal hernia with obstruction, without mention of gangrene, unilateral or unspecified, (not specified as recurrent)
550.12	Inguinal hernia with obstruction, without mention gangrene, bilateral, (not specified as recurrent)
551.00	Femoral hernia with gangrene, unilateral or unspecified (not specified as recurrent)
551.02	Femoral hernia with gangrene, bilateral, (not specified as recurrent)
551.1	Umbilical hernia with gangrene
551.2*	Ventral hernia with gangrene
551.3	Diaphragmatic hernia with gangrene
551.8	Hernia of other specified sites, with gangrene
551.9	Hernia of unspecified site, with gangrene
552.00	Unilateral or unspecified femoral hernia with obstruction
552.02	Bilateral femoral hernia with obstruction
552.1	Umbilical hernia with obstruction
552.2*	Ventral hernia with obstruction
552.3	Diaphragmatic hernia with obstruction
552.8	Hernia of other specified site, with obstruction
552.9	Hernia of unspecified site, with obstruction
557.0	Acute vascular insufficiency of intestine
558.2	Toxic gastroenteritis and colitis
560.0	Intussusception
560.1	Paralytic ileus
560.2	Volvulus
560.30	Unspecified impaction of intestine
560.32	Fecal impaction
560.39	Impaction of intestine, other
560.89	Other specified intestinal obstruction
560.9	Unspecified intestinal obstruction
566	Abscess of anal and rectal regions
567*	Peritonitis and retroperitoneal infections
568.81	Hemoperitoneum (nontraumatic)
569.3	Hemorrhage of rectum and anus
569.7*	Complications of intestinal pouch
569.83	Perforation of intestine
570	Acute and subacute necrosis of liver
572.0	Abscess of liver
572.1	Portal pyemia
572.2	Hepatic encephalopathy
572.4	Hepatorenal syndrome
573.3	Unspecified hepatitis
573.4	Hepatic infarction
576.1	Cholangitis
577.0	Acute pancreatitis
577.2	Cyst and pseudocyst of pancreas
578*	Gastrointestinal hemorrhage
579.3	Other and unspecified postsurgical nonabsorption
580*	Acute glomerulonephritis
584*	Acute kidney failure
590.1*	Acute pyelonephritis
590.2	Renal and perinephric abscess
590.3	Pyeloureteritis cystica
590.8*	Other pyelonephritis or pyonephrosis, not specified as acute or chronic
590.9	Unspecified infection of kidney
591	Hydronephrosis
593.5	Hydroureter
595.0	Acute cystitis
595.4	Cystitis in diseases classified elsewhere
595.81	Cystitis cystica
595.89	Other specified types of cystitis
595.9	Unspecified cystitis
596.0	Bladder neck obstruction
596.1	Intestinovesical fistula
596.2	Vesical fistula, not elsewhere classified
596.4	Atony of bladder
596.6	Nontraumatic rupture of bladder
596.7	Hemorrhage into bladder wall
597.0	Urethral abscess
599.0	Urinary tract infection, site not specified
599.6*	Urinary obstruction
599.7*	Hematuria
619.1	Digestive-genital tract fistula, female
619.8	Other specified fistula involving female genital tract
620.7	Hematoma of broad ligament
682*	Other cellulitis and abscess
683	Acute lymphadenitis
693.0	Dermatitis due to drugs and medicines taken internally
695.0	Toxic erythema
708.0	Allergic urticaria
733.1*	Pathologic fracture
740*	Anencephalus and similar anomalies
741*	Spina bifida
742*	Other congenital anomalies of nervous system
745.4	Ventricular septal defect
756.72	Omphalocele
756.73	Gastroschisis
759.4	Conjoined twins
779.7	Periventricular leukomalacia
780.01	Coma
780.03	Persistent vegetative state
780.31	Febrile convulsions (simple), unspecified
780.39	Other convulsions
781.7	Tetany
785.0	Unspecified tachycardia
785.4	Gangrene
785.50	Unspecified shock
788.2*	Retention of urine
790.7	Bacteremia
791.1	Chyluria
799.1	Respiratory arrest
820*	Fracture of neck of femur
821.0*	Closed fracture of shaft or unspecified part of femur
821.1*	Open fracture of shaft or unspecified part of femur
860*	Traumatic pneumothorax and hemothorax
865*	Injury to spleen
900.0*	Injury to carotid artery
900.1	Internal jugular vein injury
900.81	External jugular vein injury
901.0	Thoracic aorta injury
901.1	Innominate and subclavian artery injury
901.2	Superior vena cava injury
901.3	Innominate and subclavian vein injury
901.41	Pulmonary artery injury
901.42	Pulmonary vein injury
902.0	Abdominal aorta injury
902.10	Unspecified inferior vena cava injury
953.4	Injury to brachial plexus
958.0	Air embolism as an early complication of trauma
958.1	Fat embolism as an early complication of trauma

Surgical   Medical   CC Indicator   MCC Indicator   Procedure Proxy

MDC 15: Newborns And Other Neonates With Conditions Originating In The Perinatal Period—MEDICAL

958.2	Secondary and recurrent hemorrhage as an early complication of trauma
958.3	Posttraumatic wound infection not elsewhere classified
958.4	Traumatic shock
958.5	Traumatic anuria
958.7	Traumatic subcutaneous emphysema
995.20	Unspecified adverse effect of unspecified drug, medicinal and biological substance
995.21	Arthus phenomenon
995.22	Unspecified adverse effect of anesthesia
995.23	Unspecified adverse effect of insulin
995.27	Other drug allergy
995.29	Unspecified adverse effect of other drug, medicinal and biological substance
995.4	Shock due to anesthesia not elsewhere classified
997.0*	Nervous system complications
997.1	Cardiac complications
997.2	Peripheral vascular complications
997.3*	Respiratory complications
997.4*	Digestive system complications, not elsewhere classified
997.5	Urinary complications
997.71	Vascular complications of mesenteric artery
997.72	Vascular complications of renal artery
997.79	Vascular complications of other vessels
998.0*	Postoperative shock
998.11	Hemorrhage complicating a procedure
998.12	Hematoma complicating a procedure
998.13	Seroma complicating a procedure
998.2	Accidental puncture or laceration during procedure
998.4	Foreign body accidentally left during procedure, not elsewhere classified
998.51	Infected postoperative seroma
998.59	Other postoperative infection
998.6	Persistent postoperative fistula, not elsewhere classified
998.7	Acute reaction to foreign substance accidentally left during procedure, not elsewhere classified
998.9	Unspecified complication of procedure, not elsewhere classified
999.1	Air embolism as complication of medical care, not elsewhere classified
999.2	Other vascular complications of medical care, not elsewhere classified
999.34	Acute infection following transfusion, infusion, or injection of blood and blood products
999.39	Complications of medical care, NEC, infection following other infusion, injection, transfusion, or vaccination
999.4*	Anaphylactic reaction due to serum
999.5*	Other serum reaction, not elsewhere classified
999.6*	ABO incompatibility reaction due to transfusion of blood or blood products
999.7*	Rh and other non-ABO incompatibility reaction due to transfusion of blood or blood products
999.8*	Other and unspecified infusion and transfusion reaction

DRG 794 Neonate with Other Significant Problems
GMLOS 3.4   AMLOS 3.4   RW 1.2311   ☑

Principal or secondary diagnosis of newborn or neonate with other significant problems, not assigned to DRGs 789-793, 795 or 998

DRG 795 Normal Newborn
GMLOS 3.1   AMLOS 3.1   RW 0.1667   ☑

Principal Diagnosis

762.4	Fetus or newborn affected by prolapsed cord
762.5	Fetus or newborn affected by other compression of umbilical cord
762.6	Fetus or newborn affected by other and unspecified conditions of umbilical cord
763.0	Fetus or newborn affected by breech delivery and extraction

763.1	Fetus or newborn affected by other malpresentation, malposition, and disproportion during labor and delivery
763.2	Fetus or newborn affected by forceps delivery
763.3	Fetus or newborn affected by delivery by vacuum extractor
763.6	Fetus or newborn affected to precipitate delivery
763.9	Unspecified complication of labor and delivery affecting fetus or newborn
764.08	Light-for-dates without mention of fetal malnutrition, 2,000-2,499 grams
764.09	Light-for-dates without mention of fetal malnutrition, 2,500 or more grams
764.98	Unspecified fetal growth retardation, 2,000-2,499 grams
764.99	Unspecified fetal growth retardation, 2,500 or more grams
765.20	Unspecified weeks of gestation
765.29	37 or more completed weeks of gestation
766.0	Exceptionally large baby relating to long gestation
766.1	Other "heavy-for-dates" infants not related to gestation period
766.2*	Late infant, not "heavy-for-dates"
767.19	Birth trauma, other injuries to scalp
768.6	Mild or moderate birth asphyxia
772.6	Fetal and neonatal cutaneous hemorrhage
774.3*	Neonatal jaundice due to delayed conjugation from other causes
774.5	Perinatal jaundice from other causes
774.6	Unspecified fetal and neonatal jaundice
778.8	Other specified condition involving the integument of fetus and newborn
779.31	Feeding problems in newborn
779.33	Other vomiting in newborn
779.83	Delayed separation of umbilical cord
V30.00	Single liveborn, born in hospital, delivered without mention of cesarean delivery
V30.01	Single liveborn, born in hospital, delivered by cesarean delivery
V30.1	Single liveborn, born before admission to hospital
V31.00	Twin, mate liveborn, born in hospital, delivered without mention of cesarean delivery
V31.01	Twin, mate liveborn, born in hospital, delivered by cesarean delivery
V31.1	Twin birth, mate liveborn, born before admission to hospital
V32.00	Twin, mate stillborn, born in hospital, delivered without mention of cesarean delivery
V32.01	Twin, mate stillborn, born in hospital, delivered by cesarean delivery
V32.1	Twin birth, mate stillborn, born before admission to hospital
V33.00	Twin, unspecified whether mate stillborn or liveborn, born in hospital, delivered without mention of cesarean delivery
V33.01	Twin, unspecified whether mate stillborn or liveborn, born in hospital, delivered by cesarean delivery
V33.1	Twin birth, unspecified whether mate liveborn or stillborn, born before admission to hospital
V34.00	Other multiple, mates all liveborn, born in hospital, delivered without mention of cesarean delivery
V34.01	Other multiple, mates all liveborn, born in hospital, delivered by cesarean delivery
V34.1	Other multiple birth (three or more), mates all liveborn, born before admission to hospital
V35.00	Other multiple, mates all stillborn, born in hospital, delivered without mention of cesarean delivery
V35.01	Other multiple, mates all stillborn, born in hospital, delivered by cesarean delivery
V35.1	Other multiple birth (three or more), mates all stillborn, born before admission to hospital
V36.00	Other multiple, mates liveborn and stillborn, born in hospital, delivered without mention of cesarean delivery
V36.01	Other multiple, mates liveborn and stillborn, born in hospital, delivered by cesarean delivery
V36.1	Other multiple birth (three or more), mates liveborn and stillborn, born before admission to hospital

T Transfer DRG   SP Special Payment   ☑ Optimization Potential   ᵀᴾ Targeted Potential   * Code Range   ● New DRG   ▲ Revised DRG Title

172   Valid 10/01/2012-09/30/2013   © 2012 OptumInsight, Inc.

V37.00	Other multiple, unspecified whether mates stillborn or liveborn, born in hospital, delivered without mention of cesarean delivery
V37.01	Other multiple, unspecified whether mates stillborn or liveborn, born in hospital, delivered by cesarean delivery
V37.1	Other multiple birth (three or more), unspecified whether mates liveborn or stillborn, born before admission to hospital
V39.00	Liveborn infant, unspecified whether single, twin, or multiple, born in hospital, delivered without mention of cesarean delivery
V39.01	Liveborn infant, unspecified whether single, twin, or multiple, born in hospital, delivered by cesarean
V39.1	Liveborn, unspecified whether single, twin or multiple, born before admission to hospital

AND

No Secondary Diagnosis
OR
Only Secondary Diagnosis

478.11	Nasal mucositis (ulcerative)
478.19	Other diseases of nasal cavity and sinuses
520.6	Disturbances in tooth eruption
605	Redundant prepuce and phimosis
623.8	Other specified noninflammatory disorder of vagina
686.9	Unspecified local infection of skin and subcutaneous tissue
691.0	Diaper or napkin rash
709.00	Dyschromia, unspecified
709.01	Vitiligo
709.09	Other dyschromia
744.1	Congenital anomalies of accessory auricle
752.5*	Undescended and retractile testicle
754.61	Congenital pes planus
757.33	Congenital pigmentary anomaly of skin
757.39	Other specified congenital anomaly of skin
762.4	Fetus or newborn affected by prolapsed cord
762.5	Fetus or newborn affected by other compression of umbilical cord
762.6	Fetus or newborn affected by other and unspecified conditions of umbilical cord
763.0	Fetus or newborn affected by breech delivery and extraction
763.1	Fetus or newborn affected by other malpresentation, malposition, and disproportion during labor and delivery
763.2	Fetus or newborn affected by forceps delivery
763.3	Fetus or newborn affected by delivery by vacuum extractor
763.6	Fetus or newborn affected by precipitate delivery
763.9	Unspecified complication of labor and delivery affecting fetus or newborn
764.08	Light-for-dates without mention of fetal malnutrition, 2,000-2,499 grams
764.09	Light-for-dates without mention of fetal malnutrition, 2,500 or more grams
764.98	Unspecified fetal growth retardation, 2,000-2,499 grams
764.99	Unspecified fetal growth retardation, 2,500 or more grams
765.20	Unspecified weeks of gestation
765.29	37 or more completed weeks of gestation
766.0	Exceptionally large baby relating to long gestation
766.1	Other "heavy-for-dates" infants not related to gestation period
766.2*	Late infant, not "heavy-for-dates"
767.19	Birth trauma, other injuries to scalp
768.6	Mild or moderate birth asphyxia
772.6	Fetal and neonatal cutaneous hemorrhage
774.3*	Neonatal jaundice due to delayed conjugation from other causes
774.5	Perinatal jaundice from other causes
774.6	Unspecified fetal and neonatal jaundice
778.8	Other specified condition involving the integument of fetus and newborn
794.15	Nonspecific abnormal auditory function studies
795.4	Other nonspecific abnormal histological findings
796.4	Other abnormal clinical finding
V01.81	Contact with or exposure to anthrax
V01.89	Contact or exposure to other communicable diseases
V05.3	Need for prophylactic vaccination and inoculation against viral hepatitis
V05.4	Need for prophylactic vaccination and inoculation against varicella
V05.8	Need for prophylactic vaccination and inoculation against other specified disease
V20.1	Health supervision of other healthy infant or child receiving care
V20.2	Routine infant or child health check
V20.3*	Newborn health supervision
V29*	Observation and evaluation of newborns and infants for suspected condition not found
V30.00	Single liveborn, born in hospital, delivered without mention of cesarean delivery
V30.01	Single liveborn, born in hospital, delivered by cesarean delivery
V30.1	Single liveborn, born before admission to hospital
V31.00	Twin, mate liveborn, born in hospital, delivered without mention of cesarean delivery
V31.01	Twin, mate liveborn, born in hospital, delivered by cesarean delivery
V31.1	Twin birth, mate liveborn, born before admission to hospital
V32.00	Twin, mate stillborn, born in hospital, delivered without mention of cesarean delivery
V32.01	Twin, mate stillborn, born in hospital, delivered by cesarean delivery
V32.1	Twin birth, mate stillborn, born before admission to hospital
V33.00	Twin, unspecified whether mate stillborn or liveborn, born in hospital, delivered without mention of cesarean delivery
V33.01	Twin, unspecified whether mate stillborn or liveborn, born in hospital, delivered by cesarean delivery
V33.1	Twin birth, unspecified whether mate liveborn or stillborn, born before admission to hospital
V34.00	Other multiple, mates all liveborn, born in hospital, delivered without mention of cesarean delivery
V34.01	Other multiple, mates all liveborn, born in hospital, delivered by cesarean delivery
V34.1	Other multiple birth (three or more), mates all liveborn, born before admission to hospital
V35.00	Other multiple, mates all stillborn, born in hospital, delivered without mention of cesarean delivery
V35.01	Other multiple, mates all stillborn, born in hospital, delivered by cesarean delivery
V35.1	Other multiple birth (three or more), mates all stillborn, born before admission to hospital
V36.00	Other multiple, mates liveborn and stillborn, born in hospital, delivered without mention of cesarean delivery
V36.01	Other multiple, mates liveborn and stillborn, born in hospital, delivered by cesarean delivery
V36.1	Other multiple birth (three or more), mates liveborn and stillborn, born before admission to hospital
V37.00	Other multiple, unspecified whether mates stillborn or liveborn, born in hospital, delivered without mention of cesarean delivery
V37.01	Other multiple, unspecified whether mates stillborn or liveborn, born in hospital, delivered by cesarean delivery
V37.1	Other multiple birth (three or more), unspecified whether mates liveborn or stillborn, born before admission to hospital
V39.00	Liveborn infant, unspecified whether single, twin, or multiple, born in hospital, delivered without mention of cesarean delivery
V39.01	Liveborn infant, unspecified whether single, twin, or multiple, born in hospital, delivered by cesarean
V39.1	Liveborn, unspecified whether single, twin or multiple, born before admission to hospital

MDC 15: Newborns And Other Neonates With Conditions Originating In The Perinatal Period—MEDICAL

V50.2	Routine or ritual circumcision
V64.05	Vaccination not carried out because of caregiver refusal
V70.3	Other general medical examination for administrative purposes
V72.1*	Examination of ears and hearing
V77.3	Screening for phenylketonuria (PKU)

DRG 998 **Principal Diagnosis Invalid as Discharge Diagnosis**
GMLOS 0.0   AMLOS 0.0   RW 0.0000

Note: If there is no value in either the GMLOS or the AMLOS, the volume of cases is insufficient to determine a meaningful computation of these statistics.

Principal diagnoses listed for MDC 15 considered invalid as discharge diagnosis

V30.2	Single liveborn, born outside hospital and not hospitalized
V31.2	Twin birth, mate liveborn, born outside hospital and not hospitalized
V32.2	Twin birth, mate stillborn, born outside hospital and not hospitalized
V33.2	Twin birth, unspecified whether mate liveborn or stillborn, born outside hospital and not hospitalized
V34.2	Other multiple birth (three or more), mates all liveborn, born outside hospital and not hospitalized
V35.2	Other multiple birth (three or more), mates all stillborn, born outside of hospital and not hospitalized
V36.2	Other multiple birth (three or more), mates liveborn and stillborn, born outside hospital and not hospitalized
V37.2	Other multiple birth (three or more), unspecified whether mates liveborn or stillborn, born outside of hospital
V39.2	Liveborn, unspecified whether single, twin or multiple, born outside hospital and not hospitalized

Ⓣ *Transfer DRG*   ⓈⓅ *Special Payment*   ☑ *Optimization Potential*   ▽ *Targeted Potential*   ** Code Range*   ● *New DRG*   ▲ *Revised DRG Title*

174   Valid 10/01/2012-09/30/2013   © 2012 OptumInsight, Inc.

MDC 16
Diseases And Disorders Of The Blood And Blood-Forming Organs And Immunological Disorders

017.20	254.0	279.8	282.49	284.9	287.32	288.64	759.0	999.69
017.21	254.1	279.9	282.5	285.0	287.33	288.65	782.7	999.70
017.22	254.8	280.0	282.60	285.1	287.39	288.66	785.6	999.71
017.23	254.9	280.1	282.61	285.21	287.41	288.69	789.2	999.72
017.24	273.0	280.8	282.62	285.22	287.49	288.8	790.01	999.73
017.25	273.1	280.9	282.63	285.29	287.5	288.9	790.09	999.74
017.26	279.00	281.0	282.64	285.3	287.8	289.0	795.71	999.75
017.70	279.01	281.1	282.68	285.8	287.9	289.1	795.79	999.76
017.71	279.02	281.2	282.69	285.9	288.00	289.3	865.00	999.77
017.72	279.03	281.3	282.7	286.0	288.01	289.4	865.01	999.78
017.73	279.04	281.4	282.8	286.1	288.02	289.50	865.02	999.79
017.74	279.05	281.8	282.9	286.2	288.03	289.51	865.03	999.80
017.75	279.06	281.9	283.0	286.3	288.04	289.52	865.04	999.83
017.76	279.09	282.0	283.10	286.4	288.09	289.53	865.09	999.84
078.3	279.10	282.1	283.11	286.52	288.1	289.59	865.10	999.85
091.4	279.11	282.2	283.19	286.53	288.2	289.6	865.11	999.89
209.62	279.12	282.3	283.2	286.59	288.3	289.7	865.12	V42.81
212.6	279.13	282.40	283.9	286.6	288.4	289.81	865.13	V42.82
228.1	279.19	282.41	284.01	286.7	288.50	289.82	865.14	
229.0	279.2	282.42	284.09	286.9	288.51	289.84	865.19	
238.71	279.3	282.43	284.11	287.0	288.59	289.89	996.85	
238.72	279.50	282.44	284.12	287.1	288.60	289.9	999.60	
238.73	279.51	282.45	284.19	287.2	288.61	457.8	999.61	
238.74	279.52	282.46	284.81	287.30	288.62	457.9	999.62	
238.75	279.53	282.47	284.89	287.31	288.63	683	999.63	

MDC 16: Diseases And Disorders Of The Blood And Blood-Forming Organs And Immunological Disorders—SURGICAL

SURGICAL

DRG 799   Splenectomy with MCC
GMLOS 9.7   AMLOS 12.7   RW 5.1496   ☑

Operating Room Procedures
41.2   Splenotomy
41.33   Open biopsy of spleen
41.4*   Excision or destruction of lesion or tissue of spleen
41.5   Total splenectomy
41.93   Excision of accessory spleen
41.94   Transplantation of spleen
41.95   Repair and plastic operations on spleen
41.99   Other operations on spleen

DRG 800   Splenectomy with CC
GMLOS 5.5   AMLOS 7.1   RW 2.6372   ☑

Select operating room procedures listed under DRG 799

DRG 801   Splenectomy without CC/MCC
GMLOS 3.0   AMLOS 3.8   RW 1.5736   ☑

Select operating room procedures listed under DRG 799

DRG 802   Other O.R. Procedures of the Blood and Blood-Forming Organs with MCC
GMLOS 8.3   AMLOS 11.4   RW 3.6452   ☑

Operating Room Procedures
07.16   Biopsy of thymus
07.8*   Thymectomy
07.9*   Other operations on thymus
26.30   Sialoadenectomy, not otherwise specified
34.22   Mediastinoscopy
34.26   Open biopsy of mediastinum
38.7   Interruption of the vena cava
40.0   Incision of lymphatic structures
40.1*   Diagnostic procedures on lymphatic structures
40.2*   Simple excision of lymphatic structure
40.3   Regional lymph node excision
40.4*   Radical excision of cervical lymph nodes
40.5*   Radical excision of other lymph nodes
40.9   Other operations on lymphatic structures
50.12   Open biopsy of liver
50.14   Laparoscopic liver biopsy
50.19   Other diagnostic procedures on liver
54.11   Exploratory laparotomy
54.19   Other laparotomy
54.21   Laparoscopy
54.23   Biopsy of peritoneum
54.29   Other diagnostic procedures on abdominal region
55.24   Open biopsy of kidney
55.29   Other diagnostic procedures on kidney
77.49   Biopsy of other bone, except facial bones
83.21   Open biopsy of soft tissue
86.06   Insertion of totally implantable infusion pump
86.22   Excisional debridement of wound, infection, or burn

DRG 803   Other O.R. Procedures of the Blood and Blood-Forming Organs with CC
GMLOS 4.4   AMLOS 5.8   RW 1.7576   ☑

Select operating room procedures listed under DRG 802

DRG 804   Other O.R. Procedures of the Blood and Blood-Forming Organs without CC/MCC
GMLOS 2.3   AMLOS 3.1   RW 1.1211   ☑

Select operating room procedures listed under DRG 802

MEDICAL

DRG 808   Major Hematologic/Immunologic Diagnoses Except Sickle Cell Crisis and Coagulation with MCC
GMLOS 5.9   AMLOS 7.8   RW 2.0902

Principal Diagnosis
279.11   DiGeorge's syndrome
279.12   Wiskott-Aldrich syndrome
279.13   Nezelof's syndrome
279.19   Other deficiency of cell-mediated immunity
279.2   Combined immunity deficiency
279.5*   Graft-versus-host disease
283.0   Autoimmune hemolytic anemias
283.10   Unspecified non-autoimmune hemolytic anemia
283.19   Other non-autoimmune hemolytic anemias
283.2   Hemoglobinuria due to hemolysis from external causes
283.9   Acquired hemolytic anemia, unspecified
284.0*   Constitutional aplastic anemia
284.1*   Pancytopenia
284.8*   Other specified aplastic anemias
284.9   Unspecified aplastic anemia
288.0*   Neutropenia
288.1   Functional disorders of polymorphonuclear neutrophils
288.2   Genetic anomalies of leukocytes
996.85   Complications of bone marrow transplant

DRG 809   Major Hematologic/Immunologic Diagnoses Except Sickle Cell Crisis and Coagulation with CC
GMLOS 3.7   AMLOS 4.7   RW 1.1767   ☑

Select principal diagnosis listed under DRG 808

DRG 810   Major Hematologic/Immunologic Diagnoses Except Sickle Cell Crisis and Coagulation without CC/MCC
GMLOS 2.7   AMLOS 3.4   RW 0.8490   ☑

Select principal diagnosis listed under DRG 808

DRG 811   Red Blood Cell Disorders with MCC
GMLOS 3.7   AMLOS 5.0   RW 1.2556   ☑

Principal Diagnosis
238.72   Low grade myelodysplastic syndrome lesions
238.73   High grade myelodysplastic syndrome lesions
238.74   Myelodysplastic syndrome with 5q deletion
238.75   Myelodysplastic syndrome, unspecified
280*   Iron deficiency anemias
281*   Other deficiency anemias
282*   Hereditary hemolytic anemias
283.11   Hemolytic-uremic syndrome
285*   Other and unspecified anemias
289.7   Methemoglobinemia
790.0*   Abnormality of red blood cells
999.6*   ABO incompatibility reaction due to transfusion of blood or blood products
999.7*   Rh and other non-ABO incompatibility reaction due to transfusion of blood or blood products
999.80   Transfusion reaction, unspecified
999.83   Hemolytic transfusion reaction, incompatibility unspecified

---

Ⓣ Transfer DRG   ⓢⓟ Special Payment   ☑ Optimization Potential   ▽ Targeted Potential   * Code Range   ● New DRG   ▲ Revised DRG Title

176   Valid 10/01/2012-09/30/2013   © 2012 OptumInsight, Inc.

999.84	Acute hemolytic transfusion reaction, incompatibility unspecified
999.85	Delayed hemolytic transfusion reaction, incompatibility unspecified
999.89	Other transfusion reaction

DRG 812   Red Blood Cell Disorders without MCC

GMLOS 2.6   AMLOS 3.4   RW 0.7872   ☑

Select principal diagnosis listed under DRG 811

DRG 813   Coagulation Disorders

GMLOS 3.6   AMLOS 5.0   RW 1.5841   ☑

Principal Diagnosis

286.0	Congenital factor VIII disorder
286.1	Congenital factor IX disorder
286.2	Congenital factor XI deficiency
286.3	Congenital deficiency of other clotting factors
286.4	Von Willebrand's disease
286.52	Acquired hemophilia
286.59	Other hemorrhagic disorder due to intrinsic circulating anticoagulants, antibodies, or inhibitors
286.6	Defibrination syndrome
286.7	Acquired coagulation factor deficiency
286.9	Other and unspecified coagulation defects
287*	Purpura and other hemorrhagic conditions
289.84	Heparin-induced thrombocytopenia [HIT]
782.7	Spontaneous ecchymoses

DRG 814   Reticuloendothelial and Immunity Disorders with MCC

GMLOS 4.9   AMLOS 6.6   RW 1.6794   ☑

Principal Diagnosis

017.2*	Tuberculosis of peripheral lymph nodes
017.7*	Tuberculosis of spleen
078.3	Cat-scratch disease
091.4	Adenopathy due to secondary syphilis
209.62	Benign carcinoid tumor of the thymus
212.6	Benign neoplasm of thymus
228.1	Lymphangioma, any site
229.0	Benign neoplasm of lymph nodes
238.71	Essential thrombocythemia
254*	Diseases of thymus gland
273.0	Polyclonal hypergammaglobulinemia
273.1	Monoclonal paraproteinemia
279.0*	Deficiency of humoral immunity
279.10	Unspecified immunodeficiency with predominant T-cell defect
279.3	Unspecified immunity deficiency
279.8	Other specified disorders involving the immune mechanism
279.9	Unspecified disorder of immune mechanism
286.53	Antiphospholipid antibody with hemorrhagic disorder
288.3	Eosinophilia
288.4	Hemophagocytic syndromes
288.5*	Decreased white blood cell count
288.6*	Elevated white blood cell count
288.8	Other specified disease of white blood cells
288.9	Unspecified disease of white blood cells
289.0	Polycythemia, secondary
289.1	Chronic lymphadenitis
289.3	Lymphadenitis, unspecified, except mesenteric
289.4	Hypersplenism
289.5*	Other diseases of spleen
289.6	Familial polycythemia
289.81	Primary hypercoagulable state
289.82	Secondary hypercoagulable state
289.89	Other specified diseases of blood and blood-forming organs
289.9	Unspecified diseases of blood and blood-forming organs
457.8	Other noninfectious disorders of lymphatic channels

457.9	Unspecified noninfectious disorder of lymphatic channels
683	Acute lymphadenitis
759.0	Congenital anomalies of spleen
785.6	Enlargement of lymph nodes
789.2	Splenomegaly
795.7*	Other nonspecific immunological findings
865*	Injury to spleen
V42.81	Bone marrow replaced by transplant
V42.82	Peripheral stem cells replaced by transplant

DRG 815   Reticuloendothelial and Immunity Disorders with CC

GMLOS 3.5   AMLOS 4.5   RW 1.0102   ☑

Select principal diagnosis listed under DRG 814

DRG 816   Reticuloendothelial and Immunity Disorders without CC/MCC

GMLOS 2.5   AMLOS 3.1   RW 0.6918   ☑

Select principal diagnosis listed under DRG 814

Surgical   *Medical*   *CC Indicator*   *MCC Indicator*   *Procedure Proxy*

Myeloproliferative Diseases And Disorders And Poorly Differentiated Neoplasms

MDC 17: Myeloproliferative Diseases And Disorders And Poorly Differentiated Neoplasms

158.0	200.33	200.87	201.62	202.26	202.81	205.22	208.90	V10.3
159.1	200.34	200.88	201.63	202.27	202.82	205.30	208.91	V10.40
164.0	200.35	201.00	201.64	202.28	202.83	205.31	208.92	V10.41
176.5	200.36	201.01	201.65	202.30	202.84	205.32	209.20	V10.42
195.4	200.37	201.02	201.66	202.31	202.85	205.80	209.22	V10.43
195.5	200.38	201.03	201.67	202.32	202.86	205.81	209.29	V10.44
195.8	200.40	201.04	201.68	202.33	202.87	205.82	209.30	V10.45
196.0	200.41	201.05	201.70	202.34	202.88	205.90	209.60	V10.46
196.1	200.42	201.06	201.71	202.35	202.90	205.91	209.69	V10.47
196.2	200.43	201.07	201.72	202.36	202.91	205.92	209.70	V10.48
196.3	200.44	201.08	201.73	202.37	202.92	206.00	209.71	V10.49
196.5	200.45	201.10	201.74	202.38	202.93	206.01	209.75	V10.50
196.6	200.46	201.11	201.75	202.40	202.94	206.02	209.79	V10.51
196.8	200.47	201.12	201.76	202.41	202.95	206.10	229.8	V10.52
196.9	200.48	201.13	201.77	202.42	202.96	206.11	229.9	V10.53
198.89	200.50	201.14	201.78	202.43	202.97	206.12	234.8	V10.59
199.0	200.51	201.15	201.90	202.44	202.98	206.20	234.9	V10.60
199.1	200.52	201.16	201.91	202.45	203.00	206.21	238.4	V10.61
199.2	200.53	201.17	201.92	202.46	203.01	206.22	238.5	V10.62
200.00	200.54	201.18	201.93	202.47	203.02	206.80	238.6	V10.63
200.01	200.55	201.20	201.94	202.48	203.10	206.81	238.76	V10.69
200.02	200.56	201.21	201.95	202.50	203.11	206.82	238.79	V10.71
200.03	200.57	201.22	201.96	202.51	203.12	206.90	238.8	V10.72
200.04	200.58	201.23	201.97	202.52	203.80	206.91	238.9	V10.79
200.05	200.60	201.24	201.98	202.53	203.81	206.92	239.81	V10.81
200.06	200.61	201.25	202.00	202.54	203.82	207.00	239.89	V10.82
200.07	200.62	201.26	202.01	202.55	204.00	207.01	239.9	V10.83
200.08	200.63	201.27	202.02	202.56	204.01	207.02	273.2	V10.84
200.10	200.64	201.28	202.03	202.57	204.02	207.10	273.3	V10.85
200.11	200.65	201.40	202.04	202.58	204.10	207.11	273.8	V10.86
200.12	200.66	201.41	202.05	202.60	204.11	207.12	273.9	V10.87
200.13	200.67	201.42	202.06	202.61	204.12	207.20	284.2	V10.88
200.14	200.68	201.43	202.07	202.62	204.20	207.21	289.83	V10.89
200.15	200.70	201.44	202.08	202.63	204.21	207.22	759.6	V10.90
200.16	200.71	201.45	202.10	202.64	204.22	207.80	V10.00	V10.91
200.17	200.72	201.46	202.11	202.65	204.80	207.81	V10.01	V13.22
200.18	200.73	201.47	202.12	202.66	204.81	207.82	V10.02	V58.0
200.20	200.74	201.48	202.13	202.67	204.82	208.00	V10.03	V58.11
200.21	200.75	201.50	202.14	202.68	204.90	208.01	V10.04	V58.12
200.22	200.76	201.51	202.15	202.70	204.91	208.02	V10.05	V67.1
200.23	200.77	201.52	202.16	202.71	204.92	208.10	V10.06	V67.2
200.24	200.78	201.53	202.17	202.72	205.00	208.11	V10.07	V71.1
200.25	200.80	201.54	202.18	202.73	205.01	208.12	V10.09	
200.26	200.81	201.55	202.20	202.74	205.02	208.20	V10.11	
200.27	200.82	201.56	202.21	202.75	205.10	208.21	V10.12	
200.28	200.83	201.57	202.22	202.76	205.11	208.22	V10.20	
200.30	200.84	201.58	202.23	202.77	205.12	208.80	V10.21	
200.31	200.85	201.60	202.24	202.78	205.20	208.81	V10.22	
200.32	200.86	201.61	202.25	202.80	205.21	208.82	V10.29	

SURGICAL

DRG 820	**Lymphoma and Leukemia with Major O.R. Procedure with MCC**		
	GMLOS 12.7	AMLOS 16.9	RW 5.7228 ☑

Principal Diagnosis

159.1	Malignant neoplasm of spleen, not elsewhere classified
176.5	Kaposi's sarcoma of lymph nodes
196*	Secondary and unspecified malignant neoplasm of lymph nodes
200*	Lymphosarcoma and reticulosarcoma and other specified malignant tumors of lymphatic tissue
201*	Hodgkin's disease
202.0*	Nodular lymphoma
202.1*	Mycosis fungoides
202.2*	Sezary's disease
202.3*	Malignant histiocytosis
202.4*	Leukemic reticuloendotheliosis
202.6*	Malignant mast cell tumors
202.7*	Peripheral T-cell lymphoma
202.8*	Other malignant lymphomas
202.9*	Other and unspecified malignant neoplasms of lymphoid and histiocytic tissue
203*	Multiple myeloma and immunoproliferative neoplasms
204*	Lymphoid leukemia
205*	Myeloid leukemia
206*	Monocytic leukemia
207*	Other specified leukemia
208*	Leukemia of unspecified cell type
209.71	Secondary neuroendocrine tumor of distant lymph nodes
238.4	Neoplasm of uncertain behavior of polycythemia vera
238.5	Neoplasm of uncertain behavior of histiocytic and mast cells
238.6	Neoplasm of uncertain behavior of plasma cells
238.76	Myelofibrosis with myeloid metaplasia
238.79	Other lymphatic and hematopoietic tissues
273.2	Other paraproteinemias
273.3	Macroglobulinemia
284.2	Myelophthisis
289.83	Myelofibrosis

Operating Room Procedures

01.12	Open biopsy of cerebral meninges
01.14	Open biopsy of brain
01.18	Other diagnostic procedures on brain and cerebral meninges
01.22	Removal of intracranial neurostimulator lead(s)
01.23	Reopening of craniotomy site
01.24	Other craniotomy
01.25	Other craniectomy
01.28	Placement of intracerebral catheter(s) via burr hole(s)
01.31	Incision of cerebral meninges
01.32	Lobotomy and tractotomy
01.39	Other incision of brain
01.4*	Operations on thalamus and globus pallidus
01.5*	Other excision or destruction of brain and meninges
01.6	Excision of lesion of skull
02.2*	Ventriculostomy
02.3*	Extracranial ventricular shunt
02.42	Replacement of ventricular shunt
02.91	Lysis of cortical adhesions
02.93	Implantation or replacement of intracranial neurostimulator lead(s)
02.99	Other operations on skull, brain, and cerebral meninges
03.02	Reopening of laminectomy site
03.09	Other exploration and decompression of spinal canal
03.1	Division of intraspinal nerve root
03.2*	Chordotomy
03.32	Biopsy of spinal cord or spinal meninges
03.39	Other diagnostic procedures on spinal cord and spinal canal structures
03.4	Excision or destruction of lesion of spinal cord or spinal meninges
03.53	Repair of vertebral fracture
03.59	Other repair and plastic operations on spinal cord structures
03.6	Lysis of adhesions of spinal cord and nerve roots
03.7*	Shunt of spinal theca
03.93	Implantation or replacement of spinal neurostimulator lead(s)
03.97	Revision of spinal thecal shunt
03.99	Other operations on spinal cord and spinal canal structures
07.16	Biopsy of thymus
07.8*	Thymectomy
07.9*	Other operations on thymus
17.31	Laparoscopic multiple segmental resection of large intestine
17.33	Laparoscopic right hemicolectomy
17.34	Laparoscopic resection of transverse colon
17.35	Laparoscopic left hemicolectomy
17.36	Laparoscopic sigmoidectomy
17.39	Other laparoscopic partial excision of large intestine
17.62	Laser interstitial thermal therapy [LITT] of lesion or tissue of head and neck under guidance
17.69	Laser interstitial thermal therapy [LITT] of lesion or tissue of other and unspecified site under guidance
32.20	Thoracoscopic excision of lesion or tissue of lung
32.23	Open ablation of lung lesion or tissue
32.25	Thoracoscopic ablation of lung lesion or tissue
32.29	Other local excision or destruction of lesion or tissue of lung
32.3*	Segmental resection of lung
33.28	Open biopsy of lung
34.02	Exploratory thoracotomy
34.22	Mediastinoscopy
34.26	Open biopsy of mediastinum
34.3	Excision or destruction of lesion or tissue of mediastinum
34.4	Excision or destruction of lesion of chest wall
34.51	Decortication of lung
34.52	Thoracoscopic decortication of lung
34.6	Scarification of pleura
37.12	Pericardiotomy
37.24	Biopsy of pericardium
37.31	Pericardiectomy
37.91	Open chest cardiac massage
38.08	Incision of lower limb arteries
39.98	Control of hemorrhage, not otherwise specified
39.99	Other operations on vessels
40.3	Regional lymph node excision
40.4*	Radical excision of cervical lymph nodes
40.5*	Radical excision of other lymph nodes
40.9	Other operations on lymphatic structures
41.2	Splenotomy
41.33	Open biopsy of spleen
41.4*	Excision or destruction of lesion or tissue of spleen
41.5	Total splenectomy
41.93	Excision of accessory spleen
41.94	Transplantation of spleen
41.95	Repair and plastic operations on spleen
41.99	Other operations on spleen
42.1*	Esophagostomy
42.21	Operative esophagoscopy by incision
42.25	Open biopsy of esophagus
42.32	Local excision of other lesion or tissue of esophagus
42.39	Other destruction of lesion or tissue of esophagus
42.4*	Excision of esophagus
42.5*	Intrathoracic anastomosis of esophagus
42.6*	Antesternal anastomosis of esophagus
42.7	Esophagomyotomy
42.82	Suture of laceration of esophagus
42.83	Closure of esophagostomy
42.84	Repair of esophageal fistula, not elsewhere classified

MDC 17: Myeloproliferative Diseases And Disorders And Poorly Differentiated Neoplasms—SURGICAL

42.85	Repair of esophageal stricture
42.86	Production of subcutaneous tunnel without esophageal anastomosis
42.87	Other graft of esophagus
42.89	Other repair of esophagus
43.0	Gastrotomy
43.5	Partial gastrectomy with anastomosis to esophagus
43.6	Partial gastrectomy with anastomosis to duodenum
43.7	Partial gastrectomy with anastomosis to jejunum
43.8*	Other partial gastrectomy
43.9*	Total gastrectomy
44.11	Transabdominal gastroscopy
44.3*	Gastroenterostomy without gastrectomy
44.63	Closure of other gastric fistula
45.02	Other incision of small intestine
45.03	Incision of large intestine
45.11	Transabdominal endoscopy of small intestine
45.31	Other local excision of lesion of duodenum
45.32	Other destruction of lesion of duodenum
45.33	Local excision of lesion or tissue of small intestine, except duodenum
45.34	Other destruction of lesion of small intestine, except duodenum
45.41	Excision of lesion or tissue of large intestine
45.49	Other destruction of lesion of large intestine
45.50	Isolation of intestinal segment, not otherwise specified
45.61	Multiple segmental resection of small intestine
45.62	Other partial resection of small intestine
45.63	Total removal of small intestine
45.71	Open and other multiple segmental resection of large intestine
45.73	Open and other right hemicolectomy
45.74	Open and other resection of transverse colon
45.75	Open and other left hemicolectomy
45.76	Open and other sigmoidectomy
45.79	Other and unspecified partial excision of large intestine
45.8*	Total intra-abdominal colectomy
45.90	Intestinal anastomosis, not otherwise specified
45.91	Small-to-small intestinal anastomosis
45.92	Anastomosis of small intestine to rectal stump
45.93	Other small-to-large intestinal anastomosis
45.94	Large-to-large intestinal anastomosis
45.95	Anastomosis to anus
46.0*	Exteriorization of intestine
46.10	Colostomy, not otherwise specified
46.11	Temporary colostomy
46.13	Permanent colostomy
46.20	Ileostomy, not otherwise specified
46.21	Temporary ileostomy
46.22	Continent ileostomy
46.23	Other permanent ileostomy
46.40	Revision of intestinal stoma, not otherwise specified
46.41	Revision of stoma of small intestine
46.80	Intra-abdominal manipulation of intestine, not otherwise specified
46.81	Intra-abdominal manipulation of small intestine
46.82	Intra-abdominal manipulation of large intestine
46.99	Other operations on intestines
48.4*	Pull-through resection of rectum
48.5*	Abdominoperineal resection of rectum
48.6*	Other resection of rectum
50.12	Open biopsy of liver
50.14	Laparoscopic liver biopsy
50.19	Other diagnostic procedures on liver
51.2*	Cholecystectomy
51.3*	Anastomosis of gallbladder or bile duct
51.42	Common duct exploration for relief of other obstruction
51.43	Insertion of choledochohepatic tube for decompression
51.49	Incision of other bile ducts for relief of obstruction
51.59	Incision of other bile duct

51.93	Closure of other biliary fistula
51.94	Revision of anastomosis of biliary tract
51.95	Removal of prosthetic device from bile duct
51.99	Other operations on biliary tract
52.12	Open biopsy of pancreas
52.19	Other diagnostic procedures on pancreas
52.92	Cannulation of pancreatic duct
54.0	Incision of abdominal wall
54.11	Exploratory laparotomy
54.12	Reopening of recent laparotomy site
54.19	Other laparotomy
54.22	Biopsy of abdominal wall or umbilicus
54.29	Other diagnostic procedures on abdominal region
54.3	Excision or destruction of lesion or tissue of abdominal wall or umbilicus
54.4	Excision or destruction of peritoneal tissue
54.63	Other suture of abdominal wall
54.64	Suture of peritoneum
54.72	Other repair of abdominal wall
54.73	Other repair of peritoneum
54.74	Other repair of omentum
54.75	Other repair of mesentery
54.93	Creation of cutaneoperitoneal fistula
54.94	Creation of peritoneovascular shunt
54.95	Incision of peritoneum
55.24	Open biopsy of kidney
55.29	Other diagnostic procedures on kidney
56.5*	Cutaneous uretero-ileostomy
56.6*	Other external urinary diversion
56.71	Urinary diversion to intestine
56.72	Revision of ureterointestinal anastomosis
56.73	Nephrocystanastomosis, not otherwise specified
56.75	Transureteroureterostomy
56.83	Closure of ureterostomy
56.84	Closure of other fistula of ureter
57.18	Other suprapubic cystostomy
57.21	Vesicostomy
57.22	Revision or closure of vesicostomy
57.34	Open biopsy of bladder
57.39	Other diagnostic procedures on bladder
57.59	Open excision or destruction of other lesion or tissue of bladder
57.6	Partial cystectomy
57.7*	Total cystectomy
57.82	Closure of cystostomy
57.83	Repair of fistula involving bladder and intestine
57.84	Repair of other fistula of bladder
57.88	Other anastomosis of bladder
58.43	Closure of other fistula of urethra
59.00	Retroperitoneal dissection, not otherwise specified
59.02	Other lysis of perirenal or periureteral adhesions
59.03	Laparoscopic lysis of perirenal or periureteral adhesions
59.09	Other incision of perirenal or periureteral tissue
59.1*	Incision of perivesical tissue
59.2*	Diagnostic procedures on perirenal and perivesical tissue
59.91	Excision of perirenal or perivesical tissue
59.92	Other operations on perirenal or perivesical tissue
70.72	Repair of colovaginal fistula
70.73	Repair of rectovaginal fistula
70.74	Repair of other vaginoenteric fistula
70.75	Repair of other fistula of vagina
80.53	Repair of the anulus fibrosus with graft or prosthesis
80.54	Other and unspecified repair of the anulus fibrosus

DRG 821 **Lymphoma and Leukemia with Major O.R. Procedure with CC**

GMLOS 5.0	AMLOS 6.9	RW 2.3066	☑

Select principal diagnosis and operating room procedures listed under DRG 820

T *Transfer DRG* SP *Special Payment* ☑ *Optimization Potential* ▽ *Targeted Potential* * *Code Range* ● *New DRG* ▲ *Revised DRG Title*

Valid 10/01/2012-09/30/2013

DRG 822   Lymphoma and Leukemia with Major O.R. Procedure without CC/MCC
GMLOS 2.2   AMLOS 2.8   RW 1.1935   ☑

Select principal diagnosis and operating room procedures listed under DRG 820

DRG 823   Lymphoma and Nonacute Leukemia with Other O.R. Procedure with MCC
GMLOS 11.7   AMLOS 14.8   RW 4.5397   ☑

Select principal diagnosis listed under DRG 820
AND

Select any other operating room procedures not listed under DRG 820
OR

Nonoperating Room Procedures
92.3*   Stereotactic radiosurgery

DRG 824   Lymphoma and Nonacute Leukemia with Other O.R. Procedure with CC
GMLOS 6.2   AMLOS 8.1   RW 2.2603   ☑

Select principal diagnosis listed under DRG 820

Select any other operating room procedures not listed under DRG 820
OR

Nonoperating Room Procedures
92.3*   Stereotactic radiosurgery

DRG 825   Lymphoma and Nonacute Leukemia with Other O.R. Procedure without CC/MCC
GMLOS 2.7   AMLOS 3.8   RW 1.2712   ☑

Select principal diagnosis listed under DRG 820

Select any other operating room procedures not listed under DRG 820
OR

Nonoperating Room Procedures
92.3*   Stereotactic radiosurgery

DRG 826   Myeloproliferative Disorders or Poorly Differentiated Neoplasms with Major O.R. Procedure with MCC
GMLOS 10.9   AMLOS 14.0   RW 4.8680

Principal Diagnosis
158.0   Malignant neoplasm of retroperitoneum
164.0   Malignant neoplasm of thymus
195.4   Malignant neoplasm of upper limb
195.5   Malignant neoplasm of lower limb
195.8   Malignant neoplasm of other specified sites
198.89   Secondary malignant neoplasm of other specified sites
199.0   Disseminated malignant neoplasm
199.1   Other malignant neoplasm of unspecified site
199.2   Malignant neoplasm associated with transplanted organ
202.5*   Letterer-Siwe disease
209.20   Malignant carcinoid tumor of unknown primary site
209.22   Malignant carcinoid tumor of the thymus
209.29   Malignant carcinoid tumor of other sites
209.30   Malignant poorly differentiated neuroendocrine carcinoma, any site
209.60   Benign carcinoid tumor of unknown primary site
209.69   Benign carcinoid tumor of other sites
209.70   Secondary neuroendocrine tumor, unspecified site
209.75   Secondary Merkel cell carcinoma
209.79   Secondary neuroendocrine tumor of other sites
229.8   Benign neoplasm of other specified sites
229.9   Benign neoplasm of unspecified site

234.8   Carcinoma in situ of other specified sites
234.9   Carcinoma in situ, site unspecified
238.8   Neoplasm of uncertain behavior of other specified sites
238.9   Neoplasm of uncertain behavior, site unspecified
239.8*   Neoplasm of unspecified nature of other specified sites
239.9   Neoplasm of unspecified nature, site unspecified
273.8   Other disorders of plasma protein metabolism
273.9   Unspecified disorder of plasma protein metabolism
759.6   Other congenital hamartoses, not elsewhere classified
V10*   Personal history of malignant neoplasm
V13.22   Personal history of cervical dysplasia
V58.0   Radiotherapy
V58.1*   Encounter for antineoplastic chemotherapy and immunotherapy
V67.1   Radiotherapy follow-up examination
V67.2   Chemotherapy follow-up examination
V71.1   Observation for suspected malignant neoplasm

Select operating room procedures listed under DRG 820

DRG 827   Myeloproliferative Disorders or Poorly Differentiated Neoplasms with Major O.R. Procedure with CC
GMLOS 5.3   AMLOS 6.8   RW 2.1765   ☑

Select principal diagnosis listed under DRG 826 with operating room procedures listed under DRG 820

DRG 828   Myeloproliferative Disorders or Poorly Differentiated Neoplasms with Major O.R. Procedure without CC/MCC
GMLOS 2.8   AMLOS 3.4   RW 1.3409   ☑

Select principal diagnosis listed under DRG 826 with operating room procedures listed under DRG 820

DRG 829   Myeloproliferative Disorders or Poorly Differentiated Neoplasms with Other O.R. Procedure with CC/MCC
GMLOS 6.4   AMLOS 9.6   RW 3.0335   ☑

Select principal diagnosis listed under DRG 826

Select any other operating room procedures not listed under DRG 820
OR

Nonoperating Room Procedures
92.3*   Stereotactic radiosurgery

DRG 830   Myeloproliferative Disorders or Poorly Differentiated Neoplasms with Other O.R. Procedure without CC/MCC
GMLOS 2.5   AMLOS 3.3   RW 1.1804   ☑

Select principal diagnosis listed under DRG 826

Select any other operating room procedures not listed under DRG 820
OR

Nonoperating Room Procedures
92.3*   Stereotactic radiosurgery

MEDICAL

DRG 834   Acute Leukemia without Major O.R. Procedure with MCC
GMLOS 9.9   AMLOS 16.1   RW 5.1622   ☑

Principal Diagnosis
204.0*   Acute lymphoid leukemia
205.0*   Acute myeloid leukemia
206.0*   Acute monocytic leukemia
207.0*   Acute erythremia and erythroleukemia
208.0*   Acute leukemia of unspecified cell type

MDC 17: Myeloproliferative Diseases And Disorders And Poorly Differentiated Neoplasms—MEDICAL

DRG 835   Acute Leukemia without Major O.R. Procedure with CC
GMLOS 5.1   AMLOS 8.3   RW 2.2133   ☑

Select principal diagnosis listed under DRG 834

DRG 836   Acute Leukemia without Major O.R. Procedure without CC/MCC
GMLOS 2.8   AMLOS 4.0   RW 1.0992   ☑

Select principal diagnosis listed under DRG 834

DRG 837   Chemotherapy with Acute Leukemia as Secondary Diagnosis or with High Dose Chemotherapy Agent with MCC
GMLOS 16.7   AMLOS 22.5   RW 6.4881

Principal Diagnosis

V58.1*	Encounter for antineoplastic chemotherapy and immunotherapy
V67.2	Chemotherapy follow-up examination

AND

Secondary Diagnosis

204.0*	Acute lymphoid leukemia
205.0*	Acute myeloid leukemia
206.0*	Acute monocytic leukemia
207.0*	Acute erythremia and erythroleukemia
208.0*	Acute leukemia of unspecified cell type

OR

Nonoperating Room Procedure

00.15	High-dose infusion interleukin-2 [IL-2]

DRG 838   Chemotherapy with Acute Leukemia as Secondary Diagnosis with CC or High Dose Chemotherapy Agent
GMLOS 7.2   AMLOS 10.2   RW 2.7537   ☑

Select principal and secondary diagnosis or nonoperating procedure listed under DRG 837

DRG 839   Chemotherapy with Acute Leukemia as Secondary Diagnosis without CC/MCC
GMLOS 4.7   AMLOS 5.6   RW 1.2412   ☑

Principal Diagnosis

V58.1*	Encounter for antineoplastic chemotherapy and immunotherapy
V67.2	Chemotherapy follow-up examination

AND

Secondary Diagnosis

204.0*	Acute lymphoid leukemia
205.0*	Acute myeloid leukemia
206.0*	Acute monocytic leukemia
207.0*	Acute erythremia and erythroleukemia
208.0*	Acute leukemia of unspecified cell type

DRG 840   Lymphoma and Nonacute Leukemia with MCC
GMLOS 7.7   AMLOS 10.5   RW 3.0103   T ☑

Principal Diagnosis

159.1	Malignant neoplasm of spleen, not elsewhere classified
176.5	Kaposi's sarcoma of lymph nodes
196*	Secondary and unspecified malignant neoplasm of lymph nodes
200*	Lymphosarcoma and reticulosarcoma and other specified malignant tumors of lymphatic tissue
201*	Hodgkin's disease
202.0*	Nodular lymphoma
202.1*	Mycosis fungoides

202.2*	Sezary's disease
202.3*	Malignant histiocytosis
202.4*	Leukemic reticuloendotheliosis
202.6*	Malignant mast cell tumors
202.7*	Peripheral T-cell lymphoma
202.8*	Other malignant lymphomas
202.9*	Other and unspecified malignant neoplasms of lymphoid and histiocytic tissue
203*	Multiple myeloma and immunoproliferative neoplasms
204.1*	Chronic lymphoid leukemia
204.2*	Subacute lymphoid leukemia
204.8*	Other lymphoid leukemia
204.9*	Unspecified lymphoid leukemia
205.1*	Chronic myeloid leukemia
205.2*	Subacute myeloid leukemia
205.3*	Myeloid sarcoma
205.8*	Other myeloid leukemia
205.9*	Unspecified myeloid leukemia
206.1*	Chronic monocytic leukemia
206.2*	Subacute monocytic leukemia
206.8*	Other monocytic leukemia
206.9*	Unspecified monocytic leukemia
207.1*	Chronic erythremia
207.2*	Megakaryocytic leukemia
207.8*	Other specified leukemia
208.1*	Chronic leukemia of unspecified cell type
208.2*	Subacute leukemia of unspecified cell type
208.8*	Other leukemia of unspecified cell type
208.9*	Unspecified leukemia
209.71	Secondary neuroendocrine tumor of distant lymph nodes
238.4	Neoplasm of uncertain behavior of polycythemia vera
238.5	Neoplasm of uncertain behavior of histiocytic and mast cells
238.6	Neoplasm of uncertain behavior of plasma cells
238.76	Myelofibrosis with myeloid metaplasia
238.79	Other lymphatic and hematopoietic tissues
273.2	Other paraproteinemias
273.3	Macroglobulinemia
284.2	Myelophthisis
289.83	Myelofibrosis

DRG 841   Lymphoma and Nonacute Leukemia with CC
GMLOS 4.8   AMLOS 6.4   RW 1.6192   T ☑

Select principal diagnosis listed under DRG 840

DRG 842   Lymphoma and Nonacute Leukemia without CC/MCC
GMLOS 3.0   AMLOS 4.0   RW 1.0450   T ☑

Select principal diagnosis listed under DRG 840

DRG 843   Other Myeloproliferative Disorders or Poorly Differentiated Neoplasm Diagnoses with MCC
GMLOS 5.9   AMLOS 7.9   RW 1.8719   ☑

Principal Diagnosis

158.0	Malignant neoplasm of retroperitoneum
164.0	Malignant neoplasm of thymus
195.4	Malignant neoplasm of upper limb
195.5	Malignant neoplasm of lower limb
195.8	Malignant neoplasm of other specified sites
198.89	Secondary malignant neoplasm of other specified sites
199*	Malignant neoplasm without specification of site
202.5*	Letterer-Siwe disease
209.20	Malignant carcinoid tumor of unknown primary site
209.22	Malignant carcinoid tumor of the thymus
209.29	Malignant carcinoid tumor of other sites
209.30	Malignant poorly differentiated neuroendocrine carcinoma, any site
209.60	Benign carcinoid tumor of unknown primary site
209.69	Benign carcinoid tumor of other sites

Ⓣ *Transfer DRG*   ⓈⓅ *Special Payment*   ☑ *Optimization Potential*   ▽ᵇ *Targeted Potential*   * *Code Range*   ● *New DRG*   ▲ *Revised DRG Title*

209.70	Secondary neuroendocrine tumor, unspecified site
209.75	Secondary Merkel cell carcinoma
209.79	Secondary neuroendocrine tumor of other sites
229.8	Benign neoplasm of other specified sites
229.9	Benign neoplasm of unspecified site
234.8	Carcinoma in situ of other specified sites
234.9	Carcinoma in situ, site unspecified
238.8	Neoplasm of uncertain behavior of other specified sites
238.9	Neoplasm of uncertain behavior, site unspecified
239.8*	Neoplasm of unspecified nature of other specified sites
239.9	Neoplasm of unspecified nature, site unspecified
273.8	Other disorders of plasma protein metabolism
273.9	Unspecified disorder of plasma protein metabolism
759.6	Other congenital hamartoses, not elsewhere classified
V10*	Personal history of malignant neoplasm
V13.22	Personal history of cervical dysplasia
V71.1	Observation for suspected malignant neoplasm

DRG 844 **Other Myeloproliferative Disorders or Poorly Differentiated Neoplasm Diagnoses with CC**
GMLOS 4.3   AMLOS 5.6   RW 1.2216   ☑

Select principal diagnosis listed under DRG 843

DRG 845 **Other Myeloproliferative Disorders or Poorly Differentiated Neoplasm Diagnoses without CC/MCC**
GMLOS 2.9   AMLOS 3.8   RW 0.8612   ☑

Select principal diagnosis listed under DRG 843

DRG 846 **Chemotherapy without Acute Leukemia as Secondary Diagnosis with MCC**
GMLOS 5.7   AMLOS 8.3   RW 2.4374   ☑

Principal Diagnosis

V58.1*	Encounter for antineoplastic chemotherapy and immunotherapy
V67.2	Chemotherapy follow-up examination

DRG 847 **Chemotherapy without Acute Leukemia as Secondary Diagnosis with CC**
GMLOS 2.9   AMLOS 3.5   RW 1.0447   ☑

Select principal diagnosis listed under DRG 846

DRG 848 **Chemotherapy without Acute Leukemia as Secondary Diagnosis without CC/MCC**
GMLOS 2.4   AMLOS 3.0   RW 0.7878   ☑

Select principal diagnosis listed under DRG 846

DRG 849 **Radiotherapy**
GMLOS 4.6   AMLOS 6.2   RW 1.3396   ☑

Principal Diagnosis

V58.0	Radiotherapy
V67.1	Radiotherapy follow-up examination

MDC 17: Myeloproliferative Diseases And Disorders And Poorly Differentiated Neoplasms—MEDICAL

Surgical	*Medical*	*CC Indicator*	*MCC Indicator*	*Procedure Proxy*

MDC 18
Infectious And Parasitic Diseases

002.0	021.3	038.41	045.23	065.3	081.0	090.5	117.6	488.09
002.1	021.8	038.42	050.0	065.4	081.1	090.6	117.7	488.19
002.2	021.9	038.43	050.1	065.8	081.2	090.7	117.8	488.89
002.3	022.3	038.44	050.2	065.9	081.9	090.9	117.9	780.60
002.9	022.8	038.49	050.9	066.0	082.0	091.2	118	780.61
003.1	022.9	038.8	051.01	066.1	082.1	091.7	120.2	780.62
003.20	023.0	038.9	051.02	066.3	082.2	091.89	120.8	780.63
003.29	023.1	039.8	051.9	066.40	082.3	091.9	120.9	780.66
003.8	023.2	039.9	052.7	066.41	082.40	092.0	121.5	785.52
003.9	023.3	040.0	052.8	066.42	082.41	092.9	121.6	785.59
005.1	023.8	040.1	052.9	066.49	082.49	095.8	121.8	790.7
006.8	023.9	040.3	053.79	066.8	082.8	095.9	121.9	790.8
006.9	024	040.41	053.8	066.9	082.9	096	122.3	795.31
017.90	025	040.42	054.5	072.79	083.0	097.0	122.4	795.39
017.91	026.0	040.82	054.79	072.8	083.1	097.1	122.6	958.3
017.92	026.1	040.89	054.8	072.9	083.2	097.9	122.7	995.90
017.93	026.9	041.00	055.79	073.7	083.8	098.89	122.9	995.91
017.94	027.0	041.01	055.8	073.8	083.9	100.0	124	995.92
017.95	027.1	041.02	055.9	073.9	084.0	100.9	125.0	995.93
017.96	027.2	041.03	056.79	074.3	084.1	102.7	125.1	995.94
018.00	027.8	041.04	056.8	074.8	084.2	102.8	125.2	998.51
018.01	027.9	041.05	056.9	075	084.3	102.9	125.3	998.59
018.02	030.0	041.09	057.0	078.2	084.4	103.2	125.4	999.0
018.03	030.1	041.10	057.8	078.4	084.5	103.9	125.5	999.34
018.04	030.2	041.11	057.9	078.5	084.6	104.0	125.6	999.39
018.05	030.3	041.12	058.10	078.7	084.7	104.8	125.7	V08
018.06	030.8	041.19	058.11	078.88	084.8	104.9	125.9	V09.0
018.80	030.9	041.2	058.12	078.89	084.9	112.5	127.8	V09.1
018.81	031.2	041.3	059.00	079.0	085.0	112.89	128.0	V09.2
018.82	031.8	041.41	059.01	079.1	085.9	112.9	128.1	V09.3
018.83	031.9	041.42	059.09	079.2	086.1	114.3	128.8	V09.4
018.84	032.89	041.43	059.10	079.3	086.2	114.9	128.9	V09.50
018.85	032.9	041.49	059.11	079.4	086.3	115.00	130.7	V09.51
018.86	034.1	041.5	059.12	079.50	086.4	115.09	130.8	V09.6
018.90	036.2	041.6	059.19	079.51	086.5	115.10	130.9	V09.70
018.91	036.3	041.7	059.20	079.52	086.9	115.19	131.8	V09.71
018.92	036.89	041.81	059.21	079.53	087.0	115.90	131.9	V09.80
018.93	036.9	041.82	059.22	079.59	087.1	115.99	136.0	V09.81
018.94	037	041.83	059.8	079.6	087.9	116.0	136.21	V09.90
018.95	038.0	041.84	059.9	079.81	088.0	116.1	136.29	V09.91
018.96	038.10	041.85	060.0	079.82	088.81	116.2	136.4	
020.0	038.11	041.86	060.1	079.83	088.82	117.0	136.5	
020.1	038.12	041.89	060.9	079.88	088.89	117.1	136.8	
020.2	038.19	041.9	061	079.89	088.9	117.2	136.9	
020.8	038.2	045.20	065.0	079.98	090.0	117.3	137.4	
020.9	038.3	045.21	065.1	079.99	090.1	117.4	139.8	
021.0	038.40	045.22	065.2	080	090.2	117.5	487.8	

SURGICAL

DRG 853 **Infectious and Parasitic Diseases with O.R. Procedure with MCC**

GMLOS 11.3   AMLOS 14.6   RW 5.3431   T ☑

Select any principal diagnosis from MDC 18 excluding
958.3   Posttraumatic wound infection not elsewhere classified
998.51   Infected postoperative seroma
998.59   Other postoperative infection
999.39   Complications of medical care, NEC, infection following other infusion, injection, transfusion, or vaccination

AND

Select any operating room procedure

DRG 854 **Infectious and Parasitic Diseases with O.R. Procedure with CC**

GMLOS 7.3   AMLOS 8.8   RW 2.5583   T ☑

Select principal diagnosis and operating room procedure listed under DRG 853

DRG 855 **Infectious and Parasitic Diseases with O.R. Procedure without CC/MCC**

GMLOS 3.5   AMLOS 4.9   RW 1.5331   T ☑

Select principal diagnosis and operating room procedure listed under DRG 853

DRG 856 **Postoperative or Posttraumatic Infections with O.R. Procedure with MCC**

GMLOS 10.5   AMLOS 14.0   RW 4.8125   T ☑

Principal Diagnosis
958.3   Posttraumatic wound infection not elsewhere classified
998.51   Infected postoperative seroma
998.59   Other postoperative infection
999.34   Acute infection following transfusion, infusion, or injection of blood and blood products
999.39   Complications of medical care, NEC, infection following other infusion, injection, transfusion, or vaccination

AND

Select any operating room procedure

DRG 857 **Postoperative or Posttraumatic Infections with O.R. Procedure with CC**

GMLOS 5.8   AMLOS 7.4   RW 2.0649   T ☑

Select principal diagnosis and operating room procedure listed under DRG 856

DRG 858 **Postoperative or Posttraumatic Infections with O.R. Procedure without CC/MCC**

GMLOS 3.8   AMLOS 4.7   RW 1.2534   T ☑

Select principal diagnosis and operating room procedure listed under DRG 856

MEDICAL

DRG 862 **Postoperative and Posttraumatic Infections with MCC**

GMLOS 5.7   AMLOS 7.6   RW 2.0099   T ☑

Principal Diagnosis
958.3   Posttraumatic wound infection not elsewhere classified
998.5*   Postoperative infection, not elsewhere classified

DRG 863 **Postoperative and Posttraumatic Infections without MCC**

GMLOS 3.8   AMLOS 4.7   RW 0.9822   T ☑

Select principal diagnosis listed under DRG 862

DRG 864 **Fever**

GMLOS 2.9   AMLOS 3.7   RW 0.8443   ☑

Principal Diagnosis
780.60   Fever, unspecified
780.61   Fever presenting with conditions classified elsewhere
780.62   Postprocedural fever
780.63   Postvaccination fever
780.66   Febrile nonhemolytic transfusion reaction

DRG 865 **Viral Illness with MCC**

GMLOS 4.4   AMLOS 6.2   RW 1.5181   ☑

Principal Diagnosis
045.2*   Acute nonparalytic poliomyelitis
050*   Smallpox
051.0*   Cowpox and vaccinia not from vaccination
051.9   Unspecified paravaccinia
052.7   Chickenpox with other specified complications
052.8   Chickenpox with unspecified complication
052.9   Varicella without mention of complication
053.79   Other specified herpes zoster complications
053.8   Unspecified herpes zoster complication
054.79   Other specified herpes simplex complications
054.8   Unspecified herpes simplex complication
055.79   Other specified measles complications
055.8   Unspecified measles complication
055.9   Measles without mention of complication
056.79   Rubella with other specified complications
056.8   Unspecified rubella complications
056.9   Rubella without mention of complication
057*   Other viral exanthemata
058.10   Roseola infantum, unspecified
058.11   Roseola infantum due to human herpesvirus 6
058.12   Roseola infantum due to human herpesvirus 7
059*   Other poxvirus infections
060*   Yellow fever
061   Dengue
065*   Arthropod-borne hemorrhagic fever
066.0   Phlebotomus fever
066.1   Tick-borne fever
066.3   Other mosquito-borne fever
066.4*   West Nile fever
066.8   Other specified arthropod-borne viral diseases
066.9   Unspecified arthropod-borne viral disease
072.79   Mumps with other specified complications
072.8   Unspecified mumps complication
072.9   Mumps without mention of complication
073.7   Ornithosis with other specified complications
073.8   Ornithosis with unspecified complication
073.9   Unspecified ornithosis
074.3   Hand, foot, and mouth disease
074.8   Other specified diseases due to Coxsackievirus
075   Infectious mononucleosis

078.2	Sweating fever
078.4	Foot and mouth disease
078.5	Cytomegaloviral disease
078.7	Arenaviral hemorrhagic fever
078.88	Other specified diseases due to Chlamydiae
078.89	Other specified diseases due to viruses
079*	Viral and chlamydial infection in conditions classified elsewhere and of unspecified site
487.8	Influenza with other manifestations
488.09	Influenza due to identified avian influenza virus with other manifestations
488.19	Influenza due to identified 2009 H1N1 influenza virus with other manifestations
488.89	Influenza due to identified novel influenza A virus with other manifestations
790.8	Unspecified viremia
999.0	Generalized vaccinia as complication of medical care, not elsewhere classified
V08	Asymptomatic human immunodeficiency virus (HIV) infection status

DRG 866   **Viral Illness without MCC**

GMLOS 2.8   AMLOS 3.4   RW 0.7594   ☑

Select principal diagnosis listed under DRG 865

DRG 867   **Other Infectious and Parasitic Diseases Diagnoses with MCC**

GMLOS 7.0   AMLOS 9.4   RW 2.5861   Ⓣ☑

Principal Diagnosis

002*	Typhoid and paratyphoid fevers
003.20	Unspecified localized salmonella infection
003.29	Other localized salmonella infections
003.8	Other specified salmonella infections
003.9	Unspecified salmonella infection
005.1	Botulism food poisoning
006.8	Amebic infection of other sites
006.9	Unspecified amebiasis
017.9*	Tuberculosis of other specified organs
018.0*	Acute miliary tuberculosis
018.8*	Other specified miliary tuberculosis
018.9*	Unspecified miliary tuberculosis
020.0	Bubonic plague
020.1	Cellulocutaneous plague
020.8	Other specified types of plague
020.9	Unspecified plague
021.0	Ulceroglandular tularemia
021.3	Oculoglandular tularemia
021.8	Other specified tularemia
021.9	Unspecified tularemia
022.8	Other specified manifestations of anthrax
022.9	Unspecified anthrax
023*	Brucellosis
024	Glanders
025	Melioidosis
026*	Rat-bite fever
027*	Other zoonotic bacterial diseases
030*	Leprosy
031.2	Disseminated diseases due to other mycobacteria
031.8	Other specified diseases due to other mycobacteria
031.9	Unspecified diseases due to mycobacteria
032.89	Other specified diphtheria
032.9	Unspecified diphtheria
034.1	Scarlet fever
037	Tetanus
039.8	Actinomycotic infection of other specified sites
039.9	Actinomycotic infection of unspecified site
040.0	Gas gangrene
040.1	Rhinoscleroma

040.3	Necrobacillosis
040.41	Infant botulism
040.42	Wound botulism
040.82	Toxic shock syndrome
040.89	Other specified bacterial diseases
041*	Bacterial infection in conditions classified elsewhere and of unspecified site
080	Louse-borne (epidemic) typhus
081*	Other typhus
082*	Tick-borne rickettsioses
083*	Other rickettsioses
084*	Malaria
085.0	Visceral leishmaniasis (kala-azar)
085.9	Unspecified leishmaniasis
086.1	Chagas' disease with other organ involvement
086.2	Chagas' disease without mention of organ involvement
086.3	Gambian trypanosomiasis
086.4	Rhodesian trypanosomiasis
086.5	African trypanosomiasis, unspecified
086.9	Unspecified trypanosomiasis
087*	Relapsing fever
088*	Other arthropod-borne diseases
090.0	Early congenital syphilis, symptomatic
090.1	Early congenital syphilis, latent
090.2	Unspecified early congenital syphilis
090.5	Other late congenital syphilis, symptomatic
090.6	Late congenital syphilis, latent
090.7	Late congenital syphilis, unspecified
090.9	Congenital syphilis, unspecified
091.2	Other primary syphilis
091.7	Early syphilis, secondary syphilis, relapse
091.89	Early syphilis, other forms of secondary syphilis
091.9	Early syphilis, unspecified secondary syphilis
092*	Early syphilis, latent
095.8	Other specified forms of late symptomatic syphilis
095.9	Unspecified late symptomatic syphilis
096	Late syphilis, latent
097*	Other and unspecified syphilis
098.89	Gonococcal infection of other specified sites
100.0	Leptospirosis icterohemorrhagica
100.9	Unspecified leptospirosis
102.7	Other manifestations due to yaws
102.8	Latent yaws
102.9	Unspecified yaws
103.2	Late lesions of pinta
103.9	Unspecified pinta
104*	Other spirochetal infection
112.5	Disseminated candidiasis
112.89	Other candidiasis of other specified sites
112.9	Candidiasis of unspecified site
114.3	Other forms of progressive coccidioidomycosis
114.9	Unspecified coccidioidomycosis
115.00	Histoplasma capsulatum, without mention of manifestation
115.09	Histoplasma capsulatum, with mention of other manifestation
115.10	Histoplasma duboisii, without mention of manifestation
115.19	Histoplasma duboisii with mention of other manifestation
115.90	Unspecified Histoplasmosis without mention of manifestation
115.99	Unspecified Histoplasmosis with mention of other manifestation
116*	Blastomycotic infection
117*	Other mycoses
118	Opportunistic mycoses
120.2	Schistosomiasis due to schistosoma japonicum
120.8	Other specified schistosomiasis
120.9	Unspecified schistosomiasis
121.5	Metagonimiasis
121.6	Heterophyiasis
121.8	Other specified trematode infections

Ⓣ *Transfer DRG*   ⓈⓅ *Special Payment*   ☑ *Optimization Potential*   ▽ *Targeted Potential*   * *Code Range*   ● *New DRG*   ▲ *Revised DRG Title*

186   Valid 10/01/2012–09/30/2013   © 2012 OptumInsight, Inc.

121.9	Unspecified trematode infection
122.3	Other echinococcus granulosus infection
122.4	Unspecified echinococcus granulosus infection
122.6	Other echinococcus multilocularis infection
122.7	Unspecified echinococcus multilocularis infection
122.9	Other and unspecified echinococcosis
124	Trichinosis
125*	Filarial infection and dracontiasis
127.8	Mixed intestinal helminthiasis
128*	Other and unspecified helminthiases
130.7	Toxoplasmosis of other specified sites
130.8	Multisystemic disseminated toxoplasmosis
130.9	Unspecified toxoplasmosis
131.8	Trichomoniasis of other specified sites
131.9	Unspecified trichomoniasis
136.0	Ainhum
136.2*	Specific infections by free-living amebae
136.4	Psorospermiasis
136.5	Sarcosporidiosis
136.8	Other specified infectious and parasitic diseases
136.9	Unspecified infectious and parasitic diseases
137.4	Late effects of tuberculosis of other specified organs
139.8	Late effects of other and unspecified infectious and parasitic diseases
795.3*	Nonspecific positive culture findings
999.34	Acute infection following transfusion, infusion, or injection of blood and blood products
999.39	Complications of medical care, NEC, infection following other infusion, injection, transfusion, or vaccination
V09*	Infection with drug-resistant microorganisms

DRG 868 **Other Infectious and Parasitic Diseases Diagnoses with CC**
      GMLOS 3.9   AMLOS 4.9   RW 1.0762   T ☑

Select principal diagnosis listed under DRG 867

DRG 869 **Other Infectious and Parasitic Diseases Diagnoses without CC/MCC**
      GMLOS 2.8   AMLOS 3.5   RW 0.7415   T ☑

Select principal diagnosis listed under DRG 867

DRG 870 **Septicemia or Severe Sepsis with Mechanical Ventilation 96+ Hours**
      GMLOS 12.6   AMLOS 14.8   RW 5.8399   T ▽

Principal Diagnosis

003.1	Salmonella septicemia
020.2	Septicemic plague
022.3	Anthrax septicemia
036.2	Meningococcemia
036.3	Waterhouse-Friderichsen syndrome, meningococcal
036.89	Other specified meningococcal infections
036.9	Unspecified meningococcal infection
038*	Septicemia
054.5	Herpetic septicemia
785.52	Septic shock
785.59	Other shock without mention of trauma
790.7	Bacteremia
995.9*	Systemic inflammatory response syndrome (SIRS)

AND

Nonoperating Room Procedure

96.72	Continuous invasive mechanical ventilation for 96 consecutive hours or more

DRG 871 **Septicemia or Severe Sepsis without Mechanical Ventilation 96+ Hours with MCC**
      GMLOS 5.2   AMLOS 6.9   RW 1.8803   T ☑ ▽

Principal Diagnosis

003.1	Salmonella septicemia
020.2	Septicemic plague
022.3	Anthrax septicemia
036.2	Meningococcemia
036.3	Waterhouse-Friderichsen syndrome, meningococcal
036.89	Other specified meningococcal infections
036.9	Unspecified meningococcal infection
038*	Septicemia
054.5	Herpetic septicemia
785.52	Septic shock
785.59	Other shock without mention of trauma
790.7	Bacteremia
995.9*	Systemic inflammatory response syndrome (SIRS)

DRG 872 **Septicemia or Severe Sepsis without Mechanical Ventilation 96+ Hours without MCC**
      GMLOS 4.2   AMLOS 5.0   RW 1.0988   T ☑ ▽

Select principal diagnosis listed under DRG 871

MDC 18: Infectious And Parasitic Diseases—MEDICAL

Surgical	*Medical*	*CC Indicator*	*MCC Indicator*	*Procedure Proxy*

Mental Diseases And Disorders

290.0	295.24	296.01	296.64	300.22	302.72	308.9	313.1	327.15
290.10	295.25	296.02	296.65	300.23	302.73	309.0	313.21	327.19
290.11	295.30	296.03	296.66	300.29	302.74	309.1	313.22	388.45
290.12	295.31	296.04	296.7	300.3	302.75	309.21	313.23	758.0
290.13	295.32	296.05	296.80	300.4	302.76	309.22	313.3	758.1
290.20	295.33	296.06	296.81	300.5	302.79	309.23	313.81	758.2
290.21	295.34	296.10	296.82	300.6	302.81	309.24	313.82	758.31
290.3	295.35	296.11	296.89	300.7	302.82	309.28	313.83	758.32
290.40	295.40	296.12	296.90	300.81	302.83	309.29	313.89	758.33
290.41	295.41	296.13	296.99	300.82	302.84	309.3	313.9	758.39
290.42	295.42	296.14	297.0	300.89	302.85	309.4	314.00	759.83
290.43	295.43	296.15	297.1	300.9	302.89	309.81	314.01	780.02
290.8	295.44	296.16	297.2	301.0	302.9	309.82	314.1	780.1
290.9	295.45	296.20	297.3	301.10	306.7	309.83	314.2	780.50
293.0	295.50	296.21	297.8	301.11	306.8	309.89	314.8	780.52
293.1	295.51	296.22	297.9	301.12	306.9	309.9	314.9	780.54
293.81	295.52	296.23	298.0	301.13	307.0	310.0	315.00	780.55
293.82	295.53	296.24	298.1	301.20	307.1	310.1	315.01	780.56
293.83	295.54	296.25	298.2	301.21	307.3	310.9	315.02	780.58
293.84	295.55	296.26	298.3	301.22	307.40	311	315.09	780.59
293.89	295.60	296.30	298.4	301.3	307.41	312.00	315.1	784.60
293.9	295.61	296.31	298.8	301.4	307.42	312.01	315.2	784.61
294.0	295.62	296.32	298.9	301.50	307.43	312.02	315.31	784.69
294.10	295.63	296.33	299.00	301.51	307.44	312.03	315.32	797
294.11	295.64	296.34	299.01	301.59	307.45	312.10	315.34	799.21
294.20	295.65	296.35	299.10	301.6	307.46	312.11	315.39	799.22
294.21	295.70	296.36	299.11	301.7	307.47	312.12	315.4	799.23
294.8	295.71	296.40	299.80	301.81	307.48	312.13	315.5	799.24
294.9	295.72	296.41	299.81	301.82	307.49	312.20	315.8	799.25
295.00	295.73	296.42	299.90	301.83	307.50	312.21	315.9	799.29
295.01	295.74	296.43	299.91	301.84	307.51	312.22	316	799.51
295.02	295.75	296.44	300.00	301.89	307.52	312.23	317	799.52
295.03	295.80	296.45	300.01	301.9	307.53	312.30	318.0	799.54
295.04	295.81	296.46	300.02	302.0	307.54	312.31	318.1	799.55
295.05	295.82	296.50	300.09	302.1	307.59	312.32	318.2	799.59
295.10	295.83	296.51	300.10	302.2	307.6	312.33	319	V62.84
295.11	295.84	296.52	300.11	302.3	307.7	312.34	327.00	V71.01
295.12	295.85	296.53	300.12	302.4	307.80	312.35	327.01	V71.02
295.13	295.90	296.54	300.13	302.50	307.89	312.39	327.02	V71.09
295.14	295.91	296.55	300.14	302.51	307.9	312.4	327.09	
295.15	295.92	296.56	300.15	302.52	308.0	312.81	327.10	
295.20	295.93	296.60	300.16	302.53	308.1	312.82	327.11	
295.21	295.94	296.61	300.19	302.6	308.2	312.89	327.12	
295.22	295.95	296.62	300.20	302.70	308.3	312.9	327.13	
295.23	296.00	296.63	300.21	302.71	308.4	313.0	327.14	

SURGICAL

DRG 876　O.R. Procedure with Principal Diagnoses of Mental Illness
GMLOS 7.5　　　AMLOS 12.2　　　RW 2.7097

Select any operating room procedure

MEDICAL

DRG 880　Acute Adjustment Reaction and Psychosocial Dysfunction
GMLOS 2.2　　　AMLOS 3.0　　　RW 0.6474　☑

Principal Diagnosis
293.0　Delirium due to conditions classified elsewhere
293.1　Subacute delirium
293.9　Unspecified transient mental disorder in conditions classified elsewhere
300.0*　Anxiety states
300.10　Hysteria, unspecified
300.11　Conversion disorder
300.12　Dissociative amnesia
300.13　Dissociative fugue
300.15　Dissociative disorder or reaction, unspecified
300.16　Factitious disorder with predominantly psychological signs and symptoms
300.19　Other and unspecified factitious illness
300.9　Unspecified nonpsychotic mental disorder
308*　Acute reaction to stress
780.1　Hallucinations
799.21　Nervousness
799.22　Irritability
799.25　Demoralization and apathy
799.29　Other signs and symptoms involving emotional state
V62.84　Suicidal ideation
V71.01　Observation of adult antisocial behavior
V71.02　Observation of childhood or adolescent antisocial behavior

DRG 881　Depressive Neuroses
GMLOS 3.2　　　AMLOS 4.3　　　RW 0.6356　☑

Principal Diagnosis
300.4　Dysthymic disorder
301.12　Chronic depressive personality disorder
309.0　Adjustment disorder with depressed mood
309.1　Prolonged depressive reaction as adjustment reaction
311　Depressive disorder, not elsewhere classified

DRG 882　Neuroses Except Depressive
GMLOS 3.1　　　AMLOS 4.2　　　RW 0.6271　☑

Principal Diagnosis
300.2*　Phobic disorders
300.3　Obsessive-compulsive disorders
300.5　Neurasthenia
300.6　Depersonalization disorder
300.7　Hypochondriasis
300.8*　Somatoform disorders
306.7　Malfunction of organs of special sense arising from mental factors
306.9　Unspecified psychophysiological malfunction
307.53　Rumination disorder
307.54　Psychogenic vomiting
307.80　Psychogenic pain, site unspecified
307.89　Other pain disorder related to psychological factors
309.2*　Predominant disturbance of other emotions as adjustment reaction

309.3　Adjustment disorder with disturbance of conduct
309.4　Adjustment disorder with mixed disturbance of emotions and conduct
309.8*　Other specified adjustment reactions
309.9　Unspecified adjustment reaction
313.0　Overanxious disorder specific to childhood and adolescence
313.1　Misery and unhappiness disorder specific to childhood and adolescence
799.23　Impulsiveness

DRG 883　Disorders of Personality and Impulse Control
GMLOS 4.7　　　AMLOS 8.1　　　RW 1.3613

Principal Diagnosis
300.14　Dissociative identity disorder
301.0　Paranoid personality disorder
301.10　Affective personality disorder, unspecified
301.11　Chronic hypomanic personality disorder
301.13　Cyclothymic disorder
301.2*　Schizoid personality disorder
301.3　Explosive personality disorder
301.4　Obsessive-compulsive personality disorder
301.5*　Histrionic personality disorder
301.6　Dependent personality disorder
301.7　Antisocial personality disorder
301.8*　Other personality disorders
301.9　Unspecified personality disorder
307.1　Anorexia nervosa
312.31　Pathological gambling
312.32　Kleptomania
312.34　Intermittent explosive disorder
312.35　Isolated explosive disorder
312.39　Other disorder of impulse control
799.24　Emotional lability

DRG 884　Organic Disturbances and Mental Retardation
GMLOS 3.9　　　AMLOS 5.4　　　RW 0.9850　Ⓣ☑

Principal Diagnosis
290*　Dementias
293.8*　Other specified transient mental disorders due to conditions classified elsewhere
294*　Persistent mental disorders due to conditions classified elsewhere
299.0*　Autistic disorder
299.1*　Childhood disintegrative disorder
307.9　Other and unspecified special symptom or syndrome, not elsewhere classified
310.0　Frontal lobe syndrome
310.1　Personality change due to conditions classified elsewhere
310.9　Unspecified nonpsychotic mental disorder following organic brain damage
316　Psychic factors associated with diseases classified elsewhere
317　Mild intellectual disabilities
318*　Other specified intellectual disabilities
319　Unspecified intellectual disabilities
758.0　Down's syndrome
758.1　Patau's syndrome
758.2　Edwards' syndrome
758.3*　Autosomal deletion syndromes
759.83　Fragile X syndrome
780.02　Transient alteration of awareness
797　Senility without mention of psychosis
799.52　Cognitive communication deficit
799.54　Psychomotor deficit
799.55　Frontal lobe and executive function deficit
799.59　Other signs and symptoms involving cognition

DRG 885   Psychoses
GMLOS 5.4   AMLOS 7.4   RW 0.9539   ▽

Principal Diagnosis

295*	Schizophrenic disorders
296*	Episodic mood disorders
297*	Delusional disorders
298.0	Depressive type psychosis
298.1	Excitative type psychosis
298.3	Acute paranoid reaction
298.4	Psychogenic paranoid psychosis
298.8	Other and unspecified reactive psychosis
298.9	Unspecified psychosis
299.8*	Other specified pervasive developmental disorders
299.9*	Unspecified pervasive developmental disorder

DRG 886   Behavioral and Developmental Disorders
GMLOS 3.8   AMLOS 6.1   RW 0.7812

Principal Diagnosis

307.52	Pica
307.6	Enuresis
307.7	Encopresis
312.0*	Undersocialized conduct disorder, aggressive type
312.1*	Undersocialized conduct disorder, unaggressive type
312.2*	Socialized conduct disorder
312.30	Impulse control disorder, unspecified
312.33	Pyromania
312.4	Mixed disturbance of conduct and emotions
312.8*	Other specified disturbances of conduct, not elsewhere classified
312.9	Unspecified disturbance of conduct
313.2*	Sensitivity, shyness, and social withdrawal disorder specific to childhood and adolescence
313.3	Relationship problems specific to childhood and adolescence
313.8*	Other or mixed emotional disturbances of childhood or adolescence
313.9	Unspecified emotional disturbance of childhood or adolescence
314*	Hyperkinetic syndrome of childhood
315.00	Developmental reading disorder, unspecified
315.01	Alexia
315.02	Developmental dyslexia
315.09	Other specific developmental reading disorder
315.1	Mathematics disorder
315.2	Other specific developmental learning difficulties
315.31	Expressive language disorder
315.32	Mixed receptive-expressive language disorder
315.34	Speech and language developmental delay due to hearing loss
315.39	Other developmental speech or language disorder
315.4	Developmental coordination disorder
315.5	Mixed development disorder
315.8	Other specified delay in development
315.9	Unspecified delay in development
388.45	Acquired auditory processing disorder
784.61	Alexia and dyslexia
784.69	Other symbolic dysfunction
799.51	Attention or concentration deficit

DRG 887   Other Mental Disorder Diagnoses
GMLOS 3.1   AMLOS 4.7   RW 0.9473   ☑

Principal Diagnosis

298.2	Reactive confusion
302*	Sexual and gender identity disorders
306.8	Other specified psychophysiological malfunction
307.0	Adult onset fluency disorder
307.3	Stereotypic movement disorder
307.4*	Specific disorders of sleep of nonorganic origin
307.50	Eating disorder, unspecified
307.51	Bulimia nervosa
307.59	Other disorder of eating
327.0*	Organic disorders of initiating and maintaining sleep [Organic insomnia]
327.1*	Organic disorders of excessive somnolence [Organic hypersomnia]
780.50	Unspecified sleep disturbance
780.52	Insomnia, unspecified
780.54	Hypersomnia, unspecified
780.55	Disruption of 24 hour sleep wake cycle, unspecified
780.56	Dysfunctions associated with sleep stages or arousal from sleep
780.58	Sleep related movement disorder, unspecified
780.59	Other sleep disturbances
784.60	Symbolic dysfunction, unspecified
V71.09	Observation of other suspected mental condition

Ⓣ *Transfer DRG*   ⓢⓟ *Special Payment*   ☑ *Optimization Potential*   ▽ *Targeted Potential*   * *Code Range*   ● *New DRG*   ▲ *Revised DRG Title*

MDC 20
Alcohol/Drug Use And Alcohol/Drug-Induced Organic Mental Disorders

291.0	292.12	303.03	304.13	304.43	304.73	305.03	305.43	305.73
291.1	292.2	303.90	304.20	304.50	304.80	305.20	305.50	305.80
291.2	292.81	303.91	304.21	304.51	304.81	305.21	305.51	305.81
291.3	292.82	303.92	304.22	304.52	304.82	305.22	305.52	305.82
291.4	292.83	303.93	304.23	304.53	304.83	305.23	305.53	305.83
291.5	292.84	304.00	304.30	304.60	304.90	305.30	305.60	305.90
291.81	292.85	304.01	304.31	304.61	304.91	305.31	305.61	305.91
291.82	292.89	304.02	304.32	304.62	304.92	305.32	305.62	305.92
291.89	292.9	304.03	304.33	304.63	304.93	305.33	305.63	305.93
291.9	303.00	304.10	304.40	304.70	305.00	305.40	305.70	790.3
292.0	303.01	304.11	304.41	304.71	305.01	305.41	305.71	
292.11	303.02	304.12	304.42	304.72	305.02	305.42	305.72	

MEDICAL

DRG 894   **Alcohol/Drug Abuse or Dependence, Left Against Medical Advice**
GMLOS 2.1   AMLOS 3.0   RW 0.4278   ☑

Select principal diagnosis in MDC 20

AND

Discharge status of against medical advice (AMA)

DRG 895   **Alcohol/Drug Abuse or Dependence with Rehabilitation Therapy**
GMLOS 9.2   AMLOS 11.7   RW 1.0963   ☑

Principal Diagnosis
291*   Alcohol-induced mental disorders
292*   Drug-induced mental disorders
303.0*   Acute alcoholic intoxication
303.9*   Other and unspecified alcohol dependence
304*   Drug dependence
305.0*   Nondependent alcohol abuse
305.2*   Nondependent cannabis abuse
305.3*   Nondependent hallucinogen abuse
305.4*   Nondependent sedative, hypnotic or anxiolytic abuse
305.5*   Nondependent opioid abuse
305.6*   Nondependent cocaine abuse
305.7*   Nondependent amphetamine or related acting sympathomimetic abuse
305.8*   Nondependent antidepressant type abuse
305.9*   Other, mixed, or unspecified nondependent drug abuse
790.3   Excessive blood level of alcohol

AND

Nonoperating Room Procedures
94.61   Alcohol rehabilitation
94.63   Alcohol rehabilitation and detoxification
94.64   Drug rehabilitation
94.66   Drug rehabilitation and detoxification
94.67   Combined alcohol and drug rehabilitation
94.69   Combined alcohol and drug rehabilitation and detoxification

DRG 896   **Alcohol/Drug Abuse or Dependence without Rehabilitation Therapy with MCC**
GMLOS 4.8   AMLOS 6.7   RW 1.5271   T ☑

Select only principal diagnosis listed under DRG 895

DRG 897   **Alcohol/Drug Abuse or Dependence without Rehabilitation Therapy without MCC**
GMLOS 3.2   AMLOS 4.0   RW 0.6788   T ☑

Select only principal diagnosis listed under DRG 895

MDC 20: Alcohol/Drug Use And Alcohol/Drug-Induced Organic Mental Disorders—MEDICAL

MDC 21
Injuries, Poisonings And Toxic Effects Of Drugs

238.77	900.02	903.9	958.93	964.8	971.1	978.8	989.6	995.63
349.31	900.03	904.0	958.99	964.9	971.2	978.9	989.7	995.64
349.39	900.1	904.1	959.01	965.00	971.3	979.0	989.81	995.65
796.0	900.81	904.2	959.09	965.01	971.9	979.1	989.82	995.66
819.0	900.82	904.3	959.11	965.02	972.0	979.2	989.83	995.67
819.1	900.89	904.40	959.12	965.09	972.1	979.3	989.84	995.68
828.0	900.9	904.41	959.13	965.1	972.2	979.4	989.89	995.69
828.1	901.0	904.42	959.14	965.4	972.3	979.5	989.9	995.7
862.8	901.1	904.50	959.19	965.5	972.4	979.6	990	995.80
862.9	901.2	904.51	959.2	965.61	972.5	979.7	991.0	995.81
868.09	901.3	904.52	959.3	965.69	972.6	979.9	991.1	995.82
868.19	901.40	904.53	959.4	965.7	972.7	980.0	991.2	995.83
869.0	901.41	904.54	959.5	965.8	972.8	980.1	991.3	995.84
869.1	901.42	904.6	959.6	965.9	972.9	980.2	991.4	995.85
875.1	901.81	904.7	959.7	966.0	973.0	980.3	991.5	995.86
879.3	901.82	904.8	959.8	966.1	973.1	980.8	991.6	995.89
879.5	901.83	904.9	959.9	966.2	973.2	980.9	991.8	996.52
879.7	901.89	908.5	960.0	966.3	973.3	981	991.9	996.55
879.9	901.9	908.6	960.1	966.4	973.4	982.0	992.0	996.56
880.10	902.0	908.9	960.2	967.0	973.5	982.1	992.1	996.57
880.11	902.10	909.0	960.3	967.1	973.6	982.2	992.2	996.59
880.12	902.11	909.1	960.4	967.2	973.8	982.3	992.3	996.60
880.13	902.19	909.2	960.5	967.3	973.9	982.4	992.4	996.68
880.19	902.20	909.3	960.6	967.4	974.0	982.8	992.5	996.69
881.10	902.21	909.4	960.7	967.5	974.1	983.0	992.6	996.70
881.11	902.22	909.5	960.8	967.6	974.2	983.1	992.7	996.79
881.12	902.23	909.9	960.9	967.8	974.3	983.2	992.8	996.80
882.1	902.24	925.1	961.0	967.9	974.4	983.9	992.9	996.87
883.1	902.25	925.2	961.1	968.0	974.5	984.0	993.2	996.88
884.1	902.26	926.11	961.2	968.1	974.6	984.1	993.3	996.89
885.0	902.27	926.12	961.3	968.2	974.7	984.8	993.4	997.91
885.1	902.29	926.19	961.4	968.3	975.0	984.9	993.8	997.99
886.0	902.31	926.8	961.5	968.4	975.1	985.0	993.9	998.00
886.1	902.32	926.9	961.6	968.5	975.2	985.1	994.0	998.01
887.0	902.33	927.00	961.7	968.6	975.3	985.2	994.1	998.02
887.1	902.34	927.01	961.8	968.7	975.4	985.3	994.2	998.09
887.2	902.39	927.02	961.9	968.9	975.5	985.4	994.3	998.11
887.3	902.40	927.03	962.0	969.00	975.6	985.5	994.4	998.12
887.4	902.41	927.09	962.1	969.01	975.7	985.6	994.5	998.13
887.5	902.42	927.10	962.2	969.02	975.8	985.8	994.7	998.2
887.6	902.49	927.11	962.3	969.03	976.0	985.9	994.8	998.30
887.7	902.50	927.20	962.4	969.04	976.1	986	994.9	998.31
890.1	902.51	927.21	962.5	969.05	976.2	987.0	995.0	998.32
891.1	902.52	927.3	962.6	969.09	976.3	987.1	995.1	998.33
892.1	902.53	927.8	962.7	969.1	976.4	987.2	995.20	998.4
893.1	902.54	927.9	962.8	969.2	976.6	987.3	995.21	998.6
894.1	902.55	928.00	962.9	969.3	976.7	987.4	995.22	998.7
895.0	902.56	928.01	963.0	969.4	976.8	987.5	995.23	998.81
895.1	902.59	928.10	963.1	969.5	976.9	987.6	995.24	998.83
896.0	902.81	928.11	963.2	969.6	977.0	987.7	995.27	998.89
896.1	902.82	928.20	963.3	969.70	977.1	987.8	995.29	998.9
896.2	902.87	928.21	963.4	969.71	977.2	987.9	995.3	999.41
896.3	902.89	928.3	963.5	969.72	977.3	988.0	995.4	999.42
897.0	902.9	928.8	963.8	969.73	977.4	988.1	995.50	999.49
897.1	903.00	928.9	963.9	969.79	977.8	988.2	995.51	999.51
897.2	903.01	929.0	964.0	969.8	977.9	988.8	995.52	999.52
897.3	903.02	929.9	964.1	969.9	978.0	988.9	995.53	999.59
897.4	903.1	958.2	964.2	970.0	978.1	989.0	995.54	999.9
897.5	903.2	958.4	964.3	970.1	978.2	989.1	995.55	V71.3
897.6	903.3	958.8	964.4	970.81	978.3	989.2	995.59	V71.4
897.7	903.4	958.90	964.5	970.89	978.4	989.3	995.60	V71.6
900.00	903.5	958.91	964.6	970.9	978.5	989.4	995.61	
900.01	903.8	958.92	964.7	971.0	978.6	989.5	995.62	

SURGICAL

DRG 901   **Wound Debridements for Injuries with MCC**
GMLOS 9.9   AMLOS 14.9   RW 4.3477   ☑

Operating Room Procedure
86.22   Excisional debridement of wound, infection, or burn

DRG 902   **Wound Debridements for Injuries with CC**
GMLOS 5.0   AMLOS 6.9   RW 1.7079   ☑

Select operating room procedure listed under DRG 901

DRG 903   **Wound Debridements for Injuries without CC/MCC**
GMLOS 3.0   AMLOS 4.0   RW 0.9890   ☑

Select operating room procedure listed under DRG 901

DRG 904   **Skin Grafts for Injuries with CC/MCC**
GMLOS 7.0   AMLOS 10.1   RW 2.9145   ☑

Operating Room Procedures
85.82   Split-thickness graft to breast
85.83   Full-thickness graft to breast
85.84   Pedicle graft to breast
86.60   Free skin graft, not otherwise specified
86.63   Full-thickness skin graft to other sites
86.65   Heterograft to skin
86.66   Homograft to skin
86.67   Dermal regenerative graft
86.69   Other skin graft to other sites
86.70   Pedicle or flap graft, not otherwise specified
86.71   Cutting and preparation of pedicle grafts or flaps
86.72   Advancement of pedicle graft
86.74   Attachment of pedicle or flap graft to other sites
86.75   Revision of pedicle or flap graft
86.93   Insertion of tissue expander

DRG 905   **Skin Grafts for Injuries without CC/MCC**
GMLOS 3.4   AMLOS 4.6   RW 1.2630   ☑

Select operating room procedures listed under DRG 904

DRG 906   **Hand Procedures for Injuries**
GMLOS 2.4   AMLOS 3.6   RW 1.1596   ☑

Operating Room Procedures
04.43   Release of carpal tunnel
77.04   Sequestrectomy of carpals and metacarpals
77.14   Other incision of carpals and metacarpals without division
77.24   Wedge osteotomy of carpals and metacarpals
77.34   Other division of carpals and metacarpals
77.44   Biopsy of carpals and metacarpals
77.64   Local excision of lesion or tissue of carpals and metacarpals
77.74   Excision of carpals and metacarpals for graft
77.84   Other partial ostectomy of carpals and metacarpals
77.94   Total ostectomy of carpals and metacarpals
78.04   Bone graft of carpals and metacarpals
78.14   Application of external fixator device, carpals and metacarpals
78.24   Limb shortening procedures, carpals and metacarpals
78.34   Limb lengthening procedures, carpals and metacarpals
78.44   Other repair or plastic operations on carpals and metacarpals
78.54   Internal fixation of carpals and metacarpals without fracture reduction
78.64   Removal of implanted device from carpals and metacarpals
78.74   Osteoclasis of carpals and metacarpals

78.84   Diagnostic procedures on carpals and metacarpals, not elsewhere classified
78.94   Insertion of bone growth stimulator into carpals and metacarpals
79.13   Closed reduction of fracture of carpals and metacarpals with internal fixation
79.14   Closed reduction of fracture of phalanges of hand with internal fixation
79.23   Open reduction of fracture of carpals and metacarpals without internal fixation
79.24   Open reduction of fracture of phalanges of hand without internal fixation
79.33   Open reduction of fracture of carpals and metacarpals with internal fixation
79.34   Open reduction of fracture of phalanges of hand with internal fixation
79.63   Debridement of open fracture of carpals and metacarpals
79.64   Debridement of open fracture of phalanges of hand
79.83   Open reduction of dislocation of wrist
79.84   Open reduction of dislocation of hand and finger
79.93   Unspecified operation on bone injury of carpals and metacarpals
79.94   Unspecified operation on bone injury of phalanges of hand
80.03   Arthrotomy for removal of prosthesis without replacement, wrist
80.04   Arthrotomy for removal of prosthesis without replacement, hand and finger
80.13   Other arthrotomy of wrist
80.14   Other arthrotomy of hand and finger
80.43   Division of joint capsule, ligament, or cartilage of wrist
80.44   Division of joint capsule, ligament, or cartilage of hand and finger
80.73   Synovectomy of wrist
80.74   Synovectomy of hand and finger
80.83   Other local excision or destruction of lesion of wrist joint
80.84   Other local excision or destruction of lesion of joint of hand and finger
80.93   Other excision of wrist joint
80.94   Other excision of joint of hand and finger
81.25   Carporadial fusion
81.26   Metacarpocarpal fusion
81.27   Metacarpophalangeal fusion
81.28   Interphalangeal fusion
81.71   Arthroplasty of metacarpophalangeal and interphalangeal joint with implant
81.72   Arthroplasty of metacarpophalangeal and interphalangeal joint without implant
81.74   Arthroplasty of carpocarpal or carpometacarpal joint with implant
81.75   Arthroplasty of carpocarpal or carpometacarpal joint without implant
81.79   Other repair of hand, fingers, and wrist
82.01   Exploration of tendon sheath of hand
82.02   Myotomy of hand
82.03   Bursotomy of hand
82.09   Other incision of soft tissue of hand
82.1*   Division of muscle, tendon, and fascia of hand
82.2*   Excision of lesion of muscle, tendon, and fascia of hand
82.3*   Other excision of soft tissue of hand
82.4*   Suture of muscle, tendon, and fascia of hand
82.5*   Transplantation of muscle and tendon of hand
82.6*   Reconstruction of thumb
82.7*   Plastic operation on hand with graft or implant
82.8*   Other plastic operations on hand
82.91   Lysis of adhesions of hand
82.99   Other operations on muscle, tendon, and fascia of hand
84.01   Amputation and disarticulation of finger
84.02   Amputation and disarticulation of thumb
84.21   Thumb reattachment
84.22   Finger reattachment

Ⓣ *Transfer DRG*   ⓢ *Special Payment*   ☑ *Optimization Potential*   ⷱ *Targeted Potential*   * *Code Range*   ● *New DRG*   ▲ *Revised DRG Title*

86.61	Full-thickness skin graft to hand
86.62	Other skin graft to hand
86.73	Attachment of pedicle or flap graft to hand
86.85	Correction of syndactyly

DRG 907 Other O.R. Procedures for Injuries with MCC

GMLOS 7.7   AMLOS 10.9   RW 3.8565   T ☑

Operating Room Procedures

00.61	Percutaneous angioplasty of extracranial vessel(s)
00.62	Percutaneous angioplasty of intracranial vessel(s)
00.70	Revision of hip replacement, both acetabular and femoral components
00.71	Revision of hip replacement, acetabular component
00.72	Revision of hip replacement, femoral component
00.73	Revision of hip replacement, acetabular liner and/or femoral head only
00.8*	Other knee and hip procedures
01.18	Other diagnostic procedures on brain and cerebral meninges
01.19	Other diagnostic procedures on skull
01.23	Reopening of craniotomy site
01.24	Other craniotomy
01.25	Other craniectomy
01.28	Placement of intracerebral catheter(s) via burr hole(s)
01.3*	Incision of brain and cerebral meninges
01.41	Operations on thalamus
01.52	Hemispherectomy
01.53	Lobectomy of brain
01.59	Other excision or destruction of lesion or tissue of brain
02.0*	Cranioplasty
02.11	Simple suture of dura mater of brain
02.12	Other repair of cerebral meninges
02.13	Ligation of meningeal vessel
02.2*	Ventriculostomy
02.3*	Extracranial ventricular shunt
02.42	Replacement of ventricular shunt
02.43	Removal of ventricular shunt
02.91	Lysis of cortical adhesions
02.92	Repair of brain
02.93	Implantation or replacement of intracranial neurostimulator lead(s)
02.94	Insertion or replacement of skull tongs or halo traction device
02.99	Other operations on skull, brain, and cerebral meninges
03.0*	Exploration and decompression of spinal canal structures
03.1	Division of intraspinal nerve root
03.2*	Chordotomy
03.53	Repair of vertebral fracture
03.59	Other repair and plastic operations on spinal cord structures
03.6	Lysis of adhesions of spinal cord and nerve roots
03.93	Implantation or replacement of spinal neurostimulator lead(s)
03.94	Removal of spinal neurostimulator lead(s)
03.97	Revision of spinal thecal shunt
03.98	Removal of spinal thecal shunt
03.99	Other operations on spinal cord and spinal canal structures
04.02	Division of trigeminal nerve
04.03	Division or crushing of other cranial and peripheral nerves
04.04	Other incision of cranial and peripheral nerves
04.05	Gasserian ganglionectomy
04.06	Other cranial or peripheral ganglionectomy
04.07	Other excision or avulsion of cranial and peripheral nerves
04.12	Open biopsy of cranial or peripheral nerve or ganglion
04.19	Other diagnostic procedures on cranial and peripheral nerves and ganglia
04.3	Suture of cranial and peripheral nerves
04.41	Decompression of trigeminal nerve root
04.42	Other cranial nerve decompression
04.44	Release of tarsal tunnel
04.49	Other peripheral nerve or ganglion decompression or lysis of adhesions
04.5	Cranial or peripheral nerve graft
04.6	Transposition of cranial and peripheral nerves
04.7*	Other cranial or peripheral neuroplasty
04.9*	Other operations on cranial and peripheral nerves
05.9	Other operations on nervous system
06.02	Reopening of wound of thyroid field
06.09	Other incision of thyroid field
06.92	Ligation of thyroid vessels
06.93	Suture of thyroid gland
07.43	Ligation of adrenal vessels
07.44	Repair of adrenal gland
07.45	Reimplantation of adrenal tissue
07.49	Other operations on adrenal glands, nerves, and vessels
07.8*	Thymectomy
07.91	Exploration of thymus field
07.92	Other incision of thymus
07.93	Repair of thymus
07.95	Thoracoscopic incision of thymus
07.98	Other and unspecified thoracoscopic operations on thymus
08.11	Biopsy of eyelid
08.2*	Excision or destruction of lesion or tissue of eyelid
08.3*	Repair of blepharoptosis and lid retraction
08.4*	Repair of entropion or ectropion
08.5*	Other adjustment of lid position
08.6*	Reconstruction of eyelid with flaps or grafts
08.7*	Other reconstruction of eyelid
08.9*	Other operations on eyelids
09.11	Biopsy of lacrimal gland
09.19	Other diagnostic procedures on lacrimal system
09.21	Excision of lesion of lacrimal gland
09.22	Other partial dacryoadenectomy
09.23	Total dacryoadenectomy
09.3	Other operations on lacrimal gland
09.44	Intubation of nasolacrimal duct
09.52	Incision of lacrimal canaliculi
09.6	Excision of lacrimal sac and passage
09.7*	Repair of canaliculus and punctum
09.8*	Fistulization of lacrimal tract to nasal cavity
09.9*	Other operations on lacrimal system
10.0	Removal of embedded foreign body from conjunctiva by incision
10.3*	Excision or destruction of lesion or tissue of conjunctiva
10.4*	Conjunctivoplasty
10.6	Repair of laceration of conjunctiva
11.0	Magnetic removal of embedded foreign body from cornea
11.1	Incision of cornea
11.22	Biopsy of cornea
11.32	Excision of pterygium with corneal graft
11.42	Thermocauterization of corneal lesion
11.43	Cryotherapy of corneal lesion
11.49	Other removal or destruction of corneal lesion
11.5*	Repair of cornea
11.6*	Corneal transplant
11.7*	Other reconstructive and refractive surgery on cornea
11.9*	Other operations on cornea
12.0*	Removal of intraocular foreign body from anterior segment of eye
12.1*	Iridotomy and simple iridectomy
12.2*	Diagnostic procedures on iris, ciliary body, sclera, and anterior chamber
12.3*	Iridoplasty and coreoplasty
12.4*	Excision or destruction of lesion of iris and ciliary body
12.5*	Facilitation of intraocular circulation
12.6*	Scleral fistulization
12.8*	Operations on sclera
12.91	Therapeutic evacuation of anterior chamber
12.92	Injection into anterior chamber
12.97	Other operations on iris

Surgical   Medical   CC Indicator   MCC Indicator   Procedure Proxy

12.98	Other operations on ciliary body
12.99	Other operations on anterior chamber
13.0*	Removal of foreign body from lens
13.72	Secondary insertion of intraocular lens prosthesis
13.8	Removal of implanted lens
13.9*	Other operations on lens
14.0*	Removal of foreign body from posterior segment of eye
14.31	Repair of retinal tear by diathermy
14.4*	Repair of retinal detachment with scleral buckling and implant
14.5*	Other repair of retinal detachment
14.6	Removal of surgically implanted material from posterior segment of eye
14.7*	Operations on vitreous
14.9	Other operations on retina, choroid, and posterior chamber
15.7	Repair of injury of extraocular muscle
15.9	Other operations on extraocular muscles and tendons
16.0*	Orbitotomy
16.1	Removal of penetrating foreign body from eye, not otherwise specified
16.3*	Evisceration of eyeball
16.4*	Enucleation of eyeball
16.5*	Exenteration of orbital contents
16.6*	Secondary procedures after removal of eyeball
16.7*	Removal of ocular or orbital implant
16.8*	Repair of injury of eyeball and orbit
16.92	Excision of lesion of orbit
16.93	Excision of lesion of eye, unspecified structure
16.98	Other operations on orbit
16.99	Other operations on eyeball
17.3*	Laparoscopic partial excision of large intestine
17.53	Percutaneous atherectomy of extracranial vessel(s)
17.54	Percutaneous atherectomy of intracranial vessel(s)
17.56	Atherectomy of other non-coronary vessel(s)
18.39	Other excision of external ear
18.6	Reconstruction of external auditory canal
18.7*	Other plastic repair of external ear
18.9	Other operations on external ear
21.04	Control of epistaxis by ligation of ethmoidal arteries
21.05	Control of epistaxis by (transantral) ligation of the maxillary artery
21.06	Control of epistaxis by ligation of the external carotid artery
21.07	Control of epistaxis by excision of nasal mucosa and skin grafting of septum and lateral nasal wall
21.09	Control of epistaxis by other means
21.4	Resection of nose
21.5	Submucous resection of nasal septum
21.62	Fracture of the turbinates
21.69	Other turbinectomy
21.72	Open reduction of nasal fracture
21.83	Total nasal reconstruction
21.84	Revision rhinoplasty
21.85	Augmentation rhinoplasty
21.86	Limited rhinoplasty
21.87	Other rhinoplasty
21.88	Other septoplasty
21.89	Other repair and plastic operations on nose
21.99	Other operations on nose
24.2	Gingivoplasty
24.5	Alveoloplasty
25.59	Other repair and plastic operations on tongue
26.4*	Repair of salivary gland or duct
27.0	Drainage of face and floor of mouth
27.49	Other excision of mouth
27.53	Closure of fistula of mouth
27.54	Repair of cleft lip
27.55	Full-thickness skin graft to lip and mouth
27.56	Other skin graft to lip and mouth
27.57	Attachment of pedicle or flap graft to lip and mouth
27.59	Other plastic repair of mouth

27.61	Suture of laceration of palate
27.92	Incision of mouth, unspecified structure
27.99	Other operations on oral cavity
28.7	Control of hemorrhage after tonsillectomy and adenoidectomy
28.91	Removal of foreign body from tonsil and adenoid by incision
29.0	Pharyngotomy
29.4	Plastic operation on pharynx
29.51	Suture of laceration of pharynx
29.53	Closure of other fistula of pharynx
29.59	Other repair of pharynx
29.99	Other operations on pharynx
30.1	Hemilaryngectomy
30.2*	Other partial laryngectomy
31.61	Suture of laceration of larynx
31.64	Repair of laryngeal fracture
31.69	Other repair of larynx
31.7*	Repair and plastic operations on trachea
31.92	Lysis of adhesions of trachea or larynx
31.99	Other operations on trachea
32.1	Other excision of bronchus
32.20	Thoracoscopic excision of lesion or tissue of lung
32.3*	Segmental resection of lung
32.4*	Lobectomy of lung
32.5*	Pneumonectomy
32.9	Other excision of lung
33.0	Incision of bronchus
33.1	Incision of lung
33.4*	Repair and plastic operation on lung and bronchus
33.92	Ligation of bronchus
33.98	Other operations on bronchus
33.99	Other operations on lung
34.02	Exploratory thoracotomy
34.03	Reopening of recent thoracotomy site
34.1	Incision of mediastinum
34.21	Transpleural thoracoscopy
34.5*	Pleurectomy
34.6	Scarification of pleura
34.73	Closure of other fistula of thorax
34.79	Other repair of chest wall
34.82	Suture of laceration of diaphragm
34.83	Closure of fistula of diaphragm
34.84	Other repair of diaphragm
34.85	Implantation of diaphragmatic pacemaker
34.89	Other operations on diaphragm
34.93	Repair of pleura
34.99	Other operations on thorax
37.11	Cardiotomy
37.12	Pericardiotomy
37.31	Pericardiectomy
37.49	Other repair of heart and pericardium
37.74	Insertion or replacement of epicardial lead (electrode) into epicardium
37.75	Revision of lead (electrode)
37.76	Replacement of transvenous atrial and/or ventricular lead(s) (electrode(s))
37.77	Removal of lead(s) (electrodes) without replacement
37.79	Revision or relocation of cardiac device pocket
37.80	Insertion of permanent pacemaker, initial or replacement, type of device not specified
37.85	Replacement of any type of pacemaker device with single-chamber device, not specified as rate responsive
37.86	Replacement of any type of pacemaker device with single-chamber device, rate responsive
37.87	Replacement of any type of pacemaker device with dual-chamber device
37.89	Revision or removal of pacemaker device
37.91	Open chest cardiac massage
38.0*	Incision of vessel
38.10	Endarterectomy, unspecified site

Ⓣ *Transfer DRG*   SP *Special Payment*   ☑ *Optimization Potential*   ⱽᴿᴸⁱᵈ *Targeted Potential*   * *Code Range*   ● *New DRG*   ▲ *Revised DRG Title*

196   Valid 10/01/2012-09/30/2013   © 2012 OptumInsight, Inc.

38.12	Endarterectomy of other vessels of head and neck
38.13	Endarterectomy of upper limb vessels
38.14	Endarterectomy of aorta
38.15	Endarterectomy of other thoracic vessels
38.16	Endarterectomy of abdominal arteries
38.18	Endarterectomy of lower limb arteries
38.3*	Resection of vessel with anastomosis
38.4*	Resection of vessel with replacement
38.6*	Other excision of vessels
38.7	Interruption of the vena cava
38.8*	Other surgical occlusion of vessels
39.22	Aorta-subclavian-carotid bypass
39.23	Other intrathoracic vascular shunt or bypass
39.24	Aorta-renal bypass
39.25	Aorta-iliac-femoral bypass
39.26	Other intra-abdominal vascular shunt or bypass
39.27	Arteriovenostomy for renal dialysis
39.28	Extracranial-intracranial (EC-IC) vascular bypass
39.29	Other (peripheral) vascular shunt or bypass
39.3*	Suture of vessel
39.4*	Revision of vascular procedure
39.50	Angioplasty of other non-coronary vessel(s)
39.52	Other repair of aneurysm
39.56	Repair of blood vessel with tissue patch graft
39.57	Repair of blood vessel with synthetic patch graft
39.58	Repair of blood vessel with unspecified type of patch graft
39.59	Other repair of vessel
39.71	Endovascular implantation of other graft in abdominal aorta
39.72	Endovascular (total) embolization or occlusion of head and neck vessels
39.73	Endovascular implantation of graft in thoracic aorta
39.74	Endovascular removal of obstruction from head and neck vessel(s)
39.75	Endovascular embolization or occlusion of vessel(s) of head or neck using bare coils
39.76	Endovascular embolization or occlusion of vessel(s) of head or neck using bioactive coils
39.77	Temporary (partial) therapeutic endovascular occlusion of vessel
39.79	Other endovascular procedures on other vessels
39.91	Freeing of vessel
39.93	Insertion of vessel-to-vessel cannula
39.98	Control of hemorrhage, not otherwise specified
39.99	Other operations on vessels
40.29	Simple excision of other lymphatic structure
40.6*	Operations on thoracic duct
40.9	Other operations on lymphatic structures
41.2	Splenotomy
41.42	Excision of lesion or tissue of spleen
41.43	Partial splenectomy
41.5	Total splenectomy
41.93	Excision of accessory spleen
41.95	Repair and plastic operations on spleen
41.99	Other operations on spleen
42.09	Other incision of esophagus
42.1*	Esophagostomy
42.21	Operative esophagoscopy by incision
42.4*	Excision of esophagus
42.5*	Intrathoracic anastomosis of esophagus
42.6*	Antesternal anastomosis of esophagus
42.7	Esophagomyotomy
42.82	Suture of laceration of esophagus
42.83	Closure of esophagostomy
42.84	Repair of esophageal fistula, not elsewhere classified
42.85	Repair of esophageal stricture
42.86	Production of subcutaneous tunnel without esophageal anastomosis
42.87	Other graft of esophagus
42.89	Other repair of esophagus
43.0	Gastrotomy

43.5	Partial gastrectomy with anastomosis to esophagus
43.6	Partial gastrectomy with anastomosis to duodenum
43.7	Partial gastrectomy with anastomosis to jejunum
43.8*	Other partial gastrectomy
43.9*	Total gastrectomy
44.11	Transabdominal gastroscopy
44.5	Revision of gastric anastomosis
44.61	Suture of laceration of stomach
44.63	Closure of other gastric fistula
44.64	Gastropexy
44.65	Esophagogastroplasty
44.66	Other procedures for creation of esophagogastric sphincteric competence
44.67	Laparoscopic procedures for creation of esophagogastric sphincteric competence
44.68	Laparoscopic gastroplasty
44.69	Other repair of stomach
44.92	Intraoperative manipulation of stomach
44.99	Other operations on stomach
45.0*	Enterotomy
45.11	Transabdominal endoscopy of small intestine
45.21	Transabdominal endoscopy of large intestine
45.6*	Other excision of small intestine
45.7*	Open and other partial excision of large intestine
45.8*	Total intra-abdominal colectomy
45.9*	Intestinal anastomosis
46.0*	Exteriorization of intestine
46.10	Colostomy, not otherwise specified
46.11	Temporary colostomy
46.13	Permanent colostomy
46.20	Ileostomy, not otherwise specified
46.21	Temporary ileostomy
46.22	Continent ileostomy
46.23	Other permanent ileostomy
46.4*	Revision of intestinal stoma
46.5*	Closure of intestinal stoma
46.7*	Other repair of intestine
46.80	Intra-abdominal manipulation of intestine, not otherwise specified
46.81	Intra-abdominal manipulation of small intestine
46.82	Intra-abdominal manipulation of large intestine
46.93	Revision of anastomosis of small intestine
46.94	Revision of anastomosis of large intestine
46.99	Other operations on intestines
47.1*	Incidental appendectomy
47.92	Closure of appendiceal fistula
48.0	Proctotomy
48.1	Proctostomy
48.21	Transabdominal proctosigmoidoscopy
48.40	Pull-through resection of rectum, not otherwise specified
48.42	Laparoscopic pull-through resection of rectum
48.43	Open pull-through resection of rectum
48.49	Other pull-through resection of rectum
48.5*	Abdominoperineal resection of rectum
48.6*	Other resection of rectum
48.7*	Repair of rectum
48.8*	Incision or excision of perirectal tissue or lesion
48.91	Incision of rectal stricture
49.1*	Incision or excision of anal fistula
49.71	Suture of laceration of anus
49.73	Closure of anal fistula
49.75	Implantation or revision of artificial anal sphincter
49.76	Removal of artificial anal sphincter
49.79	Other repair of anal sphincter
49.95	Control of (postoperative) hemorrhage of anus
49.99	Other operations on anus
50.0	Hepatotomy
50.12	Open biopsy of liver
50.14	Laparoscopic liver biopsy
50.19	Other diagnostic procedures on liver

Surgical	Medical	CC Indicator	MCC Indicator	Procedure Proxy

50.22	Partial hepatectomy
50.3	Lobectomy of liver
50.4	Total hepatectomy
50.6*	Repair of liver
51.2*	Cholecystectomy
51.3*	Anastomosis of gallbladder or bile duct
51.42	Common duct exploration for relief of other obstruction
51.43	Insertion of choledochohepatic tube for decompression
51.59	Incision of other bile duct
51.61	Excision of cystic duct remnant
51.7*	Repair of bile ducts
51.81	Dilation of sphincter of Oddi
51.82	Pancreatic sphincterotomy
51.83	Pancreatic sphincteroplasty
51.89	Other operations on sphincter of Oddi
51.91	Repair of laceration of gallbladder
51.92	Closure of cholecystostomy
51.93	Closure of other biliary fistula
51.94	Revision of anastomosis of biliary tract
51.95	Removal of prosthetic device from bile duct
51.99	Other operations on biliary tract
52.12	Open biopsy of pancreas
52.19	Other diagnostic procedures on pancreas
52.5*	Partial pancreatectomy
52.6	Total pancreatectomy
52.7	Radical pancreaticoduodenectomy
52.92	Cannulation of pancreatic duct
52.95	Other repair of pancreas
52.96	Anastomosis of pancreas
52.99	Other operations on pancreas
53.43	Other laparoscopic umbilical herniorrhaphy
53.49	Other open umbilical herniorrhaphy
53.61	Other open incisional hernia repair with graft or prosthesis
53.62	Laparoscopic incisional hernia repair with graft or prosthesis
53.7*	Repair of diaphragmatic hernia, abdominal approach
53.8*	Repair of diaphragmatic hernia, thoracic approach
54.0	Incision of abdominal wall
54.1*	Laparotomy
54.21	Laparoscopy
54.22	Biopsy of abdominal wall or umbilicus
54.29	Other diagnostic procedures on abdominal region
54.5*	Lysis of peritoneal adhesions
54.6*	Suture of abdominal wall and peritoneum
54.7*	Other repair of abdominal wall and peritoneum
54.92	Removal of foreign body from peritoneal cavity
54.93	Creation of cutaneoperitoneal fistula
54.95	Incision of peritoneum
55.0*	Nephrotomy and nephrostomy
55.1*	Pyelotomy and pyelostomy
55.24	Open biopsy of kidney
55.29	Other diagnostic procedures on kidney
55.31	Marsupialization of kidney lesion
55.4	Partial nephrectomy
55.5*	Complete nephrectomy
55.61	Renal autotransplantation
55.81	Suture of laceration of kidney
55.82	Closure of nephrostomy and pyelostomy
55.83	Closure of other fistula of kidney
55.84	Reduction of torsion of renal pedicle
55.86	Anastomosis of kidney
55.87	Correction of ureteropelvic junction
55.89	Other repair of kidney
55.97	Implantation or replacement of mechanical kidney
55.98	Removal of mechanical kidney
55.99	Other operations on kidney
56.0	Transurethral removal of obstruction from ureter and renal pelvis
56.1	Ureteral meatotomy
56.2	Ureterotomy
56.4*	Ureterectomy

56.5*	Cutaneous uretero-ileostomy
56.6*	Other external urinary diversion
56.7*	Other anastomosis or bypass of ureter
56.81	Lysis of intraluminal adhesions of ureter
56.82	Suture of laceration of ureter
56.83	Closure of ureterostomy
56.84	Closure of other fistula of ureter
56.86	Removal of ligature from ureter
56.89	Other repair of ureter
56.95	Ligation of ureter
56.99	Other operations on ureter
57.12	Lysis of intraluminal adhesions with incision into bladder
57.18	Other suprapubic cystostomy
57.19	Other cystotomy
57.2*	Vesicostomy
57.39	Other diagnostic procedures on bladder
57.6	Partial cystectomy
57.79	Other total cystectomy
57.81	Suture of laceration of bladder
57.82	Closure of cystostomy
57.83	Repair of fistula involving bladder and intestine
57.84	Repair of other fistula of bladder
57.87	Reconstruction of urinary bladder
57.89	Other repair of bladder
57.93	Control of (postoperative) hemorrhage of bladder
57.99	Other operations on bladder
58.0	Urethrotomy
58.1	Urethral meatotomy
58.41	Suture of laceration of urethra
58.42	Closure of urethrostomy
58.43	Closure of other fistula of urethra
58.44	Reanastomosis of urethra
58.46	Other reconstruction of urethra
58.49	Other repair of urethra
58.5	Release of urethral stricture
58.93	Implantation of artificial urinary sphincter (AUS)
59.02	Other lysis of perirenal or periureteral adhesions
59.03	Laparoscopic lysis of perirenal or periureteral adhesions
59.09	Other incision of perirenal or periureteral tissue
59.1*	Incision of perivesical tissue
59.2*	Diagnostic procedures on perirenal and perivesical tissue
60.93	Repair of prostate
60.94	Control of (postoperative) hemorrhage of prostate
61.42	Repair of scrotal fistula
61.49	Other repair of scrotum and tunica vaginalis
61.99	Other operations on scrotum and tunica vaginalis
62.0	Incision of testis
62.3	Unilateral orchiectomy
62.4*	Bilateral orchiectomy
62.6*	Repair of testes
62.99	Other operations on testes
63.51	Suture of laceration of spermatic cord and epididymis
63.53	Transplantation of spermatic cord
63.59	Other repair of spermatic cord and epididymis
63.81	Suture of laceration of vas deferens and epididymis
63.82	Reconstruction of surgically divided vas deferens
63.89	Other repair of vas deferens and epididymis
63.94	Lysis of adhesions of spermatic cord
63.99	Other operations on spermatic card, epididymis, and vas deferens
64.41	Suture of laceration of penis
64.43	Construction of penis
64.44	Reconstruction of penis
64.45	Replantation of penis
64.49	Other repair of penis
65.7*	Repair of ovary
65.8*	Lysis of adhesions of ovary and fallopian tube
66.71	Simple suture of fallopian tube
66.79	Other repair of fallopian tube
67.5*	Repair of internal cervical os

Ⓣ Transfer DRG   ⓢ Special Payment   ☑ Optimization Potential   ▽ Targeted Potential   * Code Range   ● New DRG   ▲ Revised DRG Title

198   Valid 10/01/2012-09/30/2013   © 2012 OptumInsight, Inc.

MDC 21: Injuries, Poisonings And Toxic Effects Of Drugs—SURGICAL

67.6*	Other repair of cervix
68.0	Hysterotomy
69.23	Vaginal repair of chronic inversion of uterus
69.29	Other repair of uterus and supporting structures
69.4*	Uterine repair
69.97	Removal of other penetrating foreign body from cervix
70.13	Lysis of intraluminal adhesions of vagina
70.62	Vaginal reconstruction
70.64	Vaginal reconstruction with graft or prosthesis
70.71	Suture of laceration of vagina
70.72	Repair of colovaginal fistula
70.73	Repair of rectovaginal fistula
70.74	Repair of other vaginoenteric fistula
70.75	Repair of other fistula of vagina
70.79	Other repair of vagina
71.01	Lysis of vulvar adhesions
71.7*	Repair of vulva and perineum
76.0*	Incision of facial bone without division
76.1*	Diagnostic procedures on facial bones and joints
76.2	Local excision or destruction of lesion of facial bone
76.3*	Partial ostectomy of facial bone
76.4*	Excision and reconstruction of facial bones
76.5	Temporomandibular arthroplasty
76.6*	Other facial bone repair and orthognathic surgery
76.70	Reduction of facial fracture, not otherwise specified
76.72	Open reduction of malar and zygomatic fracture
76.74	Open reduction of maxillary fracture
76.76	Open reduction of mandibular fracture
76.77	Open reduction of alveolar fracture
76.79	Other open reduction of facial fracture
76.91	Bone graft to facial bone
76.92	Insertion of synthetic implant in facial bone
76.94	Open reduction of temporomandibular dislocation
76.97	Removal of internal fixation device from facial bone
76.99	Other operations on facial bones and joints
77.00	Sequestrectomy, unspecified site
77.01	Sequestrectomy of scapula, clavicle, and thorax (ribs and sternum)
77.02	Sequestrectomy of humerus
77.03	Sequestrectomy of radius and ulna
77.05	Sequestrectomy of femur
77.06	Sequestrectomy of patella
77.07	Sequestrectomy of tibia and fibula
77.08	Sequestrectomy of tarsals and metatarsals
77.09	Sequestrectomy of other bone, except facial bones
77.10	Other incision of bone without division, unspecified site
77.11	Other incision of scapula, clavicle, and thorax (ribs and sternum) without division
77.12	Other incision of humerus without division
77.13	Other incision of radius and ulna without division
77.15	Other incision of femur without division
77.16	Other incision of patella without division
77.17	Other incision of tibia and fibula without division
77.18	Other incision of tarsals and metatarsals without division
77.19	Other incision of other bone, except facial bones, without division
77.20	Wedge osteotomy, unspecified site
77.21	Wedge osteotomy of scapula, clavicle, and thorax (ribs and sternum)
77.22	Wedge osteotomy of humerus
77.23	Wedge osteotomy of radius and ulna
77.25	Wedge osteotomy of femur
77.26	Wedge osteotomy of patella
77.27	Wedge osteotomy of tibia and fibula
77.28	Wedge osteotomy of tarsals and metatarsals
77.29	Wedge osteotomy of other bone, except facial bones
77.30	Other division of bone, unspecified site
77.31	Other division of scapula, clavicle, and thorax (ribs and sternum)
77.32	Other division of humerus

77.33	Other division of radius and ulna
77.35	Other division of femur
77.36	Other division of patella
77.37	Other division of tibia and fibula
77.38	Other division of tarsals and metatarsals
77.39	Other division of other bone, except facial bones
77.58	Other excision, fusion, and repair of toes
77.60	Local excision of lesion or tissue of bone, unspecified site
77.61	Local excision of lesion or tissue of scapula, clavicle, and thorax (ribs and sternum)
77.62	Local excision of lesion or tissue of humerus
77.63	Local excision of lesion or tissue of radius and ulna
77.65	Local excision of lesion or tissue of femur
77.66	Local excision of lesion or tissue of patella
77.67	Local excision of lesion or tissue of tibia and fibula
77.68	Local excision of lesion or tissue of tarsals and metatarsals
77.69	Local excision of lesion or tissue of other bone, except facial bones
77.70	Excision of bone for graft, unspecified site
77.71	Excision of scapula, clavicle, and thorax (ribs and sternum) for graft
77.72	Excision of humerus for graft
77.73	Excision of radius and ulna for graft
77.75	Excision of femur for graft
77.76	Excision of patella for graft
77.77	Excision of tibia and fibula for graft
77.78	Excision of tarsals and metatarsals for graft
77.79	Excision of other bone for graft, except facial bones
77.80	Other partial ostectomy, unspecified site
77.81	Other partial ostectomy of scapula, clavicle, and thorax (ribs and sternum)
77.82	Other partial ostectomy of humerus
77.83	Other partial ostectomy of radius and ulna
77.85	Other partial ostectomy of femur
77.86	Other partial ostectomy of patella
77.87	Other partial ostectomy of tibia and fibula
77.88	Other partial ostectomy of tarsals and metatarsals
77.89	Other partial ostectomy of other bone, except facial bones
77.90	Total ostectomy, unspecified site
77.91	Total ostectomy of scapula, clavicle, and thorax (ribs and sternum)
77.92	Total ostectomy of humerus
77.93	Total ostectomy of radius and ulna
77.95	Total ostectomy of femur
77.96	Total ostectomy of patella
77.97	Total ostectomy of tibia and fibula
77.98	Total ostectomy of tarsals and metatarsals
77.99	Total ostectomy of other bone, except facial bones
78.00	Bone graft, unspecified site
78.01	Bone graft of scapula, clavicle, and thorax (ribs and sternum)
78.02	Bone graft of humerus
78.03	Bone graft of radius and ulna
78.05	Bone graft of femur
78.06	Bone graft of patella
78.07	Bone graft of tibia and fibula
78.08	Bone graft of tarsals and metatarsals
78.09	Bone graft of other bone, except facial bones
78.10	Application of external fixator device, unspecified site
78.11	Application of external fixator device, scapula, clavicle, and thorax [ribs and sternum]
78.12	Application of external fixator device, humerus
78.13	Application of external fixator device, radius and ulna
78.15	Application of external fixator device, femur
78.16	Application of external fixator device, patella
78.17	Application of external fixator device, tibia and fibula
78.18	Application of external fixator device, tarsals and metatarsals
78.19	Application of external fixator device, other
78.20	Limb shortening procedures, unspecified site
78.22	Limb shortening procedures, humerus

Surgical	Medical	CC Indicator	MCC Indicator	Procedure Proxy

MDC 21: Injuries, Poisonings And Toxic Effects Of Drugs—SURGICAL

78.23	Limb shortening procedures, radius and ulna
78.25	Limb shortening procedures, femur
78.27	Limb shortening procedures, tibia and fibula
78.28	Limb shortening procedures, tarsals and metatarsals
78.29	Limb shortening procedures, other
78.30	Limb lengthening procedures, unspecified site
78.32	Limb lengthening procedures, humerus
78.33	Limb lengthening procedures, radius and ulna
78.35	Limb lengthening procedures, femur
78.37	Limb lengthening procedures, tibia and fibula
78.38	Limb lengthening procedures, tarsals and metatarsals
78.39	Other limb lengthening procedures
78.40	Other repair or plastic operations on bone, unspecified site
78.41	Other repair or plastic operations on scapula, clavicle, and thorax (ribs and sternum)
78.42	Other repair or plastic operation on humerus
78.43	Other repair or plastic operations on radius and ulna
78.45	Other repair or plastic operations on femur
78.46	Other repair or plastic operations on patella
78.47	Other repair or plastic operations on tibia and fibula
78.48	Other repair or plastic operations on tarsals and metatarsals
78.49	Other repair or plastic operations on other bone, except facial bones
78.50	Internal fixation of bone without fracture reduction, unspecified site
78.51	Internal fixation of scapula, clavicle, and thorax (ribs and sternum) without fracture reduction
78.52	Internal fixation of humerus without fracture reduction
78.53	Internal fixation of radius and ulna without fracture reduction
78.55	Internal fixation of femur without fracture reduction
78.56	Internal fixation of patella without fracture reduction
78.57	Internal fixation of tibia and fibula without fracture reduction
78.58	Internal fixation of tarsals and metatarsals without fracture reduction
78.59	Internal fixation of other bone, except facial bones, without fracture reduction
78.60	Removal of implanted device, unspecified site
78.61	Removal of implanted device from scapula, clavicle, and thorax (ribs and sternum)
78.62	Removal of implanted device from humerus
78.63	Removal of implanted device from radius and ulna
78.65	Removal of implanted device from femur
78.66	Removal of implanted device from patella
78.67	Removal of implanted device from tibia and fibula
78.68	Removal of implanted device from tarsal and metatarsals
78.69	Removal of implanted device from other bone
78.70	Osteoclasis, unspecified site
78.71	Osteoclasis of scapula, clavicle, and thorax (ribs and sternum)
78.72	Osteoclasis of humerus
78.73	Osteoclasis of radius and ulna
78.75	Osteoclasis of femur
78.76	Osteoclasis of patella
78.77	Osteoclasis of tibia and fibula
78.78	Osteoclasis of tarsals and metatarsals
78.79	Osteoclasis of other bone, except facial bones
78.90	Insertion of bone growth stimulator, unspecified site
78.91	Insertion of bone growth stimulator into scapula, clavicle and thorax (ribs and sternum)
78.92	Insertion of bone growth stimulator into humerus
78.93	Insertion of bone growth stimulator into radius and ulna
78.95	Insertion of bone growth stimulator into femur
78.96	Insertion of bone growth stimulator into patella
78.97	Insertion of bone growth stimulator into tibia and fibula
78.98	Insertion of bone growth stimulator into tarsals and metatarsals
78.99	Insertion of bone growth stimulator into other bone
79.10	Closed reduction of fracture with internal fixation, unspecified site
79.11	Closed reduction of fracture of humerus with internal fixation
79.12	Closed reduction of fracture of radius and ulna with internal fixation
79.15	Closed reduction of fracture of femur with internal fixation
79.16	Closed reduction of fracture of tibia and fibula with internal fixation
79.17	Closed reduction of fracture of tarsals and metatarsals with internal fixation
79.18	Closed reduction of fracture of phalanges of foot with internal fixation
79.19	Closed reduction of fracture of other specified bone, except facial bones, with internal fixation
79.20	Open reduction of fracture without internal fixation, unspecified site
79.21	Open reduction of fracture of humerus without internal fixation
79.22	Open reduction of fracture of radius and ulna without internal fixation
79.25	Open reduction of fracture of femur without internal fixation
79.26	Open reduction of fracture of tibia and fibula without internal fixation
79.27	Open reduction of fracture of tarsals and metatarsals without internal fixation
79.28	Open reduction of fracture of phalanges of foot without internal fixation
79.29	Open reduction of fracture of other specified bone, except facial bones, without internal fixation
79.30	Open reduction of fracture with internal fixation, unspecified site
79.31	Open reduction of fracture of humerus with internal fixation
79.32	Open reduction of fracture of radius and ulna with internal fixation
79.35	Open reduction of fracture of femur with internal fixation
79.36	Open reduction of fracture of tibia and fibula with internal fixation
79.37	Open reduction of fracture of tarsals and metatarsals with internal fixation
79.38	Open reduction of fracture of phalanges of foot with internal fixation
79.39	Open reduction of fracture of other specified bone, except facial bones, with internal fixation
79.40	Closed reduction of separated epiphysis, unspecified site
79.41	Closed reduction of separated epiphysis of humerus
79.42	Closed reduction of separated epiphysis of radius and ulna
79.45	Closed reduction of separated epiphysis of femur
79.46	Closed reduction of separated epiphysis of tibia and fibula
79.49	Closed reduction of separated epiphysis of other specified bone
79.50	Open reduction of separated epiphysis, unspecified site
79.51	Open reduction of separated epiphysis of humerus
79.52	Open reduction of separated epiphysis of radius and ulna
79.55	Open reduction of separated epiphysis of femur
79.56	Open reduction of separated epiphysis of tibia and fibula
79.59	Open reduction of separated epiphysis of other specified bone
79.60	Debridement of open fracture, unspecified site
79.61	Debridement of open fracture of humerus
79.62	Debridement of open fracture of radius and ulna
79.65	Debridement of open fracture of femur
79.66	Debridement of open fracture of tibia and fibula
79.67	Debridement of open fracture of tarsals and metatarsals
79.68	Debridement of open fracture of phalanges of foot
79.69	Debridement of open fracture of other specified bone, except facial bones
79.80	Open reduction of dislocation of unspecified site
79.81	Open reduction of dislocation of shoulder
79.82	Open reduction of dislocation of elbow

Ⓣ *Transfer DRG*   ⓢⓟ *Special Payment*   ☑ *Optimization Potential*   ▽ *Targeted Potential*   * *Code Range*   ● *New DRG*   ▲ *Revised DRG Title*

200   Valid 10/01/2012-09/30/2013   © 2012 OptumInsight, Inc.

79.85	Open reduction of dislocation of hip
79.86	Open reduction of dislocation of knee
79.87	Open reduction of dislocation of ankle
79.88	Open reduction of dislocation of foot and toe
79.89	Open reduction of dislocation of other specified site, except temporomandibular
79.90	Unspecified operation on bone injury, unspecified site
79.91	Unspecified operation on bone injury of humerus
79.92	Unspecified operation on bone injury of radius and ulna
79.95	Unspecified operation on bone injury of femur
79.96	Unspecified operation on bone injury of tibia and fibula
79.97	Unspecified operation on bone injury of tarsals and metatarsals
79.98	Unspecified operation on bone injury of phalanges of foot
79.99	Unspecified operation on bone injury of other specified bone
80.00	Arthrotomy for removal of prosthesis without replacement, unspecified site
80.01	Arthrotomy for removal of prosthesis without replacement, shoulder
80.02	Arthrotomy for removal of prosthesis without replacement, elbow
80.05	Arthrotomy for removal of prosthesis without replacement, hip
80.06	Arthrotomy for removal of prosthesis without replacement, knee
80.07	Arthrotomy for removal of prosthesis without replacement, ankle
80.08	Arthrotomy for removal of prosthesis without replacement, foot and toe
80.09	Arthrotomy for removal of prosthesis without replacement, other specified site
80.10	Other arthrotomy, unspecified site
80.11	Other arthrotomy of shoulder
80.12	Other arthrotomy of elbow
80.15	Other arthrotomy of hip
80.16	Other arthrotomy of knee
80.17	Other arthrotomy of ankle
80.18	Other arthrotomy of foot and toe
80.19	Other arthrotomy of other specified site
80.2*	Arthroscopy
80.40	Division of joint capsule, ligament, or cartilage, unspecified site
80.41	Division of joint capsule, ligament, or cartilage of shoulder
80.42	Division of joint capsule, ligament, or cartilage of elbow
80.45	Division of joint capsule, ligament, or cartilage of hip
80.46	Division of joint capsule, ligament, or cartilage of knee
80.47	Division of joint capsule, ligament, or cartilage of ankle
80.48	Division of joint capsule, ligament, or cartilage of foot and toe
80.49	Division of joint capsule, ligament, or cartilage of other specified site
80.50	Excision or destruction of intervertebral disc, unspecified
80.51	Excision of intervertebral disc
80.53	Repair of the anulus fibrosus with graft or prosthesis
80.54	Other and unspecified repair of the anulus fibrosus
80.59	Other destruction of intervertebral disc
80.6	Excision of semilunar cartilage of knee
80.70	Synovectomy, unspecified site
80.71	Synovectomy of shoulder
80.72	Synovectomy of elbow
80.75	Synovectomy of hip
80.76	Synovectomy of knee
80.77	Synovectomy of ankle
80.78	Synovectomy of foot and toe
80.79	Synovectomy of other specified site
80.80	Other local excision or destruction of lesion of joint, unspecified site
80.81	Other local excision or destruction of lesion of shoulder joint
80.82	Other local excision or destruction of lesion of elbow joint
80.85	Other local excision or destruction of lesion of hip joint
80.86	Other local excision or destruction of lesion of knee joint
80.87	Other local excision or destruction of lesion of ankle joint
80.88	Other local excision or destruction of lesion of joint of foot and toe
80.89	Other local excision or destruction of lesion of joint of other specified site
80.90	Other excision of joint, unspecified site
80.91	Other excision of shoulder joint
80.92	Other excision of elbow joint
80.95	Other excision of hip joint
80.96	Other excision of knee joint
80.97	Other excision of ankle joint
80.98	Other excision of joint of foot and toe
80.99	Other excision of joint of other specified site
81.00	Spinal fusion, not otherwise specified
81.01	Atlas-axis spinal fusion
81.02	Other cervical fusion of the anterior column, anterior technique
81.03	Other cervical fusion of the posterior column, posterior technique
81.04	Dorsal and dorsolumbar fusion of the anterior column, anterior technique
81.05	Dorsal and dorsolumbar fusion of the posterior column, posterior technique
81.06	Lumbar and lumbosacral fusion of the anterior column, anterior technique
81.07	Lumbar and lumbosacral fusion of the posterior column, posterior technique
81.08	Lumbar and lumbosacral fusion of the anterior column, posterior technique
81.1*	Arthrodesis and arthroereisis of foot and ankle
81.20	Arthrodesis of unspecified joint
81.21	Arthrodesis of hip
81.22	Arthrodesis of knee
81.23	Arthrodesis of shoulder
81.24	Arthrodesis of elbow
81.29	Arthrodesis of other specified joint
81.3*	Refusion of spine
81.4*	Other repair of joint of lower extremity
81.5*	Joint replacement of lower extremity
81.65	Percutaneous vertebroplasty
81.66	Percutaneous vertebral augmentation
81.73	Total wrist replacement
81.8*	Arthroplasty and repair of shoulder and elbow
81.93	Suture of capsule or ligament of upper extremity
81.94	Suture of capsule or ligament of ankle and foot
81.95	Suture of capsule or ligament of other lower extremity
81.96	Other repair of joint
81.97	Revision of joint replacement of upper extremity
81.98	Other diagnostic procedures on joint structures
81.99	Other operations on joint structures
83.0*	Incision of muscle, tendon, fascia, and bursa
83.1*	Division of muscle, tendon, and fascia
83.29	Other diagnostic procedures on muscle, tendon, fascia, and bursa, including that of hand
83.3*	Excision of lesion of muscle, tendon, fascia, and bursa
83.4*	Other excision of muscle, tendon, and fascia
83.5	Bursectomy
83.6*	Suture of muscle, tendon, and fascia
83.7*	Reconstruction of muscle and tendon
83.8*	Other plastic operations on muscle, tendon, and fascia
83.91	Lysis of adhesions of muscle, tendon, fascia, and bursa
83.92	Insertion or replacement of skeletal muscle stimulator
83.93	Removal of skeletal muscle stimulator
83.99	Other operations on muscle, tendon, fascia, and bursa
84.00	Upper limb amputation, not otherwise specified
84.03	Amputation through hand
84.04	Disarticulation of wrist
84.05	Amputation through forearm

MDC 21: Injuries, Poisonings And Toxic Effects Of Drugs—SURGICAL

84.06	Disarticulation of elbow
84.07	Amputation through humerus
84.08	Disarticulation of shoulder
84.09	Interthoracoscapular amputation
84.1*	Amputation of lower limb
84.23	Forearm, wrist, or hand reattachment
84.24	Upper arm reattachment
84.25	Toe reattachment
84.26	Foot reattachment
84.27	Lower leg or ankle reattachment
84.28	Thigh reattachment
84.29	Other reattachment of extremity
84.3	Revision of amputation stump
84.40	Implantation or fitting of prosthetic limb device, not otherwise specified
84.44	Implantation of prosthetic device of arm
84.48	Implantation of prosthetic device of leg
84.59	Insertion of other spinal devices
84.6*	Replacement of spinal disc
84.8*	Insertion, replacement and revision of posterior spinal motion preservation device(s)
84.91	Amputation, not otherwise specified
84.94	Insertion of sternal fixation device with rigid plates
84.99	Other operations on musculoskeletal system
85.12	Open biopsy of breast
85.2*	Excision or destruction of breast tissue
85.3*	Reduction mammoplasty and subcutaneous mammectomy
85.4*	Mastectomy
85.50	Augmentation mammoplasty, not otherwise specified
85.53	Unilateral breast implant
85.54	Bilateral breast implant
85.6*	Mastopexy
85.7*	Total reconstruction of breast
85.85	Muscle flap graft to breast
85.86	Transposition of nipple
85.87	Other repair or reconstruction of nipple
85.89	Other mammoplasty
85.93	Revision of implant of breast
85.94	Removal of implant of breast
85.95	Insertion of breast tissue expander
85.96	Removal of breast tissue expander (s)
85.99	Other operations on the breast
86.06	Insertion of totally implantable infusion pump
86.21	Excision of pilonidal cyst or sinus
86.4	Radical excision of skin lesion
86.81	Repair for facial weakness
86.82	Facial rhytidectomy
86.83	Size reduction plastic operation
86.84	Relaxation of scar or web contracture of skin
86.86	Onychoplasty
86.87	Fat graft of skin and subcutaneous tissue
86.89	Other repair and reconstruction of skin and subcutaneous tissue
86.91	Excision of skin for graft
92.27	Implantation or insertion of radioactive elements

OR

Any of the following procedure combinations

37.70	Initial insertion of lead (electrode), not otherwise specified
AND	
37.80	Insertion of permanent pacemaker, initial or replacement, type of device not specified

OR

37.70	Initial insertion of lead (electrode), not otherwise specified
AND	
37.81	Initial insertion of single-chamber device, not specified as rate responsive

OR

37.70	Initial insertion of lead (electrode), not otherwise specified

AND

37.82	Initial insertion of single-chamber device, rate responsive

OR

37.70	Initial insertion of lead (electrode), not otherwise specified
AND	
37.85	Replacement of any type of pacemaker device with single-chamber device, not specified as rate responsive

OR

37.70	Initial insertion of lead (electrode), not otherwise specified
AND	
37.86	Replacement of any type of pacemaker device with single-chamber device, rate responsive

OR

37.70	Initial insertion of lead (electrode), not otherwise specified
AND	
37.87	Replacement of any type of pacemaker device with dual-chamber device

OR

37.71	Initial insertion of transvenous lead (electrode) into ventricle
AND	
37.80	Insertion of permanent pacemaker, initial or replacement, type of device not specified

OR

37.71	Initial insertion of transvenous lead (electrode) into ventricle
AND	
37.81	Initial insertion of single-chamber device, not specified as rate responsive

OR

37.71	Initial insertion of transvenous lead (electrode) into ventricle
AND	
37.82	Initial insertion of single-chamber device, rate responsive

OR

37.71	Initial insertion of transvenous lead (electrode) into ventricle
AND	
37.85	Replacement of any type of pacemaker device with single-chamber device, not specified as rate responsive

OR

37.71	Initial insertion of transvenous lead (electrode) into ventricle
AND	
37.86	Replacement of any type of pacemaker device with single-chamber device, rate responsive

OR

37.71	Initial insertion of transvenous lead (electrode) into ventricle
AND	
37.87	Replacement of any type of pacemaker device with dual-chamber device

OR

37.72	Initial insertion of transvenous leads (electrodes) into atrium and ventricle
AND	
37.80	Insertion of permanent pacemaker, initial or replacement, type of device not specified

OR

37.72	Initial insertion of transvenous leads (electrodes) into atrium and ventricle
AND	
37.83	Initial insertion of dual-chamber device

OR

37.73	Initial insertion of transvenous lead (electrode) into atrium
AND	
37.80	Insertion of permanent pacemaker, initial or replacement, type of device not specified

T Transfer DRG   SP Special Payment   ☑ Optimization Potential   ▽ Targeted Potential   * Code Range   ● New DRG   ▲ Revised DRG Title

202   Valid 10/01/2012–09/30/2013   © 2012 OptumInsight, Inc.

OR

37.73   Initial insertion of transvenous lead (electrode) into atrium
AND
37.81   Initial insertion of single-chamber device, not specified as rate responsive

OR

37.73   Initial insertion of transvenous lead (electrode) into atrium
AND
37.82   Initial insertion of single-chamber device, rate responsive

OR

37.73   Initial insertion of transvenous lead (electrode) into atrium
AND
37.85   Replacement of any type of pacemaker device with single-chamber device, not specified as rate responsive

OR

37.73   Initial insertion of transvenous lead (electrode) into atrium
AND
37.86   Replacement of any type of pacemaker device with single-chamber device, rate responsive

OR

37.73   Initial insertion of transvenous lead (electrode) into atrium
AND
37.87   Replacement of any type of pacemaker device with dual-chamber device

OR

37.74   Insertion or replacement of epicardial lead (electrode) into epicardium
AND
37.80   Insertion of permanent pacemaker, initial or replacement, type of device not specified

OR

37.74   Insertion or replacement of epicardial lead (electrode) into epicardium
AND
37.81   Initial insertion of single-chamber device, not specified as rate responsive

OR

37.74   Insertion or replacement of epicardial lead (electrode) into epicardium
AND
37.82   Initial insertion of single-chamber device, rate responsive

OR

37.74   Insertion or replacement of epicardial lead (electrode) into epicardium
AND
37.83   Initial insertion of dual-chamber device

OR

37.74   Insertion or replacement of epicardial lead (electrode) into epicardium
AND
37.85   Replacement of any type of pacemaker device with single-chamber device, not specified as rate responsive

OR

37.74   Insertion or replacement of epicardial lead (electrode) into epicardium
AND
37.86   Replacement of any type of pacemaker device with single-chamber device, rate responsive

OR

37.74   Insertion or replacement of epicardial lead (electrode) into epicardium
AND
37.87   Replacement of any type of pacemaker device with dual-chamber device

OR

37.76   Replacement of transvenous atrial and/or ventricular lead(s) (electrode(s))
AND
37.80   Insertion of permanent pacemaker, initial or replacement, type of device not specified

OR

37.76   Replacement of transvenous atrial and/or ventricular lead(s) (electrode(s))
AND
37.85   Replacement of any type of pacemaker device with single-chamber device, not specified as rate responsive

OR

37.76   Replacement of transvenous atrial and/or ventricular lead(s) (electrode(s))
AND
37.86   Replacement of any type of pacemaker device with single-chamber device, rate responsive

OR

37.76   Replacement of transvenous atrial and/or ventricular lead(s) (electrode(s))
AND
37.87   Replacement of any type of pacemaker device with dual-chamber device

DRG 908   Other O.R. Procedures for Injuries with CC

GMLOS 4.5   AMLOS 6.0   RW 1.9519   T ☑

Select operating room procedure and combination procedures listed under DRG 907

DRG 909   Other O.R. Procedures for Injuries without CC/MCC

GMLOS 2.6   AMLOS 3.3   RW 1.2051   T ☑

Select operating room procedure and combination procedures listed under DRG 907

MEDICAL

DRG 913   Traumatic Injury with MCC

GMLOS 3.8   AMLOS 5.1   RW 1.2273   ☑

Principal Diagnosis

819*   Multiple fractures involving both upper limbs, and upper limb with rib(s) and sternum
828*   Multiple fractures involving both lower limbs, lower with upper limb, and lower limb(s) with rib(s) and sternum
862.8   Injury to multiple and unspecified intrathoracic organs without mention of open wound into cavity
862.9   Injury to multiple and unspecified intrathoracic organs with open wound into cavity
868.09   Injury to other and multiple intra-abdominal organs without mention of open wound into cavity
868.19   Injury to other and multiple intra-abdominal organs, with open wound into cavity
869*   Internal injury to unspecified or ill-defined organs
875.1   Open wound of chest (wall), complicated
879.3   Open wound of abdominal wall, anterior, complicated
879.5   Open wound of abdominal wall, lateral, complicated
879.7   Open wound of other and unspecified parts of trunk, complicated
879.9   Open wound(s) (multiple) of unspecified site(s), complicated
880.1*   Open wound of shoulder and upper arm, complicated
881.1*   Open wound of elbow, forearm, and wrist, complicated
882.1   Open wound of hand except finger(s) alone, complicated
883.1   Open wound of finger(s), complicated

MDC 21: Injuries, Poisonings And Toxic Effects Of Drugs—MEDICAL

884.1	Multiple and unspecified open wound of upper limb, complicated
885*	Traumatic amputation of thumb (complete) (partial)
886*	Traumatic amputation of other finger(s) (complete) (partial)
887*	Traumatic amputation of arm and hand (complete) (partial)
890.1	Open wound of hip and thigh, complicated
891.1	Open wound of knee, leg (except thigh), and ankle, complicated
892.1	Open wound of foot except toe(s) alone, complicated
893.1	Open wound of toe(s), complicated
894.1	Multiple and unspecified open wound of lower limb, complicated
895*	Traumatic amputation of toe(s) (complete) (partial)
896*	Traumatic amputation of foot (complete) (partial)
897*	Traumatic amputation of leg(s) (complete) (partial)
900*	Injury to blood vessels of head and neck
901*	Injury to blood vessels of thorax
902*	Injury to blood vessels of abdomen and pelvis
903*	Injury to blood vessels of upper extremity
904*	Injury to blood vessels of lower extremity and unspecified sites
908.5	Late effect of foreign body in orifice
908.6	Late effect of certain complications of trauma
908.9	Late effect of unspecified injury
925*	Crushing injury of face, scalp, and neck
926.1*	Crushing injury of other specified sites of trunk
926.8	Crushing injury of multiple sites of trunk
926.9	Crushing injury of unspecified site of trunk
927*	Crushing injury of upper limb
928*	Crushing injury of lower limb
929*	Crushing injury of multiple and unspecified sites
959*	Injury, other and unspecified

DRG 914   Traumatic Injury without MCC
GMLOS 2.5   AMLOS 3.1   RW 0.6998   ☑

Select principal diagnosis listed under DRG 913

DRG 915   Allergic Reactions with MCC
GMLOS 3.7   AMLOS 5.1   RW 1.5168

Principal Diagnosis

995.0	Other anaphylactic reaction
995.1	Angioneurotic edema not elsewhere classified
995.3	Allergy, unspecified not elsewhere classified
995.6*	Anaphylactic reaction due to food
999.4*	Anaphylactic reaction due to serum
999.5*	Other serum reaction, not elsewhere classified

DRG 916   Allergic Reactions without MCC
GMLOS 1.7   AMLOS 2.1   RW 0.5042   ☑

Select principal diagnosis listed under DRG 915

DRG 917   Poisoning and Toxic Effects of Drugs with MCC
GMLOS 3.6   AMLOS 4.9   RW 1.4542   T ☑

Principal Diagnosis

960*	Poisoning by antibiotics
961*	Poisoning by other anti-infectives
962*	Poisoning by hormones and synthetic substitutes
963*	Poisoning by primarily systemic agents
964*	Poisoning by agents primarily affecting blood constituents
965*	Poisoning by analgesics, antipyretics, and antirheumatics
966*	Poisoning by anticonvulsants and anti-Parkinsonism drugs
967*	Poisoning by sedatives and hypnotics
968*	Poisoning by other central nervous system depressants and anesthetics
969*	Poisoning by psychotropic agents
970*	Poisoning by central nervous system stimulants

971*	Poisoning by drugs primarily affecting the autonomic nervous system
972*	Poisoning by agents primarily affecting the cardiovascular system
973*	Poisoning by agents primarily affecting the gastrointestinal system
974*	Poisoning by water, mineral, and uric acid metabolism drugs
975*	Poisoning by agents primarily acting on the smooth and skeletal muscles and respiratory system
976.0	Poisoning by local anti-infectives and anti-inflammatory drugs
976.1	Poisoning by antipruritics
976.2	Poisoning by local astringents and local detergents
976.3	Poisoning by emollients, demulcents, and protectants
976.4	Poisoning by keratolytics, keratoplastics, other hair treatment drugs and preparations
976.6	Poisoning by anti-infectives and other drugs and preparations for ear, nose, and throat
976.7	Poisoning by dental drugs topically applied
976.8	Poisoning by other agents primarily affecting skin and mucous membrane
976.9	Poisoning by unspecified agent primarily affecting skin and mucous membrane
977*	Poisoning by other and unspecified drugs and medicinal substances
978*	Poisoning by bacterial vaccines
979*	Poisoning by other vaccines and biological substances
980*	Toxic effect of alcohol
981	Toxic effect of petroleum products
982*	Toxic effect of solvents other than petroleum-based
983*	Toxic effect of corrosive aromatics, acids, and caustic alkalis
984*	Toxic effect of lead and its compounds (including fumes)
985*	Toxic effect of other metals
986	Toxic effect of carbon monoxide
987*	Toxic effect of other gases, fumes, or vapors
988*	Toxic effect of noxious substances eaten as food
989*	Toxic effect of other substances, chiefly nonmedicinal as to source
995.2*	Other and unspecified adverse effect of drug, medicinal and biological substance

DRG 918   Poisoning and Toxic Effects of Drugs without MCC
GMLOS 2.1   AMLOS 2.7   RW 0.6304   T ☑

Select principal diagnosis listed under DRG 917

DRG 919   Complications of Treatment with MCC
GMLOS 4.4   AMLOS 6.0   RW 1.6615   ☑

Principal Diagnosis

238.77	Post-transplant lymphoproliferative disorder [PTLD]
349.3*	Dural tear
996.52	Mechanical complication due to other tissue graft, not elsewhere classified
996.55	Mechanical complications due to artificial skin graft and decellularized allodermis
996.56	Mechanical complications due to peritoneal dialysis catheter
996.57	Mechanical complication due to insulin pump
996.59	Mechanical complication due to other implant and internal device, not elsewhere classified
996.60	Infection and inflammatory reaction due to unspecified device, implant, and graft
996.68	Infection and inflammatory reaction due to peritoneal dialysis catheter
996.69	Infection and inflammatory reaction due to other internal prosthetic device, implant, and graft
996.70	Other complications due to unspecified device, implant, and graft
996.79	Other complications due to other internal prosthetic device, implant, and graft

---

T *Transfer DRG*   SP *Special Payment*   ☑ *Optimization Potential*   ▽ *Targeted Potential*   * *Code Range*   ● *New DRG*   ▲ *Revised DRG Title*

996.80	Complications of transplanted organ, unspecified site
996.87	Complications of transplanted organ, intestine
996.88	Complications of transplanted organ, stem cell
996.89	Complications of other transplanted organ
997.9*	Complications affecting other specified body systems, not elsewhere classified
998.0*	Postoperative shock
998.1*	Hemorrhage or hematoma or seroma complicating procedure, not elsewhere classified
998.2	Accidental puncture or laceration during procedure
998.3*	Disruption of wound
998.4	Foreign body accidentally left during procedure, not elsewhere classified
998.6	Persistent postoperative fistula, not elsewhere classified
998.7	Acute reaction to foreign substance accidentally left during procedure, not elsewhere classified
998.81	Emphysema (subcutaneous) (surgical) resulting from a procedure
998.83	Non-healing surgical wound
998.89	Other specified complications
998.9	Unspecified complication of procedure, not elsewhere classified
999.9	Other and unspecified complications of medical care, not elsewhere classified

DRG 920   Complications of Treatment with CC
GMLOS 3.1   AMLOS 4.0   RW 0.9693   ☑

Select principal diagnosis listed under DRG 919

DRG 921   Complications of Treatment without CC/MCC
GMLOS 2.2   AMLOS 2.8   RW 0.6637   ☑

Select principal diagnosis listed under DRG 919

DRG 922   Other Injury, Poisoning and Toxic Effect Diagnoses with MCC
GMLOS 3.9   AMLOS 5.7   RW 1.4305   ☑

Principal Diagnosis

796.0	Nonspecific abnormal toxicological findings
909*	Late effects of other and unspecified external causes
958.2	Secondary and recurrent hemorrhage as an early complication of trauma
958.4	Traumatic shock
958.8	Other early complications of trauma
958.9*	Traumatic compartment syndrome
990	Effects of radiation, unspecified
991*	Effects of reduced temperature
992*	Effects of heat and light
993.2	Other and unspecified effects of high altitude
993.3	Caisson disease
993.4	Effects of air pressure caused by explosion
993.8	Other specified effects of air pressure
993.9	Unspecified effect of air pressure
994.0	Effects of lightning
994.1	Drowning and nonfatal submersion
994.2	Effects of hunger
994.3	Effects of thirst
994.4	Exhaustion due to exposure
994.5	Exhaustion due to excessive exertion
994.7	Asphyxiation and strangulation
994.8	Electrocution and nonfatal effects of electric current
994.9	Other effects of external causes
995.4	Shock due to anesthesia not elsewhere classified
995.5*	Child maltreatment syndrome
995.7	Other adverse food reactions, not elsewhere classified
995.8*	Other specified adverse effects, not elsewhere classified
V71.3	Observation following accident at work
V71.4	Observation following other accident

V71.6	Observation following other inflicted injury

DRG 923   Other Injury, Poisoning and Toxic Effect Diagnoses without MCC
GMLOS 2.2   AMLOS 2.9   RW 0.6438   ☑

Select principal diagnosis listed under DRG 922

Surgical	Medical	CC Indicator	MCC Indicator	Procedure Proxy

941.00	941.39	942.21	943.11	943.55	944.36	945.19	946.3	948.73
941.01	941.40	942.22	943.12	943.56	944.37	945.20	946.4	948.74
941.03	941.41	942.23	943.13	943.59	944.38	945.21	946.5	948.75
941.04	941.42	942.24	943.14	944.00	944.40	945.22	947.8	948.76
941.05	941.43	942.25	943.15	944.01	944.41	945.23	947.9	948.77
941.06	941.44	942.29	943.16	944.02	944.42	945.24	948.00	948.80
941.07	941.45	942.30	943.19	944.03	944.43	945.25	948.10	948.81
941.08	941.46	942.31	943.20	944.04	944.44	945.26	948.11	948.82
941.09	941.47	942.32	943.21	944.05	944.45	945.29	948.20	948.83
941.10	941.48	942.33	943.22	944.06	944.46	945.30	948.21	948.84
941.11	941.49	942.34	943.23	944.07	944.47	945.31	948.22	948.85
941.13	941.50	942.35	943.24	944.08	944.48	945.32	948.30	948.86
941.14	941.51	942.39	943.25	944.10	944.50	945.33	948.31	948.87
941.15	941.52	942.40	943.26	944.11	944.51	945.34	948.32	948.88
941.16	941.53	942.41	943.29	944.12	944.52	945.35	948.33	948.90
941.17	941.54	942.42	943.30	944.13	944.53	945.36	948.40	948.91
941.18	941.55	942.43	943.31	944.14	944.54	945.39	948.41	948.92
941.19	941.56	942.44	943.32	944.15	944.55	945.40	948.42	948.93
941.20	941.57	942.45	943.33	944.16	944.56	945.41	948.43	948.94
941.21	941.58	942.49	943.34	944.17	944.57	945.42	948.44	948.95
941.23	941.59	942.50	943.35	944.18	944.58	945.43	948.50	948.96
941.24	942.00	942.51	943.36	944.20	945.00	945.44	948.51	948.97
941.25	942.01	942.52	943.39	944.21	945.01	945.45	948.52	948.98
941.26	942.02	942.53	943.40	944.22	945.02	945.46	948.53	948.99
941.27	942.03	942.54	943.41	944.23	945.03	945.49	948.54	949.0
941.28	942.04	942.55	943.42	944.24	945.04	945.50	948.55	949.1
941.29	942.05	942.59	943.43	944.25	945.05	945.51	948.60	949.2
941.30	942.09	943.00	943.44	944.26	945.06	945.52	948.61	949.3
941.31	942.10	943.01	943.45	944.27	945.09	945.53	948.62	949.4
941.32	942.11	943.02	943.46	944.28	945.10	945.54	948.63	949.5
941.33	942.12	943.03	943.49	944.30	945.11	945.55	948.64	
941.34	942.13	943.04	943.50	944.31	945.12	945.56	948.65	
941.35	942.14	943.05	943.51	944.32	945.13	945.59	948.66	
941.36	942.15	943.06	943.52	944.33	945.14	946.0	948.70	
941.37	942.19	943.09	943.53	944.34	945.15	946.1	948.71	
941.38	942.20	943.10	943.54	944.35	945.16	946.2	948.72	

SURGICAL

DRG 927 Extensive Burns or Full Thickness Burns with Mechanical Ventilation 96+ Hours with Skin Graft
GMLOS 22.5   AMLOS 29.6   RW 16.4026

Principal or Secondary Diagnosis

941.3*   Full-thickness skin loss due to burn (third degree NOS) of face, head, and neck

941.4*   Deep necrosis of underlying tissues due to burn (deep third degree) of face, head, and neck without mention of loss of a body part

941.5*   Deep necrosis of underlying tissues due to burn (deep third degree) of face, head, and neck with loss of a body part

942.3*   Full-thickness skin loss due to burn (third degree NOS) of trunk

942.4*   Deep necrosis of underlying tissues due to burn (deep third degree) of trunk without mention of loss of a body part

942.5*   Deep necrosis of underlying tissues due to burn (deep third degree) of trunk with loss of a body part

943.3*   Full-thickness skin loss due to burn (third degree NOS) of upper limb, except wrist and hand

943.4*   Deep necrosis of underlying tissues due to burn (deep third degree) of upper limb, except wrist and hand, without mention of loss of a body part

943.5*   Deep necrosis of underlying tissues due to burn (deep third degree) of upper limb, except wrist and hand, with loss of a body part

944.3*   Full-thickness skin loss due to burn (third degree NOS) of wrist(s) and hand(s)

944.4*   Deep necrosis of underlying tissues due to burn (deep third degree) of wrist(s) and hand(s), without mention of loss of a body part

944.5*   Deep necrosis of underlying tissues due to burn (deep third degree) of wrist(s) and hand(s), with loss of a body part

945.3*   Full-thickness skin loss due to burn (third degree NOS) of lower limb(s)

945.4*   Deep necrosis of underlying tissues due to burn (deep third degree) of lower limb(s) without mention of loss of a body part

945.5*   Deep necrosis of underlying tissues due to burn (deep third degree) of lower limb(s) with loss of a body part

946.3   Full-thickness skin loss due to burn (third degree NOS) of multiple specified sites

946.4   Deep necrosis of underlying tissues due to burn (deep third degree) of multiple specified sites, without mention of loss of a body part

946.5   Deep necrosis of underlying tissues due to burn (deep third degree) of multiple specified sites, with loss of a body part

948.11   Burn (any degree) involving 10-19% of body surface with third degree burn of 10-19%

949.3   Full-thickness skin loss due to burn (third degree NOS), unspecified site

949.4   Deep necrosis of underlying tissue due to burn (deep third degree), unspecified site without mention of loss of body part

949.5   Deep necrosis of underlying tissues due to burn (deep third degree, unspecified site with loss of body part

AND

Nonoperating Room Procedure

96.72   Continuous invasive mechanical ventilation for 96 consecutive hours or more

AND

Operating Room Procedures

85.82   Split-thickness graft to breast

85.83   Full-thickness graft to breast

85.84   Pedicle graft to breast

86.60   Free skin graft, not otherwise specified

86.61   Full-thickness skin graft to hand

86.62   Other skin graft to hand

86.63   Full-thickness skin graft to other sites

86.65   Heterograft to skin

86.66   Homograft to skin

86.67   Dermal regenerative graft

86.69   Other skin graft to other sites

86.7*   Pedicle grafts or flaps

86.93   Insertion of tissue expander

OR

Principal or Secondary Diagnosis

948.21   Burn (any degree) involving 20-29% of body surface with third degree burn of 10-19%

948.22   Burn (any degree) involving 20-29% of body surface with third degree burn of 20-29%

948.31   Burn (any degree) involving 30-39% of body surface with third degree burn of 10-19%

948.32   Burn (any degree) involving 30-39% of body surface with third degree burn of 20-29%

948.33   Burn (any degree) involving 30-39% of body surface with third degree burn of 30-39%

948.41   Burn (any degree) involving 40-49% of body surface with third degree burn of 10-19%

948.42   Burn (any degree) involving 40-49% of body surface with third degree burn of 20-29%

948.43   Burn (any degree) involving 40-49% of body surface with third degree burn of 30-39%

948.44   Burn (any degree) involving 40-49% of body surface with third degree burn of 40-49%

948.51   Burn (any degree) involving 50-59% of body surface with third degree burn of 10-19%

948.52   Burn (any degree) involving 50-59% of body surface with third degree burn of 20-29%

948.53   Burn (any degree) involving 50-59% of body surface with third degree burn of 30-39%

948.54   Burn (any degree) involving 50-59% of body surface with third degree burn of 40-49%

948.55   Burn (any degree) involving 50-59% of body surface with third degree burn of 50-59%

948.61   Burn (any degree) involving 60-69% of body surface with third degree burn of 10-19%

948.62   Burn (any degree) involving 60-69% of body surface with third degree burn of 20-29%

948.63   Burn (any degree) involving 60-69% of body surface with third degree burn of 30-39%

948.64   Burn (any degree) involving 60-69% of body surface with third degree burn of 40-49%

948.65   Burn (any degree) involving 60-69% of body surface with third degree burn of 50-59%

948.66   Burn (any degree) involving 60-69% of body surface with third degree burn of 60-69%

948.71   Burn (any degree) involving 70-79% of body surface with third degree burn of 10-19%

948.72   Burn (any degree) involving 70-79% of body surface with third degree burn of 20-29%

948.73   Burn (any degree) involving 70-79% of body surface with third degree burn of 30-39%

948.74   Burn (any degree) involving 70-79% of body surface with third degree burn of 40-49%

948.75   Burn (any degree) involving 70-79% of body surface with third degree burn of 50-59%

948.76   Burn (any degree) involving 70-79% of body surface with third degree burn of 60-69%

948.77   Burn (any degree) involving 70-79% of body surface with third degree burn of 70-79%

948.81   Burn (any degree) involving 80-89% of body surface with third degree burn of 10-19%

MDC 22: Burns—SURGICAL

948.82	Burn (any degree) involving 80-89% of body surface with third degree burn of 20-29%
948.83	Burn (any degree) involving 80-89% of body surface with third degree burn of 30-39%
948.84	Burn (any degree) involving 80-89% of body surface with third degree burn of 40-49%
948.85	Burn (any degree) involving 80-89% of body surface with third degree burn of 50-59%
948.86	Burn (any degree) involving 80-89% of body surface with third degree burn of 60-69%
948.87	Burn (any degree) involving 80-89% of body surface with third degree burn of 70-79%
948.88	Burn (any degree) involving 80-89% of body surface with third degree burn of 80-89%
948.91	Burn (any degree) involving 90% or more of body surface with third degree burn of 10-19%
948.92	Burn (any degree) involving 90% or more of body surface with third degree burn of 20-29%
948.93	Burn (any degree) involving 90% or more of body surface with third degree burn of 30-39%
948.94	Burn (any degree) involving 90% or more of body surface with third degree burn of 40-49%
948.95	Burn (any degree) involving 90% or more of body surface with third degree burn of 50-59%
948.96	Burn (any degree) involving 90% or more of body surface with third degree burn of 60-69%
948.97	Burn (any degree) involving 90% or more of body surface with third degree burn of 70-79%
948.98	Burn (any degree) involving 90% or more of body surface with third degree burn of 80-89%
948.99	Burn (any degree) involving 90% or more of body surface with third degree burn of 90% or more of body surface

AND

Operating Room Procedures

85.82	Split-thickness graft to breast
85.83	Full-thickness graft to breast
85.84	Pedicle graft to breast
86.60	Free skin graft, not otherwise specified
86.61	Full-thickness skin graft to hand
86.62	Other skin graft to hand
86.63	Full-thickness skin graft to other sites
86.65	Heterograft to skin
86.66	Homograft to skin
86.67	Dermal regenerative graft
86.69	Other skin graft to other sites
86.7*	Pedicle grafts or flaps
86.93	Insertion of tissue expander

DRG 928   Full Thickness Burn with Skin Graft or Inhalation Injury with CC/MCC

GMLOS 11.2   **AMLOS 15.3**   **RW 4.7919**   ☑

Principal or Secondary Diagnosis

941.3*	Full-thickness skin loss due to burn (third degree NOS) of face, head, and neck
941.4*	Deep necrosis of underlying tissues due to burn (deep third degree) of face, head, and neck without mention of loss of a body part
941.5*	Deep necrosis of underlying tissues due to burn (deep third degree) of face, head, and neck with loss of a body part
942.3*	Full-thickness skin loss due to burn (third degree NOS) of trunk
942.4*	Deep necrosis of underlying tissues due to burn (deep third degree) of trunk without mention of loss of a body part
942.5*	Deep necrosis of underlying tissues due to burn (deep third degree) of trunk with loss of a body part
943.3*	Full-thickness skin loss due to burn (third degree NOS) of upper limb, except wrist and hand
943.4*	Deep necrosis of underlying tissues due to burn (deep third degree) of upper limb, except wrist and hand, without mention of loss of a body part
943.5*	Deep necrosis of underlying tissues due to burn (deep third degree) of upper limb, except wrist and hand, with loss of a body part
944.3*	Full-thickness skin loss due to burn (third degree NOS) of wrist(s) and hand(s)
944.4*	Deep necrosis of underlying tissues due to burn (deep third degree) of wrist(s) and hand(s), without mention of loss of a body part
944.5*	Deep necrosis of underlying tissues due to burn (deep third degree) of wrist(s) and hand(s), with loss of a body part
945.3*	Full-thickness skin loss due to burn (third degree NOS) of lower limb(s)
945.4*	Deep necrosis of underlying tissues due to burn (deep third degree) of lower limb(s) without mention of loss of a body part
945.5*	Deep necrosis of underlying tissues due to burn (deep third degree) of lower limb(s) with loss of a body part
946.3	Full-thickness skin loss due to burn (third degree NOS) of multiple specified sites
946.4	Deep necrosis of underlying tissues due to burn (deep third degree) of multiple specified sites, without mention of loss of a body part
946.5	Deep necrosis of underlying tissues due to burn (deep third degree) of multiple specified sites, with loss of a body part
948.11	Burn (any degree) involving 10-19% of body surface with third degree burn of 10-19%
949.3	Full-thickness skin loss due to burn (third degree NOS), unspecified site
949.4	Deep necrosis of underlying tissue due to burn (deep third degree), unspecified site without mention of loss of body part
949.5	Deep necrosis of underlying tissues due to burn (deep third degree, unspecified site with loss of body part

AND

Operating Room Procedures

85.82	Split-thickness graft to breast
85.83	Full-thickness graft to breast
85.84	Pedicle graft to breast
86.60	Free skin graft, not otherwise specified
86.61	Full-thickness skin graft to hand
86.62	Other skin graft to hand
86.63	Full-thickness skin graft to other sites
86.65	Heterograft to skin
86.66	Homograft to skin
86.67	Dermal regenerative graft
86.69	Other skin graft to other sites
86.7*	Pedicle grafts or flaps
86.93	Insertion of tissue expander

OR

Secondary Diagnosis

508.2	Respiratory conditions due to smoke inhalation
518.5*	Pulmonary insufficiency following trauma and surgery
518.81	Acute respiratory failure
518.84	Acute and chronic respiratory failure
947.1	Burn of larynx, trachea, and lung
987.9	Toxic effect of unspecified gas, fume, or vapor

Ⓣ *Transfer DRG*   ⓈⓅ *Special Payment*   ☑ *Optimization Potential*   ▽ *Targeted Potential*   * *Code Range*   ● *New DRG*   ▲ *Revised DRG Title*

208   Valid 10/01/2012-09/30/2013   © 2012 OptumInsight, Inc.

DRG 929 Full Thickness Burn with Skin Graft or Inhalation Injury without CC/MCC

GMLOS 5.2   AMLOS 7.3   RW 2.2420   ☑

Select principal or secondary diagnosis and operating room procedure or secondary diagnosis listed under DRG 928

Select principal or secondary diagnosis in combination with secondary diagnosis of inhalation injury and operating room procedures listed under DRG 928

MEDICAL

DRG 933 Extensive Burns or Full Thickness Burns with Mechanical Ventilation 96+ Hours without Skin Graft

GMLOS 2.5   AMLOS 5.3   RW 2.3740   ☑

Principal or Secondary Diagnosis

941.3*	Full-thickness skin loss due to burn (third degree NOS) of face, head, and neck
941.4*	Deep necrosis of underlying tissues due to burn (deep third degree) of face, head, and neck without mention of loss of a body part
941.5*	Deep necrosis of underlying tissues due to burn (deep third degree) of face, head, and neck with loss of a body part
942.3*	Full-thickness skin loss due to burn (third degree NOS) of trunk
942.4*	Deep necrosis of underlying tissues due to burn (deep third degree) of trunk without mention of loss of a body part
942.5*	Deep necrosis of underlying tissues due to burn (deep third degree) of trunk with loss of a body part
943.3*	Full-thickness skin loss due to burn (third degree NOS) of upper limb, except wrist and hand
943.4*	Deep necrosis of underlying tissues due to burn (deep third degree) of upper limb, except wrist and hand, without mention of loss of a body part
943.5*	Deep necrosis of underlying tissues due to burn (deep third degree) of upper limb, except wrist and hand, with loss of a body part
944.3*	Full-thickness skin loss due to burn (third degree NOS) of wrist(s) and hand(s)
944.4*	Deep necrosis of underlying tissues due to burn (deep third degree) of wrist(s) and hand(s), without mention of loss of a body part
944.5*	Deep necrosis of underlying tissues due to burn (deep third degree) of wrist(s) and hand(s), with loss of a body part
945.3*	Full-thickness skin loss due to burn (third degree NOS) of lower limb(s)
945.4*	Deep necrosis of underlying tissues due to burn (deep third degree) of lower limb(s) without mention of loss of a body part
945.5*	Deep necrosis of underlying tissues due to burn (deep third degree) of lower limb(s) with loss of a body part
946.3	Full-thickness skin loss due to burn (third degree NOS) of multiple specified sites
946.4	Deep necrosis of underlying tissues due to burn (deep third degree) of multiple specified sites, without mention of loss of a body part
946.5	Deep necrosis of underlying tissues due to burn (deep third degree) of multiple specified sites, with loss of a body part
948.11	Burn (any degree) involving 10-19% of body surface with third degree burn of 10-19%
949.3	Full-thickness skin loss due to burn (third degree NOS), unspecified site
949.4	Deep necrosis of underlying tissue due to burn (deep third degree), unspecified site without mention of loss of body part
949.5	Deep necrosis of underlying tissues due to burn (deep third degree, unspecified site with loss of body part

AND

Nonoperating Room Procedure

96.72	Continuous invasive mechanical ventilation for 96 consecutive hours or more

OR

Principal or Secondary Diagnosis

948.21	Burn (any degree) involving 20-29% of body surface with third degree burn of 10-19%
948.22	Burn (any degree) involving 20-29% of body surface with third degree burn of 20-29%
948.31	Burn (any degree) involving 30-39% of body surface with third degree burn of 10-19%
948.32	Burn (any degree) involving 30-39% of body surface with third degree burn of 20-29%
948.33	Burn (any degree) involving 30-39% of body surface with third degree burn of 30-39%
948.41	Burn (any degree) involving 40-49% of body surface with third degree burn of 10-19%
948.42	Burn (any degree) involving 40-49% of body surface with third degree burn of 20-29%
948.43	Burn (any degree) involving 40-49% of body surface with third degree burn of 30-39%
948.44	Burn (any degree) involving 40-49% of body surface with third degree burn of 40-49%
948.51	Burn (any degree) involving 50-59% of body surface with third degree burn of 10-19%
948.52	Burn (any degree) involving 50-59% of body surface with third degree burn of 20-29%
948.53	Burn (any degree) involving 50-59% of body surface with third degree burn of 30-39%
948.54	Burn (any degree) involving 50-59% of body surface with third degree burn of 40-49%
948.55	Burn (any degree) involving 50-59% of body surface with third degree burn of 50-59%
948.61	Burn (any degree) involving 60-69% of body surface with third degree burn of 10-19%
948.62	Burn (any degree) involving 60-69% of body surface with third degree burn of 20-29%
948.63	Burn (any degree) involving 60-69% of body surface with third degree burn of 30-39%
948.64	Burn (any degree) involving 60-69% of body surface with third degree burn of 40-49%
948.65	Burn (any degree) involving 60-69% of body surface with third degree burn of 50-59%
948.66	Burn (any degree) involving 60-69% of body surface with third degree burn of 60-69%
948.71	Burn (any degree) involving 70-79% of body surface with third degree burn of 10-19%
948.72	Burn (any degree) involving 70-79% of body surface with third degree burn of 20-29%
948.73	Burn (any degree) involving 70-79% of body surface with third degree burn of 30-39%
948.74	Burn (any degree) involving 70-79% of body surface with third degree burn of 40-49%
948.75	Burn (any degree) involving 70-79% of body surface with third degree burn of 50-59%
948.76	Burn (any degree) involving 70-79% of body surface with third degree burn of 60-69%
948.77	Burn (any degree) involving 70-79% of body surface with third degree burn of 70-79%
948.81	Burn (any degree) involving 80-89% of body surface with third degree burn of 10-19%
948.82	Burn (any degree) involving 80-89% of body surface with third degree burn of 20-29%
948.83	Burn (any degree) involving 80-89% of body surface with third degree burn of 30-39%

948.84	Burn (any degree) involving 80-89% of body surface with third degree burn of 40-49%
948.85	Burn (any degree) involving 80-89% of body surface with third degree burn of 50-59%
948.86	Burn (any degree) involving 80-89% of body surface with third degree burn of 60-69%
948.87	Burn (any degree) involving 80-89% of body surface with third degree burn of 70-79%
948.88	Burn (any degree) involving 80-89% of body surface with third degree burn of 80-89%
948.91	Burn (any degree) involving 90% or more of body surface with third degree burn of 10-19%
948.92	Burn (any degree) involving 90% or more of body surface with third degree burn of 20-29%
948.93	Burn (any degree) involving 90% or more of body surface with third degree burn of 30-39%
948.94	Burn (any degree) involving 90% or more of body surface with third degree burn of 40-49%
948.95	Burn (any degree) involving 90% or more of body surface with third degree burn of 50-59%
948.96	Burn (any degree) involving 90% or more of body surface with third degree burn of 60-69%
948.97	Burn (any degree) involving 90% or more of body surface with third degree burn of 70-79%
948.98	Burn (any degree) involving 90% or more of body surface with third degree burn of 80-89%
948.99	Burn (any degree) involving 90% or more of body surface with third degree burn of 90% or more of body surface

DRG 934 Full Thickness Burn without Skin Graft or Inhalation Injury

GMLOS 4.0   **AMLOS 5.7**   **RW 1.5123**   ☑

Principal Diagnosis

941.3*	Full-thickness skin loss due to burn (third degree NOS) of face, head, and neck
941.4*	Deep necrosis of underlying tissues due to burn (deep third degree) of face, head, and neck without mention of loss of a body part
941.5*	Deep necrosis of underlying tissues due to burn (deep third degree) of face, head, and neck with loss of a body part
942.3*	Full-thickness skin loss due to burn (third degree NOS) of trunk
942.4*	Deep necrosis of underlying tissues due to burn (deep third degree) of trunk without mention of loss of a body part
942.5*	Deep necrosis of underlying tissues due to burn (deep third degree) of trunk with loss of a body part
943.3*	Full-thickness skin loss due to burn (third degree NOS) of upper limb, except wrist and hand
943.4*	Deep necrosis of underlying tissues due to burn (deep third degree) of upper limb, except wrist and hand, without mention of loss of a body part
943.5*	Deep necrosis of underlying tissues due to burn (deep third degree) of upper limb, except wrist and hand, with loss of a body part
944.3*	Full-thickness skin loss due to burn (third degree NOS) of wrist(s) and hand(s)
944.4*	Deep necrosis of underlying tissues due to burn (deep third degree) of wrist(s) and hand(s), without mention of loss of a body part
944.5*	Deep necrosis of underlying tissues due to burn (deep third degree) of wrist(s) and hand(s), with loss of a body part
945.3*	Full-thickness skin loss due to burn (third degree NOS) of lower limb(s)
945.4*	Deep necrosis of underlying tissues due to burn (deep third degree) of lower limb(s) without mention of loss of a body part
945.5*	Deep necrosis of underlying tissues due to burn (deep third degree) of lower limb(s) with loss of a body part

946.3	Full-thickness skin loss due to burn (third degree NOS) of multiple specified sites
946.4	Deep necrosis of underlying tissues due to burn (deep third degree) of multiple specified sites, without mention of loss of a body part
946.5	Deep necrosis of underlying tissues due to burn (deep third degree) of multiple specified sites, with loss of a body part
948.11	Burn (any degree) involving 10-19% of body surface with third degree burn of 10-19%
949.3	Full-thickness skin loss due to burn (third degree NOS), unspecified site
949.4	Deep necrosis of underlying tissue due to burn (deep third degree), unspecified site without mention of loss of body part
949.5	Deep necrosis of underlying tissues due to burn (deep third degree, unspecified site with loss of body part

DRG 935 Nonextensive Burns

GMLOS 3.3   **AMLOS 5.0**   **RW 1.3410**   ☑

Principal Diagnosis

941.00	Burn of unspecified degree of unspecified site of face and head
941.01	Burn of unspecified degree of ear (any part)
941.03	Burn of unspecified degree of lip(s)
941.04	Burn of unspecified degree of chin
941.05	Burn of unspecified degree of nose (septum)
941.06	Burn of unspecified degree of scalp (any part)
941.07	Burn of unspecified degree of forehead and cheek
941.08	Burn of unspecified degree of neck
941.09	Burn of unspecified degree of multiple sites (except with eye) of face, head, and neck
941.10	Erythema due to burn (first degree) of unspecified site of face and head
941.11	Erythema due to burn (first degree) of ear (any part)
941.13	Erythema due to burn (first degree) of lip(s)
941.14	Erythema due to burn (first degree) of chin
941.15	Erythema due to burn (first degree) of nose (septum)
941.16	Erythema due to burn (first degree) of scalp (any part)
941.17	Erythema due to burn (first degree) of forehead and cheek
941.18	Erythema due to burn (first degree) of neck
941.19	Erythema due to burn (first degree) of multiple sites (except with eye) of face, head, and neck
941.20	Blisters, with epidermal loss due to burn (second degree) of face and head, unspecified site
941.21	Blisters, with epidermal loss due to burn (second degree) of ear (any part)
941.23	Blisters, with epidermal loss due to burn (second degree) of lip(s)
941.24	Blisters, with epidermal loss due to burn (second degree) of chin
941.25	Blisters, with epidermal loss due to burn (second degree) of nose (septum)
941.26	Blisters, with epidermal loss due to burn (second degree) of scalp (any part)
941.27	Blisters, with epidermal loss due to burn (second degree) of forehead and cheek
941.28	Blisters, with epidermal loss due to burn (second degree) of neck
941.29	Blisters, with epidermal loss due to burn (second degree) of multiple sites (except with eye) of face, head, and neck
942.0*	Burn of trunk, unspecified degree
942.1*	Erythema due to burn (first degree) of trunk
942.2*	Blisters with epidermal loss due to burn (second degree) of trunk
943.0*	Burn of upper limb, except wrist and hand, unspecified degree
943.1*	Erythema due to burn (first degree) of upper limb, except wrist and hand

MDC 22: Burns—MEDICAL

Ⓣ _Transfer DRG_   ⁇ _Special Payment_   ☑ _Optimization Potential_   ⁇ _Targeted Potential_   * _Code Range_   ● _New DRG_   ▲ _Revised DRG Title_

210   Valid 10/01/2012-09/30/2013   © 2012 OptumInsight, Inc.

943.2*	Blisters with epidermal loss due to burn (second degree) of upper limb, except wrist and hand
944.0*	Burn of wrist(s) and hand(s), unspecified degree
944.1*	Erythema due to burn (first degree) of wrist(s) and hand(s)
944.2*	Blisters with epidermal loss due to burn (second degree) of wrist(s) and hand(s)
945.0*	Burn of lower limb(s), unspecified degree
945.1*	Erythema due to burn (first degree) of lower limb(s)
945.2*	Blisters with epidermal loss due to burn (second degree) of lower limb(s)
946.0	Burns of multiple specified sites, unspecified degree
946.1	Erythema due to burn (first degree) of multiple specified sites
946.2	Blisters with epidermal loss due to burn (second degree) of multiple specified sites
947.8	Burn of other specified sites of internal organs
947.9	Burn of internal organs, unspecified site
948.00	Burn (any degree) involving less than 10% of body surface with third degree burn of less than 10% or unspecified amount
948.10	Burn (any degree) involving 10-19% of body surface with third degree burn of less than 10% or unspecified amount
948.20	Burn (any degree) involving 20-29% of body surface with third degree burn of less than 10% or unspecified amount
948.30	Burn (any degree) involving 30-39% of body surface with third degree burn of less than 10% or unspecified amount
948.40	Burn (any degree) involving 40-49% of body surface with third degree burn of less than 10% or unspecified amount
948.50	Burn (any degree) involving 50-59% of body surface with third degree burn of less than 10% or unspecified amount
948.60	Burn (any degree) involving 60-69% of body surface with third degree burn of less than 10% or unspecified amount
948.70	Burn (any degree) involving 70-79% of body surface with third degree burn of less than 10% or unspecified amount
948.80	Burn (any degree) involving 80-89% of body surface with third degree burn of less than 10% or unspecified amount
948.90	Burn (any degree) involving 90% or more of body surface with third degree burn of less than 10% or unspecified amount
949.0	Burn of unspecified site, unspecified degree
949.1	Erythema due to burn (first degree), unspecified site
949.2	Blisters with epidermal loss due to burn (second degree), unspecified site

MDC 22: Burns—MEDICAL

Surgical	Medical	CC Indicator	MCC Indicator	Procedure Proxy

305.1	V01.71	V07.4	V13.7	V17.1	V25.43	V42.9	V48.3	V58.2
338.11	V01.79	V07.51	V13.81	V17.2	V25.49	V43.81	V48.4	V58.30
338.12	V01.81	V07.52	V13.89	V17.3	V25.5	V43.82	V48.5	V58.31
338.18	V01.82	V07.59	V13.9	V17.41	V25.8	V43.83	V48.6	V58.32
338.19	V01.83	V07.8	V14.0	V17.49	V25.9	V43.89	V48.7	V58.41
338.3	V01.84	V07.9	V14.1	V17.5	V26.1	V44.0	V48.8	V58.42
758.4	V01.89	V11.0	V14.2	V17.6	V26.21	V44.1	V48.9	V58.43
758.5	V01.9	V11.1	V14.3	V17.7	V26.22	V44.2	V49.0	V58.44
758.9	V02.0	V11.2	V14.4	V17.81	V26.29	V44.3	V49.1	V58.49
759.9	V02.1	V11.3	V14.5	V17.89	V26.31	V44.4	V49.2	V58.5
780.64	V02.2	V11.4	V14.6	V18.0	V26.32	V44.50	V49.3	V58.61
780.65	V02.3	V11.8	V14.7	V18.11	V26.33	V44.51	V49.4	V58.62
780.71	V02.4	V11.9	V14.8	V18.19	V26.34	V44.52	V49.5	V58.63
780.79	V02.51	V12.00	V14.9	V18.2	V26.35	V44.59	V49.60	V58.64
780.91	V02.52	V12.01	V15.01	V18.3	V26.39	V44.6	V49.61	V58.65
780.92	V02.53	V12.02	V15.02	V18.4	V26.41	V44.7	V49.62	V58.66
780.93	V02.54	V12.03	V15.03	V18.51	V26.42	V44.8	V49.63	V58.67
780.94	V02.59	V12.04	V15.04	V18.59	V26.49	V44.9	V49.64	V58.68
780.95	V02.7	V12.09	V15.05	V18.61	V26.51	V45.00	V49.65	V58.69
780.96	V02.8	V12.1	V15.06	V18.69	V26.52	V45.01	V49.66	V58.71
780.97	V02.9	V12.21	V15.07	V18.7	V26.81	V45.02	V49.67	V58.72
780.99	V03.0	V12.29	V15.08	V18.8	V26.82	V45.09	V49.70	V58.73
782.3	V03.1	V12.3	V15.09	V18.9	V26.89	V45.11	V49.71	V58.74
782.5	V03.2	V12.40	V15.1	V19.0	V26.9	V45.12	V49.72	V58.75
782.61	V03.3	V12.41	V15.21	V19.11	V27.0	V45.2	V49.73	V58.76
782.62	V03.4	V12.42	V15.22	V19.19	V27.1	V45.3	V49.74	V58.77
789.51	V03.5	V12.49	V15.29	V19.2	V27.2	V45.4	V49.75	V58.78
789.59	V03.6	V12.50	V15.3	V19.3	V27.3	V45.51	V49.76	V58.81
790.1	V03.7	V12.51	V15.41	V19.4	V27.4	V45.52	V49.77	V58.82
790.4	V03.81	V12.52	V15.42	V19.5	V27.5	V45.59	V49.81	V58.83
790.5	V03.82	V12.53	V15.49	V19.6	V27.6	V45.61	V49.82	V58.89
790.6	V03.89	V12.54	V15.51	V19.7	V27.7	V45.69	V49.83	V58.9
790.91	V03.9	V12.55	V15.52	V19.8	V27.9	V45.71	V49.84	V59.01
790.92	V04.0	V12.59	V15.53	V20.0	V28.3	V45.72	V49.85	V59.02
790.93	V04.1	V12.60	V15.59	V20.1	V28.4	V45.73	V49.86	V59.09
790.94	V04.2	V12.61	V15.6	V20.2	V28.5	V45.75	V49.87	V59.3
790.95	V04.3	V12.69	V15.7	V20.31	V28.6	V45.79	V49.89	V59.5
790.99	V04.4	V12.70	V15.80	V20.32	V28.81	V45.81	V49.9	V59.70
791.3	V04.5	V12.71	V15.81	V21.0	V28.82	V45.82	V50.3	V59.71
792.5	V04.6	V12.72	V15.82	V21.1	V28.89	V45.83	V50.49	V59.72
792.9	V04.7	V12.79	V15.83	V21.2	V28.9	V45.84	V50.8	V59.73
793.91	V04.81	V13.00	V15.84	V21.30	V29.0	V45.85	V50.9	V59.74
793.99	V04.82	V13.01	V15.85	V21.31	V29.1	V45.86	V52.2	V59.8
795.2	V04.89	V13.02	V15.86	V21.32	V29.2	V45.87	V52.3	V59.9
795.4	V05.0	V13.03	V15.87	V21.33	V29.3	V45.88	V52.4	V60.0
795.81	V05.1	V13.09	V15.88	V21.34	V29.8	V45.89	V52.8	V60.1
795.82	V05.2	V13.1	V15.89	V21.35	V29.9	V46.0	V52.9	V60.2
795.89	V05.3	V13.21	V15.9	V21.8	V40.0	V46.11	V53.1	V60.3
796.4	V05.4	V13.23	V16.0	V21.9	V40.1	V46.12	V53.2	V60.4
796.6	V05.8	V13.24	V16.1	V22.0	V40.2	V46.13	V53.4	V60.5
796.9	V05.9	V13.29	V16.2	V22.1	V40.31	V46.14	V53.8	V60.6
798.9	V06.0	V13.3	V16.3	V22.2	V40.39	V46.2	V53.90	V60.81
799.3	V06.1	V13.4	V16.40	V24.1	V40.9	V46.3	V53.91	V60.89
799.4	V06.2	V13.51	V16.41	V24.2	V41.0	V46.8	V53.99	V60.9
799.81	V06.3	V13.52	V16.42	V25.01	V41.1	V46.9	V55.8	V61.01
799.82	V06.4	V13.59	V16.43	V25.02	V41.2	V47.0	V55.9	V61.02
799.89	V06.5	V13.61	V16.49	V25.03	V41.3	V47.1	V57.0	V61.03
799.9	V06.6	V13.62	V16.51	V25.04	V41.4	V47.2	V57.1	V61.04
V01.0	V06.8	V13.63	V16.52	V25.09	V41.5	V47.3	V57.21	V61.05
V01.1	V06.9	V13.64	V16.59	V25.11	V41.6	V47.4	V57.22	V61.06
V01.2	V07.0	V13.65	V16.6	V25.12	V41.7	V47.5	V57.3	V61.07
V01.3	V07.1	V13.66	V16.7	V25.13	V41.8	V47.9	V57.4	V61.08
V01.4	V07.2	V13.67	V16.8	V25.40	V41.9	V48.0	V57.81	V61.09
V01.5	V07.31	V13.68	V16.9	V25.41	V42.84	V48.1	V57.89	V61.10
V01.6	V07.39	V13.69	V17.0	V25.42	V42.89	V48.2	V57.9	V61.11

V61.12	V64.03	V66.9	V71.82	V73.89	V76.50	V81.3	V85.33	V89.03
V61.20	V64.04	V67.00	V71.83	V73.98	V76.51	V81.4	V85.34	V89.04
V61.21	V64.05	V67.01	V71.89	V73.99	V76.52	V81.5	V85.35	V89.05
V61.22	V64.06	V67.09	V71.9	V74.0	V76.81	V81.6	V85.36	V89.09
V61.23	V64.07	V67.3	V72.0	V74.1	V76.89	V82.0	V85.37	V90.01
V61.24	V64.08	V67.4	V72.11	V74.2	V76.9	V82.1	V85.38	V90.09
V61.25	V64.09	V67.51	V72.12	V74.3	V77.0	V82.2	V85.39	V90.10
V61.29	V64.1	V67.59	V72.19	V74.4	V77.1	V82.3	V85.51	V90.11
V61.3	V64.2	V67.6	V72.2	V74.5	V77.2	V82.4	V85.52	V90.12
V61.41	V64.3	V67.9	V72.31	V74.6	V77.3	V82.5	V85.53	V90.2
V61.42	V64.41	V68.01	V72.32	V74.8	V77.4	V82.6	V85.54	V90.31
V61.49	V64.42	V68.09	V72.40	V74.9	V77.5	V82.71	V86.0	V90.32
V61.8	V64.43	V68.1	V72.41	V75.0	V77.6	V82.79	V86.1	V90.33
V61.9	V65.0	V68.2	V72.42	V75.1	V77.7	V82.81	V87.01	V90.39
V62.0	V65.11	V68.81	V72.5	V75.2	V77.8	V82.89	V87.02	V90.81
V62.1	V65.19	V68.89	V72.60	V75.3	V77.91	V82.9	V87.09	V90.83
V62.21	V65.2	V68.9	V72.61	V75.4	V77.99	V83.01	V87.11	V90.89
V62.22	V65.3	V69.0	V72.62	V75.5	V78.0	V83.02	V87.12	V90.9
V62.29	V65.40	V69.1	V72.63	V75.6	V78.1	V83.81	V87.19	V91.00
V62.3	V65.41	V69.2	V72.69	V75.7	V78.2	V83.89	V87.2	V91.01
V62.4	V65.42	V69.3	V72.7	V75.8	V78.3	V84.01	V87.31	V91.02
V62.5	V65.43	V69.4	V72.81	V75.9	V78.8	V84.02	V87.32	V91.03
V62.6	V65.44	V69.5	V72.82	V76.0	V78.9	V84.03	V87.39	V91.09
V62.81	V65.45	V69.8	V72.83	V76.10	V79.0	V84.04	V87.41	V91.10
V62.82	V65.46	V69.9	V72.84	V76.11	V79.1	V84.09	V87.42	V91.11
V62.83	V65.49	V70.0	V72.85	V76.12	V79.2	V84.81	V87.43	V91.12
V62.85	V65.5	V70.1	V72.86	V76.19	V79.3	V84.89	V87.44	V91.19
V62.89	V65.8	V70.2	V72.9	V76.2	V79.8	V85.0	V87.45	V91.20
V62.9	V65.9	V70.3	V73.0	V76.3	V79.9	V85.1	V87.46	V91.21
V63.0	V66.0	V70.4	V73.1	V76.41	V80.01	V85.21	V87.49	V91.22
V63.1	V66.1	V70.5	V73.2	V76.42	V80.09	V85.22	V88.11	V91.29
V63.2	V66.2	V70.6	V73.3	V76.43	V80.1	V85.23	V88.12	V91.90
V63.8	V66.3	V70.7	V73.4	V76.44	V80.2	V85.24	V88.21	V91.91
V63.9	V66.4	V70.8	V73.5	V76.45	V80.3	V85.25	V88.22	V91.92
V64.00	V66.5	V70.9	V73.6	V76.46	V81.0	V85.30	V88.29	V91.99
V64.01	V66.6	V71.5	V73.81	V76.47	V81.1	V85.31	V89.01	
V64.02	V66.7	V71.81	V73.88	V76.49	V81.2	V85.32	V89.02	

SURGICAL

DRG 939   O.R. Procedure with Diagnoses of Other Contact with Health Services with MCC
GMLOS 6.2   AMLOS 9.1   RW 2.7769

Select any operating room procedure

DRG 940   O.R. Procedure with Diagnoses of Other Contact with Health Services with CC
GMLOS 3.6   AMLOS 5.3   RW 1.8108   ☑

Select any operating room procedure

DRG 941   O.R. Procedure with Diagnoses of Other Contact with Health Services without CC/MCC
GMLOS 2.1   AMLOS 2.7   RW 1.1776   ☑

Select any operating room procedure

MEDICAL

DRG 945   Rehabilitation with CC/MCC
GMLOS 8.3   AMLOS 10.1   RW 1.3204   ⊤☑

Principal Diagnosis
V52.8   Fitting and adjustment of other specified prosthetic device
V52.9   Fitting and adjustment of unspecified prosthetic device
V57.1   Other physical therapy
V57.2*   Occupational therapy and vocational rehabilitation
V57.3   Care involving use of rehabilitation speech-language therapy
V57.89   Other specified rehabilitation procedure
V57.9   Unspecified rehabilitation procedure

DRG 946   Rehabilitation without CC/MCC
GMLOS 6.5   AMLOS 7.4   RW 1.2530   ⊤☑

Select principal diagnosis listed under DRG 945

DRG 947   Signs and Symptoms with MCC
GMLOS 3.6   AMLOS 4.8   RW 1.1131   ⊤☑

Principal Diagnosis
338.1*   Acute pain
338.3   Neoplasm related pain (acute) (chronic)
780.64   Chills (without fever)
780.65   Hypothermia not associated with low environmental temperature
780.71   Chronic fatigue syndrome
780.79   Other malaise and fatigue
780.9*   Other general symptoms
782.3   Edema
782.5   Cyanosis
782.6*   Pallor and flushing
789.5*   Ascites
790.1   Elevated sedimentation rate
790.4   Nonspecific elevation of levels of transaminase or lactic acid dehydrogenase (LDH)
790.5   Other nonspecific abnormal serum enzyme levels
790.6   Other abnormal blood chemistry
790.9*   Other nonspecific findings on examination of blood
791.3   Myoglobinuria
792.5   Cloudy (hemodialysis) (peritoneal) dialysis affluent
792.9   Other nonspecific abnormal finding in body substances

793.9*   Other nonspecific abnormal findings on radiological and other examinations of body structure
795.4   Other nonspecific abnormal histological findings
795.8*   Abnormal tumor markers
796.4   Other abnormal clinical finding
796.6   Nonspecific abnormal findings on neonatal screening
796.9   Other nonspecific abnormal finding
799.3   Unspecified debility
799.4   Cachexia

DRG 948   Signs and Symptoms without MCC
GMLOS 2.7   AMLOS 3.3   RW 0.7010   ⊤☑

Select principal diagnosis listed under DRG 947

DRG 949   Aftercare with CC/MCC
GMLOS 2.8   AMLOS 4.2   RW 0.9372   ☑

Principal Diagnosis
V58.4*   Other aftercare following surgery
V58.5   Orthodontics aftercare
V58.6*   Long-term (current) drug use
V58.7*   Aftercare following surgery to specified body systems, not elsewhere classified
V58.8*   Other specified aftercare
V58.9   Unspecified aftercare
V67.0*   Surgery follow-up examination
V67.4   Treatment of healed fracture follow-up examination
V87.4*   Personal history of drug therapy

DRG 950   Aftercare without CC/MCC
GMLOS 2.3   AMLOS 3.3   RW 0.5693   ☑

Select principal diagnosis listed under DRG 949

DRG 951   Other Factors Influencing Health Status
GMLOS 2.4   AMLOS 5.9   RW 0.8105   ☑

Principal Diagnosis
305.1   Nondependent tobacco use disorder
758.4   Balanced autosomal translocation in normal individual
758.5   Other conditions due to autosomal anomalies
758.9   Conditions due to anomaly of unspecified chromosome
759.9   Unspecified congenital anomaly
795.2   Nonspecific abnormal findings on chromosomal analysis
798.9   Unattended death
799.8*   Other ill-defined conditions
799.9   Other unknown and unspecified cause of morbidity or mortality
V01*   Contact with or exposure to communicable diseases
V02.0   Carrier or suspected carrier of cholera
V02.1   Carrier or suspected carrier of typhoid
V02.2   Carrier or suspected carrier of amebiasis
V02.3   Carrier or suspected carrier of other gastrointestinal pathogens
V02.4   Carrier or suspected carrier of diphtheria
V02.5*   Carrier or suspected carrier of other specified bacterial diseases
V02.7   Carrier or suspected carrier of gonorrhea
V02.8   Carrier or suspected carrier of other venereal diseases
V02.9   Carrier or suspected carrier of other specified infectious organism
V03*   Need for prophylactic vaccination and inoculation against bacterial diseases
V04*   Need for prophylactic vaccination and inoculation against certain viral diseases
V05*   Need for other prophylactic vaccination and inoculation against single diseases
V06*   Need for prophylactic vaccination and inoculation against combinations of diseases

V07*	Need for isolation and other prophylactic or treatment measures
V11*	Personal history of mental disorder
V12*	Personal history of certain other diseases
V13.0*	Personal history of disorders of urinary system
V13.1	Personal history of trophoblastic disease
V13.21	Personal history of pre-term labor
V13.23	Personal history of vaginal dysplasia
V13.24	Personal history of vulvar dysplasia
V13.29	Personal history of other genital system and obstetric disorders
V13.3	Personal history of diseases of skin and subcutaneous tissue
V13.4	Personal history of arthritis
V13.5*	Personal history of other musculoskeletal disorders
V13.6*	Personal history of congenital (corrected) malformations
V13.7	Personal history of perinatal problems
V13.8*	Personal history of other specified diseases
V13.9	Personal history of unspecified disease
V14*	Personal history of allergy to medicinal agents
V15*	Other personal history presenting hazards to health
V16*	Family history of malignant neoplasm
V17*	Family history of certain chronic disabling diseases
V18*	Family history of certain other specific conditions
V19*	Family history of other conditions
V20*	Health supervision of infant or child
V21*	Constitutional states in development
V22*	Normal pregnancy
V24.1	Postpartum care and examination of lactating mother
V24.2	Routine postpartum follow-up
V25.0*	General counseling and advice for contraceptive management
V25.1*	Encounter for insertion or removal of intrauterine contraceptive device
V25.4*	Surveillance of previously prescribed contraceptive methods
V25.5	Insertion of implantable subdermal contraceptive
V25.8	Other specified contraceptive management
V25.9	Unspecified contraceptive management
V26.1	Artificial insemination
V26.2*	Investigation and testing for procreation management
V26.3*	Genetic counseling and testing
V26.4*	Procreative management, general counseling and advice
V26.5*	Sterilization status
V26.8*	Other specified procreative management
V26.9	Unspecified procreative management
V27*	Outcome of delivery
V28.3	Encounter for routine screening for malformation using ultrasonics
V28.4	Antenatal screening for fetal growth retardation using ultrasonics
V28.5	Antenatal screening for isoimmunization
V28.6	Screening of Streptococcus B
V28.8*	Encounter for other specified antenatal screening
V28.9	Unspecified antenatal screening
V29*	Observation and evaluation of newborns and infants for suspected condition not found
V40*	Mental and behavioral problems
V41*	Problems with special senses and other special functions
V42.84	Organ or tissue replaced by transplant, intestines
V42.89	Other organ or tissue replaced by transplant
V42.9	Unspecified organ or tissue replaced by transplant
V43.8*	Other organ or tissue replaced by other means
V44*	Artificial opening status
V45.0*	Postsurgical cardiac pacemaker in situ
V45.1*	Renal dialysis status
V45.2	Presence of cerebrospinal fluid drainage device
V45.3	Intestinal bypass or anastomosis status
V45.4	Arthrodesis status
V45.5*	Presence of contraceptive device
V45.61	Cataract extraction status
V45.69	Other states following surgery of eye and adnexa
V45.71	Acquired absence of breast and nipple
V45.72	Acquired absence of intestine (large) (small)
V45.73	Acquired absence of kidney
V45.75	Acquired absence of organ, stomach
V45.79	Other acquired absence of organ
V45.8*	Other postprocedural status
V46*	Other dependence on machines and devices
V47*	Other problems with internal organs
V48*	Problems with head, neck, and trunk
V49*	Problems with limbs and other problems
V50.3	Ear piercing
V50.49	Other prophylactic organ removal
V50.8	Other elective surgery for purposes other than remedying health states
V50.9	Unspecified elective surgery for purposes other than remedying health states
V52.2	Fitting and adjustment of artificial eye
V52.3	Fitting and adjustment of dental prosthetic device
V52.4	Fitting and adjustment of breast prosthesis and implant
V53.1	Fitting and adjustment of spectacles and contact lenses
V53.2	Fitting and adjustment of hearing aid
V53.4	Fitting and adjustment of orthodontic devices
V53.8	Fitting and adjustment of wheelchair
V53.9*	Fitting and adjustment of other and unspecified device
V55.8	Attention to other specified artificial opening
V55.9	Attention to unspecified artificial opening
V57.0	Care involving breathing exercises
V57.4	Orthoptic training
V57.81	Orthotic training
V58.2	Blood transfusion, without reported diagnosis
V58.3*	Attention to dressings and sutures
V59.0*	Blood donor
V59.3	Bone marrow donor
V59.5	Cornea donor
V59.7*	Egg (oocyte) (ovum) Donor
V59.8	Donor of other specified organ or tissue
V59.9	Donor of unspecified organ or tissue
V60*	Housing, household, and economic circumstances
V61.0*	Family disruption
V61.10	Counseling for marital and partner problems, unspecified
V61.11	Counseling for victim of spousal and partner abuse
V61.12	Counseling for perpetrator of spousal and partner abuse
V61.2*	Parent-child problems
V61.3	Problems with aged parents or in-laws
V61.4*	Health problems within family
V61.8	Other specified family circumstance
V61.9	Unspecified family circumstance
V62.0	Unemployment
V62.1	Adverse effects of work environment
V62.2*	Other occupational circumstances or maladjustment
V62.3	Educational circumstance
V62.4	Social maladjustment
V62.5	Legal circumstance
V62.6	Refusal of treatment for reasons of religion or conscience
V62.81	Interpersonal problem, not elsewhere classified
V62.82	Bereavement, uncomplicated
V62.83	Counseling for perpetrator of physical/sexual abuse
V62.85	Homicidal ideation
V62.89	Other psychological or physical stress, not elsewhere classified
V62.9	Unspecified psychosocial circumstance
V63*	Unavailability of other medical facilities for care
V64*	Persons encountering health services for specific procedures, not carried out
V65*	Other persons seeking consultation
V66*	Convalescence and palliative care
V67.3	Psychotherapy and other treatment for mental disorder follow-up examination
V67.5*	Other follow-up examination
V67.6	Combined treatment follow-up examination

Surgical   *Medical*   CC Indicator   MCC Indicator   *Procedure Proxy*

V67.9	Unspecified follow-up examination
V68*	Encounters for administrative purposes
V69*	Problems related to lifestyle
V70*	General medical examination
V71.5	Observation following alleged rape or seduction
V71.8*	Observation and evaluation for other specified suspected conditions
V71.9	Observation for unspecified suspected condition
V72*	Special investigations and examinations
V73*	Special screening examination for viral and chlamydial diseases
V74*	Special screening examination for bacterial and spirochetal diseases
V75*	Special screening examination for other infectious diseases
V76*	Special screening for malignant neoplasms
V77*	Special screening for endocrine, nutritional, metabolic, and immunity disorders
V78*	Special screening for disorders of blood and blood-forming organs
V79*	Special screening for mental disorders and developmental handicaps
V80*	Special screening for neurological, eye, and ear diseases
V81*	Special screening for cardiovascular, respiratory, and genitourinary diseases
V82*	Special screening for other condition
V83.01	Asymptomatic hemophilia A carrier
V83.02	Symptomatic hemophilia A carrier
V83.8*	Other genetic carrier status
V84.0*	Genetic susceptibility to malignant neoplasm
V84.8*	Genetic susceptibility to other disease
V85.0	Body Mass Index less than 19, adult
V85.1	Body Mass Index between 19-24, adult
V85.2*	Body Mass Index between 25-29, adult
V85.3*	Body Mass Index between 30-39, adult
V85.5*	Body Mass Index, pediatric
V86*	Estrogen receptor status
V87.0*	Contact with and (suspected) exposure to hazardous metals
V87.1*	Contact with and (suspected) exposure to hazardous aromatic compounds
V87.2	Contact with and (suspected) exposure to other potentially hazardous chemicals
V87.3*	Contact with and (suspected) exposure to other potentially hazardous substances
V88.1*	Acquired absence of pancreas
V88.2*	Acquired absence of joint
V89.0*	Suspected maternal and fetal conditions not found
V90.0*	Retained radioactive fragment
V90.1*	Retained metal fragments
V90.2	Retained plastic fragments
V90.3*	Retained organic fragments
V90.8*	Other specified retained foreign body
V90.9	Retained foreign body, unspecified material
V91.0*	Twin gestation placenta status
V91.1*	Triplet gestation placenta status
V91.2*	Quadruplet gestation placenta status
V91.9*	Other specified multiple gestation placenta status

MDC 24
Multiple Significant Trauma

800.00	800.83	801.66	803.15	804.00	804.83	806.28	810.00	813.31
800.01	800.84	801.69	803.16	804.01	804.84	806.29	810.01	813.32
800.02	800.85	801.70	803.19	804.02	804.85	806.30	810.02	813.33
800.03	800.86	801.71	803.20	804.03	804.86	806.31	810.03	813.40
800.04	800.89	801.72	803.21	804.04	804.89	806.32	810.10	813.41
800.05	800.90	801.73	803.22	804.05	804.90	806.33	810.11	813.42
800.06	800.91	801.74	803.23	804.06	804.91	806.34	810.12	813.43
800.09	800.92	801.75	803.24	804.09	804.92	806.35	810.13	813.44
800.10	800.93	801.76	803.25	804.10	804.93	806.36	811.00	813.45
800.11	800.94	801.79	803.26	804.11	804.94	806.37	811.01	813.46
800.12	800.95	801.80	803.29	804.12	804.95	806.38	811.02	813.47
800.13	800.96	801.81	803.30	804.13	804.96	806.39	811.03	813.50
800.14	800.99	801.82	803.31	804.14	804.99	806.4	811.09	813.51
800.15	801.00	801.83	803.32	804.15	805.00	806.5	811.10	813.52
800.16	801.01	801.84	803.33	804.16	805.01	806.60	811.11	813.53
800.19	801.02	801.85	803.34	804.19	805.02	806.61	811.12	813.54
800.20	801.03	801.86	803.35	804.20	805.03	806.62	811.13	813.80
800.21	801.04	801.89	803.36	804.21	805.04	806.69	811.19	813.81
800.22	801.05	801.90	803.39	804.22	805.05	806.70	812.00	813.82
800.23	801.06	801.91	803.40	804.23	805.06	806.71	812.01	813.83
800.24	801.09	801.92	803.41	804.24	805.07	806.72	812.02	813.90
800.25	801.10	801.93	803.42	804.25	805.08	806.79	812.03	813.91
800.26	801.11	801.94	803.43	804.26	805.10	806.8	812.09	813.92
800.29	801.12	801.95	803.44	804.29	805.11	806.9	812.10	813.93
800.30	801.13	801.96	803.45	804.30	805.12	807.00	812.11	814.00
800.31	801.14	801.99	803.46	804.31	805.13	807.01	812.12	814.01
800.32	801.15	802.0	803.49	804.32	805.14	807.02	812.13	814.02
800.33	801.16	802.1	803.50	804.33	805.15	807.03	812.19	814.03
800.34	801.19	802.20	803.51	804.34	805.16	807.04	812.20	814.04
800.35	801.20	802.21	803.52	804.35	805.17	807.05	812.21	814.05
800.36	801.21	802.22	803.53	804.36	805.18	807.06	812.30	814.06
800.39	801.22	802.23	803.54	804.39	805.2	807.07	812.31	814.07
800.40	801.23	802.24	803.55	804.40	805.3	807.08	812.40	814.08
800.41	801.24	802.25	803.56	804.41	805.4	807.09	812.41	814.09
800.42	801.25	802.26	803.59	804.42	805.5	807.10	812.42	814.10
800.43	801.26	802.27	803.60	804.43	805.6	807.11	812.43	814.11
800.44	801.29	802.28	803.61	804.44	805.7	807.12	812.44	814.12
800.45	801.30	802.29	803.62	804.45	805.8	807.13	812.49	814.13
800.46	801.31	802.30	803.63	804.46	805.9	807.14	812.50	814.14
800.49	801.32	802.31	803.64	804.49	806.00	807.15	812.51	814.15
800.50	801.33	802.32	803.65	804.50	806.01	807.16	812.52	814.16
800.51	801.34	802.33	803.66	804.51	806.02	807.17	812.53	814.17
800.52	801.35	802.34	803.69	804.52	806.03	807.18	812.54	814.18
800.53	801.36	802.35	803.70	804.53	806.04	807.19	812.59	814.19
800.54	801.39	802.36	803.71	804.54	806.05	807.2	813.00	815.00
800.55	801.40	802.37	803.72	804.55	806.06	807.3	813.01	815.01
800.56	801.41	802.38	803.73	804.56	806.07	807.4	813.02	815.02
800.59	801.42	802.39	803.74	804.59	806.08	807.5	813.03	815.03
800.60	801.43	802.4	803.75	804.60	806.09	807.6	813.04	815.04
800.61	801.44	802.5	803.76	804.61	806.10	808.0	813.05	815.09
800.62	801.45	802.6	803.79	804.62	806.11	808.1	813.06	815.10
800.63	801.46	802.7	803.80	804.63	806.12	808.2	813.07	815.11
800.64	801.49	802.8	803.81	804.64	806.13	808.3	813.08	815.12
800.65	801.50	802.9	803.82	804.65	806.14	808.41	813.10	815.13
800.66	801.51	803.00	803.83	804.66	806.15	808.42	813.11	815.14
800.69	801.52	803.01	803.84	804.69	806.16	808.43	813.12	815.19
800.70	801.53	803.02	803.85	804.70	806.17	808.44	813.13	816.00
800.71	801.54	803.03	803.86	804.71	806.18	808.49	813.14	816.01
800.72	801.55	803.04	803.89	804.72	806.19	808.51	813.15	816.02
800.73	801.56	803.05	803.90	804.73	806.20	808.52	813.16	816.03
800.74	801.59	803.06	803.91	804.74	806.21	808.53	813.17	816.10
800.75	801.60	803.09	803.92	804.75	806.22	808.54	813.18	816.11
800.76	801.61	803.10	803.93	804.76	806.23	808.59	813.20	816.12
800.79	801.62	803.11	803.94	804.79	806.24	808.8	813.21	816.13
800.80	801.63	803.12	803.95	804.80	806.25	808.9	813.22	817.0
800.81	801.64	803.13	803.96	804.81	806.26	809.0	813.23	817.1
800.82	801.65	803.14	803.99	804.82	806.27	809.1	813.30	818.0

818.1	825.24	836.1	840.4	851.02	851.94	854.06	863.93	871.5
819.0	825.25	836.2	840.5	851.03	851.95	854.09	863.94	871.6
819.1	825.29	836.3	840.6	851.04	851.96	854.10	863.95	871.7
820.00	825.30	836.4	840.7	851.05	851.99	854.11	863.99	871.9
820.01	825.31	836.50	840.8	851.06	852.00	854.12	864.00	872.00
820.02	825.32	836.51	840.9	851.09	852.01	854.13	864.01	872.01
820.03	825.33	836.52	841.0	851.10	852.02	854.14	864.02	872.02
820.09	825.34	836.53	841.1	851.11	852.03	854.15	864.03	872.10
820.10	825.35	836.54	841.2	851.12	852.04	854.16	864.04	872.11
820.11	825.39	836.59	841.3	851.13	852.05	854.19	864.05	872.12
820.12	826.0	836.60	841.8	851.14	852.06	860.0	864.09	872.61
820.13	826.1	836.61	841.9	851.15	852.09	860.1	864.10	872.62
820.19	827.0	836.62	842.00	851.16	852.10	860.2	864.11	872.63
820.20	827.1	836.63	842.01	851.19	852.11	860.3	864.12	872.64
820.21	828.0	836.64	842.02	851.20	852.12	860.4	864.13	872.69
820.22	828.1	836.69	842.09	851.21	852.13	860.5	864.14	872.71
820.30	829.0	837.0	842.10	851.22	852.14	861.00	864.15	872.72
820.31	829.1	837.1	842.11	851.23	852.15	861.01	864.19	872.73
820.32	830.0	838.00	842.12	851.24	852.16	861.02	865.00	872.74
820.8	830.1	838.01	842.13	851.25	852.19	861.03	865.01	872.79
820.9	831.00	838.02	842.19	851.26	852.20	861.10	865.02	872.8
821.00	831.01	838.03	843.0	851.29	852.21	861.11	865.03	872.9
821.01	831.02	838.04	843.1	851.30	852.22	861.12	865.04	873.0
821.10	831.03	838.05	843.8	851.31	852.23	861.13	865.09	873.1
821.11	831.04	838.06	843.9	851.32	852.24	861.20	865.10	873.20
821.20	831.09	838.09	844.0	851.33	852.25	861.21	865.11	873.22
821.21	831.10	838.10	844.1	851.34	852.26	861.22	865.12	873.23
821.22	831.11	838.11	844.2	851.35	852.29	861.30	865.13	873.29
821.23	831.12	838.12	844.3	851.36	852.30	861.31	865.14	873.30
821.29	831.13	838.13	844.8	851.39	852.31	861.32	865.19	873.31
821.30	831.14	838.14	844.9	851.40	852.32	862.0	866.00	873.32
821.31	831.19	838.15	845.00	851.41	852.33	862.1	866.01	873.33
821.32	832.00	838.16	845.01	851.42	852.34	862.21	866.02	873.39
821.33	832.01	838.19	845.02	851.43	852.35	862.22	866.03	873.40
821.39	832.02	839.00	845.03	851.44	852.36	862.29	866.10	873.41
822.0	832.03	839.01	845.09	851.45	852.39	862.31	866.11	873.42
822.1	832.04	839.02	845.10	851.46	852.40	862.32	866.12	873.43
823.00	832.09	839.03	845.11	851.49	852.41	862.39	866.13	873.44
823.01	832.10	839.04	845.12	851.50	852.42	862.8	867.0	873.49
823.02	832.11	839.05	845.13	851.51	852.43	862.9	867.1	873.50
823.10	832.12	839.06	845.19	851.52	852.44	863.0	867.2	873.51
823.11	832.13	839.07	846.0	851.53	852.45	863.1	867.3	873.52
823.12	832.14	839.08	846.1	851.54	852.46	863.20	867.4	873.53
823.20	832.19	839.10	846.2	851.55	852.49	863.21	867.5	873.54
823.21	832.2	839.11	846.3	851.56	852.50	863.29	867.6	873.59
823.22	833.00	839.12	846.8	851.59	852.51	863.30	867.7	873.60
823.30	833.01	839.13	846.9	851.60	852.52	863.31	867.8	873.61
823.31	833.02	839.14	847.0	851.61	852.53	863.39	867.9	873.62
823.32	833.03	839.15	847.1	851.62	852.54	863.40	868.00	873.63
823.40	833.04	839.16	847.2	851.63	852.55	863.41	868.01	873.64
823.41	833.05	839.17	847.3	851.64	852.56	863.42	868.02	873.65
823.42	833.09	839.18	847.4	851.65	852.59	863.43	868.03	873.69
823.80	833.10	839.20	847.9	851.66	853.00	863.44	868.04	873.70
823.81	833.11	839.21	848.0	851.69	853.01	863.45	868.09	873.71
823.82	833.12	839.30	848.1	851.70	853.02	863.46	868.10	873.72
823.90	833.13	839.31	848.2	851.71	853.03	863.49	868.11	873.73
823.91	833.14	839.40	848.3	851.72	853.04	863.50	868.12	873.74
823.92	833.15	839.41	848.40	851.73	853.05	863.51	868.13	873.75
824.0	833.19	839.42	848.41	851.74	853.06	863.52	868.14	873.79
824.1	834.00	839.49	848.42	851.75	853.09	863.53	868.19	873.8
824.2	834.01	839.50	848.49	851.76	853.10	863.54	869.0	873.9
824.3	834.02	839.51	848.5	851.79	853.11	863.55	869.1	874.00
824.4	834.10	839.52	848.8	851.80	853.12	863.56	870.0	874.01
824.5	834.11	839.59	848.9	851.81	853.13	863.59	870.1	874.02
824.6	834.12	839.61	850.0	851.82	853.14	863.80	870.2	874.10
824.7	835.00	839.69	850.11	851.83	853.15	863.81	870.3	874.11
824.8	835.01	839.71	850.12	851.84	853.16	863.82	870.4	874.12
824.9	835.02	839.79	850.2	851.85	853.19	863.83	870.8	874.2
825.0	835.03	839.8	850.3	851.86	854.00	863.84	870.9	874.3
825.1	835.10	839.9	850.4	851.89	854.01	863.85	871.0	874.4
825.20	835.11	840.0	850.5	851.90	854.02	863.89	871.1	874.5
825.21	835.12	840.1	850.9	851.91	854.03	863.90	871.2	874.8
825.22	835.13	840.2	851.00	851.92	854.04	863.91	871.3	874.9
825.23	836.0	840.3	851.01	851.93	854.05	863.92	871.4	

875.0	882.0	900.00	902.59	911.8	916.8	923.3	951.0	955.3
875.1	882.1	900.01	902.81	911.9	916.9	923.8	951.1	955.4
876.0	882.2	900.02	902.82	912.0	917.0	923.9	951.2	955.5
876.1	883.0	900.03	902.87	912.1	917.1	924.00	951.3	955.6
877.0	883.1	900.1	902.89	912.2	917.2	924.01	951.4	955.7
877.1	883.2	900.81	902.9	912.3	917.3	924.10	951.5	955.8
878.0	884.0	900.82	903.00	912.4	917.4	924.11	951.6	955.9
878.1	884.1	900.89	903.01	912.5	917.5	924.20	951.7	956.0
878.2	884.2	900.9	903.02	912.6	917.6	924.21	951.8	956.1
878.3	885.0	901.0	903.1	912.7	917.7	924.3	951.9	956.2
878.4	885.1	901.1	903.2	912.8	917.8	924.4	952.00	956.3
878.5	886.0	901.2	903.3	912.9	917.9	924.5	952.01	956.4
878.6	886.1	901.3	903.4	913.0	918.0	924.8	952.02	956.5
878.7	887.0	901.40	903.5	913.1	918.1	924.9	952.03	956.8
878.8	887.1	901.41	903.8	913.2	918.2	925.1	952.04	956.9
878.9	887.2	901.42	903.9	913.3	918.9	925.2	952.05	957.0
879.0	887.3	901.81	904.0	913.4	919.0	926.0	952.06	957.1
879.1	887.4	901.82	904.1	913.5	919.1	926.11	952.07	957.8
879.2	887.5	901.83	904.2	913.6	919.2	926.12	952.08	957.9
879.3	887.6	901.89	904.3	913.7	919.3	926.19	952.09	958.0
879.4	887.7	901.9	904.40	913.8	919.4	926.8	952.10	958.1
879.5	890.0	902.0	904.41	913.9	919.5	926.9	952.11	958.2
879.6	890.1	902.10	904.42	914.0	919.6	927.00	952.12	958.3
879.7	890.2	902.11	904.50	914.1	919.7	927.01	952.13	958.4
879.8	891.0	902.19	904.51	914.2	919.8	927.02	952.14	958.5
879.9	891.1	902.20	904.52	914.3	919.9	927.03	952.15	958.6
880.00	891.2	902.21	904.53	914.4	920	927.09	952.16	958.7
880.01	892.0	902.22	904.54	914.5	921.0	927.10	952.17	958.8
880.02	892.1	902.23	904.6	914.6	921.1	927.11	952.18	958.90
880.03	892.2	902.24	904.7	914.7	921.2	927.20	952.19	958.91
880.09	893.0	902.25	904.8	914.8	921.3	927.21	952.2	958.92
880.10	893.1	902.26	904.9	914.9	921.9	927.3	952.3	958.93
880.11	893.2	902.27	910.0	915.0	922.0	927.8	952.4	958.99
880.12	894.0	902.29	910.1	915.1	922.1	927.9	952.8	959.01
880.13	894.1	902.31	910.2	915.2	922.2	928.00	952.9	959.09
880.19	894.2	902.32	910.3	915.3	922.31	928.01	953.0	959.11
880.20	895.0	902.33	910.4	915.4	922.32	928.10	953.1	959.12
880.21	895.1	902.34	910.5	915.5	922.33	928.11	953.2	959.13
880.22	896.0	902.39	910.6	915.6	922.4	928.20	953.3	959.14
880.23	896.1	902.40	910.7	915.7	922.8	928.21	953.4	959.19
880.29	896.2	902.41	910.8	915.8	922.9	928.3	953.5	959.2
881.00	896.3	902.42	910.9	915.9	923.00	928.8	953.8	959.3
881.01	897.0	902.49	911.0	916.0	923.01	928.9	953.9	959.4
881.02	897.1	902.50	911.1	916.1	923.02	929.0	954.0	959.5
881.10	897.2	902.51	911.2	916.2	923.03	929.9	954.1	959.6
881.11	897.3	902.52	911.3	916.3	923.09	950.0	954.8	959.7
881.12	897.4	902.53	911.4	916.4	923.10	950.1	954.9	959.8
881.20	897.5	902.54	911.5	916.5	923.11	950.2	955.0	959.9
881.21	897.6	902.55	911.6	916.6	923.20	950.3	955.1	
881.22	897.7	902.56	911.7	916.7	923.21	950.9	955.2	

MDC 24: Multiple Significant Trauma

SURGICAL

MDC 24: Multiple Significant Trauma—SURGICAL

DRG 955   Craniotomy for Multiple Significant Trauma
          GMLOS 8.1   AMLOS 11.5   RW 5.4170

Select the principal diagnosis from the Trauma Diagnosis List located in DRG 963

AND

At least two different diagnoses from two different Significant Trauma Body Site Categories located in DRG 963

AND

Operating Room Procedures

01.21	Incision and drainage of cranial sinus
01.23	Reopening of craniotomy site
01.24	Other craniotomy
01.25	Other craniectomy
01.28	Placement of intracerebral catheter(s) via burr hole(s)
01.31	Incision of cerebral meninges
01.32	Lobotomy and tractotomy
01.39	Other incision of brain
01.41	Operations on thalamus
01.42	Operations on globus pallidus
01.51	Excision of lesion or tissue of cerebral meninges
01.52	Hemispherectomy
01.53	Lobectomy of brain
01.59	Other excision or destruction of lesion or tissue of brain
01.6	Excision of lesion of skull
02.01	Opening of cranial suture
02.02	Elevation of skull fracture fragments
02.03	Formation of cranial bone flap
02.04	Bone graft to skull
02.05	Insertion of skull plate
02.06	Other cranial osteoplasty
02.11	Simple suture of dura mater of brain
02.12	Other repair of cerebral meninges
02.13	Ligation of meningeal vessel
02.14	Choroid plexectomy
02.2*	Ventriculostomy
02.92	Repair of brain
02.94	Insertion or replacement of skull tongs or halo traction device
02.99	Other operations on skull, brain, and cerebral meninges
04.41	Decompression of trigeminal nerve root
38.81	Other surgical occlusion of intracranial vessels

OR

Select a principal diagnosis from one Significant Trauma Body Site Category located in DRG 963

AND

Two or more significant trauma diagnoses from different Significant Trauma Body Site Categories located in DRG 963

AND

Any operating room procedure listed above

DRG 956   Limb Reattachment, Hip and Femur Procedures for Multiple Significant Trauma
          GMLOS 6.9   AMLOS 8.4   RW 3.6372   T ☑

Select principal diagnosis from Trauma Diagnosis List located in DRG 963

AND

At least two different diagnoses from two different Significant Trauma Body Site Categories located in DRG 963

AND

Operating Room Procedures

00.70	Revision of hip replacement, both acetabular and femoral components
00.71	Revision of hip replacement, acetabular component
00.72	Revision of hip replacement, femoral component
00.73	Revision of hip replacement, acetabular liner and/or femoral head only
00.85	Resurfacing hip, total, acetabulum and femoral head
00.86	Resurfacing hip, partial, femoral head
00.87	Resurfacing hip, partial, acetabulum
77.05	Sequestrectomy of femur
77.25	Wedge osteotomy of femur
77.35	Other division of femur
77.85	Other partial ostectomy of femur
77.95	Total ostectomy of femur
78.05	Bone graft of femur
78.15	Application of external fixator device, femur
78.25	Limb shortening procedures, femur
78.35	Limb lengthening procedures, femur
78.45	Other repair or plastic operations on femur
78.55	Internal fixation of femur without fracture reduction
78.75	Osteoclasis of femur
78.95	Insertion of bone growth stimulator into femur
79.15	Closed reduction of fracture of femur with internal fixation
79.25	Open reduction of fracture of femur without internal fixation
79.35	Open reduction of fracture of femur with internal fixation
79.45	Closed reduction of separated epiphysis of femur
79.55	Open reduction of separated epiphysis of femur
79.65	Debridement of open fracture of femur
79.85	Open reduction of dislocation of hip
79.95	Unspecified operation on bone injury of femur
80.05	Arthrotomy for removal of prosthesis without replacement, hip
80.15	Other arthrotomy of hip
80.45	Division of joint capsule, ligament, or cartilage of hip
80.95	Other excision of hip joint
81.21	Arthrodesis of hip
81.40	Repair of hip, not elsewhere classified
81.51	Total hip replacement
81.52	Partial hip replacement
81.53	Revision of hip replacement, not otherwise specified
83.12	Adductor tenotomy of hip
84.23	Forearm, wrist, or hand reattachment
84.24	Upper arm reattachment
84.26	Foot reattachment
84.27	Lower leg or ankle reattachment
84.28	Thigh reattachment

OR

Select a principal diagnosis from one Significant Trauma Body Site Category located in DRG 963

AND

Two or more significant trauma diagnoses from different Significant Trauma Body Site Categories located in DRG 963

AND

Operating room procedure listed above

DRG 957   Other O.R. Procedures for Multiple Significant Trauma with MCC
          GMLOS 9.9   AMLOS 13.9   RW 6.4182

Select principal diagnosis from Trauma Diagnosis List located in DRG 963

AND

At least two different diagnoses from two different Significant Trauma Body Site Categories located in DRG 963

AND

T Transfer DRG   SP Special Payment   ☑ Optimization Potential   ▽ Targeted Potential   * Code Range   ● New DRG   ▲ Revised DRG Title

220   Valid 10/01/2012–09/30/2013   © 2012 OptumInsight, Inc.

Any operating room procedure from MDC 21

EXCLUDING

Pacemaker leads and devices and any procedure listed under DRGs 955 and 956
OR

Select a principal diagnosis from one Significant Trauma Body Site Category located in DRG 963
AND

Two or more significant trauma diagnoses from different Significant Trauma Body Site Categories located in DRG 963
AND

Any operating room procedure from MDC 21

EXCLUDING

Pacemaker leads and devices

All procedures listed under DRGs 955 and 956

DRG 958 Other O.R. Procedures for Multiple Significant Trauma with CC

| GMLOS 7.2 | AMLOS 9.1 | RW 3.9004 | ☑ |

Select principal diagnosis from Trauma Diagnosis List located in DRG 963
AND

At least two different diagnoses from two different Significant Trauma Body Site Categories located in DRG 963
AND

Any operating room procedure from MDC 21

EXCLUDING

Pacemaker leads and devices and any procedure listed under DRGs 955 and 956
OR

Select a principal diagnosis from one Significant Trauma Body Site Category located in DRG 963
AND

Two or more significant trauma diagnoses from different Significant Trauma Body Site Categories located in DRG 963
AND

Any operating room procedure from MDC 21

EXCLUDING

Pacemaker leads and devices

All procedures listed under DRGs 955 and 956

DRG 959 Other O.R. Procedures for Multiple Significant Trauma without CC/MCC

| GMLOS 4.7 | AMLOS 5.8 | RW 2.5646 | ☑ |

Select principal diagnosis from Trauma Diagnosis List located in DRG 963
AND

At least two different diagnoses from two different Significant Trauma Body Site Categories located in DRG 963
AND

Any operating room procedure from MDC 21

EXCLUDING

Pacemaker leads and devices and any procedure listed under DRGs 955 and 956

OR

Select a principal diagnosis from one Significant Trauma Body Site Category located in DRG 963
AND

Two or more significant trauma diagnoses from different Significant Trauma Body Site Categories located in DRG 963
AND

Any operating room procedure from MDC 21

EXCLUDING

Pacemaker leads and devices

All procedures listed under DRGs 955 and 956

MEDICAL

DRG 963 Other Multiple Significant Trauma with MCC

| GMLOS 5.8 | AMLOS 8.5 | RW 2.8483 | ☑ |

Select principal diagnosis from list of the Trauma Diagnosis List located below
WITH

At least two different diagnoses from two different Significant Trauma Body Site Categories located in DRG 963
OR

Select a principal diagnosis from one Significant Trauma Body Site Category
AND

Two or more significant trauma diagnoses from different Significant Trauma Body Site Categories located in DRG 963

Trauma Diagnosis

800.0*	Closed fracture of vault of skull without mention of intracranial injury
800.1*	Closed fracture of vault of skull with cerebral laceration and contusion
800.2*	Closed fracture of vault of skull with subarachnoid, subdural, and extradural hemorrhage
800.3*	Closed fracture of vault of skull with other and unspecified intracranial hemorrhage
800.4*	Closed fracture of vault of skull with intercranial injury of other and unspecified nature
800.5*	Open fracture of vault of skull without mention of intracranial injury
800.6*	Open fracture of vault of skull with cerebral laceration and contusion
800.7*	Open fracture of vault of skull with subarachnoid, subdural, and extradural hemorrhage
800.8*	Open fracture of vault of skull with other and unspecified intracranial hemorrhage
800.9*	Open fracture of vault of skull with intracranial injury of other and unspecified nature
801.0*	Closed fracture of base of skull without mention of intracranial injury
801.1*	Closed fracture of base of skull with cerebral laceration and contusion
801.2*	Closed fracture of base of skull with subarachnoid, subdural, and extradural hemorrhage
801.3*	Closed fracture of base of skull with other and unspecified intracranial hemorrhage
801.4*	Closed fracture of base of skull with intracranial injury of other and unspecified nature
801.5*	Open fracture of base of skull without mention of intracranial injury

---

801.6*	Open fracture of base of skull with cerebral laceration and contusion
801.7*	Open fracture of base of skull with subarachnoid, subdural, and extradural hemorrhage
801.8*	Open fracture of base of skull with other and unspecified intracranial hemorrhage
801.9*	Open fracture of base of skull with intracranial injury of other and unspecified nature
802.0	Nasal bones, closed fracture
802.1	Nasal bones, open fracture
802.2*	Mandible, closed fracture
802.3*	Mandible, open fracture
802.4	Malar and maxillary bones, closed fracture
802.5	Malar and maxillary bones, open fracture
802.6	Orbital floor (blow-out), closed fracture
802.7	Orbital floor (blow-out), open fracture
802.8	Other facial bones, closed fracture
802.9	Other facial bones, open fracture
803.0*	Other closed skull fracture without mention of intracranial injury
803.1*	Other closed skull fracture with cerebral laceration and contusion
803.2*	Other closed skull fracture with subarachnoid, subdural, and extradural hemorrhage
803.3*	Closed skull fracture with other and unspecified intracranial hemorrhage
803.4*	Other closed skull fracture with intracranial injury of other and unspecified nature
803.5*	Other open skull fracture without mention of intracranial injury
803.6*	Other open skull fracture with cerebral laceration and contusion
803.7*	Other open skull fracture with subarachnoid, subdural, and extradural hemorrhage
803.8*	Other open skull fracture with other and unspecified intracranial hemorrhage
803.9*	Other open skull fracture with intracranial injury of other and unspecified nature
804.0*	Closed fractures involving skull or face with other bones, without mention of intracranial injury
804.1*	Closed fractures involving skull or face with other bones, with cerebral laceration and contusion
804.2*	Closed fractures involving skull or face with other bones with subarachnoid, subdural, and extradural hemorrhage
804.3*	Closed fractures involving skull or face with other bones, with other and unspecified intracranial hemorrhage
804.4*	Closed fractures involving skull or face with other bones, with intracranial injury of other and unspecified nature
804.5*	Open fractures involving skull or face with other bones, without mention of intracranial injury
804.6*	Open fractures involving skull or face with other bones, with cerebral laceration and contusion
804.7*	Open fractures involving skull or face with other bones with subarachnoid, subdural, and extradural hemorrhage
804.8*	Open fractures involving skull or face with other bones, with other and unspecified intracranial hemorrhage
804.9*	Open fractures involving skull or face with other bones, with intracranial injury of other and unspecified nature
805.0*	Closed fracture of cervical vertebra without mention of spinal cord injury
805.1*	Open fracture of cervical vertebra without mention of spinal cord injury
805.2	Closed fracture of dorsal (thoracic) vertebra without mention of spinal cord injury
805.3	Open fracture of dorsal (thoracic) vertebra without mention of spinal cord injury
805.4	Closed fracture of lumbar vertebra without mention of spinal cord injury
805.5	Open fracture of lumbar vertebra without mention of spinal cord injury
805.6	Closed fracture of sacrum and coccyx without mention of spinal cord injury
805.7	Open fracture of sacrum and coccyx without mention of spinal cord injury
805.8	Closed fracture of unspecified part of vertebral column without mention of spinal cord injury
805.9	Open fracture of unspecified part of vertebral column without mention of spinal cord injury
806.0*	Closed fracture of cervical vertebra with spinal cord injury
806.1*	Open fracture of cervical vertebra with spinal cord injury
806.2*	Closed fracture of dorsal (thoracic) vertebra with spinal cord injury
806.3*	Open fracture of dorsal vertebra with spinal cord injury
806.4	Closed fracture of lumbar spine with spinal cord injury
806.5	Open fracture of lumbar spine with spinal cord injury
806.6*	Closed fracture of sacrum and coccyx with spinal cord injury
806.7*	Open fracture of sacrum and coccyx with spinal cord injury
806.8	Closed fracture of unspecified vertebra with spinal cord injury
806.9	Open fracture of unspecified vertebra with spinal cord injury
807.0*	Closed fracture of rib(s)
807.1*	Open fracture of rib(s)
807.2	Closed fracture of sternum
807.3	Open fracture of sternum
807.4	Flail chest
807.5	Closed fracture of larynx and trachea
807.6	Open fracture of larynx and trachea
808.0	Closed fracture of acetabulum
808.1	Open fracture of acetabulum
808.2	Closed fracture of pubis
808.3	Open fracture of pubis
808.4*	Closed fracture of other specified part of pelvis
808.5*	Open fracture of other specified part of pelvis
808.8	Unspecified closed fracture of pelvis
808.9	Unspecified open fracture of pelvis
809.0	Fracture of bones of trunk, closed
809.1	Fracture of bones of trunk, open
810.0*	Closed fracture of clavicle
810.1*	Open fracture of clavicle
811.0*	Closed fracture of scapula
811.1*	Open fracture of scapula
812.0*	Closed fracture of upper end of humerus
812.1*	Open fracture of upper end of humerus
812.2*	Closed fracture of shaft or unspecified part of humerus
812.3*	Open fracture of shaft or unspecified part of humerus
812.4*	Closed fracture of lower end of humerus
812.5*	Open fracture of lower end of humerus
813.0*	Closed fracture of upper end of radius and ulna
813.1*	Open fracture of upper end of radius and ulna
813.2*	Closed fracture of shaft of radius and ulna
813.3*	Open fracture of shaft of radius and ulna
813.4*	Closed fracture of lower end of radius and ulna
813.5*	Open fracture of lower end of radius and ulna
813.8*	Closed fracture of unspecified part of radius with ulna
813.9*	Open fracture of unspecified part of radius with ulna
814.0*	Closed fractures of carpal bones
814.1*	Open fractures of carpal bones
815.0*	Closed fracture of metacarpal bones
815.1*	Open fracture of metacarpal bones
816.0*	Closed fracture of one or more phalanges of hand
816.1*	Open fracture of one or more phalanges of hand
817.0	Multiple closed fractures of hand bones
817.1	Multiple open fractures of hand bones
818.0	Ill-defined closed fractures of upper limb
818.1	Ill-defined open fractures of upper limb
819.0	Multiple closed fractures involving both upper limbs, and upper limb with rib(s) and sternum
819.1	Multiple open fractures involving both upper limbs, and upper limb with rib(s) and sternum
820.0*	Closed transcervical fracture

MDC 24: Multiple Significant Trauma—MEDICAL

T *Transfer DRG*   SP *Special Payment*   ☑ *Optimization Potential*   ⊽ *Targeted Potential*   * *Code Range*   ● *New DRG*   ▲ *Revised DRG Title*

820.1*	Open transcervical fracture
820.2*	Closed pertrochanteric fracture of femur
820.3*	Open pertrochanteric fracture of femur
820.8	Closed fracture of unspecified part of neck of femur
820.9	Open fracture of unspecified part of neck of femur
821.0*	Closed fracture of shaft or unspecified part of femur
821.1*	Open fracture of shaft or unspecified part of femur
821.2*	Closed fracture of lower end of femur
821.3*	Open fracture of lower end of femur
822.0	Closed fracture of patella
822.1	Open fracture of patella
823.0*	Closed fracture of upper end of tibia and fibula
823.1*	Open fracture of upper end of tibia and fibula
823.2*	Closed fracture of shaft of tibia and fibula
823.3*	Open fracture of shaft of tibia and fibula
823.4*	Torus fracture of tibia and fibula
823.8*	Closed fracture of unspecified part of tibia and fibula
823.9*	Open fracture of unspecified part of tibia and fibula
824.0	Closed fracture of medial malleolus
824.1	Open fracture of medial malleolus
824.2	Closed fracture of lateral malleolus
824.3	Open fracture of lateral malleolus
824.4	Closed bimalleolar fracture
824.5	Open bimalleolar fracture
824.6	Closed trimalleolar fracture
824.7	Open trimalleolar fracture
824.8	Unspecified closed fracture of ankle
824.9	Unspecified open fracture of ankle
825.0	Closed fracture of calcaneus
825.1	Open fracture of calcaneus
825.2*	Closed fracture of other tarsal and metatarsal bones
825.3*	Open fracture of other tarsal and metatarsal bones
826.0	Closed fracture of one or more phalanges of foot
826.1	Open fracture of one or more phalanges of foot
827.0	Other, multiple and ill-defined closed fractures of lower limb
827.1	Other, multiple and ill-defined open fractures of lower limb
828.0	Multiple closed fractures involving both lower limbs, lower with upper limb, and lower limb(s) with rib(s) and sternum
828.1	Multiple fractures involving both lower limbs, lower with upper limb, and lower limb(s) with rib(s) and sternum, open
829.0	Closed fracture of unspecified bone
829.1	Open fracture of unspecified bone
830.0	Closed dislocation of jaw
830.1	Open dislocation of jaw
831.0*	Closed dislocation of shoulder, unspecified
831.1*	Open dislocation of shoulder
832.0*	Closed dislocation of elbow
832.1*	Open dislocation of elbow
832.2	Nursemaid's elbow
833.0*	Closed dislocation of wrist
833.1*	Open dislocation of wrist
834.0*	Closed dislocation of finger
834.1*	Open dislocation of finger
835.0*	Closed dislocation of hip
835.1*	Open dislocation of hip
836.0	Tear of medial cartilage or meniscus of knee, current
836.1	Tear of lateral cartilage or meniscus of knee, current
836.2	Other tear of cartilage or meniscus of knee, current
836.3	Closed dislocation of patella
836.4	Open dislocation of patella
836.5*	Other closed dislocation of knee
836.6*	Other open dislocation of knee
837.0	Closed dislocation of ankle
837.1	Open dislocation of ankle
838.0*	Closed dislocation of foot
838.1*	Open dislocation of foot
839.0*	Closed dislocation, cervical vertebra
839.1*	Open dislocation, cervical vertebra
839.2*	Closed dislocation, thoracic and lumbar vertebra
839.3*	Open dislocation, thoracic and lumbar vertebra
839.4*	Closed dislocation, other vertebra
839.5*	Open dislocation, other vertebra
839.6*	Closed dislocation, other location
839.71	Open dislocation, sternum
839.79	Open dislocation, other location
839.8	Closed dislocation, multiple and ill-defined sites
839.9	Open dislocation, multiple and ill-defined sites
840.0	Acromioclavicular (joint) (ligament) sprain and strain
840.1	Coracoclavicular (ligament) sprain and strain
840.2	Coracohumeral (ligament) sprain and strain
840.3	Infraspinatus (muscle) (tendon) sprain and strain
840.4	Rotator cuff (capsule) sprain and strain
840.5	Subscapularis (muscle) sprain and strain
840.6	Supraspinatus (muscle) (tendon) sprain and strain
840.7	Superior glenoid labrum lesions (SLAP)
840.8	Sprain and strain of other specified sites of shoulder and upper arm
840.9	Sprain and strain of unspecified site of shoulder and upper arm
841*	Sprains and strains of elbow and forearm
842*	Sprains and strains of wrist and hand
843*	Sprains and strains of hip and thigh
844*	Sprains and strains of knee and leg
845*	Sprains and strains of ankle and foot
846*	Sprains and strains of sacroiliac region
847*	Sprains and strains of other and unspecified parts of back
848*	Other and ill-defined sprains and strains
850.0	Concussion with no loss of consciousness
850.1*	Concussion with brief (less than one hour) loss of consciousness
850.2	Concussion with moderate (1-24 hours) loss of consciousness
850.3	Concussion with prolonged (more than 24 hours) loss of consciousness and return to pre-existing conscious level
850.4	Concussion with prolonged (more than 24 hours) loss of consciousness, without return to pre-existing conscious level
850.5	Concussion with loss of consciousness of unspecified duration
850.9	Unspecified concussion
851.0*	Cortex (cerebral) contusion without mention of open intracranial wound
851.1*	Cortex (cerebral) contusion with open intracranial wound
851.2*	Cortex (cerebral) laceration without mention of open intracranial wound
851.3*	Cortex (cerebral) laceration with open intracranial wound
851.4*	Cerebellar or brain stem contusion without mention of open intracranial wound
851.5*	Cerebellar or brain stem contusion with open intracranial wound
851.6*	Cerebellar or brain stem laceration without mention of open intracranial wound
851.7*	Cerebellar or brain stem laceration with open intracranial wound
851.8*	Other and unspecified cerebral laceration and contusion, without mention of open intracranial wound
851.9*	Other and unspecified cerebral laceration and contusion, with open intracranial wound
852*	Subarachnoid, subdural, and extradural hemorrhage, following injury
853*	Other and unspecified intracranial hemorrhage following injury
854*	Intracranial injury of other and unspecified nature
860*	Traumatic pneumothorax and hemothorax
861*	Injury to heart and lung
862*	Injury to other and unspecified intrathoracic organs
863.0	Stomach injury without mention of open wound into cavity
863.1	Stomach injury with open wound into cavity
863.2*	Small intestine injury without mention of open wound into cavity

MDC 24: Multiple Significant Trauma—MEDICAL

Surgical	Medical	CC Indicator	MCC Indicator	Procedure Proxy

863.3*	Small intestine injury with open wound into cavity
863.4*	Colon or rectal injury without mention of open wound into cavity
863.5*	Injury to colon or rectum with open wound into cavity
863.8*	Injury to other and unspecified gastrointestinal sites without mention of open wound into cavity
863.9*	Injury to other and unspecified gastrointestinal sites, with open wound into cavity
864.0*	Liver injury without mention of open wound into cavity
864.1*	Liver injury with open wound into cavity
865*	Injury to spleen
866*	Injury to kidney
867*	Injury to pelvic organs
868.0*	Injury to other intra-abdominal organs without mention of open wound into cavity
868.1*	Injury to other intra-abdominal organs with open wound into cavity
869*	Internal injury to unspecified or ill-defined organs
870*	Open wound of ocular adnexa
871*	Open wound of eyeball
872*	Open wound of ear
873*	Other open wound of head
874.0*	Open wound of larynx and trachea, without mention of complication
874.1*	Open wound of larynx and trachea, complicated
874.2	Open wound of thyroid gland, without mention of complication
874.3	Open wound of thyroid gland, complicated
874.4	Open wound of pharynx, without mention of complication
874.5	Open wound of pharynx, complicated
874.8	Open wound of other and unspecified parts of neck, without mention of complication
874.9	Open wound of other and unspecified parts of neck, complicated
875*	Open wound of chest (wall)
876*	Open wound of back
877*	Open wound of buttock
878*	Open wound of genital organs (external), including traumatic amputation
879*	Open wound of other and unspecified sites, except limbs
880*	Open wound of shoulder and upper arm
881*	Open wound of elbow, forearm, and wrist
882*	Open wound of hand except finger(s) alone
883*	Open wound of finger(s)
884*	Multiple and unspecified open wound of upper limb
885*	Traumatic amputation of thumb (complete) (partial)
886*	Traumatic amputation of other finger(s) (complete) (partial)
887*	Traumatic amputation of arm and hand (complete) (partial)
890*	Open wound of hip and thigh
891*	Open wound of knee, leg (except thigh), and ankle
892*	Open wound of foot except toe(s) alone
893*	Open wound of toe(s)
894*	Multiple and unspecified open wound of lower limb
895*	Traumatic amputation of toe(s) (complete) (partial)
896*	Traumatic amputation of foot (complete) (partial)
897*	Traumatic amputation of leg(s) (complete) (partial)
900.0*	Injury to carotid artery
900.1	Internal jugular vein injury
900.8*	Injury to other specified blood vessels of head and neck
900.9	Injury to unspecified blood vessel of head and neck
901.0	Thoracic aorta injury
901.1	Innominate and subclavian artery injury
901.2	Superior vena cava injury
901.3	Innominate and subclavian vein injury
901.4*	Pulmonary blood vessel injury
901.8*	Injury to other specified blood vessels of thorax
901.9	Injury to unspecified blood vessel of thorax
902*	Injury to blood vessels of abdomen and pelvis
903*	Injury to blood vessels of upper extremity
904.0	Common femoral artery injury
904.1	Superficial femoral artery injury
904.2	Femoral vein injury
904.3	Saphenous vein injury
904.4*	Popliteal blood vessel vein
904.5*	Tibial blood vessel(s) injury
904.6	Deep plantar blood vessels injury
904.7	Injury to specified blood vessels of lower extremity, other
904.8	Injury to unspecified blood vessel of lower extremity
904.9	Injury to blood vessels, unspecified site
910*	Superficial injury of face, neck, and scalp, except eye
911*	Superficial injury of trunk
912*	Superficial injury of shoulder and upper arm
913*	Superficial injury of elbow, forearm, and wrist
914*	Superficial injury of hand(s) except finger(s) alone
915*	Superficial injury of finger(s)
916*	Superficial injury of hip, thigh, leg, and ankle
917*	Superficial injury of foot and toe(s)
918*	Superficial injury of eye and adnexa
919*	Superficial injury of other, multiple, and unspecified sites
920	Contusion of face, scalp, and neck except eye(s)
921*	Contusion of eye and adnexa
922*	Contusion of trunk
923*	Contusion of upper limb
924*	Contusion of lower limb and of other and unspecified sites
925*	Crushing injury of face, scalp, and neck
926.0	Crushing injury of external genitalia
926.1*	Crushing injury of other specified sites of trunk
926.8	Crushing injury of multiple sites of trunk
926.9	Crushing injury of unspecified site of trunk
927.0*	Crushing injury of shoulder and upper arm
927.1*	Crushing injury of elbow and forearm
927.2*	Crushing injury of wrist and hand(s), except finger(s) alone
927.3	Crushing injury of finger(s)
927.8	Crushing injury of multiple sites of upper limb
927.9	Crushing injury of unspecified site of upper limb
928.0*	Crushing injury of hip and thigh
928.1*	Crushing injury of knee and lower leg
928.2*	Crushing injury of ankle and foot, excluding toe(s) alone
928.3	Crushing injury of toe(s)
928.8	Crushing injury of multiple sites of lower limb
928.9	Crushing injury of unspecified site of lower limb
929*	Crushing injury of multiple and unspecified sites
950*	Injury to optic nerve and pathways
951*	Injury to other cranial nerve(s)
952*	Spinal cord injury without evidence of spinal bone injury
953*	Injury to nerve roots and spinal plexus
953.1	Injury to dorsal nerve root
953.2	Injury to lumbar nerve root
953.3	Injury to sacral nerve root
953.4	Injury to brachial plexus
953.5	Injury to lumbosacral plexus
953.8	Injury to multiple sites of nerve roots and spinal plexus
953.9	Injury to unspecified site of nerve roots and spinal plexus
954.0	Injury to cervical sympathetic nerve, excluding shoulder and pelvic girdles
954.1	Injury to other sympathetic nerve, excluding shoulder and pelvic girdles
954.8	Injury to other specified nerve(s) of trunk, excluding shoulder and pelvic girdles
954.9	Injury to unspecified nerve of trunk, excluding shoulder and pelvic girdles
955.0	Injury to axillary nerve
955.1	Injury to median nerve
955.2	Injury to ulnar nerve
955.3	Injury to radial nerve
955.4	Injury to musculocutaneous nerve
955.5	Injury to cutaneous sensory nerve, upper limb
955.6	Injury to digital nerve, upper limb
955.7	Injury to other specified nerve(s) of shoulder girdle and upper limb

---

Ⓣ *Transfer DRG*   ⓈⓅ *Special Payment*   ☑ *Optimization Potential*   ▽ *Targeted Potential*   * *Code Range*   ● *New DRG*   ▲ *Revised DRG Title*

955.8	Injury to multiple nerves of shoulder girdle and upper limb
955.9	Injury to unspecified nerve of shoulder girdle and upper limb
956.0	Injury to sciatic nerve
956.1	Injury to femoral nerve
956.2	Injury to posterior tibial nerve
956.3	Injury to peroneal nerve
956.4	Injury to cutaneous sensory nerve, lower limb
956.5	Injury to other specified nerve(s) of pelvic girdle and lower limb
956.8	Injury to multiple nerves of pelvic girdle and lower limb
956.9	Injury to unspecified nerve of pelvic girdle and lower limb
957*	Injury to other and unspecified nerves
958.0	Air embolism as an early complication of trauma
958.1	Fat embolism as an early complication of trauma
958.2	Secondary and recurrent hemorrhage as an early complication of trauma
958.3	Posttraumatic wound infection not elsewhere classified
958.4	Traumatic shock
958.5	Traumatic anuria
958.6	Volkmann's ischemic contracture
958.7	Traumatic subcutaneous emphysema
958.8	Other early complications of trauma
958.90	Compartment syndrome, unspecified
958.91	Traumatic compartment syndrome of upper extremity
958.92	Traumatic compartment syndrome of lower extremity
958.93	Traumatic compartment syndrome of abdomen
958.99	Traumatic compartment syndrome of other sites
959.0*	Injury, other and unspecified, head, face, and neck
959.1*	Injury, other and unspecified, trunk
959.2	Injury, other and unspecified, shoulder and upper arm
959.3	Injury, other and unspecified, elbow, forearm, and wrist
959.4	Injury, other and unspecified, hand, except finger
959.5	Injury, other and unspecified, finger
959.6	Injury, other and unspecified, hip and thigh
959.7	Injury, other and unspecified, knee, leg, ankle, and foot
959.8	Injury, other and unspecified, other specified sites, including multiple
959.9	Injury, other and unspecified, unspecified site

Significant Trauma Body Site Category 1—Head

800.02	Closed fracture of vault of skull without mention of intracranial injury, brief (less than one hour) loss of consciousness
800.03	Closed fracture of vault of skull without mention of intracranial injury, moderate (1-24 hours) loss of consciousness
800.04	Closed fracture of vault of skull without mention of intracranial injury, prolonged (more than 24 hours) loss of consciousness and return to pre-existing conscious level
800.05	Closed fracture of vault of skull without mention of intracranial injury, prolonged (more than 24 hours) loss of consciousness, without return to pre-existing conscious level
800.10	Closed fracture of vault of skull with cerebral laceration and contusion, unspecified state of consciousness
800.12	Closed fracture of vault of skull with cerebral laceration and contusion, brief (less than one hour) loss of consciousness
800.13	Closed fracture of vault of skull with cerebral laceration and contusion, moderate (1-24 hours) loss of consciousness
800.14	Closed fracture of vault of skull with cerebral laceration and contusion, prolonged (more than 24 hours) loss of consciousness and return to pre-existing conscious level
800.15	Closed fracture of vault of skull with cerebral laceration and contusion, prolonged (more than 24 hours) loss of consciousness, without return to pre-existing conscious level
800.16	Closed fracture of vault of skull with cerebral laceration and contusion, loss of consciousness of unspecified duration
800.19	Closed fracture of vault of skull with cerebral laceration and contusion, unspecified concussion
800.20	Closed fracture of vault of skull with subarachnoid, subdural, and extradural hemorrhage, unspecified state of consciousness
800.22	Closed fracture of vault of skull with subarachnoid, subdural, and extradural hemorrhage, brief (less than one hour) loss of consciousness
800.23	Closed fracture of vault of skull with subarachnoid, subdural, and extradural hemorrhage, moderate (1-24 hours) loss of consciousness
800.24	Closed fracture of vault of skull with subarachnoid, subdural, and extradural hemorrhage, prolonged (more than 24 hours) loss of consciousness and return to pre-existing conscious level
800.25	Closed fracture of vault of skull with subarachnoid, subdural, and extradural hemorrhage, prolonged (more than 24 hours) loss of consciousness, without return to pre-existing conscious level
800.26	Closed fracture of vault of skull with subarachnoid, subdural, and extradural hemorrhage, loss of consciousness of unspecified duration
800.29	Closed fracture of vault of skull with subarachnoid, subdural, and extradural hemorrhage, unspecified concussion
800.30	Closed fracture of vault of skull with other and unspecified intracranial hemorrhage, unspecified state of consciousness
800.32	Closed fracture of vault of skull with other and unspecified intracranial hemorrhage, brief (less than one hour) loss of consciousness
800.33	Closed fracture of vault of skull with other and unspecified intracranial hemorrhage, moderate (1-24 hours) loss of consciousness
800.34	Closed fracture of vault of skull with other and unspecified intracranial hemorrhage, prolonged (more than 24 hours) loss of consciousness and return to pre-existing conscious level
800.35	Closed fracture of vault of skull with other and unspecified intracranial hemorrhage, prolonged (more than 24 hours) loss of consciousness, without return to pre-existing conscious level
800.36	Closed fracture of vault of skull with other and unspecified intracranial hemorrhage, loss of consciousness of unspecified duration
800.39	Closed fracture of vault of skull with other and unspecified intracranial hemorrhage, unspecified concussion
800.40	Closed fracture of vault of skull with intracranial injury of other and unspecified nature, unspecified state of consciousness
800.42	Closed fracture of vault of skull with intracranial injury of other and unspecified nature, brief (less than one hour) loss of consciousness
800.43	Closed fracture of vault of skull with intracranial injury of other and unspecified nature, moderate (1-24 hours) loss of consciousness
800.44	Closed fracture of vault of skull with intracranial injury of other and unspecified nature, prolonged (more than 24 hours) loss of consciousness and return to pre-existing conscious level
800.45	Closed fracture of vault of skull with intracranial injury of other and unspecified nature, prolonged (more than 24 hours) loss of consciousness, without return to pre-existing conscious level
800.46	Closed fracture of vault of skull with intracranial injury of other and unspecified nature, loss of consciousness of unspecified duration
800.49	Closed fracture of vault of skull with intracranial injury of other and unspecified nature, unspecified concussion
800.52	Open fracture of vault of skull without mention of intracranial injury, brief (less than one hour) loss of consciousness

MDC 24: Multiple Significant Trauma—MEDICAL

800.53	Open fracture of vault of skull without mention of intracranial injury, moderate (1-24 hours) loss of consciousness
800.54	Open fracture of vault of skull without mention of intracranial injury, prolonged (more than 24 hours) loss of consciousness and return to pre-existing conscious level
800.55	Open fracture of vault of skull without mention of intracranial injury, prolonged (more than 24 hours) loss of consciousness, without return to pre-existing conscious level
800.6*	Open fracture of vault of skull with cerebral laceration and contusion
800.7*	Open fracture of vault of skull with subarachnoid, subdural, and extradural hemorrhage
800.8*	Open fracture of vault of skull with other and unspecified intracranial hemorrhage
800.9*	Open fracture of vault of skull with intracranial injury of other and unspecified nature
801.02	Closed fracture of base of skull without mention of intracranial injury, brief (less than one hour) loss of consciousness
801.03	Closed fracture of base of skull without mention of intracranial injury, moderate (1-24 hours) loss of consciousness
801.04	Closed fracture of base of skull without mention of intracranial injury, prolonged (more than 24 hours) loss of consciousness and return to pre-existing conscious level
801.05	Closed fracture of base of skull without mention of intracranial injury, prolonged (more than 24 hours) loss of consciousness, without return to pre-existing conscious level
801.1*	Closed fracture of base of skull with cerebral laceration and contusion
801.2*	Closed fracture of base of skull with subarachnoid, subdural, and extradural hemorrhage
801.3*	Closed fracture of base of skull with other and unspecified intracranial hemorrhage
801.4*	Closed fracture of base of skull with intracranial injury of other and unspecified nature
801.52	Open fracture of base of skull without mention of intracranial injury, brief (less than one hour) loss of consciousness
801.53	Open fracture of base of skull without mention of intracranial injury, moderate (1-24 hours) loss of consciousness
801.54	Open fracture of base of skull without mention of intracranial injury, prolonged (more than 24 hours) loss of consciousness and return to pre-existing conscious level
801.55	Open fracture of base of skull without mention of intracranial injury, prolonged (more than 24 hours) loss of consciousness, without return to pre-existing conscious level
801.6*	Open fracture of base of skull with cerebral laceration and contusion
801.7*	Open fracture of base of skull with subarachnoid, subdural, and extradural hemorrhage
801.8*	Open fracture of base of skull with other and unspecified intracranial hemorrhage
801.9*	Open fracture of base of skull with intracranial injury of other and unspecified nature
803.02	Other closed skull fracture without mention of intracranial injury, brief (less than one hour) loss of consciousness
803.03	Other closed skull fracture without mention of intracranial injury, moderate (1-24 hours) loss of consciousness
803.04	Other closed skull fracture without mention of intracranial injury, prolonged (more than 24 hours) loss of consciousness and return to pre-existing conscious level
803.05	Other closed skull fracture without mention of intracranial injury, prolonged (more than 24 hours) loss of consciousness, without return to pre-existing conscious level
803.1*	Other closed skull fracture with cerebral laceration and contusion
803.2*	Other closed skull fracture with subarachnoid, subdural, and extradural hemorrhage
803.3*	Closed skull fracture with other and unspecified intracranial hemorrhage
803.4*	Other closed skull fracture with intracranial injury of other and unspecified nature
803.52	Other open skull fracture without mention of intracranial injury, brief (less than one hour) loss of consciousness
803.53	Other open skull fracture without mention of intracranial injury, moderate (1-24 hours) loss of consciousness
803.54	Other open skull fracture without mention of intracranial injury, prolonged (more than 24 hours) loss of consciousness and return to pre-existing conscious level
803.55	Other open skull fracture without mention of intracranial injury, prolonged (more than 24 hours) loss of consciousness, without return to pre-existing conscious level
803.6*	Other open skull fracture with cerebral laceration and contusion
803.7*	Other open skull fracture with subarachnoid, subdural, and extradural hemorrhage
803.8*	Other open skull fracture with other and unspecified intracranial hemorrhage
803.9*	Other open skull fracture with intracranial injury of other and unspecified nature
804.02	Closed fractures involving skull or face with other bones, without mention of intracranial injury, brief (less than one hour) loss of consciousness
804.03	Closed fractures involving skull or face with other bones, without mention of intracranial injury, moderate (1-24 hours) loss of consciousness
804.04	Closed fractures involving skull or face with other bones, without mention of intracranial injury, prolonged (more than 24 hours) loss of consciousness and return to pre-existing conscious level
804.05	Closed fractures involving skull of face with other bones, without mention of intracranial injury, prolonged (more than 24 hours) loss of consciousness, without return to pre-existing conscious level
804.06	Closed fractures involving skull of face with other bones, without mention of intracranial injury, loss of consciousness of unspecified duration
804.1*	Closed fractures involving skull or face with other bones, with cerebral laceration and contusion
804.2*	Closed fractures involving skull or face with other bones with subarachnoid, subdural, and extradural hemorrhage
804.3*	Closed fractures involving skull or face with other bones, with other and unspecified intracranial hemorrhage
804.40	Closed fractures involving skull or face with other bones, with intracranial injury of other and unspecified nature, unspecified state of consciousness
804.41	Closed fractures involving skull or face with other bones, with intracranial injury of other and unspecified nature, no loss of consciousness
804.42	Closed fractures involving skull or face with other bones, with intracranial injury of other and unspecified nature, brief (less than one hour) loss of consciousness
804.43	Closed fractures involving skull or face with other bones, with intracranial injury of other and unspecified nature, moderate (1-24 hours) loss of consciousness
804.44	Closed fractures involving skull or face with other bones, with intracranial injury of other and unspecified nature, prolonged (more than 24 hours) loss of consciousness and return to pre-existing conscious level

Ⓣ *Transfer DRG*   ˢᴾ *Special Payment*   ☑ *Optimization Potential*   ▽ *Targeted Potential*   * *Code Range*   ● *New DRG*   ▲ *Revised DRG Title*

226   Valid 10/01/2012-09/30/2013   © 2012 OptumInsight, Inc.

804.45	Closed fractures involving skull or face with other bones, with intracranial injury of other and unspecified nature, prolonged (more than 24 hours) loss of consciousness, without return to pre-existing conscious level
804.46	Closed fractures involving skull or face with other bones, with intracranial injury of other and unspecified nature, loss of consciousness of unspecified duration
804.52	Open fractures involving skull or face with other bones, without mention of intracranial injury, brief (less than one hour) loss of consciousness
804.53	Open fractures involving skull or face with other bones, without mention of intracranial injury, moderate (1-24 hours) loss of consciousness
804.54	Open fractures involving skull or face with other bones, without mention of intracranial injury, prolonged (more than 24 hours) loss of consciousness and return to pre-existing conscious level
804.55	Open fractures involving skull or face with other bones, without mention of intracranial injury, prolonged (more than 24 hours) loss of consciousness, without return to pre-existing conscious level
804.60	Open fractures involving skull or face with other bones, with cerebral laceration and contusion, unspecified state of consciousness
804.61	Open fractures involving skull or face with other bones, with cerebral laceration and contusion, no loss of consciousness
804.62	Open fractures involving skull or face with other bones, with cerebral laceration and contusion, brief (less than one hour) loss of consciousness
804.63	Open fractures involving skull or face with other bones, with cerebral laceration and contusion, moderate (1-24 hours) loss of consciousness
804.64	Open fractures involving skull or face with other bones, with cerebral laceration and contusion, prolonged (more than 24 hours) loss of consciousness and return to pre-existing conscious level
804.65	Open fractures involving skull or face with other bones, with cerebral laceration and contusion, prolonged (more than 24 hours) loss of consciousness, without return to pre-existing conscious level
804.66	Open fractures involving skull or face with other bones, with cerebral laceration and contusion, loss of consciousness of unspecified duration
804.7*	Open fractures involving skull or face with other bones with subarachnoid, subdural, and extradural hemorrhage
804.8*	Open fractures involving skull or face with other bones, with other and unspecified intracranial hemorrhage
804.9*	Open fractures involving skull or face with other bones, with intracranial injury of other and unspecified nature
850.2	Concussion with moderate (1-24 hours) loss of consciousness
850.3	Concussion with prolonged (more than 24 hours) loss of consciousness and return to pre-existing conscious level
850.4	Concussion with prolonged (more than 24 hours) loss of consciousness, without return to pre-existing conscious level
851.00	Cortex (cerebral) contusion without mention of open intracranial wound, state of consciousness unspecified
851.01	Cortex (cerebral) contusion without mention of open intracranial wound, no loss of consciousness
851.02	Cortex (cerebral) contusion without mention of open intracranial wound, brief (less than 1 hour) loss of consciousness
851.03	Cortex (cerebral) contusion without mention of open intracranial wound, moderate (1-24 hours) loss of consciousness
851.04	Cortex (cerebral) contusion without mention of open intracranial wound, prolonged (more than 24 hours) loss of consciousness and return to pre-existing conscious level
851.05	Cortex (cerebral) contusion without mention of open intracranial wound, prolonged (more than 24 hours) loss of consciousness, without return to pre-existing conscious level
851.06	Cortex (cerebral) contusion without mention of open intracranial wound, loss of consciousness of unspecified duration
851.09	Cortex (cerebral) contusion without mention of open intracranial wound, unspecified concussion
851.1*	Cortex (cerebral) contusion with open intracranial wound
851.2*	Cortex (cerebral) laceration without mention of open intracranial wound
851.3*	Cortex (cerebral) laceration with open intracranial wound
851.4*	Cerebellar or brain stem contusion without mention of open intracranial wound
851.5*	Cerebellar or brain stem contusion with open intracranial wound
851.6*	Cerebellar or brain stem laceration without mention of open intracranial wound
851.7*	Cerebellar or brain stem laceration with open intracranial wound
851.8*	Other and unspecified cerebral laceration and contusion, without mention of open intracranial wound
851.9*	Other and unspecified cerebral laceration and contusion, with open intracranial wound
852*	Subarachnoid, subdural, and extradural hemorrhage, following injury
853*	Other and unspecified intracranial hemorrhage following injury
854*	Intracranial injury of other and unspecified nature
900.01	Common carotid artery injury
900.02	External carotid artery injury
900.03	Internal carotid artery injury
900.1	Internal jugular vein injury
900.81	External jugular vein injury
900.82	Injury to multiple blood vessels of head and neck
925.1	Crushing injury of face and scalp
925.2	Crushing injury of neck

Significant Trauma Body Site Category 2—Chest

807.07	Closed fracture of seven ribs
807.08	Closed fracture of eight or more ribs
807.14	Open fracture of four ribs
807.15	Open fracture of five ribs
807.16	Open fracture of six ribs
807.17	Open fracture of seven ribs
807.18	Open fracture of eight or more ribs
807.19	Open fracture of multiple ribs, unspecified
807.3	Open fracture of sternum
807.4	Flail chest
807.5	Closed fracture of larynx and trachea
807.6	Open fracture of larynx and trachea
819.1	Multiple open fractures involving both upper limbs, and upper limb with rib(s) and sternum
839.71	Open dislocation, sternum
860*	Traumatic pneumothorax and hemothorax
861*	Injury to heart and lung
862*	Injury to other and unspecified intrathoracic organs
874.10	Open wound of larynx with trachea, complicated
874.11	Open wound of larynx, complicated
874.12	Open wound of trachea, complicated
901.0	Thoracic aorta injury
901.1	Innominate and subclavian artery injury
901.2	Superior vena cava injury
901.3	Innominate and subclavian vein injury
901.4*	Pulmonary blood vessel injury
901.83	Injury to multiple blood vessels of thorax
901.89	Injury to specified blood vessels of thorax, other
901.9	Injury to unspecified blood vessel of thorax
927.01	Crushing injury of scapular region

Surgical   *Medical*   *CC Indicator*   *MCC Indicator*   *Procedure Proxy*

MDC 24: Multiple Significant Trauma—MEDICAL

958.0	Air embolism as an early complication of trauma
958.1	Fat embolism as an early complication of trauma

Significant Trauma Body Site Category 3—Abdomen

863.0	Stomach injury without mention of open wound into cavity
863.1	Stomach injury with open wound into cavity
863.2*	Small intestine injury without mention of open wound into cavity
863.3*	Small intestine injury with open wound into cavity
863.4*	Colon or rectal injury without mention of open wound into cavity
863.5*	Injury to colon or rectum with open wound into cavity
863.81	Pancreas head injury without mention of open wound into cavity
863.82	Pancreas body injury without mention of open wound into cavity
863.83	Pancreas tail injury without mention of open wound into cavity
863.84	Pancreas injury, multiple and unspecified sites, without mention of open wound into cavity
863.85	Appendix injury without mention of open wound into cavity
863.89	Injury to other and unspecified gastrointestinal sites without mention of open wound into cavity
863.9*	Injury to other and unspecified gastrointestinal sites, with open wound into cavity
864*	Injury to liver
865*	Injury to spleen
868.02	Bile duct and gallbladder injury without mention of open wound into cavity
868.09	Injury to other and multiple intra-abdominal organs without mention of open wound into cavity
868.12	Bile duct and gallbladder injury, with open wound into cavity
868.13	Peritoneum injury with open wound into cavity
868.14	Retroperitoneum injury with open wound into cavity
868.19	Injury to other and multiple intra-abdominal organs, with open wound into cavity
902*	Injury to blood vessels of abdomen and pelvis
958.93	Traumatic compartment syndrome of abdomen

Significant Trauma Body Site Category 4—Kidney

866*	Injury to kidney
868.01	Adrenal gland injury without mention of open wound into cavity
868.11	Adrenal gland injury, with open wound into cavity

Significant Trauma Body Site Category 5—Urinary

867*	Injury to pelvic organs

Significant Trauma Body Site Category 6—Pelvis and Spine

805.6	Closed fracture of sacrum and coccyx without mention of spinal cord injury
805.7	Open fracture of sacrum and coccyx without mention of spinal cord injury
806.0*	Closed fracture of cervical vertebra with spinal cord injury
806.1*	Open fracture of cervical vertebra with spinal cord injury
806.2*	Closed fracture of dorsal (thoracic) vertebra with spinal cord injury
806.3*	Open fracture of dorsal vertebra with spinal cord injury
806.4	Closed fracture of lumbar spine with spinal cord injury
806.5	Open fracture of lumbar spine with spinal cord injury
806.60	Closed fracture of sacrum and coccyx with unspecified spinal cord injury
806.7*	Open fracture of sacrum and coccyx with spinal cord injury
806.8	Closed fracture of unspecified vertebra with spinal cord injury
806.9	Open fracture of unspecified vertebra with spinal cord injury
808*	Fracture of pelvis
809.1	Fracture of bones of trunk, open
839.0*	Closed dislocation, cervical vertebra
839.1*	Open dislocation, cervical vertebra

839.52	Open dislocation, sacrum
839.59	Open dislocation, other vertebra
868.03	Peritoneum injury without mention of open wound into cavity
868.04	Retroperitoneum injury without mention of open wound into cavity
926.11	Crushing injury of back
926.19	Crushing injury of other specified sites of trunk
926.8	Crushing injury of multiple sites of trunk
926.9	Crushing injury of unspecified site of trunk
952*	Spinal cord injury without evidence of spinal bone injury
953.5	Injury to lumbosacral plexus
953.8	Injury to multiple sites of nerve roots and spinal plexus
954.8	Injury to other specified nerve(s) of trunk, excluding shoulder and pelvic girdles
954.9	Injury to unspecified nerve of trunk, excluding shoulder and pelvic girdles

Significant Trauma Body Site Category 7—Upper Limb

812.1*	Open fracture of upper end of humerus
812.30	Open fracture of unspecified part of humerus
812.31	Open fracture of shaft of humerus
812.5*	Open fracture of lower end of humerus
813.1*	Open fracture of upper end of radius and ulna
813.3*	Open fracture of shaft of radius and ulna
813.5*	Open fracture of lower end of radius and ulna
813.9*	Open fracture of unspecified part of radius with ulna
818.1	Ill-defined open fractures of upper limb
831.1*	Open dislocation of shoulder
832.1*	Open dislocation of elbow
887*	Traumatic amputation of arm and hand (complete) (partial)
903*	Injury to blood vessels of upper extremity
927.0*	Crushing injury of shoulder and upper arm
927.1*	Crushing injury of elbow and forearm
927.8	Crushing injury of multiple sites of upper limb
927.9	Crushing injury of unspecified site of upper limb
953.4	Injury to brachial plexus
955.0	Injury to axillary nerve
955.1	Injury to median nerve
955.2	Injury to ulnar nerve
955.3	Injury to radial nerve
955.8	Injury to multiple nerves of shoulder girdle and upper limb
958.6	Volkmann's ischemic contracture
958.91	Traumatic compartment syndrome of upper extremity

Significant Trauma Body Site Category 8—Lower Limb

820*	Fracture of neck of femur
821*	Fracture of other and unspecified parts of femur
823.1*	Open fracture of upper end of tibia and fibula
823.3*	Open fracture of shaft of tibia and fibula
823.4*	Torus fracture of tibia and fibula
823.9*	Open fracture of unspecified part of tibia and fibula
828*	Multiple fractures involving both lower limbs, lower with upper limb, and lower limb(s) with rib(s) and sternum
835.1*	Open dislocation of hip
836.6*	Other open dislocation of knee
837.1	Open dislocation of ankle
896*	Traumatic amputation of foot (complete) (partial)
897*	Traumatic amputation of leg(s) (complete) (partial)
904.0	Common femoral artery injury
904.1	Superficial femoral artery injury
904.2	Femoral vein injury
904.4*	Popliteal blood vessel vein
904.5*	Tibial blood vessel(s) injury
904.7	Injury to specified blood vessels of lower extremity, other
926.12	Crushing injury of buttock
928.0*	Crushing injury of hip and thigh
928.1*	Crushing injury of knee and lower leg
928.8	Crushing injury of multiple sites of lower limb
928.9	Crushing injury of unspecified site of lower limb
956.0	Injury to sciatic nerve

T Transfer DRG　　SP Special Payment　　☑ Optimization Potential　　TP Targeted Potential　　* Code Range　　● New DRG　　▲ Revised DRG Title

956.1	Injury to femoral nerve
956.2	Injury to posterior tibial nerve
956.3	Injury to peroneal nerve
956.8	Injury to multiple nerves of pelvic girdle and lower limb
956.9	Injury to unspecified nerve of pelvic girdle and lower limb
958.92	Traumatic compartment syndrome of lower extremity

DRG 964 Other Multiple Significant Trauma with CC

GMLOS 4.4   **AMLOS** 5.5   **RW** 1.4975   ☑

Select principal diagnosis from list of the Trauma Diagnosis List under DRG 963

WITH

At least two different diagnoses from two different Significant Trauma Body Site Categories located in DRG 963

OR

Select a principal diagnosis from one Significant Trauma Body Site Category

AND

Two or more significant trauma diagnoses from different Significant Trauma Body Site Categories listed under DRG 963

DRG 965 Other Multiple Significant Trauma without CC/MCC

GMLOS 3.0   **AMLOS** 3.6   **RW** 0.9600   ☑

Select principal diagnosis from list of the Trauma Diagnosis List under DRG 963

WITH

At least two different diagnoses from two different Significant Trauma Body Site Categories located in DRG 963

OR

Select a principal diagnosis from one Significant Trauma Body Site Category

AND

Two or more significant trauma diagnoses from different Significant Trauma Body Site Categories listed under DRG 963

MDC 24: Multiple Significant Trauma—MEDICAL

Surgical	Medical	CC Indicator	MCC Indicator	Procedure Proxy

MDC 25
Human Immunodeficiency Virus Infections

Note: MDC 25 contains diagnosis code 042 only.

SURGICAL

DRG 969   HIV with Extensive O.R. Procedure with MCC
            GMLOS 12.0   AMLOS 16.3   RW 5.4815

Principal Diagnosis
042   Human immunodeficiency virus [HIV]
AND

Any operating room procedures excluding nonextensive operating room procedures (those procedures assigned to DRGs 987 - 989)
OR

Secondary Diagnosis
042   Human immunodeficiency virus [HIV]
WITH

Principal Diagnosis

Any major or significant HIV-related condition listed in DRG 974 or DRG 977
AND

Any operating room procedures excluding nonextensive operating room procedures (those procedures assigned to DRGs 987 - 989)

DRG 970   HIV with Extensive O.R. Procedure without MCC
            GMLOS 5.5   AMLOS 7.4   RW 2.6631   ☑

Principal Diagnosis
042   Human immunodeficiency virus [HIV]
AND

Any operating room procedures excluding nonextensive operating room procedures (those procedures assigned to DRGs 987 - 989)
OR

Secondary Diagnosis
042   Human immunodeficiency virus [HIV]
WITH

Principal Diagnosis

Any major or significant HIV-related condition listed in DRG 974 or DRG 977
AND

Any operating room procedures excluding nonextensive operating room procedures (those procedures assigned to DRGs 987 - 989)

MEDICAL

DRG 974   HIV with Major Related Condition with MCC
            GMLOS 6.8   AMLOS 9.6   RW 2.5943   ☑

Principal or Secondary Diagnosis
042   Human immunodeficiency virus [HIV]

AND

Major HIV-related Diagnosis
003.1   Salmonella septicemia
003.2*   Localized salmonella infections
003.8   Other specified salmonella infections
003.9   Unspecified salmonella infection
007.2   Coccidiosis
010*   Primary tuberculous infection
011*   Pulmonary tuberculosis
012*   Other respiratory tuberculosis
013*   Tuberculosis of meninges and central nervous system
014*   Tuberculosis of intestines, peritoneum, and mesenteric glands
015*   Tuberculosis of bones and joints
016*   Tuberculosis of genitourinary system
017*   Tuberculosis of other organs
018*   Miliary tuberculosis
031.2   Disseminated diseases due to other mycobacteria
031.8   Other specified diseases due to other mycobacteria
031.9   Unspecified diseases due to mycobacteria
038*   Septicemia
039*   Actinomycotic infections
046.3   Progressive multifocal leukoencephalopathy
046.7*   Other specified prion diseases of central nervous system
046.8   Other specified slow virus infection of central nervous system
046.9   Unspecified slow virus infection of central nervous system
049.8   Other specified non-arthropod-borne viral diseases of central nervous system
049.9   Unspecified non-arthropod-borne viral disease of central nervous system
053.0   Herpes zoster with meningitis
053.10   Herpes zoster with unspecified nervous system complication
053.11   Geniculate herpes zoster
053.12   Postherpetic trigeminal neuralgia
053.13   Postherpetic polyneuropathy
053.19   Other herpes zoster with nervous system complications
053.20   Herpes zoster dermatitis of eyelid
053.21   Herpes zoster keratoconjunctivitis
053.22   Herpes zoster iridocyclitis
053.29   Other ophthalmic herpes zoster complications
053.71   Otitis externa due to herpes zoster
053.79   Other specified herpes zoster complications
053.8   Unspecified herpes zoster complication
053.9   Herpes zoster without mention of complication
054.0   Eczema herpeticum
054.10   Unspecified genital herpes
054.11   Herpetic vulvovaginitis
054.12   Herpetic ulceration of vulva
054.13   Herpetic infection of penis
054.19   Other genital herpes
054.2   Herpetic gingivostomatitis
054.3   Herpetic meningoencephalitis
054.40   Unspecified ophthalmic complication herpes simplex
054.41   Herpes simplex dermatitis of eyelid
054.42   Dendritic keratitis
054.43   Herpes simplex disciform keratitis
054.44   Herpes simplex iridocyclitis
054.49   Herpes simplex with other ophthalmic complications
054.5   Herpetic septicemia
054.6   Herpetic whitlow
054.71   Visceral herpes simplex

054.72	Herpes simplex meningitis
054.73	Herpes simplex otitis externa
054.79	Other specified herpes simplex complications
054.8	Unspecified herpes simplex complication
054.9	Herpes simplex without mention of complication
058.21	Human herpesvirus 6 encephalitis
058.29	Other human herpesvirus encephalitis
078.5	Cytomegaloviral disease
112.0	Candidiasis of mouth
112.3	Candidiasis of skin and nails
112.4	Candidiasis of lung
112.5	Disseminated candidiasis
112.8*	Candidiasis of other specified sites
112.9	Candidiasis of unspecified site
114*	Coccidioidomycosis
115*	Histoplasmosis
117.5	Cryptococcosis
118	Opportunistic mycoses
127.2	Strongyloidiasis
130*	Toxoplasmosis
136.3	Pneumocystosis
136.8	Other specified infectious and parasitic diseases
176*	Kaposi's sarcoma
200.0*	Reticulosarcoma
200.2*	Burkitt's tumor or lymphoma
200.3*	Marginal zone lymphoma
200.4*	Mantle cell lymphoma
200.5*	Primary central nervous system lymphoma
200.6*	Anaplastic large cell lymphoma
200.7*	Large cell lymphoma
200.8*	Other named variants of lymphosarcoma and reticulosarcoma
202.7*	Peripheral T-cell lymphoma
202.8*	Other malignant lymphomas
290.1*	Presenile dementia
294.9	Unspecified persistent mental disorders due to conditions classified elsewhere
298.9	Unspecified psychosis
310.9	Unspecified nonpsychotic mental disorder following organic brain damage
323.81	Other causes of encephalitis and encephalomyelitis
323.82	Other causes of myelitis
323.9	Unspecified causes of encephalitis, myelitis, and encephalomyelitis
336.9	Unspecified disease of spinal cord
341.9	Unspecified demyelinating disease of central nervous system
348.3*	Encephalopathy, not elsewhere classified
348.9	Unspecified condition of brain
349.9	Unspecified disorders of nervous system
421.0	Acute and subacute bacterial endocarditis
421.9	Unspecified acute endocarditis
422.9*	Other and unspecified acute myocarditis
480.3	Pneumonia due to SARS-associated coronavirus
480.8	Pneumonia due to other virus not elsewhere classified
480.9	Unspecified viral pneumonia
481	Pneumococcal pneumonia (streptococcus pneumoniae pneumonia)
482*	Other bacterial pneumonia
486	Pneumonia, organism unspecified
488.01	Influenza due to identified avian influenza virus with pneumonia
488.11	Influenza due to identified 2009 H1N1 influenza virus with pneumonia
488.81	Influenza due to identified novel influenza A virus with pneumonia

DRG 975 **HIV with Major Related Condition with CC**
GMLOS 4.8   AMLOS 6.2   RW 1.3142   ☑

Select principal and secondary diagnoses listed under DRG 974

DRG 976 **HIV with Major Related Condition without CC/MCC**
GMLOS 3.3   AMLOS 4.1   RW 0.8416   ☑

Select principal and secondary diagnoses listed under DRG 974

DRG 977 **HIV with or without Other Related Condition**
GMLOS 3.5   AMLOS 4.7   RW 1.0517   ☑

Principal Diagnosis
042	Human immunodeficiency virus [HIV]

OR

Secondary Diagnosis of HIV Infection
042	Human immunodeficiency virus [HIV]

AND

Principal Diagnosis of Significant HIV-Related Condition
009*	Ill-defined intestinal infections
047.9	Unspecified viral meningitis
079.9*	Unspecified viral and chlamydial infections, in conditions classified elsewhere and of unspecified site
110*	Dermatophytosis
111*	Dermatomycosis, other and unspecified
260	Kwashiorkor
261	Nutritional marasmus
262	Other severe protein-calorie malnutrition
263*	Other and unspecified protein-calorie malnutrition
264*	Vitamin A deficiency
265*	Thiamine and niacin deficiency states
266*	Deficiency of B-complex components
267	Ascorbic acid deficiency
268*	Vitamin D deficiency
269*	Other nutritional deficiencies
276.5*	Volume depletion
279*	Disorders involving the immune mechanism
280*	Iron deficiency anemias
281*	Other deficiency anemias
283*	Acquired hemolytic anemias
284.8*	Other specified aplastic anemias
284.9	Unspecified aplastic anemia
285.9	Unspecified anemia
287.4*	Secondary thrombocytopenia
287.5	Unspecified thrombocytopenia
288.0*	Neutropenia
289.4	Hypersplenism
289.84	Heparin-induced thrombocytopenia [HIT]
289.9	Unspecified diseases of blood and blood-forming organs
357.0	Acute infective polyneuritis
357.9	Unspecified inflammatory and toxic neuropathy
362.1*	Other background retinopathy and retinal vascular changes
369*	Blindness and low vision
425.9	Unspecified secondary cardiomyopathy
516.30	Idiopathic interstitial pneumonia, not otherwise specified
516.35	Idiopathic lymphoid interstitial pneumonia
516.36	Cryptogenic organizing pneumonia
516.37	Desquamative interstitial pneumonia
516.8	Other specified alveolar and parietoalveolar pneumonopathies
527.9	Unspecified disease of the salivary glands
528.6	Leukoplakia of oral mucosa, including tongue
558.1	Gastroenteritis and colitis due to radiation
558.2	Toxic gastroenteritis and colitis
558.4*	Eosinophilic gastroenteritis and colitis
558.9	Other and unspecified noninfectious gastroenteritis and colitis

MDC 25: Human Immunodeficiency Virus Infections—MEDICAL

579.9	Unspecified intestinal malabsorption
580*	Acute glomerulonephritis
581*	Nephrotic syndrome
582*	Chronic glomerulonephritis
583*	Nephritis and nephropathy, not specified as acute or chronic
683	Acute lymphadenitis
709.9	Unspecified disorder of skin and subcutaneous tissue
711.0*	Pyogenic arthritis
711.9*	Unspecified infective arthritis
716.9*	Unspecified arthropathy
729.2	Unspecified neuralgia, neuritis, and radiculitis
779.34	Failure to thrive in newborn
780.60	Fever, unspecified
780.61	Fever presenting with conditions classified elsewhere
780.62	Postprocedural fever
780.63	Postvaccination fever
780.66	Febrile nonhemolytic transfusion reaction
780.7*	Malaise and fatigue
780.8	Generalized hyperhidrosis
782.1	Rash and other nonspecific skin eruption
783.2*	Abnormal loss of weight
783.4*	Lack of expected normal physiological development
785.6	Enlargement of lymph nodes
786.0*	Dyspnea and respiratory abnormalities
789.1	Hepatomegaly
789.2	Splenomegaly
799.4	Cachexia

Ⓣ *Transfer DRG*   ⓢ *Special Payment*   ☑ *Optimization Potential*   ▽ *Targeted Potential*   * *Code Range*   ● *New DRG*   ▲ *Revised DRG Title*

232   Valid 10/01/2012-09/30/2013   © 2012 OptumInsight, Inc.

DRGs Associated with All MDCs

SURGICAL

DRG 981   **Extensive O.R. Procedure Unrelated to Principal Diagnosis with MCC**

     GMLOS 10.5   AMLOS 13.7   RW 5.0270   ☐T

Discharges with all operating room procedures not listed for DRG 984 and DRG 987 that are unrelated to principal diagnosis

DRG 982   **Extensive O.R. Procedure Unrelated to Principal Diagnosis with CC**

     GMLOS 6.0   AMLOS 7.8   RW 2.8276   ☐T ☑

Discharges with all operating room procedures not listed for DRG 984 and DRG 987 that are unrelated to principal diagnosis

DRG 983   **Extensive O.R. Procedure Unrelated to Principal Diagnosis without CC/MCC**

     GMLOS 2.9   AMLOS 3.8   RW 1.7175   ☐T ☑

Discharges with all operating room procedures not listed for DRG 984 and DRG 987 that are unrelated to principal diagnosis

DRG 984   **Prostatic O.R. Procedure Unrelated to Principal Diagnosis with MCC**

     GMLOS 10.6   AMLOS 13.1   RW 3.6217

Operating Room Procedures

60.0	Incision of prostate
60.12	Open biopsy of prostate
60.15	Biopsy of periprostatic tissue
60.18	Other diagnostic procedures on prostate and periprostatic tissue
60.2*	Transurethral prostatectomy
60.61	Local excision of lesion of prostate
60.69	Other prostatectomy
60.8*	Incision or excision of periprostatic tissue
60.93	Repair of prostate
60.94	Control of (postoperative) hemorrhage of prostate
60.95	Transurethral balloon dilation of the prostatic urethra
60.96	Transurethral destruction of prostate tissue by microwave thermotherapy
60.97	Other transurethral destruction of prostate tissue by other thermotherapy
60.99	Other operations on prostate

With or without operating room procedures listed under DRG 987

DRG 985   **Prostatic O.R. Procedure Unrelated to Principal Diagnosis with CC**

     GMLOS 6.1   AMLOS 8.2   RW 2.0895   ☑

Select operating room procedures listed under DRG 984 with or without operating room procedures listed under DRG 987

DRG 986   **Prostatic O.R. Procedure Unrelated to Principal Diagnosis without CC/MCC**

     GMLOS 2.5   AMLOS 3.6   RW 1.0710   ☑

Select operating room procedures listed under DRG 984 with or without operating room procedures listed under DRG 987

DRG 987   **Nonextensive O.R. Procedure Unrelated to Principal Diagnosis with MCC**

     GMLOS 8.6   AMLOS 11.4   RW 3.3374   ☐T ☑

Operating Room Procedures

04.07	Other excision or avulsion of cranial and peripheral nerves
04.4*	Lysis of adhesions and decompression of cranial and peripheral nerves
04.99	Other operations on cranial and peripheral nerves
05.23	Lumbar sympathectomy
06.02	Reopening of wound of thyroid field
08.11	Biopsy of eyelid
08.2*	Excision or destruction of lesion or tissue of eyelid
08.3*	Repair of blepharoptosis and lid retraction
08.4*	Repair of entropion or ectropion
08.5*	Other adjustment of lid position
08.6*	Reconstruction of eyelid with flaps or grafts
08.7*	Other reconstruction of eyelid
08.9*	Other operations on eyelids
09.0	Incision of lacrimal gland
09.1*	Diagnostic procedures on lacrimal system
09.2*	Excision of lesion or tissue of lacrimal gland
09.3	Other operations on lacrimal gland
09.4*	Manipulation of lacrimal passage
09.5*	Incision of lacrimal sac and passages
09.6	Excision of lacrimal sac and passage
09.7*	Repair of canaliculus and punctum
09.8*	Fistulization of lacrimal tract to nasal cavity
09.9*	Other operations on lacrimal system
10.0	Removal of embedded foreign body from conjunctiva by incision
10.1	Other incision of conjunctiva
10.2*	Diagnostic procedures on conjunctiva
10.3*	Excision or destruction of lesion or tissue of conjunctiva
10.4*	Conjunctivoplasty
10.5	Lysis of adhesions of conjunctiva and eyelid
10.6	Repair of laceration of conjunctiva
10.9*	Other operations on conjunctiva
11.0	Magnetic removal of embedded foreign body from cornea
11.1	Incision of cornea
11.2*	Diagnostic procedures on cornea
11.3*	Excision of pterygium
11.4*	Excision or destruction of tissue or other lesion of cornea
11.5*	Repair of cornea
11.6*	Corneal transplant
11.7*	Other reconstructive and refractive surgery on cornea
11.9*	Other operations on cornea
12.0*	Removal of intraocular foreign body from anterior segment of eye
12.1*	Iridotomy and simple iridectomy
12.2*	Diagnostic procedures on iris, ciliary body, sclera, and anterior chamber
12.3*	Iridoplasty and coreoplasty
12.4*	Excision or destruction of lesion of iris and ciliary body
12.5*	Facilitation of intraocular circulation

12.61	Trephination of sclera with iridectomy
12.62	Thermocauterization of sclera with iridectomy
12.63	Iridencleisis and iridotasis
12.64	Trabeculectomy ab externo
12.65	Other scleral fistulization with iridectomy
12.66	Postoperative revision of scleral fistulization procedure
12.69	Other scleral fistulizing procedure
12.7*	Other procedures for relief of elevated intraocular pressure
12.8*	Operations on sclera
12.9*	Other operations on iris, ciliary body, and anterior chamber
13.0*	Removal of foreign body from lens
13.1*	Intracapsular extraction of lens
13.2	Extracapsular extraction of lens by linear extraction technique
13.3	Extracapsular extraction of lens by simple aspiration (and irrigation) technique
13.4*	Extracapsular extraction of lens by fragmentation and aspiration technique
13.5*	Other extracapsular extraction of lens
13.6*	Other cataract extraction
13.70	Insertion of pseudophakos, not otherwise specified
13.71	Insertion of intraocular lens prosthesis at time of cataract extraction, one-stage
13.72	Secondary insertion of intraocular lens prosthesis
13.8	Removal of implanted lens
13.9*	Other operations on lens
14.0*	Removal of foreign body from posterior segment of eye
14.1*	Diagnostic procedures on retina, choroid, vitreous, and posterior chamber
14.21	Destruction of chorioretinal lesion by diathermy
14.22	Destruction of chorioretinal lesion by cryotherapy
14.26	Destruction of chorioretinal lesion by radiation therapy
14.27	Destruction of chorioretinal lesion by implantation of radiation source
14.29	Other destruction of chorioretinal lesion
14.31	Repair of retinal tear by diathermy
14.32	Repair of retinal tear by cryotherapy
14.39	Other repair of retinal tear
14.4*	Repair of retinal detachment with scleral buckling and implant
14.5*	Other repair of retinal detachment
14.6	Removal of surgically implanted material from posterior segment of eye
14.7*	Operations on vitreous
14.9	Other operations on retina, choroid, and posterior chamber
15.0*	Diagnostic procedures on extraocular muscles or tendons
15.1*	Operations on one extraocular muscle involving temporary detachment from globe
15.2*	Other operations on one extraocular muscle
15.3	Operations on two or more extraocular muscles involving temporary detachment from globe, one or both eyes
15.4	Other operations on two or more extraocular muscles, one or both eyes
15.5	Transposition of extraocular muscles
15.6	Revision of extraocular muscle surgery
15.7	Repair of injury of extraocular muscle
15.9	Other operations on extraocular muscles and tendons
16.0*	Orbitotomy
16.1	Removal of penetrating foreign body from eye, not otherwise specified
16.22	Diagnostic aspiration of orbit
16.23	Biopsy of eyeball and orbit
16.29	Other diagnostic procedures on orbit and eyeball
16.3*	Evisceration of eyeball
16.4*	Enucleation of eyeball
16.5*	Exenteration of orbital contents
16.6*	Secondary procedures after removal of eyeball
16.7*	Removal of ocular or orbital implant
16.8*	Repair of injury of eyeball and orbit
16.92	Excision of lesion of orbit
16.93	Excision of lesion of eye, unspecified structure
16.98	Other operations on orbit
16.99	Other operations on eyeball
18.21	Excision of preauricular sinus
18.31	Radical excision of lesion of external ear
18.39	Other excision of external ear
18.5	Surgical correction of prominent ear
18.6	Reconstruction of external auditory canal
18.71	Construction of auricle of ear
18.72	Reattachment of amputated ear
18.79	Other plastic repair of external ear
18.9	Other operations on external ear
19.1*	Stapedectomy
19.4	Myringoplasty
19.9	Other repair of middle ear
20.01	Myringotomy with insertion of tube
20.2*	Incision of mastoid and middle ear
20.32	Biopsy of middle and inner ear
20.39	Other diagnostic procedures on middle and inner ear
20.51	Excision of lesion of middle ear
21.09	Control of epistaxis by other means
21.5	Submucous resection of nasal septum
21.62	Fracture of the turbinates
21.69	Other turbinectomy
21.72	Open reduction of nasal fracture
21.82	Closure of nasal fistula
21.83	Total nasal reconstruction
21.84	Revision rhinoplasty
21.85	Augmentation rhinoplasty
21.86	Limited rhinoplasty
21.87	Other rhinoplasty
21.88	Other septoplasty
21.89	Other repair and plastic operations on nose
21.99	Other operations on nose
22.63	Ethmoidectomy
24.4	Excision of dental lesion of jaw
24.5	Alveoloplasty
25.1	Excision or destruction of lesion or tissue of tongue
26.12	Open biopsy of salivary gland or duct
26.2*	Excision of lesion of salivary gland
26.3*	Sialoadenectomy
27.21	Biopsy of bony palate
27.22	Biopsy of uvula and soft palate
27.3*	Excision of lesion or tissue of bony palate
27.42	Wide excision of lesion of lip
27.43	Other excision of lesion or tissue of lip
27.49	Other excision of mouth
27.53	Closure of fistula of mouth
27.54	Repair of cleft lip
27.55	Full-thickness skin graft to lip and mouth
27.56	Other skin graft to lip and mouth
27.57	Attachment of pedicle or flap graft to lip and mouth
27.59	Other plastic repair of mouth
27.7*	Operations on uvula
27.92	Incision of mouth, unspecified structure
27.99	Other operations on oral cavity
28.11	Biopsy of tonsils and adenoids
28.2	Tonsillectomy without adenoidectomy
29.4	Plastic operation on pharynx
30.09	Other excision or destruction of lesion or tissue of larynx
31.98	Other operations on larynx
33.27	Closed endoscopic biopsy of lung
34.3	Excision or destruction of lesion or tissue of mediastinum
34.4	Excision or destruction of lesion of chest wall
37.89	Revision or removal of pacemaker device
38.00	Incision of vessel, unspecified site
38.09	Incision of lower limb veins
38.21	Biopsy of blood vessel
38.59	Ligation and stripping of lower limb varicose veins
38.86	Other surgical occlusion of abdominal arteries

Ⓣ Transfer DRG   ⓈⓅ Special Payment   ☑ Optimization Potential   ▽ Targeted Potential   * Code Range   ● New DRG   ▲ Revised DRG Title

234   Valid 10/01/2012-09/30/2013   © 2012 OptumInsight, Inc.

39.94	Replacement of vessel-to-vessel cannula
40.0	Incision of lymphatic structures
40.1*	Diagnostic procedures on lymphatic structures
40.21	Excision of deep cervical lymph node
40.23	Excision of axillary lymph node
40.24	Excision of inguinal lymph node
40.29	Simple excision of other lymphatic structure
40.3	Regional lymph node excision
43.49	Other destruction of lesion or tissue of stomach
44.15	Open biopsy of stomach
44.67	Laparoscopic procedures for creation of esophagogastric sphincteric competence
44.68	Laparoscopic gastroplasty
44.95	Laparoscopic gastric restrictive procedure
44.96	Laparoscopic revision of gastric restrictive procedure
44.97	Laparoscopic removal of gastric restrictive device(s)
44.98	(Laparoscopic) adjustment of size of adjustable gastric restrictive device
45.11	Transabdominal endoscopy of small intestine
45.21	Transabdominal endoscopy of large intestine
45.26	Open biopsy of large intestine
45.31	Other local excision of lesion of duodenum
45.32	Other destruction of lesion of duodenum
45.33	Local excision of lesion or tissue of small intestine, except duodenum
45.34	Other destruction of lesion of small intestine, except duodenum
45.41	Excision of lesion or tissue of large intestine
45.49	Other destruction of lesion of large intestine
46.41	Revision of stoma of small intestine
46.43	Other revision of stoma of large intestine
46.52	Closure of stoma of large intestine
48.25	Open biopsy of rectum
48.35	Local excision of rectal lesion or tissue
48.8*	Incision or excision of perirectal tissue or lesion
49.1*	Incision or excision of anal fistula
49.39	Other local excision or destruction of lesion or tissue of anus
49.44	Destruction of hemorrhoids by cryotherapy
49.45	Ligation of hemorrhoids
49.46	Excision of hemorrhoids
49.49	Other procedures on hemorrhoids
49.5*	Division of anal sphincter
49.6	Excision of anus
49.79	Other repair of anal sphincter
51.23	Laparoscopic cholecystectomy
51.99	Other operations on biliary tract
53.0*	Other unilateral repair of inguinal hernia
53.1*	Other bilateral repair of inguinal hernia
53.2*	Unilateral repair of femoral hernia
53.3*	Bilateral repair of femoral hernia
53.41	Other and open repair of umbilical hernia with graft or prosthesis
53.49	Other open umbilical herniorrhaphy
53.51	Incisional hernia repair
53.61	Other open incisional hernia repair with graft or prosthesis
53.69	Other and open repair of other hernia of anterior abdominal wall with graft or prosthesis
54.21	Laparoscopy
54.22	Biopsy of abdominal wall or umbilicus
54.29	Other diagnostic procedures on abdominal region
54.3	Excision or destruction of lesion or tissue of abdominal wall or umbilicus
54.4	Excision or destruction of peritoneal tissue
54.64	Suture of peritoneum
55.12	Pyelostomy
56.0	Transurethral removal of obstruction from ureter and renal pelvis
56.1	Ureteral meatotomy
56.2	Ureterotomy
56.39	Other diagnostic procedures on ureter

56.52	Revision of cutaneous uretero-ileostomy
57.22	Revision or closure of vesicostomy
57.33	Closed (transurethral) biopsy of bladder
57.39	Other diagnostic procedures on bladder
57.49	Other transurethral excision or destruction of lesion or tissue of bladder
57.59	Open excision or destruction of other lesion or tissue of bladder
57.82	Closure of cystostomy
57.91	Sphincterotomy of bladder
57.97	Replacement of electronic bladder stimulator
57.98	Removal of electronic bladder stimulator
58.0	Urethrotomy
58.1	Urethral meatotomy
58.5	Release of urethral stricture
58.99	Other operations on urethra and periurethral tissue
59.79	Other repair of urinary stress incontinence
61.2	Excision of hydrocele (of tunica vaginalis)
63.09	Other diagnostic procedures on spermatic cord, epididymis, and vas deferens
63.1	Excision of varicocele and hydrocele of spermatic cord
63.2	Excision of cyst of epididymis
63.3	Excision of other lesion or tissue of spermatic cord and epididymis
64.11	Biopsy of penis
64.2	Local excision or destruction of lesion of penis
64.49	Other repair of penis
64.92	Incision of penis
64.93	Division of penile adhesions
64.95	Insertion or replacement of non-inflatable penile prosthesis
64.96	Removal of internal prosthesis of penis
64.97	Insertion or replacement of inflatable penile prosthesis
64.98	Other operations on penis
64.99	Other operations on male genital organs
65.61	Other removal of both ovaries and tubes at same operative episode
66.2*	Bilateral endoscopic destruction or occlusion of fallopian tubes
66.3*	Other bilateral destruction or occlusion of fallopian tubes
66.92	Unilateral destruction or occlusion of fallopian tube
67.1*	Diagnostic procedures on cervix
67.2	Conization of cervix
67.3*	Other excision or destruction of lesion or tissue of cervix
68.15	Closed biopsy of uterine ligaments
68.16	Closed biopsy of uterus
68.29	Other excision or destruction of lesion of uterus
68.5*	Vaginal hysterectomy
69.01	Dilation and curettage for termination of pregnancy
69.09	Other dilation and curettage of uterus
69.51	Aspiration curettage of uterus for termination of pregnancy
69.52	Aspiration curettage following delivery or abortion
69.95	Incision of cervix
70.14	Other vaginotomy
70.23	Biopsy of cul-de-sac
70.24	Vaginal biopsy
70.29	Other diagnostic procedures on vagina and cul-de-sac
70.3*	Local excision or destruction of vagina and cul-de-sac
70.76	Hymenorrhaphy
71.09	Other incision of vulva and perineum
71.1*	Diagnostic procedures on vulva
71.22	Incision of Bartholin's gland (cyst)
71.23	Marsupialization of Bartholin's gland (cyst)
71.24	Excision or other destruction of Bartholin's gland (cyst)
71.29	Other operations on Bartholin's gland
71.3	Other local excision or destruction of vulva and perineum
71.4	Operations on clitoris
71.71	Suture of laceration of vulva or perineum
71.79	Other repair of vulva and perineum
76.11	Biopsy of facial bone
76.2	Local excision or destruction of lesion of facial bone

Surgical	Medical	CC Indicator	MCC Indicator	Procedure Proxy

77.38	Other division of tarsals and metatarsals
77.4*	Biopsy of bone
77.5*	Excision and repair of bunion and other toe deformities
77.6*	Local excision of lesion or tissue of bone
77.88	Other partial ostectomy of tarsals and metatarsals
77.98	Total ostectomy of tarsals and metatarsals
78.03	Bone graft of radius and ulna
78.6*	Removal of implanted device from bone
79.12	Closed reduction of fracture of radius and ulna with internal fixation
80.16	Other arthrotomy of knee
80.18	Other arthrotomy of foot and toe
80.26	Arthroscopy of knee
80.46	Division of joint capsule, ligament, or cartilage of knee
80.6	Excision of semilunar cartilage of knee
80.7*	Synovectomy
80.86	Other local excision or destruction of lesion of knee joint
80.88	Other local excision or destruction of lesion of joint of foot and toe
80.98	Other excision of joint of foot and toe
81.57	Replacement of joint of foot and toe
81.83	Other repair of shoulder
82.01	Exploration of tendon sheath of hand
82.09	Other incision of soft tissue of hand
82.11	Tenotomy of hand
82.21	Excision of lesion of tendon sheath of hand
82.29	Excision of other lesion of soft tissue of hand
82.41	Suture of tendon sheath of hand
82.45	Other suture of other tendon of hand
82.46	Suture of muscle or fascia of hand
83.0*	Incision of muscle, tendon, fascia, and bursa
83.13	Other tenotomy
83.19	Other division of soft tissue
83.21	Open biopsy of soft tissue
83.32	Excision of lesion of muscle
83.39	Excision of lesion of other soft tissue
83.5	Bursectomy
83.6*	Suture of muscle, tendon, and fascia
84.01	Amputation and disarticulation of finger
85.12	Open biopsy of breast
85.20	Excision or destruction of breast tissue, not otherwise specified
85.21	Local excision of lesion of breast
85.23	Subtotal mastectomy
85.50	Augmentation mammoplasty, not otherwise specified
85.53	Unilateral breast implant
85.54	Bilateral breast implant
85.93	Revision of implant of breast
85.94	Removal of implant of breast
85.95	Insertion of breast tissue expander
85.96	Removal of breast tissue expander (s)
85.99	Other operations on the breast
86.21	Excision of pilonidal cyst or sinus
86.25	Dermabrasion
86.4	Radical excision of skin lesion
86.60	Free skin graft, not otherwise specified
86.62	Other skin graft to hand
86.65	Heterograft to skin
86.82	Facial rhytidectomy
86.83	Size reduction plastic operation
86.84	Relaxation of scar or web contracture of skin
86.89	Other repair and reconstruction of skin and subcutaneous tissue
87.53	Intraoperative cholangiogram
92.27	Implantation or insertion of radioactive elements
95.04	Eye examination under anesthesia

DRG 988 **Nonextensive O.R. Procedure Unrelated to Principal Diagnosis with CC**

GMLOS 5.0   AMLOS 6.7   RW 1.8141   T ☑

Select operating room procedures listed under DRG 987

DRG 989 **Nonextensive O.R. Procedure Unrelated to Principal Diagnosis without CC/MCC**

GMLOS 2.2   AMLOS 3.0   RW 1.0150   T ☑

Select operating room procedures listed under DRG 987

DRG 999 **Ungroupable**

GMLOS 0.0   AMLOS 0.0   RW 0.0000

Discharges with invalid ICD-9-CM principal diagnosis, sex or discharge status field(s) missing or invalid and necessary for DRG assignment

---

T *Transfer DRG*   SP *Special Payment*   ☑ *Optimization Potential*   *Targeted Potential*   * *Code Range*   ● *New DRG*   ▲ *Revised DRG Title*

236   Valid 10/01/2012-09/30/2013   © 2012 OptumInsight, Inc.

Alphabetic Index to Diseases

765.22	24 completed weeks of gestation	**164**
765.23	25-26 completed weeks of gestation	**164**
765.24	27-28 completed weeks of gestation	**164 , 168**
765.25	29-30 completed weeks of gestation	**164 , 168**
765.26	31-32 completed weeks of gestation	**164 , 168**
765.27	33-34 completed weeks of gestation	**164 , 168**
765.28	35-36 completed weeks of gestation	**164 , 168**
765.29	37 or more completed weeks of gestation	**172 , 173**
039.2	Abdominal actinomycotic infection	**75**
441.4	Abdominal aneurysm without mention of rupture	**66**
441.3	Abdominal aneurysm, ruptured	**66**
902.0	Abdominal aorta injury	**167 , 171**
789.3*	Abdominal or pelvic swelling, mass, or lump	**78**
789.0*	Abdominal pain	**78**
789.4*	Abdominal rigidity	**79**
789.6*	Abdominal tenderness	**78**
786.7	Abnormal chest sounds	**54**
796.7*	Abnormal cytologic smear of anus and anal HPV	**79**
796.5	Abnormal finding on antenatal screening	**157 , 160**
790.2*	Abnormal glucose	**114**
374.43	Abnormal innervation syndrome of eyelid	**39**
781.0	Abnormal involuntary movements	**32**
783.2*	Abnormal loss of weight	**232**
648.84	Abnormal maternal glucose tolerance complicating pregnancy, childbirth, or the puerperium, postpartum condition or complication	**153**
648.83	Abnormal maternal glucose tolerance, antepartum	**155 , 157**
648.80	Abnormal maternal glucose tolerance, complicating pregnancy, childbirth, or the puerperium, unspecified as to episode of care	**160**
648.81	Abnormal maternal glucose tolerance, with delivery	**135 , 143 , 148**
648.82	Abnormal maternal glucose tolerance, with delivery, with current postpartum complication	**136 , 143 , 149**
795.0*	Abnormal Papanicolaou smear of cervix and cervical HPV	**128 , 131**
795.1*	Abnormal Papanicolaou smear of vagina and vaginal HPV	**128 , 131**
781.92	Abnormal posture	**32**
796.1	Abnormal reflex	**32**
786.4	Abnormal sputum	**54**
795.8*	Abnormal tumor markers	**214**
659.73	Abnormality in fetal heart rate or rhythm, antepartum condition or complication	**156 , 159**
659.71	Abnormality in fetal heart rate or rhythm, delivered, with or without mention of antepartum condition	**137 , 144 , 150**
659.70	Abnormality in fetal heart rate or rhythm, unspecified as to episode of care or not applicable	**137 , 144 , 150**
781.2	Abnormality of gait	**32**
790.0*	Abnormality of red blood cells	**176**
251.5	Abnormality of secretion of gastrin	**77**
251.4	Abnormality of secretion of glucagon	**115**
999.6*	ABO incompatibility reaction due to transfusion of blood or blood products	**168 , 172 , 176**
637*	Abortion, unspecified as to legality	**154**
915.0	Abrasion or friction burn of finger, without mention of infection	**108**
917.0	Abrasion or friction burn of foot and toe(s), without mention of infection	**108**
919.0	Abrasion or friction burn of other, multiple, and unspecified sites, without mention of infection	**108**
566	Abscess of anal and rectal regions	**79 , 167 , 171**
616.3	Abscess of Bartholin's gland	**128 , 131**
675.12	Abscess of breast associated with childbirth, delivered, with mention of postpartum complication	**140 , 142 , 148**
675.11	Abscess of breast associated with childbirth, delivered, with or without mention of antepartum condition	**140 , 142 , 148**
675.10	Abscess of breast associated with childbirth, unspecified as to episode of care	**162**
675.13	Abscess of breast, antepartum	**157 , 159**
675.14	Abscess of breast, postpartum condition or complication	**154**
569.5	Abscess of intestine	**76**
572.0	Abscess of liver	**167 , 171**
513*	Abscess of lung and mediastinum	**51 , 166 , 171**
254.1	Abscess of thymus	**165 , 169**
133*	Acariasis	**109**
998.2	Accidental puncture or laceration during procedure	**168 , 172 , 205**
791.6	Acetonuria	**114**
530.0	Achalasia and cardiospasm	**78**
726.71	Achilles bursitis or tendinitis	**98**
536.0	Achlorhydria	**78**
368.54	Achromatopsia	**39**
V45.71	Acquired absence of breast and nipple	**215**
V88.0*	Acquired absence of cervix and uterus	**129 , 132**
V45.72	Acquired absence of intestine (large) (small)	**215**
V88.2*	Acquired absence of joint	**216**
V45.73	Acquired absence of kidney	**215**
V45.78	Acquired absence of organ, eye	**40**
V45.77	Acquired absence of organ, genital organs	**125 , 129 , 132**
V45.76	Acquired absence of organ, lung	**54**
V45.74	Acquired absence of organ, other parts of urinary tract	**121**
V45.75	Acquired absence of organ, stomach	**215**
V88.1*	Acquired absence of pancreas	**216**
388.45	Acquired auditory processing disorder	**190**
429.71	Acquired cardiac septal defect	**69**
286.7	Acquired coagulation factor deficiency	**177**
368.55	Acquired color vision deficiencies	**38**
593.2	Acquired cyst of kidney	**121**
736.3*	Acquired deformities of hip	**100**
736.8*	Acquired deformities of other parts of limbs	**100**
735*	Acquired deformities of toe	**100**
738.3	Acquired deformity of chest and rib	**100**
736.9	Acquired deformity of limb, site unspecified	**100**
738.2	Acquired deformity of neck	**100**
738.0	Acquired deformity of nose	**47**
738.6	Acquired deformity of pelvis	**100**
736.71	Acquired equinovarus deformity	**100**
283.9	Acquired hemolytic anemia, unspecified	**165 , 170 , 176**
283*	Acquired hemolytic anemias	**231**
286.52	Acquired hemophilia	**177**
537.0	Acquired hypertrophic pyloric stenosis	**77**
244*	Acquired hypothyroidism	**115**

738.8	Acquired musculoskeletal deformity of other specified site	**100**
738.9	Acquired musculoskeletal deformity of unspecified site	**100**
738.4	Acquired spondylolisthesis	**97**
380.5*	Acquired stenosis of external ear canal	**47**
840.0	Acromioclavicular (joint) (ligament) sprain and strain	**223**
039.8	Actinomycotic infection of other specified sites	**186**
039.9	Actinomycotic infection of unspecified site	**186**
039*	Actinomycotic infections	**230**
341.2*	Acute (transverse) myelitis	**9 , 33**
341.21	Acute (transverse) myelitis in conditions classified elsewhere	**10**
341.20	Acute (transverse) myelitis NOS	**10**
571.1	Acute alcoholic hepatitis	**82**
303.0*	Acute alcoholic intoxication	**192**
006.0	Acute amebic dysentery without mention of abscess	**75**
518.84	Acute and chronic respiratory failure	**52 , 208**
421.0	Acute and subacute bacterial endocarditis	**65 , 231**
421*	Acute and subacute endocarditis	**166 , 170**
421.1	Acute and subacute infective endocarditis in diseases classified elsewhere	**65**
364.0*	Acute and subacute iridocyclitis	**39**
570	Acute and subacute necrosis of liver	**83 , 167 , 171**
540.0	Acute appendicitis with generalized peritonitis	**73 , 76**
540.1	Acute appendicitis with peritoneal abscess	**73 , 76**
540.9	Acute appendicitis without mention of peritonitis	**78**
466*	Acute bronchitis and bronchiolitis	**53**
519.11	Acute bronchospasm	**3**
375.31	Acute canaliculitis, lacrimal	**38**
517.3	Acute chest syndrome	**53**
415.0	Acute cor pulmonale	**69**
411.81	Acute coronary occlusion without myocardial infarction	**68**
595.0	Acute cystitis	**120 , 167 , 171**
375.01	Acute dacryoadenitis	**38**
375.32	Acute dacryocystitis	**38**
536.1	Acute dilatation of stomach	**78 , 166 , 171**
532.0*	Acute duodenal ulcer with hemorrhage	**76**
532.2*	Acute duodenal ulcer with hemorrhage and perforation	**76**
532.1*	Acute duodenal ulcer with perforation	**77**
532.31	Acute duodenal ulcer without mention of hemorrhage or perforation, with obstruction	**77**
532.30	Acute duodenal ulcer without mention of hemorrhage, perforation, or obstruction	**77**
333.72	Acute dystonia due to drugs	**32**
360.01	Acute endophthalmitis	**38**
464.3*	Acute epiglottitis	**3 , 46**
207.0*	Acute erythremia and erythroleukemia	**181 , 182**
446.1	Acute febrile mucocutaneous lymph node syndrome (MCLS)	**97**
531.0*	Acute gastric ulcer with hemorrhage	**76**
531.2*	Acute gastric ulcer with hemorrhage and perforation	**76**
531.1*	Acute gastric ulcer with perforation	**77**
531.31	Acute gastric ulcer without mention of hemorrhage or perforation, with obstruction	**77**
531.30	Acute gastric ulcer without mention of hemorrhage, perforation, or obstruction	**77**
535.01	Acute gastritis with hemorrhage	**76**
535.00	Acute gastritis without mention of hemorrhage	**78**
534.0*	Acute gastrojejunal ulcer with hemorrhage	**76**
534.2*	Acute gastrojejunal ulcer with hemorrhage and perforation	**76**
534.1*	Acute gastrojejunal ulcer with perforation	**77**
534.3*	Acute gastrojejunal ulcer without mention of hemorrhage or perforation	**77**

580*	Acute glomerulonephritis	**121 , 167 , 171 , 232**
999.84	Acute hemolytic transfusion reaction, incompatibility unspecified	**177**
999.34	Acute infection following transfusion, infusion, or injection of blood and blood products	**168 , 172 , 185 , 187**
357.0	Acute infective polyneuritis	**33 , 231**
584*	Acute kidney failure	**167 , 171**
669.32	Acute kidney failure following labor and delivery, delivered, with mention of postpartum complication	**139 , 142 , 147**
669.34	Acute kidney failure following labor and delivery, postpartum condition or complication	**154**
669.30	Acute kidney failure following labor and delivery, unspecified as to episode of care or not applicable	**139 , 146 , 151**
584.7	Acute kidney failure with lesion of medullary [papillary] necrosis	**119**
584.6	Acute kidney failure with lesion of renal cortical necrosis	**119**
584.5	Acute kidney failure with lesion of tubular necrosis	**119**
584.8	Acute kidney failure with other specified pathological lesion in kidney	**119**
584.9	Acute kidney failure, unspecified	**119**
464.01	Acute laryngitis, with obstruction	**3 , 46**
464.00	Acute laryngitis, without mention of obstruction	**3 , 46**
464.2*	Acute laryngotracheitis	**3 , 46**
208.0*	Acute leukemia of unspecified cell type	**181 , 182**
683	Acute lymphadenitis	**167 , 171 , 177 , 232**
204.0*	Acute lymphoid leukemia	**181 , 182**
383.0*	Acute mastoiditis	**46**
018.0*	Acute miliary tuberculosis	**186**
206.0*	Acute monocytic leukemia	**181 , 182**
205.0*	Acute myeloid leukemia	**181 , 182**
410.00	Acute myocardial infarction of anterolateral wall, episode of care unspecified	**68**
410.01	Acute myocardial infarction of anterolateral wall, initial episode of care	**56 , 65**
410.02	Acute myocardial infarction of anterolateral wall, subsequent episode of care	**68**
410.20	Acute myocardial infarction of inferolateral wall, episode of care unspecified	**68**
410.21	Acute myocardial infarction of inferolateral wall, initial episode of care	**56 , 65**
410.22	Acute myocardial infarction of inferolateral wall, subsequent episode of care	**68**
410.30	Acute myocardial infarction of inferoposterior wall, episode of care unspecified	**68**
410.31	Acute myocardial infarction of inferoposterior wall, initial episode of care	**56 , 65**
410.32	Acute myocardial infarction of inferoposterior wall, subsequent episode of care	**68**
410.10	Acute myocardial infarction of other anterior wall, episode of care unspecified	**68**
410.11	Acute myocardial infarction of other anterior wall, initial episode of care	**56 , 65**
410.12	Acute myocardial infarction of other anterior wall, subsequent episode of care	**68**
410.40	Acute myocardial infarction of other inferior wall, episode of care unspecified	**68**
410.41	Acute myocardial infarction of other inferior wall, initial episode of care	**56 , 65**
410.42	Acute myocardial infarction of other inferior wall, subsequent episode of care	**68**
410.50	Acute myocardial infarction of other lateral wall, episode of care unspecified	**68**
410.51	Acute myocardial infarction of other lateral wall, initial episode of care	**56 , 65**

410.52	Acute myocardial infarction of other lateral wall, subsequent episode of care **68**
410.80	Acute myocardial infarction of other specified sites, episode of care unspecified **69**
410.81	Acute myocardial infarction of other specified sites, initial episode of care **57 , 65**
410.82	Acute myocardial infarction of other specified sites, subsequent episode of care **69**
410.70	Acute myocardial infarction, subendocardial infarction, episode of care unspecified **69**
410.71	Acute myocardial infarction, subendocardial infarction, initial episode of care **57 , 65**
410.72	Acute myocardial infarction, subendocardial infarction, subsequent episode of care **69**
410.60	Acute myocardial infarction, true posterior wall infarction, episode of care unspecified **68**
410.61	Acute myocardial infarction, true posterior wall infarction, initial episode of care **57 , 65**
410.62	Acute myocardial infarction, true posterior wall infarction, subsequent episode of care **69**
410.90	Acute myocardial infarction, unspecified site, episode of care unspecified **69**
410.91	Acute myocardial infarction, unspecified site, initial episode of care **57 , 65**
410.92	Acute myocardial infarction, unspecified site, subsequent episode of care **69**
422*	Acute myocarditis **69**
422.0	Acute myocarditis in diseases classified elsewhere **166 , 170**
384.0*	Acute myringitis without mention of otitis media **46**
460	Acute nasopharyngitis (common cold) **3 , 46**
045.2*	Acute nonparalytic poliomyelitis **185**
381.0*	Acute nonsuppurative otitis media **46**
614.5	Acute or unspecified pelvic peritonitis, female **131**
730.0*	Acute osteomyelitis **96**
730.06	Acute osteomyelitis, lower leg **90**
730.08	Acute osteomyelitis, other specified site **87**
338.1*	Acute pain **214**
577.0	Acute pancreatitis **167 , 171**
045.0*	Acute paralytic poliomyelitis specified as bulbar **8 , 10 , 33**
614.3	Acute parametritis and pelvic cellulitis **131**
298.3	Acute paranoid reaction **190**
533.0*	Acute peptic ulcer, unspecified site, with hemorrhage **76**
533.2*	Acute peptic ulcer, unspecified site, with hemorrhage and perforation **76**
533.1*	Acute peptic ulcer, unspecified site, with perforation **77**
533.31	Acute peptic ulcer, unspecified site, without mention of hemorrhage and perforation, with obstruction **77**
533.30	Acute peptic ulcer, unspecified site, without mention of hemorrhage, perforation, or obstruction **77**
420*	Acute pericarditis **69**
420.0	Acute pericarditis in diseases classified elsewhere **166 , 170**
380.01	Acute perichondritis of pinna **100**
462	Acute pharyngitis **3 , 46**
045.1*	Acute poliomyelitis with other paralysis **8 , 10 , 33**
285.1	Acute posthemorrhagic anemia **165 , 170**
506.1	Acute pulmonary edema due to fumes and vapors **52**
415*	Acute pulmonary heart disease **166 , 170**
508.0	Acute pulmonary manifestations due to radiation **54 , 166 , 170**
590.1*	Acute pyelonephritis **167 , 171**
998.7	Acute reaction to foreign substance accidentally left during procedure, not elsewhere classified **168 , 172 , 205**
308*	Acute reaction to stress **189**

518.81	Acute respiratory failure **52 , 208**
391.1	Acute rheumatic endocarditis **67**
391.2	Acute rheumatic myocarditis **68**
391.0	Acute rheumatic pericarditis **68**
614.0	Acute salpingitis and oophoritis **131**
461*	Acute sinusitis **46**
463	Acute tonsillitis **3 , 46**
464.1*	Acute tracheitis **53**
045.9*	Acute unspecified poliomyelitis **8 , 10 , 33**
465*	Acute upper respiratory infections of multiple or unspecified sites **3 , 46**
557.0	Acute vascular insufficiency of intestine **167 , 171**
453.4*	Acute venous embolism and thrombosis of deep vessels of lower extremity **66**
453.8*	Acute venous embolism and thrombosis of other specified veins **67**
436	Acute, but ill-defined, cerebrovascular disease **20 , 166 , 170**
474.2	Adenoid vegetations **47**
091.4	Adenopathy due to secondary syphilis **177**
364.7*	Adhesions and disruptions of iris and ciliary body **39**
726.0	Adhesive capsulitis of shoulder **98**
309.0	Adjustment disorder with depressed mood **189**
309.3	Adjustment disorder with disturbance of conduct **189**
309.4	Adjustment disorder with mixed disturbance of emotions and conduct **189**
737.0	Adolescent postural kyphosis **87**
868.01	Adrenal gland injury without mention of open wound into cavity **115 , 228**
868.11	Adrenal gland injury, with open wound into cavity **115 , 228**
307.0	Adult onset fluency disorder **190**
V62.1	Adverse effects of work environment **215**
V58.7*	Aftercare following surgery to specified body systems, not elsewhere classified **214**
V54.2*	Aftercare for healing pathologic fracture **99**
V54.1*	Aftercare for healing traumatic fracture **99**
V54.0*	Aftercare involving internal fixation device **99**
V51*	Aftercare involving the use of plastic surgery **110**
136.0	Ainhum **187**
958.0	Air embolism as an early complication of trauma **51 , 167 , 171 , 225 , 228**
999.1	Air embolism as complication of medical care, not elsewhere classified **51 , 168 , 172**
291*	Alcohol-induced mental disorders **192**
571.2	Alcoholic cirrhosis of liver **82**
571.0	Alcoholic fatty liver **83**
535.31	Alcoholic gastritis with hemorrhage **76**
535.30	Alcoholic gastritis without mention of hemorrhage **78**
357.5	Alcoholic polyneuropathy **21**
315.01	Alexia **190**
784.61	Alexia and dyslexia **190**
733.7	Algoneurodystrophy **100**
518.6	Allergic bronchopulmonary aspergillosis **53**
477*	Allergic rhinitis **46**
708.0	Allergic urticaria **167 , 171**
995.3	Allergy, unspecified not elsewhere classified **204**
117.6	Allescheriosis (Petriellidiosis) **165 , 169**
282.43	Alpha thalassemia **165 , 170**
273.4	Alpha-1-antitrypsin deficiency **115**

331.0	Alzheimer's disease **19**
368.0*	Amblyopia ex anopsia **39**
006.5	Amebic brain abscess **8 , 10 , 33**
006.8	Amebic infection of other sites **186**
006.3	Amebic liver abscess **83**
006.4	Amebic lung abscess **51**
006.2	Amebic nondysenteric colitis **75**
006.6	Amebic skin ulceration **108**
673.13	Amniotic fluid embolism, antepartum condition or complication **157 , 159**
673.14	Amniotic fluid embolism, postpartum condition or complication **154**
673.10	Amniotic fluid embolism, unspecified as to episode of care **162**
673.12	Amniotic fluid embolism, with delivery, with mention of postpartum complication **139 , 142 , 147**
673.11	Amniotic fluid embolism, with delivery, with or without mention of antepartum condition **139 , 142 , 147**
997.6*	Amputation stump complication **101**
277.3*	Amyloidosis **97**
569.0	Anal and rectal polyp **79**
565*	Anal fissure and fistula **79**
564.6	Anal spasm **78**
664.61	Anal sphincter tear complicating delivery, not associated with third-degree perineal laceration, delivered, with or without mention of antepartum condition **138 , 145 , 151**
664.64	Anal sphincter tear complicating delivery, not associated with third-degree perineal laceration, postpartum condition or complication **153**
664.60	Anal sphincter tear complicating delivery, not associated with third-degree perineal laceration, unspecified as to episode of care or not applicable **138 , 145 , 151**
995.6*	Anaphylactic reaction due to food **204**
999.4*	Anaphylactic reaction due to serum **168 , 172 , 204**
200.6*	Anaplastic large cell lymphoma **231**
126*	Ancylostomiasis and necatoriasis **76**
776.6	Anemia of neonatal prematurity **164 , 169**
740*	Anencephalus and similar anomalies **32 , 167 , 171**
414.1*	Aneurysm and dissection of heart **69**
093.0	Aneurysm of aorta, specified as syphilitic **67**
442.3	Aneurysm of artery of lower extremity **66**
442.0	Aneurysm of artery of upper extremity **66**
414.10	Aneurysm of heart **166 , 170**
442.2	Aneurysm of iliac artery **66**
442.8*	Aneurysm of other specified artery **66**
442.1	Aneurysm of renal artery **121**
413.0	Angina decubitus **68**
569.84	Angiodysplasia of intestine (without mention of hemorrhage) **79**
569.85	Angiodysplasia of intestine with hemorrhage **76**
537.82	Angiodysplasia of stomach and duodenum (without mention of hemorrhage) **78**
537.83	Angiodysplasia of stomach and duodenum with hemorrhage **76**
995.1	Angioneurotic edema not elsewhere classified **204**
127.1	Anisakiasis **77**
379.41	Anisocoria **38**
367.3*	Anisometropia and aniseikonia **39**
845.0*	Ankle sprain and strain **100**
720.0	Ankylosing spondylitis **97**
718.5*	Ankylosis of joint **98**
378.85	Anomalies of divergence in binocular eye movement **40**
747.3*	Anomalies of pulmonary artery **68**
426.7	Anomalous atrioventricular excitation **166 , 170**

307.1	Anorexia nervosa **189**
348.1	Anoxic brain damage **32 , 166 , 170**
V28.4	Antenatal screening for fetal growth retardation using ultrasonics **215**
V28.5	Antenatal screening for isoimmunization **215**
641.33	Antepartum hemorrhage associated with coagulation defect, antepartum **155 , 157**
641.30	Antepartum hemorrhage associated with coagulation defects, unspecified as to episode of care **157 , 160**
641.31	Antepartum hemorrhage associated with coagulation defects, with delivery **135 , 141 , 146**
335*	Anterior horn cell disease **19**
032.2	Anterior nasal diphtheria **2 , 47**
022.3	Anthrax septicemia **187**
286.53	Antiphospholipid antibody with hemorrhagic disorder **177**
301.7	Antisocial personality disorder **189**
300.0*	Anxiety states **189**
441.9	Aortic aneurysm of unspecified site without mention of rupture **66**
441.5	Aortic aneurysm of unspecified site, ruptured **66**
447.7*	Aortic ectasia **66**
379.3*	Aphakia and other disorders of lens **40**
784.3	Aphasia **32**
541	Appendicitis, unqualified **78**
863.95	Appendix injury with open wound into cavity **79**
863.85	Appendix injury without mention of open wound into cavity **79 , 228**
078.7	Arenaviral hemorrhagic fever **186**
379.45	Argyll Robertson pupil, atypical **19**
733.91	Arrest of bone development or growth **100**
444*	Arterial embolism and thrombosis **166 , 170**
444.0*	Arterial embolism and thrombosis of abdominal aorta **66**
447.0	Arteriovenous fistula, acquired **66**
056.71	Arthritis due to rubella **98**
V45.4	Arthrodesis status **215**
711.7*	Arthropathy associated with helminthiasis **97**
711.6*	Arthropathy associated with mycoses **97**
711.4*	Arthropathy associated with other bacterial diseases **97**
713*	Arthropathy associated with other disorders classified elsewhere **98**
711.8*	Arthropathy associated with other infectious and parasitic diseases **97**
711.5*	Arthropathy associated with other viral diseases **98**
711.1*	Arthropathy associated with Reiter's disease and nonspecific urethritis **97**
711.2*	Arthropathy in Behcet's syndrome **97**
065*	Arthropod-borne hemorrhagic fever **185**
995.21	Arthus phenomenon **167 , 172**
718.07	Articular cartilage disorder, ankle and foot **99**
718.03	Articular cartilage disorder, forearm **99**
718.04	Articular cartilage disorder, hand **99**
718.09	Articular cartilage disorder, multiple sites **100**
718.08	Articular cartilage disorder, other specified site **100**
718.05	Articular cartilage disorder, pelvic region and thigh **100**
718.01	Articular cartilage disorder, shoulder region **99**
718.00	Articular cartilage disorder, site unspecified **100**
718.02	Articular cartilage disorder, upper arm **99**
V26.1	Artificial insemination **215**
V44*	Artificial opening status **215**
501	Asbestosis **53**
127.0	Ascariasis **77**

*Code Range

789.5*	Ascites **214**	
267	Ascorbic acid deficiency **114 , 231**	
733.4*	Aseptic necrosis of bone **98**	
117.3	Aspergillosis **165 , 169**	
799.0*	Asphyxia and hypoxemia **54**	
994.7	Asphyxiation and strangulation **205**	
770.86	Aspiration of postnatal stomach contents with respiratory symptoms **164 , 168**	
770.85	Aspiration of postnatal stomach contents without respiratory symptoms **164 , 168**	
493.91	Asthma, unspecified with status asthmaticus **166 , 170**	
367.2*	Astigmatism **39**	
646.53	Asymptomatic bacteriuria antepartum **155 , 158**	
646.54	Asymptomatic bacteriuria in pregnancy, postpartum condition or complication **152**	
646.50	Asymptomatic bacteriuria in pregnancy, unspecified as to episode of care **160**	
646.51	Asymptomatic bacteriuria in pregnancy, with delivery **135 ,142 , 148**	
646.52	Asymptomatic bacteriuria in pregnancy, with delivery, with current postpartum complication **135 , 142 , 148**	
V83.01	Asymptomatic hemophilia A carrier **216**	
V08	Asymptomatic human immunodeficiency virus (HIV) infection status **186**	
094.3	Asymptomatic neurosyphilis **33**	
454.9	Asymptomatic varicose veins **67**	
445.0*	Atheroembolism of extremities **66**	
445.81	Atheroembolism of kidney **121**	
445.89	Atheroembolism of other site **66**	
440.0	Atherosclerosis of aorta **66**	
440.3*	Atherosclerosis of bypass graft of extremities **66**	
440.2*	Atherosclerosis of native arteries of the extremities **66**	
440.24	Atherosclerosis of native arteries of the extremities with gangrene **166 , 170**	
440.8	Atherosclerosis of other specified arteries **66**	
440.1	Atherosclerosis of renal artery **121**	
333.71	Athetoid cerebral palsy **19**	
596.4	Atony of bladder **167 , 171**	
691*	Atopic dermatitis and related conditions **109**	
427.3*	Atrial fibrillation and flutter **68 , 166 , 170**	
426.0	Atrioventricular block, complete **166 , 170**	
535.11	Atrophic gastritis with hemorrhage **76**	
535.10	Atrophic gastritis without mention of hemorrhage **78**	
608.3	Atrophy of testis **125**	
799.51	Attention or concentration deficit **190**	
V55.7	Attention to artificial vagina **129 , 132**	
V55.3	Attention to colostomy **79**	
V55.5	Attention to cystostomy **121**	
V58.3*	Attention to dressings and sutures **215**	
V55.1	Attention to gastrostomy **79**	
V55.2	Attention to ileostomy **79**	
V55.4	Attention to other artificial opening of digestive tract **79**	
V55.6	Attention to other artificial opening of urinary tract **121**	
V55.8	Attention to other specified artificial opening **215**	
V55.0	Attention to tracheostomy **54**	
V55.9	Attention to unspecified artificial opening **215**	
299.0*	Autistic disorder **189**	
279.4*	Autoimmune disease, not elsewhere classified **97**	
283.0	Autoimmune hemolytic anemias **176**	
758.3*	Autosomal deletion syndromes **189**	

790.7	Bacteremia **167 , 171 , 187**
041*	Bacterial infection in conditions classified elsewhere and of unspecified site **186**
320*	Bacterial meningitis **9 , 10 , 33 , 165 , 170**
758.4	Balanced autosomal translocation in normal individual **214**
607.81	Balanitis xerotica obliterans **125**
607.1	Balanoposthitis **125**
649.23	Bariatric surgery status complicating pregnancy, childbirth, or the puerperium, antepartum condition or complication **155 , 158**
649.22	Bariatric surgery status complicating pregnancy, childbirth, or the puerperium, delivered, with mention of postpartum complication **136 , 143 , 149**
649.21	Bariatric surgery status complicating pregnancy, childbirth, or the puerperium, delivered, with or without mention of antepartum condition **136 , 143 , 149**
649.24	Bariatric surgery status complicating pregnancy, childbirth, or the puerperium, postpartum condition or complication **153**
649.20	Bariatric surgery status complicating pregnancy, childbirth, or the puerperium, unspecified as to episode of care or not applicable **161**
993.0	Barotrauma, otitic **46**
993.1	Barotrauma, sinus **46**
530.85	Barrett's esophagus **77**
136.1	Behcet's syndrome **97**
209.65	Benign carcinoid tumor of foregut, not otherwise specified **78**
209.67	Benign carcinoid tumor of hindgut, not otherwise specified **78**
209.66	Benign carcinoid tumor of midgut, not otherwise specified **78**
209.69	Benign carcinoid tumor of other sites **181 , 182**
209.61	Benign carcinoid tumor of the bronchus and lung **52**
209.64	Benign carcinoid tumor of the kidney **117 , 120**
209.63	Benign carcinoid tumor of the stomach **78**
209.62	Benign carcinoid tumor of the thymus **177**
209.60	Benign carcinoid tumor of unknown primary site **181 , 182**
209.5*	Benign carcinoid tumors of the appendix, large intestine, and rectum **78**
209.4*	Benign carcinoid tumors of the small intestine **78**
642.03	Benign essential hypertension antepartum **155 , 157**
642.00	Benign essential hypertension complicating pregnancy, childbirth, and the puerperium, unspecified as to episode of care **160**
642.01	Benign essential hypertension with delivery **135 , 141 , 146**
642.04	Benign essential hypertension, complicating pregnancy, childbirth, and the puerperium, postpartum condition or complication **152**
642.02	Benign essential hypertension, with delivery, with current postpartum complication **135 , 141 , 146**
402.11	Benign hypertensive heart disease with heart failure **56 , 65 , 166 , 170**
402.10	Benign hypertensive heart disease without heart failure **67**
348.2	Benign intracranial hypertension **34**
610*	Benign mammary dysplasias **107**
694.61	Benign mucous membrane pemphigoid with ocular involvement **40**
694.60	Benign mucous membrane pemphigoid without mention of ocular involvement **106**
227.0	Benign neoplasm of adrenal gland **115**
227.6	Benign neoplasm of aortic body and other paraganglia **19**
213.9	Benign neoplasm of bone and articular cartilage, site unspecified **100**
213.0	Benign neoplasm of bones of skull and face **3 , 100**
225*	Benign neoplasm of brain and other parts of nervous system **19**
217	Benign neoplasm of breast **109**
212.3	Benign neoplasm of bronchus and lung **52**

227.5	Benign neoplasm of carotid body **19**
211.3	Benign neoplasm of colon **78**
211.2	Benign neoplasm of duodenum, jejunum, and ileum **78**
216.2	Benign neoplasm of ear and external auditory canal **109**
227.9	Benign neoplasm of endocrine gland, site unspecified **115**
211.0	Benign neoplasm of esophagus **78**
224*	Benign neoplasm of eye **38**
216.1	Benign neoplasm of eyelid, including canthus **38**
210.3	Benign neoplasm of floor of mouth **48**
212.7	Benign neoplasm of heart **68**
210.8	Benign neoplasm of hypopharynx **47**
211.7	Benign neoplasm of islets of Langerhans **115**
223*	Benign neoplasm of kidney and other urinary organs **117 , 120**
212.1	Benign neoplasm of larynx **3 , 47**
210.0	Benign neoplasm of lip **48**
210*	Benign neoplasm of lip, oral cavity, and pharynx **3**
211.5	Benign neoplasm of liver and biliary passages **83**
213.7	Benign neoplasm of long bones of lower limb **100**
213.1	Benign neoplasm of lower jaw bone **3 , 48**
229.0	Benign neoplasm of lymph nodes **177**
210.2	Benign neoplasm of major salivary glands **47**
222*	Benign neoplasm of male genital organs **125**
212.5	Benign neoplasm of mediastinum **52**
212.0	Benign neoplasm of nasal cavities, middle ear, and accessory sinuses **3 , 47**
210.7	Benign neoplasm of nasopharynx **47**
210.4	Benign neoplasm of other and unspecified parts of mouth **48**
211.9	Benign neoplasm of other and unspecified site of the digestive system **78**
227.8	Benign neoplasm of other endocrine glands and related structures **115**
221*	Benign neoplasm of other female genital organs **128 , 131**
210.6	Benign neoplasm of other parts of oropharynx **47**
229.8	Benign neoplasm of other specified sites **181 , 183**
212.8	Benign neoplasm of other specified sites of respiratory and intrathoracic organs **52**
216.8	Benign neoplasm of other specified sites of skin **109**
220	Benign neoplasm of ovary **128 , 131**
211.6	Benign neoplasm of pancreas, except islets of Langerhans **83**
227.1	Benign neoplasm of parathyroid gland **115**
213.6	Benign neoplasm of pelvic bones, sacrum, and coccyx **100**
210.9	Benign neoplasm of pharynx, unspecified **47**
227.4	Benign neoplasm of pineal gland **19**
227.3	Benign neoplasm of pituitary gland and craniopharyngeal duct (pouch) **115**
212.4	Benign neoplasm of pleura **52**
211.4	Benign neoplasm of rectum and anal canal **78**
212.9	Benign neoplasm of respiratory and intrathoracic organs, site unspecified **52**
211.8	Benign neoplasm of retroperitoneum and peritoneum **78**
213.3	Benign neoplasm of ribs, sternum, and clavicle **52**
216.4	Benign neoplasm of scalp and skin of neck **109**
213.4	Benign neoplasm of scapula and long bones of upper limb **100**
213.8	Benign neoplasm of short bones of lower limb **100**
213.5	Benign neoplasm of short bones of upper limb **100**
216.0	Benign neoplasm of skin of lip **109**
216.7	Benign neoplasm of skin of lower limb, including hip **109**
216.3	Benign neoplasm of skin of other and unspecified parts of face **109**
216.5	Benign neoplasm of skin of trunk, except scrotum **109**
216.6	Benign neoplasm of skin of upper limb, including shoulder **109**
216.9	Benign neoplasm of skin, site unspecified **109**
211.1	Benign neoplasm of stomach **78**
212.6	Benign neoplasm of thymus **177**
226	Benign neoplasm of thyroid glands **3 , 115**
210.1	Benign neoplasm of tongue **48**
210.5	Benign neoplasm of tonsil **47**
212.2	Benign neoplasm of trachea **52**
229.9	Benign neoplasm of unspecified site **181 , 183**
213.2	Benign neoplasm of vertebral column, excluding sacrum and coccyx **87 , 100**
333.93	Benign shuddering attacks **32**
V62.82	Bereavement, uncomplicated **215**
282.44	Beta thalassemia **165 , 170**
552.02	Bilateral femoral hernia with obstruction **167 , 171**
868.02	Bile duct and gallbladder injury without mention of open wound into cavity **83 , 228**
868.12	Bile duct and gallbladder injury, with open wound into cavity **83 , 228**
571.6	Biliary cirrhosis **82**
779.32	Bilious vomiting in newborn **164 , 169**
791.4	Biliuria **83**
767.11	Birth trauma, epicranial subaponeurotic hemorrhage (massive) **164 , 168**
767.19	Birth trauma, other injuries to scalp **172 , 173**
921.0	Black eye, not otherwise specified **40**
867.1	Bladder and urethra injury with open wound into cavity **121**
867.0	Bladder and urethra injury without mention of open wound into cavity **121**
596.0	Bladder neck obstruction **167 , 171**
V43.5	Bladder replaced by other means **121**
116.0	Blastomycosis **165 , 169**
116*	Blastomycotic infection **186**
374.34	Blepharochalasis **39**
374.46	Blepharophimosis **39**
333.81	Blepharospasm **39**
369*	Blindness and low vision **39 , 231**
945.2*	Blisters with epidermal loss due to burn (second degree) of lower limb(s) **211**
946.2	Blisters with epidermal loss due to burn (second degree) of multiple specified sites **211**
942.2*	Blisters with epidermal loss due to burn (second degree) of trunk **210**
943.2*	Blisters with epidermal loss due to burn (second degree) of upper limb, except wrist and hand **211**
944.2*	Blisters with epidermal loss due to burn (second degree) of wrist(s) and hand(s) **211**
949.2	Blisters with epidermal loss due to burn (second degree), unspecified site **211**
941.24	Blisters, with epidermal loss due to burn (second degree) of chin **210**
941.21	Blisters, with epidermal loss due to burn (second degree) of ear (any part) **210**
941.22	Blisters, with epidermal loss due to burn (second degree) of eye (with other parts of face, head, and neck) **40**
941.20	Blisters, with epidermal loss due to burn (second degree) of face and head, unspecified site **210**
941.27	Blisters, with epidermal loss due to burn (second degree) of forehead and cheek **210**
941.23	Blisters, with epidermal loss due to burn (second degree) of lip(s) **210**
941.29	Blisters, with epidermal loss due to burn (second degree) of multiple sites (except with eye) of face, head, and neck **210**

*Code Range

© 2012 OptumInsight, Inc.

941.28	Blisters, with epidermal loss due to burn (second degree) of neck **210**
941.25	Blisters, with epidermal loss due to burn (second degree) of nose (septum) **210**
941.26	Blisters, with epidermal loss due to burn (second degree) of scalp (any part) **210**
V59.0*	Blood donor **215**
V58.2	Blood transfusion, without reported diagnosis **215**
V43.4	Blood vessel replaced by other means **69**
999.32	Bloodstream infection due to central venous catheter **69**
V85.4*	Body Mass Index 40 and over, adult **114**
V85.1	Body Mass Index between 19-24, adult **216**
V85.2*	Body Mass Index between 25-29, adult **216**
V85.3*	Body Mass Index between 30-39, adult **216**
V85.0	Body Mass Index less than 19, adult **216**
V85.5*	Body Mass Index, pediatric **216**
648.74	Bone and joint disorders of maternal back, pelvis, and lower limbs complicating pregnancy, childbirth, or the puerperium, postpartum condition or complication **153**
648.73	Bone and joint disorders of maternal back, pelvis, and lower limbs, antepartum **155 , 157**
648.70	Bone and joint disorders of maternal back, pelvis, and lower limbs, complicating pregnancy, childbirth, or the puerperium, unspecified as to episode of care **160**
648.71	Bone and joint disorders of maternal back, pelvis, and lower limbs, with delivery **135 , 143 , 148**
648.72	Bone and joint disorders of maternal back, pelvis, and lower limbs, with delivery, with current postpartum complication **135 , 143 , 148**
102.6	Bone and joint lesions due to yaws **97**
V59.2	Bone donor **101**
V59.3	Bone marrow donor **215**
V42.81	Bone marrow replaced by transplant **177**
V42.4	Bone replaced by transplant **101**
365.0*	Borderline glaucoma (glaucoma suspect) **39**
005.1	Botulism food poisoning **186**
723.4	Brachial neuritis or radiculitis NOS **21**
348.82	Brain death **21**
669.61	Breech extraction, without mention of indication, delivered, with or without mention of antepartum condition **139 , 146 , 151**
669.60	Breech extraction, without mention of indication, unspecified as to episode of care **139 , 146 , 151**
652.13	Breech or other malpresentation successfully converted to cephalic presentation, antepartum **155 , 158**
652.11	Breech or other malpresentation successfully converted to cephalic presentation, delivered **136 , 143 , 149**
652.10	Breech or other malpresentation successfully converted to cephalic presentation, unspecified as to episode of care **161**
652.23	Breech presentation without mention of version, antepartum **155 , 158**
652.21	Breech presentation without mention of version, delivered **136 , 143 , 149**
652.20	Breech presentation without mention of version, unspecified as to episode of care **161**
494*	Bronchiectasis **53**
506.0	Bronchitis and pneumonitis due to fumes and vapors **54**
490	Bronchitis, not specified as acute or chronic **53**
485	Bronchopneumonia, organism unspecified **53 , 166 , 170**
862.31	Bronchus injury with open wound into cavity **52**
862.21	Bronchus injury without mention of open wound into cavity **52**
023*	Brucellosis **186**
020.0	Bubonic plague **186**
453.0	Budd-Chiari syndrome **83**

745.0	Bulbus cordis anomalies and anomalies of cardiac septal closure, common truncus **67**
745.3	Bulbus cordis anomalies and anomalies of cardiac septal closure, common ventricle **67**
307.51	Bulimia nervosa **190**
727.1	Bunion **100**
200.2*	Burkitt's tumor or lymphoma **231**
200.21	Burkitt's tumor or lymphoma of lymph nodes of head, face, and neck **2**
948.11	Burn (any degree) involving 10-19% of body surface with third degree burn of 10-19% **207 , 208 , 209 , 210**
948.10	Burn (any degree) involving 10-19% of body surface with third degree burn of less than 10% or unspecified amount **211**
948.21	Burn (any degree) involving 20-29% of body surface with third degree burn of 10-19% **207 , 209**
948.22	Burn (any degree) involving 20-29% of body surface with third degree burn of 20-29% **207 , 209**
948.20	Burn (any degree) involving 20-29% of body surface with third degree burn of less than 10% or unspecified amount **211**
948.31	Burn (any degree) involving 30-39% of body surface with third degree burn of 10-19% **207 , 209**
948.32	Burn (any degree) involving 30-39% of body surface with third degree burn of 20-29% **207 , 209**
948.33	Burn (any degree) involving 30-39% of body surface with third degree burn of 30-39% **207 , 209**
948.30	Burn (any degree) involving 30-39% of body surface with third degree burn of less than 10% or unspecified amount **211**
948.41	Burn (any degree) involving 40-49% of body surface with third degree burn of 10-19% **207 , 209**
948.42	Burn (any degree) involving 40-49% of body surface with third degree burn of 20-29% **207 , 209**
948.43	Burn (any degree) involving 40-49% of body surface with third degree burn of 30-39% **207 , 209**
948.44	Burn (any degree) involving 40-49% of body surface with third degree burn of 40-49% **207 , 209**
948.40	Burn (any degree) involving 40-49% of body surface with third degree burn of less than 10% or unspecified amount **211**
948.51	Burn (any degree) involving 50-59% of body surface with third degree burn of 10-19% **207 , 209**
948.52	Burn (any degree) involving 50-59% of body surface with third degree burn of 20-29% **207 , 209**
948.53	Burn (any degree) involving 50-59% of body surface with third degree burn of 30-39% **207 , 209**
948.54	Burn (any degree) involving 50-59% of body surface with third degree burn of 40-49% **207 , 209**
948.55	Burn (any degree) involving 50-59% of body surface with third degree burn of 50-59% **207 , 209**
948.50	Burn (any degree) involving 50-59% of body surface with third degree burn of less than 10% or unspecified amount **211**
948.61	Burn (any degree) involving 60-69% of body surface with third degree burn of 10-19% **207 , 209**
948.62	Burn (any degree) involving 60-69% of body surface with third degree burn of 20-29% **207 , 209**
948.63	Burn (any degree) involving 60-69% of body surface with third degree burn of 30-39% **207 , 209**
948.64	Burn (any degree) involving 60-69% of body surface with third degree burn of 40-49% **207 , 209**
948.65	Burn (any degree) involving 60-69% of body surface with third degree burn of 50-59% **207 , 209**
948.66	Burn (any degree) involving 60-69% of body surface with third degree burn of 60-69% **207 , 209**
948.60	Burn (any degree) involving 60-69% of body surface with third degree burn of less than 10% or unspecified amount **211**
948.71	Burn (any degree) involving 70-79% of body surface with third degree burn of 10-19% **207 , 209**

948.72	Burn (any degree) involving 70-79% of body surface with third degree burn of 20-29% **207 , 209**
948.73	Burn (any degree) involving 70-79% of body surface with third degree burn of 30-39% **207 , 209**
948.74	Burn (any degree) involving 70-79% of body surface with third degree burn of 40-49% **207 , 209**
948.75	Burn (any degree) involving 70-79% of body surface with third degree burn of 50-59% **207 , 209**
948.76	Burn (any degree) involving 70-79% of body surface with third degree burn of 60-69% **207 , 209**
948.77	Burn (any degree) involving 70-79% of body surface with third degree burn of 70-79% **207 , 209**
948.70	Burn (any degree) involving 70-79% of body surface with third degree burn of less than 10% or unspecified amount **211**
948.81	Burn (any degree) involving 80-89% of body surface with third degree burn of 10-19% **207 , 209**
948.82	Burn (any degree) involving 80-89% of body surface with third degree burn of 20-29% **208 , 209**
948.83	Burn (any degree) involving 80-89% of body surface with third degree burn of 30-39% **208 , 209**
948.84	Burn (any degree) involving 80-89% of body surface with third degree burn of 40-49% **208 , 210**
948.85	Burn (any degree) involving 80-89% of body surface with third degree burn of 50-59% **208 , 210**
948.86	Burn (any degree) involving 80-89% of body surface with third degree burn of 60-69% **208 , 210**
948.87	Burn (any degree) involving 80-89% of body surface with third degree burn of 70-79% **208 , 210**
948.88	Burn (any degree) involving 80-89% of body surface with third degree burn of 80-89% **208 , 210**
948.80	Burn (any degree) involving 80-89% of body surface with third degree burn of less than 10% or unspecified amount **211**
948.91	Burn (any degree) involving 90% or more of body surface with third degree burn of 10-19% **208 , 210**
948.92	Burn (any degree) involving 90% or more of body surface with third degree burn of 20-29% **208 , 210**
948.93	Burn (any degree) involving 90% or more of body surface with third degree burn of 30-39% **208 , 210**
948.94	Burn (any degree) involving 90% or more of body surface with third degree burn of 40-49% **208 , 210**
948.95	Burn (any degree) involving 90% or more of body surface with third degree burn of 50-59% **208 , 210**
948.96	Burn (any degree) involving 90% or more of body surface with third degree burn of 60-69% **208 , 210**
948.97	Burn (any degree) involving 90% or more of body surface with third degree burn of 70-79% **208 , 210**
948.98	Burn (any degree) involving 90% or more of body surface with third degree burn of 80-89% **208 , 210**
948.99	Burn (any degree) involving 90% or more of body surface with third degree burn of 90% or more of body surface **208 , 210**
948.90	Burn (any degree) involving 90% or more of body surface with third degree burn of less than 10% or unspecified amount **211**
948.00	Burn (any degree) involving less than 10% of body surface with third degree burn of less than 10% or unspecified amount **211**
940*	Burn confined to eye and adnexa **40**
947.2	Burn of esophagus **75**
947.3	Burn of gastrointestinal tract **79**
947.9	Burn of internal organs, unspecified site **211**
947.1	Burn of larynx, trachea, and lung **54 , 208**
945.0*	Burn of lower limb(s), unspecified degree **211**
947.0	Burn of mouth and pharynx **4 , 48**
947.8	Burn of other specified sites of internal organs **211**
942.0*	Burn of trunk, unspecified degree **210**
941.04	Burn of unspecified degree of chin **210**
941.01	Burn of unspecified degree of ear (any part) **210**
941.02	Burn of unspecified degree of eye (with other parts of face, head, and neck) **40**
941.07	Burn of unspecified degree of forehead and cheek **210**
941.03	Burn of unspecified degree of lip(s) **210**
941.09	Burn of unspecified degree of multiple sites (except with eye) of face, head, and neck **210**
941.08	Burn of unspecified degree of neck **210**
941.05	Burn of unspecified degree of nose (septum) **210**
941.06	Burn of unspecified degree of scalp (any part) **210**
941.00	Burn of unspecified degree of unspecified site of face and head **210**
949.0	Burn of unspecified site, unspecified degree **211**
943.0*	Burn of upper limb, except wrist and hand, unspecified degree **210**
947.4	Burn of vagina and uterus **129 , 132**
944.0*	Burn of wrist(s) and hand(s), unspecified degree **211**
946.0	Burns of multiple specified sites, unspecified degree **211**
799.4	Cachexia **214 , 232**
993.3	Caisson disease **205**
726.73	Calcaneal spur **100**
594.0	Calculus in diverticulum of bladder **121**
594.2	Calculus in urethra **120**
592*	Calculus of kidney and ureter **120**
112.81	Candidal endocarditis **65 , 165 , 169**
112.83	Candidal meningitis **9 , 10 , 33 , 165 , 169**
112.82	Candidal otitis externa **47 , 165 , 169**
112.4	Candidiasis of lung **51 , 165 , 169 , 231**
112.0	Candidiasis of mouth **2 , 48 , 231**
112.8*	Candidiasis of other specified sites **231**
112.2	Candidiasis of other urogenital sites **125 , 128 , 131**
112.3	Candidiasis of skin and nails **108 , 231**
112.84	Candidiasis of the esophagus **75 , 165 , 169**
112.85	Candidiasis of the intestine **77 , 165 , 169**
112.9	Candidiasis of unspecified site **186 , 231**
112.1	Candidiasis of vulva and vagina **128 , 131**
127.5	Capillariasis **78**
680*	Carbuncle and furuncle **107**
230.5	Carcinoma in situ of anal canal **76**
230.6	Carcinoma in situ of anus, unspecified **76**
233.7	Carcinoma in situ of bladder **117 , 120**
233.0	Carcinoma in situ of breast **105 , 106**
231.2	Carcinoma in situ of bronchus and lung **52**
233.1	Carcinoma in situ of cervix uteri **127 , 130**
230.3	Carcinoma in situ of colon **76**
230.1	Carcinoma in situ of esophagus **76**
234.0	Carcinoma in situ of eye **38**
232.1	Carcinoma in situ of eyelid, including canthus **38**
231.0	Carcinoma in situ of larynx **3 , 46**
230.0	Carcinoma in situ of lip, oral cavity, and pharynx **3 , 46**
230.8	Carcinoma in situ of liver and biliary system **82**
230.9	Carcinoma in situ of other and unspecified digestive organs **76**
233.6	Carcinoma in situ of other and unspecified male genital organs **123 , 124**
230.7	Carcinoma in situ of other and unspecified parts of intestine **76**
233.2	Carcinoma in situ of other and unspecified parts of uterus **127 , 130**
233.9	Carcinoma in situ of other and unspecified urinary organs **117 , 120**
231.8	Carcinoma in situ of other specified parts of respiratory system **52**
234.8	Carcinoma in situ of other specified sites **181 , 183**

*Code Range

232.8	Carcinoma in situ of other specified sites of skin **109**	
233.5	Carcinoma in situ of penis **123 , 124**	
233.4	Carcinoma in situ of prostate **123 , 124**	
230.4	Carcinoma in situ of rectum **76**	
231.9	Carcinoma in situ of respiratory system, part unspecified **52**	
232.4	Carcinoma in situ of scalp and skin of neck **109**	
232.2	Carcinoma in situ of skin of ear and external auditory canal **109**	
232.0	Carcinoma in situ of skin of lip **109**	
232.7	Carcinoma in situ of skin of lower limb, including hip **109**	
232.3	Carcinoma in situ of skin of other and unspecified parts of face **109**	
232.5	Carcinoma in situ of skin of trunk, except scrotum **109**	
232.6	Carcinoma in situ of skin of upper limb, including shoulder **109**	
232.9	Carcinoma in situ of skin, site unspecified **109**	
230.2	Carcinoma in situ of stomach **76**	
231.1	Carcinoma in situ of trachea **52**	
233.3*	Carcinoma in situ, other and unspecified female genital organs **127 , 130**	
234.9	Carcinoma in situ, site unspecified **181 , 183**	
427.5	Cardiac arrest **66 , 166 , 170**	
779.85	Cardiac arrest of newborn **164 , 169**	
997.1	Cardiac complications **69 , 168 , 172**	
668.13	Cardiac complications of the administration of anesthesia or other sedation in labor and delivery, antepartum **156 , 159**	
668.11	Cardiac complications of the administration of anesthesia or other sedation in labor and delivery, delivered **138 , 141 , 147**	
668.12	Cardiac complications of the administration of anesthesia or other sedation in labor and delivery, delivered, with mention of postpartum complication **138 , 141 , 147**	
668.14	Cardiac complications of the administration of anesthesia or other sedation in labor and delivery, postpartum condition or complication **153**	
668.10	Cardiac complications of the administration of anesthesia or other sedation in labor and delivery, unspecified as to episode of care **138 , 145 , 151**	
785.51	Cardiogenic shock **57 , 66**	
429.3	Cardiomegaly **67**	
425*	Cardiomyopathy **69**	
425.8	Cardiomyopathy in other diseases classified elsewhere **166 , 170**	
306.2	Cardiovascular malfunction arising from mental factors **68**	
V57.0	Care involving breathing exercises **215**	
V57.3	Care involving use of rehabilitation speech-language therapy **214**	
277.82	Carnitine deficiency due to inborn errors of metabolism **115**	
V02.2	Carrier or suspected carrier of amebiasis **214**	
V02.0	Carrier or suspected carrier of cholera **214**	
V02.4	Carrier or suspected carrier of diphtheria **214**	
V02.7	Carrier or suspected carrier of gonorrhea **214**	
V02.3	Carrier or suspected carrier of other gastrointestinal pathogens **214**	
V02.5*	Carrier or suspected carrier of other specified bacterial diseases **214**	
V02.9	Carrier or suspected carrier of other specified infectious organism **214**	
V02.8	Carrier or suspected carrier of other venereal diseases **214**	
V02.1	Carrier or suspected carrier of typhoid **214**	
V02.6*	Carrier or suspected carrier of viral hepatitis **83**	
078.3	Cat-scratch disease **177**	
347*	Cataplexy and narcolepsy **32**	
366*	Cataract **39**	
V45.61	Cataract extraction status **215**	
998.82	Cataract fragments in eye following surgery **40**	

344.61	Cauda equina syndrome with neurogenic bladder **121**
344.60	Cauda equina syndrome without mention of neurogenic bladder **20**
738.7	Cauliflower ear **47**
736.75	Cavovarus deformity of foot, acquired **100**
736.73	Cavus deformity of foot, acquired **100**
447.4	Celiac artery compression syndrome **78**
682.0	Cellulitis and abscess of face **3**
681*	Cellulitis and abscess of finger and toe **104 , 107**
682.1	Cellulitis and abscess of neck **3**
478.71	Cellulitis and perichondritis of larynx **46**
478.21	Cellulitis of pharynx or nasopharynx **46**
020.1	Cellulocutaneous plague **186**
370.03	Central corneal ulcer **38**
668.23	Central nervous system complications of the administration of anesthesia or other sedation in labor and delivery, antepartum **156 , 159**
668.21	Central nervous system complications of the administration of anesthesia or other sedation in labor and delivery, delivered **138 , 142 , 147**
668.22	Central nervous system complications of the administration of anesthesia or other sedation in labor and delivery, delivered, with mention of postpartum complication **138 , 142 , 147**
668.24	Central nervous system complications of the administration of anesthesia or other sedation in labor and delivery, postpartum condition or complication **153**
668.20	Central nervous system complications of the administration of anesthesia or other sedation in labor and delivery, unspecified as to episode of care **138 , 145 , 151**
655.03	Central nervous system malformation in fetus, antepartum **156 , 158**
655.00	Central nervous system malformation in fetus, unspecified as to episode of care in pregnancy **161**
655.01	Central nervous system malformation in fetus, with delivery **136 , 144 , 149**
338.0	Central pain syndrome **32**
327.27	Central sleep apnea in conditions classified elsewhere **32**
851.5*	Cerebellar or brain stem contusion with open intracranial wound **9 , 11 , 223 , 227**
851.52	Cerebellar or brain stem contusion with open intracranial wound, brief (less than 1 hour) loss of consciousness **30**
851.56	Cerebellar or brain stem contusion with open intracranial wound, loss of consciousness of unspecified duration **26**
851.53	Cerebellar or brain stem contusion with open intracranial wound, moderate (1-24 hours) loss of consciousness **25**
851.51	Cerebellar or brain stem contusion with open intracranial wound, no loss of consciousness **30**
851.54	Cerebellar or brain stem contusion with open intracranial wound, prolonged (more than 24 hours) loss of consciousness and return to pre-existing conscious level **25**
851.55	Cerebellar or brain stem contusion with open intracranial wound, prolonged (more than 24 hours) loss of consciousness, without return to pre-existing conscious level **26**
851.59	Cerebellar or brain stem contusion with open intracranial wound, unspecified concussion **30**
851.50	Cerebellar or brain stem contusion with open intracranial wound, unspecified state of consciousness **30**
851.4*	Cerebellar or brain stem contusion without mention of open intracranial wound **223 , 227**
851.42	Cerebellar or brain stem contusion without mention of open intracranial wound, brief (less than 1 hour) loss of consciousness **30**
851.46	Cerebellar or brain stem contusion without mention of open intracranial wound, loss of consciousness of unspecified duration **25**

851.43	Cerebellar or brain stem contusion without mention of open intracranial wound, moderate (1-24 hours) loss of consciousness **25**
851.41	Cerebellar or brain stem contusion without mention of open intracranial wound, no loss of consciousness **30**
851.44	Cerebellar or brain stem contusion without mention of open intracranial wound, prolonged (more than 24 hours) loss consciousness and return to pre-existing conscious level **25**
851.45	Cerebellar or brain stem contusion without mention of open intracranial wound, prolonged (more than 24 hours) loss of consciousness, without return to pre-existing conscious level **25**
851.49	Cerebellar or brain stem contusion without mention of open intracranial wound, unspecified concussion **30**
851.40	Cerebellar or brain stem contusion without mention of open intracranial wound, unspecified state of consciousness **30**
851.7*	Cerebellar or brain stem laceration with open intracranial wound **9 , 11 , 223 , 227**
851.72	Cerebellar or brain stem laceration with open intracranial wound, brief (less than one hour) loss of consciousness **30**
851.76	Cerebellar or brain stem laceration with open intracranial wound, loss of consciousness of unspecified duration **26**
851.73	Cerebellar or brain stem laceration with open intracranial wound, moderate (1-24 hours) loss of consciousness **26**
851.71	Cerebellar or brain stem laceration with open intracranial wound, no loss of consciousness **30**
851.74	Cerebellar or brain stem laceration with open intracranial wound, prolonged (more than 24 hours) loss of consciousness and return to pre-existing conscious level **26**
851.75	Cerebellar or brain stem laceration with open intracranial wound, prolonged (more than 24 hours) loss of consciousness, without return to pre-existing conscious level **26**
851.70	Cerebellar or brain stem laceration with open intracranial wound, state of consciousness unspecified **30**
851.79	Cerebellar or brain stem laceration with open intracranial wound, unspecified concussion **30**
851.6*	Cerebellar or brain stem laceration without mention of open intracranial wound **9 , 11 , 223 , 227**
851.62	Cerebellar or brain stem laceration without mention of open intracranial wound, brief (less than 1 hour) loss of consciousness **30**
851.66	Cerebellar or brain stem laceration without mention of open intracranial wound, loss of consciousness of unspecified duration **26**
851.63	Cerebellar or brain stem laceration without mention of open intracranial wound, moderate (1-24 hours) loss of consciousness **26**
851.61	Cerebellar or brain stem laceration without mention of open intracranial wound, no loss of consciousness **30**
851.64	Cerebellar or brain stem laceration without mention of open intracranial wound, prolonged (more than 24 hours) loss of consciousness and return to pre-existing conscious level **26**
851.65	Cerebellar or brain stem laceration without mention of open intracranial wound, prolonged (more than 24 hours) loss of consciousness, without return to pre-existing conscious level **26**
851.69	Cerebellar or brain stem laceration without mention of open intracranial wound, unspecified concussion **30**
851.60	Cerebellar or brain stem laceration without mention of open intracranial wound, unspecified state of consciousness **30**
437.3	Cerebral aneurysm, nonruptured **32**
437.4	Cerebral arteritis **34**
437.0	Cerebral atherosclerosis **20**
348.0	Cerebral cysts **32**
331.7	Cerebral degeneration in diseases classified elsewhere **19**
330*	Cerebral degenerations usually manifest in childhood **19**
779.2	Cerebral depression, coma, and other abnormal cerebral signs in fetus or newborn **164 , 169**

348.5	Cerebral edema **21**
434.11	Cerebral embolism with cerebral infarction **9 , 10 , 19 , 20**
434.10	Cerebral embolism without mention of cerebral infarction **20**
434.01	Cerebral thrombosis with cerebral infarction **9 , 10 , 19 , 20**
434.00	Cerebral thrombosis without mention of cerebral infarction **20**
388.61	Cerebrospinal fluid otorrhea **32**
349.81	Cerebrospinal fluid rhinorrhea **32 , 166 , 170**
674.00	Cerebrovascular disorder occurring in pregnancy, childbirth, or the puerperium, unspecified as to episode of care **162**
674.03	Cerebrovascular disorder, antepartum **157 , 159**
674.02	Cerebrovascular disorder, with delivery, with mention of postpartum complication **139 , 142 , 148**
674.01	Cerebrovascular disorder, with delivery, with or without mention of antepartum condition **139 , 142 , 148**
674.04	Cerebrovascular disorders in the puerperium, postpartum condition or complication **154**
364.2*	Certain types of iridocyclitis **39**
370.3*	Certain types of keratoconjunctivitis **39**
654.53	Cervical incompetence, antepartum condition or complication **155 , 158**
654.51	Cervical incompetence, delivered **136 , 143 , 149**
654.52	Cervical incompetence, delivered, with mention of postpartum complication **136 , 143 , 149**
654.54	Cervical incompetence, postpartum condition or complication **153**
654.50	Cervical incompetence, unspecified as to episode of care in pregnancy **161**
756.2	Cervical rib **100**
649.73	Cervical shortening, antepartum condition or complication **155 , 158**
649.71	Cervical shortening, delivered, with or without mention of antepartum condition **136 , 143 , 149**
649.70	Cervical shortening, unspecified as to episode of care or not applicable **161**
723.1	Cervicalgia **97**
616.0	Cervicitis and endocervicitis **128 , 131**
723.3	Cervicobrachial syndrome (diffuse) **21**
723.2	Cervicocranial syndrome **21**
039.3	Cervicofacial actinomycotic infection **108**
669.71	Cesarean delivery, without mention of indication, delivered, with or without mention of antepartum condition **139 , 146 , 152**
669.70	Cesarean delivery, without mention of indication, unspecified as to episode of care **139 , 146 , 151**
086.0	Chagas' disease with heart involvement **68**
086.1	Chagas' disease with other organ involvement **186**
086.2	Chagas' disease without mention of organ involvement **186**
099.0	Chancroid **125 , 128 , 131**
782.8	Changes in skin texture **109**
V67.2	Chemotherapy follow-up examination **181 , 182 , 183**
786.59	Chest pain, other **68**
786.50	Chest pain, unspecified **68**
052.7	Chickenpox with other specified complications **165 , 169 , 185**
052.8	Chickenpox with unspecified complication **165 , 169 , 185**
995.5*	Child maltreatment syndrome **205**
299.1*	Childhood disintegrative disorder **189**
315.35	Childhood onset fluency disorder **32**
780.64	Chills (without fever) **214**
099.52	Chlamydia trachomatis infection of anus and rectum **78**
099.53	Chlamydia trachomatis infection of lower genitourinary sites **125 , 128 , 131**
099.54	Chlamydia trachomatis infection of other genitourinary sites **120**

*Code Range

© 2012 OptumInsight, Inc.

099.59	Chlamydia trachomatis infection of other specified site **125 , 128 , 131**
099.56	Chlamydia trachomatis infection of peritoneum **78**
099.51	Chlamydia trachomatis infection of pharynx **2 , 46**
099.55	Chlamydia trachomatis infection of unspecified genitourinary site **125 , 128 , 131**
099.50	Chlamydia trachomatis infection of unspecified site **125 , 128 , 131**
576.1	Cholangitis **167 , 171**
574*	Cholelithiasis **83**
567.81	Choleperitonitis **79**
001*	Cholera **75**
380.03	Chondritis of pinna **100**
756.4	Chondrodystrophy **100**
733.92	Chondromalacia **98**
717.7	Chondromalacia of patella **99**
363*	Chorioretinal inflammations, scars, and other disorders of choroid **39**
130.2	Chorioretinitis due to toxoplasmosis **38 , 165 , 169**
655.13	Chromosomal abnormality in fetus, affecting management of mother, antepartum **156 , 158**
655.10	Chromosomal abnormality in fetus, affecting management of mother, unspecified as to episode of care in pregnancy **161**
655.11	Chromosomal abnormality in fetus, affecting management of mother, with delivery **136 , 144 , 149**
474.01	Chronic adenoiditis **46**
496	Chronic airway obstruction, not elsewhere classified **53**
508.1	Chronic and other pulmonary manifestations due to radiation **53**
375.02	Chronic dacryoadenitis **39**
301.12	Chronic depressive personality disorder **189**
474*	Chronic disease of tonsils and adenoids **3**
537.2	Chronic duodenal ileus **78**
532.71	Chronic duodenal ulcer without mention of hemorrhage or perforation, with obstruction **77**
532.70	Chronic duodenal ulcer without mention of hemorrhage, perforation, or obstruction **77**
360.03	Chronic endophthalmitis **39**
375.03	Chronic enlargement of lacrimal gland **39**
207.1*	Chronic erythremia **182**
780.71	Chronic fatigue syndrome **214**
531.71	Chronic gastric ulcer without mention of hemorrhage or perforation, with obstruction **77**
531.70	Chronic gastric ulcer without mention of hemorrhage, perforation, without mention of obstruction **77**
534.7*	Chronic gastrojejunal ulcer without mention of hemorrhage or perforation **77**
582*	Chronic glomerulonephritis **121 , 232**
098.30	Chronic gonococcal infection of upper genitourinary tract, site unspecified **120**
571.4*	Chronic hepatitis **83**
301.11	Chronic hypomanic personality disorder **189**
458.1	Chronic hypotension **69**
375.4*	Chronic inflammation of lacrimal passages **39**
376.1*	Chronic inflammatory disorders of orbit **39**
595.1	Chronic interstitial cystitis **120**
006.1	Chronic intestinal amebiasis without mention of abscess **75**
364.1*	Chronic iridocyclitis **39**
585*	Chronic kidney disease (CKD) **2 , 119**
476.0	Chronic laryngitis **3**
476*	Chronic laryngitis and laryngotracheitis **46**
476.1	Chronic laryngotracheitis **3**
208.1*	Chronic leukemia of unspecified cell type **182**
289.1	Chronic lymphadenitis **177**
204.1*	Chronic lymphoid leukemia **182**
383.1	Chronic mastoiditis **46**
206.1*	Chronic monocytic leukemia **182**
381.2*	Chronic mucoid otitis media **46**
205.1*	Chronic myeloid leukemia **182**
384.1	Chronic myringitis without mention of otitis media **46**
472.2	Chronic nasopharyngitis **3**
493.21	Chronic obstructive asthma with status asthmaticus **53**
493.20	Chronic obstructive asthma, unspecified **53**
493.22	Chronic obstructive asthma, with (acute) exacerbation **53**
532.4*	Chronic or unspecified duodenal ulcer with hemorrhage **76**
532.6*	Chronic or unspecified duodenal ulcer with hemorrhage and perforation **76**
532.5*	Chronic or unspecified duodenal ulcer with perforation **77**
531.4*	Chronic or unspecified gastric ulcer with hemorrhage **76**
531.6*	Chronic or unspecified gastric ulcer with hemorrhage and perforation **76**
531.5*	Chronic or unspecified gastric ulcer with perforation **77**
534.4*	Chronic or unspecified gastrojejunal ulcer with hemorrhage **76**
534.6*	Chronic or unspecified gastrojejunal ulcer with hemorrhage and perforation **76**
534.5*	Chronic or unspecified gastrojejunal ulcer with perforation **77**
614.4	Chronic or unspecified parametritis and pelvic cellulitis **131**
533.4*	Chronic or unspecified peptic ulcer, unspecified site, with hemorrhage **76**
533.6*	Chronic or unspecified peptic ulcer, unspecified site, with hemorrhage and perforation **76**
533.5*	Chronic or unspecified peptic ulcer, unspecified site, with perforation **77**
730.1*	Chronic osteomyelitis **96**
730.16	Chronic osteomyelitis, lower leg **90**
730.18	Chronic osteomyelitis, other specified sites **87**
338.2*	Chronic pain **32**
338.4	Chronic pain syndrome **32**
573.0	Chronic passive congestion of liver **83**
533.71	Chronic peptic ulcer of unspecified site without mention of hemorrhage or perforation, with obstruction **77**
533.70	Chronic peptic ulcer, unspecified site, without mention of hemorrhage, perforation, or obstruction **77**
380.02	Chronic perichondritis of pinna **100**
472.1	Chronic pharyngitis **3**
472*	Chronic pharyngitis and nasopharyngitis **46**
714.4	Chronic postrheumatic arthropathy **98**
114.4	Chronic pulmonary coccidioidomycosis **51**
416.2	Chronic pulmonary embolism **51 , 166 , 170**
506.4	Chronic respiratory conditions due to fumes and vapors **53**
770.7	Chronic respiratory disease arising in the perinatal period **53**
518.83	Chronic respiratory failure **52**
393	Chronic rheumatic pericarditis **68**
614.1	Chronic salpingitis and oophoritis **131**
381.1*	Chronic serous otitis media **46**
473*	Chronic sinusitis **46**
474.00	Chronic tonsillitis **46**
474.02	Chronic tonsillitis and adenoiditis **46**
440.4	Chronic total occlusion of artery of the extremities **66**
414.2	Chronic total occlusion of coronary artery **67**
707*	Chronic ulcer of skin **104 , 106**
453.5*	Chronic venous embolism and thrombosis of deep vessels of lower extremity **66**

453.7*	Chronic venous embolism and thrombosis of other specified vessels **67**
459.3*	Chronic venous hypertension **67**
791.1	Chyluria **120 , 167 , 171**
327.3*	Circadian rhythm sleep disorder **3 , 32**
571.5	Cirrhosis of liver without mention of alcohol **82**
736.74	Claw foot, acquired **21**
736.06	Claw hand (acquired) **21**
749.1*	Cleft lip **3**
749.0*	Cleft palate **3**
749*	Cleft palate and cleft lip **48**
749.2*	Cleft palate with cleft lip **3**
121.1	Clonorchiasis **83**
824.4	Closed bimalleolar fracture **223**
837.0	Closed dislocation of ankle **223**
832.0*	Closed dislocation of elbow **223**
834.0*	Closed dislocation of finger **223**
838.0*	Closed dislocation of foot **223**
835.0*	Closed dislocation of hip **223**
830.0	Closed dislocation of jaw **223**
836.3	Closed dislocation of patella **223**
831.0*	Closed dislocation of shoulder, unspecified **223**
833.0*	Closed dislocation of wrist **223**
839.0*	Closed dislocation, cervical vertebra **98 , 223 , 228**
839.8	Closed dislocation, multiple and ill-defined sites **100 , 223**
839.69	Closed dislocation, other location **100**
839.6*	Closed dislocation, other location **223**
839.4*	Closed dislocation, other vertebra **98 , 223**
839.61	Closed dislocation, sternum **52**
839.2*	Closed dislocation, thoracic and lumbar vertebra **98 , 223**
808.0	Closed fracture of acetabulum **222**
811.01	Closed fracture of acromial process of scapula **99**
801.1*	Closed fracture of base of skull with cerebral laceration and contusion **221 , 226**
801.12	Closed fracture of base of skull with cerebral laceration and contusion, brief (less than one hour) loss of consciousness **28**
801.16	Closed fracture of base of skull with cerebral laceration and contusion, loss of consciousness of unspecified duration **22**
801.13	Closed fracture of base of skull with cerebral laceration and contusion, moderate (1-24 hours) loss of consciousness **22**
801.11	Closed fracture of base of skull with cerebral laceration and contusion, no loss of consciousness **28**
801.14	Closed fracture of base of skull with cerebral laceration and contusion, prolonged (more than 24 hours) loss of consciousness and return to pre-existing conscious level **22**
801.15	Closed fracture of base of skull with cerebral laceration and contusion, prolonged (more than 24 hours) loss of consciousness, without return to pre-existing conscious level **22**
801.19	Closed fracture of base of skull with cerebral laceration and contusion, unspecified concussion **28**
801.10	Closed fracture of base of skull with cerebral laceration and contusion, unspecified state of consciousness **28**
801.4*	Closed fracture of base of skull with intracranial injury of other and unspecified nature **221 , 226**
801.42	Closed fracture of base of skull with intracranial injury of other and unspecified nature, brief (less than one hour) loss of consciousness **28**
801.46	Closed fracture of base of skull with intracranial injury of other and unspecified nature, loss of consciousness of unspecified duration **23**
801.43	Closed fracture of base of skull with intracranial injury of other and unspecified nature, moderate (1-24 hours) loss of consciousness **23**
801.41	Closed fracture of base of skull with intracranial injury of other and unspecified nature, no loss of consciousness **28**
801.44	Closed fracture of base of skull with intracranial injury of other and unspecified nature, prolonged (more than 24 hours) loss of consciousness and return to pre-existing conscious level **23**
801.45	Closed fracture of base of skull with intracranial injury of other and unspecified nature, prolonged (more than 24 hours) loss of consciousness, without return to pre-existing conscious level **23**
801.49	Closed fracture of base of skull with intracranial injury of other and unspecified nature, unspecified concussion **28**
801.40	Closed fracture of base of skull with intracranial injury of other and unspecified nature, unspecified state of consciousness **28**
801.3*	Closed fracture of base of skull with other and unspecified intracranial hemorrhage **221 , 226**
801.32	Closed fracture of base of skull with other and unspecified intracranial hemorrhage, brief (less than one hour) loss of consciousness **28**
801.36	Closed fracture of base of skull with other and unspecified intracranial hemorrhage, loss of consciousness of unspecified duration **23**
801.33	Closed fracture of base of skull with other and unspecified intracranial hemorrhage, moderate (1-24 hours) loss of consciousness **22**
801.31	Closed fracture of base of skull with other and unspecified intracranial hemorrhage, no loss of consciousness **28**
801.34	Closed fracture of base of skull with other and unspecified intracranial hemorrhage, prolonged (more than 24 hours) loss of consciousness and return to pre-existing conscious level **22**
801.35	Closed fracture of base of skull with other and unspecified intracranial hemorrhage, prolonged (more than 24 hours) loss of consciousness, without return to pre-existing conscious level **23**
801.39	Closed fracture of base of skull with other and unspecified intracranial hemorrhage, unspecified concussion **28**
801.30	Closed fracture of base of skull with other and unspecified intracranial hemorrhage, unspecified state of consciousness **28**
801.2*	Closed fracture of base of skull with subarachnoid, subdural, and extradural hemorrhage **221 , 226**
801.22	Closed fracture of base of skull with subarachnoid, subdural, and extradural hemorrhage, brief (less than one hour) loss of consciousness **28**
801.26	Closed fracture of base of skull with subarachnoid, subdural, and extradural hemorrhage, loss of consciousness of unspecified duration **22**
801.23	Closed fracture of base of skull with subarachnoid, subdural, and extradural hemorrhage, moderate (1-24 hours) loss of consciousness **22**
801.21	Closed fracture of base of skull with subarachnoid, subdural, and extradural hemorrhage, no loss of consciousness **28**
801.24	Closed fracture of base of skull with subarachnoid, subdural, and extradural hemorrhage, prolonged (more than 24 hours) loss of consciousness and return to pre-existing conscious level **22**
801.25	Closed fracture of base of skull with subarachnoid, subdural, and extradural hemorrhage, prolonged (more than 24 hours) loss of consciousness, without return to pre-existing conscious level **22**
801.29	Closed fracture of base of skull with subarachnoid, subdural, and extradural hemorrhage, unspecified concussion **28**
801.20	Closed fracture of base of skull with subarachnoid, subdural, and extradural hemorrhage, unspecified state of consciousness **28**
801.0*	Closed fracture of base of skull without mention of intracranial injury **221**
801.02	Closed fracture of base of skull without mention of intracranial injury, brief (less than one hour) loss of consciousness **28 , 226**
801.06	Closed fracture of base of skull without mention of intracranial injury, loss of consciousness of unspecified duration **22**
801.03	Closed fracture of base of skull without mention of intracranial injury, moderate (1-24 hours) loss of consciousness **22 , 226**

*Code Range © 2012 OptumInsight, Inc.

801.01	Closed fracture of base of skull without mention of intracranial injury, no loss of consciousness **28**	807.03	Closed fracture of three ribs **52**
		807.02	Closed fracture of two ribs **54**
801.04	Closed fracture of base of skull without mention of intracranial injury, prolonged (more than 24 hours) loss of consciousness and return to pre-existing conscious level **22 , 226**	829.0	Closed fracture of unspecified bone **223**
		820.8	Closed fracture of unspecified part of neck of femur **223**
		813.8*	Closed fracture of unspecified part of radius with ulna **222**
801.05	Closed fracture of base of skull without mention of intracranial injury, prolonged (more than 24 hours) loss of consciousness, without return to pre-existing conscious level **22 , 226**	811.00	Closed fracture of unspecified part of scapula **99**
		823.8*	Closed fracture of unspecified part of tibia and fibula **223**
		805.8	Closed fracture of unspecified part of vertebral column without mention of spinal cord injury **222**
801.09	Closed fracture of base of skull without mention of intracranial injury, unspecified concussion **28**	806.8	Closed fracture of unspecified vertebra with spinal cord injury **222 , 228**
801.00	Closed fracture of base of skull without mention of intracranial injury, unspecified state of consciousness **28**	812.0*	Closed fracture of upper end of humerus **222**
825.0	Closed fracture of calcaneus **99 , 223**	813.0*	Closed fracture of upper end of radius and ulna **222**
806.0*	Closed fracture of cervical vertebra with spinal cord injury **222 , 228**	823.0*	Closed fracture of upper end of tibia and fibula **223**
805.0*	Closed fracture of cervical vertebra without mention of spinal cord injury **222**	800.1*	Closed fracture of vault of skull with cerebral laceration and contusion **221**
810.0*	Closed fracture of clavicle **222**	800.12	Closed fracture of vault of skull with cerebral laceration and contusion, brief (less than one hour) loss of consciousness **27 , 225**
811.02	Closed fracture of coracoid process of scapula **99**		
806.2*	Closed fracture of dorsal (thoracic) vertebra with spinal cord injury **222 , 228**	800.16	Closed fracture of vault of skull with cerebral laceration and contusion, loss of consciousness of unspecified duration **21 , 225**
805.2	Closed fracture of dorsal (thoracic) vertebra without mention of spinal cord injury **222**	800.13	Closed fracture of vault of skull with cerebral laceration and contusion, moderate (1-24 hours) loss of consciousness **21 , 225**
807.08	Closed fracture of eight or more ribs **52 , 227**	800.11	Closed fracture of vault of skull with cerebral laceration and contusion, no loss of consciousness **27**
807.05	Closed fracture of five ribs **52**		
807.04	Closed fracture of four ribs **52**	800.14	Closed fracture of vault of skull with cerebral laceration and contusion, prolonged (more than 24 hours) loss of consciousness and return to pre-existing conscious level **21 , 225**
811.03	Closed fracture of glenoid cavity and neck of scapula **99**		
807.5	Closed fracture of larynx and trachea **3 , 47 , 222 , 227**	800.15	Closed fracture of vault of skull with cerebral laceration and contusion, prolonged (more than 24 hours) loss of consciousness, without return to pre-existing conscious level **21 , 225**
824.2	Closed fracture of lateral malleolus **223**		
821.2*	Closed fracture of lower end of femur **223**		
812.4*	Closed fracture of lower end of humerus **222**	800.19	Closed fracture of vault of skull with cerebral laceration and contusion, unspecified concussion **27 , 225**
813.4*	Closed fracture of lower end of radius and ulna **222**	800.10	Closed fracture of vault of skull with cerebral laceration and contusion, unspecified state of consciousness **27 , 225**
806.4	Closed fracture of lumbar spine with spinal cord injury **222 , 228**		
805.4	Closed fracture of lumbar vertebra without mention of spinal cord injury **222**	800.4*	Closed fracture of vault of skull with intercranial injury of other and unspecified nature **221**
824.0	Closed fracture of medial malleolus **223**	800.42	Closed fracture of vault of skull with intracranial injury of other and unspecified nature, brief (less than one hour) loss of consciousness **27 , 225**
815.0*	Closed fracture of metacarpal bones **222**		
807.09	Closed fracture of multiple ribs, unspecified **52**	800.46	Closed fracture of vault of skull with intracranial injury of other and unspecified nature, loss of consciousness of unspecified duration **22 , 225**
826.0	Closed fracture of one or more phalanges of foot **223**		
816.0*	Closed fracture of one or more phalanges of hand **222**	800.43	Closed fracture of vault of skull with intracranial injury of other and unspecified nature, moderate (1-24 hours) loss of consciousness **22 , 225**
807.01	Closed fracture of one rib **54**		
811.09	Closed fracture of other part of scapula **101**	800.41	Closed fracture of vault of skull with intracranial injury of other and unspecified nature, no loss of consciousness **27**
808.4*	Closed fracture of other specified part of pelvis **222**		
825.2*	Closed fracture of other tarsal and metatarsal bones **99 , 223**	800.44	Closed fracture of vault of skull with intracranial injury of other and unspecified nature, prolonged (more than 24 hours) loss of consciousness and return to pre-existing conscious level **22 , 225**
822.0	Closed fracture of patella **223**		
808.2	Closed fracture of pubis **222**		
807.0*	Closed fracture of rib(s) **222**	800.45	Closed fracture of vault of skull with intracranial injury of other and unspecified nature, prolonged (more than 24 hours) loss of consciousness, without return to pre-existing conscious level **22 , 225**
807.00	Closed fracture of rib(s), unspecified **54**		
806.6*	Closed fracture of sacrum and coccyx with spinal cord injury **222**		
806.60	Closed fracture of sacrum and coccyx with unspecified spinal cord injury **228**	800.49	Closed fracture of vault of skull with intracranial injury of other and unspecified nature, unspecified concussion **27 , 225**
805.6	Closed fracture of sacrum and coccyx without mention of spinal cord injury **222 , 228**	800.40	Closed fracture of vault of skull with intracranial injury of other and unspecified nature, unspecified state of consciousness **27 , 225**
811.0*	Closed fracture of scapula **222**		
807.07	Closed fracture of seven ribs **52 , 227**	800.3*	Closed fracture of vault of skull with other and unspecified intracranial hemorrhage **221**
813.2*	Closed fracture of shaft of radius and ulna **222**		
823.2*	Closed fracture of shaft of tibia and fibula **223**	800.32	Closed fracture of vault of skull with other and unspecified intracranial hemorrhage, brief (less than one hour) loss of consciousness **27 , 225**
821.0*	Closed fracture of shaft or unspecified part of femur **167 , 171 , 223**		
812.2*	Closed fracture of shaft or unspecified part of humerus **222**		
807.06	Closed fracture of six ribs **52**		
807.2	Closed fracture of sternum **52 , 222**		

800.36   Closed fracture of vault of skull with other and unspecified intracranial hemorrhage, loss of consciousness of unspecified duration **22 , 225**

800.33   Closed fracture of vault of skull with other and unspecified intracranial hemorrhage, moderate (1-24 hours) loss of consciousness **22 , 225**

800.31   Closed fracture of vault of skull with other and unspecified intracranial hemorrhage, no loss of consciousness **27**

800.34   Closed fracture of vault of skull with other and unspecified intracranial hemorrhage, prolonged (more than 24 hours) loss of consciousness and return to pre-existing conscious level **22 , 225**

800.35   Closed fracture of vault of skull with other and unspecified intracranial hemorrhage, prolonged (more than 24 hours) loss of consciousness, without return to pre-existing conscious level **22 , 225**

800.39   Closed fracture of vault of skull with other and unspecified intracranial hemorrhage, unspecified concussion **27 , 225**

800.30   Closed fracture of vault of skull with other and unspecified intracranial hemorrhage, unspecified state of consciousness **27 , 225**

800.2*   Closed fracture of vault of skull with subarachnoid, subdural, and extradural hemorrhage **221**

800.22   Closed fracture of vault of skull with subarachnoid, subdural, and extradural hemorrhage, brief (less than one hour) loss of consciousness **27 , 225**

800.26   Closed fracture of vault of skull with subarachnoid, subdural, and extradural hemorrhage, loss of consciousness of unspecified duration **21 , 225**

800.23   Closed fracture of vault of skull with subarachnoid, subdural, and extradural hemorrhage, moderate (1-24 hours) loss of consciousness **21 , 225**

800.21   Closed fracture of vault of skull with subarachnoid, subdural, and extradural hemorrhage, no loss of consciousness **27**

800.24   Closed fracture of vault of skull with subarachnoid, subdural, and extradural hemorrhage, prolonged (more than 24 hours) loss of consciousness and return to pre-existing conscious level **21 , 225**

800.25   Closed fracture of vault of skull with subarachnoid, subdural, and extradural hemorrhage, prolonged (more than 24 hours) loss of consciousness, without return to pre-existing conscious level **21 , 225**

800.29   Closed fracture of vault of skull with subarachnoid, subdural, and extradural hemorrhage, unspecified concussion **27 , 225**

800.20   Closed fracture of vault of skull with subarachnoid, subdural, and extradural hemorrhage, unspecified state of consciousness **27 , 225**

800.0*   Closed fracture of vault of skull without mention of intracranial injury **221**

800.02   Closed fracture of vault of skull without mention of intracranial injury, brief (less than one hour) loss of consciousness **27 , 225**

800.06   Closed fracture of vault of skull without mention of intracranial injury, loss of consciousness of unspecified duration **21**

800.03   Closed fracture of vault of skull without mention of intracranial injury, moderate (1-24 hours) loss of consciousness **21 , 225**

800.01   Closed fracture of vault of skull without mention of intracranial injury, no loss of consciousness **27**

800.04   Closed fracture of vault of skull without mention of intracranial injury, prolonged (more than 24 hours) loss of consciousness and return to pre-existing conscious level **21 , 225**

800.05   Closed fracture of vault of skull without mention of intracranial injury, prolonged (more than 24 hours) loss of consciousness, without return to pre-existing conscious level **21 , 225**

800.09   Closed fracture of vault of skull without mention of intracranial injury, unspecified concussion **27**

800.00   Closed fracture of vault of skull without mention of intracranial injury, unspecified state of consciousness **27**

804.06   Closed fractures involving skull of face with other bones, without mention of intracranial injury, loss of consciousness of unspecified duration **24 , 226**

804.05   Closed fractures involving skull of face with other bones, without mention of intracranial injury, prolonged (more than 24 hours) loss of consciousness, without return to pre-existing conscious level **24 , 226**

804.09   Closed fractures involving skull of face with other bones, without mention of intracranial injury, unspecified concussion **29**

804.2*   Closed fractures involving skull or face with other bones with subarachnoid, subdural, and extradural hemorrhage **222 , 226**

804.22   Closed fractures involving skull or face with other bones with subarachnoid, subdural, and extradural hemorrhage, brief (less than one hour) loss of consciousness **29**

804.26   Closed fractures involving skull or face with other bones with subarachnoid, subdural, and extradural hemorrhage, loss of consciousness of unspecified duration **24**

804.23   Closed fractures involving skull or face with other bones with subarachnoid, subdural, and extradural hemorrhage, moderate (1-24 hours) loss of consciousness **24**

804.21   Closed fractures involving skull or face with other bones with subarachnoid, subdural, and extradural hemorrhage, no loss of consciousness **29**

804.24   Closed fractures involving skull or face with other bones with subarachnoid, subdural, and extradural hemorrhage, prolonged (more than 24 hours) loss of consciousness and return to pre-existing conscious level **24**

804.25   Closed fractures involving skull or face with other bones with subarachnoid, subdural, and extradural hemorrhage, prolonged (more than 24 hours) loss of consciousness, without return to pre-existing conscious level **24**

804.29   Closed fractures involving skull or face with other bones with subarachnoid, subdural, and extradural hemorrhage, unspecified concussion **29**

804.20   Closed fractures involving skull or face with other bones with subarachnoid, subdural, and extradural hemorrhage, unspecified state of consciousness **29**

804.1*   Closed fractures involving skull or face with other bones, with cerebral laceration and contusion **222 , 226**

804.12   Closed fractures involving skull or face with other bones, with cerebral laceration and contusion, brief (less than one hour) loss of consciousness **29**

804.16   Closed fractures involving skull or face with other bones, with cerebral laceration and contusion, loss of consciousness of unspecified duration **24**

804.13   Closed fractures involving skull or face with other bones, with cerebral laceration and contusion, moderate (1-24 hours) loss of consciousness **24**

804.11   Closed fractures involving skull or face with other bones, with cerebral laceration and contusion, no loss of consciousness **29**

804.14   Closed fractures involving skull or face with other bones, with cerebral laceration and contusion, prolonged (more than 24 hours) loss of consciousness and return to pre-existing conscious level **24**

804.15   Closed fractures involving skull or face with other bones, with cerebral laceration and contusion, prolonged (more than 24 hours) loss of consciousness, without return to pre-existing conscious level **24**

804.19   Closed fractures involving skull or face with other bones, with cerebral laceration and contusion, unspecified concussion **29**

804.10   Closed fractures involving skull or face with other bones, with cerebral laceration and contusion, unspecified state of consciousness **29**

804.4*   Closed fractures involving skull or face with other bones, with intracranial injury of other and unspecified nature **222**

804.42   Closed fractures involving skull or face with other bones, with intracranial injury of other and unspecified nature, brief (less than one hour) loss of consciousness **29 , 226**

804.46   Closed fractures involving skull or face with other bones, with intracranial injury of other and unspecified nature, loss of consciousness of unspecified duration **25 , 227**

*Code Range

804.43 Closed fractures involving skull or face with other bones, with intracranial injury of other and unspecified nature, moderate (1-24 hours) loss of consciousness **24 , 226**

804.41 Closed fractures involving skull or face with other bones, with intracranial injury of other and unspecified nature, no loss of consciousness **29 , 226**

804.44 Closed fractures involving skull or face with other bones, with intracranial injury of other and unspecified nature, prolonged (more than 24 hours) loss of consciousness and return to pre-existing conscious level **24 , 226**

804.45 Closed fractures involving skull or face with other bones, with intracranial injury of other and unspecified nature, prolonged (more than 24 hours) loss of consciousness, without return to pre-existing conscious level **24 , 227**

804.49 Closed fractures involving skull or face with other bones, with intracranial injury of other and unspecified nature, unspecified concussion **29**

804.40 Closed fractures involving skull or face with other bones, with intracranial injury of other and unspecified nature, unspecified state of consciousness **29 , 226**

804.3* Closed fractures involving skull or face with other bones, with other and unspecified intracranial hemorrhage **222 , 226**

804.32 Closed fractures involving skull or face with other bones, with other and unspecified intracranial hemorrhage, brief (less than one hour) loss of consciousness **29**

804.36 Closed fractures involving skull or face with other bones, with other and unspecified intracranial hemorrhage, loss of consciousness of unspecified duration **24**

804.33 Closed fractures involving skull or face with other bones, with other and unspecified intracranial hemorrhage, moderate (1-24 hours) loss of consciousness **24**

804.31 Closed fractures involving skull or face with other bones, with other and unspecified intracranial hemorrhage, no loss of consciousness **29**

804.34 Closed fractures involving skull or face with other bones, with other and unspecified intracranial hemorrhage, prolonged (more than 24 hours) loss of consciousness and return to preexisting conscious level **24**

804.35 Closed fractures involving skull or face with other bones, with other and unspecified intracranial hemorrhage, prolonged (more than 24 hours) loss of consciousness, without return to pre-existing conscious level **24**

804.39 Closed fractures involving skull or face with other bones, with other and unspecified intracranial hemorrhage, unspecified concussion **29**

804.30 Closed fractures involving skull or face with other bones, with other and unspecified intracranial hemorrhage, unspecified state of consciousness **29**

804.0* Closed fractures involving skull or face with other bones, without mention of intracranial injury **222**

804.02 Closed fractures involving skull or face with other bones, without mention of intracranial injury, brief (less than one hour) loss of consciousness **29 , 226**

804.03 Closed fractures involving skull or face with other bones, without mention of intracranial injury, moderate (1-24 hours) loss of consciousness **24 , 226**

804.01 Closed fractures involving skull or face with other bones, without mention of intracranial injury, no loss of consciousness **29**

804.00 Closed fractures involving skull or face with other bones, without mention of intracranial injury, unspecified state of consciousness **29**

804.04 Closed fractures involving skull or face with other bones, without mention or intracranial injury, prolonged (more than 24 hours) loss of consciousness and return to pre-existing conscious level **24 , 226**

814.0* Closed fractures of carpal bones **222**

820.2* Closed pertrochanteric fracture of femur **223**

803.3* Closed skull fracture with other and unspecified intracranial hemorrhage **222 , 226**

820.0* Closed transcervical fracture **222**

824.6 Closed trimalleolar fracture **223**

792.5 Cloudy (hemodialysis) (peritoneal) dialysis affluent **214**

736.07 Club hand, acquired **21**

781.5 Clubbing of fingers **54**

649.33 Coagulation defects complicating pregnancy, childbirth, or the puerperium, antepartum condition or complication **155 , 158**

649.32 Coagulation defects complicating pregnancy, childbirth, or the puerperium, delivered, with mention of postpartum complication **136 , 143 , 149**

649.31 Coagulation defects complicating pregnancy, childbirth, or the puerperium, delivered, with or without mention of antepartum condition **136 , 143 , 149**

649.34 Coagulation defects complicating pregnancy, childbirth, or the puerperium, postpartum condition or complication **153**

649.30 Coagulation defects complicating pregnancy, childbirth, or the puerperium, unspecified as to episode of care or not applicable **161**

500 Coal workers' pneumoconiosis **53**

747.1* Coarctation of aorta **68**

114.2 Coccidioidal meningitis **9 , 10 , 33 , 165 , 169**

114* Coccidioidomycosis **231**

007.2 Coccidiosis **230**

799.52 Cognitive communication deficit **189**

789.7 Colic **78**

377.23 Coloboma of optic disc **40**

863.4* Colon or rectal injury without mention of open wound into cavity **79 , 224 , 228**

569.6* Colostomy and enterostomy complications **79**

780.01 Coma **21 , 167 , 171**

279.2 Combined immunity deficiency **176**

428.4* Combined systolic and diastolic heart failure **57 , 166 , 170**

V67.6 Combined treatment follow-up examination **215**

900.01 Common carotid artery injury **227**

904.0 Common femoral artery injury **224 , 228**

331.3 Communicating hydrocephalus **19**

958.90 Compartment syndrome, unspecified **225**

518.2 Compensatory emphysema **54**

629.3* Complication of implanted vaginal mesh and other prosthetic materials **131**

997.9* Complications affecting other specified body systems, not elsewhere classified **205**

639* Complications following abortion or ectopic and molar pregnancies **152**

383.3* Complications following mastoidectomy **47**

539* Complications of bariatric procedures **78**

996.85 Complications of bone marrow transplant **176**

569.7* Complications of intestinal pouch **79 , 167 , 171**

999.39 Complications of medical care, NEC, infection following other infusion, injection, transfusion, or vaccination **168 , 172 , 185 , 187**

996.89 Complications of other transplanted organ **205**

996.9* Complications of reattached extremity or body part **99**

996.83 Complications of transplanted heart **69**

996.81 Complications of transplanted kidney **121**

996.82 Complications of transplanted liver **83**

996.84 Complications of transplanted lung **54**

996.87 Complications of transplanted organ, intestine **205**

996.88 Complications of transplanted organ, stem cell **205**

996.80 Complications of transplanted organ, unspecified site **205**

996.86	Complications of transplanted pancreas **83**
348.4	Compression of brain **21**
459.2	Compression of vein **67**
850*	Concussion **31**
850.1*	Concussion with brief (less than one hour) loss of consciousness **223**
850.5	Concussion with loss of consciousness of unspecified duration **223**
850.2	Concussion with moderate (1-24 hours) loss of consciousness **223 , 227**
850.0	Concussion with no loss of consciousness **223**
850.3	Concussion with prolonged (more than 24 hours) loss of consciousness and return to pre-existing conscious level **223 , 227**
850.4	Concussion with prolonged (more than 24 hours) loss of consciousness, without return to pre-existing conscious level **223 , 227**
758.9	Conditions due to anomaly of unspecified chromosome **214**
426*	Conduction disorders **68**
327.41	Confusional arousals **32**
654.03	Congenital abnormalities of pregnant uterus, antepartum **155 , 158**
654.01	Congenital abnormalities of pregnant uterus, delivered **136 , 143 , 149**
654.02	Congenital abnormalities of pregnant uterus, delivered, with mention of postpartum complication **136 , 143 , 149**
654.00	Congenital abnormalities of pregnant uterus, unspecified as to episode of care **161**
654.04	Congenital abnormalities of uterus, postpartum condition or complication **153**
750.21	Congenital absence of salivary gland **3 , 47**
756.13	Congenital absence of vertebra **98**
747.5	Congenital absence or hypoplasia of umbilical artery **67**
750.22	Congenital accessory salivary gland **3 , 47**
748.5	Congenital agenesis, hypoplasia, and dysplasia of lung **54**
744.1	Congenital anomalies of accessory auricle **47 , 173**
759.1	Congenital anomalies of adrenal gland **115**
752.4*	Congenital anomalies of cervix, vagina, and external female genitalia **128 , 131**
744.0*	Congenital anomalies of ear causing impairment of hearing **47**
743*	Congenital anomalies of eye **40**
752.1*	Congenital anomalies of fallopian tubes and broad ligaments **128 , 131**
747.4*	Congenital anomalies of great veins **68**
751.4	Congenital anomalies of intestinal fixation **79**
759.2	Congenital anomalies of other endocrine glands **115**
752.0	Congenital anomalies of ovaries **128 , 131**
751.7	Congenital anomalies of pancreas **83**
746.0*	Congenital anomalies of pulmonary valve **67**
756.0	Congenital anomalies of skull and face bones **100**
759.0	Congenital anomalies of spleen **177**
753*	Congenital anomalies of urinary system **121**
756.7*	Congenital anomaly of abdominal wall **79**
747.81	Congenital anomaly of cerebrovascular system **32**
756.6	Congenital anomaly of diaphragm **54**
756.10	Congenital anomaly of spine, unspecified **98**
751.2	Congenital atresia and stenosis of large intestine, rectum, and anal canal **79**
751.1	Congenital atresia and stenosis of small intestine **79**
750.23	Congenital atresia, salivary duct **3 , 47**
751.61	Congenital biliary atresia **83**
754.42	Congenital bowing of femur **100**

754.43	Congenital bowing of tibia and fibula **100**
754.44	Congenital bowing of unspecified long bones of leg **100**
744.4*	Congenital branchial cleft cyst or fistula **47**
748.61	Congenital bronchiectasis **53**
327.25	Congenital central alveolar hypoventilation syndrome **32**
748.0	Congenital choanal atresia **47**
746.85	Congenital coronary artery anomaly **67**
751.62	Congenital cystic disease of liver **83**
748.4	Congenital cystic lung **54**
771.1	Congenital cytomegalovirus infection **164 , 168**
286.3	Congenital deficiency of other clotting factors **177**
754.3*	Congenital dislocation of hip **100**
754.41	Congenital dislocation of knee (with genu recurvatum) **99**
750.27	Congenital diverticulum of pharynx **3 , 47**
752.2	Congenital doubling of uterus **128 , 131**
757.31	Congenital ectodermal dysplasia **109**
286.1	Congenital factor IX disorder **177**
286.0	Congenital factor VIII disorder **177**
286.2	Congenital factor XI deficiency **177**
750.25	Congenital fistula of lip **3 , 48**
750.24	Congenital fistula of salivary gland **3 , 47**
756.15	Congenital fusion of spine (vertebra) **98**
754.40	Congenital genu recurvatum **100**
746.86	Congenital heart block **68**
359.0	Congenital hereditary muscular dystrophy **32**
750.6	Congenital hiatus hernia **79**
750.5	Congenital hypertrophic pyloric stenosis **79**
243	Congenital hypothyroidism **115**
746.83	Congenital infundibular pulmonic stenosis **67**
746.4	Congenital insufficiency of aortic valve **67**
746.87	Congenital malposition of heart and cardiac apex **68**
746.6	Congenital mitral insufficiency **67**
746.5	Congenital mitral stenosis **67**
754.0	Congenital musculoskeletal deformities of skull, face, and jaw **100**
754.2	Congenital musculoskeletal deformity of spine **87 , 100**
754.1	Congenital musculoskeletal deformity of sternocleidomastoid muscle **100**
379.51	Congenital nystagmus **40**
746.84	Congenital obstructive anomalies of heart, not elsewhere classified **67**
654.73	Congenital or acquired abnormality of vagina, antepartum condition or complication **156 , 158**
654.72	Congenital or acquired abnormality of vagina, delivered, with mention of postpartum complication **136 , 144 , 149**
654.74	Congenital or acquired abnormality of vagina, postpartum condition or complication **153**
654.70	Congenital or acquired abnormality of vagina, unspecified as to episode of care in pregnancy **161**
654.71	Congenital or acquired abnormality of vagina, with delivery **136 , 144 , 149**
654.83	Congenital or acquired abnormality of vulva, antepartum condition or complication **156 , 158**
654.82	Congenital or acquired abnormality of vulva, delivered, with mention of postpartum complication **136 , 144 , 149**
654.84	Congenital or acquired abnormality of vulva, postpartum condition or complication **153**
654.80	Congenital or acquired abnormality of vulva, unspecified as to episode of care in pregnancy **161**
654.81	Congenital or acquired abnormality of vulva, with delivery **136 , 144 , 149**
756.5*	Congenital osteodystrophies **100**

754.61	Congenital pes planus **173**	
757.33	Congenital pigmentary anomaly of skin **109 , 173**	
770.0	Congenital pneumonia **164 , 168**	
771.0	Congenital rubella **164 , 168**	
747.82	Congenital spinal vessel anomaly **32**	
756.12	Congenital spondylolisthesis **98**	
756.11	Congenital spondylolysis, lumbosacral region **98**	
746.3	Congenital stenosis of aortic valve **67**	
746.81	Congenital subaortic stenosis **67**	
090.9	Congenital syphilis, unspecified **186**	
750.3	Congenital tracheoesophageal fistula, esophageal atresia and stenosis **75**	
746.1	Congenital tricuspid atresia and stenosis **67**	
754.6*	Congenital valgus deformities of feet **100**	
754.5*	Congenital varus deformities of feet **100**	
757.32	Congenital vascular hamartomas **109**	
748.2	Congenital web of larynx **3 , 47**	
744.5	Congenital webbing of neck **109**	
428.0	Congestive heart failure, unspecified **57 , 166 , 170**	
759.4	Conjoined twins **79 , 167 , 171**	
032.81	Conjunctival diphtheria **38**	
130.1	Conjunctivitis due to toxoplasmosis **38 , 165 , 169**	
376.31	Constant exophthalmos **39**	
564.0*	Constipation **78**	
284.0*	Constitutional aplastic anemia **176**	
V21*	Constitutional states in development **215**	
692*	Contact dermatitis and other eczema **109**	
V01.89	Contact or exposure to other communicable diseases **173**	
V87.1*	Contact with and (suspected) exposure to hazardous aromatic compounds **216**	
V87.0*	Contact with and (suspected) exposure to hazardous metals **216**	
V87.2	Contact with and (suspected) exposure to other potentially hazardous chemicals **216**	
V87.3*	Contact with and (suspected) exposure to other potentially hazardous substances **216**	
V01.81	Contact with or exposure to anthrax **173**	
V01*	Contact with or exposure to communicable diseases **214**	
051.2	Contagious pustular dermatitis **108**	
718.4*	Contracture of joint **100**	
728.6	Contracture of palmar fascia **99**	
922.2	Contusion of abdominal wall **108**	
922.0	Contusion of breast **108**	
922.1	Contusion of chest wall **108**	
921*	Contusion of eye and adnexa **224**	
921.3	Contusion of eyeball **40**	
921.1	Contusion of eyelids and periocular area **40**	
920	Contusion of face, scalp, and neck except eye(s) **108 , 224**	
922.4	Contusion of genital organs **125 , 128 , 132**	
924*	Contusion of lower limb and of other and unspecified sites **108 , 224**	
922.8	Contusion of multiple sites of trunk **108**	
921.2	Contusion of orbital tissues **40**	
922.3*	Contusion of trunk **108**	
922*	Contusion of trunk **224**	
922.9	Contusion of unspecified part of trunk **108**	
923*	Contusion of upper limb **108 , 224**	
V66*	Convalescence and palliative care **215**	
378.84	Convergence excess or spasm in binocular eye movement **40**	
378.83	Convergence insufficiency or palsy in binocular eye movement **40**	

300.11	Conversion disorder **189**	
780.3*	Convulsions **33**	
779.0	Convulsions in newborn **164 , 169**	
745.7	Cor biloculare **67**	
746.82	Cor triatriatum **67**	
840.1	Coracoclavicular (ligament) sprain and strain **223**	
840.2	Coracohumeral (ligament) sprain and strain **223**	
663.13	Cord around neck, with compression, complicating labor and delivery, antepartum **156 , 159**	
663.11	Cord around neck, with compression, complicating labor and delivery, delivered **138 , 145 , 151**	
663.10	Cord around neck, with compression, complicating labor and delivery, unspecified as to episode of care **138 , 145 , 151**	
V59.5	Cornea donor **215**	
V42.5	Cornea replaced by transplant **40**	
370.55	Corneal abscess **38**	
370.6*	Corneal neovascularization **39**	
371*	Corneal opacity and other disorders of cornea **39**	
700	Corns and callosities **109**	
414.0*	Coronary atherosclerosis **67**	
414.4	Coronary atherosclerosis due to calcified coronary lesion **67**	
414.3	Coronary atherosclerosis due to lipid rich plaque **67**	
851.1*	Cortex (cerebral) contusion with open intracranial wound **9 , 11 , 223 , 227**	
851.12	Cortex (cerebral) contusion with open intracranial wound, brief (less than 1 hour) loss of consciousness **30**	
851.16	Cortex (cerebral) contusion with open intracranial wound, loss of consciousness of unspecified duration **25**	
851.13	Cortex (cerebral) contusion with open intracranial wound, moderate (1-24 hours) loss of consciousness **25**	
851.11	Cortex (cerebral) contusion with open intracranial wound, no loss of consciousness **30**	
851.14	Cortex (cerebral) contusion with open intracranial wound, prolonged (more than 24 hours) loss of consciousness and return to pre-existing conscious level **25**	
851.15	Cortex (cerebral) contusion with open intracranial wound, prolonged (more than 24 hours) loss of consciousness, without return to pre-existing conscious level **25**	
851.19	Cortex (cerebral) contusion with open intracranial wound, unspecified concussion **30**	
851.10	Cortex (cerebral) contusion with open intracranial wound, unspecified state of consciousness **30**	
851.0*	Cortex (cerebral) contusion without mention of open intracranial wound **223**	
851.02	Cortex (cerebral) contusion without mention of open intracranial wound, brief (less than 1 hour) loss of consciousness **30 , 227**	
851.06	Cortex (cerebral) contusion without mention of open intracranial wound, loss of consciousness of unspecified duration **25 , 227**	
851.03	Cortex (cerebral) contusion without mention of open intracranial wound, moderate (1-24 hours) loss of consciousness **25 , 227**	
851.01	Cortex (cerebral) contusion without mention of open intracranial wound, no loss of consciousness **30 , 227**	
851.04	Cortex (cerebral) contusion without mention of open intracranial wound, prolonged (more than 24 hours) loss of consciousness and return to pre-existing conscious level **25 , 227**	
851.05	Cortex (cerebral) contusion without mention of open intracranial wound, prolonged (more than 24 hours) loss of consciousness, without return to pre-existing conscious level **25 , 227**	
851.00	Cortex (cerebral) contusion without mention of open intracranial wound, state of consciousness unspecified **30 , 227**	
851.09	Cortex (cerebral) contusion without mention of open intracranial wound, unspecified concussion **30 , 227**	
851.3*	Cortex (cerebral) laceration with open intracranial wound **9 , 11 , 223 , 227**	

851.32	Cortex (cerebral) laceration with open intracranial wound, brief (less than 1 hour) loss of consciousness **30**		926.12	Crushing injury of buttock **228**
851.36	Cortex (cerebral) laceration with open intracranial wound, loss of consciousness of unspecified duration **25**		927.1*	Crushing injury of elbow and forearm **224 , 228**
			926.0	Crushing injury of external genitalia **125 , 128 , 132 , 224**
851.33	Cortex (cerebral) laceration with open intracranial wound, moderate (1-24 hours) loss of consciousness **25**		925.1	Crushing injury of face and scalp **227**
851.31	Cortex (cerebral) laceration with open intracranial wound, no loss of consciousness **30**		925*	Crushing injury of face, scalp, and neck **4 , 204 , 224**
			927.3	Crushing injury of finger(s) **224**
851.34	Cortex (cerebral) laceration with open intracranial wound, prolonged (more than 24 hours) loss of consciousness and return to pre-existing conscious level **25**		928.0*	Crushing injury of hip and thigh **224 , 228**
			928.1*	Crushing injury of knee and lower leg **224 , 228**
			928*	Crushing injury of lower limb **204**
851.35	Cortex (cerebral) laceration with open intracranial wound, prolonged (more than 24 hours) loss of consciousness, without return to pre-existing conscious level **25**		929*	Crushing injury of multiple and unspecified sites **204 , 224**
			928.8	Crushing injury of multiple sites of lower limb **224 , 228**
			926.8	Crushing injury of multiple sites of trunk **204 , 224 , 228**
851.39	Cortex (cerebral) laceration with open intracranial wound, unspecified concussion **30**		927.8	Crushing injury of multiple sites of upper limb **224 , 228**
851.30	Cortex (cerebral) laceration with open intracranial wound, unspecified state of consciousness **30**		925.2	Crushing injury of neck **227**
			926.1*	Crushing injury of other specified sites of trunk **204 , 224**
851.2*	Cortex (cerebral) laceration without mention of open intracranial wound **9 , 11 , 223 , 227**		926.19	Crushing injury of other specified sites of trunk **228**
			927.01	Crushing injury of scapular region **227**
851.22	Cortex (cerebral) laceration without mention of open intracranial wound, brief (less than 1 hour) loss of consciousness **30**		927.0*	Crushing injury of shoulder and upper arm **224 , 228**
			928.3	Crushing injury of toe(s) **224**
851.26	Cortex (cerebral) laceration without mention of open intracranial wound, loss of consciousness of unspecified duration **25**		928.9	Crushing injury of unspecified site of lower limb **224 , 228**
			926.9	Crushing injury of unspecified site of trunk **204 , 224 , 228**
851.23	Cortex (cerebral) laceration without mention of open intracranial wound, moderate (1-24 hours) loss of consciousness **25**		927.9	Crushing injury of unspecified site of upper limb **224 , 228**
			927*	Crushing injury of upper limb **204**
851.21	Cortex (cerebral) laceration without mention of open intracranial wound, no loss of consciousness **30**		927.2*	Crushing injury of wrist and hand(s), except finger(s) alone **224**
			321.0	Cryptococcal meningitis **9 , 10**
851.24	Cortex (cerebral) laceration without mention of open intracranial wound, prolonged (more than 24 hours) loss of consciousness and return to pre-existing conscious level **25**		117.5	Cryptococcosis **165 , 169 , 231**
			516.36	Cryptogenic organizing pneumonia **231**
			712*	Crystal arthropathies **98**
851.25	Cortex (cerebral) laceration without mention of open intracranial wound, prolonged (more than 24 hours) loss of consciousness, without return to pre-existing conscious level **25**		736.01	Cubitus valgus (acquired) **100**
			736.02	Cubitus varus (acquired) **100**
			737*	Curvature of spine **97**
851.29	Cortex (cerebral) laceration without mention of open intracranial wound, unspecified concussion **30**		737.4*	Curvature of spine associated with other conditions **87**
			039.0	Cutaneous actinomycotic infection **108**
851.20	Cortex (cerebral) laceration without mention of open intracranial wound, unspecified state of consciousness **30**		022.0	Cutaneous anthrax **108**
			032.85	Cutaneous diphtheria **108**
331.6	Corticobasal degeneration **19**		031.1	Cutaneous diseases due to other mycobacteria **108**
365.3*	Corticosteroid-induced glaucoma **39**		085.4	Cutaneous leishmaniasis, American **108**
786.2	Cough **54**		085.2	Cutaneous leishmaniasis, Asian desert **108**
V61.10	Counseling for marital and partner problems, unspecified **215**		085.3	Cutaneous leishmaniasis, Ethiopian **108**
V62.83	Counseling for perpetrator of physical/sexual abuse **215**		085.1	Cutaneous leishmaniasis, urban **108**
			120.3	Cutaneous schistosomiasis **108**
V61.12	Counseling for perpetrator of spousal and partner abuse **215**		782.5	Cyanosis **214**
V61.11	Counseling for victim of spousal and partner abuse **215**		301.13	Cyclothymic disorder **189**
051.0*	Cowpox and vaccinia not from vaccination **185**		577.2	Cyst and pseudocyst of pancreas **167 , 171**
074.20	Coxsackie carditis, unspecified **68**		616.2	Cyst of Bartholin's gland **128 , 131**
074.22	Coxsackie endocarditis **67**		733.2*	Cyst of bone **98**
074.23	Coxsackie myocarditis **68**		478.26	Cyst of pharynx or nasopharynx **47**
074.21	Coxsackie pericarditis **68**		246.2	Cyst of thyroid **3**
676.13	Cracked nipple, antepartum condition or complication **157 , 159**		277.03	Cystic fibrosis with gastrointestinal manifestations **78**
676.12	Cracked nipple, delivered, with mention of postpartum complication **140 , 146 , 152**		277.01	Cystic fibrosis with meconium ileus **164 , 168**
			277.09	Cystic fibrosis with other manifestations **114**
676.11	Cracked nipple, delivered, with or without mention of antepartum condition **140 , 146 , 152**		277.02	Cystic fibrosis with pulmonary manifestations **51**
			277.00	Cystic fibrosis without mention of meconium ileus **114**
676.14	Cracked nipple, postpartum condition or complication **154**		123.1	Cysticercosis **75**
676.10	Cracked nipple, unspecified as to prenatal or postnatal episode of care **162**		595.81	Cystitis cystica **120 , 167 , 171**
			595.4	Cystitis in diseases classified elsewhere **120 , 167 , 171**
729.82	Cramp of limb **98**		364.6*	Cysts of iris, ciliary body, and anterior chamber **39**
377.22	Crater-like holes of optic disc **40**		078.5	Cytomegaloviral disease **186 , 231**
359.81	Critical illness myopathy **32**			
464.4	Croup **3 , 46**			
928.2*	Crushing injury of ankle and foot, excluding toe(s) alone **224**			
926.11	Crushing injury of back **228**			

665.64   Damage to pelvic joints and ligaments, postpartum condition or complication **153**

665.60   Damage to pelvic joints and ligaments, unspecified as to episode of care in pregnancy **138 , 145 , 151**

665.61   Damage to pelvic joints and ligaments, with delivery **138 , 145 , 151**

798.2   Death occurring in less than 24 hours from onset of symptoms, not otherwise explained **66**

655.73   Decreased fetal movements, affecting management of mother, antepartum condition or complication **156 , 158**

655.71   Decreased fetal movements, affecting management of mother, delivered **136 , 144 , 149**

655.70   Decreased fetal movements, unspecified as to episode of care **161**

288.5*   Decreased white blood cell count **177**

949.4   Deep necrosis of underlying tissue due to burn (deep third degree), unspecified site without mention of loss of body part **207 , 208 , 209 , 210**

949.5   Deep necrosis of underlying tissues due to burn (deep third degree, unspecified site with loss of body part **207 , 208 , 209 , 210**

941.52   Deep necrosis of underlying tissues due to burn (deep third degree) of eye (with other parts of face, head, and neck), with loss of a body part **40**

941.42   Deep necrosis of underlying tissues due to burn (deep third degree) of eye (with other parts of face, head, and neck), without mention of loss of a body part **40**

941.5*   Deep necrosis of underlying tissues due to burn (deep third degree) of face, head, and neck with loss of a body part **207 , 208 , 209 , 210**

941.4*   Deep necrosis of underlying tissues due to burn (deep third degree) of face, head, and neck without mention of loss of a body part **207 , 208 , 209 , 210**

945.5*   Deep necrosis of underlying tissues due to burn (deep third degree) of lower limb(s) with loss of a body part **207 , 208 , 209 , 210**

945.4*   Deep necrosis of underlying tissues due to burn (deep third degree) of lower limb(s) without mention of loss of a body part **207 , 208 , 209 , 210**

946.5   Deep necrosis of underlying tissues due to burn (deep third degree) of multiple specified sites, with loss of a body part **207 , 208 , 209 , 210**

946.4   Deep necrosis of underlying tissues due to burn (deep third degree) of multiple specified sites, without mention of loss of a body part **207 , 208 , 209 , 210**

942.5*   Deep necrosis of underlying tissues due to burn (deep third degree) of trunk with loss of a body part **207 , 208 , 209 , 210**

942.4*   Deep necrosis of underlying tissues due to burn (deep third degree) of trunk without mention of loss of a body part **207 , 208 , 209 , 210**

943.5*   Deep necrosis of underlying tissues due to burn (deep third degree) of upper limb, except wrist and hand, with loss of a body part **207 , 208 , 209 , 210**

943.4*   Deep necrosis of underlying tissues due to burn (deep third degree) of upper limb, except wrist and hand, without mention of loss of a body part **207 , 208 , 209 , 210**

944.5*   Deep necrosis of underlying tissues due to burn (deep third degree) of wrist(s) and hand(s), with loss of a body part **207 , 208 , 209 , 210**

944.4*   Deep necrosis of underlying tissues due to burn (deep third degree) of wrist(s) and hand(s), without mention of loss of a body part **207 , 208 , 209 , 210**

671.33   Deep phlebothrombosis, antepartum **157 , 159**

671.30   Deep phlebothrombosis, antepartum, unspecified as to episode of care **162**

671.31   Deep phlebothrombosis, antepartum, with delivery **139 , 142 , 147**

671.44   Deep phlebothrombosis, postpartum condition or complication **154**

671.40   Deep phlebothrombosis, postpartum, unspecified as to episode of care **162**

671.42   Deep phlebothrombosis, postpartum, with delivery **139 , 142 , 147**

904.6   Deep plantar blood vessels injury **224**

660.31   Deep transverse arrest and persistent occipitoposterior position during labor and deliver, delivered **137 , 144 , 150**

660.33   Deep transverse arrest and persistent occipitoposterior position during labor and delivery, antepartum **156 , 159**

660.30   Deep transverse arrest and persistent occipitoposterior position during labor and delivery, unspecified as to episode of care **137 , 144 , 150**

286.6   Defibrination syndrome **165 , 170 , 177**

266*   Deficiency of B-complex components **114 , 231**

279.0*   Deficiency of humoral immunity **177**

612*   Deformity and disproportion of reconstructed breast **107**

376.4*   Deformity of orbit **39**

360.4*   Degenerated conditions of globe **39**

362.5*   Degeneration of macula and posterior pole of retina **39**

364.5*   Degenerations of iris and ciliary body **39**

388.0*   Degenerative and vascular disorders of ear **47**

360.2*   Degenerative disorders of globe **39**

666.24   Delayed and secondary postpartum hemorrhage, postpartum condition or complication **153**

666.20   Delayed and secondary postpartum hemorrhage, unspecified as to episode of care **162**

666.22   Delayed and secondary postpartum hemorrhage, with delivery **138 , 141 , 147**

658.33   Delayed delivery after artificial rupture of membranes, antepartum **156 , 159**

658.31   Delayed delivery after artificial rupture of membranes, delivered **137 , 144 , 150**

658.30   Delayed delivery after artificial rupture of membranes, unspecified as to episode of care **137 , 144 , 150**

658.23   Delayed delivery after spontaneous or unspecified rupture of membranes, antepartum **156 , 159**

658.21   Delayed delivery after spontaneous or unspecified rupture of membranes, delivered **137 , 144 , 150**

658.20   Delayed delivery after spontaneous or unspecified rupture of membranes, unspecified as to episode of care **137 , 144 , 150**

662.33   Delayed delivery of second twin, triplet, etc., antepartum **156 , 159**

662.31   Delayed delivery of second twin, triplet, etc., delivered **137 , 145 , 150**

662.30   Delayed delivery of second twin, triplet, etc., unspecified as to episode of care **137 , 145 , 150**

999.85   Delayed hemolytic transfusion reaction, incompatibility unspecified **177**

779.83   Delayed separation of umbilical cord **172**

293.0   Delirium due to conditions classified elsewhere **189**

282.45   Delta-beta thalassemia **165 , 170**

297*   Delusional disorders **190**

331.82   Dementia with Lewy bodies **19**

290*   Dementias **189**

799.25   Demoralization and apathy **189**

054.42   Dendritic keratitis **230**

061   Dengue **185**

524*   Dentofacial anomalies, including malocclusion **3 , 48**

301.6   Dependent personality disorder **189**

300.6   Depersonalization disorder **189**

311   Depressive disorder, not elsewhere classified **189**

298.0	Depressive type psychosis	**190**
717.1	Derangement of anterior horn of medial meniscus	**99**
717.4*	Derangement of lateral meniscus	**99**
717.5	Derangement of meniscus, not elsewhere classified	**99**
717.2	Derangement of posterior horn of medial meniscus	**99**
693.0	Dermatitis due to drugs and medicines taken internally	**167 , 171**
693*	Dermatitis due to substances taken internally	**109**
698.4	Dermatitis factitia (artefacta)	**109**
694.0	Dermatitis herpetiformis	**109**
757.2	Dermatoglyphic anomalies	**109**
111*	Dermatomycosis, other and unspecified	**108 , 231**
110*	Dermatophytosis	**108 , 231**
516.37	Desquamative interstitial pneumonia	**231**
368.52	Deutan defect in color vision	**39**
315.4	Developmental coordination disorder	**190**
718.7*	Developmental dislocation of joint	**100**
315.02	Developmental dyslexia	**190**
315.00	Developmental reading disorder, unspecified	**190**
470	Deviated nasal septum	**3 , 47**
253.5	Diabetes insipidus	**165 , 169**
250.0*	Diabetes mellitus without mention of complication	**1 , 2 , 114**
250.2*	Diabetes with hyperosmolarity	**1 , 2 , 114**
250.1*	Diabetes with ketoacidosis	**1 , 2 , 114**
250.6*	Diabetes with neurological manifestations	**1 , 2 , 20**
250.5*	Diabetes with ophthalmic manifestations	**1 , 2 , 38**
250.3*	Diabetes with other coma	**1 , 2 , 114**
250.8*	Diabetes with other specified manifestations	**2 , 114**
250.7*	Diabetes with peripheral circulatory disorders	**1 , 2 , 66**
250.4*	Diabetes with renal manifestations	**1 , 2 , 121**
250.41	Diabetes with renal manifestations, type I [juvenile type], not stated as uncontrolled	**119**
250.43	Diabetes with renal manifestations, type I [juvenile type], uncontrolled	**119**
250.9*	Diabetes with unspecified complication	**2 , 114**
362.0*	Diabetic retinopathy	**39**
691.0	Diaper or napkin rash	**173**
862.1	Diaphragm injury with open wound into cavity	**52**
862.0	Diaphragm injury without mention of open wound into cavity	**52**
551.3	Diaphragmatic hernia with gangrene	**167 , 171**
552.3	Diaphragmatic hernia with obstruction	**78 , 167 , 171**
553.3	Diaphragmatic hernia without mention of obstruction or gangrene	**78**
728.84	Diastasis of muscle	**99**
428.3*	Diastolic heart failure	**57 , 166 , 170**
569.86	Dieulafoy lesion (hemorrhagic) of intestine	**79**
537.84	Dieulafoy lesion (hemorrhagic) of stomach and duodenum	**76**
719.7	Difficulty in walking	**98**
710*	Diffuse diseases of connective tissue	**97**
370.52	Diffuse interstitial keratitis	**39**
279.11	DiGeorge's syndrome	**176**
997.4*	Digestive system complications, not elsewhere classified	**79 , 168 , 172**
619.1	Digestive-genital tract fistula, female	**79 , 167 , 171**
032.84	Diphtheritic cystitis	**120**
032.82	Diphtheritic myocarditis	**68**
032.83	Diphtheritic peritonitis	**75**
123.4	Diphyllobothriasis, intestinal	**77**
388.41	Diplacusis	**47**
344.2	Diplegia of upper limbs	**18**

343.0	Diplegic infantile cerebral palsy	**18**
368.2	Diplopia	**38**
529*	Diseases and other conditions of the tongue	**3 , 48**
395*	Diseases of aortic valve	**67**
704*	Diseases of hair and hair follicles	**109**
521*	Diseases of hard tissues of teeth	**3 , 48**
396*	Diseases of mitral and aortic valves	**67**
394*	Diseases of mitral valve	**67**
703*	Diseases of nail	**109**
397*	Diseases of other endocardial structures	**67**
577*	Diseases of pancreas	**83**
522*	Diseases of pulp and periapical tissues	**3 , 48**
706*	Diseases of sebaceous glands	**109**
526*	Diseases of the jaws	**3 , 48**
528*	Diseases of the oral soft tissues, excluding lesions specific for gingiva and tongue	**3 , 48**
527*	Diseases of the salivary glands	**3 , 47**
254*	Diseases of thymus gland	**177**
837*	Dislocation of ankle	**100**
832*	Dislocation of elbow	**100**
834*	Dislocation of finger	**100**
838*	Dislocation of foot	**100**
835*	Dislocation of hip	**96**
830*	Dislocation of jaw	**3 , 48**
836*	Dislocation of knee	**100**
831*	Dislocation of shoulder	**100**
833*	Dislocation of wrist	**100**
733.90	Disorder of bone and cartilage, unspecified	**100**
279*	Disorders involving the immune mechanism	**231**
388.5	Disorders of acoustic nerve	**47**
255*	Disorders of adrenal glands	**115**
270*	Disorders of amino-acid transport and metabolism	**114**
277.4	Disorders of bilirubin excretion	**83**
275.4*	Disorders of calcium metabolism	**114**
372*	Disorders of conjunctiva	**39**
275.1	Disorders of copper metabolism	**115**
519.4	Disorders of diaphragm	**54**
277.85	Disorders of fatty acid oxidation	**115**
276*	Disorders of fluid, electrolyte, and acid-base balance	**114 , 165 , 169**
275.0*	Disorders of iron metabolism	**115**
272*	Disorders of lipoid metabolism	**114**
275.2	Disorders of magnesium metabolism	**114**
349.2	Disorders of meninges, not elsewhere classified	**32**
626*	Disorders of menstruation and other abnormal bleeding from female genital tract	**128 , 131**
277.87	Disorders of mitochondrial metabolism	**115**
377.5*	Disorders of optic chiasm	**32**
352*	Disorders of other cranial nerves	**20**
377.6*	Disorders of other visual pathways	**32**
252*	Disorders of parathyroid gland	**115**
275.3	Disorders of phosphorus metabolism	**115**
277.1	Disorders of porphyrin metabolism	**115**
705*	Disorders of sweat glands	**109**
337*	Disorders of the autonomic nervous system	**20**
253*	Disorders of the pituitary gland and its hypothalamic control	**115**
520*	Disorders of tooth development and eruption	**3 , 48**
621*	Disorders of uterus, not elsewhere classified	**128 , 131**
377.7*	Disorders of visual cortex	**32**

*Code Range

379.2*	Disorders of vitreous body **40**	
588*	Disorders resulting from impaired renal function **121**	
780.55	Disruption of 24 hour sleep wake cycle, unspecified **190**	
674.14	Disruption of cesarean wound, postpartum condition or complication **154**	
674.10	Disruption of cesarean wound, unspecified as to episode of care **162**	
674.12	Disruption of cesarean wound, with delivery, with mention of postpartum complication **139 , 142 , 148**	
674.24	Disruption of perineal wound, postpartum condition or complication **154**	
674.20	Disruption of perineal wound, unspecified as to episode of care in pregnancy **162**	
674.22	Disruption of perineal wound, with delivery, with mention of postpartum complication **139 , 142 , 148**	
998.3*	Disruption of wound **205**	
441.0*	Dissection of aorta **66**	
443.21	Dissection of carotid artery **66**	
443.22	Dissection of iliac artery **66**	
443.29	Dissection of other artery **66**	
443.23	Dissection of renal artery **121**	
443.24	Dissection of vertebral artery **66**	
112.5	Disseminated candidiasis **165 , 169 , 186 , 231**	
031.2	Disseminated diseases due to other mycobacteria **186 , 230**	
776.2	Disseminated intravascular coagulation in newborn **164 , 168**	
199.0	Disseminated malignant neoplasm **181**	
379.55	Dissociated nystagmus **38**	
300.12	Dissociative amnesia **189**	
300.15	Dissociative disorder or reaction, unspecified **189**	
300.13	Dissociative fugue **189**	
300.14	Dissociative identity disorder **189**	
782.0	Disturbance of skin sensation **32**	
520.6	Disturbances in tooth eruption **173**	
781.1	Disturbances of sensation of smell and taste **32**	
562.11	Diverticulitis of colon (without mention of hemorrhage) **78**	
562.13	Diverticulitis of colon with hemorrhage **76**	
562.01	Diverticulitis of small intestine (without mention of hemorrhage) **78**	
562.03	Diverticulitis of small intestine with hemorrhage **76**	
562.10	Diverticulosis of colon (without mention of hemorrhage) **78**	
562.12	Diverticulosis of colon with hemorrhage **76**	
562.00	Diverticulosis of small intestine (without mention of hemorrhage) **78**	
562.02	Diverticulosis of small intestine with hemorrhage **76**	
530.6	Diverticulum of esophagus, acquired **78**	
780.4	Dizziness and giddiness **46**	
V59.8	Donor of other specified organ or tissue **215**	
V59.9	Donor of unspecified organ or tissue **215**	
758.0	Down's syndrome **189**	
994.1	Drowning and nonfatal submersion **205**	
304*	Drug dependence **192**	
779.4	Drug reactions and intoxications specific to newborn **164 , 169**	
292.0	Drug withdrawal **165 , 170**	
779.5	Drug withdrawal syndrome in newborn **164 , 169**	
292*	Drug-induced mental disorders **192**	
359.24	Drug-induced myotonia **32**	
377.21	Drusen of optic disc **38**	
378.71	Duane's syndrome **40**	
532.90	Duodenal ulcer, unspecified as acute or chronic, without hemorrhage, perforation, or obstruction **77**	

532.91	Duodenal ulcer, unspecified as acute or chronic, without mention of hemorrhage or perforation, with obstruction **77**	
535.61	Duodenitis with hemorrhage **76**	
535.60	Duodenitis without mention of hemorrhage **78**	
349.3*	Dural tear **166 , 170 , 204**	
709.00	Dyschromia, unspecified **173**	
780.56	Dysfunctions associated with sleep stages or arousal from sleep **190**	
530.5	Dyskinesia of esophagus **78**	
625.3	Dysmenorrhea **131**	
277.7	Dysmetabolic Syndrome X **115**	
625.0	Dyspareunia **131**	
536.8	Dyspepsia and other specified disorders of function of stomach **78**	
786.0*	Dyspnea and respiratory abnormalities **54 , 232**	
300.4	Dysthymic disorder **189**	
788.1	Dysuria **120**	
V50.3	Ear piercing **215**	
090.1	Early congenital syphilis, latent **186**	
090.0	Early congenital syphilis, symptomatic **186**	
644.21	Early onset of delivery, delivered, with or without mention of antepartum condition **135 , 142 , 148**	
644.20	Early onset of delivery, unspecified as to episode of care **155 , 158**	
091.81	Early syphilis, acute syphilitic meningitis (secondary) **9 , 10 , 33**	
092*	Early syphilis, latent **186**	
091.89	Early syphilis, other forms of secondary syphilis **186**	
091.69	Early syphilis, secondary syphilis of other viscera **78**	
091.7	Early syphilis, secondary syphilis, relapse **186**	
091.62	Early syphilis, secondary syphilitic hepatitis **83**	
091.61	Early syphilis, secondary syphilitic periostitis **96**	
091.82	Early syphilis, syphilitic alopecia **108**	
091.9	Early syphilis, unspecified secondary syphilis **186**	
091.5*	Early syphilis, uveitis due to secondary syphilis **38**	
307.50	Eating disorder, unspecified **190**	
746.2	Ebstein's anomaly **67**	
122.0	Echinococcus granulosus infection of liver **83**	
122.1	Echinococcus granulosus infection of lung **51**	
122.2	Echinococcus granulosus infection of thyroid **115**	
122.5	Echinococcus multilocularis infection of liver **83**	
642.60	Eclampsia complicating pregnancy, childbirth or the puerperium, unspecified as to episode of care **157 , 160**	
642.63	Eclampsia, antepartum **155 , 157**	
642.64	Eclampsia, postpartum condition or complication **152**	
642.61	Eclampsia, with delivery **135 , 141 , 147**	
642.62	Eclampsia, with delivery, with current postpartum complication **135 , 141 , 147**	
633*	Ectopic pregnancy **154**	
374.1*	Ectropion **39**	
054.0	Eczema herpeticum **108 , 165 , 169 , 230**	
782.3	Edema **214**	
478.6	Edema of larynx **3 , 47**	
607.83	Edema of penis **125**	
478.25	Edema of pharynx or nasopharynx **47**	
646.10	Edema or excessive weight gain in pregnancy, unspecified as to episode of care **157 , 160**	
646.12	Edema or excessive weight gain in pregnancy, with delivery, with current postpartum complication **135 , 142 , 148**	
646.11	Edema or excessive weight gain in pregnancy, with delivery, with or without mention of antepartum complication **135 , 142 , 148**	

646.14	Edema or excessive weight gain in pregnancy, without mention of hypertension, postpartum condition or complication **152**	
646.13	Edema or excessive weight gain, antepartum **155 , 157**	
V62.3	Educational circumstance **215**	
758.2	Edwards' syndrome **189**	
993.4	Effects of air pressure caused by explosion **205**	
992*	Effects of heat and light **205**	
994.2	Effects of hunger **205**	
994.0	Effects of lightning **205**	
990	Effects of radiation, unspecified **205**	
991*	Effects of reduced temperature **205**	
994.3	Effects of thirst **205**	
719.0*	Effusion of joint **100**	
V59.7*	Egg (oocyte) (ovum) Donor **215**	
913.1	Elbow, forearm, and wrist, abrasion or friction burn, infected **107**	
913.0	Elbow, forearm, and wrist, abrasion or friction burn, without mention of infection **108**	
913.3	Elbow, forearm, and wrist, blister infected **107**	
913.2	Elbow, forearm, and wrist, blister, without mention of infection **109**	
913.5	Elbow, forearm, and wrist, insect bite, nonvenomous, infected **107**	
913.4	Elbow, forearm, and wrist, insect bite, nonvenomous, without mention of infection **109**	
913.6	Elbow, forearm, and wrist, superficial foreign body (splinter), without major open wound and without mention of infection **108**	
913.7	Elbow, forearm, and wrist, superficial foreign body (splinter), without major open wound, infected **107**	
659.61	Elderly multigravida, delivered, with mention of antepartum condition **137 , 144 , 150**	
659.60	Elderly multigravida, unspecified as to episode of care or not applicable **137 , 144 , 150**	
659.63	Elderly multigravida, with antepartum condition or complication **156 , 159**	
659.53	Elderly primigravida, antepartum **156 , 159**	
659.51	Elderly primigravida, delivered **137 , 144 , 150**	
659.50	Elderly primigravida, unspecified as to episode of care **137 , 144 , 150**	
V50.0	Elective hair transplant for purposes other than remedying health states **110**	
994.8	Electrocution and nonfatal effects of electric current **205**	
796.2	Elevated blood pressure reading without diagnosis of hypertension **69**	
790.1	Elevated sedimentation rate **214**	
288.6*	Elevated white blood cell count **177**	
444.2*	Embolism and thrombosis of arteries of the extremities **66**	
444.8*	Embolism and thrombosis of other specified artery **66**	
453.3	Embolism and thrombosis of renal vein **121**	
444.1	Embolism and thrombosis of thoracic aorta **66**	
444.9	Embolism and thrombosis of unspecified artery **66**	
453.9	Embolism and thrombosis of unspecified site **67**	
799.24	Emotional lability **189**	
998.81	Emphysema (subcutaneous) (surgical) resulting from a procedure **205**	
492.0	Emphysematous bleb **53**	
510*	Empyema **51 , 166 , 170**	
323.51	Encephalitis and encephalomyelitis following immunization procedures **10**	
323.01	Encephalitis and encephalomyelitis in viral diseases classified elsewhere **10**	
323.5*	Encephalitis, myelitis, and encephalomyelitis following immunization procedures **9 , 33**	

323.2	Encephalitis, myelitis, and encephalomyelitis in protozoal diseases classified elsewhere **9 , 10 , 33**	
323.1	Encephalitis, myelitis, and encephalomyelitis in rickettsial diseases classified elsewhere **9 , 10 , 33**	
323.0*	Encephalitis, myelitis, and encephalomyelitis in viral diseases classified elsewhere **9 , 33**	
056.01	Encephalomyelitis due to rubella **33**	
348.3*	Encephalopathy, not elsewhere classified **20 , 231**	
307.7	Encopresis **190**	
V58.1*	Encounter for antineoplastic chemotherapy and immunotherapy **181 , 182 , 183**	
V56*	Encounter for dialysis and dialysis catheter care **120**	
V25.1*	Encounter for insertion or removal of intrauterine contraceptive device **215**	
V28.8*	Encounter for other specified antenatal screening **215**	
V28.3	Encounter for routine screening for malformation using ultrasonics **215**	
V68*	Encounters for administrative purposes **216**	
603.0	Encysted hydrocele **125**	
424.9*	Endocarditis, valve unspecified **166 , 170**	
376.2*	Endocrine exophthalmos **39**	
306.6	Endocrine malfunction arising from mental factors **115**	
617.6	Endometriosis in scar of skin **109**	
617.2	Endometriosis of fallopian tube **128 , 131**	
617.5	Endometriosis of intestine **78**	
617.8	Endometriosis of other specified sites **128 , 131**	
617.1	Endometriosis of ovary **128 , 131**	
617.3	Endometriosis of pelvic peritoneum **128 , 131**	
617.4	Endometriosis of rectovaginal septum and vagina **128 , 131**	
617.0	Endometriosis of uterus **128 , 131**	
617.9	Endometriosis, site unspecified **128 , 131**	
676.23	Engorgement of breast, antepartum **157 , 159**	
676.22	Engorgement of breasts, delivered, with mention of postpartum complication **140 , 146 , 152**	
676.21	Engorgement of breasts, delivered, with or without mention of antepartum condition **140 , 146 , 152**	
676.24	Engorgement of breasts, postpartum condition or complication **154**	
676.20	Engorgement of breasts, unspecified as to prenatal or postnatal episode of care **162**	
785.6	Enlargement of lymph nodes **177 , 232**	
376.5*	Enophthalmos **39**	
021.1	Enteric tularemia **75**	
127.4	Enterobiasis **78**	
726.3*	Enthesopathy of elbow region **98**	
726.5	Enthesopathy of hip region **98**	
726.6*	Enthesopathy of knee **98**	
726.4	Enthesopathy of wrist and carpus **98**	
374.0*	Entropion and trichiasis of eyelid **39**	
307.6	Enuresis **190**	
288.3	Eosinophilia **177**	
535.71	Eosinophilic gastritis with hemorrhage **76**	
535.70	Eosinophilic gastritis without mention of hemorrhage **78**	
558.4*	Eosinophilic gastroenteritis and colitis **78 , 231**	
322.1	Eosinophilic meningitis **166 , 170**	
074.1	Epidemic pleurodynia **53**	
078.81	Epidemic vertigo **32**	
078.82	Epidemic vomiting syndrome **77**	
345*	Epilepsy and recurrent seizures **33**	
649.43	Epilepsy complicating pregnancy, childbirth, or the puerperium, antepartum condition or complication **155 , 158**	

649.42	Epilepsy complicating pregnancy, childbirth, or the puerperium, delivered, with mention of postpartum complication **136** , **143** , **149**
649.41	Epilepsy complicating pregnancy, childbirth, or the puerperium, delivered, with or without mention of antepartum condition **136** , **143** , **149**
649.44	Epilepsy complicating pregnancy, childbirth, or the puerperium, postpartum condition or complication **153**
649.40	Epilepsy complicating pregnancy, childbirth, or the puerperium, unspecified as to episode of care or not applicable **161**
375.2*	Epiphora **39**
296*	Episodic mood disorders **190**
784.7	Epistaxis **46**
736.72	Equinus deformity of foot, acquired **100**
035	Erysipelas **107**
941.14	Erythema due to burn (first degree) of chin **210**
941.11	Erythema due to burn (first degree) of ear (any part) **210**
941.12	Erythema due to burn (first degree) of eye (with other parts face, head, and neck) **40**
941.17	Erythema due to burn (first degree) of forehead and cheek **210**
941.13	Erythema due to burn (first degree) of lip(s) **210**
945.1*	Erythema due to burn (first degree) of lower limb(s) **211**
941.19	Erythema due to burn (first degree) of multiple sites (except with eye) of face, head, and neck **210**
946.1	Erythema due to burn (first degree) of multiple specified sites **211**
941.18	Erythema due to burn (first degree) of neck **210**
941.15	Erythema due to burn (first degree) of nose (septum) **210**
941.16	Erythema due to burn (first degree) of scalp (any part) **210**
942.1*	Erythema due to burn (first degree) of trunk **210**
941.10	Erythema due to burn (first degree) of unspecified site of face and head **210**
943.1*	Erythema due to burn (first degree) of upper limb, except wrist and hand **210**
944.1*	Erythema due to burn (first degree) of wrist(s) and hand(s) **211**
949.1	Erythema due to burn (first degree), unspecified site **211**
695.1*	Erythema multiforme **106**
695.2	Erythema nodosum **106**
017.1*	Erythema nodosum with hypersensitivity reaction in tuberculosis **106**
690*	Erythematosquamous dermatosis **109**
530.82	Esophageal hemorrhage **75**
530.83	Esophageal leukoplakia **78**
530.81	Esophageal reflux **78**
456.0	Esophageal varices with bleeding **75**
456.20	Esophageal varices with bleeding in diseases classified elsewhere **75**
456.1	Esophageal varices without mention of bleeding **75**
456.21	Esophageal varices without mention of bleeding in diseases classified elsewhere **78**
530.1*	Esophagitis **78**
862.32	Esophagus injury with open wound into cavity **79**
862.22	Esophagus injury without mention of open wound into cavity **75**
378.0*	Esotropia **40**
333.1	Essential and other specified forms of tremor **32**
401.1	Essential hypertension, benign **67**
401.0	Essential hypertension, malignant **67**
238.71	Essential thrombocythemia **177**
V86*	Estrogen receptor status **216**
381.5*	Eustachian salpingitis **46**
V72.1*	Examination of ears and hearing **174**
766.0	Exceptionally large baby relating to long gestation **172** , **173**

790.3	Excessive blood level of alcohol **192**
656.63	Excessive fetal growth affecting management of mother, antepartum **156** , **158**
656.61	Excessive fetal growth affecting management of mother, delivered **137** , **144** , **150**
656.60	Excessive fetal growth affecting management of mother, unspecified as to episode of care **161**
298.1	Excitative type psychosis **190**
695.5*	Exfoliation due to erythematous conditions according to extent of body surface involved **109**
994.5	Exhaustion due to excessive exertion **205**
994.4	Exhaustion due to exposure **205**
378.1*	Exotropia **40**
301.3	Explosive personality disorder **189**
315.31	Expressive language disorder **190**
900.02	External carotid artery injury **227**
900.81	External jugular vein injury **167** , **171** , **227**
852.52	Extradural hemorrhage following injury, with open intracranial wound, brief (less than 1 hour) loss of consciousness **31**
852.56	Extradural hemorrhage following injury, with open intracranial wound, loss of consciousness of unspecified duration **26**
852.53	Extradural hemorrhage following injury, with open intracranial wound, moderate (1-24 hours) loss of consciousness **26**
852.51	Extradural hemorrhage following injury, with open intracranial wound, no loss of consciousness **31**
852.54	Extradural hemorrhage following injury, with open intracranial wound, prolonged (more than 24 hours) loss of consciousness and return to pre-existing conscious level **26**
852.55	Extradural hemorrhage following injury, with open intracranial wound, prolonged (more than 24 hours) loss of consciousness, without return to pre-existing conscious level **26**
852.50	Extradural hemorrhage following injury, with open intracranial wound, state of consciousness unspecified **31**
852.59	Extradural hemorrhage following injury, with open intracranial wound, unspecified concussion **31**
852.42	Extradural hemorrhage following injury, without mention of open intracranial wound, brief (less than 1 hour) loss of consciousness **31**
852.46	Extradural hemorrhage following injury, without mention of open intracranial wound, loss of consciousness of unspecified duration **26**
852.43	Extradural hemorrhage following injury, without mention of open intracranial wound, moderate (1-24 hours) loss of consciousness **26**
852.41	Extradural hemorrhage following injury, without mention of open intracranial wound, no loss of consciousness **31**
852.44	Extradural hemorrhage following injury, without mention of open intracranial wound, prolonged (more than 24 hours) loss of consciousness and return to pre-existing conscious level **26**
852.45	Extradural hemorrhage following injury, without mention of open intracranial wound, prolonged (more than 24 hours) loss of consciousness, without return to pre-existing conscious level **26**
852.49	Extradural hemorrhage following injury, without mention of open intracranial wound, unspecified concussion **31**
852.40	Extradural hemorrhage following injury, without mention of open intracranial wound, unspecified state of consciousness **31**
999.82	Extravasation of other vesicant agent **69**
788.8	Extravasation of urine **120**
999.81	Extravasation of vesicant chemotherapy **69**
765.04	Extreme fetal immaturity, 1,000-1,249 grams **164**
765.05	Extreme fetal immaturity, 1,250-1,499 grams **164**
765.06	Extreme fetal immaturity, 1,500-1,749 grams **164** , **168**
765.07	Extreme fetal immaturity, 1,750-1,999 grams **164** , **168**
765.08	Extreme fetal immaturity, 2,000-2,499 grams **164** , **168**
765.02	Extreme fetal immaturity, 500-749 grams **164**

765.03	Extreme fetal immaturity, 750-999 grams **164**	
765.01	Extreme fetal immaturity, less than 500 grams **164**	
765.00	Extreme fetal immaturity, unspecified (weight) **164 , 168**	
495*	Extrinsic allergic alveolitis **53**	
493.0*	Extrinsic asthma **53**	
493.01	Extrinsic asthma with status asthmaticus **166 , 170**	
V43.0	Eye globe replaced by other means **40**	
374.41	Eyelid retraction or lag **39**	
910.1	Face, neck, and scalp except eye, abrasion or friction burn, infected **107**	
910.3	Face, neck, and scalp except eye, blister, infected **109**	
910.2	Face, neck, and scalp except eye, blister, without mention of infection **109**	
910.5	Face, neck, and scalp except eye, insect bite, nonvenomous, infected **107**	
910.4	Face, neck, and scalp except eye, insect bite, nonvenomous, without mention of infection **109**	
910.7	Face, neck, and scalp except eye, superficial foreign body (splinter), without major open wound, infected **107**	
910.0	Face, neck, and scalp, except eye, abrasion or friction burn, without mention of infection **108**	
910.6	Face, neck, and scalp, except eye, superficial foreign body (splinter), without major open wound or mention of infection **108**	
351*	Facial nerve disorders **20**	
781.94	Facial weakness **32**	
300.16	Factitious disorder with predominantly psychological signs and symptoms **189**	
638*	Failed attempted abortion **154**	
660.73	Failed forceps or vacuum extractor, unspecified, antepartum **156 , 159**	
659.03	Failed mechanical induction of labor, antepartum **156 , 159**	
659.01	Failed mechanical induction of labor, delivered **137 , 144 , 150**	
659.00	Failed mechanical induction of labor, unspecified as to episode of care **137 , 144 , 150**	
659.13	Failed medical or unspecified induction of labor, antepartum **156 , 159**	
659.11	Failed medical or unspecified induction of labor, delivered **137 , 144 , 150**	
659.10	Failed medical or unspecified induction of labor, unspecified as to episode of care **137 , 144 , 150**	
676.43	Failure of lactation, antepartum condition or complication **157 , 159**	
676.44	Failure of lactation, postpartum condition or complication **154**	
676.40	Failure of lactation, unspecified as to episode of care **162**	
676.42	Failure of lactation, with delivery, with mention of postpartum complication **140 , 146 , 152**	
676.41	Failure of lactation, with delivery, with or without mention of antepartum condition **140 , 146 , 152**	
779.34	Failure to thrive in newborn **114 , 232**	
795.6	False positive serological test for syphilis **97**	
289.6	Familial polycythemia **177**	
V61.0*	Family disruption **215**	
V17*	Family history of certain chronic disabling diseases **215**	
V18*	Family history of certain other specific conditions **215**	
V16*	Family history of malignant neoplasm **215**	
V19*	Family history of other conditions **215**	
121.3	Fascioliasis **83**	
121.4	Fasciolopsiasis **83**	
958.1	Fat embolism as an early complication of trauma **51 , 167 , 171 , 225 , 228**	
032.0	Faucial diphtheria **2 , 46**	
780.31	Febrile convulsions (simple), unspecified **167 , 171**	

780.66	Febrile nonhemolytic transfusion reaction **185 , 232**	
560.32	Fecal impaction **167 , 171**	
779.31	Feeding problems in newborn **172**	
714.1	Felty's syndrome **97**	
629.2*	Female genital mutilation status **131**	
628*	Female infertility **128 , 131**	
625.6	Female stress incontinence **131**	
551.02	Femoral hernia with gangrene, bilateral, (not specified as recurrent) **167 , 171**	
551.00	Femoral hernia with gangrene, unilateral or unspecified (not specified as recurrent) **167 , 171**	
552.0*	Femoral hernia with obstruction **78**	
553.0*	Femoral hernia without mention of obstruction or gangrene **79**	
904.2	Femoral vein injury **224 , 228**	
772.5	Fetal and neonatal adrenal hemorrhage **164 , 168**	
772.6	Fetal and neonatal cutaneous hemorrhage **172 , 173**	
772.4	Fetal and neonatal gastrointestinal hemorrhage **164 , 168**	
772.2	Fetal and neonatal subarachnoid hemorrhage of newborn **164 , 168**	
770.1*	Fetal and newborn aspiration **164 , 168**	
777.1	Fetal and newborn meconium obstruction **164 , 169**	
772.0	Fetal blood loss affecting newborn **164 , 168**	
679.13	Fetal complications from in utero procedure, antepartum condition or complication **157 , 160**	
679.12	Fetal complications from in utero procedure, delivered, with mention of postpartum complication **140 , 146 , 152**	
679.11	Fetal complications from in utero procedure, delivered, with or without mention of antepartum condition **140 , 146 , 152**	
679.14	Fetal complications from in utero procedure, postpartum condition or complication **154**	
679.10	Fetal complications from in utero procedure, unspecified as to episode of care or not applicable **162**	
678.13	Fetal conjoined twins, antepartum condition or complication **157 , 159**	
678.11	Fetal conjoined twins, delivered, with or without mention of antepartum condition **140 , 146 , 152**	
678.10	Fetal conjoined twins, unspecified as to episode of care or not applicable **162**	
653.83	Fetal disproportion of other origin, antepartum **155 , 158**	
653.81	Fetal disproportion of other origin, delivered **136 , 143 , 149**	
653.80	Fetal disproportion of other origin, unspecified as to episode of care **161**	
656.33	Fetal distress affecting management of mother, antepartum **156 , 158**	
656.31	Fetal distress affecting management of mother, delivered **137 , 144 , 150**	
656.30	Fetal distress affecting management of mother, unspecified as to episode of care **137 , 144 , 150**	
652.43	Fetal face or brow presentation, antepartum **155 , 158**	
652.41	Fetal face or brow presentation, delivered **136 , 143 , 149**	
652.40	Fetal face or brow presentation, unspecified as to episode of care **161**	
678.03	Fetal hematologic conditions, antepartum condition or complication **157 , 159**	
678.01	Fetal hematologic conditions, delivered, with or without mention of antepartum condition **140 , 146 , 152**	
678.00	Fetal hematologic conditions, unspecified as to episode of care or not applicable **162**	
764.24	Fetal malnutrition without mention of "light-for-dates", 1,000-1,249 grams **164 , 168**	
764.25	Fetal malnutrition without mention of "light-for-dates", 1,250-1,499 grams **164 , 168**	
764.26	Fetal malnutrition without mention of "light-for-dates", 1,500-1,749 grams **164 , 168**	

*Code Range

764.27	Fetal malnutrition without mention of "light-for-dates", 1,750-1,999 grams **164** , **168**
764.28	Fetal malnutrition without mention of "light-for-dates", 2,000-2,499 grams **164** , **168**
764.22	Fetal malnutrition without mention of "light-for-dates", 500-749 grams **164** , **168**
764.23	Fetal malnutrition without mention of "light-for-dates", 750-999 grams **164** , **168**
764.21	Fetal malnutrition without mention of "light-for-dates", less than 500 grams **164** , **168**
656.03	Fetal-maternal hemorrhage, antepartum condition or complication **156** , **158**
656.00	Fetal-maternal hemorrhage, unspecified as to episode of care in pregnancy **161**
656.01	Fetal-maternal hemorrhage, with delivery **137** , **144** , **150**
653.43	Fetopelvic disproportion, antepartum **155** , **158**
653.41	Fetopelvic disproportion, delivered **136** , **143** , **149**
653.40	Fetopelvic disproportion, unspecified as to episode of care **161**
763.0	Fetus or newborn affected by breech delivery and extraction **172** , **173**
763.4	Fetus or newborn affected by cesarean delivery **164** , **168**
763.3	Fetus or newborn affected by delivery by vacuum extractor **172** , **173**
763.2	Fetus or newborn affected by forceps delivery **172** , **173**
762.6	Fetus or newborn affected by other and unspecified conditions of umbilical cord **172** , **173**
762.5	Fetus or newborn affected by other compression of umbilical cord **172** , **173**
763.1	Fetus or newborn affected by other malpresentation, malposition, and disproportion during labor and delivery **172** , **173**
763.6	Fetus or newborn affected by precipitate delivery **172** , **173**
762.4	Fetus or newborn affected by prolapsed cord **172** , **173**
780.61	Fever presenting with conditions classified elsewhere **185** , **232**
780.60	Fever, unspecified **185** , **232**
125*	Filarial infection and dracontiasis **187**
915.1	Finger, abrasion or friction burn, infected **107**
915.3	Finger, blister, infected **107**
915.2	Finger, blister, without mention of infection **109**
915.5	Finger, insect bite, nonvenomous, infected **107**
915.4	Finger, insect bite, nonvenomous, without mention of infection **109**
915.6	Finger, superficial foreign body (splinter), without major open wound and without mention of infection **108**
915.7	Finger, superficial foreign body (splinter), without major open wound, infected **107**
664.04	First-degree perineal laceration, postpartum condition or complication **153**
664.00	First-degree perineal laceration, unspecified as to episode of care in pregnancy **138** , **145** , **151**
664.01	First-degree perineal laceration, with delivery **138** , **145** , **151**
569.81	Fistula of intestine, excluding rectum and anus **79**
537.4	Fistula of stomach or duodenum **78**
V52.0	Fitting and adjustment of artificial arm (complete) (partial) **99**
V52.2	Fitting and adjustment of artificial eye **215**
V52.1	Fitting and adjustment of artificial leg (complete) (partial) **99**
V52.4	Fitting and adjustment of breast prosthesis and implant **215**
V53.3*	Fitting and adjustment of cardiac device **69**
V52.3	Fitting and adjustment of dental prosthetic device **215**
V53.0*	Fitting and adjustment of devices related to nervous system and special senses **33**
V53.2	Fitting and adjustment of hearing aid **215**
V53.4	Fitting and adjustment of orthodontic devices **215**
V53.7	Fitting and adjustment of orthopedic device **99**

V53.9*	Fitting and adjustment of other and unspecified device **215**
V53.5*	Fitting and adjustment of other gastrointestinal appliance and device **79**
V52.8	Fitting and adjustment of other specified prosthetic device **214**
V53.1	Fitting and adjustment of spectacles and contact lenses **215**
V52.9	Fitting and adjustment of unspecified prosthetic device **214**
V53.6	Fitting and adjustment of urinary device **121**
V53.8	Fitting and adjustment of wheelchair **215**
807.4	Flail chest **52** , **222** , **227**
734	Flat foot **100**
005.2	Food poisoning due to Clostridium perfringens (C. welchii) **75**
005.3	Food poisoning due to other Clostridia **75**
005.4	Food poisoning due to Vibrio parahaemolyticus **75**
078.4	Foot and mouth disease **186**
917.1	Foot and toe(s), abrasion or friction burn, infected **107**
917.3	Foot and toe(s), blister, infected **107**
917.2	Foot and toe(s), blister, without mention of infection **109**
917.5	Foot and toe(s), insect bite, nonvenomous, infected **107**
917.4	Foot and toe(s), insect bite, nonvenomous, without mention of infection **109**
917.6	Foot and toe(s), superficial foreign body (splinter), without major open wound and without mention of infection **108**
917.7	Foot and toe(s), superficial foreign body (splinter), without major open wound, infected **107**
845.1*	Foot sprain and strain **100**
669.51	Forceps or vacuum extractor delivery without mention of indication, delivered, with or without mention of antepartum condition **139** , **146** , **151**
669.50	Forceps or vacuum extractor delivery without mention of indication, unspecified as to episode of care **139** , **146** , **151**
998.4	Foreign body accidentally left during procedure, not elsewhere classified **168** , **172** , **205**
728.82	Foreign body granuloma of muscle **99**
937	Foreign body in anus and rectum **79**
939.0	Foreign body in bladder and urethra **121**
938	Foreign body in digestive system, unspecified **79**
931	Foreign body in ear **47**
935.1	Foreign body in esophagus **79**
936	Foreign body in intestine and colon **79**
934.1	Foreign body in main bronchus **54**
935.0	Foreign body in mouth **4** , **48**
932	Foreign body in nose **48**
934.8	Foreign body in other specified parts of trachea, bronchus, and lung **54**
939.3	Foreign body in penis **125**
933*	Foreign body in pharynx and larynx **4** , **48**
934.9	Foreign body in respiratory tree, unspecified **54**
935.2	Foreign body in stomach **79**
934.0	Foreign body in trachea **54**
939.9	Foreign body in unspecified site in genitourinary tract **121**
939.1	Foreign body in uterus, any part **129** , **132**
939.2	Foreign body in vulva and vagina **129** , **132**
930*	Foreign body on external eye **40**
377.04	Foster-Kennedy syndrome **32**
664.34	Fourth-degree perineal laceration, postpartum condition or complication **153**
664.30	Fourth-degree perineal laceration, unspecified as to episode of care in pregnancy **138** , **145** , **151**
664.31	Fourth-degree perineal laceration, with delivery **138** , **145** , **151**
824*	Fracture of ankle **99**
809.0	Fracture of bones of trunk, closed **101** , **222**

809.1	Fracture of bones of trunk, open **101** , **222** , **228**	
814*	Fracture of carpal bone(s) **99**	
810*	Fracture of clavicle **99**	
812*	Fracture of humerus **99**	
815*	Fracture of metacarpal bone(s) **99**	
820*	Fracture of neck of femur **96** , **167** , **171** , **228**	
826*	Fracture of one or more phalanges of foot **99**	
816*	Fracture of one or more phalanges of hand **99**	
821*	Fracture of other and unspecified parts of femur **96** , **228**	
822*	Fracture of patella **99**	
808*	Fracture of pelvis **96** , **228**	
813*	Fracture of radius and ulna **99**	
823*	Fracture of tibia and fibula **99**	
829*	Fracture of unspecified bones **100**	
806*	Fracture of vertebral column with spinal cord injury **18**	
805*	Fracture of vertebral column without mention of spinal cord injury **98**	
759.83	Fragile X syndrome **189**	
788.4*	Frequency of urination and polyuria **120**	
799.55	Frontal lobe and executive function deficit **189**	
310.0	Frontal lobe syndrome **189**	
331.1*	Frontotemporal dementia **19**	
941.32	Full-thickness skin loss due to burn (third degree NOS) of eye (with other parts of face, head, and neck) **40**	
941.3*	Full-thickness skin loss due to burn (third degree NOS) of face, head, and neck **207** , **208** , **209** , **210**	
945.3*	Full-thickness skin loss due to burn (third degree NOS) of lower limb(s) **207** , **208** , **209** , **210**	
946.3	Full-thickness skin loss due to burn (third degree NOS) of multiple specified sites **207** , **208** , **209** , **210**	
942.3*	Full-thickness skin loss due to burn (third degree NOS) of trunk **207** , **208** , **209** , **210**	
943.3*	Full-thickness skin loss due to burn (third degree NOS) of upper limb, except wrist and hand **207** , **208** , **209** , **210**	
944.3*	Full-thickness skin loss due to burn (third degree NOS) of wrist(s) and hand(s) **207** , **208** , **209** , **210**	
949.3	Full-thickness skin loss due to burn (third degree NOS), unspecified site **207** , **208** , **209** , **210**	
564.5	Functional diarrhea **78**	
288.1	Functional disorders of polymorphonuclear neutrophils **176**	
429.4	Functional disturbances following cardiac surgery **69** , **166** , **170**	
780.72	Functional quadriplegia **18**	
676.60	Galactorrhea associated with childbirth, unspecified as to episode of care **162**	
676.63	Galactorrhea, antepartum condition or complication **157** , **159**	
676.64	Galactorrhea, postpartum condition or complication **154**	
676.62	Galactorrhea, with delivery, with mention of postpartum complication **140** , **146** , **152**	
676.61	Galactorrhea, with delivery, with or without mention of antepartum condition **140** , **146** , **152**	
271.1	Galactosemia **114**	
086.3	Gambian trypanosomiasis **186**	
727.4*	Ganglion and cyst of synovium, tendon, and bursa **99**	
102.5	Gangosa due to yaws **2** , **47**	
785.4	Gangrene **67** , **167** , **171**	
040.0	Gas gangrene **165** , **169** , **186**	
537.1	Gastric diverticulum **78**	
535.21	Gastric mucosal hypertrophy with hemorrhage **76**	
535.20	Gastric mucosal hypertrophy without mention of hemorrhage **78**	
531.91	Gastric ulcer, unspecified as acute or chronic, without mention of hemorrhage or perforation, with obstruction **77**	

531.90	Gastric ulcer, unspecified as acute or chronic, without mention of hemorrhage, perforation, or obstruction **77**
558.1	Gastroenteritis and colitis due to radiation **79** , **231**
558.3	Gastroenteritis and colitis, allergic **78**
530.7	Gastroesophageal laceration-hemorrhage syndrome **75**
022.2	Gastrointestinal anthrax **75**
578*	Gastrointestinal hemorrhage **76** , **167** , **171**
306.4	Gastrointestinal malfunction arising from mental factors **78**
538	Gastrointestinal mucositis (ulcerative) **78**
863.90	Gastrointestinal tract injury, unspecified site, with open wound into cavity **79**
863.80	Gastrointestinal tract injury, unspecified site, without mention of open wound into cavity **79**
534.9*	Gastrojejunal ulcer, unspecified as acute or chronic, without mention of hemorrhage or perforation **77**
536.3	Gastroparesis **78**
537.5	Gastroptosis **78**
756.73	Gastroschisis **167** , **171**
536.4*	Gastrostomy complications **78**
V25.0*	General counseling and advice for contraceptive management **215**
V70*	General medical examination **216**
094.1	General paresis **19**
440.9	Generalized and unspecified atherosclerosis **66**
368.45	Generalized contraction or constriction in visual field **38**
780.8	Generalized hyperhidrosis **109** , **232**
659.33	Generalized infection during labor, antepartum **156** , **159**
659.31	Generalized infection during labor, delivered **137** , **141** , **147**
659.30	Generalized infection during labor, unspecified as to episode of care **137** , **144** , **150**
999.0	Generalized vaccinia as complication of medical care, not elsewhere classified **186**
653.13	Generally contracted pelvis in pregnancy, antepartum **155** , **158**
653.11	Generally contracted pelvis in pregnancy, delivered **136** , **143** , **149**
653.10	Generally contracted pelvis in pregnancy, unspecified as to episode of care in pregnancy **161**
288.2	Genetic anomalies of leukocytes **176**
V26.3*	Genetic counseling and testing **215**
V84.0*	Genetic susceptibility to malignant neoplasm **216**
V84.8*	Genetic susceptibility to other disease **216**
333.6	Genetic torsion dystonia **19**
053.11	Geniculate herpes zoster **20** , **165** , **169** , **230**
618*	Genital prolapse **128** , **131**
091.0	Genital syphilis (primary) **125** , **128** , **130**
619.2	Genital tract-skin fistula, female **128** , **131**
016.9*	Genitourinary tuberculosis, unspecified **120**
736.5	Genu recurvatum (acquired) **100**
736.4*	Genu valgum or varum (acquired) **100**
446.5	Giant cell arteritis **97**
727.02	Giant cell tumor of tendon sheath **100**
523*	Gingival and periodontal diseases **3** , **48**
024	Glanders **186**
365.4*	Glaucoma associated with congenital anomalies, dystrophies, and systemic syndromes **39**
365.5*	Glaucoma associated with disorders of the lens **39**
365.6*	Glaucoma associated with other ocular disorders **39**
365.7*	Glaucoma stage **39**
377.14	Glaucomatous atrophy (cupping) of optic disc **40**
271.0	Glycogenosis **114**
791.5	Glycosuria **114**

758.6	Gonadal dysgenesis **125 , 128 , 131**
098.50	Gonococcal arthritis **97**
098.52	Gonococcal bursitis **97**
098.15	Gonococcal cervicitis (acute) **128 , 130**
098.35	Gonococcal cervicitis, chronic **128 , 130**
098.11	Gonococcal cystitis (acute) **120**
098.31	Gonococcal cystitis, chronic **120**
098.84	Gonococcal endocarditis **65**
098.16	Gonococcal endometritis (acute) **128 , 130**
098.36	Gonococcal endometritis, chronic **128 , 130**
098.13	Gonococcal epididymo-orchitis (acute) **125**
098.33	Gonococcal epididymo-orchitis, chronic **125**
098.0	Gonococcal infection (acute) of lower genitourinary tract **125 , 128 , 130**
098.10	Gonococcal infection (acute) of upper genitourinary tract, site unspecified **125 , 128 , 130**
098.7	Gonococcal infection of anus and rectum **78**
098.4*	Gonococcal infection of eye **38**
098.89	Gonococcal infection of other specified sites **186**
098.6	Gonococcal infection of pharynx **2 , 46**
098.2	Gonococcal infections, chronic, of lower genitourinary tract **125 , 128 , 130**
098.81	Gonococcal keratosis (blennorrhagica) **38**
098.82	Gonococcal meningitis **9 , 10 , 33**
098.83	Gonococcal pericarditis **68**
098.86	Gonococcal peritonitis **75**
098.12	Gonococcal prostatitis (acute) **125**
098.32	Gonococcal prostatitis, chronic **125**
098.37	Gonococcal salpingitis (chronic) **128 , 130**
098.17	Gonococcal salpingitis, specified as acute **128 , 130**
098.14	Gonococcal seminal vesiculitis (acute) **125**
098.34	Gonococcal seminal vesiculitis, chronic **125**
098.53	Gonococcal spondylitis **96**
098.51	Gonococcal synovitis and tenosynovitis **97**
274.8*	Gout with other specified manifestations **98**
274.9	Gout, unspecified **98**
274.0*	Gouty arthropathy **98**
274.10	Gouty nephropathy, unspecified **121**
279.5*	Graft-versus-host disease **176**
659.43	Grand multiparity with current pregnancy, antepartum **156 , 159**
659.40	Grand multiparity with current pregnancy, unspecified as to episode of care **162**
659.41	Grand multiparity, delivered, with or without mention of antepartum condition **137 , 144 , 150**
099.2	Granuloma inguinale **125 , 128 , 131**
102.4	Gummata and ulcers due to yaws **108**
780.1	Hallucinations **189**
074.3	Hand, foot, and mouth disease **185**
914.1	Hand(s) except finger(s) alone, abrasion or friction burn, infected **107**
914.0	Hand(s) except finger(s) alone, abrasion or friction burn, without mention of infection **108**
914.3	Hand(s) except finger(s) alone, blister, infected **107**
914.2	Hand(s) except finger(s) alone, blister, without mention of infection **109**
914.5	Hand(s) except finger(s) alone, insect bite, nonvenomous, infected **107**
914.4	Hand(s) except finger(s) alone, insect bite, nonvenomous, without mention of infection **109**
914.7	Hand(s) except finger(s) alone, superficial foreign body (splinter) without major open wound, infected **107**
914.6	Hand(s) except finger(s) alone, superficial foreign body (splinter), without major open wound and without mention of infection **108**
784.0	Headache **34**
V61.4*	Health problems within family **215**
V20*	Health supervision of infant or child **215**
V20.1	Health supervision of other healthy infant or child receiving care **173**
389*	Hearing loss **47**
428*	Heart failure **66**
861.1*	Heart injury, with open wound into thorax **69**
861.0*	Heart injury, without mention of open wound into thorax **69**
V43.2*	Heart replaced by other means **69**
V42.1	Heart replaced by transplant **69**
V43.3	Heart valve replaced by other means **69**
V42.2	Heart valve replaced by transplant **69**
228.04	Hemangioma of intra-abdominal structures **78**
228.02	Hemangioma of intracranial structures **32**
228.09	Hemangioma of other sites **3 , 68**
228.03	Hemangioma of retina **38**
228.01	Hemangioma of skin and subcutaneous tissue **3 , 109**
228.00	Hemangioma of unspecified site **3 , 68**
719.1*	Hemarthrosis **98**
629.0	Hematocele, female, not elsewhere classified **131**
998.12	Hematoma complicating a procedure **168 , 172**
620.7	Hematoma of broad ligament **167 , 171**
599.7*	Hematuria **120 , 167 , 171**
342*	Hemiplegia and hemiparesis **19**
343.1	Hemiplegic infantile cerebral palsy **18**
756.14	Hemivertebra **98**
282.47	Hemoglobin E-beta thalassemia **165 , 170**
791.2	Hemoglobinuria **120**
283.2	Hemoglobinuria due to hemolysis from external causes **165 , 170 , 176**
773.2	Hemolytic disease due to other and unspecified isoimmunization of fetus or newborn **164 , 168**
999.83	Hemolytic transfusion reaction, incompatibility unspecified **176**
283.11	Hemolytic-uremic syndrome **176**
423.0	Hemopericardium **166 , 170**
568.81	Hemoperitoneum (nontraumatic) **167 , 171**
288.4	Hemophagocytic syndromes **177**
786.3*	Hemoptysis **54**
246.3	Hemorrhage and infarction of thyroid **3**
998.11	Hemorrhage complicating a procedure **168 , 172**
641.13	Hemorrhage from placenta previa, antepartum **155 , 158**
641.10	Hemorrhage from placenta previa, unspecified as to episode of care **160**
641.11	Hemorrhage from placenta previa, with delivery **135 , 141 , 146**
784.8	Hemorrhage from throat **3 , 47**
596.7	Hemorrhage into bladder wall **167 , 171**
569.3	Hemorrhage of rectum and anus **76 , 167 , 171**
998.1*	Hemorrhage or hematoma or seroma complicating procedure, not elsewhere classified **205**
776.0	Hemorrhagic disease of newborn **164 , 168**
078.6	Hemorrhagic nephrosonephritis **120**
455*	Hemorrhoids **78**
289.84	Heparin-induced thrombocytopenia [HIT] **165 , 170 , 177 , 231**
572.2	Hepatic encephalopathy **167 , 171**

573.4	Hepatic infarction **83 , 167 , 171**
130.5	Hepatitis due to toxoplasmosis **83 , 165 , 169**
573.2	Hepatitis in other infectious diseases classified elsewhere **83**
573.1	Hepatitis in viral diseases classified elsewhere **83**
789.1	Hepatomegaly **83 , 232**
573.5	Hepatopulmonary syndrome **54**
572.4	Hepatorenal syndrome **167 , 171**
655.23	Hereditary disease in family possibly affecting fetus, affecting management of mother, antepartum condition or complication **156 , 158**
655.20	Hereditary disease in family possibly affecting fetus, affecting management of mother, unspecified as to episode of care in pregnancy **161**
655.21	Hereditary disease in family possibly affecting fetus, affecting management of mother, with delivery **136 , 144 , 149**
757.0	Hereditary edema of legs **109**
271.2	Hereditary fructose intolerance **78**
282*	Hereditary hemolytic anemias **176**
448.0	Hereditary hemorrhagic telangiectasia **66**
377.16	Hereditary optic atrophy **38**
356.0	Hereditary peripheral neuropathy **20**
359.1	Hereditary progressive muscular dystrophy **32**
362.7*	Hereditary retinal dystrophies **39**
356.2	Hereditary sensory neuropathy **20**
552.8	Hernia of other specified site, with obstruction **78 , 167 , 171**
553.8	Hernia of other specified sites of abdominal cavity without mention of obstruction or gangrene **79**
551.8	Hernia of other specified sites, with gangrene **167 , 171**
553.9	Hernia of unspecified site of abdominal cavity without mention of obstruction or gangrene **79**
551.9	Hernia of unspecified site, with gangrene **167 , 171**
552.9	Hernia of unspecified site, with obstruction **78 , 167 , 171**
074.0	Herpangina **2 , 46**
054.41	Herpes simplex dermatitis of eyelid **230**
054.43	Herpes simplex disciform keratitis **230**
054.44	Herpes simplex iridocyclitis **230**
054.72	Herpes simplex meningitis **8 , 10 , 21 , 165 , 169 , 231**
054.74	Herpes simplex myelitis **8 , 10 , 33**
054.73	Herpes simplex otitis externa **47 , 165 , 169 , 231**
054.4*	Herpes simplex with ophthalmic complications **38 , 165 , 169**
054.49	Herpes simplex with other ophthalmic complications **230**
054.9	Herpes simplex without mention of complication **108 , 231**
053.20	Herpes zoster dermatitis of eyelid **165 , 169 , 230**
053.22	Herpes zoster iridocyclitis **165 , 169 , 230**
053.21	Herpes zoster keratoconjunctivitis **165 , 169 , 230**
053.14	Herpes zoster myelitis **8 , 10 , 33**
053.0	Herpes zoster with meningitis **21 , 165 , 169 , 230**
053.2*	Herpes zoster with ophthalmic complications **38**
053.10	Herpes zoster with unspecified nervous system complication **20 , 165 , 169 , 230**
053.9	Herpes zoster without mention of complication **106 , 165 , 169 , 230**
054.2	Herpetic gingivostomatitis **2 , 48 , 165 , 169 , 230**
054.13	Herpetic infection of penis **125 , 230**
054.3	Herpetic meningoencephalitis **8 , 10 , 33 , 165 , 169 , 230**
054.5	Herpetic septicemia **165 , 169 , 187 , 230**
054.12	Herpetic ulceration of vulva **128 , 130 , 230**
054.11	Herpetic vulvovaginitis **128 , 130 , 230**
054.6	Herpetic whitlow **108 , 230**
368.47	Heteronymous bilateral field defects in visual field **38**
378.4*	Heterophoria **40**

121.6	Heterophyiasis **186**
786.8	Hiccough **54**
327.22	High altitude periodic breathing **54**
652.53	High fetal head at term, antepartum **155 , 158**
652.51	High fetal head at term, delivered **136 , 143 , 149**
652.50	High fetal head at term, unspecified as to episode of care **161**
238.73	High grade myelodysplastic syndrome lesions **176**
665.44	High vaginal laceration, postpartum condition or complication **153**
665.40	High vaginal laceration, unspecified as to episode of care in pregnancy **138 , 145 , 151**
665.41	High vaginal laceration, with delivery **138 , 145 , 151**
916.1	Hip, thigh, leg, and ankle, abrasion or friction burn, infected **107**
916.0	Hip, thigh, leg, and ankle, abrasion or friction burn, without mention of infection **108**
916.3	Hip, thigh, leg, and ankle, blister, infected **107**
916.2	Hip, thigh, leg, and ankle, blister, without mention of infection **109**
916.5	Hip, thigh, leg, and ankle, insect bite, nonvenomous, infected **107**
916.4	Hip, thigh, leg, and ankle, insect bite, nonvenomous, without mention of infection **109**
916.6	Hip, thigh, leg, and ankle, superficial foreign body (splinter), without major open wound and without mention of infection **108**
916.7	Hip, thigh, leg, and ankle, superficial foreign body (splinter), without major open wound, infected **107**
751.3	Hirschsprung's disease and other congenital functional disorders of colon **79**
115.04	Histoplasma capsulatum endocarditis **65 , 165 , 169**
115.01	Histoplasma capsulatum meningitis **9 , 10 , 33 , 165 , 169**
115.03	Histoplasma capsulatum pericarditis **68 , 165 , 169**
115.05	Histoplasma capsulatum pneumonia **51 , 165 , 169**
115.02	Histoplasma capsulatum retinitis **38 , 165 , 169**
115.09	Histoplasma capsulatum, with mention of other manifestation **186**
115.00	Histoplasma capsulatum, without mention of manifestation **186**
115.14	Histoplasma duboisii endocarditis **65 , 165 , 169**
115.11	Histoplasma duboisii meningitis **9 , 10 , 33 , 165 , 169**
115.13	Histoplasma duboisii pericarditis **68 , 165 , 169**
115.15	Histoplasma duboisii pneumonia **51 , 165 , 169**
115.12	Histoplasma duboisii retinitis **38 , 165 , 169**
115.19	Histoplasma duboisii with mention of other manifestation **186**
115.10	Histoplasma duboisii, without mention of manifestation **186**
115*	Histoplasmosis **231**
301.5*	Histrionic personality disorder **189**
201*	Hodgkin's disease **179 , 182**
201.71	Hodgkin's disease, lymphocytic depletion, of lymph nodes of head, face, and neck **2**
201.41	Hodgkin's disease, lymphocytic-histiocytic predominance of lymph nodes of head, face, and neck **2**
201.61	Hodgkin's disease, mixed cellularity, involving lymph nodes of head, face, and neck **2**
201.51	Hodgkin's disease, nodular sclerosis, of lymph nodes of head, face, and neck **2**
201.91	Hodgkin's disease, unspecified type, of lymph nodes of head, face, and neck **2**
201.11	Hodgkin's granuloma of lymph nodes of head, face, and neck **2**
201.01	Hodgkin's paragranuloma of lymph nodes of head, face, and neck **2**
201.21	Hodgkin's sarcoma of lymph nodes of head, face, and neck **2**
V62.85	Homicidal ideation **215**

368.46	Homonymous bilateral field defects in visual field **38**
537.6	Hourglass stricture or stenosis of stomach **78**
V60*	Housing, household, and economic circumstances **215**
058.21	Human herpesvirus 6 encephalitis **9 , 10 , 33 , 165 , 169 , 231**
042	Human immunodeficiency virus [HIV] **230 , 231**
275.5	Hungry bone syndrome **114**
333.4	Huntington's chorea **19**
630	Hydatidiform mole **155 , 158**
629.1	Hydrocele, canal of Nuck **131**
653.63	Hydrocephalic fetus causing disproportion, antepartum **155 , 158**
653.61	Hydrocephalic fetus causing disproportion, delivered **136 , 143 , 149**
653.60	Hydrocephalic fetus causing disproportion, unspecified as to episode of care **161**
591	Hydronephrosis **120 , 167 , 171**
773.3	Hydrops fetalis due to isoimmunization **164 , 168**
778.0	Hydrops fetalis not due to isoimmunization **164 , 169**
593.5	Hydroureter **120 , 167 , 171**
123.6	Hymenolepiasis **75**
388.42	Hyperacusis **47**
278.3	Hypercarotinemia **114**
643.13	Hyperemesis gravidarum with metabolic disturbance, antepartum **155 , 157**
643.11	Hyperemesis gravidarum with metabolic disturbance, delivered **135 , 142 , 148**
643.10	Hyperemesis gravidarum with metabolic disturbance, unspecified as to episode of care **157 , 160**
102.3	Hyperkeratosis due to yaws **108**
429.82	Hyperkinetic heart disease **69 , 166 , 170**
314*	Hyperkinetic syndrome of childhood **190**
367.0	Hypermetropia **39**
728.5	Hypermobility syndrome **99**
733.3	Hyperostosis of skull **100**
374.52	Hyperpigmentation of eyelid **39**
600*	Hyperplasia of prostate **124**
447.3	Hyperplasia of renal artery **121**
446.2*	Hypersensitivity angiitis **97**
780.53	Hypersomnia with sleep apnea, unspecified **3 , 47**
780.54	Hypersomnia, unspecified **190**
289.4	Hypersplenism **177 , 231**
642.13	Hypertension secondary to renal disease, antepartum **155 , 157**
642.14	Hypertension secondary to renal disease, complicating pregnancy, childbirth, and the puerperium, postpartum condition or complication **152**
642.10	Hypertension secondary to renal disease, complicating pregnancy, childbirth, and the puerperium, unspecified as to episode of care **160**
642.11	Hypertension secondary to renal disease, with delivery **135 , 141 , 146**
642.12	Hypertension secondary to renal disease, with delivery, with current postpartum complication **135 , 141 , 147**
403.10	Hypertensive chronic kidney disease, benign, with chronic kidney disease stage I through stage IV, or unspecified **119**
403.11	Hypertensive chronic kidney disease, benign, with chronic kidney disease stage V or end stage renal disease **2 , 119**
403.00	Hypertensive chronic kidney disease, malignant, with chronic kidney disease stage I through stage IV, or unspecified **119**
403.01	Hypertensive chronic kidney disease, malignant, with chronic kidney disease stage V or end stage renal disease **2 , 119**
403.90	Hypertensive chronic kidney disease, unspecified, with chronic kidney disease stage I through stage IV, or unspecified **119**
403.91	Hypertensive chronic kidney disease, unspecified, with chronic kidney disease stage V or end stage renal disease **2 , 119**
437.2	Hypertensive encephalopathy **21**
404.13	Hypertensive heart and chronic kidney disease, benign, with heart failure and chronic kidney disease stage V or end stage renal disease **2 , 56 , 66 , 166 , 170**
404.11	Hypertensive heart and chronic kidney disease, benign, with heart failure and with chronic kidney disease stage I through stage IV, or unspecified **56 , 66 , 166 , 170**
404.10	Hypertensive heart and chronic kidney disease, benign, without heart failure and with chronic kidney disease stage I through stage IV, or unspecified **67**
404.12	Hypertensive heart and chronic kidney disease, benign, without heart failure and with chronic kidney disease stage V or end stage renal disease **2 , 119**
404.01	Hypertensive heart and chronic kidney disease, malignant, with heart failure and with chronic kidney disease stage I through stage IV, or unspecified **56 , 66 , 166 , 170**
404.03	Hypertensive heart and chronic kidney disease, malignant, with heart failure and with chronic kidney disease stage V or end stage renal disease **2 , 56 , 66 , 166 , 170**
404.00	Hypertensive heart and chronic kidney disease, malignant, without heart failure and with chronic kidney disease stage I through stage IV, or unspecified **67**
404.02	Hypertensive heart and chronic kidney disease, malignant, without heart failure and with chronic kidney disease stage V or end stage renal disease **2 , 119**
404.93	Hypertensive heart and chronic kidney disease, unspecified, with heart failure and chronic kidney disease stage V or end stage renal disease **2 , 56 , 66 , 166 , 170**
404.91	Hypertensive heart and chronic kidney disease, unspecified, with heart failure and with chronic kidney disease stage I through stage IV, or unspecified **56 , 66 , 166 , 170**
404.90	Hypertensive heart and chronic kidney disease, unspecified, without heart failure and with chronic kidney disease stage I through stage IV, or unspecified **67**
404.92	Hypertensive heart and chronic kidney disease, unspecified, without heart failure and with chronic kidney disease stage V or end stage renal disease **2 , 119**
402.91	Hypertensive heart disease, unspecified, with heart failure **56 , 65 , 166 , 170**
661.43	Hypertonic, incoordinate, or prolonged uterine contractions, antepartum **156 , 159**
661.40	Hypertonic, incoordinate, or prolonged uterine contractions, unspecified as to episode of care **137 , 145 , 150**
661.41	Hypertonic, incoordinate, or prolonged uterine contractions, with delivery **137 , 145 , 150**
374.54	Hypertrichosis of eyelid **39**
593.1	Hypertrophy of kidney **121**
478.0	Hypertrophy of nasal turbinates **47**
474.1*	Hypertrophy of tonsils and adenoids **47**
278.2	Hypervitaminosis A **114**
278.4	Hypervitaminosis D **114**
364.41	Hyphema **39**
775.4	Hypocalcemia and hypomagnesemia of newborn **164 , 168**
300.7	Hypochondriasis **189**
251.2	Hypoglycemia, unspecified **114**
251.0	Hypoglycemic coma **114 , 165 , 169**
252.1	Hypoparathyroidism **165 , 169**
374.53	Hypopigmentation of eyelid **39**
746.7	Hypoplastic left heart syndrome **67**
370.04	Hypopyon ulcer **38**
752.6*	Hypospadias and epispadias and other penile anomalies **125**
780.65	Hypothermia not associated with low environmental temperature **214**

360.3*	Hypotony of eye **39**	
374.55	Hypotrichosis of eyelid **39**	
300.10	Hysteria, unspecified **189**	
277.83	Iatrogenic carnitine deficiency **115**	
458.2*	Iatrogenic hypotension **68**	
512.1	Iatrogenic pneumothorax **53**	
757.1	Ichthyosis congenita **109**	
516.30	Idiopathic interstitial pneumonia, not otherwise specified **231**	
516.35	Idiopathic lymphoid interstitial pneumonia **231**	
331.5	Idiopathic normal pressure hydrocephalus [INPH] **19**	
356.4	Idiopathic progressive polyneuropathy **21**	
327.24	Idiopathic sleep related nonobstructive alveolar hypoventilation **47**	
341.22	Idiopathic transverse myelitis **10**	
818.0	Ill-defined closed fractures of upper limb **222**	
818*	Ill-defined fractures of upper limb **99**	
009*	Ill-defined intestinal infections **77 , 231**	
818.1	Ill-defined open fractures of upper limb **222 , 228**	
636*	Illegally induced abortion **154**	
V61.6	Illegitimacy or illegitimate pregnancy **157 , 160**	
380.4	Impacted cerumen **47**	
560.39	Impaction of intestine, other **167 , 171**	
388.43	Impairment of auditory discrimination **47**	
684	Impetigo **107**	
694.3	Impetigo herpetiformis **109**	
607.84	Impotence of organic origin **125**	
312.30	Impulse control disorder, unspecified **190**	
799.23	Impulsiveness **189**	
752.7	Indeterminate sex and pseudohermaphroditism **125 , 128 , 131**	
040.41	Infant botulism **165 , 169 , 186**	
343.4	Infantile hemiplegia **18**	
603.1	Infected hydrocele **125**	
998.51	Infected postoperative seroma **168 , 172 , 185**	
996.61	Infection and inflammatory reaction due to cardiac device, implant, and graft **69**	
996.64	Infection and inflammatory reaction due to indwelling urinary catheter **121**	
996.66	Infection and inflammatory reaction due to internal joint prosthesis **90 , 99**	
996.63	Infection and inflammatory reaction due to nervous system device, implant, and graft **33**	
996.65	Infection and inflammatory reaction due to other genitourinary device, implant, and graft **121**	
996.67	Infection and inflammatory reaction due to other internal orthopedic device, implant, and graft **90 , 99**	
996.69	Infection and inflammatory reaction due to other internal prosthetic device, implant, and graft **204**	
996.62	Infection and inflammatory reaction due to other vascular device, implant, and graft **69**	
996.68	Infection and inflammatory reaction due to peritoneal dialysis catheter **204**	
996.60	Infection and inflammatory reaction due to unspecified device, implant, and graft **204**	
658.43	Infection of amniotic cavity, antepartum **156 , 159**	
658.41	Infection of amniotic cavity, delivered **137 , 144 , 150**	
658.40	Infection of amniotic cavity, unspecified as to episode of care **137 , 144 , 150**	
530.86	Infection of esophagostomy **78**	
675.02	Infection of nipple associated with childbirth, delivered with mention of postpartum complication **140 , 142 , 148**	
675.01	Infection of nipple associated with childbirth, delivered, with or without mention of antepartum condition **140 , 142 , 148**	

675.00	Infection of nipple associated with childbirth, unspecified as to episode of care **162**
675.03	Infection of nipple, antepartum **157 , 159**
675.04	Infection of nipple, postpartum condition or complication **154**
V09*	Infection with drug-resistant microorganisms **187**
646.63	Infections of genitourinary tract antepartum **155 , 157**
646.64	Infections of genitourinary tract in pregnancy, postpartum condition or complication **153**
646.60	Infections of genitourinary tract in pregnancy, unspecified as to episode of care **157 , 160**
646.61	Infections of genitourinary tract in pregnancy, with delivery **135 , 142 , 148**
646.62	Infections of genitourinary tract in pregnancy, with delivery, with current postpartum complication **135 , 142 , 148**
590*	Infections of kidney **120**
323.61	Infectious acute disseminated encephalomyelitis [ADEM] **10**
075	Infectious mononucleosis **185**
728.0	Infective myositis **99**
380.1*	Infective otitis externa **47**
379.6*	Inflammation (infection) of postprocedural bleb **40**
373*	Inflammation of eyelids **39**
359.7*	Inflammatory and immune myopathies, NEC **97**
614*	Inflammatory disease of ovary, fallopian tube, pelvic cellular tissue, and peritoneum **128**
601*	Inflammatory diseases of prostate **125**
615*	Inflammatory diseases of uterus, except cervix **128 , 131**
488.19	Influenza due to identified 2009 H1N1 influenza virus with other manifestations **186**
488.12	Influenza due to identified 2009 H1N1 influenza virus with other respiratory manifestations **53 , 166 , 170**
488.11	Influenza due to identified 2009 H1N1 influenza virus with pneumonia **53 , 166 , 170 , 231**
488.09	Influenza due to identified avian influenza virus with other manifestations **186**
488.02	Influenza due to identified avian influenza virus with other respiratory manifestations **53 , 166 , 170**
488.01	Influenza due to identified avian influenza virus with pneumonia **53 , 166 , 170 , 231**
488.89	Influenza due to identified novel influenza A virus with other manifestations **186**
488.82	Influenza due to identified novel influenza A virus with other respiratory manifestations **53 , 166 , 170**
488.81	Influenza due to identified novel influenza A virus with pneumonia **53 , 166 , 170 , 231**
487.8	Influenza with other manifestations **186**
487.1	Influenza with other respiratory manifestations **46**
487.0	Influenza with pneumonia **51 , 53**
840.3	Infraspinatus (muscle) (tendon) sprain and strain **223**
550*	Inguinal hernia **78**
550.02	Inguinal hernia with gangrene, bilateral **167 , 171**
550.00	Inguinal hernia with gangrene, unilateral or unspecified, (not specified as recurrent) **167 , 171**
550.12	Inguinal hernia with obstruction, without mention gangrene, bilateral, (not specified as recurrent) **167 , 171**
550.10	Inguinal hernia with obstruction, without mention of gangrene, unilateral or unspecified, (not specified as recurrent) **167 , 171**
102.0	Initial lesions of yaws **108**
951.3	Injury to abducens nerve **21**
951.6	Injury to accessory nerve **21**
951.5	Injury to acoustic nerve **48**
955.0	Injury to axillary nerve **224 , 228**
902*	Injury to blood vessels of abdomen and pelvis **204 , 224 , 228**
900*	Injury to blood vessels of head and neck **204**

904*	Injury to blood vessels of lower extremity and unspecified sites **204**
901*	Injury to blood vessels of thorax **204**
903*	Injury to blood vessels of upper extremity **204 , 224 , 228**
904.9	Injury to blood vessels, unspecified site **224**
953.4	Injury to brachial plexus **167 , 171 , 224 , 228**
900.0*	Injury to carotid artery **167 , 171 , 224**
954.0	Injury to cervical sympathetic nerve, excluding shoulder and pelvic girdles **224**
863.5*	Injury to colon or rectum with open wound into cavity **79 , 224 , 228**
956.4	Injury to cutaneous sensory nerve, lower limb **225**
955.5	Injury to cutaneous sensory nerve, upper limb **224**
955.6	Injury to digital nerve, upper limb **224**
953.1	Injury to dorsal nerve root **224**
951.4	Injury to facial nerve **21**
956.1	Injury to femoral nerve **225 , 229**
861*	Injury to heart and lung **223 , 227**
951.7	Injury to hypoglossal nerve **21**
866*	Injury to kidney **121 , 224 , 228**
864*	Injury to liver **83 , 228**
953.2	Injury to lumbar nerve root **224**
953.5	Injury to lumbosacral plexus **224 , 228**
955.1	Injury to median nerve **224 , 228**
862.9	Injury to multiple and unspecified intrathoracic organs with open wound into cavity **203**
862.8	Injury to multiple and unspecified intrathoracic organs without mention of open wound into cavity **203**
900.82	Injury to multiple blood vessels of head and neck **4 , 227**
901.83	Injury to multiple blood vessels of thorax **227**
956.8	Injury to multiple nerves of pelvic girdle and lower limb **225 , 229**
955.8	Injury to multiple nerves of shoulder girdle and upper limb **225 , 228**
953.8	Injury to multiple sites of nerve roots and spinal plexus **224 , 228**
955.4	Injury to musculocutaneous nerve **224**
953*	Injury to nerve roots and spinal plexus **21 , 224**
951.0	Injury to oculomotor nerve **21**
950.1	Injury to optic chiasm **33**
950*	Injury to optic nerve and pathways **224**
950.2	Injury to optic pathways **33**
868.09	Injury to other and multiple intra-abdominal organs without mention of open wound into cavity **203 , 228**
868.19	Injury to other and multiple intra-abdominal organs, with open wound into cavity **203 , 228**
863.99	Injury to other and unspecified gastrointestinal sites with open wound into cavity **79**
863.8*	Injury to other and unspecified gastrointestinal sites without mention of open wound into cavity **224**
863.89	Injury to other and unspecified gastrointestinal sites without mention of open wound into cavity **79 , 228**
863.9*	Injury to other and unspecified gastrointestinal sites, with open wound into cavity **224 , 228**
862*	Injury to other and unspecified intrathoracic organs **223 , 227**
957*	Injury to other and unspecified nerves **21 , 225**
951*	Injury to other cranial nerve(s) **224**
868.1*	Injury to other intra-abdominal organs with open wound into cavity **224**
868.0*	Injury to other intra-abdominal organs without mention of open wound into cavity **224**
954*	Injury to other nerve(s) of trunk, excluding shoulder and pelvic girdles **21**
900.8*	Injury to other specified blood vessels of head and neck **224**
900.89	Injury to other specified blood vessels of head and neck **4**
901.8*	Injury to other specified blood vessels of thorax **224**
951.8	Injury to other specified cranial nerves **21**
862.39	Injury to other specified intrathoracic organs with open wound into cavity **54**
862.29	Injury to other specified intrathoracic organs without mention of open wound into cavity **54**
956.5	Injury to other specified nerve(s) of pelvic girdle and lower limb **225**
955.7	Injury to other specified nerve(s) of shoulder girdle and upper limb **224**
954.8	Injury to other specified nerve(s) of trunk, excluding shoulder and pelvic girdles **224 , 228**
867.7	Injury to other specified pelvic organs with open wound into cavity **125 , 128 , 131**
867.6	Injury to other specified pelvic organs without mention of open wound into cavity **125 , 128 , 131**
954.1	Injury to other sympathetic nerve, excluding shoulder and pelvic girdles **224**
867*	Injury to pelvic organs **224 , 228**
956*	Injury to peripheral nerve(s) of pelvic girdle and lower limb **21**
955*	Injury to peripheral nerve(s) of shoulder girdle and upper limb **21**
956.3	Injury to peroneal nerve **225 , 229**
956.2	Injury to posterior tibial nerve **225 , 229**
955.3	Injury to radial nerve **224 , 228**
953.3	Injury to sacral nerve root **224**
956.0	Injury to sciatic nerve **225 , 228**
904.7	Injury to specified blood vessels of lower extremity, other **224 , 228**
901.89	Injury to specified blood vessels of thorax, other **227**
767.4	Injury to spine and spinal cord, birth trauma **164 , 168**
865*	Injury to spleen **167 , 171 , 177 , 224 , 228**
951.2	Injury to trigeminal nerve **21**
951.1	Injury to trochlear nerve **21**
955.2	Injury to ulnar nerve **224 , 228**
900.9	Injury to unspecified blood vessel of head and neck **4 , 224**
904.8	Injury to unspecified blood vessel of lower extremity **224**
901.9	Injury to unspecified blood vessel of thorax **224 , 227**
951.9	Injury to unspecified cranial nerve **21**
868.00	Injury to unspecified intra-abdominal organ without mention of open wound into cavity **79**
868.10	Injury to unspecified intra-abdominal organ, with open wound into cavity **79**
956.9	Injury to unspecified nerve of pelvic girdle and lower limb **225 , 229**
955.9	Injury to unspecified nerve of shoulder girdle and upper limb **225**
954.9	Injury to unspecified nerve of trunk, excluding shoulder and pelvic girdles **224 , 228**
950.9	Injury to unspecified optic nerve and pathways **33**
867.9	Injury to unspecified pelvic organ with open wound into cavity **125 , 128 , 131**
867.8	Injury to unspecified pelvic organ without mention of open wound into cavity **125 , 128 , 131**
953.9	Injury to unspecified site of nerve roots and spinal plexus **224**
950.3	Injury to visual cortex **33**
959*	Injury, other and unspecified **204**
959.3	Injury, other and unspecified, elbow, forearm, and wrist **225**
959.5	Injury, other and unspecified, finger **225**
959.4	Injury, other and unspecified, hand, except finger **225**
959.0*	Injury, other and unspecified, head, face, and neck **4 , 225**
959.6	Injury, other and unspecified, hip and thigh **225**

959.7	Injury, other and unspecified, knee, leg, ankle, and foot **225**	
959.8	Injury, other and unspecified, other specified sites, including multiple **225**	
959.2	Injury, other and unspecified, shoulder and upper arm **225**	
959.1*	Injury, other and unspecified, trunk **225**	
959.9	Injury, other and unspecified, unspecified site **225**	
653.23	Inlet contraction of pelvis in pregnancy, antepartum **155 , 158**	
653.21	Inlet contraction of pelvis in pregnancy, delivered **136 , 143 , 149**	
653.20	Inlet contraction of pelvis in pregnancy, unspecified as to episode of care in pregnancy **161**	
901.1	Innominate and subclavian artery injury **167 , 171 , 224 , 227**	
901.3	Innominate and subclavian vein injury **167 , 171 , 224 , 227**	
V25.5	Insertion of implantable subdermal contraceptive **215**	
780.51	Insomnia with sleep apnea, unspecified **3 , 47**	
780.52	Insomnia, unspecified **190**	
798.1	Instantaneous death **66**	
V23.7	Insufficient prenatal care **162**	
411.1	Intermediate coronary syndrome **68**	
103.1	Intermediate lesions of pinta **108**	
376.34	Intermittent exophthalmos **38**	
312.34	Intermittent explosive disorder **189**	
378.2*	Intermittent heterotropia **40**	
900.03	Internal carotid artery injury **227**	
869*	Internal injury to unspecified or ill-defined organs **203 , 224**	
900.1	Internal jugular vein injury **167 , 171 , 224 , 227**	
378.86	Internuclear ophthalmoplegia **32**	
V62.81	Interpersonal problem, not elsewhere classified **215**	
518.1	Interstitial emphysema **53 , 166 , 171**	
770.2	Interstitial emphysema and related conditions of newborn **164 , 168**	
516.6*	Interstitial lung diseases of childhood **166 , 171**	
728.81	Interstitial myositis **99**	
722*	Intervertebral disc disorders **97**	
V45.3	Intestinal bypass or anastomosis status **215**	
271.3	Intestinal disaccharidase deficiencies and disaccharide malabsorption **78**	
008.2	Intestinal infection due to aerobacter aerogenes **75**	
008.1	Intestinal infection due to Arizona group of paracolon bacilli **75**	
008.04	Intestinal infection due to enterohemorrhagic E. coli **75**	
008.03	Intestinal infection due to enteroinvasive E. coli **75**	
008.01	Intestinal infection due to enteropathogenic E. coli **75**	
008.02	Intestinal infection due to enterotoxigenic E. coli **75**	
008.09	Intestinal infection due to other intestinal E. coli infections **75**	
008.8	Intestinal infection due to other organism, NEC **77**	
008.49	Intestinal infection due to other organisms **75**	
008.5	Intestinal infection due to unspecified bacterial enteritis **75**	
008.00	Intestinal infection due to unspecified E. coli **75**	
008.6*	Intestinal infection, enteritis due to specified virus **77**	
008.43	Intestinal infections due to campylobacter **75**	
008.45	Intestinal infections due to clostridium difficile **75**	
008.46	Intestinal infections due to other anaerobes **75**	
008.47	Intestinal infections due to other gram-negative bacteria **75**	
008.3	Intestinal infections due to proteus (mirabilis) (morganii) **75**	
008.42	Intestinal infections due to pseudomonas **75**	
008.41	Intestinal infections due to staphylococcus **75**	
008.44	Intestinal infections due to yersinia enterocolitica **75**	
579*	Intestinal malabsorption **78**	
560*	Intestinal obstruction without mention of hernia **77**	
596.1	Intestinovesical fistula **167 , 171**	

431	Intracerebral hemorrhage **8 , 9 , 10 , 20 , 166 , 170**
324*	Intracranial and intraspinal abscess **9 , 10 , 33 , 166 , 170**
854*	Intracranial injury of other and unspecified nature **223 , 227**
854.1*	Intracranial injury of other and unspecified nature with open intracranial wound **9 , 11**
854.12	Intracranial injury of other and unspecified nature, with open intracranial wound, brief (less than 1 hour) loss of consciousness **31**
854.16	Intracranial injury of other and unspecified nature, with open intracranial wound, loss of consciousness of unspecified duration **27**
854.13	Intracranial injury of other and unspecified nature, with open intracranial wound, moderate (1-24 hours) loss of consciousness **27**
854.11	Intracranial injury of other and unspecified nature, with open intracranial wound, no loss of consciousness **31**
854.14	Intracranial injury of other and unspecified nature, with open intracranial wound, prolonged (more than 24 hours) loss of consciousness and return to pre-existing conscious level **27**
854.15	Intracranial injury of other and unspecified nature, with open intracranial wound, prolonged (more than 24 hours) loss of consciousness, without return to pre-existing conscious level **27**
854.10	Intracranial injury of other and unspecified nature, with open intracranial wound, unspecified state of consciousness **31**
854.19	Intracranial injury of other and unspecified nature, with open intracranial wound, with unspecified concussion **31**
854.02	Intracranial injury of other and unspecified nature, without mention of open intracranial wound, brief (less than 1 hour) loss of consciousness **31**
854.06	Intracranial injury of other and unspecified nature, without mention of open intracranial wound, loss of consciousness of unspecified duration **27**
854.03	Intracranial injury of other and unspecified nature, without mention of open intracranial wound, moderate (1-24 hours) loss of consciousness **27**
854.01	Intracranial injury of other and unspecified nature, without mention of open intracranial wound, no loss of consciousness **31**
854.04	Intracranial injury of other and unspecified nature, without mention of open intracranial wound, prolonged (more than 24 hours) loss of consciousness and return to pre-existing conscious level **27**
854.05	Intracranial injury of other and unspecified nature, without mention of open intracranial wound, prolonged (more than 24 hours) loss of consciousness, without return to pre-existing conscious level **27**
854.09	Intracranial injury of other and unspecified nature, without mention of open intracranial wound, unspecified concussion **31**
854.00	Intracranial injury of other and unspecified nature, without mention of open intracranial wound, unspecified state of consciousness **31**
656.43	Intrauterine death affecting management of mother, antepartum **156 , 158**
656.41	Intrauterine death affecting management of mother, delivered **137 , 144 , 150**
656.40	Intrauterine death affecting management of mother, unspecified as to episode of care **137 , 144 , 150**
772.1*	Intraventricular hemorrhage **164 , 168**
493.1*	Intrinsic asthma **53**
493.11	Intrinsic asthma with status asthmaticus **166 , 170**
560.0	Intussusception **167 , 171**
665.22	Inversion of uterus, delivered with postpartum complication **138 , 145 , 151**
665.24	Inversion of uterus, postpartum condition or complication **153**
665.20	Inversion of uterus, unspecified as to episode of care in pregnancy **138 , 145 , 151**
V26.2*	Investigation and testing for procreation management **215**

280*	Iron deficiency anemias **176 , 231**	090.7	Late congenital syphilis, unspecified **186**
595.82	Irradiation cystitis **121**	908.6	Late effect of certain complications of trauma **204**
799.22	Irritability **189**	677	Late effect of complication of pregnancy, childbirth, and the puerperium **162**
564.1	Irritable bowel syndrome **78**	905.6	Late effect of dislocation **100**
656.23	Isoimmunization from other and unspecified blood-group incompatibility, affecting management of mother, antepartum **156 , 158**	908.5	Late effect of foreign body in orifice **204**
		905.4	Late effect of fracture of lower extremities **99**
656.21	Isoimmunization from other and unspecified blood-group incompatibility, affecting management of mother, delivered **137 , 144 , 150**	905.5	Late effect of fracture of multiple and unspecified bones **99**
		905.3	Late effect of fracture of neck of femur **99**
		905.0	Late effect of fracture of skull and face bones **32**
656.20	Isoimmunization from other and unspecified blood-group incompatibility, unspecified as to episode of care in pregnancy **161**	905.1	Late effect of fracture of spine and trunk without mention of spinal cord lesion **98**
		905.2	Late effect of fracture of upper extremities **99**
312.35	Isolated explosive disorder **189**	908.3	Late effect of injury to blood vessel of head, neck, and extremities **67**
012.2*	Isolated tracheal or bronchial tuberculosis **51**	908.4	Late effect of injury to blood vessel of thorax, abdomen, and pelvis **67**
782.4	Jaundice, unspecified, not of newborn **83**		
784.92	Jaw pain **3 , 48**	907.1	Late effect of injury to cranial nerve **33**
V43.6*	Joint replaced by other means **101**	907.3	Late effect of injury to nerve root(s), spinal plexus(es), and other nerves of trunk **33**
714.3*	Juvenile chronic polyarthritis **97**		
694.2	Juvenile dermatitis herpetiformis **109**	907.9	Late effect of injury to other and unspecified nerve **33**
090.4*	Juvenile neurosyphilis **33**	907.5	Late effect of injury to peripheral nerve of pelvic girdle and lower limb **33**
732.0	Juvenile osteochondrosis of spine **87**		
176*	Kaposi's sarcoma **231**	907.4	Late effect of injury to peripheral nerve of shoulder girdle and upper limb **33**
176.3	Kaposi's sarcoma of gastrointestinal sites **76**		
176.4	Kaposi's sarcoma of lung **52**	908.0	Late effect of internal injury to chest **54**
176.5	Kaposi's sarcoma of lymph nodes **179 , 182**	908.1	Late effect of internal injury to intra-abdominal organs **79**
176.8	Kaposi's sarcoma of other specified sites **109**	908.2	Late effect of internal injury to other internal organs **125 , 128 , 132**
176.2	Kaposi's sarcoma of palate **2 , 46**		
176.0	Kaposi's sarcoma of skin **109**	907.0	Late effect of intracranial injury without mention of skull fracture **33**
176.1	Kaposi's sarcoma of soft tissue **109**		
176.9	Kaposi's sarcoma of unspecified site **109**	907.2	Late effect of spinal cord injury **18**
773.4	Kernicterus due to isoimmunization of fetus or newborn **164 , 168**	905.7	Late effect of sprain and strain without mention of tendon injury **100**
774.7	Kernicterus of fetus or newborn not due to isoimmunization **164 , 168**	905.8	Late effect of tendon injury **99**
		905.9	Late effect of traumatic amputation **99**
V59.4	Kidney donor **121**	908.9	Late effect of unspecified injury **204**
V42.0	Kidney replaced by transplant **2 , 121**	138	Late effects of acute poliomyelitis **32**
312.32	Kleptomania **189**	137.1	Late effects of central nervous system tuberculosis **32**
758.7	Klinefelter's syndrome **125**	438*	Late effects of cerebrovascular disease **19**
756.16	Klippel-Feil syndrome **100**	137.2	Late effects of genitourinary tuberculosis **120**
260	Kwashiorkor **114 , 231**	906*	Late effects of injuries to skin and subcutaneous tissues **108**
737.3*	Kyphoscoliosis and scoliosis **87**	326	Late effects of intracranial abscess or pyogenic infection **32**
416.1	Kyphoscoliotic heart disease **69**	909*	Late effects of other and unspecified external causes **205**
737.1*	Kyphosis (acquired) **87**		
386.5*	Labyrinthine dysfunction **46**	139.8	Late effects of other and unspecified infectious and parasitic diseases **187**
386.4*	Labyrinthine fistula **47**		
386.3*	Labyrinthitis **46**	137.0	Late effects of respiratory or unspecified tuberculosis **53**
665.34	Laceration of cervix, postpartum condition or complication **153**	139.1	Late effects of trachoma **38**
665.30	Laceration of cervix, unspecified as to episode of care in pregnancy **138 , 145 , 151**	137.3	Late effects of tuberculosis of bones and joints **100**
		137.4	Late effects of tuberculosis of other specified organs **187**
665.31	Laceration of cervix, with delivery **138 , 145 , 151**	139.0	Late effects of viral encephalitis **32**
781.3	Lack of coordination **32**	766.2*	Late infant, not "heavy-for-dates" **172 , 173**
783.4*	Lack of expected normal physiological development **232**	103.2	Late lesions of pinta **186**
		775.7	Late metabolic acidosis of newborn **164 , 168**
374.2*	Lagophthalmos **39**	096	Late syphilis, latent **186**
358.3*	Lambert-Eaton syndrome **19**	643.23	Late vomiting of pregnancy, antepartum **155 , 157**
200.7*	Large cell lymphoma **231**	643.21	Late vomiting of pregnancy, delivered **135 , 142 , 148**
032.3	Laryngeal diphtheria **2 , 47**	643.20	Late vomiting of pregnancy, unspecified as to episode of care **157 , 160**
478.75	Laryngeal spasm **47 , 166 , 170**		
773.5	Late anemia due to isoimmunization of fetus or newborn **164 , 168**	379.52	Latent nystagmus **38**
		102.8	Latent yaws **186**
090.6	Late congenital syphilis, latent **186**		

376.36	Lateral displacement of globe of eye **38**
728.4	Laxity of ligament **99**
428.1	Left heart failure **57** , **166** , **170**
V62.5	Legal circumstance **215**
635*	Legally induced abortion **154**
482.84	Legionnaires' disease **51**
V43.1	Lens replaced by other means **40**
030*	Leprosy **186**
100.0	Leptospirosis icterohemorrhagica **186**
765.21	Less than 24 completed weeks of gestation **164**
446.3	Lethal midline granuloma **97**
202.5*	Letterer-Siwe disease **181** , **182**
202.51	Letterer-Siwe disease of lymph nodes of head, face, and neck **3**
208*	Leukemia of unspecified cell type **179**
202.4*	Leukemic reticuloendotheliosis **179** , **182**
202.41	Leukemic reticuloendotheliosis of lymph nodes of head, face, and neck **3**
528.6	Leukoplakia of oral mucosa, including tongue **231**
607.0	Leukoplakia of penis **125**
697*	Lichen **109**
698.3	Lichenification and lichen simplex chronicus **109**
764.14	Light-for-dates with signs of fetal malnutrition, 1,000-1,249 grams **164** , **168**
764.15	Light-for-dates with signs of fetal malnutrition, 1,250-1,499 grams **164** , **168**
764.16	Light-for-dates with signs of fetal malnutrition, 1,500-1,749 grams **164** , **168**
764.17	Light-for-dates with signs of fetal malnutrition, 1,750-1,999 grams **164** , **168**
764.18	Light-for-dates with signs of fetal malnutrition, 2,000-2,499 grams **164** , **168**
764.12	Light-for-dates with signs of fetal malnutrition, 500-749 grams **164** , **168**
764.13	Light-for-dates with signs of fetal malnutrition, 750-999 grams **164** , **168**
764.11	Light-for-dates with signs of fetal malnutrition, less than 500 grams **164** , **168**
764.08	Light-for-dates without mention of fetal malnutrition, 2,000-2,499 grams **172** , **173**
764.09	Light-for-dates without mention of fetal malnutrition, 2,500 or more grams **172** , **173**
V43.7	Limb replaced by other means **101**
214.3	Lipoma of intra-abdominal organs **78**
214.2	Lipoma of intrathoracic organs **52**
214.1	Lipoma of other skin and subcutaneous tissue **109**
214.8	Lipoma of other specified sites **109**
214.0	Lipoma of skin and subcutaneous tissue of face **109**
214.4	Lipoma of spermatic cord **125**
214.9	Lipoma of unspecified site **109**
V39.01	Liveborn infant, unspecified whether single, twin, or multiple, born in hospital, delivered by cesarean **173**
V39.00	Liveborn infant, unspecified whether single, twin, or multiple, born in hospital, delivered without mention of cesarean delivery **173**
V39.1	Liveborn, unspecified whether single, twin or multiple, born before admission to hospital **173**
V39.2	Liveborn, unspecified whether single, twin, or multiple, born outside hospital and not hospitalized **174**
572*	Liver abscess and sequelae of chronic liver disease **83**
646.73	Liver and biliary tract disorders in pregnancy, antepartum condition or complication **155** , **157**
646.71	Liver and biliary tract disorders in pregnancy, delivered, with or without mention of antepartum condition **135** , **143** , **148**
646.70	Liver and biliary tract disorders in pregnancy, unspecified as to episode of care or not applicable **157** , **160**
V59.6	Liver donor **83**
864.1*	Liver injury with open wound into cavity **224**
864.0*	Liver injury without mention of open wound into cavity **224**
V42.7	Liver replaced by transplant **83**
999.33	Local infection due to central venous catheter **69**
278.1	Localized adiposity **114**
003.2*	Localized salmonella infections **230**
782.2	Localized superficial swelling, mass, or lump **109**
660.50	Locked twins during labor and delivery, unspecified as to episode of care in pregnancy **137** , **144** , **150**
660.53	Locked twins, antepartum **156** , **159**
660.51	Locked twins, delivered **137** , **144** , **150**
V58.6*	Long-term (current) drug use **214**
718.1*	Loose body in joint **100**
717.6	Loose body in knee **100**
737.2*	Lordosis (acquired) **87**
781.91	Loss of height **32**
080	Louse-borne (epidemic) typhus **186**
238.72	Low grade myelodysplastic syndrome lesions **176**
365.12	Low tension open-angle glaucoma **38**
861.31	Lung contusion with open wound into thorax **54**
861.21	Lung contusion without mention of open wound into thorax **54**
517.8	Lung involvement in other diseases classified elsewhere **53**
517.2	Lung involvement in systemic sclerosis **53**
861.32	Lung laceration with open wound into thorax **52**
861.22	Lung laceration without mention of open wound into thorax **52**
V42.6	Lung replaced by transplant **54**
695.4	Lupus erythematosus **106**
289.3	Lymphadenitis, unspecified, except mesenteric **177**
228.1	Lymphangioma, any site **177**
457.2	Lymphangitis **107** , **166** , **170**
049.0	Lymphocytic choriomeningitis **21**
099.1	Lymphogranuloma venereum **125** , **128** , **131**
204*	Lymphoid leukemia **179**
200*	Lymphosarcoma and reticulosarcoma and other specified malignant tumors of lymphatic tissue **179** , **182**
200.11	Lymphosarcoma of lymph nodes of head, face, and neck **2**
744.81	Macrocheilia **48**
273.3	Macroglobulinemia **179** , **182**
744.83	Macrostomia **48**
039.4	Madura foot **108**
653.00	Major abnormality of bony pelvis, not further specified in pregnancy, unspecified as to episode of care **161**
653.03	Major abnormality of bony pelvis, not further specified, antepartum **155** , **158**
653.01	Major abnormality of bony pelvis, not further specified, delivered **136** , **143** , **149**
670.02	Major puerperal infection, unspecified, delivered, with mention of postpartum complication **139** , **142** , **147**
670.04	Major puerperal infection, unspecified, postpartum condition or complication **154**
670.00	Major puerperal infection, unspecified, unspecified as to episode of care or not applicable **162**
780.7*	Malaise and fatigue **232**
802.4	Malar and maxillary bones, closed fracture **3** , **48** , **222**
802.5	Malar and maxillary bones, open fracture **3** , **48** , **222**
084*	Malaria **186**
606*	Male infertility **125**

*Code Range

306.7	Malfunction of organs of special sense arising from mental factors **189**
209.25	Malignant carcinoid tumor of foregut, not otherwise specified **76**
209.27	Malignant carcinoid tumor of hindgut, not otherwise specified **76**
209.26	Malignant carcinoid tumor of midgut, not otherwise specified **76**
209.29	Malignant carcinoid tumor of other sites **181 , 182**
209.11	Malignant carcinoid tumor of the appendix **73**
209.21	Malignant carcinoid tumor of the bronchus and lung **52**
209.24	Malignant carcinoid tumor of the kidney **117 , 120**
209.23	Malignant carcinoid tumor of the stomach **76**
209.22	Malignant carcinoid tumor of the thymus **181 , 182**
209.20	Malignant carcinoid tumor of unknown primary site **181 , 182**
209.1*	Malignant carcinoid tumors of the appendix, large intestine, and rectum **76**
209.0*	Malignant carcinoid tumors of the small intestine **76**
202.3*	Malignant histiocytosis **179 , 182**
202.31	Malignant histiocytosis of lymph nodes of head, face, and neck **3**
402.01	Malignant hypertensive heart disease with heart failure **56 ,65 , 166 , 170**
402.00	Malignant hypertensive heart disease without heart failure **67**
202.6*	Malignant mast cell tumors **179 , 182**
202.61	Malignant mast cell tumors of lymph nodes of head, face, and neck **3**
172.8	Malignant melanoma of other specified sites of skin **106**
172.2	Malignant melanoma of skin of ear and external auditory canal **106**
172.1	Malignant melanoma of skin of eyelid, including canthus **38**
172.0	Malignant melanoma of skin of lip **106**
172.7	Malignant melanoma of skin of lower limb, including hip **106**
172.3	Malignant melanoma of skin of other and unspecified parts of face **106**
172.4	Malignant melanoma of skin of scalp and neck **106**
172.5	Malignant melanoma of skin of trunk, except scrotum **106**
172.6	Malignant melanoma of skin of upper limb, including shoulder **106**
199.2	Malignant neoplasm associated with transplanted organ **181**
195.2	Malignant neoplasm of abdomen **76**
194.0	Malignant neoplasm of adrenal gland **115**
164.2	Malignant neoplasm of anterior mediastinum **52**
194.6	Malignant neoplasm of aortic body and other paraganglia **19**
153.5	Malignant neoplasm of appendix **73**
188*	Malignant neoplasm of bladder **117 , 120**
182*	Malignant neoplasm of body of uterus **127 , 130**
170*	Malignant neoplasm of bone and articular cartilage **97**
191*	Malignant neoplasm of brain **19**
194.5	Malignant neoplasm of carotid body **19**
180*	Malignant neoplasm of cervix uteri **127 , 130**
153*	Malignant neoplasm of colon **76**
171*	Malignant neoplasm of connective and other soft tissue **97**
194.9	Malignant neoplasm of endocrine gland, site unspecified **115**
150*	Malignant neoplasm of esophagus **76**
190*	Malignant neoplasm of eye **38**
174*	Malignant neoplasm of female breast **105 , 106**
144*	Malignant neoplasm of floor of mouth **2 , 46**
156*	Malignant neoplasm of gallbladder and extrahepatic bile ducts **82**
143*	Malignant neoplasm of gum **2 , 46**
195.0	Malignant neoplasm of head, face, and neck **2 , 46**
164.1	Malignant neoplasm of heart **68**
148*	Malignant neoplasm of hypopharynx **2 , 46**
159.9	Malignant neoplasm of ill-defined sites of digestive organs and peritoneum **76**
165.9	Malignant neoplasm of ill-defined sites within the respiratory system **52**
159.0	Malignant neoplasm of intestinal tract, part unspecified **76**
189*	Malignant neoplasm of kidney and other and unspecified urinary organs **117 , 120**
161*	Malignant neoplasm of larynx **2 , 46**
140*	Malignant neoplasm of lip **2 , 46**
155*	Malignant neoplasm of liver and intrahepatic bile ducts **82**
195.5	Malignant neoplasm of lower limb **181 , 182**
142*	Malignant neoplasm of major salivary glands **2 , 46**
175*	Malignant neoplasm of male breast **105 , 106**
170.1	Malignant neoplasm of mandible **2**
164.9	Malignant neoplasm of mediastinum, part unspecified **52**
160*	Malignant neoplasm of nasal cavities, middle ear, and accessory sinuses **2 , 46**
147*	Malignant neoplasm of nasopharynx **2 , 46**
146*	Malignant neoplasm of oropharynx **2 , 46**
149*	Malignant neoplasm of other and ill-defined sites within the lip, oral cavity, and pharynx **2 , 46**
184*	Malignant neoplasm of other and unspecified female genital organs **127 , 130**
145*	Malignant neoplasm of other and unspecified parts of mouth **2 , 46**
192*	Malignant neoplasm of other and unspecified parts of nervous system **19**
194.8	Malignant neoplasm of other endocrine glands and related structures **115**
164.8	Malignant neoplasm of other parts of mediastinum **52**
159.8	Malignant neoplasm of other sites of digestive system and intra-abdominal organs **76**
165.8	Malignant neoplasm of other sites within the respiratory system and intrathoracic organs **52**
195.8	Malignant neoplasm of other specified sites **181 , 182**
183*	Malignant neoplasm of ovary and other uterine adnexa **127 , 130**
157*	Malignant neoplasm of pancreas **82**
194.1	Malignant neoplasm of parathyroid gland **115**
195.3	Malignant neoplasm of pelvis **123 , 124 , 127 , 130**
187*	Malignant neoplasm of penis and other male genital organs **123 , 124**
158.9	Malignant neoplasm of peritoneum, unspecified **76**
194.4	Malignant neoplasm of pineal gland **19**
194.3	Malignant neoplasm of pituitary gland and craniopharyngeal duct **115**
181	Malignant neoplasm of placenta **127 , 130**
163*	Malignant neoplasm of pleura **52**
164.3	Malignant neoplasm of posterior mediastinum **52**
185	Malignant neoplasm of prostate **123 , 124**
154*	Malignant neoplasm of rectum, rectosigmoid junction, and anus **76**
158.0	Malignant neoplasm of retroperitoneum **181 , 182**
152*	Malignant neoplasm of small intestine, including duodenum **76**
158.8	Malignant neoplasm of specified parts of peritoneum **76**
159.1	Malignant neoplasm of spleen, not elsewhere classified **179 , 182**
151*	Malignant neoplasm of stomach **76**
186*	Malignant neoplasm of testis **123 , 124**
195.1	Malignant neoplasm of thorax **52**
164.0	Malignant neoplasm of thymus **181 , 182**
193	Malignant neoplasm of thyroid gland **2 , 115**

141*	Malignant neoplasm of tongue **2** , **46**
162*	Malignant neoplasm of trachea, bronchus, and lung **52**
195.4	Malignant neoplasm of upper limb **181** , **182**
165.0	Malignant neoplasm of upper respiratory tract, part unspecified **2** , **46**
179	Malignant neoplasm of uterus, part unspecified **127** , **130**
170.2	Malignant neoplasm of vertebral column, excluding sacrum and coccyx **87**
199*	Malignant neoplasm without specification of site **182**
511.81	Malignant pleural effusion **52**
209.30	Malignant poorly differentiated neuroendocrine carcinoma, any site **181** , **182**
736.1	Mallet finger **100**
263.1	Malnutrition of mild degree **165** , **169**
263.0	Malnutrition of moderate degree **165** , **169**
733.8*	Malunion and nonunion of fracture **100**
802.2*	Mandible, closed fracture **3** , **48** , **222**
802.3*	Mandible, open fracture **3** , **48** , **222**
200.4*	Mantle cell lymphoma **231**
759.82	Marfan's syndrome **68**
370.01	Marginal corneal ulcer **39**
200.3*	Marginal zone lymphoma **231**
648.24	Maternal anemia complicating pregnancy, childbirth, or the puerperium, postpartum condition or complication **153**
648.20	Maternal anemia of mother, complicating pregnancy, childbirth, or the puerperium, unspecified as to episode of care **160**
648.22	Maternal anemia with delivery, with current postpartum complication **135** , **143** , **148**
648.23	Maternal anemia, antepartum **155** , **157**
648.21	Maternal anemia, with delivery **135** , **143** , **148**
679.03	Maternal complications from in utero procedure, antepartum condition or complication **157** , **159**
679.02	Maternal complications from in utero procedure, delivered, with mention of postpartum complication **140** , **142** , **148**
679.01	Maternal complications from in utero procedure, delivered, with or without mention of antepartum condition **140** , **142** , **148**
679.04	Maternal complications from in utero procedure, postpartum condition or complication **154**
679.00	Maternal complications from in utero procedure, unspecified as to episode of care or not applicable **140** , **146** , **152**
648.54	Maternal congenital cardiovascular disorders complicating pregnancy, childbirth, or the puerperium, postpartum condition or complication **153**
648.53	Maternal congenital cardiovascular disorders, antepartum **155** , **157**
648.50	Maternal congenital cardiovascular disorders, complicating pregnancy, childbirth, or the puerperium, unspecified as to episode of care **160**
648.51	Maternal congenital cardiovascular disorders, with delivery **135** , **141** , **147**
648.52	Maternal congenital cardiovascular disorders, with delivery, with current postpartum complication **135** , **141** , **147**
648.01	Maternal diabetes mellitus with delivery **135** , **141** , **147**
648.02	Maternal diabetes mellitus with delivery, with current postpartum complication **135** , **141** , **147**
648.03	Maternal diabetes mellitus, antepartum **155** , **157**
648.04	Maternal diabetes mellitus, complicating pregnancy, childbirth, or the puerperium, postpartum condition or complication **153**
648.00	Maternal diabetes mellitus, complicating pregnancy, childbirth, or the puerperium, unspecified as to episode of care **160**
669.03	Maternal distress complicating labor and delivery, antepartum condition or complication **156** , **159**
669.04	Maternal distress complicating labor and delivery, postpartum condition or complication **154**

669.00	Maternal distress complicating labor and delivery, unspecified as to episode of care **139** , **146** , **151**
669.02	Maternal distress, with delivery, with mention of postpartum complication **139** , **146** , **151**
669.01	Maternal distress, with delivery, with or without mention of antepartum condition **139** , **146** , **151**
648.34	Maternal drug dependence complicating pregnancy, childbirth, or the puerperium, postpartum condition or complication **153**
648.30	Maternal drug dependence complicating pregnancy, childbirth, or the puerperium, unspecified as to episode of care **160**
648.33	Maternal drug dependence, antepartum **155** , **157**
648.31	Maternal drug dependence, with delivery **135** , **143** , **148**
648.32	Maternal drug dependence, with delivery, with current postpartum complication **135** , **143** , **148**
647.10	Maternal gonorrhea complicating pregnancy, childbirth, or the puerperium, unspecified as to episode of care **160**
647.14	Maternal gonorrhea complicating pregnancy, childbirth, or the puerperium, postpartum condition or complication **153**
647.11	Maternal gonorrhea with delivery **135** , **141** , **147**
647.13	Maternal gonorrhea, antepartum **155** , **157**
647.12	Maternal gonorrhea, with delivery, with current postpartum complication **135** , **141** , **147**
669.20	Maternal hypotension syndrome complicating labor and delivery, unspecified as to episode of care **139** , **146** , **151**
669.23	Maternal hypotension syndrome, antepartum **156** , **159**
669.24	Maternal hypotension syndrome, postpartum condition or complication **154**
669.22	Maternal hypotension syndrome, with delivery, with mention of postpartum complication **139** , **146** , **151**
669.21	Maternal hypotension syndrome, with delivery, with or without mention of antepartum condition **139** , **146** , **151**
647.40	Maternal malaria complicating pregnancy, childbirth or the puerperium, unspecified as to episode of care **160**
647.41	Maternal malaria with delivery **135** , **141** , **147**
647.42	Maternal malaria with delivery, with current postpartum complication **135** , **141** , **147**
647.43	Maternal malaria, antepartum **155** , **157**
647.44	Maternal malaria, complicating pregnancy, childbirth, or the puerperium, postpartum condition or complication **153**
648.44	Maternal mental disorders complicating pregnancy, childbirth, or the puerperium, postpartum condition or complication **153**
648.43	Maternal mental disorders, antepartum **155** , **157**
648.40	Maternal mental disorders, complicating pregnancy, childbirth, or the puerperium, unspecified as to episode of care **160**
648.41	Maternal mental disorders, with delivery **135** , **143** , **148**
648.42	Maternal mental disorders, with delivery, with current postpartum complication **135** , **143** , **148**
647.54	Maternal rubella complicating pregnancy, childbirth, or the puerperium, postpartum condition or complication **153**
647.50	Maternal rubella complicating pregnancy, childbirth, or the puerperium, unspecified as to episode of care **160**
647.51	Maternal rubella with delivery **135** , **141** , **147**
647.52	Maternal rubella with delivery, with current postpartum complication **135** , **141** , **147**
647.53	Maternal rubella, antepartum **155** , **157**
647.04	Maternal syphilis complicating pregnancy, childbirth, or the puerperium, postpartum condition or complication **153**
647.03	Maternal syphilis, antepartum **155** , **157**
647.00	Maternal syphilis, complicating pregnancy, childbirth, or the puerperium, unspecified as to episode of care **160**
647.01	Maternal syphilis, complicating pregnancy, with delivery **135** , **141** , **147**
647.02	Maternal syphilis, complicating pregnancy, with delivery, with current postpartum complication **135** , **141** , **147**

648.14	Maternal thyroid dysfunction complicating pregnancy, childbirth, or the puerperium, postpartum condition or complication **153**	207.2*	Megakaryocytic leukemia **182**
648.10	Maternal thyroid dysfunction complicating pregnancy, childbirth, or the puerperium, unspecified as to episode of care or not applicable **160**	172.9	Melanoma of skin, site unspecified **106**

648.14 Maternal thyroid dysfunction complicating pregnancy, childbirth, or the puerperium, postpartum condition or complication **153**

648.10 Maternal thyroid dysfunction complicating pregnancy, childbirth, or the puerperium, unspecified as to episode of care or not applicable **160**

648.12 Maternal thyroid dysfunction with delivery, with current postpartum complication **135 , 143 , 148**

648.11 Maternal thyroid dysfunction with delivery, with or without mention of antepartum condition **135 , 143 , 148**

648.13 Maternal thyroid dysfunction, antepartum condition or complication **155 , 157**

647.34 Maternal tuberculosis complicating pregnancy, childbirth, or the puerperium, postpartum condition or complication **153**

647.30 Maternal tuberculosis complicating pregnancy, childbirth, or the puerperium, unspecified as to episode of care **160**

647.31 Maternal tuberculosis with delivery **135 , 141 , 147**

647.32 Maternal tuberculosis with delivery, with current postpartum complication **135 , 141 , 147**

647.33 Maternal tuberculosis, antepartum **155 , 157**

315.1 Mathematics disorder **190**

055.71 Measles keratoconjunctivitis **38**

055.9 Measles without mention of complication **185**

055.7* Measles, with other specified complications **165 , 169**

996.04 Mechanical complication due to automatic implantable cardiac defibrillator **68**

996.54 Mechanical complication due to breast prosthesis **107**

996.01 Mechanical complication due to cardiac pacemaker (electrode) **68**

996.51 Mechanical complication due to corneal graft **40**

996.03 Mechanical complication due to coronary bypass graft **69**

996.02 Mechanical complication due to heart valve prosthesis **68**

996.57 Mechanical complication due to insulin pump **204**

996.32 Mechanical complication due to intrauterine contraceptive device **129 , 132**

996.53 Mechanical complication due to ocular lens prosthesis **40**

996.59 Mechanical complication due to other implant and internal device, not elsewhere classified **204**

996.52 Mechanical complication due to other tissue graft, not elsewhere classified **204**

996.31 Mechanical complication due to urethral (indwelling) catheter **121**

996.09 Mechanical complication of cardiac device, implant, and graft, other **69**

530.87 Mechanical complication of esophagostomy **78**

996.39 Mechanical complication of genitourinary device, implant, and graft, other **121**

996.4* Mechanical complication of internal orthopedic device, implant, and graft **99**

996.2 Mechanical complication of nervous system device, implant, and graft **33**

996.1 Mechanical complication of other vascular device, implant, and graft **69**

996.00 Mechanical complication of unspecified cardiac device, implant, and graft **69**

996.30 Mechanical complication of unspecified genitourinary device, implant, and graft **121**

996.55 Mechanical complications due to artificial skin graft and decellularized allodermis **204**

996.56 Mechanical complications due to peritoneal dialysis catheter **204**

374.33 Mechanical ptosis **39**

378.6* Mechanical strabismus **40**

751.0 Meckel's diverticulum **77**

519.2 Mediastinitis **51 , 166 , 171**

564.7 Megacolon, other than Hirschsprung's **79**

207.2* Megakaryocytic leukemia **182**

172.9 Melanoma of skin, site unspecified **106**

025 Melioidosis **186**

386.0* Meniere's disease **46**

781.6 Meningismus **32**

049.1 Meningitis due to adenovirus **21**

047* Meningitis due to enterovirus **21**

321* Meningitis due to other organisms **33 , 165 , 170**

321.3 Meningitis due to trypanosomiasis **9 , 10**

321.2 Meningitis due to viruses not elsewhere classified **9 , 10**

321.1 Meningitis in other fungal diseases **9 , 10**

322* Meningitis of unspecified cause **33**

036.82 Meningococcal arthropathy **97 , 165 , 169**

036.4* Meningococcal carditis **165 , 169**

036.40 Meningococcal carditis, unspecified **68**

036.1 Meningococcal encephalitis **8 , 10 , 33**

036.42 Meningococcal endocarditis **65**

036.0 Meningococcal meningitis **8 , 10 , 33**

036.43 Meningococcal myocarditis **68**

036.81 Meningococcal optic neuritis **38 , 165 , 169**

036.41 Meningococcal pericarditis **68**

036.2 Meningococcemia **187**

130.0 Meningoencephalitis due to toxoplasmosis **9 , 10 , 33 , 165 , 169**

627* Menopausal and postmenopausal disorders **128 , 131**

V25.3 Menstrual extraction **129 , 132**

V40* Mental and behavioral problems **215**

209.36 Merkel cell carcinoma of other sites **106**

209.31 Merkel cell carcinoma of the face **106**

209.34 Merkel cell carcinoma of the lower limb **106**

209.32 Merkel cell carcinoma of the scalp and neck **106**

209.35 Merkel cell carcinoma of the trunk **106**

209.33 Merkel cell carcinoma of the upper limb **106**

121.5 Metagonimiasis **186**

289.7 Methemoglobinemia **176**

482.42 Methicillin resistant pneumonia due to Staphylococcus aureus **51**

482.41 Methicillin susceptible pneumonia due to Staphylococcus aureus **51**

744.82 Microcheilia **48**

744.84 Microstomia **48**

346* Migraine **34**

331.83 Mild cognitive impairment, so stated **19**

643.03 Mild hyperemesis gravidarum, antepartum **155 , 157**

643.01 Mild hyperemesis gravidarum, delivered **135 , 142 , 148**

643.00 Mild hyperemesis gravidarum, unspecified as to episode of care **157 , 160**

317 Mild intellectual disabilities **189**

768.6 Mild or moderate birth asphyxia **172 , 173**

642.43 Mild or unspecified pre-eclampsia, antepartum **155 , 157**

642.44 Mild or unspecified pre-eclampsia, postpartum condition or complication **152**

642.40 Mild or unspecified pre-eclampsia, unspecified as to episode of care **160**

642.41 Mild or unspecified pre-eclampsia, with delivery **135 , 141 , 147**

642.42 Mild or unspecified pre-eclampsia, with delivery, with current postpartum complication **135 , 141 , 147**

018* Miliary tuberculosis **230**

379.42 Miosis (persistent), not due to miotics **38**

313.1 Misery and unhappiness disorder specific to childhood and adolescence **189**

632	Missed abortion **154**	
625.2	Mittelschmerz **131**	
315.5	Mixed development disorder **190**	
312.4	Mixed disturbance of conduct and emotions **190**	
127.8	Mixed intestinal helminthiasis **187**	
103.3	Mixed lesions of pinta **108**	
315.32	Mixed receptive-expressive language disorder **190**	
768.72	Moderate hypoxic-ischemic encephalopathy **164 , 168**	
078.0	Molluscum contagiosum **108**	
273.1	Monoclonal paraproteinemia **177**	
206*	Monocytic leukemia **179**	
355*	Mononeuritis of lower limb and unspecified site **20**	
354*	Mononeuritis of upper limb and mononeuritis multiplex **20**	
344.3*	Monoplegia of lower limb **32**	
344.4*	Monoplegia of upper limb **32**	
343.3	Monoplegic infantile cerebral palsy **32**	
370.07	Mooren's ulcer **39**	
278.01	Morbid obesity **114**	
062*	Mosquito-borne viral encephalitis **9 , 10 , 33**	
994.6	Motion sickness **46**	
437.5	Moyamoya disease **32**	
085.5	Mucocutaneous leishmaniasis, (American) **108**	
277.5	Mucopolysaccharidosis **115**	
491.1	Mucopurulent chronic bronchitis **53**	
V61.5	Multiparity **129 , 132**	
894*	Multiple and unspecified open wound of lower limb **224**	
894.1	Multiple and unspecified open wound of lower limb, complicated **204**	
894.2	Multiple and unspecified open wound of lower limb, with tendon involvement **101**	
894.0	Multiple and unspecified open wound of lower limb, without mention of complication **108**	
884*	Multiple and unspecified open wound of upper limb **224**	
884.1	Multiple and unspecified open wound of upper limb, complicated **204**	
884.2	Multiple and unspecified open wound of upper limb, with tendon involvement **101**	
884.0	Multiple and unspecified open wound of upper limb, without mention of complication **108**	
828.0	Multiple closed fractures involving both lower limbs, lower with upper limb, and lower limb(s) with rib(s) and sternum **223**	
819.0	Multiple closed fractures involving both upper limbs, and upper limb with rib(s) and sternum **222**	
817.0	Multiple closed fractures of hand bones **222**	
759.7	Multiple congenital anomalies, so described **101**	
828*	Multiple fractures involving both lower limbs, lower with upper limb, and lower limb(s) with rib(s) and sternum **203 , 228**	
828.1	Multiple fractures involving both lower limbs, lower with upper limb, and lower limb(s) with rib(s) and sternum, open **223**	
819*	Multiple fractures involving both upper limbs, and upper limb with rib(s) and sternum **203**	
817*	Multiple fractures of hand bones **99**	
651.73	Multiple gestation following (elective) fetal reduction, antepartum condition or complication **155 , 158**	
651.71	Multiple gestation following (elective) fetal reduction, delivered, with or without mention of antepartum condition **136 , 143 , 149**	
651.70	Multiple gestation following (elective) fetal reduction, unspecified as to episode of care or not applicable **161**	
652.63	Multiple gestation with malpresentation of one fetus or more, antepartum **155 , 158**	

652.61	Multiple gestation with malpresentation of one fetus or more, delivered **136 , 143 , 149**	
652.60	Multiple gestation with malpresentation of one fetus or more, unspecified as to episode of care **161**	
203*	Multiple myeloma and immunoproliferative neoplasms **179 , 182**	
819.1	Multiple open fractures involving both upper limbs, and upper limb with rib(s) and sternum **222 , 227**	
817.1	Multiple open fractures of hand bones **222**	
102.1	Multiple papillomata and wet crab yaws due to yaws **108**	
340	Multiple sclerosis **19**	
130.8	Multisystemic disseminated toxoplasmosis **165 , 169 , 187**	
072.2	Mumps encephalitis **9 , 10 , 33 , 165 , 169**	
072.71	Mumps hepatitis **83**	
072.1	Mumps meningitis **9 , 10 , 21 , 165 , 169**	
072.0	Mumps orchitis **125 , 165 , 169**	
072.3	Mumps pancreatitis **83 , 165 , 169**	
072.72	Mumps polyneuropathy **20**	
072.7*	Mumps with other specified complications **165 , 169**	
072.79	Mumps with other specified complications **185**	
072.9	Mumps without mention of complication **185**	
728.87	Muscle weakness (generalized) **98**	
728.1*	Muscular calcification and ossification **99**	
728.2	Muscular wasting and disuse atrophy, not elsewhere classified **99**	
306.0	Musculoskeletal malfunction arising from mental factors **98**	
358.0*	Myasthenia gravis **19**	
358.1	Myasthenic syndromes in diseases classified elsewhere **19**	
202.1*	Mycosis fungoides **179 , 182**	
202.11	Mycosis fungoides of lymph nodes of head, face, and neck **2**	
370.05	Mycotic corneal ulcer **38**	
117.4	Mycotic mycetomas **165 , 169**	
379.43	Mydriasis (persistent), not due to mydriatics **38**	
323.52	Myelitis following immunization procedures **10**	
323.02	Myelitis in viral diseases classified elsewhere **10**	
238.74	Myelodysplastic syndrome with 5q deletion **176**	
238.75	Myelodysplastic syndrome, unspecified **176**	
289.83	Myelofibrosis **179 , 182**	
238.76	Myelofibrosis with myeloid metaplasia **179 , 182**	
205*	Myeloid leukemia **179**	
205.3*	Myeloid sarcoma **182**	
336.3	Myelopathy in other diseases classified elsewhere **32**	
284.2	Myelophthisis **179 , 182**	
429.1	Myocardial degeneration **69**	
130.3	Myocarditis due to toxoplasmosis **68 , 165 , 169**	
333.2	Myoclonus **32**	
374.32	Myogenic ptosis **38**	
791.3	Myoglobinuria **214**	
359.5	Myopathy in endocrine diseases classified elsewhere **32**	
376.82	Myopathy of extraocular muscles **38**	
367.1	Myopia **39**	
359.22	Myotonia congenita **32**	
359.23	Myotonic chondrodystrophy **32**	
359.21	Myotonic muscular dystrophy **32**	
802.0	Nasal bones, closed fracture **47 , 222**	
802.1	Nasal bones, open fracture **47 , 222**	
478.11	Nasal mucositis (ulcerative) **173**	
471*	Nasal polyps **47**	
032.1	Nasopharyngeal diphtheria **2 , 47**	
040.3	Necrobacillosis **186**	
447.5	Necrosis of artery **66**	

777.5*	Necrotizing enterocolitis in newborn **164** , **169**	
728.86	Necrotizing fasciitis **99**	
V07*	Need for isolation and other prophylactic or treatment measures **215**	
V05*	Need for other prophylactic vaccination and inoculation against single diseases **214**	
V03*	Need for prophylactic vaccination and inoculation against bacterial diseases **214**	
V04*	Need for prophylactic vaccination and inoculation against certain viral diseases **214**	
V06*	Need for prophylactic vaccination and inoculation against combinations of diseases **214**	
V05.8	Need for prophylactic vaccination and inoculation against other specified disease **173**	
V05.4	Need for prophylactic vaccination and inoculation against varicella **173**	
V05.3	Need for prophylactic vaccination and inoculation against viral hepatitis **173**	
775.1	Neonatal diabetes mellitus **164** , **168**	
775.6	Neonatal hypoglycemia **164** , **168**	
771.5	Neonatal infective mastitis **164** , **168**	
777.2	Neonatal intestinal obstruction due to inspissated milk **164** , **169**	
774.3*	Neonatal jaundice due to delayed conjugation from other causes **172** , **173**	
775.2	Neonatal myasthenia gravis **164** , **168**	
775.3	Neonatal thyrotoxicosis **164** , **168**	
237.2	Neoplasm of uncertain behavior of adrenal gland **115**	
236.7	Neoplasm of uncertain behavior of bladder **117** , **120**	
238.0	Neoplasm of uncertain behavior of bone and articular cartilage **87** , **97**	
237.5	Neoplasm of uncertain behavior of brain and spinal cord **19**	
238.3	Neoplasm of uncertain behavior of breast **105** , **106**	
238.1	Neoplasm of uncertain behavior of connective and other soft tissue **100**	
238.5	Neoplasm of uncertain behavior of histiocytic and mast cells **179** , **182**	
235.6	Neoplasm of uncertain behavior of larynx **3** , **46**	
235.1	Neoplasm of uncertain behavior of lip, oral cavity, and pharynx **3** , **46**	
235.3	Neoplasm of uncertain behavior of liver and biliary passages **83**	
235.0	Neoplasm of uncertain behavior of major salivary glands **3** , **46**	
237.6	Neoplasm of uncertain behavior of meninges **19**	
235.5	Neoplasm of uncertain behavior of other and unspecified digestive organs **76**	
237.4	Neoplasm of uncertain behavior of other and unspecified endocrine glands **115**	
236.3	Neoplasm of uncertain behavior of other and unspecified female genital organs **127** , **130**	
236.6	Neoplasm of uncertain behavior of other and unspecified male genital organs **123** , **124**	
237.9	Neoplasm of uncertain behavior of other and unspecified parts of nervous system **19**	
235.9	Neoplasm of uncertain behavior of other and unspecified respiratory organs **52**	
236.9*	Neoplasm of uncertain behavior of other and unspecified urinary organs **117** , **120**	
238.8	Neoplasm of uncertain behavior of other specified sites **181** , **183**	
236.2	Neoplasm of uncertain behavior of ovary **127** , **130**	
237.3	Neoplasm of uncertain behavior of paraganglia **19**	
237.1	Neoplasm of uncertain behavior of pineal gland **19**	
237.0	Neoplasm of uncertain behavior of pituitary gland and craniopharyngeal duct **115**	

236.1	Neoplasm of uncertain behavior of placenta **127** , **130**
238.6	Neoplasm of uncertain behavior of plasma cells **179** , **182**
235.8	Neoplasm of uncertain behavior of pleura, thymus, and mediastinum **52**
238.4	Neoplasm of uncertain behavior of polycythemia vera **179** , **182**
236.5	Neoplasm of uncertain behavior of prostate **123** , **124**
235.4	Neoplasm of uncertain behavior of retroperitoneum and peritoneum **76**
238.2	Neoplasm of uncertain behavior of skin **109**
235.2	Neoplasm of uncertain behavior of stomach, intestines, and rectum **76**
236.4	Neoplasm of uncertain behavior of testis **123** , **124**
235.7	Neoplasm of uncertain behavior of trachea, bronchus, and lung **52**
236.0	Neoplasm of uncertain behavior of uterus **127** , **130**
238.9	Neoplasm of uncertain behavior, site unspecified **181** , **183**
239.4	Neoplasm of unspecified nature of bladder **117** , **120**
239.6	Neoplasm of unspecified nature of brain **19**
239.3	Neoplasm of unspecified nature of breast **106**
239.0	Neoplasm of unspecified nature of digestive system **76**
239.7	Neoplasm of unspecified nature of endocrine glands and other parts of nervous system **115**
239.5	Neoplasm of unspecified nature of other genitourinary organs **117** , **120**
239.8*	Neoplasm of unspecified nature of other specified sites **181** , **183**
239.1	Neoplasm of unspecified nature of respiratory system **52**
239.9	Neoplasm of unspecified nature, site unspecified **181** , **183**
338.3	Neoplasm related pain (acute) (chronic) **214**
239.2	Neoplasms of unspecified nature of bone, soft tissue, and skin **87** , **100**
583*	Nephritis and nephropathy, not specified as acute or chronic **121** , **232**
593.0	Nephroptosis **121**
581*	Nephrotic syndrome **121** , **232**
353*	Nerve root and plexus disorders **20**
997.0*	Nervous system complications **33** , **168** , **172**
349.1	Nervous system complications from surgically implanted device **32** , **166** , **170**
799.21	Nervousness **189**
300.5	Neurasthenia **189**
237.7*	Neurofibromatosis **32**
333.92	Neuroleptic malignant syndrome **32**
781.8	Neurological neglect syndrome **32**
341.0	Neuromyelitis optica **19**
288.0*	Neutropenia **176** , **231**
448.1	Nevus, non-neoplastic **109**
V20.3*	Newborn health supervision **173**
279.13	Nezelof's syndrome **176**
368.6*	Night blindness **39**
202.0*	Nodular lymphoma **179** , **182**
202.01	Nodular lymphoma of lymph nodes of head, face, and neck **2**
388.1*	Noise effects on inner ear **47**
283.1*	Non-autoimmune hemolytic anemias **165** , **170**
998.83	Non-healing surgical wound **205**
739.9	Nonallopathic lesion of abdomen and other sites, not elsewhere classified **98**
739.1	Nonallopathic lesion of cervical region, not elsewhere classified **97**
739.0	Nonallopathic lesion of head region, not elsewhere classified **98**
739.6	Nonallopathic lesion of lower extremities, not elsewhere classified **98**

739.3	Nonallopathic lesion of lumbar region, not elsewhere classified **98**
739.5	Nonallopathic lesion of pelvic region, not elsewhere classified **98**
739.8	Nonallopathic lesion of rib cage, not elsewhere classified **98**
739.4	Nonallopathic lesion of sacral region, not elsewhere classified **98**
739.2	Nonallopathic lesion of thoracic region not elsewhere classified **97**
739.7	Nonallopathic lesion of upper extremities, not elsewhere classified **98**
305.0*	Nondependent alcohol abuse **192**
305.7*	Nondependent amphetamine or related acting sympathomimetic abuse **192**
305.8*	Nondependent antidepressant type abuse **192**
305.2*	Nondependent cannabis abuse **192**
305.6*	Nondependent cocaine abuse **192**
305.3*	Nondependent hallucinogen abuse **192**
305.5*	Nondependent opioid abuse **192**
305.4*	Nondependent sedative, hypnotic or anxiolytic abuse **192**
305.1	Nondependent tobacco use disorder **214**
380.3*	Noninfectious disorders of pinna **47**
622*	Noninflammatory disorders of cervix **128 , 131**
620*	Noninflammatory disorders of ovary, fallopian tube, and broad ligament **128 , 131**
623*	Noninflammatory disorders of vagina **128 , 131**
624*	Noninflammatory disorders of vulva and perineum **128 , 131**
675.23	Nonpurulent mastitis, antepartum **157 , 159**
675.22	Nonpurulent mastitis, delivered, with mention of postpartum complication **140 , 142 , 148**
675.21	Nonpurulent mastitis, delivered, with or without mention of antepartum condition **140 , 142 , 148**
675.24	Nonpurulent mastitis, postpartum condition or complication **154**
675.20	Nonpurulent mastitis, unspecified as to episode of prenatal or postnatal care **162**
322.0	Nonpyogenic meningitis **165 , 170**
437.6	Nonpyogenic thrombosis of intracranial venous sinus **32**
793.6	Nonspecific (abnormal) findings on radiological and other examination of abdominal area, including retroperitoneum **78**
793.3	Nonspecific (abnormal) findings on radiological and other examination of biliary tract **83**
793.4	Nonspecific (abnormal) findings on radiological and other examination of gastrointestinal tract **78**
793.5	Nonspecific (abnormal) findings on radiological and other examination of genitourinary organs **121**
793.7	Nonspecific (abnormal) findings on radiological and other examination of musculoskeletal system **101**
793.2	Nonspecific (abnormal) findings on radiological and other examination of other intrathoracic organs **67**
793.0	Nonspecific (abnormal) findings on radiological and other examination of skull and head **32**
794.15	Nonspecific abnormal auditory function studies **47 , 173**
794.12	Nonspecific abnormal electro-oculogram (EOG) **40**
794.31	Nonspecific abnormal electrocardiogram (ECG) (EKG) **69**
794.17	Nonspecific abnormal electromyogram (EMG) **101**
792.3	Nonspecific abnormal finding in amniotic fluid **157 , 160**
792.0	Nonspecific abnormal finding in cerebrospinal fluid **32**
792.4	Nonspecific abnormal finding in saliva **47**
792.2	Nonspecific abnormal finding in semen **125**
792.1	Nonspecific abnormal finding in stool contents **78**
795.2	Nonspecific abnormal findings on chromosomal analysis **214**
796.6	Nonspecific abnormal findings on neonatal screening **214**
793.8*	Nonspecific abnormal findings on radiological and other examinations of body structure, breast **107**

794.14	Nonspecific abnormal oculomotor studies **40**
794.10	Nonspecific abnormal response to unspecified nerve stimulation **32**
794.7	Nonspecific abnormal results of basal metabolism function study **115**
794.0*	Nonspecific abnormal results of function study of brain and central nervous system **32**
794.4	Nonspecific abnormal results of kidney function study **121**
794.8	Nonspecific abnormal results of liver function study **83**
794.6	Nonspecific abnormal results of other endocrine function study **115**
794.9	Nonspecific abnormal results of other specified function study **121**
794.2	Nonspecific abnormal results of pulmonary system function study **54**
794.5	Nonspecific abnormal results of thyroid function study **115**
794.11	Nonspecific abnormal retinal function studies **40**
796.0	Nonspecific abnormal toxicological findings **205**
794.30	Nonspecific abnormal unspecified cardiovascular function study **69**
794.16	Nonspecific abnormal vestibular function studies **47**
794.13	Nonspecific abnormal visually evoked potential **40**
790.4	Nonspecific elevation of levels of transaminase or lactic acid dehydrogenase (LDH) **214**
796.3	Nonspecific low blood pressure reading **69**
289.2	Nonspecific mesenteric lymphadenitis **78**
795.3*	Nonspecific positive culture findings **187**
795.5*	Nonspecific reaction to test for tuberculosis **51**
381.4	Nonsuppurative otitis media, not specified as acute or chronic **46**
241*	Nontoxic nodular goiter **115**
729.7*	Nontraumatic compartment syndrome **99**
596.6	Nontraumatic rupture of bladder **167 , 171**
650	Normal delivery **136 , 143 , 149**
V22*	Normal pregnancy **215**
832.2	Nursemaid's elbow **223**
261	Nutritional marasmus **114 , 165 , 169 , 231**
379.54	Nystagmus associated with disorders of the vestibular system **38**
379.57	Nystagmus with deficiencies of saccadic eye movements **38**
379.58	Nystagmus with deficiencies of smooth pursuit movements **38**
649.13	Obesity complicating pregnancy, childbirth, or the puerperium, antepartum condition or complication **155 , 158**
649.12	Obesity complicating pregnancy, childbirth, or the puerperium, delivered, with mention of postpartum complication **136 , 143 , 149**
649.11	Obesity complicating pregnancy, childbirth, or the puerperium, delivered, with or without mention of antepartum condition **136 , 143 , 149**
649.14	Obesity complicating pregnancy, childbirth, or the puerperium, postpartum condition or complication **153**
649.10	Obesity complicating pregnancy, childbirth, or the puerperium, unspecified as to episode of care or not applicable **161**
278.03	Obesity hypoventilation syndrome **54**
278.00	Obesity, unspecified **114**
V71.8*	Observation and evaluation for other specified suspected conditions **216**
V29*	Observation and evaluation of newborns and infants for suspected condition not found **173 , 215**
V71.3	Observation following accident at work **205**
V71.5	Observation following alleged rape or seduction **216**
V71.4	Observation following other accident **205**
V71.6	Observation following other inflicted injury **205**
V71.7	Observation for suspected cardiovascular disease **68**

V71.1	Observation for suspected malignant neoplasm **181** , **183**
V71.2	Observation for suspected tuberculosis **51**
V71.9	Observation for unspecified suspected condition **216**
V71.01	Observation of adult antisocial behavior **189**
V71.02	Observation of childhood or adolescent antisocial behavior **189**
V71.09	Observation of other suspected mental condition **190**
300.3	Obsessive-compulsive disorders **189**
301.4	Obsessive-compulsive personality disorder **189**
673.03	Obstetrical air embolism, antepartum condition or complication **157** , **159**
673.04	Obstetrical air embolism, postpartum condition or complication **154**
673.00	Obstetrical air embolism, unspecified as to episode of care **162**
673.02	Obstetrical air embolism, with delivery, with mention of postpartum complication **139** , **142** , **147**
673.01	Obstetrical air embolism, with delivery, with or without mention of antepartum condition **139** , **142** , **147**
673.23	Obstetrical blood-clot embolism, antepartum **157** , **159**
673.24	Obstetrical blood-clot embolism, postpartum condition or complication **154**
673.20	Obstetrical blood-clot embolism, unspecified as to episode of care **162**
673.21	Obstetrical blood-clot embolism, with delivery, with or without mention of antepartum condition **139** , **142** , **147**
673.22	Obstetrical blood-clot embolism, with mention of postpartum complication **139** , **142** , **147**
673.33	Obstetrical pyemic and septic embolism, antepartum **157** , **159**
673.34	Obstetrical pyemic and septic embolism, postpartum condition or complication **154**
673.30	Obstetrical pyemic and septic embolism, unspecified as to episode of care **162**
673.32	Obstetrical pyemic and septic embolism, with delivery, with mention of postpartum complication **139** , **142** , **148**
673.31	Obstetrical pyemic and septic embolism, with delivery, with or without mention of antepartum condition **139** , **142** , **148**
660.23	Obstruction by abnormal pelvic soft tissues during labor and delivery, antepartum **156** , **159**
660.21	Obstruction by abnormal pelvic soft tissues during labor and delivery, delivered **137** , **144** , **150**
660.20	Obstruction by abnormal pelvic soft tissues during labor and delivery, unspecified as to episode of care **137** , **144** , **150**
660.13	Obstruction by bony pelvis during labor and delivery, antepartum **156** , **159**
660.11	Obstruction by bony pelvis during labor and delivery, delivered **137** , **144** , **150**
660.10	Obstruction by bony pelvis during labor and delivery, unspecified as to episode of care **137** , **144** , **150**
660.03	Obstruction caused by malposition of fetus at onset of labor, antepartum **156** , **159**
660.01	Obstruction caused by malposition of fetus at onset of labor, delivered **137** , **144** , **150**
660.00	Obstruction caused by malposition of fetus at onset of labor, unspecified as to episode of care **137** , **144** , **150**
381.6*	Obstruction of Eustachian tube **47**
491.2*	Obstructive chronic bronchitis **53**
331.4	Obstructive hydrocephalus **19**
327.23	Obstructive sleep apnea (adult) (pediatric) **47**
433.01	Occlusion and stenosis of basilar artery with cerebral infarction **9** , **10** , **19** , **20** , **166** , **170**
433.00	Occlusion and stenosis of basilar artery without mention of cerebral infarction **20**
433.11	Occlusion and stenosis of carotid artery with cerebral infarction **9** , **10** , **19** , **20** , **166** , **170**

433.10	Occlusion and stenosis of carotid artery without mention of cerebral infarction **20**
433.31	Occlusion and stenosis of multiple and bilateral precerebral arteries with cerebral infarction **9** , **10** , **19** , **20** , **166** , **170**
433.30	Occlusion and stenosis of multiple and bilateral precerebral arteries without mention of cerebral infarction **20**
433.81	Occlusion and stenosis of other specified precerebral artery with cerebral infarction **9** , **10** , **19** , **20** , **166** , **170**
433.80	Occlusion and stenosis of other specified precerebral artery without mention of cerebral infarction **20**
433.91	Occlusion and stenosis of unspecified precerebral artery with cerebral infarction **9** , **10** , **19** , **20** , **166** , **170**
433.90	Occlusion and stenosis of unspecified precerebral artery without mention of cerebral infarction **20**
433.21	Occlusion and stenosis of vertebral artery with cerebral infarction **9** , **10** , **19** , **20** , **166** , **170**
433.20	Occlusion and stenosis of vertebral artery without mention of cerebral infarction **20**
434*	Occlusion of cerebral arteries **166** , **170**
V57.2*	Occupational therapy and vocational rehabilitation **214**
781.93	Ocular torticollis **98**
021.3	Oculoglandular tularemia **186**
717.0	Old bucket handle tear of medial meniscus **99**
412	Old myocardial infarction **67**
658.03	Oligohydramnios, antepartum **156** , **159**
658.01	Oligohydramnios, delivered **137** , **144** , **150**
658.00	Oligohydramnios, unspecified as to episode of care **161**
788.5	Oliguria and anuria **119** , **120**
771.4	Omphalitis of the newborn **164** , **168**
756.72	Omphalocele **167** , **171**
649.8*	Onset (spontaneous) of labor after 37 completed weeks of gestation but before 39 completed weeks gestation, with delivery by (planned) cesarean section **136** , **141** , **149**
649.82	Onset (spontaneous) of labor after 37 completed weeks of gestation but before 39 completed weeks gestation, with delivery by (planned) cesarean section, delivered, with mention of postpartum complication **143**
649.81	Onset (spontaneous) of labor after 37 completed weeks of gestation but before 39 completed weeks gestation, with delivery by (planned) cesarean section, delivered, with or without mention of antepartum condition **143**
824.5	Open bimalleolar fracture **223**
837.1	Open dislocation of ankle **223** , **228**
832.1*	Open dislocation of elbow **223** , **228**
834.1*	Open dislocation of finger **223**
838.1*	Open dislocation of foot **223**
835.1*	Open dislocation of hip **223** , **228**
830.1	Open dislocation of jaw **223**
836.4	Open dislocation of patella **223**
831.1*	Open dislocation of shoulder **223** , **228**
833.1*	Open dislocation of wrist **223**
839.1*	Open dislocation, cervical vertebra **98** , **223** , **228**
839.9	Open dislocation, multiple and ill-defined sites **100** , **223**
839.79	Open dislocation, other location **100** , **223**
839.59	Open dislocation, other vertebra **228**
839.5*	Open dislocation, other vertebra **98** , **223**
839.52	Open dislocation, sacrum **228**
839.71	Open dislocation, sternum **52** , **223** , **227**
839.3*	Open dislocation, thoracic and lumbar vertebra **98** , **223**
808.1	Open fracture of acetabulum **222**
811.11	Open fracture of acromial process of scapula **99**
801.6*	Open fracture of base of skull with cerebral laceration and contusion **222** , **226**

801.62	Open fracture of base of skull with cerebral laceration and contusion, brief (less than one hour) loss of consciousness **28**
801.66	Open fracture of base of skull with cerebral laceration and contusion, loss of consciousness of unspecified duration **23**
801.63	Open fracture of base of skull with cerebral laceration and contusion, moderate (1-24 hours) loss of consciousness **23**
801.61	Open fracture of base of skull with cerebral laceration and contusion, no loss of consciousness **28**
801.64	Open fracture of base of skull with cerebral laceration and contusion, prolonged (more than 24 hours) loss of consciousness and return to pre-existing conscious level **23**
801.65	Open fracture of base of skull with cerebral laceration and contusion, prolonged (more than 24 hours) loss of consciousness, without return to pre-existing conscious level **23**
801.69	Open fracture of base of skull with cerebral laceration and contusion, unspecified concussion **28**
801.60	Open fracture of base of skull with cerebral laceration and contusion, unspecified state of consciousness **28**
801.9*	Open fracture of base of skull with intracranial injury of other and unspecified nature **222 , 226**
801.92	Open fracture of base of skull with intracranial injury of other and unspecified nature, brief (less than one hour) loss of consciousness **28**
801.96	Open fracture of base of skull with intracranial injury of other and unspecified nature, loss of consciousness of unspecified duration **23**
801.93	Open fracture of base of skull with intracranial injury of other and unspecified nature, moderate (1-24 hours) loss of consciousness **23**
801.91	Open fracture of base of skull with intracranial injury of other and unspecified nature, no loss of consciousness **28**
801.94	Open fracture of base of skull with intracranial injury of other and unspecified nature, prolonged (more than 24 hours) loss of consciousness and return to pre-existing conscious level **23**
801.95	Open fracture of base of skull with intracranial injury of other and unspecified nature, prolonged (more than 24 hours) loss of consciousness, without return to pre-existing conscious level **23**
801.99	Open fracture of base of skull with intracranial injury of other and unspecified nature, unspecified concussion **28**
801.90	Open fracture of base of skull with intracranial injury of other and unspecified nature, unspecified state of consciousness **28**
801.8*	Open fracture of base of skull with other and unspecified intracranial hemorrhage **222 , 226**
801.82	Open fracture of base of skull with other and unspecified intracranial hemorrhage, brief (less than one hour) loss of consciousness **28**
801.86	Open fracture of base of skull with other and unspecified intracranial hemorrhage, loss of consciousness of unspecified duration **23**
801.83	Open fracture of base of skull with other and unspecified intracranial hemorrhage, moderate (1-24 hours) loss of consciousness **23**
801.81	Open fracture of base of skull with other and unspecified intracranial hemorrhage, no loss of consciousness **28**
801.84	Open fracture of base of skull with other and unspecified intracranial hemorrhage, prolonged (more than 24 hours) loss of consciousness and return to pre-existing conscious level **23**
801.85	Open fracture of base of skull with other and unspecified intracranial hemorrhage, prolonged (more than 24 hours) loss of consciousness, without return to pre-existing conscious level **23**
801.89	Open fracture of base of skull with other and unspecified intracranial hemorrhage, unspecified concussion **28**
801.80	Open fracture of base of skull with other and unspecified intracranial hemorrhage, unspecified state of consciousness **28**
801.7*	Open fracture of base of skull with subarachnoid, subdural, and extradural hemorrhage **222 , 226**
801.72	Open fracture of base of skull with subarachnoid, subdural, and extradural hemorrhage, brief (less than one hour) loss of consciousness **28**
801.76	Open fracture of base of skull with subarachnoid, subdural, and extradural hemorrhage, loss of consciousness of unspecified duration **23**
801.73	Open fracture of base of skull with subarachnoid, subdural, and extradural hemorrhage, moderate (1-24 hours) loss of consciousness **23**
801.71	Open fracture of base of skull with subarachnoid, subdural, and extradural hemorrhage, no loss of consciousness **28**
801.74	Open fracture of base of skull with subarachnoid, subdural, and extradural hemorrhage, prolonged (more than 24 hours) loss of consciousness and return to pre-existing conscious level **23**
801.75	Open fracture of base of skull with subarachnoid, subdural, and extradural hemorrhage, prolonged (more than 24 hours) loss of consciousness, without return to pre-existing conscious level **23**
801.79	Open fracture of base of skull with subarachnoid, subdural, and extradural hemorrhage, unspecified concussion **28**
801.70	Open fracture of base of skull with subarachnoid, subdural, and extradural hemorrhage, unspecified state of consciousness **28**
801.5*	Open fracture of base of skull without mention of intracranial injury **221**
801.52	Open fracture of base of skull without mention of intracranial injury, brief (less than one hour) loss of consciousness **28 , 226**
801.56	Open fracture of base of skull without mention of intracranial injury, loss of consciousness of unspecified duration **23**
801.53	Open fracture of base of skull without mention of intracranial injury, moderate (1-24 hours) loss of consciousness **23 , 226**
801.51	Open fracture of base of skull without mention of intracranial injury, no loss of consciousness **28**
801.54	Open fracture of base of skull without mention of intracranial injury, prolonged (more than 24 hours) loss of consciousness and return to pre-existing conscious level **23 , 226**
801.55	Open fracture of base of skull without mention of intracranial injury, prolonged (more than 24 hours) loss of consciousness, without return to pre-existing conscious level **23 , 226**
801.59	Open fracture of base of skull without mention of intracranial injury, unspecified concussion **28**
801.50	Open fracture of base of skull without mention of intracranial injury, unspecified state of consciousness **28**
825.1	Open fracture of calcaneus **99 , 223**
806.1*	Open fracture of cervical vertebra with spinal cord injury **222 , 228**
805.1*	Open fracture of cervical vertebra without mention of spinal cord injury **222**
810.1*	Open fracture of clavicle **222**
811.12	Open fracture of coracoid process **99**
805.3	Open fracture of dorsal (thoracic) vertebra without mention of spinal cord injury **222**
806.3*	Open fracture of dorsal vertebra with spinal cord injury **222 , 228**
807.18	Open fracture of eight or more ribs **227**
807.15	Open fracture of five ribs **227**
807.14	Open fracture of four ribs **227**
811.13	Open fracture of glenoid cavity and neck of scapula **99**
807.6	Open fracture of larynx and trachea **3 , 47 , 222 , 227**
824.3	Open fracture of lateral malleolus **223**
821.3*	Open fracture of lower end of femur **223**
812.5*	Open fracture of lower end of humerus **222 , 228**
813.5*	Open fracture of lower end of radius and ulna **222 , 228**
806.5	Open fracture of lumbar spine with spinal cord injury **222 , 228**
805.5	Open fracture of lumbar vertebra without mention of spinal cord injury **222**
824.1	Open fracture of medial malleolus **223**
815.1*	Open fracture of metacarpal bones **222**

*Code Range

807.19	Open fracture of multiple ribs, unspecified **227**
826.1	Open fracture of one or more phalanges of foot **223**
816.1*	Open fracture of one or more phalanges of hand **222**
811.19	Open fracture of other part of scapula **101**
808.5*	Open fracture of other specified part of pelvis **222**
825.3*	Open fracture of other tarsal and metatarsal bones **99 , 223**
822.1	Open fracture of patella **223**
808.3	Open fracture of pubis **222**
807.1*	Open fracture of rib(s) **52 , 222**
806.7*	Open fracture of sacrum and coccyx with spinal cord injury **222 , 228**
805.7	Open fracture of sacrum and coccyx without mention of spinal cord injury **222 , 228**
811.1*	Open fracture of scapula **222**
807.17	Open fracture of seven ribs **227**
812.31	Open fracture of shaft of humerus **228**
813.3*	Open fracture of shaft of radius and ulna **222 , 228**
823.3*	Open fracture of shaft of tibia and fibula **223 , 228**
821.1*	Open fracture of shaft or unspecified part of femur **167 , 171 , 223**
812.3*	Open fracture of shaft or unspecified part of humerus **222**
807.16	Open fracture of six ribs **227**
807.3	Open fracture of sternum **52 , 222 , 227**
829.1	Open fracture of unspecified bone **223**
812.30	Open fracture of unspecified part of humerus **228**
820.9	Open fracture of unspecified part of neck of femur **223**
813.9*	Open fracture of unspecified part of radius with ulna **222 , 228**
811.10	Open fracture of unspecified part of scapula **99**
823.9*	Open fracture of unspecified part of tibia and fibula **223 , 228**
805.9	Open fracture of unspecified part of vertebral column without mention of spinal cord injury **222**
806.9	Open fracture of unspecified vertebra with spinal cord injury **222 , 228**
812.1*	Open fracture of upper end of humerus **222 , 228**
813.1*	Open fracture of upper end of radius and ulna **222 , 228**
823.1*	Open fracture of upper end of tibia and fibula **223 , 228**
800.6*	Open fracture of vault of skull with cerebral laceration and contusion **221 , 226**
800.62	Open fracture of vault of skull with cerebral laceration and contusion, brief (less than one hour) loss of consciousness **27**
800.66	Open fracture of vault of skull with cerebral laceration and contusion, loss of consciousness of unspecified duration **22**
800.63	Open fracture of vault of skull with cerebral laceration and contusion, moderate (1-24 hours) loss of consciousness **22**
800.61	Open fracture of vault of skull with cerebral laceration and contusion, no loss of consciousness **27**
800.64	Open fracture of vault of skull with cerebral laceration and contusion, prolonged (more than 24 hours) loss of consciousness and return to pre-existing conscious level **22**
800.65	Open fracture of vault of skull with cerebral laceration and contusion, prolonged (more than 24 hours) loss of consciousness, without return to pre-existing conscious level **22**
800.69	Open fracture of vault of skull with cerebral laceration and contusion, unspecified concussion **27**
800.60	Open fracture of vault of skull with cerebral laceration and contusion, unspecified state of consciousness **27**
800.9*	Open fracture of vault of skull with intracranial injury of other and unspecified nature **221 , 226**
800.92	Open fracture of vault of skull with intracranial injury of other and unspecified nature, brief (less than one hour) loss of consciousness **28**
800.96	Open fracture of vault of skull with intracranial injury of other and unspecified nature, loss of consciousness of unspecified duration **22**
800.93	Open fracture of vault of skull with intracranial injury of other and unspecified nature, moderate (1-24 hours) loss of consciousness **22**
800.91	Open fracture of vault of skull with intracranial injury of other and unspecified nature, no loss of consciousness **28**
800.94	Open fracture of vault of skull with intracranial injury of other and unspecified nature, prolonged (more than 24 hours) loss of consciousness and return to pre-existing conscious level **22**
800.95	Open fracture of vault of skull with intracranial injury of other and unspecified nature, prolonged (more than 24 hours) loss of consciousness, without return to pre-existing conscious level **22**
800.99	Open fracture of vault of skull with intracranial injury of other and unspecified nature, unspecified concussion **28**
800.90	Open fracture of vault of skull with intracranial injury of other and unspecified nature, unspecified state of consciousness **28**
800.8*	Open fracture of vault of skull with other and unspecified intracranial hemorrhage **221 , 226**
800.82	Open fracture of vault of skull with other and unspecified intracranial hemorrhage, brief (less than one hour) loss of consciousness **27**
800.86	Open fracture of vault of skull with other and unspecified intracranial hemorrhage, loss of consciousness of unspecified duration **22**
800.83	Open fracture of vault of skull with other and unspecified intracranial hemorrhage, moderate (1-24 hours) loss of consciousness **22**
800.81	Open fracture of vault of skull with other and unspecified intracranial hemorrhage, no loss of consciousness **27**
800.84	Open fracture of vault of skull with other and unspecified intracranial hemorrhage, prolonged (more than 24 hours) loss of consciousness and return to pre-existing conscious level **22**
800.85	Open fracture of vault of skull with other and unspecified intracranial hemorrhage, prolonged (more than 24 hours) loss of consciousness, without return to pre-existing conscious level **22**
800.89	Open fracture of vault of skull with other and unspecified intracranial hemorrhage, unspecified concussion **28**
800.80	Open fracture of vault of skull with other and unspecified intracranial hemorrhage, unspecified state of consciousness **27**
800.7*	Open fracture of vault of skull with subarachnoid, subdural, and extradural hemorrhage **221 , 226**
800.72	Open fracture of vault of skull with subarachnoid, subdural, and extradural hemorrhage, brief (less than one hour) loss of consciousness **27**
800.76	Open fracture of vault of skull with subarachnoid, subdural, and extradural hemorrhage, loss of consciousness of unspecified duration **22**
800.73	Open fracture of vault of skull with subarachnoid, subdural, and extradural hemorrhage, moderate (1-24 hours) loss of consciousness **22**
800.71	Open fracture of vault of skull with subarachnoid, subdural, and extradural hemorrhage, no loss of consciousness **27**
800.74	Open fracture of vault of skull with subarachnoid, subdural, and extradural hemorrhage, prolonged (more than 24 hours) loss of consciousness and return to pre-existing conscious level **22**
800.75	Open fracture of vault of skull with subarachnoid, subdural, and extradural hemorrhage, prolonged (more than 24 hours) loss of consciousness, without return to pre-existing conscious level **22**
800.79	Open fracture of vault of skull with subarachnoid, subdural, and extradural hemorrhage, unspecified concussion **27**
800.70	Open fracture of vault of skull with subarachnoid, subdural, and extradural hemorrhage, unspecified state of consciousness **27**
800.5*	Open fracture of vault of skull without mention of intracranial injury **221**
800.52	Open fracture of vault of skull without mention of intracranial injury, brief (less than one hour) loss of consciousness **27 , 225**

800.56   Open fracture of vault of skull without mention of intracranial injury, loss of consciousness of unspecified duration **22**

800.53   Open fracture of vault of skull without mention of intracranial injury, moderate (1-24 hours) loss of consciousness **22 , 226**

800.51   Open fracture of vault of skull without mention of intracranial injury, no loss of consciousness **27**

800.54   Open fracture of vault of skull without mention of intracranial injury, prolonged (more than 24 hours) loss of consciousness and return to pre-existing conscious level **22 , 226**

800.55   Open fracture of vault of skull without mention of intracranial injury, prolonged (more than 24 hours) loss of consciousness, without return to pre-existing conscious level **22 , 226**

800.59   Open fracture of vault of skull without mention of intracranial injury, unspecified concussion **27**

800.50   Open fracture of vault of skull without mention of intracranial injury, unspecified state of consciousness **27**

804.7*   Open fractures involving skull or face with other bones with subarachnoid, subdural, and extradural hemorrhage **222 , 227**

804.72   Open fractures involving skull or face with other bones with subarachnoid, subdural, and extradural hemorrhage, brief (less than one hour) loss of consciousness **30**

804.76   Open fractures involving skull or face with other bones with subarachnoid, subdural, and extradural hemorrhage, loss of consciousness of unspecified duration **25**

804.73   Open fractures involving skull or face with other bones with subarachnoid, subdural, and extradural hemorrhage, moderate (1-24 hours) loss of consciousness **25**

804.71   Open fractures involving skull or face with other bones with subarachnoid, subdural, and extradural hemorrhage, no loss of consciousness **29**

804.74   Open fractures involving skull or face with other bones with subarachnoid, subdural, and extradural hemorrhage, prolonged (more than 24 hours) loss of consciousness and return to pre-existing conscious level **25**

804.75   Open fractures involving skull or face with other bones with subarachnoid, subdural, and extradural hemorrhage, prolonged (more than 24 hours) loss of consciousness, without return to pre-existing conscious level **25**

804.79   Open fractures involving skull or face with other bones with subarachnoid, subdural, and extradural hemorrhage, unspecified concussion **30**

804.70   Open fractures involving skull or face with other bones with subarachnoid, subdural, and extradural hemorrhage, unspecified state of consciousness **29**

804.6*   Open fractures involving skull or face with other bones, with cerebral laceration and contusion **222**

804.62   Open fractures involving skull or face with other bones, with cerebral laceration and contusion, brief (less than one hour) loss of consciousness **29 , 227**

804.66   Open fractures involving skull or face with other bones, with cerebral laceration and contusion, loss of consciousness of unspecified duration **25 , 227**

804.63   Open fractures involving skull or face with other bones, with cerebral laceration and contusion, moderate (1-24 hours) loss of consciousness **25 , 227**

804.61   Open fractures involving skull or face with other bones, with cerebral laceration and contusion, no loss of consciousness **29 , 227**

804.64   Open fractures involving skull or face with other bones, with cerebral laceration and contusion, prolonged (more than 24 hours) loss of consciousness and return to pre-existing conscious level **25 , 227**

804.65   Open fractures involving skull or face with other bones, with cerebral laceration and contusion, prolonged (more than 24 hours) loss of consciousness, without return to pre-existing conscious level **25 , 227**

804.69   Open fractures involving skull or face with other bones, with cerebral laceration and contusion, unspecified concussion **29**

804.60   Open fractures involving skull or face with other bones, with cerebral laceration and contusion, unspecified state of consciousness **29 , 227**

804.9*   Open fractures involving skull or face with other bones, with intracranial injury of other and unspecified nature **222 , 227**

804.92   Open fractures involving skull or face with other bones, with intracranial injury of other and unspecified nature, brief (less than one hour) loss of consciousness **30**

804.96   Open fractures involving skull or face with other bones, with intracranial injury of other and unspecified nature, loss of consciousness of unspecified duration **25**

804.93   Open fractures involving skull or face with other bones, with intracranial injury of other and unspecified nature, moderate (1-24 hours) loss of consciousness **25**

804.91   Open fractures involving skull or face with other bones, with intracranial injury of other and unspecified nature, no loss of consciousness **30**

804.94   Open fractures involving skull or face with other bones, with intracranial injury of other and unspecified nature, prolonged (more than 24 hours) loss of consciousness and return to pre-existing conscious level **25**

804.95   Open fractures involving skull or face with other bones, with intracranial injury of other and unspecified nature, prolonged (more than 24 hours) loss of consciousness, without return to pre-existing level **25**

804.99   Open fractures involving skull or face with other bones, with intracranial injury of other and unspecified nature, unspecified concussion **30**

804.90   Open fractures involving skull or face with other bones, with intracranial injury of other and unspecified nature, unspecified state of consciousness **30**

804.8*   Open fractures involving skull or face with other bones, with other and unspecified intracranial hemorrhage **222 , 227**

804.82   Open fractures involving skull or face with other bones, with other and unspecified intracranial hemorrhage, brief (less than one hour) loss of consciousness **30**

804.86   Open fractures involving skull or face with other bones, with other and unspecified intracranial hemorrhage, loss of consciousness of unspecified duration **25**

804.83   Open fractures involving skull or face with other bones, with other and unspecified intracranial hemorrhage, moderate (1-24 hours) loss of consciousness **25**

804.81   Open fractures involving skull or face with other bones, with other and unspecified intracranial hemorrhage, no loss of consciousness **30**

804.84   Open fractures involving skull or face with other bones, with other and unspecified intracranial hemorrhage, prolonged (more than 24 hours) loss of consciousness and return to pre-existing conscious level **25**

804.85   Open fractures involving skull or face with other bones, with other and unspecified intracranial hemorrhage, prolonged (more than 24 hours) loss of consciousness, without return to pre-existing conscious level **25**

804.89   Open fractures involving skull or face with other bones, with other and unspecified intracranial hemorrhage, unspecified concussion **30**

804.80   Open fractures involving skull or face with other bones, with other and unspecified intracranial hemorrhage, unspecified state of consciousness **30**

804.5*   Open fractures involving skull or face with other bones, without mention of intracranial injury **222**

804.52   Open fractures involving skull or face with other bones, without mention of intracranial injury, brief (less than one hour) loss of consciousness **29 , 227**

804.56   Open fractures involving skull or face with other bones, without mention of intracranial injury, loss of consciousness of unspecified duration **25**

804.53	Open fractures involving skull or face with other bones, without mention of intracranial injury, moderate (1-24 hours) loss of consciousness **25 , 227**	
804.51	Open fractures involving skull or face with other bones, without mention of intracranial injury, no loss of consciousness **29**	
804.54	Open fractures involving skull or face with other bones, without mention of intracranial injury, prolonged (more than 24 hours) loss of consciousness and return to pre-existing conscious level **25 , 227**	
804.55	Open fractures involving skull or face with other bones, without mention of intracranial injury, prolonged (more than 24 hours) loss of consciousness, without return to pre-existing conscious level **25 , 227**	
804.59	Open fractures involving skull or face with other bones, without mention of intracranial injury, unspecified concussion **29**	
804.50	Open fractures involving skull or face with other bones, without mention of intracranial injury, unspecified state of consciousness **29**	
814.1*	Open fractures of carpal bones **222**	
820.3*	Open pertrochanteric fracture of femur **223**	
820.1*	Open transcervical fracture **223**	
824.7	Open trimalleolar fracture **223**	
879.3	Open wound of abdominal wall, anterior, complicated **203**	
879.2	Open wound of abdominal wall, anterior, without mention of complication **107**	
879.5	Open wound of abdominal wall, lateral, complicated **203**	
879.4	Open wound of abdominal wall, lateral, without mention of complication **107**	
876*	Open wound of back **107 , 224**	
879.1	Open wound of breast, complicated **107**	
879.0	Open wound of breast, without mention of complication **107**	
873.71	Open wound of buccal mucosa, complicated **3**	
873.61	Open wound of buccal mucosa, without mention of complication **3**	
877*	Open wound of buttock **107 , 224**	
873.51	Open wound of cheek, complicated **3 , 107**	
873.41	Open wound of cheek, without mention of complication **3 , 107**	
875*	Open wound of chest (wall) **224**	
875.1	Open wound of chest (wall), complicated **203**	
875.0	Open wound of chest (wall), without mention of complication **107**	
872*	Open wound of ear **47 , 224**	
881*	Open wound of elbow, forearm, and wrist **224**	
881.1*	Open wound of elbow, forearm, and wrist, complicated **203**	
881.2*	Open wound of elbow, forearm, and wrist, with tendon involvement **101**	
881.0*	Open wound of elbow, forearm, and wrist, without mention of complication **108**	
871*	Open wound of eyeball **40 , 224**	
873.59	Open wound of face, other and multiple sites, complicated **107**	
873.49	Open wound of face, other and multiple sites, without mention of complication **107**	
873.50	Open wound of face, unspecified site, complicated **3 , 107**	
873.40	Open wound of face, unspecified site, without mention of complication **3 , 107**	
883*	Open wound of finger(s) **224**	
883.1	Open wound of finger(s), complicated **203**	
883.2	Open wound of finger(s), with tendon involvement **101**	
883.0	Open wound of finger(s), without mention of complication **108**	
892*	Open wound of foot except toe(s) alone **224**	
892.1	Open wound of foot except toe(s) alone, complicated **204**	
892.2	Open wound of foot except toe(s) alone, with tendon involvement **101**	

892.0	Open wound of foot except toe(s) alone, without mention of complication **108**
873.52	Open wound of forehead, complicated **107**
873.42	Open wound of forehead, without mention of complication **107**
878*	Open wound of genital organs (external), including traumatic amputation **224**
873.72	Open wound of gum (alveolar process), complicated **4**
873.62	Open wound of gum (alveolar process), without mention of complication **3**
882*	Open wound of hand except finger(s) alone **224**
882.1	Open wound of hand except finger(s) alone, complicated **203**
882.2	Open wound of hand except finger(s) alone, with tendon involvement **101**
882.0	Open wound of hand except finger(s) alone, without mention of complication **108**
890*	Open wound of hip and thigh **224**
890.1	Open wound of hip and thigh, complicated **204**
890.2	Open wound of hip and thigh, with tendon involvement **101**
890.0	Open wound of hip and thigh, without mention of complication **108**
873.7*	Open wound of internal structure of mouth, complicated **48**
873.6*	Open wound of internal structures of mouth, without mention of complication **48**
873.54	Open wound of jaw, complicated **3 , 48**
873.44	Open wound of jaw, without mention of complication **3 , 48**
891*	Open wound of knee, leg (except thigh), and ankle **224**
891.1	Open wound of knee, leg (except thigh), and ankle, complicated **204**
891.2	Open wound of knee, leg (except thigh), and ankle, with tendon involvement **101**
891.0	Open wound of knee, leg (except thigh), and ankle, without mention of complication **108**
874.1*	Open wound of larynx and trachea, complicated **224**
874.0*	Open wound of larynx and trachea, without mention of complication **224**
874.10	Open wound of larynx with trachea, complicated **4 , 47 , 227**
874.00	Open wound of larynx with trachea, without mention of complication **4 , 47**
874.11	Open wound of larynx, complicated **4 , 47 , 227**
874.01	Open wound of larynx, without mention of complication **4 , 47**
873.53	Open wound of lip, complicated **3 , 48**
873.43	Open wound of lip, without mention of complication **3 , 48**
873.79	Open wound of mouth, other and multiple sites, complicated **4**
873.69	Open wound of mouth, other and multiple sites, without mention of complication **3**
873.70	Open wound of mouth, unspecified site, complicated **3**
873.60	Open wound of mouth, unspecified site, without mention of complication **3**
873.22	Open wound of nasal cavity, without mention of complication **47**
873.21	Open wound of nasal septum, without mention of complication **47**
873.23	Open wound of nasal sinus, without mention of complication **47**
873.3*	Open wound of nose, complicated **3 , 47**
873.29	Open wound of nose, multiple sites, without mention of complication **47**
873.20	Open wound of nose, unspecified site, without mention of complication **47**
873.2*	Open wound of nose, without mention of complication **3**
870*	Open wound of ocular adnexa **40 , 224**
878.9	Open wound of other and unspecified parts of genital organs, complicated **125 , 128 , 132**
878.8	Open wound of other and unspecified parts of genital organs, without mention of complication **125 , 128 , 131**

874.9	Open wound of other and unspecified parts of neck, complicated **4 , 107 , 224**
874.8	Open wound of other and unspecified parts of neck, without mention of complication **4 , 107 , 224**
879.7	Open wound of other and unspecified parts of trunk, complicated **203**
879.6	Open wound of other and unspecified parts of trunk, without mention of complication **107**
879*	Open wound of other and unspecified sites, except limbs **224**
873.75	Open wound of palate, complicated **4**
873.65	Open wound of palate, without mention of complication **3**
878.1	Open wound of penis, complicated **125**
878.0	Open wound of penis, without mention of complication **125**
874.5	Open wound of pharynx, complicated **4 , 47 , 224**
874.4	Open wound of pharynx, without mention of complication **4 , 47 , 224**
873.1	Open wound of scalp, complicated **107**
873.0	Open wound of scalp, without mention of complication **107**
878.3	Open wound of scrotum and testes, complicated **125**
878.2	Open wound of scrotum and testes, without mention of complication **125**
880*	Open wound of shoulder and upper arm **224**
880.1*	Open wound of shoulder and upper arm, complicated **203**
880.2*	Open wound of shoulder and upper arm, with tendon involvement **101**
880.0*	Open wound of shoulder and upper arm, without mention of complication **108**
874.3	Open wound of thyroid gland, complicated **4 , 115 , 224**
874.2	Open wound of thyroid gland, without mention of complication **4 , 115 , 224**
893*	Open wound of toe(s) **224**
893.1	Open wound of toe(s), complicated **204**
893.2	Open wound of toe(s), with tendon involvement **101**
893.0	Open wound of toe(s), without mention of complication **108**
873.74	Open wound of tongue and floor of mouth, complicated **4**
873.64	Open wound of tongue and floor of mouth, without mention of complication **3**
874.12	Open wound of trachea, complicated **4 , 52 , 227**
874.02	Open wound of trachea, without mention of complication **4 , 52**
878.7	Open wound of vagina, complicated **128 , 131**
878.6	Open wound of vagina, without mention of complication **128 , 131**
878.5	Open wound of vulva, complicated **128 , 131**
878.4	Open wound of vulva, without mention of complication **128 , 131**
879.9	Open wound(s) (multiple) of unspecified site(s), complicated **203**
879.8	Open wound(s) (multiple) of unspecified site(s), without mention of complication **108**
365.14	Open-angle glaucoma of childhood **39**
360.14	Ophthalmia nodosa **39**
121.0	Opisthorchiasis **83**
118	Opportunistic mycoses **165 , 169 , 186 , 231**
377.13	Optic atrophy associated with retinal dystrophies **40**
950.0	Optic nerve injury **40**
377.3*	Optic neuritis **38**
376.01	Orbital cellulitis **38**
376.81	Orbital cysts **40**
376.33	Orbital edema or congestion **39**
802.6	Orbital floor (blow-out), closed fracture **3 , 40 , 222**
802.7	Orbital floor (blow-out), open fracture **3 , 40 , 222**
376.32	Orbital hemorrhage **39**
376.03	Orbital osteomyelitis **38**

376.02	Orbital periostitis **38**
376.04	Orbital tenonitis **38**
604*	Orchitis and epididymitis **125**
V42.84	Organ or tissue replaced by transplant, intestines **215**
327.1*	Organic disorders of excessive somnolence [Organic hypersomnia] **190**
327.0*	Organic disorders of initiating and maintaining sleep [Organic hypersomnia] **190**
327.4*	Organic parasomnia **3**
327.40	Organic parasomnia, unspecified **47**
327.2*	Organic sleep apnea **3**
327.20	Organic sleep apnea, unspecified **47**
327.5*	Organic sleep related movement disorders **3**
333.84	Organic writers' cramp **32**
073.7	Ornithosis with other specified complications **185**
073.0	Ornithosis with pneumonia **51**
073.8	Ornithosis with unspecified complication **185**
333.82	Orofacial dyskinesia **32**
V58.5	Orthodontics aftercare **214**
V57.4	Orthoptic training **215**
458.0	Orthostatic hypotension **68**
V57.81	Orthotic training **215**
723.7	Ossification of posterior longitudinal ligament in cervical region **97**
733.5	Osteitis condensans **98**
731*	Osteitis deformans and osteopathies associated with other disorders classified elsewhere **98**
715*	Osteoarthrosis and allied disorders **98**
732*	Osteochondropathies **98**
756.51	Osteogenesis imperfecta **87**
268.2	Osteomalacia, unspecified **98**
730.7*	Osteopathy resulting from poliomyelitis **100**
733.0*	Osteoporosis **98**
745.61	Ostium primum defect **67**
745.5	Ostium secundum type atrial septal defect **67**
388.7*	Otalgia **47**
766.1	Other "heavy-for-dates" infants not related to gestation period **172 , 173**
388.44	Other abnormal auditory perception, recruitment **47**
790.6	Other abnormal blood chemistry **214**
796.4	Other abnormal clinical finding **173 , 214**
785.3	Other abnormal heart sounds **69**
631*	Other abnormal product of conception **155 , 158**
654.43	Other abnormalities in shape or position of gravid uterus and of neighboring structures, antepartum **155 , 158**
654.41	Other abnormalities in shape or position of gravid uterus and of neighboring structures, delivered **136 , 143 , 149**
654.42	Other abnormalities in shape or position of gravid uterus and of neighboring structures, delivered, with mention of postpartum complication **136 , 143 , 149**
654.44	Other abnormalities in shape or position of gravid uterus and of neighboring structures, postpartum condition or complication **153**
654.40	Other abnormalities in shape or position of gravid uterus and of neighboring structures, unspecified as to episode of care **161**
788.6*	Other abnormality of urination **120**
616.4	Other abscess of vulva **128 , 131**
V45.79	Other acquired absence of organ **215**
736.76	Other acquired calcaneus deformity **100**
736.2*	Other acquired deformities of finger **100**
736.09	Other acquired deformities of forearm, excluding fingers **100**

736.6	Other acquired deformities of knee **100**
736.79	Other acquired deformity of ankle and foot **100**
738.5	Other acquired deformity of back or spine **97**
738.1*	Other acquired deformity of head **100**
333.79	Other acquired torsion dystonia **32**
411.89	Other acute and subacute form of ischemic heart disease **68**
506.3	Other acute and subacute respiratory conditions due to fumes and vapors **54**
391.8	Other acute rheumatic heart disease **68**
995.7	Other adverse food reactions, not elsewhere classified **205**
726.2	Other affections of shoulder region, not elsewhere classified **98**
V58.4*	Other aftercare following surgery **214**
780.09	Other alteration of consciousness **21**
516*	Other alveolar and parietoalveolar pneumonopathy **53**
995.0	Other anaphylactic reaction **204**
848*	Other and ill-defined sprains and strains **223**
654.93	Other and unspecified abnormality of organs and soft tissues of pelvis, antepartum condition or complication **156 , 158**
654.92	Other and unspecified abnormality of organs and soft tissues of pelvis, delivered, with mention of postpartum complication **136 , 144 , 149**
654.94	Other and unspecified abnormality of organs and soft tissues of pelvis, postpartum condition or complication **153**
654.90	Other and unspecified abnormality of organs and soft tissues of pelvis, unspecified as to episode of care in pregnancy **161**
654.91	Other and unspecified abnormality of organs and soft tissues of pelvis, with delivery **136 , 144 , 149**
422.9*	Other and unspecified acute myocarditis **231**
995.2*	Other and unspecified adverse effect of drug, medicinal and biological substance **204**
303.9*	Other and unspecified alcohol dependence **192**
285*	Other and unspecified anemias **176**
413.9	Other and unspecified angina pectoris **68**
716*	Other and unspecified arthropathies **98**
448.9	Other and unspecified capillary diseases **66**
779.1	Other and unspecified cerebral irritability in newborn **164 , 169**
851.9*	Other and unspecified cerebral laceration and contusion, with open intracranial wound **9 , 11 , 223 , 227**
851.92	Other and unspecified cerebral laceration and contusion, with open intracranial wound, brief (less than 1 hour) loss of consciousness **30**
851.96	Other and unspecified cerebral laceration and contusion, with open intracranial wound, loss of consciousness of unspecified duration **26**
851.93	Other and unspecified cerebral laceration and contusion, with open intracranial wound, moderate (1-24 hours) loss of consciousness **26**
851.91	Other and unspecified cerebral laceration and contusion, with open intracranial wound, no loss of consciousness **30**
851.94	Other and unspecified cerebral laceration and contusion, with open intracranial wound, prolonged (more than 24 hours) loss of consciousness and return to pre-existing conscious level **26**
851.95	Other and unspecified cerebral laceration and contusion, with open intracranial wound, prolonged (more than 24 hours) loss of consciousness, without return to pre-existing conscious level **26**
851.99	Other and unspecified cerebral laceration and contusion, with open intracranial wound, unspecified concussion **30**
851.90	Other and unspecified cerebral laceration and contusion, with open intracranial wound, unspecified state of consciousness **30**
851.8*	Other and unspecified cerebral laceration and contusion, without mention of open intracranial wound **9 , 11 , 223 , 227**
851.82	Other and unspecified cerebral laceration and contusion, without mention of open intracranial wound, brief (less than 1 hour) loss of consciousness **30**
851.86	Other and unspecified cerebral laceration and contusion, without mention of open intracranial wound, loss of consciousness of unspecified duration **26**
851.83	Other and unspecified cerebral laceration and contusion, without mention of open intracranial wound, moderate (1-24 hours) loss of consciousness **26**
851.81	Other and unspecified cerebral laceration and contusion, without mention of open intracranial wound, no loss of consciousness **30**
851.84	Other and unspecified cerebral laceration and contusion, without mention of open intracranial wound, prolonged (more than 24 hours) loss of consciousness and return to preexisting conscious level **26**
851.85	Other and unspecified cerebral laceration and contusion, without mention of open intracranial wound, prolonged (more than 24 hours) loss of consciousness, without return to pre-existing conscious level **26**
851.89	Other and unspecified cerebral laceration and contusion, without mention of open intracranial wound, unspecified concussion **30**
851.80	Other and unspecified cerebral laceration and contusion, without mention of open intracranial wound, unspecified state of consciousness **30**
381.3	Other and unspecified chronic nonsuppurative otitis media **46**
286.9	Other and unspecified coagulation defects **177**
999.9	Other and unspecified complications of medical care, not elsewhere classified **205**
756.9	Other and unspecified congenital anomaly of musculoskeletal system **101**
663.23	Other and unspecified cord entanglement, with compression, complicating labor and delivery, antepartum **156 , 159**
663.21	Other and unspecified cord entanglement, with compression, complicating labor and delivery, delivered **138 , 145 , 151**
663.20	Other and unspecified cord entanglement, with compression, complicating labor and delivery, unspecified as to episode of care **138 , 145 , 151**
663.33	Other and unspecified cord entanglement, without mention of compression, complicating labor and delivery, antepartum **156 , 159**
663.31	Other and unspecified cord entanglement, without mention of compression, complicating labor and delivery, delivered **138 , 145 , 151**
663.30	Other and unspecified cord entanglement, without mention of compression, complicating labor and delivery, unspecified as to episode of care **138 , 145 , 151**
717.3	Other and unspecified derangement of medial meniscus **99**
478.9	Other and unspecified diseases of upper respiratory tract **3 , 46**
676.33	Other and unspecified disorder of breast associated with childbirth, antepartum condition or complication **157 , 159**
676.32	Other and unspecified disorder of breast associated with childbirth, delivered, with mention of postpartum complication **140 , 146 , 152**
676.31	Other and unspecified disorder of breast associated with childbirth, delivered, with or without mention of antepartum condition **140 , 146 , 152**
676.34	Other and unspecified disorder of breast associated with childbirth, postpartum condition or complication **154**
676.30	Other and unspecified disorder of breast associated with childbirth, unspecified as to episode of care **162**
724*	Other and unspecified disorders of back **97**
729.9*	Other and unspecified disorders of soft tissue **98**
122.9	Other and unspecified echinococcosis **187**
993.2	Other and unspecified effects of high altitude **205**
300.19	Other and unspecified factitious illness **189**
128*	Other and unspecified helminthiases **187**
378.3*	Other and unspecified heterotropia **40**
999.31	Other and unspecified infection due to central venous catheter **69**

999.8* Other and unspecified infusion and transfusion reaction **168 , 172**

432* Other and unspecified intracranial hemorrhage **8 , 20 , 166 , 170**

853* Other and unspecified intracranial hemorrhage following injury **223 , 227**

853.1* Other and unspecified intracranial hemorrhage following injury with open intracranial wound **9 , 11**

853.12 Other and unspecified intracranial hemorrhage following injury, with open intracranial wound, brief (less than 1 hour) loss of consciousness **31**

853.16 Other and unspecified intracranial hemorrhage following injury, with open intracranial wound, loss of consciousness of unspecified duration **27**

853.13 Other and unspecified intracranial hemorrhage following injury, with open intracranial wound, moderate (1-24 hours) loss of consciousness **27**

853.11 Other and unspecified intracranial hemorrhage following injury, with open intracranial wound, no loss of consciousness **31**

853.14 Other and unspecified intracranial hemorrhage following injury, with open intracranial wound, prolonged (more than 24 hours) loss of consciousness and return to pre-existing conscious level **27**

853.15 Other and unspecified intracranial hemorrhage following injury, with open intracranial wound, prolonged (more than 24 hours) loss of consciousness, without return to pre-existing conscious level **27**

853.19 Other and unspecified intracranial hemorrhage following injury, with open intracranial wound, unspecified concussion **31**

853.10 Other and unspecified intracranial hemorrhage following injury, with open intracranial wound, unspecified state of consciousness **31**

853.0* Other and unspecified intracranial hemorrhage following injury, without mention of open intracranial wound **9 , 11**

853.02 Other and unspecified intracranial hemorrhage following injury, without mention of open intracranial wound, brief (less than 1 hour) loss of consciousness **31**

853.06 Other and unspecified intracranial hemorrhage following injury, without mention of open intracranial wound, loss of consciousness of unspecified duration **27**

853.03 Other and unspecified intracranial hemorrhage following injury, without mention of open intracranial wound, moderate (1-24 hours) loss of consciousness **27**

853.01 Other and unspecified intracranial hemorrhage following injury, without mention of open intracranial wound, no loss of consciousness **31**

853.04 Other and unspecified intracranial hemorrhage following injury, without mention of open intracranial wound, prolonged (more than 24 hours) loss of consciousness and return to preexisting conscious level **27**

853.09 Other and unspecified intracranial hemorrhage following injury, without mention of open intracranial wound, unspecified concussion **31**

853.00 Other and unspecified intracranial hemorrhage following injury, without mention of open intracranial wound, unspecified state of consciousness **31**

853.05 Other and unspecified intracranial hemorrhage following injury. Without mention of open intracranial wound, prolonged (more than 24 hours) loss of consciousness, without return to pre-existing conscious level **27**

370.4* Other and unspecified keratoconjunctivitis **39**

173.1* Other and unspecified malignant neoplasm of eyelid, including canthus **38**

173.8* Other and unspecified malignant neoplasm of other specified sites of skin **109**

173.4* Other and unspecified malignant neoplasm of scalp and skin of neck **109**

173.2* Other and unspecified malignant neoplasm of skin of ear and external auditory canal **109**

173.0* Other and unspecified malignant neoplasm of skin of lip **2 , 109**

173.7* Other and unspecified malignant neoplasm of skin of lower limb, including hip **109**

173.3* Other and unspecified malignant neoplasm of skin of other and unspecified parts of face **109**

173.5* Other and unspecified malignant neoplasm of skin of trunk, except scrotum **109**

173.6* Other and unspecified malignant neoplasm of skin of upper limb, including shoulder **109**

173.9* Other and unspecified malignant neoplasm of skin, site unspecified **109**

202.9* Other and unspecified malignant neoplasms of lymphoid and histiocytic tissue **179 , 182**

202.91 Other and unspecified malignant neoplasms of lymphoid and histiocytic tissue of lymph nodes of head, face, and neck **3**

558.9 Other and unspecified noninfectious gastroenteritis and colitis **78 , 231**

873.8 Other and unspecified open wound of head without mention of complication **107**

873.9 Other and unspecified open wound of head, complicated **107**

386.1* Other and unspecified peripheral vertigo **46**

696.5 Other and unspecified pityriasis **109**

579.3 Other and unspecified postsurgical nonabsorption **167 , 171**

263* Other and unspecified protein-calorie malnutrition **114 , 231**

298.8 Other and unspecified reactive psychosis **190**

398.99 Other and unspecified rheumatic heart diseases **68**

307.9 Other and unspecified special symptom or syndrome, not elsewhere classified **189**

913.9 Other and unspecified superficial injury of elbow, forearm, and wrist, infected **107**

913.8 Other and unspecified superficial injury of elbow, forearm, and wrist, without mention of infection **108**

910.9 Other and unspecified superficial injury of face, neck, and scalp, infected **107**

910.8 Other and unspecified superficial injury of face, neck, and scalp, without mention of infection **108**

915.8 Other and unspecified superficial injury of finger without mention of infection **108**

915.9 Other and unspecified superficial injury of finger, infected **107**

917.9 Other and unspecified superficial injury of foot and toes, infected **107**

917.8 Other and unspecified superficial injury of foot and toes, without mention of infection **108**

914.9 Other and unspecified superficial injury of hand(s) except finger(s) alone, infected **107**

914.8 Other and unspecified superficial injury of hand(s) except finger(s) alone, without mention of infection **108**

916.9 Other and unspecified superficial injury of hip, thigh, leg, and ankle, infected **107**

916.8 Other and unspecified superficial injury of hip, thigh, leg, and ankle, without mention of infection **108**

919.9 Other and unspecified superficial injury of other, multiple, and unspecified sites, infected **107**

919.8 Other and unspecified superficial injury of other, multiple, and unspecified sites, without mention of infection **108**

912.9 Other and unspecified superficial injury of shoulder and upper arm, infected **107**

912.8 Other and unspecified superficial injury of shoulder and upper arm, without mention of infection **108**

911.9 Other and unspecified superficial injury of trunk, infected **107**

911.8 Other and unspecified superficial injury of trunk, without mention of infection **108**

097* Other and unspecified syphilis **186**

*Code Range

661.23	Other and unspecified uterine inertia, antepartum **156** , **159**	
661.20	Other and unspecified uterine inertia, unspecified as to episode of care **137** , **145** , **150**	
661.21	Other and unspecified uterine inertia, with delivery **137** , **145** , **150**	
442.9	Other aneurysm of unspecified site **66**	
379.49	Other anomaly of pupillary function **38**	
V28.2	Other antenatal screening based on amniocentesis **157** , **160**	
641.83	Other antepartum hemorrhage, antepartum **155** , **158**	
641.80	Other antepartum hemorrhage, unspecified as to episode of care **160**	
641.81	Other antepartum hemorrhage, with delivery **135** , **141** , **146**	
671.53	Other antepartum phlebitis and thrombosis **157** , **159**	
542	Other appendicitis **78**	
088*	Other arthropod-borne diseases **186**	
362.1*	Other background retinopathy and retinal vascular changes **39** , **231**	
005.8*	Other bacterial food poisoning **75**	
482*	Other bacterial pneumonia **166** , **170** , **231**	
215*	Other benign neoplasm of connective and other soft tissue **100**	
219*	Other benign neoplasm of uterus **128** , **131**	
426.53	Other bilateral bundle branch block **166** , **170**	
745.8	Other bulbus cordis anomalies and anomalies of cardiac septal closure **67**	
727.3	Other bursitis disorders **99**	
594.1	Other calculus in bladder **120**	
112.89	Other candidiasis of other specified sites **186**	
323.81	Other causes of encephalitis and encephalomyelitis **10** , **231**	
323.8*	Other causes of encephalitis, myelitis, and encephalomyelitis **9** , **33**	
323.82	Other causes of myelitis **10** , **231**	
660.83	Other causes of obstructed labor, antepartum **156** , **159**	
660.81	Other causes of obstructed labor, delivered **137** , **144** , **150**	
660.80	Other causes of obstructed labor, unspecified as to episode of care **137** , **144** , **150**	
791.7	Other cells and casts in urine **121**	
682*	Other cellulitis and abscess **104** , **107** , **167** , **171**	
331.89	Other cerebral degeneration **19**	
429.79	Other certain sequelae of myocardial infarction, not elsewhere classified **69**	
375.6*	Other changes of lacrimal passages **39**	
333.5	Other choreas **19**	
491.8	Other chronic bronchitis **53**	
595.2	Other chronic cystitis **120**	
474.8	Other chronic disease of tonsils and adenoids **47**	
098.39	Other chronic gonococcal infections of upper genitourinary tract **125** , **128** , **130**	
571.8	Other chronic nonalcoholic liver disease **83**	
614.7	Other chronic pelvic peritonitis, female **131**	
416.8	Other chronic pulmonary heart diseases **69**	
836.5*	Other closed dislocation of knee **223**	
803.1*	Other closed skull fracture with cerebral laceration and contusion **222** , **226**	
803.12	Other closed skull fracture with cerebral laceration and contusion, brief (less than one hour) loss of consciousness **28**	
803.16	Other closed skull fracture with cerebral laceration and contusion, loss of consciousness of unspecified duration **23**	
803.13	Other closed skull fracture with cerebral laceration and contusion, moderate (1-24 hours) loss of consciousness **23**	
803.11	Other closed skull fracture with cerebral laceration and contusion, no loss of consciousness **28**	

803.14	Other closed skull fracture with cerebral laceration and contusion, prolonged (more than 24 hours) loss of consciousness and return to pre-existing conscious level **23**
803.15	Other closed skull fracture with cerebral laceration and contusion, prolonged (more than 24 hours) loss of consciousness, without return to pre-existing conscious level **23**
803.19	Other closed skull fracture with cerebral laceration and contusion, unspecified concussion **28**
803.10	Other closed skull fracture with cerebral laceration and contusion, unspecified state of consciousness **28**
803.4*	Other closed skull fracture with intracranial injury of other and unspecified nature **222** , **226**
803.42	Other closed skull fracture with intracranial injury of other and unspecified nature, brief (less than one hour) loss of consciousness **29**
803.46	Other closed skull fracture with intracranial injury of other and unspecified nature, loss of consciousness of unspecified duration **24**
803.43	Other closed skull fracture with intracranial injury of other and unspecified nature, moderate (1-24 hours) loss of consciousness **23**
803.41	Other closed skull fracture with intracranial injury of other and unspecified nature, no loss of consciousness **29**
803.44	Other closed skull fracture with intracranial injury of other and unspecified nature, prolonged (more than 24 hours) loss of consciousness and return to pre-existing conscious level **24**
803.45	Other closed skull fracture with intracranial injury of other and unspecified nature, prolonged (more than 24 hours) loss of consciousness, without return to pre-existing conscious level **24**
803.49	Other closed skull fracture with intracranial injury of other and unspecified nature, unspecified concussion **29**
803.40	Other closed skull fracture with intracranial injury of other and unspecified nature, unspecified state of consciousness **29**
803.32	Other closed skull fracture with other and unspecified intracranial hemorrhage, brief (less than one hour) loss of consciousness **28**
803.36	Other closed skull fracture with other and unspecified intracranial hemorrhage, loss of consciousness of unspecified duration **23**
803.33	Other closed skull fracture with other and unspecified intracranial hemorrhage, moderate (1-24 hours) loss of consciousness **23**
803.31	Other closed skull fracture with other and unspecified intracranial hemorrhage, no loss of consciousness **28**
803.34	Other closed skull fracture with other and unspecified intracranial hemorrhage, prolonged (more than 24 hours) loss of consciousness and return to pre-existing conscious level **23**
803.35	Other closed skull fracture with other and unspecified intracranial hemorrhage, prolonged (more than 24 hours) loss of consciousness, without return to pre-existing conscious level **23**
803.39	Other closed skull fracture with other and unspecified intracranial hemorrhage, unspecified concussion **28**
803.30	Other closed skull fracture with other and unspecified intracranial hemorrhage, unspecified state of unconsciousness **28**
803.2*	Other closed skull fracture with subarachnoid, subdural, and extradural hemorrhage **222** , **226**
803.22	Other closed skull fracture with subarachnoid, subdural, and extradural hemorrhage, brief (less than one hour) loss of consciousness **28**
803.26	Other closed skull fracture with subarachnoid, subdural, and extradural hemorrhage, loss of consciousness of unspecified duration **23**
803.23	Other closed skull fracture with subarachnoid, subdural, and extradural hemorrhage, moderate (1-24 hours) loss of consciousness **23**
803.21	Other closed skull fracture with subarachnoid, subdural, and extradural hemorrhage, no loss of consciousness **28**
803.24	Other closed skull fracture with subarachnoid, subdural, and extradural hemorrhage, prolonged (more than 24 hours) loss of consciousness and return to pre-existing conscious level **23**

803.25	Other closed skull fracture with subarachnoid, subdural, and extradural hemorrhage, prolonged (more than 24 hours) loss of consciousness, without return to pre-existing conscious level **23**
803.29	Other closed skull fracture with subarachnoid, subdural, and extradural hemorrhage, unspecified concussion **28**
803.20	Other closed skull fracture with subarachnoid, subdural, and extradural hemorrhage, unspecified state of consciousness **28**
803.0*	Other closed skull fracture without mention of intracranial injury **222**
803.02	Other closed skull fracture without mention of intracranial injury, brief (less than one hour) loss of consciousness **28 , 226**
803.06	Other closed skull fracture without mention of intracranial injury, loss of consciousness of unspecified duration **23**
803.03	Other closed skull fracture without mention of intracranial injury, moderate (1-24 hours) loss of consciousness **23 , 226**
803.01	Other closed skull fracture without mention of intracranial injury, no loss of consciousness **28**
803.04	Other closed skull fracture without mention of intracranial injury, prolonged (more than 24 hours) loss of consciousness and return to pre-existing conscious level **23 , 226**
803.05	Other closed skull fracture without mention of intracranial injury, prolonged (more than 24 hours) loss of consciousness, without return to pre-existing conscious level **23 , 226**
803.09	Other closed skull fracture without mention of intracranial injury, unspecified concussion **28**
803.00	Other closed skull fracture without mention of intracranial injury, unspecified state of consciousness **28**
368.59	Other color vision deficiencies **39**
669.83	Other complication of labor and delivery, antepartum condition or complication **157 , 159**
669.82	Other complication of labor and delivery, delivered, with mention of postpartum complication **139 , 146 , 152**
669.81	Other complication of labor and delivery, delivered, with or without mention of antepartum condition **139 , 146 , 152**
669.84	Other complication of labor and delivery, postpartum condition or complication **154**
669.80	Other complication of labor and delivery, unspecified as to episode of care **139 , 146 , 152**
674.30	Other complication of obstetrical surgical wounds, unspecified as to episode of care **162**
674.32	Other complication of obstetrical surgical wounds, with delivery, with mention of postpartum complication **139 , 142 , 148**
674.80	Other complication of puerperium, unspecified as to episode of care **162**
674.82	Other complication of puerperium, with delivery, with mention of postpartum complication **139 , 142 , 148**
996.76	Other complications due to genitourinary device, implant, and graft **121**
996.71	Other complications due to heart valve prosthesis **69**
996.77	Other complications due to internal joint prosthesis **99**
996.75	Other complications due to nervous system device, implant, and graft **33**
996.72	Other complications due to other cardiac device, implant, and graft **69**
996.78	Other complications due to other internal orthopedic device, implant, and graft **99**
996.79	Other complications due to other internal prosthetic device, implant, and graft **204**
996.74	Other complications due to other vascular device, implant, and graft **69**
996.73	Other complications due to renal dialysis device, implant, and graft **69**
996.70	Other complications due to unspecified device, implant, and graft **204**
669.43	Other complications of obstetrical surgery and procedures, antepartum condition or complication **157 , 159**
669.44	Other complications of obstetrical surgery and procedures, postpartum condition or complication **154**
669.40	Other complications of obstetrical surgery and procedures, unspecified as to episode of care **139 , 146 , 151**
669.42	Other complications of obstetrical surgery and procedures, with delivery, with mention of postpartum complication **139 , 142 , 147**
669.41	Other complications of obstetrical surgery and procedures, with delivery, with or without mention of antepartum condition **139 , 142 , 147**
674.34	Other complications of obstetrical surgical wounds, postpartum condition or complication **154**
674.84	Other complications of puerperium, postpartum condition or complication **154**
668.83	Other complications of the administration of anesthesia or other sedation in labor and delivery, antepartum **156 , 159**
668.81	Other complications of the administration of anesthesia or other sedation in labor and delivery, delivered **138 , 142 , 147**
668.82	Other complications of the administration of anesthesia or other sedation in labor and delivery, delivered, with mention of postpartum complication **138 , 142 , 147**
668.84	Other complications of the administration of anesthesia or other sedation in labor and delivery, postpartum condition or complication **154**
668.80	Other complications of the administration of anesthesia or other sedation in labor and delivery, unspecified as to episode of care **138 , 145 , 151**
758.5	Other conditions due to autosomal anomalies **214**
758.8*	Other conditions due to chromosome anomalies **125 , 128 , 131**
348.89	Other conditions of brain **20**
751.5	Other congenital anomalies of intestine **79**
755*	Other congenital anomalies of limbs **100**
742*	Other congenital anomalies of nervous system **32 , 167 , 171**
750.1*	Other congenital anomalies of tongue **3 , 48**
747.2*	Other congenital anomaly of aorta **68**
751.69	Other congenital anomaly of gallbladder, bile ducts, and liver **83**
748.3	Other congenital anomaly of larynx, trachea, and bronchus **3 , 47**
748.69	Other congenital anomaly of lung **54**
748.1	Other congenital anomaly of nose **47**
747.6*	Other congenital anomaly of peripheral vascular system **67**
756.3	Other congenital anomaly of ribs and sternum **54**
756.19	Other congenital anomaly of spine **98**
752.3*	Other congenital anomaly of uterus **128 , 131**
754.7*	Other congenital deformity of feet **100**
745.69	Other congenital endocardial cushion defect **67**
759.6	Other congenital hamartoses, not elsewhere classified **181 , 183**
771.2	Other congenital infection specific to the perinatal period **164 , 168**
654.63	Other congenital or acquired abnormality of cervix, antepartum condition or complication **155 , 158**
654.62	Other congenital or acquired abnormality of cervix, delivered, with mention of postpartum complication **136 , 144 , 149**
654.64	Other congenital or acquired abnormality of cervix, postpartum condition or complication **153**
654.60	Other congenital or acquired abnormality of cervix, unspecified as to episode of care in pregnancy **161**
654.61	Other congenital or acquired abnormality of cervix, with delivery **136 , 143 , 149**
780.39	Other convulsions **167 , 171**
767.7	Other cranial and peripheral nerve injuries, birth trauma **164 , 168**
648.94	Other current maternal conditions classifiable elsewhere complicating pregnancy, childbirth, or the puerperium, postpartum condition or complication **153**

648.93	Other current maternal conditions classifiable elsewhere, antepartum **155 , 157**
648.90	Other current maternal conditions classifiable elsewhere, complicating pregnancy, childbirth, or the puerperium, unspecified as to episode of care **160**
648.91	Other current maternal conditions classifiable elsewhere, with delivery **136 , 143 , 149**
648.92	Other current maternal conditions classifiable elsewhere, with delivery, with current postpartum complication **136 , 143 , 149**
737.8	Other curvatures of spine associated with other conditions **87**
277.6	Other deficiencies of circulating enzymes **115**
281*	Other deficiency anemias **176 , 231**
279.19	Other deficiency of cell-mediated immunity **176**
333.0	Other degenerative diseases of the basal ganglia **19**
374.56	Other degenerative disorders of skin affecting eyelid **39**
341.8	Other demyelinating diseases of central nervous system **19**
V46*	Other dependence on machines and devices **215**
702*	Other dermatoses **109**
315.39	Other developmental speech or language disorder **190**
478.29	Other disease of pharynx or nasopharynx **47**
525*	Other diseases and conditions of the teeth and supporting structures **3 , 48**
543*	Other diseases of appendix **78**
077*	Other diseases of conjunctiva due to viruses and Chlamydiae **38**
424*	Other diseases of endocardium **67**
478.79	Other diseases of larynx **47**
478.7*	Other diseases of larynx, not elsewhere classified **3**
518.89	Other diseases of lung, not elsewhere classified **54**
519.3	Other diseases of mediastinum, not elsewhere classified **54**
478.19	Other diseases of nasal cavity and sinuses **173**
478.1*	Other diseases of nasal cavity and sinuses **47**
423*	Other diseases of pericardium **69**
478.2*	Other diseases of pharynx, not elsewhere classified **3**
417*	Other diseases of pulmonary circulation **69**
519.8	Other diseases of respiratory system, not elsewhere classified **54**
289.5*	Other diseases of spleen **177**
519.19	Other diseases of trachea and bronchus **3**
519.1*	Other diseases of trachea and bronchus, not elsewhere classified **54**
478.5	Other diseases of vocal cords **3 , 47**
307.59	Other disorder of eating **190**
312.39	Other disorder of impulse control **189**
676.83	Other disorder of lactation, antepartum condition or complication **157 , 159**
676.80	Other disorder of lactation, unspecified as to episode of care **162**
676.82	Other disorder of lactation, with delivery, with mention of postpartum complication **140 , 146 , 152**
676.81	Other disorder of lactation, with delivery, with or without mention of antepartum condition **140 , 146 , 152**
728.89	Other disorder of muscle, ligament, and fascia **99**
576*	Other disorders of biliary tract **83**
368.3*	Other disorders of binocular vision **39**
596*	Other disorders of bladder **121**
733.99	Other disorders of bone and cartilage **100**
611*	Other disorders of breast **107**
388.8	Other disorders of ear **47**
381.8*	Other disorders of Eustachian tube **47**
380.8*	Other disorders of external ear **47**
374.8*	Other disorders of eyelid **39**
629*	Other disorders of female genital organs **128**
575*	Other disorders of gallbladder **83**

360.8*	Other disorders of globe **39**
364.8*	Other disorders of iris and ciliary body **39**
386.8	Other disorders of labyrinth **46**
375.1*	Other disorders of lacrimal gland **39**
375.8*	Other disorders of lacrimal system **39**
676.84	Other disorders of lactation, postpartum condition or complication **154**
383.8*	Other disorders of mastoid **47**
385*	Other disorders of middle ear and mastoid **47**
377.4*	Other disorders of optic nerve **38**
429.81	Other disorders of papillary muscle **67 , 166 , 170**
568*	Other disorders of peritoneum **79**
273.8	Other disorders of plasma protein metabolism **181 , 183**
602*	Other disorders of prostate **125**
277.2	Other disorders of purine and pyrimidine metabolism **115**
367.8*	Other disorders of refraction and accommodation **39**
379.1*	Other disorders of sclera **40**
709*	Other disorders of skin and subcutaneous tissue **109**
727.8*	Other disorders of synovium, tendon, and bursa **99**
246*	Other disorders of thyroid **115**
378.87	Other dissociated deviation of eye movements **38**
995.27	Other drug allergy **167 , 172**
709.09	Other dyschromia **173**
958.8	Other early complications of trauma **205 , 225**
102.2	Other early skin lesions due to yaws **108**
122.3	Other echinococcus granulosus infection **187**
122.6	Other echinococcus multilocularis infection **187**
994.9	Other effects of external causes **205**
V50.8	Other elective surgery for purposes other than remedying health states **215**
492.8	Other emphysema **53**
323.41	Other encephalitis and encephalomyelitis due to other infections classified elsewhere **10**
323.4*	Other encephalitis, myelitis, and encephalomyelitis due to other infections classified elsewhere **9 , 33**
259*	Other endocrine disorders **115**
360.19	Other endophthalmitis **38**
048	Other enterovirus diseases of central nervous system **21**
726.79	Other enthesopathy of ankle and tarsus **98**
333.99	Other extrapyramidal disease and abnormal movement disorder **19**
802.8	Other facial bones, closed fracture **3 , 101 , 222**
802.9	Other facial bones, open fracture **3 , 101 , 222**
653.73	Other fetal abnormality causing disproportion, antepartum **155 , 158**
653.71	Other fetal abnormality causing disproportion, delivered **136 , 143 , 149**
653.70	Other fetal abnormality causing disproportion, unspecified as to episode of care **161**
728.7*	Other fibromatoses of muscle, ligament, and fascia **99**
V67.5*	Other follow-up examination **215**
493.8*	Other forms of asthma **53**
370.8	Other forms of keratitis **39**
379.56	Other forms of nystagmus **40**
114.3	Other forms of progressive coccidioidomycosis **165 , 169 , 186**
361.8*	Other forms of retinal detachment **39**
333.89	Other fragments of torsion dystonia **32**
V70.3	Other general medical examination for administrative purposes **174**
780.9*	Other general symptoms **214**
437.1	Other generalized ischemic cerebrovascular disease **20**

V83.8*	Other genetic carrier status **216**	
054.19	Other genital herpes **125** , **128** , **130** , **230**	
306.59	Other genitourinary malfunction arising from mental factors **121**	
098.85	Other gonococcal heart disease **68**	
098.59	Other gonococcal infection of joint **97**	
098.19	Other gonococcal infections (acute) of upper genitourinary tract **125** , **128** , **130**	
274.19	Other gouty nephropathy **121**	
339*	Other headache syndromes **34**	
286.59	Other hemorrhagic disorder due to intrinsic circulating anticoagulants, antibodies, or inhibitors **177**	
551*	Other hernia of abdominal cavity, with gangrene **78**	
053.19	Other herpes zoster with nervous system complications **20** , **165** , **169** , **230**	
058.29	Other human herpesvirus encephalitis **9** , **10** , **33** , **165** , **169** , **231**	
058.8*	Other human herpesvirus infections **108**	
278.8	Other hyperalimentation **114**	
701*	Other hypertrophic and atrophic conditions of skin **109**	
437.8	Other ill-defined cerebrovascular disease **20**	
799.8*	Other ill-defined conditions **214**	
429.89	Other ill-defined heart disease **67**	
666.14	Other immediate postpartum hemorrhage, postpartum condition or complication **153**	
666.10	Other immediate postpartum hemorrhage, unspecified as to episode of care **162**	
666.12	Other immediate postpartum hemorrhage, with delivery **138** , **141** , **147**	
771.8*	Other infection specific to the perinatal period **164** , **168**	
730.8*	Other infections involving bone in diseases classified elsewhere **96**	
134*	Other infestation **109**	
357.8*	Other inflammatory and toxic neuropathy **21**	
608.4	Other inflammatory disorder of male genital organs **125**	
607.2	Other inflammatory disorders of penis **125**	
720.8*	Other inflammatory spondylopathies **97**	
999.88	Other infusion reaction **69**	
665.54	Other injury to pelvic organs, postpartum condition or complication **153**	
665.50	Other injury to pelvic organs, unspecified as to episode of care in pregnancy **138** , **145** , **151**	
665.51	Other injury to pelvic organs, with delivery **138** , **145** , **151**	
717.8*	Other internal derangement of knee **99**	
370.59	Other interstitial and deep keratitis **39**	
379.59	Other irregularities of eye movements **40**	
718.8*	Other joint derangement, not elsewhere classified **100**	
655.83	Other known or suspected fetal abnormality, not elsewhere classified, affecting management of mother, antepartum condition or complication **156** , **158**	
655.81	Other known or suspected fetal abnormality, not elsewhere classified, affecting management of mother, delivery **136** , **144** , **149**	
655.80	Other known or suspected fetal abnormality, not elsewhere classified, affecting management of mother, unspecified as to episode of care **161**	
090.5	Other late congenital syphilis, symptomatic **186**	
208.8*	Other leukemia of unspecified cell type **182**	
686*	Other local infection of skin and subcutaneous tissue **107**	
003.29	Other localized salmonella infections **186**	
368.44	Other localized visual field defect **38**	
594.8	Other lower urinary tract calculus **120**	
238.79	Other lymphatic and hematopoietic tissues **179** , **182**	

204.8*	Other lymphoid leukemia **182**	
670.82	Other major puerperal infection, delivered, with mention of postpartum complication **139** , **142** , **147**	
670.84	Other major puerperal infection, postpartum condition or complication **154**	
670.80	Other major puerperal infection, unspecified as to episode of care or not applicable **162**	
780.79	Other malaise and fatigue **214**	
202.8*	Other malignant lymphomas **179** , **182** , **231**	
202.81	Other malignant lymphomas of lymph nodes of head, face, and neck **3**	
199.1	Other malignant neoplasm of unspecified site **181**	
102.7	Other manifestations due to yaws **186**	
264.8	Other manifestations of vitamin A deficiency **114**	
648.64	Other maternal cardiovascular diseases complicating pregnancy, childbirth, or the puerperium, postpartum condition or complication **153**	
648.60	Other maternal cardiovascular diseases complicating pregnancy, childbirth, or the puerperium, unspecified as to episode of care **160**	
648.63	Other maternal cardiovascular diseases, antepartum **155** , **157**	
648.61	Other maternal cardiovascular diseases, with delivery **135** , **141** , **147**	
648.62	Other maternal cardiovascular diseases, with delivery, with current postpartum complication **135** , **141** , **147**	
647.21	Other maternal venereal diseases with delivery **135** , **141** , **147**	
647.22	Other maternal venereal diseases with delivery, with current postpartum complication **135** , **141** , **147**	
647.23	Other maternal venereal diseases, antepartum condition or complication **155** , **157**	
647.20	Other maternal venereal diseases, complicating pregnancy, childbirth, or the puerperium, unspecified as to episode of care **160**	
647.60	Other maternal viral disease complicating pregnancy, childbirth, or the puerperium, unspecified as to episode of care **160**	
647.61	Other maternal viral disease with delivery **135** , **141** , **147**	
647.62	Other maternal viral disease with delivery, with current postpartum complication **135** , **141** , **147**	
647.63	Other maternal viral disease, antepartum **155** , **157**	
647.64	Other maternal viral diseases complicating pregnancy, childbirth, or the puerperium, postpartum condition or complication **153**	
206.8*	Other monocytic leukemia **182**	
066.3	Other mosquito-borne fever **185**	
V34.1	Other multiple birth (three or more), mates all liveborn, born before admission to hospital **172** , **173**	
V34.2	Other multiple birth (three or more), mates all liveborn, born outside hospital and not hospitalized **174**	
V35.1	Other multiple birth (three or more), mates all stillborn, born before admission to hospital **172** , **173**	
V35.2	Other multiple birth (three or more), mates all stillborn, born outside of hospital and not hospitalized **174**	
V36.1	Other multiple birth (three or more), mates liveborn and stillborn, born before admission to hospital **172** , **173**	
V36.2	Other multiple birth (three or more), mates liveborn and stillborn, born outside hospital and not hospitalized **174**	
V37.1	Other multiple birth (three or more), unspecified whether mates liveborn or stillborn, born before admission to hospital **173**	
V37.2	Other multiple birth (three or more), unspecified whether mates liveborn or stillborn, born outside of hospital **174**	
651.63	Other multiple pregnancy with fetal loss and retention of one or more fetus(es), antepartum **155** , **158**	
651.61	Other multiple pregnancy with fetal loss and retention of one or more fetus(es), delivered **136** , **143** , **149**	

*Code Range

651.60	Other multiple pregnancy with fetal loss and retention of one or more fetus(es), unspecified as to episode of care or not applicable **161**	
V34.01	Other multiple, mates all liveborn, born in hospital, delivered by cesarean delivery **172 , 173**	
V34.00	Other multiple, mates all liveborn, born in hospital, delivered without mention of cesarean delivery **172 , 173**	
V35.01	Other multiple, mates all stillborn, born in hospital, delivered by cesarean delivery **172 , 173**	
V35.00	Other multiple, mates all stillborn, born in hospital, delivered without mention of cesarean delivery **172 , 173**	
V36.01	Other multiple, mates liveborn and stillborn, born in hospital, delivered by cesarean delivery **172 , 173**	
V36.00	Other multiple, mates liveborn and stillborn, born in hospital, delivered without mention of cesarean delivery **172 , 173**	
V37.01	Other multiple, unspecified whether mates stillborn or liveborn, born in hospital, delivered by cesarean delivery **173**	
V37.00	Other multiple, unspecified whether mates stillborn or liveborn, born in hospital, delivered without mention of cesarean delivery **173**	

651.60 Other multiple pregnancy with fetal loss and retention of one or more fetus(es), unspecified as to episode of care or not applicable **161**

V34.01 Other multiple, mates all liveborn, born in hospital, delivered by cesarean delivery **172 , 173**

V34.00 Other multiple, mates all liveborn, born in hospital, delivered without mention of cesarean delivery **172 , 173**

V35.01 Other multiple, mates all stillborn, born in hospital, delivered by cesarean delivery **172 , 173**

V35.00 Other multiple, mates all stillborn, born in hospital, delivered without mention of cesarean delivery **172 , 173**

V36.01 Other multiple, mates liveborn and stillborn, born in hospital, delivered by cesarean delivery **172 , 173**

V36.00 Other multiple, mates liveborn and stillborn, born in hospital, delivered without mention of cesarean delivery **172 , 173**

V37.01 Other multiple, unspecified whether mates stillborn or liveborn, born in hospital, delivered by cesarean delivery **173**

V37.00 Other multiple, unspecified whether mates stillborn or liveborn, born in hospital, delivered without mention of cesarean delivery **173**

729.89 Other musculoskeletal symptoms referable to limbs **98**

117* Other mycoses **186**

323.42 Other myelitis due to other infections classified elsewhere **10**

205.8* Other myeloid leukemia **182**

336.8 Other myelopathy **32**

359.89 Other myopathies **32**

200.8* Other named variants of lymphosarcoma and reticulosarcoma **231**

200.81 Other named variants of lymphosarcoma and reticulosarcoma of lymph nodes of head, face, and neck **2**

056.09 Other neurological rubella complications **33**

283.19 Other non-autoimmune hemolytic anemias **176**

099.4* Other nongonococcal urethritis (NGU) **125 , 128 , 131**

457.8 Other noninfectious disorders of lymphatic channels **177**

457.1 Other noninfectious lymphedema **109**

794.39 Other nonspecific abnormal cardiovascular system function study **69**

796.9 Other nonspecific abnormal finding **214**

792.9 Other nonspecific abnormal finding in body substances **214**

793.19 Other nonspecific abnormal finding of lung field **54**

793.9* Other nonspecific abnormal findings on radiological and other examinations of body structure **214**

795.4 Other nonspecific abnormal histological findings **173 , 214**

794.19 Other nonspecific abnormal result of function study of peripheral nervous system and special senses **32**

790.5 Other nonspecific abnormal serum enzyme levels **214**

791.9 Other nonspecific finding on examination of urine **121**

790.9* Other nonspecific findings on examination of blood **214**

795.7* Other nonspecific immunological findings **177**

269* Other nutritional deficiencies **114 , 231**

673.83 Other obstetrical pulmonary embolism, antepartum **157 , 159**

673.84 Other obstetrical pulmonary embolism, postpartum condition or complication **154**

673.80 Other obstetrical pulmonary embolism, unspecified as to episode of care **162**

673.82 Other obstetrical pulmonary embolism, with delivery, with mention of postpartum complication **139 , 142 , 148**

673.81 Other obstetrical pulmonary embolism, with delivery, with or without mention of antepartum condition **139 , 142 , 148**

537.3 Other obstruction of duodenum **77**

V62.2* Other occupational circumstances or maladjustment **215**

264.7 Other ocular manifestations of vitamin A deficiency **39**

836.6* Other open dislocation of knee **223 , 228**

803.6* Other open skull fracture with cerebral laceration and contusion **222 , 226**

803.62 Other open skull fracture with cerebral laceration and contusion, brief (less than one hour) loss of consciousness **29**

803.66 Other open skull fracture with cerebral laceration and contusion, loss of consciousness of unspecified duration **24**

803.63 Other open skull fracture with cerebral laceration and contusion, moderate (1-24 hours) loss of consciousness **24**

803.61 Other open skull fracture with cerebral laceration and contusion, no loss of consciousness **29**

803.64 Other open skull fracture with cerebral laceration and contusion, prolonged (more than 24 hours) loss of consciousness and return to pre-existing conscious level **24**

803.65 Other open skull fracture with cerebral laceration and contusion, prolonged (more than 24 hours) loss of consciousness, without return to pre-existing conscious level **24**

803.69 Other open skull fracture with cerebral laceration and contusion, unspecified concussion **29**

803.60 Other open skull fracture with cerebral laceration and contusion, unspecified state of consciousness **29**

803.9* Other open skull fracture with intracranial injury of other and unspecified nature **222 , 226**

803.92 Other open skull fracture with intracranial injury of other and unspecified nature, brief (less than one hour) loss of consciousness **29**

803.96 Other open skull fracture with intracranial injury of other and unspecified nature, loss of consciousness of unspecified duration **24**

803.93 Other open skull fracture with intracranial injury of other and unspecified nature, moderate (1-24 hours) loss of consciousness **24**

803.91 Other open skull fracture with intracranial injury of other and unspecified nature, no loss of consciousness **29**

803.94 Other open skull fracture with intracranial injury of other and unspecified nature, prolonged (more than 24 hours) loss of consciousness and return to pre-existing conscious level **24**

803.95 Other open skull fracture with intracranial injury of other and unspecified nature, prolonged (more than 24 hours) loss of consciousness, without return to pre-existing conscious level **24**

803.99 Other open skull fracture with intracranial injury of other and unspecified nature, unspecified concussion **29**

803.90 Other open skull fracture with intracranial injury of other and unspecified nature, unspecified state of consciousness **29**

803.8* Other open skull fracture with other and unspecified intracranial hemorrhage **222 , 226**

803.82 Other open skull fracture with other and unspecified intracranial hemorrhage, brief (less than one hour) loss of consciousness **29**

803.86 Other open skull fracture with other and unspecified intracranial hemorrhage, loss of consciousness of unspecified duration **24**

803.83 Other open skull fracture with other and unspecified intracranial hemorrhage, moderate (1-24 hours) loss of consciousness **24**

803.81 Other open skull fracture with other and unspecified intracranial hemorrhage, no loss of consciousness **29**

803.84 Other open skull fracture with other and unspecified intracranial hemorrhage, prolonged (more than 24 hours) loss of consciousness and return to pre-existing conscious level **24**

803.85 Other open skull fracture with other and unspecified intracranial hemorrhage, prolonged (more than 24 hours) loss of consciousness, without return to pre-existing conscious level **24**

803.89 Other open skull fracture with other and unspecified intracranial hemorrhage, unspecified concussion **29**

803.80 Other open skull fracture with other and unspecified intracranial hemorrhage, unspecified state of consciousness **29**

803.7* Other open skull fracture with subarachnoid, subdural, and extradural hemorrhage **222 , 226**

803.72	Other open skull fracture with subarachnoid, subdural, and extradural hemorrhage, brief (less than one hour) loss of consciousness **29**
803.76	Other open skull fracture with subarachnoid, subdural, and extradural hemorrhage, loss of consciousness of unspecified duration **24**
803.73	Other open skull fracture with subarachnoid, subdural, and extradural hemorrhage, moderate (1-24 hours) loss of consciousness **24**
803.71	Other open skull fracture with subarachnoid, subdural, and extradural hemorrhage, no loss of consciousness **29**
803.74	Other open skull fracture with subarachnoid, subdural, and extradural hemorrhage, prolonged (more than 24 hours) loss of consciousness and return to pre-existing conscious level **24**
803.75	Other open skull fracture with subarachnoid, subdural, and extradural hemorrhage, prolonged (more than 24 hours) loss of consciousness, without return to pre-existing conscious level **24**
803.79	Other open skull fracture with subarachnoid, subdural, and extradural hemorrhage, unspecified concussion **29**
803.70	Other open skull fracture with subarachnoid, subdural, and extradural hemorrhage, unspecified state of consciousness **29**
803.50	Other open skull fracture without mention of injury, state of consciousness unspecified **29**
803.5*	Other open skull fracture without mention of intracranial injury **222**
803.52	Other open skull fracture without mention of intracranial injury, brief (less than one hour) loss of consciousness **29 , 226**
803.56	Other open skull fracture without mention of intracranial injury, loss of consciousness of unspecified duration **24**
803.53	Other open skull fracture without mention of intracranial injury, moderate (1-24 hours) loss of consciousness **24 , 226**
803.51	Other open skull fracture without mention of intracranial injury, no loss of consciousness **29**
803.54	Other open skull fracture without mention of intracranial injury, prolonged (more than 24 hours) loss of consciousness and return to pre-existing conscious level **24 , 226**
803.55	Other open skull fracture without mention of intracranial injury, prolonged (more than 24 hours) loss of consciousness, without return to pre-existing conscious level **24 , 226**
803.59	Other open skull fracture without mention of intracranial injury, unspecified concussion **29**
873*	Other open wound of head **224**
053.29	Other ophthalmic herpes zoster complications **165 , 169 , 230**
313.8*	Other or mixed emotional disturbances of childhood or adolescence **190**
376.89	Other orbital disorder **40**
V43.89	Other organ or tissue replaced by other means **2**
V43.8*	Other organ or tissue replaced by other means **215**
V42.89	Other organ or tissue replaced by transplant **215**
327.49	Other organic parasomnia **47**
327.29	Other organic sleep apnea **47**
327.8	Other organic sleep disorders **3 , 47**
327.59	Other organic sleep related movement disorders **47**
V54.8*	Other orthopedic aftercare **99**
380.2*	Other otitis externa **47**
388.69	Other otorrhea **47**
307.89	Other pain disorder related to psychological factors **189**
273.2	Other paraproteinemias **179 , 182**
726.8	Other peripheral enthesopathies **98**
V15*	Other personal history presenting hazards to health **215**
301.8*	Other personality disorders **189**
V65*	Other persons seeking consultation **215**
671.50	Other phlebitis and thrombosis complicating pregnancy and the puerperium, unspecified as to episode of care **162**
671.52	Other phlebitis and thrombosis with delivery, with mention of postpartum complication **139 , 142 , 147**
671.51	Other phlebitis and thrombosis with delivery, with or without mention of antepartum condition **139 , 142 , 147**
671.54	Other phlebitis and thrombosis, postpartum condition or complication **154**
V57.1	Other physical therapy **214**
656.73	Other placental conditions affecting management of mother, antepartum **156 , 158**
656.71	Other placental conditions affecting management of mother, delivered **137 , 144 , 150**
656.70	Other placental conditions affecting management of mother, unspecified as to episode of care **161**
V50.1	Other plastic surgery for unacceptable cosmetic appearance **110**
512.8*	Other pneumothorax and air leak **53**
323.62	Other postinfectious encephalitis and encephalomyelitis **10**
564.4	Other postoperative functional disorders **78**
998.59	Other postoperative infection **168 , 172 , 185**
V45.8*	Other postprocedural status **215**
059*	Other poxvirus infections **185**
642.24	Other pre-existing hypertension complicating pregnancy, childbirth, and the puerperium, postpartum condition or complication **152**
642.20	Other pre-existing hypertension complicating pregnancy, childbirth, and the puerperium, unspecified as to episode of care **160**
642.23	Other pre-existing hypertension, antepartum **155 , 157**
642.21	Other pre-existing hypertension, with delivery **135 , 141 , 147**
642.22	Other pre-existing hypertension, with delivery, with current postpartum complication **135 , 141 , 147**
765.1*	Other preterm infants **164 , 168**
091.2	Other primary syphilis **186**
658.83	Other problem associated with amniotic cavity and membranes, antepartum **156 , 159**
658.81	Other problem associated with amniotic cavity and membranes, delivered **137 , 144 , 150**
658.80	Other problem associated with amniotic cavity and membranes, unspecified as to episode of care **161**
V47*	Other problems with internal organs **215**
362.2*	Other proliferative retinopathy **39**
V50.49	Other prophylactic organ removal **215**
263.8	Other protein-calorie malnutrition **165 , 169**
007*	Other protozoal intestinal diseases **75**
696.1	Other psoriasis **106**
V62.89	Other psychological or physical stress, not elsewhere classified **215**
518.82	Other pulmonary insufficiency, not elsewhere classified **54**
518.52	Other pulmonary insufficiency, not elsewhere classified, following trauma and surgery **166 , 171**
590.8*	Other pyelonephritis or pyonephrosis, not specified as acute or chronic **167 , 171**
012*	Other respiratory tuberculosis **230**
362.8*	Other retinal disorders **39**
714.2	Other rheumatoid arthritis with visceral or systemic involvement **97**
083*	Other rickettsioses **186**
277.84	Other secondary carnitine deficiency **115**
374.45	Other sensorimotor disorders of eyelid **38**
999.5*	Other serum reaction, not elsewhere classified **168 , 172 , 204**
262	Other severe protein-calorie malnutrition **114 , 165 , 169 , 231**
785.59	Other shock without mention of trauma **187**
799.59	Other signs and symptoms involving cognition **189**
799.29	Other signs and symptoms involving emotional state **189**

780.59	Other sleep disturbances **190**
315.2	Other specific developmental learning difficulties **190**
315.09	Other specific developmental reading disorder **190**
728.3	Other specific muscle disorders **99**
309.8*	Other specified adjustment reactions **189**
995.8*	Other specified adverse effects, not elsewhere classified **205**
V58.8*	Other specified aftercare **214**
516.8	Other specified alveolar and parietoalveolar pneumonopathies **231**
752.89	Other specified anomalies of genital organs **128 , 131**
284.8*	Other specified aplastic anemias **176 , 231**
066.8	Other specified arthropod-borne viral diseases **185**
040.89	Other specified bacterial diseases **186**
694.8	Other specified bullous dermatosis **106**
427.8*	Other specified cardiac dysrhythmias **68**
093.8*	Other specified cardiovascular syphilis **68**
123.8	Other specified cestode infection **75**
459.89	Other specified circulatory system disorders **67**
646.80	Other specified complication of pregnancy, unspecified as to episode of care **157 , 160**
646.81	Other specified complication of pregnancy, with delivery **135 , 143 , 148**
646.83	Other specified complication, antepartum **155 , 157**
998.89	Other specified complications **205**
646.84	Other specified complications of pregnancy, postpartum condition or complication **153**
646.82	Other specified complications of pregnancy, with delivery, with current postpartum complication **135 , 143 , 148**
778.8	Other specified condition involving the integument of fetus and newborn **172 , 173**
426.89	Other specified conduction disorder **166 , 170**
751.8	Other specified congenital anomalies of digestive system **79**
744.2*	Other specified congenital anomalies of ear **47**
752.8*	Other specified congenital anomalies of genital organs **125**
750.26	Other specified congenital anomalies of mouth **3 , 48**
756.8*	Other specified congenital anomalies of muscle, tendon, fascia, and connective tissue **100**
750.7	Other specified congenital anomalies of stomach **79**
757.8	Other specified congenital anomalies of the integument **109**
750.8	Other specified congenital anomalies of upper alimentary tract **79**
747.89	Other specified congenital anomaly of circulatory system **67**
750.4	Other specified congenital anomaly of esophagus **75**
744.89	Other specified congenital anomaly of face and neck **47**
746.89	Other specified congenital anomaly of heart **68**
750.29	Other specified congenital anomaly of pharynx **3 , 47**
748.8	Other specified congenital anomaly of respiratory system **54**
757.39	Other specified congenital anomaly of skin **109 , 173**
V25.8	Other specified contraceptive management **215**
315.8	Other specified delay in development **190**
032.89	Other specified diphtheria **186**
288.8	Other specified disease of white blood cells **177**
078.88	Other specified diseases due to Chlamydiae **186**
074.8	Other specified diseases due to Coxsackievirus **185**
031.8	Other specified diseases due to other mycobacteria **186 , 230**
078.89	Other specified diseases due to viruses **186**
289.89	Other specified diseases of blood and blood-forming organs **177**
569.89	Other specified disorder of intestines **79**
608.8*	Other specified disorder of male genital organs **125**
349.89	Other specified disorder of nervous system **20**
607.89	Other specified disorder of penis **125**
537.89	Other specified disorder of stomach and duodenum **78**
530.89	Other specified disorder of the esophagus **78**
599.8*	Other specified disorder of urethra and urinary tract **121**
279.8	Other specified disorders involving the immune mechanism **177**
447.8	Other specified disorders of arteries and arterioles **66**
271.8	Other specified disorders of carbohydrate transport and metabolism **114**
379.8	Other specified disorders of eye and adnexa **40**
629.8*	Other specified disorders of female genital organs **131**
719.8*	Other specified disorders of joint **98**
593.8*	Other specified disorders of kidney and ureter **121**
573.8	Other specified disorders of liver **83**
277.89	Other specified disorders of metabolism **115**
275.8	Other specified disorders of mineral metabolism **115**
251.8	Other specified disorders of pancreatic internal secretion **115**
569.4*	Other specified disorders of rectum and anus **79**
246.8	Other specified disorders of thyroid **3**
384.8*	Other specified disorders of tympanic membrane **47**
312.8*	Other specified disturbances of conduct, not elsewhere classified **190**
993.8	Other specified effects of air pressure **205**
695.89	Other specified erythematous condition **109**
V61.8	Other specified family circumstance **215**
656.83	Other specified fetal and placental problems affecting management of mother, antepartum **156 , 158**
656.81	Other specified fetal and placental problems affecting management of mother, delivered **137 , 144 , 150**
656.80	Other specified fetal and placental problems affecting management of mother, unspecified as to episode of care **161**
619.8	Other specified fistula involving female genital tract **128 , 131 , 167 , 171**
414.8	Other specified forms of chronic ischemic heart disease **67**
511.89	Other specified forms of effusion, except tuberculous **52 , 166 , 171**
365.8*	Other specified forms of glaucoma **39**
095.8	Other specified forms of late symptomatic syphilis **186**
564.8*	Other specified functional disorders of intestine **78**
535.41	Other specified gastritis with hemorrhage **76**
535.40	Other specified gastritis without mention of hemorrhage **78**
640.83	Other specified hemorrhage in early pregnancy, antepartum **154**
640.81	Other specified hemorrhage in early pregnancy, delivered **135 , 142 , 148**
640.80	Other specified hemorrhage in early pregnancy, unspecified as to episode of care **154**
054.79	Other specified herpes simplex complications **165 , 169 , 185 , 231**
053.79	Other specified herpes zoster complications **165 , 169 , 185 , 230**
251.1	Other specified hypoglycemia **115**
458.8	Other specified hypotension **69**
356.8	Other specified idiopathic peripheral neuropathy **21**
659.83	Other specified indication for care or intervention related to labor and delivery, antepartum **156 , 159**
659.81	Other specified indication for care or intervention related to labor and delivery, delivered **137 , 144 , 150**
659.80	Other specified indication for care or intervention related to labor and delivery, unspecified as to episode of care **137 , 144 , 150**
343.8	Other specified infantile cerebral palsy **32**
675.82	Other specified infection of the breast and nipple associated with childbirth, delivered, with mention of postpartum complication **140 , 146 , 152**

675.81	Other specified infection of the breast and nipple associated with childbirth, delivered, with or without mention of antepartum condition **140 , 146 , 152**
675.80	Other specified infection of the breast and nipple associated with childbirth, unspecified as to episode of care **162**
675.83	Other specified infection of the breast and nipple, antepartum **157 , 159**
675.84	Other specified infections of the breast and nipple, postpartum condition or complication **154**
136.8	Other specified infectious and parasitic diseases **187 , 231**
614.8	Other specified inflammatory disease of female pelvic organs and tissues **131**
616.8*	Other specified inflammatory diseases of cervix, vagina, and vulva **128 , 131**
714.89	Other specified inflammatory polyarthropathies **97**
318*	Other specified intellectual disabilities **189**
127.7	Other specified intestinal helminthiasis **78**
560.89	Other specified intestinal obstruction **167 , 171**
100.8*	Other specified leptospiral infections **9 , 10 , 33**
207*	Other specified leukemia **179**
207.8*	Other specified leukemia **182**
652.83	Other specified malposition or malpresentation of fetus, antepartum **155 , 158**
652.81	Other specified malposition or malpresentation of fetus, delivered **136 , 143 , 149**
652.80	Other specified malposition or malpresentation of fetus, unspecified as to episode of care **161**
022.8	Other specified manifestations of anthrax **186**
647.80	Other specified maternal infectious and parasitic disease complicating pregnancy, childbirth, or the puerperium, unspecified as to episode of care **160**
647.81	Other specified maternal infectious and parasitic disease with delivery **135 , 141 , 147**
647.82	Other specified maternal infectious and parasitic disease with delivery, with current postpartum complication **135 , 141 , 147**
647.83	Other specified maternal infectious and parasitic disease, antepartum **155 , 157**
647.84	Other specified maternal infectious and parasitic diseases complicating pregnancy, childbirth, or the puerperium, postpartum condition or complication **153**
055.79	Other specified measles complications **185**
036.89	Other specified meningococcal infections **187**
018.8*	Other specified miliary tuberculosis **186**
759.89	Other specified multiple congenital anomalies, so described **101**
V91.9*	Other specified multiple gestation placenta status **216**
651.83	Other specified multiple gestation, antepartum **155 , 158**
651.81	Other specified multiple gestation, delivered **136 , 143 , 149**
651.80	Other specified multiple gestation, unspecified as to episode of care **161**
358.8	Other specified myoneural disorders **21**
359.29	Other specified myotonic disorder **32**
094.89	Other specified neurosyphilis **19**
049.8	Other specified non-arthropod-borne viral diseases of central nervous system **33 , 230**
623.8	Other specified noninflammatory disorder of vagina **173**
310.8*	Other specified nonpsychotic mental disorder following organic brain damage **19**
754.89	Other specified nonteratogenic anomalies **100**
665.83	Other specified obstetrical trauma, antepartum **156 , 159**
665.82	Other specified obstetrical trauma, delivered, with postpartum **138 , 145 , 151**
665.84	Other specified obstetrical trauma, postpartum condition or complication **153**
665.80	Other specified obstetrical trauma, unspecified as to episode of care **138 , 145 , 151**
665.81	Other specified obstetrical trauma, with delivery **138 , 145 , 151**
344.8*	Other specified paralytic syndromes **32**
443.8*	Other specified peripheral vascular diseases **66**
567.89	Other specified peritonitis **76**
299.8*	Other specified pervasive developmental disorders **190**
046.7*	Other specified prion diseases of central nervous system **230**
V26.8*	Other specified procreative management **215**
698.8	Other specified pruritic conditions **109**
306.8	Other specified psychophysiological malfunction **190**
V57.89	Other specified rehabilitation procedure **214**
012.8*	Other specified respiratory tuberculosis **51**
V90.8*	Other specified retained foreign body **216**
003.8	Other specified salmonella infections **186 , 230**
120.8	Other specified schistosomiasis **186**
848.8	Other specified sites of sprains and strains **100**
046.8	Other specified slow virus infection of central nervous system **230**
625.8	Other specified symptom associated with female genital organs **131**
293.8*	Other specified transient mental disorders due to conditions classified elsewhere **189**
664.84	Other specified trauma to perineum and vulva, postpartum condition or complication **153**
664.80	Other specified trauma to perineum and vulva, unspecified as to episode of care in pregnancy **138 , 145 , 151**
664.81	Other specified trauma to perineum and vulva, with delivery **138 , 145 , 151**
121.8	Other specified trematode infections **186**
021.8	Other specified tularemia **186**
603.8	Other specified type of hydrocele **125**
595.89	Other specified types of cystitis **120 , 167 , 171**
020.8	Other specified types of plague **186**
099.8	Other specified venereal diseases **125 , 128 , 131**
070.4*	Other specified viral hepatitis with hepatic coma **165 , 169**
070.5*	Other specified viral hepatitis without mention of hepatic coma **165 , 169**
368.8	Other specified visual disturbances **39**
784.5*	Other speech disturbance **32**
104*	Other spirochetal infection **186**
482.49	Other Staphylococcus pneumonia **51**
V45.69	Other states following surgery of eye and adnexa **215**
567.2*	Other suppurative peritonitis **76**
784.69	Other symbolic dysfunction **190**
789.9	Other symptoms involving abdomen and pelvis **78**
785.9	Other symptoms involving cardiovascular system **69**
784.99	Other symptoms involving head and neck **47**
781.99	Other symptoms involving nervous and musculoskeletal systems **32**
786.9	Other symptoms involving respiratory system and chest **54**
782.9	Other symptoms involving skin and integumentary tissues **109**
788.9*	Other symptoms involving urinary system **120**
719.6*	Other symptoms referable to joint **98**
723.8	Other syndromes affecting cervical region **97**
727.09	Other synovitis and tenosynovitis **99**
836.2	Other tear of cartilage or meniscus of knee, current **223**
727.05	Other tenosynovitis of hand and wrist **99**
282.49	Other thalassemia **165 , 170**
644.13	Other threatened labor, antepartum **154**
644.10	Other threatened labor, unspecified as to episode of care **154**

999.89	Other transfusion reaction **177**	
776.3	Other transient neonatal disorders of coagulation **164 , 169**	
775.5	Other transitory neonatal electrolyte disturbances **164 , 168**	
081*	Other typhus **186**	
663.83	Other umbilical cord complications during labor and delivery, antepartum **156 , 159**	
663.81	Other umbilical cord complications during labor and delivery, delivered **138 , 145 , 151**	
663.80	Other umbilical cord complications during labor and delivery, unspecified as to episode of care **138 , 145 , 151**	
799.9	Other unknown and unspecified cause of morbidity or mortality **214**	
V61.7	Other unwanted pregnancy **154**	
593.4	Other ureteric obstruction **120**	
131.09	Other urogenital trichomoniasis **125 , 128 , 131**	
999.2	Other vascular complications of medical care, not elsewhere classified **69 , 168 , 172**	
647.24	Other venereal diseases complicating pregnancy, childbrith, or the puerperium, postpartum condition or complication **153**	
671.80	Other venous complication of pregnancy and the puerperium, unspecified as to episode of care **162**	
671.83	Other venous complication, antepartum **157 , 159**	
671.82	Other venous complication, with delivery, with mention of postpartum complication **139 , 146 , 152**	
671.81	Other venous complication, with delivery, with or without mention of antepartum condition **139 , 146 , 152**	
671.84	Other venous complications, postpartum condition or complication **154**	
453.2	Other venous embolism and thrombosis, of inferior vena cava **66 , 166 , 170**	
057*	Other viral exanthemata **185**	
368.15	Other visual distortions and entoptic phenomena **39**	
643.83	Other vomiting complicating pregnancy, antepartum **155 , 157**	
643.81	Other vomiting complicating pregnancy, delivered **135 , 142 , 148**	
643.80	Other vomiting complicating pregnancy, unspecified as to episode of care **157 , 160**	
779.33	Other vomiting in newborn **172**	
625.79	Other vulvodynia **131**	
027*	Other zoonotic bacterial diseases **186**	
305.9*	Other, mixed, or unspecified nondependent drug abuse **192**	
827.0	Other, multiple and ill-defined closed fractures of lower limb **223**	
827.1	Other, multiple and ill-defined open fractures of lower limb **223**	
827*	Other, multiple, and ill-defined fractures of lower limb **99**	
919.1	Other, multiple, and unspecified sites, abrasion or friction burn, infected **107**	
919.3	Other, multiple, and unspecified sites, blister, infected **107**	
919.2	Other, multiple, and unspecified sites, blister, without mention of infection **109**	
919.5	Other, multiple, and unspecified sites, insect bite, nonvenomous, infected **107**	
919.4	Other, multiple, and unspecified sites, insect bite, nonvenomous, without mention of infection **110**	
919.6	Other, multiple, and unspecified sites, superficial foreign body (splinter), without major open wound and without mention of infection **108**	
919.7	Other, multiple, and unspecified sites, superficial foreign body (splinter), without major open wound, infected **107**	
053.71	Otitis externa due to herpes zoster **47 , 165 , 169 , 230**	
387*	Otosclerosis **47**	
V27*	Outcome of delivery **215**	
653.33	Outlet contraction of pelvis in pregnancy, antepartum **155 , 158**	

653.31	Outlet contraction of pelvis in pregnancy, delivered **136 , 143 , 149**
653.30	Outlet contraction of pelvis in pregnancy, unspecified as to episode of care in pregnancy **161**
256*	Ovarian dysfunction **128 , 131**
313.0	Overanxious disorder specific to childhood and adolescence **189**
278.02	Overweight **114**
625*	Pain and other symptoms associated with female genital organs **128**
719.4*	Pain in joint **98**
729.5	Pain in soft tissues of limb **98**
786.52	Painful respiration **54**
719.3*	Palindromic rheumatism **98**
782.6*	Pallor and flushing **214**
785.1	Palpitations **68**
378.81	Palsy of conjugate gaze **40**
863.92	Pancreas body injury with open wound into cavity **83**
863.82	Pancreas body injury without mention of open wound into cavity **83 , 228**
863.91	Pancreas head injury with open wound into cavity **83**
863.81	Pancreas head injury without mention of open wound into cavity **83 , 228**
863.94	Pancreas injury, multiple and unspecified sites, with open wound into cavity **83**
863.84	Pancreas injury, multiple and unspecified sites, without mention of open wound into cavity **83 , 228**
V42.83	Pancreas replaced by transplant **83**
863.93	Pancreas tail injury with open wound into cavity **83**
863.83	Pancreas tail injury without mention of open wound into cavity **83 , 228**
284.1*	Pancytopenia **176**
723.6	Panniculitis specified as affecting neck **109**
360.02	Panophthalmitis **38**
360.12	Panuveitis **39**
377.02	Papilledema associated with decreased ocular pressure **40 , 166 , 170**
377.01	Papilledema associated with increased intracranial pressure **32 , 166 , 170**
377.03	Papilledema associated with retinal disorder **40**
646.03	Papyraceous fetus, antepartum **155 , 158**
646.01	Papyraceous fetus, delivered, with or without mention of antepartum condition **135 , 142 , 148**
646.00	Papyraceous fetus, unspecified as to episode of care **135 , 142 , 148**
116.1	Paracoccidioidomycosis **165 , 169**
121.2	Paragonimiasis **51**
478.3*	Paralysis of vocal cords or larynx **3 , 47 , 166 , 170**
560.1	Paralytic ileus **167 , 171**
374.31	Paralytic ptosis **38**
378.5*	Paralytic strabismus **38**
301.0	Paranoid personality disorder **189**
478.22	Parapharyngeal abscess **46 , 166 , 170**
344.1	Paraplegia **18**
696.2	Parapsoriasis **106**
360.13	Parasitic endophthalmitis NOS **38**
327.44	Parasomnia in conditions classified elsewhere **47**
V61.2*	Parent-child problems **215**
367.51	Paresis of accommodation **39**
332*	Parkinson's disease **19**
427.0	Paroxysmal supraventricular tachycardia **68**
427.1	Paroxysmal ventricular tachycardia **68 , 166 , 170**

377.15	Partial optic atrophy **38**	
758.1	Patau's syndrome **189**	
747.0	Patent ductus arteriosus **68**	
733.1*	Pathologic fracture **97 , 167 , 171**	
733.13	Pathologic fracture of vertebrae **87**	
718.27	Pathological dislocation of ankle and foot joint **99**	
718.23	Pathological dislocation of forearm joint **99**	
718.24	Pathological dislocation of hand joint **99**	
718.29	Pathological dislocation of joint of multiple sites **100**	
718.28	Pathological dislocation of joint of other specified site **100**	
718.20	Pathological dislocation of joint, site unspecified **99**	
718.26	Pathological dislocation of lower leg joint **99**	
718.25	Pathological dislocation of pelvic region and thigh joint **100**	
718.21	Pathological dislocation of shoulder joint **99**	
718.22	Pathological dislocation of upper arm joint **99**	
312.31	Pathological gambling **189**	
381.7	Patulous Eustachian tube **47**	
754.82	Pectus carinatum **54**	
754.81	Pectus excavatum **54**	
132*	Pediculosis and phthirus infestation **108**	
625.5	Pelvic congestion syndrome **131**	
665.72	Pelvic hematoma, delivered with postpartum complication **138 , 145 , 151**	
665.74	Pelvic hematoma, postpartum condition or complication **153**	
665.70	Pelvic hematoma, unspecified as to episode of care **138 , 145 , 151**	
665.71	Pelvic hematoma, with delivery **138 , 145 , 151**	
614.6	Pelvic peritoneal adhesions, female (postoperative) (postinfection) **131**	
848.5	Pelvic sprain and strains **96**	
456.5	Pelvic varices **125 , 128 , 131**	
694.5	Pemphigoid **106**	
694.4	Pemphigus **106**	
533.91	Peptic ulcer, unspecified site, unspecified as acute or chronic, without mention of hemorrhage or perforation, with obstruction **77**	
533.90	Peptic ulcer, unspecified site, unspecified as acute or chronic, without mention of hemorrhage, perforation, or obstruction **77**	
370.06	Perforated corneal ulcer **38**	
530.4	Perforation of esophagus **75 , 166 , 171**	
569.83	Perforation of intestine **79 , 167 , 171**	
384.2*	Perforation of tympanic membrane **47**	
777.6	Perinatal intestinal perforation **164 , 169**	
774.4	Perinatal jaundice due to hepatocellular damage **164 , 168**	
774.5	Perinatal jaundice from other causes **172 , 173**	
327.51	Periodic limb movement disorder **32**	
359.3	Periodic paralysis **32**	
730.37	Periostitis, without mention of osteomyelitis, ankle and foot **100**	
730.33	Periostitis, without mention of osteomyelitis, forearm **98**	
730.34	Periostitis, without mention of osteomyelitis, hand **98**	
730.36	Periostitis, without mention of osteomyelitis, lower leg **98**	
730.39	Periostitis, without mention of osteomyelitis, multiple sites **100**	
730.38	Periostitis, without mention of osteomyelitis, other specified sites **100**	
730.35	Periostitis, without mention of osteomyelitis, pelvic region and thigh **98**	
730.31	Periostitis, without mention of osteomyelitis, shoulder region **98**	
730.30	Periostitis, without mention of osteomyelitis, unspecified site **98**	
730.32	Periostitis, without mention of osteomyelitis, upper arm **98**	
674.53	Peripartum cardiomyopathy, antepartum condition or complication **157 , 159**	

674.52	Peripartum cardiomyopathy, delivered, with mention of postpartum condition **139 , 142 , 148**
674.51	Peripartum cardiomyopathy, delivered, with or without mention of antepartum condition **139 , 142 , 148**
674.54	Peripartum cardiomyopathy, postpartum condition or complication **154**
674.50	Peripartum cardiomyopathy, unspecified as to episode of care or not applicable **162**
646.43	Peripheral neuritis antepartum **155 , 157**
646.44	Peripheral neuritis in pregnancy, postpartum condition or complication **152**
646.40	Peripheral neuritis in pregnancy, unspecified as to episode of care **160**
646.41	Peripheral neuritis in pregnancy, with delivery **135 , 142 , 148**
646.42	Peripheral neuritis in pregnancy, with delivery, with current postpartum complication **135 , 142 , 148**
362.6*	Peripheral retinal degenerations **39**
V42.82	Peripheral stem cells replaced by transplant **177**
202.7*	Peripheral T-cell lymphoma **179 , 182 , 231**
997.2	Peripheral vascular complications **67 , 168 , 172**
868.13	Peritoneum injury with open wound into cavity **79 , 228**
868.03	Peritoneum injury without mention of open wound into cavity **79 , 228**
567*	Peritonitis and retroperitoneal infections **167 , 171**
567.0	Peritonitis in infectious diseases classified elsewhere **76**
475	Peritonsillar abscess **3 , 46**
779.7	Periventricular leukomalacia **32 , 167 , 171**
356.1	Peroneal muscular atrophy **20**
277.86	Peroxisomal disorders **115**
747.83	Persistent fetal circulation **164 , 168**
294*	Persistent mental disorders due to conditions classified elsewhere **189**
998.6	Persistent postoperative fistula, not elsewhere classified **168 , 172 , 205**
780.03	Persistent vegetative state **21 , 167 , 171**
536.2	Persistent vomiting **78**
V14*	Personal history of allergy to medicinal agents **215**
V13.4	Personal history of arthritis **215**
V12*	Personal history of certain other diseases **215**
V13.22	Personal history of cervical dysplasia **181 , 183**
V13.6*	Personal history of congenital (corrected) malformations **215**
V13.3	Personal history of diseases of skin and subcutaneous tissue **215**
V13.0*	Personal history of disorders of urinary system **215**
V87.4*	Personal history of drug therapy **214**
V10*	Personal history of malignant neoplasm **181 , 183**
V10.21	Personal history of malignant neoplasm of larynx **4**
V10.02	Personal history of malignant neoplasm of other and unspecified parts of oral cavity and pharynx **4**
V10.01	Personal history of malignant neoplasm of tongue **4**
V11*	Personal history of mental disorder **215**
V13.29	Personal history of other genital system and obstetric disorders **215**
V13.5*	Personal history of other musculoskeletal disorders **215**
V13.8*	Personal history of other specified diseases **215**
V13.7	Personal history of perinatal problems **215**
V13.21	Personal history of pre-term labor **215**
V13.1	Personal history of trophoblastic disease **215**
V13.9	Personal history of unspecified disease **215**
V13.23	Personal history of vaginal dysplasia **215**
V13.24	Personal history of vulvar dysplasia **215**
310.1	Personality change due to conditions classified elsewhere **189**

*Code Range

© 2012 OptumInsight, Inc.

V64*	Persons encountering health services for specific procedures, not carried out **215**
383.2*	Petrositis **46**
607.85	Peyronie's disease **125**
451.1*	Phlebitis and thrombophlebitis of deep veins of lower extremities **66 , 166 , 170**
451.83	Phlebitis and thrombophlebitis of deep veins of upper extremities **66**
451.81	Phlebitis and thrombophlebitis of iliac vein **66 , 166 , 170**
325	Phlebitis and thrombophlebitis of intracranial venous sinuses **9 , 10 , 32**
451.2	Phlebitis and thrombophlebitis of lower extremities, unspecified **66 , 166 , 170**
451.89	Phlebitis and thrombophlebitis of other site **66**
451.82	Phlebitis and thrombophlebitis of superficial veins of upper extremities **66**
451.0	Phlebitis and thrombophlebitis of superficial vessels of lower extremities **66**
451.9	Phlebitis and thrombophlebitis of unspecified site **66**
451.84	Phlebitis and thrombophlebitis of upper extremities, unspecified **66**
066.0	Phlebotomus fever **185**
375.33	Phlegmonous dacryocystitis **39**
300.2*	Phobic disorders **189**
307.52	Pica **190**
365.13	Pigmentary open-angle glaucoma **39**
685*	Pilonidal cyst **107**
696.3	Pityriasis rosea **109**
696.4	Pityriasis rubra pilaris **109**
641.03	Placenta previa without hemorrhage, antepartum **155 , 158**
641.00	Placenta previa without hemorrhage, unspecified as to episode of care **160**
641.01	Placenta previa without hemorrhage, with delivery **135 , 141 , 146**
674.44	Placental polyp, postpartum condition or complication **154**
674.40	Placental polyp, unspecified as to episode of care **162**
674.42	Placental polyp, with delivery, with mention of postpartum complication **139 , 146 , 152**
511.1	Pleurisy with effusion, with mention of bacterial cause other than tuberculosis **51 , 166 , 171**
511.0	Pleurisy without mention of effusion or current tuberculosis **53**
567.1	Pneumococcal peritonitis **76**
481	Pneumococcal pneumonia (streptococcus pneumoniae pneumonia) **53 , 166 , 170 , 231**
503	Pneumoconiosis due to other inorganic dust **53**
502	Pneumoconiosis due to other silica or silicates **53**
136.3	Pneumocystosis **51 , 165 , 169 , 231**
482.81	Pneumonia due to anaerobes **51**
482.82	Pneumonia due to Escherichia coli (E. coli) **51**
482.2	Pneumonia due to Hemophilus influenzae (H. influenzae) **53**
482.0	Pneumonia due to Klebsiella pneumoniae **51**
482.83	Pneumonia due to other gram-negative bacteria **51**
482.8*	Pneumonia due to other specified bacteria **51**
482.89	Pneumonia due to other specified bacteria **51**
483*	Pneumonia due to other specified organism **53 , 166 , 170**
480.8	Pneumonia due to other virus not elsewhere classified **231**
482.1	Pneumonia due to Pseudomonas **51**
480.3	Pneumonia due to SARS-associated coronavirus **231**
482.4*	Pneumonia due to Staphylococcus **51**
482.40	Pneumonia due to Staphylococcus, unspecified **51**
482.3*	Pneumonia due to Streptococcus **53**
484*	Pneumonia in infectious diseases classified elsewhere **51**

486	Pneumonia, organism unspecified **53 , 166 , 170 , 231**
020.5	Pneumonic plague, unspecified **51**
507.0	Pneumonitis due to inhalation of food or vomitus **166 , 170**
507.8	Pneumonitis due to other solids and liquids **166 , 170**
507*	Pneumonitis due to solids and liquids **51**
130.4	Pneumonitis due to toxoplasmosis **51 , 165 , 169**
504	Pneumonopathy due to inhalation of other dust **53**
975*	Poisoning by agents primarily acting on the smooth and skeletal muscles and respiratory system **204**
964*	Poisoning by agents primarily affecting blood constituents **204**
972*	Poisoning by agents primarily affecting the cardiovascular system **204**
973*	Poisoning by agents primarily affecting the gastrointestinal system **204**
965*	Poisoning by analgesics, antipyretics, and antirheumatics **204**
976.6	Poisoning by anti-infectives and other drugs and preparations for ear, nose, and throat **204**
960*	Poisoning by antibiotics **204**
966*	Poisoning by anticonvulsants and anti-Parkinsonism drugs **204**
976.1	Poisoning by antipruritics **204**
978*	Poisoning by bacterial vaccines **204**
970*	Poisoning by central nervous system stimulants **204**
976.7	Poisoning by dental drugs topically applied **204**
971*	Poisoning by drugs primarily affecting the autonomic nervous system **204**
976.3	Poisoning by emollients, demulcents, and protectants **204**
976.5	Poisoning by eye anti-infectives and other eye drugs **40**
962*	Poisoning by hormones and synthetic substitutes **204**
976.4	Poisoning by keratolytics, keratoplastics, other hair treatment drugs and preparations **204**
976.0	Poisoning by local anti-infectives and anti-inflammatory drugs **204**
976.2	Poisoning by local astringents and local detergents **204**
976.8	Poisoning by other agents primarily affecting skin and mucous membrane **204**
977*	Poisoning by other and unspecified drugs and medicinal substances **204**
961*	Poisoning by other anti-infectives **204**
968*	Poisoning by other central nervous system depressants and anesthetics **204**
979*	Poisoning by other vaccines and biological substances **204**
963*	Poisoning by primarily systemic agents **204**
969*	Poisoning by psychotropic agents **204**
967*	Poisoning by sedatives and hypnotics **204**
976.9	Poisoning by unspecified agent primarily affecting skin and mucous membrane **204**
974*	Poisoning by water, mineral, and uric acid metabolism drugs **204**
446.0	Polyarteritis nodosa **97**
273.0	Polyclonal hypergammaglobulinemia **177**
289.0	Polycythemia, secondary **177**
258*	Polyglandular dysfunction and related disorders **115**
657.03	Polyhydramnios, antepartum complication **156 , 159**
657.00	Polyhydramnios, unspecified as to episode of care **161**
657.01	Polyhydramnios, with delivery **137 , 144 , 150**
725	Polymyalgia rheumatica **97**
357.6	Polyneuropathy due to drugs **21**
357.7	Polyneuropathy due to other toxic agents **21**
357.1	Polyneuropathy in collagen vascular disease **21**
357.2	Polyneuropathy in diabetes **21**
357.3	Polyneuropathy in malignant disease **21**
357.4	Polyneuropathy in other diseases classified elsewhere **21**

478.4	Polyp of vocal cord or larynx **3** , **47**	
656.53	Poor fetal growth, affecting management of mother, antepartum condition or complication **156** , **158**	
656.51	Poor fetal growth, affecting management of mother, delivered **137** , **144** , **150**	
656.50	Poor fetal growth, affecting management of mother, unspecified as to episode of care **161**	
904.4*	Popliteal blood vessel vein **224** , **228**	
572.1	Portal pyemia **167** , **171**	
452	Portal vein thrombosis **83**	
645.13	Post term pregnancy, antepartum condition or complication **155** , **158**	
645.11	Post term pregnancy, delivered, with or without mention of antepartum condition **135** , **142** , **148**	
645.10	Post term pregnancy, unspecified as to episode of care or not applicable **160**	
238.77	Post-transplant lymphoproliferative disorder [PTLD] **204**	
383.81	Postauricular fistula **166** , **170**	
310.2	Postconcussion syndrome **34**	
711.3*	Postdysenteric arthropathy **98**	
564.2	Postgastric surgery syndromes **78**	
053.13	Postherpetic polyneuropathy **20** , **165** , **169** , **230**	
053.12	Postherpetic trigeminal neuralgia **20** , **165** , **169** , **230**	
323.6*	Postinfectious encephalitis, myelitis, and encephalomyelitis **9** , **33**	
323.63	Postinfectious myelitis **10**	
377.12	Postinflammatory optic atrophy **38**	
515	Postinflammatory pulmonary fibrosis **53**	
457.0	Postmastectomy lymphedema syndrome **107**	
055.0	Postmeasles encephalitis **9** , **10** , **33** , **165** , **169**	
055.2	Postmeasles otitis media **46** , **165** , **169**	
055.1	Postmeasles pneumonia **51** , **165** , **169**	
411.0	Postmyocardial infarction syndrome **69**	
784.91	Postnasal drip **47**	
512.2	Postoperative air leak **53**	
998.5*	Postoperative infection, not elsewhere classified **185**	
998.0*	Postoperative shock **168** , **172** , **205**	
V24.0	Postpartum care and examination immediately after delivery **154**	
V24.1	Postpartum care and examination of lactating mother **215**	
666.34	Postpartum coagulation defects, postpartum condition or complication **153**	
666.30	Postpartum coagulation defects, unspecified as to episode of care **162**	
666.32	Postpartum coagulation defects, with delivery **138** , **141** , **147**	
459.1*	Postphlebitic syndrome **67**	
780.62	Postprocedural fever **185** , **232**	
V45.0*	Postsurgical cardiac pacemaker in situ **215**	
251.3	Postsurgical hypoinsulinemia **2** , **114**	
958.3	Posttraumatic wound infection not elsewhere classified **167** , **172** , **185** , **225**	
593.6	Postural proteinuria **121**	
780.63	Postvaccination fever **185** , **232**	
052.0	Postvaricella encephalitis **33** , **165** , **169**	
052.2	Postvaricella myelitis **8** , **10** , **33**	
759.81	Prader-Willi syndrome **101**	
642.73	Pre-eclampsia or eclampsia superimposed on pre-existing hypertension, antepartum **155** , **157**	
642.70	Pre-eclampsia or eclampsia superimposed on pre-existing hypertension, complicating pregnancy, childbirth, or the puerperium, unspecified as to episode of care **157** , **160**	
642.74	Pre-eclampsia or eclampsia superimposed on pre-existing hypertension, postpartum condition or complication **152**	

642.71	Pre-eclampsia or eclampsia superimposed on pre-existing hypertension, with delivery **135** , **141** , **147**
642.72	Pre-eclampsia or eclampsia superimposed on pre-existing hypertension, with delivery, with current postpartum complication **135** , **141** , **147**
661.33	Precipitate labor, antepartum **156** , **159**
661.30	Precipitate labor, unspecified as to episode of care **137** , **145** , **150**
661.31	Precipitate labor, with delivery **137** , **145** , **150**
786.51	Precordial pain **68**
309.2*	Predominant disturbance of other emotions as adjustment reaction **189**
646.33	Pregnancy complication, recurrent pregnancy loss, antepartum condition or complication **155** , **158**
646.30	Pregnancy complication, recurrent pregnancy loss, unspecified as to episode of care **160**
646.31	Pregnancy complication, recurrent pregnancy loss, with or without mention of antepartum condition **135** , **142** , **148**
V23.3	Pregnancy with grand multiparity **162**
V23.2	Pregnancy with history of abortion **162**
V23.0	Pregnancy with history of infertility **162**
V23.1	Pregnancy with history of trophoblastic disease **162**
V23.4*	Pregnancy with other poor obstetric history **162**
V23.5	Pregnancy with other poor reproductive history **162**
427.6*	Premature beats **68**
658.13	Premature rupture of membranes in pregnancy, antepartum **156** , **159**
658.11	Premature rupture of membranes in pregnancy, delivered **137** , **144** , **150**
658.10	Premature rupture of membranes in pregnancy, unspecified as to episode of care **137** , **144** , **150**
641.23	Premature separation of placenta, antepartum **155** , **158**
641.20	Premature separation of placenta, unspecified as to episode of care **160**
641.21	Premature separation of placenta, with delivery **135** , **141** , **146**
625.4	Premenstrual tension syndromes **131**
367.4	Presbyopia **39**
V45.2	Presence of cerebrospinal fluid drainage device **215**
V45.5*	Presence of contraceptive device **215**
290.1*	Presenile dementia **231**
654.23	Previous cesarean delivery, antepartum condition or complication **155** , **158**
654.21	Previous cesarean delivery, delivered, with or without mention of antepartum condition **136** , **143** , **149**
654.20	Previous cesarean delivery, unspecified as to episode of care or not applicable **161**
607.3	Priapism **125**
091.1	Primary anal syphilis **78**
365.2*	Primary angle-closure glaucoma **39**
770.4	Primary atelectasis of newborn **164** , **168**
277.81	Primary carnitine deficiency **115**
200.5*	Primary central nervous system lymphoma **231**
327.21	Primary central sleep apnea **32**
114.0	Primary coccidioidomycosis (pulmonary) **51**
114.1	Primary extrapulmonary coccidioidomycosis **108**
289.81	Primary hypercoagulable state **177**
103.0	Primary lesions of pinta **108**
365.11	Primary open-angle glaucoma **39**
377.11	Primary optic atrophy **38**
020.3	Primary pneumonic plague **51**
416.0	Primary pulmonary hypertension **69**
010*	Primary tuberculous infection **51** , **230**

*Code Range © 2012 OptumInsight, Inc.

661.03	Primary uterine inertia, antepartum **156 , 159**
661.00	Primary uterine inertia, unspecified as to episode of care **137 , 144 , 150**
661.01	Primary uterine inertia, with delivery **137 , 144 , 150**
413.1	Prinzmetal angina **68**
V69*	Problems related to lifestyle **216**
V61.3	Problems with aged parents or in-laws **215**
V48*	Problems with head, neck, and trunk **215**
V49*	Problems with limbs and other problems **215**
V41*	Problems with special senses and other special functions **215**
V26.4*	Procreative management, general counseling and advice **215**
378.72	Progressive external ophthalmoplegia **38**
046.3	Progressive multifocal leukoencephalopathy **230**
663.03	Prolapse of cord, complicating labor and delivery, antepartum **156 , 159**
663.01	Prolapse of cord, complicating labor and delivery, delivered **138 , 145 , 150**
663.00	Prolapse of cord, complicating labor and delivery, unspecified as to episode of care **137 , 145 , 150**
652.73	Prolapsed arm of fetus, antepartum condition or complication **155 , 158**
652.71	Prolapsed arm of fetus, delivered **136 , 143 , 149**
652.70	Prolapsed arm of fetus, unspecified as to episode of care **161**
599.5	Prolapsed urethral mucosa **121**
309.1	Prolonged depressive reaction as adjustment reaction **189**
662.03	Prolonged first stage of labor, antepartum **156 , 159**
662.01	Prolonged first stage of labor, delivered **137 , 145 , 150**
662.00	Prolonged first stage of labor, unspecified as to episode of care **137 , 145 , 150**
645.23	Prolonged pregnancy, antepartum condition or complication **155 , 158**
645.21	Prolonged pregnancy, delivered, with or without mention of antepartum condition **135 , 142 , 148**
645.20	Prolonged pregnancy, unspecified as to episode of care or not applicable **160**
662.23	Prolonged second stage of labor, antepartum **156 , 159**
662.21	Prolonged second stage of labor, delivered **137 , 145 , 150**
662.20	Prolonged second stage of labor, unspecified as to episode of care **137 , 145 , 150**
V50.41	Prophylactic breast removal **107**
V50.42	Prophylactic ovary removal **129 , 132**
368.51	Protan defect in color vision **39**
791.0	Proteinuria **120**
698.2	Prurigo **109**
698.0	Pruritus ani **109**
698.1	Pruritus of genital organs **125 , 128 , 131**
051.1	Pseudocowpox **108**
377.24	Pseudopapilledema **38**
696.8	Psoriasis related disease NEC **109**
696.0	Psoriatic arthropathy **97**
136.4	Psorospermiasis **187**
316	Psychic factors associated with diseases classified elsewhere **189**
306.52	Psychogenic dysmenorrhea **128 , 131**
306.53	Psychogenic dysuria **121**
306.50	Psychogenic genitourinary malfunction, unspecified **121**
307.80	Psychogenic pain, site unspecified **189**
298.4	Psychogenic paranoid psychosis **190**
306.51	Psychogenic vaginismus **128 , 131**
307.54	Psychogenic vomiting **189**
799.54	Psychomotor deficit **189**
368.16	Psychophysical visual disturbances **39**
V67.3	Psychotherapy and other treatment for mental disorder follow-up examination **215**
670.12	Puerperal endometritis, delivered, with mention of postpartum complication **139 , 142 , 147**
670.14	Puerperal endometritis, postpartum condition or complication **154**
670.10	Puerperal endometritis, unspecified as to episode of care or not applicable **162**
672.02	Puerperal pyrexia of unknown origin, delivered, with mention of postpartum complication **139 , 142 , 147**
672.04	Puerperal pyrexia of unknown origin, postpartum condition or complication **154**
672.00	Puerperal pyrexia of unknown origin, unspecified as to episode of care **162**
670.22	Puerperal sepsis, delivered, with mention of postpartum complication **139 , 142 , 147**
670.24	Puerperal sepsis, postpartum condition or complication **154**
670.20	Puerperal sepsis, unspecified as to episode of care or not applicable **162**
670.32	Puerperal septic thrombophlebitis, delivered, with mention of postpartum complication **139 , 142 , 147**
670.34	Puerperal septic thrombophlebitis, postpartum condition or complication **154**
670.30	Puerperal septic thrombophlebitis, unspecified as to episode of care or not applicable **162**
039.1	Pulmonary actinomycotic infection **51**
022.1	Pulmonary anthrax **51**
901.41	Pulmonary artery injury **167 , 171**
901.4*	Pulmonary blood vessel injury **224 , 227**
518.0	Pulmonary collapse **54 , 166 , 171**
668.03	Pulmonary complications of the administration of anesthesia or other sedation in labor and delivery, antepartum **156 , 159**
668.01	Pulmonary complications of the administration of anesthesia or other sedation in labor and delivery, delivered **138 , 141 , 147**
668.02	Pulmonary complications of the administration of anesthesia or other sedation in labor and delivery, delivered, with mention of postpartum complication **138 , 141 , 147**
668.04	Pulmonary complications of the administration of anesthesia or other sedation in labor and delivery, postpartum condition or complication **153**
668.00	Pulmonary complications of the administration of anesthesia or other sedation in labor and delivery, unspecified as to episode of care **138 , 145 , 151**
514	Pulmonary congestion and hypostasis **52**
031.0	Pulmonary diseases due to other mycobacteria **51**
415.1*	Pulmonary embolism and infarction **51**
518.3	Pulmonary eosinophilia **53**
770.3	Pulmonary hemorrhage of fetus or newborn **164 , 168**
518.5*	Pulmonary insufficiency following trauma and surgery **52 , 208**
011*	Pulmonary tuberculosis **51 , 230**
021.2	Pulmonary tularemia **51**
901.42	Pulmonary vein injury **167 , 171**
376.35	Pulsating exophthalmos **38**
287*	Purpura and other hemorrhagic conditions **177**
590.3	Pyeloureteritis cystica **167 , 171**
537.81	Pylorospasm **78**
711.0*	Pyogenic arthritis **97 , 232**
711.06	Pyogenic arthritis, lower leg **90**
312.33	Pyromania **190**
344.0*	Quadriplegia and quadriparesis **18**
343.2	Quadriplegic infantile cerebral palsy **18**
V91.2*	Quadruplet gestation placenta status **216**

651.53	Quadruplet pregnancy with fetal loss and retention of one or more, antepartum **155** , **158**	V90.1*****	Retained metal fragments **216**
651.51	Quadruplet pregnancy with fetal loss and retention of one or more, delivered **136** , **143** , **149**	V90.3*****	Retained organic fragments **216**
		667.04	Retained placenta without hemorrhage, postpartum condition or complication **153**

651.53   Quadruplet pregnancy with fetal loss and retention of one or more, antepartum **155** , **158**

651.51   Quadruplet pregnancy with fetal loss and retention of one or more, delivered **136** , **143** , **149**

651.50   Quadruplet pregnancy with fetal loss and retention of one or more, unspecified as to episode of care or not applicable **161**

651.23   Quadruplet pregnancy, antepartum **155** , **158**

651.21   Quadruplet pregnancy, delivered **136** , **143** , **149**

651.20   Quadruplet pregnancy, unspecified as to episode of care **161**

071   Rabies **9** , **10** , **33**

727.04   Radial styloid tenosynovitis **99**

V58.0   Radiotherapy **181** , **183**

V67.1   Radiotherapy follow-up examination **181** , **183**

782.1   Rash and other nonspecific skin eruption **109** , **232**

026*****   Rat-bite fever **186**

443.0   Raynaud's syndrome **97**

349.0   Reaction to spinal or lumbar puncture **34** , **166** , **170**

298.2   Reactive confusion **190**

569.1   Rectal prolapse **79**

718.37   Recurrent dislocation of ankle and foot joint **99**

718.33   Recurrent dislocation of forearm joint **99**

718.34   Recurrent dislocation of hand joint **99**

718.39   Recurrent dislocation of joint of multiple sites **100**

718.38   Recurrent dislocation of joint of other specified site **100**

718.30   Recurrent dislocation of joint, site unspecified **100**

718.36   Recurrent dislocation of lower leg joint **99**

718.35   Recurrent dislocation of pelvic region and thigh joint **100**

718.31   Recurrent dislocation of shoulder joint **99**

718.32   Recurrent dislocation of upper arm joint **99**

327.43   Recurrent isolated sleep paralysis **32**

605   Redundant prepuce and phimosis **125** , **173**

356.3   Refsum's disease **32**

V62.6   Refusal of treatment for reasons of religion or conscience **215**

555*****   Regional enteritis **77**

099.3   Reiter's disease **97**

087*****   Relapsing fever **186**

313.3   Relationship problems specific to childhood and adolescence **190**

327.42   REM sleep behavior disorder **47**

590.2   Renal and perinephric abscess **167** , **171**

788.0   Renal colic **120**

V45.1*****   Renal dialysis status **215**

271.4   Renal glycosuria **114**

729.6   Residual foreign body in soft tissue **100**

365.15   Residual stage of open angle glaucoma **39**

799.1   Respiratory arrest **54** , **167** , **171**

997.3*****   Respiratory complications **54** , **168** , **172**

508.8   Respiratory conditions due to other specified external agents **54**

508.2   Respiratory conditions due to smoke inhalation **54** , **208**

508.9   Respiratory conditions due to unspecified external agent **54**

769   Respiratory distress syndrome in newborn **164**

770.84   Respiratory failure of newborn **164** , **168**

306.1   Respiratory malfunction arising from mental factors **54**

079.6   Respiratory syncytial virus (RSV) **165** , **169**

333.94   Restless legs syndrome [RLS] **19**

376.6   Retained (old) foreign body following penetrating wound of orbit **40**

360.5*****   Retained (old) intraocular foreign body, magnetic **39**

360.6*****   Retained (old) intraocular foreign body, nonmagnetic **39**

V90.9   Retained foreign body, unspecified material **216**

V90.1*****   Retained metal fragments **216**

V90.3*****   Retained organic fragments **216**

667.04   Retained placenta without hemorrhage, postpartum condition or complication **153**

667.00   Retained placenta without hemorrhage, unspecified as to episode of care **162**

667.02   Retained placenta without hemorrhage, with delivery, with mention of postpartum complication **138** , **141** , **147**

V90.2   Retained plastic fragments **216**

667.12   Retained portions of placenta or membranes, without hemorrhage, delivered, with mention of postpartum complication **138** , **141** , **147**

667.14   Retained portions of placenta or membranes, without hemorrhage, postpartum condition or complication **153**

667.10   Retained portions of placenta or membranes, without hemorrhage, unspecified as to episode of care **162**

V90.0*****   Retained radioactive fragment **216**

788.2*****   Retention of urine **120** , **167** , **171**

200.0*****   Reticulosarcoma **231**

200.01   Reticulosarcoma of lymph nodes of head, face, and neck **2**

361.3*****   Retinal defects without detachment **39**

361.0*****   Retinal detachment with retinal defect **39**

362.3*****   Retinal vascular occlusion **38**

361.1*****   Retinoschisis and retinal cysts **39**

676.03   Retracted nipple, antepartum condition or complication **157** , **159**

676.02   Retracted nipple, delivered, with mention of postpartum complication **140** , **146** , **152**

676.01   Retracted nipple, delivered, with or without mention of antepartum condition **140** , **146** , **152**

676.04   Retracted nipple, postpartum condition or complication **154**

676.00   Retracted nipple, unspecified as to prenatal or postnatal episode of care **162**

567.3*****   Retroperitoneal infections **76**

868.14   Retroperitoneum injury with open wound into cavity **121** , **228**

868.04   Retroperitoneum injury without mention of open wound into cavity **121** , **228**

478.24   Retropharyngeal abscess **46** , **166** , **170**

654.33   Retroverted and incarcerated gravid uterus, antepartum **155** , **158**

654.31   Retroverted and incarcerated gravid uterus, delivered **136** , **143** , **149**

654.32   Retroverted and incarcerated gravid uterus, delivered, with mention of postpartum complication **136** , **143** , **149**

654.34   Retroverted and incarcerated gravid uterus, postpartum condition or complication **153**

654.30   Retroverted and incarcerated gravid uterus, unspecified as to episode of care **161**

331.81   Reye's syndrome **32**

999.7*****   Rh and other non-ABO incompatibility reaction due to transfusion of blood or blood products **168** , **172** , **176**

728.88   Rhabdomyolysis **99**

656.13   Rhesus isoimmunization affecting management of mother, antepartum condition **156** , **158**

656.11   Rhesus isoimmunization affecting management of mother, delivered **137** , **144** , **150**

656.10   Rhesus isoimmunization unspecified as to episode of care in pregnancy **161**

392*****   Rheumatic chorea **68**

390   Rheumatic fever without mention of heart involvement **97**

398.91   Rheumatic heart failure (congestive) **56** , **65** , **166** , **170**

398.0   Rheumatic myocarditis **68**

517.1   Rheumatic pneumonia **53**

729.0	Rheumatism, unspecified and fibrositis **98**	368.41	Scotoma involving central area in visual field **38**
714.0	Rheumatoid arthritis **97**	368.42	Scotoma of blind spot area in visual field **39**
714.81	Rheumatoid lung **53**	V28.0	Screening for chromosomal anomalies by amniocentesis **157 , 160**
040.1	Rhinoscleroma **186**		
086.4	Rhodesian trypanosomiasis **186**	V77.3	Screening for phenylketonuria (PKU) **174**
268.0	Rickets, active **98**	V28.1	Screening for raised alpha-fetoprotein levels in amniotic fluid **157 , 160**
268.1	Rickets, late effect **98**		
370.02	Ring corneal ulcer **39**	V28.6	Screening of Streptococcus B **215**
695.81	Ritter's disease **106**	456.4	Scrotal varices **125**
695.3	Rosacea **109**	664.14	Second-degree perineal laceration, postpartum condition or complication **153**
058.11	Roseola infantum due to human herpesvirus 6**165 , 169 , 185**		
058.12	Roseola infantum due to human herpesvirus 7**165 , 169 , 185**	664.10	Second-degree perineal laceration, unspecified as to episode of care in pregnancy **138 , 145 , 151**
058.10	Roseola infantum, unspecified **165 , 169 , 185**	664.11	Second-degree perineal laceration, with delivery **138 , 145 , 151**
840.4	Rotator cuff (capsule) sprain and strain **223**	958.2	Secondary and recurrent hemorrhage as an early complication of trauma **167 , 172 , 205 , 225**
726.1*	Rotator cuff syndrome of shoulder and allied disorders **98**		
V20.2	Routine infant or child health check **173**	196*	Secondary and unspecified malignant neoplasm of lymph nodes **179 , 182**
V50.2	Routine or ritual circumcision **125 , 174**	196.0	Secondary and unspecified malignant neoplasm of lymph nodes of head, face, and neck **2**
V24.2	Routine postpartum follow-up **215**		
056.0*	Rubella with neurological complications **165 , 169**	249*	Secondary diabetes mellitus **1 , 2**
056.7*	Rubella with other specified complications **165 , 169**	249.2*	Secondary diabetes mellitus with hyperosmolarity **114**
056.79	Rubella with other specified complications **185**	249.1*	Secondary diabetes mellitus with ketoacidosis **114**
056.9	Rubella without mention of complication **185**	249.6*	Secondary diabetes mellitus with neurological manifestations **20**
364.42	Rubeosis iridis **39**	249.5*	Secondary diabetes mellitus with ophthalmic manifestations **38**
307.53	Rumination disorder **189**	249.3*	Secondary diabetes mellitus with other coma **114**
447.2	Rupture of artery **66**	249.8*	Secondary diabetes mellitus with other specified manifestations **114**
429.5	Rupture of chordae tendineae **67**		
728.83	Rupture of muscle, nontraumatic **99**	249.7*	Secondary diabetes mellitus with peripheral circulatory disorders **66**
429.6	Rupture of papillary muscle **67**		
727.5*	Rupture of synovium **99**	249.4*	Secondary diabetes mellitus with renal manifestations **121**
727.6*	Rupture of tendon, nontraumatic **99**	249.9*	Secondary diabetes mellitus with unspecified complication **114**
665.03	Rupture of uterus before onset of labor, antepartum **156 , 159**	249.0*	Secondary diabetes mellitus without mention of complication **114**
665.00	Rupture of uterus before onset of labor, unspecified as to episode of care **138 , 145 , 151**		
		289.82	Secondary hypercoagulable state **177**
665.01	Rupture of uterus before onset of labor, with delivery **138 , 145 , 151**	405*	Secondary hypertension **67**
		198.7	Secondary malignant neoplasm of adrenal gland **115**
665.10	Rupture of uterus during labor, unspecified as to episode **138 , 145 , 151**	198.5	Secondary malignant neoplasm of bone and bone marrow **87 , 97**
665.11	Rupture of uterus during labor, with delivery **138 , 145 , 151**	198.3	Secondary malignant neoplasm of brain and spinal cord **19**
720.2	Sacroiliitis, not elsewhere classified **97**	198.81	Secondary malignant neoplasm of breast **105 , 106**
003.23	Salmonella arthritis **97**	198.82	Secondary malignant neoplasm of genital organs **123 , 124 , 127 , 130**
003.0	Salmonella gastroenteritis **75**		
003.21	Salmonella meningitis **8 , 10 , 33**	198.0	Secondary malignant neoplasm of kidney **117 , 120**
003.24	Salmonella osteomyelitis **96**	197.5	Secondary malignant neoplasm of large intestine and rectum **76**
003.22	Salmonella pneumonia **51**	197.7	Secondary malignant neoplasm of liver **82**
003.1	Salmonella septicemia **187 , 230**	197.0	Secondary malignant neoplasm of lung **52**
614.2	Salpingitis and oophoritis not specified as acute, subacute, or chronic **131**	197.1	Secondary malignant neoplasm of mediastinum **52**
		197.8	Secondary malignant neoplasm of other digestive organs and spleen **76**
904.3	Saphenous vein injury **224**		
135	Sarcoidosis **53**	198.4	Secondary malignant neoplasm of other parts of nervous system **19**
136.5	Sarcosporidiosis **187**		
034.1	Scarlet fever **186**	197.3	Secondary malignant neoplasm of other respiratory organs **52**
341.1	Schilder's disease **19**	198.89	Secondary malignant neoplasm of other specified sites **181 , 182**
120.0	Schistosomiasis due to schistosoma haematobium **120**	198.1	Secondary malignant neoplasm of other urinary organs **117 , 120**
120.2	Schistosomiasis due to schistosoma japonicum **186**		
120.1	Schistosomiasis due to schistosoma mansoni **83**	198.6	Secondary malignant neoplasm of ovary **127 , 130**
301.2*	Schizoid personality disorder **189**	197.2	Secondary malignant neoplasm of pleura **52**
295*	Schizophrenic disorders **190**	197.6	Secondary malignant neoplasm of retroperitoneum and peritoneum **76**
379.0*	Scleritis and episcleritis **40**		
370.54	Sclerosing keratitis **39**	198.2	Secondary malignant neoplasm of skin **105 , 106**
567.82	Sclerosing mesenteritis **79**		

197.4	Secondary malignant neoplasm of small intestine including duodenum **76**	
209.75	Secondary Merkel cell carcinoma **181** , **183**	
209.73	Secondary neuroendocrine tumor of bone **87** , **97**	
209.71	Secondary neuroendocrine tumor of distant lymph nodes **179** , **182**	
209.72	Secondary neuroendocrine tumor of liver **82**	
209.79	Secondary neuroendocrine tumor of other sites **181** , **183**	
209.74	Secondary neuroendocrine tumor of peritoneum **76**	
209.70	Secondary neuroendocrine tumor, unspecified site **181** , **183**	
020.4	Secondary pneumonic plague **51**	
091.3	Secondary syphilis of skin or mucous membranes **108**	
287.4*	Secondary thrombocytopenia **165** , **170** , **231**	
661.13	Secondary uterine inertia, antepartum **156** , **159**	
661.10	Secondary uterine inertia, unspecified as to episode of care **137** , **145** , **150**	
661.11	Secondary uterine inertia, with delivery **137** , **145** , **150**	
368.43	Sector or arcuate defects in visual field **38**	
608.0	Seminal vesiculitis **125**	
331.2	Senile degeneration of brain **19**	
797	Senility without mention of psychosis **189**	
313.2*	Sensitivity, shyness, and social withdrawal disorder specific to childhood and adolescence **190**	
374.44	Sensory disorders of eyelid **39**	
362.4*	Separation of retinal layers **39**	
449	Septic arterial embolism **66** , **166** , **170**	
422.92	Septic myocarditis **166** , **170**	
785.52	Septic shock **187**	
038*	Septicemia **165** , **169** , **187** , **230**	
020.2	Septicemic plague **187**	
998.13	Seroma complicating a procedure **168** , **172**	
361.2	Serous retinal detachment **39**	
768.5	Severe birth asphyxia **164** , **168**	
768.73	Severe hypoxic-ischemic encephalopathy **164** , **168**	
642.53	Severe pre-eclampsia, antepartum **155** , **157**	
642.54	Severe pre-eclampsia, postpartum condition or complication **152**	
642.50	Severe pre-eclampsia, unspecified as to episode of care **157** , **160**	
642.51	Severe pre-eclampsia, with delivery **135** , **141** , **147**	
642.52	Severe pre-eclampsia, with delivery, with current postpartum complication **135** , **141** , **147**	
302*	Sexual and gender identity disorders **190**	
202.2*	Sezary's disease **179** , **182**	
202.21	Sezary's disease of lymph nodes of head, face, and neck **3**	
004*	Shigellosis **75**	
995.4	Shock due to anesthesia not elsewhere classified **167** , **172** , **205**	
669.13	Shock during or following labor and delivery, antepartum shock **156** , **159**	
669.14	Shock during or following labor and delivery, postpartum condition or complication **154**	
669.10	Shock during or following labor and delivery, unspecified as to episode of care **139** , **146** , **151**	
669.12	Shock during or following labor and delivery, with delivery, with mention of postpartum complication **139** , **142** , **147**	
669.11	Shock during or following labor and delivery, with delivery, with or without mention of antepartum condition **139** , **142** , **147**	
663.43	Short cord complicating labor and delivery, antepartum **156** , **159**	
663.41	Short cord complicating labor and delivery, delivered **138** , **145** , **151**	

663.40	Short cord complicating labor and delivery, unspecified as to episode of care **138** , **145** , **151**
660.41	Shoulder (girdle) dystocia during labor and deliver, delivered **137** , **144** , **150**
660.43	Shoulder (girdle) dystocia during labor and delivery, antepartum **156** , **159**
660.40	Shoulder (girdle) dystocia during labor and delivery, unspecified as to episode of care **137** , **144** , **150**
912.1	Shoulder and upper arm, abrasion or friction burn, infected **107**
912.0	Shoulder and upper arm, abrasion or friction burn, without mention of infection **108**
912.3	Shoulder and upper arm, blister, infected **107**
912.2	Shoulder and upper arm, blister, without mention of infection **108**
912.5	Shoulder and upper arm, insect bite, nonvenomous, infected **107**
912.4	Shoulder and upper arm, insect bite, nonvenomous, without mention of infection **109**
912.6	Shoulder and upper arm, superficial foreign body (splinter), without major open wound and without mention of infection **108**
912.7	Shoulder and upper arm, superficial foreign body (splinter), without major open wound, infected **107**
282.42	Sickle-cell thalassemia with crisis **165** , **169**
282.41	Sickle-cell thalassemia without crisis **165** , **169**
240*	Simple and unspecified goiter **115**
491.0	Simple chronic bronchitis **53**
V30.1	Single liveborn, born before admission to hospital **172** , **173**
V30.01	Single liveborn, born in hospital, delivered by cesarean delivery **172** , **173**
V30.00	Single liveborn, born in hospital, delivered without mention of cesarean delivery **172** , **173**
V30.2	Single liveborn, born outside hospital and not hospitalized **174**
759.3	Situs inversus **79**
V59.1	Skin donor **110**
306.3	Skin malfunction arising from mental factors **109**
V42.3	Skin replaced by transplant **110**
327.53	Sleep related bruxism **47**
327.26	Sleep related hypoventilation/hypoxemia in conditions classifiable elsewhere **47**
327.52	Sleep related leg cramps **32**
780.58	Sleep related movement disorder, unspecified **190**
046*	Slow virus infections and prion diseases of central nervous system **19**
863.3*	Small intestine injury with open wound into cavity **79** , **224** , **228**
863.2*	Small intestine injury without mention of open wound into cavity **79** , **223** , **228**
589*	Small kidney of unknown cause **121**
050*	Smallpox **185**
V62.4	Social maladjustment **215**
312.2*	Socialized conduct disorder **190**
793.11	Solitary pulmonary nodule **54**
300.8*	Somatoform disorders **189**
123.5	Sparganosis (larval diphyllobothriasis) **75**
367.53	Spasm of accommodation **39**
378.82	Spasm of conjugate gaze **40**
728.85	Spasm of muscle **98**
333.83	Spasmodic torticollis **32**
V72*	Special investigations and examinations **216**
V74*	Special screening examination for bacterial and spirochetal diseases **216**
V75*	Special screening examination for other infectious diseases **216**

V73*	Special screening examination for viral and chlamydial diseases **216**	
V81*	Special screening for cardiovascular, respiratory, and genitourinary diseases **216**	
V78*	Special screening for disorders of blood and blood-forming organs **216**	
V77*	Special screening for endocrine, nutritional, metabolic, and immunity disorders **216**	
V76*	Special screening for malignant neoplasms **216**	
V79*	Special screening for mental disorders and developmental handicaps **216**	
V80*	Special screening for neurological, eye, and ear diseases **216**	
V82*	Special screening for other condition **216**	
727.2	Specific bursitides often of occupational origin **99**	
307.4*	Specific disorders of sleep of nonorganic origin **190**	
136.2*	Specific infections by free-living amebae **187**	
757.6	Specified congenital anomalies of breast **107**	
757.4	Specified congenital anomalies of hair **109**	
757.5	Specified congenital anomalies of nails **109**	
315.34	Speech and language developmental delay due to hearing loss **190**	
608.1	Spermatocele **125**	
741*	Spina bifida **32 , 167 , 171**	
756.17	Spina bifida occulta **32**	
952*	Spinal cord injury without evidence of spinal bone injury **18 , 224 , 228**	
720.1	Spinal enthesopathy **97**	
723.0	Spinal stenosis in cervical region **97**	
334*	Spinocerebellar disease **19**	
789.2	Splenomegaly **177 , 232**	
721*	Spondylosis and allied disorders **97**	
634*	Spontaneous abortion **154**	
782.7	Spontaneous ecchymoses **177**	
512.0	Spontaneous tension pneumothorax **53**	
649.53	Spotting complicating pregnancy, antepartum condition or complication **155 , 158**	
649.51	Spotting complicating pregnancy, delivered, with or without mention of antepartum condition **136 , 143 , 149**	
649.50	Spotting complicating pregnancy, unspecified as to episode of care or not applicable **161**	
848.1	Sprain and strain of jaw **48**	
840.8	Sprain and strain of other specified sites of shoulder and upper arm **223**	
848.3	Sprain and strain of ribs **54**	
848.0	Sprain and strain of septal cartilage of nose **101**	
848.4*	Sprain and strain of sternum **54**	
848.2	Sprain and strain of thyroid region **101**	
840.9	Sprain and strain of unspecified site of shoulder and upper arm **223**	
845*	Sprains and strains of ankle and foot **223**	
841*	Sprains and strains of elbow and forearm **100 , 223**	
843*	Sprains and strains of hip and thigh **96 , 223**	
844*	Sprains and strains of knee and leg **100 , 223**	
847*	Sprains and strains of other and unspecified parts of back **98 , 223**	
846*	Sprains and strains of sacroiliac region **98 , 223**	
840*	Sprains and strains of shoulder and upper arm **100**	
842*	Sprains and strains of wrist and hand **100 , 223**	
005.0	Staphylococcal food poisoning **75**	
375.5*	Stenosis and insufficiency of lacrimal passages **39**	
478.74	Stenosis of larynx **47**	
569.2	Stenosis of rectum and anus **79**	

307.3	Stereotypic movement disorder **190**	
V25.2	Sterilization **125 , 129 , 132**	
V26.5*	Sterilization status **215**	
333.91	Stiff-man syndrome **32**	
719.5*	Stiffness of joint, not elsewhere classified **98**	
863.1	Stomach injury with open wound into cavity **79 , 223 , 228**	
863.0	Stomach injury without mention of open wound into cavity **79 , 223 , 228**	
378.73	Strabismus in other neuromuscular disorders **38**	
034.0	Streptococcal sore throat **2 , 46**	
733.96	Stress fracture of femoral neck **97**	
733.95	Stress fracture of other bone **97**	
733.98	Stress fracture of pelvis **97**	
733.97	Stress fracture of shaft of femur **97**	
733.94	Stress fracture of the metatarsals **97**	
733.93	Stress fracture of tibia or fibula **97**	
530.3	Stricture and stenosis of esophagus **78**	
447.1	Stricture of artery **66**	
593.3	Stricture or kinking of ureter **120**	
786.1	Stridor **54**	
127.2	Strongyloidiasis **78 , 231**	
336.2	Subacute combined degeneration of spinal cord in diseases classified elsewhere **32**	
293.1	Subacute delirium **189**	
333.85	Subacute dyskinesia due to drugs **32**	
208.2*	Subacute leukemia of unspecified cell type **182**	
204.2*	Subacute lymphoid leukemia **182**	
206.2*	Subacute monocytic leukemia **182**	
205.2*	Subacute myeloid leukemia **182**	
046.2	Subacute sclerosing panencephalitis **165 , 169**	
430	Subarachnoid hemorrhage **8 , 9 , 10 , 20 , 166 , 170**	
852.0*	Subarachnoid hemorrhage following injury without mention of open intracranial wound **9 , 11**	
852.1*	Subarachnoid hemorrhage following injury, with open intracranial wound **9 , 11**	
852.12	Subarachnoid hemorrhage following injury, with open intracranial wound, brief (less than 1 hour) loss of consciousness **31**	
852.16	Subarachnoid hemorrhage following injury, with open intracranial wound, loss of consciousness of unspecified duration **26**	
852.13	Subarachnoid hemorrhage following injury, with open intracranial wound, moderate (1-24 hours) loss of consciousness **26**	
852.11	Subarachnoid hemorrhage following injury, with open intracranial wound, no loss of consciousness **30**	
852.14	Subarachnoid hemorrhage following injury, with open intracranial wound, prolonged (more than 24 hours) loss of consciousness and return to pre-existing conscious level **26**	
852.15	Subarachnoid hemorrhage following injury, with open intracranial wound, prolonged (more than 24 hours) loss of consciousness, without return to pre-existing conscious level **26**	
852.19	Subarachnoid hemorrhage following injury, with open intracranial wound, unspecified concussion **31**	
852.10	Subarachnoid hemorrhage following injury, with open intracranial wound, unspecified state of consciousness **30**	
852.02	Subarachnoid hemorrhage following injury, without mention of open intracranial wound, brief (less than 1 hour) loss of consciousness **30**	
852.06	Subarachnoid hemorrhage following injury, without mention of open intracranial wound, loss of consciousness of unspecified duration **26**	

852.03	Subarachnoid hemorrhage following injury, without mention of open intracranial wound, moderate (1-24 hours) loss of consciousness **26**
852.01	Subarachnoid hemorrhage following injury, without mention of open intracranial wound, no loss of consciousness **30**
852.04	Subarachnoid hemorrhage following injury, without mention of open intracranial wound, prolonged (more than 24 hours) loss of consciousness and return to pre-existing conscious level **26**
852.05	Subarachnoid hemorrhage following injury, without mention of open intracranial wound, prolonged (more than 24 hours) loss of consciousness, without return to pre-existing conscious level **26**
852.09	Subarachnoid hemorrhage following injury, without mention of open intracranial wound, unspecified concussion **30**
852.00	Subarachnoid hemorrhage following injury, without mention of open intracranial wound, unspecified state of consciousness **30**
852*	Subarachnoid, subdural, and extradural hemorrhage, following injury **223 , 227**
694.1	Subcorneal pustular dermatosis **109**
767.0	Subdural and cerebral hemorrhage, birth trauma **164 , 168**
852.3*	Subdural hemorrhage following injury, with open intracranial wound **9 , 11**
852.32	Subdural hemorrhage following injury, with open intracranial wound, brief (less than 1 hour) loss of consciousness **31**
852.36	Subdural hemorrhage following injury, with open intracranial wound, loss of consciousness of unspecified duration **26**
852.33	Subdural hemorrhage following injury, with open intracranial wound, moderate (1-24 hours) loss of consciousness **26**
852.31	Subdural hemorrhage following injury, with open intracranial wound, no loss of consciousness **31**
852.34	Subdural hemorrhage following injury, with open intracranial wound, prolonged (more than 24 hours) loss of consciousness and return to pre-existing conscious level **26**
852.35	Subdural hemorrhage following injury, with open intracranial wound, prolonged (more than 24 hours) loss of consciousness, without return to pre-existing conscious level **26**
852.30	Subdural hemorrhage following injury, with open intracranial wound, state of consciousness unspecified **31**
852.39	Subdural hemorrhage following injury, with open intracranial wound, unspecified concussion **31**
852.22	Subdural hemorrhage following injury, without mention of open intracranial wound, brief (less than one hour) loss of consciousness **31**
852.26	Subdural hemorrhage following injury, without mention of open intracranial wound, loss of consciousness of unspecified duration **26**
852.23	Subdural hemorrhage following injury, without mention of open intracranial wound, moderate (1-24 hours) loss of consciousness **26**
852.21	Subdural hemorrhage following injury, without mention of open intracranial wound, no loss of consciousness **31**
852.24	Subdural hemorrhage following injury, without mention of open intracranial wound, prolonged (more than 24 hours) loss of consciousness and return to pre-existing conscious level **26**
852.25	Subdural hemorrhage following injury, without mention of open intracranial wound, prolonged (more than 24 hours) loss of consciousness, without return to pre-existing conscious level **26**
852.29	Subdural hemorrhage following injury, without mention of open intracranial wound, unspecified concussion **31**
852.20	Subdural hemorrhage following injury, without mention of open intracranial wound, unspecified state of consciousness **31**
456.3	Sublingual varices **67**
383.01	Subperiosteal abscess of mastoid **166 , 170**
840.5	Subscapularis (muscle) sprain and strain **223**
798.0	Sudden infant death syndrome **32**
368.11	Sudden visual loss **38**
V62.84	Suicidal ideation **189**
904.1	Superficial femoral artery injury **224 , 228**
913*	Superficial injury of elbow, forearm, and wrist **224**
918*	Superficial injury of eye and adnexa **40 , 224**
910*	Superficial injury of face, neck, and scalp, except eye **224**
915*	Superficial injury of finger(s) **224**
917*	Superficial injury of foot and toe(s) **224**
914*	Superficial injury of hand(s) except finger(s) alone **224**
916*	Superficial injury of hip, thigh, leg, and ankle **224**
919*	Superficial injury of other, multiple, and unspecified sites **224**
912*	Superficial injury of shoulder and upper arm **224**
911*	Superficial injury of trunk **224**
370.2*	Superficial keratitis without conjunctivitis **39**
671.20	Superficial thrombophlebitis complicating pregnancy and the puerperium, unspecified as to episode of care **162**
671.22	Superficial thrombophlebitis with delivery, with mention of postpartum complication **139 , 146 , 152**
671.21	Superficial thrombophlebitis with delivery, with or without mention of antepartum condition **139 , 146 , 152**
671.23	Superficial thrombophlebitis, antepartum **157 , 159**
671.24	Superficial thrombophlebitis, postpartum condition or complication **154**
840.7	Superior glenoid labrum lesions (SLAP) **223**
901.2	Superior vena cava injury **167 , 171 , 224 , 227**
V23.8*	Supervision of other high-risk pregnancy **162**
676.53	Suppressed lactation, antepartum condition or complication **157 , 159**
676.54	Suppressed lactation, postpartum condition or complication **154**
676.50	Suppressed lactation, unspecified as to episode of care **162**
676.52	Suppressed lactation, with delivery, with mention of postpartum complication **140 , 146 , 152**
676.51	Suppressed lactation, with delivery, with or without mention of antepartum condition **140 , 146 , 152**
382*	Suppurative and unspecified otitis media **46**
840.6	Supraspinatus (muscle) (tendon) sprain and strain **223**
V67.0*	Surgery follow-up examination **214**
V25.4*	Surveillance of previously prescribed contraceptive methods **215**
655.53	Suspected damage to fetus from drugs, affecting management of mother, antepartum **156 , 158**
655.51	Suspected damage to fetus from drugs, affecting management of mother, delivered **136 , 144 , 149**
655.50	Suspected damage to fetus from drugs, affecting management of mother, unspecified as to episode of care **161**
655.43	Suspected damage to fetus from other disease in mother, affecting management of mother, antepartum condition or complication **156 , 158**
655.40	Suspected damage to fetus from other disease in mother, affecting management of mother, unspecified as to episode of care in pregnancy **161**
655.41	Suspected damage to fetus from other disease in mother, affecting management of mother, with delivery **136 , 144 , 149**
655.63	Suspected damage to fetus from radiation, affecting management of mother, antepartum condition or complication **156 , 158**
655.61	Suspected damage to fetus from radiation, affecting management of mother, delivered **136 , 144 , 149**
655.60	Suspected damage to fetus from radiation, affecting management of mother, unspecified as to episode of care **161**
655.33	Suspected damage to fetus from viral disease in mother, affecting management of mother, antepartum condition or complication **156 , 158**
655.30	Suspected damage to fetus from viral disease in mother, affecting management of mother, unspecified as to episode of care in pregnancy **161**

655.31	Suspected damage to fetus from viral disease in mother, affecting management of mother, with delivery **136 , 144 , 149**
V89.0*	Suspected maternal and fetal conditions not found **216**
078.2	Sweating fever **186**
729.81	Swelling of limb **98**
786.6	Swelling, mass, or lump in chest **54**
784.2	Swelling, mass, or lump in head and neck **109**
784.60	Symbolic dysfunction, unspecified **190**
360.11	Sympathetic uveitis **39**
V83.02	Symptomatic hemophilia A carrier **216**
359.6	Symptomatic inflammatory myopathy in diseases classified elsewhere **32**
783*	Symptoms concerning nutrition, metabolism, and development **114**
787*	Symptoms involving digestive system **78**
780.2	Syncope and collapse **68**
727.01	Synovitis and tenosynovitis in diseases classified elsewhere **98**
095.5	Syphilis of bone **96**
095.4	Syphilis of kidney **120**
095.3	Syphilis of liver **83**
095.1	Syphilis of lung **51**
095.6	Syphilis of muscle **98**
095.7	Syphilis of synovium, tendon, and bursa **98**
094.86	Syphilitic acoustic neuritis **47**
093.1	Syphilitic aortitis **67**
094.83	Syphilitic disseminated retinochoroiditis **38**
094.81	Syphilitic encephalitis **9 , 10 , 33**
093.22	Syphilitic endocarditis, aortic valve **67**
093.21	Syphilitic endocarditis, mitral valve **67**
093.24	Syphilitic endocarditis, pulmonary valve **67**
093.23	Syphilitic endocarditis, tricuspid valve **67**
095.0	Syphilitic episcleritis **38**
090.3	Syphilitic interstitial keratitis **38**
094.2	Syphilitic meningitis **9 , 10 , 33**
094.84	Syphilitic optic atrophy **38**
094.82	Syphilitic Parkinsonism **19**
095.2	Syphilitic peritonitis **75**
094.85	Syphilitic retrobulbar neuritis **19**
094.87	Syphilitic ruptured cerebral aneurysm **8 , 32**
336.0	Syringomyelia and syringobulbia **19**
995.9*	Systemic inflammatory response syndrome (SIRS) **187**
428.2*	Systolic heart failure **57 , 166 , 170**
094.0	Tabes dorsalis **19**
123.2	Taenia saginata infection **77**
123.0	Taenia solium infection, intestinal form **77**
123.3	Taeniasis, unspecified **77**
446.7	Takayasu's disease **97**
429.83	Takotsubo syndrome **69**
836.1	Tear of lateral cartilage or meniscus of knee, current **223**
836.0	Tear of medial cartilage or meniscus of knee, current **223**
348.81	Temporal sclerosis **20**
727.06	Tenosynovitis of foot and ankle **99**
307.81	Tension headache **34**
257*	Testicular dysfunction **115**
037	Tetanus **165 , 169 , 186**
781.7	Tetany **114 , 167 , 171**
745.2	Tetralogy of Fallot **67**
282.40	Thalassemia, unspecified **165 , 169**
265*	Thiamine and niacin deficiency states **114 , 231**

664.24	Third-degree perineal laceration, postpartum condition or complication **153**
664.20	Third-degree perineal laceration, unspecified as to episode of care in pregnancy **138 , 145 , 151**
664.21	Third-degree perineal laceration, with delivery **138 , 145 , 151**
666.04	Third-stage postpartum hemorrhage, postpartum condition or complication **153**
666.00	Third-stage postpartum hemorrhage, unspecified as to episode of care **162**
666.02	Third-stage postpartum hemorrhage, with delivery **138 , 141 , 147**
441.2	Thoracic aneurysm without mention of rupture **66**
441.1	Thoracic aneurysm, ruptured **66**
901.0	Thoracic aorta injury **167 , 171 , 224 , 227**
441.7	Thoracoabdominal aneurysm without mention of rupture **66**
441.6	Thoracoabdominal aneurysm, ruptured **66**
640.03	Threatened abortion, antepartum **154**
640.01	Threatened abortion, delivered **135 , 142 , 148**
640.00	Threatened abortion, unspecified as to episode of care **154**
644.03	Threatened premature labor, antepartum **154**
644.00	Threatened premature labor, unspecified as to episode of care **154**
784.1	Throat pain **47**
443.1	Thromboangiitis obliterans (Buerger's disease) **66**
453.1	Thrombophlebitis migrans **66**
446.6	Thrombotic microangiopathy **97**
245*	Thyroiditis **3 , 115**
242*	Thyrotoxicosis with or without goiter **3 , 115**
904.5*	Tibial blood vessel(s) injury **224 , 228**
726.72	Tibialis tendinitis **98**
066.1	Tick-borne fever **185**
082*	Tick-borne rickettsioses **186**
063*	Tick-borne viral encephalitis **9 , 10 , 33**
307.2*	Tics **32**
333.3	Tics of organic origin **32**
733.6	Tietze's disease **54**
388.3*	Tinnitus **47**
649.03	Tobacco use disorder complicating pregnancy, childbirth, or the puerperium, antepartum condition or complication **155 , 158**
649.02	Tobacco use disorder complicating pregnancy, childbirth, or the puerperium, delivered, with mention of postpartum complication **136 , 143 , 149**
649.01	Tobacco use disorder complicating pregnancy, childbirth, or the puerperium, delivered, with or without mention of antepartum condition **136 , 143 , 149**
649.04	Tobacco use disorder complicating pregnancy, childbirth, or the puerperium, postpartum condition or complication **153**
649.00	Tobacco use disorder complicating pregnancy, childbirth, or the puerperium, unspecified as to episode of care or not applicable **160**
750.0	Tongue tie **3 , 48**
379.46	Tonic pupillary reaction **38**
608.2*	Torsion of testis **125**
723.5	Torticollis, unspecified **97**
823.4*	Torus fracture of tibia and fibula **223 , 228**
367.52	Total or complete internal ophthalmoplegia **38**
980*	Toxic effect of alcohol **204**
986	Toxic effect of carbon monoxide **204**
983*	Toxic effect of corrosive aromatics, acids, and caustic alkalis **204**
984*	Toxic effect of lead and its compounds (including fumes) **204**
988*	Toxic effect of noxious substances eaten as food **204**
987*	Toxic effect of other gases, fumes, or vapors **204**

985*	Toxic effect of other metals **204**
989*	Toxic effect of other substances, chiefly nonmedicinal as to source **204**
981	Toxic effect of petroleum products **204**
982*	Toxic effect of solvents other than petroleum-based **204**
987.9	Toxic effect of unspecified gas, fume, or vapor **208**
323.71	Toxic encephalitis and encephalomyelitis **10 , 32**
323.7*	Toxic encephalitis, myelitis, and encephalomyelitis **9**
349.82	Toxic encephalopathy **32 , 166 , 170**
695.0	Toxic erythema **106 , 167 , 171**
558.2	Toxic gastroenteritis and colitis **79 , 167 , 171 , 231**
323.72	Toxic myelitis **10 , 32**
358.2	Toxic myoneural disorders **21**
359.4	Toxic myopathy **32**
040.82	Toxic shock syndrome **186**
130*	Toxoplasmosis **231**
130.7	Toxoplasmosis of other specified sites **165 , 169 , 187**
530.84	Tracheoesophageal fistula **75 , 166 , 171**
519.0*	Tracheostomy complications **3 , 54**
076*	Trachoma **38**
999.80	Transfusion reaction, unspecified **176**
518.7	Transfusion related acute lung injury [TRALI] **54**
780.02	Transient alteration of awareness **189**
435*	Transient cerebral ischemia **20**
437.7	Transient global amnesia **20**
642.33	Transient hypertension of pregnancy, antepartum **155 , 158**
642.34	Transient hypertension of pregnancy, postpartum condition or complication **152**
642.30	Transient hypertension of pregnancy, unspecified as to episode of care **160**
642.31	Transient hypertension of pregnancy, with delivery **135 , 142 , 148**
642.32	Transient hypertension of pregnancy, with delivery, with current postpartum complication **135 , 142 , 148**
776.1	Transient neonatal thrombocytopenia **164 , 168**
781.4	Transient paralysis of limb **32**
368.12	Transient visual loss **38**
745.1*	Transposition of great vessels **67**
652.33	Transverse or oblique fetal presentation, antepartum **155 , 158**
652.31	Transverse or oblique fetal presentation, delivered **136 , 143 , 149**
652.30	Transverse or oblique fetal presentation, unspecified as to episode of care **161**
887*	Traumatic amputation of arm and hand (complete) (partial) **204 , 224 , 228**
896*	Traumatic amputation of foot (complete) (partial) **204 , 224 , 228**
897*	Traumatic amputation of leg(s) (complete) (partial) **204 , 224 , 228**
886*	Traumatic amputation of other finger(s) (complete) (partial) **204 , 224**
885*	Traumatic amputation of thumb (complete) (partial) **204 , 224**
895*	Traumatic amputation of toe(s) (complete) (partial) **204 , 224**
958.5	Traumatic anuria **119 , 120 , 167 , 172 , 225**
958.9*	Traumatic compartment syndrome **205**
958.93	Traumatic compartment syndrome of abdomen **225 , 228**
958.92	Traumatic compartment syndrome of lower extremity **225 , 229**
958.99	Traumatic compartment syndrome of other sites **225**
958.91	Traumatic compartment syndrome of upper extremity **225 , 228**
860*	Traumatic pneumothorax and hemothorax **53 , 167 , 171 , 223 , 227**
958.4	Traumatic shock **167 , 172 , 205 , 225**
958.7	Traumatic subcutaneous emphysema **53 , 167 , 172 , 225**
V67.4	Treatment of healed fracture follow-up examination **214**
124	Trichinosis **187**
131.03	Trichomonal prostatitis **125**
131.02	Trichomonal urethritis **125 , 128 , 131**
131.01	Trichomonal vulvovaginitis **128 , 131**
131.8	Trichomoniasis of other specified sites **187**
127.6	Trichostrongyliasis **78**
127.3	Trichuriasis **78**
426.54	Trifascicular block **166 , 170**
350*	Trigeminal nerve disorders **20**
727.03	Trigger finger (acquired) **99**
595.3	Trigonitis **120**
V91.1*	Triplet gestation placenta status **216**
651.43	Triplet pregnancy with fetal loss and retention of one or more, antepartum **155 , 158**
651.41	Triplet pregnancy with fetal loss and retention of one or more, delivered **136 , 143 , 149**
651.40	Triplet pregnancy with fetal loss and retention of one or more, unspecified as to episode of care or not applicable **161**
651.13	Triplet pregnancy, antepartum **155 , 158**
651.11	Triplet pregnancy, delivered **136 , 143 , 149**
651.10	Triplet pregnancy, unspecified as to episode of care **161**
368.53	Tritan defect in color vision **39**
040.81	Tropical pyomyositis **98**
911.1	Trunk abrasion or friction burn, infected **107**
911.0	Trunk abrasion or friction burn, without mention of infection **108**
911.3	Trunk blister, infected **107**
911.2	Trunk blister, without mention of infection **109**
911.5	Trunk, insect bite, nonvenomous, infected **107**
911.4	Trunk, insect bite, nonvenomous, without mention of infection **109**
911.6	Trunk, superficial foreign body (splinter), without major open wound and without mention of infection **108**
911.7	Trunk, superficial foreign body (splinter), without major open wound, infected **107**
017.6*	Tuberculosis of adrenal glands **115**
016.1*	Tuberculosis of bladder **120**
015*	Tuberculosis of bones and joints **230**
017.4*	Tuberculosis of ear **46**
016.4*	Tuberculosis of epididymis **124**
017.8*	Tuberculosis of esophagus **75**
017.3*	Tuberculosis of eye **38**
016*	Tuberculosis of genitourinary system **230**
015.1*	Tuberculosis of hip **97**
014*	Tuberculosis of intestines, peritoneum, and mesenteric glands **75 , 230**
012.1*	Tuberculosis of intrathoracic lymph nodes **51**
016.0*	Tuberculosis of kidney **120**
015.2*	Tuberculosis of knee **97**
015.5*	Tuberculosis of limb bones **96**
015.6*	Tuberculosis of mastoid **46**
013*	Tuberculosis of meninges and central nervous system **8 , 10 , 33 , 230**
016.7*	Tuberculosis of other female genital organs **128 , 130**
016.5*	Tuberculosis of other male genital organs **124**
017*	Tuberculosis of other organs **230**
015.7*	Tuberculosis of other specified bone **96**
015.8*	Tuberculosis of other specified joint **97**

017.9*	Tuberculosis of other specified organs **186**
016.3*	Tuberculosis of other urinary organs **120**
017.2*	Tuberculosis of peripheral lymph nodes **177**
017.0*	Tuberculosis of skin and subcutaneous cellular tissue **108**
017.7*	Tuberculosis of spleen **177**
017.5*	Tuberculosis of thyroid gland **115**
015.9*	Tuberculosis of unspecified bones and joints **97**
016.2*	Tuberculosis of ureter **120**
015.0*	Tuberculosis of vertebral column **96**
015.02	Tuberculosis of vertebral column, bacteriological or histological examination unknown (at present) **87**
015.04	Tuberculosis of vertebral column, tubercle bacilli not found (in sputum) by microscopy, but found by bacterial culture **87**
015.05	Tuberculosis of vertebral column, tubercle bacilli not found by bacteriological examination, but tuberculosis confirmed histologically **87**
012.3*	Tuberculous laryngitis **2 , 46**
016.6*	Tuberculous oophoritis and salpingitis **128 , 130**
012.0*	Tuberculous pleurisy **51**
759.5	Tuberous sclerosis **32**
V26.0	Tuboplasty or vasoplasty after previous sterilization **125 , 129 , 132**
277.88	Tumor lysis syndrome **119 , 165 , 169**
654.10	Tumors of body of pregnant uterus, unspecified as to episode of care in pregnancy **161**
654.13	Tumors of body of uterus, antepartum condition or complication **155 , 158**
654.11	Tumors of body of uterus, delivered **136 , 143 , 149**
654.12	Tumors of body of uterus, delivered, with mention of postpartum complication **136 , 143 , 149**
654.14	Tumors of body of uterus, postpartum condition or complication **153**
V31.1	Twin birth, mate liveborn, born before admission to hospital **172 , 173**
V31.2	Twin birth, mate liveborn, born outside hospital and not hospitalized **174**
V32.1	Twin birth, mate stillborn, born before admission to hospital **172 , 173**
V32.2	Twin birth, mate stillborn, born outside hospital and not hospitalized **174**
V33.1	Twin birth, unspecified whether mate liveborn or stillborn, born before admission to hospital **172 , 173**
V33.2	Twin birth, unspecified whether mate liveborn or stillborn, born outside hospital and not hospitalized **174**
V91.0*	Twin gestation placenta status **216**
651.33	Twin pregnancy with fetal loss and retention of one fetus, antepartum **155 , 158**
651.31	Twin pregnancy with fetal loss and retention of one fetus, delivered **136 , 143 , 149**
651.30	Twin pregnancy with fetal loss and retention of one fetus, unspecified as to episode of care or not applicable **161**
651.03	Twin pregnancy, antepartum **155 , 158**
651.01	Twin pregnancy, delivered **136 , 143 , 149**
651.00	Twin pregnancy, unspecified as to episode of care **161**
V31.01	Twin, mate liveborn, born in hospital, delivered by cesarean delivery **172 , 173**
V31.00	Twin, mate liveborn, born in hospital, delivered without mention of cesarean delivery **172 , 173**
V32.01	Twin, mate stillborn, born in hospital, delivered by cesarean delivery **172 , 173**
V32.00	Twin, mate stillborn, born in hospital, delivered without mention of cesarean delivery **172 , 173**
V33.01	Twin, unspecified whether mate stillborn or liveborn, born in hospital, delivered by cesarean delivery **172 , 173**

V33.00	Twin, unspecified whether mate stillborn or liveborn, born in hospital, delivered without mention of cesarean delivery **172 , 173**
002*	Typhoid and paratyphoid fevers **186**
530.2*	Ulcer of esophagus **77**
569.82	Ulceration of intestine **79**
616.5*	Ulceration of vulva **128 , 131**
556*	Ulcerative colitis **77**
021.0	Ulceroglandular tularemia **186**
551.1	Umbilical hernia with gangrene **167 , 171**
552.1	Umbilical hernia with obstruction **78 , 167 , 171**
553.1	Umbilical hernia without mention of obstruction or gangrene **79**
798.9	Unattended death **214**
V63*	Unavailability of other medical facilities for care **215**
312.0*	Undersocialized conduct disorder, aggressive type **190**
312.1*	Undersocialized conduct disorder, unaggressive type **190**
752.5*	Undescended and retractile testicle **125 , 173**
785.2	Undiagnosed cardiac murmurs **68**
V62.0	Unemployment **215**
552.00	Unilateral or unspecified femoral hernia with obstruction **167 , 171**
388.40	Unspecified abnormal auditory perception **47**
379.40	Unspecified abnormal pupillary function **38**
661.93	Unspecified abnormality of labor, antepartum **156 , 159**
661.90	Unspecified abnormality of labor, unspecified as to episode of care **137 , 145 , 150**
661.91	Unspecified abnormality of labor, with delivery **137 , 145 , 150**
518.4	Unspecified acute edema of lung **52 , 166 , 171**
421.9	Unspecified acute endocarditis **65 , 231**
376.00	Unspecified acute inflammation of orbit **39**
391.9	Unspecified acute rheumatic heart disease **68**
309.9	Unspecified adjustment reaction **189**
995.22	Unspecified adverse effect of anesthesia **167 , 172**
995.23	Unspecified adverse effect of insulin **167 , 172**
995.29	Unspecified adverse effect of other drug, medicinal and biological substance **167 , 172**
995.20	Unspecified adverse effect of unspecified drug, medicinal and biological substance **167 , 172**
V58.9	Unspecified aftercare **214**
571.3	Unspecified alcoholic liver damage **82**
006.9	Unspecified amebiasis **186**
285.9	Unspecified anemia **231**
V28.9	Unspecified antenatal screening **215**
641.93	Unspecified antepartum hemorrhage, antepartum **155 , 158**
641.90	Unspecified antepartum hemorrhage, unspecified as to episode of care **160**
641.91	Unspecified antepartum hemorrhage, with delivery **135 , 141 , 146**
646.23	Unspecified antepartum renal disease **155 , 157**
022.9	Unspecified anthrax **186**
284.9	Unspecified aplastic anemia **176 , 231**
447.6	Unspecified arteritis **97**
716.9*	Unspecified arthropathy **232**
066.9	Unspecified arthropod-borne viral disease **185**
493.9*	Unspecified asthma **54**
482.9	Unspecified bacterial pneumonia **53**
694.9	Unspecified bullous dermatosis **106**
594.9	Unspecified calculus of lower urinary tract **120**
427.9	Unspecified cardiac dysrhythmia **68**
429.2	Unspecified cardiovascular disease **67**

093.9	Unspecified cardiovascular syphilis **68**
323.9	Unspecified causes of encephalitis, myelitis, and encephalomyelitis **9** , **10** , **33** , **231**
434.91	Unspecified cerebral artery occlusion with cerebral infarction **9** , **11** , **19** , **20**
434.90	Unspecified cerebral artery occlusion without mention of cerebral infarction **20**
331.9	Unspecified cerebral degeneration **19**
437.9	Unspecified cerebrovascular disease **20**
123.9	Unspecified cestode infection **76**
491.9	Unspecified chronic bronchitis **53**
474.9	Unspecified chronic disease of tonsils and adenoids **47**
414.9	Unspecified chronic ischemic heart disease **67**
571.9	Unspecified chronic liver disease without mention of alcohol **83**
416.9	Unspecified chronic pulmonary heart disease **69**
459.9	Unspecified circulatory system disorder **67**
824.8	Unspecified closed fracture of ankle **223**
808.8	Unspecified closed fracture of pelvis **222**
114.9	Unspecified coccidioidomycosis **186**
763.9	Unspecified complication of labor and delivery affecting fetus or newborn **172** , **173**
669.93	Unspecified complication of labor and delivery, antepartum condition or complication **157** , **159**
669.94	Unspecified complication of labor and delivery, postpartum condition or complication **154**
669.90	Unspecified complication of labor and delivery, unspecified as to episode of care **139** , **146** , **152**
669.92	Unspecified complication of labor and delivery, with delivery, with mention of postpartum complication **139** , **146** , **152**
669.91	Unspecified complication of labor and delivery, with delivery, with or without mention of antepartum condition **139** , **146** , **152**
646.93	Unspecified complication of pregnancy, antepartum **155** , **158**
646.90	Unspecified complication of pregnancy, unspecified as to episode of care **160**
646.91	Unspecified complication of pregnancy, with delivery **135** , **143** , **148**
998.9	Unspecified complication of procedure, not elsewhere classified **168** , **172** , **205**
668.93	Unspecified complication of the administration of anesthesia or other sedation in labor and delivery, antepartum **156** , **159**
668.91	Unspecified complication of the administration of anesthesia or other sedation in labor and delivery, delivered **139** , **142** , **147**
668.92	Unspecified complication of the administration of anesthesia or other sedation in labor and delivery, delivered, with mention of postpartum complication **139** , **142** , **147**
668.94	Unspecified complication of the administration of anesthesia or other sedation in labor and delivery, postpartum condition or complication **154**
668.90	Unspecified complication of the administration of anesthesia or other sedation in labor and delivery, unspecified as to episode of care **139** , **145** , **151**
674.94	Unspecified complications of puerperium, postpartum condition or complication **154**
674.90	Unspecified complications of puerperium, unspecified as to episode of care **162**
674.92	Unspecified complications of puerperium, with delivery, with mention of postpartum complication **139** , **146** , **152**
850.9	Unspecified concussion **223**
348.9	Unspecified condition of brain **20** , **231**
759.9	Unspecified congenital anomaly **214**
747.9	Unspecified congenital anomaly of circulatory system **67**
751.9	Unspecified congenital anomaly of digestive system **79**
744.3	Unspecified congenital anomaly of ear **47**
744.9	Unspecified congenital anomaly of face and neck **109**
751.60	Unspecified congenital anomaly of gallbladder, bile ducts, and liver **83**
752.9	Unspecified congenital anomaly of genital organs **125** , **128** , **131**
746.9	Unspecified congenital anomaly of heart **68**
748.60	Unspecified congenital anomaly of lung **54**
748.9	Unspecified congenital anomaly of respiratory system **54**
757.9	Unspecified congenital anomaly of the integument **109**
750.9	Unspecified congenital anomaly of upper alimentary tract **79**
745.9	Unspecified congenital defect of septal closure **67**
V25.9	Unspecified contraceptive management **215**
921.9	Unspecified contusion of eye **40**
370.00	Unspecified corneal ulcer **38**
737.9	Unspecified curvature of spine associated with other condition **87**
595.9	Unspecified cystitis **120** , **167** , **171**
375.00	Unspecified dacryoadenitis **39**
375.30	Unspecified dacryocystitis **39**
799.3	Unspecified debility **214**
736.70	Unspecified deformity of ankle and foot, acquired **100**
736.00	Unspecified deformity of forearm, excluding fingers **100**
374.50	Unspecified degenerative disorder of eyelid **39**
315.9	Unspecified delay in development **190**
341.9	Unspecified demyelinating disease of central nervous system **19** , **231**
718.9*	Unspecified derangement of joint **100**
032.9	Unspecified diphtheria **186**
478.70	Unspecified disease of larynx **47**
478.20	Unspecified disease of pharynx **47**
519.9	Unspecified disease of respiratory system **54**
336.9	Unspecified disease of spinal cord **32** , **231**
527.9	Unspecified disease of the salivary glands **231**
288.9	Unspecified disease of white blood cells **177**
031.9	Unspecified diseases due to mycobacteria **186** , **230**
289.9	Unspecified diseases of blood and blood-forming organs **177** , **231**
271.9	Unspecified disorder of carbohydrate transport and metabolism **114**
388.9	Unspecified disorder of ear **47**
530.9	Unspecified disorder of esophagus **78**
380.9	Unspecified disorder of external ear **47**
379.9*	Unspecified disorder of eye and adnexa **40**
378.9	Unspecified disorder of eye movements **40**
374.9	Unspecified disorder of eyelid **39**
629.9	Unspecified disorder of female genital organs **131**
360.9	Unspecified disorder of globe **39**
279.9	Unspecified disorder of immune mechanism **177**
569.9	Unspecified disorder of intestine **79**
364.9	Unspecified disorder of iris and ciliary body **39**
719.9*	Unspecified disorder of joint **98**
593.9	Unspecified disorder of kidney and ureter **121**
375.9	Unspecified disorder of lacrimal system **39**
676.93	Unspecified disorder of lactation, antepartum condition or complication **157** , **159**
676.94	Unspecified disorder of lactation, postpartum condition or complication **154**
676.90	Unspecified disorder of lactation, unspecified as to episode of care **162**
676.92	Unspecified disorder of lactation, with delivery, with mention of postpartum complication **140** , **146** , **152**

676.91	Unspecified disorder of lactation, with delivery, with or without mention of antepartum condition **140 , 146 , 152**
573.9	Unspecified disorder of liver **83**
608.9	Unspecified disorder of male genital organs **125**
277.9	Unspecified disorder of metabolism **115**
275.9	Unspecified disorder of mineral metabolism **115**
728.9	Unspecified disorder of muscle, ligament, and fascia **99**
377.9	Unspecified disorder of optic nerve and visual pathways **32**
376.9	Unspecified disorder of orbit **40**
251.9	Unspecified disorder of pancreatic internal secretion **115**
607.9	Unspecified disorder of penis **125**
273.9	Unspecified disorder of plasma protein metabolism **181 , 183**
367.9	Unspecified disorder of refraction and accommodation **39**
709.9	Unspecified disorder of skin and subcutaneous tissue **232**
537.9	Unspecified disorder of stomach and duodenum **78**
727.9	Unspecified disorder of synovium, tendon, and bursa **99**
246.9	Unspecified disorder of thyroid **3**
384.9	Unspecified disorder of tympanic membrane **47**
599.9	Unspecified disorder of urethra and urinary tract **121**
447.9	Unspecified disorders of arteries and arterioles **66**
349.9	Unspecified disorders of nervous system **20 , 231**
312.9	Unspecified disturbance of conduct **190**
090.2	Unspecified early congenital syphilis **186**
122.4	Unspecified echinococcus granulosus infection **187**
122.7	Unspecified echinococcus multilocularis infection **187**
122.8	Unspecified echinococcus of liver **83**
993.9	Unspecified effect of air pressure **205**
V50.9	Unspecified elective surgery for purposes other than remedying health states **215**
313.9	Unspecified emotional disturbance of childhood or adolescence **190**
726.9*	Unspecified enthesopathy **98**
726.70	Unspecified enthesopathy of ankle and tarsus **98**
695.9	Unspecified erythematous condition **109**
401.9	Unspecified essential hypertension **67**
381.9	Unspecified Eustachian tube disorder **47**
376.30	Unspecified exophthalmos **39**
333.90	Unspecified extrapyramidal disease and abnormal movement disorder **19**
660.71	Unspecified failed forceps or vacuum extractor, delivered **137 , 144 , 150**
660.70	Unspecified failed forceps or vacuum extractor, unspecified as to episode of care **137 , 144 , 150**
660.63	Unspecified failed trial of labor, antepartum **156 , 159**
660.61	Unspecified failed trial of labor, delivered **137 , 144 , 150**
660.60	Unspecified failed trial of labor, unspecified as to episode **137 , 144 , 150**
V61.9	Unspecified family circumstance **215**
729.4	Unspecified fasciitis **99**
655.93	Unspecified fetal abnormality affecting management of mother, antepartum condition or complication **156 , 158**
655.91	Unspecified fetal abnormality affecting management of mother, delivery **137 , 144 , 150**
655.90	Unspecified fetal abnormality affecting management of mother, unspecified as to episode of care **161**
774.6	Unspecified fetal and neonatal jaundice **172 , 173**
656.93	Unspecified fetal and placental problem affecting management of mother, antepartum **156 , 159**
656.91	Unspecified fetal and placental problem affecting management of mother, delivered **137 , 144 , 150**
656.90	Unspecified fetal and placental problem affecting management of mother, unspecified as to episode of care **161**

653.93	Unspecified fetal disproportion, antepartum **155 , 158**
653.91	Unspecified fetal disproportion, delivered **136 , 143 , 149**
653.90	Unspecified fetal disproportion, unspecified as to episode of care **161**
764.98	Unspecified fetal growth retardation, 2,000-2,499 grams **172 , 173**
764.99	Unspecified fetal growth retardation, 2,500 or more grams **172 , 173**
619.9	Unspecified fistula involving female genital tract **128 , 131**
V67.9	Unspecified follow-up examination **216**
005.9	Unspecified food poisoning **77**
564.9	Unspecified functional disorder of intestine **78**
536.9	Unspecified functional disorder of stomach **78**
535.51	Unspecified gastritis and gastroduodenitis with hemorrhage **76**
535.50	Unspecified gastritis and gastroduodenitis without mention of hemorrhage **78**
054.10	Unspecified genital herpes **124 , 128 , 130 , 230**
365.9	Unspecified glaucoma **39**
429.9	Unspecified heart disease **67**
428.9	Unspecified heart failure **57 , 166 , 170**
459.0	Unspecified hemorrhage **69 , 166 , 170**
640.93	Unspecified hemorrhage in early pregnancy, antepartum **154**
640.91	Unspecified hemorrhage in early pregnancy, delivered **135 , 142 , 148**
640.90	Unspecified hemorrhage in early pregnancy, unspecified as to episode of care **154**
573.3	Unspecified hepatitis **83 , 167 , 171**
356.9	Unspecified hereditary and idiopathic peripheral neuropathy **21**
054.8	Unspecified herpes simplex complication **165 , 169 , 185 , 231**
053.8	Unspecified herpes zoster complication **165 , 169 , 185 , 230**
V23.9	Unspecified high-risk pregnancy **162**
115.94	Unspecified Histoplasmosis endocarditis **65 , 165 , 169**
115.91	Unspecified Histoplasmosis meningitis **9 , 10 , 33 , 165 , 169**
115.93	Unspecified Histoplasmosis pericarditis **68 , 165 , 169**
115.95	Unspecified Histoplasmosis pneumonia **51 , 165 , 169**
115.92	Unspecified Histoplasmosis retinitis **38 , 165 , 169**
115.99	Unspecified Histoplasmosis with mention of other manifestation **186**
115.90	Unspecified Histoplasmosis without mention of manifestation **186**
603.9	Unspecified hydrocele **125**
642.93	Unspecified hypertension antepartum **155 , 157**
642.94	Unspecified hypertension complicating pregnancy, childbirth, or the puerperium, postpartum condition or complication **152**
642.90	Unspecified hypertension complicating pregnancy, childbirth, or the puerperium, unspecified as to episode of care **160**
642.91	Unspecified hypertension, with delivery **135 , 141 , 147**
642.92	Unspecified hypertension, with delivery, with current postpartum complication **135 , 141 , 147**
402.90	Unspecified hypertensive heart disease without heart failure **67**
458.9	Unspecified hypotension **69**
279.3	Unspecified immunity deficiency **177**
279.10	Unspecified immunodeficiency with predominant T-cell defect **177**
560.30	Unspecified impaction of intestine **167 , 171**
659.93	Unspecified indication for care or intervention related to labor and delivery, antepartum **156 , 159**
659.91	Unspecified indication for care or intervention related to labor and delivery, delivered **137 , 144 , 150**
659.90	Unspecified indication for care or intervention related to labor and delivery, unspecified as to episode of care **137 , 144 , 150**
343.9	Unspecified infantile cerebral palsy **32**

730.9*	Unspecified infection of bone **96**
590.9	Unspecified infection of kidney **167 , 171**
675.93	Unspecified infection of the breast and nipple, antepartum **157 , 159**
675.92	Unspecified infection of the breast and nipple, delivered, with mention of postpartum complication **140 , 146 , 152**
675.91	Unspecified infection of the breast and nipple, delivered, with or without mention of antepartum condition **140 , 146 , 152**
675.94	Unspecified infection of the breast and nipple, postpartum condition or complication **154**
675.90	Unspecified infection of the breast and nipple, unspecified as to prenatal or postnatal episode of care **162**
136.9	Unspecified infectious and parasitic diseases **187**
711.9*	Unspecified infective arthritis **97 , 232**
902.10	Unspecified inferior vena cava injury **167 , 171**
357.9	Unspecified inflammatory and toxic neuropathy **21 , 231**
616.9	Unspecified inflammatory disease of cervix, vagina, and vulva **128 , 131**
614.9	Unspecified inflammatory disease of female pelvic organs and tissues **131**
714.9	Unspecified inflammatory polyarthropathy **98**
720.9	Unspecified inflammatory spondylopathy **97**
319	Unspecified intellectual disabilities **189**
717.9	Unspecified internal derangement of knee **99**
370.50	Unspecified interstitial keratitis **39**
127.9	Unspecified intestinal helminthiasis **78**
579.9	Unspecified intestinal malabsorption **232**
560.9	Unspecified intestinal obstruction **167 , 171**
129	Unspecified intestinal parasitism **78**
432.9	Unspecified intracranial hemorrhage **9 , 10**
718.65	Unspecified intrapelvic protrusion acetabulum, pelvic region and thigh **100**
364.3	Unspecified iridocyclitis **39**
370.9	Unspecified keratitis **39**
095.9	Unspecified late symptomatic syphilis **186**
085.9	Unspecified leishmaniasis **186**
100.9	Unspecified leptospirosis **186**
208.9*	Unspecified leukemia **182**
686.9	Unspecified local infection of skin and subcutaneous tissue **173**
003.20	Unspecified localized salmonella infection **186**
861.30	Unspecified lung injury with open wound into thorax **54**
861.20	Unspecified lung injury without mention of open wound into thorax **54**
204.9*	Unspecified lymphoid leukemia **182**
652.93	Unspecified malposition or malpresentation of fetus, antepartum **155 , 158**
652.91	Unspecified malposition or malpresentation of fetus, delivered **136 , 143 , 149**
652.90	Unspecified malposition or malpresentation of fetus, unspecified as to episode of care **161**
383.9	Unspecified mastoiditis **46**
647.94	Unspecified maternal infection or infestation complicating pregnancy, childbirth, or the puerperium, postpartum condition or complication **153**
647.90	Unspecified maternal infection or infestation complicating pregnancy, childbirth, or the puerperium, unspecified as to episode of care **160**
647.91	Unspecified maternal infection or infestation with delivery **135 , 141 , 147**
647.92	Unspecified maternal infection or infestation with delivery, with current postpartum complication **135 , 141 , 147**
647.93	Unspecified maternal infection or infestation, antepartum **155 , 157**

659.21	Unspecified maternal pyrexia during labor, delivered **137 , 141 , 147**
659.20	Unspecified maternal pyrexia during labor, unspecified as to episode of care **137 , 144 , 150**
659.23	Unspecified maternal pyrexia, antepartum **156 , 159**
055.8	Unspecified measles complication **165 , 169 , 185**
322.9	Unspecified meningitis **166 , 170**
036.9	Unspecified meningococcal infection **187**
018.9*	Unspecified miliary tuberculosis **186**
206.9*	Unspecified monocytic leukemia **182**
344.5	Unspecified monoplegia **32**
651.93	Unspecified multiple gestation, antepartum **155 , 158**
651.91	Unspecified multiple gestation, delivered **136 , 143 , 149**
651.90	Unspecified multiple gestation, unspecified as to episode of care **161**
072.8	Unspecified mumps complication **165 , 169 , 185**
723.9	Unspecified musculoskeletal disorders and symptoms referable to neck **97**
729.1	Unspecified myalgia and myositis **98**
205.9*	Unspecified myeloid leukemia **182**
429.0	Unspecified myocarditis **69**
358.9	Unspecified myoneural disorders **21**
359.9	Unspecified myopathy **32**
729.2	Unspecified neuralgia, neuritis, and radiculitis **21 , 232**
094.9	Unspecified neurosyphilis **19**
049.9	Unspecified non-arthropod-borne viral disease of central nervous system **33 , 230**
283.10	Unspecified non-autoimmune hemolytic anemia **176**
457.9	Unspecified noninfectious disorder of lymphatic channels **177**
300.9	Unspecified nonpsychotic mental disorder **189**
310.9	Unspecified nonpsychotic mental disorder following organic brain damage **189 , 231**
379.50	Unspecified nystagmus **38**
665.93	Unspecified obstetrical trauma, antepartum **156 , 159**
665.92	Unspecified obstetrical trauma, delivered, with postpartum complication **138 , 145 , 151**
665.94	Unspecified obstetrical trauma, postpartum condition or complication **153**
665.90	Unspecified obstetrical trauma, unspecified as to episode of care **138 , 145 , 151**
665.91	Unspecified obstetrical trauma, with delivery **138 , 145 , 151**
660.93	Unspecified obstructed labor, antepartum **156 , 159**
660.90	Unspecified obstructed labor, unspecified as to episode of care **137 , 144 , 150**
660.91	Unspecified obstructed labor, with delivery **137 , 144 , 150**
824.9	Unspecified open fracture of ankle **223**
808.9	Unspecified open fracture of pelvis **222**
365.10	Unspecified open-angle glaucoma **39**
054.40	Unspecified ophthalmic complication herpes simplex **230**
377.10	Unspecified optic atrophy **38**
V42.9	Unspecified organ or tissue replaced by transplant **215**
073.9	Unspecified ornithosis **185**
V54.9	Unspecified orthopedic aftercare **99**
730.2*	Unspecified osteomyelitis **96**
730.26	Unspecified osteomyelitis, lower leg **90**
730.28	Unspecified osteomyelitis, other specified sites **87**
388.60	Unspecified otorrhea **47**
729.3*	Unspecified panniculitis **109**
377.00	Unspecified papilledema **32 , 166 , 170**
344.9	Unspecified paralysis **32**
051.9	Unspecified paravaccinia **185**

*Code Range

© 2012 OptumInsight, Inc.

427.2	Unspecified paroxysmal tachycardia **68**	
380.00	Unspecified perichondritis of pinna **46**	
664.44	Unspecified perineal laceration, postpartum condition or complication **153**	
664.40	Unspecified perineal laceration, unspecified as to episode of care in pregnancy **138 , 145 , 151**	
664.41	Unspecified perineal laceration, with delivery **138 , 145 , 151**	
443.9	Unspecified peripheral vascular disease **66**	
567.9	Unspecified peritonitis **76**	
294.9	Unspecified persistent mental disorders due to conditions classified elsewhere **231**	
301.9	Unspecified personality disorder **189**	
299.9*	Unspecified pervasive developmental disorder **190**	
103.9	Unspecified pinta **186**	
020.9	Unspecified plague **186**	
511.9	Unspecified pleural effusion **52 , 166 , 171**	
505	Unspecified pneumoconiosis **53**	
658.93	Unspecified problem associated with amniotic cavity and membranes, antepartum **156 , 159**	
658.91	Unspecified problem associated with amniotic cavity and membranes, delivered **137 , 144 , 150**	
658.90	Unspecified problem associated with amniotic cavity and membranes, unspecified as to episode of care **162**	
V26.9	Unspecified procreative management **215**	
662.13	Unspecified prolonged labor, antepartum **156 , 159**	
662.11	Unspecified prolonged labor, delivered **137 , 145 , 150**	
662.10	Unspecified prolonged labor, unspecified as to episode of care **137 , 145 , 150**	
263.9	Unspecified protein-calorie malnutrition **165 , 169**	
698.9	Unspecified pruritic disorder **109**	
306.9	Unspecified psychophysiological malfunction **189**	
298.9	Unspecified psychosis **190 , 231**	
V62.9	Unspecified psychosocial circumstance **215**	
374.30	Unspecified ptosis of eyelid **38**	
114.5	Unspecified pulmonary coccidioidomycosis **51**	
360.00	Unspecified purulent endophthalmitis **38**	
V57.9	Unspecified rehabilitation procedure **214**	
646.20	Unspecified renal disease in pregnancy, unspecified as to episode of care **157 , 160**	
646.21	Unspecified renal disease in pregnancy, with delivery **135 , 142 , 148**	
646.22	Unspecified renal disease in pregnancy, with delivery, with current postpartum complication **135 , 142 , 148**	
646.24	Unspecified renal disease in pregnancy, without mention of hypertension, postpartum condition or complication **152**	
586	Unspecified renal failure **119 , 120**	
587	Unspecified renal sclerosis **121**	
506.9	Unspecified respiratory conditions due to fumes and vapors **53**	
361.9	Unspecified retinal detachment **39**	
362.9	Unspecified retinal disorder **39**	
398.90	Unspecified rheumatic heart disease **68**	
056.8	Unspecified rubella complications **165 , 169 , 185**	
056.00	Unspecified rubella neurological complication **20**	
003.9	Unspecified salmonella infection **186 , 230**	
120.9	Unspecified schistosomiasis **186**	
425.9	Unspecified secondary cardiomyopathy **231**	
785.50	Unspecified shock **57 , 66 , 167 , 171**	
848.9	Unspecified site of sprain and strain **100**	
780.57	Unspecified sleep apnea **3 , 47**	
780.50	Unspecified sleep disturbance **190**	
046.9	Unspecified slow virus infection of central nervous system **230**	

368.10	Unspecified subjective visual disturbance **39**
388.2	Unspecified sudden hearing loss **47**
464.51	Unspecified supraglottis, with obstruction **3 , 46**
464.50	Unspecified supraglottis, without mention of obstruction **3 , 46**
625.9	Unspecified symptom associated with female genital organs **131**
727.00	Unspecified synovitis and tenosynovitis **98**
093.20	Unspecified syphilitic endocarditis of valve **65**
785.0	Unspecified tachycardia **68 , 167 , 171**
287.5	Unspecified thrombocytopenia **231**
130.9	Unspecified toxoplasmosis **187**
293.9	Unspecified transient mental disorder in conditions classified elsewhere **189**
664.94	Unspecified trauma to perineum and vulva, postpartum condition or complication **153**
664.90	Unspecified trauma to perineum and vulva, unspecified as to episode of care in pregnancy **138 , 145 , 151**
664.91	Unspecified trauma to perineum and vulva, with delivery **138 , 145 , 151**
121.9	Unspecified trematode infection **187**
131.9	Unspecified trichomoniasis **187**
086.9	Unspecified trypanosomiasis **186**
021.9	Unspecified tularemia **186**
745.60	Unspecified type congenital endocardial cushion defect **67**
663.93	Unspecified umbilical cord complication during labor and delivery, antepartum **156 , 159**
663.91	Unspecified umbilical cord complication during labor and delivery, delivered **138 , 145 , 151**
663.90	Unspecified umbilical cord complication during labor and delivery, unspecified as to episode of care **138 , 145 , 151**
131.00	Unspecified urogenital trichomoniasis **125 , 128 , 131**
099.9	Unspecified venereal disease **125 , 128 , 131**
459.81	Unspecified venous (peripheral) insufficiency **67**
671.90	Unspecified venous complication of pregnancy and the puerperium, unspecified as to episode of care **162**
671.93	Unspecified venous complication, antepartum **157 , 159**
671.94	Unspecified venous complication, postpartum condition or complication **154**
671.92	Unspecified venous complication, with delivery, with mention of postpartum complication **139 , 146 , 152**
671.91	Unspecified venous complication, with delivery, with or without mention of antepartum condition **139 , 146 , 152**
386.9	Unspecified vertiginous syndromes and labyrinthine disorders **46**
079.9*	Unspecified viral and chlamydial infections, in conditions classified elsewhere and of unspecified site **231**
070.6	Unspecified viral hepatitis with hepatic coma **165 , 169**
070.9	Unspecified viral hepatitis without mention of hepatic coma **165 , 169**
047.9	Unspecified viral meningitis **231**
480.9	Unspecified viral pneumonia **231**
790.8	Unspecified viremia **186**
368.9	Unspecified visual disturbance **39**
368.40	Unspecified visual field defect **38**
264.9	Unspecified vitamin A deficiency **114**
268.9	Unspecified vitamin D deficiency **114**
643.93	Unspecified vomiting of pregnancy, antepartum **155 , 157**
643.91	Unspecified vomiting of pregnancy, delivered **135 , 142 , 148**
643.90	Unspecified vomiting of pregnancy, unspecified as to episode of care **157 , 160**
765.20	Unspecified weeks of gestation **172 , 173**
102.9	Unspecified yaws **186**
652.03	Unstable lie of fetus, antepartum **155 , 158**
652.01	Unstable lie of fetus, delivered **136 , 143 , 149**

652.00	Unstable lie of fetus, unspecified as to episode of care **161**
653.53	Unusually large fetus causing disproportion, antepartum **155** , **158**
653.51	Unusually large fetus causing disproportion, delivered **136** , **143** , **149**
653.50	Unusually large fetus causing disproportion, unspecified as to episode of care **161**
506.2	Upper respiratory inflammation due to fumes and vapors **54**
478.8	Upper respiratory tract hypersensitivity reaction, site unspecified **3** , **46**
867.3	Ureter injury with open wound into cavity **121**
867.2	Ureter injury without mention of open wound into cavity **121**
597.0	Urethral abscess **167** , **171**
599.3	Urethral caruncle **121**
788.7	Urethral discharge **120**
599.2	Urethral diverticulum **121**
599.4	Urethral false passage **121**
599.1	Urethral fistula **121**
598*	Urethral stricture **121**
597*	Urethritis, not sexually transmitted, and urethral syndrome **120**
274.11	Uric acid nephrolithiasis **120**
997.5	Urinary complications **121** , **168** , **172**
788.3*	Urinary incontinence **120**
599.6*	Urinary obstruction **121** , **167** , **171**
599.0	Urinary tract infection, site not specified **120** , **167** , **171**
619.0	Urinary-genital tract fistula, female **123** , **131**
708*	Urticaria **109**
218*	Uterine leiomyoma **128** , **131**
649.63	Uterine size date discrepancy, antepartum condition or complication **155** , **158**
649.62	Uterine size date discrepancy, delivered, with mention of postpartum complication **136** , **143** , **149**
649.61	Uterine size date discrepancy, delivered, with or without mention of antepartum condition **136** , **143** , **149**
649.64	Uterine size date discrepancy, postpartum condition or complication **153**
649.60	Uterine size date discrepancy, unspecified as to episode of care or not applicable **161**
867.5	Uterus injury with open wound into cavity **128** , **131**
867.4	Uterus injury without mention of open wound into cavity **128** , **131**
V64.05	Vaccination not carried out because of caregiver refusal **174**
625.1	Vaginismus **131**
616.1*	Vaginitis and vulvovaginitis **128** , **131**
736.03	Valgus deformity of wrist (acquired) **100**
052.1	Varicella (hemorrhagic) pneumonitis **51** , **165** , **169**
052.9	Varicella without mention of complication **165** , **169** , **185**
456.8	Varices of other sites **67**
671.00	Varicose veins of legs complicating pregnancy and the puerperium, unspecified as to episode of care **162**
671.03	Varicose veins of legs, antepartum **157** , **159**
671.04	Varicose veins of legs, postpartum condition or complication **154**
671.02	Varicose veins of legs, with delivery, with mention of postpartum complication **139** , **146** , **152**
671.01	Varicose veins of legs, with delivery, with or without mention of antepartum condition **139** , **146** , **152**
454.1	Varicose veins of lower extremities with inflammation **67**
454.0	Varicose veins of lower extremities with ulcer **67**
454.2	Varicose veins of lower extremities with ulcer and inflammation **67**
454.8	Varicose veins of the lower extremities with other complications **67**

671.10	Varicose veins of vulva and perineum complicating pregnancy and the puerperium, unspecified as to episode of care **162**
671.13	Varicose veins of vulva and perineum, antepartum **157** , **159**
671.14	Varicose veins of vulva and perineum, postpartum condition or complication **154**
671.12	Varicose veins of vulva and perineum, with delivery, with mention of postpartum complication **139** , **146** , **152**
671.11	Varicose veins of vulva and perineum, with delivery, with or without mention of antepartum condition **139** , **146** , **152**
736.04	Varus deformity of wrist (acquired) **100**
663.53	Vasa previa complicating labor and delivery, antepartum **156** , **159**
663.51	Vasa previa complicating labor and delivery, delivered **138** , **145** , **151**
663.50	Vasa previa complicating labor and delivery, unspecified as to episode of care **138** , **145** , **151**
997.71	Vascular complications of mesenteric artery **79** , **168** , **172**
997.79	Vascular complications of other vessels **67** , **168** , **172**
997.72	Vascular complications of renal artery **121** , **168** , **172**
607.82	Vascular disorders of penis **125**
557*	Vascular insufficiency of intestine **79**
663.63	Vascular lesions of cord complicating labor and delivery, antepartum **156** , **159**
663.61	Vascular lesions of cord complicating labor and delivery, delivered **138** , **145** , **151**
663.60	Vascular lesions of cord complicating labor and delivery, unspecified as to episode of care **138** , **145** , **151**
336.1	Vascular myelopathies **32**
066.2	Venezuelan equine fever **9** , **10** , **33**
453.6	Venous embolism and thrombosis of superficial vessels of lower extremity **66**
551.2*	Ventral hernia with gangrene **167** , **171**
552.2*	Ventral hernia with obstruction **78** , **167** , **171**
553.2*	Ventral hernia without mention of obstruction or gangrene **79**
427.4*	Ventricular fibrillation and flutter **68** , **166** , **170**
745.4	Ventricular septal defect **67** , **167** , **171**
386.2	Vertigo of central origin **46**
596.2	Vesical fistula, not elsewhere classified **167** , **171**
593.7*	Vesicoureteral reflux **121**
719.2*	Villonodular synovitis **98**
101	Vincent's angina **2** , **46**
079*	Viral and chlamydial infection in conditions classified elsewhere and of unspecified site **186**
064	Viral encephalitis transmitted by other and unspecified arthropods **9** , **10** , **33**
070*	Viral hepatitis **83**
070.2*	Viral hepatitis B with hepatic coma **165** , **169**
070.3*	Viral hepatitis B without mention of hepatic coma **165** , **169**
480*	Viral pneumonia **53**
078.1*	Viral warts **108**
054.71	Visceral herpes simplex **78** , **165** , **169** , **230**
085.0	Visceral leishmaniasis (kala-azar) **186**
379.53	Visual deprivation nystagmus **40**
368.13	Visual discomfort **39**
368.14	Visual distortions of shape and size **39**
799.53	Visuospatial deficit **32**
264*	Vitamin A deficiency **231**
264.0	Vitamin A deficiency with conjunctival xerosis **38**
264.1	Vitamin A deficiency with conjunctival xerosis and Bitot's spot **38**
264.3	Vitamin A deficiency with corneal ulceration and xerosis **38**
264.2	Vitamin A deficiency with corneal xerosis **38**
264.4	Vitamin A deficiency with keratomalacia **39**

264.5	Vitamin A deficiency with night blindness **39**
264.6	Vitamin A deficiency with xerophthalmic scars of cornea **39**
268*	Vitamin D deficiency **231**
709.01	Vitiligo **173**
360.04	Vitreous abscess **38**
784.4*	Voice and resonance disorders **47**
958.6	Volkmann's ischemic contracture **101** , **225** , **228**
276.5*	Volume depletion **231**
560.2	Volvulus **167** , **171**
564.3	Vomiting following gastrointestinal surgery **78**
569.87	Vomiting of fecal matter **79**
286.4	Von Willebrand's disease **177**
456.6	Vulval varices **128** , **131**
664.54	Vulvar and perineal hematoma, postpartum condition or complication **153**
664.50	Vulvar and perineal hematoma, unspecified as to episode of care in pregnancy **138** , **145** , **151**
664.51	Vulvar and perineal hematoma, with delivery **138** , **145** , **151**
625.71	Vulvar vestibulitis **131**
625.70	Vulvodynia, unspecified **131**
036.3	Waterhouse-Friderichsen syndrome, meningococcal **165** , **169** , **187**
446.4	Wegener's granulomatosis **97**
066.4*	West Nile fever **185**
040.2	Whipple's disease **78**
033*	Whooping cough **53**
279.12	Wiskott-Aldrich syndrome **176**
040.42	Wound botulism **186**
736.05	Wrist drop (acquired) **21**
374.51	Xanthelasma of eyelid **109**
060*	Yellow fever **185**
117.7	Zygomycosis (Phycomycosis or Mucormycosis) **165** , **169**

Numeric Index to Diseases

001*	Cholera **75**	
002*	Typhoid and paratyphoid fevers **186**	
003.0	Salmonella gastroenteritis **75**	
003.1	Salmonella septicemia **187 , 230**	
003.2*	Localized salmonella infections **230**	
003.20	Unspecified localized salmonella infection **186**	
003.21	Salmonella meningitis **8 , 10 , 33**	
003.22	Salmonella pneumonia **51**	
003.23	Salmonella arthritis **97**	
003.24	Salmonella osteomyelitis **96**	
003.29	Other localized salmonella infections **186**	
003.8	Other specified salmonella infections **186 , 230**	
003.9	Unspecified salmonella infection **186 , 230**	
004*	Shigellosis **75**	
005.0	Staphylococcal food poisoning **75**	
005.1	Botulism food poisoning **186**	
005.2	Food poisoning due to Clostridium perfringens (C. welchii) **75**	
005.3	Food poisoning due to other Clostridia **75**	
005.4	Food poisoning due to Vibrio parahaemolyticus **75**	
005.8*	Other bacterial food poisoning **75**	
005.9	Unspecified food poisoning **77**	
006.0	Acute amebic dysentery without mention of abscess **75**	
006.1	Chronic intestinal amebiasis without mention of abscess **75**	
006.2	Amebic nondysenteric colitis **75**	
006.3	Amebic liver abscess **83**	
006.4	Amebic lung abscess **51**	
006.5	Amebic brain abscess **8 , 10 , 33**	
006.6	Amebic skin ulceration **108**	
006.8	Amebic infection of other sites **186**	
006.9	Unspecified amebiasis **186**	
007.2	Coccidiosis **230**	
007*	Other protozoal intestinal diseases **75**	
008.00	Intestinal infection due to unspecified E. coli **75**	
008.01	Intestinal infection due to enteropathogenic E. coli **75**	
008.02	Intestinal infection due to enterotoxigenic E. coli **75**	
008.03	Intestinal infection due to enteroinvasive E. coli **75**	
008.04	Intestinal infection due to enterohemorrhagic E. coli **75**	
008.09	Intestinal infection due to other intestinal E. coli infections **75**	
008.1	Intestinal infection due to Arizona group of paracolon bacilli **75**	
008.2	Intestinal infection due to aerobacter aerogenes **75**	
008.3	Intestinal infections due to proteus (mirabilis) (morganii) **75**	
008.41	Intestinal infections due to staphylococcus **75**	
008.42	Intestinal infections due to pseudomonas **75**	
008.43	Intestinal infections due to campylobacter **75**	
008.44	Intestinal infections due to yersinia enterocolitica **75**	
008.45	Intestinal infections due to clostridium difficile **75**	
008.46	Intestinal infections due to other anaerobes **75**	
008.47	Intestinal infections due to other gram-negative bacteria **75**	
008.49	Intestinal infection due to other organisms **75**	
008.5	Intestinal infection due to unspecified bacterial enteritis **75**	
008.6*	Intestinal infection, enteritis due to specified virus **77**	
008.8	Intestinal infection due to other organism, NEC **77**	
009*	Ill-defined intestinal infections **77 , 231**	
010*	Primary tuberculous infection **51 , 230**	

011*	Pulmonary tuberculosis **51 , 230**	
012.0*	Tuberculous pleurisy **51**	
012.1*	Tuberculosis of intrathoracic lymph nodes **51**	
012.2*	Isolated tracheal or bronchial tuberculosis **51**	
012.3*	Tuberculous laryngitis **2 , 46**	
012.8*	Other specified respiratory tuberculosis **51**	
012*	Other respiratory tuberculosis **230**	
013*	Tuberculosis of meninges and central nervous system **8 , 10 , 33 , 230**	
014*	Tuberculosis of intestines, peritoneum, and mesenteric glands **75 , 230**	
015.0*	Tuberculosis of vertebral column **96**	
015.02	Tuberculosis of vertebral column, bacteriological or histological examination unknown (at present) **87**	
015.04	Tuberculosis of vertebral column, tubercle bacilli not found (in sputum) by microscopy, but found by bacterial culture **87**	
015.05	Tuberculosis of vertebral column, tubercle bacilli not found by bacteriological examination, but tuberculosis confirmed histologically **87**	
015.1*	Tuberculosis of hip **97**	
015.2*	Tuberculosis of knee **97**	
015.5*	Tuberculosis of limb bones **96**	
015.6*	Tuberculosis of mastoid **46**	
015.7*	Tuberculosis of other specified bone **96**	
015.8*	Tuberculosis of other specified joint **97**	
015.9*	Tuberculosis of unspecified bones and joints **97**	
015*	Tuberculosis of bones and joints **230**	
016.0*	Tuberculosis of kidney **120**	
016.1*	Tuberculosis of bladder **120**	
016.2*	Tuberculosis of ureter **120**	
016.3*	Tuberculosis of other urinary organs **120**	
016.4*	Tuberculosis of epididymis **124**	
016.5*	Tuberculosis of other male genital organs **124**	
016.6*	Tuberculous oophoritis and salpingitis **128 , 130**	
016.7*	Tuberculosis of other female genital organs **128 , 130**	
016.9*	Genitourinary tuberculosis, unspecified **120**	
016*	Tuberculosis of genitourinary system **230**	
017.0*	Tuberculosis of skin and subcutaneous cellular tissue **108**	
017.1*	Erythema nodosum with hypersensitivity reaction in tuberculosis **106**	
017.2*	Tuberculosis of peripheral lymph nodes **177**	
017.3*	Tuberculosis of eye **38**	
017.4*	Tuberculosis of ear **46**	
017.5*	Tuberculosis of thyroid gland **115**	
017.6*	Tuberculosis of adrenal glands **115**	
017.7*	Tuberculosis of spleen **177**	
017.8*	Tuberculosis of esophagus **75**	
017.9*	Tuberculosis of other specified organs **186**	
017*	Tuberculosis of other organs **230**	
018.0*	Acute miliary tuberculosis **186**	
018.8*	Other specified miliary tuberculosis **186**	
018.9*	Unspecified miliary tuberculosis **186**	
018*	Miliary tuberculosis **230**	
020.0	Bubonic plague **186**	
020.1	Cellulocutaneous plague **186**	
020.2	Septicemic plague **187**	

*Code Range

020.3	Primary pneumonic plague **51**	
020.4	Secondary pneumonic plague **51**	
020.5	Pneumonic plague, unspecified **51**	
020.8	Other specified types of plague **186**	
020.9	Unspecified plague **186**	
021.0	Ulceroglandular tularemia **186**	
021.1	Enteric tularemia **75**	
021.2	Pulmonary tularemia **51**	
021.3	Oculoglandular tularemia **186**	
021.8	Other specified tularemia **186**	
021.9	Unspecified tularemia **186**	
022.0	Cutaneous anthrax **108**	
022.1	Pulmonary anthrax **51**	
022.2	Gastrointestinal anthrax **75**	
022.3	Anthrax septicemia **187**	
022.8	Other specified manifestations of anthrax **186**	
022.9	Unspecified anthrax **186**	
023*	Brucellosis **186**	
024	Glanders **186**	
025	Melioidosis **186**	
026*	Rat-bite fever **186**	
027*	Other zoonotic bacterial diseases **186**	
030*	Leprosy **186**	
031.0	Pulmonary diseases due to other mycobacteria **51**	
031.1	Cutaneous diseases due to other mycobacteria **108**	
031.2	Disseminated diseases due to other mycobacteria **186 , 230**	
031.8	Other specified diseases due to other mycobacteria **186 , 230**	
031.9	Unspecified diseases due to mycobacteria **186 , 230**	
032.0	Faucial diphtheria **2 , 46**	
032.1	Nasopharyngeal diphtheria **2 , 47**	
032.2	Anterior nasal diphtheria **2 , 47**	
032.3	Laryngeal diphtheria **2 , 47**	
032.81	Conjunctival diphtheria **38**	
032.82	Diphtheritic myocarditis **68**	
032.83	Diphtheritic peritonitis **75**	
032.84	Diphtheritic cystitis **120**	
032.85	Cutaneous diphtheria **108**	
032.89	Other specified diphtheria **186**	
032.9	Unspecified diphtheria **186**	
033*	Whooping cough **53**	
034.0	Streptococcal sore throat **2 , 46**	
034.1	Scarlet fever **186**	
035	Erysipelas **107**	
036.0	Meningococcal meningitis **8 , 10 , 33**	
036.1	Meningococcal encephalitis **8 , 10 , 33**	
036.2	Meningococcemia **187**	
036.3	Waterhouse-Friderichsen syndrome, meningococcal **165 , 169 , 187**	
036.4*	Meningococcal carditis **165 , 169**	
036.40	Meningococcal carditis, unspecified **68**	
036.41	Meningococcal pericarditis **68**	
036.42	Meningococcal endocarditis **65**	
036.43	Meningococcal myocarditis **68**	
036.81	Meningococcal optic neuritis **38 , 165 , 169**	
036.82	Meningococcal arthropathy **97 , 165 , 169**	
036.89	Other specified meningococcal infections **187**	
036.9	Unspecified meningococcal infection **187**	
037	Tetanus **165 , 169 , 186**	
038*	Septicemia **165 , 169 , 187 , 230**	

039.0	Cutaneous actinomycotic infection **108**	
039.1	Pulmonary actinomycotic infection **51**	
039.2	Abdominal actinomycotic infection **75**	
039.3	Cervicofacial actinomycotic infection **108**	
039.4	Madura foot **108**	
039.8	Actinomycotic infection of other specified sites **186**	
039.9	Actinomycotic infection of unspecified site **186**	
039*	Actinomycotic infections **230**	
040.0	Gas gangrene **165 , 169 , 186**	
040.1	Rhinoscleroma **186**	
040.2	Whipple's disease **78**	
040.3	Necrobacillosis **186**	
040.41	Infant botulism **165 , 169 , 186**	
040.42	Wound botulism **186**	
040.81	Tropical pyomyositis **98**	
040.82	Toxic shock syndrome **186**	
040.89	Other specified bacterial diseases **186**	
041*	Bacterial infection in conditions classified elsewhere and of unspecified site **186**	
042	Human immunodeficiency virus [HIV] **230 , 231**	
045.0*	Acute paralytic poliomyelitis specified as bulbar **8 , 10 , 33**	
045.1*	Acute poliomyelitis with other paralysis **8 , 10 , 33**	
045.2*	Acute nonparalytic poliomyelitis **185**	
045.9*	Acute unspecified poliomyelitis **8 , 10 , 33**	
046.2	Subacute sclerosing panencephalitis **165 , 169**	
046.3	Progressive multifocal leukoencephalopathy **230**	
046.7*	Other specified prion diseases of central nervous system **230**	
046.8	Other specified slow virus infection of central nervous system **230**	
046.9	Unspecified slow virus infection of central nervous system **230**	
046*	Slow virus infections and prion diseases of central nervous system **19**	
047.9	Unspecified viral meningitis **231**	
047*	Meningitis due to enterovirus **21**	
048	Other enterovirus diseases of central nervous system **21**	
049.0	Lymphocytic choriomeningitis **21**	
049.1	Meningitis due to adenovirus **21**	
049.8	Other specified non-arthropod-borne viral diseases of central nervous system **33 , 230**	
049.9	Unspecified non-arthropod-borne viral disease of central nervous system **33 , 230**	
050*	Smallpox **185**	
051.0*	Cowpox and vaccinia not from vaccination **185**	
051.1	Pseudocowpox **108**	
051.2	Contagious pustular dermatitis **108**	
051.9	Unspecified paravaccinia **185**	
052.0	Postvaricella encephalitis **33 , 165 , 169**	
052.1	Varicella (hemorrhagic) pneumonitis **51 , 165 , 169**	
052.2	Postvaricella myelitis **8 , 10 , 33**	
052.7	Chickenpox with other specified complications **165 , 169 , 185**	
052.8	Chickenpox with unspecified complication **165 , 169 , 185**	
052.9	Varicella without mention of complication **165 , 169 , 185**	
053.0	Herpes zoster with meningitis **21 , 165 , 169 , 230**	
053.10	Herpes zoster with unspecified nervous system complication **20 , 165 , 169 , 230**	
053.11	Geniculate herpes zoster **20 , 165 , 169 , 230**	
053.12	Postherpetic trigeminal neuralgia **20 , 165 , 169 , 230**	
053.13	Postherpetic polyneuropathy **20 , 165 , 169 , 230**	
053.14	Herpes zoster myelitis **8 , 10 , 33**	

*Code Range

053.19	Other herpes zoster with nervous system complications **20** , **165** , **169** , **230**	
053.2*****	Herpes zoster with ophthalmic complications **38**	
053.20	Herpes zoster dermatitis of eyelid **165** , **169** , **230**	
053.21	Herpes zoster keratoconjunctivitis **165** , **169** , **230**	
053.22	Herpes zoster iridocyclitis **165** , **169** , **230**	
053.29	Other ophthalmic herpes zoster complications **165** , **169** , **230**	
053.71	Otitis externa due to herpes zoster **47** , **165** , **169** , **230**	
053.79	Other specified herpes zoster complications **165** , **169** , **185** , **230**	
053.8	Unspecified herpes zoster complication **165** , **169** , **185** , **230**	
053.9	Herpes zoster without mention of complication **106** , **165** , **169** , **230**	
054.0	Eczema herpeticum **108** , **165** , **169** , **230**	
054.10	Unspecified genital herpes **124** , **128** , **130** , **230**	
054.11	Herpetic vulvovaginitis **128** , **130** , **230**	
054.12	Herpetic ulceration of vulva **128** , **130** , **230**	
054.13	Herpetic infection of penis **125** , **230**	
054.19	Other genital herpes **125** , **128** , **130** , **230**	
054.2	Herpetic gingivostomatitis **2** , **48** , **165** , **169** , **230**	
054.3	Herpetic meningoencephalitis **8** , **10** , **33** , **165** , **169** , **230**	
054.4*****	Herpes simplex with ophthalmic complications **38** , **165** , **169**	
054.40	Unspecified ophthalmic complication herpes simplex **230**	
054.41	Herpes simplex dermatitis of eyelid **230**	
054.42	Dendritic keratitis **230**	
054.43	Herpes simplex disciform keratitis **230**	
054.44	Herpes simplex iridocyclitis **230**	
054.49	Herpes simplex with other ophthalmic complications **230**	
054.5	Herpetic septicemia **165** , **169** , **187** , **230**	
054.6	Herpetic whitlow **108** , **230**	
054.71	Visceral herpes simplex **78** , **165** , **169** , **230**	
054.72	Herpes simplex meningitis **8** , **10** , **21** , **165** , **169** , **231**	
054.73	Herpes simplex otitis externa **47** , **165** , **169** , **231**	
054.74	Herpes simplex myelitis **8** , **10** , **33**	
054.79	Other specified herpes simplex complications **165** , **169** , **185** , **231**	
054.8	Unspecified herpes simplex complication **165** , **169** , **185** , **231**	
054.9	Herpes simplex without mention of complication **108** , **231**	
055.0	Postmeasles encephalitis **9** , **10** , **33** , **165** , **169**	
055.1	Postmeasles pneumonia **51** , **165** , **169**	
055.2	Postmeasles otitis media **46** , **165** , **169**	
055.7*****	Measles, with other specified complications **165** , **169**	
055.71	Measles keratoconjunctivitis **38**	
055.79	Other specified measles complications **185**	
055.8	Unspecified measles complication **165** , **169** , **185**	
055.9	Measles without mention of complication **185**	
056.0*****	Rubella with neurological complications **165** , **169**	
056.00	Unspecified rubella neurological complication **20**	
056.01	Encephalomyelitis due to rubella **33**	
056.09	Other neurological rubella complications **33**	
056.7*****	Rubella with other specified complications **165** , **169**	
056.71	Arthritis due to rubella **98**	
056.79	Rubella with other specified complications **185**	
056.8	Unspecified rubella complications **165** , **169** , **185**	
056.9	Rubella without mention of complication **185**	
057*****	Other viral exanthemata **185**	
058.10	Roseola infantum, unspecified **165** , **169** , **185**	
058.11	Roseola infantum due to human herpesvirus 6 **165** , **169** , **185**	
058.12	Roseola infantum due to human herpesvirus 7 **165** , **169** , **185**	
058.21	Human herpesvirus 6 encephalitis **9** , **10** , **33** , **165** , **169** , **231**	

058.29	Other human herpesvirus encephalitis **9** , **10** , **33** , **165** , **169** , **231**
058.8*****	Other human herpesvirus infections **108**
059*****	Other poxvirus infections **185**
060*****	Yellow fever **185**
061	Dengue **185**
062*****	Mosquito-borne viral encephalitis **9** , **10** , **33**
063*****	Tick-borne viral encephalitis **9** , **10** , **33**
064	Viral encephalitis transmitted by other and unspecified arthropods **9** , **10** , **33**
065*****	Arthropod-borne hemorrhagic fever **185**
066.0	Phlebotomus fever **185**
066.1	Tick-borne fever **185**
066.2	Venezuelan equine fever **9** , **10** , **33**
066.3	Other mosquito-borne fever **185**
066.4*****	West Nile fever **185**
066.8	Other specified arthropod-borne viral diseases **185**
066.9	Unspecified arthropod-borne viral disease **185**
070.2*****	Viral hepatitis B with hepatic coma **165** , **169**
070.3*****	Viral hepatitis B without mention of hepatic coma **165** , **169**
070.4*****	Other specified viral hepatitis with hepatic coma **165** , **169**
070.5*****	Other specified viral hepatitis without mention of hepatic coma **165** , **169**
070.6	Unspecified viral hepatitis with hepatic coma **165** , **169**
070.9	Unspecified viral hepatitis without mention of hepatic coma **165** , **169**
070*****	Viral hepatitis **83**
071	Rabies **9** , **10** , **33**
072.0	Mumps orchitis **125** , **165** , **169**
072.1	Mumps meningitis **9** , **10** , **21** , **165** , **169**
072.2	Mumps encephalitis **9** , **10** , **33** , **165** , **169**
072.3	Mumps pancreatitis **83** , **165** , **169**
072.7*****	Mumps with other specified complications **165** , **169**
072.71	Mumps hepatitis **83**
072.72	Mumps polyneuropathy **20**
072.79	Mumps with other specified complications **185**
072.8	Unspecified mumps complication **165** , **169** , **185**
072.9	Mumps without mention of complication **185**
073.0	Ornithosis with pneumonia **51**
073.7	Ornithosis with other specified complications **185**
073.8	Ornithosis with unspecified complication **185**
073.9	Unspecified ornithosis **185**
074.0	Herpangina **2** , **46**
074.1	Epidemic pleurodynia **53**
074.20	Coxsackie carditis, unspecified **68**
074.21	Coxsackie pericarditis **68**
074.22	Coxsackie endocarditis **67**
074.23	Coxsackie myocarditis **68**
074.3	Hand, foot, and mouth disease **185**
074.8	Other specified diseases due to Coxsackievirus **185**
075	Infectious mononucleosis **185**
076*****	Trachoma **38**
077*****	Other diseases of conjunctiva due to viruses and Chlamydiae **38**
078.0	Molluscum contagiosum **108**
078.1*****	Viral warts **108**
078.2	Sweating fever **186**
078.3	Cat-scratch disease **177**
078.4	Foot and mouth disease **186**
078.5	Cytomegaloviral disease **186** , **231**
078.6	Hemorrhagic nephrosonephritis **120**

078.7	Arenaviral hemorrhagic fever	**186**
078.81	Epidemic vertigo	**32**
078.82	Epidemic vomiting syndrome	**77**
078.88	Other specified diseases due to Chlamydiae	**186**
078.89	Other specified diseases due to viruses	**186**
079.6	Respiratory syncytial virus (RSV)	**165 , 169**
079.9*	Unspecified viral and chlamydial infections, in conditions classified elsewhere and of unspecified site	**231**
079*	Viral and chlamydial infection in conditions classified elsewhere and of unspecified site	**186**
080	Louse-borne (epidemic) typhus	**186**
081*	Other typhus	**186**
082*	Tick-borne rickettsioses	**186**
083*	Other rickettsioses	**186**
084*	Malaria	**186**
085.0	Visceral leishmaniasis (kala-azar)	**186**
085.1	Cutaneous leishmaniasis, urban	**108**
085.2	Cutaneous leishmaniasis, Asian desert	**108**
085.3	Cutaneous leishmaniasis, Ethiopian	**108**
085.4	Cutaneous leishmaniasis, American	**108**
085.5	Mucocutaneous leishmaniasis, (American)	**108**
085.9	Unspecified leishmaniasis	**186**
086.0	Chagas' disease with heart involvement	**68**
086.1	Chagas' disease with other organ involvement	**186**
086.2	Chagas' disease without mention of organ involvement	**186**
086.3	Gambian trypanosomiasis	**186**
086.4	Rhodesian trypanosomiasis	**186**
086.5	African trypanosomiasis, unspecified	**186**
086.9	Unspecified trypanosomiasis	**186**
087*	Relapsing fever	**186**
088*	Other arthropod-borne diseases	**186**
090.0	Early congenital syphilis, symptomatic	**186**
090.1	Early congenital syphilis, latent	**186**
090.2	Unspecified early congenital syphilis	**186**
090.3	Syphilitic interstitial keratitis	**38**
090.4*	Juvenile neurosyphilis	**33**
090.5	Other late congenital syphilis, symptomatic	**186**
090.6	Late congenital syphilis, latent	**186**
090.7	Late congenital syphilis, unspecified	**186**
090.9	Congenital syphilis, unspecified	**186**
091.0	Genital syphilis (primary)	**125 , 128 , 130**
091.1	Primary anal syphilis	**78**
091.2	Other primary syphilis	**186**
091.3	Secondary syphilis of skin or mucous membranes	**108**
091.4	Adenopathy due to secondary syphilis	**177**
091.5*	Early syphilis, uveitis due to secondary syphilis	**38**
091.61	Early syphilis, secondary syphilitic periostitis	**96**
091.62	Early syphilis, secondary syphilitic hepatitis	**83**
091.69	Early syphilis, secondary syphilis of other viscera	**78**
091.7	Early syphilis, secondary syphilis, relapse	**186**
091.81	Early syphilis, acute syphilitic meningitis (secondary)	**9 , 10 , 33**
091.82	Early syphilis, syphilitic alopecia	**108**
091.89	Early syphilis, other forms of secondary syphilis	**186**
091.9	Early syphilis, unspecified secondary syphilis	**186**
092*	Early syphilis, latent	**186**
093.0	Aneurysm of aorta, specified as syphilitic	**67**
093.1	Syphilitic aortitis	**67**
093.20	Unspecified syphilitic endocarditis of valve	**65**
093.21	Syphilitic endocarditis, mitral valve	**67**

093.22	Syphilitic endocarditis, aortic valve	**67**
093.23	Syphilitic endocarditis, tricuspid valve	**67**
093.24	Syphilitic endocarditis, pulmonary valve	**67**
093.8*	Other specified cardiovascular syphilis	**68**
093.9	Unspecified cardiovascular syphilis	**68**
094.0	Tabes dorsalis	**19**
094.1	General paresis	**19**
094.2	Syphilitic meningitis	**9 , 10 , 33**
094.3	Asymptomatic neurosyphilis	**33**
094.81	Syphilitic encephalitis	**9 , 10 , 33**
094.82	Syphilitic Parkinsonism	**19**
094.83	Syphilitic disseminated retinochoroiditis	**38**
094.84	Syphilitic optic atrophy	**38**
094.85	Syphilitic retrobulbar neuritis	**19**
094.86	Syphilitic acoustic neuritis	**47**
094.87	Syphilitic ruptured cerebral aneurysm	**8 , 32**
094.89	Other specified neurosyphilis	**19**
094.9	Unspecified neurosyphilis	**19**
095.0	Syphilitic episcleritis	**38**
095.1	Syphilis of lung	**51**
095.2	Syphilitic peritonitis	**75**
095.3	Syphilis of liver	**83**
095.4	Syphilis of kidney	**120**
095.5	Syphilis of bone	**96**
095.6	Syphilis of muscle	**98**
095.7	Syphilis of synovium, tendon, and bursa	**98**
095.8	Other specified forms of late symptomatic syphilis	**186**
095.9	Unspecified late symptomatic syphilis	**186**
096	Late syphilis, latent	**186**
097*	Other and unspecified syphilis	**186**
098.0	Gonococcal infection (acute) of lower genitourinary tract	**125 , 128 , 130**
098.10	Gonococcal infection (acute) of upper genitourinary tract, site unspecified	**125 , 128 , 130**
098.11	Gonococcal cystitis (acute)	**120**
098.12	Gonococcal prostatitis (acute)	**125**
098.13	Gonococcal epididymo-orchitis (acute)	**125**
098.14	Gonococcal seminal vesiculitis (acute)	**125**
098.15	Gonococcal cervicitis (acute)	**128 , 130**
098.16	Gonococcal endometritis (acute)	**128 , 130**
098.17	Gonococcal salpingitis, specified as acute	**128 , 130**
098.19	Other gonococcal infections (acute) of upper genitourinary tract	**125 , 128 , 130**
098.2	Gonococcal infections, chronic, of lower genitourinary tract	**125 , 128 , 130**
098.30	Chronic gonococcal infection of upper genitourinary tract, site unspecified	**120**
098.31	Gonococcal cystitis, chronic	**120**
098.32	Gonococcal prostatitis, chronic	**125**
098.33	Gonococcal epididymo-orchitis, chronic	**125**
098.34	Gonococcal seminal vesiculitis, chronic	**125**
098.35	Gonococcal cervicitis, chronic	**128 , 130**
098.36	Gonococcal endometritis, chronic	**128 , 130**
098.37	Gonococcal salpingitis (chronic)	**128 , 130**
098.39	Other chronic gonococcal infections of upper genitourinary tract	**125 , 128 , 130**
098.4*	Gonococcal infection of eye	**38**
098.50	Gonococcal arthritis	**97**
098.51	Gonococcal synovitis and tenosynovitis	**97**
098.52	Gonococcal bursitis	**97**

*Code Range

098.53	Gonococcal spondylitis **96**	
098.59	Other gonococcal infection of joint **97**	
098.6	Gonococcal infection of pharynx **2 , 46**	
098.7	Gonococcal infection of anus and rectum **78**	
098.81	Gonococcal keratosis (blennorrhagica) **38**	
098.82	Gonococcal meningitis **9 , 10 , 33**	
098.83	Gonococcal pericarditis **68**	
098.84	Gonococcal endocarditis **65**	
098.85	Other gonococcal heart disease **68**	
098.86	Gonococcal peritonitis **75**	
098.89	Gonococcal infection of other specified sites **186**	
099.0	Chancroid **125 , 128 , 131**	
099.1	Lymphogranuloma venereum **125 , 128 , 131**	
099.2	Granuloma inguinale **125 , 128 , 131**	
099.3	Reiter's disease **97**	
099.4*	Other nongonococcal urethritis (NGU) **125 , 128 , 131**	
099.50	Chlamydia trachomatis infection of unspecified site **125 , 128 , 131**	
099.51	Chlamydia trachomatis infection of pharynx **2 , 46**	
099.52	Chlamydia trachomatis infection of anus and rectum **78**	
099.53	Chlamydia trachomatis infection of lower genitourinary sites **125 , 128 , 131**	
099.54	Chlamydia trachomatis infection of other genitourinary sites **120**	
099.55	Chlamydia trachomatis infection of unspecified genitourinary site **125 , 128 , 131**	
099.56	Chlamydia trachomatis infection of peritoneum **78**	
099.59	Chlamydia trachomatis infection of other specified site **125 , 128 , 131**	
099.8	Other specified venereal diseases **125 , 128 , 131**	
099.9	Unspecified venereal disease **125 , 128 , 131**	
100.0	Leptospirosis icterohemorrhagica **186**	
100.8*	Other specified leptospiral infections **9 , 10 , 33**	
100.9	Unspecified leptospirosis **186**	
101	Vincent's angina **2 , 46**	
102.0	Initial lesions of yaws **108**	
102.1	Multiple papillomata and wet crab yaws due to yaws **108**	
102.2	Other early skin lesions due to yaws **108**	
102.3	Hyperkeratosis due to yaws **108**	
102.4	Gummata and ulcers due to yaws **108**	
102.5	Gangosa due to yaws **2 , 47**	
102.6	Bone and joint lesions due to yaws **97**	
102.7	Other manifestations due to yaws **186**	
102.8	Latent yaws **186**	
102.9	Unspecified yaws **186**	
103.0	Primary lesions of pinta **108**	
103.1	Intermediate lesions of pinta **108**	
103.2	Late lesions of pinta **186**	
103.3	Mixed lesions of pinta **108**	
103.9	Unspecified pinta **186**	
104*	Other spirochetal infection **186**	
110*	Dermatophytosis **108 , 231**	
111*	Dermatomycosis, other and unspecified **108 , 231**	
112.0	Candidiasis of mouth **2 , 48 , 231**	
112.1	Candidiasis of vulva and vagina **128 , 131**	
112.2	Candidiasis of other urogenital sites **125 , 128 , 131**	
112.3	Candidiasis of skin and nails **108 , 231**	
112.4	Candidiasis of lung **51 , 165 , 169 , 231**	
112.5	Disseminated candidiasis **165 , 169 , 186 , 231**	
112.8*	Candidiasis of other specified sites **231**	
112.81	Candidal endocarditis **65 , 165 , 169**	

112.82	Candidal otitis externa **47 , 165 , 169**
112.83	Candidal meningitis **9 , 10 , 33 , 165 , 169**
112.84	Candidiasis of the esophagus **75 , 165 , 169**
112.85	Candidiasis of the intestine **77 , 165 , 169**
112.89	Other candidiasis of other specified sites **186**
112.9	Candidiasis of unspecified site **186 , 231**
114.0	Primary coccidioidomycosis (pulmonary) **51**
114.1	Primary extrapulmonary coccidioidomycosis **108**
114.2	Coccidioidal meningitis **9 , 10 , 33 , 165 , 169**
114.3	Other forms of progressive coccidioidomycosis **165 , 169 , 186**
114.4	Chronic pulmonary coccidioidomycosis **51**
114.5	Unspecified pulmonary coccidioidomycosis **51**
114.9	Unspecified coccidioidomycosis **186**
114*	Coccidioidomycosis **231**
115.00	Histoplasma capsulatum, without mention of manifestation **186**
115.01	Histoplasma capsulatum meningitis **9 , 10 , 33 , 165 , 169**
115.02	Histoplasma capsulatum retinitis **38 , 165 , 169**
115.03	Histoplasma capsulatum pericarditis **68 , 165 , 169**
115.04	Histoplasma capsulatum endocarditis **65 , 165 , 169**
115.05	Histoplasma capsulatum pneumonia **51 , 165 , 169**
115.09	Histoplasma capsulatum, with mention of other manifestation **186**
115.10	Histoplasma duboisii, without mention of manifestation **186**
115.11	Histoplasma duboisii meningitis **9 , 10 , 33 , 165 , 169**
115.12	Histoplasma duboisii retinitis **38 , 165 , 169**
115.13	Histoplasma duboisii pericarditis **68 , 165 , 169**
115.14	Histoplasma duboisii endocarditis **65 , 165 , 169**
115.15	Histoplasma duboisii pneumonia **51 , 165 , 169**
115.19	Histoplasma duboisii with mention of other manifestation **186**
115.90	Unspecified Histoplasmosis without mention of manifestation **186**
115.91	Unspecified Histoplasmosis meningitis **9 , 10 , 33 , 165 , 169**
115.92	Unspecified Histoplasmosis retinitis **38 , 165 , 169**
115.93	Unspecified Histoplasmosis pericarditis **68 , 165 , 169**
115.94	Unspecified Histoplasmosis endocarditis **65 , 165 , 169**
115.95	Unspecified Histoplasmosis pneumonia **51 , 165 , 169**
115.99	Unspecified Histoplasmosis with mention of other manifestation **186**
115*	Histoplasmosis **231**
116.0	Blastomycosis **165 , 169**
116.1	Paracoccidioidomycosis **165 , 169**
116*	Blastomycotic infection **186**
117.3	Aspergillosis **165 , 169**
117.4	Mycotic mycetomas **165 , 169**
117.5	Cryptococcosis **165 , 169 , 231**
117.6	Allescheriosis (Petriellidiosis) **165 , 169**
117.7	Zygomycosis (Phycomycosis or Mucormycosis) **165 , 169**
117*	Other mycoses **186**
118	Opportunistic mycoses **165 , 169 , 186 , 231**
120.0	Schistosomiasis due to schistosoma haematobium **120**
120.1	Schistosomiasis due to schistosoma mansoni **83**
120.2	Schistosomiasis due to schistosoma japonicum **186**
120.3	Cutaneous schistosomiasis **108**
120.8	Other specified schistosomiasis **186**
120.9	Unspecified schistosomiasis **186**
121.0	Opisthorchiasis **83**
121.1	Clonorchiasis **83**
121.2	Paragonimiasis **51**
121.3	Fascioliasis **83**

Numeric Index to Diseases

Numeric Index to Diseases

121.4	Fasciolopsiasis **83**	
121.5	Metagonimiasis **186**	
121.6	Heterophyiasis **186**	
121.8	Other specified trematode infections **186**	
121.9	Unspecified trematode infection **187**	
122.0	Echinococcus granulosus infection of liver **83**	
122.1	Echinococcus granulosus infection of lung **51**	
122.2	Echinococcus granulosus infection of thyroid **115**	
122.3	Other echinococcus granulosus infection **187**	
122.4	Unspecified echinococcus granulosus infection **187**	
122.5	Echinococcus multilocularis infection of liver **83**	
122.6	Other echinococcus multilocularis infection **187**	
122.7	Unspecified echinococcus multilocularis infection **187**	
122.8	Unspecified echinococcus of liver **83**	
122.9	Other and unspecified echinococcosis **187**	
123.0	Taenia solium infection, intestinal form **77**	
123.1	Cysticercosis **75**	
123.2	Taenia saginata infection **77**	
123.3	Taeniasis, unspecified **77**	
123.4	Diphyllobothriasis, intestinal **77**	
123.5	Sparganosis (larval diphyllobothriasis) **75**	
123.6	Hymenolepiasis **75**	
123.8	Other specified cestode infection **75**	
123.9	Unspecified cestode infection **76**	
124	Trichinosis **187**	
125*	Filarial infection and dracontiasis **187**	
126*	Ancylostomiasis and necatoriasis **76**	
127.0	Ascariasis **77**	
127.1	Anisakiasis **77**	
127.2	Strongyloidiasis **78 , 231**	
127.3	Trichuriasis **78**	
127.4	Enterobiasis **78**	
127.5	Capillariasis **78**	
127.6	Trichostrongyliasis **78**	
127.7	Other specified intestinal helminthiasis **78**	
127.8	Mixed intestinal helminthiasis **187**	
127.9	Unspecified intestinal helminthiasis **78**	
128*	Other and unspecified helminthiases **187**	
129	Unspecified intestinal parasitism **78**	
130.0	Meningoencephalitis due to toxoplasmosis **9 , 10 , 33 , 165 , 169**	
130.1	Conjunctivitis due to toxoplasmosis **38 , 165 , 169**	
130.2	Chorioretinitis due to toxoplasmosis **38 , 165 , 169**	
130.3	Myocarditis due to toxoplasmosis **68 , 165 , 169**	
130.4	Pneumonitis due to toxoplasmosis **51 , 165 , 169**	
130.5	Hepatitis due to toxoplasmosis **83 , 165 , 169**	
130.7	Toxoplasmosis of other specified sites **165 , 169 , 187**	
130.8	Multisystemic disseminated toxoplasmosis **165 , 169 , 187**	
130.9	Unspecified toxoplasmosis **187**	
130*	Toxoplasmosis **231**	
131.00	Unspecified urogenital trichomoniasis **125 , 128 , 131**	
131.01	Trichomonal vulvovaginitis **128 , 131**	
131.02	Trichomonal urethritis **125 , 128 , 131**	
131.03	Trichomonal prostatitis **125**	
131.09	Other urogenital trichomoniasis **125 , 128 , 131**	
131.8	Trichomoniasis of other specified sites **187**	
131.9	Unspecified trichomoniasis **187**	
132*	Pediculosis and phthirus infestation **108**	
133*	Acariasis **109**	

134*	Other infestation **109**	
135	Sarcoidosis **53**	
136.0	Ainhum **187**	
136.1	Behcet's syndrome **97**	
136.2*	Specific infections by free-living amebae **187**	
136.3	Pneumocystosis **51 , 165 , 169 , 231**	
136.4	Psorospermiasis **187**	
136.5	Sarcosporidiosis **187**	
136.8	Other specified infectious and parasitic diseases **187 , 231**	
136.9	Unspecified infectious and parasitic diseases **187**	
137.0	Late effects of respiratory or unspecified tuberculosis **53**	
137.1	Late effects of central nervous system tuberculosis **32**	
137.2	Late effects of genitourinary tuberculosis **120**	
137.3	Late effects of tuberculosis of bones and joints **100**	
137.4	Late effects of tuberculosis of other specified organs **187**	
138	Late effects of acute poliomyelitis **32**	
139.0	Late effects of viral encephalitis **32**	
139.1	Late effects of trachoma **38**	
139.8	Late effects of other and unspecified infectious and parasitic diseases **187**	
140*	Malignant neoplasm of lip **2 , 46**	
141*	Malignant neoplasm of tongue **2 , 46**	
142*	Malignant neoplasm of major salivary glands **2 , 46**	
143*	Malignant neoplasm of gum **2 , 46**	
144*	Malignant neoplasm of floor of mouth **2 , 46**	
145*	Malignant neoplasm of other and unspecified parts of mouth **2 , 46**	
146*	Malignant neoplasm of oropharynx **2 , 46**	
147*	Malignant neoplasm of nasopharynx **2 , 46**	
148*	Malignant neoplasm of hypopharynx **2 , 46**	
149*	Malignant neoplasm of other and ill-defined sites within the lip, oral cavity, and pharynx **2 , 46**	
150*	Malignant neoplasm of esophagus **76**	
151*	Malignant neoplasm of stomach **76**	
152*	Malignant neoplasm of small intestine, including duodenum **76**	
153.5	Malignant neoplasm of appendix **73**	
153*	Malignant neoplasm of colon **76**	
154*	Malignant neoplasm of rectum, rectosigmoid junction, and anus **76**	
155*	Malignant neoplasm of liver and intrahepatic bile ducts **82**	
156*	Malignant neoplasm of gallbladder and extrahepatic bile ducts **82**	
157*	Malignant neoplasm of pancreas **82**	
158.0	Malignant neoplasm of retroperitoneum **181 , 182**	
158.8	Malignant neoplasm of specified parts of peritoneum **76**	
158.9	Malignant neoplasm of peritoneum, unspecified **76**	
159.0	Malignant neoplasm of intestinal tract, part unspecified **76**	
159.1	Malignant neoplasm of spleen, not elsewhere classified **179 , 182**	
159.8	Malignant neoplasm of other sites of digestive system and intra-abdominal organs **76**	
159.9	Malignant neoplasm of ill-defined sites of digestive organs and peritoneum **76**	
160*	Malignant neoplasm of nasal cavities, middle ear, and accessory sinuses **2 , 46**	
161*	Malignant neoplasm of larynx **2 , 46**	
162*	Malignant neoplasm of trachea, bronchus, and lung **52**	
163*	Malignant neoplasm of pleura **52**	
164.0	Malignant neoplasm of thymus **181 , 182**	
164.1	Malignant neoplasm of heart **68**	
164.2	Malignant neoplasm of anterior mediastinum **52**	

*Code Range

164.3	Malignant neoplasm of posterior mediastinum **52**	
164.8	Malignant neoplasm of other parts of mediastinum **52**	
164.9	Malignant neoplasm of mediastinum, part unspecified **52**	
165.0	Malignant neoplasm of upper respiratory tract, part unspecified **2 , 46**	
165.8	Malignant neoplasm of other sites within the respiratory system and intrathoracic organs **52**	
165.9	Malignant neoplasm of ill-defined sites within the respiratory system **52**	
170.1	Malignant neoplasm of mandible **2**	
170.2	Malignant neoplasm of vertebral column, excluding sacrum and coccyx **87**	
170*	Malignant neoplasm of bone and articular cartilage **97**	
171*	Malignant neoplasm of connective and other soft tissue **97**	
172.0	Malignant melanoma of skin of lip **106**	
172.1	Malignant melanoma of skin of eyelid, including canthus **38**	
172.2	Malignant melanoma of skin of ear and external auditory canal **106**	
172.3	Malignant melanoma of skin of other and unspecified parts of face **106**	
172.4	Malignant melanoma of skin of scalp and neck **106**	
172.5	Malignant melanoma of skin of trunk, except scrotum **106**	
172.6	Malignant melanoma of skin of upper limb, including shoulder **106**	
172.7	Malignant melanoma of skin of lower limb, including hip **106**	
172.8	Malignant melanoma of other specified sites of skin **106**	
172.9	Melanoma of skin, site unspecified **106**	
173.0*	Other and unspecified malignant neoplasm of skin of lip **2 , 109**	
173.1*	Other and unspecified malignant neoplasm of eyelid, including canthus **38**	
173.2*	Other and unspecified malignant neoplasm of skin of ear and external auditory canal **109**	
173.3*	Other and unspecified malignant neoplasm of skin of other and unspecified parts of face **109**	
173.4*	Other and unspecified malignant neoplasm of scalp and skin of neck **109**	
173.5*	Other and unspecified malignant neoplasm of skin of trunk, except scrotum **109**	
173.6*	Other and unspecified malignant neoplasm of skin of upper limb, including shoulder **109**	
173.7*	Other and unspecified malignant neoplasm of skin of lower limb, including hip **109**	
173.8*	Other and unspecified malignant neoplasm of other specified sites of skin **109**	
173.9*	Other and unspecified malignant neoplasm of skin, site unspecified **109**	
174*	Malignant neoplasm of female breast **105 , 106**	
175*	Malignant neoplasm of male breast **105 , 106**	
176.0	Kaposi's sarcoma of skin **109**	
176.1	Kaposi's sarcoma of soft tissue **109**	
176.2	Kaposi's sarcoma of palate **2 , 46**	
176.3	Kaposi's sarcoma of gastrointestinal sites **76**	
176.4	Kaposi's sarcoma of lung **52**	
176.5	Kaposi's sarcoma of lymph nodes **179 , 182**	
176.8	Kaposi's sarcoma of other specified sites **109**	
176.9	Kaposi's sarcoma of unspecified site **109**	
176*	Kaposi's sarcoma **231**	
179	Malignant neoplasm of uterus, part unspecified **127 , 130**	
180*	Malignant neoplasm of cervix uteri **127 , 130**	
181	Malignant neoplasm of placenta **127 , 130**	
182*	Malignant neoplasm of body of uterus **127 , 130**	

183*	Malignant neoplasm of ovary and other uterine adnexa **127 , 130**
184*	Malignant neoplasm of other and unspecified female genital organs **127 , 130**
185	Malignant neoplasm of prostate **123 , 124**
186*	Malignant neoplasm of testis **123 , 124**
187*	Malignant neoplasm of penis and other male genital organs **123 , 124**
188*	Malignant neoplasm of bladder **117 , 120**
189*	Malignant neoplasm of kidney and other and unspecified urinary organs **117 , 120**
190*	Malignant neoplasm of eye **38**
191*	Malignant neoplasm of brain **19**
192*	Malignant neoplasm of other and unspecified parts of nervous system **19**
193	Malignant neoplasm of thyroid gland **2 , 115**
194.0	Malignant neoplasm of adrenal gland **115**
194.1	Malignant neoplasm of parathyroid gland **115**
194.3	Malignant neoplasm of pituitary gland and craniopharyngeal duct **115**
194.4	Malignant neoplasm of pineal gland **19**
194.5	Malignant neoplasm of carotid body **19**
194.6	Malignant neoplasm of aortic body and other paraganglia **19**
194.8	Malignant neoplasm of other endocrine glands and related structures **115**
194.9	Malignant neoplasm of endocrine gland, site unspecified **115**
195.0	Malignant neoplasm of head, face, and neck **2 , 46**
195.1	Malignant neoplasm of thorax **52**
195.2	Malignant neoplasm of abdomen **76**
195.3	Malignant neoplasm of pelvis **123 , 124 , 127 , 130**
195.4	Malignant neoplasm of upper limb **181 , 182**
195.5	Malignant neoplasm of lower limb **181 , 182**
195.8	Malignant neoplasm of other specified sites **181 , 182**
196.0	Secondary and unspecified malignant neoplasm of lymph nodes of head, face, and neck **2**
196*	Secondary and unspecified malignant neoplasm of lymph nodes **179 , 182**
197.0	Secondary malignant neoplasm of lung **52**
197.1	Secondary malignant neoplasm of mediastinum **52**
197.2	Secondary malignant neoplasm of pleura **52**
197.3	Secondary malignant neoplasm of other respiratory organs **52**
197.4	Secondary malignant neoplasm of small intestine including duodenum **76**
197.5	Secondary malignant neoplasm of large intestine and rectum **76**
197.6	Secondary malignant neoplasm of retroperitoneum and peritoneum **76**
197.7	Secondary malignant neoplasm of liver **82**
197.8	Secondary malignant neoplasm of other digestive organs and spleen **76**
198.0	Secondary malignant neoplasm of kidney **117 , 120**
198.1	Secondary malignant neoplasm of other urinary organs **117 , 120**
198.2	Secondary malignant neoplasm of skin **105 , 106**
198.3	Secondary malignant neoplasm of brain and spinal cord **19**
198.4	Secondary malignant neoplasm of other parts of nervous system **19**
198.5	Secondary malignant neoplasm of bone and bone marrow **87 , 97**
198.6	Secondary malignant neoplasm of ovary **127 , 130**
198.7	Secondary malignant neoplasm of adrenal gland **115**
198.81	Secondary malignant neoplasm of breast **105 , 106**

198.82	Secondary malignant neoplasm of genital organs **123** , **124** , **127** , **130**	
198.89	Secondary malignant neoplasm of other specified sites **181** , **182**	
199.0	Disseminated malignant neoplasm **181**	
199.1	Other malignant neoplasm of unspecified site **181**	
199.2	Malignant neoplasm associated with transplanted organ **181**	
199*	Malignant neoplasm without specification of site **182**	
200.0*	Reticulosarcoma **231**	
200.01	Reticulosarcoma of lymph nodes of head, face, and neck **2**	
200.11	Lymphosarcoma of lymph nodes of head, face, and neck **2**	
200.2*	Burkitt's tumor or lymphoma **231**	
200.21	Burkitt's tumor or lymphoma of lymph nodes of head, face, and neck **2**	
200.3*	Marginal zone lymphoma **231**	
200.4*	Mantle cell lymphoma **231**	
200.5*	Primary central nervous system lymphoma **231**	
200.6*	Anaplastic large cell lymphoma **231**	
200.7*	Large cell lymphoma **231**	
200.8*	Other named variants of lymphosarcoma and reticulosarcoma **231**	
200.81	Other named variants of lymphosarcoma and reticulosarcoma of lymph nodes of head, face, and neck **2**	
200*	Lymphosarcoma and reticulosarcoma and other specified malignant tumors of lymphatic tissue **179** , **182**	
201.01	Hodgkin's paragranuloma of lymph nodes of head, face, and neck **2**	
201.11	Hodgkin's granuloma of lymph nodes of head, face, and neck **2**	
201.21	Hodgkin's sarcoma of lymph nodes of head, face, and neck **2**	
201.41	Hodgkin's disease, lymphocytic-histiocytic predominance of lymph nodes of head, face, and neck **2**	
201.51	Hodgkin's disease, nodular sclerosis, of lymph nodes of head, face, and neck **2**	
201.61	Hodgkin's disease, mixed cellularity, involving lymph nodes of head, face, and neck **2**	
201.71	Hodgkin's disease, lymphocytic depletion, of lymph nodes of head, face, and neck **2**	
201.91	Hodgkin's disease, unspecified type, of lymph nodes of head, face, and neck **2**	
201*	Hodgkin's disease **179** , **182**	
202.0*	Nodular lymphoma **179** , **182**	
202.01	Nodular lymphoma of lymph nodes of head, face, and neck **2**	
202.1*	Mycosis fungoides **179** , **182**	
202.11	Mycosis fungoides of lymph nodes of head, face, and neck **2**	
202.2*	Sezary's disease **179** , **182**	
202.21	Sezary's disease of lymph nodes of head, face, and neck **3**	
202.3*	Malignant histiocytosis **179** , **182**	
202.31	Malignant histiocytosis of lymph nodes of head, face, and neck **3**	
202.4*	Leukemic reticuloendotheliosis **179** , **182**	
202.41	Leukemic reticuloendotheliosis of lymph nodes of head, face, and neck **3**	
202.5*	Letterer-Siwe disease **181** , **182**	
202.51	Letterer-Siwe disease of lymph nodes of head, face, and neck **3**	
202.6*	Malignant mast cell tumors **179** , **182**	
202.61	Malignant mast cell tumors of lymph nodes of head, face, and neck **3**	
202.7*	Peripheral T-cell lymphoma **179** , **182** , **231**	
202.8*	Other malignant lymphomas **179** , **182** , **231**	
202.81	Other malignant lymphomas of lymph nodes of head, face, and neck **3**	
202.9*	Other and unspecified malignant neoplasms of lymphoid and histiocytic tissue **179** , **182**	

202.91	Other and unspecified malignant neoplasms of lymphoid and histiocytic tissue of lymph nodes of head, face, and neck **3**	
203*	Multiple myeloma and immunoproliferative neoplasms **179** , **182**	
204.0*	Acute lymphoid leukemia **181** , **182**	
204.1*	Chronic lymphoid leukemia **182**	
204.2*	Subacute lymphoid leukemia **182**	
204.8*	Other lymphoid leukemia **182**	
204.9*	Unspecified lymphoid leukemia **182**	
204*	Lymphoid leukemia **179**	
205.0*	Acute myeloid leukemia **181** , **182**	
205.1*	Chronic myeloid leukemia **182**	
205.2*	Subacute myeloid leukemia **182**	
205.3*	Myeloid sarcoma **182**	
205.8*	Other myeloid leukemia **182**	
205.9*	Unspecified myeloid leukemia **182**	
205*	Myeloid leukemia **179**	
206.0*	Acute monocytic leukemia **181** , **182**	
206.1*	Chronic monocytic leukemia **182**	
206.2*	Subacute monocytic leukemia **182**	
206.8*	Other monocytic leukemia **182**	
206.9*	Unspecified monocytic leukemia **182**	
206*	Monocytic leukemia **179**	
207.0*	Acute erythremia and erythroleukemia **181** , **182**	
207.1*	Chronic erythremia **182**	
207.2*	Megakaryocytic leukemia **182**	
207.8*	Other specified leukemia **182**	
207*	Other specified leukemia **179**	
208.0*	Acute leukemia of unspecified cell type **181** , **182**	
208.1*	Chronic leukemia of unspecified cell type **182**	
208.2*	Subacute leukemia of unspecified cell type **182**	
208.8*	Other leukemia of unspecified cell type **182**	
208.9*	Unspecified leukemia **182**	
208*	Leukemia of unspecified cell type **179**	
209.0*	Malignant carcinoid tumors of the small intestine **76**	
209.1*	Malignant carcinoid tumors of the appendix, large intestine, and rectum **76**	
209.11	Malignant carcinoid tumor of the appendix **73**	
209.20	Malignant carcinoid tumor of unknown primary site **181** , **182**	
209.21	Malignant carcinoid tumor of the bronchus and lung **52**	
209.22	Malignant carcinoid tumor of the thymus **181** , **182**	
209.23	Malignant carcinoid tumor of the stomach **76**	
209.24	Malignant carcinoid tumor of the kidney **117** , **120**	
209.25	Malignant carcinoid tumor of foregut, not otherwise specified **76**	
209.26	Malignant carcinoid tumor of midgut, not otherwise specified **76**	
209.27	Malignant carcinoid tumor of hindgut, not otherwise specified **76**	
209.29	Malignant carcinoid tumor of other sites **181** , **182**	
209.30	Malignant poorly differentiated neuroendocrine carcinoma, any site **181** , **182**	
209.31	Merkel cell carcinoma of the face **106**	
209.32	Merkel cell carcinoma of the scalp and neck **106**	
209.33	Merkel cell carcinoma of the upper limb **106**	
209.34	Merkel cell carcinoma of the lower limb **106**	
209.35	Merkel cell carcinoma of the trunk **106**	
209.36	Merkel cell carcinoma of other sites **106**	
209.4*	Benign carcinoid tumors of the small intestine **78**	
209.5*	Benign carcinoid tumors of the appendix, large intestine, and rectum **78**	
209.60	Benign carcinoid tumor of unknown primary site **181** , **182**	
209.61	Benign carcinoid tumor of the bronchus and lung **52**	

*Code Range

209.62	Benign carcinoid tumor of the thymus **177**	
209.63	Benign carcinoid tumor of the stomach **78**	
209.64	Benign carcinoid tumor of the kidney **117** , **120**	
209.65	Benign carcinoid tumor of foregut, not otherwise specified **78**	
209.66	Benign carcinoid tumor of midgut, not otherwise specified **78**	
209.67	Benign carcinoid tumor of hindgut, not otherwise specified **78**	
209.69	Benign carcinoid tumor of other sites **181** , **182**	
209.70	Secondary neuroendocrine tumor, unspecified site **181** , **183**	
209.71	Secondary neuroendocrine tumor of distant lymph nodes **179** , **182**	
209.72	Secondary neuroendocrine tumor of liver **82**	
209.73	Secondary neuroendocrine tumor of bone **87** , **97**	
209.74	Secondary neuroendocrine tumor of peritoneum **76**	
209.75	Secondary Merkel cell carcinoma **181** , **183**	
209.79	Secondary neuroendocrine tumor of other sites **181** , **183**	
210.0	Benign neoplasm of lip **48**	
210.1	Benign neoplasm of tongue **48**	
210.2	Benign neoplasm of major salivary glands **47**	
210.3	Benign neoplasm of floor of mouth **48**	
210.4	Benign neoplasm of other and unspecified parts of mouth **48**	
210.5	Benign neoplasm of tonsil **47**	
210.6	Benign neoplasm of other parts of oropharynx **47**	
210.7	Benign neoplasm of nasopharynx **47**	
210.8	Benign neoplasm of hypopharynx **47**	
210.9	Benign neoplasm of pharynx, unspecified **47**	
210*	Benign neoplasm of lip, oral cavity, and pharynx **3**	
211.0	Benign neoplasm of esophagus **78**	
211.1	Benign neoplasm of stomach **78**	
211.2	Benign neoplasm of duodenum, jejunum, and ileum **78**	
211.3	Benign neoplasm of colon **78**	
211.4	Benign neoplasm of rectum and anal canal **78**	
211.5	Benign neoplasm of liver and biliary passages **83**	
211.6	Benign neoplasm of pancreas, except islets of Langerhans **83**	
211.7	Benign neoplasm of islets of Langerhans **115**	
211.8	Benign neoplasm of retroperitoneum and peritoneum **78**	
211.9	Benign neoplasm of other and unspecified site of the digestive system **78**	
212.0	Benign neoplasm of nasal cavities, middle ear, and accessory sinuses **3** , **47**	
212.1	Benign neoplasm of larynx **3** , **47**	
212.2	Benign neoplasm of trachea **52**	
212.3	Benign neoplasm of bronchus and lung **52**	
212.4	Benign neoplasm of pleura **52**	
212.5	Benign neoplasm of mediastinum **52**	
212.6	Benign neoplasm of thymus **177**	
212.7	Benign neoplasm of heart **68**	
212.8	Benign neoplasm of other specified sites of respiratory and intrathoracic organs **52**	
212.9	Benign neoplasm of respiratory and intrathoracic organs, site unspecified **52**	
213.0	Benign neoplasm of bones of skull and face **3** , **100**	
213.1	Benign neoplasm of lower jaw bone **3** , **48**	
213.2	Benign neoplasm of vertebral column, excluding sacrum and coccyx **87** , **100**	
213.3	Benign neoplasm of ribs, sternum, and clavicle **52**	
213.4	Benign neoplasm of scapula and long bones of upper limb **100**	
213.5	Benign neoplasm of short bones of upper limb **100**	
213.6	Benign neoplasm of pelvic bones, sacrum, and coccyx **100**	
213.7	Benign neoplasm of long bones of lower limb **100**	
213.8	Benign neoplasm of short bones of lower limb **100**	

213.9	Benign neoplasm of bone and articular cartilage, site unspecified **100**	
214.0	Lipoma of skin and subcutaneous tissue of face **109**	
214.1	Lipoma of other skin and subcutaneous tissue **109**	
214.2	Lipoma of intrathoracic organs **52**	
214.3	Lipoma of intra-abdominal organs **78**	
214.4	Lipoma of spermatic cord **125**	
214.8	Lipoma of other specified sites **109**	
214.9	Lipoma of unspecified site **109**	
215*	Other benign neoplasm of connective and other soft tissue **100**	
216.0	Benign neoplasm of skin of lip **109**	
216.1	Benign neoplasm of eyelid, including canthus **38**	
216.2	Benign neoplasm of ear and external auditory canal **109**	
216.3	Benign neoplasm of skin of other and unspecified parts of face **109**	
216.4	Benign neoplasm of scalp and skin of neck **109**	
216.5	Benign neoplasm of skin of trunk, except scrotum **109**	
216.6	Benign neoplasm of skin of upper limb, including shoulder **109**	
216.7	Benign neoplasm of skin of lower limb, including hip **109**	
216.8	Benign neoplasm of other specified sites of skin **109**	
216.9	Benign neoplasm of skin, site unspecified **109**	
217	Benign neoplasm of breast **109**	
218*	Uterine leiomyoma **128** , **131**	
219*	Other benign neoplasm of uterus **128** , **131**	
220	Benign neoplasm of ovary **128** , **131**	
221*	Benign neoplasm of other female genital organs **128** , **131**	
222*	Benign neoplasm of male genital organs **125**	
223*	Benign neoplasm of kidney and other urinary organs **117** , **120**	
224*	Benign neoplasm of eye **38**	
225*	Benign neoplasm of brain and other parts of nervous system **19**	
226	Benign neoplasm of thyroid glands **3** , **115**	
227.0	Benign neoplasm of adrenal gland **115**	
227.1	Benign neoplasm of parathyroid gland **115**	
227.3	Benign neoplasm of pituitary gland and craniopharyngeal duct (pouch) **115**	
227.4	Benign neoplasm of pineal gland **19**	
227.5	Benign neoplasm of carotid body **19**	
227.6	Benign neoplasm of aortic body and other paraganglia **19**	
227.8	Benign neoplasm of other endocrine glands and related structures **115**	
227.9	Benign neoplasm of endocrine gland, site unspecified **115**	
228.00	Hemangioma of unspecified site **3** , **68**	
228.01	Hemangioma of skin and subcutaneous tissue **3** , **109**	
228.02	Hemangioma of intracranial structures **32**	
228.03	Hemangioma of retina **38**	
228.04	Hemangioma of intra-abdominal structures **78**	
228.09	Hemangioma of other sites **3** , **68**	
228.1	Lymphangioma, any site **177**	
229.0	Benign neoplasm of lymph nodes **177**	
229.8	Benign neoplasm of other specified sites **181** , **183**	
229.9	Benign neoplasm of unspecified site **181** , **183**	
230.0	Carcinoma in situ of lip, oral cavity, and pharynx **3** , **46**	
230.1	Carcinoma in situ of esophagus **76**	
230.2	Carcinoma in situ of stomach **76**	
230.3	Carcinoma in situ of colon **76**	
230.4	Carcinoma in situ of rectum **76**	
230.5	Carcinoma in situ of anal canal **76**	
230.6	Carcinoma in situ of anus, unspecified **76**	
230.7	Carcinoma in situ of other and unspecified parts of intestine **76**	
230.8	Carcinoma in situ of liver and biliary system **82**	

230.9	Carcinoma in situ of other and unspecified digestive organs **76**
231.0	Carcinoma in situ of larynx **3 , 46**
231.1	Carcinoma in situ of trachea **52**
231.2	Carcinoma in situ of bronchus and lung **52**
231.8	Carcinoma in situ of other specified parts of respiratory system **52**
231.9	Carcinoma in situ of respiratory system, part unspecified **52**
232.0	Carcinoma in situ of skin of lip **109**
232.1	Carcinoma in situ of eyelid, including canthus **38**
232.2	Carcinoma in situ of skin of ear and external auditory canal **109**
232.3	Carcinoma in situ of skin of other and unspecified parts of face **109**
232.4	Carcinoma in situ of scalp and skin of neck **109**
232.5	Carcinoma in situ of skin of trunk, except scrotum **109**
232.6	Carcinoma in situ of skin of upper limb, including shoulder **109**
232.7	Carcinoma in situ of skin of lower limb, including hip **109**
232.8	Carcinoma in situ of other specified sites of skin **109**
232.9	Carcinoma in situ of skin, site unspecified **109**
233.0	Carcinoma in situ of breast **105 , 106**
233.1	Carcinoma in situ of cervix uteri **127 , 130**
233.2	Carcinoma in situ of other and unspecified parts of uterus **127 , 130**
233.3*	Carcinoma in situ, other and unspecified female genital organs **127 , 130**
233.4	Carcinoma in situ of prostate **123 , 124**
233.5	Carcinoma in situ of penis **123 , 124**
233.6	Carcinoma in situ of other and unspecified male genital organs **123 , 124**
233.7	Carcinoma in situ of bladder **117 , 120**
233.9	Carcinoma in situ of other and unspecified urinary organs **117 , 120**
234.0	Carcinoma in situ of eye **38**
234.8	Carcinoma in situ of other specified sites **181 , 183**
234.9	Carcinoma in situ, site unspecified **181 , 183**
235.0	Neoplasm of uncertain behavior of major salivary glands **3 , 46**
235.1	Neoplasm of uncertain behavior of lip, oral cavity, and pharynx **3 , 46**
235.2	Neoplasm of uncertain behavior of stomach, intestines, and rectum **76**
235.3	Neoplasm of uncertain behavior of liver and biliary passages **83**
235.4	Neoplasm of uncertain behavior of retroperitoneum and peritoneum **76**
235.5	Neoplasm of uncertain behavior of other and unspecified digestive organs **76**
235.6	Neoplasm of uncertain behavior of larynx **3 , 46**
235.7	Neoplasm of uncertain behavior of trachea, bronchus, and lung **52**
235.8	Neoplasm of uncertain behavior of pleura, thymus, and mediastinum **52**
235.9	Neoplasm of uncertain behavior of other and unspecified respiratory organs **52**
236.0	Neoplasm of uncertain behavior of uterus **127 , 130**
236.1	Neoplasm of uncertain behavior of placenta **127 , 130**
236.2	Neoplasm of uncertain behavior of ovary **127 , 130**
236.3	Neoplasm of uncertain behavior of other and unspecified female genital organs **127 , 130**
236.4	Neoplasm of uncertain behavior of testis **123 , 124**
236.5	Neoplasm of uncertain behavior of prostate **123 , 124**
236.6	Neoplasm of uncertain behavior of other and unspecified male genital organs **123 , 124**
236.7	Neoplasm of uncertain behavior of bladder **117 , 120**
236.9*	Neoplasm of uncertain behavior of other and unspecified urinary organs **117 , 120**

237.0	Neoplasm of uncertain behavior of pituitary gland and craniopharyngeal duct **115**
237.1	Neoplasm of uncertain behavior of pineal gland **19**
237.2	Neoplasm of uncertain behavior of adrenal gland **115**
237.3	Neoplasm of uncertain behavior of paraganglia **19**
237.4	Neoplasm of uncertain behavior of other and unspecified endocrine glands **115**
237.5	Neoplasm of uncertain behavior of brain and spinal cord **19**
237.6	Neoplasm of uncertain behavior of meninges **19**
237.7*	Neurofibromatosis **32**
237.9	Neoplasm of uncertain behavior of other and unspecified parts of nervous system **19**
238.0	Neoplasm of uncertain behavior of bone and articular cartilage **87 , 97**
238.1	Neoplasm of uncertain behavior of connective and other soft tissue **100**
238.2	Neoplasm of uncertain behavior of skin **109**
238.3	Neoplasm of uncertain behavior of breast **105 , 106**
238.4	Neoplasm of uncertain behavior of polycythemia vera **179 , 182**
238.5	Neoplasm of uncertain behavior of histiocytic and mast cells **179 , 182**
238.6	Neoplasm of uncertain behavior of plasma cells **179 , 182**
238.71	Essential thrombocythemia **177**
238.72	Low grade myelodysplastic syndrome lesions **176**
238.73	High grade myelodysplastic syndrome lesions **176**
238.74	Myelodysplastic syndrome with 5q deletion **176**
238.75	Myelodysplastic syndrome, unspecified **176**
238.76	Myelofibrosis with myeloid metaplasia **179 , 182**
238.77	Post-transplant lymphoproliferative disorder [PTLD] **204**
238.79	Other lymphatic and hematopoietic tissues **179 , 182**
238.8	Neoplasm of uncertain behavior of other specified sites **181 , 183**
238.9	Neoplasm of uncertain behavior, site unspecified **181 , 183**
239.0	Neoplasm of unspecified nature of digestive system **76**
239.1	Neoplasm of unspecified nature of respiratory system **52**
239.2	Neoplasms of unspecified nature of bone, soft tissue, and skin **87 , 100**
239.3	Neoplasm of unspecified nature of breast **106**
239.4	Neoplasm of unspecified nature of bladder **117 , 120**
239.5	Neoplasm of unspecified nature of other genitourinary organs **117 , 120**
239.6	Neoplasm of unspecified nature of brain **19**
239.7	Neoplasm of unspecified nature of endocrine glands and other parts of nervous system **115**
239.8*	Neoplasm of unspecified nature of other specified sites **181 , 183**
239.9	Neoplasm of unspecified nature, site unspecified **181 , 183**
240*	Simple and unspecified goiter **115**
241*	Nontoxic nodular goiter **115**
242*	Thyrotoxicosis with or without goiter **3 , 115**
243	Congenital hypothyroidism **115**
244*	Acquired hypothyroidism **115**
245*	Thyroiditis **3 , 115**
246.2	Cyst of thyroid **3**
246.3	Hemorrhage and infarction of thyroid **3**
246.8	Other specified disorders of thyroid **3**
246.9	Unspecified disorder of thyroid **3**
246*	Other disorders of thyroid **115**
249.0*	Secondary diabetes mellitus without mention of complication **114**
249.1*	Secondary diabetes mellitus with ketoacidosis **114**
249.2*	Secondary diabetes mellitus with hyperosmolarity **114**

Numeric Index to Diseases

249.3*	Secondary diabetes mellitus with other coma **114**
249.4*	Secondary diabetes mellitus with renal manifestations **121**
249.5*	Secondary diabetes mellitus with ophthalmic manifestations **38**
249.6*	Secondary diabetes mellitus with neurological manifestations **20**
249.7*	Secondary diabetes mellitus with peripheral circulatory disorders **66**
249.8*	Secondary diabetes mellitus with other specified manifestations **114**
249.9*	Secondary diabetes mellitus with unspecified complication **114**
249*	Secondary diabetes mellitus **1 , 2**
250.0*	Diabetes mellitus without mention of complication **1 , 2 , 114**
250.1*	Diabetes with ketoacidosis **1 , 2 , 114**
250.2*	Diabetes with hyperosmolarity **1 , 2 , 114**
250.3*	Diabetes with other coma **1 , 2 , 114**
250.4*	Diabetes with renal manifestations **1 , 2 , 121**
250.41	Diabetes with renal manifestations, type I [juvenile type], not stated as uncontrolled **119**
250.43	Diabetes with renal manifestations, type I [juvenile type], uncontrolled **119**
250.5*	Diabetes with ophthalmic manifestations **1 , 2 , 38**
250.6*	Diabetes with neurological manifestations **1 , 2 , 20**
250.7*	Diabetes with peripheral circulatory disorders **1 , 2 , 66**
250.8*	Diabetes with other specified manifestations **2 , 114**
250.9*	Diabetes with unspecified complication **2 , 114**
251.0	Hypoglycemic coma **114 , 165 , 169**
251.1	Other specified hypoglycemia **115**
251.2	Hypoglycemia, unspecified **114**
251.3	Postsurgical hypoinsulinemia **2 , 114**
251.4	Abnormality of secretion of glucagon **115**
251.5	Abnormality of secretion of gastrin **77**
251.8	Other specified disorders of pancreatic internal secretion **115**
251.9	Unspecified disorder of pancreatic internal secretion **115**
252.1	Hypoparathyroidism **165 , 169**
252*	Disorders of parathyroid gland **115**
253.5	Diabetes insipidus **165 , 169**
253*	Disorders of the pituitary gland and its hypothalamic control **115**
254.1	Abscess of thymus **165 , 169**
254*	Diseases of thymus gland **177**
255*	Disorders of adrenal glands **115**
256*	Ovarian dysfunction **128 , 131**
257*	Testicular dysfunction **115**
258*	Polyglandular dysfunction and related disorders **115**
259*	Other endocrine disorders **115**
260	Kwashiorkor **114 , 231**
261	Nutritional marasmus **114 , 165 , 169 , 231**
262	Other severe protein-calorie malnutrition **114 , 165 , 169 , 231**
263.0	Malnutrition of moderate degree **165 , 169**
263.1	Malnutrition of mild degree **165 , 169**
263.8	Other protein-calorie malnutrition **165 , 169**
263.9	Unspecified protein-calorie malnutrition **165 , 169**
263*	Other and unspecified protein-calorie malnutrition **114 , 231**
264.0	Vitamin A deficiency with conjunctival xerosis **38**
264.1	Vitamin A deficiency with conjunctival xerosis and Bitot's spot **38**
264.2	Vitamin A deficiency with corneal xerosis **38**
264.3	Vitamin A deficiency with corneal ulceration and xerosis **38**
264.4	Vitamin A deficiency with keratomalacia **39**
264.5	Vitamin A deficiency with night blindness **39**
264.6	Vitamin A deficiency with xerophthalmic scars of cornea **39**
264.7	Other ocular manifestations of vitamin A deficiency **39**
264.8	Other manifestations of vitamin A deficiency **114**

264.9	Unspecified vitamin A deficiency **114**
264*	Vitamin A deficiency **231**
265*	Thiamine and niacin deficiency states **114 , 231**
266*	Deficiency of B-complex components **114 , 231**
267	Ascorbic acid deficiency **114 , 231**
268.0	Rickets, active **98**
268.1	Rickets, late effect **98**
268.2	Osteomalacia, unspecified **98**
268.9	Unspecified vitamin D deficiency **114**
268*	Vitamin D deficiency **231**
269*	Other nutritional deficiencies **114 , 231**
270*	Disorders of amino-acid transport and metabolism **114**
271.0	Glycogenosis **114**
271.1	Galactosemia **114**
271.2	Hereditary fructose intolerance **78**
271.3	Intestinal disaccharidase deficiencies and disaccharide malabsorption **78**
271.4	Renal glycosuria **114**
271.8	Other specified disorders of carbohydrate transport and metabolism **114**
271.9	Unspecified disorder of carbohydrate transport and metabolism **114**
272*	Disorders of lipoid metabolism **114**
273.0	Polyclonal hypergammaglobulinemia **177**
273.1	Monoclonal paraproteinemia **177**
273.2	Other paraproteinemias **179 , 182**
273.3	Macroglobulinemia **179 , 182**
273.4	Alpha-1-antitrypsin deficiency **115**
273.8	Other disorders of plasma protein metabolism **181 , 183**
273.9	Unspecified disorder of plasma protein metabolism **181 , 183**
274.0*	Gouty arthropathy **98**
274.10	Gouty nephropathy, unspecified **121**
274.11	Uric acid nephrolithiasis **120**
274.19	Other gouty nephropathy **121**
274.8*	Gout with other specified manifestations **98**
274.9	Gout, unspecified **98**
275.0*	Disorders of iron metabolism **115**
275.1	Disorders of copper metabolism **115**
275.2	Disorders of magnesium metabolism **114**
275.3	Disorders of phosphorus metabolism **115**
275.4*	Disorders of calcium metabolism **114**
275.5	Hungry bone syndrome **114**
275.8	Other specified disorders of mineral metabolism **115**
275.9	Unspecified disorder of mineral metabolism **115**
276.5*	Volume depletion **231**
276*	Disorders of fluid, electrolyte, and acid-base balance **114 , 165 , 169**
277.00	Cystic fibrosis without mention of meconium ileus **114**
277.01	Cystic fibrosis with meconium ileus **164 , 168**
277.02	Cystic fibrosis with pulmonary manifestations **51**
277.03	Cystic fibrosis with gastrointestinal manifestations **78**
277.09	Cystic fibrosis with other manifestations **114**
277.1	Disorders of porphyrin metabolism **115**
277.2	Other disorders of purine and pyrimidine metabolism **115**
277.3*	Amyloidosis **97**
277.4	Disorders of bilirubin excretion **83**
277.5	Mucopolysaccharidosis **115**
277.6	Other deficiencies of circulating enzymes **115**
277.7	Dysmetabolic Syndrome X **115**
277.81	Primary carnitine deficiency **115**

*Code Range © 2012 OptumInsight, Inc.

298.2	Reactive confusion **190**	
298.3	Acute paranoid reaction **190**	
298.4	Psychogenic paranoid psychosis **190**	
298.8	Other and unspecified reactive psychosis **190**	
298.9	Unspecified psychosis **190 , 231**	
299.0*	Autistic disorder **189**	
299.1*	Childhood disintegrative disorder **189**	
299.8*	Other specified pervasive developmental disorders **190**	
299.9*	Unspecified pervasive developmental disorder **190**	
300.0*	Anxiety states **189**	
300.10	Hysteria, unspecified **189**	
300.11	Conversion disorder **189**	
300.12	Dissociative amnesia **189**	
300.13	Dissociative fugue **189**	
300.14	Dissociative identity disorder **189**	
300.15	Dissociative disorder or reaction, unspecified **189**	
300.16	Factitious disorder with predominantly psychological signs and symptoms **189**	
300.19	Other and unspecified factitious illness **189**	
300.2*	Phobic disorders **189**	
300.3	Obsessive-compulsive disorders **189**	
300.4	Dysthymic disorder **189**	
300.5	Neurasthenia **189**	
300.6	Depersonalization disorder **189**	
300.7	Hypochondriasis **189**	
300.8*	Somatoform disorders **189**	
300.9	Unspecified nonpsychotic mental disorder **189**	
301.0	Paranoid personality disorder **189**	
301.10	Affective personality disorder, unspecified **189**	
301.11	Chronic hypomanic personality disorder **189**	
301.12	Chronic depressive personality disorder **189**	
301.13	Cyclothymic disorder **189**	
301.2*	Schizoid personality disorder **189**	
301.3	Explosive personality disorder **189**	
301.4	Obsessive-compulsive personality disorder **189**	
301.5*	Histrionic personality disorder **189**	
301.6	Dependent personality disorder **189**	
301.7	Antisocial personality disorder **189**	
301.8*	Other personality disorders **189**	
301.9	Unspecified personality disorder **189**	
302*	Sexual and gender identity disorders **190**	
303.0*	Acute alcoholic intoxication **192**	
303.9*	Other and unspecified alcohol dependence **192**	
304*	Drug dependence **192**	
305.0*	Nondependent alcohol abuse **192**	
305.1	Nondependent tobacco use disorder **214**	
305.2*	Nondependent cannabis abuse **192**	
305.3*	Nondependent hallucinogen abuse **192**	
305.4*	Nondependent sedative, hypnotic or anxiolytic abuse **192**	
305.5*	Nondependent opioid abuse **192**	
305.6*	Nondependent cocaine abuse **192**	
305.7*	Nondependent amphetamine or related acting sympathomimetic abuse **192**	
305.8*	Nondependent antidepressant type abuse **192**	
305.9*	Other, mixed, or unspecified nondependent drug abuse **192**	
306.0	Musculoskeletal malfunction arising from mental factors **98**	
306.1	Respiratory malfunction arising from mental factors **54**	
306.2	Cardiovascular malfunction arising from mental factors **68**	
306.3	Skin malfunction arising from mental factors **109**	
306.4	Gastrointestinal malfunction arising from mental factors **78**	
306.50	Psychogenic genitourinary malfunction, unspecified **121**	
306.51	Psychogenic vaginismus **128 , 131**	
306.52	Psychogenic dysmenorrhea **128 , 131**	
306.53	Psychogenic dysuria **121**	
306.59	Other genitourinary malfunction arising from mental factors **121**	
306.6	Endocrine malfunction arising from mental factors **115**	
306.7	Malfunction of organs of special sense arising from mental factors **189**	
306.8	Other specified psychophysiological malfunction **190**	
306.9	Unspecified psychophysiological malfunction **189**	
307.0	Adult onset fluency disorder **190**	
307.1	Anorexia nervosa **189**	
307.2*	Tics **32**	
307.3	Stereotypic movement disorder **190**	
307.4*	Specific disorders of sleep of nonorganic origin **190**	
307.50	Eating disorder, unspecified **190**	
307.51	Bulimia nervosa **190**	
307.52	Pica **190**	
307.53	Rumination disorder **189**	
307.54	Psychogenic vomiting **189**	
307.59	Other disorder of eating **190**	
307.6	Enuresis **190**	
307.7	Encopresis **190**	
307.80	Psychogenic pain, site unspecified **189**	
307.81	Tension headache **34**	
307.89	Other pain disorder related to psychological factors **189**	
307.9	Other and unspecified special symptom or syndrome, not elsewhere classified **189**	
308*	Acute reaction to stress **189**	
309.0	Adjustment disorder with depressed mood **189**	
309.1	Prolonged depressive reaction as adjustment reaction **189**	
309.2*	Predominant disturbance of other emotions as adjustment reaction **189**	
309.3	Adjustment disorder with disturbance of conduct **189**	
309.4	Adjustment disorder with mixed disturbance of emotions and conduct **189**	
309.8*	Other specified adjustment reactions **189**	
309.9	Unspecified adjustment reaction **189**	
310.0	Frontal lobe syndrome **189**	
310.1	Personality change due to conditions classified elsewhere **189**	
310.2	Postconcussion syndrome **34**	
310.8*	Other specified nonpsychotic mental disorder following organic brain damage **19**	
310.9	Unspecified nonpsychotic mental disorder following organic brain damage **189 , 231**	
311	Depressive disorder, not elsewhere classified **189**	
312.0*	Undersocialized conduct disorder, aggressive type **190**	
312.1*	Undersocialized conduct disorder, unaggressive type **190**	
312.2*	Socialized conduct disorder **190**	
312.30	Impulse control disorder, unspecified **190**	
312.31	Pathological gambling **189**	
312.32	Kleptomania **189**	
312.33	Pyromania **190**	
312.34	Intermittent explosive disorder **189**	
312.35	Isolated explosive disorder **189**	
312.39	Other disorder of impulse control **189**	
312.4	Mixed disturbance of conduct and emotions **190**	
312.8*	Other specified disturbances of conduct, not elsewhere classified **190**	

312.9	Unspecified disturbance of conduct **190**	
313.0	Overanxious disorder specific to childhood and adolescence **189**	
313.1	Misery and unhappiness disorder specific to childhood and adolescence **189**	
313.2*	Sensitivity, shyness, and social withdrawal disorder specific to childhood and adolescence **190**	
313.3	Relationship problems specific to childhood and adolescence **190**	
313.8*	Other or mixed emotional disturbances of childhood or adolescence **190**	
313.9	Unspecified emotional disturbance of childhood or adolescence **190**	
314*	Hyperkinetic syndrome of childhood **190**	
315.00	Developmental reading disorder, unspecified **190**	
315.01	Alexia **190**	
315.02	Developmental dyslexia **190**	
315.09	Other specific developmental reading disorder **190**	
315.1	Mathematics disorder **190**	
315.2	Other specific developmental learning difficulties **190**	
315.31	Expressive language disorder **190**	
315.32	Mixed receptive-expressive language disorder **190**	
315.34	Speech and language developmental delay due to hearing loss **190**	
315.35	Childhood onset fluency disorder **32**	
315.39	Other developmental speech or language disorder **190**	
315.4	Developmental coordination disorder **190**	
315.5	Mixed development disorder **190**	
315.8	Other specified delay in development **190**	
315.9	Unspecified delay in development **190**	
316	Psychic factors associated with diseases classified elsewhere **189**	
317	Mild intellectual disabilities **189**	
318*	Other specified intellectual disabilities **189**	
319	Unspecified intellectual disabilities **189**	
320*	Bacterial meningitis **9 , 10 , 33 , 165 , 170**	
321.0	Cryptococcal meningitis **9 , 10**	
321.1	Meningitis in other fungal diseases **9 , 10**	
321.2	Meningitis due to viruses not elsewhere classified **9 , 10**	
321.3	Meningitis due to trypanosomiasis **9 , 10**	
321*	Meningitis due to other organisms **33 , 165 , 170**	
322.0	Nonpyogenic meningitis **165 , 170**	
322.1	Eosinophilic meningitis **166 , 170**	
322.9	Unspecified meningitis **166 , 170**	
322*	Meningitis of unspecified cause **33**	
323.0*	Encephalitis, myelitis, and encephalomyelitis in viral diseases classified elsewhere **9 , 33**	
323.01	Encephalitis and encephalomyelitis in viral diseases classified elsewhere **10**	
323.02	Myelitis in viral diseases classified elsewhere **10**	
323.1	Encephalitis, myelitis, and encephalomyelitis in rickettsial diseases classified elsewhere **9 , 10 , 33**	
323.2	Encephalitis, myelitis, and encephalomyelitis in protozoal diseases classified elsewhere **9 , 10 , 33**	
323.4*	Other encephalitis, myelitis, and encephalomyelitis due to other infections classified elsewhere **9 , 33**	
323.41	Other encephalitis and encephalomyelitis due to other infections classified elsewhere **10**	
323.42	Other myelitis due to other infections classified elsewhere **10**	
323.5*	Encephalitis, myelitis, and encephalomyelitis following immunization procedures **9 , 33**	
323.51	Encephalitis and encephalomyelitis following immunization procedures **10**	
323.52	Myelitis following immunization procedures **10**	

323.6*	Postinfectious encephalitis, myelitis, and encephalomyelitis **9 , 33**	
323.61	Infectious acute disseminated encephalomyelitis [ADEM] **10**	
323.62	Other postinfectious encephalitis and encephalomyelitis **10**	
323.63	Postinfectious myelitis **10**	
323.7*	Toxic encephalitis, myelitis, and encephalomyelitis **9**	
323.71	Toxic encephalitis and encephalomyelitis **10 , 32**	
323.72	Toxic myelitis **10 , 32**	
323.8*	Other causes of encephalitis, myelitis, and encephalomyelitis **9 , 33**	
323.81	Other causes of encephalitis and encephalomyelitis **10 , 231**	
323.82	Other causes of myelitis **10 , 231**	
323.9	Unspecified causes of encephalitis, myelitis, and encephalomyelitis **9 , 10 , 33 , 231**	
324*	Intracranial and intraspinal abscess **9 , 10 , 33 , 166 , 170**	
325	Phlebitis and thrombophlebitis of intracranial venous sinuses **9 , 10 , 32**	
326	Late effects of intracranial abscess or pyogenic infection **32**	
327.0*	Organic disorders of initiating and maintaining sleep [Organic hypersomnia] **190**	
327.1*	Organic disorders of excessive somnolence [Organic hypersomnia] **190**	
327.2*	Organic sleep apnea **3**	
327.20	Organic sleep apnea, unspecified **47**	
327.21	Primary central sleep apnea **32**	
327.22	High altitude periodic breathing **54**	
327.23	Obstructive sleep apnea (adult) (pediatric) **47**	
327.24	Idiopathic sleep related nonobstructive alveolar hypoventilation **47**	
327.25	Congenital central alveolar hypoventilation syndrome **32**	
327.26	Sleep related hypoventilation/hypoxemia in conditions classifiable elsewhere **47**	
327.27	Central sleep apnea in conditions classified elsewhere **32**	
327.29	Other organic sleep apnea **47**	
327.3*	Circadian rhythm sleep disorder **3 , 32**	
327.4*	Organic parasomnia **3**	
327.40	Organic parasomnia, unspecified **47**	
327.41	Confusional arousals **32**	
327.42	REM sleep behavior disorder **47**	
327.43	Recurrent isolated sleep paralysis **32**	
327.44	Parasomnia in conditions classified elsewhere **47**	
327.49	Other organic parasomnia **47**	
327.5*	Organic sleep related movement disorders **3**	
327.51	Periodic limb movement disorder **32**	
327.52	Sleep related leg cramps **32**	
327.53	Sleep related bruxism **47**	
327.59	Other organic sleep related movement disorders **47**	
327.8	Other organic sleep disorders **3 , 47**	
330*	Cerebral degenerations usually manifest in childhood **19**	
331.0	Alzheimer's disease **19**	
331.1*	Frontotemporal dementia **19**	
331.2	Senile degeneration of brain **19**	
331.3	Communicating hydrocephalus **19**	
331.4	Obstructive hydrocephalus **19**	
331.5	Idiopathic normal pressure hydrocephalus [INPH] **19**	
331.6	Corticobasal degeneration **19**	
331.7	Cerebral degeneration in diseases classified elsewhere **19**	
331.81	Reye's syndrome **32**	
331.82	Dementia with Lewy bodies **19**	
331.83	Mild cognitive impairment, so stated **19**	

*Code Range

331.89	Other cerebral degeneration	**19**
331.9	Unspecified cerebral degeneration	**19**
332*	Parkinson's disease	**19**
333.0	Other degenerative diseases of the basal ganglia	**19**
333.1	Essential and other specified forms of tremor	**32**
333.2	Myoclonus	**32**
333.3	Tics of organic origin	**32**
333.4	Huntington's chorea	**19**
333.5	Other choreas	**19**
333.6	Genetic torsion dystonia	**19**
333.71	Athetoid cerebral palsy	**19**
333.72	Acute dystonia due to drugs	**32**
333.79	Other acquired torsion dystonia	**32**
333.81	Blepharospasm	**39**
333.82	Orofacial dyskinesia	**32**
333.83	Spasmodic torticollis	**32**
333.84	Organic writers' cramp	**32**
333.85	Subacute dyskinesia due to drugs	**32**
333.89	Other fragments of torsion dystonia	**32**
333.90	Unspecified extrapyramidal disease and abnormal movement disorder	**19**
333.91	Stiff-man syndrome	**32**
333.92	Neuroleptic malignant syndrome	**32**
333.93	Benign shuddering attacks	**32**
333.94	Restless legs syndrome [RLS]	**19**
333.99	Other extrapyramidal disease and abnormal movement disorder	**19**
334*	Spinocerebellar disease	**19**
335*	Anterior horn cell disease	**19**
336.0	Syringomyelia and syringobulbia	**19**
336.1	Vascular myelopathies	**32**
336.2	Subacute combined degeneration of spinal cord in diseases classified elsewhere	**32**
336.3	Myelopathy in other diseases classified elsewhere	**32**
336.8	Other myelopathy	**32**
336.9	Unspecified disease of spinal cord	**32 , 231**
337*	Disorders of the autonomic nervous system	**20**
338.0	Central pain syndrome	**32**
338.1*	Acute pain	**214**
338.2*	Chronic pain	**32**
338.3	Neoplasm related pain (acute) (chronic)	**214**
338.4	Chronic pain syndrome	**32**
339*	Other headache syndromes	**34**
340	Multiple sclerosis	**19**
341.0	Neuromyelitis optica	**19**
341.1	Schilder's disease	**19**
341.2*	Acute (transverse) myelitis	**9 , 33**
341.20	Acute (transverse) myelitis NOS	**10**
341.21	Acute (transverse) myelitis in conditions classified elsewhere	**10**
341.22	Idiopathic transverse myelitis	**10**
341.8	Other demyelinating diseases of central nervous system	**19**
341.9	Unspecified demyelinating disease of central nervous system	**19 , 231**
342*	Hemiplegia and hemiparesis	**19**
343.0	Diplegic infantile cerebral palsy	**18**
343.1	Hemiplegic infantile cerebral palsy	**18**
343.2	Quadriplegic infantile cerebral palsy	**18**
343.3	Monoplegic infantile cerebral palsy	**32**
343.4	Infantile hemiplegia	**18**
343.8	Other specified infantile cerebral palsy	**32**

343.9	Unspecified infantile cerebral palsy	**32**
344.0*	Quadriplegia and quadriparesis	**18**
344.1	Paraplegia	**18**
344.2	Diplegia of upper limbs	**18**
344.3*	Monoplegia of lower limb	**32**
344.4*	Monoplegia of upper limb	**32**
344.5	Unspecified monoplegia	**32**
344.60	Cauda equina syndrome without mention of neurogenic bladder **20**
344.61	Cauda equina syndrome with neurogenic bladder	**121**
344.8*	Other specified paralytic syndromes	**32**
344.9	Unspecified paralysis	**32**
345*	Epilepsy and recurrent seizures	**33**
346*	Migraine	**34**
347*	Cataplexy and narcolepsy	**32**
348.0	Cerebral cysts	**32**
348.1	Anoxic brain damage	**32 , 166 , 170**
348.2	Benign intracranial hypertension	**34**
348.3*	Encephalopathy, not elsewhere classified	**20 , 231**
348.4	Compression of brain	**21**
348.5	Cerebral edema	**21**
348.81	Temporal sclerosis	**20**
348.82	Brain death	**21**
348.89	Other conditions of brain	**20**
348.9	Unspecified condition of brain	**20 , 231**
349.0	Reaction to spinal or lumbar puncture	**34 , 166 , 170**
349.1	Nervous system complications from surgically implanted device **32 , 166 , 170**
349.2	Disorders of meninges, not elsewhere classified	**32**
349.3*	Dural tear	**166 , 170 , 204**
349.81	Cerebrospinal fluid rhinorrhea	**32 , 166 , 170**
349.82	Toxic encephalopathy	**32 , 166 , 170**
349.89	Other specified disorder of nervous system	**20**
349.9	Unspecified disorders of nervous system	**20 , 231**
350*	Trigeminal nerve disorders	**20**
351*	Facial nerve disorders	**20**
352*	Disorders of other cranial nerves	**20**
353*	Nerve root and plexus disorders	**20**
354*	Mononeuritis of upper limb and mononeuritis multiplex	**20**
355*	Mononeuritis of lower limb and unspecified site	**20**
356.0	Hereditary peripheral neuropathy	**20**
356.1	Peroneal muscular atrophy	**20**
356.2	Hereditary sensory neuropathy	**20**
356.3	Refsum's disease	**32**
356.4	Idiopathic progressive polyneuropathy	**21**
356.8	Other specified idiopathic peripheral neuropathy	**21**
356.9	Unspecified hereditary and idiopathic peripheral neuropathy	**21**
357.0	Acute infective polyneuritis	**33 , 231**
357.1	Polyneuropathy in collagen vascular disease	**21**
357.2	Polyneuropathy in diabetes	**21**
357.3	Polyneuropathy in malignant disease	**21**
357.4	Polyneuropathy in other diseases classified elsewhere	**21**
357.5	Alcoholic polyneuropathy	**21**
357.6	Polyneuropathy due to drugs	**21**
357.7	Polyneuropathy due to other toxic agents	**21**
357.8*	Other inflammatory and toxic neuropathy	**21**
357.9	Unspecified inflammatory and toxic neuropathy	**21 , 231**
358.0*	Myasthenia gravis	**19**
358.1	Myasthenic syndromes in diseases classified elsewhere	**19**

358.2	Toxic myoneural disorders	**21**
358.3*	Lambert-Eaton syndrome	**19**
358.8	Other specified myoneural disorders	**21**
358.9	Unspecified myoneural disorders	**21**
359.0	Congenital hereditary muscular dystrophy	**32**
359.1	Hereditary progressive muscular dystrophy	**32**
359.21	Myotonic muscular dystrophy	**32**
359.22	Myotonia congenita	**32**
359.23	Myotonic chondrodystrophy	**32**
359.24	Drug-induced myotonia	**32**
359.29	Other specified myotonic disorder	**32**
359.3	Periodic paralysis	**32**
359.4	Toxic myopathy	**32**
359.5	Myopathy in endocrine diseases classified elsewhere	**32**
359.6	Symptomatic inflammatory myopathy in diseases classified elsewhere	**32**
359.7*	Inflammatory and immune myopathies, NEC	**97**
359.81	Critical illness myopathy	**32**
359.89	Other myopathies	**32**
359.9	Unspecified myopathy	**32**
360.00	Unspecified purulent endophthalmitis	**38**
360.01	Acute endophthalmitis	**38**
360.02	Panophthalmitis	**38**
360.03	Chronic endophthalmitis	**39**
360.04	Vitreous abscess	**38**
360.11	Sympathetic uveitis	**39**
360.12	Panuveitis	**39**
360.13	Parasitic endophthalmitis NOS	**38**
360.14	Ophthalmia nodosa	**39**
360.19	Other endophthalmitis	**38**
360.2*	Degenerative disorders of globe	**39**
360.3*	Hypotony of eye	**39**
360.4*	Degenerated conditions of globe	**39**
360.5*	Retained (old) intraocular foreign body, magnetic	**39**
360.6*	Retained (old) intraocular foreign body, nonmagnetic	**39**
360.8*	Other disorders of globe	**39**
360.9	Unspecified disorder of globe	**39**
361.0*	Retinal detachment with retinal defect	**39**
361.1*	Retinoschisis and retinal cysts	**39**
361.2	Serous retinal detachment	**39**
361.3*	Retinal defects without detachment	**39**
361.8*	Other forms of retinal detachment	**39**
361.9	Unspecified retinal detachment	**39**
362.0*	Diabetic retinopathy	**39**
362.1*	Other background retinopathy and retinal vascular changes	**39**, **231**
362.2*	Other proliferative retinopathy	**39**
362.3*	Retinal vascular occlusion	**38**
362.4*	Separation of retinal layers	**39**
362.5*	Degeneration of macula and posterior pole of retina	**39**
362.6*	Peripheral retinal degenerations	**39**
362.7*	Hereditary retinal dystrophies	**39**
362.8*	Other retinal disorders	**39**
362.9	Unspecified retinal disorder	**39**
363*	Chorioretinal inflammations, scars, and other disorders of choroid	**39**
364.0*	Acute and subacute iridocyclitis	**39**
364.1*	Chronic iridocyclitis	**39**
364.2*	Certain types of iridocyclitis	**39**
364.3	Unspecified iridocyclitis	**39**
364.41	Hyphema	**39**
364.42	Rubeosis iridis	**39**
364.5*	Degenerations of iris and ciliary body	**39**
364.6*	Cysts of iris, ciliary body, and anterior chamber	**39**
364.7*	Adhesions and disruptions of iris and ciliary body	**39**
364.8*	Other disorders of iris and ciliary body	**39**
364.9	Unspecified disorder of iris and ciliary body	**39**
365.0*	Borderline glaucoma (glaucoma suspect)	**39**
365.10	Unspecified open-angle glaucoma	**39**
365.11	Primary open-angle glaucoma	**39**
365.12	Low tension open-angle glaucoma	**38**
365.13	Pigmentary open-angle glaucoma	**39**
365.14	Open-angle glaucoma of childhood	**39**
365.15	Residual stage of open angle glaucoma	**39**
365.2*	Primary angle-closure glaucoma	**39**
365.3*	Corticosteroid-induced glaucoma	**39**
365.4*	Glaucoma associated with congenital anomalies, dystrophies, and systemic syndromes	**39**
365.5*	Glaucoma associated with disorders of the lens	**39**
365.6*	Glaucoma associated with other ocular disorders	**39**
365.7*	Glaucoma stage	**39**
365.8*	Other specified forms of glaucoma	**39**
365.9	Unspecified glaucoma	**39**
366*	Cataract	**39**
367.0	Hypermetropia	**39**
367.1	Myopia	**39**
367.2*	Astigmatism	**39**
367.3*	Anisometropia and aniseikonia	**39**
367.4	Presbyopia	**39**
367.51	Paresis of accommodation	**39**
367.52	Total or complete internal ophthalmoplegia	**38**
367.53	Spasm of accommodation	**39**
367.8*	Other disorders of refraction and accommodation	**39**
367.9	Unspecified disorder of refraction and accommodation	**39**
368.0*	Amblyopia ex anopsia	**39**
368.10	Unspecified subjective visual disturbance	**39**
368.11	Sudden visual loss	**38**
368.12	Transient visual loss	**38**
368.13	Visual discomfort	**39**
368.14	Visual distortions of shape and size	**39**
368.15	Other visual distortions and entoptic phenomena	**39**
368.16	Psychophysical visual disturbances	**39**
368.2	Diplopia	**38**
368.3*	Other disorders of binocular vision	**39**
368.40	Unspecified visual field defect	**38**
368.41	Scotoma involving central area in visual field	**38**
368.42	Scotoma of blind spot area in visual field	**39**
368.43	Sector or arcuate defects in visual field	**38**
368.44	Other localized visual field defect	**38**
368.45	Generalized contraction or constriction in visual field	**38**
368.46	Homonymous bilateral field defects in visual field	**38**
368.47	Heteronymous bilateral field defects in visual field	**38**
368.51	Protan defect in color vision	**39**
368.52	Deutan defect in color vision	**39**
368.53	Tritan defect in color vision	**39**
368.54	Achromatopsia	**39**
368.55	Acquired color vision deficiencies	**38**
368.59	Other color vision deficiencies	**39**

*Code Range

368.6*	Night blindness	39
368.8	Other specified visual disturbances	39
368.9	Unspecified visual disturbance	39
369*	Blindness and low vision	39 , 231
370.00	Unspecified corneal ulcer	38
370.01	Marginal corneal ulcer	39
370.02	Ring corneal ulcer	39
370.03	Central corneal ulcer	38
370.04	Hypopyon ulcer	38
370.05	Mycotic corneal ulcer	38
370.06	Perforated corneal ulcer	38
370.07	Mooren's ulcer	39
370.2*	Superficial keratitis without conjunctivitis	39
370.3*	Certain types of keratoconjunctivitis	39
370.4*	Other and unspecified keratoconjunctivitis	39
370.50	Unspecified interstitial keratitis	39
370.52	Diffuse interstitial keratitis	39
370.54	Sclerosing keratitis	39
370.55	Corneal abscess	38
370.59	Other interstitial and deep keratitis	39
370.6*	Corneal neovascularization	39
370.8	Other forms of keratitis	39
370.9	Unspecified keratitis	39
371*	Corneal opacity and other disorders of cornea	39
372*	Disorders of conjunctiva	39
373*	Inflammation of eyelids	39
374.0*	Entropion and trichiasis of eyelid	39
374.1*	Ectropion	39
374.2*	Lagophthalmos	39
374.30	Unspecified ptosis of eyelid	38
374.31	Paralytic ptosis	38
374.32	Myogenic ptosis	38
374.33	Mechanical ptosis	39
374.34	Blepharochalasis	39
374.41	Eyelid retraction or lag	39
374.43	Abnormal innervation syndrome of eyelid	39
374.44	Sensory disorders of eyelid	39
374.45	Other sensorimotor disorders of eyelid	38
374.46	Blepharophimosis	39
374.50	Unspecified degenerative disorder of eyelid	39
374.51	Xanthelasma of eyelid	109
374.52	Hyperpigmentation of eyelid	39
374.53	Hypopigmentation of eyelid	39
374.54	Hypertrichosis of eyelid	39
374.55	Hypotrichosis of eyelid	39
374.56	Other degenerative disorders of skin affecting eyelid	39
374.8*	Other disorders of eyelid	39
374.9	Unspecified disorder of eyelid	39
375.00	Unspecified dacryoadenitis	39
375.01	Acute dacryoadenitis	38
375.02	Chronic dacryoadenitis	39
375.03	Chronic enlargement of lacrimal gland	39
375.1*	Other disorders of lacrimal gland	39
375.2*	Epiphora	39
375.30	Unspecified dacryocystitis	39
375.31	Acute canaliculitis, lacrimal	38
375.32	Acute dacryocystitis	38
375.33	Phlegmonous dacryocystitis	39
375.4*	Chronic inflammation of lacrimal passages	39

375.5*	Stenosis and insufficiency of lacrimal passages	39
375.6*	Other changes of lacrimal passages	39
375.8*	Other disorders of lacrimal system	39
375.9	Unspecified disorder of lacrimal system	39
376.00	Unspecified acute inflammation of orbit	39
376.01	Orbital cellulitis	38
376.02	Orbital periostitis	38
376.03	Orbital osteomyelitis	38
376.04	Orbital tenonitis	38
376.1*	Chronic inflammatory disorders of orbit	39
376.2*	Endocrine exophthalmos	39
376.30	Unspecified exophthalmos	39
376.31	Constant exophthalmos	39
376.32	Orbital hemorrhage	39
376.33	Orbital edema or congestion	39
376.34	Intermittent exophthalmos	38
376.35	Pulsating exophthalmos	38
376.36	Lateral displacement of globe of eye	38
376.4*	Deformity of orbit	39
376.5*	Enophthalmos	39
376.6	Retained (old) foreign body following penetrating wound of orbit 40
376.81	Orbital cysts	40
376.82	Myopathy of extraocular muscles	38
376.89	Other orbital disorder	40
376.9	Unspecified disorder of orbit	40
377.00	Unspecified papilledema	32 , 166 , 170
377.01	Papilledema associated with increased intracranial pressure 32 , 166 , 170
377.02	Papilledema associated with decreased ocular pressure 40 , 166 , 170
377.03	Papilledema associated with retinal disorder	40
377.04	Foster-Kennedy syndrome	32
377.10	Unspecified optic atrophy	38
377.11	Primary optic atrophy	38
377.12	Postinflammatory optic atrophy	38
377.13	Optic atrophy associated with retinal dystrophies	40
377.14	Glaucomatous atrophy (cupping) of optic disc	40
377.15	Partial optic atrophy	38
377.16	Hereditary optic atrophy	38
377.21	Drusen of optic disc	38
377.22	Crater-like holes of optic disc	40
377.23	Coloboma of optic disc	40
377.24	Pseudopapilledema	38
377.3*	Optic neuritis	38
377.4*	Other disorders of optic nerve	38
377.5*	Disorders of optic chiasm	32
377.6*	Disorders of other visual pathways	32
377.7*	Disorders of visual cortex	32
377.9	Unspecified disorder of optic nerve and visual pathways	32
378.0*	Esotropia	40
378.1*	Exotropia	40
378.2*	Intermittent heterotropia	40
378.3*	Other and unspecified heterotropia	40
378.4*	Heterophoria	40
378.5*	Paralytic strabismus	38
378.6*	Mechanical strabismus	40
378.71	Duane's syndrome	40
378.72	Progressive external ophthalmoplegia	38

*Code Range

378.73	Strabismus in other neuromuscular disorders **38**	
378.81	Palsy of conjugate gaze **40**	
378.82	Spasm of conjugate gaze **40**	
378.83	Convergence insufficiency or palsy in binocular eye movement **40**	
378.84	Convergence excess or spasm in binocular eye movement **40**	
378.85	Anomalies of divergence in binocular eye movement **40**	
378.86	Internuclear ophthalmoplegia **32**	
378.87	Other dissociated deviation of eye movements **38**	
378.9	Unspecified disorder of eye movements **40**	
379.0*	Scleritis and episcleritis **40**	
379.1*	Other disorders of sclera **40**	
379.2*	Disorders of vitreous body **40**	
379.3*	Aphakia and other disorders of lens **40**	
379.40	Unspecified abnormal pupillary function **38**	
379.41	Anisocoria **38**	
379.42	Miosis (persistent), not due to miotics **38**	
379.43	Mydriasis (persistent), not due to mydriatics **38**	
379.45	Argyll Robertson pupil, atypical **19**	
379.46	Tonic pupillary reaction **38**	
379.49	Other anomaly of pupillary function **33**	
379.50	Unspecified nystagmus **38**	
379.51	Congenital nystagmus **40**	
379.52	Latent nystagmus **38**	
379.53	Visual deprivation nystagmus **40**	
379.54	Nystagmus associated with disorders of the vestibular system **38**	
379.55	Dissociated nystagmus **38**	
379.56	Other forms of nystagmus **40**	
379.57	Nystagmus with deficiencies of saccadic eye movements **38**	
379.58	Nystagmus with deficiencies of smooth pursuit movements **38**	
379.59	Other irregularities of eye movements **40**	
379.6*	Inflammation (infection) of postprocedural bleb **40**	
379.8	Other specified disorders of eye and adnexa **40**	
379.9*	Unspecified disorder of eye and adnexa **40**	
380.00	Unspecified perichondritis of pinna **46**	
380.01	Acute perichondritis of pinna **100**	
380.02	Chronic perichondritis of pinna **100**	
380.03	Chondritis of pinna **100**	
380.1*	Infective otitis externa **47**	
380.2*	Other otitis externa **47**	
380.3*	Noninfectious disorders of pinna **47**	
380.4	Impacted cerumen **47**	
380.5*	Acquired stenosis of external ear canal **47**	
380.8*	Other disorders of external ear **47**	
380.9	Unspecified disorder of external ear **47**	
381.0*	Acute nonsuppurative otitis media **46**	
381.1*	Chronic serous otitis media **46**	
381.2*	Chronic mucoid otitis media **46**	
381.3	Other and unspecified chronic nonsuppurative otitis media **46**	
381.4	Nonsuppurative otitis media, not specified as acute or chronic **46**	
381.5*	Eustachian salpingitis **46**	
381.6*	Obstruction of Eustachian tube **47**	
381.7	Patulous Eustachian tube **47**	
381.8*	Other disorders of Eustachian tube **47**	
381.9	Unspecified Eustachian tube disorder **47**	
382*	Suppurative and unspecified otitis media **46**	
383.0*	Acute mastoiditis **46**	
383.01	Subperiosteal abscess of mastoid **166 , 170**	
383.1	Chronic mastoiditis **46**	

383.2*	Petrositis **46**
383.3*	Complications following mastoidectomy **47**
383.8*	Other disorders of mastoid **47**
383.81	Postauricular fistula **166 , 170**
383.9	Unspecified mastoiditis **46**
384.0*	Acute myringitis without mention of otitis media **46**
384.1	Chronic myringitis without mention of otitis media **46**
384.2*	Perforation of tympanic membrane **47**
384.8*	Other specified disorders of tympanic membrane **47**
384.9	Unspecified disorder of tympanic membrane **47**
385*	Other disorders of middle ear and mastoid **47**
386.0*	Meniere's disease **46**
386.1*	Other and unspecified peripheral vertigo **46**
386.2	Vertigo of central origin **46**
386.3*	Labyrinthitis **46**
386.4*	Labyrinthine fistula **47**
386.5*	Labyrinthine dysfunction **46**
386.8	Other disorders of labyrinth **46**
386.9	Unspecified vertiginous syndromes and labyrinthine disorders **46**
387*	Otosclerosis **47**
388.0*	Degenerative and vascular disorders of ear **47**
388.1*	Noise effects on inner ear **47**
388.2	Unspecified sudden hearing loss **47**
388.3*	Tinnitus **47**
388.40	Unspecified abnormal auditory perception **47**
388.41	Diplacusis **47**
388.42	Hyperacusis **47**
388.43	Impairment of auditory discrimination **47**
388.44	Other abnormal auditory perception, recruitment **47**
388.45	Acquired auditory processing disorder **190**
388.5	Disorders of acoustic nerve **47**
388.60	Unspecified otorrhea **47**
388.61	Cerebrospinal fluid otorrhea **32**
388.69	Other otorrhea **47**
388.7*	Otalgia **47**
388.8	Other disorders of ear **47**
388.9	Unspecified disorder of ear **47**
389*	Hearing loss **47**
390	Rheumatic fever without mention of heart involvement **97**
391.0	Acute rheumatic pericarditis **68**
391.1	Acute rheumatic endocarditis **67**
391.2	Acute rheumatic myocarditis **68**
391.8	Other acute rheumatic heart disease **68**
391.9	Unspecified acute rheumatic heart disease **68**
392*	Rheumatic chorea **68**
393	Chronic rheumatic pericarditis **68**
394*	Diseases of mitral valve **67**
395*	Diseases of aortic valve **67**
396*	Diseases of mitral and aortic valves **67**
397*	Diseases of other endocardial structures **67**
398.0	Rheumatic myocarditis **68**
398.90	Unspecified rheumatic heart disease **68**
398.91	Rheumatic heart failure (congestive) **56 , 65 , 166 , 170**
398.99	Other and unspecified rheumatic heart diseases **68**
401.0	Essential hypertension, malignant **67**
401.1	Essential hypertension, benign **67**
401.9	Unspecified essential hypertension **67**
402.00	Malignant hypertensive heart disease without heart failure **67**

402.01	Malignant hypertensive heart disease with heart failure **56**, **65**, **166**, **170**	
402.10	Benign hypertensive heart disease without heart failure **67**	
402.11	Benign hypertensive heart disease with heart failure **56**, **65**, **166**, **170**	
402.90	Unspecified hypertensive heart disease without heart failure **67**	
402.91	Hypertensive heart disease, unspecified, with heart failure **56**, **65**, **166**, **170**	
403.00	Hypertensive chronic kidney disease, malignant, with chronic kidney disease stage I through stage IV, or unspecified **119**	
403.01	Hypertensive chronic kidney disease, malignant, with chronic kidney disease stage V or end stage renal disease **2**, **119**	
403.10	Hypertensive chronic kidney disease, benign, with chronic kidney disease stage I through stage IV, or unspecified **119**	
403.11	Hypertensive chronic kidney disease, benign, with chronic kidney disease stage V or end stage renal disease **2**, **119**	
403.90	Hypertensive chronic kidney disease, unspecified, with chronic kidney disease stage I through stage IV, or unspecified **119**	
403.91	Hypertensive chronic kidney disease, unspecified, with chronic kidney disease stage V or end stage renal disease **2**, **119**	
404.00	Hypertensive heart and chronic kidney disease, malignant, without heart failure and with chronic kidney disease stage I through stage IV, or unspecified **67**	
404.01	Hypertensive heart and chronic kidney disease, malignant, with heart failure and with chronic kidney disease stage I through stage IV, or unspecified **56**, **66**, **166**, **170**	
404.02	Hypertensive heart and chronic kidney disease, malignant, without heart failure and with chronic kidney disease stage V or end stage renal disease **2**, **119**	
404.03	Hypertensive heart and chronic kidney disease, malignant, with heart failure and with chronic kidney disease stage V or end stage renal disease **2**, **56**, **66**, **166**, **170**	
404.10	Hypertensive heart and chronic kidney disease, benign, without heart failure and with chronic kidney disease stage I through stage IV, or unspecified **67**	
404.11	Hypertensive heart and chronic kidney disease, benign, with heart failure and with chronic kidney disease stage I through stage IV, or unspecified **56**, **66**, **166**, **170**	
404.12	Hypertensive heart and chronic kidney disease, benign, without heart failure and with chronic kidney disease stage V or end stage renal disease **2**, **119**	
404.13	Hypertensive heart and chronic kidney disease, benign, with heart failure and chronic kidney disease stage V or end stage renal disease **2**, **56**, **66**, **166**, **170**	
404.90	Hypertensive heart and chronic kidney disease, unspecified, without heart failure and with chronic kidney disease stage I through stage IV, or unspecified **67**	
404.91	Hypertensive heart and chronic kidney disease, unspecified, with heart failure and with chronic kidney disease stage I through stage IV, or unspecified **56**, **66**, **166**, **170**	
404.92	Hypertensive heart and chronic kidney disease, unspecified, without heart failure and with chronic kidney disease stage V or end stage renal disease **2**, **119**	
404.93	Hypertensive heart and chronic kidney disease, unspecified, with heart failure and chronic kidney disease stage V or end stage renal disease **2**, **56**, **66**, **166**, **170**	
405*	Secondary hypertension **67**	
410.00	Acute myocardial infarction of anterolateral wall, episode of care unspecified **68**	
410.01	Acute myocardial infarction of anterolateral wall, initial episode of care **56**, **65**	
410.02	Acute myocardial infarction of anterolateral wall, subsequent episode of care **68**	
410.10	Acute myocardial infarction of other anterior wall, episode of care unspecified **68**	
410.11	Acute myocardial infarction of other anterior wall, initial episode of care **56**, **65**	

410.12	Acute myocardial infarction of other anterior wall, subsequent episode of care **68**
410.20	Acute myocardial infarction of inferolateral wall, episode of care unspecified **68**
410.21	Acute myocardial infarction of inferolateral wall, initial episode of care **56**, **65**
410.22	Acute myocardial infarction of inferolateral wall, subsequent episode of care **68**
410.30	Acute myocardial infarction of inferoposterior wall, episode of care unspecified **68**
410.31	Acute myocardial infarction of inferoposterior wall, initial episode of care **56**, **65**
410.32	Acute myocardial infarction of inferoposterior wall, subsequent episode of care **68**
410.40	Acute myocardial infarction of other inferior wall, episode of care unspecified **68**
410.41	Acute myocardial infarction of other inferior wall, initial episode of care **56**, **65**
410.42	Acute myocardial infarction of other inferior wall, subsequent episode of care **68**
410.50	Acute myocardial infarction of other lateral wall, episode of care unspecified **68**
410.51	Acute myocardial infarction of other lateral wall, initial episode of care **56**, **65**
410.52	Acute myocardial infarction of other lateral wall, subsequent episode of care **68**
410.60	Acute myocardial infarction, true posterior wall infarction, episode of care unspecified **68**
410.61	Acute myocardial infarction, true posterior wall infarction, initial episode of care **57**, **65**
410.62	Acute myocardial infarction, true posterior wall infarction, subsequent episode of care **69**
410.70	Acute myocardial infarction, subendocardial infarction, episode of care unspecified **69**
410.71	Acute myocardial infarction, subendocardial infarction, initial episode of care **57**, **65**
410.72	Acute myocardial infarction, subendocardial infarction, subsequent episode of care **69**
410.80	Acute myocardial infarction of other specified sites, episode of care unspecified **69**
410.81	Acute myocardial infarction of other specified sites, initial episode of care **57**, **65**
410.82	Acute myocardial infarction of other specified sites, subsequent episode of care **69**
410.90	Acute myocardial infarction, unspecified site, episode of care unspecified **69**
410.91	Acute myocardial infarction, unspecified site, initial episode of care **57**, **65**
410.92	Acute myocardial infarction, unspecified site, subsequent episode of care **69**
411.0	Postmyocardial infarction syndrome **69**
411.1	Intermediate coronary syndrome **68**
411.81	Acute coronary occlusion without myocardial infarction **68**
411.89	Other acute and subacute form of ischemic heart disease **68**
412	Old myocardial infarction **67**
413.0	Angina decubitus **68**
413.1	Prinzmetal angina **68**
413.9	Other and unspecified angina pectoris **68**
414.0*	Coronary atherosclerosis **67**
414.1*	Aneurysm and dissection of heart **69**
414.10	Aneurysm of heart **166**, **170**
414.2	Chronic total occlusion of coronary artery **67**
414.3	Coronary atherosclerosis due to lipid rich plaque **67**
414.4	Coronary atherosclerosis due to calcified coronary lesion **67**

Numeric Index to Diseases

414.8	Other specified forms of chronic ischemic heart disease	**67**
414.9	Unspecified chronic ischemic heart disease	**67**
415.0	Acute cor pulmonale	**69**
415.1*	Pulmonary embolism and infarction	**51**
415*	Acute pulmonary heart disease	**166 , 170**
416.0	Primary pulmonary hypertension	**69**
416.1	Kyphoscoliotic heart disease	**69**
416.2	Chronic pulmonary embolism	**51 , 166 , 170**
416.8	Other chronic pulmonary heart diseases	**69**
416.9	Unspecified chronic pulmonary heart disease	**69**
417*	Other diseases of pulmonary circulation	**69**
420.0	Acute pericarditis in diseases classified elsewhere	**166 , 170**
420*	Acute pericarditis	**69**
421.0	Acute and subacute bacterial endocarditis	**65 , 231**
421.1	Acute and subacute infective endocarditis in diseases classified elsewhere	**65**
421.9	Unspecified acute endocarditis	**65 , 231**
421*	Acute and subacute endocarditis	**166 , 170**
422.0	Acute myocarditis in diseases classified elsewhere	**166 , 170**
422.9*	Other and unspecified acute myocarditis	**231**
422.92	Septic myocarditis	**166 , 170**
422*	Acute myocarditis	**69**
423.0	Hemopericardium	**166 , 170**
423*	Other diseases of pericardium	**69**
424.9*	Endocarditis, valve unspecified	**166 , 170**
424*	Other diseases of endocardium	**67**
425.8	Cardiomyopathy in other diseases classified elsewhere	**166 , 170**
425.9	Unspecified secondary cardiomyopathy	**231**
425*	Cardiomyopathy	**69**
426.0	Atrioventricular block, complete	**166 , 170**
426.53	Other bilateral bundle branch block	**166 , 170**
426.54	Trifascicular block	**166 , 170**
426.7	Anomalous atrioventricular excitation	**166 , 170**
426.89	Other specified conduction disorder	**166 , 170**
426*	Conduction disorders	**68**
427.0	Paroxysmal supraventricular tachycardia	**68**
427.1	Paroxysmal ventricular tachycardia	**68 , 166 , 170**
427.2	Unspecified paroxysmal tachycardia	**68**
427.3*	Atrial fibrillation and flutter	**68 , 166 , 170**
427.4*	Ventricular fibrillation and flutter	**68 , 166 , 170**
427.5	Cardiac arrest	**66 , 166 , 170**
427.6*	Premature beats	**68**
427.8*	Other specified cardiac dysrhythmias	**68**
427.9	Unspecified cardiac dysrhythmia	**68**
428.0	Congestive heart failure, unspecified	**57 , 166 , 170**
428.1	Left heart failure	**57 , 166 , 170**
428.2*	Systolic heart failure	**57 , 166 , 170**
428.3*	Diastolic heart failure	**57 , 166 , 170**
428.4*	Combined systolic and diastolic heart failure	**57 , 166 , 170**
428.9	Unspecified heart failure	**57 , 166 , 170**
428*	Heart failure	**66**
429.0	Unspecified myocarditis	**69**
429.1	Myocardial degeneration	**69**
429.2	Unspecified cardiovascular disease	**67**
429.3	Cardiomegaly	**67**
429.4	Functional disturbances following cardiac surgery	**69 , 166 , 170**
429.5	Rupture of chordae tendineae	**67**
429.6	Rupture of papillary muscle	**67**
429.71	Acquired cardiac septal defect	**69**

429.79	Other certain sequelae of myocardial infarction, not elsewhere classified	**69**
429.81	Other disorders of papillary muscle	**67 , 166 , 170**
429.82	Hyperkinetic heart disease	**69 , 166 , 170**
429.83	Takotsubo syndrome	**69**
429.89	Other ill-defined heart disease	**67**
429.9	Unspecified heart disease	**67**
430	Subarachnoid hemorrhage	**8 , 9 , 10 , 20 , 166 , 170**
431	Intracerebral hemorrhage	**8 , 9 , 10 , 20 , 166 , 170**
432.9	Unspecified intracranial hemorrhage	**9 , 10**
432*	Other and unspecified intracranial hemorrhage	**8 , 20 , 166 , 170**
433.00	Occlusion and stenosis of basilar artery without mention of cerebral infarction	**20**
433.01	Occlusion and stenosis of basilar artery with cerebral infarction	**9 , 10 , 19 , 20 , 166 , 170**
433.10	Occlusion and stenosis of carotid artery without mention of cerebral infarction	**20**
433.11	Occlusion and stenosis of carotid artery with cerebral infarction	**9 , 10 , 19 , 20 , 166 , 170**
433.20	Occlusion and stenosis of vertebral artery without mention of cerebral infarction	**20**
433.21	Occlusion and stenosis of vertebral artery with cerebral infarction	**9 , 10 , 19 , 20 , 166 , 170**
433.30	Occlusion and stenosis of multiple and bilateral precerebral arteries without mention of cerebral infarction	**20**
433.31	Occlusion and stenosis of multiple and bilateral precerebral arteries with cerebral infarction	**9 , 10 , 19 , 20 , 166 , 170**
433.80	Occlusion and stenosis of other specified precerebral artery without mention of cerebral infarction	**20**
433.81	Occlusion and stenosis of other specified precerebral artery with cerebral infarction	**9 , 10 , 19 , 20 , 166 , 170**
433.90	Occlusion and stenosis of unspecified precerebral artery without mention of cerebral infarction	**20**
433.91	Occlusion and stenosis of unspecified precerebral artery with cerebral infarction	**9 , 10 , 19 , 20 , 166 , 170**
434.00	Cerebral thrombosis without mention of cerebral infarction	**20**
434.01	Cerebral thrombosis with cerebral infarction	**9 , 10 , 19 , 20**
434.10	Cerebral embolism without mention of cerebral infarction	**20**
434.11	Cerebral embolism with cerebral infarction	**9 , 10 , 19 , 20**
434.90	Unspecified cerebral artery occlusion without mention of cerebral infarction	**20**
434.91	Unspecified cerebral artery occlusion with cerebral infarction	**9 , 11 , 19 , 20**
434*	Occlusion of cerebral arteries	**166 , 170**
435*	Transient cerebral ischemia	**20**
436	Acute, but ill-defined, cerebrovascular disease	**20 , 166 , 170**
437.0	Cerebral atherosclerosis	**20**
437.1	Other generalized ischemic cerebrovascular disease	**20**
437.2	Hypertensive encephalopathy	**21**
437.3	Cerebral aneurysm, nonruptured	**32**
437.4	Cerebral arteritis	**34**
437.5	Moyamoya disease	**32**
437.6	Nonpyogenic thrombosis of intracranial venous sinus	**32**
437.7	Transient global amnesia	**20**
437.8	Other ill-defined cerebrovascular disease	**20**
437.9	Unspecified cerebrovascular disease	**20**
438*	Late effects of cerebrovascular disease	**19**
440.0	Atherosclerosis of aorta	**66**
440.1	Atherosclerosis of renal artery	**121**
440.2*	Atherosclerosis of native arteries of the extremities	**66**

*Code Range

440.24	Atherosclerosis of native arteries of the extremities with gangrene **166**, **170**	448.1	Nevus, non-neoplastic **109**
440.3*	Atherosclerosis of bypass graft of extremities **66**	448.9	Other and unspecified capillary diseases **66**
440.4	Chronic total occlusion of artery of the extremities **66**	449	Septic arterial embolism **66**, **166**, **170**
440.8	Atherosclerosis of other specified arteries **66**	451.0	Phlebitis and thrombophlebitis of superficial vessels of lower extremities **66**
440.9	Generalized and unspecified atherosclerosis **66**	451.1*	Phlebitis and thrombophlebitis of deep veins of lower extremities **66**, **166**, **170**
441.0*	Dissection of aorta **66**		
441.1	Thoracic aneurysm, ruptured **66**	451.2	Phlebitis and thrombophlebitis of lower extremities, unspecified **66**, **166**, **170**
441.2	Thoracic aneurysm without mention of rupture **66**		
441.3	Abdominal aneurysm, ruptured **66**	451.81	Phlebitis and thrombophlebitis of iliac vein **66**, **166**, **170**
441.4	Abdominal aneurysm without mention of rupture **66**	451.82	Phlebitis and thrombophlebitis of superficial veins of upper extremities **66**
441.5	Aortic aneurysm of unspecified site, ruptured **66**		
441.6	Thoracoabdominal aneurysm, ruptured **66**	451.83	Phlebitis and thrombophlebitis of deep veins of upper extremities **66**
441.7	Thoracoabdominal aneurysm without mention of rupture **66**		
441.9	Aortic aneurysm of unspecified site without mention of rupture **66**	451.84	Phlebitis and thrombophlebitis of upper extremities, unspecified **66**
		451.89	Phlebitis and thrombophlebitis of other site **66**
442.0	Aneurysm of artery of upper extremity **66**	451.9	Phlebitis and thrombophlebitis of unspecified site **66**
442.1	Aneurysm of renal artery **121**	452	Portal vein thrombosis **83**
442.2	Aneurysm of iliac artery **66**	453.0	Budd-Chiari syndrome **83**
442.3	Aneurysm of artery of lower extremity **66**	453.1	Thrombophlebitis migrans **66**
442.8*	Aneurysm of other specified artery **66**	453.2	Other venous embolism and thrombosis, of inferior vena cava **66**, **166**, **170**
442.9	Other aneurysm of unspecified site **66**		
443.0	Raynaud's syndrome **97**	453.3	Embolism and thrombosis of renal vein **121**
443.1	Thromboangiitis obliterans (Buerger's disease) **66**	453.4*	Acute venous embolism and thrombosis of deep vessels of lower extremity **66**
443.21	Dissection of carotid artery **66**		
443.22	Dissection of iliac artery **66**	453.5*	Chronic venous embolism and thrombosis of deep vessels of lower extremity **66**
443.23	Dissection of renal artery **121**		
443.24	Dissection of vertebral artery **66**	453.6	Venous embolism and thrombosis of superficial vessels of lower extremity **66**
443.29	Dissection of other artery **66**		
443.8*	Other specified peripheral vascular diseases **66**	453.7*	Chronic venous embolism and thrombosis of other specified vessels **67**
443.9	Unspecified peripheral vascular disease **66**		
444.0*	Arterial embolism and thrombosis of abdominal aorta **66**	453.8*	Acute venous embolism and thrombosis of other specified veins **67**
444.1	Embolism and thrombosis of thoracic aorta **66**	453.9	Embolism and thrombosis of unspecified site **67**
444.2*	Embolism and thrombosis of arteries of the extremities **66**	454.0	Varicose veins of lower extremities with ulcer **67**
444.8*	Embolism and thrombosis of other specified artery **66**	454.1	Varicose veins of lower extremities with inflammation **67**
444.9	Embolism and thrombosis of unspecified artery **66**	454.2	Varicose veins of lower extremities with ulcer and inflammation **67**
444*	Arterial embolism and thrombosis **166**, **170**		
445.0*	Atheroembolism of extremities **66**	454.8	Varicose veins of the lower extremities with other complications **67**
445.81	Atheroembolism of kidney **121**		
445.89	Atheroembolism of other site **66**	454.9	Asymptomatic varicose veins **67**
446.0	Polyarteritis nodosa **97**	455*	Hemorrhoids **78**
446.1	Acute febrile mucocutaneous lymph node syndrome (MCLS) **97**	456.0	Esophageal varices with bleeding **75**
		456.1	Esophageal varices without mention of bleeding **75**
446.2*	Hypersensitivity angiitis **97**	456.20	Esophageal varices with bleeding in diseases classified elsewhere **75**
446.3	Lethal midline granuloma **97**		
446.4	Wegener's granulomatosis **97**	456.21	Esophageal varices without mention of bleeding in diseases classified elsewhere **78**
446.5	Giant cell arteritis **97**		
446.6	Thrombotic microangiopathy **97**	456.3	Sublingual varices **67**
446.7	Takayasu's disease **97**	456.4	Scrotal varices **125**
447.0	Arteriovenous fistula, acquired **66**	456.5	Pelvic varices **125**, **128**, **131**
447.1	Stricture of artery **66**	456.6	Vulval varices **128**, **131**
447.2	Rupture of artery **66**	456.8	Varices of other sites **67**
447.3	Hyperplasia of renal artery **121**	457.0	Postmastectomy lymphedema syndrome **107**
447.4	Celiac artery compression syndrome **78**	457.1	Other noninfectious lymphedema **109**
447.5	Necrosis of artery **66**	457.2	Lymphangitis **107**, **166**, **170**
447.6	Unspecified arteritis **97**	457.8	Other noninfectious disorders of lymphatic channels **177**
447.7*	Aortic ectasia **66**	457.9	Unspecified noninfectious disorder of lymphatic channels **177**
447.8	Other specified disorders of arteries and arterioles **66**	458.0	Orthostatic hypotension **68**
447.9	Unspecified disorders of arteries and arterioles **66**	458.1	Chronic hypotension **69**
448.0	Hereditary hemorrhagic telangiectasia **66**	458.2*	Iatrogenic hypotension **68**

458.8	Other specified hypotension	**69**
458.9	Unspecified hypotension	**69**
459.0	Unspecified hemorrhage	**69 , 166 , 170**
459.1*	Postphlebitic syndrome	**67**
459.2	Compression of vein	**67**
459.3*	Chronic venous hypertension	**67**
459.81	Unspecified venous (peripheral) insufficiency	**67**
459.89	Other specified circulatory system disorders	**67**
459.9	Unspecified circulatory system disorder	**67**
460	Acute nasopharyngitis (common cold)	**3 , 46**
461*	Acute sinusitis	**46**
462	Acute pharyngitis	**3 , 46**
463	Acute tonsillitis	**3 , 46**
464.00	Acute laryngitis, without mention of obstruction	**3 , 46**
464.01	Acute laryngitis, with obstruction	**3 , 46**
464.1*	Acute tracheitis	**53**
464.2*	Acute laryngotracheitis	**3 , 46**
464.3*	Acute epiglottitis	**3 , 46**
464.4	Croup	**3 , 46**
464.50	Unspecified supraglottis, without mention of obstruction	**3 , 46**
464.51	Unspecified supraglottis, with obstruction	**3 , 46**
465*	Acute upper respiratory infections of multiple or unspecified sites	**3 , 46**
466*	Acute bronchitis and bronchiolitis	**53**
470	Deviated nasal septum	**3 , 47**
471*	Nasal polyps	**47**
472.1	Chronic pharyngitis	**3**
472.2	Chronic nasopharyngitis	**3**
472*	Chronic pharyngitis and nasopharyngitis	**46**
473*	Chronic sinusitis	**46**
474.00	Chronic tonsillitis	**46**
474.01	Chronic adenoiditis	**46**
474.02	Chronic tonsillitis and adenoiditis	**46**
474.1*	Hypertrophy of tonsils and adenoids	**47**
474.2	Adenoid vegetations	**47**
474.8	Other chronic disease of tonsils and adenoids	**47**
474.9	Unspecified chronic disease of tonsils and adenoids	**47**
474*	Chronic disease of tonsils and adenoids	**3**
475	Peritonsillar abscess	**3 , 46**
476.0	Chronic laryngitis	**3**
476.1	Chronic laryngotracheitis	**3**
476*	Chronic laryngitis and laryngotracheitis	**46**
477*	Allergic rhinitis	**46**
478.0	Hypertrophy of nasal turbinates	**47**
478.1*	Other diseases of nasal cavity and sinuses	**47**
478.11	Nasal mucositis (ulcerative)	**173**
478.19	Other diseases of nasal cavity and sinuses	**173**
478.2*	Other diseases of pharynx, not elsewhere classified	**3**
478.20	Unspecified disease of pharynx	**47**
478.21	Cellulitis of pharynx or nasopharynx	**46**
478.22	Parapharyngeal abscess	**46 , 166 , 170**
478.24	Retropharyngeal abscess	**46 , 166 , 170**
478.25	Edema of pharynx or nasopharynx	**47**
478.26	Cyst of pharynx or nasopharynx	**47**
478.29	Other disease of pharynx or nasopharynx	**47**
478.3*	Paralysis of vocal cords or larynx	**3 , 47 , 166 , 170**
478.4	Polyp of vocal cord or larynx	**3 , 47**
478.5	Other diseases of vocal cords	**3 , 47**
478.6	Edema of larynx	**3 , 47**

478.7*	Other diseases of larynx, not elsewhere classified	**3**
478.70	Unspecified disease of larynx	**47**
478.71	Cellulitis and perichondritis of larynx	**46**
478.74	Stenosis of larynx	**47**
478.75	Laryngeal spasm	**47 , 166 , 170**
478.79	Other diseases of larynx	**47**
478.8	Upper respiratory tract hypersensitivity reaction, site unspecified	**3 , 46**
478.9	Other and unspecified diseases of upper respiratory tract	**3 , 46**
480.3	Pneumonia due to SARS-associated coronavirus	**231**
480.8	Pneumonia due to other virus not elsewhere classified	**231**
480.9	Unspecified viral pneumonia	**231**
480*	Viral pneumonia	**53**
481	Pneumococcal pneumonia (streptococcus pneumoniae pneumonia)	**53 , 166 , 170 , 231**
482.0	Pneumonia due to Klebsiella pneumoniae	**51**
482.1	Pneumonia due to Pseudomonas	**51**
482.2	Pneumonia due to Hemophilus influenzae (H. influenzae)	**53**
482.3*	Pneumonia due to Streptococcus	**53**
482.4*	Pneumonia due to Staphylococcus	**51**
482.40	Pneumonia due to Staphylococcus, unspecified	**51**
482.41	Methicillin susceptible pneumonia due to Staphylococcus aureus	**51**
482.42	Methicillin resistant pneumonia due to Staphylococcus aureus	**51**
482.49	Other Staphylococcus pneumonia	**51**
482.8*	Pneumonia due to other specified bacteria	**51**
482.81	Pneumonia due to anaerobes	**51**
482.82	Pneumonia due to Escherichia coli (E. coli)	**51**
482.83	Pneumonia due to other gram-negative bacteria	**51**
482.84	Legionnaires' disease	**51**
482.89	Pneumonia due to other specified bacteria	**51**
482.9	Unspecified bacterial pneumonia	**53**
482*	Other bacterial pneumonia	**166 , 170 , 231**
483*	Pneumonia due to other specified organism	**53 , 166 , 170**
484*	Pneumonia in infectious diseases classified elsewhere	**51**
485	Bronchopneumonia, organism unspecified	**53 , 166 , 170**
486	Pneumonia, organism unspecified	**53 , 166 , 170 , 231**
487.0	Influenza with pneumonia	**51 , 53**
487.1	Influenza with other respiratory manifestations	**46**
487.8	Influenza with other manifestations	**186**
488.01	Influenza due to identified avian influenza virus with pneumonia	**53 , 166 , 170 , 231**
488.02	Influenza due to identified avian influenza virus with other respiratory manifestations	**53 , 166 , 170**
488.09	Influenza due to identified avian influenza virus with other manifestations	**186**
488.11	Influenza due to identified 2009 H1N1 influenza virus with pneumonia	**53 , 166 , 170 , 231**
488.12	Influenza due to identified 2009 H1N1 influenza virus with other respiratory manifestations	**53 , 166 , 170**
488.19	Influenza due to identified 2009 H1N1 influenza virus with other manifestations	**186**
488.81	Influenza due to identified novel influenza A virus with pneumonia	**53 , 166 , 170 , 231**
488.82	Influenza due to identified novel influenza A virus with other respiratory manifestations	**53 , 166 , 170**
488.89	Influenza due to identified novel influenza A virus with other manifestations	**186**
490	Bronchitis, not specified as acute or chronic	**53**
491.0	Simple chronic bronchitis	**53**
491.1	Mucopurulent chronic bronchitis	**53**

*Code Range

© 2012 OptumInsight, Inc.

491.2*	Obstructive chronic bronchitis **53**	
491.8	Other chronic bronchitis **53**	
491.9	Unspecified chronic bronchitis **53**	
492.0	Emphysematous bleb **53**	
492.8	Other emphysema **53**	
493.0*	Extrinsic asthma **53**	
493.01	Extrinsic asthma with status asthmaticus **166 , 170**	
493.1*	Intrinsic asthma **53**	
493.11	Intrinsic asthma with status asthmaticus **166 , 170**	
493.20	Chronic obstructive asthma, unspecified **53**	
493.21	Chronic obstructive asthma with status asthmaticus **53**	
493.22	Chronic obstructive asthma, with (acute) exacerbation **53**	
493.8*	Other forms of asthma **53**	
493.9*	Unspecified asthma **54**	
493.91	Asthma, unspecified with status asthmaticus **166 , 170**	
494*	Bronchiectasis **53**	
495*	Extrinsic allergic alveolitis **53**	
496	Chronic airway obstruction, not elsewhere classified **53**	
500	Coal workers' pneumoconiosis **53**	
501	Asbestosis **53**	
502	Pneumoconiosis due to other silica or silicates **53**	
503	Pneumoconiosis due to other inorganic dust **53**	
504	Pneumonopathy due to inhalation of other dust **53**	
505	Unspecified pneumoconiosis **53**	
506.0	Bronchitis and pneumonitis due to fumes and vapors **54**	
506.1	Acute pulmonary edema due to fumes and vapors **52**	
506.2	Upper respiratory inflammation due to fumes and vapors **54**	
506.3	Other acute and subacute respiratory conditions due to fumes and vapors **54**	
506.4	Chronic respiratory conditions due to fumes and vapors **53**	
506.9	Unspecified respiratory conditions due to fumes and vapors **53**	
507.0	Pneumonitis due to inhalation of food or vomitus **166 , 170**	
507.8	Pneumonitis due to other solids and liquids **166 , 170**	
507*	Pneumonitis due to solids and liquids **51**	
508.0	Acute pulmonary manifestations due to radiation **54 , 166 , 170**	
508.1	Chronic and other pulmonary manifestations due to radiation **53**	
508.2	Respiratory conditions due to smoke inhalation **54 , 208**	
508.8	Respiratory conditions due to other specified external agents **54**	
508.9	Respiratory conditions due to unspecified external agent **54**	
510*	Empyema **51 , 166 , 170**	
511.0	Pleurisy without mention of effusion or current tuberculosis **53**	
511.1	Pleurisy with effusion, with mention of bacterial cause other than tuberculosis **51 , 166 , 171**	
511.81	Malignant pleural effusion **52**	
511.89	Other specified forms of effusion, except tuberculous **52 , 166 , 171**	
511.9	Unspecified pleural effusion **52 , 166 , 171**	
512.0	Spontaneous tension pneumothorax **53**	
512.1	Iatrogenic pneumothorax **53**	
512.2	Postoperative air leak **53**	
512.8*	Other pneumothorax and air leak **53**	
513*	Abscess of lung and mediastinum **51 , 166 , 171**	
514	Pulmonary congestion and hypostasis **52**	
515	Postinflammatory pulmonary fibrosis **53**	
516.30	Idiopathic interstitial pneumonia, not otherwise specified **231**	
516.35	Idiopathic lymphoid interstitial pneumonia **231**	
516.36	Cryptogenic organizing pneumonia **231**	
516.37	Desquamative interstitial pneumonia **231**	
516.6*	Interstitial lung diseases of childhood **166 , 171**	

516.8	Other specified alveolar and parietoalveolar pneumonopathies **231**	
516*	Other alveolar and parietoalveolar pneumonopathy **53**	
517.1	Rheumatic pneumonia **53**	
517.2	Lung involvement in systemic sclerosis **53**	
517.3	Acute chest syndrome **53**	
517.8	Lung involvement in other diseases classified elsewhere **53**	
518.0	Pulmonary collapse **54 , 166 , 171**	
518.1	Interstitial emphysema **53 , 166 , 171**	
518.2	Compensatory emphysema **54**	
518.3	Pulmonary eosinophilia **53**	
518.4	Unspecified acute edema of lung **52 , 166 , 171**	
518.5*	Pulmonary insufficiency following trauma and surgery **52 , 208**	
518.52	Other pulmonary insufficiency, not elsewhere classified, following trauma and surgery **166 , 171**	
518.6	Allergic bronchopulmonary aspergillosis **53**	
518.7	Transfusion related acute lung injury [TRALI] **54**	
518.81	Acute respiratory failure **52 , 208**	
518.82	Other pulmonary insufficiency, not elsewhere classified **54**	
518.83	Chronic respiratory failure **52**	
518.84	Acute and chronic respiratory failure **52 , 208**	
518.89	Other diseases of lung, not elsewhere classified **54**	
519.0*	Tracheostomy complications **3 , 54**	
519.1*	Other diseases of trachea and bronchus, not elsewhere classified **54**	
519.11	Acute bronchospasm **3**	
519.19	Other diseases of trachea and bronchus **3**	
519.2	Mediastinitis **51 , 166 , 171**	
519.3	Other diseases of mediastinum, not elsewhere classified **54**	
519.4	Disorders of diaphragm **54**	
519.8	Other diseases of respiratory system, not elsewhere classified **54**	
519.9	Unspecified disease of respiratory system **54**	
520.6	Disturbances in tooth eruption **173**	
520*	Disorders of tooth development and eruption **3 , 48**	
521*	Diseases of hard tissues of teeth **3 , 48**	
522*	Diseases of pulp and periapical tissues **3 , 48**	
523*	Gingival and periodontal diseases **3 , 48**	
524*	Dentofacial anomalies, including malocclusion **3 , 48**	
525*	Other diseases and conditions of the teeth and supporting structures **3 , 48**	
526*	Diseases of the jaws **3 , 48**	
527.9	Unspecified disease of the salivary glands **231**	
527*	Diseases of the salivary glands **3 , 47**	
528.6	Leukoplakia of oral mucosa, including tongue **231**	
528*	Diseases of the oral soft tissues, excluding lesions specific for gingiva and tongue **3 , 48**	
529*	Diseases and other conditions of the tongue **3 , 48**	
530.0	Achalasia and cardiospasm **78**	
530.1*	Esophagitis **78**	
530.2*	Ulcer of esophagus **77**	
530.3	Stricture and stenosis of esophagus **78**	
530.4	Perforation of esophagus **75 , 166 , 171**	
530.5	Dyskinesia of esophagus **78**	
530.6	Diverticulum of esophagus, acquired **78**	
530.7	Gastroesophageal laceration-hemorrhage syndrome **75**	
530.81	Esophageal reflux **78**	
530.82	Esophageal hemorrhage **75**	
530.83	Esophageal leukoplakia **78**	
530.84	Tracheoesophageal fistula **75 , 166 , 171**	
530.85	Barrett's esophagus **77**	

530.86	Infection of esophagostomy **78**	
530.87	Mechanical complication of esophagostomy **78**	
530.89	Other specified disorder of the esophagus **78**	
530.9	Unspecified disorder of esophagus **78**	
531.0*	Acute gastric ulcer with hemorrhage **76**	
531.1*	Acute gastric ulcer with perforation **77**	
531.2*	Acute gastric ulcer with hemorrhage and perforation **76**	
531.30	Acute gastric ulcer without mention of hemorrhage, perforation, or obstruction **77**	
531.31	Acute gastric ulcer without mention of hemorrhage or perforation, with obstruction **77**	
531.4*	Chronic or unspecified gastric ulcer with hemorrhage **76**	
531.5*	Chronic or unspecified gastric ulcer with perforation **77**	
531.6*	Chronic or unspecified gastric ulcer with hemorrhage and perforation **76**	
531.70	Chronic gastric ulcer without mention of hemorrhage, perforation, without mention of obstruction **77**	
531.71	Chronic gastric ulcer without mention of hemorrhage or perforation, with obstruction **77**	
531.90	Gastric ulcer, unspecified as acute or chronic, without mention of hemorrhage, perforation, or obstruction **77**	
531.91	Gastric ulcer, unspecified as acute or chronic, without mention of hemorrhage or perforation, with obstruction **77**	
532.0*	Acute duodenal ulcer with hemorrhage **76**	
532.1*	Acute duodenal ulcer with perforation **77**	
532.2*	Acute duodenal ulcer with hemorrhage and perforation **76**	
532.30	Acute duodenal ulcer without mention of hemorrhage, perforation, or obstruction **77**	
532.31	Acute duodenal ulcer without mention of hemorrhage or perforation, with obstruction **77**	
532.4*	Chronic or unspecified duodenal ulcer with hemorrhage **76**	
532.5*	Chronic or unspecified duodenal ulcer with perforation **77**	
532.6*	Chronic or unspecified duodenal ulcer with hemorrhage and perforation **76**	
532.70	Chronic duodenal ulcer without mention of hemorrhage, perforation, or obstruction **77**	
532.71	Chronic duodenal ulcer without mention of hemorrhage or perforation, with obstruction **77**	
532.90	Duodenal ulcer, unspecified as acute or chronic, without hemorrhage, perforation, or obstruction **77**	
532.91	Duodenal ulcer, unspecified as acute or chronic, without mention of hemorrhage or perforation, with obstruction **77**	
533.0*	Acute peptic ulcer, unspecified site, with hemorrhage **76**	
533.1*	Acute peptic ulcer, unspecified site, with perforation **77**	
533.2*	Acute peptic ulcer, unspecified site, with hemorrhage and perforation **76**	
533.30	Acute peptic ulcer, unspecified site, without mention of hemorrhage, perforation, or obstruction **77**	
533.31	Acute peptic ulcer, unspecified site, without mention of hemorrhage and perforation, with obstruction **77**	
533.4*	Chronic or unspecified peptic ulcer, unspecified site, with hemorrhage **76**	
533.5*	Chronic or unspecified peptic ulcer, unspecified site, with perforation **77**	
533.6*	Chronic or unspecified peptic ulcer, unspecified site, with hemorrhage and perforation **76**	
533.70	Chronic peptic ulcer, unspecified site, without mention of hemorrhage, perforation, or obstruction **77**	
533.71	Chronic peptic ulcer of unspecified site without mention of hemorrhage or perforation, with obstruction **77**	
533.90	Peptic ulcer, unspecified site, unspecified as acute or chronic, without mention of hemorrhage, perforation, or obstruction **77**	

533.91	Peptic ulcer, unspecified site, unspecified as acute or chronic, without mention of hemorrhage or perforation, with obstruction **77**
534.0*	Acute gastrojejunal ulcer with hemorrhage **76**
534.1*	Acute gastrojejunal ulcer with perforation **77**
534.2*	Acute gastrojejunal ulcer with hemorrhage and perforation **76**
534.3*	Acute gastrojejunal ulcer without mention of hemorrhage or perforation **77**
534.4*	Chronic or unspecified gastrojejunal ulcer with hemorrhage **76**
534.5*	Chronic or unspecified gastrojejunal ulcer with perforation **77**
534.6*	Chronic or unspecified gastrojejunal ulcer with hemorrhage and perforation **76**
534.7*	Chronic gastrojejunal ulcer without mention of hemorrhage or perforation **77**
534.9*	Gastrojejunal ulcer, unspecified as acute or chronic, without mention of hemorrhage or perforation **77**
535.00	Acute gastritis without mention of hemorrhage **78**
535.01	Acute gastritis with hemorrhage **76**
535.10	Atrophic gastritis without mention of hemorrhage **78**
535.11	Atrophic gastritis with hemorrhage **76**
535.20	Gastric mucosal hypertrophy without mention of hemorrhage **78**
535.21	Gastric mucosal hypertrophy with hemorrhage **76**
535.30	Alcoholic gastritis without mention of hemorrhage **78**
535.31	Alcoholic gastritis with hemorrhage **76**
535.40	Other specified gastritis without mention of hemorrhage **78**
535.41	Other specified gastritis with hemorrhage **76**
535.50	Unspecified gastritis and gastroduodenitis without mention of hemorrhage **78**
535.51	Unspecified gastritis and gastroduodenitis with hemorrhage **76**
535.60	Duodenitis without mention of hemorrhage **78**
535.61	Duodenitis with hemorrhage **76**
535.70	Eosinophilic gastritis without mention of hemorrhage **78**
535.71	Eosinophilic gastritis with hemorrhage **76**
536.0	Achlorhydria **78**
536.1	Acute dilatation of stomach **78 , 166 , 171**
536.2	Persistent vomiting **78**
536.3	Gastroparesis **78**
536.4*	Gastrostomy complications **78**
536.8	Dyspepsia and other specified disorders of function of stomach **78**
536.9	Unspecified functional disorder of stomach **78**
537.0	Acquired hypertrophic pyloric stenosis **77**
537.1	Gastric diverticulum **78**
537.2	Chronic duodenal ileus **78**
537.3	Other obstruction of duodenum **77**
537.4	Fistula of stomach or duodenum **78**
537.5	Gastroptosis **78**
537.6	Hourglass stricture or stenosis of stomach **78**
537.81	Pylorospasm **78**
537.82	Angiodysplasia of stomach and duodenum (without mention of hemorrhage) **78**
537.83	Angiodysplasia of stomach and duodenum with hemorrhage **76**
537.84	Dieulafoy lesion (hemorrhagic) of stomach and duodenum **76**
537.89	Other specified disorder of stomach and duodenum **78**
537.9	Unspecified disorder of stomach and duodenum **78**
538	Gastrointestinal mucositis (ulcerative) **78**
539*	Complications of bariatric procedures **78**
540.0	Acute appendicitis with generalized peritonitis **73 , 76**
540.1	Acute appendicitis with peritoneal abscess **73 , 76**
540.9	Acute appendicitis without mention of peritonitis **78**
541	Appendicitis, unqualified **78**

542	Other appendicitis **78**	
543*	Other diseases of appendix **78**	
550.00	Inguinal hernia with gangrene, unilateral or unspecified, (not specified as recurrent) **167 , 171**	
550.02	Inguinal hernia with gangrene, bilateral **167 , 171**	
550.10	Inguinal hernia with obstruction, without mention of gangrene, unilateral or unspecified, (not specified as recurrent) **167 , 171**	
550.12	Inguinal hernia with obstruction, without mention gangrene, bilateral, (not specified as recurrent) **167 , 171**	
550*	Inguinal hernia **78**	
551.00	Femoral hernia with gangrene, unilateral or unspecified (not specified as recurrent) **167 , 171**	
551.02	Femoral hernia with gangrene, bilateral, (not specified as recurrent) **167 , 171**	
551.1	Umbilical hernia with gangrene **167 , 171**	
551.2*	Ventral hernia with gangrene **167 , 171**	
551.3	Diaphragmatic hernia with gangrene **167 , 171**	
551.8	Hernia of other specified sites, with gangrene **167 , 171**	
551.9	Hernia of unspecified site, with gangrene **167 , 171**	
551*	Other hernia of abdominal cavity, with gangrene **78**	
552.0*	Femoral hernia with obstruction **78**	
552.00	Unilateral or unspecified femoral hernia with obstruction **167 , 171**	
552.02	Bilateral femoral hernia with obstruction **167 , 171**	
552.1	Umbilical hernia with obstruction **78 , 167 , 171**	
552.2*	Ventral hernia with obstruction **78 , 167 , 171**	
552.3	Diaphragmatic hernia with obstruction **78 , 167 , 171**	
552.8	Hernia of other specified site, with obstruction **78 , 167 , 171**	
552.9	Hernia of unspecified site, with obstruction **78 , 167 , 171**	
553.0*	Femoral hernia without mention of obstruction or gangrene **79**	
553.1	Umbilical hernia without mention of obstruction or gangrene **79**	
553.2*	Ventral hernia without mention of obstruction or gangrene **79**	
553.3	Diaphragmatic hernia without mention of obstruction or gangrene **78**	
553.8	Hernia of other specified sites of abdominal cavity without mention of obstruction or gangrene **79**	
553.9	Hernia of unspecified site of abdominal cavity without mention of obstruction or gangrene **79**	
555*	Regional enteritis **77**	
556*	Ulcerative colitis **77**	
557.0	Acute vascular insufficiency of intestine **167 , 171**	
557*	Vascular insufficiency of intestine **79**	
558.1	Gastroenteritis and colitis due to radiation **79 , 231**	
558.2	Toxic gastroenteritis and colitis **79 , 167 , 171 , 231**	
558.3	Gastroenteritis and colitis, allergic **78**	
558.4*	Eosinophilic gastroenteritis and colitis **78 , 231**	
558.9	Other and unspecified noninfectious gastroenteritis and colitis **78 , 231**	
560.0	Intussusception **167 , 171**	
560.1	Paralytic ileus **167 , 171**	
560.2	Volvulus **167 , 171**	
560.30	Unspecified impaction of intestine **167 , 171**	
560.32	Fecal impaction **167 , 171**	
560.39	Impaction of intestine, other **167 , 171**	
560.89	Other specified intestinal obstruction **167 , 171**	
560.9	Unspecified intestinal obstruction **167 , 171**	
560*	Intestinal obstruction without mention of hernia **77**	
562.00	Diverticulosis of small intestine (without mention of hemorrhage) **78**	
562.01	Diverticulitis of small intestine (without mention of hemorrhage) **78**	

562.02	Diverticulosis of small intestine with hemorrhage **76**
562.03	Diverticulitis of small intestine with hemorrhage **76**
562.10	Diverticulosis of colon (without mention of hemorrhage) **78**
562.11	Diverticulitis of colon (without mention of hemorrhage) **78**
562.12	Diverticulosis of colon with hemorrhage **76**
562.13	Diverticulitis of colon with hemorrhage **76**
564.0*	Constipation **78**
564.1	Irritable bowel syndrome **78**
564.2	Postgastric surgery syndromes **78**
564.3	Vomiting following gastrointestinal surgery **78**
564.4	Other postoperative functional disorders **78**
564.5	Functional diarrhea **78**
564.6	Anal spasm **78**
564.7	Megacolon, other than Hirschsprung's **79**
564.8*	Other specified functional disorders of intestine **78**
564.9	Unspecified functional disorder of intestine **78**
565*	Anal fissure and fistula **79**
566	Abscess of anal and rectal regions **79 , 167 , 171**
567.0	Peritonitis in infectious diseases classified elsewhere **76**
567.1	Pneumococcal peritonitis **76**
567.2*	Other suppurative peritonitis **76**
567.3*	Retroperitoneal infections **76**
567.81	Choleperitonitis **79**
567.82	Sclerosing mesenteritis **79**
567.89	Other specified peritonitis **76**
567.9	Unspecified peritonitis **76**
567*	Peritonitis and retroperitoneal infections **167 , 171**
568.81	Hemoperitoneum (nontraumatic) **167 , 171**
568*	Other disorders of peritoneum **79**
569.0	Anal and rectal polyp **79**
569.1	Rectal prolapse **79**
569.2	Stenosis of rectum and anus **79**
569.3	Hemorrhage of rectum and anus **76 , 167 , 171**
569.4*	Other specified disorders of rectum and anus **79**
569.5	Abscess of intestine **76**
569.6*	Colostomy and enterostomy complications **79**
569.7*	Complications of intestinal pouch **79 , 167 , 171**
569.81	Fistula of intestine, excluding rectum and anus **79**
569.82	Ulceration of intestine **79**
569.83	Perforation of intestine **79 , 167 , 171**
569.84	Angiodysplasia of intestine (without mention of hemorrhage) **79**
569.85	Angiodysplasia of intestine with hemorrhage **76**
569.86	Dieulafoy lesion (hemorrhagic) of intestine **79**
569.87	Vomiting of fecal matter **79**
569.89	Other specified disorder of intestines **79**
569.9	Unspecified disorder of intestine **79**
570	Acute and subacute necrosis of liver **83 , 167 , 171**
571.0	Alcoholic fatty liver **83**
571.1	Acute alcoholic hepatitis **82**
571.2	Alcoholic cirrhosis of liver **82**
571.3	Unspecified alcoholic liver damage **82**
571.4*	Chronic hepatitis **83**
571.5	Cirrhosis of liver without mention of alcohol **82**
571.6	Biliary cirrhosis **82**
571.8	Other chronic nonalcoholic liver disease **83**
571.9	Unspecified chronic liver disease without mention of alcohol **83**
572.0	Abscess of liver **167 , 171**
572.1	Portal pyemia **167 , 171**
572.2	Hepatic encephalopathy **167 , 171**

572.4	Hepatorenal syndrome **167 , 171**	
572*	Liver abscess and sequelae of chronic liver disease **83**	
573.0	Chronic passive congestion of liver **83**	
573.1	Hepatitis in viral diseases classified elsewhere **83**	
573.2	Hepatitis in other infectious diseases classified elsewhere **83**	
573.3	Unspecified hepatitis **83 , 167 , 171**	
573.4	Hepatic infarction **83 , 167 , 171**	
573.5	Hepatopulmonary syndrome **54**	
573.8	Other specified disorders of liver **83**	
573.9	Unspecified disorder of liver **83**	
574*	Cholelithiasis **83**	
575*	Other disorders of gallbladder **83**	
576.1	Cholangitis **167 , 171**	
576*	Other disorders of biliary tract **83**	
577.0	Acute pancreatitis **167 , 171**	
577.2	Cyst and pseudocyst of pancreas **167 , 171**	
577*	Diseases of pancreas **83**	
578*	Gastrointestinal hemorrhage **76 , 167 , 171**	
579.3	Other and unspecified postsurgical nonabsorption **167 , 171**	
579.9	Unspecified intestinal malabsorption **232**	
579*	Intestinal malabsorption **78**	
580*	Acute glomerulonephritis **121 , 167 , 171 , 232**	
581*	Nephrotic syndrome **121 , 232**	
582*	Chronic glomerulonephritis **121 , 232**	
583*	Nephritis and nephropathy, not specified as acute or chronic **121 , 232**	
584*	Acute kidney failure **167 , 171**	
584.5	Acute kidney failure with lesion of tubular necrosis **119**	
584.6	Acute kidney failure with lesion of renal cortical necrosis **119**	
584.8	Acute kidney failure with other specified pathological lesion in kidney **119**	
584.9	Acute kidney failure, unspecified **119**	
584.7	Acute kidney failure with lesion of medullary [papillary] necrosis **119**	
585*	Chronic kidney disease (CKD) **2 , 119**	
586	Unspecified renal failure **119 , 120**	
587	Unspecified renal sclerosis **121**	
588*	Disorders resulting from impaired renal function **121**	
589*	Small kidney of unknown cause **121**	
590.1*	Acute pyelonephritis **167 , 171**	
590.2	Renal and perinephric abscess **167 , 171**	
590.3	Pyeloureteritis cystica **167 , 171**	
590.8*	Other pyelonephritis or pyonephrosis, not specified as acute or chronic **167 , 171**	
590.9	Unspecified infection of kidney **167 , 171**	
590*	Infections of kidney **120**	
591	Hydronephrosis **120 , 167 , 171**	
592*	Calculus of kidney and ureter **120**	
593.0	Nephroptosis **121**	
593.1	Hypertrophy of kidney **121**	
593.2	Acquired cyst of kidney **121**	
593.3	Stricture or kinking of ureter **120**	
593.4	Other ureteric obstruction **120**	
593.5	Hydroureter **120 , 167 , 171**	
593.6	Postural proteinuria **121**	
593.7*	Vesicoureteral reflux **121**	
593.8*	Other specified disorders of kidney and ureter **121**	
593.9	Unspecified disorder of kidney and ureter **121**	
594.0	Calculus in diverticulum of bladder **121**	
594.1	Other calculus in bladder **120**	

594.2	Calculus in urethra **120**	
594.8	Other lower urinary tract calculus **120**	
594.9	Unspecified calculus of lower urinary tract **120**	
595.0	Acute cystitis **120 , 167 , 171**	
595.1	Chronic interstitial cystitis **120**	
595.2	Other chronic cystitis **120**	
595.3	Trigonitis **120**	
595.4	Cystitis in diseases classified elsewhere **120 , 167 , 171**	
595.81	Cystitis cystica **120 , 167 , 171**	
595.82	Irradiation cystitis **121**	
595.89	Other specified types of cystitis **120 , 167 , 171**	
595.9	Unspecified cystitis **120 , 167 , 171**	
596.0	Bladder neck obstruction **167 , 171**	
596.1	Intestinovesical fistula **167 , 171**	
596.2	Vesical fistula, not elsewhere classified **167 , 171**	
596.4	Atony of bladder **167 , 171**	
596.6	Nontraumatic rupture of bladder **167 , 171**	
596.7	Hemorrhage into bladder wall **167 , 171**	
596*	Other disorders of bladder **121**	
597.0	Urethral abscess **167 , 171**	
597*	Urethritis, not sexually transmitted, and urethral syndrome **120**	
598*	Urethral stricture **121**	
599.0	Urinary tract infection, site not specified **120 , 167 , 171**	
599.1	Urethral fistula **121**	
599.2	Urethral diverticulum **121**	
599.3	Urethral caruncle **121**	
599.4	Urethral false passage **121**	
599.5	Prolapsed urethral mucosa **121**	
599.6*	Urinary obstruction **121 , 167 , 171**	
599.7*	Hematuria **120 , 167 , 171**	
599.8*	Other specified disorder of urethra and urinary tract **121**	
599.9	Unspecified disorder of urethra and urinary tract **121**	
600*	Hyperplasia of prostate **124**	
601*	Inflammatory diseases of prostate **125**	
602*	Other disorders of prostate **125**	
603.0	Encysted hydrocele **125**	
603.1	Infected hydrocele **125**	
603.8	Other specified type of hydrocele **125**	
603.9	Unspecified hydrocele **125**	
604*	Orchitis and epididymitis **125**	
605	Redundant prepuce and phimosis **125 , 173**	
606*	Male infertility **125**	
607.0	Leukoplakia of penis **125**	
607.1	Balanoposthitis **125**	
607.2	Other inflammatory disorders of penis **125**	
607.3	Priapism **125**	
607.81	Balanitis xerotica obliterans **125**	
607.82	Vascular disorders of penis **125**	
607.83	Edema of penis **125**	
607.84	Impotence of organic origin **125**	
607.85	Peyronie's disease **125**	
607.89	Other specified disorder of penis **125**	
607.9	Unspecified disorder of penis **125**	
608.0	Seminal vesiculitis **125**	
608.1	Spermatocele **125**	
608.2*	Torsion of testis **125**	
608.3	Atrophy of testis **125**	
608.4	Other inflammatory disorder of male genital organs **125**	
608.8*	Other specified disorder of male genital organs **125**	

*Code Range

608.9	Unspecified disorder of male genital organs **125**	625.6	Female stress incontinence **131**
610*	Benign mammary dysplasias **107**	625.70	Vulvodynia, unspecified **131**
611*	Other disorders of breast **107**	625.71	Vulvar vestibulitis **131**
612*	Deformity and disproportion of reconstructed breast **107**	625.79	Other vulvodynia **131**
614.0	Acute salpingitis and oophoritis **131**	625.8	Other specified symptom associated with female genital organs **131**
614.1	Chronic salpingitis and oophoritis **131**	625.9	Unspecified symptom associated with female genital organs **131**
614.2	Salpingitis and oophoritis not specified as acute, subacute, or chronic **131**	625*	Pain and other symptoms associated with female genital organs **128**
614.3	Acute parametritis and pelvic cellulitis **131**	626*	Disorders of menstruation and other abnormal bleeding from female genital tract **128 , 131**
614.4	Chronic or unspecified parametritis and pelvic cellulitis **131**	627*	Menopausal and postmenopausal disorders **128 , 131**
614.5	Acute or unspecified pelvic peritonitis, female **131**	628*	Female infertility **128 , 131**
614.6	Pelvic peritoneal adhesions, female (postoperative) (postinfection) **131**	629.0	Hematocele, female, not elsewhere classified **131**
614.7	Other chronic pelvic peritonitis, female **131**	629.1	Hydrocele, canal of Nuck **131**
614.8	Other specified inflammatory disease of female pelvic organs and tissues **131**	629.2*	Female genital mutilation status **131**
614.9	Unspecified inflammatory disease of female pelvic organs and tissues **131**	629.3*	Complication of implanted vaginal mesh and other prosthetic materials **131**
614*	Inflammatory disease of ovary, fallopian tube, pelvic cellular tissue, and peritoneum **128**	629.8*	Other specified disorders of female genital organs **131**
615*	Inflammatory diseases of uterus, except cervix **128 , 131**	629.9	Unspecified disorder of female genital organs **131**
616.0	Cervicitis and endocervicitis **128 , 131**	629*	Other disorders of female genital organs **128**
616.1*	Vaginitis and vulvovaginitis **128 , 131**	630	Hydatidiform mole **155 , 158**
616.2	Cyst of Bartholin's gland **128 , 131**	631*	Other abnormal product of conception **155 , 158**
616.3	Abscess of Bartholin's gland **128 , 131**	632	Missed abortion **154**
616.4	Other abscess of vulva **128 , 131**	633*	Ectopic pregnancy **154**
616.5*	Ulceration of vulva **128 , 131**	634*	Spontaneous abortion **154**
616.8*	Other specified inflammatory diseases of cervix, vagina, and vulva **128 , 131**	635*	Legally induced abortion **154**
		636*	Illegally induced abortion **154**
616.9	Unspecified inflammatory disease of cervix, vagina, and vulva **128 , 131**	637*	Abortion, unspecified as to legality **154**
		638*	Failed attempted abortion **154**
617.0	Endometriosis of uterus **128 , 131**	639*	Complications following abortion or ectopic and molar pregnancies **152**
617.1	Endometriosis of ovary **128 , 131**	640.00	Threatened abortion, unspecified as to episode of care **154**
617.2	Endometriosis of fallopian tube **128 , 131**	640.01	Threatened abortion, delivered **135 , 142 , 148**
617.3	Endometriosis of pelvic peritoneum **128 , 131**	640.03	Threatened abortion, antepartum **154**
617.4	Endometriosis of rectovaginal septum and vagina **128 , 131**	640.80	Other specified hemorrhage in early pregnancy, unspecified as to episode of care **154**
617.5	Endometriosis of intestine **78**	640.81	Other specified hemorrhage in early pregnancy, delivered **135 , 142 , 148**
617.6	Endometriosis in scar of skin **109**	640.83	Other specified hemorrhage in early pregnancy, antepartum **154**
617.8	Endometriosis of other specified sites **128 , 131**	640.90	Unspecified hemorrhage in early pregnancy, unspecified as to episode of care **154**
617.9	Endometriosis, site unspecified **128 , 131**	640.91	Unspecified hemorrhage in early pregnancy, delivered **135 , 142 , 148**
618*	Genital prolapse **128 , 131**	640.93	Unspecified hemorrhage in early pregnancy, antepartum **154**
619.0	Urinary-genital tract fistula, female **128 , 131**	641.00	Placenta previa without hemorrhage, unspecified as to episode of care **160**
619.1	Digestive-genital tract fistula, female **79 , 167 , 171**	641.01	Placenta previa without hemorrhage, with delivery **135 , 141 , 146**
619.2	Genital tract-skin fistula, female **128 , 131**	641.03	Placenta previa without hemorrhage, antepartum **155 , 158**
619.8	Other specified fistula involving female genital tract **128 , 131 , 167 , 171**	641.10	Hemorrhage from placenta previa, unspecified as to episode of care **160**
619.9	Unspecified fistula involving female genital tract **128 , 131**	641.11	Hemorrhage from placenta previa, with delivery **135 , 141 , 146**
620.7	Hematoma of broad ligament **167 , 171**	641.13	Hemorrhage from placenta previa, antepartum **155 , 158**
620*	Noninflammatory disorders of ovary, fallopian tube, and broad ligament **128 , 131**	641.20	Premature separation of placenta, unspecified as to episode of care **160**
621*	Disorders of uterus, not elsewhere classified **128 , 131**	641.21	Premature separation of placenta, with delivery **135 , 141 , 146**
622*	Noninflammatory disorders of cervix **128 , 131**	641.23	Premature separation of placenta, antepartum **155 , 158**
623.8	Other specified noninflammatory disorder of vagina **173**	641.30	Antepartum hemorrhage associated with coagulation defects, unspecified as to episode of care **157 , 160**
623*	Noninflammatory disorders of vagina **128 , 131**		
624*	Noninflammatory disorders of vulva and perineum **128 , 131**	641.31	Antepartum hemorrhage associated with coagulation defects, with delivery **135 , 141 , 146**
625.0	Dyspareunia **131**		
625.1	Vaginismus **131**		
625.2	Mittelschmerz **131**		
625.3	Dysmenorrhea **131**		
625.4	Premenstrual tension syndromes **131**		
625.5	Pelvic congestion syndrome **131**		

Numeric Index to Diseases

641.33 Antepartum hemorrhage associated with coagulation defect, antepartum **155** , **157**

641.80 Other antepartum hemorrhage, unspecified as to episode of care **160**

641.81 Other antepartum hemorrhage, with delivery **135** , **141** , **146**

641.83 Other antepartum hemorrhage, antepartum **155** , **158**

641.90 Unspecified antepartum hemorrhage, unspecified as to episode of care **160**

641.91 Unspecified antepartum hemorrhage, with delivery **135** , **141** , **146**

641.93 Unspecified antepartum hemorrhage, antepartum **155** , **158**

642.00 Benign essential hypertension complicating pregnancy, childbirth, and the puerperium, unspecified as to episode of care **160**

642.01 Benign essential hypertension with delivery **135** , **141** , **146**

642.02 Benign essential hypertension, with delivery, with current postpartum complication **135** , **141** , **146**

642.03 Benign essential hypertension antepartum **155** , **157**

642.04 Benign essential hypertension, complicating pregnancy, childbirth, and the puerperium, postpartum condition or complication **152**

642.10 Hypertension secondary to renal disease, complicating pregnancy, childbirth, and the puerperium, unspecified as to episode of care **160**

642.11 Hypertension secondary to renal disease, with delivery **135** , **141** , **146**

642.12 Hypertension secondary to renal disease, with delivery, with current postpartum complication **135** , **141** , **147**

642.13 Hypertension secondary to renal disease, antepartum **155** , **157**

642.14 Hypertension secondary to renal disease, complicating pregnancy, childbirth, and the puerperium, postpartum condition or complication **152**

642.20 Other pre-existing hypertension complicating pregnancy, childbirth, and the puerperium, unspecified as to episode of care **160**

642.21 Other pre-existing hypertension, with delivery **135** , **141** , **147**

642.22 Other pre-existing hypertension, with delivery, with current postpartum complication **135** , **141** , **147**

642.23 Other pre-existing hypertension, antepartum **155** , **157**

642.24 Other pre-existing hypertension complicating pregnancy, childbirth, and the puerperium, postpartum condition or complication **152**

642.30 Transient hypertension of pregnancy, unspecified as to episode of care **160**

642.31 Transient hypertension of pregnancy, with delivery **135** , **142** , **148**

642.32 Transient hypertension of pregnancy, with delivery, with current postpartum complication **135** , **142** , **148**

642.33 Transient hypertension of pregnancy, antepartum **155** , **158**

642.34 Transient hypertension of pregnancy, postpartum condition or complication **152**

642.40 Mild or unspecified pre-eclampsia, unspecified as to episode of care **160**

642.41 Mild or unspecified pre-eclampsia, with delivery **135** , **141** , **147**

642.42 Mild or unspecified pre-eclampsia, with delivery, with current postpartum complication **135** , **141** , **147**

642.43 Mild or unspecified pre-eclampsia, antepartum **155** , **157**

642.44 Mild or unspecified pre-eclampsia, postpartum condition or complication **152**

642.50 Severe pre-eclampsia, unspecified as to episode of care **157** , **160**

642.51 Severe pre-eclampsia, with delivery **135** , **141** , **147**

642.52 Severe pre-eclampsia, with delivery, with current postpartum complication **135** , **141** , **147**

642.53 Severe pre-eclampsia, antepartum **155** , **157**

642.54 Severe pre-eclampsia, postpartum condition or complication **152**

642.60 Eclampsia complicating pregnancy, childbirth or the puerperium, unspecified as to episode of care **157** , **160**

642.61 Eclampsia, with delivery **135** , **141** , **147**

642.62 Eclampsia, with delivery, with current postpartum complication **135** , **141** , **147**

642.63 Eclampsia, antepartum **155** , **157**

642.64 Eclampsia, postpartum condition or complication **152**

642.70 Pre-eclampsia or eclampsia superimposed on pre-existing hypertension, complicating pregnancy, childbirth, or the puerperium, unspecified as to episode of care **157** , **160**

642.71 Pre-eclampsia or eclampsia superimposed on pre-existing hypertension, with delivery **135** , **141** , **147**

642.72 Pre-eclampsia or eclampsia superimposed on pre-existing hypertension, with delivery, with current postpartum complication **135** , **141** , **147**

642.73 Pre-eclampsia or eclampsia superimposed on pre-existing hypertension, antepartum **155** , **157**

642.74 Pre-eclampsia or eclampsia superimposed on pre-existing hypertension, postpartum condition or complication **152**

642.90 Unspecified hypertension complicating pregnancy, childbirth, or the puerperium, unspecified as to episode of care **160**

642.91 Unspecified hypertension, with delivery **135** , **141** , **147**

642.92 Unspecified hypertension, with delivery, with current postpartum complication **135** , **141** , **147**

642.93 Unspecified hypertension antepartum **155** , **157**

642.94 Unspecified hypertension complicating pregnancy, childbirth, or the puerperium, postpartum condition or complication **152**

643.00 Mild hyperemesis gravidarum, unspecified as to episode of care **157** , **160**

643.01 Mild hyperemesis gravidarum, delivered **135** , **142** , **148**

643.03 Mild hyperemesis gravidarum, antepartum **155** , **157**

643.10 Hyperemesis gravidarum with metabolic disturbance, unspecified as to episode of care **157** , **160**

643.11 Hyperemesis gravidarum with metabolic disturbance, delivered **135** , **142** , **148**

643.13 Hyperemesis gravidarum with metabolic disturbance, antepartum **155** , **157**

643.20 Late vomiting of pregnancy, unspecified as to episode of care **157** , **160**

643.21 Late vomiting of pregnancy, delivered **135** , **142** , **148**

643.23 Late vomiting of pregnancy, antepartum **155** , **157**

643.80 Other vomiting complicating pregnancy, unspecified as to episode of care **157** , **160**

643.81 Other vomiting complicating pregnancy, delivered **135** , **142** , **148**

643.83 Other vomiting complicating pregnancy, antepartum **155** , **157**

643.90 Unspecified vomiting of pregnancy, unspecified as to episode of care **157** , **160**

643.91 Unspecified vomiting of pregnancy, delivered **135** , **142** , **148**

643.93 Unspecified vomiting of pregnancy, antepartum **155** , **157**

644.00 Threatened premature labor, unspecified as to episode of care **154**

644.03 Threatened premature labor, antepartum **154**

644.10 Other threatened labor, unspecified as to episode of care **154**

644.13 Other threatened labor, antepartum **154**

644.20 Early onset of delivery, unspecified as to episode of care **155** , **158**

644.21 Early onset of delivery, delivered, with or without mention of antepartum condition **135** , **142** , **148**

645.10 Post term pregnancy, unspecified as to episode of care or not applicable **160**

645.11 Post term pregnancy, delivered, with or without mention of antepartum condition **135 , 142 , 148**

645.13 Post term pregnancy, antepartum condition or complication **155 , 158**

645.20 Prolonged pregnancy, unspecified as to episode of care or not applicable **160**

645.21 Prolonged pregnancy, delivered, with or without mention of antepartum condition **135 , 142 , 148**

645.23 Prolonged pregnancy, antepartum condition or complication **155 , 158**

646.00 Papyraceous fetus, unspecified as to episode of care **135 , 142 , 148**

646.01 Papyraceous fetus, delivered, with or without mention of antepartum condition **135 , 142 , 148**

646.03 Papyraceous fetus, antepartum **155 , 158**

646.10 Edema or excessive weight gain in pregnancy, unspecified as to episode of care **157 , 160**

646.11 Edema or excessive weight gain in pregnancy, with delivery, with or without mention of antepartum complication **135 , 142 , 148**

646.12 Edema or excessive weight gain in pregnancy, with delivery, with current postpartum complication **135 , 142 , 148**

646.13 Edema or excessive weight gain, antepartum **155 , 157**

646.14 Edema or excessive weight gain in pregnancy, without mention of hypertension, postpartum condition or complication **152**

646.20 Unspecified renal disease in pregnancy, unspecified as to episode of care **157 , 160**

646.21 Unspecified renal disease in pregnancy, with delivery **135 , 142 , 148**

646.22 Unspecified renal disease in pregnancy, with delivery, with current postpartum complication **135 , 142 , 148**

646.23 Unspecified antepartum renal disease **155 , 157**

646.24 Unspecified renal disease in pregnancy, without mention of hypertension, postpartum condition or complication **152**

646.30 Pregnancy complication, recurrent pregnancy loss, unspecified as to episode of care **160**

646.31 Pregnancy complication, recurrent pregnancy loss, with or without mention of antepartum condition **135 , 142 , 148**

646.33 Pregnancy complication, recurrent pregnancy loss, antepartum condition or complication **155 , 158**

646.40 Peripheral neuritis in pregnancy, unspecified as to episode of care **160**

646.41 Peripheral neuritis in pregnancy, with delivery **135 , 142 , 148**

646.42 Peripheral neuritis in pregnancy, with delivery, with current postpartum complication **135 , 142 , 148**

646.43 Peripheral neuritis antepartum **155 , 157**

646.44 Peripheral neuritis in pregnancy, postpartum condition or complication **152**

646.50 Asymptomatic bacteriuria in pregnancy, unspecified as to episode of care **160**

646.51 Asymptomatic bacteriuria in pregnancy, with delivery **135 , 142 , 148**

646.52 Asymptomatic bacteriuria in pregnancy, with delivery, with current postpartum complication **135 , 142 , 148**

646.53 Asymptomatic bacteriuria antepartum **155 , 158**

646.54 Asymptomatic bacteriuria in pregnancy, postpartum condition or complication **152**

646.60 Infections of genitourinary tract in pregnancy, unspecified as to episode of care **157 , 160**

646.61 Infections of genitourinary tract in pregnancy, with delivery **135 , 142 , 148**

646.62 Infections of genitourinary tract in pregnancy, with delivery, with current postpartum complication **135 , 142 , 148**

646.63 Infections of genitourinary tract antepartum **155 , 157**

646.64 Infections of genitourinary tract in pregnancy, postpartum condition or complication **153**

646.70 Liver and biliary tract disorders in pregnancy, unspecified as to episode of care or not applicable **157 , 160**

646.71 Liver and biliary tract disorders in pregnancy, delivered, with or without mention of antepartum condition **135 , 143 , 148**

646.73 Liver and biliary tract disorders in pregnancy, antepartum condition or complication **155 , 157**

646.80 Other specified complication of pregnancy, unspecified as to episode of care **157 , 160**

646.81 Other specified complication of pregnancy, with delivery **135 , 143 , 148**

646.82 Other specified complications of pregnancy, with delivery, with current postpartum complication **135 , 143 , 148**

646.83 Other specified complication, antepartum **155 , 157**

646.84 Other specified complications of pregnancy, postpartum condition or complication **153**

646.90 Unspecified complication of pregnancy, unspecified as to episode of care **160**

646.91 Unspecified complication of pregnancy, with delivery **135 , 143 , 148**

646.93 Unspecified complication of pregnancy, antepartum **155 , 158**

647.00 Maternal syphilis, complicating pregnancy, childbirth, or the puerperium, unspecified as to episode of care **160**

647.01 Maternal syphilis, complicating pregnancy, with delivery **135 , 141 , 147**

647.02 Maternal syphilis, complicating pregnancy, with delivery, with current postpartum complication **135 , 141 , 147**

647.03 Maternal syphilis, antepartum **155 , 157**

647.04 Maternal syphilis complicating pregnancy, childbrith, or the puerperium, postpartum condition or complication **153**

647.10 Maternal gonorrhea complicating pregnancy, childbirth, or the puerperium, unspecified as to episode of care **160**

647.11 Maternal gonorrhea with delivery **135 , 141 , 147**

647.12 Maternal gonorrhea, with delivery, with current postpartum complication **135 , 141 , 147**

647.13 Maternal gonorrhea, antepartum **155 , 157**

647.14 Maternal gonorrhea complicating pregnancy, childbrith, or the puerperium, postpartum condition or complication **153**

647.20 Other maternal venereal diseases, complicating pregnancy, childbirth, or the puerperium, unspecified as to episode of care **160**

647.21 Other maternal venereal diseases with delivery **135 , 141 , 147**

647.22 Other maternal venereal diseases with delivery, with current postpartum complication **135 , 141 , 147**

647.23 Other maternal venereal diseases, antepartum condition or complication **155 , 157**

647.24 Other venereal diseases complicating pregnancy, childbrith, or the puerperium, postpartum condition or complication **153**

647.30 Maternal tuberculosis complicating pregnancy, childbirth, or the puerperium, unspecified as to episode of care **160**

647.31 Maternal tuberculosis with delivery **135 , 141 , 147**

647.32 Maternal tuberculosis with delivery, with current postpartum complication **135 , 141 , 147**

647.33 Maternal tuberculosis, antepartum **155 , 157**

647.34 Maternal tuberculosis complicating pregnancy, childbirth, or the puerperium, postpartum condition or complication **153**

647.40 Maternal malaria complicating pregnancy, childbirth or the puerperium, unspecified as to episode of care **160**

647.41 Maternal malaria with delivery **135 , 141 , 147**

647.42 Maternal malaria with delivery, with current postpartum complication **135 , 141 , 147**

647.43 Maternal malaria, antepartum **155 , 157**

647.44 Maternal malaria, complicating pregnancy, childbirth, or the puerperium, postpartum condition or complication **153**

647.50 Maternal rubella complicating pregnancy, childbirth, or the puerperium, unspecified as to episode of care **160**

647.51	Maternal rubella with delivery **135 , 141 , 147**
647.52	Maternal rubella with delivery, with current postpartum complication **135 , 141 , 147**
647.53	Maternal rubella, antepartum **155 , 157**
647.54	Maternal rubella complicating pregnancy, childbirth, or the puerperium, postpartum condition or complication **153**
647.60	Other maternal viral disease complicating pregnancy, childbirth, or the puerperium, unspecified as to episode of care **160**
647.61	Other maternal viral disease with delivery **135 , 141 , 147**
647.62	Other maternal viral disease with delivery, with current postpartum complication **135 , 141 , 147**
647.63	Other maternal viral disease, antepartum **155 , 157**
647.64	Other maternal viral diseases complicating pregnancy, childbirth, or the puerperium, postpartum condition or complication **153**
647.80	Other specified maternal infectious and parasitic disease complicating pregnancy, childbirth, or the puerperium, unspecified as to episode of care **160**
647.81	Other specified maternal infectious and parasitic disease with delivery **135 , 141 , 147**
647.82	Other specified maternal infectious and parasitic disease with delivery, with current postpartum complication **135 , 141 , 147**
647.83	Other specified maternal infectious and parasitic disease, antepartum **155 , 157**
647.84	Other specified maternal infectious and parasitic diseases complicating pregnancy, childbirth, or the puerperium, postpartum condition or complication **153**
647.90	Unspecified maternal infection or infestation complicating pregnancy, childbirth, or the puerperium, unspecified as to episode of care **160**
647.91	Unspecified maternal infection or infestation with delivery **135 , 141 , 147**
647.92	Unspecified maternal infection or infestation with delivery, with current postpartum complication **135 , 141 , 147**
647.93	Unspecified maternal infection or infestation, antepartum **155 , 157**
647.94	Unspecified maternal infection or infestation complicating pregnancy, childbirth, or the puerperium, postpartum condition or complication **153**
648.00	Maternal diabetes mellitus, complicating pregnancy, childbirth, or the puerperium, unspecified as to episode of care **160**
648.01	Maternal diabetes mellitus with delivery **135 , 141 , 147**
648.02	Maternal diabetes mellitus with delivery, with current postpartum complication **135 , 141 , 147**
648.03	Maternal diabetes mellitus, antepartum **155 , 157**
648.04	Maternal diabetes mellitus, complicating pregnancy, childbirth, or the puerperium, postpartum condition or complication **153**
648.10	Maternal thyroid dysfunction complicating pregnancy, childbirth, or the puerperium, unspecified as to episode of care or not applicable **160**
648.11	Maternal thyroid dysfunction with delivery, with or without mention of antepartum condition **135 , 143 , 148**
648.12	Maternal thyroid dysfunction with delivery, with current postpartum complication **135 , 143 , 148**
648.13	Maternal thyroid dysfunction, antepartum condition or complication **155 , 157**
648.14	Maternal thyroid dysfunction complicating pregnancy, childbirth, or the puerperium, postpartum condition or complication **153**
648.20	Maternal anemia of mother, complicating pregnancy, childbirth, or the puerperium, unspecified as to episode of care **160**
648.21	Maternal anemia, with delivery **135 , 143 , 148**
648.22	Maternal anemia with delivery, with current postpartum complication **135 , 143 , 148**
648.23	Maternal anemia, antepartum **155 , 157**
648.24	Maternal anemia complicating pregnancy, childbirth, or the puerperium, postpartum condition or complication **153**
648.30	Maternal drug dependence complicating pregnancy, childbirth, or the puerperium, unspecified as to episode of care **160**
648.31	Maternal drug dependence, with delivery **135 , 143 , 148**
648.32	Maternal drug dependence, with delivery, with current postpartum complication **135 , 143 , 148**
648.33	Maternal drug dependence, antepartum **155 , 157**
648.34	Maternal drug dependence complicating pregnancy, childbirth, or the puerperium, postpartum condition or complication **153**
648.40	Maternal mental disorders, complicating pregnancy, childbirth, or the puerperium, unspecified as to episode of care **160**
648.41	Maternal mental disorders, with delivery **135 , 143 , 148**
648.42	Maternal mental disorders, with delivery, with current postpartum complication **135 , 143 , 148**
648.43	Maternal mental disorders, antepartum **155 , 157**
648.44	Maternal mental disorders complicating pregnancy, childbirth, or the puerperium, postpartum condition or complication **153**
648.50	Maternal congenital cardiovascular disorders, complicating pregnancy, childbirth, or the puerperium, unspecified as to episode of care **160**
648.51	Maternal congenital cardiovascular disorders, with delivery **135 , 141 , 147**
648.52	Maternal congenital cardiovascular disorders, with delivery, with current postpartum complication **135 , 141 , 147**
648.53	Maternal congenital cardiovascular disorders, antepartum **155 , 157**
648.54	Maternal congenital cardiovascular disorders complicating pregnancy, childbirth, or the puerperium, postpartum condition or complication **153**
648.60	Other maternal cardiovascular diseases complicating pregnancy, childbirth, or the puerperium, unspecified as to episode of care **160**
648.61	Other maternal cardiovascular diseases, with delivery **135 , 141 , 147**
648.62	Other maternal cardiovascular diseases, with delivery, with current postpartum complication **135 , 141 , 147**
648.63	Other maternal cardiovascular diseases, antepartum **155 , 157**
648.64	Other maternal cardiovascular diseases complicating pregnancy, childbirth, or the puerperium, postpartum condition or complication **153**
648.70	Bone and joint disorders of maternal back, pelvis, and lower limbs, complicating pregnancy, childbirth, or the puerperium, unspecified as to episode of care **160**
648.71	Bone and joint disorders of maternal back, pelvis, and lower limbs, with delivery **135 , 143 , 148**
648.72	Bone and joint disorders of maternal back, pelvis, and lower limbs, with delivery, with current postpartum complication **135 , 143 , 148**
648.73	Bone and joint disorders of maternal back, pelvis, and lower limbs, antepartum **155 , 157**
648.74	Bone and joint disorders of maternal back, pelvis, and lower limbs complicating pregnancy, childbirth, or the puerperium, postpartum condition or complication **153**
648.80	Abnormal maternal glucose tolerance, complicating pregnancy, childbirth, or the puerperium, unspecified as to episode of care **160**
648.81	Abnormal maternal glucose tolerance, with delivery **135 , 143 , 148**
648.82	Abnormal maternal glucose tolerance, with delivery, with current postpartum complication **136 , 143 , 149**
648.83	Abnormal maternal glucose tolerance, antepartum **155 , 157**
648.84	Abnormal maternal glucose tolerance complicating pregnancy, childbirth, or the puerperium, postpartum condition or complication **153**
648.90	Other current maternal conditions classifiable elsewhere, complicating pregnancy, childbirth, or the puerperium, unspecified as to episode of care **160**

648.91 Other current maternal conditions classifiable elsewhere, with delivery **136 , 143 , 149**

648.92 Other current maternal conditions classifiable elsewhere, with delivery, with current postpartum complication **136 , 143 , 149**

648.93 Other current maternal conditions classifiable elsewhere, antepartum **155 , 157**

648.94 Other current maternal conditions classifiable elsewhere complicating pregnancy, childbirth, or the puerperium, postpartum condition or complication **153**

649.00 Tobacco use disorder complicating pregnancy, childbirth, or the puerperium, unspecified as to episode of care or not applicable **160**

649.01 Tobacco use disorder complicating pregnancy, childbirth, or the puerperium, delivered, with or without mention of antepartum condition **136 , 143 , 149**

649.02 Tobacco use disorder complicating pregnancy, childbirth, or the puerperium, delivered, with mention of postpartum complication **136 , 143 , 149**

649.03 Tobacco use disorder complicating pregnancy, childbirth, or the puerperium, antepartum condition or complication **155 , 158**

649.04 Tobacco use disorder complicating pregnancy, childbirth, or the puerperium, postpartum condition or complication **153**

649.10 Obesity complicating pregnancy, childbirth, or the puerperium, unspecified as to episode of care or not applicable **161**

649.11 Obesity complicating pregnancy, childbirth, or the puerperium, delivered, with or without mention of antepartum condition **136 , 143 , 149**

649.12 Obesity complicating pregnancy, childbirth, or the puerperium, delivered, with mention of postpartum complication **136 , 143 , 149**

649.13 Obesity complicating pregnancy, childbirth, or the puerperium, antepartum condition or complication **155 , 158**

649.14 Obesity complicating pregnancy, childbirth, or the puerperium, postpartum condition or complication **153**

649.20 Bariatric surgery status complicating pregnancy, childbirth, or the puerperium, unspecified as to episode of care or not applicable **161**

649.21 Bariatric surgery status complicating pregnancy, childbirth, or the puerperium, delivered, with or without mention of antepartum condition **136 , 143 , 149**

649.22 Bariatric surgery status complicating pregnancy, childbirth, or the puerperium, delivered, with mention of postpartum complication **136 , 143 , 149**

649.23 Bariatric surgery status complicating pregnancy, childbirth, or the puerperium, antepartum condition or complication **155 , 158**

649.24 Bariatric surgery status complicating pregnancy, childbirth, or the puerperium, postpartum condition or complication **153**

649.30 Coagulation defects complicating pregnancy, childbirth, or the puerperium, unspecified as to episode of care or not applicable **161**

649.31 Coagulation defects complicating pregnancy, childbirth, or the puerperium, delivered, with or without mention of antepartum condition **136 , 143 , 149**

649.32 Coagulation defects complicating pregnancy, childbirth, or the puerperium, delivered, with mention of postpartum complication **136 , 143 , 149**

649.33 Coagulation defects complicating pregnancy, childbirth, or the puerperium, antepartum condition or complication **155 , 158**

649.34 Coagulation defects complicating pregnancy, childbirth, or the puerperium, postpartum condition or complication **153**

649.40 Epilepsy complicating pregnancy, childbirth, or the puerperium, unspecified as to episode of care or not applicable **161**

649.41 Epilepsy complicating pregnancy, childbirth, or the puerperium, delivered, with or without mention of antepartum condition **136 , 143 , 149**

649.42 Epilepsy complicating pregnancy, childbirth, or the puerperium, delivered, with mention of postpartum complication **136 , 143 , 149**

649.43 Epilepsy complicating pregnancy, childbirth, or the puerperium, antepartum condition or complication **155 , 158**

649.44 Epilepsy complicating pregnancy, childbirth, or the puerperium, postpartum condition or complication **153**

649.50 Spotting complicating pregnancy, unspecified as to episode of care or not applicable **161**

649.51 Spotting complicating pregnancy, delivered, with or without mention of antepartum condition **136 , 143 , 149**

649.53 Spotting complicating pregnancy, antepartum condition or complication **155 , 158**

649.60 Uterine size date discrepancy, unspecified as to episode of care or not applicable **161**

649.61 Uterine size date discrepancy, delivered, with or without mention of antepartum condition **136 , 143 , 149**

649.62 Uterine size date discrepancy, delivered, with mention of postpartum complication **136 , 143 , 149**

649.63 Uterine size date discrepancy, antepartum condition or complication **155 , 158**

649.64 Uterine size date discrepancy, postpartum condition or complication **153**

649.70 Cervical shortening, unspecified as to episode of care or not applicable **161**

649.71 Cervical shortening, delivered, with or without mention of antepartum condition **136 , 143 , 149**

649.73 Cervical shortening, antepartum condition or complication **155 , 158**

649.8* Onset (spontaneous) of labor after 37 completed weeks of gestation but before 39 completed weeks gestation, with delivery by (planned) cesarean section **136 , 141 , 149**

649.81 Onset (spontaneous) of labor after 37 completed weeks of gestation but before 39 completed weeks gestation, with delivery by (planned) cesarean section, delivered, with or without mention of antepartum condition **143**

649.82 Onset (spontaneous) of labor after 37 completed weeks of gestation but before 39 completed weeks gestation, with delivery by (planned) cesarean section, delivered, with mention of postpartum complication **143**

650 Normal delivery **136 , 143 , 149**

651.00 Twin pregnancy, unspecified as to episode of care **161**

651.01 Twin pregnancy, delivered **136 , 143 , 149**

651.03 Twin pregnancy, antepartum **155 , 158**

651.10 Triplet pregnancy, unspecified as to episode of care **161**

651.11 Triplet pregnancy, delivered **136 , 143 , 149**

651.13 Triplet pregnancy, antepartum **155 , 158**

651.20 Quadruplet pregnancy, unspecified as to episode of care **161**

651.21 Quadruplet pregnancy, delivered **136 , 143 , 149**

651.23 Quadruplet pregnancy, antepartum **155 , 158**

651.30 Twin pregnancy with fetal loss and retention of one fetus, unspecified as to episode of care or not applicable **161**

651.31 Twin pregnancy with fetal loss and retention of one fetus, delivered **136 , 143 , 149**

651.33 Twin pregnancy with fetal loss and retention of one fetus, antepartum **155 , 158**

651.40 Triplet pregnancy with fetal loss and retention of one or more, unspecified as to episode of care or not applicable **161**

651.41 Triplet pregnancy with fetal loss and retention of one or more, delivered **136 , 143 , 149**

651.43 Triplet pregnancy with fetal loss and retention of one or more, antepartum **155 , 158**

651.50 Quadruplet pregnancy with fetal loss and retention of one or more, unspecified as to episode of care or not applicable **161**

651.51 Quadruplet pregnancy with fetal loss and retention of one or more, delivered **136 , 143 , 149**

651.53 Quadruplet pregnancy with fetal loss and retention of one or more, antepartum **155 , 158**

651.60	Other multiple pregnancy with fetal loss and retention of one or more fetus(es), unspecified as to episode of care or not applicable **161**
651.61	Other multiple pregnancy with fetal loss and retention of one or more fetus(es), delivered **136 , 143 , 149**
651.63	Other multiple pregnancy with fetal loss and retention of one or more fetus(es), antepartum **155 , 158**
651.70	Multiple gestation following (elective) fetal reduction, unspecified as to episode of care or not applicable **161**
651.71	Multiple gestation following (elective) fetal reduction, delivered, with or without mention of antepartum condition **136 , 143 , 149**
651.73	Multiple gestation following (elective) fetal reduction, antepartum condition or complication **155 , 158**
651.80	Other specified multiple gestation, unspecified as to episode of care **161**
651.81	Other specified multiple gestation, delivered **136 , 143 , 149**
651.83	Other specified multiple gestation, antepartum **155 , 158**
651.90	Unspecified multiple gestation, unspecified as to episode of care **161**
651.91	Unspecified multiple gestation, delivered **136 , 143 , 149**
651.93	Unspecified multiple gestation, antepartum **155 , 158**
652.00	Unstable lie of fetus, unspecified as to episode of care **161**
652.01	Unstable lie of fetus, delivered **136 , 143 , 149**
652.03	Unstable lie of fetus, antepartum **155 , 158**
652.10	Breech or other malpresentation successfully converted to cephalic presentation, unspecified as to episode of care **161**
652.11	Breech or other malpresentation successfully converted to cephalic presentation, delivered **136 , 143 , 149**
652.13	Breech or other malpresentation successfully converted to cephalic presentation, antepartum **155 , 158**
652.20	Breech presentation without mention of version, unspecified as to episode of care **161**
652.21	Breech presentation without mention of version, delivered **136 , 143 , 149**
652.23	Breech presentation without mention of version, antepartum **155 , 158**
652.30	Transverse or oblique fetal presentation, unspecified as to episode of care **161**
652.31	Transverse or oblique fetal presentation, delivered **136 , 143 , 149**
652.33	Transverse or oblique fetal presentation, antepartum **155 , 158**
652.40	Fetal face or brow presentation, unspecified as to episode of care **161**
652.41	Fetal face or brow presentation, delivered **136 , 143 , 149**
652.43	Fetal face or brow presentation, antepartum **155 , 158**
652.50	High fetal head at term, unspecified as to episode of care **161**
652.51	High fetal head at term, delivered **136 , 143 , 149**
652.53	High fetal head at term, antepartum **155 , 158**
652.60	Multiple gestation with malpresentation of one fetus or more, unspecified as to episode of care **161**
652.61	Multiple gestation with malpresentation of one fetus or more, delivered **136 , 143 , 149**
652.63	Multiple gestation with malpresentation of one fetus or more, antepartum **155 , 158**
652.70	Prolapsed arm of fetus, unspecified as to episode of care **161**
652.71	Prolapsed arm of fetus, delivered **136 , 143 , 149**
652.73	Prolapsed arm of fetus, antepartum condition or complication **155 , 158**
652.80	Other specified malposition or malpresentation of fetus, unspecified as to episode of care **161**
652.81	Other specified malposition or malpresentation of fetus, delivered **136 , 143 , 149**
652.83	Other specified malposition or malpresentation of fetus, antepartum **155 , 158**
652.90	Unspecified malposition or malpresentation of fetus, unspecified as to episode of care **161**
652.91	Unspecified malposition or malpresentation of fetus, delivered **136 , 143 , 149**
652.93	Unspecified malposition or malpresentation of fetus, antepartum **155 , 158**
653.00	Major abnormality of bony pelvis, not further specified in pregnancy, unspecified as to episode of care **161**
653.01	Major abnormality of bony pelvis, not further specified, delivered **136 , 143 , 149**
653.03	Major abnormality of bony pelvis, not further specified, antepartum **155 , 158**
653.10	Generally contracted pelvis in pregnancy, unspecified as to episode of care in pregnancy **161**
653.11	Generally contracted pelvis in pregnancy, delivered **136 , 143 , 149**
653.13	Generally contracted pelvis in pregnancy, antepartum **155 , 158**
653.20	Inlet contraction of pelvis in pregnancy, unspecified as to episode of care in pregnancy **161**
653.21	Inlet contraction of pelvis in pregnancy, delivered **136 , 143 , 149**
653.23	Inlet contraction of pelvis in pregnancy, antepartum **155 , 158**
653.30	Outlet contraction of pelvis in pregnancy, unspecified as to episode of care in pregnancy **161**
653.31	Outlet contraction of pelvis in pregnancy, delivered **136 , 143 , 149**
653.33	Outlet contraction of pelvis in pregnancy, antepartum **155 , 158**
653.40	Fetopelvic disproportion, unspecified as to episode of care **161**
653.41	Fetopelvic disproportion, delivered **136 , 143 , 149**
653.43	Fetopelvic disproportion, antepartum **155 , 158**
653.50	Unusually large fetus causing disproportion, unspecified as to episode of care **161**
653.51	Unusually large fetus causing disproportion, delivered **136 , 143 , 149**
653.53	Unusually large fetus causing disproportion, antepartum **155 , 158**
653.60	Hydrocephalic fetus causing disproportion, unspecified as to episode of care **161**
653.61	Hydrocephalic fetus causing disproportion, delivered **136 , 143 , 149**
653.63	Hydrocephalic fetus causing disproportion, antepartum **155 , 158**
653.70	Other fetal abnormality causing disproportion, unspecified as to episode of care **161**
653.71	Other fetal abnormality causing disproportion, delivered **136 , 143 , 149**
653.73	Other fetal abnormality causing disproportion, antepartum **155 , 158**
653.80	Fetal disproportion of other origin, unspecified as to episode of care **161**
653.81	Fetal disproportion of other origin, delivered **136 , 143 , 149**
653.83	Fetal disproportion of other origin, antepartum **155 , 158**
653.90	Unspecified fetal disproportion, unspecified as to episode of care **161**
653.91	Unspecified fetal disproportion, delivered **136 , 143 , 149**
653.93	Unspecified fetal disproportion, antepartum **155 , 158**
654.00	Congenital abnormalities of pregnant uterus, unspecified as to episode of care **161**
654.01	Congenital abnormalities of pregnant uterus, delivered **136 , 143 , 149**
654.02	Congenital abnormalities of pregnant uterus, delivered, with mention of postpartum complication **136 , 143 , 149**

654.03	Congenital abnormalities of pregnant uterus, antepartum **155** , **158**	
654.04	Congenital abnormalities of uterus, postpartum condition or complication **153**	
654.10	Tumors of body of pregnant uterus, unspecified as to episode of care in pregnancy **161**	
654.11	Tumors of body of uterus, delivered **136** , **143** , **149**	
654.12	Tumors of body of uterus, delivered, with mention of postpartum complication **136** , **143** , **149**	
654.13	Tumors of body of uterus, antepartum condition or complication **155** , **158**	
654.14	Tumors of body of uterus, postpartum condition or complication **153**	

654.03 Congenital abnormalities of pregnant uterus, antepartum **155** , **158**

654.04 Congenital abnormalities of uterus, postpartum condition or complication **153**

654.10 Tumors of body of pregnant uterus, unspecified as to episode of care in pregnancy **161**

654.11 Tumors of body of uterus, delivered **136** , **143** , **149**

654.12 Tumors of body of uterus, delivered, with mention of postpartum complication **136** , **143** , **149**

654.13 Tumors of body of uterus, antepartum condition or complication **155** , **158**

654.14 Tumors of body of uterus, postpartum condition or complication **153**

654.20 Previous cesarean delivery, unspecified as to episode of care or not applicable **161**

654.21 Previous cesarean delivery, delivered, with or without mention of antepartum condition **136** , **143** , **149**

654.23 Previous cesarean delivery, antepartum condition or complication **155** , **158**

654.30 Retroverted and incarcerated gravid uterus, unspecified as to episode of care **161**

654.31 Retroverted and incarcerated gravid uterus, delivered **136** , **143** , **149**

654.32 Retroverted and incarcerated gravid uterus, delivered, with mention of postpartum complication **136** , **143** , **149**

654.33 Retroverted and incarcerated gravid uterus, antepartum **155** , **158**

654.34 Retroverted and incarcerated gravid uterus, postpartum condition or complication **153**

654.40 Other abnormalities in shape or position of gravid uterus and of neighboring structures, unspecified as to episode of care **161**

654.41 Other abnormalities in shape or position of gravid uterus and of neighboring structures, delivered **136** , **143** , **149**

654.42 Other abnormalities in shape or position of gravid uterus and of neighboring structures, delivered, with mention of postpartum complication **136** , **143** , **149**

654.43 Other abnormalities in shape or position of gravid uterus and of neighboring structures, antepartum **155** , **158**

654.44 Other abnormalities in shape or position of gravid uterus and of neighboring structures, postpartum condition or complication **153**

654.50 Cervical incompetence, unspecified as to episode of care in pregnancy **161**

654.51 Cervical incompetence, delivered **136** , **143** , **149**

654.52 Cervical incompetence, delivered, with mention of postpartum complication **136** , **143** , **149**

654.53 Cervical incompetence, antepartum condition or complication **155** , **158**

654.54 Cervical incompetence, postpartum condition or complication **153**

654.60 Other congenital or acquired abnormality of cervix, unspecified as to episode of care in pregnancy **161**

654.61 Other congenital or acquired abnormality of cervix, with delivery **136** , **143** , **149**

654.62 Other congenital or acquired abnormality of cervix, delivered, with mention of postpartum complication **136** , **144** , **149**

654.63 Other congenital or acquired abnormality of cervix, antepartum condition or complication **155** , **158**

654.64 Other congenital or acquired abnormality of cervix, postpartum condition or complication **153**

654.70 Congenital or acquired abnormality of vagina, unspecified as to episode of care in pregnancy **161**

654.71 Congenital or acquired abnormality of vagina, with delivery **136** , **144** , **149**

654.72 Congenital or acquired abnormality of vagina, delivered, with mention of postpartum complication **136** , **144** , **149**

654.73 Congenital or acquired abnormality of vagina, antepartum condition or complication **156** , **158**

654.74 Congenital or acquired abnormality of vagina, postpartum condition or complication **153**

654.80 Congenital or acquired abnormality of vulva, unspecified as to episode of care in pregnancy **161**

654.81 Congenital or acquired abnormality of vulva, with delivery **136** , **144** , **149**

654.82 Congenital or acquired abnormality of vulva, delivered, with mention of postpartum complication **136** , **144** , **149**

654.83 Congenital or acquired abnormality of vulva, antepartum condition or complication **156** , **158**

654.84 Congenital or acquired abnormality of vulva, postpartum condition or complication **153**

654.90 Other and unspecified abnormality of organs and soft tissues of pelvis, unspecified as to episode of care in pregnancy **161**

654.91 Other and unspecified abnormality of organs and soft tissues of pelvis, with delivery **136** , **144** , **149**

654.92 Other and unspecified abnormality of organs and soft tissues of pelvis, delivered, with mention of postpartum complication **136** , **144** , **149**

654.93 Other and unspecified abnormality of organs and soft tissues of pelvis, antepartum condition or complication **156** , **158**

654.94 Other and unspecified abnormality of organs and soft tissues of pelvis, postpartum condition or complication **153**

655.00 Central nervous system malformation in fetus, unspecified as to episode of care in pregnancy **161**

655.01 Central nervous system malformation in fetus, with delivery **136** , **144** , **149**

655.03 Central nervous system malformation in fetus, antepartum **156** , **158**

655.10 Chromosomal abnormality in fetus, affecting management of mother, unspecified as to episode of care in pregnancy **161**

655.11 Chromosomal abnormality in fetus, affecting management of mother, with delivery **136** , **144** , **149**

655.13 Chromosomal abnormality in fetus, affecting management of mother, antepartum **156** , **158**

655.20 Hereditary disease in family possibly affecting fetus, affecting management of mother, unspecified as to episode of care in pregnancy **161**

655.21 Hereditary disease in family possibly affecting fetus, affecting management of mother, with delivery **136** , **144** , **149**

655.23 Hereditary disease in family possibly affecting fetus, affecting management of mother, antepartum condition or complication **156** , **158**

655.30 Suspected damage to fetus from viral disease in mother, affecting management of mother, unspecified as to episode of care in pregnancy **161**

655.31 Suspected damage to fetus from viral disease in mother, affecting management of mother, with delivery **136** , **144** , **149**

655.33 Suspected damage to fetus from viral disease in mother, affecting management of mother, antepartum condition or complication **156** , **158**

655.40 Suspected damage to fetus from other disease in mother, affecting management of mother, unspecified as to episode of care in pregnancy **161**

655.41 Suspected damage to fetus from other disease in mother, affecting management of mother, with delivery **136** , **144** , **149**

655.43 Suspected damage to fetus from other disease in mother, affecting management of mother, antepartum condition or complication **156** , **158**

655.50 Suspected damage to fetus from drugs, affecting management of mother, unspecified as to episode of care **161**

655.51 Suspected damage to fetus from drugs, affecting management of mother, delivered **136** , **144** , **149**

655.53 Suspected damage to fetus from drugs, affecting management of mother, antepartum **156** , **158**

Numeric Index to Diseases

655.60	Suspected damage to fetus from radiation, affecting management of mother, unspecified as to episode of care **161**
655.61	Suspected damage to fetus from radiation, affecting management of mother, delivered **136** , **144** , **149**
655.63	Suspected damage to fetus from radiation, affecting management of mother, antepartum condition or complication **156** , **158**
655.70	Decreased fetal movements, unspecified as to episode of care **161**
655.71	Decreased fetal movements, affecting management of mother, delivered **136** , **144** , **149**
655.73	Decreased fetal movements, affecting management of mother, antepartum condition or complication **156** , **158**
655.80	Other known or suspected fetal abnormality, not elsewhere classified, affecting management of mother, unspecified as to episode of care **161**
655.81	Other known or suspected fetal abnormality, not elsewhere classified, affecting management of mother, delivery **136** , **144** , **149**
655.83	Other known or suspected fetal abnormality, not elsewhere classified, affecting management of mother, antepartum condition or complication **156** , **158**
655.90	Unspecified fetal abnormality affecting management of mother, unspecified as to episode of care **161**
655.91	Unspecified fetal abnormality affecting management of mother, delivery **137** , **144** , **150**
655.93	Unspecified fetal abnormality affecting management of mother, antepartum condition or complication **156** , **158**
656.00	Fetal-maternal hemorrhage, unspecified as to episode of care in pregnancy **161**
656.01	Fetal-maternal hemorrhage, with delivery **137** , **144** , **150**
656.03	Fetal-maternal hemorrhage, antepartum condition or complication **156** , **158**
656.10	Rhesus isoimmunization unspecified as to episode of care in pregnancy **161**
656.11	Rhesus isoimmunization affecting management of mother, delivered **137** , **144** , **150**
656.13	Rhesus isoimmunization affecting management of mother, antepartum condition **156** , **158**
656.20	Isoimmunization from other and unspecified blood-group incompatibility, unspecified as to episode of care in pregnancy **161**
656.21	Isoimmunization from other and unspecified blood-group incompatibility, affecting management of mother, delivered **137** , **144** , **150**
656.23	Isoimmunization from other and unspecified blood-group incompatibility, affecting management of mother, antepartum **156** , **158**
656.30	Fetal distress affecting management of mother, unspecified as to episode of care **137** , **144** , **150**
656.31	Fetal distress affecting management of mother, delivered **137** , **144** , **150**
656.33	Fetal distress affecting management of mother, antepartum **156** , **158**
656.40	Intrauterine death affecting management of mother, unspecified as to episode of care **137** , **144** , **150**
656.41	Intrauterine death affecting management of mother, delivered **137** , **144** , **150**
656.43	Intrauterine death affecting management of mother, antepartum **156** , **158**
656.50	Poor fetal growth, affecting management of mother, unspecified as to episode of care **161**
656.51	Poor fetal growth, affecting management of mother, delivered **137** , **144** , **150**
656.53	Poor fetal growth, affecting management of mother, antepartum condition or complication **156** , **158**
656.60	Excessive fetal growth affecting management of mother, unspecified as to episode of care **161**
656.61	Excessive fetal growth affecting management of mother, delivered **137** , **144** , **150**
656.63	Excessive fetal growth affecting management of mother, antepartum **156** , **158**
656.70	Other placental conditions affecting management of mother, unspecified as to episode of care **161**
656.71	Other placental conditions affecting management of mother, delivered **137** , **144** , **150**
656.73	Other placental conditions affecting management of mother, antepartum **156** , **158**
656.80	Other specified fetal and placental problems affecting management of mother, unspecified as to episode of care **161**
656.81	Other specified fetal and placental problems affecting management of mother, delivered **137** , **144** , **150**
656.83	Other specified fetal and placental problems affecting management of mother, antepartum **156** , **158**
656.90	Unspecified fetal and placental problem affecting management of mother, unspecified as to episode of care **161**
656.91	Unspecified fetal and placental problem affecting management of mother, delivered **137** , **144** , **150**
656.93	Unspecified fetal and placental problem affecting management of mother, antepartum **156** , **159**
657.00	Polyhydramnios, unspecified as to episode of care **161**
657.01	Polyhydramnios, with delivery **137** , **144** , **150**
657.03	Polyhydramnios, antepartum complication **156** , **159**
658.00	Oligohydramnios, unspecified as to episode of care **161**
658.01	Oligohydramnios, delivered **137** , **144** , **150**
658.03	Oligohydramnios, antepartum **156** , **159**
658.10	Premature rupture of membranes in pregnancy, unspecified as to episode of care **137** , **144** , **150**
658.11	Premature rupture of membranes in pregnancy, delivered **137** , **144** , **150**
658.13	Premature rupture of membranes in pregnancy, antepartum **156** , **159**
658.20	Delayed delivery after spontaneous or unspecified rupture of membranes, unspecified as to episode of care **137** , **144** , **150**
658.21	Delayed delivery after spontaneous or unspecified rupture of membranes, delivered **137** , **144** , **150**
658.23	Delayed delivery after spontaneous or unspecified rupture of membranes, antepartum **156** , **159**
658.30	Delayed delivery after artificial rupture of membranes, unspecified as to episode of care **137** , **144** , **150**
658.31	Delayed delivery after artificial rupture of membranes, delivered **137** , **144** , **150**
658.33	Delayed delivery after artificial rupture of membranes, antepartum **156** , **159**
658.40	Infection of amniotic cavity, unspecified as to episode of care **137** , **144** , **150**
658.41	Infection of amniotic cavity, delivered **137** , **144** , **150**
658.43	Infection of amniotic cavity, antepartum **156** , **159**
658.80	Other problem associated with amniotic cavity and membranes, unspecified as to episode of care **161**
658.81	Other problem associated with amniotic cavity and membranes, delivered **137** , **144** , **150**
658.83	Other problem associated with amniotic cavity and membranes, antepartum **156** , **159**
658.90	Unspecified problem associated with amniotic cavity and membranes, unspecified as to episode of care **162**
658.91	Unspecified problem associated with amniotic cavity and membranes, delivered **137** , **144** , **150**
658.93	Unspecified problem associated with amniotic cavity and membranes, antepartum **156** , **159**

*Code Range

659.00 Failed mechanical induction of labor, unspecified as to episode of care **137 , 144 , 150**

659.01 Failed mechanical induction of labor, delivered **137 , 144 , 150**

659.03 Failed mechanical induction of labor, antepartum **156 , 159**

659.10 Failed medical or unspecified induction of labor, unspecified as to episode of care **137 , 144 , 150**

659.11 Failed medical or unspecified induction of labor, delivered **137 , 144 , 150**

659.13 Failed medical or unspecified induction of labor, antepartum **156 , 159**

659.20 Unspecified maternal pyrexia during labor, unspecified as to episode of care **137 , 144 , 150**

659.21 Unspecified maternal pyrexia during labor, delivered **137 , 141 , 147**

659.23 Unspecified maternal pyrexia, antepartum **156 , 159**

659.30 Generalized infection during labor, unspecified as to episode of care **137 , 144 , 150**

659.31 Generalized infection during labor, delivered **137 , 141 , 147**

659.33 Generalized infection during labor, antepartum **156 , 159**

659.40 Grand multiparity with current pregnancy, unspecified as to episode of care **162**

659.41 Grand multiparity, delivered, with or without mention of antepartum condition **137 , 144 , 150**

659.43 Grand multiparity with current pregnancy, antepartum **156 , 159**

659.50 Elderly primigravida, unspecified as to episode of care **137 , 144 , 150**

659.51 Elderly primigravida, delivered **137 , 144 , 150**

659.53 Elderly primigravida, antepartum **156 , 159**

659.60 Elderly multigravida, unspecified as to episode of care or not applicable **137 , 144 , 150**

659.61 Elderly multigravida, delivered, with mention of antepartum condition **137 , 144 , 150**

659.63 Elderly multigravida, with antepartum condition or complication **156 , 159**

659.70 Abnormality in fetal heart rate or rhythm, unspecified as to episode of care or not applicable **137 , 144 , 150**

659.71 Abnormality in fetal heart rate or rhythm, delivered, with or without mention of antepartum condition **137 , 144 , 150**

659.73 Abnormality in fetal heart rate or rhythm, antepartum condition or complication **156 , 159**

659.80 Other specified indication for care or intervention related to labor and delivery, unspecified as to episode of care **137 , 144 , 150**

659.81 Other specified indication for care or intervention related to labor and delivery, delivered **137 , 144 , 150**

659.83 Other specified indication for care or intervention related to labor and delivery, antepartum **156 , 159**

659.90 Unspecified indication for care or intervention related to labor and delivery, unspecified as to episode of care **137 , 144 , 150**

659.91 Unspecified indication for care or intervention related to labor and delivery, delivered **137 , 144 , 150**

659.93 Unspecified indication for care or intervention related to labor and delivery, antepartum **156 , 159**

660.00 Obstruction caused by malposition of fetus at onset of labor, unspecified as to episode of care **137 , 144 , 150**

660.01 Obstruction caused by malposition of fetus at onset of labor, delivered **137 , 144 , 150**

660.03 Obstruction caused by malposition of fetus at onset of labor, antepartum **156 , 159**

660.10 Obstruction by bony pelvis during labor and delivery, unspecified as to episode of care **137 , 144 , 150**

660.11 Obstruction by bony pelvis during labor and delivery, delivered **137 , 144 , 150**

660.13 Obstruction by bony pelvis during labor and delivery, antepartum **156 , 159**

660.20 Obstruction by abnormal pelvic soft tissues during labor and delivery, unspecified as to episode of care **137 , 144 , 150**

660.21 Obstruction by abnormal pelvic soft tissues during labor and delivery, delivered **137 , 144 , 150**

660.23 Obstruction by abnormal pelvic soft tissues during labor and delivery, antepartum **156 , 159**

660.30 Deep transverse arrest and persistent occipitoposterior position during labor and delivery, unspecified as to episode of care **137 , 144 , 150**

660.31 Deep transverse arrest and persistent occipitoposterior position during labor and deliver, delivered **137 , 144 , 150**

660.33 Deep transverse arrest and persistent occipitoposterior position during labor and delivery, antepartum **156 , 159**

660.40 Shoulder (girdle) dystocia during labor and delivery, unspecified as to episode of care **137 , 144 , 150**

660.41 Shoulder (girdle) dystocia during labor and deliver, delivered **137 , 144 , 150**

660.43 Shoulder (girdle) dystocia during labor and delivery, antepartum **156 , 159**

660.50 Locked twins during labor and delivery, unspecified as to episode of care in pregnancy **137 , 144 , 150**

660.51 Locked twins, delivered **137 , 144 , 150**

660.53 Locked twins, antepartum **156 , 159**

660.60 Unspecified failed trial of labor, unspecified as to episode **137 , 144 , 150**

660.61 Unspecified failed trial of labor, delivered **137 , 144 , 150**

660.63 Unspecified failed trial of labor, antepartum **156 , 159**

660.70 Unspecified failed forceps or vacuum extractor, unspecified as to episode of care **137 , 144 , 150**

660.71 Unspecified failed forceps or vacuum extractor, delivered **137 , 144 , 150**

660.73 Failed forceps or vacuum extractor, unspecified, antepartum **156 , 159**

660.80 Other causes of obstructed labor, unspecified as to episode of care **137 , 144 , 150**

660.81 Other causes of obstructed labor, delivered **137 , 144 , 150**

660.83 Other causes of obstructed labor, antepartum **156 , 159**

660.90 Unspecified obstructed labor, unspecified as to episode of care **137 , 144 , 150**

660.91 Unspecified obstructed labor, with delivery **137 , 144 , 150**

660.93 Unspecified obstructed labor, antepartum **156 , 159**

661.00 Primary uterine inertia, unspecified as to episode of care **137 , 144 , 150**

661.01 Primary uterine inertia, with delivery **137 , 144 , 150**

661.03 Primary uterine inertia, antepartum **156 , 159**

661.10 Secondary uterine inertia, unspecified as to episode of care **137 , 145 , 150**

661.11 Secondary uterine inertia, with delivery **137 , 145 , 150**

661.13 Secondary uterine inertia, antepartum **156 , 159**

661.20 Other and unspecified uterine inertia, unspecified as to episode of care **137 , 145 , 150**

661.21 Other and unspecified uterine inertia, with delivery **137 , 145 , 150**

661.23 Other and unspecified uterine inertia, antepartum **156 , 159**

661.30 Precipitate labor, unspecified as to episode of care **137 , 145 , 150**

661.31 Precipitate labor, with delivery **137 , 145 , 150**

661.33 Precipitate labor, antepartum **156 , 159**

661.40 Hypertonic, incoordinate, or prolonged uterine contractions, unspecified as to episode of care **137 , 145 , 150**

661.41 Hypertonic, incoordinate, or prolonged uterine contractions, with delivery **137 , 145 , 150**

661.43 Hypertonic, incoordinate, or prolonged uterine contractions, antepartum **156 , 159**

Numeric Index to Diseases

661.90	Unspecified abnormality of labor, unspecified as to episode of care **137**, **145**, **150**
661.91	Unspecified abnormality of labor, with delivery **137**, **145**, **150**
661.93	Unspecified abnormality of labor, antepartum **156**, **159**
662.00	Prolonged first stage of labor, unspecified as to episode of care **137**, **145**, **150**
662.01	Prolonged first stage of labor, delivered **137**, **145**, **150**
662.03	Prolonged first stage of labor, antepartum **156**, **159**
662.10	Unspecified prolonged labor, unspecified as to episode of care **137**, **145**, **150**
662.11	Unspecified prolonged labor, delivered **137**, **145**, **150**
662.13	Unspecified prolonged labor, antepartum **156**, **159**
662.20	Prolonged second stage of labor, unspecified as to episode of care **137**, **145**, **150**
662.21	Prolonged second stage of labor, delivered **137**, **145**, **150**
662.23	Prolonged second stage of labor, antepartum **156**, **159**
662.30	Delayed delivery of second twin, triplet, etc., unspecified as to episode of care **137**, **145**, **150**
662.31	Delayed delivery of second twin, triplet, etc., delivered **137**, **145**, **150**
662.33	Delayed delivery of second twin, triplet, etc., antepartum **156**, **159**
663.00	Prolapse of cord, complicating labor and delivery, unspecified as to episode of care **137**, **145**, **150**
663.01	Prolapse of cord, complicating labor and delivery, delivered **138**, **145**, **150**
663.03	Prolapse of cord, complicating labor and delivery, antepartum **156**, **159**
663.10	Cord around neck, with compression, complicating labor and delivery, unspecified as to episode of care **138**, **145**, **151**
663.11	Cord around neck, with compression, complicating labor and delivery, delivered **138**, **145**, **151**
663.13	Cord around neck, with compression, complicating labor and delivery, antepartum **156**, **159**
663.20	Other and unspecified cord entanglement, with compression, complicating labor and delivery, unspecified as to episode of care **138**, **145**, **151**
663.21	Other and unspecified cord entanglement, with compression, complicating labor and delivery, delivered **138**, **145**, **151**
663.23	Other and unspecified cord entanglement, with compression, complicating labor and delivery, antepartum **156**, **159**
663.30	Other and unspecified cord entanglement, without mention of compression, complicating labor and delivery, unspecified as to episode of care **138**, **145**, **151**
663.31	Other and unspecified cord entanglement, without mention of compression, complicating labor and delivery, delivered **138**, **145**, **151**
663.33	Other and unspecified cord entanglement, without mention of compression, complicating labor and delivery, antepartum **156**, **159**
663.40	Short cord complicating labor and delivery, unspecified as to episode of care **138**, **145**, **151**
663.41	Short cord complicating labor and delivery, delivered **138**, **145**, **151**
663.43	Short cord complicating labor and delivery, antepartum **156**, **159**
663.50	Vasa previa complicating labor and delivery, unspecified as to episode of care **138**, **145**, **151**
663.51	Vasa previa complicating labor and delivery, delivered **138**, **145**, **151**
663.53	Vasa previa complicating labor and delivery, antepartum **156**, **159**
663.60	Vascular lesions of cord complicating labor and delivery, unspecified as to episode of care **138**, **145**, **151**
663.61	Vascular lesions of cord complicating labor and delivery, delivered **138**, **145**, **151**
663.63	Vascular lesions of cord complicating labor and delivery, antepartum **156**, **159**
663.80	Other umbilical cord complications during labor and delivery, unspecified as to episode of care **138**, **145**, **151**
663.81	Other umbilical cord complications during labor and delivery, delivered **138**, **145**, **151**
663.83	Other umbilical cord complications during labor and delivery, antepartum **156**, **159**
663.90	Unspecified umbilical cord complication during labor and delivery, unspecified as to episode of care **138**, **145**, **151**
663.91	Unspecified umbilical cord complication during labor and delivery, delivered **138**, **145**, **151**
663.93	Unspecified umbilical cord complication during labor and delivery, antepartum **156**, **159**
664.00	First-degree perineal laceration, unspecified as to episode of care in pregnancy **138**, **145**, **151**
664.01	First-degree perineal laceration, with delivery **138**, **145**, **151**
664.04	First-degree perineal laceration, postpartum condition or complication **153**
664.10	Second-degree perineal laceration, unspecified as to episode of care in pregnancy **138**, **145**, **151**
664.11	Second-degree perineal laceration, with delivery **138**, **145**, **151**
664.14	Second-degree perineal laceration, postpartum condition or complication **153**
664.20	Third-degree perineal laceration, unspecified as to episode of care in pregnancy **138**, **145**, **151**
664.21	Third-degree perineal laceration, with delivery **138**, **145**, **151**
664.24	Third-degree perineal laceration, postpartum condition or complication **153**
664.30	Fourth-degree perineal laceration, unspecified as to episode of care in pregnancy **138**, **145**, **151**
664.31	Fourth-degree perineal laceration, with delivery **138**, **145**, **151**
664.34	Fourth-degree perineal laceration, postpartum condition or complication **153**
664.40	Unspecified perineal laceration, unspecified as to episode of care in pregnancy **138**, **145**, **151**
664.41	Unspecified perineal laceration, with delivery **138**, **145**, **151**
664.44	Unspecified perineal laceration, postpartum condition or complication **153**
664.50	Vulvar and perineal hematoma, unspecified as to episode of care in pregnancy **138**, **145**, **151**
664.51	Vulvar and perineal hematoma, with delivery **138**, **145**, **151**
664.54	Vulvar and perineal hematoma, postpartum condition or complication **153**
664.60	Anal sphincter tear complicating delivery, not associated with third-degree perineal laceration, unspecified as to episode of care or not applicable **138**, **145**, **151**
664.61	Anal sphincter tear complicating delivery, not associated with third-degree perineal laceration, delivered, with or without mention of antepartum condition **138**, **145**, **151**
664.64	Anal sphincter tear complicating delivery, not associated with third-degree perineal laceration, postpartum condition or complication **153**
664.80	Other specified trauma to perineum and vulva, unspecified as to episode of care in pregnancy **138**, **145**, **151**
664.81	Other specified trauma to perineum and vulva, with delivery **138**, **145**, **151**
664.84	Other specified trauma to perineum and vulva, postpartum condition or complication **153**
664.90	Unspecified trauma to perineum and vulva, unspecified as to episode of care in pregnancy **138**, **145**, **151**
664.91	Unspecified trauma to perineum and vulva, with delivery **138**, **145**, **151**

664.94	Unspecified trauma to perineum and vulva, postpartum condition or complication **153**	

665.00   Rupture of uterus before onset of labor, unspecified as to episode of care **138** , **145** , **151**

665.01   Rupture of uterus before onset of labor, with delivery **138** , **145** , **151**

665.03   Rupture of uterus before onset of labor, antepartum **156** , **159**

665.10   Rupture of uterus during labor, unspecified as to episode **138** , **145** , **151**

665.11   Rupture of uterus during labor, with delivery **138** , **145** , **151**

665.20   Inversion of uterus, unspecified as to episode of care in pregnancy **138** , **145** , **151**

665.22   Inversion of uterus, delivered with postpartum complication **138** , **145** , **151**

665.24   Inversion of uterus, postpartum condition or complication **153**

665.30   Laceration of cervix, unspecified as to episode of care in pregnancy **138** , **145** , **151**

665.31   Laceration of cervix, with delivery **138** , **145** , **151**

665.34   Laceration of cervix, postpartum condition or complication **153**

665.40   High vaginal laceration, unspecified as to episode of care in pregnancy **138** , **145** , **151**

665.41   High vaginal laceration, with delivery **138** , **145** , **151**

665.44   High vaginal laceration, postpartum condition or complication **153**

665.50   Other injury to pelvic organs, unspecified as to episode of care in pregnancy **138** , **145** , **151**

665.51   Other injury to pelvic organs, with delivery **138** , **145** , **151**

665.54   Other injury to pelvic organs, postpartum condition or complication **153**

665.60   Damage to pelvic joints and ligaments, unspecified as to episode of care in pregnancy **138** , **145** , **151**

665.61   Damage to pelvic joints and ligaments, with delivery **138** , **145** , **151**

665.64   Damage to pelvic joints and ligaments, postpartum condition or complication **153**

665.70   Pelvic hematoma, unspecified as to episode of care **138** , **145** , **151**

665.71   Pelvic hematoma, with delivery **138** , **145** , **151**

665.72   Pelvic hematoma, delivered with postpartum complication **138** , **145** , **151**

665.74   Pelvic hematoma, postpartum condition or complication **153**

665.80   Other specified obstetrical trauma, unspecified as to episode of care **138** , **145** , **151**

665.81   Other specified obstetrical trauma, with delivery **138** , **145** , **151**

665.82   Other specified obstetrical trauma, delivered, with postpartum **138** , **145** , **151**

665.83   Other specified obstetrical trauma, antepartum **156** , **159**

665.84   Other specified obstetrical trauma, postpartum condition or complication **153**

665.90   Unspecified obstetrical trauma, unspecified as to episode of care **138** , **145** , **151**

665.91   Unspecified obstetrical trauma, with delivery **138** , **145** , **151**

665.92   Unspecified obstetrical trauma, delivered, with postpartum complication **138** , **145** , **151**

665.93   Unspecified obstetrical trauma, antepartum **156** , **159**

665.94   Unspecified obstetrical trauma, postpartum condition or complication **153**

666.00   Third-stage postpartum hemorrhage, unspecified as to episode of care **162**

666.02   Third-stage postpartum hemorrhage, with delivery **138** , **141** , **147**

666.04   Third-stage postpartum hemorrhage, postpartum condition or complication **153**

666.10   Other immediate postpartum hemorrhage, unspecified as to episode of care **162**

666.12   Other immediate postpartum hemorrhage, with delivery **138** , **141** , **147**

666.14   Other immediate postpartum hemorrhage, postpartum condition or complication **153**

666.20   Delayed and secondary postpartum hemorrhage, unspecified as to episode of care **162**

666.22   Delayed and secondary postpartum hemorrhage, with delivery **138** , **141** , **147**

666.24   Delayed and secondary postpartum hemorrhage, postpartum condition or complication **153**

666.30   Postpartum coagulation defects, unspecified as to episode of care **162**

666.32   Postpartum coagulation defects, with delivery **138** , **141** , **147**

666.34   Postpartum coagulation defects, postpartum condition or complication **153**

667.00   Retained placenta without hemorrhage, unspecified as to episode of care **162**

667.02   Retained placenta without hemorrhage, with delivery, with mention of postpartum complication **138** , **141** , **147**

667.04   Retained placenta without hemorrhage, postpartum condition or complication **153**

667.10   Retained portions of placenta or membranes, without hemorrhage, unspecified as to episode of care **162**

667.12   Retained portions of placenta or membranes, without hemorrhage, delivered, with mention of postpartum complication **138** , **141** , **147**

667.14   Retained portions of placenta or membranes, without hemorrhage, postpartum condition or complication **153**

668.00   Pulmonary complications of the administration of anesthesia or other sedation in labor and delivery, unspecified as to episode of care **138** , **145** , **151**

668.01   Pulmonary complications of the administration of anesthesia or other sedation in labor and delivery, delivered **138** , **141** , **147**

668.02   Pulmonary complications of the administration of anesthesia or other sedation in labor and delivery, delivered, with mention of postpartum complication **138** , **141** , **147**

668.03   Pulmonary complications of the administration of anesthesia or other sedation in labor and delivery, antepartum **156** , **159**

668.04   Pulmonary complications of the administration of anesthesia or other sedation in labor and delivery, postpartum condition or complication **153**

668.10   Cardiac complications of the administration of anesthesia or other sedation in labor and delivery, unspecified as to episode of care **138** , **145** , **151**

668.11   Cardiac complications of the administration of anesthesia or other sedation in labor and delivery, delivered **138** , **141** , **147**

668.12   Cardiac complications of the administration of anesthesia or other sedation in labor and delivery, delivered, with mention of postpartum complication **138** , **141** , **147**

668.13   Cardiac complications of the administration of anesthesia or other sedation in labor and delivery, antepartum **156** , **159**

668.14   Cardiac complications of the administration of anesthesia or other sedation in labor and delivery, postpartum condition or complication **153**

668.20   Central nervous system complications of the administration of anesthesia or other sedation in labor and delivery, unspecified as to episode of care **138** , **145** , **151**

668.21   Central nervous system complications of the administration of anesthesia or other sedation in labor and delivery, delivered **138** , **142** , **147**

668.22   Central nervous system complications of the administration of anesthesia or other sedation in labor and delivery, delivered, with mention of postpartum complication **138** , **142** , **147**

668.23　Central nervous system complications of the administration of anesthesia or other sedation in labor and delivery, antepartum **156 , 159**

668.24　Central nervous system complications of the administration of anesthesia or other sedation in labor and delivery, postpartum condition or complication **153**

668.80　Other complications of the administration of anesthesia or other sedation in labor and delivery, unspecified as to episode of care **138 , 145 , 151**

668.81　Other complications of the administration of anesthesia or other sedation in labor and delivery, delivered **138 , 142 , 147**

668.82　Other complications of the administration of anesthesia or other sedation in labor and delivery, delivered, with mention of postpartum complication **138 , 142 , 147**

668.83　Other complications of the administration of anesthesia or other sedation in labor and delivery, antepartum **156 , 159**

668.84　Other complications of the administration of anesthesia or other sedation in labor and delivery, postpartum condition or complication **154**

668.90　Unspecified complication of the administration of anesthesia or other sedation in labor and delivery, unspecified as to episode of care **139 , 145 , 151**

668.91　Unspecified complication of the administration of anesthesia or other sedation in labor and delivery, delivered **139 , 142 , 147**

668.92　Unspecified complication of the administration of anesthesia or other sedation in labor and delivery, delivered, with mention of postpartum complication **139 , 142 , 147**

668.93　Unspecified complication of the administration of anesthesia or other sedation in labor and delivery, antepartum **156 , 159**

668.94　Unspecified complication of the administration of anesthesia or other sedation in labor and delivery, postpartum condition or complication **154**

669.00　Maternal distress complicating labor and delivery, unspecified as to episode of care **139 , 146 , 151**

669.01　Maternal distress, with delivery, with or without mention of antepartum condition **139 , 146 , 151**

669.02　Maternal distress, with delivery, with mention of postpartum complication **139 , 146 , 151**

669.03　Maternal distress complicating labor and delivery, antepartum condition or complication **156 , 159**

669.04　Maternal distress complicating labor and delivery, postpartum condition or complication **154**

669.10　Shock during or following labor and delivery, unspecified as to episode of care **139 , 146 , 151**

669.11　Shock during or following labor and delivery, with delivery, with or without mention of antepartum condition **139 , 142 , 147**

669.12　Shock during or following labor and delivery, with delivery, with mention of postpartum complication **139 , 142 , 147**

669.13　Shock during or following labor and delivery, antepartum shock **156 , 159**

669.14　Shock during or following labor and delivery, postpartum condition or complication **154**

669.20　Maternal hypotension syndrome complicating labor and delivery, unspecified as to episode of care **139 , 146 , 151**

669.21　Maternal hypotension syndrome, with delivery, with or without mention of antepartum condition **139 , 146 , 151**

669.22　Maternal hypotension syndrome, with delivery, with mention of postpartum complication **139 , 146 , 151**

669.23　Maternal hypotension syndrome, antepartum **156 , 159**

669.24　Maternal hypotension syndrome, postpartum condition or complication **154**

669.30　Acute kidney failure following labor and delivery, unspecified as to episode of care or not applicable **139 , 146 , 151**

669.32　Acute kidney failure following labor and delivery, delivered, with mention of postpartum complication **139 , 142 , 147**

669.34　Acute kidney failure following labor and delivery, postpartum condition or complication **154**

669.40　Other complications of obstetrical surgery and procedures, unspecified as to episode of care **139 , 146 , 151**

669.41　Other complications of obstetrical surgery and procedures, with delivery, with or without mention of antepartum condition **139 , 142 , 147**

669.42　Other complications of obstetrical surgery and procedures, with delivery, with mention of postpartum complication **139 , 142 , 147**

669.43　Other complications of obstetrical surgery and procedures, antepartum condition or complication **157 , 159**

669.44　Other complications of obstetrical surgery and procedures, postpartum condition or complication **154**

669.50　Forceps or vacuum extractor delivery without mention of indication, unspecified as to episode of care **139 , 146 , 151**

669.51　Forceps or vacuum extractor delivery without mention of indication, delivered, with or without mention of antepartum condition **139 , 146 , 151**

669.60　Breech extraction, without mention of indication, unspecified as to episode of care **139 , 146 , 151**

669.61　Breech extraction, without mention of indication, delivered, with or without mention of antepartum condition **139 , 146 , 151**

669.70　Cesarean delivery, without mention of indication, unspecified as to episode of care **139 , 146 , 151**

669.71　Cesarean delivery, without mention of indication, delivered, with or without mention of antepartum condition **139 , 146 , 152**

669.80　Other complication of labor and delivery, unspecified as to episode of care **139 , 146 , 152**

669.81　Other complication of labor and delivery, delivered, with or without mention of antepartum condition **139 , 146 , 152**

669.82　Other complication of labor and delivery, delivered, with mention of postpartum complication **139 , 146 , 152**

669.83　Other complication of labor and delivery, antepartum condition or complication **157 , 159**

669.84　Other complication of labor and delivery, postpartum condition or complication **154**

669.90　Unspecified complication of labor and delivery, unspecified as to episode of care **139 , 146 , 152**

669.91　Unspecified complication of labor and delivery, with delivery, with or without mention of antepartum condition **139 , 146 , 152**

669.92　Unspecified complication of labor and delivery, with delivery, with mention of postpartum complication **139 , 146 , 152**

669.93　Unspecified complication of labor and delivery, antepartum condition or complication **157 , 159**

669.94　Unspecified complication of labor and delivery, postpartum condition or complication **154**

670.00　Major puerperal infection, unspecified, unspecified as to episode of care or not applicable **162**

670.02　Major puerperal infection, unspecified, delivered, with mention of postpartum complication **139 , 142 , 147**

670.04　Major puerperal infection, unspecified, postpartum condition or complication **154**

670.10　Puerperal endometritis, unspecified as to episode of care or not applicable **162**

670.12　Puerperal endometritis, delivered, with mention of postpartum complication **139 , 142 , 147**

670.14　Puerperal endometritis, postpartum condition or complication **154**

670.20　Puerperal sepsis, unspecified as to episode of care or not applicable **162**

670.22　Puerperal sepsis, delivered, with mention of postpartum complication **139 , 142 , 147**

670.24　Puerperal sepsis, postpartum condition or complication **154**

670.30　Puerperal septic thrombophlebitis, unspecified as to episode of care or not applicable **162**

670.32　Puerperal septic thrombophlebitis, delivered, with mention of postpartum complication **139 , 142 , 147**

670.34	Puerperal septic thrombophlebitis, postpartum condition or complication **154**	
670.80	Other major puerperal infection, unspecified as to episode of care or not applicable **162**	
670.82	Other major puerperal infection, delivered, with mention of postpartum complication **139 , 142 , 147**	
670.84	Other major puerperal infection, postpartum condition or complication **154**	
671.00	Varicose veins of legs complicating pregnancy and the puerperium, unspecified as to episode of care **162**	
671.01	Varicose veins of legs, with delivery, with or without mention of antepartum condition **139 , 146 , 152**	
671.02	Varicose veins of legs, with delivery, with mention of postpartum complication **139 , 146 , 152**	
671.03	Varicose veins of legs, antepartum **157 , 159**	
671.04	Varicose veins of legs, postpartum condition or complication **154**	
671.10	Varicose veins of vulva and perineum complicating pregnancy and the puerperium, unspecified as to episode of care **162**	
671.11	Varicose veins of vulva and perineum, with delivery, with or without mention of antepartum condition **139 , 146 , 152**	
671.12	Varicose veins of vulva and perineum, with delivery, with mention of postpartum complication **139 , 146 , 152**	
671.13	Varicose veins of vulva and perineum, antepartum **157 , 159**	
671.14	Varicose veins of vulva and perineum, postpartum condition or complication **154**	
671.20	Superficial thrombophlebitis complicating pregnancy and the puerperium, unspecified as to episode of care **162**	
671.21	Superficial thrombophlebitis with delivery, with or without mention of antepartum condition **139 , 146 , 152**	
671.22	Superficial thrombophlebitis with delivery, with mention of postpartum complication **139 , 146 , 152**	
671.23	Superficial thrombophlebitis, antepartum **157 , 159**	
671.24	Superficial thrombophlebitis, postpartum condition or complication **154**	
671.30	Deep phlebothrombosis, antepartum, unspecified as to episode of care **162**	
671.31	Deep phlebothrombosis, antepartum, with delivery **139 , 142 , 147**	
671.33	Deep phlebothrombosis, antepartum **157 , 159**	
671.40	Deep phlebothrombosis, postpartum, unspecified as to episode of care **162**	
671.42	Deep phlebothrombosis, postpartum, with delivery **139 , 142 , 147**	
671.44	Deep phlebothrombosis, postpartum condition or complication **154**	
671.50	Other phlebitis and thrombosis complicating pregnancy and the puerperium, unspecified as to episode of care **162**	
671.51	Other phlebitis and thrombosis with delivery, with or without mention of antepartum condition **139 , 142 , 147**	
671.52	Other phlebitis and thrombosis with delivery, with mention of postpartum complication **139 , 142 , 147**	
671.53	Other antepartum phlebitis and thrombosis **157 , 159**	
671.54	Other phlebitis and thrombosis, postpartum condition or complication **154**	
671.80	Other venous complication of pregnancy and the puerperium, unspecified as to episode of care **162**	
671.81	Other venous complication, with delivery, with or without mention of antepartum condition **139 , 146 , 152**	
671.82	Other venous complication, with delivery, with mention of postpartum complication **139 , 146 , 152**	
671.83	Other venous complication, antepartum **157 , 159**	
671.84	Other venous complications, postpartum condition or complication **154**	
671.90	Unspecified venous complication of pregnancy and the puerperium, unspecified as to episode of care **162**	

671.91	Unspecified venous complication, with delivery, with or without mention of antepartum condition **139 , 146 , 152**	
671.92	Unspecified venous complication, with delivery, with mention of postpartum complication **139 , 146 , 152**	
671.93	Unspecified venous complication, antepartum **157 , 159**	
671.94	Unspecified venous complication, postpartum condition or complication **154**	
672.00	Puerperal pyrexia of unknown origin, unspecified as to episode of care **162**	
672.02	Puerperal pyrexia of unknown origin, delivered, with mention of postpartum complication **139 , 142 , 147**	
672.04	Puerperal pyrexia of unknown origin, postpartum condition or complication **154**	
673.00	Obstetrical air embolism, unspecified as to episode of care **162**	
673.01	Obstetrical air embolism, with delivery, with or without mention of antepartum condition **139 , 142 , 147**	
673.02	Obstetrical air embolism, with delivery, with mention of postpartum complication **139 , 142 , 147**	
673.03	Obstetrical air embolism, antepartum condition or complication **157 , 159**	
673.04	Obstetrical air embolism, postpartum condition or complication **154**	
673.10	Amniotic fluid embolism, unspecified as to episode of care **162**	
673.11	Amniotic fluid embolism, with delivery, with or without mention of antepartum condition **139 , 142 , 147**	
673.12	Amniotic fluid embolism, with delivery, with mention of postpartum complication **139 , 142 , 147**	
673.13	Amniotic fluid embolism, antepartum condition or complication **157 , 159**	
673.14	Amniotic fluid embolism, postpartum condition or complication **154**	
673.20	Obstetrical blood-clot embolism, unspecified as to episode of care **162**	
673.21	Obstetrical blood-clot embolism, with delivery, with or without mention of antepartum condition **139 , 142 , 147**	
673.22	Obstetrical blood-clot embolism, with mention of postpartum complication **139 , 142 , 147**	
673.23	Obstetrical blood-clot embolism, antepartum **157 , 159**	
673.24	Obstetrical blood-clot embolism, postpartum condition or complication **154**	
673.30	Obstetrical pyemic and septic embolism, unspecified as to episode of care **162**	
673.31	Obstetrical pyemic and septic embolism, with delivery, with or without mention of antepartum condition **139 , 142 , 148**	
673.32	Obstetrical pyemic and septic embolism, with delivery, with mention of postpartum complication **139 , 142 , 148**	
673.33	Obstetrical pyemic and septic embolism, antepartum **157 , 159**	
673.34	Obstetrical pyemic and septic embolism, postpartum condition or complication **154**	
673.80	Other obstetrical pulmonary embolism, unspecified as to episode of care **162**	
673.81	Other obstetrical pulmonary embolism, with delivery, with or without mention of antepartum condition **139 , 142 , 148**	
673.82	Other obstetrical pulmonary embolism, with delivery, with mention of postpartum complication **139 , 142 , 148**	
673.83	Other obstetrical pulmonary embolism, antepartum **157 , 159**	
673.84	Other obstetrical pulmonary embolism, postpartum condition or complication **154**	
674.00	Cerebrovascular disorder occurring in pregnancy, childbirth, or the puerperium, unspecified as to episode of care **162**	
674.01	Cerebrovascular disorder, with delivery, with or without mention of antepartum condition **139 , 142 , 148**	
674.02	Cerebrovascular disorder, with delivery, with mention of postpartum complication **139 , 142 , 148**	
674.03	Cerebrovascular disorder, antepartum **157 , 159**	

674.04	Cerebrovascular disorders in the puerperium, postpartum condition or complication **154**
674.10	Disruption of cesarean wound, unspecified as to episode of care **162**
674.12	Disruption of cesarean wound, with delivery, with mention of postpartum complication **139 , 142 , 148**
674.14	Disruption of cesarean wound, postpartum condition or complication **154**
674.20	Disruption of perineal wound, unspecified as to episode of care in pregnancy **162**
674.22	Disruption of perineal wound, with delivery, with mention of postpartum complication **139 , 142 , 148**
674.24	Disruption of perineal wound, postpartum condition or complication **154**
674.30	Other complication of obstetrical surgical wounds, unspecified as to episode of care **162**
674.32	Other complication of obstetrical surgical wounds, with delivery, with mention of postpartum complication **139 , 142 , 148**
674.34	Other complications of obstetrical surgical wounds, postpartum condition or complication **154**
674.40	Placental polyp, unspecified as to episode of care **162**
674.42	Placental polyp, with delivery, with mention of postpartum complication **139 , 146 , 152**
674.44	Placental polyp, postpartum condition or complication **154**
674.50	Peripartum cardiomyopathy, unspecified as to episode of care or not applicable **162**
674.51	Peripartum cardiomyopathy, delivered, with or without mention of antepartum condition **139 , 142 , 148**
674.52	Peripartum cardiomyopathy, delivered, with mention of postpartum condition **139 , 142 , 148**
674.53	Peripartum cardiomyopathy, antepartum condition or complication **157 , 159**
674.54	Peripartum cardiomyopathy, postpartum condition or complication **154**
674.80	Other complication of puerperium, unspecified as to episode of care **162**
674.82	Other complication of puerperium, with delivery, with mention of postpartum complication **139 , 142 , 148**
674.84	Other complications of puerperium, postpartum condition or complication **154**
674.90	Unspecified complications of puerperium, unspecified as to episode of care **162**
674.92	Unspecified complications of puerperium, with delivery, with mention of postpartum complication **139 , 146 , 152**
674.94	Unspecified complications of puerperium, postpartum condition or complication **154**
675.00	Infection of nipple associated with childbirth, unspecified as to episode of care **162**
675.01	Infection of nipple associated with childbirth, delivered, with or without mention of antepartum condition **140 , 142 , 148**
675.02	Infection of nipple associated with childbirth, delivered with mention of postpartum complication **140 , 142 , 148**
675.03	Infection of nipple, antepartum **157 , 159**
675.04	Infection of nipple, postpartum condition or complication **154**
675.10	Abscess of breast associated with childbirth, unspecified as to episode of care **162**
675.11	Abscess of breast associated with childbirth, delivered, with or without mention of antepartum condition **140 , 142 , 148**
675.12	Abscess of breast associated with childbirth, delivered, with mention of postpartum complication **140 , 142 , 148**
675.13	Abscess of breast, antepartum **157 , 159**
675.14	Abscess of breast, postpartum condition or complication **154**
675.20	Nonpurulent mastitis, unspecified as to episode of prenatal or postnatal care **162**
675.21	Nonpurulent mastitis, delivered, with or without mention of antepartum condition **140 , 142 , 148**
675.22	Nonpurulent mastitis, delivered, with mention of postpartum complication **140 , 142 , 148**
675.23	Nonpurulent mastitis, antepartum **157 , 159**
675.24	Nonpurulent mastitis, postpartum condition or complication **154**
675.80	Other specified infection of the breast and nipple associated with childbirth, unspecified as to episode of care **162**
675.81	Other specified infection of the breast and nipple associated with childbirth, delivered, with or without mention of antepartum condition **140 , 146 , 152**
675.82	Other specified infection of the breast and nipple associated with childbirth, delivered, with mention of postpartum complication **140 , 146 , 152**
675.83	Other specified infection of the breast and nipple, antepartum **157 , 159**
675.84	Other specified infections of the breast and nipple, postpartum condition or complication **154**
675.90	Unspecified infection of the breast and nipple, unspecified as to prenatal or postnatal episode of care **162**
675.91	Unspecified infection of the breast and nipple, delivered, with or without mention of antepartum condition **140 , 146 , 152**
675.92	Unspecified infection of the breast and nipple, delivered, with mention of postpartum complication **140 , 146 , 152**
675.93	Unspecified infection of the breast and nipple, antepartum **157 , 159**
675.94	Unspecified infection of the breast and nipple, postpartum condition or complication **154**
676.00	Retracted nipple, unspecified as to prenatal or postnatal episode of care **162**
676.01	Retracted nipple, delivered, with or without mention of antepartum condition **140 , 146 , 152**
676.02	Retracted nipple, delivered, with mention of postpartum complication **140 , 146 , 152**
676.03	Retracted nipple, antepartum condition or complication **157 , 159**
676.04	Retracted nipple, postpartum condition or complication **154**
676.10	Cracked nipple, unspecified as to prenatal or postnatal episode of care **162**
676.11	Cracked nipple, delivered, with or without mention of antepartum condition **140 , 146 , 152**
676.12	Cracked nipple, delivered, with mention of postpartum complication **140 , 146 , 152**
676.13	Cracked nipple, antepartum condition or complication **157 , 159**
676.14	Cracked nipple, postpartum condition or complication **154**
676.20	Engorgement of breasts, unspecified as to prenatal or postnatal episode of care **162**
676.21	Engorgement of breasts, delivered, with or without mention of antepartum condition **140 , 146 , 152**
676.22	Engorgement of breasts, delivered, with mention of postpartum complication **140 , 146 , 152**
676.23	Engorgement of breast, antepartum **157 , 159**
676.24	Engorgement of breasts, postpartum condition or complication **154**
676.30	Other and unspecified disorder of breast associated with childbirth, unspecified as to episode of care **162**
676.31	Other and unspecified disorder of breast associated with childbirth, delivered, with or without mention of antepartum condition **140 , 146 , 152**
676.32	Other and unspecified disorder of breast associated with childbirth, delivered, with mention of postpartum complication **140 , 146 , 152**
676.33	Other and unspecified disorder of breast associated with childbirth, antepartum condition or complication **157 , 159**
676.34	Other and unspecified disorder of breast associated with childbirth, postpartum condition or complication **154**

*Code Range

676.40	Failure of lactation, unspecified as to episode of care **162**	
676.41	Failure of lactation, with delivery, with or without mention of antepartum condition **140 , 146 , 152**	
676.42	Failure of lactation, with delivery, with mention of postpartum complication **140 , 146 , 152**	
676.43	Failure of lactation, antepartum condition or complication **157 , 159**	
676.44	Failure of lactation, postpartum condition or complication **154**	
676.50	Suppressed lactation, unspecified as to episode of care **162**	
676.51	Suppressed lactation, with delivery, with or without mention of antepartum condition **140 , 146 , 152**	
676.52	Suppressed lactation, with delivery, with mention of postpartum complication **140 , 146 , 152**	
676.53	Suppressed lactation, antepartum condition or complication **157 , 159**	
676.54	Suppressed lactation, postpartum condition or complication **154**	
676.60	Galactorrhea associated with childbirth, unspecified as to episode of care **162**	
676.61	Galactorrhea, with delivery, with or without mention of antepartum condition **140 , 146 , 152**	
676.62	Galactorrhea, with delivery, with mention of postpartum complication **140 , 146 , 152**	
676.63	Galactorrhea, antepartum condition or complication **157 , 159**	
676.64	Galactorrhea, postpartum condition or complication **154**	
676.80	Other disorder of lactation, unspecified as to episode of care **162**	
676.81	Other disorder of lactation, with delivery, with or without mention of antepartum condition **140 , 146 , 152**	
676.82	Other disorder of lactation, with delivery, with mention of postpartum complication **140 , 146 , 152**	
676.83	Other disorder of lactation, antepartum condition or complication **157 , 159**	
676.84	Other disorders of lactation, postpartum condition or complication **154**	
676.90	Unspecified disorder of lactation, unspecified as to episode of care **162**	
676.91	Unspecified disorder of lactation, with delivery, with or without mention of antepartum condition **140 , 146 , 152**	
676.92	Unspecified disorder of lactation, with delivery, with mention of postpartum complication **140 , 146 , 152**	
676.93	Unspecified disorder of lactation, antepartum condition or complication **157 , 159**	
676.94	Unspecified disorder of lactation, postpartum condition or complication **154**	
677	Late effect of complication of pregnancy, childbirth, and the puerperium **162**	
678.00	Fetal hematologic conditions, unspecified as to episode of care or not applicable **162**	
678.01	Fetal hematologic conditions, delivered, with or without mention of antepartum condition **140 , 146 , 152**	
678.03	Fetal hematologic conditions, antepartum condition or complication **157 , 159**	
678.10	Fetal conjoined twins, unspecified as to episode of care or not applicable **162**	
678.11	Fetal conjoined twins, delivered, with or without mention of antepartum condition **140 , 146 , 152**	
678.13	Fetal conjoined twins, antepartum condition or complication **157 , 159**	
679.00	Maternal complications from in utero procedure, unspecified as to episode of care or not applicable **140 , 146 , 152**	
679.01	Maternal complications from in utero procedure, delivered, with or without mention of antepartum condition **140 , 142 , 148**	
679.02	Maternal complications from in utero procedure, delivered, with mention of postpartum complication **140 , 142 , 148**	
679.03	Maternal complications from in utero procedure, antepartum condition or complication **157 , 159**	

679.04	Maternal complications from in utero procedure, postpartum condition or complication **154**	
679.10	Fetal complications from in utero procedure, unspecified as to episode of care or not applicable **162**	
679.11	Fetal complications from in utero procedure, delivered, with or without mention of antepartum condition **140 , 146 , 152**	
679.12	Fetal complications from in utero procedure, delivered, with mention of postpartum complication **140 , 146 , 152**	
679.13	Fetal complications from in utero procedure, antepartum condition or complication **157 , 160**	
679.14	Fetal complications from in utero procedure, postpartum condition or complication **154**	
680*	Carbuncle and furuncle **107**	
681*	Cellulitis and abscess of finger and toe **104 , 107**	
682.0	Cellulitis and abscess of face **3**	
682.1	Cellulitis and abscess of neck **3**	
682*	Other cellulitis and abscess **104 , 107 , 167 , 171**	
683	Acute lymphadenitis **167 , 171 , 177 , 232**	
684	Impetigo **107**	
685*	Pilonidal cyst **107**	
686.9	Unspecified local infection of skin and subcutaneous tissue **173**	
686*	Other local infection of skin and subcutaneous tissue **107**	
690*	Erythematosquamous dermatosis **109**	
691.0	Diaper or napkin rash **173**	
691*	Atopic dermatitis and related conditions **109**	
692*	Contact dermatitis and other eczema **109**	
693.0	Dermatitis due to drugs and medicines taken internally **167 , 171**	
693*	Dermatitis due to substances taken internally **109**	
694.0	Dermatitis herpetiformis **109**	
694.1	Subcorneal pustular dermatosis **109**	
694.2	Juvenile dermatitis herpetiformis **109**	
694.3	Impetigo herpetiformis **109**	
694.4	Pemphigus **106**	
694.5	Pemphigoid **106**	
694.60	Benign mucous membrane pemphigoid without mention of ocular involvement **106**	
694.61	Benign mucous membrane pemphigoid with ocular involvement **40**	
694.8	Other specified bullous dermatosis **106**	
694.9	Unspecified bullous dermatosis **106**	
695.0	Toxic erythema **106 , 167 , 171**	
695.1*	Erythema multiforme **106**	
695.2	Erythema nodosum **106**	
695.3	Rosacea **109**	
695.4	Lupus erythematosus **106**	
695.5*	Exfoliation due to erythematous conditions according to extent of body surface involved **109**	
695.81	Ritter's disease **106**	
695.89	Other specified erythematous condition **109**	
695.9	Unspecified erythematous condition **109**	
696.0	Psoriatic arthropathy **97**	
696.1	Other psoriasis **106**	
696.2	Parapsoriasis **106**	
696.3	Pityriasis rosea **109**	
696.4	Pityriasis rubra pilaris **109**	
696.5	Other and unspecified pityriasis **109**	
696.8	Psoriasis related disease NEC **109**	
697*	Lichen **109**	
698.0	Pruritus ani **109**	
698.1	Pruritus of genital organs **125 , 128 , 131**	

698.2	Prurigo	**109**
698.3	Lichenification and lichen simplex chronicus	**109**
698.4	Dermatitis factitia (artefacta)	**109**
698.8	Other specified pruritic conditions	**109**
698.9	Unspecified pruritic disorder	**109**
700	Corns and callosities	**109**
701*	Other hypertrophic and atrophic conditions of skin	**109**
702*	Other dermatoses	**109**
703*	Diseases of nail	**109**
704*	Diseases of hair and hair follicles	**109**
705*	Disorders of sweat glands	**109**
706*	Diseases of sebaceous glands	**109**
707*	Chronic ulcer of skin	**104** , **106**
708.0	Allergic urticaria	**167** , **171**
708*	Urticaria	**109**
709.00	Dyschromia, unspecified	**173**
709.01	Vitiligo	**173**
709.09	Other dyschromia	**173**
709.9	Unspecified disorder of skin and subcutaneous tissue	**232**
709*	Other disorders of skin and subcutaneous tissue	**109**
710*	Diffuse diseases of connective tissue	**97**
711.0*	Pyogenic arthritis	**97** , **232**
711.06	Pyogenic arthritis, lower leg	**90**
711.1*	Arthropathy associated with Reiter's disease and nonspecific urethritis	**97**
711.2*	Arthropathy in Behcet's syndrome	**97**
711.3*	Postdysenteric arthropathy	**98**
711.4*	Arthropathy associated with other bacterial diseases	**97**
711.5*	Arthropathy associated with other viral diseases	**98**
711.6*	Arthropathy associated with mycoses	**97**
711.7*	Arthropathy associated with helminthiasis	**97**
711.8*	Arthropathy associated with other infectious and parasitic diseases	**97**
711.9*	Unspecified infective arthritis	**97** , **232**
712*	Crystal arthropathies	**98**
713*	Arthropathy associated with other disorders classified elsewhere	**98**
714.0	Rheumatoid arthritis	**97**
714.1	Felty's syndrome	**97**
714.2	Other rheumatoid arthritis with visceral or systemic involvement	**97**
714.3*	Juvenile chronic polyarthritis	**97**
714.4	Chronic postrheumatic arthropathy	**98**
714.81	Rheumatoid lung	**53**
714.89	Other specified inflammatory polyarthropathies	**97**
714.9	Unspecified inflammatory polyarthropathy	**98**
715*	Osteoarthrosis and allied disorders	**98**
716.9*	Unspecified arthropathy	**232**
716*	Other and unspecified arthropathies	**98**
717.0	Old bucket handle tear of medial meniscus	**99**
717.1	Derangement of anterior horn of medial meniscus	**99**
717.2	Derangement of posterior horn of medial meniscus	**99**
717.3	Other and unspecified derangement of medial meniscus	**99**
717.4*	Derangement of lateral meniscus	**99**
717.5	Derangement of meniscus, not elsewhere classified	**99**
717.6	Loose body in knee	**100**
717.7	Chondromalacia of patella	**99**
717.8*	Other internal derangement of knee	**99**
717.9	Unspecified internal derangement of knee	**99**
718.00	Articular cartilage disorder, site unspecified	**100**

718.01	Articular cartilage disorder, shoulder region	**99**
718.02	Articular cartilage disorder, upper arm	**99**
718.03	Articular cartilage disorder, forearm	**99**
718.04	Articular cartilage disorder, hand	**99**
718.05	Articular cartilage disorder, pelvic region and thigh	**100**
718.07	Articular cartilage disorder, ankle and foot	**99**
718.08	Articular cartilage disorder, other specified site	**100**
718.09	Articular cartilage disorder, multiple sites	**100**
718.1*	Loose body in joint	**100**
718.20	Pathological dislocation of joint, site unspecified	**99**
718.21	Pathological dislocation of shoulder joint	**99**
718.22	Pathological dislocation of upper arm joint	**99**
718.23	Pathological dislocation of forearm joint	**99**
718.24	Pathological dislocation of hand joint	**99**
718.25	Pathological dislocation of pelvic region and thigh joint	**100**
718.26	Pathological dislocation of lower leg joint	**99**
718.27	Pathological dislocation of ankle and foot joint	**99**
718.28	Pathological dislocation of joint of other specified site	**100**
718.29	Pathological dislocation of joint of multiple sites	**100**
718.30	Recurrent dislocation of joint, site unspecified	**100**
718.31	Recurrent dislocation of shoulder joint	**99**
718.32	Recurrent dislocation of upper arm joint	**99**
718.33	Recurrent dislocation of forearm joint	**99**
718.34	Recurrent dislocation of hand joint	**99**
718.35	Recurrent dislocation of pelvic region and thigh joint	**100**
718.36	Recurrent dislocation of lower leg joint	**99**
718.37	Recurrent dislocation of ankle and foot joint	**99**
718.38	Recurrent dislocation of joint of other specified site	**100**
718.39	Recurrent dislocation of joint of multiple sites	**100**
718.4*	Contracture of joint	**100**
718.5*	Ankylosis of joint	**98**
718.65	Unspecified intrapelvic protrusion acetabulum, pelvic region and thigh	**100**
718.7*	Developmental dislocation of joint	**100**
718.8*	Other joint derangement, not elsewhere classified	**100**
718.9*	Unspecified derangement of joint	**100**
719.0*	Effusion of joint	**100**
719.1*	Hemarthrosis	**98**
719.2*	Villonodular synovitis	**98**
719.3*	Palindromic rheumatism	**98**
719.4*	Pain in joint	**98**
719.5*	Stiffness of joint, not elsewhere classified	**98**
719.6*	Other symptoms referable to joint	**98**
719.7	Difficulty in walking	**98**
719.8*	Other specified disorders of joint	**98**
719.9*	Unspecified disorder of joint	**98**
720.0	Ankylosing spondylitis	**97**
720.1	Spinal enthesopathy	**97**
720.2	Sacroiliitis, not elsewhere classified	**97**
720.8*	Other inflammatory spondylopathies	**97**
720.9	Unspecified inflammatory spondylopathy	**97**
721*	Spondylosis and allied disorders	**97**
722*	Intervertebral disc disorders	**97**
723.0	Spinal stenosis in cervical region	**97**
723.1	Cervicalgia	**97**
723.2	Cervicocranial syndrome	**21**
723.3	Cervicobrachial syndrome (diffuse)	**21**
723.4	Brachial neuritis or radiculitis NOS	**21**
723.5	Torticollis, unspecified	**97**

*Code Range

© 2012 OptumInsight, Inc.

723.6	Panniculitis specified as affecting neck **109**	
723.7	Ossification of posterior longitudinal ligament in cervical region **97**	
723.8	Other syndromes affecting cervical region **97**	
723.9	Unspecified musculoskeletal disorders and symptoms referable to neck **97**	
724*	Other and unspecified disorders of back **97**	
725	Polymyalgia rheumatica **97**	
726.0	Adhesive capsulitis of shoulder **98**	
726.1*	Rotator cuff syndrome of shoulder and allied disorders **98**	
726.2	Other affections of shoulder region, not elsewhere classified **98**	
726.3*	Enthesopathy of elbow region **98**	
726.4	Enthesopathy of wrist and carpus **98**	
726.5	Enthesopathy of hip region **98**	
726.6*	Enthesopathy of knee **98**	
726.70	Unspecified enthesopathy of ankle and tarsus **98**	
726.71	Achilles bursitis or tendinitis **98**	
726.72	Tibialis tendinitis **98**	
726.73	Calcaneal spur **100**	
726.79	Other enthesopathy of ankle and tarsus **98**	
726.8	Other peripheral enthesopathies **98**	
726.9*	Unspecified enthesopathy **98**	
727.00	Unspecified synovitis and tenosynovitis **98**	
727.01	Synovitis and tenosynovitis in diseases classified elsewhere **98**	
727.02	Giant cell tumor of tendon sheath **100**	
727.03	Trigger finger (acquired) **99**	
727.04	Radial styloid tenosynovitis **99**	
727.05	Other tenosynovitis of hand and wrist **99**	
727.06	Tenosynovitis of foot and ankle **99**	
727.09	Other synovitis and tenosynovitis **99**	
727.1	Bunion **100**	
727.2	Specific bursitides often of occupational origin **99**	
727.3	Other bursitis disorders **99**	
727.4*	Ganglion and cyst of synovium, tendon, and bursa **99**	
727.5*	Rupture of synovium **99**	
727.6*	Rupture of tendon, nontraumatic **99**	
727.8*	Other disorders of synovium, tendon, and bursa **99**	
727.9	Unspecified disorder of synovium, tendon, and bursa **99**	
728.0	Infective myositis **99**	
728.1*	Muscular calcification and ossification **99**	
728.2	Muscular wasting and disuse atrophy, not elsewhere classified **99**	
728.3	Other specific muscle disorders **99**	
728.4	Laxity of ligament **99**	
728.5	Hypermobility syndrome **99**	
728.6	Contracture of palmar fascia **99**	
728.7*	Other fibromatoses of muscle, ligament, and fascia **99**	
728.81	Interstitial myositis **99**	
728.82	Foreign body granuloma of muscle **99**	
728.83	Rupture of muscle, nontraumatic **99**	
728.84	Diastasis of muscle **99**	
728.85	Spasm of muscle **98**	
728.86	Necrotizing fasciitis **99**	
728.87	Muscle weakness (generalized) **98**	
728.88	Rhabdomyolysis **99**	
728.89	Other disorder of muscle, ligament, and fascia **99**	
728.9	Unspecified disorder of muscle, ligament, and fascia **99**	
729.0	Rheumatism, unspecified and fibrositis **98**	
729.1	Unspecified myalgia and myositis **98**	
729.2	Unspecified neuralgia, neuritis, and radiculitis **21 , 232**	

729.3*	Unspecified panniculitis **109**
729.4	Unspecified fasciitis **99**
729.5	Pain in soft tissues of limb **98**
729.6	Residual foreign body in soft tissue **100**
729.7*	Nontraumatic compartment syndrome **99**
729.81	Swelling of limb **98**
729.82	Cramp of limb **98**
729.89	Other musculoskeletal symptoms referable to limbs **98**
729.9*	Other and unspecified disorders of soft tissue **98**
730.0*	Acute osteomyelitis **96**
730.06	Acute osteomyelitis, lower leg **90**
730.08	Acute osteomyelitis, other specified site **87**
730.1*	Chronic osteomyelitis **96**
730.16	Chronic osteomyelitis, lower leg **90**
730.18	Chronic osteomyelitis, other specified sites **87**
730.2*	Unspecified osteomyelitis **96**
730.26	Unspecified osteomyelitis, lower leg **90**
730.28	Unspecified osteomyelitis, other specified sites **87**
730.30	Periostitis, without mention of osteomyelitis, unspecified site **98**
730.31	Periostitis, without mention of osteomyelitis, shoulder region **98**
730.32	Periostitis, without mention of osteomyelitis, upper arm **98**
730.33	Periostitis, without mention of osteomyelitis, forearm **98**
730.34	Periostitis, without mention of osteomyelitis, hand **98**
730.35	Periostitis, without mention of osteomyelitis, pelvic region and thigh **98**
730.36	Periostitis, without mention of osteomyelitis, lower leg **98**
730.37	Periostitis, without mention of osteomyelitis, ankle and foot **100**
730.38	Periostitis, without mention of osteomyelitis, other specified sites **100**
730.39	Periostitis, without mention of osteomyelitis, multiple sites **100**
730.7*	Osteopathy resulting from poliomyelitis **100**
730.8*	Other infections involving bone in diseases classified elsewhere **96**
730.9*	Unspecified infection of bone **96**
731*	Osteitis deformans and osteopathies associated with other disorders classified elsewhere **98**
732.0	Juvenile osteochondrosis of spine **87**
732*	Osteochondropathies **98**
733.0*	Osteoporosis **98**
733.1*	Pathologic fracture **97 , 167 , 171**
733.13	Pathologic fracture of vertebrae **87**
733.2*	Cyst of bone **98**
733.3	Hyperostosis of skull **100**
733.4*	Aseptic necrosis of bone **98**
733.5	Osteitis condensans **98**
733.6	Tietze's disease **54**
733.7	Algoneurodystrophy **100**
733.8*	Malunion and nonunion of fracture **100**
733.90	Disorder of bone and cartilage, unspecified **100**
733.91	Arrest of bone development or growth **100**
733.92	Chondromalacia **98**
733.93	Stress fracture of tibia or fibula **97**
733.94	Stress fracture of the metatarsals **97**
733.95	Stress fracture of other bone **97**
733.96	Stress fracture of femoral neck **97**
733.97	Stress fracture of shaft of femur **97**
733.98	Stress fracture of pelvis **97**
733.99	Other disorders of bone and cartilage **100**
734	Flat foot **100**
735*	Acquired deformities of toe **100**

Numeric Index to Diseases

736.00	Unspecified deformity of forearm, excluding fingers **100**	
736.01	Cubitus valgus (acquired) **100**	
736.02	Cubitus varus (acquired) **100**	
736.03	Valgus deformity of wrist (acquired) **100**	
736.04	Varus deformity of wrist (acquired) **100**	
736.05	Wrist drop (acquired) **21**	
736.06	Claw hand (acquired) **21**	
736.07	Club hand, acquired **21**	
736.09	Other acquired deformities of forearm, excluding fingers **100**	
736.1	Mallet finger **100**	
736.2*	Other acquired deformities of finger **100**	
736.3*	Acquired deformities of hip **100**	
736.4*	Genu valgum or varum (acquired) **100**	
736.5	Genu recurvatum (acquired) **100**	
736.6	Other acquired deformities of knee **100**	
736.70	Unspecified deformity of ankle and foot, acquired **100**	
736.71	Acquired equinovarus deformity **100**	
736.72	Equinus deformity of foot, acquired **100**	
736.73	Cavus deformity of foot, acquired **100**	
736.74	Claw foot, acquired **21**	
736.75	Cavovarus deformity of foot, acquired **100**	
736.76	Other acquired calcaneus deformity **100**	
736.79	Other acquired deformity of ankle and foot **100**	
736.8*	Acquired deformities of other parts of limbs **100**	
736.9	Acquired deformity of limb, site unspecified **100**	
737.0	Adolescent postural kyphosis **87**	
737.1*	Kyphosis (acquired) **87**	
737.2*	Lordosis (acquired) **87**	
737.3*	Kyphoscoliosis and scoliosis **87**	
737.4*	Curvature of spine associated with other conditions **87**	
737.8	Other curvatures of spine associated with other conditions **87**	
737.9	Unspecified curvature of spine associated with other condition **87**	
737*	Curvature of spine **97**	
738.0	Acquired deformity of nose **47**	
738.1*	Other acquired deformity of head **100**	
738.2	Acquired deformity of neck **100**	
738.3	Acquired deformity of chest and rib **100**	
738.4	Acquired spondylolisthesis **97**	
738.5	Other acquired deformity of back or spine **97**	
738.6	Acquired deformity of pelvis **100**	
738.7	Cauliflower ear **47**	
738.8	Acquired musculoskeletal deformity of other specified site **100**	
738.9	Acquired musculoskeletal deformity of unspecified site **100**	
739.0	Nonallopathic lesion of head region, not elsewhere classified **98**	
739.1	Nonallopathic lesion of cervical region, not elsewhere classified **97**	
739.2	Nonallopathic lesion of thoracic region, not elsewhere classified **97**	
739.3	Nonallopathic lesion of lumbar region, not elsewhere classified **98**	
739.4	Nonallopathic lesion of sacral region, not elsewhere classified **98**	
739.5	Nonallopathic lesion of pelvic region, not elsewhere classified **98**	
739.6	Nonallopathic lesion of lower extremities, not elsewhere classified **98**	
739.7	Nonallopathic lesion of upper extremities, not elsewhere classified **98**	
739.8	Nonallopathic lesion of rib cage, not elsewhere classified **98**	
739.9	Nonallopathic lesion of abdomen and other sites, not elsewhere classified **98**	

740*	Anencephalus and similar anomalies **32 , 167 , 171**
741*	Spina bifida **32 , 167 , 171**
742*	Other congenital anomalies of nervous system **32 , 167 , 171**
743*	Congenital anomalies of eye **40**
744.0*	Congenital anomalies of ear causing impairment of hearing **47**
744.1	Congenital anomalies of accessory auricle **47 , 173**
744.2*	Other specified congenital anomalies of ear **47**
744.3	Unspecified congenital anomaly of ear **47**
744.4*	Congenital branchial cleft cyst or fistula **47**
744.5	Congenital webbing of neck **109**
744.81	Macrocheilia **48**
744.82	Microcheilia **48**
744.83	Macrostomia **48**
744.84	Microstomia **48**
744.89	Other specified congenital anomaly of face and neck **47**
744.9	Unspecified congenital anomaly of face and neck **109**
745.0	Bulbus cordis anomalies and anomalies of cardiac septal closure, common truncus **67**
745.1*	Transposition of great vessels **67**
745.2	Tetralogy of Fallot **67**
745.3	Bulbus cordis anomalies and anomalies of cardiac septal closure, common ventricle **67**
745.4	Ventricular septal defect **67 , 167 , 171**
745.5	Ostium secundum type atrial septal defect **67**
745.60	Unspecified type congenital endocardial cushion defect **67**
745.61	Ostium primum defect **67**
745.69	Other congenital endocardial cushion defect **67**
745.7	Cor biloculare **67**
745.8	Other bulbus cordis anomalies and anomalies of cardiac septal closure **67**
745.9	Unspecified congenital defect of septal closure **67**
746.0*	Congenital anomalies of pulmonary valve **67**
746.1	Congenital tricuspid atresia and stenosis **67**
746.2	Ebstein's anomaly **67**
746.3	Congenital stenosis of aortic valve **67**
746.4	Congenital insufficiency of aortic valve **67**
746.5	Congenital mitral stenosis **67**
746.6	Congenital mitral insufficiency **67**
746.7	Hypoplastic left heart syndrome **67**
746.81	Congenital subaortic stenosis **67**
746.82	Cor triatriatum **67**
746.83	Congenital infundibular pulmonic stenosis **67**
746.84	Congenital obstructive anomalies of heart, not elsewhere classified **67**
746.85	Congenital coronary artery anomaly **67**
746.86	Congenital heart block **68**
746.87	Congenital malposition of heart and cardiac apex **68**
746.89	Other specified congenital anomaly of heart **68**
746.9	Unspecified congenital anomaly of heart **68**
747.0	Patent ductus arteriosus **68**
747.1*	Coarctation of aorta **68**
747.2*	Other congenital anomaly of aorta **68**
747.3*	Anomalies of pulmonary artery **68**
747.4*	Congenital anomalies of great veins **68**
747.5	Congenital absence or hypoplasia of umbilical artery **67**
747.6*	Other congenital anomaly of peripheral vascular system **67**
747.81	Congenital anomaly of cerebrovascular system **32**
747.82	Congenital spinal vessel anomaly **32**
747.83	Persistent fetal circulation **164 , 168**
747.89	Other specified congenital anomaly of circulatory system **67**

*Code Range © 2012 OptumInsight, Inc.

747.9	Unspecified congenital anomaly of circulatory system **67**	
748.0	Congenital choanal atresia **47**	
748.1	Other congenital anomaly of nose **47**	
748.2	Congenital web of larynx **3 , 47**	
748.3	Other congenital anomaly of larynx, trachea, and bronchus **3 , 47**	
748.4	Congenital cystic lung **54**	
748.5	Congenital agenesis, hypoplasia, and dysplasia of lung **54**	
748.60	Unspecified congenital anomaly of lung **54**	
748.61	Congenital bronchiectasis **53**	
748.69	Other congenital anomaly of lung **54**	
748.8	Other specified congenital anomaly of respiratory system **54**	
748.9	Unspecified congenital anomaly of respiratory system **54**	
749.0*	Cleft palate **3**	
749.1*	Cleft lip **3**	
749.2*	Cleft palate with cleft lip **3**	
749*	Cleft palate and cleft lip **48**	
750.0	Tongue tie **3 , 48**	
750.1*	Other congenital anomalies of tongue **3 , 48**	
750.21	Congenital absence of salivary gland **3 , 47**	
750.22	Congenital accessory salivary gland **3 , 47**	
750.23	Congenital atresia, salivary duct **3 , 47**	
750.24	Congenital fistula of salivary gland **3 , 47**	
750.25	Congenital fistula of lip **3 , 48**	
750.26	Other specified congenital anomalies of mouth **3 , 48**	
750.27	Congenital diverticulum of pharynx **3 , 47**	
750.29	Other specified congenital anomaly of pharynx **3 , 47**	
750.3	Congenital tracheoesophageal fistula, esophageal atresia and stenosis **75**	
750.4	Other specified congenital anomaly of esophagus **75**	
750.5	Congenital hypertrophic pyloric stenosis **79**	
750.6	Congenital hiatus hernia **79**	
750.7	Other specified congenital anomalies of stomach **79**	
750.8	Other specified congenital anomalies of upper alimentary tract **79**	
750.9	Unspecified congenital anomaly of upper alimentary tract **79**	
751.0	Meckel's diverticulum **77**	
751.1	Congenital atresia and stenosis of small intestine **79**	
751.2	Congenital atresia and stenosis of large intestine, rectum, and anal canal **79**	
751.3	Hirschsprung's disease and other congenital functional disorders of colon **79**	
751.4	Congenital anomalies of intestinal fixation **79**	
751.5	Other congenital anomalies of intestine **79**	
751.60	Unspecified congenital anomaly of gallbladder, bile ducts, and liver **83**	
751.61	Congenital biliary atresia **83**	
751.62	Congenital cystic disease of liver **83**	
751.69	Other congenital anomaly of gallbladder, bile ducts, and liver **83**	
751.7	Congenital anomalies of pancreas **83**	
751.8	Other specified congenital anomalies of digestive system **79**	
751.9	Unspecified congenital anomaly of digestive system **79**	
752.0	Congenital anomalies of ovaries **128 , 131**	
752.1*	Congenital anomalies of fallopian tubes and broad ligaments **128 , 131**	
752.2	Congenital doubling of uterus **128 , 131**	
752.3*	Other congenital anomaly of uterus **128 , 131**	
752.4*	Congenital anomalies of cervix, vagina, and external female genitalia **128 , 131**	
752.5*	Undescended and retractile testicle **125 , 173**	
752.6*	Hypospadias and epispadias and other penile anomalies **125**	

752.7	Indeterminate sex and pseudohermaphroditism **125 , 128 , 131**
752.8*	Other specified congenital anomalies of genital organs **125**
752.89	Other specified anomalies of genital organs **128 , 131**
752.9	Unspecified congenital anomaly of genital organs **125 , 128 , 131**
753*	Congenital anomalies of urinary system **121**
754.0	Congenital musculoskeletal deformities of skull, face, and jaw **100**
754.1	Congenital musculoskeletal deformity of sternocleidomastoid muscle **100**
754.2	Congenital musculoskeletal deformity of spine **87 , 100**
754.3*	Congenital dislocation of hip **100**
754.40	Congenital genu recurvatum **100**
754.41	Congenital dislocation of knee (with genu recurvatum) **99**
754.42	Congenital bowing of femur **100**
754.43	Congenital bowing of tibia and fibula **100**
754.44	Congenital bowing of unspecified long bones of leg **100**
754.5*	Congenital varus deformities of feet **100**
754.6*	Congenital valgus deformities of feet **100**
754.61	Congenital pes planus **173**
754.7*	Other congenital deformity of feet **100**
754.81	Pectus excavatum **54**
754.82	Pectus carinatum **54**
754.89	Other specified nonteratogenic anomalies **100**
755*	Other congenital anomalies of limbs **100**
756.0	Congenital anomalies of skull and face bones **100**
756.10	Congenital anomaly of spine, unspecified **98**
756.11	Congenital spondylolysis, lumbosacral region **98**
756.12	Congenital spondylolisthesis **98**
756.13	Congenital absence of vertebra **98**
756.14	Hemivertebra **98**
756.15	Congenital fusion of spine (vertebra) **98**
756.16	Klippel-Feil syndrome **100**
756.17	Spina bifida occulta **32**
756.19	Other congenital anomaly of spine **98**
756.2	Cervical rib **100**
756.3	Other congenital anomaly of ribs and sternum **54**
756.4	Chondrodystrophy **100**
756.5*	Congenital osteodystrophies **100**
756.51	Osteogenesis imperfecta **87**
756.6	Congenital anomaly of diaphragm **54**
756.7*	Congenital anomaly of abdominal wall **79**
756.72	Omphalocele **167 , 171**
756.73	Gastroschisis **167 , 171**
756.8*	Other specified congenital anomalies of muscle, tendon, fascia, and connective tissue **100**
756.9	Other and unspecified congenital anomaly of musculoskeletal system **101**
757.0	Hereditary edema of legs **109**
757.1	Ichthyosis congenita **109**
757.2	Dermatoglyphic anomalies **109**
757.31	Congenital ectodermal dysplasia **109**
757.32	Congenital vascular hamartomas **109**
757.33	Congenital pigmentary anomaly of skin **109 , 173**
757.39	Other specified congenital anomaly of skin **109 , 173**
757.4	Specified congenital anomalies of hair **109**
757.5	Specified congenital anomalies of nails **109**
757.6	Specified congenital anomalies of breast **107**
757.8	Other specified congenital anomalies of the integument **109**
757.9	Unspecified congenital anomaly of the integument **109**

Numeric Index to Diseases

758.0	Down's syndrome **189**	764.23	Fetal malnutrition without mention of "light-for-dates", 750-999 grams **164 , 168**
758.1	Patau's syndrome **189**	764.24	Fetal malnutrition without mention of "light-for-dates", 1,000-1,249 grams **164 , 168**
758.2	Edwards' syndrome **189**		
758.3*	Autosomal deletion syndromes **189**	764.25	Fetal malnutrition without mention of "light-for-dates", 1,250-1,499 grams **164 , 168**
758.4	Balanced autosomal translocation in normal individual **214**	764.26	Fetal malnutrition without mention of "light-for-dates", 1,500-1,749 grams **164 , 168**
758.5	Other conditions due to autosomal anomalies **214**		
758.6	Gonadal dysgenesis **125 , 128 , 131**	764.27	Fetal malnutrition without mention of "light-for-dates", 1,750-1,999 grams **164 , 168**
758.7	Klinefelter's syndrome **125**	764.28	Fetal malnutrition without mention of "light-for-dates", 2,000-2,499 grams **164 , 168**
758.8*	Other conditions due to chromosome anomalies **125 ,128 ,131**		
758.9	Conditions due to anomaly of unspecified chromosome **214**	764.98	Unspecified fetal growth retardation, 2,000-2,499 grams **172 , 173**
759.0	Congenital anomalies of spleen **177**	764.99	Unspecified fetal growth retardation, 2,500 or more grams **172 , 173**
759.1	Congenital anomalies of adrenal gland **115**		
759.2	Congenital anomalies of other endocrine glands **115**	765.00	Extreme fetal immaturity, unspecified (weight) **164 , 168**
759.3	Situs inversus **79**	765.01	Extreme fetal immaturity, less than 500 grams **164**
759.4	Conjoined twins **79 , 167 , 171**	765.02	Extreme fetal immaturity, 500-749 grams **164**
759.5	Tuberous sclerosis **32**	765.03	Extreme fetal immaturity, 750-999 grams **164**
759.6	Other congenital hamartoses, not elsewhere classified **181 , 183**	765.04	Extreme fetal immaturity, 1,000-1,249 grams **164**
759.7	Multiple congenital anomalies, so described **101**	765.05	Extreme fetal immaturity, 1,250-1,499 grams **164**
759.81	Prader-Willi syndrome **101**	765.06	Extreme fetal immaturity, 1,500-1,749 grams **164 , 168**
759.82	Marfan's syndrome **68**	765.07	Extreme fetal immaturity, 1,750-1,999 grams **164 , 168**
759.83	Fragile X syndrome **189**	765.08	Extreme fetal immaturity, 2,000-2,499 grams **164 , 168**
759.89	Other specified multiple congenital anomalies, so described **101**	765.1*	Other preterm infants **164 , 168**
759.9	Unspecified congenital anomaly **214**	765.20	Unspecified weeks of gestation **172 , 173**
762.4	Fetus or newborn affected by prolapsed cord **172 , 173**	765.21	Less than 24 completed weeks of gestation **164**
762.5	Fetus or newborn affected by other compression of umbilical cord **172 , 173**	765.22	24 completed weeks of gestation **164**
		765.23	25-26 completed weeks of gestation **164**
762.6	Fetus or newborn affected by other and unspecified conditions of umbilical cord **172 , 173**	765.24	27-28 completed weeks of gestation **164 , 168**
		765.25	29-30 completed weeks of gestation **164 , 168**
763.0	Fetus or newborn affected by breech delivery and extraction **172 , 173**	765.26	31-32 completed weeks of gestation **164 , 168**
		765.27	33-34 completed weeks of gestation **164 , 168**
763.1	Fetus or newborn affected by other malpresentation, malposition, and disproportion during labor and delivery **172 , 173**	765.28	35-36 completed weeks of gestation **164 , 168**
		765.29	37 or more completed weeks of gestation **172 , 173**
763.2	Fetus or newborn affected by forceps delivery **172 , 173**	766.0	Exceptionally large baby relating to long gestation **172 , 173**
763.3	Fetus or newborn affected by delivery by vacuum extractor **172 , 173**	766.1	Other "heavy-for-dates" infants not related to gestation period **172 , 173**
763.4	Fetus or newborn affected by cesarean delivery **164 , 168**	766.2*	Late infant, not "heavy-for-dates" **172 , 173**
763.6	Fetus or newborn affected by precipitate delivery **172 , 173**	767.0	Subdural and cerebral hemorrhage, birth trauma **164 , 168**
763.9	Unspecified complication of labor and delivery affecting fetus or newborn **172 , 173**	767.11	Birth trauma, epicranial subaponeurotic hemorrhage (massive) **164 , 168**
764.08	Light-for-dates without mention of fetal malnutrition, 2,000-2,499 grams **172 , 173**	767.19	Birth trauma, other injuries to scalp **172 , 173**
		767.4	Injury to spine and spinal cord, birth trauma **164 , 168**
764.09	Light-for-dates without mention of fetal malnutrition, 2,500 or more grams **172 , 173**	767.7	Other cranial and peripheral nerve injuries, birth trauma **164 , 168**
764.11	Light-for-dates with signs of fetal malnutrition, less than 500 grams **164 , 168**	768.5	Severe birth asphyxia **164 , 168**
		768.6	Mild or moderate birth asphyxia **172 , 173**
764.12	Light-for-dates with signs of fetal malnutrition, 500-749 grams **164 , 168**	768.72	Moderate hypoxic-ischemic encephalopathy **164 , 168**
764.13	Light-for-dates with signs of fetal malnutrition, 750-999 grams **164 , 168**	768.73	Severe hypoxic-ischemic encephalopathy **164 , 168**
		769	Respiratory distress syndrome in newborn **164**
764.14	Light-for-dates with signs of fetal malnutrition, 1,000-1,249 grams **164 , 168**	770.0	Congenital pneumonia **164 , 168**
		770.1*	Fetal and newborn aspiration **164 , 168**
764.15	Light-for-dates with signs of fetal malnutrition, 1,250-1,499 grams **164 , 168**	770.2	Interstitial emphysema and related conditions of newborn **164 , 168**
764.16	Light-for-dates with signs of fetal malnutrition, 1,500-1,749 grams **164 , 168**	770.3	Pulmonary hemorrhage of fetus or newborn **164 , 168**
		770.4	Primary atelectasis of newborn **164 , 168**
764.17	Light-for-dates with signs of fetal malnutrition, 1,750-1,999 grams **164 , 168**	770.7	Chronic respiratory disease arising in the perinatal period **53**
764.18	Light-for-dates with signs of fetal malnutrition, 2,000-2,499 grams **164 , 168**	770.84	Respiratory failure of newborn **164 , 168**
764.21	Fetal malnutrition without mention of "light-for-dates", less than 500 grams **164 , 168**	770.85	Aspiration of postnatal stomach contents without respiratory symptoms **164 , 168**
764.22	Fetal malnutrition without mention of "light-for-dates", 500-749 grams **164 , 168**		

770.86	Aspiration of postnatal stomach contents with respiratory symptoms **164**, **168**		779.85	Cardiac arrest of newborn **164**, **169**
771.0	Congenital rubella **164**, **168**		780.01	Coma **21**, **167**, **171**
771.1	Congenital cytomegalovirus infection **164**, **168**		780.02	Transient alteration of awareness **189**
771.2	Other congenital infection specific to the perinatal period **164**, **168**		780.03	Persistent vegetative state **21**, **167**, **171**
771.4	Omphalitis of the newborn **164**, **168**		780.09	Other alteration of consciousness **21**
771.5	Neonatal infective mastitis **164**, **168**		780.1	Hallucinations **189**
771.8*	Other infection specific to the perinatal period **164**, **168**		780.2	Syncope and collapse **68**
772.0	Fetal blood loss affecting newborn **164**, **168**		780.3*	Convulsions **33**
772.1*	Intraventricular hemorrhage **164**, **168**		780.31	Febrile convulsions (simple), unspecified **167**, **171**
772.2	Fetal and neonatal subarachnoid hemorrhage of newborn **164**, **168**		780.39	Other convulsions **167**, **171**
772.4	Fetal and neonatal gastrointestinal hemorrhage **164**, **168**		780.4	Dizziness and giddiness **46**
772.5	Fetal and neonatal adrenal hemorrhage **164**, **168**		780.50	Unspecified sleep disturbance **190**
772.6	Fetal and neonatal cutaneous hemorrhage **172**, **173**		780.51	Insomnia with sleep apnea, unspecified **3**, **47**
773.2	Hemolytic disease due to other and unspecified isoimmunization of fetus or newborn **164**, **168**		780.52	Insomnia, unspecified **190**
			780.53	Hypersomnia with sleep apnea, unspecified **3**, **47**
773.3	Hydrops fetalis due to isoimmunization **164**, **168**		780.54	Hypersomnia, unspecified **190**
773.4	Kernicterus due to isoimmunization of fetus or newborn **164**, **168**		780.55	Disruption of 24 hour sleep wake cycle, unspecified **190**
773.5	Late anemia due to isoimmunization of fetus or newborn **164**, **168**		780.56	Dysfunctions associated with sleep stages or arousal from sleep **190**
774.3*	Neonatal jaundice due to delayed conjugation from other causes **172**, **173**		780.57	Unspecified sleep apnea **3**, **47**
			780.58	Sleep related movement disorder, unspecified **190**
774.4	Perinatal jaundice due to hepatocellular damage **164**, **168**		780.59	Other sleep disturbances **190**
774.5	Perinatal jaundice from other causes **172**, **173**		780.60	Fever, unspecified **185**, **232**
774.6	Unspecified fetal and neonatal jaundice **172**, **173**		780.61	Fever presenting with conditions classified elsewhere **185**, **232**
774.7	Kernicterus of fetus or newborn not due to isoimmunization **164**, **168**		780.62	Postprocedural fever **185**, **232**
			780.63	Postvaccination fever **185**, **232**
775.1	Neonatal diabetes mellitus **164**, **168**		780.64	Chills (without fever) **214**
775.2	Neonatal myasthenia gravis **164**, **168**		780.65	Hypothermia not associated with low environmental temperature **214**
775.3	Neonatal thyrotoxicosis **164**, **168**			
775.4	Hypocalcemia and hypomagnesemia of newborn **164**, **168**		780.66	Febrile nonhemolytic transfusion reaction **185**, **232**
775.5	Other transitory neonatal electrolyte disturbances **164**, **168**		780.7*	Malaise and fatigue **232**
775.6	Neonatal hypoglycemia **164**, **168**		780.71	Chronic fatigue syndrome **214**
775.7	Late metabolic acidosis of newborn **164**, **168**		780.72	Functional quadriplegia **18**
776.0	Hemorrhagic disease of newborn **164**, **168**		780.79	Other malaise and fatigue **214**
776.1	Transient neonatal thrombocytopenia **164**, **168**		780.8	Generalized hyperhidrosis **109**, **232**
776.2	Disseminated intravascular coagulation in newborn **164**, **168**		780.9*	Other general symptoms **214**
			781.0	Abnormal involuntary movements **32**
776.3	Other transient neonatal disorders of coagulation **164**, **169**		781.1	Disturbances of sensation of smell and taste **32**
776.6	Anemia of neonatal prematurity **164**, **169**		781.2	Abnormality of gait **32**
777.1	Fetal and newborn meconium obstruction **164**, **169**		781.3	Lack of coordination **32**
777.2	Neonatal intestinal obstruction due to inspissated milk **164**, **169**		781.4	Transient paralysis of limb **32**
			781.5	Clubbing of fingers **54**
777.5*	Necrotizing enterocolitis in newborn **164**, **169**		781.6	Meningismus **32**
777.6	Perinatal intestinal perforation **164**, **169**		781.7	Tetany **114**, **167**, **171**
778.0	Hydrops fetalis not due to isoimmunization **164**, **169**		781.8	Neurological neglect syndrome **32**
778.8	Other specified condition involving the integument of fetus and newborn **172**, **173**		781.91	Loss of height **32**
			781.92	Abnormal posture **32**
779.0	Convulsions in newborn **164**, **169**		781.93	Ocular torticollis **98**
779.1	Other and unspecified cerebral irritability in newborn **164**, **169**		781.94	Facial weakness **32**
779.2	Cerebral depression, coma, and other abnormal cerebral signs in fetus or newborn **164**, **169**		781.99	Other symptoms involving nervous and musculoskeletal systems **32**
			782.0	Disturbance of skin sensation **32**
779.31	Feeding problems in newborn **172**		782.1	Rash and other nonspecific skin eruption **109**, **232**
779.32	Bilious vomiting in newborn **164**, **169**		782.2	Localized superficial swelling, mass, or lump **109**
779.33	Other vomiting in newborn **172**		782.3	Edema **214**
779.34	Failure to thrive in newborn **114**, **232**		782.4	Jaundice, unspecified, not of newborn **83**
779.4	Drug reactions and intoxications specific to newborn **164**, **169**		782.5	Cyanosis **214**
779.5	Drug withdrawal syndrome in newborn **164**, **169**		782.6*	Pallor and flushing **214**
779.7	Periventricular leukomalacia **32**, **167**, **171**		782.7	Spontaneous ecchymoses **177**
779.83	Delayed separation of umbilical cord **172**			

782.8	Changes in skin texture **109**	
782.9	Other symptoms involving skin and integumentary tissues **109**	
783.2*	Abnormal loss of weight **232**	
783.4*	Lack of expected normal physiological development **232**	
783*	Symptoms concerning nutrition, metabolism, and development **114**	
784.0	Headache **34**	
784.1	Throat pain **47**	
784.2	Swelling, mass, or lump in head and neck **109**	
784.3	Aphasia **32**	
784.4*	Voice and resonance disorders **47**	
784.5*	Other speech disturbance **32**	
784.60	Symbolic dysfunction, unspecified **190**	
784.61	Alexia and dyslexia **190**	
784.69	Other symbolic dysfunction **190**	
784.7	Epistaxis **46**	
784.8	Hemorrhage from throat **3 , 47**	
784.91	Postnasal drip **47**	
784.92	Jaw pain **3 , 48**	
784.99	Other symptoms involving head and neck **47**	
785.0	Unspecified tachycardia **68 , 167 , 171**	
785.1	Palpitations **68**	
785.2	Undiagnosed cardiac murmurs **68**	
785.3	Other abnormal heart sounds **69**	
785.4	Gangrene **67 , 167 , 171**	
785.50	Unspecified shock **57 , 66 , 167 , 171**	
785.51	Cardiogenic shock **57 , 66**	
785.52	Septic shock **187**	
785.59	Other shock without mention of trauma **187**	
785.6	Enlargement of lymph nodes **177 , 232**	
785.9	Other symptoms involving cardiovascular system **69**	
786.0*	Dyspnea and respiratory abnormalities **54 , 232**	
786.1	Stridor **54**	
786.2	Cough **54**	
786.3*	Hemoptysis **54**	
786.4	Abnormal sputum **54**	
786.50	Chest pain, unspecified **68**	
786.51	Precordial pain **68**	
786.52	Painful respiration **54**	
786.59	Chest pain, other **68**	
786.6	Swelling, mass, or lump in chest **54**	
786.7	Abnormal chest sounds **54**	
786.8	Hiccough **54**	
786.9	Other symptoms involving respiratory system and chest **54**	
787*	Symptoms involving digestive system **78**	
788.0	Renal colic **120**	
788.1	Dysuria **120**	
788.2*	Retention of urine **120 , 167 , 171**	
788.3*	Urinary incontinence **120**	
788.4*	Frequency of urination and polyuria **120**	
788.5	Oliguria and anuria **119 , 120**	
788.6*	Other abnormality of urination **120**	
788.7	Urethral discharge **120**	
788.8	Extravasation of urine **120**	
788.9*	Other symptoms involving urinary system **120**	
789.0*	Abdominal pain **78**	
789.1	Hepatomegaly **83 , 232**	
789.2	Splenomegaly **177 , 232**	
789.3*	Abdominal or pelvic swelling, mass, or lump **78**	

789.4*	Abdominal rigidity **79**
789.5*	Ascites **214**
789.6*	Abdominal tenderness **78**
789.7	Colic **78**
789.9	Other symptoms involving abdomen and pelvis **78**
790.0*	Abnormality of red blood cells **176**
790.1	Elevated sedimentation rate **214**
790.2*	Abnormal glucose **114**
790.3	Excessive blood level of alcohol **192**
790.4	Nonspecific elevation of levels of transaminase or lactic acid dehydrogenase (LDH) **214**
790.5	Other nonspecific abnormal serum enzyme levels **214**
790.6	Other abnormal blood chemistry **214**
790.7	Bacteremia **167 , 171 , 187**
790.8	Unspecified viremia **186**
790.9*	Other nonspecific findings on examination of blood **214**
791.0	Proteinuria **120**
791.1	Chyluria **120 , 167 , 171**
791.2	Hemoglobinuria **120**
791.3	Myoglobinuria **214**
791.4	Biliuria **83**
791.5	Glycosuria **114**
791.6	Acetonuria **114**
791.7	Other cells and casts in urine **121**
791.9	Other nonspecific finding on examination of urine **121**
792.0	Nonspecific abnormal finding in cerebrospinal fluid **32**
792.1	Nonspecific abnormal finding in stool contents **78**
792.2	Nonspecific abnormal finding in semen **125**
792.3	Nonspecific abnormal finding in amniotic fluid **157 , 160**
792.4	Nonspecific abnormal finding in saliva **47**
792.5	Cloudy (hemodialysis) (peritoneal) dialysis affluent **214**
792.9	Other nonspecific abnormal finding in body substances **214**
793.0	Nonspecific (abnormal) findings on radiological and other examination of skull and head **32**
793.11	Solitary pulmonary nodule **54**
793.19	Other nonspecific abnormal finding of lung field **54**
793.2	Nonspecific (abnormal) findings on radiological and other examination of other intrathoracic organs **67**
793.3	Nonspecific (abnormal) findings on radiological and other examination of biliary tract **83**
793.4	Nonspecific (abnormal) findings on radiological and other examination of gastrointestinal tract **78**
793.5	Nonspecific (abnormal) findings on radiological and other examination of genitourinary organs **121**
793.6	Nonspecific (abnormal) findings on radiological and other examination of abdominal area, including retroperitoneum **78**
793.7	Nonspecific (abnormal) findings on radiological and other examination of musculoskeletal system **101**
793.8*	Nonspecific abnormal findings on radiological and other examinations of body structure, breast **107**
793.9*	Other nonspecific abnormal findings on radiological and other examinations of body structure **214**
794.0*	Nonspecific abnormal results of function study of brain and central nervous system **32**
794.10	Nonspecific abnormal response to unspecified nerve stimulation **32**
794.11	Nonspecific abnormal retinal function studies **40**
794.12	Nonspecific abnormal electro-oculogram (EOG) **40**
794.13	Nonspecific abnormal visually evoked potential **40**
794.14	Nonspecific abnormal oculomotor studies **40**
794.15	Nonspecific abnormal auditory function studies **47 , 173**

*Code Range

794.16	Nonspecific abnormal vestibular function studies **47**	
794.17	Nonspecific abnormal electromyogram (EMG) **101**	
794.19	Other nonspecific abnormal result of function study of peripheral nervous system and special senses **32**	
794.2	Nonspecific abnormal results of pulmonary system function study **54**	
794.30	Nonspecific abnormal unspecified cardiovascular function study **69**	
794.31	Nonspecific abnormal electrocardiogram (ECG) (EKG) **69**	
794.39	Other nonspecific abnormal cardiovascular system function study **69**	
794.4	Nonspecific abnormal results of kidney function study **121**	
794.5	Nonspecific abnormal results of thyroid function study **115**	
794.6	Nonspecific abnormal results of other endocrine function study **115**	
794.7	Nonspecific abnormal results of basal metabolism function study **115**	
794.8	Nonspecific abnormal results of liver function study **83**	
794.9	Nonspecific abnormal results of other specified function study **121**	
795.0*	Abnormal Papanicolaou smear of cervix and cervical HPV **128 , 131**	
795.1*	Abnormal Papanicolaou smear of vagina and vaginal HPV **128 , 131**	
795.2	Nonspecific abnormal findings on chromosomal analysis **214**	
795.3*	Nonspecific positive culture findings **187**	
795.4	Other nonspecific abnormal histological findings **173 , 214**	
795.5*	Nonspecific reaction to test for tuberculosis **51**	
795.6	False positive serological test for syphilis **97**	
795.7*	Other nonspecific immunological findings **177**	
795.8*	Abnormal tumor markers **214**	
796.0	Nonspecific abnormal toxicological findings **205**	
796.1	Abnormal reflex **32**	
796.2	Elevated blood pressure reading without diagnosis of hypertension **69**	
796.3	Nonspecific low blood pressure reading **69**	
796.4	Other abnormal clinical finding **173 , 214**	
796.5	Abnormal finding on antenatal screening **157 , 160**	
796.6	Nonspecific abnormal findings on neonatal screening **214**	
796.7*	Abnormal cytologic smear of anus and anal HPV **79**	
796.9	Other nonspecific abnormal finding **214**	
797	Senility without mention of psychosis **189**	
798.0	Sudden infant death syndrome **32**	
798.1	Instantaneous death **66**	
798.2	Death occurring in less than 24 hours from onset of symptoms, not otherwise explained **66**	
798.9	Unattended death **214**	
799.0*	Asphyxia and hypoxemia **54**	
799.1	Respiratory arrest **54 , 167 , 171**	
799.21	Nervousness **189**	
799.22	Irritability **189**	
799.23	Impulsiveness **189**	
799.24	Emotional lability **189**	
799.25	Demoralization and apathy **189**	
799.29	Other signs and symptoms involving emotional state **189**	
799.3	Unspecified debility **214**	
799.4	Cachexia **214 , 232**	
799.51	Attention or concentration deficit **190**	
799.52	Cognitive communication deficit **189**	
799.53	Visuospatial deficit **32**	
799.54	Psychomotor deficit **189**	

799.55	Frontal lobe and executive function deficit **189**
799.59	Other signs and symptoms involving cognition **189**
799.8*	Other ill-defined conditions **214**
799.9	Other unknown and unspecified cause of morbidity or mortality **214**
800.0*	Closed fracture of vault of skull without mention of intracranial injury **221**
800.00	Closed fracture of vault of skull without mention of intracranial injury, unspecified state of consciousness **27**
800.01	Closed fracture of vault of skull without mention of intracranial injury, no loss of consciousness **27**
800.02	Closed fracture of vault of skull without mention of intracranial injury, brief (less than one hour) loss of consciousness **27 , 225**
800.03	Closed fracture of vault of skull without mention of intracranial injury, moderate (1-24 hours) loss of consciousness **21 , 225**
800.04	Closed fracture of vault of skull without mention of intracranial injury, prolonged (more than 24 hours) loss of consciousness and return to pre-existing conscious level **21 , 225**
800.05	Closed fracture of vault of skull without mention of intracranial injury, prolonged (more than 24 hours) loss of consciousness, without return to pre-existing conscious level **21 , 225**
800.06	Closed fracture of vault of skull without mention of intracranial injury, loss of consciousness of unspecified duration **21**
800.09	Closed fracture of vault of skull without mention of intracranial injury, unspecified concussion **27**
800.1*	Closed fracture of vault of skull with cerebral laceration and contusion **221**
800.10	Closed fracture of vault of skull with cerebral laceration and contusion, unspecified state of consciousness **27 , 225**
800.11	Closed fracture of vault of skull with cerebral laceration and contusion, no loss of consciousness **27**
800.12	Closed fracture of vault of skull with cerebral laceration and contusion, brief (less than one hour) loss of consciousness **27 , 225**
800.13	Closed fracture of vault of skull with cerebral laceration and contusion, moderate (1-24 hours) loss of consciousness **21 , 225**
800.14	Closed fracture of vault of skull with cerebral laceration and contusion, prolonged (more than 24 hours) loss of consciousness and return to pre-existing conscious level **21 , 225**
800.15	Closed fracture of vault of skull with cerebral laceration and contusion, prolonged (more than 24 hours) loss of consciousness, without return to pre-existing conscious level **21 , 225**
800.16	Closed fracture of vault of skull with cerebral laceration and contusion, loss of consciousness of unspecified duration **21 , 225**
800.19	Closed fracture of vault of skull with cerebral laceration and contusion, unspecified concussion **27 , 225**
800.2*	Closed fracture of vault of skull with subarachnoid, subdural, and extradural hemorrhage **221**
800.20	Closed fracture of vault of skull with subarachnoid, subdural, and extradural hemorrhage, unspecified state of consciousness **27 , 225**
800.21	Closed fracture of vault of skull with subarachnoid, subdural, and extradural hemorrhage, no loss of consciousness **27**
800.22	Closed fracture of vault of skull with subarachnoid, subdural, and extradural hemorrhage, brief (less than one hour) loss of consciousness **27 , 225**
800.23	Closed fracture of vault of skull with subarachnoid, subdural, and extradural hemorrhage, moderate (1-24 hours) loss of consciousness **21 , 225**
800.24	Closed fracture of vault of skull with subarachnoid, subdural, and extradural hemorrhage, prolonged (more than 24 hours) loss of consciousness and return to pre-existing conscious level **21 , 225**
800.25	Closed fracture of vault of skull with subarachnoid, subdural, and extradural hemorrhage, prolonged (more than 24 hours) loss of consciousness, without return to pre-existing conscious level **21 , 225**

Numeric Index to Diseases

800.26	Closed fracture of vault of skull with subarachnoid, subdural, and extradural hemorrhage, loss of consciousness of unspecified duration **21 , 225**
800.29	Closed fracture of vault of skull with subarachnoid, subdural, and extradural hemorrhage, unspecified concussion **27 , 225**
800.3*	Closed fracture of vault of skull with other and unspecified intracranial hemorrhage **221**
800.30	Closed fracture of vault of skull with other and unspecified intracranial hemorrhage, unspecified state of consciousness **27 , 225**
800.31	Closed fracture of vault of skull with other and unspecified intracranial hemorrhage, no loss of consciousness **27**
800.32	Closed fracture of vault of skull with other and unspecified intracranial hemorrhage, brief (less than one hour) loss of consciousness **27 , 225**
800.33	Closed fracture of vault of skull with other and unspecified intracranial hemorrhage, moderate (1-24 hours) loss of consciousness **22 , 225**
800.34	Closed fracture of vault of skull with other and unspecified intracranial hemorrhage, prolonged (more than 24 hours) loss of consciousness and return to pre-existing conscious level **22 , 225**
800.35	Closed fracture of vault of skull with other and unspecified intracranial hemorrhage, prolonged (more than 24 hours) loss of consciousness, without return to pre-existing conscious level **22 , 225**
800.36	Closed fracture of vault of skull with other and unspecified intracranial hemorrhage, loss of consciousness of unspecified duration **22 , 225**
800.39	Closed fracture of vault of skull with other and unspecified intracranial hemorrhage, unspecified concussion **27 , 225**
800.4*	Closed fracture of vault of skull with intercranial injury of other and unspecified nature **221**
800.40	Closed fracture of vault of skull with intracranial injury of other and unspecified nature, unspecified state of consciousness **27 , 225**
800.41	Closed fracture of vault of skull with intracranial injury of other and unspecified nature, no loss of consciousness **27**
800.42	Closed fracture of vault of skull with intracranial injury of other and unspecified nature, brief (less than one hour) loss of consciousness **27 , 225**
800.43	Closed fracture of vault of skull with intracranial injury of other and unspecified nature, moderate (1-24 hours) loss of consciousness **22 , 225**
800.44	Closed fracture of vault of skull with intracranial injury of other and unspecified nature, prolonged (more than 24 hours) loss of consciousness and return to pre-existing conscious level **22 , 225**
800.45	Closed fracture of vault of skull with intracranial injury of other and unspecified nature, prolonged (more than 24 hours) loss of consciousness, without return to pre-existing conscious level **22 , 225**
800.46	Closed fracture of vault of skull with intracranial injury of other and unspecified nature, loss of consciousness of unspecified duration **22 , 225**
800.49	Closed fracture of vault of skull with intracranial injury of other and unspecified nature, unspecified concussion **27 , 225**
800.5*	Open fracture of vault of skull without mention of intracranial injury **221**
800.50	Open fracture of vault of skull without mention of intracranial injury, unspecified state of consciousness **27**
800.51	Open fracture of vault of skull without mention of intracranial injury, no loss of consciousness **27**
800.52	Open fracture of vault of skull without mention of intracranial injury, brief (less than one hour) loss of consciousness **27 , 225**
800.53	Open fracture of vault of skull without mention of intracranial injury, moderate (1-24 hours) loss of consciousness **22 , 226**
800.54	Open fracture of vault of skull without mention of intracranial injury, prolonged (more than 24 hours) loss of consciousness and return to pre-existing conscious level **22 , 226**
800.55	Open fracture of vault of skull without mention of intracranial injury, prolonged (more than 24 hours) loss of consciousness, without return to pre-existing conscious level **22 , 226**
800.56	Open fracture of vault of skull without mention of intracranial injury, loss of consciousness of unspecified duration **22**
800.59	Open fracture of vault of skull without mention of intracranial injury, unspecified concussion **27**
800.6*	Open fracture of vault of skull with cerebral laceration and contusion **221 , 226**
800.60	Open fracture of vault of skull with cerebral laceration and contusion, unspecified state of consciousness **27**
800.61	Open fracture of vault of skull with cerebral laceration and contusion, no loss of consciousness **27**
800.62	Open fracture of vault of skull with cerebral laceration and contusion, brief (less than one hour) loss of consciousness **27**
800.63	Open fracture of vault of skull with cerebral laceration and contusion, moderate (1-24 hours) loss of consciousness **22**
800.64	Open fracture of vault of skull with cerebral laceration and contusion, prolonged (more than 24 hours) loss of consciousness and return to pre-existing conscious level **22**
800.65	Open fracture of vault of skull with cerebral laceration and contusion, prolonged (more than 24 hours) loss of consciousness, without return to pre-existing conscious level **22**
800.66	Open fracture of vault of skull with cerebral laceration and contusion, loss of consciousness of unspecified duration **22**
800.69	Open fracture of vault of skull with cerebral laceration and contusion, unspecified concussion **27**
800.7*	Open fracture of vault of skull with subarachnoid, subdural, and extradural hemorrhage **221 , 226**
800.70	Open fracture of vault of skull with subarachnoid, subdural, and extradural hemorrhage, unspecified state of consciousness **27**
800.71	Open fracture of vault of skull with subarachnoid, subdural, and extradural hemorrhage, no loss of consciousness **27**
800.72	Open fracture of vault of skull with subarachnoid, subdural, and extradural hemorrhage, brief (less than one hour) loss of consciousness **27**
800.73	Open fracture of vault of skull with subarachnoid, subdural, and extradural hemorrhage, moderate (1-24 hours) loss of consciousness **22**
800.74	Open fracture of vault of skull with subarachnoid, subdural, and extradural hemorrhage, prolonged (more than 24 hours) loss of consciousness and return to pre-existing conscious level **22**
800.75	Open fracture of vault of skull with subarachnoid, subdural, and extradural hemorrhage, prolonged (more than 24 hours) loss of consciousness, without return to pre-existing conscious level **22**
800.76	Open fracture of vault of skull with subarachnoid, subdural, and extradural hemorrhage, loss of consciousness of unspecified duration **22**
800.79	Open fracture of vault of skull with subarachnoid, subdural, and extradural hemorrhage, unspecified concussion **27**
800.8*	Open fracture of vault of skull with other and unspecified intracranial hemorrhage **221 , 226**
800.80	Open fracture of vault of skull with other and unspecified intracranial hemorrhage, unspecified state of consciousness **27**
800.81	Open fracture of vault of skull with other and unspecified intracranial hemorrhage, no loss of consciousness **27**
800.82	Open fracture of vault of skull with other and unspecified intracranial hemorrhage, brief (less than one hour) loss of consciousness **27**
800.83	Open fracture of vault of skull with other and unspecified intracranial hemorrhage, moderate (1-24 hours) loss of consciousness **22**
800.84	Open fracture of vault of skull with other and unspecified intracranial hemorrhage, prolonged (more than 24 hours) loss of consciousness and return to pre-existing conscious level **22**

*Code Range

© 2012 OptumInsight, Inc.

800.85	Open fracture of vault of skull with other and unspecified intracranial hemorrhage, prolonged (more than 24 hours) loss of consciousness, without return to pre-existing conscious level **22**
800.86	Open fracture of vault of skull with other and unspecified intracranial hemorrhage, loss of consciousness of unspecified duration **22**
800.89	Open fracture of vault of skull with other and unspecified intracranial hemorrhage, unspecified concussion **28**
800.9*	Open fracture of vault of skull with intracranial injury of other and unspecified nature **221 , 226**
800.90	Open fracture of vault of skull with intracranial injury of other and unspecified nature, unspecified state of consciousness **28**
800.91	Open fracture of vault of skull with intracranial injury of other and unspecified nature, no loss of consciousness **28**
800.92	Open fracture of vault of skull with intracranial injury of other and unspecified nature, brief (less than one hour) loss of consciousness **28**
800.93	Open fracture of vault of skull with intracranial injury of other and unspecified nature, moderate (1-24 hours) loss of consciousness **22**
800.94	Open fracture of vault of skull with intracranial injury of other and unspecified nature, prolonged (more than 24 hours) loss of consciousness and return to pre-existing conscious level **22**
800.95	Open fracture of vault of skull with intracranial injury of other and unspecified nature, prolonged (more than 24 hours) loss of consciousness, without return to pre-existing conscious level **22**
800.96	Open fracture of vault of skull with intracranial injury of other and unspecified nature, loss of consciousness of unspecified duration **22**
800.99	Open fracture of vault of skull with intracranial injury of other and unspecified nature, unspecified concussion **28**
801.0*	Closed fracture of base of skull without mention of intracranial injury **221**
801.00	Closed fracture of base of skull without mention of intracranial injury, unspecified state of consciousness **28**
801.01	Closed fracture of base of skull without mention of intracranial injury, no loss of consciousness **28**
801.02	Closed fracture of base of skull without mention of intracranial injury, brief (less than one hour) loss of consciousness **28 , 226**
801.03	Closed fracture of base of skull without mention of intracranial injury, moderate (1-24 hours) loss of consciousness **22 , 226**
801.04	Closed fracture of base of skull without mention of intracranial injury, prolonged (more than 24 hours) loss of consciousness and return to pre-existing conscious level **22 , 226**
801.05	Closed fracture of base of skull without mention of intracranial injury, prolonged (more than 24 hours) loss of consciousness, without return to pre-existing conscious level **22 , 226**
801.06	Closed fracture of base of skull without mention of intracranial injury, loss of consciousness of unspecified duration **22**
801.09	Closed fracture of base of skull without mention of intracranial injury, unspecified concussion **28**
801.1*	Closed fracture of base of skull with cerebral laceration and contusion **221 , 226**
801.10	Closed fracture of base of skull with cerebral laceration and contusion, unspecified state of consciousness **28**
801.11	Closed fracture of base of skull with cerebral laceration and contusion, no loss of consciousness **28**
801.12	Closed fracture of base of skull with cerebral laceration and contusion, brief (less than one hour) loss of consciousness **28**
801.13	Closed fracture of base of skull with cerebral laceration and contusion, moderate (1-24 hours) loss of consciousness **22**
801.14	Closed fracture of base of skull with cerebral laceration and contusion, prolonged (more than 24 hours) loss of consciousness and return to pre-existing conscious level **22**
801.15	Closed fracture of base of skull with cerebral laceration and contusion, prolonged (more than 24 hours) loss of consciousness, without return to pre-existing conscious level **22**
801.16	Closed fracture of base of skull with cerebral laceration and contusion, loss of consciousness of unspecified duration **22**
801.19	Closed fracture of base of skull with cerebral laceration and contusion, unspecified concussion **28**
801.2*	Closed fracture of base of skull with subarachnoid, subdural, and extradural hemorrhage **221 , 226**
801.20	Closed fracture of base of skull with subarachnoid, subdural, and extradural hemorrhage, unspecified state of consciousness **28**
801.21	Closed fracture of base of skull with subarachnoid, subdural, and extradural hemorrhage, no loss of consciousness **28**
801.22	Closed fracture of base of skull with subarachnoid, subdural, and extradural hemorrhage, brief (less than one hour) loss of consciousness **28**
801.23	Closed fracture of base of skull with subarachnoid, subdural, and extradural hemorrhage, moderate (1-24 hours) loss of consciousness **22**
801.24	Closed fracture of base of skull with subarachnoid, subdural, and extradural hemorrhage, prolonged (more than 24 hours) loss of consciousness and return to pre-existing conscious level **22**
801.25	Closed fracture of base of skull with subarachnoid, subdural, and extradural hemorrhage, prolonged (more than 24 hours) loss of consciousness, without return to pre-existing conscious level **22**
801.26	Closed fracture of base of skull with subarachnoid, subdural, and extradural hemorrhage, loss of consciousness of unspecified duration **22**
801.29	Closed fracture of base of skull with subarachnoid, subdural, and extradural hemorrhage, unspecified concussion **28**
801.3*	Closed fracture of base of skull with other and unspecified intracranial hemorrhage **221 , 226**
801.30	Closed fracture of base of skull with other and unspecified intracranial hemorrhage, unspecified state of consciousness **28**
801.31	Closed fracture of base of skull with other and unspecified intracranial hemorrhage, no loss of consciousness **28**
801.32	Closed fracture of base of skull with other and unspecified intracranial hemorrhage, brief (less than one hour) loss of consciousness **28**
801.33	Closed fracture of base of skull with other and unspecified intracranial hemorrhage, moderate (1-24 hours) loss of consciousness **22**
801.34	Closed fracture of base of skull with other and unspecified intracranial hemorrhage, prolonged (more than 24 hours) loss of consciousness and return to pre-existing conscious level **22**
801.35	Closed fracture of base of skull with other and unspecified intracranial hemorrhage, prolonged (more than 24 hours) loss of consciousness, without return to pre-existing conscious level **23**
801.36	Closed fracture of base of skull with other and unspecified intracranial hemorrhage, loss of consciousness of unspecified duration **23**
801.39	Closed fracture of base of skull with other and unspecified intracranial hemorrhage, unspecified concussion **28**
801.4*	Closed fracture of base of skull with intracranial injury of other and unspecified nature **221 , 226**
801.40	Closed fracture of base of skull with intracranial injury of other and unspecified nature, unspecified state of consciousness **28**
801.41	Closed fracture of base of skull with intracranial injury of other and unspecified nature, no loss of consciousness **28**
801.42	Closed fracture of base of skull with intracranial injury of other and unspecified nature, brief (less than one hour) loss of consciousness **28**
801.43	Closed fracture of base of skull with intracranial injury of other and unspecified nature, moderate (1-24 hours) loss of consciousness **23**
801.44	Closed fracture of base of skull with intracranial injury of other and unspecified nature, prolonged (more than 24 hours) loss of consciousness and return to pre-existing conscious level **23**
801.45	Closed fracture of base of skull with intracranial injury of other and unspecified nature, prolonged (more than 24 hours) loss of consciousness, without return to pre-existing conscious level **23**

801.46	Closed fracture of base of skull with intracranial injury of other and unspecified nature, loss of consciousness of unspecified duration **23**
801.49	Closed fracture of base of skull with intracranial injury of other and unspecified nature, unspecified concussion **28**
801.5*	Open fracture of base of skull without mention of intracranial injury **221**
801.50	Open fracture of base of skull without mention of intracranial injury, unspecified state of consciousness **28**
801.51	Open fracture of base of skull without mention of intracranial injury, no loss of consciousness **28**
801.52	Open fracture of base of skull without mention of intracranial injury, brief (less than one hour) loss of consciousness **28 , 226**
801.53	Open fracture of base of skull without mention of intracranial injury, moderate (1-24 hours) loss of consciousness **23 , 226**
801.54	Open fracture of base of skull without mention of intracranial injury, prolonged (more than 24 hours) loss of consciousness and return to pre-existing conscious level **23 , 226**
801.55	Open fracture of base of skull without mention of intracranial injury, prolonged (more than 24 hours) loss of consciousness, without return to pre-existing conscious level **23 , 226**
801.56	Open fracture of base of skull without mention of intracranial injury, loss of consciousness of unspecified duration **23**
801.59	Open fracture of base of skull without mention of intracranial injury, unspecified concussion **28**
801.6*	Open fracture of base of skull with cerebral laceration and contusion **222 , 226**
801.60	Open fracture of base of skull with cerebral laceration and contusion, unspecified state of consciousness **28**
801.61	Open fracture of base of skull with cerebral laceration and contusion, no loss of consciousness **28**
801.62	Open fracture of base of skull with cerebral laceration and contusion, brief (less than one hour) loss of consciousness **28**
801.63	Open fracture of base of skull with cerebral laceration and contusion, moderate (1-24 hours) loss of consciousness **23**
801.64	Open fracture of base of skull with cerebral laceration and contusion, prolonged (more than 24 hours) loss of consciousness and return to pre-existing conscious level **23**
801.65	Open fracture of base of skull with cerebral laceration and contusion, prolonged (more than 24 hours) loss of consciousness, without return to pre-existing conscious level **23**
801.66	Open fracture of base of skull with cerebral laceration and contusion, loss of consciousness of unspecified duration **23**
801.69	Open fracture of base of skull with cerebral laceration and contusion, unspecified concussion **28**
801.7*	Open fracture of base of skull with subarachnoid, subdural, and extradural hemorrhage **222 , 226**
801.70	Open fracture of base of skull with subarachnoid, subdural, and extradural hemorrhage, unspecified state of consciousness **28**
801.71	Open fracture of base of skull with subarachnoid, subdural, and extradural hemorrhage, no loss of consciousness **28**
801.72	Open fracture of base of skull with subarachnoid, subdural, and extradural hemorrhage, brief (less than one hour) loss of consciousness **28**
801.73	Open fracture of base of skull with subarachnoid, subdural, and extradural hemorrhage, moderate (1-24 hours) loss of consciousness **23**
801.74	Open fracture of base of skull with subarachnoid, subdural, and extradural hemorrhage, prolonged (more than 24 hours) loss of consciousness and return to pre-existing conscious level **23**
801.75	Open fracture of base of skull with subarachnoid, subdural, and extradural hemorrhage, prolonged (more than 24 hours) loss of consciousness, without return to pre-existing conscious level **23**
801.76	Open fracture of base of skull with subarachnoid, subdural, and extradural hemorrhage, loss of consciousness of unspecified duration **23**
801.79	Open fracture of base of skull with subarachnoid, subdural, and extradural hemorrhage, unspecified concussion **28**
801.8*	Open fracture of base of skull with other and unspecified intracranial hemorrhage **222 , 226**
801.80	Open fracture of base of skull with other and unspecified intracranial hemorrhage, unspecified state of consciousness **28**
801.81	Open fracture of base of skull with other and unspecified intracranial hemorrhage, no loss of consciousness **28**
801.82	Open fracture of base of skull with other and unspecified intracranial hemorrhage, brief (less than one hour) loss of consciousness **28**
801.83	Open fracture of base of skull with other and unspecified intracranial hemorrhage, moderate (1-24 hours) loss of consciousness **23**
801.84	Open fracture of base of skull with other and unspecified intracranial hemorrhage, prolonged (more than 24 hours) loss of consciousness and return to pre-existing conscious level **23**
801.85	Open fracture of base of skull with other and unspecified intracranial hemorrhage, prolonged (more than 24 hours) loss of consciousness, without return to pre-existing conscious level **23**
801.86	Open fracture of base of skull with other and unspecified intracranial hemorrhage, loss of consciousness of unspecified duration **23**
801.89	Open fracture of base of skull with other and unspecified intracranial hemorrhage, unspecified concussion **28**
801.9*	Open fracture of base of skull with intracranial injury of other and unspecified nature **222 , 226**
801.90	Open fracture of base of skull with intracranial injury of other and unspecified nature, unspecified state of consciousness **28**
801.91	Open fracture of base of skull with intracranial injury of other and unspecified nature, no loss of consciousness **28**
801.92	Open fracture of base of skull with intracranial injury of other and unspecified nature, brief (less than one hour) loss of consciousness **28**
801.93	Open fracture of base of skull with intracranial injury of other and unspecified nature, moderate (1-24 hours) loss of consciousness **23**
801.94	Open fracture of base of skull with intracranial injury of other and unspecified nature, prolonged (more than 24 hours) loss of consciousness and return to pre-existing conscious level **23**
801.95	Open fracture of base of skull with intracranial injury of other and unspecified nature, prolonged (more than 24 hours) loss of consciousness, without return to pre-existing conscious level **23**
801.96	Open fracture of base of skull with intracranial injury of other and unspecified nature, loss of consciousness of unspecified duration **23**
801.99	Open fracture of base of skull with intracranial injury of other and unspecified nature, unspecified concussion **28**
802.0	Nasal bones, closed fracture **47 , 222**
802.1	Nasal bones, open fracture **47 , 222**
802.2*	Mandible, closed fracture **3 , 48 , 222**
802.3*	Mandible, open fracture **3 , 48 , 222**
802.4	Malar and maxillary bones, closed fracture **3 , 48 , 222**
802.5	Malar and maxillary bones, open fracture **3 , 48 , 222**
802.6	Orbital floor (blow-out), closed fracture **3 , 40 , 222**
802.7	Orbital floor (blow-out), open fracture **3 , 40 , 222**
802.8	Other facial bones, closed fracture **3 , 101 , 222**
802.9	Other facial bones, open fracture **3 , 101 , 222**
803.0*	Other closed skull fracture without mention of intracranial injury **222**
803.00	Other closed skull fracture without mention of intracranial injury, unspecified state of consciousness **28**
803.01	Other closed skull fracture without mention of intracranial injury, no loss of consciousness **28**
803.02	Other closed skull fracture without mention of intracranial injury, brief (less than one hour) loss of consciousness **28 , 226**

*Code Range

© 2012 OptumInsight, Inc.

803.03 Other closed skull fracture without mention of intracranial injury, moderate (1-24 hours) loss of consciousness **23** , **226**

803.04 Other closed skull fracture without mention of intracranial injury, prolonged (more than 24 hours) loss of consciousness and return to pre-existing conscious level **23** , **226**

803.05 Other closed skull fracture without mention of intracranial injury, prolonged (more than 24 hours) loss of consciousness, without return to pre-existing conscious level **23** , **226**

803.06 Other closed skull fracture without mention of intracranial injury, loss of consciousness of unspecified duration **23**

803.09 Other closed skull fracture without mention of intracranial injury, unspecified concussion **28**

803.1* Other closed skull fracture with cerebral laceration and contusion **222** , **226**

803.10 Other closed skull fracture with cerebral laceration and contusion, unspecified state of consciousness **28**

803.11 Other closed skull fracture with cerebral laceration and contusion, no loss of consciousness **28**

803.12 Other closed skull fracture with cerebral laceration and contusion, brief (less than one hour) loss of consciousness **28**

803.13 Other closed skull fracture with cerebral laceration and contusion, moderate (1-24 hours) loss of consciousness **23**

803.14 Other closed skull fracture with cerebral laceration and contusion, prolonged (more than 24 hours) loss of consciousness and return to pre-existing conscious level **23**

803.15 Other closed skull fracture with cerebral laceration and contusion, prolonged (more than 24 hours) loss of consciousness, without return to pre-existing conscious level **23**

803.16 Other closed skull fracture with cerebral laceration and contusion, loss of consciousness of unspecified duration **23**

803.19 Other closed skull fracture with cerebral laceration and contusion, unspecified concussion **28**

803.2* Other closed skull fracture with subarachnoid, subdural, and extradural hemorrhage **222** , **226**

803.20 Other closed skull fracture with subarachnoid, subdural, and extradural hemorrhage, unspecified state of consciousness **28**

803.21 Other closed skull fracture with subarachnoid, subdural, and extradural hemorrhage, no loss of consciousness **28**

803.22 Other closed skull fracture with subarachnoid, subdural, and extradural hemorrhage, brief (less than one hour) loss of consciousness **28**

803.23 Other closed skull fracture with subarachnoid, subdural, and extradural hemorrhage, moderate (1-24 hours) loss of consciousness **23**

803.24 Other closed skull fracture with subarachnoid, subdural, and extradural hemorrhage, prolonged (more than 24 hours) loss of consciousness and return to pre-existing conscious level **23**

803.25 Other closed skull fracture with subarachnoid, subdural, and extradural hemorrhage, prolonged (more than 24 hours) loss of consciousness, without return to pre-existing conscious level **23**

803.26 Other closed skull fracture with subarachnoid, subdural, and extradural hemorrhage, loss of consciousness of unspecified duration **23**

803.29 Other closed skull fracture with subarachnoid, subdural, and extradural hemorrhage, unspecified concussion **28**

803.3* Closed skull fracture with other and unspecified intracranial hemorrhage **222** , **226**

803.30 Other closed skull fracture with other and unspecified intracranial hemorrhage, unspecified state of unconsciousness **28**

803.31 Other closed skull fracture with other and unspecified intracranial hemorrhage, no loss of consciousness **28**

803.32 Other closed skull fracture with other and unspecified intracranial hemorrhage, brief (less than one hour) loss of consciousness **28**

803.33 Other closed skull fracture with other and unspecified intracranial hemorrhage, moderate (1-24 hours) loss of consciousness **23**

803.34 Other closed skull fracture with other and unspecified intracranial hemorrhage, prolonged (more than 24 hours) loss of consciousness and return to pre-existing conscious level **23**

803.35 Other closed skull fracture with other and unspecified intracranial hemorrhage, prolonged (more than 24 hours) loss of consciousness, without return to pre-existing conscious level **23**

803.36 Other closed skull fracture with other and unspecified intracranial hemorrhage, loss of consciousness of unspecified duration **23**

803.39 Other closed skull fracture with other and unspecified intracranial hemorrhage, unspecified concussion **28**

803.4* Other closed skull fracture with intracranial injury of other and unspecified nature **222** , **226**

803.40 Other closed skull fracture with intracranial injury of other and unspecified nature, unspecified state of consciousness **29**

803.41 Other closed skull fracture with intracranial injury of other and unspecified nature, no loss of consciousness **29**

803.42 Other closed skull fracture with intracranial injury of other and unspecified nature, brief (less than one hour) loss of consciousness **29**

803.43 Other closed skull fracture with intracranial injury of other and unspecified nature, moderate (1-24 hours) loss of consciousness **23**

803.44 Other closed skull fracture with intracranial injury of other and unspecified nature, prolonged (more than 24 hours) loss of consciousness and return to pre-existing conscious level **24**

803.45 Other closed skull fracture with intracranial injury of other and unspecified nature, prolonged (more than 24 hours) loss of consciousness, without return to pre-existing conscious level **24**

803.46 Other closed skull fracture with intracranial injury of other and unspecified nature, loss of consciousness of unspecified duration **24**

803.49 Other closed skull fracture with intracranial injury of other and unspecified nature, unspecified concussion **29**

803.5* Other open skull fracture without mention of intracranial injury **222**

803.50 Other open skull fracture without mention of injury, state of consciousness unspecified **29**

803.51 Other open skull fracture without mention of intracranial injury, no loss of consciousness **29**

803.52 Other open skull fracture without mention of intracranial injury, brief (less than one hour) loss of consciousness **29** , **226**

803.53 Other open skull fracture without mention of intracranial injury, moderate (1-24 hours) loss of consciousness **24** , **226**

803.54 Other open skull fracture without mention of intracranial injury, prolonged (more than 24 hours) loss of consciousness and return to pre-existing conscious level **24** , **226**

803.55 Other open skull fracture without mention of intracranial injury, prolonged (more than 24 hours) loss of consciousness, without return to pre-existing conscious level **24** , **226**

803.56 Other open skull fracture without mention of intracranial injury, loss of consciousness of unspecified duration **24**

803.59 Other open skull fracture without mention of intracranial injury, unspecified concussion **29**

803.6* Other open skull fracture with cerebral laceration and contusion **222** , **226**

803.60 Other open skull fracture with cerebral laceration and contusion, unspecified state of consciousness **29**

803.61 Other open skull fracture with cerebral laceration and contusion, no loss of consciousness **29**

803.62 Other open skull fracture with cerebral laceration and contusion, brief (less than one hour) loss of consciousness **29**

803.63 Other open skull fracture with cerebral laceration and contusion, moderate (1-24 hours) loss of consciousness **24**

803.64 Other open skull fracture with cerebral laceration and contusion, prolonged (more than 24 hours) loss of consciousness and return to pre-existing conscious level **24**

803.65 Other open skull fracture with cerebral laceration and contusion, prolonged (more than 24 hours) loss of consciousness, without return to pre-existing conscious level **24**

803.66 Other open skull fracture with cerebral laceration and contusion, loss of consciousness of unspecified duration **24**

803.69 Other open skull fracture with cerebral laceration and contusion, unspecified concussion **29**

803.7* Other open skull fracture with subarachnoid, subdural, and extradural hemorrhage **222 , 226**

803.70 Other open skull fracture with subarachnoid, subdural, and extradural hemorrhage, unspecified state of consciousness **29**

803.71 Other open skull fracture with subarachnoid, subdural, and extradural hemorrhage, no loss of consciousness **29**

803.72 Other open skull fracture with subarachnoid, subdural, and extradural hemorrhage, brief (less than one hour) loss of consciousness **29**

803.73 Other open skull fracture with subarachnoid, subdural, and extradural hemorrhage, moderate (1-24 hours) loss of consciousness **24**

803.74 Other open skull fracture with subarachnoid, subdural, and extradural hemorrhage, prolonged (more than 24 hours) loss of consciousness and return to pre-existing conscious level **24**

803.75 Other open skull fracture with subarachnoid, subdural, and extradural hemorrhage, prolonged (more than 24 hours) loss of consciousness, without return to pre-existing conscious level **24**

803.76 Other open skull fracture with subarachnoid, subdural, and extradural hemorrhage, loss of consciousness of unspecified duration **24**

803.79 Other open skull fracture with subarachnoid, subdural, and extradural hemorrhage, unspecified concussion **29**

803.8* Other open skull fracture with other and unspecified intracranial hemorrhage **222 , 226**

803.80 Other open skull fracture with other and unspecified intracranial hemorrhage, unspecified state of consciousness **29**

803.81 Other open skull fracture with other and unspecified intracranial hemorrhage, no loss of consciousness **29**

803.82 Other open skull fracture with other and unspecified intracranial hemorrhage, brief (less than one hour) loss of consciousness **29**

803.83 Other open skull fracture with other and unspecified intracranial hemorrhage, moderate (1-24 hours) loss of consciousness **24**

803.84 Other open skull fracture with other and unspecified intracranial hemorrhage, prolonged (more than 24 hours) loss of consciousness and return to pre-existing conscious level **24**

803.85 Other open skull fracture with other and unspecified intracranial hemorrhage, prolonged (more than 24 hours) loss of consciousness, without return to pre-existing conscious level **24**

803.86 Other open skull fracture with other and unspecified intracranial hemorrhage, loss of consciousness of unspecified duration **24**

803.89 Other open skull fracture with other and unspecified intracranial hemorrhage, unspecified concussion **29**

803.9* Other open skull fracture with intracranial injury of other and unspecified nature **222 , 226**

803.90 Other open skull fracture with intracranial injury of other and unspecified nature, unspecified state of consciousness **29**

803.91 Other open skull fracture with intracranial injury of other and unspecified nature, no loss of consciousness **29**

803.92 Other open skull fracture with intracranial injury of other and unspecified nature, brief (less than one hour) loss of consciousness **29**

803.93 Other open skull fracture with intracranial injury of other and unspecified nature, moderate (1-24 hours) loss of consciousness **24**

803.94 Other open skull fracture with intracranial injury of other and unspecified nature, prolonged (more than 24 hours) loss of consciousness and return to pre-existing conscious level **24**

803.95 Other open skull fracture with intracranial injury of other and unspecified nature, prolonged (more than 24 hours) loss of consciousness, without return to pre-existing conscious level **24**

803.96 Other open skull fracture with intracranial injury of other and unspecified nature, loss of consciousness of unspecified duration **24**

803.99 Other open skull fracture with intracranial injury of other and unspecified nature, unspecified concussion **29**

804.0* Closed fractures involving skull or face with other bones, without mention of intracranial injury **222**

804.00 Closed fractures involving skull or face with other bones, without mention of intracranial injury, unspecified state of consciousness **29**

804.01 Closed fractures involving skull or face with other bones, without mention of intracranial injury, no loss of consciousness **29**

804.02 Closed fractures involving skull or face with other bones, without mention of intracranial injury, brief (less than one hour) loss of consciousness **29 , 226**

804.03 Closed fractures involving skull or face with other bones, without mention of intracranial injury, moderate (1-24 hours) loss of consciousness **24 , 226**

804.04 Closed fractures involving skull or face with other bones, without mention or intracranial injury, prolonged (more than 24 hours) loss of consciousness and return to pre-existing conscious level **24 , 226**

804.05 Closed fractures involving skull of face with other bones, without mention of intracranial injury, prolonged (more than 24 hours) loss of consciousness, without return to pre-existing conscious level **24 , 226**

804.06 Closed fractures involving skull of face with other bones, without mention of intracranial injury, loss of consciousness of unspecified duration **24 , 226**

804.09 Closed fractures involving skull of face with other bones, without mention of intracranial injury, unspecified concussion **29**

804.1* Closed fractures involving skull or face with other bones, with cerebral laceration and contusion **222 , 226**

804.10 Closed fractures involving skull or face with other bones, with cerebral laceration and contusion, unspecified state of consciousness **29**

804.11 Closed fractures involving skull or face with other bones, with cerebral laceration and contusion, no loss of consciousness **29**

804.12 Closed fractures involving skull or face with other bones, with cerebral laceration and contusion, brief (less than one hour) loss of consciousness **29**

804.13 Closed fractures involving skull or face with other bones, with cerebral laceration and contusion, moderate (1-24 hours) loss of consciousness **24**

804.14 Closed fractures involving skull or face with other bones, with cerebral laceration and contusion, prolonged (more than 24 hours) loss of consciousness and return to pre-existing conscious level **24**

804.15 Closed fractures involving skull or face with other bones, with cerebral laceration and contusion, prolonged (more than 24 hours) loss of consciousness, without return to pre-existing conscious level **24**

804.16 Closed fractures involving skull or face with other bones, with cerebral laceration and contusion, loss of consciousness of unspecified duration **24**

804.19 Closed fractures involving skull or face with other bones, with cerebral laceration and contusion, unspecified concussion **29**

804.2* Closed fractures involving skull or face with other bones with subarachnoid, subdural, and extradural hemorrhage **222 , 226**

804.20 Closed fractures involving skull or face with other bones with subarachnoid, subdural, and extradural hemorrhage, unspecified state of consciousness **29**

804.21 Closed fractures involving skull or face with other bones with subarachnoid, subdural, and extradural hemorrhage, no loss of consciousness **29**

804.22   Closed fractures involving skull or face with other bones with subarachnoid, subdural, and extradural hemorrhage, brief (less than one hour) loss of consciousness **29**

804.23   Closed fractures involving skull or face with other bones with subarachnoid, subdural, and extradural hemorrhage, moderate (1-24 hours) loss of consciousness **24**

804.24   Closed fractures involving skull or face with other bones with subarachnoid, subdural, and extradural hemorrhage, prolonged (more than 24 hours) loss of consciousness and return to pre-existing conscious level **24**

804.25   Closed fractures involving skull or face with other bones with subarachnoid, subdural, and extradural hemorrhage, prolonged (more than 24 hours) loss of consciousness, without return to pre-existing conscious level **24**

804.26   Closed fractures involving skull or face with other bones with subarachnoid, subdural, and extradural hemorrhage, loss of consciousness of unspecified duration **24**

804.29   Closed fractures involving skull or face with other bones with subarachnoid, subdural, and extradural hemorrhage, unspecified concussion **29**

804.3*   Closed fractures involving skull or face with other bones, with other and unspecified intracranial hemorrhage **222 , 226**

804.30   Closed fractures involving skull or face with other bones, with other and unspecified intracranial hemorrhage, unspecified state of consciousness **29**

804.31   Closed fractures involving skull or face with other bones, with other and unspecified intracranial hemorrhage, no loss of consciousness **29**

804.32   Closed fractures involving skull or face with other bones, with other and unspecified intracranial hemorrhage, brief (less than one hour) loss of consciousness **29**

804.33   Closed fractures involving skull or face with other bones, with other and unspecified intracranial hemorrhage, moderate (1-24 hours) loss of consciousness **24**

804.34   Closed fractures involving skull or face with other bones, with other and unspecified intracranial hemorrhage, prolonged (more than 24 hours) loss of consciousness and return to preexisting conscious level **24**

804.35   Closed fractures involving skull or face with other bones, with other and unspecified intracranial hemorrhage, prolonged (more than 24 hours) loss of consciousness, without return to pre-existing conscious level **24**

804.36   Closed fractures involving skull or face with other bones, with other and unspecified intracranial hemorrhage, loss of consciousness of unspecified duration **24**

804.39   Closed fractures involving skull or face with other bones, with other and unspecified intracranial hemorrhage, unspecified concussion **29**

804.4*   Closed fractures involving skull or face with other bones, with intracranial injury of other and unspecified nature **222**

804.40   Closed fractures involving skull or face with other bones, with intracranial injury of other and unspecified nature, unspecified state of consciousness **29 , 226**

804.41   Closed fractures involving skull or face with other bones, with intracranial injury of other and unspecified nature, no loss of consciousness **29 , 226**

804.42   Closed fractures involving skull or face with other bones, with intracranial injury of other and unspecified nature, brief (less than one hour) loss of consciousness **29 , 226**

804.43   Closed fractures involving skull or face with other bones, with intracranial injury of other and unspecified nature, moderate (1-24 hours) loss of consciousness **24 , 226**

804.44   Closed fractures involving skull or face with other bones, with intracranial injury of other and unspecified nature, prolonged (more than 24 hours) loss of consciousness and return to pre-existing conscious level **24 , 226**

804.45   Closed fractures involving skull or face with other bones, with intracranial injury of other and unspecified nature, prolonged (more than 24 hours) loss of consciousness, without return to pre-existing conscious level **24 , 227**

804.46   Closed fractures involving skull or face with other bones, with intracranial injury of other and unspecified nature, loss of consciousness of unspecified duration **25 , 227**

804.49   Closed fractures involving skull or face with other bones, with intracranial injury of other and unspecified nature, unspecified concussion **29**

804.5*   Open fractures involving skull or face with other bones, without mention of intracranial injury **222**

804.50   Open fractures involving skull or face with other bones, without mention of intracranial injury, unspecified state of consciousness **29**

804.51   Open fractures involving skull or face with other bones, without mention of intracranial injury, no loss of consciousness **29**

804.52   Open fractures involving skull or face with other bones, without mention of intracranial injury, brief (less than one hour) loss of consciousness **29 , 227**

804.53   Open fractures involving skull or face with other bones, without mention of intracranial injury, moderate (1-24 hours) loss of consciousness **25 , 227**

804.54   Open fractures involving skull or face with other bones, without mention of intracranial injury, prolonged (more than 24 hours) loss of consciousness and return to pre-existing conscious level **25 , 227**

804.55   Open fractures involving skull or face with other bones, without mention of intracranial injury, prolonged (more than 24 hours) loss of consciousness, without return to pre-existing conscious level **25 , 227**

804.56   Open fractures involving skull or face with other bones, without mention of intracranial injury, loss of consciousness of unspecified duration **25**

804.59   Open fractures involving skull or face with other bones, without mention of intracranial injury, unspecified concussion **29**

804.6*   Open fractures involving skull or face with other bones, with cerebral laceration and contusion **222**

804.60   Open fractures involving skull or face with other bones, with cerebral laceration and contusion, unspecified state of consciousness **29 , 227**

804.61   Open fractures involving skull or face with other bones, with cerebral laceration and contusion, no loss of consciousness **29 , 227**

804.62   Open fractures involving skull or face with other bones, with cerebral laceration and contusion, brief (less than one hour) loss of consciousness **29 , 227**

804.63   Open fractures involving skull or face with other bones, with cerebral laceration and contusion, moderate (1-24 hours) loss of consciousness **25 , 227**

804.64   Open fractures involving skull or face with other bones, with cerebral laceration and contusion, prolonged (more than 24 hours) loss of consciousness and return to pre-existing conscious level **25 , 227**

804.65   Open fractures involving skull or face with other bones, with cerebral laceration and contusion, prolonged (more than 24 hours) loss of consciousness, without return to pre-existing conscious level **25 , 227**

804.66   Open fractures involving skull or face with other bones, with cerebral laceration and contusion, loss of consciousness of unspecified duration **25 , 227**

804.69   Open fractures involving skull or face with other bones, with cerebral laceration and contusion, unspecified concussion **29**

804.7*   Open fractures involving skull or face with other bones with subarachnoid, subdural, and extradural hemorrhage **222 , 227**

804.70   Open fractures involving skull or face with other bones with subarachnoid, subdural, and extradural hemorrhage, unspecified state of consciousness **29**

804.71	Open fractures involving skull or face with other bones with subarachnoid, subdural, and extradural hemorrhage, no loss of consciousness **29**
804.72	Open fractures involving skull or face with other bones with subarachnoid, subdural, and extradural hemorrhage, brief (less than one hour) loss of consciousness **30**
804.73	Open fractures involving skull or face with other bones with subarachnoid, subdural, and extradural hemorrhage, moderate (1-24 hours) loss of consciousness **25**
804.74	Open fractures involving skull or face with other bones with subarachnoid, subdural, and extradural hemorrhage, prolonged (more than 24 hours) loss of consciousness and return to pre-existing conscious level **25**
804.75	Open fractures involving skull or face with other bones with subarachnoid, subdural, and extradural hemorrhage, prolonged (more than 24 hours) loss of consciousness, without return to pre-existing conscious level **25**
804.76	Open fractures involving skull or face with other bones with subarachnoid, subdural, and extradural hemorrhage, loss of consciousness of unspecified duration **25**
804.79	Open fractures involving skull or face with other bones with subarachnoid, subdural, and extradural hemorrhage, unspecified concussion **30**
804.8*	Open fractures involving skull or face with other bones, with other and unspecified intracranial hemorrhage **222 , 227**
804.80	Open fractures involving skull or face with other bones, with other and unspecified intracranial hemorrhage, unspecified state of consciousness **30**
804.81	Open fractures involving skull or face with other bones, with other and unspecified intracranial hemorrhage, no loss of consciousness **30**
804.82	Open fractures involving skull or face with other bones, with other and unspecified intracranial hemorrhage, brief (less than one hour) loss of consciousness **30**
804.83	Open fractures involving skull or face with other bones, with other and unspecified intracranial hemorrhage, moderate (1-24 hours) loss of consciousness **25**
804.84	Open fractures involving skull or face with other bones, with other and unspecified intracranial hemorrhage, prolonged (more than 24 hours) loss of consciousness and return to pre-existing conscious level **25**
804.85	Open fractures involving skull or face with other bones, with other and unspecified intracranial hemorrhage, prolonged (more than 24 hours) loss of consciousness, without return to pre-existing conscious level **25**
804.86	Open fractures involving skull or face with other bones, with other and unspecified intracranial hemorrhage, loss of consciousness of unspecified duration **25**
804.89	Open fractures involving skull or face with other bones, with other and unspecified intracranial hemorrhage, unspecified concussion **30**
804.9*	Open fractures involving skull or face with other bones, with intracranial injury of other and unspecified nature **222 , 227**
804.90	Open fractures involving skull or face with other bones, with intracranial injury of other and unspecified nature, unspecified state of consciousness **30**
804.91	Open fractures involving skull or face with other bones, with intracranial injury of other and unspecified nature, no loss of consciousness **30**
804.92	Open fractures involving skull or face with other bones, with intracranial injury of other and unspecified nature, brief (less than one hour) loss of consciousness **30**
804.93	Open fractures involving skull or face with other bones, with intracranial injury of other and unspecified nature, moderate (1-24 hours) loss of consciousness **25**
804.94	Open fractures involving skull or face with other bones, with intracranial injury of other and unspecified nature, prolonged (more than 24 hours) loss of consciousness and return to pre-existing conscious level **25**
804.95	Open fractures involving skull or face with other bones, with intracranial injury of other and unspecified nature, prolonged (more than 24 hours) loss of consciousness, without return to pre-existing level **25**
804.96	Open fractures involving skull or face with other bones, with intracranial injury of other and unspecified nature, loss of consciousness of unspecified duration **25**
804.99	Open fractures involving skull or face with other bones, with intracranial injury of other and unspecified nature, unspecified concussion **30**
805.0*	Closed fracture of cervical vertebra without mention of spinal cord injury **222**
805.1*	Open fracture of cervical vertebra without mention of spinal cord injury **222**
805.2	Closed fracture of dorsal (thoracic) vertebra without mention of spinal cord injury **222**
805.3	Open fracture of dorsal (thoracic) vertebra without mention of spinal cord injury **222**
805.4	Closed fracture of lumbar vertebra without mention of spinal cord injury **222**
805.5	Open fracture of lumbar vertebra without mention of spinal cord injury **222**
805.6	Closed fracture of sacrum and coccyx without mention of spinal cord injury **222 , 228**
805.7	Open fracture of sacrum and coccyx without mention of spinal cord injury **222 , 228**
805.8	Closed fracture of unspecified part of vertebral column without mention of spinal cord injury **222**
805.9	Open fracture of unspecified part of vertebral column without mention of spinal cord injury **222**
805*	Fracture of vertebral column without mention of spinal cord injury **98**
806.0*	Closed fracture of cervical vertebra with spinal cord injury **222 , 228**
806.1*	Open fracture of cervical vertebra with spinal cord injury **222 , 228**
806.2*	Closed fracture of dorsal (thoracic) vertebra with spinal cord injury **222 , 228**
806.3*	Open fracture of dorsal vertebra with spinal cord injury **222 , 228**
806.4	Closed fracture of lumbar spine with spinal cord injury **222 , 228**
806.5	Open fracture of lumbar spine with spinal cord injury **222 , 228**
806.6*	Closed fracture of sacrum and coccyx with spinal cord injury **222**
806.60	Closed fracture of sacrum and coccyx with unspecified spinal cord injury **228**
806.7*	Open fracture of sacrum and coccyx with spinal cord injury **222 , 228**
806.8	Closed fracture of unspecified vertebra with spinal cord injury **222 , 228**
806.9	Open fracture of unspecified vertebra with spinal cord injury **222 , 228**
806*	Fracture of vertebral column with spinal cord injury **18**
807.0*	Closed fracture of rib(s) **222**
807.00	Closed fracture of rib(s), unspecified **54**
807.01	Closed fracture of one rib **54**
807.02	Closed fracture of two ribs **54**
807.03	Closed fracture of three ribs **52**
807.04	Closed fracture of four ribs **52**
807.05	Closed fracture of five ribs **52**
807.06	Closed fracture of six ribs **52**
807.07	Closed fracture of seven ribs **52 , 227**
807.08	Closed fracture of eight or more ribs **52 , 227**
807.09	Closed fracture of multiple ribs, unspecified **52**
807.1*	Open fracture of rib(s) **52 , 222**
807.14	Open fracture of four ribs **227**

807.15	Open fracture of five ribs **227**	
807.16	Open fracture of six ribs **227**	
807.17	Open fracture of seven ribs **227**	
807.18	Open fracture of eight or more ribs **227**	
807.19	Open fracture of multiple ribs, unspecified **227**	
807.2	Closed fracture of sternum **52 , 222**	
807.3	Open fracture of sternum **52 , 222 , 227**	
807.4	Flail chest **52 , 222 , 227**	
807.5	Closed fracture of larynx and trachea **3 , 47 , 222 , 227**	
807.6	Open fracture of larynx and trachea **3 , 47 , 222 , 227**	
808.0	Closed fracture of acetabulum **222**	
808.1	Open fracture of acetabulum **222**	
808.2	Closed fracture of pubis **222**	
808.3	Open fracture of pubis **222**	
808.4*	Closed fracture of other specified part of pelvis **222**	
808.5*	Open fracture of other specified part of pelvis **222**	
808.8	Unspecified closed fracture of pelvis **222**	
808.9	Unspecified open fracture of pelvis **222**	
808*	Fracture of pelvis **96 , 228**	
809.0	Fracture of bones of trunk, closed **101 , 222**	
809.1	Fracture of bones of trunk, open **101 , 222 , 228**	
810.0*	Closed fracture of clavicle **222**	
810.1*	Open fracture of clavicle **222**	
810*	Fracture of clavicle **99**	
811.0*	Closed fracture of scapula **222**	
811.00	Closed fracture of unspecified part of scapula **99**	
811.01	Closed fracture of acromial process of scapula **99**	
811.02	Closed fracture of coracoid process of scapula **99**	
811.03	Closed fracture of glenoid cavity and neck of scapula **99**	
811.09	Closed fracture of other part of scapula **101**	
811.1*	Open fracture of scapula **222**	
811.10	Open fracture of unspecified part of scapula **99**	
811.11	Open fracture of acromial process of scapula **99**	
811.12	Open fracture of coracoid process **99**	
811.13	Open fracture of glenoid cavity and neck of scapula **99**	
811.19	Open fracture of other part of scapula **101**	
812.0*	Closed fracture of upper end of humerus **222**	
812.1*	Open fracture of upper end of humerus **222 , 228**	
812.2*	Closed fracture of shaft or unspecified part of humerus **222**	
812.3*	Open fracture of shaft or unspecified part of humerus **222**	
812.30	Open fracture of unspecified part of humerus **228**	
812.31	Open fracture of shaft of humerus **228**	
812.4*	Closed fracture of lower end of humerus **222**	
812.5*	Open fracture of lower end of humerus **222 , 228**	
812*	Fracture of humerus **99**	
813.0*	Closed fracture of upper end of radius and ulna **222**	
813.1*	Open fracture of upper end of radius and ulna **222 , 228**	
813.2*	Closed fracture of shaft of radius and ulna **222**	
813.3*	Open fracture of shaft of radius and ulna **222 , 228**	
813.4*	Closed fracture of lower end of radius and ulna **222**	
813.5*	Open fracture of lower end of radius and ulna **222 , 228**	
813.8*	Closed fracture of unspecified part of radius with ulna **222**	
813.9*	Open fracture of unspecified part of radius with ulna **222 , 228**	
813*	Fracture of radius and ulna **99**	
814.0*	Closed fractures of carpal bones **222**	
814.1*	Open fractures of carpal bones **222**	
814*	Fracture of carpal bone(s) **99**	
815.0*	Closed fracture of metacarpal bones **222**	
815.1*	Open fracture of metacarpal bones **222**	

815*	Fracture of metacarpal bone(s) **99**	
816.0*	Closed fracture of one or more phalanges of hand **222**	
816.1*	Open fracture of one or more phalanges of hand **222**	
816*	Fracture of one or more phalanges of hand **99**	
817.0	Multiple closed fractures of hand bones **222**	
817.1	Multiple open fractures of hand bones **222**	
817*	Multiple fractures of hand bones **99**	
818.0	Ill-defined closed fractures of upper limb **222**	
818.1	Ill-defined open fractures of upper limb **222 , 228**	
818*	Ill-defined fractures of upper limb **99**	
819.0	Multiple closed fractures involving both upper limbs, and upper limb with rib(s) and sternum **222**	
819.1	Multiple open fractures involving both upper limbs, and upper limb with rib(s) and sternum **222 , 227**	
819*	Multiple fractures involving both upper limbs, and upper limb with rib(s) and sternum **203**	
820.0*	Closed transcervical fracture **222**	
820.1*	Open transcervical fracture **223**	
820.2*	Closed pertrochanteric fracture of femur **223**	
820.3*	Open pertrochanteric fracture of femur **223**	
820.8	Closed fracture of unspecified part of neck of femur **223**	
820.9	Open fracture of unspecified part of neck of femur **223**	
820*	Fracture of neck of femur **96 , 167 , 171 , 228**	
821.0*	Closed fracture of shaft or unspecified part of femur **167 , 171 , 223**	
821.1*	Open fracture of shaft or unspecified part of femur **167 , 171 , 223**	
821.2*	Closed fracture of lower end of femur **223**	
821.3*	Open fracture of lower end of femur **223**	
821*	Fracture of other and unspecified parts of femur **96 , 228**	
822.0	Closed fracture of patella **223**	
822.1	Open fracture of patella **223**	
822*	Fracture of patella **99**	
823.0*	Closed fracture of upper end of tibia and fibula **223**	
823.1*	Open fracture of upper end of tibia and fibula **223 , 228**	
823.2*	Closed fracture of shaft of tibia and fibula **223**	
823.3*	Open fracture of shaft of tibia and fibula **223 , 228**	
823.4*	Torus fracture of tibia and fibula **223 , 228**	
823.8*	Closed fracture of unspecified part of tibia and fibula **223**	
823.9*	Open fracture of unspecified part of tibia and fibula **223 , 228**	
823*	Fracture of tibia and fibula **99**	
824.0	Closed fracture of medial malleolus **223**	
824.1	Open fracture of medial malleolus **223**	
824.2	Closed fracture of lateral malleolus **223**	
824.3	Open fracture of lateral malleolus **223**	
824.4	Closed bimalleolar fracture **223**	
824.5	Open bimalleolar fracture **223**	
824.6	Closed trimalleolar fracture **223**	
824.7	Open trimalleolar fracture **223**	
824.8	Unspecified closed fracture of ankle **223**	
824.9	Unspecified open fracture of ankle **223**	
824*	Fracture of ankle **99**	
825.0	Closed fracture of calcaneus **99 , 223**	
825.1	Open fracture of calcaneus **99 , 223**	
825.2*	Closed fracture of other tarsal and metatarsal bones **99 , 223**	
825.3*	Open fracture of other tarsal and metatarsal bones **99 , 223**	
826.0	Closed fracture of one or more phalanges of foot **223**	
826.1	Open fracture of one or more phalanges of foot **223**	
826*	Fracture of one or more phalanges of foot **99**	
827.0	Other, multiple and ill-defined closed fractures of lower limb **223**	

827.1	Other, multiple and ill-defined open fractures of lower limb **223**
827*	Other, multiple, and ill-defined fractures of lower limb **99**
828.0	Multiple closed fractures involving both lower limbs, lower with upper limb, and lower limb(s) with rib(s) and sternum **223**
828.1	Multiple fractures involving both lower limbs, lower with upper limb, and lower limb(s) with rib(s) and sternum, open **223**
828*	Multiple fractures involving both lower limbs, lower with upper limb, and lower limb(s) with rib(s) and sternum **203 , 228**
829.0	Closed fracture of unspecified bone **223**
829.1	Open fracture of unspecified bone **223**
829*	Fracture of unspecified bones **100**
830.0	Closed dislocation of jaw **223**
830.1	Open dislocation of jaw **223**
830*	Dislocation of jaw **3 , 48**
831.0*	Closed dislocation of shoulder, unspecified **223**
831.1*	Open dislocation of shoulder **223 , 228**
831*	Dislocation of shoulder **100**
832.0*	Closed dislocation of elbow **223**
832.1*	Open dislocation of elbow **223 , 228**
832.2	Nursemaid's elbow **223**
832*	Dislocation of elbow **100**
833.0*	Closed dislocation of wrist **223**
833.1*	Open dislocation of wrist **223**
833*	Dislocation of wrist **100**
834.0*	Closed dislocation of finger **223**
834.1*	Open dislocation of finger **223**
834*	Dislocation of finger **100**
835.0*	Closed dislocation of hip **223**
835.1*	Open dislocation of hip **223 , 228**
835*	Dislocation of hip **96**
836.0	Tear of medial cartilage or meniscus of knee, current **223**
836.1	Tear of lateral cartilage or meniscus of knee, current **223**
836.2	Other tear of cartilage or meniscus of knee, current **223**
836.3	Closed dislocation of patella **223**
836.4	Open dislocation of patella **223**
836.5*	Other closed dislocation of knee **223**
836.6*	Other open dislocation of knee **223 , 228**
836*	Dislocation of knee **100**
837.0	Closed dislocation of ankle **223**
837.1	Open dislocation of ankle **223 , 228**
837*	Dislocation of ankle **100**
838.0*	Closed dislocation of foot **223**
838.1*	Open dislocation of foot **223**
838*	Dislocation of foot **100**
839.0*	Closed dislocation, cervical vertebra **98 , 223 , 228**
839.1*	Open dislocation, cervical vertebra **98 , 223 , 228**
839.2*	Closed dislocation, thoracic and lumbar vertebra **98 , 223**
839.3*	Open dislocation, thoracic and lumbar vertebra **98 , 223**
839.4*	Closed dislocation, other vertebra **98 , 223**
839.5*	Open dislocation, other vertebra **98 , 223**
839.52	Open dislocation, sacrum **228**
839.59	Open dislocation, other vertebra **228**
839.6*	Closed dislocation, other location **223**
839.61	Closed dislocation, sternum **52**
839.69	Closed dislocation, other location **100**
839.71	Open dislocation, sternum **52 , 223 , 227**
839.79	Open dislocation, other location **100 , 223**
839.8	Closed dislocation, multiple and ill-defined sites **100 , 223**
839.9	Open dislocation, multiple and ill-defined sites **100 , 223**
840.0	Acromioclavicular (joint) (ligament) sprain and strain **223**
840.1	Coracoclavicular (ligament) sprain and strain **223**
840.2	Coracohumeral (ligament) sprain and strain **223**
840.3	Infraspinatus (muscle) (tendon) sprain and strain **223**
840.4	Rotator cuff (capsule) sprain and strain **223**
840.5	Subscapularis (muscle) sprain and strain **223**
840.6	Supraspinatus (muscle) (tendon) sprain and strain **223**
840.7	Superior glenoid labrum lesions (SLAP) **223**
840.8	Sprain and strain of other specified sites of shoulder and upper arm **223**
840.9	Sprain and strain of unspecified site of shoulder and upper arm **223**
840*	Sprains and strains of shoulder and upper arm **100**
841*	Sprains and strains of elbow and forearm **100 , 223**
842*	Sprains and strains of wrist and hand **100 , 223**
843*	Sprains and strains of hip and thigh **96 , 223**
844*	Sprains and strains of knee and leg **100 , 223**
845.0*	Ankle sprain and strain **100**
845.1*	Foot sprain and strain **100**
845*	Sprains and strains of ankle and foot **223**
846*	Sprains and strains of sacroiliac region **98 , 223**
847*	Sprains and strains of other and unspecified parts of back **98 , 223**
848.0	Sprain and strain of septal cartilage of nose **101**
848.1	Sprain and strain of jaw **48**
848.2	Sprain and strain of thyroid region **101**
848.3	Sprain and strain of ribs **54**
848.4*	Sprain and strain of sternum **54**
848.5	Pelvic sprain and strains **96**
848.8	Other specified sites of sprains and strains **100**
848.9	Unspecified site of sprain and strain **100**
848*	Other and ill-defined sprains and strains **223**
850.0	Concussion with no loss of consciousness **223**
850.1*	Concussion with brief (less than one hour) loss of consciousness **223**
850.2	Concussion with moderate (1-24 hours) loss of consciousness **223 , 227**
850.3	Concussion with prolonged (more than 24 hours) loss of consciousness and return to pre-existing conscious level **223 , 227**
850.4	Concussion with prolonged (more than 24 hours) loss of consciousness, without return to pre-existing conscious level **223 , 227**
850.5	Concussion with loss of consciousness of unspecified duration **223**
850.9	Unspecified concussion **223**
850*	Concussion **31**
851.0*	Cortex (cerebral) contusion without mention of open intracranial wound **223**
851.00	Cortex (cerebral) contusion without mention of open intracranial wound, state of consciousness unspecified **30 , 227**
851.01	Cortex (cerebral) contusion without mention of open intracranial wound, no loss of consciousness **30 , 227**
851.02	Cortex (cerebral) contusion without mention of open intracranial wound, brief (less than 1 hour) loss of consciousness **30 , 227**
851.03	Cortex (cerebral) contusion without mention of open intracranial wound, moderate (1-24 hours) loss of consciousness **25 , 227**
851.04	Cortex (cerebral) contusion without mention of open intracranial wound, prolonged (more than 24 hours) loss of consciousness and return to pre-existing conscious level **25 , 227**
851.05	Cortex (cerebral) contusion without mention of open intracranial wound, prolonged (more than 24 hours) loss of consciousness, without return to pre-existing conscious level **25 , 227**

851.06	Cortex (cerebral) contusion without mention of open intracranial wound, loss of consciousness of unspecified duration **25 , 227**
851.09	Cortex (cerebral) contusion without mention of open intracranial wound, unspecified concussion **30 , 227**
851.1*	Cortex (cerebral) contusion with open intracranial wound **9 , 11 , 223 , 227**
851.10	Cortex (cerebral) contusion with open intracranial wound, unspecified state of consciousness **30**
851.11	Cortex (cerebral) contusion with open intracranial wound, no loss of consciousness **30**
851.12	Cortex (cerebral) contusion with open intracranial wound, brief (less than 1 hour) loss of consciousness **30**
851.13	Cortex (cerebral) contusion with open intracranial wound, moderate (1-24 hours) loss of consciousness **25**
851.14	Cortex (cerebral) contusion with open intracranial wound, prolonged (more than 24 hours) loss of consciousness and return to pre-existing conscious level **25**
851.15	Cortex (cerebral) contusion with open intracranial wound, prolonged (more than 24 hours) loss of consciousness, without return to pre-existing conscious level **25**
851.16	Cortex (cerebral) contusion with open intracranial wound, loss of consciousness of unspecified duration **25**
851.19	Cortex (cerebral) contusion with open intracranial wound, unspecified concussion **30**
851.2*	Cortex (cerebral) laceration without mention of open intracranial wound **9 , 11 , 223 , 227**
851.20	Cortex (cerebral) laceration without mention of open intracranial wound, unspecified state of consciousness **30**
851.21	Cortex (cerebral) laceration without mention of open intracranial wound, no loss of consciousness **30**
851.22	Cortex (cerebral) laceration without mention of open intracranial wound, brief (less than 1 hour) loss of consciousness **30**
851.23	Cortex (cerebral) laceration without mention of open intracranial wound, moderate (1-24 hours) loss of consciousness **25**
851.24	Cortex (cerebral) laceration without mention of open intracranial wound, prolonged (more than 24 hours) loss of consciousness and return to pre-existing conscious level **25**
851.25	Cortex (cerebral) laceration without mention of open intracranial wound, prolonged (more than 24 hours) loss of consciousness, without return to pre-existing conscious level **25**
851.26	Cortex (cerebral) laceration without mention of open intracranial wound, loss of consciousness of unspecified duration **25**
851.29	Cortex (cerebral) laceration without mention of open intracranial wound, unspecified concussion **30**
851.3*	Cortex (cerebral) laceration with open intracranial wound **9 , 11 , 223 , 227**
851.30	Cortex (cerebral) laceration with open intracranial wound, unspecified state of consciousness **30**
851.31	Cortex (cerebral) laceration with open intracranial wound, no loss of consciousness **30**
851.32	Cortex (cerebral) laceration with open intracranial wound, brief (less than 1 hour) loss of consciousness **30**
851.33	Cortex (cerebral) laceration with open intracranial wound, moderate (1-24 hours) loss of consciousness **25**
851.34	Cortex (cerebral) laceration with open intracranial wound, prolonged (more than 24 hours) loss of consciousness and return to pre-existing conscious level **25**
851.35	Cortex (cerebral) laceration with open intracranial wound, prolonged (more than 24 hours) loss of consciousness, without return to pre-existing conscious level **25**
851.36	Cortex (cerebral) laceration with open intracranial wound, loss of consciousness of unspecified duration **25**
851.39	Cortex (cerebral) laceration with open intracranial wound, unspecified concussion **30**
851.4*	Cerebellar or brain stem contusion without mention of open intracranial wound **223 , 227**
851.40	Cerebellar or brain stem contusion without mention of open intracranial wound, unspecified state of consciousness **30**
851.41	Cerebellar or brain stem contusion without mention of open intracranial wound, no loss of consciousness **30**
851.42	Cerebellar or brain stem contusion without mention of open intracranial wound, brief (less than 1 hour) loss of consciousness **30**
851.43	Cerebellar or brain stem contusion without mention of open intracranial wound, moderate (1-24 hours) loss of consciousness **25**
851.44	Cerebellar or brain stem contusion without mention of open intracranial wound, prolonged (more than 24 hours) loss consciousness and return to pre-existing conscious level **25**
851.45	Cerebellar or brain stem contusion without mention of open intracranial wound, prolonged (more than 24 hours) loss of consciousness, without return to pre-existing conscious level **25**
851.46	Cerebellar or brain stem contusion without mention of open intracranial wound, loss of consciousness of unspecified duration **25**
851.49	Cerebellar or brain stem contusion without mention of open intracranial wound, unspecified concussion **30**
851.5*	Cerebellar or brain stem contusion with open intracranial wound **9 , 11 , 223 , 227**
851.50	Cerebellar or brain stem contusion with open intracranial wound, unspecified state of consciousness **30**
851.51	Cerebellar or brain stem contusion with open intracranial wound, no loss of consciousness **30**
851.52	Cerebellar or brain stem contusion with open intracranial wound, brief (less than 1 hour) loss of consciousness **30**
851.53	Cerebellar or brain stem contusion with open intracranial wound, moderate (1-24 hours) loss of consciousness **25**
851.54	Cerebellar or brain stem contusion with open intracranial wound, prolonged (more than 24 hours) loss of consciousness and return to pre-existing conscious level **25**
851.55	Cerebellar or brain stem contusion with open intracranial wound, prolonged (more than 24 hours) loss of consciousness, without return to pre-existing conscious level **26**
851.56	Cerebellar or brain stem contusion with open intracranial wound, loss of consciousness of unspecified duration **26**
851.59	Cerebellar or brain stem contusion with open intracranial wound, unspecified concussion **30**
851.6*	Cerebellar or brain stem laceration without mention of open intracranial wound **9 , 11 , 223 , 227**
851.60	Cerebellar or brain stem laceration without mention of open intracranial wound, unspecified state of consciousness **30**
851.61	Cerebellar or brain stem laceration without mention of open intracranial wound, no loss of consciousness **30**
851.62	Cerebellar or brain stem laceration without mention of open intracranial wound, brief (less than 1 hour) loss of consciousness **30**
851.63	Cerebellar or brain stem laceration without mention of open intracranial wound, moderate (1-24 hours) loss of consciousness **26**
851.64	Cerebellar or brain stem laceration without mention of open intracranial wound, prolonged (more than 24 hours) loss of consciousness and return to pre-existing conscious level **26**
851.65	Cerebellar or brain stem laceration without mention of open intracranial wound, prolonged (more than 24 hours) loss of consciousness, without return to pre-existing conscious level **26**
851.66	Cerebellar or brain stem laceration without mention of open intracranial wound, loss of consciousness of unspecified duration **26**
851.69	Cerebellar or brain stem laceration without mention of open intracranial wound, unspecified concussion **30**
851.7*	Cerebellar or brain stem laceration with open intracranial wound **9 , 11 , 223 , 227**

851.70   Cerebellar or brain stem laceration with open intracranial wound, state of consciousness unspecified **30**

851.71   Cerebellar or brain stem laceration with open intracranial wound, no loss of consciousness **30**

851.72   Cerebellar or brain stem laceration with open intracranial wound, brief (less than one hour) loss of consciousness **30**

851.73   Cerebellar or brain stem laceration with open intracranial wound, moderate (1-24 hours) loss of consciousness **26**

851.74   Cerebellar or brain stem laceration with open intracranial wound, prolonged (more than 24 hours) loss of consciousness and return to pre-existing conscious level **26**

851.75   Cerebellar or brain stem laceration with open intracranial wound, prolonged (more than 24 hours) loss of consciousness, without return to pre-existing conscious level **26**

851.76   Cerebellar or brain stem laceration with open intracranial wound, loss of consciousness of unspecified duration **26**

851.79   Cerebellar or brain stem laceration with open intracranial wound, unspecified concussion **30**

851.8*   Other and unspecified cerebral laceration and contusion, without mention of open intracranial wound **9 , 11 , 223 , 227**

851.80   Other and unspecified cerebral laceration and contusion, without mention of open intracranial wound, unspecified state of consciousness **30**

851.81   Other and unspecified cerebral laceration and contusion, without mention of open intracranial wound, no loss of consciousness **30**

851.82   Other and unspecified cerebral laceration and contusion, without mention of open intracranial wound, brief (less than 1 hour) loss of consciousness **30**

851.83   Other and unspecified cerebral laceration and contusion, without mention of open intracranial wound, moderate (1-24 hours) loss of consciousness **26**

851.84   Other and unspecified cerebral laceration and contusion, without mention of open intracranial wound, prolonged (more than 24 hours) loss of consciousness and return to preexisting conscious level **26**

851.85   Other and unspecified cerebral laceration and contusion, without mention of open intracranial wound, prolonged (more than 24 hours) loss of consciousness, without return to pre-existing conscious level **26**

851.86   Other and unspecified cerebral laceration and contusion, without mention of open intracranial wound, loss of consciousness of unspecified duration **26**

851.89   Other and unspecified cerebral laceration and contusion, without mention of open intracranial wound, unspecified concussion **30**

851.9*   Other and unspecified cerebral laceration and contusion, with open intracranial wound **9 , 11 , 223 , 227**

851.90   Other and unspecified cerebral laceration and contusion, with open intracranial wound, unspecified state of consciousness **30**

851.91   Other and unspecified cerebral laceration and contusion, with open intracranial wound, no loss of consciousness **30**

851.92   Other and unspecified cerebral laceration and contusion, with open intracranial wound, brief (less than 1 hour) loss of consciousness **30**

851.93   Other and unspecified cerebral laceration and contusion, with open intracranial wound, moderate (1-24 hours) loss of consciousness **26**

851.94   Other and unspecified cerebral laceration and contusion, with open intracranial wound, prolonged (more than 24 hours) loss of consciousness and return to pre-existing conscious level **26**

851.95   Other and unspecified cerebral laceration and contusion, with open intracranial wound, prolonged (more than 24 hours) loss of consciousness, without return to pre-existing conscious level **26**

851.96   Other and unspecified cerebral laceration and contusion, with open intracranial wound, loss of consciousness of unspecified duration **26**

851.99   Other and unspecified cerebral laceration and contusion, with open intracranial wound, unspecified concussion **30**

852.0*   Subarachnoid hemorrhage following injury without mention of open intracranial wound **9 , 11**

852.00   Subarachnoid hemorrhage following injury, without mention of open intracranial wound, unspecified state of consciousness **30**

852.01   Subarachnoid hemorrhage following injury, without mention of open intracranial wound, no loss of consciousness **30**

852.02   Subarachnoid hemorrhage following injury, without mention of open intracranial wound, brief (less than 1 hour) loss of consciousness **30**

852.03   Subarachnoid hemorrhage following injury, without mention of open intracranial wound, moderate (1-24 hours) loss of consciousness **26**

852.04   Subarachnoid hemorrhage following injury, without mention of open intracranial wound, prolonged (more than 24 hours) loss of consciousness and return to pre-existing conscious level **26**

852.05   Subarachnoid hemorrhage following injury, without mention of open intracranial wound, prolonged (more than 24 hours) loss of consciousness, without return to pre-existing conscious level **26**

852.06   Subarachnoid hemorrhage following injury, without mention of open intracranial wound, loss of consciousness of unspecified duration **26**

852.09   Subarachnoid hemorrhage following injury, without mention of open intracranial wound, unspecified concussion **30**

852.1*   Subarachnoid hemorrhage following injury, with open intracranial wound **9 , 11**

852.10   Subarachnoid hemorrhage following injury, with open intracranial wound, unspecified state of consciousness **30**

852.11   Subarachnoid hemorrhage following injury, with open intracranial wound, no loss of consciousness **30**

852.12   Subarachnoid hemorrhage following injury, with open intracranial wound, brief (less than 1 hour) loss of consciousness **31**

852.13   Subarachnoid hemorrhage following injury, with open intracranial wound, moderate (1-24 hours) loss of consciousness **26**

852.14   Subarachnoid hemorrhage following injury, with open intracranial wound, prolonged (more than 24 hours) loss of consciousness and return to pre-existing conscious level **26**

852.15   Subarachnoid hemorrhage following injury, with open intracranial wound, prolonged (more than 24 hours) loss of consciousness, without return to pre-existing conscious level **26**

852.16   Subarachnoid hemorrhage following injury, with open intracranial wound, loss of consciousness of unspecified duration **26**

852.19   Subarachnoid hemorrhage following injury, with open intracranial wound, unspecified concussion **31**

852.20   Subdural hemorrhage following injury, without mention of open intracranial wound, unspecified state of consciousness **31**

852.21   Subdural hemorrhage following injury, without mention of open intracranial wound, no loss of consciousness **31**

852.22   Subdural hemorrhage following injury, without mention of open intracranial wound, brief (less than one hour) loss of consciousness **31**

852.23   Subdural hemorrhage following injury, without mention of open intracranial wound, moderate (1-24 hours) loss of consciousness **26**

852.24   Subdural hemorrhage following injury, without mention of open intracranial wound, prolonged (more than 24 hours) loss of consciousness and return to pre-existing conscious level **26**

852.25   Subdural hemorrhage following injury, without mention of open intracranial wound, prolonged (more than 24 hours) loss of consciousness, without return to pre-existing conscious level **26**

852.26   Subdural hemorrhage following injury, without mention of open intracranial wound, loss of consciousness of unspecified duration **26**

852.29   Subdural hemorrhage following injury, without mention of open intracranial wound, unspecified concussion **31**

852.3*   Subdural hemorrhage following injury, with open intracranial wound **9 , 11**

852.30   Subdural hemorrhage following injury, with open intracranial wound, state of consciousness unspecified **31**

852.31   Subdural hemorrhage following injury, with open intracranial wound, no loss of consciousness **31**

852.32   Subdural hemorrhage following injury, with open intracranial wound, brief (less than 1 hour) loss of consciousness **31**

852.33   Subdural hemorrhage following injury, with open intracranial wound, moderate (1-24 hours) loss of consciousness **26**

852.34   Subdural hemorrhage following injury, with open intracranial wound, prolonged (more than 24 hours) loss of consciousness and return to pre-existing conscious level **26**

852.35   Subdural hemorrhage following injury, with open intracranial wound, prolonged (more than 24 hours) loss of consciousness, without return to pre-existing conscious level **26**

852.36   Subdural hemorrhage following injury, with open intracranial wound, loss of consciousness of unspecified duration **26**

852.39   Subdural hemorrhage following injury, with open intracranial wound, unspecified concussion **31**

852.40   Extradural hemorrhage following injury, without mention of open intracranial wound, unspecified state of consciousness **31**

852.41   Extradural hemorrhage following injury, without mention of open intracranial wound, no loss of consciousness **31**

852.42   Extradural hemorrhage following injury, without mention of open intracranial wound, brief (less than 1 hour) loss of consciousness **31**

852.43   Extradural hemorrhage following injury, without mention of open intracranial wound, moderate (1-24 hours) loss of consciousness **26**

852.44   Extradural hemorrhage following injury, without mention of open intracranial wound, prolonged (more than 24 hours) loss of consciousness and return to pre-existing conscious level **26**

852.45   Extradural hemorrhage following injury, without mention of open intracranial wound, prolonged (more than 24 hours) loss of consciousness, without return to pre-existing conscious level **26**

852.46   Extradural hemorrhage following injury, without mention of open intracranial wound, loss of consciousness of unspecified duration **26**

852.49   Extradural hemorrhage following injury, without mention of open intracranial wound, unspecified concussion **31**

852.50   Extradural hemorrhage following injury, with open intracranial wound, state of consciousness unspecified **31**

852.51   Extradural hemorrhage following injury, with open intracranial wound, no loss of consciousness **31**

852.52   Extradural hemorrhage following injury, with open intracranial wound, brief (less than 1 hour) loss of consciousness **31**

852.53   Extradural hemorrhage following injury, with open intracranial wound, moderate (1-24 hours) loss of consciousness **26**

852.54   Extradural hemorrhage following injury, with open intracranial wound, prolonged (more than 24 hours) loss of consciousness and return to pre-existing conscious level **26**

852.55   Extradural hemorrhage following injury, with open intracranial wound, prolonged (more than 24 hours) loss of consciousness, without return to pre-existing conscious level **26**

852.56   Extradural hemorrhage following injury, with open intracranial wound, loss of consciousness of unspecified duration **26**

852.59   Extradural hemorrhage following injury, with open intracranial wound, unspecified concussion **31**

852*   Subarachnoid, subdural, and extradural hemorrhage, following injury **223 , 227**

853.0*   Other and unspecified intracranial hemorrhage following injury, without mention of open intracranial wound **9 , 11**

853.00   Other and unspecified intracranial hemorrhage following injury, without mention of open intracranial wound, unspecified state of consciousness **31**

853.01   Other and unspecified intracranial hemorrhage following injury, without mention of open intracranial wound, no loss of consciousness **31**

853.02   Other and unspecified intracranial hemorrhage following injury, without mention of open intracranial wound, brief (less than 1 hour) loss of consciousness **31**

853.03   Other and unspecified intracranial hemorrhage following injury, without mention of open intracranial wound, moderate (1-24 hours) loss of consciousness **27**

853.04   Other and unspecified intracranial hemorrhage following injury, without mention of open intracranial wound, prolonged (more than 24 hours) loss of consciousness and return to preexisting conscious level **27**

853.05   Other and unspecified intracranial hemorrhage following injury. Without mention of open intracranial wound, prolonged (more than 24 hours) loss of consciousness, without return to pre-existing conscious level **27**

853.06   Other and unspecified intracranial hemorrhage following injury, without mention of open intracranial wound, loss of consciousness of unspecified duration **27**

853.09   Other and unspecified intracranial hemorrhage following injury, without mention of open intracranial wound, unspecified concussion **31**

853.1*   Other and unspecified intracranial hemorrhage following injury with open intracranial wound **9 , 11**

853.10   Other and unspecified intracranial hemorrhage following injury, with open intracranial wound, unspecified state of consciousness **31**

853.11   Other and unspecified intracranial hemorrhage following injury, with open intracranial wound, no loss of consciousness **31**

853.12   Other and unspecified intracranial hemorrhage following injury, with open intracranial wound, brief (less than 1 hour) loss of consciousness **31**

853.13   Other and unspecified intracranial hemorrhage following injury, with open intracranial wound, moderate (1-24 hours) loss of consciousness **27**

853.14   Other and unspecified intracranial hemorrhage following injury, with open intracranial wound, prolonged (more than 24 hours) loss of consciousness and return to pre-existing conscious level **27**

853.15   Other and unspecified intracranial hemorrhage following injury, with open intracranial wound, prolonged (more than 24 hours) loss of consciousness, without return to pre-existing conscious level **27**

853.16   Other and unspecified intracranial hemorrhage following injury, with open intracranial wound, loss of consciousness of unspecified duration **27**

853.19   Other and unspecified intracranial hemorrhage following injury, with open intracranial wound, unspecified concussion **31**

853*   Other and unspecified intracranial hemorrhage following injury **223 , 227**

854.00   Intracranial injury of other and unspecified nature, without mention of open intracranial wound, unspecified state of consciousness **31**

854.01   Intracranial injury of other and unspecified nature, without mention of open intracranial wound, no loss of consciousness **31**

854.02   Intracranial injury of other and unspecified nature, without mention of open intracranial wound, brief (less than 1 hour) loss of consciousness **31**

854.03   Intracranial injury of other and unspecified nature, without mention of open intracranial wound, moderate (1-24 hours) loss of consciousness **27**

854.04   Intracranial injury of other and unspecified nature, without mention of open intracranial wound, prolonged (more than 24 hours) loss of consciousness and return to pre-existing conscious level **27**

854.05 Intracranial injury of other and unspecified nature, without mention of open intracranial wound, prolonged (more than 24 hours) loss of consciousness, without return to pre-existing conscious level **27**

854.06 Intracranial injury of other and unspecified nature, without mention of open intracranial wound, loss of consciousness of unspecified duration **27**

854.09 Intracranial injury of other and unspecified nature, without mention of open intracranial wound, unspecified concussion **31**

854.1* Intracranial injury of other and unspecified nature with open intracranial wound **9 , 11**

854.10 Intracranial injury of other and unspecified nature, with open intracranial wound, unspecified state of consciousness **31**

854.11 Intracranial injury of other and unspecified nature, with open intracranial wound, no loss of consciousness **31**

854.12 Intracranial injury of other and unspecified nature, with open intracranial wound, brief (less than 1 hour) loss of consciousness **31**

854.13 Intracranial injury of other and unspecified nature, with open intracranial wound, moderate (1-24 hours) loss of consciousness **27**

854.14 Intracranial injury of other and unspecified nature, with open intracranial wound, prolonged (more than 24 hours) loss of consciousness and return to pre-existing conscious level **27**

854.15 Intracranial injury of other and unspecified nature, with open intracranial wound, prolonged (more than 24 hours) loss of consciousness, without return to pre-existing conscious level **27**

854.16 Intracranial injury of other and unspecified nature, with open intracranial wound, loss of consciousness of unspecified duration **27**

854.19 Intracranial injury of other and unspecified nature, with open intracranial wound, with unspecified concussion **31**

854* Intracranial injury of other and unspecified nature **223 , 227**

860* Traumatic pneumothorax and hemothorax **53 , 167 , 171 , 223 , 227**

861.0* Heart injury, without mention of open wound into thorax **69**

861.1* Heart injury, with open wound into thorax **69**

861.20 Unspecified lung injury without mention of open wound into thorax **54**

861.21 Lung contusion without mention of open wound into thorax **54**

861.22 Lung laceration without mention of open wound into thorax **52**

861.30 Unspecified lung injury with open wound into thorax **54**

861.31 Lung contusion with open wound into thorax **54**

861.32 Lung laceration with open wound into thorax **52**

861* Injury to heart and lung **223 , 227**

862.0 Diaphragm injury without mention of open wound into cavity **52**

862.1 Diaphragm injury with open wound into cavity **52**

862.21 Bronchus injury without mention of open wound into cavity **52**

862.22 Esophagus injury without mention of open wound into cavity **75**

862.29 Injury to other specified intrathoracic organs without mention of open wound into cavity **54**

862.31 Bronchus injury with open wound into cavity **52**

862.32 Esophagus injury with open wound into cavity **79**

862.39 Injury to other specified intrathoracic organs with open wound into cavity **54**

862.8 Injury to multiple and unspecified intrathoracic organs without mention of open wound into cavity **203**

862.9 Injury to multiple and unspecified intrathoracic organs with open wound into cavity **203**

862* Injury to other and unspecified intrathoracic organs **223 , 227**

863.0 Stomach injury without mention of open wound into cavity **79 , 223 , 228**

863.1 Stomach injury with open wound into cavity **79 , 223 , 228**

863.2* Small intestine injury without mention of open wound into cavity **79 , 223 , 228**

863.3* Small intestine injury with open wound into cavity **79 , 224 , 228**

863.4* Colon or rectal injury without mention of open wound into cavity **79 , 224 , 228**

863.5* Injury to colon or rectum with open wound into cavity **79 , 224 , 228**

863.8* Injury to other and unspecified gastrointestinal sites without mention of open wound into cavity **224**

863.80 Gastrointestinal tract injury, unspecified site, without mention of open wound into cavity **79**

863.81 Pancreas head injury without mention of open wound into cavity **83 , 228**

863.82 Pancreas body injury without mention of open wound into cavity **83 , 228**

863.83 Pancreas tail injury without mention of open wound into cavity **83 , 228**

863.84 Pancreas injury, multiple and unspecified sites, without mention of open wound into cavity **83 , 228**

863.85 Appendix injury without mention of open wound into cavity **79 , 228**

863.89 Injury to other and unspecified gastrointestinal sites without mention of open wound into cavity **79 , 228**

863.9* Injury to other and unspecified gastrointestinal sites, with open wound into cavity **224 , 228**

863.90 Gastrointestinal tract injury, unspecified site, with open wound into cavity **79**

863.91 Pancreas head injury with open wound into cavity **83**

863.92 Pancreas body injury with open wound into cavity **83**

863.93 Pancreas tail injury with open wound into cavity **83**

863.94 Pancreas injury, multiple and unspecified sites, with open wound into cavity **83**

863.95 Appendix injury with open wound into cavity **79**

863.99 Injury to other and unspecified gastrointestinal sites with open wound into cavity **79**

864.0* Liver injury without mention of open wound into cavity **224**

864.1* Liver injury with open wound into cavity **224**

864* Injury to liver **83 , 228**

865* Injury to spleen **167 , 171 , 177 , 224 , 228**

866* Injury to kidney **121 , 224 , 228**

867.0 Bladder and urethra injury without mention of open wound into cavity **121**

867.1 Bladder and urethra injury with open wound into cavity **121**

867.2 Ureter injury without mention of open wound into cavity **121**

867.3 Ureter injury with open wound into cavity **121**

867.4 Uterus injury without mention of open wound into cavity **128 , 131**

867.5 Uterus injury with open wound into cavity **128 , 131**

867.6 Injury to other specified pelvic organs without mention of open wound into cavity **125 , 128 , 131**

867.7 Injury to other specified pelvic organs with open wound into cavity **125 , 128 , 131**

867.8 Injury to unspecified pelvic organ without mention of open wound into cavity **125 , 128 , 131**

867.9 Injury to unspecified pelvic organ with open wound into cavity **125 , 128 , 131**

867* Injury to pelvic organs **224 , 228**

868.0* Injury to other intra-abdominal organs without mention of open wound into cavity **224**

868.00 Injury to unspecified intra-abdominal organ without mention of open wound into cavity **79**

868.01 Adrenal gland injury without mention of open wound into cavity **115 , 228**

868.02 Bile duct and gallbladder injury without mention of open wound into cavity **83 , 228**

868.03   Peritoneum injury without mention of open wound into cavity **79 , 228**

868.04   Retroperitoneum injury without mention of open wound into cavity **121 , 228**

868.09   Injury to other and multiple intra-abdominal organs without mention of open wound into cavity **203 , 228**

868.1*   Injury to other intra-abdominal organs with open wound into cavity **224**

868.10   Injury to unspecified intra-abdominal organ, with open wound into cavity **79**

868.11   Adrenal gland injury, with open wound into cavity **115 , 228**

868.12   Bile duct and gallbladder injury, with open wound into cavity **83 , 228**

868.13   Peritoneum injury with open wound into cavity **79 , 228**

868.14   Retroperitoneum injury with open wound into cavity **121 , 228**

868.19   Injury to other and multiple intra-abdominal organs, with open wound into cavity **203 , 228**

869*   Internal injury to unspecified or ill-defined organs **203 , 224**

870*   Open wound of ocular adnexa **40 , 224**

871*   Open wound of eyeball **40 , 224**

872*   Open wound of ear **47 , 224**

873.0   Open wound of scalp, without mention of complication **107**

873.1   Open wound of scalp, complicated **107**

873.2*   Open wound of nose, without mention of complication **3**

873.20   Open wound of nose, unspecified site, without mention of complication **47**

873.21   Open wound of nasal septum, without mention of complication **47**

873.22   Open wound of nasal cavity, without mention of complication **47**

873.23   Open wound of nasal sinus, without mention of complication **47**

873.29   Open wound of nose, multiple sites, without mention of complication **47**

873.3*   Open wound of nose, complicated **3 , 47**

873.40   Open wound of face, unspecified site, without mention of complication **3 , 107**

873.41   Open wound of cheek, without mention of complication **3 , 107**

873.42   Open wound of forehead, without mention of complication **107**

873.43   Open wound of lip, without mention of complication **3 , 48**

873.44   Open wound of jaw, without mention of complication **3 , 48**

873.49   Open wound of face, other and multiple sites, without mention of complication **107**

873.50   Open wound of face, unspecified site, complicated **3 , 107**

873.51   Open wound of cheek, complicated **3 , 107**

873.52   Open wound of forehead, complicated **107**

873.53   Open wound of lip, complicated **3 , 48**

873.54   Open wound of jaw, complicated **3 , 48**

873.59   Open wound of face, other and multiple sites, complicated **107**

873.6*   Open wound of internal structures of mouth, without mention of complication **48**

873.60   Open wound of mouth, unspecified site, without mention of complication **3**

873.61   Open wound of buccal mucosa, without mention of complication **3**

873.62   Open wound of gum (alveolar process), without mention of complication **3**

873.64   Open wound of tongue and floor of mouth, without mention of complication **3**

873.65   Open wound of palate, without mention of complication **3**

873.69   Open wound of mouth, other and multiple sites, without mention of complication **3**

873.7*   Open wound of internal structure of mouth, complicated **48**

873.70   Open wound of mouth, unspecified site, complicated **3**

873.71   Open wound of buccal mucosa, complicated **3**

873.72   Open wound of gum (alveolar process), complicated **4**

873.74   Open wound of tongue and floor of mouth, complicated **4**

873.75   Open wound of palate, complicated **4**

873.79   Open wound of mouth, other and multiple sites, complicated **4**

873.8   Other and unspecified open wound of head without mention of complication **107**

873.9   Other and unspecified open wound of head, complicated **107**

873*   Other open wound of head **224**

874.0*   Open wound of larynx and trachea, without mention of complication **224**

874.00   Open wound of larynx with trachea, without mention of complication **4 , 47**

874.01   Open wound of larynx, without mention of complication **4 , 47**

874.02   Open wound of trachea, without mention of complication **4 , 52**

874.1*   Open wound of larynx and trachea, complicated **224**

874.10   Open wound of larynx with trachea, complicated **4 , 47 , 227**

874.11   Open wound of larynx, complicated **4 , 47 , 227**

874.12   Open wound of trachea, complicated **4 , 52 , 227**

874.2   Open wound of thyroid gland, without mention of complication **4 , 115 , 224**

874.3   Open wound of thyroid gland, complicated **4 , 115 , 224**

874.4   Open wound of pharynx, without mention of complication **4 , 47 , 224**

874.5   Open wound of pharynx, complicated **4 , 47 , 224**

874.8   Open wound of other and unspecified parts of neck, without mention of complication **4 , 107 , 224**

874.9   Open wound of other and unspecified parts of neck, complicated **4 , 107 , 224**

875.0   Open wound of chest (wall), without mention of complication **107**

875.1   Open wound of chest (wall), complicated **203**

875*   Open wound of chest (wall) **224**

876*   Open wound of back **107 , 224**

877*   Open wound of buttock **107 , 224**

878.0   Open wound of penis, without mention of complication **125**

878.1   Open wound of penis, complicated **125**

878.2   Open wound of scrotum and testes, without mention of complication **125**

878.3   Open wound of scrotum and testes, complicated **125**

878.4   Open wound of vulva, without mention of complication **128 , 131**

878.5   Open wound of vulva, complicated **128 , 131**

878.6   Open wound of vagina, without mention of complication **128 , 131**

878.7   Open wound of vagina, complicated **128 , 131**

878.8   Open wound of other and unspecified parts of genital organs, without mention of complication **125 , 128 , 131**

878.9   Open wound of other and unspecified parts of genital organs, complicated **125 , 128 , 132**

878*   Open wound of genital organs (external), including traumatic amputation **224**

879.0   Open wound of breast, without mention of complication **107**

879.1   Open wound of breast, complicated **107**

879.2   Open wound of abdominal wall, anterior, without mention of complication **107**

879.3   Open wound of abdominal wall, anterior, complicated **203**

879.4   Open wound of abdominal wall, lateral, without mention of complication **107**

879.5   Open wound of abdominal wall, lateral, complicated **203**

879.6   Open wound of other and unspecified parts of trunk, without mention of complication **107**

879.7   Open wound of other and unspecified parts of trunk, complicated **203**

879.8	Open wound(s) (multiple) of unspecified site(s), without mention of complication **108**
879.9	Open wound(s) (multiple) of unspecified site(s), complicated **203**
879*	Open wound of other and unspecified sites, except limbs **224**
880.0*	Open wound of shoulder and upper arm, without mention of complication **108**
880.1*	Open wound of shoulder and upper arm, complicated **203**
880.2*	Open wound of shoulder and upper arm, with tendon involvement **101**
880*	Open wound of shoulder and upper arm **224**
881.0*	Open wound of elbow, forearm, and wrist, without mention of complication **108**
881.1*	Open wound of elbow, forearm, and wrist, complicated **203**
881.2*	Open wound of elbow, forearm, and wrist, with tendon involvement **101**
881*	Open wound of elbow, forearm, and wrist **224**
882.0	Open wound of hand except finger(s) alone, without mention of complication **108**
882.1	Open wound of hand except finger(s) alone, complicated **203**
882.2	Open wound of hand except finger(s) alone, with tendon involvement **101**
882*	Open wound of hand except finger(s) alone **224**
883.0	Open wound of finger(s), without mention of complication **108**
883.1	Open wound of finger(s), complicated **203**
883.2	Open wound of finger(s), with tendon involvement **101**
883*	Open wound of finger(s) **224**
884.0	Multiple and unspecified open wound of upper limb, without mention of complication **108**
884.1	Multiple and unspecified open wound of upper limb, complicated **204**
884.2	Multiple and unspecified open wound of upper limb, with tendon involvement **101**
884*	Multiple and unspecified open wound of upper limb **224**
885*	Traumatic amputation of thumb (complete) (partial) **204 , 224**
886*	Traumatic amputation of other finger(s) (complete) (partial) **204 , 224**
887*	Traumatic amputation of arm and hand (complete) (partial) **204 , 224 , 228**
890.0	Open wound of hip and thigh, without mention of complication **108**
890.1	Open wound of hip and thigh, complicated **204**
890.2	Open wound of hip and thigh, with tendon involvement **101**
890*	Open wound of hip and thigh **224**
891.0	Open wound of knee, leg (except thigh), and ankle, without mention of complication **108**
891.1	Open wound of knee, leg (except thigh), and ankle, complicated **204**
891.2	Open wound of knee, leg (except thigh), and ankle, with tendon involvement **101**
891*	Open wound of knee, leg (except thigh), and ankle **224**
892.0	Open wound of foot except toe(s) alone, without mention of complication **108**
892.1	Open wound of foot except toe(s) alone, complicated **204**
892.2	Open wound of foot except toe(s) alone, with tendon involvement **101**
892*	Open wound of foot except toe(s) alone **224**
893.0	Open wound of toe(s), without mention of complication **108**
893.1	Open wound of toe(s), complicated **204**
893.2	Open wound of toe(s), with tendon involvement **101**
893*	Open wound of toe(s) **224**
894.0	Multiple and unspecified open wound of lower limb, without mention of complication **108**

894.1	Multiple and unspecified open wound of lower limb, complicated **204**
894.2	Multiple and unspecified open wound of lower limb, with tendon involvement **101**
894*	Multiple and unspecified open wound of lower limb **224**
895*	Traumatic amputation of toe(s) (complete) (partial) **204 , 224**
896*	Traumatic amputation of foot (complete) (partial) **204 , 224 , 228**
897*	Traumatic amputation of leg(s) (complete) (partial) **204 , 224 , 228**
900.0*	Injury to carotid artery **167 , 171 , 224**
900.01	Common carotid artery injury **227**
900.02	External carotid artery injury **227**
900.03	Internal carotid artery injury **227**
900.1	Internal jugular vein injury **167 , 171 , 224 , 227**
900.8*	Injury to other specified blood vessels of head and neck **224**
900.81	External jugular vein injury **167 , 171 , 227**
900.82	Injury to multiple blood vessels of head and neck **4 , 227**
900.89	Injury to other specified blood vessels of head and neck **4**
900.9	Injury to unspecified blood vessel of head and neck **4 , 224**
900*	Injury to blood vessels of head and neck **204**
901.0	Thoracic aorta injury **167 , 171 , 224 , 227**
901.1	Innominate and subclavian artery injury **167 , 171 , 224 , 227**
901.2	Superior vena cava injury **167 , 171 , 224 , 227**
901.3	Innominate and subclavian vein injury **167 , 171 , 224 , 227**
901.4*	Pulmonary blood vessel injury **224 , 227**
901.41	Pulmonary artery injury **167 , 171**
901.42	Pulmonary vein injury **167 , 171**
901.8*	Injury to other specified blood vessels of thorax **224**
901.83	Injury to multiple blood vessels of thorax **227**
901.89	Injury to specified blood vessels of thorax, other **227**
901.9	Injury to unspecified blood vessel of thorax **224 , 227**
901*	Injury to blood vessels of thorax **204**
902.0	Abdominal aorta injury **167 , 171**
902.10	Unspecified inferior vena cava injury **167 , 171**
902*	Injury to blood vessels of abdomen and pelvis **204 , 224 , 228**
903*	Injury to blood vessels of upper extremity **204 , 224 , 228**
904.0	Common femoral artery injury **224 , 228**
904.1	Superficial femoral artery injury **224 , 228**
904.2	Femoral vein injury **224 , 228**
904.3	Saphenous vein injury **224**
904.4*	Popliteal blood vessel vein **224 , 228**
904.5*	Tibial blood vessel(s) injury **224 , 228**
904.6	Deep plantar blood vessels injury **224**
904.7	Injury to specified blood vessels of lower extremity, other **224 , 228**
904.8	Injury to unspecified blood vessel of lower extremity **224**
904.9	Injury to blood vessels, unspecified site **224**
904*	Injury to blood vessels of lower extremity and unspecified sites **204**
905.0	Late effect of fracture of skull and face bones **32**
905.1	Late effect of fracture of spine and trunk without mention of spinal cord lesion **98**
905.2	Late effect of fracture of upper extremities **99**
905.3	Late effect of fracture of neck of femur **99**
905.4	Late effect of fracture of lower extremities **99**
905.5	Late effect of fracture of multiple and unspecified bones **99**
905.6	Late effect of dislocation **100**
905.7	Late effect of sprain and strain without mention of tendon injury **100**

*Code Range

905.8	Late effect of tendon injury **99**
905.9	Late effect of traumatic amputation **99**
906*	Late effects of injuries to skin and subcutaneous tissues **108**
907.0	Late effect of intracranial injury without mention of skull fracture **33**
907.1	Late effect of injury to cranial nerve **33**
907.2	Late effect of spinal cord injury **18**
907.3	Late effect of injury to nerve root(s), spinal plexus(es), and other nerves of trunk **33**
907.4	Late effect of injury to peripheral nerve of shoulder girdle and upper limb **33**
907.5	Late effect of injury to peripheral nerve of pelvic girdle and lower limb **33**
907.9	Late effect of injury to other and unspecified nerve **33**
908.0	Late effect of internal injury to chest **54**
908.1	Late effect of internal injury to intra-abdominal organs **79**
908.2	Late effect of internal injury to other internal organs **125** , **128** , **132**
908.3	Late effect of injury to blood vessel of head, neck, and extremities **67**
908.4	Late effect of injury to blood vessel of thorax, abdomen, and pelvis **67**
908.5	Late effect of foreign body in orifice **204**
908.6	Late effect of certain complications of trauma **204**
908.9	Late effect of unspecified injury **204**
909*	Late effects of other and unspecified external causes **205**
910.0	Face, neck, and scalp, except eye, abrasion or friction burn, without mention of infection **108**
910.1	Face, neck, and scalp except eye, abrasion or friction burn, infected **107**
910.2	Face, neck, and scalp except eye, blister, without mention of infection **109**
910.3	Face, neck, and scalp except eye, blister, infected **109**
910.4	Face, neck, and scalp except eye, insect bite, nonvenomous, without mention of infection **109**
910.5	Face, neck, and scalp except eye, insect bite, nonvenomous, infected **107**
910.6	Face, neck, and scalp, except eye, superficial foreign body (splinter), without major open wound or mention of infection **108**
910.7	Face, neck, and scalp except eye, superficial foreign body (splinter), without major open wound, infected **107**
910.8	Other and unspecified superficial injury of face, neck, and scalp, without mention of infection **108**
910.9	Other and unspecified superficial injury of face, neck, and scalp, infected **107**
910*	Superficial injury of face, neck, and scalp, except eye **224**
911.0	Trunk abrasion or friction burn, without mention of infection **108**
911.1	Trunk abrasion or friction burn, infected **107**
911.2	Trunk blister, without mention of infection **109**
911.3	Trunk blister, infected **107**
911.4	Trunk, insect bite, nonvenomous, without mention of infection **109**
911.5	Trunk, insect bite, nonvenomous, infected **107**
911.6	Trunk, superficial foreign body (splinter), without major open wound and without mention of infection **108**
911.7	Trunk, superficial foreign body (splinter), without major open wound, infected **107**
911.8	Other and unspecified superficial injury of trunk, without mention of infection **108**
911.9	Other and unspecified superficial injury of trunk, infected **107**
911*	Superficial injury of trunk **224**

912.0	Shoulder and upper arm, abrasion or friction burn, without mention of infection **108**
912.1	Shoulder and upper arm, abrasion or friction burn, infected **107**
912.2	Shoulder and upper arm, blister, without mention of infection **108**
912.3	Shoulder and upper arm, blister, infected **107**
912.4	Shoulder and upper arm, insect bite, nonvenomous, without mention of infection **109**
912.5	Shoulder and upper arm, insect bite, nonvenomous, infected **107**
912.6	Shoulder and upper arm, superficial foreign body (splinter), without major open wound and without mention of infection **108**
912.7	Shoulder and upper arm, superficial foreign body (splinter), without major open wound, infected **107**
912.8	Other and unspecified superficial injury of shoulder and upper arm, without mention of infection **108**
912.9	Other and unspecified superficial injury of shoulder and upper arm, infected **107**
912*	Superficial injury of shoulder and upper arm **224**
913.0	Elbow, forearm, and wrist, abrasion or friction burn, without mention of infection **108**
913.1	Elbow, forearm, and wrist, abrasion or friction burn, infected **107**
913.2	Elbow, forearm, and wrist, blister, without mention of infection **109**
913.3	Elbow, forearm, and wrist, blister infected **107**
913.4	Elbow, forearm, and wrist, insect bite, nonvenomous, without mention of infection **109**
913.5	Elbow, forearm, and wrist, insect bite, nonvenomous, infected **107**
913.6	Elbow, forearm, and wrist, superficial foreign body (splinter), without major open wound and without mention of infection **108**
913.7	Elbow, forearm, and wrist, superficial foreign body (splinter), without major open wound, infected **107**
913.8	Other and unspecified superficial injury of elbow, forearm, and wrist, without mention of infection **108**
913.9	Other and unspecified superficial injury of elbow, forearm, and wrist, infected **107**
913*	Superficial injury of elbow, forearm, and wrist **224**
914.0	Hand(s) except finger(s) alone, abrasion or friction burn, without mention of infection **108**
914.1	Hand(s) except finger(s) alone, abrasion or friction burn, infected **107**
914.2	Hand(s) except finger(s) alone, blister, without mention of infection **109**
914.3	Hand(s) except finger(s) alone, blister, infected **107**
914.4	Hand(s) except finger(s) alone, insect bite, nonvenomous, without mention of infection **109**
914.5	Hand(s) except finger(s) alone, insect bite, nonvenomous, infected **107**
914.6	Hand(s) except finger(s) alone, superficial foreign body (splinter), without major open wound and without mention of infection **108**
914.7	Hand(s) except finger(s) alone, superficial foreign body (splinter) without major open wound, infected **107**
914.8	Other and unspecified superficial injury of hand(s) except finger(s) alone, without mention of infection **108**
914.9	Other and unspecified superficial injury of hand(s) except finger(s) alone, infected **107**
914*	Superficial injury of hand(s) except finger(s) alone **224**
915.0	Abrasion or friction burn of finger, without mention of infection **108**
915.1	Finger, abrasion or friction burn, infected **107**
915.2	Finger, blister, without mention of infection **109**
915.3	Finger, blister, infected **107**

Numeric Index to Diseases

915.4	Finger, insect bite, nonvenomous, without mention of infection **109**
915.5	Finger, insect bite, nonvenomous, infected **107**
915.6	Finger, superficial foreign body (splinter), without major open wound and without mention of infection **108**
915.7	Finger, superficial foreign body (splinter), without major open wound, infected **107**
915.8	Other and unspecified superficial injury of finger without mention of infection **108**
915.9	Other and unspecified superficial injury of finger, infected **107**
915*	Superficial injury of finger(s) **224**
916.0	Hip, thigh, leg, and ankle, abrasion or friction burn, without mention of infection **108**
916.1	Hip, thigh, leg, and ankle, abrasion or friction burn, infected **107**
916.2	Hip, thigh, leg, and ankle, blister, without mention of infection **109**
916.3	Hip, thigh, leg, and ankle, blister, infected **107**
916.4	Hip, thigh, leg, and ankle, insect bite, nonvenomous, without mention of infection **109**
916.5	Hip, thigh, leg, and ankle, insect bite, nonvenomous, infected **107**
916.6	Hip, thigh, leg, and ankle, superficial foreign body (splinter), without major open wound and without mention of infection **108**
916.7	Hip, thigh, leg, and ankle, superficial foreign body (splinter), without major open wound, infected **107**
916.8	Other and unspecified superficial injury of hip, thigh, leg, and ankle, without mention of infection **108**
916.9	Other and unspecified superficial injury of hip, thigh, leg, and ankle, infected **107**
916*	Superficial injury of hip, thigh, leg, and ankle **224**
917.0	Abrasion or friction burn of foot and toe(s), without mention of infection **108**
917.1	Foot and toe(s), abrasion or friction burn, infected **107**
917.2	Foot and toe(s), blister, without mention of infection **109**
917.3	Foot and toe(s), blister, infected **107**
917.4	Foot and toe(s), insect bite, nonvenomous, without mention of infection **109**
917.5	Foot and toe(s), insect bite, nonvenomous, infected **107**
917.6	Foot and toe(s), superficial foreign body (splinter), without major open wound and without mention of infection **108**
917.7	Foot and toe(s), superficial foreign body (splinter), without major open wound, infected **107**
917.8	Other and unspecified superficial injury of foot and toes, without mention of infection **108**
917.9	Other and unspecified superficial injury of foot and toes, infected **107**
917*	Superficial injury of foot and toe(s) **224**
918*	Superficial injury of eye and adnexa **40** , **224**
919.0	Abrasion or friction burn of other, multiple, and unspecified sites, without mention of infection **108**
919.1	Other, multiple, and unspecified sites, abrasion or friction burn, infected **107**
919.2	Other, multiple, and unspecified sites, blister, without mention of infection **109**
919.3	Other, multiple, and unspecified sites, blister, infected **107**
919.4	Other, multiple, and unspecified sites, insect bite, nonvenomous, without mention of infection **110**
919.5	Other, multiple, and unspecified sites, insect bite, nonvenomous, infected **107**
919.6	Other, multiple, and unspecified sites, superficial foreign body (splinter), without major open wound and without mention of infection **108**
919.7	Other, multiple, and unspecified sites, superficial foreign body (splinter), without major open wound, infected **107**
919.8	Other and unspecified superficial injury of other, multiple, and unspecified sites, without mention of infection **108**
919.9	Other and unspecified superficial injury of other, multiple, and unspecified sites, infected **107**
919*	Superficial injury of other, multiple, and unspecified sites **224**
920	Contusion of face, scalp, and neck except eye(s) **108** , **224**
921.0	Black eye, not otherwise specified **40**
921.1	Contusion of eyelids and periocular area **40**
921.2	Contusion of orbital tissues **40**
921.3	Contusion of eyeball **40**
921.9	Unspecified contusion of eye **40**
921*	Contusion of eye and adnexa **224**
922.0	Contusion of breast **108**
922.1	Contusion of chest wall **108**
922.2	Contusion of abdominal wall **108**
922.3*	Contusion of trunk **108**
922.4	Contusion of genital organs **125** , **128** , **132**
922.8	Contusion of multiple sites of trunk **108**
922.9	Contusion of unspecified part of trunk **108**
922*	Contusion of trunk **224**
923*	Contusion of upper limb **108** , **224**
924*	Contusion of lower limb and of other and unspecified sites **108** , **224**
925.1	Crushing injury of face and scalp **227**
925.2	Crushing injury of neck **227**
925*	Crushing injury of face, scalp, and neck **4** , **204** , **224**
926.0	Crushing injury of external genitalia **125** , **128** , **132** , **224**
926.1*	Crushing injury of other specified sites of trunk **204** , **224**
926.11	Crushing injury of back **228**
926.12	Crushing injury of buttock **228**
926.19	Crushing injury of other specified sites of trunk **228**
926.8	Crushing injury of multiple sites of trunk **204** , **224** , **228**
926.9	Crushing injury of unspecified site of trunk **204** , **224** , **228**
927.0*	Crushing injury of shoulder and upper arm **224** , **228**
927.01	Crushing injury of scapular region **227**
927.1*	Crushing injury of elbow and forearm **224** , **228**
927.2*	Crushing injury of wrist and hand(s), except finger(s) alone **224**
927.3	Crushing injury of finger(s) **224**
927.8	Crushing injury of multiple sites of upper limb **224** , **228**
927.9	Crushing injury of unspecified site of upper limb **224** , **228**
927*	Crushing injury of upper limb **204**
928.0*	Crushing injury of hip and thigh **224** , **228**
928.1*	Crushing injury of knee and lower leg **224** , **228**
928.2*	Crushing injury of ankle and foot, excluding toe(s) alone **224**
928.3	Crushing injury of toe(s) **224**
928.8	Crushing injury of multiple sites of lower limb **224** , **228**
928.9	Crushing injury of unspecified site of lower limb **224** , **228**
928*	Crushing injury of lower limb **204**
929*	Crushing injury of multiple and unspecified sites **204** , **224**
930*	Foreign body on external eye **40**
931	Foreign body in ear **47**
932	Foreign body in nose **48**
933*	Foreign body in pharynx and larynx **4** , **48**
934.0	Foreign body in trachea **54**
934.1	Foreign body in main bronchus **54**
934.8	Foreign body in other specified parts of trachea, bronchus, and lung **54**
934.9	Foreign body in respiratory tree, unspecified **54**
935.0	Foreign body in mouth **4** , **48**
935.1	Foreign body in esophagus **79**

*Code Range

935.2	Foreign body in stomach **79**	
936	Foreign body in intestine and colon **79**	
937	Foreign body in anus and rectum **79**	
938	Foreign body in digestive system, unspecified **79**	
939.0	Foreign body in bladder and urethra **121**	
939.1	Foreign body in uterus, any part **129 , 132**	
939.2	Foreign body in vulva and vagina **129 , 132**	
939.3	Foreign body in penis **125**	
939.9	Foreign body in unspecified site in genitourinary tract **121**	
940*	Burn confined to eye and adnexa **40**	

941.00 Burn of unspecified degree of unspecified site of face and head **210**

941.01 Burn of unspecified degree of ear (any part) **210**

941.02 Burn of unspecified degree of eye (with other parts of face, head, and neck) **40**

941.03 Burn of unspecified degree of lip(s) **210**

941.04 Burn of unspecified degree of chin **210**

941.05 Burn of unspecified degree of nose (septum) **210**

941.06 Burn of unspecified degree of scalp (any part) **210**

941.07 Burn of unspecified degree of forehead and cheek **210**

941.08 Burn of unspecified degree of neck **210**

941.09 Burn of unspecified degree of multiple sites (except with eye) of face, head, and neck **210**

941.10 Erythema due to burn (first degree) of unspecified site of face and head **210**

941.11 Erythema due to burn (first degree) of ear (any part) **210**

941.12 Erythema due to burn (first degree) of eye (with other parts face, head, and neck) **40**

941.13 Erythema due to burn (first degree) of lip(s) **210**

941.14 Erythema due to burn (first degree) of chin **210**

941.15 Erythema due to burn (first degree) of nose (septum) **210**

941.16 Erythema due to burn (first degree) of scalp (any part) **210**

941.17 Erythema due to burn (first degree) of forehead and cheek **210**

941.18 Erythema due to burn (first degree) of neck **210**

941.19 Erythema due to burn (first degree) of multiple sites (except with eye) of face, head, and neck **210**

941.20 Blisters, with epidermal loss due to burn (second degree) of face and head, unspecified site **210**

941.21 Blisters, with epidermal loss due to burn (second degree) of ear (any part) **210**

941.22 Blisters, with epidermal loss due to burn (second degree) of eye (with other parts of face, head, and neck) **40**

941.23 Blisters, with epidermal loss due to burn (second degree) of lip(s) **210**

941.24 Blisters, with epidermal loss due to burn (second degree) of chin **210**

941.25 Blisters, with epidermal loss due to burn (second degree) of nose (septum) **210**

941.26 Blisters, with epidermal loss due to burn (second degree) of scalp (any part) **210**

941.27 Blisters, with epidermal loss due to burn (second degree) of forehead and cheek **210**

941.28 Blisters, with epidermal loss due to burn (second degree) of neck **210**

941.29 Blisters, with epidermal loss due to burn (second degree) of multiple sites (except with eye) of face, head, and neck **210**

941.3* Full-thickness skin loss due to burn (third degree NOS) of face, head, and neck **207 , 208 , 209 , 210**

941.32 Full-thickness skin loss due to burn (third degree NOS) of eye (with other parts of face, head, and neck) **40**

941.4* Deep necrosis of underlying tissues due to burn (deep third degree) of face, head, and neck without mention of loss of a body part **207 , 208 , 209 , 210**

941.42 Deep necrosis of underlying tissues due to burn (deep third degree) of eye (with other parts of face, head, and neck), without mention of loss of a body part **40**

941.5* Deep necrosis of underlying tissues due to burn (deep third degree) of face, head, and neck with loss of a body part **207 , 208 , 209 , 210**

941.52 Deep necrosis of underlying tissues due to burn (deep third degree) of eye (with other parts of face, head, and neck), with loss of a body part **40**

942.0* Burn of trunk, unspecified degree **210**

942.1* Erythema due to burn (first degree) of trunk **210**

942.2* Blisters with epidermal loss due to burn (second degree) of trunk **210**

942.3* Full-thickness skin loss due to burn (third degree NOS) of trunk **207 , 208 , 209 , 210**

942.4* Deep necrosis of underlying tissues due to burn (deep third degree) of trunk without mention of loss of a body part **207 , 208 , 209 , 210**

942.5* Deep necrosis of underlying tissues due to burn (deep third degree) of trunk with loss of a body part **207 , 208 , 209 , 210**

943.0* Burn of upper limb, except wrist and hand, unspecified degree **210**

943.1* Erythema due to burn (first degree) of upper limb, except wrist and hand **210**

943.2* Blisters with epidermal loss due to burn (second degree) of upper limb, except wrist and hand **211**

943.3* Full-thickness skin loss due to burn (third degree NOS) of upper limb, except wrist and hand **207 , 208 , 209 , 210**

943.4* Deep necrosis of underlying tissues due to burn (deep third degree) of upper limb, except wrist and hand, without mention of loss of a body part **207 , 208 , 209 , 210**

943.5* Deep necrosis of underlying tissues due to burn (deep third degree) of upper limb, except wrist and hand, with loss of a body part **207 , 208 , 209 , 210**

944.0* Burn of wrist(s) and hand(s), unspecified degree **211**

944.1* Erythema due to burn (first degree) of wrist(s) and hand(s) **211**

944.2* Blisters with epidermal loss due to burn (second degree) of wrist(s) and hand(s) **211**

944.3* Full-thickness skin loss due to burn (third degree NOS) of wrist(s) and hand(s) **207 , 208 , 209 , 210**

944.4* Deep necrosis of underlying tissues due to burn (deep third degree) of wrist(s) and hand(s), without mention of loss of a body part **207 , 208 , 209 , 210**

944.5* Deep necrosis of underlying tissues due to burn (deep third degree) of wrist(s) and hand(s), with loss of a body part **207 , 208 , 209 , 210**

945.0* Burn of lower limb(s), unspecified degree **211**

945.1* Erythema due to burn (first degree) of lower limb(s) **211**

945.2* Blisters with epidermal loss due to burn (second degree) of lower limb(s) **211**

945.3* Full-thickness skin loss due to burn (third degree NOS) of lower limb(s) **207 , 208 , 209 , 210**

945.4* Deep necrosis of underlying tissues due to burn (deep third degree) of lower limb(s) without mention of loss of a body part **207 , 208 , 209 , 210**

945.5* Deep necrosis of underlying tissues due to burn (deep third degree) of lower limb(s) with loss of a body part **207 , 208 , 209 , 210**

946.0 Burns of multiple specified sites, unspecified degree **211**

946.1 Erythema due to burn (first degree) of multiple specified sites **211**

946.2 Blisters with epidermal loss due to burn (second degree) of multiple specified sites **211**

946.3 Full-thickness skin loss due to burn (third degree NOS) of multiple specified sites **207 , 208 , 209 , 210**

946.4	Deep necrosis of underlying tissues due to burn (deep third degree) of multiple specified sites, without mention of loss of a body part **207 , 208 , 209 , 210**
946.5	Deep necrosis of underlying tissues due to burn (deep third degree) of multiple specified sites, with loss of a body part **207 , 208 , 209 , 210**
947.0	Burn of mouth and pharynx **4 , 48**
947.1	Burn of larynx, trachea, and lung **54 , 208**
947.2	Burn of esophagus **75**
947.3	Burn of gastrointestinal tract **79**
947.4	Burn of vagina and uterus **129 , 132**
947.8	Burn of other specified sites of internal organs **211**
947.9	Burn of internal organs, unspecified site **211**
948.00	Burn (any degree) involving less than 10% of body surface with third degree burn of less than 10% or unspecified amount **211**
948.10	Burn (any degree) involving 10-19% of body surface with third degree burn of less than 10% or unspecified amount **211**
948.11	Burn (any degree) involving 10-19% of body surface with third degree burn of 10-19% **207 , 208 , 209 , 210**
948.20	Burn (any degree) involving 20-29% of body surface with third degree burn of less than 10% or unspecified amount **211**
948.21	Burn (any degree) involving 20-29% of body surface with third degree burn of 10-19% **207 , 209**
948.22	Burn (any degree) involving 20-29% of body surface with third degree burn of 20-29% **207 , 209**
948.30	Burn (any degree) involving 30-39% of body surface with third degree burn of less than 10% or unspecified amount **211**
948.31	Burn (any degree) involving 30-39% of body surface with third degree burn of 10-19% **207 , 209**
948.32	Burn (any degree) involving 30-39% of body surface with third degree burn of 20-29% **207 , 209**
948.33	Burn (any degree) involving 30-39% of body surface with third degree burn of 30-39% **207 , 209**
948.40	Burn (any degree) involving 40-49% of body surface with third degree burn of less than 10% or unspecified amount **211**
948.41	Burn (any degree) involving 40-49% of body surface with third degree burn of 10-19% **207 , 209**
948.42	Burn (any degree) involving 40-49% of body surface with third degree burn of 20-29% **207 , 209**
948.43	Burn (any degree) involving 40-49% of body surface with third degree burn of 30-39% **207 , 209**
948.44	Burn (any degree) involving 40-49% of body surface with third degree burn of 40-49% **207 , 209**
948.50	Burn (any degree) involving 50-59% of body surface with third degree burn of less than 10% or unspecified amount **211**
948.51	Burn (any degree) involving 50-59% of body surface with third degree burn of 10-19% **207 , 209**
948.52	Burn (any degree) involving 50-59% of body surface with third degree burn of 20-29% **207 , 209**
948.53	Burn (any degree) involving 50-59% of body surface with third degree burn of 30-39% **207 , 209**
948.54	Burn (any degree) involving 50-59% of body surface with third degree burn of 40-49% **207 , 209**
948.55	Burn (any degree) involving 50-59% of body surface with third degree burn of 50-59% **207 , 209**
948.60	Burn (any degree) involving 60-69% of body surface with third degree burn of less than 10% or unspecified amount **211**
948.61	Burn (any degree) involving 60-69% of body surface with third degree burn of 10-19% **207 , 209**
948.62	Burn (any degree) involving 60-69% of body surface with third degree burn of 20-29% **207 , 209**
948.63	Burn (any degree) involving 60-69% of body surface with third degree burn of 30-39% **207 , 209**
948.64	Burn (any degree) involving 60-69% of body surface with third degree burn of 40-49% **207 , 209**
948.65	Burn (any degree) involving 60-69% of body surface with third degree burn of 50-59% **207 , 209**
948.66	Burn (any degree) involving 60-69% of body surface with third degree burn of 60-69% **207 , 209**
948.70	Burn (any degree) involving 70-79% of body surface with third degree burn of less than 10% or unspecified amount **211**
948.71	Burn (any degree) involving 70-79% of body surface with third degree burn of 10-19% **207 , 209**
948.72	Burn (any degree) involving 70-79% of body surface with third degree burn of 20-29% **207 , 209**
948.73	Burn (any degree) involving 70-79% of body surface with third degree burn of 30-39% **207 , 209**
948.74	Burn (any degree) involving 70-79% of body surface with third degree burn of 40-49% **207 , 209**
948.75	Burn (any degree) involving 70-79% of body surface with third degree burn of 50-59% **207 , 209**
948.76	Burn (any degree) involving 70-79% of body surface with third degree burn of 60-69% **207 , 209**
948.77	Burn (any degree) involving 70-79% of body surface with third degree burn of 70-79% **207 , 209**
948.80	Burn (any degree) involving 80-89% of body surface with third degree burn of less than 10% or unspecified amount **211**
948.81	Burn (any degree) involving 80-89% of body surface with third degree burn of 10-19% **207 , 209**
948.82	Burn (any degree) involving 80-89% of body surface with third degree burn of 20-29% **208 , 209**
948.83	Burn (any degree) involving 80-89% of body surface with third degree burn of 30-39% **208 , 209**
948.84	Burn (any degree) involving 80-89% of body surface with third degree burn of 40-49% **208 , 210**
948.85	Burn (any degree) involving 80-89% of body surface with third degree burn of 50-59% **208 , 210**
948.86	Burn (any degree) involving 80-89% of body surface with third degree burn of 60-69% **208 , 210**
948.87	Burn (any degree) involving 80-89% of body surface with third degree burn of 70-79% **208 , 210**
948.88	Burn (any degree) involving 80-89% of body surface with third degree burn of 80-89% **208 , 210**
948.90	Burn (any degree) involving 90% or more of body surface with third degree burn of less than 10% or unspecified amount **211**
948.91	Burn (any degree) involving 90% or more of body surface with third degree burn of 10-19% **208 , 210**
948.92	Burn (any degree) involving 90% or more of body surface with third degree burn of 20-29% **208 , 210**
948.93	Burn (any degree) involving 90% or more of body surface with third degree burn of 30-39% **208 , 210**
948.94	Burn (any degree) involving 90% or more of body surface with third degree burn of 40-49% **208 , 210**
948.95	Burn (any degree) involving 90% or more of body surface with third degree burn of 50-59% **208 , 210**
948.96	Burn (any degree) involving 90% or more of body surface with third degree burn of 60-69% **208 , 210**
948.97	Burn (any degree) involving 90% or more of body surface with third degree burn of 70-79% **208 , 210**
948.98	Burn (any degree) involving 90% or more of body surface with third degree burn of 80-89% **208 , 210**
948.99	Burn (any degree) involving 90% or more of body surface with third degree burn of 90% or more of body surface **208 , 210**
949.0	Burn of unspecified site, unspecified degree **211**
949.1	Erythema due to burn (first degree), unspecified site **211**
949.2	Blisters with epidermal loss due to burn (second degree), unspecified site **211**
949.3	Full-thickness skin loss due to burn (third degree NOS), unspecified site **207 , 208 , 209 , 210**

949.4	Deep necrosis of underlying tissue due to burn (deep third degree), unspecified site without mention of loss of body part **207** , **208** , **209** , **210**	956.5	Injury to other specified nerve(s) of pelvic girdle and lower limb **225**
949.5	Deep necrosis of underlying tissues due to burn (deep third degree, unspecified site with loss of body part **207** , **208** , **209** , **210**	956.8	Injury to multiple nerves of pelvic girdle and lower limb **225** , **229**
950.0	Optic nerve injury **40**	956.9	Injury to unspecified nerve of pelvic girdle and lower limb **225** , **229**
950.1	Injury to optic chiasm **33**	956*	Injury to peripheral nerve(s) of pelvic girdle and lower limb **21**
950.2	Injury to optic pathways **33**	957*	Injury to other and unspecified nerves **21** , **225**
950.3	Injury to visual cortex **33**	958.0	Air embolism as an early complication of trauma **51** , **167** , **171** , **225** , **228**
950.9	Injury to unspecified optic nerve and pathways **33**	958.1	Fat embolism as an early complication of trauma **51** , **167** , **171** , **225** , **228**
950*	Injury to optic nerve and pathways **224**	958.2	Secondary and recurrent hemorrhage as an early complication of trauma **167** , **172** , **205** , **225**
951.0	Injury to oculomotor nerve **21**	958.3	Posttraumatic wound infection not elsewhere classified **167** , **172** , **185** , **225**
951.1	Injury to trochlear nerve **21**	958.4	Traumatic shock **167** , **172** , **205** , **225**
951.2	Injury to trigeminal nerve **21**	958.5	Traumatic anuria **119** , **120** , **167** , **172** , **225**
951.3	Injury to abducens nerve **21**	958.6	Volkmann's ischemic contracture **101** , **225** , **228**
951.4	Injury to facial nerve **21**	958.7	Traumatic subcutaneous emphysema **53** , **167** , **172** , **225**
951.5	Injury to acoustic nerve **48**	958.8	Other early complications of trauma **205** , **225**
951.6	Injury to accessory nerve **21**	958.9*	Traumatic compartment syndrome **205**
951.7	Injury to hypoglossal nerve **21**	958.90	Compartment syndrome, unspecified **225**
951.8	Injury to other specified cranial nerves **21**	958.91	Traumatic compartment syndrome of upper extremity **225** , **228**
951.9	Injury to unspecified cranial nerve **21**	958.92	Traumatic compartment syndrome of lower extremity **225** , **229**
951*	Injury to other cranial nerve(s) **224**	958.93	Traumatic compartment syndrome of abdomen **225** , **228**
952*	Spinal cord injury without evidence of spinal bone injury **18** , **224** , **228**	958.99	Traumatic compartment syndrome of other sites **225**
953.1	Injury to dorsal nerve root **224**	959.0*	Injury, other and unspecified, head, face, and neck **4** , **225**
953.2	Injury to lumbar nerve root **224**	959.1*	Injury, other and unspecified, trunk **225**
953.3	Injury to sacral nerve root **224**	959.2	Injury, other and unspecified, shoulder and upper arm **225**
953.4	Injury to brachial plexus **167** , **171** , **224** , **228**	959.3	Injury, other and unspecified, elbow, forearm, and wrist **225**
953.5	Injury to lumbosacral plexus **224** , **228**	959.4	Injury, other and unspecified, hand, except finger **225**
953.8	Injury to multiple sites of nerve roots and spinal plexus **224** , **228**	959.5	Injury, other and unspecified, finger **225**
953.9	Injury to unspecified site of nerve roots and spinal plexus **224**	959.6	Injury, other and unspecified, hip and thigh **225**
953*	Injury to nerve roots and spinal plexus **21** , **224**	959.7	Injury, other and unspecified, knee, leg, ankle, and foot **225**
954.0	Injury to cervical sympathetic nerve, excluding shoulder and pelvic girdles **224**	959.8	Injury, other and unspecified, other specified sites, including multiple **225**
954.1	Injury to other sympathetic nerve, excluding shoulder and pelvic girdles **224**	959.9	Injury, other and unspecified, unspecified site **225**
954.8	Injury to other specified nerve(s) of trunk, excluding shoulder and pelvic girdles **224** , **228**	959*	Injury, other and unspecified **204**
954.9	Injury to unspecified nerve of trunk, excluding shoulder and pelvic girdles **224** , **228**	960*	Poisoning by antibiotics **204**
954*	Injury to other nerve(s) of trunk, excluding shoulder and pelvic girdles **21**	961*	Poisoning by other anti-infectives **204**
955.0	Injury to axillary nerve **224** , **228**	962*	Poisoning by hormones and synthetic substitutes **204**
955.1	Injury to median nerve **224** , **228**	963*	Poisoning by primarily systemic agents **204**
955.2	Injury to ulnar nerve **224** , **228**	964*	Poisoning by agents primarily affecting blood constituents **204**
955.3	Injury to radial nerve **224** , **228**	965*	Poisoning by analgesics, antipyretics, and antirheumatics **204**
955.4	Injury to musculocutaneous nerve **224**	966*	Poisoning by anticonvulsants and anti-Parkinsonism drugs **204**
955.5	Injury to cutaneous sensory nerve, upper limb **224**	967*	Poisoning by sedatives and hypnotics **204**
955.6	Injury to digital nerve, upper limb **224**	968*	Poisoning by other central nervous system depressants and anesthetics **204**
955.7	Injury to other specified nerve(s) of shoulder girdle and upper limb **224**	969*	Poisoning by psychotropic agents **204**
955.8	Injury to multiple nerves of shoulder girdle and upper limb **225** , **228**	970*	Poisoning by central nervous system stimulants **204**
955.9	Injury to unspecified nerve of shoulder girdle and upper limb **225**	971*	Poisoning by drugs primarily affecting the autonomic nervous system **204**
955*	Injury to peripheral nerve(s) of shoulder girdle and upper limb **21**	972*	Poisoning by agents primarily affecting the cardiovascular system **204**
956.0	Injury to sciatic nerve **225** , **228**	973*	Poisoning by agents primarily affecting the gastrointestinal system **204**
956.1	Injury to femoral nerve **225** , **229**	974*	Poisoning by water, mineral, and uric acid metabolism drugs **204**
956.2	Injury to posterior tibial nerve **225** , **229**	975*	Poisoning by agents primarily acting on the smooth and skeletal muscles and respiratory system **204**
956.3	Injury to peroneal nerve **225** , **229**	976.0	Poisoning by local anti-infectives and anti-inflammatory drugs **204**
956.4	Injury to cutaneous sensory nerve, lower limb **225**		

976.1	Poisoning by antipruritics **204**	
976.2	Poisoning by local astringents and local detergents **204**	
976.3	Poisoning by emollients, demulcents, and protectants **204**	
976.4	Poisoning by keratolytics, keratoplastics, other hair treatment drugs and preparations **204**	
976.5	Poisoning by eye anti-infectives and other eye drugs **40**	
976.6	Poisoning by anti-infectives and other drugs and preparations for ear, nose, and throat **204**	
976.7	Poisoning by dental drugs topically applied **204**	
976.8	Poisoning by other agents primarily affecting skin and mucous membrane **204**	
976.9	Poisoning by unspecified agent primarily affecting skin and mucous membrane **204**	
977*	Poisoning by other and unspecified drugs and medicinal substances **204**	
978*	Poisoning by bacterial vaccines **204**	
979*	Poisoning by other vaccines and biological substances **204**	
980*	Toxic effect of alcohol **204**	
981	Toxic effect of petroleum products **204**	
982*	Toxic effect of solvents other than petroleum-based **204**	
983*	Toxic effect of corrosive aromatics, acids, and caustic alkalis **204**	
984*	Toxic effect of lead and its compounds (including fumes) **204**	
985*	Toxic effect of other metals **204**	
986	Toxic effect of carbon monoxide **204**	
987.9	Toxic effect of unspecified gas, fume, or vapor **208**	
987*	Toxic effect of other gases, fumes, or vapors **204**	
988*	Toxic effect of noxious substances eaten as food **204**	
989*	Toxic effect of other substances, chiefly nonmedicinal as to source **204**	
990	Effects of radiation, unspecified **205**	
991*	Effects of reduced temperature **205**	
992*	Effects of heat and light **205**	
993.0	Barotrauma, otitic **46**	
993.1	Barotrauma, sinus **46**	
993.2	Other and unspecified effects of high altitude **205**	
993.3	Caisson disease **205**	
993.4	Effects of air pressure caused by explosion **205**	
993.8	Other specified effects of air pressure **205**	
993.9	Unspecified effect of air pressure **205**	
994.0	Effects of lightning **205**	
994.1	Drowning and nonfatal submersion **205**	
994.2	Effects of hunger **205**	
994.3	Effects of thirst **205**	
994.4	Exhaustion due to exposure **205**	
994.5	Exhaustion due to excessive exertion **205**	
994.6	Motion sickness **46**	
994.7	Asphyxiation and strangulation **205**	
994.8	Electrocution and nonfatal effects of electric current **205**	
994.9	Other effects of external causes **205**	
995.0	Other anaphylactic reaction **204**	
995.1	Angioneurotic edema not elsewhere classified **204**	
995.2*	Other and unspecified adverse effect of drug, medicinal and biological substance **204**	
995.20	Unspecified adverse effect of unspecified drug, medicinal and biological substance **167 , 172**	
995.21	Arthus phenomenon **167 , 172**	
995.22	Unspecified adverse effect of anesthesia **167 , 172**	
995.23	Unspecified adverse effect of insulin **167 , 172**	
995.27	Other drug allergy **167 , 172**	
995.29	Unspecified adverse effect of other drug, medicinal and biological substance **167 , 172**	

995.3	Allergy, unspecified not elsewhere classified **204**
995.4	Shock due to anesthesia not elsewhere classified **167 , 172 , 205**
995.5*	Child maltreatment syndrome **205**
995.6*	Anaphylactic reaction due to food **204**
995.7	Other adverse food reactions, not elsewhere classified **205**
995.8*	Other specified adverse effects, not elsewhere classified **205**
995.9*	Systemic inflammatory response syndrome (SIRS) **187**
996.00	Mechanical complication of unspecified cardiac device, implant, and graft **69**
996.01	Mechanical complication due to cardiac pacemaker (electrode) **68**
996.02	Mechanical complication due to heart valve prosthesis **68**
996.03	Mechanical complication due to coronary bypass graft **69**
996.04	Mechanical complication due to automatic implantable cardiac defibrillator **68**
996.09	Mechanical complication of cardiac device, implant, and graft, other **69**
996.1	Mechanical complication of other vascular device, implant, and graft **69**
996.2	Mechanical complication of nervous system device, implant, and graft **33**
996.30	Mechanical complication of unspecified genitourinary device, implant, and graft **121**
996.31	Mechanical complication due to urethral (indwelling) catheter **121**
996.32	Mechanical complication due to intrauterine contraceptive device **129 , 132**
996.39	Mechanical complication of genitourinary device, implant, and graft, other **121**
996.4*	Mechanical complication of internal orthopedic device, implant, and graft **99**
996.51	Mechanical complication due to corneal graft **40**
996.52	Mechanical complication due to other tissue graft, not elsewhere classified **204**
996.53	Mechanical complication due to ocular lens prosthesis **40**
996.54	Mechanical complication due to breast prosthesis **107**
996.55	Mechanical complications due to artificial skin graft and decellularized allodermis **204**
996.56	Mechanical complications due to peritoneal dialysis catheter **204**
996.57	Mechanical complication due to insulin pump **204**
996.59	Mechanical complication due to other implant and internal device, not elsewhere classified **204**
996.60	Infection and inflammatory reaction due to unspecified device, implant, and graft **204**
996.61	Infection and inflammatory reaction due to cardiac device, implant, and graft **69**
996.62	Infection and inflammatory reaction due to other vascular device, implant, and graft **69**
996.63	Infection and inflammatory reaction due to nervous system device, implant, and graft **33**
996.64	Infection and inflammatory reaction due to indwelling urinary catheter **121**
996.65	Infection and inflammatory reaction due to other genitourinary device, implant, and graft **121**
996.66	Infection and inflammatory reaction due to internal joint prosthesis **90 , 99**
996.67	Infection and inflammatory reaction due to other internal orthopedic device, implant, and graft **90 , 99**
996.68	Infection and inflammatory reaction due to peritoneal dialysis catheter **204**
996.69	Infection and inflammatory reaction due to other internal prosthetic device, implant, and graft **204**
996.70	Other complications due to unspecified device, implant, and graft **204**

996.71	Other complications due to heart valve prosthesis **69**	
996.72	Other complications due to other cardiac device, implant, and graft **69**	
996.73	Other complications due to renal dialysis device, implant, and graft **69**	
996.74	Other complications due to other vascular device, implant, and graft **69**	
996.75	Other complications due to nervous system device, implant, and graft **33**	
996.76	Other complications due to genitourinary device, implant, and graft **121**	
996.77	Other complications due to internal joint prosthesis **99**	
996.78	Other complications due to other internal orthopedic device, implant, and graft **99**	
996.79	Other complications due to other internal prosthetic device, implant, and graft **204**	
996.80	Complications of transplanted organ, unspecified site **205**	
996.81	Complications of transplanted kidney **121**	
996.82	Complications of transplanted liver **83**	
996.83	Complications of transplanted heart **69**	
996.84	Complications of transplanted lung **54**	
996.85	Complications of bone marrow transplant **176**	
996.86	Complications of transplanted pancreas **83**	
996.87	Complications of transplanted organ, intestine **205**	
996.88	Complications of transplanted organ, stem cell **205**	
996.89	Complications of other transplanted organ **205**	
996.9*	Complications of reattached extremity or body part **99**	
997.0*	Nervous system complications **33 , 168 , 172**	
997.1	Cardiac complications **69 , 168 , 172**	
997.2	Peripheral vascular complications **67 , 168 , 172**	
997.3*	Respiratory complications **54 , 168 , 172**	
997.4*	Digestive system complications, not elsewhere classified **79 , 168 , 172**	
997.5	Urinary complications **121 , 168 , 172**	
997.6*	Amputation stump complication **101**	
997.71	Vascular complications of mesenteric artery **79 , 168 , 172**	
997.72	Vascular complications of renal artery **121 , 168 , 172**	
997.79	Vascular complications of other vessels **67 , 168 , 172**	
997.9*	Complications affecting other specified body systems, not elsewhere classified **205**	
998.0*	Postoperative shock **168 , 172 , 205**	
998.1*	Hemorrhage or hematoma or seroma complicating procedure, not elsewhere classified **205**	
998.11	Hemorrhage complicating a procedure **168 , 172**	
998.12	Hematoma complicating a procedure **168 , 172**	
998.13	Seroma complicating a procedure **168 , 172**	
998.2	Accidental puncture or laceration during procedure **168 , 172 , 205**	
998.3*	Disruption of wound **205**	
998.4	Foreign body accidentally left during procedure, not elsewhere classified **168 , 172 , 205**	
998.5*	Postoperative infection, not elsewhere classified **185**	
998.51	Infected postoperative seroma **168 , 172 , 185**	
998.59	Other postoperative infection **168 , 172 , 185**	
998.6	Persistent postoperative fistula, not elsewhere classified **168 , 172 , 205**	
998.7	Acute reaction to foreign substance accidentally left during procedure, not elsewhere classified **168 , 172 , 205**	
998.81	Emphysema (subcutaneous) (surgical) resulting from a procedure **205**	
998.82	Cataract fragments in eye following surgery **40**	
998.83	Non-healing surgical wound **205**	

998.89	Other specified complications **205**
998.9	Unspecified complication of procedure, not elsewhere classified **168 , 172 , 205**
999.0	Generalized vaccinia as complication of medical care, not elsewhere classified **186**
999.1	Air embolism as complication of medical care, not elsewhere classified **51 , 168 , 172**
999.2	Other vascular complications of medical care, not elsewhere classified **69 , 168 , 172**
999.31	Other and unspecified infection due to central venous catheter **69**
999.32	Bloodstream infection due to central venous catheter **69**
999.33	Local infection due to central venous catheter **69**
999.34	Acute infection following transfusion, infusion, or injection of blood and blood products **168 , 172 , 185 , 187**
999.39	Complications of medical care, NEC, infection following other infusion, injection, transfusion, or vaccination **168 , 172 , 185 , 187**
999.4*	Anaphylactic reaction due to serum **168 , 172 , 204**
999.5*	Other serum reaction, not elsewhere classified **168 , 172 , 204**
999.6*	ABO incompatibility reaction due to transfusion of blood or blood products **168 , 172 , 176**
999.7*	Rh and other non-ABO incompatibility reaction due to transfusion of blood or blood products **168 , 172 , 176**
999.8*	Other and unspecified infusion and transfusion reaction **168 , 172**
999.80	Transfusion reaction, unspecified **176**
999.81	Extravasation of vesicant chemotherapy **69**
999.82	Extravasation of other vesicant agent **69**
999.83	Hemolytic transfusion reaction, incompatibility unspecified **176**
999.84	Acute hemolytic transfusion reaction, incompatibility unspecified **177**
999.85	Delayed hemolytic transfusion reaction, incompatibility unspecified **177**
999.88	Other infusion reaction **69**
999.89	Other transfusion reaction **177**
999.9	Other and unspecified complications of medical care, not elsewhere classified **205**
V01.81	Contact with or exposure to anthrax **173**
V01.89	Contact or exposure to other communicable diseases **173**
V01*	Contact with or exposure to communicable diseases **214**
V02.0	Carrier or suspected carrier of cholera **214**
V02.1	Carrier or suspected carrier of typhoid **214**
V02.2	Carrier or suspected carrier of amebiasis **214**
V02.3	Carrier or suspected carrier of other gastrointestinal pathogens **214**
V02.4	Carrier or suspected carrier of diphtheria **214**
V02.5*	Carrier or suspected carrier of other specified bacterial diseases **214**
V02.6*	Carrier or suspected carrier of viral hepatitis **83**
V02.7	Carrier or suspected carrier of gonorrhea **214**
V02.8	Carrier or suspected carrier of other venereal diseases **214**
V02.9	Carrier or suspected carrier of other specified infectious organism **214**
V03*	Need for prophylactic vaccination and inoculation against bacterial diseases **214**
V04*	Need for prophylactic vaccination and inoculation against certain viral diseases **214**
V05.3	Need for prophylactic vaccination and inoculation against viral hepatitis **173**
V05.4	Need for prophylactic vaccination and inoculation against varicella **173**

V05.8	Need for prophylactic vaccination and inoculation against other specified disease **173**	
V05*	Need for other prophylactic vaccination and inoculation against single diseases **214**	
V06*	Need for prophylactic vaccination and inoculation against combinations of diseases **214**	
V07*	Need for isolation and other prophylactic or treatment measures **215**	
V08	Asymptomatic human immunodeficiency virus (HIV) infection status **186**	
V09*	Infection with drug-resistant microorganisms **187**	
V10.01	Personal history of malignant neoplasm of tongue **4**	
V10.02	Personal history of malignant neoplasm of other and unspecified parts of oral cavity and pharynx **4**	
V10.21	Personal history of malignant neoplasm of larynx **4**	
V10*	Personal history of malignant neoplasm **181** , **183**	
V11*	Personal history of mental disorder **215**	
V12*	Personal history of certain other diseases **215**	
V13.0*	Personal history of disorders of urinary system **215**	
V13.1	Personal history of trophoblastic disease **215**	
V13.21	Personal history of pre-term labor **215**	
V13.22	Personal history of cervical dysplasia **131** , **183**	
V13.23	Personal history of vaginal dysplasia **215**	
V13.24	Personal history of vulvar dysplasia **215**	
V13.29	Personal history of other genital system and obstetric disorders **215**	
V13.3	Personal history of diseases of skin and subcutaneous tissue **215**	
V13.4	Personal history of arthritis **215**	
V13.5*	Personal history of other musculoskeletal disorders **215**	
V13.6*	Personal history of congenital (corrected) malformations **215**	
V13.7	Personal history of perinatal problems **215**	
V13.8*	Personal history of other specified diseases **215**	
V13.9	Personal history of unspecified disease **215**	
V14*	Personal history of allergy to medicinal agents **215**	
V15*	Other personal history presenting hazards to health **215**	
V16*	Family history of malignant neoplasm **215**	
V17*	Family history of certain chronic disabling diseases **215**	
V18*	Family history of certain other specific conditions **215**	
V19*	Family history of other conditions **215**	
V20.1	Health supervision of other healthy infant or child receiving care **173**	
V20.2	Routine infant or child health check **173**	
V20.3*	Newborn health supervision **173**	
V20*	Health supervision of infant or child **215**	
V21*	Constitutional states in development **215**	
V22*	Normal pregnancy **215**	
V23.0	Pregnancy with history of infertility **162**	
V23.1	Pregnancy with history of trophoblastic disease **162**	
V23.2	Pregnancy with history of abortion **162**	
V23.3	Pregnancy with grand multiparity **162**	
V23.4*	Pregnancy with other poor obstetric history **162**	
V23.5	Pregnancy with other poor reproductive history **162**	
V23.7	Insufficient prenatal care **162**	
V23.8*	Supervision of other high-risk pregnancy **162**	
V23.9	Unspecified high-risk pregnancy **162**	
V24.0	Postpartum care and examination immediately after delivery **154**	
V24.1	Postpartum care and examination of lactating mother **215**	
V24.2	Routine postpartum follow-up **215**	
V25.0*	General counseling and advice for contraceptive management **215**	

V25.1*	Encounter for insertion or removal of intrauterine contraceptive device **215**
V25.2	Sterilization **125** , **129** , **132**
V25.3	Menstrual extraction **129** , **132**
V25.4*	Surveillance of previously prescribed contraceptive methods **215**
V25.5	Insertion of implantable subdermal contraceptive **215**
V25.8	Other specified contraceptive management **215**
V25.9	Unspecified contraceptive management **215**
V26.0	Tuboplasty or vasoplasty after previous sterilization **125** , **129** , **132**
V26.1	Artificial insemination **215**
V26.2*	Investigation and testing for procreation management **215**
V26.3*	Genetic counseling and testing **215**
V26.4*	Procreative management, general counseling and advice **215**
V26.5*	Sterilization status **215**
V26.8*	Other specified procreative management **215**
V26.9	Unspecified procreative management **215**
V27*	Outcome of delivery **215**
V28.0	Screening for chromosomal anomalies by amniocentesis **157** , **160**
V28.1	Screening for raised alpha-fetoprotein levels in amniotic fluid **157** , **160**
V28.2	Other antenatal screening based on amniocentesis **157** , **160**
V28.3	Encounter for routine screening for malformation using ultrasonics **215**
V28.4	Antenatal screening for fetal growth retardation using ultrasonics **215**
V28.5	Antenatal screening for isoimmunization **215**
V28.6	Screening of Streptococcus B **215**
V28.8*	Encounter for other specified antenatal screening **215**
V28.9	Unspecified antenatal screening **215**
V29*	Observation and evaluation of newborns and infants for suspected condition not found **173** , **215**
V30.00	Single liveborn, born in hospital, delivered without mention of cesarean delivery **172** , **173**
V30.01	Single liveborn, born in hospital, delivered by cesarean delivery **172** , **173**
V30.1	Single liveborn, born before admission to hospital **172** , **173**
V30.2	Single liveborn, born outside hospital and not hospitalized **174**
V31.00	Twin, mate liveborn, born in hospital, delivered without mention of cesarean delivery **172** , **173**
V31.01	Twin, mate liveborn, born in hospital, delivered by cesarean delivery **172** , **173**
V31.1	Twin birth, mate liveborn, born before admission to hospital **172** , **173**
V31.2	Twin birth, mate liveborn, born outside hospital and not hospitalized **174**
V32.00	Twin, mate stillborn, born in hospital, delivered without mention of cesarean delivery **172** , **173**
V32.01	Twin, mate stillborn, born in hospital, delivered by cesarean delivery **172** , **173**
V32.1	Twin birth, mate stillborn, born before admission to hospital **172** , **173**
V32.2	Twin birth, mate stillborn, born outside hospital and not hospitalized **174**
V33.00	Twin, unspecified whether mate stillborn or liveborn, born in hospital, delivered without mention of cesarean delivery **172** , **173**
V33.01	Twin, unspecified whether mate stillborn or liveborn, born in hospital, delivered by cesarean delivery **172** , **173**
V33.1	Twin birth, unspecified whether mate liveborn or stillborn, born before admission to hospital **172** , **173**
V33.2	Twin birth, unspecified whether mate liveborn or stillborn, born outside hospital and not hospitalized **174**

*Code Range

V34.00	Other multiple, mates all liveborn, born in hospital, delivered without mention of cesarean delivery **172 , 173**	
V34.01	Other multiple, mates all liveborn, born in hospital, delivered by cesarean delivery **172 , 173**	
V34.1	Other multiple birth (three or more), mates all liveborn, born before admission to hospital **172 , 173**	
V34.2	Other multiple birth (three or more), mates all liveborn, born outside hospital and not hospitalized **174**	
V35.00	Other multiple, mates all stillborn, born in hospital, delivered without mention of cesarean delivery **172 , 173**	
V35.01	Other multiple, mates all stillborn, born in hospital, delivered by cesarean delivery **172 , 173**	
V35.1	Other multiple birth (three or more), mates all stillborn, born before admission to hospital **172 , 173**	
V35.2	Other multiple birth (three or more), mates all stillborn, born outside of hospital and not hospitalized **174**	
V36.00	Other multiple, mates liveborn and stillborn, born in hospital, delivered without mention of cesarean delivery **172 , 173**	
V36.01	Other multiple, mates liveborn and stillborn, born in hospital, delivered by cesarean delivery **172 , 173**	
V36.1	Other multiple birth (three or more), mates liveborn and stillborn, born before admission to hospital **172 , 173**	
V36.2	Other multiple birth (three or more), mates liveborn and stillborn, born outside hospital and not hospitalized **174**	
V37.00	Other multiple, unspecified whether mates stillborn or liveborn, born in hospital, delivered without mention of cesarean delivery **173**	
V37.01	Other multiple, unspecified whether mates stillborn or liveborn, born in hospital, delivered by cesarean delivery **173**	
V37.1	Other multiple birth (three or more), unspecified whether mates liveborn or stillborn, born before admission to hospital **173**	
V37.2	Other multiple birth (three or more), unspecified whether mates liveborn or stillborn, born outside of hospital **174**	
V39.00	Liveborn infant, unspecified whether single, twin, or multiple, born in hospital, delivered without mention of cesarean delivery **173**	
V39.01	Liveborn infant, unspecified whether single, twin, or multiple, born in hospital, delivered by cesarean **173**	
V39.1	Liveborn, unspecified whether single, twin or multiple, born before admission to hospital **173**	
V39.2	Liveborn, unspecified whether single, twin, or multiple, born outside hospital and not hospitalized **174**	
V40*	Mental and behavioral problems **215**	
V41*	Problems with special senses and other special functions **215**	
V42.0	Kidney replaced by transplant **2 , 121**	
V42.1	Heart replaced by transplant **69**	
V42.2	Heart valve replaced by transplant **69**	
V42.3	Skin replaced by transplant **110**	
V42.4	Bone replaced by transplant **101**	
V42.5	Cornea replaced by transplant **40**	
V42.6	Lung replaced by transplant **54**	
V42.7	Liver replaced by transplant **83**	
V42.81	Bone marrow replaced by transplant **177**	
V42.82	Peripheral stem cells replaced by transplant **177**	
V42.83	Pancreas replaced by transplant **83**	
V42.84	Organ or tissue replaced by transplant, intestines **215**	
V42.89	Other organ or tissue replaced by transplant **215**	
V42.9	Unspecified organ or tissue replaced by transplant **215**	
V43.0	Eye globe replaced by other means **40**	
V43.1	Lens replaced by other means **40**	
V43.2*	Heart replaced by other means **69**	
V43.3	Heart valve replaced by other means **69**	
V43.4	Blood vessel replaced by other means **69**	

V43.5	Bladder replaced by other means **121**
V43.6*	Joint replaced by other means **101**
V43.7	Limb replaced by other means **101**
V43.8*	Other organ or tissue replaced by other means **215**
V43.89	Other organ or tissue replaced by other means **2**
V44*	Artificial opening status **215**
V45.0*	Postsurgical cardiac pacemaker in situ **215**
V45.1*	Renal dialysis status **215**
V45.2	Presence of cerebrospinal fluid drainage device **215**
V45.3	Intestinal bypass or anastomosis status **215**
V45.4	Arthrodesis status **215**
V45.5*	Presence of contraceptive device **215**
V45.61	Cataract extraction status **215**
V45.69	Other states following surgery of eye and adnexa **215**
V45.71	Acquired absence of breast and nipple **215**
V45.72	Acquired absence of intestine (large) (small) **215**
V45.73	Acquired absence of kidney **215**
V45.74	Acquired absence of organ, other parts of urinary tract **121**
V45.75	Acquired absence of organ, stomach **215**
V45.76	Acquired absence of organ, lung **54**
V45.77	Acquired absence of organ, genital organs **125 , 129 , 132**
V45.78	Acquired absence of organ, eye **40**
V45.79	Other acquired absence of organ **215**
V45.8*	Other postprocedural status **215**
V46*	Other dependence on machines and devices **215**
V47*	Other problems with internal organs **215**
V48*	Problems with head, neck, and trunk **215**
V49*	Problems with limbs and other problems **215**
V50.0	Elective hair transplant for purposes other than remedying health states **110**
V50.1	Other plastic surgery for unacceptable cosmetic appearance **110**
V50.2	Routine or ritual circumcision **125 , 174**
V50.3	Ear piercing **215**
V50.41	Prophylactic breast removal **107**
V50.42	Prophylactic ovary removal **129 , 132**
V50.49	Other prophylactic organ removal **215**
V50.8	Other elective surgery for purposes other than remedying health states **215**
V50.9	Unspecified elective surgery for purposes other than remedying health states **215**
V51*	Aftercare involving the use of plastic surgery **110**
V52.0	Fitting and adjustment of artificial arm (complete) (partial) **99**
V52.1	Fitting and adjustment of artificial leg (complete) (partial) **99**
V52.2	Fitting and adjustment of artificial eye **215**
V52.3	Fitting and adjustment of dental prosthetic device **215**
V52.4	Fitting and adjustment of breast prosthesis and implant **215**
V52.8	Fitting and adjustment of other specified prosthetic device **214**
V52.9	Fitting and adjustment of unspecified prosthetic device **214**
V53.0*	Fitting and adjustment of devices related to nervous system and special senses **33**
V53.1	Fitting and adjustment of spectacles and contact lenses **215**
V53.2	Fitting and adjustment of hearing aid **215**
V53.3*	Fitting and adjustment of cardiac device **69**
V53.4	Fitting and adjustment of orthodontic devices **215**
V53.5*	Fitting and adjustment of other gastrointestinal appliance and device **79**
V53.6	Fitting and adjustment of urinary device **121**
V53.7	Fitting and adjustment of orthopedic device **99**
V53.8	Fitting and adjustment of wheelchair **215**
V53.9*	Fitting and adjustment of other and unspecified device **215**

*Code Range

V78* Special screening for disorders of blood and blood-forming organs **216**

V79* Special screening for mental disorders and developmental handicaps **216**

V80* Special screening for neurological, eye, and ear diseases **216**

V81* Special screening for cardiovascular, respiratory, and genitourinary diseases **216**

V82* Special screening for other condition **216**

V83.01 Asymptomatic hemophilia A carrier **216**

V83.02 Symptomatic hemophilia A carrier **216**

V83.8* Other genetic carrier status **216**

V84.0* Genetic susceptibility to malignant neoplasm **216**

V84.8* Genetic susceptibility to other disease **216**

V85.0 Body Mass Index less than 19, adult **216**

V85.1 Body Mass Index between 19-24, adult **216**

V85.2* Body Mass Index between 25-29, adult **216**

V85.3* Body Mass Index between 30-39, adult **216**

V85.4* Body Mass Index 40 and over, adult **114**

V85.5* Body Mass Index, pediatric **216**

V86* Estrogen receptor status **216**

V87.0* Contact with and (suspected) exposure to hazardous metals **216**

V87.1* Contact with and (suspected) exposure to hazardous aromatic compounds **216**

V87.2 Contact with and (suspected) exposure to other potentially hazardous chemicals **216**

V87.3* Contact with and (suspected) exposure to other potentially hazardous substances **216**

V87.4* Personal history of drug therapy **214**

V88.0* Acquired absence of cervix and uterus **129 , 132**

V88.1* Acquired absence of pancreas **216**

V88.2* Acquired absence of joint **216**

V89.0* Suspected maternal and fetal conditions not found **216**

V90.0* Retained radioactive fragment **216**

V90.1* Retained metal fragments **216**

V90.2 Retained plastic fragments **216**

V90.3* Retained organic fragments **216**

V90.8* Other specified retained foreign body **216**

V90.9 Retained foreign body, unspecified material **216**

V91.0* Twin gestation placenta status **216**

V91.1* Triplet gestation placenta status **216**

V91.2* Quadruplet gestation placenta status **216**

V91.9* Other specified multiple gestation placenta status **216**

Numeric Index to Diseases

Alphabetic Index to Procedures

44.98	(Laparoscopic) adjustment of size of adjustable gastric restrictive device **112, 235**
48.75	Abdominal proctopexy **72**
84.19	Abdominopelvic amputation **60, 89**
48.5*	Abdominoperineal resection of rectum **73, 180, 197**
04.72	Accessory-facial anastomosis **43**
04.73	Accessory-hypoglossal anastomosis **43**
83.11	Achillotenotomy **93**
83.12	Adductor tenotomy of hip **90, 220**
28.6	Adenoidectomy without tonsillectomy **44**
86.72	Advancement of pedicle graft **14, 17, 45, 64, 75, 88, 112, 194**
83.71	Advancement of tendon **105**
94.61	Alcohol rehabilitation **192**
94.63	Alcohol rehabilitation and detoxification **192**
41.02	Allogeneic bone marrow transplant with purging **4**
41.03	Allogeneic bone marrow transplant without purging **4**
41.08	Allogeneic hematopoietic stem cell transplant with purging **4**
41.05	Allogeneic hematopoietic stem cell transplant without purging **4**
52.85	Allotransplantation of cells of islets of Langerhans **119**
24.5	Alveoloplasty **45, 196, 234**
84.17	Amputation above knee **14, 17, 60, 89, 112**
84.01	Amputation and disarticulation of finger **94, 194, 236**
84.02	Amputation and disarticulation of thumb **94, 194**
84.14	Amputation of ankle through malleoli of tibia and fibula **14, 17, 60, 89, 112**
67.4	Amputation of cervix **129**
84.1*	Amputation of lower limb **105, 202**
64.3	Amputation of penis **123**
84.11	Amputation of toe **14, 16, 63, 93, 112**
84.0*	Amputation of upper limb **63, 105**
84.12	Amputation through foot **14, 17, 60, 89, 112**
84.05	Amputation through forearm **89, 201**
84.03	Amputation through hand **89, 201**
84.07	Amputation through humerus **89, 202**
84.91	Amputation, not otherwise specified **60, 89, 105, 202**
49.72	Anal cerclage **74, 105**
49.12	Anal fistulectomy **105**
49.11	Anal fistulotomy **105**
51.3*	Anastomosis of gallbladder or bile duct **81, 180, 198**
51.32	Anastomosis of gallbladder to intestine **75**
51.37	Anastomosis of hepatic duct to gastrointestinal tract **75**
55.86	Anastomosis of kidney **198**
52.96	Anastomosis of pancreas **81, 198**
45.92	Anastomosis of small intestine to rectal stump **180**
45.95	Anastomosis to anus **180**
88.53	Angiocardiography of left heart structures **56, 57, 59, 65**
88.52	Angiocardiography of right heart structures **56, 57, 59, 65**
39.50	Angioplasty of other non-coronary vessel(s) **13, 50, 63, 74, 82, 95, 105, 113, 118, 197**
81.11	Ankle fusion **91, 114**
35.33	Annuloplasty **56**
48.62	Anterior resection of rectum with synchronous colostomy **64**
42.6*	Antesternal anastomosis of esophagus **72, 179, 197**
42.65	Antesternal esophageal anastomosis with interposition of colon **45**

42.63	Antesternal esophageal anastomosis with interposition of small bowel **45**
42.61	Antesternal esophagoesophagostomy **45**
42.62	Antesternal esophagogastrostomy **45**
39.25	Aorta-iliac-femoral bypass **59, 105, 113, 197**
39.24	Aorta-renal bypass **59, 117, 197**
39.22	Aorta-subclavian-carotid bypass **13, 59, 197**
47.0*	Appendectomy **73**
47.91	Appendicostomy **73**
78.14	Application of external fixator device, carpals and metacarpals **94, 194**
78.15	Application of external fixator device, femur **89, 199, 220**
78.12	Application of external fixator device, humerus **91, 199**
78.19	Application of external fixator device, other **95, 199**
78.16	Application of external fixator device, patella **90, 199**
78.13	Application of external fixator device, radius and ulna **94, 199**
78.11	Application of external fixator device, scapula, clavicle, and thorax [ribs and sternum] **51, 95, 199**
78.18	Application of external fixator device, tarsals and metatarsals **93, 199**
78.17	Application of external fixator device, tibia and fibula **91, 199**
78.10	Application of external fixator device, unspecified site **95, 199**
39.27	Arteriovenostomy for renal dialysis **64, 74, 113, 118, 197**
81.1*	Arthrodesis and arthroereisis of foot and ankle **201**
81.24	Arthrodesis of elbow **93, 201**
81.21	Arthrodesis of hip **90, 201, 220**
81.22	Arthrodesis of knee **90, 201**
81.29	Arthrodesis of other specified joint **96, 201**
81.23	Arthrodesis of shoulder **93, 114, 201**
81.20	Arthrodesis of unspecified joint **96, 201**
81.8*	Arthroplasty and repair of shoulder and elbow **201**
81.74	Arthroplasty of carpocarpal or carpometacarpal joint with implant **14, 16, 93, 194**
81.75	Arthroplasty of carpocarpal or carpometacarpal joint without implant **14, 16, 93, 194**
81.71	Arthroplasty of metacarpophalangeal and interphalangeal joint with implant **14, 16, 93, 194**
81.72	Arthroplasty of metacarpophalangeal and interphalangeal joint without implant **14, 16, 93, 194**
80.2*	Arthroscopy **93, 201**
80.26	Arthroscopy of knee **114, 236**
80.07	Arthrotomy for removal of prosthesis without replacement, ankle **92, 201**
80.02	Arthrotomy for removal of prosthesis without replacement, elbow **92, 201**
80.08	Arthrotomy for removal of prosthesis without replacement, foot and toe **92, 201**
80.04	Arthrotomy for removal of prosthesis without replacement, hand and finger **92, 194**
80.05	Arthrotomy for removal of prosthesis without replacement, hip **88, 201, 220**
80.06	Arthrotomy for removal of prosthesis without replacement, knee **88, 201**
80.09	Arthrotomy for removal of prosthesis without replacement, other specified site **92, 201**
80.01	Arthrotomy for removal of prosthesis without replacement, shoulder **92, 201**

*Code Range

79.11	Closed reduction of fracture of humerus with internal fixation **91, 200**
79.19	Closed reduction of fracture of other specified bone, except facial bones, with internal fixation **95, 200**
79.18	Closed reduction of fracture of phalanges of foot with internal fixation **93, 200**
79.14	Closed reduction of fracture of phalanges of hand with internal fixation **94, 194**
79.12	Closed reduction of fracture of radius and ulna with internal fixation **94, 200, 236**
79.17	Closed reduction of fracture of tarsals and metatarsals with internal fixation **93, 200**
79.16	Closed reduction of fracture of tibia and fibula with internal fixation **91, 200**
79.10	Closed reduction of fracture with internal fixation, unspecified site **95, 200**
79.45	Closed reduction of separated epiphysis of femur **90, 200, 220**
79.41	Closed reduction of separated epiphysis of humerus **91, 200**
79.49	Closed reduction of separated epiphysis of other specified bone **96, 200**
79.42	Closed reduction of separated epiphysis of radius and ulna **94, 200**
79.46	Closed reduction of separated epiphysis of tibia and fibula **91, 200**
79.40	Closed reduction of separated epiphysis, unspecified site **96, 200**
49.73	Closure of anal fistula **74, 105, 197**
47.92	Closure of appendiceal fistula **72, 197**
29.52	Closure of branchial cleft fistula **44, 104**
51.92	Closure of cholecystostomy **81, 198**
57.82	Closure of cystostomy **117, 124, 130, 180, 198, 235**
42.83	Closure of esophagostomy **45, 72, 179, 197**
31.72	Closure of external fistula of trachea **44, 50, 64, 104**
34.83	Closure of fistula of diaphragm **196**
46.72	Closure of fistula of duodenum **72**
46.76	Closure of fistula of large intestine **72**
27.53	Closure of fistula of mouth **45, 196, 234**
46.74	Closure of fistula of small intestine, except duodenum **72**
69.42	Closure of fistula of uterus **73**
46.5*	Closure of intestinal stoma **73, 197**
50.61	Closure of laceration of liver **81**
21.82	Closure of nasal fistula **44, 234**
55.82	Closure of nephrostomy and pyelostomy **198**
51.93	Closure of other biliary fistula **81, 180, 198**
55.83	Closure of other fistula of kidney **198**
29.53	Closure of other fistula of pharynx **44, 196**
34.73	Closure of other fistula of thorax **50, 196**
31.73	Closure of other fistula of trachea **44, 50, 72**
56.84	Closure of other fistula of ureter **73, 124, 130, 180, 198**
58.43	Closure of other fistula of urethra **123, 130, 180, 198**
44.63	Closure of other gastric fistula **72, 82, 180, 197**
48.73	Closure of other rectal fistula **74, 105, 129**
48.72	Closure of proctostomy **72**
46.52	Closure of stoma of large intestine **235**
56.83	Closure of ureterostomy **124, 130, 180, 198**
58.42	Closure of urethrostomy **198**
46.10	Colostomy, not otherwise specified **72, 180, 197**
94.67	Combined alcohol and drug rehabilitation **192**
94.69	Combined alcohol and drug rehabilitation and detoxification **192**
33.6	Combined heart-lung transplantation **1**
88.54	Combined right and left heart angiocardiography **56, 57, 59, 65**
37.23	Combined right and left heart cardiac catheterization **56, 57, 58, 65**
51.42	Common duct exploration for relief of other obstruction **81, 180, 198**
51.41	Common duct exploration for removal of calculus **81**
25.3	Complete glossectomy **43**
30.3	Complete laryngectomy **2**
55.5*	Complete nephrectomy **117, 198**
06.4	Complete thyroidectomy **112**
67.2	Conization of cervix **129, 140, 235**
10.4*	Conjunctivoplasty **195, 233**
18.71	Construction of auricle of ear **104, 234**
64.43	Construction of penis **198**
46.22	Continent ileostomy **72, 180, 197**
96.72	Continuous invasive mechanical ventilation for 96 consecutive hours or more **1, 54, 187, 207, 209**
96.71	Continuous invasive mechanical ventilation for less than 96 consecutive hours **54**
96.70	Continuous invasive mechanical ventilation of unspecified duration **54**
49.95	Control of (postoperative) hemorrhage of anus **197**
57.93	Control of (postoperative) hemorrhage of bladder **117, 198**
60.94	Control of (postoperative) hemorrhage of prostate **124, 198, 233**
21.05	Control of epistaxis by (transantral) ligation of the maxillary artery **44, 64, 196**
21.07	Control of epistaxis by excision of nasal mucosa and skin grafting of septum and lateral nasal wall **44, 64, 196**
21.04	Control of epistaxis by ligation of ethmoidal arteries **44, 64, 196**
21.06	Control of epistaxis by ligation of the external carotid artery **44, 64, 196**
21.09	Control of epistaxis by other means **44, 64, 196, 234**
28.7	Control of hemorrhage after tonsillectomy and adenoidectomy **44, 196**
39.41	Control of hemorrhage following vascular surgery **63, 113**
39.98	Control of hemorrhage, not otherwise specified **44, 50, 64, 74, 82, 95, 105, 113, 119, 124, 130, 140, 179, 197**
41.06	Cord blood stem cell transplant **4**
12.35	Coreoplasty **37**
11.6*	Corneal transplant **195, 233**
11.60	Corneal transplant, not otherwise specified **37**
88.55	Coronary arteriography using single catheter **56, 57, 59, 65**
88.56	Coronary arteriography using two catheters **56, 57, 59, 65**
27.62	Correction of cleft palate **14, 16, 44**
75.36	Correction of fetal defect **141**
08.38	Correction of lid retraction **104, 113**
86.85	Correction of syndactyly **94, 195**
55.87	Correction of ureteropelvic junction **198**
01.20	Cranial implantation or replacement of neurostimulator pulse generator **9, 11, 13, 16**
04.5	Cranial or peripheral nerve graft **14, 16, 195**
02.0*	Cranioplasty **8, 10, 95, 195**
35.94	Creation of conduit between atrium and pulmonary artery **58**
35.93	Creation of conduit between left ventricle and aorta **58**
35.92	Creation of conduit between right ventricle and pulmonary artery **58**
54.93	Creation of cutaneoperitoneal fistula **64, 75, 82, 119, 180, 198**
54.94	Creation of peritoneovascular shunt **75, 81, 180**
35.42	Creation of septal defect in heart **58**
29.31	Cricopharyngeal myotomy **44**
11.43	Cryotherapy of corneal lesion **195**
70.12	Culdotomy **130, 141**

Alphabetic Index to Procedures

*Code Range

38.16	Endarterectomy of abdominal arteries **59, 74, 118, 197**
38.14	Endarterectomy of aorta **59, 74, 197**
38.11	Endarterectomy of intracranial vessels **8, 10, 11**
38.18	Endarterectomy of lower limb arteries **63, 113, 197**
38.15	Endarterectomy of other thoracic vessels **50, 59, 197**
38.12	Endarterectomy of other vessels of head and neck **13, 44, 63, 113, 197**
38.13	Endarterectomy of upper limb vessels **63, 113, 197**
38.10	Endarterectomy, unspecified site **13, 63, 196**
68.23	Endometrial ablation **127, 129**
39.72	Endovascular (total) embolization or occlusion of head and neck vessels **8, 10, 11, 59, 60, 118, 197**
39.75	Endovascular embolization or occlusion of vessel(s) of head or neck using bare coils **8, 10, 11, 59, 60, 118, 197**
39.76	Endovascular embolization or occlusion of vessel(s) of head or neck using bioactive coils **8, 10, 11, 59, 60, 119, 197**
39.78	Endovascular implantation of branching or fenestrated graft(s) in aorta **59, 60**
39.73	Endovascular implantation of graft in thoracic aorta **56, 118, 197**
39.71	Endovascular implantation of other graft in abdominal aorta **59, 60, 118, 197**
39.74	Endovascular removal of obstruction from head and neck vessel(s) **8, 10, 11, 197**
35.05	Endovascular replacement of aortic valve **56**
35.07	Endovascular replacement of pulmonary valve **56**
35.09	Endovascular replacement of unspecified heart valve **56**
45.0*	Enterotomy **197**
16.4*	Enucleation of eyeball **37, 196, 234**
63.4	Epididymectomy **123**
63.92	Epididymotomy **123**
63.83	Epididymovasostomy **123**
30.21	Epiglottidectomy **44**
11.76	Epikeratophakia **37**
42.40	Esophagectomy, not otherwise specified **44**
44.65	Esophagogastroplasty **72, 197**
42.7	Esophagomyotomy **45, 72, 179, 197**
42.1*	Esophagostomy **72, 179, 197**
42.10	Esophagostomy, not otherwise specified **44**
22.63	Ethmoidectomy **234**
16.3*	Evisceration of eyeball **37, 196, 234**
76.4*	Excision and reconstruction of facial bones **95, 199**
77.5*	Excision and repair of bunion and other toe deformities **93, 236**
41.93	Excision of accessory spleen **176, 179, 197**
04.01	Excision of acoustic neuroma **8, 10, 11, 43**
51.62	Excision of ampulla of Vater (with reimplantation of common duct) **75, 81**
37.32	Excision of aneurysm of heart **58**
49.6	Excision of anus **74, 235**
40.23	Excision of axillary lymph node **44, 50, 64, 74, 95, 235**
77.70	Excision of bone for graft, unspecified site **92, 199**
29.2	Excision of branchial cleft cyst or vestige **44, 104**
77.74	Excision of carpals and metacarpals for graft **94, 194**
63.2	Excision of cyst of epididymis **123, 235**
51.61	Excision of cystic duct remnant **81, 198**
40.21	Excision of deep cervical lymph node **44, 50, 64, 74, 95, 113, 235**
24.4	Excision of dental lesion of jaw **45, 234**
85.24	Excision of ectopic breast tissue **106**
42.4*	Excision of esophagus **72, 179, 197**
77.75	Excision of femur for graft **92, 199**
49.46	Excision of hemorrhoids **74, 140, 235**
77.72	Excision of humerus for graft **92, 199**

61.2	Excision of hydrocele (of tunica vaginalis) **123, 235**
40.24	Excision of inguinal lymph node **50, 64, 74, 95, 119, 124, 130, 140, 235**
40.22	Excision of internal mammary lymph node **50**
80.51	Excision of intervertebral disc **12, 13, 90, 91, 201**
09.6	Excision of lacrimal sac and passage **195, 233**
12.44	Excision of lesion of ciliary body **37**
16.93	Excision of lesion of eye, unspecified structure **37, 104, 196, 234**
12.42	Excision of lesion of iris **37**
09.21	Excision of lesion of lacrimal gland **195**
22.62	Excision of lesion of maxillary sinus with other approach **95**
20.51	Excision of lesion of middle ear **234**
83.32	Excision of lesion of muscle **105, 236**
82.2*	Excision of lesion of muscle, tendon, and fascia of hand **94, 194**
83.3*	Excision of lesion of muscle, tendon, fascia, and bursa **92, 201**
16.92	Excision of lesion of orbit **37, 43, 196, 234**
83.39	Excision of lesion of other soft tissue **45, 105, 114, 236**
26.2*	Excision of lesion of salivary gland **45, 234**
01.6	Excision of lesion of skull **8, 10, 11, 43, 92, 179, 220**
83.31	Excision of lesion of tendon sheath **114**
82.21	Excision of lesion of tendon sheath of hand **105, 114, 236**
28.92	Excision of lesion of tonsil and adenoid **44**
61.92	Excision of lesion of tunica vaginalis other than hydrocele **123**
27.3*	Excision of lesion or tissue of bony palate **234**
01.51	Excision of lesion or tissue of cerebral meninges **8, 10, 11, 220**
34.81	Excision of lesion or tissue of diaphragm **95**
09.2*	Excision of lesion or tissue of lacrimal gland **233**
45.41	Excision of lesion or tissue of large intestine **74, 113, 180, 235**
41.42	Excision of lesion or tissue of spleen **197**
06.6	Excision of lingual thyroid **44, 112**
28.5	Excision of lingual tonsil **44**
08.24	Excision of major lesion of eyelid, full-thickness **104**
08.23	Excision of major lesion of eyelid, partial-thickness **104**
83.43	Excision of muscle or fascia for graft **14, 16**
85.25	Excision of nipple **106**
51.69	Excision of other bile duct **75, 81**
77.79	Excision of other bone for graft, except facial bones **45, 92, 199**
82.29	Excision of other lesion of soft tissue of hand **105, 236**
63.3	Excision of other lesion or tissue of spermatic cord and epididymis **123, 235**
08.22	Excision of other minor lesion of eyelid **104**
77.76	Excision of patella for graft **92, 199**
59.91	Excision of perirenal or perivesical tissue **118, 124, 180**
58.92	Excision of periurethral tissue **118**
86.21	Excision of pilonidal cyst or sinus **105, 202, 236**
18.21	Excision of preauricular sinus **44, 104, 234**
11.3*	Excision of pterygium **37, 233**
11.32	Excision of pterygium with corneal graft **195**
77.73	Excision of radius and ulna for graft **92, 199**
77.71	Excision of scapula, clavicle, and thorax (ribs and sternum) for graft **51, 92, 199**
80.6	Excision of semilunar cartilage of knee **90, 114, 201, 236**
60.73	Excision of seminal vesicle **124**
86.91	Excision of skin for graft **14, 17, 45, 65, 104, 112, 202**
77.78	Excision of tarsals and metatarsals for graft **93, 199**
83.41	Excision of tendon for graft **14, 16**
06.7	Excision of thyroglossal duct or tract **44, 112**
77.77	Excision of tibia and fibula for graft **92, 199**
28.4	Excision of tonsil tag **44**

Alphabetic Index to Procedures

63.1	Excision of varicocele and hydrocele of spermatic cord **123, 235**	
85.2*	Excision or destruction of breast tissue **202**	
85.20	Excision or destruction of breast tissue, not otherwise specified **106, 236**	
80.50	Excision or destruction of intervertebral disc, unspecified **12, 13, 90, 91, 201**	
34.4	Excision or destruction of lesion of chest wall **50, 92, 104, 113, 179, 234**	
70.32	Excision or destruction of lesion of cul-de-sac **141**	
66.61	Excision or destruction of lesion of fallopian tube **127, 129**	
12.4*	Excision or destruction of lesion of iris and ciliary body **195, 233**	
12.84	Excision or destruction of lesion of sclera **37**	
03.4	Excision or destruction of lesion of spinal cord or spinal meninges **12, 13, 90, 91, 179**	
70.33	Excision or destruction of lesion of vagina **105, 148**	
54.3	Excision or destruction of lesion or tissue of abdominal wall or umbilicus **75, 92, 105, 113, 180, 235**	
10.3*	Excision or destruction of lesion or tissue of conjunctiva **195, 233**	
08.2*	Excision or destruction of lesion or tissue of eyelid **37, 195, 233**	
30.0*	Excision or destruction of lesion or tissue of larynx **44**	
34.3	Excision or destruction of lesion or tissue of mediastinum **50, 113, 179, 234**	
29.3*	Excision or destruction of lesion or tissue of pharynx **72**	
41.4*	Excision or destruction of lesion or tissue of spleen **176, 179**	
25.1	Excision or destruction of lesion or tissue of tongue **45, 64, 234**	
37.34	Excision or destruction of other lesion or tissue of heart, endovascular approach **62, 63**	
37.33	Excision or destruction of other lesion or tissue of heart, open approach **58**	
37.37	Excision or destruction of other lesion or tissue of heart, thoracoscopic approach **58**	
54.4	Excision or destruction of peritoneal tissue **75, 82, 113, 130, 180, 235**	
62.2	Excision or destruction of testicular lesion **123**	
11.4*	Excision or destruction of tissue or other lesion of cornea **37, 233**	
71.24	Excision or other destruction of Bartholin's gland (cyst) **105, 129, 141, 235**	
86.22	Excisional debridement of wound, infection, or burn **14, 17, 37, 45, 51, 64, 75, 82, 88, 104, 112, 119, 124, 130, 176, 194**	
16.51	Exenteration of orbit with removal of adjacent structures **43, 95**	
16.52	Exenteration of orbit with therapeutic removal of orbital bone **43**	
16.5*	Exenteration of orbital contents **37, 196, 234**	
03.0*	Exploration and decompression of spinal canal structures **12, 13, 195**	
07.0*	Exploration of adrenal field **112**	
51.51	Exploration of common bile duct **81**	
82.01	Exploration of tendon sheath of hand **94, 194, 236**	
07.91	Exploration of thymus field **195**	
54.11	Exploratory laparotomy **50, 64, 82, 105, 113, 123, 140, 176, 180**	
34.02	Exploratory thoracotomy **50, 64, 118, 179, 196**	
42.12	Exteriorization of esophageal pouch **44**	
46.0*	Exteriorization of intestine **72, 180, 197**	
46.03	Exteriorization of large intestine **64**	
22.3*	External maxillary antrotomy **45**	
13.4*	Extracapsular extraction of lens by fragmentation and aspiration technique **234**	
13.2	Extracapsular extraction of lens by linear extraction technique **234**	
13.3	Extracapsular extraction of lens by simple aspiration (and irrigation) technique **234**	
39.65	Extracorporeal membrane oxygenation (ECMO) **1**	

98.51	Extracorporeal shockwave lithotripsy (ESWL) of the kidney, ureter and/or bladder **120**
02.3*	Extracranial ventricular shunt **13, 179, 195**
39.28	Extracranial-intracranial (EC-IC) vascular bypass **8, 10, 11, 197**
86.90	Extraction of fat for graft or banking **105**
74.2	Extraperitoneal cesarean section **140**
95.04	Eye examination under anesthesia **37, 236**
86.82	Facial rhytidectomy **45, 202, 236**
12.5*	Facilitation of intraocular circulation **195, 233**
83.14	Fasciotomy **14, 16, 92, 105**
86.87	Fat graft of skin and subcutaneous tissue **45, 112, 202**
85.55	Fat graft to breast **106**
20.6*	Fenestration of inner ear **44**
84.22	Finger reattachment **94, 194**
09.8*	Fistulization of lacrimal tract to nasal cavity **195, 233**
81.42	Five-in-one repair of knee **90**
46.6*	Fixation of intestine **73**
84.26	Foot reattachment **89, 202, 220**
84.23	Forearm, wrist, or hand reattachment **90, 202, 220**
02.03	Formation of cranial bone flap **11, 43, 220**
21.62	Fracture of the turbinates **196, 234**
86.60	Free skin graft, not otherwise specified **14, 17, 64, 75, 88, 104, 112, 194, 207, 208, 236**
39.91	Freeing of vessel **63, 74, 113, 197**
22.4*	Frontal sinusotomy and sinusectomy **45**
85.83	Full-thickness graft to breast **104, 194, 207, 208**
86.61	Full-thickness skin graft to hand **14, 17, 64, 94, 104, 195, 207, 208**
27.55	Full-thickness skin graft to lip and mouth **45, 104, 196, 234**
86.63	Full-thickness skin graft to other sites **14, 17, 45, 64, 75, 88, 104, 112, 194, 207, 208**
81.64	Fusion or refusion of 9 or more vertebrae **87, 88**
04.05	Gasserian ganglionectomy **14, 16, 43, 195**
44.3*	Gastroenterostomy without gastrectomy **72, 112, 180**
44.64	Gastropexy **72, 197**
43.0	Gastrotomy **72, 82, 113, 180, 197**
24.2	Gingivoplasty **45, 196**
12.51	Goniopuncture without goniotomy **37**
12.53	Goniotomy with goniopuncture **37**
12.52	Goniotomy without goniopuncture **37**
49.74	Gracilis muscle transplant for anal incontinence **74**
83.82	Graft of muscle or fascia **14, 16, 93, 105**
36.2	Heart revascularization by arterial implant **58**
37.51	Heart transplantation **1**
30.1	Hemilaryngectomy **43, 50, 196**
01.52	Hemispherectomy **8, 10, 11, 195, 220**
50.0	Hepatotomy **81, 197**
86.65	Heterograft to skin **14, 17, 64, 75, 88, 104, 194, 207, 208, 236**
52.83	Heterotransplant of pancreas **81, 113**
00.15	High-dose infusion interleukin-2 [IL-2] **182**
86.66	Homograft to skin **14, 17, 45, 64, 75, 88, 104, 194, 207, 208**
52.82	Homotransplant of pancreas **2, 81, 113**
70.31	Hymenectomy **148**
70.76	Hymenorrhaphy **129, 235**
04.71	Hypoglossal-facial anastomosis **43**
07.6*	Hypophysectomy **8, 10, 11, 112**
68.0	Hysterotomy **127, 129, 140, 199**
74.91	Hysterotomy to terminate pregnancy **141**
46.20	Ileostomy, not otherwise specified **72, 180, 197**
37.61	Implant of pulsation balloon **59**

*Code Range

37.65	Implant of single ventricular (extracorporeal) external heart assist system **1**, **56**
58.93	Implantation of artificial urinary sphincter (AUS) **118**, **198**
37.95	Implantation of automatic cardioverter/defibrillator leads(s) only **57**, **58**, **65**
37.96	Implantation of automatic cardioverter/defibrillator pulse generator only **57**, **58**, **62**
00.51	Implantation of cardiac resynchronization defibrillator, total system (CRT-D) **57**
00.50	Implantation of cardiac resynchronization pacemaker without mention of defibrillation, total system (CRT-P) **60**
37.67	Implantation of cardiomyostimulation system **59**
00.10	Implantation of chemotherapeutic agent **9**
34.85	Implantation of diaphragmatic pacemaker **196**
20.95	Implantation of electromagnetic hearing device **44**
57.96	Implantation of electronic bladder stimulator **118**
56.92	Implantation of electronic ureteral stimulator **117**
84.44	Implantation of prosthetic device of arm **94**, **202**
84.48	Implantation of prosthetic device of leg **92**, **202**
17.51	Implantation of rechargeable cardiac contractility modulation [CCM], total system **57**
37.52	Implantation of total internal biventricular heart replacement system **1**
84.40	Implantation or fitting of prosthetic limb device, not otherwise specified **96**, **202**
37.60	Implantation or insertion of biventricular external heart assist system **1**, **56**
92.27	Implantation or insertion of radioactive elements **14**, **17**, **45**, **51**, **62**, **65**, **75**, **105**, **114**, **119**, **124**, **129**, **202**, **236**
37.94	Implantation or replacement of automatic cardioverter/ defibrillator, total system (AICD) **57**
17.52	Implantation or replacement of cardiac contractility modulation [CCM] rechargeable pulse generator only **62**
00.54	Implantation or replacement of cardiac resynchronization defibrillator pulse generator device only (CRT-D) **57**, **58**, **62**
00.53	Implantation or replacement of cardiac resynchronization pacemaker pulse generator only (CRT-P) **60**, **61**, **63**
20.98	Implantation or replacement of cochlear prosthetic device, multiple channel **43**
20.96	Implantation or replacement of cochlear prosthetic device, not otherwise specified **43**
20.97	Implantation or replacement of cochlear prosthetic device, single channel **43**
02.93	Implantation or replacement of intracranial neurostimulator lead(s) **8**, **9**, **10**, **11**, **179**, **195**
55.97	Implantation or replacement of mechanical kidney **117**, **198**
04.92	Implantation or replacement of peripheral neurostimulator lead(s) **14**, **16**, **18**, **43**, **63**, **95**, **118**, **124**, **130**
66.93	Implantation or replacement of prosthesis of fallopian tube **127**, **129**
03.93	Implantation or replacement of spinal neurostimulator lead(s) **12**, **13**, **90**, **91**, **118**, **123**, **130**, **179**, **195**
00.57	Implantation or replacement of subcutaneous device for intracardiac or great vessel hemodynamic monitoring **63**, **65**
00.52	Implantation or replacement of transvenous lead (electrode) into left ventricular coronary venous system **57**, **60**, **65**
49.75	Implantation or revision of artificial anal sphincter **73**, **105**, **197**
47.1*	Incidental appendectomy **130**, **197**
01.21	Incision and drainage of cranial sinus **8**, **9**, **11**, **220**
28.0	Incision and drainage of tonsil and peritonsillar structures **44**
38.06	Incision of abdominal arteries **59**, **74**, **118**
38.07	Incision of abdominal veins **59**, **74**, **118**
54.0	Incision of abdominal wall **64**, **75**, **82**, **105**, **119**, **180**, **198**
38.04	Incision of aorta **59**, **74**

71.22	Incision of Bartholin's gland (cyst) **129**, **141**, **235**
01.3*	Incision of brain and cerebral meninges **195**
33.0	Incision of bronchus **50**, **196**
01.31	Incision of cerebral meninges **8**, **9**, **11**, **179**, **220**
69.95	Incision of cervix **129**, **140**, **235**
11.1	Incision of cornea **37**, **195**, **233**
45.01	Incision of duodenum **72**, **82**
42.01	Incision of esophageal web **44**, **72**
76.0*	Incision of facial bone without division **199**
37.10	Incision of heart, not otherwise specified **58**
45.00	Incision of intestine, not otherwise specified **73**
38.01	Incision of intracranial vessels **8**, **10**, **11**
09.52	Incision of lacrimal canaliculi **195**
09.0	Incision of lacrimal gland **233**
09.5*	Incision of lacrimal sac and passages **233**
45.03	Incision of large intestine **73**, **180**
38.08	Incision of lower limb arteries **63**, **113**, **179**
38.09	Incision of lower limb veins **64**, **234**
33.1	Incision of lung **50**, **196**
40.0	Incision of lymphatic structures **105**, **176**, **235**
20.21	Incision of mastoid **45**
20.2*	Incision of mastoid and middle ear **234**
34.1	Incision of mediastinum **50**, **64**, **196**
20.23	Incision of middle ear **44**
27.92	Incision of mouth, unspecified structure **45**, **104**, **196**, **234**
83.0*	Incision of muscle, tendon, fascia, and bursa **92**, **201**, **236**
51.59	Incision of other bile duct **75**, **81**, **180**, **198**
51.49	Incision of other bile ducts for relief of obstruction **81**, **180**
38.05	Incision of other thoracic vessels **50**, **59**, **72**
38.02	Incision of other vessels of head and neck **14**, **16**, **44**, **63**, **113**
27.1	Incision of palate **45**
64.92	Incision of penis **123**, **235**
49.01	Incision of perianal abscess **74**, **105**
54.95	Incision of peritoneum **14**, **16**, **64**, **75**, **82**, **119**, **180**, **198**
58.91	Incision of periurethral tissue **118**
59.1*	Incision of perivesical tissue **118**, **124**, **130**, **180**, **198**
20.22	Incision of petrous pyramid air cells **45**
07.72	Incision of pituitary gland **104**
60.0	Incision of prostate **124**, **233**
48.91	Incision of rectal stricture **197**
60.72	Incision of seminal vesicle **124**
63.93	Incision of spermatic cord **123**
62.0	Incision of testis **123**, **198**
38.03	Incision of upper limb vessels **63**, **113**
38.0*	Incision of vessel **196**
38.00	Incision of vessel, unspecified site **44**, **63**, **113**, **234**
71.0*	Incision of vulva and perineum **129**, **148**
49.1*	Incision or excision of anal fistula **74**, **197**, **235**
68.22	Incision or excision of congenital septum of uterus **129**
60.8*	Incision or excision of periprostatic tissue **124**, **233**
48.8*	Incision or excision of perirectal tissue or lesion **74**, **105**, **197**, **235**
20.7*	Incision, excision, and destruction of inner ear **44**
53.51	Incisional hernia repair **235**
35.34	Infundibulectomy **58**
37.83	Initial insertion of dual-chamber device **15**, **17**, **18**, **61**, **202**, **203**
37.70	Initial insertion of lead (electrode), not otherwise specified **14**, **15**, **17**, **60**, **202**
37.81	Initial insertion of single-chamber device, not specified as rate responsive **15**, **17**, **18**, **60**, **61**, **202**, **203**

*Code Range

37.91	Open chest cardiac massage **50**, **59**, **179**, **196**
36.03	Open chest coronary artery angioplasty **58**
57.59	Open excision or destruction of other lesion or tissue of bladder **180**, **235**
35.1*	Open heart valvuloplasty without replacement **56**
48.43	Open pull-through resection of rectum **197**
76.77	Open reduction of alveolar fracture **43**, **95**, **199**
79.87	Open reduction of dislocation of ankle **91**, **201**
79.82	Open reduction of dislocation of elbow **94**, **200**
79.88	Open reduction of dislocation of foot and toe **93**, **201**
79.84	Open reduction of dislocation of hand and finger **94**, **194**
79.85	Open reduction of dislocation of hip **90**, **201**, **220**
79.86	Open reduction of dislocation of knee **90**, **201**
79.89	Open reduction of dislocation of other specified site, except temporomandibular **96**, **201**
79.81	Open reduction of dislocation of shoulder **94**, **200**
79.80	Open reduction of dislocation of unspecified site **96**, **200**
79.83	Open reduction of dislocation of wrist **94**, **194**
79.33	Open reduction of fracture of carpals and metacarpals with internal fixation **94**, **194**
79.23	Open reduction of fracture of carpals and metacarpals without internal fixation **94**, **194**
79.35	Open reduction of fracture of femur with internal fixation **90**, **113**, **200**, **220**
79.25	Open reduction of fracture of femur without internal fixation **89**, **200**, **220**
79.31	Open reduction of fracture of humerus with internal fixation **91**, **200**
79.21	Open reduction of fracture of humerus without internal fixation **91**, **200**
79.39	Open reduction of fracture of other specified bone, except facial bones, with internal fixation **45**, **96**, **200**
79.29	Open reduction of fracture of other specified bone, except facial bones, without internal fixation **45**, **96**, **200**
79.38	Open reduction of fracture of phalanges of foot with internal fixation **93**, **200**
79.28	Open reduction of fracture of phalanges of foot without internal fixation **93**, **200**
79.34	Open reduction of fracture of phalanges of hand with internal fixation **94**, **194**
79.24	Open reduction of fracture of phalanges of hand without internal fixation **94**, **194**
79.32	Open reduction of fracture of radius and ulna with internal fixation **94**, **200**
79.22	Open reduction of fracture of radius and ulna without internal fixation **94**, **200**
79.37	Open reduction of fracture of tarsals and metatarsals with internal fixation **93**, **200**
79.27	Open reduction of fracture of tarsals and metatarsals without internal fixation **93**, **200**
79.36	Open reduction of fracture of tibia and fibula with internal fixation **91**, **200**
79.26	Open reduction of fracture of tibia and fibula without internal fixation **91**, **200**
79.30	Open reduction of fracture with internal fixation, unspecified site **96**, **200**
79.20	Open reduction of fracture without internal fixation, unspecified site **96**, **200**
76.72	Open reduction of malar and zygomatic fracture **43**, **95**, **199**
76.76	Open reduction of mandibular fracture **43**, **95**, **199**
76.74	Open reduction of maxillary fracture **43**, **95**, **199**
21.72	Open reduction of nasal fracture **43**, **95**, **104**, **196**, **234**
79.55	Open reduction of separated epiphysis of femur **90**, **200**, **220**
79.51	Open reduction of separated epiphysis of humerus **91**, **200**
79.59	Open reduction of separated epiphysis of other specified bone **96**, **200**
79.52	Open reduction of separated epiphysis of radius and ulna **94**, **200**
79.56	Open reduction of separated epiphysis of tibia and fibula **91**, **200**
79.50	Open reduction of separated epiphysis, unspecified site **96**, **200**
76.94	Open reduction of temporomandibular dislocation **43**, **95**, **199**
02.01	Opening of cranial suture **11**, **43**, **220**
64.5	Operations for sex transformation, not elsewhere classified **123**, **129**
39.8*	Operations on carotid body, carotid sinus and other vascular bodies **63**
35.32	Operations on chordae tendineae **58**
71.4	Operations on clitoris **129**, **235**
10*	Operations on conjunctiva **37**
34.8*	Operations on diaphragm **50**
15*	Operations on extraocular muscles **37**
01.42	Operations on globus pallidus **8**, **10**, **11**, **220**
09*	Operations on lacrimal system **37**
13*	Operations on lens **37**
15.1*	Operations on one extraocular muscle involving temporary detachment from globe **234**
35.39	Operations on other structures adjacent to valves of heart **58**
65*	Operations on ovary **127**, **129**
35.31	Operations on papillary muscle **58**
07.5*	Operations on pineal gland **8**, **10**, **11**, **112**
12.8*	Operations on sclera **195**, **234**
01.41	Operations on thalamus **8**, **9**, **11**, **195**, **220**
01.4*	Operations on thalamus and globus pallidus **179**
40.6*	Operations on thoracic duct **50**, **197**
35.35	Operations on trabeculae carneae cordis **58**
15.3	Operations on two or more extraocular muscles involving temporary detachment from globe, one or both eyes **234**
27.7*	Operations on uvula **45**, **234**
14.7*	Operations on vitreous **38**, **196**, **234**
42.21	Operative esophagoscopy by incision **44**, **72**, **179**, **197**
16.0*	Orbitotomy **37**, **196**, **234**
16.01	Orbitotomy with bone flap **43**
16.02	Orbitotomy with insertion of orbital implant **43**
62.5	Orchiopexy **123**
78.74	Osteoclasis of carpals and metacarpals **94**, **194**
78.75	Osteoclasis of femur **89**, **200**, **220**
78.72	Osteoclasis of humerus **91**, **200**
78.79	Osteoclasis of other bone, except facial bones **95**, **200**
78.76	Osteoclasis of patella **90**, **200**
78.73	Osteoclasis of radius and ulna **94**, **200**
78.71	Osteoclasis of scapula, clavicle, and thorax (ribs and sternum) **51**, **95**, **200**
78.78	Osteoclasis of tarsals and metatarsals **93**, **200**
78.77	Osteoclasis of tibia and fibula **91**, **200**
78.70	Osteoclasis, unspecified site **95**, **200**
39.29	Other (peripheral) vascular shunt or bypass **13**, **50**, **63**, **82**, **105**, **113**, **197**
08.5*	Other adjustment of lid position **14**, **16**, **37**, **104**, **195**, **233**
84.15	Other amputation below knee **14**, **17**, **60**, **89**, **112**
49.59	Other anal sphincterotomy **148**
57.88	Other anastomosis of bladder **117**, **124**, **180**
04.74	Other anastomosis of cranial or peripheral nerve **43**
56.7*	Other anastomosis or bypass of ureter **117**, **198**
53.69	Other and open repair of other hernia of anterior abdominal wall with graft or prosthesis **235**

53.41	Other and open repair of umbilical hernia with graft or prosthesis **235**
50.26	Other and unspecified ablation of liver lesion or tissue **74**, **81**
32.26	Other and unspecified ablation of lung lesion or tissue **50**
88.57	Other and unspecified coronary arteriography **56**, **57**, **59**, **65**
68.9	Other and unspecified hysterectomy **127**, **129**, **140**
45.79	Other and unspecified partial excision of large intestine **64**, **180**
68.69	Other and unspecified radical abdominal hysterectomy **127**, **140**
68.79	Other and unspecified radical vaginal hysterectomy **127**, **140**
35.7*	Other and unspecified repair of atrial and ventricular septa **58**
80.54	Other and unspecified repair of the anulus fibrosus **12**, **13**, **90**, **91**, **180**, **201**
07.98	Other and unspecified thoracoscopic operations on thymus **14**, **16**, **195**
68.49	Other and unspecified total abdominal hysterectomy **127**, **129**, **140**
48.63	Other anterior resection of rectum **64**
42.69	Other antesternal anastomosis of esophagus **45**
42.68	Other antesternal esophageal anastomosis with interposition **45**
42.66	Other antesternal esophagocolostomy **45**
42.64	Other antesternal esophagoenterostomy **45**
47.09	Other appendectomy **64**
80.17	Other arthrotomy of ankle **91**, **201**
80.12	Other arthrotomy of elbow **93**, **114**, **201**
80.18	Other arthrotomy of foot and toe **93**, **201**, **236**
80.14	Other arthrotomy of hand and finger **93**, **194**
80.15	Other arthrotomy of hip **90**, **201**, **220**
80.16	Other arthrotomy of knee **90**, **114**, **201**, **236**
80.19	Other arthrotomy of other specified site **96**, **201**
80.11	Other arthrotomy of shoulder **93**, **201**
80.13	Other arthrotomy of wrist **93**, **194**
80.10	Other arthrotomy, unspecified site **96**, **113**, **201**
66.3*	Other bilateral destruction or occlusion of fallopian tubes **129**, **140**, **235**
53.1*	Other bilateral repair of inguinal hernia **74**, **235**
13.6*	Other cataract extraction **234**
81.02	Other cervical fusion of the anterior column, anterior technique **12**, **13**, **87**, **89**, **201**
81.03	Other cervical fusion of the posterior column, posterior technique **12**, **13**, **87**, **89**, **201**
74.99	Other cesarean section of unspecified type **140**
83.85	Other change in muscle or tendon length **14**, **16**, **93**
51.03	Other cholecystostomy **74**, **81**
51.04	Other cholecystotomy **81**
11.69	Other corneal transplant **37**
04.42	Other cranial nerve decompression **14**, **16**, **43**, **195**
04.06	Other cranial or peripheral ganglionectomy **14**, **16**, **43**, **95**, **195**
04.7*	Other cranial or peripheral neuroplasty **14**, **16**, **195**
02.06	Other cranial osteoplasty **11**, **43**, **220**
01.25	Other craniectomy **8**, **9**, **11**, **43**, **95**, **179**, **195**, **220**
01.24	Other craniotomy **8**, **9**, **11**, **43**, **179**, **195**, **220**
57.19	Other cystotomy **117**, **198**
14.29	Other destruction of chorioretinal lesion **37**, **234**
80.59	Other destruction of intervertebral disc **12**, **13**, **91**, **201**
45.32	Other destruction of lesion of duodenum **72**, **82**, **180**, **235**
45.49	Other destruction of lesion of large intestine **73**, **180**, **235**
50.29	Other destruction of lesion of liver **74**, **81**
45.34	Other destruction of lesion of small intestine, except duodenum **73**, **180**, **235**
42.39	Other destruction of lesion or tissue of esophagus **44**, **72**, **179**
43.49	Other destruction of lesion or tissue of stomach **72**, **235**
54.29	Other diagnostic procedures on abdominal region **75**, **82**, **130**, **176**, **180**, **198**, **235**
07.19	Other diagnostic procedures on adrenal glands, pituitary gland, pineal gland, and thymus **14**, **16**, **112**
51.19	Other diagnostic procedures on biliary tract **74**, **82**
57.39	Other diagnostic procedures on bladder **117**, **124**, **180**, **198**, **235**
38.29	Other diagnostic procedures on blood vessels **63**, **113**
01.18	Other diagnostic procedures on brain and cerebral meninges **8**, **9**, **11**, **179**, **195**
34.28	Other diagnostic procedures on chest wall, pleura, and diaphragm **50**
04.19	Other diagnostic procedures on cranial and peripheral nerves and ganglia **14**, **16**, **43**, **95**, **195**
76.19	Other diagnostic procedures on facial bones and joints **43**
12.29	Other diagnostic procedures on iris, ciliary body, sclera, and anterior chamber **37**
81.98	Other diagnostic procedures on joint structures **89**, **201**
55.29	Other diagnostic procedures on kidney **117**, **176**, **180**, **198**
09.19	Other diagnostic procedures on lacrimal system **44**, **195**
50.19	Other diagnostic procedures on liver **74**, **82**, **105**, **119**, **176**, **180**, **197**
33.29	Other diagnostic procedures on lung or bronchus **50**
40.19	Other diagnostic procedures on lymphatic structures **44**, **50**, **119**
34.29	Other diagnostic procedures on mediastinum **50**, **64**
20.39	Other diagnostic procedures on middle and inner ear **44**, **234**
83.29	Other diagnostic procedures on muscle, tendon, fascia, and bursa, including that of hand **201**
16.29	Other diagnostic procedures on orbit and eyeball **37**, **234**
52.19	Other diagnostic procedures on pancreas **75**, **82**, **113**, **180**, **198**
60.18	Other diagnostic procedures on prostate and periprostatic tissue **124**, **233**
60.19	Other diagnostic procedures on seminal vesicles **124**
01.19	Other diagnostic procedures on skull **8**, **9**, **11**, **89**, **195**
63.09	Other diagnostic procedures on spermatic cord, epididymis, and vas deferens **123**, **235**
03.39	Other diagnostic procedures on spinal cord and spinal canal structures **12**, **13**, **90**, **91**, **179**
62.19	Other diagnostic procedures on testes **123**
06.19	Other diagnostic procedures on thyroid and parathyroid glands **95**, **112**
28.19	Other diagnostic procedures on tonsils and adenoids **44**
56.39	Other diagnostic procedures on ureter **117**, **235**
68.19	Other diagnostic procedures on uterus and supporting structures **127**, **129**
70.29	Other diagnostic procedures on vagina and cul-de-sac **129**, **141**, **235**
69.09	Other dilation and curettage of uterus **129**, **140**, **235**
77.30	Other division of bone, unspecified site **45**, **95**, **199**
77.34	Other division of carpals and metacarpals **94**, **194**
77.35	Other division of femur **89**, **199**, **220**
77.32	Other division of humerus **91**, **199**
77.39	Other division of other bone, except facial bones **95**, **199**
77.36	Other division of patella **90**, **199**
77.33	Other division of radius and ulna **94**, **199**
77.31	Other division of scapula, clavicle, and thorax (ribs and sternum) **51**, **95**, **199**
83.19	Other division of soft tissue **14**, **16**, **92**, **236**
77.38	Other division of tarsals and metatarsals **93**, **113**, **199**, **236**
77.37	Other division of tibia and fibula **91**, **199**
39.79	Other endovascular procedures on other vessels **8**, **10**, **11**, **59**, **60**, **119**, **197**
38.64	Other excision of abdominal aorta **59**, **74**

*Code Range

38.66	Other excision of abdominal arteries **59**, **74**, **118**
38.67	Other excision of abdominal veins **59**, **74**, **118**
80.97	Other excision of ankle joint **91**, **201**
32.1	Other excision of bronchus **50**, **196**
51.63	Other excision of common duct **75**, **81**
80.92	Other excision of elbow joint **94**, **201**
18.39	Other excision of external ear **196**, **234**
18.3*	Other excision of external ear **44**, **104**
80.95	Other excision of hip joint **90**, **201**, **220**
38.61	Other excision of intracranial vessels **8**, **10**, **11**
80.98	Other excision of joint of foot and toe **93**, **114**, **201**, **236**
80.94	Other excision of joint of hand and finger **94**, **194**
80.99	Other excision of joint of other specified site **91**, **201**
80.90	Other excision of joint, unspecified site **96**, **201**
80.96	Other excision of knee joint **90**, **201**
27.43	Other excision of lesion or tissue of lip **45**, **104**, **234**
38.68	Other excision of lower limb arteries **63**, **113**
38.69	Other excision of lower limb veins **64**
32.9	Other excision of lung **50**, **196**
20.5*	Other excision of middle ear **44**
27.49	Other excision of mouth **45**, **196**, **234**
83.4*	Other excision of muscle, tendon, and fascia **92**, **201**
38.65	Other excision of other thoracic vessel **50**, **59**, **72**
38.62	Other excision of other vessels of head and neck **13**, **44**, **63**
49.04	Other excision of perianal tissue **74**, **105**
80.91	Other excision of shoulder joint **94**, **201**
45.6*	Other excision of small intestine **72**, **197**
83.49	Other excision of soft tissue **14**, **16**, **45**, **105**
82.39	Other excision of soft tissue of hand **105**
82.3*	Other excision of soft tissue of hand **94**, **194**
38.63	Other excision of upper limb vessels **63**, **113**
38.6*	Other excision of vessels **197**
38.60	Other excision of vessels, unspecified site **63**, **113**
80.93	Other excision of wrist joint **94**, **194**
04.07	Other excision or avulsion of cranial and peripheral nerves **14**, **16**, **43**, **95**, **195**, **233**
57.5*	Other excision or destruction of bladder tissue **117**, **124**, **130**
01.5*	Other excision or destruction of brain and meninges **179**
68.29	Other excision or destruction of lesion of uterus **127**, **129**, **235**
01.59	Other excision or destruction of lesion or tissue of brain **8**, **10**, **11**, **195**, **220**
67.39	Other excision or destruction of lesion or tissue of cervix **105**
67.3*	Other excision or destruction of lesion or tissue of cervix **129**, **140**, **235**
30.09	Other excision or destruction of lesion or tissue of larynx **50**, **234**
52.22	Other excision or destruction of lesion or tissue of pancreas or pancreatic duct **81**, **113**
29.39	Other excision or destruction of lesion or tissue of pharynx **44**
69.19	Other excision or destruction of uterus and supporting structures **127**, **129**
77.58	Other excision, fusion, and repair of toes **199**
16.59	Other exenteration of orbit **43**, **95**
03.09	Other exploration and decompression of spinal canal **90**, **91**, **179**
42.19	Other external fistulization of esophagus **44**
56.6*	Other external urinary diversion **117**, **124**, **130**, **180**, **198**
13.59	Other extracapsular extraction of lens **113**
13.5*	Other extracapsular extraction of lens **234**
76.6*	Other facial bone repair and orthognathic surgery **43**, **95**, **199**
12.59	Other facilitation of intraocular circulation **37**
83.44	Other fasciectomy **105**
81.17	Other fusion of foot **93**
44.39	Other gastroenterostomy without gastrectomy **64**, **82**
12.79	Other glaucoma procedures **113**
25.94	Other glossotomy **45**
42.87	Other graft of esophagus **45**, **72**, **180**, **197**
36.3*	Other heart revascularization **58**
53.9	Other hernia repair **74**
77.10	Other incision of bone without division, unspecified site **92**, **199**
01.39	Other incision of brain **8**, **9**, **11**, **179**, **220**
77.14	Other incision of carpals and metacarpals without division **94**, **194**
10.1	Other incision of conjunctiva **233**
04.04	Other incision of cranial and peripheral nerves **14**, **16**, **43**, **95**, **195**
42.09	Other incision of esophagus **44**, **72**, **197**
76.09	Other incision of facial bone **45**, **92**
77.15	Other incision of femur without division **92**, **199**
77.12	Other incision of humerus without division **92**, **199**
31.3	Other incision of larynx or trachea **44**, **50**
77.19	Other incision of other bone, except facial bones, without division **45**, **92**, **199**
77.16	Other incision of patella without division **92**, **199**
49.02	Other incision of perianal tissue **74**, **105**
59.09	Other incision of perirenal or periureteral tissue **117**, **124**, **130**, **180**, **198**
77.13	Other incision of radius and ulna without division **92**, **199**
77.11	Other incision of scapula, clavicle, and thorax (ribs and sternum) without division **51**, **92**, **199**
86.09	Other incision of skin and subcutaneous tissue **105**
45.02	Other incision of small intestine **73**, **180**
83.09	Other incision of soft tissue **105**
82.09	Other incision of soft tissue of hand **94**, **105**, **194**, **236**
77.18	Other incision of tarsals and metatarsals without division **93**, **199**
07.92	Other incision of thymus **195**
06.09	Other incision of thyroid field **43**, **104**, **112**, **195**
77.17	Other incision of tibia and fibula without division **92**, **199**
71.09	Other incision of vulva and perineum **105**, **235**
39.26	Other intra-abdominal vascular shunt or bypass **59**, **74**, **82**, **117**, **197**
42.59	Other intrathoracic anastomosis of esophagus **44**
42.56	Other intrathoracic esophagocolostomy **44**
42.54	Other intrathoracic esophagoenterostomy **44**
39.23	Other intrathoracic vascular shunt or bypass **59**, **197**
12.39	Other iridoplasty **37**
55.69	Other kidney transplantation **2**, **117**
00.8*	Other knee and hip procedures **195**
11.62	Other lamellar keratoplasty **37**
17.39	Other laparoscopic partial excision of large intestine **64**, **179**
53.43	Other laparoscopic umbilical herniorrhaphy **198**
54.19	Other laparotomy **64**, **82**, **176**, **180**
78.39	Other limb lengthening procedures **95**, **200**
45.31	Other local excision of lesion of duodenum **72**, **82**, **180**, **235**
80.87	Other local excision or destruction of lesion of ankle joint **91**, **201**
80.82	Other local excision or destruction of lesion of elbow joint **92**, **114**, **201**
80.85	Other local excision or destruction of lesion of hip joint **92**, **201**
80.88	Other local excision or destruction of lesion of joint of foot and toe **93**, **114**, **201**, **236**
80.84	Other local excision or destruction of lesion of joint of hand and finger **94**, **194**
80.89	Other local excision or destruction of lesion of joint of other specified site **92**, **201**

*Code Range

80.80	Other local excision or destruction of lesion of joint, unspecified site **92**, **201**
80.86	Other local excision or destruction of lesion of knee joint **92**, **201**, **236**
80.81	Other local excision or destruction of lesion of shoulder joint **92**, **201**
80.83	Other local excision or destruction of lesion of wrist joint **94**, **105**, **194**
49.39	Other local excision or destruction of lesion or tissue of anus **74**, **105**, **235**
32.09	Other local excision or destruction of lesion or tissue of bronchus **50**
32.29	Other local excision or destruction of lesion or tissue of lung **50**, **179**
86.3	Other local excision or destruction of lesion or tissue of skin and subcutaneous tissue **105**
71.3	Other local excision or destruction of vulva and perineum **105**, **129**, **148**, **235**
59.02	Other lysis of perirenal or periureteral adhesions **117**, **124**, **130**, **180**, **198**
54.59	Other lysis of peritoneal adhesions **113**
85.89	Other mammoplasty **106**, **202**
14.74	Other mechanical vitrectomy **113**
83.79	Other muscle transposition **114**
83.45	Other myectomy **14**, **16**, **105**
22.6*	Other nasal sinusectomy **45**
22.5*	Other nasal sinusotomy **45**
75.99	Other obstetric operations **141**
53.61	Other open incisional hernia repair with graft or prosthesis **198**, **235**
76.79	Other open reduction of facial fracture **37**, **43**, **95**, **199**
53.49	Other open umbilical herniorrhaphy **198**, **235**
07.4*	Other operations on adrenal glands, nerves, and vessels **112**
07.49	Other operations on adrenal glands, nerves, and vessels **195**
12.99	Other operations on anterior chamber **37**, **196**
49.99	Other operations on anus **197**
49.9*	Other operations on anus **74**
47.99	Other operations on appendix **73**
71.29	Other operations on Bartholin's gland **129**, **141**, **235**
51.99	Other operations on biliary tract **81**, **180**, **198**, **235**
57.99	Other operations on bladder **118**, **198**
33.98	Other operations on bronchus **50**, **196**
69.99	Other operations on cervix and uterus **130**
12.98	Other operations on ciliary body **37**, **196**
10.9*	Other operations on conjunctiva **233**
11.9*	Other operations on cornea **195**, **233**
11.99	Other operations on cornea **37**
04.99	Other operations on cranial and peripheral nerves **14**, **16**, **43**, **95**, **233**
04.9*	Other operations on cranial and peripheral nerves **195**
70.92	Other operations on cul-de-sac **129**
70.93	Other operations on cul-de-sac with graft or prosthesis **129**
34.89	Other operations on diaphragm **196**
18.9	Other operations on external ear **44**, **104**, **196**, **234**
15.9	Other operations on extraocular muscles and tendons **196**, **234**
16.99	Other operations on eyeball **37**, **113**, **196**, **234**
08.99	Other operations on eyelids **104**
08.9*	Other operations on eyelids **37**, **195**, **233**
76.99	Other operations on facial bones and joints **43**, **95**, **199**
66.99	Other operations on fallopian tubes **127**, **129**
71.9	Other operations on female genital organs **130**
37.99	Other operations on heart and pericardium **59**
07.79	Other operations on hypophysis **104**
07.7*	Other operations on hypophysis **8**, **10**, **11**, **112**
46.99	Other operations on intestines **72**, **82**, **180**, **197**
12.97	Other operations on iris **37**, **195**
12.9*	Other operations on iris, ciliary body, and anterior chamber **234**
81.99	Other operations on joint structures **96**, **201**
55.99	Other operations on kidney **117**, **198**
09.3	Other operations on lacrimal gland **195**, **233**
09.9*	Other operations on lacrimal system **195**, **233**
09.99	Other operations on lacrimal system **44**
31.98	Other operations on larynx **44**, **50**, **234**
13.9*	Other operations on lens **196**, **234**
33.99	Other operations on lung **50**, **196**
40.9	Other operations on lymphatic structures **44**, **74**, **105**, **119**, **124**, **176**, **179**, **197**
64.99	Other operations on male genital organs **123**, **235**
20.99	Other operations on middle and inner ear **44**
82.99	Other operations on muscle, tendon, and fascia of hand **94**, **194**
83.99	Other operations on muscle, tendon, fascia, and bursa **93**, **201**
84.99	Other operations on musculoskeletal system **96**, **202**
22.9	Other operations on nasal sinuses **45**
05.9	Other operations on nervous system **14**, **16**, **195**
21.99	Other operations on nose **44**, **104**, **196**, **234**
15.2*	Other operations on one extraocular muscle **234**
27.99	Other operations on oral cavity **45**, **196**, **234**
16.98	Other operations on orbit **37**, **43**, **196**, **234**
52.99	Other operations on pancreas **75**, **81**, **198**
06.99	Other operations on parathyroid glands **113**
64.98	Other operations on penis **123**, **235**
59.92	Other operations on perirenal or perivesical tissue **118**, **124**, **180**
29.99	Other operations on pharynx **44**, **196**
60.99	Other operations on prostate **124**, **233**
48.9*	Other operations on rectum and perirectal tissue **74**
14.9	Other operations on retina, choroid, and posterior chamber **38**, **196**, **234**
26.99	Other operations on salivary gland or duct **45**
12.89	Other operations on sclera **37**
61.99	Other operations on scrotum and tunica vaginalis **123**, **198**
60.79	Other operations on seminal vesicles **124**
35.98	Other operations on septa of heart **58**
02.99	Other operations on skull, brain, and cerebral meninges **8**, **10**, **11**, **43**, **95**, **179**, **195**, **220**
63.99	Other operations on spermatic cord, epididymis, and vas deferens **123**, **198**
51.89	Other operations on sphincter of Oddi **81**, **198**
03.99	Other operations on spinal cord and spinal canal structures **12**, **13**, **90**, **91**, **179**, **195**
41.99	Other operations on spleen **176**, **179**, **197**
44.99	Other operations on stomach **72**, **112**, **197**
69.98	Other operations on supporting structures of uterus **129**
05.8*	Other operations on sympathetic nerves or ganglia **14**, **16**
05.89	Other operations on sympathetic nerves or ganglia **64**
62.99	Other operations on testes **123**, **198**
85.99	Other operations on the breast **106**, **202**, **236**
34.99	Other operations on thorax **50**, **196**
07.9*	Other operations on thymus **50**, **113**, **176**, **179**
06.98	Other operations on thyroid glands **113**
25.99	Other operations on tongue **45**
28.99	Other operations on tonsils and adenoids **44**

81.46	Other repair of the collateral ligaments **90**	
81.45	Other repair of the cruciate ligaments **90**	
56.89	Other repair of ureter **198**	
58.49	Other repair of urethra **123, 130, 198**	
59.79	Other repair of urinary stress incontinence **118, 129, 235**	
69.49	Other repair of uterus **140**	
69.29	Other repair of uterus and supporting structures **199**	
70.79	Other repair of vagina **129, 148, 199**	
63.89	Other repair of vas deferens and epididymis **123, 198**	
39.59	Other repair of vessel **13, 63, 105, 113, 118, 197**	
71.79	Other repair of vulva and perineum **148, 235**	
78.42	Other repair or plastic operation on humerus **91, 200**	
78.40	Other repair or plastic operations on bone, unspecified site **95, 200**	
78.44	Other repair or plastic operations on carpals and metacarpals **94, 194**	
78.45	Other repair or plastic operations on femur **89, 200, 220**	
78.49	Other repair or plastic operations on other bone, except facial bones **95, 200**	
78.46	Other repair or plastic operations on patella **90, 200**	
78.43	Other repair or plastic operations on radius and ulna **94, 200**	
78.41	Other repair or plastic operations on scapula, clavicle, and thorax (ribs and sternum) **51, 95, 200**	
78.48	Other repair or plastic operations on tarsals and metatarsals **93, 200**	
78.47	Other repair or plastic operations on tibia and fibula **91, 200**	
85.87	Other repair or reconstruction of nipple **106, 202**	
48.69	Other resection of rectum **64, 123**	
48.6*	Other resection of rectum **73, 180, 197**	
16.64	Other revision of enucleation socket **43**	
16.66	Other revision of exenteration cavity **44**	
46.43	Other revision of stoma of large intestine **235**	
39.49	Other revision of vascular procedure **63, 74, 82, 113, 118**	
21.87	Other rhinoplasty **44, 95, 104, 196, 234**	
14.49	Other scleral buckling **113**	
12.65	Other scleral fistulization with iridectomy **234**	
12.69	Other scleral fistulizing procedure **234**	
12.88	Other scleral reinforcement **37**	
21.88	Other septoplasty **44, 95, 104, 196, 234**	
86.62	Other skin graft to hand **14, 17, 64, 94, 104, 195, 207, 208, 236**	
27.56	Other skin graft to lip and mouth **45, 104, 196, 234**	
86.69	Other skin graft to other sites **14, 17, 45, 51, 64, 75, 88, 104, 112, 194, 207, 208**	
45.93	Other small-to-large intestinal anastomosis **64, 113, 180**	
57.18	Other suprapubic cystostomy **117, 124, 129, 180, 198**	
33.39	Other surgical collapse of lung **50**	
38.84	Other surgical occlusion of abdominal aorta **59, 74**	
38.86	Other surgical occlusion of abdominal arteries **59, 74, 118, 234**	
38.87	Other surgical occlusion of abdominal veins **59, 74, 118**	
38.81	Other surgical occlusion of intracranial vessels **8, 10, 11, 220**	
38.88	Other surgical occlusion of lower limb arteries **63, 113**	
38.89	Other surgical occlusion of lower limb veins **64**	
38.85	Other surgical occlusion of other thoracic vessel **50, 59, 72**	
38.82	Other surgical occlusion of other vessels of head and neck **14, 16, 44, 63**	
38.83	Other surgical occlusion of upper limb vessels **63, 113**	
38.8*	Other surgical occlusion of vessels **197**	
38.80	Other surgical occlusion of vessels, unspecified site **63**	
54.63	Other suture of abdominal wall **105, 180**	
83.65	Other suture of muscle or fascia **92, 105, 114**	

82.45	Other suture of other tendon of hand **105, 236**
83.64	Other suture of tendon **92**
82.33	Other tenonectomy of hand **114**
83.13	Other tenotomy **14, 16, 92, 114, 236**
57.79	Other total cystectomy **198**
43.99	Other total gastrectomy **64**
76.42	Other total mandibulectomy **43**
76.45	Other total ostectomy of other facial bone **43**
81.80	Other total shoulder replacement **90**
50.59	Other transplant of liver **1**
60.97	Other transurethral destruction of prostate tissue by other thermotherapy **118, 123, 233**
57.49	Other transurethral excision or destruction of lesion or tissue of bladder **124, 235**
21.69	Other turbinectomy **196, 234**
53.0*	Other unilateral repair of inguinal hernia **74, 235**
70.14	Other vaginotomy **129, 148, 235**
71.6*	Other vulvectomy **129**
51.83	Pancreatic sphincteroplasty **72, 81, 198**
51.82	Pancreatic sphincterotomy **72, 81, 198**
52.80	Pancreatic transplant, not otherwise specified **2, 81, 113**
52.0*	Pancreatotomy **81**
69.3	Paracervical uterine denervation **127, 129**
06.95	Parathyroid tissue reimplantation **113**
06.8*	Parathyroidectomy **112, 118**
59.6	Paraurethral suspension **118, 129**
07.2*	Partial adrenalectomy **112**
57.6	Partial cystectomy **117, 123, 130, 180, 198**
42.41	Partial esophagectomy **44**
07.63	Partial excision of pituitary gland, unspecified approach **104**
43.6	Partial gastrectomy with anastomosis to duodenum **64, 72, 180, 197**
43.5	Partial gastrectomy with anastomosis to esophagus **72, 180, 197**
43.7	Partial gastrectomy with anastomosis to jejunum **64, 72, 113, 180, 197**
25.2	Partial glossectomy **45**
50.22	Partial hepatectomy **81, 198**
81.52	Partial hip replacement **88, 89, 114, 220**
76.31	Partial mandibulectomy **43, 95**
55.4	Partial nephrectomy **117, 198**
76.3*	Partial ostectomy of facial bone **199**
76.39	Partial ostectomy of other facial bone **43, 95**
52.5*	Partial pancreatectomy **81, 113, 198**
81.81	Partial shoulder replacement **90**
41.43	Partial splenectomy **95, 197**
56.41	Partial ureterectomy **124, 130**
37.35	Partial ventriculectomy **58**
81.44	Patellar stabilization **90**
85.84	Pedicle graft to breast **104, 194, 207, 208**
86.7*	Pedicle grafts or flaps **104, 207, 208**
86.70	Pedicle or flap graft, not otherwise specified **14, 17, 45, 64, 75, 88, 112, 194**
68.8	Pelvic evisceration **73, 127**
11.63	Penetrating keratoplasty with autograft **37**
44.32	Percutaneous [endoscopic] gastrojejunostomy **82**
50.24	Percutaneous ablation of liver lesion or tissue **74, 81**
32.24	Percutaneous ablation of lung lesion or tissue **50**
00.61	Percutaneous angioplasty of extracranial vessel(s) **13, 63, 195**
00.62	Percutaneous angioplasty of intracranial vessel(s) **8, 9, 11, 63, 195**

17.53	Percutaneous atherectomy of extracranial vessel(s) **13, 63, 196**
17.54	Percutaneous atherectomy of intracranial vessel(s) **8, 10, 11, 63, 196**
35.96	Percutaneous balloon valvuloplasty **58, 62, 63**
00.63	Percutaneous insertion of carotid artery stent(s) **13**
35.97	Percutaneous mitral valve repair with implant **58, 62, 63**
00.66	Percutaneous transluminal coronary angioplasty [PTCA] **58, 62**
81.66	Percutaneous vertebral augmentation **96, 201**
81.65	Percutaneous vertebroplasty **96, 201**
37.31	Pericardiectomy **50, 59, 179, 196**
37.12	Pericardiotomy **50, 59, 179, 196**
60.62	Perineal prostatectomy **118, 123**
46.13	Permanent colostomy **64, 72, 180, 197**
29.32	Pharyngeal diverticulectomy **44**
29.33	Pharyngectomy (partial) **44**
29.0	Pharyngotomy **44, 196**
01.28	Placement of intracerebral catheter(s) via burr hole(s) **8, 9, 11, 179, 195, 220**
82.72	Plastic operation on hand with graft of muscle or fascia **105**
82.7*	Plastic operation on hand with graft or implant **14, 16, 94, 194**
82.79	Plastic operation on hand with other graft or implant **105**
29.4	Plastic operation on pharynx **14, 16, 44, 196, 234**
03.5*	Plastic operations on spinal cord structures **12, 13**
34.5*	Pleurectomy **50, 196**
32.21	Plication of emphysematous bleb **50**
59.3	Plication of urethrovesical junction **118**
32.5*	Pneumonectomy **50, 196**
12.66	Postoperative revision of scleral fistulization procedure **234**
05.24	Presacral sympathectomy **130**
09.43	Probing of nasolacrimal duct **44**
00.43	Procedure on four or more vessels **62**
48.1	Proctostomy **72, 197**
48.0	Proctotomy **73, 197**
42.86	Production of subcutaneous tunnel without esophageal anastomosis **45, 72, 180, 197**
73.94	Pubiotomy to assist delivery **141**
48.4*	Pull-through resection of rectum **73, 180**
48.40	Pull-through resection of rectum, not otherwise specified **197**
33.93	Puncture of lung **50**
55.12	Pyelostomy **235**
55.1*	Pyelotomy and pyelostomy **117, 198**
43.3	Pyloromyotomy **72**
83.86	Quadricepsplasty **93**
11.75	Radial keratotomy **37**
32.6	Radical dissection of thoracic structures **50**
40.51	Radical excision of axillary lymph nodes **95**
40.4*	Radical excision of cervical lymph nodes **50, 105, 113, 176, 179**
40.53	Radical excision of iliac lymph nodes **95, 113, 117, 123, 127**
18.31	Radical excision of lesion of external ear **234**
40.50	Radical excision of lymph nodes, not otherwise specified **43, 50, 119, 124, 127**
40.59	Radical excision of other lymph nodes **43, 50, 95, 117, 123, 127**
40.5*	Radical excision of other lymph nodes **74, 105, 176, 179**
40.52	Radical excision of periaortic lymph nodes **50, 95, 113, 117, 123, 127**
86.4	Radical excision of skin lesion **14, 17, 37, 45, 64, 93, 104, 202, 236**
25.4	Radical glossectomy **43**
40.54	Radical groin dissection **95, 117, 123, 127**
30.4	Radical laryngectomy **2**

40.42	Radical neck dissection, bilateral **43**
40.40	Radical neck dissection, not otherwise specified **43**
40.41	Radical neck dissection, unilateral **43**
52.7	Radical pancreaticoduodenectomy **72, 81, 198**
60.5	Radical prostatectomy **118, 123**
71.5	Radical vulvectomy **127**
39.54	Re-entry operation (aorta) **50, 59**
58.44	Reanastomosis of urethra **198**
18.72	Reattachment of amputated ear **234**
54.61	Reclosure of postoperative disruption of abdominal wall **82, 130**
18.6	Reconstruction of external auditory canal **44, 104, 196, 234**
08.6*	Reconstruction of eyelid with flaps or grafts **37, 104, 195, 233**
08.70	Reconstruction of eyelid, not otherwise specified **113**
83.7*	Reconstruction of muscle and tendon **14, 16, 92, 201**
64.44	Reconstruction of penis **198**
63.82	Reconstruction of surgically divided vas deferens **123, 198**
82.6*	Reconstruction of thumb **14, 16, 93, 194**
31.75	Reconstruction of trachea and construction of artificial larynx **44, 50**
57.87	Reconstruction of urinary bladder **117, 198**
19*	Reconstructive operations on middle ear **44**
48.74	Rectorectostomy **72**
85.3*	Reduction mammoplasty and subcutaneous mammectomy **105, 106, 202**
76.70	Reduction of facial fracture, not otherwise specified **43, 95, 199**
55.84	Reduction of torsion of renal pedicle **198**
81.31	Refusion of Atlas-axis spine **89**
81.34	Refusion of dorsal and dorsolumbar spine, anterior column, anterior technique **87, 88**
81.35	Refusion of dorsal and dorsolumbar spine, posterior column, posterior technique **87, 88**
81.36	Refusion of lumbar and lumbosacral spine, anterior column, anterior technique **87, 88**
81.38	Refusion of lumbar and lumbosacral spine, anterior column, posterior technique **87, 88**
81.37	Refusion of lumbar and lumbosacral spine, posterior column, posterior technique **87, 88**
81.32	Refusion of other cervical spine, anterior column, anterior technique **87, 89**
81.33	Refusion of other cervical spine, posterior column, posterior technique **87, 89**
81.3*	Refusion of spine **12, 13, 201**
81.39	Refusion of spine, not elsewhere classified **87, 88**
81.30	Refusion of spine, not otherwise specified **87, 88**
40.3	Regional lymph node excision **44, 50, 64, 74, 95, 105, 113, 119, 124, 130, 140, 176, 179, 235**
39.55	Reimplantation of aberrant renal vessel **63, 117**
07.45	Reimplantation of adrenal tissue **195**
52.81	Reimplantation of pancreatic tissue **81**
86.84	Relaxation of scar or web contracture of skin **45, 202, 236**
04.43	Release of carpal tunnel **14, 16, 94, 194**
83.84	Release of clubfoot, not elsewhere classified **93**
04.44	Release of tarsal tunnel **14, 16, 93, 195**
58.5	Release of urethral stricture **118, 123, 130, 198, 235**
39.43	Removal of arteriovenous shunt for renal dialysis **64, 118**
49.76	Removal of artificial anal sphincter **73, 105, 197**
11.92	Removal of artificial implant from cornea **37**
62.41	Removal of both testes at same operative episode **95**
85.96	Removal of breast tissue expander (s) **106, 202, 236**
01.29	Removal of cranial neurostimulator pulse generator **13, 16**
57.98	Removal of electronic bladder stimulator **118, 235**

56.94	Removal of electronic ureteral stimulator **117**
10.0	Removal of embedded foreign body from conjunctiva by incision **195**, **233**
37.64	Removal of external heart assist system(s) or device(s) **1**, **59**
74.3	Removal of extratubal ectopic pregnancy **141**
13.0*	Removal of foreign body from lens **196**, **234**
54.92	Removal of foreign body from peritoneal cavity **75**, **119**, **198**
14.0*	Removal of foreign body from posterior segment of eye **37**, **196**, **234**
28.91	Removal of foreign body from tonsil and adenoid by incision **44**, **196**
85.94	Removal of implant of breast **106**, **202**, **236**
78.6*	Removal of implanted device from bone **236**
78.64	Removal of implanted device from carpals and metacarpals **92**, **194**
78.65	Removal of implanted device from femur **92**, **113**, **200**
78.62	Removal of implanted device from humerus **92**, **200**
78.69	Removal of implanted device from other bone **92**, **200**
78.66	Removal of implanted device from patella **92**, **200**
78.63	Removal of implanted device from radius and ulna **92**, **200**
78.61	Removal of implanted device from scapula, clavicle, and thorax (ribs and sternum) **51**, **92**, **200**
78.68	Removal of implanted device from tarsal and metatarsals **92**, **200**
78.67	Removal of implanted device from tibia and fibula **92**, **200**
78.60	Removal of implanted device, unspecified site **92**, **200**
13.8	Removal of implanted lens **196**, **234**
37.55	Removal of internal biventricular heart replacement system **59**
76.97	Removal of internal fixation device from facial bone **43**, **92**, **199**
64.96	Removal of internal prosthesis of penis **119**, **123**, **235**
01.22	Removal of intracranial neurostimulator lead(s) **8**, **9**, **11**, **179**
12.0*	Removal of intraocular foreign body from anterior segment of eye **37**, **195**, **233**
37.77	Removal of lead(s) (electrodes) without replacement **14**, **16**, **64**, **196**
12.40	Removal of lesion of anterior segment of eye, not otherwise specified **37**
08.20	Removal of lesion of eyelid, not otherwise specified **104**, **113**
56.86	Removal of ligature from ureter **198**
55.98	Removal of mechanical kidney **117**, **198**
16.7*	Removal of ocular or orbital implant **37**, **196**, **234**
69.97	Removal of other penetrating foreign body from cervix **129**, **199**
16.1	Removal of penetrating foreign body from eye, not otherwise specified **38**, **196**, **234**
04.93	Removal of peripheral neurostimulator lead(s) **14**, **16**, **43**, **95**, **124**, **130**
66.94	Removal of prosthesis of fallopian tube **127**, **129**
51.95	Removal of prosthetic device from bile duct **81**, **180**, **198**
83.93	Removal of skeletal muscle stimulator **14**, **16**, **93**, **201**
02.07	Removal of skull plate **11**, **43**
03.94	Removal of spinal neurostimulator lead(s) **12**, **13**, **90**, **91**, **118**, **123**, **130**, **195**
03.98	Removal of spinal thecal shunt **12**, **13**, **90**, **91**, **195**
14.6	Removal of surgically implanted material from posterior segment of eye **37**, **113**, **196**, **234**
63.85	Removal of valve from vas deferens **123**
02.43	Removal of ventricular shunt **13**, **195**
12.93	Removal or destruction of epithelial downgrowth from anterior chamber **37**
55.61	Renal autotransplantation **117**, **198**
01.23	Reopening of craniotomy site **8**, **9**, **11**, **43**, **179**, **195**, **220**
03.02	Reopening of laminectomy site **90**, **91**, **179**
54.12	Reopening of recent laparotomy site **82**, **180**
34.03	Reopening of recent thoracotomy site **50**, **64**, **196**
06.02	Reopening of wound of thyroid field **112**, **195**, **233**
33.4*	Repair and plastic operation on lung and bronchus **50**, **196**
64.4*	Repair and plastic operation on penis **123**
41.95	Repair and plastic operations on spleen **176**, **179**, **197**
31.7*	Repair and plastic operations on trachea **196**
86.81	Repair for facial weakness **14**, **17**, **45**, **93**, **202**
07.44	Repair of adrenal gland **195**
39.53	Repair of arteriovenous fistula **8**, **10**, **11**, **63**
35.6*	Repair of atrial and ventricular septa with tissue graft **58**
35.52	Repair of atrial septal defect with prosthesis, closed technique **63**
35.51	Repair of atrial septal defect with prosthesis, open technique **58**
51.7*	Repair of bile ducts **81**, **198**
57.86	Repair of bladder exstrophy **117**
08.3*	Repair of blepharoptosis and lid retraction **37**, **195**, **233**
39.57	Repair of blood vessel with synthetic patch graft **13**, **63**, **113**, **118**, **197**
39.56	Repair of blood vessel with tissue patch graft **13**, **63**, **113**, **118**, **197**
39.58	Repair of blood vessel with unspecified type of patch graft **13**, **63**, **113**, **118**, **197**
02.92	Repair of brain **8**, **10**, **11**, **195**, **220**
09.73	Repair of canaliculus **104**
09.7*	Repair of canaliculus and punctum **195**, **233**
02.1*	Repair of cerebral meninges **8**, **10**, **11**
27.54	Repair of cleft lip **44**, **104**, **196**, **234**
70.72	Repair of colovaginal fistula **72**, **129**, **180**, **199**
11.5*	Repair of cornea **37**, **195**, **233**
75.61	Repair of current obstetric laceration of bladder and urethra **148**
75.51	Repair of current obstetric laceration of cervix **148**
75.52	Repair of current obstetric laceration of corpus uteri **141**
75.50	Repair of current obstetric laceration of uterus, not otherwise specified **148**
70.51	Repair of cystocele **118**
70.5*	Repair of cystocele and rectocele **130**
70.50	Repair of cystocele and rectocele **75**, **118**
70.53	Repair of cystocele and rectocele with graft or prosthesis **72**, **117**
70.54	Repair of cystocele with graft or prosthesis **118**
53.7*	Repair of diaphragmatic hernia, abdominal approach **50**, **72**, **198**
53.8*	Repair of diaphragmatic hernia, thoracic approach **50**, **72**, **198**
35.54	Repair of endocardial cushion defect with prosthesis **58**
08.4*	Repair of entropion or ectropion **37**, **195**, **233**
08.44	Repair of entropion or ectropion with lid reconstruction **104**
42.84	Repair of esophageal fistula, not elsewhere classified **45**, **72**, **179**, **197**
42.85	Repair of esophageal stricture **72**, **180**, **197**
66.7*	Repair of fallopian tube **127**, **129**
57.83	Repair of fistula involving bladder and intestine **73**, **117**, **124**, **130**, **180**, **198**
67.62	Repair of fistula of cervix **140**
71.72	Repair of fistula of vulva or perineum **73**
54.71	Repair of gastroschisis **74**
37.4*	Repair of heart and pericardium **59**
37.63	Repair of heart assist system **1**, **56**
81.40	Repair of hip, not elsewhere classified **90**, **220**
58.45	Repair of hypospadias or epispadias **123**
15.7	Repair of injury of extraocular muscle **196**, **234**
16.8*	Repair of injury of eyeball and orbit **37**, **196**, **234**
67.5*	Repair of internal cervical os **198**
10.6	Repair of laceration of conjunctiva **195**, **233**

*Code Range © 2012 OptumInsight, Inc.

51.91	Repair of laceration of gallbladder **81**, **198**
31.64	Repair of laryngeal fracture **196**
31.6*	Repair of larynx **44**, **50**
50.6*	Repair of liver **198**
22.7*	Repair of nasal sinus **45**
04.76	Repair of old traumatic injury of cranial and peripheral nerves **43**
57.84	Repair of other fistula of bladder **117**, **124**, **130**, **180**, **198**
70.75	Repair of other fistula of vagina **73**, **129**, **180**, **199**
53.5*	Repair of other hernia of anterior abdominal wall (without graft or prosthesis) **74**
53.6*	Repair of other hernia of anterior abdominal wall with graft or prosthesis **74**
70.74	Repair of other vaginoenteric fistula **72**, **129**, **180**, **199**
20.93	Repair of oval and round windows **44**
65.7*	Repair of ovary **198**
34.74	Repair of pectus deformity **50**, **95**
34.93	Repair of pleura **50**, **196**
60.93	Repair of prostate **124**, **198**, **233**
70.52	Repair of rectocele **72**
70.55	Repair of rectocele with graft or prosthesis **72**
70.73	Repair of rectovaginal fistula **72**, **129**, **180**, **199**
48.7*	Repair of rectum **197**
81.82	Repair of recurrent dislocation of shoulder **94**
14.54	Repair of retinal detachment with laser photocoagulation **113**
14.4*	Repair of retinal detachment with scleral buckling and implant **37**, **196**, **234**
14.32	Repair of retinal tear by cryotherapy **37**, **234**
14.31	Repair of retinal tear by diathermy **37**, **196**, **234**
26.4*	Repair of salivary gland or duct **45**, **196**
12.82	Repair of scleral fistula **37**
12.85	Repair of scleral staphyloma with graft **37**
61.42	Repair of scrotal fistula **123**, **198**
62.6*	Repair of testes **123**, **198**
80.53	Repair of the anulus fibrosus with graft or prosthesis **12**, **13**, **90**, **91**, **180**, **201**
07.93	Repair of thymus **195**
53.4*	Repair of umbilical hernia **74**
35.50	Repair of unspecified septal defect of heart with prosthesis **58**
56.8*	Repair of ureter **117**
58.4*	Repair of urethra **118**
69.2*	Repair of uterine supporting structures **129**
35.55	Repair of ventricular septal defect with prosthesis, closed technique **58**
35.53	Repair of ventricular septal defect with prosthesis, open technique **58**
03.53	Repair of vertebral fracture **90**, **91**, **179**, **195**
71.7*	Repair of vulva and perineum **129**, **199**
37.87	Replacement of any type of pacemaker device with dual-chamber device **14**, **15**, **16**, **17**, **18**, **60**, **61**, **63**, **196**, **202**, **203**
37.85	Replacement of any type of pacemaker device with single-chamber device, not specified as rate responsive **14**, **15**, **16**, **17**, **18**, **60**, **61**, **63**, **196**, **202**, **203**
37.86	Replacement of any type of pacemaker device with single-chamber device, rate responsive **14**, **15**, **16**, **17**, **18**, **60**, **61**, **63**, **196**, **202**, **203**
37.97	Replacement of automatic cardioverter/defibrillator leads(s) only **57**, **58**, **65**
37.98	Replacement of automatic cardioverter/defibrillator pulse generator only **57**, **58**, **62**
57.97	Replacement of electronic bladder stimulator **118**, **235**
56.93	Replacement of electronic ureteral stimulator **117**
81.57	Replacement of joint of foot and toe **93**, **236**
84.6*	Replacement of spinal disc **12**, **13**, **91**, **202**
37.76	Replacement of transvenous atrial and/or ventricular lead(s) (electrode(s)) **14**, **16**, **18**, **61**, **64**, **196**, **203**
02.42	Replacement of ventricular shunt **13**, **179**, **195**
39.94	Replacement of vessel-to-vessel cannula **63**, **119**, **235**
37.54	Replacement or repair of other implantable component of (total) replacement heart system **56**
37.53	Replacement or repair of thoracic unit of (total) replacement heart system **56**
64.45	Replantation of penis **198**
38.44	Resection of abdominal aorta with replacement **59**
38.36	Resection of abdominal arteries with anastomosis **59**, **74**, **118**
38.46	Resection of abdominal arteries with replacement **59**, **74**, **118**
38.37	Resection of abdominal veins with anastomosis **59**, **74**, **118**
38.47	Resection of abdominal veins with replacement **59**, **74**, **118**
38.34	Resection of aorta with anastomosis **59**, **74**
38.31	Resection of intracranial vessels with anastomosis **8**, **10**, **11**
38.41	Resection of intracranial vessels with replacement **8**, **10**, **11**
38.38	Resection of lower limb arteries with anastomosis **63**, **113**
38.48	Resection of lower limb arteries with replacement **63**, **113**
38.39	Resection of lower limb veins with anastomosis **64**
38.49	Resection of lower limb veins with replacement **64**
21.4	Resection of nose **43**, **104**, **196**
38.35	Resection of other thoracic vessels with anastomosis **50**, **59**, **72**
38.45	Resection of other thoracic vessels with replacement **50**, **56**, **72**
38.32	Resection of other vessels of head and neck with anastomosis **13**, **44**, **63**
38.42	Resection of other vessels of head and neck with replacement **14**, **16**, **44**, **63**
85.22	Resection of quadrant of breast **105**, **106**
38.33	Resection of upper limb vessels with anastomosis **63**, **113**
38.43	Resection of upper limb vessels with replacement **63**, **113**
38.3*	Resection of vessel with anastomosis **197**
38.30	Resection of vessel with anastomosis, unspecified site **63**, **113**
38.4*	Resection of vessel with replacement **197**
38.40	Resection of vessel with replacement, unspecified site **63**
00.87	Resurfacing hip, partial, acetabulum **88**, **113**, **220**
00.86	Resurfacing hip, partial, femoral head **88**, **113**, **220**
00.85	Resurfacing hip, total, acetabulum and femoral head **88**, **220**
59.00	Retroperitoneal dissection, not otherwise specified **95**, **105**, **117**, **123**, **130**, **180**
60.4	Retropubic prostatectomy **118**, **123**
59.5	Retropubic urethral suspension **118**, **129**
81.88	Reverse total shoulder replacement **90**
84.3	Revision of amputation stump **63**, **89**, **105**, **112**, **202**
51.94	Revision of anastomosis of biliary tract **81**, **180**, **198**
46.94	Revision of anastomosis of large intestine **72**, **197**
46.93	Revision of anastomosis of small intestine **72**, **197**
39.42	Revision of arteriovenous shunt for renal dialysis **64**, **113**, **118**
27.63	Revision of cleft palate repair **44**, **104**
35.95	Revision of corrective procedure on heart **58**
56.52	Revision of cutaneous uretero-ileostomy **235**
16.63	Revision of enucleation socket with graft **43**
15.6	Revision of extraocular muscle surgery **234**
84.85	Revision of facet replacement device(s) **96**
44.5	Revision of gastric anastomosis **72**, **112**, **197**
00.71	Revision of hip replacement, acetabular component **88**, **113**, **195**, **220**
00.73	Revision of hip replacement, acetabular liner and/or femoral head only **88**, **113**, **195**, **220**

00.70	Revision of hip replacement, both acetabular and femoral components **88, 113, 195, 220**
00.72	Revision of hip replacement, femoral component **88, 113, 195, 220**
81.53	Revision of hip replacement, not otherwise specified **88, 114, 220**
85.93	Revision of implant of breast **106, 202, 236**
84.81	Revision of interspinous process device(s) **96**
46.4*	Revision of intestinal stoma **74, 197**
46.40	Revision of intestinal stoma, not otherwise specified **180**
81.59	Revision of joint replacement of lower extremity, not elsewhere classified **96**
81.97	Revision of joint replacement of upper extremity **96, 201**
00.82	Revision of knee replacement, femoral component **88**
81.55	Revision of knee replacement, not otherwise specified **88**
00.83	Revision of knee replacement, patellar component **90**
00.81	Revision of knee replacement, tibial component **88**
00.80	Revision of knee replacement, total (all components) **88**
37.75	Revision of lead (electrode) **14, 16, 64, 196**
20.92	Revision of mastoidectomy **45**
12.83	Revision of operative wound of anterior segment, not elsewhere classified **37**
86.75	Revision of pedicle or flap graft **14, 17, 45, 64, 75, 88, 112, 194**
84.83	Revision of pedicle-based dynamic stabilization device(s) **96**
04.75	Revision of previous repair of cranial and peripheral nerves **43**
03.97	Revision of spinal thecal shunt **12, 13, 90, 91, 179, 195**
46.41	Revision of stoma of small intestine **180, 235**
00.84	Revision of total knee replacement, tibial insert (liner) **90**
31.74	Revision of tracheostomy **44, 50, 64, 104**
56.72	Revision of ureterointestinal anastomosis **124, 130, 180**
39.4*	Revision of vascular procedure **197**
57.22	Revision or closure of vesicostomy **130, 180, 235**
37.79	Revision or relocation of cardiac device pocket **14, 16, 64, 104, 196**
37.89	Revision or removal of pacemaker device **14, 16, 64, 196, 234**
84.66	Revision or replacement of artificial spinal disc prosthesis, cervical **91**
84.68	Revision or replacement of artificial spinal disc prosthesis, lumbosacral **91**
84.69	Revision or replacement of artificial spinal disc prosthesis, not otherwise specified **91**
84.67	Revision or replacement of artificial spinal disc prosthesis, thoracic **91**
21.84	Revision rhinoplasty **44, 95, 104, 196, 234**
37.21	Right heart cardiac catheterization **56, 57, 58, 65**
83.63	Rotator cuff repair **94**
66.62	Salpingectomy with removal of tubal pregnancy **127, 129, 140**
66.0*	Salpingotomy **127, 129**
34.6	Scarification of pleura **50, 179, 196**
12.6*	Scleral fistulization **37, 195**
12.87	Scleral reinforcement with graft **37**
16.65	Secondary graft to exenteration cavity **44**
13.72	Secondary insertion of intraocular lens prosthesis **196, 234**
16.6*	Secondary procedures after removal of eyeball **37, 196, 234**
32.3*	Segmental resection of lung **50, 179, 196**
84.92	Separation of equal conjoined twins **96**
84.93	Separation of unequal conjoined twins **96**
77.04	Sequestrectomy of carpals and metacarpals **94, 194**
76.01	Sequestrectomy of facial bone **43, 95**
77.05	Sequestrectomy of femur **89, 199, 220**
77.02	Sequestrectomy of humerus **91, 199**
77.09	Sequestrectomy of other bone, except facial bones **95, 199**

77.06	Sequestrectomy of patella **90, 199**
77.03	Sequestrectomy of radius and ulna **94, 199**
77.01	Sequestrectomy of scapula, clavicle, and thorax (ribs and sternum) **50, 95, 199**
77.08	Sequestrectomy of tarsals and metatarsals **93, 199**
77.07	Sequestrectomy of tibia and fibula **91, 199**
77.00	Sequestrectomy, unspecified site **95, 199**
03.7*	Shunt of spinal theca **12, 13, 179**
26.3*	Sialoadenectomy **45, 234**
26.30	Sialoadenectomy, not otherwise specified **176**
40.2*	Simple excision of lymphatic structure **105, 176**
40.29	Simple excision of other lymphatic structure **44, 50, 64, 74, 95, 113, 119, 124, 130, 197, 235**
02.11	Simple suture of dura mater of brain **195, 220**
66.71	Simple suture of fallopian tube **198**
86.83	Size reduction plastic operation **112, 202, 236**
45.91	Small-to-small intestinal anastomosis **112, 180**
05.21	Sphenopalatine ganglionectomy **43**
57.91	Sphincterotomy of bladder **117, 235**
81.00	Spinal fusion, not otherwise specified **12, 13, 87, 88, 201**
41.2	Splenotomy **176, 179, 197**
85.82	Split-thickness graft to breast **104, 194, 207, 208**
19.1*	Stapedectomy **234**
92.3*	Stereotactic radiosurgery **16, 18, 114, 181**
21.5	Submucous resection of nasal septum **44, 196, 234**
06.5*	Substernal thyroidectomy **112**
81.13	Subtalar fusion **93**
81.18	Subtalar joint arthroereisis **96**
68.3*	Subtotal abdominal hysterectomy **127, 129, 140**
85.23	Subtotal mastectomy **105, 106, 236**
60.3	Suprapubic prostatectomy **118, 123**
59.4	Suprapubic sling operation **118, 129**
75.93	Surgical correction of inverted uterus **141**
18.5	Surgical correction of prominent ear **44, 104, 234**
54.6*	Suture of abdominal wall and peritoneum **75, 198**
39.31	Suture of artery **50, 63, 105, 113**
81.94	Suture of capsule or ligament of ankle and foot **93, 201**
81.95	Suture of capsule or ligament of other lower extremity **92, 201**
81.93	Suture of capsule or ligament of upper extremity **94, 201**
04.3	Suture of cranial and peripheral nerves **14, 16, 195**
44.42	Suture of duodenal ulcer site **72**
44.41	Suture of gastric ulcer site **72**
49.71	Suture of laceration of anus **74, 105, 197**
57.81	Suture of laceration of bladder **117, 198**
67.61	Suture of laceration of cervix **148**
34.82	Suture of laceration of diaphragm **196**
46.71	Suture of laceration of duodenum **72**
42.82	Suture of laceration of esophagus **45, 72, 179, 197**
55.81	Suture of laceration of kidney **198**
46.75	Suture of laceration of large intestine **72**
31.61	Suture of laceration of larynx **196**
27.61	Suture of laceration of palate **45, 196**
64.41	Suture of laceration of penis **198**
29.51	Suture of laceration of pharynx **44, 196**
48.71	Suture of laceration of rectum **72, 148**
12.81	Suture of laceration of sclera **37**
46.73	Suture of laceration of small intestine, except duodenum **72**
63.51	Suture of laceration of spermatic cord and epididymis **123, 198**
44.61	Suture of laceration of stomach **72, 197**

*Code Range   © 2012 OptumInsight, Inc.

31.71	Suture of laceration of trachea **44**, **50**
56.82	Suture of laceration of ureter **198**
58.41	Suture of laceration of urethra **198**
69.41	Suture of laceration of uterus **140**
70.71	Suture of laceration of vagina **105**, **129**, **148**, **199**
63.81	Suture of laceration of vas deferens and epididymis **123**, **198**
71.71	Suture of laceration of vulva or perineum **105**, **148**, **235**
82.46	Suture of muscle or fascia of hand **236**
83.6*	Suture of muscle, tendon, and fascia **201**, **236**
82.4*	Suture of muscle, tendon, and fascia of hand **94**, **194**
44.40	Suture of peptic ulcer, not otherwise specified **72**
54.64	Suture of peritoneum **82**, **180**, **235**
83.61	Suture of tendon sheath **92**
82.41	Suture of tendon sheath of hand **236**
06.93	Suture of thyroid gland **113**, **195**
39.30	Suture of unspecified blood vessel **63**
39.32	Suture of vein **64**
39.3*	Suture of vessel **13**, **197**
05.2*	Sympathectomy **14**, **16**, **64**
80.7*	Synovectomy **236**
80.77	Synovectomy of ankle **91**, **201**
80.72	Synovectomy of elbow **94**, **201**
80.78	Synovectomy of foot and toe **93**, **201**
80.74	Synovectomy of hand and finger **94**, **194**
80.75	Synovectomy of hip **90**, **201**
80.76	Synovectomy of knee **90**, **201**
80.79	Synovectomy of other specified site **92**, **201**
80.71	Synovectomy of shoulder **94**, **201**
80.73	Synovectomy of wrist **94**, **194**
80.70	Synovectomy, unspecified site **92**, **201**
39.0	Systemic to pulmonary artery shunt **59**
81.15	Tarsometatarsal fusion **93**
11.91	Tattooing of cornea **37**
39.77	Temporary (partial) therapeutic endovascular occlusion of vessel **13**, **63**, **197**
46.11	Temporary colostomy **72**, **180**, **197**
46.21	Temporary ileostomy **72**, **180**, **197**
31.1	Temporary tracheostomy **1**, **4**
76.5	Temporomandibular arthroplasty **45**, **95**, **199**
83.81	Tendon graft **14**, **16**, **92**
83.83	Tendon pulley reconstruction on muscle, tendon, and fascia **14**, **16**, **93**
83.75	Tendon transfer or transplantation **114**
82.11	Tenotomy of hand **236**
12.91	Therapeutic evacuation of anterior chamber **37**, **195**
11.42	Thermocauterization of corneal lesion **195**
12.62	Thermocauterization of sclera with iridectomy **234**
11.74	Thermokeratoplasty **37**
84.28	Thigh reattachment **89**, **202**, **220**
33.34	Thoracoplasty **50**
32.25	Thoracoscopic ablation of lung lesion or tissue **50**, **179**
34.52	Thoracoscopic decortication of lung **179**
34.06	Thoracoscopic drainage of pleural cavity **50**
32.20	Thoracoscopic excision of lesion or tissue of lung **50**, **179**, **196**
07.95	Thoracoscopic incision of thymus **14**, **16**, **195**
33.20	Thoracoscopic lung biopsy **50**, **64**, **95**, **118**
34.20	Thoracoscopic pleural biopsy **50**
84.21	Thumb reattachment **94**, **194**
07.8*	Thymectomy **14**, **16**, **50**, **113**, **176**, **179**, **195**
06.94	Thyroid tissue reimplantation **113**
84.25	Toe reattachment **93**, **202**
28.3	Tonsillectomy with adenoidectomy **44**
28.2	Tonsillectomy without adenoidectomy **44**, **234**
81.56	Total ankle replacement **88**, **89**
66.5*	Total bilateral salpingectomy **127**, **129**, **140**
57.7*	Total cystectomy **117**, **123**, **130**, **180**
09.23	Total dacryoadenectomy **195**
81.84	Total elbow replacement **90**
42.42	Total esophagectomy **44**
07.68	Total excision of pituitary gland, other specified approach **104**
07.64	Total excision of pituitary gland, transfrontal approach **104**
07.65	Total excision of pituitary gland, transsphenoidal approach **104**
07.69	Total excision of pituitary gland, unspecified approach **104**
43.9*	Total gastrectomy **72**, **180**, **197**
50.4	Total hepatectomy **81**, **198**
81.51	Total hip replacement **88**, **89**, **220**
45.8*	Total intra-abdominal colectomy **64**, **72**, **180**, **197**
81.54	Total knee replacement **88**, **89**
76.41	Total mandibulectomy with synchronous reconstruction **43**
21.83	Total nasal reconstruction **44**, **95**, **104**, **196**, **234**
77.94	Total ostectomy of carpals and metacarpals **94**, **194**
77.95	Total ostectomy of femur **89**, **199**, **220**
77.92	Total ostectomy of humerus **91**, **199**
77.99	Total ostectomy of other bone, except facial bones **45**, **95**, **199**
76.44	Total ostectomy of other facial bone with synchronous reconstruction **43**
77.96	Total ostectomy of patella **90**, **199**
77.93	Total ostectomy of radius and ulna **94**, **199**
77.91	Total ostectomy of scapula, clavicle, and thorax (ribs and sternum) **12**, **13**, **51**, **95**, **199**
77.98	Total ostectomy of tarsals and metatarsals **93**, **199**, **236**
77.97	Total ostectomy of tibia and fibula **91**, **199**
77.90	Total ostectomy, unspecified site **95**, **199**
52.6	Total pancreatectomy **81**, **198**
85.7*	Total reconstruction of breast **105**, **106**, **202**
45.63	Total removal of small intestine **180**
35.8*	Total repair of certain congenital cardiac anomalies **58**
41.5	Total splenectomy **64**, **74**, **95**, **176**, **179**, **197**
66.4	Total unilateral salpingectomy **127**, **129**, **140**
81.73	Total wrist replacement **90**, **201**
12.64	Trabeculectomy ab externo **113**, **234**
12.54	Trabeculotomy ab externo **37**
67.51	Transabdominal cerclage of cervix **129**, **148**
45.21	Transabdominal endoscopy of large intestine **73**, **197**, **235**
45.11	Transabdominal endoscopy of small intestine **73**, **180**, **197**, **235**
44.11	Transabdominal gastroscopy **72**, **82**, **180**, **197**
48.21	Transabdominal proctosigmoidoscopy **73**, **197**
35.06	Transapical replacement of aortic valve **56**
35.08	Transapical replacement of pulmonary valve **56**
17.55	Transluminal coronary atherectomy **58**, **62**
46.97	Transplant of intestine **1**
82.5*	Transplantation of muscle and tendon of hand **14**, **16**, **94**, **194**
63.53	Transplantation of spermatic cord **123**, **198**
41.94	Transplantation of spleen **176**, **179**
34.21	Transpleural thoracoscopy **50**, **64**, **196**
04.6	Transposition of cranial and peripheral nerves **14**, **16**, **195**
15.5	Transposition of extraocular muscles **234**
85.86	Transposition of nipple **106**, **202**

Alphabetic Index to Procedures

Numeric Index to Procedures

00.10	Implantation of chemotherapeutic agent **9**
00.15	High-dose infusion interleukin-2 [IL-2] **182**
00.43	Procedure on four or more vessels **62**
00.48	Insertion of four or more vascular stents **62**
00.50	Implantation of cardiac resynchronization pacemaker without mention of defibrillation, total system (CRT-P) **60**
00.51	Implantation of cardiac resynchronization defibrillator, total system (CRT-D) **57**
00.52	Implantation or replacement of transvenous lead (electrode) into left ventricular coronary venous system **57 , 60 , 65**
00.53	Implantation or replacement of cardiac resynchronization pacemaker pulse generator only (CRT-P) **60 , 61 , 63**
00.54	Implantation or replacement of cardiac resynchronization defibrillator pulse generator device only (CRT-D) **57 , 58 , 62**
00.56	Insertion or replacement of implantable pressure sensor with lead for intracardiac or great vessel hemodynamic monitoring **64 , 65**
00.57	Implantation or replacement of subcutaneous device for intracardiac or great vessel hemodynamic monitoring **63 , 65**
00.61	Percutaneous angioplasty of extracranial vessel(s) **13 , 63 , 195**
00.62	Percutaneous angioplasty of intracranial vessel(s) **8 , 9 , 11 , 63 , 195**
00.63	Percutaneous insertion of carotid artery stent(s) **13**
00.66	Percutaneous transluminal coronary angioplasty [PTCA] **58 , 62**
00.70	Revision of hip replacement, both acetabular and femoral components **88 , 113 , 195 , 220**
00.71	Revision of hip replacement, acetabular component **88 , 113 , 195 , 220**
00.72	Revision of hip replacement, femoral component **88 , 113 , 195 , 220**
00.73	Revision of hip replacement, acetabular liner and/or femoral head only **88 , 113 , 195 , 220**
00.8*	Other knee and hip procedures **195**
00.80	Revision of knee replacement, total (all components) **88**
00.81	Revision of knee replacement, tibial component **88**
00.82	Revision of knee replacement, femoral component **88**
00.83	Revision of knee replacement, patellar component **90**
00.84	Revision of total knee replacement, tibial insert (liner) **90**
00.85	Resurfacing hip, total, acetabulum and femoral head **88 , 220**
00.86	Resurfacing hip, partial, femoral head **88 , 113 , 220**
00.87	Resurfacing hip, partial, acetabulum **88 , 113 , 220**
01.12	Open biopsy of cerebral meninges **8 , 9 , 11 , 179**
01.14	Open biopsy of brain **8 , 9 , 11 , 179**
01.15	Biopsy of skull **8 , 9 , 11 , 89 , 113**
01.18	Other diagnostic procedures on brain and cerebral meninges **8 , 9 , 11 , 179 , 195**
01.19	Other diagnostic procedures on skull **8 , 9 , 11 , 89 , 195**
01.20	Cranial implantation or replacement of neurostimulator pulse generator **9 , 11 , 13 , 16**
01.21	Incision and drainage of cranial sinus **8 , 9 , 11 , 220**
01.22	Removal of intracranial neurostimulator lead(s) **8 , 9 , 11 , 179**
01.23	Reopening of craniotomy site **8 , 9 , 11 , 43 , 179 , 195 , 220**
01.24	Other craniotomy **8 , 9 , 11 , 43 , 179 , 195 , 220**
01.25	Other craniectomy **8 , 9 , 11 , 43 , 95 , 179 , 195 , 220**
01.28	Placement of intracerebral catheter(s) via burr hole(s) **8 , 9 , 11 , 179 , 195 , 220**
01.29	Removal of cranial neurostimulator pulse generator **13 , 16**
01.3*	Incision of brain and cerebral meninges **195**

01.31	Incision of cerebral meninges **8 , 9 , 11 , 179 , 220**
01.32	Lobotomy and tractotomy **8 , 9 , 11 , 179 , 220**
01.39	Other incision of brain **8 , 9 , 11 , 179 , 220**
01.4*	Operations on thalamus and globus pallidus **179**
01.41	Operations on thalamus **8 , 9 , 11 , 195 , 220**
01.42	Operations on globus pallidus **8 , 10 , 11 , 220**
01.5*	Other excision or destruction of brain and meninges **179**
01.51	Excision of lesion or tissue of cerebral meninges **8 , 10 , 11 , 220**
01.52	Hemispherectomy **8 , 10 , 11 , 195 , 220**
01.53	Lobectomy of brain **8 , 10 , 11 , 195 , 220**
01.59	Other excision or destruction of lesion or tissue of brain **8 , 10 , 11 , 195 , 220**
01.6	Excision of lesion of skull **8 , 10 , 11 , 43 , 92 , 179 , 220**
02.0*	Cranioplasty **8 , 10 , 95 , 195**
02.01	Opening of cranial suture **11 , 43 , 220**
02.02	Elevation of skull fracture fragments **11 , 43 , 220**
02.03	Formation of cranial bone flap **11 , 43 , 220**
02.04	Bone graft to skull **11 , 43 , 220**
02.05	Insertion of skull plate **11 , 43 , 220**
02.06	Other cranial osteoplasty **11 , 43 , 220**
02.07	Removal of skull plate **11 , 43**
02.1*	Repair of cerebral meninges **8 , 10 , 11**
02.11	Simple suture of dura mater of brain **195 , 220**
02.12	Other repair of cerebral meninges **195 , 220**
02.13	Ligation of meningeal vessel **8 , 195 , 220**
02.14	Choroid plexectomy **220**
02.2*	Ventriculostomy **8 , 10 , 11 , 179 , 195 , 220**
02.3*	Extracranial ventricular shunt **13 , 179 , 195**
02.42	Replacement of ventricular shunt **13 , 179 , 195**
02.43	Removal of ventricular shunt **13 , 195**
02.91	Lysis of cortical adhesions **8 , 10 , 11 , 179 , 195**
02.92	Repair of brain **8 , 10 , 11 , 195 , 220**
02.93	Implantation or replacement of intracranial neurostimulator lead(s) **8 , 9 , 10 , 11 , 179 , 195**
02.94	Insertion or replacement of skull tongs or halo traction device **8 , 10 , 11 , 95 , 195 , 220**
02.99	Other operations on skull, brain, and cerebral meninges **8 , 10 , 11 , 43 , 95 , 179 , 195 , 220**
03.0*	Exploration and decompression of spinal canal structures **12 , 13 , 195**
03.02	Reopening of laminectomy site **90 , 91 , 179**
03.09	Other exploration and decompression of spinal canal **90 , 91 , 179**
03.1	Division of intraspinal nerve root **12 , 13 , 90 , 91 , 179 , 195**
03.2*	Chordotomy **12 , 13 , 82 , 179 , 195**
03.32	Biopsy of spinal cord or spinal meninges **12 , 13 , 90 , 91 , 179**
03.39	Other diagnostic procedures on spinal cord and spinal canal structures **12 , 13 , 90 , 91 , 179**
03.4	Excision or destruction of lesion of spinal cord or spinal meninges **12 , 13 , 90 , 91 , 179**
03.5*	Plastic operations on spinal cord structures **12 , 13**
03.53	Repair of vertebral fracture **90 , 91 , 179 , 195**
03.59	Other repair and plastic operations on spinal cord structures **90 , 91 , 179 , 195**
03.6	Lysis of adhesions of spinal cord and nerve roots **12 , 13 , 90 , 91 , 179 , 195**
03.7*	Shunt of spinal theca **12 , 13 , 179**

*Code Range

03.93	Implantation or replacement of spinal neurostimulator lead(s) **12 , 13 , 90 , 91 , 118 , 123 , 130 , 179 , 195**	
03.94	Removal of spinal neurostimulator lead(s) **12 , 13 , 90 , 91 , 118 , 123 , 130 , 195**	
03.97	Revision of spinal thecal shunt **12 , 13 , 90 , 91 , 179 , 195**	
03.98	Removal of spinal thecal shunt **12 , 13 , 90 , 91 , 195**	
03.99	Other operations on spinal cord and spinal canal structures **12 , 13 , 90 , 91 , 179 , 195**	
04.01	Excision of acoustic neuroma **8 , 10 , 11 , 43**	
04.02	Division of trigeminal nerve **14 , 16 , 43 , 195**	
04.03	Division or crushing of other cranial and peripheral nerves **14 , 16 , 43 , 95 , 195**	
04.04	Other incision of cranial and peripheral nerves **14 , 16 , 43 , 95 , 195**	
04.05	Gasserian ganglionectomy **14 , 16 , 43 , 195**	
04.06	Other cranial or peripheral ganglionectomy **14 , 16 , 43 , 95 , 195**	
04.07	Other excision or avulsion of cranial and peripheral nerves **14 , 16 , 43 , 95 , 195 , 233**	
04.12	Open biopsy of cranial or peripheral nerve or ganglion **14 , 16 , 43 , 95 , 195**	
04.19	Other diagnostic procedures on cranial and peripheral nerves and ganglia **14 , 16 , 43 , 95 , 195**	
04.3	Suture of cranial and peripheral nerves **14 , 16 , 195**	
04.4*	Lysis of adhesions and decompression of cranial and peripheral nerves **233**	
04.41	Decompression of trigeminal nerve root **8 , 10 , 11 , 43 , 195 , 220**	
04.42	Other cranial nerve decompression **14 , 16 , 43 , 195**	
04.43	Release of carpal tunnel **14 , 16 , 94 , 194**	
04.44	Release of tarsal tunnel **14 , 16 , 93 , 195**	
04.49	Other peripheral nerve or ganglion decompression or lysis of adhesions **14 , 16 , 43 , 95 , 195**	
04.5	Cranial or peripheral nerve graft **14 , 16 , 195**	
04.6	Transposition of cranial and peripheral nerves **14 , 16 , 195**	
04.7*	Other cranial or peripheral neuroplasty **14 , 16 , 195**	
04.71	Hypoglossal-facial anastomosis **43**	
04.72	Accessory-facial anastomosis **43**	
04.73	Accessory-hypoglossal anastomosis **43**	
04.74	Other anastomosis of cranial or peripheral nerve **43**	
04.75	Revision of previous repair of cranial and peripheral nerves **43**	
04.76	Repair of old traumatic injury of cranial and peripheral nerves **43**	
04.9*	Other operations on cranial and peripheral nerves **195**	
04.91	Neurectasis **14 , 16**	
04.92	Implantation or replacement of peripheral neurostimulator lead(s) **14 , 16 , 18 , 43 , 63 , 95 , 118 , 124 , 130**	
04.93	Removal of peripheral neurostimulator lead(s) **14 , 16 , 43 , 95 , 124 , 130**	
04.99	Other operations on cranial and peripheral nerves **14 , 16 , 43 , 95 , 233**	
05.0	Division of sympathetic nerve or ganglion **14 , 16 , 64**	
05.1*	Diagnostic procedures on sympathetic nerves or ganglia **14 , 16**	
05.2*	Sympathectomy **14 , 16 , 64**	
05.21	Sphenopalatine ganglionectomy **43**	
05.22	Cervical sympathectomy **43**	
05.23	Lumbar sympathectomy **233**	
05.24	Presacral sympathectomy **130**	
05.8*	Other operations on sympathetic nerves or ganglia **14 , 16**	
05.89	Other operations on sympathetic nerves or ganglia **64**	
05.9	Other operations on nervous system **14 , 16 , 195**	
06.02	Reopening of wound of thyroid field **112 , 195 , 233**	
06.09	Other incision of thyroid field **43 , 104 , 112 , 195**	

06.12	Open biopsy of thyroid gland **112**
06.13	Biopsy of parathyroid gland **95 , 112**
06.19	Other diagnostic procedures on thyroid and parathyroid glands **95 , 112**
06.2	Unilateral thyroid lobectomy **112**
06.3*	Other partial thyroidectomy **112**
06.4	Complete thyroidectomy **112**
06.5*	Substernal thyroidectomy **112**
06.6	Excision of lingual thyroid **44 , 112**
06.7	Excision of thyroglossal duct or tract **44 , 112**
06.8*	Parathyroidectomy **112 , 118**
06.91	Division of thyroid isthmus **112**
06.92	Ligation of thyroid vessels **113 , 195**
06.93	Suture of thyroid gland **113 , 195**
06.94	Thyroid tissue reimplantation **113**
06.95	Parathyroid tissue reimplantation **113**
06.98	Other operations on thyroid glands **113**
06.99	Other operations on parathyroid glands **113**
07.0*	Exploration of adrenal field **112**
07.12	Open biopsy of adrenal gland **112**
07.13	Biopsy of pituitary gland, transfrontal approach **8 , 10 , 11 , 112**
07.14	Biopsy of pituitary gland, transsphenoidal approach **8 , 10 , 11 , 112**
07.15	Biopsy of pituitary gland, unspecified approach **8 , 10 , 11 , 112**
07.16	Biopsy of thymus **50 , 113 , 176 , 179**
07.17	Biopsy of pineal gland **8 , 10 , 11 , 112**
07.19	Other diagnostic procedures on adrenal glands, pituitary gland, pineal gland, and thymus **14 , 16 , 112**
07.2*	Partial adrenalectomy **112**
07.22	Unilateral adrenalectomy **104**
07.3	Bilateral adrenalectomy **104 , 112**
07.4*	Other operations on adrenal glands, nerves, and vessels **112**
07.43	Ligation of adrenal vessels **195**
07.44	Repair of adrenal gland **195**
07.45	Reimplantation of adrenal tissue **195**
07.49	Other operations on adrenal glands, nerves, and vessels **195**
07.5*	Operations on pineal gland **8 , 10 , 11 , 112**
07.6*	Hypophysectomy **8 , 10 , 11 , 112**
07.63	Partial excision of pituitary gland, unspecified approach **104**
07.64	Total excision of pituitary gland, transfrontal approach **104**
07.65	Total excision of pituitary gland, transsphenoidal approach **104**
07.68	Total excision of pituitary gland, other specified approach **104**
07.69	Total excision of pituitary gland, unspecified approach **104**
07.7*	Other operations on hypophysis **8 , 10 , 11 , 112**
07.72	Incision of pituitary gland **104**
07.79	Other operations on hypophysis **104**
07.8*	Thymectomy **14 , 16 , 50 , 113 , 176 , 179 , 195**
07.9*	Other operations on thymus **50 , 113 , 176 , 179**
07.91	Exploration of thymus field **195**
07.92	Other incision of thymus **195**
07.93	Repair of thymus **195**
07.95	Thoracoscopic incision of thymus **14 , 16 , 195**
07.98	Other and unspecified thoracoscopic operations on thymus **14 , 16 , 195**
08.11	Biopsy of eyelid **37 , 195 , 233**
08.2*	Excision or destruction of lesion or tissue of eyelid **37 , 195 , 233**
08.20	Removal of lesion of eyelid, not otherwise specified **104 , 113**
08.22	Excision of other minor lesion of eyelid **104**
08.23	Excision of major lesion of eyelid, partial-thickness **104**
08.24	Excision of major lesion of eyelid, full-thickness **104**

*Code Range

08.25	Destruction of lesion of eyelid **104**	
08.3*	Repair of blepharoptosis and lid retraction **37 , 195 , 233**	
08.38	Correction of lid retraction **104 , 113**	
08.4*	Repair of entropion or ectropion **37 , 195 , 233**	
08.44	Repair of entropion or ectropion with lid reconstruction **104**	
08.5*	Other adjustment of lid position **14 , 16 , 37 , 104 , 195 , 233**	
08.6*	Reconstruction of eyelid with flaps or grafts **37 , 104 , 195 , 233**	
08.7*	Other reconstruction of eyelid **37 , 104 , 195 , 233**	
08.70	Reconstruction of eyelid, not otherwise specified **113**	
08.9*	Other operations on eyelids **37 , 195 , 233**	
08.99	Other operations on eyelids **104**	
09.0	Incision of lacrimal gland **233**	
09.1*	Diagnostic procedures on lacrimal system **233**	
09.11	Biopsy of lacrimal gland **195**	
09.12	Biopsy of lacrimal sac **44**	
09.19	Other diagnostic procedures on lacrimal system **44 , 195**	
09.2*	Excision of lesion or tissue of lacrimal gland **233**	
09.21	Excision of lesion of lacrimal gland **195**	
09.22	Other partial dacryoadenectomy **195**	
09.23	Total dacryoadenectomy **195**	
09.3	Other operations on lacrimal gland **195 , 233**	
09.4*	Manipulation of lacrimal passage **233**	
09.43	Probing of nasolacrimal duct **44**	
09.44	Intubation of nasolacrimal duct **44 , 195**	
09.5*	Incision of lacrimal sac and passages **233**	
09.52	Incision of lacrimal canaliculi **195**	
09.6	Excision of lacrimal sac and passage **195 , 233**	
09.7*	Repair of canaliculus and punctum **195 , 233**	
09.73	Repair of canaliculus **104**	
09.8*	Fistulization of lacrimal tract to nasal cavity **195 , 233**	
09.81	Dacryocystorhinostomy (DCR) **44**	
09.9*	Other operations on lacrimal system **195 , 233**	
09.99	Other operations on lacrimal system **44**	
09*	Operations on lacrimal system **37**	
10.0	Removal of embedded foreign body from conjunctiva by incision **195 , 233**	
10.1	Other incision of conjunctiva **233**	
10.2*	Diagnostic procedures on conjunctiva **233**	
10.3*	Excision or destruction of lesion or tissue of conjunctiva **195 , 233**	
10.4*	Conjunctivoplasty **195 , 233**	
10.5	Lysis of adhesions of conjunctiva and eyelid **233**	
10.6	Repair of laceration of conjunctiva **195 , 233**	
10.9*	Other operations on conjunctiva **233**	
10*	Operations on conjunctiva **37**	
11.0	Magnetic removal of embedded foreign body from cornea **37 , 195 , 233**	
11.1	Incision of cornea **37 , 195 , 233**	
11.2*	Diagnostic procedures on cornea **37 , 233**	
11.22	Biopsy of cornea **195**	
11.3*	Excision of pterygium **37 , 233**	
11.32	Excision of pterygium with corneal graft **195**	
11.4*	Excision or destruction of tissue or other lesion of cornea **37 , 233**	
11.42	Thermocauterization of corneal lesion **195**	
11.43	Cryotherapy of corneal lesion **195**	
11.49	Other removal or destruction of corneal lesion **195**	
11.5*	Repair of cornea **37 , 195 , 233**	
11.6*	Corneal transplant **195 , 233**	
11.60	Corneal transplant, not otherwise specified **37**	
11.61	Lamellar keratoplasty with autograft **37**	

11.62	Other lamellar keratoplasty **37**
11.63	Penetrating keratoplasty with autograft **37**
11.64	Other penetrating keratoplasty **37**
11.69	Other corneal transplant **37**
11.7*	Other reconstructive and refractive surgery on cornea **195 , 233**
11.71	Keratomileusis **37**
11.72	Keratophakia **37**
11.73	Keratoprosthesis **37**
11.74	Thermokeratoplasty **37**
11.75	Radial keratotomy **37**
11.76	Epikeratophakia **37**
11.79	Other reconstructive surgery on cornea **37**
11.9*	Other operations on cornea **195 , 233**
11.91	Tattooing of cornea **37**
11.92	Removal of artificial implant from cornea **37**
11.99	Other operations on cornea **37**
12.0*	Removal of intraocular foreign body from anterior segment of eye **37 , 195 , 233**
12.1*	Iridotomy and simple iridectomy **37 , 195 , 233**
12.2*	Diagnostic procedures on iris, ciliary body, sclera, and anterior chamber **195 , 233**
12.21	Diagnostic aspiration of anterior chamber of eye **37**
12.22	Biopsy of iris **37**
12.29	Other diagnostic procedures on iris, ciliary body, sclera, and anterior chamber **37**
12.3*	Iridoplasty and coreoplasty **195 , 233**
12.31	Lysis of goniosynechiae **37**
12.32	Lysis of other anterior synechiae **37**
12.33	Lysis of posterior synechiae **37**
12.34	Lysis of corneovitreal adhesions **37**
12.35	Coreoplasty **37**
12.39	Other iridoplasty **37**
12.4*	Excision or destruction of lesion of iris and ciliary body **195 , 233**
12.40	Removal of lesion of anterior segment of eye, not otherwise specified **37**
12.41	Destruction of lesion of iris, nonexcisional **37**
12.42	Excision of lesion of iris **37**
12.43	Destruction of lesion of ciliary body, nonexcisional **37**
12.44	Excision of lesion of ciliary body **37**
12.5*	Facilitation of intraocular circulation **195 , 233**
12.51	Goniopuncture without goniotomy **37**
12.52	Goniotomy without goniopuncture **37**
12.53	Goniotomy with goniopuncture **37**
12.54	Trabeculotomy ab externo **37**
12.55	Cyclodialysis **37**
12.59	Other facilitation of intraocular circulation **37**
12.6*	Scleral fistulization **37 , 195**
12.61	Trephination of sclera with iridectomy **234**
12.62	Thermocauterization of sclera with iridectomy **234**
12.63	Iridencleisis and iridotasis **234**
12.64	Trabeculectomy ab externo **113 , 234**
12.65	Other scleral fistulization with iridectomy **234**
12.66	Postoperative revision of scleral fistulization procedure **234**
12.69	Other scleral fistulizing procedure **234**
12.7*	Other procedures for relief of elevated intraocular pressure **37 , 234**
12.72	Cyclocryotherapy **113**
12.79	Other glaucoma procedures **113**
12.8*	Operations on sclera **195 , 234**
12.81	Suture of laceration of sclera **37**

Numeric Index to Procedures

17.61	Laser interstitial thermal therapy [LITT] of lesion or tissue of brain under guidance **8 , 10 , 11**	
17.62	Laser interstitial thermal therapy [LITT] of lesion or tissue of head and neck under guidance **113 , 179**	
17.63	Laser interstitial thermal therapy [LITT] of lesion or tissue of liver under guidance **74 , 81**	
17.69	Laser interstitial thermal therapy [LITT] of lesion or tissue of other and unspecified site under guidance **50 , 106 , 124 , 179**	
18.21	Excision of preauricular sinus **44 , 104 , 234**	
18.3*	Other excision of external ear **44 , 104**	
18.31	Radical excision of lesion of external ear **234**	
18.39	Other excision of external ear **196 , 234**	
18.5	Surgical correction of prominent ear **44 , 104 , 234**	
18.6	Reconstruction of external auditory canal **44 , 104 , 196 , 234**	
18.7*	Other plastic repair of external ear **44 , 196**	
18.71	Construction of auricle of ear **104 , 234**	
18.72	Reattachment of amputated ear **234**	
18.79	Other plastic repair of external ear **104 , 234**	
18.9	Other operations on external ear **44 , 104 , 196 , 234**	
19.1*	Stapedectomy **234**	
19.4	Myringoplasty **234**	
19.9	Other repair of middle ear **234**	
19*	Reconstructive operations on middle ear **44**	
20.01	Myringotomy with insertion of tube **44 , 234**	
20.2*	Incision of mastoid and middle ear **234**	
20.21	Incision of mastoid **45**	
20.22	Incision of petrous pyramid air cells **45**	
20.23	Incision of middle ear **44**	
20.32	Biopsy of middle and inner ear **44 , 234**	
20.39	Other diagnostic procedures on middle and inner ear **44 , 234**	
20.4*	Mastoidectomy **45**	
20.5*	Other excision of middle ear **44**	
20.51	Excision of lesion of middle ear **234**	
20.6*	Fenestration of inner ear **44**	
20.7*	Incision, excision, and destruction of inner ear **44**	
20.91	Tympanosympathectomy **44**	
20.92	Revision of mastoidectomy **45**	
20.93	Repair of oval and round windows **44**	
20.95	Implantation of electromagnetic hearing device **44**	
20.96	Implantation or replacement of cochlear prosthetic device, not otherwise specified **43**	
20.97	Implantation or replacement of cochlear prosthetic device, single channel **43**	
20.98	Implantation or replacement of cochlear prosthetic device, multiple channel **43**	
20.99	Other operations on middle and inner ear **44**	
21.04	Control of epistaxis by ligation of ethmoidal arteries **44 , 64 , 196**	
21.05	Control of epistaxis by (transantral) ligation of the maxillary artery **44 , 64 , 196**	
21.06	Control of epistaxis by ligation of the external carotid artery **44 , 64 , 196**	
21.07	Control of epistaxis by excision of nasal mucosa and skin grafting of septum and lateral nasal wall **44 , 64 , 196**	
21.09	Control of epistaxis by other means **44 , 64 , 196 , 234**	
21.4	Resection of nose **43 , 104 , 196**	
21.5	Submucous resection of nasal septum **44 , 196 , 234**	
21.6*	Turbinectomy **44**	
21.62	Fracture of the turbinates **196 , 234**	
21.69	Other turbinectomy **196 , 234**	
21.72	Open reduction of nasal fracture **43 , 95 , 104 , 196 , 234**	
21.82	Closure of nasal fistula **44 , 234**	

21.83	Total nasal reconstruction **44 , 95 , 104 , 196 , 234**
21.84	Revision rhinoplasty **44 , 95 , 104 , 196 , 234**
21.85	Augmentation rhinoplasty **44 , 95 , 104 , 196 , 234**
21.86	Limited rhinoplasty **44 , 95 , 104 , 196 , 234**
21.87	Other rhinoplasty **44 , 95 , 104 , 196 , 234**
21.88	Other septoplasty **44 , 95 , 104 , 196 , 234**
21.89	Other repair and plastic operations on nose **44 , 95 , 104 , 196 , 234**
21.99	Other operations on nose **44 , 104 , 196 , 234**
22.12	Open biopsy of nasal sinus **45**
22.3*	External maxillary antrotomy **45**
22.4*	Frontal sinusotomy and sinusectomy **45**
22.5*	Other nasal sinusotomy **45**
22.6*	Other nasal sinusectomy **45**
22.62	Excision of lesion of maxillary sinus with other approach **95**
22.63	Ethmoidectomy **234**
22.7*	Repair of nasal sinus **45**
22.9	Other operations on nasal sinuses **45**
24.2	Gingivoplasty **45 , 196**
24.4	Excision of dental lesion of jaw **45 , 234**
24.5	Alveoloplasty **45 , 196 , 234**
25.02	Open biopsy of tongue **45**
25.1	Excision or destruction of lesion or tissue of tongue **45 , 64 , 234**
25.2	Partial glossectomy **45**
25.3	Complete glossectomy **43**
25.4	Radical glossectomy **43**
25.59	Other repair and plastic operations on tongue **45 , 196**
25.94	Other glossotomy **45**
25.99	Other operations on tongue **45**
26.12	Open biopsy of salivary gland or duct **45 , 234**
26.2*	Excision of lesion of salivary gland **45 , 234**
26.3*	Sialoadenectomy **45 , 234**
26.30	Sialoadenectomy, not otherwise specified **176**
26.4*	Repair of salivary gland or duct **45 , 196**
26.99	Other operations on salivary gland or duct **45**
27.0	Drainage of face and floor of mouth **45 , 104 , 196**
27.1	Incision of palate **45**
27.21	Biopsy of bony palate **45 , 234**
27.22	Biopsy of uvula and soft palate **45 , 234**
27.3*	Excision of lesion or tissue of bony palate **234**
27.31	Local excision or destruction of lesion or tissue of bony palate **45**
27.32	Wide excision or destruction of lesion or tissue of bony palate **43**
27.42	Wide excision of lesion of lip **45 , 104 , 234**
27.43	Other excision of lesion or tissue of lip **45 , 104 , 234**
27.49	Other excision of mouth **45 , 196 , 234**
27.53	Closure of fistula of mouth **45 , 196 , 234**
27.54	Repair of cleft lip **44 , 104 , 196 , 234**
27.55	Full-thickness skin graft to lip and mouth **45 , 104 , 196 , 234**
27.56	Other skin graft to lip and mouth **45 , 104 , 196 , 234**
27.57	Attachment of pedicle or flap graft to lip and mouth **45 , 104 , 196 , 234**
27.59	Other plastic repair of mouth **45 , 104 , 196 , 234**
27.61	Suture of laceration of palate **45 , 196**
27.62	Correction of cleft palate **14 , 16 , 44**
27.63	Revision of cleft palate repair **44 , 104**
27.69	Other plastic repair of palate **14 , 16 , 44 , 104**
27.7*	Operations on uvula **45 , 234**
27.92	Incision of mouth, unspecified structure **45 , 104 , 196 , 234**
27.99	Other operations on oral cavity **45 , 196 , 234**

28.0	Incision and drainage of tonsil and peritonsillar structures	**44**
28.11	Biopsy of tonsils and adenoids	**44 , 234**
28.19	Other diagnostic procedures on tonsils and adenoids	**44**
28.2	Tonsillectomy without adenoidectomy	**44 , 234**
28.3	Tonsillectomy with adenoidectomy	**44**
28.4	Excision of tonsil tag	**44**
28.5	Excision of lingual tonsil	**44**
28.6	Adenoidectomy without tonsillectomy	**44**
28.7	Control of hemorrhage after tonsillectomy and adenoidectomy **44 , 196**	
28.91	Removal of foreign body from tonsil and adenoid by incision **44 , 196**	
28.92	Excision of lesion of tonsil and adenoid	**44**
28.99	Other operations on tonsils and adenoids	**44**
29.0	Pharyngotomy	**44 , 196**
29.2	Excision of branchial cleft cyst or vestige	**44 , 104**
29.3*	Excision or destruction of lesion or tissue of pharynx	**72**
29.31	Cricopharyngeal myotomy	**44**
29.32	Pharyngeal diverticulectomy	**44**
29.33	Pharyngectomy (partial)	**44**
29.39	Other excision or destruction of lesion or tissue of pharynx	**44**
29.4	Plastic operation on pharynx	**14 , 16 , 44 , 196 , 234**
29.51	Suture of laceration of pharynx	**44 , 196**
29.52	Closure of branchial cleft fistula	**44 , 104**
29.53	Closure of other fistula of pharynx	**44 , 196**
29.54	Lysis of pharyngeal adhesions	**44**
29.59	Other repair of pharynx	**14 , 16 , 44 , 196**
29.92	Division of glossopharyngeal nerve	**8 , 10 , 11 , 44**
29.99	Other operations on pharynx	**44 , 196**
30.0*	Excision or destruction of lesion or tissue of larynx	**44**
30.01	Marsupialization of laryngeal cyst	**50**
30.09	Other excision or destruction of lesion or tissue of larynx	**50 , 234**
30.1	Hemilaryngectomy	**43 , 50 , 196**
30.2*	Other partial laryngectomy	**50 , 196**
30.21	Epiglottidectomy	**44**
30.22	Vocal cordectomy	**44**
30.29	Other partial laryngectomy	**43**
30.3	Complete laryngectomy	**2**
30.4	Radical laryngectomy	**2**
31.1	Temporary tracheostomy	**1 , 4**
31.21	Mediastinal tracheostomy	**1 , 4**
31.29	Other permanent tracheostomy	**1 , 4**
31.3	Other incision of larynx or trachea	**44 , 50**
31.45	Open biopsy of larynx or trachea	**44 , 50**
31.5	Local excision or destruction of lesion or tissue of trachea	**44 , 50**
31.6*	Repair of larynx	**44 , 50**
31.61	Suture of laceration of larynx	**196**
31.64	Repair of laryngeal fracture	**196**
31.69	Other repair of larynx	**196**
31.7*	Repair and plastic operations on trachea	**196**
31.71	Suture of laceration of trachea	**44 , 50**
31.72	Closure of external fistula of trachea	**44 , 50 , 64 , 104**
31.73	Closure of other fistula of trachea	**44 , 50 , 72**
31.74	Revision of tracheostomy	**44 , 50 , 64 , 104**
31.75	Reconstruction of trachea and construction of artificial larynx **44 , 50**	
31.79	Other repair and plastic operations on trachea	**44 , 50**
31.91	Division of laryngeal nerve	**44 , 50**
31.92	Lysis of adhesions of trachea or larynx	**44 , 50 , 196**

31.98	Other operations on larynx	**44 , 50 , 234**
31.99	Other operations on trachea	**44 , 50 , 196**
32.09	Other local excision or destruction of lesion or tissue of bronchus **50**	
32.1	Other excision of bronchus	**50 , 196**
32.20	Thoracoscopic excision of lesion or tissue of lung	**50 , 179 , 196**
32.21	Plication of emphysematous bleb	**50**
32.22	Lung volume reduction surgery	**50**
32.23	Open ablation of lung lesion or tissue	**50 , 179**
32.24	Percutaneous ablation of lung lesion or tissue	**50**
32.25	Thoracoscopic ablation of lung lesion or tissue	**50 , 179**
32.26	Other and unspecified ablation of lung lesion or tissue	**50**
32.27	Bronchoscopic bronchial thermoplasty, ablation of airway smooth muscle **50**	
32.29	Other local excision or destruction of lesion or tissue of lung **50 , 179**	
32.3*	Segmental resection of lung	**50 , 179 , 196**
32.4*	Lobectomy of lung	**50 , 196**
32.5*	Pneumonectomy	**50 , 196**
32.6	Radical dissection of thoracic structures	**50**
32.9	Other excision of lung	**50 , 196**
33.0	Incision of bronchus	**50 , 196**
33.1	Incision of lung	**50 , 196**
33.20	Thoracoscopic lung biopsy	**50 , 64 , 95 , 118**
33.25	Open biopsy of bronchus	**50**
33.27	Closed endoscopic biopsy of lung	**50 , 64 , 234**
33.28	Open biopsy of lung	**50 , 64 , 95 , 118 , 179**
33.29	Other diagnostic procedures on lung or bronchus	**50**
33.34	Thoracoplasty	**50**
33.39	Other surgical collapse of lung	**50**
33.4*	Repair and plastic operation on lung and bronchus	**50 , 196**
33.5*	Lung transplant	**1**
33.6	Combined heart-lung transplantation	**1**
33.92	Ligation of bronchus	**50 , 196**
33.93	Puncture of lung	**50**
33.98	Other operations on bronchus	**50 , 196**
33.99	Other operations on lung	**50 , 196**
34.02	Exploratory thoracotomy	**50 , 64 , 118 , 179 , 196**
34.03	Reopening of recent thoracotomy site	**50 , 64 , 196**
34.06	Thoracoscopic drainage of pleural cavity	**50**
34.1	Incision of mediastinum	**50 , 64 , 196**
34.20	Thoracoscopic pleural biopsy	**50**
34.21	Transpleural thoracoscopy	**50 , 64 , 196**
34.22	Mediastinoscopy	**44 , 50 , 64 , 176 , 179**
34.26	Open biopsy of mediastinum	**50 , 64 , 113 , 176 , 179**
34.27	Biopsy of diaphragm	**50**
34.28	Other diagnostic procedures on chest wall, pleura, and diaphragm **50**	
34.29	Other diagnostic procedures on mediastinum	**50 , 64**
34.3	Excision or destruction of lesion or tissue of mediastinum **50 , 113 , 179 , 234**	
34.4	Excision or destruction of lesion of chest wall **50 , 92 , 104 , 113 , 179 , 234**	
34.5*	Pleurectomy	**50 , 196**
34.51	Decortication of lung	**179**
34.52	Thoracoscopic decortication of lung	**179**
34.6	Scarification of pleura	**50 , 179 , 196**
34.73	Closure of other fistula of thorax	**50 , 196**
34.74	Repair of pectus deformity	**50 , 95**
34.79	Other repair of chest wall	**50 , 95 , 104 , 196**

*Code Range

© 2012 OptumInsight, Inc.

Numeric Index to Procedures

34.8*	Operations on diaphragm **50**	
34.81	Excision of lesion or tissue of diaphragm **95**	
34.82	Suture of laceration of diaphragm **196**	
34.83	Closure of fistula of diaphragm **196**	
34.84	Other repair of diaphragm **196**	
34.85	Implantation of diaphragmatic pacemaker **196**	
34.89	Other operations on diaphragm **196**	
34.93	Repair of pleura **50 , 196**	
34.99	Other operations on thorax **50 , 196**	
35.0*	Closed heart valvotomy or transcatheter replacement of heart valve **59**	
35.05	Endovascular replacement of aortic valve **56**	
35.06	Transapical replacement of aortic valve **56**	
35.07	Endovascular replacement of pulmonary valve **56**	
35.08	Transapical replacement of pulmonary valve **56**	
35.09	Endovascular replacement of unspecified heart valve **56**	
35.1*	Open heart valvuloplasty without replacement **56**	
35.2*	Open and other replacement of heart valve **56**	
35.31	Operations on papillary muscle **58**	
35.32	Operations on chordae tendineae **58**	
35.33	Annuloplasty **56**	
35.34	Infundibulectomy **58**	
35.35	Operations on trabeculae carneae cordis **58**	
35.39	Operations on other structures adjacent to valves of heart **58**	
35.42	Creation of septal defect in heart **58**	
35.50	Repair of unspecified septal defect of heart with prosthesis **58**	
35.51	Repair of atrial septal defect with prosthesis, open technique **58**	
35.52	Repair of atrial septal defect with prosthesis, closed technique **63**	
35.53	Repair of ventricular septal defect with prosthesis, open technique **58**	
35.54	Repair of endocardial cushion defect with prosthesis **58**	
35.55	Repair of ventricular septal defect with prosthesis, closed technique **58**	
35.6*	Repair of atrial and ventricular septa with tissue graft **58**	
35.7*	Other and unspecified repair of atrial and ventricular septa **58**	
35.8*	Total repair of certain congenital cardiac anomalies **58**	
35.91	Interatrial transposition of venous return **58**	
35.92	Creation of conduit between right ventricle and pulmonary artery **58**	
35.93	Creation of conduit between left ventricle and aorta **58**	
35.94	Creation of conduit between atrium and pulmonary artery **58**	
35.95	Revision of corrective procedure on heart **58**	
35.96	Percutaneous balloon valvuloplasty **58 , 62 , 63**	
35.97	Percutaneous mitral valve repair with implant **58 , 62 , 63**	
35.98	Other operations on septa of heart **58**	
35.99	Other operations on valves of heart **58**	
36.03	Open chest coronary artery angioplasty **58**	
36.06	Insertion of non-drug-eluting coronary artery stent(s) **62**	
36.07	Insertion of drug-eluting coronary artery stent(s) **62**	
36.09	Other removal of coronary artery obstruction **62 , 63**	
36.1*	Bypass anastomosis for heart revascularization **58 , 59**	
36.2	Heart revascularization by arterial implant **58**	
36.3*	Other heart revascularization **58**	
36.9*	Other operations on vessels of heart **58**	
37.10	Incision of heart, not otherwise specified **58**	
37.11	Cardiotomy **58 , 196**	
37.12	Pericardiotomy **50 , 59 , 179 , 196**	
37.21	Right heart cardiac catheterization **56 , 57 , 58 , 65**	
37.22	Left heart cardiac catheterization **56 , 57 , 58 , 65**	

37.23	Combined right and left heart cardiac catheterization **56 , 57 , 58 , 65**
37.24	Biopsy of pericardium **50 , 59 , 179**
37.26	Catheter based invasive electrophysiologic testing **56 , 62 , 63**
37.27	Cardiac mapping **62 , 63**
37.31	Pericardiectomy **50 , 59 , 179 , 196**
37.32	Excision of aneurysm of heart **58**
37.33	Excision or destruction of other lesion or tissue of heart, open approach **58**
37.34	Excision or destruction of other lesion or tissue of heart, endovascular approach **62 , 63**
37.35	Partial ventriculectomy **58**
37.37	Excision or destruction of other lesion or tissue of heart, thoracoscopic approach **58**
37.4*	Repair of heart and pericardium **59**
37.49	Other repair of heart and pericardium **196**
37.51	Heart transplantation **1**
37.52	Implantation of total internal biventricular heart replacement system **1**
37.53	Replacement or repair of thoracic unit of (total) replacement heart system **56**
37.54	Replacement or repair of other implantable component of (total) replacement heart system **56**
37.55	Removal of internal biventricular heart replacement system **59**
37.60	Implantation or insertion of biventricular external heart assist system **1 , 56**
37.61	Implant of pulsation balloon **59**
37.62	Insertion of temporary non-implantable extracorporeal circulatory assist device **56**
37.63	Repair of heart assist system **1 , 56**
37.64	Removal of external heart assist system(s) or device(s) **1 , 59**
37.65	Implant of single ventricular (extracorporeal) external heart assist system **1 , 56**
37.66	Insertion of implantable heart assist system **1**
37.67	Implantation of cardiomyostimulation system **59**
37.68	Insertion of percutaneous external heart assist device **56**
37.70	Initial insertion of lead (electrode), not otherwise specified **14 , 15 , 17 , 60 , 202**
37.71	Initial insertion of transvenous lead (electrode) into ventricle **15 , 17 , 60 , 202**
37.72	Initial insertion of transvenous leads (electrodes) into atrium and ventricle **15 , 17 , 60 , 61 , 202**
37.73	Initial insertion of transvenous lead (electrode) into atrium **15 , 17 , 18 , 61 , 202 , 203**
37.74	Insertion or replacement of epicardial lead (electrode) into epicardium **14 , 15 , 16 , 18 , 57 , 58 , 61 , 64 , 196 , 203**
37.75	Revision of lead (electrode) **14 , 16 , 64 , 196**
37.76	Replacement of transvenous atrial and/or ventricular lead(s) (electrode(s)) **14 , 16 , 18 , 61 , 64 , 196 , 203**
37.77	Removal of lead(s) (electrodes) without replacement **14 , 16 , 64 , 196**
37.79	Revision or relocation of cardiac device pocket **14 , 16 , 64 , 104 , 196**
37.80	Insertion of permanent pacemaker, initial or replacement, type of device not specified **14 , 15 , 16 , 17 , 18 , 60 , 61 , 63 , 196 , 202 , 203**
37.81	Initial insertion of single-chamber device, not specified as rate responsive **15 , 17 , 18 , 60 , 61 , 202 , 203**
37.82	Initial insertion of single-chamber device, rate responsive **15 , 17 , 18 , 60 , 61 , 202 , 203**
37.83	Initial insertion of dual-chamber device **15 , 17 , 18 , 61 , 202 , 203**

37.85	Replacement of any type of pacemaker device with single-chamber device, not specified as rate responsive **14 , 15 , 16 , 17 , 18 , 60 , 61 , 63 , 196 , 202 , 203**
37.86	Replacement of any type of pacemaker device with single-chamber device, rate responsive **14 , 15 , 16 , 17 , 18 , 60 , 61 , 63 , 196 , 202 , 203**
37.87	Replacement of any type of pacemaker device with dual-chamber device **14 , 15 , 16 , 17 , 18 , 60 , 61 , 63 , 196 , 202 , 203**
37.89	Revision or removal of pacemaker device **14 , 16 , 64 , 196 , 234**
37.90	Insertion of left atrial appendage device **63**
37.91	Open chest cardiac massage **50 , 59 , 179 , 196**
37.94	Implantation or replacement of automatic cardioverter/defibrillator, total system (AICD) **57**
37.95	Implantation of automatic cardioverter/defibrillator leads(s) only **57 , 58 , 65**
37.96	Implantation of automatic cardioverter/defibrillator pulse generator only **57 , 58 , 62**
37.97	Replacement of automatic cardioverter/defibrillator leads(s) only **57 , 58 , 65**
37.98	Replacement of automatic cardioverter/defibrillator pulse generator only **57 , 58 , 62**
37.99	Other operations on heart and pericardium **59**
38.0*	Incision of vessel **196**
38.00	Incision of vessel, unspecified site **44 , 63 , 113 , 234**
38.01	Incision of intracranial vessels **8 , 10 , 11**
38.02	Incision of other vessels of head and neck **14 , 16 , 44 , 63 , 113**
38.03	Incision of upper limb vessels **63 , 113**
38.04	Incision of aorta **59 , 74**
38.05	Incision of other thoracic vessels **50 , 59 , 72**
38.06	Incision of abdominal arteries **59 , 74 , 118**
38.07	Incision of abdominal veins **59 , 74 , 118**
38.08	Incision of lower limb arteries **63 , 113 , 179**
38.09	Incision of lower limb veins **64 , 234**
38.10	Endarterectomy, unspecified site **13 , 63 , 196**
38.11	Endarterectomy of intracranial vessels **8 , 10 , 11**
38.12	Endarterectomy of other vessels of head and neck **13 , 44 , 63 , 113 , 197**
38.13	Endarterectomy of upper limb vessels **63 , 113 , 197**
38.14	Endarterectomy of aorta **59 , 74 , 197**
38.15	Endarterectomy of other thoracic vessels **50 , 59 , 197**
38.16	Endarterectomy of abdominal arteries **59 , 74 , 118 , 197**
38.18	Endarterectomy of lower limb arteries **63 , 113 , 197**
38.21	Biopsy of blood vessel **14 , 16 , 37 , 44 , 50 , 63 , 95 , 113 , 118 , 234**
38.26	Insertion of implantable pressure sensor without lead for intracardiac or great vessel hemodynamic monitoring **64**
38.29	Other diagnostic procedures on blood vessels **63 , 113**
38.3*	Resection of vessel with anastomosis **197**
38.30	Resection of vessel with anastomosis, unspecified site **63 , 113**
38.31	Resection of intracranial vessels with anastomosis **8 , 10 , 11**
38.32	Resection of other vessels of head and neck with anastomosis **13 , 44 , 63**
38.33	Resection of upper limb vessels with anastomosis **63 , 113**
38.34	Resection of aorta with anastomosis **59 , 74**
38.35	Resection of other thoracic vessels with anastomosis **50 , 59 , 72**
38.36	Resection of abdominal arteries with anastomosis **59 , 74 , 118**
38.37	Resection of abdominal veins with anastomosis **59 , 74 , 118**
38.38	Resection of lower limb arteries with anastomosis **63 , 113**
38.39	Resection of lower limb veins with anastomosis **64**
38.4*	Resection of vessel with replacement **197**
38.40	Resection of vessel with replacement, unspecified site **63**
38.41	Resection of intracranial vessels with replacement **8 , 10 , 11**

38.42	Resection of other vessels of head and neck with replacement **14 , 16 , 44 , 63**
38.43	Resection of upper limb vessels with replacement **63 , 113**
38.44	Resection of abdominal aorta with replacement **59**
38.45	Resection of other thoracic vessels with replacement **50 , 56 , 72**
38.46	Resection of abdominal arteries with replacement **59 , 74 , 118**
38.47	Resection of abdominal veins with replacement **59 , 74 , 118**
38.48	Resection of lower limb arteries with replacement **63 , 113**
38.49	Resection of lower limb veins with replacement **64**
38.50	Ligation and stripping of varicose veins, unspecified site **64**
38.51	Ligation and stripping of varicose veins of intracranial vessels **8 , 10 , 11**
38.52	Ligation and stripping of varicose veins of other vessels of head and neck **63**
38.53	Ligation and stripping of varicose veins of upper limb vessels **64**
38.55	Ligation and stripping of varicose veins of other thoracic vessel **50 , 59 , 113**
38.57	Ligation and stripping of abdominal varicose veins **63 , 74**
38.59	Ligation and stripping of lower limb varicose veins **64 , 234**
38.6*	Other excision of vessels **197**
38.60	Other excision of vessels, unspecified site **63 , 113**
38.61	Other excision of intracranial vessels **8 , 10 , 11**
38.62	Other excision of other vessels of head and neck **13 , 44 , 63**
38.63	Other excision of upper limb vessels **63 , 113**
38.64	Other excision of abdominal aorta **59 , 74**
38.65	Other excision of other thoracic vessel **50 , 59 , 72**
38.66	Other excision of abdominal arteries **59 , 74 , 118**
38.67	Other excision of abdominal veins **59 , 74 , 118**
38.68	Other excision of lower limb arteries **63 , 113**
38.69	Other excision of lower limb veins **64**
38.7	Interruption of the vena cava **14 , 16 , 50 , 63 , 74 , 82 , 95 , 113 , 118 , 124 , 130 , 140 , 176 , 197**
38.8*	Other surgical occlusion of vessels **197**
38.80	Other surgical occlusion of vessels, unspecified site **63**
38.81	Other surgical occlusion of intracranial vessels **8 , 10 , 11 , 220**
38.82	Other surgical occlusion of other vessels of head and neck **14 , 16 , 44 , 63**
38.83	Other surgical occlusion of upper limb vessels **63 , 113**
38.84	Other surgical occlusion of abdominal aorta **59 , 74**
38.85	Other surgical occlusion of other thoracic vessel **50 , 59 , 72**
38.86	Other surgical occlusion of abdominal arteries **59 , 74 , 118 , 234**
38.87	Other surgical occlusion of abdominal veins **59 , 74 , 118**
38.88	Other surgical occlusion of lower limb arteries **63 , 113**
38.89	Other surgical occlusion of lower limb veins **64**
39.0	Systemic to pulmonary artery shunt **59**
39.1	Intra-abdominal venous shunt **59 , 72 , 81**
39.21	Caval-pulmonary artery anastomosis **59**
39.22	Aorta-subclavian-carotid bypass **13 , 59 , 197**
39.23	Other intrathoracic vascular shunt or bypass **59 , 197**
39.24	Aorta-renal bypass **59 , 117 , 197**
39.25	Aorta-iliac-femoral bypass **59 , 105 , 113 , 197**
39.26	Other intra-abdominal vascular shunt or bypass **59 , 74 , 82 , 117 , 197**
39.27	Arteriovenostomy for renal dialysis **64 , 74 , 113 , 118 , 197**
39.28	Extracranial-intracranial (EC-IC) vascular bypass **8 , 10 , 11 , 197**
39.29	Other (peripheral) vascular shunt or bypass **13 , 50 , 63 , 82 , 105 , 113 , 197**
39.3*	Suture of vessel **13 , 197**
39.30	Suture of unspecified blood vessel **63**
39.31	Suture of artery **50 , 63 , 105 , 113**

*Code Range

© 2012 OptumInsight, Inc.

39.32	Suture of vein **64**	
39.4*	Revision of vascular procedure **197**	
39.41	Control of hemorrhage following vascular surgery **63 , 113**	
39.42	Revision of arteriovenous shunt for renal dialysis **64 , 113 , 118**	
39.43	Removal of arteriovenous shunt for renal dialysis **64 , 118**	
39.49	Other revision of vascular procedure **63 , 74 , 82 , 113 , 118**	
39.50	Angioplasty of other non-coronary vessel(s) **13 , 50 , 63 , 74 , 82 , 95 , 105 , 113 , 118 , 197**	
39.51	Clipping of aneurysm **8 , 10 , 11 , 63**	
39.52	Other repair of aneurysm **8 , 10 , 11 , 59 , 118 , 197**	
39.53	Repair of arteriovenous fistula **8 , 10 , 11 , 63**	
39.54	Re-entry operation (aorta) **50 , 59**	
39.55	Reimplantation of aberrant renal vessel **63 , 117**	
39.56	Repair of blood vessel with tissue patch graft **13 , 63 , 113 , 118 , 197**	
39.57	Repair of blood vessel with synthetic patch graft **13 , 63 , 113 , 118 , 197**	
39.58	Repair of blood vessel with unspecified type of patch graft **13 , 63 , 113 , 118 , 197**	
39.59	Other repair of vessel **13 , 63 , 105 , 113 , 118 , 197**	
39.65	Extracorporeal membrane oxygenation (ECMO) **1**	
39.71	Endovascular implantation of other graft in abdominal aorta **59 , 60 , 118 , 197**	
39.72	Endovascular (total) embolization or occlusion of head and neck vessels **8 , 10 , 11 , 59 , 60 , 118 , 197**	
39.73	Endovascular implantation of graft in thoracic aorta **56 , 118 , 197**	
39.74	Endovascular removal of obstruction from head and neck vessel(s) **8 , 10 , 11 , 197**	
39.75	Endovascular embolization or occlusion of vessel(s) of head or neck using bare coils **8 , 10 , 11 , 59 , 60 , 118 , 197**	
39.76	Endovascular embolization or occlusion of vessel(s) of head or neck using bioactive coils **8 , 10 , 11 , 59 , 60 , 119 , 197**	
39.77	Temporary (partial) therapeutic endovascular occlusion of vessel **13 , 63 , 197**	
39.78	Endovascular implantation of branching or fenestrated graft(s) in aorta **59 , 60**	
39.79	Other endovascular procedures on other vessels **8 , 10 , 11 , 59 , 60 , 119 , 197**	
39.8*	Operations on carotid body, carotid sinus and other vascular bodies **63**	
39.91	Freeing of vessel **63 , 74 , 113 , 197**	
39.92	Injection of sclerosing agent into vein **13 , 64**	
39.93	Insertion of vessel-to-vessel cannula **64 , 113 , 119 , 197**	
39.94	Replacement of vessel-to-vessel cannula **63 , 119 , 235**	
39.98	Control of hemorrhage, not otherwise specified **44 , 50 , 64 , 74 , 82 , 95 , 105 , 113 , 119 , 124 , 130 , 140 , 179 , 197**	
39.99	Other operations on vessels **44 , 50 , 63 , 74 , 140 , 179 , 197**	
40.0	Incision of lymphatic structures **105 , 176 , 235**	
40.1*	Diagnostic procedures on lymphatic structures **64 , 74 , 95 , 105 , 113 , 124 , 176 , 235**	
40.11	Biopsy of lymphatic structure **14 , 16 , 44 , 50 , 82 , 119 , 130**	
40.19	Other diagnostic procedures on lymphatic structures **44 , 50 , 119**	
40.2*	Simple excision of lymphatic structure **105 , 176**	
40.21	Excision of deep cervical lymph node **44 , 50 , 64 , 74 , 95 , 113 , 235**	
40.22	Excision of internal mammary lymph node **50**	
40.23	Excision of axillary lymph node **44 , 50 , 64 , 74 , 95 , 235**	
40.24	Excision of inguinal lymph node **50 , 64 , 74 , 95 , 119 , 124 , 130 , 140 , 235**	
40.29	Simple excision of other lymphatic structure **44 , 50 , 64 , 74 , 95 , 113 , 119 , 124 , 130 , 197 , 235**	

40.3	Regional lymph node excision **44 , 50 , 64 , 74 , 95 , 105 , 113 , 119 , 124 , 130 , 140 , 176 , 179 , 235**
40.4*	Radical excision of cervical lymph nodes **50 , 105 , 113 , 176 , 179**
40.40	Radical neck dissection, not otherwise specified **43**
40.41	Radical neck dissection, unilateral **43**
40.42	Radical neck dissection, bilateral **43**
40.5*	Radical excision of other lymph nodes **74 , 105 , 176 , 179**
40.50	Radical excision of lymph nodes, not otherwise specified **43 , 50 , 119 , 124 , 127**
40.51	Radical excision of axillary lymph nodes **95**
40.52	Radical excision of periaortic lymph nodes **50 , 95 , 113 , 117 , 123 , 127**
40.53	Radical excision of iliac lymph nodes **95 , 113 , 117 , 123 , 127**
40.54	Radical groin dissection **95 , 117 , 123 , 127**
40.59	Radical excision of other lymph nodes **43 , 50 , 95 , 117 , 123 , 127**
40.6*	Operations on thoracic duct **50 , 197**
40.9	Other operations on lymphatic structures **44 , 74 , 105 , 119 , 124 , 176 , 179 , 197**
41.00	Bone marrow transplant, not otherwise specified **4**
41.01	Autologous bone marrow transplant without purging **4**
41.02	Allogeneic bone marrow transplant with purging **4**
41.03	Allogeneic bone marrow transplant without purging **4**
41.04	Autologous hematopoietic stem cell transplant without purging **4**
41.05	Allogeneic hematopoietic stem cell transplant without purging **4**
41.06	Cord blood stem cell transplant **4**
41.07	Autologous hematopoietic stem cell transplant with purging **4**
41.08	Allogeneic hematopoietic stem cell transplant with purging **4**
41.09	Autologous bone marrow transplant with purging **4**
41.2	Splenotomy **176 , 179 , 197**
41.33	Open biopsy of spleen **176 , 179**
41.4*	Excision or destruction of lesion or tissue of spleen **176 , 179**
41.42	Excision of lesion or tissue of spleen **197**
41.43	Partial splenectomy **95 , 197**
41.5	Total splenectomy **64 , 74 , 95 , 176 , 179 , 197**
41.93	Excision of accessory spleen **176 , 179 , 197**
41.94	Transplantation of spleen **176 , 179**
41.95	Repair and plastic operations on spleen **176 , 179 , 197**
41.99	Other operations on spleen **176 , 179 , 197**
42.01	Incision of esophageal web **44 , 72**
42.09	Other incision of esophagus **44 , 72 , 197**
42.1*	Esophagostomy **72 , 179 , 197**
42.10	Esophagostomy, not otherwise specified **44**
42.11	Cervical esophagostomy **44**
42.12	Exteriorization of esophageal pouch **44**
42.19	Other external fistulization of esophagus **44**
42.21	Operative esophagoscopy by incision **44 , 72 , 179 , 197**
42.25	Open biopsy of esophagus **44 , 72 , 179**
42.31	Local excision of esophageal diverticulum **44 , 72**
42.32	Local excision of other lesion or tissue of esophagus **44 , 72 , 179**
42.39	Other destruction of lesion or tissue of esophagus **44 , 72 , 179**
42.4*	Excision of esophagus **72 , 179 , 197**
42.40	Esophagectomy, not otherwise specified **44**
42.41	Partial esophagectomy **44**
42.42	Total esophagectomy **44**
42.5*	Intrathoracic anastomosis of esophagus **72 , 179 , 197**
42.51	Intrathoracic esophagoesophagostomy **44**
42.52	Intrathoracic esophagogastrostomy **44**

42.53	Intrathoracic esophageal anastomosis with interposition of small bowel **44**
42.54	Other intrathoracic esophagoenterostomy **44**
42.55	Intrathoracic esophageal anastomosis with interposition of colon **44**
42.56	Other intrathoracic esophagocolostomy **44**
42.58	Intrathoracic esophageal anastomosis with other interposition **44**
42.59	Other intrathoracic anastomosis of esophagus **44**
42.6*	Antesternal anastomosis of esophagus **72 , 179 , 197**
42.61	Antesternal esophagoesophagostomy **45**
42.62	Antesternal esophagogastrostomy **45**
42.63	Antesternal esophageal anastomosis with interposition of small bowel **45**
42.64	Other antesternal esophagoenterostomy **45**
42.65	Antesternal esophageal anastomosis with interposition of colon **45**
42.66	Other antesternal esophagocolostomy **45**
42.68	Other antesternal esophageal anastomosis with interposition **45**
42.69	Other antesternal anastomosis of esophagus **45**
42.7	Esophagomyotomy **45 , 72 , 179 , 197**
42.82	Suture of laceration of esophagus **45 , 72 , 179 , 197**
42.83	Closure of esophagostomy **45 , 72 , 179 , 197**
42.84	Repair of esophageal fistula, not elsewhere classified **45 , 72 , 179 , 197**
42.85	Repair of esophageal stricture **72 , 180 , 197**
42.86	Production of subcutaneous tunnel without esophageal anastomosis **45 , 72 , 180 , 197**
42.87	Other graft of esophagus **45 , 72 , 180 , 197**
42.89	Other repair of esophagus **45 , 72 , 180 , 197**
42.91	Ligation of esophageal varices **72 , 82**
43.0	Gastrotomy **72 , 82 , 113 , 180 , 197**
43.3	Pyloromyotomy **72**
43.42	Local excision of other lesion or tissue of stomach **72 , 82 , 113**
43.49	Other destruction of lesion or tissue of stomach **72 , 235**
43.5	Partial gastrectomy with anastomosis to esophagus **72 , 180 , 197**
43.6	Partial gastrectomy with anastomosis to duodenum **64 , 72 , 180 , 197**
43.7	Partial gastrectomy with anastomosis to jejunum **64 , 72 , 113 , 180 , 197**
43.8*	Other partial gastrectomy **72 , 180 , 197**
43.82	Laparoscopic vertical (sleeve) gastrectomy **64 , 112**
43.89	Open and other partial gastrectomy **64 , 112**
43.9*	Total gastrectomy **72 , 180 , 197**
43.99	Other total gastrectomy **64**
44.0*	Vagotomy **72**
44.00	Vagotomy, not otherwise specified **14 , 16**
44.11	Transabdominal gastroscopy **72 , 82 , 180 , 197**
44.15	Open biopsy of stomach **72 , 235**
44.21	Dilation of pylorus by incision **72**
44.29	Other pyloroplasty **72**
44.3*	Gastroenterostomy without gastrectomy **72 , 112 , 180**
44.32	Percutaneous [endoscopic] gastrojejunostomy **82**
44.38	Laparoscopic gastroenterostomy **64 , 82**
44.39	Other gastroenterostomy without gastrectomy **64 , 82**
44.40	Suture of peptic ulcer, not otherwise specified **72**
44.41	Suture of gastric ulcer site **72**
44.42	Suture of duodenal ulcer site **72**
44.5	Revision of gastric anastomosis **72 , 112 , 197**
44.61	Suture of laceration of stomach **72 , 197**
44.63	Closure of other gastric fistula **72 , 82 , 180 , 197**
44.64	Gastropexy **72 , 197**
44.65	Esophagogastroplasty **72 , 197**
44.66	Other procedures for creation of esophagogastric sphincteric competence **72 , 197**
44.67	Laparoscopic procedures for creation of esophagogastric sphincteric competence **72 , 197 , 235**
44.68	Laparoscopic gastroplasty **72 , 112 , 197 , 235**
44.69	Other repair of stomach **72 , 112 , 197**
44.91	Ligation of gastric varices **72 , 82**
44.92	Intraoperative manipulation of stomach **72 , 82 , 113 , 197**
44.95	Laparoscopic gastric restrictive procedure **112 , 235**
44.96	Laparoscopic revision of gastric restrictive procedure **112 , 235**
44.97	Laparoscopic removal of gastric restrictive device(s) **112 , 235**
44.98	(Laparoscopic) adjustment of size of adjustable gastric restrictive device **112 , 235**
44.99	Other operations on stomach **72 , 112 , 197**
45.0*	Enterotomy **197**
45.00	Incision of intestine, not otherwise specified **73**
45.01	Incision of duodenum **72 , 82**
45.02	Other incision of small intestine **73 , 180**
45.03	Incision of large intestine **73 , 180**
45.11	Transabdominal endoscopy of small intestine **73 , 180 , 197 , 235**
45.15	Open biopsy of small intestine **73**
45.21	Transabdominal endoscopy of large intestine **73 , 197 , 235**
45.26	Open biopsy of large intestine **73 , 235**
45.31	Other local excision of lesion of duodenum **72 , 82 , 180 , 235**
45.32	Other destruction of lesion of duodenum **72 , 82 , 180 , 235**
45.33	Local excision of lesion or tissue of small intestine, except duodenum **74 , 180 , 235**
45.34	Other destruction of lesion of small intestine, except duodenum **73 , 180 , 235**
45.41	Excision of lesion or tissue of large intestine **74 , 113 , 180 , 235**
45.49	Other destruction of lesion of large intestine **73 , 180 , 235**
45.5*	Isolation of intestinal segment **72**
45.50	Isolation of intestinal segment, not otherwise specified **180**
45.6*	Other excision of small intestine **72 , 197**
45.61	Multiple segmental resection of small intestine **64 , 180**
45.62	Other partial resection of small intestine **64 , 113 , 180**
45.63	Total removal of small intestine **180**
45.7*	Open and other partial excision of large intestine **72 , 197**
45.71	Open and other multiple segmental resection of large intestine **180**
45.72	Open and other cecectomy **64**
45.73	Open and other right hemicolectomy **64 , 180**
45.74	Open and other resection of transverse colon **64 , 180**
45.75	Open and other left hemicolectomy **64 , 113 , 180**
45.76	Open and other sigmoidectomy **180**
45.79	Other and unspecified partial excision of large intestine **64 , 180**
45.8*	Total intra-abdominal colectomy **64 , 72 , 180 , 197**
45.9*	Intestinal anastomosis **72 , 197**
45.90	Intestinal anastomosis, not otherwise specified **112 , 180**
45.91	Small-to-small intestinal anastomosis **112 , 180**
45.92	Anastomosis of small intestine to rectal stump **180**
45.93	Other small-to-large intestinal anastomosis **64 , 113 , 180**
45.94	Large-to-large intestinal anastomosis **113 , 180**
45.95	Anastomosis to anus **180**
46.0*	Exteriorization of intestine **72 , 180 , 197**
46.03	Exteriorization of large intestine **64**
46.10	Colostomy, not otherwise specified **72 , 180 , 197**

*Code Range

46.11	Temporary colostomy **72 , 180 , 197**	
46.13	Permanent colostomy **64 , 72 , 180 , 197**	
46.20	Ileostomy, not otherwise specified **72 , 180 , 197**	
46.21	Temporary ileostomy **72 , 180 , 197**	
46.22	Continent ileostomy **72 , 180 , 197**	
46.23	Other permanent ileostomy **72 , 180 , 197**	
46.4*	Revision of intestinal stoma **74 , 197**	
46.40	Revision of intestinal stoma, not otherwise specified **180**	
46.41	Revision of stoma of small intestine **180 , 235**	
46.43	Other revision of stoma of large intestine **235**	
46.5*	Closure of intestinal stoma **73 , 197**	
46.52	Closure of stoma of large intestine **235**	
46.6*	Fixation of intestine **73**	
46.7*	Other repair of intestine **197**	
46.71	Suture of laceration of duodenum **72**	
46.72	Closure of fistula of duodenum **72**	
46.73	Suture of laceration of small intestine, except duodenum **72**	
46.74	Closure of fistula of small intestine, except duodenum **72**	
46.75	Suture of laceration of large intestine **72**	
46.76	Closure of fistula of large intestine **72**	
46.79	Other repair of intestine **72**	
46.80	Intra-abdominal manipulation of intestine, not otherwise specified **72 , 82 , 180 , 197**	
46.81	Intra-abdominal manipulation of small intestine **72 , 82 , 180 , 197**	
46.82	Intra-abdominal manipulation of large intestine **72 , 82 , 180 , 197**	
46.91	Myotomy of sigmoid colon **72**	
46.92	Myotomy of other parts of colon **72**	
46.93	Revision of anastomosis of small intestine **72 , 197**	
46.94	Revision of anastomosis of large intestine **72 , 197**	
46.97	Transplant of intestine **1**	
46.99	Other operations on intestines **72 , 82 , 180 , 197**	
47.0*	Appendectomy **73**	
47.09	Other appendectomy **64**	
47.1*	Incidental appendectomy **130 , 197**	
47.2	Drainage of appendiceal abscess **73**	
47.91	Appendicostomy **73**	
47.92	Closure of appendiceal fistula **72 , 197**	
47.99	Other operations on appendix **73**	
48.0	Proctotomy **73 , 197**	
48.1	Proctostomy **72 , 197**	
48.21	Transabdominal proctosigmoidoscopy **73 , 197**	
48.25	Open biopsy of rectum **64 , 73 , 235**	
48.35	Local excision of rectal lesion or tissue **64 , 74 , 105 , 235**	
48.4*	Pull-through resection of rectum **73 , 180**	
48.40	Pull-through resection of rectum, not otherwise specified **197**	
48.42	Laparoscopic pull-through resection of rectum **197**	
48.43	Open pull-through resection of rectum **197**	
48.49	Other pull-through resection of rectum **197**	
48.5*	Abdominoperineal resection of rectum **73 , 180 , 197**	
48.6*	Other resection of rectum **73 , 180 , 197**	
48.62	Anterior resection of rectum with synchronous colostomy **64**	
48.63	Other anterior resection of rectum **64**	
48.69	Other resection of rectum **64 , 123**	
48.7*	Repair of rectum **197**	
48.71	Suture of laceration of rectum **72 , 148**	
48.72	Closure of proctostomy **72**	
48.73	Closure of other rectal fistula **74 , 105 , 129**	

48.74	Rectorectostomy **72**
48.75	Abdominal proctopexy **72**
48.76	Other proctopexy **72**
48.79	Other repair of rectum **74 , 140**
48.8*	Incision or excision of perirectal tissue or lesion **74 , 105 , 197 , 235**
48.9*	Other operations on rectum and perirectal tissue **74**
48.91	Incision of rectal stricture **197**
49.01	Incision of perianal abscess **74 , 105**
49.02	Other incision of perianal tissue **74 , 105**
49.04	Other excision of perianal tissue **74 , 105**
49.1*	Incision or excision of anal fistula **74 , 197 , 235**
49.11	Anal fistulotomy **105**
49.12	Anal fistulectomy **105**
49.39	Other local excision or destruction of lesion or tissue of anus **74 , 105 , 235**
49.44	Destruction of hemorrhoids by cryotherapy **74 , 235**
49.45	Ligation of hemorrhoids **74 , 235**
49.46	Excision of hemorrhoids **74 , 140 , 235**
49.49	Other procedures on hemorrhoids **74 , 235**
49.5*	Division of anal sphincter **74 , 235**
49.59	Other anal sphincterotomy **148**
49.6	Excision of anus **74 , 235**
49.71	Suture of laceration of anus **74 , 105 , 197**
49.72	Anal cerclage **74 , 105**
49.73	Closure of anal fistula **74 , 105 , 197**
49.74	Gracilis muscle transplant for anal incontinence **74**
49.75	Implantation or revision of artificial anal sphincter **73 , 105 , 197**
49.76	Removal of artificial anal sphincter **73 , 105 , 197**
49.79	Other repair of anal sphincter **74 , 105 , 197 , 235**
49.9*	Other operations on anus **74**
49.95	Control of (postoperative) hemorrhage of anus **197**
49.99	Other operations on anus **197**
50.0	Hepatotomy **81 , 197**
50.12	Open biopsy of liver **45 , 50 , 64 , 74 , 82 , 95 , 105 , 113 , 119 , 124 , 130 , 176 , 180 , 197**
50.14	Laparoscopic liver biopsy **74 , 82 , 105 , 119 , 176 , 180 , 197**
50.19	Other diagnostic procedures on liver **74 , 82 , 105 , 119 , 176 , 180 , 197**
50.21	Marsupialization of lesion of liver **81**
50.22	Partial hepatectomy **81 , 198**
50.23	Open ablation of liver lesion or tissue **74 , 81**
50.24	Percutaneous ablation of liver lesion or tissue **74 , 81**
50.25	Laparoscopic ablation of liver lesion or tissue **74 , 81**
50.26	Other and unspecified ablation of liver lesion or tissue **74 , 81**
50.29	Other destruction of lesion of liver **74 , 81**
50.3	Lobectomy of liver **81 , 198**
50.4	Total hepatectomy **81 , 198**
50.51	Auxiliary liver transplant **1**
50.59	Other transplant of liver **1**
50.6*	Repair of liver **198**
50.61	Closure of laceration of liver **81**
50.69	Other repair of liver **81**
51.02	Trocar cholecystostomy **81**
51.03	Other cholecystostomy **74 , 81**
51.04	Other cholecystotomy **81**
51.13	Open biopsy of gallbladder or bile ducts **74 , 82**
51.19	Other diagnostic procedures on biliary tract **74 , 82**
51.2*	Cholecystectomy **81 , 180 , 198**
51.21	Other partial cholecystectomy **81**

Numeric Index to Procedures *(side tab)*

51.22	Cholecystectomy **74** , **81**
51.23	Laparoscopic cholecystectomy **74** , **82** , **235**
51.24	Laparoscopic partial cholecystectomy **82**
51.3*	Anastomosis of gallbladder or bile duct **81** , **180** , **198**
51.32	Anastomosis of gallbladder to intestine **75**
51.36	Choledochoenterostomy **75**
51.37	Anastomosis of hepatic duct to gastrointestinal tract **75**
51.41	Common duct exploration for removal of calculus **81**
51.42	Common duct exploration for relief of other obstruction **81** , **180** , **198**
51.43	Insertion of choledochohepatic tube for decompression **81** , **180** , **198**
51.49	Incision of other bile ducts for relief of obstruction **81** , **180**
51.51	Exploration of common bile duct **81**
51.59	Incision of other bile duct **75** , **81** , **180** , **198**
51.61	Excision of cystic duct remnant **81** , **198**
51.62	Excision of ampulla of Vater (with reimplantation of common duct) **75** , **81**
51.63	Other excision of common duct **75** , **81**
51.69	Excision of other bile duct **75** , **81**
51.7*	Repair of bile ducts **81** , **198**
51.81	Dilation of sphincter of Oddi **75** , **81** , **198**
51.82	Pancreatic sphincterotomy **72** , **81** , **198**
51.83	Pancreatic sphincteroplasty **72** , **81** , **198**
51.89	Other operations on sphincter of Oddi **81** , **198**
51.91	Repair of laceration of gallbladder **81** , **198**
51.92	Closure of cholecystostomy **81** , **198**
51.93	Closure of other biliary fistula **81** , **180** , **198**
51.94	Revision of anastomosis of biliary tract **81** , **180** , **198**
51.95	Removal of prosthetic device from bile duct **81** , **180** , **198**
51.99	Other operations on biliary tract **81** , **180** , **198** , **235**
52.0*	Pancreatotomy **81**
52.12	Open biopsy of pancreas **75** , **82** , **113** , **180** , **198**
52.19	Other diagnostic procedures on pancreas **75** , **82** , **113** , **180** , **198**
52.22	Other excision or destruction of lesion or tissue of pancreas or pancreatic duct **81** , **113**
52.3	Marsupialization of pancreatic cyst **81**
52.4	Internal drainage of pancreatic cyst **81**
52.5*	Partial pancreatectomy **81** , **113** , **198**
52.6	Total pancreatectomy **81** , **198**
52.7	Radical pancreaticoduodenectomy **72** , **81** , **198**
52.80	Pancreatic transplant, not otherwise specified **2** , **81** , **113**
52.81	Reimplantation of pancreatic tissue **81**
52.82	Homotransplant of pancreas **2** , **81** , **113**
52.83	Heterotransplant of pancreas **81** , **113**
52.84	Autotransplantation of cells of islets of Langerhans **119**
52.85	Allotransplantation of cells of islets of Langerhans **119**
52.92	Cannulation of pancreatic duct **75** , **81** , **180** , **198**
52.95	Other repair of pancreas **81** , **198**
52.96	Anastomosis of pancreas **81** , **198**
52.99	Other operations on pancreas **75** , **81** , **198**
53.0*	Other unilateral repair of inguinal hernia **74** , **235**
53.1*	Other bilateral repair of inguinal hernia **74** , **235**
53.2*	Unilateral repair of femoral hernia **74** , **235**
53.3*	Bilateral repair of femoral hernia **74** , **235**
53.4*	Repair of umbilical hernia **74**
53.41	Other and open repair of umbilical hernia with graft or prosthesis **235**
53.43	Other laparoscopic umbilical herniorrhaphy **198**
53.49	Other open umbilical herniorrhaphy **198** , **235**
53.5*	Repair of other hernia of anterior abdominal wall (without graft or prosthesis) **74**
53.51	Incisional hernia repair **235**
53.6*	Repair of other hernia of anterior abdominal wall with graft or prosthesis **74**
53.61	Other open incisional hernia repair with graft or prosthesis **198** , **235**
53.62	Laparoscopic incisional hernia repair with graft or prosthesis **198**
53.69	Other and open repair of other hernia of anterior abdominal wall with graft or prosthesis **235**
53.7*	Repair of diaphragmatic hernia, abdominal approach **50** , **72** , **198**
53.8*	Repair of diaphragmatic hernia, thoracic approach **50** , **72** , **198**
53.9	Other hernia repair **74**
54.0	Incision of abdominal wall **64** , **75** , **82** , **105** , **119** , **180** , **198**
54.1*	Laparotomy **75** , **119** , **130** , **198**
54.11	Exploratory laparotomy **50** , **64** , **82** , **105** , **113** , **123** , **140** , **176** , **180**
54.12	Reopening of recent laparotomy site **82** , **180**
54.19	Other laparotomy **64** , **82** , **176** , **180**
54.21	Laparoscopy **75** , **82** , **105** , **119** , **129** , **140** , **176** , **198** , **235**
54.22	Biopsy of abdominal wall or umbilicus **75** , **105** , **180** , **198** , **235**
54.23	Biopsy of peritoneum **75** , **82** , **130** , **176**
54.29	Other diagnostic procedures on abdominal region **75** , **82** , **130** , **176** , **180** , **198** , **235**
54.3	Excision or destruction of lesion or tissue of abdominal wall or umbilicus **75** , **92** , **105** , **113** , **180** , **235**
54.4	Excision or destruction of peritoneal tissue **75** , **82** , **113** , **130** , **180** , **235**
54.5*	Lysis of peritoneal adhesions **73** , **82** , **119** , **130** , **198**
54.59	Other lysis of peritoneal adhesions **113**
54.6*	Suture of abdominal wall and peritoneum **75** , **198**
54.61	Reclosure of postoperative disruption of abdominal wall **82** , **130**
54.62	Delayed closure of granulating abdominal wound **82** , **130**
54.63	Other suture of abdominal wall **105** , **180**
54.64	Suture of peritoneum **82** , **180** , **235**
54.7*	Other repair of abdominal wall and peritoneum **198**
54.71	Repair of gastroschisis **74**
54.72	Other repair of abdominal wall **74** , **82** , **105** , **180**
54.73	Other repair of peritoneum **75** , **82** , **180**
54.74	Other repair of omentum **75** , **82** , **180**
54.75	Other repair of mesentery **75** , **82** , **180**
54.92	Removal of foreign body from peritoneal cavity **75** , **119** , **198**
54.93	Creation of cutaneoperitoneal fistula **64** , **75** , **82** , **119** , **180** , **198**
54.94	Creation of peritoneovascular shunt **75** , **81** , **180**
54.95	Incision of peritoneum **14** , **16** , **64** , **75** , **82** , **119** , **180** , **198**
55.0*	Nephrotomy and nephrostomy **117** , **198**
55.1*	Pyelotomy and pyelostomy **117** , **198**
55.12	Pyelostomy **235**
55.24	Open biopsy of kidney **95** , **117** , **176** , **180** , **198**
55.29	Other diagnostic procedures on kidney **117** , **176** , **180** , **198**
55.3*	Local excision or destruction of lesion or tissue of kidney **117**
55.31	Marsupialization of kidney lesion **198**
55.4	Partial nephrectomy **117** , **198**
55.5*	Complete nephrectomy **117** , **198**
55.61	Renal autotransplantation **117** , **198**
55.69	Other kidney transplantation **2** , **117**
55.7	Nephropexy **117**
55.8*	Other repair of kidney **117**

*Code Range

55.81	Suture of laceration of kidney **198**	
55.82	Closure of nephrostomy and pyelostomy **198**	
55.83	Closure of other fistula of kidney **198**	
55.84	Reduction of torsion of renal pedicle **198**	
55.86	Anastomosis of kidney **198**	
55.87	Correction of ureteropelvic junction **198**	
55.89	Other repair of kidney **198**	
55.91	Decapsulation of kidney **64 , 117**	
55.97	Implantation or replacement of mechanical kidney **117 , 198**	
55.98	Removal of mechanical kidney **117 , 198**	
55.99	Other operations on kidney **117 , 198**	
56.0	Transurethral removal of obstruction from ureter and renal pelvis **118 , 198 , 235**	
56.1	Ureteral meatotomy **117 , 198 , 235**	
56.2	Ureterotomy **117 , 198 , 235**	
56.34	Open biopsy of ureter **117**	
56.39	Other diagnostic procedures on ureter **117 , 235**	
56.4*	Ureterectomy **117 , 198**	
56.41	Partial ureterectomy **124 , 130**	
56.5*	Cutaneous uretero-ileostomy **117 , 124 , 130 , 180 , 198**	
56.52	Revision of cutaneous uretero-ileostomy **235**	
56.6*	Other external urinary diversion **117 , 124 , 130 , 180 , 198**	
56.7*	Other anastomosis or bypass of ureter **117 , 198**	
56.71	Urinary diversion to intestine **124 , 130 , 180**	
56.72	Revision of ureterointestinal anastomosis **124 , 130 , 180**	
56.73	Nephrocystanastomosis, not otherwise specified **124 , 130 , 180**	
56.75	Transureteroureterostomy **124 , 130 , 180**	
56.8*	Repair of ureter **117**	
56.81	Lysis of intraluminal adhesions of ureter **198**	
56.82	Suture of laceration of ureter **198**	
56.83	Closure of ureterostomy **124 , 130 , 180 , 198**	
56.84	Closure of other fistula of ureter **73 , 124 , 130 , 180 , 198**	
56.86	Removal of ligature from ureter **198**	
56.89	Other repair of ureter **198**	
56.92	Implantation of electronic ureteral stimulator **117**	
56.93	Replacement of electronic ureteral stimulator **117**	
56.94	Removal of electronic ureteral stimulator **117**	
56.95	Ligation of ureter **117 , 198**	
56.99	Other operations on ureter **117 , 198**	
57.12	Lysis of intraluminal adhesions with incision into bladder **117 , 198**	
57.18	Other suprapubic cystostomy **117 , 124 , 129 , 180 , 198**	
57.19	Other cystotomy **117 , 198**	
57.2*	Vesicostomy **117 , 124 , 198**	
57.21	Vesicostomy **129 , 180**	
57.22	Revision or closure of vesicostomy **130 , 180 , 235**	
57.33	Closed (transurethral) biopsy of bladder **118 , 124 , 130 , 235**	
57.34	Open biopsy of bladder **117 , 124 , 130 , 180**	
57.39	Other diagnostic procedures on bladder **117 , 124 , 180 , 198 , 235**	
57.4*	Transurethral excision or destruction of bladder tissue **118**	
57.49	Other transurethral excision or destruction of lesion or tissue of bladder **124 , 235**	
57.5*	Other excision or destruction of bladder tissue **117 , 124 , 130**	
57.59	Open excision or destruction of other lesion or tissue of bladder **180 , 235**	
57.6	Partial cystectomy **117 , 123 , 130 , 180 , 198**	
57.7*	Total cystectomy **117 , 123 , 130 , 180**	
57.79	Other total cystectomy **198**	
57.81	Suture of laceration of bladder **117 , 198**	

57.82	Closure of cystostomy **117 , 124 , 130 , 180 , 198 , 235**
57.83	Repair of fistula involving bladder and intestine **73 , 117 , 124 , 130 , 180 , 198**
57.84	Repair of other fistula of bladder **117 , 124 , 130 , 180 , 198**
57.85	Cystourethroplasty and plastic repair of bladder neck **117 , 129**
57.86	Repair of bladder exstrophy **117**
57.87	Reconstruction of urinary bladder **117 , 198**
57.88	Other anastomosis of bladder **117 , 124 , 180**
57.89	Other repair of bladder **117 , 130 , 198**
57.91	Sphincterotomy of bladder **117 , 235**
57.93	Control of (postoperative) hemorrhage of bladder **117 , 198**
57.96	Implantation of electronic bladder stimulator **118**
57.97	Replacement of electronic bladder stimulator **118 , 235**
57.98	Removal of electronic bladder stimulator **118 , 235**
57.99	Other operations on bladder **118 , 198**
58.0	Urethrotomy **118 , 130 , 198 , 235**
58.1	Urethral meatotomy **118 , 124 , 198 , 235**
58.4*	Repair of urethra **118**
58.41	Suture of laceration of urethra **198**
58.42	Closure of urethrostomy **198**
58.43	Closure of other fistula of urethra **123 , 130 , 180 , 198**
58.44	Reanastomosis of urethra **198**
58.45	Repair of hypospadias or epispadias **123**
58.46	Other reconstruction of urethra **123 , 198**
58.47	Urethral meatoplasty **124**
58.49	Other repair of urethra **123 , 130 , 198**
58.5	Release of urethral stricture **118 , 123 , 130 , 198 , 235**
58.91	Incision of periurethral tissue **118**
58.92	Excision of periurethral tissue **118**
58.93	Implantation of artificial urinary sphincter (AUS) **118 , 198**
58.99	Other operations on urethra and periurethral tissue **118 , 124 , 130 , 235**
59.00	Retroperitoneal dissection, not otherwise specified **95 , 105 , 117 , 123 , 130 , 180**
59.02	Other lysis of perirenal or periureteral adhesions **117 , 124 , 130 , 180 , 198**
59.03	Laparoscopic lysis of perirenal or periureteral adhesions **117 , 124 , 130 , 180 , 198**
59.09	Other incision of perirenal or periureteral tissue **117 , 124 , 130 , 180 , 198**
59.1*	Incision of perivesical tissue **118 , 124 , 130 , 180 , 198**
59.2*	Diagnostic procedures on perirenal and perivesical tissue **118 , 124 , 180 , 198**
59.3	Plication of urethrovesical junction **118**
59.4	Suprapubic sling operation **118 , 129**
59.5	Retropubic urethral suspension **118 , 129**
59.6	Paraurethral suspension **118 , 129**
59.71	Levator muscle operation for urethrovesical suspension **118 , 129**
59.79	Other repair of urinary stress incontinence **118 , 129 , 235**
59.91	Excision of perirenal or perivesical tissue **118 , 124 , 180**
59.92	Other operations on perirenal or perivesical tissue **118 , 124 , 180**
60.0	Incision of prostate **124 , 233**
60.12	Open biopsy of prostate **118 , 124 , 233**
60.14	Open biopsy of seminal vesicles **124**
60.15	Biopsy of periprostatic tissue **124 , 233**
60.18	Other diagnostic procedures on prostate and periprostatic tissue **124 , 233**
60.19	Other diagnostic procedures on seminal vesicles **124**
60.2*	Transurethral prostatectomy **118 , 123 , 233**

*Code Range

© 2012 OptumInsight, Inc.

67.61	Suture of laceration of cervix **148**	
67.62	Repair of fistula of cervix **140**	
67.69	Other repair of cervix **148**	
68.0	Hysterotomy **127 , 129 , 140 , 199**	
68.13	Open biopsy of uterus **127 , 129**	
68.14	Open biopsy of uterine ligaments **127 , 129**	
68.15	Closed biopsy of uterine ligaments **129 , 235**	
68.16	Closed biopsy of uterus **129 , 235**	
68.19	Other diagnostic procedures on uterus and supporting structures **127 , 129**	
68.21	Division of endometrial synechiae **129**	
68.22	Incision or excision of congenital septum of uterus **129**	
68.23	Endometrial ablation **127 , 129**	
68.24	Uterine artery embolization [UAE] with coils **130**	
68.25	Uterine artery embolization [UAE] without coils **130**	
68.29	Other excision or destruction of lesion of uterus **127 , 129 , 235**	
68.3*	Subtotal abdominal hysterectomy **127 , 129 , 140**	
68.41	Laparoscopic total abdominal hysterectomy **127 , 129 , 140**	
68.49	Other and unspecified total abdominal hysterectomy **127 , 129 , 140**	
68.5*	Vaginal hysterectomy **127 , 129 , 140 , 235**	
68.61	Laparoscopic radical abdominal hysterectomy **127 , 140**	
68.69	Other and unspecified radical abdominal hysterectomy **127 , 140**	
68.71	Laparoscopic radical vaginal hysterectomy [LRVH] **127 , 140**	
68.79	Other and unspecified radical vaginal hysterectomy **127 , 140**	
68.8	Pelvic evisceration **73 , 127**	
68.9	Other and unspecified hysterectomy **127 , 129 , 140**	
69.0*	Dilation and curettage of uterus **141**	
69.01	Dilation and curettage for termination of pregnancy **235**	
69.02	Dilation and curettage following delivery or abortion **140**	
69.09	Other dilation and curettage of uterus **129 , 140 , 235**	
69.19	Other excision or destruction of uterus and supporting structures **127 , 129**	
69.2*	Repair of uterine supporting structures **129**	
69.23	Vaginal repair of chronic inversion of uterus **199**	
69.29	Other repair of uterus and supporting structures **199**	
69.3	Paracervical uterine denervation **127 , 129**	
69.4*	Uterine repair **127 , 129 , 199**	
69.41	Suture of laceration of uterus **140**	
69.42	Closure of fistula of uterus **73**	
69.49	Other repair of uterus **140**	
69.51	Aspiration curettage of uterus for termination of pregnancy **141 , 235**	
69.52	Aspiration curettage following delivery or abortion **140 , 141 , 235**	
69.95	Incision of cervix **129 , 140 , 235**	
69.97	Removal of other penetrating foreign body from cervix **129 , 199**	
69.98	Other operations on supporting structures of uterus **129**	
69.99	Other operations on cervix and uterus **130**	
70.12	Culdotomy **130 , 141**	
70.13	Lysis of intraluminal adhesions of vagina **129 , 148 , 199**	
70.14	Other vaginotomy **129 , 148 , 235**	
70.23	Biopsy of cul-de-sac **129 , 141 , 235**	
70.24	Vaginal biopsy **105 , 129 , 148 , 235**	
70.29	Other diagnostic procedures on vagina and cul-de-sac **129 , 141 , 235**	
70.3*	Local excision or destruction of vagina and cul-de-sac **129 , 235**	
70.31	Hymenectomy **148**	
70.32	Excision or destruction of lesion of cul-de-sac **141**	
70.33	Excision or destruction of lesion of vagina **105 , 148**	

70.4	Obliteration and total excision of vagina **129**
70.5*	Repair of cystocele and rectocele **130**
70.50	Repair of cystocele and rectocele **75 , 118**
70.51	Repair of cystocele **118**
70.52	Repair of rectocele **72**
70.53	Repair of cystocele and rectocele with graft or prosthesis **72 , 117**
70.54	Repair of cystocele with graft or prosthesis **118**
70.55	Repair of rectocele with graft or prosthesis **72**
70.6*	Vaginal construction and reconstruction **130**
70.62	Vaginal reconstruction **199**
70.64	Vaginal reconstruction with graft or prosthesis **199**
70.71	Suture of laceration of vagina **105 , 129 , 148 , 199**
70.72	Repair of colovaginal fistula **72 , 129 , 180 , 199**
70.73	Repair of rectovaginal fistula **72 , 129 , 180 , 199**
70.74	Repair of other vaginoenteric fistula **72 , 129 , 180 , 199**
70.75	Repair of other fistula of vagina **73 , 129 , 180 , 199**
70.76	Hymenorrhaphy **129 , 235**
70.77	Vaginal suspension and fixation **118 , 130**
70.78	Vaginal suspension and fixation with graft or prosthesis **118 , 130**
70.79	Other repair of vagina **129 , 148 , 199**
70.8	Obliteration of vaginal vault **130**
70.91	Other operations on vagina **129**
70.92	Other operations on cul-de-sac **129**
70.93	Other operations on cul-de-sac with graft or prosthesis **129**
71.0*	Incision of vulva and perineum **129 , 148**
71.01	Lysis of vulvar adhesions **199**
71.09	Other incision of vulva and perineum **105 , 235**
71.1*	Diagnostic procedures on vulva **105 , 129 , 148 , 235**
71.22	Incision of Bartholin's gland (cyst) **129 , 141 , 235**
71.23	Marsupialization of Bartholin's gland (cyst) **129 , 141 , 235**
71.24	Excision or other destruction of Bartholin's gland (cyst) **105 , 129 , 141 , 235**
71.29	Other operations on Bartholin's gland **129 , 141 , 235**
71.3	Other local excision or destruction of vulva and perineum **105 , 129 , 148 , 235**
71.4	Operations on clitoris **129 , 235**
71.5	Radical vulvectomy **127**
71.6*	Other vulvectomy **129**
71.62	Bilateral vulvectomy **105**
71.7*	Repair of vulva and perineum **129 , 199**
71.71	Suture of laceration of vulva or perineum **105 , 148 , 235**
71.72	Repair of fistula of vulva or perineum **73**
71.79	Other repair of vulva and perineum **148 , 235**
71.8	Other operations on vulva **129**
71.9	Other operations on female genital organs **130**
73.94	Pubiotomy to assist delivery **141**
73.99	Other operations to assist delivery **148**
74.0	Classical cesarean section **140**
74.1	Low cervical cesarean section **140**
74.2	Extraperitoneal cesarean section **140**
74.3	Removal of extratubal ectopic pregnancy **141**
74.4	Cesarean section of other specified type **140**
74.91	Hysterotomy to terminate pregnancy **141**
74.99	Other cesarean section of unspecified type **140**
75.36	Correction of fetal defect **141**
75.50	Repair of current obstetric laceration of uterus, not otherwise specified **148**
75.51	Repair of current obstetric laceration of cervix **148**
75.52	Repair of current obstetric laceration of corpus uteri **141**

*Code Range

© 2012 OptumInsight, Inc.

77.80	Other partial ostectomy, unspecified site **95** , **199**
77.81	Other partial ostectomy of scapula, clavicle, and thorax (ribs and sternum) **12** , **13** , **51** , **95** , **199**
77.82	Other partial ostectomy of humerus **91** , **199**
77.83	Other partial ostectomy of radius and ulna **94** , **199**
77.84	Other partial ostectomy of carpals and metacarpals **94** , **194**
77.85	Other partial ostectomy of femur **89** , **199** , **220**
77.86	Other partial ostectomy of patella **90** , **199**
77.87	Other partial ostectomy of tibia and fibula **91** , **199**
77.88	Other partial ostectomy of tarsals and metatarsals **93** , **113** , **199** , **236**
77.89	Other partial ostectomy of other bone, except facial bones **45** , **95** , **113** , **199**
77.90	Total ostectomy, unspecified site **95** , **199**
77.91	Total ostectomy of scapula, clavicle, and thorax (ribs and sternum) **12** , **13** , **51** , **95** , **199**
77.92	Total ostectomy of humerus **91** , **199**
77.93	Total ostectomy of radius and ulna **94** , **199**
77.94	Total ostectomy of carpals and metacarpals **94** , **194**
77.95	Total ostectomy of femur **89** , **199** , **220**
77.96	Total ostectomy of patella **90** , **199**
77.97	Total ostectomy of tibia and fibula **91** , **199**
77.98	Total ostectomy of tarsals and metatarsals **93** , **199** , **236**
77.99	Total ostectomy of other bone, except facial bones **45** , **95** , **199**
78.00	Bone graft, unspecified site **95** , **199**
78.01	Bone graft of scapula, clavicle, and thorax (ribs and sternum) **51** , **95** , **199**
78.02	Bone graft of humerus **91** , **199**
78.03	Bone graft of radius and ulna **94** , **199** , **236**
78.04	Bone graft of carpals and metacarpals **94** , **194**
78.05	Bone graft of femur **89** , **199** , **220**
78.06	Bone graft of patella **90** , **199**
78.07	Bone graft of tibia and fibula **91** , **199**
78.08	Bone graft of tarsals and metatarsals **93** , **199**
78.09	Bone graft of other bone, except facial bones **95** , **199**
78.10	Application of external fixator device, unspecified site **95** , **199**
78.11	Application of external fixator device, scapula, clavicle, and thorax [ribs and sternum] **51** , **95** , **199**
78.12	Application of external fixator device, humerus **91** , **199**
78.13	Application of external fixator device, radius and ulna **94** , **199**
78.14	Application of external fixator device, carpals and metacarpals **94** , **194**
78.15	Application of external fixator device, femur **89** , **199** , **220**
78.16	Application of external fixator device, patella **90** , **199**
78.17	Application of external fixator device, tibia and fibula **91** , **199**
78.18	Application of external fixator device, tarsals and metatarsals **93** , **199**
78.19	Application of external fixator device, other **95** , **199**
78.20	Limb shortening procedures, unspecified site **95** , **199**
78.22	Limb shortening procedures, humerus **91** , **199**
78.23	Limb shortening procedures, radius and ulna **94** , **200**
78.24	Limb shortening procedures, carpals and metacarpals **94** , **194**
78.25	Limb shortening procedures, femur **89** , **200** , **220**
78.27	Limb shortening procedures, tibia and fibula **91** , **200**
78.28	Limb shortening procedures, tarsals and metatarsals **93** , **200**
78.29	Limb shortening procedures, other **95** , **200**
78.30	Limb lengthening procedures, unspecified site **95** , **200**
78.32	Limb lengthening procedures, humerus **91** , **200**
78.33	Limb lengthening procedures, radius and ulna **94** , **200**
78.34	Limb lengthening procedures, carpals and metacarpals **94** , **194**
78.35	Limb lengthening procedures, femur **89** , **200** , **220**
78.37	Limb lengthening procedures, tibia and fibula **91** , **200**
78.38	Limb lengthening procedures, tarsals and metatarsals **93** , **200**
78.39	Other limb lengthening procedures **95** , **200**
78.40	Other repair or plastic operations on bone, unspecified site **95** , **200**
78.41	Other repair or plastic operations on scapula, clavicle, and thorax (ribs and sternum) **51** , **95** , **200**
78.42	Other repair or plastic operation on humerus **91** , **200**
78.43	Other repair or plastic operations on radius and ulna **94** , **200**
78.44	Other repair or plastic operations on carpals and metacarpals **94** , **194**
78.45	Other repair or plastic operations on femur **89** , **200** , **220**
78.46	Other repair or plastic operations on patella **90** , **200**
78.47	Other repair or plastic operations on tibia and fibula **91** , **200**
78.48	Other repair or plastic operations on tarsals and metatarsals **93** , **200**
78.49	Other repair or plastic operations on other bone, except facial bones **95** , **200**
78.50	Internal fixation of bone without fracture reduction, unspecified site **95** , **200**
78.51	Internal fixation of scapula, clavicle, and thorax (ribs and sternum) without fracture reduction **51** , **95** , **200**
78.52	Internal fixation of humerus without fracture reduction **91** , **200**
78.53	Internal fixation of radius and ulna without fracture reduction **94** , **200**
78.54	Internal fixation of carpals and metacarpals without fracture reduction **94** , **194**
78.55	Internal fixation of femur without fracture reduction **89** , **200** , **220**
78.56	Internal fixation of patella without fracture reduction **90** , **200**
78.57	Internal fixation of tibia and fibula without fracture reduction **91** , **200**
78.58	Internal fixation of tarsals and metatarsals without fracture reduction **93** , **200**
78.59	Internal fixation of other bone, except facial bones, without fracture reduction **95** , **200**
78.6*	Removal of implanted device from bone **236**
78.60	Removal of implanted device, unspecified site **92** , **200**
78.61	Removal of implanted device from scapula, clavicle, and thorax (ribs and sternum) **51** , **92** , **200**
78.62	Removal of implanted device from humerus **92** , **200**
78.63	Removal of implanted device from radius and ulna **92** , **200**
78.64	Removal of implanted device from carpals and metacarpals **92** , **194**
78.65	Removal of implanted device from femur **92** , **113** , **200**
78.66	Removal of implanted device from patella **92** , **200**
78.67	Removal of implanted device from tibia and fibula **92** , **200**
78.68	Removal of implanted device from tarsal and metatarsals **92** , **200**
78.69	Removal of implanted device from other bone **92** , **200**
78.70	Osteoclasis, unspecified site **95** , **200**
78.71	Osteoclasis of scapula, clavicle, and thorax (ribs and sternum) **51** , **95** , **200**
78.72	Osteoclasis of humerus **91** , **200**
78.73	Osteoclasis of radius and ulna **94** , **200**
78.74	Osteoclasis of carpals and metacarpals **94** , **194**
78.75	Osteoclasis of femur **89** , **200** , **220**
78.76	Osteoclasis of patella **90** , **200**
78.77	Osteoclasis of tibia and fibula **91** , **200**
78.78	Osteoclasis of tarsals and metatarsals **93** , **200**
78.79	Osteoclasis of other bone, except facial bones **95** , **200**

78.80	Diagnostic procedures on bone, not elsewhere classified, unspecified site **89**
78.81	Diagnostic procedures on scapula, clavicle, and thorax (ribs and sternum) not elsewhere classified **51 , 89**
78.82	Diagnostic procedures on humerus, not elsewhere classified **89**
78.83	Diagnostic procedures on radius and ulna, not elsewhere classified **89**
78.84	Diagnostic procedures on carpals and metacarpals, not elsewhere classified **94 , 194**
78.85	Diagnostic procedures on femur, not elsewhere classified **89**
78.86	Diagnostic procedures on patella, not elsewhere classified **89**
78.87	Diagnostic procedures on tibia and fibula, not elsewhere classified **89**
78.88	Diagnostic procedures on tarsals and metatarsals, not elsewhere classified **93**
78.89	Diagnostic procedures on other bone, except facial bones, not elsewhere classified **89**
78.90	Insertion of bone growth stimulator, unspecified site **95 , 200**
78.91	Insertion of bone growth stimulator into scapula, clavicle and thorax (ribs and sternum) **51 , 95 , 200**
78.92	Insertion of bone growth stimulator into humerus **91 , 200**
78.93	Insertion of bone growth stimulator into radius and ulna **94 , 200**
78.94	Insertion of bone growth stimulator into carpals and metacarpals **94 , 194**
78.95	Insertion of bone growth stimulator into femur **89 , 200 , 220**
78.96	Insertion of bone growth stimulator into patella **90 , 200**
78.97	Insertion of bone growth stimulator into tibia and fibula **91 , 200**
78.98	Insertion of bone growth stimulator into tarsals and metatarsals **93 , 200**
78.99	Insertion of bone growth stimulator into other bone **95 , 200**
79.10	Closed reduction of fracture with internal fixation, unspecified site **95 , 200**
79.11	Closed reduction of fracture of humerus with internal fixation **91 , 200**
79.12	Closed reduction of fracture of radius and ulna with internal fixation **94 , 200 , 236**
79.13	Closed reduction of fracture of carpals and metacarpals with internal fixation **94 , 194**
79.14	Closed reduction of fracture of phalanges of hand with internal fixation **94 , 194**
79.15	Closed reduction of fracture of femur with internal fixation **89 , 200 , 220**
79.16	Closed reduction of fracture of tibia and fibula with internal fixation **91 , 200**
79.17	Closed reduction of fracture of tarsals and metatarsals with internal fixation **93 , 200**
79.18	Closed reduction of fracture of phalanges of foot with internal fixation **93 , 200**
79.19	Closed reduction of fracture of other specified bone, except facial bones, with internal fixation **95 , 200**
79.20	Open reduction of fracture without internal fixation, unspecified site **96 , 200**
79.21	Open reduction of fracture of humerus without internal fixation **91 , 200**
79.22	Open reduction of fracture of radius and ulna without internal fixation **94 , 200**
79.23	Open reduction of fracture of carpals and metacarpals without internal fixation **94 , 194**
79.24	Open reduction of fracture of phalanges of hand without internal fixation **94 , 194**
79.25	Open reduction of fracture of femur without internal fixation **89 , 200 , 220**
79.26	Open reduction of fracture of tibia and fibula without internal fixation **91 , 200**
79.27	Open reduction of fracture of tarsals and metatarsals without internal fixation **93 , 200**
79.28	Open reduction of fracture of phalanges of foot without internal fixation **93 , 200**
79.29	Open reduction of fracture of other specified bone, except facial bones, without internal fixation **45 , 96 , 200**
79.30	Open reduction of fracture with internal fixation, unspecified site **96 , 200**
79.31	Open reduction of fracture of humerus with internal fixation **91 , 200**
79.32	Open reduction of fracture of radius and ulna with internal fixation **94 , 200**
79.33	Open reduction of fracture of carpals and metacarpals with internal fixation **94 , 194**
79.34	Open reduction of fracture of phalanges of hand with internal fixation **94 , 194**
79.35	Open reduction of fracture of femur with internal fixation **90 , 113 , 200 , 220**
79.36	Open reduction of fracture of tibia and fibula with internal fixation **91 , 200**
79.37	Open reduction of fracture of tarsals and metatarsals with internal fixation **93 , 200**
79.38	Open reduction of fracture of phalanges of foot with internal fixation **93 , 200**
79.39	Open reduction of fracture of other specified bone, except facial bones, with internal fixation **45 , 96 , 200**
79.40	Closed reduction of separated epiphysis, unspecified site **96 , 200**
79.41	Closed reduction of separated epiphysis of humerus **91 , 200**
79.42	Closed reduction of separated epiphysis of radius and ulna **94 , 200**
79.45	Closed reduction of separated epiphysis of femur **90 , 200 , 220**
79.46	Closed reduction of separated epiphysis of tibia and fibula **91 , 200**
79.49	Closed reduction of separated epiphysis of other specified bone **96 , 200**
79.50	Open reduction of separated epiphysis, unspecified site **96 , 200**
79.51	Open reduction of separated epiphysis of humerus **91 , 200**
79.52	Open reduction of separated epiphysis of radius and ulna **94 , 200**
79.55	Open reduction of separated epiphysis of femur **90 , 200 , 220**
79.56	Open reduction of separated epiphysis of tibia and fibula **91 , 200**
79.59	Open reduction of separated epiphysis of other specified bone **96 , 200**
79.60	Debridement of open fracture, unspecified site **96 , 200**
79.61	Debridement of open fracture of humerus **91 , 200**
79.62	Debridement of open fracture of radius and ulna **94 , 200**
79.63	Debridement of open fracture of carpals and metacarpals **94 , 194**
79.64	Debridement of open fracture of phalanges of hand **94 , 194**
79.65	Debridement of open fracture of femur **90 , 200 , 220**
79.66	Debridement of open fracture of tibia and fibula **91 , 200**
79.67	Debridement of open fracture of tarsals and metatarsals **93 , 200**
79.68	Debridement of open fracture of phalanges of foot **93 , 200**
79.69	Debridement of open fracture of other specified bone, except facial bones **45 , 96 , 200**
79.80	Open reduction of dislocation of unspecified site **96 , 200**
79.81	Open reduction of dislocation of shoulder **94 , 200**
79.82	Open reduction of dislocation of elbow **94 , 200**
79.83	Open reduction of dislocation of wrist **94 , 194**
79.84	Open reduction of dislocation of hand and finger **94 , 194**
79.85	Open reduction of dislocation of hip **90 , 201 , 220**
79.86	Open reduction of dislocation of knee **90 , 201**
79.87	Open reduction of dislocation of ankle **91 , 201**

*Code Range

© 2012 OptumInsight, Inc.

79.88	Open reduction of dislocation of foot and toe **93 , 201**	
79.89	Open reduction of dislocation of other specified site, except temporomandibular **96 , 201**	
79.90	Unspecified operation on bone injury, unspecified site **96 , 201**	
79.91	Unspecified operation on bone injury of humerus **91 , 201**	
79.92	Unspecified operation on bone injury of radius and ulna **94 , 201**	
79.93	Unspecified operation on bone injury of carpals and metacarpals **94 , 194**	
79.94	Unspecified operation on bone injury of phalanges of hand **94 , 194**	
79.95	Unspecified operation on bone injury of femur **90 , 201 , 220**	
79.96	Unspecified operation on bone injury of tibia and fibula **91 , 201**	
79.97	Unspecified operation on bone injury of tarsals and metatarsals **91 , 201**	
79.98	Unspecified operation on bone injury of phalanges of foot **93 , 201**	
79.99	Unspecified operation on bone injury of other specified bone **96 , 201**	
80.00	Arthrotomy for removal of prosthesis without replacement, unspecified site **92 , 201**	
80.01	Arthrotomy for removal of prosthesis without replacement, shoulder **92 , 201**	
80.02	Arthrotomy for removal of prosthesis without replacement, elbow **92 , 201**	
80.03	Arthrotomy for removal of prosthesis without replacement, wrist **92 , 194**	
80.04	Arthrotomy for removal of prosthesis without replacement, hand and finger **92 , 194**	
80.05	Arthrotomy for removal of prosthesis without replacement, hip **88 , 201 , 220**	
80.06	Arthrotomy for removal of prosthesis without replacement, knee **88 , 201**	
80.07	Arthrotomy for removal of prosthesis without replacement, ankle **92 , 201**	
80.08	Arthrotomy for removal of prosthesis without replacement, foot and toe **92 , 201**	
80.09	Arthrotomy for removal of prosthesis without replacement, other specified site **92 , 201**	
80.10	Other arthrotomy, unspecified site **96 , 113 , 201**	
80.11	Other arthrotomy of shoulder **93 , 201**	
80.12	Other arthrotomy of elbow **93 , 114 , 201**	
80.13	Other arthrotomy of wrist **93 , 194**	
80.14	Other arthrotomy of hand and finger **93 , 194**	
80.15	Other arthrotomy of hip **90 , 201 , 220**	
80.16	Other arthrotomy of knee **90 , 114 , 201 , 236**	
80.17	Other arthrotomy of ankle **91 , 201**	
80.18	Other arthrotomy of foot and toe **93 , 201 , 236**	
80.19	Other arthrotomy of other specified site **96 , 201**	
80.2*	Arthroscopy **93 , 201**	
80.26	Arthroscopy of knee **114 , 236**	
80.40	Division of joint capsule, ligament, or cartilage, unspecified site **96 , 201**	
80.41	Division of joint capsule, ligament, or cartilage of shoulder **94 , 201**	
80.42	Division of joint capsule, ligament, or cartilage of elbow **94 , 201**	
80.43	Division of joint capsule, ligament, or cartilage of wrist **94 , 194**	
80.44	Division of joint capsule, ligament, or cartilage of hand and finger **94 , 194**	
80.45	Division of joint capsule, ligament, or cartilage of hip **90 , 201 , 220**	
80.46	Division of joint capsule, ligament, or cartilage of knee **90 , 201 , 236**	
80.47	Division of joint capsule, ligament, or cartilage of ankle **91 , 201**	
80.48	Division of joint capsule, ligament, or cartilage of foot and toe **93 , 201**	
80.49	Division of joint capsule, ligament, or cartilage of other specified site **96 , 201**	
80.50	Excision or destruction of intervertebral disc, unspecified **12 , 13 , 90 , 91 , 201**	
80.51	Excision of intervertebral disc **12 , 13 , 90 , 91 , 201**	
80.53	Repair of the anulus fibrosus with graft or prosthesis **12 , 13 , 90 , 91 , 180 , 201**	
80.54	Other and unspecified repair of the anulus fibrosus **12 , 13 , 90 , 91 , 180 , 201**	
80.59	Other destruction of intervertebral disc **12 , 13 , 91 , 201**	
80.6	Excision of semilunar cartilage of knee **90 , 114 , 201 , 236**	
80.7*	Synovectomy **236**	
80.70	Synovectomy, unspecified site **92 , 201**	
80.71	Synovectomy of shoulder **94 , 201**	
80.72	Synovectomy of elbow **94 , 201**	
80.73	Synovectomy of wrist **94 , 194**	
80.74	Synovectomy of hand and finger **94 , 194**	
80.75	Synovectomy of hip **90 , 201**	
80.76	Synovectomy of knee **90 , 201**	
80.77	Synovectomy of ankle **91 , 201**	
80.78	Synovectomy of foot and toe **93 , 201**	
80.79	Synovectomy of other specified site **92 , 201**	
80.80	Other local excision or destruction of lesion of joint, unspecified site **92 , 201**	
80.81	Other local excision or destruction of lesion of shoulder joint **92 , 201**	
80.82	Other local excision or destruction of lesion of elbow joint **92 , 114 , 201**	
80.83	Other local excision or destruction of lesion of wrist joint **94 , 105 , 194**	
80.84	Other local excision or destruction of lesion of joint of hand and finger **94 , 194**	
80.85	Other local excision or destruction of lesion of hip joint **92 , 201**	
80.86	Other local excision or destruction of lesion of knee joint **92 , 201 , 236**	
80.87	Other local excision or destruction of lesion of ankle joint **91 , 201**	
80.88	Other local excision or destruction of lesion of joint of foot and toe **93 , 114 , 201 , 236**	
80.89	Other local excision or destruction of lesion of joint of other specified site **92 , 201**	
80.90	Other excision of joint, unspecified site **96 , 201**	
80.91	Other excision of shoulder joint **94 , 201**	
80.92	Other excision of elbow joint **94 , 201**	
80.93	Other excision of wrist joint **94 , 194**	
80.94	Other excision of joint of hand and finger **94 , 194**	
80.95	Other excision of hip joint **90 , 201 , 220**	
80.96	Other excision of knee joint **90 , 201**	
80.97	Other excision of ankle joint **91 , 201**	
80.98	Other excision of joint of foot and toe **93 , 114 , 201 , 236**	
80.99	Other excision of joint of other specified site **91 , 201**	
81.00	Spinal fusion, not otherwise specified **12 , 13 , 87 , 88 , 201**	
81.01	Atlas-axis spinal fusion **12 , 13 , 89 , 201**	
81.02	Other cervical fusion of the anterior column, anterior technique **12 , 13 , 87 , 89 , 201**	
81.03	Other cervical fusion of the posterior column, posterior technique **12 , 13 , 87 , 89 , 201**	
81.04	Dorsal and dorsolumbar fusion of the anterior column, anterior technique **12 , 13 , 87 , 88 , 201**	
81.05	Dorsal and dorsolumbar fusion of the posterior column, posterior technique **12 , 13 , 87 , 88 , 201**	

Numeric Index to Procedures

81.06	Lumbar and lumbosacral fusion of the anterior column, anterior technique **12** , **13** , **87** , **88** , **201**
81.07	Lumbar and lumbosacral fusion of the posterior column, posterior technique **12** , **13** , **87** , **88** , **201**
81.08	Lumbar and lumbosacral fusion of the anterior column, posterior technique **12** , **13** , **87** , **88** , **201**
81.1*	Arthrodesis and arthroereisis of foot and ankle **201**
81.11	Ankle fusion **91** , **114**
81.12	Triple arthrodesis **91**
81.13	Subtalar fusion **93**
81.14	Midtarsal fusion **93**
81.15	Tarsometatarsal fusion **93**
81.16	Metatarsophalangeal fusion **93**
81.17	Other fusion of foot **93**
81.18	Subtalar joint arthroereisis **96**
81.20	Arthrodesis of unspecified joint **96** , **201**
81.21	Arthrodesis of hip **90** , **201** , **220**
81.22	Arthrodesis of knee **90** , **201**
81.23	Arthrodesis of shoulder **93** , **114** , **201**
81.24	Arthrodesis of elbow **93** , **201**
81.25	Carporadial fusion **94** , **194**
81.26	Metacarpocarpal fusion **94** , **194**
81.27	Metacarpophalangeal fusion **94** , **194**
81.28	Interphalangeal fusion **94** , **194**
81.29	Arthrodesis of other specified joint **96** , **201**
81.3*	Refusion of spine **12** , **13** , **201**
81.30	Refusion of spine, not otherwise specified **87** , **88**
81.31	Refusion of Atlas-axis spine **89**
81.32	Refusion of other cervical spine, anterior column, anterior technique **87** , **89**
81.33	Refusion of other cervical spine, posterior column, posterior technique **87** , **89**
81.34	Refusion of dorsal and dorsolumbar spine, anterior column, anterior technique **87** , **88**
81.35	Refusion of dorsal and dorsolumbar spine, posterior column, posterior technique **87** , **88**
81.36	Refusion of lumbar and lumbosacral spine, anterior column, anterior technique **87** , **88**
81.37	Refusion of lumbar and lumbosacral spine, posterior column, posterior technique **87** , **88**
81.38	Refusion of lumbar and lumbosacral spine, anterior column, posterior technique **87** , **88**
81.39	Refusion of spine, not elsewhere classified **87** , **88**
81.4*	Other repair of joint of lower extremity **201**
81.40	Repair of hip, not elsewhere classified **90** , **220**
81.42	Five-in-one repair of knee **90**
81.43	Triad knee repair **90**
81.44	Patellar stabilization **90**
81.45	Other repair of the cruciate ligaments **90**
81.46	Other repair of the collateral ligaments **90**
81.47	Other repair of knee **90**
81.49	Other repair of ankle **91**
81.5*	Joint replacement of lower extremity **201**
81.51	Total hip replacement **88** , **89** , **220**
81.52	Partial hip replacement **88** , **89** , **114** , **220**
81.53	Revision of hip replacement, not otherwise specified **88** , **114** , **220**
81.54	Total knee replacement **88** , **89**
81.55	Revision of knee replacement, not otherwise specified **88**
81.56	Total ankle replacement **88** , **89**
81.57	Replacement of joint of foot and toe **93** , **236**

81.59	Revision of joint replacement of lower extremity, not elsewhere classified **96**
81.64	Fusion or refusion of 9 or more vertebrae **87** , **88**
81.65	Percutaneous vertebroplasty **96** , **201**
81.66	Percutaneous vertebral augmentation **96** , **201**
81.71	Arthroplasty of metacarpophalangeal and interphalangeal joint with implant **14** , **16** , **93** , **194**
81.72	Arthroplasty of metacarpophalangeal and interphalangeal joint without implant **14** , **16** , **93** , **194**
81.73	Total wrist replacement **90** , **201**
81.74	Arthroplasty of carpocarpal or carpometacarpal joint with implant **14** , **16** , **93** , **194**
81.75	Arthroplasty of carpocarpal or carpometacarpal joint without implant **14** , **16** , **93** , **194**
81.79	Other repair of hand, fingers, and wrist **14** , **16** , **93** , **194**
81.8*	Arthroplasty and repair of shoulder and elbow **201**
81.80	Other total shoulder replacement **90**
81.81	Partial shoulder replacement **90**
81.82	Repair of recurrent dislocation of shoulder **94**
81.83	Other repair of shoulder **93** , **236**
81.84	Total elbow replacement **90**
81.85	Other repair of elbow **93**
81.88	Reverse total shoulder replacement **90**
81.93	Suture of capsule or ligament of upper extremity **94** , **201**
81.94	Suture of capsule or ligament of ankle and foot **93** , **201**
81.95	Suture of capsule or ligament of other lower extremity **92** , **201**
81.96	Other repair of joint **96** , **201**
81.97	Revision of joint replacement of upper extremity **96** , **201**
81.98	Other diagnostic procedures on joint structures **89** , **201**
81.99	Other operations on joint structures **96** , **201**
82.01	Exploration of tendon sheath of hand **94** , **194** , **236**
82.02	Myotomy of hand **94** , **194**
82.03	Bursotomy of hand **94** , **194**
82.09	Other incision of soft tissue of hand **94** , **105** , **194** , **236**
82.1*	Division of muscle, tendon, and fascia of hand **94** , **194**
82.11	Tenotomy of hand **236**
82.2*	Excision of lesion of muscle, tendon, and fascia of hand **94** , **194**
82.21	Excision of lesion of tendon sheath of hand **105** , **114** , **236**
82.29	Excision of other lesion of soft tissue of hand **105** , **236**
82.3*	Other excision of soft tissue of hand **94** , **194**
82.33	Other tenonectomy of hand **114**
82.39	Other excision of soft tissue of hand **105**
82.4*	Suture of muscle, tendon, and fascia of hand **94** , **194**
82.41	Suture of tendon sheath of hand **236**
82.45	Other suture of other tendon of hand **105** , **236**
82.46	Suture of muscle or fascia of hand **236**
82.5*	Transplantation of muscle and tendon of hand **14** , **16** , **94** , **194**
82.6*	Reconstruction of thumb **14** , **16** , **93** , **194**
82.7*	Plastic operation on hand with graft or implant **14** , **16** , **94** , **194**
82.72	Plastic operation on hand with graft of muscle or fascia **105**
82.79	Plastic operation on hand with other graft or implant **105**
82.8*	Other plastic operations on hand **14** , **16** , **94** , **194**
82.89	Other plastic operations on hand **105**
82.91	Lysis of adhesions of hand **94** , **105** , **194**
82.99	Other operations on muscle, tendon, and fascia of hand **94** , **194**
83.0*	Incision of muscle, tendon, fascia, and bursa **92** , **201** , **236**
83.02	Myotomy **45** , **105**
83.09	Other incision of soft tissue **105**
83.1*	Division of muscle, tendon, and fascia **201**
83.11	Achillotenotomy **93**

*Code Range

© 2012 OptumInsight, Inc.

83.12	Adductor tenotomy of hip **90 , 220**	
83.13	Other tenotomy **14 , 16 , 92 , 114 , 236**	
83.14	Fasciotomy **14 , 16 , 92 , 105**	
83.19	Other division of soft tissue **14 , 16 , 92 , 236**	
83.2*	Diagnostic procedures on muscle, tendon, fascia, and bursa, including that of hand **92**	
83.21	Open biopsy of soft tissue **14 , 16 , 51 , 105 , 176 , 236**	
83.29	Other diagnostic procedures on muscle, tendon, fascia, and bursa, including that of hand **201**	
83.3*	Excision of lesion of muscle, tendon, fascia, and bursa **92 , 201**	
83.31	Excision of lesion of tendon sheath **114**	
83.32	Excision of lesion of muscle **105 , 236**	
83.39	Excision of lesion of other soft tissue **45 , 105 , 114 , 236**	
83.4*	Other excision of muscle, tendon, and fascia **92 , 201**	
83.41	Excision of tendon for graft **14 , 16**	
83.43	Excision of muscle or fascia for graft **14 , 16**	
83.44	Other fasciectomy **105**	
83.45	Other myectomy **14 , 16 , 105**	
83.49	Other excision of soft tissue **14 , 16 , 45 , 105**	
83.5	Bursectomy **92 , 201 , 236**	
83.6*	Suture of muscle, tendon, and fascia **201 , 236**	
83.61	Suture of tendon sheath **92**	
83.62	Delayed suture of tendon **92**	
83.63	Rotator cuff repair **94**	
83.64	Other suture of tendon **92**	
83.65	Other suture of muscle or fascia **92 , 105 , 114**	
83.7*	Reconstruction of muscle and tendon **14 , 16 , 92 , 201**	
83.71	Advancement of tendon **105**	
83.75	Tendon transfer or transplantation **114**	
83.79	Other muscle transposition **114**	
83.8*	Other plastic operations on muscle, tendon, and fascia **201**	
83.81	Tendon graft **14 , 16 , 92**	
83.82	Graft of muscle or fascia **14 , 16 , 93 , 105**	
83.83	Tendon pulley reconstruction on muscle, tendon, and fascia **14 , 16 , 93**	
83.84	Release of clubfoot, not elsewhere classified **93**	
83.85	Other change in muscle or tendon length **14 , 16 , 93**	
83.86	Quadricepsplasty **93**	
83.87	Other plastic operations on muscle **14 , 16 , 93 , 105**	
83.88	Other plastic operations on tendon **14 , 16 , 93 , 105**	
83.89	Other plastic operations on fascia **14 , 16 , 93 , 105**	
83.91	Lysis of adhesions of muscle, tendon, fascia, and bursa **93 , 201**	
83.92	Insertion or replacement of skeletal muscle stimulator **14 , 16 , 93 , 201**	
83.93	Removal of skeletal muscle stimulator **14 , 16 , 93 , 201**	
83.99	Other operations on muscle, tendon, fascia, and bursa **93 , 201**	
84.0*	Amputation of upper limb **63 , 105**	
84.00	Upper limb amputation, not otherwise specified **89 , 201**	
84.01	Amputation and disarticulation of finger **94 , 194 , 236**	
84.02	Amputation and disarticulation of thumb **94 , 194**	
84.03	Amputation through hand **89 , 201**	
84.04	Disarticulation of wrist **89 , 201**	
84.05	Amputation through forearm **89 , 201**	
84.06	Disarticulation of elbow **89 , 202**	
84.07	Amputation through humerus **89 , 202**	
84.08	Disarticulation of shoulder **89 , 202**	
84.09	Interthoracoscapular amputation **89 , 202**	
84.1*	Amputation of lower limb **105 , 202**	
84.10	Lower limb amputation, not otherwise specified **60 , 89 , 112**	
84.11	Amputation of toe **14 , 16 , 63 , 93 , 112**	

84.12	Amputation through foot **14 , 17 , 60 , 89 , 112**
84.13	Disarticulation of ankle **14 , 17 , 60 , 89 , 112**
84.14	Amputation of ankle through malleoli of tibia and fibula **14 , 17 , 60 , 89 , 112**
84.15	Other amputation below knee **14 , 17 , 60 , 89 , 112**
84.16	Disarticulation of knee **14 , 17 , 60 , 89 , 112**
84.17	Amputation above knee **14 , 17 , 60 , 89 , 112**
84.18	Disarticulation of hip **60 , 89**
84.19	Abdominopelvic amputation **60 , 89**
84.21	Thumb reattachment **94 , 194**
84.22	Finger reattachment **94 , 194**
84.23	Forearm, wrist, or hand reattachment **90 , 202 , 220**
84.24	Upper arm reattachment **90 , 202 , 220**
84.25	Toe reattachment **93 , 202**
84.26	Foot reattachment **89 , 202 , 220**
84.27	Lower leg or ankle reattachment **89 , 202 , 220**
84.28	Thigh reattachment **89 , 202 , 220**
84.29	Other reattachment of extremity **96 , 202**
84.3	Revision of amputation stump **63 , 89 , 105 , 112 , 202**
84.40	Implantation or fitting of prosthetic limb device, not otherwise specified **96 , 202**
84.44	Implantation of prosthetic device of arm **94 , 202**
84.48	Implantation of prosthetic device of leg **92 , 202**
84.59	Insertion of other spinal devices **12 , 13 , 91 , 202**
84.6*	Replacement of spinal disc **12 , 13 , 91 , 202**
84.60	Insertion of spinal disc prosthesis, not otherwise specified **91**
84.61	Insertion of partial spinal disc prosthesis, cervical **91**
84.63	Insertion of spinal disc prosthesis, thoracic **91**
84.64	Insertion of partial spinal disc prosthesis, lumbosacral **91**
84.66	Revision or replacement of artificial spinal disc prosthesis, cervical **91**
84.67	Revision or replacement of artificial spinal disc prosthesis, thoracic **91**
84.68	Revision or replacement of artificial spinal disc prosthesis, lumbosacral **91**
84.69	Revision or replacement of artificial spinal disc prosthesis, not otherwise specified **91**
84.8*	Insertion, replacement and revision of posterior spinal motion preservation device(s) **202**
84.80	Insertion or replacement of interspinous process device(s) **12 , 13 , 91**
84.81	Revision of interspinous process device(s) **96**
84.82	Insertion or replacement of pedicle-based dynamic stabilization device(s) **12 , 13 , 91**
84.83	Revision of pedicle-based dynamic stabilization device(s) **96**
84.84	Insertion or replacement of facet replacement device(s) **12 , 13 , 91**
84.85	Revision of facet replacement device(s) **96**
84.91	Amputation, not otherwise specified **60 , 89 , 105 , 202**
84.92	Separation of equal conjoined twins **96**
84.93	Separation of unequal conjoined twins **96**
84.94	Insertion of sternal fixation device with rigid plates **51 , 64 , 96 , 202**
84.99	Other operations on musculoskeletal system **96 , 202**
85.12	Open biopsy of breast **106 , 114 , 202 , 236**
85.2*	Excision or destruction of breast tissue **202**
85.20	Excision or destruction of breast tissue, not otherwise specified **106 , 236**
85.21	Local excision of lesion of breast **106 , 114 , 236**
85.22	Resection of quadrant of breast **105 , 106**
85.23	Subtotal mastectomy **105 , 106 , 236**

85.24	Excision of ectopic breast tissue **106**
85.25	Excision of nipple **106**
85.3*	Reduction mammoplasty and subcutaneous mammectomy **105**, **106**, **202**
85.31	Unilateral reduction mammoplasty **112**
85.32	Bilateral reduction mammoplasty **112**
85.4*	Mastectomy **105**, **106**, **202**
85.50	Augmentation mammoplasty, not otherwise specified **106**, **202**, **236**
85.53	Unilateral breast implant **106**, **202**, **236**
85.54	Bilateral breast implant **106**, **202**, **236**
85.55	Fat graft to breast **106**
85.6	Mastopexy **106**, **202**
85.7*	Total reconstruction of breast **105**, **106**, **202**
85.82	Split-thickness graft to breast **104**, **194**, **207**, **208**
85.83	Full-thickness graft to breast **104**, **194**, **207**, **208**
85.84	Pedicle graft to breast **104**, **194**, **207**, **208**
85.85	Muscle flap graft to breast **104**, **202**
85.86	Transposition of nipple **106**, **202**
85.87	Other repair or reconstruction of nipple **106**, **202**
85.89	Other mammoplasty **106**, **202**
85.93	Revision of implant of breast **106**, **202**, **236**
85.94	Removal of implant of breast **106**, **202**, **236**
85.95	Insertion of breast tissue expander **106**, **202**, **236**
85.96	Removal of breast tissue expander (s) **106**, **202**, **236**
85.99	Other operations on the breast **106**, **202**, **236**
86.06	Insertion of totally implantable infusion pump **14**, **17**, **51**, **64**, **75**, **82**, **96**, **105**, **114**, **119**, **124**, **130**, **176**, **202**
86.07	Insertion of totally implantable vascular access device (VAD) **105**, **119**
86.09	Other incision of skin and subcutaneous tissue **105**
86.21	Excision of pilonidal cyst or sinus **105**, **202**, **236**
86.22	Excisional debridement of wound, infection, or burn **14**, **17**, **37**, **45**, **51**, **64**, **75**, **82**, **88**, **104**, **112**, **119**, **124**, **130**, **176**, **194**
86.25	Dermabrasion **105**, **236**
86.3	Other local excision or destruction of lesion or tissue of skin and subcutaneous tissue **105**
86.4	Radical excision of skin lesion **14**, **17**, **37**, **45**, **64**, **93**, **104**, **202**, **236**
86.60	Free skin graft, not otherwise specified **14**, **17**, **64**, **75**, **88**, **104**, **112**, **194**, **207**, **208**, **236**
86.61	Full-thickness skin graft to hand **14**, **17**, **64**, **94**, **104**, **195**, **207**, **208**
86.62	Other skin graft to hand **14**, **17**, **64**, **94**, **104**, **195**, **207**, **208**, **236**
86.63	Full-thickness skin graft to other sites **14**, **17**, **45**, **64**, **75**, **88**, **104**, **112**, **194**, **207**, **208**
86.65	Heterograft to skin **14**, **17**, **64**, **75**, **88**, **104**, **194**, **207**, **208**, **236**
86.66	Homograft to skin **14**, **17**, **45**, **64**, **75**, **88**, **104**, **194**, **207**, **208**
86.67	Dermal regenerative graft **14**, **17**, **45**, **64**, **75**, **88**, **104**, **112**, **194**, **207**, **208**
86.69	Other skin graft to other sites **14**, **17**, **45**, **51**, **64**, **75**, **88**, **104**, **112**, **194**, **207**, **208**
86.7*	Pedicle grafts or flaps **104**, **207**, **208**
86.70	Pedicle or flap graft, not otherwise specified **14**, **17**, **45**, **64**, **75**, **88**, **112**, **194**
86.71	Cutting and preparation of pedicle grafts or flaps **14**, **17**, **45**, **64**, **75**, **88**, **112**, **194**
86.72	Advancement of pedicle graft **14**, **17**, **45**, **64**, **75**, **88**, **112**, **194**
86.73	Attachment of pedicle or flap graft to hand **94**, **195**
86.74	Attachment of pedicle or flap graft to other sites **14**, **17**, **45**, **64**, **75**, **88**, **112**, **194**
86.75	Revision of pedicle or flap graft **14**, **17**, **45**, **64**, **75**, **88**, **112**, **194**
86.8*	Other repair and reconstruction of skin and subcutaneous tissue **105**
86.81	Repair for facial weakness **14**, **17**, **45**, **93**, **202**
86.82	Facial rhytidectomy **45**, **202**, **236**
86.83	Size reduction plastic operation **112**, **202**, **236**
86.84	Relaxation of scar or web contracture of skin **45**, **202**, **236**
86.85	Correction of syndactyly **94**, **195**
86.86	Onychoplasty **202**
86.87	Fat graft of skin and subcutaneous tissue **45**, **112**, **202**
86.89	Other repair and reconstruction of skin and subcutaneous tissue **45**, **112**, **202**, **236**
86.90	Extraction of fat for graft or banking **105**
86.91	Excision of skin for graft **14**, **17**, **45**, **65**, **104**, **112**, **202**
86.93	Insertion of tissue expander **14**, **17**, **45**, **65**, **75**, **88**, **104**, **112**, **194**, **207**, **208**
86.94	Insertion or replacement of single array neurostimulator pulse generator, not specified as rechargeable **12**, **14**, **17**, **18**, **91**
86.95	Insertion or replacement of multiple array neurostimulator pulse generator, not specified as rechargeable **9**, **11**, **12**, **14**, **17**, **18**, **91**
86.96	Insertion or replacement of other neurostimulator pulse generator **14**, **17**, **63**
86.97	Insertion or replacement of single array rechargeable neurostimulator pulse generator **12**, **14**, **17**, **18**, **91**
86.98	Insertion or replacement of multiple array (two or more) rechargeable neurostimulator pulse generator **9**, **11**, **12**, **14**, **17**, **18**, **91**
87.53	Intraoperative cholangiogram **82**, **236**
88.52	Angiocardiography of right heart structures **56**, **57**, **59**, **65**
88.53	Angiocardiography of left heart structures **56**, **57**, **59**, **65**
88.54	Combined right and left heart angiocardiography **56**, **57**, **59**, **65**
88.55	Coronary arteriography using single catheter **56**, **57**, **59**, **65**
88.56	Coronary arteriography using two catheters **56**, **57**, **59**, **65**
88.57	Other and unspecified coronary arteriography **56**, **57**, **59**, **65**
88.58	Negative-contrast cardiac roentgenography **56**, **57**, **59**, **65**
92.27	Implantation or insertion of radioactive elements **14**, **17**, **45**, **51**, **62**, **65**, **75**, **105**, **114**, **119**, **124**, **129**, **202**, **236**
92.3*	Stereotactic radiosurgery **16**, **18**, **114**, **181**
94.61	Alcohol rehabilitation **192**
94.63	Alcohol rehabilitation and detoxification **192**
94.64	Drug rehabilitation **192**
94.66	Drug rehabilitation and detoxification **192**
94.67	Combined alcohol and drug rehabilitation **192**
94.69	Combined alcohol and drug rehabilitation and detoxification **192**
95.04	Eye examination under anesthesia **37**, **236**
96.70	Continuous invasive mechanical ventilation of unspecified duration **54**
96.71	Continuous invasive mechanical ventilation for less than 96 consecutive hours **54**
96.72	Continuous invasive mechanical ventilation for 96 consecutive hours or more **1**, **54**, **187**, **207**, **209**
98.51	Extracorporeal shockwave lithotripsy (ESWL) of the kidney, ureter and/or bladder **120**
99.10	Injection or infusion of thrombolytic agent **19**

*Code Range

© 2012 OptumInsight, Inc.

Appendix A — Lists of CCs and MCCs

Numeric CC List

001.0	Cholera due to Vibrio cholerae
001.1	Cholera due to Vibrio cholerae el tor
001.9	Unspecified cholera
002.0	Typhoid fever
002.1	Paratyphoid fever A
002.2	Paratyphoid fever B
002.3	Paratyphoid fever C
002.9	Unspecified paratyphoid fever
003.0	Salmonella gastroenteritis
003.23	Salmonella arthritis
003.24	Salmonella osteomyelitis
003.29	Other localized salmonella infections
003.8	Other specified salmonella infections
003.9	Unspecified salmonella infection
004.0	Shigella dysenteriae
005.0	Staphylococcal food poisoning
005.1	Botulism food poisoning
005.2	Food poisoning due to Clostridium perfringens (C. welchii)
005.3	Food poisoning due to other Clostridia
005.4	Food poisoning due to Vibrio parahaemolyticus
005.81	Food poisoning due to Vibrio vulnificus
005.89	Other bacterial food poisoning
006.0	Acute amebic dysentery without mention of abscess
006.1	Chronic intestinal amebiasis without mention of abscess
006.2	Amebic nondysenteric colitis
006.8	Amebic infection of other sites
007.1	Giardiasis
007.2	Coccidiosis
007.4	Cryptosporidiosis
007.5	Cyclosporiasis
007.8	Other specified protozoal intestinal diseases
007.9	Unspecified protozoal intestinal disease
008.00	Intestinal infection due to unspecified E. coli
008.01	Intestinal infection due to enteropathogenic E. coli
008.02	Intestinal infection due to enterotoxigenic E. coli
008.03	Intestinal infection due to enteroinvasive E. coli
008.04	Intestinal infection due to enterohemorrhagic E. coli
008.09	Intestinal infection due to other intestinal E. coli infections
008.1	Intestinal infection due to Arizona group of paracolon bacilli
008.2	Intestinal infection due to aerobacter aerogenes
008.3	Intestinal infections due to proteus (mirabilis) (morganii)
008.41	Intestinal infections due to staphylococcus
008.42	Intestinal infections due to pseudomonas
008.43	Intestinal infections due to campylobacter
008.44	Intestinal infections due to yersinia enterocolitica
008.45	Intestinal infections due to clostridium difficile
008.46	Intestinal infections due to other anaerobes
008.47	Intestinal infections due to other gram-negative bacteria
008.49	Intestinal infection due to other organisms
008.5	Intestinal infection due to unspecified bacterial enteritis
008.61	Intestinal infection, enteritis due to rotavirus
008.62	Intestinal infection, enteritis due to adenovirus
008.63	Intestinal infection, enteritis due to Norwalk virus
008.64	Intestinal infection, enteritis due to other small round viruses (SRVs)
008.65	Enteritis due to calicivirus
008.66	Intestinal infection, enteritis due to astrovirus
008.67	Intestinal infection, enteritis due to enterovirus not elsewhere classified
008.69	Intestinal infection, enteritis due to other viral enteritis
009.0	Infectious colitis, enteritis, and gastroenteritis
009.1	Colitis, enteritis, and gastroenteritis of presumed infectious origin
009.2	Infectious diarrhea
009.3	Diarrhea of presumed infectious origin
010.00	Primary tuberculous complex, confirmation unspecified
010.01	Primary tuberculous complex, bacteriological or histological examination not done
010.02	Primary tuberculous complex, bacteriological or histological examination unknown (at present)
010.03	Primary tuberculous complex, tubercle bacilli found (in sputum) by microscopy
010.04	Primary tuberculous complex, tubercle bacilli not found (in sputum) by microscopy, but found by bacterial culture
010.05	Primary tuberculous complex, tubercle bacilli not found by bacteriological examination, but tuberculosis confirmed histologically
010.06	Primary tuberculous complex, tubercle bacilli not found by bacteriological or histological examination, but tuberculosis confirmed by other methods [inoculation of animals]
010.10	Tuberculous pleurisy in primary progressive tuberculosis, confirmation unspecified
010.11	Tuberculous pleurisy in primary progressive tuberculosis, bacteriological or histological examination not done
010.12	Tuberculous pleurisy in primary progressive tuberculosis, bacteriological or histological examination results unknown (at present)
010.13	Tuberculous pleurisy in primary progressive tuberculosis, tubercle bacilli found (in sputum) by microscopy
010.14	Tuberculous pleurisy in primary progressive tuberculosis, tubercle bacilli not found (in sputum) by microscopy, but found by bacterial culture
010.15	Tuberculous pleurisy in primary progressive tuberculosis, tubercle bacilli not found by bacteriological examination, but tuberculosis confirmed histologically
010.16	Tuberculous pleurisy in primary progressive tuberculosis, tubercle bacilli not found by bacteriological or histological examination, but tuberculosis confirmed by other methods [inoculation of animals]
010.80	Other primary progressive tuberculosis infection, confirmation unspecified
010.81	Other primary progressive tuberculosis infection, bacteriological or histological examination not done
010.82	Other primary progressive tuberculosis infection, bacteriological or histological examination unknown (at present)
010.83	Other primary progressive tuberculosis infection, tubercle bacilli found (in sputum) by microscopy
010.84	Other primary progressive tuberculosis infection, tubercle bacilli not found (in sputum) by microscopy, but found by bacterial culture
010.85	Other primary progressive tuberculosis infection, tubercle bacilli not found by bacteriological examination, but tuberculosis confirmed histologically
010.86	Other primary progressive tuberculosis infection, tubercle bacilli not found by bacteriological or histological examination, but tuberculosis confirmed by other methods [inoculation of animals]
010.90	Primary tuberculous infection, unspecified, confirmation unspecified

010.91 Primary tuberculous infection, unspecified, bacteriological or histological examination not done

010.92 Primary tuberculous infection, unspecified, bacteriological or histological examination unknown (at present)

010.93 Primary tuberculous infection, unspecified, tubercle bacilli found (in sputum) by microscopy

010.94 Primary tuberculous infection, unspecified, tubercle bacilli not found (in sputum) by microscopy, but found by bacterial culture

010.95 Primary tuberculous infection, unspecified, tubercle bacilli not found by bacteriological examination, but tuberculosis confirmed histologically

010.96 Primary tuberculous infection, unspecified, tubercle bacilli not found by bacteriological or histological examination, but tuberculosis confirmed by other methods [inoculation of animals]

011.00 Tuberculosis of lung, infiltrative, confirmation unspecified

011.01 Tuberculosis of lung, infiltrative, bacteriological or histological examination not done

011.02 Tuberculosis of lung, infiltrative, bacteriological or histological examination unknown (at present)

011.03 Tuberculosis of lung, infiltrative, tubercle bacilli found (in sputum) by microscopy

011.04 Tuberculosis of lung, infiltrative, tubercle bacilli not found (in sputum) by microscopy, but found by bacterial culture

011.05 Tuberculosis of lung, infiltrative, tubercle bacilli not found by bacteriological examination, but tuberculosis confirmed histologically

011.06 Tuberculosis of lung, infiltrative, tubercle bacilli not found bacteriological or histological examination, but tuberculosis confirmed by other methods (inoculation of animals)

011.10 Tuberculosis of lung, nodular, confirmation unspecified

011.11 Tuberculosis of lung, nodular, bacteriological or histological examination not done

011.12 Tuberculosis of lung, nodular, bacteriological or histological examination unknown (at present)

011.13 Tuberculosis of lung, nodular, tubercle bacilli found (in sputum) by microscopy

011.14 Tuberculosis of lung, nodular, tubercle bacilli not found (in sputum) by microscopy, but found by bacterial culture

011.15 Tuberculosis of lung, nodular, tubercle bacilli not found by bacteriological examination, but tuberculosis confirmed histologically

011.16 Tuberculosis of lung, nodular, tubercle bacilli not found by bacteriological or histological examination, but tuberculosis confirmed by other methods [inoculation of animals]

011.20 Tuberculosis of lung with cavitation, confirmation unspecified

011.21 Tuberculosis of lung with cavitation, bacteriological or histological examination not done

011.22 Tuberculosis of lung with cavitation, bacteriological or histological examination unknown (at present)

011.23 Tuberculosis of lung with cavitation, tubercle bacilli found (in sputum) by microscopy

011.24 Tuberculosis of lung with cavitation, tubercle bacilli not found (in sputum) by microscopy, but found by bacterial culture

011.25 Tuberculosis of lung with cavitation, tubercle bacilli not found by bacteriological examination, but tuberculosis confirmed histologically

011.26 Tuberculosis of lung with cavitation, tubercle bacilli not found by bacteriological or histological examination, but tuberculosis confirmed by other methods [inoculation of animals]

011.30 Tuberculosis of bronchus, confirmation unspecified

011.31 Tuberculosis of bronchus, bacteriological or histological examination not done

011.32 Tuberculosis of bronchus, bacteriological or histological examination unknown (at present)

011.33 Tuberculosis of bronchus, tubercle bacilli found (in sputum) by microscopy

011.34 Tuberculosis of bronchus, tubercle bacilli not found (in sputum) by microscopy, but found in bacterial culture

011.35 Tuberculosis of bronchus, tubercle bacilli not found by bacteriological examination, but tuberculosis confirmed histologically

011.36 Tuberculosis of bronchus, tubercle bacilli not found by bacteriological or histological examination, but tuberculosis confirmed by other methods [inoculation of animals]

011.40 Tuberculous fibrosis of lung, confirmation unspecified

011.41 Tuberculous fibrosis of lung, bacteriological or histological examination not done

011.42 Tuberculous fibrosis of lung, bacteriological or histological examination unknown (at present)

011.43 Tuberculous fibrosis of lung, tubercle bacilli found (in sputum) by microscopy

011.44 Tuberculous fibrosis of lung, tubercle bacilli not found (in sputum) by microscopy, but found by bacterial culture

011.45 Tuberculous fibrosis of lung, tubercle bacilli not found by bacteriological examination, but tuberculosis confirmed histologically

011.46 Tuberculous fibrosis of lung, tubercle bacilli not found by bacteriological or histological examination, but tuberculosis confirmed by other methods [inoculation of animals]

011.50 Tuberculous bronchiectasis, confirmation unspecified

011.51 Tuberculous bronchiectasis, bacteriological or histological examination not done

011.52 Tuberculous bronchiectasis, bacteriological or histological examination unknown (at present)

011.53 Tuberculous bronchiectasis, tubercle bacilli found (in sputum) by microscopy

011.54 Tuberculous bronchiectasis, tubercle bacilli not found (in sputum) by microscopy, but found by bacterial culture

011.55 Tuberculous bronchiectasis, tubercle bacilli not found by bacteriological examination, but tuberculosis confirmed histologically

011.56 Tuberculous bronchiectasis, tubercle bacilli not found by bacteriological or histological examination, but tuberculosis confirmed by other methods [inoculation of animals]

011.70 Tuberculous pneumothorax, confirmation unspecified

011.71 Tuberculous pneumothorax, bacteriological or histological examination not done

011.72 Tuberculous pneumothorax, bacteriological or histological examination unknown (at present)

011.73 Tuberculous pneumothorax, tubercle bacilli not found (in sputum) by microscopy

011.74 Tuberculous pneumothorax, tubercle bacilli not found (in sputum) by microscopy, but found by bacterial culture

011.75 Tuberculous pneumothorax, tubercle bacilli not found by bacteriological examination, but tuberculosis confirmed histologically

011.76 Tuberculous pneumothorax, tubercle bacilli not found by bacteriological or histological examination but tuberculosis confirmed by other methods [inoculation of animals]

011.80 Other specified pulmonary tuberculosis, confirmation unspecified

011.81 Other specified pulmonary tuberculosis, bacteriological or histological examination not done

011.82 Other specified pulmonary tuberculosis, bacteriological or histological examination unknown (at present)

011.83 Other specified pulmonary tuberculosis, tubercle bacilli found (in sputum) by microscopy

011.84 Other specified pulmonary tuberculosis, tubercle bacilli not found (in sputum) by microscopy, but found by bacterial culture

011.85 Other specified pulmonary tuberculosis, tubercle bacilli not found by bacteriological examination, but tuberculosis confirmed histologically

011.86 Other specified pulmonary tuberculosis, tubercle bacilli not found by bacteriological or histological examination, but tuberculosis confirmed by other methods [inoculation of animals]

011.90 Unspecified pulmonary tuberculosis, confirmation unspecified

011.91 Unspecified pulmonary tuberculosis, bacteriological or histological examination not done

011.92 Unspecified pulmonary tuberculosis, bacteriological or histological examination unknown (at present)

011.93 Unspecified pulmonary tuberculosis, tubercle bacilli found (in sputum) by microscopy

011.94 Unspecified pulmonary tuberculosis, tubercle bacilli not found (in sputum) by microscopy, but found by bacterial culture

011.95 Unspecified pulmonary tuberculosis, tubercle bacilli not found by bacteriological examination, but tuberculosis confirmed histologically

011.96 Unspecified pulmonary tuberculosis, tubercle bacilli not found by bacteriological or histological examination, but tuberculosis confirmed by other methods [inoculation of animals]

012.00 Tuberculous pleurisy, confirmation unspecified

012.01 Tuberculous pleurisy, bacteriological or histological examination not done

012.02 Tuberculous pleurisy, bacteriological or histological examination unknown (at present)

012.03 Tuberculous pleurisy, tubercle bacilli found (in sputum) by microscopy

012.04 Tuberculous pleurisy, tubercle bacilli not found (in sputum) by microscopy, but found by bacterial culture

012.05 Tuberculous pleurisy, tubercle bacilli not found by bacteriological examination, but tuberculosis confirmed histologically

012.06 Tuberculous pleurisy, tubercle bacilli not found by bacteriological or histological examination, but tuberculosis confirmed by other methods [inoculation of animals]

012.10 Tuberculosis of intrathoracic lymph nodes, confirmation unspecified

012.11 Tuberculosis of intrathoracic lymph nodes, bacteriological or histological examination not done

012.12 Tuberculosis of intrathoracic lymph nodes, bacteriological or histological examination unknown (at present)

012.13 Tuberculosis of intrathoracic lymph nodes, tubercle bacilli found (in sputum) by microscopy

012.14 Tuberculosis of intrathoracic lymph nodes, tubercle bacilli not found (in sputum) by microscopy, but found by bacterial culture

012.15 Tuberculosis of intrathoracic lymph nodes, tubercle bacilli not found by bacteriological examination, but tuberculosis confirmed histologically

012.16 Tuberculosis of intrathoracic lymph nodes, tubercle bacilli not found by bacteriological or histological examination but tuberculosis confirmed by other methods

012.20 Isolated tracheal or bronchial tuberculosis, unspecified

012.21 Isolated tracheal or bronchial tuberculosis, bacteriological or histological examination not done

012.22 Isolated tracheal or bronchial tuberculosis, bacteriological or histological examination unknown (at present)

012.23 Isolated tracheal or bronchial tuberculosis, tubercle bacilli found (in sputum) by microscopy

012.24 Isolated tracheal or bronchial tuberculosis, tubercle bacilli not found (in sputum) by microscopy, but found by bacterial culture

012.25 Isolated tracheal or bronchial tuberculosis, tubercle bacilli not found by bacteriological examination, but tuberculosis confirmed histologically

012.26 Isolated tracheal or bronchial tuberculosis, tubercle bacilli not found by bacteriological or histological examination, but tuberculosis confirmed by other methods [inoculation of animals]

012.30 Tuberculous laryngitis, confirmation unspecified

012.31 Tuberculous laryngitis, bacteriological or histological examination not done

012.32 Tuberculous laryngitis, bacteriological or histological examination unknown (at present)

012.33 Tuberculous laryngitis, tubercle bacilli found (in sputum) by microscopy

012.34 Tuberculous laryngitis, tubercle bacilli not found (in sputum) by microscopy, but found by bacterial culture

012.35 Tuberculous laryngitis, tubercle bacilli not found by bacteriological examination, but tuberculosis confirmed histologically

012.36 Tuberculous laryngitis, tubercle bacilli not found by bacteriological or histological examination, but tuberculosis confirmed by other methods [inoculation of animals]

012.80 Other specified respiratory tuberculosis, confirmation unspecified

012.81 Other specified respiratory tuberculosis, bacteriological or histological examination not done

012.82 Other specified respiratory tuberculosis, bacteriological or histological examination unknown (at present)

012.83 Other specified respiratory tuberculosis, tubercle bacilli found (in sputum) by microscopy

012.84 Other specified respiratory tuberculosis, tubercle bacilli not found (in sputum) by microscopy, but found by bacterial culture

012.85 Other specified respiratory tuberculosis, tubercle bacilli not found by bacteriological examination, but tuberculosis confirmed histologically

012.86 Other specified respiratory tuberculosis, tubercle bacilli not found by bacteriological or histological examination, but tuberculosis confirmed by other methods [inoculation of animals]

014.80 Tuberculosis of intestines, peritoneum, and mesenteric glands, other, confirmation unspecified

014.81 Tuberculosis of intestines, peritoneum, and mesenteric glands, other, bacteriological or histological examination not done

014.82 Tuberculosis of intestines, peritoneum, and mesenteric glands, other, bacteriological or histological examination unknown (at present)

014.83 Tuberculosis of intestines, peritoneum, and mesenteric glands, other, tubercle bacilli found (in sputum) by microscopy

014.84 Tuberculosis of intestines, peritoneum, and mesenteric glands, other, tubercle bacilli not found (in sputum) by microscopy, but found by bacterial culture

014.85 Tuberculosis of intestines, peritoneum, and mesenteric glands, other, tubercle bacilli not found by bacteriological examination, but tuberculosis confirmed histologically

014.86 Tuberculosis of intestines, peritoneum, and mesenteric glands, other, tubercle bacilli not found by bacteriological or histological examination, but tuberculosis confirmed by other methods [inoculation of animals]

015.00 Tuberculosis of vertebral column, confirmation unspecified

015.01 Tuberculosis of vertebral column, bacteriological or histological examination not done

015.02 Tuberculosis of vertebral column, bacteriological or histological examination unknown (at present)

015.03 Tuberculosis of vertebral column, tubercle bacilli found (in sputum) by microscopy

015.04 Tuberculosis of vertebral column, tubercle bacilli not found (in sputum) by microscopy, but found by bacterial culture

015.05 Tuberculosis of vertebral column, tubercle bacilli not found by bacteriological examination, but tuberculosis confirmed histologically

015.06 Tuberculosis of vertebral column, tubercle bacilli not found by bacteriological or histological examination, but tuberculosis confirmed by other methods [inoculation of animals]

015.10 Tuberculosis of hip, confirmation unspecified

015.11 Tuberculosis of hip, bacteriological or histological examination not done

015.12 Tuberculosis of hip, bacteriological or histological examination unknown (at present)

015.13 Tuberculosis of hip, tubercle bacilli found (in sputum) by microscopy

015.14	Tuberculosis of hip, tubercle bacilli not found (in sputum) by microscopy, but found by bacterial culture
015.15	Tuberculosis of hip, tubercle bacilli not found by bacteriological examination, but tuberculosis confirmed histologically
015.16	Tuberculosis of hip, tubercle bacilli not found by bacteriological or histological examination, but tuberculosis confirmed by other methods [inoculation of animals]
015.20	Tuberculosis of knee, confirmation unspecified
015.21	Tuberculosis of knee, bacteriological or histological examination not done
015.22	Tuberculosis of knee, bacteriological or histological examination unknown (at present)
015.23	Tuberculosis of knee, tubercle bacilli found (in sputum) by microscopy
015.24	Tuberculosis of knee, tubercle bacilli not found (in sputum) by microscopy, but found by bacterial culture
015.25	Tuberculosis of knee, tubercle bacilli not found by bacteriological examination, but tuberculosis confirmed histologically
015.26	Tuberculosis of knee, tubercle bacilli not found by bacteriological or histological examination, but tuberculosis confirmed by other methods [inoculation of animals]
015.50	Tuberculosis of limb bones, confirmation unspecified
015.51	Tuberculosis of limb bones, bacteriological or histological examination not done
015.52	Tuberculosis of limb bones, bacteriological or histological examination unknown (at present)
015.53	Tuberculosis of limb bones, tubercle bacilli found (in sputum) by microscopy
015.54	Tuberculosis of limb bones, tubercle bacilli not found (in sputum) by microscopy, but found by bacterial culture
015.55	Tuberculosis of limb bones, tubercle bacilli not found by bacteriological examination, but tuberculosis confirmed histologically
015.56	Tuberculosis of limb bones, tubercle bacilli not found by bacteriological or histological examination, but tuberculosis confirmed by other methods [inoculation of animals]
015.60	Tuberculosis of mastoid, confirmation unspecified
015.61	Tuberculosis of mastoid, bacteriological or histological examination not done
015.62	Tuberculosis of mastoid, bacteriological or histological examination unknown (at present)
015.63	Tuberculosis of mastoid, tubercle bacilli found (in sputum) by microscopy
015.64	Tuberculosis of mastoid, tubercle bacilli not found (in sputum) by microscopy, but found by bacterial culture
015.65	Tuberculosis of mastoid, tubercle bacilli not found by bacteriological examination, but tuberculosis confirmed histologically
015.66	Tuberculosis of mastoid, tubercle bacilli not found by bacteriological or histological examination but tuberculosis confirmed by other methods [inoculation of animals]
015.70	Tuberculosis of other specified bone, unspecified
015.71	Tuberculosis of other specified bone, bacteriological or histological examination not done
015.72	Tuberculosis of other specified bone, bacteriological or histological examination unknown (at present)
015.73	Tuberculosis of other specified bone, tubercle bacilli found (in sputum) by microscopy
015.74	Tuberculosis of other specified bone, tubercle bacilli not found (in sputum) by microscopy, but found by bacterial culture
015.75	Tuberculosis of other specified bone, tubercle bacilli not found by bacteriological examination, but tuberculosis confirmed histologically
015.76	Tuberculosis of other specified bone, tubercle bacilli not found by bacteriological or histological examination, but tuberculosis confirmed by other methods [inoculation of animals]
015.80	Tuberculosis of other specified joint, confirmation unspecified
015.81	Tuberculosis of other specified joint, bacteriological or histological examination not done
015.82	Tuberculosis of other specified joint, bacteriological or histological examination unknown (at present)
015.83	Tuberculosis of other specified joint, tubercle bacilli found (in sputum) by microscopy
015.84	Tuberculosis of other specified joint, tubercle bacilli not found (in sputum) by microscopy, but found by bacterial culture
015.85	Tuberculosis of other specified joint, tubercle bacilli not found by bacteriological examination, but tuberculosis confirmed histologically
015.86	Tuberculosis of other specified joint, tubercle bacilli not found by bacteriological or histological examination, but tuberculosis confirmed by other methods [inoculation of animals]
015.90	Tuberculosis of unspecified bones and joints, confirmation unspecified
015.91	Tuberculosis of unspecified bones and joints, bacteriological or histological examination not done
015.92	Tuberculosis of unspecified bones and joints, bacteriological or histological examination unknown (at present)
015.93	Tuberculosis of unspecified bones and joints, tubercle bacilli found (in sputum) by microscopy
015.94	Tuberculosis of unspecified bones and joints, tubercle bacilli not found (in sputum) by microscopy, but found by bacterial culture
015.95	Tuberculosis of unspecified bones and joints, tubercle bacilli not found by bacteriological examination, but tuberculosis confirmed histologically
015.96	Tuberculosis of unspecified bones and joints, tubercle bacilli not found by bacteriological or histological examination, but tuberculosis confirmed by other methods [inoculation of animals]
016.00	Tuberculosis of kidney, confirmation unspecified
016.01	Tuberculosis of kidney, bacteriological or histological examination not done
016.02	Tuberculosis of kidney, bacteriological or histological examination unknown (at present)
016.03	Tuberculosis of kidney, tubercle bacilli found (in sputum) by microscopy
016.04	Tuberculosis of kidney, tubercle bacilli not found (in sputum) by microscopy, but found by bacterial culture
016.05	Tuberculosis of kidney, tubercle bacilli not found by bacteriological examination, but tuberculosis confirmed histologically
016.06	Tuberculosis of kidney, tubercle bacilli not found by bacteriological or histological examination, but tuberculosis confirmed by other methods [inoculation of animals]
016.10	Tuberculosis of bladder, confirmation unspecified
016.11	Tuberculosis of bladder, bacteriological or histological examination not done
016.12	Tuberculosis of bladder, bacteriological or histological examination unknown (at present)
016.13	Tuberculosis of bladder, tubercle bacilli found (in sputum) by microscopy
016.14	Tuberculosis of bladder, tubercle bacilli not found (in sputum) by microscopy, but found by bacterial culture
016.15	Tuberculosis of bladder, tubercle bacilli not found by bacteriological examination, but tuberculosis confirmed histologically
016.16	Tuberculosis of bladder, tubercle bacilli not found by bacteriological or histological examination, but tuberculosis confirmed by other methods [inoculation of animals]
016.20	Tuberculosis of ureter, confirmation unspecified
016.21	Tuberculosis of ureter, bacteriological or histological examination not done
016.22	Tuberculosis of ureter, bacteriological or histological examination unknown (at present)

016.23 Tuberculosis of ureter, tubercle bacilli found (in sputum) by microscopy

016.24 Tuberculosis of ureter, tubercle bacilli not found (in sputum) by microscopy, but found by bacterial culture

016.25 Tuberculosis of ureter, tubercle bacilli not found by bacteriological examination, but tuberculosis confirmed histologically

016.26 Tuberculosis of ureter, tubercle bacilli not found by bacteriological or histological examination, but tuberculosis confirmed by other methods [inoculation of animals]

016.30 Tuberculosis of other urinary organs, confirmation unspecified

016.31 Tuberculosis of other urinary organs, bacteriological or histological examination not done

016.32 Tuberculosis of other urinary organs, bacteriological or histological examination unknown (at present)

016.33 Tuberculosis of other urinary organs, tubercle bacilli found (in sputum) by microscopy

016.34 Tuberculosis of other urinary organs, tubercle bacilli not found (in sputum) by microscopy, but found by bacterial culture

016.35 Tuberculosis of other urinary organs, tubercle bacilli not found by bacteriological examination, but tuberculosis confirmed histologically

016.36 Tuberculosis of other urinary organs, tubercle bacilli not found by bacteriological or histological examination, but tuberculosis confirmed by other methods [inoculation of animals]

016.40 Tuberculosis of epididymis, confirmation unspecified

016.41 Tuberculosis of epididymis, bacteriological or histological examination not done

016.42 Tuberculosis of epididymis, bacteriological or histological examination unknown (at present)

016.43 Tuberculosis of epididymis, tubercle bacilli found (in sputum) by microscopy

016.44 Tuberculosis of epididymis, tubercle bacilli not found (in sputum) by microscopy, but found by bacterial culture

016.45 Tuberculosis of epididymis, tubercle bacilli not found by bacteriological examination, but tuberculosis confirmed histologically

016.46 Tuberculosis of epididymis, tubercle bacilli not found by bacteriological or histological examination, but tuberculosis confirmed by other methods [inoculation of animals]

016.50 Tuberculosis of other male genital organs, confirmation unspecified

016.51 Tuberculosis of other male genital organs, bacteriological or histological examination not done

016.52 Tuberculosis of other male genital organs, bacteriological or histological examination unknown (at present)

016.53 Tuberculosis of other male genital organs, tubercle bacilli found (in sputum) by microscopy

016.54 Tuberculosis of other male genital organs, tubercle bacilli not found (in sputum) by microscopy, but found by bacterial culture

016.55 Tuberculosis of other male genital organs, tubercle bacilli not found by bacteriological examination, but tuberculosis confirmed histologically

016.56 Tuberculosis of other male genital organs, tubercle bacilli not found by bacteriological or histological examination, but tuberculosis confirmed by other methods [inoculation of animals]

016.60 Tuberculous oophoritis and salpingitis, confirmation unspecified

016.61 Tuberculous oophoritis and salpingitis, bacteriological or histological examination not done

016.62 Tuberculous oophoritis and salpingitis, bacteriological or histological examination unknown (at present)

016.63 Tuberculous oophoritis and salpingitis, tubercle bacilli found (in sputum) by microscopy

016.64 Tuberculous oophoritis and salpingitis, tubercle bacilli not found (in sputum) by microscopy, but found by bacterial culture

016.65 Tuberculous oophoritis and salpingitis, tubercle bacilli not found by bacteriological examination, but tuberculosis confirmed histologically

016.66 Tuberculous oophoritis and salpingitis, tubercle bacilli not found by bacteriological or histological examination, but tuberculosis confirmed by other methods [inoculation of animals]

016.70 Tuberculosis of other female genital organs, confirmation unspecified

016.71 Tuberculosis of other female genital organs, bacteriological or histological examination not done

016.72 Tuberculosis of other female genital organs, bacteriological or histological examination unknown (at present)

016.73 Tuberculosis of other female genital organs, tubercle bacilli found (in sputum) by microscopy

016.74 Tuberculosis of other female genital organs, tubercle bacilli not found (in sputum) by microscopy, but found by bacterial culture

016.75 Tuberculosis of other female genital organs, tubercle bacilli not found by bacteriological examination, but tuberculosis confirmed histologically

016.76 Tuberculosis of other female genital organs, tubercle bacilli not found by bacteriological or histological examination, but tuberculosis confirmed by other methods [inoculation of animals]

016.90 Unspecified genitourinary tuberculosis, confirmation unspecified

016.91 Unspecified genitourinary tuberculosis, bacteriological or histological examination not done

016.92 Unspecified genitourinary tuberculosis, bacteriological or histological examination unknown (at present)

016.93 Unspecified genitourinary tuberculosis, tubercle bacilli found (in sputum) by microscopy

016.94 Unspecified genitourinary tuberculosis, tubercle bacilli not found (in sputum) by microscopy, but found by bacterial culture

016.95 Unspecified genitourinary tuberculosis, tubercle bacilli not found by bacteriological examination, but tuberculosis confirmed histologically

016.96 Unspecified genitourinary tuberculosis, tubercle bacilli not found by bacteriological or histological examination, but tuberculosis confirmed by other methods [inoculation of animals]

017.00 Tuberculosis of skin and subcutaneous cellular tissue, confirmation unspecified

017.01 Tuberculosis of skin and subcutaneous cellular tissue, bacteriological or histological examination not done

017.02 Tuberculosis of skin and subcutaneous cellular tissue, bacteriological or histological examination unknown (at present)

017.03 Tuberculosis of skin and subcutaneous cellular tissue, tubercle bacilli found (in sputum) by microscopy

017.04 Tuberculosis of skin and subcutaneous cellular tissue, tubercle bacilli not found (in sputum) by microscopy, but found by bacterial culture

017.05 Tuberculosis of skin and subcutaneous cellular tissue, tubercle bacilli not found by bacteriological examination, but tuberculosis confirmed histologically

017.06 Tuberculosis of skin and subcutaneous cellular tissue, tubercle bacilli not found by bacteriological or histological examination, but tuberculosis confirmed by other methods [inoculation of animals]

017.20 Tuberculosis of peripheral lymph nodes, confirmation unspecified

017.21 Tuberculosis of peripheral lymph nodes, bacteriological or histological examination not done

017.22 Tuberculosis of peripheral lymph nodes, bacteriological or histological examination unknown (at present)

017.23 Tuberculosis of peripheral lymph nodes, tubercle bacilli found (in sputum) by microscopy

017.24 Tuberculosis of peripheral lymph nodes, tubercle bacilli not found (in sputum) by microscopy, but found by bacterial culture

017.25 Tuberculosis of peripheral lymph nodes, tubercle bacilli not found by bacteriological examination, but tuberculosis confirmed histologically

017.26 Tuberculosis of peripheral lymph nodes, tubercle bacilli not found by bacteriological or histological examination, but tuberculosis confirmed by other methods [inoculation of animals]

017.30 Tuberculosis of eye, confirmation unspecified

017.31	Tuberculosis of eye, bacteriological or histological examination not done
017.32	Tuberculosis of eye, bacteriological or histological examination unknown (at present)
017.33	Tuberculosis of eye, tubercle bacilli found (in sputum) by microscopy
017.34	Tuberculosis of eye, tubercle bacilli not found (in sputum) by microscopy, but found by bacterial culture
017.35	Tuberculosis of eye, tubercle bacilli not found by bacteriological examination, but tuberculosis confirmed histologically
017.36	Tuberculosis of eye, tubercle bacilli not found by bacteriological or histological examination, but tuberculosis confirmed by other methods [inoculation of animals]
017.40	Tuberculosis of ear, confirmation unspecified
017.41	Tuberculosis of ear, bacteriological or histological examination not done
017.42	Tuberculosis of ear, bacteriological or histological examination unknown (at present)
017.43	Tuberculosis of ear, tubercle bacilli found (in sputum) by microscopy
017.44	Tuberculosis of ear, tubercle bacilli not found (in sputum) by microscopy, but found by bacterial culture
017.45	Tuberculosis of ear, tubercle bacilli not found by bacteriological examination, but tuberculosis confirmed histologically
017.46	Tuberculosis of ear, tubercle bacilli not found by bacteriological or histological examination, but tuberculosis confirmed by other methods [inoculation of animals]
017.50	Tuberculosis of thyroid gland, confirmation unspecified
017.51	Tuberculosis of thyroid gland, bacteriological or histological examination not done
017.52	Tuberculosis of thyroid gland, bacteriological or histological examination unknown (at present)
017.53	Tuberculosis of thyroid gland, tubercle bacilli found (in sputum) by microscopy
017.54	Tuberculosis of thyroid gland, tubercle bacilli not found (in sputum) by microscopy, but found by bacterial culture
017.55	Tuberculosis of thyroid gland, tubercle bacilli not found by bacteriological examination, but tuberculosis confirmed histologically
017.56	Tuberculosis of thyroid gland, tubercle bacilli not found by bacteriological or histological examination, but tuberculosis confirmed by other methods [inoculation of animals]
017.60	Tuberculosis of adrenal glands, confirmation unspecified
017.61	Tuberculosis of adrenal glands, bacteriological or histological examination not done
017.62	Tuberculosis of adrenal glands, bacteriological or histological examination unknown (at present)
017.63	Tuberculosis of adrenal glands, tubercle bacilli found (in sputum) by microscopy
017.64	Tuberculosis of adrenal glands, tubercle bacilli not found (in sputum) by microscopy, but found by bacterial culture
017.65	Tuberculosis of adrenal glands, tubercle bacilli not found by bacteriological examination, but tuberculosis confirmed histologically
017.66	Tuberculosis of adrenal glands, tubercle bacilli not found by bacteriological or histological examination, but tuberculosis confirmed by other methods [inoculation of animals]
017.70	Tuberculosis of spleen, confirmation unspecified
017.71	Tuberculosis of spleen, bacteriological or histological examination not done
017.72	Tuberculosis of spleen, bacteriological or histological examination unknown (at present)
017.73	Tuberculosis of spleen, tubercle bacilli found (in sputum) by microscopy
017.74	Tuberculosis of spleen, tubercle bacilli not found (in sputum) by microscopy, but found by bacterial culture
017.75	Tuberculosis of spleen, tubercle bacilli not found by bacteriological examination, but tuberculosis confirmed histologically
017.76	Tuberculosis of spleen, tubercle bacilli not found by bacteriological or histological examination, but tuberculosis confirmed by other methods [inoculation of animals]
017.80	Tuberculosis of esophagus, confirmation unspecified
017.81	Tuberculosis of esophagus, bacteriological or histological examination not done
017.82	Tuberculosis of esophagus, bacteriological or histological examination unknown (at present)
017.83	Tuberculosis of esophagus, tubercle bacilli found (in sputum) by microscopy
017.84	Tuberculosis of esophagus, tubercle bacilli not found (in sputum) by microscopy, but found by bacterial culture
017.85	Tuberculosis of esophagus, tubercle bacilli not found by bacteriological examination, but tuberculosis confirmed histologically
017.86	Tuberculosis of esophagus, tubercle bacilli not found by bacteriological or histological examination, but tuberculosis confirmed by other methods [inoculation of animals]
017.90	Tuberculosis of other specified organs, confirmation unspecified
017.91	Tuberculosis of other specified organs, bacteriological or histological examination not done
017.92	Tuberculosis of other specified organs, bacteriological or histological examination unknown (at present)
017.93	Tuberculosis of other specified organs, tubercle bacilli found (in sputum) by microscopy
017.94	Tuberculosis of other specified organs, tubercle bacilli not found (in sputum) by microscopy, but found by bacterial culture
017.95	Tuberculosis of other specified organs, tubercle bacilli not found by bacteriological examination, but tuberculosis confirmed histologically
017.96	Tuberculosis of other specified organs, tubercle bacilli not found by bacteriological or histological examination but tuberculosis confirmed by other methods [inoculation of animals]
021.0	Ulceroglandular tularemia
021.1	Enteric tularemia
021.2	Pulmonary tularemia
021.3	Oculoglandular tularemia
021.8	Other specified tularemia
021.9	Unspecified tularemia
022.0	Cutaneous anthrax
022.2	Gastrointestinal anthrax
022.8	Other specified manifestations of anthrax
022.9	Unspecified anthrax
023.8	Other brucellosis
023.9	Brucellosis, unspecified
024	Glanders
025	Melioidosis
026.0	Spirillary fever
026.1	Streptobacillary fever
026.9	Unspecified rat-bite fever
027.0	Listeriosis
027.2	Pasteurellosis
027.8	Other specified zoonotic bacterial diseases
027.9	Unspecified zoonotic bacterial disease
030.0	Lepromatous leprosy (type L)
030.1	Tuberculoid leprosy (type T)
030.2	Indeterminate leprosy (group I)
030.3	Borderline leprosy (group B)
030.8	Other specified leprosy
030.9	Unspecified leprosy
031.0	Pulmonary diseases due to other mycobacteria

031.1	Cutaneous diseases due to other mycobacteria
031.2	Disseminated diseases due to other mycobacteria
031.8	Other specified diseases due to other mycobacteria
031.9	Unspecified diseases due to mycobacteria
032.0	Faucial diphtheria
032.1	Nasopharyngeal diphtheria
032.2	Anterior nasal diphtheria
032.3	Laryngeal diphtheria
032.81	Conjunctival diphtheria
032.82	Diphtheritic myocarditis
032.83	Diphtheritic peritonitis
032.84	Diphtheritic cystitis
032.85	Cutaneous diphtheria
032.89	Other specified diphtheria
032.9	Unspecified diphtheria
033.0	Whooping cough due to Bordetella pertussis (P. pertussis)
033.1	Whooping cough due to Bordetella parapertussis (B. parapertussis)
033.8	Whooping cough due to other specified organism
033.9	Whooping cough, unspecified organism
034.1	Scarlet fever
036.81	Meningococcal optic neuritis
036.82	Meningococcal arthropathy
036.89	Other specified meningococcal infections
036.9	Unspecified meningococcal infection
039.0	Cutaneous actinomycotic infection
039.1	Pulmonary actinomycotic infection
039.2	Abdominal actinomycotic infection
039.3	Cervicofacial actinomycotic infection
039.4	Madura foot
039.8	Actinomycotic infection of other specified sites
039.9	Actinomycotic infection of unspecified site
040.2	Whipple's disease
040.3	Necrobacillosis
040.41	Infant botulism
040.42	Wound botulism
040.81	Tropical pyomyositis
046.0	Kuru
046.11	Variant Creutzfeldt-Jakob disease
046.19	Other and unspecified Creutzfeldt-Jakob disease
046.2	Subacute sclerosing panencephalitis
046.3	Progressive multifocal leukoencephalopathy
046.71	Gerstmann-Straussler-Scheinker syndrome
046.72	Fatal familial insomnia
046.79	Other and unspecified prion disease of central nervous system
046.8	Other specified slow virus infection of central nervous system
046.9	Unspecified slow virus infection of central nervous system
047.0	Meningitis due to coxsackie virus
047.1	Meningitis due to ECHO virus
047.8	Other specified viral meningitis
047.9	Unspecified viral meningitis
048	Other enterovirus diseases of central nervous system
049.0	Lymphocytic choriomeningitis
049.1	Meningitis due to adenovirus
049.8	Other specified non-arthropod-borne viral diseases of central nervous system
049.9	Unspecified non-arthropod-borne viral disease of central nervous system
050.0	Variola major
050.1	Alastrim

050.2	Modified smallpox
050.9	Unspecified smallpox
052.7	Chickenpox with other specified complications
052.8	Chickenpox with unspecified complication
052.9	Varicella without mention of complication
053.10	Herpes zoster with unspecified nervous system complication
053.11	Geniculate herpes zoster
053.12	Postherpetic trigeminal neuralgia
053.13	Postherpetic polyneuropathy
053.19	Other herpes zoster with nervous system complications
053.20	Herpes zoster dermatitis of eyelid
053.21	Herpes zoster keratoconjunctivitis
053.22	Herpes zoster iridocyclitis
053.29	Other ophthalmic herpes zoster complications
053.71	Otitis externa due to herpes zoster
053.79	Other specified herpes zoster complications
053.8	Unspecified herpes zoster complication
054.2	Herpetic gingivostomatitis
054.40	Unspecified ophthalmic complication herpes simplex
054.41	Herpes simplex dermatitis of eyelid
054.42	Dendritic keratitis
054.43	Herpes simplex disciform keratitis
054.44	Herpes simplex iridocyclitis
054.49	Herpes simplex with other ophthalmic complications
054.71	Visceral herpes simplex
054.79	Other specified herpes simplex complications
055.71	Measles keratoconjunctivitis
055.79	Other specified measles complications
056.00	Unspecified rubella neurological complication
056.09	Other neurological rubella complications
056.71	Arthritis due to rubella
056.79	Rubella with other specified complications
057.0	Erythema infectiosum (fifth disease)
059.01	Monkeypox
059.21	Tanapox
060.0	Sylvatic yellow fever
060.1	Urban yellow fever
060.9	Unspecified yellow fever
061	Dengue
065.0	Crimean hemorrhagic fever (CHF Congo virus)
065.1	Omsk hemorrhagic fever
065.2	Kyasanur Forest disease
065.3	Other tick-borne hemorrhagic fever
065.4	Mosquito-borne hemorrhagic fever
065.8	Other specified arthropod-borne hemorrhagic fever
065.9	Unspecified arthropod-borne hemorrhagic fever
066.0	Phlebotomus fever
066.1	Tick-borne fever
066.2	Venezuelan equine fever
066.3	Other mosquito-borne fever
066.8	Other specified arthropod-borne viral diseases
066.9	Unspecified arthropod-borne viral disease
070.1	Viral hepatitis A without mention of hepatic coma
070.30	Viral hepatitis B without mention of hepatic coma, acute or unspecified, without mention of hepatitis delta
070.31	Viral hepatitis B without mention of hepatic coma, acute or unspecified, with hepatitis delta
070.32	Viral hepatitis B without mention of hepatic coma, chronic, without mention of hepatitis delta

070.33	Viral hepatitis B without mention of hepatic coma, chronic, with hepatitis delta
070.51	Acute hepatitis C without mention of hepatic coma
070.52	Hepatitis delta without mention of active hepatitis B disease or hepatic coma
070.53	Hepatitis E without mention of hepatic coma
070.59	Other specified viral hepatitis without mention of hepatic coma
070.9	Unspecified viral hepatitis without mention of hepatic coma
071	Rabies
072.0	Mumps orchitis
072.3	Mumps pancreatitis
072.71	Mumps hepatitis
072.72	Mumps polyneuropathy
072.79	Mumps with other specified complications
072.8	Unspecified mumps complication
073.7	Ornithosis with other specified complications
073.8	Ornithosis with unspecified complication
073.9	Unspecified ornithosis
074.20	Coxsackie carditis, unspecified
074.21	Coxsackie pericarditis
074.22	Coxsackie endocarditis
074.23	Coxsackie myocarditis
078.3	Cat-scratch disease
078.5	Cytomegaloviral disease
078.6	Hemorrhagic nephrosonephritis
078.7	Arenaviral hemorrhagic fever
079.51	Human t-cell lymphotrophic virus, type I (HTLV-I), in conditions classified elsewhere and of unspecified site
079.52	Human t-cell lymphotrophic virus, type II (HTLV-II), in conditions classified elsewhere and of unspecified site
079.53	Human immunodeficiency virus, type 2 (HIV 2), in conditions classified elsewhere and of unspecified site
079.81	Hantavirus infection
079.82	SARS-associated coronavirus
079.83	Parvovirus B19
080	Louse-borne (epidemic) typhus
081.0	Murine (endemic) typhus
081.1	Brill's disease
081.2	Scrub typhus
081.9	Unspecified typhus
082.0	Spotted fevers
082.1	Boutonneuse fever
082.2	North Asian tick fever
082.3	Queensland tick typhus
082.40	Ehrlichiosis, unspecified
082.41	Ehrlichiosis chaffeensis [E. chaffeensis]
082.49	Other ehrlichiosis
082.8	Other specified tick-borne rickettsioses
082.9	Unspecified tick-borne rickettsiosis
083.0	Q fever
083.1	Trench fever
083.2	Rickettsialpox
083.8	Other specified rickettsioses
083.9	Unspecified rickettsiosis
084.1	Vivax malaria (benign tertian)
084.2	Quartan malaria
084.3	Ovale malaria
084.4	Other malaria
084.5	Mixed malaria
084.6	Unspecified malaria
084.7	Induced malaria
084.8	Blackwater fever
084.9	Other pernicious complications of malaria
085.0	Visceral leishmaniasis (kala-azar)
085.1	Cutaneous leishmaniasis, urban
085.2	Cutaneous leishmaniasis, Asian desert
085.3	Cutaneous leishmaniasis, Ethiopian
085.4	Cutaneous leishmaniasis, American
085.5	Mucocutaneous leishmaniasis, (American)
085.9	Unspecified leishmaniasis
086.0	Chagas' disease with heart involvement
086.1	Chagas' disease with other organ involvement
086.2	Chagas' disease without mention of organ involvement
086.3	Gambian trypanosomiasis
086.4	Rhodesian trypanosomiasis
086.5	African trypanosomiasis, unspecified
086.9	Unspecified trypanosomiasis
087.0	Louse-borne relapsing fever
087.1	Tick-borne relapsing fever
087.9	Unspecified relapsing fever
088.0	Bartonellosis
088.81	Lyme disease
088.82	Babesiosis
090.0	Early congenital syphilis, symptomatic
090.2	Unspecified early congenital syphilis
090.3	Syphilitic interstitial keratitis
090.40	Unspecified juvenile neurosyphilis
090.49	Other juvenile neurosyphilis
090.5	Other late congenital syphilis, symptomatic
091.3	Secondary syphilis of skin or mucous membranes
091.4	Adenopathy due to secondary syphilis
091.50	Early syphilis, syphilitic uveitis, unspecified
091.51	Early syphilis, syphilitic chorioretinitis (secondary)
091.52	Early syphilis, syphilitic iridocyclitis (secondary)
091.61	Early syphilis, secondary syphilitic periostitis
091.62	Early syphilis, secondary syphilitic hepatitis
091.69	Early syphilis, secondary syphilis of other viscera
091.7	Early syphilis, secondary syphilis, relapse
091.82	Early syphilis, syphilitic alopecia
091.89	Early syphilis, other forms of secondary syphilis
091.9	Early syphilis, unspecified secondary syphilis
093.0	Aneurysm of aorta, specified as syphilitic
093.1	Syphilitic aortitis
093.20	Unspecified syphilitic endocarditis of valve
093.21	Syphilitic endocarditis, mitral valve
093.22	Syphilitic endocarditis, aortic valve
093.23	Syphilitic endocarditis, tricuspid valve
093.24	Syphilitic endocarditis, pulmonary valve
093.81	Syphilitic pericarditis
093.82	Syphilitic myocarditis
093.89	Other specified cardiovascular syphilis
093.9	Unspecified cardiovascular syphilis
094.0	Tabes dorsalis
094.1	General paresis
094.3	Asymptomatic neurosyphilis
094.82	Syphilitic Parkinsonism
094.83	Syphilitic disseminated retinochoroiditis
094.84	Syphilitic optic atrophy
094.85	Syphilitic retrobulbar neuritis

094.86	Syphilitic acoustic neuritis
094.89	Other specified neurosyphilis
094.9	Unspecified neurosyphilis
095.0	Syphilitic episcleritis
095.1	Syphilis of lung
095.2	Syphilitic peritonitis
095.3	Syphilis of liver
095.4	Syphilis of kidney
095.5	Syphilis of bone
095.6	Syphilis of muscle
095.7	Syphilis of synovium, tendon, and bursa
095.8	Other specified forms of late symptomatic syphilis
095.9	Unspecified late symptomatic syphilis
098.0	Gonococcal infection (acute) of lower genitourinary tract
098.10	Gonococcal infection (acute) of upper genitourinary tract, site unspecified
098.11	Gonococcal cystitis (acute)
098.12	Gonococcal prostatitis (acute)
098.13	Gonococcal epididymo-orchitis (acute)
098.14	Gonococcal seminal vesiculitis (acute)
098.15	Gonococcal cervicitis (acute)
098.16	Gonococcal endometritis (acute)
098.17	Gonococcal salpingitis, specified as acute
098.19	Other gonococcal infections (acute) of upper genitourinary tract
098.40	Gonococcal conjunctivitis (neonatorum)
098.41	Gonococcal iridocyclitis
098.42	Gonococcal endophthalmia
098.43	Gonococcal keratitis
098.49	Other gonococcal infection of eye
098.50	Gonococcal arthritis
098.51	Gonococcal synovitis and tenosynovitis
098.52	Gonococcal bursitis
098.53	Gonococcal spondylitis
098.59	Other gonococcal infection of joint
098.81	Gonococcal keratosis (blennorrhagica)
098.85	Other gonococcal heart disease
098.86	Gonococcal peritonitis
098.89	Gonococcal infection of other specified sites
099.56	Chlamydia trachomatis infection of peritoneum
100.0	Leptospirosis icterohemorrhagica
100.89	Other specified leptospiral infections
100.9	Unspecified leptospirosis
101	Vincent's angina
112.0	Candidiasis of mouth
112.2	Candidiasis of other urogenital sites
112.82	Candidal otitis externa
112.84	Candidiasis of the esophagus
112.85	Candidiasis of the intestine
112.89	Other candidiasis of other specified sites
114.0	Primary coccidioidomycosis (pulmonary)
114.1	Primary extrapulmonary coccidioidomycosis
114.3	Other forms of progressive coccidioidomycosis
114.4	Chronic pulmonary coccidioidomycosis
114.5	Unspecified pulmonary coccidioidomycosis
114.9	Unspecified coccidioidomycosis
115.02	Histoplasma capsulatum retinitis
115.09	Histoplasma capsulatum, with mention of other manifestation
115.12	Histoplasma duboisii retinitis
115.19	Histoplasma duboisii with mention of other manifestation

115.92	Unspecified Histoplasmosis retinitis
116.0	Blastomycosis
116.1	Paracoccidioidomycosis
117.3	Aspergillosis
117.4	Mycotic mycetomas
117.5	Cryptococcosis
117.6	Allescheriosis (Petriellidiosis)
117.8	Infection by dematiaceous fungi (Phaeohyphomycosis)
117.9	Other and unspecified mycoses
118	Opportunistic mycoses
120.0	Schistosomiasis due to schistosoma haematobium
120.1	Schistosomiasis due to schistosoma mansoni
120.2	Schistosomiasis due to schistosoma japonicum
120.3	Cutaneous schistosomiasis
120.8	Other specified schistosomiasis
120.9	Unspecified schistosomiasis
121.0	Opisthorchiasis
121.1	Clonorchiasis
121.2	Paragonimiasis
121.3	Fascioliasis
121.4	Fasciolopsiasis
121.5	Metagonimiasis
121.6	Heterophyiasis
121.8	Other specified trematode infections
122.0	Echinococcus granulosus infection of liver
122.1	Echinococcus granulosus infection of lung
122.2	Echinococcus granulosus infection of thyroid
122.3	Other echinococcus granulosus infection
122.4	Unspecified echinococcus granulosus infection
122.5	Echinococcus multilocularis infection of liver
122.6	Other echinococcus multilocularis infection
122.7	Unspecified echinococcus multilocularis infection
122.8	Unspecified echinococcus of liver
122.9	Other and unspecified echinococcosis
123.0	Taenia solium infection, intestinal form
123.1	Cysticercosis
123.2	Taenia saginata infection
123.3	Taeniasis, unspecified
123.4	Diphyllobothriasis, intestinal
123.5	Sparganosis (larval diphyllobothriasis)
123.6	Hymenolepiasis
123.8	Other specified cestode infection
124	Trichinosis
125.0	Bancroftian filariasis
125.1	Malayan filariasis
125.2	Loiasis
125.3	Onchocerciasis
125.4	Dipetalonemiasis
125.5	Mansonella ozzardi infection
125.6	Other specified filariasis
125.7	Dracontiasis
125.9	Unspecified filariasis
126.0	Ancylostomiasis and necatoriasis due to ancylostoma duodenale
126.1	Ancylostomiasis and necatoriasis due to necator americanus
126.2	Ancylostomiasis and necatoriasis due to ancylostoma braziliense
126.3	Ancylostomiasis and necatoriasis due to ancylostoma ceylanicum
126.8	Ancylostomiasis and necatoriasis due to other specified ancylostoma
126.9	Unspecified ancylostomiasis and necatoriasis

© 2012 OptumInsight, Inc.

127.0	Ascariasis
127.1	Anisakiasis
127.2	Strongyloidiasis
127.3	Trichuriasis
127.4	Enterobiasis
127.5	Capillariasis
127.6	Trichostrongyliasis
127.7	Other specified intestinal helminthiasis
127.8	Mixed intestinal helminthiasis
127.9	Unspecified intestinal helminthiasis
130.1	Conjunctivitis due to toxoplasmosis
130.2	Chorioretinitis due to toxoplasmosis
130.5	Hepatitis due to toxoplasmosis
130.7	Toxoplasmosis of other specified sites
130.9	Unspecified toxoplasmosis
136.29	Other specific infections by free-living amebae
136.4	Psorospermiasis
136.5	Sarcosporidiosis
150.0	Malignant neoplasm of cervical esophagus
150.1	Malignant neoplasm of thoracic esophagus
150.2	Malignant neoplasm of abdominal esophagus
150.3	Malignant neoplasm of upper third of esophagus
150.4	Malignant neoplasm of middle third of esophagus
150.5	Malignant neoplasm of lower third of esophagus
150.8	Malignant neoplasm of other specified part of esophagus
150.9	Malignant neoplasm of esophagus, unspecified site
151.0	Malignant neoplasm of cardia
151.1	Malignant neoplasm of pylorus
151.2	Malignant neoplasm of pyloric antrum
151.3	Malignant neoplasm of fundus of stomach
151.4	Malignant neoplasm of body of stomach
151.5	Malignant neoplasm of lesser curvature of stomach, unspecified
151.6	Malignant neoplasm of greater curvature of stomach, unspecified
151.8	Malignant neoplasm of other specified sites of stomach
151.9	Malignant neoplasm of stomach, unspecified site
152.0	Malignant neoplasm of duodenum
152.1	Malignant neoplasm of jejunum
152.2	Malignant neoplasm of ileum
152.3	Malignant neoplasm of Meckel's diverticulum
152.8	Malignant neoplasm of other specified sites of small intestine
152.9	Malignant neoplasm of small intestine, unspecified site
153.0	Malignant neoplasm of hepatic flexure
153.1	Malignant neoplasm of transverse colon
153.2	Malignant neoplasm of descending colon
153.3	Malignant neoplasm of sigmoid colon
153.4	Malignant neoplasm of cecum
153.5	Malignant neoplasm of appendix
153.6	Malignant neoplasm of ascending colon
153.7	Malignant neoplasm of splenic flexure
153.8	Malignant neoplasm of other specified sites of large intestine
153.9	Malignant neoplasm of colon, unspecified site
154.0	Malignant neoplasm of rectosigmoid junction
154.1	Malignant neoplasm of rectum
154.2	Malignant neoplasm of anal canal
154.3	Malignant neoplasm of anus, unspecified site
154.8	Malignant neoplasm of other sites of rectum, rectosigmoid junction, and anus
155.0	Malignant neoplasm of liver, primary
155.1	Malignant neoplasm of intrahepatic bile ducts

155.2	Malignant neoplasm of liver, not specified as primary or secondary
156.0	Malignant neoplasm of gallbladder
156.1	Malignant neoplasm of extrahepatic bile ducts
156.2	Malignant neoplasm of ampulla of Vater
156.8	Malignant neoplasm of other specified sites of gallbladder and extrahepatic bile ducts
156.9	Malignant neoplasm of biliary tract, part unspecified site
157.0	Malignant neoplasm of head of pancreas
157.1	Malignant neoplasm of body of pancreas
157.2	Malignant neoplasm of tail of pancreas
157.3	Malignant neoplasm of pancreatic duct
157.4	Malignant neoplasm of islets of Langerhans
157.8	Malignant neoplasm of other specified sites of pancreas
157.9	Malignant neoplasm of pancreas, part unspecified
158.0	Malignant neoplasm of retroperitoneum
158.8	Malignant neoplasm of specified parts of peritoneum
158.9	Malignant neoplasm of peritoneum, unspecified
162.0	Malignant neoplasm of trachea
162.2	Malignant neoplasm of main bronchus
162.3	Malignant neoplasm of upper lobe, bronchus, or lung
162.4	Malignant neoplasm of middle lobe, bronchus, or lung
162.5	Malignant neoplasm of lower lobe, bronchus, or lung
162.8	Malignant neoplasm of other parts of bronchus or lung
162.9	Malignant neoplasm of bronchus and lung, unspecified site
163.0	Malignant neoplasm of parietal pleura
163.1	Malignant neoplasm of visceral pleura
163.8	Malignant neoplasm of other specified sites of pleura
163.9	Malignant neoplasm of pleura, unspecified site
164.0	Malignant neoplasm of thymus
164.1	Malignant neoplasm of heart
164.2	Malignant neoplasm of anterior mediastinum
164.3	Malignant neoplasm of posterior mediastinum
164.8	Malignant neoplasm of other parts of mediastinum
164.9	Malignant neoplasm of mediastinum, part unspecified
170.0	Malignant neoplasm of bones of skull and face, except mandible
170.1	Malignant neoplasm of mandible
170.2	Malignant neoplasm of vertebral column, excluding sacrum and coccyx
170.3	Malignant neoplasm of ribs, sternum, and clavicle
170.4	Malignant neoplasm of scapula and long bones of upper limb
170.5	Malignant neoplasm of short bones of upper limb
170.6	Malignant neoplasm of pelvic bones, sacrum, and coccyx
170.7	Malignant neoplasm of long bones of lower limb
170.8	Malignant neoplasm of short bones of lower limb
170.9	Malignant neoplasm of bone and articular cartilage, site unspecified
171.0	Malignant neoplasm of connective and other soft tissue of head, face, and neck
171.2	Malignant neoplasm of connective and other soft tissue of upper limb, including shoulder
171.3	Malignant neoplasm of connective and other soft tissue of lower limb, including hip
171.4	Malignant neoplasm of connective and other soft tissue of thorax
171.5	Malignant neoplasm of connective and other soft tissue of abdomen
171.6	Malignant neoplasm of connective and other soft tissue of pelvis
171.7	Malignant neoplasm of connective and other soft tissue of trunk, unspecified site
171.8	Malignant neoplasm of other specified sites of connective and other soft tissue

171.9	Malignant neoplasm of connective and other soft tissue, site unspecified	197.2	Secondary malignant neoplasm of pleura
176.0	Kaposi's sarcoma of skin	197.3	Secondary malignant neoplasm of other respiratory organs
176.1	Kaposi's sarcoma of soft tissue	197.4	Secondary malignant neoplasm of small intestine including duodenum
176.2	Kaposi's sarcoma of palate		
176.3	Kaposi's sarcoma of gastrointestinal sites	197.5	Secondary malignant neoplasm of large intestine and rectum
176.4	Kaposi's sarcoma of lung	197.6	Secondary malignant neoplasm of retroperitoneum and peritoneum
176.5	Kaposi's sarcoma of lymph nodes		
176.8	Kaposi's sarcoma of other specified sites	197.7	Secondary malignant neoplasm of liver
176.9	Kaposi's sarcoma of unspecified site	197.8	Secondary malignant neoplasm of other digestive organs and spleen
183.0	Malignant neoplasm of ovary		
189.0	Malignant neoplasm of kidney, except pelvis	198.0	Secondary malignant neoplasm of kidney
189.1	Malignant neoplasm of renal pelvis	198.1	Secondary malignant neoplasm of other urinary organs
189.2	Malignant neoplasm of ureter	198.2	Secondary malignant neoplasm of skin
189.3	Malignant neoplasm of urethra	198.3	Secondary malignant neoplasm of brain and spinal cord
189.4	Malignant neoplasm of paraurethral glands	198.4	Secondary malignant neoplasm of other parts of nervous system
189.8	Malignant neoplasm of other specified sites of urinary organs	198.5	Secondary malignant neoplasm of bone and bone marrow
189.9	Malignant neoplasm of urinary organ, site unspecified	198.6	Secondary malignant neoplasm of ovary
191.0	Malignant neoplasm of cerebrum, except lobes and ventricles	198.7	Secondary malignant neoplasm of adrenal gland
191.1	Malignant neoplasm of frontal lobe of brain	198.81	Secondary malignant neoplasm of breast
191.2	Malignant neoplasm of temporal lobe of brain	198.82	Secondary malignant neoplasm of genital organs
191.3	Malignant neoplasm of parietal lobe of brain	198.89	Secondary malignant neoplasm of other specified sites
191.4	Malignant neoplasm of occipital lobe of brain	199.0	Disseminated malignant neoplasm
191.5	Malignant neoplasm of ventricles of brain	199.2	Malignant neoplasm associated with transplanted organ
191.6	Malignant neoplasm of cerebellum NOS	200.00	Reticulosarcoma, unspecified site, extranodal and solid organ sites
191.7	Malignant neoplasm of brain stem		
191.8	Malignant neoplasm of other parts of brain	200.01	Reticulosarcoma of lymph nodes of head, face, and neck
191.9	Malignant neoplasm of brain, unspecified site	200.02	Reticulosarcoma of intrathoracic lymph nodes
192.0	Malignant neoplasm of cranial nerves	200.03	Reticulosarcoma of intra-abdominal lymph nodes
192.1	Malignant neoplasm of cerebral meninges	200.04	Reticulosarcoma of lymph nodes of axilla and upper limb
192.2	Malignant neoplasm of spinal cord	200.05	Reticulosarcoma of lymph nodes of inguinal region and lower limb
192.3	Malignant neoplasm of spinal meninges		
192.8	Malignant neoplasm of other specified sites of nervous system	200.06	Reticulosarcoma of intrapelvic lymph nodes
192.9	Malignant neoplasm of nervous system, part unspecified	200.07	Reticulosarcoma of spleen
		200.08	Reticulosarcoma of lymph nodes of multiple sites
194.0	Malignant neoplasm of adrenal gland	200.10	Lymphosarcoma, unspecified site, extranodal and solid organ sites
194.1	Malignant neoplasm of parathyroid gland		
194.3	Malignant neoplasm of pituitary gland and craniopharyngeal duct	200.11	Lymphosarcoma of lymph nodes of head, face, and neck
194.4	Malignant neoplasm of pineal gland	200.12	Lymphosarcoma of intrathoracic lymph nodes
194.5	Malignant neoplasm of carotid body	200.13	Lymphosarcoma of intra-abdominal lymph nodes
194.6	Malignant neoplasm of aortic body and other paraganglia	200.14	Lymphosarcoma of lymph nodes of axilla and upper limb
194.8	Malignant neoplasm of other endocrine glands and related structures	200.15	Lymphosarcoma of lymph nodes of inguinal region and lower limb
		200.16	Lymphosarcoma of intrapelvic lymph nodes
194.9	Malignant neoplasm of endocrine gland, site unspecified	200.17	Lymphosarcoma of spleen
196.0	Secondary and unspecified malignant neoplasm of lymph nodes of head, face, and neck	200.18	Lymphosarcoma of lymph nodes of multiple sites
		200.20	Burkitt's tumor or lymphoma, unspecified site, extranodal and solid organ sites
196.1	Secondary and unspecified malignant neoplasm of intrathoracic lymph nodes		
		200.21	Burkitt's tumor or lymphoma of lymph nodes of head, face, and neck
196.2	Secondary and unspecified malignant neoplasm of intra-abdominal lymph nodes		
		200.22	Burkitt's tumor or lymphoma of intrathoracic lymph nodes
196.3	Secondary and unspecified malignant neoplasm of lymph nodes of axilla and upper limb	200.23	Burkitt's tumor or lymphoma of intra-abdominal lymph nodes
		200.24	Burkitt's tumor or lymphoma of lymph nodes of axilla and upper limb
196.5	Secondary and unspecified malignant neoplasm of lymph nodes of inguinal region and lower limb		
		200.25	Burkitt's tumor or lymphoma of lymph nodes of inguinal region and lower limb
196.6	Secondary and unspecified malignant neoplasm of intrapelvic lymph nodes		
		200.26	Burkitt's tumor or lymphoma of intrapelvic lymph nodes
196.8	Secondary and unspecified malignant neoplasm of lymph nodes of multiple sites	200.27	Burkitt's tumor or lymphoma of spleen
		200.28	Burkitt's tumor or lymphoma of lymph nodes of multiple sites
196.9	Secondary and unspecified malignant neoplasm of lymph nodes, site unspecified	200.30	Marginal zone lymphoma, unspecified site, extranodal and solid organ sites
197.0	Secondary malignant neoplasm of lung	200.31	Marginal zone lymphoma, lymph nodes of head, face, and neck
197.1	Secondary malignant neoplasm of mediastinum	200.32	Marginal zone lymphoma, intrathoracic lymph nodes
		200.33	Marginal zone lymphoma, intra-abdominal lymph nodes
		200.34	Marginal zone lymphoma, lymph nodes of axilla and upper limb

Appendix A — Numeric CC List

200.35	Marginal zone lymphoma, lymph nodes of inguinal region and lower limb
200.36	Marginal zone lymphoma, intrapelvic lymph nodes
200.37	Marginal zone lymphoma, spleen
200.38	Marginal zone lymphoma, lymph nodes of multiple sites
200.40	Mantle cell lymphoma, unspecified site, extranodal and solid organ sites
200.41	Mantle cell lymphoma, lymph nodes of head, face, and neck
200.42	Mantle cell lymphoma, intrathoracic lymph nodes
200.43	Mantle cell lymphoma, intra-abdominal lymph nodes
200.44	Mantle cell lymphoma, lymph nodes of axilla and upper limb
200.45	Mantle cell lymphoma, lymph nodes of inguinal region and lower limb
200.46	Mantle cell lymphoma, intrapelvic lymph nodes
200.47	Mantle cell lymphoma, spleen
200.48	Mantle cell lymphoma, lymph nodes of multiple sites
200.50	Primary central nervous system lymphoma, unspecified site, extranodal and solid organ sites
200.51	Primary central nervous system lymphoma, lymph nodes of head, face, and neck
200.52	Primary central nervous system lymphoma, intrathoracic lymph nodes
200.53	Primary central nervous system lymphoma, intra-abdominal lymph nodes
200.54	Primary central nervous system lymphoma, lymph nodes of axilla and upper limb
200.55	Primary central nervous system lymphoma, lymph nodes of inguinal region and lower limb
200.56	Primary central nervous system lymphoma, intrapelvic lymph nodes
200.57	Primary central nervous system lymphoma, spleen
200.58	Primary central nervous system lymphoma, lymph nodes of multiple sites
200.60	Anaplastic large cell lymphoma, unspecified site, extranodal and solid organ sites
200.61	Anaplastic large cell lymphoma, lymph nodes of head, face, and neck
200.62	Anaplastic large cell lymphoma, intrathoracic lymph nodes
200.63	Anaplastic large cell lymphoma, intra-abdominal lymph nodes
200.64	Anaplastic large cell lymphoma, lymph nodes of axilla and upper limb
200.65	Anaplastic large cell lymphoma, lymph nodes of inguinal region and lower limb
200.66	Anaplastic large cell lymphoma, intrapelvic lymph nodes
200.67	Anaplastic large cell lymphoma, spleen
200.68	Anaplastic large cell lymphoma, lymph nodes of multiple sites
200.70	Large cell lymphoma, unspecified site, extranodal and solid organ sites
200.71	Large cell lymphoma, lymph nodes of head, face, and neck
200.72	Large cell lymphoma, intrathoracic lymph nodes
200.73	Large cell lymphoma, intra-abdominal lymph nodes
200.74	Large cell lymphoma, lymph nodes of axilla and upper limb
200.75	Large cell lymphoma, lymph nodes of inguinal region and lower limb
200.76	Large cell lymphoma, intrapelvic lymph nodes
200.77	Large cell lymphoma, spleen
200.78	Large cell lymphoma, lymph nodes of multiple sites
200.80	Other named variants, unspecified site, extranodal and solid organ sites
200.81	Other named variants of lymphosarcoma and reticulosarcoma of lymph nodes of head, face, and neck
200.82	Other named variants of lymphosarcoma and reticulosarcoma of intrathoracic lymph nodes
200.83	Other named variants of lymphosarcoma and reticulosarcoma of intra-abdominal lymph nodes
200.84	Other named variants of lymphosarcoma and reticulosarcoma of lymph nodes of axilla and upper limb
200.85	Other named variants of lymphosarcoma and reticulosarcoma of lymph nodes of inguinal region and lower limb
200.86	Other named variants of lymphosarcoma and reticulosarcoma of intrapelvic lymph nodes
200.87	Other named variants of lymphosarcoma and reticulosarcoma of spleen
200.88	Other named variants of lymphosarcoma and reticulosarcoma of lymph nodes of multiple sites
201.00	Hodgkin's paragranuloma, unspecified site, extranodal and solid organ sites
201.01	Hodgkin's paragranuloma of lymph nodes of head, face, and neck
201.02	Hodgkin's paragranuloma of intrathoracic lymph nodes
201.03	Hodgkin's paragranuloma of intra-abdominal lymph nodes
201.04	Hodgkin's paragranuloma of lymph nodes of axilla and upper limb
201.05	Hodgkin's paragranuloma of lymph nodes of inguinal region and lower limb
201.06	Hodgkin's paragranuloma of intrapelvic lymph nodes
201.07	Hodgkin's paragranuloma of spleen
201.08	Hodgkin's paragranuloma of lymph nodes of multiple sites
201.10	Hodgkin's granuloma, unspecified site, extranodal and solid organ sites
201.11	Hodgkin's granuloma of lymph nodes of head, face, and neck
201.12	Hodgkin's granuloma of intrathoracic lymph nodes
201.13	Hodgkin's granuloma of intra-abdominal lymph nodes
201.14	Hodgkin's granuloma of lymph nodes of axilla and upper limb
201.15	Hodgkin's granuloma of lymph nodes of inguinal region and lower limb
201.16	Hodgkin's granuloma of intrapelvic lymph nodes
201.17	Hodgkin's granuloma of spleen
201.18	Hodgkin's granuloma of lymph nodes of multiple sites
201.20	Hodgkin's sarcoma, unspecified site, extranodal and solid organ sites
201.21	Hodgkin's sarcoma of lymph nodes of head, face, and neck
201.22	Hodgkin's sarcoma of intrathoracic lymph nodes
201.23	Hodgkin's sarcoma of intra-abdominal lymph nodes
201.24	Hodgkin's sarcoma of lymph nodes of axilla and upper limb
201.25	Hodgkin's sarcoma of lymph nodes of inguinal region and lower limb
201.26	Hodgkin's sarcoma of intrapelvic lymph nodes
201.27	Hodgkin's sarcoma of spleen
201.28	Hodgkin's sarcoma of lymph nodes of multiple sites
201.40	Hodgkin's disease, lymphocytic-histiocytic predominance, unspecified site, extranodal and solid organ sites
201.41	Hodgkin's disease, lymphocytic-histiocytic predominance of lymph nodes of head, face, and neck
201.42	Hodgkin's disease, lymphocytic-histiocytic predominance of intrathoracic lymph nodes
201.43	Hodgkin's disease, lymphocytic-histiocytic predominance of intra-abdominal lymph nodes
201.44	Hodgkin's disease, lymphocytic-histiocytic predominance of lymph nodes of axilla and upper limb
201.45	Hodgkin's disease, lymphocytic-histiocytic predominance of lymph nodes of inguinal region and lower limb
201.46	Hodgkin's disease, lymphocytic-histiocytic predominance of intrapelvic lymph nodes
201.47	Hodgkin's disease, lymphocytic-histiocytic predominance of spleen
201.48	Hodgkin's disease, lymphocytic-histiocytic predominance of lymph nodes of multiple sites

201.50   Hodgkin's disease, nodular sclerosis, unspecified site, extranodal and solid organ sites

201.51   Hodgkin's disease, nodular sclerosis, of lymph nodes of head, face, and neck

201.52   Hodgkin's disease, nodular sclerosis, of intrathoracic lymph nodes

201.53   Hodgkin's disease, nodular sclerosis, of intra-abdominal lymph nodes

201.54   Hodgkin's disease, nodular sclerosis, of lymph nodes of axilla and upper limb

201.55   Hodgkin's disease, nodular sclerosis, of lymph nodes of inguinal region and lower limb

201.56   Hodgkin's disease, nodular sclerosis, of intrapelvic lymph nodes

201.57   Hodgkin's disease, nodular sclerosis, of spleen

201.58   Hodgkin's disease, nodular sclerosis, of lymph nodes of multiple sites

201.60   Hodgkin's disease, mixed cellularity, unspecified site, extranodal and solid organ sites

201.61   Hodgkin's disease, mixed cellularity, involving lymph nodes of head, face, and neck

201.62   Hodgkin's disease, mixed cellularity, of intrathoracic lymph nodes

201.63   Hodgkin's disease, mixed cellularity, of intra-abdominal lymph nodes

201.64   Hodgkin's disease, mixed cellularity, of lymph nodes of axilla and upper limb

201.65   Hodgkin's disease, mixed cellularity, of lymph nodes of inguinal region and lower limb

201.66   Hodgkin's disease, mixed cellularity, of intrapelvic lymph nodes

201.67   Hodgkin's disease, mixed cellularity, of spleen

201.68   Hodgkin's disease, mixed cellularity, of lymph nodes of multiple sites

201.70   Hodgkin's disease, lymphocytic depletion, unspecified site, extranodal and solid organ sites

201.71   Hodgkin's disease, lymphocytic depletion, of lymph nodes of head, face, and neck

201.72   Hodgkin's disease, lymphocytic depletion, of intrathoracic lymph nodes

201.73   Hodgkin's disease, lymphocytic depletion, of intra-abdominal lymph nodes

201.74   Hodgkin's disease, lymphocytic depletion, of lymph nodes of axilla and upper limb

201.75   Hodgkin's disease, lymphocytic depletion, of lymph nodes of inguinal region and lower limb

201.76   Hodgkin's disease, lymphocytic depletion, of intrapelvic lymph nodes

201.77   Hodgkin's disease, lymphocytic depletion, of spleen

201.78   Hodgkin's disease, lymphocytic depletion, of lymph nodes of multiple sites

201.90   Hodgkin's disease, unspecified type, unspecified site, extranodal and solid organ sites

201.91   Hodgkin's disease, unspecified type, of lymph nodes of head, face, and neck

201.92   Hodgkin's disease, unspecified type, of intrathoracic lymph nodes

201.93   Hodgkin's disease, unspecified type, of intra-abdominal lymph nodes

201.94   Hodgkin's disease, unspecified type, of lymph nodes of axilla and upper limb

201.95   Hodgkin's disease, unspecified type, of lymph nodes of inguinal region and lower limb

201.96   Hodgkin's disease, unspecified type, of intrapelvic lymph nodes

201.97   Hodgkin's disease, unspecified type, of spleen

201.98   Hodgkin's disease, unspecified type, of lymph nodes of multiple sites

202.00   Nodular lymphoma, unspecified site, extranodal and solid organ sites

202.01   Nodular lymphoma of lymph nodes of head, face, and neck

202.02   Nodular lymphoma of intrathoracic lymph nodes

202.03   Nodular lymphoma of intra-abdominal lymph nodes

202.04   Nodular lymphoma of lymph nodes of axilla and upper limb

202.05   Nodular lymphoma of lymph nodes of inguinal region and lower limb

202.06   Nodular lymphoma of intrapelvic lymph nodes

202.07   Nodular lymphoma of spleen

202.08   Nodular lymphoma of lymph nodes of multiple sites

202.10   Mycosis fungoides, unspecified site, extranodal and solid organ sites

202.11   Mycosis fungoides of lymph nodes of head, face, and neck

202.12   Mycosis fungoides of intrathoracic lymph nodes

202.13   Mycosis fungoides of intra-abdominal lymph nodes

202.14   Mycosis fungoides of lymph nodes of axilla and upper limb

202.15   Mycosis fungoides of lymph nodes of inguinal region and lower limb

202.16   Mycosis fungoides of intrapelvic lymph nodes

202.17   Mycosis fungoides of spleen

202.18   Mycosis fungoides of lymph nodes of multiple sites

202.20   Sezary's disease, unspecified site, extranodal and solid organ sites

202.21   Sezary's disease of lymph nodes of head, face, and neck

202.22   Sezary's disease of intrathoracic lymph nodes

202.23   Sezary's disease of intra-abdominal lymph nodes

202.24   Sezary's disease of lymph nodes of axilla and upper limb

202.25   Sezary's disease of lymph nodes of inguinal region and lower limb

202.26   Sezary's disease of intrapelvic lymph nodes

202.27   Sezary's disease of spleen

202.28   Sezary's disease of lymph nodes of multiple sites

202.30   Malignant histiocytosis, unspecified site, extranodal and solid organ sites

202.31   Malignant histiocytosis of lymph nodes of head, face, and neck

202.32   Malignant histiocytosis of intrathoracic lymph nodes

202.33   Malignant histiocytosis of intra-abdominal lymph nodes

202.34   Malignant histiocytosis of lymph nodes of axilla and upper limb

202.35   Malignant histiocytosis of lymph nodes of inguinal region and lower limb

202.36   Malignant histiocytosis of intrapelvic lymph nodes

202.37   Malignant histiocytosis of spleen

202.38   Malignant histiocytosis of lymph nodes of multiple sites

202.40   Leukemic reticuloendotheliosis, unspecified site, extranodal and solid organ sites

202.41   Leukemic reticuloendotheliosis of lymph nodes of head, face, and neck

202.42   Leukemic reticuloendotheliosis of intrathoracic lymph nodes

202.43   Leukemic reticuloendotheliosis of intra-abdominal lymph nodes

202.44   Leukemic reticuloendotheliosis of lymph nodes of axilla and upper limb

202.45   Leukemic reticuloendotheliosis of lymph nodes of inguinal region and lower limb

202.46   Leukemic reticuloendotheliosis of intrapelvic lymph nodes

202.47   Leukemic reticuloendotheliosis of spleen

202.48   Leukemic reticuloendotheliosis of lymph nodes of multiple sites

202.50   Letterer-Siwe disease, unspecified site, extranodal and solid organ sites

202.51   Letterer-Siwe disease of lymph nodes of head, face, and neck

202.52   Letterer-Siwe disease of intrathoracic lymph nodes

202.53   Letterer-Siwe disease of intra-abdominal lymph nodes

202.54   Letterer-Siwe disease of lymph nodes of axilla and upper limb

202.55   Letterer-Siwe disease of lymph nodes of inguinal region and lower limb

202.56   Letterer-Siwe disease of intrapelvic lymph nodes

202.57	Letterer-Siwe disease of spleen
202.58	Letterer-Siwe disease of lymph nodes of multiple sites
202.60	Malignant mast cell tumors, unspecified site, extranodal and solid organ sites
202.61	Malignant mast cell tumors of lymph nodes of head, face, and neck
202.62	Malignant mast cell tumors of intrathoracic lymph nodes
202.63	Malignant mast cell tumors of intra-abdominal lymph nodes
202.64	Malignant mast cell tumors of lymph nodes of axilla and upper limb
202.65	Malignant mast cell tumors of lymph nodes of inguinal region and lower limb
202.66	Malignant mast cell tumors of intrapelvic lymph nodes
202.67	Malignant mast cell tumors of spleen
202.68	Malignant mast cell tumors of lymph nodes of multiple sites
202.70	Peripheral T-cell lymphoma, unspecified site, extranodal and solid organ sites
202.71	Peripheral T-cell lymphoma, lymph nodes of head, face, and neck
202.72	Peripheral T-cell lymphoma, intrathoracic lymph nodes
202.73	Peripheral T-cell lymphoma, intra-abdominal lymph nodes
202.74	Peripheral T-cell lymphoma, lymph nodes of axilla and upper limb
202.75	Peripheral T-cell lymphoma, lymph nodes of inguinal region and lower limb
202.76	Peripheral T-cell lymphoma, intrapelvic lymph nodes
202.77	Peripheral T-cell lymphoma, spleen
202.78	Peripheral T-cell lymphoma, lymph nodes of multiple sites
202.80	Other malignant lymphomas, unspecified site, extranodal and solid organ sites
202.81	Other malignant lymphomas of lymph nodes of head, face, and neck
202.82	Other malignant lymphomas of intrathoracic lymph nodes
202.83	Other malignant lymphomas of intra-abdominal lymph nodes
202.84	Other malignant lymphomas of lymph nodes of axilla and upper limb
202.85	Other malignant lymphomas of lymph nodes of inguinal region and lower limb
202.86	Other malignant lymphomas of intrapelvic lymph nodes
202.87	Other malignant lymphomas of spleen
202.88	Other malignant lymphomas of lymph nodes of multiple sites
202.90	Other and unspecified malignant neoplasms of lymphoid and histiocytic tissue, unspecified site, extranodal and solid organ sites
202.91	Other and unspecified malignant neoplasms of lymphoid and histiocytic tissue of lymph nodes of head, face, and neck
202.92	Other and unspecified malignant neoplasms of lymphoid and histiocytic tissue of intrathoracic lymph nodes
202.93	Other and unspecified malignant neoplasms of lymphoid and histiocytic tissue of intra-abdominal lymph nodes
202.94	Other and unspecified malignant neoplasms of lymphoid and histiocytic tissue of lymph nodes of axilla and upper limb
202.95	Other and unspecified malignant neoplasms of lymphoid and histiocytic tissue of lymph nodes of inguinal region and lower limb
202.96	Other and unspecified malignant neoplasms of lymphoid and histiocytic tissue of intrapelvic lymph nodes
202.97	Other and unspecified malignant neoplasms of lymphoid and histiocytic tissue of spleen
202.98	Other and unspecified malignant neoplasms of lymphoid and histiocytic tissue of lymph nodes of multiple sites
203.00	Multiple myeloma, without mention of having achieved remission
203.01	Multiple myeloma in remission
203.02	Multiple myeloma, in relapse
203.10	Plasma cell leukemia, without mention of having achieved remission
203.11	Plasma cell leukemia in remission
203.12	Plasma cell leukemia, in relapse
203.80	Other immunoproliferative neoplasms, without mention of having achieved remission
203.81	Other immunoproliferative neoplasms in remission
203.82	Other immunoproliferative neoplasms, in relapse
204.00	Acute lymphoid leukemia, without mention of having achieved remission
204.01	Acute lymphoid leukemia in remission
204.02	Acute lymphoid leukemia, in relapse
204.10	Chronic lymphoid leukemia, without mention of having achieved remission
204.11	Chronic lymphoid leukemia in remission
204.12	Chronic lymphoid leukemia, in relapse
204.20	Subacute lymphoid leukemia, without mention of having achieved remission
204.21	Subacute lymphoid leukemia in remission
204.22	Subacute lymphoid leukemia, in relapse
204.80	Other lymphoid leukemia, without mention of having achieved remission
204.81	Other lymphoid leukemia in remission
204.82	Other lymphoid leukemia, in relapse
204.90	Unspecified lymphoid leukemia, without mention of having achieved remission
204.91	Unspecified lymphoid leukemia in remission
204.92	Unspecified lymphoid leukemia, in relapse
205.00	Acute myeloid leukemia, without mention of having achieved remission
205.01	Acute myeloid leukemia in remission
205.02	Acute myeloid leukemia, in relapse
205.10	Chronic myeloid leukemia, without mention of having achieved remission
205.11	Chronic myeloid leukemia in remission
205.12	Chronic myeloid leukemia, in relapse
205.20	Subacute myeloid leukemia, without mention of having achieved remission
205.21	Subacute myeloid leukemia in remission
205.22	Subacute myeloid leukemia, in relapse
205.30	Myeloid sarcoma, without mention of having achieved remission
205.31	Myeloid sarcoma in remission
205.32	Myeloid sarcoma, in relapse
205.80	Other myeloid leukemia, without mention of having achieved remission
205.81	Other myeloid leukemia in remission
205.82	Other myeloid leukemia, in relapse
205.90	Unspecified myeloid leukemia, without mention of having achieved remission
205.91	Unspecified myeloid leukemia in remission
205.92	Unspecified myeloid leukemia, in relapse
206.00	Acute monocytic leukemia, without mention of having achieved remission
206.01	Acute monocytic leukemia in remission
206.02	Acute monocytic leukemia, in relapse
206.10	Chronic monocytic leukemia, without mention of having achieved remission
206.11	Chronic monocytic leukemia in remission
206.12	Chronic monocytic leukemia, in relapse
206.20	Subacute monocytic leukemia, without mention of having achieved remission
206.21	Subacute monocytic leukemia in remission
206.22	Subacute monocytic leukemia, in relapse
206.80	Other monocytic leukemia, without mention of having achieved remission
206.81	Other monocytic leukemia in remission

Appendix A — Numeric CC List

206.82	Other monocytic leukemia, in relapse
206.90	Unspecified monocytic leukemia, without mention of having achieved remission
206.91	Unspecified monocytic leukemia in remission
206.92	Unspecified monocytic leukemia, in relapse
207.00	Acute erythremia and erythroleukemia, without mention of having achieved remission
207.01	Acute erythremia and erythroleukemia in remission
207.02	Acute erythremia and erythroleukemia, in relapse
207.10	Chronic erythremia, without mention of having achieved remission
207.11	Chronic erythremia in remission
207.12	Chronic erythremia, in relapse
207.20	Megakaryocytic leukemia, without mention of having achieved remission
207.21	Megakaryocytic leukemia in remission
207.22	Megakaryocytic leukemia, in relapse
207.80	Other specified leukemia, without mention of having achieved remission
207.81	Other specified leukemia in remission
207.82	Other specified leukemia, in relapse
208.00	Acute leukemia of unspecified cell type, without mention of having achieved remission
208.01	Acute leukemia of unspecified cell type in remission
208.02	Acute leukemia of unspecified cell type, in relapse
208.10	Chronic leukemia of unspecified cell type, without mention of having achieved remission
208.11	Chronic leukemia of unspecified cell type in remission
208.12	Chronic leukemia of unspecified cell type, in relapse
208.20	Subacute leukemia of unspecified cell type, without mention of having achieved remission
208.21	Subactue leukemia of unspecified cell type in remission
208.22	Subacute leukemia of unspecified cell type, in relapse
208.80	Other leukemia of unspecified cell type, without mention of having achieved remission
208.81	Other leukemia of unspecified cell type in remission
208.82	Other leukemia of unspecified cell type, in relapse
208.90	Unspecified leukemia, without mention of having achieved remission
208.91	Unspecified leukemia in remission
208.92	Unspecified leukemia, in relapse
209.00	Malignant carcinoid tumor of the small intestine, unspecified portion
209.01	Malignant carcinoid tumor of the duodenum
209.02	Malignant carcinoid tumor of the jejunum
209.03	Malignant carcinoid tumor of the ileum
209.10	Malignant carcinoid tumor of the large intestine, unspecified portion
209.11	Malignant carcinoid tumor of the appendix
209.12	Malignant carcinoid tumor of the cecum
209.13	Malignant carcinoid tumor of the ascending colon
209.14	Malignant carcinoid tumor of the transverse colon
209.15	Malignant carcinoid tumor of the descending colon
209.16	Malignant carcinoid tumor of the sigmoid colon
209.17	Malignant carcinoid tumor of the rectum
209.20	Malignant carcinoid tumor of unknown primary site
209.21	Malignant carcinoid tumor of the bronchus and lung
209.22	Malignant carcinoid tumor of the thymus
209.23	Malignant carcinoid tumor of the stomach
209.24	Malignant carcinoid tumor of the kidney
209.25	Malignant carcinoid tumor of foregut, not otherwise specified
209.26	Malignant carcinoid tumor of midgut, not otherwise specified

209.27	Malignant carcinoid tumor of hindgut, not otherwise specified
209.29	Malignant carcinoid tumor of other sites
209.30	Malignant poorly differentiated neuroendocrine carcinoma, any site
209.71	Secondary neuroendocrine tumor of distant lymph nodes
209.72	Secondary neuroendocrine tumor of liver
209.73	Secondary neuroendocrine tumor of bone
209.74	Secondary neuroendocrine tumor of peritoneum
209.79	Secondary neuroendocrine tumor of other sites
238.5	Neoplasm of uncertain behavior of histiocytic and mast cells
238.6	Neoplasm of uncertain behavior of plasma cells
238.73	High grade myelodysplastic syndrome lesions
238.74	Myelodysplastic syndrome with 5q deletion
238.76	Myelofibrosis with myeloid metaplasia
238.77	Post-transplant lymphoproliferative disorder [PTLD]
238.79	Other lymphatic and hematopoietic tissues
245.0	Acute thyroiditis
246.3	Hemorrhage and infarction of thyroid
251.0	Hypoglycemic coma
251.3	Postsurgical hypoinsulinemia
253.1	Other and unspecified anterior pituitary hyperfunction
253.2	Panhypopituitarism
253.5	Diabetes insipidus
253.6	Other disorders of neurohypophysis
254.1	Abscess of thymus
255.0	Cushing's syndrome
255.3	Other corticoadrenal overactivity
255.41	Glucocorticoid deficiency
255.42	Mineralocorticoid deficiency
255.5	Other adrenal hypofunction
255.6	Medulloadrenal hyperfunction
259.2	Carcinoid syndrome
263.0	Malnutrition of moderate degree
263.1	Malnutrition of mild degree
263.2	Arrested development following protein-calorie malnutrition
263.8	Other protein-calorie malnutrition
263.9	Unspecified protein-calorie malnutrition
265.0	Beriberi
265.1	Other and unspecified manifestations of thiamine deficiency
266.0	Ariboflavinosis
268.0	Rickets, active
270.0	Disturbances of amino-acid transport
270.1	Phenylketonuria (PKU)
270.2	Other disturbances of aromatic amino-acid metabolism
270.3	Disturbances of branched-chain amino-acid metabolism
270.4	Disturbances of sulphur-bearing amino-acid metabolism
270.5	Disturbances of histidine metabolism
270.6	Disorders of urea cycle metabolism
270.7	Other disturbances of straight-chain amino-acid metabolism
270.8	Other specified disorders of amino-acid metabolism
270.9	Unspecified disorder of amino-acid metabolism
271.0	Glycogenosis
271.1	Galactosemia
271.8	Other specified disorders of carbohydrate transport and metabolism
274.11	Uric acid nephrolithiasis
276.0	Hyperosmolality and/or hypernatremia
276.1	Hyposmolality and/or hyponatremia
276.2	Acidosis

276.3	Alkalosis
276.4	Mixed acid-base balance disorder
277.00	Cystic fibrosis without mention of meconium ileus
277.03	Cystic fibrosis with gastrointestinal manifestations
277.09	Cystic fibrosis with other manifestations
277.1	Disorders of porphyrin metabolism
277.2	Other disorders of purine and pyrimidine metabolism
277.30	Amyloidosis, unspecified
277.31	Familial Mediterranean fever
277.39	Other amyloidosis
277.5	Mucopolysaccharidosis
277.85	Disorders of fatty acid oxidation
277.86	Peroxisomal disorders
277.87	Disorders of mitochondrial metabolism
277.89	Other specified disorders of metabolism
278.03	Obesity hypoventilation syndrome
279.00	Unspecified hypogammaglobulinemia
279.01	Selective IgA immunodeficiency
279.02	Selective IgM immunodeficiency
279.03	Other selective immunoglobulin deficiencies
279.04	Congenital hypogammaglobulinemia
279.05	Immunodeficiency with increased IgM
279.06	Common variable immunodeficiency
279.09	Other deficiency of humoral immunity
279.10	Unspecified immunodeficiency with predominant T-cell defect
279.11	DiGeorge's syndrome
279.12	Wiskott-Aldrich syndrome
279.13	Nezelof's syndrome
279.19	Other deficiency of cell-mediated immunity
279.2	Combined immunity deficiency
279.3	Unspecified immunity deficiency
279.50	Graft-versus-host disease, unspecified
279.51	Acute graft-versus-host disease
279.52	Chronic graft-versus-host disease
279.53	Acute on chronic graft-versus-host disease
282.8	Other specified hereditary hemolytic anemias
282.9	Unspecified hereditary hemolytic anemia
283.0	Autoimmune hemolytic anemias
283.10	Unspecified non-autoimmune hemolytic anemia
283.19	Other non-autoimmune hemolytic anemias
283.9	Acquired hemolytic anemia, unspecified
284.01	Constitutional red blood cell aplasia
284.09	Other constitutional aplastic anemia
284.19	Other pancytopenia
284.2	Myelophthisis
284.9	Unspecified aplastic anemia
285.1	Acute posthemorrhagic anemia
286.2	Congenital factor XI deficiency
286.3	Congenital deficiency of other clotting factors
286.4	Von Willebrand's disease
286.52	Acquired hemophilia
286.53	Antiphospholipid antibody with hemorrhagic disorder
286.59	Other hemorrhagic disorder due to intrinsic circulating anticoagulants, antibodies, or inhibitors
286.7	Acquired coagulation factor deficiency
286.9	Other and unspecified coagulation defects
287.0	Allergic purpura
287.31	Immune thrombocytopenic purpura
287.32	Evans' syndrome
287.33	Congenital and hereditary thrombocytopenic purpura
288.4	Hemophagocytic syndromes
289.7	Methemoglobinemia
289.81	Primary hypercoagulable state
289.82	Secondary hypercoagulable state
289.83	Myelofibrosis
290.11	Presenile dementia with delirium
290.12	Presenile dementia with delusional features
290.13	Presenile dementia with depressive features
290.20	Senile dementia with delusional features
290.21	Senile dementia with depressive features
290.3	Senile dementia with delirium
290.41	Vascular dementia, with delirium
290.42	Vascular dementia, with delusions
290.43	Vascular dementia, with depressed mood
290.8	Other specified senile psychotic conditions
290.9	Unspecified senile psychotic condition
291.0	Alcohol withdrawal delirium
291.2	Alcohol-induced persisting dementia
291.3	Alcohol-induced psychotic disorder with hallucinations
291.81	Alcohol withdrawal
291.89	Other specified alcohol-induced mental disorders
291.9	Unspecified alcohol-induced mental disorders
292.0	Drug withdrawal
292.11	Drug-induced psychotic disorder with delusions
292.12	Drug-induced psychotic disorder with hallucinations
292.81	Drug-induced delirium
292.82	Drug-induced persisting dementia
293.0	Delirium due to conditions classified elsewhere
293.1	Subacute delirium
293.81	Psychotic disorder with delusions in conditions classified elsewhere
293.82	Psychotic disorder with hallucinations in conditions classified elsewhere
293.9	Unspecified transient mental disorder in conditions classified elsewhere
294.11	Dementia in conditions classified elsewhere with behavioral disturbance
294.21	Dementia, unspecified, with behavioral disturbance
295.00	Simple schizophrenia, unspecified condition
295.01	Simple schizophrenia, subchronic condition
295.02	Simple schizophrenia, chronic condition
295.03	Simple schizophrenia, subchronic condition with acute exacerbation
295.04	Simple schizophrenia, chronic condition with acute exacerbation
295.10	Disorganized schizophrenia, unspecified condition
295.11	Disorganized schizophrenia, subchronic condition
295.12	Disorganized schizophrenia, chronic condition
295.13	Disorganized schizophrenia, subchronic condition with acute exacerbation
295.14	Disorganized schizophrenia, chronic condition with acute exacerbation
295.20	Catatonic schizophrenia, unspecified condition
295.21	Catatonic schizophrenia, subchronic condition
295.22	Catatonic schizophrenia, chronic condition
295.23	Catatonic schizophrenia, subchronic condition with acute exacerbation
295.24	Catatonic schizophrenia, chronic condition with acute exacerbation
295.30	Paranoid schizophrenia, unspecified condition
295.31	Paranoid schizophrenia, subchronic condition
295.32	Paranoid schizophrenia, chronic condition

295.33	Paranoid schizophrenia, subchronic condition with acute exacerbation
295.34	Paranoid schizophrenia, chronic condition with acute exacerbation
295.40	Schizophreniform disorder, unspecified
295.41	Schizophreniform disorder, subchronic
295.42	Schizophreniform disorder, chronic
295.43	Schizophreniform disorder, subchronic with acute exacerbation
295.44	Schizophreniform disorder, chronic with acute exacerbation
295.53	Latent schizophrenia, subchronic condition with acute exacerbation
295.54	Latent schizophrenia, chronic condition with acute exacerbation
295.60	Schizophrenic disorders, residual type, unspecified
295.61	Schizophrenic disorders, residual type, subchronic
295.62	Schizophrenic disorders, residual type, chronic
295.63	Schizophrenic disorders, residual type, subchronic with acute exacerbation
295.64	Schizophrenic disorders, residual type, chronic with acute exacerbation
295.71	Schizoaffective disorder, subchronic
295.72	Schizoaffective disorder, chronic
295.73	Schizoaffective disorder, subchronic with acute exacerbation
295.74	Schizoaffective disorder, chronic with acute exacerbation
295.80	Other specified types of schizophrenia, unspecified condition
295.81	Other specified types of schizophrenia, subchronic condition
295.82	Other specified types of schizophrenia, chronic condition
295.83	Other specified types of schizophrenia, subchronic condition with acute exacerbation
295.84	Other specified types of schizophrenia, chronic condition with acute exacerbation
295.91	Unspecified schizophrenia, subchronic condition
295.92	Unspecified schizophrenia, chronic condition
295.93	Unspecified schizophrenia, subchronic condition with acute exacerbation
295.94	Unspecified schizophrenia, chronic condition with acute exacerbation
296.00	Bipolar I disorder, single manic episode, unspecified
296.01	Bipolar I disorder, single manic episode, mild
296.02	Bipolar I disorder, single manic episode, moderate
296.03	Bipolar I disorder, single manic episode, severe, without mention of psychotic behavior
296.04	Bipolar I disorder, single manic episode, severe, specified as with psychotic behavior
296.10	Manic disorder, recurrent episode, unspecified
296.11	Manic disorder, recurrent episode, mild
296.12	Manic disorder, recurrent episode, moderate
296.13	Manic disorder, recurrent episode, severe, without mention of psychotic behavior
296.14	Manic disorder, recurrent episode, severe, specified as with psychotic behavior
296.20	Major depressive disorder, single episode, unspecified
296.21	Major depressive disorder, single episode, mild
296.22	Major depressive disorder, single episode, moderate
296.23	Major depressive disorder, single episode, severe, without mention of psychotic behavior
296.24	Major depressive disorder, single episode, severe, specified as with psychotic behavior
296.30	Major depressive disorder, recurrent episode, unspecified
296.31	Major depressive disorder, recurrent episode, mild
296.32	Major depressive disorder, recurrent episode, moderate
296.33	Major depressive disorder, recurrent episode, severe, without mention of psychotic behavior

296.34	Major depressive disorder, recurrent episode, severe, specified as with psychotic behavior
296.40	Bipolar I disorder, most recent episode (or current) manic, unspecified
296.41	Bipolar I disorder, most recent episode (or current) manic, mild
296.42	Bipolar I disorder, most recent episode (or current) manic, moderate
296.43	Bipolar I disorder, most recent episode (or current) manic, severe, without mention of psychotic behavior
296.44	Bipolar I disorder, most recent episode (or current) manic, severe, specified as with psychotic behavior
296.50	Bipolar I disorder, most recent episode (or current) depressed, unspecified
296.51	Bipolar I disorder, most recent episode (or current) depressed, mild
296.52	Bipolar I disorder, most recent episode (or current) depressed, moderate
296.53	Bipolar I disorder, most recent episode (or current) depressed, severe, without mention of psychotic behavior
296.54	Bipolar I disorder, most recent episode (or current) depressed, severe, specified as with psychotic behavior
296.60	Bipolar I disorder, most recent episode (or current) mixed, unspecified
296.61	Bipolar I disorder, most recent episode (or current) mixed, mild
296.62	Bipolar I disorder, most recent episode (or current) mixed, moderate
296.63	Bipolar I disorder, most recent episode (or current) mixed, severe, without mention of psychotic behavior
296.64	Bipolar I disorder, most recent episode (or current) mixed, severe, specified as with psychotic behavior
296.89	Other and unspecified bipolar disorders
296.99	Other specified episodic mood disorder
298.0	Depressive type psychosis
298.1	Excitative type psychosis
298.3	Acute paranoid reaction
298.4	Psychogenic paranoid psychosis
299.00	Autistic disorder, current or active state
299.01	Autistic disorder, residual state
299.10	Childhood disintegrative disorder, current or active state
299.11	Childhood disintegrative disorder, residual state
299.80	Other specified pervasive developmental disorders, current or active state
299.81	Other specified pervasive developmental disorders, residual state
299.90	Unspecified pervasive developmental disorder, current or active state
299.91	Unspecified pervasive developmental disorder, residual state
301.51	Chronic factitious illness with physical symptoms
304.01	Opioid type dependence, continuous pattern of use
304.11	Sedative, hypnotic or anxiolytic dependence, continuous pattern of use
304.21	Cocaine dependence, continuous pattern of use
304.41	Amphetamine and other psychostimulant dependence, continuous pattern of use
304.51	Hallucinogen dependence, continuous pattern of use
304.61	Other specified drug dependence, continuous pattern of use
304.71	Combinations of opioid type drug with any other drug dependence, continuous pattern of use
304.81	Combinations of drug dependence excluding opioid type drug, continuous pattern of use
304.91	Unspecified drug dependence, continuous pattern of use
307.1	Anorexia nervosa
307.51	Bulimia nervosa
318.1	Severe intellectual disabilities
318.2	Profound intellectual disabilities
322.2	Chronic meningitis

330.0	Leukodystrophy
330.1	Cerebral lipidoses
330.2	Cerebral degeneration in generalized lipidoses
330.3	Cerebral degeneration of childhood in other diseases classified elsewhere
330.8	Other specified cerebral degenerations in childhood
330.9	Unspecified cerebral degeneration in childhood
331.3	Communicating hydrocephalus
331.4	Obstructive hydrocephalus
331.5	Idiopathic normal pressure hydrocephalus [INPH]
332.1	Secondary Parkinsonism
333.0	Other degenerative diseases of the basal ganglia
333.4	Huntington's chorea
333.71	Athetoid cerebral palsy
333.72	Acute dystonia due to drugs
333.79	Other acquired torsion dystonia
333.90	Unspecified extrapyramidal disease and abnormal movement disorder
333.91	Stiff-man syndrome
334.0	Friedreich's ataxia
334.1	Hereditary spastic paraplegia
334.2	Primary cerebellar degeneration
334.3	Other cerebellar ataxia
334.4	Cerebellar ataxia in diseases classified elsewhere
334.8	Other spinocerebellar diseases
334.9	Unspecified spinocerebellar disease
335.0	Werdnig-Hoffmann disease
335.10	Unspecified spinal muscular atrophy
335.11	Kugelberg-Welander disease
335.19	Other spinal muscular atrophy
335.20	Amyotrophic lateral sclerosis
335.21	Progressive muscular atrophy
335.22	Progressive bulbar palsy
335.23	Pseudobulbar palsy
335.24	Primary lateral sclerosis
335.29	Other motor neuron diseases
335.8	Other anterior horn cell diseases
335.9	Unspecified anterior horn cell disease
336.0	Syringomyelia and syringobulbia
336.2	Subacute combined degeneration of spinal cord in diseases classified elsewhere
336.3	Myelopathy in other diseases classified elsewhere
336.8	Other myelopathy
336.9	Unspecified disease of spinal cord
337.1	Peripheral autonomic neuropathy in disorders classified elsewhere
337.20	Unspecified reflex sympathetic dystrophy
337.21	Reflex sympathetic dystrophy of the upper limb
337.22	Reflex sympathetic dystrophy of the lower limb
337.29	Reflex sympathetic dystrophy of other specified site
341.0	Neuromyelitis optica
341.1	Schilder's disease
341.20	Acute (transverse) myelitis NOS
341.21	Acute (transverse) myelitis in conditions classified elsewhere
341.22	Idiopathic transverse myelitis
341.8	Other demyelinating diseases of central nervous system
341.9	Unspecified demyelinating disease of central nervous system
342.00	Flaccid hemiplegia affecting unspecified side
342.01	Flaccid hemiplegia affecting dominant side
342.02	Flaccid hemiplegia affecting nondominant side
342.10	Spastic hemiplegia affecting unspecified side
342.11	Spastic hemiplegia affecting dominant side
342.12	Spastic hemiplegia affecting nondominant side
342.80	Other specified hemiplegia affecting unspecified side
342.81	Other specified hemiplegia affecting dominant side
342.82	Other specified hemiplegia affecting nondominant side
342.90	Unspecified hemiplegia affecting unspecified side
342.91	Unspecified hemiplegia affecting dominant side
342.92	Unspecified hemiplegia affecting nondominant side
343.0	Diplegic infantile cerebral palsy
343.1	Hemiplegic infantile cerebral palsy
343.4	Infantile hemiplegia
344.1	Paraplegia
344.2	Diplegia of upper limbs
344.60	Cauda equina syndrome without mention of neurogenic bladder
344.61	Cauda equina syndrome with neurogenic bladder
345.01	Generalized nonconvulsive epilepsy with intractable epilepsy
345.11	Generalized convulsive epilepsy with intractable epilepsy
345.40	Localization-related (focal) (partial) epilepsy and epileptic syndromes with complex partial seizures, without mention of intractable epilepsy
345.41	Localization-related (focal) (partial) epilepsy and epileptic syndromes with complex partial seizures, with intractable epilepsy
345.50	Localization-related (focal) (partial) epilepsy and epileptic syndromes with simple partial seizures, without mention of intractable epilepsy
345.51	Localization-related (focal) (partial) epilepsy and epileptic syndromes with simple partial seizures, with intractable epilepsy
345.60	Infantile spasms without mention of intractable epilepsy
345.61	Infantile spasms with intractable epilepsy
345.70	Epilepsia partialis continua without mention of intractable epilepsy
345.80	Other forms of epilepsy and recurrent seizures, without mention of intractable epilepsy
345.81	Other forms of epilepsy and recurrent seizures, with intractable epilepsy
345.91	Unspecified epilepsy with intractable epilepsy
346.60	Persistent migraine aura with cerebral infarction, without mention of intractable migraine without mention of status migrainosus
346.61	Persistent migraine aura with cerebral infarction, with intractable migraine, so stated, without mention of status migrainosus
346.62	Persistent migraine aura with cerebral infarction, without mention of intractable migraine with status migrainosus
346.63	Persistent migraine aura with cerebral infarction, with intractable migraine, so stated, with status migrainosus
348.1	Anoxic brain damage
349.1	Nervous system complications from surgically implanted device
349.31	Accidental puncture or laceration of dura during a procedure
349.39	Other dural tear
349.81	Cerebrospinal fluid rhinorrhea
356.3	Refsum's disease
357.0	Acute infective polyneuritis
357.81	Chronic inflammatory demyelinating polyneuritis
357.82	Critical illness polyneuropathy
358.1	Myasthenic syndromes in diseases classified elsewhere
358.30	Lambert-Eaton syndrome, unspecified
358.31	Lambert-Eaton syndrome in neoplastic disease
358.39	Lambert-Eaton syndrome in other diseases classified elsewhere
359.0	Congenital hereditary muscular dystrophy
359.1	Hereditary progressive muscular dystrophy
359.4	Toxic myopathy
359.6	Symptomatic inflammatory myopathy in diseases classified elsewhere

359.81	Critical illness myopathy
360.00	Unspecified purulent endophthalmitis
360.01	Acute endophthalmitis
360.02	Panophthalmitis
360.04	Vitreous abscess
360.11	Sympathetic uveitis
360.12	Panuveitis
360.13	Parasitic endophthalmitis NOS
360.19	Other endophthalmitis
361.2	Serous retinal detachment
361.81	Traction detachment of retina
361.89	Other forms of retinal detachment
361.9	Unspecified retinal detachment
362.30	Unspecified retinal vascular occlusion
362.31	Central artery occlusion of retina
362.32	Arterial branch occlusion of retina
362.33	Partial arterial occlusion of retina
362.34	Transient arterial occlusion of retina
362.35	Central vein occlusion of retina
362.40	Unspecified retinal layer separation
362.42	Serous detachment of retinal pigment epithelium
362.43	Hemorrhagic detachment of retinal pigment epithelium
362.84	Retinal ischemia
363.10	Unspecified disseminated chorioretinitis
363.11	Disseminated choroiditis and chorioretinitis, posterior pole
363.12	Disseminated choroiditis and chorioretinitis, peripheral
363.13	Disseminated choroiditis and chorioretinitis, generalized
363.14	Disseminated retinitis and retinochoroiditis, metastatic
363.15	Disseminated retinitis and retinochoroiditis, pigment epitheliopathy
363.20	Unspecified chorioretinitis
363.63	Choroidal rupture
363.70	Unspecified choroidal detachment
363.71	Serous choroidal detachment
363.72	Hemorrhagic choroidal detachment
364.00	Unspecified acute and subacute iridocyclitis
364.01	Primary iridocyclitis
364.02	Recurrent iridocyclitis
364.03	Secondary iridocyclitis, infectious
364.22	Glaucomatocyclitic crises
364.3	Unspecified iridocyclitis
365.22	Acute angle-closure glaucoma
368.11	Sudden visual loss
368.12	Transient visual loss
376.01	Orbital cellulitis
376.02	Orbital periostitis
376.03	Orbital osteomyelitis
377.00	Unspecified papilledema
377.01	Papilledema associated with increased intracranial pressure
377.30	Unspecified optic neuritis
377.31	Optic papillitis
377.32	Retrobulbar neuritis (acute)
377.39	Other optic neuritis
377.51	Disorders of optic chiasm associated with pituitary neoplasms and disorders
377.52	Disorders of optic chiasm associated with other neoplasms
377.53	Disorders of optic chiasm associated with vascular disorders
377.54	Disorders of optic chiasm associated with inflammatory disorders
377.61	Disorders of other visual pathways associated with neoplasms
377.62	Disorders of other visual pathways associated with vascular disorders
377.63	Disorders of other visual pathways associated with inflammatory disorders
377.71	Disorders of visual cortex associated with neoplasms
377.72	Disorders of visual cortex associated with vascular disorders
377.73	Disorders of visual cortex associated with inflammatory disorders
380.14	Malignant otitis externa
383.00	Acute mastoiditis without complications
383.01	Subperiosteal abscess of mastoid
383.02	Acute mastoiditis with other complications
388.61	Cerebrospinal fluid otorrhea
391.0	Acute rheumatic pericarditis
391.1	Acute rheumatic endocarditis
391.2	Acute rheumatic myocarditis
391.8	Other acute rheumatic heart disease
391.9	Unspecified acute rheumatic heart disease
392.0	Rheumatic chorea with heart involvement
392.9	Rheumatic chorea without mention of heart involvement
393	Chronic rheumatic pericarditis
398.0	Rheumatic myocarditis
398.91	Rheumatic heart failure (congestive)
401.0	Essential hypertension, malignant
402.00	Malignant hypertensive heart disease without heart failure
402.01	Malignant hypertensive heart disease with heart failure
403.00	Hypertensive chronic kidney disease, malignant, with chronic kidney disease stage I through stage IV, or unspecified
403.01	Hypertensive chronic kidney disease, malignant, with chronic kidney disease stage V or end stage renal disease
403.11	Hypertensive chronic kidney disease, benign, with chronic kidney disease stage V or end stage renal disease
403.91	Hypertensive chronic kidney disease, unspecified, with chronic kidney disease stage V or end stage renal disease
404.00	Hypertensive heart and chronic kidney disease, malignant, without heart failure and with chronic kidney disease stage I through stage IV, or unspecified
404.01	Hypertensive heart and chronic kidney disease, malignant, with heart failure and with chronic kidney disease stage I through stage IV, or unspecified
404.02	Hypertensive heart and chronic kidney disease, malignant, without heart failure and with chronic kidney disease stage V or end stage renal disease
404.03	Hypertensive heart and chronic kidney disease, malignant, with heart failure and with chronic kidney disease stage V or end stage renal disease
404.11	Hypertensive heart and chronic kidney disease, benign, with heart failure and with chronic kidney disease stage I through stage IV, or unspecified
404.12	Hypertensive heart and chronic kidney disease, benign, without heart failure and with chronic kidney disease stage V or end stage renal disease
404.13	Hypertensive heart and chronic kidney disease, benign, with heart failure and chronic kidney disease stage V or end stage renal disease
404.91	Hypertensive heart and chronic kidney disease, unspecified, with heart failure and with chronic kidney disease stage I through stage IV, or unspecified
404.92	Hypertensive heart and chronic kidney disease, unspecified, without heart failure and with chronic kidney disease stage V or end stage renal disease
404.93	Hypertensive heart and chronic kidney disease, unspecified, with heart failure and chronic kidney disease stage V or end stage renal disease
405.01	Secondary renovascular hypertension, malignant
405.09	Other secondary hypertension, malignant

411.0	Postmyocardial infarction syndrome
411.1	Intermediate coronary syndrome
411.81	Acute coronary occlusion without myocardial infarction
411.89	Other acute and subacute form of ischemic heart disease
413.0	Angina decubitus
413.1	Prinzmetal angina
414.02	Coronary atherosclerosis of autologous vein bypass graft
414.03	Coronary atherosclerosis of nonautologous biological bypass graft
414.04	Coronary atherosclerosis of artery bypass graft
414.06	Coronary atherosclerosis, of native coronary artery of transplanted heart
414.07	Coronary atherosclerosis, of bypass graft (artery) (vein) of transplanted heart
414.10	Aneurysm of heart
414.19	Other aneurysm of heart
416.0	Primary pulmonary hypertension
416.1	Kyphoscoliotic heart disease
416.2	Chronic pulmonary embolism
417.0	Arteriovenous fistula of pulmonary vessels
417.1	Aneurysm of pulmonary artery
420.0	Acute pericarditis in diseases classified elsewhere
420.90	Unspecified acute pericarditis
420.91	Acute idiopathic pericarditis
420.99	Other acute pericarditis
423.0	Hemopericardium
423.1	Adhesive pericarditis
423.2	Constrictive pericarditis
423.3	Cardiac tamponade
423.8	Other specified diseases of pericardium
423.9	Unspecified disease of pericardium
424.90	Endocarditis, valve unspecified, unspecified cause
424.91	Endocarditis in diseases classified elsewhere
424.99	Other endocarditis, valve unspecified
425.0	Endomyocardial fibrosis
425.11	Hypertrophic obstructive cardiomyopathy
425.18	Other hypertrophic cardiomyopathy
425.2	Obscure cardiomyopathy of Africa
425.3	Endocardial fibroelastosis
425.4	Other primary cardiomyopathies
425.5	Alcoholic cardiomyopathy
425.7	Nutritional and metabolic cardiomyopathy
425.8	Cardiomyopathy in other diseases classified elsewhere
425.9	Unspecified secondary cardiomyopathy
426.0	Atrioventricular block, complete
426.12	Mobitz (type) II atrioventricular block
426.53	Other bilateral bundle branch block
426.54	Trifascicular block
426.89	Other specified conduction disorder
427.0	Paroxysmal supraventricular tachycardia
427.1	Paroxysmal ventricular tachycardia
427.32	Atrial flutter
428.1	Left heart failure
428.20	Unspecified systolic heart failure
428.22	Chronic systolic heart failure
428.30	Unspecified diastolic heart failure
428.32	Chronic diastolic heart failure
428.40	Unspecified combined systolic and diastolic heart failure
428.42	Chronic combined systolic and diastolic heart failure
429.71	Acquired cardiac septal defect
429.79	Other certain sequelae of myocardial infarction, not elsewhere classified
429.81	Other disorders of papillary muscle
429.82	Hyperkinetic heart disease
429.83	Takotsubo syndrome
432.9	Unspecified intracranial hemorrhage
435.0	Basilar artery syndrome
435.1	Vertebral artery syndrome
435.2	Subclavian steal syndrome
435.3	Vertebrobasilar artery syndrome
435.8	Other specified transient cerebral ischemias
435.9	Unspecified transient cerebral ischemia
436	Acute, but ill-defined, cerebrovascular disease
437.1	Other generalized ischemic cerebrovascular disease
437.2	Hypertensive encephalopathy
437.4	Cerebral arteritis
437.5	Moyamoya disease
437.6	Nonpyogenic thrombosis of intracranial venous sinus
438.20	Hemiplegia affecting unspecified side due to cerebrovascular disease
438.21	Hemiplegia affecting dominant side due to cerebrovascular disease
438.22	Hemiplegia affecting nondominant side due to cerebrovascular disease
440.24	Atherosclerosis of native arteries of the extremities with gangrene
440.4	Chronic total occlusion of artery of the extremities
444.09	Other arterial embolism and thrombosis of abdominal aorta
444.1	Embolism and thrombosis of thoracic aorta
444.21	Embolism and thrombosis of arteries of upper extremity
444.22	Embolism and thrombosis of arteries of lower extremity
444.81	Embolism and thrombosis of iliac artery
444.89	Embolism and thrombosis of other specified artery
444.9	Embolism and thrombosis of unspecified artery
445.01	Atheroembolism of upper extremity
445.02	Atheroembolism of lower extremity
445.81	Atheroembolism of kidney
445.89	Atheroembolism of other site
446.0	Polyarteritis nodosa
446.1	Acute febrile mucocutaneous lymph node syndrome (MCLS)
446.20	Unspecified hypersensitivity angiitis
446.21	Goodpasture's syndrome
446.29	Other specified hypersensitivity angiitis
446.3	Lethal midline granuloma
446.4	Wegener's granulomatosis
446.7	Takayasu's disease
447.2	Rupture of artery
447.4	Celiac artery compression syndrome
447.5	Necrosis of artery
449	Septic arterial embolism
451.11	Phlebitis and thrombophlebitis of femoral vein (deep) (superficial)
451.19	Phlebitis and thrombophlebitis of other deep vessels of lower extremities
451.81	Phlebitis and thrombophlebitis of iliac vein
451.83	Phlebitis and thrombophlebitis of deep veins of upper extremities
451.89	Phlebitis and thrombophlebitis of other site
453.1	Thrombophlebitis migrans
453.3	Embolism and thrombosis of renal vein
453.40	Acute venous embolism and thrombosis of unspecified deep vessels of lower extremity
453.41	Acute venous embolism and thrombosis of deep vessels of proximal lower extremity

453.42	Acute venous embolism and thrombosis of deep vessels of distal lower extremity
453.50	Chronic venous embolism and thrombosis of unspecified deep vessels of lower extremity
453.51	Chronic venous embolism and thrombosis of deep vessels of proximal lower extremity
453.52	Chronic venous embolism and thrombosis of deep vessels of distal lower extremity
453.6	Venous embolism and thrombosis of superficial vessels of lower extremity
453.71	Chronic venous embolism and thrombosis of superficial veins of upper extremity
453.72	Chronic venous embolism and thrombosis of deep veins of upper extremity
453.73	Chronic venous embolism and thrombosis of upper extremity, unspecified
453.74	Chronic venous embolism and thrombosis of axillary veins
453.75	Chronic venous embolism and thrombosis of subclavian veins
453.76	Chronic venous embolism and thrombosis of internal jugular veins
453.77	Chronic venous embolism and thrombosis of other thoracic veins
453.79	Chronic venous embolism and thrombosis of other specified veins
453.81	Acute venous embolism and thrombosis of superficial veins of upper extremity
453.82	Acute venous embolism and thrombosis of deep veins of upper extremity
453.83	Acute venous embolism and thrombosis of upper extremity, unspecified
453.84	Acute venous embolism and thrombosis of axillary veins
453.85	Acute venous embolism and thrombosis of subclavian veins
453.86	Acute venous embolism and thrombosis of internal jugular veins
453.87	Acute venous embolism and thrombosis of other thoracic veins
453.89	Acute venous embolism and thrombosis of other specified veins
453.9	Embolism and thrombosis of unspecified site
454.2	Varicose veins of lower extremities with ulcer and inflammation
456.1	Esophageal varices without mention of bleeding
456.21	Esophageal varices without mention of bleeding in diseases classified elsewhere
459.11	Postphlebitic syndrome with ulcer
459.13	Postphlebitic syndrome with ulcer and inflammation
459.2	Compression of vein
459.31	Chronic venous hypertension with ulcer
459.33	Chronic venous hypertension with ulcer and inflammation
464.30	Acute epiglottitis without mention of obstruction
466.11	Acute bronchiolitis due to respiratory syncytial virus (RSV)
466.19	Acute bronchiolitis due to other infectious organisms
475	Peritonsillar abscess
478.21	Cellulitis of pharynx or nasopharynx
478.22	Parapharyngeal abscess
478.24	Retropharyngeal abscess
478.34	Bilateral complete paralysis of vocal cords or larynx
478.71	Cellulitis and perichondritis of larynx
488.02	Influenza due to identified avian influenza virus with other respiratory manifestations
488.09	Influenza due to identified avian influenza virus with other manifestations
491.21	Obstructive chronic bronchitis, with (acute) exacerbation
491.22	Obstructive chronic bronchitis with acute bronchitis
493.01	Extrinsic asthma with status asthmaticus
493.02	Extrinsic asthma, with (acute) exacerbation
493.11	Intrinsic asthma with status asthmaticus
493.12	Intrinsic asthma, with (acute) exacerbation
493.21	Chronic obstructive asthma with status asthmaticus

493.22	Chronic obstructive asthma, with (acute) exacerbation
493.91	Asthma, unspecified with status asthmaticus
493.92	Asthma, unspecified, with (acute) exacerbation
494.1	Bronchiectasis with acute exacerbation
495.7	Ventilation pneumonitis
495.8	Other specified allergic alveolitis and pneumonitis
495.9	Unspecified allergic alveolitis and pneumonitis
506.0	Bronchitis and pneumonitis due to fumes and vapors
508.0	Acute pulmonary manifestations due to radiation
508.1	Chronic and other pulmonary manifestations due to radiation
511.81	Malignant pleural effusion
511.89	Other specified forms of effusion, except tuberculous
511.9	Unspecified pleural effusion
512.1	Iatrogenic pneumothorax
512.2	Postoperative air leak
512.81	Primary spontaneous pneumothorax
512.82	Secondary spontaneous pneumothorax
512.83	Chronic pneumothorax
512.84	Other air leak
512.89	Other pneumothorax
514	Pulmonary congestion and hypostasis
516.0	Pulmonary alveolar proteinosis
516.1	Idiopathic pulmonary hemosiderosis
516.2	Pulmonary alveolar microlithiasis
516.33	Acute interstitial pneumonitis
516.35	Idiopathic lymphoid interstitial pneumonia
516.36	Cryptogenic organizing pneumonia
516.37	Desquamative interstitial pneumonia
516.5	Adult pulmonary Langerhans cell histiocytosis
516.8	Other specified alveolar and parietoalveolar pneumonopathies
516.9	Unspecified alveolar and parietoalveolar pneumonopathy
517.1	Rheumatic pneumonia
517.2	Lung involvement in systemic sclerosis
517.3	Acute chest syndrome
518.0	Pulmonary collapse
518.3	Pulmonary eosinophilia
518.6	Allergic bronchopulmonary aspergillosis
518.7	Transfusion related acute lung injury [TRALI]
518.82	Other pulmonary insufficiency, not elsewhere classified
518.83	Chronic respiratory failure
519.00	Unspecified tracheostomy complication
519.01	Infection of tracheostomy
519.02	Mechanical complication of tracheostomy
519.09	Other tracheostomy complications
522.0	Pulpitis
522.4	Acute apical periodontitis of pulpal origin
527.3	Abscess of salivary gland
527.4	Fistula of salivary gland
528.3	Cellulitis and abscess of oral soft tissues
530.12	Acute esophagitis
530.20	Ulcer of esophagus without bleeding
530.86	Infection of esophagostomy
530.87	Mechanical complication of esophagostomy
531.30	Acute gastric ulcer without mention of hemorrhage, perforation, or obstruction
532.30	Acute duodenal ulcer without mention of hemorrhage, perforation, or obstruction
533.30	Acute peptic ulcer, unspecified site, without mention of hemorrhage, perforation, or obstruction

534.30	Acute gastrojejunal ulcer without mention of hemorrhage, perforation, or obstruction
536.1	Acute dilatation of stomach
536.41	Infection of gastrostomy
536.42	Mechanical complication of gastrostomy
537.0	Acquired hypertrophic pyloric stenosis
537.3	Other obstruction of duodenum
537.4	Fistula of stomach or duodenum
538	Gastrointestinal mucositis (ulcerative)
539.01	Infection due to gastric band procedure
539.09	Other complications of gastric band procedure
539.81	Infection due to other bariatric procedure
539.89	Other complications of other bariatric procedure
540.9	Acute appendicitis without mention of peritonitis
550.10	Inguinal hernia with obstruction, without mention of gangrene, unilateral or unspecified, (not specified as recurrent)
550.11	Inguinal hernia with obstruction, without mention of gangrene, recurrent unilateral or unspecified
550.12	Inguinal hernia with obstruction, without mention gangrene, bilateral, (not specified as recurrent)
550.13	Inguinal hernia with obstruction, without mention of gangrene, recurrent bilateral
552.00	Unilateral or unspecified femoral hernia with obstruction
552.01	Recurrent unilateral or unspecified femoral hernia with obstruction
552.02	Bilateral femoral hernia with obstruction
552.03	Recurrent bilateral femoral hernia with obstruction
552.1	Umbilical hernia with obstruction
552.20	Unspecified ventral hernia with obstruction
552.21	Incisional hernia with obstruction
552.29	Other ventral hernia with obstruction
552.3	Diaphragmatic hernia with obstruction
552.8	Hernia of other specified site, with obstruction
552.9	Hernia of unspecified site, with obstruction
555.0	Regional enteritis of small intestine
555.1	Regional enteritis of large intestine
555.2	Regional enteritis of small intestine with large intestine
555.9	Regional enteritis of unspecified site
556.0	Ulcerative (chronic) enterocolitis
556.1	Ulcerative (chronic) ileocolitis
556.2	Ulcerative (chronic) proctitis
556.3	Ulcerative (chronic) proctosigmoiditis
556.4	Pseudopolyposis of colon
556.5	Left sided ulcerative (chronic) colitis
556.6	Universal ulcerative (chronic) colitis
556.8	Other ulcerative colitis
556.9	Unspecified ulcerative colitis
557.1	Chronic vascular insufficiency of intestine
557.9	Unspecified vascular insufficiency of intestine
558.1	Gastroenteritis and colitis due to radiation
558.2	Toxic gastroenteritis and colitis
560.0	Intussusception
560.1	Paralytic ileus
560.30	Unspecified impaction of intestine
560.31	Gallstone ileus
560.39	Impaction of intestine, other
560.81	Intestinal or peritoneal adhesions with obstruction (postoperative) (postinfection)
560.89	Other specified intestinal obstruction
560.9	Unspecified intestinal obstruction
562.01	Diverticulitis of small intestine (without mention of hemorrhage)

562.11	Diverticulitis of colon (without mention of hemorrhage)
564.7	Megacolon, other than Hirschsprung's
564.81	Neurogenic bowel
566	Abscess of anal and rectal regions
567.82	Sclerosing mesenteritis
568.82	Peritoneal effusion (chronic)
569.3	Hemorrhage of rectum and anus
569.41	Ulcer of anus and rectum
569.5	Abscess of intestine
569.61	Infection of colostomy or enterostomy
569.62	Mechanical complication of colostomy and enterostomy
569.69	Other complication of colostomy or enterostomy
569.71	Pouchitis
569.79	Other complications of intestinal pouch
569.81	Fistula of intestine, excluding rectum and anus
569.82	Ulceration of intestine
572.3	Portal hypertension
573.1	Hepatitis in viral diseases classified elsewhere
573.2	Hepatitis in other infectious diseases classified elsewhere
574.00	Calculus of gallbladder with acute cholecystitis, without mention of obstruction
574.01	Calculus of gallbladder with acute cholecystitis and obstruction
574.10	Calculus of gallbladder with other cholecystitis, without mention of obstruction
574.11	Calculus of gallbladder with other cholecystitis and obstruction
574.21	Calculus of gallbladder without mention of cholecystitis, with obstruction
574.30	Calculus of bile duct with acute cholecystitis without mention of obstruction
574.31	Calculus of bile duct with acute cholecystitis and obstruction
574.40	Calculus of bile duct with other cholecystitis, without mention of obstruction
574.41	Calculus of bile duct with other cholecystitis and obstruction
574.51	Calculus of bile duct without mention of cholecystitis, with obstruction
574.60	Calculus of gallbladder and bile duct with acute cholecystitis, without mention of obstruction
574.61	Calculus of gallbladder and bile duct with acute cholecystitis, with obstruction
574.70	Calculus of gallbladder and bile duct with other cholecystitis, without mention of obstruction
574.71	Calculus of gallbladder and bile duct with other cholecystitis, with obstruction
574.80	Calculus of gallbladder and bile duct with acute and chronic cholecystitis, without mention of obstruction
574.91	Calculus of gallbladder and bile duct without cholecystitis, with obstruction
575.0	Acute cholecystitis
575.12	Acute and chronic cholecystitis
575.2	Obstruction of gallbladder
575.3	Hydrops of gallbladder
575.5	Fistula of gallbladder
576.1	Cholangitis
576.4	Fistula of bile duct
577.1	Chronic pancreatitis
577.2	Cyst and pseudocyst of pancreas
578.0	Hematemesis
578.1	Blood in stool
578.9	Hemorrhage of gastrointestinal tract, unspecified
579.1	Tropical sprue
579.2	Blind loop syndrome

579.3	Other and unspecified postsurgical nonabsorption
579.4	Pancreatic steatorrhea
579.8	Other specified intestinal malabsorption
579.9	Unspecified intestinal malabsorption
581.0	Nephrotic syndrome with lesion of proliferative glomerulonephritis
581.1	Nephrotic syndrome with lesion of membranous glomerulonephritis
581.2	Nephrotic syndrome with lesion of membranoproliferative glomerulonephritis
581.3	Nephrotic syndrome with lesion of minimal change glomerulonephritis
581.81	Nephrotic syndrome with other specified pathological lesion in kidney in diseases classified elsewhere
581.89	Other nephrotic syndrome with specified pathological lesion in kidney
581.9	Nephrotic syndrome with unspecified pathological lesion in kidney
582.0	Chronic glomerulonephritis with lesion of proliferative glomerulonephritis
582.1	Chronic glomerulonephritis with lesion of membranous glomerulonephritis
582.2	Chronic glomerulonephritis with lesion of membranoproliferative glomerulonephritis
582.4	Chronic glomerulonephritis with lesion of rapidly progressive glomerulonephritis
582.81	Chronic glomerulonephritis with other specified pathological lesion in kidney in diseases classified elsewhere
582.89	Other chronic glomerulonephritis with specified pathological lesion in kidney
582.9	Chronic glomerulonephritis with unspecified pathological lesion in kidney
583.0	Nephritis and nephropathy, not specified as acute or chronic, with lesion of proliferative glomerulonephritis
583.1	Nephritis and nephropathy, not specified as acute or chronic, with lesion of membranous glomerulonephritis
583.2	Nephritis and nephropathy, not specified as acute or chronic, with lesion of membranoproliferative glomerulonephritis
583.7	Nephritis and nephropathy, not specified as acute or chronic, with lesion of renal medullary necrosis
584.8	Acute kidney failure with other specified pathological lesion in kidney
584.9	Acute kidney failure, unspecified
585.4	Chronic kidney disease, Stage IV (severe)
585.5	Chronic kidney disease, Stage V
588.1	Nephrogenic diabetes insipidus
588.81	Secondary hyperparathyroidism (of renal origin)
590.01	Chronic pyelonephritis with lesion of renal medullary necrosis
590.10	Acute pyelonephritis without lesion of renal medullary necrosis
590.3	Pyeloureteritis cystica
590.80	Unspecified pyelonephritis
590.81	Pyelitis or pyelonephritis in diseases classified elsewhere
591	Hydronephrosis
592.1	Calculus of ureter
593.4	Other ureteric obstruction
593.5	Hydroureter
593.81	Vascular disorders of kidney
593.82	Ureteral fistula
595.0	Acute cystitis
595.82	Irradiation cystitis
596.1	Intestinovesical fistula
596.2	Vesical fistula, not elsewhere classified
596.7	Hemorrhage into bladder wall
596.81	Infection of cystostomy

596.82	Mechanical complication of cystostomy
596.83	Other complication of cystostomy
597.0	Urethral abscess
599.0	Urinary tract infection, site not specified
599.1	Urethral fistula
601.0	Acute prostatitis
601.2	Abscess of prostate
603.1	Infected hydrocele
604.0	Orchitis, epididymitis, and epididymo-orchitis, with abscess
607.3	Priapism
607.82	Vascular disorders of penis
608.20	Torsion of testis, unspecified
608.21	Extravaginal torsion of spermatic cord
608.22	Intravaginal torsion of spermatic cord
608.23	Torsion of appendix testis
608.24	Torsion of appendix epididymis
614.0	Acute salpingitis and oophoritis
614.3	Acute parametritis and pelvic cellulitis
614.7	Other chronic pelvic peritonitis, female
615.0	Acute inflammatory disease of uterus, except cervix
616.3	Abscess of Bartholin's gland
616.4	Other abscess of vulva
616.81	Mucositis (ulcerative) of cervix, vagina, and vulva
619.0	Urinary-genital tract fistula, female
619.1	Digestive-genital tract fistula, female
619.2	Genital tract-skin fistula, female
619.8	Other specified fistula involving female genital tract
619.9	Unspecified fistula involving female genital tract
620.5	Torsion of ovary, ovarian pedicle, or fallopian tube
633.00	Abdominal pregnancy without intrauterine pregnancy
633.01	Abdominal pregnancy with intrauterine pregnancy
633.10	Tubal pregnancy without intrauterine pregnancy
633.11	Tubal pregnancy with intrauterine pregnancy
633.20	Ovarian pregnancy without intrauterine pregnancy
633.21	Ovarian pregnancy with intrauterine pregnancy
633.80	Other ectopic pregnancy without intrauterine pregnancy
633.81	Other ectopic pregnancy with intrauterine pregnancy
633.90	Unspecified ectopic pregnancy without intrauterine pregnancy
633.91	Unspecified ectopic pregnancy with intrauterine pregnancy
634.00	Unspecified spontaneous abortion complicated by genital tract and pelvic infection
634.01	Incomplete spontaneous abortion complicated by genital tract and pelvic infection
634.02	Complete spontaneous abortion complicated by genital tract and pelvic infection
634.20	Unspecified spontaneous abortion complicated by damage to pelvic organs or tissues
634.21	Incomplete spontaneous abortion complicated by damage to pelvic organs or tissues
634.22	Complete spontaneous abortion complicated by damage to pelvic organs or tissues
634.40	Unspecified spontaneous abortion complicated by metabolic disorder
634.41	Incomplete spontaneous abortion complicated by metabolic disorder
634.42	Complete spontaneous abortion complicated by metabolic disorder
634.60	Unspecified spontaneous abortion complicated by embolism
634.70	Unspecified spontaneous abortion with other specified complications

634.71	Incomplete spontaneous abortion with other specified complications
634.72	Complete spontaneous abortion with other specified complications
634.80	Unspecified spontaneous abortion with unspecified complication
634.81	Incomplete spontaneous abortion with unspecified complication
634.82	Complete spontaneous abortion with unspecified complication
635.00	Unspecified legally induced abortion complicated by genital tract and pelvic infection
635.01	Incomplete legally induced abortion complicated by genital tract and pelvic infection
635.02	Complete legally induced abortion complicated by genital tract and pelvic infection
635.20	Unspecified legally induced abortion complicated by damage to pelvic organs or tissues
635.21	Legally induced abortion complicated by damage to pelvic organs or tissues, incomplete
635.22	Complete legally induced abortion complicated by damage to pelvic organs or tissues
635.40	Unspecified legally induced abortion complicated by metabolic disorder
635.41	Incomplete legally induced abortion complicated by metabolic disorder
635.42	Complete legally induced abortion complicated by metabolic disorder
635.70	Unspecified legally induced abortion with other specified complications
635.71	Incomplete legally induced abortion with other specified complications
635.72	Complete legally induced abortion with other specified complications
635.80	Unspecified legally induced abortion with unspecified complication
635.81	Incomplete legally induced abortion with unspecified complication
635.82	Complete legally induced abortion with unspecified complication
636.00	Unspecified illegally induced abortion complicated by genital tract and pelvic infection
636.01	Incomplete illegally induced abortion complicated by genital tract and pelvic infection
636.02	Complete illegally induced abortion complicated by genital tract and pelvic infection
636.20	Unspecified illegally induced abortion complicated by damage to pelvic organs or tissues
636.21	Incomplete illegally induced abortion complicated by damage to pelvic organs or tissues
636.22	Complete illegally induced abortion complicated by damage to pelvic organs or tissues
636.40	Unspecified illegally induced abortion complicated by metabolic disorder
636.41	Incomplete illegally induced abortion complicated by metabolic disorder
636.42	Complete illegally induced abortion complicated by metabolic disorder
636.70	Unspecified illegally induced abortion with other specified complications
636.71	Incomplete illegally induced abortion with other specified complications
636.72	Complete illegally induced abortion with other specified complications
636.80	Unspecified illegally induced abortion with unspecified complication
636.81	Incomplete illegally induced abortion with unspecified complication
636.82	Complete illegally induced abortion with unspecified complication

637.00	Abortion, unspecified as to completion or legality, complicated by genital tract and pelvic infection
637.01	Abortion, unspecified as to legality, incomplete, complicated by genital tract and pelvic infection
637.02	Abortion, unspecified as to legality, complete, complicated by genital tract and pelvic infection
637.20	Abortion, unspecified as to completion or legality, complicated by damage to pelvic organs or tissues
637.21	Abortion, unspecified as to legality, incomplete, complicated by damage to pelvic organs or tissues
637.22	Abortion, unspecified as to legality, complete, complicated by damage to pelvic organs or tissues
637.40	Abortion, unspecified as to completeness or legality, complicated by metabolic disorder
637.41	Abortion, unspecified as to legality, incomplete, complicated by metabolic disorder
637.42	Abortion, unspecified as to legality, complete, complicated by metabolic disorder
637.70	Abortion, unspecified as to completion or legality, with other specified complications
637.71	Abortion, unspecified as to legality, incomplete, with other specified complications
637.72	Abortion, unspecified as to legality, complete, with other specified complications
637.80	Abortion, unspecified as to completion or legality, with unspecified complication
637.81	Abortion, unspecified as to legality, incomplete, with unspecified complication
637.82	Abortion, unspecified as to legality, complete, with unspecified complication
638.0	Failed attempted abortion complicated by genital tract and pelvic infection
638.1	Failed attempted abortion complicated by delayed or excessive hemorrhage
638.2	Failed attempted abortion complicated by damage to pelvic organs or tissues
638.4	Failed attempted abortion complicated by metabolic disorder
638.7	Failed attempted abortion with other specified complication
638.8	Failed attempted abortion with unspecified complication
639.0	Genital tract and pelvic infection following abortion or ectopic and molar pregnancies
639.1	Delayed or excessive hemorrhage following abortion or ectopic and molar pregnancies
639.2	Damage to pelvic organs and tissues following abortion or ectopic and molar pregnancies
639.4	Metabolic disorders following abortion or ectopic and molar pregnancies
639.8	Other specified complication following abortion or ectopic and molar pregnancies
639.9	Unspecified complication following abortion or ectopic and molar pregnancies
640.01	Threatened abortion, delivered
640.03	Threatened abortion, antepartum
640.93	Unspecified hemorrhage in early pregnancy, antepartum
641.01	Placenta previa without hemorrhage, with delivery
641.03	Placenta previa without hemorrhage, antepartum
641.23	Premature separation of placenta, antepartum
642.01	Benign essential hypertension with delivery
642.02	Benign essential hypertension, with delivery, with current postpartum complication
642.03	Benign essential hypertension antepartum
642.13	Hypertension secondary to renal disease, antepartum
642.14	Hypertension secondary to renal disease, complicating pregnancy, childbirth, and the puerperium, postpartum condition or complication

642.31	Transient hypertension of pregnancy, with delivery
642.32	Transient hypertension of pregnancy, with delivery, with current postpartum complication
642.41	Mild or unspecified pre-eclampsia, with delivery
642.43	Mild or unspecified pre-eclampsia, antepartum
642.44	Mild or unspecified pre-eclampsia, postpartum condition or complication
642.91	Unspecified hypertension, with delivery
642.92	Unspecified hypertension, with delivery, with current postpartum complication
642.93	Unspecified hypertension antepartum
642.94	Unspecified hypertension complicating pregnancy, childbirth, or the puerperium, postpartum condition or complication
644.13	Other threatened labor, antepartum
644.20	Early onset of delivery, unspecified as to episode of care
646.21	Unspecified renal disease in pregnancy, with delivery
646.22	Unspecified renal disease in pregnancy, with delivery, with current postpartum complication
646.23	Unspecified antepartum renal disease
646.24	Unspecified renal disease in pregnancy, without mention of hypertension, postpartum condition or complication
646.31	Pregnancy complication, recurrent pregnancy loss, with or without mention of antepartum condition
646.61	Infections of genitourinary tract in pregnancy, with delivery
646.62	Infections of genitourinary tract in pregnancy, with delivery, with current postpartum complication
646.63	Infections of genitourinary tract antepartum
646.64	Infections of genitourinary tract in pregnancy, postpartum condition or complication
646.71	Liver and biliary tract disorders in pregnancy, delivered, with or without mention of antepartum condition
646.73	Liver and biliary tract disorders in pregnancy, antepartum condition or complication
647.01	Maternal syphilis, complicating pregnancy, with delivery
647.02	Maternal syphilis, complicating pregnancy, with delivery, with current postpartum complication
647.03	Maternal syphilis, antepartum
647.04	Maternal syphilis complicating pregnancy, childbirth, or the puerperium, postpartum condition or complication
647.11	Maternal gonorrhea with delivery
647.12	Maternal gonorrhea, with delivery, with current postpartum complication
647.13	Maternal gonorrhea, antepartum
647.14	Maternal gonorrhea complicating pregnancy, childbirth, or the puerperium, postpartum condition or complication
647.21	Other maternal venereal diseases with delivery
647.22	Other maternal venereal diseases with delivery, with current postpartum complication
647.23	Other maternal venereal diseases, antepartum condition or complication
647.24	Other venereal diseases complicating pregnancy, childbirth, or the puerperium, postpartum condition or complication
647.31	Maternal tuberculosis with delivery
647.32	Maternal tuberculosis with delivery, with current postpartum complication
647.33	Maternal tuberculosis, antepartum
647.34	Maternal tuberculosis complicating pregnancy, childbirth, or the puerperium, postpartum condition or complication
647.41	Maternal malaria with delivery
647.42	Maternal malaria with delivery, with current postpartum complication
647.43	Maternal malaria, antepartum
647.44	Maternal malaria, complicating pregnancy, childbirth, or the puerperium, postpartum condition or complication
647.51	Maternal rubella with delivery
647.52	Maternal rubella with delivery, with current postpartum complication
647.53	Maternal rubella, antepartum
647.54	Maternal rubella complicating pregnancy, childbirth, or the puerperium, postpartum condition or complication
647.61	Other maternal viral disease with delivery
647.62	Other maternal viral disease with delivery, with current postpartum complication
647.63	Other maternal viral disease, antepartum
647.64	Other maternal viral diseases complicating pregnancy, childbirth, or the puerperium, postpartum condition or complication
647.81	Other specified maternal infectious and parasitic disease with delivery
647.82	Other specified maternal infectious and parasitic disease with delivery, with current postpartum complication
647.83	Other specified maternal infectious and parasitic disease, antepartum
647.84	Other specified maternal infectious and parasitic diseases complicating pregnancy, childbirth, or the puerperium, postpartum condition or complication
647.91	Unspecified maternal infection or infestation with delivery
647.92	Unspecified maternal infection or infestation with delivery, with current postpartum complication
647.93	Unspecified maternal infection or infestation, antepartum
647.94	Unspecified maternal infection or infestation complicating pregnancy, childbirth, or the puerperium, postpartum condition or complication
648.00	Maternal diabetes mellitus, complicating pregnancy, childbirth, or the puerperium, unspecified as to episode of care
648.03	Maternal diabetes mellitus, antepartum
648.04	Maternal diabetes mellitus, complicating pregnancy, childbirth, or the puerperium, postpartum condition or complication
648.31	Maternal drug dependence, with delivery
648.32	Maternal drug dependence, with delivery, with current postpartum complication
648.33	Maternal drug dependence, antepartum
648.34	Maternal drug dependence complicating pregnancy, childbirth, or the puerperium, postpartum condition or complication
648.51	Maternal congenital cardiovascular disorders, with delivery
648.52	Maternal congenital cardiovascular disorders, with delivery, with current postpartum complication
648.53	Maternal congenital cardiovascular disorders, antepartum
648.54	Maternal congenital cardiovascular disorders complicating pregnancy, childbirth, or the puerperium, postpartum condition or complication
648.61	Other maternal cardiovascular diseases, with delivery
648.62	Other maternal cardiovascular diseases, with delivery, with current postpartum complication
648.63	Other maternal cardiovascular diseases, antepartum
648.64	Other maternal cardiovascular diseases complicating pregnancy, childbirth, or the puerperium, postpartum condition or complication
648.71	Bone and joint disorders of maternal back, pelvis, and lower limbs, with delivery
648.72	Bone and joint disorders of maternal back, pelvis, and lower limbs, with delivery, with current postpartum complication
648.73	Bone and joint disorders of maternal back, pelvis, and lower limbs, antepartum
648.74	Bone and joint disorders of maternal back, pelvis, and lower limbs complicating pregnancy, childbirth, or the puerperium, postpartum condition or complication

649.30	Coagulation defects complicating pregnancy, childbirth, or the puerperium, unspecified as to episode of care or not applicable
649.31	Coagulation defects complicating pregnancy, childbirth, or the puerperium, delivered, with or without mention of antepartum condition
649.32	Coagulation defects complicating pregnancy, childbirth, or the puerperium, delivered, with mention of postpartum complication
649.33	Coagulation defects complicating pregnancy, childbirth, or the puerperium, antepartum condition or complication
649.34	Coagulation defects complicating pregnancy, childbirth, or the puerperium, postpartum condition or complication
649.41	Epilepsy complicating pregnancy, childbirth, or the puerperium, delivered, with or without mention of antepartum condition
649.42	Epilepsy complicating pregnancy, childbirth, or the puerperium, delivered, with mention of postpartum complication
649.43	Epilepsy complicating pregnancy, childbirth, or the puerperium, antepartum condition or complication
649.44	Epilepsy complicating pregnancy, childbirth, or the puerperium, postpartum condition or complication
649.70	Cervical shortening, unspecified as to episode of care or not applicable
649.71	Cervical shortening, delivered, with or without mention of antepartum condition
649.73	Cervical shortening, antepartum condition or complication
651.01	Twin pregnancy, delivered
651.11	Triplet pregnancy, delivered
651.13	Triplet pregnancy, antepartum
651.21	Quadruplet pregnancy, delivered
651.23	Quadruplet pregnancy, antepartum
651.41	Triplet pregnancy with fetal loss and retention of one or more, delivered
651.43	Triplet pregnancy with fetal loss and retention of one or more, antepartum
651.51	Quadruplet pregnancy with fetal loss and retention of one or more, delivered
651.53	Quadruplet pregnancy with fetal loss and retention of one or more, antepartum
651.81	Other specified multiple gestation, delivered
651.83	Other specified multiple gestation, antepartum
656.13	Rhesus isoimmunization affecting management of mother, antepartum condition
656.31	Fetal distress affecting management of mother, delivered
656.41	Intrauterine death affecting management of mother, delivered
656.43	Intrauterine death affecting management of mother, antepartum
656.51	Poor fetal growth, affecting management of mother, delivered
657.01	Polyhydramnios, with delivery
658.01	Oligohydramnios, delivered
658.03	Oligohydramnios, antepartum
658.81	Other problem associated with amniotic cavity and membranes, delivered
659.21	Unspecified maternal pyrexia during labor, delivered
660.03	Obstruction caused by malposition of fetus at onset of labor, antepartum
662.11	Unspecified prolonged labor, delivered
664.21	Third-degree perineal laceration, with delivery
664.31	Fourth-degree perineal laceration, with delivery
664.61	Anal sphincter tear complicating delivery, not associated with third-degree perineal laceration, delivered, with or without mention of antepartum condition
664.64	Anal sphincter tear complicating delivery, not associated with third-degree perineal laceration, postpartum condition or complication
665.22	Inversion of uterus, delivered with postpartum complication
665.31	Laceration of cervix, with delivery
665.41	High vaginal laceration, with delivery
665.51	Other injury to pelvic organs, with delivery
665.61	Damage to pelvic joints and ligaments, with delivery
665.71	Pelvic hematoma, with delivery
665.72	Pelvic hematoma, delivered with postpartum complication
666.02	Third-stage postpartum hemorrhage, with delivery
666.04	Third-stage postpartum hemorrhage, postpartum condition or complication
666.12	Other immediate postpartum hemorrhage, with delivery
666.14	Other immediate postpartum hemorrhage, postpartum condition or complication
666.22	Delayed and secondary postpartum hemorrhage, with delivery
666.24	Delayed and secondary postpartum hemorrhage, postpartum condition or complication
666.32	Postpartum coagulation defects, with delivery
669.24	Maternal hypotension syndrome, postpartum condition or complication
670.10	Puerperal endometritis, unspecified as to episode of care or not applicable
670.12	Puerperal endometritis, delivered, with mention of postpartum complication
670.14	Puerperal endometritis, postpartum condition or complication
670.20	Puerperal sepsis, unspecified as to episode of care or not applicable
670.30	Puerperal septic thrombophlebitis, unspecified as to episode of care or not applicable
671.20	Superficial thrombophlebitis complicating pregnancy and the puerperium, unspecified as to episode of care
671.21	Superficial thrombophlebitis with delivery, with or without mention of antepartum condition
671.22	Superficial thrombophlebitis with delivery, with mention of postpartum complication
671.23	Superficial thrombophlebitis, antepartum
671.24	Superficial thrombophlebitis, postpartum condition or complication
671.30	Deep phlebothrombosis, antepartum, unspecified as to episode of care
671.40	Deep phlebothrombosis, postpartum, unspecified as to episode of care
671.50	Other phlebitis and thrombosis complicating pregnancy and the puerperium, unspecified as to episode of care
671.51	Other phlebitis and thrombosis with delivery, with or without mention of antepartum condition
671.52	Other phlebitis and thrombosis with delivery, with mention of postpartum complication
671.53	Other antepartum phlebitis and thrombosis
671.54	Other phlebitis and thrombosis, postpartum condition or complication
671.80	Other venous complication of pregnancy and the puerperium, unspecified as to episode of care
671.81	Other venous complication, with delivery, with or without mention of antepartum condition
671.82	Other venous complication, with delivery, with mention of postpartum complication
671.83	Other venous complication, antepartum
671.84	Other venous complications, postpartum condition or complication
671.90	Unspecified venous complication of pregnancy and the puerperium, unspecified as to episode of care
671.91	Unspecified venous complication, with delivery, with or without mention of antepartum condition
671.92	Unspecified venous complication, with delivery, with mention of postpartum complication
672.02	Puerperal pyrexia of unknown origin, delivered, with mention of postpartum complication

672.04	Puerperal pyrexia of unknown origin, postpartum condition or complication
673.30	Obstetrical pyemic and septic embolism, unspecified as to episode of care
674.02	Cerebrovascular disorder, with delivery, with mention of postpartum complication
674.03	Cerebrovascular disorder, antepartum
674.04	Cerebrovascular disorders in the puerperium, postpartum condition or complication
675.11	Abscess of breast associated with childbirth, delivered, with or without mention of antepartum condition
675.12	Abscess of breast associated with childbirth, delivered, with mention of postpartum complication
682.0	Cellulitis and abscess of face
682.1	Cellulitis and abscess of neck
682.2	Cellulitis and abscess of trunk
682.3	Cellulitis and abscess of upper arm and forearm
682.4	Cellulitis and abscess of hand, except fingers and thumb
682.5	Cellulitis and abscess of buttock
682.6	Cellulitis and abscess of leg, except foot
682.7	Cellulitis and abscess of foot, except toes
682.8	Cellulitis and abscess of other specified site
682.9	Cellulitis and abscess of unspecified site
685.0	Pilonidal cyst with abscess
686.01	Pyoderma gangrenosum
694.4	Pemphigus
694.5	Pemphigoid
695.0	Toxic erythema
695.12	Erythema multiforme major
695.13	Stevens-Johnson syndrome
695.14	Stevens-Johnson syndrome-toxic epidermal necrolysis overlap syndrome
695.15	Toxic epidermal necrolysis
695.53	Exfoliation due to erythematous condition involving 30-39 percent of body surface
695.54	Exfoliation due to erythematous condition involving 40-49 percent of body surface
695.55	Exfoliation due to erythematous condition involving 50-59 percent of body surface
695.56	Exfoliation due to erythematous condition involving 60-69 percent of body surface
695.57	Exfoliation due to erythematous condition involving 70-79 percent of body surface
695.58	Exfoliation due to erythematous condition involving 80-89 percent of body surface
695.59	Exfoliation due to erythematous condition involving 90 percent or more of body surface
707.00	Pressure ulcer, unspecified site
707.01	Pressure ulcer, elbow
707.09	Pressure ulcer, other site
707.10	Ulcer of lower limb, unspecified
707.11	Ulcer of thigh
707.12	Ulcer of calf
707.13	Ulcer of ankle
707.14	Ulcer of heel and midfoot
707.19	Ulcer of other part of lower limb
710.3	Dermatomyositis
710.4	Polymyositis
710.5	Eosinophilia myalgia syndrome
710.8	Other specified diffuse disease of connective tissue
711.00	Pyogenic arthritis, site unspecified
711.01	Pyogenic arthritis, shoulder region

711.02	Pyogenic arthritis, upper arm
711.03	Pyogenic arthritis, forearm
711.04	Pyogenic arthritis, hand
711.05	Pyogenic arthritis, pelvic region and thigh
711.06	Pyogenic arthritis, lower leg
711.07	Pyogenic arthritis, ankle and foot
711.08	Pyogenic arthritis, other specified sites
711.09	Pyogenic arthritis, multiple sites
711.10	Arthropathy associated with Reiter's disease and nonspecific urethritis, site unspecified
711.11	Arthropathy associated with Reiter's disease and nonspecific urethritis, shoulder region
711.12	Arthropathy associated with Reiter's disease and nonspecific urethritis, upper arm
711.13	Arthropathy associated with Reiter's disease and nonspecific urethritis, forearm
711.14	Arthropathy associated with Reiter's disease and nonspecific urethritis, hand
711.15	Arthropathy associated with Reiter's disease and nonspecific urethritis, pelvic region and thigh
711.16	Arthropathy associated with Reiter's disease and nonspecific urethritis, lower leg
711.17	Arthropathy associated with Reiter's disease and nonspecific urethritis, ankle and foot
711.18	Arthropathy associated with Reiter's disease and nonspecific urethritis, other specified site
711.19	Arthropathy associated with Reiter's disease and nonspecific urethritis, multiple sites
711.20	Arthropathy in Behcet's syndrome, site unspecified
711.21	Arthropathy in Behcet's syndrome, shoulder region
711.22	Arthropathy in Behcet's syndrome, upper arm
711.23	Arthropathy in Behcet's syndrome, forearm
711.24	Arthropathy in Behcet's syndrome, hand
711.25	Arthropathy in Behcet's syndrome, pelvic region and thigh
711.26	Arthropathy in Behcet's syndrome, lower leg
711.27	Arthropathy in Behcet's syndrome, ankle and foot
711.28	Arthropathy in Behcet's syndrome, other specified sites
711.29	Arthropathy in Behcet's syndrome, multiple sites
711.30	Postdysenteric arthropathy, site unspecified
711.31	Postdysenteric arthropathy, shoulder region
711.32	Postdysenteric arthropathy, upper arm
711.33	Postdysenteric arthropathy, forearm
711.34	Postdysenteric arthropathy, hand
711.35	Postdysenteric arthropathy, pelvic region and thigh
711.36	Postdysenteric arthropathy, lower leg
711.37	Postdysenteric arthropathy, ankle and foot
711.38	Postdysenteric arthropathy, other specified sites
711.39	Postdysenteric arthropathy, multiple sites
711.40	Arthropathy associated with other bacterial diseases, site unspecified
711.41	Arthropathy associated with other bacterial diseases, shoulder region
711.42	Arthropathy associated with other bacterial diseases, upper arm
711.43	Arthropathy associated with other bacterial diseases, forearm
711.44	Arthropathy, associated with other bacterial diseases, hand
711.45	Arthropathy associated with other bacterial diseases, pelvic region and thigh
711.46	Arthropathy associated with other bacterial diseases, lower leg
711.47	Arthropathy associated with other bacterial disease, ankle and foot
711.48	Arthropathy associated with other bacterial diseases, other specific sites
711.49	Arthropathy associated with other bacterial diseases, multiple sites

711.50	Arthropathy associated with other viral diseases, site unspecified
711.51	Arthropathy associated with other viral diseases, shoulder region
711.52	Arthropathy associated with other viral diseases, upper arm
711.53	Arthropathy associated with other viral diseases, forearm
711.54	Arthropathy associated with other viral diseases, hand
711.55	Arthropathy associated with other viral diseases, pelvic region and thigh
711.56	Arthropathy associated with other viral diseases, lower leg
711.57	Arthropathy associated with other viral diseases, ankle and foot
711.58	Arthropathy associated with other viral diseases, other specified sites
711.59	Arthropathy associated with other viral diseases, of multiple sites
711.60	Arthropathy associated with mycoses, site unspecified
711.61	Arthropathy associated with mycoses, shoulder region
711.62	Arthropathy associated with mycoses, upper arm
711.63	Arthropathy associated with mycoses, forearm
711.64	Arthropathy associated with mycoses, hand
711.65	Arthropathy associated with mycoses, pelvic region and thigh
711.66	Arthropathy associated with mycoses, lower leg
711.67	Arthropathy associated with mycoses, ankle and foot
711.68	Arthropathy associated with mycoses, other specified site
711.69	Arthropathy associated with mycoses, multiple sites
711.70	Arthropathy associated with helminthiasis, site unspecified
711.71	Arthropathy associated with helminthiasis, shoulder region
711.72	Arthropathy associated with helminthiasis, upper arm
711.73	Arthropathy associated with helminthiasis, forearm
711.74	Arthropathy associated with helminthiasis, hand
711.75	Arthropathy associated with helminthiasis, pelvic region and thigh
711.76	Arthropathy associated with helminthiasis, lower leg
711.77	Arthropathy associated with helminthiasis, ankle and foot
711.78	Arthropathy associated with helminthiasis, other specified site
711.79	Arthropathy associated with helminthiasis, multiple sites
711.80	Arthropathy associated with other infectious and parasitic diseases, site unspecified
711.81	Arthropathy associated with other infectious and parasitic diseases, shoulder region
711.82	Arthropathy associated with other infectious and parasitic diseases, upper arm
711.83	Arthropathy associated with other infectious and parasitic diseases, forearm
711.84	Arthropathy associated with other infectious and parasitic diseases, hand
711.85	Arthropathy associated with other infectious and parasitic diseases, pelvic region and thigh
711.86	Arthropathy associated with other infectious and parasitic diseases, lower leg
711.87	Arthropathy associated with other infectious and parasitic diseases, ankle and foot
711.88	Arthropathy associated with other infectious and parasitic diseases, other specific site
711.89	Arthropathy associated with other infectious and parasitic diseases, multiple sites
711.90	Unspecified infective arthritis, site unspecified
711.91	Unspecified infective arthritis, shoulder region
711.92	Unspecified infective arthritis, upper arm
711.93	Unspecified infective arthritis, forearm
711.94	Unspecified infective arthritis, hand
711.95	Unspecified infective arthritis, pelvic region and thigh
711.96	Unspecified infective arthritis, lower leg
711.97	Unspecified infective arthritis, ankle and foot
711.98	Unspecified infective arthritis, other specified sites
711.99	Unspecified infective arthritis, multiple sites
714.31	Polyarticular juvenile rheumatoid arthritis, acute
719.10	Hemarthrosis, site unspecified
719.11	Hemarthrosis, shoulder region
719.12	Hemarthrosis, upper arm
719.13	Hemarthrosis, forearm
719.14	Hemarthrosis, hand
719.15	Hemarthrosis, pelvic region and thigh
719.16	Hemarthrosis, lower leg
719.17	Hemarthrosis, ankle and foot
719.18	Hemarthrosis, other specified site
719.19	Hemarthrosis, multiple sites
721.1	Cervical spondylosis with myelopathy
721.41	Spondylosis with myelopathy, thoracic region
721.42	Spondylosis with myelopathy, lumbar region
721.7	Traumatic spondylopathy
721.91	Spondylosis of unspecified site with myelopathy
722.71	Intervertebral cervical disc disorder with myelopathy, cervical region
722.72	Intervertebral thoracic disc disorder with myelopathy, thoracic region
722.73	Intervertebral lumbar disc disorder with myelopathy, lumbar region
728.0	Infective myositis
728.88	Rhabdomyolysis
729.71	Nontraumatic compartment syndrome of upper extremity
729.72	Nontraumatic compartment syndrome of lower extremity
729.73	Nontraumatic compartment syndrome of abdomen
729.79	Nontraumatic compartment syndrome of other sites
730.00	Acute osteomyelitis, site unspecified
730.01	Acute osteomyelitis, shoulder region
730.02	Acute osteomyelitis, upper arm
730.03	Acute osteomyelitis, forearm
730.04	Acute osteomyelitis, hand
730.05	Acute osteomyelitis, pelvic region and thigh
730.06	Acute osteomyelitis, lower leg
730.07	Acute osteomyelitis, ankle and foot
730.08	Acute osteomyelitis, other specified site
730.09	Acute osteomyelitis, multiple sites
730.10	Chronic osteomyelitis, site unspecified
730.11	Chronic osteomyelitis, shoulder region
730.12	Chronic osteomyelitis, upper arm
730.13	Chronic osteomyelitis, forearm
730.14	Chronic osteomyelitis, hand
730.15	Chronic osteomyelitis, pelvic region and thigh
730.16	Chronic osteomyelitis, lower leg
730.17	Chronic osteomyelitis, ankle and foot
730.18	Chronic osteomyelitis, other specified sites
730.19	Chronic osteomyelitis, multiple sites
730.20	Unspecified osteomyelitis, site unspecified
730.21	Unspecified osteomyelitis, shoulder region
730.22	Unspecified osteomyelitis, upper arm
730.23	Unspecified osteomyelitis, forearm
730.24	Unspecified osteomyelitis, hand
730.25	Unspecified osteomyelitis, pelvic region and thigh
730.26	Unspecified osteomyelitis, lower leg
730.27	Unspecified osteomyelitis, ankle and foot
730.28	Unspecified osteomyelitis, other specified sites
730.29	Unspecified osteomyelitis, multiple sites

730.80	Other infections involving bone in diseases classified elsewhere, site unspecified
730.81	Other infections involving bone diseases classified elsewhere, shoulder region
730.82	Other infections involving bone diseases classified elsewhere, upper arm
730.83	Other infections involving bone in diseases classified elsewhere, forearm
730.84	Other infections involving diseases classified elsewhere, hand bone
730.85	Other infections involving bone diseases classified elsewhere, pelvic region and thigh
730.86	Other infections involving bone diseases classified elsewhere, lower leg
730.87	Other infections involving bone diseases classified elsewhere, ankle and foot
730.88	Other infections involving bone diseases classified elsewhere, other specified sites
730.89	Other infections involving bone diseases classified elsewhere, multiple sites
730.90	Unspecified infection of bone, site unspecified
730.91	Unspecified infection of bone, shoulder region
730.92	Unspecified infection of bone, upper arm
730.93	Unspecified infection of bone, forearm
730.94	Unspecified infection of bone, hand
730.95	Unspecified infection of bone, pelvic region and thigh
730.96	Unspecified infection of bone, lower leg
730.97	Unspecified infection of bone, ankle and foot
730.98	Unspecified infection of bone of other specified site
730.99	Unspecified infection of bone in multiple sites
733.10	Pathologic fracture, unspecified site
733.11	Pathologic fracture of humerus
733.12	Pathologic fracture of distal radius and ulna
733.13	Pathologic fracture of vertebrae
733.14	Pathologic fracture of neck of femur
733.15	Pathologic fracture of other specified part of femur
733.16	Pathologic fracture of tibia and fibula
733.19	Pathologic fracture of other specified site
733.40	Aseptic necrosis of bone, site unspecified
733.41	Aseptic necrosis of head of humerus
733.42	Aseptic necrosis of head and neck of femur
733.43	Aseptic necrosis of medial femoral condyle
733.44	Aseptic necrosis of talus
733.45	Aseptic necrosis of bone, jaw
733.49	Aseptic necrosis of other bone site
733.81	Malunion of fracture
733.82	Nonunion of fracture
741.00	Spina bifida with hydrocephalus, unspecified region
741.01	Spina bifida with hydrocephalus, cervical region
741.02	Spina bifida with hydrocephalus, dorsal (thoracic) region
741.03	Spina bifida with hydrocephalus, lumbar region
742.0	Encephalocele
742.4	Other specified congenital anomalies of brain
745.12	Corrected transposition of great vessels
745.4	Ventricular septal defect
745.5	Ostium secundum type atrial septal defect
745.60	Unspecified type congenital endocardial cushion defect
745.61	Ostium primum defect
745.69	Other congenital endocardial cushion defect
746.00	Unspecified congenital pulmonary valve anomaly
746.02	Congenital stenosis of pulmonary valve
746.09	Other congenital anomalies of pulmonary valve

746.3	Congenital stenosis of aortic valve
746.4	Congenital insufficiency of aortic valve
746.5	Congenital mitral stenosis
746.6	Congenital mitral insufficiency
746.83	Congenital infundibular pulmonic stenosis
746.85	Congenital coronary artery anomaly
746.87	Congenital malposition of heart and cardiac apex
747.0	Patent ductus arteriosus
747.10	Coarctation of aorta (preductal) (postductal)
747.20	Unspecified congenital anomaly of aorta
747.21	Congenital anomaly of aortic arch
747.22	Congenital atresia and stenosis of aorta
747.29	Other congenital anomaly of aorta
747.40	Congenital anomaly of great veins unspecified
747.41	Total congenital anomalous pulmonary venous connection
747.42	Partial congenital anomalous pulmonary venous connection
747.49	Other congenital anomalies of great veins
747.82	Congenital spinal vessel anomaly
747.89	Other specified congenital anomaly of circulatory system
747.9	Unspecified congenital anomaly of circulatory system
748.3	Other congenital anomaly of larynx, trachea, and bronchus
748.4	Congenital cystic lung
748.61	Congenital bronchiectasis
750.4	Other specified congenital anomaly of esophagus
751.1	Congenital atresia and stenosis of small intestine
751.2	Congenital atresia and stenosis of large intestine, rectum, and anal canal
751.3	Hirschsprung's disease and other congenital functional disorders of colon
751.4	Congenital anomalies of intestinal fixation
751.5	Other congenital anomalies of intestine
751.60	Unspecified congenital anomaly of gallbladder, bile ducts, and liver
751.62	Congenital cystic disease of liver
751.69	Other congenital anomaly of gallbladder, bile ducts, and liver
751.7	Congenital anomalies of pancreas
753.0	Congenital renal agenesis and dysgenesis
753.10	Unspecified congenital cystic kidney disease
753.11	Congenital single renal cyst
753.12	Congenital polycystic kidney, unspecified type
753.13	Congenital polycystic kidney, autosomal dominant
753.14	Congenital polycystic kidney, autosomal recessive
753.15	Congenital renal dysplasia
753.16	Congenital medullary cystic kidney
753.17	Congenital medullary sponge kidney
753.19	Other specified congenital cystic kidney disease
753.20	Unspecified obstructive defect of renal pelvis and ureter
753.21	Congenital obstruction of ureteropelvic junction
753.22	Congenital obstruction of ureterovesical junction
753.23	Congenital ureterocele
753.29	Other obstructive defect of renal pelvis and ureter
753.5	Exstrophy of urinary bladder
753.6	Congenital atresia and stenosis of urethra and bladder neck
754.2	Congenital musculoskeletal deformity of spine
754.89	Other specified nonteratogenic anomalies
756.13	Congenital absence of vertebra
756.3	Other congenital anomaly of ribs and sternum
756.51	Osteogenesis imperfecta
756.52	Osteopetrosis
756.83	Ehlers-Danlos syndrome

758.1	Patau's syndrome
758.2	Edwards' syndrome
758.31	Cri-du-chat syndrome
758.33	Autosomal deletion syndromes, other microdeletions
758.39	Autosomal deletion syndromes, other autosomal deletions
759.0	Congenital anomalies of spleen
759.3	Situs inversus
759.5	Tuberous sclerosis
759.6	Other congenital hamartoses, not elsewhere classified
759.7	Multiple congenital anomalies, so described
759.81	Prader-Willi syndrome
759.82	Marfan's syndrome
759.89	Other specified multiple congenital anomalies, so described
767.11	Birth trauma, epicranial subaponeurotic hemorrhage (massive)
768.70	Hypoxic-ischemic encephalopathy, unspecified
768.71	Mild hypoxic-ischemic encephalopathy
768.72	Moderate hypoxic-ischemic encephalopathy
770.4	Primary atelectasis of newborn
770.5	Other and unspecified atelectasis of newborn
770.81	Primary apnea of newborn
770.82	Other apnea of newborn
770.83	Cyanotic attacks of newborn
771.0	Congenital rubella
771.4	Omphalitis of the newborn
771.5	Neonatal infective mastitis
771.82	Urinary tract infection of newborn
771.83	Bacteremia of newborn
771.89	Other infections specific to the perinatal period
772.10	Intraventricular hemorrhage, unspecified grade
772.11	Intraventricular hemorrhage, Grade I
772.12	Intraventricular hemorrhage, Grade II
772.5	Fetal and neonatal adrenal hemorrhage
775.1	Neonatal diabetes mellitus
775.2	Neonatal myasthenia gravis
775.3	Neonatal thyrotoxicosis
775.4	Hypocalcemia and hypomagnesemia of newborn
775.81	Other acidosis of newborn
775.89	Other neonatal endocrine and metabolic disturbances
776.0	Hemorrhagic disease of newborn
776.3	Other transient neonatal disorders of coagulation
776.5	Congenital anemia
776.6	Anemia of neonatal prematurity
777.4	Transitory ileus of newborn
778.1	Sclerema neonatorum
778.5	Other and unspecified edema of newborn
779.4	Drug reactions and intoxications specific to newborn
779.5	Drug withdrawal syndrome in newborn
780.03	Persistent vegetative state
780.1	Hallucinations
780.31	Febrile convulsions (simple), unspecified
780.32	Complex febrile convulsions
780.33	Post traumatic seizures
781.4	Transient paralysis of limb
781.6	Meningismus
781.7	Tetany
781.8	Neurological neglect syndrome
782.4	Jaundice, unspecified, not of newborn
784.3	Aphasia
785.4	Gangrene

785.50	Unspecified shock
786.04	Cheyne-Stokes respiration
786.30	Hemoptysis, unspecified
786.31	Acute idiopathic pulmonary hemorrhage in infants [AIPHI]
786.39	Other hemoptysis
788.8	Extravasation of urine
789.51	Malignant ascites
789.59	Other ascites
790.01	Precipitous drop in hematocrit
790.7	Bacteremia
791.1	Chyluria
791.3	Myoglobinuria
799.01	Asphyxia
799.4	Cachexia
800.00	Closed fracture of vault of skull without mention of intracranial injury, unspecified state of consciousness
800.01	Closed fracture of vault of skull without mention of intracranial injury, no loss of consciousness
800.02	Closed fracture of vault of skull without mention of intracranial injury, brief (less than one hour) loss of consciousness
800.06	Closed fracture of vault of skull without mention of intracranial injury, loss of consciousness of unspecified duration
800.09	Closed fracture of vault of skull without mention of intracranial injury, unspecified concussion
800.40	Closed fracture of vault of skull with intracranial injury of other and unspecified nature, unspecified state of consciousness
800.41	Closed fracture of vault of skull with intracranial injury of other and unspecified nature, no loss of consciousness
800.42	Closed fracture of vault of skull with intracranial injury of other and unspecified nature, brief (less than one hour) loss of consciousness
800.46	Closed fracture of vault of skull with intracranial injury of other and unspecified nature, loss of consciousness of unspecified duration
800.49	Closed fracture of vault of skull with intracranial injury of other and unspecified nature, unspecified concussion
801.00	Closed fracture of base of skull without mention of intracranial injury, unspecified state of consciousness
801.01	Closed fracture of base of skull without mention of intracranial injury, no loss of consciousness
801.02	Closed fracture of base of skull without mention of intracranial injury, brief (less than one hour) loss of consciousness
801.06	Closed fracture of base of skull without mention of intracranial injury, loss of consciousness of unspecified duration
801.09	Closed fracture of base of skull without mention of intracranial injury, unspecified concussion
801.40	Closed fracture of base of skull with intracranial injury of other and unspecified nature, unspecified state of consciousness
801.41	Closed fracture of base of skull with intracranial injury of other and unspecified nature, no loss of consciousness
801.42	Closed fracture of base of skull with intracranial injury of other and unspecified nature, brief (less than one hour) loss of consciousness
801.46	Closed fracture of base of skull with intracranial injury of other and unspecified nature, loss of consciousness of unspecified duration
801.49	Closed fracture of base of skull with intracranial injury of other and unspecified nature, unspecified concussion
802.1	Nasal bones, open fracture
802.20	Closed fracture of unspecified site of mandible
802.21	Closed fracture of condylar process of mandible
802.22	Closed fracture of subcondylar process of mandible
802.23	Closed fracture of coronoid process of mandible
802.24	Closed fracture of unspecified part of ramus of mandible
802.25	Closed fracture of angle of jaw
802.26	Closed fracture of symphysis of body of mandible
802.27	Closed fracture of alveolar border of body of mandible

802.28	Closed fracture of other and unspecified part of body of mandible
802.29	Closed fracture of multiple sites of mandible
802.30	Open fracture of unspecified site of mandible
802.31	Open fracture of condylar process of mandible
802.32	Open fracture of subcondylar process of mandible
802.33	Open fracture of coronoid process of mandible
802.34	Open fracture of unspecified part of ramus of mandible
802.35	Open fracture of angle of jaw
802.36	Open fracture of symphysis of body of mandible
802.37	Open fracture of alveolar border of body of mandible
802.38	Open fracture of other and unspecified part of body of mandible
802.39	Open fracture of multiple sites of mandible
802.4	Malar and maxillary bones, closed fracture
802.5	Malar and maxillary bones, open fracture
802.6	Orbital floor (blow-out), closed fracture
802.7	Orbital floor (blow-out), open fracture
802.8	Other facial bones, closed fracture
802.9	Other facial bones, open fracture
803.00	Other closed skull fracture without mention of intracranial injury, unspecified state of consciousness
803.01	Other closed skull fracture without mention of intracranial injury, no loss of consciousness
803.02	Other closed skull fracture without mention of intracranial injury, brief (less than one hour) loss of consciousness
803.06	Other closed skull fracture without mention of intracranial injury, loss of consciousness of unspecified duration
803.09	Other closed skull fracture without mention of intracranial injury, unspecified concussion
803.40	Other closed skull fracture with intracranial injury of other and unspecified nature, unspecified state of consciousness
803.41	Other closed skull fracture with intracranial injury of other and unspecified nature, no loss of consciousness
803.42	Other closed skull fracture with intracranial injury of other and unspecified nature, brief (less than one hour) loss of consciousness
803.46	Other closed skull fracture with intracranial injury of other and unspecified nature, loss of consciousness of unspecified duration
803.49	Other closed skull fracture with intracranial injury of other and unspecified nature, unspecified concussion
804.00	Closed fractures involving skull or face with other bones, without mention of intracranial injury, unspecified state of consciousness
804.01	Closed fractures involving skull or face with other bones, without mention of intracranial injury, no loss of consciousness
804.02	Closed fractures involving skull or face with other bones, without mention of intracranial injury, brief (less than one hour) loss of consciousness
804.06	Closed fractures involving skull of face with other bones, without mention of intracranial injury, loss of consciousness of unspecified duration
804.09	Closed fractures involving skull of face with other bones, without mention of intracranial injury, unspecified concussion
804.40	Closed fractures involving skull or face with other bones, with intracranial injury of other and unspecified nature, unspecified state of consciousness
804.41	Closed fractures involving skull or face with other bones, with intracranial injury of other and unspecified nature, no loss of consciousness
804.42	Closed fractures involving skull or face with other bones, with intracranial injury of other and unspecified nature, brief (less than one hour) loss of consciousness
804.46	Closed fractures involving skull or face with other bones, with intracranial injury of other and unspecified nature, loss of consciousness of unspecified duration
804.49	Closed fractures involving skull or face with other bones, with intracranial injury of other and unspecified nature, unspecified concussion
804.50	Open fractures involving skull or face with other bones, without mention of intracranial injury, unspecified state of consciousness
804.51	Open fractures involving skull or face with other bones, without mention of intracranial injury, no loss of consciousness
804.52	Open fractures involving skull or face with other bones, without mention of intracranial injury, brief (less than one hour) loss of consciousness
804.56	Open fractures involving skull or face with other bones, without mention of intracranial injury, loss of consciousness of unspecified duration
804.59	Open fractures involving skull or face with other bones, without mention of intracranial injury, unspecified concussion
804.90	Open fractures involving skull or face with other bones, with intracranial injury of other and unspecified nature, unspecified state of consciousness
804.91	Open fractures involving skull or face with other bones, with intracranial injury of other and unspecified nature, no loss of consciousness
804.92	Open fractures involving skull or face with other bones, with intracranial injury of other and unspecified nature, brief (less than one hour) loss of consciousness
804.96	Open fractures involving skull or face with other bones, with intracranial injury of other and unspecified nature, loss of consciousness of unspecified duration
804.99	Open fractures involving skull or face with other bones, with intracranial injury of other and unspecified nature, unspecified concussion
805.00	Closed fracture of cervical vertebra, unspecified level without mention of spinal cord injury
805.01	Closed fracture of first cervical vertebra without mention of spinal cord injury
805.02	Closed fracture of second cervical vertebra without mention of spinal cord injury
805.03	Closed fracture of third cervical vertebra without mention of spinal cord injury
805.04	Closed fracture of fourth cervical vertebra without mention of spinal cord injury
805.05	Closed fracture of fifth cervical vertebra without mention of spinal cord injury
805.06	Closed fracture of sixth cervical vertebra without mention of spinal cord injury
805.07	Closed fracture of seventh cervical vertebra without mention of spinal cord injury
805.08	Closed fracture of multiple cervical vertebrae without mention of spinal cord injury
805.2	Closed fracture of dorsal (thoracic) vertebra without mention of spinal cord injury
805.4	Closed fracture of lumbar vertebra without mention of spinal cord injury
805.6	Closed fracture of sacrum and coccyx without mention of spinal cord injury
805.8	Closed fracture of unspecified part of vertebral column without mention of spinal cord injury
807.00	Closed fracture of rib(s), unspecified
807.01	Closed fracture of one rib
807.02	Closed fracture of two ribs
807.03	Closed fracture of three ribs
807.04	Closed fracture of four ribs
807.05	Closed fracture of five ribs
807.06	Closed fracture of six ribs
807.07	Closed fracture of seven ribs
807.08	Closed fracture of eight or more ribs
807.09	Closed fracture of multiple ribs, unspecified
807.2	Closed fracture of sternum
808.2	Closed fracture of pubis

808.41	Closed fracture of ilium
808.42	Closed fracture of ischium
808.43	Multiple closed pelvic fractures with disruption of pelvic circle
808.44	Multiple closed pelvic fractures without disruption of pelvic circle
808.49	Closed fracture of other specified part of pelvis
808.8	Unspecified closed fracture of pelvis
809.0	Fracture of bones of trunk, closed
810.10	Unspecified part of open fracture of clavicle
810.11	Open fracture of sternal end of clavicle
810.12	Open fracture of shaft of clavicle
810.13	Open fracture of acromial end of clavicle
811.10	Open fracture of unspecified part of scapula
811.11	Open fracture of acromial process of scapula
811.12	Open fracture of coracoid process
811.13	Open fracture of glenoid cavity and neck of scapula
811.19	Open fracture of other part of scapula
812.00	Closed fracture of unspecified part of upper end of humerus
812.01	Closed fracture of surgical neck of humerus
812.02	Closed fracture of anatomical neck of humerus
812.03	Closed fracture of greater tuberosity of humerus
812.09	Other closed fractures of upper end of humerus
812.20	Closed fracture of unspecified part of humerus
812.21	Closed fracture of shaft of humerus
812.40	Closed fracture of unspecified part of lower end of humerus
812.41	Closed fracture of supracondylar humerus
812.42	Closed fracture of lateral condyle of humerus
812.43	Closed fracture of medial condyle of humerus
812.44	Closed fracture of unspecified condyle(s) of humerus
812.49	Other closed fracture of lower end of humerus
813.20	Unspecified closed fracture of shaft of radius or ulna
813.21	Closed fracture of shaft of radius (alone)
813.22	Closed fracture of shaft of ulna (alone)
813.23	Closed fracture of shaft of radius with ulna
813.40	Unspecified closed fracture of lower end of forearm
813.41	Closed Colles' fracture
813.42	Other closed fractures of distal end of radius (alone)
813.43	Closed fracture of distal end of ulna (alone)
813.44	Closed fracture of lower end of radius with ulna
813.45	Torus fracture of radius (alone)
813.46	Torus fracture of ulna (alone)
813.47	Torus fracture of radius and ulna
813.80	Closed fracture of unspecified part of forearm
813.82	Closed fracture of unspecified part of ulna (alone)
813.83	Closed fracture of unspecified part of radius with ulna
814.10	Unspecified open fracture of carpal bone
814.11	Open fracture of navicular (scaphoid) bone of wrist
814.12	Open fracture of lunate (semilunar) bone of wrist
814.13	Open fracture of triquetral (cuneiform) bone of wrist
814.14	Open fracture of pisiform bone of wrist
814.15	Open fracture of trapezium bone (larger multangular) of wrist
814.16	Open fracture of trapezoid bone (smaller multangular) of wrist
814.17	Open fracture of capitate bone (os magnum) of wrist
814.18	Open fracture of hamate (unciform) bone of wrist
814.19	Open fracture of other bone of wrist
815.10	Open fracture of metacarpal bone(s), site unspecified
815.11	Open fracture of base of thumb (first) metacarpal bone(s)
815.12	Open fracture of base of other metacarpal bone(s)
815.13	Open fracture of shaft of metacarpal bone(s)
815.14	Open fracture of neck of metacarpal bone(s)
815.19	Open fracture of multiple sites of metacarpus
816.10	Open fracture of phalanx or phalanges of hand, unspecified
816.11	Open fracture of middle or proximal phalanx or phalanges of hand
816.12	Open fracture of distal phalanx or phalanges of hand
816.13	Open fractures of multiple sites of phalanx or phalanges of hand
817.1	Multiple open fractures of hand bones
818.1	Ill-defined open fractures of upper limb
819.0	Multiple closed fractures involving both upper limbs, and upper limb with rib(s) and sternum
819.1	Multiple open fractures involving both upper limbs, and upper limb with rib(s) and sternum
821.20	Closed fracture of unspecified part of lower end of femur
821.21	Closed fracture of femoral condyle
821.22	Closed fracture of lower epiphysis of femur
821.23	Closed supracondylar fracture of femur
821.29	Other closed fracture of lower end of femur
822.0	Closed fracture of patella
822.1	Open fracture of patella
823.00	Closed fracture of upper end of tibia
823.02	Closed fracture of upper end of fibula with tibia
823.20	Closed fracture of shaft of tibia
823.22	Closed fracture of shaft of fibula with tibia
823.40	Torus fracture of tibia alone
823.42	Torus fracture of fibula with tibia
823.80	Closed fracture of unspecified part of tibia
823.82	Closed fracture of unspecified part of fibula with tibia
824.1	Open fracture of medial malleolus
824.3	Open fracture of lateral malleolus
824.5	Open bimalleolar fracture
824.7	Open trimalleolar fracture
824.9	Unspecified open fracture of ankle
825.1	Open fracture of calcaneus
825.30	Open fracture of unspecified bone(s) of foot (except toes)
825.31	Open fracture of astragalus
825.32	Open fracture of navicular (scaphoid) bone of foot
825.33	Open fracture of cuboid bone
825.34	Open fracture of cuneiform bone of foot,
825.35	Open fracture of metatarsal bone(s)
825.39	Other open fractures of tarsal and metatarsal bones
827.1	Other, multiple and ill-defined open fractures of lower limb
830.1	Open dislocation of jaw
831.10	Open unspecified dislocation of shoulder
831.11	Open anterior dislocation of humerus
831.12	Open posterior dislocation of humerus
831.13	Open inferior dislocation of humerus
831.14	Open dislocation of acromioclavicular (joint)
831.19	Open dislocation of other site of shoulder
832.10	Open unspecified dislocation of elbow
832.11	Open anterior dislocation of elbow
832.12	Open posterior dislocation of elbow
832.13	Open medial dislocation of elbow
832.14	Open lateral dislocation of elbow
832.19	Open dislocation of other site of elbow
833.10	Open dislocation of wrist, unspecified part
833.11	Open dislocation of distal radioulnar (joint)
833.12	Open dislocation of radiocarpal (joint)
833.13	Open dislocation of midcarpal (joint)
833.14	Open dislocation of carpometacarpal (joint)
833.15	Open dislocation of proximal end of metacarpal (bone)

833.19	Open dislocation of other part of wrist
835.00	Closed dislocation of hip, unspecified site
835.01	Closed posterior dislocation of hip
835.02	Closed obturator dislocation of hip
835.03	Other closed anterior dislocation of hip
836.4	Open dislocation of patella
836.60	Open dislocation of knee unspecified part
836.61	Open anterior dislocation of tibia, proximal end
836.62	Open posterior dislocation of tibia, proximal end
836.63	Open medial dislocation of tibia, proximal end
836.64	Open lateral dislocation of tibia, proximal end
836.69	Other open dislocation of knee
837.1	Open dislocation of ankle
839.00	Closed dislocation, unspecified cervical vertebra
839.01	Closed dislocation, first cervical vertebra
839.02	Closed dislocation, second cervical vertebra
839.03	Closed dislocation, third cervical vertebra
839.04	Closed dislocation, fourth cervical vertebra
839.05	Closed dislocation, fifth cervical vertebra
839.06	Closed dislocation, sixth cervical vertebra
839.07	Closed dislocation, seventh cervical vertebra
839.08	Closed dislocation, multiple cervical vertebrae
839.51	Open dislocation, coccyx
839.52	Open dislocation, sacrum
839.61	Closed dislocation, sternum
839.79	Open dislocation, other location
839.9	Open dislocation, multiple and ill-defined sites
850.11	Concussion, with loss of consciousness of 30 minutes or less
850.12	Concussion, with loss of consciousness 31 to 59 minutes
850.2	Concussion with moderate (1-24 hours) loss of consciousness
850.3	Concussion with prolonged (more than 24 hours) loss of consciousness and return to pre-existing conscious level
850.5	Concussion with loss of consciousness of unspecified duration
851.02	Cortex (cerebral) contusion without mention of open intracranial wound, brief (less than 1 hour) loss of consciousness
851.03	Cortex (cerebral) contusion without mention of open intracranial wound, moderate (1-24 hours) loss of consciousness
851.04	Cortex (cerebral) contusion without mention of open intracranial wound, prolonged (more than 24 hours) loss of consciousness and return to pre-existing conscious level
851.06	Cortex (cerebral) contusion without mention of open intracranial wound, loss of consciousness of unspecified duration
851.42	Cerebellar or brain stem contusion without mention of open intracranial wound, brief (less than 1 hour) loss of consciousness
851.43	Cerebellar or brain stem contusion without mention of open intracranial wound, moderate (1-24 hours) loss of consciousness
851.44	Cerebellar or brain stem contusion without mention of open intracranial wound, prolonged (more than 24 hours) loss consciousness and return to pre-existing conscious level
851.46	Cerebellar or brain stem contusion without mention of open intracranial wound, loss of consciousness of unspecified duration
854.02	Intracranial injury of other and unspecified nature, without mention of open intracranial wound, brief (less than 1 hour) loss of consciousness
854.03	Intracranial injury of other and unspecified nature, without mention of open intracranial wound, moderate (1-24 hours) loss of consciousness
854.04	Intracranial injury of other and unspecified nature, without mention of open intracranial wound, prolonged (more than 24 hours) loss of consciousness and return to pre-existing conscious level
854.06	Intracranial injury of other and unspecified nature, without mention of open intracranial wound, loss of consciousness of unspecified duration
860.0	Traumatic pneumothorax without mention of open wound into thorax
861.00	Unspecified injury to heart without mention of open wound into thorax
861.01	Heart contusion without mention of open wound into thorax
861.20	Unspecified lung injury without mention of open wound into thorax
861.21	Lung contusion without mention of open wound into thorax
862.0	Diaphragm injury without mention of open wound into cavity
862.29	Injury to other specified intrathoracic organs without mention of open wound into cavity
862.8	Injury to multiple and unspecified intrathoracic organs without mention of open wound into cavity
863.0	Stomach injury without mention of open wound into cavity
863.20	Small intestine injury, unspecified site, without mention of open wound into cavity
863.21	Duodenum injury without mention of open wound into cavity
863.29	Other injury to small intestine without mention of open wound into cavity
863.40	Colon injury unspecified site, without mention of open wound into cavity
863.41	Ascending (right) colon injury without mention of open wound into cavity
863.42	Transverse colon injury without mention of open wound into cavity
863.43	Descending (left) colon injury without mention of open wound into cavity
863.44	Sigmoid colon injury without mention of open wound into cavity
863.45	Rectum injury without mention of open wound into cavity
863.46	Injury to multiple sites in colon and rectum without mention of open wound into cavity
863.49	Other colon and rectum injury, without mention of open wound into cavity
863.80	Gastrointestinal tract injury, unspecified site, without mention of open wound into cavity
863.81	Pancreas head injury without mention of open wound into cavity
863.82	Pancreas body injury without mention of open wound into cavity
863.83	Pancreas tail injury without mention of open wound into cavity
863.84	Pancreas injury, multiple and unspecified sites, without mention of open wound into cavity
863.85	Appendix injury without mention of open wound into cavity
863.89	Injury to other and unspecified gastrointestinal sites without mention of open wound into cavity
864.00	Unspecified injury to liver without mention of open wound into cavity
864.01	Liver hematoma and contusion without mention of open wound into cavity
864.02	Liver laceration, minor, without mention of open wound into cavity
864.05	Liver injury without mention of open wound into cavity, unspecified laceration
864.09	Other liver injury without mention of open wound into cavity
865.00	Unspecified spleen injury without mention of open wound into cavity
865.01	Spleen hematoma, without rupture of capsule or mention of open wound into cavity
865.02	Capsular tears to spleen, without major disruption of parenchyma or mention of open wound into cavity
865.09	Other spleen injury without mention of open wound into cavity
866.00	Unspecified kidney injury without mention of open wound into cavity
866.01	Kidney hematoma without rupture of capsule or mention of open wound into cavity

866.02	Kidney laceration without mention of open wound into cavity
867.0	Bladder and urethra injury without mention of open wound into cavity
867.2	Ureter injury without mention of open wound into cavity
867.4	Uterus injury without mention of open wound into cavity
867.6	Injury to other specified pelvic organs without mention of open wound into cavity
867.8	Injury to unspecified pelvic organ without mention of open wound into cavity
868.00	Injury to unspecified intra-abdominal organ without mention of open wound into cavity
868.01	Adrenal gland injury without mention of open wound into cavity
868.02	Bile duct and gallbladder injury without mention of open wound into cavity
868.03	Peritoneum injury without mention of open wound into cavity
868.04	Retroperitoneum injury without mention of open wound into cavity
868.09	Injury to other and multiple intra-abdominal organs without mention of open wound into cavity
869.0	Internal injury to unspecified or ill-defined organs without mention of open wound into cavity
870.2	Laceration of eyelid involving lacrimal passages
870.3	Penetrating wound of orbit, without mention of foreign body
870.4	Penetrating wound of orbit with foreign body
870.8	Other specified open wound of ocular adnexa
870.9	Unspecified open wound of ocular adnexa
871.0	Ocular laceration without prolapse of intraocular tissue
871.1	Ocular laceration with prolapse or exposure of intraocular tissue
871.2	Rupture of eye with partial loss of intraocular tissue
871.3	Avulsion of eye
871.5	Penetration of eyeball with magnetic foreign body
871.6	Penetration of eyeball with (nonmagnetic) foreign body
871.9	Unspecified open wound of eyeball
872.12	Open wound of auditory canal, complicated
872.61	Open wound of ear drum, without mention of complication
872.62	Open wound of ossicles, without mention of complication
872.63	Open wound of Eustachian tube, without mention of complication
872.64	Open wound of cochlea, without mention of complication
872.69	Open wound of other and multiple sites, without mention of complication
872.71	Open wound of ear drum, complicated
872.72	Open wound of ossicles, complicated
872.73	Open wound of Eustachian tube, complicated
872.74	Open wound of cochlea, complicated
872.79	Open wound of other and multiple sites, complicated
873.23	Open wound of nasal sinus, without mention of complication
873.33	Open wound of nasal sinus, complicated
874.2	Open wound of thyroid gland, without mention of complication
874.3	Open wound of thyroid gland, complicated
874.4	Open wound of pharynx, without mention of complication
874.5	Open wound of pharynx, complicated
875.0	Open wound of chest (wall), without mention of complication
875.1	Open wound of chest (wall), complicated
880.20	Open wound of shoulder region, with tendon involvement
880.21	Open wound of scapular region, with tendon involvement
880.22	Open wound of axillary region, with tendon involvement
880.23	Open wound of upper arm, with tendon involvement
880.29	Open wound of multiple sites of shoulder and upper arm, with tendon involvement
881.20	Open wound of forearm, with tendon involvement
881.21	Open wound of elbow, with tendon involvement
881.22	Open wound of wrist, with tendon involvement
882.2	Open wound of hand except finger(s) alone, with tendon involvement
883.2	Open wound of finger(s), with tendon involvement
884.2	Multiple and unspecified open wound of upper limb, with tendon involvement
887.0	Traumatic amputation of arm and hand (complete) (partial), unilateral, below elbow, without mention of complication
887.1	Traumatic amputation of arm and hand (complete) (partial), unilateral, below elbow, complicated
887.2	Traumatic amputation of arm and hand (complete) (partial), unilateral, at or above elbow, without mention of complication
887.3	Traumatic amputation of arm and hand (complete) (partial), unilateral, at or above elbow, complicated
887.4	Traumatic amputation of arm and hand (complete) (partial), unilateral, level not specified, without mention of complication
887.5	Traumatic amputation of arm and hand (complete) (partial), unilateral, level not specified, complicated
890.2	Open wound of hip and thigh, with tendon involvement
891.2	Open wound of knee, leg (except thigh), and ankle, with tendon involvement
892.2	Open wound of foot except toe(s) alone, with tendon involvement
893.2	Open wound of toe(s), with tendon involvement
894.2	Multiple and unspecified open wound of lower limb, with tendon involvement
896.0	Traumatic amputation of foot (complete) (partial), unilateral, without mention of complication
896.1	Traumatic amputation of foot (complete) (partial), unilateral, complicated
897.0	Traumatic amputation of leg(s) (complete) (partial), unilateral, below knee, without mention of complication
897.1	Traumatic amputation of leg(s) (complete) (partial), unilateral, below knee, complicated
897.2	Traumatic amputation of leg(s) (complete) (partial), unilateral, at or above knee, without mention of complication
897.3	Traumatic amputation of leg(s) (complete) (partial), unilateral, at or above knee, complicated
897.4	Traumatic amputation of leg(s) (complete) (partial), unilateral, level not specified, without mention of complication
897.5	Traumatic amputation of leg(s) (complete) (partial), unilateral, level not specified, complicated
900.00	Injury to carotid artery, unspecified
900.01	Common carotid artery injury
900.02	External carotid artery injury
900.03	Internal carotid artery injury
900.1	Internal jugular vein injury
900.81	External jugular vein injury
900.82	Injury to multiple blood vessels of head and neck
900.89	Injury to other specified blood vessels of head and neck
900.9	Injury to unspecified blood vessel of head and neck
901.81	Intercostal artery or vein injury
901.82	Internal mammary artery or vein injury
901.89	Injury to specified blood vessels of thorax, other
901.9	Injury to unspecified blood vessel of thorax
902.55	Uterine artery injury
902.56	Uterine vein injury
902.81	Ovarian artery injury
902.82	Ovarian vein injury
902.89	Injury to specified blood vessels of abdomen and pelvis, other
902.9	Injury to blood vessel of abdomen and pelvis, unspecified
903.1	Brachial blood vessels injury
903.2	Radial blood vessels injury
903.3	Ulnar blood vessels injury

903.4	Palmar artery injury
903.5	Digital blood vessels injury
903.8	Injury to specified blood vessels of upper extremity, other
903.9	Injury to unspecified blood vessel of upper extremity
904.3	Saphenous vein injury
904.50	Unspecified tibial vessel(s) injury
904.51	Anterior tibial artery injury
904.52	Anterior tibial vein injury
904.53	Posterior tibial artery injury
904.54	Posterior tibial vein injury
904.6	Deep plantar blood vessels injury
904.7	Injury to specified blood vessels of lower extremity, other
904.8	Injury to unspecified blood vessel of lower extremity
904.9	Injury to blood vessels, unspecified site
925.1	Crushing injury of face and scalp
925.2	Crushing injury of neck
928.00	Crushing injury of thigh
928.01	Crushing injury of hip
934.0	Foreign body in trachea
934.1	Foreign body in main bronchus
934.8	Foreign body in other specified parts of trachea, bronchus, and lung
940.5	Burn with resulting rupture and destruction of eyeball
941.30	Full-thickness skin loss due to burn (third degree NOS) of unspecified site of face and head
941.31	Full-thickness skin loss due to burn (third degree NOS) of ear (any part)
941.32	Full-thickness skin loss due to burn (third degree NOS) of eye (with other parts of face, head, and neck)
941.33	Full-thickness skin loss due to burn (third degree NOS) of lip(s)
941.34	Full-thickness skin loss due to burn (third degree NOS) of chin
941.35	Full-thickness skin loss due to burn (third degree NOS) of nose (septum)
941.36	Full-thickness skin loss due to burn (third degree NOS) of scalp (any part)
941.37	Full-thickness skin loss due to burn (third degree NOS) of forehead and cheek
941.38	Full-thickness skin loss due to burn (third degree NOS) of neck
941.39	Full-thickness skin loss due to burn (third degree NOS) of multiple sites (except with eye) of face, head, and neck
941.40	Deep necrosis of underlying tissues due to burn (deep third degree) of unspecified site of face and head, without mention of loss of a body part
941.41	Deep necrosis of underlying tissues due to burn (deep third degree) of ear (any part), without mention of loss of a body part
941.42	Deep necrosis of underlying tissues due to burn (deep third degree) of eye (with other parts of face, head, and neck), without mention of loss of a body part
941.43	Deep necrosis of underlying tissues due to burn (deep third degree) of lip(s), without mention of loss of a body part
941.44	Deep necrosis of underlying tissues due to burn (deep third degree) of chin, without mention of loss of a body part
941.45	Deep necrosis of underlying tissues due to burn (deep third degree) of nose (septum), without mention of loss of a body part
941.46	Deep necrosis of underlying tissues due to burn (deep third degree) of scalp (any part), without mention of loss of a body part
941.47	Deep necrosis of underlying tissues due to burn (deep third degree) of forehead and cheek, without mention of loss of a body part
941.48	Deep necrosis of underlying tissues due to burn (deep third degree) of neck, without mention of loss of a body part
941.49	Deep necrosis of underlying tissues due to burn (deep third degree) of multiple sites (except with eye) of face, head, and neck, without mention of loss of a body part
941.50	Deep necrosis of underlying tissues due to burn (deep third degree) of face and head, unspecified site, with loss of a body part
941.51	Deep necrosis of underlying tissues due to burn (deep third degree) of ear (any part), with loss of a body part
941.52	Deep necrosis of underlying tissues due to burn (deep third degree) of eye (with other parts of face, head, and neck), with loss of a body part
941.53	Deep necrosis of underlying tissues due to burn (deep third degree) of lip(s), with loss of a body part
941.54	Deep necrosis of underlying tissues due to burn (deep third degree) of chin, with loss of a body part
941.55	Deep necrosis of underlying tissues due to burn (deep third degree) of nose (septum), with loss of a body part
941.56	Deep necrosis of underlying tissues due to burn (deep third degree) of scalp (any part), with loss of a body part
941.57	Deep necrosis of underlying tissues due to burn (deep third degree) of forehead and cheek, with loss of a body part
941.58	Deep necrosis of underlying tissues due to burn (deep third degree) of neck, with loss of a body part
941.59	Deep necrosis of underlying tissues due to burn (deep third degree) of multiple sites (except eye) of face, head, and neck, with loss of a body part
942.30	Full-thickness skin loss due to burn (third degree NOS) of unspecified site of trunk
942.31	Full-thickness skin loss due to burn (third degree NOS) of breast
942.32	Full-thickness skin loss due to burn (third degree NOS) of chest wall, excluding breast and nipple
942.33	Full-thickness skin loss due to burn (third degree NOS) of abdominal wall
942.34	Full-thickness skin loss due to burn (third degree NOS) of back (any part)
942.35	Full-thickness skin loss due to burn (third degree NOS) of genitalia
942.39	Full-thickness skin loss due to burn (third degree NOS) of other and multiple sites of trunk
942.40	Deep necrosis of underlying tissues due to burn (deep third degree) of trunk, unspecified site, without mention of loss of a body part
942.41	Deep necrosis of underlying tissues due to burn (deep third degree) of breast, without mention of loss of a body part
942.42	Deep necrosis of underlying tissues due to burn (deep third degree) of chest wall, excluding breast and nipple, without mention of loss of a body part
942.43	Deep necrosis of underlying tissues due to burn (deep third degree) of abdominal wall, without mention of loss of a body part
942.44	Deep necrosis of underlying tissues due to burn (deep third degree) of back (any part), without mention of loss of a body part
942.45	Deep necrosis of underlying tissues due to burn (deep third degree) of genitalia, without mention of loss of a body part
942.49	Deep necrosis of underlying tissues due to burn (deep third degree) of other and multiple sites of trunk, without mention of loss of a body part
942.50	Deep necrosis of underlying tissues due to burn (deep third degree) of unspecified site of trunk, with loss of a body part
942.51	Deep necrosis of underlying tissues due to burn (deep third degree) of breast, with loss of a body part
942.52	Deep necrosis of underlying tissues due to burn (deep third degree) of chest wall, excluding breast and nipple, with loss of a body part
942.53	Deep necrosis of underlying tissues due to burn (deep third degree) of abdominal wall with loss of a body part
942.54	Deep necrosis of underlying tissues due to burn (deep third degree) of back (any part), with loss of a body part
942.55	Deep necrosis of underlying tissues due to burn (deep third degree) of genitalia, with loss of a body part
942.59	Deep necrosis of underlying tissues due to burn (deep third degree) of other and multiple sites of trunk, with loss of a body part
943.30	Full-thickness skin loss due to burn (third degree NOS) of unspecified site of upper limb

943.31   Full-thickness skin loss due to burn (third degree NOS) of forearm

943.32   Full-thickness skin loss due to burn (third degree NOS) of elbow

943.33   Full-thickness skin loss due to burn (third degree NOS) of upper arm

943.34   Full-thickness skin loss due to burn (third degree NOS) of axilla

943.35   Full-thickness skin loss due to burn (third degree NOS) of shoulder

943.36   Full-thickness skin loss due to burn (third degree NOS) of scapular region

943.39   Full-thickness skin loss due to burn (third degree NOS) of multiple sites of upper limb, except wrist and hard

943.40   Deep necrosis of underlying tissues due to burn (deep third degree) of unspecified site of upper limb, without mention of loss of a body part

943.41   Deep necrosis of underlying tissues due to burn (deep third degree) of forearm, without mention of loss of a body part

943.42   Deep necrosis of underlying tissues due to burn (deep third degree) of elbow, without mention of loss of a body part

943.43   Deep necrosis of underlying tissues due to burn (deep third degree) of upper arm, without mention of loss of a body part

943.44   Deep necrosis of underlying tissues due to burn (deep third degree) of axilla, without mention of loss of a body part

943.45   Deep necrosis of underlying tissues due to burn (deep third degree) of shoulder, without mention of loss of a body part

943.46   Deep necrosis of underlying tissues due to burn (deep third degree) of scapular region, without mention of loss of a body part

943.49   Deep necrosis of underlying tissues due to burn (deep third degree) of multiple sites of upper limb, except wrist and hand, without mention of loss of a body part

943.50   Deep necrosis of underlying tissues due to burn (deep third degree) of unspecified site of upper limb, with loss of a body part

943.51   Deep necrosis of underlying tissues due to burn (deep third degree) of forearm, with loss of a body part

943.52   Deep necrosis of underlying tissues due to burn (deep third degree) of elbow, with loss of a body part

943.53   Deep necrosis of underlying tissues due to burn (deep third degree) of upper arm, with loss of upper a body part

943.54   Deep necrosis of underlying tissues due to burn (deep third degree) of axilla, with loss of a body part

943.55   Deep necrosis of underlying tissues due to burn (deep third degree) of shoulder, with loss of a body part

943.56   Deep necrosis of underlying tissues due to burn (deep third degree) of scapular region, with loss of a body part

943.59   Deep necrosis of underlying tissues due to burn (deep third degree) of multiple sites of upper limb, except wrist and hand, with loss of a body part

944.30   Full-thickness skin loss due to burn (third degree NOS) of unspecified site of hand

944.31   Full-thickness skin loss due to burn (third degree NOS) of single digit [finger (nail)] other than thumb

944.32   Full-thickness skin loss due to burn (third degree NOS) of thumb (nail)

944.33   Full-thickness skin loss due to burn (third degree NOS) of two or more digits of hand, not including thumb

944.34   Full-thickness skin loss due to burn (third degree NOS) of two or more digits of hand including thumb

944.35   Full-thickness skin loss due to burn (third degree NOS) of palm of hand

944.36   Full-thickness skin loss due to burn (third degree NOS) of back of hand

944.37   Full-thickness skin loss due to burn (third degree NOS) of wrist

944.38   Full-thickness skin loss due to burn (third degree NOS) of multiple sites of wrist(s) and hand(s)

944.40   Deep necrosis of underlying tissues due to burn (deep third degree) of unspecified site of hand, without mention of loss of a body part

944.41   Deep necrosis of underlying tissues due to burn (deep third degree) of single digit [finger (nail)] other than thumb, without mention of loss of a body part

944.42   Deep necrosis of underlying tissues due to burn (deep third degree) of thumb (nail), without mention of loss of a body part

944.43   Deep necrosis of underlying tissues due to burn (deep third degree) of two or more digits of hand, not including thumb, without mention of loss of a body part

944.44   Deep necrosis of underlying tissues due to burn (deep third degree) of two or more digits of hand including thumb, without mention of loss of a body part

944.45   Deep necrosis of underlying tissues due to burn (deep third degree) of palm of hand, without mention of loss of a body part

944.46   Deep necrosis of underlying tissues due to burn (deep third degree) of back of hand, without mention of loss of a body part

944.47   Deep necrosis of underlying tissues due to burn (deep third degree) of wrist, without mention of loss of a body part

944.48   Deep necrosis of underlying tissues due to burn (deep third degree) of multiple sites of wrist(s) and hand(s), without mention of loss of a body part

944.50   Deep necrosis of underlying tissues due to burn (deep third degree) of unspecified site of hand, with loss of a body part

944.51   Deep necrosis of underlying tissues due to burn (deep third degree) of single digit (finger (nail)) other than thumb, with loss of a body part

944.52   Deep necrosis of underlying tissues due to burn (deep third degree) of thumb (nail), with loss of a body part

944.53   Deep necrosis of underlying tissues due to burn (deep third degree) of two or more digits of hand, not including thumb, with loss of a body part

944.54   Deep necrosis of underlying tissues due to burn (deep third degree) of two or more digits of hand including thumb, with loss of a body part

944.55   Deep necrosis of underlying tissues due to burn (deep third degree) of palm of hand, with loss of a body part

944.56   Deep necrosis of underlying tissues due to burn (deep third degree) of back of hand, with loss of a body part

944.57   Deep necrosis of underlying tissues due to burn (deep third degree) of wrist, with loss of a body part

944.58   Deep necrosis of underlying tissues due to burn (deep third degree) of multiple sites of wrist(s) and hand(s), with loss of a body part

945.30   Full-thickness skin loss due to burn (third degree NOS) of unspecified site of lower limb

945.31   Full-thickness skin loss due to burn (third degree NOS) of toe(s) (nail)

945.32   Full-thickness skin loss due to burn (third degree NOS) of foot

945.33   Full-thickness skin loss due to burn (third degree NOS) of ankle

945.34   Full-thickness skin loss due to burn (third degree NOS) of lower leg

945.35   Full-thickness skin loss due to burn (third degree NOS) of knee

945.36   Full-thickness skin loss due to burn (third degree NOS) of thigh (any part)

945.39   Full-thickness skin loss due to burn (third degree NOS) of multiple sites of lower limb(s)

945.40   Deep necrosis of underlying tissues due to burn (deep third degree) of unspecified site of lower limb (leg), without mention of loss of a body part

945.41   Deep necrosis of underlying tissues due to burn (deep third degree) of toe(s) (nail), without mention of loss of a body part

945.42   Deep necrosis of underlying tissues due to burn (deep third degree) of foot, without mention of loss of a body part

945.43   Deep necrosis of underlying tissues due to burn (deep third degree) of ankle, without mention of loss of a body part

945.44   Deep necrosis of underlying tissues due to burn (deep third degree) of lower leg, without mention of loss of a body part

945.45   Deep necrosis of underlying tissues due to burn (deep third degree) of knee, without mention of loss of a body part

945.46   Deep necrosis of underlying tissues due to burn (deep third degree) of thigh (any part), without mention of loss of a body part

945.49	Deep necrosis of underlying tissues due to burn (deep third degree) of multiple sites of lower limb(s), without mention of loss of a body part	951.4	Injury to facial nerve
		951.5	Injury to acoustic nerve
945.50	Deep necrosis of underlying tissues due to burn (deep third degree) of unspecified site lower limb (leg), with loss of a body part	951.6	Injury to accessory nerve
		951.7	Injury to hypoglossal nerve
		951.8	Injury to other specified cranial nerves
945.51	Deep necrosis of underlying tissues due to burn (deep third degree) of toe(s) (nail), with loss of a body part	951.9	Injury to unspecified cranial nerve
		958.2	Secondary and recurrent hemorrhage as an early complication of trauma
945.52	Deep necrosis of underlying tissues due to burn (deep third degree) of foot, with loss of a body part		
		958.3	Posttraumatic wound infection not elsewhere classified
945.53	Deep necrosis of underlying tissues due to burn (deep third degree) of ankle, with loss of a body part	958.7	Traumatic subcutaneous emphysema
		958.90	Compartment syndrome, unspecified
945.54	Deep necrosis of underlying tissues due to burn (deep third degree) of lower leg, with loss of a body part	958.91	Traumatic compartment syndrome of upper extremity
		958.92	Traumatic compartment syndrome of lower extremity
945.55	Deep necrosis of underlying tissues due to burn (deep third degree) of knee, with loss of a body part	958.93	Traumatic compartment syndrome of abdomen
		958.99	Traumatic compartment syndrome of other sites
945.56	Deep necrosis of underlying tissues due to burn (deep third degree) of thigh (any part), with loss of a body part	991.0	Frostbite of face
		991.1	Frostbite of hand
945.59	Deep necrosis of underlying tissues due to burn (deep third degree) of multiple sites of lower limb(s), with loss of a body part	991.2	Frostbite of foot
		991.3	Frostbite of other and unspecified sites
		991.4	Effects of immersion of foot
946.3	Full-thickness skin loss due to burn (third degree NOS) of multiple specified sites	992.0	Heat stroke and sunstroke
		993.3	Caisson disease
946.4	Deep necrosis of underlying tissues due to burn (deep third degree) of multiple specified sites, without mention of loss of a body part	994.1	Drowning and nonfatal submersion
		994.7	Asphyxiation and strangulation
		995.0	Other anaphylactic reaction
946.5	Deep necrosis of underlying tissues due to burn (deep third degree) of multiple specified sites, with loss of a body part	995.4	Shock due to anesthesia not elsewhere classified
		995.50	Child abuse, unspecified
947.1	Burn of larynx, trachea, and lung	995.51	Child emotional/psychological abuse
947.2	Burn of esophagus	995.52	Child neglect (nutritional)
947.3	Burn of gastrointestinal tract	995.53	Child sexual abuse
947.4	Burn of vagina and uterus	995.54	Child physical abuse
948.10	Burn (any degree) involving 10-19% of body surface with third degree burn of less than 10% or unspecified amount	995.55	Shaken infant syndrome
		995.59	Other child abuse and neglect
		995.60	Anaphylactic reaction due to unspecified food
948.11	Burn (any degree) involving 10-19% of body surface with third degree burn of 10-19%	995.61	Anaphylactic reaction due to peanuts
		995.62	Anaphylactic reaction due to crustaceans
948.20	Burn (any degree) involving 20-29% of body surface with third degree burn of less than 10% or unspecified amount	995.63	Anaphylactic reaction due to fruits and vegetables
		995.64	Anaphylactic reaction due to tree nuts and seeds
948.30	Burn (any degree) involving 30-39% of body surface with third degree burn of less than 10% or unspecified amount	995.65	Anaphylactic reaction due to fish
		995.66	Anaphylactic reaction due to food additives
948.40	Burn (any degree) involving 40-49% of body surface with third degree burn of less than 10% or unspecified amount	995.67	Anaphylactic reaction due to milk products
		995.68	Anaphylactic reaction due to eggs
948.50	Burn (any degree) involving 50-59% of body surface with third degree burn of less than 10% or unspecified amount	995.69	Anaphylactic reaction due to other specified food
		995.80	Adult maltreatment, unspecified
948.60	Burn (any degree) involving 60-69% of body surface with third degree burn of less than 10% or unspecified amount	995.81	Adult physical abuse
		995.83	Adult sexual abuse
948.70	Burn (any degree) involving 70-79% of body surface with third degree burn of less than 10% or unspecified amount	995.84	Adult neglect (nutritional)
		995.85	Other adult abuse and neglect
948.80	Burn (any degree) involving 80-89% of body surface with third degree burn of less than 10% or unspecified amount	995.86	Malignant hyperthermia
		995.90	Systemic inflammatory response syndrome, unspecified
948.90	Burn (any degree) involving 90% or more of body surface with third degree burn of less than 10% or unspecified amount	995.93	Systemic inflammatory response syndrome due to noninfectious process without acute organ dysfunction
949.3	Full-thickness skin loss due to burn (third degree NOS), unspecified site	996.00	Mechanical complication of unspecified cardiac device, implant, and graft
949.4	Deep necrosis of underlying tissue due to burn (deep third degree), unspecified site without mention of loss of body part		
		996.01	Mechanical complication due to cardiac pacemaker (electrode)
949.5	Deep necrosis of underlying tissues due to burn (deep third degree, unspecified site with loss of body part	996.02	Mechanical complication due to heart valve prosthesis
		996.03	Mechanical complication due to coronary bypass graft
950.0	Optic nerve injury	996.04	Mechanical complication due to automatic implantable cardiac defibrillator
950.1	Injury to optic chiasm		
950.2	Injury to optic pathways		
950.3	Injury to visual cortex		
950.9	Injury to unspecified optic nerve and pathways		
951.0	Injury to oculomotor nerve		
951.1	Injury to trochlear nerve		
951.2	Injury to trigeminal nerve		
951.3	Injury to abducens nerve		

Appendix A — Numeric CC List

996.09	Mechanical complication of cardiac device, implant, and graft, other
996.1	Mechanical complication of other vascular device, implant, and graft
996.2	Mechanical complication of nervous system device, implant, and graft
996.30	Mechanical complication of unspecified genitourinary device, implant, and graft
996.39	Mechanical complication of genitourinary device, implant, and graft, other
996.40	Unspecified mechanical complication of internal orthopedic device, implant, and graft
996.41	Mechanical loosening of prosthetic joint
996.42	Dislocation of prosthetic joint
996.43	Broken prosthetic joint implant
996.44	Peri-prosthetic fracture around prosthetic joint
996.45	Peri-prosthetic osteolysis
996.46	Articular bearing surface wear of prosthetic joint
996.47	Other mechanical complication of prosthetic joint implant
996.49	Other mechanical complication of other internal orthopedic device, implant, and graft
996.51	Mechanical complication due to corneal graft
996.52	Mechanical complication due to other tissue graft, not elsewhere classified
996.53	Mechanical complication due to ocular lens prosthesis
996.54	Mechanical complication due to breast prosthesis
996.55	Mechanical complications due to artificial skin graft and decellularized allodermis
996.56	Mechanical complications due to peritoneal dialysis catheter
996.57	Mechanical complication due to insulin pump
996.59	Mechanical complication due to other implant and internal device, not elsewhere classified
996.60	Infection and inflammatory reaction due to unspecified device, implant, and graft
996.61	Infection and inflammatory reaction due to cardiac device, implant, and graft
996.62	Infection and inflammatory reaction due to other vascular device, implant, and graft
996.63	Infection and inflammatory reaction due to nervous system device, implant, and graft
996.64	Infection and inflammatory reaction due to indwelling urinary catheter
996.65	Infection and inflammatory reaction due to other genitourinary device, implant, and graft
996.66	Infection and inflammatory reaction due to internal joint prosthesis
996.67	Infection and inflammatory reaction due to other internal orthopedic device, implant, and graft
996.68	Infection and inflammatory reaction due to peritoneal dialysis catheter
996.69	Infection and inflammatory reaction due to other internal prosthetic device, implant, and graft
996.71	Other complications due to heart valve prosthesis
996.72	Other complications due to other cardiac device, implant, and graft
996.73	Other complications due to renal dialysis device, implant, and graft
996.74	Other complications due to other vascular device, implant, and graft
996.75	Other complications due to nervous system device, implant, and graft
996.76	Other complications due to genitourinary device, implant, and graft
996.77	Other complications due to internal joint prosthesis
996.78	Other complications due to other internal orthopedic device, implant, and graft
996.79	Other complications due to other internal prosthetic device, implant, and graft
996.80	Complications of transplanted organ, unspecified site
996.81	Complications of transplanted kidney
996.82	Complications of transplanted liver
996.83	Complications of transplanted heart
996.84	Complications of transplanted lung
996.85	Complications of bone marrow transplant
996.86	Complications of transplanted pancreas
996.87	Complications of transplanted organ, intestine
996.88	Complications of transplanted organ, stem cell
996.89	Complications of other transplanted organ
996.90	Complications of unspecified reattached extremity
996.91	Complications of reattached forearm
996.92	Complications of reattached hand
996.93	Complications of reattached finger(s)
996.94	Complications of reattached upper extremity, other and unspecified
996.95	Complications of reattached foot and toe(s)
996.96	Complications of reattached lower extremity, other and unspecified
996.99	Complications of other specified reattached body part
997.01	Central nervous system complication
997.02	Iatrogenic cerebrovascular infarction or hemorrhage
997.09	Other nervous system complications
997.1	Cardiac complications
997.2	Peripheral vascular complications
997.31	Ventilator associated pneumonia
997.32	Postprocedural aspiration pneumonia
997.39	Other respiratory complications
997.41	Retained cholelithiasis following cholecystectomy
997.49	Other digestive system complications
997.62	Infection (chronic) of amputation stump
997.71	Vascular complications of mesenteric artery
997.72	Vascular complications of renal artery
997.79	Vascular complications of other vessels
997.99	Other complications affecting other specified body systems, NEC
998.00	Postoperative shock, unspecified
998.11	Hemorrhage complicating a procedure
998.12	Hematoma complicating a procedure
998.13	Seroma complicating a procedure
998.2	Accidental puncture or laceration during procedure
998.30	Disruption of wound, unspecified
998.31	Disruption of internal operation (surgical) wound
998.32	Disruption of external operation (surgical) wound
998.33	Disruption of traumatic injury wound repair
998.4	Foreign body accidentally left during procedure, not elsewhere classified
998.51	Infected postoperative seroma
998.59	Other postoperative infection
998.6	Persistent postoperative fistula, not elsewhere classified
998.7	Acute reaction to foreign substance accidentally left during procedure, not elsewhere classified
998.83	Non-healing surgical wound
999.0	Generalized vaccinia as complication of medical care, not elsewhere classified
999.2	Other vascular complications of medical care, not elsewhere classified
999.31	Other and unspecified infection due to central venous catheter
999.32	Bloodstream infection due to central venous catheter
999.33	Local infection due to central venous catheter
999.34	Acute infection following transfusion, infusion, or injection of blood and blood products

999.39   Complications of medical care, NEC, infection following other infusion, injection, transfusion, or vaccination

999.41   Anaphylactic reaction due to administration of blood and blood products

999.42   Anaphylactic reaction due to vaccination

999.49   Anaphylactic reaction due to other serum

999.51   Other serum reaction due to administration of blood and blood products

999.52   Other serum reaction due to vaccination

999.59   Other serum reaction

999.60   ABO incompatibility reaction, unspecified

999.61   ABO incompatibility with hemolytic transfusion reaction not specified as acute or delayed

999.62   ABO incompatibility with acute hemolytic transfusion reaction

999.63   ABO incompatibility with delayed hemolytic transfusion reaction

999.69   Other ABO incompatibility reaction

999.70   Rh incompatibility reaction, unspecified

999.71   Rh incompatibility with hemolytic transfusion reaction not specified as acute or delayed

999.72   Rh incompatibility with acute hemolytic transfusion reaction

999.73   Rh incompatibility with delayed hemolytic transfusion reaction

999.74   Other Rh incompatibility reaction

999.75   Non-ABO incompatibility reaction, unspecified

999.76   Non-ABO incompatibility with hemolytic transfusion reaction not specified as acute or delayed

999.77   Non-ABO incompatibility with acute hemolytic transfusion reaction

999.78   Non-ABO incompatibility with delayed hemolytic transfusion reaction

999.79   Other non-ABO incompatibility reaction

999.81   Extravasation of vesicant chemotherapy

999.82   Extravasation of other vesicant agent

999.83   Hemolytic transfusion reaction, incompatibility unspecified

999.84   Acute hemolytic transfusion reaction, incompatibility unspecified

999.85   Delayed hemolytic transfusion reaction, incompatibility unspecified

V42.0   Kidney replaced by transplant

V42.1   Heart replaced by transplant

V42.6   Lung replaced by transplant

V42.7   Liver replaced by transplant

V42.81   Bone marrow replaced by transplant

V42.82   Peripheral stem cells replaced by transplant

V42.83   Pancreas replaced by transplant

V42.84   Organ or tissue replaced by transplant, intestines

V43.21   Organ or tissue replaced by other means, Heart assist device

V43.22   Organ or tissue replaced by other means, Fully implantable artificial heart

V46.11   Dependence on respirator, status

V46.12   Encounter for respirator dependence during power failure

V46.13   Encounter for weaning from respirator [ventilator]

V46.14   Mechanical complication of respirator [ventilator]

V55.1   Attention to gastrostomy

V62.84   Suicidal ideation

V85.0   Body Mass Index less than 19, adult

V85.41   Body Mass Index 40.0-44.9, adult

V85.42   Body Mass Index 45.0-49.9, adult

V85.43   Body Mass Index 50.0-59.9, adult

V85.44   Body Mass Index 60.0-69.9, adult

V85.45   Body Mass Index 70 and over, adult

Appendix A — Numeric CC List

Alphabetic CC List

039.2	Abdominal actinomycotic infection
633.01	Abdominal pregnancy with intrauterine pregnancy
633.00	Abdominal pregnancy without intrauterine pregnancy
999.60	ABO incompatibility reaction, unspecified
999.62	ABO incompatibility with acute hemolytic transfusion reaction
999.63	ABO incompatibility with delayed hemolytic transfusion reaction
999.61	ABO incompatibility with hemolytic transfusion reaction not specified as acute or delayed
637.40	Abortion, unspecified as to completeness or legality, complicated by metabolic disorder
637.20	Abortion, unspecified as to completion or legality, complicated by damage to pelvic organs or tissues
637.00	Abortion, unspecified as to completion or legality, complicated by genital tract and pelvic infection
637.70	Abortion, unspecified as to completion or legality, with other specified complications
637.80	Abortion, unspecified as to completion or legality, with unspecified complication
637.22	Abortion, unspecified as to legality, complete, complicated by damage to pelvic organs or tissues
637.02	Abortion, unspecified as to legality, complete, complicated by genital tract and pelvic infection
637.42	Abortion, unspecified as to legality, complete, complicated by metabolic disorder
637.72	Abortion, unspecified as to legality, complete, with other specified complications
637.82	Abortion, unspecified as to legality, complete, with unspecified complication
637.21	Abortion, unspecified as to legality, incomplete, complicated by damage to pelvic organs or tissues
637.01	Abortion, unspecified as to legality, incomplete, complicated by genital tract and pelvic infection
637.41	Abortion, unspecified as to legality, incomplete, complicated by metabolic disorder
637.71	Abortion, unspecified as to legality, incomplete, with other specified complications
637.81	Abortion, unspecified as to legality, incomplete, with unspecified complication
566	Abscess of anal and rectal regions
616.3	Abscess of Bartholin's gland
675.12	Abscess of breast associated with childbirth, delivered, with mention of postpartum complication
675.11	Abscess of breast associated with childbirth, delivered, with or without mention of antepartum condition
569.5	Abscess of intestine
601.2	Abscess of prostate
527.3	Abscess of salivary gland
254.1	Abscess of thymus
998.2	Accidental puncture or laceration during procedure
349.31	Accidental puncture or laceration of dura during a procedure
276.2	Acidosis
429.71	Acquired cardiac septal defect
286.7	Acquired coagulation factor deficiency
283.9	Acquired hemolytic anemia, unspecified
286.52	Acquired hemophilia
537.0	Acquired hypertrophic pyloric stenosis
039.8	Actinomycotic infection of other specified sites
039.9	Actinomycotic infection of unspecified site
341.21	Acute (transverse) myelitis in conditions classified elsewhere
341.20	Acute (transverse) myelitis NOS
006.0	Acute amebic dysentery without mention of abscess

575.12	Acute and chronic cholecystitis
365.22	Acute angle-closure glaucoma
522.4	Acute apical periodontitis of pulpal origin
540.9	Acute appendicitis without mention of peritonitis
466.19	Acute bronchiolitis due to other infectious organisms
466.11	Acute bronchiolitis due to respiratory syncytial virus (RSV)
517.3	Acute chest syndrome
575.0	Acute cholecystitis
411.81	Acute coronary occlusion without myocardial infarction
595.0	Acute cystitis
536.1	Acute dilatation of stomach
532.30	Acute duodenal ulcer without mention of hemorrhage, perforation, or obstruction
333.72	Acute dystonia due to drugs
360.01	Acute endophthalmitis
464.30	Acute epiglottitis without mention of obstruction
207.01	Acute erythremia and erythroleukemia in remission
207.02	Acute erythremia and erythroleukemia, in relapse
207.00	Acute erythremia and erythroleukemia, without mention of having achieved remission
530.12	Acute esophagitis
446.1	Acute febrile mucocutaneous lymph node syndrome (MCLS)
531.30	Acute gastric ulcer without mention of hemorrhage, perforation, or obstruction
534.30	Acute gastrojejunal ulcer without mention of hemorrhage, perforation, or obstruction
279.51	Acute graft-versus-host disease
999.84	Acute hemolytic transfusion reaction, incompatibility unspecified
070.51	Acute hepatitis C without mention of hepatic coma
420.91	Acute idiopathic pericarditis
786.31	Acute idiopathic pulmonary hemorrhage in infants [AIPHI]
999.34	Acute infection following transfusion, infusion, or injection of blood and blood products
357.0	Acute infective polyneuritis
615.0	Acute inflammatory disease of uterus, except cervix
516.33	Acute interstitial pneumonitis
584.8	Acute kidney failure with other specified pathological lesion in kidney
584.9	Acute kidney failure, unspecified
208.01	Acute leukemia of unspecified cell type in remission
208.02	Acute leukemia of unspecified cell type, in relapse
208.00	Acute leukemia of unspecified cell type, without mention of having achieved remission
204.01	Acute lymphoid leukemia in remission
204.02	Acute lymphoid leukemia, in relapse
204.00	Acute lymphoid leukemia, without mention of having achieved remission
383.02	Acute mastoiditis with other complications
383.00	Acute mastoiditis without complications
206.01	Acute monocytic leukemia in remission
206.02	Acute monocytic leukemia, in relapse
206.00	Acute monocytic leukemia, without mention of having achieved remission
205.01	Acute myeloid leukemia in remission
205.02	Acute myeloid leukemia, in relapse
205.00	Acute myeloid leukemia, without mention of having achieved remission
279.53	Acute on chronic graft-versus-host disease
730.07	Acute osteomyelitis, ankle and foot
730.03	Acute osteomyelitis, forearm
730.04	Acute osteomyelitis, hand

730.06	Acute osteomyelitis, lower leg
730.09	Acute osteomyelitis, multiple sites
730.08	Acute osteomyelitis, other specified site
730.05	Acute osteomyelitis, pelvic region and thigh
730.01	Acute osteomyelitis, shoulder region
730.00	Acute osteomyelitis, site unspecified
730.02	Acute osteomyelitis, upper arm
614.3	Acute parametritis and pelvic cellulitis
298.3	Acute paranoid reaction
533.30	Acute peptic ulcer, unspecified site, without mention of hemorrhage, perforation, or obstruction
420.0	Acute pericarditis in diseases classified elsewhere
285.1	Acute posthemorrhagic anemia
601.0	Acute prostatitis
508.0	Acute pulmonary manifestations due to radiation
590.10	Acute pyelonephritis without lesion of renal medullary necrosis
998.7	Acute reaction to foreign substance accidentally left during procedure, not elsewhere classified
391.1	Acute rheumatic endocarditis
391.2	Acute rheumatic myocarditis
391.0	Acute rheumatic pericarditis
614.0	Acute salpingitis and oophoritis
245.0	Acute thyroiditis
453.84	Acute venous embolism and thrombosis of axillary veins
453.82	Acute venous embolism and thrombosis of deep veins of upper extremity
453.42	Acute venous embolism and thrombosis of deep vessels of distal lower extremity
453.41	Acute venous embolism and thrombosis of deep vessels of proximal lower extremity
453.86	Acute venous embolism and thrombosis of internal jugular veins
453.89	Acute venous embolism and thrombosis of other specified veins
453.87	Acute venous embolism and thrombosis of other thoracic veins
453.85	Acute venous embolism and thrombosis of subclavian veins
453.81	Acute venous embolism and thrombosis of superficial veins of upper extremity
453.40	Acute venous embolism and thrombosis of unspecified deep vessels of lower extremity
453.83	Acute venous embolism and thrombosis of upper extremity, unspecified
436	Acute, but ill-defined, cerebrovascular disease
091.4	Adenopathy due to secondary syphilis
423.1	Adhesive pericarditis
868.01	Adrenal gland injury without mention of open wound into cavity
995.80	Adult maltreatment, unspecified
995.84	Adult neglect (nutritional)
995.81	Adult physical abuse
516.5	Adult pulmonary Langerhans cell histiocytosis
995.83	Adult sexual abuse
086.5	African trypanosomiasis, unspecified
050.1	Alastrim
291.81	Alcohol withdrawal
291.0	Alcohol withdrawal delirium
291.2	Alcohol-induced persisting dementia
291.3	Alcohol-induced psychotic disorder with hallucinations
425.5	Alcoholic cardiomyopathy
276.3	Alkalosis
518.6	Allergic bronchopulmonary aspergillosis
287.0	Allergic purpura
117.6	Allescheriosis (Petriellidiosis)

006.8	Amebic infection of other sites
006.2	Amebic nondysenteric colitis
304.41	Amphetamine and other psychostimulant dependence, continuous pattern of use
277.30	Amyloidosis, unspecified
335.20	Amyotrophic lateral sclerosis
664.61	Anal sphincter tear complicating delivery, not associated with third-degree perineal laceration, delivered, with or without mention of antepartum condition
664.64	Anal sphincter tear complicating delivery, not associated with third-degree perineal laceration, postpartum condition or complication
999.41	Anaphylactic reaction due to administration of blood and blood products
995.62	Anaphylactic reaction due to crustaceans
995.68	Anaphylactic reaction due to eggs
995.65	Anaphylactic reaction due to fish
995.66	Anaphylactic reaction due to food additives
995.63	Anaphylactic reaction due to fruits and vegetables
995.67	Anaphylactic reaction due to milk products
999.49	Anaphylactic reaction due to other serum
995.69	Anaphylactic reaction due to other specified food
995.61	Anaphylactic reaction due to peanuts
995.64	Anaphylactic reaction due to tree nuts and seeds
995.60	Anaphylactic reaction due to unspecified food
999.42	Anaphylactic reaction due to vaccination
200.63	Anaplastic large cell lymphoma, intra-abdominal lymph nodes
200.66	Anaplastic large cell lymphoma, intrapelvic lymph nodes
200.62	Anaplastic large cell lymphoma, intrathoracic lymph nodes
200.64	Anaplastic large cell lymphoma, lymph nodes of axilla and upper limb
200.61	Anaplastic large cell lymphoma, lymph nodes of head, face, and neck
200.65	Anaplastic large cell lymphoma, lymph nodes of inguinal region and lower limb
200.68	Anaplastic large cell lymphoma, lymph nodes of multiple sites
200.67	Anaplastic large cell lymphoma, spleen
200.60	Anaplastic large cell lymphoma, unspecified site, extranodal and solid organ sites
126.2	Ancylostomiasis and necatoriasis due to ancylostoma braziliense
126.3	Ancylostomiasis and necatoriasis due to ancylostoma ceylanicum
126.0	Ancylostomiasis and necatoriasis due to ancylostoma duodenale
126.1	Ancylostomiasis and necatoriasis due to necator americanus
126.8	Ancylostomiasis and necatoriasis due to other specified ancylostoma
776.6	Anemia of neonatal prematurity
093.0	Aneurysm of aorta, specified as syphilitic
414.10	Aneurysm of heart
417.1	Aneurysm of pulmonary artery
413.0	Angina decubitus
127.1	Anisakiasis
307.1	Anorexia nervosa
348.1	Anoxic brain damage
032.2	Anterior nasal diphtheria
904.51	Anterior tibial artery injury
904.52	Anterior tibial vein injury
286.53	Antiphospholipid antibody with hemorrhagic disorder
784.3	Aphasia
863.85	Appendix injury without mention of open wound into cavity
078.7	Arenaviral hemorrhagic fever
266.0	Ariboflavinosis

263.2	Arrested development following protein-calorie malnutrition
362.32	Arterial branch occlusion of retina
417.0	Arteriovenous fistula of pulmonary vessels
056.71	Arthritis due to rubella
711.77	Arthropathy associated with helminthiasis, ankle and foot
711.73	Arthropathy associated with helminthiasis, forearm
711.74	Arthropathy associated with helminthiasis, hand
711.76	Arthropathy associated with helminthiasis, lower leg
711.79	Arthropathy associated with helminthiasis, multiple sites
711.78	Arthropathy associated with helminthiasis, other specified site
711.75	Arthropathy associated with helminthiasis, pelvic region and thigh
711.71	Arthropathy associated with helminthiasis, shoulder region
711.70	Arthropathy associated with helminthiasis, site unspecified
711.72	Arthropathy associated with helminthiasis, upper arm
711.67	Arthropathy associated with mycoses, ankle and foot
711.63	Arthropathy associated with mycoses, forearm
711.64	Arthropathy associated with mycoses, hand
711.66	Arthropathy associated with mycoses, lower leg
711.69	Arthropathy associated with mycoses, multiple sites
711.68	Arthropathy associated with mycoses, other specified site
711.65	Arthropathy associated with mycoses, pelvic region and thigh
711.61	Arthropathy associated with mycoses, shoulder region
711.60	Arthropathy associated with mycoses, site unspecified
711.62	Arthropathy associated with mycoses, upper arm
711.47	Arthropathy associated with other bacterial disease, ankle and foot
711.43	Arthropathy associated with other bacterial diseases, forearm
711.46	Arthropathy associated with other bacterial diseases, lower leg
711.49	Arthropathy associated with other bacterial diseases, multiple sites
711.48	Arthropathy associated with other bacterial diseases, other specific sites
711.45	Arthropathy associated with other bacterial diseases, pelvic region and thigh
711.41	Arthropathy associated with other bacterial diseases, shoulder region
711.40	Arthropathy associated with other bacterial diseases, site unspecified
711.42	Arthropathy associated with other bacterial diseases, upper arm
711.87	Arthropathy associated with other infectious and parasitic diseases, ankle and foot
711.83	Arthropathy associated with other infectious and parasitic diseases, forearm
711.84	Arthropathy associated with other infectious and parasitic diseases, hand
711.86	Arthropathy associated with other infectious and parasitic diseases, lower leg
711.89	Arthropathy associated with other infectious and parasitic diseases, multiple sites
711.88	Arthropathy associated with other infectious and parasitic diseases, other specific site
711.85	Arthropathy associated with other infectious and parasitic diseases, pelvic region and thigh
711.81	Arthropathy associated with other infectious and parasitic diseases, shoulder region
711.80	Arthropathy associated with other infectious and parasitic diseases, site unspecified
711.82	Arthropathy associated with other infectious and parasitic diseases, upper arm
711.57	Arthropathy associated with other viral diseases, ankle and foot
711.53	Arthropathy associated with other viral diseases, forearm
711.54	Arthropathy associated with other viral diseases, hand
711.56	Arthropathy associated with other viral diseases, lower leg
711.59	Arthropathy associated with other viral diseases, of multiple sites
711.58	Arthropathy associated with other viral diseases, other specified sites
711.55	Arthropathy associated with other viral diseases, pelvic region and thigh
711.51	Arthropathy associated with other viral diseases, shoulder region
711.50	Arthropathy associated with other viral diseases, site unspecified
711.52	Arthropathy associated with other viral diseases, upper arm
711.17	Arthropathy associated with Reiter's disease and nonspecific urethritis, ankle and foot
711.13	Arthropathy associated with Reiter's disease and nonspecific urethritis, forearm
711.14	Arthropathy associated with Reiter's disease and nonspecific urethritis, hand
711.16	Arthropathy associated with Reiter's disease and nonspecific urethritis, lower leg
711.19	Arthropathy associated with Reiter's disease and nonspecific urethritis, multiple sites
711.18	Arthropathy associated with Reiter's disease and nonspecific urethritis, other specified site
711.15	Arthropathy associated with Reiter's disease and nonspecific urethritis, pelvic region and thigh
711.11	Arthropathy associated with Reiter's disease and nonspecific urethritis, shoulder region
711.10	Arthropathy associated with Reiter's disease and nonspecific urethritis, site unspecified
711.12	Arthropathy associated with Reiter's disease and nonspecific urethritis, upper arm
711.27	Arthropathy in Behcet's syndrome, ankle and foot
711.23	Arthropathy in Behcet's syndrome, forearm
711.24	Arthropathy in Behcet's syndrome, hand
711.26	Arthropathy in Behcet's syndrome, lower leg
711.29	Arthropathy in Behcet's syndrome, multiple sites
711.28	Arthropathy in Behcet's syndrome, other specified sites
711.25	Arthropathy in Behcet's syndrome, pelvic region and thigh
711.21	Arthropathy in Behcet's syndrome, shoulder region
711.20	Arthropathy in Behcet's syndrome, site unspecified
711.22	Arthropathy in Behcet's syndrome, upper arm
711.44	Arthropathy, associated with other bacterial diseases, hand
996.46	Articular bearing surface wear of prosthetic joint
127.0	Ascariasis
863.41	Ascending (right) colon injury without mention of open wound into cavity
733.45	Aseptic necrosis of bone, jaw
733.40	Aseptic necrosis of bone, site unspecified
733.42	Aseptic necrosis of head and neck of femur
733.41	Aseptic necrosis of head of humerus
733.43	Aseptic necrosis of medial femoral condyle
733.49	Aseptic necrosis of other bone site
733.44	Aseptic necrosis of talus
117.3	Aspergillosis
799.01	Asphyxia
994.7	Asphyxiation and strangulation
493.91	Asthma, unspecified with status asthmaticus
493.92	Asthma, unspecified, with (acute) exacerbation
094.3	Asymptomatic neurosyphilis
445.81	Atheroembolism of kidney
445.02	Atheroembolism of lower extremity
445.89	Atheroembolism of other site
445.01	Atheroembolism of upper extremity
440.24	Atherosclerosis of native arteries of the extremities with gangrene
333.71	Athetoid cerebral palsy
427.32	Atrial flutter

426.0	Atrioventricular block, complete
V55.1	Attention to gastrostomy
299.00	Autistic disorder, current or active state
299.01	Autistic disorder, residual state
283.0	Autoimmune hemolytic anemias
758.39	Autosomal deletion syndromes, other autosomal deletions
758.33	Autosomal deletion syndromes, other microdeletions
871.3	Avulsion of eye
088.82	Babesiosis
790.7	Bacteremia
771.83	Bacteremia of newborn
125.0	Bancroftian filariasis
088.0	Bartonellosis
435.0	Basilar artery syndrome
642.03	Benign essential hypertension antepartum
642.01	Benign essential hypertension with delivery
642.02	Benign essential hypertension, with delivery, with current postpartum complication
265.0	Beriberi
478.34	Bilateral complete paralysis of vocal cords or larynx
552.02	Bilateral femoral hernia with obstruction
868.02	Bile duct and gallbladder injury without mention of open wound into cavity
296.51	Bipolar I disorder, most recent episode (or current) depressed, mild
296.52	Bipolar I disorder, most recent episode (or current) depressed, moderate
296.54	Bipolar I disorder, most recent episode (or current) depressed, severe, specified as with psychotic behavior
296.53	Bipolar I disorder, most recent episode (or current) depressed, severe, without mention of psychotic behavior
296.50	Bipolar I disorder, most recent episode (or current) depressed, unspecified
296.41	Bipolar I disorder, most recent episode (or current) manic, mild
296.42	Bipolar I disorder, most recent episode (or current) manic, moderate
296.44	Bipolar I disorder, most recent episode (or current) manic, severe, specified as with psychotic behavior
296.43	Bipolar I disorder, most recent episode (or current) manic, severe, without mention of psychotic behavior
296.40	Bipolar I disorder, most recent episode (or current) manic, unspecified
296.61	Bipolar I disorder, most recent episode (or current) mixed, mild
296.62	Bipolar I disorder, most recent episode (or current) mixed, moderate
296.64	Bipolar I disorder, most recent episode (or current) mixed, severe, specified as with psychotic behavior
296.63	Bipolar I disorder, most recent episode (or current) mixed, severe, without mention of psychotic behavior
296.60	Bipolar I disorder, most recent episode (or current) mixed, unspecified
296.01	Bipolar I disorder, single manic episode, mild
296.02	Bipolar I disorder, single manic episode, moderate
296.04	Bipolar I disorder, single manic episode, severe, specified as with psychotic behavior
296.03	Bipolar I disorder, single manic episode, severe, without mention of psychotic behavior
296.00	Bipolar I disorder, single manic episode, unspecified
767.11	Birth trauma, epicranial subaponeurotic hemorrhage (massive)
084.8	Blackwater fever
867.0	Bladder and urethra injury without mention of open wound into cavity
116.0	Blastomycosis
579.2	Blind loop syndrome

578.1	Blood in stool
999.32	Bloodstream infection due to central venous catheter
V85.41	Body Mass Index 40.0-44.9, adult
V85.42	Body Mass Index 45.0-49.9, adult
V85.43	Body Mass Index 50.0-59.9, adult
V85.44	Body Mass Index 60.0-69.9, adult
V85.45	Body Mass Index 70 and over, adult
V85.0	Body Mass Index less than 19, adult
648.74	Bone and joint disorders of maternal back, pelvis, and lower limbs complicating pregnancy, childbirth, or the puerperium, postpartum condition or complication
648.73	Bone and joint disorders of maternal back, pelvis, and lower limbs, antepartum
648.71	Bone and joint disorders of maternal back, pelvis, and lower limbs, with delivery
648.72	Bone and joint disorders of maternal back, pelvis, and lower limbs, with delivery, with current postpartum complication
V42.81	Bone marrow replaced by transplant
030.3	Borderline leprosy (group B)
005.1	Botulism food poisoning
082.1	Boutonneuse fever
903.1	Brachial blood vessels injury
081.1	Brill's disease
996.43	Broken prosthetic joint implant
494.1	Bronchiectasis with acute exacerbation
506.0	Bronchitis and pneumonitis due to fumes and vapors
023.9	Brucellosis, unspecified
307.51	Bulimia nervosa
200.23	Burkitt's tumor or lymphoma of intra-abdominal lymph nodes
200.26	Burkitt's tumor or lymphoma of intrapelvic lymph nodes
200.22	Burkitt's tumor or lymphoma of intrathoracic lymph nodes
200.24	Burkitt's tumor or lymphoma of lymph nodes of axilla and upper limb
200.21	Burkitt's tumor or lymphoma of lymph nodes of head, face, and neck
200.25	Burkitt's tumor or lymphoma of lymph nodes of inguinal region and lower limb
200.28	Burkitt's tumor or lymphoma of lymph nodes of multiple sites
200.27	Burkitt's tumor or lymphoma of spleen
200.20	Burkitt's tumor or lymphoma, unspecified site, extranodal and solid organ sites
948.11	Burn (any degree) involving 10-19% of body surface with third degree burn of 10-19%
948.10	Burn (any degree) involving 10-19% of body surface with third degree burn of less than 10% or unspecified amount
948.20	Burn (any degree) involving 20-29% of body surface with third degree burn of less than 10% or unspecified amount
948.30	Burn (any degree) involving 30-39% of body surface with third degree burn of less than 10% or unspecified amount
948.40	Burn (any degree) involving 40-49% of body surface with third degree burn of less than 10% or unspecified amount
948.50	Burn (any degree) involving 50-59% of body surface with third degree burn of less than 10% or unspecified amount
948.60	Burn (any degree) involving 60-69% of body surface with third degree burn of less than 10% or unspecified amount
948.70	Burn (any degree) involving 70-79% of body surface with third degree burn of less than 10% or unspecified amount
948.80	Burn (any degree) involving 80-89% of body surface with third degree burn of less than 10% or unspecified amount
948.90	Burn (any degree) involving 90% or more of body surface with third degree burn of less than 10% or unspecified amount
947.2	Burn of esophagus
947.3	Burn of gastrointestinal tract

Appendix A — Alphabetic CC List

947.1	Burn of larynx, trachea, and lung
947.4	Burn of vagina and uterus
940.5	Burn with resulting rupture and destruction of eyeball
799.4	Cachexia
993.3	Caisson disease
574.31	Calculus of bile duct with acute cholecystitis and obstruction
574.30	Calculus of bile duct with acute cholecystitis without mention of obstruction
574.41	Calculus of bile duct with other cholecystitis and obstruction
574.40	Calculus of bile duct with other cholecystitis, without mention of obstruction
574.51	Calculus of bile duct without mention of cholecystitis, with obstruction
574.80	Calculus of gallbladder and bile duct with acute and chronic cholecystitis, without mention of obstruction
574.61	Calculus of gallbladder and bile duct with acute cholecystitis, with obstruction
574.60	Calculus of gallbladder and bile duct with acute cholecystitis, without mention of obstruction
574.71	Calculus of gallbladder and bile duct with other cholecystitis, with obstruction
574.70	Calculus of gallbladder and bile duct with other cholecystitis, without mention of obstruction
574.91	Calculus of gallbladder and bile duct without cholecystitis, with obstruction
574.01	Calculus of gallbladder with acute cholecystitis and obstruction
574.00	Calculus of gallbladder with acute cholecystitis, without mention of obstruction
574.11	Calculus of gallbladder with other cholecystitis and obstruction
574.10	Calculus of gallbladder with other cholecystitis, without mention of obstruction
574.21	Calculus of gallbladder without mention of cholecystitis, with obstruction
592.1	Calculus of ureter
112.82	Candidal otitis externa
112.0	Candidiasis of mouth
112.2	Candidiasis of other urogenital sites
112.84	Candidiasis of the esophagus
112.85	Candidiasis of the intestine
127.5	Capillariasis
865.02	Capsular tears to spleen, without major disruption of parenchyma or mention of open wound into cavity
259.2	Carcinoid syndrome
997.1	Cardiac complications
423.3	Cardiac tamponade
425.8	Cardiomyopathy in other diseases classified elsewhere
078.3	Cat-scratch disease
295.22	Catatonic schizophrenia, chronic condition
295.24	Catatonic schizophrenia, chronic condition with acute exacerbation
295.21	Catatonic schizophrenia, subchronic condition
295.23	Catatonic schizophrenia, subchronic condition with acute exacerbation
295.20	Catatonic schizophrenia, unspecified condition
344.61	Cauda equina syndrome with neurogenic bladder
344.60	Cauda equina syndrome without mention of neurogenic bladder
447.4	Celiac artery compression syndrome
682.5	Cellulitis and abscess of buttock
682.0	Cellulitis and abscess of face
682.7	Cellulitis and abscess of foot, except toes
682.4	Cellulitis and abscess of hand, except fingers and thumb
682.6	Cellulitis and abscess of leg, except foot
682.1	Cellulitis and abscess of neck

528.3	Cellulitis and abscess of oral soft tissues
682.8	Cellulitis and abscess of other specified site
682.2	Cellulitis and abscess of trunk
682.9	Cellulitis and abscess of unspecified site
682.3	Cellulitis and abscess of upper arm and forearm
478.71	Cellulitis and perichondritis of larynx
478.21	Cellulitis of pharynx or nasopharynx
362.31	Central artery occlusion of retina
997.01	Central nervous system complication
362.35	Central vein occlusion of retina
334.4	Cerebellar ataxia in diseases classified elsewhere
851.42	Cerebellar or brain stem contusion without mention of open intracranial wound, brief (less than 1 hour) loss of consciousness
851.46	Cerebellar or brain stem contusion without mention of open intracranial wound, loss of consciousness of unspecified duration
851.43	Cerebellar or brain stem contusion without mention of open intracranial wound, moderate (1-24 hours) loss of consciousness
851.44	Cerebellar or brain stem contusion without mention of open intracranial wound, prolonged (more than 24 hours) loss consciousness and return to pre-existing conscious level
437.4	Cerebral arteritis
330.2	Cerebral degeneration in generalized lipidoses
330.3	Cerebral degeneration of childhood in other diseases classified elsewhere
330.1	Cerebral lipidoses
388.61	Cerebrospinal fluid otorrhea
349.81	Cerebrospinal fluid rhinorrhea
674.03	Cerebrovascular disorder, antepartum
674.02	Cerebrovascular disorder, with delivery, with mention of postpartum complication
674.04	Cerebrovascular disorders in the puerperium, postpartum condition or complication
649.73	Cervical shortening, antepartum condition or complication
649.71	Cervical shortening, delivered, with or without mention of antepartum condition
649.70	Cervical shortening, unspecified as to episode of care or not applicable
721.1	Cervical spondylosis with myelopathy
039.3	Cervicofacial actinomycotic infection
086.0	Chagas' disease with heart involvement
086.1	Chagas' disease with other organ involvement
086.2	Chagas' disease without mention of organ involvement
786.04	Cheyne-Stokes respiration
052.7	Chickenpox with other specified complications
052.8	Chickenpox with unspecified complication
995.50	Child abuse, unspecified
995.51	Child emotional/psychological abuse
995.52	Child neglect (nutritional)
995.54	Child physical abuse
995.53	Child sexual abuse
299.10	Childhood disintegrative disorder, current or active state
299.11	Childhood disintegrative disorder, residual state
099.56	Chlamydia trachomatis infection of peritoneum
576.1	Cholangitis
001.0	Cholera due to Vibrio cholerae
001.1	Cholera due to Vibrio cholerae el tor
130.2	Chorioretinitis due to toxoplasmosis
363.63	Choroidal rupture
508.1	Chronic and other pulmonary manifestations due to radiation
428.42	Chronic combined systolic and diastolic heart failure
428.32	Chronic diastolic heart failure

207.11	Chronic erythremia in remission
207.12	Chronic erythremia, in relapse
207.10	Chronic erythremia, without mention of having achieved remission
301.51	Chronic factitious illness with physical symptoms
582.2	Chronic glomerulonephritis with lesion of membranoproliferative glomerulonephritis
582.1	Chronic glomerulonephritis with lesion of membranous glomerulonephritis
582.0	Chronic glomerulonephritis with lesion of proliferative glomerulonephritis
582.4	Chronic glomerulonephritis with lesion of rapidly progressive glomerulonephritis
582.81	Chronic glomerulonephritis with other specified pathological lesion in kidney in diseases classified elsewhere
582.9	Chronic glomerulonephritis with unspecified pathological lesion in kidney
279.52	Chronic graft-versus-host disease
357.81	Chronic inflammatory demyelinating polyneuritis
006.1	Chronic intestinal amebiasis without mention of abscess
585.4	Chronic kidney disease, Stage IV (severe)
585.5	Chronic kidney disease, Stage V
208.11	Chronic leukemia of unspecified cell type in remission
208.12	Chronic leukemia of unspecified cell type, in relapse
208.10	Chronic leukemia of unspecified cell type, without mention of having achieved remission
204.11	Chronic lymphoid leukemia in remission
204.12	Chronic lymphoid leukemia, in relapse
204.10	Chronic lymphoid leukemia, without mention of having achieved remission
322.2	Chronic meningitis
206.11	Chronic monocytic leukemia in remission
206.12	Chronic monocytic leukemia, in relapse
206.10	Chronic monocytic leukemia, without mention of having achieved remission
205.11	Chronic myeloid leukemia in remission
205.12	Chronic myeloid leukemia, in relapse
205.10	Chronic myeloid leukemia, without mention of having achieved remission
493.21	Chronic obstructive asthma with status asthmaticus
493.22	Chronic obstructive asthma, with (acute) exacerbation
730.17	Chronic osteomyelitis, ankle and foot
730.13	Chronic osteomyelitis, forearm
730.14	Chronic osteomyelitis, hand
730.16	Chronic osteomyelitis, lower leg
730.19	Chronic osteomyelitis, multiple sites
730.18	Chronic osteomyelitis, other specified sites
730.15	Chronic osteomyelitis, pelvic region and thigh
730.11	Chronic osteomyelitis, shoulder region
730.10	Chronic osteomyelitis, site unspecified
730.12	Chronic osteomyelitis, upper arm
577.1	Chronic pancreatitis
512.83	Chronic pneumothorax
114.4	Chronic pulmonary coccidioidomycosis
416.2	Chronic pulmonary embolism
590.01	Chronic pyelonephritis with lesion of renal medullary necrosis
518.83	Chronic respiratory failure
393	Chronic rheumatic pericarditis
428.22	Chronic systolic heart failure
440.4	Chronic total occlusion of artery of the extremities
557.1	Chronic vascular insufficiency of intestine
453.74	Chronic venous embolism and thrombosis of axillary veins
453.72	Chronic venous embolism and thrombosis of deep veins of upper extremity
453.52	Chronic venous embolism and thrombosis of deep vessels of distal lower extremity
453.51	Chronic venous embolism and thrombosis of deep vessels of proximal lower extremity
453.76	Chronic venous embolism and thrombosis of internal jugular veins
453.79	Chronic venous embolism and thrombosis of other specified veins
453.77	Chronic venous embolism and thrombosis of other thoracic veins
453.75	Chronic venous embolism and thrombosis of subclavian veins
453.71	Chronic venous embolism and thrombosis of superficial veins of upper extremity
453.50	Chronic venous embolism and thrombosis of unspecified deep vessels of lower extremity
453.73	Chronic venous embolism and thrombosis of upper extremity, unspecified
459.31	Chronic venous hypertension with ulcer
459.33	Chronic venous hypertension with ulcer and inflammation
791.1	Chyluria
121.1	Clonorchiasis
813.41	Closed Colles' fracture
835.00	Closed dislocation of hip, unspecified site
839.05	Closed dislocation, fifth cervical vertebra
839.01	Closed dislocation, first cervical vertebra
839.04	Closed dislocation, fourth cervical vertebra
839.08	Closed dislocation, multiple cervical vertebrae
839.02	Closed dislocation, second cervical vertebra
839.07	Closed dislocation, seventh cervical vertebra
839.06	Closed dislocation, sixth cervical vertebra
839.61	Closed dislocation, sternum
839.03	Closed dislocation, third cervical vertebra
839.00	Closed dislocation, unspecified cervical vertebra
802.27	Closed fracture of alveolar border of body of mandible
812.02	Closed fracture of anatomical neck of humerus
802.25	Closed fracture of angle of jaw
801.42	Closed fracture of base of skull with intracranial injury of other and unspecified nature, brief (less than one hour) loss of consciousness
801.46	Closed fracture of base of skull with intracranial injury of other and unspecified nature, loss of consciousness of unspecified duration
801.41	Closed fracture of base of skull with intracranial injury of other and unspecified nature, no loss of consciousness
801.49	Closed fracture of base of skull with intracranial injury of other and unspecified nature, unspecified concussion
801.40	Closed fracture of base of skull with intracranial injury of other and unspecified nature, unspecified state of consciousness
801.02	Closed fracture of base of skull without mention of intracranial injury, brief (less than one hour) loss of consciousness
801.06	Closed fracture of base of skull without mention of intracranial injury, loss of consciousness of unspecified duration
801.01	Closed fracture of base of skull without mention of intracranial injury, no loss of consciousness
801.09	Closed fracture of base of skull without mention of intracranial injury, unspecified concussion
801.00	Closed fracture of base of skull without mention of intracranial injury, unspecified state of consciousness
805.00	Closed fracture of cervical vertebra, unspecified level without mention of spinal cord injury
802.21	Closed fracture of condylar process of mandible
802.23	Closed fracture of coronoid process of mandible
813.43	Closed fracture of distal end of ulna (alone)
805.2	Closed fracture of dorsal (thoracic) vertebra without mention of spinal cord injury
807.08	Closed fracture of eight or more ribs

821.21	Closed fracture of femoral condyle
805.05	Closed fracture of fifth cervical vertebra without mention of spinal cord injury
805.01	Closed fracture of first cervical vertebra without mention of spinal cord injury
807.05	Closed fracture of five ribs
807.04	Closed fracture of four ribs
805.04	Closed fracture of fourth cervical vertebra without mention of spinal cord injury
812.03	Closed fracture of greater tuberosity of humerus
808.41	Closed fracture of ilium
808.42	Closed fracture of ischium
812.42	Closed fracture of lateral condyle of humerus
813.44	Closed fracture of lower end of radius with ulna
821.22	Closed fracture of lower epiphysis of femur
805.4	Closed fracture of lumbar vertebra without mention of spinal cord injury
812.43	Closed fracture of medial condyle of humerus
805.08	Closed fracture of multiple cervical vertebrae without mention of spinal cord injury
807.09	Closed fracture of multiple ribs, unspecified
802.29	Closed fracture of multiple sites of mandible
807.01	Closed fracture of one rib
802.28	Closed fracture of other and unspecified part of body of mandible
808.49	Closed fracture of other specified part of pelvis
822.0	Closed fracture of patella
808.2	Closed fracture of pubis
807.00	Closed fracture of rib(s), unspecified
805.6	Closed fracture of sacrum and coccyx without mention of spinal cord injury
805.02	Closed fracture of second cervical vertebra without mention of spinal cord injury
807.07	Closed fracture of seven ribs
805.07	Closed fracture of seventh cervical vertebra without mention of spinal cord injury
823.22	Closed fracture of shaft of fibula with tibia
812.21	Closed fracture of shaft of humerus
813.21	Closed fracture of shaft of radius (alone)
813.23	Closed fracture of shaft of radius with ulna
823.20	Closed fracture of shaft of tibia
813.22	Closed fracture of shaft of ulna (alone)
807.06	Closed fracture of six ribs
805.06	Closed fracture of sixth cervical vertebra without mention of spinal cord injury
807.2	Closed fracture of sternum
802.22	Closed fracture of subcondylar process of mandible
812.41	Closed fracture of supracondylar humerus
812.01	Closed fracture of surgical neck of humerus
802.26	Closed fracture of symphysis of body of mandible
805.03	Closed fracture of third cervical vertebra without mention of spinal cord injury
807.03	Closed fracture of three ribs
807.02	Closed fracture of two ribs
812.44	Closed fracture of unspecified condyle(s) of humerus
823.82	Closed fracture of unspecified part of fibula with tibia
813.80	Closed fracture of unspecified part of forearm
812.20	Closed fracture of unspecified part of humerus
821.20	Closed fracture of unspecified part of lower end of femur
812.40	Closed fracture of unspecified part of lower end of humerus
813.83	Closed fracture of unspecified part of radius with ulna
802.24	Closed fracture of unspecified part of ramus of mandible
823.80	Closed fracture of unspecified part of tibia
813.82	Closed fracture of unspecified part of ulna (alone)
812.00	Closed fracture of unspecified part of upper end of humerus
805.8	Closed fracture of unspecified part of vertebral column without mention of spinal cord injury
802.20	Closed fracture of unspecified site of mandible
823.02	Closed fracture of upper end of fibula with tibia
823.00	Closed fracture of upper end of tibia
800.42	Closed fracture of vault of skull with intracranial injury of other and unspecified nature, brief (less than one hour) loss of consciousness
800.46	Closed fracture of vault of skull with intracranial injury of other and unspecified nature, loss of consciousness of unspecified duration
800.41	Closed fracture of vault of skull with intracranial injury of other and unspecified nature, no loss of consciousness
800.49	Closed fracture of vault of skull with intracranial injury of other and unspecified nature, unspecified concussion
800.40	Closed fracture of vault of skull with intracranial injury of other and unspecified nature, unspecified state of consciousness
800.02	Closed fracture of vault of skull without mention of intracranial injury, brief (less than one hour) loss of consciousness
800.06	Closed fracture of vault of skull without mention of intracranial injury, loss of consciousness of unspecified duration
800.01	Closed fracture of vault of skull without mention of intracranial injury, no loss of consciousness
800.09	Closed fracture of vault of skull without mention of intracranial injury, unspecified concussion
800.00	Closed fracture of vault of skull without mention of intracranial injury, unspecified state of consciousness
804.06	Closed fractures involving skull of face with other bones, without mention of intracranial injury, loss of consciousness of unspecified duration
804.09	Closed fractures involving skull of face with other bones, without mention of intracranial injury, unspecified concussion
804.42	Closed fractures involving skull or face with other bones, with intracranial injury of other and unspecified nature, brief (less than one hour) loss of consciousness
804.46	Closed fractures involving skull or face with other bones, with intracranial injury of other and unspecified nature, loss of consciousness of unspecified duration
804.41	Closed fractures involving skull or face with other bones, with intracranial injury of other and unspecified nature, no loss of consciousness
804.49	Closed fractures involving skull or face with other bones, with intracranial injury of other and unspecified nature, unspecified concussion
804.40	Closed fractures involving skull or face with other bones, with intracranial injury of other and unspecified nature, unspecified state of consciousness
804.02	Closed fractures involving skull or face with other bones, without mention of intracranial injury, brief (less than one hour) loss of consciousness
804.01	Closed fractures involving skull or face with other bones, without mention of intracranial injury, no loss of consciousness
804.00	Closed fractures involving skull or face with other bones, without mention of intracranial injury, unspecified state of consciousness
835.02	Closed obturator dislocation of hip
835.01	Closed posterior dislocation of hip
821.23	Closed supracondylar fracture of femur
649.33	Coagulation defects complicating pregnancy, childbirth, or the puerperium, antepartum condition or complication
649.32	Coagulation defects complicating pregnancy, childbirth, or the puerperium, delivered, with mention of postpartum complication
649.31	Coagulation defects complicating pregnancy, childbirth, or the puerperium, delivered, with or without mention of antepartum condition

649.34	Coagulation defects complicating pregnancy, childbirth, or the puerperium, postpartum condition or complication
649.30	Coagulation defects complicating pregnancy, childbirth, or the puerperium, unspecified as to episode of care or not applicable
747.10	Coarctation of aorta (preductal) (postductal)
304.21	Cocaine dependence, continuous pattern of use
007.2	Coccidiosis
009.1	Colitis, enteritis, and gastroenteritis of presumed infectious origin
863.40	Colon injury unspecified site, without mention of open wound into cavity
304.81	Combinations of drug dependence excluding opioid type drug, continuous pattern of use
304.71	Combinations of opioid type drug with any other drug dependence, continuous pattern of use
279.2	Combined immunity deficiency
900.01	Common carotid artery injury
279.06	Common variable immunodeficiency
331.3	Communicating hydrocephalus
958.90	Compartment syndrome, unspecified
636.22	Complete illegally induced abortion complicated by damage to pelvic organs or tissues
636.02	Complete illegally induced abortion complicated by genital tract and pelvic infection
636.42	Complete illegally induced abortion complicated by metabolic disorder
636.72	Complete illegally induced abortion with other specified complications
636.82	Complete illegally induced abortion with unspecified complication
635.22	Complete legally induced abortion complicated by damage to pelvic organs or tissues
635.02	Complete legally induced abortion complicated by genital tract and pelvic infection
635.42	Complete legally induced abortion complicated by metabolic disorder
635.72	Complete legally induced abortion with other specified complications
635.82	Complete legally induced abortion with unspecified complication
634.22	Complete spontaneous abortion complicated by damage to pelvic organs or tissues
634.02	Complete spontaneous abortion complicated by genital tract and pelvic infection
634.42	Complete spontaneous abortion complicated by metabolic disorder
634.72	Complete spontaneous abortion with other specified complications
634.82	Complete spontaneous abortion with unspecified complication
780.32	Complex febrile convulsions
996.85	Complications of bone marrow transplant
999.39	Complications of medical care, NEC, infection following other infusion, injection, transfusion, or vaccination
996.99	Complications of other specified reattached body part
996.89	Complications of other transplanted organ
996.93	Complications of reattached finger(s)
996.95	Complications of reattached foot and toe(s)
996.91	Complications of reattached forearm
996.92	Complications of reattached hand
996.96	Complications of reattached lower extremity, other and unspecified
996.94	Complications of reattached upper extremity, other and unspecified
996.83	Complications of transplanted heart
996.81	Complications of transplanted kidney
996.82	Complications of transplanted liver
996.84	Complications of transplanted lung
996.87	Complications of transplanted organ, intestine
996.88	Complications of transplanted organ, stem cell
996.80	Complications of transplanted organ, unspecified site
996.86	Complications of transplanted pancreas
996.90	Complications of unspecified reattached extremity
459.2	Compression of vein
850.5	Concussion with loss of consciousness of unspecified duration
850.2	Concussion with moderate (1-24 hours) loss of consciousness
850.3	Concussion with prolonged (more than 24 hours) loss of consciousness and return to pre-existing conscious level
850.12	Concussion, with loss of consciousness 31 to 59 minutes
850.11	Concussion, with loss of consciousness of 30 minutes or less
756.13	Congenital absence of vertebra
287.33	Congenital and hereditary thrombocytopenic purpura
776.5	Congenital anemia
751.4	Congenital anomalies of intestinal fixation
751.7	Congenital anomalies of pancreas
759.0	Congenital anomalies of spleen
747.21	Congenital anomaly of aortic arch
747.40	Congenital anomaly of great veins unspecified
747.22	Congenital atresia and stenosis of aorta
751.2	Congenital atresia and stenosis of large intestine, rectum, and anal canal
751.1	Congenital atresia and stenosis of small intestine
753.6	Congenital atresia and stenosis of urethra and bladder neck
748.61	Congenital bronchiectasis
746.85	Congenital coronary artery anomaly
751.62	Congenital cystic disease of liver
748.4	Congenital cystic lung
286.3	Congenital deficiency of other clotting factors
286.2	Congenital factor XI deficiency
359.0	Congenital hereditary muscular dystrophy
279.04	Congenital hypogammaglobulinemia
746.83	Congenital infundibular pulmonic stenosis
746.4	Congenital insufficiency of aortic valve
746.87	Congenital malposition of heart and cardiac apex
753.16	Congenital medullary cystic kidney
753.17	Congenital medullary sponge kidney
746.6	Congenital mitral insufficiency
746.5	Congenital mitral stenosis
754.2	Congenital musculoskeletal deformity of spine
753.21	Congenital obstruction of ureteropelvic junction
753.22	Congenital obstruction of ureterovesical junction
753.13	Congenital polycystic kidney, autosomal dominant
753.14	Congenital polycystic kidney, autosomal recessive
753.12	Congenital polycystic kidney, unspecified type
753.0	Congenital renal agenesis and dysgenesis
753.15	Congenital renal dysplasia
771.0	Congenital rubella
753.11	Congenital single renal cyst
747.82	Congenital spinal vessel anomaly
746.3	Congenital stenosis of aortic valve
746.02	Congenital stenosis of pulmonary valve
753.23	Congenital ureterocele
032.81	Conjunctival diphtheria
130.1	Conjunctivitis due to toxoplasmosis
284.01	Constitutional red blood cell aplasia
423.2	Constrictive pericarditis
414.04	Coronary atherosclerosis of artery bypass graft

414.02	Coronary atherosclerosis of autologous vein bypass graft
414.03	Coronary atherosclerosis of nonautologous biological bypass graft
414.07	Coronary atherosclerosis, of bypass graft (artery) (vein) of transplanted heart
414.06	Coronary atherosclerosis, of native coronary artery of transplanted heart
745.12	Corrected transposition of great vessels
851.02	Cortex (cerebral) contusion without mention of open intracranial wound, brief (less than 1 hour) loss of consciousness
851.06	Cortex (cerebral) contusion without mention of open intracranial wound, loss of consciousness of unspecified duration
851.03	Cortex (cerebral) contusion without mention of open intracranial wound, moderate (1-24 hours) loss of consciousness
851.04	Cortex (cerebral) contusion without mention of open intracranial wound, prolonged (more than 24 hours) loss of consciousness and return to pre-existing conscious level
074.20	Coxsackie carditis, unspecified
074.22	Coxsackie endocarditis
074.23	Coxsackie myocarditis
074.21	Coxsackie pericarditis
758.31	Cri-du-chat syndrome
065.0	Crimean hemorrhagic fever (CHF Congo virus)
359.81	Critical illness myopathy
357.82	Critical illness polyneuropathy
925.1	Crushing injury of face and scalp
928.01	Crushing injury of hip
925.2	Crushing injury of neck
928.00	Crushing injury of thigh
117.5	Cryptococcosis
516.36	Cryptogenic organizing pneumonia
007.4	Cryptosporidiosis
255.0	Cushing's syndrome
039.0	Cutaneous actinomycotic infection
022.0	Cutaneous anthrax
032.85	Cutaneous diphtheria
031.1	Cutaneous diseases due to other mycobacteria
085.4	Cutaneous leishmaniasis, American
085.2	Cutaneous leishmaniasis, Asian desert
085.3	Cutaneous leishmaniasis, Ethiopian
085.1	Cutaneous leishmaniasis, urban
120.3	Cutaneous schistosomiasis
770.83	Cyanotic attacks of newborn
007.5	Cyclosporiasis
577.2	Cyst and pseudocyst of pancreas
277.03	Cystic fibrosis with gastrointestinal manifestations
277.09	Cystic fibrosis with other manifestations
277.00	Cystic fibrosis without mention of meconium ileus
123.1	Cysticercosis
078.5	Cytomegaloviral disease
665.61	Damage to pelvic joints and ligaments, with delivery
639.2	Damage to pelvic organs and tissues following abortion or ectopic and molar pregnancies
949.4	Deep necrosis of underlying tissue due to burn (deep third degree), unspecified site without mention of loss of body part
949.5	Deep necrosis of underlying tissues due to burn (deep third degree, unspecified site with loss of body part
942.53	Deep necrosis of underlying tissues due to burn (deep third degree) of abdominal wall with loss of a body part
942.43	Deep necrosis of underlying tissues due to burn (deep third degree) of abdominal wall, without mention of loss of a body part
945.53	Deep necrosis of underlying tissues due to burn (deep third degree) of ankle, with loss of a body part
945.43	Deep necrosis of underlying tissues due to burn (deep third degree) of ankle, without mention of loss of a body part
943.54	Deep necrosis of underlying tissues due to burn (deep third degree) of axilla, with loss of a body part
943.44	Deep necrosis of underlying tissues due to burn (deep third degree) of axilla, without mention of loss of a body part
942.54	Deep necrosis of underlying tissues due to burn (deep third degree) of back (any part), with loss of a body part
942.44	Deep necrosis of underlying tissues due to burn (deep third degree) of back (any part), without mention of loss of a body part
944.56	Deep necrosis of underlying tissues due to burn (deep third degree) of back of hand, with loss of a body part
944.46	Deep necrosis of underlying tissues due to burn (deep third degree) of back of hand, without mention of loss of a body part
942.51	Deep necrosis of underlying tissues due to burn (deep third degree) of breast, with loss of a body part
942.41	Deep necrosis of underlying tissues due to burn (deep third degree) of breast, without mention of loss of a body part
942.52	Deep necrosis of underlying tissues due to burn (deep third degree) of chest wall, excluding breast and nipple, with loss of a body part
942.42	Deep necrosis of underlying tissues due to burn (deep third degree) of chest wall, excluding breast and nipple, without mention of loss of a body part
941.54	Deep necrosis of underlying tissues due to burn (deep third degree) of chin, with loss of a body part
941.44	Deep necrosis of underlying tissues due to burn (deep third degree) of chin, without mention of loss of a body part
941.51	Deep necrosis of underlying tissues due to burn (deep third degree) of ear (any part), with loss of a body part
941.41	Deep necrosis of underlying tissues due to burn (deep third degree) of ear (any part), without mention of loss of a body part
943.52	Deep necrosis of underlying tissues due to burn (deep third degree) of elbow, with loss of a body part
943.42	Deep necrosis of underlying tissues due to burn (deep third degree) of elbow, without mention of loss of a body part
941.52	Deep necrosis of underlying tissues due to burn (deep third degree) of eye (with other parts of face, head, and neck), with loss of a body part
941.42	Deep necrosis of underlying tissues due to burn (deep third degree) of eye (with other parts of face, head, and neck), without mention of loss of a body part
941.50	Deep necrosis of underlying tissues due to burn (deep third degree) of face and head, unspecified site, with loss of a body part
945.52	Deep necrosis of underlying tissues due to burn (deep third degree) of foot, with loss of a body part
945.42	Deep necrosis of underlying tissues due to burn (deep third degree) of foot, without mention of loss of a body part
943.51	Deep necrosis of underlying tissues due to burn (deep third degree) of forearm, with loss of a body part
943.41	Deep necrosis of underlying tissues due to burn (deep third degree) of forearm, without mention of loss of a body part
941.57	Deep necrosis of underlying tissues due to burn (deep third degree) of forehead and cheek, with loss of a body part
941.47	Deep necrosis of underlying tissues due to burn (deep third degree) of forehead and cheek, without mention of loss of a body part
942.55	Deep necrosis of underlying tissues due to burn (deep third degree) of genitalia, with loss of a body part
942.45	Deep necrosis of underlying tissues due to burn (deep third degree) of genitalia, without mention of loss of a body part
945.55	Deep necrosis of underlying tissues due to burn (deep third degree) of knee, with loss of a body part
945.45	Deep necrosis of underlying tissues due to burn (deep third degree) of knee, without mention of loss of a body part
941.53	Deep necrosis of underlying tissues due to burn (deep third degree) of lip(s), with loss of a body part

941.43	Deep necrosis of underlying tissues due to burn (deep third degree) of lip(s), without mention of loss of a body part
945.54	Deep necrosis of underlying tissues due to burn (deep third degree) of lower leg, with loss of a body part
945.44	Deep necrosis of underlying tissues due to burn (deep third degree) of lower leg, without mention of loss of a body part
941.59	Deep necrosis of underlying tissues due to burn (deep third degree) of multiple sites (except eye) of face, head, and neck, with loss of a body part
941.49	Deep necrosis of underlying tissues due to burn (deep third degree) of multiple sites (except with eye) of face, head, and neck, without mention of loss of a body part
945.59	Deep necrosis of underlying tissues due to burn (deep third degree) of multiple sites of lower limb(s), with loss of a body part
945.49	Deep necrosis of underlying tissues due to burn (deep third degree) of multiple sites of lower limb(s), without mention of loss of a body part
943.59	Deep necrosis of underlying tissues due to burn (deep third degree) of multiple sites of upper limb, except wrist and hand, with loss of a body part
943.49	Deep necrosis of underlying tissues due to burn (deep third degree) of multiple sites of upper limb, except wrist and hand, without mention of loss of a body part
944.58	Deep necrosis of underlying tissues due to burn (deep third degree) of multiple sites of wrist(s) and hand(s), with loss of a body part
944.48	Deep necrosis of underlying tissues due to burn (deep third degree) of multiple sites of wrist(s) and hand(s), without mention of loss of a body part
946.5	Deep necrosis of underlying tissues due to burn (deep third degree) of multiple specified sites, with loss of a body part
946.4	Deep necrosis of underlying tissues due to burn (deep third degree) of multiple specified sites, without mention of loss of a body part
941.58	Deep necrosis of underlying tissues due to burn (deep third degree) of neck, with loss of a body part
941.48	Deep necrosis of underlying tissues due to burn (deep third degree) of neck, without mention of loss of a body part
941.55	Deep necrosis of underlying tissues due to burn (deep third degree) of nose (septum), with loss of a body part
941.45	Deep necrosis of underlying tissues due to burn (deep third degree) of nose (septum), without mention of loss of a body part
942.59	Deep necrosis of underlying tissues due to burn (deep third degree) of other and multiple sites of trunk, with loss of a body part
942.49	Deep necrosis of underlying tissues due to burn (deep third degree) of other and multiple sites of trunk, without mention of loss of a body part
944.55	Deep necrosis of underlying tissues due to burn (deep third degree) of palm of hand, with loss of a body part
944.45	Deep necrosis of underlying tissues due to burn (deep third degree) of palm of hand, without mention of loss of a body part
941.56	Deep necrosis of underlying tissues due to burn (deep third degree) of scalp (any part), with loss of a body part
941.46	Deep necrosis of underlying tissues due to burn (deep third degree) of scalp (any part), without mention of loss of a body part
943.56	Deep necrosis of underlying tissues due to burn (deep third degree) of scapular region, with loss of a body part
943.46	Deep necrosis of underlying tissues due to burn (deep third degree) of scapular region, without mention of loss of a body part
943.55	Deep necrosis of underlying tissues due to burn (deep third degree) of shoulder, with loss of a body part
943.45	Deep necrosis of underlying tissues due to burn (deep third degree) of shoulder, without mention of loss of a body part
944.51	Deep necrosis of underlying tissues due to burn (deep third degree) of single digit (finger (nail)) other than thumb, with loss of a body part
944.41	Deep necrosis of underlying tissues due to burn (deep third degree) of single digit [finger (nail)] other than thumb, without mention of loss of a body part
945.56	Deep necrosis of underlying tissues due to burn (deep third degree) of thigh (any part), with loss of a body part
945.46	Deep necrosis of underlying tissues due to burn (deep third degree) of thigh (any part), without mention of loss of a body part
944.52	Deep necrosis of underlying tissues due to burn (deep third degree) of thumb (nail), with loss of a body part
944.42	Deep necrosis of underlying tissues due to burn (deep third degree) of thumb (nail), without mention of loss of a body part
945.51	Deep necrosis of underlying tissues due to burn (deep third degree) of toe(s) (nail), with loss of a body part
945.41	Deep necrosis of underlying tissues due to burn (deep third degree) of toe(s) (nail), without mention of loss of a body part
942.40	Deep necrosis of underlying tissues due to burn (deep third degree) of trunk, unspecified site, without mention of loss of a body part
944.54	Deep necrosis of underlying tissues due to burn (deep third degree) of two or more digits of hand including thumb, with loss of a body part
944.44	Deep necrosis of underlying tissues due to burn (deep third degree) of two or more digits of hand including thumb, without mention of loss of a body part
944.53	Deep necrosis of underlying tissues due to burn (deep third degree) of two or more digits of hand, not including thumb, with loss of a body part
944.43	Deep necrosis of underlying tissues due to burn (deep third degree) of two or more digits of hand, not including thumb, without mention of loss of a body part
945.50	Deep necrosis of underlying tissues due to burn (deep third degree) of unspecified site lower limb (leg), with loss of a body part
941.40	Deep necrosis of underlying tissues due to burn (deep third degree) of unspecified site of face and head, without mention of loss of a body part
944.50	Deep necrosis of underlying tissues due to burn (deep third degree) of unspecified site of hand, with loss of a body part
944.40	Deep necrosis of underlying tissues due to burn (deep third degree) of unspecified site of hand, without mention of loss of a body part
945.40	Deep necrosis of underlying tissues due to burn (deep third degree) of unspecified site of lower limb (leg), without mention of loss of a body part
942.50	Deep necrosis of underlying tissues due to burn (deep third degree) of unspecified site of trunk, with loss of a body part
943.50	Deep necrosis of underlying tissues due to burn (deep third degree) of unspecified site of upper limb, with loss of a body part
943.40	Deep necrosis of underlying tissues due to burn (deep third degree) of unspecified site of upper limb, without mention of loss of a body part
943.53	Deep necrosis of underlying tissues due to burn (deep third degree) of upper arm, with loss of upper a body part
943.43	Deep necrosis of underlying tissues due to burn (deep third degree) of upper arm, without mention of loss of a body part
944.57	Deep necrosis of underlying tissues due to burn (deep third degree) of wrist, with loss of a body part
944.47	Deep necrosis of underlying tissues due to burn (deep third degree) of wrist, without mention of loss of a body part
671.30	Deep phlebothrombosis, antepartum, unspecified as to episode of care
671.40	Deep phlebothrombosis, postpartum, unspecified as to episode of care
904.6	Deep plantar blood vessels injury
666.24	Delayed and secondary postpartum hemorrhage, postpartum condition or complication
666.22	Delayed and secondary postpartum hemorrhage, with delivery
999.85	Delayed hemolytic transfusion reaction, incompatibility unspecified
639.1	Delayed or excessive hemorrhage following abortion or ectopic and molar pregnancies
293.0	Delirium due to conditions classified elsewhere

294.11	Dementia in conditions classified elsewhere with behavioral disturbance
294.21	Dementia, unspecified, with behavioral disturbance
054.42	Dendritic keratitis
061	Dengue
V46.11	Dependence on respirator, status
298.0	Depressive type psychosis
710.3	Dermatomyositis
863.43	Descending (left) colon injury without mention of open wound into cavity
516.37	Desquamative interstitial pneumonia
253.5	Diabetes insipidus
862.0	Diaphragm injury without mention of open wound into cavity
552.3	Diaphragmatic hernia with obstruction
009.3	Diarrhea of presumed infectious origin
279.11	DiGeorge's syndrome
619.1	Digestive-genital tract fistula, female
903.5	Digital blood vessels injury
125.4	Dipetalonemiasis
032.84	Diphtheritic cystitis
032.82	Diphtheritic myocarditis
032.83	Diphtheritic peritonitis
123.4	Diphyllobothriasis, intestinal
344.2	Diplegia of upper limbs
343.0	Diplegic infantile cerebral palsy
996.42	Dislocation of prosthetic joint
277.85	Disorders of fatty acid oxidation
277.87	Disorders of mitochondrial metabolism
377.54	Disorders of optic chiasm associated with inflammatory disorders
377.52	Disorders of optic chiasm associated with other neoplasms
377.51	Disorders of optic chiasm associated with pituitary neoplasms and disorders
377.53	Disorders of optic chiasm associated with vascular disorders
377.63	Disorders of other visual pathways associated with inflammatory disorders
377.61	Disorders of other visual pathways associated with neoplasms
377.62	Disorders of other visual pathways associated with vascular disorders
277.1	Disorders of porphyrin metabolism
270.6	Disorders of urea cycle metabolism
377.73	Disorders of visual cortex associated with inflammatory disorders
377.71	Disorders of visual cortex associated with neoplasms
377.72	Disorders of visual cortex associated with vascular disorders
295.12	Disorganized schizophrenia, chronic condition
295.14	Disorganized schizophrenia, chronic condition with acute exacerbation
295.11	Disorganized schizophrenia, subchronic condition
295.13	Disorganized schizophrenia, subchronic condition with acute exacerbation
295.10	Disorganized schizophrenia, unspecified condition
998.32	Disruption of external operation (surgical) wound
998.31	Disruption of internal operation (surgical) wound
998.33	Disruption of traumatic injury wound repair
998.30	Disruption of wound, unspecified
363.13	Disseminated choroiditis and chorioretinitis, generalized
363.12	Disseminated choroiditis and chorioretinitis, peripheral
363.11	Disseminated choroiditis and chorioretinitis, posterior pole
031.2	Disseminated diseases due to other mycobacteria
199.0	Disseminated malignant neoplasm
363.14	Disseminated retinitis and retinochoroiditis, metastatic
363.15	Disseminated retinitis and retinochoroiditis, pigment epitheliopathy
270.0	Disturbances of amino-acid transport
270.3	Disturbances of branched-chain amino-acid metabolism
270.5	Disturbances of histidine metabolism
270.4	Disturbances of sulphur-bearing amino-acid metabolism
562.11	Diverticulitis of colon (without mention of hemorrhage)
562.01	Diverticulitis of small intestine (without mention of hemorrhage)
125.7	Dracontiasis
994.1	Drowning and nonfatal submersion
779.4	Drug reactions and intoxications specific to newborn
292.0	Drug withdrawal
779.5	Drug withdrawal syndrome in newborn
292.81	Drug-induced delirium
292.82	Drug-induced persisting dementia
292.11	Drug-induced psychotic disorder with delusions
292.12	Drug-induced psychotic disorder with hallucinations
863.21	Duodenum injury without mention of open wound into cavity
090.0	Early congenital syphilis, symptomatic
644.20	Early onset of delivery, unspecified as to episode of care
091.89	Early syphilis, other forms of secondary syphilis
091.69	Early syphilis, secondary syphilis of other viscera
091.7	Early syphilis, secondary syphilis, relapse
091.62	Early syphilis, secondary syphilitic hepatitis
091.61	Early syphilis, secondary syphilitic periostitis
091.82	Early syphilis, syphilitic alopecia
091.51	Early syphilis, syphilitic chorioretinitis (secondary)
091.52	Early syphilis, syphilitic iridocyclitis (secondary)
091.50	Early syphilis, syphilitic uveitis, unspecified
091.9	Early syphilis, unspecified secondary syphilis
122.0	Echinococcus granulosus infection of liver
122.1	Echinococcus granulosus infection of lung
122.2	Echinococcus granulosus infection of thyroid
122.5	Echinococcus multilocularis infection of liver
758.2	Edwards' syndrome
991.4	Effects of immersion of foot
756.83	Ehlers-Danlos syndrome
082.41	Ehrlichiosis chaffeensis [E. chaffeensis]
082.40	Ehrlichiosis, unspecified
444.22	Embolism and thrombosis of arteries of lower extremity
444.21	Embolism and thrombosis of arteries of upper extremity
444.81	Embolism and thrombosis of iliac artery
444.89	Embolism and thrombosis of other specified artery
453.3	Embolism and thrombosis of renal vein
444.1	Embolism and thrombosis of thoracic aorta
444.9	Embolism and thrombosis of unspecified artery
453.9	Embolism and thrombosis of unspecified site
742.0	Encephalocele
V46.12	Encounter for respirator dependence during power failure
V46.13	Encounter for weaning from respirator [ventilator]
425.3	Endocardial fibroelastosis
424.91	Endocarditis in diseases classified elsewhere
424.90	Endocarditis, valve unspecified, unspecified cause
425.0	Endomyocardial fibrosis
021.1	Enteric tularemia
008.65	Enteritis due to calicivirus
127.4	Enterobiasis
710.5	Eosinophilia myalgia syndrome
345.70	Epilepsia partialis continua without mention of intractable epilepsy

649.43	Epilepsy complicating pregnancy, childbirth, or the puerperium, antepartum condition or complication
649.42	Epilepsy complicating pregnancy, childbirth, or the puerperium, delivered, with mention of postpartum complication
649.41	Epilepsy complicating pregnancy, childbirth, or the puerperium, delivered, with or without mention of antepartum condition
649.44	Epilepsy complicating pregnancy, childbirth, or the puerperium, postpartum condition or complication
057.0	Erythema infectiosum (fifth disease)
695.12	Erythema multiforme major
456.1	Esophageal varices without mention of bleeding
456.21	Esophageal varices without mention of bleeding in diseases classified elsewhere
401.0	Essential hypertension, malignant
287.32	Evans' syndrome
298.1	Excitative type psychosis
695.53	Exfoliation due to erythematous condition involving 30-39 percent of body surface
695.54	Exfoliation due to erythematous condition involving 40-49 percent of body surface
695.55	Exfoliation due to erythematous condition involving 50-59 percent of body surface
695.56	Exfoliation due to erythematous condition involving 60-69 percent of body surface
695.57	Exfoliation due to erythematous condition involving 70-79 percent of body surface
695.58	Exfoliation due to erythematous condition involving 80-89 percent of body surface
695.59	Exfoliation due to erythematous condition involving 90 percent or more of body surface
753.5	Exstrophy of urinary bladder
900.02	External carotid artery injury
900.81	External jugular vein injury
608.21	Extravaginal torsion of spermatic cord
999.82	Extravasation of other vesicant agent
788.8	Extravasation of urine
999.81	Extravasation of vesicant chemotherapy
493.01	Extrinsic asthma with status asthmaticus
493.02	Extrinsic asthma, with (acute) exacerbation
638.2	Failed attempted abortion complicated by damage to pelvic organs or tissues
638.1	Failed attempted abortion complicated by delayed or excessive hemorrhage
638.0	Failed attempted abortion complicated by genital tract and pelvic infection
638.4	Failed attempted abortion complicated by metabolic disorder
638.7	Failed attempted abortion with other specified complication
638.8	Failed attempted abortion with unspecified complication
277.31	Familial Mediterranean fever
121.3	Fascioliasis
121.4	Fasciolopsiasis
046.72	Fatal familial insomnia
032.0	Faucial diphtheria
780.31	Febrile convulsions (simple), unspecified
772.5	Fetal and neonatal adrenal hemorrhage
656.31	Fetal distress affecting management of mother, delivered
576.4	Fistula of bile duct
575.5	Fistula of gallbladder
569.81	Fistula of intestine, excluding rectum and anus
527.4	Fistula of salivary gland
537.4	Fistula of stomach or duodenum
342.01	Flaccid hemiplegia affecting dominant side

342.02	Flaccid hemiplegia affecting nondominant side
342.00	Flaccid hemiplegia affecting unspecified side
005.2	Food poisoning due to Clostridium perfringens (C. welchii)
005.3	Food poisoning due to other Clostridia
005.4	Food poisoning due to Vibrio parahaemolyticus
005.81	Food poisoning due to Vibrio vulnificus
998.4	Foreign body accidentally left during procedure, not elsewhere classified
934.1	Foreign body in main bronchus
934.8	Foreign body in other specified parts of trachea, bronchus, and lung
934.0	Foreign body in trachea
664.31	Fourth-degree perineal laceration, with delivery
809.0	Fracture of bones of trunk, closed
334.0	Friedreich's ataxia
991.0	Frostbite of face
991.2	Frostbite of foot
991.1	Frostbite of hand
991.3	Frostbite of other and unspecified sites
942.33	Full-thickness skin loss due to burn (third degree NOS) of abdominal wall
945.33	Full-thickness skin loss due to burn (third degree NOS) of ankle
943.34	Full-thickness skin loss due to burn (third degree NOS) of axilla
942.34	Full-thickness skin loss due to burn (third degree NOS) of back (any part)
944.36	Full-thickness skin loss due to burn (third degree NOS) of back of hand
942.31	Full-thickness skin loss due to burn (third degree NOS) of breast
942.32	Full-thickness skin loss due to burn (third degree NOS) of chest wall, excluding breast and nipple
941.34	Full-thickness skin loss due to burn (third degree NOS) of chin
941.31	Full-thickness skin loss due to burn (third degree NOS) of ear (any part)
943.32	Full-thickness skin loss due to burn (third degree NOS) of elbow
941.32	Full-thickness skin loss due to burn (third degree NOS) of eye (with other parts of face, head, and neck)
945.32	Full-thickness skin loss due to burn (third degree NOS) of foot
943.31	Full-thickness skin loss due to burn (third degree NOS) of forearm
941.37	Full-thickness skin loss due to burn (third degree NOS) of forehead and cheek
942.35	Full-thickness skin loss due to burn (third degree NOS) of genitalia
945.35	Full-thickness skin loss due to burn (third degree NOS) of knee
941.33	Full-thickness skin loss due to burn (third degree NOS) of lip(s)
945.34	Full-thickness skin loss due to burn (third degree NOS) of lower leg
941.39	Full-thickness skin loss due to burn (third degree NOS) of multiple sites (except with eye) of face, head, and neck
945.39	Full-thickness skin loss due to burn (third degree NOS) of multiple sites of lower limb(s)
943.39	Full-thickness skin loss due to burn (third degree NOS) of multiple sites of upper limb, except wrist and hand
944.38	Full-thickness skin loss due to burn (third degree NOS) of multiple sites of wrist(s) and hand(s)
946.3	Full-thickness skin loss due to burn (third degree NOS) of multiple specified sites
941.38	Full-thickness skin loss due to burn (third degree NOS) of neck
941.35	Full-thickness skin loss due to burn (third degree NOS) of nose (septum)
942.39	Full-thickness skin loss due to burn (third degree NOS) of other and multiple sites of trunk
944.35	Full-thickness skin loss due to burn (third degree NOS) of palm of hand
941.36	Full-thickness skin loss due to burn (third degree NOS) of scalp (any part)

Appendix A — Alphabetic CC List

943.36	Full-thickness skin loss due to burn (third degree NOS) of scapular region
943.35	Full-thickness skin loss due to burn (third degree NOS) of shoulder
944.31	Full-thickness skin loss due to burn (third degree NOS) of single digit [finger (nail)] other than thumb
945.36	Full-thickness skin loss due to burn (third degree NOS) of thigh (any part)
944.32	Full-thickness skin loss due to burn (third degree NOS) of thumb (nail)
945.31	Full-thickness skin loss due to burn (third degree NOS) of toe(s) (nail)
944.34	Full-thickness skin loss due to burn (third degree NOS) of two or more digits of hand including thumb
944.33	Full-thickness skin loss due to burn (third degree NOS) of two or more digits of hand, not including thumb
941.30	Full-thickness skin loss due to burn (third degree NOS) of unspecified site of face and head
944.30	Full-thickness skin loss due to burn (third degree NOS) of unspecified site of hand
945.30	Full-thickness skin loss due to burn (third degree NOS) of unspecified site of lower limb
942.30	Full-thickness skin loss due to burn (third degree NOS) of unspecified site of trunk
943.30	Full-thickness skin loss due to burn (third degree NOS) of unspecified site of upper limb
943.33	Full-thickness skin loss due to burn (third degree NOS) of upper arm
944.37	Full-thickness skin loss due to burn (third degree NOS) of wrist
949.3	Full-thickness skin loss due to burn (third degree NOS), unspecified site
271.1	Galactosemia
560.31	Gallstone ileus
086.3	Gambian trypanosomiasis
785.4	Gangrene
558.1	Gastroenteritis and colitis due to radiation
022.2	Gastrointestinal anthrax
538	Gastrointestinal mucositis (ulcerative)
863.80	Gastrointestinal tract injury, unspecified site, without mention of open wound into cavity
094.1	General paresis
345.11	Generalized convulsive epilepsy with intractable epilepsy
345.01	Generalized nonconvulsive epilepsy with intractable epilepsy
999.0	Generalized vaccinia as complication of medical care, not elsewhere classified
053.11	Geniculate herpes zoster
639.0	Genital tract and pelvic infection following abortion or ectopic and molar pregnancies
619.2	Genital tract-skin fistula, female
046.71	Gerstmann-Straussler-Scheinker syndrome
007.1	Giardiasis
024	Glanders
364.22	Glaucomatocyclitic crises
255.41	Glucocorticoid deficiency
271.0	Glycogenosis
098.50	Gonococcal arthritis
098.52	Gonococcal bursitis
098.15	Gonococcal cervicitis (acute)
098.40	Gonococcal conjunctivitis (neonatorum)
098.11	Gonococcal cystitis (acute)
098.16	Gonococcal endometritis (acute)
098.42	Gonococcal endophthalmia
098.13	Gonococcal epididymo-orchitis (acute)
098.0	Gonococcal infection (acute) of lower genitourinary tract
098.10	Gonococcal infection (acute) of upper genitourinary tract, site unspecified
098.89	Gonococcal infection of other specified sites
098.41	Gonococcal iridocyclitis
098.43	Gonococcal keratitis
098.81	Gonococcal keratosis (blennorrhagica)
098.86	Gonococcal peritonitis
098.12	Gonococcal prostatitis (acute)
098.17	Gonococcal salpingitis, specified as acute
098.14	Gonococcal seminal vesiculitis (acute)
098.53	Gonococcal spondylitis
098.51	Gonococcal synovitis and tenosynovitis
446.21	Goodpasture's syndrome
279.50	Graft-versus-host disease, unspecified
780.1	Hallucinations
304.51	Hallucinogen dependence, continuous pattern of use
079.81	Hantavirus infection
861.01	Heart contusion without mention of open wound into thorax
V42.1	Heart replaced by transplant
992.0	Heat stroke and sunstroke
719.17	Hemarthrosis, ankle and foot
719.13	Hemarthrosis, forearm
719.14	Hemarthrosis, hand
719.16	Hemarthrosis, lower leg
719.19	Hemarthrosis, multiple sites
719.18	Hemarthrosis, other specified site
719.15	Hemarthrosis, pelvic region and thigh
719.11	Hemarthrosis, shoulder region
719.10	Hemarthrosis, site unspecified
719.12	Hemarthrosis, upper arm
578.0	Hematemesis
998.12	Hematoma complicating a procedure
438.21	Hemiplegia affecting dominant side due to cerebrovascular disease
438.22	Hemiplegia affecting nondominant side due to cerebrovascular disease
438.20	Hemiplegia affecting unspecified side due to cerebrovascular disease
343.1	Hemiplegic infantile cerebral palsy
999.83	Hemolytic transfusion reaction, incompatibility unspecified
423.0	Hemopericardium
288.4	Hemophagocytic syndromes
786.30	Hemoptysis, unspecified
246.3	Hemorrhage and infarction of thyroid
998.11	Hemorrhage complicating a procedure
596.7	Hemorrhage into bladder wall
578.9	Hemorrhage of gastrointestinal tract, unspecified
569.3	Hemorrhage of rectum and anus
363.72	Hemorrhagic choroidal detachment
362.43	Hemorrhagic detachment of retinal pigment epithelium
776.0	Hemorrhagic disease of newborn
078.6	Hemorrhagic nephrosonephritis
070.52	Hepatitis delta without mention of active hepatitis B disease or hepatic coma
130.5	Hepatitis due to toxoplasmosis
070.53	Hepatitis E without mention of hepatic coma
573.2	Hepatitis in other infectious diseases classified elsewhere
573.1	Hepatitis in viral diseases classified elsewhere
359.1	Hereditary progressive muscular dystrophy
334.1	Hereditary spastic paraplegia
552.8	Hernia of other specified site, with obstruction

552.9	Hernia of unspecified site, with obstruction
054.41	Herpes simplex dermatitis of eyelid
054.43	Herpes simplex disciform keratitis
054.44	Herpes simplex iridocyclitis
054.49	Herpes simplex with other ophthalmic complications
053.20	Herpes zoster dermatitis of eyelid
053.22	Herpes zoster iridocyclitis
053.21	Herpes zoster keratoconjunctivitis
053.10	Herpes zoster with unspecified nervous system complication
054.2	Herpetic gingivostomatitis
121.6	Heterophyiasis
238.73	High grade myelodysplastic syndrome lesions
665.41	High vaginal laceration, with delivery
751.3	Hirschsprung's disease and other congenital functional disorders of colon
115.02	Histoplasma capsulatum retinitis
115.09	Histoplasma capsulatum, with mention of other manifestation
115.12	Histoplasma duboisii retinitis
115.19	Histoplasma duboisii with mention of other manifestation
201.73	Hodgkin's disease, lymphocytic depletion, of intra-abdominal lymph nodes
201.76	Hodgkin's disease, lymphocytic depletion, of intrapelvic lymph nodes
201.72	Hodgkin's disease, lymphocytic depletion, of intrathoracic lymph nodes
201.74	Hodgkin's disease, lymphocytic depletion, of lymph nodes of axilla and upper limb
201.71	Hodgkin's disease, lymphocytic depletion, of lymph nodes of head, face, and neck
201.75	Hodgkin's disease, lymphocytic depletion, of lymph nodes of inguinal region and lower limb
201.78	Hodgkin's disease, lymphocytic depletion, of lymph nodes of multiple sites
201.77	Hodgkin's disease, lymphocytic depletion, of spleen
201.70	Hodgkin's disease, lymphocytic depletion, unspecified site, extranodal and solid organ sites
201.43	Hodgkin's disease, lymphocytic-histiocytic predominance of intra-abdominal lymph nodes
201.46	Hodgkin's disease, lymphocytic-histiocytic predominance of intrapelvic lymph nodes
201.42	Hodgkin's disease, lymphocytic-histiocytic predominance of intrathoracic lymph nodes
201.44	Hodgkin's disease, lymphocytic-histiocytic predominance of lymph nodes of axilla and upper limb
201.41	Hodgkin's disease, lymphocytic-histiocytic predominance of lymph nodes of head, face, and neck
201.45	Hodgkin's disease, lymphocytic-histiocytic predominance of lymph nodes of inguinal region and lower limb
201.48	Hodgkin's disease, lymphocytic-histiocytic predominance of lymph nodes of multiple sites
201.47	Hodgkin's disease, lymphocytic-histiocytic predominance of spleen
201.40	Hodgkin's disease, lymphocytic-histiocytic predominance, unspecified site, extranodal and solid organ sites
201.61	Hodgkin's disease, mixed cellularity, involving lymph nodes of head, face, and neck
201.63	Hodgkin's disease, mixed cellularity, of intra-abdominal lymph nodes
201.66	Hodgkin's disease, mixed cellularity, of intrapelvic lymph nodes
201.62	Hodgkin's disease, mixed cellularity, of intrathoracic lymph nodes
201.64	Hodgkin's disease, mixed cellularity, of lymph nodes of axilla and upper limb
201.65	Hodgkin's disease, mixed cellularity, of lymph nodes of inguinal region and lower limb
201.68	Hodgkin's disease, mixed cellularity, of lymph nodes of multiple sites
201.67	Hodgkin's disease, mixed cellularity, of spleen
201.60	Hodgkin's disease, mixed cellularity, unspecified site, extranodal and solid organ sites
201.53	Hodgkin's disease, nodular sclerosis, of intra-abdominal lymph nodes
201.56	Hodgkin's disease, nodular sclerosis, of intrapelvic lymph nodes
201.52	Hodgkin's disease, nodular sclerosis, of intrathoracic lymph nodes
201.54	Hodgkin's disease, nodular sclerosis, of lymph nodes of axilla and upper limb
201.51	Hodgkin's disease, nodular sclerosis, of lymph nodes of head, face, and neck
201.55	Hodgkin's disease, nodular sclerosis, of lymph nodes of inguinal region and lower limb
201.58	Hodgkin's disease, nodular sclerosis, of lymph nodes of multiple sites
201.57	Hodgkin's disease, nodular sclerosis, of spleen
201.50	Hodgkin's disease, nodular sclerosis, unspecified site, extranodal and solid organ sites
201.93	Hodgkin's disease, unspecified type, of intra-abdominal lymph nodes
201.96	Hodgkin's disease, unspecified type, of intrapelvic lymph nodes
201.92	Hodgkin's disease, unspecified type, of intrathoracic lymph nodes
201.94	Hodgkin's disease, unspecified type, of lymph nodes of axilla and upper limb
201.91	Hodgkin's disease, unspecified type, of lymph nodes of head, face, and neck
201.95	Hodgkin's disease, unspecified type, of lymph nodes of inguinal region and lower limb
201.98	Hodgkin's disease, unspecified type, of lymph nodes of multiple sites
201.97	Hodgkin's disease, unspecified type, of spleen
201.90	Hodgkin's disease, unspecified type, unspecified site, extranodal and solid organ sites
201.13	Hodgkin's granuloma of intra-abdominal lymph nodes
201.16	Hodgkin's granuloma of intrapelvic lymph nodes
201.12	Hodgkin's granuloma of intrathoracic lymph nodes
201.14	Hodgkin's granuloma of lymph nodes of axilla and upper limb
201.11	Hodgkin's granuloma of lymph nodes of head, face, and neck
201.15	Hodgkin's granuloma of lymph nodes of inguinal region and lower limb
201.18	Hodgkin's granuloma of lymph nodes of multiple sites
201.17	Hodgkin's granuloma of spleen
201.10	Hodgkin's granuloma, unspecified site, extranodal and solid organ sites
201.03	Hodgkin's paragranuloma of intra-abdominal lymph nodes
201.06	Hodgkin's paragranuloma of intrapelvic lymph nodes
201.02	Hodgkin's paragranuloma of intrathoracic lymph nodes
201.04	Hodgkin's paragranuloma of lymph nodes of axilla and upper limb
201.01	Hodgkin's paragranuloma of lymph nodes of head, face, and neck
201.05	Hodgkin's paragranuloma of lymph nodes of inguinal region and lower limb
201.08	Hodgkin's paragranuloma of lymph nodes of multiple sites
201.07	Hodgkin's paragranuloma of spleen
201.00	Hodgkin's paragranuloma, unspecified site, extranodal and solid organ sites
201.23	Hodgkin's sarcoma of intra-abdominal lymph nodes
201.26	Hodgkin's sarcoma of intrapelvic lymph nodes
201.22	Hodgkin's sarcoma of intrathoracic lymph nodes
201.24	Hodgkin's sarcoma of lymph nodes of axilla and upper limb
201.21	Hodgkin's sarcoma of lymph nodes of head, face, and neck

201.25	Hodgkin's sarcoma of lymph nodes of inguinal region and lower limb
201.28	Hodgkin's sarcoma of lymph nodes of multiple sites
201.27	Hodgkin's sarcoma of spleen
201.20	Hodgkin's sarcoma, unspecified site, extranodal and solid organ sites
079.53	Human immunodeficiency virus, type 2 (HIV 2), in conditions classified elsewhere and of unspecified site
079.51	Human t-cell lymphotrophic virus, type I (HTLV-I), in conditions classified elsewhere and of unspecified site
079.52	Human t-cell lymphotrophic virus, type II (HTLV-II), in conditions classified elsewhere and of unspecified site
333.4	Huntington's chorea
591	Hydronephrosis
575.3	Hydrops of gallbladder
593.5	Hydroureter
123.6	Hymenolepiasis
429.82	Hyperkinetic heart disease
276.0	Hyperosmolality and/or hypernatremia
642.13	Hypertension secondary to renal disease, antepartum
642.14	Hypertension secondary to renal disease, complicating pregnancy, childbirth, and the puerperium, postpartum condition or complication
403.11	Hypertensive chronic kidney disease, benign, with chronic kidney disease stage V or end stage renal disease
403.00	Hypertensive chronic kidney disease, malignant, with chronic kidney disease stage I through stage IV, or unspecified
403.01	Hypertensive chronic kidney disease, malignant, with chronic kidney disease stage V or end stage renal disease
403.91	Hypertensive chronic kidney disease, unspecified, with chronic kidney disease stage V or end stage renal disease
437.2	Hypertensive encephalopathy
404.13	Hypertensive heart and chronic kidney disease, benign, with heart failure and chronic kidney disease stage V or end stage renal disease
404.11	Hypertensive heart and chronic kidney disease, benign, with heart failure and with chronic kidney disease stage I through stage IV, or unspecified
404.12	Hypertensive heart and chronic kidney disease, benign, without heart failure and with chronic kidney disease stage V or end stage renal disease
404.01	Hypertensive heart and chronic kidney disease, malignant, with heart failure and with chronic kidney disease stage I through stage IV, or unspecified
404.03	Hypertensive heart and chronic kidney disease, malignant, with heart failure and with chronic kidney disease stage V or end stage renal disease
404.00	Hypertensive heart and chronic kidney disease, malignant, without heart failure and with chronic kidney disease stage I through stage IV, or unspecified
404.02	Hypertensive heart and chronic kidney disease, malignant, without heart failure and with chronic kidney disease stage V or end stage renal disease
404.93	Hypertensive heart and chronic kidney disease, unspecified, with heart failure and chronic kidney disease stage V or end stage renal disease
404.91	Hypertensive heart and chronic kidney disease, unspecified, with heart failure and with chronic kidney disease stage I through stage IV, or unspecified
404.92	Hypertensive heart and chronic kidney disease, unspecified, without heart failure and with chronic kidney disease stage V or end stage renal disease
425.11	Hypertrophic obstructive cardiomyopathy
775.4	Hypocalcemia and hypomagnesemia of newborn
251.0	Hypoglycemic coma
276.1	Hyposmolality and/or hyponatremia
768.70	Hypoxic-ischemic encephalopathy, unspecified
997.02	Iatrogenic cerebrovascular infarction or hemorrhage
512.1	Iatrogenic pneumothorax
516.35	Idiopathic lymphoid interstitial pneumonia
331.5	Idiopathic normal pressure hydrocephalus [INPH]
516.1	Idiopathic pulmonary hemosiderosis
341.22	Idiopathic transverse myelitis
818.1	Ill-defined open fractures of upper limb
287.31	Immune thrombocytopenic purpura
279.05	Immunodeficiency with increased IgM
560.39	Impaction of intestine, other
552.21	Incisional hernia with obstruction
636.21	Incomplete illegally induced abortion complicated by damage to pelvic organs or tissues
636.01	Incomplete illegally induced abortion complicated by genital tract and pelvic infection
636.41	Incomplete illegally induced abortion complicated by metabolic disorder
636.71	Incomplete illegally induced abortion with other specified complications
636.81	Incomplete illegally induced abortion with unspecified complication
635.01	Incomplete legally induced abortion complicated by genital tract and pelvic infection
635.41	Incomplete legally induced abortion complicated by metabolic disorder
635.71	Incomplete legally induced abortion with other specified complications
635.81	Incomplete legally induced abortion with unspecified complication
634.21	Incomplete spontaneous abortion complicated by damage to pelvic organs or tissues
634.01	Incomplete spontaneous abortion complicated by genital tract and pelvic infection
634.41	Incomplete spontaneous abortion complicated by metabolic disorder
634.71	Incomplete spontaneous abortion with other specified complications
634.81	Incomplete spontaneous abortion with unspecified complication
030.2	Indeterminate leprosy (group I)
084.7	Induced malaria
040.41	Infant botulism
343.4	Infantile hemiplegia
345.61	Infantile spasms with intractable epilepsy
345.60	Infantile spasms without mention of intractable epilepsy
603.1	Infected hydrocele
998.51	Infected postoperative seroma
997.62	Infection (chronic) of amputation stump
996.61	Infection and inflammatory reaction due to cardiac device, implant, and graft
996.64	Infection and inflammatory reaction due to indwelling urinary catheter
996.66	Infection and inflammatory reaction due to internal joint prosthesis
996.63	Infection and inflammatory reaction due to nervous system device, implant, and graft
996.65	Infection and inflammatory reaction due to other genitourinary device, implant, and graft
996.67	Infection and inflammatory reaction due to other internal orthopedic device, implant, and graft
996.69	Infection and inflammatory reaction due to other internal prosthetic device, implant, and graft
996.62	Infection and inflammatory reaction due to other vascular device, implant, and graft

996.68	Infection and inflammatory reaction due to peritoneal dialysis catheter
996.60	Infection and inflammatory reaction due to unspecified device, implant, and graft
117.8	Infection by dematiaceous fungi (Phaeohyphomycosis)
539.01	Infection due to gastric band procedure
539.81	Infection due to other bariatric procedure
569.61	Infection of colostomy or enterostomy
596.81	Infection of cystostomy
530.86	Infection of esophagostomy
536.41	Infection of gastrostomy
519.01	Infection of tracheostomy
646.63	Infections of genitourinary tract antepartum
646.64	Infections of genitourinary tract in pregnancy, postpartum condition or complication
646.61	Infections of genitourinary tract in pregnancy, with delivery
646.62	Infections of genitourinary tract in pregnancy, with delivery, with current postpartum complication
009.0	Infectious colitis, enteritis, and gastroenteritis
009.2	Infectious diarrhea
728.0	Infective myositis
488.09	Influenza due to identified avian influenza virus with other manifestations
488.02	Influenza due to identified avian influenza virus with other respiratory manifestations
550.12	Inguinal hernia with obstruction, without mention gangrene, bilateral, (not specified as recurrent)
550.13	Inguinal hernia with obstruction, without mention of gangrene, recurrent bilateral
550.11	Inguinal hernia with obstruction, without mention of gangrene, recurrent unilateral or unspecified
550.10	Inguinal hernia with obstruction, without mention of gangrene, unilateral or unspecified, (not specified as recurrent)
951.3	Injury to abducens nerve
951.6	Injury to accessory nerve
951.5	Injury to acoustic nerve
902.9	Injury to blood vessel of abdomen and pelvis, unspecified
904.9	Injury to blood vessels, unspecified site
900.00	Injury to carotid artery, unspecified
951.4	Injury to facial nerve
951.7	Injury to hypoglossal nerve
862.8	Injury to multiple and unspecified intrathoracic organs without mention of open wound into cavity
900.82	Injury to multiple blood vessels of head and neck
863.46	Injury to multiple sites in colon and rectum without mention of open wound into cavity
951.0	Injury to oculomotor nerve
950.1	Injury to optic chiasm
950.2	Injury to optic pathways
868.09	Injury to other and multiple intra-abdominal organs without mention of open wound into cavity
863.89	Injury to other and unspecified gastrointestinal sites without mention of open wound into cavity
900.89	Injury to other specified blood vessels of head and neck
951.8	Injury to other specified cranial nerves
862.29	Injury to other specified intrathoracic organs without mention of open wound into cavity
867.6	Injury to other specified pelvic organs without mention of open wound into cavity
902.89	Injury to specified blood vessels of abdomen and pelvis, other
904.7	Injury to specified blood vessels of lower extremity, other
901.89	Injury to specified blood vessels of thorax, other

903.8	Injury to specified blood vessels of upper extremity, other
951.2	Injury to trigeminal nerve
951.1	Injury to trochlear nerve
900.9	Injury to unspecified blood vessel of head and neck
904.8	Injury to unspecified blood vessel of lower extremity
901.9	Injury to unspecified blood vessel of thorax
903.9	Injury to unspecified blood vessel of upper extremity
951.9	Injury to unspecified cranial nerve
868.00	Injury to unspecified intra-abdominal organ without mention of open wound into cavity
950.9	Injury to unspecified optic nerve and pathways
867.8	Injury to unspecified pelvic organ without mention of open wound into cavity
950.3	Injury to visual cortex
901.81	Intercostal artery or vein injury
411.1	Intermediate coronary syndrome
900.03	Internal carotid artery injury
869.0	Internal injury to unspecified or ill-defined organs without mention of open wound into cavity
900.1	Internal jugular vein injury
901.82	Internal mammary artery or vein injury
722.71	Intervertebral cervical disc disorder with myelopathy, cervical region
722.73	Intervertebral lumbar disc disorder with myelopathy, lumbar region
722.72	Intervertebral thoracic disc disorder with myelopathy, thoracic region
008.2	Intestinal infection due to aerobacter aerogenes
008.1	Intestinal infection due to Arizona group of paracolon bacilli
008.04	Intestinal infection due to enterohemorrhagic E. coli
008.03	Intestinal infection due to enteroinvasive E. coli
008.01	Intestinal infection due to enteropathogenic E. coli
008.02	Intestinal infection due to enterotoxigenic E. coli
008.09	Intestinal infection due to other intestinal E. coli infections
008.49	Intestinal infection due to other organisms
008.5	Intestinal infection due to unspecified bacterial enteritis
008.00	Intestinal infection due to unspecified E. coli
008.62	Intestinal infection, enteritis due to adenovirus
008.66	Intestinal infection, enteritis due to astrovirus
008.67	Intestinal infection, enteritis due to enterovirus not elsewhere classified
008.63	Intestinal infection, enteritis due to Norwalk virus
008.64	Intestinal infection, enteritis due to other small round viruses (SRVs)
008.69	Intestinal infection, enteritis due to other viral enteritis
008.61	Intestinal infection, enteritis due to rotavirus
008.43	Intestinal infections due to campylobacter
008.45	Intestinal infections due to clostridium difficile
008.46	Intestinal infections due to other anaerobes
008.47	Intestinal infections due to other gram-negative bacteria
008.3	Intestinal infections due to proteus (mirabilis) (morganii)
008.42	Intestinal infections due to pseudomonas
008.41	Intestinal infections due to staphylococcus
008.44	Intestinal infections due to yersinia enterocolitica
560.81	Intestinal or peritoneal adhesions with obstruction (postoperative) (postinfection)
596.1	Intestinovesical fistula
854.02	Intracranial injury of other and unspecified nature, without mention of open intracranial wound, brief (less than 1 hour) loss of consciousness

854.06 Intracranial injury of other and unspecified nature, without mention of open intracranial wound, loss of consciousness of unspecified duration

854.03 Intracranial injury of other and unspecified nature, without mention of open intracranial wound, moderate (1-24 hours) loss of consciousness

854.04 Intracranial injury of other and unspecified nature, without mention of open intracranial wound, prolonged (more than 24 hours) loss of consciousness and return to pre-existing conscious level

656.43 Intrauterine death affecting management of mother, antepartum

656.41 Intrauterine death affecting management of mother, delivered

608.22 Intravaginal torsion of spermatic cord

772.11 Intraventricular hemorrhage, Grade I

772.12 Intraventricular hemorrhage, Grade II

772.10 Intraventricular hemorrhage, unspecified grade

493.11 Intrinsic asthma with status asthmaticus

493.12 Intrinsic asthma, with (acute) exacerbation

560.0 Intussusception

665.22 Inversion of uterus, delivered with postpartum complication

595.82 Irradiation cystitis

012.21 Isolated tracheal or bronchial tuberculosis, bacteriological or histological examination not done

012.22 Isolated tracheal or bronchial tuberculosis, bacteriological or histological examination unknown (at present)

012.23 Isolated tracheal or bronchial tuberculosis, tubercle bacilli found (in sputum) by microscopy

012.24 Isolated tracheal or bronchial tuberculosis, tubercle bacilli not found (in sputum) by microscopy, but found by bacterial culture

012.25 Isolated tracheal or bronchial tuberculosis, tubercle bacilli not found by bacteriological examination, but tuberculosis confirmed histologically

012.26 Isolated tracheal or bronchial tuberculosis, tubercle bacilli not found by bacteriological or histological examination, but tuberculosis confirmed by other methods [inoculation of animals]

012.20 Isolated tracheal or bronchial tuberculosis, unspecified

782.4 Jaundice, unspecified, not of newborn

176.3 Kaposi's sarcoma of gastrointestinal sites

176.4 Kaposi's sarcoma of lung

176.5 Kaposi's sarcoma of lymph nodes

176.8 Kaposi's sarcoma of other specified sites

176.2 Kaposi's sarcoma of palate

176.0 Kaposi's sarcoma of skin

176.1 Kaposi's sarcoma of soft tissue

176.9 Kaposi's sarcoma of unspecified site

866.01 Kidney hematoma without rupture of capsule or mention of open wound into cavity

866.02 Kidney laceration without mention of open wound into cavity

V42.0 Kidney replaced by transplant

335.11 Kugelberg-Welander disease

046.0 Kuru

065.2 Kyasanur Forest disease

416.1 Kyphoscoliotic heart disease

665.31 Laceration of cervix, with delivery

870.2 Laceration of eyelid involving lacrimal passages

358.31 Lambert-Eaton syndrome in neoplastic disease

358.39 Lambert-Eaton syndrome in other diseases classified elsewhere

358.30 Lambert-Eaton syndrome, unspecified

200.73 Large cell lymphoma, intra-abdominal lymph nodes

200.76 Large cell lymphoma, intrapelvic lymph nodes

200.72 Large cell lymphoma, intrathoracic lymph nodes

200.74 Large cell lymphoma, lymph nodes of axilla and upper limb

200.71 Large cell lymphoma, lymph nodes of head, face, and neck

200.75 Large cell lymphoma, lymph nodes of inguinal region and lower limb

200.78 Large cell lymphoma, lymph nodes of multiple sites

200.77 Large cell lymphoma, spleen

200.70 Large cell lymphoma, unspecified site, extranodal and solid organ sites

032.3 Laryngeal diphtheria

295.54 Latent schizophrenia, chronic condition with acute exacerbation

295.53 Latent schizophrenia, subchronic condition with acute exacerbation

428.1 Left heart failure

556.5 Left sided ulcerative (chronic) colitis

635.21 Legally induced abortion complicated by damage to pelvic organs or tissues, incomplete

030.0 Lepromatous leprosy (type L)

100.0 Leptospirosis icterohemorrhagica

446.3 Lethal midline granuloma

202.53 Letterer-Siwe disease of intra-abdominal lymph nodes

202.56 Letterer-Siwe disease of intrapelvic lymph nodes

202.52 Letterer-Siwe disease of intrathoracic lymph nodes

202.54 Letterer-Siwe disease of lymph nodes of axilla and upper limb

202.51 Letterer-Siwe disease of lymph nodes of head, face, and neck

202.55 Letterer-Siwe disease of lymph nodes of inguinal region and lower limb

202.58 Letterer-Siwe disease of lymph nodes of multiple sites

202.57 Letterer-Siwe disease of spleen

202.50 Letterer-Siwe disease, unspecified site, extranodal and solid organ sites

202.43 Leukemic reticuloendotheliosis of intra-abdominal lymph nodes

202.46 Leukemic reticuloendotheliosis of intrapelvic lymph nodes

202.42 Leukemic reticuloendotheliosis of intrathoracic lymph nodes

202.44 Leukemic reticuloendotheliosis of lymph nodes of axilla and upper limb

202.41 Leukemic reticuloendotheliosis of lymph nodes of head, face, and neck

202.45 Leukemic reticuloendotheliosis of lymph nodes of inguinal region and lower limb

202.48 Leukemic reticuloendotheliosis of lymph nodes of multiple sites

202.47 Leukemic reticuloendotheliosis of spleen

202.40 Leukemic reticuloendotheliosis, unspecified site, extranodal and solid organ sites

330.0 Leukodystrophy

027.0 Listeriosis

646.73 Liver and biliary tract disorders in pregnancy, antepartum condition or complication

646.71 Liver and biliary tract disorders in pregnancy, delivered, with or without mention of antepartum condition

864.01 Liver hematoma and contusion without mention of open wound into cavity

864.05 Liver injury without mention of open wound into cavity, unspecified laceration

864.02 Liver laceration, minor, without mention of open wound into cavity

V42.7 Liver replaced by transplant

999.33 Local infection due to central venous catheter

345.41 Localization-related (focal) (partial) epilepsy and epileptic syndromes with complex partial seizures, with intractable epilepsy

345.40 Localization-related (focal) (partial) epilepsy and epileptic syndromes with complex partial seizures, without mention of intractable epilepsy

345.51 Localization-related (focal) (partial) epilepsy and epileptic syndromes with simple partial seizures, with intractable epilepsy

345.50	Localization-related (focal) (partial) epilepsy and epileptic syndromes with simple partial seizures, without mention of intractable epilepsy
125.2	Loiasis
080	Louse-borne (epidemic) typhus
087.0	Louse-borne relapsing fever
861.21	Lung contusion without mention of open wound into thorax
517.2	Lung involvement in systemic sclerosis
V42.6	Lung replaced by transplant
088.81	Lyme disease
049.0	Lymphocytic choriomeningitis
200.13	Lymphosarcoma of intra-abdominal lymph nodes
200.16	Lymphosarcoma of intrapelvic lymph nodes
200.12	Lymphosarcoma of intrathoracic lymph nodes
200.14	Lymphosarcoma of lymph nodes of axilla and upper limb
200.11	Lymphosarcoma of lymph nodes of head, face, and neck
200.15	Lymphosarcoma of lymph nodes of inguinal region and lower limb
200.18	Lymphosarcoma of lymph nodes of multiple sites
200.17	Lymphosarcoma of spleen
200.10	Lymphosarcoma, unspecified site, extranodal and solid organ sites
039.4	Madura foot
296.31	Major depressive disorder, recurrent episode, mild
296.32	Major depressive disorder, recurrent episode, moderate
296.34	Major depressive disorder, recurrent episode, severe, specified as with psychotic behavior
296.33	Major depressive disorder, recurrent episode, severe, without mention of psychotic behavior
296.30	Major depressive disorder, recurrent episode, unspecified
296.21	Major depressive disorder, single episode, mild
296.22	Major depressive disorder, single episode, moderate
296.24	Major depressive disorder, single episode, severe, specified as with psychotic behavior
296.23	Major depressive disorder, single episode, severe, without mention of psychotic behavior
296.20	Major depressive disorder, single episode, unspecified
802.4	Malar and maxillary bones, closed fracture
802.5	Malar and maxillary bones, open fracture
125.1	Malayan filariasis
789.51	Malignant ascites
209.25	Malignant carcinoid tumor of foregut, not otherwise specified
209.27	Malignant carcinoid tumor of hindgut, not otherwise specified
209.26	Malignant carcinoid tumor of midgut, not otherwise specified
209.29	Malignant carcinoid tumor of other sites
209.11	Malignant carcinoid tumor of the appendix
209.13	Malignant carcinoid tumor of the ascending colon
209.21	Malignant carcinoid tumor of the bronchus and lung
209.12	Malignant carcinoid tumor of the cecum
209.15	Malignant carcinoid tumor of the descending colon
209.01	Malignant carcinoid tumor of the duodenum
209.03	Malignant carcinoid tumor of the ileum
209.02	Malignant carcinoid tumor of the jejunum
209.24	Malignant carcinoid tumor of the kidney
209.10	Malignant carcinoid tumor of the large intestine, unspecified portion
209.17	Malignant carcinoid tumor of the rectum
209.16	Malignant carcinoid tumor of the sigmoid colon
209.00	Malignant carcinoid tumor of the small intestine, unspecified portion
209.23	Malignant carcinoid tumor of the stomach
209.22	Malignant carcinoid tumor of the thymus
209.14	Malignant carcinoid tumor of the transverse colon
209.20	Malignant carcinoid tumor of unknown primary site
202.33	Malignant histiocytosis of intra-abdominal lymph nodes
202.36	Malignant histiocytosis of intrapelvic lymph nodes
202.32	Malignant histiocytosis of intrathoracic lymph nodes
202.34	Malignant histiocytosis of lymph nodes of axilla and upper limb
202.31	Malignant histiocytosis of lymph nodes of head, face, and neck
202.35	Malignant histiocytosis of lymph nodes of inguinal region and lower limb
202.38	Malignant histiocytosis of lymph nodes of multiple sites
202.37	Malignant histiocytosis of spleen
202.30	Malignant histiocytosis, unspecified site, extranodal and solid organ sites
402.01	Malignant hypertensive heart disease with heart failure
402.00	Malignant hypertensive heart disease without heart failure
995.86	Malignant hyperthermia
202.63	Malignant mast cell tumors of intra-abdominal lymph nodes
202.66	Malignant mast cell tumors of intrapelvic lymph nodes
202.62	Malignant mast cell tumors of intrathoracic lymph nodes
202.64	Malignant mast cell tumors of lymph nodes of axilla and upper limb
202.61	Malignant mast cell tumors of lymph nodes of head, face, and neck
202.65	Malignant mast cell tumors of lymph nodes of inguinal region and lower limb
202.68	Malignant mast cell tumors of lymph nodes of multiple sites
202.67	Malignant mast cell tumors of spleen
202.60	Malignant mast cell tumors, unspecified site, extranodal and solid organ sites
199.2	Malignant neoplasm associated with transplanted organ
150.2	Malignant neoplasm of abdominal esophagus
194.0	Malignant neoplasm of adrenal gland
156.2	Malignant neoplasm of ampulla of Vater
164.2	Malignant neoplasm of anterior mediastinum
154.3	Malignant neoplasm of anus, unspecified site
194.6	Malignant neoplasm of aortic body and other paraganglia
153.5	Malignant neoplasm of appendix
153.6	Malignant neoplasm of ascending colon
156.9	Malignant neoplasm of biliary tract, part unspecified site
157.1	Malignant neoplasm of body of pancreas
151.4	Malignant neoplasm of body of stomach
170.9	Malignant neoplasm of bone and articular cartilage, site unspecified
170.0	Malignant neoplasm of bones of skull and face, except mandible
191.7	Malignant neoplasm of brain stem
191.9	Malignant neoplasm of brain, unspecified site
162.9	Malignant neoplasm of bronchus and lung, unspecified site
151.0	Malignant neoplasm of cardia
194.5	Malignant neoplasm of carotid body
153.4	Malignant neoplasm of cecum
191.6	Malignant neoplasm of cerebellum NOS
192.1	Malignant neoplasm of cerebral meninges
191.0	Malignant neoplasm of cerebrum, except lobes and ventricles
150.0	Malignant neoplasm of cervical esophagus
153.9	Malignant neoplasm of colon, unspecified site
171.5	Malignant neoplasm of connective and other soft tissue of abdomen
171.0	Malignant neoplasm of connective and other soft tissue of head, face, and neck
171.3	Malignant neoplasm of connective and other soft tissue of lower limb, including hip

171.6	Malignant neoplasm of connective and other soft tissue of pelvis
171.4	Malignant neoplasm of connective and other soft tissue of thorax
171.7	Malignant neoplasm of connective and other soft tissue of trunk, unspecified site
171.2	Malignant neoplasm of connective and other soft tissue of upper limb, including shoulder
171.9	Malignant neoplasm of connective and other soft tissue, site unspecified
192.0	Malignant neoplasm of cranial nerves
153.2	Malignant neoplasm of descending colon
152.0	Malignant neoplasm of duodenum
194.9	Malignant neoplasm of endocrine gland, site unspecified
150.9	Malignant neoplasm of esophagus, unspecified site
156.1	Malignant neoplasm of extrahepatic bile ducts
191.1	Malignant neoplasm of frontal lobe of brain
151.3	Malignant neoplasm of fundus of stomach
156.0	Malignant neoplasm of gallbladder
151.6	Malignant neoplasm of greater curvature of stomach, unspecified
157.0	Malignant neoplasm of head of pancreas
164.1	Malignant neoplasm of heart
153.0	Malignant neoplasm of hepatic flexure
152.2	Malignant neoplasm of ileum
155.1	Malignant neoplasm of intrahepatic bile ducts
157.4	Malignant neoplasm of islets of Langerhans
152.1	Malignant neoplasm of jejunum
189.0	Malignant neoplasm of kidney, except pelvis
151.5	Malignant neoplasm of lesser curvature of stomach, unspecified
155.2	Malignant neoplasm of liver, not specified as primary or secondary
155.0	Malignant neoplasm of liver, primary
170.7	Malignant neoplasm of long bones of lower limb
162.5	Malignant neoplasm of lower lobe, bronchus, or lung
150.5	Malignant neoplasm of lower third of esophagus
162.2	Malignant neoplasm of main bronchus
170.1	Malignant neoplasm of mandible
152.3	Malignant neoplasm of Meckel's diverticulum
164.9	Malignant neoplasm of mediastinum, part unspecified
162.4	Malignant neoplasm of middle lobe, bronchus, or lung
150.4	Malignant neoplasm of middle third of esophagus
192.9	Malignant neoplasm of nervous system, part unspecified
191.4	Malignant neoplasm of occipital lobe of brain
194.8	Malignant neoplasm of other endocrine glands and related structures
191.8	Malignant neoplasm of other parts of brain
162.8	Malignant neoplasm of other parts of bronchus or lung
164.8	Malignant neoplasm of other parts of mediastinum
154.8	Malignant neoplasm of other sites of rectum, rectosigmoid junction, and anus
150.8	Malignant neoplasm of other specified part of esophagus
171.8	Malignant neoplasm of other specified sites of connective and other soft tissue
156.8	Malignant neoplasm of other specified sites of gallbladder and extrahepatic bile ducts
153.8	Malignant neoplasm of other specified sites of large intestine
192.8	Malignant neoplasm of other specified sites of nervous system
157.8	Malignant neoplasm of other specified sites of pancreas
163.8	Malignant neoplasm of other specified sites of pleura
152.8	Malignant neoplasm of other specified sites of small intestine
151.8	Malignant neoplasm of other specified sites of stomach
189.8	Malignant neoplasm of other specified sites of urinary organs
183.0	Malignant neoplasm of ovary
157.9	Malignant neoplasm of pancreas, part unspecified
157.3	Malignant neoplasm of pancreatic duct
194.1	Malignant neoplasm of parathyroid gland
189.4	Malignant neoplasm of paraurethral glands
191.3	Malignant neoplasm of parietal lobe of brain
163.0	Malignant neoplasm of parietal pleura
170.6	Malignant neoplasm of pelvic bones, sacrum, and coccyx
158.9	Malignant neoplasm of peritoneum, unspecified
194.4	Malignant neoplasm of pineal gland
194.3	Malignant neoplasm of pituitary gland and craniopharyngeal duct
163.9	Malignant neoplasm of pleura, unspecified site
164.3	Malignant neoplasm of posterior mediastinum
151.2	Malignant neoplasm of pyloric antrum
151.1	Malignant neoplasm of pylorus
154.0	Malignant neoplasm of rectosigmoid junction
154.1	Malignant neoplasm of rectum
189.1	Malignant neoplasm of renal pelvis
158.0	Malignant neoplasm of retroperitoneum
170.3	Malignant neoplasm of ribs, sternum, and clavicle
170.4	Malignant neoplasm of scapula and long bones of upper limb
170.8	Malignant neoplasm of short bones of lower limb
170.5	Malignant neoplasm of short bones of upper limb
153.3	Malignant neoplasm of sigmoid colon
152.9	Malignant neoplasm of small intestine, unspecified site
158.8	Malignant neoplasm of specified parts of peritoneum
192.2	Malignant neoplasm of spinal cord
192.3	Malignant neoplasm of spinal meninges
153.7	Malignant neoplasm of splenic flexure
151.9	Malignant neoplasm of stomach, unspecified site
157.2	Malignant neoplasm of tail of pancreas
191.2	Malignant neoplasm of temporal lobe of brain
150.1	Malignant neoplasm of thoracic esophagus
164.0	Malignant neoplasm of thymus
162.0	Malignant neoplasm of trachea
153.1	Malignant neoplasm of transverse colon
162.3	Malignant neoplasm of upper lobe, bronchus, or lung
150.3	Malignant neoplasm of upper third of esophagus
189.2	Malignant neoplasm of ureter
189.3	Malignant neoplasm of urethra
189.9	Malignant neoplasm of urinary organ, site unspecified
191.5	Malignant neoplasm of ventricles of brain
170.2	Malignant neoplasm of vertebral column, excluding sacrum and coccyx
163.1	Malignant neoplasm of visceral pleura
380.14	Malignant otitis externa
511.81	Malignant pleural effusion
209.30	Malignant poorly differentiated neuroendocrine carcinoma, any site
263.1	Malnutrition of mild degree
263.0	Malnutrition of moderate degree
733.81	Malunion of fracture
296.11	Manic disorder, recurrent episode, mild
296.12	Manic disorder, recurrent episode, moderate
296.14	Manic disorder, recurrent episode, severe, specified as with psychotic behavior
296.13	Manic disorder, recurrent episode, severe, without mention of psychotic behavior
296.10	Manic disorder, recurrent episode, unspecified
125.5	Mansonella ozzardi infection
200.43	Mantle cell lymphoma, intra-abdominal lymph nodes

200.46	Mantle cell lymphoma, intrapelvic lymph nodes
200.42	Mantle cell lymphoma, intrathoracic lymph nodes
200.44	Mantle cell lymphoma, lymph nodes of axilla and upper limb
200.41	Mantle cell lymphoma, lymph nodes of head, face, and neck
200.45	Mantle cell lymphoma, lymph nodes of inguinal region and lower limb
200.48	Mantle cell lymphoma, lymph nodes of multiple sites
200.47	Mantle cell lymphoma, spleen
200.40	Mantle cell lymphoma, unspecified site, extranodal and solid organ sites
759.82	Marfan's syndrome
200.33	Marginal zone lymphoma, intra-abdominal lymph nodes
200.36	Marginal zone lymphoma, intrapelvic lymph nodes
200.32	Marginal zone lymphoma, intrathoracic lymph nodes
200.34	Marginal zone lymphoma, lymph nodes of axilla and upper limb
200.31	Marginal zone lymphoma, lymph nodes of head, face, and neck
200.35	Marginal zone lymphoma, lymph nodes of inguinal region and lower limb
200.38	Marginal zone lymphoma, lymph nodes of multiple sites
200.37	Marginal zone lymphoma, spleen
200.30	Marginal zone lymphoma, unspecified site, extranodal and solid organ sites
648.54	Maternal congenital cardiovascular disorders complicating pregnancy, childbirth, or the puerperium, postpartum condition or complication
648.53	Maternal congenital cardiovascular disorders, antepartum
648.51	Maternal congenital cardiovascular disorders, with delivery
648.52	Maternal congenital cardiovascular disorders, with delivery, with current postpartum complication
648.03	Maternal diabetes mellitus, antepartum
648.04	Maternal diabetes mellitus, complicating pregnancy, childbirth, or the puerperium, postpartum condition or complication
648.00	Maternal diabetes mellitus, complicating pregnancy, childbirth, or the puerperium, unspecified as to episode of care
648.34	Maternal drug dependence complicating pregnancy, childbirth, or the puerperium, postpartum condition or complication
648.33	Maternal drug dependence, antepartum
648.31	Maternal drug dependence, with delivery
648.32	Maternal drug dependence, with delivery, with current postpartum complication
647.14	Maternal gonorrhea complicating pregnancy, childbrith, or the puerperium, postpartum condition or complication
647.11	Maternal gonorrhea with delivery
647.13	Maternal gonorrhea, antepartum
647.12	Maternal gonorrhea, with delivery, with current postpartum complication
669.24	Maternal hypotension syndrome, postpartum condition or complication
647.41	Maternal malaria with delivery
647.42	Maternal malaria with delivery, with current postpartum complication
647.43	Maternal malaria, antepartum
647.44	Maternal malaria, complicating pregnancy, childbirth, or the puerperium, postpartum condition or complication
647.54	Maternal rubella complicating pregnancy, childbirth, or the puerperium, postpartum condition or complication
647.51	Maternal rubella with delivery
647.52	Maternal rubella with delivery, with current postpartum complication
647.53	Maternal rubella, antepartum
647.04	Maternal syphilis complicating pregnancy, childbrith, or the puerperium, postpartum condition or complication
647.03	Maternal syphilis, antepartum

647.01	Maternal syphilis, complicating pregnancy, with delivery
647.02	Maternal syphilis, complicating pregnancy, with delivery, with current postpartum complication
647.34	Maternal tuberculosis complicating pregnancy, childbirth, or the puerperium, postpartum condition or complication
647.31	Maternal tuberculosis with delivery
647.32	Maternal tuberculosis with delivery, with current postpartum complication
647.33	Maternal tuberculosis, antepartum
055.71	Measles keratoconjunctivitis
996.04	Mechanical complication due to automatic implantable cardiac defibrillator
996.54	Mechanical complication due to breast prosthesis
996.01	Mechanical complication due to cardiac pacemaker (electrode)
996.51	Mechanical complication due to corneal graft
996.03	Mechanical complication due to coronary bypass graft
996.02	Mechanical complication due to heart valve prosthesis
996.57	Mechanical complication due to insulin pump
996.53	Mechanical complication due to ocular lens prosthesis
996.59	Mechanical complication due to other implant and internal device, not elsewhere classified
996.52	Mechanical complication due to other tissue graft, not elsewhere classified
996.09	Mechanical complication of cardiac device, implant, and graft, other
569.62	Mechanical complication of colostomy and enterostomy
596.82	Mechanical complication of cystostomy
530.87	Mechanical complication of esophagostomy
536.42	Mechanical complication of gastrostomy
996.39	Mechanical complication of genitourinary device, implant, and graft, other
996.2	Mechanical complication of nervous system device, implant, and graft
996.1	Mechanical complication of other vascular device, implant, and graft
V46.14	Mechanical complication of respirator [ventilator]
519.02	Mechanical complication of tracheostomy
996.00	Mechanical complication of unspecified cardiac device, implant, and graft
996.30	Mechanical complication of unspecified genitourinary device, implant, and graft
996.55	Mechanical complications due to artificial skin graft and decellularized allodermis
996.56	Mechanical complications due to peritoneal dialysis catheter
996.41	Mechanical loosening of prosthetic joint
255.6	Medulloadrenal hyperfunction
564.7	Megacolon, other than Hirschsprung's
207.21	Megakaryocytic leukemia in remission
207.22	Megakaryocytic leukemia, in relapse
207.20	Megakaryocytic leukemia, without mention of having achieved remission
025	Melioidosis
781.6	Meningismus
049.1	Meningitis due to adenovirus
047.0	Meningitis due to coxsackie virus
047.1	Meningitis due to ECHO virus
036.82	Meningococcal arthropathy
036.81	Meningococcal optic neuritis
639.4	Metabolic disorders following abortion or ectopic and molar pregnancies
121.5	Metagonimiasis
289.7	Methemoglobinemia

Appendix A — Alphabetic CC List

768.71	Mild hypoxic-ischemic encephalopathy
642.43	Mild or unspecified pre-eclampsia, antepartum
642.44	Mild or unspecified pre-eclampsia, postpartum condition or complication
642.41	Mild or unspecified pre-eclampsia, with delivery
255.42	Mineralocorticoid deficiency
276.4	Mixed acid-base balance disorder
127.8	Mixed intestinal helminthiasis
084.5	Mixed malaria
426.12	Mobitz (type) II atrioventricular block
768.72	Moderate hypoxic-ischemic encephalopathy
050.2	Modified smallpox
059.01	Monkeypox
065.4	Mosquito-borne hemorrhagic fever
437.5	Moyamoya disease
085.5	Mucocutaneous leishmaniasis, (American)
277.5	Mucopolysaccharidosis
616.81	Mucositis (ulcerative) of cervix, vagina, and vulva
894.2	Multiple and unspecified open wound of lower limb, with tendon involvement
884.2	Multiple and unspecified open wound of upper limb, with tendon involvement
819.0	Multiple closed fractures involving both upper limbs, and upper limb with rib(s) and sternum
808.43	Multiple closed pelvic fractures with disruption of pelvic circle
808.44	Multiple closed pelvic fractures without disruption of pelvic circle
759.7	Multiple congenital anomalies, so described
203.01	Multiple myeloma in remission
203.02	Multiple myeloma, in relapse
203.00	Multiple myeloma, without mention of having achieved remission
819.1	Multiple open fractures involving both upper limbs, and upper limb with rib(s) and sternum
817.1	Multiple open fractures of hand bones
072.71	Mumps hepatitis
072.0	Mumps orchitis
072.3	Mumps pancreatitis
072.72	Mumps polyneuropathy
072.79	Mumps with other specified complications
081.0	Murine (endemic) typhus
358.1	Myasthenic syndromes in diseases classified elsewhere
202.13	Mycosis fungoides of intra-abdominal lymph nodes
202.16	Mycosis fungoides of intrapelvic lymph nodes
202.12	Mycosis fungoides of intrathoracic lymph nodes
202.14	Mycosis fungoides of lymph nodes of axilla and upper limb
202.11	Mycosis fungoides of lymph nodes of head, face, and neck
202.15	Mycosis fungoides of lymph nodes of inguinal region and lower limb
202.18	Mycosis fungoides of lymph nodes of multiple sites
202.17	Mycosis fungoides of spleen
202.10	Mycosis fungoides, unspecified site, extranodal and solid organ sites
117.4	Mycotic mycetomas
238.74	Myelodysplastic syndrome with 5q deletion
289.83	Myelofibrosis
238.76	Myelofibrosis with myeloid metaplasia
205.31	Myeloid sarcoma in remission
205.32	Myeloid sarcoma, in relapse
205.30	Myeloid sarcoma, without mention of having achieved remission
336.3	Myelopathy in other diseases classified elsewhere
284.2	Myelophthisis

791.3	Myoglobinuria
802.1	Nasal bones, open fracture
032.1	Nasopharyngeal diphtheria
040.3	Necrobacillosis
447.5	Necrosis of artery
775.1	Neonatal diabetes mellitus
771.5	Neonatal infective mastitis
775.2	Neonatal myasthenia gravis
775.3	Neonatal thyrotoxicosis
238.5	Neoplasm of uncertain behavior of histiocytic and mast cells
238.6	Neoplasm of uncertain behavior of plasma cells
583.2	Nephritis and nephropathy, not specified as acute or chronic, with lesion of membranoproliferative glomerulonephritis
583.1	Nephritis and nephropathy, not specified as acute or chronic, with lesion of membranous glomerulonephritis
583.0	Nephritis and nephropathy, not specified as acute or chronic, with lesion of proliferative glomerulonephritis
583.7	Nephritis and nephropathy, not specified as acute or chronic, with lesion of renal medullary necrosis
588.1	Nephrogenic diabetes insipidus
581.2	Nephrotic syndrome with lesion of membranoproliferative glomerulonephritis
581.1	Nephrotic syndrome with lesion of membranous glomerulonephritis
581.3	Nephrotic syndrome with lesion of minimal change glomerulonephritis
581.0	Nephrotic syndrome with lesion of proliferative glomerulonephritis
581.81	Nephrotic syndrome with other specified pathological lesion in kidney in diseases classified elsewhere
581.9	Nephrotic syndrome with unspecified pathological lesion in kidney
349.1	Nervous system complications from surgically implanted device
564.81	Neurogenic bowel
781.8	Neurological neglect syndrome
341.0	Neuromyelitis optica
279.13	Nezelof's syndrome
202.03	Nodular lymphoma of intra-abdominal lymph nodes
202.06	Nodular lymphoma of intrapelvic lymph nodes
202.02	Nodular lymphoma of intrathoracic lymph nodes
202.04	Nodular lymphoma of lymph nodes of axilla and upper limb
202.01	Nodular lymphoma of lymph nodes of head, face, and neck
202.05	Nodular lymphoma of lymph nodes of inguinal region and lower limb
202.08	Nodular lymphoma of lymph nodes of multiple sites
202.07	Nodular lymphoma of spleen
202.00	Nodular lymphoma, unspecified site, extranodal and solid organ sites
999.75	Non-ABO incompatibility reaction, unspecified
999.77	Non-ABO incompatibility with acute hemolytic transfusion reaction
999.78	Non-ABO incompatibility with delayed hemolytic transfusion reaction
999.76	Non-ABO incompatibility with hemolytic transfusion reaction not specified as acute or delayed
998.83	Non-healing surgical wound
437.6	Nonpyogenic thrombosis of intracranial venous sinus
729.73	Nontraumatic compartment syndrome of abdomen
729.72	Nontraumatic compartment syndrome of lower extremity
729.79	Nontraumatic compartment syndrome of other sites
729.71	Nontraumatic compartment syndrome of upper extremity
733.82	Nonunion of fracture
082.2	North Asian tick fever
425.7	Nutritional and metabolic cardiomyopathy

278.03	Obesity hypoventilation syndrome
425.2	Obscure cardiomyopathy of Africa
673.30	Obstetrical pyemic and septic embolism, unspecified as to episode of care
660.03	Obstruction caused by malposition of fetus at onset of labor, antepartum
575.2	Obstruction of gallbladder
491.22	Obstructive chronic bronchitis with acute bronchitis
491.21	Obstructive chronic bronchitis, with (acute) exacerbation
331.4	Obstructive hydrocephalus
871.1	Ocular laceration with prolapse or exposure of intraocular tissue
871.0	Ocular laceration without prolapse of intraocular tissue
021.3	Oculoglandular tularemia
658.03	Oligohydramnios, antepartum
658.01	Oligohydramnios, delivered
771.4	Omphalitis of the newborn
065.1	Omsk hemorrhagic fever
125.3	Onchocerciasis
832.11	Open anterior dislocation of elbow
831.11	Open anterior dislocation of humerus
836.61	Open anterior dislocation of tibia, proximal end
824.5	Open bimalleolar fracture
831.14	Open dislocation of acromioclavicular (joint)
837.1	Open dislocation of ankle
833.14	Open dislocation of carpometacarpal (joint)
833.11	Open dislocation of distal radioulnar (joint)
830.1	Open dislocation of jaw
836.60	Open dislocation of knee unspecified part
833.13	Open dislocation of midcarpal (joint)
833.19	Open dislocation of other part of wrist
832.19	Open dislocation of other site of elbow
831.19	Open dislocation of other site of shoulder
836.4	Open dislocation of patella
833.15	Open dislocation of proximal end of metacarpal (bone)
833.12	Open dislocation of radiocarpal (joint)
833.10	Open dislocation of wrist, unspecified part
839.51	Open dislocation, coccyx
839.9	Open dislocation, multiple and ill-defined sites
839.79	Open dislocation, other location
839.52	Open dislocation, sacrum
810.13	Open fracture of acromial end of clavicle
811.11	Open fracture of acromial process of scapula
802.37	Open fracture of alveolar border of body of mandible
802.35	Open fracture of angle of jaw
825.31	Open fracture of astragalus
815.12	Open fracture of base of other metacarpal bone(s)
815.11	Open fracture of base of thumb (first) metacarpal bone(s)
825.1	Open fracture of calcaneus
814.17	Open fracture of capitate bone (os magnum) of wrist
802.31	Open fracture of condylar process of mandible
811.12	Open fracture of coracoid process
802.33	Open fracture of coronoid process of mandible
825.33	Open fracture of cuboid bone
825.34	Open fracture of cuneiform bone of foot,
816.12	Open fracture of distal phalanx or phalanges of hand
811.13	Open fracture of glenoid cavity and neck of scapula
814.18	Open fracture of hamate (unciform) bone of wrist
824.3	Open fracture of lateral malleolus
814.12	Open fracture of lunate (semilunar) bone of wrist

824.1	Open fracture of medial malleolus
815.10	Open fracture of metacarpal bone(s), site unspecified
825.35	Open fracture of metatarsal bone(s)
816.11	Open fracture of middle or proximal phalanx or phalanges of hand
802.39	Open fracture of multiple sites of mandible
815.19	Open fracture of multiple sites of metacarpus
825.32	Open fracture of navicular (scaphoid) bone of foot
814.11	Open fracture of navicular (scaphoid) bone of wrist
815.14	Open fracture of neck of metacarpal bone(s)
802.38	Open fracture of other and unspecified part of body of mandible
814.19	Open fracture of other bone of wrist
811.19	Open fracture of other part of scapula
822.1	Open fracture of patella
816.10	Open fracture of phalanx or phalanges of hand, unspecified
814.14	Open fracture of pisiform bone of wrist
810.12	Open fracture of shaft of clavicle
815.13	Open fracture of shaft of metacarpal bone(s)
810.11	Open fracture of sternal end of clavicle
802.32	Open fracture of subcondylar process of mandible
802.36	Open fracture of symphysis of body of mandible
814.15	Open fracture of trapezium bone (larger multangular) of wrist
814.16	Open fracture of trapezoid bone (smaller multangular) of wrist
814.13	Open fracture of triquetral (cuneiform) bone of wrist
825.30	Open fracture of unspecified bone(s) of foot (except toes)
802.34	Open fracture of unspecified part of ramus of mandible
811.10	Open fracture of unspecified part of scapula
802.30	Open fracture of unspecified site of mandible
804.92	Open fractures involving skull or face with other bones, with intracranial injury of other and unspecified nature, brief (less than one hour) loss of consciousness
804.96	Open fractures involving skull or face with other bones, with intracranial injury of other and unspecified nature, loss of consciousness of unspecified duration
804.91	Open fractures involving skull or face with other bones, with intracranial injury of other and unspecified nature, no loss of consciousness
804.99	Open fractures involving skull or face with other bones, with intracranial injury of other and unspecified nature, unspecified concussion
804.90	Open fractures involving skull or face with other bones, with intracranial injury of other and unspecified nature, unspecified state of consciousness
804.52	Open fractures involving skull or face with other bones, without mention of intracranial injury, brief (less than one hour) loss of consciousness
804.56	Open fractures involving skull or face with other bones, without mention of intracranial injury, loss of consciousness of unspecified duration
804.51	Open fractures involving skull or face with other bones, without mention of intracranial injury, no loss of consciousness
804.59	Open fractures involving skull or face with other bones, without mention of intracranial injury, unspecified concussion
804.50	Open fractures involving skull or face with other bones, without mention of intracranial injury, unspecified state of consciousness
816.13	Open fractures of multiple sites of phalanx or phalanges of hand
831.13	Open inferior dislocation of humerus
832.14	Open lateral dislocation of elbow
836.64	Open lateral dislocation of tibia, proximal end
832.13	Open medial dislocation of elbow
836.63	Open medial dislocation of tibia, proximal end
832.12	Open posterior dislocation of elbow
831.12	Open posterior dislocation of humerus

836.62	Open posterior dislocation of tibia, proximal end
824.7	Open trimalleolar fracture
832.10	Open unspecified dislocation of elbow
831.10	Open unspecified dislocation of shoulder
872.12	Open wound of auditory canal, complicated
880.22	Open wound of axillary region, with tendon involvement
875.1	Open wound of chest (wall), complicated
875.0	Open wound of chest (wall), without mention of complication
872.74	Open wound of cochlea, complicated
872.64	Open wound of cochlea, without mention of complication
872.71	Open wound of ear drum, complicated
872.61	Open wound of ear drum, without mention of complication
881.21	Open wound of elbow, with tendon involvement
872.73	Open wound of Eustachian tube, complicated
872.63	Open wound of Eustachian tube, without mention of complication
883.2	Open wound of finger(s), with tendon involvement
892.2	Open wound of foot except toe(s) alone, with tendon involvement
881.20	Open wound of forearm, with tendon involvement
882.2	Open wound of hand except finger(s) alone, with tendon involvement
890.2	Open wound of hip and thigh, with tendon involvement
891.2	Open wound of knee, leg (except thigh), and ankle, with tendon involvement
880.29	Open wound of multiple sites of shoulder and upper arm, with tendon involvement
873.33	Open wound of nasal sinus, complicated
873.23	Open wound of nasal sinus, without mention of complication
872.72	Open wound of ossicles, complicated
872.62	Open wound of ossicles, without mention of complication
872.79	Open wound of other and multiple sites, complicated
872.69	Open wound of other and multiple sites, without mention of complication
874.5	Open wound of pharynx, complicated
874.4	Open wound of pharynx, without mention of complication
880.21	Open wound of scapular region, with tendon involvement
880.20	Open wound of shoulder region, with tendon involvement
874.3	Open wound of thyroid gland, complicated
874.2	Open wound of thyroid gland, without mention of complication
893.2	Open wound of toe(s), with tendon involvement
880.23	Open wound of upper arm, with tendon involvement
881.22	Open wound of wrist, with tendon involvement
304.01	Opioid type dependence, continuous pattern of use
121.0	Opisthorchiasis
118	Opportunistic mycoses
950.0	Optic nerve injury
377.31	Optic papillitis
376.01	Orbital cellulitis
802.6	Orbital floor (blow-out), closed fracture
802.7	Orbital floor (blow-out), open fracture
376.03	Orbital osteomyelitis
376.02	Orbital periostitis
604.0	Orchitis, epididymitis, and epididymo-orchitis, with abscess
V43.22	Organ or tissue replaced by other means, Fully implantable artificial heart
V43.21	Organ or tissue replaced by other means, Heart assist device
V42.84	Organ or tissue replaced by transplant, intestines
073.7	Ornithosis with other specified complications
073.8	Ornithosis with unspecified complication
756.51	Osteogenesis imperfecta
756.52	Osteopetrosis

745.61	Ostium primum defect
745.5	Ostium secundum type atrial septal defect
999.69	Other ABO incompatibility reaction
616.4	Other abscess of vulva
775.81	Other acidosis of newborn
333.79	Other acquired torsion dystonia
411.89	Other acute and subacute form of ischemic heart disease
420.99	Other acute pericarditis
391.8	Other acute rheumatic heart disease
255.5	Other adrenal hypofunction
995.85	Other adult abuse and neglect
512.84	Other air leak
277.39	Other amyloidosis
995.0	Other anaphylactic reaction
253.1	Other and unspecified anterior pituitary hyperfunction
770.5	Other and unspecified atelectasis of newborn
296.89	Other and unspecified bipolar disorders
286.9	Other and unspecified coagulation defects
046.19	Other and unspecified Creutzfeldt-Jakob disease
122.9	Other and unspecified echinococcosis
778.5	Other and unspecified edema of newborn
999.31	Other and unspecified infection due to central venous catheter
202.93	Other and unspecified malignant neoplasms of lymphoid and histiocytic tissue of intra-abdominal lymph nodes
202.96	Other and unspecified malignant neoplasms of lymphoid and histiocytic tissue of intrapelvic lymph nodes
202.92	Other and unspecified malignant neoplasms of lymphoid and histiocytic tissue of intrathoracic lymph nodes
202.94	Other and unspecified malignant neoplasms of lymphoid and histiocytic tissue of lymph nodes of axilla and upper limb
202.91	Other and unspecified malignant neoplasms of lymphoid and histiocytic tissue of lymph nodes of head, face, and neck
202.95	Other and unspecified malignant neoplasms of lymphoid and histiocytic tissue of lymph nodes of inguinal region and lower limb
202.98	Other and unspecified malignant neoplasms of lymphoid and histiocytic tissue of lymph nodes of multiple sites
202.97	Other and unspecified malignant neoplasms of lymphoid and histiocytic tissue of spleen
202.90	Other and unspecified malignant neoplasms of lymphoid and histiocytic tissue, unspecified site, extranodal and solid organ sites
265.1	Other and unspecified manifestations of thiamine deficiency
117.9	Other and unspecified mycoses
579.3	Other and unspecified postsurgical nonabsorption
046.79	Other and unspecified prion disease of central nervous system
414.19	Other aneurysm of heart
671.53	Other antepartum phlebitis and thrombosis
335.8	Other anterior horn cell diseases
770.82	Other apnea of newborn
444.09	Other arterial embolism and thrombosis of abdominal aorta
789.59	Other ascites
005.89	Other bacterial food poisoning
426.53	Other bilateral bundle branch block
023.8	Other brucellosis
112.89	Other candidiasis of other specified sites
334.3	Other cerebellar ataxia
429.79	Other certain sequelae of myocardial infarction, not elsewhere classified
995.59	Other child abuse and neglect
582.89	Other chronic glomerulonephritis with specified pathological lesion in kidney
614.7	Other chronic pelvic peritonitis, female

835.03	Other closed anterior dislocation of hip
821.29	Other closed fracture of lower end of femur
812.49	Other closed fracture of lower end of humerus
813.42	Other closed fractures of distal end of radius (alone)
812.09	Other closed fractures of upper end of humerus
803.42	Other closed skull fracture with intracranial injury of other and unspecified nature, brief (less than one hour) loss of consciousness
803.46	Other closed skull fracture with intracranial injury of other and unspecified nature, loss of consciousness of unspecified duration
803.41	Other closed skull fracture with intracranial injury of other and unspecified nature, no loss of consciousness
803.49	Other closed skull fracture with intracranial injury of other and unspecified nature, unspecified concussion
803.40	Other closed skull fracture with intracranial injury of other and unspecified nature, unspecified state of consciousness
803.02	Other closed skull fracture without mention of intracranial injury, brief (less than one hour) loss of consciousness
803.06	Other closed skull fracture without mention of intracranial injury, loss of consciousness of unspecified duration
803.01	Other closed skull fracture without mention of intracranial injury, no loss of consciousness
803.09	Other closed skull fracture without mention of intracranial injury, unspecified concussion
803.00	Other closed skull fracture without mention of intracranial injury, unspecified state of consciousness
863.49	Other colon and rectum injury, without mention of open wound into cavity
569.69	Other complication of colostomy or enterostomy
596.83	Other complication of cystostomy
997.99	Other complications affecting other specified body systems, NEC
996.76	Other complications due to genitourinary device, implant, and graft
996.71	Other complications due to heart valve prosthesis
996.77	Other complications due to internal joint prosthesis
996.75	Other complications due to nervous system device, implant, and graft
996.72	Other complications due to other cardiac device, implant, and graft
996.78	Other complications due to other internal orthopedic device, implant, and graft
996.79	Other complications due to other internal prosthetic device, implant, and graft
996.74	Other complications due to other vascular device, implant, and graft
996.73	Other complications due to renal dialysis device, implant, and graft
539.09	Other complications of gastric band procedure
569.79	Other complications of intestinal pouch
539.89	Other complications of other bariatric procedure
747.49	Other congenital anomalies of great veins
751.5	Other congenital anomalies of intestine
746.09	Other congenital anomalies of pulmonary valve
747.29	Other congenital anomaly of aorta
751.69	Other congenital anomaly of gallbladder, bile ducts, and liver
748.3	Other congenital anomaly of larynx, trachea, and bronchus
756.3	Other congenital anomaly of ribs and sternum
745.69	Other congenital endocardial cushion defect
759.6	Other congenital hamartoses, not elsewhere classified
284.09	Other constitutional aplastic anemia
255.3	Other corticoadrenal overactivity
279.19	Other deficiency of cell-mediated immunity
279.09	Other deficiency of humoral immunity
333.0	Other degenerative diseases of the basal ganglia
341.8	Other demyelinating diseases of central nervous system
997.49	Other digestive system complications

253.6	Other disorders of neurohypophysis
429.81	Other disorders of papillary muscle
277.2	Other disorders of purine and pyrimidine metabolism
270.2	Other disturbances of aromatic amino-acid metabolism
270.7	Other disturbances of straight-chain amino-acid metabolism
349.39	Other dural tear
122.3	Other echinococcus granulosus infection
122.6	Other echinococcus multilocularis infection
633.81	Other ectopic pregnancy with intrauterine pregnancy
633.80	Other ectopic pregnancy without intrauterine pregnancy
082.49	Other ehrlichiosis
424.99	Other endocarditis, valve unspecified
360.19	Other endophthalmitis
048	Other enterovirus diseases of central nervous system
802.8	Other facial bones, closed fracture
802.9	Other facial bones, open fracture
345.81	Other forms of epilepsy and recurrent seizures, with intractable epilepsy
345.80	Other forms of epilepsy and recurrent seizures, without mention of intractable epilepsy
114.3	Other forms of progressive coccidioidomycosis
361.89	Other forms of retinal detachment
437.1	Other generalized ischemic cerebrovascular disease
098.85	Other gonococcal heart disease
098.49	Other gonococcal infection of eye
098.59	Other gonococcal infection of joint
098.19	Other gonococcal infections (acute) of upper genitourinary tract
786.39	Other hemoptysis
286.59	Other hemorrhagic disorder due to intrinsic circulating anticoagulants, antibodies, or inhibitors
053.19	Other herpes zoster with nervous system complications
425.18	Other hypertrophic cardiomyopathy
666.14	Other immediate postpartum hemorrhage, postpartum condition or complication
666.12	Other immediate postpartum hemorrhage, with delivery
203.81	Other immunoproliferative neoplasms in remission
203.82	Other immunoproliferative neoplasms, in relapse
203.80	Other immunoproliferative neoplasms, without mention of having achieved remission
730.87	Other infections involving bone diseases classified elsewhere, ankle and foot
730.86	Other infections involving bone diseases classified elsewhere, lower leg
730.89	Other infections involving bone diseases classified elsewhere, multiple sites
730.88	Other infections involving bone diseases classified elsewhere, other specified sites
730.85	Other infections involving bone diseases classified elsewhere, pelvic region and thigh
730.81	Other infections involving bone diseases classified elsewhere, shoulder region
730.82	Other infections involving bone diseases classified elsewhere, upper arm
730.83	Other infections involving bone in diseases classified elsewhere, forearm
730.80	Other infections involving bone in diseases classified elsewhere, site unspecified
730.84	Other infections involving diseases classified elsewhere, hand bone
771.89	Other infections specific to the perinatal period
665.51	Other injury to pelvic organs, with delivery
863.29	Other injury to small intestine without mention of open wound into cavity

090.49	Other juvenile neurosyphilis
090.5	Other late congenital syphilis, symptomatic
208.81	Other leukemia of unspecified cell type in remission
208.82	Other leukemia of unspecified cell type, in relapse
208.80	Other leukemia of unspecified cell type, without mention of having achieved remission
864.09	Other liver injury without mention of open wound into cavity
003.29	Other localized salmonella infections
238.79	Other lymphatic and hematopoietic tissues
204.81	Other lymphoid leukemia in remission
204.82	Other lymphoid leukemia, in relapse
204.80	Other lymphoid leukemia, without mention of having achieved remission
084.4	Other malaria
202.83	Other malignant lymphomas of intra-abdominal lymph nodes
202.86	Other malignant lymphomas of intrapelvic lymph nodes
202.82	Other malignant lymphomas of intrathoracic lymph nodes
202.84	Other malignant lymphomas of lymph nodes of axilla and upper limb
202.81	Other malignant lymphomas of lymph nodes of head, face, and neck
202.85	Other malignant lymphomas of lymph nodes of inguinal region and lower limb
202.88	Other malignant lymphomas of lymph nodes of multiple sites
202.87	Other malignant lymphomas of spleen
202.80	Other malignant lymphomas, unspecified site, extranodal and solid organ sites
648.64	Other maternal cardiovascular diseases complicating pregnancy, childbirth, or the puerperium, postpartum condition or complication
648.63	Other maternal cardiovascular diseases, antepartum
648.61	Other maternal cardiovascular diseases with delivery
648.62	Other maternal cardiovascular diseases, with delivery, with current postpartum complication
647.21	Other maternal venereal diseases with delivery
647.22	Other maternal venereal diseases with delivery, with current postpartum complication
647.23	Other maternal venereal diseases, antepartum condition or complication
647.61	Other maternal viral disease with delivery
647.62	Other maternal viral disease with delivery, with current postpartum complication
647.63	Other maternal viral disease, antepartum
647.64	Other maternal viral diseases complicating pregnancy, childbirth, or the puerperium, postpartum condition or complication
996.49	Other mechanical complication of other internal orthopedic device, implant, and graft
996.47	Other mechanical complication of prosthetic joint implant
206.81	Other monocytic leukemia in remission
206.82	Other monocytic leukemia, in relapse
206.80	Other monocytic leukemia, without mention of having achieved remission
066.3	Other mosquito-borne fever
335.29	Other motor neuron diseases
205.81	Other myeloid leukemia in remission
205.82	Other myeloid leukemia, in relapse
205.80	Other myeloid leukemia, without mention of having achieved remission
336.8	Other myelopathy
200.83	Other named variants of lymphosarcoma and reticulosarcoma of intra-abdominal lymph nodes
200.86	Other named variants of lymphosarcoma and reticulosarcoma of intrapelvic lymph nodes
200.82	Other named variants of lymphosarcoma and reticulosarcoma of intrathoracic lymph nodes
200.84	Other named variants of lymphosarcoma and reticulosarcoma of lymph nodes of axilla and upper limb
200.81	Other named variants of lymphosarcoma and reticulosarcoma of lymph nodes of head, face, and neck
200.85	Other named variants of lymphosarcoma and reticulosarcoma of lymph nodes of inguinal region and lower limb
200.88	Other named variants of lymphosarcoma and reticulosarcoma of lymph nodes of multiple sites
200.87	Other named variants of lymphosarcoma and reticulosarcoma of spleen
200.80	Other named variants, unspecified site, extranodal and solid organ sites
775.89	Other neonatal endocrine and metabolic disturbances
581.89	Other nephrotic syndrome with specified pathological lesion in kidney
997.09	Other nervous system complications
056.09	Other neurological rubella complications
999.79	Other non-ABO incompatibility reaction
283.19	Other non-autoimmune hemolytic anemias
537.3	Other obstruction of duodenum
753.29	Other obstructive defect of renal pelvis and ureter
836.69	Other open dislocation of knee
825.39	Other open fractures of tarsal and metatarsal bones
053.29	Other ophthalmic herpes zoster complications
377.39	Other optic neuritis
284.19	Other pancytopenia
084.9	Other pernicious complications of malaria
671.50	Other phlebitis and thrombosis complicating pregnancy and the puerperium, unspecified as to episode of care
671.52	Other phlebitis and thrombosis with delivery, with mention of postpartum complication
671.51	Other phlebitis and thrombosis with delivery, with or without mention of antepartum condition
671.54	Other phlebitis and thrombosis, postpartum condition or complication
512.89	Other pneumothorax
998.59	Other postoperative infection
425.4	Other primary cardiomyopathies
010.81	Other primary progressive tuberculosis infection, bacteriological or histological examination not done
010.82	Other primary progressive tuberculosis infection, bacteriological or histological examination unknown (at present)
010.80	Other primary progressive tuberculosis infection, confirmation unspecified
010.83	Other primary progressive tuberculosis infection, tubercle bacilli found (in sputum) by microscopy
010.84	Other primary progressive tuberculosis infection, tubercle bacilli not found (in sputum) by microscopy, but found by bacterial culture
010.85	Other primary progressive tuberculosis infection, tubercle bacilli not found by bacteriological examination, but tuberculosis confirmed histologically
010.86	Other primary progressive tuberculosis infection, tubercle bacilli not found by bacteriological or histological examination, but tuberculosis confirmed by other methods [inoculation of animals]
658.81	Other problem associated with amniotic cavity and membranes, delivered
263.8	Other protein-calorie malnutrition
518.82	Other pulmonary insufficiency, not elsewhere classified
997.39	Other respiratory complications
999.74	Other Rh incompatibility reaction
405.09	Other secondary hypertension, malignant

279.03	Other selective immunoglobulin deficiencies	055.79	Other specified measles complications
999.59	Other serum reaction	036.89	Other specified meningococcal infections
999.51	Other serum reaction due to administration of blood and blood products	759.89	Other specified multiple congenital anomalies, so described
999.52	Other serum reaction due to vaccination	651.83	Other specified multiple gestation, antepartum
136.29	Other specific infections by free-living amebae	651.81	Other specified multiple gestation, delivered
291.89	Other specified alcohol-induced mental disorders	094.89	Other specified neurosyphilis
495.8	Other specified allergic alveolitis and pneumonitis	049.8	Other specified non-arthropod-borne viral diseases of central nervous system
516.8	Other specified alveolar and parietoalveolar pneumonopathies	754.89	Other specified nonteratogenic anomalies
065.8	Other specified arthropod-borne hemorrhagic fever	870.8	Other specified open wound of ocular adnexa
066.8	Other specified arthropod-borne viral diseases	299.80	Other specified pervasive developmental disorders, current or active state
093.89	Other specified cardiovascular syphilis	299.81	Other specified pervasive developmental disorders, residual state
330.8	Other specified cerebral degenerations in childhood	007.8	Other specified protozoal intestinal diseases
123.8	Other specified cestode infection	011.81	Other specified pulmonary tuberculosis, bacteriological or histological examination not done
639.8	Other specified complication following abortion or ectopic and molar pregnancies	011.82	Other specified pulmonary tuberculosis, bacteriological or histological examination unknown (at present)
426.89	Other specified conduction disorder	011.80	Other specified pulmonary tuberculosis, confirmation unspecified
742.4	Other specified congenital anomalies of brain	011.83	Other specified pulmonary tuberculosis, tubercle bacilli found (in sputum) by microscopy
747.89	Other specified congenital anomaly of circulatory system	011.84	Other specified pulmonary tuberculosis, tubercle bacilli not found (in sputum) by microscopy, but found by bacterial culture
750.4	Other specified congenital anomaly of esophagus		
753.19	Other specified congenital cystic kidney disease	011.85	Other specified pulmonary tuberculosis, tubercle bacilli not found by bacteriological examination, but tuberculosis confirmed histologically
710.8	Other specified diffuse disease of connective tissue		
032.89	Other specified diphtheria	011.86	Other specified pulmonary tuberculosis, tubercle bacilli not found by bacteriological or histological examination, but tuberculosis confirmed by other methods [inoculation of animals]
031.8	Other specified diseases due to other mycobacteria		
423.8	Other specified diseases of pericardium		
270.8	Other specified disorders of amino-acid metabolism		
271.8	Other specified disorders of carbohydrate transport and metabolism	012.81	Other specified respiratory tuberculosis, bacteriological or histological examination not done
277.89	Other specified disorders of metabolism	012.82	Other specified respiratory tuberculosis, bacteriological or histological examination unknown (at present)
304.61	Other specified drug dependence, continuous pattern of use	012.80	Other specified respiratory tuberculosis, confirmation unspecified
296.99	Other specified episodic mood disorder	012.83	Other specified respiratory tuberculosis, tubercle bacilli found (in sputum) by microscopy
125.6	Other specified filariasis		
619.8	Other specified fistula involving female genital tract	012.84	Other specified respiratory tuberculosis, tubercle bacilli not found (in sputum) by microscopy, but found by bacterial culture
511.89	Other specified forms of effusion, except tuberculous		
095.8	Other specified forms of late symptomatic syphilis	012.85	Other specified respiratory tuberculosis, tubercle bacilli not found by bacteriological examination, but tuberculosis confirmed histologically
342.81	Other specified hemiplegia affecting dominant side		
342.82	Other specified hemiplegia affecting nondominant side	012.86	Other specified respiratory tuberculosis, tubercle bacilli not found by bacteriological or histological examination, but tuberculosis confirmed by other methods [inoculation of animals]
342.80	Other specified hemiplegia affecting unspecified side		
282.8	Other specified hereditary hemolytic anemias		
054.79	Other specified herpes simplex complications	083.8	Other specified rickettsioses
053.79	Other specified herpes zoster complications	003.8	Other specified salmonella infections
446.29	Other specified hypersensitivity angiitis	120.8	Other specified schistosomiasis
127.7	Other specified intestinal helminthiasis	290.8	Other specified senile psychotic conditions
579.8	Other specified intestinal malabsorption	046.8	Other specified slow virus infection of central nervous system
560.89	Other specified intestinal obstruction	082.8	Other specified tick-borne rickettsioses
030.8	Other specified leprosy	435.8	Other specified transient cerebral ischemias
100.89	Other specified leptospiral infections	121.8	Other specified trematode infections
207.81	Other specified leukemia in remission	021.8	Other specified tularemia
207.82	Other specified leukemia, in relapse	295.82	Other specified types of schizophrenia, chronic condition
207.80	Other specified leukemia, without mention of having achieved remission	295.84	Other specified types of schizophrenia, chronic condition with acute exacerbation
022.8	Other specified manifestations of anthrax	295.81	Other specified types of schizophrenia, subchronic condition
647.81	Other specified maternal infectious and parasitic disease with delivery	295.83	Other specified types of schizophrenia, subchronic condition with acute exacerbation
647.82	Other specified maternal infectious and parasitic disease with delivery, with current postpartum complication	295.80	Other specified types of schizophrenia, unspecified condition
647.83	Other specified maternal infectious and parasitic disease, antepartum	070.59	Other specified viral hepatitis without mention of hepatic coma
647.84	Other specified maternal infectious and parasitic diseases complicating pregnancy, childbirth, or the puerperium, postpartum condition or complication	047.8	Other specified viral meningitis
		027.8	Other specified zoonotic bacterial diseases

335.19	Other spinal muscular atrophy
334.8	Other spinocerebellar diseases
865.09	Other spleen injury without mention of open wound into cavity
644.13	Other threatened labor, antepartum
065.3	Other tick-borne hemorrhagic fever
519.09	Other tracheostomy complications
776.3	Other transient neonatal disorders of coagulation
556.8	Other ulcerative colitis
593.4	Other ureteric obstruction
999.2	Other vascular complications of medical care, not elsewhere classified
647.24	Other venereal diseases complicating pregnancy, childbrith, or the puerperium, postpartum condition or complication
671.80	Other venous complication of pregnancy and the puerperium, unspecified as to episode of care
671.83	Other venous complication, antepartum
671.82	Other venous complication, with delivery, with mention of postpartum complication
671.81	Other venous complication, with delivery, with or without mention of antepartum condition
671.84	Other venous complications, postpartum condition or complication
552.29	Other ventral hernia with obstruction
827.1	Other, multiple and ill-defined open fractures of lower limb
053.71	Otitis externa due to herpes zoster
084.3	Ovale malaria
902.81	Ovarian artery injury
633.21	Ovarian pregnancy with intrauterine pregnancy
633.20	Ovarian pregnancy without intrauterine pregnancy
902.82	Ovarian vein injury
903.4	Palmar artery injury
863.82	Pancreas body injury without mention of open wound into cavity
863.81	Pancreas head injury without mention of open wound into cavity
863.84	Pancreas injury, multiple and unspecified sites, without mention of open wound into cavity
V42.83	Pancreas replaced by transplant
863.83	Pancreas tail injury without mention of open wound into cavity
579.4	Pancreatic steatorrhea
253.2	Panhypopituitarism
360.02	Panophthalmitis
360.12	Panuveitis
377.01	Papilledema associated with increased intracranial pressure
116.1	Paracoccidioidomycosis
121.2	Paragonimiasis
560.1	Paralytic ileus
295.32	Paranoid schizophrenia, chronic condition
295.34	Paranoid schizophrenia, chronic condition with acute exacerbation
295.31	Paranoid schizophrenia, subchronic condition
295.33	Paranoid schizophrenia, subchronic condition with acute exacerbation
295.30	Paranoid schizophrenia, unspecified condition
478.22	Parapharyngeal abscess
344.1	Paraplegia
360.13	Parasitic endophthalmitis NOS
002.1	Paratyphoid fever A
002.2	Paratyphoid fever B
002.3	Paratyphoid fever C
427.0	Paroxysmal supraventricular tachycardia
427.1	Paroxysmal ventricular tachycardia
362.33	Partial arterial occlusion of retina
747.42	Partial congenital anomalous pulmonary venous connection

079.83	Parvovirus B19
027.2	Pasteurellosis
758.1	Patau's syndrome
747.0	Patent ductus arteriosus
733.12	Pathologic fracture of distal radius and ulna
733.11	Pathologic fracture of humerus
733.14	Pathologic fracture of neck of femur
733.15	Pathologic fracture of other specified part of femur
733.19	Pathologic fracture of other specified site
733.16	Pathologic fracture of tibia and fibula
733.13	Pathologic fracture of vertebrae
733.10	Pathologic fracture, unspecified site
665.72	Pelvic hematoma, delivered with postpartum complication
665.71	Pelvic hematoma, with delivery
694.5	Pemphigoid
694.4	Pemphigus
870.4	Penetrating wound of orbit with foreign body
870.3	Penetrating wound of orbit, without mention of foreign body
871.6	Penetration of eyeball with (nonmagnetic) foreign body
871.5	Penetration of eyeball with magnetic foreign body
996.44	Peri-prosthetic fracture around prosthetic joint
996.45	Peri-prosthetic osteolysis
337.1	Peripheral autonomic neuropathy in disorders classified elsewhere
V42.82	Peripheral stem cells replaced by transplant
202.73	Peripheral T-cell lymphoma, intra-abdominal lymph nodes
202.76	Peripheral T-cell lymphoma, intrapelvic lymph nodes
202.72	Peripheral T-cell lymphoma, intrathoracic lymph nodes
202.74	Peripheral T-cell lymphoma, lymph nodes of axilla and upper limb
202.71	Peripheral T-cell lymphoma, lymph nodes of head, face, and neck
202.75	Peripheral T-cell lymphoma, lymph nodes of inguinal region and lower limb
202.78	Peripheral T-cell lymphoma, lymph nodes of multiple sites
202.77	Peripheral T-cell lymphoma, spleen
202.70	Peripheral T-cell lymphoma, unspecified site, extranodal and solid organ sites
997.2	Peripheral vascular complications
568.82	Peritoneal effusion (chronic)
868.03	Peritoneum injury without mention of open wound into cavity
475	Peritonsillar abscess
277.86	Peroxisomal disorders
346.63	Persistent migraine aura with cerebral infarction, with intractable migraine, so stated, with status migrainosus
346.61	Persistent migraine aura with cerebral infarction, with intractable migraine, so stated, without mention of status migrainosus
346.62	Persistent migraine aura with cerebral infarction, without mention of intractable migraine with status migrainosus
346.60	Persistent migraine aura with cerebral infarction, without mention of intractable migraine without mention of status migrainosus
998.6	Persistent postoperative fistula, not elsewhere classified
780.03	Persistent vegetative state
270.1	Phenylketonuria (PKU)
451.83	Phlebitis and thrombophlebitis of deep veins of upper extremities
451.11	Phlebitis and thrombophlebitis of femoral vein (deep) (superficial)
451.81	Phlebitis and thrombophlebitis of iliac vein
451.19	Phlebitis and thrombophlebitis of other deep vessels of lower extremities
451.89	Phlebitis and thrombophlebitis of other site
066.0	Phlebotomus fever
685.0	Pilonidal cyst with abscess
641.03	Placenta previa without hemorrhage, antepartum

641.01	Placenta previa without hemorrhage, with delivery
203.11	Plasma cell leukemia in remission
203.12	Plasma cell leukemia, in relapse
203.10	Plasma cell leukemia, without mention of having achieved remission
446.0	Polyarteritis nodosa
714.31	Polyarticular juvenile rheumatoid arthritis, acute
657.01	Polyhydramnios, with delivery
710.4	Polymyositis
656.51	Poor fetal growth, affecting management of mother, delivered
572.3	Portal hypertension
780.33	Post traumatic seizures
238.77	Post-transplant lymphoproliferative disorder [PTLD]
711.37	Postdysenteric arthropathy, ankle and foot
711.33	Postdysenteric arthropathy, forearm
711.34	Postdysenteric arthropathy, hand
711.36	Postdysenteric arthropathy, lower leg
711.39	Postdysenteric arthropathy, multiple sites
711.38	Postdysenteric arthropathy, other specified sites
711.35	Postdysenteric arthropathy, pelvic region and thigh
711.31	Postdysenteric arthropathy, shoulder region
711.30	Postdysenteric arthropathy, site unspecified
711.32	Postdysenteric arthropathy, upper arm
904.53	Posterior tibial artery injury
904.54	Posterior tibial vein injury
053.13	Postherpetic polyneuropathy
053.12	Postherpetic trigeminal neuralgia
411.0	Postmyocardial infarction syndrome
512.2	Postoperative air leak
998.00	Postoperative shock, unspecified
666.32	Postpartum coagulation defects, with delivery
459.11	Postphlebitic syndrome with ulcer
459.13	Postphlebitic syndrome with ulcer and inflammation
997.32	Postprocedural aspiration pneumonia
251.3	Postsurgical hypoinsulinemia
958.3	Posttraumatic wound infection not elsewhere classified
569.71	Pouchitis
759.81	Prader-Willi syndrome
790.01	Precipitous drop in hematocrit
646.31	Pregnancy complication, recurrent pregnancy loss, with or without mention of antepartum condition
641.23	Premature separation of placenta, antepartum
290.11	Presenile dementia with delirium
290.12	Presenile dementia with delusional features
290.13	Presenile dementia with depressive features
707.01	Pressure ulcer, elbow
707.09	Pressure ulcer, other site
707.00	Pressure ulcer, unspecified site
607.3	Priapism
770.81	Primary apnea of newborn
770.4	Primary atelectasis of newborn
200.53	Primary central nervous system lymphoma, intra-abdominal lymph nodes
200.56	Primary central nervous system lymphoma, intrapelvic lymph nodes
200.52	Primary central nervous system lymphoma, intrathoracic lymph nodes
200.54	Primary central nervous system lymphoma, lymph nodes of axilla and upper limb
200.51	Primary central nervous system lymphoma, lymph nodes of head, face, and neck
200.55	Primary central nervous system lymphoma, lymph nodes of inguinal region and lower limb
200.58	Primary central nervous system lymphoma, lymph nodes of multiple sites
200.57	Primary central nervous system lymphoma, spleen
200.50	Primary central nervous system lymphoma, unspecified site, extranodal and solid organ sites
334.2	Primary cerebellar degeneration
114.0	Primary coccidioidomycosis (pulmonary)
114.1	Primary extrapulmonary coccidioidomycosis
289.81	Primary hypercoagulable state
364.01	Primary iridocyclitis
335.24	Primary lateral sclerosis
416.0	Primary pulmonary hypertension
512.81	Primary spontaneous pneumothorax
010.01	Primary tuberculous complex, bacteriological or histological examination not done
010.02	Primary tuberculous complex, bacteriological or histological examination unknown (at present)
010.00	Primary tuberculous complex, confirmation unspecified
010.03	Primary tuberculous complex, tubercle bacilli found (in sputum) by microscopy
010.04	Primary tuberculous complex, tubercle bacilli not found (in sputum) by microscopy, but found by bacterial culture
010.05	Primary tuberculous complex, tubercle bacilli not found by bacteriological examination, but tuberculosis confirmed histologically
010.06	Primary tuberculous complex, tubercle bacilli not found by bacteriological or histological examination, but tuberculosis confirmed by other methods [inoculation of animals]
010.91	Primary tuberculous infection, unspecified, bacteriological or histological examination not done
010.92	Primary tuberculous infection, unspecified, bacteriological or histological examination unknown (at present)
010.90	Primary tuberculous infection, unspecified, confirmation unspecified
010.93	Primary tuberculous infection, unspecified, tubercle bacilli found (in sputum) by microscopy
010.94	Primary tuberculous infection, unspecified, tubercle bacilli not found (in sputum) by microscopy, but found by bacterial culture
010.95	Primary tuberculous infection, unspecified, tubercle bacilli not found by bacteriological examination, but tuberculosis confirmed histologically
010.96	Primary tuberculous infection, unspecified, tubercle bacilli not found by bacteriological or histological examination, but tuberculosis confirmed by other methods [inoculation of animals]
413.1	Prinzmetal angina
318.2	Profound intellectual disabilities
335.22	Progressive bulbar palsy
046.3	Progressive multifocal leukoencephalopathy
335.21	Progressive muscular atrophy
335.23	Pseudobulbar palsy
556.4	Pseudopolyposis of colon
136.4	Psorospermiasis
298.4	Psychogenic paranoid psychosis
293.81	Psychotic disorder with delusions in conditions classified elsewhere
293.82	Psychotic disorder with hallucinations in conditions classified elsewhere
670.12	Puerperal endometritis, delivered, with mention of postpartum complication
670.14	Puerperal endometritis, postpartum condition or complication

670.10	Puerperal endometritis, unspecified as to episode of care or not applicable
672.02	Puerperal pyrexia of unknown origin, delivered, with mention of postpartum complication
672.04	Puerperal pyrexia of unknown origin, postpartum condition or complication
670.20	Puerperal sepsis, unspecified as to episode of care or not applicable
670.30	Puerperal septic thrombophlebitis, unspecified as to episode of care or not applicable
039.1	Pulmonary actinomycotic infection
516.2	Pulmonary alveolar microlithiasis
516.0	Pulmonary alveolar proteinosis
518.0	Pulmonary collapse
514	Pulmonary congestion and hypostasis
031.0	Pulmonary diseases due to other mycobacteria
518.3	Pulmonary eosinophilia
021.2	Pulmonary tularemia
522.0	Pulpitis
590.81	Pyelitis or pyelonephritis in diseases classified elsewhere
590.3	Pyeloureteritis cystica
686.01	Pyoderma gangrenosum
711.07	Pyogenic arthritis, ankle and foot
711.03	Pyogenic arthritis, forearm
711.04	Pyogenic arthritis, hand
711.06	Pyogenic arthritis, lower leg
711.09	Pyogenic arthritis, multiple sites
711.08	Pyogenic arthritis, other specified sites
711.05	Pyogenic arthritis, pelvic region and thigh
711.01	Pyogenic arthritis, shoulder region
711.00	Pyogenic arthritis, site unspecified
711.02	Pyogenic arthritis, upper arm
083.0	Q fever
651.53	Quadruplet pregnancy with fetal loss and retention of one or more, antepartum
651.51	Quadruplet pregnancy with fetal loss and retention of one or more, delivered
651.23	Quadruplet pregnancy, antepartum
651.21	Quadruplet pregnancy, delivered
084.2	Quartan malaria
082.3	Queensland tick typhus
071	Rabies
903.2	Radial blood vessels injury
863.45	Rectum injury without mention of open wound into cavity
552.03	Recurrent bilateral femoral hernia with obstruction
364.02	Recurrent iridocyclitis
552.01	Recurrent unilateral or unspecified femoral hernia with obstruction
337.29	Reflex sympathetic dystrophy of other specified site
337.22	Reflex sympathetic dystrophy of the lower limb
337.21	Reflex sympathetic dystrophy of the upper limb
356.3	Refsum's disease
555.1	Regional enteritis of large intestine
555.0	Regional enteritis of small intestine
555.2	Regional enteritis of small intestine with large intestine
555.9	Regional enteritis of unspecified site
997.41	Retained cholelithiasis following cholecystectomy
200.03	Reticulosarcoma of intra-abdominal lymph nodes
200.06	Reticulosarcoma of intrapelvic lymph nodes
200.02	Reticulosarcoma of intrathoracic lymph nodes
200.04	Reticulosarcoma of lymph nodes of axilla and upper limb
200.01	Reticulosarcoma of lymph nodes of head, face, and neck
200.05	Reticulosarcoma of lymph nodes of inguinal region and lower limb
200.08	Reticulosarcoma of lymph nodes of multiple sites
200.07	Reticulosarcoma of spleen
200.00	Reticulosarcoma, unspecified site, extranodal and solid organ sites
362.84	Retinal ischemia
377.32	Retrobulbar neuritis (acute)
868.04	Retroperitoneum injury without mention of open wound into cavity
478.24	Retropharyngeal abscess
999.70	Rh incompatibility reaction, unspecified
999.72	Rh incompatibility with acute hemolytic transfusion reaction
999.73	Rh incompatibility with delayed hemolytic transfusion reaction
999.71	Rh incompatibility with hemolytic transfusion reaction not specified as acute or delayed
728.88	Rhabdomyolysis
656.13	Rhesus isoimmunization affecting management of mother, antepartum condition
392.0	Rheumatic chorea with heart involvement
392.9	Rheumatic chorea without mention of heart involvement
398.91	Rheumatic heart failure (congestive)
398.0	Rheumatic myocarditis
517.1	Rheumatic pneumonia
086.4	Rhodesian trypanosomiasis
268.0	Rickets, active
083.2	Rickettsialpox
056.79	Rubella with other specified complications
447.2	Rupture of artery
871.2	Rupture of eye with partial loss of intraocular tissue
003.23	Salmonella arthritis
003.0	Salmonella gastroenteritis
003.24	Salmonella osteomyelitis
904.3	Saphenous vein injury
136.5	Sarcosporidiosis
079.82	SARS-associated coronavirus
034.1	Scarlet fever
341.1	Schilder's disease
120.0	Schistosomiasis due to schistosoma haematobium
120.2	Schistosomiasis due to schistosoma japonicum
120.1	Schistosomiasis due to schistosoma mansoni
295.72	Schizoaffective disorder, chronic
295.74	Schizoaffective disorder, chronic with acute exacerbation
295.71	Schizoaffective disorder, subchronic
295.73	Schizoaffective disorder, subchronic with acute exacerbation
295.62	Schizophrenic disorders, residual type, chronic
295.64	Schizophrenic disorders, residual type, chronic with acute exacerbation
295.61	Schizophrenic disorders, residual type, subchronic
295.63	Schizophrenic disorders, residual type, subchronic with acute exacerbation
295.60	Schizophrenic disorders, residual type, unspecified
295.42	Schizophreniform disorder, chronic
295.44	Schizophreniform disorder, chronic with acute exacerbation
295.41	Schizophreniform disorder, subchronic
295.43	Schizophreniform disorder, subchronic with acute exacerbation
295.40	Schizophreniform disorder, unspecified
778.1	Sclerema neonatorum
567.82	Sclerosing mesenteritis
081.2	Scrub typhus
958.2	Secondary and recurrent hemorrhage as an early complication of trauma

196.2	Secondary and unspecified malignant neoplasm of intra-abdominal lymph nodes
196.6	Secondary and unspecified malignant neoplasm of intrapelvic lymph nodes
196.1	Secondary and unspecified malignant neoplasm of intrathoracic lymph nodes
196.3	Secondary and unspecified malignant neoplasm of lymph nodes of axilla and upper limb
196.0	Secondary and unspecified malignant neoplasm of lymph nodes of head, face, and neck
196.5	Secondary and unspecified malignant neoplasm of lymph nodes of inguinal region and lower limb
196.8	Secondary and unspecified malignant neoplasm of lymph nodes of multiple sites
196.9	Secondary and unspecified malignant neoplasm of lymph nodes, site unspecified
289.82	Secondary hypercoagulable state
588.81	Secondary hyperparathyroidism (of renal origin)
364.03	Secondary iridocyclitis, infectious
198.7	Secondary malignant neoplasm of adrenal gland
198.5	Secondary malignant neoplasm of bone and bone marrow
198.3	Secondary malignant neoplasm of brain and spinal cord
198.81	Secondary malignant neoplasm of breast
198.82	Secondary malignant neoplasm of genital organs
198.0	Secondary malignant neoplasm of kidney
197.5	Secondary malignant neoplasm of large intestine and rectum
197.7	Secondary malignant neoplasm of liver
197.0	Secondary malignant neoplasm of lung
197.1	Secondary malignant neoplasm of mediastinum
197.8	Secondary malignant neoplasm of other digestive organs and spleen
198.4	Secondary malignant neoplasm of other parts of nervous system
197.3	Secondary malignant neoplasm of other respiratory organs
198.89	Secondary malignant neoplasm of other specified sites
198.1	Secondary malignant neoplasm of other urinary organs
198.6	Secondary malignant neoplasm of ovary
197.2	Secondary malignant neoplasm of pleura
197.6	Secondary malignant neoplasm of retroperitoneum and peritoneum
198.2	Secondary malignant neoplasm of skin
197.4	Secondary malignant neoplasm of small intestine including duodenum
209.73	Secondary neuroendocrine tumor of bone
209.71	Secondary neuroendocrine tumor of distant lymph nodes
209.72	Secondary neuroendocrine tumor of liver
209.79	Secondary neuroendocrine tumor of other sites
209.74	Secondary neuroendocrine tumor of peritoneum
332.1	Secondary Parkinsonism
405.01	Secondary renovascular hypertension, malignant
512.82	Secondary spontaneous pneumothorax
091.3	Secondary syphilis of skin or mucous membranes
304.11	Sedative, hypnotic or anxiolytic dependence, continuous pattern of use
279.01	Selective IgA immunodeficiency
279.02	Selective IgM immunodeficiency
290.3	Senile dementia with delirium
290.20	Senile dementia with delusional features
290.21	Senile dementia with depressive features
449	Septic arterial embolism
998.13	Seroma complicating a procedure
363.71	Serous choroidal detachment

362.42	Serous detachment of retinal pigment epithelium
361.2	Serous retinal detachment
318.1	Severe intellectual disabilities
202.23	Sezary's disease of intra-abdominal lymph nodes
202.26	Sezary's disease of intrapelvic lymph nodes
202.22	Sezary's disease of intrathoracic lymph nodes
202.24	Sezary's disease of lymph nodes of axilla and upper limb
202.21	Sezary's disease of lymph nodes of head, face, and neck
202.25	Sezary's disease of lymph nodes of inguinal region and lower limb
202.28	Sezary's disease of lymph nodes of multiple sites
202.27	Sezary's disease of spleen
202.20	Sezary's disease, unspecified site, extranodal and solid organ sites
995.55	Shaken infant syndrome
004.0	Shigella dysenteriae
995.4	Shock due to anesthesia not elsewhere classified
863.44	Sigmoid colon injury without mention of open wound into cavity
295.02	Simple schizophrenia, chronic condition
295.04	Simple schizophrenia, chronic condition with acute exacerbation
295.01	Simple schizophrenia, subchronic condition
295.03	Simple schizophrenia, subchronic condition with acute exacerbation
295.00	Simple schizophrenia, unspecified condition
759.3	Situs inversus
863.20	Small intestine injury, unspecified site, without mention of open wound into cavity
123.5	Sparganosis (larval diphyllobothriasis)
342.11	Spastic hemiplegia affecting dominant side
342.12	Spastic hemiplegia affecting nondominant side
342.10	Spastic hemiplegia affecting unspecified side
741.01	Spina bifida with hydrocephalus, cervical region
741.02	Spina bifida with hydrocephalus, dorsal (thoracic) region
741.03	Spina bifida with hydrocephalus, lumbar region
741.00	Spina bifida with hydrocephalus, unspecified region
026.0	Spirillary fever
865.01	Spleen hematoma, without rupture of capsule or mention of open wound into cavity
721.91	Spondylosis of unspecified site with myelopathy
721.42	Spondylosis with myelopathy, lumbar region
721.41	Spondylosis with myelopathy, thoracic region
082.0	Spotted fevers
005.0	Staphylococcal food poisoning
695.13	Stevens-Johnson syndrome
695.14	Stevens-Johnson syndrome-toxic epidermal necrolysis overlap syndrome
333.91	Stiff-man syndrome
863.0	Stomach injury without mention of open wound into cavity
026.1	Streptobacillary fever
127.2	Strongyloidiasis
208.21	Subactue leukemia of unspecified cell type in remission
336.2	Subacute combined degeneration of spinal cord in diseases classified elsewhere
293.1	Subacute delirium
208.22	Subacute leukemia of unspecified cell type, in relapse
208.20	Subacute leukemia of unspecified cell type, without mention of having achieved remission
204.21	Subacute lymphoid leukemia in remission
204.22	Subacute lymphoid leukemia, in relapse
204.20	Subacute lymphoid leukemia, without mention of having achieved remission
206.21	Subacute monocytic leukemia in remission

206.22	Subacute monocytic leukemia, in relapse
206.20	Subacute monocytic leukemia, without mention of having achieved remission
205.21	Subacute myeloid leukemia in remission
205.22	Subacute myeloid leukemia, in relapse
205.20	Subacute myeloid leukemia, without mention of having achieved remission
046.2	Subacute sclerosing panencephalitis
435.2	Subclavian steal syndrome
383.01	Subperiosteal abscess of mastoid
368.11	Sudden visual loss
V62.84	Suicidal ideation
671.20	Superficial thrombophlebitis complicating pregnancy and the puerperium, unspecified as to episode of care
671.22	Superficial thrombophlebitis with delivery, with mention of postpartum complication
671.21	Superficial thrombophlebitis with delivery, with or without mention of antepartum condition
671.23	Superficial thrombophlebitis, antepartum
671.24	Superficial thrombophlebitis, postpartum condition or complication
060.0	Sylvatic yellow fever
360.11	Sympathetic uveitis
359.6	Symptomatic inflammatory myopathy in diseases classified elsewhere
095.5	Syphilis of bone
095.4	Syphilis of kidney
095.3	Syphilis of liver
095.1	Syphilis of lung
095.6	Syphilis of muscle
095.7	Syphilis of synovium, tendon, and bursa
094.86	Syphilitic acoustic neuritis
093.1	Syphilitic aortitis
094.83	Syphilitic disseminated retinochoroiditis
093.22	Syphilitic endocarditis, aortic valve
093.21	Syphilitic endocarditis, mitral valve
093.24	Syphilitic endocarditis, pulmonary valve
093.23	Syphilitic endocarditis, tricuspid valve
095.0	Syphilitic episcleritis
090.3	Syphilitic interstitial keratitis
093.82	Syphilitic myocarditis
094.84	Syphilitic optic atrophy
094.82	Syphilitic Parkinsonism
093.81	Syphilitic pericarditis
095.2	Syphilitic peritonitis
094.85	Syphilitic retrobulbar neuritis
336.0	Syringomyelia and syringobulbia
995.93	Systemic inflammatory response syndrome due to noninfectious process without acute organ dysfunction
995.90	Systemic inflammatory response syndrome, unspecified
094.0	Tabes dorsalis
123.2	Taenia saginata infection
123.0	Taenia solium infection, intestinal form
123.3	Taeniasis, unspecified
446.7	Takayasu's disease
429.83	Takotsubo syndrome
059.21	Tanapox
781.7	Tetany
664.21	Third-degree perineal laceration, with delivery
666.04	Third-stage postpartum hemorrhage, postpartum condition or complication

666.02	Third-stage postpartum hemorrhage, with delivery
640.03	Threatened abortion, antepartum
640.01	Threatened abortion, delivered
453.1	Thrombophlebitis migrans
066.1	Tick-borne fever
087.1	Tick-borne relapsing fever
608.24	Torsion of appendix epididymis
608.23	Torsion of appendix testis
620.5	Torsion of ovary, ovarian pedicle, or fallopian tube
608.20	Torsion of testis, unspecified
823.42	Torus fracture of fibula with tibia
813.45	Torus fracture of radius (alone)
813.47	Torus fracture of radius and ulna
823.40	Torus fracture of tibia alone
813.46	Torus fracture of ulna (alone)
747.41	Total congenital anomalous pulmonary venous connection
695.15	Toxic epidermal necrolysis
695.0	Toxic erythema
558.2	Toxic gastroenteritis and colitis
359.4	Toxic myopathy
130.7	Toxoplasmosis of other specified sites
361.81	Traction detachment of retina
518.7	Transfusion related acute lung injury [TRALI]
362.34	Transient arterial occlusion of retina
642.31	Transient hypertension of pregnancy, with delivery
642.32	Transient hypertension of pregnancy, with delivery, with current postpartum complication
781.4	Transient paralysis of limb
368.12	Transient visual loss
777.4	Transitory ileus of newborn
863.42	Transverse colon injury without mention of open wound into cavity
887.3	Traumatic amputation of arm and hand (complete) (partial), unilateral, at or above elbow, complicated
887.2	Traumatic amputation of arm and hand (complete) (partial), unilateral, at or above elbow, without mention of complication
887.1	Traumatic amputation of arm and hand (complete) (partial), unilateral, below elbow, complicated
887.0	Traumatic amputation of arm and hand (complete) (partial), unilateral, below elbow, without mention of complication
887.5	Traumatic amputation of arm and hand (complete) (partial), unilateral, level not specified, complicated
887.4	Traumatic amputation of arm and hand (complete) (partial), unilateral, level not specified, without mention of complication
896.1	Traumatic amputation of foot (complete) (partial), unilateral, complicated
896.0	Traumatic amputation of foot (complete) (partial), unilateral, without mention of complication
897.3	Traumatic amputation of leg(s) (complete) (partial), unilateral, at or above knee, complicated
897.2	Traumatic amputation of leg(s) (complete) (partial), unilateral, at or above knee, without mention of complication
897.1	Traumatic amputation of leg(s) (complete) (partial), unilateral, below knee, complicated
897.0	Traumatic amputation of leg(s) (complete) (partial), unilateral, below knee, without mention of complication
897.5	Traumatic amputation of leg(s) (complete) (partial), unilateral, level not specified, complicated
897.4	Traumatic amputation of leg(s) (complete) (partial), unilateral, level not specified, without mention of complication
958.93	Traumatic compartment syndrome of abdomen
958.92	Traumatic compartment syndrome of lower extremity
958.99	Traumatic compartment syndrome of other sites

958.91	Traumatic compartment syndrome of upper extremity
860.0	Traumatic pneumothorax without mention of open wound into thorax
721.7	Traumatic spondylopathy
958.7	Traumatic subcutaneous emphysema
083.1	Trench fever
124	Trichinosis
127.6	Trichostrongyliasis
127.3	Trichuriasis
426.54	Trifascicular block
651.43	Triplet pregnancy with fetal loss and retention of one or more, antepartum
651.41	Triplet pregnancy with fetal loss and retention of one or more, delivered
651.13	Triplet pregnancy, antepartum
651.11	Triplet pregnancy, delivered
040.81	Tropical pyomyositis
579.1	Tropical sprue
633.11	Tubal pregnancy with intrauterine pregnancy
633.10	Tubal pregnancy without intrauterine pregnancy
030.1	Tuberculoid leprosy (type T)
017.61	Tuberculosis of adrenal glands, bacteriological or histological examination not done
017.62	Tuberculosis of adrenal glands, bacteriological or histological examination unknown (at present)
017.60	Tuberculosis of adrenal glands, confirmation unspecified
017.63	Tuberculosis of adrenal glands, tubercle bacilli found (in sputum) by microscopy
017.64	Tuberculosis of adrenal glands, tubercle bacilli not found (in sputum) by microscopy, but found by bacterial culture
017.65	Tuberculosis of adrenal glands, tubercle bacilli not found by bacteriological examination, but tuberculosis confirmed histologically
017.66	Tuberculosis of adrenal glands, tubercle bacilli not found by bacteriological or histological examination, but tuberculosis confirmed by other methods [inoculation of animals]
016.11	Tuberculosis of bladder, bacteriological or histological examination not done
016.12	Tuberculosis of bladder, bacteriological or histological examination unknown (at present)
016.10	Tuberculosis of bladder, confirmation unspecified
016.13	Tuberculosis of bladder, tubercle bacilli found (in sputum) by microscopy
016.14	Tuberculosis of bladder, tubercle bacilli not found (in sputum) by microscopy, but found by bacterial culture
016.15	Tuberculosis of bladder, tubercle bacilli not found by bacteriological examination, but tuberculosis confirmed histologically
016.16	Tuberculosis of bladder, tubercle bacilli not found by bacteriological or histological examination, but tuberculosis confirmed by other methods [inoculation of animals]
011.31	Tuberculosis of bronchus, bacteriological or histological examination not done
011.32	Tuberculosis of bronchus, bacteriological or histological examination unknown (at present)
011.30	Tuberculosis of bronchus, confirmation unspecified
011.33	Tuberculosis of bronchus, tubercle bacilli found (in sputum) by microscopy
011.34	Tuberculosis of bronchus, tubercle bacilli not found (in sputum) by microscopy, but found in bacterial culture
011.35	Tuberculosis of bronchus, tubercle bacilli not found by bacteriological examination, but tuberculosis confirmed histologically
011.36	Tuberculosis of bronchus, tubercle bacilli not found by bacteriological or histological examination, but tuberculosis confirmed by other methods [inoculation of animals]
017.41	Tuberculosis of ear, bacteriological or histological examination not done
017.42	Tuberculosis of ear, bacteriological or histological examination unknown (at present)
017.40	Tuberculosis of ear, confirmation unspecified
017.43	Tuberculosis of ear, tubercle bacilli found (in sputum) by microscopy
017.44	Tuberculosis of ear, tubercle bacilli not found (in sputum) by microscopy, but found by bacterial culture
017.45	Tuberculosis of ear, tubercle bacilli not found by bacteriological examination, but tuberculosis confirmed histologically
017.46	Tuberculosis of ear, tubercle bacilli not found by bacteriological or histological examination, but tuberculosis confirmed by other methods [inoculation of animals]
016.41	Tuberculosis of epididymis, bacteriological or histological examination not done
016.42	Tuberculosis of epididymis, bacteriological or histological examination unknown (at present)
016.40	Tuberculosis of epididymis, confirmation unspecified
016.43	Tuberculosis of epididymis, tubercle bacilli found (in sputum) by microscopy
016.44	Tuberculosis of epididymis, tubercle bacilli not found (in sputum) by microscopy, but found by bacterial culture
016.45	Tuberculosis of epididymis, tubercle bacilli not found by bacteriological examination, but tuberculosis confirmed histologically
016.46	Tuberculosis of epididymis, tubercle bacilli not found by bacteriological or histological examination, but tuberculosis confirmed by other methods [inoculation of animals]
017.81	Tuberculosis of esophagus, bacteriological or histological examination not done
017.82	Tuberculosis of esophagus, bacteriological or histological examination unknown (at present)
017.80	Tuberculosis of esophagus, confirmation unspecified
017.83	Tuberculosis of esophagus, tubercle bacilli found (in sputum) by microscopy
017.84	Tuberculosis of esophagus, tubercle bacilli not found (in sputum) by microscopy, but found by bacterial culture
017.85	Tuberculosis of esophagus, tubercle bacilli not found by bacteriological examination, but tuberculosis confirmed histologically
017.86	Tuberculosis of esophagus, tubercle bacilli not found by bacteriological or histological examination, but tuberculosis confirmed by other methods [inoculation of animals]
017.31	Tuberculosis of eye, bacteriological or histological examination not done
017.32	Tuberculosis of eye, bacteriological or histological examination unknown (at present)
017.30	Tuberculosis of eye, confirmation unspecified
017.33	Tuberculosis of eye, tubercle bacilli found (in sputum) by microscopy
017.34	Tuberculosis of eye, tubercle bacilli not found (in sputum) by microscopy, but found by bacterial culture
017.35	Tuberculosis of eye, tubercle bacilli not found by bacteriological examination, but tuberculosis confirmed histologically
017.36	Tuberculosis of eye, tubercle bacilli not found by bacteriological or histological examination, but tuberculosis confirmed by other methods [inoculation of animals]
015.11	Tuberculosis of hip, bacteriological or histological examination not done
015.12	Tuberculosis of hip, bacteriological or histological examination unknown (at present)
015.10	Tuberculosis of hip, confirmation unspecified

015.13 Tuberculosis of hip, tubercle bacilli found (in sputum) by microscopy

015.14 Tuberculosis of hip, tubercle bacilli not found (in sputum) by microscopy, but found by bacterial culture

015.15 Tuberculosis of hip, tubercle bacilli not found by bacteriological examination, but tuberculosis confirmed histologically

015.16 Tuberculosis of hip, tubercle bacilli not found by bacteriological or histological examination, but tuberculosis confirmed by other methods [inoculation of animals]

014.81 Tuberculosis of intestines, peritoneum, and mesenteric glands, other, bacteriological or histological examination not done

014.82 Tuberculosis of intestines, peritoneum, and mesenteric glands, other, bacteriological or histological examination unknown (at present)

014.80 Tuberculosis of intestines, peritoneum, and mesenteric glands, other, confirmation unspecified

014.83 Tuberculosis of intestines, peritoneum, and mesenteric glands, other, tubercle bacilli found (in sputum) by microscopy

014.84 Tuberculosis of intestines, peritoneum, and mesenteric glands, other, tubercle bacilli not found (in sputum) by microscopy, but found by bacterial culture

014.85 Tuberculosis of intestines, peritoneum, and mesenteric glands, other, tubercle bacilli not found by bacteriological examination, but tuberculosis confirmed histologically

014.86 Tuberculosis of intestines, peritoneum, and mesenteric glands, other, tubercle bacilli not found by bacteriological or histological examination, but tuberculosis confirmed by other methods [inoculation of animals]

012.11 Tuberculosis of intrathoracic lymph nodes, bacteriological or histological examination not done

012.12 Tuberculosis of intrathoracic lymph nodes, bacteriological or histological examination unknown (at present)

012.10 Tuberculosis of intrathoracic lymph nodes, confirmation unspecified

012.13 Tuberculosis of intrathoracic lymph nodes, tubercle bacilli found (in sputum) by microscopy

012.14 Tuberculosis of intrathoracic lymph nodes, tubercle bacilli not found (in sputum) by microscopy, but found by bacterial culture

012.15 Tuberculosis of intrathoracic lymph nodes, tubercle bacilli not found by bacteriological examination, but tuberculosis confirmed histologically

012.16 Tuberculosis of intrathoracic lymph nodes, tubercle bacilli not found by bacteriological or histological examination but tuberculosis confirmed by other methods

016.01 Tuberculosis of kidney, bacteriological or histological examination not done

016.02 Tuberculosis of kidney, bacteriological or histological examination unknown (at present)

016.00 Tuberculosis of kidney, confirmation unspecified

016.03 Tuberculosis of kidney, tubercle bacilli found (in sputum) by microscopy

016.04 Tuberculosis of kidney, tubercle bacilli not found (in sputum) by microscopy, but found by bacterial culture

016.05 Tuberculosis of kidney, tubercle bacilli not found by bacteriological examination, but tuberculosis confirmed histologically

016.06 Tuberculosis of kidney, tubercle bacilli not found by bacteriological or histological examination, but tuberculosis confirmed by other methods [inoculation of animals]

015.21 Tuberculosis of knee, bacteriological or histological examination not done

015.22 Tuberculosis of knee, bacteriological or histological examination unknown (at present)

015.20 Tuberculosis of knee, confirmation unspecified

015.23 Tuberculosis of knee, tubercle bacilli found (in sputum) by microscopy

015.24 Tuberculosis of knee, tubercle bacilli not found (in sputum) by microscopy, but found by bacterial culture

015.25 Tuberculosis of knee, tubercle bacilli not found by bacteriological examination, but tuberculosis confirmed histologically

015.26 Tuberculosis of knee, tubercle bacilli not found by bacteriological or histological examination, but tuberculosis confirmed by other methods [inoculation of animals]

015.51 Tuberculosis of limb bones, bacteriological or histological examination not done

015.52 Tuberculosis of limb bones, bacteriological or histological examination unknown (at present)

015.50 Tuberculosis of limb bones, confirmation unspecified

015.53 Tuberculosis of limb bones, tubercle bacilli found (in sputum) by microscopy

015.54 Tuberculosis of limb bones, tubercle bacilli not found (in sputum) by microscopy, but found by bacterial culture

015.55 Tuberculosis of limb bones, tubercle bacilli not found by bacteriological examination, but tuberculosis confirmed histologically

015.56 Tuberculosis of limb bones, tubercle bacilli not found by bacteriological or histological examination, but tuberculosis confirmed by other methods [inoculation of animals]

011.21 Tuberculosis of lung with cavitation, bacteriological or histological examination not done

011.22 Tuberculosis of lung with cavitation, bacteriological or histological examination unknown (at present)

011.20 Tuberculosis of lung with cavitation, confirmation unspecified

011.23 Tuberculosis of lung with cavitation, tubercle bacilli found (in sputum) by microscopy

011.24 Tuberculosis of lung with cavitation, tubercle bacilli not found (in sputum) by microscopy, but found by bacterial culture

011.25 Tuberculosis of lung with cavitation, tubercle bacilli not found by bacteriological examination, but tuberculosis confirmed histologically

011.26 Tuberculosis of lung with cavitation, tubercle bacilli not found by bacteriological or histological examination, but tuberculosis confirmed by other methods [inoculation of animals]

011.01 Tuberculosis of lung, infiltrative, bacteriological or histological examination not done

011.02 Tuberculosis of lung, infiltrative, bacteriological or histological examination unknown (at present)

011.00 Tuberculosis of lung, infiltrative, confirmation unspecified

011.03 Tuberculosis of lung, infiltrative, tubercle bacilli found (in sputum) by microscopy

011.04 Tuberculosis of lung, infiltrative, tubercle bacilli not found (in sputum) by microscopy, but found by bacterial culture

011.06 Tuberculosis of lung, infiltrative, tubercle bacilli not found bacteriological or histological examination, but tuberculosis confirmed by other methods (inoculation of animals)

011.05 Tuberculosis of lung, infiltrative, tubercle bacilli not found by bacteriological examination, but tuberculosis confirmed histologically

011.11 Tuberculosis of lung, nodular, bacteriological or histological examination not done

011.12 Tuberculosis of lung, nodular, bacteriological or histological examination unknown (at present)

011.10 Tuberculosis of lung, nodular, confirmation unspecified

011.13 Tuberculosis of lung, nodular, tubercle bacilli found (in sputum) by microscopy

011.14 Tuberculosis of lung, nodular, tubercle bacilli not found (in sputum) by microscopy, but found by bacterial culture

011.15 Tuberculosis of lung, nodular, tubercle bacilli not found by bacteriological examination, but tuberculosis confirmed histologically

011.16 Tuberculosis of lung, nodular, tubercle bacilli not found by bacteriological or histological examination, but tuberculosis confirmed by other methods [inoculation of animals]

015.61 Tuberculosis of mastoid, bacteriological or histological examination not done

015.62   Tuberculosis of mastoid, bacteriological or histological examination unknown (at present)

015.60   Tuberculosis of mastoid, confirmation unspecified

015.63   Tuberculosis of mastoid, tubercle bacilli found (in sputum) by microscopy

015.64   Tuberculosis of mastoid, tubercle bacilli not found (in sputum) by microscopy, but found by bacterial culture

015.65   Tuberculosis of mastoid, tubercle bacilli not found by bacteriological examination, but tuberculosis confirmed histologically

015.66   Tuberculosis of mastoid, tubercle bacilli not found by bacteriological or histological examination but tuberculosis confirmed by other methods [inoculation of animals]

016.71   Tuberculosis of other female genital organs, bacteriological or histological examination not done

016.72   Tuberculosis of other female genital organs, bacteriological or histological examination unknown (at present)

016.70   Tuberculosis of other female genital organs, confirmation unspecified

016.73   Tuberculosis of other female genital organs, tubercle bacilli found (in sputum) by microscopy

016.74   Tuberculosis of other female genital organs, tubercle bacilli not found (in sputum) by microscopy, but found by bacterial culture

016.75   Tuberculosis of other female genital organs, tubercle bacilli not found by bacteriological examination, but tuberculosis confirmed histologically

016.76   Tuberculosis of other female genital organs, tubercle bacilli not found by bacteriological or histological examination, but tuberculosis confirmed by other methods [inoculation of animals]

016.51   Tuberculosis of other male genital organs, bacteriological or histological examination not done

016.52   Tuberculosis of other male genital organs, bacteriological or histological examination unknown (at present)

016.50   Tuberculosis of other male genital organs, confirmation unspecified

016.53   Tuberculosis of other male genital organs, tubercle bacilli found (in sputum) by microscopy

016.54   Tuberculosis of other male genital organs, tubercle bacilli not found (in sputum) by microscopy, but found by bacterial culture

016.55   Tuberculosis of other male genital organs, tubercle bacilli not found by bacteriological examination, but tuberculosis confirmed histologically

016.56   Tuberculosis of other male genital organs, tubercle bacilli not found by bacteriological or histological examination, but tuberculosis confirmed by other methods [inoculation of animals]

015.71   Tuberculosis of other specified bone, bacteriological or histological examination not done

015.72   Tuberculosis of other specified bone, bacteriological or histological examination unknown (at present)

015.73   Tuberculosis of other specified bone, tubercle bacilli found (in sputum) by microscopy

015.74   Tuberculosis of other specified bone, tubercle bacilli not found (in sputum) by microscopy, but found by bacterial culture

015.75   Tuberculosis of other specified bone, tubercle bacilli not found by bacteriological examination, but tuberculosis confirmed histologically

015.76   Tuberculosis of other specified bone, tubercle bacilli not found by bacteriological or histological examination, but tuberculosis confirmed by other methods [inoculation of animals]

015.70   Tuberculosis of other specified bone, unspecified

015.81   Tuberculosis of other specified joint, bacteriological or histological examination not done

015.82   Tuberculosis of other specified joint, bacteriological or histological examination unknown (at present)

015.80   Tuberculosis of other specified joint, confirmation unspecified

015.83   Tuberculosis of other specified joint, tubercle bacilli found (in sputum) by microscopy

015.84   Tuberculosis of other specified joint, tubercle bacilli not found (in sputum) by microscopy, but found by bacterial culture

015.85   Tuberculosis of other specified joint, tubercle bacilli not found by bacteriological examination, but tuberculosis confirmed histologically

015.86   Tuberculosis of other specified joint, tubercle bacilli not found by bacteriological or histological examination, but tuberculosis confirmed by other methods [inoculation of animals]

017.91   Tuberculosis of other specified organs, bacteriological or histological examination not done

017.92   Tuberculosis of other specified organs, bacteriological or histological examination unknown (at present)

017.90   Tuberculosis of other specified organs, confirmation unspecified

017.93   Tuberculosis of other specified organs, tubercle bacilli found (in sputum) by microscopy

017.94   Tuberculosis of other specified organs, tubercle bacilli not found (in sputum) by microscopy, but found by bacterial culture

017.95   Tuberculosis of other specified organs, tubercle bacilli not found by bacteriological examination, but tuberculosis confirmed histologically

017.96   Tuberculosis of other specified organs, tubercle bacilli not found by bacteriological or histological examination but tuberculosis confirmed by other methods [inoculation of animals]

016.31   Tuberculosis of other urinary organs, bacteriological or histological examination not done

016.32   Tuberculosis of other urinary organs, bacteriological or histological examination unknown (at present)

016.30   Tuberculosis of other urinary organs, confirmation unspecified

016.33   Tuberculosis of other urinary organs, tubercle bacilli found (in sputum) by microscopy

016.34   Tuberculosis of other urinary organs, tubercle bacilli not found (in sputum) by microscopy, but found by bacterial culture

016.35   Tuberculosis of other urinary organs, tubercle bacilli not found by bacteriological examination, but tuberculosis confirmed histologically

016.36   Tuberculosis of other urinary organs, tubercle bacilli not found by bacteriological or histological examination, but tuberculosis confirmed by other methods [inoculation of animals]

017.21   Tuberculosis of peripheral lymph nodes, bacteriological or histological examination not done

017.22   Tuberculosis of peripheral lymph nodes, bacteriological or histological examination unknown (at present)

017.20   Tuberculosis of peripheral lymph nodes, confirmation unspecified

017.23   Tuberculosis of peripheral lymph nodes, tubercle bacilli found (in sputum) by microscopy

017.24   Tuberculosis of peripheral lymph nodes, tubercle bacilli not found (in sputum) by microscopy, but found by bacterial culture

017.25   Tuberculosis of peripheral lymph nodes, tubercle bacilli not found by bacteriological examination, but tuberculosis confirmed histologically

017.26   Tuberculosis of peripheral lymph nodes, tubercle bacilli not found by bacteriological or histological examination, but tuberculosis confirmed by other methods [inoculation of animals]

017.01   Tuberculosis of skin and subcutaneous cellular tissue, bacteriological or histological examination not done

017.02   Tuberculosis of skin and subcutaneous cellular tissue, bacteriological or histological examination unknown (at present)

017.00   Tuberculosis of skin and subcutaneous cellular tissue, confirmation unspecified

017.03   Tuberculosis of skin and subcutaneous cellular tissue, tubercle bacilli found (in sputum) by microscopy

017.04   Tuberculosis of skin and subcutaneous cellular tissue, tubercle bacilli not found (in sputum) by microscopy, but found by bacterial culture

017.05   Tuberculosis of skin and subcutaneous cellular tissue, tubercle bacilli not found by bacteriological examination, but tuberculosis confirmed histologically

017.06 Tuberculosis of skin and subcutaneous cellular tissue, tubercle bacilli not found by bacteriological or histological examination, but tuberculosis confirmed by other methods [inoculation of animals]

017.71 Tuberculosis of spleen, bacteriological or histological examination not done

017.72 Tuberculosis of spleen, bacteriological or histological examination unknown (at present)

017.70 Tuberculosis of spleen, confirmation unspecified

017.73 Tuberculosis of spleen, tubercle bacilli found (in sputum) by microscopy

017.74 Tuberculosis of spleen, tubercle bacilli not found (in sputum) by microscopy, but found by bacterial culture

017.75 Tuberculosis of spleen, tubercle bacilli not found by bacteriological examination, but tuberculosis confirmed histologically

017.76 Tuberculosis of spleen, tubercle bacilli not found by bacteriological or histological examination, but tuberculosis confirmed by other methods [inoculation of animals]

017.51 Tuberculosis of thyroid gland, bacteriological or histological examination not done

017.52 Tuberculosis of thyroid gland, bacteriological or histological examination unknown (at present)

017.50 Tuberculosis of thyroid gland, confirmation unspecified

017.53 Tuberculosis of thyroid gland, tubercle bacilli found (in sputum) by microscopy

017.54 Tuberculosis of thyroid gland, tubercle bacilli not found (in sputum) by microscopy, but found by bacterial culture

017.55 Tuberculosis of thyroid gland, tubercle bacilli not found by bacteriological examination, but tuberculosis confirmed histologically

017.56 Tuberculosis of thyroid gland, tubercle bacilli not found by bacteriological or histological examination, but tuberculosis confirmed by other methods [inoculation of animals]

015.91 Tuberculosis of unspecified bones and joints, bacteriological or histological examination not done

015.92 Tuberculosis of unspecified bones and joints, bacteriological or histological examination unknown (at present)

015.90 Tuberculosis of unspecified bones and joints, confirmation unspecified

015.93 Tuberculosis of unspecified bones and joints, tubercle bacilli found (in sputum) by microscopy

015.94 Tuberculosis of unspecified bones and joints, tubercle bacilli not found (in sputum) by microscopy, but found by bacterial culture

015.95 Tuberculosis of unspecified bones and joints, tubercle bacilli not found by bacteriological examination, but tuberculosis confirmed histologically

015.96 Tuberculosis of unspecified bones and joints, tubercle bacilli not found by bacteriological or histological examination, but tuberculosis confirmed by other methods [inoculation of animals]

016.21 Tuberculosis of ureter, bacteriological or histological examination not done

016.22 Tuberculosis of ureter, bacteriological or histological examination unknown (at present)

016.20 Tuberculosis of ureter, confirmation unspecified

016.23 Tuberculosis of ureter, tubercle bacilli found (in sputum) by microscopy

016.24 Tuberculosis of ureter, tubercle bacilli not found (in sputum) by microscopy, but found by bacterial culture

016.25 Tuberculosis of ureter, tubercle bacilli not found by bacteriological examination, but tuberculosis confirmed histologically

016.26 Tuberculosis of ureter, tubercle bacilli not found by bacteriological or histological examination, but tuberculosis confirmed by other methods [inoculation of animals]

015.01 Tuberculosis of vertebral column, bacteriological or histological examination not done

015.02 Tuberculosis of vertebral column, bacteriological or histological examination unknown (at present)

015.00 Tuberculosis of vertebral column, confirmation unspecified

015.03 Tuberculosis of vertebral column, tubercle bacilli found (in sputum) by microscopy

015.04 Tuberculosis of vertebral column, tubercle bacilli not found (in sputum) by microscopy, but found by bacterial culture

015.05 Tuberculosis of vertebral column, tubercle bacilli not found by bacteriological examination, but tuberculosis confirmed histologically

015.06 Tuberculosis of vertebral column, tubercle bacilli not found by bacteriological or histological examination, but tuberculosis confirmed by other methods [inoculation of animals]

011.51 Tuberculous bronchiectasis, bacteriological or histological examination not done

011.52 Tuberculous bronchiectasis, bacteriological or histological examination unknown (at present)

011.50 Tuberculous bronchiectasis, confirmation unspecified

011.53 Tuberculous bronchiectasis, tubercle bacilli found (in sputum) by microscopy

011.54 Tuberculous bronchiectasis, tubercle bacilli not found (in sputum) by microscopy, but found by bacterial culture

011.55 Tuberculous bronchiectasis, tubercle bacilli not found by bacteriological examination, but tuberculosis confirmed histologically

011.56 Tuberculous bronchiectasis, tubercle bacilli not found by bacteriological or histological examination, but tuberculosis confirmed by other methods [inoculation of animals]

011.41 Tuberculous fibrosis of lung, bacteriological or histological examination not done

011.42 Tuberculous fibrosis of lung, bacteriological or histological examination unknown (at present)

011.40 Tuberculous fibrosis of lung, confirmation unspecified

011.43 Tuberculous fibrosis of lung, tubercle bacilli found (in sputum) by microscopy

011.44 Tuberculous fibrosis of lung, tubercle bacilli not found (in sputum) by microscopy, but found by bacterial culture

011.45 Tuberculous fibrosis of lung, tubercle bacilli not found by bacteriological examination, but tuberculosis confirmed histologically

011.46 Tuberculous fibrosis of lung, tubercle bacilli not found by bacteriological or histological examination, but tuberculosis confirmed by other methods [inoculation of animals]

012.31 Tuberculous laryngitis, bacteriological or histological examination not done

012.32 Tuberculous laryngitis, bacteriological or histological examination unknown (at present)

012.30 Tuberculous laryngitis, confirmation unspecified

012.33 Tuberculous laryngitis, tubercle bacilli found (in sputum) by microscopy

012.34 Tuberculous laryngitis, tubercle bacilli not found (in sputum) by microscopy, but found by bacterial culture

012.35 Tuberculous laryngitis, tubercle bacilli not found by bacteriological examination, but tuberculosis confirmed histologically

012.36 Tuberculous laryngitis, tubercle bacilli not found by bacteriological or histological examination, but tuberculosis confirmed by other methods [inoculation of animals]

016.61 Tuberculous oophoritis and salpingitis, bacteriological or histological examination not done

016.62 Tuberculous oophoritis and salpingitis, bacteriological or histological examination unknown (at present)

016.60 Tuberculous oophoritis and salpingitis, confirmation unspecified

016.63 Tuberculous oophoritis and salpingitis, tubercle bacilli found (in sputum) by microscopy

016.64 Tuberculous oophoritis and salpingitis, tubercle bacilli not found (in sputum) by microscopy, but found by bacterial culture

016.65	Tuberculous oophoritis and salpingitis, tubercle bacilli not found by bacteriological examination, but tuberculosis confirmed histologically
016.66	Tuberculous oophoritis and salpingitis, tubercle bacilli not found by bacteriological or histological examination, but tuberculosis confirmed by other methods [inoculation of animals]
010.11	Tuberculous pleurisy in primary progressive tuberculosis, bacteriological or histological examination not done
010.12	Tuberculous pleurisy in primary progressive tuberculosis, bacteriological or histological examination results unknown (at present)
010.10	Tuberculous pleurisy in primary progressive tuberculosis, confirmation unspecified
010.13	Tuberculous pleurisy in primary progressive tuberculosis, tubercle bacilli found (in sputum) by microscopy
010.14	Tuberculous pleurisy in primary progressive tuberculosis, tubercle bacilli not found (in sputum) by microscopy, but found by bacterial culture
010.15	Tuberculous pleurisy in primary progressive tuberculosis, tubercle bacilli not found by bacteriological examination, but tuberculosis confirmed histologically
010.16	Tuberculous pleurisy in primary progressive tuberculosis, tubercle bacilli not found by bacteriological or histological examination, but tuberculosis confirmed by other methods [inoculation of animals]
012.01	Tuberculous pleurisy, bacteriological or histological examination not done
012.02	Tuberculous pleurisy, bacteriological or histological examination unknown (at present)
012.00	Tuberculous pleurisy, confirmation unspecified
012.03	Tuberculous pleurisy, tubercle bacilli found (in sputum) by microscopy
012.04	Tuberculous pleurisy, tubercle bacilli not found (in sputum) by microscopy, but found by bacterial culture
012.05	Tuberculous pleurisy, tubercle bacilli not found by bacteriological examination, but tuberculosis confirmed histologically
012.06	Tuberculous pleurisy, tubercle bacilli not found by bacteriological or histological examination, but tuberculosis confirmed by other methods [inoculation of animals]
011.71	Tuberculous pneumothorax, bacteriological or histological examination not done
011.72	Tuberculous pneumothorax, bacteriological or histological examination unknown (at present)
011.70	Tuberculous pneumothorax, confirmation unspecified
011.73	Tuberculous pneumothorax, tubercle bacilli not found (in sputum) by microscopy
011.74	Tuberculous pneumothorax, tubercle bacilli not found (in sputum) by microscopy, but found by bacterial culture
011.75	Tuberculous pneumothorax, tubercle bacilli not found by bacteriological examination, but tuberculosis confirmed histologically
011.76	Tuberculous pneumothorax, tubercle bacilli not found by bacteriological or histological examination but tuberculosis confirmed by other methods [inoculation of animals]
759.5	Tuberous sclerosis
651.01	Twin pregnancy, delivered
002.0	Typhoid fever
707.13	Ulcer of ankle
569.41	Ulcer of anus and rectum
707.12	Ulcer of calf
530.20	Ulcer of esophagus without bleeding
707.14	Ulcer of heel and midfoot
707.10	Ulcer of lower limb, unspecified
707.19	Ulcer of other part of lower limb
707.11	Ulcer of thigh
569.82	Ulceration of intestine
556.0	Ulcerative (chronic) enterocolitis
556.1	Ulcerative (chronic) ileocolitis
556.2	Ulcerative (chronic) proctitis
556.3	Ulcerative (chronic) proctosigmoiditis
021.0	Ulceroglandular tularemia
903.3	Ulnar blood vessels injury
552.1	Umbilical hernia with obstruction
552.00	Unilateral or unspecified femoral hernia with obstruction
556.6	Universal ulcerative (chronic) colitis
364.00	Unspecified acute and subacute iridocyclitis
420.90	Unspecified acute pericarditis
391.9	Unspecified acute rheumatic heart disease
291.9	Unspecified alcohol-induced mental disorders
495.9	Unspecified allergic alveolitis and pneumonitis
516.9	Unspecified alveolar and parietoalveolar pneumonopathy
126.9	Unspecified ancylostomiasis and necatoriasis
646.23	Unspecified antepartum renal disease
335.9	Unspecified anterior horn cell disease
022.9	Unspecified anthrax
284.9	Unspecified aplastic anemia
065.9	Unspecified arthropod-borne hemorrhagic fever
066.9	Unspecified arthropod-borne viral disease
093.9	Unspecified cardiovascular syphilis
330.9	Unspecified cerebral degeneration in childhood
001.9	Unspecified cholera
363.20	Unspecified chorioretinitis
363.70	Unspecified choroidal detachment
813.40	Unspecified closed fracture of lower end of forearm
808.8	Unspecified closed fracture of pelvis
813.20	Unspecified closed fracture of shaft of radius or ulna
114.9	Unspecified coccidioidomycosis
428.40	Unspecified combined systolic and diastolic heart failure
639.9	Unspecified complication following abortion or ectopic and molar pregnancies
747.20	Unspecified congenital anomaly of aorta
747.9	Unspecified congenital anomaly of circulatory system
751.60	Unspecified congenital anomaly of gallbladder, bile ducts, and liver
753.10	Unspecified congenital cystic kidney disease
746.00	Unspecified congenital pulmonary valve anomaly
341.9	Unspecified demyelinating disease of central nervous system
428.30	Unspecified diastolic heart failure
032.9	Unspecified diphtheria
423.9	Unspecified disease of pericardium
336.9	Unspecified disease of spinal cord
031.9	Unspecified diseases due to mycobacteria
270.9	Unspecified disorder of amino-acid metabolism
363.10	Unspecified disseminated chorioretinitis
304.91	Unspecified drug dependence, continuous pattern of use
090.2	Unspecified early congenital syphilis
122.4	Unspecified echinococcus granulosus infection
122.7	Unspecified echinococcus multilocularis infection
122.8	Unspecified echinococcus of liver
633.91	Unspecified ectopic pregnancy with intrauterine pregnancy
633.90	Unspecified ectopic pregnancy without intrauterine pregnancy
345.91	Unspecified epilepsy with intractable epilepsy
333.90	Unspecified extrapyramidal disease and abnormal movement disorder
125.9	Unspecified filariasis
619.9	Unspecified fistula involving female genital tract

016.91	Unspecified genitourinary tuberculosis, bacteriological or histological examination not done
016.92	Unspecified genitourinary tuberculosis, bacteriological or histological examination unknown (at present)
016.90	Unspecified genitourinary tuberculosis, confirmation unspecified
016.93	Unspecified genitourinary tuberculosis, tubercle bacilli found (in sputum) by microscopy
016.94	Unspecified genitourinary tuberculosis, tubercle bacilli not found (in sputum) by microscopy, but found by bacterial culture
016.95	Unspecified genitourinary tuberculosis, tubercle bacilli not found by bacteriological examination, but tuberculosis confirmed histologically
016.96	Unspecified genitourinary tuberculosis, tubercle bacilli not found by bacteriological or histological examination, but tuberculosis confirmed by other methods [inoculation of animals]
342.91	Unspecified hemiplegia affecting dominant side
342.92	Unspecified hemiplegia affecting nondominant side
342.90	Unspecified hemiplegia affecting unspecified side
640.93	Unspecified hemorrhage in early pregnancy, antepartum
282.9	Unspecified hereditary hemolytic anemia
053.8	Unspecified herpes zoster complication
115.92	Unspecified Histoplasmosis retinitis
446.20	Unspecified hypersensitivity angiitis
642.93	Unspecified hypertension antepartum
642.94	Unspecified hypertension complicating pregnancy, childbirth, or the puerperium, postpartum condition or complication
642.91	Unspecified hypertension, with delivery
642.92	Unspecified hypertension, with delivery, with current postpartum complication
279.00	Unspecified hypogammaglobulinemia
636.20	Unspecified illegally induced abortion complicated by damage to pelvic organs or tissues
636.00	Unspecified illegally induced abortion complicated by genital tract and pelvic infection
636.40	Unspecified illegally induced abortion complicated by metabolic disorder
636.70	Unspecified illegally induced abortion with other specified complications
636.80	Unspecified illegally induced abortion with unspecified complication
279.3	Unspecified immunity deficiency
279.10	Unspecified immunodeficiency with predominant T-cell defect
560.30	Unspecified impaction of intestine
730.99	Unspecified infection of bone in multiple sites
730.98	Unspecified infection of bone of other specified site
730.97	Unspecified infection of bone, ankle and foot
730.93	Unspecified infection of bone, forearm
730.94	Unspecified infection of bone, hand
730.96	Unspecified infection of bone, lower leg
730.95	Unspecified infection of bone, pelvic region and thigh
730.91	Unspecified infection of bone, shoulder region
730.90	Unspecified infection of bone, site unspecified
730.92	Unspecified infection of bone, upper arm
711.97	Unspecified infective arthritis, ankle and foot
711.93	Unspecified infective arthritis, forearm
711.94	Unspecified infective arthritis, hand
711.96	Unspecified infective arthritis, lower leg
711.99	Unspecified infective arthritis, multiple sites
711.98	Unspecified infective arthritis, other specified sites
711.95	Unspecified infective arthritis, pelvic region and thigh
711.91	Unspecified infective arthritis, shoulder region
711.90	Unspecified infective arthritis, site unspecified
711.92	Unspecified infective arthritis, upper arm
861.00	Unspecified injury to heart without mention of open wound into thorax
864.00	Unspecified injury to liver without mention of open wound into cavity
127.9	Unspecified intestinal helminthiasis
579.9	Unspecified intestinal malabsorption
560.9	Unspecified intestinal obstruction
432.9	Unspecified intracranial hemorrhage
364.3	Unspecified iridocyclitis
090.40	Unspecified juvenile neurosyphilis
866.00	Unspecified kidney injury without mention of open wound into cavity
095.9	Unspecified late symptomatic syphilis
635.20	Unspecified legally induced abortion complicated by damage to pelvic organs or tissues
635.00	Unspecified legally induced abortion complicated by genital tract and pelvic infection
635.40	Unspecified legally induced abortion complicated by metabolic disorder
635.70	Unspecified legally induced abortion with other specified complications
635.80	Unspecified legally induced abortion with unspecified complication
085.9	Unspecified leishmaniasis
030.9	Unspecified leprosy
100.9	Unspecified leptospirosis
208.91	Unspecified leukemia in remission
208.92	Unspecified leukemia, in relapse
208.90	Unspecified leukemia, without mention of having achieved remission
861.20	Unspecified lung injury without mention of open wound into thorax
204.91	Unspecified lymphoid leukemia in remission
204.92	Unspecified lymphoid leukemia, in relapse
204.90	Unspecified lymphoid leukemia, without mention of having achieved remission
084.6	Unspecified malaria
647.94	Unspecified maternal infection or infestation complicating pregnancy, childbirth, or the puerperium, postpartum condition or complication
647.91	Unspecified maternal infection or infestation with delivery
647.92	Unspecified maternal infection or infestation with delivery, with current postpartum complication
647.93	Unspecified maternal infection or infestation, antepartum
659.21	Unspecified maternal pyrexia during labor, delivered
996.40	Unspecified mechanical complication of internal orthopedic device, implant, and graft
036.9	Unspecified meningococcal infection
206.91	Unspecified monocytic leukemia in remission
206.92	Unspecified monocytic leukemia, in relapse
206.90	Unspecified monocytic leukemia, without mention of having achieved remission
072.8	Unspecified mumps complication
205.91	Unspecified myeloid leukemia in remission
205.92	Unspecified myeloid leukemia, in relapse
205.90	Unspecified myeloid leukemia, without mention of having achieved remission
094.9	Unspecified neurosyphilis
049.9	Unspecified non-arthropod-borne viral disease of central nervous system
283.10	Unspecified non-autoimmune hemolytic anemia
753.20	Unspecified obstructive defect of renal pelvis and ureter

824.9	Unspecified open fracture of ankle
814.10	Unspecified open fracture of carpal bone
871.9	Unspecified open wound of eyeball
870.9	Unspecified open wound of ocular adnexa
054.40	Unspecified ophthalmic complication herpes simplex
377.30	Unspecified optic neuritis
073.9	Unspecified ornithosis
730.27	Unspecified osteomyelitis, ankle and foot
730.23	Unspecified osteomyelitis, forearm
730.24	Unspecified osteomyelitis, hand
730.26	Unspecified osteomyelitis, lower leg
730.29	Unspecified osteomyelitis, multiple sites
730.28	Unspecified osteomyelitis, other specified sites
730.25	Unspecified osteomyelitis, pelvic region and thigh
730.21	Unspecified osteomyelitis, shoulder region
730.20	Unspecified osteomyelitis, site unspecified
730.22	Unspecified osteomyelitis, upper arm
377.00	Unspecified papilledema
002.9	Unspecified paratyphoid fever
810.10	Unspecified part of open fracture of clavicle
299.90	Unspecified pervasive developmental disorder, current or active state
299.91	Unspecified pervasive developmental disorder, residual state
511.9	Unspecified pleural effusion
662.11	Unspecified prolonged labor, delivered
263.9	Unspecified protein-calorie malnutrition
007.9	Unspecified protozoal intestinal disease
114.5	Unspecified pulmonary coccidioidomycosis
011.91	Unspecified pulmonary tuberculosis, bacteriological or histological examination not done
011.92	Unspecified pulmonary tuberculosis, bacteriological or histological examination unknown (at present)
011.90	Unspecified pulmonary tuberculosis, confirmation unspecified
011.93	Unspecified pulmonary tuberculosis, tubercle bacilli found (in sputum) by microscopy
011.94	Unspecified pulmonary tuberculosis, tubercle bacilli not found (in sputum) by microscopy, but found by bacterial culture
011.95	Unspecified pulmonary tuberculosis, tubercle bacilli not found by bacteriological examination, but tuberculosis confirmed histologically
011.96	Unspecified pulmonary tuberculosis, tubercle bacilli not found by bacteriological or histological examination, but tuberculosis confirmed by other methods [inoculation of animals]
360.00	Unspecified purulent endophthalmitis
590.80	Unspecified pyelonephritis
026.9	Unspecified rat-bite fever
337.20	Unspecified reflex sympathetic dystrophy
087.9	Unspecified relapsing fever
646.21	Unspecified renal disease in pregnancy, with delivery
646.22	Unspecified renal disease in pregnancy, with delivery, with current postpartum complication
646.24	Unspecified renal disease in pregnancy, without mention of hypertension, postpartum condition or complication
361.9	Unspecified retinal detachment
362.40	Unspecified retinal layer separation
362.30	Unspecified retinal vascular occlusion
083.9	Unspecified rickettsiosis
056.00	Unspecified rubella neurological complication
003.9	Unspecified salmonella infection
120.9	Unspecified schistosomiasis
295.92	Unspecified schizophrenia, chronic condition

295.94	Unspecified schizophrenia, chronic condition with acute exacerbation
295.91	Unspecified schizophrenia, subchronic condition
295.93	Unspecified schizophrenia, subchronic condition with acute exacerbation
425.9	Unspecified secondary cardiomyopathy
290.9	Unspecified senile psychotic condition
785.50	Unspecified shock
046.9	Unspecified slow virus infection of central nervous system
050.9	Unspecified smallpox
335.10	Unspecified spinal muscular atrophy
334.9	Unspecified spinocerebellar disease
865.00	Unspecified spleen injury without mention of open wound into cavity
634.20	Unspecified spontaneous abortion complicated by damage to pelvic organs or tissues
634.60	Unspecified spontaneous abortion complicated by embolism
634.00	Unspecified spontaneous abortion complicated by genital tract and pelvic infection
634.40	Unspecified spontaneous abortion complicated by metabolic disorder
634.70	Unspecified spontaneous abortion with other specified complications
634.80	Unspecified spontaneous abortion with unspecified complication
093.20	Unspecified syphilitic endocarditis of valve
428.20	Unspecified systolic heart failure
904.50	Unspecified tibial vessel(s) injury
082.9	Unspecified tick-borne rickettsiosis
130.9	Unspecified toxoplasmosis
519.00	Unspecified tracheostomy complication
435.9	Unspecified transient cerebral ischemia
293.9	Unspecified transient mental disorder in conditions classified elsewhere
086.9	Unspecified trypanosomiasis
021.9	Unspecified tularemia
745.60	Unspecified type congenital endocardial cushion defect
081.9	Unspecified typhus
556.9	Unspecified ulcerative colitis
557.9	Unspecified vascular insufficiency of intestine
671.90	Unspecified venous complication of pregnancy and the puerperium, unspecified as to episode of care
671.92	Unspecified venous complication, with delivery, with mention of postpartum complication
671.91	Unspecified venous complication, with delivery, with or without mention of antepartum condition
552.20	Unspecified ventral hernia with obstruction
070.9	Unspecified viral hepatitis without mention of hepatic coma
047.9	Unspecified viral meningitis
060.9	Unspecified yellow fever
027.9	Unspecified zoonotic bacterial disease
060.1	Urban yellow fever
867.2	Ureter injury without mention of open wound into cavity
593.82	Ureteral fistula
597.0	Urethral abscess
599.1	Urethral fistula
274.11	Uric acid nephrolithiasis
771.82	Urinary tract infection of newborn
599.0	Urinary tract infection, site not specified
619.0	Urinary-genital tract fistula, female
902.55	Uterine artery injury
902.56	Uterine vein injury

867.4	Uterus injury without mention of open wound into cavity
046.11	Variant Creutzfeldt-Jakob disease
052.9	Varicella without mention of complication
454.2	Varicose veins of lower extremities with ulcer and inflammation
050.0	Variola major
997.71	Vascular complications of mesenteric artery
997.79	Vascular complications of other vessels
997.72	Vascular complications of renal artery
290.41	Vascular dementia, with delirium
290.42	Vascular dementia, with delusions
290.43	Vascular dementia, with depressed mood
593.81	Vascular disorders of kidney
607.82	Vascular disorders of penis
066.2	Venezuelan equine fever
453.6	Venous embolism and thrombosis of superficial vessels of lower extremity
495.7	Ventilation pneumonitis
997.31	Ventilator associated pneumonia
745.4	Ventricular septal defect
435.1	Vertebral artery syndrome
435.3	Vertebrobasilar artery syndrome
596.2	Vesical fistula, not elsewhere classified
101	Vincent's angina
070.1	Viral hepatitis A without mention of hepatic coma
070.31	Viral hepatitis B without mention of hepatic coma, acute or unspecified, with hepatitis delta
070.30	Viral hepatitis B without mention of hepatic coma, acute or unspecified, without mention of hepatitis delta
070.33	Viral hepatitis B without mention of hepatic coma, chronic, with hepatitis delta
070.32	Viral hepatitis B without mention of hepatic coma, chronic, without mention of hepatitis delta
054.71	Visceral herpes simplex
085.0	Visceral leishmaniasis (kala-azar)
360.04	Vitreous abscess
084.1	Vivax malaria (benign tertian)
286.4	Von Willebrand's disease
446.4	Wegener's granulomatosis
335.0	Werdnig-Hoffmann disease
040.2	Whipple's disease
033.1	Whooping cough due to Bordetella parapertussis (B. parapertussis)
033.0	Whooping cough due to Bordetella pertussis (P. pertussis)
033.8	Whooping cough due to other specified organism
033.9	Whooping cough, unspecified organism
279.12	Wiskott-Aldrich syndrome
040.42	Wound botulism

Numeric MCC List

003.1	Salmonella septicemia
003.21	Salmonella meningitis
003.22	Salmonella pneumonia
006.3	Amebic liver abscess
006.4	Amebic lung abscess
006.5	Amebic brain abscess
011.60	Tuberculous pneumonia (any form), confirmation unspecified
011.61	Tuberculous pneumonia (any form), bacteriological or histological examination not done
011.62	Tuberculous pneumonia (any form), bacteriological or histological examination unknown (at present)
011.63	Tuberculous pneumonia (any form), tubercle bacilli found (in sputum) by microscopy
011.64	Tuberculous pneumonia (any form), tubercle bacilli not found (in sputum) by microscopy, but found by bacterial culture
011.65	Tuberculous pneumonia (any form), tubercle bacilli not found by bacteriological examination, but tuberculosis confirmed histologically
011.66	Tuberculous pneumonia (any form), tubercle bacilli not found by bacteriological or histological examination, but tuberculosis confirmed by other methods [inoculation of animals]
013.00	Tuberculous meningitis, confirmation unspecified
013.01	Tuberculous meningitis, bacteriological or histological examination not done
013.02	Tuberculous meningitis, bacteriological or histological examination unknown (at present)
013.03	Tuberculous meningitis, tubercle bacilli found (in sputum) by microscopy
013.04	Tuberculous meningitis, tubercle bacilli not found (in sputum) by microscopy, but found by bacterial culture
013.05	Tuberculous meningitis, tubercle bacilli not found by bacteriological examination, but tuberculosis confirmed histologically
013.06	Tuberculous meningitis, tubercle bacilli not found by bacteriological or histological examination, but tuberculosis confirmed by other methods [inoculation of animals]
013.10	Tuberculoma of meninges, confirmation unspecified
013.11	Tuberculoma of meninges, bacteriological or histological examination not done
013.12	Tuberculoma of meninges, bacteriological or histological examination unknown (at present)
013.13	Tuberculoma of meninges, tubercle bacilli found (in sputum) by microscopy
013.14	Tuberculoma of meninges, tubercle bacilli not found (in sputum) by microscopy, but found by bacterial culture
013.15	Tuberculoma of meninges, tubercle bacilli not found by bacteriological examination, but tuberculosis confirmed histologically
013.16	Tuberculoma of meninges, tubercle bacilli not found by bacteriological or histological examination but tuberculosis confirmed by other methods [inoculation of animals]
013.20	Tuberculoma of brain, confirmation unspecified
013.21	Tuberculoma of brain, bacteriological or histological examination not done
013.22	Tuberculoma of brain, bacteriological or histological examination unknown (at present)
013.23	Tuberculoma of brain, tubercle bacilli found (in sputum) by microscopy
013.24	Tuberculoma of brain, tubercle bacilli not found (in sputum) by microscopy, but found by bacterial culture
013.25	Tuberculoma of brain, tubercle bacilli not found by bacteriological examination, but tuberculosis confirmed histologically
013.26	Tuberculoma of brain, tubercle bacilli not found by bacteriological or histological examination, but tuberculosis confirmed by other methods [inoculation of animals]
013.30	Tuberculous abscess of brain, confirmation unspecified
013.31	Tuberculous abscess of brain, bacteriological or histological examination not done
013.32	Tuberculous abscess of brain, bacteriological or histological examination unknown (at present)
013.33	Tuberculous abscess of brain, tubercle bacilli found (in sputum) by microscopy
013.34	Tuberculous abscess of brain, tubercle bacilli not found (in sputum) by microscopy, but found by bacterial culture
013.35	Tuberculous abscess of brain, tubercle bacilli not found by bacteriological examination, but tuberculosis confirmed histologically
013.36	Tuberculous abscess of brain, tubercle bacilli not found by bacteriological or histological examination, but tuberculosis confirmed by other methods [inoculation of animals]
013.40	Tuberculoma of spinal cord, confirmation unspecified
013.41	Tuberculoma of spinal cord, bacteriological or histological examination not done
013.42	Tuberculoma of spinal cord, bacteriological or histological examination unknown (at present)
013.43	Tuberculoma of spinal cord, tubercle bacilli found (in sputum) by microscopy
013.44	Tuberculoma of spinal cord, tubercle bacilli not found (in sputum) by microscopy, but found by bacterial culture
013.45	Tuberculoma of spinal cord, tubercle bacilli not found by bacteriological examination, but tuberculosis confirmed histologically
013.46	Tuberculoma of spinal cord, tubercle bacilli not found by bacteriological or histological examination, but tuberculosis confirmed by other methods [inoculation of animals]
013.50	Tuberculous abscess of spinal cord, confirmation unspecified
013.51	Tuberculous abscess of spinal cord, bacteriological or histological examination not done
013.52	Tuberculous abscess of spinal cord, bacteriological or histological examination unknown (at present)
013.53	Tuberculous abscess of spinal cord, tubercle bacilli found (in sputum) by microscopy
013.54	Tuberculous abscess of spinal cord, tubercle bacilli not found (in sputum) by microscopy, but found by bacterial culture
013.55	Tuberculous abscess of spinal cord, tubercle bacilli not found by bacteriological examination, but tuberculosis confirmed histologically
013.56	Tuberculous abscess of spinal cord, tubercle bacilli not found by bacteriological or histological examination, but tuberculosis confirmed by other methods [inoculation of animals]
013.60	Tuberculous encephalitis or myelitis, confirmation unspecified
013.61	Tuberculous encephalitis or myelitis, bacteriological or histological examination not done
013.62	Tuberculous encephalitis or myelitis, bacteriological or histological examination unknown (at present)
013.63	Tuberculous encephalitis or myelitis, tubercle bacilli found (in sputum) by microscopy
013.64	Tuberculous encephalitis or myelitis, tubercle bacilli not found (in sputum) by microscopy, but found by bacterial culture
013.65	Tuberculous encephalitis or myelitis, tubercle bacilli not found by bacteriological examination, but tuberculosis confirmed histologically
013.66	Tuberculous encephalitis or myelitis, tubercle bacilli not found by bacteriological or histological examination, but tuberculosis confirmed by other methods [inoculation of animals]
013.80	Other specified tuberculosis of central nervous system, confirmation unspecified

013.81	Other specified tuberculosis of central nervous system, bacteriological or histological examination not done
013.82	Other specified tuberculosis of central nervous system, bacteriological or histological examination unknown (at present)
013.83	Other specified tuberculosis of central nervous system, tubercle bacilli found (in sputum) by microscopy
013.84	Other specified tuberculosis of central nervous system, tubercle bacilli not found (in sputum) by microscopy, but found by bacterial culture
013.85	Other specified tuberculosis of central nervous system, tubercle bacilli not found by bacteriological examination, but tuberculosis confirmed histologically
013.86	Other specified tuberculosis of central nervous system, tubercle bacilli not found by bacteriological or histological examination, but tuberculosis confirmed by other methods [inoculation of animals]
013.90	Unspecified tuberculosis of central nervous system, confirmation unspecified
013.91	Unspecified tuberculosis of central nervous system, bacteriological or histological examination not done
013.92	Unspecified tuberculosis of central nervous system, bacteriological or histological examination unknown (at present)
013.93	Unspecified tuberculosis of central nervous system, tubercle bacilli found (in sputum) by microscopy
013.94	Unspecified tuberculosis of central nervous system, tubercle bacilli not found (in sputum) by microscopy, but found by bacterial culture
013.95	Unspecified tuberculosis of central nervous system, tubercle bacilli not found by bacteriological examination, but tuberculosis confirmed histologically
013.96	Unspecified tuberculosis of central nervous system, tubercle bacilli not found by bacteriological or histological examination but tuberculosis confirmed by other methods [inoculation of animals]
014.00	Tuberculous peritonitis, unspecified
014.01	Tuberculous peritonitis, bacteriological or histological examination not done
014.02	Tuberculous peritonitis, bacteriological or histological examination unknown (at present)
014.03	Tuberculous peritonitis, tubercle bacilli found (in sputum) by microscopy
014.04	Tuberculous peritonitis, tubercle bacilli not found (in sputum) by microscopy, but found by bacterial culture
014.05	Tuberculous peritonitis, tubercle bacilli not found by bacteriological examination, but tuberculosis confirmed histologically
014.06	Tuberculous peritonitis, tubercle bacilli not found by bacteriological or histological examination, but tuberculosis confirmed by other methods [inoculation of animals]
018.00	Acute miliary tuberculosis, unspecified
018.01	Acute miliary tuberculosis, bacteriological or histological examination not done
018.02	Acute miliary tuberculosis, bacteriological or histological examination unknown (at present)
018.03	Acute miliary tuberculosis, tubercle bacilli found (in sputum) by microscopy
018.04	Acute miliary tuberculosis, tubercle bacilli not found (in sputum) by microscopy, but found by bacterial culture
018.05	Acute miliary tuberculosis, tubercle bacilli not found by bacteriological examination, but tuberculosis confirmed histologically
018.06	Acute miliary tuberculosis, tubercle bacilli not found by bacteriological or histological examination, but tuberculosis confirmed by other methods [inoculation of animals]
018.80	Other specified miliary tuberculosis, confirmation unspecified
018.81	Other specified miliary tuberculosis, bacteriological or histological examination not done
018.82	Other specified miliary tuberculosis, bacteriological or histological examination unknown (at present)
018.83	Other specified miliary tuberculosis, tubercle bacilli found (in sputum) by microscopy
018.84	Other specified miliary tuberculosis, tubercle bacilli not found (in sputum) by microscopy, but found by bacterial culture
018.85	Other specified miliary tuberculosis, tubercle bacilli not found by bacteriological examination, but tuberculosis confirmed histologically
018.86	Other specified miliary tuberculosis, tubercle bacilli not found by bacteriological or histological examination, but tuberculosis confirmed by other methods [inoculation of animals]
018.90	Unspecified miliary tuberculosis, unspecified
018.91	Unspecified miliary tuberculosis, bacteriological or histological examination not done
018.92	Unspecified miliary tuberculosis, bacteriological or histological examination unknown (at present)
018.93	Unspecified miliary tuberculosis, tubercle bacilli found (in sputum) by microscopy
018.94	Unspecified miliary tuberculosis, tubercle bacilli not found (in sputum) by microscopy, but found by bacterial culture
018.95	Unspecified miliary tuberculosis, tubercle bacilli not found by bacteriological examination, but tuberculosis confirmed histologically
018.96	Unspecified miliary tuberculosis, tubercle bacilli not found by bacteriological or histological examination, but tuberculosis confirmed by other methods [inoculation of animals]
020.0	Bubonic plague
020.1	Cellulocutaneous plague
020.2	Septicemic plague
020.3	Primary pneumonic plague
020.4	Secondary pneumonic plague
020.5	Pneumonic plague, unspecified
020.8	Other specified types of plague
020.9	Unspecified plague
022.1	Pulmonary anthrax
022.3	Anthrax septicemia
036.0	Meningococcal meningitis
036.1	Meningococcal encephalitis
036.2	Meningococcemia
036.3	Waterhouse-Friderichsen syndrome, meningococcal
036.40	Meningococcal carditis, unspecified
036.41	Meningococcal pericarditis
036.42	Meningococcal endocarditis
036.43	Meningococcal myocarditis
037	Tetanus
038.0	Streptococcal septicemia
038.10	Unspecified staphylococcal septicemia
038.11	Methicillin susceptible Staphylococcus aureus septicemia
038.12	Methicillin resistant Staphylococcus aureus septicemia
038.19	Other staphylococcal septicemia
038.2	Pneumococcal septicemia
038.3	Septicemia due to anaerobes
038.40	Septicemia due to unspecified gram-negative organism
038.41	Septicemia due to hemophilus influenzae (H. influenzae)
038.42	Septicemia due to Escherichia coli (E. coli)
038.43	Septicemia due to pseudomonas
038.44	Septicemia due to serratia
038.49	Other septicemia due to gram-negative organism
038.8	Other specified septicemia
038.9	Unspecified septicemia
040.0	Gas gangrene
040.82	Toxic shock syndrome
042	Human immunodeficiency virus [HIV]

045.00	Acute paralytic poliomyelitis specified as bulbar, unspecified poliovirus
045.01	Acute paralytic poliomyelitis specified as bulbar, poliovirus type I
045.02	Acute paralytic poliomyelitis specified as bulbar, poliovirus type II
045.03	Acute paralytic poliomyelitis specified as bulbar, poliovirus type III
045.10	Acute poliomyelitis with other paralysis, unspecified poliovirus
045.11	Acute poliomyelitis with other paralysis, poliovirus type I
045.12	Acute poliomyelitis with other paralysis, poliovirus type II
045.13	Acute poliomyelitis with other paralysis, poliovirus type III
052.0	Postvaricella encephalitis
052.1	Varicella (hemorrhagic) pneumonitis
052.2	Postvaricella myelitis
053.0	Herpes zoster with meningitis
053.14	Herpes zoster myelitis
054.3	Herpetic meningoencephalitis
054.5	Herpetic septicemia
054.72	Herpes simplex meningitis
054.74	Herpes simplex myelitis
055.0	Postmeasles encephalitis
055.1	Postmeasles pneumonia
056.01	Encephalomyelitis due to rubella
058.21	Human herpesvirus 6 encephalitis
058.29	Other human herpesvirus encephalitis
062.0	Japanese encephalitis
062.1	Western equine encephalitis
062.2	Eastern equine encephalitis
062.3	St. Louis encephalitis
062.4	Australian encephalitis
062.5	California virus encephalitis
062.8	Other specified mosquito-borne viral encephalitis
062.9	Unspecified mosquito-borne viral encephalitis
063.0	Russian spring-summer (taiga) encephalitis
063.1	Louping ill
063.2	Central European encephalitis
063.8	Other specified tick-borne viral encephalitis
063.9	Unspecified tick-borne viral encephalitis
064	Viral encephalitis transmitted by other and unspecified arthropods
066.40	West Nile fever, unspecified
066.41	West Nile fever with encephalitis
066.42	West Nile fever with other neurologic manifestation
066.49	West Nile fever with other complications
070.0	Viral hepatitis A with hepatic coma
070.20	Viral hepatitis B with hepatic coma, acute or unspecified, without mention of hepatitis delta
070.21	Viral hepatitis B with hepatic coma, acute or unspecified, with hepatitis delta
070.22	Viral hepatitis B with hepatic coma, chronic, without mention of hepatitis delta
070.23	Viral hepatitis B with hepatic coma, chronic, with hepatitis delta
070.41	Acute hepatitis C with hepatic coma
070.42	Hepatitis delta without mention of active hepatitis B disease with hepatic coma
070.43	Hepatitis E with hepatic coma
070.44	Chronic hepatitis C with hepatic coma
070.49	Other specified viral hepatitis with hepatic coma
070.6	Unspecified viral hepatitis with hepatic coma
070.71	Unspecified viral hepatitis C with hepatic coma
072.1	Mumps meningitis
072.2	Mumps encephalitis
073.0	Ornithosis with pneumonia

084.0	Falciparum malaria (malignant tertian)
090.41	Congenital syphilitic encephalitis
090.42	Congenital syphilitic meningitis
091.81	Early syphilis, acute syphilitic meningitis (secondary)
094.2	Syphilitic meningitis
094.81	Syphilitic encephalitis
094.87	Syphilitic ruptured cerebral aneurysm
098.82	Gonococcal meningitis
098.83	Gonococcal pericarditis
098.84	Gonococcal endocarditis
100.81	Leptospiral meningitis (aseptic)
112.4	Candidiasis of lung
112.5	Disseminated candidiasis
112.81	Candidal endocarditis
112.83	Candidal meningitis
114.2	Coccidioidal meningitis
115.01	Histoplasma capsulatum meningitis
115.03	Histoplasma capsulatum pericarditis
115.04	Histoplasma capsulatum endocarditis
115.05	Histoplasma capsulatum pneumonia
115.11	Histoplasma duboisii meningitis
115.13	Histoplasma duboisii pericarditis
115.14	Histoplasma duboisii endocarditis
115.15	Histoplasma duboisii pneumonia
115.91	Unspecified Histoplasmosis meningitis
115.93	Unspecified Histoplasmosis pericarditis
115.94	Unspecified Histoplasmosis endocarditis
115.95	Unspecified Histoplasmosis pneumonia
117.7	Zygomycosis (Phycomycosis or Mucormycosis)
130.0	Meningoencephalitis due to toxoplasmosis
130.3	Myocarditis due to toxoplasmosis
130.4	Pneumonitis due to toxoplasmosis
130.8	Multisystemic disseminated toxoplasmosis
136.3	Pneumocystosis
242.01	Toxic diffuse goiter with mention of thyrotoxic crisis or storm
242.11	Toxic uninodular goiter with mention of thyrotoxic crisis or storm
242.21	Toxic multinodular goiter with mention of thyrotoxic crisis or storm
242.31	Toxic nodular goiter, unspecified type, with mention of thyrotoxic crisis or storm
242.41	Thyrotoxicosis from ectopic thyroid nodule with mention of thyrotoxic crisis or storm
242.81	Thyrotoxicosis of other specified origin with mention of thyrotoxic crisis or storm
242.91	Thyrotoxicosis without mention of goiter or other cause, with mention of thyrotoxic crisis or storm
249.10	Secondary diabetes mellitus with ketoacidosis, not stated as uncontrolled, or unspecified
249.11	Secondary diabetes mellitus with ketoacidosis, uncontrolled
249.20	Secondary diabetes mellitus with hyperosmolarity, not stated as uncontrolled, or unspecified
249.21	Secondary diabetes mellitus with hyperosmolarity, uncontrolled
249.30	Secondary diabetes mellitus with other coma, not stated as uncontrolled, or unspecified
249.31	Secondary diabetes mellitus with other coma, uncontrolled
250.10	Diabetes with ketoacidosis, type II or unspecified type, not stated as uncontrolled
250.11	Diabetes with ketoacidosis, type I [juvenile type], not stated as uncontrolled
250.12	Diabetes with ketoacidosis, type II or unspecified type, uncontrolled
250.13	Diabetes with ketoacidosis, type I [juvenile type], uncontrolled

250.20	Diabetes with hyperosmolarity, type II or unspecified type, not stated as uncontrolled
250.21	Diabetes with hyperosmolarity, type I [juvenile type], not stated as uncontrolled
250.22	Diabetes with hyperosmolarity, type II or unspecified type, uncontrolled
250.23	Diabetes with hyperosmolarity, type I [juvenile type], uncontrolled
250.30	Diabetes with other coma, type II or unspecified type, not stated as uncontrolled
250.31	Diabetes with other coma, type I [juvenile type], not stated as uncontrolled
250.32	Diabetes with other coma, type II or unspecified type, uncontrolled
250.33	Diabetes with other coma, type I [juvenile type], uncontrolled
260	Kwashiorkor
261	Nutritional marasmus
262	Other severe protein-calorie malnutrition
277.01	Cystic fibrosis with meconium ileus
277.02	Cystic fibrosis with pulmonary manifestations
277.88	Tumor lysis syndrome
282.42	Sickle-cell thalassemia with crisis
282.62	Hb-SS disease with crisis
282.64	Sickle-cell/Hb-C disease with crisis
282.69	Other sickle-cell disease with crisis
283.11	Hemolytic-uremic syndrome
284.11	Antineoplastic chemotherapy induced pancytopenia
284.12	Other drug induced pancytopenia
284.81	Red cell aplasia (acquired) (adult) (with thymoma)
284.89	Other specified aplastic anemias
286.0	Congenital factor VIII disorder
286.1	Congenital factor IX disorder
286.6	Defibrination syndrome
320.0	Hemophilus meningitis
320.1	Pneumococcal meningitis
320.2	Streptococcal meningitis
320.3	Staphylococcal meningitis
320.7	Meningitis in other bacterial diseases classified elsewhere
320.81	Anaerobic meningitis
320.82	Meningitis due to gram-negative bacteria, not elsewhere classified
320.89	Meningitis due to other specified bacteria
320.9	Meningitis due to unspecified bacterium
321.0	Cryptococcal meningitis
321.1	Meningitis in other fungal diseases
321.2	Meningitis due to viruses not elsewhere classified
321.3	Meningitis due to trypanosomiasis
321.4	Meningitis in sarcoidosis
321.8	Meningitis due to other nonbacterial organisms classified elsewhere
322.0	Nonpyogenic meningitis
322.1	Eosinophilic meningitis
322.9	Unspecified meningitis
323.01	Encephalitis and encephalomyelitis in viral diseases classified elsewhere
323.02	Myelitis in viral diseases classified elsewhere
323.1	Encephalitis, myelitis, and encephalomyelitis in rickettsial diseases classified elsewhere
323.2	Encephalitis, myelitis, and encephalomyelitis in protozoal diseases classified elsewhere
323.41	Other encephalitis and encephalomyelitis due to other infections classified elsewhere
323.42	Other myelitis due to other infections classified elsewhere

323.51	Encephalitis and encephalomyelitis following immunization procedures
323.52	Myelitis following immunization procedures
323.61	Infectious acute disseminated encephalomyelitis [ADEM]
323.62	Other postinfectious encephalitis and encephalomyelitis
323.63	Postinfectious myelitis
323.71	Toxic encephalitis and encephalomyelitis
323.72	Toxic myelitis
323.81	Other causes of encephalitis and encephalomyelitis
323.82	Other causes of myelitis
323.9	Unspecified causes of encephalitis, myelitis, and encephalomyelitis
324.0	Intracranial abscess
324.1	Intraspinal abscess
324.9	Intracranial and intraspinal abscess of unspecified site
325	Phlebitis and thrombophlebitis of intracranial venous sinuses
331.81	Reye's syndrome
333.92	Neuroleptic malignant syndrome
336.1	Vascular myelopathies
343.2	Quadriplegic infantile cerebral palsy
344.00	Unspecified quadriplegia
344.01	Quadriplegia and quadriparesis, C1-C4, complete
344.02	Quadriplegia and quadriparesis, C1-C4, incomplete
344.03	Quadriplegia and quadriparesis, C5-C7, complete
344.04	C5-C7, incomplete
344.09	Other quadriplegia and quadriparesis
344.81	Locked-in state
345.2	Epileptic petit mal status
345.3	Epileptic grand mal status
345.71	Epilepsia partialis continua with intractable epilepsy
348.30	Encephalopathy, unspecified
348.31	Metabolic encephalopathy
348.39	Other encephalopathy
348.4	Compression of brain
348.5	Cerebral edema
348.82	Brain death
349.82	Toxic encephalopathy
358.01	Myasthenia gravis with (acute) exacerbation
410.01	Acute myocardial infarction of anterolateral wall, initial episode of care
410.11	Acute myocardial infarction of other anterior wall, initial episode of care
410.21	Acute myocardial infarction of inferolateral wall, initial episode of care
410.31	Acute myocardial infarction of inferoposterior wall, initial episode of care
410.41	Acute myocardial infarction of other inferior wall, initial episode of care
410.51	Acute myocardial infarction of other lateral wall, initial episode of care
410.61	Acute myocardial infarction, true posterior wall infarction, initial episode of care
410.71	Acute myocardial infarction, subendocardial infarction, initial episode of care
410.81	Acute myocardial infarction of other specified sites, initial episode of care
410.91	Acute myocardial infarction, unspecified site, initial episode of care
414.12	Dissection of coronary artery
415.0	Acute cor pulmonale
415.11	Iatrogenic pulmonary embolism and infarction
415.12	Septic pulmonary embolism
415.13	Saddle embolus of pulmonary artery

415.19	Other pulmonary embolism and infarction
421.0	Acute and subacute bacterial endocarditis
421.1	Acute and subacute infective endocarditis in diseases classified elsewhere
421.9	Unspecified acute endocarditis
422.0	Acute myocarditis in diseases classified elsewhere
422.90	Unspecified acute myocarditis
422.91	Idiopathic myocarditis
422.92	Septic myocarditis
422.93	Toxic myocarditis
422.99	Other acute myocarditis
427.41	Ventricular fibrillation
427.42	Ventricular flutter
427.5	Cardiac arrest
428.21	Acute systolic heart failure
428.23	Acute on chronic systolic heart failure
428.31	Acute diastolic heart failure
428.33	Acute on chronic diastolic heart failure
428.41	Acute combined systolic and diastolic heart failure
428.43	Acute on chronic combined systolic and diastolic heart failure
429.5	Rupture of chordae tendineae
429.6	Rupture of papillary muscle
430	Subarachnoid hemorrhage
431	Intracerebral hemorrhage
432.0	Nontraumatic extradural hemorrhage
432.1	Subdural hemorrhage
433.01	Occlusion and stenosis of basilar artery with cerebral infarction
433.11	Occlusion and stenosis of carotid artery with cerebral infarction
433.21	Occlusion and stenosis of vertebral artery with cerebral infarction
433.31	Occlusion and stenosis of multiple and bilateral precerebral arteries with cerebral infarction
433.81	Occlusion and stenosis of other specified precerebral artery with cerebral infarction
433.91	Occlusion and stenosis of unspecified precerebral artery with cerebral infarction
434.01	Cerebral thrombosis with cerebral infarction
434.11	Cerebral embolism with cerebral infarction
434.91	Unspecified cerebral artery occlusion with cerebral infarction
441.00	Dissecting aortic aneurysm (any part), unspecified site
441.01	Dissecting aortic aneurysm (any part), thoracic
441.02	Dissecting aortic aneurysm (any part), abdominal
441.03	Dissecting aortic aneurysm (any part), thoracoabdominal
441.1	Thoracic aneurysm, ruptured
441.3	Abdominal aneurysm, ruptured
441.5	Aortic aneurysm of unspecified site, ruptured
441.6	Thoracoabdominal aneurysm, ruptured
443.21	Dissection of carotid artery
443.22	Dissection of iliac artery
443.23	Dissection of renal artery
443.24	Dissection of vertebral artery
443.29	Dissection of other artery
444.01	Saddle embolus of abdominal aorta
446.6	Thrombotic microangiopathy
452	Portal vein thrombosis
453.0	Budd-Chiari syndrome
453.2	Other venous embolism and thrombosis, of inferior vena cava
456.0	Esophageal varices with bleeding
456.20	Esophageal varices with bleeding in diseases classified elsewhere
464.01	Acute laryngitis, with obstruction
464.11	Acute tracheitis with obstruction

464.21	Acute laryngotracheitis with obstruction
464.31	Acute epiglottitis with obstruction
464.51	Unspecified supraglottis, with obstruction
480.0	Pneumonia due to adenovirus
480.1	Pneumonia due to respiratory syncytial virus
480.2	Pneumonia due to parainfluenza virus
480.3	Pneumonia due to SARS-associated coronavirus
480.8	Pneumonia due to other virus not elsewhere classified
480.9	Unspecified viral pneumonia
481	Pneumococcal pneumonia (streptococcus pneumoniae pneumonia)
482.0	Pneumonia due to Klebsiella pneumoniae
482.1	Pneumonia due to Pseudomonas
482.2	Pneumonia due to Hemophilus influenzae (H. influenzae)
482.30	Pneumonia due to unspecified Streptococcus
482.31	Pneumonia due to Streptococcus, group A
482.32	Pneumonia due to Streptococcus, group B
482.39	Pneumonia due to other Streptococcus
482.40	Pneumonia due to Staphylococcus, unspecified
482.41	Methicillin susceptible pneumonia due to Staphylococcus aureus
482.42	Methicillin resistant pneumonia due to Staphylococcus aureus
482.49	Other Staphylococcus pneumonia
482.81	Pneumonia due to anaerobes
482.82	Pneumonia due to Escherichia coli (E. coli)
482.83	Pneumonia due to other gram-negative bacteria
482.84	Legionnaires' disease
482.89	Pneumonia due to other specified bacteria
482.9	Unspecified bacterial pneumonia
483.0	Pneumonia due to Mycoplasma pneumoniae
483.1	Pneumonia due to Chlamydia
483.8	Pneumonia due to other specified organism
484.1	Pneumonia in cytomegalic inclusion disease
484.3	Pneumonia in whooping cough
484.5	Pneumonia in anthrax
484.6	Pneumonia in aspergillosis
484.7	Pneumonia in other systemic mycoses
484.8	Pneumonia in other infectious diseases classified elsewhere
485	Bronchopneumonia, organism unspecified
486	Pneumonia, organism unspecified
487.0	Influenza with pneumonia
488.01	Influenza due to identified avian influenza virus with pneumonia
488.11	Influenza due to identified 2009 H1N1 influenza virus with pneumonia
488.81	Influenza due to identified novel influenza A virus with pneumonia
506.1	Acute pulmonary edema due to fumes and vapors
507.0	Pneumonitis due to inhalation of food or vomitus
507.1	Pneumonitis due to inhalation of oils and essences
507.8	Pneumonitis due to other solids and liquids
510.0	Empyema with fistula
510.9	Empyema without mention of fistula
511.1	Pleurisy with effusion, with mention of bacterial cause other than tuberculosis
512.0	Spontaneous tension pneumothorax
513.0	Abscess of lung
513.1	Abscess of mediastinum
516.4	Lymphangioleiomyomatosis
516.61	Neuroendocrine cell hyperplasia of infancy
516.62	Pulmonary interstitial glycogenosis
516.63	Surfactant mutations of the lung

516.64	Alveolar capillary dysplasia with vein misalignment
516.69	Other interstitial lung diseases of childhood
518.4	Unspecified acute edema of lung
518.51	Acute respiratory failure following trauma and surgery
518.52	Other pulmonary insufficiency, not elsewhere classified, following trauma and surgery
518.53	Acute and chronic respiratory failure following trauma and surgery
518.81	Acute respiratory failure
518.84	Acute and chronic respiratory failure
519.2	Mediastinitis
530.21	Ulcer of esophagus with bleeding
530.4	Perforation of esophagus
530.7	Gastroesophageal laceration-hemorrhage syndrome
530.82	Esophageal hemorrhage
530.84	Tracheoesophageal fistula
531.00	Acute gastric ulcer with hemorrhage, without mention of obstruction
531.01	Acute gastric ulcer with hemorrhage and obstruction
531.10	Acute gastric ulcer with perforation, without mention of obstruction
531.11	Acute gastric ulcer with perforation and obstruction
531.20	Acute gastric ulcer with hemorrhage and perforation, without mention of obstruction
531.21	Acute gastric ulcer with hemorrhage, perforation, and obstruction
531.31	Acute gastric ulcer without mention of hemorrhage or perforation, with obstruction
531.40	Chronic or unspecified gastric ulcer with hemorrhage, without mention of obstruction
531.41	Chronic or unspecified gastric ulcer with hemorrhage and obstruction
531.50	Chronic or unspecified gastric ulcer with perforation, without mention of obstruction
531.51	Chronic or unspecified gastric ulcer with perforation and obstruction
531.60	Chronic or unspecified gastric ulcer with hemorrhage and perforation, without mention of obstruction
531.61	Chronic or unspecified gastric ulcer with hemorrhage, perforation, and obstruction
531.71	Chronic gastric ulcer without mention of hemorrhage or perforation, with obstruction
531.91	Gastric ulcer, unspecified as acute or chronic, without mention of hemorrhage or perforation, with obstruction
532.00	Acute duodenal ulcer with hemorrhage, without mention of obstruction
532.01	Acute duodenal ulcer with hemorrhage and obstruction
532.10	Acute duodenal ulcer with perforation, without mention of obstruction
532.11	Acute duodenal ulcer with perforation and obstruction
532.20	Acute duodenal ulcer with hemorrhage and perforation, without mention of obstruction
532.21	Acute duodenal ulcer with hemorrhage, perforation, and obstruction
532.31	Acute duodenal ulcer without mention of hemorrhage or perforation, with obstruction
532.40	Duodenal ulcer, chronic or unspecified, with hemorrhage, without mention of obstruction
532.41	Chronic or unspecified duodenal ulcer with hemorrhage and obstruction
532.50	Chronic or unspecified duodenal ulcer with perforation, without mention of obstruction
532.51	Chronic or unspecified duodenal ulcer with perforation and obstruction
532.60	Chronic or unspecified duodenal ulcer with hemorrhage and perforation, without mention of obstruction
532.61	Chronic or unspecified duodenal ulcer with hemorrhage, perforation, and obstruction
532.71	Chronic duodenal ulcer without mention of hemorrhage or perforation, with obstruction
532.91	Duodenal ulcer, unspecified as acute or chronic, without mention of hemorrhage or perforation, with obstruction
533.00	Acute peptic ulcer, unspecified site, with hemorrhage, without mention of obstruction
533.01	Acute peptic ulcer, unspecified site, with hemorrhage and obstruction
533.10	Acute peptic ulcer, unspecified site, with perforation, without mention of obstruction
533.11	Acute peptic ulcer, unspecified site, with perforation and obstruction
533.20	Acute peptic ulcer, unspecified site, with hemorrhage and perforation, without mention of obstruction
533.21	Acute peptic ulcer, unspecified site, with hemorrhage, perforation, and obstruction
533.31	Acute peptic ulcer, unspecified site, without mention of hemorrhage and perforation, with obstruction
533.40	Chronic or unspecified peptic ulcer, unspecified site, with hemorrhage, without mention of obstruction
533.41	Chronic or unspecified peptic ulcer, unspecified site, with hemorrhage and obstruction
533.50	Chronic or unspecified peptic ulcer, unspecified site, with perforation, without mention of obstruction
533.51	Chronic or unspecified peptic ulcer, unspecified site, with perforation and obstruction
533.60	Chronic or unspecified peptic ulcer, unspecified site, with hemorrhage and perforation, without mention of obstruction
533.61	Chronic or unspecified peptic ulcer, unspecified site, with hemorrhage, perforation, and obstruction
533.71	Chronic peptic ulcer of unspecified site without mention of hemorrhage or perforation, with obstruction
533.91	Peptic ulcer, unspecified site, unspecified as acute or chronic, without mention of hemorrhage or perforation, with obstruction
534.00	Acute gastrojejunal ulcer with hemorrhage, without mention of obstruction
534.01	Acute gastrojejunal ulcer, with hemorrhage and obstruction
534.10	Acute gastrojejunal ulcer with perforation, without mention of obstruction
534.11	Acute gastrojejunal ulcer with perforation and obstruction
534.20	Acute gastrojejunal ulcer with hemorrhage and perforation, without mention of obstruction
534.21	Acute gastrojejunal ulcer with hemorrhage, perforation, and obstruction
534.31	Acute gastrojejunal ulcer without mention of hemorrhage or perforation, with obstruction
534.40	Chronic or unspecified gastrojejunal ulcer with hemorrhage, without mention of obstruction
534.41	Chronic or unspecified gastrojejunal ulcer, with hemorrhage and obstruction
534.50	Chronic or unspecified gastrojejunal ulcer with perforation, without mention of obstruction
534.51	Chronic or unspecified gastrojejunal ulcer with perforation and obstruction
534.60	Chronic or unspecified gastrojejunal ulcer with hemorrhage and perforation, without mention of obstruction
534.61	Chronic or unspecified gastrojejunal ulcer with hemorrhage, perforation, and obstruction
534.71	Chronic gastrojejunal ulcer without mention of hemorrhage or perforation, with obstruction
534.91	Gastrojejunal ulcer, unspecified as acute or chronic, without mention of hemorrhage or perforation, with obstruction
535.01	Acute gastritis with hemorrhage

535.11	Atrophic gastritis with hemorrhage
535.21	Gastric mucosal hypertrophy with hemorrhage
535.31	Alcoholic gastritis with hemorrhage
535.41	Other specified gastritis with hemorrhage
535.51	Unspecified gastritis and gastroduodenitis with hemorrhage
535.61	Duodenitis with hemorrhage
535.71	Eosinophilic gastritis with hemorrhage
537.83	Angiodysplasia of stomach and duodenum with hemorrhage
537.84	Dieulafoy lesion (hemorrhagic) of stomach and duodenum
540.0	Acute appendicitis with generalized peritonitis
540.1	Acute appendicitis with peritoneal abscess
550.00	Inguinal hernia with gangrene, unilateral or unspecified, (not specified as recurrent)
550.01	Inguinal hernia with gangrene, recurrent unilateral or unspecified inguinal hernia
550.02	Inguinal hernia with gangrene, bilateral
550.03	Inguinal hernia with gangrene, recurrent bilateral
551.00	Femoral hernia with gangrene, unilateral or unspecified (not specified as recurrent)
551.01	Femoral hernia with gangrene, recurrent unilateral or unspecified
551.02	Femoral hernia with gangrene, bilateral, (not specified as recurrent)
551.03	Femoral hernia with gangrene, recurrent bilateral
551.1	Umbilical hernia with gangrene
551.20	Unspecified ventral hernia with gangrene
551.21	Incisional ventral hernia, with gangrene
551.29	Other ventral hernia with gangrene
551.3	Diaphragmatic hernia with gangrene
551.8	Hernia of other specified sites, with gangrene
551.9	Hernia of unspecified site, with gangrene
557.0	Acute vascular insufficiency of intestine
560.2	Volvulus
562.02	Diverticulosis of small intestine with hemorrhage
562.03	Diverticulitis of small intestine with hemorrhage
562.12	Diverticulosis of colon with hemorrhage
562.13	Diverticulitis of colon with hemorrhage
567.0	Peritonitis in infectious diseases classified elsewhere
567.1	Pneumococcal peritonitis
567.21	Peritonitis (acute) generalized
567.22	Peritoneal abscess
567.23	Spontaneous bacterial peritonitis
567.29	Other suppurative peritonitis
567.31	Psoas muscle abscess
567.38	Other retroperitoneal abscess
567.39	Other retroperitoneal infections
567.81	Choleperitonitis
567.89	Other specified peritonitis
567.9	Unspecified peritonitis
568.81	Hemoperitoneum (nontraumatic)
569.83	Perforation of intestine
569.85	Angiodysplasia of intestine with hemorrhage
569.86	Dieulafoy lesion (hemorrhagic) of intestine
570	Acute and subacute necrosis of liver
572.0	Abscess of liver
572.1	Portal pyemia
572.2	Hepatic encephalopathy
572.4	Hepatorenal syndrome
573.4	Hepatic infarction
574.81	Calculus of gallbladder and bile duct with acute and chronic cholecystitis, with obstruction
575.4	Perforation of gallbladder
576.2	Obstruction of bile duct
576.3	Perforation of bile duct
577.0	Acute pancreatitis
580.0	Acute glomerulonephritis with lesion of proliferative glomerulonephritis
580.4	Acute glomerulonephritis with lesion of rapidly progressive glomerulonephritis
580.81	Acute glomerulonephritis with other specified pathological lesion in kidney in disease classified elsewhere
580.89	Other acute glomerulonephritis with other specified pathological lesion in kidney
580.9	Acute glomerulonephritis with unspecified pathological lesion in kidney
583.4	Nephritis and nephropathy, not specified as acute or chronic, with lesion of rapidly progressive glomerulonephritis
583.6	Nephritis and nephropathy, not specified as acute or chronic, with lesion of renal cortical necrosis
584.5	Acute kidney failure with lesion of tubular necrosis
584.6	Acute kidney failure with lesion of renal cortical necrosis
584.7	Acute kidney failure with lesion of medullary [papillary] necrosis
585.6	End stage renal disease
590.11	Acute pyelonephritis with lesion of renal medullary necrosis
590.2	Renal and perinephric abscess
596.6	Nontraumatic rupture of bladder
614.5	Acute or unspecified pelvic peritonitis, female
634.30	Unspecified spontaneous abortion complicated by renal failure
634.31	Incomplete spontaneous abortion complicated by renal failure
634.32	Complete spontaneous abortion complicated by renal failure
634.50	Unspecified spontaneous abortion complicated by shock
634.51	Incomplete spontaneous abortion complicated by shock
634.52	Complete spontaneous abortion complicated by shock
634.61	Incomplete spontaneous abortion complicated by embolism
634.62	Complete spontaneous abortion complicated by embolism
635.30	Unspecified legally induced abortion complicated by renal failure
635.31	Incomplete legally induced abortion complicated by renal failure
635.32	Complete legally induced abortion complicated by renal failure
635.50	Unspecified legally induced abortion complicated by shock
635.51	Legally induced abortion, complicated by shock, incomplete
635.52	Complete legally induced abortion complicated by shock
635.60	Unspecified legally induced abortion complicated by embolism
635.61	Incomplete legally induced abortion complicated by embolism
635.62	Complete legally induced abortion complicated by embolism
636.30	Unspecified illegally induced abortion complicated by renal failure
636.31	Incomplete illegally induced abortion complicated by renal failure
636.32	Complete illegally induced abortion complicated by renal failure
636.50	Unspecified illegally induced abortion complicated by shock
636.51	Incomplete illegally induced abortion complicated by shock
636.52	Complete illegally induced abortion complicated by shock
636.60	Unspecified illegally induced abortion complicated by embolism
636.61	Incomplete illegally induced abortion complicated by embolism
636.62	Complete illegally induced abortion complicated by embolism
637.30	Abortion, unspecified as to completion or legality, complicated by renal failure
637.31	Abortion, unspecified as to legality, incomplete, complicated by renal failure
637.32	Abortion, unspecified as to legality, complete, complicated by renal failure
637.50	Abortion, unspecified as to completion or legality, complicated by shock
637.51	Abortion, unspecified as to legality, incomplete, complicated by shock

Appendix A — Numeric MCC List

Appendix A — Numeric MCC List

637.52	Abortion, unspecified as to legality, complete, complicated by shock
637.60	Abortion, unspecified as to completion or legality, complicated by embolism
637.61	Abortion, unspecified as to legality, incomplete, complicated by embolism
637.62	Abortion, unspecified as to legality, complete, complicated by embolism
638.3	Failed attempted abortion complicated by renal failure
638.5	Failed attempted abortion complicated by shock
638.6	Failed attempted abortion complicated by embolism
639.3	Complications following abortion and ectopic and molar pregnancies, kidney failure
639.5	Shock following abortion or ectopic and molar pregnancies
639.6	Embolism following abortion or ectopic and molar pregnancies
641.11	Hemorrhage from placenta previa, with delivery
641.13	Hemorrhage from placenta previa, antepartum
641.21	Premature separation of placenta, with delivery
641.31	Antepartum hemorrhage associated with coagulation defects, with delivery
641.33	Antepartum hemorrhage associated with coagulation defect, antepartum
642.11	Hypertension secondary to renal disease, with delivery
642.12	Hypertension secondary to renal disease, with delivery, with current postpartum complication
642.42	Mild or unspecified pre-eclampsia, with delivery, with current postpartum complication
642.51	Severe pre-eclampsia, with delivery
642.52	Severe pre-eclampsia, with delivery, with current postpartum complication
642.53	Severe pre-eclampsia, antepartum
642.54	Severe pre-eclampsia, postpartum condition or complication
642.61	Eclampsia, with delivery
642.62	Eclampsia, with delivery, with current postpartum complication
642.63	Eclampsia, antepartum
642.64	Eclampsia, postpartum condition or complication
642.71	Pre-eclampsia or eclampsia superimposed on pre-existing hypertension, with delivery
642.72	Pre-eclampsia or eclampsia superimposed on pre-existing hypertension, with delivery, with current postpartum complication
642.73	Pre-eclampsia or eclampsia superimposed on pre-existing hypertension, antepartum
642.74	Pre-eclampsia or eclampsia superimposed on pre-existing hypertension, postpartum condition or complication
644.03	Threatened premature labor, antepartum
644.21	Early onset of delivery, delivered, with or without mention of antepartum condition
648.01	Maternal diabetes mellitus with delivery
648.02	Maternal diabetes mellitus with delivery, with current postpartum complication
654.51	Cervical incompetence, delivered
654.52	Cervical incompetence, delivered, with mention of postpartum complication
654.53	Cervical incompetence, antepartum condition or complication
654.54	Cervical incompetence, postpartum condition or complication
658.41	Infection of amniotic cavity, delivered
658.43	Infection of amniotic cavity, antepartum
659.31	Generalized infection during labor, delivered
659.33	Generalized infection during labor, antepartum
665.01	Rupture of uterus before onset of labor, with delivery
665.03	Rupture of uterus before onset of labor, antepartum
665.11	Rupture of uterus during labor, with delivery

669.11	Shock during or following labor and delivery, with delivery, with or without mention of antepartum condition
669.12	Shock during or following labor and delivery, with delivery, with mention of postpartum complication
669.13	Shock during or following labor and delivery, antepartum shock
669.14	Shock during or following labor and delivery, postpartum condition or complication
669.21	Maternal hypotension syndrome, with delivery, with or without mention of antepartum condition
669.22	Maternal hypotension syndrome, with delivery, with mention of postpartum complication
669.32	Acute kidney failure following labor and delivery, delivered, with mention of postpartum complication
669.34	Acute kidney failure following labor and delivery, postpartum condition or complication
670.02	Major puerperal infection, unspecified, delivered, with mention of postpartum complication
670.04	Major puerperal infection, unspecified, postpartum condition or complication
670.22	Puerperal sepsis, delivered, with mention of postpartum complication
670.24	Puerperal sepsis, postpartum condition or complication
670.32	Puerperal septic thrombophlebitis, delivered, with mention of postpartum complication
670.34	Puerperal septic thrombophlebitis, postpartum condition or complication
670.80	Other major puerperal infection, unspecified as to episode of care or not applicable
670.82	Other major puerperal infection, delivered, with mention of postpartum complication
670.84	Other major puerperal infection, postpartum condition or complication
671.31	Deep phlebothrombosis, antepartum, with delivery
671.33	Deep phlebothrombosis, antepartum
671.42	Deep phlebothrombosis, postpartum, with delivery
671.44	Deep phlebothrombosis, postpartum condition or complication
673.01	Obstetrical air embolism, with delivery, with or without mention of antepartum condition
673.02	Obstetrical air embolism, with delivery, with mention of postpartum complication
673.03	Obstetrical air embolism, antepartum condition or complication
673.04	Obstetrical air embolism, postpartum condition or complication
673.11	Amniotic fluid embolism, with delivery, with or without mention of antepartum condition
673.12	Amniotic fluid embolism, with delivery, with mention of postpartum complication
673.13	Amniotic fluid embolism, antepartum condition or complication
673.14	Amniotic fluid embolism, postpartum condition or complication
673.21	Obstetrical blood-clot embolism, with delivery, with or without mention of antepartum condition
673.22	Obstetrical blood-clot embolism, with mention of postpartum complication
673.23	Obstetrical blood-clot embolism, antepartum
673.24	Obstetrical blood-clot embolism, postpartum condition or complication
673.31	Obstetrical pyemic and septic embolism, with delivery, with or without mention of antepartum condition
673.32	Obstetrical pyemic and septic embolism, with delivery, with mention of postpartum complication
673.33	Obstetrical pyemic and septic embolism, antepartum
673.34	Obstetrical pyemic and septic embolism, postpartum condition or complication
673.81	Other obstetrical pulmonary embolism, with delivery, with or without mention of antepartum condition

673.82	Other obstetrical pulmonary embolism, with delivery, with mention of postpartum complication
673.83	Other obstetrical pulmonary embolism, antepartum
673.84	Other obstetrical pulmonary embolism, postpartum condition or complication
674.01	Cerebrovascular disorder, with delivery, with or without mention of antepartum condition
674.50	Peripartum cardiomyopathy, unspecified as to episode of care or not applicable
674.51	Peripartum cardiomyopathy, delivered, with or without mention of antepartum condition
674.52	Peripartum cardiomyopathy, delivered, with mention of postpartum condition
674.53	Peripartum cardiomyopathy, antepartum condition or complication
674.54	Peripartum cardiomyopathy, postpartum condition or complication
707.23	Pressure ulcer stage III
707.24	Pressure ulcer stage IV
728.86	Necrotizing fasciitis
740.0	Anencephalus
740.1	Craniorachischisis
740.2	Iniencephaly
742.2	Congenital reduction deformities of brain
745.0	Bulbus cordis anomalies and anomalies of cardiac septal closure, common truncus
745.10	Complete transposition of great vessels
745.11	Transposition of great vessels, double outlet right ventricle
745.19	Other transposition of great vessels
745.2	Tetralogy of Fallot
745.3	Bulbus cordis anomalies and anomalies of cardiac septal closure, common ventricle
745.7	Cor biloculare
746.01	Congenital atresia of pulmonary valve
746.1	Congenital tricuspid atresia and stenosis
746.2	Ebstein's anomaly
746.7	Hypoplastic left heart syndrome
746.81	Congenital subaortic stenosis
746.82	Cor triatriatum
746.84	Congenital obstructive anomalies of heart, not elsewhere classified
746.86	Congenital heart block
747.11	Congenital interruption of aortic arch
747.31	Pulmonary artery coarctation and atresia
747.32	Pulmonary arteriovenous malformation
747.39	Other anomalies of pulmonary artery and pulmonary circulation
747.81	Congenital anomaly of cerebrovascular system
747.83	Persistent fetal circulation
748.5	Congenital agenesis, hypoplasia, and dysplasia of lung
750.3	Congenital tracheoesophageal fistula, esophageal atresia and stenosis
751.61	Congenital biliary atresia
755.55	Acrocephalosyndactyly
756.6	Congenital anomaly of diaphragm
756.70	Unspecified congenital anomaly of abdominal wall
756.71	Prune belly syndrome
756.72	Omphalocele
756.73	Gastroschisis
756.79	Other congenital anomalies of abdominal wall
758.32	Velo-cardio-facial syndrome
759.4	Conjoined twins
767.0	Subdural and cerebral hemorrhage, birth trauma

768.5	Severe birth asphyxia
768.73	Severe hypoxic-ischemic encephalopathy
769	Respiratory distress syndrome in newborn
770.0	Congenital pneumonia
770.12	Meconium aspiration with respiratory symptoms, of fetus and newborn
770.14	Aspiration of clear amniotic fluid with respiratory symptoms, of fetus and newborn
770.16	Aspiration of blood with respiratory symptoms, of fetus and newborn
770.18	Other fetal and newborn aspiration with respiratory symptoms
770.2	Interstitial emphysema and related conditions of newborn
770.3	Pulmonary hemorrhage of fetus or newborn
770.7	Chronic respiratory disease arising in the perinatal period
770.84	Respiratory failure of newborn
770.86	Aspiration of postnatal stomach contents with respiratory symptoms
770.87	Respiratory arrest of newborn
771.1	Congenital cytomegalovirus infection
771.2	Other congenital infection specific to the perinatal period
771.3	Tetanus neonatorum
771.81	Septicemia (sepsis) of newborn
772.13	Intraventricular hemorrhage, Grade III
772.14	Intraventricular hemorrhage, Grade IV
772.2	Fetal and neonatal subarachnoid hemorrhage of newborn
772.4	Fetal and neonatal gastrointestinal hemorrhage
773.3	Hydrops fetalis due to isoimmunization
773.4	Kernicterus due to isoimmunization of fetus or newborn
774.4	Perinatal jaundice due to hepatocellular damage
774.7	Kernicterus of fetus or newborn not due to isoimmunization
775.7	Late metabolic acidosis of newborn
776.1	Transient neonatal thrombocytopenia
776.2	Disseminated intravascular coagulation in newborn
776.7	Transient neonatal neutropenia
777.50	Necrotizing enterocolitis in newborn, unspecified
777.51	Stage I necrotizing enterocolitis in newborn
777.52	Stage II necrotizing enterocolitis in newborn
777.53	Stage III necrotizing enterocolitis in newborn
777.6	Perinatal intestinal perforation
778.0	Hydrops fetalis not due to isoimmunization
779.0	Convulsions in newborn
779.2	Cerebral depression, coma, and other abnormal cerebral signs in fetus or newborn
779.32	Bilious vomiting in newborn
779.7	Periventricular leukomalacia
779.85	Cardiac arrest of newborn
780.01	Coma
780.72	Functional quadriplegia
785.51	Cardiogenic shock
785.52	Septic shock
785.59	Other shock without mention of trauma
799.1	Respiratory arrest
800.03	Closed fracture of vault of skull without mention of intracranial injury, moderate (1-24 hours) loss of consciousness
800.04	Closed fracture of vault of skull without mention of intracranial injury, prolonged (more than 24 hours) loss of consciousness and return to pre-existing conscious level
800.05	Closed fracture of vault of skull without mention of intracranial injury, prolonged (more than 24 hours) loss of consciousness, without return to pre-existing conscious level

800.10	Closed fracture of vault of skull with cerebral laceration and contusion, unspecified state of consciousness
800.11	Closed fracture of vault of skull with cerebral laceration and contusion, no loss of consciousness
800.12	Closed fracture of vault of skull with cerebral laceration and contusion, brief (less than one hour) loss of consciousness
800.13	Closed fracture of vault of skull with cerebral laceration and contusion, moderate (1-24 hours) loss of consciousness
800.14	Closed fracture of vault of skull with cerebral laceration and contusion, prolonged (more than 24 hours) loss of consciousness and return to pre-existing conscious level
800.15	Closed fracture of vault of skull with cerebral laceration and contusion, prolonged (more than 24 hours) loss of consciousness, without return to pre-existing conscious level
800.16	Closed fracture of vault of skull with cerebral laceration and contusion, loss of consciousness of unspecified duration
800.19	Closed fracture of vault of skull with cerebral laceration and contusion, unspecified concussion
800.20	Closed fracture of vault of skull with subarachnoid, subdural, and extradural hemorrhage, unspecified state of consciousness
800.21	Closed fracture of vault of skull with subarachnoid, subdural, and extradural hemorrhage, no loss of consciousness
800.22	Closed fracture of vault of skull with subarachnoid, subdural, and extradural hemorrhage, brief (less than one hour) loss of consciousness
800.23	Closed fracture of vault of skull with subarachnoid, subdural, and extradural hemorrhage, moderate (1-24 hours) loss of consciousness
800.24	Closed fracture of vault of skull with subarachnoid, subdural, and extradural hemorrhage, prolonged (more than 24 hours) loss of consciousness and return to pre-existing conscious level
800.25	Closed fracture of vault of skull with subarachnoid, subdural, and extradural hemorrhage, prolonged (more than 24 hours) loss of consciousness, without return to pre-existing conscious level
800.26	Closed fracture of vault of skull with subarachnoid, subdural, and extradural hemorrhage, loss of consciousness of unspecified duration
800.29	Closed fracture of vault of skull with subarachnoid, subdural, and extradural hemorrhage, unspecified concussion
800.30	Closed fracture of vault of skull with other and unspecified intracranial hemorrhage, unspecified state of consciousness
800.31	Closed fracture of vault of skull with other and unspecified intracranial hemorrhage, no loss of consciousness
800.32	Closed fracture of vault of skull with other and unspecified intracranial hemorrhage, brief (less than one hour) loss of consciousness
800.33	Closed fracture of vault of skull with other and unspecified intracranial hemorrhage, moderate (1-24 hours) loss of consciousness
800.34	Closed fracture of vault of skull with other and unspecified intracranial hemorrhage, prolonged (more than 24 hours) loss of consciousness and return to pre-existing conscious level
800.35	Closed fracture of vault of skull with other and unspecified intracranial hemorrhage, prolonged (more than 24 hours) loss of consciousness, without return to pre-existing conscious level
800.36	Closed fracture of vault of skull with other and unspecified intracranial hemorrhage, loss of consciousness of unspecified duration
800.39	Closed fracture of vault of skull with other and unspecified intracranial hemorrhage, unspecified concussion
800.43	Closed fracture of vault of skull with intracranial injury of other and unspecified nature, moderate (1-24 hours) loss of consciousness
800.44	Closed fracture of vault of skull with intracranial injury of other and unspecified nature, prolonged (more than 24 hours) loss of consciousness and return to pre-existing conscious level
800.45	Closed fracture of vault of skull with intracranial injury of other and unspecified nature, prolonged (more than 24 hours) loss of consciousness, without return to pre-existing conscious level
800.50	Open fracture of vault of skull without mention of intracranial injury, unspecified state of consciousness
800.51	Open fracture of vault of skull without mention of intracranial injury, no loss of consciousness
800.52	Open fracture of vault of skull without mention of intracranial injury, brief (less than one hour) loss of consciousness
800.53	Open fracture of vault of skull without mention of intracranial injury, moderate (1-24 hours) loss of consciousness
800.54	Open fracture of vault of skull without mention of intracranial injury, prolonged (more than 24 hours) loss of consciousness and return to pre-existing conscious level
800.55	Open fracture of vault of skull without mention of intracranial injury, prolonged (more than 24 hours) loss of consciousness, without return to pre-existing conscious level
800.56	Open fracture of vault of skull without mention of intracranial injury, loss of consciousness of unspecified duration
800.59	Open fracture of vault of skull without mention of intracranial injury, unspecified concussion
800.60	Open fracture of vault of skull with cerebral laceration and contusion, unspecified state of consciousness
800.61	Open fracture of vault of skull with cerebral laceration and contusion, no loss of consciousness
800.62	Open fracture of vault of skull with cerebral laceration and contusion, brief (less than one hour) loss of consciousness
800.63	Open fracture of vault of skull with cerebral laceration and contusion, moderate (1-24 hours) loss of consciousness
800.64	Open fracture of vault of skull with cerebral laceration and contusion, prolonged (more than 24 hours) loss of consciousness and return to pre-existing conscious level
800.65	Open fracture of vault of skull with cerebral laceration and contusion, prolonged (more than 24 hours) loss of consciousness, without return to pre-existing conscious level
800.66	Open fracture of vault of skull with cerebral laceration and contusion, loss of consciousness of unspecified duration
800.69	Open fracture of vault of skull with cerebral laceration and contusion, unspecified concussion
800.70	Open fracture of vault of skull with subarachnoid, subdural, and extradural hemorrhage, unspecified state of consciousness
800.71	Open fracture of vault of skull with subarachnoid, subdural, and extradural hemorrhage, no loss of consciousness
800.72	Open fracture of vault of skull with subarachnoid, subdural, and extradural hemorrhage, brief (less than one hour) loss of consciousness
800.73	Open fracture of vault of skull with subarachnoid, subdural, and extradural hemorrhage, moderate (1-24 hours) loss of consciousness
800.74	Open fracture of vault of skull with subarachnoid, subdural, and extradural hemorrhage, prolonged (more than 24 hours) loss of consciousness and return to pre-existing conscious level
800.75	Open fracture of vault of skull with subarachnoid, subdural, and extradural hemorrhage, prolonged (more than 24 hours) loss of consciousness, without return to pre-existing conscious level
800.76	Open fracture of vault of skull with subarachnoid, subdural, and extradural hemorrhage, loss of consciousness of unspecified duration
800.79	Open fracture of vault of skull with subarachnoid, subdural, and extradural hemorrhage, unspecified concussion
800.80	Open fracture of vault of skull with other and unspecified intracranial hemorrhage, unspecified state of consciousness
800.81	Open fracture of vault of skull with other and unspecified intracranial hemorrhage, no loss of consciousness
800.82	Open fracture of vault of skull with other and unspecified intracranial hemorrhage, brief (less than one hour) loss of consciousness
800.83	Open fracture of vault of skull with other and unspecified intracranial hemorrhage, moderate (1-24 hours) loss of consciousness

800.84   Open fracture of vault of skull with other and unspecified intracranial hemorrhage, prolonged (more than 24 hours) loss of consciousness and return to pre-existing conscious level

800.85   Open fracture of vault of skull with other and unspecified intracranial hemorrhage, prolonged (more than 24 hours) loss of consciousness, without return to pre-existing conscious level

800.86   Open fracture of vault of skull with other and unspecified intracranial hemorrhage, loss of consciousness of unspecified duration

800.89   Open fracture of vault of skull with other and unspecified intracranial hemorrhage, unspecified concussion

800.90   Open fracture of vault of skull with intracranial injury of other and unspecified nature, unspecified state of consciousness

800.91   Open fracture of vault of skull with intracranial injury of other and unspecified nature, no loss of consciousness

800.92   Open fracture of vault of skull with intracranial injury of other and unspecified nature, brief (less than one hour) loss of consciousness

800.93   Open fracture of vault of skull with intracranial injury of other and unspecified nature, moderate (1-24 hours) loss of consciousness

800.94   Open fracture of vault of skull with intracranial injury of other and unspecified nature, prolonged (more than 24 hours) loss of consciousness and return to pre-existing conscious level

800.95   Open fracture of vault of skull with intracranial injury of other and unspecified nature, prolonged (more than 24 hours) loss of consciousness, without return to pre-existing conscious level

800.96   Open fracture of vault of skull with intracranial injury of other and unspecified nature, loss of consciousness of unspecified duration

800.99   Open fracture of vault of skull with intracranial injury of other and unspecified nature, unspecified concussion

801.03   Closed fracture of base of skull without mention of intracranial injury, moderate (1-24 hours) loss of consciousness

801.04   Closed fracture of base of skull without mention of intracranial injury, prolonged (more than 24 hours) loss of consciousness and return to pre-existing conscious level

801.05   Closed fracture of base of skull without mention of intracranial injury, prolonged (more than 24 hours) loss of consciousness, without return to pre-existing conscious level

801.10   Closed fracture of base of skull with cerebral laceration and contusion, unspecified state of consciousness

801.11   Closed fracture of base of skull with cerebral laceration and contusion, no loss of consciousness

801.12   Closed fracture of base of skull with cerebral laceration and contusion, brief (less than one hour) loss of consciousness

801.13   Closed fracture of base of skull with cerebral laceration and contusion, moderate (1-24 hours) loss of consciousness

801.14   Closed fracture of base of skull with cerebral laceration and contusion, prolonged (more than 24 hours) loss of consciousness and return to pre-existing conscious level

801.15   Closed fracture of base of skull with cerebral laceration and contusion, prolonged (more than 24 hours) loss of consciousness, without return to pre-existing conscious level

801.16   Closed fracture of base of skull with cerebral laceration and contusion, loss of consciousness of unspecified duration

801.19   Closed fracture of base of skull with cerebral laceration and contusion, unspecified concussion

801.20   Closed fracture of base of skull with subarachnoid, subdural, and extradural hemorrhage, unspecified state of consciousness

801.21   Closed fracture of base of skull with subarachnoid, subdural, and extradural hemorrhage, no loss of consciousness

801.22   Closed fracture of base of skull with subarachnoid, subdural, and extradural hemorrhage, brief (less than one hour) loss of consciousness

801.23   Closed fracture of base of skull with subarachnoid, subdural, and extradural hemorrhage, moderate (1-24 hours) loss of consciousness

801.24   Closed fracture of base of skull with subarachnoid, subdural, and extradural hemorrhage, prolonged (more than 24 hours) loss of consciousness and return to pre-existing conscious level

801.25   Closed fracture of base of skull with subarachnoid, subdural, and extradural hemorrhage, prolonged (more than 24 hours) loss of consciousness, without return to pre-existing conscious level

801.26   Closed fracture of base of skull with subarachnoid, subdural, and extradural hemorrhage, loss of consciousness of unspecified duration

801.29   Closed fracture of base of skull with subarachnoid, subdural, and extradural hemorrhage, unspecified concussion

801.30   Closed fracture of base of skull with other and unspecified intracranial hemorrhage, unspecified state of consciousness

801.31   Closed fracture of base of skull with other and unspecified intracranial hemorrhage, no loss of consciousness

801.32   Closed fracture of base of skull with other and unspecified intracranial hemorrhage, brief (less than one hour) loss of consciousness

801.33   Closed fracture of base of skull with other and unspecified intracranial hemorrhage, moderate (1-24 hours) loss of consciousness

801.34   Closed fracture of base of skull with other and unspecified intracranial hemorrhage, prolonged (more than 24 hours) loss of consciousness and return to pre-existing conscious level

801.35   Closed fracture of base of skull with other and unspecified intracranial hemorrhage, prolonged (more than 24 hours) loss of consciousness, without return to pre-existing conscious level

801.36   Closed fracture of base of skull with other and unspecified intracranial hemorrhage, loss of consciousness of unspecified duration

801.39   Closed fracture of base of skull with other and unspecified intracranial hemorrhage, unspecified concussion

801.43   Closed fracture of base of skull with intracranial injury of other and unspecified nature, moderate (1-24 hours) loss of consciousness

801.44   Closed fracture of base of skull with intracranial injury of other and unspecified nature, prolonged (more than 24 hours) loss of consciousness and return to pre-existing conscious level

801.45   Closed fracture of base of skull with intracranial injury of other and unspecified nature, prolonged (more than 24 hours) loss of consciousness, without return to pre-existing conscious level

801.50   Open fracture of base of skull without mention of intracranial injury, unspecified state of consciousness

801.51   Open fracture of base of skull without mention of intracranial injury, no loss of consciousness

801.52   Open fracture of base of skull without mention of intracranial injury, brief (less than one hour) loss of consciousness

801.53   Open fracture of base of skull without mention of intracranial injury, moderate (1-24 hours) loss of consciousness

801.54   Open fracture of base of skull without mention of intracranial injury, prolonged (more than 24 hours) loss of consciousness and return to pre-existing conscious level

801.55   Open fracture of base of skull without mention of intracranial injury, prolonged (more than 24 hours) loss of consciousness, without return to pre-existing conscious level

801.56   Open fracture of base of skull without mention of intracranial injury, loss of consciousness of unspecified duration

801.59   Open fracture of base of skull without mention of intracranial injury, unspecified concussion

801.60   Open fracture of base of skull with cerebral laceration and contusion, unspecified state of consciousness

801.61   Open fracture of base of skull with cerebral laceration and contusion, no loss of consciousness

801.62   Open fracture of base of skull with cerebral laceration and contusion, brief (less than one hour) loss of consciousness

801.63   Open fracture of base of skull with cerebral laceration and contusion, moderate (1-24 hours) loss of consciousness

801.64 Open fracture of base of skull with cerebral laceration and contusion, prolonged (more than 24 hours) loss of consciousness and return to pre-existing conscious level

801.65 Open fracture of base of skull with cerebral laceration and contusion, prolonged (more than 24 hours) loss of consciousness, without return to pre-existing conscious level

801.66 Open fracture of base of skull with cerebral laceration and contusion, loss of consciousness of unspecified duration

801.69 Open fracture of base of skull with cerebral laceration and contusion, unspecified concussion

801.70 Open fracture of base of skull with subarachnoid, subdural, and extradural hemorrhage, unspecified state of consciousness

801.71 Open fracture of base of skull with subarachnoid, subdural, and extradural hemorrhage, no loss of consciousness

801.72 Open fracture of base of skull with subarachnoid, subdural, and extradural hemorrhage, brief (less than one hour) loss of consciousness

801.73 Open fracture of base of skull with subarachnoid, subdural, and extradural hemorrhage, moderate (1-24 hours) loss of consciousness

801.74 Open fracture of base of skull with subarachnoid, subdural, and extradural hemorrhage, prolonged (more than 24 hours) loss of consciousness and return to pre-existing conscious level

801.75 Open fracture of base of skull with subarachnoid, subdural, and extradural hemorrhage, prolonged (more than 24 hours) loss of consciousness, without return to pre-existing conscious level

801.76 Open fracture of base of skull with subarachnoid, subdural, and extradural hemorrhage, loss of consciousness of unspecified duration

801.79 Open fracture of base of skull with subarachnoid, subdural, and extradural hemorrhage, unspecified concussion

801.80 Open fracture of base of skull with other and unspecified intracranial hemorrhage, unspecified state of consciousness

801.81 Open fracture of base of skull with other and unspecified intracranial hemorrhage, no loss of consciousness

801.82 Open fracture of base of skull with other and unspecified intracranial hemorrhage, brief (less than one hour) loss of consciousness

801.83 Open fracture of base of skull with other and unspecified intracranial hemorrhage, moderate (1-24 hours) loss of consciousness

801.84 Open fracture of base of skull with other and unspecified intracranial hemorrhage, prolonged (more than 24 hours) loss of consciousness and return to pre-existing conscious level

801.85 Open fracture of base of skull with other and unspecified intracranial hemorrhage, prolonged (more than 24 hours) loss of consciousness, without return to pre-existing conscious level

801.86 Open fracture of base of skull with other and unspecified intracranial hemorrhage, loss of consciousness of unspecified duration

801.89 Open fracture of base of skull with other and unspecified intracranial hemorrhage, unspecified concussion

801.90 Open fracture of base of skull with intracranial injury of other and unspecified nature, unspecified state of consciousness

801.91 Open fracture of base of skull with intracranial injury of other and unspecified nature, no loss of consciousness

801.92 Open fracture of base of skull with intracranial injury of other and unspecified nature, brief (less than one hour) loss of consciousness

801.93 Open fracture of base of skull with intracranial injury of other and unspecified nature, moderate (1-24 hours) loss of consciousness

801.94 Open fracture of base of skull with intracranial injury of other and unspecified nature, prolonged (more than 24 hours) loss of consciousness and return to pre-existing conscious level

801.95 Open fracture of base of skull with intracranial injury of other and unspecified nature, prolonged (more than 24 hours) loss of consciousness, without return to pre-existing conscious level

801.96 Open fracture of base of skull with intracranial injury of other and unspecified nature, loss of consciousness of unspecified duration

801.99 Open fracture of base of skull with intracranial injury of other and unspecified nature, unspecified concussion

803.03 Other closed skull fracture without mention of intracranial injury, moderate (1-24 hours) loss of consciousness

803.04 Other closed skull fracture without mention of intracranial injury, prolonged (more than 24 hours) loss of consciousness and return to pre-existing conscious level

803.05 Other closed skull fracture without mention of intracranial injury, prolonged (more than 24 hours) loss of consciousness, without return to pre-existing conscious level

803.10 Other closed skull fracture with cerebral laceration and contusion, unspecified state of consciousness

803.11 Other closed skull fracture with cerebral laceration and contusion, no loss of consciousness

803.12 Other closed skull fracture with cerebral laceration and contusion, brief (less than one hour) loss of consciousness

803.13 Other closed skull fracture with cerebral laceration and contusion, moderate (1-24 hours) loss of consciousness

803.14 Other closed skull fracture with cerebral laceration and contusion, prolonged (more than 24 hours) loss of consciousness and return to pre-existing conscious level

803.15 Other closed skull fracture with cerebral laceration and contusion, prolonged (more than 24 hours) loss of consciousness, without return to pre-existing conscious level

803.16 Other closed skull fracture with cerebral laceration and contusion, loss of consciousness of unspecified duration

803.19 Other closed skull fracture with cerebral laceration and contusion, unspecified concussion

803.20 Other closed skull fracture with subarachnoid, subdural, and extradural hemorrhage, unspecified state of consciousness

803.21 Other closed skull fracture with subarachnoid, subdural, and extradural hemorrhage, no loss of consciousness

803.22 Other closed skull fracture with subarachnoid, subdural, and extradural hemorrhage, brief (less than one hour) loss of consciousness

803.23 Other closed skull fracture with subarachnoid, subdural, and extradural hemorrhage, moderate (1-24 hours) loss of consciousness

803.24 Other closed skull fracture with subarachnoid, subdural, and extradural hemorrhage, prolonged (more than 24 hours) loss of consciousness and return to pre-existing conscious level

803.25 Other closed skull fracture with subarachnoid, subdural, and extradural hemorrhage, prolonged (more than 24 hours) loss of consciousness, without return to pre-existing conscious level

803.26 Other closed skull fracture with subarachnoid, subdural, and extradural hemorrhage, loss of consciousness of unspecified duration

803.29 Other closed skull fracture with subarachnoid, subdural, and extradural hemorrhage, unspecified concussion

803.30 Other closed skull fracture with other and unspecified intracranial hemorrhage, unspecified state of unconsciousness

803.31 Other closed skull fracture with other and unspecified intracranial hemorrhage, no loss of consciousness

803.32 Other closed skull fracture with other and unspecified intracranial hemorrhage, brief (less than one hour) loss of consciousness

803.33 Other closed skull fracture with other and unspecified intracranial hemorrhage, moderate (1-24 hours) loss of consciousness

803.34 Other closed skull fracture with other and unspecified intracranial hemorrhage, prolonged (more than 24 hours) loss of consciousness and return to pre-existing conscious level

803.35 Other closed skull fracture with other and unspecified intracranial hemorrhage, prolonged (more than 24 hours) loss of consciousness, without return to pre-existing conscious level

803.36 Other closed skull fracture with other and unspecified intracranial hemorrhage, loss of consciousness of unspecified duration

803.39 Other closed skull fracture with other and unspecified intracranial hemorrhage, unspecified concussion

803.43 Other closed skull fracture with intracranial injury of other and unspecified nature, moderate (1-24 hours) loss of consciousness

803.44 Other closed skull fracture with intracranial injury of other and unspecified nature, prolonged (more than 24 hours) loss of consciousness and return to pre-existing conscious level

803.45 Other closed skull fracture with intracranial injury of other and unspecified nature, prolonged (more than 24 hours) loss of consciousness, without return to pre-existing conscious level

803.50 Other open skull fracture without mention of injury, state of consciousness unspecified

803.51 Other open skull fracture without mention of intracranial injury, no loss of consciousness

803.52 Other open skull fracture without mention of intracranial injury, brief (less than one hour) loss of consciousness

803.53 Other open skull fracture without mention of intracranial injury, moderate (1-24 hours) loss of consciousness

803.54 Other open skull fracture without mention of intracranial injury, prolonged (more than 24 hours) loss of consciousness and return to pre-existing conscious level

803.55 Other open skull fracture without mention of intracranial injury, prolonged (more than 24 hours) loss of consciousness, without return to pre-existing conscious level

803.56 Other open skull fracture without mention of intracranial injury, loss of consciousness of unspecified duration

803.59 Other open skull fracture without mention of intracranial injury, unspecified concussion

803.60 Other open skull fracture with cerebral laceration and contusion, unspecified state of consciousness

803.61 Other open skull fracture with cerebral laceration and contusion, no loss of consciousness

803.62 Other open skull fracture with cerebral laceration and contusion, brief (less than one hour) loss of consciousness

803.63 Other open skull fracture with cerebral laceration and contusion, moderate (1-24 hours) loss of consciousness

803.64 Other open skull fracture with cerebral laceration and contusion, prolonged (more than 24 hours) loss of consciousness and return to pre-existing conscious level

803.65 Other open skull fracture with cerebral laceration and contusion, prolonged (more than 24 hours) loss of consciousness, without return to pre-existing conscious level

803.66 Other open skull fracture with cerebral laceration and contusion, loss of consciousness of unspecified duration

803.69 Other open skull fracture with cerebral laceration and contusion, unspecified concussion

803.70 Other open skull fracture with subarachnoid, subdural, and extradural hemorrhage, unspecified state of consciousness

803.71 Other open skull fracture with subarachnoid, subdural, and extradural hemorrhage, no loss of consciousness

803.72 Other open skull fracture with subarachnoid, subdural, and extradural hemorrhage, brief (less than one hour) loss of consciousness

803.73 Other open skull fracture with subarachnoid, subdural, and extradural hemorrhage, moderate (1-24 hours) loss of consciousness

803.74 Other open skull fracture with subarachnoid, subdural, and extradural hemorrhage, prolonged (more than 24 hours) loss of consciousness and return to pre-existing conscious level

803.75 Other open skull fracture with subarachnoid, subdural, and extradural hemorrhage, prolonged (more than 24 hours) loss of consciousness, without return to pre-existing conscious level

803.76 Other open skull fracture with subarachnoid, subdural, and extradural hemorrhage, loss of consciousness of unspecified duration

803.79 Other open skull fracture with subarachnoid, subdural, and extradural hemorrhage, unspecified concussion

803.80 Other open skull fracture with other and unspecified intracranial hemorrhage, unspecified state of consciousness

803.81 Other open skull fracture with other and unspecified intracranial hemorrhage, no loss of consciousness

803.82 Other open skull fracture with other and unspecified intracranial hemorrhage, brief (less than one hour) loss of consciousness

803.83 Other open skull fracture with other and unspecified intracranial hemorrhage, moderate (1-24 hours) loss of consciousness

803.84 Other open skull fracture with other and unspecified intracranial hemorrhage, prolonged (more than 24 hours) loss of consciousness and return to pre-existing conscious level

803.85 Other open skull fracture with other and unspecified intracranial hemorrhage, prolonged (more than 24 hours) loss of consciousness, without return to pre-existing conscious level

803.86 Other open skull fracture with other and unspecified intracranial hemorrhage, loss of consciousness of unspecified duration

803.89 Other open skull fracture with other and unspecified intracranial hemorrhage, unspecified concussion

803.90 Other open skull fracture with intracranial injury of other and unspecified nature, unspecified state of consciousness

803.91 Other open skull fracture with intracranial injury of other and unspecified nature, no loss of consciousness

803.92 Other open skull fracture with intracranial injury of other and unspecified nature, brief (less than one hour) loss of consciousness

803.93 Other open skull fracture with intracranial injury of other and unspecified nature, moderate (1-24 hours) loss of consciousness

803.94 Other open skull fracture with intracranial injury of other and unspecified nature, prolonged (more than 24 hours) loss of consciousness and return to pre-existing conscious level

803.95 Other open skull fracture with intracranial injury of other and unspecified nature, prolonged (more than 24 hours) loss of consciousness, without return to pre-existing conscious level

803.96 Other open skull fracture with intracranial injury of other and unspecified nature, loss of consciousness of unspecified duration

803.99 Other open skull fracture with intracranial injury of other and unspecified nature, unspecified concussion

804.03 Closed fractures involving skull or face with other bones, without mention of intracranial injury, moderate (1-24 hours) loss of consciousness

804.04 Closed fractures involving skull or face with other bones, without mention or intracranial injury, prolonged (more than 24 hours) loss of consciousness and return to pre-existing conscious level

804.05 Closed fractures involving skull or face with other bones, without mention of intracranial injury, prolonged (more than 24 hours) loss of consciousness, without return to pre-existing conscious level

804.10 Closed fractures involving skull or face with other bones, with cerebral laceration and contusion, unspecified state of consciousness

804.11 Closed fractures involving skull or face with other bones, with cerebral laceration and contusion, no loss of consciousness

804.12 Closed fractures involving skull or face with other bones, with cerebral laceration and contusion, brief (less than one hour) loss of consciousness

804.13 Closed fractures involving skull or face with other bones, with cerebral laceration and contusion, moderate (1-24 hours) loss of consciousness

804.14 Closed fractures involving skull or face with other bones, with cerebral laceration and contusion, prolonged (more than 24 hours) loss of consciousness and return to pre-existing conscious level

804.15 Closed fractures involving skull or face with other bones, with cerebral laceration and contusion, prolonged (more than 24 hours) loss of consciousness, without return to pre-existing conscious level

804.16 Closed fractures involving skull or face with other bones, with cerebral laceration and contusion, loss of consciousness of unspecified duration

804.19 Closed fractures involving skull or face with other bones, with cerebral laceration and contusion, unspecified concussion

804.20 Closed fractures involving skull or face with other bones with subarachnoid, subdural, and extradural hemorrhage, unspecified state of consciousness

804.21   Closed fractures involving skull or face with other bones with subarachnoid, subdural, and extradural hemorrhage, no loss of consciousness

804.22   Closed fractures involving skull or face with other bones with subarachnoid, subdural, and extradural hemorrhage, brief (less than one hour) loss of consciousness

804.23   Closed fractures involving skull or face with other bones with subarachnoid, subdural, and extradural hemorrhage, moderate (1-24 hours) loss of consciousness

804.24   Closed fractures involving skull or face with other bones with subarachnoid, subdural, and extradural hemorrhage, prolonged (more than 24 hours) loss of consciousness and return to pre-existing conscious level

804.25   Closed fractures involving skull or face with other bones with subarachnoid, subdural, and extradural hemorrhage, prolonged (more than 24 hours) loss of consciousness, without return to pre-existing conscious level

804.26   Closed fractures involving skull or face with other bones with subarachnoid, subdural, and extradural hemorrhage, loss of consciousness of unspecified duration

804.29   Closed fractures involving skull or face with other bones with subarachnoid, subdural, and extradural hemorrhage, unspecified concussion

804.30   Closed fractures involving skull or face with other bones, with other and unspecified intracranial hemorrhage, unspecified state of consciousness

804.31   Closed fractures involving skull or face with other bones, with other and unspecified intracranial hemorrhage, no loss of consciousness

804.32   Closed fractures involving skull or face with other bones, with other and unspecified intracranial hemorrhage, brief (less than one hour) loss of consciousness

804.33   Closed fractures involving skull or face with other bones, with other and unspecified intracranial hemorrhage, moderate (1-24 hours) loss of consciousness

804.34   Closed fractures involving skull or face with other bones, with other and unspecified intracranial hemorrhage, prolonged (more than 24 hours) loss of consciousness and return to preexisting conscious level

804.35   Closed fractures involving skull or face with other bones, with other and unspecified intracranial hemorrhage, prolonged (more than 24 hours) loss of consciousness, without return to pre-existing conscious level

804.36   Closed fractures involving skull or face with other bones, with other and unspecified intracranial hemorrhage, loss of consciousness of unspecified duration

804.39   Closed fractures involving skull or face with other bones, with other and unspecified intracranial hemorrhage, unspecified concussion

804.43   Closed fractures involving skull or face with other bones, with intracranial injury of other and unspecified nature, moderate (1-24 hours) loss of consciousness

804.44   Closed fractures involving skull or face with other bones, with intracranial injury of other and unspecified nature, prolonged (more than 24 hours) loss of consciousness and return to pre-existing conscious level

804.45   Closed fractures involving skull or face with other bones, with intracranial injury of other and unspecified nature, prolonged (more than 24 hours) loss of consciousness, without return to pre-existing conscious level

804.53   Open fractures involving skull or face with other bones, without mention of intracranial injury, moderate (1-24 hours) loss of consciousness

804.54   Open fractures involving skull or face with other bones, without mention of intracranial injury, prolonged (more than 24 hours) loss of consciousness and return to pre-existing conscious level

804.55   Open fractures involving skull or face with other bones, without mention of intracranial injury, prolonged (more than 24 hours) loss of consciousness, without return to pre-existing conscious level

804.60   Open fractures involving skull or face with other bones, with cerebral laceration and contusion, unspecified state of consciousness

804.61   Open fractures involving skull or face with other bones, with cerebral laceration and contusion, no loss of consciousness

804.62   Open fractures involving skull or face with other bones, with cerebral laceration and contusion, brief (less than one hour) loss of consciousness

804.63   Open fractures involving skull or face with other bones, with cerebral laceration and contusion, moderate (1-24 hours) loss of consciousness

804.64   Open fractures involving skull or face with other bones, with cerebral laceration and contusion, prolonged (more than 24 hours) loss of consciousness and return to pre-existing conscious level

804.65   Open fractures involving skull or face with other bones, with cerebral laceration and contusion, prolonged (more than 24 hours) loss of consciousness, without return to pre-existing conscious level

804.66   Open fractures involving skull or face with other bones, with cerebral laceration and contusion, loss of consciousness of unspecified duration

804.69   Open fractures involving skull or face with other bones, with cerebral laceration and contusion, unspecified concussion

804.70   Open fractures involving skull or face with other bones with subarachnoid, subdural, and extradural hemorrhage, unspecified state of consciousness

804.71   Open fractures involving skull or face with other bones with subarachnoid, subdural, and extradural hemorrhage, no loss of consciousness

804.72   Open fractures involving skull or face with other bones with subarachnoid, subdural, and extradural hemorrhage, brief (less than one hour) loss of consciousness

804.73   Open fractures involving skull or face with other bones with subarachnoid, subdural, and extradural hemorrhage, moderate (1-24 hours) loss of consciousness

804.74   Open fractures involving skull or face with other bones with subarachnoid, subdural, and extradural hemorrhage, prolonged (more than 24 hours) loss of consciousness and return to pre-existing conscious level

804.75   Open fractures involving skull or face with other bones with subarachnoid, subdural, and extradural hemorrhage, prolonged (more than 24 hours) loss of consciousness, without return to pre-existing conscious level

804.76   Open fractures involving skull or face with other bones with subarachnoid, subdural, and extradural hemorrhage, loss of consciousness of unspecified duration

804.79   Open fractures involving skull or face with other bones with subarachnoid, subdural, and extradural hemorrhage, unspecified concussion

804.80   Open fractures involving skull or face with other bones, with other and unspecified intracranial hemorrhage, unspecified state of consciousness

804.81   Open fractures involving skull or face with other bones, with other and unspecified intracranial hemorrhage, no loss of consciousness

804.82   Open fractures involving skull or face with other bones, with other and unspecified intracranial hemorrhage, brief (less than one hour) loss of consciousness

804.83   Open fractures involving skull or face with other bones, with other and unspecified intracranial hemorrhage, moderate (1-24 hours) loss of consciousness

804.84   Open fractures involving skull or face with other bones, with other and unspecified intracranial hemorrhage, prolonged (more than 24 hours) loss of consciousness and return to pre-existing conscious level

804.85   Open fractures involving skull or face with other bones, with other and unspecified intracranial hemorrhage, prolonged (more than 24 hours) loss of consciousness, without return to pre-existing conscious level

804.86	Open fractures involving skull or face with other bones, with other and unspecified intracranial hemorrhage, loss of consciousness of unspecified duration
804.89	Open fractures involving skull or face with other bones, with other and unspecified intracranial hemorrhage, unspecified concussion
804.93	Open fractures involving skull or face with other bones, with intracranial injury of other and unspecified nature, moderate (1-24 hours) loss of consciousness
804.94	Open fractures involving skull or face with other bones, with intracranial injury of other and unspecified nature, prolonged (more than 24 hours) loss of consciousness and return to pre-existing conscious level
804.95	Open fractures involving skull or face with other bones, with intracranial injury of other and unspecified nature, prolonged (more than 24 hours) loss of consciousness, without return to pre-existing level
805.10	Open fracture of cervical vertebra, unspecified level without mention of spinal cord injury
805.11	Open fracture of first cervical vertebra without mention of spinal cord injury
805.12	Open fracture of second cervical vertebra without mention of spinal cord injury
805.13	Open fracture of third cervical vertebra without mention of spinal cord injury
805.14	Open fracture of fourth cervical vertebra without mention of spinal cord injury
805.15	Open fracture of fifth cervical vertebra without mention of spinal cord injury
805.16	Open fracture of sixth cervical vertebra without mention of spinal cord injury
805.17	Open fracture of seventh cervical vertebra without mention of spinal cord injury
805.18	Open fracture of multiple cervical vertebrae without mention of spinal cord injury
805.3	Open fracture of dorsal (thoracic) vertebra without mention of spinal cord injury
805.5	Open fracture of lumbar vertebra without mention of spinal cord injury
805.7	Open fracture of sacrum and coccyx without mention of spinal cord injury
805.9	Open fracture of unspecified part of vertebral column without mention of spinal cord injury
806.00	Closed fracture of C1-C4 level with unspecified spinal cord injury
806.01	Closed fracture of C1-C4 level with complete lesion of cord
806.02	Closed fracture of C1-C4 level with anterior cord syndrome
806.03	Closed fracture of C1-C4 level with central cord syndrome
806.04	Closed fracture of C1-C4 level with other specified spinal cord injury
806.05	Closed fracture of C5-C7 level with unspecified spinal cord injury
806.06	Closed fracture of C5-C7 level with complete lesion of cord
806.07	Closed fracture of C5-C7 level with anterior cord syndrome
806.08	Closed fracture of C5-C7 level with central cord syndrome
806.09	Closed fracture of C5-C7 level with other specified spinal cord injury
806.10	Open fracture of C1-C4 level with unspecified spinal cord injury
806.11	Open fracture of C1-C4 level with complete lesion of cord
806.12	Open fracture of C1-C4 level with anterior cord syndrome
806.13	Open fracture of C1-C4 level with central cord syndrome
806.14	Open fracture of C1-C4 level with other specified spinal cord injury
806.15	Open fracture of C5-C7 level with unspecified spinal cord injury
806.16	Open fracture of C5-C7 level with complete lesion of cord
806.17	Open fracture of C5-C7 level with anterior cord syndrome
806.18	Open fracture of C5-C7 level with central cord syndrome
806.19	Open fracture of C5-C7 level with other specified spinal cord injury
806.20	Closed fracture of T1-T6 level with unspecified spinal cord injury
806.21	Closed fracture of T1-T6 level with complete lesion of cord
806.22	Closed fracture of T1-T6 level with anterior cord syndrome
806.23	Closed fracture of T1-T6 level with central cord syndrome
806.24	Closed fracture of T1-T6 level with other specified spinal cord injury
806.25	Closed fracture of T7-T12 level with unspecified spinal cord injury
806.26	Closed fracture of T7-T12 level with complete lesion of cord
806.27	Closed fracture of T7-T12 level with anterior cord syndrome
806.28	Closed fracture of T7-T12 level with central cord syndrome
806.29	Closed fracture of T7-T12 level with other specified spinal cord injury
806.30	Open fracture of T1-T6 level with unspecified spinal cord injury
806.31	Open fracture of T1-T6 level with complete lesion of cord
806.32	Open fracture of T1-T6 level with anterior cord syndrome
806.33	Open fracture of T1-T6 level with central cord syndrome
806.34	Open fracture of T1-T6 level with other specified spinal cord injury
806.35	Open fracture of T7-T12 level with unspecified spinal cord injury
806.36	Open fracture of T7-T12 level with complete lesion of cord
806.37	Open fracture of T7-T12 level with anterior cord syndrome
806.38	Open fracture of T7-T12 level with central cord syndrome
806.39	Open fracture of T7-T12 level with other specified spinal cord injury
806.4	Closed fracture of lumbar spine with spinal cord injury
806.5	Open fracture of lumbar spine with spinal cord injury
806.60	Closed fracture of sacrum and coccyx with unspecified spinal cord injury
806.61	Closed fracture of sacrum and coccyx with complete cauda equina lesion
806.62	Closed fracture of sacrum and coccyx with other cauda equina injury
806.69	Closed fracture of sacrum and coccyx with other spinal cord injury
806.70	Open fracture of sacrum and coccyx with unspecified spinal cord injury
806.71	Open fracture of sacrum and coccyx with complete cauda equina lesion
806.72	Open fracture of sacrum and coccyx with other cauda equina injury
806.79	Open fracture of sacrum and coccyx with other spinal cord injury
806.8	Closed fracture of unspecified vertebra with spinal cord injury
806.9	Open fracture of unspecified vertebra with spinal cord injury
807.10	Open fracture of rib(s), unspecified
807.11	Open fracture of one rib
807.12	Open fracture of two ribs
807.13	Open fracture of three ribs
807.14	Open fracture of four ribs
807.15	Open fracture of five ribs
807.16	Open fracture of six ribs
807.17	Open fracture of seven ribs
807.18	Open fracture of eight or more ribs
807.19	Open fracture of multiple ribs, unspecified
807.3	Open fracture of sternum
807.4	Flail chest
807.5	Closed fracture of larynx and trachea
807.6	Open fracture of larynx and trachea
808.0	Closed fracture of acetabulum
808.1	Open fracture of acetabulum
808.3	Open fracture of pubis
808.51	Open fracture of ilium
808.52	Open fracture of ischium
808.53	Multiple open pelvic fractures with disruption of pelvic circle
808.54	Multiple open pelvic fractures without disruption of pelvic circle
808.59	Open fracture of other specified part of pelvis
808.9	Unspecified open fracture of pelvis
809.1	Fracture of bones of trunk, open

812.10	Open fracture of unspecified part of upper end of humerus
812.11	Open fracture of surgical neck of humerus
812.12	Open fracture of anatomical neck of humerus
812.13	Open fracture of greater tuberosity of humerus
812.19	Other open fracture of upper end of humerus
812.30	Open fracture of unspecified part of humerus
812.31	Open fracture of shaft of humerus
812.50	Open fracture of unspecified part of lower end of humerus
812.51	Open fracture of supracondylar humerus
812.52	Open fracture of lateral condyle of humerus
812.53	Open fracture of medial condyle of humerus
812.54	Open fracture of unspecified condyle(s) of humerus
812.59	Other open fracture of lower end of humerus
813.10	Unspecified open fracture of upper end of forearm
813.11	Open fracture of olecranon process of ulna
813.12	Open fracture of coronoid process of ulna
813.13	Open Monteggia's fracture
813.14	Other and unspecified open fractures of proximal end of ulna (alone)
813.15	Open fracture of head of radius
813.16	Open fracture of neck of radius
813.17	Other and unspecified open fractures of proximal end of radius (alone)
813.18	Open fracture of radius with ulna, upper end (any part)
813.30	Unspecified open fracture of shaft of radius or ulna
813.31	Open fracture of shaft of radius (alone)
813.32	Open fracture of shaft of ulna (alone)
813.33	Open fracture of shaft of radius with ulna
813.50	Unspecified open fracture of lower end of forearm
813.51	Open Colles' fracture
813.52	Other open fractures of distal end of radius (alone)
813.53	Open fracture of distal end of ulna (alone)
813.54	Open fracture of lower end of radius with ulna
813.90	Open fracture of unspecified part of forearm
813.91	Open fracture of unspecified part of radius (alone)
813.92	Open fracture of unspecified part of ulna (alone)
813.93	Open fracture of unspecified part of radius with ulna
820.00	Closed fracture of unspecified intracapsular section of neck of femur
820.01	Closed fracture of epiphysis (separation) (upper) of neck of femur
820.02	Closed fracture of midcervical section of femur
820.03	Closed fracture of base of neck of femur
820.09	Other closed transcervical fracture of femur
820.10	Open fracture of unspecified intracapsular section of neck of femur
820.11	Open fracture of epiphysis (separation) (upper) of neck of femur
820.12	Open fracture of midcervical section of femur
820.13	Open fracture of base of neck of femur
820.19	Other open transcervical fracture of femur
820.20	Closed fracture of unspecified trochanteric section of femur
820.21	Closed fracture of intertrochanteric section of femur
820.22	Closed fracture of subtrochanteric section of femur
820.30	Open fracture of unspecified trochanteric section of femur
820.31	Open fracture of intertrochanteric section of femur
820.32	Open fracture of subtrochanteric section of femur
820.8	Closed fracture of unspecified part of neck of femur
820.9	Open fracture of unspecified part of neck of femur
821.00	Closed fracture of unspecified part of femur
821.01	Closed fracture of shaft of femur
821.10	Open fracture of unspecified part of femur

821.11	Open fracture of shaft of femur
821.30	Open fracture of unspecified part of lower end of femur
821.31	Open fracture of femoral condyle
821.32	Open fracture of lower epiphysis of femur
821.33	Open supracondylar fracture of femur
821.39	Other open fracture of lower end of femur
823.10	Open fracture of upper end of tibia
823.11	Open fracture of upper end of fibula
823.12	Open fracture of upper end of fibula with tibia
823.30	Open fracture of shaft of tibia
823.31	Open fracture of shaft of fibula
823.32	Open fracture of shaft of fibula with tibia
823.90	Open fracture of unspecified part of tibia
823.91	Open fracture of unspecified part of fibula
823.92	Open fracture of unspecified part of fibula with tibia
828.0	Multiple closed fractures involving both lower limbs, lower with upper limb, and lower limb(s) with rib(s) and sternum
828.1	Multiple fractures involving both lower limbs, lower with upper limb, and lower limb(s) with rib(s) and sternum, open
835.10	Open dislocation of hip, unspecified site
835.11	Open posterior dislocation of hip
835.12	Open obturator dislocation of hip
835.13	Other open anterior dislocation of hip
839.10	Open dislocation, unspecified cervical vertebra
839.11	Open dislocation, first cervical vertebra
839.12	Open dislocation, second cervical vertebra
839.13	Open dislocation, third cervical vertebra
839.14	Open dislocation, fourth cervical vertebra
839.15	Open dislocation, fifth cervical vertebra
839.16	Open dislocation, sixth cervical vertebra
839.17	Open dislocation, seventh cervical vertebra
839.18	Open dislocation, multiple cervical vertebrae
839.30	Open dislocation, lumbar vertebra
839.31	Open dislocation, thoracic vertebra
839.50	Open dislocation, vertebra, unspecified site
839.59	Open dislocation, other vertebra
839.71	Open dislocation, sternum
850.4	Concussion with prolonged (more than 24 hours) loss of consciousness, without return to pre-existing conscious level
851.05	Cortex (cerebral) contusion without mention of open intracranial wound, prolonged (more than 24 hours) loss of consciousness, without return to pre-existing conscious level
851.10	Cortex (cerebral) contusion with open intracranial wound, unspecified state of consciousness
851.11	Cortex (cerebral) contusion with open intracranial wound, no loss of consciousness
851.12	Cortex (cerebral) contusion with open intracranial wound, brief (less than 1 hour) loss of consciousness
851.13	Cortex (cerebral) contusion with open intracranial wound, moderate (1-24 hours) loss of consciousness
851.14	Cortex (cerebral) contusion with open intracranial wound, prolonged (more than 24 hours) loss of consciousness and return to pre-existing conscious level
851.15	Cortex (cerebral) contusion with open intracranial wound, prolonged (more than 24 hours) loss of consciousness, without return to pre-existing conscious level
851.16	Cortex (cerebral) contusion with open intracranial wound, loss of consciousness of unspecified duration
851.19	Cortex (cerebral) contusion with open intracranial wound, unspecified concussion
851.20	Cortex (cerebral) laceration without mention of open intracranial wound, unspecified state of consciousness

851.21 Cortex (cerebral) laceration without mention of open intracranial wound, no loss of consciousness

851.22 Cortex (cerebral) laceration without mention of open intracranial wound, brief (less than 1 hour) loss of consciousness

851.23 Cortex (cerebral) laceration without mention of open intracranial wound, moderate (1-24 hours) loss of consciousness

851.24 Cortex (cerebral) laceration without mention of open intracranial wound, prolonged (more than 24 hours) loss of consciousness and return to pre-existing conscious level

851.25 Cortex (cerebral) laceration without mention of open intracranial wound, prolonged (more than 24 hours) loss of consciousness, without return to pre-existing conscious level

851.26 Cortex (cerebral) laceration without mention of open intracranial wound, loss of consciousness of unspecified duration

851.29 Cortex (cerebral) laceration without mention of open intracranial wound, unspecified concussion

851.30 Cortex (cerebral) laceration with open intracranial wound, unspecified state of consciousness

851.31 Cortex (cerebral) laceration with open intracranial wound, no loss of consciousness

851.32 Cortex (cerebral) laceration with open intracranial wound, brief (less than 1 hour) loss of consciousness

851.33 Cortex (cerebral) laceration with open intracranial wound, moderate (1-24 hours) loss of consciousness

851.34 Cortex (cerebral) laceration with open intracranial wound, prolonged (more than 24 hours) loss of consciousness and return to pre-existing conscious level

851.35 Cortex (cerebral) laceration with open intracranial wound, prolonged (more than 24 hours) loss of consciousness, without return to pre-existing conscious level

851.36 Cortex (cerebral) laceration with open intracranial wound, loss of consciousness of unspecified duration

851.39 Cortex (cerebral) laceration with open intracranial wound, unspecified concussion

851.45 Cerebellar or brain stem contusion without mention of open intracranial wound, prolonged (more than 24 hours) loss of consciousness, without return to pre-existing conscious level

851.50 Cerebellar or brain stem contusion with open intracranial wound, unspecified state of consciousness

851.51 Cerebellar or brain stem contusion with open intracranial wound, no loss of consciousness

851.52 Cerebellar or brain stem contusion with open intracranial wound, brief (less than 1 hour) loss of consciousness

851.53 Cerebellar or brain stem contusion with open intracranial wound, moderate (1-24 hours) loss of consciousness

851.54 Cerebellar or brain stem contusion with open intracranial wound, prolonged (more than 24 hours) loss of consciousness and return to pre-existing conscious level

851.55 Cerebellar or brain stem contusion with open intracranial wound, prolonged (more than 24 hours) loss of consciousness, without return to pre-existing conscious level

851.56 Cerebellar or brain stem contusion with open intracranial wound, loss of consciousness of unspecified duration

851.59 Cerebellar or brain stem contusion with open intracranial wound, unspecified concussion

851.60 Cerebellar or brain stem laceration without mention of open intracranial wound, unspecified state of consciousness

851.61 Cerebellar or brain stem laceration without mention of open intracranial wound, no loss of consciousness

851.62 Cerebellar or brain stem laceration without mention of open intracranial wound, brief (less than 1 hour) loss of consciousness

851.63 Cerebellar or brain stem laceration without mention of open intracranial wound, moderate (1-24 hours) loss of consciousness

851.64 Cerebellar or brain stem laceration without mention of open intracranial wound, prolonged (more than 24 hours) loss of consciousness and return to pre-existing conscious level

851.65 Cerebellar or brain stem laceration without mention of open intracranial wound, prolonged (more than 24 hours) loss of consciousness, without return to pre-existing conscious level

851.66 Cerebellar or brain stem laceration without mention of open intracranial wound, loss of consciousness of unspecified duration

851.69 Cerebellar or brain stem laceration without mention of open intracranial wound, unspecified concussion

851.70 Cerebellar or brain stem laceration with open intracranial wound, state of consciousness unspecified

851.71 Cerebellar or brain stem laceration with open intracranial wound, no loss of consciousness

851.72 Cerebellar or brain stem laceration with open intracranial wound, brief (less than one hour) loss of consciousness

851.73 Cerebellar or brain stem laceration with open intracranial wound, moderate (1-24 hours) loss of consciousness

851.74 Cerebellar or brain stem laceration with open intracranial wound, prolonged (more than 24 hours) loss of consciousness and return to pre-existing conscious level

851.75 Cerebellar or brain stem laceration with open intracranial wound, prolonged (more than 24 hours) loss of consciousness, without return to pre-existing conscious level

851.76 Cerebellar or brain stem laceration with open intracranial wound, loss of consciousness of unspecified duration

851.79 Cerebellar or brain stem laceration with open intracranial wound, unspecified concussion

851.80 Other and unspecified cerebral laceration and contusion, without mention of open intracranial wound, unspecified state of consciousness

851.81 Other and unspecified cerebral laceration and contusion, without mention of open intracranial wound, no loss of consciousness

851.82 Other and unspecified cerebral laceration and contusion, without mention of open intracranial wound, brief (less than 1 hour) loss of consciousness

851.83 Other and unspecified cerebral laceration and contusion, without mention of open intracranial wound, moderate (1-24 hours) loss of consciousness

851.84 Other and unspecified cerebral laceration and contusion, without mention of open intracranial wound, prolonged (more than 24 hours) loss of consciousness and return to preexisting conscious level

851.85 Other and unspecified cerebral laceration and contusion, without mention of open intracranial wound, prolonged (more than 24 hours) loss of consciousness, without return to pre-existing conscious level

851.86 Other and unspecified cerebral laceration and contusion, without mention of open intracranial wound, loss of consciousness of unspecified duration

851.89 Other and unspecified cerebral laceration and contusion, without mention of open intracranial wound, unspecified concussion

851.90 Other and unspecified cerebral laceration and contusion, with open intracranial wound, unspecified state of consciousness

851.91 Other and unspecified cerebral laceration and contusion, with open intracranial wound, no loss of consciousness

851.92 Other and unspecified cerebral laceration and contusion, with open intracranial wound, brief (less than 1 hour) loss of consciousness

851.93 Other and unspecified cerebral laceration and contusion, with open intracranial wound, moderate (1-24 hours) loss of consciousness

851.94 Other and unspecified cerebral laceration and contusion, with open intracranial wound, prolonged (more than 24 hours) loss of consciousness and return to pre-existing conscious level

851.95 Other and unspecified cerebral laceration and contusion, with open intracranial wound, prolonged (more than 24 hours) loss of consciousness, without return to pre-existing conscious level

851.96 Other and unspecified cerebral laceration and contusion, with open intracranial wound, loss of consciousness of unspecified duration

851.99 Other and unspecified cerebral laceration and contusion, with open intracranial wound, unspecified concussion

852.00 Subarachnoid hemorrhage following injury, without mention of open intracranial wound, unspecified state of consciousness

852.01 Subarachnoid hemorrhage following injury, without mention of open intracranial wound, no loss of consciousness

852.02 Subarachnoid hemorrhage following injury, without mention of open intracranial wound, brief (less than 1 hour) loss of consciousness

852.03 Subarachnoid hemorrhage following injury, without mention of open intracranial wound, moderate (1-24 hours) loss of consciousness

852.04 Subarachnoid hemorrhage following injury, without mention of open intracranial wound, prolonged (more than 24 hours) loss of consciousness and return to pre-existing conscious level

852.05 Subarachnoid hemorrhage following injury, without mention of open intracranial wound, prolonged (more than 24 hours) loss of consciousness, without return to pre-existing conscious level

852.06 Subarachnoid hemorrhage following injury, without mention of open intracranial wound, loss of consciousness of unspecified duration

852.09 Subarachnoid hemorrhage following injury, without mention of open intracranial wound, unspecified concussion

852.10 Subarachnoid hemorrhage following injury, with open intracranial wound, unspecified state of consciousness

852.11 Subarachnoid hemorrhage following injury, with open intracranial wound, no loss of consciousness

852.12 Subarachnoid hemorrhage following injury, with open intracranial wound, brief (less than 1 hour) loss of consciousness

852.13 Subarachnoid hemorrhage following injury, with open intracranial wound, moderate (1-24 hours) loss of consciousness

852.14 Subarachnoid hemorrhage following injury, with open intracranial wound, prolonged (more than 24 hours) loss of consciousness and return to pre-existing conscious level

852.15 Subarachnoid hemorrhage following injury, with open intracranial wound, prolonged (more than 24 hours) loss of consciousness, without return to pre-existing conscious level

852.16 Subarachnoid hemorrhage following injury, with open intracranial wound, loss of consciousness of unspecified duration

852.19 Subarachnoid hemorrhage following injury, with open intracranial wound, unspecified concussion

852.20 Subdural hemorrhage following injury, without mention of open intracranial wound, unspecified state of consciousness

852.21 Subdural hemorrhage following injury, without mention of open intracranial wound, no loss of consciousness

852.22 Subdural hemorrhage following injury, without mention of open intracranial wound, brief (less than one hour) loss of consciousness

852.23 Subdural hemorrhage following injury, without mention of open intracranial wound, moderate (1-24 hours) loss of consciousness

852.24 Subdural hemorrhage following injury, without mention of open intracranial wound, prolonged (more than 24 hours) loss of consciousness and return to pre-existing conscious level

852.25 Subdural hemorrhage following injury, without mention of open intracranial wound, prolonged (more than 24 hours) loss of consciousness, without return to pre-existing conscious level

852.26 Subdural hemorrhage following injury, without mention of open intracranial wound, loss of consciousness of unspecified duration

852.29 Subdural hemorrhage following injury, without mention of open intracranial wound, unspecified concussion

852.30 Subdural hemorrhage following injury, with open intracranial wound, state of consciousness unspecified

852.31 Subdural hemorrhage following injury, with open intracranial wound, no loss of consciousness

852.32 Subdural hemorrhage following injury, with open intracranial wound, brief (less than 1 hour) loss of consciousness

852.33 Subdural hemorrhage following injury, with open intracranial wound, moderate (1-24 hours) loss of consciousness

852.34 Subdural hemorrhage following injury, with open intracranial wound, prolonged (more than 24 hours) loss of consciousness and return to pre-existing conscious level

852.35 Subdural hemorrhage following injury, with open intracranial wound, prolonged (more than 24 hours) loss of consciousness, without return to pre-existing conscious level

852.36 Subdural hemorrhage following injury, with open intracranial wound, loss of consciousness of unspecified duration

852.39 Subdural hemorrhage following injury, with open intracranial wound, unspecified concussion

852.40 Extradural hemorrhage following injury, without mention of open intracranial wound, unspecified state of consciousness

852.41 Extradural hemorrhage following injury, without mention of open intracranial wound, no loss of consciousness

852.42 Extradural hemorrhage following injury, without mention of open intracranial wound, brief (less than 1 hour) loss of consciousness

852.43 Extradural hemorrhage following injury, without mention of open intracranial wound, moderate (1-24 hours) loss of consciousness

852.44 Extradural hemorrhage following injury, without mention of open intracranial wound, prolonged (more than 24 hours) loss of consciousness and return to pre-existing conscious level

852.45 Extradural hemorrhage following injury, without mention of open intracranial wound, prolonged (more than 24 hours) loss of consciousness, without return to pre-existing conscious level

852.46 Extradural hemorrhage following injury, without mention of open intracranial wound, loss of consciousness of unspecified duration

852.49 Extradural hemorrhage following injury, without mention of open intracranial wound, unspecified concussion

852.50 Extradural hemorrhage following injury, with open intracranial wound, state of consciousness unspecified

852.51 Extradural hemorrhage following injury, with open intracranial wound, no loss of consciousness

852.52 Extradural hemorrhage following injury, with open intracranial wound, brief (less than 1 hour) loss of consciousness

852.53 Extradural hemorrhage following injury, with open intracranial wound, moderate (1-24 hours) loss of consciousness

852.54 Extradural hemorrhage following injury, with open intracranial wound, prolonged (more than 24 hours) loss of consciousness and return to pre-existing conscious level

852.55 Extradural hemorrhage following injury, with open intracranial wound, prolonged (more than 24 hours) loss of consciousness, without return to pre-existing conscious level

852.56 Extradural hemorrhage following injury, with open intracranial wound, loss of consciousness of unspecified duration

852.59 Extradural hemorrhage following injury, with open intracranial wound, unspecified concussion

853.00 Other and unspecified intracranial hemorrhage following injury, without mention of open intracranial wound, unspecified state of consciousness

853.01 Other and unspecified intracranial hemorrhage following injury, without mention of open intracranial wound, no loss of consciousness

853.02 Other and unspecified intracranial hemorrhage following injury, without mention of open intracranial wound, brief (less than 1 hour) loss of consciousness

853.03 Other and unspecified intracranial hemorrhage following injury, without mention of open intracranial wound, moderate (1-24 hours) loss of consciousness

853.04 Other and unspecified intracranial hemorrhage following injury, without mention of open intracranial wound, prolonged (more than 24 hours) loss of consciousness and return to preexisting conscious level

853.05 Other and unspecified intracranial hemorrhage following injury. Without mention of open intracranial wound, prolonged (more than 24 hours) loss of consciousness, without return to pre-existing conscious level

853.06 Other and unspecified intracranial hemorrhage following injury, without mention of open intracranial wound, loss of consciousness of unspecified duration

853.09 Other and unspecified intracranial hemorrhage following injury, without mention of open intracranial wound, unspecified concussion

853.10 Other and unspecified intracranial hemorrhage following injury, with open intracranial wound, unspecified state of consciousness

853.11 Other and unspecified intracranial hemorrhage following injury, with open intracranial wound, no loss of consciousness

853.12 Other and unspecified intracranial hemorrhage following injury, with open intracranial wound, brief (less than 1 hour) loss of consciousness

853.13 Other and unspecified intracranial hemorrhage following injury, with open intracranial wound, moderate (1-24 hours) loss of consciousness

853.14 Other and unspecified intracranial hemorrhage following injury, with open intracranial wound, prolonged (more than 24 hours) loss of consciousness and return to pre-existing conscious level

853.15 Other and unspecified intracranial hemorrhage following injury, with open intracranial wound, prolonged (more than 24 hours) loss of consciousness, without return to pre-existing conscious level

853.16 Other and unspecified intracranial hemorrhage following injury, with open intracranial wound, loss of consciousness of unspecified duration

853.19 Other and unspecified intracranial hemorrhage following injury, with open intracranial wound, unspecified concussion

854.05 Intracranial injury of other and unspecified nature, without mention of open intracranial wound, prolonged (more than 24 hours) loss of consciousness, without return to pre-existing conscious level

854.10 Intracranial injury of other and unspecified nature, with open intracranial wound, unspecified state of consciousness

854.11 Intracranial injury of other and unspecified nature, with open intracranial wound, no loss of consciousness

854.12 Intracranial injury of other and unspecified nature, with open intracranial wound, brief (less than 1 hour) loss of consciousness

854.13 Intracranial injury of other and unspecified nature, with open intracranial wound, moderate (1-24 hours) loss of consciousness

854.14 Intracranial injury of other and unspecified nature, with open intracranial wound, prolonged (more than 24 hours) loss of consciousness and return to pre-existing conscious level

854.15 Intracranial injury of other and unspecified nature, with open intracranial wound, prolonged (more than 24 hours) loss of consciousness, without return to pre-existing conscious level

854.16 Intracranial injury of other and unspecified nature, with open intracranial wound, loss of consciousness of unspecified duration

854.19 Intracranial injury of other and unspecified nature, with open intracranial wound, with unspecified concussion

860.1   Traumatic pneumothorax with open wound into thorax

860.2   Traumatic hemothorax without mention of open wound into thorax

860.3   Traumatic hemothorax with open wound into thorax

860.4   Traumatic pneumohemothorax without mention of open wound into thorax

860.5   Traumatic pneumohemothorax with open wound into thorax

861.02 Heart laceration without penetration of heart chambers or mention of open wound into thorax

861.03 Heart laceration with penetration of heart chambers, without mention of open wound into thorax

861.10 Unspecified injury to heart with open wound into thorax

861.11 Heart contusion with open wound into thorax

861.12 Heart laceration without penetration of heart chambers, with open wound into thorax

861.13 Heart laceration with penetration of heart chambers and open wound into thorax

861.22 Lung laceration without mention of open wound into thorax

861.30 Unspecified lung injury with open wound into thorax

861.31 Lung contusion with open wound into thorax

861.32 Lung laceration with open wound into thorax

862.1   Diaphragm injury with open wound into cavity

862.21 Bronchus injury without mention of open wound into cavity

862.22 Esophagus injury without mention of open wound into cavity

862.31 Bronchus injury with open wound into cavity

862.32 Esophagus injury with open wound into cavity

862.39 Injury to other specified intrathoracic organs with open wound into cavity

862.9   Injury to multiple and unspecified intrathoracic organs with open wound into cavity

863.1   Stomach injury with open wound into cavity

863.30 Small intestine injury, unspecified site, with open wound into cavity

863.31 Duodenum injury with open wound into cavity

863.39 Other injury to small intestine with open wound into cavity

863.50 Colon injury, unspecified site, with open wound into cavity

863.51 Ascending (right) colon injury with open wound into cavity

863.52 Transverse colon injury with open wound into cavity

863.53 Descending (left) colon injury with open wound into cavity

863.54 Sigmoid colon injury with open wound into cavity

863.55 Rectum injury with open wound into cavity

863.56 Injury to multiple sites in colon and rectum with open wound into cavity

863.59 Other injury to colon and rectum with open wound into cavity

863.90 Gastrointestinal tract injury, unspecified site, with open wound into cavity

863.91 Pancreas head injury with open wound into cavity

863.92 Pancreas body injury with open wound into cavity

863.93 Pancreas tail injury with open wound into cavity

863.94 Pancreas injury, multiple and unspecified sites, with open wound into cavity

863.95 Appendix injury with open wound into cavity

863.99 Injury to other and unspecified gastrointestinal sites with open wound into cavity

864.03 Liver laceration, moderate, without mention of open wound into cavity

864.04 Liver laceration, major, without mention of open wound into cavity

864.10 Unspecified liver injury with open wound into cavity

864.11 Liver hematoma and contusion with open wound into cavity

864.12 Liver laceration, minor, with open wound into cavity

864.13 Liver laceration, moderate, with open wound into cavity

864.14 Liver laceration, major, with open wound into cavity

864.15 Liver injury with open wound into cavity, unspecified laceration

864.19 Other liver injury with open wound into cavity

865.03 Spleen laceration extending into parenchyma without mention of open wound into cavity

865.04 Massive parenchymal disruption of spleen without mention of open wound into cavity

865.10 Unspecified spleen injury with open wound into cavity

865.11 Spleen hematoma, without rupture of capsule, with open wound into cavity

865.12 Capsular tears to spleen, without major disruption of parenchyma, with open wound into cavity

865.13 Spleen laceration extending into parenchyma, with open wound into cavity

865.14 Massive parenchyma disruption of spleen with open wound into cavity

865.19 Other spleen injury with open wound into cavity

866.03 Complete disruption of kidney parenchyma, without mention of open wound into cavity

866.10	Unspecified kidney injury with open wound into cavity
866.11	Kidney hematoma, without rupture of capsule, with open wound into cavity
866.12	Kidney laceration with open wound into cavity
866.13	Complete disruption of kidney parenchyma, with open wound into cavity
867.1	Bladder and urethra injury with open wound into cavity
867.3	Ureter injury with open wound into cavity
867.5	Uterus injury with open wound into cavity
867.7	Injury to other specified pelvic organs with open wound into cavity
867.9	Injury to unspecified pelvic organ with open wound into cavity
868.10	Injury to unspecified intra-abdominal organ, with open wound into cavity
868.11	Adrenal gland injury, with open wound into cavity
868.12	Bile duct and gallbladder injury, with open wound into cavity
868.13	Peritoneum injury with open wound into cavity
868.14	Retroperitoneum injury with open wound into cavity
868.19	Injury to other and multiple intra-abdominal organs, with open wound into cavity
869.1	Internal injury to unspecified or ill-defined organs with open wound into cavity
874.00	Open wound of larynx with trachea, without mention of complication
874.01	Open wound of larynx, without mention of complication
874.02	Open wound of trachea, without mention of complication
874.10	Open wound of larynx with trachea, complicated
874.11	Open wound of larynx, complicated
874.12	Open wound of trachea, complicated
887.6	Traumatic amputation of arm and hand (complete) (partial), bilateral (any level), without mention of complication
887.7	Traumatic amputation of arm and hand (complete) (partial), bilateral (any level), complicated
896.2	Traumatic amputation of foot (complete) (partial), bilateral, without mention of complication
896.3	Traumatic amputation of foot (complete) (partial), bilateral, complicated
897.6	Traumatic amputation of leg(s) (complete) (partial), bilateral (any level), without mention of complication
897.7	Traumatic amputation of leg(s) (complete) (partial), bilateral (any level), complicated
901.0	Thoracic aorta injury
901.1	Innominate and subclavian artery injury
901.2	Superior vena cava injury
901.3	Innominate and subclavian vein injury
901.40	Injury to unspecified pulmonary vessel(s)
901.41	Pulmonary artery injury
901.42	Pulmonary vein injury
901.83	Injury to multiple blood vessels of thorax
902.0	Abdominal aorta injury
902.10	Unspecified inferior vena cava injury
902.11	Hepatic vein injury
902.19	Injury to specified branches of inferior vena cava, other
902.20	Unspecified celiac and mesenteric artery injury
902.21	Gastric artery injury
902.22	Hepatic artery injury
902.23	Splenic artery injury
902.24	Injury to specified branches of celiac axis, other
902.25	Superior mesenteric artery (trunk) injury
902.26	Injury to primary branches of superior mesenteric artery
902.27	Inferior mesenteric artery injury
902.29	Injury to celiac and mesenteric arteries, other
902.31	Injury to superior mesenteric vein and primary subdivisions
902.32	Inferior mesenteric vein injury
902.33	Portal vein injury
902.34	Splenic vein injury
902.39	Injury to portal and splenic veins, other
902.40	Renal vessel(s) injury, unspecified
902.41	Renal artery injury
902.42	Renal vein injury
902.49	Renal blood vessel injury, other
902.50	Unspecified iliac vessel(s) injury
902.51	Hypogastric artery injury
902.52	Hypogastric vein injury
902.53	Iliac artery injury
902.54	Iliac vein injury
902.59	Injury to iliac blood vessels, other
902.87	Injury to multiple blood vessels of abdomen and pelvis
903.00	Axillary vessel(s) injury, unspecified
903.01	Axillary artery injury
903.02	Axillary vein injury
904.0	Common femoral artery injury
904.1	Superficial femoral artery injury
904.2	Femoral vein injury
904.40	Unspecified popliteal vessel(s) injury
904.41	Popliteal artery injury
904.42	Popliteal vein injury
948.21	Burn (any degree) involving 20-29% of body surface with third degree burn of 10-19%
948.22	Burn (any degree) involving 20-29% of body surface with third degree burn of 20-29%
948.31	Burn (any degree) involving 30-39% of body surface with third degree burn of 10-19%
948.32	Burn (any degree) involving 30-39% of body surface with third degree burn of 20-29%
948.33	Burn (any degree) involving 30-39% of body surface with third degree burn of 30-39%
948.41	Burn (any degree) involving 40-49% of body surface with third degree burn of 10-19%
948.42	Burn (any degree) involving 40-49% of body surface with third degree burn of 20-29%
948.43	Burn (any degree) involving 40-49% of body surface with third degree burn of 30-39%
948.44	Burn (any degree) involving 40-49% of body surface with third degree burn of 40-49%
948.51	Burn (any degree) involving 50-59% of body surface with third degree burn of 10-19%
948.52	Burn (any degree) involving 50-59% of body surface with third degree burn of 20-29%
948.53	Burn (any degree) involving 50-59% of body surface with third degree burn of 30-39%
948.54	Burn (any degree) involving 50-59% of body surface with third degree burn of 40-49%
948.55	Burn (any degree) involving 50-59% of body surface with third degree burn of 50-59%
948.61	Burn (any degree) involving 60-69% of body surface with third degree burn of 10-19%
948.62	Burn (any degree) involving 60-69% of body surface with third degree burn of 20-29%
948.63	Burn (any degree) involving 60-69% of body surface with third degree burn of 30-39%
948.64	Burn (any degree) involving 60-69% of body surface with third degree burn of 40-49%
948.65	Burn (any degree) involving 60-69% of body surface with third degree burn of 50-59%

948.66 Burn (any degree) involving 60-69% of body surface with third degree burn of 60-69%

948.71 Burn (any degree) involving 70-79% of body surface with third degree burn of 10-19%

948.72 Burn (any degree) involving 70-79% of body surface with third degree burn of 20-29%

948.73 Burn (any degree) involving 70-79% of body surface with third degree burn of 30-39%

948.74 Burn (any degree) involving 70-79% of body surface with third degree burn of 40-49%

948.75 Burn (any degree) involving 70-79% of body surface with third degree burn of 50-59%

948.76 Burn (any degree) involving 70-79% of body surface with third degree burn of 60-69%

948.77 Burn (any degree) involving 70-79% of body surface with third degree burn of 70-79%

948.81 Burn (any degree) involving 80-89% of body surface with third degree burn of 10-19%

948.82 Burn (any degree) involving 80-89% of body surface with third degree burn of 20-29%

948.83 Burn (any degree) involving 80-89% of body surface with third degree burn of 30-39%

948.84 Burn (any degree) involving 80-89% of body surface with third degree burn of 40-49%

948.85 Burn (any degree) involving 80-89% of body surface with third degree burn of 50-59%

948.86 Burn (any degree) involving 80-89% of body surface with third degree burn of 60-69%

948.87 Burn (any degree) involving 80-89% of body surface with third degree burn of 70-79%

948.88 Burn (any degree) involving 80-89% of body surface with third degree burn of 80-89%

948.91 Burn (any degree) involving 90% or more of body surface with third degree burn of 10-19%

948.92 Burn (any degree) involving 90% or more of body surface with third degree burn of 20-29%

948.93 Burn (any degree) involving 90% or more of body surface with third degree burn of 30-39%

948.94 Burn (any degree) involving 90% or more of body surface with third degree burn of 40-49%

948.95 Burn (any degree) involving 90% or more of body surface with third degree burn of 50-59%

948.96 Burn (any degree) involving 90% or more of body surface with third degree burn of 60-69%

948.97 Burn (any degree) involving 90% or more of body surface with third degree burn of 70-79%

948.98 Burn (any degree) involving 90% or more of body surface with third degree burn of 80-89%

948.99 Burn (any degree) involving 90% or more of body surface with third degree burn of 90% or more of body surface

952.00 C1-C4 level spinal cord injury, unspecified

952.01 C1-C4 level with complete lesion of spinal cord

952.02 C1-C4 level with anterior cord syndrome

952.03 C1-C4 level with central cord syndrome

952.04 C1-C4 level with other specified spinal cord injury

952.05 C5-C7 level spinal cord injury, unspecified

952.06 C5-C7 level with complete lesion of spinal cord

952.07 C5-C7 level with anterior cord syndrome

952.08 C5-C7 level with central cord syndrome

952.09 C5-C7 level with other specified spinal cord injury

952.10 T1-T6 level spinal cord injury, unspecified

952.11 T1-T6 level with complete lesion of spinal cord

952.12 T1-T6 level with anterior cord syndrome

952.13 T1-T6 level with central cord syndrome

952.14 T1-T6 level with other specified spinal cord injury

952.15 T7-T12 level spinal cord injury, unspecified

952.16 T7-T12 level with complete lesion of spinal cord

952.17 T7-T12 level with anterior cord syndrome

952.18 T7-T12 level with central cord syndrome

952.19 T7-T12 level with other specified spinal cord injury

952.2   Lumbar spinal cord injury without spinal bone injury

952.3   Sacral spinal cord injury without spinal bone injury

952.4   Cauda equina spinal cord injury without spinal bone injury

952.8   Multiple sites of spinal cord injury without spinal bone injury

958.0   Air embolism as an early complication of trauma

958.1   Fat embolism as an early complication of trauma

958.4   Traumatic shock

958.5   Traumatic anuria

995.91 Sepsis

995.92 Severe sepsis

995.94 Systemic inflammatory response syndrome due to noninfectious process with acute organ dysfunction

998.01 Postoperative shock, cardiogenic

998.02 Postoperative shock, septic

998.09 Postoperative shock, other

999.1   Air embolism as complication of medical care, not elsewhere classified

Alphabetic MCC List

441.3	Abdominal aneurysm, ruptured
902.0	Abdominal aorta injury
637.60	Abortion, unspecified as to completion or legality, complicated by embolism
637.30	Abortion, unspecified as to completion or legality, complicated by renal failure
637.50	Abortion, unspecified as to completion or legality, complicated by shock
637.62	Abortion, unspecified as to legality, complete, complicated by embolism
637.32	Abortion, unspecified as to legality, complete, complicated by renal failure
637.52	Abortion, unspecified as to legality, complete, complicated by shock
637.61	Abortion, unspecified as to legality, incomplete, complicated by embolism
637.31	Abortion, unspecified as to legality, incomplete, complicated by renal failure
637.51	Abortion, unspecified as to legality, incomplete, complicated by shock
572.0	Abscess of liver
513.0	Abscess of lung
513.1	Abscess of mediastinum
755.55	Acrocephalosyndactyly
518.84	Acute and chronic respiratory failure
518.53	Acute and chronic respiratory failure following trauma and surgery
421.0	Acute and subacute bacterial endocarditis
421.1	Acute and subacute infective endocarditis in diseases classified elsewhere
570	Acute and subacute necrosis of liver
540.0	Acute appendicitis with generalized peritonitis
540.1	Acute appendicitis with peritoneal abscess
428.41	Acute combined systolic and diastolic heart failure
415.0	Acute cor pulmonale
428.31	Acute diastolic heart failure
532.01	Acute duodenal ulcer with hemorrhage and obstruction
532.20	Acute duodenal ulcer with hemorrhage and perforation, without mention of obstruction
532.21	Acute duodenal ulcer with hemorrhage, perforation, and obstruction
532.00	Acute duodenal ulcer with hemorrhage, without mention of obstruction
532.11	Acute duodenal ulcer with perforation and obstruction
532.10	Acute duodenal ulcer with perforation, without mention of obstruction
532.31	Acute duodenal ulcer without mention of hemorrhage or perforation, with obstruction
464.31	Acute epiglottitis with obstruction
531.01	Acute gastric ulcer with hemorrhage and obstruction
531.20	Acute gastric ulcer with hemorrhage and perforation, without mention of obstruction
531.21	Acute gastric ulcer with hemorrhage, perforation, and obstruction
531.00	Acute gastric ulcer with hemorrhage, without mention of obstruction
531.11	Acute gastric ulcer with perforation and obstruction
531.10	Acute gastric ulcer with perforation, without mention of obstruction
531.31	Acute gastric ulcer without mention of hemorrhage or perforation, with obstruction
535.01	Acute gastritis with hemorrhage
534.20	Acute gastrojejunal ulcer with hemorrhage and perforation, without mention of obstruction
534.21	Acute gastrojejunal ulcer with hemorrhage, perforation, and obstruction
534.00	Acute gastrojejunal ulcer with hemorrhage, without mention of obstruction
534.11	Acute gastrojejunal ulcer with perforation and obstruction
534.10	Acute gastrojejunal ulcer with perforation, without mention of obstruction
534.31	Acute gastrojejunal ulcer without mention of hemorrhage or perforation, with obstruction
534.01	Acute gastrojejunal ulcer, with hemorrhage and obstruction
580.0	Acute glomerulonephritis with lesion of proliferative glomerulonephritis
580.4	Acute glomerulonephritis with lesion of rapidly progressive glomerulonephritis
580.81	Acute glomerulonephritis with other specified pathological lesion in kidney in disease classified elsewhere
580.9	Acute glomerulonephritis with unspecified pathological lesion in kidney
070.41	Acute hepatitis C with hepatic coma
669.32	Acute kidney failure following labor and delivery, delivered, with mention of postpartum complication
669.34	Acute kidney failure following labor and delivery, postpartum condition or complication
584.7	Acute kidney failure with lesion of medullary [papillary] necrosis
584.6	Acute kidney failure with lesion of renal cortical necrosis
584.5	Acute kidney failure with lesion of tubular necrosis
464.01	Acute laryngitis, with obstruction
464.21	Acute laryngotracheitis with obstruction
018.01	Acute miliary tuberculosis, bacteriological or histological examination not done
018.02	Acute miliary tuberculosis, bacteriological or histological examination unknown (at present)
018.03	Acute miliary tuberculosis, tubercle bacilli found (in sputum) by microscopy
018.04	Acute miliary tuberculosis, tubercle bacilli not found (in sputum) by microscopy, but found by bacterial culture
018.05	Acute miliary tuberculosis, tubercle bacilli not found by bacteriological examination, but tuberculosis confirmed histologically
018.06	Acute miliary tuberculosis, tubercle bacilli not found by bacteriological or histological examination, but tuberculosis confirmed by other methods [inoculation of animals]
018.00	Acute miliary tuberculosis, unspecified
410.01	Acute myocardial infarction of anterolateral wall, initial episode of care
410.21	Acute myocardial infarction of inferolateral wall, initial episode of care
410.31	Acute myocardial infarction of inferoposterior wall, initial episode of care
410.11	Acute myocardial infarction of other anterior wall, initial episode of care
410.41	Acute myocardial infarction of other inferior wall, initial episode of care
410.51	Acute myocardial infarction of other lateral wall, initial episode of care
410.81	Acute myocardial infarction of other specified sites, initial episode of care
410.71	Acute myocardial infarction, subendocardial infarction, initial episode of care
410.61	Acute myocardial infarction, true posterior wall infarction, initial episode of care
410.91	Acute myocardial infarction, unspecified site, initial episode of care
422.0	Acute myocarditis in diseases classified elsewhere
428.43	Acute on chronic combined systolic and diastolic heart failure
428.33	Acute on chronic diastolic heart failure

Appendix A — Alphabetic MCC List

428.23	Acute on chronic systolic heart failure
614.5	Acute or unspecified pelvic peritonitis, female
577.0	Acute pancreatitis
045.01	Acute paralytic poliomyelitis specified as bulbar, poliovirus type I
045.02	Acute paralytic poliomyelitis specified as bulbar, poliovirus type II
045.03	Acute paralytic poliomyelitis specified as bulbar, poliovirus type III
045.00	Acute paralytic poliomyelitis specified as bulbar, unspecified poliovirus
533.01	Acute peptic ulcer, unspecified site, with hemorrhage and obstruction
533.20	Acute peptic ulcer, unspecified site, with hemorrhage and perforation, without mention of obstruction
533.21	Acute peptic ulcer, unspecified site, with hemorrhage, perforation, and obstruction
533.00	Acute peptic ulcer, unspecified site, with hemorrhage, without mention of obstruction
533.11	Acute peptic ulcer, unspecified site, with perforation and obstruction
533.10	Acute peptic ulcer, unspecified site, with perforation, without mention of obstruction
533.31	Acute peptic ulcer, unspecified site, without mention of hemorrhage and perforation, with obstruction
045.11	Acute poliomyelitis with other paralysis, poliovirus type I
045.12	Acute poliomyelitis with other paralysis, poliovirus type II
045.13	Acute poliomyelitis with other paralysis, poliovirus type III
045.10	Acute poliomyelitis with other paralysis, unspecified poliovirus
506.1	Acute pulmonary edema due to fumes and vapors
590.11	Acute pyelonephritis with lesion of renal medullary necrosis
518.81	Acute respiratory failure
518.51	Acute respiratory failure following trauma and surgery
428.21	Acute systolic heart failure
464.11	Acute tracheitis with obstruction
557.0	Acute vascular insufficiency of intestine
868.11	Adrenal gland injury, with open wound into cavity
958.0	Air embolism as an early complication of trauma
999.1	Air embolism as complication of medical care, not elsewhere classified
535.31	Alcoholic gastritis with hemorrhage
516.64	Alveolar capillary dysplasia with vein misalignment
006.5	Amebic brain abscess
006.3	Amebic liver abscess
006.4	Amebic lung abscess
673.13	Amniotic fluid embolism, antepartum condition or complication
673.14	Amniotic fluid embolism, postpartum condition or complication
673.12	Amniotic fluid embolism, with delivery, with mention of postpartum complication
673.11	Amniotic fluid embolism, with delivery, with or without mention of antepartum condition
320.81	Anaerobic meningitis
740.0	Anencephalus
569.85	Angiodysplasia of intestine with hemorrhage
537.83	Angiodysplasia of stomach and duodenum with hemorrhage
641.33	Antepartum hemorrhage associated with coagulation defect, antepartum
641.31	Antepartum hemorrhage associated with coagulation defects, with delivery
022.3	Anthrax septicemia
284.11	Antineoplastic chemotherapy induced pancytopenia
441.5	Aortic aneurysm of unspecified site, ruptured
863.95	Appendix injury with open wound into cavity
863.51	Ascending (right) colon injury with open wound into cavity

770.16	Aspiration of blood with respiratory symptoms, of fetus and newborn
770.14	Aspiration of clear amniotic fluid with respiratory symptoms, of fetus and newborn
770.86	Aspiration of postnatal stomach contents with respiratory symptoms
535.11	Atrophic gastritis with hemorrhage
062.4	Australian encephalitis
903.01	Axillary artery injury
903.02	Axillary vein injury
903.00	Axillary vessel(s) injury, unspecified
868.12	Bile duct and gallbladder injury, with open wound into cavity
779.32	Bilious vomiting in newborn
867.1	Bladder and urethra injury with open wound into cavity
348.82	Brain death
485	Bronchopneumonia, organism unspecified
862.31	Bronchus injury with open wound into cavity
862.21	Bronchus injury without mention of open wound into cavity
020.0	Bubonic plague
453.0	Budd-Chiari syndrome
745.0	Bulbus cordis anomalies and anomalies of cardiac septal closure, common truncus
745.3	Bulbus cordis anomalies and anomalies of cardiac septal closure, common ventricle
948.21	Burn (any degree) involving 20-29% of body surface with third degree burn of 10-19%
948.22	Burn (any degree) involving 20-29% of body surface with third degree burn of 20-29%
948.31	Burn (any degree) involving 30-39% of body surface with third degree burn of 10-19%
948.32	Burn (any degree) involving 30-39% of body surface with third degree burn of 20-29%
948.33	Burn (any degree) involving 30-39% of body surface with third degree burn of 30-39%
948.41	Burn (any degree) involving 40-49% of body surface with third degree burn of 10-19%
948.42	Burn (any degree) involving 40-49% of body surface with third degree burn of 20-29%
948.43	Burn (any degree) involving 40-49% of body surface with third degree burn of 30-39%
948.44	Burn (any degree) involving 40-49% of body surface with third degree burn of 40-49%
948.51	Burn (any degree) involving 50-59% of body surface with third degree burn of 10-19%
948.52	Burn (any degree) involving 50-59% of body surface with third degree burn of 20-29%
948.53	Burn (any degree) involving 50-59% of body surface with third degree burn of 30-39%
948.54	Burn (any degree) involving 50-59% of body surface with third degree burn of 40-49%
948.55	Burn (any degree) involving 50-59% of body surface with third degree burn of 50-59%
948.61	Burn (any degree) involving 60-69% of body surface with third degree burn of 10-19%
948.62	Burn (any degree) involving 60-69% of body surface with third degree burn of 20-29%
948.63	Burn (any degree) involving 60-69% of body surface with third degree burn of 30-39%
948.64	Burn (any degree) involving 60-69% of body surface with third degree burn of 40-49%
948.65	Burn (any degree) involving 60-69% of body surface with third degree burn of 50-59%
948.66	Burn (any degree) involving 60-69% of body surface with third degree burn of 60-69%

Appendix A — Alphabetic MCC List

948.71	Burn (any degree) involving 70-79% of body surface with third degree burn of 10-19%
948.72	Burn (any degree) involving 70-79% of body surface with third degree burn of 20-29%
948.73	Burn (any degree) involving 70-79% of body surface with third degree burn of 30-39%
948.74	Burn (any degree) involving 70-79% of body surface with third degree burn of 40-49%
948.75	Burn (any degree) involving 70-79% of body surface with third degree burn of 50-59%
948.76	Burn (any degree) involving 70-79% of body surface with third degree burn of 60-69%
948.77	Burn (any degree) involving 70-79% of body surface with third degree burn of 70-79%
948.81	Burn (any degree) involving 80-89% of body surface with third degree burn of 10-19%
948.82	Burn (any degree) involving 80-89% of body surface with third degree burn of 20-29%
948.83	Burn (any degree) involving 80-89% of body surface with third degree burn of 30-39%
948.84	Burn (any degree) involving 80-89% of body surface with third degree burn of 40-49%
948.85	Burn (any degree) involving 80-89% of body surface with third degree burn of 50-59%
948.86	Burn (any degree) involving 80-89% of body surface with third degree burn of 60-69%
948.87	Burn (any degree) involving 80-89% of body surface with third degree burn of 70-79%
948.88	Burn (any degree) involving 80-89% of body surface with third degree burn of 80-89%
948.91	Burn (any degree) involving 90% or more of body surface with third degree burn of 10-19%
948.92	Burn (any degree) involving 90% or more of body surface with third degree burn of 20-29%
948.93	Burn (any degree) involving 90% or more of body surface with third degree burn of 30-39%
948.94	Burn (any degree) involving 90% or more of body surface with third degree burn of 40-49%
948.95	Burn (any degree) involving 90% or more of body surface with third degree burn of 50-59%
948.96	Burn (any degree) involving 90% or more of body surface with third degree burn of 60-69%
948.97	Burn (any degree) involving 90% or more of body surface with third degree burn of 70-79%
948.98	Burn (any degree) involving 90% or more of body surface with third degree burn of 80-89%
948.99	Burn (any degree) involving 90% or more of body surface with third degree burn of 90% or more of body surface
952.00	C1-C4 level spinal cord injury, unspecified
952.02	C1-C4 level with anterior cord syndrome
952.03	C1-C4 level with central cord syndrome
952.01	C1-C4 level with complete lesion of spinal cord
952.04	C1-C4 level with other specified spinal cord injury
952.05	C5-C7 level spinal cord injury, unspecified
952.07	C5-C7 level with anterior cord syndrome
952.08	C5-C7 level with central cord syndrome
952.06	C5-C7 level with complete lesion of spinal cord
952.09	C5-C7 level with other specified spinal cord injury
344.04	C5-C7, incomplete
574.81	Calculus of gallbladder and bile duct with acute and chronic cholecystitis, with obstruction
062.5	California virus encephalitis
112.81	Candidal endocarditis
112.83	Candidal meningitis
112.4	Candidiasis of lung
865.12	Capsular tears to spleen, without major disruption of parenchyma, with open wound into cavity
427.5	Cardiac arrest
779.85	Cardiac arrest of newborn
785.51	Cardiogenic shock
952.4	Cauda equina spinal cord injury without spinal bone injury
020.1	Cellulocutaneous plague
063.2	Central European encephalitis
851.52	Cerebellar or brain stem contusion with open intracranial wound, brief (less than 1 hour) loss of consciousness
851.56	Cerebellar or brain stem contusion with open intracranial wound, loss of consciousness of unspecified duration
851.53	Cerebellar or brain stem contusion with open intracranial wound, moderate (1-24 hours) loss of consciousness
851.51	Cerebellar or brain stem contusion with open intracranial wound, no loss of consciousness
851.54	Cerebellar or brain stem contusion with open intracranial wound, prolonged (more than 24 hours) loss of consciousness and return to pre-existing conscious level
851.55	Cerebellar or brain stem contusion with open intracranial wound, prolonged (more than 24 hours) loss of consciousness, without return to pre-existing conscious level
851.59	Cerebellar or brain stem contusion with open intracranial wound, unspecified concussion
851.50	Cerebellar or brain stem contusion with open intracranial wound, unspecified state of consciousness
851.45	Cerebellar or brain stem contusion without mention of open intracranial wound, prolonged (more than 24 hours) loss of consciousness, without return to pre-existing conscious level
851.72	Cerebellar or brain stem laceration with open intracranial wound, brief (less than one hour) loss of consciousness
851.76	Cerebellar or brain stem laceration with open intracranial wound, loss of consciousness of unspecified duration
851.73	Cerebellar or brain stem laceration with open intracranial wound, moderate (1-24 hours) loss of consciousness
851.71	Cerebellar or brain stem laceration with open intracranial wound, no loss of consciousness
851.74	Cerebellar or brain stem laceration with open intracranial wound, prolonged (more than 24 hours) loss of consciousness and return to pre-existing conscious level
851.75	Cerebellar or brain stem laceration with open intracranial wound, prolonged (more than 24 hours) loss of consciousness, without return to pre-existing conscious level
851.70	Cerebellar or brain stem laceration with open intracranial wound, state of consciousness unspecified
851.79	Cerebellar or brain stem laceration with open intracranial wound, unspecified concussion
851.62	Cerebellar or brain stem laceration without mention of open intracranial wound, brief (less than 1 hour) loss of consciousness
851.66	Cerebellar or brain stem laceration without mention of open intracranial wound, loss of consciousness of unspecified duration
851.63	Cerebellar or brain stem laceration without mention of open intracranial wound, moderate (1-24 hours) loss of consciousness
851.61	Cerebellar or brain stem laceration without mention of open intracranial wound, no loss of consciousness
851.64	Cerebellar or brain stem laceration without mention of open intracranial wound, prolonged (more than 24 hours) loss of consciousness and return to pre-existing conscious level
851.65	Cerebellar or brain stem laceration without mention of open intracranial wound, prolonged (more than 24 hours) loss of consciousness, without return to pre-existing conscious level
851.69	Cerebellar or brain stem laceration without mention of open intracranial wound, unspecified concussion
851.60	Cerebellar or brain stem laceration without mention of open intracranial wound, unspecified state of consciousness

779.2	Cerebral depression, coma, and other abnormal cerebral signs in fetus or newborn
348.5	Cerebral edema
434.11	Cerebral embolism with cerebral infarction
434.01	Cerebral thrombosis with cerebral infarction
674.01	Cerebrovascular disorder, with delivery, with or without mention of antepartum condition
654.53	Cervical incompetence, antepartum condition or complication
654.51	Cervical incompetence, delivered
654.52	Cervical incompetence, delivered, with mention of postpartum complication
654.54	Cervical incompetence, postpartum condition or complication
567.81	Choleperitonitis
532.71	Chronic duodenal ulcer without mention of hemorrhage or perforation, with obstruction
531.71	Chronic gastric ulcer without mention of hemorrhage or perforation, with obstruction
534.71	Chronic gastrojejunal ulcer without mention of hemorrhage or perforation, with obstruction
070.44	Chronic hepatitis C with hepatic coma
532.41	Chronic or unspecified duodenal ulcer with hemorrhage and obstruction
532.60	Chronic or unspecified duodenal ulcer with hemorrhage and perforation, without mention of obstruction
532.61	Chronic or unspecified duodenal ulcer with hemorrhage, perforation, and obstruction
532.51	Chronic or unspecified duodenal ulcer with perforation and obstruction
532.50	Chronic or unspecified duodenal ulcer with perforation, without mention of obstruction
531.41	Chronic or unspecified gastric ulcer with hemorrhage and obstruction
531.60	Chronic or unspecified gastric ulcer with hemorrhage and perforation, without mention of obstruction
531.61	Chronic or unspecified gastric ulcer with hemorrhage, perforation, and obstruction
531.40	Chronic or unspecified gastric ulcer with hemorrhage, without mention of obstruction
531.51	Chronic or unspecified gastric ulcer with perforation and obstruction
531.50	Chronic or unspecified gastric ulcer with perforation, without mention of obstruction
534.60	Chronic or unspecified gastrojejunal ulcer with hemorrhage and perforation, without mention of obstruction
534.61	Chronic or unspecified gastrojejunal ulcer with hemorrhage, perforation, and obstruction
534.40	Chronic or unspecified gastrojejunal ulcer with hemorrhage, without mention of obstruction
534.51	Chronic or unspecified gastrojejunal ulcer with perforation and obstruction
534.50	Chronic or unspecified gastrojejunal ulcer with perforation, without mention of obstruction
534.41	Chronic or unspecified gastrojejunal ulcer, with hemorrhage and obstruction
533.41	Chronic or unspecified peptic ulcer, unspecified site, with hemorrhage and obstruction
533.60	Chronic or unspecified peptic ulcer, unspecified site, with hemorrhage and perforation, without mention of obstruction
533.61	Chronic or unspecified peptic ulcer, unspecified site, with hemorrhage, perforation, and obstruction
533.40	Chronic or unspecified peptic ulcer, unspecified site, with hemorrhage, without mention of obstruction
533.51	Chronic or unspecified peptic ulcer, unspecified site, with perforation and obstruction

533.50	Chronic or unspecified peptic ulcer, unspecified site, with perforation, without mention of obstruction
533.71	Chronic peptic ulcer of unspecified site without mention of hemorrhage or perforation, with obstruction
770.7	Chronic respiratory disease arising in the perinatal period
808.0	Closed fracture of acetabulum
820.03	Closed fracture of base of neck of femur
801.12	Closed fracture of base of skull with cerebral laceration and contusion, brief (less than one hour) loss of consciousness
801.16	Closed fracture of base of skull with cerebral laceration and contusion, loss of consciousness of unspecified duration
801.13	Closed fracture of base of skull with cerebral laceration and contusion, moderate (1-24 hours) loss of consciousness
801.11	Closed fracture of base of skull with cerebral laceration and contusion, no loss of consciousness
801.14	Closed fracture of base of skull with cerebral laceration and contusion, prolonged (more than 24 hours) loss of consciousness and return to pre-existing conscious level
801.15	Closed fracture of base of skull with cerebral laceration and contusion, prolonged (more than 24 hours) loss of consciousness, without return to pre-existing conscious level
801.19	Closed fracture of base of skull with cerebral laceration and contusion, unspecified concussion
801.10	Closed fracture of base of skull with cerebral laceration and contusion, unspecified state of consciousness
801.43	Closed fracture of base of skull with intracranial injury of other and unspecified nature, moderate (1-24 hours) loss of consciousness
801.44	Closed fracture of base of skull with intracranial injury of other and unspecified nature, prolonged (more than 24 hours) loss of consciousness and return to pre-existing conscious level
801.45	Closed fracture of base of skull with intracranial injury of other and unspecified nature, prolonged (more than 24 hours) loss of consciousness, without return to pre-existing conscious level
801.32	Closed fracture of base of skull with other and unspecified intracranial hemorrhage, brief (less than one hour) loss of consciousness
801.36	Closed fracture of base of skull with other and unspecified intracranial hemorrhage, loss of consciousness of unspecified duration
801.33	Closed fracture of base of skull with other and unspecified intracranial hemorrhage, moderate (1-24 hours) loss of consciousness
801.31	Closed fracture of base of skull with other and unspecified intracranial hemorrhage, no loss of consciousness
801.34	Closed fracture of base of skull with other and unspecified intracranial hemorrhage, prolonged (more than 24 hours) loss of consciousness and return to pre-existing conscious level
801.35	Closed fracture of base of skull with other and unspecified intracranial hemorrhage, prolonged (more than 24 hours) loss of consciousness, without return to pre-existing conscious level
801.39	Closed fracture of base of skull with other and unspecified intracranial hemorrhage, unspecified concussion
801.30	Closed fracture of base of skull with other and unspecified intracranial hemorrhage, unspecified state of consciousness
801.22	Closed fracture of base of skull with subarachnoid, subdural, and extradural hemorrhage, brief (less than one hour) loss of consciousness
801.26	Closed fracture of base of skull with subarachnoid, subdural, and extradural hemorrhage, loss of consciousness of unspecified duration
801.23	Closed fracture of base of skull with subarachnoid, subdural, and extradural hemorrhage, moderate (1-24 hours) loss of consciousness
801.21	Closed fracture of base of skull with subarachnoid, subdural, and extradural hemorrhage, no loss of consciousness

801.24	Closed fracture of base of skull with subarachnoid, subdural, and extradural hemorrhage, prolonged (more than 24 hours) loss of consciousness and return to pre-existing conscious level
801.25	Closed fracture of base of skull with subarachnoid, subdural, and extradural hemorrhage, prolonged (more than 24 hours) loss of consciousness, without return to pre-existing conscious level
801.29	Closed fracture of base of skull with subarachnoid, subdural, and extradural hemorrhage, unspecified concussion
801.20	Closed fracture of base of skull with subarachnoid, subdural, and extradural hemorrhage, unspecified state of consciousness
801.03	Closed fracture of base of skull without mention of intracranial injury, moderate (1-24 hours) loss of consciousness
801.04	Closed fracture of base of skull without mention of intracranial injury, prolonged (more than 24 hours) loss of consciousness and return to pre-existing conscious level
801.05	Closed fracture of base of skull without mention of intracranial injury, prolonged (more than 24 hours) loss of consciousness, without return to pre-existing conscious level
806.02	Closed fracture of C1-C4 level with anterior cord syndrome
806.03	Closed fracture of C1-C4 level with central cord syndrome
806.01	Closed fracture of C1-C4 level with complete lesion of cord
806.04	Closed fracture of C1-C4 level with other specified spinal cord injury
806.00	Closed fracture of C1-C4 level with unspecified spinal cord injury
806.07	Closed fracture of C5-C7 level with anterior cord syndrome
806.08	Closed fracture of C5-C7 level with central cord syndrome
806.06	Closed fracture of C5-C7 level with complete lesion of cord
806.09	Closed fracture of C5-C7 level with other specified spinal cord injury
806.05	Closed fracture of C5-C7 level with unspecified spinal cord injury
820.01	Closed fracture of epiphysis (separation) (upper) of neck of femur
820.21	Closed fracture of intertrochanteric section of femur
807.5	Closed fracture of larynx and trachea
806.4	Closed fracture of lumbar spine with spinal cord injury
820.02	Closed fracture of midcervical section of femur
806.61	Closed fracture of sacrum and coccyx with complete cauda equina lesion
806.62	Closed fracture of sacrum and coccyx with other cauda equina injury
806.69	Closed fracture of sacrum and coccyx with other spinal cord injury
806.60	Closed fracture of sacrum and coccyx with unspecified spinal cord injury
821.01	Closed fracture of shaft of femur
820.22	Closed fracture of subtrochanteric section of femur
806.22	Closed fracture of T1-T6 level with anterior cord syndrome
806.23	Closed fracture of T1-T6 level with central cord syndrome
806.21	Closed fracture of T1-T6 level with complete lesion of cord
806.24	Closed fracture of T1-T6 level with other specified spinal cord injury
806.20	Closed fracture of T1-T6 level with unspecified spinal cord injury
806.27	Closed fracture of T7-T12 level with anterior cord syndrome
806.28	Closed fracture of T7-T12 level with central cord syndrome
806.26	Closed fracture of T7-T12 level with complete lesion of cord
806.29	Closed fracture of T7-T12 level with other specified spinal cord injury
806.25	Closed fracture of T7-T12 level with unspecified spinal cord injury
820.00	Closed fracture of unspecified intracapsular section of neck of femur
821.00	Closed fracture of unspecified part of femur
820.8	Closed fracture of unspecified part of neck of femur
820.20	Closed fracture of unspecified trochanteric section of femur
806.8	Closed fracture of unspecified vertebra with spinal cord injury
800.12	Closed fracture of vault of skull with cerebral laceration and contusion, brief (less than one hour) loss of consciousness
800.16	Closed fracture of vault of skull with cerebral laceration and contusion, loss of consciousness of unspecified duration

800.13	Closed fracture of vault of skull with cerebral laceration and contusion, moderate (1-24 hours) loss of consciousness
800.11	Closed fracture of vault of skull with cerebral laceration and contusion, no loss of consciousness
800.14	Closed fracture of vault of skull with cerebral laceration and contusion, prolonged (more than 24 hours) loss of consciousness and return to pre-existing conscious level
800.15	Closed fracture of vault of skull with cerebral laceration and contusion, prolonged (more than 24 hours) loss of consciousness, without return to pre-existing conscious level
800.19	Closed fracture of vault of skull with cerebral laceration and contusion, unspecified concussion
800.10	Closed fracture of vault of skull with cerebral laceration and contusion, unspecified state of consciousness
800.43	Closed fracture of vault of skull with intracranial injury of other and unspecified nature, moderate (1-24 hours) loss of consciousness
800.44	Closed fracture of vault of skull with intracranial injury of other and unspecified nature, prolonged (more than 24 hours) loss of consciousness and return to pre-existing conscious level
800.45	Closed fracture of vault of skull with intracranial injury of other and unspecified nature, prolonged (more than 24 hours) loss of consciousness, without return to pre-existing conscious level
800.32	Closed fracture of vault of skull with other and unspecified intracranial hemorrhage, brief (less than one hour) loss of consciousness
800.36	Closed fracture of vault of skull with other and unspecified intracranial hemorrhage, loss of consciousness of unspecified duration
800.33	Closed fracture of vault of skull with other and unspecified intracranial hemorrhage, moderate (1-24 hours) loss of consciousness
800.31	Closed fracture of vault of skull with other and unspecified intracranial hemorrhage, no loss of consciousness
800.34	Closed fracture of vault of skull with other and unspecified intracranial hemorrhage, prolonged (more than 24 hours) loss of consciousness and return to pre-existing conscious level
800.35	Closed fracture of vault of skull with other and unspecified intracranial hemorrhage, prolonged (more than 24 hours) loss of consciousness, without return to pre-existing conscious level
800.39	Closed fracture of vault of skull with other and unspecified intracranial hemorrhage, unspecified concussion
800.30	Closed fracture of vault of skull with other and unspecified intracranial hemorrhage, unspecified state of consciousness
800.22	Closed fracture of vault of skull with subarachnoid, subdural, and extradural hemorrhage, brief (less than one hour) loss of consciousness
800.26	Closed fracture of vault of skull with subarachnoid, subdural, and extradural hemorrhage, loss of consciousness of unspecified duration
800.23	Closed fracture of vault of skull with subarachnoid, subdural, and extradural hemorrhage, moderate (1-24 hours) loss of consciousness
800.21	Closed fracture of vault of skull with subarachnoid, subdural, and extradural hemorrhage, no loss of consciousness
800.24	Closed fracture of vault of skull with subarachnoid, subdural, and extradural hemorrhage, prolonged (more than 24 hours) loss of consciousness and return to pre-existing conscious level
800.25	Closed fracture of vault of skull with subarachnoid, subdural, and extradural hemorrhage, prolonged (more than 24 hours) loss of consciousness, without return to pre-existing conscious level
800.29	Closed fracture of vault of skull with subarachnoid, subdural, and extradural hemorrhage, unspecified concussion
800.20	Closed fracture of vault of skull with subarachnoid, subdural, and extradural hemorrhage, unspecified state of consciousness
800.03	Closed fracture of vault of skull without mention of intracranial injury, moderate (1-24 hours) loss of consciousness

Appendix A — Alphabetic MCC List

800.04	Closed fracture of vault of skull without mention of intracranial injury, prolonged (more than 24 hours) loss of consciousness and return to pre-existing conscious level
800.05	Closed fracture of vault of skull without mention of intracranial injury, prolonged (more than 24 hours) loss of consciousness, without return to pre-existing conscious level
804.05	Closed fractures involving skull of face with other bones, without mention of intracranial injury, prolonged (more than 24 hours) loss of consciousness, without return to pre-existing conscious level
804.22	Closed fractures involving skull or face with other bones with subarachnoid, subdural, and extradural hemorrhage, brief (less than one hour) loss of consciousness
804.26	Closed fractures involving skull or face with other bones with subarachnoid, subdural, and extradural hemorrhage, loss of consciousness of unspecified duration
804.23	Closed fractures involving skull or face with other bones with subarachnoid, subdural, and extradural hemorrhage, moderate (1-24 hours) loss of consciousness
804.21	Closed fractures involving skull or face with other bones with subarachnoid, subdural, and extradural hemorrhage, no loss of consciousness
804.24	Closed fractures involving skull or face with other bones with subarachnoid, subdural, and extradural hemorrhage, prolonged (more than 24 hours) loss of consciousness and return to pre-existing conscious level
804.25	Closed fractures involving skull or face with other bones with subarachnoid, subdural, and extradural hemorrhage, prolonged (more than 24 hours) loss of consciousness, without return to pre-existing conscious level
804.29	Closed fractures involving skull or face with other bones with subarachnoid, subdural, and extradural hemorrhage, unspecified concussion
804.20	Closed fractures involving skull or face with other bones with subarachnoid, subdural, and extradural hemorrhage, unspecified state of consciousness
804.12	Closed fractures involving skull or face with other bones, with cerebral laceration and contusion, brief (less than one hour) loss of consciousness
804.16	Closed fractures involving skull or face with other bones, with cerebral laceration and contusion, loss of consciousness of unspecified duration
804.13	Closed fractures involving skull or face with other bones, with cerebral laceration and contusion, moderate (1-24 hours) loss of consciousness
804.11	Closed fractures involving skull or face with other bones, with cerebral laceration and contusion, no loss of consciousness
804.14	Closed fractures involving skull or face with other bones, with cerebral laceration and contusion, prolonged (more than 24 hours) loss of consciousness and return to pre-existing conscious level
804.15	Closed fractures involving skull or face with other bones, with cerebral laceration and contusion, prolonged (more than 24 hours) loss of consciousness, without return to pre-existing conscious level
804.19	Closed fractures involving skull or face with other bones, with cerebral laceration and contusion, unspecified concussion
804.10	Closed fractures involving skull or face with other bones, with cerebral laceration and contusion, unspecified state of consciousness
804.43	Closed fractures involving skull or face with other bones, with intracranial injury of other and unspecified nature, moderate (1-24 hours) loss of consciousness
804.44	Closed fractures involving skull or face with other bones, with intracranial injury of other and unspecified nature, prolonged (more than 24 hours) loss of consciousness and return to pre-existing conscious level
804.45	Closed fractures involving skull or face with other bones, with intracranial injury of other and unspecified nature, prolonged (more than 24 hours) loss of consciousness, without return to pre-existing conscious level
804.32	Closed fractures involving skull or face with other and unspecified intracranial hemorrhage, brief (less than one hour) loss of consciousness
804.36	Closed fractures involving skull or face with other and unspecified intracranial hemorrhage, loss of consciousness of unspecified duration
804.33	Closed fractures involving skull or face with other bones, with other and unspecified intracranial hemorrhage, moderate (1-24 hours) loss of consciousness
804.31	Closed fractures involving skull or face with other bones, with other and unspecified intracranial hemorrhage, no loss of consciousness
804.34	Closed fractures involving skull or face with other bones, with other and unspecified intracranial hemorrhage, prolonged (more than 24 hours) loss of consciousness and return to preexisting conscious level
804.35	Closed fractures involving skull or face with other bones, with other and unspecified intracranial hemorrhage, prolonged (more than 24 hours) loss of consciousness, without return to pre-existing conscious level
804.39	Closed fractures involving skull or face with other bones, with other and unspecified intracranial hemorrhage, unspecified concussion
804.30	Closed fractures involving skull or face with other bones, with other and unspecified intracranial hemorrhage, unspecified state of consciousness
804.03	Closed fractures involving skull or face with other bones, without mention of intracranial injury, moderate (1-24 hours) loss of consciousness
804.04	Closed fractures involving skull or face with other bones, without mention or intracranial injury, prolonged (more than 24 hours) loss of consciousness and return to pre-existing conscious level
114.2	Coccidioidal meningitis
863.50	Colon injury, unspecified site, with open wound into cavity
780.01	Coma
904.0	Common femoral artery injury
866.13	Complete disruption of kidney parenchyma, with open wound into cavity
866.03	Complete disruption of kidney parenchyma, without mention of open wound into cavity
636.62	Complete illegally induced abortion complicated by embolism
636.32	Complete illegally induced abortion complicated by renal failure
636.52	Complete illegally induced abortion complicated by shock
635.62	Complete legally induced abortion complicated by embolism
635.32	Complete legally induced abortion complicated by renal failure
635.52	Complete legally induced abortion complicated by shock
634.62	Complete spontaneous abortion complicated by embolism
634.32	Complete spontaneous abortion complicated by renal failure
634.52	Complete spontaneous abortion complicated by shock
745.10	Complete transposition of great vessels
639.3	Complications following abortion and ectopic and molar pregnancies, kidney failure
348.4	Compression of brain
850.4	Concussion with prolonged (more than 24 hours) loss of consciousness, without return to pre-existing conscious level
748.5	Congenital agenesis, hypoplasia, and dysplasia of lung
747.81	Congenital anomaly of cerebrovascular system
756.6	Congenital anomaly of diaphragm
746.01	Congenital atresia of pulmonary valve
751.61	Congenital biliary atresia
771.1	Congenital cytomegalovirus infection
286.1	Congenital factor IX disorder
286.0	Congenital factor VIII disorder
746.86	Congenital heart block
747.11	Congenital interruption of aortic arch
746.84	Congenital obstructive anomalies of heart, not elsewhere classified

Appendix A — Alphabetic MCC List

770.0	Congenital pneumonia
742.2	Congenital reduction deformities of brain
746.81	Congenital subaortic stenosis
090.41	Congenital syphilitic encephalitis
090.42	Congenital syphilitic meningitis
750.3	Congenital tracheoesophageal fistula, esophageal atresia and stenosis
746.1	Congenital tricuspid atresia and stenosis
759.4	Conjoined twins
779.0	Convulsions in newborn
745.7	Cor biloculare
746.82	Cor triatriatum
851.12	Cortex (cerebral) contusion with open intracranial wound, brief (less than 1 hour) loss of consciousness
851.16	Cortex (cerebral) contusion with open intracranial wound, loss of consciousness of unspecified duration
851.13	Cortex (cerebral) contusion with open intracranial wound, moderate (1-24 hours) loss of consciousness
851.11	Cortex (cerebral) contusion with open intracranial wound, no loss of consciousness
851.14	Cortex (cerebral) contusion with open intracranial wound, prolonged (more than 24 hours) loss of consciousness and return to pre-existing conscious level
851.15	Cortex (cerebral) contusion with open intracranial wound, prolonged (more than 24 hours) loss of consciousness, without return to pre-existing conscious level
851.19	Cortex (cerebral) contusion with open intracranial wound, unspecified concussion
851.10	Cortex (cerebral) contusion with open intracranial wound, unspecified state of consciousness
851.05	Cortex (cerebral) contusion without mention of open intracranial wound, prolonged (more than 24 hours) loss of consciousness, without return to pre-existing conscious level
851.32	Cortex (cerebral) laceration with open intracranial wound, brief (less than 1 hour) loss of consciousness
851.36	Cortex (cerebral) laceration with open intracranial wound, loss of consciousness of unspecified duration
851.33	Cortex (cerebral) laceration with open intracranial wound, moderate (1-24 hours) loss of consciousness
851.31	Cortex (cerebral) laceration with open intracranial wound, no loss of consciousness
851.34	Cortex (cerebral) laceration with open intracranial wound, prolonged (more than 24 hours) loss of consciousness and return to pre-existing conscious level
851.35	Cortex (cerebral) laceration with open intracranial wound, prolonged (more than 24 hours) loss of consciousness, without return to pre-existing conscious level
851.39	Cortex (cerebral) laceration with open intracranial wound, unspecified concussion
851.30	Cortex (cerebral) laceration with open intracranial wound, unspecified state of consciousness
851.22	Cortex (cerebral) laceration without mention of open intracranial wound, brief (less than 1 hour) loss of consciousness
851.26	Cortex (cerebral) laceration without mention of open intracranial wound, loss of consciousness of unspecified duration
851.23	Cortex (cerebral) laceration without mention of open intracranial wound, moderate (1-24 hours) loss of consciousness
851.21	Cortex (cerebral) laceration without mention of open intracranial wound, no loss of consciousness
851.24	Cortex (cerebral) laceration without mention of open intracranial wound, prolonged (more than 24 hours) loss of consciousness and return to pre-existing conscious level
851.25	Cortex (cerebral) laceration without mention of open intracranial wound, prolonged (more than 24 hours) loss of consciousness, without return to pre-existing conscious level
851.29	Cortex (cerebral) laceration without mention of open intracranial wound, unspecified concussion
851.20	Cortex (cerebral) laceration without mention of open intracranial wound, unspecified state of consciousness
740.1	Craniorachischisis
321.0	Cryptococcal meningitis
277.01	Cystic fibrosis with meconium ileus
277.02	Cystic fibrosis with pulmonary manifestations
671.33	Deep phlebothrombosis, antepartum
671.31	Deep phlebothrombosis, antepartum, with delivery
671.44	Deep phlebothrombosis, postpartum condition or complication
671.42	Deep phlebothrombosis, postpartum, with delivery
286.6	Defibrination syndrome
863.53	Descending (left) colon injury with open wound into cavity
250.21	Diabetes with hyperosmolarity, type I [juvenile type], not stated as uncontrolled
250.23	Diabetes with hyperosmolarity, type I [juvenile type], uncontrolled
250.20	Diabetes with hyperosmolarity, type II or unspecified type, not stated as uncontrolled
250.22	Diabetes with hyperosmolarity, type II or unspecified type, uncontrolled
250.11	Diabetes with ketoacidosis, type I [juvenile type], not stated as uncontrolled
250.13	Diabetes with ketoacidosis, type I [juvenile type], uncontrolled
250.10	Diabetes with ketoacidosis, type II or unspecified type, not stated as uncontrolled
250.12	Diabetes with ketoacidosis, type II or unspecified type, uncontrolled
250.31	Diabetes with other coma, type I [juvenile type], not stated as uncontrolled
250.33	Diabetes with other coma, type I [juvenile type], uncontrolled
250.30	Diabetes with other coma, type II or unspecified type, not stated as uncontrolled
250.32	Diabetes with other coma, type II or unspecified type, uncontrolled
862.1	Diaphragm injury with open wound into cavity
551.3	Diaphragmatic hernia with gangrene
569.86	Dieulafoy lesion (hemorrhagic) of intestine
537.84	Dieulafoy lesion (hemorrhagic) of stomach and duodenum
441.02	Dissecting aortic aneurysm (any part), abdominal
441.01	Dissecting aortic aneurysm (any part), thoracic
441.03	Dissecting aortic aneurysm (any part), thoracoabdominal
441.00	Dissecting aortic aneurysm (any part), unspecified site
443.21	Dissection of carotid artery
414.12	Dissection of coronary artery
443.22	Dissection of iliac artery
443.29	Dissection of other artery
443.23	Dissection of renal artery
443.24	Dissection of vertebral artery
112.5	Disseminated candidiasis
776.2	Disseminated intravascular coagulation in newborn
562.13	Diverticulitis of colon with hemorrhage
562.03	Diverticulitis of small intestine with hemorrhage
562.12	Diverticulosis of colon with hemorrhage
562.02	Diverticulosis of small intestine with hemorrhage
532.40	Duodenal ulcer, chronic or unspecified, with hemorrhage, without mention of obstruction
532.91	Duodenal ulcer, unspecified as acute or chronic, without mention of hemorrhage or perforation, with obstruction
535.61	Duodenitis with hemorrhage
863.31	Duodenum injury with open wound into cavity
644.21	Early onset of delivery, delivered, with or without mention of antepartum condition

091.81	Early syphilis, acute syphilitic meningitis (secondary)
062.2	Eastern equine encephalitis
746.2	Ebstein's anomaly
642.63	Eclampsia, antepartum
642.64	Eclampsia, postpartum condition or complication
642.61	Eclampsia, with delivery
642.62	Eclampsia, with delivery, with current postpartum complication
639.6	Embolism following abortion or ectopic and molar pregnancies
510.0	Empyema with fistula
510.9	Empyema without mention of fistula
323.51	Encephalitis and encephalomyelitis following immunization procedures
323.01	Encephalitis and encephalomyelitis in viral diseases classified elsewhere
323.2	Encephalitis, myelitis, and encephalomyelitis in protozoal diseases classified elsewhere
323.1	Encephalitis, myelitis, and encephalomyelitis in rickettsial diseases classified elsewhere
056.01	Encephalomyelitis due to rubella
348.30	Encephalopathy, unspecified
585.6	End stage renal disease
535.71	Eosinophilic gastritis with hemorrhage
322.1	Eosinophilic meningitis
345.71	Epilepsia partialis continua with intractable epilepsy
345.3	Epileptic grand mal status
345.2	Epileptic petit mal status
530.82	Esophageal hemorrhage
456.0	Esophageal varices with bleeding
456.20	Esophageal varices with bleeding in diseases classified elsewhere
862.32	Esophagus injury with open wound into cavity
862.22	Esophagus injury without mention of open wound into cavity
852.52	Extradural hemorrhage following injury, with open intracranial wound, brief (less than 1 hour) loss of consciousness
852.56	Extradural hemorrhage following injury, with open intracranial wound, loss of consciousness of unspecified duration
852.53	Extradural hemorrhage following injury, with open intracranial wound, moderate (1-24 hours) loss of consciousness
852.51	Extradural hemorrhage following injury, with open intracranial wound, no loss of consciousness
852.54	Extradural hemorrhage following injury, with open intracranial wound, prolonged (more than 24 hours) loss of consciousness and return to pre-existing conscious level
852.55	Extradural hemorrhage following injury, with open intracranial wound, prolonged (more than 24 hours) loss of consciousness, without return to pre-existing conscious level
852.50	Extradural hemorrhage following injury, with open intracranial wound, state of consciousness unspecified
852.59	Extradural hemorrhage following injury, with open intracranial wound, unspecified concussion
852.42	Extradural hemorrhage following injury, without mention of open intracranial wound, brief (less than 1 hour) loss of consciousness
852.46	Extradural hemorrhage following injury, without mention of open intracranial wound, loss of consciousness of unspecified duration
852.43	Extradural hemorrhage following injury, without mention of open intracranial wound, moderate (1-24 hours) loss of consciousness
852.41	Extradural hemorrhage following injury, without mention of open intracranial wound, no loss of consciousness
852.44	Extradural hemorrhage following injury, without mention of open intracranial wound, prolonged (more than 24 hours) loss of consciousness and return to pre-existing conscious level
852.45	Extradural hemorrhage following injury, without mention of open intracranial wound, prolonged (more than 24 hours) loss of consciousness, without return to pre-existing conscious level

852.49	Extradural hemorrhage following injury, without mention of open intracranial wound, unspecified concussion
852.40	Extradural hemorrhage following injury, without mention of open intracranial wound, unspecified state of consciousness
638.6	Failed attempted abortion complicated by embolism
638.3	Failed attempted abortion complicated by renal failure
638.5	Failed attempted abortion complicated by shock
084.0	Falciparum malaria (malignant tertian)
958.1	Fat embolism as an early complication of trauma
551.02	Femoral hernia with gangrene, bilateral, (not specified as recurrent)
551.03	Femoral hernia with gangrene, recurrent bilateral
551.01	Femoral hernia with gangrene, recurrent unilateral or unspecified
551.00	Femoral hernia with gangrene, unilateral or unspecified (not specified as recurrent)
904.2	Femoral vein injury
772.4	Fetal and neonatal gastrointestinal hemorrhage
772.2	Fetal and neonatal subarachnoid hemorrhage of newborn
807.4	Flail chest
809.1	Fracture of bones of trunk, open
780.72	Functional quadriplegia
040.0	Gas gangrene
902.21	Gastric artery injury
535.21	Gastric mucosal hypertrophy with hemorrhage
531.91	Gastric ulcer, unspecified as acute or chronic, without mention of hemorrhage or perforation, with obstruction
530.7	Gastroesophageal laceration-hemorrhage syndrome
863.90	Gastrointestinal tract injury, unspecified site, with open wound into cavity
534.91	Gastrojejunal ulcer, unspecified as acute or chronic, without mention of hemorrhage or perforation, with obstruction
756.73	Gastroschisis
659.33	Generalized infection during labor, antepartum
659.31	Generalized infection during labor, delivered
098.84	Gonococcal endocarditis
098.82	Gonococcal meningitis
098.83	Gonococcal pericarditis
282.62	Hb-SS disease with crisis
861.11	Heart contusion with open wound into thorax
861.13	Heart laceration with penetration of heart chambers and open wound into thorax
861.03	Heart laceration with penetration of heart chambers, without mention of open wound into thorax
861.02	Heart laceration without penetration of heart chambers or mention of open wound into thorax
861.12	Heart laceration without penetration of heart chambers, with open wound into thorax
283.11	Hemolytic-uremic syndrome
568.81	Hemoperitoneum (nontraumatic)
320.0	Hemophilus meningitis
641.13	Hemorrhage from placenta previa, antepartum
641.11	Hemorrhage from placenta previa, with delivery
902.22	Hepatic artery injury
572.2	Hepatic encephalopathy
573.4	Hepatic infarction
902.11	Hepatic vein injury
070.42	Hepatitis delta without mention of active hepatitis B disease with hepatic coma
070.43	Hepatitis E with hepatic coma
572.4	Hepatorenal syndrome
551.8	Hernia of other specified sites, with gangrene
551.9	Hernia of unspecified site, with gangrene

054.72	Herpes simplex meningitis
054.74	Herpes simplex myelitis
053.14	Herpes zoster myelitis
053.0	Herpes zoster with meningitis
054.3	Herpetic meningoencephalitis
054.5	Herpetic septicemia
115.04	Histoplasma capsulatum endocarditis
115.01	Histoplasma capsulatum meningitis
115.03	Histoplasma capsulatum pericarditis
115.05	Histoplasma capsulatum pneumonia
115.14	Histoplasma duboisii endocarditis
115.11	Histoplasma duboisii meningitis
115.13	Histoplasma duboisii pericarditis
115.15	Histoplasma duboisii pneumonia
058.21	Human herpesvirus 6 encephalitis
042	Human immunodeficiency virus [HIV]
773.3	Hydrops fetalis due to isoimmunization
778.0	Hydrops fetalis not due to isoimmunization
642.11	Hypertension secondary to renal disease, with delivery
642.12	Hypertension secondary to renal disease, with delivery, with current postpartum complication
902.51	Hypogastric artery injury
902.52	Hypogastric vein injury
746.7	Hypoplastic left heart syndrome
415.11	Iatrogenic pulmonary embolism and infarction
422.91	Idiopathic myocarditis
902.53	Iliac artery injury
902.54	Iliac vein injury
551.21	Incisional ventral hernia, with gangrene
636.61	Incomplete illegally induced abortion complicated by embolism
636.31	Incomplete illegally induced abortion complicated by renal failure
636.51	Incomplete illegally induced abortion complicated by shock
635.61	Incomplete legally induced abortion complicated by embolism
635.31	Incomplete legally induced abortion complicated by renal failure
634.61	Incomplete spontaneous abortion complicated by embolism
634.31	Incomplete spontaneous abortion complicated by renal failure
634.51	Incomplete spontaneous abortion complicated by shock
658.43	Infection of amniotic cavity, antepartum
658.41	Infection of amniotic cavity, delivered
323.61	Infectious acute disseminated encephalomyelitis [ADEM]
902.27	Inferior mesenteric artery injury
902.32	Inferior mesenteric vein injury
488.11	Influenza due to identified 2009 H1N1 influenza virus with pneumonia
488.01	Influenza due to identified avian influenza virus with pneumonia
488.81	Influenza due to identified novel influenza A virus with pneumonia
487.0	Influenza with pneumonia
550.02	Inguinal hernia with gangrene, bilateral
550.03	Inguinal hernia with gangrene, recurrent bilateral
550.01	Inguinal hernia with gangrene, recurrent unilateral or unspecified inguinal hernia
550.00	Inguinal hernia with gangrene, unilateral or unspecified, (not specified as recurrent)
740.2	Iniencephaly
902.29	Injury to celiac and mesenteric arteries, other
902.59	Injury to iliac blood vessels, other
862.9	Injury to multiple and unspecified intrathoracic organs with open wound into cavity
902.87	Injury to multiple blood vessels of abdomen and pelvis
901.83	Injury to multiple blood vessels of thorax

863.56	Injury to multiple sites in colon and rectum with open wound into cavity
868.19	Injury to other and multiple intra-abdominal organs, with open wound into cavity
863.99	Injury to other and unspecified gastrointestinal sites with open wound into cavity
862.39	Injury to other specified intrathoracic organs with open wound into cavity
867.7	Injury to other specified pelvic organs with open wound into cavity
902.39	Injury to portal and splenic veins, other
902.26	Injury to primary branches of superior mesenteric artery
902.24	Injury to specified branches of celiac axis, other
902.19	Injury to specified branches of inferior vena cava, other
902.31	Injury to superior mesenteric vein and primary subdivisions
868.10	Injury to unspecified intra-abdominal organ, with open wound into cavity
867.9	Injury to unspecified pelvic organ with open wound into cavity
901.40	Injury to unspecified pulmonary vessel(s)
901.1	Innominate and subclavian artery injury
901.3	Innominate and subclavian vein injury
869.1	Internal injury to unspecified or ill-defined organs with open wound into cavity
770.2	Interstitial emphysema and related conditions of newborn
431	Intracerebral hemorrhage
324.0	Intracranial abscess
324.9	Intracranial and intraspinal abscess of unspecified site
854.12	Intracranial injury of other and unspecified nature, with open intracranial wound, brief (less than 1 hour) loss of consciousness
854.16	Intracranial injury of other and unspecified nature, with open intracranial wound, loss of consciousness of unspecified duration
854.13	Intracranial injury of other and unspecified nature, with open intracranial wound, moderate (1-24 hours) loss of consciousness
854.11	Intracranial injury of other and unspecified nature, with open intracranial wound, no loss of consciousness
854.14	Intracranial injury of other and unspecified nature, with open intracranial wound, prolonged (more than 24 hours) loss of consciousness and return to pre-existing conscious level
854.15	Intracranial injury of other and unspecified nature, with open intracranial wound, prolonged (more than 24 hours) loss of consciousness, without return to pre-existing conscious level
854.10	Intracranial injury of other and unspecified nature, with open intracranial wound, unspecified state of consciousness
854.19	Intracranial injury of other and unspecified nature, with open intracranial wound, with unspecified concussion
854.05	Intracranial injury of other and unspecified nature, without mention of open intracranial wound, prolonged (more than 24 hours) loss of consciousness, without return to pre-existing conscious level
324.1	Intraspinal abscess
772.13	Intraventricular hemorrhage, Grade III
772.14	Intraventricular hemorrhage, Grade IV
062.0	Japanese encephalitis
773.4	Kernicterus due to isoimmunization of fetus or newborn
774.7	Kernicterus of fetus or newborn not due to isoimmunization
866.11	Kidney hematoma, without rupture of capsule, with open wound into cavity
866.12	Kidney laceration with open wound into cavity
260	Kwashiorkor
775.7	Late metabolic acidosis of newborn
635.51	Legally induced abortion, complicated by shock, incomplete
482.84	Legionnaires' disease
100.81	Leptospiral meningitis (aseptic)
864.11	Liver hematoma and contusion with open wound into cavity

864.15	Liver injury with open wound into cavity, unspecified laceration
864.14	Liver laceration, major, with open wound into cavity
864.04	Liver laceration, major, without mention of open wound into cavity
864.12	Liver laceration, minor, with open wound into cavity
864.13	Liver laceration, moderate, with open wound into cavity
864.03	Liver laceration, moderate, without mention of open wound into cavity
344.81	Locked-in state
063.1	Louping ill
952.2	Lumbar spinal cord injury without spinal bone injury
861.31	Lung contusion with open wound into thorax
861.32	Lung laceration with open wound into thorax
861.22	Lung laceration without mention of open wound into thorax
516.4	Lymphangioleiomyomatosis
670.02	Major puerperal infection, unspecified, delivered, with mention of postpartum complication
670.04	Major puerperal infection, unspecified, postpartum condition or complication
865.14	Massive parenchyma disruption of spleen with open wound into cavity
865.04	Massive parenchymal disruption of spleen without mention of open wound into cavity
648.01	Maternal diabetes mellitus with delivery
648.02	Maternal diabetes mellitus with delivery, with current postpartum complication
669.22	Maternal hypotension syndrome, with delivery, with mention of postpartum complication
669.21	Maternal hypotension syndrome, with delivery, with or without mention of antepartum condition
770.12	Meconium aspiration with respiratory symptoms, of fetus and newborn
519.2	Mediastinitis
320.82	Meningitis due to gram-negative bacteria, not elsewhere classified
321.8	Meningitis due to other nonbacterial organisms classified elsewhere
320.89	Meningitis due to other specified bacteria
321.3	Meningitis due to trypanosomiasis
320.9	Meningitis due to unspecified bacterium
321.2	Meningitis due to viruses not elsewhere classified
320.7	Meningitis in other bacterial diseases classified elsewhere
321.1	Meningitis in other fungal diseases
321.4	Meningitis in sarcoidosis
036.40	Meningococcal carditis, unspecified
036.1	Meningococcal encephalitis
036.42	Meningococcal endocarditis
036.0	Meningococcal meningitis
036.43	Meningococcal myocarditis
036.41	Meningococcal pericarditis
036.2	Meningococcemia
130.0	Meningoencephalitis due to toxoplasmosis
348.31	Metabolic encephalopathy
482.42	Methicillin resistant pneumonia due to Staphylococcus aureus
038.12	Methicillin resistant Staphylococcus aureus septicemia
482.41	Methicillin susceptible pneumonia due to Staphylococcus aureus
038.11	Methicillin susceptible Staphylococcus aureus septicemia
642.42	Mild or unspecified pre-eclampsia, with delivery, with current postpartum complication
828.0	Multiple closed fractures involving both lower limbs, lower with upper limb, and lower limb(s) with rib(s) and sternum
828.1	Multiple fractures involving both lower limbs, lower with upper limb, and lower limb(s) with rib(s) and sternum, open

808.53	Multiple open pelvic fractures with disruption of pelvic circle
808.54	Multiple open pelvic fractures without disruption of pelvic circle
952.8	Multiple sites of spinal cord injury without spinal bone injury
130.8	Multisystemic disseminated toxoplasmosis
072.2	Mumps encephalitis
072.1	Mumps meningitis
358.01	Myasthenia gravis with (acute) exacerbation
323.52	Myelitis following immunization procedures
323.02	Myelitis in viral diseases classified elsewhere
130.3	Myocarditis due to toxoplasmosis
777.50	Necrotizing enterocolitis in newborn, unspecified
728.86	Necrotizing fasciitis
583.4	Nephritis and nephropathy, not specified as acute or chronic, with lesion of rapidly progressive glomerulonephritis
583.6	Nephritis and nephropathy, not specified as acute or chronic, with lesion of renal cortical necrosis
516.61	Neuroendocrine cell hyperplasia of infancy
333.92	Neuroleptic malignant syndrome
322.0	Nonpyogenic meningitis
432.0	Nontraumatic extradural hemorrhage
596.6	Nontraumatic rupture of bladder
261	Nutritional marasmus
673.03	Obstetrical air embolism, antepartum condition or complication
673.04	Obstetrical air embolism, postpartum condition or complication
673.02	Obstetrical air embolism, with delivery, with mention of postpartum complication
673.01	Obstetrical air embolism, with delivery, with or without mention of antepartum condition
673.23	Obstetrical blood-clot embolism, antepartum
673.24	Obstetrical blood-clot embolism, postpartum condition or complication
673.21	Obstetrical blood-clot embolism, with delivery, with or without mention of antepartum condition
673.22	Obstetrical blood-clot embolism, with mention of postpartum complication
673.33	Obstetrical pyemic and septic embolism, antepartum
673.34	Obstetrical pyemic and septic embolism, postpartum condition or complication
673.32	Obstetrical pyemic and septic embolism, with delivery, with mention of postpartum complication
673.31	Obstetrical pyemic and septic embolism, with delivery, with or without mention of antepartum condition
576.2	Obstruction of bile duct
433.01	Occlusion and stenosis of basilar artery with cerebral infarction
433.11	Occlusion and stenosis of carotid artery with cerebral infarction
433.31	Occlusion and stenosis of multiple and bilateral precerebral arteries with cerebral infarction
433.81	Occlusion and stenosis of other specified precerebral artery with cerebral infarction
433.91	Occlusion and stenosis of unspecified precerebral artery with cerebral infarction
433.21	Occlusion and stenosis of vertebral artery with cerebral infarction
756.72	Omphalocele
813.51	Open Colles' fracture
835.10	Open dislocation of hip, unspecified site
839.15	Open dislocation, fifth cervical vertebra
839.11	Open dislocation, first cervical vertebra
839.14	Open dislocation, fourth cervical vertebra
839.30	Open dislocation, lumbar vertebra
839.18	Open dislocation, multiple cervical vertebrae
839.59	Open dislocation, other vertebra

839.12	Open dislocation, second cervical vertebra
839.17	Open dislocation, seventh cervical vertebra
839.16	Open dislocation, sixth cervical vertebra
839.71	Open dislocation, sternum
839.13	Open dislocation, third cervical vertebra
839.31	Open dislocation, thoracic vertebra
839.10	Open dislocation, unspecified cervical vertebra
839.50	Open dislocation, vertebra, unspecified site
808.1	Open fracture of acetabulum
812.12	Open fracture of anatomical neck of humerus
820.13	Open fracture of base of neck of femur
801.62	Open fracture of base of skull with cerebral laceration and contusion, brief (less than one hour) loss of consciousness
801.66	Open fracture of base of skull with cerebral laceration and contusion, loss of consciousness of unspecified duration
801.63	Open fracture of base of skull with cerebral laceration and contusion, moderate (1-24 hours) loss of consciousness
801.61	Open fracture of base of skull with cerebral laceration and contusion, no loss of consciousness
801.64	Open fracture of base of skull with cerebral laceration and contusion, prolonged (more than 24 hours) loss of consciousness and return to pre-existing conscious level
801.65	Open fracture of base of skull with cerebral laceration and contusion, prolonged (more than 24 hours) loss of consciousness, without return to pre-existing conscious level
801.69	Open fracture of base of skull with cerebral laceration and contusion, unspecified concussion
801.60	Open fracture of base of skull with cerebral laceration and contusion, unspecified state of consciousness
801.92	Open fracture of base of skull with intracranial injury of other and unspecified nature, brief (less than one hour) loss of consciousness
801.96	Open fracture of base of skull with intracranial injury of other and unspecified nature, loss of consciousness of unspecified duration
801.93	Open fracture of base of skull with intracranial injury of other and unspecified nature, moderate (1-24 hours) loss of consciousness
801.91	Open fracture of base of skull with intracranial injury of other and unspecified nature, no loss of consciousness
801.94	Open fracture of base of skull with intracranial injury of other and unspecified nature, prolonged (more than 24 hours) loss of consciousness and return to pre-existing conscious level
801.95	Open fracture of base of skull with intracranial injury of other and unspecified nature, prolonged (more than 24 hours) loss of consciousness, without return to pre-existing conscious level
801.99	Open fracture of base of skull with intracranial injury of other and unspecified nature, unspecified concussion
801.90	Open fracture of base of skull with intracranial injury of other and unspecified nature, unspecified state of consciousness
801.82	Open fracture of base of skull with other and unspecified intracranial hemorrhage, brief (less than one hour) loss of consciousness
801.86	Open fracture of base of skull with other and unspecified intracranial hemorrhage, loss of consciousness of unspecified duration
801.83	Open fracture of base of skull with other and unspecified intracranial hemorrhage, moderate (1-24 hours) loss of consciousness
801.81	Open fracture of base of skull with other and unspecified intracranial hemorrhage, no loss of consciousness
801.84	Open fracture of base of skull with other and unspecified intracranial hemorrhage, prolonged (more than 24 hours) loss of consciousness and return to pre-existing conscious level
801.85	Open fracture of base of skull with other and unspecified intracranial hemorrhage, prolonged (more than 24 hours) loss of consciousness, without return to pre-existing conscious level
801.89	Open fracture of base of skull with other and unspecified intracranial hemorrhage, unspecified concussion
801.80	Open fracture of base of skull with other and unspecified intracranial hemorrhage, unspecified state of consciousness
801.72	Open fracture of base of skull with subarachnoid, subdural, and extradural hemorrhage, brief (less than one hour) loss of consciousness
801.76	Open fracture of base of skull with subarachnoid, subdural, and extradural hemorrhage, loss of consciousness of unspecified duration
801.73	Open fracture of base of skull with subarachnoid, subdural, and extradural hemorrhage, moderate (1-24 hours) loss of consciousness
801.71	Open fracture of base of skull with subarachnoid, subdural, and extradural hemorrhage, no loss of consciousness
801.74	Open fracture of base of skull with subarachnoid, subdural, and extradural hemorrhage, prolonged (more than 24 hours) loss of consciousness and return to pre-existing conscious level
801.75	Open fracture of base of skull with subarachnoid, subdural, and extradural hemorrhage, prolonged (more than 24 hours) loss of consciousness, without return to pre-existing conscious level
801.79	Open fracture of base of skull with subarachnoid, subdural, and extradural hemorrhage, unspecified concussion
801.70	Open fracture of base of skull with subarachnoid, subdural, and extradural hemorrhage, unspecified state of consciousness
801.52	Open fracture of base of skull without mention of intracranial injury, brief (less than one hour) loss of consciousness
801.56	Open fracture of base of skull without mention of intracranial injury, loss of consciousness of unspecified duration
801.53	Open fracture of base of skull without mention of intracranial injury, moderate (1-24 hours) loss of consciousness
801.51	Open fracture of base of skull without mention of intracranial injury, no loss of consciousness
801.54	Open fracture of base of skull without mention of intracranial injury, prolonged (more than 24 hours) loss of consciousness and return to pre-existing conscious level
801.55	Open fracture of base of skull without mention of intracranial injury, prolonged (more than 24 hours) loss of consciousness, without return to pre-existing conscious level
801.59	Open fracture of base of skull without mention of intracranial injury, unspecified concussion
801.50	Open fracture of base of skull without mention of intracranial injury, unspecified state of consciousness
806.12	Open fracture of C1-C4 level with anterior cord syndrome
806.13	Open fracture of C1-C4 level with central cord syndrome
806.11	Open fracture of C1-C4 level with complete lesion of cord
806.14	Open fracture of C1-C4 level with other specified spinal cord injury
806.10	Open fracture of C1-C4 level with unspecified spinal cord injury
806.17	Open fracture of C5-C7 level with anterior cord syndrome
806.18	Open fracture of C5-C7 level with central cord syndrome
806.16	Open fracture of C5-C7 level with complete lesion of cord
806.19	Open fracture of C5-C7 level with other specified spinal cord injury
806.15	Open fracture of C5-C7 level with unspecified spinal cord injury
805.10	Open fracture of cervical vertebra, unspecified level without mention of spinal cord injury
813.12	Open fracture of coronoid process of ulna
813.53	Open fracture of distal end of ulna (alone)
805.3	Open fracture of dorsal (thoracic) vertebra without mention of spinal cord injury
807.18	Open fracture of eight or more ribs
820.11	Open fracture of epiphysis (separation) (upper) of neck of femur
821.31	Open fracture of femoral condyle
805.15	Open fracture of fifth cervical vertebra without mention of spinal cord injury
805.11	Open fracture of first cervical vertebra without mention of spinal cord injury
807.15	Open fracture of five ribs

807.14	Open fracture of four ribs
805.14	Open fracture of fourth cervical vertebra without mention of spinal cord injury
812.13	Open fracture of greater tuberosity of humerus
813.15	Open fracture of head of radius
808.51	Open fracture of ilium
820.31	Open fracture of intertrochanteric section of femur
808.52	Open fracture of ischium
807.6	Open fracture of larynx and trachea
812.52	Open fracture of lateral condyle of humerus
813.54	Open fracture of lower end of radius with ulna
821.32	Open fracture of lower epiphysis of femur
806.5	Open fracture of lumbar spine with spinal cord injury
805.5	Open fracture of lumbar vertebra without mention of spinal cord injury
812.53	Open fracture of medial condyle of humerus
820.12	Open fracture of midcervical section of femur
805.18	Open fracture of multiple cervical vertebrae without mention of spinal cord injury
807.19	Open fracture of multiple ribs, unspecified
813.16	Open fracture of neck of radius
813.11	Open fracture of olecranon process of ulna
807.11	Open fracture of one rib
808.59	Open fracture of other specified part of pelvis
808.3	Open fracture of pubis
813.18	Open fracture of radius with ulna, upper end (any part)
807.10	Open fracture of rib(s), unspecified
806.71	Open fracture of sacrum and coccyx with complete cauda equina lesion
806.72	Open fracture of sacrum and coccyx with other cauda equina injury
806.79	Open fracture of sacrum and coccyx with other spinal cord injury
806.70	Open fracture of sacrum and coccyx with unspecified spinal cord injury
805.7	Open fracture of sacrum and coccyx without mention of spinal cord injury
805.12	Open fracture of second cervical vertebra without mention of spinal cord injury
807.17	Open fracture of seven ribs
805.17	Open fracture of seventh cervical vertebra without mention of spinal cord injury
821.11	Open fracture of shaft of femur
823.31	Open fracture of shaft of fibula
823.32	Open fracture of shaft of fibula with tibia
812.31	Open fracture of shaft of humerus
813.31	Open fracture of shaft of radius (alone)
813.33	Open fracture of shaft of radius with ulna
823.30	Open fracture of shaft of tibia
813.32	Open fracture of shaft of ulna (alone)
807.16	Open fracture of six ribs
805.16	Open fracture of sixth cervical vertebra without mention of spinal cord injury
807.3	Open fracture of sternum
820.32	Open fracture of subtrochanteric section of femur
812.51	Open fracture of supracondylar humerus
812.11	Open fracture of surgical neck of humerus
806.32	Open fracture of T1-T6 level with anterior cord syndrome
806.33	Open fracture of T1-T6 level with central cord syndrome
806.31	Open fracture of T1-T6 level with complete lesion of cord
806.34	Open fracture of T1-T6 level with other specified spinal cord injury
806.30	Open fracture of T1-T6 level with unspecified spinal cord injury
806.37	Open fracture of T7-T12 level with anterior cord syndrome

806.38	Open fracture of T7-T12 level with central cord syndrome
806.36	Open fracture of T7-T12 level with complete lesion of cord
806.39	Open fracture of T7-T12 level with other specified spinal cord injury
806.35	Open fracture of T7-T12 level with unspecified spinal cord injury
805.13	Open fracture of third cervical vertebra without mention of spinal cord injury
807.13	Open fracture of three ribs
807.12	Open fracture of two ribs
812.54	Open fracture of unspecified condyle(s) of humerus
820.10	Open fracture of unspecified intracapsular section of neck of femur
821.10	Open fracture of unspecified part of femur
823.91	Open fracture of unspecified part of fibula
823.92	Open fracture of unspecified part of fibula with tibia
813.90	Open fracture of unspecified part of forearm
812.30	Open fracture of unspecified part of humerus
821.30	Open fracture of unspecified part of lower end of femur
812.50	Open fracture of unspecified part of lower end of humerus
820.9	Open fracture of unspecified part of neck of femur
813.91	Open fracture of unspecified part of radius (alone)
813.93	Open fracture of unspecified part of radius with ulna
823.90	Open fracture of unspecified part of tibia
813.92	Open fracture of unspecified part of ulna (alone)
812.10	Open fracture of unspecified part of upper end of humerus
805.9	Open fracture of unspecified part of vertebral column without mention of spinal cord injury
820.30	Open fracture of unspecified trochanteric section of femur
806.9	Open fracture of unspecified vertebra with spinal cord injury
823.11	Open fracture of upper end of fibula
823.12	Open fracture of upper end of fibula with tibia
823.10	Open fracture of upper end of tibia
800.62	Open fracture of vault of skull with cerebral laceration and contusion, brief (less than one hour) loss of consciousness
800.66	Open fracture of vault of skull with cerebral laceration and contusion, loss of consciousness of unspecified duration
800.63	Open fracture of vault of skull with cerebral laceration and contusion, moderate (1-24 hours) loss of consciousness
800.61	Open fracture of vault of skull with cerebral laceration and contusion, no loss of consciousness
800.64	Open fracture of vault of skull with cerebral laceration and contusion, prolonged (more than 24 hours) loss of consciousness and return to pre-existing conscious level
800.65	Open fracture of vault of skull with cerebral laceration and contusion, prolonged (more than 24 hours) loss of consciousness, without return to pre-existing conscious level
800.69	Open fracture of vault of skull with cerebral laceration and contusion, unspecified concussion
800.60	Open fracture of vault of skull with cerebral laceration and contusion, unspecified state of consciousness
800.92	Open fracture of vault of skull with intracranial injury of other and unspecified nature, brief (less than one hour) loss of consciousness
800.96	Open fracture of vault of skull with intracranial injury of other and unspecified nature, loss of consciousness of unspecified duration
800.93	Open fracture of vault of skull with intracranial injury of other and unspecified nature, moderate (1-24 hours) loss of consciousness
800.91	Open fracture of vault of skull with intracranial injury of other and unspecified nature, no loss of consciousness
800.94	Open fracture of vault of skull with intracranial injury of other and unspecified nature, prolonged (more than 24 hours) loss of consciousness and return to pre-existing conscious level
800.95	Open fracture of vault of skull with intracranial injury of other and unspecified nature, prolonged (more than 24 hours) loss of consciousness, without return to pre-existing conscious level

800.99 Open fracture of vault of skull with intracranial injury of other and unspecified nature, unspecified concussion

800.90 Open fracture of vault of skull with intracranial injury of other and unspecified nature, unspecified state of consciousness

800.82 Open fracture of vault of skull with other and unspecified intracranial hemorrhage, brief (less than one hour) loss of consciousness

800.86 Open fracture of vault of skull with other and unspecified intracranial hemorrhage, loss of consciousness of unspecified duration

800.83 Open fracture of vault of skull with other and unspecified intracranial hemorrhage, moderate (1-24 hours) loss of consciousness

800.81 Open fracture of vault of skull with other and unspecified intracranial hemorrhage, no loss of consciousness

800.84 Open fracture of vault of skull with other and unspecified intracranial hemorrhage, prolonged (more than 24 hours) loss of consciousness and return to pre-existing conscious level

800.85 Open fracture of vault of skull with other and unspecified intracranial hemorrhage, prolonged (more than 24 hours) loss of consciousness, without return to pre-existing conscious level

800.89 Open fracture of vault of skull with other and unspecified intracranial hemorrhage, unspecified concussion

800.80 Open fracture of vault of skull with other and unspecified intracranial hemorrhage, unspecified state of consciousness

800.72 Open fracture of vault of skull with subarachnoid, subdural, and extradural hemorrhage, brief (less than one hour) loss of consciousness

800.76 Open fracture of vault of skull with subarachnoid, subdural, and extradural hemorrhage, loss of consciousness of unspecified duration

800.73 Open fracture of vault of skull with subarachnoid, subdural, and extradural hemorrhage, moderate (1-24 hours) loss of consciousness

800.71 Open fracture of vault of skull with subarachnoid, subdural, and extradural hemorrhage, no loss of consciousness

800.74 Open fracture of vault of skull with subarachnoid, subdural, and extradural hemorrhage, prolonged (more than 24 hours) loss of consciousness and return to pre-existing conscious level

800.75 Open fracture of vault of skull with subarachnoid, subdural, and extradural hemorrhage, prolonged (more than 24 hours) loss of consciousness, without return to pre-existing conscious level

800.79 Open fracture of vault of skull with subarachnoid, subdural, and extradural hemorrhage, unspecified concussion

800.70 Open fracture of vault of skull with subarachnoid, subdural, and extradural hemorrhage, unspecified state of consciousness

800.52 Open fracture of vault of skull without mention of intracranial injury, brief (less than one hour) loss of consciousness

800.56 Open fracture of vault of skull without mention of intracranial injury, loss of consciousness of unspecified duration

800.53 Open fracture of vault of skull without mention of intracranial injury, moderate (1-24 hours) loss of consciousness

800.51 Open fracture of vault of skull without mention of intracranial injury, no loss of consciousness

800.54 Open fracture of vault of skull without mention of intracranial injury, prolonged (more than 24 hours) loss of consciousness and return to pre-existing conscious level

800.55 Open fracture of vault of skull without mention of intracranial injury, prolonged (more than 24 hours) loss of consciousness, without return to pre-existing conscious level

800.59 Open fracture of vault of skull without mention of intracranial injury, unspecified concussion

800.50 Open fracture of vault of skull without mention of intracranial injury, unspecified state of consciousness

804.72 Open fractures involving skull or face with other bones with subarachnoid, subdural, and extradural hemorrhage, brief (less than one hour) loss of consciousness

804.76 Open fractures involving skull or face with other bones with subarachnoid, subdural, and extradural hemorrhage, loss of consciousness of unspecified duration

804.73 Open fractures involving skull or face with other bones with subarachnoid, subdural, and extradural hemorrhage, moderate (1-24 hours) loss of consciousness

804.71 Open fractures involving skull or face with other bones with subarachnoid, subdural, and extradural hemorrhage, no loss of consciousness

804.74 Open fractures involving skull or face with other bones with subarachnoid, subdural, and extradural hemorrhage, prolonged (more than 24 hours) loss of consciousness and return to pre-existing conscious level

804.75 Open fractures involving skull or face with other bones with subarachnoid, subdural, and extradural hemorrhage, prolonged (more than 24 hours) loss of consciousness, without return to pre-existing conscious level

804.79 Open fractures involving skull or face with other bones with subarachnoid, subdural, and extradural hemorrhage, unspecified concussion

804.70 Open fractures involving skull or face with other bones with subarachnoid, subdural, and extradural hemorrhage, unspecified state of consciousness

804.62 Open fractures involving skull or face with other bones, with cerebral laceration and contusion, brief (less than one hour) loss of consciousness

804.66 Open fractures involving skull or face with other bones, with cerebral laceration and contusion, loss of consciousness of unspecified duration

804.63 Open fractures involving skull or face with other bones, with cerebral laceration and contusion, moderate (1-24 hours) loss of consciousness

804.61 Open fractures involving skull or face with other bones, with cerebral laceration and contusion, no loss of consciousness

804.64 Open fractures involving skull or face with other bones, with cerebral laceration and contusion, prolonged (more than 24 hours) loss of consciousness and return to pre-existing conscious level

804.65 Open fractures involving skull or face with other bones, with cerebral laceration and contusion, prolonged (more than 24 hours) loss of consciousness, without return to pre-existing conscious level

804.69 Open fractures involving skull or face with other bones, with cerebral laceration and contusion, unspecified concussion

804.60 Open fractures involving skull or face with other bones, with cerebral laceration and contusion, unspecified state of consciousness

804.93 Open fractures involving skull or face with other bones, with intracranial injury of other and unspecified nature, moderate (1-24 hours) loss of consciousness

804.94 Open fractures involving skull or face with other bones, with intracranial injury of other and unspecified nature, prolonged (more than 24 hours) loss of consciousness and return to pre-existing conscious level

804.95 Open fractures involving skull or face with other bones, with intracranial injury of other and unspecified nature, prolonged (more than 24 hours) loss of consciousness, without return to pre-existing level

804.82 Open fractures involving skull or face with other bones, with other and unspecified intracranial hemorrhage, brief (less than one hour) loss of consciousness

804.86 Open fractures involving skull or face with other bones, with other and unspecified intracranial hemorrhage, loss of consciousness of unspecified duration

804.83 Open fractures involving skull or face with other bones, with other and unspecified intracranial hemorrhage, moderate (1-24 hours) loss of consciousness

804.81 Open fractures involving skull or face with other bones, with other and unspecified intracranial hemorrhage, no loss of consciousness

804.84 Open fractures involving skull or face with other bones, with other and unspecified intracranial hemorrhage, prolonged (more than 24 hours) loss of consciousness and return to pre-existing conscious level

804.85 Open fractures involving skull or face with other bones, with other and unspecified intracranial hemorrhage, prolonged (more than 24 hours) loss of consciousness, without return to pre-existing conscious level

804.89 Open fractures involving skull or face with other bones, with other and unspecified intracranial hemorrhage, unspecified concussion

804.80 Open fractures involving skull or face with other bones, with other and unspecified intracranial hemorrhage, unspecified state of consciousness

804.53 Open fractures involving skull or face with other bones, without mention of intracranial injury, moderate (1-24 hours) loss of consciousness

804.54 Open fractures involving skull or face with other bones, without mention of intracranial injury, prolonged (more than 24 hours) loss of consciousness and return to pre-existing conscious level

804.55 Open fractures involving skull or face with other bones, without mention of intracranial injury, prolonged (more than 24 hours) loss of consciousness, without return to pre-existing conscious level

813.13 Open Monteggia's fracture

835.12 Open obturator dislocation of hip

835.11 Open posterior dislocation of hip

821.33 Open supracondylar fracture of femur

874.10 Open wound of larynx with trachea, complicated

874.00 Open wound of larynx with trachea, without mention of complication

874.11 Open wound of larynx, complicated

874.01 Open wound of larynx, without mention of complication

874.12 Open wound of trachea, complicated

874.02 Open wound of trachea, without mention of complication

073.0 Ornithosis with pneumonia

580.89 Other acute glomerulonephritis with other specified pathological lesion in kidney

422.99 Other acute myocarditis

851.92 Other and unspecified cerebral laceration and contusion, with open intracranial wound, brief (less than 1 hour) loss of consciousness

851.96 Other and unspecified cerebral laceration and contusion, with open intracranial wound, loss of consciousness of unspecified duration

851.93 Other and unspecified cerebral laceration and contusion, with open intracranial wound, moderate (1-24 hours) loss of consciousness

851.91 Other and unspecified cerebral laceration and contusion, with open intracranial wound, no loss of consciousness

851.94 Other and unspecified cerebral laceration and contusion, with open intracranial wound, prolonged (more than 24 hours) loss of consciousness and return to pre-existing conscious level

851.95 Other and unspecified cerebral laceration and contusion, with open intracranial wound, prolonged (more than 24 hours) loss of consciousness, without return to pre-existing conscious level

851.99 Other and unspecified cerebral laceration and contusion, with open intracranial wound, unspecified concussion

851.90 Other and unspecified cerebral laceration and contusion, with open intracranial wound, unspecified state of consciousness

851.82 Other and unspecified cerebral laceration and contusion, without mention of open intracranial wound, brief (less than 1 hour) loss of consciousness

851.86 Other and unspecified cerebral laceration and contusion, without mention of open intracranial wound, loss of consciousness of unspecified duration

851.83 Other and unspecified cerebral laceration and contusion, without mention of open intracranial wound, moderate (1-24 hours) loss of consciousness

851.81 Other and unspecified cerebral laceration and contusion, without mention of open intracranial wound, no loss of consciousness

851.84 Other and unspecified cerebral laceration and contusion, without mention of open intracranial wound, prolonged (more than 24 hours) loss of consciousness and return to preexisting conscious level

851.85 Other and unspecified cerebral laceration and contusion, without mention of open intracranial wound, prolonged (more than 24 hours) loss of consciousness, without return to pre-existing conscious level

851.89 Other and unspecified cerebral laceration and contusion, without mention of open intracranial wound, unspecified concussion

851.80 Other and unspecified cerebral laceration and contusion, without mention of open intracranial wound, unspecified state of consciousness

853.12 Other and unspecified intracranial hemorrhage following injury, with open intracranial wound, brief (less than 1 hour) loss of consciousness

853.16 Other and unspecified intracranial hemorrhage following injury, with open intracranial wound, loss of consciousness of unspecified duration

853.13 Other and unspecified intracranial hemorrhage following injury, with open intracranial wound, moderate (1-24 hours) loss of consciousness

853.11 Other and unspecified intracranial hemorrhage following injury, with open intracranial wound, no loss of consciousness

853.14 Other and unspecified intracranial hemorrhage following injury, with open intracranial wound, prolonged (more than 24 hours) loss of consciousness and return to pre-existing conscious level

853.15 Other and unspecified intracranial hemorrhage following injury, with open intracranial wound, prolonged (more than 24 hours) loss of consciousness, without return to pre-existing conscious level

853.19 Other and unspecified intracranial hemorrhage following injury, with open intracranial wound, unspecified concussion

853.10 Other and unspecified intracranial hemorrhage following injury, with open intracranial wound, unspecified state of consciousness

853.02 Other and unspecified intracranial hemorrhage following injury, without mention of open intracranial wound, brief (less than 1 hour) loss of consciousness

853.06 Other and unspecified intracranial hemorrhage following injury, without mention of open intracranial wound, loss of consciousness of unspecified duration

853.03 Other and unspecified intracranial hemorrhage following injury, without mention of open intracranial wound, moderate (1-24 hours) loss of consciousness

853.01 Other and unspecified intracranial hemorrhage following injury, without mention of open intracranial wound, no loss of consciousness

853.04 Other and unspecified intracranial hemorrhage following injury, without mention of open intracranial wound, prolonged (more than 24 hours) loss of consciousness and return to preexisting conscious level

853.09 Other and unspecified intracranial hemorrhage following injury, without mention of open intracranial wound, unspecified concussion

853.00 Other and unspecified intracranial hemorrhage following injury, without mention of open intracranial wound, unspecified state of consciousness

853.05 Other and unspecified intracranial hemorrhage following injury. Without mention of open intracranial wound, prolonged (more than 24 hours) loss of consciousness, without return to pre-existing conscious level

813.17 Other and unspecified open fractures of proximal end of radius (alone)

813.14 Other and unspecified open fractures of proximal end of ulna (alone)

747.39 Other anomalies of pulmonary artery and pulmonary circulation

323.81 Other causes of encephalitis and encephalomyelitis

323.82 Other causes of myelitis

803.12 Other closed skull fracture with cerebral laceration and contusion, brief (less than one hour) loss of consciousness

803.16 Other closed skull fracture with cerebral laceration and contusion, loss of consciousness of unspecified duration

803.13 Other closed skull fracture with cerebral laceration and contusion, moderate (1-24 hours) loss of consciousness

803.11 Other closed skull fracture with cerebral laceration and contusion, no loss of consciousness

803.14 Other closed skull fracture with cerebral laceration and contusion, prolonged (more than 24 hours) loss of consciousness and return to pre-existing conscious level

803.15 Other closed skull fracture with cerebral laceration and contusion, prolonged (more than 24 hours) loss of consciousness, without return to pre-existing conscious level

803.19 Other closed skull fracture with cerebral laceration and contusion, unspecified concussion

803.10 Other closed skull fracture with cerebral laceration and contusion, unspecified state of consciousness

803.43 Other closed skull fracture with intracranial injury of other and unspecified nature, moderate (1-24 hours) loss of consciousness

803.44 Other closed skull fracture with intracranial injury of other and unspecified nature, prolonged (more than 24 hours) loss of consciousness and return to pre-existing conscious level

803.45 Other closed skull fracture with intracranial injury of other and unspecified nature, prolonged (more than 24 hours) loss of consciousness, without return to pre-existing conscious level

803.32 Other closed skull fracture with other and unspecified intracranial hemorrhage, brief (less than one hour) loss of consciousness

803.36 Other closed skull fracture with other and unspecified intracranial hemorrhage, loss of consciousness of unspecified duration

803.33 Other closed skull fracture with other and unspecified intracranial hemorrhage, moderate (1-24 hours) loss of consciousness

803.31 Other closed skull fracture with other and unspecified intracranial hemorrhage, no loss of consciousness

803.34 Other closed skull fracture with other and unspecified intracranial hemorrhage, prolonged (more than 24 hours) loss of consciousness and return to pre-existing conscious level

803.35 Other closed skull fracture with other and unspecified intracranial hemorrhage, prolonged (more than 24 hours) loss of consciousness, without return to pre-existing conscious level

803.39 Other closed skull fracture with other and unspecified intracranial hemorrhage, unspecified concussion

803.30 Other closed skull fracture with other and unspecified intracranial hemorrhage, unspecified state of unconsciousness

803.22 Other closed skull fracture with subarachnoid, subdural, and extradural hemorrhage, brief (less than one hour) loss of consciousness

803.26 Other closed skull fracture with subarachnoid, subdural, and extradural hemorrhage, loss of consciousness of unspecified duration

803.23 Other closed skull fracture with subarachnoid, subdural, and extradural hemorrhage, moderate (1-24 hours) loss of consciousness

803.21 Other closed skull fracture with subarachnoid, subdural, and extradural hemorrhage, no loss of consciousness

803.24 Other closed skull fracture with subarachnoid, subdural, and extradural hemorrhage, prolonged (more than 24 hours) loss of consciousness and return to pre-existing conscious level

803.25 Other closed skull fracture with subarachnoid, subdural, and extradural hemorrhage, prolonged (more than 24 hours) loss of consciousness, without return to pre-existing conscious level

803.29 Other closed skull fracture with subarachnoid, subdural, and extradural hemorrhage, unspecified concussion

803.20 Other closed skull fracture with subarachnoid, subdural, and extradural hemorrhage, unspecified state of consciousness

803.03 Other closed skull fracture without mention of intracranial injury, moderate (1-24 hours) loss of consciousness

803.04 Other closed skull fracture without mention of intracranial injury, prolonged (more than 24 hours) loss of consciousness and return to pre-existing conscious level

803.05 Other closed skull fracture without mention of intracranial injury, prolonged (more than 24 hours) loss of consciousness, without return to pre-existing conscious level

820.09 Other closed transcervical fracture of femur

756.79 Other congenital anomalies of abdominal wall

771.2 Other congenital infection specific to the perinatal period

284.12 Other drug induced pancytopenia

323.41 Other encephalitis and encephalomyelitis due to other infections classified elsewhere

348.39 Other encephalopathy

770.18 Other fetal and newborn aspiration with respiratory symptoms

058.29 Other human herpesvirus encephalitis

863.59 Other injury to colon and rectum with open wound into cavity

863.39 Other injury to small intestine with open wound into cavity

516.69 Other interstitial lung diseases of childhood

864.19 Other liver injury with open wound into cavity

670.82 Other major puerperal infection, delivered, with mention of postpartum complication

670.84 Other major puerperal infection, postpartum condition or complication

670.80 Other major puerperal infection, unspecified as to episode of care or not applicable

323.42 Other myelitis due to other infections classified elsewhere

673.83 Other obstetrical pulmonary embolism, antepartum

673.84 Other obstetrical pulmonary embolism, postpartum condition or complication

673.82 Other obstetrical pulmonary embolism, with delivery, with mention of postpartum complication

673.81 Other obstetrical pulmonary embolism, with delivery, with or without mention of antepartum condition

835.13 Other open anterior dislocation of hip

821.39 Other open fracture of lower end of femur

812.59 Other open fracture of lower end of humerus

812.19 Other open fracture of upper end of humerus

813.52 Other open fractures of distal end of radius (alone)

803.62 Other open skull fracture with cerebral laceration and contusion, brief (less than one hour) loss of consciousness

803.66 Other open skull fracture with cerebral laceration and contusion, loss of consciousness of unspecified duration

803.63 Other open skull fracture with cerebral laceration and contusion, moderate (1-24 hours) loss of consciousness

803.61 Other open skull fracture with cerebral laceration and contusion, no loss of consciousness

803.64 Other open skull fracture with cerebral laceration and contusion, prolonged (more than 24 hours) loss of consciousness and return to pre-existing conscious level

803.65 Other open skull fracture with cerebral laceration and contusion, prolonged (more than 24 hours) loss of consciousness, without return to pre-existing conscious level

803.69 Other open skull fracture with cerebral laceration and contusion, unspecified concussion

803.60 Other open skull fracture with cerebral laceration and contusion, unspecified state of consciousness

803.92 Other open skull fracture with intracranial injury of other and unspecified nature, brief (less than one hour) loss of consciousness

803.96 Other open skull fracture with intracranial injury of other and unspecified nature, loss of consciousness of unspecified duration

803.93 Other open skull fracture with intracranial injury of other and unspecified nature, moderate (1-24 hours) loss of consciousness

803.91 Other open skull fracture with intracranial injury of other and unspecified nature, no loss of consciousness

803.94	Other open skull fracture with intracranial injury of other and unspecified nature, prolonged (more than 24 hours) loss of consciousness and return to pre-existing conscious level
803.95	Other open skull fracture with intracranial injury of other and unspecified nature, prolonged (more than 24 hours) loss of consciousness, without return to pre-existing conscious level
803.99	Other open skull fracture with intracranial injury of other and unspecified nature, unspecified concussion
803.90	Other open skull fracture with intracranial injury of other and unspecified nature, unspecified state of consciousness
803.82	Other open skull fracture with other and unspecified intracranial hemorrhage, brief (less than one hour) loss of consciousness
803.86	Other open skull fracture with other and unspecified intracranial hemorrhage, loss of consciousness of unspecified duration
803.83	Other open skull fracture with other and unspecified intracranial hemorrhage, moderate (1-24 hours) loss of consciousness
803.81	Other open skull fracture with other and unspecified intracranial hemorrhage, no loss of consciousness
803.84	Other open skull fracture with other and unspecified intracranial hemorrhage, prolonged (more than 24 hours) loss of consciousness and return to pre-existing conscious level
803.85	Other open skull fracture with other and unspecified intracranial hemorrhage, prolonged (more than 24 hours) loss of consciousness, without return to pre-existing conscious level
803.89	Other open skull fracture with other and unspecified intracranial hemorrhage, unspecified concussion
803.80	Other open skull fracture with other and unspecified intracranial hemorrhage, unspecified state of consciousness
803.72	Other open skull fracture with subarachnoid, subdural, and extradural hemorrhage, brief (less than one hour) loss of consciousness
803.76	Other open skull fracture with subarachnoid, subdural, and extradural hemorrhage, loss of consciousness of unspecified duration
803.73	Other open skull fracture with subarachnoid, subdural, and extradural hemorrhage, moderate (1-24 hours) loss of consciousness
803.71	Other open skull fracture with subarachnoid, subdural, and extradural hemorrhage, no loss of consciousness
803.74	Other open skull fracture with subarachnoid, subdural, and extradural hemorrhage, prolonged (more than 24 hours) loss of consciousness and return to pre-existing conscious level
803.75	Other open skull fracture with subarachnoid, subdural, and extradural hemorrhage, prolonged (more than 24 hours) loss of consciousness, without return to pre-existing conscious level
803.79	Other open skull fracture with subarachnoid, subdural, and extradural hemorrhage, unspecified concussion
803.70	Other open skull fracture with subarachnoid, subdural, and extradural hemorrhage, unspecified state of consciousness
803.50	Other open skull fracture without mention of injury, state of consciousness unspecified
803.52	Other open skull fracture without mention of intracranial injury, brief (less than one hour) loss of consciousness
803.56	Other open skull fracture without mention of intracranial injury, loss of consciousness of unspecified duration
803.53	Other open skull fracture without mention of intracranial injury, moderate (1-24 hours) loss of consciousness
803.51	Other open skull fracture without mention of intracranial injury, no loss of consciousness
803.54	Other open skull fracture without mention of intracranial injury, prolonged (more than 24 hours) loss of consciousness and return to pre-existing conscious level
803.55	Other open skull fracture without mention of intracranial injury, prolonged (more than 24 hours) loss of consciousness, without return to pre-existing conscious level
803.59	Other open skull fracture without mention of intracranial injury, unspecified concussion
820.19	Other open transcervical fracture of femur
323.62	Other postinfectious encephalitis and encephalomyelitis
415.19	Other pulmonary embolism and infarction
518.52	Other pulmonary insufficiency, not elsewhere classified, following trauma and surgery
344.09	Other quadriplegia and quadriparesis
567.38	Other retroperitoneal abscess
567.39	Other retroperitoneal infections
038.49	Other septicemia due to gram-negative organism
262	Other severe protein-calorie malnutrition
785.59	Other shock without mention of trauma
282.69	Other sickle-cell disease with crisis
284.89	Other specified aplastic anemias
535.41	Other specified gastritis with hemorrhage
018.81	Other specified miliary tuberculosis, bacteriological or histological examination not done
018.82	Other specified miliary tuberculosis, bacteriological or histological examination unknown (at present)
018.80	Other specified miliary tuberculosis, confirmation unspecified
018.83	Other specified miliary tuberculosis, tubercle bacilli found (in sputum) by microscopy
018.84	Other specified miliary tuberculosis, tubercle bacilli not found (in sputum) by microscopy, but found by bacterial culture
018.85	Other specified miliary tuberculosis, tubercle bacilli not found by bacteriological examination, but tuberculosis confirmed histologically
018.86	Other specified miliary tuberculosis, tubercle bacilli not found by bacteriological or histological examination, but tuberculosis confirmed by other methods [inoculation of animals]
062.8	Other specified mosquito-borne viral encephalitis
567.89	Other specified peritonitis
038.8	Other specified septicemia
063.8	Other specified tick-borne viral encephalitis
013.81	Other specified tuberculosis of central nervous system, bacteriological or histological examination not done
013.82	Other specified tuberculosis of central nervous system, bacteriological or histological examination unknown (at present)
013.80	Other specified tuberculosis of central nervous system, confirmation unspecified
013.83	Other specified tuberculosis of central nervous system, tubercle bacilli found (in sputum) by microscopy
013.84	Other specified tuberculosis of central nervous system, tubercle bacilli not found (in sputum) by microscopy, but found by bacterial culture
013.85	Other specified tuberculosis of central nervous system, tubercle bacilli not found by bacteriological examination, but tuberculosis confirmed histologically
013.86	Other specified tuberculosis of central nervous system, tubercle bacilli not found by bacteriological or histological examination, but tuberculosis confirmed by other methods [inoculation of animals]
020.8	Other specified types of plague
070.49	Other specified viral hepatitis with hepatic coma
865.19	Other spleen injury with open wound into cavity
038.19	Other staphylococcal septicemia
482.49	Other Staphylococcus pneumonia
567.29	Other suppurative peritonitis
745.19	Other transposition of great vessels
453.2	Other venous embolism and thrombosis, of inferior vena cava
551.29	Other ventral hernia with gangrene
863.92	Pancreas body injury with open wound into cavity
863.91	Pancreas head injury with open wound into cavity
863.94	Pancreas injury, multiple and unspecified sites, with open wound into cavity

863.93	Pancreas tail injury with open wound into cavity
533.91	Peptic ulcer, unspecified site, unspecified as acute or chronic, without mention of hemorrhage or perforation, with obstruction
576.3	Perforation of bile duct
530.4	Perforation of esophagus
575.4	Perforation of gallbladder
569.83	Perforation of intestine
777.6	Perinatal intestinal perforation
774.4	Perinatal jaundice due to hepatocellular damage
674.53	Peripartum cardiomyopathy, antepartum condition or complication
674.52	Peripartum cardiomyopathy, delivered, with mention of postpartum condition
674.51	Peripartum cardiomyopathy, delivered, with or without mention of antepartum condition
674.54	Peripartum cardiomyopathy, postpartum condition or complication
674.50	Peripartum cardiomyopathy, unspecified as to episode of care or not applicable
567.22	Peritoneal abscess
868.13	Peritoneum injury with open wound into cavity
567.21	Peritonitis (acute) generalized
567.0	Peritonitis in infectious diseases classified elsewhere
779.7	Periventricular leukomalacia
747.83	Persistent fetal circulation
325	Phlebitis and thrombophlebitis of intracranial venous sinuses
511.1	Pleurisy with effusion, with mention of bacterial cause other than tuberculosis
320.1	Pneumococcal meningitis
567.1	Pneumococcal peritonitis
481	Pneumococcal pneumonia (streptococcus pneumoniae pneumonia)
038.2	Pneumococcal septicemia
136.3	Pneumocystosis
480.0	Pneumonia due to adenovirus
482.81	Pneumonia due to anaerobes
483.1	Pneumonia due to Chlamydia
482.82	Pneumonia due to Escherichia coli (E. coli)
482.2	Pneumonia due to Hemophilus influenzae (H. influenzae)
482.0	Pneumonia due to Klebsiella pneumoniae
483.0	Pneumonia due to Mycoplasma pneumoniae
482.83	Pneumonia due to other gram-negative bacteria
482.89	Pneumonia due to other specified bacteria
483.8	Pneumonia due to other specified organism
482.39	Pneumonia due to other Streptococcus
480.8	Pneumonia due to other virus not elsewhere classified
480.2	Pneumonia due to parainfluenza virus
482.1	Pneumonia due to Pseudomonas
480.1	Pneumonia due to respiratory syncytial virus
480.3	Pneumonia due to SARS-associated coronavirus
482.40	Pneumonia due to Staphylococcus, unspecified
482.31	Pneumonia due to Streptococcus, group A
482.32	Pneumonia due to Streptococcus, group B
482.30	Pneumonia due to unspecified Streptococcus
484.5	Pneumonia in anthrax
484.6	Pneumonia in aspergillosis
484.1	Pneumonia in cytomegalic inclusion disease
484.8	Pneumonia in other infectious diseases classified elsewhere
484.7	Pneumonia in other systemic mycoses
484.3	Pneumonia in whooping cough

486	Pneumonia, organism unspecified
020.5	Pneumonic plague, unspecified
507.0	Pneumonitis due to inhalation of food or vomitus
507.1	Pneumonitis due to inhalation of oils and essences
507.8	Pneumonitis due to other solids and liquids
130.4	Pneumonitis due to toxoplasmosis
904.41	Popliteal artery injury
904.42	Popliteal vein injury
572.1	Portal pyemia
902.33	Portal vein injury
452	Portal vein thrombosis
323.63	Postinfectious myelitis
055.0	Postmeasles encephalitis
055.1	Postmeasles pneumonia
998.01	Postoperative shock, cardiogenic
998.09	Postoperative shock, other
998.02	Postoperative shock, septic
052.0	Postvaricella encephalitis
052.2	Postvaricella myelitis
642.73	Pre-eclampsia or eclampsia superimposed on pre-existing hypertension, antepartum
642.74	Pre-eclampsia or eclampsia superimposed on pre-existing hypertension, postpartum condition or complication
642.71	Pre-eclampsia or eclampsia superimposed on pre-existing hypertension, with delivery
642.72	Pre-eclampsia or eclampsia superimposed on pre-existing hypertension, with delivery, with current postpartum complication
641.21	Premature separation of placenta, with delivery
707.23	Pressure ulcer stage III
707.24	Pressure ulcer stage IV
020.3	Primary pneumonic plague
756.71	Prune belly syndrome
567.31	Psoas muscle abscess
670.22	Puerperal sepsis, delivered, with mention of postpartum complication
670.24	Puerperal sepsis, postpartum condition or complication
670.32	Puerperal septic thrombophlebitis, delivered, with mention of postpartum complication
670.34	Puerperal septic thrombophlebitis, postpartum condition or complication
022.1	Pulmonary anthrax
747.32	Pulmonary arteriovenous malformation
747.31	Pulmonary artery coarctation and atresia
901.41	Pulmonary artery injury
770.3	Pulmonary hemorrhage of fetus or newborn
516.62	Pulmonary interstitial glycogenosis
901.42	Pulmonary vein injury
344.01	Quadriplegia and quadriparesis, C1-C4, complete
344.02	Quadriplegia and quadriparesis, C1-C4, incomplete
344.03	Quadriplegia and quadriparesis, C5-C7, complete
343.2	Quadriplegic infantile cerebral palsy
863.55	Rectum injury with open wound into cavity
284.81	Red cell aplasia (acquired) (adult) (with thymoma)
590.2	Renal and perinephric abscess
902.41	Renal artery injury
902.49	Renal blood vessel injury, other
902.42	Renal vein injury
902.40	Renal vessel(s) injury, unspecified
799.1	Respiratory arrest
770.87	Respiratory arrest of newborn

769	Respiratory distress syndrome in newborn
770.84	Respiratory failure of newborn
868.14	Retroperitoneum injury with open wound into cavity
331.81	Reye's syndrome
429.5	Rupture of chordae tendineae
429.6	Rupture of papillary muscle
665.03	Rupture of uterus before onset of labor, antepartum
665.01	Rupture of uterus before onset of labor, with delivery
665.11	Rupture of uterus during labor, with delivery
063.0	Russian spring-summer (taiga) encephalitis
952.3	Sacral spinal cord injury without spinal bone injury
444.01	Saddle embolus of abdominal aorta
415.13	Saddle embolus of pulmonary artery
003.21	Salmonella meningitis
003.22	Salmonella pneumonia
003.1	Salmonella septicemia
249.20	Secondary diabetes mellitus with hyperosmolarity, not stated as uncontrolled, or unspecified
249.21	Secondary diabetes mellitus with hyperosmolarity, uncontrolled
249.10	Secondary diabetes mellitus with ketoacidosis, not stated as uncontrolled, or unspecified
249.11	Secondary diabetes mellitus with ketoacidosis, uncontrolled
249.30	Secondary diabetes mellitus with other coma, not stated as uncontrolled, or unspecified
249.31	Secondary diabetes mellitus with other coma, uncontrolled
020.4	Secondary pneumonic plague
995.91	Sepsis
422.92	Septic myocarditis
415.12	Septic pulmonary embolism
785.52	Septic shock
771.81	Septicemia (sepsis) of newborn
038.3	Septicemia due to anaerobes
038.42	Septicemia due to Escherichia coli (E. coli)
038.41	Septicemia due to hemophilus influenzae (H. influenzae)
038.43	Septicemia due to pseudomonas
038.44	Septicemia due to serratia
038.40	Septicemia due to unspecified gram-negative organism
020.2	Septicemic plague
768.5	Severe birth asphyxia
768.73	Severe hypoxic-ischemic encephalopathy
642.53	Severe pre-eclampsia, antepartum
642.54	Severe pre-eclampsia, postpartum condition or complication
642.51	Severe pre-eclampsia, with delivery
642.52	Severe pre-eclampsia, with delivery, with current postpartum complication
995.92	Severe sepsis
669.13	Shock during or following labor and delivery, antepartum shock
669.14	Shock during or following labor and delivery, postpartum condition or complication
669.12	Shock during or following labor and delivery, with delivery, with mention of postpartum complication
669.11	Shock during or following labor and delivery, with delivery, with or without mention of antepartum condition
639.5	Shock following abortion or ectopic and molar pregnancies
282.42	Sickle-cell thalassemia with crisis
282.64	Sickle-cell/Hb-C disease with crisis
863.54	Sigmoid colon injury with open wound into cavity
863.30	Small intestine injury, unspecified site, with open wound into cavity
865.11	Spleen hematoma, without rupture of capsule, with open wound into cavity

865.03	Spleen laceration extending into parenchyma without mention of open wound into cavity
865.13	Spleen laceration extending into parenchyma, with open wound into cavity
902.23	Splenic artery injury
902.34	Splenic vein injury
567.23	Spontaneous bacterial peritonitis
512.0	Spontaneous tension pneumothorax
062.3	St. Louis encephalitis
777.51	Stage I necrotizing enterocolitis in newborn
777.52	Stage II necrotizing enterocolitis in newborn
777.53	Stage III necrotizing enterocolitis in newborn
320.3	Staphylococcal meningitis
863.1	Stomach injury with open wound into cavity
320.2	Streptococcal meningitis
038.0	Streptococcal septicemia
430	Subarachnoid hemorrhage
852.12	Subarachnoid hemorrhage following injury, with open intracranial wound, brief (less than 1 hour) loss of consciousness
852.16	Subarachnoid hemorrhage following injury, with open intracranial wound, loss of consciousness of unspecified duration
852.13	Subarachnoid hemorrhage following injury, with open intracranial wound, moderate (1-24 hours) loss of consciousness
852.11	Subarachnoid hemorrhage following injury, with open intracranial wound, no loss of consciousness
852.14	Subarachnoid hemorrhage following injury, with open intracranial wound, prolonged (more than 24 hours) loss of consciousness and return to pre-existing conscious level
852.15	Subarachnoid hemorrhage following injury, with open intracranial wound, prolonged (more than 24 hours) loss of consciousness, without return to pre-existing conscious level
852.19	Subarachnoid hemorrhage following injury, with open intracranial wound, unspecified concussion
852.10	Subarachnoid hemorrhage following injury, with open intracranial wound, unspecified state of consciousness
852.02	Subarachnoid hemorrhage following injury, without mention of open intracranial wound, brief (less than 1 hour) loss of consciousness
852.06	Subarachnoid hemorrhage following injury, without mention of open intracranial wound, loss of consciousness of unspecified duration
852.03	Subarachnoid hemorrhage following injury, without mention of open intracranial wound, moderate (1-24 hours) loss of consciousness
852.01	Subarachnoid hemorrhage following injury, without mention of open intracranial wound, no loss of consciousness
852.04	Subarachnoid hemorrhage following injury, without mention of open intracranial wound, prolonged (more than 24 hours) loss of consciousness and return to pre-existing conscious level
852.05	Subarachnoid hemorrhage following injury, without mention of open intracranial wound, prolonged (more than 24 hours) loss of consciousness, without return to pre-existing conscious level
852.09	Subarachnoid hemorrhage following injury, without mention of open intracranial wound, unspecified concussion
852.00	Subarachnoid hemorrhage following injury, without mention of open intracranial wound, unspecified state of consciousness
767.0	Subdural and cerebral hemorrhage, birth trauma
432.1	Subdural hemorrhage
852.32	Subdural hemorrhage following injury, with open intracranial wound, brief (less than 1 hour) loss of consciousness
852.36	Subdural hemorrhage following injury, with open intracranial wound, loss of consciousness of unspecified duration
852.33	Subdural hemorrhage following injury, with open intracranial wound, moderate (1-24 hours) loss of consciousness

852.31	Subdural hemorrhage following injury, with open intracranial wound, no loss of consciousness
852.34	Subdural hemorrhage following injury, with open intracranial wound, prolonged (more than 24 hours) loss of consciousness and return to pre-existing conscious level
852.35	Subdural hemorrhage following injury, with open intracranial wound, prolonged (more than 24 hours) loss of consciousness, without return to pre-existing conscious level
852.30	Subdural hemorrhage following injury, with open intracranial wound, state of consciousness unspecified
852.39	Subdural hemorrhage following injury, with open intracranial wound, unspecified concussion
852.22	Subdural hemorrhage following injury, without mention of open intracranial wound, brief (less than one hour) loss of consciousness
852.26	Subdural hemorrhage following injury, without mention of open intracranial wound, loss of consciousness of unspecified duration
852.23	Subdural hemorrhage following injury, without mention of open intracranial wound, moderate (1-24 hours) loss of consciousness
852.21	Subdural hemorrhage following injury, without mention of open intracranial wound, no loss of consciousness
852.24	Subdural hemorrhage following injury, without mention of open intracranial wound, prolonged (more than 24 hours) loss of consciousness and return to pre-existing conscious level
852.25	Subdural hemorrhage following injury, without mention of open intracranial wound, prolonged (more than 24 hours) loss of consciousness, without return to pre-existing conscious level
852.29	Subdural hemorrhage following injury, without mention of open intracranial wound, unspecified concussion
852.20	Subdural hemorrhage following injury, without mention of open intracranial wound, unspecified state of consciousness
904.1	Superficial femoral artery injury
902.25	Superior mesenteric artery (trunk) injury
901.2	Superior vena cava injury
516.63	Surfactant mutations of the lung
094.81	Syphilitic encephalitis
094.2	Syphilitic meningitis
094.87	Syphilitic ruptured cerebral aneurysm
995.94	Systemic inflammatory response syndrome due to noninfectious process with acute organ dysfunction
952.10	T1-T6 level spinal cord injury, unspecified
952.12	T1-T6 level with anterior cord syndrome
952.13	T1-T6 level with central cord syndrome
952.11	T1-T6 level with complete lesion of spinal cord
952.14	T1-T6 level with other specified spinal cord injury
952.15	T7-T12 level spinal cord injury, unspecified
952.17	T7-T12 level with anterior cord syndrome
952.18	T7-T12 level with central cord syndrome
952.16	T7-T12 level with complete lesion of spinal cord
952.19	T7-T12 level with other specified spinal cord injury
037	Tetanus
771.3	Tetanus neonatorum
745.2	Tetralogy of Fallot
441.1	Thoracic aneurysm, ruptured
901.0	Thoracic aorta injury
441.6	Thoracoabdominal aneurysm, ruptured
644.03	Threatened premature labor, antepartum
446.6	Thrombotic microangiopathy
242.41	Thyrotoxicosis from ectopic thyroid nodule with mention of thyrotoxic crisis or storm
242.81	Thyrotoxicosis of other specified origin with mention of thyrotoxic crisis or storm
242.91	Thyrotoxicosis without mention of goiter or other cause, with mention of thyrotoxic crisis or storm

242.01	Toxic diffuse goiter with mention of thyrotoxic crisis or storm
323.71	Toxic encephalitis and encephalomyelitis
349.82	Toxic encephalopathy
242.21	Toxic multinodular goiter with mention of thyrotoxic crisis or storm
323.72	Toxic myelitis
422.93	Toxic myocarditis
242.31	Toxic nodular goiter, unspecified type, with mention of thyrotoxic crisis or storm
040.82	Toxic shock syndrome
242.11	Toxic uninodular goiter with mention of thyrotoxic crisis or storm
530.84	Tracheoesophageal fistula
776.7	Transient neonatal neutropenia
776.1	Transient neonatal thrombocytopenia
745.11	Transposition of great vessels, double outlet right ventricle
863.52	Transverse colon injury with open wound into cavity
887.7	Traumatic amputation of arm and hand (complete) (partial), bilateral (any level), complicated
887.6	Traumatic amputation of arm and hand (complete) (partial), bilateral (any level), without mention of complication
896.3	Traumatic amputation of foot (complete) (partial), bilateral, complicated
896.2	Traumatic amputation of foot (complete) (partial), bilateral, without mention of complication
897.7	Traumatic amputation of leg(s) (complete) (partial), bilateral (any level), complicated
897.6	Traumatic amputation of leg(s) (complete) (partial), bilateral (any level), without mention of complication
958.5	Traumatic anuria
860.3	Traumatic hemothorax with open wound into thorax
860.2	Traumatic hemothorax without mention of open wound into thorax
860.5	Traumatic pneumohemothorax with open wound into thorax
860.4	Traumatic pneumohemothorax without mention of open wound into thorax
860.1	Traumatic pneumothorax with open wound into thorax
958.4	Traumatic shock
013.21	Tuberculoma of brain, bacteriological or histological examination not done
013.22	Tuberculoma of brain, bacteriological or histological examination unknown (at present)
013.20	Tuberculoma of brain, confirmation unspecified
013.23	Tuberculoma of brain, tubercle bacilli found (in sputum) by microscopy
013.24	Tuberculoma of brain, tubercle bacilli not found (in sputum) by microscopy, but found by bacterial culture
013.25	Tuberculoma of brain, tubercle bacilli not found by bacteriological examination, but tuberculosis confirmed histologically
013.26	Tuberculoma of brain, tubercle bacilli not found by bacteriological or histological examination, but tuberculosis confirmed by other methods [inoculation of animals]
013.11	Tuberculoma of meninges, bacteriological or histological examination not done
013.12	Tuberculoma of meninges, bacteriological or histological examination unknown (at present)
013.10	Tuberculoma of meninges, confirmation unspecified
013.13	Tuberculoma of meninges, tubercle bacilli found (in sputum) by microscopy
013.14	Tuberculoma of meninges, tubercle bacilli not found (in sputum) by microscopy, but found by bacterial culture
013.15	Tuberculoma of meninges, tubercle bacilli not found by bacteriological examination, but tuberculosis confirmed histologically

013.16	Tuberculoma of meninges, tubercle bacilli not found by bacteriological or histological examination but tuberculosis confirmed by other methods [inoculation of animals]
013.41	Tuberculoma of spinal cord, bacteriological or histological examination not done
013.42	Tuberculoma of spinal cord, bacteriological or histological examination unknown (at present)
013.40	Tuberculoma of spinal cord, confirmation unspecified
013.43	Tuberculoma of spinal cord, tubercle bacilli found (in sputum) by microscopy
013.44	Tuberculoma of spinal cord, tubercle bacilli not found (in sputum) by microscopy, but found by bacterial culture
013.45	Tuberculoma of spinal cord, tubercle bacilli not found by bacteriological examination, but tuberculosis confirmed histologically
013.46	Tuberculoma of spinal cord, tubercle bacilli not found by bacteriological or histological examination, but tuberculosis confirmed by other methods [inoculation of animals]
013.31	Tuberculous abscess of brain, bacteriological or histological examination not done
013.32	Tuberculous abscess of brain, bacteriological or histological examination unknown (at present)
013.30	Tuberculous abscess of brain, confirmation unspecified
013.33	Tuberculous abscess of brain, tubercle bacilli found (in sputum) by microscopy
013.34	Tuberculous abscess of brain, tubercle bacilli not found (in sputum) by microscopy, but found by bacterial culture
013.35	Tuberculous abscess of brain, tubercle bacilli not found by bacteriological examination, but tuberculosis confirmed histologically
013.36	Tuberculous abscess of brain, tubercle bacilli not found by bacteriological or histological examination, but tuberculosis confirmed by other methods [inoculation of animals]
013.51	Tuberculous abscess of spinal cord, bacteriological or histological examination not done
013.52	Tuberculous abscess of spinal cord, bacteriological or histological examination unknown (at present)
013.50	Tuberculous abscess of spinal cord, confirmation unspecified
013.53	Tuberculous abscess of spinal cord, tubercle bacilli found (in sputum) by microscopy
013.54	Tuberculous abscess of spinal cord, tubercle bacilli not found (in sputum) by microscopy, but found by bacterial culture
013.55	Tuberculous abscess of spinal cord, tubercle bacilli not found by bacteriological examination, but tuberculosis confirmed histologically
013.56	Tuberculous abscess of spinal cord, tubercle bacilli not found by bacteriological or histological examination, but tuberculosis confirmed by other methods [inoculation of animals]
013.61	Tuberculous encephalitis or myelitis, bacteriological or histological examination not done
013.62	Tuberculous encephalitis or myelitis, bacteriological or histological examination unknown (at present)
013.60	Tuberculous encephalitis or myelitis, confirmation unspecified
013.63	Tuberculous encephalitis or myelitis, tubercle bacilli found (in sputum) by microscopy
013.64	Tuberculous encephalitis or myelitis, tubercle bacilli not found (in sputum) by microscopy, but found by bacterial culture
013.65	Tuberculous encephalitis or myelitis, tubercle bacilli not found by bacteriological examination, but tuberculosis confirmed histologically
013.66	Tuberculous encephalitis or myelitis, tubercle bacilli not found by bacteriological or histological examination, but tuberculosis confirmed by other methods [inoculation of animals]
013.01	Tuberculous meningitis, bacteriological or histological examination not done
013.02	Tuberculous meningitis, bacteriological or histological examination unknown (at present)
013.00	Tuberculous meningitis, confirmation unspecified
013.03	Tuberculous meningitis, tubercle bacilli found (in sputum) by microscopy
013.04	Tuberculous meningitis, tubercle bacilli not found (in sputum) by microscopy, but found by bacterial culture
013.05	Tuberculous meningitis, tubercle bacilli not found by bacteriological examination, but tuberculosis confirmed histologically
013.06	Tuberculous meningitis, tubercle bacilli not found by bacteriological or histological examination, but tuberculosis confirmed by other methods [inoculation of animals]
014.01	Tuberculous peritonitis, bacteriological or histological examination not done
014.02	Tuberculous peritonitis, bacteriological or histological examination unknown (at present)
014.03	Tuberculous peritonitis, tubercle bacilli found (in sputum) by microscopy
014.04	Tuberculous peritonitis, tubercle bacilli not found (in sputum) by microscopy, but found by bacterial culture
014.05	Tuberculous peritonitis, tubercle bacilli not found by bacteriological examination, but tuberculosis confirmed histologically
014.06	Tuberculous peritonitis, tubercle bacilli not found by bacteriological or histological examination, but tuberculosis confirmed by other methods [inoculation of animals]
014.00	Tuberculous peritonitis, unspecified
011.61	Tuberculous pneumonia (any form), bacteriological or histological examination not done
011.62	Tuberculous pneumonia (any form), bacteriological or histological examination unknown (at present)
011.60	Tuberculous pneumonia (any form), confirmation unspecified
011.63	Tuberculous pneumonia (any form), tubercle bacilli found (in sputum) by microscopy
011.64	Tuberculous pneumonia (any form), tubercle bacilli not found (in sputum) by microscopy, but found by bacterial culture
011.65	Tuberculous pneumonia (any form), tubercle bacilli not found by bacteriological examination, but tuberculosis confirmed histologically
011.66	Tuberculous pneumonia (any form), tubercle bacilli not found by bacteriological or histological examination, but tuberculosis confirmed by other methods [inoculation of animals]
277.88	Tumor lysis syndrome
530.21	Ulcer of esophagus with bleeding
551.1	Umbilical hernia with gangrene
518.4	Unspecified acute edema of lung
421.9	Unspecified acute endocarditis
422.90	Unspecified acute myocarditis
482.9	Unspecified bacterial pneumonia
323.9	Unspecified causes of encephalitis, myelitis, and encephalomyelitis
902.20	Unspecified celiac and mesenteric artery injury
434.91	Unspecified cerebral artery occlusion with cerebral infarction
756.70	Unspecified congenital anomaly of abdominal wall
535.51	Unspecified gastritis and gastroduodenitis with hemorrhage
115.94	Unspecified Histoplasmosis endocarditis
115.91	Unspecified Histoplasmosis meningitis
115.93	Unspecified Histoplasmosis pericarditis
115.95	Unspecified Histoplasmosis pneumonia
902.50	Unspecified iliac vessel(s) injury
636.60	Unspecified illegally induced abortion complicated by embolism
636.30	Unspecified illegally induced abortion complicated by renal failure
636.50	Unspecified illegally induced abortion complicated by shock
902.10	Unspecified inferior vena cava injury

861.10	Unspecified injury to heart with open wound into thorax
866.10	Unspecified kidney injury with open wound into cavity
635.60	Unspecified legally induced abortion complicated by embolism
635.30	Unspecified legally induced abortion complicated by renal failure
635.50	Unspecified legally induced abortion complicated by shock
864.10	Unspecified liver injury with open wound into cavity
861.30	Unspecified lung injury with open wound into thorax
322.9	Unspecified meningitis
018.91	Unspecified miliary tuberculosis, bacteriological or histological examination not done
018.92	Unspecified miliary tuberculosis, bacteriological or histological examination unknown (at present)
018.93	Unspecified miliary tuberculosis, tubercle bacilli found (in sputum) by microscopy
018.94	Unspecified miliary tuberculosis, tubercle bacilli not found (in sputum) by microscopy, but found by bacterial culture
018.95	Unspecified miliary tuberculosis, tubercle bacilli not found by bacteriological examination, but tuberculosis confirmed histologically
018.96	Unspecified miliary tuberculosis, tubercle bacilli not found by bacteriological or histological examination, but tuberculosis confirmed by other methods [inoculation of animals]
018.90	Unspecified miliary tuberculosis, unspecified
062.9	Unspecified mosquito-borne viral encephalitis
813.50	Unspecified open fracture of lower end of forearm
808.9	Unspecified open fracture of pelvis
813.30	Unspecified open fracture of shaft of radius or ulna
813.10	Unspecified open fracture of upper end of forearm
567.9	Unspecified peritonitis
020.9	Unspecified plague
904.40	Unspecified popliteal vessel(s) injury
344.00	Unspecified quadriplegia
038.9	Unspecified septicemia
865.10	Unspecified spleen injury with open wound into cavity
634.30	Unspecified spontaneous abortion complicated by renal failure
634.50	Unspecified spontaneous abortion complicated by shock
038.10	Unspecified staphylococcal septicemia
464.51	Unspecified supraglottis, with obstruction
063.9	Unspecified tick-borne viral encephalitis
013.91	Unspecified tuberculosis of central nervous system, bacteriological or histological examination not done
013.92	Unspecified tuberculosis of central nervous system, bacteriological or histological examination unknown (at present)
013.90	Unspecified tuberculosis of central nervous system, confirmation unspecified
013.93	Unspecified tuberculosis of central nervous system, tubercle bacilli found (in sputum) by microscopy
013.94	Unspecified tuberculosis of central nervous system, tubercle bacilli not found (in sputum) by microscopy, but found by bacterial culture
013.95	Unspecified tuberculosis of central nervous system, tubercle bacilli not found by bacteriological examination, but tuberculosis confirmed histologically
013.96	Unspecified tuberculosis of central nervous system, tubercle bacilli not found by bacteriological or histological examination but tuberculosis confirmed by other methods [inoculation of animals]
551.20	Unspecified ventral hernia with gangrene
070.71	Unspecified viral hepatitis C with hepatic coma
070.6	Unspecified viral hepatitis with hepatic coma
480.9	Unspecified viral pneumonia
867.3	Ureter injury with open wound into cavity
867.5	Uterus injury with open wound into cavity
052.1	Varicella (hemorrhagic) pneumonitis
336.1	Vascular myelopathies
758.32	Velo-cardio-facial syndrome
427.41	Ventricular fibrillation
427.42	Ventricular flutter
064	Viral encephalitis transmitted by other and unspecified arthropods
070.0	Viral hepatitis A with hepatic coma
070.21	Viral hepatitis B with hepatic coma, acute or unspecified, with hepatitis delta
070.20	Viral hepatitis B with hepatic coma, acute or unspecified, without mention of hepatitis delta
070.23	Viral hepatitis B with hepatic coma, chronic, with hepatitis delta
070.22	Viral hepatitis B with hepatic coma, chronic, without mention of hepatitis delta
560.2	Volvulus
036.3	Waterhouse-Friderichsen syndrome, meningococcal
066.41	West Nile fever with encephalitis
066.49	West Nile fever with other complications
066.42	West Nile fever with other neurologic manifestation
066.40	West Nile fever, unspecified
062.1	Western equine encephalitis
117.7	Zygomycosis (Phycomycosis or Mucormycosis)

Appendix A — Alphabetic MCC List

Appendix B — MS-DRG Surgical Hierarchy Table

The surgical hierarchy reflects the relative resources requirement of the various surgical procedures of each major diagnostic category (MDC). The hierarchy is based upon variables such as principal diagnosis, surgical class, complications and comorbidities.

Arranging the surgical DRGs in this manner allows for the assignment of patients with multiple procedures related to the principal diagnosis to a surgical DRG that best reflects the resources used in the care of that patient. Since patients can be assigned to only one surgical class for each inpatient stay, patients with multiple procedures related to the principal diagnosis are assigned to the DRG associated with the most resource-intensive surgical class.

Pre MDC

Heart transplant or implant of heart assist system w MCC; w/o MCC	001–002
ECMO or trach w MV 96+ hrs or PDX exc face, mouth & neck w maj O.R.; w/o maj O.R.	003–004
Liver transplant w MCC; w/o MCC or intestinal transplant	005–006
Allogeneic bone marrow transplant	014
Lung transplant	007
Simultaneous pancreas/kidney transplant	008
Autologous bone marrow transplant w CC/MCC; w/o CC/MCC	016–017
Pancreas transplant	010
Tracheostomy for face, mouth & neck diagnoses w MCC; w CC; w/o CC/MCC	011–013
Multiple Significant Trauma	955-959
HIV Infections	969–970

MDC 1   DISEASES & DISORDERS OF THE NERVOUS SYSTEM

Intracranial vascular procedures w PDX hemorrhage w MCC; w CC; w/o CC/MCC	020–022
Cranio w major dev impl/acute complex CNS PDX w MCC or chemo implant	023
Cranio w major dev impl/acute complex CNS PDX w/o MCC	024
Craniotomy & endovascular intracranial procedures w MCC; w CC; w/o CC/MCC	025–027
Spinal procedures w MCC; w CC or spinal neurostimulators; w/o CC/MCC	028-030
Ventricular shunt procedures w MCC; w CC; w/o CC/MCC	031–033
Carotid artery stent procedure w MCC; w CC; w/o CC/MCC	034–036
Extracranial procedures w MCC; w CC; w/o CC/MCC	037–039
Periph/cranial nerve & other nerv syst proc w MCC; w CC or periph neurostim; w/o CC/MCC	040-042

MDC 2   DISEASES & DISORDERS OF THE EYE

Orbital procedures w CC/MCC; w/o CC/MCC	113–114
Extraocular procedures except orbit	115
Intraocular procedures w CC/MCC; w/o CC/MCC	116–117

MDC 3   DISEASES & DISORDERS OF THE EAR, NOSE, MOUTH & THROAT

Major head & neck procedures w CC/MCC or major device; w/o CC/MCC	129–130
Cranial/facial procedures w CC/MCC; w/o CC/MCC	131–132
Other ear, nose, mouth & throat O.R. procedures w CC/MCC; w/o CC/MCC	133–134
Sinus & mastoid procedures w CC/MCC; w/o CC/MCC	135–136
Mouth procedures w CC/MCC; w/o CC/MCC	137–138
Salivary gland procedures	139

MDC 4   DISEASES & DISORDERS OF THE RESPIRATORY SYSTEM

Major chest procedures w MCC; w CC; w/o CC/MCC	163–165
Other resp system O.R. procedures w MCC; w CC; w/o CC/MCC	166–168

MDC 5   DISEASES & DISORDERS OF THE CIRCULATORY SYSTEM

Other heart assist system implant	215
Cardiac valve & oth maj cardiothoracic proc w or w/o card cath w MCC; w CC; w/o CC/MCC	216–221
Cardiac defib implant w cardiac cath w; w/o AMI/HF/shock w MCC; w/o MCC	222–225
Cardiac defibrillator implant w/o cardiac cath w MCC; w/o MCC	226–227
Other cardiothoracic procedures w MCC; w CC; w/o CC/MCC	228–230
Coronary bypass w PTCA w MCC; w/o MCC	231–232
Coronary bypass w cardiac cath w MCC; w/o MCC	233–234
Coronary bypass w/o cardiac cath w MCC; w/o MCC	235–236
Major cardiovasc procedures w MCC	237
Major cardiovasc procedures w/o MCC	238
Amputation for circ sys disorders exc upper limb & toe w MCC; w CC; w/o CC/MCC	239–241
Permanent cardiac pacemaker implant w MCC; w CC; w/o CC/MCC	242–244
AICD generator procedures	245
AICD lead procedures	265
Perc cardiovasc proc w drug-eluting stent w MCC or 4+ vessels/stents	246
Perc cardiovasc proc w drug-eluting stent w/o MCC	247
Perc cardiovasc proc w non-drug-eluting stent w MCC or 4+ vessels/stents	248
Perc cardiovasc proc w non-drug-eluting stent w/o MCC	249
Perc cardiovasc proc w/o coronary artery stent w MCC; w/o MCC	250–251
Other vascular procedures w MCC; w CC; w/o CC/MCC	252–254
Upper limb & toe amputation for circ system disorders w MCC; w CC; w/o CC/MCC	255–257
Cardiac pacemaker device replacement w MCC; w/o MCC	258–259
Cardiac pacemaker revision except device replacement w MCC; w CC; w/o CC/MCC	260–262
Vein ligation & stripping	263
Other circulatory system O.R. procedures	264

MDC 6   DISEASES & DISORDERS OF THE DIGESTIVE SYSTEM

Stomach, esophageal & duodenal proc w MCC; w CC; w/o CC/MCC	326–328
Major small & large bowel procedures w MCC; w CC; w/o CC/MCC	329–331
Rectal resection w MCC; w CC; w/o CC/MCC	332–334
Peritoneal adhesiolysis w MCC; w CC; w/o CC/MCC	335–337
Appendectomy w; w/o complicated principal diag w MCC; w CC; w/o CC/MCC	338–343
Minor small & large bowel procedures w MCC; w CC; w/o CC/MCC	344–346
Anal & stomal procedures w MCC; w CC; w/o CC/MCC	347–349
Inguinal & femoral hernia procedures w MCC; w CC; w/o CC/MCC	350–352
Hernia procedures except inguinal & femoral w MCC; w CC; w/o CC/MCC	353–355
Other digestive system O.R. procedures w MCC; w CC; w/o CC/MCC	356–358

MDC 7   DISEASES & DISORDERS OF THE HEPATOBILIARY SYSTEM & PANCREAS

Pancreas, liver & shunt procedures w MCC; w CC; w/o CC/MCC	405–407
Biliary tract proc except only cholecyst w or w/o c.d.e. w MCC; w CC; w/o CC/MCC	408–410
Cholecystectomy w c.d.e. w MCC; w CC; w/o CC/MCC	411–413
Cholecystectomy except by laparoscope w/o c.d.e. w MCC; w CC; w/o CC/MCC	414–416
Laparoscopic cholecystectomy w/o c.d.e. w MCC; w CC; w/o CC/MCC	417–419
Hepatobiliary diagnostic procedures w MCC; w CC; w/o CC/MCC	420–422
Other hepatobiliary or pancreas O.R. procedures w MCC; w CC; w/o CC/MCC	423–425

MDC 8   DISEASES & DISORDERS OF THE MUSCULOSKELETAL SYSTEM & CONNECTIVE TISSUE

Combined anterior/posterior spinal fusion w MCC; w CC; w/o CC/MCC	453–455
Spinal fus exc cerv w spinal curv/malig/infec or 9+ fus w MCC; w CC; w/o CC/MCC	456–458
Spinal fusion except cervical w MCC; w/o MCC	459–460
Bilateral or multiple major joint procs of lower extremity w MCC; w/o MCC	461–462
Wnd debrid & skn graft exc hand, for musculo-conn tiss dis w MCC; w CC; w/o CC/MCC	463–465
Revision of hip or knee replacement w MCC; w CC; w/o CC/MCC	466–468
Major joint replacement or reattachment of lower extremity w MCC; w/o MCC	469–470
Cervical spinal fusion w MCC; w CC; w/o CC/MCC	471–473
Amputation for musculoskeletal sys & conn tissue dis w MCC; w CC; w/o CC/MCC	474–476
Biopsies of musculoskeletal system & connective tissue w MCC; w CC; w/o CC/MCC	477–479
Hip & femur procedures except major joint w MCC; w CC; w/o CC/MCC	480–482
Major joint & limb reattachment proc of upper extremity w CC/MCC; w/o CC/MCC	483–484
Knee procedures w pdx of infection w MCC; w CC; w/o CC/MCC	485–487
Knee procedures w/o pdx of infection w CC/MCC; w/o CC/MCC	488–489
Back & neck proc exc spinal fusion w CC/MCC; w/o CC/MCC or disc device/neurostim	490–491

MDC 8— Continued

Lower extrem & humer proc except hip,foot,femur w MCC; w CC; w/o CC/MCC	492–494
Local excision & removal int fix devices exc hip & femur w MCC; w CC; w/o CC/MCC	495–497
Local excision & removal int fix devices of hip & femur w CC/MCC; w/o CC/MCC	498–499
Soft tissue procedures w MCC; w CC; w/o CC/MCC	500–502
Foot procedures w MCC; w CC; w/o CC/MCC	503–505
Major thumb or joint procedures	506
Major shoulder or elbow joint procedures w CC/MCC; w/o CC/MCC	507–508
Arthroscopy	509
Shoulder,elbow or forearm proc,exc major joint proc w MCC; w CC; w/o CC/MCC	510–512
Hand or wrist proc, except major thumb or joint proc w CC/MCC; w/o CC/MCC	513–514
Other musculoskelet sys & conn tiss O.R. proc w MCC; w CC; w/o CC/MCC	515–517

MDC 9   DISEASES & DISORDERS OF THE SKIN, SUBCUTANEOUS TISSUE, & BREAST

Skin graft for skin ulcer or cellulitis w MCC; w CC; w/o CC/MCC	573–575
Skin graft exc for skin ulcer or cellulitis w MCC; w CC; w/o CC/MCC	576–578
Skin debridement w MCC; w CC; w/o MCC/CC	570–572
Other skin, subcut tiss & breast proc w MCC; w CC; w/o CC/MCC	579–581
Mastectomy for malignancy w CC/MCC; w/o CC/MCC	582–583
Breast biopsy, local excision & other breast procedures w CC/MCC; w/o CC/MCC	584–585

MDC 10 ENDOCRINE, NUTRITIONAL, & METABOLIC DISEASES & DISORDERS

Amputat of lower limb for endocrine, nutrit, & metabol dis w MCC; w CC; w/o CC/MCC	616–618
O.R. procedures for obesity w MCC; w CC; w/o CC/MCC	619–621
Skin grafts & wound debrid for endoc, nutrit & metab dis w MCC; w CC; w/o CC/MCC	622–624
Adrenal & pituitary procedures w CC/MCC; w/o CC/MCC	614–615
Thyroid, parathyroid & thyroglossal procedures w MCC; w CC; w/o CC/MCC	625–627
Other endocrine, nutrit & metab O.R. proc w MCC; w CC; w/o CC/MCC	628–630

MDC 11   DISEASES AND DISORDERS OF THE KIDNEY & URINARY TRACT

Kidney transplant	652
Major bladder procedures w MCC; w CC; w/o CC/MCC	653–655
Kidney & ureter procedures for neoplasm or non-neoplasm w MCC; w CC; w/o CC/MCC	656–661
Minor bladder procedures w MCC; w CC; w/o CC/MCC	662–664
Prostatectomy w MCC; w CC; w/o CC/MCC	665–667
Transurethral procedures w MCC; w CC; w/o CC/MCC	668–670
Urethral procedures w CC/MCC; w/o CC/MCC	671–672
Other kidney & urinary tract procedures w MCC; w CC; w/o CC/MCC	673–675

MDC 12   DISEASES & DISORDERS OF THE MALE REPRODUCTIVE SYSTEM

Major male pelvic procedures w CC/MCC; w/o CC/MCC	707–708
Penis procedures w CC/MCC; w/o CC/MCC	709–710
Testes procedures w CC/MCC; w/o CC/MCC	711–712
Transurethral prostatectomy w CC/MCC; w/o CC/MCC	713–714
Other male reproductive system O.R. proc for malignancy w CC/MCC; w/o CC/MCC	715–716
Other male reproductive system O.R. proc exc malignancy w CC/MCC; w/o CC/MCC	717–718

MDC 13   DISEASES & DISORDERS OF THE FEMALE REPRODUCTIVE SYSTEM

Pelvic evisceration, rad hysterectomy & rad vulvectomy w CC/MCC; w/o CC/MCC	734–735
Uterine & adnexa proc for ovarian or adnexal malignancy w MCC; w CC; w/o CC/MCC	736–738
Uterine,adnexa proc for non-ovarian/adnexal malig w MCC; w CC; w/o CC/MCC	739–741
Uterine & adnexa proc for non-malignancy w CC/MCC; w/o CC/MCC	742–743
D&C, conization, laparoscopy & tubal interruption w CC/MCC; w/o CC/MCC	744–745
Vagina, cervix & vulva procedures w CC/MCC; w/o CC/MCC	746–747
Female reproductive system reconstructive procedures	748
Other female reproductive system O.R. procedures w CC/MCC; w/o CC/MCC	749–750

MDC 14   PREGNANCY, CHILDBIRTH, & THE PUERPERIUM

Cesarean section w CC/MCC; w/o CC/MCC	765–766
Vaginal delivery w sterilization &/or D&C	767
Vaginal delivery w O.R. proc except steril &/or D&C	768
Postpartum & post abortion diagnoses w O.R. procedure	769
Abortion w D&C, aspiration curettage or hysterotomy	770

MDC 15   NEWBORNS & OTHER NEONATES W CONDITIONS ORIGINATING IN THE PERINATAL PERIOD

None	

MDC 16   DISEASES & DISORDERS OF THE BLOOD AND BLOOD FORMING ORGANS & IMMUNOLOGICAL DISORDERS

Splenectomy w MCC; w CC; w/o CC/MCC	799–801
Other O.R. proc of the blood & blood forming organs w MCC; w CC; w/o CC/MCC	802–804

MDC 17   MYELOPROLIFERATIVE DISEASES & DISORDERS, POORLY DIFFERENTIATED NEOPLASM

Lymphoma & leukemia w major O.R. procedure w MCC; w CC; w/o CC/MCC	820–822
Lymphoma & non-acute leukemia w other O.R. proc w MCC; w CC; w/o CC/MCC	823–825
Myeloprolif disord or poorly diff neopl w maj O.R. proc w MCC; w CC; w/o CC/MCC	826–828
Myeloprolif disord or poorly diff neopl w other O.R. proc w CC/MCC; w/o CC/MCC	829–830

MDC 18   INFECTIOUS & PARASITIC DISEASES, SYSTEMIC OR UNSPECIFIED SITES

Postoperative or posttraumatic infections w O.R. proc w MCC; w CC; w/o CC/MCC	856–858
Infectious & parasitic diseases w O.R. procedure w MCC; w CC; w/o CC/MCC	853–855

MDC 19   MENTAL DISEASES & DISORDERS

O.R. procedure w principal diagnoses of mental illness	876

MDC 20   ALCOHOL/DRUG USE & ALCOHOL/DRUG INDUCED ORGANIC MENTAL DISORDERS

None	

MDC 21   INJURIES, POISONINGS, & TOXIC EFFECTS OF DRUGS

Wound debridements for injuries w MCC; w CC; w/o CC/MCC	901–903
Skin grafts for injuries w CC/MCC; w/o CC/MCC	904–905
Hand procedures for injuries	906
Other O.R. procedures for injuries w MCC; w CC; w/o CC/MCC	907–909

MDC 22   BURNS

Extensive burns or full thickness burns w MV 96+ hrs w skin graft	927
Full thickness burn w skin graft or inhal inj w CC/MCC; w/o CC/MCC	928–929

MDC 23   FACTORS INFLUENCING HEALTH STATUS & OTHER CONTACTS WITH HEALTH SERVICES

O.R. proc w diagnoses of other contact w health services w MCC; w CC; w/o CC/MCC	939–941

MDC 24   MULTIPLE SIGNIFICANT TRAUMA

Craniotomy for multiple significant trauma	955
Limb reattachment, hip & femur proc for multiple significant trauma	956
Other O.R. procedures for multiple significant trauma w MCC; w CC; w/o CC/MCC	957–959

MDC 25   HUMAN IMMUNODEFICIENCY VIRUS INFECTIONS

HIV w extensive O.R. procedure w MCC; w/o MCC	969–970

Appendix C — MS-LTC-DRG Crosswalk

1 The SSO Threshold is calculated as 5/6th of the geometric average length of stay of the MS-LTC-DRG (as specified in §412.529(a) in conjunction with §412.503).

* In determining the MS-LTC-DRG relative weights for FY 2013, these MS-LTC-DRGs were adjusted for nonmonotonicity as discussed in section VII.B.3.g. (step 6) of the preamble of this final rule.

MS-LTC-DRG	MS-LTC-DRG Title	FY 2011 LTCH Cases	Relative Weight	Geometric Avg Length of Stay	Short-Stay Outlier (SSO) Threshold[1]
001	Heart transplant or implant of heart assist system w MCC	0	0.0000	0.0	0.0
002	Heart transplant or implant of heart assist system w/o MCC	0	0.0000	0.0	0.0
003	ECMO or trach w MV 96+ hrs or PDX exc face, mouth & neck w maj O.R.	362	4.1537	60.1	50.1
004	Trach w MV 96+ hrs or PDX exc face, mouth & neck w/o maj O.R.	1,861	2.9793	43.0	35.8
005	Liver transplant w MCC or intestinal transplant	0	0.0000	0.0	0.0
006	Liver transplant w/o MCC	0	0.0000	0.0	0.0
007	Lung transplant	0	0.0000	0.0	0.0
008	Simultaneous pancreas/kidney transplant	0	0.0000	0.0	0.0
010	Pancreas transplant	0	0.0000	0.0	0.0
011	Tracheostomy for face,mouth & neck diagnoses w MCC	1	1.1124	28.4	23.7
012	Tracheostomy for face,mouth & neck diagnoses w CC	3	0.8646	24.0	20.0
013	Tracheostomy for face,mouth & neck diagnoses w/o CC/MCC	0	0.4570	17.7	14.8
014	Allogeneic bone marrow transplant	0	0.7127	20.6	17.2
016	Autologous bone marrow transplant w CC/MCC	0	0.7127	20.6	17.2
017	Autologous bone marrow transplant w/o CC/MCC	0	0.7127	20.6	17.2
020	Intracranial vascular procedures w PDX hemorrhage w MCC	0	0.8315	23.8	19.8
021	Intracranial vascular procedures w PDX hemorrhage w CC	0	0.5687	21.0	17.5
022	Intracranial vascular procedures w PDX hemorrhage w/o CC/MCC	0	0.4570	17.7	14.8
023	Craniotomy w major device implant or acute complex CNS PDX w MCC	1	1.6342	33.5	27.9
024	Craniotomy w major device implant or acute complex CNS PDX w/o MCC	1	0.8646	24.0	20.0
025	Craniotomy & endovascular intracranial procedures w MCC	4	1.6342	33.5	27.9
026	Craniotomy & endovascular intracranial procedures w CC	1	0.4570	17.7	14.8
027	Craniotomy & endovascular intracranial procedures w/o CC/MCC	0	0.4570	17.7	14.8
028	Spinal procedures w MCC	13	1.1124	28.4	23.7
029	Spinal procedures w CC	9	1.1124	28.4	23.7
030	Spinal procedures w/o CC/MCC	0	0.6298	20.9	17.4
031	Ventricular shunt procedures w MCC*	3	1.1124	28.4	23.7
032	Ventricular shunt procedures w CC*	1	1.1124	28.4	23.7
033	Ventricular shunt procedures w/o CC/MCC	0	0.6298	20.9	17.4
034	Carotid artery stent procedure w MCC	0	0.6468	20.7	17.3
035	Carotid artery stent procedurew CC	0	0.6468	20.7	17.3
036	Carotid artery stent procedure w/o CC/MCC	0	0.6468	20.7	17.3
037	Extracranial procedures w MCC	23	1.6342	33.5	27.9
038	Extracranial procedures w CC	3	1.1124	28.4	23.7
039	Extracranial procedures w/o CC/MCC	0	0.6468	20.7	17.3
040	Periph & cranial nerve & other nerv syst proc w MCC	155	1.3376	32.8	27.3
041	Periph & cranial nerve & other nerv syst proc w CC	58	0.9288	28.0	23.3

MS-LTC-DRG	MS-LTC-DRG Title	FY 2011 LTCH Cases	Relative Weight	Geometric Avg Length of Stay	Short-Stay Outlier (SSO) Threshold[1]
042	Periph & cranial nerve & other nerv sys proc w/o CC/MCC	2	0.6468	20.7	17.3
052	Spinal disorders & injuries w CC/MCC*	46	1.2224	34.7	28.9
053	Spinal disorders & injuries w/o CC/MCC*	6	1.2224	34.7	28.9
054	Nervous system neoplasms w MCC	30	0.9078	25.2	21.0
055	Nervous system neoplasms w/o MCC	13	0.4570	17.7	14.8
056	Degenerative nervous system disorders w MCC	1,094	0.8383	24.9	20.8
057	Degenerative nervous system disorders w/o MCC	885	0.5767	23.1	19.3
058	Multiple sclerosis & cerebellar ataxia w MCC	20	0.8646	24.0	20.0
059	Multiple sclerosis & cerebellar ataxia w CC	14	0.8646	24.0	20.0
060	Multiple sclerosis & cerebellar ataxia w/o CC/MCC	4	0.4570	17.7	14.8
061	Acute ischemic stroke w use of thrombolytic agent w MCC	0	0.8209	23.6	19.7
062	Acute ischemic stroke w use of thrombolytic agent w CC	0	0.6539	22.7	18.9
063	Acute ischemic stroke w use of thrombolytic agent w/o CC/MCC	0	0.6468	20.7	17.3
064	Intracranial hemorrhage or cerebral infarction w MCC	145	0.8315	23.8	19.8
065	Intracranial hemorrhage or cerebral infarction w CC	48	0.5687	21.0	17.5
066	Intracranial hemorrhage or cerebral infarction w/o CC/MCC	5	0.4570	17.7	14.8
067	Nonspecific cva & precerebral occlusion w/o infarct w MCC*	1	1.1124	28.4	23.7
068	Nonspecific cva & precerebral occlusion w/o infarct w/o MCC	1	1.1124	28.4	23.7
069	Transient ischemia	15	0.6468	20.7	17.3
070	Nonspecific cerebrovascular disorders w MCC	268	0.8209	23.6	19.7
071	Nonspecific cerebrovascular disorders w CC	109	0.6539	22.7	18.9
072	Nonspecific cerebrovascular disorders w/o CC/MCC	9	0.6468	20.7	17.3
073	Cranial & peripheral nerve disorders w MCC	137	0.8888	24.7	20.6
074	Cranial & peripheral nerve disorders w/o MCC	105	0.6298	20.9	17.4
075	Viral meningitis w CC/MCC	14	0.8646	24.0	20.0
076	Viral meningitis w/o CC/MCC	1	0.4570	17.7	14.8
077	Hypertensive encephalopathy w MCC	6	0.6468	20.7	17.3
078	Hypertensive encephalopathy w CC	2	0.6468	20.7	17.3
079	Hypertensive encephalopathy w/o CC/MCC	0	0.6468	20.7	17.3
080	Nontraumatic stupor & coma w MCC	7	1.1124	28.4	23.7
081	Nontraumatic stupor & coma w/o MCC	2	0.6468	20.7	17.3
082	Traumatic stupor & coma, coma >1 hr w MCC	20	0.8646	24.0	20.0
083	Traumatic stupor & coma, coma >1 hr w CC	12	0.8646	24.0	20.0
084	Traumatic stupor & coma, coma >1 hr w/o CC/MCC	0	0.4570	17.7	14.8
085	Traumatic stupor & coma, coma <1 hr w MCC	110	0.8620	26.8	22.3
086	Traumatic stupor & coma, coma <1 hr w CC	47	0.6587	22.2	18.5
087	Traumatic stupor & coma, coma <1 hr w/o CC/MCC	8	0.4570	17.7	14.8
088	Concussion w MCC	0	0.8620	26.8	22.3
089	Concussion w CC	1	0.4570	17.7	14.8
090	Concussion w/o CC/MCC	0	0.4570	17.7	14.8
091	Other disorders of nervous system w MCC	223	0.9237	24.3	20.3
092	Other disorders of nervous system w CC	97	0.7012	23.4	19.5
093	Other disorders of nervous system w/o CC/MCC	12	0.6468	20.7	17.3

MS-LTC-DRG	MS-LTC-DRG Title	FY 2011 LTCH Cases	Relative Weight	Geometric Avg Length of Stay	Short-Stay Outlier (SSO) Threshold[1]
094	Bacterial & tuberculous infections of nervous system w MCC	246	1.0743	26.9	22.4
095	Bacterial & tuberculous infections of nervous system w CC	85	0.8569	27.2	22.7
096	Bacterial & tuberculous infections of nervous system w/o CC/MCC	13	0.6468	20.7	17.3
097	Non-bacterial infect of nervous sys exc viral meningitis w MCC	62	0.9514	23.1	19.3
098	Non-bacterial infect of nervous sys exc viral meningitis w CC	29	0.6082	19.5	16.3
099	Non-bacterial infect of nervous sys exc viral meningitis w/o CC/MCC	1	0.4570	17.7	14.8
100	Seizures w MCC	58	0.7555	22.6	18.8
101	Seizures w/o MCC	24	0.6468	20.7	17.3
102	Headaches w MCC	4	0.8646	24.0	20.0
103	Headaches w/o MCC	0	0.6468	20.7	17.3
113	Orbital procedures w CC/MCC	0	1.1124	28.4	23.7
114	Orbital procedures w/o CC/MCC	0	0.6468	20.7	17.3
115	Extraocular procedures except orbit	1	1.6342	33.5	27.9
116	Intraocular procedures w CC/MCC	0	1.1124	28.4	23.7
117	Intraocular procedures w/o CC/MCC	0	0.6468	20.7	17.3
121	Acute major eye infections w CC/MCC	14	0.8646	24.0	20.0
122	Acute major eye infections w/o CC/MCC	0	0.6468	20.7	17.3
123	Neurological eye disorders	2	1.1124	28.4	23.7
124	Other disorders of the eye w MCC	7	1.1124	28.4	23.7
125	Other disorders of the eye w/o MCC	8	0.6468	20.7	17.3
129	Major head & neck procedures w CC/MCC or major device	1	1.6342	33.5	27.9
130	Major head & neck procedures w/o CC/MCC	0	0.4570	17.7	14.8
131	Cranial/facial procedures w CC/MCC	0	1.1124	28.4	23.7
132	Cranial/facial procedures w/o CC/MCC	0	0.6468	20.7	17.3
133	Other ear, nose, mouth & throat O.R. procedures w CC/MCC	11	1.6342	33.5	27.9
134	Other ear, nose, mouth & throat O.R. procedures w/o CC/MCC	1	0.8646	24.0	20.0
135	Sinus & mastoid procedures w CC/MCC	2	1.1124	28.4	23.7
136	Sinus & mastoid procedures w/o CC/MCC	0	0.4570	17.7	14.8
137	Mouth procedures w CC/MCC	1	0.4570	17.7	14.8
138	Mouth procedures w/o CC/MCC	0	0.4570	17.7	14.8
139	Salivary gland procedures	0	0.6468	20.7	17.3
146	Ear, nose, mouth & throat malignancy w MCC	48	1.3919	29.0	24.2
147	Ear, nose, mouth & throat malignancy w CC	22	0.8646	24.0	20.0
148	Ear, nose, mouth & throat malignancy w/o CC/MCC	2	0.4570	17.7	14.8
149	Dysequilibrium	2	0.4570	17.7	14.8
150	Epistaxis w MCC	2	0.8646	24.0	20.0
151	Epistaxis w/o MCC	0	0.6468	20.7	17.3
152	Otitis media & URI w MCC	28	0.8209	20.7	17.3
153	Otitis media & URI w/o MCC	22	0.6468	20.7	17.3
154	Nasal trauma & deformity w MCC	80	0.8298	22.1	18.4
155	Nasal trauma & deformity w CC	19	0.6468	20.7	17.3
156	Nasal trauma & deformity w/o CC/MCC	4	0.6468	20.7	17.3
157	Dental & Oral Diseases w MCC	36	0.8378	24.4	20.3

MS-LTC-DRG	MS-LTC-DRG Title	FY 2011 LTCH Cases	Relative Weight	Geometric Avg Length of Stay	Short-Stay Outlier (SSO) Threshold[1]
158	Dental & Oral Diseases w CC	21	0.6468	20.7	17.3
159	Dental & Oral Diseases w/o CC/MCC	3	0.6468	20.7	17.3
163	Major chest procedures w MCC	45	2.1820	36.9	30.8
164	Major chest procedures w CC	3	0.8646	24.0	20.0
165	Major chest procedures w/o CC/MCC	0	0.8646	24.0	20.0
166	Other resp system O.R. procedures w MCC	1,981	2.4181	40.4	33.7
167	Other resp system O.R. procedures w CC	156	1.3492	28.8	24.0
168	Other resp system O.R. procedures w/o CC/MCC	1	0.4570	17.7	14.8
175	Pulmonary embolism w MCC	138	0.8189	21.4	17.8
176	Pulmonary embolism w/o MCC	48	0.5128	17.8	14.8
177	Respiratory infections & inflammations w MCC	4,683	0.8829	22.7	18.9
178	Respiratory infections & inflammations w CC	1,498	0.6907	19.8	16.5
179	Respiratory infections & inflammations w/o CC/MCC	91	0.6050	18.1	15.1
180	Respiratory neoplasms w MCC	111	0.7558	18.7	15.6
181	Respiratory neoplasms w CC*	45	0.5986	17.7	14.8
182	Respiratory neoplasms w/o CC/MCC*	1	0.5986	17.7	14.8
183	Major chest trauma w MCC*	4	1.1124	28.4	23.7
184	Major chest trauma w CC*	1	1.1124	28.4	23.7
185	Major chest trauma w/o CC/MCC	0	0.8646	24.0	20.0
186	Pleural effusion w MCC	128	0.8033	21.3	17.8
187	Pleural effusion w CC	24	0.6468	20.7	17.3
188	Pleural effusion w/o CC/MCC*	3	0.6468	20.7	17.3
189	Pulmonary edema & respiratory failure	11,689	0.9317	22.0	18.3
190	Chronic obstructive pulmonary disease w MCC	2,568	0.7484	19.8	16.5
191	Chronic obstructive pulmonary disease w CC	938	0.6132	17.8	14.8
192	Chronic obstructive pulmonary disease w/o CC/MCC	194	0.4982	15.6	13.0
193	Simple pneumonia & pleurisy w MCC	2,330	0.7476	20.1	16.8
194	Simple pneumonia & pleurisy w CC	1,091	0.6102	18.4	15.3
195	Simple pneumonia & pleurisy w/o CC/MCC	95	0.4838	16.1	13.4
196	Interstitial lung disease w MCC	109	0.7529	20.4	17.0
197	Interstitial lung disease w CC	52	0.6194	18.9	15.8
198	Interstitial lung disease w/o CC/MCC	2	0.4570	17.7	14.8
199	Pneumothorax w MCC	93	0.7444	20.9	17.4
200	Pneumothorax w CC	28	0.6159	20.2	16.8
201	Pneumothorax w/o CC/MCC	1	0.4570	17.7	14.8
202	Bronchitis & asthma w CC/MCC	114	0.6679	19.0	15.8
203	Bronchitis & asthma w/o CC/MCC	4	0.6468	20.7	17.3
204	Respiratory signs & symptoms	129	0.7824	20.3	16.9
205	Other respiratory system diagnoses w MCC	317	0.8824	22.1	18.4
206	Other respiratory system diagnoses w/o MCC	81	0.6963	19.1	15.9
207	Respiratory system diagnosis w ventilator support 96+ hours	15,538	1.9549	32.0	26.7
208	Respiratory system diagnosis w ventilator support <96 hours	2,059	1.0818	21.3	17.8
215	Other heart assist system implant	0	0.8646	24.0	20.0

MS-LTC-DRG	MS-LTC-DRG Title	FY 2011 LTCH Cases	Relative Weight	Geometric Avg Length of Stay	Short-Stay Outlier (SSO) Threshold[1]
216	Cardiac valve & oth maj cardiothoracic proc w card cath w MCC	1	1.6342	33.5	27.9
217	Cardiac valve & oth maj cardiothoracic proc w card cath w CC	0	1.0896	31.2	26.0
218	Cardiac valve & oth maj cardiothoracic proc w card cath w/o CC/MCC	0	0.6468	20.7	17.3
219	Cardiac valve & oth maj cardiothoracic proc w/o card cath w MCC	0	1.1124	28.4	23.7
220	Cardiac valve & oth maj cardiothoracic proc w/o card cath w CC	0	1.1124	28.4	23.7
221	Cardiac valve & oth maj cardiothoracic proc w/o card cath w/o CC/MCC	0	0.6468	20.7	17.3
222	Cardiac defib implant w cardiac cath w AMI/HF/shock w MCC	0	1.6342	33.5	27.9
223	Cardiac defib implant w cardiac cath w AMI/HF/shock w/o MCC	0	1.1124	28.4	23.7
224	Cardiac defib implant w cardiac cath w/o AMI/HF/shock w MCC	0	1.6342	33.5	27.9
225	Cardiac defib implant w cardiac cath w/o AMI/HF/shock w/o MCC	1	1.6342	33.5	27.9
226	Cardiac defibrillator implant w/o cardiac cath w MCC	7	1.6342	33.5	27.9
227	Cardiac defibrillator implant w/o cardiac cath w/o MCC	2	1.6342	33.5	27.9
228	Other cardiothoracic procedures w MCC	0	1.4633	31.2	26.0
229	Other cardiothoracic procedures w CC	0	1.0896	31.2	26.0
230	Other cardiothoracic procedures w/o CC/MCC	0	0.6468	20.7	17.3
231	Coronary bypass w PTCA w MCC	0	1.1124	28.4	23.7
232	Coronary bypass w PTCA w/o MCC	0	0.6468	20.7	17.3
233	Coronary bypass w cardiac cath w MCC	0	1.1124	28.4	23.7
234	Coronary bypass w cardiac cath w/o MCC	0	0.6468	20.7	17.3
235	Coronary bypass w/o cardiac cath w MCC	0	1.1124	28.4	23.7
236	Coronary bypass w/o cardiac cath w/o MCC	0	0.6468	20.7	17.3
237	Major cardiovascular procedures w MCC	9	1.1124	28.4	23.7
238	Major cardiovascular procedures w/o MCC	3	0.6468	20.7	17.3
239	Amputation for circ sys disorders exc upper limb & toe w MCC	151	1.7462	39.7	33.1
240	Amputation for circ sys disorders exc upper limb & toe w CC	55	1.1514	31.8	26.5
241	Amputation for circ sys disorders exc upper limb & toe w/o CC/MCC	0	0.6468	20.7	17.3
242	Permanent cardiac pacemaker implant w MCC	15	1.6342	33.5	27.9
243	Permanent cardiac pacemaker implant w CC	3	1.1124	28.4	23.7
244	Permanent cardiac pacemaker implant w/o CC/MCC	0	1.1124	28.4	23.7
245	AICD generator procedures	1	0.8646	24.0	20.0
246	Percutaneous cardiovascular proc w drug-eluting stent w MCC	7	1.6342	33.5	27.9
247	Percutaneous cardiovascular proc w drug-eluting stent w/o MCC	0	0.6468	20.7	17.3
248	Percutaneous cardiovasc proc w non-drug-eluting stent w MCC	4	1.6342	33.5	27.9
249	Percutaneous cardiovasc proc w non-drug-eluting stent w/o MCC	0	1.6342	33.5	27.9
250	Perc cardiovasc proc w/o coronary artery stent or AMI w MCC	1	1.6342	33.5	27.9
251	Perc cardiovasc proc w/o coronary artery stent or AMI w/o MCC	1	0.8646	24.0	20.0
252	Other vascular procedures w MCC	161	1.4633	31.2	26.0
253	Other vascular procedures w CC	48	1.0896	31.2	26.0
254	Other vascular procedures w/o CC/MCC	0	0.6468	20.7	17.3
255	Upper limb & toe amputation for circ system disorders w MCC	65	1.3863	34.8	29.0
256	Upper limb & toe amputation for circ system disorders w CC	36	0.9482	29.0	24.2
257	Upper limb & toe amputation for circ system disorders w/o CC/MCC	1	0.4570	17.7	14.8
258	Cardiac pacemaker device replacement w MCC	3	1.1124	28.4	23.7

MS-LTC-DRG	MS-LTC-DRG Title	FY 2011 LTCH Cases	Relative Weight	Geometric Avg Length of Stay	Short-Stay Outlier (SSO) Threshold[1]
259	Cardiac pacemaker device replacement w/o MCC	0	0.4570	17.7	14.8
260	Cardiac pacemaker revision except device replacement w MCC	5	1.1124	28.4	23.7
261	Cardiac pacemaker revision except device replacement w CC	2	1.1124	28.4	23.7
262	Cardiac pacemaker revision except device replacement w/o CC/MCC	1	0.4570	17.7	14.8
263	Vein ligation & stripping	4	1.6342	33.5	27.9
264	Other circulatory system O.R. procedures	732	1.1375	30.1	25.1
265	AICD lead procedures	0	1.1124	28.4	23.7
280	Circulatory disorders w AMI, discharged alive w MCC	263	0.7971	21.5	17.9
281	Circulatory disorders w AMI, discharged alive w CC	65	0.6521	20.1	16.8
282	Circulatory disorders w AMI, discharged alive w/o CC/MCC	3	0.4570	17.7	14.8
283	Circulatory disorders w AMI, expired w MCC	52	0.9079	18.1	15.1
284	Circulatory disorders w AMI, expired w CC	9	0.6468	20.7	17.3
285	Circulatory disorders w AMI, expired w/o CC/MCC	0	0.6468	20.7	17.3
286	Circulatory disorders except AMI, w card cath w MCC	10	1.6342	33.5	27.9
287	Circulatory disorders except AMI, w card cath w/o MCC	2	1.1124	28.4	23.7
288	Acute & subacute endocarditis w MCC	619	1.0850	27.1	22.6
289	Acute & subacute endocarditis w CC	184	0.8405	25.3	21.1
290	Acute & subacute endocarditis w/o CC/MCC	13	0.6468	20.7	17.3
291	Heart failure & shock w MCC	1,548	0.7962	20.9	17.4
292	Heart failure & shock w CC	658	0.5976	18.9	15.8
293	Heart failure & shock w/o CC/MCC	44	0.4745	16.8	14.0
294	Deep vein thrombophlebitis w CC/MCC	7	1.1124	28.4	23.7
295	Deep vein thrombophlebitis w/o CC/MCC	0	0.4570	17.7	14.8
296	Cardiac arrest, unexplained w MCC	0	0.7962	20.9	17.4
297	Cardiac arrest, unexplained w CC	0	0.5976	18.9	15.8
298	Cardiac arrest, unexplained w/o CC/MCC	0	0.4745	16.8	14.0
299	Peripheral vascular disorders w MCC	849	0.7967	22.8	19.0
300	Peripheral vascular disorders w CC	648	0.5932	21.1	17.6
301	Peripheral vascular disorders w/o CC/MCC	18	0.4570	17.7	14.8
302	Atherosclerosis w MCC	50	0.8194	21.5	17.9
303	Atherosclerosis w/o MCC	23	0.6468	20.7	17.3
304	Hypertension w MCC	7	1.1124	28.4	23.7
305	Hypertension w/o MCC	9	0.6468	20.7	17.3
306	Cardiac congenital & valvular disorders w MCC	44	1.0197	23.8	19.8
307	Cardiac congenital & valvular disorders w/o MCC	30	0.6446	20.9	17.4
308	Cardiac arrhythmia & conduction disorders w MCC	103	0.6881	20.6	17.2
309	Cardiac arrhythmia & conduction disorders w CC	46	0.5333	17.9	14.9
310	Cardiac arrhythmia & conduction disorders w/o CC/MCC	7	0.4570	17.7	14.8
311	Angina pectoris	6	0.6468	20.7	17.3
312	Syncope & collapse	13	0.4570	17.7	14.8
313	Chest pain	5	0.8646	24.0	20.0
314	Other circulatory system diagnoses w MCC	1,897	0.9645	23.6	19.7
315	Other circulatory system diagnoses w CC	242	0.6837	20.6	17.2

MS-LTC-DRG	MS-LTC-DRG Title	FY 2011 LTCH Cases	Relative Weight	Geometric Avg Length of Stay	Short-Stay Outlier (SSO) Threshold[1]
316	Other circulatory system diagnoses w/o CC/MCC	17	0.6468	20.7	17.3
326	Stomach, esophageal & duodenal proc w MCC	24	1.6342	33.5	27.9
327	Stomach, esophageal & duodenal proc w CC	3	1.6342	33.5	27.9
328	Stomach, esophageal & duodenal proc w/o CC/MCC	0	1.6342	33.5	27.9
329	Major small & large bowel procedures w MCC	36	2.1889	42.2	35.2
330	Major small & large bowel procedures w CC	9	1.1124	28.4	23.7
331	Major small & large bowel procedures w/o CC/MCC	1	0.4570	17.7	14.8
332	Rectal resection w MCC	1	1.6342	33.5	27.9
333	Rectal resection w CC	0	0.6468	20.7	17.3
334	Rectal resection w/o CC/MCC	0	0.6468	20.7	17.3
335	Peritoneal adhesiolysis w MCC	11	1.6342	33.5	27.9
336	Peritoneal adhesiolysis w CC	4	1.1124	28.4	23.7
337	Peritoneal adhesiolysis w/o CC/MCC	0	0.8646	24.0	20.0
338	Appendectomy w complicated principal diag w MCC	0	0.9360	23.9	19.9
339	Appendectomy w complicated principal diag w CC	0	0.6940	21.2	17.7
340	Appendectomy w complicated principal diag w/o CC/MCC	0	0.4570	17.7	14.8
341	Appendectomy w/o complicated principal diag w MCC	0	0.9360	23.9	19.9
342	Appendectomy w/o complicated principal diag w CC	0	0.6940	21.2	17.7
343	Appendectomy w/o complicated principal diag w/o CC/MCC	0	0.4570	17.7	14.8
344	Minor small & large bowel procedures w MCC	1	1.6342	33.5	27.9
345	Minor small & large bowel procedures w CC	1	0.8646	24.0	20.0
346	Minor small & large bowel procedures w/o CC/MCC	0	0.4570	17.7	14.8
347	Anal & stomal procedures w MCC	9	1.6342	33.5	27.9
348	Anal & stomal procedures w CC	3	0.6468	20.7	17.3
349	Anal & stomal procedures w/o CC/MCC	0	0.6468	20.7	17.3
350	Inguinal & femoral hernia procedures w MCC	1	1.1124	28.4	23.7
351	Inguinal & femoral hernia procedures w CC	0	0.4570	17.7	14.8
352	Inguinal & femoral hernia procedures w/o CC/MCC	1	1.1124	28.4	23.7
353	Hernia procedures except inguinal & femoral w MCC	1	1.6342	33.5	27.9
354	Hernia procedures except inguinal & femoral w CC	0	0.6940	21.2	17.7
355	Hernia procedures except inguinal & femoral w/o CC/MCC	0	0.4570	17.7	14.8
356	Other digestive system O.R. procedures w MCC	198	1.5253	36.0	30.0
357	Other digestive system O.R. procedures w CC	31	1.0171	28.2	23.5
358	Other digestive system O.R. procedures w/o CC/MCC	2	0.8646	24.0	20.0
368	Major esophageal disorders w MCC	44	0.8093	21.5	17.9
369	Major esophageal disorders w CC	6	0.6468	20.7	17.3
370	Major esophageal disorders w/o CC/MCC	0	0.4570	17.7	14.8
371	Major gastrointestinal disorders & peritoneal infections w MCC	1,177	0.9360	23.9	19.9
372	Major gastrointestinal disorders & peritoneal infections w CC	306	0.6940	21.2	17.7
373	Major gastrointestinal disorders & peritoneal infections w/o CC/MCC	12	0.4570	17.7	14.8
374	Digestive malignancy w MCC	96	0.8104	21.2	17.7
375	Digestive malignancy w CC*	28	0.5925	19.0	15.8
376	Digestive malignancy w/o CC/MCC*	3	0.5925	19.0	15.8

MS-LTC-DRG	MS-LTC-DRG Title	FY 2011 LTCH Cases	Relative Weight	Geometric Avg Length of Stay	Short-Stay Outlier (SSO) Threshold[1]
377	G.I. hemorrhage w MCC	87	0.7378	21.3	17.8
378	G.I. hemorrhage w CC	35	0.5235	17.5	14.6
379	G.I. hemorrhage w/o CC/MCC	3	0.4570	17.7	14.8
380	Complicated peptic ulcer w MCC	52	0.9321	24.5	20.4
381	Complicated peptic ulcer w CC	17	0.6468	20.7	17.3
382	Complicated peptic ulcer w/o CC/MCC	1	0.4570	17.7	14.8
383	Uncomplicated peptic ulcer w MCC	1	0.4570	17.7	14.8
384	Uncomplicated peptic ulcer w/o MCC	2	0.4570	17.7	14.8
385	Inflammatory bowel disease w MCC*	54	0.8246	20.9	17.4
386	Inflammatory bowel disease w CC*	17	0.8246	20.9	17.4
387	Inflammatory bowel disease w/o CC/MCC	1	0.4570	17.7	14.8
388	G.I. obstruction w MCC	273	0.9551	22.9	19.1
389	G.I. obstruction w CC	56	0.7665	20.9	17.4
390	G.I. obstruction w/o CC/MCC	3	0.4570	17.7	14.8
391	Esophagitis, gastroent & misc digest disorders w MCC	548	0.8787	23.0	19.2
392	Esophagitis, gastroent & misc digest disorders w/o MCC	200	0.6011	19.2	16.0
393	Other digestive system diagnoses w MCC	1,141	1.0599	26.0	21.7
394	Other digestive system diagnoses w CC	369	0.7168	21.8	18.2
395	Other digestive system diagnoses w/o CC/MCC	20	0.4570	17.7	14.8
405	Pancreas, liver & shunt procedures w MCC	15	1.6342	33.5	27.9
406	Pancreas, liver & shunt procedures w CC	1	1.6342	33.5	27.9
407	Pancreas, liver & shunt procedures w/o CC/MCC	0	0.8646	24.0	20.0
408	Biliary tract proc except only cholecyst w or w/o c.d.e. w MCC	1	0.8646	24.0	20.0
409	Biliary tract proc except only cholecyst w or w/o c.d.e. w CC	0	0.8646	24.0	20.0
410	Biliary tract proc except only cholecyst w or w/o c.d.e. w/o CC/MCC	0	0.8646	24.0	20.0
411	Cholecystectomy w c.d.e. w MCC	0	0.8646	24.0	20.0
412	Cholecystectomy w c.d.e. w CC	0	0.8646	24.0	20.0
413	Cholecystectomy w c.d.e. w/o CC/MCC	0	0.8646	24.0	20.0
414	Cholecystectomy except by laparoscope w/o c.d.e. w MCC	2	1.6342	33.5	27.9
415	Cholecystectomy except by laparoscope w/o c.d.e. w CC	1	1.1124	28.4	23.7
416	Cholecystectomy except by laparoscope w/o c.d.e. w/o CC/MCC	1	0.4570	17.7	14.8
417	Laparoscopic cholecystectomy w/o c.d.e. w MCC	15	1.6342	33.5	27.9
418	Laparoscopic cholecystectomy w/o c.d.e. w CC	3	0.6468	20.7	17.3
419	Laparoscopic cholecystectomy w/o c.d.e. w/o CC/MCC	0	0.6468	20.7	17.3
420	Hepatobiliary diagnostic procedures w MCC	1	1.6342	33.5	27.9
421	Hepatobiliary diagnostic procedures w CC	0	0.8646	24.0	20.0
422	Hepatobiliary diagnostic procedures w/o CC/MCC	0	0.8646	24.0	20.0
423	Other hepatobiliary or pancreas O.R. procedures w MCC	28	1.5480	36.6	30.5
424	Other hepatobiliary or pancreas O.R. procedures w CC	2	0.8646	24.0	20.0
425	Other hepatobiliary or pancreas O.R. procedures w/o CC/MCC	0	0.8646	24.0	20.0
432	Cirrhosis & alcoholic hepatitis w MCC	67	0.7153	21.5	17.9
433	Cirrhosis & alcoholic hepatitis w CC	13	0.4570	17.7	14.8
434	Cirrhosis & alcoholic hepatitis w/o CC/MCC	1	0.4570	17.7	14.8

MS-LTC-DRG	MS-LTC-DRG Title	FY 2011 LTCH Cases	Relative Weight	Geometric Avg Length of Stay	Short-Stay Outlier (SSO) Threshold[1]
435	Malignancy of hepatobiliary system or pancreas w MCC	44	0.7529	19.1	15.9
436	Malignancy of hepatobiliary system or pancreas w CC	6	0.4570	17.7	14.8
437	Malignancy of hepatobiliary system or pancreas w/o CC/MCC	0	0.4570	17.7	14.8
438	Disorders of pancreas except malignancy w MCC	370	0.9724	23.3	19.4
439	Disorders of pancreas except malignancy w CC*	111	0.7102	20.1	16.8
440	Disorders of pancreas except malignancy w/o CC/MCC*	4	0.7102	20.1	16.8
441	Disorders of liver except malig,cirr,alc hepa w MCC	194	0.8074	22.5	18.8
442	Disorders of liver except malig,cirr,alc hepa w CC*	73	0.6104	20.6	17.2
443	Disorders of liver except malig,cirr,alc hepa w/o CC/MCC*	10	0.6104	20.6	17.2
444	Disorders of the biliary tract w MCC	150	0.8067	21.1	17.6
445	Disorders of the biliary tract w CC	36	0.5704	19.3	16.1
446	Disorders of the biliary tract w/o CC/MCC	3	0.4570	17.7	14.8
453	Combined anterior/posterior spinal fusion w MCC	1	1.6342	33.5	27.9
454	Combined anterior/posterior spinal fusion w CC	1	1.6342	33.5	27.9
455	Combined anterior/posterior spinal fusion w/o CC/MCC	0	1.6342	33.5	27.9
456	Spinal fusion exc cerv w spinal curv, malig or 9+ fusions w MCC	1	1.6342	33.5	27.9
457	Spinal fusion exc cerv w spinal curv, malig or 9+ fusions w CC	5	1.6342	33.5	27.9
458	Spinal fusion exc cerv w spinal curv, malig or 9+ fusions w/o CC/MCC	0	1.6342	33.5	27.9
459	Spinal fusion except cervical w MCC	0	1.1124	28.4	23.7
460	Spinal fusion except cervical w/o MCC	2	1.6342	33.5	27.9
461	Bilateral or multiple major joint procs of lower extremity w MCC	0	1.6342	33.5	27.9
462	Bilateral or multiple major joint procs of lower extremity w/o MCC	1	1.6342	33.5	27.9
463	Wnd debrid & skn grft exc hand, for musculo-conn tiss dis w MCC	1,148	1.4494	39.0	32.5
464	Wnd debrid & skn grft exc hand, for musculo-conn tiss dis w CC	360	1.1134	33.3	27.8
465	Wnd debrid & skn grft exc hand, for musculo-conn tiss dis w/o CC/MCC	25	0.8583	28.0	23.3
466	Revision of hip or knee replacement w MCC	8	1.1124	28.4	23.7
467	Revision of hip or knee replacement w CC	4	1.1124	28.4	23.7
468	Revision of hip or knee replacement w/o CC/MCC	0	0.8646	24.0	20.0
469	Major joint replacement or reattachment of lower extremity w MCC	2	1.1124	28.4	23.7
470	Major joint replacement or reattachment of lower extremity w/o MCC*	2	1.1124	28.4	23.7
471	Cervical spinal fusion w MCC	1	1.1124	28.4	23.7
472	Cervical spinal fusion w CC	1	1.1124	28.4	23.7
473	Cervical spinal fusion w/o CC/MCC	0	1.1124	28.4	23.7
474	Amputation for musculoskeletal sys & conn tissue dis w MCC	130	1.3907	36.1	30.1
475	Amputation for musculoskeletal sys & conn tissue dis w CC	51	1.0838	34.5	28.8
476	Amputation for musculoskeletal sys & conn tissue dis w/o CC/MCC	1	0.6468	20.7	17.3
477	Biopsies of musculoskeletal system & connective tissue w MCC*	36	1.2940	35.1	29.3
478	Biopsies of musculoskeletal system & connective tissue w CC*	18	1.2940	35.1	29.3
479	Biopsies of musculoskeletal system & connective tissue w/o CC/MCC	2	0.8646	24.0	20.0
480	Hip & femur procedures except major joint w MCC	16	1.6342	33.5	27.9
481	Hip & femur procedures except major joint w CC	8	1.1124	28.4	23.7
482	Hip & femur procedures except major joint w/o CC/MCC	2	0.8646	24.0	20.0
483	Major joint & limb reattachment proc of upper extremity w CC/MCC	2	1.6342	33.5	27.9

MS-LTC-DRG	MS-LTC-DRG Title	FY 2011 LTCH Cases	Relative Weight	Geometric Avg Length of Stay	Short-Stay Outlier (SSO) Threshold[1]
484	Major joint & limb reattachment proc of upper extremity w/o CC/MCC	0	1.6342	33.5	27.9
485	Knee procedures w pdx of infection w MCC*	10	1.1124	28.4	23.7
486	Knee procedures w pdx of infection w CC	17	1.1124	28.4	23.7
487	Knee procedures w pdx of infection w/o CC/MCC	0	0.8646	24.0	20.0
488	Knee procedures w/o pdx of infection w CC/MCC	3	0.8646	24.0	20.0
489	Knee procedures w/o pdx of infection w/o CC/MCC	0	0.8646	24.0	20.0
490	Back & neck procedures except spinal fusion w CC/MCC or disc devices	6	1.6342	33.5	27.9
491	Back & neck procedures except spinal fusion w/o CC/MCC	0	1.6342	33.5	27.9
492	Lower extrem & humer proc except hip,foot,femur w MCC	14	1.1124	28.4	23.7
493	Lower extrem & humer proc except hip,foot,femur w CC	7	1.1124	28.4	23.7
494	Lower extrem & humer proc except hip,foot,femur w/o CC/MCC	4	1.1124	28.4	23.7
495	Local excision & removal int fix devices exc hip & femur w MCC	133	1.4450	38.9	32.4
496	Local excision & removal int fix devices exc hip & femur w CC	37	1.0553	35.0	29.2
497	Local excision & removal int fix devices exc hip & femur w/o CC/MCC	3	0.8646	24.0	20.0
498	Local excision & removal int fix devices of hip & femur w CC/MCC	30	1.3244	38.6	32.2
499	Local excision & removal int fix devices of hip & femur w/o CC/MCC	0	0.8646	24.0	20.0
500	Soft tissue procedures w MCC	243	1.2804	34.8	29.0
501	Soft tissue procedures w CC	49	1.0046	30.7	25.6
502	Soft tissue procedures w/o CC/MCC	4	0.4570	17.7	14.8
503	Foot procedures w MCC	41	1.1973	33.1	27.6
504	Foot procedures w CC*	27	0.9416	29.6	24.7
505	Foot procedures w/o CC/MCC*	3	0.9416	29.6	24.7
506	Major thumb or joint procedures	0	0.4570	17.7	14.8
507	Major shoulder or elbow joint procedures w CC/MCC	2	1.1124	28.4	23.7
508	Major shoulder or elbow joint procedures w/o CC/MCC	0	0.8646	24.0	20.0
509	Arthroscopy	0	0.4570	17.7	14.8
510	Shoulder,elbow or forearm proc,exc major joint proc w MCC	1	0.6468	20.7	17.3
511	Shoulder,elbow or forearm proc,exc major joint proc w CC	1	0.4570	17.7	14.8
512	Shoulder,elbow or forearm proc,exc major joint proc w/o CC/MCC	0	0.4570	17.7	14.8
513	Hand or wrist proc, except major thumb or joint proc w CC/MCC	9	0.8646	24.0	20.0
514	Hand or wrist proc, except major thumb or joint proc w/o CC/MCC	0	0.8646	24.0	20.0
515	Other musculoskelet sys & conn tiss O.R. proc w MCC	89	1.3864	34.3	28.6
516	Other musculoskelet sys & conn tiss O.R. proc w CC	18	1.1124	28.4	23.7
517	Other musculoskelet sys & conn tiss O.R. proc w/o CC/MCC	0	0.4570	17.7	14.8
533	Fractures of femur w MCC	3	0.8646	24.0	20.0
534	Fractures of femur w/o MCC	4	0.8646	24.0	20.0
535	Fractures of hip & pelvis w MCC	8	0.8646	24.0	20.0
536	Fractures of hip & pelvis w/o MCC	7	0.6468	20.7	17.3
537	Sprains, strains, & dislocations of hip, pelvis & thigh w CC/MCC	0	0.4570	17.7	14.8
538	Sprains, strains, & dislocations of hip, pelvis & thigh w/o CC/MCC	0	0.4570	17.7	14.8
539	Osteomyelitis w MCC	2,453	1.0422	30.0	25.0
540	Osteomyelitis w CC	886	0.7950	26.6	22.2
541	Osteomyelitis w/o CC/MCC	108	0.7158	24.9	20.8

MS-LTC-DRG	MS-LTC-DRG Title	FY 2011 LTCH Cases	Relative Weight	Geometric Avg Length of Stay	Short-Stay Outlier (SSO) Threshold[1]
542	Pathological fractures & musculoskelet & conn tiss malig w MCC	36	1.0483	23.3	19.4
543	Pathological fractures & musculoskelet & conn tiss malig w CC*	28	0.6009	19.3	16.1
544	Pathological fractures & musculoskelet & conn tiss malig w/o CC/MCC*	3	0.6009	19.3	16.1
545	Connective tissue disorders w MCC	50	0.9134	24.0	20.0
546	Connective tissue disorders w CC	25	0.6526	24.1	20.1
547	Connective tissue disorders w/o CC/MCC	3	0.4570	17.7	14.8
548	Septic arthritis w MCC	319	0.9142	26.7	22.3
549	Septic arthritis w CC	228	0.7673	25.3	21.1
550	Septic arthritis w/o CC/MCC	23	0.6468	20.7	17.3
551	Medical back problems w MCC	168	1.0333	27.9	23.3
552	Medical back problems w/o MCC	102	0.6809	23.4	19.5
553	Bone diseases & arthropathies w MCC	7	1.1124	28.4	23.7
554	Bone diseases & arthropathies w/o MCC	7	0.4570	17.7	14.8
555	Signs & symptoms of musculoskeletal system & conn tissue w MCC	14	0.8646	24.0	20.0
556	Signs & symptoms of musculoskeletal system & conn tissue w/o MCC	9	0.6468	20.7	17.3
557	Tendonitis, myositis & bursitis w MCC	166	0.9386	25.7	21.4
558	Tendonitis, myositis & bursitis w/o MCC	109	0.7119	23.4	19.5
559	Aftercare, musculoskeletal system & connective tissue w MCC	1,729	0.9194	26.5	22.1
560	Aftercare, musculoskeletal system & connective tissue w CC	1,326	0.7266	25.1	20.9
561	Aftercare, musculoskeletal system & connective tissue w/o CC/MCC	147	0.5913	22.3	18.6
562	Fx, sprn, strn & disl except femur, hip, pelvis & thigh w MCC	11	0.8646	24.0	20.0
563	Fx, sprn, strn & disl except femur, hip, pelvis & thigh w/o MCC	16	0.6468	20.7	17.3
564	Other musculoskeletal sys & connective tissue diagnoses w MCC	372	0.8350	23.6	19.7
565	Other musculoskeletal sys & connective tissue diagnoses w CC	192	0.6488	22.3	18.6
566	Other musculoskeletal sys & connective tissue diagnoses w/o CC/MCC	22	0.4570	17.7	14.8
570	Skin debridement w MCC	2,082	1.2594	34.9	29.1
571	Skin debridement w CC	347	0.9442	29.8	24.8
572	Skin debridement w/o CC/MCC	29	0.6742	24.7	20.6
573	Skin graft &/or debrid for skn ulcer or cellulitis w MCC	641	1.4358	40.7	33.9
574	Skin graft &/or debrid for skn ulcer or cellulitis w CC	87	1.2734	36.7	30.6
575	Skin graft &/or debrid for skn ulcer or cellulitis w/o CC/MCC	4	1.1124	28.4	23.7
576	Skin graft &/or debrid exc for skin ulcer or cellulitis w MCC	17	1.6342	33.5	27.9
577	Skin graft &/or debrid exc for skin ulcer or cellulitis w CC	7	1.1124	28.4	23.7
578	Skin graft &/or debrid exc for skin ulcer or cellulitis w/o CC/MCC	1	0.6468	20.7	17.3
579	Other skin, subcut tiss & breast proc w MCC	975	1.2054	33.0	27.5
580	Other skin, subcut tiss & breast proc w CC	112	0.8478	28.2	23.5
581	Other skin, subcut tiss & breast proc w/o CC/MCC	11	0.6468	20.7	17.3
582	Mastectomy for malignancy w CC/MCC	0	0.8478	28.2	23.5
583	Mastectomy for malignancy w/o CC/MCC	0	0.8646	24.0	20.0
584	Breast biopsy, local excision & other breast procedures w CC/MCC	3	0.8646	24.0	20.0
585	Breast biopsy, local excision & other breast procedures w/o CC/MCC	0	0.6003	21.0	17.5
592	Skin ulcers w MCC	4,116	0.8708	25.9	21.6
593	Skin ulcers w CC	668	0.6544	23.0	19.2

MS-LTC-DRG	MS-LTC-DRG Title	FY 2011 LTCH Cases	Relative Weight	Geometric Avg Length of Stay	Short-Stay Outlier (SSO) Threshold[1]
594	Skin ulcers w/o CC/MCC	34	0.5715	22.3	18.6
595	Major skin disorders w MCC	47	0.7516	22.4	18.7
596	Major skin disorders w/o MCC	33	0.5237	20.8	17.3
597	Malignant breast disorders w MCC	13	0.8646	24.0	20.0
598	Malignant breast disorders w CC	8	0.8646	24.0	20.0
599	Malignant breast disorders w/o CC/MCC	0	0.5237	20.8	17.3
600	Non-malignant breast disorders w CC/MCC	17	1.1124	28.4	23.7
601	Non-malignant breast disorders w/o CC/MCC	1	0.4570	17.7	14.8
602	Cellulitis w MCC	1,385	0.7676	22.6	18.8
603	Cellulitis w/o MCC	1,454	0.5261	18.5	15.4
604	Trauma to the skin, subcut tiss & breast w MCC	29	0.7304	23.1	19.3
605	Trauma to the skin, subcut tiss & breast w/o MCC	41	0.5661	20.7	17.3
606	Minor skin disorders w MCC	87	0.8285	22.9	19.1
607	Minor skin disorders w/o MCC	91	0.6003	21.0	17.5
614	Adrenal & pituitary procedures w CC/MCC	0	1.0484	30.7	25.6
615	Adrenal & pituitary procedures w/o CC/MCC	0	1.0484	30.7	25.6
616	Amputat of lower limb for endocrine,nutrit,& metabol dis w MCC	157	1.4585	37.0	30.8
617	Amputat of lower limb for endocrine,nutrit,& metabol dis w CC	127	1.0529	30.7	25.6
618	Amputat of lower limb for endocrine,nutrit,& metabol dis w/o CC/MCC	2	0.6468	20.7	17.3
619	O.R. procedures for obesity w MCC	1	1.6342	33.5	27.9
620	O.R. procedures for obesity w CC	1	1.1124	28.4	23.7
621	O.R. procedures for obesity w/o CC/MCC	0	1.1124	28.4	23.7
622	Skin grafts & wound debrid for endoc, nutrit & metab dis w MCC	425	1.2884	34.8	29.0
623	Skin grafts & wound debrid for endoc, nutrit & metab dis w CC	425	1.0175	30.7	25.6
624	Skin grafts & wound debrid for endoc, nutrit & metab dis w/o CC/MCC	10	0.6468	20.7	17.3
625	Thyroid, parathyroid & thyroglossal procedures w MCC	1	1.6342	33.5	27.9
626	Thyroid, parathyroid & thyroglossal procedures w CC	0	1.0484	30.7	25.6
627	Thyroid, parathyroid & thyroglossal procedures w/o CC/MCC	0	1.0484	30.7	25.6
628	Other endocrine, nutrit & metab O.R. proc w MCC	129	1.3058	33.4	27.8
629	Other endocrine, nutrit & metab O.R. proc w CC	109	1.0484	30.7	25.6
630	Other endocrine, nutrit & metab O.R. proc w/o CC/MCC	3	0.8646	24.0	20.0
637	Diabetes w MCC	860	0.9127	26.2	21.8
638	Diabetes w CC	1,244	0.7199	23.6	19.7
639	Diabetes w/o CC/MCC	16	0.6468	20.7	17.3
640	Nutritional & misc metabolic disorders w MCC	746	0.8837	22.8	19.0
641	Nutritional & misc metabolic disorders w/o MCC	375	0.6296	20.8	17.3
642	Inborn errors of metabolism	7	1.6342	33.5	27.9
643	Endocrine disorders w MCC	16	0.8646	24.0	20.0
644	Endocrine disorders w CC	12	0.6468	20.7	17.3
645	Endocrine disorders w/o CC/MCC	3	0.4570	17.7	14.8
652	Kidney transplant	0	0.0000	0.0	0.0
653	Major bladder procedures w MCC	0	0.6468	20.7	17.3
654	Major bladder procedures w CC	0	1.1124	28.4	23.7

MS-LTC-DRG	MS-LTC-DRG Title	FY 2011 LTCH Cases	Relative Weight	Geometric Avg Length of Stay	Short-Stay Outlier (SSO) Threshold[1]
655	Major bladder procedures w/o CC/MCC	0	1.1124	28.4	23.7
656	Kidney & ureter procedures for neoplasm w MCC	0	0.8646	24.0	20.0
657	Kidney & ureter procedures forneoplasm w CC	0	0.4570	17.7	14.8
658	Kidney & ureter procedures for neoplasm w/o CC/MCC	0	0.4570	17.7	14.8
659	Kidney & ureter procedures for non-neoplasm w MCC	11	1.6342	33.5	27.9
660	Kidney & ureter procedures for non-neoplasm w CC	3	1.1124	28.4	23.7
661	Kidney & ureter procedures for non-neoplasm w/o CC/MCC	0	1.1124	28.4	23.7
662	Minor bladder procedures w MCC	4	1.1124	28.4	23.7
663	Minor bladder procedures w CC	0	0.8646	24.0	20.0
664	Minor bladder procedures w/o CC/MCC	0	0.6468	20.7	17.3
665	Prostatectomy w MCC	5	1.1124	28.4	23.7
666	Prostatectomy w CC	1	1.1124	28.4	23.7
667	Prostatectomy w/o CC/MCC	0	1.1124	28.4	23.7
668	Transurethral procedures w MCC	10	1.1124	28.4	23.7
669	Transurethral procedures w CC	3	1.1124	28.4	23.7
670	Transurethral procedures w/o CC/MCC	0	1.1124	28.4	23.7
671	Urethral procedures w CC/MCC	0	0.8646	24.0	20.0
672	Urethral procedures w/o CC/MCC	0	1.1124	28.4	23.7
673	Other kidney & urinary tract procedures w MCC	236	1.3480	31.3	26.1
674	Other kidney & urinary tract procedures w CC	35	1.0928	29.1	24.3
675	Other kidney & urinary tract procedures w/o CC/MCC	3	0.8646	24.0	20.0
682	Renal failure w MCC	1,798	0.9172	23.2	19.3
683	Renal failure w CC	456	0.6996	20.4	17.0
684	Renal failure w/o CC/MCC	21	0.4570	17.7	14.8
685	Admit for renal dialysis	10	1.6342	33.5	27.9
686	Kidney & urinary tract neoplasms w MCC	25	0.9133	24.0	20.0
687	Kidney & urinary tract neoplasms w CC	8	0.6468	20.7	17.3
688	Kidney & urinary tract neoplasms w/o CC/MCC	1	0.4570	17.7	14.8
689	Kidney & urinary tract infections w MCC	1,158	0.7067	21.8	18.2
690	Kidney & urinary tract infections w/o MCC	703	0.5306	18.7	15.6
691	Urinary stones w esw lithotripsy w CC/MCC	0	0.8646	24.0	20.0
692	Urinary stones w esw lithotripsy w/o CC/MCC	0	0.4570	17.7	14.8
693	Urinary stones w/o esw lithotripsy w MCC	2	0.8646	24.0	20.0
694	Urinary stones w/ot esw lithotripsy w/o MCC	4	0.4570	17.7	14.8
695	Kidney & urinary tract signs & symptoms w MCC	2	1.1124	28.4	23.7
696	Kidney & urinary tract signs & symptoms w/o MCC	3	0.4570	17.7	14.8
697	Urethral stricture	0	0.4570	17.7	14.8
698	Other kidney & urinary tract diagnoses w MCC	347	0.9025	22.7	18.9
699	Other kidney & urinary tract diagnoses w CC	122	0.6831	20.9	17.4
700	Other kidney & urinary tract diagnoses w/o CC/MCC	9	0.4570	17.7	14.8
707	Major male pelvic procedures w CC/MCC	0	0.6468	20.7	17.3
708	Major male pelvic procedures w/o CC/MCC	0	0.6468	20.7	17.3
709	Penis procedures w CC/MCC	9	1.6342	33.5	27.9

MS-LTC-DRG	MS-LTC-DRG Title	FY 2011 LTCH Cases	Relative Weight	Geometric Avg Length of Stay	Short-Stay Outlier (SSO) Threshold[1]
710	Penis procedures w/o CC/MCC	0	1.6342	33.5	27.9
711	Testes procedures w CC/MCC	14	1.1124	28.4	23.7
712	Testes procedures w/o CC/MCC	0	1.1124	28.4	23.7
713	Transurethral prostatectomy w CC/MCC	1	0.6468	20.7	17.3
714	Transurethral prostatectomy w/o CC/MCC	0	0.6468	20.7	17.3
715	Other male reproductive system O.R. proc for malignancy w CC/MCC	2	0.6468	20.7	17.3
716	Other male reproductive system O.R. proc for malignancy w/o CC/MCC	0	0.6468	20.7	17.3
717	Other male reproductive system O.R. proc exc malignancy w CC/MCC	16	1.1124	28.4	23.7
718	Other male reproductive system O.R. proc exc malignancy w/o CC/MCC	1	0.4570	17.7	14.8
722	Malignancy, male reproductive system w MCC	7	0.8646	24.0	20.0
723	Malignancy, male reproductive system w CC	2	0.6468	20.7	17.3
724	Malignancy, male reproductive system w/o CC/MCC	0	0.6468	20.7	17.3
725	Benign prostatic hypertrophy w MCC	3	1.1124	28.4	23.7
726	Benign prostatic hypertrophy w/o MCC	5	0.6468	20.7	17.3
727	Inflammation of the male reproductive system w MCC	99	0.7168	21.9	18.3
728	Inflammation of the male reproductive system w/o MCC	40	0.4853	17.8	14.8
729	Other male reproductive system diagnoses w CC/MCC	60	0.7771	25.0	20.8
730	Other male reproductive system diagnoses w/o CC/MCC	0	0.6468	20.7	17.3
734	Pelvic evisceration, rad hysterectomy & rad vulvectomy w CC/MCC	0	1.1124	28.4	23.7
735	Pelvic evisceration, rad hysterectomy & rad vulvectomy w/o CC/MCC	0	1.1124	28.4	23.7
736	Uterine & adnexa proc for ovarian or adnexal malignancy w MCC	0	1.1124	28.4	23.7
737	Uterine & adnexa proc for ovarian or adnexal malignancy w CC	0	0.4570	17.7	14.8
738	Uterine & adnexa proc for ovarian or adnexal malignancy w/o CC/MCC	0	0.4570	17.7	14.8
739	Uterine,adnexa proc for non-ovarian/adnexal malig w MCC	0	1.3058	33.4	27.8
740	Uterine,adnexa proc for non-ovarian/adnexal malig w CC	0	1.0484	30.7	25.6
741	Uterine,adnexa proc for non-ovarian/adnexal malig w/o CC/MCC	0	0.8646	24.0	20.0
742	Uterine & adnexa proc for non-malignancy w CC/MCC	1	1.1124	28.4	23.7
743	Uterine & adnexa proc for non-malignancy w/o CC/MCC	0	0.8646	24.0	20.0
744	D&C, conization, laparascopy & tubal interruption w CC/MCC	0	1.1124	28.4	23.7
745	D&C, conization, laparascopy & tubal interruption w/o CC/MCC	0	1.1124	28.4	23.7
746	Vagina, cervix & vulva procedures w CC/MCC	6	1.6342	33.5	27.9
747	Vagina, cervix & vulva procedures w/o CC/MCC	1	0.8646	24.0	20.0
748	Female reproductive system reconstructive procedures	0	1.1124	28.4	23.7
749	Other female reproductive system O.R. procedures w CC/MCC	7	1.1124	28.4	23.7
750	Other female reproductive system O.R. procedures w/o CC/MCC	0	1.1124	28.4	23.7
754	Malignancy, female reproductive system w MCC	20	0.8646	24.0	20.0
755	Malignancy, female reproductive system w CC	5	0.4570	17.7	14.8
756	Malignancy, female reproductive system w/o CC/MCC	1	0.4570	17.7	14.8
757	Infections, female reproductive system w MCC	90	0.9842	25.6	21.3
758	Infections, female reproductive system w CC*	48	0.6171	19.9	16.6
759	Infections, female reproductive system w/o CC/MCC*	6	0.6171	19.9	16.6
760	Menstrual & other female reproductive system disorders w CC/MCC	7	0.8646	24.0	20.0
761	Menstrual & other female reproductive system disorders w/o CC/MCC	0	0.8646	24.0	20.0

MS-LTC-DRG	MS-LTC-DRG Title	FY 2011 LTCH Cases	Relative Weight	Geometric Avg Length of Stay	Short-Stay Outlier (SSO) Threshold[1]
765	Cesarean section w CC/MCC	0	1.1124	28.4	23.7
766	Cesarean section w/o CC/MCC	0	1.1124	28.4	23.7
767	Vaginal delivery w sterilization &/or D&C	0	1.1124	28.4	23.7
768	Vaginal delivery w O.R. proc except steril &/or D&C	0	1.1124	28.4	23.7
769	Postpartum & post abortion diagnoses w O.R. procedure	1	0.8646	24.0	20.0
770	Abortion w D&C, aspiration curettage or hysterotomy	0	1.1124	28.4	23.7
774	Vaginal delivery w complicating diagnoses	0	1.1124	28.4	23.7
775	Vaginal delivery w/o complicating diagnoses	0	1.1124	28.4	23.7
776	Postpartum & post abortion diagnoses w/o O.R. procedure	1	0.6468	20.7	17.3
777	Ectopic pregnancy	0	0.6468	20.7	17.3
778	Threatened abortion	0	0.6468	20.7	17.3
779	Abortion w/o D&C	0	0.6468	20.7	17.3
780	False labor	0	0.6468	20.7	17.3
781	Other antepartum diagnoses w medical complications	0	1.1124	28.4	23.7
782	Other antepartum diagnoses w/o medical complications	0	0.6468	20.7	17.3
789	Neonates, died or transferred to another acute care facility	0	0.6468	20.7	17.3
790	Extreme immaturity or respiratory distress syndrome, neonate	0	0.6468	20.7	17.3
791	Prematurity w major problems	0	0.6468	20.7	17.3
792	Prematurity w/o major problems	0	0.6468	20.7	17.3
793	Full term neonate w major problems	0	0.6468	20.7	17.3
794	Neonate w other significant problems	0	0.6468	20.7	17.3
795	Normal newborn	0	0.6468	20.7	17.3
799	Splenectomy w MCC	1	1.1124	28.4	23.7
800	Splenectomy w CC	1	0.6468	20.7	17.3
801	Splenectomy w/o CC/MCC	0	0.6468	20.7	17.3
802	Other O.R. proc of the blood & blood forming organs w MCC	5	1.6342	33.5	27.9
803	Other O.R. proc of the blood & blood forming organs w CC	3	1.1124	28.4	23.7
804	Other O.R. proc of the blood & blood forming organs w/o CC/MCC	0	1.1124	28.4	23.7
808	Major hematol/immun diag exc sickle cell crisis & coagul w MCC	38	1.0849	24.0	20.0
809	Major hematol/immun diag exc sickle cell crisis & coagul w CC	15	0.6468	20.7	17.3
810	Major hematol/immun diag exc sickle cell crisis & coagul w/o CC/MCC	2	0.4570	17.7	14.8
811	Red blood cell disorders w MCC*	83	0.7127	20.6	17.2
812	Red blood cell disorders w/o MCC*	27	0.7127	20.6	17.2
813	Coagulation disorders	25	0.8188	19.5	16.3
814	Reticuloendothelial & immunity disorders w MCC	37	0.9983	25.6	21.3
815	Reticuloendothelial & immunity disorders w CC	6	0.6468	20.7	17.3
816	Reticuloendothelial & immunity disorders w/o CC/MCC	0	0.6468	20.7	17.3
820	Lymphoma & leukemia w major O.R. procedure w MCC	0	1.1124	28.4	23.7
821	Lymphoma & leukemia w major O.R. procedure w CC	0	1.1124	28.4	23.7
822	Lymphoma & leukemia w major O.R. procedure w/o CC/MCC	0	1.1124	28.4	23.7
823	Lymphoma & non-acute leukemia w other O.R. proc w MCC	2	1.1124	28.4	23.7
824	Lymphoma & non-acute leukemia w other O.R. proc w CC	0	0.6468	20.7	17.3
825	Lymphoma & non-acute leukemia w other O.R. proc w/o CC/MCC	0	1.1124	28.4	23.7

MS-LTC-DRG	MS-LTC-DRG Title	FY 2011 LTCH Cases	Relative Weight	Geometric Avg Length of Stay	Short-Stay Outlier (SSO) Threshold[1]
826	Myeloprolif disord or poorly diff neopl w maj O.R. proc w MCC	0	1.1124	28.4	23.7
827	Myeloprolif disord or poorly diff neopl w maj O.R. proc w CC	0	0.6468	20.7	17.3
828	Myeloprolif disord or poorly diff neopl w maj O.R. proc w/o CC/MCC	0	1.1124	28.4	23.7
829	Myeloprolif disord or poorly diff neopl w other O.R. proc w CC/MCC	2	1.6342	33.5	27.9
830	Myeloprolif disord or poorly diff neopl w other O.R. proc w/o CC/MCC	0	1.1124	28.4	23.7
834	Acute leukemia w/o major O.R. procedure w MCC	20	1.1124	28.4	23.7
835	Acute leukemia w/o major O.R. procedure w CC	9	0.8646	24.0	20.0
836	Acute leukemia w/o major O.R. procedure w/o CC/MCC	1	0.4570	17.7	14.8
837	Chemo w acute leukemia as sdx or w high dose chemo agent w MCC	3	0.8646	24.0	20.0
838	Chemo w acute leukemia as sdx or w high dose chemo agent w CC	2	0.8646	24.0	20.0
839	Chemo w acute leukemia as sdx or w high dose chemo agent w/o CC/MCC	0	0.4570	17.7	14.8
840	Lymphoma & non-acute leukemia w MCC	72	0.9022	21.3	17.8
841	Lymphoma & non-acute leukemia w CC	34	0.6590	19.3	16.1
842	Lymphoma & non-acute leukemia w/o CC/MCC	1	0.6468	20.7	17.3
843	Other myeloprolif dis or poorly diff neopl diag w MCC	9	0.8646	24.0	20.0
844	Other myeloprolif dis or poorly diff neopl diag w CC	15	0.6468	20.7	17.3
845	Other myeloprolif dis or poorly diff neopl diag w/o CC/MCC	0	0.6468	20.7	17.3
846	Chemotherapy w/o acute leukemia as secondary diagnosis w MCC	47	1.4284	30.3	25.3
847	Chemotherapy w/o acute leukemia as secondary diagnosis w CC	31	1.2279	28.3	23.6
848	Chemotherapy w/o acute leukemia as secondary diagnosis w/o CC/MCC	0	1.2279	28.3	23.6
849	Radiotherapy	55	0.8002	22.0	18.3
853	Infectious & parasitic diseases w O.R. procedure w MCC	1,338	1.7545	37.5	31.3
854	Infectious & parasitic diseases w O.R. procedure w CC	77	1.0186	28.3	23.6
855	Infectious & parasitic diseases w O.R. procedure w/o CC/MCC	3	0.4570	17.7	14.8
856	Postoperative or post-traumatic infections w O.R. proc w MCC	449	1.4618	34.0	28.3
857	Postoperative or post-traumatic infections w O.R. proc w CC	164	0.9792	29.3	24.4
858	Postoperative or post-traumatic infections w O.R. proc w/o CC/MCC	8	0.8646	24.0	20.0
862	Postoperative & post-traumatic infections w MCC	1,878	0.9760	25.1	20.9
863	Postoperative & post-traumatic infections w/o MCC	889	0.7052	22.6	18.8
864	Fever of unknown origin	6	1.6342	33.5	27.9
865	Viral illness w MCC	36	0.8633	21.3	17.8
866	Viral illness w/o MCC	16	0.6468	20.7	17.3
867	Other infectious & parasitic diseases diagnoses w MCC	446	1.0800	23.8	19.8
868	Other infectious & parasitic diseases diagnoses w CC	46	0.5939	19.2	16.0
869	Other infectious & parasitic diseases diagnoses w/o CC/MCC	0	0.5939	19.2	16.0
870	Septicemia w MV 96+ hours	1,699	2.0726	29.6	24.7
871	Septicemia w/o MV 96+ hours w MCC	7,604	0.8781	22.9	19.1
872	Septicemia w/o MV 96+ hours w/o MCC	1,068	0.5912	19.7	16.4
876	O.R. procedure w principal diagnoses of mental illness	4	1.6342	33.5	27.9
880	Acute adjustment reaction & psychosocial dysfunction	13	0.4570	17.7	14.8
881	Depressive neuroses	30	0.3610	20.7	17.3
882	Neuroses except depressive	14	0.4570	17.7	14.8
883	Disorders of personality & impulse control	10	0.4570	17.7	14.8

MS-LTC-DRG	MS-LTC-DRG Title	FY 2011 LTCH Cases	Relative Weight	Geometric Avg Length of Stay	Short-Stay Outlier (SSO) Threshold[1]
884	Organic disturbances & mental retardation	89	0.5408	27.3	22.8
885	Psychoses	907	0.4889	23.9	19.9
886	Behavioral & developmental disorders	8	0.4570	17.7	14.8
887	Other mental disorder diagnoses	1	1.6342	33.5	27.9
894	Alcohol/drug abuse or dependence, left ama	1	0.4570	17.7	14.8
895	Alcohol/drug abuse or dependence w rehabilitation therapy	5	0.4570	17.7	14.8
896	Alcohol/drug abuse or dependence w/o rehabilitation therapy w MCC	69	0.4886	24.5	20.4
897	Alcohol/drug abuse or dependence w/o rehabilitation therapy w/o MCC	248	0.4139	24.9	20.8
901	Wound debridements for injuries w MCC	380	1.3428	33.2	27.7
902	Wound debridements for injuries w CC	165	0.9748	28.5	23.8
903	Wound debridements for injuries w/o CC/MCC	13	0.6468	20.7	17.3
904	Skin grafts for injuries w CC/MCC	96	1.2054	36.1	30.1
905	Skin grafts for injuries w/o CC/MCC	2	0.6468	20.7	17.3
906	Hand procedures for injuries	2	1.6342	33.5	27.9
907	Other O.R. procedures for injuries w MCC	173	1.6541	36.7	30.6
908	Other O.R. procedures for injuries w CC	55	0.9848	29.6	24.7
909	Other O.R. procedures for injuries w/o CC/MCC	1	0.8646	24.0	20.0
913	Traumatic injury w MCC	65	0.8344	23.6	19.7
914	Traumatic injury w/o MCC	52	0.5496	19.9	16.6
915	Allergic reactions w MCC	3	1.6342	33.5	27.9
916	Allergic reactions w/o MCC	2	0.4570	17.7	14.8
917	Poisoning & toxic effects of drugs w MCC	33	0.8413	26.0	21.7
918	Poisoning & toxic effects of drugs w/o MCC	4	0.4570	17.7	14.8
919	Complications of treatment w MCC	1,911	1.1253	26.6	22.2
920	Complications of treatment w CC	810	0.7751	23.6	19.7
921	Complications of treatment w/o CC/MCC	45	0.4928	18.6	15.5
922	Other injury, poisoning & toxic effect diag w MCC	12	0.6468	20.7	17.3
923	Other injury, poisoning & toxic effect diag w/o MCC*	2	0.6468	20.7	17.3
927	Extensive burns or full thickness burns w MV 96+ hrs w skin graft	0	0.8646	24.0	20.0
928	Full thickness burn w skin graft or inhal inj w CC/MCC	11	0.8646	24.0	20.0
929	Full thickness burn w skin graft or inhal inj w/o CC/MCC	0	0.8646	24.0	20.0
933	Extensive burns or full thickness burns w MV 96+ hrs w/o skin graft	4	1.1124	28.4	23.7
934	Full thickness burn w/o skin grft or inhal inj	43	0.6829	23.7	19.8
935	Non-extensive burns	60	0.6487	21.6	18.0
939	O.R. proc w diagnoses of other contact w health services w MCC	236	1.4272	33.7	28.1
940	O.R. proc w diagnoses of other contact w health services w CC	79	0.9889	28.2	23.5
941	O.R. proc w diagnoses of other contact w health services w/o CC/MCC	5	0.4570	17.7	14.8
945	Rehabilitation w CC/MCC	851	0.6406	20.5	17.1
946	Rehabilitation w/o CC/MCC	58	0.4280	18.7	15.6
947	Signs & symptoms w MCC	42	0.7858	21.2	17.7
948	Signs & symptoms w/o MCC	15	0.6468	20.7	17.3
949	Aftercare w CC/MCC	2,766	0.7087	21.7	18.1
950	Aftercare w/o CC/MCC	94	0.4491	16.6	13.8

MS-LTC-DRG	MS-LTC-DRG Title	FY 2011 LTCH Cases	Relative Weight	Geometric Avg Length of Stay	Short-Stay Outlier (SSO) Threshold[1]
951	Other factors influencing health status	66	1.7421	30.7	25.6
955	Craniotomy for multiple significant trauma	0	1.6342	33.5	27.9
956	Limb reattachment, hip & femur proc for multiple significant trauma	0	1.1124	28.4	23.7
957	Other O.R. procedures for multiple significant trauma w MCC	1	1.6342	33.5	27.9
958	Other O.R. procedures for multiple significant trauma w CC	1	0.8646	24.0	20.0
959	Other O.R. procedures for multiple significant trauma w/o CC/MCC	0	0.8646	24.0	20.0
963	Other multiple significant trauma w MCC	22	1.1124	28.4	23.7
964	Other multiple significant trauma w CC	12	0.6468	20.7	17.3
965	Other multiple significant trauma w/o CC/MCC	0	0.6468	20.7	17.3
969	HIV w extensive O.R. procedure w MCC	19	1.6342	33.5	27.9
970	HIV w extensive O.R. procedure w/o MCC	0	1.0144	22.7	18.9
974	HIV w major related condition w MCC	251	1.0144	22.7	18.9
975	HIV w major related condition w CC*	52	0.6294	18.3	15.3
976	HIV w major related condition w/o CC/MCC*	2	0.6294	18.3	15.3
977	HIV w or w/o other related condition	30	0.6145	18.5	15.4
981	Extensive O.R. procedure unrelated to principal diagnosis w MCC	1,253	2.1449	39.7	33.1
982	Extensive O.R. procedure unrelated to principal diagnosis w CC	169	1.1182	31.2	26.0
983	Extensive O.R. procedure unrelated to principal diagnosis w/o CC/MCC	6	1.1124	28.4	23.7
984	Prostatic O.R. procedure unrelated to principal diagnosis w MCC	14	1.1124	28.4	23.7
985	Prostatic O.R. procedure unrelated to principal diagnosis w CC	8	1.1124	28.4	23.7
986	Prostatic O.R. procedure unrelated to principal diagnosis w/o CC/MCC	1	0.6468	20.7	17.3
987	Non-extensive O.R. proc unrelated to principal diagnosis w MCC	638	1.7659	36.8	30.7
988	Non-extensive O.R. proc unrelated to principal diagnosis w CC*	115	1.0389	29.5	24.6
989	Non-extensive O.R. proc unrelated to principal diagnosis w/o CC/MCC*	3	1.0389	29.5	24.6
998	Principal Diagnosis Invalid as Discharge Diagnosis	0	0	0.0	0.0
999	Ungroupable	0	0	0.0	0.0

Appendix D — National Average Payment Table

The national average payment for each DRG is calculated by multiplying the current relative weight of the DRG by the national average hospital Medicare base rate. The national average hospital Medicare base rate is the sum of the full update labor-related and nonlabor-related amounts published in the *Federal Register*, FY 2013 Final Rule, Table 1A. National Adjusted Operating Standardized Amounts; Labor/Nonlabor (if wage index greater than 1) or Table 1B. National Adjusted Operating Standardized Amounts; Labor/Nonlabor (if wage index less than or equal to 1). This information is provided as a benchmark reference only. There is no official publication of the average hospital base rate; therefore the national average payments provided in this table are approximate.

DRG		Description	GMLOS	AMLOS	Relative Weight	National Payment Rate
	001	HEART TRANSPLANT OR IMPLANT OF HEART ASSIST SYSTEM W MCC	29.3523	38.4688	26.0295	$139,225.55
	002	HEART TRANSPLANT OR IMPLANT OF HEART ASSIST SYSTEM W/O MCC	15.5281	19.736	13.9131	$74,417.83
T	003	ECMO OR TRACH W MV 96+ HRS OR PDX EXC FACE, MOUTH & NECK W MAJ O.R.	28.2386	34.4649	17.7369	$94,870.42
T	004	TRACH W MV 96+ HRS OR PDX EXC FACE, MOUTH & NECK W/O MAJ O.R.	20.8683	25.5295	10.8833	$58,212.16
	005	LIVER TRANSPLANT W MCC OR INTESTINAL TRANSPLANT	16.0086	21.6633	10.9894	$58,779.66
	006	LIVER TRANSPLANT W/O MCC	7.9985	8.8863	4.7178	$25,234.38
	007	LUNG TRANSPLANT	14.7175	18.2065	9.6127	$51,416.03
	008	SIMULTANEOUS PANCREAS/KIDNEY TRANSPLANT	9.8469	11.3882	5.111	$27,337.51
	010	PANCREAS TRANSPLANT	8.0017	8.6064	3.8954	$20,835.56
	011	TRACHEOSTOMY FOR FACE,MOUTH & NECK DIAGNOSES W MCC	11.889	14.8922	4.8434	$25,906.18
	012	TRACHEOSTOMY FOR FACE,MOUTH & NECK DIAGNOSES W CC	8.5024	9.9821	3.1576	$16,889.24
	013	TRACHEOSTOMY FOR FACE,MOUTH & NECK DIAGNOSES W/O CC/MCC	5.5902	6.4667	1.9566	$10,465.38
	014	ALLOGENEIC BONE MARROW TRANSPLANT	18.6482	25.7956	10.5255	$56,298.37
	016	AUTOLOGOUS BONE MARROW TRANSPLANT W CC/MCC	17.8665	19.931	6.0932	$32,591.06
	017	AUTOLOGOUS BONE MARROW TRANSPLANT W/O CC/MCC	11.0214	14.1589	4.5817	$24,506.41
	020	INTRACRANIAL VASCULAR PROCEDURES W PDX HEMORRHAGE W MCC	14.473	17.5655	9.1016	$48,682.27
	021	INTRACRANIAL VASCULAR PROCEDURES W PDX HEMORRHAGE W CC	11.7505	13.533	6.64	$35,515.77
	022	INTRACRANIAL VASCULAR PROCEDURES W PDX HEMORRHAGE W/O CC/MCC	6.4908	8.0082	4.5056	$24,099.37
T	023	CRANIO W MAJOR DEV IMPL/ACUTE COMPLEX CNS PDX W MCC OR CHEMO IMPLANT	7.9188	11.122	5.2378	$28,015.74
T	024	CRANIO W MAJOR DEV IMPL/ACUTE COMPLEX CNS PDX W/O MCC	4.3294	6.5076	3.5279	$18,869.89
T	025	CRANIOTOMY & ENDOVASCULAR INTRACRANIAL PROCEDURES W MCC	8.1463	10.5416	4.5958	$24,581.83
T	026	CRANIOTOMY & ENDOVASCULAR INTRACRANIAL PROCEDURES W CC	5.3396	6.7972	2.9555	$15,808.26
T	027	CRANIOTOMY & ENDOVASCULAR INTRACRANIAL PROCEDURES W/O CC/MCC	2.7698	3.6327	2.1631	$11,569.90
SP	028	SPINAL PROCEDURES W MCC	9.8874	12.874	5.6028	$29,968.03
SP	029	SPINAL PROCEDURES W CC OR SPINAL NEUROSTIMULATORS	4.6829	6.4115	2.9277	$15,659.56
SP	030	SPINAL PROCEDURES W/O CC/MCC	2.4323	3.202	1.7854	$9,549.68
T	031	VENTRICULAR SHUNT PROCEDURES W MCC	8.5275	11.9631	4.2645	$22,809.79
T	032	VENTRICULAR SHUNT PROCEDURES W CC	3.5887	5.3267	2.0348	$10,883.66
T	033	VENTRICULAR SHUNT PROCEDURES W/O CC/MCC	2.0414	2.6005	1.4381	$7,692.05

Calculated with an average hospital Medicare base rate of $5,348.76. Each hospital's base rate and corresponding payment will vary. The national average hospital Medicare base rate is the sum of the full update labor-related and nonlabor-related amounts published in the Federal Register, FY 2013 Final Rule, Table 1A. National Adjusted Operating Standardized Amounts; Labor/Nonlabor (if wage index greater than 1) or Table 1B. National Adjusted Operating Standardized Amounts; Labor/Nonlabor (if wage index less than or equal to 1).

MS-DRGs 998 and 999 contain cases that could not be assigned to valid DRGs.

Note: If there is no value in either the geometric mean length of stay or the arithmetic mean length of stay columns, the volume of cases is insufficient to determine a meaningful computation of these statistics.

DRG		Description	GMLOS	AMLOS	Relative Weight	National Payment Rate
	034	CAROTID ARTERY STENT PROCEDURE W MCC	4.6966	7.0335	3.6918	$19,746.55
	035	CAROTID ARTERY STENT PROCEDURE W CC	2.1289	3.1736	2.1965	$11,748.55
	036	CAROTID ARTERY STENT PROCEDURE W/O CC/MCC	1.2736	1.5262	1.661	$8,884.29
	037	EXTRACRANIAL PROCEDURES W MCC	5.6434	8.3144	3.187	$17,046.50
	038	EXTRACRANIAL PROCEDURES W CC	2.4285	3.4663	1.5741	$8,419.48
	039	EXTRACRANIAL PROCEDURES W/O CC/MCC	1.3607	1.6293	1.0285	$5,501.20
SP	040	PERIPH/CRANIAL NERVE & OTHER NERV SYST PROC W MCC	8.8522	11.7424	3.868	$20,689.00
SP	041	PERIPH/CRANIAL NERVE & OTHER NERV SYST PROC W CC OR PERIPH NEUROSTIM	5.0374	6.419	2.133	$11,408.91
SP	042	PERIPH/CRANIAL NERVE & OTHER NERV SYST PROC W/O CC/MCC	2.614	3.4373	1.7744	$9,490.84
	052	SPINAL DISORDERS & INJURIES W CC/MCC	4.2659	5.7567	1.4903	$7,971.26
	053	SPINAL DISORDERS & INJURIES W/O CC/MCC	2.9055	3.5073	0.9046	$4,838.49
T	054	NERVOUS SYSTEM NEOPLASMS W MCC	4.2004	5.6827	1.3962	$7,467.94
T	055	NERVOUS SYSTEM NEOPLASMS W/O MCC	3.1932	4.3026	1.0486	$5,608.71
T	056	DEGENERATIVE NERVOUS SYSTEM DISORDERS W MCC	5.3655	7.123	1.7194	$9,196.66
T	057	DEGENERATIVE NERVOUS SYSTEM DISORDERS W/O MCC	3.6393	4.7499	0.968	$5,177.60
	058	MULTIPLE SCLEROSIS & CEREBELLAR ATAXIA W MCC	5.3797	6.9718	1.6472	$8,810.48
	059	MULTIPLE SCLEROSIS & CEREBELLAR ATAXIA W CC	3.8757	4.7303	1.0088	$5,395.83
	060	MULTIPLE SCLEROSIS & CEREBELLAR ATAXIA W/O CC/MCC	3.1012	3.6375	0.7807	$4,175.78
	061	ACUTE ISCHEMIC STROKE W USE OF THROMBOLYTIC AGENT W MCC	5.9662	7.8203	2.8668	$15,333.83
	062	ACUTE ISCHEMIC STROKE W USE OF THROMBOLYTIC AGENT W CC	4.4534	5.2004	1.9551	$10,457.36
	063	ACUTE ISCHEMIC STROKE W USE OF THROMBOLYTIC AGENT W/O CC/MCC	3.2454	3.6983	1.5366	$8,218.90
T	064	INTRACRANIAL HEMORRHAGE OR CEREBRAL INFARCTION W MCC	4.8404	6.6394	1.8424	$9,854.56
T	065	INTRACRANIAL HEMORRHAGE OR CEREBRAL INFARCTION W CC	3.6701	4.4569	1.1345	$6,068.17
T	066	INTRACRANIAL HEMORRHAGE OR CEREBRAL INFARCTION W/O CC/MCC	2.5659	3.0562	0.8135	$4,351.22
	067	NONSPECIFIC CVA & PRECEREBRAL OCCLUSION W/O INFARCT W MCC	4.1454	5.3893	1.5074	$8,062.72
	068	NONSPECIFIC CVA & PRECEREBRAL OCCLUSION W/O INFARCT W/O MCC	2.5794	3.2135	0.8899	$4,759.86
	069	TRANSIENT ISCHEMIA	2.2185	2.6959	0.7449	$3,984.29
T	070	NONSPECIFIC CEREBROVASCULAR DISORDERS W MCC	5.1194	6.8153	1.7056	$9,122.85
T	071	NONSPECIFIC CEREBROVASCULAR DISORDERS W CC	3.7075	4.6823	1.0174	$5,441.83
T	072	NONSPECIFIC CEREBROVASCULAR DISORDERS W/O CC/MCC	2.4528	3.0403	0.7506	$4,014.78
	073	CRANIAL & PERIPHERAL NERVE DISORDERS W MCC	4.0517	5.4049	1.282	$6,857.11
	074	CRANIAL & PERIPHERAL NERVE DISORDERS W/O MCC	3.1476	3.957	0.8837	$4,726.70
	075	VIRAL MENINGITIS W CC/MCC	5.5358	6.9879	1.7611	$9,419.70
	076	VIRAL MENINGITIS W/O CC/MCC	3.2475	3.897	0.8947	$4,785.54
	077	HYPERTENSIVE ENCEPHALOPATHY W MCC	4.7594	6.0142	1.6426	$8,785.87
	078	HYPERTENSIVE ENCEPHALOPATHY W CC	3.2471	4.0205	0.979	$5,236.44
	079	HYPERTENSIVE ENCEPHALOPATHY W/O CC/MCC	2.3618	2.8718	0.7297	$3,902.99
	080	NONTRAUMATIC STUPOR & COMA W MCC	3.7356	5.2224	1.2616	$6,748.00
	081	NONTRAUMATIC STUPOR & COMA W/O MCC	2.6535	3.354	0.7416	$3,966.64

Calculated with an average hospital Medicare base rate of $5,348.76. Each hospital's base rate and corresponding payment will vary. The national average hospital Medicare base rate is the sum of the full update labor-related and nonlabor-related amounts published in the Federal Register, FY 2013 Final Rule, Table 1A. National Adjusted Operating Standardized Amounts; Labor/Nonlabor (if wage index greater than 1) or Table 1B. National Adjusted Operating Standardized Amounts; Labor/Nonlabor (if wage index less than or equal to 1).

MS-DRGs 998 and 999 contain cases that could not be assigned to valid DRGs.

Note: If there is no value in either the geometric mean length of stay or the arithmetic mean length of stay columns, the volume of cases is insufficient to determine a meaningful computation of these statistics.

T *Transfer DRG*   SP *Special Payment*   © 2012 OptumInsight, Inc.

DRG		Description	GMLOS	AMLOS	Relative Weight	National Payment Rate
	082	TRAUMATIC STUPOR & COMA, COMA >1 HR W MCC	3.2658	5.6021	1.9249	$10,295.83
	083	TRAUMATIC STUPOR & COMA, COMA >1 HR W CC	3.3896	4.4527	1.3458	$7,198.36
	084	TRAUMATIC STUPOR & COMA, COMA >1 HR W/O CC/MCC	2.1779	2.7496	0.8696	$4,651.28
T	085	TRAUMATIC STUPOR & COMA, COMA <1 HR W MCC	5.0125	6.8486	2.0387	$10,904.52
T	086	TRAUMATIC STUPOR & COMA, COMA <1 HR W CC	3.3959	4.3172	1.1874	$6,351.12
T	087	TRAUMATIC STUPOR & COMA, COMA <1 HR W/O CC/MCC	2.1839	2.6985	0.7605	$4,067.73
	088	CONCUSSION W MCC	4.0842	5.2852	1.5687	$8,390.60
	089	CONCUSSION W CC	2.7305	3.4071	0.9791	$5,236.97
	090	CONCUSSION W/O CC/MCC	1.7886	2.1717	0.7218	$3,860.73
T	091	OTHER DISORDERS OF NERVOUS SYSTEM W MCC	4.2896	6.0468	1.6583	$8,869.85
T	092	OTHER DISORDERS OF NERVOUS SYSTEM W CC	3.136	3.9848	0.9214	$4,928.35
T	093	OTHER DISORDERS OF NERVOUS SYSTEM W/O CC/MCC	2.2514	2.7648	0.6938	$3,710.97
	094	BACTERIAL & TUBERCULOUS INFECTIONS OF NERVOUS SYSTEM W MCC	8.9102	11.461	3.5656	$19,071.54
	095	BACTERIAL & TUBERCULOUS INFECTIONS OF NERVOUS SYSTEM W CC	6.2788	7.8573	2.4627	$13,172.39
	096	BACTERIAL & TUBERCULOUS INFECTIONS OF NERVOUS SYSTEM W/O CC/MCC	4.4128	5.4906	2.0158	$10,782.03
	097	NON-BACTERIAL INFECT OF NERVOUS SYS EXC VIRAL MENINGITIS W MCC	8.9079	11.5207	3.3714	$18,032.81
	098	NON-BACTERIAL INFECT OF NERVOUS SYS EXC VIRAL MENINGITIS W CC	6.0945	7.6978	1.8418	$9,851.35
	099	NON-BACTERIAL INFECT OF NERVOUS SYS EXC VIRAL MENINGITIS W/O CC/MCC	4.0539	4.9489	1.2427	$6,646.90
T	100	SEIZURES W MCC	4.3196	5.7784	1.557	$8,328.02
T	101	SEIZURES W/O MCC	2.6359	3.2837	0.7643	$4,088.06
	102	HEADACHES W MCC	2.974	4.0938	1.0209	$5,460.55
	103	HEADACHES W/O MCC	2.3106	2.9092	0.6893	$3,686.90
	113	ORBITAL PROCEDURES W CC/MCC	4.142	5.6217	1.8587	$9,941.74
	114	ORBITAL PROCEDURES W/O CC/MCC	2.2352	2.8926	0.9589	$5,128.93
	115	EXTRAOCULAR PROCEDURES EXCEPT ORBIT	3.4219	4.5141	1.2407	$6,636.21
	116	INTRAOCULAR PROCEDURES W CC/MCC	3.4571	5.0969	1.5022	$8,034.91
	117	INTRAOCULAR PROCEDURES W/O CC/MCC	1.743	2.3316	0.7234	$3,869.29
	121	ACUTE MAJOR EYE INFECTIONS W CC/MCC	3.9415	4.8914	0.9589	$5,128.93
	122	ACUTE MAJOR EYE INFECTIONS W/O CC/MCC	3.2225	3.8646	0.6533	$3,494.34
	123	NEUROLOGICAL EYE DISORDERS	2.156	2.6931	0.7542	$4,034.03
	124	OTHER DISORDERS OF THE EYE W MCC	3.5594	4.9211	1.1885	$6,357.00
	125	OTHER DISORDERS OF THE EYE W/O MCC	2.5259	3.1924	0.685	$3,663.90
	129	MAJOR HEAD & NECK PROCEDURES W CC/MCC OR MAJOR DEVICE	3.7186	5.3678	2.15	$11,499.83
	130	MAJOR HEAD & NECK PROCEDURES W/O CC/MCC	2.3199	2.8831	1.2065	$6,453.28
	131	CRANIAL/FACIAL PROCEDURES W CC/MCC	4.239	6.061	2.3443	$12,539.10
	132	CRANIAL/FACIAL PROCEDURES W/O CC/MCC	2.1005	2.6696	1.2362	$6,612.14
	133	OTHER EAR, NOSE, MOUTH & THROAT O.R. PROCEDURES W CC/MCC	3.5961	5.4043	1.7818	$9,530.42
	134	OTHER EAR, NOSE, MOUTH & THROAT O.R. PROCEDURES W/O CC/MCC	1.777	2.2377	0.9177	$4,908.56
	135	SINUS & MASTOID PROCEDURES W CC/MCC	4.0495	5.8928	2.0002	$10,698.59

Calculated with an average hospital Medicare base rate of $5,348.76. Each hospital's base rate and corresponding payment will vary. The national average hospital Medicare base rate is the sum of the full update labor-related and nonlabor-related amounts published in the Federal Register, FY 2013 Final Rule, Table 1A. National Adjusted Operating Standardized Amounts; Labor/Nonlabor (if wage index greater than 1) or Table 1B. National Adjusted Operating Standardized Amounts; Labor/Nonlabor (if wage index less than or equal to 1).

MS-DRGs 998 and 999 contain cases that could not be assigned to valid DRGs.

Note: If there is no value in either the geometric mean length of stay or the arithmetic mean length of stay columns, the volume of cases is insufficient to determine a meaningful computation of these statistics.

DRG		Description	GMLOS	AMLOS	Relative Weight	National Payment Rate
	136	SINUS & MASTOID PROCEDURES W/O CC/MCC	1.765	2.3441	1.0697	$5,721.57
	137	MOUTH PROCEDURES W CC/MCC	3.8222	5.0435	1.3192	$7,056.08
	138	MOUTH PROCEDURES W/O CC/MCC	1.8728	2.3366	0.7388	$3,951.66
	139	SALIVARY GLAND PROCEDURES	1.4204	1.7827	0.8922	$4,772.16
	146	EAR, NOSE, MOUTH & THROAT MALIGNANCY W MCC	6.3227	9.1309	2.2347	$11,952.87
	147	EAR, NOSE, MOUTH & THROAT MALIGNANCY W CC	3.9019	5.3971	1.2486	$6,678.46
	148	EAR, NOSE, MOUTH & THROAT MALIGNANCY W/O CC/MCC	2.4142	3.1523	0.7488	$4,005.15
	149	DYSEQUILIBRIUM	2.0768	2.5208	0.6462	$3,456.37
	150	EPISTAXIS W MCC	3.8197	5.195	1.389	$7,429.43
	151	EPISTAXIS W/O MCC	2.2409	2.7809	0.6458	$3,454.23
	152	OTITIS MEDIA & URI W MCC	3.4353	4.3508	1.0166	$5,437.55
	153	OTITIS MEDIA & URI W/O MCC	2.5263	3.0697	0.6605	$3,532.86
	154	OTHER EAR, NOSE, MOUTH & THROAT DIAGNOSES W MCC	4.3078	5.7036	1.4138	$7,562.08
	155	OTHER EAR, NOSE, MOUTH & THROAT DIAGNOSES W CC	3.2222	4.0519	0.9137	$4,887.16
	156	OTHER EAR, NOSE, MOUTH & THROAT DIAGNOSES W/O CC/MCC	2.2777	2.8094	0.6349	$3,395.93
	157	DENTAL & ORAL DISEASES W MCC	4.6572	6.5589	1.601	$8,563.36
	158	DENTAL & ORAL DISEASES W CC	3.2053	4.1128	0.8988	$4,807.47
	159	DENTAL & ORAL DISEASES W/O CC/MCC	2.1084	2.6172	0.5969	$3,192.67
T	163	MAJOR CHEST PROCEDURES W MCC	11.2791	13.698	5.1193	$27,381.91
T	164	MAJOR CHEST PROCEDURES W CC	5.7767	6.9839	2.6191	$14,008.94
T	165	MAJOR CHEST PROCEDURES W/O CC/MCC	3.4541	4.1391	1.7922	$9,586.05
T	166	OTHER RESP SYSTEM O.R. PROCEDURES W MCC	9.0799	11.4826	3.7513	$20,064.80
T	167	OTHER RESP SYSTEM O.R. PROCEDURES W CC	5.3936	6.793	2.0043	$10,720.52
T	168	OTHER RESP SYSTEM O.R. PROCEDURES W/O CC/MCC	3.1279	4.0947	1.3153	$7,035.22
T	175	PULMONARY EMBOLISM W MCC	5.4917	6.5594	1.587	$8,488.48
T	176	PULMONARY EMBOLISM W/O MCC	3.8676	4.5874	1.0379	$5,551.48
T	177	RESPIRATORY INFECTIONS & INFLAMMATIONS W MCC	6.5882	8.1916	2.0549	$10,991.17
T	178	RESPIRATORY INFECTIONS & INFLAMMATIONS W CC	5.2713	6.3768	1.4403	$7,703.82
T	179	RESPIRATORY INFECTIONS & INFLAMMATIONS W/O CC/MCC	3.8081	4.6274	0.9799	$5,241.25
	180	RESPIRATORY NEOPLASMS W MCC	5.6011	7.2852	1.7567	$9,396.17
	181	RESPIRATORY NEOPLASMS W CC	3.9297	5.1485	1.2108	$6,476.28
	182	RESPIRATORY NEOPLASMS W/O CC/MCC	2.6689	3.448	0.8275	$4,426.10
	183	MAJOR CHEST TRAUMA W MCC	5.0288	6.2189	1.4804	$7,918.30
	184	MAJOR CHEST TRAUMA W CC	3.4928	4.1846	1.0171	$5,440.22
	185	MAJOR CHEST TRAUMA W/O CC/MCC	2.4362	2.9086	0.6961	$3,723.27
T	186	PLEURAL EFFUSION W MCC	4.9412	6.4144	1.5746	$8,422.16
T	187	PLEURAL EFFUSION W CC	3.7231	4.7141	1.1169	$5,974.03
T	188	PLEURAL EFFUSION W/O CC/MCC	2.6437	3.3001	0.7544	$4,035.10
	189	PULMONARY EDEMA & RESPIRATORY FAILURE	4.0767	5.204	1.2461	$6,665.09

Calculated with an average hospital Medicare base rate of $5,348.76. Each hospital's base rate and corresponding payment will vary. The national average hospital Medicare base rate is the sum of the full update labor-related and nonlabor-related amounts published in the Federal Register, FY 2013 Final Rule, Table 1A. National Adjusted Operating Standardized Amounts; Labor/Nonlabor (if wage index greater than 1) or Table 1B. National Adjusted Operating Standardized Amounts; Labor/Nonlabor (if wage index less than or equal to 1).

MS-DRGs 998 and 999 contain cases that could not be assigned to valid DRGs.

Note: If there is no value in either the geometric mean length of stay or the arithmetic mean length of stay columns, the volume of cases is insufficient to determine a meaningful computation of these statistics.

T *Transfer DRG*   SP *Special Payment*   © 2012 OptumInsight, Inc.

DRG		Description	GMLOS	AMLOS	Relative Weight	National Payment Rate
T	190	CHRONIC OBSTRUCTIVE PULMONARY DISEASE W MCC	4.3226	5.2606	1.186	$6,343.63
T	191	CHRONIC OBSTRUCTIVE PULMONARY DISEASE W CC	3.6035	4.3563	0.9521	$5,092.55
T	192	CHRONIC OBSTRUCTIVE PULMONARY DISEASE W/O CC/MCC	2.8697	3.4315	0.7072	$3,782.64
T	193	SIMPLE PNEUMONIA & PLEURISY W MCC	5.1068	6.2678	1.4893	$7,965.91
T	194	SIMPLE PNEUMONIA & PLEURISY W CC	3.9488	4.7244	0.9996	$5,346.62
T	195	SIMPLE PNEUMONIA & PLEURISY W/O CC/MCC	2.99	3.5163	0.7078	$3,785.85
T	196	INTERSTITIAL LUNG DISEASE W MCC	5.4856	6.9071	1.682	$8,996.61
T	197	INTERSTITIAL LUNG DISEASE W CC	3.9284	4.8396	1.1209	$5,995.43
T	198	INTERSTITIAL LUNG DISEASE W/O CC/MCC	2.9082	3.5812	0.7879	$4,214.29
	199	PNEUMOTHORAX W MCC	6.1283	7.8339	1.8915	$10,117.18
	200	PNEUMOTHORAX W CC	3.4818	4.4523	1.0242	$5,478.20
	201	PNEUMOTHORAX W/O CC/MCC	2.6016	3.314	0.6792	$3,632.88
	202	BRONCHITIS & ASTHMA W CC/MCC	3.2523	4.0067	0.8704	$4,655.56
	203	BRONCHITIS & ASTHMA W/O CC/MCC	2.5237	3.0426	0.6228	$3,331.21
	204	RESPIRATORY SIGNS & SYMPTOMS	2.1128	2.6881	0.6822	$3,648.92
T	205	OTHER RESPIRATORY SYSTEM DIAGNOSES W MCC	4.0205	5.334	1.3809	$7,386.10
T	206	OTHER RESPIRATORY SYSTEM DIAGNOSES W/O MCC	2.5367	3.2124	0.7763	$4,152.24
T	207	RESPIRATORY SYSTEM DIAGNOSIS W VENTILATOR SUPPORT 96+ HOURS	12.4954	14.5938	5.3619	$28,679.52
	208	RESPIRATORY SYSTEM DIAGNOSIS W VENTILATOR SUPPORT <96 HOURS	5.0692	6.9693	2.2899	$12,248.13
	215	OTHER HEART ASSIST SYSTEM IMPLANT	8.5492	14.989	14.1036	$75,436.77
SP	216	CARDIAC VALVE & OTH MAJ CARDIOTHORACIC PROC W CARD CATH W MCC	13.7792	16.4498	9.519	$50,914.85
SP	217	CARDIAC VALVE & OTH MAJ CARDIOTHORACIC PROC W CARD CATH W CC	8.996	10.1818	6.3495	$33,961.95
SP	218	CARDIAC VALVE & OTH MAJ CARDIOTHORACIC PROC W CARD CATH W/O CC/MCC	6.547	7.4257	5.3429	$28,577.89
SP	219	CARDIAC VALVE & OTH MAJ CARDIOTHORACIC PROC W/O CARD CATH W MCC	10.3443	12.5084	7.839	$41,928.93
SP	220	CARDIAC VALVE & OTH MAJ CARDIOTHORACIC PROC W/O CARD CATH W CC	6.8194	7.5221	5.2438	$28,047.83
SP	221	CARDIAC VALVE & OTH MAJ CARDIOTHORACIC PROC W/O CARD CATH W/O CC/MCC	5.0702	5.577	4.4232	$23,658.64
	222	CARDIAC DEFIB IMPLANT W CARDIAC CATH W AMI/HF/SHOCK W MCC	9.8815	11.9953	8.5506	$45,735.11
	223	CARDIAC DEFIB IMPLANT W CARDIAC CATH W AMI/HF/SHOCK W/O MCC	4.3653	5.9273	6.1065	$32,662.20
	224	CARDIAC DEFIB IMPLANT W CARDIAC CATH W/O AMI/HF/SHOCK W MCC	8.0883	10.0416	7.6758	$41,056.01
	225	CARDIAC DEFIB IMPLANT W CARDIAC CATH W/O AMI/HF/SHOCK W/O MCC	4.0349	5.0052	5.7605	$30,811.53
	226	CARDIAC DEFIBRILLATOR IMPLANT W/O CARDIAC CATH W MCC	6.1097	8.7367	6.7354	$36,026.04
	227	CARDIAC DEFIBRILLATOR IMPLANT W/O CARDIAC CATH W/O MCC	2.094	3.1437	5.1886	$27,752.58
	228	OTHER CARDIOTHORACIC PROCEDURES W MCC	11.2274	13.4457	7.0815	$37,877.24
	229	OTHER CARDIOTHORACIC PROCEDURES W CC	7.0969	7.9703	4.6279	$24,753.53
	230	OTHER CARDIOTHORACIC PROCEDURES W/O CC/MCC	4.8116	5.5571	3.8111	$20,384.66
	231	CORONARY BYPASS W PTCA W MCC	10.3363	12.0911	7.5297	$40,274.56
	232	CORONARY BYPASS W PTCA W/O MCC	8.2539	9.1272	5.7151	$30,568.70
T	233	CORONARY BYPASS W CARDIAC CATH W MCC	11.8506	13.3515	7.2292	$38,667.26

Calculated with an average hospital Medicare base rate of $5,348.76. Each hospital's base rate and corresponding payment will vary. The national average hospital Medicare base rate is the sum of the full update labor-related and nonlabor-related amounts published in the Federal Register, FY 2013 Final Rule, Table 1A. National Adjusted Operating Standardized Amounts; Labor/Nonlabor (if wage index greater than 1) or Table 1B. National Adjusted Operating Standardized Amounts; Labor/Nonlabor (if wage index less than or equal to 1).

MS-DRGs 998 and 999 contain cases that could not be assigned to valid DRGs.

Note: If there is no value in either the geometric mean length of stay or the arithmetic mean length of stay columns, the volume of cases is insufficient to determine a meaningful computation of these statistics.

Appendix D — National Average Payment Table

DRG		Description	GMLOS	AMLOS	Relative Weight	National Payment Rate
T	234	CORONARY BYPASS W CARDIAC CATH W/O MCC	8.1115	8.7103	4.8413	$25,894.95
T	235	CORONARY BYPASS W/O CARDIAC CATH W MCC	9.1873	10.653	5.8014	$31,030.30
T	236	CORONARY BYPASS W/O CARDIAC CATH W/O MCC	6.0112	6.4798	3.7777	$20,206.01
	237	MAJOR CARDIOVASC PROCEDURES W MCC	7.0768	10.0441	5.117	$27,369.60
	238	MAJOR CARDIOVASC PROCEDURES W/O MCC	2.7204	3.9234	3.1863	$17,042.75
T	239	AMPUTATION FOR CIRC SYS DISORDERS EXC UPPER LIMB & TOE W MCC	11.1269	14.0751	4.6194	$24,708.06
T	240	AMPUTATION FOR CIRC SYS DISORDERS EXC UPPER LIMB & TOE W CC	7.4073	9.1044	2.6531	$14,190.80
T	241	AMPUTATION FOR CIRC SYS DISORDERS EXC UPPER LIMB & TOE W/O CC/MCC	4.6943	5.6591	1.4825	$7,929.54
T	242	PERMANENT CARDIAC PACEMAKER IMPLANT W MCC	6.1055	7.8225	3.7314	$19,958.36
T	243	PERMANENT CARDIAC PACEMAKER IMPLANT W CC	3.7197	4.6964	2.6204	$14,015.89
T	244	PERMANENT CARDIAC PACEMAKER IMPLANT W/O CC/MCC	2.2952	2.8358	2.0624	$11,031.28
	245	AICD GENERATOR PROCEDURES	2.8909	4.3113	4.254	$22,753.63
	246	PERC CARDIOVASC PROC W DRUG-ELUTING STENT W MCC OR 4+ VESSELS/STENTS	3.7975	5.2273	3.1566	$16,883.90
	247	PERC CARDIOVASC PROC W DRUG-ELUTING STENT W/O MCC	1.9995	2.4655	1.9911	$10,649.92
	248	PERC CARDIOVASC PROC W NON-DRUG-ELUTING STENT W MCC OR 4+ VES/STENTS	4.7095	6.3581	3.0003	$16,047.88
	249	PERC CARDIOVASC PROC W NON-DRUG-ELUTING STENT W/O MCC	2.3401	2.9139	1.7961	$9,606.91
	250	PERC CARDIOVASC PROC W/O CORONARY ARTERY STENT W MCC	5.2364	7.0958	2.9988	$16,039.86
	251	PERC CARDIOVASC PROC W/O CORONARY ARTERY STENT W/O MCC	2.2371	2.9723	1.9237	$10,289.41
	252	OTHER VASCULAR PROCEDURES W MCC	5.2548	7.762	3.0224	$16,166.09
	253	OTHER VASCULAR PROCEDURES W CC	4.3953	5.9142	2.4739	$13,232.30
	254	OTHER VASCULAR PROCEDURES W/O CC/MCC	2.1102	2.7361	1.6609	$8,883.76
T	255	UPPER LIMB & TOE AMPUTATION FOR CIRC SYSTEM DISORDERS W MCC	6.6772	8.7941	2.4381	$13,040.81
T	256	UPPER LIMB & TOE AMPUTATION FOR CIRC SYSTEM DISORDERS W CC	5.4744	6.7791	1.5934	$8,522.71
T	257	UPPER LIMB & TOE AMPUTATION FOR CIRC SYSTEM DISORDERS W/O CC/MCC	3.2091	4.1549	0.9535	$5,100.04
	258	CARDIAC PACEMAKER DEVICE REPLACEMENT W MCC	4.9962	6.518	2.6945	$14,412.23
	259	CARDIAC PACEMAKER DEVICE REPLACEMENT W/O MCC	2.5292	3.3066	1.859	$9,943.34
	260	CARDIAC PACEMAKER REVISION EXCEPT DEVICE REPLACEMENT W MCC	7.68	10.5026	3.6624	$19,589.30
	261	CARDIAC PACEMAKER REVISION EXCEPT DEVICE REPLACEMENT W CC	3.3614	4.4227	1.6769	$8,969.34
	262	CARDIAC PACEMAKER REVISION EXCEPT DEVICE REPLACEMENT W/O CC/MCC	2.1455	2.7125	1.2343	$6,601.97
	263	VEIN LIGATION & STRIPPING	3.8012	5.9466	1.9091	$10,211.32
T	264	OTHER CIRCULATORY SYSTEM O.R. PROCEDURES	5.6343	8.3205	2.6674	$14,267.28
	265	AICD LEAD PROCEDURES	2.5423	3.7702	2.4394	$13,047.77
T	280	ACUTE MYOCARDIAL INFARCTION, DISCHARGED ALIVE W MCC	4.9497	6.2896	1.7999	$9,627.23
T	281	ACUTE MYOCARDIAL INFARCTION, DISCHARGED ALIVE W CC	3.2442	4.0045	1.0961	$5,862.78
T	282	ACUTE MYOCARDIAL INFARCTION, DISCHARGED ALIVE W/O CC/MCC	2.1318	2.5845	0.7736	$4,137.80
	283	ACUTE MYOCARDIAL INFARCTION, EXPIRED W MCC	3.1769	5.1127	1.7539	$9,381.19
	284	ACUTE MYOCARDIAL INFARCTION, EXPIRED W CC	1.8562	2.6026	0.8042	$4,301.47

Calculated with an average hospital Medicare base rate of $5,348.76. Each hospital's base rate and corresponding payment will vary. The national average hospital Medicare base rate is the sum of the full update labor-related and nonlabor-related amounts published in the Federal Register, FY 2013 Final Rule, Table 1A. National Adjusted Operating Standardized Amounts; Labor/Nonlabor (if wage index greater than 1) or Table 1B. National Adjusted Operating Standardized Amounts; Labor/Nonlabor (if wage index less than or equal to 1).

MS-DRGs 998 and 999 contain cases that could not be assigned to valid DRGs.

Note: If there is no value in either the geometric mean length of stay or the arithmetic mean length of stay columns, the volume of cases is insufficient to determine a meaningful computation of these statistics.

T *Transfer DRG*   SP *Special Payment*   © 2012 OptumInsight, Inc.

DRG		Description	GMLOS	AMLOS	Relative Weight	National Payment Rate
	285	ACUTE MYOCARDIAL INFARCTION, EXPIRED W/O CC/MCC	1.3867	1.7299	0.5353	$2,863.19
	286	CIRCULATORY DISORDERS EXCEPT AMI, W CARD CATH W MCC	4.9226	6.595	2.0617	$11,027.54
	287	CIRCULATORY DISORDERS EXCEPT AMI, W CARD CATH W/O MCC	2.4029	3.1152	1.0709	$5,727.99
T	288	ACUTE & SUBACUTE ENDOCARDITIS W MCC	7.8808	9.9017	2.8229	$15,099.01
T	289	ACUTE & SUBACUTE ENDOCARDITIS W CC	5.9475	7.2208	1.8145	$9,705.33
T	290	ACUTE & SUBACUTE ENDOCARDITIS W/O CC/MCC	4.0701	5.0217	1.2092	$6,467.72
T	291	HEART FAILURE & SHOCK W MCC	4.7198	6.0485	1.5174	$8,116.21
T	292	HEART FAILURE & SHOCK W CC	3.8036	4.6094	1.0034	$5,366.95
T	293	HEART FAILURE & SHOCK W/O CC/MCC	2.6792	3.1612	0.6751	$3,610.95
	294	DEEP VEIN THROMBOPHLEBITIS W CC/MCC	4.1756	5.0527	1.0229	$5,471.25
	295	DEEP VEIN THROMBOPHLEBITIS W/O CC/MCC	3.4566	4.0177	0.6476	$3,463.86
	296	CARDIAC ARREST, UNEXPLAINED W MCC	1.8731	2.7963	1.2878	$6,888.13
	297	CARDIAC ARREST, UNEXPLAINED W CC	1.2793	1.5395	0.6455	$3,452.62
	298	CARDIAC ARREST, UNEXPLAINED W/O CC/MCC	1.09	1.1955	0.4571	$2,444.92
T	299	PERIPHERAL VASCULAR DISORDERS W MCC	4.5385	5.8334	1.4186	$7,587.75
T	300	PERIPHERAL VASCULAR DISORDERS W CC	3.7063	4.6077	0.9679	$5,177.06
T	301	PERIPHERAL VASCULAR DISORDERS W/O CC/MCC	2.7252	3.3567	0.6679	$3,572.44
	302	ATHEROSCLEROSIS W MCC	2.9175	3.9403	1.0142	$5,424.71
	303	ATHEROSCLEROSIS W/O MCC	1.8989	2.3401	0.5773	$3,087.84
	304	HYPERTENSION W MCC	3.384	4.4111	1.0503	$5,617.80
	305	HYPERTENSION W/O MCC	2.1251	2.633	0.6187	$3,309.28
	306	CARDIAC CONGENITAL & VALVULAR DISORDERS W MCC	3.9741	5.2344	1.3122	$7,018.64
	307	CARDIAC CONGENITAL & VALVULAR DISORDERS W/O MCC	2.5665	3.2541	0.784	$4,193.43
	308	CARDIAC ARRHYTHMIA & CONDUCTION DISORDERS W MCC	3.9459	5.04	1.2285	$6,570.95
	309	CARDIAC ARRHYTHMIA & CONDUCTION DISORDERS W CC	2.7966	3.4774	0.8098	$4,331.43
	310	CARDIAC ARRHYTHMIA & CONDUCTION DISORDERS W/O CC/MCC	1.9548	2.3402	0.5541	$2,963.75
	311	ANGINA PECTORIS	1.7749	2.1773	0.5207	$2,785.10
	312	SYNCOPE & COLLAPSE	2.3736	2.9376	0.7339	$3,925.45
	313	CHEST PAIN	1.6987	2.0686	0.5617	$3,004.40
T	314	OTHER CIRCULATORY SYSTEM DIAGNOSES W MCC	4.9265	6.7127	1.8508	$9,899.49
T	315	OTHER CIRCULATORY SYSTEM DIAGNOSES W CC	3.0917	3.9666	0.9527	$5,095.76
T	316	OTHER CIRCULATORY SYSTEM DIAGNOSES W/O CC/MCC	2.0459	2.5153	0.6224	$3,329.07
T	326	STOMACH, ESOPHAGEAL & DUODENAL PROC W MCC	12.016	15.3734	5.6118	$30,016.17
T	327	STOMACH, ESOPHAGEAL & DUODENAL PROC W CC	6.3095	8.212	2.6811	$14,340.56
T	328	STOMACH, ESOPHAGEAL & DUODENAL PROC W/O CC/MCC	2.52	3.3369	1.4413	$7,709.17
T	329	MAJOR SMALL & LARGE BOWEL PROCEDURES W MCC	12.0697	14.868	5.2599	$28,133.94
T	330	MAJOR SMALL & LARGE BOWEL PROCEDURES W CC	7.4089	8.6365	2.5731	$13,762.89
T	331	MAJOR SMALL & LARGE BOWEL PROCEDURES W/O CC/MCC	4.4919	5.0257	1.6361	$8,751.11

Calculated with an average hospital Medicare base rate of $5,348.76. Each hospital's base rate and corresponding payment will vary. The national average hospital Medicare base rate is the sum of the full update labor-related and nonlabor-related amounts published in the Federal Register, FY 2013 Final Rule, Table 1A. National Adjusted Operating Standardized Amounts; Labor/Nonlabor (if wage index greater than 1) or Table 1B. National Adjusted Operating Standardized Amounts; Labor/Nonlabor (if wage index less than or equal to 1).

MS-DRGs 998 and 999 contain cases that could not be assigned to valid DRGs.

Note: If there is no value in either the geometric mean length of stay or the arithmetic mean length of stay columns, the volume of cases is insufficient to determine a meaningful computation of these statistics.

Appendix D — National Average Payment Table

DRG		Description	GMLOS	AMLOS	Relative Weight	National Payment Rate
T	332	RECTAL RESECTION W MCC	11.1702	13.3637	4.6143	$24,680.78
T	333	RECTAL RESECTION W CC	6.7216	7.8234	2.4814	$13,272.41
T	334	RECTAL RESECTION W/O CC/MCC	3.9526	4.5677	1.6181	$8,654.83
T	335	PERITONEAL ADHESIOLYSIS W MCC	11.153	13.3877	4.3146	$23,077.76
T	336	PERITONEAL ADHESIOLYSIS W CC	7.0367	8.4326	2.3529	$12,585.10
T	337	PERITONEAL ADHESIOLYSIS W/O CC/MCC	3.9684	4.988	1.5538	$8,310.90
	338	APPENDECTOMY W COMPLICATED PRINCIPAL DIAG W MCC	8.2739	10.0335	3.2008	$17,120.31
	339	APPENDECTOMY W COMPLICATED PRINCIPAL DIAG W CC	5.4125	6.36	1.8675	$9,988.81
	340	APPENDECTOMY W COMPLICATED PRINCIPAL DIAG W/O CC/MCC	3.0468	3.607	1.2024	$6,431.35
	341	APPENDECTOMY W/O COMPLICATED PRINCIPAL DIAG W MCC	4.8389	6.6251	2.3116	$12,364.19
	342	APPENDECTOMY W/O COMPLICATED PRINCIPAL DIAG W CC	2.8514	3.6934	1.3516	$7,229.38
	343	APPENDECTOMY W/O COMPLICATED PRINCIPAL DIAG W/O CC/MCC	1.6223	1.9028	0.9547	$5,106.46
	344	MINOR SMALL & LARGE BOWEL PROCEDURES W MCC	9.0322	11.5076	3.4094	$18,236.06
	345	MINOR SMALL & LARGE BOWEL PROCEDURES W CC	5.6047	6.594	1.7123	$9,158.68
	346	MINOR SMALL & LARGE BOWEL PROCEDURES W/O CC/MCC	3.9007	4.357	1.1608	$6,208.84
	347	ANAL & STOMAL PROCEDURES W MCC	6.4214	8.6429	2.5169	$13,462.29
	348	ANAL & STOMAL PROCEDURES W CC	4.1745	5.3782	1.39	$7,434.78
	349	ANAL & STOMAL PROCEDURES W/O CC/MCC	2.3013	2.8339	0.8343	$4,462.47
	350	INGUINAL & FEMORAL HERNIA PROCEDURES W MCC	5.8579	7.789	2.5082	$13,415.76
	351	INGUINAL & FEMORAL HERNIA PROCEDURES W CC	3.4214	4.3686	1.3755	$7,357.22
	352	INGUINAL & FEMORAL HERNIA PROCEDURES W/O CC/MCC	1.9502	2.4	0.9043	$4,836.88
	353	HERNIA PROCEDURES EXCEPT INGUINAL & FEMORAL W MCC	6.342	8.2373	2.8192	$15,079.22
	354	HERNIA PROCEDURES EXCEPT INGUINAL & FEMORAL W CC	4.0131	4.9505	1.5976	$8,545.18
	355	HERNIA PROCEDURES EXCEPT INGUINAL & FEMORAL W/O CC/MCC	2.3729	2.8915	1.1172	$5,975.63
T	356	OTHER DIGESTIVE SYSTEM O.R. PROCEDURES W MCC	8.8841	11.9896	3.9463	$21,107.81
T	357	OTHER DIGESTIVE SYSTEM O.R. PROCEDURES W CC	5.4978	7.0918	2.1747	$11,631.95
T	358	OTHER DIGESTIVE SYSTEM O.R. PROCEDURES W/O CC/MCC	3.1499	4.0119	1.3629	$7,289.83
	368	MAJOR ESOPHAGEAL DISORDERS W MCC	5.0733	6.5713	1.8327	$9,802.67
	369	MAJOR ESOPHAGEAL DISORDERS W CC	3.5089	4.2346	1.0664	$5,703.92
	370	MAJOR ESOPHAGEAL DISORDERS W/O CC/MCC	2.4719	2.9877	0.7593	$4,061.31
T	371	MAJOR GASTROINTESTINAL DISORDERS & PERITONEAL INFECTIONS W MCC	6.5011	8.3893	2.02	$10,804.50
T	372	MAJOR GASTROINTESTINAL DISORDERS & PERITONEAL INFECTIONS W CC	4.9267	5.9442	1.2275	$6,565.60
T	373	MAJOR GASTROINTESTINAL DISORDERS & PERITONEAL INFECTIONS W/O CC/MCC	3.6403	4.2648	0.8401	$4,493.49
T	374	DIGESTIVE MALIGNANCY W MCC	6.2661	8.4981	2.1284	$11,384.30
T	375	DIGESTIVE MALIGNANCY W CC	4.2627	5.5354	1.2738	$6,813.25
T	376	DIGESTIVE MALIGNANCY W/O CC/MCC	2.7976	3.5197	0.8809	$4,711.72
T	377	G.I. HEMORRHAGE W MCC	4.8983	6.2689	1.7817	$9,529.89
T	378	G.I. HEMORRHAGE W CC	3.3611	3.9935	1.0168	$5,438.62

Calculated with an average hospital Medicare base rate of $5,348.76. Each hospital's base rate and corresponding payment will vary. The national average hospital Medicare base rate is the sum of the full update labor-related and nonlabor-related amounts published in the Federal Register, FY 2013 Final Rule, Table 1A. National Adjusted Operating Standardized Amounts; Labor/Nonlabor (if wage index greater than 1) or Table 1B. National Adjusted Operating Standardized Amounts; Labor/Nonlabor (if wage index less than or equal to 1).

MS-DRGs 998 and 999 contain cases that could not be assigned to valid DRGs.

Note: If there is no value in either the geometric mean length of stay or the arithmetic mean length of stay columns, the volume of cases is insufficient to determine a meaningful computation of these statistics.

DRG	Description	GMLOS	AMLOS	Relative Weight	National Payment Rate
T 379	G.I. HEMORRHAGE W/O CC/MCC	2.434	2.8649	0.7015	$3,752.16
T 380	COMPLICATED PEPTIC ULCER W MCC	5.5561	7.1819	1.9311	$10,328.99
T 381	COMPLICATED PEPTIC ULCER W CC	3.7201	4.5551	1.113	$5,953.17
T 382	COMPLICATED PEPTIC ULCER W/O CC/MCC	2.8133	3.3942	0.7917	$4,234.61
383	UNCOMPLICATED PEPTIC ULCER W MCC	4.4113	5.5828	1.3384	$7,158.78
384	UNCOMPLICATED PEPTIC ULCER W/O MCC	2.9131	3.4801	0.8365	$4,474.24
385	INFLAMMATORY BOWEL DISEASE W MCC	6.2635	8.2962	1.9078	$10,204.36
386	INFLAMMATORY BOWEL DISEASE W CC	4.1035	5.0711	1.0505	$5,618.87
387	INFLAMMATORY BOWEL DISEASE W/O CC/MCC	3.1455	3.8228	0.7878	$4,213.75
T 388	G.I. OBSTRUCTION W MCC	5.4215	7.1388	1.6564	$8,859.69
T 389	G.I. OBSTRUCTION W CC	3.707	4.5739	0.9217	$4,929.95
T 390	G.I. OBSTRUCTION W/O CC/MCC	2.7349	3.249	0.6372	$3,408.23
391	ESOPHAGITIS, GASTROENT & MISC DIGEST DISORDERS W MCC	3.8807	5.133	1.1897	$6,363.42
392	ESOPHAGITIS, GASTROENT & MISC DIGEST DISORDERS W/O MCC	2.779	3.4337	0.7375	$3,944.71
393	OTHER DIGESTIVE SYSTEM DIAGNOSES W MCC	4.7965	6.6467	1.6666	$8,914.24
394	OTHER DIGESTIVE SYSTEM DIAGNOSES W CC	3.5065	4.4294	0.9837	$5,261.58
395	OTHER DIGESTIVE SYSTEM DIAGNOSES W/O CC/MCC	2.4349	2.9829	0.6791	$3,632.34
T 405	PANCREAS, LIVER & SHUNT PROCEDURES W MCC	11.3327	15.1509	5.5575	$29,725.73
T 406	PANCREAS, LIVER & SHUNT PROCEDURES W CC	6.1602	7.8519	2.7303	$14,603.72
T 407	PANCREAS, LIVER & SHUNT PROCEDURES W/O CC/MCC	4.1197	5.0466	1.828	$9,777.53
408	BILIARY TRACT PROC EXCEPT ONLY CHOLECYST W OR W/O C.D.E. W MCC	10.2514	12.7546	3.8375	$20,525.87
409	BILIARY TRACT PROC EXCEPT ONLY CHOLECYST W OR W/O C.D.E. W CC	6.8855	8.2776	2.268	$12,130.99
410	BILIARY TRACT PROC EXCEPT ONLY CHOLECYST W OR W/O C.D.E. W/O CC/MCC	4.8038	5.7099	1.6875	$9,026.03
411	CHOLECYSTECTOMY W C.D.E. W MCC	9.7331	11.675	3.804	$20,346.68
412	CHOLECYSTECTOMY W C.D.E. W CC	7.0347	8.2367	2.5989	$13,900.89
413	CHOLECYSTECTOMY W C.D.E. W/O CC/MCC	4.557	5.3016	1.8582	$9,939.07
T 414	CHOLECYSTECTOMY EXCEPT BY LAPAROSCOPE W/O C.D.E. W MCC	9.0407	10.873	3.5643	$19,064.59
T 415	CHOLECYSTECTOMY EXCEPT BY LAPAROSCOPE W/O C.D.E. W CC	5.9604	6.9268	2.0728	$11,086.91
T 416	CHOLECYSTECTOMY EXCEPT BY LAPAROSCOPE W/O C.D.E. W/O CC/MCC	3.7361	4.3722	1.3354	$7,142.73
417	LAPAROSCOPIC CHOLECYSTECTOMY W/O C.D.E. W MCC	6.1362	7.7119	2.5189	$13,472.99
418	LAPAROSCOPIC CHOLECYSTECTOMY W/O C.D.E. W CC	4.2144	5.1036	1.7007	$9,096.64
419	LAPAROSCOPIC CHOLECYSTECTOMY W/O C.D.E. W/O CC/MCC	2.5189	3.0444	1.205	$6,445.26
420	HEPATOBILIARY DIAGNOSTIC PROCEDURES W MCC	8.6916	12.2587	3.8509	$20,597.54
421	HEPATOBILIARY DIAGNOSTIC PROCEDURES W CC	4.5849	6.2153	1.7381	$9,296.68
422	HEPATOBILIARY DIAGNOSTIC PROCEDURES W/O CC/MCC	3.1925	4.016	1.3006	$6,956.60
423	OTHER HEPATOBILIARY OR PANCREAS O.R. PROCEDURES W MCC	10.1927	13.591	4.3308	$23,164.41
424	OTHER HEPATOBILIARY OR PANCREAS O.R. PROCEDURES W CC	6.3447	8.2861	2.4081	$12,880.35
425	OTHER HEPATOBILIARY OR PANCREAS O.R. PROCEDURES W/O CC/MCC	3.7627	4.8646	1.5756	$8,427.51
432	CIRRHOSIS & ALCOHOLIC HEPATITIS W MCC	4.7885	6.2968	1.6792	$8,981.64

Calculated with an average hospital Medicare base rate of $5,348.76. Each hospital's base rate and corresponding payment will vary. The national average hospital Medicare base rate is the sum of the full update labor-related and nonlabor-related amounts published in the Federal Register, FY 2013 Final Rule, Table 1A. National Adjusted Operating Standardized Amounts; Labor/Nonlabor (if wage index greater than 1) or Table 1B. National Adjusted Operating Standardized Amounts; Labor/Nonlabor (if wage index less than or equal to 1).

MS-DRGs 998 and 999 contain cases that could not be assigned to valid DRGs.

Note: If there is no value in either the geometric mean length of stay or the arithmetic mean length of stay columns, the volume of cases is insufficient to determine a meaningful computation of these statistics.

Appendix D — National Average Payment Table

DRG	Description	GMLOS	AMLOS	Relative Weight	National Payment Rate
433	CIRRHOSIS & ALCOHOLIC HEPATITIS W CC	3.3703	4.2302	0.9316	$4,982.90
434	CIRRHOSIS & ALCOHOLIC HEPATITIS W/O CC/MCC	2.6241	3.2086	0.6343	$3,392.72
435	MALIGNANCY OF HEPATOBILIARY SYSTEM OR PANCREAS W MCC	5.4211	7.068	1.7816	$9,529.35
436	MALIGNANCY OF HEPATOBILIARY SYSTEM OR PANCREAS W CC	4.0413	5.2083	1.1934	$6,383.21
437	MALIGNANCY OF HEPATOBILIARY SYSTEM OR PANCREAS W/O CC/MCC	2.7911	3.6078	0.9537	$5,101.11
438	DISORDERS OF PANCREAS EXCEPT MALIGNANCY W MCC	5.3166	7.216	1.7844	$9,544.33
439	DISORDERS OF PANCREAS EXCEPT MALIGNANCY W CC	3.7446	4.6237	0.9603	$5,136.41
440	DISORDERS OF PANCREAS EXCEPT MALIGNANCY W/O CC/MCC	2.7918	3.3248	0.679	$3,631.81
T 441	DISORDERS OF LIVER EXCEPT MALIG,CIRR,ALC HEPA W MCC	5.0549	6.9632	1.8767	$10,038.02
T 442	DISORDERS OF LIVER EXCEPT MALIG,CIRR,ALC HEPA W CC	3.488	4.4099	0.9545	$5,105.39
T 443	DISORDERS OF LIVER EXCEPT MALIG,CIRR,ALC HEPA W/O CC/MCC	2.5804	3.1629	0.6473	$3,462.25
444	DISORDERS OF THE BILIARY TRACT W MCC	4.7327	6.2052	1.6039	$8,578.88
445	DISORDERS OF THE BILIARY TRACT W CC	3.493	4.3117	1.072	$5,733.87
446	DISORDERS OF THE BILIARY TRACT W/O CC/MCC	2.4375	2.9816	0.7583	$4,055.96
453	COMBINED ANTERIOR/POSTERIOR SPINAL FUSION W MCC	10.1392	12.6207	10.5952	$56,671.18
454	COMBINED ANTERIOR/POSTERIOR SPINAL FUSION W CC	5.2917	6.3024	7.7979	$41,709.10
455	COMBINED ANTERIOR/POSTERIOR SPINAL FUSION W/O CC/MCC	3.071	3.5959	5.8705	$31,399.90
456	SPINAL FUS EXC CERV W SPINAL CURV/MALIG/INFEC OR 9+ FUS W MCC	10.6072	13.0629	9.5204	$50,922.33
457	SPINAL FUS EXC CERV W SPINAL CURV/MALIG/INFEC OR 9+ FUS W CC	5.5592	6.4563	6.4171	$34,323.53
458	SPINAL FUS EXC CERV W SPINAL CURV/MALIG/INFEC OR 9+ FUS W/O CC/MCC	3.2626	3.7117	4.9491	$26,471.55
T 459	SPINAL FUSION EXCEPT CERVICAL W MCC	7.2817	9.0922	6.539	$34,975.54
T 460	SPINAL FUSION EXCEPT CERVICAL W/O MCC	3.1185	3.6483	3.8783	$20,744.10
461	BILATERAL OR MULTIPLE MAJOR JOINT PROCS OF LOWER EXTREMITY W MCC	6.3746	7.6882	4.9062	$26,242.09
462	BILATERAL OR MULTIPLE MAJOR JOINT PROCS OF LOWER EXTREMITY W/O MCC	3.5421	3.8132	3.3745	$18,049.39
T 463	WND DEBRID & SKN GRFT EXC HAND, FOR MUSCULO-CONN TISS DIS W MCC	10.9297	15.0576	5.4443	$29,120.25
T 464	WND DEBRID & SKN GRFT EXC HAND, FOR MUSCULO-CONN TISS DIS W CC	6.4793	8.1572	2.9406	$15,728.56
T 465	WND DEBRID & SKN GRFT EXC HAND, FOR MUSCULO-CONN TISS DIS W/O CC/MCC	3.9332	4.9525	1.8802	$10,056.74
T 466	REVISION OF HIP OR KNEE REPLACEMENT W MCC	7.039	8.6607	5.0078	$26,785.52
T 467	REVISION OF HIP OR KNEE REPLACEMENT W CC	4.0568	4.5783	3.2516	$17,392.03
T 468	REVISION OF HIP OR KNEE REPLACEMENT W/O CC/MCC	3.0663	3.3111	2.607	$13,944.22
T 469	MAJOR JOINT REPLACEMENT OR REATTACHMENT OF LOWER EXTREMITY W MCC	6.413	7.5966	3.4196	$18,290.62
T 470	MAJOR JOINT REPLACEMENT OR REATTACHMENT OF LOWER EXTREMITY W/O MCC	3.2261	3.467	2.0953	$11,207.26
471	CERVICAL SPINAL FUSION W MCC	6.4715	9.0238	4.7075	$25,179.29
472	CERVICAL SPINAL FUSION W CC	2.5457	3.6301	2.8041	$14,998.46
473	CERVICAL SPINAL FUSION W/O CC/MCC	1.4658	1.7814	2.1254	$11,368.25
T 474	AMPUTATION FOR MUSCULOSKELETAL SYS & CONN TISSUE DIS W MCC	8.9469	11.5935	3.5676	$19,082.24
T 475	AMPUTATION FOR MUSCULOSKELETAL SYS & CONN TISSUE DIS W CC	5.8696	7.4237	2.0071	$10,735.50

Calculated with an average hospital Medicare base rate of $5,348.76. Each hospital's base rate and corresponding payment will vary. The national average hospital Medicare base rate is the sum of the full update labor-related and nonlabor-related amounts published in the Federal Register, FY 2013 Final Rule, Table 1A. National Adjusted Operating Standardized Amounts; Labor/Nonlabor (if wage index greater than 1) or Table 1B. National Adjusted Operating Standardized Amounts; Labor/Nonlabor (if wage index less than or equal to 1).

MS-DRGs 998 and 999 contain cases that could not be assigned to valid DRGs.

Note: If there is no value in either the geometric mean length of stay or the arithmetic mean length of stay columns, the volume of cases is insufficient to determine a meaningful computation of these statistics.

DRG		Description	GMLOS	AMLOS	Relative Weight	National Payment Rate
T	476	AMPUTATION FOR MUSCULOSKELETAL SYS & CONN TISSUE DIS W/O CC/MCC	3.0419	3.936	1.0171	$5,440.22
SP	477	BIOPSIES OF MUSCULOSKELETAL SYSTEM & CONNECTIVE TISSUE W MCC	8.892	11.0204	3.2681	$17,480.28
SP	478	BIOPSIES OF MUSCULOSKELETAL SYSTEM & CONNECTIVE TISSUE W CC	5.5015	6.8043	2.2663	$12,121.89
SP	479	BIOPSIES OF MUSCULOSKELETAL SYSTEM & CONNECTIVE TISSUE W/O CC/MCC	3.174	4.1264	1.6922	$9,051.17
SP	480	HIP & FEMUR PROCEDURES EXCEPT MAJOR JOINT W MCC	7.2097	8.4552	3.0367	$16,242.58
SP	481	HIP & FEMUR PROCEDURES EXCEPT MAJOR JOINT W CC	4.882	5.3178	1.9345	$10,347.18
SP	482	HIP & FEMUR PROCEDURES EXCEPT MAJOR JOINT W/O CC/MCC	3.9648	4.2827	1.566	$8,376.16
T	483	MAJOR JOINT & LIMB REATTACHMENT PROC OF UPPER EXTREMITY W CC/MCC	2.8554	3.4773	2.5314	$13,539.85
T	484	MAJOR JOINT & LIMB REATTACHMENT PROC OF UPPER EXTREMITY W/O CC/MCC	1.8565	2.0832	2.095	$11,205.65
	485	KNEE PROCEDURES W PDX OF INFECTION W MCC	8.6452	10.276	3.0583	$16,358.11
	486	KNEE PROCEDURES W PDX OF INFECTION W CC	5.825	6.7713	2.0808	$11,129.70
	487	KNEE PROCEDURES W PDX OF INFECTION W/O CC/MCC	4.2369	4.8813	1.4863	$7,949.86
T	488	KNEE PROCEDURES W/O PDX OF INFECTION W CC/MCC	3.5474	4.3285	1.6865	$9,020.68
T	489	KNEE PROCEDURES W/O PDX OF INFECTION W/O CC/MCC	2.4417	2.7629	1.2486	$6,678.46
	490	BACK & NECK PROC EXC SPINAL FUSION W CC/MCC OR DISC DEVICE/NEUROSTIM	3.1845	4.4585	1.8154	$9,710.14
	491	BACK & NECK PROC EXC SPINAL FUSION W/O CC/MCC	1.7216	2.0928	1.0354	$5,538.11
SP	492	LOWER EXTREM & HUMER PROC EXCEPT HIP,FOOT,FEMUR W MCC	6.6589	8.2554	3.1039	$16,602.02
SP	493	LOWER EXTREM & HUMER PROC EXCEPT HIP,FOOT,FEMUR W CC	4.0326	4.8007	1.931	$10,328.46
SP	494	LOWER EXTREM & HUMER PROC EXCEPT HIP,FOOT,FEMUR W/O CC/MCC	2.5925	3.051	1.3938	$7,455.10
SP	495	LOCAL EXCISION & REMOVAL INT FIX DEVICES EXC HIP & FEMUR W MCC	7.4634	9.7944	2.9977	$16,033.98
SP	496	LOCAL EXCISION & REMOVAL INT FIX DEVICES EXC HIP & FEMUR W CC	3.9576	5.1912	1.6306	$8,721.69
SP	497	LOCAL EXCISION & REMOVAL INT FIX DEVICES EXC HIP & FEMUR W/O CC/MCC	1.9993	2.5277	1.1202	$5,991.68
	498	LOCAL EXCISION & REMOVAL INT FIX DEVICES OF HIP & FEMUR W CC/MCC	5.3172	7.2272	2.1304	$11,395.00
	499	LOCAL EXCISION & REMOVAL INT FIX DEVICES OF HIP & FEMUR W/O CC/MCC	2.0536	2.6445	1.0106	$5,405.46
SP	500	SOFT TISSUE PROCEDURES W MCC	7.7626	10.2327	3.1368	$16,777.99
SP	501	SOFT TISSUE PROCEDURES W CC	4.4985	5.682	1.594	$8,525.92
SP	502	SOFT TISSUE PROCEDURES W/O CC/MCC	2.3641	2.9076	1.067	$5,707.13
	503	FOOT PROCEDURES W MCC	6.8195	8.7188	2.3006	$12,305.36
	504	FOOT PROCEDURES W CC	4.7944	5.8781	1.5641	$8,366.00
	505	FOOT PROCEDURES W/O CC/MCC	2.5592	3.1747	1.1478	$6,139.31
	506	MAJOR THUMB OR JOINT PROCEDURES	2.956	4.0283	1.3003	$6,954.99
	507	MAJOR SHOULDER OR ELBOW JOINT PROCEDURES W CC/MCC	4.0146	5.5728	1.8689	$9,996.30
	508	MAJOR SHOULDER OR ELBOW JOINT PROCEDURES W/O CC/MCC	1.77	2.182	1.2071	$6,456.49
	509	ARTHROSCOPY	2.5621	3.7341	1.3494	$7,217.62
T	510	SHOULDER,ELBOW OR FOREARM PROC,EXC MAJOR JOINT PROC W MCC	4.9825	6.2815	2.2963	$12,282.36
T	511	SHOULDER,ELBOW OR FOREARM PROC,EXC MAJOR JOINT PROC W CC	3.171	3.7878	1.5222	$8,141.88
T	512	SHOULDER,ELBOW OR FOREARM PROC,EXC MAJOR JOINT PROC W/O CC/MCC	1.8785	2.2348	1.1201	$5,991.15
	513	HAND OR WRIST PROC, EXCEPT MAJOR THUMB OR JOINT PROC W CC/MCC	3.595	4.753	1.3409	$7,172.15

Calculated with an average hospital Medicare base rate of $5,348.76. Each hospital's base rate and corresponding payment will vary. The national average hospital Medicare base rate is the sum of the full update labor-related and nonlabor-related amounts published in the Federal Register, FY 2013 Final Rule, Table 1A. National Adjusted Operating Standardized Amounts; Labor/Nonlabor (if wage index greater than 1) or Table 1B. National Adjusted Operating Standardized Amounts; Labor/Nonlabor (if wage index less than or equal to 1).

MS-DRGs 998 and 999 contain cases that could not be assigned to valid DRGs.

Note: If there is no value in either the geometric mean length of stay or the arithmetic mean length of stay columns, the volume of cases is insufficient to determine a meaningful computation of these statistics.

Appendix D — National Average Payment Table

Appendix D — National Average Payment Table

DRG		Description	GMLOS	AMLOS	Relative Weight	National Payment Rate
	514	HAND OR WRIST PROC, EXCEPT MAJOR THUMB OR JOINT PROC W/O CC/MCC	2.0671	2.6098	0.8655	$4,629.35
SP	515	OTHER MUSCULOSKELET SYS & CONN TISS O.R. PROC W MCC	7.664	9.7307	3.2831	$17,560.51
SP	516	OTHER MUSCULOSKELET SYS & CONN TISS O.R. PROC W CC	4.6317	5.6497	1.9744	$10,560.59
SP	517	OTHER MUSCULOSKELET SYS & CONN TISS O.R. PROC W/O CC/MCC	2.7804	3.4649	1.5767	$8,433.39
T	533	FRACTURES OF FEMUR W MCC	4.5079	6.0788	1.4725	$7,876.05
T	534	FRACTURES OF FEMUR W/O MCC	3.006	3.6644	0.7366	$3,939.90
T	535	FRACTURES OF HIP & PELVIS W MCC	4.1966	5.3694	1.279	$6,841.06
T	536	FRACTURES OF HIP & PELVIS W/O MCC	3.0667	3.5456	0.7146	$3,822.22
	537	SPRAINS, STRAINS, & DISLOCATIONS OF HIP, PELVIS & THIGH W CC/MCC	3.3615	3.9896	0.8638	$4,620.26
	538	SPRAINS, STRAINS, & DISLOCATIONS OF HIP, PELVIS & THIGH W/O CC/MCC	2.4102	2.8373	0.6405	$3,425.88
T	539	OSTEOMYELITIS W MCC	6.6372	8.6635	1.9982	$10,687.89
T	540	OSTEOMYELITIS W CC	4.9561	6.1057	1.2692	$6,788.65
T	541	OSTEOMYELITIS W/O CC/MCC	3.7941	4.7928	0.977	$5,225.74
T	542	PATHOLOGICAL FRACTURES & MUSCULOSKELET & CONN TISS MALIG W MCC	6.2702	8.2295	2.0293	$10,854.24
T	543	PATHOLOGICAL FRACTURES & MUSCULOSKELET & CONN TISS MALIG W CC	4.2913	5.3738	1.1749	$6,284.26
T	544	PATHOLOGICAL FRACTURES & MUSCULOSKELET & CONN TISS MALIG W/O CC/MCC	3.3014	3.8672	0.8012	$4,285.43
T	545	CONNECTIVE TISSUE DISORDERS W MCC	6.089	8.6505	2.4785	$13,256.90
T	546	CONNECTIVE TISSUE DISORDERS W CC	4.0986	5.1966	1.1767	$6,293.89
T	547	CONNECTIVE TISSUE DISORDERS W/O CC/MCC	2.8683	3.5162	0.7581	$4,054.89
	548	SEPTIC ARTHRITIS W MCC	5.8097	7.5613	1.7465	$9,341.61
	549	SEPTIC ARTHRITIS W CC	4.563	5.5672	1.1683	$6,248.96
	550	SEPTIC ARTHRITIS W/O CC/MCC	3.1288	3.8438	0.7723	$4,130.85
T	551	MEDICAL BACK PROBLEMS W MCC	4.9721	6.4318	1.6345	$8,742.55
T	552	MEDICAL BACK PROBLEMS W/O MCC	3.21	3.8791	0.8533	$4,564.10
	553	BONE DISEASES & ARTHROPATHIES W MCC	4.2998	5.5695	1.2087	$6,465.05
	554	BONE DISEASES & ARTHROPATHIES W/O MCC	2.9321	3.5621	0.6916	$3,699.20
	555	SIGNS & SYMPTOMS OF MUSCULOSKELETAL SYSTEM & CONN TISSUE W MCC	3.7504	5.0998	1.2348	$6,604.65
	556	SIGNS & SYMPTOMS OF MUSCULOSKELETAL SYSTEM & CONN TISSUE W/O MCC	2.5728	3.2081	0.7039	$3,764.99
T	557	TENDONITIS, MYOSITIS & BURSITIS W MCC	5.2388	6.5373	1.5613	$8,351.02
T	558	TENDONITIS, MYOSITIS & BURSITIS W/O MCC	3.4553	4.1003	0.8594	$4,596.72
T	559	AFTERCARE, MUSCULOSKELETAL SYSTEM & CONNECTIVE TISSUE W MCC	5.1619	6.9981	1.8741	$10,024.11
T	560	AFTERCARE, MUSCULOSKELETAL SYSTEM & CONNECTIVE TISSUE W CC	3.5162	4.434	1.03	$5,509.22
T	561	AFTERCARE, MUSCULOSKELETAL SYSTEM & CONNECTIVE TISSUE W/O CC/MCC	1.9734	2.4669	0.6115	$3,270.77
T	562	FX, SPRN, STRN & DISL EXCEPT FEMUR, HIP, PELVIS & THIGH W MCC	4.4206	5.6466	1.3989	$7,482.38
T	563	FX, SPRN, STRN & DISL EXCEPT FEMUR, HIP, PELVIS & THIGH W/O MCC	2.9709	3.5033	0.7463	$3,991.78
	564	OTHER MUSCULOSKELETAL SYS & CONNECTIVE TISSUE DIAGNOSES W MCC	4.6825	6.1903	1.4459	$7,733.77
	565	OTHER MUSCULOSKELETAL SYS & CONNECTIVE TISSUE DIAGNOSES W CC	3.6265	4.5178	0.9386	$5,020.35
	566	OTHER MUSCULOSKELETAL SYS & CONNECTIVE TISSUE DIAGNOSES W/O CC/MCC	2.556	3.207	0.6786	$3,629.67

Calculated with an average hospital Medicare base rate of $5,348.76. Each hospital's base rate and corresponding payment will vary. The national average hospital Medicare base rate is the sum of the full update labor-related and nonlabor-related amounts published in the Federal Register, FY 2013 Final Rule, Table 1A. National Adjusted Operating Standardized Amounts; Labor/Nonlabor (if wage index greater than 1) or Table 1B. National Adjusted Operating Standardized Amounts; Labor/Nonlabor (if wage index less than or equal to 1).

MS-DRGs 998 and 999 contain cases that could not be assigned to valid DRGs.

Note: If there is no value in either the geometric mean length of stay or the arithmetic mean length of stay columns, the volume of cases is insufficient to determine a meaningful computation of these statistics.

T *Transfer DRG*   SP *Special Payment*   © 2012 OptumInsight, Inc.

DRG		Description	GMLOS	AMLOS	Relative Weight	National Payment Rate
T	570	SKIN DEBRIDEMENT W MCC	7.5233	9.85	2.4688	$13,205.02
T	571	SKIN DEBRIDEMENT W CC	5.5401	6.6539	1.4969	$8,006.56
T	572	SKIN DEBRIDEMENT W/O CC/MCC	3.8899	4.684	1.0036	$5,368.02
T	573	SKIN GRAFT FOR SKIN ULCER OR CELLULITIS W MCC	8.575	13.0421	3.5637	$19,061.38
T	574	SKIN GRAFT FOR SKIN ULCER OR CELLULITIS W CC	7.171	9.5125	2.4469	$13,087.88
T	575	SKIN GRAFT FOR SKIN ULCER OR CELLULITIS W/O CC/MCC	4.0051	5.3368	1.3266	$7,095.67
	576	SKIN GRAFT EXC FOR SKIN ULCER OR CELLULITIS W MCC	8.4717	12.8663	4.2457	$22,709.23
	577	SKIN GRAFT EXC FOR SKIN ULCER OR CELLULITIS W CC	3.9254	5.7882	1.8963	$10,142.85
	578	SKIN GRAFT EXC FOR SKIN ULCER OR CELLULITIS W/O CC/MCC	2.3278	3.1812	1.1312	$6,050.52
T	579	OTHER SKIN, SUBCUT TISS & BREAST PROC W MCC	7.2752	9.5629	2.7186	$14,541.14
T	580	OTHER SKIN, SUBCUT TISS & BREAST PROC W CC	3.7447	5.1479	1.4875	$7,956.28
T	581	OTHER SKIN, SUBCUT TISS & BREAST PROC W/O CC/MCC	1.9641	2.5499	0.9916	$5,303.83
	582	MASTECTOMY FOR MALIGNANCY W CC/MCC	2.0074	2.6997	1.1283	$6,035.01
	583	MASTECTOMY FOR MALIGNANCY W/O CC/MCC	1.4995	1.7217	0.8992	$4,809.60
	584	BREAST BIOPSY, LOCAL EXCISION & OTHER BREAST PROCEDURES W CC/MCC	3.7174	5.3248	1.655	$8,852.20
	585	BREAST BIOPSY, LOCAL EXCISION & OTHER BREAST PROCEDURES W/O CC/MCC	1.7914	2.2158	1.1381	$6,087.42
T	592	SKIN ULCERS W MCC	5.3359	6.9401	1.4632	$7,826.31
T	593	SKIN ULCERS W CC	4.3695	5.2994	0.9912	$5,301.69
T	594	SKIN ULCERS W/O CC/MCC	3.1724	3.9499	0.6782	$3,627.53
	595	MAJOR SKIN DISORDERS W MCC	5.8866	7.6802	1.8803	$10,057.27
	596	MAJOR SKIN DISORDERS W/O MCC	3.6123	4.5332	0.888	$4,749.70
	597	MALIGNANT BREAST DISORDERS W MCC	5.3981	7.2256	1.6026	$8,571.92
	598	MALIGNANT BREAST DISORDERS W CC	4.1396	5.4716	1.228	$6,568.28
	599	MALIGNANT BREAST DISORDERS W/O CC/MCC	2.3114	3.1208	0.665	$3,556.93
	600	NON-MALIGNANT BREAST DISORDERS W CC/MCC	4.0058	5.0458	0.9968	$5,331.64
	601	NON-MALIGNANT BREAST DISORDERS W/O CC/MCC	2.9742	3.5862	0.6247	$3,341.37
T	602	CELLULITIS W MCC	5.1757	6.4742	1.4883	$7,960.56
T	603	CELLULITIS W/O MCC	3.6361	4.3371	0.8392	$4,488.68
	604	TRAUMA TO THE SKIN, SUBCUT TISS & BREAST W MCC	3.9485	5.2874	1.3297	$7,112.25
	605	TRAUMA TO THE SKIN, SUBCUT TISS & BREAST W/O MCC	2.5921	3.2151	0.7552	$4,039.38
	606	MINOR SKIN DISORDERS W MCC	4.2216	6.0006	1.3936	$7,454.03
	607	MINOR SKIN DISORDERS W/O MCC	2.8128	3.5857	0.6892	$3,686.37
	614	ADRENAL & PITUITARY PROCEDURES W CC/MCC	4.2212	5.7401	2.3998	$12,835.95
	615	ADRENAL & PITUITARY PROCEDURES W/O CC/MCC	2.3366	2.7188	1.4036	$7,507.52
T	616	AMPUTAT OF LOWER LIMB FOR ENDOCRINE,NUTRIT,& METABOL DIS W MCC	11.4674	14.1094	4.3525	$23,280.48
T	617	AMPUTAT OF LOWER LIMB FOR ENDOCRINE,NUTRIT,& METABOL DIS W CC	6.1607	7.4713	1.9716	$10,545.62
T	618	AMPUTAT OF LOWER LIMB FOR ENDOCRINE,NUTRIT,& METABOL DIS W/O CC/MCC	3.972	5.0155	1.1287	$6,037.15
	619	O.R. PROCEDURES FOR OBESITY W MCC	4.6189	7.2521	3.4876	$18,654.34

Calculated with an average hospital Medicare base rate of $5,348.76. Each hospital's base rate and corresponding payment will vary. The national average hospital Medicare base rate is the sum of the full update labor-related and nonlabor-related amounts published in the Federal Register, FY 2013 Final Rule, Table 1A. National Adjusted Operating Standardized Amounts; Labor/Nonlabor (if wage index greater than 1) or Table 1B. National Adjusted Operating Standardized Amounts; Labor/Nonlabor (if wage index less than or equal to 1).

MS-DRGs 998 and 999 contain cases that could not be assigned to valid DRGs.

Note: If there is no value in either the geometric mean length of stay or the arithmetic mean length of stay columns, the volume of cases is insufficient to determine a meaningful computation of these statistics.

Appendix D — National Average Payment Table

DRG		Description	GMLOS	AMLOS	Relative Weight	National Payment Rate
	620	O.R. PROCEDURES FOR OBESITY W CC	2.4884	3.0566	1.8601	$9,949.23
	621	O.R. PROCEDURES FOR OBESITY W/O CC/MCC	1.649	1.8627	1.5026	$8,037.05
T	622	SKIN GRAFTS & WOUND DEBRID FOR ENDOC, NUTRIT & METAB DIS W MCC	9.6557	12.7617	3.5668	$19,077.96
T	623	SKIN GRAFTS & WOUND DEBRID FOR ENDOC, NUTRIT & METAB DIS W CC	5.9472	7.2955	1.8221	$9,745.98
T	624	SKIN GRAFTS & WOUND DEBRID FOR ENDOC, NUTRIT & METAB DIS W/O CC/MCC	3.5992	4.3575	0.9662	$5,167.97
	625	THYROID, PARATHYROID & THYROGLOSSAL PROCEDURES W MCC	4.3711	6.8145	2.3606	$12,626.28
	626	THYROID, PARATHYROID & THYROGLOSSAL PROCEDURES W CC	2.0218	2.9451	1.2163	$6,505.70
	627	THYROID, PARATHYROID & THYROGLOSSAL PROCEDURES W/O CC/MCC	1.2342	1.3934	0.8217	$4,395.08
T	628	OTHER ENDOCRINE, NUTRIT & METAB O.R. PROC W MCC	6.8418	10.0302	3.2936	$17,616.68
T	629	OTHER ENDOCRINE, NUTRIT & METAB O.R. PROC W CC	6.1251	7.4301	2.144	$11,467.74
T	630	OTHER ENDOCRINE, NUTRIT & METAB O.R. PROC W/O CC/MCC	3.0719	4.138	1.2266	$6,560.79
T	637	DIABETES W MCC	4.2959	5.653	1.407	$7,525.71
T	638	DIABETES W CC	3.074	3.8314	0.8218	$4,395.61
T	639	DIABETES W/O CC/MCC	2.1943	2.6503	0.5558	$2,972.84
T	640	MISC DISORDERS OF NUTRITION,METABOLISM,FLUIDS/ELECTROLYTES W MCC	3.4069	4.7001	1.1076	$5,924.29
T	641	MISC DISORDERS OF NUTRITION,METABOLISM,FLUIDS/ELECTROLYTES W/O MCC	2.7411	3.4028	0.692	$3,701.34
	642	INBORN AND OTHER DISORDERS OF METABOLISM	3.3456	4.6153	1.1233	$6,008.26
T	643	ENDOCRINE DISORDERS W MCC	5.6572	7.1345	1.7094	$9,143.17
T	644	ENDOCRINE DISORDERS W CC	3.9704	4.918	1.0508	$5,620.48
T	645	ENDOCRINE DISORDERS W/O CC/MCC	2.8207	3.4069	0.7233	$3,868.76
	652	KIDNEY TRANSPLANT	6.0064	7.0131	3.0825	$16,487.55
T	653	MAJOR BLADDER PROCEDURES W MCC	13.076	16.0052	6.1649	$32,974.57
T	654	MAJOR BLADDER PROCEDURES W CC	7.885	9.017	3.1279	$16,730.39
T	655	MAJOR BLADDER PROCEDURES W/O CC/MCC	4.7361	5.5545	2.0913	$11,185.86
	656	KIDNEY & URETER PROCEDURES FOR NEOPLASM W MCC	7.3328	9.5272	3.5136	$18,793.40
	657	KIDNEY & URETER PROCEDURES FOR NEOPLASM W CC	4.5967	5.4262	1.9904	$10,646.17
	658	KIDNEY & URETER PROCEDURES FOR NEOPLASM W/O CC/MCC	2.8754	3.2435	1.4836	$7,935.42
T	659	KIDNEY & URETER PROCEDURES FOR NON-NEOPLASM W MCC	7.9444	10.8115	3.5192	$18,823.36
T	660	KIDNEY & URETER PROCEDURES FOR NON-NEOPLASM W CC	4.3514	5.7634	1.8829	$10,071.18
T	661	KIDNEY & URETER PROCEDURES FOR NON-NEOPLASM W/O CC/MCC	2.3269	2.8502	1.3335	$7,132.57
	662	MINOR BLADDER PROCEDURES W MCC	7.5497	10.2683	2.9941	$16,014.72
	663	MINOR BLADDER PROCEDURES W CC	3.7715	5.2202	1.5295	$8,180.93
	664	MINOR BLADDER PROCEDURES W/O CC/MCC	1.6097	2.0092	1.126	$6,022.70
	665	PROSTATECTOMY W MCC	9.532	11.9406	3.0737	$16,440.48
	666	PROSTATECTOMY W CC	4.4888	6.191	1.6602	$8,880.01
	667	PROSTATECTOMY W/O CC/MCC	1.9792	2.6061	0.876	$4,685.51
	668	TRANSURETHRAL PROCEDURES W MCC	6.7363	8.7684	2.4731	$13,228.02
	669	TRANSURETHRAL PROCEDURES W CC	3.101	4.2443	1.3015	$6,961.41

Calculated with an average hospital Medicare base rate of $5,348.76. Each hospital's base rate and corresponding payment will vary. The national average hospital Medicare base rate is the sum of the full update labor-related and nonlabor-related amounts published in the Federal Register, FY 2013 Final Rule, Table 1A. National Adjusted Operating Standardized Amounts; Labor/Nonlabor (if wage index greater than 1) or Table 1B. National Adjusted Operating Standardized Amounts; Labor/Nonlabor (if wage index less than or equal to 1).

MS-DRGs 998 and 999 contain cases that could not be assigned to valid DRGs.

Note: If there is no value in either the geometric mean length of stay or the arithmetic mean length of stay columns, the volume of cases is insufficient to determine a meaningful computation of these statistics.

T *Transfer DRG*   SP *Special Payment*

DRG		Description	GMLOS	AMLOS	Relative Weight	National Payment Rate
	670	TRANSURETHRAL PROCEDURES W/O CC/MCC	1.9082	2.4431	0.8326	$4,453.38
	671	URETHRAL PROCEDURES W CC/MCC	3.7313	5.191	1.4513	$7,762.66
	672	URETHRAL PROCEDURES W/O CC/MCC	1.8446	2.2986	0.8383	$4,483.87
	673	OTHER KIDNEY & URINARY TRACT PROCEDURES W MCC	6.4349	9.7949	3.0591	$16,362.39
	674	OTHER KIDNEY & URINARY TRACT PROCEDURES W CC	5.1087	6.9937	2.1887	$11,706.83
	675	OTHER KIDNEY & URINARY TRACT PROCEDURES W/O CC/MCC	1.7995	2.5219	1.3558	$7,251.85
T	682	RENAL FAILURE W MCC	4.863	6.4654	1.5862	$8,484.20
T	683	RENAL FAILURE W CC	3.7908	4.6553	0.9958	$5,326.30
T	684	RENAL FAILURE W/O CC/MCC	2.6184	3.1378	0.6432	$3,440.32
	685	ADMIT FOR RENAL DIALYSIS	2.5332	3.4995	0.8899	$4,759.86
	686	KIDNEY & URINARY TRACT NEOPLASMS W MCC	5.4095	7.1591	1.6823	$8,998.22
	687	KIDNEY & URINARY TRACT NEOPLASMS W CC	3.6373	4.708	1.0499	$5,615.66
	688	KIDNEY & URINARY TRACT NEOPLASMS W/O CC/MCC	2.2391	2.8658	0.6805	$3,639.83
T	689	KIDNEY & URINARY TRACT INFECTIONS W MCC	4.4503	5.494	1.1784	$6,302.98
T	690	KIDNEY & URINARY TRACT INFECTIONS W/O MCC	3.249	3.8866	0.781	$4,177.38
	691	URINARY STONES W ESW LITHOTRIPSY W CC/MCC	3.0185	4.0256	1.5632	$8,361.18
	692	URINARY STONES W ESW LITHOTRIPSY W/O CC/MCC	1.7216	2.0977	1.0563	$5,649.90
	693	URINARY STONES W/O ESW LITHOTRIPSY W MCC	4.0283	5.2376	1.4169	$7,578.66
	694	URINARY STONES W/O ESW LITHOTRIPSY W/O MCC	1.9626	2.4362	0.7017	$3,753.22
	695	KIDNEY & URINARY TRACT SIGNS & SYMPTOMS W MCC	4.1817	5.4872	1.2944	$6,923.43
	696	KIDNEY & URINARY TRACT SIGNS & SYMPTOMS W/O MCC	2.5207	3.1073	0.6639	$3,551.04
	697	URETHRAL STRICTURE	2.4688	3.206	0.8246	$4,410.59
T	698	OTHER KIDNEY & URINARY TRACT DIAGNOSES W MCC	5.1733	6.5971	1.5995	$8,555.34
T	699	OTHER KIDNEY & URINARY TRACT DIAGNOSES W CC	3.5801	4.5043	0.9998	$5,347.69
T	700	OTHER KIDNEY & URINARY TRACT DIAGNOSES W/O CC/MCC	2.6331	3.2773	0.6854	$3,666.04
	707	MAJOR MALE PELVIC PROCEDURES W CC/MCC	3.0394	4.073	1.8134	$9,699.44
	708	MAJOR MALE PELVIC PROCEDURES W/O CC/MCC	1.502	1.7249	1.2936	$6,919.16
	709	PENIS PROCEDURES W CC/MCC	3.9606	6.444	2.0087	$10,744.05
	710	PENIS PROCEDURES W/O CC/MCC	1.4794	1.8457	1.2991	$6,948.57
	711	TESTES PROCEDURES W CC/MCC	5.5133	7.8213	1.9631	$10,500.15
	712	TESTES PROCEDURES W/O CC/MCC	2.3014	3.2023	0.8418	$4,502.59
	713	TRANSURETHRAL PROSTATECTOMY W CC/MCC	3.1209	4.3994	1.3234	$7,078.55
	714	TRANSURETHRAL PROSTATECTOMY W/O CC/MCC	1.6035	1.8436	0.6983	$3,735.04
	715	OTHER MALE REPRODUCTIVE SYSTEM O.R. PROC FOR MALIGNANCY W CC/MCC	4.3865	6.6	1.9149	$10,242.34
	716	OTHER MALE REPRODUCTIVE SYSTEM O.R. PROC FOR MALIGNANCY W/O CC/MCC	1.298	1.5213	0.9656	$5,164.76
	717	OTHER MALE REPRODUCTIVE SYSTEM O.R. PROC EXC MALIGNANCY W CC/MCC	4.5312	6.1748	1.7261	$9,232.49
	718	OTHER MALE REPRODUCTIVE SYSTEM O.R. PROC EXC MALIGNANCY W/O CC/MCC	2.2183	2.9768	0.8657	$4,630.42
	722	MALIGNANCY, MALE REPRODUCTIVE SYSTEM W MCC	5.3549	7.1951	1.669	$8,927.08
	723	MALIGNANCY, MALE REPRODUCTIVE SYSTEM W CC	3.957	5.1062	1.1066	$5,918.94

Calculated with an average hospital Medicare base rate of $5,348.76. Each hospital's base rate and corresponding payment will vary. The national average hospital Medicare base rate is the sum of the full update labor-related and nonlabor-related amounts published in the Federal Register, FY 2013 Final Rule, Table 1A. National Adjusted Operating Standardized Amounts; Labor/Nonlabor (if wage index greater than 1) or Table 1B. National Adjusted Operating Standardized Amounts; Labor/Nonlabor (if wage index less than or equal to 1).

MS-DRGs 998 and 999 contain cases that could not be assigned to valid DRGs.

Note: If there is no value in either the geometric mean length of stay or the arithmetic mean length of stay columns, the volume of cases is insufficient to determine a meaningful computation of these statistics.

DRG	Description	GMLOS	AMLOS	Relative Weight	National Payment Rate
724	MALIGNANCY, MALE REPRODUCTIVE SYSTEM W/O CC/MCC	2.0256	2.603	0.6509	$3,481.51
725	BENIGN PROSTATIC HYPERTROPHY W MCC	4.6156	5.8506	1.2976	$6,940.55
726	BENIGN PROSTATIC HYPERTROPHY W/O MCC	2.6948	3.371	0.7085	$3,789.60
727	INFLAMMATION OF THE MALE REPRODUCTIVE SYSTEM W MCC	5.0053	6.3185	1.4014	$7,495.75
728	INFLAMMATION OF THE MALE REPRODUCTIVE SYSTEM W/O MCC	3.2624	3.9485	0.7721	$4,129.78
729	OTHER MALE REPRODUCTIVE SYSTEM DIAGNOSES W CC/MCC	3.3656	4.3683	1.0357	$5,539.71
730	OTHER MALE REPRODUCTIVE SYSTEM DIAGNOSES W/O CC/MCC	1.9912	2.5206	0.6113	$3,269.70
734	PELVIC EVISCERATION, RAD HYSTERECTOMY & RAD VULVECTOMY W CC/MCC	5.0073	7.1179	2.6652	$14,255.52
735	PELVIC EVISCERATION, RAD HYSTERECTOMY & RAD VULVECTOMY W/O CC/MCC	1.8686	2.2662	1.1682	$6,248.42
736	UTERINE & ADNEXA PROC FOR OVARIAN OR ADNEXAL MALIGNANCY W MCC	10.7108	13.0083	4.414	$23,609.43
737	UTERINE & ADNEXA PROC FOR OVARIAN OR ADNEXAL MALIGNANCY W CC	5.4429	6.4	2.0049	$10,723.73
738	UTERINE & ADNEXA PROC FOR OVARIAN OR ADNEXAL MALIGNANCY W/O CC/MCC	2.9592	3.3592	1.2853	$6,874.76
739	UTERINE,ADNEXA PROC FOR NON-OVARIAN/ADNEXAL MALIG W MCC	6.8001	9.2346	3.3219	$17,768.05
740	UTERINE,ADNEXA PROC FOR NON-OVARIAN/ADNEXAL MALIG W CC	3.2752	4.1654	1.5688	$8,391.13
741	UTERINE,ADNEXA PROC FOR NON-OVARIAN/ADNEXAL MALIG W/O CC/MCC	1.8298	2.1516	1.1499	$6,150.54
742	UTERINE & ADNEXA PROC FOR NON-MALIGNANCY W CC/MCC	2.927	3.8666	1.4157	$7,572.24
743	UTERINE & ADNEXA PROC FOR NON-MALIGNANCY W/O CC/MCC	1.7215	1.9372	0.9653	$5,163.16
744	D&C, CONIZATION, LAPAROSCOPY & TUBAL INTERRUPTION W CC/MCC	4.0977	5.892	1.5573	$8,329.62
745	D&C, CONIZATION, LAPAROSCOPY & TUBAL INTERRUPTION W/O CC/MCC	1.7923	2.1756	0.8109	$4,337.31
746	VAGINA, CERVIX & VULVA PROCEDURES W CC/MCC	3.0344	4.3721	1.385	$7,408.03
747	VAGINA, CERVIX & VULVA PROCEDURES W/O CC/MCC	1.4979	1.7514	0.8818	$4,716.54
748	FEMALE REPRODUCTIVE SYSTEM RECONSTRUCTIVE PROCEDURES	1.4312	1.68	0.9773	$5,227.34
749	OTHER FEMALE REPRODUCTIVE SYSTEM O.R. PROCEDURES W CC/MCC	6.0986	8.6313	2.5755	$13,775.73
750	OTHER FEMALE REPRODUCTIVE SYSTEM O.R. PROCEDURES W/O CC/MCC	2.3809	2.9772	1.0675	$5,709.80
754	MALIGNANCY, FEMALE REPRODUCTIVE SYSTEM W MCC	5.9084	8.1105	1.9833	$10,608.20
755	MALIGNANCY, FEMALE REPRODUCTIVE SYSTEM W CC	3.7844	5.0027	1.099	$5,878.29
756	MALIGNANCY, FEMALE REPRODUCTIVE SYSTEM W/O CC/MCC	2.0976	2.6807	0.5777	$3,089.98
757	INFECTIONS, FEMALE REPRODUCTIVE SYSTEM W MCC	6.0308	7.8434	1.6945	$9,063.47
758	INFECTIONS, FEMALE REPRODUCTIVE SYSTEM W CC	4.3902	5.4185	1.079	$5,771.31
759	INFECTIONS, FEMALE REPRODUCTIVE SYSTEM W/O CC/MCC	3.0692	3.6872	0.7173	$3,836.67
760	MENSTRUAL & OTHER FEMALE REPRODUCTIVE SYSTEM DISORDERS W CC/MCC	2.7762	3.6041	0.8062	$4,312.17
761	MENSTRUAL & OTHER FEMALE REPRODUCTIVE SYSTEM DISORDERS W/O CC/MCC	1.7877	2.2162	0.4951	$2,648.17
765	CESAREAN SECTION W CC/MCC	3.8071	4.7939	1.2194	$6,522.28
766	CESAREAN SECTION W/O CC/MCC	2.874	3.0827	0.8586	$4,592.45
767	VAGINAL DELIVERY W STERILIZATION &/OR D&C	2.5244	3.1955	0.9225	$4,934.23
768	VAGINAL DELIVERY W O.R. PROC EXCEPT STERIL &/OR D&C	4.7	5.8	1.8304	$9,790.37
769	POSTPARTUM & POST ABORTION DIAGNOSES W O.R. PROCEDURE	3.2839	4.9561	1.4668	$7,845.56
770	ABORTION W D&C, ASPIRATION CURETTAGE OR HYSTEROTOMY	1.565	2.0173	0.6489	$3,470.81
774	VAGINAL DELIVERY W COMPLICATING DIAGNOSES	2.6073	3.3039	0.7217	$3,860.20

Calculated with an average hospital Medicare base rate of $5,348.76. Each hospital's base rate and corresponding payment will vary. The national average hospital Medicare base rate is the sum of the full update labor-related and nonlabor-related amounts published in the Federal Register, FY 2013 Final Rule, Table 1A. National Adjusted Operating Standardized Amounts; Labor/Nonlabor (if wage index greater than 1) or Table 1B. National Adjusted Operating Standardized Amounts; Labor/Nonlabor (if wage index less than or equal to 1).

MS-DRGs 998 and 999 contain cases that could not be assigned to valid DRGs.

Note: If there is no value in either the geometric mean length of stay or the arithmetic mean length of stay columns, the volume of cases is insufficient to determine a meaningful computation of these statistics.

DRG	Description	GMLOS	AMLOS	Relative Weight	National Payment Rate
775	VAGINAL DELIVERY W/O COMPLICATING DIAGNOSES	2.1092	2.3553	0.5755	$3,078.21
776	POSTPARTUM & POST ABORTION DIAGNOSES W/O O.R. PROCEDURE	2.5384	3.2237	0.6565	$3,511.46
777	ECTOPIC PREGNANCY	1.8784	2.3143	0.8777	$4,694.61
778	THREATENED ABORTION	2.1019	3.1116	0.5049	$2,700.59
779	ABORTION W/O D&C	1.5534	1.8829	0.4962	$2,654.05
780	FALSE LABOR	1.1073	1.186	0.1896	$1,014.12
781	OTHER ANTEPARTUM DIAGNOSES W MEDICAL COMPLICATIONS	2.6348	3.7533	0.6687	$3,576.72
782	OTHER ANTEPARTUM DIAGNOSES W/O MEDICAL COMPLICATIONS	1.8208	2.5888	0.405	$2,166.25
789	NEONATES, DIED OR TRANSFERRED TO ANOTHER ACUTE CARE FACILITY	1.8	1.8	1.5035	$8,041.86
790	EXTREME IMMATURITY OR RESPIRATORY DISTRESS SYNDROME, NEONATE	17.9	17.9	4.9579	$26,518.62
791	PREMATURITY W MAJOR PROBLEMS	13.3	13.3	3.3861	$18,111.44
792	PREMATURITY W/O MAJOR PROBLEMS	8.6	8.6	2.0431	$10,928.05
793	FULL TERM NEONATE W MAJOR PROBLEMS	4.7	4.7	3.4783	$18,604.59
794	NEONATE W OTHER SIGNIFICANT PROBLEMS	3.4	3.4	1.2311	$6,584.86
795	NORMAL NEWBORN	3.1	3.1	0.1667	$891.64
799	SPLENECTOMY W MCC	9.6686	12.6592	5.1496	$27,543.97
800	SPLENECTOMY W CC	5.4681	7.0919	2.6372	$14,105.75
801	SPLENECTOMY W/O CC/MCC	2.9747	3.7944	1.5736	$8,416.81
802	OTHER O.R. PROC OF THE BLOOD & BLOOD FORMING ORGANS W MCC	8.3115	11.4201	3.6452	$19,497.30
803	OTHER O.R. PROC OF THE BLOOD & BLOOD FORMING ORGANS W CC	4.386	5.7587	1.7576	$9,400.98
804	OTHER O.R. PROC OF THE BLOOD & BLOOD FORMING ORGANS W/O CC/MCC	2.3118	3.0577	1.1211	$5,996.49
808	MAJOR HEMATOL/IMMUN DIAG EXC SICKLE CELL CRISIS & COAGUL W MCC	5.9184	7.7693	2.0902	$11,179.98
809	MAJOR HEMATOL/IMMUN DIAG EXC SICKLE CELL CRISIS & COAGUL W CC	3.7444	4.7443	1.1767	$6,293.89
810	MAJOR HEMATOL/IMMUN DIAG EXC SICKLE CELL CRISIS & COAGUL W/O CC/MCC	2.693	3.3933	0.849	$4,541.10
811	RED BLOOD CELL DISORDERS W MCC	3.6828	4.9904	1.2556	$6,715.90
812	RED BLOOD CELL DISORDERS W/O MCC	2.619	3.3911	0.7872	$4,210.54
813	COAGULATION DISORDERS	3.5515	4.969	1.5841	$8,472.97
814	RETICULOENDOTHELIAL & IMMUNITY DISORDERS W MCC	4.866	6.5678	1.6794	$8,982.71
815	RETICULOENDOTHELIAL & IMMUNITY DISORDERS W CC	3.4962	4.4646	1.0102	$5,403.32
816	RETICULOENDOTHELIAL & IMMUNITY DISORDERS W/O CC/MCC	2.5032	3.0702	0.6918	$3,700.27
820	LYMPHOMA & LEUKEMIA W MAJOR O.R. PROCEDURE W MCC	12.6927	16.9376	5.7228	$30,609.88
821	LYMPHOMA & LEUKEMIA W MAJOR O.R. PROCEDURE W CC	4.9785	6.9327	2.3066	$12,337.45
822	LYMPHOMA & LEUKEMIA W MAJOR O.R. PROCEDURE W/O CC/MCC	2.2023	2.836	1.1935	$6,383.75
823	LYMPHOMA & NON-ACUTE LEUKEMIA W OTHER O.R. PROC W MCC	11.6922	14.8256	4.5397	$24,281.77
824	LYMPHOMA & NON-ACUTE LEUKEMIA W OTHER O.R. PROC W CC	6.1869	8.0945	2.2603	$12,089.80
825	LYMPHOMA & NON-ACUTE LEUKEMIA W OTHER O.R. PROC W/O CC/MCC	2.7051	3.7631	1.2712	$6,799.34
826	MYELOPROLIF DISORD OR POORLY DIFF NEOPL W MAJ O.R. PROC W MCC	10.929	14.005	4.868	$26,037.76
827	MYELOPROLIF DISORD OR POORLY DIFF NEOPL W MAJ O.R. PROC W CC	5.2652	6.8101	2.1765	$11,641.58
828	MYELOPROLIF DISORD OR POORLY DIFF NEOPL W MAJ O.R. PROC W/O CC/MCC	2.7725	3.4166	1.3409	$7,172.15

Calculated with an average hospital Medicare base rate of $5,348.76. Each hospital's base rate and corresponding payment will vary. The national average hospital Medicare base rate is the sum of the full update labor-related and nonlabor-related amounts published in the Federal Register, FY 2013 Final Rule, Table 1A. National Adjusted Operating Standardized Amounts; Labor/Nonlabor (if wage index greater than 1) or Table 1B. National Adjusted Operating Standardized Amounts; Labor/Nonlabor (if wage index less than or equal to 1).

MS-DRGs 998 and 999 contain cases that could not be assigned to valid DRGs.

Note: If there is no value in either the geometric mean length of stay or the arithmetic mean length of stay columns, the volume of cases is insufficient to determine a meaningful computation of these statistics.

Appendix D — National Average Payment Table

DRG		Description	GMLOS	AMLOS	Relative Weight	National Payment Rate
	829	MYELOPROLIF DISORD OR POORLY DIFF NEOPL W OTHER O.R. PROC W CC/MCC	6.379	9.6257	3.0335	$16,225.46
	830	MYELOPROLIF DISORD OR POORLY DIFF NEOPL W OTHER O.R. PROC W/O CC/MCC	2.4964	3.285	1.1804	$6,313.68
	834	ACUTE LEUKEMIA W/O MAJOR O.R. PROCEDURE W MCC	9.8558	16.0961	5.1622	$27,611.37
	835	ACUTE LEUKEMIA W/O MAJOR O.R. PROCEDURE W CC	5.0721	8.2507	2.2133	$11,838.41
	836	ACUTE LEUKEMIA W/O MAJOR O.R. PROCEDURE W/O CC/MCC	2.7654	4.0088	1.0992	$5,879.36
	837	CHEMO W ACUTE LEUKEMIA AS SDX OR W HIGH DOSE CHEMO AGENT W MCC	16.6602	22.4882	6.4881	$34,703.29
	838	CHEMO W ACUTE LEUKEMIA AS SDX W CC OR HIGH DOSE CHEMO AGENT	7.2106	10.1812	2.7537	$14,728.88
	839	CHEMO W ACUTE LEUKEMIA AS SDX W/O CC/MCC	4.7232	5.5505	1.2412	$6,638.88
T	840	LYMPHOMA & NON-ACUTE LEUKEMIA W MCC	7.7158	10.5167	3.0103	$16,101.37
T	841	LYMPHOMA & NON-ACUTE LEUKEMIA W CC	4.8295	6.3679	1.6192	$8,660.71
T	842	LYMPHOMA & NON-ACUTE LEUKEMIA W/O CC/MCC	3.024	3.9514	1.045	$5,589.45
	843	OTHER MYELOPROLIF DIS OR POORLY DIFF NEOPL DIAG W MCC	5.8993	7.8756	1.8719	$10,012.34
	844	OTHER MYELOPROLIF DIS OR POORLY DIFF NEOPL DIAG W CC	4.2553	5.5639	1.2216	$6,534.05
	845	OTHER MYELOPROLIF DIS OR POORLY DIFF NEOPL DIAG W/O CC/MCC	2.8809	3.7556	0.8612	$4,606.35
	846	CHEMOTHERAPY W/O ACUTE LEUKEMIA AS SECONDARY DIAGNOSIS W MCC	5.7048	8.2586	2.4374	$13,037.07
	847	CHEMOTHERAPY W/O ACUTE LEUKEMIA AS SECONDARY DIAGNOSIS W CC	2.8795	3.5181	1.0447	$5,587.85
	848	CHEMOTHERAPY W/O ACUTE LEUKEMIA AS SECONDARY DIAGNOSIS W/O CC/MCC	2.4261	2.975	0.7878	$4,213.75
	849	RADIOTHERAPY	4.6067	6.1715	1.3396	$7,165.20
T	853	INFECTIOUS & PARASITIC DISEASES W O.R. PROCEDURE W MCC	11.3468	14.5849	5.3431	$28,578.96
T	854	INFECTIOUS & PARASITIC DISEASES W O.R. PROCEDURE W CC	7.3364	8.8226	2.5583	$13,683.73
T	855	INFECTIOUS & PARASITIC DISEASES W O.R. PROCEDURE W/O CC/MCC	3.53	4.9399	1.5331	$8,200.18
T	856	POSTOPERATIVE OR POST-TRAUMATIC INFECTIONS W O.R. PROC W MCC	10.5184	13.9737	4.8125	$25,740.91
T	857	POSTOPERATIVE OR POST-TRAUMATIC INFECTIONS W O.R. PROC W CC	5.8137	7.3841	2.0649	$11,044.65
T	858	POSTOPERATIVE OR POST-TRAUMATIC INFECTIONS W O.R. PROC W/O CC/MCC	3.8409	4.7315	1.2534	$6,704.14
T	862	POSTOPERATIVE & POST-TRAUMATIC INFECTIONS W MCC	5.7162	7.5628	2.0099	$10,750.47
T	863	POSTOPERATIVE & POST-TRAUMATIC INFECTIONS W/O MCC	3.821	4.6792	0.9822	$5,253.55
	864	FEVER	2.9415	3.6711	0.8443	$4,515.96
	865	VIRAL ILLNESS W MCC	4.4275	6.247	1.5181	$8,119.95
	866	VIRAL ILLNESS W/O MCC	2.781	3.4282	0.7594	$4,061.85
T	867	OTHER INFECTIOUS & PARASITIC DISEASES DIAGNOSES W MCC	6.9691	9.383	2.5861	$13,832.43
T	868	OTHER INFECTIOUS & PARASITIC DISEASES DIAGNOSES W CC	3.9139	4.8943	1.0762	$5,756.34
T	869	OTHER INFECTIOUS & PARASITIC DISEASES DIAGNOSES W/O CC/MCC	2.8357	3.453	0.7415	$3,966.11
T	870	SEPTICEMIA OR SEVERE SEPSIS W MV 96+ HOURS	12.6227	14.8151	5.8399	$31,236.22
T	871	SEPTICEMIA OR SEVERE SEPSIS W/O MV 96+ HOURS W MCC	5.2273	6.9073	1.8803	$10,057.27
T	872	SEPTICEMIA OR SEVERE SEPSIS W/O MV 96+ HOURS W/O MCC	4.1861	5.033	1.0988	$5,877.22
	876	O.R. PROCEDURE W PRINCIPAL DIAGNOSES OF MENTAL ILLNESS	7.4538	12.2042	2.7097	$14,493.53
	880	ACUTE ADJUSTMENT REACTION & PSYCHOSOCIAL DYSFUNCTION	2.2084	2.9829	0.6474	$3,462.79
	881	DEPRESSIVE NEUROSES	3.1942	4.3292	0.6356	$3,399.67

Calculated with an average hospital Medicare base rate of $5,348.76. Each hospital's base rate and corresponding payment will vary. The national average hospital Medicare base rate is the sum of the full update labor-related and nonlabor-related amounts published in the Federal Register, FY 2013 Final Rule, Table 1A. National Adjusted Operating Standardized Amounts; Labor/Nonlabor (if wage index greater than 1) or Table 1B. National Adjusted Operating Standardized Amounts; Labor/Nonlabor (if wage index less than or equal to 1).

MS-DRGs 998 and 999 contain cases that could not be assigned to valid DRGs.

Note: If there is no value in either the geometric mean length of stay or the arithmetic mean length of stay columns, the volume of cases is insufficient to determine a meaningful computation of these statistics.

T *Transfer DRG*   SP *Special Payment*

DRG		Description	GMLOS	AMLOS	Relative Weight	National Payment Rate
	882	NEUROSES EXCEPT DEPRESSIVE	3.1001	4.2326	0.6271	$3,354.21
	883	DISORDERS OF PERSONALITY & IMPULSE CONTROL	4.679	8.1041	1.3613	$7,281.27
T	884	ORGANIC DISTURBANCES & MENTAL RETARDATION	3.9165	5.3944	0.985	$5,268.53
	885	PSYCHOSES	5.4144	7.4024	0.9539	$5,102.18
	886	BEHAVIORAL & DEVELOPMENTAL DISORDERS	3.7959	6.0959	0.7812	$4,178.45
	887	OTHER MENTAL DISORDER DIAGNOSES	3.1049	4.7494	0.9473	$5,066.88
	894	ALCOHOL/DRUG ABUSE OR DEPENDENCE, LEFT AMA	2.1036	2.9649	0.4278	$2,288.20
	895	ALCOHOL/DRUG ABUSE OR DEPENDENCE W REHABILITATION THERAPY	9.1678	11.6848	1.0963	$5,863.85
T	896	ALCOHOL/DRUG ABUSE OR DEPENDENCE W/O REHABILITATION THERAPY W MCC	4.7928	6.6914	1.5271	$8,168.09
T	897	ALCOHOL/DRUG ABUSE OR DEPENDENCE W/O REHABILITATION THERAPY W/O MCC	3.2026	3.9951	0.6788	$3,630.74
	901	WOUND DEBRIDEMENTS FOR INJURIES W MCC	9.863	14.874	4.3477	$23,254.80
	902	WOUND DEBRIDEMENTS FOR INJURIES W CC	5.0433	6.883	1.7079	$9,135.15
	903	WOUND DEBRIDEMENTS FOR INJURIES W/O CC/MCC	3.0128	3.9887	0.989	$5,289.92
	904	SKIN GRAFTS FOR INJURIES W CC/MCC	6.9611	10.0843	2.9145	$15,588.96
	905	SKIN GRAFTS FOR INJURIES W/O CC/MCC	3.418	4.5816	1.263	$6,755.48
	906	HAND PROCEDURES FOR INJURIES	2.357	3.6224	1.1596	$6,202.42
T	907	OTHER O.R. PROCEDURES FOR INJURIES W MCC	7.7198	10.884	3.8565	$20,627.49
T	908	OTHER O.R. PROCEDURES FOR INJURIES W CC	4.5121	5.9858	1.9519	$10,440.24
T	909	OTHER O.R. PROCEDURES FOR INJURIES W/O CC/MCC	2.6253	3.3403	1.2051	$6,445.79
	913	TRAUMATIC INJURY W MCC	3.7891	5.1164	1.2273	$6,564.53
	914	TRAUMATIC INJURY W/O MCC	2.4659	3.0794	0.6998	$3,743.06
	915	ALLERGIC REACTIONS W MCC	3.736	5.1105	1.5168	$8,113.00
	916	ALLERGIC REACTIONS W/O MCC	1.6835	2.0927	0.5042	$2,696.84
T	917	POISONING & TOXIC EFFECTS OF DRUGS W MCC	3.571	4.9263	1.4542	$7,778.17
T	918	POISONING & TOXIC EFFECTS OF DRUGS W/O MCC	2.0637	2.7007	0.6304	$3,371.86
	919	COMPLICATIONS OF TREATMENT W MCC	4.3842	6.0463	1.6615	$8,886.96
	920	COMPLICATIONS OF TREATMENT W CC	3.0952	3.9966	0.9693	$5,184.55
	921	COMPLICATIONS OF TREATMENT W/O CC/MCC	2.2174	2.783	0.6637	$3,549.97
	922	OTHER INJURY, POISONING & TOXIC EFFECT DIAG W MCC	3.9083	5.6969	1.4305	$7,651.40
	923	OTHER INJURY, POISONING & TOXIC EFFECT DIAG W/O MCC	2.195	2.9029	0.6438	$3,443.53
	927	EXTENSIVE BURNS OR FULL THICKNESS BURNS W MV 96+ HRS W SKIN GRAFT	22.4719	29.6	16.4026	$87,733.57
	928	FULL THICKNESS BURN W SKIN GRAFT OR INHAL INJ W CC/MCC	11.2102	15.3353	4.7919	$25,630.72
	929	FULL THICKNESS BURN W SKIN GRAFT OR INHAL INJ W/O CC/MCC	5.2038	7.2579	2.242	$11,991.92
	933	EXTENSIVE BURNS OR FULL THICKNESS BURNS W MV 96+ HRS W/O SKIN GRAFT	2.5217	5.3224	2.374	$12,697.96
	934	FULL THICKNESS BURN W/O SKIN GRFT OR INHAL INJ	4.0428	5.7492	1.5123	$8,088.93
	935	NON-EXTENSIVE BURNS	3.347	5.025	1.341	$7,172.69
	939	O.R. PROC W DIAGNOSES OF OTHER CONTACT W HEALTH SERVICES W MCC	6.2252	9.0688	2.7769	$14,852.97
	940	O.R. PROC W DIAGNOSES OF OTHER CONTACT W HEALTH SERVICES W CC	3.6338	5.267	1.8108	$9,685.53

Calculated with an average hospital Medicare base rate of $5,348.76. Each hospital's base rate and corresponding payment will vary. The national average hospital Medicare base rate is the sum of the full update labor-related and nonlabor-related amounts published in the Federal Register, FY 2013 Final Rule, Table 1A. National Adjusted Operating Standardized Amounts; Labor/Nonlabor (if wage index greater than 1) or Table 1B. National Adjusted Operating Standardized Amounts; Labor/Nonlabor (if wage index less than or equal to 1).

MS-DRGs 998 and 999 contain cases that could not be assigned to valid DRGs.

Note: If there is no value in either the geometric mean length of stay or the arithmetic mean length of stay columns, the volume of cases is insufficient to determine a meaningful computation of these statistics.

DRG		Description	GMLOS	AMLOS	Relative Weight	National Payment Rate
	941	O.R. PROC W DIAGNOSES OF OTHER CONTACT W HEALTH SERVICES W/O CC/MCC	2.0518	2.6939	1.1776	$6,298.70
T	945	REHABILITATION W CC/MCC	8.346	10.0823	1.3204	$7,062.50
T	946	REHABILITATION W/O CC/MCC	6.5405	7.4368	1.253	$6,702.00
T	947	SIGNS & SYMPTOMS W MCC	3.5935	4.7542	1.1131	$5,953.70
T	948	SIGNS & SYMPTOMS W/O MCC	2.654	3.3334	0.701	$3,749.48
	949	AFTERCARE W CC/MCC	2.8453	4.159	0.9372	$5,012.86
	950	AFTERCARE W/O CC/MCC	2.3221	3.2682	0.5693	$3,045.05
	951	OTHER FACTORS INFLUENCING HEALTH STATUS	2.3542	5.9459	0.8105	$4,335.17
	955	CRANIOTOMY FOR MULTIPLE SIGNIFICANT TRAUMA	8.1179	11.5411	5.417	$28,974.23
T	956	LIMB REATTACHMENT, HIP & FEMUR PROC FOR MULTIPLE SIGNIFICANT TRAUMA	6.8978	8.3999	3.6372	$19,454.51
	957	OTHER O.R. PROCEDURES FOR MULTIPLE SIGNIFICANT TRAUMA W MCC	9.9161	13.8933	6.4182	$34,329.41
	958	OTHER O.R. PROCEDURES FOR MULTIPLE SIGNIFICANT TRAUMA W CC	7.2134	9.1284	3.9004	$20,862.30
	959	OTHER O.R. PROCEDURES FOR MULTIPLE SIGNIFICANT TRAUMA W/O CC/MCC	4.6894	5.8205	2.5646	$13,717.43
	963	OTHER MULTIPLE SIGNIFICANT TRAUMA W MCC	5.8433	8.5488	2.8483	$15,234.87
	964	OTHER MULTIPLE SIGNIFICANT TRAUMA W CC	4.4049	5.4504	1.4975	$8,009.77
	965	OTHER MULTIPLE SIGNIFICANT TRAUMA W/O CC/MCC	3.0418	3.6469	0.96	$5,134.81
	969	HIV W EXTENSIVE O.R. PROCEDURE W MCC	12.0334	16.3116	5.4815	$29,319.23
	970	HIV W EXTENSIVE O.R. PROCEDURE W/O MCC	5.5187	7.3671	2.6631	$14,244.28
	974	HIV W MAJOR RELATED CONDITION W MCC	6.8134	9.575	2.5943	$13,876.29
	975	HIV W MAJOR RELATED CONDITION W CC	4.781	6.2204	1.3142	$7,029.34
	976	HIV W MAJOR RELATED CONDITION W/O CC/MCC	3.2643	4.0645	0.8416	$4,501.52
	977	HIV W OR W/O OTHER RELATED CONDITION	3.4874	4.6777	1.0517	$5,625.29
T	981	EXTENSIVE O.R. PROCEDURE UNRELATED TO PRINCIPAL DIAGNOSIS W MCC	10.5075	13.676	5.027	$26,888.22
T	982	EXTENSIVE O.R. PROCEDURE UNRELATED TO PRINCIPAL DIAGNOSIS W CC	6.0048	7.7942	2.8276	$15,124.15
T	983	EXTENSIVE O.R. PROCEDURE UNRELATED TO PRINCIPAL DIAGNOSIS W/O CC/MCC	2.8624	3.8484	1.7175	$9,186.50
	984	PROSTATIC O.R. PROCEDURE UNRELATED TO PRINCIPAL DIAGNOSIS W MCC	10.5817	13.1431	3.6217	$19,371.60
	985	PROSTATIC O.R. PROCEDURE UNRELATED TO PRINCIPAL DIAGNOSIS W CC	6.0666	8.1748	2.0895	$11,176.23
	986	PROSTATIC O.R. PROCEDURE UNRELATED TO PRINCIPAL DIAGNOSIS W/O CC/MCC	2.5119	3.551	1.071	$5,728.52
T	987	NON-EXTENSIVE O.R. PROC UNRELATED TO PRINCIPAL DIAGNOSIS W MCC	8.5976	11.4354	3.3374	$17,850.95
T	988	NON-EXTENSIVE O.R. PROC UNRELATED TO PRINCIPAL DIAGNOSIS W CC	4.9863	6.7278	1.8141	$9,703.19
T	989	NON-EXTENSIVE O.R. PROC UNRELATED TO PRINCIPAL DIAGNOSIS W/O CC/MCC	2.243	3.0495	1.015	$5,428.99
	998	PRINCIPAL DIAGNOSIS INVALID AS DISCHARGE DIAGNOSIS	0	0	0	$0.00
	999	UNGROUPABLE	0	0	0	$0.00

Calculated with an average hospital Medicare base rate of $5,348.76. Each hospital's base rate and corresponding payment will vary. The national average hospital Medicare base rate is the sum of the full update labor-related and nonlabor-related amounts published in the Federal Register, FY 2013 Final Rule, Table 1A. National Adjusted Operating Standardized Amounts; Labor/Nonlabor (if wage index greater than 1) or Table 1B. National Adjusted Operating Standardized Amounts; Labor/Nonlabor (if wage index less than or equal to 1).

MS-DRGs 998 and 999 contain cases that could not be assigned to valid DRGs.

Note: If there is no value in either the geometric mean length of stay or the arithmetic mean length of stay columns, the volume of cases is insufficient to determine a meaningful computation of these statistics.

T *Transfer DRG*   SP *Special Payment*

Appendix E — 2011 MedPAR National Data

Peer Grouping	MS-DRG	Description	Discharges	Average Age	Average Length of Stay	Average Total Charge	Average Allowed
National	001	HEART TRANSPLANT OR IMPLANT OF HEART ASSIST SYSTEM W MCC	1597	60.91	37.69	$801,956	$188,234
National	002	HEART TRANSPLANT OR IMPLANT OF HEART ASSIST SYSTEM W/O MCC	411	59.59	19.56	$472,790	$101,028
National	003	ECMO OR TRACH W MV 96+ HRS OR PDX EXC FACE, MOUTH & NECK W MAJ O.R.	23534	70.30	35.21	$458,274	$105,100
National	004	TRACH W MV 96+ HRS OR PDX EXC FACE, MOUTH & NECK W/O MAJ O.R.	25389	69.43	27.55	$275,186	$65,546
National	005	LIVER TRANSPLANT W MCC OR INTESTINAL TRANSPLANT	1108	58.05	21.81	$464,193	$82,219
National	006	LIVER TRANSPLANT W/O MCC	376	59.19	9.12	$253,509	$34,763
National	007	LUNG TRANSPLANT	631	59.58	18.92	$438,552	$68,784
National	008	SIMULTANEOUS PANCREAS/KIDNEY TRANSPLANT	443	42.58	11.31	$326,982	$34,890
National	010	PANCREAS TRANSPLANT	91	42.91	8.36	$216,959	$27,334
National	011	TRACHEOSTOMY FOR FACE,MOUTH & NECK DIAGNOSES W MCC	2052	69.94	14.90	$143,571	$31,789
National	012	TRACHEOSTOMY FOR FACE,MOUTH & NECK DIAGNOSES W CC	2331	69.07	10.22	$96,833	$20,392
National	013	TRACHEOSTOMY FOR FACE,MOUTH & NECK DIAGNOSES W/O CC/MCC	1134	69.68	6.60	$61,260	$11,452
National	014	ALLOGENEIC BONE MARROW TRANSPLANT	783	60.42	25.92	$322,463	$80,024
National	020	INTRACRANIAL VASCULAR PROCEDURES W PDX HEMORRHAGE W MCC	1535	70.98	17.59	$274,084	$56,832
National	021	INTRACRANIAL VASCULAR PROCEDURES W PDX HEMORRHAGE W CC	535	68.24	13.79	$195,979	$39,459
National	022	INTRACRANIAL VASCULAR PROCEDURES W PDX HEMORRHAGE W/O CC/MCC	152	66.18	8.36	$138,554	$22,350
National	023	CRANIO W MAJOR DEV IMPL/ACUTE COMPLEX CNS PDX W MCC OR CHEMO IMPLANT	5757	72.12	11.21	$150,077	$31,185
National	024	CRANIO W MAJOR DEV IMPL/ACUTE COMPLEX CNS PDX W/O MCC	2304	71.88	6.66	$99,578	$20,116
National	025	CRANIOTOMY & ENDOVASCULAR INTRACRANIAL PROCEDURES W MCC	16733	72.41	10.54	$125,216	$27,656
National	026	CRANIOTOMY & ENDOVASCULAR INTRACRANIAL PROCEDURES W CC	12069	71.78	6.84	$82,388	$16,782
National	027	CRANIOTOMY & ENDOVASCULAR INTRACRANIAL PROCEDURES W/O CC/MCC	13588	69.64	3.67	$63,669	$11,800
National	028	SPINAL PROCEDURES W MCC	2314	67.49	13.00	$148,322	$32,856
National	029	SPINAL PROCEDURES W CC OR SPINAL NEUROSTIMULATORS	4376	66.10	6.58	$81,399	$16,493
National	030	SPINAL PROCEDURES W/O CC/MCC	3878	65.89	3.27	$46,893	$8,869
National	031	VENTRICULAR SHUNT PROCEDURES W MCC	1552	67.41	12.07	$115,237	$25,703
National	032	VENTRICULAR SHUNT PROCEDURES W CC	2763	65.18	5.37	$54,700	$10,969
National	033	VENTRICULAR SHUNT PROCEDURES W/O CC/MCC	3352	73.04	2.59	$38,584	$7,262
National	034	CAROTID ARTERY STENT PROCEDURE W MCC	1052	72.99	7.28	$104,271	$19,842
National	035	CAROTID ARTERY STENT PROCEDURE W CC	2944	73.77	3.25	$60,952	$11,411
National	036	CAROTID ARTERY STENT PROCEDURE W/O CC/MCC	6565	73.95	1.56	$45,086	$8,259
National	037	EXTRACRANIAL PROCEDURES W MCC	5593	71.37	8.52	$89,457	$18,434
National	038	EXTRACRANIAL PROCEDURES W CC	14985	74.47	3.52	$44,024	$7,553

Peer Grouping	MS-DRG	Description	Discharges	Average Age	Average Length of Stay	Average Total Charge	Average Allowed
National	039	EXTRACRANIAL PROCEDURES W/O CC/MCC	43665	74.33	1.64	$29,034	$4,596
National	040	PERIPH/CRANIAL NERVE & OTHER NERV SYST PROC W MCC	5631	69.72	12.57	$103,968	$23,481
National	041	PERIPH/CRANIAL NERVE & OTHER NERV SYST PROC W CC OR PERIPH NEUROSTIM	7992	68.85	6.72	$56,644	$11,731
National	042	PERIPH/CRANIAL NERVE & OTHER NERV SYST PROC W/O CC/MCC	3594	66.93	3.37	$47,595	$8,587
National	052	SPINAL DISORDERS & INJURIES W CC/MCC	1733	72.40	9.91	$49,588	$13,108
National	053	SPINAL DISORDERS & INJURIES W/O CC/MCC	630	69.67	9.49	$29,368	$5,974
National	054	NERVOUS SYSTEM NEOPLASMS W MCC	11304	72.61	6.03	$39,253	$8,250
National	055	NERVOUS SYSTEM NEOPLASMS W/O MCC	12435	72.16	4.62	$29,436	$5,774
National	056	DEGENERATIVE NERVOUS SYSTEM DISORDERS W MCC	15138	77.61	10.24	$43,119	$11,287
National	057	DEGENERATIVE NERVOUS SYSTEM DISORDERS W/O MCC	82171	79.00	9.47	$26,013	$7,729
National	058	MULTIPLE SCLEROSIS & CEREBELLAR ATAXIA W MCC	1135	57.35	7.88	$43,941	$10,539
National	059	MULTIPLE SCLEROSIS & CEREBELLAR ATAXIA W CC	3937	54.51	6.60	$30,797	$5,754
National	060	MULTIPLE SCLEROSIS & CEREBELLAR ATAXIA W/O CC/MCC	4092	51.99	4.38	$23,748	$4,016
National	061	ACUTE ISCHEMIC STROKE W USE OF THROMBOLYTIC AGENT W MCC	3894	79.12	8.00	$83,279	$16,458
National	062	ACUTE ISCHEMIC STROKE W USE OF THROMBOLYTIC AGENT W CC	6191	77.54	5.28	$56,206	$10,000
National	063	ACUTE ISCHEMIC STROKE W USE OF THROMBOLYTIC AGENT W/O CC/MCC	1797	75.91	3.69	$46,152	$7,500
National	064	INTRACRANIAL HEMORRHAGE OR CEREBRAL INFARCTION W MCC	79588	77.80	6.85	$48,649	$10,385
National	065	INTRACRANIAL HEMORRHAGE OR CEREBRAL INFARCTION W CC	132669	78.21	4.74	$30,118	$5,994
National	066	INTRACRANIAL HEMORRHAGE OR CEREBRAL INFARCTION W/O CC/MCC	76028	77.54	3.22	$22,703	$3,914
National	067	NONSPECIFIC CVA & PRECEREBRAL OCCLUSION W/O INFARCT W MCC	1406	75.40	5.46	$40,763	$7,934
National	068	NONSPECIFIC CVA & PRECEREBRAL OCCLUSION W/O INFARCT W/O MCC	10267	77.32	3.25	$25,286	$4,282
National	069	TRANSIENT ISCHEMIA	104708	77.38	2.63	$20,725	$3,264
National	070	NONSPECIFIC CEREBROVASCULAR DISORDERS W MCC	14928	72.14	7.33	$43,913	$10,491
National	071	NONSPECIFIC CEREBROVASCULAR DISORDERS W CC	18678	76.29	5.21	$26,445	$5,852
National	072	NONSPECIFIC CEREBROVASCULAR DISORDERS W/O CC/MCC	7035	74.93	3.22	$20,688	$3,571
National	073	CRANIAL & PERIPHERAL NERVE DISORDERS W MCC	10154	57.39	5.85	$34,884	$7,747
National	074	CRANIAL & PERIPHERAL NERVE DISORDERS W/O MCC	35540	65.57	4.03	$23,610	$4,494
National	075	VIRAL MENINGITIS W CC/MCC	1680	66.83	7.24	$50,815	$9,649
National	076	VIRAL MENINGITIS W/O CC/MCC	754	62.36	3.89	$24,319	$4,335
National	077	HYPERTENSIVE ENCEPHALOPATHY W MCC	1912	65.53	6.21	$45,303	$10,234
National	078	HYPERTENSIVE ENCEPHALOPATHY W CC	2881	76.30	4.07	$26,724	$5,050
National	079	HYPERTENSIVE ENCEPHALOPATHY W/O CC/MCC	987	76.69	2.86	$20,255	$3,592
National	080	NONTRAUMATIC STUPOR & COMA W MCC	2197	72.26	5.46	$32,306	$6,885
National	081	NONTRAUMATIC STUPOR & COMA W/O MCC	7876	75.94	3.66	$18,908	$3,986
National	082	TRAUMATIC STUPOR & COMA, COMA >1 HR W MCC	3406	76.20	5.91	$55,871	$12,228
National	083	TRAUMATIC STUPOR & COMA, COMA >1 HR W CC	3319	77.14	5.05	$39,032	$7,457
National	084	TRAUMATIC STUPOR & COMA, COMA >1 HR W/O CC/MCC	3129	76.49	2.90	$25,575	$4,556

Peer Grouping	MS-DRG	Description	Discharges	Average Age	Average Length of Stay	Average Total Charge	Average Allowed
National	085	TRAUMATIC STUPOR & COMA, COMA <1 HR W MCC	10745	78.31	7.76	$55,713	$12,495
National	086	TRAUMATIC STUPOR & COMA, COMA <1 HR W CC	18981	80.27	4.65	$31,291	$6,395
National	087	TRAUMATIC STUPOR & COMA, COMA <1 HR W/O CC/MCC	16560	79.82	2.88	$21,193	$3,921
National	088	CONCUSSION W MCC	1001	75.62	5.28	$41,524	$8,412
National	089	CONCUSSION W CC	3474	76.53	3.47	$27,657	$4,829
National	090	CONCUSSION W/O CC/MCC	2557	74.31	2.20	$21,291	$3,184
National	091	OTHER DISORDERS OF NERVOUS SYSTEM W MCC	12136	70.01	6.90	$44,095	$9,968
National	092	OTHER DISORDERS OF NERVOUS SYSTEM W CC	23369	72.23	4.48	$24,913	$5,106
National	093	OTHER DISORDERS OF NERVOUS SYSTEM W/O CC/MCC	14565	71.61	2.92	$19,575	$3,382
National	094	BACTERIAL & TUBERCULOUS INFECTIONS OF NERVOUS SYSTEM W MCC	1864	69.01	14.09	$98,332	$23,591
National	095	BACTERIAL & TUBERCULOUS INFECTIONS OF NERVOUS SYSTEM W CC	1579	69.34	9.19	$68,425	$13,769
National	096	BACTERIAL & TUBERCULOUS INFECTIONS OF NERVOUS SYSTEM W/O CC/MCC	657	67.83	6.07	$57,382	$10,526
National	097	NON-BACTERIAL INFECT OF NERVOUS SYS EXC VIRAL MENINGITIS W MCC	1586	70.98	12.05	$90,235	$19,648
National	098	NON-BACTERIAL INFECT OF NERVOUS SYS EXC VIRAL MENINGITIS W CC	1327	69.73	8.06	$51,052	$10,945
National	099	NON-BACTERIAL INFECT OF NERVOUS SYS EXC VIRAL MENINGITIS W/O CC/MCC	602	67.58	5.24	$36,013	$6,458
National	100	SEIZURES W MCC	24076	65.67	5.95	$41,955	$8,763
National	101	SEIZURES W/O MCC	62965	64.39	3.34	$21,442	$3,892
National	102	HEADACHES W MCC	1610	59.58	4.18	$28,663	$5,645
National	103	HEADACHES W/O MCC	15420	62.14	2.84	$19,357	$3,027
National	113	ORBITAL PROCEDURES W CC/MCC	755	73.89	5.64	$57,687	$11,450
National	114	ORBITAL PROCEDURES W/O CC/MCC	479	74.36	2.89	$31,644	$4,920
National	115	EXTRAOCULAR PROCEDURES EXCEPT ORBIT	993	73.07	4.42	$36,388	$6,895
National	116	INTRAOCULAR PROCEDURES W CC/MCC	525	71.98	4.84	$41,789	$7,708
National	117	INTRAOCULAR PROCEDURES W/O CC/MCC	535	73.66	2.20	$21,361	$3,575
National	121	ACUTE MAJOR EYE INFECTIONS W CC/MCC	871	69.70	5.15	$25,755	$5,410
National	122	ACUTE MAJOR EYE INFECTIONS W/O CC/MCC	564	70.28	3.83	$16,345	$3,125
National	123	NEUROLOGICAL EYE DISORDERS	3568	71.98	2.69	$23,011	$3,340
National	124	OTHER DISORDERS OF THE EYE W MCC	1029	69.63	5.25	$33,197	$6,969
National	125	OTHER DISORDERS OF THE EYE W/O MCC	5149	74.40	3.43	$18,676	$3,403
National	129	MAJOR HEAD & NECK PROCEDURES W CC/MCC OR MAJOR DEVICE	1928	71.95	5.35	$65,984	$13,683
National	130	MAJOR HEAD & NECK PROCEDURES W/O CC/MCC	1280	72.69	2.95	$39,407	$6,735
National	131	CRANIAL/FACIAL PROCEDURES W CC/MCC	1404	67.17	5.83	$67,450	$13,032
National	132	CRANIAL/FACIAL PROCEDURES W/O CC/MCC	864	64.91	2.58	$38,106	$6,954
National	133	OTHER EAR, NOSE, MOUTH & THROAT O.R. PROCEDURES W CC/MCC	2738	68.47	5.73	$52,613	$10,600
National	134	OTHER EAR, NOSE, MOUTH & THROAT O.R. PROCEDURES W/O CC/MCC	2705	67.79	2.15	$28,351	$4,092
National	135	SINUS & MASTOID PROCEDURES W CC/MCC	450	67.02	5.96	$59,897	$11,245
National	136	SINUS & MASTOID PROCEDURES W/O CC/MCC	331	70.22	2.24	$33,186	$5,186
National	137	MOUTH PROCEDURES W CC/MCC	1040	67.02	5.07	$36,700	$7,151

Peer Grouping	MS-DRG	Description	Discharges	Average Age	Average Length of Stay	Average Total Charge	Average Allowed
National	138	MOUTH PROCEDURES W/O CC/MCC	910	71.02	2.32	$22,661	$3,907
National	139	SALIVARY GLAND PROCEDURES	1322	71.32	1.68	$27,392	$4,123
National	146	EAR, NOSE, MOUTH & THROAT MALIGNANCY W MCC	896	70.69	10.69	$66,790	$15,926
National	147	EAR, NOSE, MOUTH & THROAT MALIGNANCY W CC	1595	70.73	6.15	$35,309	$7,448
National	148	EAR, NOSE, MOUTH & THROAT MALIGNANCY W/O CC/MCC	643	71.40	3.49	$21,323	$4,446
National	149	DYSEQUILIBRIUM	37956	76.80	2.51	$17,967	$2,829
National	150	EPISTAXIS W MCC	1512	71.61	5.34	$34,638	$7,368
National	151	EPISTAXIS W/O MCC	6811	77.25	2.79	$15,673	$2,958
National	152	OTITIS MEDIA & URI W MCC	3436	66.58	4.55	$27,204	$5,428
National	153	OTITIS MEDIA & URI W/O MCC	17930	72.81	3.08	$16,950	$3,015
National	154	OTHER EAR, NOSE, MOUTH & THROAT DIAGNOSES W MCC	3044	72.62	6.20	$38,499	$8,605
National	155	OTHER EAR, NOSE, MOUTH & THROAT DIAGNOSES W CC	7004	74.49	4.11	$24,076	$4,694
National	156	OTHER EAR, NOSE, MOUTH & THROAT DIAGNOSES W/O CC/MCC	3819	73.82	2.81	$16,909	$2,937
National	157	DENTAL & ORAL DISEASES W MCC	1665	70.12	6.94	$44,317	$10,156
National	158	DENTAL & ORAL DISEASES W CC	4491	70.27	4.17	$23,707	$4,800
National	159	DENTAL & ORAL DISEASES W/O CC/MCC	1802	69.94	2.64	$16,163	$2,754
National	163	MAJOR CHEST PROCEDURES W MCC	14929	70.12	13.77	$130,912	$28,537
National	164	MAJOR CHEST PROCEDURES W CC	21404	71.72	6.93	$67,986	$13,765
National	165	MAJOR CHEST PROCEDURES W/O CC/MCC	12812	71.35	4.15	$48,496	$9,144
National	166	OTHER RESP SYSTEM O.R. PROCEDURES W MCC	25697	72.07	14.47	$110,770	$25,695
National	167	OTHER RESP SYSTEM O.R. PROCEDURES W CC	18993	73.53	6.99	$53,394	$11,034
National	168	OTHER RESP SYSTEM O.R. PROCEDURES W/O CC/MCC	4405	72.26	4.05	$35,706	$6,461
National	175	PULMONARY EMBOLISM W MCC	19213	73.98	6.68	$40,067	$8,454
National	176	PULMONARY EMBOLISM W/O MCC	47117	73.54	4.57	$25,894	$5,196
National	177	RESPIRATORY INFECTIONS & INFLAMMATIONS W MCC	83188	77.44	9.08	$53,087	$12,412
National	178	RESPIRATORY INFECTIONS & INFLAMMATIONS W CC	71829	77.85	6.65	$35,258	$8,290
National	179	RESPIRATORY INFECTIONS & INFLAMMATIONS W/O CC/MCC	17891	78.39	4.70	$22,877	$5,367
National	180	RESPIRATORY NEOPLASMS W MCC	23931	74.41	7.41	$47,041	$9,769
National	181	RESPIRATORY NEOPLASMS W CC	26277	74.78	5.28	$32,534	$6,455
National	182	RESPIRATORY NEOPLASMS W/O CC/MCC	2959	75.17	3.49	$21,871	$3,957
National	183	MAJOR CHEST TRAUMA W MCC	3491	78.64	6.24	$38,122	$7,913
National	184	MAJOR CHEST TRAUMA W CC	6739	78.95	4.20	$26,674	$4,687
National	185	MAJOR CHEST TRAUMA W/O CC/MCC	2622	79.98	2.92	$18,082	$2,979
National	186	PLEURAL EFFUSION W MCC	11788	73.30	6.60	$40,004	$8,607
National	187	PLEURAL EFFUSION W CC	11644	76.83	4.73	$28,488	$5,671
National	188	PLEURAL EFFUSION W/O CC/MCC	3404	78.65	3.32	$19,284	$3,784
National	189	PULMONARY EDEMA & RESPIRATORY FAILURE	124918	71.81	7.30	$39,408	$9,203
National	190	CHRONIC OBSTRUCTIVE PULMONARY DISEASE W MCC	176354	73.00	5.47	$30,180	$6,443
National	191	CHRONIC OBSTRUCTIVE PULMONARY DISEASE W CC	177084	72.38	4.40	$23,739	$4,958
National	192	CHRONIC OBSTRUCTIVE PULMONARY DISEASE W/O CC/MCC	146209	71.52	3.44	$17,125	$3,505
National	193	SIMPLE PNEUMONIA & PLEURISY W MCC	148808	74.77	6.52	$37,505	$8,122
National	194	SIMPLE PNEUMONIA & PLEURISY W CC	241364	76.94	4.73	$24,165	$5,348
National	195	SIMPLE PNEUMONIA & PLEURISY W/O CC/MCC	109241	77.55	3.55	$16,540	$3,639

Peer Grouping	MS-DRG	Description	Discharges	Average Age	Average Length of Stay	Average Total Charge	Average Allowed
National	196	INTERSTITIAL LUNG DISEASE W MCC	8333	74.65	7.13	$42,400	$8,938
National	197	INTERSTITIAL LUNG DISEASE W CC	7066	73.85	4.92	$28,905	$5,854
National	198	INTERSTITIAL LUNG DISEASE W/O CC/MCC	3269	73.94	3.54	$20,154	$4,059
National	199	PNEUMOTHORAX W MCC	4629	74.62	7.98	$47,066	$10,113
National	200	PNEUMOTHORAX W CC	10202	74.40	4.47	$26,192	$5,147
National	201	PNEUMOTHORAX W/O CC/MCC	3492	71.71	3.34	$17,410	$3,453
National	202	BRONCHITIS & ASTHMA W CC/MCC	47324	71.65	4.03	$22,068	$4,213
National	203	BRONCHITIS & ASTHMA W/O CC/MCC	32709	70.47	3.06	$15,372	$2,748
National	204	RESPIRATORY SIGNS & SYMPTOMS	26170	73.04	2.85	$18,910	$3,394
National	205	OTHER RESPIRATORY SYSTEM DIAGNOSES W MCC	9314	69.95	6.00	$39,863	$8,001
National	206	OTHER RESPIRATORY SYSTEM DIAGNOSES W/O MCC	23078	73.90	3.25	$20,897	$3,782
National	207	RESPIRATORY SYSTEM DIAGNOSIS W VENTILATOR SUPPORT 96+ HOURS	54091	70.40	21.26	$160,254	$40,142
National	208	RESPIRATORY SYSTEM DIAGNOSIS W VENTILATOR SUPPORT <96 HOURS	84760	71.09	7.40	$62,392	$13,265
National	215	OTHER HEART ASSIST SYSTEM IMPLANT	216	66.69	14.52	$395,167	$82,524
National	216	CARDIAC VALVE & OTH MAJ CARDIOTHORACIC PROC W CARD CATH W MCC	11613	73.90	16.52	$258,727	$57,683
National	217	CARDIAC VALVE & OTH MAJ CARDIOTHORACIC PROC W CARD CATH W CC	6838	75.45	10.32	$173,211	$36,984
National	218	CARDIAC VALVE & OTH MAJ CARDIOTHORACIC PROC W CARD CATH W/O CC/MCC	1243	75.23	7.72	$146,460	$27,381
National	219	CARDIAC VALVE & OTH MAJ CARDIOTHORACIC PROC W/O CARD CATH W MCC	17167	73.77	12.55	$210,891	$47,643
National	220	CARDIAC VALVE & OTH MAJ CARDIOTHORACIC PROC W/O CARD CATH W CC	21767	74.60	7.56	$140,179	$29,117
National	221	CARDIAC VALVE & OTH MAJ CARDIOTHORACIC PROC W/O CARD CATH W/O CC/MCC	5077	74.16	5.81	$116,912	$22,895
National	222	CARDIAC DEFIB IMPLANT W CARDIAC CATH W AMI/HF/SHOCK W MCC	2242	71.30	12.12	$228,322	$48,345
National	223	CARDIAC DEFIB IMPLANT W CARDIAC CATH W AMI/HF/SHOCK W/O MCC	3072	72.15	6.03	$161,452	$34,740
National	224	CARDIAC DEFIB IMPLANT W CARDIAC CATH W/O AMI/HF/SHOCK W MCC	3018	70.89	10.17	$205,424	$43,534
National	225	CARDIAC DEFIB IMPLANT W CARDIAC CATH W/O AMI/HF/SHOCK W/O MCC	4024	72.74	5.08	$151,400	$32,829
National	226	CARDIAC DEFIBRILLATOR IMPLANT W/O CARDIAC CATH W MCC	6521	70.80	8.86	$173,177	$37,872
National	227	CARDIAC DEFIBRILLATOR IMPLANT W/O CARDIAC CATH W/O MCC	26227	72.90	3.17	$130,074	$27,961
National	228	OTHER CARDIOTHORACIC PROCEDURES W MCC	2489	70.20	13.81	$210,758	$43,660
National	229	OTHER CARDIOTHORACIC PROCEDURES W CC	2840	70.72	8.13	$128,789	$25,335
National	230	OTHER CARDIOTHORACIC PROCEDURES W/O CC/MCC	794	70.02	5.69	$106,696	$18,077
National	231	CORONARY BYPASS W PTCA W MCC	1394	70.96	12.28	$212,676	$44,182
National	232	CORONARY BYPASS W PTCA W/O MCC	1248	71.18	9.04	$157,249	$30,259
National	233	CORONARY BYPASS W CARDIAC CATH W MCC	16233	71.31	13.45	$189,828	$38,006
National	234	CORONARY BYPASS W CARDIAC CATH W/O MCC	26156	71.54	8.78	$128,384	$23,470
National	235	CORONARY BYPASS W/O CARDIAC CATH W MCC	10352	70.27	10.79	$154,100	$31,813
National	236	CORONARY BYPASS W/O CARDIAC CATH W/O MCC	25689	71.21	6.52	$100,889	$18,997

Peer Grouping	MS-DRG	Description	Discharges	Average Age	Average Length of Stay	Average Total Charge	Average Allowed
National	237	MAJOR CARDIOVASC PROCEDURES W MCC	26184	72.40	10.09	$146,406	$31,587
National	238	MAJOR CARDIOVASC PROCEDURES W/O MCC	44714	74.08	4.00	$82,757	$16,458
National	239	AMPUTATION FOR CIRC SYS DISORDERS EXC UPPER LIMB & TOE W MCC	11389	68.22	14.67	$110,054	$26,070
National	240	AMPUTATION FOR CIRC SYS DISORDERS EXC UPPER LIMB & TOE W CC	11247	74.01	9.35	$63,174	$13,752
National	241	AMPUTATION FOR CIRC SYS DISORDERS EXC UPPER LIMB & TOE W/O CC/MCC	1682	75.64	5.82	$35,526	$7,242
National	242	PERMANENT CARDIAC PACEMAKER IMPLANT W MCC	20431	79.49	7.90	$92,546	$20,580
National	243	PERMANENT CARDIAC PACEMAKER IMPLANT W CC	40422	80.54	4.72	$66,272	$14,017
National	244	PERMANENT CARDIAC PACEMAKER IMPLANT W/O CC/MCC	39367	79.59	2.83	$52,123	$10,345
National	245	AICD GENERATOR PROCEDURES	3569	72.96	4.20	$109,129	$23,106
National	246	PERC CARDIOVASC PROC W DRUG-ELUTING STENT W MCC OR 4+ VESSELS/STENTS	35267	71.04	5.17	$91,339	$17,468
National	247	PERC CARDIOVASC PROC W DRUG-ELUTING STENT W/O MCC	138984	71.89	2.36	$60,474	$9,355
National	248	PERC CARDIOVASC PROC W NON-DRUG-ELUTING STENT W MCC OR 4+ VES/STENTS	15981	73.43	6.39	$88,557	$16,800
National	249	PERC CARDIOVASC PROC W NON-DRUG-ELUTING STENT W/O MCC	42729	73.73	2.86	$55,996	$8,818
National	250	PERC CARDIOVASC PROC W/O CORONARY ARTERY STENT W MCC	9990	72.10	7.17	$90,723	$17,419
National	251	PERC CARDIOVASC PROC W/O CORONARY ARTERY STENT W/O MCC	37962	72.36	2.96	$63,026	$9,700
National	252	OTHER VASCULAR PROCEDURES W MCC	42894	66.16	7.93	$82,943	$18,669
National	253	OTHER VASCULAR PROCEDURES W CC	48190	74.22	5.96	$67,201	$13,242
National	254	OTHER VASCULAR PROCEDURES W/O CC/MCC	38121	73.34	2.70	$46,181	$8,146
National	255	UPPER LIMB & TOE AMPUTATION FOR CIRC SYSTEM DISORDERS W MCC	2684	63.11	9.65	$63,018	$15,031
National	256	UPPER LIMB & TOE AMPUTATION FOR CIRC SYSTEM DISORDERS W CC	3673	71.56	6.98	$40,136	$8,405
National	257	UPPER LIMB & TOE AMPUTATION FOR CIRC SYSTEM DISORDERS W/O CC/MCC	458	72.95	4.18	$23,218	$4,871
National	258	CARDIAC PACEMAKER DEVICE REPLACEMENT W MCC	788	82.02	6.53	$69,490	$16,588
National	259	CARDIAC PACEMAKER DEVICE REPLACEMENT W/O MCC	3954	82.20	3.25	$47,646	$10,005
National	260	CARDIAC PACEMAKER REVISION EXCEPT DEVICE REPLACEMENT W MCC	2230	70.89	10.72	$100,437	$22,113
National	261	CARDIAC PACEMAKER REVISION EXCEPT DEVICE REPLACEMENT W CC	4065	74.45	4.42	$45,279	$9,138
National	262	CARDIAC PACEMAKER REVISION EXCEPT DEVICE REPLACEMENT W/O CC/MCC	2319	76.71	2.70	$33,536	$5,776
National	263	VEIN LIGATION & STRIPPING	475	69.10	5.85	$49,472	$10,695
National	264	OTHER CIRCULATORY SYSTEM O.R. PROCEDURES	23542	64.35	9.06	$70,067	$15,870
National	265	AICD LEAD PROCEDURES	1530	71.31	3.67	$64,512	$12,950
National	280	ACUTE MYOCARDIAL INFARCTION, DISCHARGED ALIVE W MCC	79155	78.02	6.37	$44,998	$9,802
National	281	ACUTE MYOCARDIAL INFARCTION, DISCHARGED ALIVE W CC	56508	78.38	4.04	$29,037	$5,833
National	282	ACUTE MYOCARDIAL INFARCTION, DISCHARGED ALIVE W/O CC/MCC	36845	77.39	2.59	$21,340	$3,713
National	283	ACUTE MYOCARDIAL INFARCTION, EXPIRED W MCC	13727	80.09	5.23	$48,876	$10,098
National	284	ACUTE MYOCARDIAL INFARCTION, EXPIRED W CC	3402	83.75	2.68	$21,874	$4,511

Peer Grouping	MS-DRG	Description	Discharges	Average Age	Average Length of Stay	Average Total Charge	Average Allowed
National	285	ACUTE MYOCARDIAL INFARCTION, EXPIRED W/O CC/MCC	1395	85.54	1.75	$13,931	$2,555
National	286	CIRCULATORY DISORDERS EXCEPT AMI, W CARD CATH W MCC	30227	69.10	6.74	$60,254	$11,424
National	287	CIRCULATORY DISORDERS EXCEPT AMI, W CARD CATH W/O MCC	136071	70.65	3.13	$33,541	$5,195
National	288	ACUTE & SUBACUTE ENDOCARDITIS W MCC	3229	68.41	13.64	$77,154	$19,536
National	289	ACUTE & SUBACUTE ENDOCARDITIS W CC	1431	73.70	10.00	$50,034	$11,647
National	290	ACUTE & SUBACUTE ENDOCARDITIS W/O CC/MCC	245	73.34	6.42	$30,827	$7,473
National	291	HEART FAILURE & SHOCK W MCC	214824	76.11	6.17	$37,586	$8,258
National	292	HEART FAILURE & SHOCK W CC	265055	78.15	4.62	$24,445	$5,285
National	293	HEART FAILURE & SHOCK W/O CC/MCC	117005	79.86	3.17	$16,408	$3,351
National	294	DEEP VEIN THROMBOPHLEBITIS W CC/MCC	1254	73.73	5.17	$23,484	$5,581
National	295	DEEP VEIN THROMBOPHLEBITIS W/O CC/MCC	554	76.19	3.96	$13,162	$3,277
National	296	CARDIAC ARREST, UNEXPLAINED W MCC	2660	72.69	2.81	$37,220	$6,341
National	297	CARDIAC ARREST, UNEXPLAINED W CC	825	76.74	1.57	$17,948	$3,302
National	298	CARDIAC ARREST, UNEXPLAINED W/O CC/MCC	507	78.92	1.27	$12,391	$2,178
National	299	PERIPHERAL VASCULAR DISORDERS W MCC	24860	72.02	6.56	$37,255	$8,378
National	300	PERIPHERAL VASCULAR DISORDERS W CC	54468	74.68	4.86	$23,938	$5,204
National	301	PERIPHERAL VASCULAR DISORDERS W/O CC/MCC	31506	75.75	3.41	$16,143	$3,200
National	302	ATHEROSCLEROSIS W MCC	7043	70.20	4.23	$26,556	$5,715
National	303	ATHEROSCLEROSIS W/O MCC	45652	74.25	2.47	$15,917	$2,841
National	304	HYPERTENSION W MCC	3531	73.90	4.49	$28,140	$5,477
National	305	HYPERTENSION W/O MCC	40027	74.32	2.65	$16,870	$2,794
National	306	CARDIAC CONGENITAL & VALVULAR DISORDERS W MCC	3736	79.20	5.49	$33,679	$8,875
National	307	CARDIAC CONGENITAL & VALVULAR DISORDERS W/O MCC	6806	82.18	3.61	$21,038	$4,536
National	308	CARDIAC ARRHYTHMIA & CONDUCTION DISORDERS W MCC	76141	76.78	5.09	$31,367	$6,608
National	309	CARDIAC ARRHYTHMIA & CONDUCTION DISORDERS W CC	124593	77.57	3.48	$20,833	$4,117
National	310	CARDIAC ARRHYTHMIA & CONDUCTION DISORDERS W/O CC/MCC	139994	76.66	2.35	$14,608	$2,437
National	311	ANGINA PECTORIS	14996	73.20	2.16	$13,685	$2,233
National	312	SYNCOPE & COLLAPSE	182418	77.51	2.85	$19,520	$3,314
National	313	CHEST PAIN	169737	70.67	2.01	$16,188	$2,338
National	314	OTHER CIRCULATORY SYSTEM DIAGNOSES W MCC	64071	62.90	7.34	$49,782	$11,124
National	315	OTHER CIRCULATORY SYSTEM DIAGNOSES W CC	31612	71.63	4.11	$25,274	$5,159
National	316	OTHER CIRCULATORY SYSTEM DIAGNOSES W/O CC/MCC	10713	73.39	2.59	$16,762	$2,992
National	326	STOMACH, ESOPHAGEAL & DUODENAL PROC W MCC	12870	73.26	15.57	$147,075	$33,914
National	327	STOMACH, ESOPHAGEAL & DUODENAL PROC W CC	12197	71.20	8.30	$72,646	$14,968
National	328	STOMACH, ESOPHAGEAL & DUODENAL PROC W/O CC/MCC	11733	69.84	3.42	$39,721	$7,280
National	329	MAJOR SMALL & LARGE BOWEL PROCEDURES W MCC	50065	74.75	14.95	$130,976	$30,033
National	330	MAJOR SMALL & LARGE BOWEL PROCEDURES W CC	66222	73.60	8.65	$64,312	$13,572
National	331	MAJOR SMALL & LARGE BOWEL PROCEDURES W/O CC/MCC	29072	72.53	5.04	$41,272	$7,943
National	332	RECTAL RESECTION W MCC	1744	74.82	13.62	$117,196	$25,970
National	333	RECTAL RESECTION W CC	5508	74.03	7.84	$63,164	$13,074
National	334	RECTAL RESECTION W/O CC/MCC	3613	75.10	4.60	$41,732	$7,838
National	335	PERITONEAL ADHESIOLYSIS W MCC	8123	73.35	13.51	$110,240	$24,582

Peer Grouping	MS-DRG	Description	Discharges	Average Age	Average Length of Stay	Average Total Charge	Average Allowed
National	336	PERITONEAL ADHESIOLYSIS W CC	14607	71.24	8.46	$60,066	$12,577
National	337	PERITONEAL ADHESIOLYSIS W/O CC/MCC	8975	69.17	5.02	$39,934	$7,390
National	338	APPENDECTOMY W COMPLICATED PRINCIPAL DIAG W MCC	1437	71.56	9.90	$84,890	$18,187
National	339	APPENDECTOMY W COMPLICATED PRINCIPAL DIAG W CC	3577	71.42	6.39	$48,903	$9,629
National	340	APPENDECTOMY W COMPLICATED PRINCIPAL DIAG W/O CC/MCC	3587	69.53	3.64	$32,278	$5,858
National	341	APPENDECTOMY W/O COMPLICATED PRINCIPAL DIAG W MCC	971	67.04	6.86	$63,118	$13,108
National	342	APPENDECTOMY W/O COMPLICATED PRINCIPAL DIAG W CC	3179	68.21	3.70	$36,358	$6,471
National	343	APPENDECTOMY W/O COMPLICATED PRINCIPAL DIAG W/O CC/MCC	7100	66.45	1.91	$26,619	$4,242
National	344	MINOR SMALL & LARGE BOWEL PROCEDURES W MCC	1043	69.67	11.62	$90,499	$19,423
National	345	MINOR SMALL & LARGE BOWEL PROCEDURES W CC	3761	70.30	6.67	$44,569	$9,270
National	346	MINOR SMALL & LARGE BOWEL PROCEDURES W/O CC/MCC	3161	70.02	4.35	$29,492	$5,863
National	347	ANAL & STOMAL PROCEDURES W MCC	1847	66.41	8.85	$67,291	$14,930
National	348	ANAL & STOMAL PROCEDURES W CC	4946	68.94	5.32	$35,962	$7,307
National	349	ANAL & STOMAL PROCEDURES W/O CC/MCC	4235	68.87	2.77	$22,173	$3,618
National	350	INGUINAL & FEMORAL HERNIA PROCEDURES W MCC	1907	76.58	7.79	$66,810	$14,456
National	351	INGUINAL & FEMORAL HERNIA PROCEDURES W CC	4979	78.15	4.35	$36,387	$6,983
National	352	INGUINAL & FEMORAL HERNIA PROCEDURES W/O CC/MCC	6610	77.37	2.36	$24,566	$3,927
National	353	HERNIA PROCEDURES EXCEPT INGUINAL & FEMORAL W MCC	3888	67.58	8.34	$75,605	$16,365
National	354	HERNIA PROCEDURES EXCEPT INGUINAL & FEMORAL W CC	11168	68.16	4.92	$41,510	$7,974
National	355	HERNIA PROCEDURES EXCEPT INGUINAL & FEMORAL W/O CC/MCC	13568	69.09	2.83	$28,715	$4,723
National	356	OTHER DIGESTIVE SYSTEM O.R. PROCEDURES W MCC	9111	70.82	12.84	$104,261	$24,137
National	357	OTHER DIGESTIVE SYSTEM O.R. PROCEDURES W CC	8796	73.62	7.17	$57,326	$11,797
National	358	OTHER DIGESTIVE SYSTEM O.R. PROCEDURES W/O CC/MCC	2292	70.05	3.99	$37,748	$6,476
National	368	MAJOR ESOPHAGEAL DISORDERS W MCC	3847	69.60	6.86	$49,341	$10,523
National	369	MAJOR ESOPHAGEAL DISORDERS W CC	6263	72.55	4.25	$27,840	$5,473
National	370	MAJOR ESOPHAGEAL DISORDERS W/O CC/MCC	1822	72.37	2.96	$20,435	$3,553
National	371	MAJOR GASTROINTESTINAL DISORDERS & PERITONEAL INFECTIONS W MCC	27857	72.23	9.19	$51,643	$12,605
National	372	MAJOR GASTROINTESTINAL DISORDERS & PERITONEAL INFECTIONS W CC	42422	76.32	6.04	$29,591	$6,909
National	373	MAJOR GASTROINTESTINAL DISORDERS & PERITONEAL INFECTIONS W/O CC/MCC	13747	75.92	4.30	$19,989	$4,443
National	374	DIGESTIVE MALIGNANCY W MCC	9816	74.81	8.75	$56,547	$12,626
National	375	DIGESTIVE MALIGNANCY W CC	20046	75.89	5.70	$33,703	$7,019
National	376	DIGESTIVE MALIGNANCY W/O CC/MCC	2856	76.55	3.57	$23,150	$4,383
National	377	G.I. HEMORRHAGE W MCC	61280	74.20	6.33	$44,879	$9,883
National	378	G.I. HEMORRHAGE W CC	163884	78.00	3.99	$25,431	$5,122
National	379	G.I. HEMORRHAGE W/O CC/MCC	51386	77.70	2.84	$17,563	$3,302
National	380	COMPLICATED PEPTIC ULCER W MCC	3539	72.34	7.57	$51,011	$11,330
National	381	COMPLICATED PEPTIC ULCER W CC	6617	73.78	4.60	$28,740	$5,811
National	382	COMPLICATED PEPTIC ULCER W/O CC/MCC	2770	71.35	3.38	$21,367	$3,966
National	383	UNCOMPLICATED PEPTIC ULCER W MCC	1314	69.54	5.53	$35,432	$6,508
National	384	UNCOMPLICATED PEPTIC ULCER W/O MCC	8437	72.69	3.46	$23,146	$3,924

Peer Grouping	MS-DRG	Description	Discharges	Average Age	Average Length of Stay	Average Total Charge	Average Allowed
National	385	INFLAMMATORY BOWEL DISEASE W MCC	2419	65.75	8.77	$51,058	$11,283
National	386	INFLAMMATORY BOWEL DISEASE W CC	10147	63.44	5.09	$27,525	$5,342
National	387	INFLAMMATORY BOWEL DISEASE W/O CC/MCC	5028	59.75	3.82	$20,332	$3,779
National	388	G.I. OBSTRUCTION W MCC	21623	74.03	7.35	$42,425	$9,481
National	389	G.I. OBSTRUCTION W CC	62637	74.77	4.56	$23,366	$4,715
National	390	G.I. OBSTRUCTION W/O CC/MCC	47500	74.30	3.24	$16,357	$2,913
National	391	ESOPHAGITIS, GASTROENT & MISC DIGEST DISORDERS W MCC	57133	68.53	5.32	$31,657	$6,609
National	392	ESOPHAGITIS, GASTROENT & MISC DIGEST DISORDERS W/O MCC	303295	72.30	3.35	$19,259	$3,339
National	393	OTHER DIGESTIVE SYSTEM DIAGNOSES W MCC	26950	72.68	7.59	$47,113	$10,729
National	394	OTHER DIGESTIVE SYSTEM DIAGNOSES W CC	55942	74.08	4.54	$25,963	$5,260
National	395	OTHER DIGESTIVE SYSTEM DIAGNOSES W/O CC/MCC	23058	74.16	2.98	$18,068	$3,112
National	405	PANCREAS, LIVER & SHUNT PROCEDURES W MCC	5298	69.60	15.23	$155,945	$34,559
National	406	PANCREAS, LIVER & SHUNT PROCEDURES W CC	6383	70.56	7.85	$79,484	$16,409
National	407	PANCREAS, LIVER & SHUNT PROCEDURES W/O CC/MCC	2587	70.90	5.09	$55,016	$10,596
National	408	BILIARY TRACT PROC EXCEPT ONLY CHOLECYST W OR W/O C.D.E. W MCC	1464	74.44	12.76	$107,843	$24,063
National	409	BILIARY TRACT PROC EXCEPT ONLY CHOLECYST W OR W/O C.D.E. W CC	1365	74.21	8.19	$61,929	$13,732
National	410	BILIARY TRACT PROC EXCEPT ONLY CHOLECYST W OR W/O C.D.E. W/O CC/MCC	495	73.15	5.69	$47,707	$8,799
National	411	CHOLECYSTECTOMY W C.D.E. W MCC	587	75.38	11.71	$101,087	$20,952
National	412	CHOLECYSTECTOMY W C.D.E. W CC	721	74.30	8.28	$67,573	$13,782
National	413	CHOLECYSTECTOMY W C.D.E. W/O CC/MCC	402	73.27	5.25	$48,966	$8,921
National	414	CHOLECYSTECTOMY EXCEPT BY LAPAROSCOPE W/O C.D.E. W MCC	4716	72.85	10.88	$92,635	$20,598
National	415	CHOLECYSTECTOMY EXCEPT BY LAPAROSCOPE W/O C.D.E. W CC	5765	71.87	6.92	$54,048	$10,761
National	416	CHOLECYSTECTOMY EXCEPT BY LAPAROSCOPE W/O C.D.E. W/O CC/MCC	3941	70.44	4.35	$35,076	$6,488
National	417	LAPAROSCOPIC CHOLECYSTECTOMY W/O C.D.E. W MCC	19839	72.51	7.74	$67,962	$13,925
National	418	LAPAROSCOPIC CHOLECYSTECTOMY W/O C.D.E. W CC	30628	72.23	5.08	$46,050	$8,487
National	419	LAPAROSCOPIC CHOLECYSTECTOMY W/O C.D.E. W/O CC/MCC	29914	70.19	3.00	$32,966	$5,340
National	420	HEPATOBILIARY DIAGNOSTIC PROCEDURES W MCC	673	72.21	12.47	$109,047	$21,637
National	421	HEPATOBILIARY DIAGNOSTIC PROCEDURES W CC	1022	71.90	5.98	$48,666	$10,326
National	422	HEPATOBILIARY DIAGNOSTIC PROCEDURES W/O CC/MCC	242	70.55	4.13	$39,401	$6,943
National	423	OTHER HEPATOBILIARY OR PANCREAS O.R. PROCEDURES W MCC	1724	68.40	14.10	$120,625	$28,902
National	424	OTHER HEPATOBILIARY OR PANCREAS O.R. PROCEDURES W CC	858	70.30	8.32	$64,614	$13,365
National	425	OTHER HEPATOBILIARY OR PANCREAS O.R. PROCEDURES W/O CC/MCC	109	69.38	4.78	$44,232	$8,900
National	432	CIRRHOSIS & ALCOHOLIC HEPATITIS W MCC	12889	64.24	6.42	$45,701	$10,033
National	433	CIRRHOSIS & ALCOHOLIC HEPATITIS W CC	8487	65.20	4.27	$25,395	$5,097
National	434	CIRRHOSIS & ALCOHOLIC HEPATITIS W/O CC/MCC	400	61.85	3.44	$17,432	$3,127
National	435	MALIGNANCY OF HEPATOBILIARY SYSTEM OR PANCREAS W MCC	14482	74.61	7.19	$49,195	$10,344
National	436	MALIGNANCY OF HEPATOBILIARY SYSTEM OR PANCREAS W CC	14372	74.74	5.22	$32,110	$6,353

Appendix E — 2011 MedPAR National Data

Peer Grouping	MS-DRG	Description	Discharges	Average Age	Average Length of Stay	Average Total Charge	Average Allowed
National	437	MALIGNANCY OF HEPATOBILIARY SYSTEM OR PANCREAS W/O CC/MCC	2352	74.93	3.64	$26,783	$4,486
National	438	DISORDERS OF PANCREAS EXCEPT MALIGNANCY W MCC	17626	65.66	7.70	$49,953	$11,303
National	439	DISORDERS OF PANCREAS EXCEPT MALIGNANCY W CC	32787	67.04	4.64	$25,793	$5,192
National	440	DISORDERS OF PANCREAS EXCEPT MALIGNANCY W/O CC/MCC	24107	66.20	3.31	$18,069	$3,194
National	441	DISORDERS OF LIVER EXCEPT MALIG,CIRR,ALC HEPA W MCC	20231	64.15	7.22	$51,113	$11,148
National	442	DISORDERS OF LIVER EXCEPT MALIG,CIRR,ALC HEPA W CC	22438	64.97	4.46	$25,718	$5,289
National	443	DISORDERS OF LIVER EXCEPT MALIG,CIRR,ALC HEPA W/O CC/MCC	5422	65.63	3.43	$17,974	$3,319
National	444	DISORDERS OF THE BILIARY TRACT W MCC	14614	75.44	6.36	$43,494	$8,873
National	445	DISORDERS OF THE BILIARY TRACT W CC	22564	76.29	4.30	$29,349	$5,483
National	446	DISORDERS OF THE BILIARY TRACT W/O CC/MCC	13884	75.16	2.94	$20,758	$3,393
National	453	COMBINED ANTERIOR/POSTERIOR SPINAL FUSION W MCC	1550	67.26	12.68	$277,153	$64,672
National	454	COMBINED ANTERIOR/POSTERIOR SPINAL FUSION W CC	3988	66.54	6.28	$195,116	$43,741
National	455	COMBINED ANTERIOR/POSTERIOR SPINAL FUSION W/O CC/MCC	3523	65.52	3.66	$143,606	$30,624
National	456	SPINAL FUS EXC CERV W SPINAL CURV/MALIG/INFEC OR 9+ FUS W MCC	1430	68.45	13.05	$256,447	$59,426
National	457	SPINAL FUS EXC CERV W SPINAL CURV/MALIG/INFEC OR 9+ FUS W CC	4153	70.20	6.53	$162,560	$38,066
National	458	SPINAL FUS EXC CERV W SPINAL CURV/MALIG/INFEC OR 9+ FUS W/O CC/MCC	1909	69.78	3.75	$118,216	$28,357
National	459	SPINAL FUSION EXCEPT CERVICAL W MCC	4906	70.18	9.23	$154,572	$35,071
National	460	SPINAL FUSION EXCEPT CERVICAL W/O MCC	76346	68.47	3.69	$91,533	$20,245
National	461	BILATERAL OR MULTIPLE MAJOR JOINT PROCS OF LOWER EXTREMITY W MCC	646	71.28	8.15	$123,097	$24,668
National	462	BILATERAL OR MULTIPLE MAJOR JOINT PROCS OF LOWER EXTREMITY W/O MCC	11777	70.56	3.83	$78,585	$16,871
National	463	WND DEBRID & SKN GRFT EXC HAND, FOR MUSCULO-CONN TISS DIS W MCC	6402	67.17	19.75	$133,343	$31,996
National	464	WND DEBRID & SKN GRFT EXC HAND, FOR MUSCULO-CONN TISS DIS W CC	9860	69.23	9.25	$73,842	$15,758
National	465	WND DEBRID & SKN GRFT EXC HAND, FOR MUSCULO-CONN TISS DIS W/O CC/MCC	2839	69.59	5.77	$48,773	$9,682
National	466	REVISION OF HIP OR KNEE REPLACEMENT W MCC	4491	73.39	8.82	$117,988	$26,474
National	467	REVISION OF HIP OR KNEE REPLACEMENT W CC	25784	72.00	4.59	$78,444	$16,728
National	468	REVISION OF HIP OR KNEE REPLACEMENT W/O CC/MCC	18955	70.58	3.32	$63,305	$13,169
National	469	MAJOR JOINT REPLACEMENT OR REATTACHMENT OF LOWER EXTREMITY W MCC	31509	77.70	7.63	$78,719	$17,468
National	470	MAJOR JOINT REPLACEMENT OR REATTACHMENT OF LOWER EXTREMITY W/O MCC	484630	73.52	3.47	$49,064	$10,236
National	471	CERVICAL SPINAL FUSION W MCC	3569	68.92	9.18	$127,301	$28,352
National	472	CERVICAL SPINAL FUSION W CC	11403	66.05	3.73	$73,114	$14,985
National	473	CERVICAL SPINAL FUSION W/O CC/MCC	31214	64.33	1.82	$53,283	$10,347
National	474	AMPUTATION FOR MUSCULOSKELETAL SYS & CONN TISSUE DIS W MCC	3450	64.16	12.76	$90,327	$20,683
National	475	AMPUTATION FOR MUSCULOSKELETAL SYS & CONN TISSUE DIS W CC	4454	67.63	7.92	$50,876	$10,541

Peer Grouping	MS-DRG	Description	Discharges	Average Age	Average Length of Stay	Average Total Charge	Average Allowed
National	476	AMPUTATION FOR MUSCULOSKELETAL SYS & CONN TISSUE DIS W/O CC/MCC	1353	65.72	4.09	$27,466	$5,111
National	477	BIOPSIES OF MUSCULOSKELETAL SYSTEM & CONNECTIVE TISSUE W MCC	3026	73.37	11.54	$84,727	$18,901
National	478	BIOPSIES OF MUSCULOSKELETAL SYSTEM & CONNECTIVE TISSUE W CC	8569	76.68	6.91	$58,655	$11,864
National	479	BIOPSIES OF MUSCULOSKELETAL SYSTEM & CONNECTIVE TISSUE W/O CC/MCC	4134	78.19	4.17	$43,297	$8,247
National	480	HIP & FEMUR PROCEDURES EXCEPT MAJOR JOINT W MCC	28757	80.27	8.54	$74,711	$16,979
National	481	HIP & FEMUR PROCEDURES EXCEPT MAJOR JOINT W CC	91525	81.95	5.34	$47,482	$9,816
National	482	HIP & FEMUR PROCEDURES EXCEPT MAJOR JOINT W/O CC/MCC	33393	80.23	4.32	$38,914	$7,845
National	483	MAJOR JOINT & LIMB REATTACHMENT PROC OF UPPER EXTREMITY W CC/MCC	14415	74.04	3.49	$61,245	$12,509
National	484	MAJOR JOINT & LIMB REATTACHMENT PROC OF UPPER EXTREMITY W/O CC/MCC	24520	73.04	2.08	$50,221	$9,785
National	485	KNEE PROCEDURES W PDX OF INFECTION W MCC	1290	70.07	10.59	$84,533	$19,126
National	486	KNEE PROCEDURES W PDX OF INFECTION W CC	2982	70.62	7.02	$54,364	$10,984
National	487	KNEE PROCEDURES W PDX OF INFECTION W/O CC/MCC	1200	70.09	4.89	$37,527	$7,596
National	488	KNEE PROCEDURES W/O PDX OF INFECTION W CC/MCC	4063	69.35	4.36	$43,188	$8,882
National	489	KNEE PROCEDURES W/O PDX OF INFECTION W/O CC/MCC	5250	69.59	2.71	$31,140	$5,664
National	490	BACK & NECK PROC EXC SPINAL FUSION W CC/MCC OR DISC DEVICE/NEUROSTIM	22460	71.85	4.50	$48,979	$9,540
National	491	BACK & NECK PROC EXC SPINAL FUSION W/O CC/MCC	44949	71.19	2.07	$28,750	$4,448
National	492	LOWER EXTREM & HUMER PROC EXCEPT HIP,FOOT,FEMUR W MCC	6432	69.85	8.40	$78,809	$17,115
National	493	LOWER EXTREM & HUMER PROC EXCEPT HIP,FOOT,FEMUR W CC	24133	71.65	4.83	$49,870	$9,674
National	494	LOWER EXTREM & HUMER PROC EXCEPT HIP,FOOT,FEMUR W/O CC/MCC	27522	70.29	3.06	$35,776	$6,414
National	495	LOCAL EXCISION & REMOVAL INT FIX DEVICES EXC HIP & FEMUR W MCC	2057	65.87	11.95	$83,291	$18,730
National	496	LOCAL EXCISION & REMOVAL INT FIX DEVICES EXC HIP & FEMUR W CC	5854	67.50	5.35	$44,050	$8,914
National	497	LOCAL EXCISION & REMOVAL INT FIX DEVICES EXC HIP & FEMUR W/O CC/MCC	5118	66.69	2.55	$30,843	$5,369
National	498	LOCAL EXCISION & REMOVAL INT FIX DEVICES OF HIP & FEMUR W CC/MCC	1712	69.70	7.65	$58,497	$12,424
National	499	LOCAL EXCISION & REMOVAL INT FIX DEVICES OF HIP & FEMUR W/O CC/MCC	906	69.41	2.66	$27,957	$5,108
National	500	SOFT TISSUE PROCEDURES W MCC	2528	66.18	13.01	$89,112	$21,018
National	501	SOFT TISSUE PROCEDURES W CC	5973	69.13	5.83	$41,873	$8,480
National	502	SOFT TISSUE PROCEDURES W/O CC/MCC	5965	70.17	2.84	$28,154	$4,937
National	503	FOOT PROCEDURES W MCC	1084	66.26	9.72	$63,452	$14,380
National	504	FOOT PROCEDURES W CC	3479	70.27	6.08	$40,469	$8,343
National	505	FOOT PROCEDURES W/O CC/MCC	2534	68.87	3.29	$30,090	$5,345
National	506	MAJOR THUMB OR JOINT PROCEDURES	782	70.50	3.93	$34,146	$6,205
National	507	MAJOR SHOULDER OR ELBOW JOINT PROCEDURES W CC/MCC	728	69.45	5.54	$49,271	$10,558
National	508	MAJOR SHOULDER OR ELBOW JOINT PROCEDURES W/O CC/MCC	811	69.41	2.19	$32,331	$6,581

Peer Grouping	MS-DRG	Description	Discharges	Average Age	Average Length of Stay	Average Total Charge	Average Allowed
National	509	ARTHROSCOPY	296	68.62	3.71	$36,116	$6,904
National	510	SHOULDER,ELBOW OR FOREARM PROC,EXC MAJOR JOINT PROC W MCC	1283	74.71	6.34	$60,489	$11,680
National	511	SHOULDER,ELBOW OR FOREARM PROC,EXC MAJOR JOINT PROC W CC	4839	76.00	3.79	$39,690	$7,284
National	512	SHOULDER,ELBOW OR FOREARM PROC,EXC MAJOR JOINT PROC W/O CC/MCC	7473	74.26	2.22	$29,809	$4,948
National	513	HAND OR WRIST PROC, EXCEPT MAJOR THUMB OR JOINT PROC W CC/MCC	1551	67.60	4.87	$37,171	$7,074
National	514	HAND OR WRIST PROC, EXCEPT MAJOR THUMB OR JOINT PROC W/O CC/MCC	1053	68.50	2.59	$23,236	$3,754
National	515	OTHER MUSCULOSKELET SYS & CONN TISS O.R. PROC W MCC	4388	75.00	10.30	$86,017	$18,552
National	516	OTHER MUSCULOSKELET SYS & CONN TISS O.R. PROC W CC	11564	78.31	5.71	$50,774	$10,036
National	517	OTHER MUSCULOSKELET SYS & CONN TISS O.R. PROC W/O CC/MCC	9262	76.71	3.40	$40,168	$7,269
National	533	FRACTURES OF FEMUR W MCC	937	76.10	6.44	$36,080	$8,510
National	534	FRACTURES OF FEMUR W/O MCC	3771	81.06	4.22	$17,578	$4,275
National	535	FRACTURES OF HIP & PELVIS W MCC	8871	81.30	5.66	$31,074	$7,382
National	536	FRACTURES OF HIP & PELVIS W/O MCC	39579	83.88	4.14	$17,167	$4,207
National	537	SPRAINS, STRAINS, & DISLOCATIONS OF HIP, PELVIS & THIGH W CC/MCC	1002	80.12	4.07	$22,092	$4,290
National	538	SPRAINS, STRAINS, & DISLOCATIONS OF HIP, PELVIS & THIGH W/O CC/MCC	701	79.46	2.97	$15,735	$2,968
National	539	OSTEOMYELITIS W MCC	5864	66.73	18.84	$75,505	$20,416
National	540	OSTEOMYELITIS W CC	5417	70.03	9.77	$39,782	$10,105
National	541	OSTEOMYELITIS W/O CC/MCC	1362	69.64	7.03	$27,046	$6,417
National	542	PATHOLOGICAL FRACTURES & MUSCULOSKELET & CONN TISS MALIG W MCC	6157	75.23	8.55	$52,025	$11,177
National	543	PATHOLOGICAL FRACTURES & MUSCULOSKELET & CONN TISS MALIG W CC	17453	77.89	5.49	$30,021	$6,172
National	544	PATHOLOGICAL FRACTURES & MUSCULOSKELET & CONN TISS MALIG W/O CC/MCC	6225	81.80	3.98	$19,268	$3,978
National	545	CONNECTIVE TISSUE DISORDERS W MCC	4364	64.68	9.10	$67,191	$15,890
National	546	CONNECTIVE TISSUE DISORDERS W CC	6880	67.41	5.28	$30,705	$6,441
National	547	CONNECTIVE TISSUE DISORDERS W/O CC/MCC	3590	68.91	3.61	$19,859	$3,781
National	548	SEPTIC ARTHRITIS W MCC	1000	69.37	14.44	$64,712	$17,591
National	549	SEPTIC ARTHRITIS W CC	1654	71.65	8.66	$35,917	$8,634
National	550	SEPTIC ARTHRITIS W/O CC/MCC	689	72.45	4.72	$19,820	$4,834
National	551	MEDICAL BACK PROBLEMS W MCC	14267	75.76	6.86	$41,329	$9,048
National	552	MEDICAL BACK PROBLEMS W/O MCC	86960	77.29	3.97	$21,398	$4,052
National	553	BONE DISEASES & ARTHROPATHIES W MCC	3063	72.35	5.90	$35,270	$7,263
National	554	BONE DISEASES & ARTHROPATHIES W/O MCC	25078	76.08	4.44	$17,269	$4,590
National	555	SIGNS & SYMPTOMS OF MUSCULOSKELETAL SYSTEM & CONN TISSUE W MCC	3629	69.92	5.22	$32,775	$6,626
National	556	SIGNS & SYMPTOMS OF MUSCULOSKELETAL SYSTEM & CONN TISSUE W/O MCC	21845	75.24	3.22	$18,004	$3,297
National	557	TENDONITIS, MYOSITIS & BURSITIS W MCC	5450	74.84	7.43	$40,170	$9,348
National	558	TENDONITIS, MYOSITIS & BURSITIS W/O MCC	20277	75.63	4.32	$22,014	$4,516

Peer Grouping	MS-DRG	Description	Discharges	Average Age	Average Length of Stay	Average Total Charge	Average Allowed
National	559	AFTERCARE, MUSCULOSKELETAL SYSTEM & CONNECTIVE TISSUE W MCC	4244	73.04	15.83	$67,277	$17,596
National	560	AFTERCARE, MUSCULOSKELETAL SYSTEM & CONNECTIVE TISSUE W CC	7855	74.02	8.75	$34,041	$8,930
National	561	AFTERCARE, MUSCULOSKELETAL SYSTEM & CONNECTIVE TISSUE W/O CC/MCC	5797	74.46	3.77	$17,243	$4,152
National	562	FX, SPRN, STRN & DISL EXCEPT FEMUR, HIP, PELVIS & THIGH W MCC	6983	76.37	5.82	$34,364	$7,483
National	563	FX, SPRN, STRN & DISL EXCEPT FEMUR, HIP, PELVIS & THIGH W/O MCC	35356	79.31	3.62	$18,233	$3,563
National	564	OTHER MUSCULOSKELETAL SYS & CONNECTIVE TISSUE DIAGNOSES W MCC	2578	65.30	8.99	$46,528	$11,471
National	565	OTHER MUSCULOSKELETAL SYS & CONNECTIVE TISSUE DIAGNOSES W CC	5083	70.64	5.45	$25,903	$5,685
National	566	OTHER MUSCULOSKELETAL SYS & CONNECTIVE TISSUE DIAGNOSES W/O CC/MCC	1866	72.08	3.93	$18,176	$4,001
National	573	SKIN GRAFT FOR SKIN ULCER OR CELLULITIS W MCC	6390	67.22	21.23	$101,755	$26,861
National	574	SKIN GRAFT FOR SKIN ULCER OR CELLULITIS W CC	10548	68.12	10.57	$49,323	$11,889
National	575	SKIN GRAFT FOR SKIN ULCER OR CELLULITIS W/O CC/MCC	3656	68.66	5.40	$27,407	$5,686
National	576	SKIN GRAFT EXC FOR SKIN ULCER OR CELLULITIS W MCC	819	69.07	14.33	$110,062	$26,827
National	577	SKIN GRAFT EXC FOR SKIN ULCER OR CELLULITIS W CC	2807	73.37	6.11	$51,630	$10,316
National	578	SKIN GRAFT EXC FOR SKIN ULCER OR CELLULITIS W/O CC/MCC	2710	73.57	3.26	$32,174	$5,503
National	579	OTHER SKIN, SUBCUT TISS & BREAST PROC W MCC	5700	66.75	13.91	$84,307	$19,996
National	580	OTHER SKIN, SUBCUT TISS & BREAST PROC W CC	14016	69.67	5.88	$40,432	$8,041
National	581	OTHER SKIN, SUBCUT TISS & BREAST PROC W/O CC/MCC	12009	70.63	2.51	$28,012	$4,195
National	582	MASTECTOMY FOR MALIGNANCY W CC/MCC	4644	73.51	2.65	$31,601	$5,191
National	583	MASTECTOMY FOR MALIGNANCY W/O CC/MCC	7120	74.33	1.69	$24,928	$3,777
National	584	BREAST BIOPSY, LOCAL EXCISION & OTHER BREAST PROCEDURES W CC/MCC	932	64.72	5.28	$44,460	$8,367
National	585	BREAST BIOPSY, LOCAL EXCISION & OTHER BREAST PROCEDURES W/O CC/MCC	1623	64.97	2.20	$32,248	$4,921
National	592	SKIN ULCERS W MCC	7434	70.37	17.03	$68,379	$17,942
National	593	SKIN ULCERS W CC	12364	72.16	8.16	$30,120	$7,647
National	594	SKIN ULCERS W/O CC/MCC	1902	75.27	5.49	$18,751	$5,054
National	595	MAJOR SKIN DISORDERS W MCC	1344	73.55	8.32	$51,076	$12,130
National	596	MAJOR SKIN DISORDERS W/O MCC	5731	74.84	4.63	$22,536	$4,816
National	597	MALIGNANT BREAST DISORDERS W MCC	751	71.63	9.15	$47,337	$10,347
National	598	MALIGNANT BREAST DISORDERS W CC	1817	73.34	6.12	$31,463	$6,371
National	599	MALIGNANT BREAST DISORDERS W/O CC/MCC	223	74.36	3.68	$16,618	$4,179
National	600	NON-MALIGNANT BREAST DISORDERS W CC/MCC	1310	63.96	5.28	$26,411	$5,471
National	601	NON-MALIGNANT BREAST DISORDERS W/O CC/MCC	970	64.96	3.44	$14,962	$3,227
National	602	CELLULITIS W MCC	31109	69.58	7.29	$38,321	$8,816
National	603	CELLULITIS W/O MCC	170042	71.06	4.44	$19,753	$4,253
National	604	TRAUMA TO THE SKIN, SUBCUT TISS & BREAST W MCC	3228	76.08	5.44	$35,573	$7,324
National	605	TRAUMA TO THE SKIN, SUBCUT TISS & BREAST W/O MCC	22365	80.07	3.23	$19,332	$3,575
National	606	MINOR SKIN DISORDERS W MCC	2019	66.22	6.97	$38,852	$8,809
National	607	MINOR SKIN DISORDERS W/O MCC	8444	69.90	3.76	$17,587	$3,649

Peer Grouping	MS-DRG	Description	Discharges	Average Age	Average Length of Stay	Average Total Charge	Average Allowed
National	614	ADRENAL & PITUITARY PROCEDURES W CC/MCC	1962	67.98	5.77	$72,706	$14,823
National	615	ADRENAL & PITUITARY PROCEDURES W/O CC/MCC	1587	68.52	2.80	$43,171	$7,234
National	616	AMPUTAT OF LOWER LIMB FOR ENDOCRINE,NUTRIT,& METABOL DIS W MCC	2088	66.18	16.16	$109,536	$26,122
National	617	AMPUTAT OF LOWER LIMB FOR ENDOCRINE,NUTRIT,& METABOL DIS W CC	9468	65.45	7.81	$49,296	$10,498
National	618	AMPUTAT OF LOWER LIMB FOR ENDOCRINE,NUTRIT,& METABOL DIS W/O CC/MCC	155	65.31	5.15	$28,449	$6,309
National	619	O.R. PROCEDURES FOR OBESITY W MCC	944	54.51	6.99	$94,454	$20,236
National	620	O.R. PROCEDURES FOR OBESITY W CC	3787	54.89	3.11	$51,843	$9,226
National	621	O.R. PROCEDURES FOR OBESITY W/O CC/MCC	12466	55.64	1.88	$40,572	$6,839
National	622	SKIN GRAFTS & WOUND DEBRID FOR ENDOC, NUTRIT & METAB DIS W MCC	1603	67.84	19.18	$101,494	$25,913
National	623	SKIN GRAFTS & WOUND DEBRID FOR ENDOC, NUTRIT & METAB DIS W CC	3483	63.90	10.30	$53,118	$12,729
National	624	SKIN GRAFTS & WOUND DEBRID FOR ENDOC, NUTRIT & METAB DIS W/O CC/MCC	261	65.30	5.06	$26,819	$5,579
National	625	THYROID, PARATHYROID & THYROGLOSSAL PROCEDURES W MCC	1296	61.26	7.00	$68,845	$14,119
National	626	THYROID, PARATHYROID & THYROGLOSSAL PROCEDURES W CC	3388	68.25	2.86	$35,590	$5,987
National	627	THYROID, PARATHYROID & THYROGLOSSAL PROCEDURES W/O CC/MCC	12307	69.85	1.38	$24,632	$3,446
National	628	OTHER ENDOCRINE, NUTRIT & METAB O.R. PROC W MCC	4392	64.20	11.27	$90,094	$21,374
National	629	OTHER ENDOCRINE, NUTRIT & METAB O.R. PROC W CC	6203	66.01	8.00	$55,663	$12,222
National	630	OTHER ENDOCRINE, NUTRIT & METAB O.R. PROC W/O CC/MCC	483	69.24	4.24	$35,359	$7,184
National	637	DIABETES W MCC	25316	66.16	6.46	$38,467	$8,633
National	638	DIABETES W CC	65623	66.16	4.22	$21,913	$4,564
National	639	DIABETES W/O CC/MCC	27472	67.20	2.74	$14,147	$2,602
National	640	MISC DISORDERS OF NUTRITION,METABOLISM,FLUIDS/ELECTROLYTES W MCC	70761	68.36	4.99	$28,682	$6,672
National	641	MISC DISORDERS OF NUTRITION,METABOLISM,FLUIDS/ELECTROLYTES W/O MCC	188900	76.58	3.42	$17,006	$3,496
National	642	INBORN AND OTHER DISORDERS OF METABOLISM	1832	57.14	7.28	$34,077	$6,100
National	643	ENDOCRINE DISORDERS W MCC	7795	74.35	7.19	$43,104	$9,914
National	644	ENDOCRINE DISORDERS W CC	15545	74.74	4.96	$26,812	$5,590
National	645	ENDOCRINE DISORDERS W/O CC/MCC	7436	74.77	3.40	$18,819	$3,467
National	652	KIDNEY TRANSPLANT	10139	51.72	7.06	$182,234	$24,030
National	653	MAJOR BLADDER PROCEDURES W MCC	2055	72.43	16.08	$155,626	$34,691
National	654	MAJOR BLADDER PROCEDURES W CC	4573	73.07	9.19	$86,009	$16,791
National	655	MAJOR BLADDER PROCEDURES W/O CC/MCC	1715	73.07	5.63	$61,459	$10,699
National	656	KIDNEY & URETER PROCEDURES FOR NEOPLASM W MCC	3920	70.99	9.65	$97,375	$21,653
National	657	KIDNEY & URETER PROCEDURES FOR NEOPLASM W CC	10296	72.99	5.42	$54,485	$10,529
National	658	KIDNEY & URETER PROCEDURES FOR NEOPLASM W/O CC/MCC	8246	71.85	3.23	$41,158	$7,033
National	659	KIDNEY & URETER PROCEDURES FOR NON-NEOPLASM W MCC	4658	63.42	11.01	$93,528	$21,877
National	660	KIDNEY & URETER PROCEDURES FOR NON-NEOPLASM W CC	9985	68.74	5.77	$50,899	$10,375

Peer Grouping	MS-DRG	Description	Discharges	Average Age	Average Length of Stay	Average Total Charge	Average Allowed
National	661	KIDNEY & URETER PROCEDURES FOR NON-NEOPLASM W/O CC/MCC	4779	69.01	2.78	$37,320	$6,300
National	662	MINOR BLADDER PROCEDURES W MCC	941	71.83	10.31	$77,997	$18,872
National	663	MINOR BLADDER PROCEDURES W CC	2005	74.47	5.17	$39,843	$7,861
National	664	MINOR BLADDER PROCEDURES W/O CC/MCC	2698	73.12	1.92	$30,560	$4,999
National	665	PROSTATECTOMY W MCC	688	79.01	12.14	$79,009	$16,077
National	666	PROSTATECTOMY W CC	2179	78.52	6.21	$43,652	$8,931
National	667	PROSTATECTOMY W/O CC/MCC	2166	77.29	2.48	$23,081	$3,514
National	668	TRANSURETHRAL PROCEDURES W MCC	3933	74.55	8.86	$65,210	$14,494
National	669	TRANSURETHRAL PROCEDURES W CC	17598	74.46	4.21	$34,362	$6,283
National	670	TRANSURETHRAL PROCEDURES W/O CC/MCC	8552	76.14	2.33	$22,133	$3,402
National	671	URETHRAL PROCEDURES W CC/MCC	821	71.75	5.25	$39,690	$8,180
National	672	URETHRAL PROCEDURES W/O CC/MCC	701	72.54	2.19	$25,401	$3,811
National	673	OTHER KIDNEY & URINARY TRACT PROCEDURES W MCC	12954	66.36	10.24	$82,090	$18,630
National	674	OTHER KIDNEY & URINARY TRACT PROCEDURES W CC	9231	67.56	7.07	$57,645	$11,798
National	675	OTHER KIDNEY & URINARY TRACT PROCEDURES W/O CC/MCC	2259	71.86	2.43	$38,345	$6,585
National	682	RENAL FAILURE W MCC	118961	72.46	6.82	$40,487	$9,396
National	683	RENAL FAILURE W CC	178455	75.77	4.69	$24,853	$5,191
National	684	RENAL FAILURE W/O CC/MCC	34687	76.29	3.17	$16,135	$3,067
National	685	ADMIT FOR RENAL DIALYSIS	3210	62.64	3.46	$21,207	$4,749
National	686	KIDNEY & URINARY TRACT NEOPLASMS W MCC	1523	74.82	7.83	$46,519	$11,216
National	687	KIDNEY & URINARY TRACT NEOPLASMS W CC	3654	77.40	5.07	$27,716	$5,985
National	688	KIDNEY & URINARY TRACT NEOPLASMS W/O CC/MCC	693	77.50	3.63	$18,782	$3,328
National	689	KIDNEY & URINARY TRACT INFECTIONS W MCC	82966	78.15	5.75	$29,103	$6,661
National	690	KIDNEY & URINARY TRACT INFECTIONS W/O MCC	247521	78.76	3.90	$19,001	$3,992
National	691	URINARY STONES W ESW LITHOTRIPSY W CC/MCC	1089	68.22	3.94	$38,080	$7,985
National	692	URINARY STONES W ESW LITHOTRIPSY W/O CC/MCC	357	67.28	2.05	$25,471	$4,983
National	693	URINARY STONES W/O ESW LITHOTRIPSY W MCC	2567	70.40	5.26	$37,360	$7,178
National	694	URINARY STONES W/O ESW LITHOTRIPSY W/O MCC	21275	70.21	2.40	$19,203	$3,044
National	695	KIDNEY & URINARY TRACT SIGNS & SYMPTOMS W MCC	1587	77.27	5.50	$32,340	$6,848
National	696	KIDNEY & URINARY TRACT SIGNS & SYMPTOMS W/O MCC	13150	77.77	3.08	$16,178	$3,169
National	697	URETHRAL STRICTURE	610	74.74	3.09	$21,385	$3,799
National	698	OTHER KIDNEY & URINARY TRACT DIAGNOSES W MCC	32262	69.00	6.82	$41,118	$9,408
National	699	OTHER KIDNEY & URINARY TRACT DIAGNOSES W CC	36106	69.03	4.53	$26,264	$5,577
National	700	OTHER KIDNEY & URINARY TRACT DIAGNOSES W/O CC/MCC	8755	72.90	3.24	$17,442	$3,512
National	707	MAJOR MALE PELVIC PROCEDURES W CC/MCC	6247	69.18	4.03	$50,100	$8,683
National	708	MAJOR MALE PELVIC PROCEDURES W/O CC/MCC	20798	68.71	1.89	$37,787	$5,618
National	709	PENIS PROCEDURES W CC/MCC	878	66.26	6.68	$57,440	$11,826
National	710	PENIS PROCEDURES W/O CC/MCC	1433	68.75	1.77	$36,121	$6,282
National	711	TESTES PROCEDURES W CC/MCC	801	69.00	8.22	$53,918	$10,701
National	712	TESTES PROCEDURES W/O CC/MCC	396	69.41	3.01	$23,345	$3,873
National	713	TRANSURETHRAL PROSTATECTOMY W CC/MCC	9182	77.24	4.25	$33,924	$6,095
National	714	TRANSURETHRAL PROSTATECTOMY W/O CC/MCC	18392	75.64	1.80	$18,642	$2,737

Peer Grouping	MS-DRG	Description	Discharges	Average Age	Average Length of Stay	Average Total Charge	Average Allowed
National	715	OTHER MALE REPRODUCTIVE SYSTEM O.R. PROC FOR MALIGNANCY W CC/MCC	547	76.32	6.51	$51,241	$9,977
National	716	OTHER MALE REPRODUCTIVE SYSTEM O.R. PROC FOR MALIGNANCY W/O CC/MCC	534	72.20	1.45	$30,419	$4,414
National	717	OTHER MALE REPRODUCTIVE SYSTEM O.R. PROC EXC MALIGNANCY W CC/MCC	924	76.08	6.77	$47,439	$10,170
National	718	OTHER MALE REPRODUCTIVE SYSTEM O.R. PROC EXC MALIGNANCY W/O CC/MCC	448	76.05	2.93	$22,998	$3,793
National	722	MALIGNANCY, MALE REPRODUCTIVE SYSTEM W MCC	672	78.23	8.40	$44,447	$10,093
National	723	MALIGNANCY, MALE REPRODUCTIVE SYSTEM W CC	1984	78.75	5.53	$28,223	$5,981
National	724	MALIGNANCY, MALE REPRODUCTIVE SYSTEM W/O CC/MCC	283	74.71	2.80	$17,237	$2,991
National	725	BENIGN PROSTATIC HYPERTROPHY W MCC	751	79.65	6.18	$34,044	$7,475
National	726	BENIGN PROSTATIC HYPERTROPHY W/O MCC	4777	78.87	3.37	$17,837	$3,474
National	727	INFLAMMATION OF THE MALE REPRODUCTIVE SYSTEM W MCC	1842	68.43	7.21	$38,601	$8,787
National	728	INFLAMMATION OF THE MALE REPRODUCTIVE SYSTEM W/O MCC	7185	70.05	4.00	$19,418	$3,724
National	729	OTHER MALE REPRODUCTIVE SYSTEM DIAGNOSES W CC/MCC	955	65.78	5.97	$31,096	$6,980
National	730	OTHER MALE REPRODUCTIVE SYSTEM DIAGNOSES W/O CC/MCC	322	68.11	2.75	$16,357	$3,241
National	734	PELVIC EVISCERATION, RAD HYSTERECTOMY & RAD VULVECTOMY W CC/MCC	1941	71.41	7.30	$76,863	$14,604
National	735	PELVIC EVISCERATION, RAD HYSTERECTOMY & RAD VULVECTOMY W/O CC/MCC	1412	71.77	2.32	$35,107	$5,611
National	736	UTERINE & ADNEXA PROC FOR OVARIAN OR ADNEXAL MALIGNANCY W MCC	1024	73.51	13.08	$121,256	$26,477
National	737	UTERINE & ADNEXA PROC FOR OVARIAN OR ADNEXAL MALIGNANCY W CC	3737	72.31	6.37	$55,826	$10,788
National	738	UTERINE & ADNEXA PROC FOR OVARIAN OR ADNEXAL MALIGNANCY W/O CC/MCC	832	71.45	3.41	$37,735	$6,189
National	739	UTERINE,ADNEXA PROC FOR NON-OVARIAN/ADNEXAL MALIG W MCC	1028	71.38	9.40	$95,387	$21,073
National	740	UTERINE,ADNEXA PROC FOR NON-OVARIAN/ADNEXAL MALIG W CC	5290	71.44	4.20	$45,803	$7,901
National	741	UTERINE,ADNEXA PROC FOR NON-OVARIAN/ADNEXAL MALIG W/O CC/MCC	5915	71.67	2.16	$34,272	$5,129
National	742	UTERINE & ADNEXA PROC FOR NON-MALIGNANCY W CC/MCC	10958	61.69	3.88	$39,976	$7,312
National	743	UTERINE & ADNEXA PROC FOR NON-MALIGNANCY W/O CC/MCC	27328	63.96	1.92	$26,844	$4,004
National	744	D&C, CONIZATION, LAPAROSCOPY & TUBAL INTERRUPTION W CC/MCC	1811	69.75	5.96	$44,162	$8,882
National	745	D&C, CONIZATION, LAPAROSCOPY & TUBAL INTERRUPTION W/O CC/MCC	1158	70.32	2.16	$24,449	$3,937
National	746	VAGINA, CERVIX & VULVA PROCEDURES W CC/MCC	2684	71.36	4.37	$37,957	$7,322
National	747	VAGINA, CERVIX & VULVA PROCEDURES W/O CC/MCC	6693	72.67	1.70	$24,400	$3,685
National	748	FEMALE REPRODUCTIVE SYSTEM RECONSTRUCTIVE PROCEDURES	15221	71.99	1.64	$25,876	$3,950
National	749	OTHER FEMALE REPRODUCTIVE SYSTEM O.R. PROCEDURES W CC/MCC	1197	70.11	8.96	$71,317	$14,792
National	750	OTHER FEMALE REPRODUCTIVE SYSTEM O.R. PROCEDURES W/O CC/MCC	366	62.77	2.98	$30,517	$4,548

Peer Grouping	MS-DRG	Description	Discharges	Average Age	Average Length of Stay	Average Total Charge	Average Allowed
National	754	MALIGNANCY, FEMALE REPRODUCTIVE SYSTEM W MCC	1425	73.41	9.38	$54,225	$13,063
National	755	MALIGNANCY, FEMALE REPRODUCTIVE SYSTEM W CC	3918	74.53	5.38	$29,077	$6,367
National	756	MALIGNANCY, FEMALE REPRODUCTIVE SYSTEM W/O CC/MCC	460	73.87	3.09	$15,970	$3,502
National	757	INFECTIONS, FEMALE REPRODUCTIVE SYSTEM W MCC	1759	74.98	8.79	$46,574	$10,891
National	758	INFECTIONS, FEMALE REPRODUCTIVE SYSTEM W CC	2636	72.66	5.68	$28,328	$6,309
National	759	INFECTIONS, FEMALE REPRODUCTIVE SYSTEM W/O CC/MCC	1133	67.10	3.80	$18,578	$3,852
National	760	MENSTRUAL & OTHER FEMALE REPRODUCTIVE SYSTEM DISORDERS W CC/MCC	2523	65.80	3.65	$21,809	$4,455
National	761	MENSTRUAL & OTHER FEMALE REPRODUCTIVE SYSTEM DISORDERS W/O CC/MCC	1181	63.69	2.19	$13,018	$2,354
National	765	CESAREAN SECTION W CC/MCC	3815	32.25	4.77	$26,230	$6,561
National	766	CESAREAN SECTION W/O CC/MCC	2883	31.32	3.11	$16,843	$4,024
National	767	VAGINAL DELIVERY W STERILIZATION &/OR D&C	285	32.68	3.12	$17,044	$3,880
National	769	POSTPARTUM & POST ABORTION DIAGNOSES W O.R. PROCEDURE	125	32.47	5.13	$44,205	$13,520
National	770	ABORTION W D&C, ASPIRATION CURETTAGE OR HYSTEROTOMY	186	33.88	2.04	$19,945	$3,788
National	774	VAGINAL DELIVERY W COMPLICATING DIAGNOSES	1957	31.67	3.34	$15,984	$3,837
National	775	VAGINAL DELIVERY W/O COMPLICATING DIAGNOSES	6422	30.62	2.35	$11,272	$2,444
National	776	POSTPARTUM & POST ABORTION DIAGNOSES W/O O.R. PROCEDURE	785	32.09	3.85	$18,228	$4,163
National	777	ECTOPIC PREGNANCY	186	33.57	2.30	$25,207	$3,948
National	778	THREATENED ABORTION	486	30.56	3.10	$11,627	$2,498
National	779	ABORTION W/O D&C	131	33.08	1.95	$14,138	$2,506
National	780	FALSE LABOR	48	33.17	1.17	$5,056	$719
National	781	OTHER ANTEPARTUM DIAGNOSES W MEDICAL COMPLICATIONS	3961	31.50	4.39	$17,760	$4,273
National	782	OTHER ANTEPARTUM DIAGNOSES W/O MEDICAL COMPLICATIONS	203	32.29	2.59	$10,405	$2,441
National	799	SPLENECTOMY W MCC	553	68.27	12.71	$140,495	$30,703
National	800	SPLENECTOMY W CC	671	68.98	6.98	$68,976	$14,236
National	801	SPLENECTOMY W/O CC/MCC	417	68.96	3.81	$42,394	$7,962
National	802	OTHER O.R. PROC OF THE BLOOD & BLOOD FORMING ORGANS W MCC	1016	71.08	12.07	$102,901	$23,189
National	803	OTHER O.R. PROC OF THE BLOOD & BLOOD FORMING ORGANS W CC	1295	71.16	5.72	$47,222	$10,209
National	804	OTHER O.R. PROC OF THE BLOOD & BLOOD FORMING ORGANS W/O CC/MCC	772	69.44	3.00	$32,440	$5,007
National	808	MAJOR HEMATOL/IMMUN DIAG EXC SICKLE CELL CRISIS & COAGUL W MCC	10056	70.91	8.03	$57,210	$13,506
National	809	MAJOR HEMATOL/IMMUN DIAG EXC SICKLE CELL CRISIS & COAGUL W CC	16274	71.02	4.88	$31,448	$6,805
National	810	MAJOR HEMATOL/IMMUN DIAG EXC SICKLE CELL CRISIS & COAGUL W/O CC/MCC	2400	72.36	3.54	$23,887	$4,886
National	811	RED BLOOD CELL DISORDERS W MCC	37653	70.98	5.13	$32,621	$7,065
National	812	RED BLOOD CELL DISORDERS W/O MCC	117536	70.99	3.44	$20,040	$3,966
National	813	COAGULATION DISORDERS	11797	72.71	5.03	$53,434	$11,206
National	814	RETICULOENDOTHELIAL & IMMUNITY DISORDERS W MCC	1768	69.35	6.97	$46,782	$9,999

Appendix E — 2011 MedPAR National Data

Peer Grouping	MS-DRG	Description	Discharges	Average Age	Average Length of Stay	Average Total Charge	Average Allowed
National	815	RETICULOENDOTHELIAL & IMMUNITY DISORDERS W CC	4096	71.61	4.45	$26,977	$5,331
National	816	RETICULOENDOTHELIAL & IMMUNITY DISORDERS W/O CC/MCC	1536	72.19	3.12	$17,833	$3,318
National	820	LYMPHOMA & LEUKEMIA W MAJOR O.R. PROCEDURE W MCC	1453	72.74	17.00	$164,456	$37,219
National	821	LYMPHOMA & LEUKEMIA W MAJOR O.R. PROCEDURE W CC	2262	72.61	6.88	$65,472	$13,883
National	822	LYMPHOMA & LEUKEMIA W MAJOR O.R. PROCEDURE W/O CC/MCC	1812	72.00	2.85	$35,905	$6,360
National	823	LYMPHOMA & NON-ACUTE LEUKEMIA W OTHER O.R. PROC W MCC	2078	74.01	15.10	$128,585	$28,871
National	824	LYMPHOMA & NON-ACUTE LEUKEMIA W OTHER O.R. PROC W CC	3246	74.26	8.08	$64,600	$12,952
National	825	LYMPHOMA & NON-ACUTE LEUKEMIA W OTHER O.R. PROC W/O CC/MCC	1387	73.28	3.73	$36,342	$6,274
National	826	MYELOPROLIF DISORD OR POORLY DIFF NEOPL W MAJ O.R. PROC W MCC	735	71.70	13.76	$135,606	$29,684
National	827	MYELOPROLIF DISORD OR POORLY DIFF NEOPL W MAJ O.R. PROC W CC	1743	71.73	6.91	$63,647	$12,557
National	828	MYELOPROLIF DISORD OR POORLY DIFF NEOPL W MAJ O.R. PROC W/O CC/MCC	1096	72.10	3.65	$41,396	$7,665
National	829	MYELOPROLIF DISORD OR POORLY DIFF NEOPL W OTHER O.R. PROC W CC/MCC	1640	72.19	9.57	$85,962	$17,555
National	830	MYELOPROLIF DISORD OR POORLY DIFF NEOPL W OTHER O.R. PROC W/O CC/MCC	472	71.71	3.27	$35,646	$6,154
National	834	ACUTE LEUKEMIA W/O MAJOR O.R. PROCEDURE W MCC	4535	73.23	16.75	$149,929	$34,725
National	835	ACUTE LEUKEMIA W/O MAJOR O.R. PROCEDURE W CC	3476	74.58	8.66	$63,407	$15,788
National	836	ACUTE LEUKEMIA W/O MAJOR O.R. PROCEDURE W/O CC/MCC	1247	75.46	4.45	$32,378	$6,996
National	837	CHEMO W ACUTE LEUKEMIA AS SDX OR W HIGH DOSE CHEMO AGENT W MCC	1846	68.23	22.27	$181,068	$46,188
National	838	CHEMO W ACUTE LEUKEMIA AS SDX W CC OR HIGH DOSE CHEMO AGENT	1937	66.32	10.40	$83,576	$21,100
National	839	CHEMO W ACUTE LEUKEMIA AS SDX W/O CC/MCC	1698	66.76	5.60	$36,294	$8,315
National	840	LYMPHOMA & NON-ACUTE LEUKEMIA W MCC	9161	74.34	10.90	$81,914	$18,540
National	841	LYMPHOMA & NON-ACUTE LEUKEMIA W CC	11609	75.00	6.54	$44,567	$9,379
National	842	LYMPHOMA & NON-ACUTE LEUKEMIA W/O CC/MCC	3868	74.35	4.06	$30,031	$5,494
National	843	OTHER MYELOPROLIF DIS OR POORLY DIFF NEOPL DIAG W MCC	1871	73.23	7.97	$50,308	$10,973
National	844	OTHER MYELOPROLIF DIS OR POORLY DIFF NEOPL DIAG W CC	3414	73.81	5.67	$32,783	$6,621
National	845	OTHER MYELOPROLIF DIS OR POORLY DIFF NEOPL DIAG W/O CC/MCC	743	73.98	3.92	$23,446	$4,385
National	846	CHEMOTHERAPY W/O ACUTE LEUKEMIA AS SECONDARY DIAGNOSIS W MCC	3167	66.64	8.63	$72,983	$16,239
National	847	CHEMOTHERAPY W/O ACUTE LEUKEMIA AS SECONDARY DIAGNOSIS W CC	24253	68.63	3.54	$32,473	$6,084
National	848	CHEMOTHERAPY W/O ACUTE LEUKEMIA AS SECONDARY DIAGNOSIS W/O CC/MCC	1290	68.69	2.93	$22,839	$4,738
National	849	RADIOTHERAPY	988	70.04	7.23	$44,760	$8,695
National	853	INFECTIOUS & PARASITIC DISEASES W O.R. PROCEDURE W MCC	51922	71.07	15.46	$139,832	$32,898
National	854	INFECTIOUS & PARASITIC DISEASES W O.R. PROCEDURE W CC	10766	71.91	9.05	$65,319	$14,686
National	855	INFECTIOUS & PARASITIC DISEASES W O.R. PROCEDURE W/O CC/MCC	394	71.80	5.22	$41,865	$7,358

Peer Grouping	MS-DRG	Description	Discharges	Average Age	Average Length of Stay	Average Total Charge	Average Allowed
National	856	POSTOPERATIVE OR POST-TRAUMATIC INFECTIONS W O.R. PROC W MCC	7419	67.40	15.35	$120,440	$29,379
National	857	POSTOPERATIVE OR POST-TRAUMATIC INFECTIONS W O.R. PROC W CC	10875	67.88	7.81	$52,720	$11,512
National	858	POSTOPERATIVE OR POST-TRAUMATIC INFECTIONS W O.R. PROC W/O CC/MCC	2408	67.44	4.85	$31,933	$6,690
National	862	POSTOPERATIVE & POST-TRAUMATIC INFECTIONS W MCC	13630	68.64	10.31	$58,840	$13,813
National	863	POSTOPERATIVE & POST-TRAUMATIC INFECTIONS W/O MCC	24566	68.29	5.38	$25,855	$5,807
National	864	FEVER	22303	71.17	3.64	$21,999	$4,304
National	865	VIRAL ILLNESS W MCC	2534	67.16	6.51	$42,682	$10,024
National	866	VIRAL ILLNESS W/O MCC	8606	72.33	3.43	$20,079	$3,620
National	867	OTHER INFECTIOUS & PARASITIC DISEASES DIAGNOSES W MCC	6328	68.67	10.64	$73,122	$17,113
National	868	OTHER INFECTIOUS & PARASITIC DISEASES DIAGNOSES W CC	3107	71.77	5.10	$27,278	$6,482
National	869	OTHER INFECTIOUS & PARASITIC DISEASES DIAGNOSES W/O CC/MCC	933	72.24	3.46	$17,382	$3,961
National	870	SEPTICEMIA OR SEVERE SEPSIS W MV 96+ HOURS	34981	71.46	15.92	$161,031	$36,654
National	871	SEPTICEMIA OR SEVERE SEPSIS W/O MV 96+ HOURS W MCC	364317	75.50	7.28	$49,450	$11,061
National	872	SEPTICEMIA OR SEVERE SEPSIS W/O MV 96+ HOURS W/O MCC	134696	76.14	5.13	$27,476	$5,988
National	876	O.R. PROCEDURE W PRINCIPAL DIAGNOSES OF MENTAL ILLNESS	1246	64.50	17.17	$70,200	$17,509
National	880	ACUTE ADJUSTMENT REACTION & PSYCHOSOCIAL DYSFUNCTION	11834	65.60	4.54	$17,176	$3,887
National	881	DEPRESSIVE NEUROSES	21974	56.69	7.01	$14,893	$4,392
National	882	NEUROSES EXCEPT DEPRESSIVE	7432	50.90	7.11	$14,422	$4,489
National	883	DISORDERS OF PERSONALITY & IMPULSE CONTROL	3017	46.15	12.95	$25,752	$7,400
National	884	ORGANIC DISTURBANCES & MENTAL RETARDATION	50743	79.67	10.58	$25,583	$7,794
National	885	PSYCHOSES	443213	52.72	13.02	$24,202	$7,321
National	886	BEHAVIORAL & DEVELOPMENTAL DISORDERS	3163	61.85	13.31	$24,217	$7,146
National	887	OTHER MENTAL DISORDER DIAGNOSES	942	56.10	15.21	$26,892	$6,080
National	894	ALCOHOL/DRUG ABUSE OR DEPENDENCE, LEFT AMA	6748	49.57	3.06	$9,229	$2,243
National	895	ALCOHOL/DRUG ABUSE OR DEPENDENCE W REHABILITATION THERAPY	13754	50.07	11.55	$16,983	$7,200
National	896	ALCOHOL/DRUG ABUSE OR DEPENDENCE W/O REHABILITATION THERAPY W MCC	9145	62.30	7.17	$36,435	$8,411
National	897	ALCOHOL/DRUG ABUSE OR DEPENDENCE W/O REHABILITATION THERAPY W/O MCC	65397	56.15	5.46	$14,853	$3,792
National	901	WOUND DEBRIDEMENTS FOR INJURIES W MCC	1182	66.20	21.20	$120,629	$33,013
National	902	WOUND DEBRIDEMENTS FOR INJURIES W CC	2013	68.76	9.01	$48,143	$12,649
National	903	WOUND DEBRIDEMENTS FOR INJURIES W/O CC/MCC	842	68.73	4.43	$26,577	$5,749
National	904	SKIN GRAFTS FOR INJURIES W CC/MCC	2490	66.11	11.27	$85,351	$20,059
National	905	SKIN GRAFTS FOR INJURIES W/O CC/MCC	993	69.38	4.72	$34,869	$6,823
National	906	HAND PROCEDURES FOR INJURIES	864	67.77	3.68	$34,097	$5,817
National	907	OTHER O.R. PROCEDURES FOR INJURIES W MCC	9759	64.77	11.61	$105,050	$24,229
National	908	OTHER O.R. PROCEDURES FOR INJURIES W CC	11074	68.99	6.16	$51,188	$10,535
National	909	OTHER O.R. PROCEDURES FOR INJURIES W/O CC/MCC	5490	68.35	3.35	$32,246	$5,758
National	913	TRAUMATIC INJURY W MCC	1209	75.24	6.53	$34,943	$8,733

Peer Grouping	MS-DRG	Description	Discharges	Average Age	Average Length of Stay	Average Total Charge	Average Allowed
National	914	TRAUMATIC INJURY W/O MCC	6609	77.51	3.38	$18,095	$3,828
National	915	ALLERGIC REACTIONS W MCC	2023	68.37	5.26	$41,722	$8,105
National	916	ALLERGIC REACTIONS W/O MCC	7475	70.84	2.08	$13,024	$2,020
National	917	POISONING & TOXIC EFFECTS OF DRUGS W MCC	27470	59.21	5.00	$38,871	$8,259
National	918	POISONING & TOXIC EFFECTS OF DRUGS W/O MCC	42709	59.67	2.75	$16,756	$3,079
National	919	COMPLICATIONS OF TREATMENT W MCC	14232	65.41	9.35	$55,861	$13,024
National	920	COMPLICATIONS OF TREATMENT W CC	18956	70.84	4.97	$27,742	$6,107
National	921	COMPLICATIONS OF TREATMENT W/O CC/MCC	7762	70.47	2.88	$17,201	$3,173
National	922	OTHER INJURY, POISONING & TOXIC EFFECT DIAG W MCC	1556	72.02	5.88	$39,992	$8,434
National	923	OTHER INJURY, POISONING & TOXIC EFFECT DIAG W/O MCC	4289	74.44	2.95	$17,774	$3,445
National	927	EXTENSIVE BURNS OR FULL THICKNESS BURNS W MV 96+ HRS W SKIN GRAFT	207	66.77	29.28	$470,374	$107,602
National	928	FULL THICKNESS BURN W SKIN GRAFT OR INHAL INJ W CC/MCC	1210	66.08	15.70	$140,252	$34,904
National	929	FULL THICKNESS BURN W SKIN GRAFT OR INHAL INJ W/O CC/MCC	507	65.64	7.52	$61,092	$13,784
National	933	EXTENSIVE BURNS OR FULL THICKNESS BURNS W MV 96+ HRS W/O SKIN GRAFT	189	73.62	6.29	$74,368	$19,192
National	934	FULL THICKNESS BURN W/O SKIN GRFT OR INHAL INJ	795	67.17	7.24	$43,280	$9,694
National	935	NON-EXTENSIVE BURNS	2709	65.26	5.40	$35,254	$8,537
National	939	O.R. PROC W DIAGNOSES OF OTHER CONTACT W HEALTH SERVICES W MCC	2426	68.47	17.56	$88,326	$24,023
National	940	O.R. PROC W DIAGNOSES OF OTHER CONTACT W HEALTH SERVICES W CC	3316	71.76	10.97	$58,877	$15,040
National	941	O.R. PROC W DIAGNOSES OF OTHER CONTACT W HEALTH SERVICES W/O CC/MCC	1512	68.51	3.68	$32,744	$7,046
National	945	REHABILITATION W CC/MCC	291315	75.45	13.35	$37,818	$16,603
National	946	REHABILITATION W/O CC/MCC	67703	76.42	10.69	$27,659	$13,266
National	947	SIGNS & SYMPTOMS W MCC	16265	70.40	4.92	$28,077	$6,169
National	948	SIGNS & SYMPTOMS W/O MCC	71372	74.95	3.37	$17,547	$3,565
National	949	AFTERCARE W CC/MCC	3818	70.61	18.63	$59,865	$18,893
National	950	AFTERCARE W/O CC/MCC	468	70.58	8.16	$23,172	$6,446
National	951	OTHER FACTORS INFLUENCING HEALTH STATUS	1816	70.47	14.03	$27,954	$9,729
National	955	CRANIOTOMY FOR MULTIPLE SIGNIFICANT TRAUMA	494	73.77	11.64	$164,018	$36,038
National	956	LIMB REATTACHMENT, HIP & FEMUR PROC FOR MULTIPLE SIGNIFICANT TRAUMA	5205	80.67	8.45	$89,974	$19,201
National	957	OTHER O.R. PROCEDURES FOR MULTIPLE SIGNIFICANT TRAUMA W MCC	1866	69.35	13.89	$187,620	$41,516
National	958	OTHER O.R. PROCEDURES FOR MULTIPLE SIGNIFICANT TRAUMA W CC	1414	69.61	9.13	$113,021	$22,256
National	959	OTHER O.R. PROCEDURES FOR MULTIPLE SIGNIFICANT TRAUMA W/O CC/MCC	214	67.11	5.85	$71,585	$13,848
National	963	OTHER MULTIPLE SIGNIFICANT TRAUMA W MCC	2329	76.22	9.05	$80,261	$17,998
National	964	OTHER MULTIPLE SIGNIFICANT TRAUMA W CC	3637	77.16	6.01	$42,472	$8,061
National	965	OTHER MULTIPLE SIGNIFICANT TRAUMA W/O CC/MCC	1064	78.98	4.06	$26,828	$4,986
National	969	HIV W EXTENSIVE O.R. PROCEDURE W MCC	587	52.28	16.79	$166,448	$42,951
National	970	HIV W EXTENSIVE O.R. PROCEDURE W/O MCC	93	50.10	7.19	$70,541	$17,625
National	974	HIV W MAJOR RELATED CONDITION W MCC	5629	51.09	10.47	$78,470	$20,031

Peer Grouping	MS-DRG	Description	Discharges	Average Age	Average Length of Stay	Average Total Charge	Average Allowed
National	975	HIV W MAJOR RELATED CONDITION W CC	4214	50.96	7.91	$41,305	$9,373
National	976	HIV W MAJOR RELATED CONDITION W/O CC/MCC	1454	49.32	6.43	$27,792	$5,838
National	977	HIV W OR W/O OTHER RELATED CONDITION	3308	51.09	6.78	$33,665	$7,056
National	981	EXTENSIVE O.R. PROCEDURE UNRELATED TO PRINCIPAL DIAGNOSIS W MCC	28528	71.37	15.23	$135,124	$30,989
National	982	EXTENSIVE O.R. PROCEDURE UNRELATED TO PRINCIPAL DIAGNOSIS W CC	20187	73.37	8.08	$73,074	$15,836
National	983	EXTENSIVE O.R. PROCEDURE UNRELATED TO PRINCIPAL DIAGNOSIS W/O CC/MCC	5505	70.10	3.78	$45,480	$8,503
National	984	PROSTATIC O.R. PROCEDURE UNRELATED TO PRINCIPAL DIAGNOSIS W MCC	566	78.10	13.68	$92,521	$20,649
National	985	PROSTATIC O.R. PROCEDURE UNRELATED TO PRINCIPAL DIAGNOSIS W CC	991	78.54	8.50	$55,199	$12,264
National	986	PROSTATIC O.R. PROCEDURE UNRELATED TO PRINCIPAL DIAGNOSIS W/O CC/MCC	464	77.28	3.64	$28,717	$5,633
National	987	NON-EXTENSIVE O.R. PROC UNRELATED TO PRINCIPAL DIAGNOSIS W MCC	9107	69.93	14.06	$95,770	$22,060
National	988	NON-EXTENSIVE O.R. PROC UNRELATED TO PRINCIPAL DIAGNOSIS W CC	11218	71.25	7.37	$48,505	$10,255
National	989	NON-EXTENSIVE O.R. PROC UNRELATED TO PRINCIPAL DIAGNOSIS W/O CC/MCC	3692	70.46	3.62	$29,783	$5,817

Appendix F — Medicare Case Mix Index Data

2013 IPPS Impact File

State	Average Daily Census	Average Number of Beds	Average CMI V30
AK	54	117	1.43
AL	77	144	1.28
AR	82	157	1.38
AZ	118	196	1.61
CA	123	204	1.56
CO	97	163	1.59
CT	147	207	1.44
DC	233	331	1.69
DE	217	333	1.58
FL	175	290	1.49
GA	101	171	1.43
HI	98	157	1.57
IA	89	169	1.47
ID	75	152	1.71
IL	126	212	1.44
IN	93	170	1.50
KS	57	110	1.55
KY	106	184	1.34
LA	72	135	1.44
MA	147	216	1.36
MD	181	253	1.44
ME	74	129	1.34
MI	138	216	1.48
MN	104	173	1.44
MO	110	200	1.45
MS	70	146	1.23
MT	64	120	1.59
NC	139	212	1.46
ND	106	180	1.71
NE	89	155	1.68
NH	87	149	1.53
NJ	199	287	1.51
NM	58	109	1.32
NV	134	198	1.58
NY	193	258	1.41
OH	115	191	1.49
OK	59	111	1.38
OR	102	166	1.58

For acute care hospitals where case mix index (CMI) > 0
No critical access hospital (CAH)

State	Average Daily Census	Average Number of Beds	Average CMI V30
PA	133	205	1.46
PR	113	156	1.40
RI	144	209	1.43
SC	115	189	1.44
SD	45	91	1.59
TN	101	175	1.37
TX	93	165	1.51
UT	66	127	1.55
VA	117	200	1.40
VT	76	124	1.41
WA	121	195	1.55
WI	87	159	1.56
WV	91	164	1.34
WY	31	78	1.41

For acute care hospitals where case mix index (CMI) > 0
No critical access hospital (CAH)